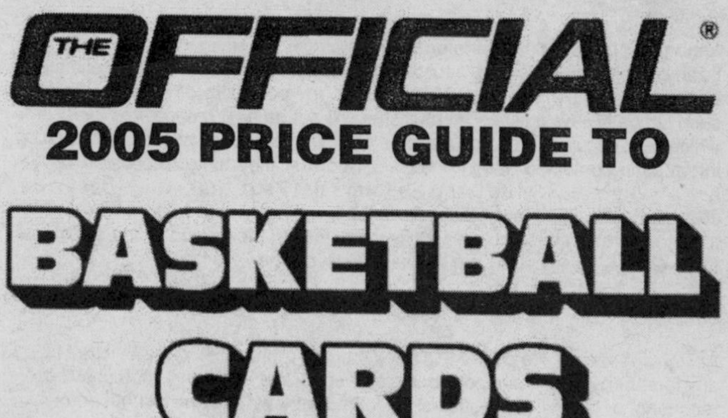

THE OFFICIAL® 2005 PRICE GUIDE TO BASKETBALL CARDS

DR. JAMES BECKETT

FOURTEENTH EDITION

HOUSE OF COLLECTIBLES
Random House Reference
New York

Important Notice: All of the information, including valuations, in this book has been compiled from reliable sources, and efforts have been made to eliminate errors and questionable data. Nevertheless, the possibility of error in a work of such scope always exists. The publisher will not be held responsible for losses which may occur in the purchase, sale or other transaction of items because of information contained herein. Readers who feel they have discovered errors are invited to write and inform us, so that they may be corrected in subsequent editions. Those seeking further information on the topics covered in this book are advised to refer to the complete line of *Official Price Guides* published by the House of Collectibles.

Published by:
House of Collectibles
Random House Information Group
New York, New York

www.houseofcollectibles.com

Distributed by The Random House Information Group,
a division of Random House, Inc.,
New York, and simultaneously in Canada by
Random House of Canada Limited, Toronto.

www.randomhouse.com

Printed in the United States of America

ISSN: 1062-6980

ISBN: 0-375-72059-6

10 9 8 7 6 5 4 3 2 1

Fourteenth Edition: November 2004

Table of Contents

Table of Contents

Table of Contents

Table of Contents

Table of Contents

Table of Contents

About the Author

Jim Beckett, the leading authority on sports card values in the United States, conducts a wide range of activities in the world of sports. He possesses one of the finest collections of sports cards and autographs in the world, has made numerous appearances on radio and television, and has been frequently cited in many national publications. He was awarded the first "Special Achievement Award" for Contributions to the Hobby by the National Sports Collectors Convention in 1980, the "Jock Jaspersen Award" for Hobby Dedication in 1983, and the "Buck Barker Spirit of the Hobby Award" in 1991.

Dr. Beckett is the author of *Beckett Baseball Card Price Guide, The Official Price Guide to Baseball Cards, The Sport Americana Price Guide to Baseball Collectibles, The Sport Americana Baseball Memorabilia and Autograph Price Guide, Beckett Football Card Price Guide, The Official Price Guide to Football Cards, Beckett Hockey Card Price Guide, The Official Price Guide to Hockey Cards, Beckett Basketball Card Price Guide, The Official Price Guide to Basketball Cards,* and *The Sport Americana Baseball Card Alphabetical Checklist.* In addition, he is the founder, publisher, and editor of *Beckett Baseball, Beckett Basketball, Beckett Football, Beckett Hockey,* and *Beckett Racing* magazines.

Jim Beckett received his Ph.D. in Statistics from Southern Methodist University in 1975. Prior to starting Beckett Publications in 1984, Dr. Beckett served as an Associate Professor of Statistics at Bowling Green State University and as a vice president of a consulting firm in Dallas, Texas. He currently resides in Dallas.

How to Use This Book

Isn't it great? Every year this book gets bigger and bigger with all the new sets coming out. But even more exciting is that every year there are more attractive choices and, subsequently, more interest in the cards we love so much. This edition has been enhanced and expanded from the previous edition. The cards you collect—who appears on them, what they look like, where they are from, and (most important to most of you) what their current values are—are enumerated within. Many of the features contained in the other Beckett Price Guides have been incorporated into this volume since condition grading, terminology, and many other aspects of collecting are common to card collecting in general. We hope you find the book both interesting and useful in your collecting pursuits.

The Beckett Guide has been successful where other attempts have failed because it is complete, current, and valid: This price guide contains not just one, but two prices by condition for all the basketball cards listed, which account for most of the basketball cards in existence. The prices were added to the card lists just prior to printing and reflect not the author's opinions or desires but the going retail prices for each card, based on the marketplace (sports memorabilia conventions and shows, sports card shops, hobby papers, internet autions, current mail-order catalogs, local club meetings, auction results, and other firsthand reports of actually realized prices).

What is the best price guide available on the market today? Of course, card sellers will prefer the price guide with the highest prices, while card buyers will naturally prefer the one with the lowest prices. Accuracy, however, is the true test. Use the price guide used by more collectors and dealers than all the others combined. Look for the Beckett name. I won't put my name on anything I won't stake my reputation on. Not the lowest and not the highest—but the most accurate, with integrity.

To facilitate your use of this book, read the complete introductory section on the following pages before going to the pricing pages. Every collectible field has its own terminology; we've tried to capture most of these terms and definitions in our glossary. Please read carefully the section on grading and the condition of your cards, as you will not be able to determine which price column is appropriate for a given card without first knowing its condition.

Introduction

Welcome to the exciting world of sports card collecting, one of America's most popular avocations. You have made a good choice in buying this book, since it will open up to you the entire spectrum of this field in the simplest, most concise way.

The growth of *Beckett Baseball, Beckett Basketball, Beckett Football, Beckett Hockey*, and *Beckett Racing* is another indication of the unprecedented popularity of sports cards. Founded in 1984 by Dr. James Beckett—the author of this price guide—*Beckett Baseball* contains the most extensive and accepted monthly Price Guide, collectible glossy superstar covers, colorful feature articles, a "Hot List," Convention Calendar, tips for beginners, "Readers Write" letters to and responses from the editor, information on errors and varieties, autograph collecting tips and profiles of the sport's hottest stars. Published every month, BB is the hobby's largest paid circulation periodical. The other five magazines were built on the success of BB.

So collecting sports cards—while still pursued as a hobby with youthful exuberance by kids in the neighborhood—has also taken on the trappings of an industry, with thousands of full- and part-time card dealers, as well as vendors of supplies, clubs, and conventions. In fact, each year since 1980 thousands of hobbyists have assembled for a National Sports Collectors Convention, at which hundreds of dealers have displayed their wares, seminars have been conducted, autographs penned by sports notables, and millions of cards changed hands.

The Beckett Guide is the best annual guide available to the exciting world of basketball cards. Read it and use it. May your enjoyment and your card collection increase in the coming months and years.

How to Collect

Each collection is personal and reflects the individuality of its owner. There are no set rules on how to collect cards. Since card collecting is a hobby or leisurely pastime, what you collect, how much you collect, and how much time and money you spend collecting are entirely up to you. The funds you have available for collecting and your own personal taste should determine how you collect. The information and ideas presented here are intended to help you get the most enjoyment from this hobby.

It is impossible to collect every card ever produced. Therefore, beginners as well as intermediate and advanced collectors usually specialize their collections in some way. One of the reasons this hobby is popular is that individual collectors can define and tailor their collecting methods to match their own tastes. To give you some ideas of the various approaches to collecting, we will list some of the more popular areas of specialization.

Many collectors select complete sets from particular years. For example, they may concentrate on assembling complete sets from all the years since their birth or from when they became avid sports fans. They may try to collect a card for every player during that specified period of time. Many others wish to acquire only certain players. Usually such players are the superstars of the sport, but occasionally collectors will specialize in all the cards of players who attended a particular college or came from a certain town. Some collectors are only interested in the first cards or Rookie cards of certain players.

Another fun way to collect cards is by team. Most fans have a favorite team, and it is natural for that loyalty to be translated into a desire for cards of the players on that particular team. For most of the recent years, team sets (all the cards from a given team for that year) are readily available at a reasonable price. *The Sport Americana Team Football and Basketball Card Checklist* will open up this aspect of the field to the collector.

Obtaining Cards

Several avenues are open to card collectors. Cards still can be purchased in the traditional way: by the pack at the local discount, grocery, or convenience store. But there are also thousands of card shops across the country that specialize in selling cards individually or by the pack, box, or set. Another alternative is the thousands of card shows held each month around the country, which feature anywhere from five to 800 tables of sports cards and memorabilia for sale.

For many years, it has been possible to purchase complete sets of cards through mail-order advertisers found in traditional sports media publications, such as *The Sporting News, Basketball Digest, Street & Smith* yearbooks, and others. These sets also are advertised in the card collecting periodicals. Many collectors will begin by subscribing to at least one of the hobby periodicals, all of which have good up-to-date information. In fact, subscription offers can be found in the advertising section of this book.

Most serious card collectors obtain old (and new) cards from one or more of several main sources: (1) trading or buying from other collectors or dealers; (2) responding to sale or auction ads in the hobby publications; (3) buying at a local hobby store; (4) attending sports collectibles shows or conventions; and/or (5) purchasing cards over the Internet.

We advise that you try all five methods since each has its own distinct advantages: (1) trading is a great way to make new friends; (2) hobby periodicals help you keep up with what's going on (including when and where the conventions are happening); (3) stores provide the opportunity to enjoy personalized service and to consider a great diversity of material in a relaxed sports-oriented atmosphere; (4) shows allow you to choose from multiple dealers and thousands of cards under one roof in a competitive situation; and (5) the Internet allows a collector to purchase cards from just about anywhere in the world.

Preserving Your Cards

Cards are fragile. They must be handled properly in order to retain their value. Careless handling can easily result in creased or bent cards. It is, however, not recommended that tweezers or tongs be used to pick up your cards since such utensils might mar or indent card surfaces and thus reduce those cards' conditions and values. In general, your cards should be directly handled as little as possible. This is sometimes easier said than done.

Although there are still many who use custom boxes, storage trays, or even shoeboxes, plastic sheets are the preferred method of many collectors for storing cards. A collection stored in plastic pages in a three-ring album allows you to view your collection at any time without the need to touch the card itself. Cards can also be kept in single holders (of various types and thicknesses) designed for the enjoyment of each card individually. For a large collection, some collectors may use a combination of the above methods. When purchasing plastic sheets for your cards, be sure that you find the pocket size that fits the cards snugly. Don't put your 1969-70 Topps in a sheet designed to fit 1992-93 Topps.

Most hobby and collectibles shops and virtually all collectors' conventions will have these plastic pages available in quantity for the various sizes offered, or you can purchase them directly from the advertisers at the back of this book. Also, remember that pocket size isn't the only factor to consider when looking for plastic sheets. Other factors such as safety, economy, appearance, availability, or personal preference also may indicate which types of sheets a collector may want to buy.

Damp, sunny, and/or hot conditions—no, this is not a weather forecast—are three elements to avoid in extremes if you are interested in preserving your collection. Too much (or too little) humidity can cause gradual deterioration of a card. Direct, bright sun (or fluorescent light) over time will bleach out the color of a card. Extreme heat accelerates the decomposition of the card. On the other hand, many cards have lasted more than 50 years without much scientific intervention. So be cautious, even if the above factors typically present a problem only when in the extreme. It never hurts to be prudent.

Collecting vs. Investing

Collecting individual players and collecting complete sets are both popular vehicles for investment and speculation. Most investors and speculators stock up on complete sets or on quantities of players that they think have good investment potential.

There is obviously no guarantee in this book, or anywhere else for that matter, that cards will outperform the stock market or other investment alternatives in the future. After all, basketball cards do not pay quarterly dividends and cards cannot be sold at their "current values" as easily as stocks or bonds.

Nevertheless, investors have noticed a favorable long-term trend in the past performance of sports collectibles, and certain cards and sets have outperformed just about any other investment in certain years. Many hobbyists maintain that the best investment is and always will be the building of a collection, which traditionally has held up better than outright speculation.

Some of the obvious questions are, Which cards? When to buy? When to sell? The best investment you can make is in your own education. The more you know about your collection and collecting in general, the more informed the decisions you will be able to make. We're not selling investment tips. We're selling information about the current value of basketball cards. It's up to you to use that information to your best advantage.

Glossary/Legend

Our glossary defines terms frequently used in card collecting. Many of these terms are also common to other types of sports memorabilia collecting. Some terms may have several meanings depending on use and context.

ABA—American Basketball Association.

ACC—Accomplishment.

ACO—Assistant Coach Card.

AL—Active Leader.

ART—All-Rookie Team.

AS—All-Star.

ASA—All-Star Advice.

ASW—All-Star Weekend.

AUTO/AU—Autograph.

AW—Award Winner.

B—Bronze.

BC—Bonus Card.

BRICK—A group or "lot" or cards, usually 50 or more having common characteristics, that is, intended to be bought, sold, or traded as a unit.

BT—Beam Team or Breakaway Threats.

CB—Collegiate Best.

CBA—Continental Basketball Association.

CL—Checklist Card. A card that lists in order the cards and players in the set or series. Older checklist cards in mint condition that have not been checked off are very desirable and command large premiums.

CO—Coach Card.

COIN—A small disc of metal or plastic portraying a player in its center.

COLLECTOR—A person who engages in the hobby of collecting cards primarily for his/her own enjoyment, with any profit motive being secondary.

COMBINATION CARD—A single card depicting two, or more players (not including team cards).

COMMON CARD—The typical card of any set.

CONVENTION ISSUE—A set produced in conjunction with a sports collectibles convention to commemorate or promote the show. Most recent convention issues could also be classified as promo sets.

COR—Corrected Card. A version of an error card that was fixed by the manufacturer.

COUPON—See Tab.

CY—City Lights.

DEALER—A person who engages in buying, selling, and trading sports collectibles or supplies. A dealer may also be a collector, but as a dealer, he anticipates a profit.

DIE-CUT—A card with part of its stock partially cut for ornamental reasons.

DISC—A circular-shaped card.

DISPLAY SHEET—A clear, plastic page that is punched for insertion into a binder (with standard three-ring spacing) containing pockets for displaying cards. Many different styles of sheets exist with pockets of varying sizes to hold the many differing card formats. The vast majority of current cards measure 2 1/2 by 3 1/2 inches and fit in nine-pocket sheets.

DP—Double Print. A card that was printed in approximately double the quantity compared to other cards in the same series. Or, Draft Pick card.

ERR—Error card. A card with erroneous information, spelling, or depiction on either side of the card. Most errors are never corrected by the producing card company.

EXCH—A Card that is inserted into packs that can be redeemed for something else—usually a set or autograph.

FIN—Finals.

FLB—Flashback.

FPM—Future Playoff MVPs.

FSL—Future Scoring Leaders.

FULL SHEET—A complete sheet of cards that has not been cut into individual cards by the manufacturer. Also called an uncut sheet.

G—Gold.

GQ—Gentleman's Quarterly.

GRA—Grace.

HL—Highlight Card.

HOF—Hall of Fame, or Hall of Famer (also abbreviated HOFer).

HOR—Horizontal pose on a card, as opposed to the standard vertical orientation found on most cards.

IA—In Action Card. A special type of card depicting a player in an action photo, such as the 1982 Topps cards.

INSERT—A card of a different type, e.g., a poster, or any other sports collectible contained and sold in the same package along with a card or cards of a major set.

IS—Inside Stuff.

ISSUE—Synonymous with set, but usually used in conjunction with a manufacturer, e.g., a Topps issue.

JSY—Jersey Card.

JWA—John Wooden Award.

KID—Kid Picture Card.

LEGITIMATE ISSUE—A set produced to promote or boost sales of a product or service, e.g., bubble gum, cereal, cigarettes, etc. Most collector issues are not legitimate issues in this sense.

LID—A circular-shaped card (possibly with tab) that forms the top of the container for the product being promoted.

MAG—Magic of SkyBox cards.
MAJOR SET—A set produced by a national manufacturer of cards, containing a large number of cards. Usually 100 or more different cards comprise a major set.
MC—Members Choice.
MEM—Memorial.
MINI—A small card or stamp (the 1991-92 SkyBox Canadian set, for example).
MO—McDonald's Open.
MVP—Most Valuable Player.
NNO—No Number on Back.
NY—New York.
OBVERSE—The front, face, or pictured side of the card.
OLY—Olympic Card.
PANEL—An extended card that is composed of multiple individual cards.
PC—Poster Card.
PERIPHERAL SET—A loosely defined term that applies to any nonregular issue set. This term most often is used to describe food issue, giveaway, regional, or sendaway sets that contain a fairly small number of cards and are not accepted by the hobby as major sets.
PF—Pacific Finest.
POY—Player of the Year.
PREMIUM—A card, sometimes on photographic stock, that is purchased or obtained in conjunction with (or redeemed for) another card or product. This term applies mainly to older products, as newer cards distributed in this manner are generally lumped together as peripheral sets.
PREMIUM CARDS—A class of products introduced recently, intended to have higher-quality card stock and photography than regular cards, but with more limited production and higher cost. Detrmining what is and isn't a premium card is somewhat subjective.
PROMOTIONAL SET—A set, usually containing a small number of cards, issued by a national card producer and distributed in limited quantities or to a select group of people, such as major show attendees or dealers with wholesale accounts. Presumably, the purpose of a promo set is to stir up demand for an upcoming set. Also called a preview, prototype, promo, or test set.
QP—Quadruple Print. A card that was printed in approximately four times the quantity compared to other cards in the same series.
RARE—A card or series of cards of very limited availability. Unfortunately, "rare" is a subjective term sometimes used indiscriminately. Using strict definitions, rare cards are harder to obtain than scarce cards.
RC—Rookie Card.
REGIONAL—A card issued and distributed only in a limited geographical area of the country. The producer may or may not be a major, national producer of trading cards. The key is whether the set was distributed nationally in any form or not.
REVERSE—The back or narrative side of the card.
REV NEG—Reversed or flopped photo side of the card. This is a common type of error card, but only some are corrected.
RIS—Rising Star.
ROY—Rookie of the Year.
S—Silver.
SA—Super Action Card. Similar to an In Action Card.
SAL—SkyBox Salutes.
SASE—Self-addressed, stamped envelope.
SCARCE—A card or series of cards of limited availability. This subjective term is sometimes used indiscriminately to promote or hype value. Using strict

definitions, scarce cards are easier to obtain than rare cards.

SERIES—The entire set of cards issued by a particular producer in a particular year, e.g., the 1978-79 Topps series. Also, within a particular set, series can refer to a group of (consecutively numbered) cards printed at the same time, e.g., the first series of the 1972-73 Topps set (#1 through #132).

SET—One each of an entire run of cards of the same type, produced by a particular manufacturer during a single season. In other words, if you have a complete set of 1989-90 Fleer cards, then you have every card from #1 up to and including #132; i.e., all the different cards that were produced.

SHOOT—Shooting Star.

SHOW—A large gathering of dealers and collectors at a single location for the purpose of buying, selling, and trading sports cards and memorabilia. Conventions are open to the public and sometimes also feature autograph guests, door prizes, films, contests, etc. (Or, Showcase, as in 1996-97 Flair Showcase.)

SKED—Schedules.

SP—Single or Short Print. A card which was printed in a lesser quantity compared to the other cards in the same series (also see Double Print). This term can be used only in a relative sense and in reference to one particular set. For instance, the 1989-90 Hoops Pistons Championship card (#353A) is less common than the other cards in that set, but it isn't necessarily scarcer than regular cards of any other set.

SPECIAL CARD—A card that portrays something other than a single player or team.

SS—Star Stats.

STANDARD SIZE—The standard size for sports cards is 2 1/2 by 3 1/2 inches. All exceptions, such as 1969-70 Topps, are noted in card descriptions.

STAR CARD—A card that portrays a player of some repute, usually determined by his ability, but sometimes referring to sheer popularity.

STAY—Stay in School.

STICKER—A card-like item with a removable layer that can be affixed to another surface. Example: 1986-87 through 1989-90 Fleer bonus cards.

STOCK—The cardboard or paper on which the card is printed.

STY—Style.

SUPERSTAR CARD—A card that portrays a superstar, e.g., a Hall of Fame member or a player whose current performance may eventually warrant serious Hall of Fame consideration.

SY—Schoolyard Stars.

TC—Team Card or Team Checklist Card.

TD—Triple Double. A term used for having double-digit totals in three categories.

TAB — A card portion set off from the rest of the card, usually with perforations, that may be removed without damaging the central character or event depicted by the card.

TEAM CARD—A card that depicts an entire team, notably the 1989-90 and 1990-91 NBA Hoops Detroit Pistons championship cards and the 1991-92 NBA Hoops subset.

TEST SET—A set, usually containing a small number of cards, issued by a national producer and distributed in a limited section of the country or to a select group of people. Presumably, the purpose of a test set is to measure market appeal for a particular type of card. Also called a promo or prototype set.

TFC—Team Fact Card.

TL—Team Leader.

TO—Tip-Off.

TR—Traded Card.

TRIB—Tribune.

TRV—Trivia.
TT—Team Tickets Card.
UER—Uncorrected Error Card.
USA—Team USA.
VAR—Variation Card. One of two or more cards from the same series, with the same card number (or player with identical pose, if the series is unnumbered) differing from one another in some aspect, from the printing, stock, or other feature of the card. This is often caused when the manufacturer of the cards notices an error in a particular card, corrects the error, and then resumes the print run. In this case there will be two versions or variations of the same card. Sometimes one of the variations is relatively scarce. Variations also can result from accidental or deliberate design changes, information updates, photo substitutions, etc.
VERT—Vertical pose on a card.
XRC—Extended Rookie Card. A player's first appearance on a card, but issued in a set that was not distributed nationally or in packs. In basketball sets, this term refers only to the 1983, '84, and '85 Star Company sets.
YB—Yearbook.
20A—Twenty Assist Club.
50P—Fifty point Club.
6M—Sixth Man.
!—Condition-sensitive card or set (see Grading Your Cards).
*****—Multisport set.

Understanding Card Values

Determining Value

Why are some cards more valuable than others? Obviously, the economic laws of supply and demand are applicable to card collecting, just as they are to any other field where a commodity is bought, sold, or traded in a free, unregulated market.

Supply (the number of cards available on the market) is less than the total number of cards originally produced, since attrition diminishes that original quantity of cards. Each year a percentage of cards is typically thrown away, destroyed, or otherwise lost to collectors. This percentage is much, much smaller today than it was in the past, because more and more people have become increasingly aware of the value of their cards.

For those who collect only mint condition cards, the supply of older cards can be quite small indeed. Until recently, collectors were not so conscious of the need to preserve the condition of their cards. For this reason, it is difficult to know exactly how many 1957-58 Topps cards are currently available, mint or otherwise. It is generally accepted that there are fewer 1957-58 Topps cards available than 1969-70, 1979-80, or 1992-93 Topps cards. If demand were equal for each of these sets, the law of supply and demand would increase the price for the least available sets.

Demand, however, is never equal for all sets, so price correlations can be complicated. The demand for a card is influenced by many factors. These include (1) the age of the card; (2) the number of cards printed; (3) the player(s) portrayed on the card; (4) the attractiveness and popularity of the set; and (5) the physical condition of the card.

In general, (1) the older the card, (2) the fewer the number of the cards printed, (3) the more famous, popular, and talented the player, (4) the more attractive and popular the set, and (5) the better the condition of the card, the higher the value of the card will be. There are exceptions to all but one of these factors: the condition of the card. Given two cards similar in all respects except condition, the one in the best condition will always be valued higher.

While those guidelines help to establish the value of a card, the countless exceptions and peculiarities make it impossible to develop any simple, direct mathematical formula to determine card values.

Regional Variation

Since the market for cards varies from region to region, card prices of local players may be higher. This is known as a regional premium. How significant the premium is—and if there is any premium at all—depends on the local popularity of the team and the player.

The largest regional premiums usually do not apply to superstars, who often are so well-known nationwide that the prices of their key cards are too high for local dealers to realize a premium.

Lesser stars often command the strongest premiums. Their popularity is concentrated in their home region, creating local demand that greatly exceeds overall demand.

Regional premiums can apply to popular retired players, and sometimes can be found in the areas where the players grew up or starred in college in addition to where they played.

A regional discount is the converse of a regional premium. Regional discounts occur when a player has been so popular in his region for so long that local collectors and dealers have accumulated quantities of his cards. The abundant supply may make the cards available in that area at the lowest prices anywhere.

Set Prices

A somewhat paradoxical situation exists in the price of a complete set versus the combined cost of the individual cards in the set. In nearly every case, the sum of the prices for the individual cards is higher than the cost for the complete set. This is prevalent especially in cards of the past few years. The reasons for this apparent anomaly stem from the habits of collectors and from the carrying costs to dealers. Today, each card in a set normally is produced in the same quantity as all others in its set.

Many collectors pick up only stars, superstars, and particular teams. As a result, the dealer is left with a shortage of certain player cards and an abundance of others. He therefore incurs an expense in simply "carrying" these less desirable cards in stock. On the other hand, if he sells a complete set, he gets rid of large numbers of cards at one time. For this reason, he generally is willing to receive less money for a complete set. By doing this, he recovers all of his costs and also makes a profit.

Set prices do not include rare card varieties, unless specifically stated. Of course, the prices for sets do include one example of each type for the given set, but this is the least expensive variety.

For some sets, a complete set price is not listed. This is due to sets currently not trading on the market as such. Usually, the sets that have low serial number print runs do not have complete set prices.

Scarce Series

Only a select few pre-1990 basketball sets contain scarce series: 1948 Bowman; 1970-71 and 1972-73 Topps; and 1983-84, 1984-85, and 1985-86 Star. The 1948 Bowman set was printed on two 36-card sheets, the second of which was issued in significantly lower quantities. The two Topps scarce series are only marginally tougher to aquire than the set as a whole. The Star Company scarcities relate to particular team sets that, to different extents, were less widely distributed.

We are always looking for information or photographs of printing sheets of cards for research. Each year, we try to update the hobby's knowledge of distribution anomalies. Please contact us at the address in this book if you have firsthand knowledge that would be helpful in this pursuit.

Grading Your Cards

Each hobby has its own grading terminology—stamps, coins, comic books, record collecting, etc. Collectors of sports cards are no exception. The one invariable criterion for determining the value of a card is its condition: The better the condition of the card, the more valuable it is. Condition grading, however, is subjective. Individual card dealers and collectors differ in the strictness of their grading, but the stated condition of a card should be determined without regard to whether it is being bought or sold.

No allowance is made for age. A 1961-62 Fleer card is judged by the same standards as a 1991-92 Fleer card. But there are specific sets and cards that are condition-sensitive (marked with "!" in the price guide) because of their border color, consistently poor centering, or other factors. Such cards and sets sometimes command premiums above the listed percentages in Mint condition.

Centering

Current centering terminology uses numbers representing the percentage of border on either side of the main design. Obviously, centering is diminished in importance for borderless cards such as Stadium Club.

Slightly Off-Center (60/40) - A slightly off-center card is one that upon close inspection is found to have one border wider than the opposite border. This degree once was offensive only to purists, but now some hobbyists try to avoid cards that are anything other than perfectly centered.

Off-Center (70/30) - An off-center card has one border that is noticeably more than twice as wide as the opposite border.

Badly Off-Center (80/20 or worse) - A badly off-center card has virtually no border on one side of the card.

Miscut - A miscut card actually shows part of the adjacent card in its larger border, and consequently a corresponding amount of its card is cut off.

Corner Wear

Corner wear is the most scrutinized grading criteria in the hobby. These are the major categories of corner wear:

Corner with a slight touch of wear - The corner still is sharp, but there is a slight touch of wear showing. On a dark-bordered card, this shows as a dot of white.

Fuzzy corner - The corner still comes to a point, but the point has just begun to fray. A slightly "dinged" corner is considered the same as a fuzzy corner.

Slightly rounded corner - The fraying of the corner has increased to where there is only a hint of a point. Mild layering may be evident. A "dinged" corner is considered the same as a slightly rounded corner.

Rounded corner - The point is completely gone. Some layering is noticeable.

Badly rounded corner - The corner is completely round and rough. Severe layering is evident.

Creases

A third common defect is the crease. The degree of creasing in a card is difficult to show in a drawing or picture. On giving the specific condition of an expensive card for sale, the seller should also note any creases. Creases can be categorized by severity according to the following scale:

Light Crease - A light crease is a crease that is barely noticeable upon close inspection. In fact, when cards are in plastic sheets or holders, a light crease may not be seen (until the card is taken out of the holder). A light crease on the front is much more serious than a light crease only on the back of the card.

Medium Crease - A medium crease is noticeable when held and studied at arm's length by the naked eye, but does not overly detract from the appearance of the card. It is an obvious crease, but not one that breaks the picture surface of the card.

Centering

Well-center

Slightly off-center

Off-center

Badly off-center

Miscut

Corner Wear

The partial cards here have been photographed at 300%. This was done in order to magnify each card's corner wear to such a degree that differences could be shown on a printed page.

This 1986-87 Fleer Mark Aguirre card has a slight touch of wear. Notice the extremely slight fraying on the corner.

This 1986-87 Fleer Isiah Thomas card has a fuzzy corner. Notice that there is no longer a sharp corner.

This 1986-87 Fleer Wayman Tisdale card has a slightly rounded corner evident by the lack of a sharp point and heavy wear on both edges.

This 1986-87 Fleer Herb Williams card displays a badly rounded corner. Notice a large portion of missing cardboard accompanied by heavy wear and excessive fraying.

This 1986-87 Fleer Maurice Cheeks card displays several creases of varying degrees. Light creases (middle of the card) may not break the card's surface, while heavy creases (right side) will.

Heavy Crease - A heavy crease is one that has torn or broken through the card's picture surface, e.g., puts a tear in the photo surface.

Alterations

Deceptive Trimming - This occurs when someone alters the card in order to (1) shave off edge wear, (2) improve the sharpness of the corners, or (3) improve centering. Obviously, the objective is to falsely increase the perceived value of the card to an unsuspecting buyer. The shrinkage is usually evident only if the trimmed card is compared to an adjacent full-size card or if the trimmed card is itself measured.

Obvious Trimming - Obvious trimming is noticeable and unfortunate. It is usually performed by non-collectors who give no thought to the present or future value of their cards.

Deceptively Retouched Borders - This occurs when the borders (especially on those cards with dark borders) are touched up on the edges and corners with Magic Marker or crayons of appropriate color in order to make the card appear to be in mint condition.

Categorization of Defects

Miscellaneous Flaws

The following are common minor flaws that, depending on severity, lower a card's condition by one to four grades and often render it no better than Excellent-Mint (see Condition Guide): bubbles (lumps in surface), gum and wax stains, diamond cutting (slanted borders), notching, off-centered backs, paper wrinkles, scratched-off cartoons or puzzles on back, rubber band marks, scratches, surface impressions, and warping.

The following are common serious flaws that, depending on severity, lower a card's condition at least four grades and often render it no better than Good: chemical or sun fading, erasure marks, mildew, miscutting (severe off-centering), holes, bleached or retouched borders, tape marks, tears, trimming, water or coffee stains, and writing.

Condition Guide

Grades

Mint (Mt) - A card with no flaws or wear. The card has four perfect corners, 55/45 or better centering from top to bottom and from left to right, original gloss, smooth edges, and original color borders. A mint card does not have print spots, or color or focus imperfections.

Near Mint-Mint (NrMt-Mt) - A card with one minor flaw. Any one of the following would lower a mint card to near mint-mint: one corner with a slight touch of wear, barely noticeable print spots, or color or focus imperfections. The card must have 60/40 or better centering in both directions, original gloss, smooth edges, and original color borders.

Near Mint (NrMt) - A card with one minor flaw. Any one of the following would lower a mint card to near mint: one fuzzy corner or two to four corners with slight touches of wear, 70/30 to 60/40 centering, slightly rough edges, minor print spots, or color or focus imperfections. The card must have original gloss and original color borders.

Excellent-Mint (ExMt) - A card with two or three fuzzy, but not rounded, corners and centering no worse than 80/20. The card may have no more than two of the following: slightly rough edges, very slightly discolored borders, minor print spots, or color or focus imperfections. The card must have original gloss.

Excellent (Ex) - A card with four fuzzy but definitely not rounded corners and centering no worse than 80/20. The card may have a small amount of original gloss lost, rough edges, slightly discolored borders and minor print spots, color or focus imperfections.

Very Good (Vg) - A card that has been handled but not abused: Factors may include slightly rounded corners with slight layering, slight notching on edges, a significant amount of gloss lost from the surface but no scuffing, and moderate discoloration of borders. The card may have a few light creases.

Good (G), Fair (F), Poor (P) - A well-worn, mishandled, or abused card: Factors may include badly rounded and layered corners, scuffing, most or all original gloss missing, seriously discolored borders, moderate or heavy creases, and one or more serious flaws. The grade of good, fair, or poor depends on the severity of wear and flaws. Good, fair, and poor cards generally are used only as fillers.

The most widely used grades are defined above. Obviously, many cards will not perfectly fit one of these definitions. Therefore, categories between the major grades known as in-between grades are used, such as Good to Very Good (G-Vg), Very Good to Excellent (VgEx), and Excellent-Mint to Near Mint (ExMt-NrMt). Such grades indicate a card with all qualities of the lower category but with at least a few qualities of the higher category.

This price guide book lists each card and set in two grades, with the bottom grade valued at about 40-45% of the top grade.

The value of cards that fall between the listed columns can also be calculated using a percentage of the top grade. For example, a card that falls between the top and middle grades (Ex, ExMt, or NrMt in most cases) will generally be valued at anywhere from 50% to 90% of the top grade.

Similarly, a card that falls between the middle and bottom grades (G-Vg, Vg, or VgEx in most cases) will generally be valued at anywhere from 20% to 40% of the top grade.

There are also cases where cards are in better condition than the top grade or worse than the bottom grade. Cards that grade worse than the lowest grade are generally valued at 5-10% of the top grade.

When a card exceeds the top grade by one—such as NrMt-Mt when the top grade is NrMt, or mint when the top grade is NrMt-Mt—a premium of up to 50% is possible, with 10-20% the usual norm.

When a card exceeds the top grade by two—such as mint when the top grade is NrMt, or NrMt-Mt when the top grade is ExMt—a premium of 25-50% is the usual norm. But certain condition-sensitive cards or sets, particularly those from the pre-war era, can bring premiums of up to 100% or even more.

Unopened packs, boxes, and factory-collated sets are considered mint in their unknown (and presumed perfect) state. Once opened, however, each card can be graded (and valued) in its own right by taking into account any defects that may be present in spite of the fact that the card has never been handled.

Selling Your Cards

Just about every collector sells cards or will sell cards at some point. Someday you may be interested in selling your duplicates or maybe even your whole collection. You may sell to other collectors, friends, or dealers. You may even sell cards you purchased from a certain dealer back to that same dealer. In any event, it helps to know some of the mechanics of the typical transaction between buyer and seller.

Dealers will buy cards in order to resell them to other collectors who are interested in them. Dealers will always pay a higher percentage for items that (in their opinion) can be resold quickly, and a much lower percentage for those items that are perceived as having low demand and hence are slow moving. In either case, dealers must buy at a price that allows for business expense and a profit margin.

If you have cards for sale, the best advice I can give is that you get several offers for your cards—either from card shops or at a card show—and take the best offer, all things considered. Note, the "best" offer may not be the one for the highest amount. And remember, if a dealer really wants your cards, he won't let you get away without making his best competitive offer. Another alternative is to place your cards in an auction as one or several lots.

Many people think nothing of going into a department store and paying $15 for an item of clothing for which the store paid $5. But if you were selling your $15 card to a dealer and he offered you $5 for it, you might think his markup unreasonable. To complete the analogy, most department stores (and card dealers) that consistently pay $10 for $15 items eventually go out of business. An exception is when the dealer has lined up a willing buyer for the item(s) you are attempting to sell, or if the cards are so hot that it's likely he'll have to hold the cards for only a short period of time.

In those cases, an offer of up to 75% of book value still will allow the dealer to make a reasonable profit considering the short time he will need to hold the merchandise. In general, however, most cards and collections will bring offers in the range of 25-50% of retail price. Also consider that most material from the past five to 10 years is plentiful. If that's what you're selling, don't be surprised if your best offer is well below that range.

Interesting Notes

The first card numerically of an issue is the single card most likely to obtain excessive wear. Consequently, you typically will find the price on the #1 card (in NrMt or mint condition) somewhat higher than might otherwise be the case. Similarly, but to a lesser extent (because normally the less important, reverse side of the card is the one exposed), the last card numerically in an issue also is prone to abnormal wear. This extra wear and tear occurs because the first and last cards are exposed to the elements (human element included) more than any other cards. They are generally end cards in any brick formations, rubber bandings, stackings on wet surfaces, and similar arrangements.

Sports cards have no intrinsic value. The value of a card, like the value of other collectibles, can be determined only by you and your enjoyment in viewing and possessing these cardboard treasures.

Remember, the buyer ultimately determines the price of each card. You are the determining price factor because you have the ability to say "no" to the price of any card by not exchanging your hard-earned money for a given card. When the cost of a trading card exceeds the enjoyment you will receive from it, your answer should be "no." We assess and report the prices. You set them!

We are always interested in receiving the price input of collectors and dealers from around the country. We happily credit all contributors. We welcome your opinions, since your contributions assist us in ensuring a better guide each year. If you would like to join our survey list for future editions of this book and others authored by Dr. Beckett, please send your name and address to Dr. James Beckett, 15850 Dallas Parkway, Dallas, Texas 75248.

History of Basketball Cards

The earliest basketball collectibles known are team postcards issued at the turn of the twentieth century. Many of these postcards feature collegiate or high school teams of that day. Postcards were intermittently issued throughout the first half of the twentieth century, with the bulk of them coming out in the 1920s and '30s. Unfortunately, the cataloging of these collectibles is sporadic at best. In addition, many collectors consider these postcards as more memorabilia than trading cards, thus their exclusion from this book.

In 1910, College Athlete felts (catalog number B-33) made their debut. Of a total of 270 felts, 20 featured basketball players.

The first true basketball trading cards were issued by Murad cigarettes in 1911. The "College Series" cards depict a number of various sports and colleges, including four basketball cards (Luther, Northwestern, Williams, and Xavier). In addition to these small (2-by-3-inch) cards, Murad issued a large (8-by-5-inch) basketball card featuring Williams College (catalog number T-6) as part of another multisport set.

The first basketball cards ever to be issued in gum packs were distributed in 1933 by Goudey in its multisport Sport Kings set, which was the first issue to list individual and professional players. Four cards from the complete 48-card set feature original Celtics basketball players Nat Holman, Ed Wachter, Joe Lapchick, and Eddie Burke.

The period of growth that the National Basketball Association experienced from 1948 to 1951 marked the first initial boom, both for that sport and the cards that chronicle it. In 1948, Bowman created the first trading card set exclusively devoted to basketball cards, ushering in the modern era of hoops collectibles. The 72-card Bowman set contains the Rookie card of HOFer George Mikan, one of the most valuable, and important, basketball cards in the hobby. Mikan, pro basketball's first dominant big man, set the stage for Bill Russell, Wilt Chamberlain, and all the other legendary centers who have played the game since.

In addition to the Bowman release, Topps included 11 basketball cards in its 252-card multisport 1948 Magic Photo set. Five of the cards feature individual players (including collegiate great "Easy" Ed Macauley), another five feature colleges, and one additional card highlights a Manhattan-Dartmouth game. These 11 cards represent Topp's first effort to produce basketball trading cards. Kellogg's also created an 18-card multisport set of trading cards in 1948 that was inserted into boxes of Pep cereal. The only basketball card in the set features Mikan. Throughout 1948 and 1949, the Exhibit Supply Company of Chicago issued oversized thick-stock multisport trading cards in conjunction with the 1948 Olympic games. Six basketball players were featured, including HOFers Mikan and Joe Fulks, among others. The cards were distributed through penny arcade machines.

In 1950-51, Scott's Chips issued a 13-card set featuring the Minneapolis Lakers. The cards were issued in Scott's Potato and Cheese Potato Chip boxes. The cards are extremely scarce today due to the fact that many were redeemed back in 1950-51 in exchange for game tickets and signed team pictures. This set contains possibly the scarcest Mikan issue in existence. In 1951, a Philadelphia-based meat company called Berk Ross issued a four-series, 72-card multisport set. The set contains five different basketball players, including the first cards of HOFers Bob Cousy and Bill Sharman.

General Mills issued an oversized six-card multisport set on the backs of Wheaties cereal boxes in 1951. The only basketball player featured in the set is Mikan.

In 1952, Wheaties expanded the cereal box set to 30 cards, including six issues featuring basketball players of that day. Of these six cards, two feature Mikan (a portrait and an action shot). The 1952 cards are significantly smaller than the previous year's issue. That same year, the 32-card Bread for Health set was issued. The set was one of the few trading card issues of that decade exclusively devoted to the sport of basketball. The cards are actually bread end labels and were probably meant to be housed in an album. To date, the only companies known to have issued this set are Fisher's Bread in the New Jersey, New York, and Pennsylvania areas and NBC Bread in the Michigan area.

One must skip ahead to 1957-58 to find the next major basketball issue, again produced by Topps. Its 80-card basketball set from that year is recognized within the hobby as the second major modern basketball issue, including Rookie cards of all-time greats such as Bill Russell, Bob Cousy, and Bob Pettit.

In 1960, Post cereal created a nine-card multisport set by devoting most of the back of the actual cereal boxes to full-color picture frames of the athletes. HOFers Cousy and Pettit are the two featured basketball players.

In 1961-62, Fleer issued the third major modern basketball set. The 66-card set contains the Rookie cards of all-time greats such as Wilt Chamberlain, Oscar Robertson, and Jerry West. That same year, Bell Brand Potato Chips inserted trading cards (one per bag) featuring the L.A. Lakers team of that year and including scarce, early issues of HOFers West and Elgin Baylor.

From 1963 to 1968 no major companies manufactured basketball cards. Kahn's (an Ohio-based meat company) issued small regional basketball sets from 1957-58 through 1965-66 (including the first cards of Jerry West and Oscar Robertson in its 1960-61 set). All the Kahn's sets feature members of the Cincinnati Royals, except for the few issues featuring the Lakers' West.

In 1968, Topps printed a very limited quantity of standard-size black-and-white test issue cards, preluding its 1969-70 nationwide return to the basketball card market.

The 1969-70 Topps set began a 13-year run of producing nationally distributed basketball card sets which ended in 1981-82. This was about the time the league's popularity bottomed out and was about to begin its ascent to the lofty level it's at today. Topp's run included several sets that are troublesome for today's collectors. The 1969-70, 1970-71, and 1976-77 sets are larger than standard size, thus making them hard to store and preserve. The 1980-81 set consists of standard-size panels containing three cards each. Completing and cataloging the 1980-81 set (which features the classic Larry Bird RC/Magic Johnson RC/Julius Erving panel) is challenging, to say the least.

In 1983, this basketball card void was filled by the Star Company, a small company which issued three attractive sets of basketball cards, along with a plethora of peripheral sets. Star's 1983-84 premiere offering was issued in four groups, with the first series (cards 1-100) very difficult to obtain, as many of the early team subsets were miscut and destroyed before release. The 1984-85 and 1985-86 sets were more widely and evenly distributed. Even so, players' initial appearances on any of the three Star Company sets are considered Extended Rookie cards, not regular Rookie cards, because of the relatively limited distribution. Chief among these is Michael Jordan's 1984-85 Star XRC, the most valuable sports card issued in a 1980s major set.

Then, in 1986, Fleer took over the rights to produce cards for the NBA. Their 1986-87, 1987-88, and 1988-89 sets each contain 132 attractive, colorful cards depicting mostly stars and superstars. They were sold in the familiar wax pack format (12 cards and one sticker per pack). Fleer increased its set size to 168 in 1989-90, and was joined by NBA Hoops, which produced a 300-card first series (containing David Robinson's only Rookie card) and a 52-card second series. The demand for all three Star Company sets, along with the first four Fleer sets and the premiere NBA Hoops set, skyrocketed during the early part of 1990.

The basketball card market stabilized somewhat in 1990-91, with both Fleer and Hoops stepping up production substantially. A new major set, SkyBox, also made a splash in the market with its unique "high-tech" cards featuring computer-generated backgrounds. Because of overproduction, none of the three major 1990-91 sets have experienced significant price growth, although the increased competition has led to higher quality and more innovative products.

Another milestone in 1990-91 was the first-time inclusion of current rookies in update sets (NBA Hoops and SkyBox Series II, Fleer Update). The NBA Hoops and SkyBox issues contain just the 11 lottery picks, while Fleer's 100-card boxed set includes all rookies of any significance. A small company called "Star Pics" (not to be confused with Star Company) tried to fill this niche by printing a 70-card set in late 1990, but because the set was not licensed by the NBA, it is not considered a major set by the majority of collectors. It does, however, contain the first nationally distributed cards of 1990-91 rookies such as Derrick Coleman and Kendall Gill, among others.

In 1991-92, the draft pick set market that Star Pics opened in 1990-91 expanded to include several competitors. More significantly, that season brought with it the three established NBA card brands plus Upper Deck, known throughout the hobby for its high-quality card stock and photography in other sports. Upper Deck's first basketball set probably captured NBA action better than any previous set. But its value—like all other major 1990-91 and 1991-92 NBA sets—declined because of overproduction.

On the bright side, the historic entrance of NBA players to Olympic competition kept interest in basketball cards going long after the Chicago Bulls won their second straight NBA championship. So for at least one year, the basketball card market—probably the most seasonal of the four major team sports—remained in the spotlight for an extended period of time.

The 1992-93 season will be remembered as the year of Shaq—the debut campaign of the most heralded rookie in many years. Shaquille O'Neal headlined the most promising rookie class in NBA history, sparking unprecedented interest in basketball cards. Among O'Neal's many talented rookie companions were Alonzo Mourning, Jim Jackson, and Latrell Sprewell.

Classic Games, known primarily for producing draft picks and minor league baseball cards, signed O'Neal to an exclusive contract through 1992, thus postponing the appearances of O'Neal's NBA-licensed cards.

Shaquille's Classic and NBA cards, particularly the inserts, became some of the most sought-after collectibles in years. As a direct result of O'Neal and his fellow rookie standouts, the basketball card market achieved a new level of popularity in 1993.

The hobby rode that crest of popularity throughout the 1993-94 season. Michael Jordan may have retired, but his absence only spurred interest in some of his tougher inserts. Another strong rookie class followed Shaq, and Reggie Miller elevated his collectibility to a superstar level. Hakeem Olajuwon, by leading the Rockets to an NBA title, boosted his early cards to levels surpassed only by Jordan.

No new cardmakers came on board, but super premium Topps Finest raised the stakes, and the parallel set came into its own.

In 1994-95, the return of Michael Jordan, coupled with the high impact splash of Detroit Pistons rookie Grant Hill, kept collector interest high. In addition, the NBA granted all the licensed manufacturers the opportunity to create a fourth brand of basketball cards that year, allowing each company to create a selection of clearly defined niche products at different price points. The manufacturers also expanded the calendar release dates, with 1994-95 cards being released on a consistent basis from August, 1994, all the way through June, 1995. The super-premium card market expanded greatly as the battle for the best-selling five-dollar (or more) pack reached epic levels by season's end. The key new super premium products included the premier, of SP, Embossed, and Emotion. This has continued through 1996 with the release of SPx, which contained only one card per pack.

The collecting year of 1996-97 brought even more to the table with a prominent motif of tough parallel sets and an influx of autographs available at lower ratio pulls. One of the greatest rookie classes in some time also carried the collecting season with players showing great promise: Allen Iverson, Kobe Bryant, Stephon Marbury, Antoine Walker, and Shareef Abdur-Rahim. Topps Chrome was also introduced, bringing about a rookie frenzy not seen since the 1986-87 Fleer set.

In 1997-98, Kobe Bryant was deemed the next Michael Jordan and his cards escalated in value throughout the year. In addition, a stronger than expected rookie class gave collectors some new blood to chase after, including Tim Duncan, Keith Van Horn, Ron Mercer, and Tim Thomas. Autographs and serial-numbered inserts were the key inserts to chase featuring numbering as low as one of one.

The 1998-99 season brought about a huge change in basketball. The players' strike crushed a growing basketball market and sent manufacturers scrambling. On top of this, Michael Jordan decided to retire (again), sending another direct hit to the hobby. Many releases were cut back—or cut period. There was a bright spot once the season began though—a great rookie class led by Vince Carter. The hobby benefited by combining the great class with shorter print run products. The top of the class was the 1998-99 SP Authentic release, which serially numbered the rookies to 3500. The San Antonio Spurs were crowned NBA Champions, leading to a spike in Tim Duncan cards. The top hobby card of the season was the SP Authentic Vince Carter RC.

If the beginning of the 1998-99 season was at rock bottom, the 1999-00 season was one of transition. Vince Carter became the new hobby hero and the NBA Champion L.A. Lakers helped the state of the hobby with their two horses, Kobe Bryant and Shaquille O'Neal. Another solid rookie class emerged, led by Steve Francis and Elton Brand, who shared Rookie of the Year honors. The 1999-00 card releases all combined elements of short-printed or serially numbered rookies, autographs, and game-worn materials. SP Authentic again led the way for consumer dollars, but many other brands also did extremely well, including E-X, Flair Showcase, and SPx, which combined rookie serial-numbered cards with autographs. The top hobby card of the season was the SPx Steve Francis RC, which was autographed to 500.

The year of 2000-01 releases will definitely leave its mark on the face of basketball cards for years to come. Noteworthy points of interest include the first one-per-pack graded insert in Upper Deck Ultimate Collection, the first one-per-pack memorabilia release in SP Game Floor, and the first one-per-box autographed jersey in Fleer Legacy. While these concepts have become commonplace over the course of the last year and a half, more than two years ago, notions such as these were unheard of.

Rookie cards were all the rage this year, and were available in several different formats and pricing tiers. It looks as though the sequentially numbered rookie has worked its way in as a hobby staple, as have autographed and memorabilia rookie issues. The uniqueness of 2000-01's releases is both staggering and impressive, as it is comforting to know that our hobby is still pointed in the right direction.

It also appears that 2000-01 marks a changing of the guard as far as basketball heroes are concerned. It is rather unfeasible to compare anyone in today's basketball game to the stature and legend that Michael Jordan has built for himself throughout the past two decades, but several young heroes are working their way up into our daily sports repertoire. As Michael Jordan sales begin to slow, Kobe Bryant, the L.A. Lakers' cast and crew, and Allen Iverson continue to build steam and fill the derelict space left by our hobby idol.

The release year of 2001-02 followed in the footsteps of previous years, as nearly every set issued had some type of memorabilia and/or autographed element to it. The hobby was shaken into somewhat of a frenzy as Michael Jordan rose up out of retirement (again), this time as a mentor and a player of the young Washington Wizards squad. Base Michael Jordan card values dominated sets, and at one point, $10 to $12 was a common value on the high end; and the explosive volume of sales provided the biggest boost as far as hobby dollars is concerned. Notable releases this year include Topps Pristine for its pack-in-a-pack-in-a-pack concept, encased uncirculated cards, and the use of new playoff-related materials such as towels. Upper Deck followed the comeback of Michael Jordan with several commemorative issues such as MJ Jersey Collection, and MJ's Back Jerseys which was inserted in several brands at the beginning of the release season. Fleer and Topps rejuvenated the market for parallel sets as Fleer issued two memorabilia parallels with its E-X release, and Topps made waves with the Topps Chrome Refractors Black Border set. A soft rookie crop as of the end of 2001-02 card releases had an impact on newer sales; the emergence of young stars such as Mike Bibby, Dirk Nowitzki, and Paul Pierce had collectors stammering for cardboard of players, who, since their rookie issues, had gone unnoticed, and dominated the market toward the end of the season.

2002-03 paved the way for the globalization of basketball trading cards. The 2002 NBA Draft boasts the highest number of foreign players drafted in the first round with ten, and the biggest push towards international card collecting was the number one draft choice, Yao Ming. Unlike most big men drafted, Ming had the ability to come in right away and put up good numbers for his Houston squad. Then, Ming coupled with Amare Stoudemire, a high-school draftee for Phoenix provided the perfect one-two punch to breathe some life back into the hobby, which had died off after the retirement of Michael Jordan in 1997 and the NBA lockout in 1998.

Additional Reading

Each year Beckett Publications produces comprehensive annual price guides for each of the five major sports: *Beckett Baseball Card Price Guide, Beckett Football Card Price Guide, Beckett Basketball Card Price Guide, Beckett Hockey Card Price Guide and Alpahabetical Checklist*, and *Beckett Racing Card and Die Cast Price Guide*. The aim of these annual guides is to provide information and accurate pricing on a wide array of sports cards, ranging from main issues by the major card manufacturers to various regional, promotional, and food issues. Also, alphabetical checklists, such as *Beckett Basketball Card Alphabetical Checklist #1*, are published to assist the collector in identifying all the cards of a particular player. The seasoned collector will find these tools valuable sources of information that will enable him/her to pursue his/her hobby interests.

In addition, abridged editions of the Beckett Price Guides have been published for each of three major sports as part of the House of Collectibles series: *The Official Price Guide to Baseball Cards, The Official Price Guide to Football Cards*, and *The Official Price Guide to Basketball Cards*. Published in a convenient mass-market paperback format, these price guides provide information and accurate pricing on all the main issues by the major card manufacturers.

Prices in This Guide

Prices found in this guide reflect current retail rates just prior to the printing of this book. They do not reflect the FOR SALE prices of the author, the publisher, the distributors, the advertisers, or any card dealers associated with this guide. No one is obligated in any way to buy, sell, or trade his or her cards based on these prices. The price listings were compiled by the author from actual buy/sell transactions at sports conventions, sports card shops, buy/sell advertisements in the hobby papers, for-sale prices from dealer catalogs and price lists, and discussions with leading hobbyists in the U.S. and Canada. All prices are in U.S. dollars.

Acknowledgments

A great deal of diligence, hard work, and dedicated effort went into this year's volume. The high standards to which we hold ourselves, however, could not have been met without the expert input and generous amount of time contributed by many people. Our sincere thanks are extended to each and every one of them.

A complete list of these invaluable contributors appears after the price guide.

1998-99 Black Diamond

	Nm-Mt	Ex-Mt
COMPLETE SET (120)	80.00	24.00
COMPLETE SET w/o RC (90)	40.00	12.00
COMMON MJ (1-13/22)	3.00	.90
COMMON CARD (14-90)	.30	.09
COMMON ROOKIE (91-120)	.50	.15
❑ 1 Michael Jordan	3.00	.90
❑ 2 Michael Jordan	3.00	.90
❑ 3 Michael Jordan	3.00	.90
❑ 4 Michael Jordan	3.00	.90
❑ 5 Michael Jordan	3.00	.90
❑ 6 Michael Jordan	3.00	.90
❑ 7 Michael Jordan	3.00	.90
❑ 8 Michael Jordan	3.00	.90
❑ 9 Michael Jordan	3.00	.90
❑ 10 Michael Jordan	3.00	.90
❑ 11 Michael Jordan	3.00	.90
❑ 12 Michael Jordan	3.00	.90
❑ 13 Michael Jordan	3.00	.90
❑ 14 Dikembe Mutombo	.60	.18
❑ 15 Steve Smith	.60	.18
❑ 16 Mookie Blaylock	.30	.09
❑ 17 Antoine Walker	1.00	.30
❑ 18 Kenny Anderson	.60	.18
❑ 19 Ron Mercer	.60	.18
❑ 20 Glen Rice	.60	.18
❑ 21 Derrick Coleman	.30	.09
❑ 22 Michael Jordan	3.00	.90
❑ 23 Toni Kukoc	.60	.18
❑ 24 Brent Barry	.60	.18
❑ 25 Brevin Knight	.30	.09
❑ 26 Derek Anderson	1.00	.30
❑ 27 Shawn Kemp	.60	.18
❑ 28 Shawn Bradley	.30	.09
❑ 29 Michael Finley	1.00	.30
❑ 30 Nick Van Exel	1.00	.30
❑ 31 Chauncey Billups	.60	.18
❑ 32 Antonio McDyess	.60	.18
❑ 33 Grant Hill	1.00	.30
❑ 34 Jerry Stackhouse	1.00	.30
❑ 35 Bison Dele	.30	.09
❑ 36 John Starks	.60	.18
❑ 37 Chris Mills	.30	.09
❑ 38 Scottie Pippen	1.50	.45
❑ 39 Hakeem Olajuwon	1.00	.30
❑ 40 Charles Barkley	1.25	.35
❑ 41 Antonio Davis	.30	.09
❑ 42 Reggie Miller	1.00	.30
❑ 43 Mark Jackson	.60	.18
❑ 44 Eddie Jones	1.00	.30
❑ 45 Shaquille O'Neal	2.50	.75
❑ 46 Kobe Bryant	4.00	1.20
❑ 47 Rodney Rogers	.30	.09
❑ 48 Maurice Taylor	.60	.18
❑ 49 Tim Hardaway	.60	.18
❑ 50 Jamal Mashburn	.60	.18
❑ 51 Alonzo Mourning	.60	.18
❑ 52 Ray Allen	1.00	.30
❑ 53 Terrell Brandon	.60	.18
❑ 54 Glenn Robinson	.60	.18
❑ 55 Joe Smith	.60	.18
❑ 56 Stephon Marbury	1.00	.30
❑ 57 Kevin Garnett	2.00	.60
❑ 58 Kerry Kittles	.30	.09
❑ 59 Jayson Williams	.30	.09
❑ 60 Keith Van Horn	1.00	.30
❑ 61 Patrick Ewing	1.00	.30
❑ 62 Allan Houston	.60	.18
❑ 63 Latrell Sprewell	1.00	.30
❑ 64 Anfernee Hardaway	1.00	.30
❑ 65 Horace Grant	.60	.18
❑ 66 Allen Iverson	2.00	.60
❑ 67 Tim Thomas	.60	.18
❑ 68 Jason Kidd	1.50	.45
❑ 69 Danny Manning	.30	.09
❑ 70 Tom Gugliotta	.30	.09
❑ 71 Damon Stoudamire	.60	.18
❑ 72 Rasheed Wallace	1.00	.30
❑ 73 Isaiah Rider	.30	.09
❑ 74 Corliss Williamson	.60	.18
❑ 75 Chris Webber	1.00	.30
❑ 76 Tim Duncan	1.50	.45
❑ 77 David Robinson	1.00	.30
❑ 78 Sean Elliott	.60	.18
❑ 79 Gary Payton	1.00	.30
❑ 80 Vin Baker	.60	.18
❑ 81 John Wallace	.30	.09
❑ 82 Tracy McGrady	2.50	.75
❑ 83 Jeff Hornacek	.60	.18
❑ 84 Karl Malone	1.00	.30
❑ 85 John Stockton	1.00	.30
❑ 86 Bryant Reeves	.30	.09
❑ 87 Shareef Abdur-Rahim	1.00	.30
❑ 88 Rod Strickland	.30	.09
❑ 89 Juwan Howard	.60	.18
❑ 90 Mitch Richmond	.60	.18
❑ 91 Michael Olowokandi RC	2.00	.60
❑ 92 Dirk Nowitzki RC	12.00	3.60
❑ 93 Raef LaFrentz RC	2.00	.60
❑ 94 Mike Bibby RC	6.00	1.80
❑ 95 Ricky Davis RC	4.00	1.20
❑ 96 Jason Williams RC	5.00	1.50
❑ 97 Al Harrington RC	3.00	.90
❑ 98 Bonzi Wells RC	5.00	1.50
❑ 99 Keon Clark RC	2.00	.60
❑ 100 Rashard Lewis RC	5.00	1.50
❑ 101 Paul Pierce RC	6.00	1.80
❑ 102 Antawn Jamison RC	6.00	1.80
❑ 103 Nazr Mohammed RC	.60	.18
❑ 104 Brian Skinner RC	1.25	.35
❑ 105 Corey Benjamin RC	1.25	.35
❑ 106 Peja Stojakovic RC	5.00	1.50
❑ 107 Bryce Drew RC	1.25	.35
❑ 108 Matt Harpring RC	2.50	.75
❑ 109 Toby Bailey RC	.50	.15
❑ 110 Tyronn Lue RC	1.50	.45
❑ 111 Michael Dickerson RC	2.50	.75
❑ 112 Roshown McLeod RC	.60	.18
❑ 113 Felipe Lopez RC	1.50	.45
❑ 114 Michael Doleac RC	1.25	.35
❑ 115 Ruben Patterson RC	2.50	.75
❑ 116 Robert Traylor RC	1.25	.35
❑ 117 Sam Jacobson RC	.50	.15
❑ 118 Larry Hughes RC	4.00	1.20
❑ 119 Pat Garrity RC	.60	.18
❑ 120 Vince Carter RC	15.00	4.50

1999-00 Black Diamond

	Nm-Mt	Ex-Mt
COMPLETE SET (120)	50.00	15.00
COMPLETE SET w/o RC (90)	25.00	7.50
COMMON CARD (1-90)	.25	.07
COMMON ROOKIE (91-120)	.50	.15
❑ 1 Dikembe Mutombo	.50	.15
❑ 2 Alan Henderson	.25	.07
❑ 3 Roshown McLeod	.25	.07
❑ 4 Kenny Anderson	.50	.15
❑ 5 Paul Pierce	1.00	.30
❑ 6 Antoine Walker	.75	.23
❑ 7 Eddie Jones	.75	.23
❑ 8 Elden Campbell	.25	.07
❑ 9 David Wesley	.25	.07
❑ 10 Toni Kukoc	.50	.15
❑ 11 Randy Brown	.25	.07
❑ 12 Dickey Simpkins	.25	.07
❑ 13 Shawn Kemp	.50	.15
❑ 14 Zydrunas Ilgauskas	.50	.15
❑ 15 Brevin Knight	.25	.07
❑ 16 Michael Finley	.75	.23
❑ 17 Dirk Nowitzki	1.50	.45
❑ 18 Robert Pack	.25	.07
❑ 19 Antonio McDyess	.50	.15
❑ 20 Nick Van Exel	.75	.23
❑ 21 Ron Mercer	.50	.15
❑ 22 Grant Hill	.75	.23
❑ 23 Lindsey Hunter	.25	.07
❑ 24 Jerry Stackhouse	.75	.23
❑ 25 Antawn Jamison	1.25	.35
❑ 26 John Starks	.50	.15
❑ 27 Donyell Marshall	.50	.15
❑ 28 Hakeem Olajuwon	.75	.23
❑ 29 Charles Barkley	1.00	.30
❑ 30 Cuttino Mobley	.75	.23
❑ 31 Reggie Miller	.75	.23
❑ 32 Rik Smits	.50	.15
❑ 33 Jalen Rose	.75	.23
❑ 34 Maurice Taylor	.50	.15
❑ 35 Tyrone Nesby RC	.25	.07
❑ 36 Michael Olowokandi	.50	.15
❑ 37 Shaquille O'Neal	2.00	.60
❑ 38 Kobe Bryant	3.00	.90
❑ 39 Glen Rice	.50	.15
❑ 40 P.J. Brown	.25	.07
❑ 41 Tim Hardaway	.50	.15
❑ 42 Alonzo Mourning	.50	.15
❑ 43 Jamal Mashburn	.50	.15
❑ 44 Glenn Robinson	.75	.23
❑ 45 Ray Allen	.75	.23
❑ 46 Tim Thomas	.50	.15
❑ 47 Kevin Garnett	1.50	.45
❑ 48 Joe Smith	.50	.15
❑ 49 Terrell Brandon	.50	.15
❑ 50 Stephon Marbury	.75	.23
❑ 51 Jayson Williams	.25	.07
❑ 52 Keith Van Horn	.75	.23
❑ 53 Latrell Sprewell	.75	.23
❑ 54 Allan Houston	.50	.15
❑ 55 Patrick Ewing	.75	.23
❑ 56 Marcus Camby	.50	.15
❑ 57 Darrell Armstrong	.25	.07
❑ 58 Bo Outlaw	.25	.07
❑ 59 Michael Doleac	.25	.07
❑ 60 Allen Iverson	1.50	.45
❑ 61 Theo Ratliff	.50	.15
❑ 62 Larry Hughes	.75	.23
❑ 63 Anfernee Hardaway	.75	.23
❑ 64 Jason Kidd	1.25	.35
❑ 65 Tom Gugliotta	.25	.07
❑ 66 Brian Grant	.50	.15
❑ 67 Damon Stoudamire	.50	.15
❑ 68 Rasheed Wallace	.75	.23
❑ 69 Jason Williams	.75	.23
❑ 70 Chris Webber	.75	.23
❑ 71 Vlade Divac	.50	.15
❑ 72 Tim Duncan	1.50	.45
❑ 73 David Robinson	.75	.23
❑ 74 Avery Johnson	.25	.07
❑ 75 Sean Elliott	.50	.15
❑ 76 Gary Payton	.75	.23
❑ 77 Vin Baker	.50	.15
❑ 78 Brent Barry	.50	.15
❑ 79 Vince Carter	2.00	.60
❑ 80 Tracy McGrady	2.00	.60
❑ 81 Doug Christie	.50	.15
❑ 82 Karl Malone	.75	.23
❑ 83 John Stockton	.75	.23
❑ 84 Bryon Russell	.25	.07
❑ 85 Shareef Abdur-Rahim	.75	.23
❑ 86 Mike Bibby	.75	.23
❑ 87 Felipe Lopez	.25	.07

❑ 88	Juwan Howard	.50	.15
❑ 89	Rod Strickland	.25	.07
❑ 90	Mitch Richmond	.50	.15
❑ 91	Elton Brand RC	3.00	.90
❑ 92	Steve Francis RC	4.00	1.20
❑ 93	Baron Davis RC	2.50	.75
❑ 94	Lamar Odom RC	2.50	.75
❑ 95	Jonathan Bender RC	2.50	.75
❑ 96	Wally Szczerbiak RC	2.50	.75
❑ 97	Richard Hamilton RC	2.50	.75
❑ 98	Andre Miller RC	2.50	.75
❑ 99	Shawn Marion RC	3.00	.90
❑ 100	Jason Terry RC	1.50	.45
❑ 101	Trajan Langdon RC	1.00	.30
❑ 102	Aleksandar Radojevic RC	.50	.15
❑ 103	Corey Maggette RC	2.50	.75
❑ 104	William Avery RC	1.00	.30
❑ 105	Ron Artest RC	1.50	.45
❑ 106	Adrian Griffin RC	.75	.23
❑ 107	James Posey RC	1.50	.45
❑ 108	Quincy Lewis RC	.75	.23
❑ 109	Dion Glover RC	.75	.23
❑ 110	Jeff Foster RC	.75	.23
❑ 111	Kenny Thomas RC	1.00	.30
❑ 112	Devean George RC	1.25	.35
❑ 113	Tim James RC	.75	.23
❑ 114	Vonteego Cummings RC	1.00	.30
❑ 115	Jumaine Jones RC	1.25	.35
❑ 116	Scott Padgett RC	.75	.23
❑ 117	Obinna Ekezie RC	.60	.18
❑ 118	Ryan Robertson RC	.60	.18
❑ 119	Chucky Atkins RC	1.00	.30
❑ 120	A.J. Bramlett RC	.50	.15

2000-01 Black Diamond

	Nm-Mt	Ex-Mt
COMP.SET w/o SP's (90)	20.00	6.00
COMMON CARD (1-90)	.25	.07
COMMON GEM (91-100)	3.00	.90
COMMON GEM (101-110)	4.00	1.20
COMMON GEM (111-120)	4.00	1.20
COMMON JSY (121-126)	12.00	3.60
COMMON JSY (127-132)	15.00	4.50

❑ 1	Dikembe Mutombo	.50	.15
❑ 2	Alan Henderson	.25	.07
❑ 3	Jason Terry	.75	.23
❑ 4	Paul Pierce	.75	.23
❑ 5	Antoine Walker	.75	.23
❑ 6	Kenny Anderson	.50	.15
❑ 7	Jamal Mashburn	.50	.15
❑ 8	Derrick Coleman	.25	.07
❑ 9	Baron Davis	.75	.23
❑ 10	Elton Brand	.75	.23
❑ 11	Ron Artest	.50	.15
❑ 12	Ron Mercer	.50	.15
❑ 13	Lamond Murray	.25	.07
❑ 14	Andre Miller	.50	.15
❑ 15	Matt Harpring	.75	.23
❑ 16	Michael Finley	.75	.23
❑ 17	Dirk Nowitzki	1.25	.35
❑ 18	Steve Nash	.75	.23
❑ 19	Antonio McDyess	.50	.15
❑ 20	Nick Van Exel	.75	.23
❑ 21	Raef LaFrentz	.50	.15
❑ 22	Jerry Stackhouse	.75	.23
❑ 23	Joe Smith	.50	.15
❑ 24	Chucky Atkins	.25	.07
❑ 25	Antawn Jamison	.75	.23
❑ 26	Larry Hughes	.50	.15
❑ 27	Chris Mills	.25	.07
❑ 28	Steve Francis	.75	.23
❑ 29	Hakeem Olajuwon	.75	.23
❑ 30	Cuttino Mobley	.50	.15
❑ 31	Reggie Miller	.75	.23
❑ 32	Jalen Rose	.75	.23
❑ 33	Jermaine O'Neal	.75	.23
❑ 34	Austin Croshere	.50	.15
❑ 35	Lamar Odom	.75	.23
❑ 36	Corey Maggette	.50	.15
❑ 37	Jeff McInnis	.25	.07
❑ 38	Kobe Bryant	3.00	.90
❑ 39	Shaquille O'Neal	2.00	.60
❑ 40	Ron Harper	.50	.15
❑ 41	Isaiah Rider	.50	.15
❑ 42	Eddie Jones	.75	.23
❑ 43	Tim Hardaway	.50	.15
❑ 44	Brian Grant	.50	.15
❑ 45	Glenn Robinson	.50	.15
❑ 46	Sam Cassell	.75	.23
❑ 47	Ray Allen	.75	.23
❑ 48	Kevin Garnett	1.50	.45
❑ 49	Terrell Brandon	.50	.15
❑ 50	Wally Szczerbiak	.50	.15
❑ 51	Stephon Marbury	.75	.23
❑ 52	Keith Van Horn	.75	.23
❑ 53	Kendall Gill	.25	.07
❑ 54	Latrell Sprewell	.75	.23
❑ 55	Allan Houston	.50	.15
❑ 56	Marcus Camby	.50	.15
❑ 57	Grant Hill	.75	.23
❑ 58	Tracy McGrady	2.00	.60
❑ 59	Darrell Armstrong	.25	.07
❑ 60	Allen Iverson	1.50	.45
❑ 61	Toni Kukoc	.50	.15
❑ 62	Theo Ratliff	.50	.15
❑ 63	Jason Kidd	1.25	.35
❑ 64	Shawn Marion	.75	.23
❑ 65	Anfernee Hardaway	.75	.23
❑ 66	Scottie Pippen	1.25	.35
❑ 67	Rasheed Wallace	.75	.23
❑ 68	Damon Stoudamire	.50	.15
❑ 69	Steve Smith	.50	.15
❑ 70	Chris Webber	.75	.23
❑ 71	Jason Williams	.50	.15
❑ 72	Peja Stojakovic	.75	.23
❑ 73	Tim Duncan	1.50	.45
❑ 74	David Robinson	.75	.23
❑ 75	Derek Anderson	.50	.15
❑ 76	Gary Payton	.75	.23
❑ 77	Patrick Ewing	.75	.23
❑ 78	Rashard Lewis	.50	.15
❑ 79	Vince Carter	2.00	.60
❑ 80	Mark Jackson	.25	.07
❑ 81	Antonio Davis	.25	.07
❑ 82	Karl Malone	.75	.23
❑ 83	John Stockton	.75	.23
❑ 84	Bryon Russell	.25	.07
❑ 85	Shareef Abdur-Rahim	.75	.23
❑ 86	Michael Dickerson	.50	.15
❑ 87	Mike Bibby	.75	.23
❑ 88	Mitch Richmond	.50	.15
❑ 89	Richard Hamilton	.50	.15
❑ 90	Juwan Howard	.50	.15
❑ 91	Eduardo Najera RC	4.00	1.20
❑ 92	Eddie House RC	3.00	.90
❑ 93	Michael Redd RC	5.00	1.50
❑ 94	Ruben Wolkowyski RC	3.00	.90
❑ 95	Dan Langhi RC	3.00	.90
❑ 96	Mark Madsen RC	3.00	.90
❑ 97	Speedy Claxton RC	3.00	.90
❑ 98	Iakovos Tsakalidis RC	3.00	.90
❑ 99	Dragan Tarlac RC	3.00	.90
❑ 100	Donnell Harvey RC	3.00	.90
❑ 101	Etan Thomas RC	4.00	1.20
❑ 102	Hidayet Turkoglu RC	6.00	1.80
❑ 103	Mike Penberthy RC	4.00	1.20
❑ 104	Paul McPherson RC	4.00	1.20
❑ 105	Jason Collier RC	4.00	1.20
❑ 106	Hanno Mottola RC	4.00	1.20
❑ 107	A.J. Guyton RC	4.00	1.20
❑ 108	Daniel Santiago RC	4.00	1.20
❑ 109	Lavor Postell RC	4.00	1.20
❑ 110	Erick Barkley RC	4.00	1.20
❑ 111	Chris Porter RC	4.00	1.20
❑ 112	Mateen Cleaves RC	4.00	1.20
❑ 113	Marc Jackson RC	4.00	1.20
❑ 114	Joel Przybilla RC	4.00	1.20
❑ 115	Courtney Alexander RC	4.00	1.20
❑ 116	Khalid El-Amin RC	4.00	1.20
❑ 117	Keyon Dooling RC	4.00	1.20
❑ 118	Desmond Mason RC	4.00	1.20
❑ 119	Stephen Jackson RC	5.00	1.50
❑ 120	Morris Peterson RC	6.00	1.80
❑ 121	Jerome Moiso JSY RC	12.00	3.60
❑ 122	Jamal Crawford JSY RC	15.00	4.50
❑ 123	D.Stevenson JSY RC	12.00	3.60
❑ 124	Q.Richardson JSY RC	15.00	4.50
❑ 125	Marcus Fizer JSY RC	12.00	3.60
❑ 126	Mike Miller JSY RC	15.00	4.50
❑ 127	Jamaal Magloire JSY RC	15.00	4.50
❑ 128	Chris Mihm JSY RC	15.00	4.50
❑ 129	DerMarr Johnson JSY RC	15.00	4.50
❑ 130	Stromile Swift JSY RC	15.00	4.50
❑ 131	Darius Miles JSY RC	15.00	4.50
❑ 132	Kenyon Martin JSY RC	25.00	7.50

2003-04 Black Diamond

	MINT	NRMT
COMMON CARD (1-84)	.20	.09
COMMON CARD (85-117)	.25	.11
COMMON ROOKIE (118-126)	4.00	1.80
COMMON CARD (127-147)	2.00	.90
COMMON ROOKIE (148-168)	5.00	2.20
COMMON CARD (169-183)	8.00	3.60
COMMON ROOKIE (184-198)	12.00	5.50
KORVER AND KITTLES HAVE 2 CARDS		-

❑ 1	Carlos Boozer	.60	.25
❑ 2	Dajuan Wagner	.40	.18
❑ 3	Steve Francis	.60	.25
❑ 4	Michael Finley	.60	.25
❑ 5	Jalen Rose	.60	.25
❑ 6	Kenyon Martin	.60	.25
❑ 7	Quentin Richardson	.40	.18
❑ 8	Antoine Walker	.60	.25
❑ 9	Drew Gooden	.40	.18
❑ 10	Mike Bibby	.60	.25
❑ 11	Zydrunas Ilgauskas	.40	.18
❑ 12	Dan Dickau	.20	.09
❑ 13	Steve Nash	.60	.25
❑ 14	Eduardo Najera	.40	.18
❑ 15	Joe Smith	.40	.18
❑ 16	Pau Gasol	.60	.25
❑ 17	Anthony Mason	.20	.09
❑ 18	Lamar Odom	.60	.25
❑ 19	Sam Cassell	.60	.25
❑ 20	Marko Jaric	.40	.18
❑ 21	Marcus Fizer	.40	.18
❑ 22	Jay Williams	.40	.18
❑ 23	Jason Richardson	.60	.25
❑ 24	Richard Jefferson	.40	.18
❑ 25	Gerald Wallace	.40	.18
❑ 26	Reggie Evans	.20	.09
❑ 27	Jerome Williams	.20	.09
❑ 28	Grant Hill	.60	.25
❑ 29	Darrell Armstrong	.20	.09
❑ 30	Rasheed Wallace	.60	.25
❑ 31	Shane Battier	.60	.25
❑ 32	Richard Hamilton	.40	.18
❑ 33	Antonio Davis	.20	.09
❑ 34	Ray Allen	.60	.25
❑ 35	Terrell Brandon	.20	.09
❑ 36	Tim Thomas	.40	.18

❑ 37 Al Harrington .40 .18
❑ 38 Brian Grant .40 .18
❑ 39 Zeljko Rebraca .20 .09
❑ 40 Kerry Kittles .20 .09
❑ 41 Maurice Taylor .20 .09
❑ 42 Jerry Stackhouse .60 .25
❑ 43 Nikoloz Tskitishvili .40 .18
❑ 44 Derrick Coleman .20 .09
❑ 45 Raef LaFrentz .40 .18
❑ 46 Dale Davis .40 .18
❑ 47 Andrei Kirilenko .60 .25
❑ 48 Melvin Ely .20 .09
❑ 49 Speedy Claxton .20 .09
❑ 50 Mike Miller .60 .25
❑ 51 Scot Pollard .20 .09
❑ 52 Popeye Jones .20 .09
❑ 53 Wesley Person .20 .09
❑ 54 Chris Wilcox .40 .18
❑ 55 Dikembe Mutombo .40 .18
❑ 56 Toni Kukoc .40 .18
❑ 57 Eddie Griffin .40 .18
❑ 58 Kedrick Brown .20 .09
❑ 59 Eddie Jones .60 .25
❑ 60 Jon Barry .20 .09
❑ 61 Jonathan Bender .40 .18
❑ 62 Larry Hughes .40 .18
❑ 63 Rodney White .20 .09
❑ 64 Eddy Curry .40 .18
❑ 65 Theo Ratliff .40 .18
❑ 66 Jamaal Tinsley .60 .25
❑ 67 Zach Randolph .60 .25
❑ 68 Alvin Williams .20 .09
❑ 69 Derek Fisher .60 .25
❑ 70 Vin Baker .40 .18
❑ 71 Juan Dixon .40 .18
❑ 72 Devean George .40 .18
❑ 73 Damon Stoudamire .40 .18
❑ 74 Joe Johnson .20 .09
❑ 75 Jared Jeffries .20 .09
❑ 76 Cuttino Mobley .40 .18
❑ 77 Vladimir Radmanovic .20 .09
❑ 78 Ron Mercer .20 .09
❑ 79 Kenny Thomas .20 .09
❑ 80 Nazr Mohammed .20 .09
❑ 81 Donyell Marshall .60 .25
❑ 82 Lorenzen Wright .20 .09
❑ 83 Nick Van Exel .60 .25
❑ 84 Jason Terry .60 .25
❑ 85 Ben Wallace 1.00 .45
❑ 86 Glenn Robinson 1.00 .45
❑ 87 Gilbert Arenas 1.00 .45
❑ 88 Caron Butler 1.00 .45
❑ 89 Marcus Camby .40 .18
❑ 90 Jason Kidd 1.50 .70
❑ 91 Antawn Jamison 1.00 .45
❑ 92 Rashard Lewis 1.00 .45
❑ 93 Juwan Howard .60 .25
❑ 94 Andre Miller .60 .25
❑ 95 Hedo Turkoglu 1.00 .45
❑ 96 Jason Williams .60 .25
❑ 97 Chauncey Billups .60 .25
❑ 98 P.J. Brown .25 .11
❑ 99 Tyson Chandler 1.00 .45
❑ 100 Jamal Mashburn .60 .25
❑ 101 Bonzi Wells .60 .25
❑ 102 Brad Miller 1.00 .45
❑ 103 Gordan Giricek .60 .25
❑ 104 Nene .60 .25
❑ 105 Mike Dunleavy .60 .25
❑ 106 Kerry Kittles .25 .11
❑ 107 Jamaal Magloire .25 .11
❑ 108 Desmond Mason .60 .25
❑ 109 Corey Maggette .60 .25
❑ 110 Michael Olowokandi .25 .11
❑ 111 Tayshaun Prince .60 .25
❑ 112 Earl Boykins .60 .25
❑ 113 Allan Houston .60 .25
❑ 114 Morris Peterson .60 .25
❑ 115 Ricky Davis 1.00 .45
❑ 116 Keith Van Horn 1.00 .45
❑ 117 Shareef Abdur-Rahim 1.00 .45
❑ 118 Willie Green RC 4.00 1.80
❑ 119 Kyle Korver RC 5.00 2.20
❑ 120 Brandon Hunter RC 4.00 1.80
❑ 121 Keith Bogans RC 4.00 1.80
❑ 122 Maurice Williams RC 4.00 1.80
❑ 123 James Lang RC 4.00 1.80
❑ 124 Zaur Pachulia RC 4.00 1.80
❑ 125 Slavko Vranes RC 4.00 1.80
❑ 126 Theron Smith RC 4.00 1.80
❑ 127 Paul Pierce 2.00 .90
❑ 128 Alonzo Mourning 2.00 .90
❑ 129 Elton Brand 2.00 .90
❑ 130 Manu Ginobili 2.00 .90
❑ 131 Peja Stojakovic 2.00 .90
❑ 132 Latrell Sprewell 2.00 .90
❑ 133 Baron Davis 2.00 .90
❑ 134 Stephon Marbury 2.00 .90
❑ 135 Darius Miles 2.00 .90
❑ 136 Antonio McDyess 2.00 .90
❑ 137 Jermaine O'Neal 2.00 .90
❑ 138 Scottie Pippen 3.00 1.35
❑ 139 Wally Szczerbiak 2.00 .90
❑ 140 Chris Webber 2.00 .90
❑ 141 Reggie Miller 2.00 .90
❑ 142 Tony Parker 2.00 .90
❑ 143 Karl Malone 2.00 .90
❑ 144 David Robinson 2.00 .90
❑ 145 Matt Harpring 2.00 .90
❑ 146 Shawn Marion 2.00 .90
❑ 147 Tim Duncan 4.00 1.80
❑ 148 Dwyane Wade RC 12.00 5.50
❑ 149 Chris Kaman RC 5.00 2.20
❑ 150 Chris Bosh RC 10.00 4.50
❑ 151 Mickael Pietrus RC 5.00 2.20
❑ 152 Boris Diaw RC 5.00 2.20
❑ 153 Marcus Banks RC 5.00 2.20
❑ 154 Troy Bell RC 5.00 2.20
❑ 155 Zarko Cabarkapa RC 5.00 2.20
❑ 156 David West RC 5.00 2.20
❑ 157 Zoran Planinic RC 5.00 2.20
❑ 158 Aleksandar Pavlovic RC 5.00 2.20
❑ 159 Jerome Beasley RC 5.00 2.20
❑ 160 Kyle Korver 5.00 2.20
❑ 161 Travis Hansen RC 5.00 2.20
❑ 162 Steve Blake RC 5.00 2.20
❑ 163 Leandro Barbosa RC 5.00 2.20
❑ 164 Kendrick Perkins RC 5.00 2.20
❑ 165 Kirk Penney RC 5.00 2.20
❑ 166 Maciej Lampe RC 5.00 2.20
❑ 167 Jason Kapono RC 5.00 2.20
❑ 168 Luke Walton RC 6.00 2.70
❑ 169 Gary Payton 8.00 3.60
❑ 170 Wilt Chamberlain 10.00 4.50
❑ 171 Tracy McGrady 10.00 4.50
❑ 172 Amare Stoudemire 8.00 3.60
❑ 173 Vince Carter 10.00 4.50
❑ 174 Shaquille O'Neal 10.00 4.50
❑ 175 Larry Bird 20.00 9.00
❑ 176 Julius Erving 10.00 4.50
❑ 177 Magic Johnson 10.00 4.50
❑ 178 Dirk Nowitzki 8.00 3.60
❑ 179 Yao Ming 10.00 4.50
❑ 180 Allen Iverson 10.00 4.50
❑ 181 Kevin Garnett 10.00 4.50
❑ 182 Kobe Bryant 15.00 6.75
❑ 183 Michael Jordan 25.00 11.00
❑ 184 LeBron James RC 100.00 45.00
❑ 185 Darko Milicic RC 12.00 5.50
❑ 186 Carmelo Anthony RC 60.00 27.00
❑ 187 T.J. Ford RC 12.00 5.50
❑ 188 Mike Sweetney RC 12.00 5.50
❑ 189 Kirk Hinrich RC 15.00 6.75
❑ 190 Nick Collison RC 12.00 5.50
❑ 191 Travis Outlaw RC 12.00 5.50
❑ 192 Jarvis Hayes RC 12.00 5.50
❑ 193 Luke Ridnour RC 12.00 5.50
❑ 194 Reece Gaines RC 12.00 5.50
❑ 195 Ndudi Ebi RC 12.00 5.50
❑ 196 Dahntay Jones RC 12.00 5.50
❑ 197 Brian Cook RC 12.00 5.50
❑ 198 Josh Howard RC 15.00 6.75

1948 Bowman

	Ex-Mt	VG
COMPLETE SET (72)	8,000.00	4,000.00
COMMON CARD (1-36)	60.00	30.00
COMMON CARD (37-72)	90.00	45.00

❑ 1 Ernie Calverley RC 175.00 52.50
❑ 2 Ralph Hamilton 60.00 30.00
❑ 3 Gale Bishop 60.00 30.00
❑ 4 Fred Lewis CO RC 75.00 38.00
❑ 5 Basketball Play 50.00 25.00
Single cut off post
❑ 6 Bob Ferrick RC 75.00 38.00
❑ 7 John Logan 60.00 30.00
❑ 8 Mel Riebe 60.00 30.00
❑ 9 Andy Phillip RC 125.00 60.00
❑ 10 Bob Davies RC 125.00 60.00
❑ 11 Basketball Play 50.00 25.00
Single cut with return pass to post
❑ 12 Kenny Sailors RC 75.00 38.00
❑ 13 Paul Armstrong 60.00 30.00
❑ 14 Howard Dallmar RC 75.00 38.00
❑ 15 Bruce Hale RC 75.00 38.00
❑ 16 Sid Hertzberg 75.00 38.00
❑ 17 Basketball Play 50.00 25.00
Single cut
❑ 18 Red Rocha 60.00 30.00
❑ 19 Eddie Ehlers 60.00 30.00
❑ 20 Ellis(Gene) Vance 60.00 30.00
❑ 21 Andrew(Fuzzy) Levane RC 75.00 38.00
❑ 22 Earl Shannon 60.00 30.00
❑ 23 Basketball Play 50.00 25.00
Double cut off post
❑ 24 Leo(Crystal) Klier 60.00 30.00
❑ 25 George Senesky 60.00 30.00
❑ 26 Price Brookfield 60.00 30.00
❑ 27 John Norlander 60.00 30.00
❑ 28 Don Putman 60.00 30.00
❑ 29 Basketball Play 50.00 25.00
Double post
❑ 30 Jack Garfinkel 60.00 30.00
❑ 31 Chuck Gilmur 60.00 30.00
❑ 32 Red Holzman RC 225.00 110.00
❑ 33 Jack Smiley 60.00 30.00
❑ 34 Joe Fulks RC 150.00 75.00
❑ 35 Basketball Play 50.00 25.00
Screen play
❑ 36 Hal Tidrick 60.00 30.00
❑ 37 Don(Swede) Carlson 90.00 45.00
❑ 38 Buddy Jeanette RC CO 135.00 70.00
❑ 39 Ray Kuka 90.00 45.00
❑ 40 Stan Miasek 90.00 45.00
❑ 41 Basketball Play 75.00 38.00
Double screen
❑ 42 George Nostrand 90.00 45.00
❑ 43 Chuck Halbert RC 125.00 60.00
❑ 44 Arnie Johnson 90.00 45.00
❑ 45 Bob Doll 90.00 45.00
❑ 46 Horace McKinney RC 135.00 70.00
❑ 47 Basketball Play 75.00 38.00
Out of bounds
❑ 48 Ed Sadowski 125.00 60.00
❑ 49 Bob Kinney 90.00 45.00
❑ 50 Charles(Hawk) Black 90.00 45.00
❑ 51 Jack Dwan 75.00 38.00
❑ 52 Cornelius Simmons RC 125.00 60.00
❑ 53 Basketball Play 75.00 38.00
Out of bounds
❑ 54 Bud Palmer RC 150.00 75.00
❑ 55 Max Zaslofsky RC 200.00 100.00
❑ 56 Lee Roy Robbins 90.00 45.00
❑ 57 Arthur Spector 90.00 45.00
❑ 58 Arnie Risen RC 150.00 75.00
❑ 59 Basketball Play 75.00 38.00
Out of bounds play
❑ 60 Ariel Maughan 90.00 45.00
❑ 61 Dick O'Keefe 90.00 45.00
❑ 62 Herman Schaefer 90.00 45.00

Card		
❑ 63 John Mahnken	90.00	45.00
❑ 64 Tommy Byrnes	90.00	45.00
❑ 65 Basketball Play Held ball	75.00	38.00
❑ 66 Jim Pollard RC	300.00	150.00
❑ 67 Lee Mogus	90.00	45.00
❑ 68 Lee Knorek	90.00	45.00
❑ 69 George Mikan RC	2,500.00	1,250.00
❑ 70 Walter Budko	90.00	45.00
❑ 71 Basketball Play Guards Play	75.00	38.00
❑ 72 Carl Braun RC	450.00	135.00

2003-04 Bowman

	MINT	NRMT
COMP.SET w/o RC's (110)	40.00	18.00
COMMON CARD (1-110)	.20	.09
COMMON ROOKIE (111-146)	4.00	1.80
COMMON AU RC (148-156)	20.00	9.00
CARD 147 NOT RELEASED	-	
❑ 1 Yao Ming	2.00	.90
❑ 2 Glenn Robinson	.75	.35
❑ 3 Antoine Walker	.75	.35
❑ 4 Jalen Rose	.75	.35
❑ 5 Ricky Davis	.75	.35
❑ 6 Juwan Howard	.50	.23
❑ 7 Kwame Brown	.50	.23
❑ 8 Mike Bibby	.75	.35
❑ 9 Wally Szczerbiak	.50	.23
❑ 10 Allen Iverson	1.50	.70
❑ 11 Shareef Abdur-Rahim	.75	.35
❑ 12 Jamal Mashburn	.50	.23
❑ 13 Stephon Marbury	.75	.35
❑ 14 Desmond Mason	.50	.23
❑ 15 Gordan Giricek	.50	.23
❑ 16 Caron Butler	.75	.35
❑ 17 Jermaine O'Neal	.75	.35
❑ 18 Kenyon Martin	.75	.35
❑ 19 Andrei Kirilenko	.75	.35
❑ 20 Dirk Nowitzki	1.25	.55
❑ 21 Richard Hamilton	.50	.23
❑ 22 Troy Murphy	.75	.35
❑ 23 Shawn Marion	.75	.35
❑ 24 Allan Houston	.50	.23
❑ 25 Keith Van Horn	.75	.35
❑ 26 Brian Grant	.50	.23
❑ 27 Mike Miller	.75	.35
❑ 28 Chris Webber	.75	.35
❑ 29 Brent Barry	.50	.23
❑ 30 Elton Brand	.75	.35
❑ 31 Juan Dixon	.50	.23
❑ 32 Karl Malone	.75	.35
❑ 33 Darrell Armstrong	.20	.09
❑ 34 Rasheed Wallace	.75	.35
❑ 35 Michael Redd	.75	.35
❑ 36 Rashard Lewis	.75	.35
❑ 37 Ron Artest	.50	.23
❑ 38 P.J. Brown	.20	.09
❑ 39 Eddie Griffin	.50	.23
❑ 40 Tim Duncan	1.50	.70
❑ 41 Kurt Thomas	.50	.23
❑ 42 Raef Lafrentz	.50	.23
❑ 43 Ben Wallace	.75	.35
❑ 44 Lamar Odom	.75	.35
❑ 45 Vince Carter	2.00	.90
❑ 46 Derek Anderson	.50	.23
❑ 47 Stromile Swift	.50	.23
❑ 48 Bobby Jackson	.50	.23
❑ 49 Richard Jefferson	.50	.23
❑ 50 Shaquille O'Neal	2.00	.90
❑ 51 Calbert Cheaney	.20	.09
❑ 52 Troy Hudson	.20	.09
❑ 53 Ray Allen	.75	.35
❑ 54 Howard Eisley	.20	.09
❑ 55 Alonzo Mourning	.50	.23
❑ 56 Sam Cassell	.75	.35
❑ 57 Derrick Coleman	.20	.09
❑ 58 Andre Miller	.50	.23
❑ 59 Antawn Jamison	.75	.35
❑ 60 Kevin Garnett	1.50	.70
❑ 61 Steve Francis	.75	.35
❑ 62 Tyson Chandler	.75	.35
❑ 63 Drew Gooden	.50	.23
❑ 64 Scottie Pippen	1.25	.55
❑ 65 Pau Gasol	.75	.35
❑ 66 Steve Nash	.75	.35
❑ 67 DaJuan Wagner	.50	.23
❑ 68 Jason Terry	.75	.35
❑ 69 Reggie Miller	.75	.35
❑ 70 Tracy McGrady	2.00	.90
❑ 71 Nene Hilario	.50	.23
❑ 72 Morris Peterson	.50	.23
❑ 73 Peja Stojakovic	.75	.35
❑ 74 Eddie Jones	.75	.35
❑ 75 Tony Parker	.75	.35
❑ 76 Corliss Williamson	.50	.23
❑ 77 Vladimir Radmanovic	.20	.09
❑ 78 Amare Stoudemire	1.50	.70
❑ 79 Tony Delk	.20	.09
❑ 80 Jason Kidd	1.25	.55
❑ 81 Gary Payton	.75	.35
❑ 82 Corey Maggette	.50	.23
❑ 83 Darius Miles	.75	.35
❑ 84 Cuttino Mobley	.50	.23
❑ 85 Eric Snow	.50	.23
❑ 86 Matt Harpring	.75	.35
❑ 87 Manu Ginobili	.75	.35
❑ 88 Latrell Sprewell	.75	.35
❑ 89 Alvin Williams	.20	.09
❑ 90 Paul Pierce	.75	.35
❑ 91 Anfernee Hardaway	.75	.35
❑ 92 Gilbert Arenas	.75	.35
❑ 93 Jerry Stackhouse	.75	.35
❑ 94 Tim Thomas	.50	.23
❑ 95 Nikoloz Tskitishvili	.20	.09
❑ 96 Doug Christie	.50	.23
❑ 97 Zydrunas Ilgauskas	.50	.23
❑ 98 Jamaal Tinsley	.75	.35
❑ 99 Theo Ratliff	.50	.23
❑ 100 Kobe Bryant	3.00	1.35
❑ 101 Chauncey Billups	.50	.23
❑ 102 Michael Finley	.75	.35
❑ 103 Jason Williams	.50	.23
❑ 104 Bonzi Wells	.50	.23
❑ 105 Voshon Lenard	.20	.09
❑ 106 Jason Richardson	.75	.35
❑ 107 Baron Davis	.75	.35
❑ 108 Radoslav Nesterovic	.50	.23
❑ 109 Eddy Curry	.50	.23
❑ 110 Michael Olowokandi	.20	.09
❑ 111 Josh Howard RC	5.00	2.20
❑ 112 Mario Austin RC	4.00	1.80
❑ 113 Rick Rickert RC	4.00	1.80
❑ 114 Tommy Smith RC	4.00	1.80
❑ 115 Dahntay Jones RC	4.00	1.80
❑ 116 Ndudi Ebi RC	4.00	1.80
❑ 117 Maurice Williams RC	4.00	1.80
❑ 118 Kendrick Perkins RC	4.00	1.80
❑ 119 Steve Blake RC	4.00	1.80
❑ 120 David West RC	4.00	1.80
❑ 121 Chris Kaman RC	4.00	1.80
❑ 122 Keith Bogans RC	4.00	1.80
❑ 123 LeBron James RC	35.00	16.00
❑ 124 Devin Brown RC	4.00	1.80
❑ 125 Jason Kapono RC	4.00	1.80
❑ 126 Zoran Planinic RC	4.00	1.80
❑ 127 Zaur Pachulia RC	4.00	1.80
❑ 128 Malick Badiane RC	4.00	1.80
❑ 129 Kyle Korver RC	5.00	2.20
❑ 130 Darko Milicic RC	5.00	2.20
❑ 131 Troy Bell RC	4.00	1.80
❑ 132 Luke Walton RC	4.00	1.80
❑ 133 Mike Sweetney RC	4.00	1.80
❑ 134 Jarvis Hayes RC	4.00	1.80
❑ 135 Leandro Barbosa RC	4.00	1.80
❑ 136 Carlos Delfino RC	4.00	1.80
❑ 137 Sofoklis Schortsanitis RC	4.00	1.80
❑ 138 Slavko Vranes RC	4.00	1.80
❑ 139 Travis Hansen RC	4.00	1.80
❑ 140 Carmelo Anthony RC	20.00	9.00
❑ 141 Reece Gaines RC	4.00	1.80
❑ 142 Maciej Lampe RC	4.00	1.80
❑ 143 Travis Outlaw RC	4.00	1.80
❑ 144 Jerome Beasley RC	4.00	1.80
❑ 145 Mickael Pietrus RC	4.00	1.80
❑ 146 Brian Cook RC	4.00	1.80
❑ 148 Kirk Hinrich AU RC	40.00	18.00
❑ 149 Dwyane Wade AU RC	60.00	27.00
❑ 150 Marcus Banks AU RC	30.00	13.50
❑ 151 Nick Collison AU RC	25.00	11.00
❑ 152 Boris Diaw AU RC	20.00	9.00
❑ 153 Chris Bosh AU RC	50.00	22.00
❑ 154 T.J. Ford AU RC	30.00	13.50
❑ 155 Luke Ridnour AU RC	30.00	13.50
❑ 156 A.Pavlovic AU RC	20.00	9.00
❑ 157 Z.Cabarkapa AU RC	20.00	9.00

2002-03 Bowman Signature Edition

	Nm-Mt	Ex-Mt
COMMON CARD	.60	.18
COMMON ROOKIE	12.00	3.60
❑ SE-AI Allen Iverson	4.00	1.20
❑ SE-AJ Antawn Jamison	2.00	.60
❑ SE-AK Andrei Kirilenko	2.00	.60
❑ SE-AM Alonzo Mourning	1.25	.35
❑ SE-AS Stoudemire JSY AU RC	150.00	45.00
❑ SE-AW Antoine Walker	2.00	.60
❑ SE-AKM Antonio McDyess	1.25	.35
❑ SE-ALM Andre Miller	1.25	.35
❑ SE-BD Baron Davis	2.00	.60
❑ SE-BN Bostjan Nachbar AU RC	12.00	3.60
❑ SE-BW Ben Wallace	2.00	.60
❑ SE-CB Curtis Borchardt AU RC	12.00	3.60
❑ SE-CM Cuttino Mobley	1.25	.35
❑ SE-CO Chris Owens AU RC	12.00	3.60
❑ SE-CT Cezary Trybanski AU RC	12.00	3.60
❑ SE-CW Chris Wilcox JSY AU RC	25.00	7.50
❑ SE-CBO C.Boozer JSY AU RC	40.00	12.00
❑ SE-CBU Caron Butler JSY AU RC	30.00	9.00
❑ SE-CJA C.Jacobsen JSY AU RC	20.00	6.00
❑ SE-CJE C.Jefferies JSY AU RC	12.00	3.60
❑ SE-DD Dan Dickau AU RC	12.00	3.60
❑ SE-DN Dirk Nowitzki	3.00	.90
❑ SE-DW D.Wagner JSY AU RC	25.00	7.50
❑ SE-DGA D.Gadzuric JSY AU RC	12.00	3.60
❑ SE-DGO D.Gooden JSY AU RC	40.00	12.00
❑ SE-DLM Darius Miles	2.00	.60
❑ SE-EB Elton Brand	2.00	.60
❑ SE-EC Eddy Curry	2.00	.60
❑ SE-EG Manu Ginobili AU RC	40.00	12.00
❑ SE-EJ Eddie Jones	2.00	.60
❑ SE-ER E.Rentzias AU RC	12.00	3.60
❑ SE-FJ Fred Jones JSY AU RC	15.00	4.50
❑ SE-FR Frank Williams AU RC	12.00	3.60
❑ SE-GG Gordan Giricek AU RC	25.00	7.50
❑ SE-GP Gary Payton	2.00	.60
❑ SE-GR Glenn Robinson	2.00	.60
❑ SE-JB J.R. Bremer AU RC	15.00	4.50
❑ SE-JD Juan Dixon JSY AU RC	30.00	9.00
❑ SE-JJ J.Jeffries JSY AU RC	20.00	6.00

❑ SE-JK Jason Kidd .... 3.00 .90
❑ SE-JM Jamal Mashburn .... 1.25 .35
❑ SE-JO Jermaine O'Neal .... 2.00 .60
❑ SE-JP Jannero Pargo AU RC 15.00 4.50
❑ SE-JS John Salmons JSY AU RC 12.00 3.60
❑ SE-JT Jamaal Tinsley .... 1.50 .45
❑ SE-JAW Jay Williams/1249 RC 8.00 2.40
❑ SE-JDS Jerry Stackhouse.. 2.00 .60
❑ SE-JOS John Stockton ...... 2.00 .60
❑ SE-JWE Jiri Welsch AU RC 12.00 3.60
❑ SE-JWI Jerome Williams...... .60 .18
❑ SE-KB Kobe Bryant............ 8.00 2.40
❑ SE-KG Kevin Garnett 4.00 1.20
❑ SE-KM Karl Malone............ 2.00 .60
❑ SE-KR K.Rush JSY AU RC 30.00 9.00
❑ SE-KS Kenny Satterfield...... .60 .18
❑ SE-KLM Kenyon Martin...... 2.00 .60
❑ SE-LS Latrell Sprewell ...... 2.00 .60
❑ SE-MB Mike Bibby .... 2.00 .60
❑ SE-MD M.Dunleavy JSY AU RC 30.00 9.00
❑ SE-ME Melvin Ely JSY AU RC 15.00 4.50
❑ SE-MH M.Haislip JSY AU RC 12.00 3.60
❑ SE-MO Mehmet Okur AU RC 12.00 3.60
❑ SE-MCW Chris Webber .... 2.00 .60
❑ SE-MJA Marko Jaric AU RC 15.00 4.50
❑ SE-MJJ Michael Jordan .. 12.00 3.60
❑ SE-NH N.Hilario JSY AU RC 40.00 12.00
❑ SE-NT N.Tskitishvili JSY AU RC 20.00 6.00
❑ SE-PG Pau Gasol .... 2.00 .60
❑ SE-PP Paul Pierce .... 2.00 .60
❑ SE-PS Peja Stojakovic ...... 2.00 .60
❑ SE-PSA P.Savovic JSY AU RC 15.00 4.50
❑ SE-QR Quentin Richardson 1.25 .35
❑ SE-RA Ray Allen.............. 2.00 .60
❑ SE-RA R.Archibald JSY AU RC 12.00 3.60
❑ SE-RB Rasual Butler AU RC 15.00 4.50
❑ SE-RJ Richard Jefferson.... 1.25 .35
❑ SE-RL Rashard Lewis........ 1.25 .35
❑ SE-RW Rasheed Wallace.. 2.00 .60
❑ SE-RCH Richard Hamilton 1.25 .35
❑ SE-RHU R.Humphrey JSY AU RC 12.00 3.60
❑ SE-RMA R.Mason JSY AU RC 12.00 3.60
❑ SE-RMU R.Murray JSY AU RC 40.00 12.00
❑ SE-SA Shareef Abdur-Rahim 2.00 .60
❑ SE-SC Sam Clancy JSY AU RC 12.00 3.60
❑ SE-SF Steve Francis.......... 2.00 .60
❑ SE-SM Stephon Marbury .. 2.00 .60
❑ SE-SN Steve Nash .... 2.00 .60
❑ SE-SO Shaquille O'Neal 5.00 1.50
❑ SE-SCB Shane Battier ...... 2.00 .60
❑ SE-SDM Shawn Marion .... 2.00 .60
❑ SE-TC Tyson Chandler...... 2.00 .60
❑ SE-TD Tim Duncan............ 5.00 1.50
❑ SE-TP T.Prince JSY AU RC 25.00 7.50
❑ SE-TP Tony Parker............ 2.00 .60
❑ SE-TS Tamar Slay AU RC 12.00 3.60
❑ SE-TLM Tracy McGrady 5.00 1.50
❑ SE-VC Vince Carter 5.00 1.50
❑ SE-VY V.Yarbrough JSY AU RC 12.00 3.60
❑ SE-WS Wally Szczerbiak .. 1.25 .35
❑ SE-YM Yao Ming AU RC 180.00 55.00

2003-04 Bowman Signature Edition

	MINT	NRMT
COMP.SET w/o SP's (55)	60.00	27.00
COMMON CARD (1-55)	.60	.25
SEMISTARS 1-55	1.25	.55
UNLISTED STARS 1-55	2.00	.90
COMMON ROOKIE (56-60)	6.00	2.70
UNLESS NOTED BELOW	-	
COMMON AU RC (61-76)......	12.00	5.50
COMMON JSY AU RC (77-105)	15.00	6.75
COMMON AU RC (106-118) ..	12.00	5.50

❑ 1 Tracy McGrady.............. 5.00 2.20
❑ 2 Baron Davis .... 2.00 .90
❑ 3 Allen Iverson 4.00 1.80
❑ 4 Bonzi Wells .... 2.00 .90
❑ 5 Tony Parker .... 2.00 .90
❑ 6 Morris Peterson .... 1.25 .55
❑ 7 Jerry Stackhouse .... 2.00 .90
❑ 8 Jason Terry .... 2.00 .90
❑ 9 Tyson Chandler .... 2.00 .90
❑ 10 Dirk Nowitzki 3.00 1.35
❑ 11 Nene............................ 1.25 .55
❑ 12 Antawn Jamison.......... 2.00 .90
❑ 13 Richard Hamilton .... 1.25 .55
❑ 14 Steve Francis.............. 2.00 .90
❑ 15 Jermaine O'Neal.......... 2.00 .90
❑ 16 Elton Brand .... 2.00 .90
❑ 17 Mike Miller .... 2.00 .90
❑ 18 Caron Butler................ 2.00 .90
❑ 19 Gary Payton................ 2.00 .90
❑ 20 Shaquille O'Neal.......... 5.00 2.20
❑ 21 Kevin Garnett 4.00 1.80
❑ 22 Desmond Mason .... 1.25 .55
❑ 23 Jamal Mashburn.......... 1.25 .55
❑ 24 Drew Gooden.............. 1.25 .55
❑ 25 Eric Snow.................... 1.25 .55
❑ 26 Shawn Marion .... 2.00 .90
❑ 27 Peja Stojakovic............ 2.00 .90
❑ 28 Karl Malone .... 2.00 .90
❑ 29 Shareef Abdur-Rahim .. 2.00 .90
❑ 30 Paul Pierce.................. 2.00 .90
❑ 31 Dajuan Wagner .... 1.25 .55
❑ 32 Steve Nash.................. 2.00 .90
❑ 33 Ben Wallace................ 2.00 .90
❑ 34 Jason Richardson .... 2.00 .90
❑ 35 Yao Ming 5.00 2.20
❑ 36 Ron Artest .... 1.25 .55
❑ 37 Andre Miller .... 1.25 .55
❑ 38 Kobe Bryant 8.00 3.60
❑ 39 Pau Gasol .... 2.00 .90
❑ 40 Tim Duncan 4.00 1.80
❑ 41 Ray Allen .... 2.00 .90
❑ 42 Vince Carter 5.00 2.20
❑ 43 Andrei Kirilenko .... 2.00 .90
❑ 44 Chris Webber .... 2.00 .90
❑ 45 Rasheed Wallace.......... 2.00 .90
❑ 46 Amare Stoudemire 4.00 1.80
❑ 47 Latrell Sprewell............ 2.00 .90
❑ 48 Kenyon Martin .... 2.00 .90
❑ 49 Wally Szczerbiak .... 1.25 .55
❑ 50 Jason Kidd 3.00 1.35
❑ 51 Eddie Jones .... 2.00 .90
❑ 52 Jalen Rose .... 2.00 .90
❑ 53 Ricky Davis .... 2.00 .90
❑ 54 Antoine Walker.............. 2.00 .90
❑ 55 Allan Houston................ 1.25 .55
❑ 56 Lebron James RC 80.00 36.00
❑ 57 Darko Milicic RC.......... 10.00 4.50
❑ 58 Chris Kaman RC 6.00 2.70
❑ 59 Kyle Korver RC 8.00 3.60
❑ 60 Willie Green RC 6.00 2.70
❑ 61 James Lang AU RC 12.00 5.50
❑ 62 Carl English AU RC 12.00 5.50
❑ 63 Devin Brown AU RC.... 12.00 5.50
❑ 64 Theron Smith AU RC .. 12.00 5.50
❑ 65 Rick Rickert AU RC 12.00 5.50
❑ 66 Z.Cabarkapa AU RC .. 12.00 5.50
❑ 67 D.Zimmerman AU RC 12.00 5.50
❑ 68 A.Pavlovic AU RC 12.00 5.50
❑ 69 Malick Badiane AU RC 12.00 5.50
❑ 70 Boris Diaw AU RC 12.00 5.50
❑ 71 Zaur Pachulia AU RC.. 12.00 5.50
❑ 72 Zoran Planinic AU RC 12.00 5.50
❑ 73 Carlos Delfino AU RC 12.00 5.50
❑ 74 Maciej Lampe AU RC.. 12.00 5.50
❑ 75 S.Schortsanitis AU RC 12.00 5.50
❑ 76 Mario Austin AU RC.... 12.00 5.50
❑ 77 C.Anthony/1170 JSY AU RC 160.00 70.00
❑ 78 Chris Bosh JSY AU RC 50.00 22.00
❑ 79 D.Wade JSY AU RC .. 60.00 27.00
❑ 80 Kirk Hinrich JSY AU RC 50.00 22.00
❑ 81 T.J. Ford JSY AU RC.. 40.00 18.00
❑ 82 D.West/1245 JSY AU RC 15.00 6.75
❑ 83 Marcus Banks JSY AU RC 15.00 6.75
❑ 84 Dahntay Jones JSY AU RC 15.00 6.75
❑ 85 Luke Ridnour JSY AU RC 30.00 13.50
❑ 86 Reece Gaines JSY AU RC 15.00 6.75
❑ 87 T.Outlaw/1075 JSY AU RC 15.00 6.75
❑ 88 B.Cook/1063 JSY AU RC 15.00 6.75
❑ 89 Troy Bell JSY AU RC .. 15.00 6.75
❑ 90 Ndudi Ebi JSY AU RC 20.00 9.00
❑ 91 K.Perkins/1238 JSY AU RC 15.00 6.75
❑ 92 L.Barbosa JSY AU RC 15.00 6.75
❑ 93 J.Howard/1111 JSY AU RC 30.00 13.50
❑ 94 Slavko Vranes JSY AU RC 15.00 6.75
❑ 95 Jason Kapono JSY AU RC 15.00 6.75
❑ 96 Luke Walton JSY AU RC 30.00 13.50
❑ 97 M.Williams/1172 JSY AU RC 15.00 6.75
❑ 98 M.Bonner/960 JSY AU RC 15.00 6.75
❑ 99 Travis Hansen JSY AU RC 15.00 6.75
❑ 100 Steve Blake JSY AU RC 15.00 6.75
❑ 101 Keith Bogans JSY AU RC 15.00 6.75
❑ 102 Mike Sweetney JSY AU RC 15.00 6.75
❑ 103 Jarvis Hayes JSY AU RC 30.00 13.50
❑ 104 Mickael Pietrus JSY AU RC 20.00 9.00
❑ 105 Nick Collison JSY AU RC 20.00 9.00
❑ 106 Jerome Beasley AU RC 12.00 5.50
❑ 107 James Jones AU RC 12.00 5.50
❑ 108 Brandon Hunter AU RC 12.00 5.50
❑ 109 Tommy Smith AU RC 12.00 5.50
❑ 110 Marcus Hatten AU RC 12.00 5.50
❑ 111 Koko Archibong AU RC 12.00 5.50
❑ 112 Ime Udoka AU RC 12.00 5.50
❑ 113 Eric Chenowith AU RC 12.00 5.50
❑ 114 Stephane Pelle AU RC 12.00 5.50
❑ 115 Marquis Daniels AU RC 50.00 22.00
❑ 116 Paccelis Morlende AU RC 12.00 5.50
❑ 117 George Williams AU RC 12.00 5.50
❑ 118 Udonis Haslem AU RC 15.00 6.75

1996-97 Bowman's Best

	Nm-Mt	Ex-Mt
COMPLETE SET (125)	50.00	15.00
COMMON CARD (1-80/TB1-20)	.40	.12
COMMON ROOKIE (R1-R25)....	.50	.15

❑ 1 Scottie Pippen .... 2.00 .60
❑ 2 Glen Rice .... .75 .23
❑ 3 Bryant Stith...................... .40 .12
❑ 4 Dino Radja .... .40 .12
❑ 5 Horace Grant .... .75 .23
❑ 6 Mahmoud Abdul-Rauf ...... .40 .12
❑ 7 Mookie Blaylock .... .40 .12
❑ 8 Clifford Robinson .... .40 .12
❑ 9 Vin Baker .... .75 .23
❑ 10 Grant Hill .... 1.25 .35
❑ 11 Terrell Brandon .... .75 .23
❑ 12 P.J. Brown .... .40 .12
❑ 13 Kendall Gill .... .40 .12
❑ 14 Brent Barry .... .40 .12
❑ 15 Hakeem Olajuwon .... 1.25 .35
❑ 16 Allan Houston.................. .75 .23
❑ 17 Elden Campbell .... .40 .12
❑ 18 Latrell Sprewell.............. 1.25 .35
❑ 19 Jerry Stackhouse .... 1.50 .45
❑ 20 Robert Horry.................. .75 .23
❑ 21 Mitch Richmond .... .75 .23
❑ 22 Gary Payton.................. 1.25 .35
❑ 23 Rik Smits .... .75 .23

Card		
❑ 24 Jim Jackson	.40	.12
❑ 25 Damon Stoudamire	1.25	.35
❑ 26 Bobby Phills	.40	.12
❑ 27 Chris Webber	1.25	.35
❑ 28 Shawn Bradley	.40	.12
❑ 29 Arvydas Sabonis	.75	.23
❑ 30 John Stockton	1.25	.35
❑ 31 Anfernee Hardaway	1.25	.35
❑ 32 Christian Laettner	.75	.23
❑ 33 Juwan Howard	.75	.23
❑ 34 Anthony Mason	.75	.23
❑ 35 Tom Gugliotta	.40	.12
❑ 36 Avery Johnson	.40	.12
❑ 37 Cedric Ceballos	.40	.12
❑ 38 Patrick Ewing	1.25	.35
❑ 39 Joe Smith	.75	.23
❑ 40 Dennis Rodman	.75	.23
❑ 41 Alonzo Mourning	.75	.23
❑ 42 Kevin Garnett	2.50	.75
❑ 43 Antonio McDyess	1.25	.35
❑ 44 Detlef Schrempf	.75	.23
❑ 45 Reggie Miller	1.25	.35
❑ 46 Charles Barkley	1.50	.45
❑ 47 Derrick Coleman	.75	.23
❑ 48 Brian Grant	1.25	.35
❑ 49 Kenny Anderson	.40	.12
❑ 50 Otis Thorpe	.40	.12
❑ 51 Rod Strickland	.40	.12
❑ 52 Eric Williams	.40	.12
❑ 53 Rony Seikaly	.40	.12
❑ 54 Danny Manning	.75	.23
❑ 55 Karl Malone	1.25	.35
❑ 56 B.J. Armstrong	.40	.12
❑ 57 Greg Anthony	.40	.12
❑ 58 Larry Johnson	.75	.23
❑ 59 Loy Vaught	.40	.12
❑ 60 Sean Elliott	.75	.23
❑ 61 Dikembe Mutombo	.75	.23
❑ 62 Clarence Weatherspoon	.40	.12
❑ 63 Jamal Mashburn	.75	.23
❑ 64 Bryant Reeves	.40	.12
❑ 65 Vlade Divac	.40	.12
❑ 66 Shawn Kemp	.75	.23
❑ 67 LaPhonso Ellis	.40	.12
❑ 68 Tyrone Hill	.40	.12
❑ 69 David Robinson	1.25	.35
❑ 70 Shaquille O'Neal	3.00	.90
❑ 71 Doug Christie	.75	.23
❑ 72 Jayson Williams	.75	.23
❑ 73 Michael Finley	1.50	.45
❑ 74 Tim Hardaway	.75	.23
❑ 75 Clyde Drexler	1.25	.35
❑ 76 Joe Dumars	1.25	.35
❑ 77 Glenn Robinson	1.25	.35
❑ 78 Dana Barros	.40	.12
❑ 79 Jason Kidd	2.00	.60
❑ 80 Michael Jordan	8.00	2.40
❑ R1 Allen Iverson RC	12.00	3.60
❑ R2 Stephon Marbury RC	4.00	1.20
❑ R3 Shareef Abdur-Rahim RC	4.00	1.20
❑ R4 Marcus Camby RC	2.00	.60
❑ R5 Ray Allen RC	5.00	1.50
❑ R6 Antoine Walker RC	4.00	1.20
❑ R7 Lorenzen Wright RC	.50	.15
❑ R8 Kerry Kittles RC	1.50	.45
❑ R9 Samaki Walker RC	.50	.15
❑ R10 Tony Delk RC	.50	.15
❑ R11 Vitaly Potapenko RC	.50	.15
❑ R12 Jerome Williams RC	1.50	.45
❑ R13 Todd Fuller RC	.50	.15
❑ R14 Erick Dampier RC	1.50	.45
❑ R15 Derek Fisher RC	2.50	.75
❑ R16 Donald Whiteside RC	.50	.15
❑ R17 John Wallace RC	.50	.15
❑ R18 Steve Nash RC	3.00	.90
❑ R19 Brian Evans RC	.50	.15
❑ R20 Jermaine O'Neal RC	4.00	1.20
❑ R21 Roy Rogers RC	.50	.15
❑ R22 Priest Lauderdale RC	.50	.15
❑ R23 Kobe Bryant RC	20.00	6.00
❑ R24 Martin Muursepp RC	.50	.15
❑ R25 Zydrunas Ilgauskas RC	1.00	.30
❑ TB1 Avery Johnson RET	.40	.12
❑ TB2 Chris Webber RET	1.25	.35
❑ TB3 Sean Elliott RET	.40	.12
❑ TB4 Joe Dumars RET	.75	.23
❑ TB5 Grant Hill RET	1.25	.35
❑ TB6 Gary Payton RET	.75	.23
❑ TB7 Shawn Kemp RET	.40	.12
❑ TB8 Shaquille O'Neal	1.25	.35
❑ TB9 Eddie Jones RET	.75	.23
❑ TB10 John Wallace RET	.75	.23
❑ TB11 Patrick Ewing RET	.75	.23
❑ TB12 Jerry Stackhouse RET	.50	.15
❑ TB13 Allen Iverson RET	2.50	.75
❑ TB14 Latrell Sprewell RET	1.25	.35
❑ TB15 Dino Radja RET	.40	.12
❑ TB16 David Wesley RET	.40	.12
❑ TB17 Joe Smith RET	.40	.12
❑ TB18 D.Stoudamire RET	.75	.23
❑ TB19 Marcus Camby RET	.75	.23
❑ TB20 Juwan Howard RET	.40	.12

1997-98 Bowman's Best

	Nm-Mt	Ex-Mt
COMPLETE SET (125)	40.00	12.00
COMMON CARD (1-100)	.25	.07
COMMON ROOKIE (101-125)	.30	.09
❑ 1 Scottie Pippen	1.25	.35
❑ 2 Michael Finley	.75	.23
❑ 3 David Wesley	.25	.07
❑ 4 Brent Barry	.50	.15
❑ 5 Gary Payton	.75	.23
❑ 6 Christian Laettner	.50	.15
❑ 7 Grant Hill	.75	.23
❑ 8 Glenn Robinson	.75	.23
❑ 9 Reggie Miller	.75	.23
❑ 10 Tyus Edney	.25	.07
❑ 11 Jim Jackson	.25	.07
❑ 12 John Stockton	.75	.23
❑ 13 Karl Malone	.75	.23
❑ 14 Samaki Walker	.25	.07
❑ 15 Bryant Stith	.25	.07
❑ 16 Clyde Drexler	.75	.23
❑ 17 Danny Ferry	.25	.07
❑ 18 Shawn Bradley	.25	.07
❑ 19 Bryant Reeves	.25	.07
❑ 20 John Starks	.25	.07
❑ 21 Joe Dumars	.75	.23
❑ 22 Checklist	.25	.07
❑ 23 Antonio McDyess	.50	.15
❑ 24 Jeff Hornacek	.50	.15
❑ 25 Terrell Brandon	.50	.15
❑ 26 Kendall Gill	.25	.07
❑ 27 LaPhonso Ellis	.25	.07
❑ 28 Shaquille O'Neal	2.00	.60
❑ 29 Mahmoud Abdul-Rauf	.25	.07
❑ 30 Eric Williams	.25	.07
❑ 31 Lorenzen Wright	.25	.07
❑ 32 Shareef Abdur-Rahim	1.25	.35
❑ 33 Avery Johnson	.25	.07
❑ 34 Juwan Howard	.50	.15
❑ 35 Vin Baker	.50	.15
❑ 36 Dikembe Mutombo	.50	.15
❑ 37 Patrick Ewing	.75	.23
❑ 38 Allen Iverson	2.00	.60
❑ 39 Alonzo Mourning	.50	.15
❑ 40 Travis Knight	.25	.07
❑ 41 Ray Allen	.75	.23
❑ 42 Detlef Schrempf	.50	.15
❑ 43 Kevin Johnson	.50	.15
❑ 44 David Robinson	.75	.23
❑ 45 Tim Hardaway	.50	.15
❑ 46 Shawn Kemp	.50	.15
❑ 47 Marcus Camby	.75	.23
❑ 48 Rony Seikaly	.25	.07
❑ 49 Eddie Jones	.75	.23
❑ 50 Rik Smits	.50	.15
❑ 51 Jayson Williams	.25	.07
❑ 52 Malik Sealy	.25	.07
❑ 53 Chris Mullin	.75	.23
❑ 54 Larry Johnson	.50	.15
❑ 55 Isaiah Rider	.50	.15
❑ 56 Dennis Rodman	.50	.15
❑ 57 Bob Sura	.25	.07
❑ 58 Hakeem Olajuwon	.75	.23
❑ 59 Steve Smith	.50	.15
❑ 60 Michael Jordan	5.00	1.50
❑ 61 Jerry Stackhouse	.75	.23
❑ 62 Joe Smith	.50	.15
❑ 63 Walt Williams	.25	.07
❑ 64 Anthony Peeler	.25	.07
❑ 65 Charles Barkley	1.00	.30
❑ 66 Erick Dampier	.50	.15
❑ 67 Horace Grant	.50	.15
❑ 68 Anthony Mason	.50	.15
❑ 69 Anfernee Hardaway	.75	.23
❑ 70 Elden Campbell	.25	.07
❑ 71 Cedric Ceballos	.25	.07
❑ 72 Allan Houston	.50	.15
❑ 73 Kerry Kittles	.75	.23
❑ 74 Antoine Walker	1.00	.30
❑ 75 Sean Elliott	.50	.15
❑ 76 Jamal Mashburn	.50	.15
❑ 77 Mitch Richmond	.50	.15
❑ 78 Damon Stoudamire	.50	.15
❑ 79 Tom Gugliotta	.50	.15
❑ 80 Jason Kidd	1.25	.35
❑ 81 Chris Webber	.75	.23
❑ 82 Glen Rice	.50	.15
❑ 83 Loy Vaught	.25	.07
❑ 84 Olden Polynice	.25	.07
❑ 85 Kenny Anderson	.50	.15
❑ 86 Stephon Marbury	1.00	.30
❑ 87 Calbert Cheaney	.25	.07
❑ 88 Kobe Bryant	3.00	.90
❑ 89 Arvydas Sabonis	.50	.15
❑ 90 Kevin Garnett	1.50	.45
❑ 91 Grant Hill BP	.75	.23
❑ 92 Clyde Drexler BP	.50	.15
❑ 93 Patrick Ewing BP	.50	.15
❑ 94 Shawn Kemp BP	.25	.07
❑ 95 Shaquille O'Neal BP	.75	.23
❑ 96 Michael Jordan BP	2.50	.75
❑ 97 Karl Malone BP	.75	.23
❑ 98 Allen Iverson BP	1.00	.30
❑ 99 Shareef Abdur-Rahim BP	.60	.18
❑ 100 Dikembe Mutombo BP	.25	.07
❑ 101 Bobby Jackson RC	1.00	.30
❑ 102 Tony Battie RC	.60	.18
❑ 103 Keith Booth RC	.30	.09
❑ 104 Keith Van Horn RC	2.00	.60
❑ 105 Paul Grant RC	.30	.09
❑ 106 Tim Duncan RC	5.00	1.50
❑ 107 Scot Pollard RC	.50	.15
❑ 108 Maurice Taylor RC	1.25	.35
❑ 109 Antonio Daniels RC	.60	.18
❑ 110 Austin Croshere RC	1.25	.35
❑ 111 Tracy McGrady RC	8.00	2.40
❑ 112 Charles O'Bannon RC	.30	.09
❑ 113 Rodrick Rhodes RC	.30	.09
❑ 114 Johnny Taylor RC	.30	.09
❑ 115 Danny Fortson RC	.75	.23
❑ 116 Chauncey Billups RC	1.25	.35
❑ 117 Tim Thomas RC	2.00	.60
❑ 118 Derek Anderson RC	2.50	.75
❑ 119 Ed Gray RC	.30	.09
❑ 120 Jacque Vaughn RC	.50	.15
❑ 121 Kelvin Cato RC	.60	.18
❑ 122 Tariq Abdul-Wahad RC	.50	.15
❑ 123 Ron Mercer RC	1.50	.45
❑ 124 Brevin Knight RC	.75	.23
❑ 125 Adonal Foyle RC	.50	.15

1998-99 Bowman's Best

	Nm-Mt	Ex-Mt
COMPLETE SET (125)	100.00	30.00
COMPLETE SET w/o SP (100)	20.00	6.00
COMMON CARD (1-100)	.25	.07
COMMON ROOKIE (101-125)	.75	.23

❑ 1 Jason Kidd 1.25 .35
❑ 2 Dikembe Mutombo .50 .15
❑ 3 Chris Mullin .75 .23
❑ 4 Terrell Brandon .50 .15
❑ 5 Cedric Ceballos .25 .07
❑ 6 Rod Strickland .25 .07
❑ 7 Darrell Armstrong .25 .07
❑ 8 Anfernee Hardaway .75 .23
❑ 9 Eddie Jones .75 .23
❑ 10 Allen Iverson 1.50 .45
❑ 11 Kenny Anderson .50 .15
❑ 12 Toni Kukoc .50 .15
❑ 13 Lawrence Funderburke .25 .07
❑ 14 P.J. Brown .25 .07
❑ 15 Jeff Hornacek .50 .15
❑ 16 Mookie Blaylock .25 .07
❑ 17 Avery Johnson .25 .07
❑ 18 Donyell Marshall .50 .15
❑ 19 Detlef Schrempf .50 .15
❑ 20 Joe Dumars .75 .23
❑ 21 Charles Barkley 1.00 .30
❑ 22 Maurice Taylor .50 .15
❑ 23 Chauncey Billups .50 .15
❑ 24 Lee Mayberry .25 .07
❑ 25 Glen Rice .50 .15
❑ 26 John Stockton .75 .23
❑ 27 Rik Smits .50 .15
❑ 28 Laphonso Ellis .25 .07
❑ 29 Kerry Kittles .25 .07
❑ 30 Damon Stoudamire .50 .15
❑ 31 Kevin Garnett 1.50 .45
❑ 32 Chris Mills .25 .07
❑ 33 Kendall Gill .25 .07
❑ 34 Tim Thomas .50 .15
❑ 35 Derek Anderson .75 .23
❑ 36 Billy Owens .25 .07
❑ 37 Bobby Jackson .50 .15
❑ 38 Allan Houston .50 .15
❑ 39 Horace Grant .50 .15
❑ 40 Ray Allen .75 .23
❑ 41 Shawn Bradley .25 .07
❑ 42 Arvydas Sabonis .50 .15
❑ 43 Rex Chapman .25 .07
❑ 44 Larry Johnson .50 .15
❑ 45 Jayson Williams .25 .07
❑ 46 Joe Smith .50 .15
❑ 47 Ron Mercer .50 .15
❑ 48 Rodney Rogers .25 .07
❑ 49 Corliss Williamson .50 .15
❑ 50 Tim Duncan 1.25 .35
❑ 51 Rasheed Wallace .75 .23
❑ 52 Vin Baker .50 .15
❑ 53 Reggie Miller .75 .23
❑ 54 Patrick Ewing .75 .23
❑ 55 Michael Finley .75 .23
❑ 56 Bryant Reeves .25 .07
❑ 57 Glenn Robinson .50 .15
❑ 58 Walter McCarty .25 .07
❑ 59 Brent Barry .50 .15
❑ 60 John Starks .50 .15
❑ 61 Clarence Weatherspoon .25 .07
❑ 62 Calbert Cheaney .25 .07
❑ 63 Lamond Murray .25 .07
❑ 64 Zydrunas Ilgauskas .50 .15
❑ 65 Anthony Mason .50 .15
❑ 66 Bryon Russell .25 .07
❑ 67 Dean Garrett .25 .07
❑ 68 Tom Gugliotta .25 .07
❑ 69 Dennis Rodman .50 .15
❑ 70 Keith Van Horn .75 .23
❑ 71 Jamal Mashburn .50 .15
❑ 72 Steve Smith .50 .15
❑ 73 David Wesley .25 .07
❑ 74 Chris Webber .75 .23
❑ 75 Isaiah Rider .25 .07
❑ 76 Stephon Marbury .75 .23
❑ 77 Tim Hardaway .50 .15
❑ 78 Jerry Stackhouse .75 .23
❑ 79 John Wallace .25 .07
❑ 80 Karl Malone .75 .23
❑ 81 Juwan Howard .50 .15
❑ 82 Antonio McDyess .50 .15
❑ 83 David Robinson .75 .23
❑ 84 Bobby Phills .25 .07
❑ 85 Scottie Pippen 1.25 .35
❑ 86 Brevin Knight .25 .07
❑ 87 Alan Henderson .25 .07
❑ 88 Kobe Bryant 3.00 .90
❑ 89 Shawn Kemp .50 .15
❑ 90 Antoine Walker .75 .23
❑ 91 Tracy McGrady 2.00 .60
❑ 92 Hakeem Olajuwon .75 .23
❑ 93 Mark Jackson .50 .15
❑ 94 Bison Dele .25 .07
❑ 95 Gary Payton .75 .23
❑ 96 Ron Harper .50 .15
❑ 97 Shareef Abdur-Rahim .75 .23
❑ 98 Alonzo Mourning .50 .15
❑ 99 Grant Hill .75 .23
❑ 100 Shaquille O'Neal 2.00 .60
❑ 101 Michael Olowokandi RC 2.50 .75
❑ 102 Mike Bibby RC 8.00 2.40
❑ 103 Raef LaFrentz RC 2.50 .75
❑ 104 Antawn Jamison RC 8.00 2.40
❑ 105 Vince Carter RC 20.00 6.00
❑ 106 Robert Traylor RC 1.50 .45
❑ 107 Jason Williams RC 6.00 1.80
❑ 108 Larry Hughes RC 5.00 1.50
❑ 109 Dirk Nowitzki RC 15.00 4.50
❑ 110 Paul Pierce RC 8.00 2.40
❑ 111 Bonzi Wells RC 6.00 1.80
❑ 112 Michael Doleac RC 1.50 .45
❑ 113 Keon Clark RC 2.50 .75
❑ 114 Michael Dickerson RC 3.00 .90
❑ 115 Matt Harpring RC 2.50 .75
❑ 116 Bryce Drew RC 1.50 .45
❑ 117 Pat Garrity RC 1.00 .30
❑ 118 Roshown McLeod RC 1.00 .30
❑ 119 Ricky Davis RC 5.00 1.50
❑ 120 Brian Skinner RC 1.50 .45
❑ 121 Tyronn Lue RC 2.00 .60
❑ 122 Felipe Lopez RC 2.00 .60
❑ 123 Al Harrington RC 4.00 1.20
❑ 124 Corey Benjamin RC 1.50 .45
❑ 125 Nazr Mohammed RC .75 .23

1999-00 Bowman's Best

	Nm-Mt	Ex-Mt
COMPLETE SET (133)	60.00	18.00
COMMON CARD (1-100)	.25	.07
COMMON ROOKIE (101-133)	.50	.15

❑ 1 Vince Carter 2.00 .60
❑ 2 Dikembe Mutombo .50 .15
❑ 3 Steve Nash .75 .23
❑ 4 Matt Harpring .75 .23
❑ 5 Stephon Marbury .75 .23
❑ 6 Chris Webber .75 .23
❑ 7 Jason Kidd 1.25 .35
❑ 8 Theo Ratliff .50 .15
❑ 9 Damon Stoudamire .50 .15
❑ 10 Shareef Abdur-Rahim .75 .23
❑ 11 Rod Strickland .25 .07
❑ 12 Jeff Hornacek .50 .15
❑ 13 Vin Baker .50 .15
❑ 14 Joe Smith .50 .15
❑ 15 Alonzo Mourning .50 .15
❑ 16 Isaiah Rider .25 .07
❑ 17 Shaquille O'Neal 2.00 .60
❑ 18 Chris Mullin .75 .23
❑ 19 Charles Barkley 1.00 .30
❑ 20 Grant Hill .75 .23
❑ 21 Chris Mills .25 .07
❑ 22 Antonio McDyess .50 .15
❑ 23 Brevin Knight .25 .07
❑ 24 Toni Kukoc .50 .15
❑ 25 Antoine Walker .75 .23
❑ 26 Eddie Jones .75 .23
❑ 27 Tim Thomas .50 .15
❑ 28 Latrell Sprewell .75 .23
❑ 29 Larry Hughes .75 .23
❑ 30 Tim Duncan 1.50 .45
❑ 31 Horace Grant .50 .15
❑ 32 John Stockton .75 .23
❑ 33 Mike Bibby .75 .23
❑ 34 Mitch Richmond .50 .15
❑ 35 Allan Houston .50 .15
❑ 36 Terrell Brandon .50 .15
❑ 37 Glenn Robinson .75 .23
❑ 38 Tyrone Nesby RC .25 .07
❑ 39 Glen Rice .50 .15
❑ 40 Hakeem Olajuwon .75 .23
❑ 41 Jerry Stackhouse .75 .23
❑ 42 Elden Campbell .25 .07
❑ 43 Ron Harper .50 .15
❑ 44 Kenny Anderson .50 .15
❑ 45 Michael Finley .75 .23
❑ 46 Scottie Pippen 1.25 .35
❑ 47 Lindsey Hunter .25 .07
❑ 48 Michael Olowokandi .50 .15
❑ 49 P.J. Brown .25 .07
❑ 50 Keith Van Horn .75 .23
❑ 51 Michael Doleac .25 .07
❑ 52 Anfernee Hardaway .75 .23
❑ 53 Rasheed Wallace .75 .23
❑ 54 Nick Anderson .25 .07
❑ 55 Gary Payton .75 .23
❑ 56 Tracy McGrady 2.00 .60
❑ 57 Ray Allen .75 .23
❑ 58 Kobe Bryant 3.00 .90
❑ 59 Ron Mercer .50 .15
❑ 60 Shawn Kemp .50 .15
❑ 61 Anthony Mason .50 .15
❑ 62 Tim Hardaway .50 .15
❑ 63 Antawn Jamison 1.25 .35
❑ 64 Mark Jackson .50 .15
❑ 65 Tom Gugliotta .25 .07
❑ 66 Marcus Camby .50 .15
❑ 67 Kerry Kittles .25 .07
❑ 68 Vlade Divac .50 .15
❑ 69 Avery Johnson .25 .07
❑ 70 Karl Malone .75 .23
❑ 71 Juwan Howard .50 .15
❑ 72 Alan Henderson .25 .07
❑ 73 Hersey Hawkins .50 .15
❑ 74 Darrell Armstrong .25 .07
❑ 75 Allen Iverson 1.50 .45
❑ 76 Maurice Taylor .50 .15
❑ 77 Gary Trent .25 .07
❑ 78 John Starks .50 .15
❑ 79 Paul Pierce .75 .23
❑ 80 Kevin Garnett 1.50 .45
❑ 81 Patrick Ewing .75 .23
❑ 82 Steve Smith .50 .15
❑ 83 Jason Williams .75 .23
❑ 84 David Robinson .75 .23
❑ 85 Charles Oakley .25 .07
❑ 86 Bryant Reeves .25 .07
❑ 87 Nick Van Exel .75 .23
❑ 88 Reggie Miller .75 .23
❑ 89 Chris Gatling .25 .07
❑ 90 Brian Grant .50 .15
❑ 91 Allen Iverson BP .75 .23

Card	Nm-Mt	Ex-Mt
❑ 92 Tim Duncan BP	.75	.23
❑ 93 Keith Van Horn BP	.25	.07
❑ 94 Kevin Garnett BP	.75	.23
❑ 95 Kobe Bryant BP	1.50	.45
❑ 96 Elton Brand BP	1.50	.45
❑ 97 Baron Davis BP	1.50	.45
❑ 98 Lamar Odom BP	1.25	.35
❑ 99 Wally Szczerbiak BP	1.25	.35
❑ 100 Jason Terry BP	.75	.23
❑ 101 Elton Brand RC	3.00	.90
❑ 102 Steve Francis RC	4.00	1.20
❑ 103 Baron Davis RC	2.50	.75
❑ 104 Lamar Odom RC	2.50	.75
❑ 105 Jonathan Bender RC	2.50	.75
❑ 106 Wally Szczerbiak RC	2.50	.75
❑ 107 Richard Hamilton RC	2.50	.75
❑ 108 Andre Miller RC	2.50	.75
❑ 109 Shawn Marion RC	3.00	.90
❑ 110 Jason Terry RC	1.50	.45
❑ 111 Trajan Langdon RC	1.00	.30
❑ 112 Aleksandar Radojevic RC	.50	.15
❑ 113 Corey Maggette RC	2.50	.75
❑ 114 William Avery RC	1.00	.30
❑ 115 DeMarco Johnson RC	.60	.18
❑ 116 Ron Artest RC	1.50	.45
❑ 117 Cal Bowdler RC	.75	.23
❑ 118 James Posey RC	1.50	.45
❑ 119 Quincy Lewis RC	.75	.23
❑ 120 Dion Glover RC	.75	.23
❑ 121 Jeff Foster RC	.75	.23
❑ 122 Kenny Thomas RC	1.00	.30
❑ 123 Devean George RC	1.25	.35
❑ 124 Tim James RC	.75	.23
❑ 125 Vonteego Cummings RC	1.00	.30
❑ 126 Jumaine Jones RC	1.25	.35
❑ 127 Scott Padgett RC	.75	.23
❑ 128 Anthony Carter RC	1.50	.45
❑ 129 Chris Herren RC	.50	.15
❑ 130 Todd MacCulloch RC	.75	.23
❑ 131 John Celestand RC	.75	.23
❑ 132 Adrian Griffin RC	.75	.23
❑ 133 Mirsad Turkcan RC	.50	.15

2000-01 Bowman's Best

	Nm-Mt	Ex-Mt
COMPLETE SET w/o RC (100)	30.00	9.00
COMMON CARD (1-100)	.25	.07
COMMON ROOKIE (101-133)	3.00	.90
❑ 1 Allen Iverson	1.50	.45
❑ 2 Darrell Armstrong	.25	.07
❑ 3 Kendall Gill	.25	.07
❑ 4 Marcus Camby	.50	.15
❑ 5 Glen Rice	.50	.15
❑ 6 Eddie Jones	.75	.23
❑ 7 Wally Szczerbiak	.50	.15
❑ 8 Antawn Jamison	.75	.23
❑ 9 Raef LaFrentz	.50	.15
❑ 10 Steve Francis	.75	.23
❑ 11 Tracy McGrady	2.00	.60
❑ 12 Brian Grant	.50	.15
❑ 13 Vlade Divac	.50	.15
❑ 14 Gary Payton	.75	.23
❑ 15 Vince Carter	2.00	.60
❑ 16 John Stockton	.75	.23
❑ 17 Mike Bibby	.75	.23
❑ 18 Derek Anderson	.50	.15
❑ 19 Juwan Howard	.50	.15
❑ 20 Allan Houston	.50	.15
❑ 21 Kevin Garnett	1.50	.45
❑ 22 Michael Olowokandi	.25	.07
❑ 23 Maurice Taylor	.25	.07
❑ 24 Jerry Stackhouse	.75	.23
❑ 25 Nick Van Exel	.75	.23
❑ 26 Andre Miller	.50	.15
❑ 27 Michael Finley	.75	.23
❑ 28 Jamal Mashburn	.50	.15
❑ 29 Ron Mercer	.50	.15
❑ 30 Jim Jackson	.25	.07
❑ 31 Kenny Anderson	.50	.15
❑ 32 Karl Malone	.75	.23
❑ 33 Rod Strickland	.25	.07
❑ 34 Shaquille O'Neal	2.00	.60
❑ 35 Glenn Robinson	.50	.15
❑ 36 Keith Van Horn	.75	.23
❑ 37 Grant Hill	.75	.23
❑ 38 Eric Snow	.50	.15
❑ 39 Anfernee Hardaway	.75	.23
❑ 40 Scottie Pippen	1.25	.35
❑ 41 Jason Williams	.50	.15
❑ 42 Elton Brand	.75	.23
❑ 43 Stephon Marbury	.75	.23
❑ 44 David Robinson	.75	.23
❑ 45 Antonio Davis	.25	.07
❑ 46 Michael Dickerson	.50	.15
❑ 47 Mitch Richmond	.50	.15
❑ 48 Rashard Lewis	.50	.15
❑ 49 Jermaine O'Neal	.75	.23
❑ 50 Tim Duncan	1.50	.45
❑ 51 Tom Gugliotta	.25	.07
❑ 52 Theo Ratliff	.50	.15
❑ 53 Joe Smith	.50	.15
❑ 54 Tim Thomas	.50	.15
❑ 55 Brevin Knight	.25	.07
❑ 56 Dale Davis	.25	.07
❑ 57 Cuttino Mobley	.50	.15
❑ 58 Cedric Ceballos	.25	.07
❑ 59 Christian Laettner	.50	.15
❑ 60 Dirk Nowitzki	1.25	.35
❑ 61 Paul Pierce	.75	.23
❑ 62 Derrick Coleman	.25	.07
❑ 63 Dikembe Mutombo	.50	.15
❑ 64 Lamond Murray	.25	.07
❑ 65 Antonio McDyess	.50	.15
❑ 66 Reggie Miller	.75	.23
❑ 67 Hakeem Olajuwon	.75	.23
❑ 68 Corey Maggette	.50	.15
❑ 69 Lamar Odom	.75	.23
❑ 70 Larry Hughes	.50	.15
❑ 71 Anthony Mason	.50	.15
❑ 72 Sam Cassell	.75	.23
❑ 73 Terrell Brandon	.50	.15
❑ 74 Latrell Sprewell	.75	.23
❑ 75 Kobe Bryant	3.00	.90
❑ 76 Tim Hardaway	.50	.15
❑ 77 Mark Jackson	.25	.07
❑ 78 Vin Baker	.50	.15
❑ 79 Jonathan Bender	.50	.15
❑ 80 Chris Webber	.75	.23
❑ 81 Rasheed Wallace	.75	.23
❑ 82 Shawn Marion	.75	.23
❑ 83 Toni Kukoc	.50	.15
❑ 84 Patrick Ewing	.75	.23
❑ 85 Ray Allen	.75	.23
❑ 86 Isaiah Rider	.50	.15
❑ 87 Danny Fortson	.25	.07
❑ 88 Jerome Williams	.25	.07
❑ 89 Shawn Kemp	.50	.15
❑ 90 Ron Artest	.50	.15
❑ 91 P.J. Brown	.25	.07
❑ 92 Baron Davis	.75	.23
❑ 93 Antoine Walker	.75	.23
❑ 94 Jason Terry	.75	.23
❑ 95 Jalen Rose	.75	.23
❑ 96 Avery Johnson	.25	.07
❑ 97 Shareef Abdur-Rahim	.75	.23
❑ 98 Bryon Russell	.25	.07
❑ 99 Richard Hamilton	.50	.15
❑ 100 Jason Kidd	1.25	.35
❑ 101A Kenyon Martin RC	15.00	4.50
❑ 101B Kenyon Martin RC	15.00	4.50
❑ 101C Kenyon Martin RC	15.00	4.50
❑ 102A Stromile Swift RC	8.00	2.40
❑ 102B Stromile Swift RC	8.00	2.40
❑ 102C Stromile Swift RC	8.00	2.40
❑ 103A Darius Miles RC	15.00	4.50
❑ 103B Darius Miles RC	15.00	4.50
❑ 103C Darius Miles RC	15.00	4.50
❑ 104A Marcus Fizer RC	3.00	.90
❑ 104B Marcus Fizer RC	3.00	.90
❑ 104C Marcus Fizer RC	3.00	.90
❑ 105A Mike Miller RC	3.00	.90
❑ 105B Mike Miller RC	3.00	.90
❑ 105C Mike Miller RC	3.00	.90
❑ 106A DerMarr Johnson RC	3.00	.90
❑ 106B DerMarr Johnson RC	3.00	.90
❑ 106C DerMarr Johnson RC	3.00	.90
❑ 107A Chris Mihm RC	3.00	.90
❑ 107B Chris Mihm RC	3.00	.90
❑ 107C Chris Mihm RC	3.00	.90
❑ 108A Jamal Crawford RC	4.00	1.20
❑ 108B Jamal Crawford RC	4.00	1.20
❑ 108C Jamal Crawford RC	4.00	1.20
❑ 109A Joel Przybilla RC	3.00	.90
❑ 109B Joel Przybilla RC	3.00	.90
❑ 109C Joel Przybilla RC	3.00	.90
❑ 110A Keyon Dooling RC	3.00	.90
❑ 110B Keyon Dooling RC	3.00	.90
❑ 110C Keyon Dooling RC	3.00	.90
❑ 111A Jerome Moiso RC	3.00	.90
❑ 111B Jerome Moiso RC	3.00	.90
❑ 111C Jerome Moiso RC	3.00	.90
❑ 112A Etan Thomas RC	3.00	.90
❑ 112B Etan Thomas RC	3.00	.90
❑ 112C Etan Thomas RC	3.00	.90
❑ 113A Courtney Alexander RC	6.00	1.80
❑ 113B Courtney Alexander RC	6.00	1.80
❑ 113C Courtney Alexander RC	6.00	1.80
❑ 114A Mateen Cleaves RC	3.00	.90
❑ 114B Mateen Cleaves RC	3.00	.90
❑ 114C Mateen Cleaves RC	3.00	.90
❑ 115A Jason Collier RC	3.00	.90
❑ 115B Jason Collier RC	3.00	.90
❑ 115C Jason Collier RC	3.00	.90
❑ 116A Hidayet Turkoglu RC	10.00	3.00
❑ 116B Hidayet Turkoglu RC	10.00	3.00
❑ 116C Hidayet Turkoglu RC	10.00	3.00
❑ 117A Desmond Mason RC	3.00	.90
❑ 117B Desmond Mason RC	3.00	.90
❑ 117C Desmond Mason RC	3.00	.90
❑ 118A Quentin Richardson RC	12.00	3.60
❑ 118B Quentin Richardson RC	12.00	3.60
❑ 118C Quentin Richardson RC	12.00	3.60
❑ 119A Jamaal Magloire RC	3.00	.90
❑ 119B Jamaal Magloire RC	3.00	.90
❑ 119C Jamaal Magloire RC	3.00	.90
❑ 120A Speedy Claxton RC	3.00	.90
❑ 120B Speedy Claxton RC	3.00	.90
❑ 120C Speedy Claxton RC	3.00	.90
❑ 121A Morris Peterson RC	8.00	2.40
❑ 121B Morris Peterson RC	8.00	2.40
❑ 121C Morris Peterson RC	8.00	2.40
❑ 122A Donnell Harvey RC	3.00	.90
❑ 122B Donnell Harvey RC	3.00	.90
❑ 122C Donnell Harvey RC	3.00	.90
❑ 123A D.Stevenson RC	3.00	.90
❑ 123B D.Stevenson RC	3.00	.90
❑ 123C D.Stevenson RC	3.00	.90
❑ 124A Dalibor Bagaric RC	3.00	.90
❑ 124B Dalibor Bagaric RC	3.00	.90
❑ 124C Dalibor Bagaric RC	3.00	.90
❑ 125A Iakovos Tsakalidis RC	3.00	.90
❑ 125B Iakovos Tsakalidis RC	3.00	.90
❑ 125C Iakovos Tsakalidis RC	3.00	.90
❑ 126A Mamadou N'Diaye RC	3.00	.90
❑ 126B Mamadou N'Diaye RC	3.00	.90
❑ 126C Mamadou N'Diaye RC	3.00	.90
❑ 127A Lavor Postell RC	3.00	.90
❑ 127B Lavor Postell RC	3.00	.90
❑ 127C Lavor Postell RC	3.00	.90
❑ 128A Erick Barkley RC	3.00	.90
❑ 128B Erick Barkley RC	3.00	.90
❑ 128C Erick Barkley RC	3.00	.90
❑ 129A Mark Madsen RC	3.00	.90
❑ 129B Mark Madsen RC	3.00	.90
❑ 129C Mark Madsen RC	3.00	.90
❑ 130A Khalid El-Amin RC	3.00	.90
❑ 130B Khalid El-Amin RC	3.00	.90
❑ 130C Khalid El-Amin RC	3.00	.90
❑ 131A A.J. Guyton RC	3.00	.90
❑ 131B A.J. Guyton RC	3.00	.90

❑ 131C A.J. Guyton RC	3.00	.90
❑ 132A Stephen Jackson RC	6.00	1.80
❑ 132B Stephen Jackson RC	6.00	1.80
❑ 132C Stephen Jackson RC	6.00	1.80
❑ 133A Michael Redd RC	8.00	2.40
❑ 133B Michael Redd RC	8.00	2.40
❑ 133C Michael Redd RC	8.00	2.40
❑ LCP1 Kenyon Martin	10.00	3.00
Stromile Swift		
Darius Miles		
Marcus Fizer		
Mike Miller		
DerMarr Johnson		
Chris Mihm		
Jamal Crawford		
Joel Przybilla		
Keyon Dooling		
Jerome Moiso		
Etan Thomas		
Courtney Alexander		

2003-04 Bowman Chrome

	MINT	NRMT
COMP.SET w/o RC's (110)	80.00	36.00
COMMON CARD (1-110)	.40	.18
COMMON ROOKIE (111-147)	8.00	3.60
COMMON AU RC (148-157)	30.00	13.50
148-157 AU RC STATED ODDS 1:385		-
148-157 AU PRINT RUN 250 SER.#'d SETS		-
CARD 147 NOT RELEASED	-	
❑ 1 Yao Ming	4.00	1.80
❑ 2 Glenn Robinson	1.25	.55
❑ 3 Antoine Walker	1.25	.55
❑ 4 Jalen Rose	1.25	.55
❑ 5 Ricky Davis	1.25	.55
❑ 6 Juwan Howard	.75	.35
❑ 7 Kwame Brown	1.25	.55
❑ 8 Mike Bibby	1.25	.55
❑ 9 Wally Szczerbiak	.75	.35
❑ 10 Allen Iverson	2.50	1.10
❑ 11 Shareef Abdur-Rahim	1.25	.55
❑ 12 Jamal Mashburn	.75	.35
❑ 13 Stephon Marbury	1.25	.55
❑ 14 Desmond Mason	.75	.35
❑ 15 Gordan Giricek	.75	.35
❑ 16 Caron Butler	1.25	.55
❑ 17 Jermaine O'Neal	1.25	.55
❑ 18 Kenyon Martin	1.25	.55
❑ 19 Andrei Kirilenko	1.25	.55
❑ 20 Dirk Nowitzki	2.00	.90
❑ 21 Richard Hamilton	.75	.35
❑ 22 Troy Murphy	1.25	.55
❑ 23 Shawn Marion	1.25	.55
❑ 24 Allan Houston	.75	.35
❑ 25 Keith Van Horn	1.25	.55
❑ 26 Brian Grant	.75	.35
❑ 27 Mike Miller	1.25	.55
❑ 28 Chris Webber	1.25	.55
❑ 29 Brent Barry	.75	.35
❑ 30 Elton Brand	1.25	.55
❑ 31 Juan Dixon	.75	.35
❑ 32 Karl Malone	1.25	.55
❑ 33 Darrell Armstrong	.40	.18
❑ 34 Rasheed Wallace	1.25	.55
❑ 35 Michael Redd	1.25	.55
❑ 36 Rashard Lewis	1.25	.55
❑ 37 Ron Artest	.75	.35
❑ 38 P.J. Brown	.40	.18
❑ 39 Eddie Griffin	.75	.35
❑ 40 Tim Duncan	2.50	1.10
❑ 41 Kurt Thomas	.75	.35
❑ 42 Raef Lafrentz	.75	.35
❑ 43 Ben Wallace	1.25	.55
❑ 44 Lamar Odom	1.25	.55
❑ 45 Vince Carter	3.00	1.35
❑ 46 Derek Anderson	.75	.35
❑ 47 Stromile Swift	.75	.35
❑ 48 Bobby Jackson	.75	.35
❑ 49 Richard Jefferson	.75	.35
❑ 50 Shaquille O'Neal	3.00	1.35
❑ 51 Calbert Cheaney	.40	.18
❑ 52 Troy Hudson	.40	.18
❑ 53 Ray Allen	1.25	.55
❑ 54 Howard Eisley	.40	.18
❑ 55 Alonzo Mourning	.75	.35
❑ 56 Sam Cassell	1.25	.55
❑ 57 Derrick Coleman	.40	.18
❑ 58 Andre Miller	.75	.35
❑ 59 Antawn Jamison	1.25	.55
❑ 60 Kevin Garnett	2.50	1.10
❑ 61 Steve Francis	1.25	.55
❑ 62 Tyson Chandler	1.25	.55
❑ 63 Drew Gooden	.75	.35
❑ 64 Scottie Pippen	2.00	.90
❑ 65 Pau Gasol	1.25	.55
❑ 66 Steve Nash	1.25	.55
❑ 67 DaJuan Wagner	.75	.35
❑ 68 Jason Terry	1.25	.55
❑ 69 Reggie Miller	1.25	.55
❑ 70 Tracy McGrady	3.00	1.35
❑ 71 Nene Hilario	.75	.35
❑ 72 Morris Peterson	.75	.35
❑ 73 Peja Stojakovic	1.25	.55
❑ 74 Eddie Jones	1.25	.55
❑ 75 Tony Parker	1.25	.55
❑ 76 Corliss Williamson	.75	.35
❑ 77 Vladimir Radmanovic	.40	.18
❑ 78 Amare Stoudemire	4.00	1.80
❑ 79 Tony Delk	.40	.18
❑ 80 Jason Kidd	2.00	.90
❑ 81 Gary Payton	1.25	.55
❑ 82 Corey Maggette	.75	.35
❑ 83 Darius Miles	1.25	.55
❑ 84 Cuttino Mobley	.75	.35
❑ 85 Eric Snow	.75	.35
❑ 86 Matt Harpring	1.25	.55
❑ 87 Manu Ginobili	1.25	.55
❑ 88 Latrell Sprewell	1.25	.55
❑ 89 Alvin Williams	.40	.18
❑ 90 Paul Pierce	1.25	.55
❑ 91 Anfernee Hardaway	1.25	.55
❑ 92 Gilbert Arenas	1.25	.55
❑ 93 Jerry Stackhouse	1.25	.55
❑ 94 Tim Thomas	.75	.35
❑ 95 Nikoloz Tskitishvili	.40	.18
❑ 96 Doug Christie	.75	.35
❑ 97 Zydrunas Ilgauskas	.75	.35
❑ 98 Jamaal Tinsley	1.25	.55
❑ 99 Theo Ratliff	.75	.35
❑ 100 Kobe Bryant	5.00	2.20
❑ 101 Chauncey Billups	.75	.35
❑ 102 Michael Finley	1.25	.55
❑ 103 Jason Williams	.75	.35
❑ 104 Bonzi Wells	.75	.35
❑ 105 Voshon Lenard	.40	.18
❑ 106 Jason Richardson	1.25	.55
❑ 107 Baron Davis	1.25	.55
❑ 108 Radoslav Nesterovic	.75	.35
❑ 109 Eddy Curry	.75	.35
❑ 110 Michael Olowokandi	.40	.18
❑ 111 Josh Howard RC	10.00	4.50
❑ 112 Mario Austin RC	8.00	3.60
❑ 113 Rick Rickert RC	8.00	3.60
❑ 114 Tommy Smith RC	8.00	3.60
❑ 115 Dahntay Jones RC	8.00	3.60
❑ 116 Ndudi Ebi RC	8.00	3.60
❑ 117 Maurice Williams RC	8.00	3.60
❑ 118 Kendrick Perkins RC	8.00	3.60
❑ 119 Steve Blake RC	8.00	3.60
❑ 120 David West RC	8.00	3.60
❑ 121 Chris Kaman RC	8.00	3.60
❑ 122 Keith Bogans RC	8.00	3.60
❑ 123 LeBron James RC	80.00	36.00
❑ 124 Devin Brown RC	8.00	3.60
❑ 125 Jason Kapono RC	8.00	3.60
❑ 126 Zoran Planinic RC	8.00	3.60
❑ 127 Zaur Pachulia RC	8.00	3.60
❑ 128 Malick Badiane RC	8.00	3.60
❑ 129 Kyle Korver RC	10.00	4.50
❑ 130 Darko Milicic RC	12.00	5.50
❑ 131 Troy Bell RC	8.00	3.60
❑ 132 Luke Walton RC	8.00	3.60
❑ 133 Mike Sweetney RC	8.00	3.60
❑ 134 Jarvis Hayes RC	8.00	3.60
❑ 135 Leandro Barbosa RC	8.00	3.60
❑ 136 Carlos Delfino RC	8.00	3.60
❑ 137 Sofoklis Schortsanitis RC	8.00	3.60
❑ 138 Slavko Vranes RC	8.00	3.60
❑ 139 Travis Hansen RC	8.00	3.60
❑ 140 Carmelo Anthony RC	40.00	18.00
❑ 141 Reece Gaines RC	8.00	3.60
❑ 142 Maciej Lampe RC	8.00	3.60
❑ 143 Travis Outlaw RC	8.00	3.60
❑ 144 Jerome Beasley RC	8.00	3.60
❑ 145 Mickael Pietrus RC	8.00	3.60
❑ 146 Brian Cook RC	8.00	3.60
❑ 148 Kirk Hinrich AU EXCH	50.00	22.00
❑ 149 Dwyane Wade AU RC	100.00	45.00
❑ 150 Marcus Banks AU RC	50.00	22.00
❑ 151 Nick Collison AU RC	40.00	18.00
❑ 152 Boris Diaw AU RC	30.00	13.50
❑ 153 Chris Bosh AU RC	60.00	27.00
❑ 154 T.J. Ford AU RC	50.00	22.00
❑ 155 Luke Ridnour AU RC	50.00	22.00
❑ 156 Aleksander Pavlovic AU RC	30.00	13.50
❑ 157 Zarko Cabarkapa AU RC	30.00	13.50

1996-97 E-X2000

	Nm-Mt	Ex-Mt
COMPLETE SET (82)	120.00	36.00
COMMON CARD (1-82)	.60	.18
COMMON ROOKIE	2.00	.60
❑ 1 Christian Laettner	1.50	.45
❑ 2 Dikembe Mutombo	1.50	.45
❑ 3 Steve Smith	1.50	.45
❑ 4 Antoine Walker RC	10.00	3.00
❑ 5 David Wesley	.60	.18
❑ 6 Tony Delk RC	2.00	.60
❑ 7 Anthony Mason	1.50	.45
❑ 8 Glen Rice	1.50	.45
❑ 9 Michael Jordan	15.00	4.50
❑ 10 Scottie Pippen	3.00	.90
❑ 11 Dennis Rodman	1.50	.45
❑ 12 Terrell Brandon	1.50	.45
❑ 13 Chris Mills	.60	.18
❑ 14 Shawn Bradley	.60	.18
❑ 15 Michael Finley	2.50	.75
❑ 16 Dale Ellis	.60	.18
❑ 17 Antonio McDyess	1.50	.45
❑ 18 Joe Dumars	2.00	.60
❑ 19 Grant Hill	2.00	.60
❑ 20 Chris Mullin	2.00	.60
❑ 21 Joe Smith	1.50	.45
❑ 22 Latrell Sprewell	2.00	.60
❑ 23 Charles Barkley	2.50	.75
❑ 24 Clyde Drexler	2.00	.60
❑ 25 Hakeem Olajuwon	2.00	.60
❑ 26 Erick Dampier RC	2.50	.75
❑ 27 Reggie Miller	2.00	.60

Card	Nm-Mt	Ex-Mt
❑ 28 Loy Vaught	.60	.18
❑ 29 Lorenzen Wright RC	2.00	.60
❑ 30 Kobe Bryant RC	60.00	18.00
❑ 31 Eddie Jones	2.00	.60
❑ 32 Shaquille O'Neal	5.00	1.50
❑ 33 Nick Van Exel	2.00	.60
❑ 34 Tim Hardaway	1.50	.45
❑ 35 Jamal Mashburn	1.50	.45
❑ 36 Alonzo Mourning	1.50	.45
❑ 37 Ray Allen RC	10.00	3.00
❑ 38 Vin Baker	1.50	.45
❑ 39 Glenn Robinson	2.00	.60
❑ 40 Kevin Garnett	4.00	1.20
❑ 41 Tom Gugliotta	.60	.18
❑ 42 Stephon Marbury RC	8.00	2.40
❑ 43 Kendall Gill	.60	.18
❑ 44 Jim Jackson	.60	.18
❑ 45 Kerry Kittles RC	2.50	.75
❑ 46 Patrick Ewing	2.00	.60
❑ 47 Larry Johnson	1.50	.45
❑ 48 John Wallace RC	2.00	.60
❑ 49 Nick Anderson	.60	.18
❑ 50 Horace Grant	1.50	.45
❑ 51 Anfernee Hardaway	2.00	.60
❑ 52 Derrick Coleman	1.50	.45
❑ 53 Allen Iverson RC	25.00	7.50
❑ 54 Jerry Stackhouse	3.00	.90
❑ 55 Cedric Ceballos	.60	.18
❑ 56 Kevin Johnson	1.50	.45
❑ 57 Jason Kidd	3.00	.90
❑ 58 Clifford Robinson	.60	.18
❑ 59 Arvydas Sabonis	1.50	.45
❑ 60 Rasheed Wallace	2.50	.75
❑ 61 Mahmoud Abdul-Rauf	.60	.18
❑ 62 Brian Grant	2.00	.60
❑ 63 Mitch Richmond	1.50	.45
❑ 64 Sean Elliott	1.50	.45
❑ 65 David Robinson	2.00	.60
❑ 66 Dominique Wilkins	2.00	.60
❑ 67 Shawn Kemp	1.50	.45
❑ 68 Gary Payton	2.00	.60
❑ 69 Detlef Schrempf	1.50	.45
❑ 70 Marcus Camby RC	4.00	1.20
❑ 71 Damon Stoudamire	2.00	.60
❑ 72 Walt Williams	.60	.18
❑ 73 Shandon Anderson RC	2.50	.75
❑ 74 Karl Malone	2.00	.60
❑ 75 John Stockton	2.00	.60
❑ 76 Shareef Abdur-Rahim RC	10.00	3.00
❑ 77 Bryant Reeves	.60	.18
❑ 78 Roy Rogers RC	2.00	.60
❑ 79 Juwan Howard	1.50	.45
❑ 80 Chris Webber	2.00	.60
❑ 81 Checklist	.60	.18
❑ 82 Checklist	.60	.18
❑ NNO Grant Hill Blow-Up/3000	15.00	4.50
❑ NNO Grant Hill Autographed ball	200.00	60.00
❑ NNO Grant Hill Promo	2.50	.75

1997-98 E-X2001

	Nm-Mt	Ex-Mt
COMPLETE SET (82)	60.00	18.00
COMMON CARD (1-61)	.40	.12
COMMON ROOKIE (62-80)	.75	.23

Card	Nm-Mt	Ex-Mt
❑ 1 Grant Hill	1.25	.35
❑ 2 Kevin Garnett	2.50	.75
❑ 3 Allen Iverson	3.00	.90
❑ 4 Anfernee Hardaway	1.25	.35
❑ 5 Dennis Rodman	.75	.23
❑ 6 Shawn Kemp	.75	.23
❑ 7 Shaquille O'Neal	3.00	.90
❑ 8 Kobe Bryant	6.00	1.80
❑ 9 Michael Jordan	8.00	2.40
❑ 10 Marcus Camby	1.25	.35
❑ 11 Scottie Pippen	2.00	.60
❑ 12 Antoine Walker	1.50	.45
❑ 13 Stephon Marbury	1.50	.45
❑ 14 Shareef Abdur-Rahim	2.00	.60
❑ 15 Jerry Stackhouse	1.25	.35
❑ 16 Eddie Jones	1.25	.35
❑ 17 Charles Barkley	1.50	.45
❑ 18 David Robinson	1.25	.35
❑ 19 Karl Malone	1.25	.35
❑ 20 Damon Stoudamire	.75	.23
❑ 21 Patrick Ewing	1.25	.35
❑ 22 Kerry Kittles	1.25	.35
❑ 23 Gary Payton	1.25	.35
❑ 24 Glenn Robinson	1.25	.35
❑ 25 Hakeem Olajuwon	1.25	.35
❑ 26 John Starks	.75	.23
❑ 27 John Stockton	1.25	.35
❑ 28 Vin Baker	.75	.23
❑ 29 Reggie Miller	1.25	.35
❑ 30 Clyde Drexler	1.25	.35
❑ 31 Alonzo Mourning	.75	.23
❑ 32 Juwan Howard	.75	.23
❑ 33 Ray Allen	1.25	.35
❑ 34 Christian Laettner	.75	.23
❑ 35 Terrell Brandon	.75	.23
❑ 36 Sean Elliott	.75	.23
❑ 37 Rod Strickland	.40	.12
❑ 38 Rodney Rogers	.40	.12
❑ 39 Donyell Marshall	.75	.23
❑ 40 David Wesley	.40	.12
❑ 41 Sam Cassell	1.25	.35
❑ 42 Cedric Ceballos	.40	.12
❑ 43 Mahmoud Abdul-Rauf	.40	.12
❑ 44 Rik Smits	.75	.23
❑ 45 Lindsey Hunter	.40	.12
❑ 46 Michael Finley	1.25	.35
❑ 47 Steve Smith	.75	.23
❑ 48 Larry Johnson	.75	.23
❑ 49 Dikembe Mutombo	.75	.23
❑ 50 Tom Gugliotta	.75	.23
❑ 51 Joe Dumars	1.25	.35
❑ 52 Glen Rice	.75	.23
❑ 53 Bryant Reeves	.40	.12
❑ 54 Tim Hardaway	.75	.23
❑ 55 Isaiah Rider	.75	.23
❑ 56 Rasheed Wallace	1.25	.35
❑ 57 Jason Kidd	2.00	.60
❑ 58 Joe Smith	.75	.23
❑ 59 Chris Webber	1.25	.35
❑ 60 Mitch Richmond	.75	.23
❑ 61 Antonio McDyess	.75	.23
❑ 62 Bobby Jackson RC	2.50	.75
❑ 63 Derek Anderson RC	5.00	1.50
❑ 64 Kelvin Cato RC	1.25	.35
❑ 65 Jacque Vaughn RC	1.00	.30
❑ 66 Tariq Abdul-Wahad RC	1.00	.30
❑ 67 Johnny Taylor RC	.75	.23
❑ 68 Chris Anstey RC	.75	.23
❑ 69 Maurice Taylor RC	2.50	.75
❑ 70 Antonio Daniels RC	1.25	.35
❑ 71 Chauncey Billups RC	2.50	.75
❑ 72 Austin Croshere RC	2.50	.75
❑ 73 Brevin Knight RC	1.25	.35
❑ 74 Keith Van Horn RC	4.00	1.20
❑ 75 Tim Duncan RC	12.00	3.60
❑ 76 Danny Fortson RC	1.50	.45
❑ 77 Tim Thomas RC	4.00	1.20
❑ 78 Tony Battie RC	1.25	.35
❑ 79 Tracy McGrady RC	12.00	3.60
❑ 80 Ron Mercer RC	3.00	.90
❑ 81 Checklist (1-82)	.40	.12
❑ 82 Checklist (inserts)	.40	.12
❑ S1 Grant Hill SAMPLE	3.00	.90

1998-99 E-X Century

	Nm-Mt	Ex-Mt
COMPLETE SET (1-90)	100.00	30.00
COMMON CARD (1-60)	.30	.09
COMMON ROOKIE (61-90)	.75	.23
❑ 1 Keith Van Horn	1.00	.30
❑ 2 Scottie Pippen	1.50	.45
❑ 3 Tim Thomas	.60	.18
❑ 4 Stephon Marbury	1.00	.30
❑ 5 Allen Iverson	2.00	.60
❑ 6 Grant Hill	1.00	.30
❑ 7 Tim Duncan	1.50	.45
❑ 8 Latrell Sprewell	1.00	.30
❑ 9 Ron Mercer	.60	.18
❑ 10 Kobe Bryant	4.00	1.20
❑ 11 Antoine Walker	1.00	.30
❑ 12 Reggie Miller	1.00	.30
❑ 13 Kevin Garnett	2.00	.60
❑ 14 Shaquille O'Neal	2.50	.75
❑ 15 Karl Malone	1.00	.30
❑ 16 Dennis Rodman	.60	.18
❑ 17 Tracy McGrady	2.50	.75
❑ 18 Anfernee Hardaway	1.00	.30
❑ 19 Shareef Abdur-Rahim	1.00	.30
❑ 20 Marcus Camby	.60	.18
❑ 21 Eddie Jones	1.00	.30
❑ 22 Vin Baker	.60	.18
❑ 23 Charles Barkley	1.25	.35
❑ 24 Patrick Ewing	1.00	.30
❑ 25 Jason Kidd	1.50	.45
❑ 26 Mitch Richmond	.60	.18
❑ 27 Tim Hardaway	.60	.18
❑ 28 Glen Rice	.60	.18
❑ 29 Shawn Kemp	.60	.18
❑ 30 John Stockton	1.00	.30
❑ 31 Ray Allen	1.00	.30
❑ 32 Brevin Knight	.30	.09
❑ 33 David Robinson	1.00	.30
❑ 34 Juwan Howard	.60	.18
❑ 35 Alonzo Mourning	.60	.18
❑ 36 Hakeem Olajuwon	1.00	.30
❑ 37 Gary Payton	1.00	.30
❑ 38 Damon Stoudamire	.60	.18
❑ 39 Steve Smith	.60	.18
❑ 40 Chris Webber	1.00	.30
❑ 41 Michael Finley	1.00	.30
❑ 42 Jayson Williams	.30	.09
❑ 43 Maurice Taylor	.60	.18
❑ 44 Jalen Rose	1.00	.30
❑ 45 Sam Cassell	1.00	.30
❑ 46 Jerry Stackhouse	1.00	.30
❑ 47 Toni Kukoc	.60	.18
❑ 48 Charles Oakley	.30	.09
❑ 49 Jim Jackson	.30	.09
❑ 50 Dikembe Mutombo	.60	.18
❑ 51 Wesley Person	.30	.09
❑ 52 Antonio Daniels	.30	.09
❑ 53 Isaiah Rider	.30	.09
❑ 54 Tom Gugliotta	.30	.09
❑ 55 Antonio McDyess	.60	.18
❑ 56 Jeff Hornacek	.60	.18
❑ 57 Joe Dumars	1.00	.30
❑ 58 Jamal Mashburn	.60	.18
❑ 59 Donyell Marshall	.60	.18
❑ 60 Glenn Robinson	.60	.18
❑ 61 Jelani McCoy RC	.75	.23
❑ 62 Peja Stojakovic RC	6.00	1.80

Card	Nm-Mt	Ex-Mt
❑ 63 Randell Jackson RC	.75	.23
❑ 64 Brad Miller RC	8.00	2.40
❑ 65 Corey Benjamin RC	1.50	.45
❑ 66 Toby Bailey RC	.75	.23
❑ 67 Nazr Mohammed RC	1.00	.30
❑ 68 Dirk Nowitzki RC	15.00	4.50
❑ 69 Andrae Patterson RC	.75	.23
❑ 70 Michael Dickerson RC	3.00	.90
❑ 71 Cory Carr RC	.75	.23
❑ 72 Brian Skinner RC	1.50	.45
❑ 73 Pat Garrity RC	1.00	.30
❑ 74 Ricky Davis RC	5.00	1.50
❑ 75 Roshown McLeod RC	1.00	.30
❑ 76 Matt Harpring RC	2.50	.75
❑ 77 Jason Williams RC	6.00	1.80
❑ 78 Keon Clark RC	2.50	.75
❑ 79 Al Harrington RC	4.00	1.20
❑ 80 Felipe Lopez RC	2.00	.60
❑ 81 Michael Doleac RC	1.50	.45
❑ 82 Paul Pierce RC	8.00	2.40
❑ 83 Robert Traylor RC	1.50	.45
❑ 84 Raef LaFrentz RC	2.50	.75
❑ 85 Michael Olowokandi RC	2.50	.75
❑ 86 Mike Bibby RC	8.00	2.40
❑ 87 Antawn Jamison RC	8.00	2.40
❑ 88 Bonzi Wells RC	6.00	1.80
❑ 89 Vince Carter RC	25.00	7.50
❑ 90 Larry Hughes RC	5.00	1.50

1999-00 E-X

	Nm-Mt	Ex-Mt
COMPLETE SET (90)	120.00	36.00
COMPLETE SET w/o RC (60)	30.00	9.00
COMMON CARD (1-60)	.30	.09
COMMON ROOKIE (61-90)	1.25	.35
❑ 1 Stephon Marbury	1.00	.30
❑ 2 Antawn Jamison	1.50	.45
❑ 3 Patrick Ewing	1.00	.30
❑ 4 Nick Anderson	.30	.09
❑ 5 Charles Barkley	1.25	.35
❑ 6 Marcus Camby	.60	.18
❑ 7 Ron Mercer	.60	.18
❑ 8 Avery Johnson	.30	.09
❑ 9 Maurice Taylor	.60	.18
❑ 10 Isaiah Rider	.30	.09
❑ 11 Dirk Nowitzki	2.00	.60
❑ 12 Damon Stoudamire	.60	.18
❑ 13 Alonzo Mourning	.60	.18
❑ 14 Jason Kidd	1.50	.45
❑ 15 Juwan Howard	.60	.18
❑ 16 Vince Carter	2.50	.75
❑ 17 Tim Duncan	2.00	.60
❑ 18 Paul Pierce	1.00	.30
❑ 19 Tim Hardaway	.60	.18
❑ 20 Grant Hill	1.00	.30
❑ 21 Keith Van Horn	1.00	.30
❑ 22 Shaquille O'Neal	2.50	.75
❑ 23 Jason Williams	1.00	.30
❑ 24 Shareef Abdur-Rahim	1.00	.30
❑ 25 Kobe Bryant	4.00	1.20
❑ 26 David Robinson	1.00	.30
❑ 27 Anfernee Hardaway	1.00	.30
❑ 28 Vin Baker	.60	.18
❑ 29 Hakeem Olajuwon	1.00	.30
❑ 30 Michael Olowokandi	.60	.18
❑ 31 Mike Bibby	1.00	.30
❑ 32 Tracy McGrady	2.50	.75
❑ 33 Antoine Walker	1.00	.30
❑ 34 Larry Hughes	1.00	.30
❑ 35 Chris Webber	1.00	.30
❑ 36 Ray Allen	1.00	.30
❑ 37 Danny Fortson	.30	.09
❑ 38 Shawn Kemp	.60	.18
❑ 39 Michael Doleac	.30	.09
❑ 40 Gary Payton	1.00	.30
❑ 41 Toni Kukoc	.60	.18
❑ 42 Kevin Garnett	2.00	.60
❑ 43 Steve Smith	.60	.18
❑ 44 Scottie Pippen	1.50	.45
❑ 45 Allen Iverson	2.00	.60
❑ 46 Latrell Sprewell	1.00	.30
❑ 47 Matt Harpring	1.00	.30
❑ 48 Lindsey Hunter	.30	.09
❑ 49 Karl Malone	1.00	.30
❑ 50 Michael Finley	1.00	.30
❑ 51 Jerry Stackhouse	1.00	.30
❑ 52 Cedric Ceballos	.30	.09
❑ 53 Brent Barry	.60	.18
❑ 54 Elden Campbell	.30	.09
❑ 55 Glenn Robinson	1.00	.30
❑ 56 Eddie Jones	1.00	.30
❑ 57 Reggie Miller	1.00	.30
❑ 58 Mitch Richmond	.60	.18
❑ 59 Raef LaFrentz	.60	.18
❑ 60 John Starks	.60	.18
❑ 61 Elton Brand RC	8.00	2.40
❑ 62 William Avery RC	2.50	.75
❑ 63 Cal Bowdler RC	2.00	.60
❑ 64 Dion Glover RC	2.00	.60
❑ 65 Lamar Odom RC	6.00	1.80
❑ 66 Richard Hamilton RC	6.00	1.80
❑ 67 Kenny Thomas RC	2.50	.75
❑ 68 Shawn Marion RC	8.00	2.40
❑ 69 Baron Davis RC	6.00	1.80
❑ 70 Wally Szczerbiak RC	8.00	2.40
❑ 71 Scott Padgett RC	2.00	.60
❑ 72 Jason Terry RC	4.00	1.20
❑ 73 Trajan Langdon RC	2.50	.75
❑ 74 Andre Miller RC	6.00	1.80
❑ 75 Jeff Foster RC	2.00	.60
❑ 76 Tim James RC	2.00	.60
❑ 77 Aleksandar Radojevic RC	1.25	.35
❑ 78 Quincy Lewis RC	2.00	.60
❑ 79 James Posey RC	4.00	1.20
❑ 80 Steve Francis RC	10.00	3.00
❑ 81 Jonathan Bender RC	6.00	1.80
❑ 82 Corey Maggette RC	6.00	1.80
❑ 83 Obinna Ekezie RC	1.50	.45
❑ 84 Laron Profit RC	2.00	.60
❑ 85 Devean George RC	3.00	.90
❑ 86 Ron Artest RC	4.00	1.20
❑ 87 Rafer Alston RC	2.50	.75
❑ 88 Vonteego Cummings RC	2.50	.75
❑ 89 Evan Eschmeyer RC	1.25	.35
❑ 90 Jumaine Jones RC	3.00	.90
❑ S16 Vince Carter PROMO	2.50	.75

2000-01 E-X

	Nm-Mt	Ex-Mt
COMPLETE SET w/o RC (100)	40.00	12.00
COMMON CARD (1-100)	.30	.09
COMMON ROOKIE (101-130)	4.00	1.20
❑ 1 Dikembe Mutombo	.60	.18
❑ 2 Jim Jackson	.30	.09
❑ 3 Jason Terry	1.00	.30
❑ 4 Kenny Anderson	.60	.18
❑ 5 Antoine Walker	1.00	.30
❑ 6 Paul Pierce	1.00	.30
❑ 7 Jamal Mashburn	.60	.18
❑ 8 Baron Davis	1.00	.30
❑ 9 Derrick Coleman	.30	.09
❑ 10 Elton Brand	1.00	.30
❑ 11 Ron Artest	.60	.18
❑ 12 Andre Miller	.60	.18
❑ 13 Brevin Knight	.30	.09
❑ 14 Trajan Langdon	.60	.18
❑ 15 Lamond Murray	.30	.09
❑ 16 Dirk Nowitzki	1.50	.45
❑ 17 Michael Finley	1.00	.30
❑ 18 Nick Van Exel	1.00	.30
❑ 19 Antonio McDyess	.60	.18
❑ 20 Raef LaFrentz	.60	.18
❑ 21 Tariq Abdul-Wahad	.30	.09
❑ 22 Cedric Ceballos	.30	.09
❑ 23 Jerry Stackhouse	1.00	.30
❑ 24 Jerome Williams	.30	.09
❑ 25 Larry Hughes	.60	.18
❑ 26 Antawn Jamison	1.00	.30
❑ 27 Mookie Blaylock	.30	.09
❑ 28 Steve Francis	1.00	.30
❑ 29 Hakeem Olajuwon	1.00	.30
❑ 30 Maurice Taylor	.30	.09
❑ 31 Jonathan Bender	.60	.18
❑ 32 Reggie Miller	1.00	.30
❑ 33 Austin Croshere	.60	.18
❑ 34 Travis Best	.30	.09
❑ 35 Jalen Rose	1.00	.30
❑ 36 Lamar Odom	1.00	.30
❑ 37 Corey Maggette	.60	.18
❑ 38 Shaquille O'Neal	2.50	.75
❑ 39 Kobe Bryant	4.00	1.20
❑ 40 Horace Grant	.60	.18
❑ 41 Isaiah Rider	.60	.18
❑ 42 Brian Grant	.60	.18
❑ 43 Eddie Jones	1.00	.30
❑ 44 Tim Hardaway	.60	.18
❑ 45 Anthony Mason	.60	.18
❑ 46 Glenn Robinson	.60	.18
❑ 47 Ray Allen	1.00	.30
❑ 48 Sam Cassell	1.00	.30
❑ 49 Tim Thomas	.60	.18
❑ 50 Kevin Garnett	2.00	.60
❑ 51 Terrell Brandon	.60	.18
❑ 52 Joe Smith	.60	.18
❑ 53 Wally Szczerbiak	.60	.18
❑ 54 Chauncey Billups	.60	.18
❑ 55 Stephon Marbury	1.00	.30
❑ 56 Keith Van Horn	1.00	.30
❑ 57 Kerry Kittles	.30	.09
❑ 58 Allan Houston	.60	.18
❑ 59 Latrell Sprewell	1.00	.30
❑ 60 Larry Johnson	.60	.18
❑ 61 Glen Rice	.60	.18
❑ 62 Grant Hill	1.00	.30
❑ 63 Tracy McGrady	2.50	.75
❑ 64 Darrell Armstrong	.30	.09
❑ 65 Allen Iverson	2.00	.60
❑ 66 Toni Kukoc	.60	.18
❑ 67 Theo Ratliff	.60	.18
❑ 68 Jason Kidd	1.50	.45
❑ 69 Anfernee Hardaway	1.00	.30
❑ 70 Tom Gugliotta	.30	.09
❑ 71 Clifford Robinson	.30	.09
❑ 72 Shawn Kemp	.60	.18
❑ 73 Scottie Pippen	1.50	.45
❑ 74 Rasheed Wallace	1.00	.30
❑ 75 Steve Smith	.60	.18
❑ 76 Chris Webber	1.00	.30
❑ 77 Jason Williams	.60	.18
❑ 78 Peja Stojakovic	1.00	.30
❑ 79 Tim Duncan	2.00	.60
❑ 80 David Robinson	1.00	.30
❑ 81 Sean Elliott	.60	.18
❑ 82 Derek Anderson	.60	.18
❑ 83 Vin Baker	.60	.18
❑ 84 Rashard Lewis	.60	.18
❑ 85 Gary Payton	1.00	.30
❑ 86 Patrick Ewing	1.00	.30
❑ 87 Vince Carter	2.50	.75
❑ 88 Mark Jackson	.30	.09
❑ 89 Antonio Davis	.30	.09
❑ 90 Karl Malone	1.00	.30

Card	Nm-Mt	Ex-Mt
❑ 91 John Stockton	1.00	.30
❑ 92 Bryon Russell	.30	.09
❑ 93 Donyell Marshall	.60	.18
❑ 94 Shareef Abdur-Rahim	1.00	.30
❑ 95 Mike Bibby	1.00	.30
❑ 96 Michael Dickerson	.60	.18
❑ 97 Mitch Richmond	.60	.18
❑ 98 Juwan Howard	.60	.18
❑ 99 Richard Hamilton	.60	.18
❑ 100 Rod Strickland	.30	.09
❑ 101 DerMarr Johnson RC	4.00	1.20
❑ 102 Kenyon Martin RC	15.00	4.50
❑ 103 Marcus Fizer RC	4.00	1.20
❑ 104 Courtney Alexander RC	6.00	1.80
❑ 105 Stromile Swift RC	8.00	2.40
❑ 106 Darius Miles RC	15.00	4.50
❑ 107 Mike Miller RC	12.00	3.60
❑ 108 Jamal Crawford RC	4.00	1.20
❑ 109 Speedy Claxton RC	4.00	1.20
❑ 110 Quentin Richardson RC	15.00	4.50
❑ 111 Keyon Dooling RC	4.00	1.20
❑ 112 Desmond Mason RC	4.00	1.20
❑ 113 Mateen Cleaves RC	4.00	1.20
❑ 114 Morris Peterson RC	8.00	2.40
❑ 115 Hidayet Turkoglu RC	10.00	3.00
❑ 116 Donnell Harvey RC	4.00	1.20
❑ 117 Jerome Moiso RC	4.00	1.20
❑ 118 Jason Collier RC	4.00	1.20
❑ 119 Jamaal Magloire RC	4.00	1.20
❑ 120 Erick Barkley RC	4.00	1.20
❑ 121 Etan Thomas RC	4.00	1.20
❑ 122 DeShawn Stevenson RC	4.00	1.20
❑ 123 Dan Langhi RC	4.00	1.20
❑ 124 Mark Madsen RC	4.00	1.20
❑ 125 Khalid El-Amin RC	4.00	1.20
❑ 126 Lavor Postell RC	4.00	1.20
❑ 127 Eddie House RC	4.00	1.20
❑ 128 Michael Redd RC	6.00	1.80
❑ 129 Chris Porter RC	4.00	1.20
❑ 130 Mike Smith RC	4.00	1.20

2001-02 E-X

	Nm-Mt	Ex-Mt
COMPLETE SET (130)	500.00	150.00
COMP.SET w/o SP's (100)	50.00	15.00
COMMON CARD (1-100)	.30	.09
COMMON ROOKIE (101-130)	3.00	.90
❑ 1 Shareef Abdur-Rahim	1.00	.30
❑ 2 DerMarr Johnson	.60	.18
❑ 3 Jason Terry	1.00	.30
❑ 4 Paul Pierce	1.00	.30
❑ 5 Antoine Walker	1.00	.30
❑ 6 Baron Davis	1.00	.30
❑ 7 Jamal Mashburn	.60	.18
❑ 8 Chris Mihm	.60	.18
❑ 9 Andre Miller	.60	.18
❑ 10 Dirk Nowitzki	1.50	.45
❑ 11 Michael Finley	1.00	.30
❑ 12 Raef LaFrentz	.60	.18
❑ 13 Antonio McDyess	.60	.18
❑ 14 Jerry Stackhouse	1.00	.30
❑ 15 Antawn Jamison	1.00	.30
❑ 16 Steve Francis	1.00	.30
❑ 17 Jalen Rose	1.00	.30
❑ 18 Elton Brand	1.00	.30
❑ 19 Darius Miles	1.25	.35
❑ 20 Lamar Odom	1.00	.30
❑ 21 Mitch Richmond	.60	.18
❑ 22 Michael Dickerson	.60	.18
❑ 23 Stromile Swift	.60	.18
❑ 24 Alonzo Mourning	.60	.18
❑ 25 Courtney Alexander	.60	.18
❑ 26 Ray Allen	1.00	.30
❑ 27 Glenn Robinson	.60	.18
❑ 28 Terrell Brandon	.60	.18
❑ 29 Wally Szczerbiak	.60	.18
❑ 30 Joe Smith	.60	.18
❑ 31 Jason Kidd	1.50	.45
❑ 32 Kenyon Martin	1.00	.30
❑ 33 Keith Van Horn	1.00	.30
❑ 34 Grant Hill	1.00	.30
❑ 35 Tracy McGrady	2.50	.75
❑ 36 Mike Miller	1.00	.30
❑ 37 Allen Iverson	2.00	.60
❑ 38 Speedy Claxton	.60	.18
❑ 39 Dikembe Mutombo	.60	.18
❑ 40 Tom Gugliotta	.30	.09
❑ 41 Penny Hardaway	1.00	.30
❑ 42 Stephon Marbury	1.00	.30
❑ 43 Shawn Marion	1.00	.30
❑ 44 Rasheed Wallace	1.00	.30
❑ 45 Peja Stojakovic	1.00	.30
❑ 46 Mike Bibby	1.00	.30
❑ 47 Chris Webber	1.00	.30
❑ 48 David Robinson	1.00	.30
❑ 49 Vin Baker	.60	.18
❑ 50 Rashard Lewis	.60	.18
❑ 51 Desmond Mason	.60	.18
❑ 52 Gary Payton	1.00	.30
❑ 53 Vince Carter	2.50	.75
❑ 54 Antonio Davis	.30	.09
❑ 55 Hakeem Olajuwon	1.00	.30
❑ 56 Morris Peterson	.60	.18
❑ 57 Karl Malone	1.00	.30
❑ 58 DeShawn Stevenson	.60	.18
❑ 59 John Stockton	1.00	.30
❑ 60 Richard Hamilton	.60	.18
❑ 61 Corey Maggette	.60	.18
❑ 62 Steve Smith	.60	.18
❑ 63 Tim Thomas	.60	.18
❑ 64 Lindsey Hunter	.30	.09
❑ 65 Jermaine O'Neal	1.00	.30
❑ 66 Cuttino Mobley	.60	.18
❑ 67 Nick Van Exel	1.00	.30
❑ 68 Juwan Howard	.60	.18
❑ 69 James Posey	.60	.18
❑ 70 David Wesley	.30	.09
❑ 71 Marcus Fizer	.60	.18
❑ 72 Jumaine Jones	.60	.18
❑ 73 Tim Hardaway	.60	.18
❑ 74 Danny Fortson	.30	.09
❑ 75 Jonathan Bender	.60	.18
❑ 76 Quentin Richardson	.60	.18
❑ 77 Eddie House	.60	.18
❑ 78 Kurt Thomas	.60	.18
❑ 79 Anthony Mason	.60	.18
❑ 80 Theo Ratliff	.60	.18
❑ 81 Allan Houston	.60	.18
❑ 82 Latrell Sprewell	1.00	.30
❑ 83 Jason Williams	.60	.18
❑ 84 Eddie Jones	1.00	.30
❑ 85 Damon Stoudamire	.60	.18
❑ 86 Sam Cassell	1.00	.30
❑ 87 Cliff Robinson	.60	.18
❑ 88 Patrick Ewing	1.00	.30
❑ 89 Tim Duncan	1.00	.30
❑ 90 Marcus Camby	.60	.18
❑ 91 Brian Grant	.60	.18
❑ 92 Kobe Bryant	4.00	1.20
❑ 93 Ron Mercer	.60	.18
❑ 94 Reggie Miller	1.00	.30
❑ 95 Shaquille O'Neal	2.50	.75
❑ 96 Kevin Garnett	2.00	.60
❑ 97 Scottie Pippen	1.50	.45
❑ 98 Michael Jordan	15.00	4.50
❑ 99 Steve Nash	1.00	.30
❑ 100 Derek Anderson	.60	.18
❑ 101 Kedrick Brown/1750 RC	3.00	.90
❑ 102 Joseph Forte/1750 RC	8.00	2.40
❑ 103 Joe Johnson/1250 RC	6.00	1.80
❑ 104 Kirk Haston/1750 RC	3.00	.90
❑ 105 Tyson Chandler/750 RC	15.00	4.50
❑ 106 Eddy Curry/1250 RC	8.00	2.40
❑ 107 D.Diop/1750 RC	3.00	.90
❑ 108 T.Hassell/1250 RC	3.00	.90
❑ 109 Z.Rebraca/1250 RC	3.00	.90
❑ 110 Rodney White/1750 RC	4.00	1.20
❑ 111 Troy Murphy/1250 RC	8.00	2.40
❑ 112 J.Richardson/750 RC	15.00	4.50
❑ 113 Eddie Griffin/750 RC	10.00	3.00
❑ 114 Terence Morris/1750 RC	3.00	.90
❑ 115 Oscar Torres/1250 RC	4.00	1.20
❑ 116 Jamaal Tinsley/750 RC	10.00	3.00
❑ 117 Pau Gasol/750 RC	25.00	7.50
❑ 118 Shane Battier/750 RC	10.00	3.00
❑ 119 B.Armstrong/1250 RC	5.00	1.50
❑ 120 R.Jefferson/750 RC	10.00	3.00
❑ 121 Steven Hunter/1250 RC	4.00	1.20
❑ 122 S.Dalembert/1750 RC	3.00	.90
❑ 123 Z.Randolph/1250 RC	12.00	3.60
❑ 124 G.Wallace/1750 RC	6.00	1.80
❑ 125 Tony Parker/750 RC	25.00	7.50
❑ 126 V.Radmanovic/1250 RC	5.00	1.50
❑ 127 Michael Bradley/1750 RC	3.00	.90
❑ 128 Jarron Collins/1750 RC	3.00	.90
❑ 129 Andrei Kirilenko/750 RC	20.00	6.00
❑ 130 Kwame Brown/750 RC	10.00	3.00

2003-04 E-X

	Nm-Mt	Ex-Mt
COMP.SET w/o SP's (72)	50.00	15.00
COMMON CARD (1-72)	.25	.07
COMMON ROOKIE (73-102)	6.00	1.80
❑ 1 Shareef Abdur-Rahim	1.00	.30
❑ 2 Ray Allen	1.00	.30
❑ 3 Gilbert Arenas	1.00	.30
❑ 4 Ron Artest	.60	.18
❑ 5 Mike Bibby	1.00	.30
❑ 6 Chauncey Billups	.60	.18
❑ 7 Elton Brand	1.00	.30
❑ 8 Kwame Brown	.60	.18
❑ 9 Kobe Bryant	4.00	1.20
❑ 10 Caron Butler	1.00	.30
❑ 11 Vince Carter	2.50	.75
❑ 12 Eddy Curry	1.00	.30
❑ 13 Ricky Davis	1.00	.30
❑ 14 Baron Davis	1.00	.30
❑ 15 Tim Duncan	2.00	.60
❑ 16 Michael Finley	1.00	.30
❑ 17 Steve Francis	1.00	.30
❑ 18 Kevin Garnett	2.00	.60
❑ 19 Pau Gasol	1.00	.30
❑ 20 Manu Ginobili	1.00	.30
❑ 21 Drew Gooden	.60	.18
❑ 22 Nene	.60	.18
❑ 23 Grant Hill	1.00	.30
❑ 24 Allan Houston	.60	.18
❑ 25 Juwan Howard	.60	.18
❑ 26 Zydrunas Ilgauskas	.60	.18
❑ 27 Allen Iverson	2.00	.60
❑ 28 Antawn Jamison	1.00	.30
❑ 29 Richard Jefferson	.60	.18
❑ 30 Eddie Jones	1.00	.30
❑ 31 Jason Kidd	1.50	.45
❑ 32 Andrei Kirilenko	1.00	.30
❑ 33 Rashard Lewis	1.00	.30
❑ 34 Corey Maggette	.60	.18
❑ 35 Karl Malone	1.00	.30
❑ 36 Stephon Marbury	1.00	.30
❑ 37 Shawn Marion	1.00	.30
❑ 38 Kenyon Martin	1.00	.30
❑ 39 Jamal Mashburn	.60	.18

Card	Nm-Mt	Ex-Mt
❑ 40 Tracy McGrady	2.50	.75
❑ 41 Reggie Miller	1.00	.30
❑ 42 Mike Miller	1.00	.30
❑ 43 Yao Ming	2.50	.75
❑ 44 Cuttino Mobley	.60	.18
❑ 45 Steve Nash	.60	.18
❑ 46 Dirk Nowitzki	1.50	.45
❑ 47 Jermaine O'Neal	1.00	.30
❑ 48 Shaquille O'Neal	2.50	.75
❑ 49 Tony Parker	1.00	.30
❑ 50 Gary Payton	1.00	.30
❑ 51 Morris Peterson	.60	.18
❑ 52 Paul Pierce	1.00	.30
❑ 53 Scottie Pippen	1.50	.45
❑ 54 Tayshaun Prince	.60	.18
❑ 55 Vladimir Radmanovic	.25	.07
❑ 56 Michael Redd	1.00	.30
❑ 57 Jason Richardson	1.00	.30
❑ 58 Glenn Robinson	1.00	.30
❑ 59 Jalen Rose	1.00	.30
❑ 60 Latrell Sprewell	1.00	.30
❑ 61 Jerry Stackhouse	.60	.18
❑ 62 Peja Stojakovic	1.00	.30
❑ 63 Amare Stoudemire	2.00	.60
❑ 64 Wally Szczerbiak	.60	.18
❑ 65 Jason Terry	1.00	.30
❑ 66 Keith Van Horn	1.00	.30
❑ 67 Dajuan Wagner	.60	.18
❑ 68 Antoine Walker	1.00	.30
❑ 69 Ben Wallace	1.00	.30
❑ 70 Rasheed Wallace	1.00	.30
❑ 71 Chris Webber	1.00	.30
❑ 72 Bonzi Wells	.60	.18
❑ 73 Carmelo Anthony RC	40.00	12.00
❑ 74 Ndudi Ebi RC	6.00	1.80
❑ 75 Luke Ridnour RC	8.00	2.40
❑ 76 Josh Howard RC	8.00	2.40
❑ 77 Marcus Banks RC	6.00	1.80
❑ 78 Zarko Cabarkapa RC	6.00	1.80
❑ 79 Kendrick Perkins RC	6.00	1.80
❑ 80 Leandro Barbosa RC	6.00	1.80
❑ 81 David West RC	6.00	1.80
❑ 82 Boris Diaw RC	6.00	1.80
❑ 83 Carlos Delfino RC	6.00	1.80
❑ 84 Mickael Pietrus RC	6.00	1.80
❑ 85 Troy Bell RC	6.00	1.80
❑ 86 Reece Gaines RC	6.00	1.80
❑ 87 Brian Cook RC	6.00	1.80
❑ 88 Kirk Hinrich RC	8.00	2.40
❑ 89 Travis Outlaw RC	6.00	1.80
❑ 90 Dwyane Wade RC	15.00	4.50
❑ 91 Luke Walton RC	8.00	2.40
❑ 92 Chris Bosh RC	12.00	3.60
❑ 93 Jarvis Hayes RC	6.00	1.80
❑ 94 Maciej Lampe RC	6.00	1.80
❑ 95 Mike Sweetney RC	6.00	1.80
❑ 96 Sofoklis Schortsanitis RC	6.00	1.80
❑ 97 Dahntay Jones RC	6.00	1.80
❑ 98 Nick Collison RC	6.00	1.80
❑ 99 Chris Kaman RC	6.00	1.80
❑ 100 Darko Milicic RC	10.00	3.00
❑ 101 T.J. Ford RC	8.00	2.40
❑ 102 LeBron James RC	80.00	24.00

1993-94 Finest

	Nm-Mt	Ex-Mt
COMPLETE SET (220)	100.00	30.00
❑ 1 Michael Jordan	12.00	3.60
❑ 2 Larry Bird	2.50	.75
❑ 3 Shaquille O'Neal	5.00	1.50
❑ 4 Benoit Benjamin	.25	.07
❑ 5 Ricky Pierce	.25	.07
❑ 6 Ken Norman	.25	.07
❑ 7 Victor Alexander	.25	.07
❑ 8 Mark Jackson	.40	.12
❑ 9 Mark West	.25	.07
❑ 10 Don MacLean	.25	.07
❑ 11 Reggie Miller	.75	.23
❑ 12 Sarunas Marciulionis	.25	.07
❑ 13 Craig Ehlo	.25	.07
❑ 14 Toni Kukoc RC	4.00	1.20
❑ 15 Glen Rice	.40	.12
❑ 16 Otis Thorpe	.40	.12
❑ 17 Reggie Williams	.25	.07
❑ 18 Charles Smith	.25	.07
❑ 19 Micheal Williams	.25	.07
❑ 20 Tom Chambers	.25	.07
❑ 21 David Robinson	1.50	.45
❑ 22 Jamal Mashburn RC	5.00	1.50
❑ 23 Clifford Robinson	.40	.12
❑ 24 Acie Earl RC	.25	.07
❑ 25 Danny Ferry	.25	.07
❑ 26 Bobby Hurley RC	.40	.12
❑ 27 Eddie Johnson	.25	.07
❑ 28 Detlef Schrempf	.40	.12
❑ 29 Mike Brown	.25	.07
❑ 30 Latrell Sprewell	2.50	.75
❑ 31 Derek Harper	.40	.12
❑ 32 Stacey Augmon	.25	.07
❑ 33 Pooh Richardson	.25	.07
❑ 34 Larry Krystkowiak	.25	.07
❑ 35 Pervis Ellison	.25	.07
❑ 36 Jeff Malone	.25	.07
❑ 37 Sean Elliott	.40	.12
❑ 38 John Paxson	.25	.07
❑ 39 Robert Parish	.40	.12
❑ 40 Mark Aguirre	.25	.07
❑ 41 Danny Ainge	.40	.12
❑ 42 Brian Shaw	.25	.07
❑ 43 LaPhonso Ellis	.25	.07
❑ 44 Carl Herrera	.25	.07
❑ 45 Terry Cummings	.25	.07
❑ 46 Chris Dudley	.25	.07
❑ 47 Anthony Mason	.40	.12
❑ 48 Chris Morris	.25	.07
❑ 49 Todd Day	.25	.07
❑ 50 Nick Van Exel RC	6.00	1.80
❑ 51 Larry Nance	.25	.07
❑ 52 Derrick McKey	.25	.07
❑ 53 Muggsy Bogues	.40	.12
❑ 54 Andrew Lang	.25	.07
❑ 55 Chuck Person	.25	.07
❑ 56 Michael Adams	.25	.07
❑ 57 Spud Webb	.40	.12
❑ 58 Scott Skiles	.25	.07
❑ 59 A.C. Green	.40	.12
❑ 60 Terry Mills	.25	.07
❑ 61 Xavier McDaniel	.25	.07
❑ 62 B.J. Armstrong	.25	.07
❑ 63 Donald Hodge	.25	.07
❑ 64 Gary Grant	.25	.07
❑ 65 Billy Owens	.25	.07
❑ 66 Greg Anthony	.25	.07
❑ 67 Jay Humphries	.25	.07
❑ 68 Lionel Simmons	.25	.07
❑ 69 Dana Barros	.25	.07
❑ 70 Steve Smith	.75	.23
❑ 71 Ervin Johnson RC	.40	.12
❑ 72 Sleepy Floyd	.25	.07
❑ 73 Blue Edwards	.25	.07
❑ 74 Clyde Drexler	.75	.23
❑ 75 Elden Campbell	.25	.07
❑ 76 Hakeem Olajuwon	1.50	.45
❑ 77 Clarence Weatherspoon	.25	.07
❑ 78 Kevin Willis	.25	.07
❑ 79 Isaiah Rider RC	4.00	1.20
❑ 80 Derrick Coleman	.40	.12
❑ 81 Nick Anderson	.40	.12
❑ 82 Bryant Stith	.25	.07
❑ 83 Johnny Newman	.25	.07
❑ 84 Calbert Cheaney RC	1.50	.45
❑ 85 Oliver Miller	.25	.07
❑ 86 Loy Vaught	.25	.07
❑ 87 Isiah Thomas	.75	.23
❑ 88 Dee Brown	.25	.07
❑ 89 Horace Grant	.40	.12
❑ 90 Patrick Ewing AF	.40	.12
❑ 91 Clarence Weatherspoon AF	.25	.07
❑ 92 Rony Seikaly AF	.25	.07
❑ 93 Dino Radja AF	.25	.07
❑ 94 Kenny Anderson AF	.25	.07
❑ 95 John Starks AF	.25	.07
❑ 96 Tom Gugliotta AF	.40	.12
❑ 97 Steve Smith AF	.40	.12
❑ 98 Derrick Coleman AF	.25	.07
❑ 99 Shaquille O'Neal AF	3.00	.90
❑ 100 Brad Daugherty CF	.25	.07
❑ 101 Horace Grant CF	.25	.07
❑ 102 Dominique Wilkins CF	.40	.12
❑ 103 Joe Dumars CF	.40	.12
❑ 104 Alonzo Mourning CF	.75	.23
❑ 105 Scottie Pippen CF	2.50	.75
❑ 106 Reggie Miller CF	.40	.12
❑ 107 Mark Price CF	.25	.07
❑ 108 Ken Norman CF	.25	.07
❑ 109 Larry Johnson CF	.40	.12
❑ 110 Jamal Mashburn MF	.75	.23
❑ 111 Christian Laettner MF	.25	.07
❑ 112 Karl Malone MF	.75	.23
❑ 113 Dennis Rodman MF	.75	.23
❑ 114 Mahmoud Abdul-Rauf MF	.25	.07
❑ 115 Hakeem Olajuwon MF	.75	.23
❑ 116 Jim Jackson MF	.25	.07
❑ 117 John Stockton MF	.40	.12
❑ 118 David Robinson MF	.75	.23
❑ 119 Dikembe Mutombo MF	.40	.12
❑ 120 Vlade Divac PF	.25	.07
❑ 121 Dan Majerle PF	.25	.07
❑ 122 Chris Mullin PF	.40	.12
❑ 123 Shawn Kemp PF	.75	.23
❑ 124 Danny Manning PF	.25	.07
❑ 125 Charles Barkley PF	.75	.23
❑ 126 Mitch Richmond PF	.40	.12
❑ 127 Tim Hardaway PF	.40	.12
❑ 128 Detlef Schrempf PF	.25	.07
❑ 129 Clyde Drexler PF	.40	.12
❑ 130 Christian Laettner	.40	.12
❑ 131 Rodney Rogers RC	2.00	.60
❑ 132 Rik Smits	.40	.12
❑ 133 Chris Mills RC	2.00	.60
❑ 134 Corie Blount RC	.25	.07
❑ 135 Mookie Blaylock	.40	.12
❑ 136 Jim Jackson	.40	.12
❑ 137 Tom Gugliotta	.75	.23
❑ 138 Dennis Scott	.25	.07
❑ 139 Vin Baker RC	4.00	1.20
❑ 140 Gary Payton	1.50	.45
❑ 141 Sedale Threatt	.25	.07
❑ 142 Orlando Woolridge	.25	.07
❑ 143 Avery Johnson	.25	.07
❑ 144 Charles Oakley	.40	.12
❑ 145 Harvey Grant	.25	.07
❑ 146 Bimbo Coles	.25	.07
❑ 147 Vernon Maxwell	.25	.07
❑ 148 Danny Manning	.40	.12
❑ 149 Hersey Hawkins	.40	.12
❑ 150 Kevin Gamble	.25	.07
❑ 151 Johnny Dawkins	.25	.07
❑ 152 Olden Polynice	.25	.07
❑ 153 Kevin Edwards	.25	.07
❑ 154 Willie Anderson	.25	.07
❑ 155 Wayman Tisdale	.25	.07
❑ 156 Popeye Jones RC	.25	.07
❑ 157 Dan Majerle	.40	.12
❑ 158 Rex Chapman	.25	.07
❑ 159 Shawn Kemp	1.50	.45
❑ 160 Eric Murdock	.25	.07
❑ 161 Randy White	.25	.07
❑ 162 Larry Johnson	.75	.23
❑ 163 Dominique Wilkins	.75	.23
❑ 164 Dikembe Mutombo	.75	.23
❑ 165 Patrick Ewing	.75	.23
❑ 166 Jerome Kersey	.25	.07
❑ 167 Dale Davis	.25	.07
❑ 168 Ron Harper	.40	.12
❑ 169 Sam Cassell RC	6.00	1.80
❑ 170 Bill Cartwright	.25	.07
❑ 171 John Williams	.25	.07
❑ 172 Dino Radja RC	.25	.07

Card	Nm-Mt	Ex-Mt
❑ 173 Dennis Rodman	2.00	.60
❑ 174 Kenny Anderson	.40	.12
❑ 175 Robert Horry	.40	.12
❑ 176 Chris Mullin	.75	.23
❑ 177 John Salley	.25	.07
❑ 178 Scott Burrell RC	1.50	.45
❑ 179 Mitch Richmond	.75	.23
❑ 180 Lee Mayberry	.25	.07
❑ 181 James Worthy	.75	.23
❑ 182 Rick Fox	.25	.07
❑ 183 Kevin Johnson	.40	.12
❑ 184 Lindsey Hunter RC	2.00	.60
❑ 185 Marlon Maxey	.25	.07
❑ 186 Sam Perkins	.40	.12
❑ 187 Kevin Duckworth	.25	.07
❑ 188 Jeff Hornacek	.40	.12
❑ 189 Anfernee Hardaway RC	12.00	3.60
❑ 190 Rex Walters RC	.25	.07
❑ 191 Mahmoud Abdul-Rauf	.25	.07
❑ 192 Terry Dehere RC	.25	.07
❑ 193 Brad Daugherty	.25	.07
❑ 194 John Starks	.40	.12
❑ 195 Rod Strickland	.40	.12
❑ 196 Luther Wright RC	.25	.07
❑ 197 Vlade Divac	.40	.12
❑ 198 Tim Hardaway	.75	.23
❑ 199 Joe Dumars	.75	.23
❑ 200 Charles Barkley	1.50	.45
❑ 201 Alonzo Mourning	1.50	.45
❑ 202 Doug West	.25	.07
❑ 203 Anthony Avent	.25	.07
❑ 204 Lloyd Daniels	.25	.07
❑ 205 Mark Price	.25	.07
❑ 206 Rumeal Robinson	.25	.07
❑ 207 Kendall Gill	.40	.12
❑ 208 Scottie Pippen	3.00	.90
❑ 209 Kenny Smith	.25	.07
❑ 210 Walt Williams	.25	.07
❑ 211 Hubert Davis	.25	.07
❑ 212 Chris Webber RC	25.00	7.50
❑ 213 Rony Seikaly	.25	.07
❑ 214 Sam Bowie	.25	.07
❑ 215 Karl Malone	1.50	.45
❑ 216 Malik Sealy	.25	.07
❑ 217 Dale Ellis	.25	.07
❑ 218 Harold Miner	.25	.07
❑ 219 John Stockton	.75	.23
❑ 220 Shawn Bradley RC	2.00	.60

1994-95 Finest

	Nm-Mt	Ex-Mt
COMPLETE SET (1-331)	250.00	75.00
COMPLETE SERIES 1 (165)	100.00	30.00
COMPLETE SERIES 2 (166)	150.00	45.00
COMMON CARD (1-165)	.60	.18
COMMON CARD (166-331)	.30	.09
❑ 1 Chris Mullin CY	1.25	.35
❑ 2 Anthony Mason CY	.60	.18
❑ 3 John Salley CY	.60	.18
❑ 4 Jamal Mashburn CY	1.25	.35
❑ 5 Mark Jackson CY	.60	.18
❑ 6 Mario Elie CY	.60	.18
❑ 7 Kenny Anderson CY	.60	.18
❑ 8 Rod Strickland CY	.60	.18
❑ 9 Kenny Smith CY	.60	.18
❑ 10 Olden Polynice CY	.60	.18
❑ 11 Derek Harper	.60	.18
❑ 12 Danny Ainge	.60	.18
❑ 13 Dino Radja	.60	.18
❑ 14 Eric Murdock	.60	.18
❑ 15 Sean Rooks	.60	.18
❑ 16 Dell Curry	.60	.18
❑ 17 Victor Alexander	.60	.18
❑ 18 Rodney Rogers	.60	.18
❑ 19 John Salley	.60	.18
❑ 20 Brad Daugherty	.60	.18
❑ 21 Elmore Spencer	.60	.18
❑ 22 Mitch Richmond	2.50	.75
❑ 23 Rex Walters	.60	.18
❑ 24 Antonio Davis	.60	.18
❑ 25 B.J. Armstrong	.60	.18
❑ 26 Andrew Lang	.60	.18
❑ 27 Carl Herrera	.60	.18
❑ 28 Kevin Edwards	.60	.18
❑ 29 Micheal Williams	.60	.18
❑ 30 Clyde Drexler	2.50	.75
❑ 31 Dana Barros	.60	.18
❑ 32 Shaquille O'Neal	12.00	3.60
❑ 33 Patrick Ewing	2.50	.75
❑ 34 Charles Barkley	4.00	1.20
❑ 35 J.R. Reid	.60	.18
❑ 36 Lindsey Hunter	1.25	.35
❑ 37 Jeff Malone	.60	.18
❑ 38 Rik Smits	.60	.18
❑ 39 Brian Williams	.60	.18
❑ 40 Shawn Kemp	4.00	1.20
❑ 41 Terry Porter	.60	.18
❑ 42 James Worthy	2.50	.75
❑ 43 Rex Chapman	.60	.18
❑ 44 Stanley Roberts	.60	.18
❑ 45 Chris Smith	.60	.18
❑ 46 Dee Brown	.60	.18
❑ 47 Chris Gatling	.60	.18
❑ 48 Donald Hodge	.60	.18
❑ 49 Bimbo Coles	.60	.18
❑ 50 Derrick Coleman	1.25	.35
❑ 51 Muggsy Bogues CY	.60	.18
❑ 52 Reggie Williams CY	.60	.18
❑ 53 David Wingate CY	.60	.18
❑ 54 Sam Cassell CY	2.50	.75
❑ 55 Sherman Douglas CY	.60	.18
❑ 56 Keith Jennings	.60	.18
❑ 57 Kenny Gattison	.60	.18
❑ 58 Brent Price	.60	.18
❑ 59 Luc Longley	.60	.18
❑ 60 Jamal Mashburn	2.50	.75
❑ 61 Doug West	.60	.18
❑ 62 Walt Williams	.60	.18
❑ 63 Tracy Murray	.60	.18
❑ 64 Robert Pack	.60	.18
❑ 65 Johnny Dawkins	.60	.18
❑ 66 Vin Baker	2.50	.75
❑ 67 Sam Cassell	2.50	.75
❑ 68 Dale Davis	.60	.18
❑ 69 Terrell Brandon	1.25	.35
❑ 70 Billy Owens	.60	.18
❑ 71 Ervin Johnson	.60	.18
❑ 72 Allan Houston	4.00	1.20
❑ 73 Craig Ehlo	.60	.18
❑ 74 Loy Vaught	.60	.18
❑ 75 Scottie Pippen	8.00	2.40
❑ 76 Sam Bowie	.60	.18
❑ 77 Anthony Mason	1.25	.35
❑ 78 Felton Spencer	.60	.18
❑ 79 P.J. Brown	.60	.18
❑ 80 Christian Laettner	1.25	.35
❑ 81 Todd Day	.60	.18
❑ 82 Sean Elliott	1.25	.35
❑ 83 Grant Long	.60	.18
❑ 84 Xavier McDaniel	.60	.18
❑ 85 David Benoit	.60	.18
❑ 86 Larry Stewart	.60	.18
❑ 87 Donald Royal	.60	.18
❑ 88 Duane Causwell	.60	.18
❑ 89 Vlade Divac	.60	.18
❑ 90 Derrick McKey	.60	.18
❑ 91 Kevin Johnson	1.25	.35
❑ 92 LaPhonso Ellis	.60	.18
❑ 93 Jerome Kersey	.60	.18
❑ 94 Muggsy Bogues	1.25	.35
❑ 95 Tom Gugliotta	1.25	.35
❑ 96 Jeff Hornacek	1.25	.35
❑ 97 Kevin Willis	.60	.18
❑ 98 Chris Mills	1.25	.35
❑ 99 Sam Perkins	1.25	.35
❑ 100 Alonzo Mourning	3.00	.90
❑ 101 Derrick Coleman CY	.60	.18
❑ 102 Glen Rice CY	.60	.18
❑ 103 Kevin Willis CY	.60	.18
❑ 104 Chris Webber CY	3.00	.90
❑ 105 Terry Mills CY	.60	.18
❑ 106 Tim Hardaway CY	1.25	.35
❑ 107 Nick Anderson CY	.60	.18
❑ 108 Terry Cummings CY	.60	.18
❑ 109 Hersey Hawkins CY	.60	.18
❑ 110 Ken Norman CY	.60	.18
❑ 111 Nick Anderson	.60	.18
❑ 112 Tim Perry	.60	.18
❑ 113 Terry Dehere	.60	.18
❑ 114 Chris Morris	.60	.18
❑ 115 John Williams	.60	.18
❑ 116 Jon Barry	.60	.18
❑ 117 Rony Seikaly	.60	.18
❑ 118 Detlef Schrempf	1.25	.35
❑ 119 Terry Cummings	.60	.18
❑ 120 Chris Webber	6.00	1.80
❑ 121 David Wingate	.60	.18
❑ 122 Popeye Jones	.60	.18
❑ 123 Sherman Douglas	.60	.18
❑ 124 Greg Anthony	.60	.18
❑ 125 Mookie Blaylock	.60	.18
❑ 126 Don MacLean	.60	.18
❑ 127 Lionel Simmons	.60	.18
❑ 128 Scott Brooks	.60	.18
❑ 129 Jeff Turner	.60	.18
❑ 130 Bryant Stith	.60	.18
❑ 131 Shawn Bradley	.60	.18
❑ 132 Byron Scott	1.25	.35
❑ 133 Doug Christie	1.25	.35
❑ 134 Dennis Rodman	5.00	1.50
❑ 135 Dan Majerle	1.25	.35
❑ 136 Gary Grant	.60	.18
❑ 137 Bryon Russell	.60	.18
❑ 138 Will Perdue	.60	.18
❑ 139 Gheorghe Muresan	.60	.18
❑ 140 Kendall Gill	1.25	.35
❑ 141 Isaiah Rider	1.25	.35
❑ 142 Terry Mills	.60	.18
❑ 143 Willie Anderson	.60	.18
❑ 144 Hubert Davis	.60	.18
❑ 145 Lucious Harris	.60	.18
❑ 146 Spud Webb	.60	.18
❑ 147 Glen Rice	1.25	.35
❑ 148 Dennis Scott	.60	.18
❑ 149 Robert Horry	1.25	.35
❑ 150 John Stockton	2.50	.75
❑ 151 Stacey Augmon CY	.60	.18
❑ 152 Chris Mills CY	.60	.18
❑ 153 Elden Campbell CY	.60	.18
❑ 154 Jay Humphries CY	.60	.18
❑ 155 Reggie Miller CY	1.25	.35
❑ 156 George Lynch	.60	.18
❑ 157 Tyrone Hill	.60	.18
❑ 158 Lee Mayberry	.60	.18
❑ 159 Jon Koncak	.60	.18
❑ 160 Joe Dumars	2.50	.75
❑ 161 Vernon Maxwell	.60	.18
❑ 162 Joe Kleine	.60	.18
❑ 163 Acie Earl	.60	.18
❑ 164 Steve Kerr	.60	.18
❑ 165 Rod Strickland	1.25	.35
❑ 166 Glenn Robinson RC	10.00	3.00
❑ 167 Anfernee Hardaway	4.00	1.20
❑ 168 Latrell Sprewell	2.50	.75
❑ 169 Sergei Bazarevich	.30	.09
❑ 170 Hakeem Olajuwon	2.00	.60
❑ 171 Nick Van Exel	1.25	.35
❑ 172 Buck Williams	.30	.09
❑ 173 Antoine Carr	.30	.09
❑ 174 Corie Blount	.30	.09
❑ 175 Dominique Wilkins	1.25	.35
❑ 176 Yinka Dare	.30	.09
❑ 177 Byron Houston	.30	.09
❑ 178 LaSalle Thompson	.30	.09
❑ 179 Doug Smith	.30	.09
❑ 180 David Robinson	2.00	.60
❑ 181 Eric Piatkowski RC	.30	.09
❑ 182 Scott Skiles	.30	.09
❑ 183 Scott Burrell	.30	.09
❑ 184 Mark West	.30	.09

Card	Nm-Mt	Ex-Mt
❑ 185 Billy Owens	.30	.09
❑ 186 Brian Grant RC	5.00	1.50
❑ 187 Scott Williams	.30	.09
❑ 188 Gerald Madkins	.30	.09
❑ 189 Reggie Williams	.30	.09
❑ 190 Danny Manning	.60	.18
❑ 191 Mike Brown	.30	.09
❑ 192 Charles Smith	.30	.09
❑ 193 Elden Campbell	.30	.09
❑ 194 Ricky Pierce	.30	.09
❑ 195 Karl Malone	2.00	.60
❑ 196 Brooks Thompson	.30	.09
❑ 197 Alaa Abdelnaby	.30	.09
❑ 198 Tyrone Corbin	.30	.09
❑ 199 Johnny Newman	.30	.09
❑ 200 Grant Hill CB	6.00	1.80
❑ 201 Kenny Anderson CB	.30	.09
❑ 202 Olden Polynice CB	.30	.09
❑ 203 Horace Grant CB	.30	.09
❑ 204 Muggsy Bogues CB	.30	.09
❑ 205 Mark Price CB	.30	.09
❑ 206 Tom Gugliotta CB	.30	.09
❑ 207 Christian Laettner CB	.30	.09
❑ 208 Eric Montross CB	.30	.09
❑ 209 Sam Cassell CB	1.25	.35
❑ 210 Charles Oakley	.30	.09
❑ 211 Harold Ellis	.30	.09
❑ 212 Nate McMillan	.30	.09
❑ 213 Chuck Person	.30	.09
❑ 214 Harold Miner	.30	.09
❑ 215 Clarence Weatherspoon	.30	.09
❑ 216 Robert Parish	.60	.18
❑ 217 Michael Cage	.30	.09
❑ 218 Kenny Smith	.30	.09
❑ 219 Larry Krystkowiak	.30	.09
❑ 220 Dikembe Mutombo	.60	.18
❑ 221 Wayman Tisdale	.30	.09
❑ 222 Kevin Duckworth	.30	.09
❑ 223 Vern Fleming	.30	.09
❑ 224 Eric Mobley RC	.30	.09
❑ 225 Patrick Ewing CB	.60	.18
❑ 226 Clifford Robinson CB	.30	.09
❑ 227 Eric Murdock CB	.30	.09
❑ 228 Derrick Coleman CB	.30	.09
❑ 229 Otis Thorpe CB	.30	.09
❑ 230 Alonzo Mourning CB	1.25	.35
❑ 231 Donyell Marshall CB	.60	.18
❑ 232 Dikembe Mutombo CB	.30	.09
❑ 233 Rony Seikaly CB	.30	.09
❑ 234 Chris Mullin CB	.60	.18
❑ 235 Reggie Miller	1.25	.35
❑ 236 Benoit Benjamin	.30	.09
❑ 237 Sean Rooks	.30	.09
❑ 238 Terry Davis	.30	.09
❑ 239 Anthony Avent	.30	.09
❑ 240 Grant Hill RC	30.00	9.00
❑ 241 Randy Woods	.30	.09
❑ 242 Tom Chambers	.30	.09
❑ 243 Michael Adams	.30	.09
❑ 244 Monty Williams RC	.30	.09
❑ 245 Chris Mullin	1.25	.35
❑ 246 Bill Wennington	.30	.09
❑ 247 Mark Jackson	.30	.09
❑ 248 Blue Edwards	.30	.09
❑ 249 Jalen Rose RC	10.00	3.00
❑ 250 Glenn Robinson CB	1.50	.45
❑ 251 Kevin Willis CB	.30	.09
❑ 252 B.J. Armstrong CB	.30	.09
❑ 253 Jim Jackson CB	.30	.09
❑ 254 Steve Smith CB	.30	.09
❑ 255 Chris Webber CB	1.50	.45
❑ 256 Glen Rice CB	.30	.09
❑ 257 Derek Harper CB	.30	.09
❑ 258 Jalen Rose CB	2.00	.60
❑ 259 Juwan Howard CB	1.25	.35
❑ 260 Kenny Anderson	.60	.18
❑ 261 Calbert Cheaney	.30	.09
❑ 262 Bill Cartwright	.30	.09
❑ 263 Mario Elie	.30	.09
❑ 264 Chris Dudley	.30	.09
❑ 265 Jim Jackson	.60	.18
❑ 266 Antonio Harvey	.30	.09
❑ 267 Bill Curley RC	.30	.09
❑ 268 Moses Malone	1.25	.35
❑ 269 A.C. Green	.60	.18
❑ 270 Larry Johnson	.60	.18
❑ 271 Marty Conlon	.30	.09
❑ 272 Greg Graham	.30	.09
❑ 273 Eric Montross RC	.30	.09
❑ 274 Stacey King	.30	.09
❑ 275 Charles Barkley CB	1.25	.35
❑ 276 Chris Morris CB	.30	.09
❑ 277 Robert Horry CB	.60	.18
❑ 278 Dominique Wilkins CB	.60	.18
❑ 279 Latrell Sprewell CB	1.25	.35
❑ 280 Shaquille O'Neal CB	3.00	.90
❑ 281 Wesley Person CB	.60	.18
❑ 282 Mahmoud Abdul-Rauf CB	.30	.09
❑ 283 Jamal Mashburn CB	.60	.18
❑ 284 Dale Ellis CB	.30	.09
❑ 285 Gary Payton	2.00	.60
❑ 286 Jason Kidd RC	25.00	7.50
❑ 287 Ken Norman	.30	.09
❑ 288 Juwan Howard RC	5.00	1.50
❑ 289 Lamond Murray RC	2.00	.60
❑ 290 Clifford Robinson	.60	.18
❑ 291 Frank Brickowski	.30	.09
❑ 292 Adam Keefe	.30	.09
❑ 293 Ron Harper	.60	.18
❑ 294 Tom Hammonds	.30	.09
❑ 295 Otis Thorpe	.30	.09
❑ 296 Rick Mahorn	.30	.09
❑ 297 Alton Lister	.30	.09
❑ 298 Vinny Del Negro	.30	.09
❑ 299 Danny Ferry	.30	.09
❑ 300 John Starks	.30	.09
❑ 301 Duane Ferrell	.30	.09
❑ 302 Hersey Hawkins	.60	.18
❑ 303 Khalid Reeves RC	.30	.09
❑ 304 Anthony Peeler	.30	.09
❑ 305 Tim Hardaway	1.25	.35
❑ 306 Rick Fox	.30	.09
❑ 307 Jay Humphries	.30	.09
❑ 308 Brian Shaw	.30	.09
❑ 309 Danny Schayes	.30	.09
❑ 310 Stacey Augmon	.30	.09
❑ 311 Oliver Miller	.30	.09
❑ 312 Pooh Richardson	.30	.09
❑ 313 Donyell Marshall RC	5.00	1.50
❑ 314 Aaron McKie RC	5.00	1.50
❑ 315 Mark Price	.30	.09
❑ 316 B.J. Tyler RC	.30	.09
❑ 317 Olden Polynice	.30	.09
❑ 318 Avery Johnson	.30	.09
❑ 319 Derek Strong	.30	.09
❑ 320 Toni Kukoc	2.00	.60
❑ 321 Charlie Ward RC	4.00	1.20
❑ 322 Wesley Person RC	4.00	1.20
❑ 323 Eddie Jones RC	10.00	3.00
❑ 324 Horace Grant	.60	.18
❑ 325 Mahmoud Abdul-Rauf	.30	.09
❑ 326 Sharone Wright RC	.30	.09
❑ 327 Kevin Gamble	.30	.09
❑ 328 Sarunas Marciulionis	.30	.09
❑ 329 Harvey Grant	.30	.09
❑ 330 Bobby Hurley	.30	.09
❑ 331 Michael Jordan	15.00	4.50

1995-96 Finest

	Nm-Mt	Ex-Mt
COMPLETE SET (251)	220.00	65.00
COMPLETE SERIES 1 (140)	180.00	55.00
COMPLETE SERIES 2 (111)	40.00	12.00
COMMON CARD (1-250/252)	.75	.23
COMMON ROOKIE	1.50	.45
❑ 1 Hakeem Olajuwon	2.50	.75
❑ 2 Stacey Augmon	.75	.23
❑ 3 John Starks	1.50	.45
❑ 4 Sharone Wright	.75	.23
❑ 5 Jason Kidd	8.00	2.40
❑ 6 Lamond Murray	.75	.23
❑ 7 Kenny Anderson	1.50	.45
❑ 8 James Robinson	.75	.23
❑ 9 Wesley Person	.75	.23
❑ 10 Latrell Sprewell	2.50	.75
❑ 11 Sean Elliott	1.50	.45
❑ 12 Greg Anthony	.75	.23
❑ 13 Kendall Gill	.75	.23
❑ 14 Mark Jackson	1.50	.45
❑ 15 John Stockton	3.00	.90
❑ 16 Steve Smith	1.50	.45
❑ 17 Bobby Hurley	.75	.23
❑ 18 Ervin Johnson	.75	.23
❑ 19 Elden Campbell	.75	.23
❑ 20 Vin Baker	1.50	.45
❑ 21 Micheal Williams	.75	.23
❑ 22 Steve Kerr	1.50	.45
❑ 23 Kevin Duckworth	.75	.23
❑ 24 Willie Anderson	.75	.23
❑ 25 Joe Dumars	2.50	.75
❑ 26 Dale Ellis	.75	.23
❑ 27 Bimbo Coles	.75	.23
❑ 28 Nick Anderson	.75	.23
❑ 29 Dee Brown	.75	.23
❑ 30 Tyrone Hill	.75	.23
❑ 31 Reggie Miller	2.50	.75
❑ 32 Shaquille O'Neal	6.00	1.80
❑ 33 Brian Grant	2.50	.75
❑ 34 Charles Barkley	3.00	.90
❑ 35 Cedric Ceballos	.75	.23
❑ 36 Rex Walters	.75	.23
❑ 37 Kenny Smith	.75	.23
❑ 38 Popeye Jones	.75	.23
❑ 39 Harvey Grant	.75	.23
❑ 40 Gary Payton	2.50	.75
❑ 41 John Williams	.75	.23
❑ 42 Sherman Douglas	.75	.23
❑ 43 Oliver Miller	.75	.23
❑ 44 Kevin Willis	1.50	.45
❑ 45 Isaiah Rider	.75	.23
❑ 46 Gheorghe Muresan	.75	.23
❑ 47 Blue Edwards	.75	.23
❑ 48 Jeff Hornacek	1.50	.45
❑ 49 J.R. Reid	.75	.23
❑ 50 Glenn Robinson	2.50	.75
❑ 51 Dell Curry	.75	.23
❑ 52 Greg Graham	.75	.23
❑ 53 Ron Harper	1.50	.45
❑ 54 Derek Harper	1.50	.45
❑ 55 Dikembe Mutombo	1.50	.45
❑ 56 Terry Mills	.75	.23
❑ 57 Victor Alexander	.75	.23
❑ 58 Malik Sealy	.75	.23
❑ 59 Vincent Askew	.75	.23
❑ 60 Mitch Richmond	1.50	.45
❑ 61 Duane Ferrell	.75	.23
❑ 62 Dickey Simpkins	.75	.23
❑ 63 Pooh Richardson	.75	.23
❑ 64 Khalid Reeves	.75	.23
❑ 65 Dino Radja	.75	.23
❑ 66 Lee Mayberry	.75	.23
❑ 67 Kenny Gattison	.75	.23
❑ 68 Joe Kleine	.75	.23
❑ 69 Tony Dumas	.75	.23
❑ 70 Nick Van Exel	2.50	.75
❑ 71 Armon Gilliam	.75	.23
❑ 72 Craig Ehlo	.75	.23
❑ 73 Adam Keefe	.75	.23
❑ 74 Chris Dudley	.75	.23
❑ 75 Clyde Drexler	2.50	.75
❑ 76 Jeff Turner	.75	.23
❑ 77 Calbert Cheaney	.75	.23
❑ 78 Vinny Del Negro	.75	.23
❑ 79 Tim Perry	.75	.23
❑ 80 Tim Hardaway	1.50	.45
❑ 81 B.J. Armstrong	.75	.23
❑ 82 Muggsy Bogues	1.50	.45
❑ 83 Mark Macon	.75	.23
❑ 84 Doug West	.75	.23

Card	Player	Nm-Mt	Ex-Mt
❑ 85	Jalen Rose	3.00	.90
❑ 86	Chris Mills	.75	.23
❑ 87	Charles Oakley	.75	.23
❑ 88	Andrew Lang	.75	.23
❑ 89	Olden Polynice	.75	.23
❑ 90	Sam Cassell	2.50	.75
❑ 91	Todd Day	.75	.23
❑ 92	P.J. Brown	.75	.23
❑ 93	Benoit Benjamin	.75	.23
❑ 94	Sam Perkins	1.50	.45
❑ 95	Eddie Jones	3.00	.90
❑ 96	Robert Parish	1.50	.45
❑ 97	Avery Johnson	.75	.23
❑ 98	Lindsey Hunter	.75	.23
❑ 99	Billy Owens	.75	.23
❑ 100	Shawn Bradley	.75	.23
❑ 101	Dale Davis	.75	.23
❑ 102	Terry Dehere	.75	.23
❑ 103	A.C. Green	1.50	.45
❑ 104	Christian Laettner	1.50	.45
❑ 105	Horace Grant	1.50	.45
❑ 106	Rony Seikaly	.75	.23
❑ 107	Reggie Williams	.75	.23
❑ 108	Toni Kukoc	1.50	.45
❑ 109	Terrell Brandon	1.50	.45
❑ 110	Clifford Robinson	.75	.23
❑ 111	Joe Smith RC	5.00	1.50
❑ 112	Antonio McDyess RC	10.00	3.00
❑ 113	Jerry Stackhouse RC	15.00	4.50
❑ 114	Rasheed Wallace RC	12.00	3.60
❑ 115	Kevin Garnett RC	70.00	21.00
❑ 116	Bryant Reeves RC	2.50	.75
❑ 117	Damon Stoudamire RC	6.00	1.80
❑ 118	Shawn Respert RC	.75	.23
❑ 119	Ed O'Bannon RC	1.50	.45
❑ 120	Kurt Thomas RC	1.50	.45
❑ 121	Gary Trent RC	3.00	.90
❑ 122	Cherokee Parks RC	1.50	.45
❑ 123	Corliss Williamson RC	3.00	.90
❑ 124	Eric Williams RC	1.50	.45
❑ 125	Brent Barry RC	2.50	.75
❑ 126	Alan Henderson RC	3.00	.90
❑ 127	Bob Sura RC	1.50	.45
❑ 128	Theo Ratliff RC	5.00	1.50
❑ 129	Randolph Childress RC	1.50	.45
❑ 130	Jason Caffey RC	1.50	.45
❑ 131	Michael Finley RC	12.00	3.60
❑ 132	George Zidek RC	1.50	.45
❑ 133	Travis Best RC	1.50	.45
❑ 134	Loren Meyer RC	1.50	.45
❑ 135	David Vaughn RC	1.50	.45
❑ 136	Sherrell Ford RC	1.50	.45
❑ 137	Mario Bennett RC	1.50	.45
❑ 138	Greg Ostertag RC	1.50	.45
❑ 139	Cory Alexander RC	1.50	.45
❑ 140	Checklist UER #111	.75	.23
❑ 141	Chucky Brown	.75	.23
❑ 142	Eric Mobley	.75	.23
❑ 143	Tom Hammonds	.75	.23
❑ 144	Chris Webber	3.00	.90
❑ 145	Carlos Rogers	.75	.23
❑ 146	Chuck Person	.75	.23
❑ 147	Brian Williams	.75	.23
❑ 148	Kevin Gamble	.75	.23
❑ 149	Dennis Rodman	1.50	.45
❑ 150	Pervis Ellison	.75	.23
❑ 151	Jayson Williams	.75	.23
❑ 152	Buck Williams	.75	.23
❑ 153	Allan Houston	1.50	.45
❑ 154	Tom Gugliotta	.75	.23
❑ 155	Charles Smith	.75	.23
❑ 156	Chris Gatling	.75	.23
❑ 157	Darrin Hancock	.75	.23
❑ 158	Blue Edwards	.75	.23
❑ 159	Shawn Kemp	1.50	.45
❑ 160	Michael Cage	.75	.23
❑ 161	Sedale Threatt	.75	.23
❑ 162	Byron Scott	.75	.23
❑ 163	Elliot Perry	.75	.23
❑ 164	Jim Jackson	.75	.23
❑ 165	Wayman Tisdale	.75	.23
❑ 166	Vernon Maxwell	.75	.23
❑ 167	Brian Shaw	.75	.23
❑ 168	Haywoode Workman	.75	.23
❑ 169	Mookie Blaylock	.75	.23
❑ 170	Donald Royal	.75	.23
❑ 171	Lorenzo Williams	.75	.23
❑ 172	Eric Piatkowski UER Name spelled Paitkowski on back	1.50	.45
❑ 173	Sarunas Marciulionis	.75	.23
❑ 174	Otis Thorpe	.75	.23
❑ 175	Rex Chapman	.75	.23
❑ 176	Felton Spencer	.75	.23
❑ 177	John Salley	.75	.23
❑ 178	Pete Chilcutt	.75	.23
❑ 179	Scottie Pippen	4.00	1.20
❑ 180	Robert Pack	.75	.23
❑ 181	Dana Barros	.75	.23
❑ 182	Mahmoud Abdul-Rauf	.75	.23
❑ 183	Eric Murdock	.75	.23
❑ 184	Anthony Mason	1.50	.45
❑ 185	Will Perdue	.75	.23
❑ 186	Jeff Malone	.75	.23
❑ 187	Anthony Peeler	.75	.23
❑ 188	Chris Childs	.75	.23
❑ 189	Glen Rice	1.50	.45
❑ 190	Grant Hill	3.00	.90
❑ 191	Michael Smith	.75	.23
❑ 192	Sean Rooks	.75	.23
❑ 193	Clifford Rozier	.75	.23
❑ 194	Rik Smits	1.50	.45
❑ 195	Spud Webb	1.50	.45
❑ 196	Aaron McKie	1.50	.45
❑ 197	Nate McMillan	.75	.23
❑ 198	Bobby Phills	.75	.23
❑ 199	Dennis Scott	.75	.23
❑ 200	Mark West	.75	.23
❑ 201	George McCloud	.75	.23
❑ 202	B.J. Tyler	.75	.23
❑ 203	Lionel Simmons	.75	.23
❑ 204	Loy Vaught	.75	.23
❑ 205	Kevin Edwards	.75	.23
❑ 206	Eric Montross	.75	.23
❑ 207	Kenny Gattison	.75	.23
❑ 208	Mario Elie	.75	.23
❑ 209	Karl Malone	3.00	.90
❑ 210	Ken Norman	.75	.23
❑ 211	Antonio Davis	.75	.23
❑ 212	Doc Rivers	1.50	.45
❑ 213	Hubert Davis	.75	.23
❑ 214	Jamal Mashburn	1.50	.45
❑ 215	Donyell Marshall	1.50	.45
❑ 216	Sasha Danilovic RC	.75	.23
❑ 217	Danny Manning	1.50	.45
❑ 218	Scott Burrell	.75	.23
❑ 219	Vlade Divac	1.50	.45
❑ 220	Marty Conlon	.75	.23
❑ 221	Clarence Weatherspoon	.75	.23
❑ 222	Terry Porter	.75	.23
❑ 223	Luc Longley	.75	.23
❑ 224	Juwan Howard	2.50	.75
❑ 225	Danny Ferry	.75	.23
❑ 226	Rod Strickland	.75	.23
❑ 227	Bryant Stith	.75	.23
❑ 228	Derrick McKey	.75	.23
❑ 229	Michael Jordan	15.00	4.50
❑ 230	Jamie Watson	.75	.23
❑ 231	Rick Fox	1.50	.45
❑ 232	Scott Williams	.75	.23
❑ 233	Larry Johnson	1.50	.45
❑ 234	Anfernee Hardaway	2.50	.75
❑ 235	Hersey Hawkins	.75	.23
❑ 236	Robert Horry	1.50	.45
❑ 237	Kevin Johnson	1.50	.45
❑ 238	Rodney Rogers	.75	.23
❑ 239	Detlef Schrempf	1.50	.45
❑ 240	Derrick Coleman	.75	.23
❑ 241	Walt Williams	.75	.23
❑ 242	LaPhonso Ellis	.75	.23
❑ 243	Patrick Ewing	2.50	.75
❑ 244	Grant Long	.75	.23
❑ 245	David Robinson	2.50	.75
❑ 246	Chris Mullin	2.50	.75
❑ 247	Alonzo Mourning	1.50	.45
❑ 248	Dan Majerle	1.50	.45
❑ 249	Johnny Newman	.75	.23
❑ 250	Chris Morris	.75	.23
❑ 252	Magic Johnson	4.00	1.20

1996-97 Finest

	Nm-Mt	Ex-Mt
COMPLETE SET (291)	600.00	180.00
COMPLETE SERIES 1 (146)	350.00	105.00
COMPLETE SERIES 2 (145)	300.00	90.00
COMP.BRONZE SET (200)	140.00	42.50
COMP.BRONZE SER.1 (100)	100.00	30.00
COMP.BRONZE SER.2 (100)	40.00	12.00
COMMON BRONZE	.40	.12
COMMON BRONZE RC	1.25	.35
COMP.SILVER SET (54)	120.00	36.00
COMP.SILVER SER.1 (27)	40.00	12.00
COMP.SILVER SER.2 (27)	80.00	24.00
COMMON SILVER	1.25	.35
COMP.GOLD SET (37)	400.00	120.00
COMP.GOLD SER.1 (19)	200.00	60.00
COMP.GOLD SER.2 (18)	200.00	60.00
COMMON GOLD	4.00	1.20

Card	Player	Nm-Mt	Ex-Mt
❑ 1	Scottie Pippen B	2.00	.60
❑ 2	Tim Legler B	.40	.12
❑ 3	Rex Walters B	.40	.12
❑ 4	Calbert Cheaney B	.40	.12
❑ 5	Dennis Rodman B	.75	.23
❑ 6	Tyrone Hill B	.40	.12
❑ 8	Dell Curry B	.40	.12
❑ 9	Olden Polynice B	.40	.12
❑ 10	John Wallace B RC	1.50	.45
❑ 11	Martin Muursepp B RC	1.25	.35
❑ 12	Chuck Person B	.40	.12
❑ 13	Grant Hill B	1.25	.35
❑ 14	Shawn Kemp B	.75	.23
❑ 15	B.J. Armstrong B	.40	.12
❑ 16	Gary Trent B	.40	.12
❑ 17	Scott Williams B	.40	.12
❑ 18	Dino Radja B	.40	.12
❑ 19	Roy Rogers B RC	1.25	.35
❑ 20	Tony Delk B RC	2.50	.75
❑ 21	Clifford Robinson B	.40	.12
❑ 22	Ray Allen B RC	8.00	2.40
❑ 23	Clyde Drexler B	1.25	.35
❑ 24	Elliot Perry B	.40	.12
❑ 25	Gary Payton B	1.25	.35
❑ 26	Dale Davis B	.40	.12
❑ 27	Horace Grant B	.75	.23
❑ 28	Brian Evans B RC	1.25	.35
❑ 29	Joe Smith B	.75	.23
❑ 30	Reggie Miller B	1.25	.35
❑ 31	Jermaine O'Neal B RC	8.00	2.40
❑ 32	Avery Johnson B	.40	.12
❑ 33	Ed O'Bannon B	.40	.12
❑ 34	Cedric Ceballos B	.40	.12
❑ 35	Jamal Mashburn B	.75	.23
❑ 36	Micheal Williams B	.40	.12
❑ 37	Detlef Schrempf B	.75	.23
❑ 38	Damon Stoudamire B	1.25	.35
❑ 39	Jason Kidd B	2.00	.60
❑ 40	Tom Gugliotta B	.40	.12
❑ 41	Arvydas Sabonis B	.75	.23
❑ 42	Samaki Walker B RC	1.25	.35
❑ 43	Derek Fisher B RC	4.00	1.20
❑ 44	Patrick Ewing B	1.25	.35
❑ 45	Bryant Reeves B	.40	.12

Card		
❑ 46 Mookie Blaylock B	.40	.12
❑ 47 George Zidek B	.40	.12
❑ 48 Jerry Stackhouse B	1.50	.45
❑ 49 Vin Baker B	.75	.23
❑ 50 Michael Jordan B	8.00	2.40
❑ 51 Terrell Brandon B	.75	.23
❑ 52 Karl Malone B	1.25	.35
❑ 53 Lorenzen Wright B RC	1.25	.35
❑ 54 S.Abdur-Rahim B RC	5.00	1.50
❑ 55 Kurt Thomas B	.75	.23
❑ 56 Glen Rice B	.75	.23
❑ 57 Shawn Bradley B	.40	.12
❑ 58 Todd Fuller B RC	1.25	.35
❑ 59 Dale Ellis B	.40	.12
❑ 60 David Robinson B	1.25	.35
❑ 61 Doug Christie B	.75	.23
❑ 62 Stephon Marbury B RC	8.00	2.40
❑ 63 Hakeem Olajuwon B	1.25	.35
❑ 64 Lindsey Hunter B	.40	.12
❑ 65 Anfernee Hardaway B	1.25	.35
❑ 66 Kevin Garnett B	2.50	.75
❑ 67 Kendall Gill B	.40	.12
❑ 68 Sean Elliott B	.75	.23
❑ 69 Allen Iverson B RC	15.00	4.50
❑ 70 Erick Dampier B RC	2.50	.75
❑ 71 Jerome Williams B RC	2.50	.75
❑ 72 Charles Jones B	.40	.12
❑ 73 Danny Manning B	.75	.23
❑ 74 Kobe Bryant B RC	30.00	9.00
❑ 75 Steve Nash B RC	8.00	2.40
❑ 76 Sam Perkins B	.75	.23
❑ 77 Horace Grant B	.75	.23
❑ 78 Alonzo Mourning B	.75	.23
❑ 79 Kerry Kittles B RC	2.50	.75
❑ 80 LaPhonso Ellis B	.40	.12
❑ 81 Michael Finley B	1.50	.45
❑ 82 Marcus Camby B RC	3.00	.90
❑ 83 Antonio McDyess B	.75	.23
❑ 84 Antoine Walker B RC	8.00	2.40
❑ 85 Juwan Howard B	.75	.23
❑ 86 Bryon Russell B	.40	.12
❑ 87 Walter McCarty B RC	1.25	.35
❑ 88 Priest Lauderdale B RC	1.25	.35
❑ 89 Clarence Weatherspoon B	.40	.12
❑ 90 John Stockton B	1.25	.35
❑ 91 Mitch Richmond B	.75	.23
❑ 92 Dontae' Jones B RC	1.25	.35
❑ 93 Michael Smith B	.40	.12
❑ 94 Brent Barry B	.40	.12
❑ 95 Chris Mills B	.40	.12
❑ 96 Dee Brown B	.40	.12
❑ 97 Terry Dehere B	.40	.12
❑ 98 Danny Ferry B	.40	.12
❑ 99 Gheorghe Muresan B	.40	.12
❑ 100 Checklist B	.40	.12
❑ 101 Jim Jackson S	1.25	.35
❑ 102 Cedric Ceballos S	1.25	.35
❑ 103 Glen Rice S	2.50	.75
❑ 104 Tom Gugliotta S	1.25	.35
❑ 105 Mario Elie S	1.25	.35
❑ 106 Nick Anderson S	1.25	.35
❑ 107 Glenn Robinson S	2.50	.75
❑ 108 Terrell Brandon S	2.50	.75
❑ 109 Tim Hardaway S	2.50	.75
❑ 110 John Stockton S	4.00	1.20
❑ 111 Brent Barry S	1.25	.35
❑ 112 Mookie Blaylock S	1.25	.35
❑ 113 Tyus Edney S	1.25	.35
❑ 114 Gary Payton S	4.00	1.20
❑ 115 Joe Smith S	2.50	.75
❑ 116 Karl Malone S	4.00	1.20
❑ 117 Dino Radja S	1.25	.35
❑ 118 Alonzo Mourning S	2.50	.75
❑ 119 Bryant Stith S	1.25	.35
❑ 120 Derrick McKey S	1.25	.35
❑ 121 Clyde Drexler S	4.00	1.20
❑ 122 Michael Finley S	5.00	1.50
❑ 123 Sean Elliott S	2.50	.75
❑ 124 Hakeem Olajuwon S	4.00	1.20
❑ 125 Joe Dumars S	4.00	1.20
❑ 126 Shawn Bradley S	1.25	.35
❑ 127 Michael Jordan S	25.00	7.50
❑ 128 Latrell Sprewell G	10.00	3.00
❑ 129 Anfernee Hardaway G	10.00	3.00
❑ 130 Grant Hill G	10.00	3.00
❑ 131 Damon Stoudamire G	10.00	3.00
❑ 132 David Robinson G	10.00	3.00
❑ 133 Scottie Pippen G	15.00	4.50
❑ 135 Jason Kidd G	15.00	4.50
❑ 136A Jeff Hornacek G	4.00	1.20
❑ 136B Patrick Ewing G UER	10.00	3.00
Should be card number 134		
❑ 136C C. Laettner B UER	6.00	1.80
Should be card number 7		
❑ 137 Jerry Stackhouse G	12.00	3.60
❑ 138 Kevin Garnett G	20.00	6.00
❑ 139 Mitch Richmond G	6.00	1.80
❑ 140 Juwan Howard G	6.00	1.80
❑ 141 Reggie Miller G	10.00	3.00
❑ 142 Christian Laettner G	6.00	1.80
❑ 143 Vin Baker G	6.00	1.80
❑ 144 Shawn Kemp G	6.00	1.80
❑ 145 Dennis Rodman G	6.00	1.80
❑ 146 Shaquille O'Neal G	25.00	7.50
❑ 147 Mookie Blaylock B	.40	.12
❑ 148 Derek Harper B	.40	.12
❑ 149 Gerald Wilkins B	.40	.12
❑ 150 Adam Keefe B	.40	.12
❑ 151 Billy Owens B	.40	.12
❑ 152 Terrell Brandon B	.75	.23
❑ 153 Antonio Davis B	.40	.12
❑ 154 Muggsy Bogues B	.40	.12
❑ 155 Cherokee Parks B	.40	.12
❑ 156 Rasheed Wallace B	1.50	.45
❑ 157 Lee Mayberry B	.40	.12
❑ 158 Craig Ehlo B	.40	.12
❑ 159 Todd Fuller B	.40	.12
❑ 160 Charles Barkley B	1.50	.45
❑ 161 Glenn Robinson B	1.25	.35
❑ 162 Charles Oakley B	.40	.12
❑ 163 Chris Webber B	1.25	.35
❑ 164 Frank Brickowski B	.40	.12
❑ 165 Mark Jackson B	.40	.12
❑ 166 Jayson Williams B	.75	.23
❑ 167 C. Weatherspoon B	.40	.12
❑ 168 Toni Kukoc B	.75	.23
❑ 169 Alan Henderson B	.40	.12
❑ 170 Tony Delk B	.75	.23
❑ 171 Jamal Mashburn B	.75	.23
❑ 172 Vinny Del Negro B	.40	.12
❑ 173 Greg Ostertag B	.40	.12
❑ 174 Shawn Bradley B	.40	.12
❑ 175 Gheorghe Muresan B	.40	.12
❑ 176 Brent Price B	.40	.12
❑ 177 Rick Fox B	.40	.12
❑ 178 Stacey Augmon B	.40	.12
❑ 179 P.J. Brown B	.40	.12
❑ 180 Jim Jackson B	.40	.12
❑ 181 Hersey Hawkins B	.75	.23
❑ 182 Danny Manning B	.75	.23
❑ 183 Dennis Scott B	.40	.12
❑ 184 Tom Gugliotta B	.40	.12
❑ 185 Tyrone Hill B	.40	.12
❑ 186 Malik Sealy B	.40	.12
❑ 187 John Starks B	.75	.23
❑ 188 Mark Price B	.75	.23
❑ 189 Elden Campbell B	.40	.12
❑ 190 Mahmoud Abdul-Rauf B	.40	.12
❑ 191 Will Perdue B	.40	.12
❑ 192 Nate McMillan B	.40	.12
❑ 193 Robert Horry B	.75	.23
❑ 194 Dino Radja B	.40	.12
❑ 195 Loy Vaught B	.40	.12
❑ 196 Dikembe Mutombo B	.75	.23
❑ 197 Eric Montross B	.40	.12
❑ 198 Sasha Danilovic B	.40	.12
❑ 199 Kenny Anderson B	.40	.12
❑ 200 Sean Elliott B	.75	.23
❑ 201 Mark West B	.40	.12
❑ 202 Vlade Divac B	.40	.12
❑ 203 Joe Dumars B	1.25	.35
❑ 204 Allan Houston B	.75	.23
❑ 205 Kevin Garnett B	2.50	.75
❑ 206 Rod Strickland B	.40	.12
❑ 207 Robert Parish B	.75	.23
❑ 208 Jalen Rose B	1.25	.35
❑ 209 Armon Gilliam B	.40	.12
❑ 210 Kerry Kittles B	1.25	.35
❑ 211 Derrick Coleman B	.75	.23
❑ 212 Greg Anthony B	.40	.12
❑ 213 Joe Smith B	.75	.23
❑ 214 Steve Smith B	.75	.23
❑ 215 Tim Hardaway B	.75	.23
❑ 216 Tyus Edney B	.40	.12
❑ 217 Steve Nash B	1.25	.35
❑ 218 Anthony Mason B	.75	.23
❑ 219 Otis Thorpe B	.40	.12
❑ 220 Eddie Jones B	1.25	.35
❑ 221 Rik Smits B	.75	.23
❑ 222 Isaiah Rider B	.75	.23
❑ 223 Bobby Phills B	.40	.12
❑ 224 Antoine Walker B	1.25	.35
❑ 225 Rod Strickland B	.40	.12
❑ 226 Hubert Davis B	.40	.12
❑ 227 Eric Williams B	.40	.12
❑ 228 Danny Manning B	.75	.23
❑ 229 Dominique Wilkins B	1.25	.35
❑ 230 Brian Shaw B	.40	.12
❑ 231 Larry Johnson B	.75	.23
❑ 232 Kevin Willis B	.40	.12
❑ 233 Bryant Stith B	.40	.12
❑ 234 Blue Edwards B	.40	.12
❑ 235 Robert Pack B	.40	.12
❑ 236 Brian Grant B	1.25	.35
❑ 237 Latrell Sprewell B	1.25	.35
❑ 238 Glen Rice B	.75	.23
❑ 239 Jerome Williams B	1.25	.35
❑ 240 Allen Iverson B	4.00	1.20
❑ 241 Popeye Jones B	.40	.12
❑ 242 Clifford Robinson B	.40	.12
❑ 243 Shaquille O'Neal B	4.00	1.20
❑ 244 Vitaly Potapenko B RC	1.25	.35
❑ 245 Ervin Johnson B	.40	.12
❑ 246 Checklist	.40	.12
❑ 247 Scottie Pippen S	6.00	1.80
❑ 248 Jason Kidd S	6.00	1.80
❑ 249 Antonio McDyess S	2.50	.75
❑ 250 Latrell Sprewell S	4.00	1.20
❑ 251 Lorenzen Wright S	1.25	.35
❑ 252 Ray Allen S	8.00	2.40
❑ 253 Stephon Marbury S	6.00	1.80
❑ 254 Patrick Ewing S	4.00	1.20
❑ 255 Anfernee Hardaway S	4.00	1.20
❑ 256 Kenny Anderson S	1.25	.35
❑ 257 David Robinson S	4.00	1.20
❑ 258 Marcus Camby S	4.00	1.20
❑ 259 Shareef Abdur-Rahim S	8.00	2.40
❑ 260 Dennis Rodman S	2.50	.75
❑ 261 Juwan Howard S	2.50	.75
❑ 262 Damon Stoudamire S	4.00	1.20
❑ 263 Shawn Kemp S	2.50	.75
❑ 264 Mitch Richmond S	2.50	.75
❑ 265 Jerry Stackhouse S	5.00	1.50
❑ 266 Horace Grant S	2.50	.75
❑ 267 Kerry Kittles S	1.25	.35
❑ 268 Vin Baker S	2.50	.75
❑ 269 Kobe Bryant G	60.00	18.00
❑ 270 Reggie Miller S	4.00	1.20
❑ 271 Grant Hill S	4.00	1.20
❑ 272 Oliver Miller S	1.25	.35
❑ 273 Chris Webber S	2.50	.75
❑ 274 Dikembe Mutombo G	6.00	1.80
❑ 275 Antonio McDyess G	6.00	1.80
❑ 276 Clyde Drexler G	10.00	3.00

Card	Nm-Mt	Ex-Mt
❑ 277 Brent Barry G	4.00	1.20
❑ 278 Tim Hardaway G	6.00	1.80
❑ 279 Glenn Robinson G	6.00	1.80
❑ 280 Allen Iverson G	25.00	7.50
❑ 281 Hakeem Olajuwon G	10.00	3.00
❑ 282 Marcus Camby G	10.00	3.00
❑ 283 John Stockton G	10.00	3.00
❑ 284 Shareef Abdur-Rahim G	15.00	4.50
❑ 285 Karl Malone G	10.00	3.00
❑ 286 Gary Payton G	10.00	3.00
❑ 287 Stephon Marbury G	12.00	3.60
❑ 288 Alonzo Mourning G	6.00	1.80
❑ 289 Shaquille O'Neal S	8.00	2.40
❑ 290 Charles Barkley G	12.00	3.60
❑ 291 Michael Jordan G	60.00	18.00

1997-98 Finest

	Nm-Mt	Ex-Mt
COMPLETE SET (326)	750.00	220.00
COMPLETE SERIES 1 (173)	350.00	105.00
COMPLETE SERIES 2 (153)	400.00	120.00
COMP.BRONZE SET (220)	100.00	30.00
COMP.BRONZE SER.1 (120)	60.00	18.00
COMP.BRONZE SER.2 (100)	50.00	15.00
COMMON BRONZE	.30	.09
COMMON BRONZE RC	.60	.18
COMP.SILVER SET (66)	150.00	45.00
COMP.SILVER SER.1 (33)	80.00	24.00
COMP.SILVER SER.2 (33)	60.00	18.00
COMMON SILVER	1.00	.30
COMP.GOLD SET (40)	500.00	150.00
COMP.GOLD SER.1 (20)	200.00	60.00
COMP.GOLD SER.2 (20)	300.00	90.00
COMMON GOLD	4.00	1.20
❑ 1 Scottie Pippen B	1.50	.45
❑ 2 Tim Hardaway B	.60	.18
❑ 3 Bo Outlaw	.30	.09
❑ 4 Rik Smits B	.60	.18
❑ 5 Dale Ellis B	.30	.09
❑ 6 Clyde Drexler B	1.00	.30
❑ 7 Steve Smith B	.60	.18
❑ 8 Nick Anderson B	.30	.09
❑ 9 Juwan Howard B	.60	.18
❑ 10 Cedric Ceballos B	.30	.09
❑ 11 Shawn Bradley B	.30	.09
❑ 12 Loy Vaught B	.30	.09
❑ 13 Todd Day B	.30	.09
❑ 14 Glen Rice B	.60	.18
❑ 15 Bryant Stith B	.30	.09
❑ 16 Bob Sura B	.30	.09
❑ 17 Derrick McKey B	.30	.09
❑ 18 Ray Allen B	1.00	.30
❑ 19 Stephon Marbury B	1.25	.35
❑ 20 David Robinson B	1.00	.30
❑ 21 Anthony Peeler B	.30	.09
❑ 22 Isaiah Rider B	.60	.18
❑ 23 Mookie Blaylock B	.30	.09
❑ 24 Damon Stoudamire B	.60	.18
❑ 25 Rod Strickland B	.30	.09
❑ 26 Glenn Robinson B	1.00	.30
❑ 27 Chris Webber B	1.00	.30
❑ 28 Christian Laettner B	.60	.18
❑ 29 Joe Dumars B	1.00	.30
❑ 30 Mark Price B	.60	.18
❑ 31 Jamal Mashburn B	.60	.18
❑ 32 Danny Manning B	.60	.18
❑ 33 John Stockton B	1.00	.30

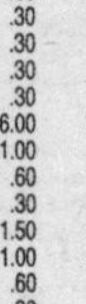

Card	Nm-Mt	Ex-Mt
❑ 34 Detlef Schrempf B	.60	.18
❑ 35 Tyus Edney B	.30	.09
❑ 36 Chris Childs B	.30	.09
❑ 37 Dana Barros B	.30	.09
❑ 38 Bobby Phills B	.30	.09
❑ 39 Michael Jordan B	6.00	1.80
❑ 40 Grant Hill B	1.00	.30
❑ 41 Brent Barry B	.60	.18
❑ 42 Rony Seikaly B	.30	.09
❑ 43 Shareef Abdur-Rahim B	1.50	.45
❑ 44 Dominique Wilkins B	1.00	.30
❑ 45 Vin Baker B	.60	.18
❑ 46 Kendall Gill B	.30	.09
❑ 47 Muggsy Bogues B	.60	.18
❑ 48 Hakeem Olajuwon B	1.00	.30
❑ 49 Reggie Miller B	1.00	.30
❑ 50 Shaquille O'Neal B	2.50	.75
❑ 51 Antonio McDyess B	.60	.18
❑ 52 Michael Finley B	1.00	.30
❑ 53 Jerry Stackhouse B	1.00	.30
❑ 54 Brian Grant B	.60	.18
❑ 55 Greg Anthony B	.30	.09
❑ 56 Patrick Ewing B	1.00	.30
❑ 57 Allen Iverson B	2.50	.75
❑ 58 Rasheed Wallace B	1.00	.30
❑ 59 Shawn Kemp B	.60	.18
❑ 60 Bryant Reeves B	.30	.09
❑ 61 Kevin Garnett B	2.00	.60
❑ 62 Allan Houston B	.60	.18
❑ 63 Stacey Augmon B	.30	.09
❑ 64 Rick Fox B	.60	.18
❑ 65 Derek Harper B	.60	.18
❑ 66 Lindsey Hunter B	.30	.09
❑ 67 Eddie Jones B	1.00	.30
❑ 68 Joe Smith B	.60	.18
❑ 69 Alonzo Mourning B	.60	.18
❑ 70 LaPhonso Ellis B	.30	.09
❑ 71 Tyrone Hill B	.30	.09
❑ 72 Charles Barkley B	1.25	.35
❑ 73 Malik Sealy B	.30	.09
❑ 74 Shandon Anderson B	.30	.09
❑ 75 Arvydas Sabonis B	.60	.18
❑ 76 Tom Gugliotta B	.60	.18
❑ 77 Anfernee Hardaway B	1.00	.30
❑ 78 Sean Elliott B	.60	.18
❑ 79 Marcus Camby B	1.00	.30
❑ 80 Gary Payton B	1.00	.30
❑ 81 Kerry Kittles B	1.00	.30
❑ 82 Dikembe Mutombo B	.60	.18
❑ 83 Antoine Walker B	1.25	.35
❑ 84 Terrell Brandon B	.60	.18
❑ 85 Otis Thorpe B	.30	.09
❑ 86 Mark Jackson B	.60	.18
❑ 87 A.C. Green B	.60	.18
❑ 88 John Starks B	.60	.18
❑ 89 Kenny Anderson B	.60	.18
❑ 90 Karl Malone B	1.00	.30
❑ 91 Mitch Richmond B	.60	.18
❑ 92 Derrick Coleman B	.30	.09
❑ 93 Horace Grant B	.60	.18
❑ 94 John Williams B	.30	.09
❑ 95 Jason Kidd B	1.50	.45
❑ 96 Mahmoud Abdul-Rauf B	.30	.09
❑ 97 Walt Williams B	.30	.09
❑ 98 Anthony Mason B	.60	.18
❑ 99 Latrell Sprewell B	1.00	.30
❑ 100 Checklist	.30	.09
❑ 101 Tim Duncan B RC	12.00	3.60
❑ 102 Keith Van Horn B RC	3.00	.90
❑ 103 Chauncey Billups B RC	2.50	.75
❑ 104 Antonio Daniels B RC	1.25	.35
❑ 105 Tony Battie B RC	1.25	.35
❑ 106 Tim Thomas B RC	4.00	1.20
❑ 107 Tracy McGrady B RC	15.00	4.50
❑ 108 Adonal Foyle B RC	.75	.23
❑ 109 Maurice Taylor B RC	2.50	.75
❑ 110 Austin Croshere B RC	2.50	.75
❑ 111 Bobby Jackson B RC	2.00	.60
❑ 112 Olivier Saint-Jean B RC	.60	.18
❑ 113 John Thomas B RC	.60	.18
❑ 114 Derek Anderson B RC	5.00	1.50
❑ 115 Brevin Knight B RC	1.50	.45
❑ 116 Charles Smith B RC	.60	.18
❑ 117 Johnny Taylor B RC	.60	.18
❑ 118 Jacque Vaughn B RC	.75	.23
❑ 119 Anthony Parker B RC	.60	.18

Card	Nm-Mt	Ex-Mt
❑ 120 Paul Grant B RC	.60	.18
❑ 121 Stephon Marbury S	4.00	1.20
❑ 122 Terrell Brandon S	2.00	.60
❑ 123 Dikembe Mutombo S	2.00	.60
❑ 124 Patrick Ewing S	3.00	.90
❑ 125 Scottie Pippen S	5.00	1.50
❑ 126 Antoine Walker S	4.00	1.20
❑ 127 Karl Malone S	3.00	.90
❑ 128 Sean Elliott S	2.00	.60
❑ 129 Chris Webber S	3.00	.90
❑ 130 Shawn Kemp S	2.00	.60
❑ 131 Hakeem Olajuwon S	3.00	.90
❑ 132 Tim Hardaway S	2.00	.60
❑ 133 Glen Rice S	2.00	.60
❑ 134 Vin Baker S	2.00	.60
❑ 135 Jim Jackson S	1.00	.30
❑ 136 Kevin Garnett S	6.00	1.80
❑ 137 Kobe Bryant S	15.00	4.50
❑ 138 Damon Stoudamire S	2.00	.60
❑ 139 Larry Johnson S	2.00	.60
❑ 140 Latrell Sprewell S	3.00	.90
❑ 141 Lorenzen Wright S	1.00	.30
❑ 142 Toni Kukoc S	2.00	.60
❑ 143 Allen Iverson S	8.00	2.40
❑ 144 Elden Campbell S	1.00	.30
❑ 145 Tom Gugliotta S	2.00	.60
❑ 146 David Robinson S	3.00	.90
❑ 147 Jayson Williams S	1.00	.30
❑ 148 Shaquille O'Neal S	8.00	2.40
❑ 149 Grant Hill S	3.00	.90
❑ 150 Reggie Miller S	3.00	.90
❑ 151 Clyde Drexler S	3.00	.90
❑ 152 Ray Allen S	1.25	.35
❑ 153 Eddie Jones S	3.00	.90
❑ 154 Michael Jordan G	80.00	24.00
❑ 155 Dominique Wilkins G	12.00	3.60
❑ 156 Charles Barkley G	15.00	4.50
❑ 157 Jerry Stackhouse G	12.00	3.60
❑ 158 Juwan Howard G	8.00	2.40
❑ 159 Marcus Camby G	12.00	3.60
❑ 160 Christian Laettner G	8.00	2.40
❑ 161 Anthony Mason G	8.00	2.40
❑ 162 Joe Smith G	8.00	2.40
❑ 163 Kerry Kittles G	12.00	3.60
❑ 164 Mitch Richmond G	8.00	2.40
❑ 165 Shareef Abdur-Rahim G	20.00	6.00
❑ 166 Alonzo Mourning G	8.00	2.40
❑ 167 Dennis Rodman G	8.00	2.40
❑ 168 Antonio McDyess G	8.00	2.40
❑ 169 Shawn Bradley G	4.00	1.20
❑ 170 Anfernee Hardaway G	12.00	3.60
❑ 171 Jason Kidd G	20.00	6.00
❑ 172 Gary Payton G	12.00	3.60
❑ 173 John Stockton G	12.00	3.60
❑ 174 Allan Houston B	.60	.18
❑ 175 Bob Sura B	.30	.09
❑ 176 Clyde Drexler B	1.00	.30
❑ 177 Glenn Robinson B	1.00	.30
❑ 178 Joe Smith B	.60	.18
❑ 179 Larry Johnson B	.60	.18
❑ 180 Mitch Richmond B	.60	.18
❑ 181 Rony Seikaly B	.30	.09
❑ 182 Tyrone Hill B	.30	.09
❑ 183 Allen Iverson B	2.50	.75
❑ 184 Brent Barry B	.60	.18
❑ 185 Damon Stoudamire B	.60	.18
❑ 186 Grant Hill B	1.00	.30
❑ 187 John Stockton B	1.00	.30
❑ 188 Latrell Sprewell B	1.00	.30
❑ 189 Mookie Blaylock B	.30	.09
❑ 190 Samaki Walker B	.30	.09
❑ 191 Vin Baker B	.60	.18
❑ 192 Alonzo Mourning B	.60	.18
❑ 193 Brevin Knight B	.60	.18
❑ 194 Danny Manning B	.60	.18
❑ 195 Hakeem Olajuwon B	1.00	.30
❑ 196 Johnny Taylor B	.30	.09
❑ 197 Lorenzen Wright B	.30	.09
❑ 198 Olden Polynice B	.30	.09
❑ 199 Scottie Pippen B	1.50	.45
❑ 200 Lindsey Hunter B	.30	.09
❑ 201 Anfernee Hardaway B	1.00	.30
❑ 202 Greg Anthony B	.30	.09
❑ 203 David Robinson B	1.00	.30
❑ 204 Horace Grant B	.60	.18
❑ 205 Calbert Cheaney B	.30	.09

❑ 206 Loy Vaught B .30 .09
❑ 207 Tariq Abdul-Wahad B .30 .09
❑ 208 Sean Elliott B .60 .18
❑ 209 Rodney Rogers B .30 .09
❑ 210 Anthony Mason B .60 .18
❑ 211 Bryant Reeves B .30 .09
❑ 212 David Wesley B .30 .09
❑ 213 Isaiah Rider B .60 .18
❑ 214 Karl Malone B 1.00 .30
❑ 215 Mahmoud Abdul-Rauf B .30 .09
❑ 216 Patrick Ewing B 1.00 .30
❑ 217 Shaquille O'Neal B 2.50 .75
❑ 218 Antoine Walker B 1.25 .35
❑ 219 Charles Barkley B 1.25 .35
❑ 220 Dennis Rodman B .60 .18
❑ 221 Jamal Mashburn B .60 .18
❑ 222 Kendall Gill B .30 .09
❑ 223 Malik Sealy B .30 .09
❑ 224 Rasheed Wallace B 1.00 .30
❑ 225 Shareef Abdur-Rahim B 1.50 .45
❑ 226 Antonio Daniels B .60 .18
❑ 227 Charles Oakley B .60 .18
❑ 228 Derek Anderson B 1.25 .35
❑ 229 Jason Kidd B 1.50 .45
❑ 230 Kenny Anderson B .60 .18
❑ 231 Marcus Camby B 1.00 .30
❑ 232 Ray Allen B 1.00 .30
❑ 233 Shawn Bradley B .30 .09
❑ 234 Antonio McDyess B .60 .18
❑ 235 Chauncey Billups B .60 .18
❑ 236 Detlef Schrempf B .60 .18
❑ 237 Jayson Williams B .30 .09
❑ 238 Kerry Kittles B 1.00 .30
❑ 239 Jalen Rose B 1.00 .30
❑ 240 Reggie Miller B 1.00 .30
❑ 241 Shawn Kemp B .60 .18
❑ 242 Arvydas Sabonis B .60 .18
❑ 243 Tom Gugliotta B .60 .18
❑ 244 Dikembe Mutombo B .60 .18
❑ 245 Jeff Hornacek B .60 .18
❑ 246 Kevin Garnett B 2.00 .60
❑ 247 Matt Maloney B .30 .09
❑ 248 Rex Chapman B .30 .09
❑ 249 Stephon Marbury B 1.25 .35
❑ 250 Austin Croshere B .60 .18
❑ 251 Chris Childs B .30 .09
❑ 252 Eddie Jones B 1.00 .30
❑ 253 Jerry Stackhouse B 1.00 .30
❑ 254 Kevin Johnson B .60 .18
❑ 255 Maurice Taylor B 1.00 .30
❑ 256 Chris Mullin B 1.00 .30
❑ 257 Terrell Brandon B .60 .18
❑ 258 Avery Johnson B .30 .09
❑ 259 Chris Webber B 1.00 .30
❑ 260 Gary Payton B 1.00 .30
❑ 261 Jim Jackson B .30 .09
❑ 262 Kobe Bryant B 5.00 1.50
❑ 263 Michael Finley B 1.00 .30
❑ 264 Rod Strickland B .30 .09
❑ 265 Tim Hardaway B .60 .18
❑ 266 B.J. Armstrong B .30 .09
❑ 267 Christian Laettner B .60 .18
❑ 268 Glen Rice B .60 .18
❑ 269 Joe Dumars B 1.00 .30
❑ 270 LaPhonso Ellis B .30 .09
❑ 271 Michael Jordan B 6.00 1.80
❑ 272 Ron Mercer B RC 2.50 .75
❑ 273 Checklist B .30 .09
❑ 274 Anfernee Hardaway S 3.00 .90
❑ 275 Dennis Rodman S 2.00 .60
❑ 276 Gary Payton S 3.00 .90
❑ 277 Jamal Mashburn S 2.00 .60
❑ 278 Shareef Abdur-Rahim S 5.00 1.50
❑ 279 Steve Smith S 2.00 .60
❑ 280 Tony Battie S 2.00 .60
❑ 281 Alonzo Mourning S 2.00 .60
❑ 282 Bobby Jackson S 1.00 .30
❑ 283 Christian Laettner S 2.00 .60
❑ 284 Jerry Stackhouse S 3.00 .90
❑ 285 Terrell Brandon S 2.00 .60
❑ 286 Chauncey Billups S 2.00 .60
❑ 287 Michael Jordan S 20.00 6.00
❑ 288 Glenn Robinson S 3.00 .90
❑ 289 Jason Kidd S 5.00 1.50
❑ 290 Joe Smith S 2.00 .60
❑ 291 Michael Finley S 3.00 .90
❑ 292 Rod Strickland S 1.00 .30
❑ 293 Ron Mercer S 2.00 .60
❑ 294 Tracy McGrady S 6.00 1.80
❑ 295 Adonal Foyle S 1.00 .30
❑ 296 Marcus Camby S 3.00 .90
❑ 297 John Stockton S 3.00 .90
❑ 298 Kerry Kittles S 3.00 .90
❑ 299 Mitch Richmond S 2.00 .60
❑ 300 Shawn Bradley S 1.00 .30
❑ 301 Anthony Mason S 2.00 .60
❑ 302 Antonio Daniels S 2.00 .60
❑ 303 Antonio McDyess S 2.00 .60
❑ 304 Charles Barkley S 4.00 1.20
❑ 305 Keith Van Horn S 3.00 .90
❑ 306 Tim Duncan S 5.00 1.50
❑ 307 Dikembe Mutombo G 8.00 2.40
❑ 308 Grant Hill G 12.00 3.60
❑ 309 Shaquille O'Neal G 30.00 9.00
❑ 310 Keith Van Horn G 12.00 3.60
❑ 311 Shawn Kemp G 8.00 2.40
❑ 312 Antoine Walker G 15.00 4.50
❑ 313 Hakeem Olajuwon G 12.00 3.60
❑ 314 Vin Baker G 8.00 2.40
❑ 315 Patrick Ewing G 12.00 3.60
❑ 316 Tracy McGrady G 20.00 6.00
❑ 317 Glen Rice G 8.00 2.40
❑ 318 Reggie Miller G 12.00 3.60
❑ 319 Kevin Garnett G 25.00 7.50
❑ 320 Allen Iverson G 30.00 9.00
❑ 321 Karl Malone G 12.00 3.60
❑ 322 Scottie Pippen G 20.00 6.00
❑ 323 Kobe Bryant G 50.00 15.00
❑ 324 Stephon Marbury G 15.00 4.50
❑ 325 Tim Duncan G 15.00 4.50
❑ 326 Chris Webber G 12.00 3.60
❑ P68 Joe Smith 2.00 .60

1998-99 Finest

	Nm-Mt	Ex-Mt
COMPLETE SET (250)	100.00	30.00
COMPLETE SERIES 1 (125)	30.00	9.00
COMPLETE SERIES 2 (125)	60.00	18.00
COMMON CARD (1-225)	.30	.09
COMMON ROOKIE (226-250)	.60	.18

❑ 1 Chris Mills .30 .09
❑ 2 Matt Maloney .30 .09
❑ 3 Sam Mitchell .30 .09
❑ 4 Corliss Williamson .60 .18
❑ 5 Bryant Reeves .30 .09
❑ 6 Juwan Howard .60 .18
❑ 7 Eddie Jones 1.00 .30
❑ 8 Ray Allen 1.00 .30
❑ 9 Larry Johnson .60 .18
❑ 10 Travis Best .30 .09
❑ 11 Isaiah Rider .30 .09
❑ 12 Hakeem Olajuwon 1.00 .30
❑ 13 Gary Trent .30 .09
❑ 14 Kevin Garnett 2.00 .60
❑ 15 Dikembe Mutombo .60 .18
❑ 16 Brevin Knight .30 .09
❑ 17 Keith Van Horn 1.00 .30
❑ 18 Theo Ratliff .60 .18
❑ 19 Tim Hardaway .60 .18
❑ 20 Blue Edwards .30 .09
❑ 21 David Wesley .30 .09
❑ 22 Jaren Jackson .30 .09
❑ 23 Nick Anderson .30 .09
❑ 24 Rodney Rogers .30 .09
❑ 25 Antonio Davis .30 .09
❑ 26 Clarence Weatherspoon .30 .09
❑ 27 Kelvin Cato .30 .09
❑ 28 Tracy McGrady 2.50 .75
❑ 29 Mookie Blaylock .30 .09
❑ 30 Ron Harper .60 .18
❑ 31 Allan Houston .60 .18
❑ 32 Brian Williams .30 .09
❑ 33 John Stockton 1.00 .30
❑ 34 Hersey Hawkins .30 .09
❑ 35 Donyell Marshall .60 .18
❑ 36 Mark Strickland .30 .09
❑ 37 Rod Strickland .30 .09
❑ 38 Cedric Ceballos .30 .09
❑ 39 Danny Fortson .30 .09
❑ 40 Shaquille O'Neal 2.50 .75
❑ 41 Kendall Gill .30 .09
❑ 42 Allen Iverson 2.00 .60
❑ 43 Travis Knight .30 .09
❑ 44 Cedric Henderson .30 .09
❑ 45 Steve Kerr .60 .18
❑ 46 Antonio McDyess .60 .18
❑ 47 Darrick Martin .30 .09
❑ 48 Shandon Anderson .30 .09
❑ 49 Shareef Abdur-Rahim 1.00 .30
❑ 50 Antoine Carr .30 .09
❑ 51 Jason Kidd 1.50 .45
❑ 52 Calbert Cheaney .30 .09
❑ 53 Antoine Walker 1.00 .30
❑ 54 Greg Anthony .30 .09
❑ 55 Jeff Hornacek .60 .18
❑ 56 Reggie Miller 1.00 .30
❑ 57 Lawrence Funderburke .30 .09
❑ 58 Derek Strong .30 .09
❑ 59 Robert Horry .60 .18
❑ 60 Shawn Bradley .30 .09
❑ 61 Matt Bullard .30 .09
❑ 62 Terrell Brandon .60 .18
❑ 63 Dan Majerle .60 .18
❑ 64 Jim Jackson .30 .09
❑ 65 Anthony Peeler .30 .09
❑ 66 Bo Outlaw .30 .09
❑ 67 Khalid Reeves .30 .09
❑ 68 Toni Kukoç .60 .18
❑ 69 Mario Elie .30 .09
❑ 70 Derek Anderson 1.00 .30
❑ 71 Jalen Rose 1.00 .30
❑ 72 Tyrone Corbin .30 .09
❑ 73 Anthony Mason .60 .18
❑ 74 Lamond Murray .30 .09
❑ 75 Tom Gugliotta .30 .09
❑ 76 Arvydas Sabonis .60 .18
❑ 77 Brian Shaw .30 .09
❑ 78 Rick Fox .60 .18
❑ 79 Danny Manning .30 .09
❑ 80 Lindsey Hunter .30 .09
❑ 81 Michael Jordan 6.00 1.80
❑ 82 LaPhonso Ellis .30 .09
❑ 83 David Robinson 1.00 .30
❑ 84 Christian Laettner .60 .18
❑ 85 Armon Gilliam .30 .09
❑ 86 Sherman Douglas .30 .09
❑ 87 Charlie Ward .30 .09
❑ 88 Shawn Kemp .60 .18
❑ 89 Gary Payton 1.00 .30
❑ 90 Doug Christie .60 .18
❑ 91 Voshon Lenard .30 .09
❑ 92 Detlef Schrempf .60 .18
❑ 93 Walter McCarty .30 .09
❑ 94 Sam Cassell 1.00 .30
❑ 95 Jerry Stackhouse 1.00 .30
❑ 96 Billy Owens .30 .09
❑ 97 Matt Geiger .30 .09
❑ 98 Avery Johnson .30 .09
❑ 99 Bobby Jackson .60 .18
❑ 100 Rex Chapman .30 .09
❑ 101 Andrew DeClercq .30 .09
❑ 102 Vlade Divac .60 .18
❑ 103 Erick Strickland .30 .09
❑ 104 Dean Garrett .30 .09
❑ 105 Grant Long .30 .09
❑ 106 Adonal Foyle .30 .09
❑ 107 Isaac Austin .30 .09
❑ 108 Michael Curry .30 .09
❑ 109 Darrell Armstrong .30 .09
❑ 110 Aaron McKie .60 .18

❑ 111 Stacey Augmon .30 .09
❑ 112 Anthony Johnson .30 .09
❑ 113 Vinny Del Negro .30 .09
❑ 114 Reggie Slater .30 .09
❑ 115 Lee Mayberry .30 .09
❑ 116 Tracy Murray .30 .09
❑ 117 Scottie Pippen 1.50 .45
❑ 118 Sam Perkins .30 .09
❑ 119 Derek Fisher 1.00 .30
❑ 120 Mark Bryant .30 .09
❑ 121 Dale Davis .60 .18
❑ 122 B.J. Armstrong .30 .09
❑ 123 Charles Barkley 1.25 .35
❑ 124 Horace Grant .60 .18
❑ 125 Checklist .30 .09
❑ 126 Alonzo Mourning .60 .18
❑ 127 Kerry Kittles .30 .09
❑ 128 Eldridge Recasner .30 .09
❑ 129 Dell Curry .30 .09
❑ 130 Jamal Mashburn .60 .18
❑ 131 Eric Piatkowski .60 .18
❑ 132 Othella Harrington .30 .09
❑ 133 Pete Chilcutt .30 .09
❑ 134 Dennis Rodman .60 .18
❑ 135 Patrick Ewing 1.00 .30
❑ 136 Danny Schayes .30 .09
❑ 137 John Williams .30 .09
❑ 138 Joe Smith .60 .18
❑ 139 Tariq Abdul-Wahad .30 .09
❑ 140 Vin Baker .60 .18
❑ 141 Elden Campbell .30 .09
❑ 142 Chris Carr .30 .09
❑ 143 John Starks .60 .18
❑ 144 Felton Spencer .30 .09
❑ 145 Mark Jackson .60 .18
❑ 146 Dana Barros .30 .09
❑ 147 Eric Williams .30 .09
❑ 148 Wesley Person .30 .09
❑ 149 Joe Dumars 1.00 .30
❑ 150 Steve Smith .60 .18
❑ 151 Randy Brown .30 .09
❑ 152 A.C. Green .60 .18
❑ 153 Dee Brown .30 .09
❑ 154 Brian Grant .60 .18
❑ 155 Tim Thomas .60 .18
❑ 156 Howard Eisley .30 .09
❑ 157 Malik Sealy .30 .09
❑ 158 Maurice Taylor .60 .18
❑ 159 Tyrone Hill .30 .09
❑ 160 Chris Gatling .30 .09
❑ 161 Rodrick Rhodes .30 .09
❑ 162 Muggsy Bogues .60 .18
❑ 163 Kenny Anderson .60 .18
❑ 164 Zydrunas Ilgauskas .60 .18
❑ 165 Grant Hill 1.00 .30
❑ 166 Lorenzen Wright .30 .09
❑ 167 Tony Battie .30 .09
❑ 168 Bobby Phills .30 .09
❑ 169 Michael Finley 1.00 .30
❑ 170 Anfernee Hardaway 1.00 .30
❑ 171 Terry Porter .30 .09
❑ 172 P.J. Brown .30 .09
❑ 173 Clifford Robinson .30 .09
❑ 174 Olden Polynice .30 .09
❑ 175 Kobe Bryant 4.00 1.20
❑ 176 Sean Elliott .60 .18
❑ 177 Latrell Sprewell 1.00 .30
❑ 178 Rik Smits .60 .18
❑ 179 Darrell Armstrong .30 .09
❑ 180 Stephon Marbury 1.00 .30
❑ 181 Brent Price .30 .09
❑ 182 Danny Fortson .30 .09
❑ 183 Vitaly Potapenko .30 .09
❑ 184 Anthony Parker .30 .09
❑ 185 Glenn Robinson .60 .18
❑ 186 Erick Dampier .60 .18
❑ 187 George McCloud .30 .09
❑ 188 Rasheed Wallace 1.00 .30
❑ 189 Aaron Williams .30 .09
❑ 190 Tim Duncan 1.50 .45
❑ 191 Chauncey Billups .60 .18
❑ 192 Jim McIlvaine .30 .09
❑ 193 Chris Mullin 1.00 .30
❑ 194 George Lynch .30 .09
❑ 195 Damon Stoudamire .60 .18
❑ 196 Bryon Russell .30 .09
❑ 197 Luc Longley .30 .09
❑ 198 Ron Mercer .60 .18
❑ 199 Alan Henderson .30 .09
❑ 200 Jayson Williams .30 .09
❑ 201 Ben Wallace 1.00 .30
❑ 202 Elliot Perry .30 .09
❑ 203 Walt Williams .30 .09
❑ 204 Cherokee Parks .30 .09
❑ 205 Brent Barry .60 .18
❑ 206 Hubert Davis .30 .09
❑ 207 Terry Davis .30 .09
❑ 208 Loy Vaught .30 .09
❑ 209 Adam Keefe .30 .09
❑ 210 Karl Malone 1.00 .30
❑ 211 Chuck Person .30 .09
❑ 212 Chris Childs .30 .09
❑ 213 Rony Seikaly .30 .09
❑ 214 Ervin Johnson .30 .09
❑ 215 Derrick McKey .30 .09
❑ 216 Jerome Williams .30 .09
❑ 217 Glen Rice .60 .18
❑ 218 Steve Nash 1.00 .30
❑ 219 Nick Van Exel 1.00 .30
❑ 220 Chris Webber 1.00 .30
❑ 221 Marcus Camby .60 .18
❑ 222 Antonio Daniels .30 .09
❑ 223 Mitch Richmond .60 .18
❑ 224 Otis Thorpe .30 .09
❑ 225 Charles Oakley .30 .09
❑ 226 Michael Olowokandi RC 1.50 .45
❑ 227 Mike Bibby RC 8.00 2.40
❑ 228 Raef LaFrentz RC 1.50 .45
❑ 229 Antawn Jamison RC 5.00 1.50
❑ 230 Vince Carter RC 15.00 4.50
❑ 231 Robert Traylor RC 1.25 .35
❑ 232 Jason Williams RC 4.00 1.20
❑ 233 Larry Hughes RC 3.00 .90
❑ 234 Dirk Nowitzki RC 10.00 3.00
❑ 235 Paul Pierce RC 5.00 1.50
❑ 236 Bonzi Wells RC 4.00 1.20
❑ 237 Michael Doleac RC 1.25 .35
❑ 238 Keon Clark RC 1.50 .45
❑ 239 Michael Dickerson RC 2.00 .60
❑ 240 Matt Harpring RC 2.50 .75
❑ 241 Bryce Drew RC 1.25 .35
❑ 242 Pat Garrity RC .75 .23
❑ 243 Roshown McLeod RC .75 .23
❑ 244 Ricky Davis RC 3.00 .90
❑ 245 Brian Skinner RC 1.25 .35
❑ 246 Tyronn Lue RC 1.25 .35
❑ 247 Felipe Lopez RC 1.25 .35
❑ 248 Sam Jacobson RC .60 .18
❑ 249 Corey Benjamin RC 1.25 .35
❑ 250 Nazr Mohammed RC .75 .23

1999-00 Finest

	Nm-Mt	Ex-Mt
COMPLETE SET (266)	280.00	85.00
COMPLETE SERIES 1 (133)	80.00	24.00
COMPLETE SERIES 2 (133)	200.00	60.00
COMP.SERIES 2 w/o RC (118)	50.00	15.00
COMMON CARD (1-266)	.30	.09
COMMON ROOKIE (110-124)	1.00	.30
COMMON ROOKIE (252-266)	4.00	1.20
COMMON SUBSET	.40	.12

❑ 1 Shareef Abdur-Rahim 1.00 .30
❑ 2 Kevin Willis .30 .09
❑ 3 Sean Elliott .60 .18
❑ 4 Vlade Divac .60 .18
❑ 5 Tom Gugliotta .30 .09
❑ 6 Matt Harpring 1.00 .30
❑ 7 Kerry Kittles .30 .09
❑ 8 Joe Smith .60 .18
❑ 9 Jamal Mashburn .60 .18
❑ 10 Tyrone Nesby RC .30 .09
❑ 11 Alan Henderson .30 .09
❑ 12 Vitaly Potapenko .30 .09
❑ 13 Dickey Simpkins .30 .09
❑ 14 Michael Finley 1.00 .30
❑ 15 Lindsey Hunter .30 .09
❑ 16 Antawn Jamison 1.50 .45
❑ 17 Reggie Miller 1.00 .30
❑ 18 Maurice Taylor .60 .18
❑ 19 Clarence Weatherspoon .30 .09
❑ 20 Sam Mitchell .30 .09
❑ 21 Latrell Sprewell 1.00 .30
❑ 22 Michael Doleac .30 .09
❑ 23 Rex Chapman .30 .09
❑ 24 Peja Stojakovic 1.25 .35
❑ 25 Vladimir Stepania .30 .09
❑ 26 Tracy McGrady 2.50 .75
❑ 27 Cherokee Parks .30 .09
❑ 28 LaPhonso Ellis .30 .09
❑ 29 Hakeem Olajuwon 1.00 .30
❑ 30 Adonal Foyle .30 .09
❑ 31 Bryant Stith .30 .09
❑ 32 Andrew DeClercq .30 .09
❑ 33 Toni Kukoc .60 .18
❑ 34 Kenny Anderson .60 .18
❑ 35 Mike Bibby 1.00 .30
❑ 36 Glen Rice .60 .18
❑ 37 Avery Johnson .30 .09
❑ 38 Arvydas Sabonis .60 .18
❑ 39 Kornel David RC .30 .09
❑ 40 Hubert Davis .30 .09
❑ 41 Grant Hill 1.00 .30
❑ 42 Donyell Marshall .60 .18
❑ 43 Jalen Rose 1.00 .30
❑ 44 Derrick Coleman .60 .18
❑ 45 P.J. Brown .30 .09
❑ 46 Vin Baker .60 .18
❑ 47 Clifford Robinson .30 .09
❑ 48 Allan Houston .60 .18
❑ 49 Kendall Gill .30 .09
❑ 50 Matt Geiger .30 .09
❑ 51 Larry Hughes 1.00 .30
❑ 52 Corliss Williamson .60 .18
❑ 53 Darrell Armstrong .30 .09
❑ 54 Bobby Jackson .60 .18
❑ 55 Bryon Russell .30 .09
❑ 56 Juwan Howard .60 .18
❑ 57 Dikembe Mutombo .60 .18
❑ 58 Eddie Jones 1.00 .30
❑ 59 Randy Brown .30 .09
❑ 60 Dirk Nowitzki 2.00 .60
❑ 61 Jerome Williams .30 .09
❑ 62 Scottie Pippen 1.50 .45
❑ 63 Dale Davis .30 .09
❑ 64 Kobe Bryant 4.00 1.20
❑ 65 Robert Traylor .30 .09
❑ 66 Tim Hardaway .60 .18
❑ 67 Michael Olowokandi .60 .18
❑ 68 Walter McCarty .30 .09
❑ 69 Damon Stoudamire .60 .18
❑ 70 Othella Harrington .30 .09
❑ 71 Chauncey Billups .60 .18
❑ 72 John Starks .60 .18
❑ 73 Ricky Davis .60 .18
❑ 74 Glenn Robinson 1.00 .30
❑ 75 Dean Garrett .30 .09
❑ 76 Chris Childs .30 .09
❑ 77 Shawn Kemp .60 .18
❑ 78 Allen Iverson 2.00 .60
❑ 79 Brian Grant .60 .18
❑ 80 David Robinson 1.00 .30
❑ 81 Tracy Murray .30 .09
❑ 82 Howard Eisley .30 .09
❑ 83 Doug Christie .60 .18
❑ 84 Gary Payton 1.00 .30
❑ 85 John Stockton 1.00 .30
❑ 86 Rod Strickland .30 .09
❑ 87 Tyrone Corbin .30 .09
❑ 88 Antonio Daniels .30 .09
❑ 89 Dee Brown .30 .09

	Card	Nm-Mt	Ex-Mt
❑ 90	Antoine Walker	1.00	.30
❑ 91	Theo Ratliff	.60	.18
❑ 92	Larry Johnson	.60	.18
❑ 93	Stephon Marbury	1.00	.30
❑ 94	Brevin Knight	.30	.09
❑ 95	Antonio McDyess	.60	.18
❑ 96	Bison Dele	.30	.09
❑ 97	Cuttino Mobley	1.00	.30
❑ 98	Haywoode Workman	.30	.09
❑ 99	J.R. Reid	.30	.09
❑ 100	Travis Best	.30	.09
❑ 101	Chris Webber GEM	1.50	.45
❑ 102	Grant Hill GEM	.75	.23
❑ 103	Kevin Garnett GEM	3.00	.90
❑ 104	Jason Kidd GEM	2.50	.75
❑ 105	Gary Payton GEM	1.00	.30
❑ 106	Shaquille O'Neal GEM	4.00	1.20
❑ 107	Alonzo Mourning GEM	.75	.23
❑ 108	Karl Malone GEM	1.50	.45
❑ 109	John Stockton GEM	.75	.23
❑ 110	Elton Brand RC	6.00	1.80
❑ 111	Baron Davis RC	5.00	1.50
❑ 112	Aleksandar Radojevic RC	1.00	.30
❑ 113	Cal Bowdler RC	1.50	.45
❑ 114	Jumaine Jones RC	1.50	.45
❑ 115	Jason Terry RC	3.00	.90
❑ 116	Trajan Langdon RC	2.00	.60
❑ 117	Dion Glover RC	1.50	.45
❑ 118	Jeff Foster RC	1.50	.45
❑ 119	Lamar Odom RC	5.00	1.50
❑ 120	Wally Szczerbiak RC	5.00	1.50
❑ 121	Shawn Marion RC	6.00	1.80
❑ 122	Kenny Thomas RC	2.00	.60
❑ 123	Devean George RC	2.50	.75
❑ 124	Scott Padgett RC	1.50	.45
❑ 125	Tim Duncan SEN	3.00	.90
❑ 126	Jason Williams SEN	.60	.18
❑ 127	Paul Pierce SEN	1.00	.30
❑ 128	Kobe Bryant SEN	6.00	1.80
❑ 129	Keith Van Horn SEN	1.00	.30
❑ 130	Vince Carter SEN	4.00	1.20
❑ 131	Matt Harpring SEN	.75	.23
❑ 132	Antawn Jamison SEN	2.50	.75
❑ 133	Tracy McGrady SEN	4.00	1.20
❑ 134	Tim Duncan	2.00	.60
❑ 135	Tariq Abdul-Wahad	.30	.09
❑ 136	Luc Longley	.30	.09
❑ 137	Steve Smith	.60	.18
❑ 138	Alonzo Mourning	.60	.18
❑ 139	Kevin Garnett	2.00	.60
❑ 140	Christian Laettner	.60	.18
❑ 141	Rik Smits	.60	.18
❑ 142	Cedric Henderson	.30	.09
❑ 143	Jim Jackson	.30	.09
❑ 144	Dan Majerle	.60	.18
❑ 145	Bryant Reeves	.30	.09
❑ 146	Antonio Davis	.30	.09
❑ 147	Michael Smith	.30	.09
❑ 148	Charlie Ward	.30	.09
❑ 149	Chris Mullin	1.00	.30
❑ 150	Danny Manning	.30	.09
❑ 151	Eric Williams	.30	.09
❑ 152	Hersey Hawkins	.60	.18
❑ 153	Isaiah Rider	.30	.09
❑ 154	Shandon Anderson	.30	.09
❑ 155	Jason Kidd	1.50	.45
❑ 156	Chris Whitney	.30	.09
❑ 157	Brent Barry	.60	.18
❑ 158	Patrick Ewing	1.00	.30
❑ 159	George Lynch	.30	.09
❑ 160	Dickey Simpkins	.30	.09
❑ 161	Derek Anderson	.60	.18
❑ 162	Ron Mercer	.60	.18
❑ 163	David Wesley	.30	.09
❑ 164	Mookie Blaylock	.30	.09
❑ 165	Terrell Brandon	.60	.18
❑ 166	Detlef Schrempf	.60	.18
❑ 167	Olden Polynice	.30	.09
❑ 168	Jayson Williams	.30	.09
❑ 169	Eric Piatkowski	.60	.18
❑ 170	A.C. Green	.60	.18
❑ 171	Chris Mills	.30	.09
❑ 172	Chris Webber	1.00	.30
❑ 173	Jeff Hornacek	.60	.18
❑ 174	Calbert Cheaney	.30	.09
❑ 175	Wesley Person	.30	.09
❑ 176	Corey Benjamin	.30	.09
❑ 177	Loy Vaught	.30	.09
❑ 178	Keith Closs	.30	.09
❑ 179	Bo Outlaw	.30	.09
❑ 180	Mitch Richmond	.60	.18
❑ 181	Charles Oakley	.30	.09
❑ 182	Felipe Lopez	.30	.09
❑ 183	Eric Snow	.60	.18
❑ 184	Paul Pierce	1.00	.30
❑ 185	Elden Campbell	.30	.09
❑ 186	Shaquille O'Neal	2.50	.75
❑ 187	Charles Barkley	1.25	.35
❑ 188	Mark Jackson	.60	.18
❑ 189	Scott Burrell	.30	.09
❑ 190	Anfernee Hardaway	1.00	.30
❑ 191	Samaki Walker	.30	.09
❑ 192	Karl Malone	1.00	.30
❑ 193	Jermaine O'Neal	1.00	.30
❑ 194	Mario Elie	.30	.09
❑ 195	Malik Sealy	.30	.09
❑ 196	Voshon Lenard	.30	.09
❑ 197	Chris Gatling	.30	.09
❑ 198	Walt Williams	.30	.09
❑ 199	Nick Van Exel	1.00	.30
❑ 200	Bimbo Coles	.30	.09
❑ 201	John Wallace	.30	.09
❑ 202	Anthony Mason	.60	.18
❑ 203	Steve Nash	1.00	.30
❑ 204	Erick Dampier	.60	.18
❑ 205	Cedric Ceballos	.30	.09
❑ 206	Derek Fisher	1.00	.30
❑ 207	Marcus Camby	.60	.18
❑ 208	Tyrone Hill	.30	.09
❑ 209	Nick Anderson	.30	.09
❑ 210	Sam Cassell	1.00	.30
❑ 211	Raef LaFrentz	.60	.18
❑ 212	Ruben Patterson	.60	.18
❑ 213	Rick Fox	.60	.18
❑ 214	Jason Williams	1.00	.30
❑ 215	Vince Carter	2.50	.75
❑ 216	Michael Dickerson	.60	.18
❑ 217	Steve Kerr	.60	.18
❑ 218	Rasheed Wallace	1.00	.30
❑ 219	Keith Van Horn	1.00	.30
❑ 220	Bob Sura	.30	.09
❑ 221	Ray Allen	1.00	.30
❑ 222	Jerry Stackhouse	1.00	.30
❑ 223	Shawn Bradley	.30	.09
❑ 224	Horace Grant	.60	.18
❑ 225	Tim Duncan USA	3.00	.90
❑ 226	Kevin Garnett USA	3.00	.90
❑ 227	Jason Kidd USA	2.50	.75
❑ 228	Steve Smith USA	.40	.12
❑ 229	Allan Houston USA	.75	.23
❑ 230	Tom Gugliotta USA	.40	.12
❑ 231	Gary Payton USA	.75	.23
❑ 232	Tim Hardaway USA	.75	.23
❑ 233	Vin Baker USA	.40	.12
❑ 234	Karl Malone CAT	1.00	.30
❑ 235	Vince Carter CAT	4.00	1.20
❑ 236	Jason Williams CAT	.75	.23
❑ 237	Alonzo Mourning CAT	.75	.23
❑ 238	Anfernee Hardaway CAT	2.00	.60
❑ 239	Mitch Richmond CAT	.75	.23
❑ 240	Steve Smith CAT	.75	.23
❑ 241	Charles Barkley CAT	1.25	.35
❑ 242	Ron Mercer CAT	.75	.23
❑ 243	Shaquille O'Neal EDGE	4.00	1.20
❑ 244	Jason Kidd EDGE	2.50	.75
❑ 245	Kevin Garnett EDGE	3.00	.90
❑ 246	Tim Duncan EDGE	3.00	.90
❑ 247	Ray Allen EDGE	1.50	.45
❑ 248	Chris Webber EDGE	1.50	.45
❑ 249	Jerry Stackhouse EDGE	.75	.23
❑ 250	Keith Van Horn EDGE	.75	.23
❑ 251	Patrick Ewing EDGE	.75	.23
❑ 252	Steve Francis RC	40.00	12.00
❑ 253	Jonathan Bender RC	20.00	6.00
❑ 254	Richard Hamilton RC	20.00	6.00
❑ 255	Andre Miller RC	20.00	6.00
❑ 256	Corey Maggette RC	20.00	6.00
❑ 257	William Avery RC	8.00	2.40
❑ 258	Ron Artest RC	12.00	3.60
❑ 259	James Posey RC	10.00	3.00
❑ 260	Quincy Lewis RC	5.00	1.50
❑ 261	Tim James RC	6.00	1.80
❑ 262	Vonteego Cummings RC	8.00	2.40
❑ 263	Anthony Carter RC	12.00	3.60
❑ 264	Mirsad Turkcan RC	4.00	1.20
❑ 265	Adrian Griffin RC	6.00	1.80
❑ 266	Ryan Robertson RC	5.00	1.50
❑ PP1	Reggie Miller Promo	1.00	.30

2000-01 Finest

	Nm-Mt	Ex-Mt
COMPLETE SET (173)	275.00	80.00
COMPLETE SET w/o SP (125)	40.00	12.00
COMMON CARD (1-173)	.30	.09
COMMON ROOKIE (126-150)	6.00	1.80

	Card	Nm-Mt	Ex-Mt
❑ 1	Shaquille O'Neal	2.50	.75
❑ 2	P.J. Brown	.30	.09
❑ 3	Joe Smith	.60	.18
❑ 4	Kendall Gill	.30	.09
❑ 5	Corey Maggette	.60	.18
❑ 6	Marcus Camby	.60	.18
❑ 7	Toni Kukoc	.60	.18
❑ 8	Kobe Bryant	1.00	.30
❑ 9	David Robinson	1.00	.30
❑ 10	Ruben Patterson	.60	.18
❑ 11	Allen Iverson	2.00	.60
❑ 12	Glenn Robinson	.60	.18
❑ 13	Anthony Carter	.60	.18
❑ 14	Jonathan Bender	.60	.18
❑ 15	Vince Carter	2.50	.75
❑ 16	Jerry Stackhouse	1.00	.30
❑ 17	Raef LaFrentz	.60	.18
❑ 18	Dikembe Mutombo	.60	.18
❑ 19	Baron Davis	1.00	.30
❑ 20	Kenny Anderson	.60	.18
❑ 21	Corey Benjamin	.30	.09
❑ 22	Andre Miller	.60	.18
❑ 23	Cedric Ceballos	.30	.09
❑ 24	Christian Laettner	.60	.18
❑ 25	Shandon Anderson	.30	.09
❑ 26	Rik Smits	.30	.09
❑ 27	Michael Olowokandi	.30	.09
❑ 28	Sam Cassell	1.00	.30
❑ 29	Tom Gugliotta	.30	.09
❑ 30	Jason Williams	.60	.18
❑ 31	Avery Johnson	.30	.09
❑ 32	Karl Malone	1.00	.30
❑ 33	Grant Hill	1.00	.30
❑ 34	Paul Pierce	1.00	.30
❑ 35	Antonio Davis	.30	.09
❑ 36	Nick Anderson	.30	.09
❑ 37	Alan Henderson	.30	.09
❑ 38	Eddie Jones	1.00	.30
❑ 39	Ron Artest	.60	.18
❑ 40	Brevin Knight	.30	.09
❑ 41	Keon Clark	.60	.18
❑ 42	Elton Brand	1.00	.30
❑ 43	Reggie Miller	1.00	.30
❑ 44	Steve Francis	1.00	.30
❑ 45	Derek Anderson	.60	.18
❑ 46	Alonzo Mourning	.60	.18
❑ 47	Terrell Brandon	.60	.18
❑ 48	Larry Johnson	.60	.18
❑ 49	Keith Van Horn	1.00	.30
❑ 50	Jason Kidd	1.50	.45
❑ 51	Scottie Pippen	1.50	.45
❑ 52	Gary Payton	1.00	.30
❑ 53	Robert Pack	.30	.09
❑ 54	Adrian Griffin	.30	.09
❑ 55	Jim Jackson	.30	.09

❑ 56 Lamond Murray .30 .09
❑ 57 Larry Hughes .60 .18
❑ 58 Dirk Nowitzki 1.50 .45
❑ 59 Vonteego Cummings .30 .09
❑ 60 Jalen Rose 1.00 .30
❑ 61 Arvydas Sabonis .60 .18
❑ 62 Kerry Kittles .30 .09
❑ 63 Kevin Garnett 2.00 .60
❑ 64 Latrell Sprewell 1.00 .30
❑ 65 Shawn Marion 1.00 .30
❑ 66 Darrell Armstrong .30 .09
❑ 67 Ron Mercer .60 .18
❑ 68 Damon Stoudamire .60 .18
❑ 69 Tracy McGrady 2.50 .75
❑ 70 Theo Ratliff .60 .18
❑ 71 Lamar Odom 1.00 .30
❑ 72 Charlie Ward .30 .09
❑ 73 John Amaechi .30 .09
❑ 74 Quincy Lewis .30 .09
❑ 75 Othella Harrington .30 .09
❑ 76 Doug Christie .60 .18
❑ 77 Richard Hamilton .60 .18
❑ 78 Donyell Marshall .60 .18
❑ 79 Vlade Divac .60 .18
❑ 80 Clifford Robinson .30 .09
❑ 81 Sean Elliott .60 .18
❑ 82 Rashard Lewis .60 .18
❑ 83 Wally Szczerbiak .60 .18
❑ 84 Dale Davis .30 .09
❑ 85 Kelvin Cato .30 .09
❑ 86 Cuttino Mobley .60 .18
❑ 87 Travis Best .30 .09
❑ 88 Robert Horry .60 .18
❑ 89 Maurice Taylor .30 .09
❑ 90 Jamal Mashburn .60 .18
❑ 91 Tim Thomas .60 .18
❑ 92 Stephon Marbury 1.00 .30
❑ 93 Patrick Ewing 1.00 .30
❑ 94 Eric Snow .60 .18
❑ 95 Anfernee Hardaway 1.00 .30
❑ 96 Steve Smith .60 .18
❑ 97 Chris Webber 1.00 .30
❑ 98 Rodney Rogers .30 .09
❑ 99 John Stockton 1.00 .30
❑ 100 Tim Duncan 2.00 .60
❑ 101 Ray Allen 1.00 .30
❑ 102 Glen Rice .60 .18
❑ 103 Bryon Russell .30 .09
❑ 104 Tim Hardaway .60 .18
❑ 105 Allan Houston .60 .18
❑ 106 Rasheed Wallace 1.00 .30
❑ 107 Vin Baker .60 .18
❑ 108 Michael Dickerson .60 .18
❑ 109 Juwan Howard .60 .18
❑ 110 Hakeem Olajuwon 1.00 .30
❑ 111 Shareef Abdur-Rahim 1.00 .30
❑ 112 Rod Strickland .30 .09
❑ 113 Hersey Hawkins .30 .09
❑ 114 Jason Terry 1.00 .30
❑ 115 Anthony Mason .60 .18
❑ 116 Mike Bibby 1.00 .30
❑ 117 Shawn Kemp .60 .18
❑ 118 Derrick Coleman .30 .09
❑ 119 Antoine Walker 1.00 .30
❑ 120 Antawn Jamison 1.00 .30
❑ 121 Michael Finley 1.00 .30
❑ 122 Antonio McDyess .60 .18
❑ 123 Nick Van Exel 1.00 .30
❑ 124 Mitch Richmond .60 .18
❑ 125 Lindsey Hunter .30 .09
❑ 126 Kenyon Martin RC 15.00 4.50
❑ 127 Stromile Swift RC 8.00 2.40
❑ 128 Darius Miles RC 15.00 4.50
❑ 129 Marcus Fizer RC 6.00 1.80
❑ 130 Mike Miller RC 12.00 3.60
❑ 131 DerMarr Johnson RC 6.00 1.80
❑ 132 Chris Mihm RC 6.00 1.80
❑ 133 Jamal Crawford RC 8.00 2.40
❑ 134 Joel Przybilla RC 6.00 1.80
❑ 135 Keyon Dooling RC 6.00 1.80
❑ 136 Jerome Moiso RC 6.00 1.80
❑ 137 Etan Thomas RC 6.00 1.80
❑ 138 Courtney Alexander RC 6.00 1.80
❑ 139 Mateen Cleaves RC 6.00 1.80
❑ 140 Jason Collier RC 6.00 1.80
❑ 141 Desmond Mason RC 6.00 1.80
❑ 142 Quentin Richardson RC 12.00 3.60
❑ 143 Jamaal Magloire RC 6.00 1.80
❑ 144 Speedy Claxton RC 6.00 1.80
❑ 145 Morris Peterson RC 8.00 2.40
❑ 146 Donnell Harvey RC 6.00 1.80
❑ 147 DeShawn Stevenson RC 6.00 1.80
❑ 148 Mamadou N'diaye RC 6.00 1.80
❑ 149 Erick Barkley RC 6.00 1.80
❑ 150 Mark Madsen RC 6.00 1.80
❑ 151 Allen Iverson 1.50 .45
Stephon Marbury OTM
❑ 152 Vince Carter 3.00 .90
Kobe Bryant OTM
❑ 153 Kevin Garnett 2.50 .75
Shareef Abdur-Rahim OTM
❑ 154 Tracy McGrady 4.00 1.20
Scottie Pippen OTM
❑ 155 Tim Duncan 3.00 .90
Elton Brand OTM
❑ 156 Steve Francis 2.50 .75
Gary Payton OTM
❑ 157 Chris Webber 1.00 .30
Karl Malone OTM
❑ 158 Alonzo Mourning 1.00 .30
Patrick Ewing OTM
❑ 159 Latrell Sprewell 1.00 .30
Eddie Jones OTM
❑ 160 Jason Kidd 1.50 .45
John Stockton OTM
❑ 161 Reggie Miller 1.00 .30
Allan Houston OTM
❑ 162 Rasheed Wallace 1.00 .30
Antoine Walker OTM
❑ 163 Jerry Stackhouse 1.00 .30
Jalen Rose OTM
❑ 164 Shaquille O'Neal GEM 6.00 1.80
❑ 165 Kobe Bryant GEM 10.00 3.00
❑ 166 Vince Carter GEM 6.00 1.80
❑ 167 Kevin Garnett GEM 5.00 1.50
❑ 168 Jason Williams GEM 2.00 .60
❑ 169 Tracy McGrady GEM 5.00 1.50
❑ 170 Steve Francis GEM 3.00 .90
❑ 171 Tim Duncan GEM 5.00 1.50
❑ 172 Elton Brand GEM 2.00 .60
❑ 173 Grant Hill GEM 2.50 .75

2002-03 Finest

	Nm-Mt	Ex-Mt
COMP.DRAFT SET (10)	450.00	135.00
COMMON CARD (1-100)	.25	.07
COMMON AU RC (101-120)	12.00	3.60
COMMON JSY (121-156)	12.00	3.60
COMMON AU RC (157-177)	12.00	3.60

❑ 1 Dirk Nowitzki 1.50 .45
❑ 2 Jason Terry 1.00 .30
❑ 3 Marcus Camby .60 .18
❑ 4 Joe Johnson 1.00 .30
❑ 5 Shawn Marion 1.00 .30
❑ 6 Andrei Kirilenko 1.00 .30
❑ 7 Jamal Mashburn .60 .18
❑ 8 Andre Miller .60 .18
❑ 9 Jason Williams .60 .18
❑ 10 Tony Delk .25 .07
❑ 11 Tyson Chandler 1.00 .30
❑ 12 Jason Richardson 1.00 .30
❑ 13 Derek Fisher 1.00 .30
❑ 14 Troy Hudson .25 .07
❑ 15 Kerry Kittles .25 .07
❑ 16 Peja Stojakovic 1.00 .30
❑ 17 Kurt Thomas .60 .18
❑ 18 Jamaal Tinsley 1.00 .30
❑ 19 Matt Harpring 1.00 .30
❑ 20 Kenny Thomas .25 .07
❑ 21 Kwame Brown .60 .18
❑ 22 Antonio Davis .25 .07
❑ 23 David Robinson 1.00 .30
❑ 24 Keith Van Horn 1.00 .30
❑ 25 Howard Eisley .25 .07
❑ 26 Jalen Rose 1.00 .30
❑ 27 Chauncey Billups .25 .07
❑ 28 Corey Maggette .60 .18
❑ 29 Pau Gasol 1.00 .30
❑ 30 Desmond Mason .60 .18
❑ 31 Brian Grant .60 .18
❑ 32 Eddie Griffin .60 .18
❑ 33 Voshon Lenard .25 .07
❑ 34 Al Harrington .60 .18
❑ 35 Calbert Cheaney .25 .07
❑ 36 Malik Rose .25 .07
❑ 37 Bonzi Wells .60 .18
❑ 38 Pat Garrity .25 .07
❑ 39 P.J. Brown .25 .07
❑ 40 Ray Allen 1.00 .30
❑ 41 Karl Malone 1.00 .30
❑ 42 Steve Nash 1.00 .30
❑ 43 Antawn Jamison 1.00 .30
❑ 44 Ron Artest .60 .18
❑ 45 Shane Battier 1.00 .30
❑ 46 Gary Payton 1.00 .30
❑ 47 Kobe Bryant 4.00 1.20
❑ 48 Lucious Harris .25 .07
❑ 49 Richard Hamilton .60 .18
❑ 50 Darius Miles 1.00 .30
❑ 51 Marcus Fizer .60 .18
❑ 52 Antoine Walker 1.00 .30
❑ 53 Juwan Howard .60 .18
❑ 54 Eddie Jones 1.00 .30
❑ 55 Kenyon Martin 1.00 .30
❑ 56 Derek Anderson .60 .18
❑ 57 Stephen Jackson .25 .07
❑ 58 Vince Carter 2.00 .60
❑ 59 Larry Hughes .60 .18
❑ 60 Doug Christie .60 .18
❑ 61 Derrick Coleman .25 .07
❑ 62 Michael Finley 1.00 .30
❑ 63 Wally Szczerbiak .60 .18
❑ 64 David Wesley .25 .07
❑ 65 Brad Miller 1.00 .30
❑ 66 Clifford Robinson .25 .07
❑ 67 Shandon Anderson .25 .07
❑ 68 Stephon Marbury 1.00 .30
❑ 69 Bobby Jackson .60 .18
❑ 70 Brent Barry .60 .18
❑ 71 Ruben Patterson .60 .18
❑ 72 Rashard Lewis 1.00 .30
❑ 73 Tony Battie .25 .07
❑ 74 Ben Wallace 1.00 .30
❑ 75 Theo Ratliff .60 .18
❑ 76 Ricky Davis 1.00 .30
❑ 77 Nick Van Exel 1.00 .30
❑ 78 Mike Miller 1.00 .30
❑ 79 Sam Cassell 1.00 .30
❑ 80 Malik Allen .25 .07
❑ 81 Mike Bibby 1.00 .30
❑ 82 Scottie Pippen 1.50 .45
❑ 83 Dikembe Mutombo .60 .18
❑ 84 Latrell Sprewell 1.00 .30
❑ 85 Predrag Drobnjak .25 .07
❑ 86 Joe Smith .60 .18
❑ 87 Aaron Mckie .60 .18
❑ 88 Jamaal Magloire .60 .18
❑ 89 Keon Clark .60 .18
❑ 90 Eric Williams .25 .07
❑ 91 Raef Lafrentz .60 .18
❑ 92 Troy Murphy 1.00 .30
❑ 93 Rick Fox .60 .18
❑ 94 Michael Redd 1.00 .30
❑ 95 Radoslav Nesterovic .60 .18
❑ 96 Donyell Marshall 1.00 .30
❑ 97 Elton Brand 1.00 .30
❑ 98 Robert Horry .60 .18
❑ 99 Zydrunas Ilgauskas .60 .18
❑ 100 Michael Jordan 8.00 2.40
❑ 101 Juaquin Hawkins AU RC 12.00 3.60

❑ 102 Dan Dickau AU RC .. 15.00 4.50
❑ 103 Jiri Welsh AU EXCH.. 12.00 3.60
❑ 104 John Salmons AU 12.00 3.60
❑ 105 Tamar Slay AU RC.... 12.00 3.60
❑ 106 Melvin Ely AU RC...... 12.00 3.60
❑ 107 Jared Jeffries AU RC 20.00 6.00
❑ 108 J.Harrington AU RC .. 12.00 3.60
❑ 109 M.Haislip AU EXCH .. 12.00 3.60
❑ 110 Qyntel Woods AU RC 20.00 6.00
❑ 111 R.Humphrey AU RC.. 12.00 3.60
❑ 112 J.R. Bremer AU RC .. 12.00 3.60
❑ 113 A.Rigadeau AU RC .. 12.00 3.60
❑ 114 Jay Williams RC *........ 6.00 1.80
❑ 115 Pat Burke AU RC 12.00 3.60
❑ 116 Smush Parker AU RC 12.00 3.60
❑ 117 Juan Dixon AU RC.... 30.00 9.00
❑ 118 V.Yarbrough AU RC.. 12.00 3.60
❑ 119 M.Okur AU EXCH 20.00 6.00
❑ 120 Rasual Butler AU RC 15.00 4.50
❑ 121 Baron Davis JSY 12.00 3.60
❑ 122 S.Abdur-Rahim JSY .. 12.00 3.60
❑ 123 Gilbert Arenas JSY.... 12.00 3.60
❑ 124 Travis Best JSY 12.00 3.60
❑ 125 Vlade Divac JSY 12.00 3.60
❑ 126 Tim Duncan JSY 20.00 6.00
❑ 127 Jason Kidd JSY 15.00 4.50
❑ 128 Kevin Garnett JSY 20.00 6.00
❑ 129 A.Hardaway JSY 12.00 3.60
❑ 130 Allen Iverson JSY...... 20.00 6.00
❑ 131 Cuttino Mobley JSY .. 12.00 3.60
❑ 132 Steve Francis JSY 12.00 3.60
❑ 133 Jermaine O'Neal JSY 12.00 3.60
❑ 134 Lamar Odom JSY...... 12.00 3.60
❑ 135 M.Olowokandi JSY.... 12.00 3.60
❑ 136 Paul Pierce JSY 12.00 3.60
❑ 137 Reggie Miller JSY...... 12.00 3.60
❑ 138 Chris Webber JSY 12.00 3.60
❑ 139 Richard Jefferson JSY 12.00 3.60
❑ 140 Allan Houston JSY 12.00 3.60
❑ 141 Glenn Robinson JSY 12.00 3.60
❑ 142 Jerome Williams JSY 12.00 3.60
❑ 143 John Stockton JSY.... 12.00 3.60
❑ 144 Rasheed Wallace JSY 12.00 3.60
❑ 145 Eric Snow JSY 12.00 3.60
❑ 146 Tracy McGrady JSY .. 25.00 7.50
❑ 147 S.O'Neal JSY 25.00 7.50
❑ 148 J.Stackhouse JSY 12.00 3.60
❑ 149 Morris Peterson JSY 12.00 3.60
❑ 150 D.Armstrong JSY 12.00 3.60
❑ 151 Tony Parker JSY 12.00 3.60
❑ 152 V.Radmanovic JSY .. 12.00 3.60
❑ 153 Anthony Mason JSY.. 12.00 3.60
❑ 154 Charles Oakley JSY .. 12.00 3.60
❑ 155 Grant Hill JSY............ 12.00 3.60
❑ 156 Vin Baker JSY 12.00 3.60
❑ 157 Chris Jefferies AU RC 15.00 4.50
❑ 158 Drew Gooden AU RC 40.00 12.00
❑ 159 C.Jacobsen AU RC ... 15.00 4.50
❑ 160 Kareem Rush AU RC 25.00 7.50
❑ 161 B.Nachbar AU RC 12.00 3.60
❑ 162 T.Prince AU RC 25.00 7.50
❑ 163 Manu Ginobili RC* 30.00 9.00
❑ 164 Gordan Giricek AU RC 25.00 7.50
❑ 165 Raul Lopez AU RC.... 12.00 3.60
❑ 166 Dan Gadzuric AU RC 12.00 3.60
❑ 167 Marko Jaric AU RC .. 15.00 4.50
❑ 168 Lonny Baxter AU RC 12.00 3.60
❑ 169 Y.Ming AU EXCH.... 100.00 30.00
❑ 170 Mike Dunleavy AU RC 30.00 9.00
❑ 171 Caron Butler AU RC.. 40.00 12.00
❑ 172 Nene Hilario AU RC.. 25.00 7.50
❑ 173 A.Stoudemire AU RC 100.00 30.00
❑ 174 N.Tskitishvili AU RC.. 20.00 6.00
❑ 175 Fred Jones AU RC 15.00 4.50
❑ 176 D.Wagner AU RC...... 30.00 9.00
❑ 177 Carlos Boozer AU RC 40.00 12.00
❑ 178 LeBron James XRC 150.00 45.00
❑ 179 Darko Milicic XRC 25.00 7.50
❑ 180 Carmelo Anthony XRC 60.00 18.00
❑ 181 Chris Bosh XRC........ 25.00 7.50
❑ 182 Dwyane Wade XRC .. 40.00 12.00
❑ 183 Chris Kaman XRC 12.00 3.60
❑ 184 Kirk Hinrich XRC 20.00 6.00
❑ 185 T.J. Ford XRC 15.00 4.50
❑ 186 Mike Sweetney XRC 12.00 3.60
❑ 187 Jarvis Hayes XRC 12.00 3.60

2003-04 Finest

	Nm-Mt	Ex-Mt
COMP.SET w/o SP's (100)	40.00	12.00
COMMON CARD (1-100)	.25	.07
COMMON JSY (101-130)	10.00	3.00
COMMON ROOKIE (131-143)	6.00	1.80
COMMON AU RC (144-172)..	12.00	3.60
COMMON DRAFT EXCH	10.00	3.00

❑ 1 Zach Randolph.............. 1.00 .30
❑ 2 Keith Van Horn............... 1.00 .30
❑ 3 Steve Francis .... 1.00 .30
❑ 4 Al Harrington .... .60 .18
❑ 5 Jason Kidd .... 1.50 .45
❑ 6 Jamaal Tinsley .... 1.00 .30
❑ 7 Lamar Odom .... 1.00 .30
❑ 8 Antoine Walker............... 1.00 .30
❑ 9 Tony Parker .... 1.00 .30
❑ 10 Jamal Mashburn............ .60 .18
❑ 11 Desmond Mason .... .60 .18
❑ 12 Carlos Arroyo .... 1.50 .45
❑ 13 Chris Andersen .... .25 .07
❑ 14 Chris Wilcox .... .60 .18
❑ 15 Vince Carter .... 2.50 .75
❑ 16 Peja Stojakovic............. 1.00 .30
❑ 17 Qyntel Woods................. .25 .07
❑ 18 Mike Dunleavy .... .60 .18
❑ 19 Sam Cassell .... 1.00 .30
❑ 20 Allan Houston................ .60 .18
❑ 21 Speedy Claxton .... .25 .07
❑ 22 Rafer Alston .... .25 .07
❑ 23 Michael Finley .... 1.00 .30
❑ 24 Richard Jefferson........... .60 .18
❑ 25 Larry Hughes .... .60 .18
❑ 26 Pau Gasol .... 1.00 .30
❑ 27 Maurice Taylor .... .25 .07
❑ 28 Donyell Marshall............ 1.00 .30
❑ 29 Darrell Armstrong .... .25 .07
❑ 30 Latrell Sprewell.............. 1.00 .30
❑ 31 Reggie Miller .... 1.00 .30
❑ 32 Stephon Marbury .... 1.00 .30
❑ 33 Antawn Jamison............ 1.00 .30
❑ 34 DerMarr Johnson........... .25 .07
❑ 35 Shareef Abdur-Rahim .. 1.00 .30
❑ 36 Tony Battie .... .25 .07
❑ 37 Kwame Brown .... .60 .18
❑ 38 Fred Jones .... .25 .07
❑ 39 Jamal Crawford .... .60 .18
❑ 40 Kurt Thomas.................. .60 .18
❑ 41 Eric Snow...................... .60 .18
❑ 42 Andre Miller .... .60 .18
❑ 43 Ray Allen .... 1.00 .30
❑ 44 Caron Butler.................. 1.00 .30
❑ 45 Corliss Williamson .... .60 .18
❑ 46 Kenny Thomas............... .25 .07
❑ 47 Jason Terry .... 1.00 .30
❑ 48 Ronald Murray .... .25 .07
❑ 49 Richard Hamilton .... .60 .18
❑ 50 Elton Brand .... 1.00 .30
❑ 51 Ron Artest .... .60 .18
❑ 52 Jerome Williams............. .25 .07
❑ 53 Ricky Davis .... 1.00 .30
❑ 54 Brent Barry.................... .60 .18
❑ 55 Dikembe Mutombo.......... .60 .18
❑ 56 Earl Boykins.................. .60 .18
❑ 57 Brad Miller .... 1.00 .30
❑ 58 Shane Battier .... 1.00 .30
❑ 59 Tyson Chandler .... 1.00 .30
❑ 60 Kelvin Cato.................... .25 .07
❑ 61 Shawn Marion .... 1.00 .30
❑ 62 Bobby Jackson............... .60 .18
❑ 63 Corey Maggette .... .60 .18
❑ 64 Antonio McDyess .... .60 .18
❑ 65 Drew Gooden................. .60 .18
❑ 66 Mike Miller .... 1.00 .30
❑ 67 Darius Miles .... 1.00 .30
❑ 68 Stephen Jackson .... .25 .07
❑ 69 Cuttino Mobley .... .60 .18
❑ 70 Gary Payton .... 1.00 .30
❑ 71 Toni Kukoc.................... .60 .18
❑ 72 Eddie Jones .... 1.00 .30
❑ 73 Gilbert Arenas .... 1.00 .30
❑ 74 Matt Harpring .... 1.00 .30
❑ 75 Marko Jaric................... .60 .18
❑ 76 Bonzi Wells .... .60 .18
❑ 77 Nick Van Exel............... 1.00 .30
❑ 78 Quentin Richardson .... .60 .18
❑ 79 Rasho Nesterovic........... .60 .18
❑ 80 Steve Nash................... 1.00 .30
❑ 81 Morris Peterson .... .60 .18
❑ 82 Nikoloz Tskitishvili .... .25 .07
❑ 83 Damon Stoudamire .... .60 .18
❑ 84 Bruce Bowen .... .25 .07
❑ 85 Brian Grant................... .60 .18
❑ 86 Jalen Rose .... 1.00 .30
❑ 87 Jerry Stackhouse .... 1.00 .30
❑ 88 Kobe Bryant 4.00 1.20
❑ 89 Eddy Curry .... .60 .18
❑ 90 Tim Thomas .... .60 .18
❑ 91 Erick Dampier................ .60 .18
❑ 92 Jason Williams .... .60 .18
❑ 93 Troy Murphy .... 1.00 .30
❑ 94 Kerry Kittles .... .25 .07
❑ 95 Zydrunas Ilgauskas .... .60 .18
❑ 96 Theo Ratliff................... .60 .18
❑ 97 Samuel Dalembert .... .25 .07
❑ 98 Jeff McInnis .... .25 .07
❑ 99 Juwan Howard .... .60 .18
❑ 100 Joe Johnson................ .60 .18
❑ 101 Paul Pierce JSY 10.00 3.00
❑ 102 Ben Wallace JSY 10.00 3.00
❑ 103 Yao Ming JSY 15.00 4.50
❑ 104 Jermaine O'Neal JSY 10.00 3.00
❑ 105 Rashard Lewis JSY .. 10.00 3.00
❑ 106 Karl Malone JSY 10.00 3.00
❑ 107 Allen Iverson JSY...... 12.00 3.60
❑ 108 Mike Bibby JSY 10.00 3.00
❑ 109 Rasheed Wallace JSY 10.00 3.00
❑ 110 Nene JSY 10.00 3.00
❑ 111 Tracy McGrady JSY .. 15.00 4.50
❑ 112 Andrei Kirilenko JSY 10.00 3.00
❑ 113 Manu Ginobili JSY 10.00 3.00
❑ 114 Kenyon Martin JSY .. 10.00 3.00
❑ 115 Amare Stoudemire JSY 12.00 3.60
❑ 116 Baron Davis JSY 10.00 3.00
❑ 117 Michael Olowokandi JSY 10.00 3.00
❑ 118 Carlos Boozer JSY.... 10.00 3.00
❑ 119 Jason Richardson JSY 10.00 3.00
❑ 120 Dirk Nowitzki JSY...... 12.00 3.60
❑ 121 Chauncey Billups JSY 10.00 3.00
❑ 122 Chris Webber JSY 10.00 3.00
❑ 123 Glenn Robinson JSY/807 10.00 3.00
❑ 124 Kevin Garnett JSY 12.00 3.60
❑ 125 Michael Redd JSY 10.00 3.00
❑ 126 David Wesley JSY 10.00 3.00
❑ 127 Tayshaun Prince JSY 10.00 3.00
❑ 128 Jamaal Magloire JSY 10.00 3.00
❑ 129 Tim Duncan JSY 12.00 3.60
❑ 130 Shaquille O'Neal JSY 15.00 4.50
❑ 131 Darko Milicic RC........ 10.00 3.00
❑ 132 Chris Kaman RC 6.00 1.80
❑ 133 LeBron James RC .. 100.00 30.00
❑ 134 Richie Frahm RC 6.00 1.80
❑ 135 Steve Blake RC 6.00 1.80
❑ 136 Zaza Pachulia RC 6.00 1.80
❑ 137 Keith Bogans RC 6.00 1.80
❑ 138 Kirk Hinrich AU RC.... 40.00 12.00
❑ 139 Jarvis Hayes RC 6.00 1.80
❑ 140 Zarko Cabarkapa AU RC 12.00 3.60
❑ 141 Zoran Planinic AU RC 12.00 3.60
❑ 142 Udonis Haslem RC...... 6.00 1.80
❑ 143 David West RC............ 6.00 1.80
❑ 144 Boris Diaw AU RC 12.00 3.60
❑ 145 Travis Outlaw AU RC EXCH 12.00 3.60

❑ 146 Brian Cook AU RC	12.00	3.60
❑ 147 Ndudi Ebi AU RC	12.00	3.60
❑ 148 Josh Howard AU RC	25.00	7.50
❑ 149 Jason Kapono AU RC	12.00	3.60
❑ 150 Luke Walton AU RC ..	25.00	7.50
❑ 151 Travis Hansen AU RC	12.00	3.60
❑ 152 Willie Green AU RC ..	12.00	3.60
❑ 153 Maurice Williams AU RC	12.00	3.60
❑ 154 Francisco Elson AU RC	12.00	3.60
❑ 155 Kyle Korver AU RC ..	20.00	6.00
❑ 156 Marquis Daniels AU RC	30.00	9.00
❑ 157 Chris Bosh AU RC	30.00	9.00
❑ 158 Dwyane Wade AU RC	60.00	18.00
❑ 159 Aleksandar Pavlovic AU RC	12.00	3.60
❑ 160 Mike Sweetney AU RC	12.00	3.60
❑ 161 Marcus Banks AU RC	12.00	3.60
❑ 162 Luke Ridnour AU RC	25.00	7.50
❑ 163 Carmelo Anthony AU RC	150.00	45.00
❑ 164 Mickael Pietrus AU RC	12.00	3.60
❑ 165 Reece Gaines AU RC	12.00	3.60
❑ 166 Kendrick Perkins AU RC	12.00	3.60
❑ 167 Troy Bell AU RC	12.00	3.60
❑ 168 Leandro Barbosa AU RC	12.00	3.60
❑ 169 Dahntay Jones AU RC	12.00	3.60
❑ 170 T.J. Ford AU RC	25.00	7.50
❑ 171 Nick Collison AU RC	12.00	3.60
❑ 172 Theron Smith AU RC	12.00	3.60
❑ NNO Draft Pick 1 EXCH ..	50.00	15.00
❑ NNO Draft Pick 2 EXCH ..	50.00	15.00
❑ NNO Draft Pick 3 EXCH ..	30.00	9.00
❑ NNO Draft Pick 4 EXCH ..	30.00	9.00
❑ NNO Draft Pick 5 EXCH ..	20.00	6.00
❑ NNO Draft Pick 6 EXCH ..	12.00	3.60
❑ NNO Draft Pick 7 EXCH ..	15.00	4.50
❑ NNO Draft Pick 8 EXCH ..	12.00	3.60
❑ NNO Draft Pick 9 EXCH ..	12.00	3.60
❑ NNO Draft Pick 10 EXCH	15.00	4.50
❑ NNO Draft Pick 11 EXCH	10.00	3.00
❑ NNO Draft Pick 12 EXCH	10.00	3.00
❑ NNO Draft Pick 13 EXCH	20.00	6.00

1994-95 Flair

	Nm-Mt	Ex-Mt
COMPLETE SET (326)	50.00	15.00
COMPLETE SERIES 1 (175)	15.00	4.50
COMPLETE SERIES 2 (151)	30.00	9.00
❑ 1 Stacey Augmon	.15	.04
❑ 2 Mookie Blaylock	.15	.04
❑ 3 Craig Ehlo	.15	.04
❑ 4 Jon Koncak	.15	.04
❑ 5 Andrew Lang	.15	.04
❑ 6 Dee Brown	.15	.04
❑ 7 Sherman Douglas	.15	.04
❑ 8 Acie Earl	.15	.04
❑ 9 Rick Fox	.15	.04
❑ 10 Kevin Gamble	.15	.04
❑ 11 Xavier McDaniel	.15	.04
❑ 12 Dino Radja	.15	.04
❑ 13 Tony Bennett	.15	.04
❑ 14 Dell Curry	.15	.04
❑ 15 Kenny Gattison	.15	.04
❑ 16 Hersey Hawkins	.30	.09
❑ 17 Larry Johnson	.30	.09
❑ 18 Alonzo Mourning	.60	.18
❑ 19 David Wingate	.15	.04
❑ 20 B.J. Armstrong	.15	.04
❑ 21 Steve Kerr	.15	.04
❑ 22 Toni Kukoc	.75	.23
❑ 23 Pete Myers	.15	.04
❑ 24 Scottie Pippen	1.50	.45
❑ 25 Bill Wennington	.15	.04
❑ 26 Terrell Brandon	.30	.09
❑ 27 Brad Daugherty	.15	.04
❑ 28 Tyrone Hill	.15	.04
❑ 29 Bobby Phills	.15	.04
❑ 30 Mark Price	.15	.04
❑ 31 Gerald Wilkins	.15	.04
❑ 32 John Williams	.15	.04
❑ 33 Lucious Harris	.15	.04
❑ 34 Jim Jackson	.30	.09
❑ 35 Jamal Mashburn	.50	.15
❑ 36 Sean Rooks	.15	.04
❑ 37 Doug Smith	.15	.04
❑ 38 Mahmoud Abdul-Rauf	.15	.04
❑ 39 LaPhonso Ellis	.15	.04
❑ 40 Dikembe Mutombo	.30	.09
❑ 41 Robert Pack	.15	.04
❑ 42 Rodney Rogers	.15	.04
❑ 43 Brian Williams	.15	.04
❑ 44 Reggie Williams	.15	.04
❑ 45 Joe Dumars	.50	.15
❑ 46 Allan Houston	.75	.23
❑ 47 Lindsey Hunter	.30	.09
❑ 48 Terry Mills	.15	.04
❑ 49 Victor Alexander	.15	.04
❑ 50 Chris Gatling	.15	.04
❑ 51 Billy Owens	.15	.04
❑ 52 Latrell Sprewell	.50	.15
❑ 53 Chris Webber	1.25	.35
❑ 54 Sam Cassell	.50	.15
❑ 55 Carl Herrera	.15	.04
❑ 56 Robert Horry	.30	.09
❑ 57 Hakeem Olajuwon	.75	.23
❑ 58 Kenny Smith	.15	.04
❑ 59 Otis Thorpe	.15	.04
❑ 60 Antonio Davis	.15	.04
❑ 61 Dale Davis	.15	.04
❑ 62 Reggie Miller	.50	.15
❑ 63 Byron Scott	.30	.09
❑ 64 Rik Smits	.15	.04
❑ 65 Haywoode Workman	.15	.04
❑ 66 Terry Dehere	.15	.04
❑ 67 Harold Ellis	.15	.04
❑ 68 Gary Grant	.15	.04
❑ 69 Elmore Spencer	.15	.04
❑ 70 Loy Vaught	.15	.04
❑ 71 Elden Campbell	.15	.04
❑ 72 Doug Christie	.30	.09
❑ 73 Vlade Divac	.15	.04
❑ 74 George Lynch	.15	.04
❑ 75 Anthony Peeler	.15	.04
❑ 76 Nick Van Exel	.50	.15
❑ 77 James Worthy	.50	.15
❑ 78 Bimbo Coles	.15	.04
❑ 79 Harold Miner	.15	.04
❑ 80 John Salley	.15	.04
❑ 81 Rony Seikaly	.15	.04
❑ 82 Steve Smith	.30	.09
❑ 83 Vin Baker	.50	.15
❑ 84 Jon Barry	.15	.04
❑ 85 Todd Day	.15	.04
❑ 86 Lee Mayberry	.15	.04
❑ 87 Eric Murdock	.15	.04
❑ 88 Mike Brown	.15	.04
❑ 89 Christian Laettner	.30	.09
❑ 90 Isaiah Rider	.30	.09
❑ 91 Doug West	.15	.04
❑ 92 Micheal Williams	.15	.04
❑ 93 Kenny Anderson	.30	.09
❑ 94 Benoit Benjamin	.15	.04
❑ 95 P.J. Brown	.15	.04
❑ 96 Derrick Coleman	.30	.09
❑ 97 Kevin Edwards	.15	.04
❑ 98 Hubert Davis	.15	.04
❑ 99 Patrick Ewing	.50	.15
❑ 100 Derek Harper	.15	.04
❑ 101 Anthony Mason	.30	.09
❑ 102 Charles Oakley	.15	.04
❑ 103 Charles Smith	.15	.04
❑ 104 John Starks	.15	.04
❑ 105 Nick Anderson	.15	.04
❑ 106 Anfernee Hardaway	1.25	.35
❑ 107 Shaquille O'Neal	2.50	.75
❑ 108 Dennis Scott	.15	.04
❑ 109 Jeff Turner	.15	.04
❑ 110 Dana Barros	.15	.04
❑ 111 Shawn Bradley	.15	.04
❑ 112 Jeff Malone	.15	.04
❑ 113 Tim Perry	.15	.04
❑ 114 Clarence Weatherspoon	.15	.04
❑ 115 Danny Ainge	.15	.04
❑ 116 Charles Barkley	.75	.23
❑ 117 A.C. Green	.30	.09
❑ 118 Kevin Johnson	.30	.09
❑ 119 Dan Majerle	.30	.09
❑ 120 Clyde Drexler	.50	.15
❑ 121 Harvey Grant	.15	.04
❑ 122 Jerome Kersey	.15	.04
❑ 123 Clifford Robinson	.30	.09
❑ 124 Rod Strickland	.30	.09
❑ 125 Buck Williams	.15	.04
❑ 126 Randy Brown	.15	.04
❑ 127 Olden Polynice	.15	.04
❑ 128 Mitch Richmond	.50	.15
❑ 129 Lionel Simmons	.15	.04
❑ 130 Spud Webb	.15	.04
❑ 131 Walt Williams	.15	.04
❑ 132 Willie Anderson	.15	.04
❑ 133 Vinny Del Negro	.15	.04
❑ 134 Sean Elliott	.30	.09
❑ 135 Avery Johnson	.15	.04
❑ 136 J.R. Reid	.15	.04
❑ 137 David Robinson	.75	.23
❑ 138 Dennis Rodman	1.00	.30
❑ 139 Kendall Gill	.30	.09
❑ 140 Ervin Johnson	.15	.04
❑ 141 Shawn Kemp	.75	.23
❑ 142 Nate McMillan	.15	.04
❑ 143 Gary Payton	.75	.23
❑ 144 Sam Perkins	.30	.09
❑ 145 David Benoit	.15	.04
❑ 146 Jeff Hornacek	.30	.09
❑ 147 Jay Humphries	.15	.04
❑ 148 Karl Malone	.75	.23
❑ 149 Bryon Russell	.15	.04
❑ 150 Felton Spencer	.15	.04
❑ 151 John Stockton	.50	.15
❑ 152 Rex Chapman	.15	.04
❑ 153 Calbert Cheaney	.15	.04
❑ 154 Tom Gugliotta	.30	.09
❑ 155 Don MacLean	.15	.04
❑ 156 Gheorghe Muresan	.15	.04
❑ 157 Doug Overton	.15	.04
❑ 158 Brent Price	.15	.04
❑ 159 Derrick Coleman USA ..	.15	.04
❑ 160 Joe Dumars USA	.30	.09
❑ 161 Tim Hardaway USA	.30	.09
❑ 162 Kevin Johnson USA	.15	.04
❑ 163 Larry Johnson USA	.15	.04
❑ 164 Shawn Kemp USA	.50	.15
❑ 165 Dan Majerle USA	.15	.04
❑ 166 Reggie Miller USA	.30	.09
❑ 167 Alonzo Mourning USA ..	.50	.15
❑ 168 Shaquille O'Neal USA	1.00	.30
❑ 169 Mark Price USA	.15	.04
❑ 170 Steve Smith USA	.15	.04
❑ 171 Isiah Thomas USA	.30	.09
❑ 172 Dominique Wilkins USA	.30	.09
❑ 173 Checklist	.15	.04
❑ 174 Checklist	.15	.04
❑ 175 Checklist	.15	.04
❑ 176 Tyrone Corbin	.15	.04
❑ 177 Grant Long	.15	.04
❑ 178 Ken Norman	.15	.04
❑ 179 Steve Smith	.30	.09
❑ 180 Blue Edwards	.15	.04
❑ 181 Pervis Ellison	.15	.04
❑ 182 Greg Minor RC	.15	.04
❑ 183 Eric Montross RC	.15	.04
❑ 184 Derek Strong	.15	.04
❑ 185 David Wesley	.15	.04
❑ 186 Dominique Wilkins	.50	.15
❑ 187 Michael Adams	.15	.04
❑ 188 Muggsy Bogues	.30	.09
❑ 189 Scott Burrell	.15	.04
❑ 190 Darrin Hancock	.15	.04
❑ 191 Robert Parish	.30	.09
❑ 192 Jud Buechler	.15	.04
❑ 193 Ron Harper	.30	.09
❑ 194 Larry Krystkowiak	.15	.04

Card	Nm-Mt	Ex-Mt
❑ 195 Will Perdue	.15	.04
❑ 196 Dickey Simpkins RC	.15	.04
❑ 197 Michael Cage	.15	.04
❑ 198 Tony Campbell	.15	.04
❑ 199 Danny Ferry	.15	.04
❑ 200 Chris Mills	.30	.09
❑ 201 Popeye Jones	.15	.04
❑ 202 Jason Kidd RC	5.00	1.50
❑ 203 Roy Tarpley	.15	.04
❑ 204 Lorenzo Williams	.15	.04
❑ 205 Dale Ellis	.15	.04
❑ 206 Tom Hammonds	.15	.04
❑ 207 Jalen Rose RC	2.00	.60
❑ 208 Reggie Slater	.15	.04
❑ 209 Bryant Stith	.15	.04
❑ 210 Rafael Addison	.15	.04
❑ 211 Bill Curley RC	.15	.04
❑ 212 Johnny Dawkins	.15	.04
❑ 213 Grant Hill RC	3.00	.90
❑ 214 Mark Macon	.15	.04
❑ 215 Oliver Miller	.15	.04
❑ 216 Ivano Newbill	.15	.04
❑ 217 Mark West	.15	.04
❑ 218 Tom Gugliotta	.30	.09
❑ 219 Tim Hardaway	.50	.15
❑ 220 Keith Jennings	.15	.04
❑ 221 Dwayne Morton	.15	.04
❑ 222 Chris Mullin	.50	.15
❑ 223 Ricky Pierce	.15	.04
❑ 224 Carlos Rogers RC	.15	.04
❑ 225 Clifford Rozier RC	.15	.04
❑ 226 Rony Seikaly	.15	.04
❑ 227 Tim Breaux	.15	.04
❑ 228 Scott Brooks	.15	.04
❑ 229 Mario Elie	.15	.04
❑ 230 Vernon Maxwell	.15	.04
❑ 231 Zan Tabak	.15	.04
❑ 232 Mark Jackson	.15	.04
❑ 233 Derrick McKey	.15	.04
❑ 234 Tony Massenburg	.15	.04
❑ 235 Lamond Murray RC	.30	.09
❑ 236 Bo Outlaw	.15	.04
❑ 237 Eric Piatkowski RC	.15	.04
❑ 238 Pooh Richardson	.15	.04
❑ 239 Malik Sealy	.15	.04
❑ 240 Cedric Ceballos	.15	.04
❑ 241 Eddie Jones RC	2.50	.75
❑ 242 Anthony Miller	.15	.04
❑ 243 Tony Smith	.15	.04
❑ 244 Sedale Threatt	.15	.04
❑ 245 Ledell Eackles	.15	.04
❑ 246 Kevin Gamble	.15	.04
❑ 247 Matt Geiger	.15	.04
❑ 248 Brad Lohaus	.15	.04
❑ 249 Billy Owens	.15	.04
❑ 250 Khalid Reeves RC	.15	.04
❑ 251 Glen Rice	.30	.09
❑ 252 Kevin Willis	.15	.04
❑ 253 Marty Conlon	.15	.04
❑ 254 Eric Mobley RC	.15	.04
❑ 255 Johnny Newman	.15	.04
❑ 256 Ed Pinckney	.15	.04
❑ 257 Glenn Robinson RC	1.50	.45
❑ 258 Pat Durham	.15	.04
❑ 259 Howard Eisley	.15	.04
❑ 260 Winston Garland	.15	.04
❑ 261 Stacey King	.15	.04
❑ 262 Donyell Marshall RC	.50	.15
❑ 263 Sean Rooks	.15	.04
❑ 264 Chris Smith	.15	.04
❑ 265 Chris Childs RC	.50	.15
❑ 266 Sleepy Floyd	.15	.04
❑ 267 Armon Gilliam	.15	.04
❑ 268 Sean Higgins	.15	.04
❑ 269 Rex Walters	.15	.04
❑ 270 Greg Anthony	.15	.04
❑ 271 Charlie Ward RC	.50	.15
❑ 272 Herb Williams	.15	.04
❑ 273 Monty Williams RC	.15	.04
❑ 274 Anthony Avent	.15	.04
❑ 275 Anthony Bowie	.15	.04
❑ 276 Horace Grant	.30	.09
❑ 277 Donald Royal	.15	.04
❑ 278 Brian Shaw	.15	.04
❑ 279 Brooks Thompson	.15	.04
❑ 280 Derrick Alston	.15	.04
❑ 281 Willie Burton	.15	.04
❑ 282 Greg Graham	.15	.04
❑ 283 B.J. Tyler RC	.15	.04
❑ 284 Scott Williams	.15	.04
❑ 285 Sharone Wright RC	.15	.04
❑ 286 Joe Kleine	.15	.04
❑ 287 Danny Manning	.30	.09
❑ 288 Elliot Perry	.15	.04
❑ 289 Wesley Person RC	.50	.15
❑ 290 Trevor Ruffin RC	.15	.04
❑ 291 Wayman Tisdale	.15	.04
❑ 292 Mark Bryant	.15	.04
❑ 293 Chris Dudley	.15	.04
❑ 294 Aaron McKie RC	1.00	.30
❑ 295 Tracy Murray	.15	.04
❑ 296 Terry Porter	.15	.04
❑ 297 James Robinson	.15	.04
❑ 298 Alaa Abdelnaby	.15	.04
❑ 299 Duane Causwell	.15	.04
❑ 300 Brian Grant RC	1.25	.35
❑ 301 Bobby Hurley	.15	.04
❑ 302 Michael Smith RC	.15	.04
❑ 303 Terry Cummings	.15	.04
❑ 304 Moses Malone	.50	.15
❑ 305 Julius Nwosu	.15	.04
❑ 306 Chuck Person	.15	.04
❑ 307 Doc Rivers	.30	.09
❑ 308 Vincent Askew	.15	.04
❑ 309 Sarunas Marciulionis	.15	.04
❑ 310 Detlef Schrempf	.30	.09
❑ 311 Dontonio Wingfield	.15	.04
❑ 312 Antoine Carr	.15	.04
❑ 313 Tom Chambers	.15	.04
❑ 314 John Crotty	.15	.04
❑ 315 Adam Keefe	.15	.04
❑ 316 Jamie Watson RC	.15	.04
❑ 317 Mitchell Butler	.15	.04
❑ 318 Kevin Duckworth	.15	.04
❑ 319 Juwan Howard RC	1.25	.35
❑ 320 Jim McIlvaine	.15	.04
❑ 321 Scott Skiles	.15	.04
❑ 322 Anthony Tucker RC	.15	.04
❑ 323 Chris Webber	1.25	.35
❑ 324 Checklist	.15	.04
❑ 325 Checklist	.15	.04
❑ 326 Michael Jordan	10.00	3.00

1995-96 Flair

	Nm-Mt	Ex-Mt
COMPLETE SET (250)	80.00	24.00
COMPLETE SERIES 1 (150)	40.00	12.00
COMPLETE SERIES 2 (100)	40.00	12.00
COMMON CARD (1-150)	.60	.18
COMMON CARD (151-250)	.40	.12
❑ 1 Stacey Augmon	.60	.18
❑ 2 Mookie Blaylock	.60	.18
❑ 3 Grant Long	.60	.18
❑ 4 Steve Smith	1.50	.45
❑ 5 Dee Brown	.60	.18
❑ 6 Sherman Douglas	.60	.18
❑ 7 Eric Montross	.60	.18
❑ 8 Dino Radja	.60	.18
❑ 9 David Wesley	.60	.18
❑ 10 Muggsy Bogues	1.50	.45
❑ 11 Scott Burrell	.60	.18
❑ 12 Dell Curry	.60	.18
❑ 13 Larry Johnson	1.50	.45
❑ 14 Alonzo Mourning	1.50	.45
❑ 15 Michael Jordan	12.00	3.60
❑ 16 Steve Kerr	1.50	.45
❑ 17 Toni Kukoc	1.50	.45
❑ 18 Scottie Pippen	3.00	.90
❑ 19 Terrell Brandon	1.50	.45
❑ 20 Tyrone Hill	.60	.18
❑ 21 Chris Mills	.60	.18
❑ 22 Bobby Phills	.60	.18
❑ 23 Mark Price	1.50	.45
❑ 24 John Williams	.60	.18
❑ 25 Jim Jackson	.60	.18
❑ 26 Popeye Jones	.60	.18
❑ 27 Jason Kidd	6.00	1.80
❑ 28 Jamal Mashburn	1.50	.45
❑ 29 Lorenzo Williams	.60	.18
❑ 30 Mahmoud Abdul-Rauf	.60	.18
❑ 31 Dikembe Mutombo	1.50	.45
❑ 32 Robert Pack	.60	.18
❑ 33 Jalen Rose	2.50	.75
❑ 34 Bryant Stith	.60	.18
❑ 35 Reggie Williams	.60	.18
❑ 36 Joe Dumars	2.00	.60
❑ 37 Grant Hill	2.50	.75
❑ 38 Allan Houston	1.50	.45
❑ 39 Lindsey Hunter	.60	.18
❑ 40 Terry Mills	.60	.18
❑ 41 Chris Gatling	.60	.18
❑ 42 Tim Hardaway	1.50	.45
❑ 43 Donyell Marshall	1.50	.45
❑ 44 Chris Mullin	2.00	.60
❑ 45 Carlos Rogers	.60	.18
❑ 46 Clifford Rozier	.60	.18
❑ 47 Latrell Sprewell	2.00	.60
❑ 48 Sam Cassell	2.00	.60
❑ 49 Clyde Drexler	2.00	.60
❑ 50 Mario Elie	.60	.18
❑ 51 Robert Horry	1.50	.45
❑ 52 Hakeem Olajuwon	2.00	.60
❑ 53 Kenny Smith	.60	.18
❑ 54 Antonio Davis	.60	.18
❑ 55 Dale Davis	.60	.18
❑ 56 Mark Jackson	1.50	.45
❑ 57 Derrick McKey	.60	.18
❑ 58 Reggie Miller	2.00	.60
❑ 59 Rik Smits	1.50	.45
❑ 60 Lamond Murray	.60	.18
❑ 61 Pooh Richardson	.60	.18
❑ 62 Malik Sealy	.60	.18
❑ 63 Loy Vaught	.60	.18
❑ 64 Elden Campbell	.60	.18
❑ 65 Cedric Ceballos	.60	.18
❑ 66 Vlade Divac	1.50	.45
❑ 67 Eddie Jones	2.50	.75
❑ 68 Nick Van Exel	2.00	.60
❑ 69 Bimbo Coles	.60	.18
❑ 70 Billy Owens	.60	.18
❑ 71 Khalid Reeves	.60	.18
❑ 72 Glen Rice	1.50	.45
❑ 73 Kevin Willis	1.50	.45
❑ 74 Vin Baker	1.50	.45
❑ 75 Todd Day	.60	.18
❑ 76 Eric Murdock	.60	.18
❑ 77 Glenn Robinson	2.00	.60
❑ 78 Tom Gugliotta	.60	.18
❑ 79 Christian Laettner	1.50	.45
❑ 80 Isaiah Rider	.60	.18
❑ 81 Doug West	.60	.18
❑ 82 Kenny Anderson	1.50	.45
❑ 83 P.J. Brown	.60	.18
❑ 84 Derrick Coleman	.60	.18
❑ 85 Armon Gilliam	.60	.18
❑ 86 Chris Morris	.60	.18
❑ 87 Hubert Davis	.60	.18
❑ 88 Patrick Ewing	2.00	.60
❑ 89 Derek Harper	1.50	.45
❑ 90 Anthony Mason	1.50	.45
❑ 91 Charles Oakley	.60	.18
❑ 92 Charles Smith	.60	.18
❑ 93 John Starks	1.50	.45
❑ 94 Nick Anderson	.60	.18
❑ 95 Horace Grant	1.50	.45
❑ 96 Anfernee Hardaway	2.00	.60
❑ 97 Shaquille O'Neal	5.00	1.50
❑ 98 Dennis Scott	.60	.18
❑ 99 Brian Shaw	.60	.18
❑ 100 Dana Barros	.60	.18

❑ 101 Shawn Bradley .60 .18
❑ 102 Clarence Weatherspoon .60 .18
❑ 103 Sharone Wright .60 .18
❑ 104 Charles Barkley 2.50 .75
❑ 105 A.C. Green 1.50 .45
❑ 106 Kevin Johnson 1.50 .45
❑ 107 Dan Majerle 1.50 .45
❑ 108 Danny Manning 1.50 .45
❑ 109 Elliot Perry .60 .18
❑ 110 Wesley Person .60 .18
❑ 111 Terry Porter .60 .18
❑ 112 Clifford Robinson .60 .18
❑ 113 Rod Strickland .60 .18
❑ 114 Otis Thorpe .60 .18
❑ 115 Buck Williams .60 .18
❑ 116 Brian Grant 2.00 .60
❑ 117 Bobby Hurley .60 .18
❑ 118 Olden Polynice .60 .18
❑ 119 Mitch Richmond 1.50 .45
❑ 120 Walt Williams .60 .18
❑ 121 Vinny Del Negro .60 .18
❑ 122 Sean Elliott 1.50 .45
❑ 123 Avery Johnson .60 .18
❑ 124 David Robinson 2.00 .60
❑ 125 Dennis Rodman 1.50 .45
❑ 126 Shawn Kemp 1.50 .45
❑ 127 Nate McMillan .60 .18
❑ 128 Gary Payton 2.00 .60
❑ 129 Sam Perkins 1.50 .45
❑ 130 Detlef Schrempf 1.50 .45
❑ 131 B.J. Armstrong .60 .18
❑ 132 Jerome Kersey .60 .18
❑ 133 Oliver Miller .60 .18
❑ 134 John Salley .60 .18
❑ 135 David Benoit .60 .18
❑ 136 Antoine Carr .60 .18
❑ 137 Jeff Hornacek 1.50 .45
❑ 138 Karl Malone 2.50 .75
❑ 139 John Stockton 2.50 .75
❑ 140 Greg Anthony .60 .18
❑ 141 Benoit Benjamin .60 .18
❑ 142 Blue Edwards .60 .18
❑ 143 Byron Scott .60 .18
❑ 144 Calbert Cheaney .60 .18
❑ 145 Juwan Howard 2.00 .60
❑ 146 Gheorghe Muresan .60 .18
❑ 147 Scott Skiles .60 .18
❑ 148 Chris Webber 2.50 .75
❑ 149 Checklist .60 .18
❑ 150 Checklist .60 .18
❑ 151 Stacey Augmon .40 .12
❑ 152 Mookie Blaylock .40 .12
❑ 153 Andrew Lang .40 .12
❑ 154 Steve Smith .75 .23
❑ 155 Dana Barros .40 .12
❑ 156 Rick Fox .75 .23
❑ 157 Kendall Gill .40 .12
❑ 158 Khalid Reeves .40 .12
❑ 159 Glen Rice .75 .23
❑ 160 Dennis Rodman 1.50 .45
❑ 161 Dan Majerle .75 .23
❑ 162 Tony Dumas .40 .12
❑ 163 Dale Ellis .40 .12
❑ 164 Otis Thorpe .40 .12
❑ 165 Rony Seikaly .40 .12
❑ 166 Sam Cassell 1.25 .35
❑ 167 Clyde Drexler 1.25 .35
❑ 168 Robert Horry .75 .23
❑ 169 Hakeem Olajuwon 2.00 .60
❑ 170 Ricky Pierce .40 .12
❑ 171 Rodney Rogers .60 .18
❑ 172 Brian Williams .40 .12
❑ 173 Magic Johnson 2.00 .60
❑ 174 Alonzo Mourning .75 .23
❑ 175 Lee Mayberry .40 .12
❑ 176 Terry Porter .40 .12
❑ 177 Shawn Bradley .40 .12
❑ 178 Jayson Williams .40 .12
❑ 179 Gary Grant .40 .12
❑ 180 Jon Koncak .40 .12
❑ 181 Derrick Coleman .60 .18
❑ 182 Vernon Maxwell .40 .12
❑ 183 John Williams .40 .12
❑ 184 Aaron McKie 1.50 .45
❑ 185 Michael Smith .40 .12
❑ 186 Chuck Person .40 .12
❑ 187 Hersey Hawkins .40 .12
❑ 188 Shawn Kemp 1.50 .45
❑ 189 Gary Payton 2.00 .60
❑ 190 Detlef Schrempf .75 .23
❑ 191 Chris Morris .40 .12
❑ 192 Robert Pack .40 .12
❑ 193 Willie Anderson EXP .40 .12
❑ 194 Oliver Miller EXP .40 .12
❑ 195 Alvin Robertson EXP .40 .12
❑ 196 Greg Anthony EXP .40 .12
❑ 197 Blue Edwards EXP .40 .12
❑ 198 Byron Scott EXP .40 .12
❑ 199 Cory Alexander RC .40 .12
❑ 200 Brent Barry RC 1.25 .35
❑ 201 Travis Best RC .60 .18
❑ 202 Jason Caffey RC .75 .23
❑ 203 Sasha Danilovic RC .40 .12
❑ 204 Tyus Edney RC .40 .12
❑ 205 Michael Finley RC 3.00 .90
❑ 206 Kevin Garnett RC 6.00 1.80
❑ 207 Alan Henderson RC 1.25 .35
❑ 208 Antonio McDyess RC 2.50 .75
❑ 209 Loren Meyer RC .40 .12
❑ 210 Lawrence Moten RC .40 .12
❑ 211 Ed O'Bannon RC .40 .12
❑ 212 Greg Ostertag RC .40 .12
❑ 213 Cherokee Parks RC .40 .12
❑ 214 Theo Ratliff RC 1.50 .45
❑ 215 Bryant Reeves RC 1.25 .35
❑ 216 Shawn Respert RC .60 .18
❑ 217 Arvydas Sabonis RC 1.50 .45
❑ 218 Joe Smith RC 2.00 .60
❑ 219 Jerry Stackhouse RC 4.00 1.20
❑ 220 Damon Stoudamire RC 2.50 .75
❑ 221 Bob Sura RC .75 .23
❑ 222 Kurt Thomas RC .75 .23
❑ 223 Gary Trent RC .40 .12
❑ 224 David Vaughn RC .40 .12
❑ 225 Rasheed Wallace RC 3.00 .90
❑ 226 Eric Williams RC .75 .23
❑ 227 Corliss Williamson RC 1.25 .35
❑ 228 George Zidek RC .40 .12
❑ 229 Vin Baker STY .40 .12
❑ 230 Charles Barkley STY 1.25 .35
❑ 231 Patrick Ewing STY .75 .23
❑ 232 Anfernee Hardaway STY 1.50 .45
❑ 233 Grant Hill STY 1.25 .35
❑ 234 Larry Johnson STY .40 .12
❑ 235 Michael Jordan STY 4.00 1.20
❑ 236 Jason Kidd STY 2.00 .60
❑ 237 Karl Malone STY 1.25 .35
❑ 238 Jamal Mashburn STY .40 .12
❑ 239 Reggie Miller STY .75 .23
❑ 240 Shaquille O'Neal STY 1.50 .45
❑ 241 Scottie Pippen STY 1.25 .35
❑ 242 Mitch Richmond STY .40 .12
❑ 243 Clifford Robinson STY .40 .12
❑ 244 David Robinson STY .75 .23
❑ 245 Glenn Robinson STY .75 .23
❑ 246 John Stockton STY 1.25 .35
❑ 247 Nick Van Exel STY .40 .12
❑ 248 Chris Webber STY 1.25 .35
❑ 249 Checklist .40 .12
❑ 250 Checklist .40 .12

1996-97 Flair Showcase Row 2

	Nm-Mt	Ex-Mt
COMPLETE SET (90)	60.00	18.00
❑ 1 Anfernee Hardaway	1.50	.45
❑ 2 Mitch Richmond	1.00	.30
❑ 3 Allen Iverson RC	8.00	2.40
❑ 4 Charles Barkley	2.00	.60
❑ 5 Juwan Howard	1.00	.30
❑ 6 David Robinson	1.50	.45
❑ 7 Gary Payton	1.50	.45
❑ 8 Kerry Kittles RC	1.50	.45
❑ 9 Dennis Rodman	1.00	.30
❑ 10 Shaquille O'Neal	4.00	1.20
❑ 11 Stephon Marbury RC	4.00	1.20
❑ 12 John Stockton	1.50	.45
❑ 13 Glenn Robinson	1.50	.45
❑ 14 Hakeem Olajuwon	1.50	.45
❑ 15 Jason Kidd	2.50	.75
❑ 16 Jerry Stackhouse	2.00	.60
❑ 17 Joe Smith	1.00	.30
❑ 18 Reggie Miller	1.50	.45
❑ 19 Grant Hill	1.50	.45
❑ 20 Damon Stoudamire	1.50	.45
❑ 21 Kevin Garnett	3.00	.90
❑ 22 Clyde Drexler	1.50	.45
❑ 23 Michael Jordan	10.00	3.00
❑ 24 Antonio McDyess	1.00	.30
❑ 25 Chris Webber	1.50	.45
❑ 26 Antoine Walker RC	4.00	1.20
❑ 27 Scottie Pippen	2.50	.75
❑ 28 Karl Malone	1.50	.45
❑ 29 Shareef Abdur-Rahim RC	4.00	1.20
❑ 30 Shawn Kemp	1.00	.30
❑ 31 Kobe Bryant RC	12.00	3.60
❑ 32 Derrick Coleman	1.00	.30
❑ 33 Alonzo Mourning	1.00	.30
❑ 34 Anthony Mason	1.00	.30
❑ 35 Ray Allen RC	3.00	.90
❑ 36 Arvydas Sabonis	1.00	.30
❑ 37 Brian Grant	1.50	.45
❑ 38 Bryant Reeves	.50	.15
❑ 39 Christian Laettner	1.00	.30
❑ 40 Tom Gugliotta	.50	.15
❑ 41 Latrell Sprewell	1.50	.45
❑ 42 Erick Dampier RC	1.50	.45
❑ 43 Gheorghe Muresan	.50	.15
❑ 44 Glen Rice	1.00	.30
❑ 45 Patrick Ewing	1.50	.45
❑ 46 Jim Jackson	.50	.15
❑ 47 Michael Finley	2.00	.60
❑ 48 Toni Kukoc	1.00	.30
❑ 49 Marcus Camby RC	2.00	.60
❑ 50 Kenny Anderson	.50	.15
❑ 51 Mark Price	1.00	.30
❑ 52 Tim Hardaway	1.00	.30
❑ 53 Mookie Blaylock	.50	.15
❑ 54 Steve Smith	1.00	.30
❑ 55 Terrell Brandon	1.00	.30
❑ 56 Lorenzen Wright RC	1.00	.30
❑ 57 Sasha Danilovic	.50	.15
❑ 58 Jeff Hornacek	1.00	.30
❑ 59 Eddie Jones	1.50	.45
❑ 60 Vin Baker	1.00	.30
❑ 61 Chris Childs	.50	.15
❑ 62 Clifford Robinson	.50	.15
❑ 63 Anthony Peeler	.50	.15
❑ 64 Dino Radja	.50	.15
❑ 65 Joe Dumars	1.50	.45
❑ 66 Loy Vaught	.50	.15
❑ 67 Rony Seikaly	.50	.15
❑ 68 Vitaly Potapenko RC	.50	.15
❑ 69 Chris Gatling	.50	.15
❑ 70 Dale Ellis	.50	.15
❑ 71 Allan Houston	1.00	.30
❑ 72 Doug Christie	1.00	.30
❑ 73 LaPhonso Ellis	.50	.15
❑ 74 Kendall Gill	.50	.15
❑ 75 Rik Smits	1.00	.30
❑ 76 Bobby Phills	.50	.15
❑ 77 Malik Sealy	.50	.15
❑ 78 Sean Elliott	1.00	.30
❑ 79 Vlade Divac	.50	.15
❑ 80 David Wesley	.50	.15
❑ 81 Dominique Wilkins	1.50	.45
❑ 82 Danny Manning	1.00	.30
❑ 83 Detlef Schrempf	1.00	.30

❑ 84 Hersey Hawkins	1.00	.30
❑ 85 Lindsey Hunter	.50	.15
❑ 86 Mahmoud Abdul-Rauf	.50	.15
❑ 87 Shawn Bradley	.50	.15
❑ 88 Horace Grant	1.00	.30
❑ 89 Cedric Ceballos	.50	.15
❑ 90 Jamal Mashburn	1.00	.30
❑ NNO Jerry Stackhouse Promo 3-card strip	3.00	.90

1997-98 Flair Showcase Row 3

	Nm-Mt	Ex-Mt
COMPLETE SET (80)	50.00	15.00
❑ 1 Michael Jordan	10.00	3.00
❑ 2 Grant Hill	1.50	.45
❑ 3 Allen Iverson	4.00	1.20
❑ 4 Kevin Garnett	3.00	.90
❑ 5 Tim Duncan RC	6.00	1.80
❑ 6 Shawn Kemp	1.00	.30
❑ 7 Shaquille O'Neal	4.00	1.20
❑ 8 Antoine Walker	2.00	.60
❑ 9 Shareef Abdur-Rahim	2.50	.75
❑ 10 Damon Stoudamire	1.00	.30
❑ 11 Anfernee Hardaway	1.50	.45
❑ 12 Keith Van Horn RC	2.50	.75
❑ 13 Dennis Rodman	1.00	.30
❑ 14 Ron Mercer RC	2.00	.60
❑ 15 Stephon Marbury	2.00	.60
❑ 16 Scottie Pippen	2.50	.75
❑ 17 Kerry Kittles	1.50	.45
❑ 18 Kobe Bryant	6.00	1.80
❑ 19 Marcus Camby	1.50	.45
❑ 20 Chauncey Billups RC	1.50	.45
❑ 21 Tracy McGrady RC	8.00	2.40
❑ 22 Joe Smith	1.00	.30
❑ 23 Brevin Knight RC	1.00	.30
❑ 24 Danny Fortson RC	1.00	.30
❑ 25 Tim Thomas RC	2.50	.75
❑ 26 Gary Payton	1.50	.45
❑ 27 David Robinson	1.50	.45
❑ 28 Hakeem Olajuwon	1.50	.45
❑ 29 Antonio Daniels RC	1.50	.45
❑ 30 Antonio McDyess	1.00	.30
❑ 31 Eddie Jones	1.50	.45
❑ 32 Adonal Foyle RC	1.00	.30
❑ 33 Glenn Robinson	1.50	.45
❑ 34 Charles Barkley	2.00	.60
❑ 35 Vin Baker	1.00	.30
❑ 36 Jerry Stackhouse	1.50	.45
❑ 37 Ray Allen	1.50	.45
❑ 38 Derek Anderson RC	3.00	.90
❑ 39 Isaac Austin	.50	.15
❑ 40 Tony Battie RC	1.50	.45
❑ 41 Tariq Abdul-Wahad RC	1.00	.30
❑ 42 Dikembe Mutombo	1.00	.30
❑ 43 Clyde Drexler	1.50	.45
❑ 44 Chris Mullin	1.50	.45
❑ 45 Tim Hardaway	1.00	.30
❑ 46 Terrell Brandon	1.00	.30
❑ 47 John Stockton	1.50	.45
❑ 48 Patrick Ewing	1.50	.45
❑ 49 Horace Grant	1.00	.30
❑ 50 Tom Gugliotta	1.00	.30
❑ 51 Mookie Blaylock	.50	.15
❑ 52 Mitch Richmond	1.00	.30
❑ 53 Anthony Mason	1.00	.30
❑ 54 Michael Finley	1.50	.45
❑ 55 Jason Kidd	2.50	.75
❑ 56 Karl Malone	1.50	.45
❑ 57 Reggie Miller	1.50	.45
❑ 58 Steve Smith	1.00	.30
❑ 59 Glen Rice	1.00	.30
❑ 60 Bryant Stith	.50	.15
❑ 61 Loy Vaught	.50	.15
❑ 62 Brian Grant	1.00	.30
❑ 63 Joe Dumars	1.50	.45
❑ 64 Juwan Howard	1.00	.30
❑ 65 Rik Smits	1.00	.30
❑ 66 Alonzo Mourning	1.00	.30
❑ 67 Allan Houston	1.00	.30
❑ 68 Chris Webber	1.50	.45
❑ 69 Kendall Gill	.50	.15
❑ 70 Rony Seikaly	.50	.15
❑ 71 Kenny Anderson	1.00	.30
❑ 72 John Wallace	.50	.15
❑ 73 Bryant Reeves	.50	.15
❑ 74 Brian Williams	.50	.15
❑ 75 Larry Johnson	1.00	.30
❑ 76 Shawn Bradley	.50	.15
❑ 77 Kevin Johnson	1.00	.30
❑ 78 Rod Strickland	.50	.15
❑ 79 Rodney Rogers	.50	.15
❑ 80 Rasheed Wallace	1.50	.45
❑ NNO Grant Hill Promo 4-card strip	1.50	.45

1998-99 Flair Showcase Row 3

	Nm-Mt	Ex-Mt
COMPLETE SET (90)	50.00	15.00
COMMON CARD (1-90)	.25	.07
COMMON ROOKIE	.50	.15
❑ 1 Keith Van Horn	.75	.23
❑ 1A K.Van Horn Promo	1.00	.30
❑ 2 Kobe Bryant	3.00	.90
❑ 3 Tim Duncan	1.25	.35
❑ 4 Kevin Garnett	1.50	.45
❑ 5 Grant Hill	.75	.23
❑ 6 Allen Iverson	1.50	.45
❑ 7 Shaquille O'Neal	2.00	.60
❑ 8 Antoine Walker	.75	.23
❑ 9 Shareef Abdur-Rahim	.75	.23
❑ 10 Stephon Marbury	.75	.23
❑ 11 Ray Allen	.75	.23
❑ 12 Shawn Kemp	.50	.15
❑ 13 Tim Thomas	.50	.15
❑ 14 Scottie Pippen	1.25	.35
❑ 15 Latrell Sprewell	.75	.23
❑ 16 Dirk Nowitzki RC	8.00	2.40
❑ 17 Antawn Jamison RC	4.00	1.20
❑ 18 Anfernee Hardaway	.75	.23
❑ 19 Larry Hughes RC	2.50	.75
❑ 20 Robert Traylor RC	1.00	.30
❑ 21 Kerry Kittles	.25	.07
❑ 22 Ron Mercer	.50	.15
❑ 23 Michael Olowokandi RC	1.25	.35
❑ 24 Jason Kidd	1.00	.30
❑ 25 Vince Carter RC	10.00	3.00
❑ 26 Charles Barkley	.75	.23
❑ 27 Antonio McDyess	.50	.15
❑ 28 Mike Bibby RC	4.00	1.20
❑ 29 Paul Pierce RC	4.00	1.20
❑ 30 Raef LaFrentz RC	1.25	.35
❑ 31 Reggie Miller	.75	.23
❑ 32 Michael Finley	.75	.23
❑ 33 Eddie Jones	.75	.23
❑ 34 Tim Hardaway	.50	.15
❑ 35 Glenn Robinson	.50	.15
❑ 36 Brevin Knight	.25	.07
❑ 37 Gary Payton	.75	.23
❑ 38 David Robinson	.75	.23
❑ 39 Karl Malone	.75	.23
❑ 40 Derek Anderson	.75	.23
❑ 41 Patrick Ewing	.75	.23
❑ 42 Juwan Howard	.50	.15
❑ 43 Jayson Williams	.25	.07
❑ 44 Terrell Brandon	.50	.15
❑ 45 Hakeem Olajuwon	.75	.23
❑ 46 Isaac Austin	.25	.07
❑ 47 Glen Rice	.50	.15
❑ 48 Maurice Taylor	.50	.15
❑ 49 Damon Stoudamire	.50	.15
❑ 50 Brian Skinner RC	1.00	.30
❑ 51 Nazr Mohammed RC	.50	.15
❑ 52 Tom Gugliotta	.25	.07
❑ 53 Al Harrington RC	2.00	.60
❑ 54 Pat Garrity RC	.60	.18
❑ 55 Jason Williams RC	3.00	.90
❑ 56 Tracy McGrady	1.50	.45
❑ 57 Keon Clark RC	1.25	.35
❑ 58 Vin Baker	.50	.15
❑ 59 Bonzi Wells RC	3.00	.90
❑ 60 John Stockton	.75	.23
❑ 61 Isaiah Rider	.25	.07
❑ 62 Alonzo Mourning	.50	.15
❑ 63 Allan Houston	.50	.15
❑ 64 Dennis Rodman	.50	.15
❑ 65 Felipe Lopez RC	1.00	.30
❑ 66 Joe Smith	.50	.15
❑ 67 Chris Webber	.75	.23
❑ 68 Mitch Richmond	.50	.15
❑ 69 Brent Barry	.50	.15
❑ 70 Mookie Blaylock	.25	.07
❑ 71 Donyell Marshall	.50	.15
❑ 72 Anthony Mason	.50	.15
❑ 73 Rod Strickland	.25	.07
❑ 74 Roshown McLeod RC	.60	.18
❑ 75 Matt Harpring RC	2.00	.60
❑ 76 Detlef Schrempf	.50	.15
❑ 77 Michael Dickerson RC	1.50	.45
❑ 78 Michael Doleac RC	1.00	.30
❑ 79 John Starks	.50	.15
❑ 80 Ricky Davis RC	2.00	.60
❑ 81 Steve Smith	.50	.15
❑ 82 Voshon Lenard	.25	.07
❑ 83 Toni Kukoc	.50	.15
❑ 84 Steve Nash	.75	.23
❑ 85 Vlade Divac	.50	.15
❑ 86 Rasheed Wallace	.75	.23
❑ 87 Bryon Russell	.25	.07
❑ 88 Antonio Daniels	.25	.07
❑ 89 Rik Smits	.50	.15
❑ 90 Joe Dumars	.75	.23

1999-00 Flair Showcase

	Nm-Mt	Ex-Mt
COMPLETE SET (130)	300.00	90.00
COMPLETE SET w/o RC (100)	30.00	9.00
COMMON CARD (1-100)	.30	.09
COMMON ROOKIE (101-130)	2.00	.60
❑ 1 Vince Carter	2.50	.75

Card		
❑ 2 Anfernee Hardaway	1.00	.30
❑ 3 Nick Van Exel	1.00	.30
❑ 4 Kerry Kittles	.30	.09
❑ 5 Michael Doleac	.30	.09
❑ 6 Sean Elliott	.60	.18
❑ 7 Shaquille O'Neal	2.50	.75
❑ 8 Avery Johnson	.30	.09
❑ 9 Brian Grant	.60	.18
❑ 10 Jerome Williams	.30	.09
❑ 11 Larry Hughes	1.00	.30
❑ 12 Jerry Stackhouse	1.00	.30
❑ 13 Alonzo Mourning	.60	.18
❑ 14 Antonio McDyess	.60	.18
❑ 15 Jason Kidd	1.50	.45
❑ 16 Bryon Russell	.30	.09
❑ 17 Hakeem Olajuwon	1.00	.30
❑ 18 Juwan Howard	.60	.18
❑ 19 Paul Pierce	1.00	.30
❑ 20 Vin Baker	.60	.18
❑ 21 Larry Johnson	.60	.18
❑ 22 Gary Trent	.30	.09
❑ 23 Jayson Williams	.30	.09
❑ 24 Tim Hardaway	.60	.18
❑ 25 Dirk Nowitzki	2.00	.60
❑ 26 Jamal Mashburn	.60	.18
❑ 27 Glenn Robinson	1.00	.30
❑ 28 Shawn Bradley	.30	.09
❑ 29 Tom Gugliotta	.30	.09
❑ 30 Vlade Divac	.60	.18
❑ 31 David Robinson	1.00	.30
❑ 32 Matt Geiger	.30	.09
❑ 33 Grant Hill	1.00	.30
❑ 34 Maurice Taylor	.60	.18
❑ 35 Toni Kukoc	.60	.18
❑ 36 Cedric Ceballos	.30	.09
❑ 37 Patrick Ewing	1.00	.30
❑ 38 Ray Allen	1.00	.30
❑ 39 Michael Finley	1.00	.30
❑ 40 Robert Traylor	.30	.09
❑ 41 Brevin Knight	.30	.09
❑ 42 Marcus Camby	.60	.18
❑ 43 Sam Cassell	1.00	.30
❑ 44 Antawn Jamison	1.50	.45
❑ 45 Steve Smith	.60	.18
❑ 46 Darrell Armstrong	.30	.09
❑ 47 Mookie Blaylock	.30	.09
❑ 48 Derek Anderson	.60	.18
❑ 49 Hersey Hawkins	.60	.18
❑ 50 Kobe Bryant	4.00	1.20
❑ 51 Shawn Kemp	.60	.18
❑ 52 Scottie Pippen	1.50	.45
❑ 53 Chris Webber	1.00	.30
❑ 54 Damon Stoudamire	.60	.18
❑ 55 Donyell Marshall	.60	.18
❑ 56 Isaiah Rider	.30	.09
❑ 57 Karl Malone	1.00	.30
❑ 58 Kevin Garnett	2.00	.60
❑ 59 Mario Elie	.30	.09
❑ 60 Michael Dickerson	.60	.18
❑ 61 Jahidi White	.30	.09
❑ 62 Joe Smith	.60	.18
❑ 63 Kenny Anderson	.60	.18
❑ 64 Reggie Miller	1.00	.30
❑ 65 Ruben Patterson	.60	.18
❑ 66 Shareef Abdur-Rahim	1.00	.30
❑ 67 Allen Iverson	2.00	.60
❑ 68 Glen Rice	.60	.18
❑ 69 Nick Anderson	.30	.09
❑ 70 Rex Chapman	.30	.09
❑ 71 Ron Mercer	.60	.18
❑ 72 Tim Duncan	2.00	.60
❑ 73 Al Harrington	1.00	.30
❑ 74 Brent Barry	.60	.18
❑ 75 Eddie Jones	1.00	.30
❑ 76 Mike Bibby	1.00	.30
❑ 77 Anthony Mason	.60	.18
❑ 78 Michael Olowokandi	.60	.18
❑ 79 Matt Harpring	1.00	.30
❑ 80 Stephon Marbury	1.00	.30
❑ 81 Tracy McGrady	2.50	.75
❑ 82 Allan Houston	.60	.18
❑ 83 Lindsey Hunter	.30	.09
❑ 84 Tariq Abdul-Wahad	.30	.09
❑ 85 Antoine Walker	1.00	.30
❑ 86 Charles Barkley	1.25	.35
❑ 87 Gary Payton	1.00	.30
❑ 88 John Stockton	1.00	.30
❑ 89 Mitch Richmond	.60	.18
❑ 90 Terrell Brandon	.60	.18
❑ 91 Charles Oakley	.30	.09
❑ 92 Bryant Reeves	.30	.09
❑ 93 Dikembe Mutombo	.60	.18
❑ 94 Elden Campbell	.30	.09
❑ 95 Jalen Rose	1.00	.30
❑ 96 Jason Williams	1.00	.30
❑ 97 Keith Van Horn	1.00	.30
❑ 98 Latrell Sprewell	1.00	.30
❑ 99 Raef LaFrentz	.60	.18
❑ 100 Rasheed Wallace	1.00	.30
❑ 101 Cal Bowdler RC	3.00	.90
❑ 102 Dion Glover RC	3.00	.90
❑ 103 Jason Terry RC	6.00	1.80
❑ 104 Adrian Griffin RC	3.00	.90
❑ 105 Baron Davis RC	10.00	3.00
❑ 106 Michael Ruffin RC	2.50	.75
❑ 107 Elton Brand RC	12.00	3.60
❑ 108 Ron Artest RC	6.00	1.80
❑ 109 Andre Miller RC	10.00	3.00
❑ 110 Trajan Langdon RC	4.00	1.20
❑ 111 James Posey RC	6.00	1.80
❑ 112 Vonteego Cummings RC	4.00	1.20
❑ 113 Kenny Thomas RC	4.00	1.20
❑ 114 Steve Francis RC	15.00	4.50
❑ 115 Jonathan Bender RC	10.00	3.00
❑ 116 Lamar Odom RC	10.00	3.00
❑ 117 Devean George RC	5.00	1.50
❑ 118 Tim James RC	3.00	.90
❑ 119 Anthony Carter RC	6.00	1.80
❑ 120 Wally Szczerbiak RC	10.00	3.00
❑ 121 William Avery RC	4.00	1.20
❑ 122 Evan Eschmeyer RC	2.00	.60
❑ 123 Corey Maggette RC	10.00	3.00
❑ 124 Jumaine Jones RC	3.00	.90
❑ 125 Shawn Marion RC	15.00	4.50
❑ 126 Ryan Robertson RC	2.50	.75
❑ 127 Aleksandar Radojevic RC	2.00	.60
❑ 128 Quincy Lewis RC	3.00	.90
❑ 129 Scott Padgett RC	3.00	.90
❑ 130 Richard Hamilton RC	10.00	3.00
❑ P1 Vince Carter PROMO	2.50	.75

2001-02 Flair

	Nm-Mt	Ex-Mt
COMP.SET w/o SP's (90)	50.00	15.00
COMMON CARDS (1-121)	.30	.09
COMMON ROOKIE (91-120)	2.00	.60
❑ 1 Tracy McGrady	2.50	.75
❑ 2 Derek Fisher	1.00	.30
❑ 3 Allen Iverson	2.00	.60
❑ 4 Chris Webber	1.00	.30
❑ 5 Jalen Rose	1.00	.30
❑ 6 Kenyon Martin	1.00	.30
❑ 7 Jermaine O'Neal	1.00	.30
❑ 8 Kobe Bryant	4.00	1.20
❑ 9 Bryon Russell	.30	.09
❑ 10 Wally Szczerbiak	.60	.18
❑ 11 Damon Stoudamire	.60	.18
❑ 12 John Stockton	1.00	.30
❑ 13 Glenn Robinson	.60	.18
❑ 14 Steve Francis	1.00	.30
❑ 15 Vince Carter	2.50	.75
❑ 16 Peja Stojakovic	1.00	.30
❑ 17 Rick Fox	.60	.18
❑ 18 Allan Houston	.60	.18
❑ 19 Danny Fortson	.30	.09
❑ 20 Gary Payton	1.00	.30
❑ 21 Darius Miles	1.00	.30
❑ 22 Kevin Garnett	2.00	.60
❑ 23 Marcus Camby	.60	.18
❑ 24 Desmond Mason	.60	.18
❑ 25 Tim Duncan	2.00	.60
❑ 26 Jamal Mashburn	.60	.18
❑ 27 Andre Miller	.60	.18
❑ 28 Antonio McDyess	.60	.18
❑ 29 Morris Peterson	.60	.18
❑ 30 Rasheed Wallace	1.00	.30
❑ 31 Shawn Marion	1.00	.30
❑ 32 Karl Malone	1.00	.30
❑ 33 Grant Hill	1.00	.30
❑ 34 Shaquille O'Neal	2.50	.75
❑ 35 Hakeem Olajuwon	1.00	.30
❑ 36 Corliss Williamson	.60	.18
❑ 37 Paul Pierce	1.00	.30
❑ 38 Antonio Davis	.30	.09
❑ 39 Antonio Daniels	.30	.09
❑ 40 Ray Allen	1.00	.30
❑ 41 Dirk Nowitzki	1.50	.45
❑ 42 Jerry Stackhouse	1.00	.30
❑ 43 Donyell Marshall	.60	.18
❑ 44 Brian Grant	.60	.18
❑ 45 Raef LaFrentz	.60	.18
❑ 46 Corey Maggette	.60	.18
❑ 47 Mike Miller	1.00	.30
❑ 48 Jason Williams	.60	.18
❑ 49 Jahidi White	.30	.09
❑ 50 David Robinson	1.00	.30
❑ 51 Shareef Abdur-Rahim	1.00	.30
❑ 52 Anfernee Hardaway	1.00	.30
❑ 53 Baron Davis	1.00	.30
❑ 54 DerMarr Johnson	.60	.18
❑ 55 Dikembe Mutombo	.60	.18
❑ 56 David Wesley	.30	.09
❑ 57 Chris Mihm	.60	.18
❑ 58 Michael Finley	1.00	.30
❑ 59 Eddie House	.60	.18
❑ 60 Stromile Swift	.60	.18
❑ 61 Courtney Alexander	.60	.18
❑ 62 Ron Mercer	.60	.18
❑ 63 Cuttino Mobley	.60	.18
❑ 64 Tim Thomas	.60	.18
❑ 65 Eddie Jones	1.00	.30
❑ 66 Lamar Odom	1.00	.30
❑ 67 Terrell Brandon	.60	.18
❑ 68 Rashard Lewis	.60	.18
❑ 69 Antoine Walker	1.00	.30
❑ 70 Latrell Sprewell	1.00	.30
❑ 71 Sam Cassell	1.00	.30
❑ 72 Mike Bibby	1.00	.30
❑ 73 Speedy Claxton	.60	.18
❑ 74 Steve Nash	1.00	.30
❑ 75 Mark Jackson	.60	.18
❑ 76 Ron Artest	.60	.18
❑ 77 Matt Harpring	1.00	.30
❑ 78 Wang Zhizhi	1.00	.30
❑ 79 Nazr Mohammed	.30	.09
❑ 80 Jason Terry	1.00	.30
❑ 81 Nick Van Exel	1.00	.30
❑ 82 Reggie Miller	1.00	.30
❑ 83 Joe Smith	.60	.18
❑ 84 Jason Kidd	1.50	.45
❑ 85 Richard Hamilton	.60	.18
❑ 86 Antawn Jamison	1.00	.30
❑ 87 Alonzo Mourning	.60	.18
❑ 88 Stephon Marbury	1.00	.30
❑ 89 Scottie Pippen	1.50	.45
❑ 90 Elton Brand	1.00	.30
❑ 91 Kwame Brown RC	6.00	1.80
❑ 92 Eddie Griffin RC	5.00	1.50
❑ 93 Tyson Chandler RC	10.00	3.00
❑ 94 Omar Cook	2.00	.60
❑ 95 Loren Woods RC	2.00	.60
❑ 96 Alton Ford RC	2.00	.60
❑ 97 Shane Battier RC	5.00	1.50
❑ 98 Joe Johnson RC	5.00	1.50
❑ 99 Rodney White RC	3.00	.90
❑ 100 Pau Gasol RC	12.00	3.60
❑ 101 Zach Randolph RC	10.00	3.00
❑ 102 Vladimir Radmanovic RC	2.50	.75
❑ 103 Brendan Haywood RC	4.00	1.20
❑ 104 Michael Bradley RC	2.00	.60

❑ 105 Tony Parker RC	15.00	4.50
❑ 106 Jason Richardson RC	10.00	3.00
❑ 107 Gerald Wallace RC	6.00	1.80
❑ 108 Damone Brown RC	2.00	.60
❑ 109 Richard Jefferson RC	10.00	3.00
❑ 110 Rookie Exchange		
❑ 111 DeSagana Diop RC	2.00	.60
❑ 112 Brandon Armstrong RC	4.00	1.20
❑ 113 Troy Murphy RC	5.00	1.50
❑ 114 Kedrick Brown RC	2.00	.60
❑ 115 Kirk Haston RC	3.00	.90
❑ 116 Gilbert Arenas RC	8.00	2.40
❑ 117 Jeryl Sasser RC	3.00	.90
❑ 118 Jamaal Tinsley RC	5.00	1.50
❑ 119 Terence Morris RC	3.00	.90
❑ 120 Michael Wright	2.00	.60
❑ 121 Michael Jordan	15.00	4.50

2002-03 Flair

	Nm-Mt	Ex-Mt
COMP.SET w/o SP's (90)	50.00	15.00
COMMON CARD (1-90)	.30	.09
COMMON ROOKIE (91-120)	6.00	1.80
❑ 1 Tracy McGrady	2.50	.75
❑ 2 Jamal Mashburn	.60	.18
❑ 3 Allen Iverson	2.00	.60
❑ 4 Alonzo Mourning	.60	.18
❑ 5 Joe Smith	.60	.18
❑ 6 Wang Zhizhi	1.00	.30
❑ 7 Karl Malone	1.00	.30
❑ 8 Keith Van Horn	1.00	.30
❑ 9 Joseph Forte	.60	.18
❑ 10 Peja Stojakovic	.60	.18
❑ 11 Juwan Howard	.60	.18
❑ 12 Brian Grant	.60	.18
❑ 13 Glenn Robinson	1.00	.30
❑ 14 Antonio McDyess	.60	.18
❑ 15 Vince Carter	2.50	.75
❑ 16 Pau Gasol	1.00	.30
❑ 17 Bonzi Wells	.60	.18
❑ 18 Chucky Atkins	.30	.09
❑ 19 Shane Battier	1.00	.30
❑ 20 Steve Francis	1.00	.30
❑ 21 Kevin Garnett	2.00	.60
❑ 22 Antawn Jamison	1.00	.30
❑ 23 Hidayet Turkoglu	1.00	.30
❑ 24 Kenyon Martin	1.00	.30
❑ 25 Cuttino Mobley	.60	.18
❑ 26 Steve Nash	1.00	.30
❑ 27 Morris Peterson	.60	.18
❑ 28 Jason Richardson	1.00	.30
❑ 29 Antoine Walker	1.00	.30
❑ 30 Rasheed Wallace	1.00	.30
❑ 31 Tim Duncan	2.00	.60
❑ 32 Paul Pierce	1.00	.30
❑ 33 Ben Wallace	1.00	.30
❑ 34 Jason Kidd	1.50	.45
❑ 35 Gary Payton	1.00	.30
❑ 36 Mike Miller	1.00	.30
❑ 37 Kobe Bryant	4.00	1.20
❑ 38 Baron Davis	1.00	.30
❑ 39 Steve Smith	.60	.18
❑ 40 Reggie Miller	1.00	.30
❑ 41 Dirk Nowitzki	1.50	.45
❑ 42 Rashard Lewis	.60	.18
❑ 43 Andre Miller	.60	.18
❑ 44 David Wesley	.30	.09
❑ 45 Ray Allen	1.00	.30

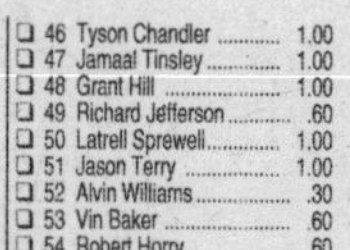

❑ 46 Tyson Chandler	1.00	.30
❑ 47 Jamaal Tinsley	1.00	.30
❑ 48 Grant Hill	1.00	.30
❑ 49 Richard Jefferson	.60	.18
❑ 50 Latrell Sprewell	1.00	.30
❑ 51 Jason Terry	1.00	.30
❑ 52 Alvin Williams	.30	.09
❑ 53 Vin Baker	.60	.18
❑ 54 Robert Horry	.60	.18
❑ 55 Eddie Jones	1.00	.30
❑ 56 Andrei Kirilenko	1.00	.30
❑ 57 Darius Miles	1.00	.30
❑ 58 Kedrick Brown	.60	.18
❑ 59 Jermaine O'Neal	1.00	.30
❑ 60 David Robinson	1.00	.30
❑ 61 Jason Williams	.60	.18
❑ 62 Wally Szczerbiak	.60	.18
❑ 63 Mike Bibby	1.00	.30
❑ 64 Shawn Marion	1.00	.30
❑ 65 Shaquille O'Neal	2.50	.75
❑ 66 Michael Redd	1.00	.30
❑ 67 Chris Webber	1.00	.30
❑ 68 Quentin Richardson	.60	.18
❑ 69 Michael Jordan	8.00	2.40
❑ 70 Jamaal Magloire	.30	.09
❑ 71 Radoslav Nesterovic	.60	.18
❑ 72 Eddy Curry	1.00	.30
❑ 73 Michael Finley	1.00	.30
❑ 74 Eddie Griffin	.60	.18
❑ 75 Aaron McKie	.60	.18
❑ 76 Tony Parker	1.00	.30
❑ 77 Shareef Abdur-Rahim	1.00	.30
❑ 78 Jalen Rose	1.00	.30
❑ 79 Jerry Stackhouse	1.00	.30
❑ 80 Jumaine Jones	.60	.18
❑ 81 Toni Kukoc	.60	.18
❑ 82 Vladimir Radmanovic	.60	.18
❑ 83 Zach Randolph	1.00	.30
❑ 84 John Stockton	1.00	.30
❑ 85 Mengke Bateer	1.00	.30
❑ 86 Dikembe Mutombo	.60	.18
❑ 87 Elton Brand	1.00	.30
❑ 88 Allan Houston	.60	.18
❑ 89 Joe Johnson	1.00	.30
❑ 90 Kwame Brown	.60	.18
❑ 91 Rookie Exchange	30.00	9.00
❑ 92 Jay Williams RC	8.00	2.40
❑ 93 Mike Dunleavy RC	12.00	3.60
❑ 94 Drew Gooden RC	20.00	6.00
❑ 95 DaJuan Wagner RC	10.00	3.00
❑ 96 Caron Butler RC	12.00	3.60
❑ 97 Jared Jeffries RC	8.00	2.40
❑ 98 Nene Hilario RC	10.00	3.00
❑ 99 Chris Wilcox RC	10.00	3.00
❑ 100 Nikoloz Tskitishvili RC	10.00	3.00
❑ 101 Kareem Rush RC	10.00	3.00
❑ 102 Curtis Borchardt RC	6.00	1.80
❑ 103 Qyntel Woods RC	8.00	2.40
❑ 104 Melvin Ely RC	6.00	1.80
❑ 105 Marcus Haislip RC	6.00	1.80
❑ 106 Carlos Boozer RC	15.00	4.50
❑ 107 Bostjan Nachbar RC	6.00	1.80
❑ 108 Amare Stoudemire RC	30.00	9.00
❑ 109 Frank Williams RC	6.00	1.80
❑ 110 Jiri Welsch RC	6.00	1.80
❑ 111 Fred Jones RC	8.00	2.40
❑ 112 Juan Dixon RC	12.00	3.60
❑ 113 Ryan Humphrey RC	6.00	1.80
❑ 114 Casey Jacobsen RC	6.00	1.80
❑ 115 Tayshaun Prince RC	10.00	3.00
❑ 116 Dan Dickau RC	6.00	1.80
❑ 117 Rookie Exchange	6.00	1.80
❑ 118 John Salmons RC	6.00	1.80
❑ 119 Manu Ginobili RC	15.00	4.50
❑ 119B Rookie Exchange	6.00	1.80
❑ 120 Rookie Exchange	6.00	1.80

2003-04 Flair

	MINT	NRMT
COMP.SET w/o SP's (90)	40.00	18.00
COMMON CARD (1-90)	.20	.09
COMMON ROOKIE (91-120)	6.00	2.70
❑ 1 Jerry Stackhouse	.75	.35
❑ 2 Eddie Griffin	.50	.23
❑ 3 Jermaine O'Neal	.75	.35

❑ 4 Kobe Bryant	3.00	1.35
❑ 5 Juwan Howard	.50	.23
❑ 6 Alonzo Mourning	.50	.23
❑ 7 Kenny Thomas	.20	.09
❑ 8 Chris Webber	.75	.35
❑ 9 Radoslav Nesterovic	.50	.23
❑ 10 Morris Peterson	.50	.23
❑ 11 DeShawn Stevenson	.20	.09
❑ 12 Steve Francis	.75	.35
❑ 13 Andrei Kirilenko	.75	.35
❑ 14 Kwame Brown	.50	.23
❑ 15 Tim Duncan	1.50	.70
❑ 16 Yao Ming	2.00	.90
❑ 17 Jamaal Tinsley	.75	.35
❑ 18 Shaquille O'Neal	2.00	.90
❑ 19 Tracy McGrady	2.00	.90
❑ 20 Dirk Nowitzki	1.25	.55
❑ 21 Marcus Camby	.50	.23
❑ 22 Elton Brand	.75	.35
❑ 23 Latrell Sprewell	.75	.35
❑ 24 Grant Hill	.75	.35
❑ 25 Shawn Marion	.75	.35
❑ 26 Rasheed Wallace	.75	.35
❑ 27 Ray Allen	.75	.35
❑ 28 Antonio Davis	.20	.09
❑ 29 Antoine Walker	.75	.35
❑ 30 Ricky Davis	.75	.35
❑ 31 Jason Kidd	1.25	.55
❑ 32 Tony Parker	.75	.35
❑ 33 Paul Pierce	.75	.35
❑ 34 Gary Payton	.75	.35
❑ 35 Kenyon Martin	.75	.35
❑ 36 Dale Davis	.50	.23
❑ 37 Vladimir Radmanovic	.20	.09
❑ 38 Matt Harpring	.75	.35
❑ 39 Shareef Abdur-Rahim	.75	.35
❑ 40 Antawn Jamison	.75	.35
❑ 41 Eddie Jones	.75	.35
❑ 42 Jamaal Magloire	.20	.09
❑ 43 Jason Richardson	.75	.35
❑ 44 Jonathan Bender	.50	.23
❑ 45 Chris Wilcox	.50	.23
❑ 46 Manu Ginobili	.75	.35
❑ 47 Chauncey Billups	.50	.23
❑ 48 Jamal Mashburn	.50	.23
❑ 49 Joe Smith	.50	.23
❑ 50 Aaron McKie	.50	.23
❑ 51 Theo Ratliff	.50	.23
❑ 52 Eddy Curry	.50	.23
❑ 53 Ron Artest	.50	.23
❑ 54 Quentin Richardson	.50	.23
❑ 55 Karl Malone	.75	.35
❑ 56 Pau Gasol	.75	.35
❑ 57 Dan Dickau	.20	.09
❑ 58 Darius Miles	.75	.35
❑ 59 Ben Wallace	.75	.35
❑ 60 Cuttino Mobley	.50	.23
❑ 61 Lamar Odom	.75	.35
❑ 62 Shane Battier	.75	.35
❑ 63 Allan Houston	.50	.23
❑ 64 Peja Stojakovic	.75	.35
❑ 65 Dajuan Wagner	.50	.23
❑ 66 Caron Butler	.75	.35
❑ 67 Keith Van Horn	.75	.35
❑ 68 Vincent Yarbrough	.20	.09
❑ 69 Tim Thomas	.50	.23
❑ 70 Troy Hudson	.20	.09
❑ 71 Amare Stoudemire	1.50	.70

❑ 72 Bobby Jackson .50 .23
❑ 73 Bonzi Wells .50 .23
❑ 74 Steve Nash .75 .35
❑ 75 Gilbert Arenas .75 .35
❑ 76 Glenn Robinson .75 .35
❑ 77 Jalen Rose .75 .35
❑ 78 Michael Finley .75 .35
❑ 79 Nene .50 .23
❑ 80 Kevin Garnett 1.50 .70
❑ 81 Richard Jefferson .50 .23
❑ 82 Baron Davis .75 .35
❑ 83 Mike Bibby .75 .35
❑ 84 Tyson Chandler .75 .35
❑ 85 Michael Redd .75 .35
❑ 86 Mike Dunleavy .50 .23
❑ 87 Drew Gooden .50 .23
❑ 88 Allen Iverson 1.50 .70
❑ 89 Vince Carter 2.00 .90
❑ 90 Larry Hughes .50 .23
❑ 91 Josh Howard RC 8.00 3.60
❑ 92 Maciej Lampe RC 6.00 2.70
❑ 93 Zarko Cabarkapa RC 6.00 2.70
❑ 94 LeBron James RC 80.00 36.00
❑ 95 Reece Gaines RC 6.00 2.70
❑ 96 Jarvis Hayes RC 6.00 2.70
❑ 97 Mickael Pietrus RC 6.00 2.70
❑ 98 T.J. Ford RC 8.00 3.60
❑ 99 Zoran Planinic RC 6.00 2.70
❑ 100 Luke Ridnour RC 8.00 3.60
❑ 101 Boris Diaw RC 6.00 2.70
❑ 102 Nick Collison RC 6.00 2.70
❑ 103 Travis Outlaw RC 6.00 2.70
❑ 104 Carmelo Anthony RC 40.00 18.00
❑ 105 Chris Kaman RC 6.00 2.70
❑ 106 Mike Sweetney RC 6.00 2.70
❑ 107 Kendrick Perkins RC 6.00 2.70
❑ 108 Jason Kapono RC 6.00 2.70
❑ 109 Troy Bell RC 6.00 2.70
❑ 110 Chris Bosh RC 12.00 5.50
❑ 111 Jerome Beasley RC 6.00 2.70
❑ 112 Darko Milicic RC 10.00 4.50
❑ 113 Dwyane Wade RC 15.00 6.75
❑ 114 David West RC 6.00 2.70
❑ 115 Kirk Hinrich RC 10.00 4.50
❑ 116 Dahntay Jones RC 6.00 2.70
❑ 117 Leandro Barbosa RC 6.00 2.70
❑ 118 Marcus Banks RC 6.00 2.70
❑ 119 Luke Walton RC 8.00 3.60
❑ 120 Ndudi Ebi RC 6.00 2.70

2003-04 Flair Final Edition

	Nm-Mt	Ex-Mt
COMP.SET w/o SP's (65)	30.00	9.00
COMMON CARD (1-65)	.20	.06
COMMON ROOKIE (66-90)	6.00	1.80

❑ 1 Allen Iverson 1.50 .45
❑ 2 Juwan Howard .50 .15
❑ 3 Stephen Jackson .20 .06
❑ 4 Manu Ginobili .75 .23
❑ 5 Steve Nash .75 .23
❑ 6 Jason Terry .75 .23
❑ 7 Tayshaun Prince .50 .15
❑ 8 Stephon Marbury .75 .23
❑ 9 Eddie Jones .75 .23
❑ 10 Reggie Miller .75 .23
❑ 11 Baron Davis .75 .23
❑ 12 Donyell Marshall .75 .23
❑ 13 Mike Bibby .75 .23
❑ 14 Kobe Bryant 3.00 .90
❑ 15 Jason Richardson .75 .23
❑ 16 Cuttino Mobley .50 .15
❑ 17 Andre Miller .50 .15
❑ 18 Corey Maggette .50 .15
❑ 19 Michael Finley .75 .23
❑ 20 Jason Kidd 1.25 .35
❑ 21 Lamar Odom .75 .23
❑ 22 Tracy McGrady 2.00 .60
❑ 23 Peja Stojakovic .75 .23
❑ 24 Richard Jefferson .50 .15
❑ 25 Rasheed Wallace .75 .23
❑ 26 Eddy Curry .50 .15
❑ 27 Ben Wallace .75 .23
❑ 28 Rashard Lewis .75 .23
❑ 29 Sam Cassell .75 .23
❑ 30 Anfernee Hardaway .75 .23
❑ 31 Carlos Boozer .75 .23
❑ 32 Jamal Crawford .50 .15
❑ 33 Dirk Nowitzki 1.25 .35
❑ 34 Steve Francis .75 .23
❑ 35 Chris Webber .75 .23
❑ 36 Elton Brand .75 .23
❑ 37 Michael Redd .50 .15
❑ 38 Jason Williams .50 .15
❑ 39 Nene .50 .15
❑ 40 Nick Van Exel .75 .23
❑ 41 Amare Stoudemire 1.50 .45
❑ 42 Latrell Sprewell .75 .23
❑ 43 Tony Parker .75 .23
❑ 44 Keith Van Horn .75 .23
❑ 45 Pau Gasol .75 .23
❑ 46 Andrei Kirilenko .75 .23
❑ 47 Shareef Abdur-Rahim .75 .23
❑ 48 Tim Thomas .50 .15
❑ 49 Jerry Stackhouse .75 .23
❑ 50 Jermaine O'Neal .75 .23
❑ 51 Jamal Mashburn .50 .15
❑ 52 Matt Harpring .75 .23
❑ 53 Damon Stoudamire .50 .15
❑ 54 Zydrunas Ilgauskas .50 .15
❑ 55 Kevin Garnett 1.50 .45
❑ 56 Tim Duncan 1.50 .45
❑ 57 Yao Ming 2.00 .60
❑ 58 Kenyon Martin .75 .23
❑ 59 Paul Pierce .75 .23
❑ 60 Ron Artest .50 .15
❑ 61 Vince Carter 2.00 .60
❑ 62 Shaquille O'Neal 2.00 .60
❑ 63 Shawn Marion .75 .23
❑ 64 Gilbert Arenas .75 .23
❑ 65 Ray Allen .75 .23
❑ 66 Chris Bosh RC 15.00 4.50
❑ 67 Brian Cook RC 6.00 1.80
❑ 68 Luke Ridnour RC 10.00 3.00
❑ 69 Willie Green RC 6.00 1.80
❑ 70 Zarko Cabarkapa RC 6.00 1.80
❑ 71 Maurice Williams RC 6.00 1.80
❑ 72 Luke Walton RC 10.00 3.00
❑ 73 David West RC 6.00 1.80
❑ 74 Mickael Pietrus RC 6.00 1.80
❑ 75 LeBron James RC 80.00 24.00
❑ 76 Marcus Banks RC 6.00 1.80
❑ 77 Keith Bogans RC 6.00 1.80
❑ 78 Darko Milicic RC 12.00 3.60
❑ 79 Jarvis Hayes RC 6.00 1.80
❑ 80 Josh Howard RC 10.00 3.00
❑ 81 Chris Kaman RC 6.00 1.80
❑ 82 Mike Sweetney RC 6.00 1.80
❑ 83 Carmelo Anthony RC 40.00 12.00
❑ 84 Travis Outlaw RC 6.00 1.80
❑ 85 Kyle Korver RC 10.00 3.00
❑ 86 Boris Diaw RC 6.00 1.80
❑ 87 Dwyane Wade RC 20.00 6.00
❑ 88 Troy Bell RC 6.00 1.80
❑ 89 T.J. Ford RC 10.00 3.00
❑ 90 Kirk Hinrich RC 12.00 3.60

1961-62 Fleer

	NM	Ex
COMPLETE SET (66)	4,000.00	1,600.00

❑ 1 Al Attles RC 125.00 38.00
❑ 2 Paul Arizin 50.00 20.00

❑ 3 Elgin Baylor RC 250.00 100.00
❑ 4 Walt Bellamy RC 60.00 24.00
❑ 5 Arlen Bockhorn 15.00 6.00
❑ 6 Bob Boozer RC 25.00 10.00
❑ 7 Carl Braun 30.00 12.00
❑ 8 Wilt Chamberlain RC 900.00 350.00
❑ 9 Larry Costello 20.00 8.00
❑ 10 Bob Cousy 200.00 80.00
❑ 11 Walter Dukes 20.00 8.00
❑ 12 Wayne Embry RC 40.00
❑ 13 Dave Gambee 15.00 6.00
❑ 14 Tom Gola 40.00 16.00
❑ 15 Sihugo Green RC 20.00
❑ 16 Hal Greer RC 80.00 32.00
❑ 17 Richie Guerin RC 40.00
❑ 18 Cliff Hagan 50.00 20.00
❑ 19 Tom Heinsohn 100.00 40.00
❑ 20 Bailey Howell RC 50.00
❑ 21 Rod Hundley 75.00 30.00
❑ 22 K.C. Jones RC 110.0
❑ 23 Sam Jones RC 110.0
❑ 24 Phil Jordan 15.00 6.00
❑ 25 John Kerr 50.00 20.00
❑ 26 Rudy LaRusso RC 40.00
❑ 27 George Lee 15.00 6.00
❑ 28 Bob Leonard 20.00 8.00
❑ 29 Clyde Lovellette 50.00
❑ 30 John McCarthy 15.00
❑ 31 Tom Meschery RC 25.00
❑ 32 Willie Naulls 25.00 10.00
❑ 33 Don Ohl RC 25.00 10.00
❑ 34 Bob Pettit 90.00 36.00
❑ 35 Frank Ramsey 40.00 16.00
❑ 36 Oscar Robertson RC 400.0
❑ 37 Guy Rodgers RC 25.00
❑ 38 Bill Russell 400.00 160.00
❑ 39 Dolph Schayes 55.00
❑ 40 Frank Selvy 20.00 8.00
❑ 41 Gene Shue 25.00 10.00
❑ 42 Jack Twyman 40.00 16.00
❑ 43 Jerry West RC 500.00 200.00
❑ 44 Len Wilkens RC UER 175.0
(Misspelled Wilkins on card front)
❑ 45 Paul Arizin IA 25.00 10.00
❑ 46 Elgin Baylor IA 100.00 40.00
❑ 47 Wilt Chamberlain IA 400.00 160.00
❑ 48 Larry Costello IA 20.00 8.00
❑ 49 Bob Cousy IA 125.00 50.00
❑ 50 Walter Dukes IA 15.00 6.00
❑ 51 Tom Gola IA 25.00 10.00
❑ 52 Richie Guerin IA 20.00 8.00
❑ 53 Cliff Hagan IA 25.00 10.00
❑ 54 Tom Heinsohn IA 50.00 20.00
❑ 55 Bailey Howell IA 25.00 10.00
❑ 56 John Kerr IA 30.00 12.00
❑ 57 Rudy LaRusso IA 20.00 8.00
❑ 58 Clyde Lovellette IA 30.00 12.00
❑ 59 Bob Pettit IA 50.00 20.00
❑ 60 Frank Ramsey IA 25.00 10.00
❑ 61 Oscar Robertson IA 175.00 70.00
❑ 62 Bill Russell IA 200.00 80.00
❑ 63 Dolph Schayes IA 35.00 14.00
❑ 64 Gene Shue IA 20.00 8.00
❑ 65 Jack Twyman IA 25.00 10.00
❑ 66 Jerry West IA 300.00 90.00

1986-87 Fleer

	Nm-Mt	Ex-Mt
COMP.w/Stickers (143)	2,100.00	850.00
COMPLETE SET (132)	1,800.00	700.00
❑ 1 Kareem Abdul-Jabbar	12.00	4.80
❑ 2 Alvan Adams	2.00	.80
❑ 3 Mark Aguirre RC	3.00	1.20
❑ 4 Danny Ainge RC	8.00	3.20
❑ 5 John Bagley RC**	2.00	.80
❑ 6 Thurl Bailey RC**	2.00	.80
❑ 7 Charles Barkley RC	50.00	20.00
❑ 8 Benoit Benjamin RC	2.50	1.00
❑ 9 Larry Bird	30.00	12.00
❑ 10 Otis Birdsong	2.00	.80
❑ 11 Rolando Blackman RC	2.50	1.00
❑ 12 Manute Bol RC	2.00	.80
❑ 14 Joe Barry Carroll	2.00	.80
❑ 15 Tom Chambers RC	4.00	1.60
❑ 16 Maurice Cheeks	2.00	.80
❑ 17 Michael Cooper	2.50	1.00
❑ 18 Wayne Cooper	2.00	.80
❑ 19 Pat Cummings	2.00	.80
❑ 20 Terry Cummings RC	3.00	1.20
❑ 21 Adrian Dantley	2.50	1.00
❑ 22 Brad Davis RC**	2.00	.80
❑ 23 Walter Davis	2.00	.80
❑ 24 Darryl Dawkins	2.50	1.00
❑ 25 Larry Drew	2.00	.80
❑ 26 Clyde Drexler RC	40.00	16.00
❑ 27 Joe Dumars RC	20.00	8.00
❑ 28 Mark Eaton RC**	2.00	.80
❑ 29 James Edwards	2.00	.80
❑ 30 Alex English	2.50	1.00
❑ 31 Julius Erving	15.00	6.00
❑ 32 Patrick Ewing RC	30.00	12.00
❑ 33 Vern Fleming RC**	2.00	.80
❑ 34 Sleepy Floyd RC**	2.00	.80
❑ 35 World B. Free	2.00	.80
❑ 36 George Gervin	4.00	1.60
❑ 37 Artis Gilmore	2.50	1.00
❑ 38 Mike Gminski	2.00	.80
❑ 39 Rickey Green	2.00	.80
❑ 40 Sidney Green	2.00	.80
❑ 41 David Greenwood	2.00	.80
❑ 42 Darrell Griffith	2.00	.80
❑ 43 Bill Hanzlik	2.00	.80
❑ 44 Derek Harper RC	6.00	2.40
❑ 45 Gerald Henderson	2.00	.80
❑ 46 Roy Hinson	2.00	.80
❑ 47 Craig Hodges RC**	2.00	.80
❑ 48 Phil Hubbard	2.00	.80
❑ 49 Jay Humphries RC**	2.00	.80
❑ 50 Dennis Johnson	2.00	.80
❑ 51 Eddie Johnson RC	3.00	1.20
❑ 52 Frank Johnson RC**	2.00	.80
❑ 53 Magic Johnson	20.00	8.00
❑ 54 Marques Johnson (Decimal point missing, rookie year scoring avg.)	2.00	.80
❑ 55 Steve Johnson UER (photo actually David Greenwood)	2.00	.80
❑ 56 Vinnie Johnson	2.00	.80
❑ 57 Michael Jordan RC	800.00	325.00
❑ 58 Clark Kellogg RC**	2.00	.80
❑ 59 Albert King	2.00	.80
❑ 60 Bernard King	2.50	1.00
❑ 61 Bill Laimbeer	2.50	1.00
❑ 62 Allen Leavell	2.00	.80
❑ 63 Lafayette Lever RC**	2.00	.80
❑ 64 Alton Lister	2.00	.80
❑ 65 Lewis Lloyd	2.00	.80
❑ 66 Maurice Lucas	2.00	.80
❑ 67 Jeff Malone RC	2.00	.80
❑ 68 Karl Malone RC	50.00	20.00
❑ 69 Moses Malone	3.00	1.20
❑ 70 Cedric Maxwell	2.00	.80
❑ 71 Rodney McCray RC**	2.00	.80
❑ 72 Xavier McDaniel RC	2.50	1.00
❑ 73 Kevin McHale	3.00	1.20
❑ 74 Mike Mitchell	2.00	.80
❑ 75 Sidney Moncrief	2.50	1.00
❑ 76 Johnny Moore	2.00	.80
❑ 77 Chris Mullin RC	15.00	6.00
❑ 78 Larry Nance RC	4.00	1.60
❑ 79 Calvin Natt	2.00	.80
❑ 80 Norm Nixon	2.00	.80
❑ 81 Charles Oakley RC	6.00	2.40
❑ 82 Hakeem Olajuwon RC	40.00	16.00
❑ 83 Louis Orr	2.00	.80
❑ 84 Robert Parish UER (Misspelled Parrish on both sides)	3.00	1.20
❑ 85 Jim Paxson	2.00	.80
❑ 86 Sam Perkins RC	6.00	2.40
❑ 87 Ricky Pierce RC	2.50	1.00
❑ 88 Paul Pressey RC**	2.00	.80
❑ 89 Kurt Rambis RC	2.00	.80
❑ 90 Robert Reid	2.00	.80
❑ 91 Doc Rivers RC	6.00	2.40
❑ 92 Alvin Robertson RC	2.00	.80
❑ 93 Cliff Robinson	2.00	.80
❑ 94 Tree Rollins	2.00	.80
❑ 95 Dan Roundfield	2.00	.80
❑ 96 Jeff Ruland	2.00	.80
❑ 97 Ralph Sampson RC	2.50	1.00
❑ 98 Danny Schayes RC**	2.00	.80
❑ 99 Byron Scott RC	4.00	1.60
❑ 100 Purvis Short	2.00	.80
❑ 101 Jerry Sichting	2.00	.80
❑ 102 Jack Sikma	2.00	.80
❑ 103 Derek Smith	2.00	.80
❑ 104 Larry Smith	2.00	.80
❑ 105 Rory Sparrow	2.00	.80
❑ 106 Steve Stipanovich	2.00	.80
❑ 107 Terry Teagle	2.00	.80
❑ 108 Reggie Theus	2.50	1.00
❑ 109 Isiah Thomas RC	25.00	10.00
❑ 110 LaSalle Thompson RC**	2.00	.80
❑ 111 Mychal Thompson	2.00	.80
❑ 112 Sedale Threatt RC**	2.00	.80
❑ 113 Wayman Tisdale RC	2.50	1.00
❑ 114 Andrew Toney	2.00	.80
❑ 115 Kelly Tripucka RC	2.00	.80
❑ 116 Mel Turpin	2.00	.80
❑ 117 Kiki Vandeweghe RC	2.50	1.00
❑ 118 Jay Vincent	2.00	.80
❑ 119 Bill Walton (Missing decimal points on four lines of FG Percentage)	4.00	1.60
❑ 120 Spud Webb RC	6.00	2.40
❑ 121 Dominique Wilkins RC	25.00	10.00
❑ 122 Gerald Wilkins RC	2.50	1.00
❑ 123 Buck Williams RC	4.00	1.60
❑ 124 Gus Williams	2.00	.80
❑ 125 Herb Williams RC**	2.00	.80
❑ 126 Kevin Willis RC	6.00	2.40
❑ 127 Randy Wittman	2.00	.80
❑ 128 Al Wood	2.00	.80
❑ 129 Mike Woodson	2.00	.80
❑ 130 Orlando Woolridge RC**	2.00	.80
❑ 131 James Worthy RC	20.00	8.00
❑ 132 Checklist 1-132	2.50	1.00

1987-88 Fleer

	Nm-Mt	Ex-Mt
COMPLETE w/Stickers (143)	300.00	120.00
COMPLETE SET (132)	200.00	80.00
❑ 1 Kareem Abdul-Jabbar	8.00	3.20
❑ 2 Alvan Adams	1.50	.60
❑ 3 Mark Aguirre	2.00	.80
❑ 4 Danny Ainge	2.00	.80
❑ 5 John Bagley	1.50	.60
❑ 6 Thurl Bailey UER (reverse negative)	1.50	.60
❑ 7 Greg Ballard	1.50	.60
❑ 8 Gene Banks	1.50	.60
❑ 9 Charles Barkley	15.00	6.00
❑ 10 Benoit Benjamin	1.50	.60
❑ 11 Larry Bird	20.00	8.00
❑ 12 Rolando Blackman	1.50	.60
❑ 13 Manute Bol	1.50	.60
❑ 14 Tony Brown	1.50	.60
❑ 15 Michael Cage RC**	1.50	.60
❑ 16 Joe Barry Carroll	1.50	.60
❑ 17 Bill Cartwright	2.00	.80
❑ 18 Terry Catledge RC	1.50	.60
❑ 19 Tom Chambers	1.50	.60
❑ 20 Maurice Cheeks	1.50	.60
❑ 21 Michael Cooper	2.00	.80
❑ 22 Dave Corzine	1.50	.60
❑ 23 Terry Cummings	2.00	.80
❑ 24 Adrian Dantley	1.50	.60
❑ 25 Brad Daugherty RC	2.50	1.00
❑ 26 Walter Davis	1.50	.60
❑ 27 Johnny Dawkins RC	1.50	.60
❑ 28 James Donaldson	1.50	.60
❑ 29 Larry Drew	1.50	.60
❑ 30 Clyde Drexler	12.00	4.80
❑ 31 Joe Dumars	4.00	1.60
❑ 32 Mark Eaton	1.50	.60
❑ 33 Dale Ellis RC	2.50	1.00
❑ 34 Alex English	2.00	.80
❑ 35 Julius Erving	12.00	4.80
❑ 36 Mike Evans	1.50	.60
❑ 37 Patrick Ewing	10.00	4.00
❑ 38 Vern Fleming	1.50	.60
❑ 39 Sleepy Floyd	1.50	.60
❑ 40 Artis Gilmore	2.00	.80
❑ 41 Mike Gminski UER (reversed negative)	1.50	.60
❑ 42 A.C. Green RC	6.00	2.40
❑ 43 Rickey Green	1.50	.60
❑ 44 Sidney Green	1.50	.60
❑ 45 David Greenwood	1.50	.60
❑ 46 Darrell Griffith	1.50	.60
❑ 47 Bill Hanzlik	1.50	.60
❑ 48 Derek Harper	2.00	.80
❑ 49 Ron Harper RC	6.00	2.40
❑ 50 Gerald Henderson	1.50	.60
❑ 51 Roy Hinson	1.50	.60
❑ 52 Craig Hodges	1.50	.60
❑ 53 Phil Hubbard	1.50	.60
❑ 54 Dennis Johnson	1.50	.60
❑ 55 Eddie Johnson	2.00	.80
❑ 56 Magic Johnson	25.00	10.00
❑ 57 Steve Johnson	1.50	.60
❑ 58 Vinnie Johnson	1.50	.60
❑ 59 Michael Jordan	100.00	40.00
❑ 60 Jerome Kersey RC**	1.50	.60
❑ 61 Bill Laimbeer	2.00	.80
❑ 62 Lafayette Lever UER (Photo actually Otis Smith)	1.50	.60
❑ 63 Cliff Levingston RC**	1.50	.60
❑ 64 Alton Lister	1.50	.60
❑ 65 John Long	1.50	.60
❑ 66 John Lucas	1.50	.60
❑ 67 Jeff Malone	1.50	.60

#	Player	Nm-Mt	Ex-Mt
❑ 68	Karl Malone	15.00	6.00
❑ 69	Moses Malone	2.50	1.00
❑ 70	Cedric Maxwell	1.50	.60
❑ 71	Tim McCormick	1.50	.60
❑ 72	Rodney McCray	1.50	.60
❑ 73	Xavier McDaniel	1.50	.60
❑ 74	Kevin McHale	2.50	1.00
❑ 75	Nate McMillan RC	2.50	1.00
❑ 76	Sidney Moncrief	1.50	.60
❑ 77	Chris Mullin	4.00	1.60
❑ 78	Larry Nance	2.00	.80
❑ 79	Charles Oakley	2.50	1.00
❑ 80	Hakeem Olajuwon	15.00	6.00
❑ 81	Robert Parish UER (Misspelled Parrish on both sides)	2.50	1.00
❑ 82	Jim Paxson	1.50	.60
❑ 83	John Paxson RC	2.50	1.00
❑ 84	Sam Perkins	2.50	1.00
❑ 85	Chuck Person RC	2.50	1.00
❑ 86	Jim Petersen	1.50	.60
❑ 87	Ricky Pierce	1.50	.60
❑ 88	Ed Pinckney RC	1.50	.60
❑ 89	Terry Porter RC (College Wisconsin, should be Wisconsin - Stevens Point)	2.50	1.00
❑ 90	Paul Pressey	1.50	.60
❑ 91	Robert Reid	1.50	.60
❑ 92	Doc Rivers	2.50	1.00
❑ 93	Alvin Robertson	1.50	.60
❑ 94	Tree Rollins	1.50	.60
❑ 95	Ralph Sampson	1.50	.60
❑ 96	Mike Sanders	1.50	.60
❑ 97	Detlef Schrempf RC	10.00	4.00
❑ 98	Byron Scott	2.00	.80
❑ 99	Jerry Sichting	1.50	.60
❑ 100	Jack Sikma	1.50	.60
❑ 101	Larry Smith	1.50	.60
❑ 102	Rory Sparrow	1.50	.60
❑ 103	Steve Stipanovich	1.50	.60
❑ 104	Jon Sundvold	1.50	.60
❑ 105	Reggie Theus	2.00	.80
❑ 106	Isiah Thomas	6.00	2.40
❑ 107	LaSalle Thompson	1.50	.60
❑ 108	Mychal Thompson	1.50	.60
❑ 109	Otis Thorpe RC	5.00	2.00
❑ 110	Sedale Threatt	1.50	.60
❑ 111	Waymon Tisdale	1.50	.60
❑ 112	Kelly Tripucka	1.50	.60
❑ 113	Trent Tucker RC**	1.50	.60
❑ 114	Terry Tyler	1.50	.60
❑ 115	Darnell Valentine	1.50	.60
❑ 116	Kiki Vandeweghe	1.50	.60
❑ 117	Darrell Walker RC**	1.50	.60
❑ 118	Dominique Wilkins	4.00	1.60
❑ 119	Gerald Wilkins	1.50	.60
❑ 120	Buck Williams	2.00	.80
❑ 121	Herb Williams	1.50	.60
❑ 122	John Williams RC	1.50	.60
❑ 123	John Williams RC	2.00	.80
❑ 124	Kevin Willis	2.00	.80
❑ 125	David Wingate RC	1.50	.60
❑ 126	Randy Wittman	1.50	.60
❑ 127	Leon Wood	1.50	.60
❑ 128	Mike Woodson	1.50	.60
❑ 129	Orlando Woolridge	1.50	.60
❑ 130	James Worthy	4.00	1.60
❑ 131	Danny Young RC**	1.50	.60
❑ 132	Checklist 1-132	3.00	1.20

1988-89 Fleer

		Nm-Mt	Ex-Mt
	COMPLETE w/Stickers (143)	200.00	80.00
	COMPLETE SET (132)	150.00	60.00
❑ 1	Antoine Carr RC**	.75	.30
❑ 2	Cliff Levingston	.50	.20
❑ 3	Doc Rivers	.75	.30
❑ 4	Spud Webb	.75	.30
❑ 5	Dominique Wilkins	1.50	.60
❑ 6	Kevin Willis	.75	.30
❑ 7	Randy Wittman	.50	.20
❑ 8	Danny Ainge	.75	.30
❑ 9	Larry Bird	12.00	4.80
❑ 10	Dennis Johnson	.50	.20
❑ 11	Kevin McHale	1.50	.60
❑ 12	Robert Parish	1.50	.60
❑ 13	Tyrone Bogues RC	2.00	.80
❑ 14	Dell Curry RC	1.50	.60
❑ 15	Dave Corzine	.50	.20
❑ 16	Horace Grant RC	5.00	2.00
❑ 17	Michael Jordan	40.00	16.00
❑ 18	Charles Oakley	.75	.30
❑ 19	John Paxson	.75	.30
❑ 20	Scottie Pippen RC UER (Misspelled Pippin on card back)	30.00	12.00
❑ 21	Brad Sellers RC	.50	.20
❑ 22	Brad Daugherty	.50	.20
❑ 23	Ron Harper	.75	.30
❑ 24	Larry Nance	.50	.20
❑ 25	Mark Price RC	2.00	.80
❑ 26	Hot Rod Williams	.50	.20
❑ 27	Mark Aguirre	.50	.20
❑ 28	Rolando Blackman	.50	.20
❑ 29	James Donaldson	.50	.20
❑ 30	Derek Harper	.75	.30
❑ 31	Sam Perkins	.75	.30
❑ 32	Roy Tarpley RC	.50	.20
❑ 33	Michael Adams RC	.50	.20
❑ 34	Alex English	.75	.30
❑ 35	Lafayette Lever	.50	.20
❑ 36	Blair Rasmussen RC	.50	.20
❑ 37	Danny Schayes	.50	.20
❑ 38	Jay Vincent	.50	.20
❑ 39	Adrian Dantley	.50	.20
❑ 40	Joe Dumars	1.50	.60
❑ 41	Vinnie Johnson	.50	.20
❑ 42	Bill Laimbeer	.75	.30
❑ 43	Dennis Rodman RC	12.00	4.80
❑ 44	John Salley RC	.75	.30
❑ 45	Isiah Thomas	1.50	.60
❑ 46	Winston Garland RC	.50	.20
❑ 47	Rod Higgins	.50	.20
❑ 48	Chris Mullin	1.50	.60
❑ 49	Ralph Sampson	.50	.20
❑ 50	Joe Barry Carroll	.50	.20
❑ 51	Sleepy Floyd	.50	.20
❑ 52	Rodney McCray	.50	.20
❑ 53	Hakeem Olajuwon	5.00	2.00
❑ 54	Purvis Short	.50	.20
❑ 55	Vern Fleming	.50	.20
❑ 56	John Long	.50	.20
❑ 57	Reggie Miller RC	25.00	10.00
❑ 58	Chuck Person	.75	.30
❑ 59	Steve Stipanovich	.50	.20
❑ 60	Waymon Tisdale	.50	.20
❑ 61	Benoit Benjamin	.50	.20
❑ 62	Michael Cage	.50	.20
❑ 63	Mike Woodson	.50	.20
❑ 64	Kareem Abdul-Jabbar	4.00	1.60
❑ 65	Michael Cooper	.50	.20
❑ 66	A.C. Green	.75	.30
❑ 67	Magic Johnson	10.00	4.00
❑ 68	Byron Scott	.75	.30
❑ 69	Mychal Thompson	.50	.20
❑ 70	James Worthy	1.50	.60
❑ 71	Duane Washington	.50	.20
❑ 72	Kevin Williams	.50	.20
❑ 73	Randy Breuer RC**	.50	.20
❑ 74	Terry Cummings	.75	.30
❑ 75	Paul Pressey	.50	.20
❑ 76	Jack Sikma	.50	.20
❑ 77	John Bagley	.50	.20
❑ 78	Roy Hinson	.50	.20
❑ 79	Buck Williams	.75	.30
❑ 80	Patrick Ewing	3.00	1.20
❑ 81	Sidney Green	.50	.20
❑ 82	Mark Jackson RC	2.50	1.00
❑ 83	Kenny Walker RC	.50	.20
❑ 84	Gerald Wilkins	.50	.20
❑ 85	Charles Barkley	5.00	2.00
❑ 86	Maurice Cheeks	.50	.20
❑ 87	Mike Gminski	.50	.20
❑ 88	Cliff Robinson	.50	.20
❑ 89	Armon Gilliam RC	1.50	.60
❑ 90	Eddie Johnson	.50	.20
❑ 91	Mark West RC	.50	.20
❑ 92	Clyde Drexler	3.00	1.20
❑ 93	Kevin Duckworth RC	.50	.20
❑ 94	Steve Johnson	.50	.20
❑ 95	Jerome Kersey	.50	.20
❑ 96	Terry Porter (College Wisconsin, should be Wisconsin Stevens Point)	.50	.20
❑ 97	Joe Kleine RC	.50	.20
❑ 98	Reggie Theus	.75	.30
❑ 99	Otis Thorpe	.75	.30
❑ 100	Kenny Smith RC (College NC State, should be North Carolina)	1.50	.60
❑ 101	Greg Anderson RC	.50	.20
❑ 102	Walter Berry RC	.50	.20
❑ 103	Frank Brickowski RC	.50	.20
❑ 104	Johnny Dawkins	.50	.20
❑ 105	Alvin Robertson	.50	.20
❑ 106	Tom Chambers (Born 6/2/59, should be 6/21/59)	.50	.20
❑ 107	Dale Ellis	.75	.30
❑ 108	Xavier McDaniel	.50	.20
❑ 109	Derrick McKey RC	1.50	.60
❑ 110	Nate McMillan UER (Photo actually Kevin Williams)	.50	.20
❑ 111	Thurl Bailey	.50	.20
❑ 112	Mark Eaton	.50	.20
❑ 113	Bobby Hansen RC**	.50	.20
❑ 114	Karl Malone	5.00	2.00
❑ 115	John Stockton RC	25.00	10.00
❑ 116	Bernard King	.50	.20
❑ 117	Jeff Malone	.50	.20
❑ 118	Moses Malone	1.50	.60
❑ 119	John Williams	.50	.20
❑ 120	Michael Jordan AS	20.00	8.00
❑ 121	Mark Jackson AS	1.50	.60
❑ 122	Byron Scott AS	.50	.20
❑ 123	Magic Johnson AS	4.00	1.60
❑ 124	Larry Bird AS	5.00	2.00
❑ 125	Dominique Wilkins AS	.75	.30
❑ 126	Hakeem Olajuwon AS	2.00	.80
❑ 127	John Stockton AS	5.00	2.00
❑ 128	Alvin Robertson AS	.50	.20
❑ 129	Charles Barkley AS (Back says Buck Williams is member of Jets, should be Nets)	2.00	.80
❑ 130	Patrick Ewing AS	1.50	.60
❑ 131	Mark Eaton AS	.50	.20
❑ 132	Checklist 1-132	.50	.20

1989-90 Fleer

		Nm-Mt	Ex-Mt
	COMPLETE w/Stickers (179)	50.00	20.00
	COMPLETE SET (168)	30.00	12.00
❑ 1	John Battle RC	.15	.06
❑ 2	Jon Koncak RC	.15	.06
❑ 3	Cliff Levingston	.15	.06
❑ 4	Moses Malone	.50	.20
❑ 5	Doc Rivers	.25	.10
❑ 6	Spud Webb UER (Points per 48 minutes incorrect at 2.6)	.25	.10
❑ 7	Dominique Wilkins	.50	.20
❑ 8	Larry Bird	3.00	1.20
❑ 9	Dennis Johnson	.15	.06
❑ 10	Reggie Lewis RC	.75	.30

❑ 11 Kevin McHale .50 .20
❑ 12 Robert Parish .25 .10
❑ 13 Ed Pinckney .15 .06
❑ 14 Brian Shaw RC .50 .20
❑ 15 Rex Chapman RC .75 .30
❑ 16 Kurt Rambis .15 .06
❑ 17 Robert Reid .15 .06
❑ 18 Kelly Tripucka .15 .06
❑ 19 Bill Cartwright UER .15 .06
(First season 1978-80, should be 1979-80)
❑ 20 Horace Grant .25 .10
❑ 21 Michael Jordan 15.00 6.00
❑ 22 John Paxson .15 .06
❑ 23 Scottie Pippen 5.00 2.00
❑ 24 Brad Sellers .15 .06
❑ 25 Brad Daugherty .15 .06
❑ 26 Craig Ehlo RC** .15 .06
❑ 27 Ron Harper .25 .10
❑ 28 Larry Nance .25 .10
❑ 29 Mark Price .25 .10
❑ 30 Mike Sanders .15 .06
❑ 31A John Williams ERR - -
❑ 31B John Williams COR .15 .06
❑ 32 Rolando Blackman UER .15 .06
(Career blocks and points listed as 1961 and 2127, should be 196 and 12,127)
❑ 33 Adrian Dantley .15 .06
❑ 34 James Donaldson .15 .06
❑ 35 Derek Harper .25 .10
❑ 36 Sam Perkins .25 .10
❑ 37 Herb Williams .15 .06
❑ 38 Michael Adams .15 .06
❑ 39 Walter Davis .15 .06
❑ 40 Alex English .15 .06
❑ 41 Lafayette Lever .15 .06
❑ 42 Blair Rasmussen .15 .06
❑ 43 Danny Schayes .15 .06
❑ 44 Mark Aguirre .15 .06
❑ 45 Joe Dumars .50 .20
❑ 46 James Edwards .15 .06
❑ 47 Vinnie Johnson .15 .06
❑ 48 Bill Laimbeer .25 .10
❑ 49 Dennis Rodman 3.00 1.20
❑ 50 Isiah Thomas .50 .20
❑ 51 John Salley .15 .06
❑ 52 Manute Bol .15 .06
❑ 53 Winston Garland .15 .06
❑ 54 Rod Higgins .15 .06
❑ 55 Chris Mullin .50 .20
❑ 56 Mitch Richmond RC 4.00 1.60
❑ 57 Terry Teagle .15 .06
❑ 58 Derrick Chievous UER .15 .06
(Stats correctly say 81 games in '88-89, text says 82)
❑ 59 Sleepy Floyd .15 .06
❑ 60 Tim McCormick .15 .06
❑ 61 Hakeem Olajuwon 1.25 .50
❑ 62 Otis Thorpe .25 .10
❑ 63 Mike Woodson .15 .06
❑ 64 Vern Fleming .15 .06
❑ 65 Reggie Miller 2.00 .80
❑ 66 Chuck Person .25 .10
❑ 67 Detlef Schrempf .25 .10
❑ 68 Rik Smits RC 1.00 .40
❑ 69 Benoit Benjamin .15 .06
❑ 70 Gary Grant RC .15 .06
❑ 71 Danny Manning RC 1.00 .40
❑ 72 Ken Norman RC .15 .06
❑ 73 Charles Smith RC .50 .20
❑ 74 Reggie Williams RC .15 .06
❑ 75 Michael Cooper .15 .06
❑ 76 A.C. Green .25 .10
❑ 77 Magic Johnson 2.50 1.00
❑ 78 Byron Scott .25 .10
❑ 79 Mychal Thompson .15 .06
❑ 80 James Worthy .50 .20
❑ 81 Kevin Edwards RC .15 .06
❑ 82 Grant Long RC .15 .06
❑ 83 Rony Seikaly RC .50 .20
❑ 84 Rory Sparrow .15 .06
❑ 85 Greg Anderson UER .15 .06
(Stats show 1988-89 as 19888-89)
❑ 86 Jay Humphries .15 .06
❑ 87 Larry Krystkowiak RC .15 .06
❑ 88 Ricky Pierce .15 .06
❑ 89 Paul Pressey .15 .06
❑ 90 Alvin Robertson .15 .06
❑ 91 Jack Sikma .15 .06
❑ 92 Steve Johnson .15 .06
❑ 93 Rick Mahorn .15 .06
❑ 94 David Rivers .15 .06
❑ 95 Joe Barry Carroll .15 .06
❑ 96 Lester Conner UER .15 .06
(Garden State in stats, should be Golden State)
❑ 97 Roy Hinson .15 .06
❑ 98 Mike McGee .15 .06
❑ 99 Chris Morris RC .25 .10
❑ 100 Patrick Ewing .75 .30
❑ 101 Mark Jackson .25 .10
❑ 102 Johnny Newman RC .15 .06
❑ 103 Charles Oakley .25 .10
❑ 104 Rod Strickland RC 2.50 1.00
❑ 105 Trent Tucker .15 .06
❑ 106 Kiki Vandeweghe .15 .06
❑ 107A Gerald Wilkins .15 .06
(U. of Tennessee)
❑ 107B Gerald Wilkins .15 .06
(U. of Tenn.)
❑ 108 Terry Catledge .15 .06
❑ 109 Dave Corzine .15 .06
❑ 110 Scott Skiles RC .25 .10
❑ 111 Reggie Theus .25 .10
❑ 112 Ron Anderson RC** .15 .06
❑ 113 Charles Barkley 1.25 .50
❑ 114 Scott Brooks RC .15 .06
❑ 115 Maurice Cheeks .15 .06
❑ 116 Mike Gminski .15 .06
❑ 117 Hersey Hawkins RC UER 1.00 .40
(Born 9/29/65, should be 9/9/65)
❑ 118 Christian Welp .15 .06
❑ 119 Tom Chambers .15 .06
❑ 120 Armon Gilliam .15 .06
❑ 121 Jeff Hornacek RC 1.00 .40
❑ 122 Eddie Johnson .25 .10
❑ 123 Kevin Johnson RC 1.50 .60
❑ 124 Dan Majerle RC 1.00 .40
❑ 125 Mark West .15 .06
❑ 126 Richard Anderson .15 .06
❑ 127 Mark Bryant RC .15 .06
❑ 128 Clyde Drexler .75 .30
❑ 129 Kevin Duckworth .15 .06
❑ 130 Jerome Kersey .15 .06
❑ 131 Terry Porter .15 .06
❑ 132 Buck Williams .25 .10
❑ 133 Danny Ainge .25 .10
❑ 134 Ricky Berry .15 .06
❑ 135 Rodney McCray .15 .06
❑ 136 Jim Petersen .15 .06
❑ 137 Harold Pressley .15 .06
❑ 138 Kenny Smith .15 .06
❑ 139 Wayman Tisdale .15 .06
❑ 140 Willie Anderson RC .15 .06
❑ 141 Frank Brickowski .15 .06
❑ 142 Terry Cummings .25 .10
❑ 143 Johnny Dawkins .15 .06
❑ 144 Vernon Maxwell RC .75 .30
❑ 145 Michael Cage .15 .06
❑ 146 Dale Ellis .25 .10
❑ 147 Alton Lister .15 .06
❑ 148 Xavier McDaniel UER .15 .06
(All-Rookie team in 1985, not 1988)
❑ 149 Derrick McKey .15 .06
❑ 150 Nate McMillan .25 .10
❑ 151 Thurl Bailey .15 .06
❑ 152 Mark Eaton .15 .06
❑ 153 Darrell Griffith .15 .06
❑ 154 Eric Leckner .15 .06
❑ 155 Karl Malone 1.25 .50
❑ 156 John Stockton 2.00 .80
❑ 157 Mark Alarie .15 .06
❑ 158 Ledell Eackles RC .15 .06
❑ 159 Bernard King .15 .06
❑ 160 Jeff Malone .15 .06
❑ 161 Darrell Walker .15 .06
❑ 162A John Williams ERR - -
❑ 162B John Williams COR .15 .06
❑ 163 Karl Malone AS .50 .20
John Stockton
Mark Eaton
❑ 164 Hakeem Olajuwon AS .50 .20
Clyde Drexler AS
❑ 165 Dominique Wilkins AS .50 .20
Moses Malone AS
❑ 166 Brad Daugherty AS .15 .06
Mark Price AS
Larry Nance AS UER
Bio says Nance had 204 blocks, should be 206)
❑ 167 Patrick Ewing AS .50 .20
Mark Jackson AS
❑ 168 Checklist 1-168 .15 .06

1990-91 Fleer

	Nm-Mt	Ex-Mt
COMPLETE SET (198)	6.00	1.80

❑ 1 John Battle UER .05 .02
(Drafted in '84, should be '85)
❑ 2 Cliff Levingston .05 .02
❑ 3 Moses Malone .15 .04
❑ 4 Kenny Smith .05 .02
❑ 5 Spud Webb .08 .02
❑ 6 Dominique Wilkins .15 .04
❑ 7 Kevin Willis .08 .02
❑ 8 Larry Bird .60 .18
❑ 9 Dennis Johnson .05 .02
❑ 10 Joe Kleine .05 .02
❑ 11 Reggie Lewis .08 .02
❑ 12 Kevin McHale .08 .02
❑ 13 Robert Parish .08 .02
❑ 14 Jim Paxson .08 .02
❑ 15 Ed Pinckney .05 .02
❑ 16 Muggsy Bogues .08 .02
❑ 17 Rex Chapman .15 .04
❑ 18 Dell Curry .05 .02
❑ 19 Armon Gilliam .05 .02
❑ 20 J.R. Reid RC .05 .02
❑ 21 Kelly Tripucka .05 .02
❑ 22 B.J. Armstrong RC .05 .02
❑ 23A Bill Cartwright ERR - -
(No decimal points in FGP and FTP)
❑ 23B Bill Cartwright COR .05 .02
❑ 24 Horace Grant .08 .02
❑ 25 Craig Hodges .05 .02

❑ 26 Michael Jordan UER 4.00 1.20
(Led NBA in scoring 4 years, not 3)
❑ 27 Stacey King RC UER ...... .05 .02
(Comma missing between progressed and Stacy)
❑ 28 John Paxson .... .08 .02
❑ 29 Will Perdue................. .05 .02
❑ 30 Scottie Pippen UER .... .60 .18
(Born AR, not AK)
❑ 31 Brad Daugherty .... .05 .02
❑ 32 Craig Ehlo .... .05 .02
❑ 33 Danny Ferry RC............. .08 .02
❑ 34 Steve Kerr .... .15 .04
❑ 35 Larry Nance .... .05 .02
❑ 36 Mark Price UER .... .08 .02
(Drafted by Cleveland, should be Dallas)
❑ 37 Hot Rod Williams .... .05 .02
❑ 38 Rolando Blackman .... .05 .02
❑ 39A Adrian Dantley ERR .... - -
(No decimal points in FGP and FTP)
❑ 39B Adrian Dantley COR .... .05 .02
❑ 40 Brad Davis .... .05 .02
❑ 41 James Donaldson UER .. .05 .02
(Text says in committed,& should be is committed)
❑ 42 Derek Harper .... .08 .02
❑ 43 Sam Perkins UER .... .08 .02
(First line of text should be intact)
❑ 44 Bill Wennington .... .05 .02
❑ 45 Herb Williams.............. .05 .02
❑ 46 Michael Adams.............. .05 .02
❑ 47 Walter Davis............... .05 .02
❑ 48 Alex English UER........... .05 .02
(Stats missing from '76-77 through '79-80)
❑ 49 Bill Hanzlik .... .05 .02
❑ 50 Lafayette Lever UER ...... .05 .02
(Born AR, not AK)
❑ 51 Todd Lichti RC .... .05 .02
❑ 52 Blair Rasmussen .... .05 .02
❑ 53 Danny Schayes .... .05 .02
❑ 54 Mark Aguirre................ .05 .02
❑ 55 Joe Dumars .... .15 .04
❑ 56 James Edwards .... .05 .02
❑ 57 Vinnie Johnson.............. .05 .02
❑ 58 Bill Laimbeer .... .08 .02
❑ 59 Dennis Rodman UER...... .40 .12
(College misspelled as coilege on back)
❑ 60 John Salley.................. .05 .02
❑ 61 Isiah Thomas .... .15 .04
❑ 62 Manute Bol.................. .05 .02
❑ 63 Tim Hardaway RC .... 1.00 .30
❑ 64 Rod Higgins .... .05 .02
❑ 65 Sarunas Marciulionis RC .05 .02
❑ 66 Chris Mullin .... .15 .04
❑ 67 Mitch Richmond .... .20 .06
❑ 68 Terry Teagle................ .05 .02
❑ 69 Anthony Bowie RC UER .05 .02
(Seasons, not seeasons)
❑ 70 Sleepy Floyd .... .05 .02
❑ 71 Buck Johnson............... .05 .02
❑ 72 Vernon Maxwell .... .05 .02
❑ 73 Hakeem Olajuwon .... .25 .07
❑ 74 Otis Thorpe .... .08 .02
❑ 75 Mitchell Wiggins............ .05 .02
❑ 76 Vern Fleming .... .05 .02
❑ 77 George McCloud RC ...... .15 .04
❑ 78 Reggie Miller .... .20 .06
❑ 79 Chuck Person............... .08 .02
❑ 80 Mike Sanders............... .05 .02
❑ 81 Detlef Schrempf............ .08 .02
❑ 82 Rik Smits .... .15 .04
❑ 83 LaSalle Thompson......... .05 .02
❑ 84 Benoit Benjamin............ .05 .02
❑ 85 Winston Garland .... .05 .02
❑ 86 Ron Harper.................. .08 .02
❑ 87 Danny Manning .... .08 .02
❑ 88 Ken Norman .... .05 .02
❑ 89 Charles Smith............... .05 .02
❑ 90 Michael Cooper .... .05 .02
❑ 91 Vlade Divac RC .... .40 .12
❑ 92 A.C. Green .... .08 .02
❑ 93 Magic Johnson.............. .50 .15
❑ 94 Byron Scott.................. .08 .02
❑ 95 Mychal Thompson UER .. .05 .02
(Missing '78-79 stats from Portland)
❑ 96 Orlando Woolridge .... .05 .02
❑ 97 James Worthy .... .15 .04
❑ 98 Sherman Douglas RC .... .08 .02
❑ 99 Kevin Edwards.............. .05 .02
❑ 100 Grant Long .... .05 .02
❑ 101 Glen Rice RC .... .60 .18
❑ 102 Rony Seikaly UER .... .08 .02
(Ron on front)
❑ 103 Billy Thompson............. .05 .02
❑ 104 Jeff Grayer RC .... .05 .02
❑ 105 Jay Humphries .... .05 .02
❑ 106 Ricky Pierce .... .05 .02
❑ 107 Paul Pressey .... .05 .02
❑ 108 Fred Roberts .... .05 .02
❑ 109 Alvin Robertson .... .05 .02
❑ 110 Jack Sikma................. .05 .02
❑ 111 Randy Breuer.............. .05 .02
❑ 112 Tony Campbell .... .05 .02
❑ 113 Tyrone Corbin .... .05 .02
❑ 114 Sam Mitchell RC UER .. .05 .02
(Mercer University, not Mercer College)
❑ 115 Tod Murphy UER .... .05 .02
(Born Long Beach, not Lakewood)
❑ 116 Pooh Richardson RC ..... .08 .02
❑ 117 Mookie Blaylock RC ...... .25 .07
❑ 118 Sam Bowie .... .05 .02
❑ 119 Lester Conner .... .05 .02
❑ 120 Dennis Hopson............. .05 .02
❑ 121 Chris Morris .... .08 .02
❑ 122 Charles Shackleford...... .05 .02
❑ 123 Purvis Short .... .05 .02
❑ 124 Maurice Cheeks .... .05 .02
❑ 125 Patrick Ewing .... .15 .04
❑ 126 Mark Jackson.............. .08 .02
❑ 127A Johnny Newman ERR .40 .12
(Jr. misprinted as J. on card back)
❑ 127B Johnny Newman COR .05 .02
❑ 128 Charles Oakley............. .08 .02
❑ 129 Trent Tucker............... .05 .02
❑ 130 Kenny Walker.............. .05 .02
❑ 131 Gerald Wilkins .... .05 .02
❑ 132 Nick Anderson RC .... .25 .07
❑ 133 Terry Catledge .... .05 .02
❑ 134 Sidney Green .... .05 .02
❑ 135 Otis Smith.................. .05 .02
❑ 136 Reggie Theus.............. .08 .02
❑ 137 Sam Vincent............... .05 .02
❑ 138 Ron Anderson .... .05 .02
❑ 139 Charles Barkley UER .... .25 .07
(FG Percentage .545.)
❑ 140 Scott Brooks UER .... .05 .02
('89-89 Philadelphia in wrong typeface)
❑ 141 Johnny Dawkins........... .05 .02
❑ 142 Mike Gminski .... .05 .02
❑ 143 Hersey Hawkins .... .08 .02
❑ 144 Rick Mahorn .... .05 .02
❑ 145 Derek Smith .... .05 .02
❑ 146 Tom Chambers .... .05 .02
❑ 147 Jeff Hornacek.............. .08 .02
❑ 148 Eddie Johnson .... .08 .02
❑ 149 Kevin Johnson .... .15 .04
❑ 150A Dan Majerle ERR........ .75 .23
(Award in 1988; three-time selection)
❑ 150B Dan Majerle COR ...... .15 .04
(Award in 1989; three-time selection)
❑ 151 Tim Perry .... .05 .02
❑ 152 Kurt Rambis .... .05 .02
❑ 153 Mark West .... .05 .02
❑ 154 Clyde Drexler .... .15 .04
❑ 155 Kevin Duckworth .... .05 .02
❑ 156 Byron Irvin .... .05 .02
❑ 157 Jerome Kersey .... .05 .02
❑ 158 Terry Porter .... .05 .02
❑ 159 Clifford Robinson RC .... .25 .07
❑ 160 Buck Williams.............. .05 .02
❑ 161 Danny Young .... .05 .02
❑ 162 Danny Ainge............... .08 .02
❑ 163 Antoine Carr .... .05 .02
❑ 164 Pervis Ellison RC .... .08 .02
❑ 165 Rodney McCray .... .05 .02
❑ 166 Harold Pressley .... .05 .02
❑ 167 Wayman Tisdale .... .05 .02
❑ 168 Willie Anderson .... .05 .02
❑ 169 Frank Brickowski .... .05 .02
❑ 170 Terry Cummings........... .05 .02
❑ 171 Sean Elliott RC............ .30 .09
❑ 172 David Robinson .... .50 .15
❑ 173 Rod Strickland .... .15 .04
❑ 174 David Wingate .... .05 .02
❑ 175 Dana Barros RC........... .15 .04
❑ 176 Michael Cage UER........ .05 .02
(Born AR, not AK)
❑ 177 Dale Ellis .... .08 .02
❑ 178 Shawn Kemp RC .... 1.50 .45
❑ 179 Xavier McDaniel .... .05 .02
❑ 180 Derrick McKey .... .05 .02
❑ 181 Nate McMillan .... .08 .02
❑ 182 Thurl Bailey .... .05 .02
❑ 183 Mike Brown .... .05 .02
❑ 184 Mark Eaton................. .05 .02
❑ 185 Blue Edwards RC......... .05 .02
❑ 186 Bobby Hansen .... .05 .02
❑ 187 Eric Leckner .... .05 .02
❑ 188 Karl Malone .... .25 .07
❑ 189 John Stockton .... .20 .06
❑ 190 Mark Alarie................. .05 .02
❑ 191 Ledell Eackles .... .05 .02
❑ 192A Harvey Grant .... .75 .23
(First name on card front in black)
❑ 192B Harvey Grant .... .05 .02
(First name on card front in white)
❑ 193 Tom Hammonds RC .... .05 .02
❑ 194 Bernard King .... .05 .02
❑ 195 Jeff Malone................. .05 .02
❑ 196 Darrell Walker .... .05 .02
❑ 197 Checklist 1-99 .... .05 .02
❑ 198 Checklist 100-198 .... .05 .02

1990-91 Fleer Update

	Nm-Mt	Ex-Mt
COM. FACT SET (100)	8.00	2.40

❑ U1 Jon Koncak .... .05 .02
❑ U2 Tim McCormick .... .05 .02
❑ U3 Doc Rivers.................. .15 .04
❑ U4 Rumeal Robinson RC .... .05 .02
❑ U5 Trevor Wilson .... .05 .02
❑ U6 Dee Brown RC............. .30 .09
❑ U7 Dave Popson............... .05 .02
❑ U8 Kevin Gamble .... .05 .02
❑ U9 Brian Shaw .... .30 .09
❑ U10 Michael Smith .... .05 .02
❑ U11 Kendall Gill RC .... .60 .18
❑ U12 Johnny Newman .... .05 .02
❑ U13 Steve Scheffler RC ...... .05 .02
❑ U14 Dennis Hopson .... .05 .02
❑ U15 Cliff Levingston .... .05 .02
❑ U16 Chucky Brown RC........ .05 .02
❑ U17 John Morton................ .05 .02
❑ U18 Gerald Paddio RC .... .05 .02
❑ U19 Alex English................ .05 .02

❑ U20 Fat Lever	.05	.02
❑ U21 Rodney McCray	.05	.02
❑ U22 Roy Tarpley	.05	.02
❑ U23 Randy White RC	.05	.02
❑ U24 Anthony Cook RC	.05	.02
❑ U25 Chris Jackson RC	.30	.09
❑ U26 Marcus Liberty RC	.05	.02
❑ U27 Orlando Woolridge	.05	.02
❑ U28 William Bedford RC	.05	.02
❑ U29 Lance Blanks RC	.05	.02
❑ U30 Scott Hastings	.05	.02
❑ U31 Tyrone Hill RC	.15	.04
❑ U32 Les Jepsen	.05	.02
❑ U33 Steve Johnson	.05	.02
❑ U34 Kevin Pritchard	.05	.02
❑ U35 Dave Jamerson RC	.05	.02
❑ U36 Kenny Smith	.05	.02
❑ U37 Greg Dreiling RC	.05	.02
❑ U38 Kenny Williams RC	.05	.02
❑ U39 Micheal Williams UER	.15	.04
❑ U40 Gary Grant	.05	.02
❑ U41 Bo Kimble RC	.05	.02
❑ U42 Loy Vaught RC	.50	.15
❑ U43 Elden Campbell RC	.60	.18
❑ U44 Sam Perkins	.15	.04
❑ U45 Tony Smith RC	.05	.02
❑ U46 Terry Teagle	.05	.02
❑ U47 Willie Burton RC	.05	.02
❑ U48 Bimbo Coles RC	.30	.09
❑ U49 Terry Davis RC	.05	.02
❑ U50 Alec Kessler RC	.05	.02
❑ U51 Greg Anderson	.05	.02
❑ U52 Frank Brickowski	.05	.02
❑ U53 Steve Henson RC	.05	.02
❑ U54 Brad Lohaus	.05	.02
❑ U55 Danny Schayes	.05	.02
❑ U56 Gerald Glass RC	.05	.02
❑ U57 Felton Spencer RC	.15	.04
❑ U58 Doug West RC	.15	.04
❑ U59 Jud Buechler RC	.15	.04
❑ U60 Derrick Coleman RC	.60	.18
❑ U61 Tate George RC	.05	.02
❑ U62 Reggie Theus	.15	.04
❑ U63 Greg Grant RC	.05	.02
❑ U64 Jerrod Mustaf RC	.05	.02
❑ U65 Eddie Lee Wilkins RC**	.05	.02
❑ U66 Michael Ansley	.05	.02
❑ U67 Jerry Reynolds	.05	.02
❑ U68 Dennis Scott RC	.40	.12
❑ U69 Manute Bol	.05	.02
❑ U70 Armon Gilliam	.05	.02
❑ U71 Brian Oliver	.05	.02
❑ U72 Kenny Payne RC	.05	.02
❑ U73 Jayson Williams RC	1.00	.30
❑ U74 Kenny Battle RC	.05	.02
❑ U75 Cedric Ceballos RC	.50	.15
❑ U76 Negele Knight RC	.05	.02
❑ U77 Xavier McDaniel	.05	.02
❑ U78 Alaa Abdelnaby RC	.05	.02
❑ U79 Danny Ainge	.15	.04
❑ U80 Mark Bryant	.05	.02
❑ U81 Drazen Petrovic RC	.15	.04
❑ U82 Anthony Bonner RC	.05	.02
❑ U83 Duane Causwell RC	.05	.02
❑ U84 Bobby Hansen	.05	.02
❑ U85 Eric Leckner	.05	.02
❑ U86 Travis Mays RC	.05	.02
❑ U87 Lionel Simmons RC	.15	.04
❑ U88 Sidney Green	.05	.02
❑ U89 Tony Massenburg	.05	.02
❑ U90 Paul Pressey	.05	.02
❑ U91 Dwayne Schintzius RC	.05	.02
❑ U92 Gary Payton RC	6.00	1.80
❑ U93 Olden Polynice	.05	.02
❑ U94 Jeff Malone	.05	.02
❑ U95 Walter Palmer	.05	.02
❑ U96 Delaney Rudd	.05	.02
❑ U97 Pervis Ellison	.15	.04
❑ U98 A.J. English RC	.05	.02
❑ U99 Greg Foster RC	.15	.04
❑ U100 Checklist 1-100	.05	.02

1991-92 Fleer

	Nm-Mt	Ex-Mt
COMPLETE SET (400)	10.00	3.00
COMPLETE SERIES 1 (240)	5.00	1.50
COMPLETE SERIES 2 (160)	5.00	1.50

❑ 1 John Battle	.05	.02
❑ 2 Jon Koncak	.05	.02
❑ 3 Rumeal Robinson	.05	.02
❑ 4 Spud Webb	.08	.02
❑ 5 Bob Weiss CO	.05	.02
❑ 6 Dominique Wilkins	.15	.04
❑ 7 Kevin Willis	.05	.02
❑ 8 Larry Bird	.60	.18
❑ 9 Dee Brown	.05	.02
❑ 10 Chris Ford CO	.05	.02
❑ 11 Kevin Gamble	.05	.02
❑ 12 Reggie Lewis	.08	.02
❑ 13 Kevin McHale	.08	.02
❑ 14 Robert Parish	.08	.02
❑ 15 Ed Pinckney	.05	.02
❑ 16 Brian Shaw	.05	.02
❑ 17 Muggsy Bogues	.08	.02
❑ 18 Rex Chapman	.08	.02
❑ 19 Dell Curry	.05	.02
❑ 20 Kendall Gill	.08	.02
❑ 21 Eric Leckner	.05	.02
❑ 22 Gene Littles CO	.05	.02
❑ 23 Johnny Newman	.05	.02
❑ 24 J.R. Reid	.05	.02
❑ 25 B.J. Armstrong	.05	.02
❑ 26 Bill Cartwright	.05	.02
❑ 27 Horace Grant	.08	.02
❑ 28 Phil Jackson CO	.08	.02
❑ 29 Michael Jordan	2.00	.60
❑ 30 Cliff Levingston	.05	.02
❑ 31 John Paxson	.05	.02
❑ 32 Will Perdue	.05	.02
❑ 33 Scottie Pippen	.50	.15
❑ 34 Brad Daugherty	.05	.02
❑ 35 Craig Ehlo	.05	.02
❑ 36 Danny Ferry	.05	.02
❑ 37 Larry Nance	.08	.02
❑ 38 Mark Price	.05	.02
❑ 39 Darnell Valentine	.05	.02
❑ 40 Hot Rod Williams	.05	.02
❑ 41 Lenny Wilkens CO	.08	.02
❑ 42 Richie Adubato CO	.05	.02
❑ 43 Rolando Blackman	.05	.02
❑ 44 James Donaldson	.05	.02
❑ 45 Derek Harper	.08	.02
❑ 46 Rodney McCray	.05	.02
❑ 47 Randy White	.05	.02
❑ 48 Herb Williams	.05	.02
❑ 49 Chris Jackson	.05	.02
❑ 50 Marcus Liberty	.05	.02
❑ 51 Todd Lichti	.05	.02
❑ 52 Blair Rasmussen	.05	.02
❑ 53 Paul Westhead CO	.05	.02
❑ 54 Reggie Williams	.05	.02
❑ 55 Joe Wolf	.05	.02
❑ 56 Orlando Woolridge	.05	.02
❑ 57 Mark Aguirre	.05	.02
❑ 58 Chuck Daly CO	.08	.02
❑ 59 Joe Dumars	.15	.04
❑ 60 James Edwards	.05	.02
❑ 61 Vinnie Johnson	.05	.02
❑ 62 Bill Laimbeer	.08	.02
❑ 63 Dennis Rodman	.30	.09
❑ 64 Isiah Thomas	.15	.04
❑ 65 Tim Hardaway	.25	.07
❑ 66 Rod Higgins	.05	.02
❑ 67 Tyrone Hill	.08	.02
❑ 68 Sarunas Marciulionis	.05	.02
❑ 69 Chris Mullin	.15	.04
❑ 70 Don Nelson CO	.08	.02
❑ 71 Mitch Richmond	.15	.04
❑ 72 Tom Tolbert	.05	.02
❑ 73 Don Chaney CO	.05	.02
❑ 74 Eric(Sleepy) Floyd	.05	.02
❑ 75 Buck Johnson	.05	.02
❑ 76 Vernon Maxwell	.05	.02
❑ 77 Hakeem Olajuwon	.25	.07
❑ 78 Kenny Smith	.05	.02
❑ 79 Larry Smith	.05	.02
❑ 80 Otis Thorpe	.08	.02
❑ 81 Vern Fleming	.05	.02
❑ 82 Bob Hill CO RC	.05	.02
❑ 83 Reggie Miller	.15	.04
❑ 84 Chuck Person	.05	.02
❑ 85 Detlef Schrempf	.08	.02
❑ 86 Rik Smits	.08	.02
❑ 87 LaSalle Thompson	.05	.02
❑ 88 Micheal Williams	.05	.02
❑ 89 Gary Grant	.05	.02
❑ 90 Ron Harper	.08	.02
❑ 91 Bo Kimble	.05	.02
❑ 92 Danny Manning	.08	.02
❑ 93 Ken Norman	.05	.02
❑ 94 Olden Polynice	.05	.02
❑ 95 Mike Schuler CO	.05	.02
❑ 96 Charles Smith	.05	.02
❑ 97 Vlade Divac	.08	.02
❑ 98 Mike Dunleavy CO	.05	.02
❑ 99 A.C. Green	.08	.02
❑ 100 Magic Johnson	.50	.15
❑ 101 Sam Perkins	.08	.02
❑ 102 Byron Scott	.08	.02
❑ 103 Terry Teagle	.05	.02
❑ 104 James Worthy	.15	.04
❑ 105 Willie Burton	.05	.02
❑ 106 Bimbo Coles	.05	.02
❑ 107 Sherman Douglas	.05	.02
❑ 108 Kevin Edwards	.05	.02
❑ 109 Grant Long	.05	.02
❑ 110 Kevin Loughery CO	.05	.02
❑ 111 Glen Rice	.15	.04
❑ 112 Rony Seikaly	.05	.02
❑ 113 Frank Brickowski	.05	.02
❑ 114 Dale Ellis	.08	.02
❑ 115 Del Harris CO	.05	.02
❑ 116 Jay Humphries	.05	.02
❑ 117 Fred Roberts	.05	.02
❑ 118 Alvin Robertson	.05	.02
❑ 119 Danny Schayes	.05	.02
❑ 120 Jack Sikma	.05	.02
❑ 121 Tony Campbell	.05	.02
❑ 122 Tyrone Corbin	.05	.02
❑ 123 Sam Mitchell	.05	.02
❑ 124 Tod Murphy	.05	.02
❑ 125 Pooh Richardson	.05	.02
❑ 126 Jimmy Rodgers CO	.05	.02
❑ 127 Felton Spencer	.05	.02
❑ 128 Mookie Blaylock	.08	.02
❑ 129 Sam Bowie	.05	.02
❑ 130 Derrick Coleman	.08	.02
❑ 131 Chris Dudley	.05	.02
❑ 132 Bill Fitch CO	.05	.02
❑ 133 Chris Morris	.05	.02
❑ 134 Drazen Petrovic	.08	.02
❑ 135 Maurice Cheeks	.05	.02
❑ 136 Patrick Ewing	.15	.04
❑ 137 Mark Jackson	.08	.02
❑ 138 Charles Oakley	.08	.02
❑ 139 Pat Riley CO	.08	.02
❑ 140 Trent Tucker	.05	.02
❑ 141 Kiki Vandeweghe	.05	.02
❑ 142 Gerald Wilkins	.05	.02
❑ 143 Nick Anderson	.08	.02
❑ 144 Terry Catledge	.05	.02
❑ 145 Matt Guokas CO	.05	.02
❑ 146 Jerry Reynolds	.05	.02
❑ 147 Dennis Scott	.08	.02
❑ 148 Scott Skiles	.05	.02
❑ 149 Otis Smith	.05	.02
❑ 150 Ron Anderson	.05	.02
❑ 151 Charles Barkley	.25	.07
❑ 152 Johnny Dawkins	.05	.02
❑ 153 Armon Gilliam	.05	.02

- ❑ 154 Hersey Hawkins .08 .02
- ❑ 155 Jim Lynam CO .05 .02
- ❑ 156 Rick Mahorn .05 .02
- ❑ 157 Brian Oliver .05 .02
- ❑ 158 Tom Chambers .05 .02
- ❑ 159 Cotton Fitzsimmons CO .05 .02
- ❑ 160 Jeff Hornacek .08 .02
- ❑ 161 Kevin Johnson .15 .04
- ❑ 162 Negele Knight .05 .02
- ❑ 163 Dan Majerle .08 .02
- ❑ 164 Xavier McDaniel .05 .02
- ❑ 165 Mark West .05 .02
- ❑ 166 Rick Adelman CO .05 .02
- ❑ 167 Danny Ainge .08 .02
- ❑ 168 Clyde Drexler .15 .04
- ❑ 169 Kevin Duckworth .05 .02
- ❑ 170 Jerome Kersey .05 .02
- ❑ 171 Terry Porter .05 .02
- ❑ 172 Clifford Robinson .08 .02
- ❑ 173 Buck Williams .05 .02
- ❑ 174 Antoine Carr .05 .02
- ❑ 175 Duane Causwell .05 .02
- ❑ 176 Jim Les RC .05 .02
- ❑ 177 Travis Mays .05 .02
- ❑ 178 Dick Motta CO .05 .02
- ❑ 179 Lionel Simmons .05 .02
- ❑ 180 Rory Sparrow .05 .02
- ❑ 181 Wayman Tisdale .05 .02
- ❑ 182 Willie Anderson .05 .02
- ❑ 183 Larry Brown CO .05 .02
- ❑ 184 Terry Cummings .05 .02
- ❑ 185 Sean Elliott .08 .02
- ❑ 186 Paul Pressey .05 .02
- ❑ 187 David Robinson .30 .09
- ❑ 188 Rod Strickland .15 .04
- ❑ 189 Benoit Benjamin .05 .02
- ❑ 190 Eddie Johnson .08 .02
- ❑ 191 K.C. Jones CO .08 .02
- ❑ 192 Shawn Kemp .40 .12
- ❑ 193 Derrick McKey .05 .02
- ❑ 194 Gary Payton .40 .12
- ❑ 195 Ricky Pierce .05 .02
- ❑ 196 Sedale Threatt .05 .02
- ❑ 197 Thurl Bailey .05 .02
- ❑ 198 Mark Eaton .05 .02
- ❑ 199 Blue Edwards .05 .02
- ❑ 200 Jeff Malone .05 .02
- ❑ 201 Karl Malone .25 .07
- ❑ 202 Jerry Sloan CO .08 .02
- ❑ 203 John Stockton .15 .04
- ❑ 204 Ledell Eackles .05 .02
- ❑ 205 Pervis Ellison .05 .02
- ❑ 206 A.J. English .05 .02
- ❑ 207 Harvey Grant .05 .02
- ❑ 208 Bernard King .05 .02
- ❑ 209 Wes Unseld CO .08 .02
- ❑ 210 Kevin Johnson AS .08 .02
- ❑ 211 Michael Jordan AS 1.00 .30
- ❑ 212 Dominique Wilkins AS .08 .02
- ❑ 213 Charles Barkley AS .15 .04
- ❑ 214 Hakeem Olajuwon AS .15 .04
- ❑ 215 Patrick Ewing AS .08 .02
- ❑ 216 Tim Hardaway AS .15 .04
- ❑ 217 John Stockton AS .08 .02
- ❑ 218 Chris Mullin AS .08 .02
- ❑ 219 Karl Malone AS .15 .04
- ❑ 220 Michael Jordan LL 1.00 .30
- ❑ 221 John Stockton LL .08 .02
- ❑ 222 Alvin Robertson LL .05 .02
- ❑ 223 Hakeem Olajuwon LL .15 .04
- ❑ 224 Buck Williams LL .05 .02
- ❑ 225 David Robinson LL .15 .04
- ❑ 226 Reggie Miller LL .08 .02
- ❑ 227 Blue Edwards SD .05 .02
- ❑ 228 Dee Brown SD .05 .02
- ❑ 229 Rex Chapman SD .05 .02
- ❑ 230 Kenny Smith SD .05 .02
- ❑ 231 Shawn Kemp SD .15 .04
- ❑ 232 Kendall Gill SD .05 .02
- ❑ 233 '91 All Star Game .50 .15
  Enemies - A Love Story
  (East Bench Scene)
- ❑ 234 Clyde Drexler ASG .15 .04
  Kevin McHale ASG
- ❑ 235 Alvin Robertson ASG .05 .02
- ❑ 236 Patrick Ewing ASG .08 .02
  Karl Malone ASG
- ❑ 237 Michael Jordan .25 .07
  Magic Johnson
  David Robinson
  Patrick Ewing
- ❑ 238 Michael Jordan ASG .50 .15
- ❑ 239 Checklist 1-120 .05 .02
- ❑ 240 Checklist 121-240 .05 .02
- ❑ 241 Stacey Augmon RC .15 .04
- ❑ 242 Maurice Cheeks .05 .02
- ❑ 243 Paul Graham RC .05 .02
- ❑ 244 Rodney Monroe RC .05 .02
- ❑ 245 Blair Rasmussen .05 .02
- ❑ 246 Alexander Volkov .05 .02
- ❑ 247 John Bagley .05 .02
- ❑ 248 Rick Fox RC .15 .04
- ❑ 249 Rickey Green .05 .02
- ❑ 250 Joe Kleine .05 .02
- ❑ 251 Stojko Vrankovic .05 .02
- ❑ 252 Allan Bristow CO .05 .02
- ❑ 253 Kenny Gattison .05 .02
- ❑ 254 Mike Gminski .05 .02
- ❑ 255 Larry Johnson RC .60 .18
- ❑ 256 Bobby Hansen .05 .02
- ❑ 257 Craig Hodges .05 .02
- ❑ 258 Stacey King .05 .02
- ❑ 259 Scott Williams RC .05 .02
- ❑ 260 John Battle .05 .02
- ❑ 261 Winston Bennett .05 .02
- ❑ 262 Terrell Brandon RC .50 .15
- ❑ 263 Henry James .05 .02
- ❑ 264 Steve Kerr .08 .02
- ❑ 265 Jimmy Oliver RC .05 .02
- ❑ 266 Brad Davis .05 .02
- ❑ 267 Terry Davis .05 .02
- ❑ 268 Donald Hodge RC .05 .02
- ❑ 269 Mike Iuzzolino RC .05 .02
- ❑ 270 Fat Lever .05 .02
- ❑ 271 Doug Smith RC .05 .02
- ❑ 272 Greg Anderson .05 .02
- ❑ 273 Kevin Brooks RC .05 .02
- ❑ 274 Walter Davis .05 .02
- ❑ 275 Winston Garland .05 .02
- ❑ 276 Mark Macon RC .05 .02
- ❑ 277 Dikembe Mutombo RC .60 .18
  (Fleer '91 on front)
- ❑ 277B Dikembe Mutombo RC .60 .18
  (Fleer '91-92 on front)
- ❑ 278 William Bedford .05 .02
- ❑ 279 Lance Blanks .05 .02
- ❑ 280 John Salley .05 .02
- ❑ 281 Charles Thomas RC .05 .02
- ❑ 282 Darrell Walker .05 .02
- ❑ 283 Orlando Woolridge .05 .02
- ❑ 284 Victor Alexander RC .05 .02
- ❑ 285 Vincent Askew RC .05 .02
- ❑ 286 Mario Elie RC .15 .04
- ❑ 287 Alton Lister .05 .02
- ❑ 288 Billy Owens RC .15 .04
- ❑ 289 Matt Bullard RC .05 .02
- ❑ 290 Carl Herrera RC .05 .02
- ❑ 291 Tree Rollins .05 .02
- ❑ 292 John Turner .05 .02
- ❑ 293 Dale Davis RC UER .15 .04
  (Photo on back act-
  ually Sean Green)
- ❑ 294 Sean Green RC .05 .02
- ❑ 295 Kenny Williams .05 .02
- ❑ 296 James Edwards .05 .02
- ❑ 297 LeRon Ellis RC .05 .02
- ❑ 298 Doc Rivers .08 .02
- ❑ 299 Loy Vaught .05 .02
- ❑ 300 Elden Campbell .08 .02
- ❑ 301 Jack Haley .05 .02
- ❑ 302 Keith Owens .05 .02
- ❑ 303 Tony Smith .05 .02
- ❑ 304 Sedale Threatt .05 .02
- ❑ 305 Keith Askins RC .05 .02
- ❑ 306 Alec Kessler .05 .02
- ❑ 307 John Morton .05 .02
- ❑ 308 Alan Ogg .05 .02
- ❑ 309 Steve Smith RC .60 .18
- ❑ 310 Lester Conner .05 .02
- ❑ 311 Jeff Grayer .05 .02
- ❑ 312 Frank Hamblen CO .05 .02
- ❑ 313 Steve Henson .05 .02
- ❑ 314 Larry Krystkowiak .05 .02
- ❑ 315 Moses Malone .15 .04
- ❑ 316 Thurl Bailey .05 .02
- ❑ 317 Randy Breuer .05 .02
- ❑ 318 Scott Brooks .05 .02
- ❑ 319 Gerald Glass .05 .02
- ❑ 320 Luc Longley RC .15 .04
- ❑ 321 Doug West .05 .02
- ❑ 322 Kenny Anderson RC .30 .09
- ❑ 323 Tate George .05 .02
- ❑ 324 Terry Mills RC .15 .04
- ❑ 325 Greg Anthony RC .15 .04
- ❑ 326 Anthony Mason RC .30 .09
- ❑ 327 Tim McCormick .05 .02
- ❑ 328 Xavier McDaniel .05 .02
- ❑ 329 Brian Quinnett .05 .02
- ❑ 330 John Starks RC .15 .04
- ❑ 331 Stanley Roberts RC .05 .02
- ❑ 332 Jeff Turner .05 .02
- ❑ 333 Sam Vincent .05 .02
- ❑ 334 Brian Williams RC .15 .04
- ❑ 335 Manute Bol .05 .02
- ❑ 336 Kenny Payne .05 .02
- ❑ 337 Charles Shackleford .05 .02
- ❑ 338 Jayson Williams .15 .04
- ❑ 339 Cedric Ceballos .08 .02
- ❑ 340 Andrew Lang .05 .02
- ❑ 341 Jerrod Mustaf .05 .02
- ❑ 342 Tim Perry .05 .02
- ❑ 343 Kurt Rambis .05 .02
- ❑ 344 Alaa Abdelnaby .05 .02
- ❑ 345 Robert Pack RC .08 .02
- ❑ 346 Danny Young .05 .02
- ❑ 347 Anthony Bonner .05 .02
- ❑ 348 Pete Chilcutt RC .05 .02
- ❑ 349 Rex Hughes CO .05 .02
- ❑ 350 Mitch Richmond .15 .04
- ❑ 351 Dwayne Schintzius .05 .02
- ❑ 352 Spud Webb .08 .02
- ❑ 353 Antoine Carr .05 .02
- ❑ 354 Sidney Green .05 .02
- ❑ 355 Vinnie Johnson .05 .02
- ❑ 356 Greg Sutton .05 .02
- ❑ 357 Dana Barros .05 .02
- ❑ 358 Michael Cage .05 .02
- ❑ 359 Marty Conlon RC .05 .02
- ❑ 360 Rich King RC .05 .02
- ❑ 361 Nate McMillan .05 .02
- ❑ 362 David Benoit RC .08 .02
- ❑ 363 Mike Brown .05 .02
- ❑ 364 Tyrone Corbin .05 .02
- ❑ 365 Eric Murdock RC .05 .02
- ❑ 366 Delaney Rudd .05 .02
- ❑ 367 Michael Adams .05 .02
- ❑ 368 Tom Hammonds .05 .02
- ❑ 369 Larry Stewart RC .05 .02
- ❑ 370 Andre Turner .05 .02
- ❑ 371 David Wingate .05 .02
- ❑ 372 Dominique Wilkins TL .08 .02
- ❑ 373 Larry Bird TL .30 .09
- ❑ 374 Rex Chapman TL .05 .02
- ❑ 375 Michael Jordan TL 1.00 .30
- ❑ 376 Brad Daugherty TL .05 .02
- ❑ 377 Derek Harper TL .05 .02
- ❑ 378 Dikembe Mutombo TL .15 .04
- ❑ 379 Joe Dumars TL .08 .02
- ❑ 380 Chris Mullin TL .08 .02
- ❑ 381 Hakeem Olajuwon TL .15 .04
- ❑ 382 Chuck Person TL .05 .02
- ❑ 383 Charles Smith TL .05 .02
- ❑ 384 James Worthy TL .08 .02
- ❑ 385 Glen Rice TL .08 .02
- ❑ 386 Alvin Robertson TL .05 .02
- ❑ 387 Tony Campbell TL .05 .02
- ❑ 388 Derrick Coleman TL .05 .02
- ❑ 389 Patrick Ewing TL .08 .02
- ❑ 390 Scott Skiles TL .05 .02
- ❑ 391 Charles Barkley TL .15 .04

❑ 392 Kevin Johnson TL .08 .02
❑ 393 Clyde Drexler TL .08 .02
❑ 394 Lionel Simmons TL .05 .02
❑ 395 David Robinson TL .15 .04
❑ 396 Ricky Pierce TL .05 .02
❑ 397 John Stockton TL .08 .02
❑ 398 Michael Adams TL .05 .02
❑ 399 Checklist .05 .02
❑ 400 Checklist .05 .02

1992-93 Fleer

	Nm-Mt	Ex-Mt
COMPLETE SET (444)	30.00	9.00
COMPLETE SERIES 1 (264)	15.00	4.50
COMPLETE SERIES 2 (180)	15.00	4.50

❑ 1 Stacey Augmon .10 .03
❑ 2 Duane Ferrell .05 .02
❑ 3 Paul Graham .05 .02
❑ 4A Jon Koncak .05 .02
(Shooting pose on back)
❑ 4B Jon Koncak .05 .02
(No ball visible in photo on back)
❑ 5 Blair Rasmussen .05 .02
❑ 6 Rumeal Robinson .05 .02
❑ 7 Bob Weiss CO .05 .02
❑ 8 Dominique Wilkins .25 .07
❑ 9 Kevin Willis .05 .02
❑ 10 John Bagley .05 .02
❑ 11 Larry Bird 1.00 .30
❑ 12 Dee Brown .05 .02
❑ 13 Chris Ford CO .05 .02
❑ 14 Rick Fox .10 .03
❑ 15 Kevin Gamble .05 .02
❑ 16 Reggie Lewis .10 .03
❑ 17 Kevin McHale .25 .07
❑ 18 Robert Parish .10 .03
❑ 19 Ed Pinckney .05 .02
❑ 20 Muggsy Bogues .10 .03
❑ 21 Allan Bristow CO .05 .02
❑ 22 Dell Curry .05 .02
❑ 23 Kenny Gattison .05 .02
❑ 24 Kendall Gill .10 .03
❑ 25 Larry Johnson .30 .09
❑ 26 Johnny Newman .05 .02
❑ 27 J.R. Reid .05 .02
❑ 28 B.J. Armstrong .05 .02
❑ 29 Bill Cartwright .05 .02
❑ 30 Horace Grant .10 .03
❑ 31 Phil Jackson CO .10 .03
❑ 32 Michael Jordan 3.00 .90
❑ 33 Stacey King .05 .02
❑ 34 Cliff Levingston .05 .02
❑ 35 John Paxson .05 .02
❑ 36 Scottie Pippen .75 .23
❑ 37 Scott Williams .05 .02
❑ 38 John Battle .05 .02
❑ 39 Terrell Brandon .25 .07
❑ 40 Brad Daugherty .05 .02
❑ 41 Craig Ehlo .05 .02
❑ 42 Larry Nance .05 .02
❑ 43 Mark Price .05 .02
❑ 44 Mike Sanders .05 .02
❑ 45 Lenny Wilkens CO .10 .03
❑ 46 John Hot Rod Williams .05 .02
❑ 47 Richie Adubato CO .05 .02
❑ 48 Terry Davis .05 .02
❑ 49 Derek Harper .10 .03
❑ 50 Donald Hodge .05 .02
❑ 51 Mike Iuzzolino .05 .02
❑ 52 Rodney McCray .05 .02
❑ 53 Doug Smith .05 .02
❑ 54 Greg Anderson .05 .02
❑ 55 Winston Garland .05 .02
❑ 56 Dan Issel CO .05 .02
❑ 57 Chris Jackson .05 .02
❑ 58 Marcus Liberty .05 .02
❑ 59 Mark Macon .05 .02
❑ 60 Dikembe Mutombo .30 .09
❑ 61 Reggie Williams .05 .02
❑ 62 Mark Aguirre .05 .02
❑ 63 Joe Dumars .25 .07
❑ 64 Bill Laimbeer .10 .03
❑ 65 Olden Polynice .05 .02
❑ 66 Dennis Rodman .50 .15
❑ 67 Ron Rothstein CO .05 .02
❑ 68 John Salley .05 .02
❑ 69 Isiah Thomas .25 .07
❑ 70 Darrell Walker .05 .02
❑ 71 Orlando Woolridge .05 .02
❑ 72 Victor Alexander .05 .02
❑ 73 Mario Elie .10 .03
❑ 74 Tim Hardaway .30 .09
❑ 75 Tyrone Hill .05 .02
❑ 76 Sarunas Marciulionis .05 .02
❑ 77 Chris Mullin .25 .07
❑ 78 Don Nelson CO .10 .03
❑ 79 Billy Owens .10 .03
❑ 80 Sleepy Floyd UER .05 .02
(Went past 4000 assist mark& not 2000)
❑ 81 Avery Johnson .05 .02
❑ 82 Buck Johnson .05 .02
❑ 83 Vernon Maxwell .05 .02
❑ 84 Hakeem Olajuwon .40 .12
❑ 85 Kenny Smith .05 .02
❑ 86 Otis Thorpe .10 .03
❑ 87 Rudy Tomjanovich CO .10 .03
❑ 88 Dale Davis .05 .02
❑ 89 Vern Fleming .05 .02
❑ 90 Bob Hill CO .05 .02
❑ 91 Reggie Miller .25 .07
❑ 92 Chuck Person .05 .02
❑ 93 Detlef Schrempf .10 .03
❑ 94 Rik Smits .10 .03
❑ 95 LaSalle Thompson .05 .02
❑ 96 Micheal Williams .05 .02
❑ 97 Larry Brown CO .10 .03
❑ 98 James Edwards .05 .02
❑ 99 Gary Grant .05 .02
❑ 100 Ron Harper .10 .03
❑ 101 Danny Manning .10 .03
❑ 102 Ken Norman .05 .02
❑ 103 Doc Rivers .10 .03
❑ 104 Charles Smith .05 .02
❑ 105 Loy Vaught .05 .02
❑ 106 Elden Campbell .10 .03
❑ 107 Vlade Divac .10 .03
❑ 108 A.C. Green .10 .03
❑ 109 Sam Perkins .10 .03
❑ 110 Randy Pfund CO RC .05 .02
❑ 111 Byron Scott .10 .03
❑ 112 Terry Teagle .05 .02
❑ 113 Sedale Threatt .05 .02
❑ 114 James Worthy .25 .07
❑ 115 Willie Burton .05 .02
❑ 116 Bimbo Coles .05 .02
❑ 117 Kevin Edwards .05 .02
❑ 118 Grant Long .05 .02
❑ 119 Kevin Loughery CO .05 .02
❑ 120 Glen Rice .25 .07
❑ 121 Rony Seikaly .05 .02
❑ 122 Brian Shaw .05 .02
❑ 123 Steve Smith .30 .09
❑ 124 Frank Brickowski .05 .02
❑ 125 Mike Dunleavy CO .05 .02
❑ 126 Blue Edwards .05 .02
❑ 127 Moses Malone .25 .07
❑ 128 Eric Murdock .05 .02
❑ 129 Fred Roberts .05 .02
❑ 130 Alvin Robertson .05 .02
❑ 131 Thurl Bailey .05 .02
❑ 132 Tony Campbell .05 .02
❑ 133 Gerald Glass .05 .02
❑ 134 Luc Longley .10 .03
❑ 135 Sam Mitchell .05 .02
❑ 136 Pooh Richardson .05 .02
❑ 137 Jimmy Rodgers CO .05 .02
❑ 138 Felton Spencer .05 .02
❑ 139 Doug West .05 .02
❑ 140 Kenny Anderson .25 .07
❑ 141 Mookie Blaylock .10 .03
❑ 142 Sam Bowie .05 .02
❑ 143 Derrick Coleman .10 .03
❑ 144 Chuck Daly CO .10 .03
❑ 145 Terry Mills .05 .02
❑ 146 Chris Morris .05 .02
❑ 147 Drazen Petrovic .05 .02
❑ 148 Greg Anthony .05 .02
❑ 149 Rolando Blackman .05 .02
❑ 150 Patrick Ewing .25 .07
❑ 151 Mark Jackson .10 .03
❑ 152 Anthony Mason .25 .07
❑ 153 Xavier McDaniel .05 .02
❑ 154 Charles Oakley .10 .03
❑ 155 Pat Riley CO .10 .03
❑ 156 John Starks .10 .03
❑ 157 Gerald Wilkins .05 .02
❑ 158 Nick Anderson .10 .03
❑ 159 Anthony Bowie .05 .02
❑ 160 Terry Catledge .05 .02
❑ 161 Matt Guokas CO .05 .02
❑ 162 Stanley Roberts .05 .02
❑ 163 Dennis Scott .10 .03
❑ 164 Scott Skiles .05 .02
❑ 165 Brian Williams .05 .02
❑ 166 Ron Anderson .05 .02
❑ 167 Manute Bol .05 .02
❑ 168 Johnny Dawkins .05 .02
❑ 169 Armon Gilliam .05 .02
❑ 170 Hersey Hawkins .10 .03
❑ 171 Jeff Hornacek .10 .03
❑ 172 Andrew Lang .05 .02
❑ 173 Doug Moe CO .05 .02
❑ 174 Tim Perry .05 .02
❑ 175 Jeff Ruland .05 .02
❑ 176 Charles Shackleford .05 .02
❑ 177 Danny Ainge .10 .03
❑ 178 Charles Barkley .40 .12
❑ 179 Cedric Ceballos .10 .03
❑ 180 Tom Chambers .05 .02
❑ 181 Kevin Johnson .25 .07
❑ 182 Dan Majerle .10 .03
❑ 183 Mark West UER .05 .02
(Needs 33 blocks to reach 1000& not 31)
❑ 184 Paul Westphal CO .05 .02
❑ 185 Rick Adelman CO .05 .02
❑ 186 Clyde Drexler .25 .07
❑ 187 Kevin Duckworth .05 .02
❑ 188 Jerome Kersey .05 .02
❑ 189 Robert Pack .05 .02
❑ 190 Terry Porter .05 .02
❑ 191 Clifford Robinson .10 .03
❑ 192 Rod Strickland .25 .07
❑ 193 Buck Williams .10 .03
❑ 194 Anthony Bonner .05 .02
❑ 195 Duane Causwell .05 .02
❑ 196 Mitch Richmond .25 .07
❑ 197 Garry St. Jean CO RC .05 .02
❑ 198 Lionel Simmons .05 .02
❑ 199 Wayman Tisdale .05 .02
❑ 200 Spud Webb .10 .03
❑ 201 Willie Anderson .05 .02
❑ 202 Antoine Carr .05 .02
❑ 203 Terry Cummings .10 .03
❑ 204 Sean Elliott .10 .03
❑ 205 Dale Ellis .05 .02
❑ 206 Vinnie Johnson .05 .02
❑ 207 David Robinson .40 .12
❑ 208 Jerry Tarkanian CO RC .05 .02
❑ 209 Benoit Benjamin .05 .02
❑ 210 Michael Cage .05 .02
❑ 211 Eddie Johnson .05 .02
❑ 212 George Karl CO .10 .03
❑ 213 Shawn Kemp .50 .15
❑ 214 Derrick McKey .05 .02
❑ 215 Nate McMillan .05 .02
❑ 216 Gary Payton .50 .15

❑ 217 Ricky Pierce .05 .02
❑ 218 David Benoit .05 .02
❑ 219 Mike Brown .05 .02
❑ 220 Tyrone Corbin .05 .02
❑ 221 Mark Eaton .05 .02
❑ 222 Jay Humphries .05 .02
❑ 223 Larry Krystkowiak .05 .02
❑ 224 Jeff Malone .05 .02
❑ 225 Karl Malone .40 .12
❑ 226 Jerry Sloan CO .10 .03
❑ 227 John Stockton .25 .07
❑ 228 Michael Adams .05 .02
❑ 229 Rex Chapman .05 .02
❑ 230 Ledell Eackles .05 .02
❑ 231 Pervis Ellison .05 .02
❑ 232 A.J. English .05 .02
❑ 233 Harvey Grant .05 .02
❑ 234 LaBradford Smith .05 .02
❑ 235 Larry Stewart .05 .02
❑ 236 Wes Unseld CO .10 .03
❑ 237 David Wingate .05 .02
❑ 238 Michael Jordan LL 1.50 .45
Scoring
❑ 239 Dennis Rodman LL .25 .07
Rebounding
❑ 240 John Stockton LL .10 .03
Assists/Steals
❑ 241 Buck Williams LL .05 .02
Field Goal Percentage
❑ 242 Mark Price LL .05 .02
Free Throw Percentage
❑ 243 Dana Barros LL .05 .02
Three Point Percentage
❑ 244 David Robinson LL .25 .07
Shots Blocked
❑ 245 Chris Mullin LL .10 .03
Minutes Played
❑ 246 Michael Jordan MVP .. 1.50 .45
❑ 247 Larry Johnson ROY UER .25 .07
(Scoring average was
19.2, not 19.7)
❑ 248 David Robinson .25 .07
Defensive Player
of the Year
❑ 249 Detlef Schrempf .05 .02
Sixth Man of the Year
❑ 250 Clyde Drexler PV .10 .03
❑ 251 Tim Hardaway PV .25 .07
❑ 252 Kevin Johnson PV .10 .03
❑ 253 Larry Johnson PV UER .25 .07
(Scoring average was
19.2& not 19.7)
❑ 254 Scottie Pippen PV .40 .12
❑ 255 Isiah Thomas PV .10 .03
❑ 256 Larry Bird SY .50 .15
❑ 257 Brad Daugherty SY .05 .02
❑ 258 Kevin Johnson SY .10 .03
❑ 259 Larry Johnson SY .25 .07
❑ 260 Scottie Pippen SY .40 .12
❑ 261 Dennis Rodman SY .25 .07
❑ 262 Checklist 1 .05 .02
❑ 263 Checklist 2 .05 .02
❑ 264 Checklist 3 .05 .02
❑ 265 Charles Barkley SD .25 .07
❑ 266 Shawn Kemp SD .25 .07
❑ 267 Dan Majerle SD .05 .02
❑ 268 Karl Malone SD .25 .07
❑ 269 Buck Williams SD .05 .02
❑ 270 Clyde Drexler SD .10 .03
❑ 271 Sean Elliott SD .05 .02
❑ 272 Ron Harper SD .05 .02
❑ 273 Michael Jordan SD 1.50 .45
❑ 274 James Worthy SD .10 .03
❑ 275 Cedric Ceballos SD .05 .02
❑ 276 Larry Nance SD .05 .02
❑ 277 Kenny Walker SD .05 .02
❑ 278 Spud Webb SD .05 .02
❑ 279 Dominique Wilkins SD .. .10 .03
❑ 280 Terrell Brandon SD .10 .03
❑ 281 Dee Brown SD .05 .02
❑ 282 Kevin Johnson SD .10 .03
❑ 283 Doc Rivers SD .05 .02
❑ 284 Byron Scott SD .05 .02
❑ 285 Manute Bol SD .05 .02
❑ 286 Dikembe Mutombo SD .. .25 .07
❑ 287 Robert Parish SD .05 .02
❑ 288 David Robinson SD .25 .07
❑ 289 Dennis Rodman SD .25 .07
❑ 290 Blue Edwards SD .05 .02
❑ 291 Patrick Ewing SD .10 .03
❑ 292 Larry Johnson SD .25 .07
❑ 293 Jerome Kersey SD .05 .02
❑ 294 Hakeem Olajuwon SD .. .25 .07
❑ 295 Stacey Augmon SD .05 .02
❑ 296 Derrick Coleman SD .05 .02
❑ 297 Kendall Gill SD .05 .02
❑ 298 Shaquille O'Neal SD 3.00 .90
❑ 299 Scottie Pippen SD .40 .12
❑ 300 Darryl Dawkins SD .10 .03
❑ 301 Mookie Blaylock .10 .03
❑ 302 Adam Keefe RC .05 .02
❑ 303 Travis Mays .05 .02
❑ 304 Morlon Wiley .05 .02
❑ 305 Sherman Douglas .05 .02
❑ 306 Joe Kleine .05 .02
❑ 307 Xavier McDaniel .05 .02
❑ 308 Tony Bennett RC .05 .02
❑ 309 Tom Hammonds .05 .02
❑ 310 Kevin Lynch .05 .02
❑ 311 Alonzo Mourning RC .. 1.50 .45
❑ 312 David Wingate .05 .02
❑ 313 Rodney McCray .05 .02
❑ 314 Will Perdue .05 .02
❑ 315 Trent Tucker .05 .02
❑ 316 Corey Williams RC .05 .02
❑ 317 Danny Ferry .05 .02
❑ 318 Jay Guidinger RC .05 .02
❑ 319 Jerome Lane .05 .02
❑ 320 Gerald Wilkins .05 .02
❑ 321 Steve Bardo RC .05 .02
❑ 322 Walter Bond RC .05 .02
❑ 323 Brian Howard RC .05 .02
❑ 324 Tracy Moore RC .05 .02
❑ 325 Sean Rooks RC .05 .02
❑ 326 Randy White .05 .02
❑ 327 Kevin Brooks .05 .02
❑ 328 LaPhonso Ellis RC .25 .07
❑ 329 Scott Hastings .05 .02
❑ 330 Todd Lichti .05 .02
❑ 331 Robert Pack .05 .02
❑ 332 Bryant Stith RC .10 .03
❑ 333 Gerald Glass .05 .02
❑ 334 Terry Mills .05 .02
❑ 335 Isaiah Morris RC .05 .02
❑ 336 Mark Randall .05 .02
❑ 337 Danny Young .05 .02
❑ 338 Chris Gatling .05 .02
❑ 339 Jeff Grayer .05 .02
❑ 340 Byron Houston RC .05 .02
❑ 341 Keith Jennings RC .05 .02
❑ 342 Alton Lister .05 .02
❑ 343 Latrell Sprewell RC 2.00 .60
❑ 344 Scott Brooks .05 .02
❑ 345 Matt Bullard .05 .02
❑ 346 Carl Herrera .05 .02
❑ 347 Robert Horry RC .25 .07
❑ 348 Tree Rollins .05 .02
❑ 349 Greg Dreiling .05 .02
❑ 350 George McCloud .05 .02
❑ 351 Sam Mitchell .05 .02
❑ 352 Pooh Richardson .05 .02
❑ 353 Malik Sealy RC .10 .03
❑ 354 Kenny Williams .05 .02
❑ 355 Jaren Jackson RC .10 .03
❑ 356 Mark Jackson .10 .03
❑ 357 Stanley Roberts .05 .02
❑ 358 Elmore Spencer RC .05 .02
❑ 359 Kiki Vandeweghe .05 .02
❑ 360 John S. Williams .05 .02
❑ 361 Randy Woods RC .05 .02
❑ 362 Duane Cooper RC .05 .02
❑ 363 James Edwards .05 .02
❑ 364 Anthony Peeler RC .10 .03
❑ 365 Tony Smith .05 .02
❑ 366 Keith Askins .05 .02
❑ 367 Matt Geiger RC .10 .03
❑ 368 Alec Kessler .05 .02
❑ 369 Harold Miner RC .10 .03
❑ 370 John Salley .05 .02
❑ 371 Anthony Avent RC .05 .02
❑ 372 Todd Day RC .10 .03
❑ 373 Blue Edwards .05 .02
❑ 374 Brad Lohaus .05 .02
❑ 375 Lee Mayberry RC .05 .02
❑ 376 Eric Murdock .05 .02
❑ 377 Danny Schayes .05 .02
❑ 378 Lance Blanks .05 .02
❑ 379 Christian Laettner RC .50 .15
❑ 380 Bob McCann RC .05 .02
❑ 381 Chuck Person .05 .02
❑ 382 Brad Sellers .05 .02
❑ 383 Chris Smith RC .05 .02
❑ 384 Micheal Williams .05 .02
❑ 385 Rafael Addison .05 .02
❑ 386 Chucky Brown .05 .02
❑ 387 Chris Dudley .05 .02
❑ 388 Tate George .05 .02
❑ 389 Rick Mahorn .05 .02
❑ 390 Rumeal Robinson .05 .02
❑ 391 Jayson Williams .10 .03
❑ 392 Eric Anderson RC .05 .02
❑ 393 Rolando Blackman .05 .02
❑ 394 Tony Campbell .05 .02
❑ 395 Hubert Davis RC .10 .03
❑ 396 Doc Rivers .10 .03
❑ 397 Charles Smith .05 .02
❑ 398 Herb Williams .05 .02
❑ 399 Litterial Green RC .05 .02
❑ 400 Greg Kite .05 .02
❑ 401 Shaquille O'Neal RC .. 6.00 1.80
❑ 402 Jerry Reynolds .05 .02
❑ 403 Jeff Turner .05 .02
❑ 404 Greg Grant .05 .02
❑ 405 Jeff Hornacek .10 .03
❑ 406 Andrew Lang .05 .02
❑ 407 Kenny Payne .05 .02
❑ 408 Tim Perry .05 .02
❑ 409 C.Weatherspoon RC .25 .07
❑ 410 Danny Ainge .10 .03
❑ 411 Charles Barkley .40 .12
❑ 412 Negele Knight .05 .02
❑ 413 Oliver Miller RC .10 .03
❑ 414 Jerrod Mustaf .05 .02
❑ 415 Mark Bryant .05 .02
❑ 416 Mario Elie .10 .03
❑ 417 Dave Johnson RC .05 .02
❑ 418 Tracy Murray RC .10 .03
❑ 419 Reggie Smith RC .05 .02
❑ 420 Rod Strickland .25 .07
❑ 421 Randy Brown .05 .02
❑ 422 Pete Chilcutt .05 .02
❑ 423 Jim Les .05 .02
❑ 424 Walt Williams RC .25 .07
❑ 425 Lloyd Daniels RC .05 .02
❑ 426 Vinny Del Negro .05 .02
❑ 427 Dale Ellis .05 .02
❑ 428 Sidney Green .05 .02
❑ 429 Avery Johnson .05 .02
❑ 430 Dana Barros .05 .02
❑ 431 Rich King .05 .02
❑ 432 Isaac Austin RC .10 .03
❑ 433 John Crotty RC .05 .02
❑ 434 Stephen Howard RC .05 .02
❑ 435 Jay Humphries .05 .02
❑ 436 Larry Krystkowiak .05 .02
❑ 437 Tom Gugliotta RC .75 .23
❑ 438 Buck Johnson .05 .02
❑ 439 Charles Jones .05 .02
❑ 440 Don MacLean RC .05 .02
❑ 441 Doug Overton .05 .02
❑ 442 Brent Price RC .10 .03
❑ 443 Checklist 1 .05 .02
❑ 444 Checklist 2 .05 .02
❑ SD266 Shawn Kemp AU 150.00 45.00
(Certified Autograph)
❑ SD277 Darrell Walker AU 30.00 9.00
(Certified Autograph)
❑ SD300 Darryl Dawkins AU 40.00 12.00
(Certified Autograph)
❑ NNO Slam Dunk Wrapper.. 3.00 .90
Exchange

1993-94 Fleer

	Nm-Mt	Ex-Mt
COMPLETE SET (400)	20.00	6.00
COMPLETE SERIES 1 (240)	10.00	3.00
COMPLETE SERIES 2 (160)	10.00	3.00

	#	Player		
❑	1	Stacey Augmon	.05	.02
❑	2	Mookie Blaylock	.10	.03
❑	3	Duane Ferrell	.05	.02
❑	4	Paul Graham	.05	.02
❑	5	Adam Keefe	.05	.02
❑	6	Jon Koncak	.05	.02
❑	7	Dominique Wilkins	.25	.07
❑	8	Kevin Willis	.05	.02
❑	9	Alaa Abdelnaby	.05	.02
❑	10	Dee Brown	.05	.02
❑	11	Sherman Douglas	.05	.02
❑	12	Rick Fox	.05	.02
❑	13	Kevin Gamble	.05	.02
❑	14	Reggie Lewis	.10	.03
❑	15	Xavier McDaniel	.05	.02
❑	16	Robert Parish	.10	.03
❑	17	Muggsy Bogues	.10	.03
❑	18	Dell Curry	.05	.02
❑	19	Kenny Gattison	.05	.02
❑	20	Kendall Gill	.10	.03
❑	21	Larry Johnson	.25	.07
❑	22	Alonzo Mourning	.40	.12
❑	23	Johnny Newman	.05	.02
❑	24	David Wingate	.05	.02
❑	25	B.J. Armstrong	.05	.02
❑	26	Bill Cartwright	.05	.02
❑	27	Horace Grant	.10	.03
❑	28	Michael Jordan	3.00	.90
❑	29	Stacey King	.05	.02
❑	30	John Paxson	.05	.02
❑	31	Will Perdue	.05	.02
❑	32	Scottie Pippen	.75	.23
❑	33	Scott Williams	.05	.02
❑	34	Terrell Brandon	.10	.03
❑	35	Brad Daugherty	.05	.02
❑	36	Craig Ehlo	.05	.02
❑	37	Danny Ferry	.05	.02
❑	38	Larry Nance	.05	.02
❑	39	Mark Price	.05	.02
❑	40	Mike Sanders	.05	.02
❑	41	Gerald Wilkins	.05	.02
❑	42	John Williams	.05	.02
❑	43	Terry Davis	.05	.02
❑	44	Derek Harper	.10	.03
❑	45	Mike Iuzzolino	.05	.02
❑	46	Jim Jackson	.10	.03
❑	47	Sean Rooks	.05	.02
❑	48	Doug Smith	.05	.02
❑	49	Randy White	.05	.02
❑	50	Mahmoud Abdul-Rauf	.05	.02
❑	51	LaPhonso Ellis	.05	.02
❑	52	Marcus Liberty	.05	.02
❑	53	Mark Macon	.05	.02
❑	54	Dikembe Mutombo	.25	.07
❑	55	Robert Pack	.05	.02
❑	56	Bryant Stith	.05	.02
❑	57	Reggie Williams	.05	.02
❑	58	Mark Aguirre	.05	.02
❑	59	Joe Dumars	.25	.07
❑	60	Bill Laimbeer	.05	.02
❑	61	Terry Mills	.05	.02
❑	62	Olden Polynice	.05	.02
❑	63	Alvin Robertson	.05	.02
❑	64	Dennis Rodman	.50	.15
❑	65	Isiah Thomas	.25	.07
❑	66	Victor Alexander	.05	.02
❑	67	Tim Hardaway	.25	.07
❑	68	Tyrone Hill	.05	.02
❑	69	Byron Houston	.05	.02
❑	70	Sarunas Marciulionis	.05	.02
❑	71	Chris Mullin	.25	.07
❑	72	Billy Owens	.05	.02
❑	73	Latrell Sprewell	.60	.18
❑	74	Scott Brooks	.05	.02
❑	75	Matt Bullard	.05	.02
❑	76	Carl Herrera	.05	.02
❑	77	Robert Horry	.10	.03
❑	78	Vernon Maxwell	.05	.02
❑	79	Hakeem Olajuwon	.40	.12
❑	80	Kenny Smith	.05	.02
❑	81	Otis Thorpe	.10	.03
❑	82	Dale Davis	.05	.02
❑	83	Vern Fleming	.05	.02
❑	84	George McCloud	.05	.02
❑	85	Reggie Miller	.25	.07
❑	86	Sam Mitchell	.05	.02
❑	87	Pooh Richardson	.05	.02
❑	88	Detlef Schrempf	.10	.03
❑	89	Rik Smits	.10	.03
❑	90	Gary Grant	.05	.02
❑	91	Ron Harper	.10	.03
❑	92	Mark Jackson	.10	.03
❑	93	Danny Manning	.10	.03
❑	94	Ken Norman	.05	.02
❑	95	Stanley Roberts	.05	.02
❑	96	Loy Vaught	.05	.02
❑	97	John Williams	.05	.02
❑	98	Elden Campbell	.05	.02
❑	99	Doug Christie	.10	.03
❑	100	Duane Cooper	.05	.02
❑	101	Vlade Divac	.10	.03
❑	102	A.C. Green	.10	.03
❑	103	Anthony Peeler	.05	.02
❑	104	Sedale Threatt	.05	.02
❑	105	James Worthy	.25	.07
❑	106	Bimbo Coles	.05	.02
❑	107	Grant Long	.05	.02
❑	108	Harold Miner	.05	.02
❑	109	Glen Rice	.10	.03
❑	110	John Salley	.05	.02
❑	111	Rony Seikaly	.05	.02
❑	112	Brian Shaw	.05	.02
❑	113	Steve Smith	.25	.07
❑	114	Anthony Avent	.05	.02
❑	115	Jon Barry	.05	.02
❑	116	Frank Brickowski	.05	.02
❑	117	Todd Day	.05	.02
❑	118	Blue Edwards	.05	.02
❑	119	Brad Lohaus	.05	.02
❑	120	Lee Mayberry	.05	.02
❑	121	Eric Murdock	.05	.02
❑	122	Thurl Bailey	.05	.02
❑	123	Christian Laettner	.10	.03
❑	124	Luc Longley	.10	.03
❑	125	Chuck Person	.05	.02
❑	126	Felton Spencer	.05	.02
❑	127	Doug West	.05	.02
❑	128	Micheal Williams	.05	.02
❑	129	Rafael Addison	.05	.02
❑	130	Kenny Anderson	.10	.03
❑	131	Sam Bowie	.05	.02
❑	132	Chucky Brown	.05	.02
❑	133	Derrick Coleman	.10	.03
❑	134	Chris Dudley	.05	.02
❑	135	Chris Morris	.05	.02
❑	136	Rumeal Robinson	.05	.02
❑	137	Greg Anthony	.05	.02
❑	138	Rolando Blackman	.05	.02
❑	139	Tony Campbell	.05	.02
❑	140	Hubert Davis	.05	.02
❑	141	Patrick Ewing	.25	.07
❑	142	Anthony Mason	.10	.03
❑	143	Charles Oakley	.10	.03
❑	144	Doc Rivers	.10	.03
❑	145	Charles Smith	.05	.02
❑	146	John Starks	.10	.03
❑	147	Nick Anderson	.10	.03
❑	148	Anthony Bowie	.05	.02
❑	149	Shaquille O'Neal	1.25	.35
❑	150	Donald Royal	.05	.02
❑	151	Dennis Scott	.05	.02
❑	152	Scott Skiles	.05	.02
❑	153	Tom Tolbert	.05	.02
❑	154	Jeff Turner	.05	.02
❑	155	Ron Anderson	.05	.02
❑	156	Johnny Dawkins	.05	.02
❑	157	Hersey Hawkins	.10	.03
❑	158	Jeff Hornacek	.10	.03
❑	159	Andrew Lang	.05	.02
❑	160	Tim Perry	.05	.02
❑	161	Clarence Weatherspoon	.05	.02
❑	162	Danny Ainge	.10	.03
❑	163	Charles Barkley	.40	.12
❑	164	Cedric Ceballos	.10	.03
❑	165	Tom Chambers	.05	.02
❑	166	Richard Dumas	.05	.02
❑	167	Kevin Johnson	.10	.03
❑	168	Negele Knight	.05	.02
❑	169	Dan Majerle	.10	.03
❑	170	Oliver Miller	.05	.02
❑	171	Mark West	.05	.02
❑	172	Mark Bryant	.05	.02
❑	173	Clyde Drexler	.25	.07
❑	174	Kevin Duckworth	.05	.02
❑	175	Mario Elie	.05	.02
❑	176	Jerome Kersey	.05	.02
❑	177	Terry Porter	.05	.02
❑	178	Clifford Robinson	.10	.03
❑	179	Rod Strickland	.10	.03
❑	180	Buck Williams	.05	.02
❑	181	Anthony Bonner	.05	.02
❑	182	Duane Causwell	.05	.02
❑	183	Mitch Richmond	.25	.07
❑	184	Lionel Simmons	.05	.02
❑	185	Wayman Tisdale	.05	.02
❑	186	Spud Webb	.10	.03
❑	187	Walt Williams	.05	.02
❑	188	Antoine Carr	.05	.02
❑	189	Terry Cummings	.05	.02
❑	190	Lloyd Daniels	.05	.02
❑	191	Vinny Del Negro	.05	.02
❑	192	Sean Elliott	.10	.03
❑	193	Dale Ellis	.05	.02
❑	194	Avery Johnson	.05	.02
❑	195	J.R. Reid	.05	.02
❑	196	David Robinson	.40	.12
❑	197	Michael Cage	.05	.02
❑	198	Eddie Johnson	.05	.02
❑	199	Shawn Kemp	.40	.12
❑	200	Derrick McKey	.05	.02
❑	201	Nate McMillan	.05	.02
❑	202	Gary Payton	.40	.12
❑	203	Sam Perkins	.10	.03
❑	204	Ricky Pierce	.05	.02
❑	205	David Benoit	.05	.02
❑	206	Tyrone Corbin	.05	.02
❑	207	Mark Eaton	.05	.02
❑	208	Jay Humphries	.05	.02
❑	209	Larry Krystkowiak	.05	.02
❑	210	Jeff Malone	.05	.02
❑	211	Karl Malone	.40	.12
❑	212	John Stockton	.25	.07
❑	213	Michael Adams	.05	.02
❑	214	Rex Chapman	.05	.02
❑	215	Pervis Ellison	.05	.02
❑	216	Harvey Grant	.05	.02
❑	217	Tom Gugliotta	.25	.07
❑	218	Buck Johnson	.05	.02
❑	219	LaBradford Smith	.05	.02
❑	220	Larry Stewart	.05	.02
❑	221	B.J. Armstrong LL 3-Pt Field Goal Percentage Leader	.05	.02
❑	222	Cedric Ceballos LL FG Percentage Leader	.05	.02
❑	223	Larry Johnson LL Minutes Played Leader	.10	.03
❑	224	Michael Jordan LL Scoring/Steals Leader	1.50	.45
❑	225	Hakeem Olajuwon LL Shot Block Leader	.25	.07
❑	226	Mark Price LL FT Percentage Leader	.05	.02
❑	227	Dennis Rodman LL Rebounding Leader	.25	.07
❑	228	John Stockton LL Assists Leader	.10	.03
❑	229	Charles Barkley AW Most Valuable Player	.25	.07
❑	230	Hakeem Olajuwon AW	.25	.07

	No.	Card	Nm-Mt	Ex-Mt
		Defensive POY		
❑	231	Shaquille O'Neal AW	.50	.15
		Rookie of the Year		
❑	232	Clifford Robinson AW	.05	.02
		Sixth Man Award		
❑	233	Shawn Kemp PV	.25	.07
❑	234	Alonzo Mourning PV	.25	.07
❑	235	Hakeem Olajuwon PV	.25	.07
❑	236	John Stockton PV	.10	.03
❑	237	Dominique Wilkins PV	.10	.03
❑	238	Checklist 1-85	.05	.02
❑	239	Checklist 86-165	.05	.02
❑	240	Checklist 166-240 UER (237 listed as Cliff Robinson; should be Dominique Wilkins)	.05	.02
❑	241	Doug Edwards RC	.05	.02
❑	242	Craig Ehlo	.05	.02
❑	243	Andrew Lang	.05	.02
❑	244	Ennis Whatley	.05	.02
❑	245	Chris Corchiani	.05	.02
❑	246	Acie Earl RC	.05	.02
❑	247	Jimmy Oliver	.05	.02
❑	248	Ed Pinckney	.05	.02
❑	249	Dino Radja RC	.05	.02
❑	250	Matt Wenstrom RC	.05	.02
❑	251	Tony Bennett	.05	.02
❑	252	Scott Burrell RC	.25	.07
❑	253	LeRon Ellis	.05	.02
❑	254	Hersey Hawkins	.10	.03
❑	255	Eddie Johnson	.05	.02
❑	256	Corie Blount RC	.05	.02
❑	257	Jo Jo English RC	.05	.02
❑	258	Dave Johnson	.05	.02
❑	259	Steve Kerr	.10	.03
❑	260	Toni Kukoc RC	1.00	.30
❑	261	Pete Myers	.05	.02
❑	262	Bill Wennington	.05	.02
❑	263	John Battle	.05	.02
❑	264	Tyrone Hill	.05	.02
❑	265	Gerald Madkins RC	.05	.02
❑	266	Chris Mills RC	.25	.07
❑	267	Bobby Phills	.05	.02
❑	268	Greg Dreiling	.05	.02
❑	269	Lucious Harris RC	.05	.02
❑	270	Donald Hodge	.05	.02
❑	271	Popeye Jones RC	.05	.02
❑	272	Tim Legler RC	.05	.02
❑	273	Fat Lever	.05	.02
❑	274	Jamal Mashburn RC	.60	.18
❑	275	Darren Morningstar RC	.05	.02
❑	276	Tom Hammonds	.05	.02
❑	277	Darnell Mee RC	.05	.02
❑	278	Rodney Rogers RC	.25	.07
❑	279	Brian Williams	.05	.02
❑	280	Greg Anderson	.05	.02
❑	281	Sean Elliott	.10	.03
❑	282	Allan Houston RC	1.00	.30
❑	283	Lindsey Hunter RC	.25	.07
❑	284	Marcus Liberty	.05	.02
❑	285	Mark Macon	.05	.02
❑	286	David Wood	.05	.02
❑	287	Jud Buechler	.05	.02
❑	288	Chris Gatling	.05	.02
❑	289	Josh Grant RC	.05	.02
❑	290	Jeff Grayer	.05	.02
❑	291	Avery Johnson	.05	.02
❑	292	Chris Webber RC	2.50	.75
❑	293	Sam Cassell RC	1.00	.30
❑	294	Mario Elie	.05	.02
❑	295	Richard Petruska RC	.05	.02
❑	296	Eric Riley RC	.05	.02
❑	297	Antonio Davis RC	.30	.09
❑	298	Scott Haskin RC	.05	.02
❑	299	Derrick McKey	.05	.02
❑	300	Byron Scott	.10	.03
❑	301	Malik Sealy	.05	.02
❑	302	LaSalle Thompson	.05	.02
❑	303	Kenny Williams	.05	.02
❑	304	Haywoode Workman	.05	.02
❑	305	Mark Aguirre	.05	.02
❑	306	Terry Dehere RC	.05	.02
❑	307	Bob Martin RC	.05	.02
❑	308	Elmore Spencer	.05	.02
❑	309	Tom Tolbert	.05	.02
❑	310	Randy Woods	.05	.02
❑	311	Sam Bowie	.05	.02
❑	312	James Edwards	.05	.02
❑	313	Antonio Harvey RC	.05	.02
❑	314	George Lynch RC	.05	.02
❑	315	Tony Smith	.05	.02
❑	316	Nick Van Exel RC	.75	.23
❑	317	Manute Bol	.05	.02
❑	318	Willie Burton	.05	.02
❑	319	Matt Geiger	.05	.02
❑	320	Alec Kessler	.05	.02
❑	321	Vin Baker RC	.60	.18
❑	322	Ken Norman	.05	.02
❑	323	Danny Schayes	.05	.02
❑	324	Derek Strong RC	.05	.02
❑	325	Mike Brown	.05	.02
❑	326	Brian Davis RC	.05	.02
❑	327	Tellis Frank	.05	.02
❑	328	Marlon Maxey	.05	.02
❑	329	Isaiah Rider RC	.50	.15
❑	330	Chris Smith	.05	.02
❑	331	Benoit Benjamin	.05	.02
❑	332	P.J. Brown RC	.25	.07
❑	333	Kevin Edwards	.05	.02
❑	334	Armon Gilliam	.05	.02
❑	335	Rick Mahorn	.05	.02
❑	336	Dwayne Schintzius	.05	.02
❑	337	Rex Walters RC	.05	.02
❑	338	David Wesley RC	.25	.07
❑	339	Jayson Williams	.10	.03
❑	340	Anthony Bonner	.05	.02
❑	341	Herb Williams	.05	.02
❑	342	Litterial Green	.05	.02
❑	343	Anfernee Hardaway RC	2.00	.60
❑	344	Greg Kite	.05	.02
❑	345	Larry Krystkowiak	.05	.02
❑	346	Todd Lichti	.05	.02
❑	347	Keith Tower RC	.05	.02
❑	348	Dana Barros	.05	.02
❑	349	Shawn Bradley RC	.25	.07
❑	350	Michael Curry RC	.05	.02
❑	351	Greg Graham RC	.05	.02
❑	352	Warren Kidd RC	.05	.02
❑	353	Moses Malone	.25	.07
❑	354	Orlando Woolridge	.05	.02
❑	355	Duane Cooper	.05	.02
❑	356	Joe Courtney RC	.05	.02
❑	357	A.C. Green	.10	.03
❑	358	Frank Johnson	.05	.02
❑	359	Joe Kleine	.05	.02
❑	360	Malcolm Mackey RC	.05	.02
❑	361	Jerrod Mustaf	.05	.02
❑	362	Chris Dudley	.05	.02
❑	363	Harvey Grant	.05	.02
❑	364	Tracy Murray	.05	.02
❑	365	James Robinson RC	.05	.02
❑	366	Reggie Smith	.05	.02
❑	367	Kevin Thompson RC	.05	.02
❑	368	Randy Breuer	.05	.02
❑	369	Randy Brown	.05	.02
❑	370	Evers Burns RC	.05	.02
❑	371	Pete Chilcutt	.05	.02
❑	372	Bobby Hurley RC	.10	.03
❑	373	Jim Les	.05	.02
❑	374	Mike Peplowski RC	.05	.02
❑	375	Willie Anderson	.05	.02
❑	376	Sleepy Floyd	.05	.02
❑	377	Negele Knight	.05	.02
❑	378	Dennis Rodman	.50	.15
❑	379	Chris Whitney RC	.05	.02
❑	380	Vincent Askew	.05	.02
❑	381	Kendall Gill	.10	.03
❑	382	Ervin Johnson RC	.10	.03
❑	383	Chris King RC	.05	.02
❑	384	Rich King	.05	.02
❑	385	Steve Scheffler	.05	.02
❑	386	Detlef Schrempf	.10	.03
❑	387	Tom Chambers	.05	.02
❑	388	John Crotty	.05	.02
❑	389	Bryon Russell RC	.25	.07
❑	390	Felton Spencer	.05	.02
❑	391	Luther Wright RC	.05	.02
❑	392	Mitchell Butler RC	.05	.02
❑	393	Calbert Cheaney RC	.10	.03
❑	394	Kevin Duckworth	.05	.02
❑	395	Don MacLean	.05	.02
❑	396	Gheorghe Muresan RC	.25	.07
❑	397	Doug Overton	.05	.02
❑	398	Brent Price	.05	.02
❑	399	Checklist	.05	.02
❑	400	Checklist	.05	.02

1994-95 Fleer

	No.	Card	Nm-Mt	Ex-Mt
		COMPLETE SET (390)	24.00	7.25
		COMPLETE SERIES 1 (240)	12.00	3.60
		COMPLETE SERIES 2 (150)	12.00	3.60
❑	1	Stacey Augmon	.05	.02
❑	2	Mookie Blaylock	.05	.02
❑	3	Craig Ehlo	.05	.02
❑	4	Duane Ferrell	.05	.02
❑	5	Adam Keefe	.05	.02
❑	6	Jon Koncak	.05	.02
❑	7	Andrew Lang	.05	.02
❑	8	Danny Manning	.10	.03
❑	9	Kevin Willis	.05	.02
❑	10	Dee Brown	.05	.02
❑	11	Sherman Douglas	.05	.02
❑	12	Acie Earl	.05	.02
❑	13	Rick Fox	.05	.02
❑	14	Kevin Gamble	.05	.02
❑	15	Xavier McDaniel	.05	.02
❑	16	Robert Parish	.10	.03
❑	17	Ed Pinckney	.05	.02
❑	18	Dino Radja	.05	.02
❑	19	Muggsy Bogues	.10	.03
❑	20	Frank Brickowski	.05	.02
❑	21	Scott Burrell	.05	.02
❑	22	Dell Curry	.05	.02
❑	23	Kenny Gattison	.05	.02
❑	24	Hersey Hawkins	.10	.03
❑	25	Eddie Johnson	.05	.02
❑	26	Larry Johnson	.10	.03
❑	27	Alonzo Mourning	.30	.09
❑	28	David Wingate	.05	.02
❑	29	B.J. Armstrong	.05	.02
❑	30	Horace Grant	.10	.03
❑	31	Steve Kerr	.05	.02
❑	32	Toni Kukoc	.40	.12
❑	33	Luc Longley	.05	.02
❑	34	Pete Myers	.05	.02
❑	35	Scottie Pippen	.75	.23
❑	36	Bill Wennington	.05	.02
❑	37	Scott Williams	.05	.02
❑	38	Terrell Brandon	.10	.03
❑	39	Brad Daugherty	.05	.02
❑	40	Tyrone Hill	.05	.02
❑	41	Chris Mills	.10	.03
❑	42	Larry Nance	.05	.02
❑	43	Bobby Phills	.05	.02
❑	44	Mark Price	.05	.02
❑	45	Gerald Wilkins	.05	.02
❑	46	John Williams	.05	.02
❑	47	Lucious Harris	.05	.02
❑	48	Donald Hodge	.05	.02
❑	49	Jim Jackson	.10	.03
❑	50	Popeye Jones	.05	.02
❑	51	Tim Legler	.05	.02
❑	52	Fat Lever	.05	.02
❑	53	Jamal Mashburn	.25	.07
❑	54	Sean Rooks	.05	.02
❑	55	Doug Smith	.05	.02
❑	56	Mahmoud Abdul-Rauf	.05	.02
❑	57	LaPhonso Ellis	.05	.02
❑	58	Dikembe Mutombo	.10	.03
❑	59	Robert Pack	.05	.02

	No.	Player		
❑	60	Rodney Rogers	.05	.02
❑	61	Bryant Stith	.05	.02
❑	62	Brian Williams	.05	.02
❑	63	Reggie Williams	.05	.02
❑	64	Greg Anderson	.05	.02
❑	65	Joe Dumars	.25	.07
❑	66	Sean Elliott	.10	.03
❑	67	Allan Houston	.40	.12
❑	68	Lindsey Hunter	.10	.03
❑	69	Terry Mills	.05	.02
❑	70	Victor Alexander	.05	.02
❑	71	Chris Gatling	.05	.02
❑	72	Tim Hardaway	.25	.07
❑	73	Keith Jennings	.05	.02
❑	74	Avery Johnson	.05	.02
❑	75	Chris Mullin	.25	.07
❑	76	Billy Owens	.05	.02
❑	77	Latrell Sprewell	.25	.07
❑	78	Chris Webber	.60	.18
❑	79	Scott Brooks	.05	.02
❑	80	Sam Cassell	.25	.07
❑	81	Mario Elie	.05	.02
❑	82	Carl Herrera	.05	.02
❑	83	Robert Horry	.10	.03
❑	84	Vernon Maxwell	.05	.02
❑	85	Hakeem Olajuwon	.40	.12
❑	86	Kenny Smith	.05	.02
❑	87	Otis Thorpe	.05	.02
❑	88	Antonio Davis	.05	.02
❑	89	Dale Davis	.05	.02
❑	90	Vern Fleming	.05	.02
❑	91	Derrick McKey	.05	.02
❑	92	Reggie Miller	.25	.07
❑	93	Pooh Richardson	.05	.02
❑	94	Byron Scott	.10	.03
❑	95	Rik Smits	.05	.02
❑	96	Haywoode Workman	.05	.02
❑	97	Terry Dehere	.05	.02
❑	98	Harold Ellis	.05	.02
❑	99	Gary Grant	.05	.02
❑	100	Ron Harper	.10	.03
❑	101	Mark Jackson	.05	.02
❑	102	Stanley Roberts	.05	.02
❑	103	Elmore Spencer	.05	.02
❑	104	Loy Vaught	.05	.02
❑	105	Dominique Wilkins	.25	.07
❑	106	Elden Campbell	.05	.02
❑	107	Doug Christie	.10	.03
❑	108	Vlade Divac	.05	.02
❑	109	George Lynch	.05	.02
❑	110	Anthony Peeler	.05	.02
❑	111	Tony Smith	.05	.02
❑	112	Sedale Threatt	.05	.02
❑	113	Nick Van Exel	.25	.07
❑	114	James Worthy	.25	.07
❑	115	Bimbo Coles	.05	.02
❑	116	Grant Long	.05	.02
❑	117	Harold Miner	.05	.02
❑	118	Glen Rice	.10	.03
❑	119	John Salley	.05	.02
❑	120	Rony Seikaly	.05	.02
❑	121	Brian Shaw	.05	.02
❑	122	Steve Smith	.10	.03
❑	123	Vin Baker	.25	.07
❑	124	Jon Barry	.05	.02
❑	125	Todd Day	.05	.02
❑	126	Blue Edwards	.05	.02
❑	127	Lee Mayberry	.05	.02
❑	128	Eric Murdock	.05	.02
❑	129	Ken Norman	.05	.02
❑	130	Derek Strong	.05	.02
❑	131	Thurl Bailey	.05	.02
❑	132	Stacey King	.05	.02
❑	133	Christian Laettner	.10	.03
❑	134	Chuck Person	.05	.02
❑	135	Isaiah Rider	.10	.03
❑	136	Chris Smith	.05	.02
❑	137	Doug West	.05	.02
❑	138	Micheal Williams	.05	.02
❑	139	Kenny Anderson	.10	.03
❑	140	Benoit Benjamin	.05	.02
❑	141	P.J. Brown	.05	.02
❑	142	Derrick Coleman	.10	.03
❑	143	Kevin Edwards	.05	.02
❑	144	Armon Gilliam	.05	.02
❑	145	Chris Morris	.05	.02
❑	146	Johnny Newman	.05	.02
❑	147	Greg Anthony	.05	.02
❑	148	Anthony Bonner	.05	.02
❑	149	Hubert Davis	.05	.02
❑	150	Patrick Ewing	.25	.07
❑	151	Derek Harper	.05	.02
❑	152	Anthony Mason	.10	.03
❑	153	Charles Oakley	.05	.02
❑	154	Doc Rivers	.10	.03
❑	155	Charles Smith	.05	.02
❑	156	John Starks	.05	.02
❑	157	Nick Anderson	.05	.02
❑	158	Anthony Avent	.05	.02
❑	159	Anfernee Hardaway	.60	.18
❑	160	Shaquille O'Neal	1.25	.35
❑	161	Donald Royal	.05	.02
❑	162	Dennis Scott	.05	.02
❑	163	Scott Skiles	.05	.02
❑	164	Jeff Turner	.05	.02
❑	165	Dana Barros	.05	.02
❑	166	Shawn Bradley	.05	.02
❑	167	Greg Graham	.05	.02
❑	168	Eric Leckner	.05	.02
❑	169	Jeff Malone	.05	.02
❑	170	Moses Malone	.25	.07
❑	171	Tim Perry	.05	.02
❑	172	Clarence Weatherspoon	.05	.02
❑	173	Orlando Woolridge	.05	.02
❑	174	Danny Ainge	.05	.02
❑	175	Charles Barkley	.40	.12
❑	176	Cedric Ceballos	.05	.02
❑	177	A.C. Green	.10	.03
❑	178	Kevin Johnson	.10	.03
❑	179	Joe Kleine	.05	.02
❑	180	Dan Majerle	.10	.03
❑	181	Oliver Miller	.05	.02
❑	182	Mark West	.05	.02
❑	183	Clyde Drexler	.25	.07
❑	184	Harvey Grant	.05	.02
❑	185	Jerome Kersey	.05	.02
❑	186	Tracy Murray	.05	.02
❑	187	Terry Porter	.05	.02
❑	188	Clifford Robinson	.10	.03
❑	189	James Robinson	.05	.02
❑	190	Rod Strickland	.10	.03
❑	191	Buck Williams	.05	.02
❑	192	Duane Causwell	.05	.02
❑	193	Bobby Hurley	.05	.02
❑	194	Olden Polynice	.05	.02
❑	195	Mitch Richmond	.25	.07
❑	196	Lionel Simmons	.05	.02
❑	197	Wayman Tisdale	.05	.02
❑	198	Spud Webb	.05	.02
❑	199	Walt Williams	.05	.02
❑	200	Trevor Wilson	.05	.02
❑	201	Willie Anderson	.05	.02
❑	202	Antoine Carr	.05	.02
❑	203	Terry Cummings	.05	.02
❑	204	Vinny Del Negro	.05	.02
❑	205	Dale Ellis	.05	.02
❑	206	Negele Knight	.05	.02
❑	207	J.R. Reid	.05	.02
❑	208	David Robinson	.40	.12
❑	209	Dennis Rodman	.50	.15
❑	210	Vincent Askew	.05	.02
❑	211	Michael Cage	.05	.02
❑	212	Kendall Gill	.10	.03
❑	213	Shawn Kemp	.40	.12
❑	214	Nate McMillan	.05	.02
❑	215	Gary Payton	.40	.12
❑	216	Sam Perkins	.10	.03
❑	217	Ricky Pierce	.05	.02
❑	218	Detlef Schrempf	.10	.03
❑	219	David Benoit	.05	.02
❑	220	Tom Chambers	.05	.02
❑	221	Tyrone Corbin	.05	.02
❑	222	Jeff Hornacek	.10	.03
❑	223	Jay Humphries	.05	.02
❑	224	Karl Malone	.40	.12
❑	225	Bryon Russell	.05	.02
❑	226	Felton Spencer	.05	.02
❑	227	John Stockton	.25	.07
❑	228	Michael Adams	.05	.02
❑	229	Rex Chapman	.05	.02
❑	230	Calbert Cheaney	.05	.02
❑	231	Kevin Duckworth	.05	.02
❑	232	Pervis Ellison	.05	.02
❑	233	Tom Gugliotta	.10	.03
❑	234	Don MacLean	.05	.02
❑	235	Gheorghe Muresan	.05	.02
❑	236	Brent Price	.05	.02
❑	237	Toronto Raptors Logo Card	.05	.02
❑	238	Checklist	.05	.02
❑	239	Checklist	.05	.02
❑	240	Checklist	.05	.02
❑	241	Sergei Bazarevich	.05	.02
❑	242	Tyrone Corbin	.05	.02
❑	243	Grant Long	.05	.02
❑	244	Ken Norman	.05	.02
❑	245	Steve Smith	.10	.03
❑	246	Fred Vinson	.05	.02
❑	247	Blue Edwards	.05	.02
❑	248	Greg Minor RC	.05	.02
❑	249	Eric Montross RC	.05	.02
❑	250	Derek Strong	.05	.02
❑	251	David Wesley	.05	.02
❑	252	Dominique Wilkins	.25	.07
❑	253	Michael Adams	.05	.02
❑	254	Tony Bennett	.05	.02
❑	255	Darrin Hancock RC	.05	.02
❑	256	Robert Parish	.10	.03
❑	257	Corie Blount	.05	.02
❑	258	Jud Buechler	.05	.02
❑	259	Greg Foster	.05	.02
❑	260	Ron Harper	.10	.03
❑	261	Larry Krystkowiak	.05	.02
❑	262	Will Perdue	.05	.02
❑	263	Dickey Simpkins RC	.05	.02
❑	264	Michael Cage	.05	.02
❑	265	Tony Campbell	.05	.02
❑	266	Terry Davis	.05	.02
❑	267	Tony Dumas RC	.05	.02
❑	268	Jason Kidd RC	2.50	.75
❑	269	Roy Tarpley	.05	.02
❑	270	Morlon Wiley	.05	.02
❑	271	Lorenzo Williams	.05	.02
❑	272	Dale Ellis	.05	.02
❑	273	Tom Hammonds	.05	.02
❑	274	Cliff Levingston	.05	.02
❑	275	Darnell Mee	.05	.02
❑	276	Jalen Rose RC	1.00	.30
❑	277	Reggie Slater	.05	.02
❑	278	Bill Curley RC	.05	.02
❑	279	Johnny Dawkins	.05	.02
❑	280	Grant Hill RC	1.25	.35
❑	281	Eric Leckner	.05	.02
❑	282	Mark Macon	.05	.02
❑	283	Oliver Miller	.05	.02
❑	284	Mark West	.05	.02
❑	285	Manute Bol	.05	.02
❑	286	Tom Gugliotta	.10	.03
❑	287	Ricky Pierce	.05	.02
❑	288	Carlos Rogers RC	.05	.02
❑	289	Clifford Rozier RC	.05	.02
❑	290	Rony Seikaly	.05	.02
❑	291	Tim Breaux	.05	.02
❑	292	Chris Jent	.05	.02
❑	293	Eric Riley	.05	.02
❑	294	Zan Tabak	.05	.02
❑	295	Duane Ferrell	.05	.02
❑	296	Mark Jackson	.05	.02
❑	297	John Williams	.05	.02
❑	298	Matt Fish	.05	.02
❑	299	Tony Massenburg	.05	.02
❑	300	Lamond Murray RC	.10	.03
❑	301	Bo Outlaw RC	.05	.02
❑	302	Eric Piatkowski RC	.05	.02
❑	303	Pooh Richardson	.05	.02
❑	304	Randy Woods	.05	.02
❑	305	Sam Bowie	.05	.02
❑	306	Cedric Ceballos	.05	.02
❑	307	Antonio Harvey	.05	.02
❑	308	Eddie Jones RC	1.25	.35
❑	309	Anthony Miller RC	.05	.02
❑	310	Ledell Eackles	.05	.02
❑	311	Kevin Gamble	.05	.02
❑	312	Brad Lohaus	.05	.02
❑	313	Billy Owens	.05	.02
❑	314	Khalid Reeves RC	.05	.02
❑	315	Kevin Willis	.05	.02
❑	316	Marty Conlon	.05	.02

❑ 317 Eric Mobley RC	.05	.02
❑ 318 Johnny Newman	.05	.02
❑ 319 Ed Pinckney	.05	.02
❑ 320 Glenn Robinson RC	.75	.23
❑ 321 Mike Brown	.05	.02
❑ 322 Pat Durham	.05	.02
❑ 323 Howard Eisley RC	.05	.02
❑ 324 Andres Guibert	.05	.02
❑ 325 Donyell Marshall RC	.25	.07
❑ 326 Sean Rooks	.05	.02
❑ 327 Yinka Dare RC	.05	.02
❑ 328 Sleepy Floyd	.05	.02
❑ 329 Sean Higgins	.05	.02
❑ 330 Rick Mahorn	.05	.02
❑ 331 Rex Walters	.05	.02
❑ 332 Jayson Williams	.10	.03
❑ 333 Charlie Ward RC	.25	.07
❑ 334 Herb Williams	.05	.02
❑ 335 Monty Williams RC	.05	.02
❑ 336 Anthony Bowie	.05	.02
❑ 337 Horace Grant	.10	.03
❑ 338 Geert Hammink	.05	.02
❑ 339 Tree Rollins	.05	.02
❑ 340 Brian Shaw	.05	.02
❑ 341 Brooks Thompson RC	.05	.02
❑ 342 Derrick Alston RC	.05	.02
❑ 343 Willie Burton	.05	.02
❑ 344 Jaren Jackson	.05	.02
❑ 345 B.J. Tyler RC	.05	.02
❑ 346 Scott Williams	.05	.02
❑ 347 Sharone Wright RC	.05	.02
❑ 348 Antonio Lang RC	.05	.02
❑ 349 Danny Manning	.10	.03
❑ 350 Elliot Perry	.05	.02
❑ 351 Wesley Person RC	.25	.07
❑ 352 Trevor Ruffin	.05	.02
❑ 353 Danny Schayes	.05	.02
❑ 354 Aaron Swinson RC	.05	.02
❑ 355 Wayman Tisdale	.05	.02
❑ 356 Mark Bryant	.05	.02
❑ 357 Chris Dudley	.05	.02
❑ 358 James Edwards	.05	.02
❑ 359 Aaron McKie RC	.50	.15
❑ 360 Alaa Abdelnaby	.05	.02
❑ 361 Frank Brickowski	.05	.02
❑ 362 Randy Brown	.05	.02
❑ 363 Brian Grant RC	.60	.18
❑ 364 Michael Smith RC	.05	.02
❑ 365 Henry Turner	.05	.02
❑ 366 Sean Elliott	.10	.03
❑ 367 Avery Johnson	.05	.02
❑ 368 Moses Malone	.25	.07
❑ 369 Julius Nwosu	.05	.02
❑ 370 Chuck Person	.05	.02
❑ 371 Chris Whitney	.05	.02
❑ 372 Bill Cartwright	.05	.02
❑ 373 Byron Houston	.05	.02
❑ 374 Ervin Johnson	.05	.02
❑ 375 Sarunas Marciulionis	.05	.02
❑ 376 Antoine Carr	.05	.02
❑ 377 John Crotty	.05	.02
❑ 378 Adam Keefe	.05	.02
❑ 379 Jamie Watson RC	.05	.02
❑ 380 Mitchell Butler	.05	.02
❑ 381 Juwan Howard RC	.60	.18
❑ 382 Jim McIlvaine RC	.05	.02
❑ 383 Doug Overton	.05	.02
❑ 384 Scott Skiles	.05	.02
❑ 385 Larry Stewart	.05	.02
❑ 386 Kenny Walker	.05	.02
❑ 387 Chris Webber	.60	.18
❑ 388 Vancouver Grizzlies Logo Card	.05	.02
❑ 389 Checklist	.05	.02
❑ 390 Checklist	.05	.02

1995-96 Fleer

	Nm-Mt	Ex-Mt
COMPLETE SET (350)	40.00	12.00
COMPLETE SERIES 1 (200)	20.00	6.00
COMPLETE SERIES 2 (150)	20.00	6.00
❑ 1 Stacey Augmon	.15	.04
❑ 2 Mookie Blaylock	.15	.04
❑ 3 Craig Ehlo	.15	.04
❑ 4 Andrew Lang	.15	.04
❑ 5 Grant Long	.15	.04
❑ 6 Ken Norman	.15	.04
❑ 7 Steve Smith	.30	.09
❑ 8 Dee Brown	.15	.04
❑ 9 Sherman Douglas	.15	.04
❑ 10 Eric Montross	.15	.04
❑ 11 Dino Radja	.15	.04
❑ 12 David Wesley	.15	.04
❑ 13 Dominique Wilkins	.50	.15
❑ 14 Muggsy Bogues	.30	.09
❑ 15 Scott Burrell	.15	.04
❑ 16 Dell Curry	.15	.04
❑ 17 Hersey Hawkins	.15	.04
❑ 18 Larry Johnson	.30	.09
❑ 19 Alonzo Mourning	.30	.09
❑ 20 Robert Parish	.30	.09
❑ 21 B.J. Armstrong	.15	.04
❑ 22 Michael Jordan	3.00	.90
❑ 23 Steve Kerr	.30	.09
❑ 24 Toni Kukoc	.30	.09
❑ 25 Will Perdue	.15	.04
❑ 26 Scottie Pippen	.75	.23
❑ 27 Terrell Brandon	.30	.09
❑ 28 Tyrone Hill	.15	.04
❑ 29 Chris Mills	.15	.04
❑ 30 Bobby Phills	.15	.04
❑ 31 Mark Price	.30	.09
❑ 32 John Williams	.15	.04
❑ 33 Lucious Harris	.15	.04
❑ 34 Jim Jackson	.15	.04
❑ 35 Popeye Jones	.15	.04
❑ 36 Jason Kidd	1.50	.45
❑ 37 Jamal Mashburn	.30	.09
❑ 38 George McCloud	.15	.04
❑ 39 Roy Tarpley	.15	.04
❑ 40 Lorenzo Williams	.15	.04
❑ 41 Mahmoud Abdul-Rauf	.15	.04
❑ 42 Dale Ellis	.15	.04
❑ 43 LaPhonso Ellis	.15	.04
❑ 44 Dikembe Mutombo	.30	.09
❑ 45 Robert Pack	.15	.04
❑ 46 Rodney Rogers	.15	.04
❑ 47 Jalen Rose	.60	.18
❑ 48 Bryant Stith	.15	.04
❑ 49 Reggie Williams	.15	.04
❑ 50 Joe Dumars	.50	.15
❑ 51 Grant Hill	.60	.18
❑ 52 Allan Houston	.30	.09
❑ 53 Lindsey Hunter	.15	.04
❑ 54 Oliver Miller	.15	.04
❑ 55 Terry Mills	.15	.04
❑ 56 Mark West	.15	.04
❑ 57 Chris Gatling	.15	.04
❑ 58 Tim Hardaway	.30	.09
❑ 59 Donyell Marshall	.30	.09
❑ 60 Chris Mullin	.50	.15
❑ 61 Carlos Rogers	.15	.04
❑ 62 Clifford Rozier	.15	.04
❑ 63 Rony Seikaly	.15	.04
❑ 64 Latrell Sprewell	.50	.15
❑ 65 Sam Cassell	.50	.15
❑ 66 Clyde Drexler	.50	.15
❑ 67 Mario Elie	.15	.04
❑ 68 Carl Herrera	.15	.04
❑ 69 Robert Horry	.30	.09
❑ 70 Vernon Maxwell	.15	.04
❑ 71 Hakeem Olajuwon	.50	.15
❑ 72 Kenny Smith	.15	.04
❑ 73 Dale Davis	.15	.04
❑ 74 Mark Jackson	.30	.09
❑ 75 Derrick McKey	.15	.04
❑ 76 Reggie Miller	.50	.15
❑ 77 Sam Mitchell	.15	.04
❑ 78 Byron Scott	.15	.04
❑ 79 Rik Smits	.30	.09
❑ 80 Terry Dehere	.15	.04
❑ 81 Tony Massenburg	.15	.04
❑ 82 Lamond Murray	.15	.04
❑ 83 Pooh Richardson	.15	.04
❑ 84 Malik Sealy	.15	.04
❑ 85 Loy Vaught	.15	.04
❑ 86 Elden Campbell	.15	.04
❑ 87 Cedric Ceballos	.15	.04
❑ 88 Vlade Divac	.30	.09
❑ 89 Eddie Jones	.60	.18
❑ 90 Anthony Peeler	.15	.04
❑ 91 Sedale Threatt	.15	.04
❑ 92 Nick Van Exel	.50	.15
❑ 93 Bimbo Coles	.15	.04
❑ 94 Matt Geiger	.15	.04
❑ 95 Billy Owens	.15	.04
❑ 96 Khalid Reeves	.15	.04
❑ 97 Glen Rice	.30	.09
❑ 98 John Salley	.15	.04
❑ 99 Kevin Willis	.30	.09
❑ 100 Vin Baker	.30	.09
❑ 101 Marty Conlon	.15	.04
❑ 102 Todd Day	.15	.04
❑ 103 Lee Mayberry	.15	.04
❑ 104 Eric Murdock	.15	.04
❑ 105 Glenn Robinson	.50	.15
❑ 106 Winston Garland	.15	.04
❑ 107 Tom Gugliotta	.15	.04
❑ 108 Christian Laettner	.30	.09
❑ 109 Isaiah Rider	.15	.04
❑ 110 Sean Rooks	.15	.04
❑ 111 Doug West	.15	.04
❑ 112 Kenny Anderson	.30	.09
❑ 113 Benoit Benjamin	.15	.04
❑ 114 P.J. Brown	.15	.04
❑ 115 Derrick Coleman	.15	.04
❑ 116 Armon Gilliam	.15	.04
❑ 117 Chris Morris	.15	.04
❑ 118 Rex Walters	.15	.04
❑ 119 Hubert Davis	.15	.04
❑ 120 Patrick Ewing	.50	.15
❑ 121 Derek Harper	.30	.09
❑ 122 Anthony Mason	.30	.09
❑ 123 Charles Oakley	.15	.04
❑ 124 Charles Smith	.15	.04
❑ 125 John Starks	.30	.09
❑ 126 Nick Anderson	.15	.04
❑ 127 Anthony Bowie	.15	.04
❑ 128 Horace Grant	.30	.09
❑ 129 Anfernee Hardaway	.50	.15
❑ 130 Shaquille O'Neal	1.25	.35
❑ 131 Donald Royal	.15	.04
❑ 132 Dennis Scott	.15	.04
❑ 133 Brian Shaw	.15	.04
❑ 134 Derrick Alston	.15	.04
❑ 135 Dana Barros	.15	.04
❑ 136 Shawn Bradley	.15	.04
❑ 137 Willie Burton	.15	.04
❑ 138 Clarence Weatherspoon	.15	.04
❑ 139 Scott Williams	.15	.04
❑ 140 Sharone Wright	.15	.04
❑ 141 Danny Ainge	.15	.04
❑ 142 Charles Barkley	.60	.18
❑ 143 A.C. Green	.30	.09
❑ 144 Kevin Johnson	.30	.09
❑ 145 Dan Majerle	.30	.09
❑ 146 Danny Manning	.30	.09
❑ 147 Elliot Perry	.15	.04
❑ 148 Wesley Person	.15	.04
❑ 149 Wayman Tisdale	.15	.04
❑ 150 Chris Dudley	.15	.04
❑ 151 Jerome Kersey	.15	.04
❑ 152 Aaron McKie	.30	.09
❑ 153 Terry Porter	.15	.04
❑ 154 Clifford Robinson	.15	.04
❑ 155 James Robinson	.15	.04
❑ 156 Rod Strickland	.15	.04
❑ 157 Otis Thorpe	.15	.04
❑ 158 Buck Williams	.15	.04

- ❑ 159 Brian Grant .50 .15
- ❑ 160 Bobby Hurley .15 .04
- ❑ 161 Olden Polynice .15 .04
- ❑ 162 Mitch Richmond .30 .09
- ❑ 163 Michael Smith .15 .04
- ❑ 164 Spud Webb .30 .09
- ❑ 165 Walt Williams .15 .04
- ❑ 166 Terry Cummings .15 .04
- ❑ 167 Vinny Del Negro .15 .04
- ❑ 168 Sean Elliott .30 .09
- ❑ 169 Avery Johnson .15 .04
- ❑ 170 Chuck Person .15 .04
- ❑ 171 J.R. Reid .15 .04
- ❑ 172 Doc Rivers .30 .09
- ❑ 173 David Robinson .50 .15
- ❑ 174 Dennis Rodman .30 .09
- ❑ 175 Vincent Askew .15 .04
- ❑ 176 Kendall Gill .15 .04
- ❑ 177 Shawn Kemp .30 .09
- ❑ 178 Sarunas Marciulionis .15 .04
- ❑ 179 Nate McMillan .15 .04
- ❑ 180 Gary Payton .50 .15
- ❑ 181 Sam Perkins .30 .09
- ❑ 182 Detlef Schrempf .30 .09
- ❑ 183 David Benoit .15 .04
- ❑ 184 Antoine Carr .15 .04
- ❑ 185 Blue Edwards .15 .04
- ❑ 186 Jeff Hornacek .30 .09
- ❑ 187 Adam Keefe .15 .04
- ❑ 188 Karl Malone .60 .18
- ❑ 189 Felton Spencer .15 .04
- ❑ 190 John Stockton .60 .18
- ❑ 191 Rex Chapman .15 .04
- ❑ 192 Calbert Cheaney .15 .04
- ❑ 193 Juwan Howard .50 .15
- ❑ 194 Don MacLean .15 .04
- ❑ 195 Gheorghe Muresan .15 .04
- ❑ 196 Scott Skiles .15 .04
- ❑ 197 Chris Webber .60 .18
- ❑ 198 Checklist .15 .04
- ❑ 199 Checklist .15 .04
- ❑ 200 Checklist .15 .04
- ❑ 201 Stacey Augmon .15 .04
- ❑ 202 Mookie Blaylock .15 .04
- ❑ 203 Grant Long .15 .04
- ❑ 204 Ken Norman .15 .04
- ❑ 205 Steve Smith .30 .09
- ❑ 206 Spud Webb .30 .09
- ❑ 207 Dana Barros .15 .04
- ❑ 208 Rick Fox .30 .09
- ❑ 209 Kendall Gill .15 .04
- ❑ 210 Khalid Reeves .15 .04
- ❑ 211 Glen Rice .30 .09
- ❑ 212 Luc Longley .15 .04
- ❑ 213 Dennis Rodman .30 .09
- ❑ 214 Dan Majerle .30 .09
- ❑ 215 Tony Dumas .15 .04
- ❑ 216 Tom Hammonds .15 .04
- ❑ 217 Elmore Spencer .15 .04
- ❑ 218 Otis Thorpe .15 .04
- ❑ 219 B.J. Armstrong .15 .04
- ❑ 220 Sam Cassell .50 .15
- ❑ 221 Clyde Drexler .50 .15
- ❑ 222 Mario Elie .15 .04
- ❑ 223 Robert Horry .30 .09
- ❑ 224 Hakeem Olajuwon .50 .15
- ❑ 225 Kenny Smith .15 .04
- ❑ 226 Antonio Davis .15 .04
- ❑ 227 Eddie Johnson .15 .04
- ❑ 228 Ricky Pierce .15 .04
- ❑ 229 Eric Piatkowski .10 .03
- ❑ 230 Rodney Rogers .15 .04
- ❑ 231 Brian Williams .15 .04
- ❑ 232 Corie Blount .15 .04
- ❑ 233 George Lynch .15 .04
- ❑ 234 Kevin Gamble .15 .04
- ❑ 235 Alonzo Mourning .30 .09
- ❑ 236 Eric Mobley .15 .04
- ❑ 237 Terry Porter .15 .04
- ❑ 238 Micheal Williams .15 .04
- ❑ 239 Kevin Edwards .15 .04
- ❑ 240 Vern Fleming .15 .04
- ❑ 241 Charlie Ward .15 .04
- ❑ 242 Jon Koncak .15 .04
- ❑ 243 Richard Dumas .15 .04
- ❑ 244 Jeff Malone .15 .04
- ❑ 245 Vernon Maxwell .15 .04
- ❑ 246 John Williams .15 .04
- ❑ 247 Harvey Grant .15 .04
- ❑ 248 Dontonio Wingfield .15 .04
- ❑ 249 Tyrone Corbin .15 .04
- ❑ 250 Sarunas Marciulionis .15 .04
- ❑ 251 Will Perdue .15 .04
- ❑ 252 Hersey Hawkins .15 .04
- ❑ 253 Ervin Johnson .15 .04
- ❑ 254 Shawn Kemp .30 .09
- ❑ 255 Gary Payton .50 .15
- ❑ 256 Sam Perkins .30 .09
- ❑ 257 Detlef Schrempf .30 .09
- ❑ 258 Chris Morris .15 .04
- ❑ 259 Robert Pack .15 .04
- ❑ 260 Willie Anderson ET .15 .04
- ❑ 261 Jimmy King ET .15 .04
- ❑ 262 Oliver Miller ET .15 .04
- ❑ 263 Tracy Murray ET .15 .04
- ❑ 264 Ed Pinckney ET .15 .04
- ❑ 265 Alvin Robertson ET .15 .04
- ❑ 266 Carlos Rogers ET .15 .04
- ❑ 267 John Salley ET .15 .04
- ❑ 268 Damon Stoudamire ET .60 .18
- ❑ 269 Zan Tabak ET .15 .04
- ❑ 270 Ashraf Amaya ET .15 .04
- ❑ 271 Greg Anthony ET .15 .04
- ❑ 272 Benoit Benjamin ET .15 .04
- ❑ 273 Blue Edwards ET .15 .04
- ❑ 274 Kenny Gattison ET .15 .04
- ❑ 275 Antonio Harvey ET .15 .04
- ❑ 276 Chris King ET .15 .04
- ❑ 277 Lawrence Moten ET .15 .04
- ❑ 278 Bryant Reeves ET .30 .09
- ❑ 279 Byron Scott ET .15 .04
- ❑ 280 Cory Alexander RC .15 .04
- ❑ 281 Jerome Allen RC .15 .04
- ❑ 282 Brent Barry RC .50 .15
- ❑ 283 Mario Bennett RC .15 .04
- ❑ 284 Travis Best RC .15 .04
- ❑ 285 Junior Burrough RC .15 .04
- ❑ 286 Jason Caffey RC .30 .09
- ❑ 287 Randolph Childress RC .15 .04
- ❑ 288 Sasha Danilovic RC .15 .04
- ❑ 289 Mark Davis RC .15 .04
- ❑ 290 Tyus Edney RC .15 .04
- ❑ 291 Michael Finley RC 1.25 .35
- ❑ 292 Sherrell Ford RC .15 .04
- ❑ 293 Kevin Garnett RC 2.50 .75
- ❑ 294 Alan Henderson RC .50 .15
- ❑ 295 Frankie King RC .15 .04
- ❑ 296 Jimmy King RC .15 .04
- ❑ 297 Donny Marshall RC .30 .09
- ❑ 298 Antonio McDyess RC 1.00 .30
- ❑ 299 Loren Meyer RC .15 .04
- ❑ 300 Lawrence Moten RC .15 .04
- ❑ 301 Ed O'Bannon RC .15 .04
- ❑ 302 Greg Ostertag RC .15 .04
- ❑ 303 Cherokee Parks RC .15 .04
- ❑ 304 Theo Ratliff RC .60 .18
- ❑ 305 Bryant Reeves RC .50 .15
- ❑ 306 Shawn Respert RC .15 .04
- ❑ 307 Lou Roe RC .15 .04
- ❑ 308 Arvydas Sabonis RC .60 .18
- ❑ 309 Joe Smith RC .75 .23
- ❑ 310 Jerry Stackhouse RC 1.50 .45
- ❑ 311 Damon Stoudamire RC 1.00 .30
- ❑ 312 Bob Sura RC .30 .09
- ❑ 313 Kurt Thomas RC .30 .09
- ❑ 314 Gary Trent RC .15 .04
- ❑ 315 David Vaughn RC .15 .04
- ❑ 316 Rasheed Wallace RC 1.25 .35
- ❑ 317 Eric Williams RC .30 .09
- ❑ 318 Corliss Williamson RC .50 .15
- ❑ 319 George Zidek RC .15 .04
- ❑ 320 Mookie Blaylock FF .15 .04
- ❑ 321 Dino Radja FF .15 .04
- ❑ 322 Larry Johnson FF .15 .04
- ❑ 323 Michael Jordan FF 1.50 .45
- ❑ 324 Tyrone Hill FF .15 .04
- ❑ 325 Jason Kidd FF .75 .23
- ❑ 326 Dikembe Mutombo FF .15 .04
- ❑ 327 Grant Hill FF .50 .15
- ❑ 328 Joe Smith FF .30 .09
- ❑ 329 Hakeem Olajuwon FF .30 .09
- ❑ 330 Reggie Miller FF .30 .09
- ❑ 331 Loy Vaught FF .15 .04
- ❑ 332 Nick Van Exel FF .15 .04
- ❑ 333 Alonzo Mourning FF .15 .04
- ❑ 334 Glenn Robinson FF .30 .09
- ❑ 335 Kevin Garnett FF 1.00 .30
- ❑ 336 Kenny Anderson FF .15 .04
- ❑ 337 Patrick Ewing FF .30 .09
- ❑ 338 Shaquille O'Neal FF .50 .15
- ❑ 339 Jerry Stackhouse FF .75 .23
- ❑ 340 Charles Barkley FF .50 .15
- ❑ 341 Clifford Robinson FF .15 .04
- ❑ 342 Mitch Richmond FF .15 .04
- ❑ 343 David Robinson FF .30 .09
- ❑ 344 Shawn Kemp FF .15 .04
- ❑ 345 Damon Stoudamire FF .60 .18
- ❑ 346 Karl Malone FF .50 .15
- ❑ 347 Bryant Reeves FF .30 .09
- ❑ 348 Chris Webber FF .30 .09
- ❑ 349 Checklist (201-319) .15 .04
- ❑ 350 Checklist (320-350/ins.) .15 .04

1996-97 Fleer

	Nm-Mt	Ex-Mt
COMPLETE SET (300)	35.00	10.50
COMPLETE SERIES 1 (150)	15.00	4.50
COMPLETE SERIES 2 (150)	20.00	6.00

- ❑ 1 Stacey Augmon .15 .04
- ❑ 2 Mookie Blaylock .15 .04
- ❑ 3 Christian Laettner .30 .09
- ❑ 4 Grant Long .15 .04
- ❑ 5 Steve Smith .30 .09
- ❑ 6 Rick Fox .15 .04
- ❑ 7 Dino Radja .15 .04
- ❑ 8 Eric Williams .15 .04
- ❑ 9 Kenny Anderson .15 .04
- ❑ 10 Dell Curry .15 .04
- ❑ 11 Larry Johnson .30 .09
- ❑ 12 Glen Rice .30 .09
- ❑ 13 Michael Jordan 3.00 .90
- ❑ 14 Toni Kukoc .30 .09
- ❑ 15 Scottie Pippen .75 .23
- ❑ 16 Dennis Rodman .30 .09
- ❑ 17 Terrell Brandon .30 .09
- ❑ 18 Chris Mills .15 .04
- ❑ 19 Bobby Phills .15 .04
- ❑ 20 Bob Sura .15 .04
- ❑ 21 Jim Jackson .15 .04
- ❑ 22 Jason Kidd .75 .23
- ❑ 23 Jamal Mashburn .30 .09
- ❑ 24 George McCloud .15 .04
- ❑ 25 Mahmoud Abdul-Rauf .15 .04
- ❑ 26 Antonio McDyess .30 .09
- ❑ 27 Dikembe Mutombo .30 .09
- ❑ 28 Jalen Rose .50 .15
- ❑ 29 Bryant Stith .15 .04
- ❑ 30 Joe Dumars .50 .15
- ❑ 31 Grant Hill .50 .15
- ❑ 32 Allan Houston .30 .09
- ❑ 33 Theo Ratliff .30 .09
- ❑ 34 Otis Thorpe .15 .04
- ❑ 35 Chris Mullin .50 .15
- ❑ 36 Joe Smith .30 .09
- ❑ 37 Latrell Sprewell .50 .15
- ❑ 38 Kevin Willis .15 .04
- ❑ 39 Sam Cassell .50 .15
- ❑ 40 Clyde Drexler .50 .15
- ❑ 41 Robert Horry .30 .09
- ❑ 42 Hakeem Olajuwon .50 .15

	No.	Player		
❑	43	Dale Davis	.15	.04
❑	44	Mark Jackson	.15	.04
❑	45	Derrick McKey	.15	.04
❑	46	Reggie Miller	.50	.15
❑	47	Rik Smits	.30	.09
❑	48	Brent Barry	.15	.04
❑	49	Malik Sealy	.15	.04
❑	50	Loy Vaught	.15	.04
❑	51	Brian Williams	.15	.04
❑	52	Elden Campbell	.15	.04
❑	53	Cedric Ceballos	.15	.04
❑	54	Vlade Divac	.15	.04
❑	55	Eddie Jones	.50	.15
❑	56	Nick Van Exel	.50	.15
❑	57	Tim Hardaway	.30	.09
❑	58	Alonzo Mourning	.30	.09
❑	59	Kurt Thomas	.30	.09
❑	60	Walt Williams	.15	.04
❑	61	Vin Baker	.30	.09
❑	62	Sherman Douglas	.15	.04
❑	63	Glenn Robinson	.50	.15
❑	64	Kevin Garnett	1.00	.30
❑	65	Tom Gugliotta	.15	.04
❑	66	Isaiah Rider	.30	.09
❑	67	Shawn Bradley	.15	.04
❑	68	Chris Childs	.15	.04
❑	69	Armon Gilliam	.15	.04
❑	70	Ed O'Bannon	.15	.04
❑	71	Patrick Ewing	.50	.15
❑	72	Derek Harper	.15	.04
❑	73	Anthony Mason	.30	.09
❑	74	Charles Oakley	.15	.04
❑	75	John Starks	.30	.09
❑	76	Nick Anderson	.15	.04
❑	77	Horace Grant	.30	.09
❑	78	Anfernee Hardaway	.50	.15
❑	79	Shaquille O'Neal	1.25	.35
❑	80	Dennis Scott	.15	.04
❑	81	Derrick Coleman	.30	.09
❑	82	Vernon Maxwell	.15	.04
❑	83	Jerry Stackhouse	.60	.18
❑	84	Clarence Weatherspoon	.15	.04
❑	85	Charles Barkley	.60	.18
❑	86	Michael Finley	.60	.18
❑	87	Kevin Johnson	.30	.09
❑	88	Wesley Person	.15	.04
❑	89	Clifford Robinson	.15	.04
❑	90	Arvydas Sabonis	.30	.09
❑	91	Rod Strickland	.15	.04
❑	92	Gary Trent	.15	.04
❑	93	Tyus Edney	.15	.04
❑	94	Brian Grant	.50	.15
❑	95	Billy Owens	.15	.04
❑	96	Mitch Richmond	.30	.09
❑	97	Vinny Del Negro	.15	.04
❑	98	Sean Elliott	.30	.09
❑	99	Avery Johnson	.15	.04
❑	100	David Robinson	.50	.15
❑	101	Hersey Hawkins	.30	.09
❑	102	Shawn Kemp	.30	.09
❑	103	Gary Payton	.50	.15
❑	104	Detlef Schrempf	.30	.09
❑	105	Oliver Miller	.15	.04
❑	106	Tracy Murray	.15	.04
❑	107	Damon Stoudamire	.50	.15
❑	108	Sharone Wright	.15	.04
❑	109	Jeff Hornacek	.30	.09
❑	110	Karl Malone	.50	.15
❑	111	John Stockton	.50	.15
❑	112	Greg Anthony	.15	.04
❑	113	Bryant Reeves	.15	.04
❑	114	Byron Scott	.15	.04
❑	115	Calbert Cheaney	.15	.04
❑	116	Juwan Howard	.30	.09
❑	117	Gheorghe Muresan	.15	.04
❑	118	Rasheed Wallace	.60	.18
❑	119	Chris Webber	.50	.15
❑	120	Mookie Blaylock HL	.15	.04
❑	121	Dino Radja HL	.15	.04
❑	122	Larry Johnson HL	.15	.04
❑	123	Michael Jordan HL	1.50	.45
❑	124	Terrell Brandon HL	.15	.04
❑	125	Jason Kidd HL	.40	.12
❑	126	Antonio McDyess HL	.30	.09
❑	127	Grant Hill HL	.30	.09
❑	128	Latrell Sprewell HL	.50	.15
❑	129	Hakeem Olajuwon HL	.30	.09
❑	130	Reggie Miller HL	.30	.09
❑	131	Loy Vaught HL	.15	.04
❑	132	Cedric Ceballos HL	.15	.04
❑	133	Alonzo Mourning HL	.15	.04
❑	134	Vin Baker HL	.15	.04
❑	135	Isaiah Rider HL	.15	.04
❑	136	Armon Gilliam HL	.15	.04
❑	137	Patrick Ewing HL	.30	.09
❑	138	Shaquille O'Neal HL	.50	.15
❑	139	Jerry Stackhouse HL	.30	.09
❑	140	Charles Barkley HL	.50	.15
❑	141	Clifford Robinson HL	.15	.04
❑	142	Mitch Richmond HL	.15	.04
❑	143	David Robinson HL	.30	.09
❑	144	Shawn Kemp HL	.15	.04
❑	145	Damon Stoudamire HL	.30	.09
❑	146	Karl Malone HL	.30	.09
❑	147	Bryant Reeves HL	.15	.04
❑	148	Juwan Howard HL	.15	.04
❑	149	Checklist	.15	.04
❑	150	Checklist	.15	.04
❑	151	Alan Henderson	.15	.04
❑	152	Priest Lauderdale RC	.15	.04
❑	153	Dikembe Mutombo	.30	.09
❑	154	Dana Barros	.15	.04
❑	155	Todd Day	.15	.04
❑	156	Brett Szabo RC	.15	.04
❑	157	Antoine Walker RC	1.00	.30
❑	158	Scott Burrell	.15	.04
❑	159	Tony Delk RC	.50	.15
❑	160	Vlade Divac	.15	.04
❑	161	Matt Geiger	.15	.04
❑	162	Anthony Mason	.30	.09
❑	163	Malik Rose RC	.30	.09
❑	164	Ron Harper	.30	.09
❑	165	Steve Kerr	.30	.09
❑	166	Luc Longley	.15	.04
❑	167	Danny Ferry	.15	.04
❑	168	Tyrone Hill	.15	.04
❑	169	Vitaly Potapenko RC	.15	.04
❑	170	Tony Dumas	.15	.04
❑	171	Chris Gatling	.15	.04
❑	172	Oliver Miller	.15	.04
❑	173	Eric Montross	.15	.04
❑	174	Samaki Walker RC	.15	.04
❑	175	Darvin Ham RC	.15	.04
❑	176	Mark Jackson	.15	.04
❑	177	Ervin Johnson	.15	.04
❑	178	Stacey Augmon	.15	.04
❑	179	Joe Dumars	.50	.15
❑	180	Grant Hill	.50	.15
❑	181	Grant Long	.15	.04
❑	182	Terry Mills	.15	.04
❑	183	Otis Thorpe	.15	.04
❑	184	Jerome Williams RC	.50	.15
❑	185	B.J. Armstrong	.15	.04
❑	186	Todd Fuller RC	.15	.04
❑	187	Ray Owes RC	.15	.04
❑	188	Mark Price	.30	.09
❑	189	Felton Spencer	.15	.04
❑	190	Charles Barkley	.60	.18
❑	191	Mario Elie	.15	.04
❑	192	Othella Harrington RC	.50	.15
❑	193	Matt Maloney RC	.30	.09
❑	194	Brent Price	.15	.04
❑	195	Kevin Willis	.15	.04
❑	196	Travis Best	.15	.04
❑	197	Erick Dampier RC	.50	.15
❑	198	Antonio Davis	.15	.04
❑	199	Jalen Rose	.50	.15
❑	200	Pooh Richardson	.15	.04
❑	201	Rodney Rogers	.15	.04
❑	202	Lorenzen Wright RC	.30	.09
❑	203	Kobe Bryant RC	6.00	1.80
❑	204	Derek Fisher RC	.75	.23
❑	205	Travis Knight RC	.15	.04
❑	206	Shaquille O'Neal	1.25	.35
❑	207	Byron Scott	.15	.04
❑	208	P.J. Brown	.15	.04
❑	209	Sasha Danilovic	.15	.04
❑	210	Dan Majerle	.30	.09
❑	211	Martin Muursepp RC	.15	.04
❑	212	Ray Allen RC	1.50	.45
❑	213	Armon Gilliam	.15	.04
❑	214	Andrew Lang	.15	.04
❑	215	Moochie Norris RC	.30	.09
❑	216	Kevin Garnett	1.00	.30
❑	217	Tom Gugliotta	.15	.04
❑	218	Shane Heal RC	.15	.04
❑	219	Stephon Marbury RC	1.50	.45
❑	220	Stojko Vrankovic	.15	.04
❑	221	Kerry Kittles RC	.50	.15
❑	222	Robert Pack	.15	.04
❑	223	Jayson Williams	.30	.09
❑	224	Allan Houston	.30	.09
❑	225	Larry Johnson	.30	.09
❑	226	Dontae' Jones RC	.15	.04
❑	227	Walter McCarty RC	.15	.04
❑	228	John Wallace RC	.50	.15
❑	229	Charlie Ward	.15	.04
❑	230	Brian Evans RC	.15	.04
❑	231	Amal McCaskill RC	.15	.04
❑	232	Brian Shaw	.15	.04
❑	233	Mark Davis	.15	.04
❑	234	Lucious Harris	.15	.04
❑	235	Allen Iverson RC	2.50	.75
❑	236	Sam Cassell	.50	.15
❑	237	Robert Horry	.30	.09
❑	238	Danny Manning	.30	.09
❑	239	Steve Nash RC	1.50	.45
❑	240	Kenny Anderson	.15	.04
❑	241	Aleksandar Djordjevic RC	.15	.04
❑	242	Jermaine O'Neal RC	1.50	.45
❑	243	Isaiah Rider	.30	.09
❑	244	Rasheed Wallace	.60	.18
❑	245	Mahmoud Abdul-Rauf	.15	.04
❑	246	Michael Smith	.15	.04
❑	247	Corliss Williamson	.30	.09
❑	248	Vernon Maxwell	.15	.04
❑	249	Charles Smith	.15	.04
❑	250	Dominique Wilkins	.50	.15
❑	251	Craig Ehlo	.15	.04
❑	252	Jim McIlvaine	.15	.04
❑	253	Sam Perkins	.30	.09
❑	254	Marcus Camby RC	.60	.18
❑	255	Popeye Jones	.15	.04
❑	256	Donald Whiteside RC	.15	.04
❑	257	Walt Williams	.15	.04
❑	258	Jeff Hornacek	.30	.09
❑	259	Karl Malone	.50	.15
❑	260	Bryon Russell	.15	.04
❑	261	John Stockton	.50	.15
❑	262	Shareef Abdur-Rahim RC	1.50	.45
❑	263	Anthony Peeler	.15	.04
❑	264	Roy Rogers RC	.15	.04
❑	265	Tim Legler	.15	.04
❑	266	Tracy Murray	.15	.04
❑	267	Rod Strickland	.15	.04
❑	268	Ben Wallace RC	3.00	.90
❑	269	Kevin Garnett CB	.50	.15
❑	270	Allan Houston CB	.15	.04
❑	271	Eddie Jones CB	.30	.09
❑	272	Jamal Mashburn CB	.15	.04
❑	273	Antonio McDyess CB	.30	.09
❑	274	Glenn Robinson CB	.30	.09
❑	275	Joe Smith CB	.15	.04
❑	276	Steve Smith CB	.15	.04
❑	277	Jerry Stackhouse CB	.50	.15
❑	278	Damon Stoudamire CB	.30	.09
❑	279	Hakeem Olajuwon AS	.30	.09
❑	280	Charles Barkley AS	.30	.09
❑	281	Patrick Ewing AS	.30	.09
❑	282	Michael Jordan AS	1.50	.45
❑	283	Clyde Drexler AS	.30	.09
❑	284	Karl Malone AS	.30	.09
❑	285	John Stockton AS	.30	.09
❑	286	David Robinson AS	.30	.09
❑	287	Scottie Pippen AS	.40	.12
❑	288	Shawn Kemp AS	.15	.04
❑	289	Shaquille O'Neal AS	.50	.15
❑	290	Mitch Richmond AS	.15	.04
❑	291	Reggie Miller AS	.30	.09
❑	292	Alonzo Mourning AS	.15	.04
❑	293	Gary Payton AS	.30	.09
❑	294	Anfernee Hardaway AS	.30	.09
❑	295	Grant Hill AS	.30	.09
❑	296	Dennis Rodman AS	.15	.04
❑	297	Juwan Howard AS	.15	.04
❑	298	Jason Kidd AS	.40	.12
❑	299	Checklist	.15	.04
❑	300	Checklist	.15	.04

1997-98 Fleer

	Nm-Mt	Ex-Mt
COMPLETE SET (350)	40.00	12.00
COMPLETE SERIES 1 (200)	20.00	6.00
COMPLETE SERIES 2 (150)	20.00	6.00
❑ 1 Anfernee Hardaway	.50	.15
❑ 2 Mitch Richmond	.30	.09
❑ 3 Allen Iverson	1.25	.35
❑ 4 Chris Webber	.50	.15
❑ 5 Sasha Danilovic	.15	.04
❑ 6 Avery Johnson	.15	.04
❑ 7 Kenny Anderson	.30	.09
❑ 8 Antoine Walker	.60	.18
❑ 9 Nick Van Exel	.50	.15
❑ 10 Mookie Blaylock	.15	.04
❑ 11 Wesley Person	.15	.04
❑ 12 Vlade Divac	.30	.09
❑ 13 Glenn Robinson	.50	.15
❑ 14 Chris Mills	.15	.04
❑ 15 Latrell Sprewell	.50	.15
❑ 16 Jayson Williams	.15	.04
❑ 17 Travis Best	.15	.04
❑ 18 Charlie Ward	.15	.04
❑ 19 Theo Ratliff	.15	.04
❑ 20 Gary Payton	.50	.15
❑ 21 Marcus Camby	.50	.15
❑ 22 Clyde Drexler	.50	.15
❑ 23 Michael Jordan	3.00	.90
❑ 24 Antonio McDyess	.30	.09
❑ 25 Stephon Marbury	.60	.18
❑ 26 Isaac Austin	.15	.04
❑ 27 Shareef Abdur-Rahim	.75	.23
❑ 28 Malik Sealy	.15	.04
❑ 29 Arvydas Sabonis	.30	.09
❑ 30 Kerry Kittles	.50	.15
❑ 31 Reggie Miller	.50	.15
❑ 32 Karl Malone	.50	.15
❑ 33 Grant Hill	.50	.15
❑ 34 Hakeem Olajuwon	.50	.15
❑ 35 Danny Ferry	.15	.04
❑ 36 Dominique Wilkins	.50	.15
❑ 37 Armon Gilliam	.15	.04
❑ 38 Danny Manning	.30	.09
❑ 39 Larry Johnson	.30	.09
❑ 40 Dino Radja	.15	.04
❑ 41 Jason Caffey	.15	.04
❑ 42 Jerry Stackhouse	.50	.15
❑ 43 Alonzo Mourning	.30	.09
❑ 44 Shawn Bradley	.15	.04
❑ 45 Bo Outlaw	.15	.04
❑ 46 Bryon Russell	.15	.04
❑ 47 Doug West	.15	.04
❑ 48 Lawrence Moten	.15	.04
❑ 49 Dale Ellis	.15	.04
❑ 50 Kobe Bryant	2.00	.60
❑ 51 Carlos Rogers	.15	.04
❑ 52 Todd Fuller	.15	.04
❑ 53 Tyus Edney	.15	.04
❑ 54 Horace Grant	.30	.09
❑ 55 Dikembe Mutombo	.30	.09
❑ 56 Jim McIlvaine	.15	.04
❑ 57 Harvey Grant	.15	.04
❑ 58 Dean Garrett	.15	.04
❑ 59 Samaki Walker	.15	.04
❑ 60 Johnny Newman	.15	.04
❑ 61 Antonio Davis	.15	.04
❑ 62 Jamal Mashburn	.30	.09
❑ 63 Muggsy Bogues	.30	.09
❑ 64 Rod Strickland	.15	.04
❑ 65 Craig Ehlo	.15	.04
❑ 66 Rex Walters	.15	.04
❑ 67 Bob Sura	.15	.04
❑ 68 Travis Knight	.15	.04
❑ 69 Toni Kukoc	.30	.09
❑ 70 Antoine Carr	.15	.04
❑ 71 Mario Elie	.15	.04
❑ 72 Popeye Jones	.15	.04
❑ 73 David Wesley	.15	.04
❑ 74 John Wallace	.15	.04
❑ 75 Calbert Cheaney	.15	.04
❑ 76 Grant Long	.15	.04
❑ 77 Will Perdue	.15	.04
❑ 78 Rasheed Wallace	.50	.15
❑ 79 Chris Gatling	.15	.04
❑ 80 Corliss Williamson	.30	.09
❑ 81 B.J. Armstrong	.15	.04
❑ 82 Brian Shaw	.15	.04
❑ 83 Darrick Martin	.15	.04
❑ 84 Vinny Del Negro	.15	.04
❑ 85 Tony Delk	.15	.04
❑ 86 Greg Anthony	.15	.04
❑ 87 Mark Davis	.15	.04
❑ 88 Anthony Goldwire	.15	.04
❑ 89 Rex Chapman	.15	.04
❑ 90 Stojko Vrankovic	.15	.04
❑ 91 Dennis Rodman	.30	.09
❑ 92 Detlef Schrempf	.30	.09
❑ 93 Henry James	.15	.04
❑ 94 Tracy Murray	.15	.04
❑ 95 Voshon Lenard	.15	.04
❑ 96 Sharone Wright	.15	.04
❑ 97 Ed O'Bannon	.15	.04
❑ 98 Gerald Wilkins	.15	.04
❑ 99 Kevin Willis	.30	.09
❑ 100 Shaquille O'Neal	1.25	.35
❑ 101 Jim Jackson	.15	.04
❑ 102 Mark Price	.30	.09
❑ 103 Patrick Ewing	.50	.15
❑ 104 Lorenzen Wright	.15	.04
❑ 105 Tyrone Hill	.15	.04
❑ 106 Ray Allen	.50	.15
❑ 107 Jermaine O'Neal	.75	.23
❑ 108 Anthony Mason	.30	.09
❑ 109 Mahmoud Abdul-Rauf	.15	.04
❑ 110 Terry Mills	.15	.04
❑ 111 Gheorghe Muresan	.15	.04
❑ 112 Mark Jackson	.30	.09
❑ 113 Greg Ostertag	.15	.04
❑ 114 Kevin Johnson	.30	.09
❑ 115 Anthony Peeler	.15	.04
❑ 116 Rony Seikaly	.15	.04
❑ 117 Keith Askins	.15	.04
❑ 118 Todd Day	.15	.04
❑ 119 Chris Childs	.15	.04
❑ 120 Chris Carr	.15	.04
❑ 121 Erick Strickland RC	.30	.09
❑ 122 Elden Campbell	.15	.04
❑ 123 Elliot Perry	.15	.04
❑ 124 Pooh Richardson	.15	.04
❑ 125 Juwan Howard	.30	.09
❑ 126 Ervin Johnson	.15	.04
❑ 127 Eric Montross	.15	.04
❑ 128 Otis Thorpe	.15	.04
❑ 129 Hersey Hawkins	.15	.04
❑ 130 Bimbo Coles	.15	.04
❑ 131 Olden Polynice	.15	.04
❑ 132 Christian Laettner	.30	.09
❑ 133 Sean Elliott	.30	.09
❑ 134 Othella Harrington	.15	.04
❑ 135 Erick Dampier	.30	.09
❑ 136 Vitaly Potapenko	.15	.04
❑ 137 Doug Christie	.30	.09
❑ 138 Luc Longley	.15	.04
❑ 139 Clarence Weatherspoon	.15	.04
❑ 140 Gary Trent	.15	.04
❑ 141 Shandon Anderson	.15	.04
❑ 142 Sam Perkins	.30	.09
❑ 143 Derek Harper	.30	.09
❑ 144 Robert Horry	.30	.09
❑ 145 Roy Rogers	.15	.04
❑ 146 John Starks	.30	.09
❑ 147 Tyrone Corbin	.15	.04
❑ 148 Andrew Lang	.15	.04
❑ 149 Derek Strong	.15	.04
❑ 150 Joe Smith	.30	.09
❑ 151 Ron Harper	.30	.09
❑ 152 Sam Cassell	.50	.15
❑ 153 Brent Barry	.30	.09
❑ 154 LaPhonso Ellis	.15	.04
❑ 155 Matt Geiger	.15	.04
❑ 156 Steve Nash	.50	.15
❑ 157 Michael Smith	.15	.04
❑ 158 Eric Williams	.15	.04
❑ 159 Tom Gugliotta	.30	.09
❑ 160 Monty Williams	.15	.04
❑ 161 Lindsey Hunter	.15	.04
❑ 162 Oliver Miller	.15	.04
❑ 163 Brent Price	.15	.04
❑ 164 Derrick McKey	.15	.04
❑ 165 Robert Pack	.15	.04
❑ 166 Derrick Coleman	.15	.04
❑ 167 Isaiah Rider	.30	.09
❑ 168 Dan Majerle	.30	.09
❑ 169 Jeff Hornacek	.30	.09
❑ 170 Terrell Brandon	.30	.09
❑ 171 Nate McMillan	.15	.04
❑ 172 Cedric Ceballos	.15	.04
❑ 173 Derek Fisher	.50	.15
❑ 174 Rodney Rogers	.15	.04
❑ 175 Blue Edwards	.15	.04
❑ 176 Brooks Thompson	.15	.04
❑ 177 Sherman Douglas	.15	.04
❑ 178 Sam Mitchell	.15	.04
❑ 179 Charles Oakley	.30	.09
❑ 180 Greg Minor	.15	.04
❑ 181 Chris Mullin	.50	.15
❑ 182 P.J. Brown	.15	.04
❑ 183 Stacey Augmon	.15	.04
❑ 184 Don MacLean	.15	.04
❑ 185 Aaron McKie	.30	.09
❑ 186 Dale Davis	.15	.04
❑ 187 Vernon Maxwell	.15	.04
❑ 188 Dell Curry	.15	.04
❑ 189 Kendall Gill	.15	.04
❑ 190 Billy Owens	.15	.04
❑ 191 Steve Kerr	.30	.09
❑ 192 Matt Maloney	.15	.04
❑ 193 Dennis Scott	.15	.04
❑ 194 A.C. Green	.30	.09
❑ 195 George McCloud	.15	.04
❑ 196 Walt Williams	.15	.04
❑ 197 Eldridge Recasner	.15	.04
❑ 198 Checklist (Hawks/Bucks)	.15	.04
❑ 199 Checklist (T'wolves/Wizards)	.15	.04
❑ 200 Checklist (inserts)	.15	.04
❑ 201 Tim Duncan RC	2.00	.60
❑ 202 Tim Thomas RC	.75	.23
❑ 203 Clifford Rozier	.15	.04
❑ 204 Bryant Reeves	.15	.04
❑ 205 Glen Rice	.30	.09
❑ 206 Darrell Armstrong	.15	.04
❑ 207 Juwan Howard	.30	.09
❑ 208 John Stockton	.50	.15
❑ 209 Antonio McDyess	.30	.09
❑ 210 James Cotton RC	.15	.04
❑ 211 Brian Grant	.30	.09
❑ 212 Chris Whitney	.15	.04
❑ 213 Antonio Davis	.15	.04
❑ 214 Kendall Gill	.15	.04
❑ 215 Adonal Foyle RC	.30	.09
❑ 216 Dean Garrett	.15	.04
❑ 217 Dennis Scott	.15	.04
❑ 218 Zydrunas Ilgauskas	.30	.09
❑ 219 Antonio Daniels RC	.50	.15
❑ 220 Derek Harper	.30	.09
❑ 221 Travis Knight	.15	.04
❑ 222 Bobby Hurley	.15	.04
❑ 223 Greg Anderson	.15	.04
❑ 224 Rod Strickland	.15	.04
❑ 225 David Benoit	.15	.04
❑ 226 Tracy McGrady RC	2.50	.75
❑ 227 Brian Williams	.15	.04
❑ 228 James Robinson	.15	.04
❑ 229 Randy Brown	.15	.04
❑ 230 Greg Foster	.15	.04
❑ 231 Reggie Miller	.50	.15

❑ 232 Eric Montross	.15	.04
❑ 233 Malik Rose	.15	.04
❑ 234 Charles Barkley	.60	.18
❑ 235 Tony Battie RC	.50	.15
❑ 236 Terry Mills	.15	.04
❑ 237 Jerald Honeycutt RC	.15	.04
❑ 238 Bubba Wells RC	.15	.04
❑ 239 John Wallace	.15	.04
❑ 240 Jason Kidd	.75	.23
❑ 241 Mark Price	.30	.09
❑ 242 Ron Mercer RC	.60	.18
❑ 243 Derrick Coleman	.15	.04
❑ 244 Fred Hoiberg	.15	.04
❑ 245 Wesley Person	.15	.04
❑ 246 Eddie Jones	.50	.15
❑ 247 Allan Houston	.30	.09
❑ 248 Keith Van Horn RC	.75	.23
❑ 249 Johnny Newman	.15	.04
❑ 250 Kevin Garnett	1.00	.30
❑ 251 Latrell Sprewell	.50	.15
❑ 252 Tracy Murray	.15	.04
❑ 253 Charles O'Bannon RC	.15	.04
❑ 254 Lamond Murray	.15	.04
❑ 255 Jerry Stackhouse	.50	.15
❑ 256 Rik Smits	.30	.09
❑ 257 Alan Henderson	.15	.04
❑ 258 Tariq Abdul-Wahad RC	.30	.09
❑ 259 Nick Anderson	.15	.04
❑ 260 Calbert Cheaney	.15	.04
❑ 261 Scottie Pippen	.75	.23
❑ 262 Rodrick Rhodes RC	.15	.04
❑ 263 Derek Anderson RC	1.00	.30
❑ 264 Dana Barros	.15	.04
❑ 265 Todd Day	.15	.04
❑ 266 Michael Finley	.50	.15
❑ 267 Kevin Edwards	.15	.04
❑ 268 Terrell Brandon	.30	.09
❑ 269 Bobby Phills	.15	.04
❑ 270 Kelvin Cato RC	.50	.15
❑ 271 Vin Baker	.30	.09
❑ 272 Eric Washington RC	.50	.15
❑ 273 Jim Jackson	.15	.04
❑ 274 Joe Dumars	.50	.15
❑ 275 David Robinson	.50	.15
❑ 276 Jayson Williams	.15	.04
❑ 277 Travis Best	.15	.04
❑ 278 Kurt Thomas	.30	.09
❑ 279 Otis Thorpe	.15	.04
❑ 280 Damon Stoudamire	.30	.09
❑ 281 John Williams	.15	.04
❑ 282 Loy Vaught	.15	.04
❑ 283 Bo Outlaw	.15	.04
❑ 284 Todd Fuller	.15	.04
❑ 285 Terry Dehere	.15	.04
❑ 286 Clarence Weatherspoon	.15	.04
❑ 287 Danny Fortson RC	.30	.09
❑ 288 Howard Eisley	.15	.04
❑ 289 Steve Smith	.30	.09
❑ 290 Chris Webber	.50	.15
❑ 291 Shawn Kemp	.30	.09
❑ 292 Sam Cassell	.50	.15
❑ 293 Rick Fox	.30	.09
❑ 294 Walter McCarty	.15	.04
❑ 295 Mark Jackson	.30	.09
❑ 296 Chris Mills	.15	.04
❑ 297 Jacque Vaughn RC	.30	.09
❑ 298 Shawn Respert	.15	.04
❑ 299 Scott Burrell	.15	.04
❑ 300 Allen Iverson	1.25	.35
❑ 301 Charles Smith RC	.15	.04
❑ 302 Ervin Johnson	.15	.04
❑ 303 Hubert Davis	.15	.04
❑ 304 Eddie Johnson	.15	.04
❑ 305 Erick Dampier	.30	.09
❑ 306 Eric Williams	.15	.04
❑ 307 Anthony Johnson RC	.15	.04
❑ 308 David Wesley	.15	.04
❑ 309 Eric Piatkowski	.30	.09
❑ 310 Austin Croshere RC	.50	.15
❑ 311 Malik Sealy	.15	.04
❑ 312 George McCloud	.15	.04
❑ 313 Anthony Parker RC	.15	.04
❑ 314 Cedric Henderson RC	.30	.09
❑ 315 John Thomas RC	.15	.04
❑ 316 Cory Alexander	.15	.04
❑ 317 Johnny Taylor RC	.15	.04
❑ 318 Chris Mullin	.50	.15
❑ 319 J.R. Reid	.15	.04
❑ 320 George Lynch	.15	.04
❑ 321 L.Funderburke RC	.30	.09
❑ 322 God Shammgod RC	.15	.04
❑ 323 Bobby Jackson RC	.75	.23
❑ 324 Khalid Reeves	.15	.04
❑ 325 Zan Tabak	.15	.04
❑ 326 Chris Gatling	.15	.04
❑ 327 Alvin Williams RC	.15	.04
❑ 328 Scot Pollard RC	.30	.09
❑ 329 Kerry Kittles	.50	.15
❑ 330 Tim Hardaway	.30	.09
❑ 331 Maurice Taylor RC	.50	.15
❑ 332 Keith Booth RC	.15	.04
❑ 333 Chris Morris	.15	.04
❑ 334 Bryant Stith	.15	.04
❑ 335 Terry Cummings	.15	.04
❑ 336 Ed Gray RC	.15	.04
❑ 337 Eric Snow	.30	.09
❑ 338 Clifford Robinson	.15	.04
❑ 339 Chris Dudley	.15	.04
❑ 340 Chauncey Billups RC	.50	.15
❑ 341 Paul Grant RC	.15	.04
❑ 342 Tyrone Hill	.15	.04
❑ 343 Joe Smith	.30	.09
❑ 344 Sean Rooks	.15	.04
❑ 345 Harvey Grant	.15	.04
❑ 346 Dale Davis	.15	.04
❑ 347 Brevin Knight RC	.30	.09
❑ 348 Serge Zwikker RC	.15	.04
❑ 349 Checklist (Hawks/Kings)	.15	.04
❑ 350 Checklist (Spurs/Wizards/Inserts)	.15	.04

1999-00 Fleer

	Nm-Mt	Ex-Mt
COMPLETE SET (220)	30.00	9.00
COMMON CARD (1-200)	.15	.04
COMMON ROOKIE (201-220)	.25	.07
❑ 1 Vince Carter	1.25	.35
❑ 2 Kobe Bryant	2.00	.60
❑ 3 Keith Van Horn	.50	.15
❑ 4 Tim Duncan	1.00	.30
❑ 5 Grant Hill	.50	.15
❑ 6 Kevin Garnett	1.00	.30
❑ 7 Anfernee Hardaway	.50	.15
❑ 8 Jason Williams	.50	.15
❑ 9 Paul Pierce	.50	.15
❑ 10 Mookie Blaylock	.15	.04
❑ 11 Shawn Bradley	.15	.04
❑ 12 Kenny Anderson	.30	.09
❑ 13 Chauncey Billups	.30	.09
❑ 14 Elden Campbell	.15	.04
❑ 15 Jason Caffey	.15	.04
❑ 16 Brent Barry	.30	.09
❑ 17 Charles Barkley	.60	.18
❑ 18 Derek Anderson	.30	.09
❑ 19 Darrick Martin	.15	.04
❑ 20 Bison Dele	.15	.04
❑ 21 Rick Fox	.30	.09
❑ 22 Antonio Davis	.15	.04
❑ 23 Terrell Brandon	.30	.09
❑ 24 P.J. Brown	.15	.04
❑ 25 Toby Bailey	.15	.04
❑ 26 Ray Allen	.50	.15
❑ 27 Brian Grant	.30	.09
❑ 28 Scott Burrell	.15	.04
❑ 29 Tariq Abdul-Wahad	.15	.04
❑ 30 Marcus Camby	.30	.09
❑ 31 John Stockton	.50	.15
❑ 32 Nick Anderson	.15	.04
❑ 33 Antonio Daniels	.15	.04
❑ 34 Matt Geiger	.15	.04
❑ 35 Vin Baker	.30	.09
❑ 36 Dee Brown	.15	.04
❑ 37 Shandon Anderson	.15	.04
❑ 38 Calbert Cheaney	.15	.04
❑ 39 Shareef Abdur-Rahim	.50	.15
❑ 40 LaPhonso Ellis	.15	.04
❑ 41 Cedric Ceballos	.15	.04
❑ 42 Tony Battie	.15	.04
❑ 43 Keon Clark	.30	.09
❑ 44 Derrick Coleman	.30	.09
❑ 45 Erick Dampier	.30	.09
❑ 46 Corey Benjamin	.15	.04
❑ 47 Michael Dickerson	.30	.09
❑ 48 Cedric Henderson	.15	.04
❑ 49 Lamond Murray	.15	.04
❑ 50 Horace Grant	.30	.09
❑ 51 Shaquille O'Neal	1.25	.35
❑ 52 Dale Davis	.15	.04
❑ 53 Dean Garrett	.15	.04
❑ 54 Tim Hardaway	.30	.09
❑ 55 Gerald Brown RC	.15	.04
❑ 56 Sam Cassell	.50	.15
❑ 57 Jim Jackson	.15	.04
❑ 58 Kendall Gill	.15	.04
❑ 59 Eric Williams	.15	.04
❑ 60 Chris Childs	.15	.04
❑ 61 Vlade Divac	.30	.09
❑ 62 Darrell Armstrong	.15	.04
❑ 63 Mario Elie	.15	.04
❑ 64 Tyrone Hill	.15	.04
❑ 65 Dale Ellis	.15	.04
❑ 66 Doug Christie	.30	.09
❑ 67 Howard Eisley	.15	.04
❑ 68 Juwan Howard	.30	.09
❑ 69 Mike Bibby	.50	.15
❑ 70 Alan Henderson	.15	.04
❑ 71 Michael Finley	.50	.15
❑ 72 Dana Barros	.15	.04
❑ 73 Danny Fortson	.15	.04
❑ 74 Ricky Davis	.30	.09
❑ 75 Adonal Foyle	.15	.04
❑ 76 Cory Carr	.15	.04
❑ 77 Bryce Drew	.15	.04
❑ 78 Shawn Kemp	.30	.09
❑ 79 Tyrone Nesby RC	.15	.04
❑ 80 Lindsey Hunter	.15	.04
❑ 81 Ruben Patterson	.30	.09
❑ 82 Al Harrington	.50	.15
❑ 83 Bobby Jackson	.30	.09
❑ 84 Dan Majerle	.30	.09
❑ 85 Rex Chapman	.15	.04
❑ 86 Dell Curry	.15	.04
❑ 87 Walt Williams	.15	.04
❑ 88 Kerry Kittles	.15	.04
❑ 89 Isaiah Rider	.15	.04
❑ 90 Patrick Ewing	.50	.15
❑ 91 Lawrence Funderburke	.15	.04
❑ 92 Isaac Austin	.15	.04
❑ 93 Sean Elliott	.30	.09
❑ 94 Larry Hughes	.50	.15
❑ 95 Hersey Hawkins	.30	.09
❑ 96 Tracy McGrady	1.25	.35
❑ 97 Jeff Hornacek	.30	.09
❑ 98 Randell Jackson	.15	.04
❑ 99 J.R. Henderson	.15	.04
❑ 100 Roshown McLeod	.15	.04
❑ 101 Steve Nash	.50	.15
❑ 102 Ron Mercer	.30	.09
❑ 103 Raef LaFrentz	.30	.09
❑ 104 Eddie Jones	.50	.15
❑ 105 Antawn Jamison	.75	.23
❑ 106 Kornel David RC	.15	.04
❑ 107 Othella Harrington	.15	.04
❑ 108 Brevin Knight	.15	.04
❑ 109 Michael Olowokandi	.30	.09
❑ 110 Christian Laettner	.30	.09
❑ 111 J.R. Reid	.15	.04
❑ 112 Reggie Miller	.50	.15
❑ 113 Andrae Patterson	.15	.04

#	Player	Nm-Mt	Ex-Mt
❑ 114	Jamal Mashburn	.30	.09
❑ 115	Glenn Robinson	.50	.15
❑ 116	Pat Garrity	.15	.04
❑ 117	Stephon Marbury	.50	.15
❑ 118	Arvydas Sabonis	.30	.09
❑ 119	Allan Houston	.30	.09
❑ 120	Peja Stojakovic	.60	.18
❑ 121	Michael Doleac	.15	.04
❑ 122	Avery Johnson	.15	.04
❑ 123	Allen Iverson	1.00	.30
❑ 124	Rashard Lewis	.50	.15
❑ 125	Charles Oakley	.15	.04
❑ 126	Karl Malone	.50	.15
❑ 127	Tracy Murray	.15	.04
❑ 128	Felipe Lopez	.15	.04
❑ 129	Dikembe Mutombo	.30	.09
❑ 130	Dirk Nowitzki	1.00	.30
❑ 131	Vitaly Potapenko	.15	.04
❑ 132	Antonio McDyess	.30	.09
❑ 133	Anthony Mason	.30	.09
❑ 134	Donyell Marshall	.30	.09
❑ 135	Ron Harper	.30	.09
❑ 136	Cuttino Mobley	.50	.15
❑ 137	Wesley Person	.15	.04
❑ 138	Rodney Rogers	.15	.04
❑ 139	Jerry Stackhouse	.50	.15
❑ 140	Glen Rice	.30	.09
❑ 141	Chris Mullin	.50	.15
❑ 142	Anthony Peeler	.15	.04
❑ 143	Alonzo Mourning	.30	.09
❑ 144	Tom Gugliotta	.15	.04
❑ 145	Tim Thomas	.30	.09
❑ 146	Damon Stoudamire	.30	.09
❑ 147	Jayson Williams	.15	.04
❑ 148	Larry Johnson	.30	.09
❑ 149	Chris Webber	.50	.15
❑ 150	Matt Harpring	.50	.15
❑ 151	David Robinson	.50	.15
❑ 152	George Lynch	.15	.04
❑ 153	Gary Payton	.50	.15
❑ 154	John Wallace	.15	.04
❑ 155	Greg Ostertag	.15	.04
❑ 156	Mitch Richmond	.30	.09
❑ 157	Cherokee Parks	.15	.04
❑ 158	Steve Smith	.30	.09
❑ 159	Gary Trent	.15	.04
❑ 160	Antoine Walker	.50	.15
❑ 161	Johnny Taylor	.15	.04
❑ 162	Brad Miller	.50	.15
❑ 163	Chris Mills	.15	.04
❑ 164	Charles Jones	.15	.04
❑ 165	Hakeem Olajuwon	.50	.15
❑ 166	Bob Sura	.15	.04
❑ 167	Brian Skinner	.15	.04
❑ 168	Korleone Young	.15	.04
❑ 169	Tyronn Lue	.30	.09
❑ 170	Jalen Rose	.50	.15
❑ 171	Joe Smith	.30	.09
❑ 172	Clarence Weatherspoon	.15	.04
❑ 173	Jason Kidd	.75	.23
❑ 174	Robert Traylor	.15	.04
❑ 175	Rasheed Wallace	.50	.15
❑ 176	Latrell Sprewell	.50	.15
❑ 177	Corliss Williamson	.30	.09
❑ 178	Bo Outlaw	.15	.04
❑ 179	Malik Rose	.15	.04
❑ 180	Nazr Mohammed	.15	.04
❑ 181	Olden Polynice	.15	.04
❑ 182	Kevin Willis	.15	.04
❑ 183	Bryon Russell	.15	.04
❑ 184	Bryant Reeves	.15	.04
❑ 185	Rod Strickland	.15	.04
❑ 186	Samaki Walker	.15	.04
❑ 187	Nick Van Exel	.50	.15
❑ 188	David Wesley	.15	.04
❑ 189	John Starks	.30	.09
❑ 190	Toni Kukoc	.30	.09
❑ 191	Scottie Pippen	.75	.23
❑ 192	Zydrunas Ilgauskas	.30	.09
❑ 193	Maurice Taylor	.30	.09
❑ 194	Rik Smits	.30	.09
❑ 195	Clifford Robinson	.15	.04
❑ 196	Bonzi Wells	.50	.15
❑ 197	Charlie Ward	.15	.04
❑ 198	Detlef Schrempf	.30	.09
❑ 199	Theo Ratliff	.30	.09
❑ 200	Rodrick Rhodes	.15	.04
❑ 201	Ron Artest RC	.75	.23
❑ 202	William Avery RC	.50	.15
❑ 203	Elton Brand RC	1.50	.45
❑ 204	Baron Davis RC	1.25	.35
❑ 205	Jumaine Jones RC	.75	.23
❑ 206	Andre Miller RC	1.25	.35
❑ 207	Lee Nailon RC	.25	.07
❑ 208	James Posey RC	.75	.23
❑ 209	Jason Terry RC	.75	.23
❑ 210	Kenny Thomas RC	.50	.15
❑ 211	Steve Francis RC	2.00	.60
❑ 212	Wally Szczerbiak RC	1.25	.35
❑ 213	Richard Hamilton RC	1.25	.35
❑ 214	Jonathan Bender RC	1.25	.35
❑ 215	Shawn Marion RC	1.50	.45
❑ 216	Aleksandar Radojevic RC	.25	.07
❑ 217	Tim James RC	.40	.12
❑ 218	Trajan Langdon RC	.50	.15
❑ 219	Lamar Odom RC	1.25	.35
❑ 220	Corey Maggette RC	1.50	.45
❑ NNO	Checklist #3	.15	.04
❑ NNO	Checklist #2	.15	.04
❑ NNO	Checklist #1	.15	.04

2000-01 Fleer

#	Player	Nm-Mt	Ex-Mt
	COMMON CARD (1-300)	.15	.04
	COMMON ROOKIE (227-271)	.50	.15
❑ 1	Lamar Odom	.50	.15
❑ 2	Christian Laettner	.30	.09
❑ 3	Michael Olowokandi	.15	.04
❑ 4	Anthony Carter	.30	.09
❑ 5	Steve Francis	.50	.15
❑ 6	Darvin Ham	.15	.04
❑ 7	Mitch Richmond	.30	.09
❑ 8	Corliss Williamson	.30	.09
❑ 9	Jason Terry	.50	.15
❑ 10	Brian Grant	.30	.09
❑ 11	Peja Stojakovic	.50	.15
❑ 12	Rick Fox	.30	.09
❑ 13	Tyrone Hill	.15	.04
❑ 14	Chauncey Billups	.30	.09
❑ 15	Otis Thorpe	.15	.04
❑ 16	Richard Hamilton	.30	.09
❑ 17	Ervin Johnson	.15	.04
❑ 18	Jim Jackson	.15	.04
❑ 19	Theo Ratliff	.30	.09
❑ 20	Doug Christie	.30	.09
❑ 21	Jalen Rose	.50	.15
❑ 22	John Wallace	.15	.04
❑ 23	Ruben Patterson	.30	.09
❑ 24	Steve Nash	.50	.15
❑ 25	Toni Kukoc	.30	.09
❑ 26	Anthony Peeler	.15	.04
❑ 27	Ray Allen	.50	.15
❑ 28	Adonal Foyle	.15	.04
❑ 29	Chris Whitney	.15	.04
❑ 30	Nick Van Exel	.50	.15
❑ 31	Sean Elliott	.30	.09
❑ 32	Erick Strickland	.15	.04
❑ 33	Jerry Stackhouse	.50	.15
❑ 34	Antawn Jamison	.50	.15
❑ 35	Grant Hill	.50	.15
❑ 36	Antonio Daniels	.15	.04
❑ 37	Karl Malone	.50	.15
❑ 38	Keith Van Horn	.50	.15
❑ 39	Ron Harper	.30	.09
❑ 40	Stephon Marbury	.50	.15
❑ 41	Bryon Russell	.15	.04
❑ 42	Corey Maggette	.30	.09
❑ 43	Hersey Hawkins	.15	.04
❑ 44	Vince Carter	1.25	.35
❑ 45	Paul Pierce	.50	.15
❑ 46	Mikki Moore	.15	.04
❑ 47	Othella Harrington	.15	.04
❑ 48	Erick Dampier	.30	.09
❑ 49	Jerome Williams	.15	.04
❑ 50	Nick Anderson	.15	.04
❑ 51	Tim Hardaway	.30	.09
❑ 52	Allan Houston	.30	.09
❑ 53	Tyrone Nesby	.15	.04
❑ 54	Brevin Knight	.15	.04
❑ 55	Chris Mills	.15	.04
❑ 56	Ron Artest	.30	.09
❑ 57	Walt Williams	.15	.04
❑ 58	Duane Causwell	.15	.04
❑ 59	Bonzi Wells	.30	.09
❑ 60	Rasheed Wallace	.50	.15
❑ 61	Dikembe Mutombo	.30	.09
❑ 62	Jahidi White	.15	.04
❑ 63	Chris Webber	.50	.15
❑ 64	Tony Battie	.15	.04
❑ 65	Mahmoud Abdul-Rauf	.15	.04
❑ 66	Monty Williams	.15	.04
❑ 67	Charlie Ward	.15	.04
❑ 68	David Robinson	.50	.15
❑ 69	Eric Snow	.30	.09
❑ 70	Jermaine O'Neal	.50	.15
❑ 71	Kurt Thomas	.30	.09
❑ 72	James Posey	.30	.09
❑ 73	Travis Best	.15	.04
❑ 74	Jonathan Bender	.30	.09
❑ 75	John Stockton	.50	.15
❑ 76	Jacque Vaughn	.15	.04
❑ 77	Ron Mercer	.30	.09
❑ 78	Shawn Marion	.50	.15
❑ 79	Larry Johnson	.30	.09
❑ 80	Maurice Taylor	.15	.04
❑ 81	Clifford Robinson	.15	.04
❑ 82	Scot Pollard	.15	.04
❑ 83	Patrick Ewing	.50	.15
❑ 84	Terrell Brandon	.30	.09
❑ 85	Horace Grant	.30	.09
❑ 86	Vin Baker	.30	.09
❑ 87	Al Harrington	.30	.09
❑ 88	Larry Hughes	.30	.09
❑ 89	David Wesley	.15	.04
❑ 90	Wally Szczerbiak	.30	.09
❑ 91	Charles Oakley	.15	.04
❑ 92	Tim Thomas	.30	.09
❑ 93	Mookie Blaylock	.15	.04
❑ 94	Jamal Mashburn	.30	.09
❑ 95	Roshown McLeod	.15	.04
❑ 96	John Starks	.30	.09
❑ 97	Rodney Rogers	.15	.04
❑ 98	Juwan Howard	.30	.09
❑ 99	Isaiah Rider	.30	.09
❑ 100	Rashard Lewis	.30	.09
❑ 101	Dion Glover	.15	.04
❑ 102	Johnny Newman	.15	.04
❑ 103	Avery Johnson	.15	.04
❑ 104	Darrell Armstrong	.15	.04
❑ 105	Eric Williams	.15	.04
❑ 106	Gary Payton	.50	.15
❑ 107	Antonio Davis	.15	.04
❑ 108	Dirk Nowitzki	.75	.23
❑ 109	Trajan Langdon	.30	.09
❑ 110	Michael Dickerson	.30	.09
❑ 111	Joe Smith	.30	.09
❑ 112	Rod Strickland	.15	.04
❑ 113	Shawn Kemp	.30	.09
❑ 114	Voshon Lenard	.15	.04
❑ 115	Marcus Camby	.30	.09
❑ 116	Matt Harpring	.50	.15
❑ 117	Isaac Austin	.15	.04
❑ 118	Malik Rose	.15	.04
❑ 119	Pat Garrity	.15	.04
❑ 120	Kenny Thomas	.15	.04
❑ 121	LaPhonso Ellis	.15	.04
❑ 122	Danny Fortson	.15	.04
❑ 123	Elton Brand	.50	.15
❑ 124	Jason Williams	.30	.09
❑ 125	Kobe Bryant	2.00	.60

❑ 126 Tariq Abdul-Wahad ...... .15 .04
❑ 127 Tracy McGrady........... 1.25 .35
❑ 128 Matt Geiger .... .15 .04
❑ 129 Antoine Walker............ .50 .15
❑ 130 Michael Finley .... .50 .15
❑ 131 Andre Miller .... .30 .09
❑ 132 Robert Horry................. .30 .09
❑ 133 Donyell Marshall........... .30 .09
❑ 134 Shareef Abdur-Rahim .. .50 .15
❑ 135 Vonteego Cummings .... .15 .04
❑ 136 Anthony Mason .... .30 .09
❑ 137 Mike Bibby .... .50 .15
❑ 138 Raef LaFrentz .... .30 .09
❑ 139 Glen Rice .... .30 .09
❑ 140 Chris Gatling .... .15 .04
❑ 141 Latrell Sprewell............ .50 .15
❑ 142 Austin Croshere .... .30 .09
❑ 143 Kenny Anderson........... .30 .09
❑ 144 Elden Campbell .... .15 .04
❑ 145 Jason Kidd .... .75 .23
❑ 146 Michael Doleac............. .15 .04
❑ 147 Muggsy Bogues .... .30 .09
❑ 148 Tim Duncan .... 1.00 .30
❑ 149 Samaki Walker............. .15 .04
❑ 150 Gary Trent .... .15 .04
❑ 151 Kevin Garnett .... 1.00 .30
❑ 152 Allen Iverson .... 1.00 .30
❑ 153 Anfernee Hardaway ...... .50 .15
❑ 154 Robert Traylor .... .15 .04
❑ 155 Scottie Pippen .... .75 .23
❑ 156 Shaquille O'Neal......... 1.25 .35
❑ 157 Vlade Divac .... .30 .09
❑ 158 Lucious Harris .... .15 .04
❑ 159 Keon Clark .... .30 .09
❑ 160 Bo Outlaw..................... .15 .04
❑ 161 P.J. Brown .... .15 .04
❑ 162 Derrick Coleman .... .15 .04
❑ 163 Mark Jackson................ .15 .04
❑ 164 Lamond Murray .... .15 .04
❑ 165 Dan Majerle .... .30 .09
❑ 166 Eddie Jones .... .50 .15
❑ 167 Cedric Ceballos .... .15 .04
❑ 168 Kendall Gill .... .15 .04
❑ 169 Tom Gugliotta.............. .15 .04
❑ 170 Jeff McInnis .... .15 .04
❑ 171 Steve Smith .... .30 .09
❑ 172 Kevin Willis.................. .15 .04
❑ 173 Lindsey Hunter............. .15 .04
❑ 174 Derek Anderson .... .30 .09
❑ 175 Shandon Anderson ...... .15 .04
❑ 176 Adrian Griffin .... .15 .04
❑ 177 Baron Davis .... .50 .15
❑ 178 Radoslav Nesterovic .... .30 .09
❑ 179 Glenn Robinson .... .30 .09
❑ 180 Sam Cassell................. .50 .15
❑ 181 Chucky Atkins .... .15 .04
❑ 182 Arvydas Sabonis .... .30 .09
❑ 183 Damon Stoudamire ...... .30 .09
❑ 184 Antonio McDyess......... .30 .09
❑ 185 Derek Fisher................. .50 .15
❑ 186 Bryant Reeves .... .15 .04
❑ 187 Hakeem Olajuwon .... .50 .15
❑ 188 Kerry Kittles .... .15 .04
❑ 189 Alan Henderson .... .15 .04
❑ 190 Sam Perkins.................. .30 .09
❑ 191 Felipe Lopez................. .15 .04
❑ 192 Tracy Murray .... .15 .04
❑ 193 Shammond Williams .... .15 .04
❑ 194 Vitaly Potapenko .... .15 .04
❑ 195 John Amaechi .... .15 .04
❑ 196 Quincy Lewis .... .15 .04
❑ 197 Reggie Miller .... .50 .15
❑ 198 Cuttino Mobley .... .30 .09
❑ 199 Rex Chapman .... .15 .04
❑ 200 Dale Davis .... .15 .04
❑ 201 Andrew DeClercq......... .15 .04
❑ 202 Kelvin Cato................... .15 .04
❑ 203 Jon Barry .... .15 .04
❑ 204 Greg Anthony............... .15 .04
❑ 205 Brent Barry................... .30 .09
❑ 206 Derrick McKey .... .15 .04
❑ 207 Vince Carter UH .... .60 .18
❑ 208 David Robinson UH ...... .30 .09
❑ 209 Eric Snow UH................ .15 .04
❑ 210 Ray Allen UH .... .30 .09
❑ 211 Lamar Odom UH .... .50 .15
❑ 212 Dikembe Mutombo UH.. .15 .04
❑ 213 Brevin Knight UH .... .15 .04
❑ 214 Vin Baker UH .... .30 .09
❑ 215 Antoine Walker UH....... .30 .09
❑ 216 Mitch Richmond UH ...... .15 .04
❑ 217 Elton Brand UH .... .50 .15
❑ 218 Jerome Williams UH...... .15 .04
❑ 219 Keith Van Horn UH........ .15 .04
❑ 220 Nick Van Exel UH.......... .15 .04
❑ 221 Shaquille O'Neal UH .... .60 .18
❑ 222 Allan Houston UH......... .30 .09
❑ 223 Shareef Abdur-Rahim UH .30 .09
❑ 224 Karl Malone UH .... .50 .15
❑ 225 Terrell Brandon UH ...... .15 .04
❑ 226 Eddie Jones UH .... .30 .09
❑ 227 Stromile Swift RC........ 1.00 .30
❑ 228 Dalibor Bagaric RC ...... .50 .15
❑ 229 Erick Barkley RC .... .50 .15
❑ 230 Mike Miller RC .... 1.50 .45
❑ 231 Kenyon Martin RC ...... 2.00 .60
❑ 232 Michael Redd RC .... 1.25 .35
❑ 233 Darius Miles RC .... 1.50 .45
❑ 234 Chris Mihm RC............. .50 .15
❑ 235 Brian Cardinal RC .... .50 .15
❑ 236 Khalid El-Amin RC .... .50 .15
❑ 237 Hanno Mottola RC .... .50 .15
❑ 238 Jamaal Magloire RC...... .50 .15
❑ 239 Courtney Alexander RC .50 .15
❑ 240 Mamadou N'Diaye RC .. .50 .15
❑ 241 Chris Porter RC .... .50 .15
❑ 242 Quentin Richardson RC 1.25 .35
❑ 243 Eddie House RC .... .50 .15
❑ 244 Joel Przybilla RC .... .50 .15
❑ 245 Soumaila Samake RC .. .50 .15
❑ 246 Speedy Claxton RC ...... .50 .15
❑ 247 Desmond Mason RC .... .50 .15
❑ 248 Mike Smith RC .... .50 .15
❑ 249 Lavor Postell RC .... .50 .15
❑ 250 Ruben Garces RC .... .50 .15
❑ 251 DeShawn Stevenson RC .50 .15
❑ 252 Hidayet Turkoglu RC .. 1.50 .45
❑ 253 Keyon Dooling RC .... .50 .15
❑ 254 Dan Langhi RC............. .50 .15
❑ 255 Mateen Cleaves RC...... .50 .15
❑ 256 Donnell Harvey RC ...... .50 .15
❑ 257 DerMarr Johnson RC.... .50 .15
❑ 258 Jason Collier RC .... .50 .15
❑ 259 Jake Voskuhl RC .... .50 .15
❑ 260 Mark Madsen RC.......... .50 .15
❑ 261 Pepe Sanchez RC .... .50 .15
❑ 262 Morris Peterson RC .... 1.00 .30
❑ 263 Daniel Santiago RC ...... .50 .15
❑ 264 Etan Thomas RC .... .50 .15
❑ 265 A.J. Guyton RC .... .50 .15
❑ 266 Marcus Fizer RC .... .50 .15
❑ 267 Jamal Crawford RC ...... .60 .18
❑ 268 Jerome Moiso RC .... .50 .15
❑ 269 Olumide Oyedeji RC .... .50 .15
❑ 270 Paul McPherson RC..... .50 .15
❑ 271 Eduardo Najera RC ...... .75 .23
❑ 272 Gary Trent .... .15 .04
Steve Nash
Christian Laettner
Michael Finley
Dirk Nowitzki
❑ 273 Antonio McDyess.......... .15 .04
Raef LaFrentz
Tariq Abdul-Wahad
Nick Van Exel
James Posey
❑ 274 Steve Francis .... .30 .09
Maurice Taylor
Shandon Anderson
Walt Williams
Hakeem Olajuwon
❑ 275 Terrell Brandon .... .30 .09
Kevin Garnett
Wally Szczerbiak
Radoslav Nesterovic
Chauncey Billups
❑ 276 Sean Elliott.................... .30 .09
Avery Johnson
David Robinson
Tim Duncan
Derek Anderson
❑ 277 Olden Polynice............. .30 .09
John Stockton
Karl Malone
Bryon Russell
John Starks
❑ 278 Othella Harrington .... .50 .15
Mike Bibby
Michael Dickerson
Bryant Reeves
Shareef Abdur-Rahim
❑ 279 Mookie Blaylock .... .30 .09
Erick Dampier
Danny Fortson
Larry Hughes
Antawn Jamison
❑ 280 Keyon Dooling .... .50 .15
Quentin Richardson
Darius Miles
Michael Olowokandi
Lamar Odom
❑ 281 Ron Harper.................... .50 .15
Isaiah Rider
Kobe Bryant
Shaquille O'Neal
Robert Horry
❑ 282 Anfernee Hardaway ...... .30 .09
Tom Gugliotta
Jason Kidd
Rodney Rogers
Clifford Robinson
❑ 283 Scottie Pippen .... .30 .09
Damon Stoudamire
Steve Smith
Arvydas Sabonis
Rasheed Wallace
❑ 284 Nick Anderson .... .30 .09
Peja Stojakovic
Vlade Divac
Jason Williams
Chris Webber
❑ 285 Gary Payton .... .30 .09
Desmond Mason
Patrick Ewing
Vin Baker
Rashard Lewis
❑ 286 Vitaly Potapenko .... .15 .04
Kenny Anderson
Adrian Griffin
Antoine Walker
Paul Pierce
❑ 287 Anthony Mason .... .15 .04
Eddie Jones
Tim Hardaway
Brian Grant
Dan Majerle
❑ 288 Kendall Gil .... .30 .09
Stephon Marbury
Kenyon Martin
Jim McIlvaine
Keith Van Horn
❑ 289 Latrell Sprewell............. .30 .09
Glen Rice
Marcus Camby
Larry Johnson
Allan Houston
❑ 290 Tracy McGrady.............. .50 .15
John Amaechi
Darrell Armstrong
Grant Hill
Charles Outlaw
❑ 291 Tyrone Hill .... .30 .09
Theo Ratliff
Allen Iverson
Eric Snow
Toni Kukoc
❑ 292 Jahidi White .... .15 .04
Mike Smith
Mitch Richmond
Juwan Howard
Rod Strickland
❑ 293 DerMarr Johnson .... .15 .04
Jason Terry
Jim Jackson
Alan Henderson
Dikembe Mutombo
❑ 294 Elden Campbell .... .15 .04
David Wesley

Card	Nm-Mt	Ex-Mt
P.J. Brown		
Jamal Mashburn		
Derrick Coleman		
❑ 295 Ron Mercer	.30	.09
Jamal Crawford		
Elton Brand		
Marcus Fizer		
Dragan Tarlac		
❑ 296 Brevin Knight	.15	.04
Robert Traylor		
Andre Miller		
Chris Mihm		
Lamond Murray		
❑ 297 Chucky Atkins	.15	.04
Jerry Stackhouse		
Cedric Ceballos		
Jerome Williams		
John Wallace		
❑ 298 Jermaine O'Neal	.30	.09
Jalen Rose		
Austin Croshere		
Jonathan Bender		
Reggie Miller		
❑ 299 Tim Thomas	.15	.04
Ervin Johnson		
Sam Cassell		
Ray Allen		
Glenn Robinson		
❑ 300 Vince Carter	.50	.15
Corliss Williamson		
Morris Peterson		
Mark Jackson		
Antonio Davis		
❑ NNO V.Carter OSR Retail	-	-
❑ NNO V.Carter OSR Sticker	5.00	1.50
❑ NNO V.Carter OSR/1986	20.00	6.00
❑ NNO V.Carter OSR AU/15	-	-

2001-02 Fleer Authentix

	Nm-Mt	Ex-Mt
COMP.SET w/o SP'S	40.00	12.00
COMMON CARD (1-100)	.25	.07
COMMON ROOKIE (101-135)	4.00	1.20
❑ 1 Vince Carter	2.00	.60
❑ 2 Terrell Brandon	.50	.15
❑ 3 Raef LaFrentz	.50	.15
❑ 4 Iakovos Tsakalidis	.25	.07
❑ 5 Elton Brand	.75	.23
❑ 6 David Robinson	.75	.23
❑ 7 Lamar Odom	.75	.23
❑ 8 Larry Hughes	.50	.15
❑ 9 Gary Payton	.75	.23
❑ 10 Rick Fox	.50	.15
❑ 11 Jamal Mashburn	.50	.15
❑ 12 Brian Grant	.50	.15
❑ 13 David Wesley	.25	.07
❑ 14 Steve Smith	.50	.15
❑ 15 Corey Maggette	.50	.15
❑ 16 Michael Jordan	12.00	3.60
❑ 17 Wally Szczerbiak	.50	.15
❑ 18 Antoine Walker	.75	.23
❑ 19 Marcus Camby	.50	.15
❑ 20 Rasheed Wallace	.75	.23
❑ 21 Travis Best	.25	.07
❑ 22 Theo Ratliff	.50	.15
❑ 23 LaPhonso Ellis	.25	.07
❑ 24 Dirk Nowitzki	1.25	.35
❑ 25 Kurt Thomas	.50	.15
❑ 26 Steve Francis	.75	.23
❑ 27 Tim Duncan	1.50	.45
❑ 28 Eddie House	.50	.15
❑ 29 Ron Mercer	.50	.15
❑ 30 Allan Houston	.50	.15
❑ 31 Trajan Langdon	.25	.07
❑ 32 Karl Malone	.75	.23
❑ 33 Glenn Robinson	.75	.23
❑ 34 Wang Zhizhi	.75	.23
❑ 35 Jason Kidd	1.25	.35
❑ 36 Maurice Taylor	.50	.15
❑ 37 Chris Webber	.75	.23
❑ 38 Michael Dickerson	.50	.15
❑ 39 Paul Pierce	.75	.23
❑ 40 Bonzi Wells	.50	.15
❑ 41 Antawn Jamison	.75	.23
❑ 42 Rashard Lewis	.50	.15
❑ 43 Reggie Miller	.75	.23
❑ 44 Patrick Ewing	.75	.23
❑ 45 Marcus Fizer	.50	.15
❑ 46 Aaron McKie	.50	.15
❑ 47 Marc Jackson	.50	.15
❑ 48 Desmond Mason	.50	.15
❑ 49 Jermaine O'Neal	.75	.23
❑ 50 DeShawn Stevenson	.50	.15
❑ 51 John Stockton	.75	.23
❑ 52 Tim Thomas	.50	.15
❑ 53 Andre Miller	.50	.15
❑ 54 Jumaine Jones	.50	.15
❑ 55 Nick Van Exel	.75	.23
❑ 56 Damon Stoudamire	.50	.15
❑ 57 Stephon Marbury	.75	.23
❑ 58 Clifford Robinson	.25	.07
❑ 59 Hidayet Turkoglu	.50	.15
❑ 60 Kobe Bryant	3.00	.90
❑ 61 Richard Hamilton	.50	.15
❑ 62 Stromile Swift	.50	.15
❑ 63 Chris Mihm	.50	.15
❑ 64 Tracy McGrady	2.00	.60
❑ 65 Jalen Rose	.75	.23
❑ 66 Morris Peterson	.50	.15
❑ 67 Alonzo Mourning	.50	.15
❑ 68 Courtney Alexander	.50	.15
❑ 69 Michael Finley	.75	.23
❑ 70 Shawn Marion	.75	.23
❑ 71 Darius Miles	.75	.23
❑ 72 Antonio Davis	.25	.07
❑ 73 Ray Allen	.75	.23
❑ 74 Shareef Abdur-Rahim	.75	.23
❑ 75 Kevin Garnett	1.50	.45
❑ 76 Latrell Sprewell	.75	.23
❑ 77 Antonio McDyess	.50	.15
❑ 78 Derek Anderson	.50	.15
❑ 79 Derek Fisher	.75	.23
❑ 80 Jason Terry	.75	.23
❑ 81 Eddie Jones	.75	.23
❑ 82 Hakeem Olajuwon	.75	.23
❑ 83 Toni Kukoc	.50	.15
❑ 84 Sam Cassell	.75	.23
❑ 85 Jamal Crawford	.50	.15
❑ 86 Allen Iverson	1.50	.45
❑ 87 Steve Nash	.75	.23
❑ 88 Dikembe Mutombo	.50	.15
❑ 89 Shaquille O'Neal	2.00	.60
❑ 90 Jerome Moiso	.50	.15
❑ 91 Kenyon Martin	.75	.23
❑ 92 Chucky Atkins	.25	.07
❑ 93 Grant Hill	.75	.23
❑ 94 Jerry Stackhouse	.75	.23
❑ 95 Jason Williams	.50	.15
❑ 96 Baron Davis	.75	.23
❑ 97 Mike Miller	.75	.23
❑ 98 Joe Smith	.50	.15
❑ 99 Peja Stojakovic	.75	.23
❑ 100 Cuttino Mobley	.50	.15
❑ 101 Kwame Brown RC	8.00	2.40
❑ 102 Jason Collins RC	4.00	1.20
❑ 103 Willie Solomon RC	4.00	1.20
❑ 104 Brendan Haywood RC	5.00	1.50
❑ 105 Jeff Trepagnier RC	4.00	1.20
❑ 106 Eddie Griffin RC	6.00	1.80
❑ 107 Joseph Forte RC	8.00	2.40
❑ 108 Rodney White RC	5.00	1.50
❑ 109 Jeryl Sasser RC	4.00	1.20
❑ 110 Samuel Dalembert RC	4.00	1.20
❑ 111 Shane Battier RC	6.00	1.80
❑ 112 Tony Parker RC	15.00	4.50
❑ 113 DeSagana Diop RC	4.00	1.20
❑ 114 Steven Hunter RC	4.00	1.20
❑ 115 Trenton Hassell RC	6.00	1.80
❑ 116 Michael Bradley RC	4.00	1.20
❑ 117 Brian Scalabrine RC	4.00	1.20
❑ 118 Troy Murphy RC	8.00	2.40
❑ 119 Brandon Armstrong RC	5.00	1.50
❑ 120 Pau Gasol RC	15.00	4.50
❑ 121 Gerald Wallace RC	8.00	2.40
❑ 122 Jason Richardson RC	12.00	3.60
❑ 123 Joe Johnson RC	6.00	1.80
❑ 124 Loren Woods RC	4.00	1.20
❑ 125 Vladimir Radmanovic RC	5.00	1.50
❑ 126 Jamaal Tinsley RC	6.00	1.80
❑ 127 Omar Cook RC	4.00	1.20
❑ 128 Kedrick Brown RC	4.00	1.20
❑ 129 Terence Morris RC	4.00	1.20
❑ 130 Richard Jefferson RC	12.00	3.60
❑ 131 Gilbert Arenas RC	10.00	3.00
❑ 132 Tyson Chandler RC	10.00	3.00
❑ 133 Kirk Haston RC	4.00	1.20
❑ 134 Eddy Curry RC	10.00	3.00
❑ 135 Zach Randolph RC	12.00	3.60

2002-03 Fleer Authentix

	Nm-Mt	Ex-Mt
COMPLETE SET (135)	250.00	75.00
COMP.SET w/o SP's (100)	40.00	12.00
COMMON CARD (1-100)	.20	.06
COMMON ROOKIE (101-135)	5.00	1.50
❑ 1 Vince Carter	2.00	.60
❑ 2 Bobby Jackson	.20	.06
❑ 3 Cuttino Mobley	.50	.15
❑ 4 John Stockton	.75	.23
❑ 5 Jamal Mashburn	.50	.15
❑ 6 Ben Wallace	.75	.23
❑ 7 Tim Duncan	1.50	.45
❑ 8 Richard Jefferson	.50	.15
❑ 9 Clifford Robinson	.20	.06
❑ 10 Gary Payton	.75	.23
❑ 11 Terrell Brandon	.50	.15
❑ 12 Michael Finley	.75	.23
❑ 13 Rasheed Wallace	.75	.23
❑ 14 Jason Williams	.50	.15
❑ 15 Andre Miller	.50	.15
❑ 16 Shawn Marion	.75	.23
❑ 17 Kobe Bryant	3.00	.90
❑ 18 Jason Terry	.75	.23
❑ 19 Latrell Sprewell	.75	.23
❑ 20 Jerry Stackhouse	.75	.23
❑ 21 Tony Parker	.75	.23
❑ 22 Ray Allen	.75	.23
❑ 23 Dirk Nowitzki	1.25	.35
❑ 24 Chris Webber	.75	.23
❑ 25 Rick Fox	.50	.15
❑ 26 Jermaine O'Neal	.75	.23
❑ 27 Karl Malone	.75	.23
❑ 28 Allan Houston	.50	.15
❑ 29 Jason Richardson	.75	.23
❑ 30 Morris Peterson	.50	.15
❑ 31 Kevin Garnett	1.50	.45
❑ 32 Antawn Jamison	.75	.23
❑ 33 Rashard Lewis	.50	.15
❑ 34 Jason Kidd	1.25	.35
❑ 35 Joe Smith	.50	.15
❑ 36 David Robinson	.75	.23
❑ 37 Brian Grant	.50	.15

❑ 38 Lamond Murray .20 .06
❑ 39 Damon Stoudamire .50 .15
❑ 40 Shane Battier .75 .23
❑ 41 Eddy Curry .75 .23
❑ 42 Dikembe Mutombo .50 .15
❑ 43 Jamaal Tinsley .75 .23
❑ 44 Courtney Alexander .50 .15
❑ 45 Wally Szczerbiak .50 .15
❑ 46 Antonio McDyess .50 .15
❑ 47 Mike Bibby .75 .23
❑ 48 Alonzo Mourning .50 .15
❑ 49 Tyson Chandler .75 .23
❑ 50 Stephon Marbury .75 .23
❑ 51 Sam Cassell .75 .23
❑ 52 Steve Nash .75 .23
❑ 53 Bonzi Wells .50 .15
❑ 54 Pau Gasol .75 .23
❑ 55 Rodney Rogers .20 .06
❑ 56 Allen Iverson 1.50 .45
❑ 57 Derek Fisher .75 .23
❑ 58 Travis Best .20 .06
❑ 59 Aaron McKie .50 .15
❑ 60 Darius Miles .75 .23
❑ 61 Richard Hamilton .50 .15
❑ 62 Marcus Camby .50 .15
❑ 63 Eddie Griffin .50 .15
❑ 64 Antonio Davis .20 .06
❑ 65 David Wesley .20 .06
❑ 66 Stromile Swift .50 .15
❑ 67 Brent Barry .50 .15
❑ 68 Glenn Robinson .75 .23
❑ 69 Antoine Walker .75 .23
❑ 70 Tracy McGrady 2.00 .60
❑ 71 Steve Smith .50 .15
❑ 72 Michael Jordan 6.00 1.80
❑ 73 Mike Miller .75 .23
❑ 74 DeShawn Stevenson .20 .06
❑ 75 Raef LaFrentz .50 .15
❑ 76 Al Harrington .50 .15
❑ 77 Vlade Divac .50 .15
❑ 78 Eddie Jones .75 .23
❑ 79 Wesley Person .20 .06
❑ 80 Kenny Anderson .50 .15
❑ 81 Elton Brand .75 .23
❑ 82 Jalen Rose .75 .23
❑ 83 Joe Johnson .75 .23
❑ 84 Shaquille O'Neal 2.00 .60
❑ 85 Paul Pierce .75 .23
❑ 86 Grant Hill .75 .23
❑ 87 Steve Francis .75 .23
❑ 88 Keon Clark .50 .15
❑ 89 Baron Davis .75 .23
❑ 90 Tim Thomas .50 .15
❑ 91 Shareef Abdur-Rahim .75 .23
❑ 92 Kenyon Martin .75 .23
❑ 93 Juwan Howard .50 .15
❑ 94 Peja Stojakovic .75 .23
❑ 95 Lamar Odom .75 .23
❑ 96 Toni Kukoc .50 .15
❑ 97 Darrell Armstrong .20 .06
❑ 98 Reggie Miller .75 .23
❑ 99 Andrei Kirilenko .75 .23
❑ 100 Keith Van Horn .75 .23
❑ 101 Rookie Exchange 30.00 9.00
❑ 102 Jay Williams RC 6.00 1.80
❑ 103 Mike Dunleavy RC 8.00 2.40
❑ 104 Drew Gooden RC 12.00 3.60
❑ 105 Nikoloz Tskitishvili RC 5.00 1.50
❑ 106 Caron Butler RC 10.00 3.00
❑ 107 Chris Wilcox RC 6.00 1.80
❑ 108 DaJuan Wagner RC 8.00 2.40
❑ 109 Nene Hilario RC 6.00 1.80
❑ 110 Qyntel Woods RC 5.00 1.50
❑ 111 Jared Jeffries RC 5.00 1.50
❑ 112 Tamar Slay RC 6.00 1.80
❑ 113 Marcus Haislip RC 5.00 1.50
❑ 114 Kareem Rush RC 6.00 1.80
❑ 115 Bostjan Nachbar RC 5.00 1.50
❑ 116 Melvin Ely RC 5.00 1.50
❑ 117 Jiri Welsch RC 5.00 1.50
❑ 118 Amare Stoudemire RC 25.00 7.50
❑ 119 Frank Williams RC 5.00 1.50
❑ 120 Rasual Butler RC 5.00 1.50
❑ 121 Dan Dickau RC 5.00 1.50
❑ 122 Carlos Boozer RC 10.00 3.00
❑ 123 Roger Mason RC 5.00 1.50
❑ 124 Corsley Edwards RC 5.00 1.50
❑ 125 Robert Archibald RC 5.00 1.50
❑ 126 John Salmons RC 5.00 1.50
❑ 127 Rod Grizzard RC 5.00 1.50
❑ 128 Dan Gadzuric RC 5.00 1.50
❑ 129 Sam Clancy RC 5.00 1.50
❑ 130 Fred Jones RC 5.00 1.50
❑ 131 Casey Jacobsen RC 5.00 1.50
❑ 132 Ryan Humphrey RC 5.00 1.50
❑ 133 Vincent Yarbrough RC 5.00 1.50
❑ 134 Juan Dixon RC 8.00 2.40
❑ 135 Tayshaun Prince RC 8.00 2.40

2003-04 Fleer Authentix

	MINT	NRMT
COMP.SET w/o SP's (1-100)	40.00	18.00
COMMON CARD (1-100)	.20	.09
COMMON ROOKIE (101-130)	5.00	2.20

❑ 1 Vince Carter 2.00 .90
❑ 2 David Wesley .20 .09
❑ 3 Eddie Griffin .50 .23
❑ 4 Andrei Kirilenko .75 .35
❑ 5 Kerry Kittles .20 .09
❑ 6 Tayshaun Prince .50 .23
❑ 7 Tim Duncan 1.50 .70
❑ 8 Troy Hudson .20 .09
❑ 9 Ben Wallace .75 .35
❑ 10 Manu Ginobili .75 .35
❑ 11 Gary Payton .75 .35
❑ 12 Dajuan Wagner .50 .23
❑ 13 Stephon Marbury .75 .35
❑ 14 Shane Battier .75 .35
❑ 15 Zydrunas Ilgauskas .50 .23
❑ 16 Eric Snow .50 .23
❑ 17 Andre Miller .50 .23
❑ 18 Shareef Abdur-Rahim .75 .35
❑ 19 Kurt Thomas .50 .23
❑ 20 Vincent Yarbrough .20 .09
❑ 21 Mike Bibby .75 .35
❑ 22 Desmond Mason .50 .23
❑ 23 Steve Nash .75 .35
❑ 24 Rasheed Wallace .75 .35
❑ 25 Kobe Bryant 3.00 1.35
❑ 26 Cuttino Mobley .50 .23
❑ 27 Matt Harpring .75 .35
❑ 28 Jamal Mashburn .50 .23
❑ 29 Mike Dunleavy .50 .23
❑ 30 Antonio Davis .20 .09
❑ 31 Michael Redd .75 .35
❑ 32 Richard Hamilton .50 .23
❑ 33 Predrag Drobnjak .20 .09
❑ 34 Kevin Garnett 1.50 .70
❑ 35 Nene .50 .23
❑ 36 Bobby Jackson .50 .23
❑ 37 Jason Williams .50 .23
❑ 38 Ricky Davis .75 .35
❑ 39 Shawn Marion .75 .35
❑ 40 Kareem Rush .50 .23
❑ 41 Eddy Curry .50 .23
❑ 42 Gordan Giricek .50 .23
❑ 43 Brad Miller .75 .35
❑ 44 Kwame Brown .50 .23
❑ 45 Sam Cassell .75 .35
❑ 46 Juwan Howard .50 .23
❑ 47 Peja Stojakovic .75 .35
❑ 48 Brian Grant .50 .23
❑ 49 Al Harrington .50 .23
❑ 50 Allen Iverson 1.50 .70
❑ 51 Caron Butler .75 .35
❑ 52 Dirk Nowitzki 1.25 .55
❑ 53 Zach Randolph .75 .35
❑ 54 Pau Gasol .75 .35
❑ 55 Tony Delk .20 .09
❑ 56 Grant Hill .75 .35
❑ 57 Shaquille O'Neal 2.00 .90
❑ 58 Tyson Chandler .75 .35
❑ 59 Tracy McGrady 2.00 .90
❑ 60 Ron Artest .50 .23
❑ 61 Jerry Stackhouse .75 .35
❑ 62 Jamaal Magloire .20 .09
❑ 63 Jason Richardson .75 .35
❑ 64 Morris Peterson .50 .23
❑ 65 Richard Jefferson .50 .23
❑ 66 Kenny Thomas .20 .09
❑ 67 Tony Parker .75 .35
❑ 68 Eddie Jones .75 .35
❑ 69 Paul Pierce .75 .35
❑ 70 Drew Gooden .50 .23
❑ 71 Jermaine O'Neal .75 .35
❑ 72 Juan Dixon .50 .23
❑ 73 Baron Davis .75 .35
❑ 74 Antawn Jamison .75 .35
❑ 75 Rashard Lewis .75 .35
❑ 76 Nick Van Exel .75 .35
❑ 77 Bonzi Wells .50 .23
❑ 78 Speedy Claxton .50 .23
❑ 79 Carlos Boozer .75 .35
❑ 80 Amare Stoudemire 1.50 .70
❑ 81 Elton Brand .75 .35
❑ 82 Jalen Rose .75 .35
❑ 83 Keith Van Horn .75 .35
❑ 84 Corey Maggette .50 .23
❑ 85 Antoine Walker .75 .35
❑ 86 Latrell Sprewell .75 .35
❑ 87 Yao Ming 2.00 .90
❑ 88 Glenn Robinson .75 .35
❑ 89 Jason Kidd 1.25 .55
❑ 90 Gilbert Arenas .75 .35
❑ 91 Ray Allen .75 .35
❑ 92 Wally Szczerbiak .50 .23
❑ 93 Michael Finley .75 .35
❑ 94 Chris Webber .75 .35
❑ 95 Reggie Miller .75 .35
❑ 96 Jason Terry .75 .35
❑ 97 Allan Houston .50 .23
❑ 98 Steve Francis .75 .35
❑ 99 Karl Malone .75 .35
❑ 100 Kenyon Martin .75 .35
❑ 101 Carmelo Anthony RC 40.00 18.00
❑ 102 Troy Bell RC 5.00 2.20
❑ 103 T.J. Ford RC 6.00 2.70
❑ 104 LeBron James RC 80.00 36.00
❑ 105 Travis Outlaw RC 5.00 2.20
❑ 106 Mike Sweetney RC 5.00 2.20
❑ 107 Aleksandar Pavlovic RC 5.00 2.20
❑ 108 Dahntay Jones RC 5.00 2.20
❑ 109 Chris Bosh RC 10.00 4.50
❑ 110 Boris Diaw RC 5.00 2.20
❑ 111 Jarvis Hayes RC 5.00 2.20
❑ 112 Brian Cook RC 5.00 2.20
❑ 113 Luke Ridnour RC 6.00 2.70
❑ 114 David West RC 5.00 2.20
❑ 115 Zoran Planinic RC 5.00 2.20
❑ 116 Zarko Cabarkapa RC 5.00 2.20
❑ 117 Marcus Banks RC 5.00 2.20
❑ 118 Kirk Hinrich RC 8.00 3.60
❑ 119 Darko Milicic RC 8.00 3.60
❑ 120 Sofoklis Schortsanitis RC 5.00 2.20
❑ 121 Ndudi Ebi RC 5.00 2.20
❑ 122 Kendrick Perkins RC 5.00 2.20
❑ 123 Leandro Barbosa RC 5.00 2.20
❑ 124 Nick Collison RC 5.00 2.20
❑ 125 Reece Gaines RC 5.00 2.20
❑ 126 Chris Kaman RC 5.00 2.20
❑ 127 Mickael Pietrus RC 5.00 2.20
❑ 128 Dwyane Wade RC 12.00 5.50
❑ 129 Josh Howard RC 6.00 2.70
❑ 130 Carlos Delfino RC 5.00 2.20

2000-01 Fleer Authority

	Nm-Mt	Ex-Mt
COMPLETE SET (141)	160.00	47.50
COMP.SET w/o SP's (110)	25.00	7.50
COMMON CARD (1-110)	.15	.04

COMMON ROOKIE (111-141)	6.00	1.80
❑ 1 Dikembe Mutombo	.20	.06
❑ 2 Cuttino Mobley	.20	.06
❑ 3 Brian Grant	.20	.06
❑ 4 Grant Hill	.40	.12
❑ 5 Jim Jackson	.15	.04
❑ 6 Derek Anderson	.20	.06
❑ 7 Jerry Stackhouse	.40	.12
❑ 8 Eddie Jones	.40	.12
❑ 9 Tracy McGrady	2.00	.60
❑ 10 Vin Baker	.20	.06
❑ 11 Jason Terry	.40	.12
❑ 12 Jerome Williams	.15	.04
❑ 13 Tim Hardaway	.20	.06
❑ 14 Darrell Armstrong	.15	.04
❑ 15 Rashard Lewis	.20	.06
❑ 16 Kenny Anderson	.20	.06
❑ 17 Larry Hughes	.20	.06
❑ 18 Anthony Mason	.20	.06
❑ 19 Allen Iverson	1.50	.45
❑ 20 Gary Payton	.40	.12
❑ 21 Antoine Walker	.40	.12
❑ 22 Antawn Jamison	.40	.12
❑ 23 Glenn Robinson	.20	.06
❑ 24 Toni Kukoc	.20	.06
❑ 25 Ruben Patterson	.20	.06
❑ 26 Paul Pierce	.40	.12
❑ 27 Mookie Blaylock	.15	.04
❑ 28 Ray Allen	.40	.12
❑ 29 Theo Ratliff	.20	.06
❑ 30 Vince Carter	2.00	.60
❑ 31 Jamal Mashburn	.20	.06
❑ 32 Steve Francis	.40	.12
❑ 33 Sam Cassell	.40	.12
❑ 34 Jason Kidd	1.25	.35
❑ 35 Mark Jackson	.15	.04
❑ 36 Baron Davis	.40	.12
❑ 37 Hakeem Olajuwon	.40	.12
❑ 38 Darvin Ham	.15	.04
❑ 39 Anfernee Hardaway	.40	.12
❑ 40 Antonio Davis	.15	.04
❑ 41 Derrick Coleman	.15	.04
❑ 42 Maurice Taylor	.15	.04
❑ 43 Kevin Garnett	1.50	.45
❑ 44 Tom Gugliotta	.15	.04
❑ 45 Karl Malone	.40	.12
❑ 46 Elton Brand	.40	.12
❑ 47 Jonathan Bender	.20	.06
❑ 48 Terrell Brandon	.20	.06
❑ 49 Clifford Robinson	.15	.04
❑ 50 John Stockton	.40	.12
❑ 51 Ron Artest	.20	.06
❑ 52 Reggie Miller	.40	.12
❑ 53 Joe Smith	.20	.06
❑ 54 Shawn Kemp	.20	.06
❑ 55 Bryon Russell	.15	.04
❑ 56 Andre Miller	.20	.06
❑ 57 Austin Croshere	.20	.06
❑ 58 Wally Szczerbiak	.20	.06
❑ 59 Scottie Pippen	1.25	.35
❑ 60 Donyell Marshall	.20	.06
❑ 61 Brevin Knight	.15	.04
❑ 62 Travis Best	.15	.04
❑ 63 Chauncey Billups	.20	.06
❑ 64 Rasheed Wallace	.40	.12
❑ 65 Shareef Abdur-Rahim	.40	.12
❑ 66 Trajan Langdon	.20	.06
❑ 67 Jalen Rose	.40	.12
❑ 68 Stephon Marbury	.40	.12
❑ 69 Steve Smith	.20	.06
❑ 70 Mike Bibby	.40	.12
❑ 71 Lamond Murray	.15	.04
❑ 72 Lamar Odom	.40	.12
❑ 73 Keith Van Horn	.40	.12
❑ 74 Chris Webber	.40	.12
❑ 75 Michael Dickerson	.20	.06
❑ 76 Dirk Nowitzki	1.25	.35
❑ 77 Corey Maggette	.20	.06
❑ 78 Kerry Kittles	.15	.04
❑ 79 Jason Williams	.20	.06
❑ 80 Mitch Richmond	.20	.06
❑ 81 Michael Finley	.40	.12
❑ 82 Shaquille O'Neal	2.00	.60
❑ 83 Allan Houston	.20	.06
❑ 84 Peja Stojakovic	.40	.12
❑ 85 Juwan Howard	.20	.06
❑ 86 Nick Van Exel	.40	.12
❑ 87 Kobe Bryant	3.00	.90
❑ 88 Latrell Sprewell	.40	.12
❑ 89 Tim Duncan	1.50	.45
❑ 90 Richard Hamilton	.20	.06
❑ 91 Antonio McDyess	.20	.06
❑ 92 Glen Rice	.20	.06
❑ 93 Larry Johnson	.20	.06
❑ 94 David Robinson	.40	.12
❑ 95 Rod Strickland	.15	.04
❑ 96 Raef LaFrentz	.20	.06
❑ 97 Ron Harper	.20	.06
❑ 98 Patrick Ewing	.40	.12
❑ 99 Sean Elliott	.20	.06
❑ 100 Tariq Abdul-Wahad	.15	.04
❑ 101 Chucky Atkins	.15	.04
❑ 102 Marcus Camby	.20	.06
❑ 103 Corliss Williamson	.20	.06
❑ 104 Rodney Rogers	.15	.04
❑ 105 Othella Harrington	.15	.04
❑ 106 Alan Henderson	.15	.04
❑ 107 David Wesley	.15	.04
❑ 108 Michael Doleac	.20	.06
❑ 109 Doug Christie	.20	.06
❑ 110 Vitaly Potapenko	.15	.04
❑ 111 DerMarr Johnson RC	6.00	1.80
❑ 112 Jamal Crawford RC	8.00	2.40
❑ 113 Morris Peterson RC	8.00	2.40
❑ 114 Erick Barkley RC	6.00	1.80
❑ 115 Kenyon Martin RC	15.00	4.50
❑ 116 Joel Przybilla RC	6.00	1.80
❑ 117 Speedy Claxton RC	6.00	1.80
❑ 118 Hidayet Turkoglu RC	10.00	3.00
❑ 119 Etan Thomas RC	6.00	1.80
❑ 120 Eddie House RC	6.00	1.80
❑ 121 Marcus Fizer RC	6.00	1.80
❑ 122 Quentin Richardson RC	10.00	3.00
❑ 123 Donnell Harvey RC	6.00	1.80
❑ 124 DeShawn Stevenson RC	6.00	1.80
❑ 125 Chris Mihm RC	6.00	1.80
❑ 126 Courtney Alexander RC	6.00	1.80
❑ 127 Keyon Dooling RC	6.00	1.80
❑ 128 Jerome Moiso RC	6.00	1.80
❑ 129 Stephen Jackson RC	8.00	2.40
❑ 130 Chris Porter RC	6.00	1.80
❑ 131 Stromile Swift RC	8.00	2.40
❑ 132 Desmond Mason RC	6.00	1.80
❑ 133 Jason Collier RC	6.00	1.80
❑ 134 Mark Madsen RC	6.00	1.80
❑ 135 Mamadou N'Diaye RC	6.00	1.80
❑ 136 Darius Miles RC	15.00	4.50
❑ 137 Mateen Cleaves RC	6.00	1.80
❑ 138 Jamaal Magloire RC	6.00	1.80
❑ 139 Khalid El-Amin RC	6.00	1.80
❑ 140 Mike Miller RC	12.00	3.60
❑ 141 Marc Jackson RC	6.00	1.80
❑ NNO Fleer/BGS Redemption	8.00	2.40

2003-04 Fleer Avant

	Nm-Mt	Ex-Mt
COMP.SET w/o SP's	40.00	12.00
COMMON USA (57-64)	5.00	1.50
COMMON ROOKIE (65-90)	5.00	1.50
❑ 1 Ben Wallace	1.50	.45
❑ 2 Glenn Robinson	1.50	.45
❑ 3 Pau Gasol	1.50	.45
❑ 4 Keon Clark	.50	.15

❑ 5 Kobe Bryant	6.00	1.80
❑ 6 Morris Peterson	1.00	.30
❑ 7 Steve Francis	1.50	.45
❑ 8 Amare Stoudemire	3.00	.90
❑ 9 Mike Dunleavy Jr.	1.00	.30
❑ 10 Kevin Garnett	3.00	.90
❑ 11 Yao Ming	4.00	1.20
❑ 12 Stephon Marbury	1.50	.45
❑ 13 Jason Richardson	1.50	.45
❑ 14 Rasheed Wallace	1.50	.45
❑ 15 Tayshaun Prince	1.00	.30
❑ 16 Steve Nash	1.50	.45
❑ 17 Jamal Mashburn	1.00	.30
❑ 18 Reggie Miller	1.50	.45
❑ 19 Chris Webber	1.50	.45
❑ 20 Andre Miller	1.50	.45
❑ 21 Peja Stojakovic	1.50	.45
❑ 22 Nene	1.00	.30
❑ 23 Manu Ginobili	1.50	.45
❑ 24 Bonzi Wells	1.00	.30
❑ 25 Lamar Odom	1.50	.45
❑ 26 Kwame Brown	1.00	.30
❑ 27 Caron Butler	1.50	.45
❑ 28 Gilbert Arenas	1.50	.45
❑ 29 Dirk Nowitzki	2.50	.75
❑ 30 Allan Houston	1.00	.30
❑ 31 Michael Finley	1.50	.45
❑ 32 Drew Gooden	1.00	.30
❑ 33 Shareef Abdur-Rahim	1.50	.45
❑ 34 Michael Redd	1.50	.45
❑ 35 Jerry Stackhouse	1.50	.45
❑ 36 Scottie Pippen	2.50	.75
❑ 37 Latrell Sprewell	1.50	.45
❑ 38 Ron Artest	1.00	.30
❑ 39 Derrick Coleman	.50	.15
❑ 40 Eddy Curry	1.00	.30
❑ 41 Wally Szczerbiak	1.00	.30
❑ 42 Dajuan Wagner	1.00	.30
❑ 43 Baron Davis	1.50	.45
❑ 44 Karl Malone	1.50	.45
❑ 45 Andrei Kirilenko	1.50	.45
❑ 46 Paul Pierce	1.50	.45
❑ 47 Desmond Mason	1.00	.30
❑ 48 Shaquille O'Neal	4.00	1.20
❑ 49 Rashard Lewis	1.50	.45
❑ 50 Ricky Davis	1.50	.45
❑ 51 Kerry Kittles	.50	.15
❑ 52 Quentin Richardson	1.00	.30
❑ 53 Tony Parker	1.50	.45
❑ 54 Elton Brand	1.50	.45
❑ 55 Richard Jefferson	1.00	.30
❑ 56 Kenyon Martin	1.50	.45
❑ 57 Ray Allen	1.50	.45
❑ 58 Mike Bibby	1.50	.45
❑ 59 Tim Duncan	8.00	2.40
❑ 60 Allen Iverson	8.00	2.40
❑ 61 Jason Kidd	6.00	1.80
❑ 62 Tracy McGrady	10.00	3.00
❑ 63 Jermaine O'Neal	1.50	.45
❑ 64 Larry Brown EXCH	8.00	2.40
❑ 65 LeBron James RC	100.00	30.00
❑ 66 Darko Milicic RC	10.00	3.00
❑ 67 Carmelo Anthony RC	40.00	12.00
❑ 68 Chris Bosh RC	12.00	3.60
❑ 69 Dwyane Wade RC	15.00	4.50
❑ 70 Chris Kaman RC	5.00	1.50
❑ 71 Kirk Hinrich RC	10.00	3.00
❑ 72 T.J. Ford RC	8.00	2.40

❑ 73 Mike Sweetney RC	5.00	1.50
❑ 74 Jarvis Hayes RC	5.00	1.50
❑ 75 Mickael Pietrus RC	5.00	1.50
❑ 76 Travis Hansen RC	5.00	1.50
❑ 77 Marcus Banks RC	5.00	1.50
❑ 78 Luke Ridnour RC	8.00	2.40
❑ 79 Reece Gaines RC	5.00	1.50
❑ 80 Troy Bell RC	5.00	1.50
❑ 81 Zarko Cabarkapa RC	5.00	1.50
❑ 82 David West RC	5.00	1.50
❑ 83 Aleksandar Pavlovic RC	5.00	1.50
❑ 84 Dahntay Jones RC	5.00	1.50
❑ 85 Boris Diaw RC	5.00	1.50
❑ 86 Zoran Planinic RC	5.00	1.50
❑ 87 Travis Outlaw RC	5.00	1.50
❑ 88 Brian Cook RC	5.00	1.50
❑ 89 Maciej Lampe RC	5.00	1.50
❑ 90 Nick Collison RC	5.00	1.50

2002-03 Fleer Box Score

	Nm-Mt	Ex-Mt
COMP.SET w/o SP's (135)	30.00	9.00
COMMON CARD (1-135)	.25	.07
COMMON RC (136-150)	2.50	.75
RS SEALED SET (151-180)	25.00	7.50
COMMON RS (151-180)	2.50	.75
AS SEALED SET (181-210)	20.00	6.00
AW SEALED SET (211-240)	20.00	6.00
❑ 1 Kwame Brown	.60	.18
❑ 2 Eddy Curry	1.00	.30
❑ 3 Allen Iverson	2.00	.60
❑ 4 Elton Brand	1.00	.30
❑ 5 Jason Kidd	1.50	.45
❑ 6 Kedrick Brown	.60	.18
❑ 7 Elden Campbell	.25	.07
❑ 8 Jason Richardson	1.00	.30
❑ 9 Shawn Marion	1.00	.30
❑ 10 John Stockton	1.00	.30
❑ 11 Theo Ratliff	.60	.18
❑ 12 Marcus Fizer	.60	.18
❑ 13 Tony Parker	1.00	.30
❑ 14 Michael Redd	1.00	.30
❑ 15 Vince Carter	2.50	.75
❑ 16 Aaron McKie	.60	.18
❑ 17 Michael Finley	1.00	.30
❑ 18 Rashard Lewis	.60	.18
❑ 19 Steve Nash	1.00	.30
❑ 20 Reggie Miller	1.00	.30
❑ 21 Tim Duncan	2.00	.60
❑ 22 Marcus Camby	.60	.18
❑ 23 Michael Jordan	8.00	2.40
❑ 24 Donnell Harvey	.25	.07
❑ 25 Michael Dickerson	.25	.07
❑ 26 James Posey	.60	.18
❑ 27 Vin Baker	.60	.18
❑ 28 Antonio McDyess	.60	.18
❑ 29 Mike Miller	1.00	.30
❑ 30 Karl Malone	1.00	.30
❑ 31 Corliss Williamson	.60	.18
❑ 32 Derek Anderson	.60	.18
❑ 33 Scottie Pippen	1.50	.45
❑ 34 Paul Pierce	1.00	.30
❑ 35 Steve Francis	1.00	.30
❑ 36 Terrell Brandon	.25	.07
❑ 37 Cuttino Mobley	.60	.18
❑ 38 Ron Artest	.60	.18
❑ 39 Jonathan Bender	.60	.18
❑ 40 Ron Mercer	.60	.18
❑ 41 Dirk Nowitzki	1.50	.45
❑ 42 Jermaine O'Neal	1.00	.30
❑ 43 Ray Allen	1.00	.30
❑ 44 Jason Terry	1.00	.30
❑ 45 Pau Gasol	1.00	.30
❑ 46 Lamar Odom	1.00	.30
❑ 47 P.J. Brown	.25	.07
❑ 48 Kurt Thomas	.60	.18
❑ 49 Grant Hill	1.00	.30
❑ 50 David Robinson	1.00	.30
❑ 51 Rasheed Wallace	1.00	.30
❑ 52 Antawn Jamison	1.00	.30
❑ 53 Juwan Howard	.60	.18
❑ 54 Andre Miller	1.00	.30
❑ 55 Kenyon Martin	1.00	.30
❑ 56 Jason Williams	.60	.18
❑ 57 Travis Best	.25	.07
❑ 58 Brian Grant	.60	.18
❑ 59 Keith Van Horn	1.00	.30
❑ 60 Alonzo Mourning	.60	.18
❑ 61 Rod Strickland	.25	.07
❑ 62 Jamaal Tinsley	1.00	.30
❑ 63 Sam Cassell	1.00	.30
❑ 64 Jalen Rose	1.00	.30
❑ 65 Tim Thomas	.60	.18
❑ 66 Eddie Griffin	.60	.18
❑ 67 Kevin Garnett	2.00	.60
❑ 68 Darrell Armstrong	.25	.07
❑ 69 Joe Smith	.60	.18
❑ 70 Wally Szczerbiak	.60	.18
❑ 71 Richard Jefferson	.60	.18
❑ 72 Chauncey Billups	.60	.18
❑ 73 Kerry Kittles	.25	.07
❑ 74 Stromile Swift	.60	.18
❑ 75 Dikembe Mutombo	.60	.18
❑ 76 Courtney Alexander	.60	.18
❑ 77 Tony Delk	.25	.07
❑ 78 Baron Davis	1.00	.30
❑ 79 Ricky Davis	.60	.18
❑ 80 Vlade Divac	.60	.18
❑ 81 Allan Houston	.60	.18
❑ 82 Richard Hamilton	.60	.18
❑ 83 Moochie Norris	.25	.07
❑ 84 Quentin Richardson	.60	.18
❑ 85 Charlie Ward	.25	.07
❑ 86 Troy Hudson	.25	.07
❑ 87 Pat Garrity	.25	.07
❑ 88 Kobe Bryant	4.00	1.20
❑ 89 Tracy McGrady	2.50	.75
❑ 90 Clifford Robinson	.25	.07
❑ 91 Glenn Robinson	1.00	.30
❑ 92 Todd MacCulloch	.25	.07
❑ 93 Lamond Murray	.25	.07
❑ 94 Eric Snow	.60	.18
❑ 95 Eddie Jones	1.00	.30
❑ 96 Tom Gugliotta	.25	.07
❑ 97 Anfernee Hardaway	1.00	.30
❑ 98 Stephon Marbury	1.00	.30
❑ 99 Antoine Walker	1.00	.30
❑ 100 Gilbert Arenas	1.00	.30
❑ 101 Ruben Patterson	.60	.18
❑ 102 Shane Battier	1.00	.30
❑ 103 David Wesley	.25	.07
❑ 104 Damon Stoudamire	.60	.18
❑ 105 Shaquille O'Neal	2.50	.75
❑ 106 Bonzi Wells	.60	.18
❑ 107 Mike Bibby	1.00	.30
❑ 108 Jamal Mashburn	.60	.18
❑ 109 Peja Stojakovic	1.00	.30
❑ 110 Latrell Sprewell	1.00	.30
❑ 111 Chris Webber	1.00	.30
❑ 112 Alvin Williams	.25	.07
❑ 113 Trenton Hassell	.60	.18
❑ 114 Derek Fisher	1.00	.30
❑ 115 Malik Rose	.25	.07
❑ 116 Kenny Anderson	.60	.18
❑ 117 Zydrunas Ilgauskas	.60	.18
❑ 118 Raef LaFrentz	.60	.18
❑ 119 Gary Payton	1.00	.30
❑ 120 Vladimir Radmanovic	.60	.18
❑ 121 Darius Miles	1.00	.30
❑ 122 Antonio Davis	.25	.07
❑ 123 Larry Hughes	.60	.18
❑ 124 Maurice Taylor	.25	.07
❑ 125 Morris Peterson	.60	.18
❑ 126 Nick Van Exel	1.00	.30
❑ 127 Ira Newble	.25	.07
❑ 128 Eric Williams	.25	.07
❑ 129 Andrei Kirilenko	1.00	.30
❑ 130 Ben Wallace	1.00	.30
❑ 131 Tyson Chandler	1.00	.30
❑ 132 Desmond Mason	.60	.18
❑ 133 Shareef Abdur-Rahim	1.00	.30
❑ 134 Danny Fortson	.25	.07
❑ 135 Jerry Stackhouse	1.00	.30
❑ 136 Yao Ming RC	20.00	6.00
❑ 137 Juan Dixon RC	5.00	1.50
❑ 138 Caron Butler RC	6.00	1.80
❑ 139 Drew Gooden RC	8.00	2.40
❑ 140 DaJuan Wagner RC	5.00	1.50
❑ 141 Jared Jeffries RC	4.00	1.20
❑ 142 Pat Burke RC	2.50	.75
❑ 143 Kareem Rush RC	4.00	1.20
❑ 144 Ryan Humphrey RC	2.50	.75
❑ 145 Manu Ginobili RC	8.00	2.40
❑ 146 Predrag Savovic RC	2.50	.75
❑ 147 Marcus Haislip RC	2.50	.75
❑ 148 John Salmons RC	2.50	.75
❑ 149 Fred Jones RC	2.50	.75
❑ 150 Roger Mason RC	2.50	.75
❑ 151 Jay Williams RS RC	4.00	1.20
❑ 152 Mike Dunleavy RS RC	4.00	1.20
❑ 153 Carlos Boozer RS RC	5.00	1.50
❑ 154 Dan Dickau RS RC	2.50	.75
❑ 155 Tayshaun Prince RS RC	3.00	.90
❑ 156 Nene Hilario RS RC	3.00	.90
❑ 157 Amare Stoudemire RS RC	12.00	3.60
❑ 158 Frank Williams RS RC	2.50	.75
❑ 159 Chris Wilcox RS RC	3.00	.90
❑ 160 Robert Archibald RS RC	2.50	.75
❑ 161 Lonny Baxter RS RC	2.50	.75
❑ 162 Curtis Borchardt RS RC	2.50	.75
❑ 163 Sam Clancy RS RC	2.50	.75
❑ 164 Melvin Ely RS RC	2.50	.75
❑ 165 Dan Gadzuric RS RC	2.50	.75
❑ 166 Smush Parker RS RC	2.50	.75
❑ 167 Chris Jefferies RS RC	2.50	.75
❑ 168 Nikoloz Tskitishvili RS RC	2.50	.75
❑ 169 Casey Jacobsen RS RC	2.50	.75
❑ 170 Ronald Murray RS RC	5.00	1.50
❑ 171 Gordan Giricek RS RC	3.00	.90
❑ 172 Rasual Butler RS RC	2.50	.75
❑ 173 Jannero Pargo RS RC	2.50	.75
❑ 174 Bostjan Nachbar RS RC	2.50	.75
❑ 175 Jiri Welsch RS RC	2.50	.75
❑ 176 Qyntel Woods RS RC	2.50	.75
❑ 177 Vincent Yarbrough RS RC	2.50	.75
❑ 178 Raul Lopez RS RC	2.50	.75
❑ 179 Mehmet Okur RS RC	2.50	.75
❑ 180 Reggie Evans RS RC	2.50	.75
❑ 181 Karl Malone AS	1.00	.30
❑ 182 Michael Jordan AS	8.00	2.40
❑ 183 Glen Rice AS	.60	.18
❑ 184 John Stockton AS	1.00	.30
❑ 185 David Robinson AS	1.00	.30
❑ 186 Shaquille O'Neal AS	2.50	.75
❑ 187 Dikembe Mutombo AS	.60	.18
❑ 188 Gary Payton AS	1.00	.30
❑ 189 Alonzo Mourning AS	.60	.18
❑ 190 Scottie Pippen AS	1.50	.45
❑ 191 Grant Hill AS	1.00	.30
❑ 192 Vin Baker AS	.60	.18
❑ 193 Kevin Garnett AS	2.00	.60
❑ 194 Jason Kidd AS	1.50	.45
❑ 195 Reggie Miller AS	1.00	.30
❑ 196 Ray Allen AS	1.00	.30
❑ 197 Kobe Bryant AS	4.00	1.20
❑ 198 Tim Duncan AS	2.00	.60
❑ 199 Chris Webber AS	.60	.18
❑ 200 Anfernee Hardaway AS	1.00	.30
❑ 201 Latrell Sprewell AS	1.00	.30
❑ 202 Vince Carter AS	2.50	.75
❑ 203 Allen Iverson AS	2.00	.60
❑ 204 Eddie Jones AS	1.00	.30
❑ 205 Antoine Walker AS	1.00	.30
❑ 206 Michael Finley AS	1.00	.30
❑ 207 Tracy McGrady AS	2.50	.75
❑ 208 Jerry Stackhouse AS	1.00	.30
❑ 209 Glenn Robinson AS	1.00	.30
❑ 210 Allan Houston AS	.60	.18

Card	Nm-Mt	Ex-Mt
❑ 211 Baron Davis AW	1.00	.30
❑ 212 Tony Parker AW	1.00	.30
❑ 213 Rick Fox AW	.60	.18
❑ 214 Steve Nash AW	1.00	.30
❑ 215 Jamaal Magloire AW	.60	.18
❑ 216 Wang Zhizhi AW	1.00	.30
❑ 217 Mengke Bateer AW	1.00	.30
❑ 218 Dirk Nowitzki AW	1.50	.45
❑ 219 Jake Tsakalidis AW	.25	.07
❑ 220 Adonal Foyle AW	.25	.07
❑ 221 Marko Jaric AW	.25	.07
❑ 222 Arvydas Sabonis AW	.25	.07
❑ 223 Eduardo Najera AW	.60	.18
❑ 224 Michael Olowokandi AW	.25	.07
❑ 225 Darius Miles AW	1.00	.30
❑ 226 Andrei Kirilenko AW	1.00	.30
❑ 227 Mamadou N'diaye AW	.25	.07
❑ 228 DeSagana Diop AW	.25	.07
❑ 229 Rasho Nesterovic AW	.60	.18
❑ 230 Pau Gasol AW	1.00	.30
❑ 231 Vladimir Radmanovic AW	.60	.18
❑ 232 Hidayet Turkoglu AW	.60	.18
❑ 233 Tim Duncan AW	2.00	.60
❑ 234 Peja Stojakovic AW	1.00	.30
❑ 235 Toni Kukoc AW	.60	.18
❑ 236 Zeljko Rebraca AW	.60	.18
❑ 237 Vlade Divac AW	.60	.18
❑ 238 Dikembe Mutombo AW	.60	.18
❑ 239 Shareef Abdur-Rahim AW	1.00	.30
❑ 240 Jason Richardson AW	1.00	.30

2001-02 Fleer Exclusive

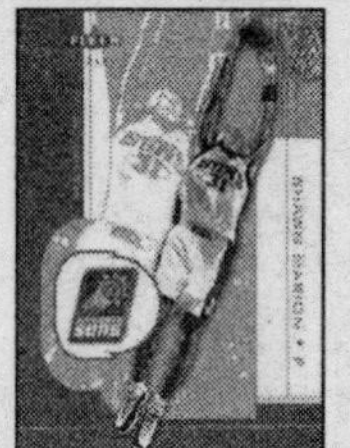

	Nm-Mt	Ex-Mt
COMPLETE SET (149)	700.00	210.00
COMP.SET w/o SP's (120)	60.00	18.00
COMMON CARD (1-100)	.30	.09
COMMON MO (101-120)	.25	.07
❑ 1 Vince Carter	2.50	.75
❑ 2 Tracy McGrady	2.50	.75
❑ 3 Dikembe Mutombo	.60	.18
❑ 4 Kobe Bryant	4.00	1.20
❑ 5 Baron Davis	1.00	.30
❑ 6 Alonzo Mourning	.60	.18
❑ 7 Allan Houston	.60	.18
❑ 8 Paul Pierce	1.00	.30
❑ 9 Jason Williams	.60	.18
❑ 10 Marcus Camby	.60	.18
❑ 11 Jason Terry	1.00	.30
❑ 12 Anfernee Hardaway	1.00	.30
❑ 13 Cuttino Mobley	.60	.18
❑ 14 Kenyon Martin	1.00	.30
❑ 15 Rashard Lewis	.60	.18
❑ 16 Darius Miles	1.00	.30
❑ 17 Jamal Mashburn	.60	.18
❑ 18 Derek Fisher	1.00	.30
❑ 19 Sam Cassell	1.00	.30
❑ 20 Antonio McDyess	.60	.18
❑ 21 John Stockton	1.00	.30
❑ 22 Andre Miller	.60	.18
❑ 23 Shawn Marion	1.00	.30
❑ 24 Steve Nash	1.00	.30
❑ 25 Kevin Garnett	2.00	.60
❑ 26 Peja Stojakovic	1.00	.30
❑ 27 Dirk Nowitzki	1.50	.45
❑ 28 Chris Webber	1.00	.30
❑ 29 Shaquille O'Neal	2.50	.75
❑ 30 Stephon Marbury	1.00	.30
❑ 31 Eddie Jones	1.00	.30
❑ 32 Raef LaFrentz	.60	.18
❑ 33 Wally Szczerbiak	.60	.18
❑ 34 Richard Hamilton	.60	.18
❑ 35 Michael Finley	1.00	.30
❑ 36 Jason Kidd	1.50	.45
❑ 37 Courtney Alexander	.60	.18
❑ 38 Glenn Robinson	1.00	.30
❑ 39 Tim Duncan	2.00	.60
❑ 40 Steve Francis	1.00	.30
❑ 41 Stromile Swift	.60	.18
❑ 42 Desmond Mason	.60	.18
❑ 43 Shareef Abdur-Rahim	1.00	.30
❑ 44 Terrell Brandon	.60	.18
❑ 45 Antawn Jamison	1.00	.30
❑ 46 Latrell Sprewell	1.00	.30
❑ 47 Mateen Cleaves	.60	.18
❑ 48 Karl Malone	1.00	.30
❑ 49 Lamar Odom	1.00	.30
❑ 50 Grant Hill	1.00	.30
❑ 51 Reggie Miller	1.00	.30
❑ 52 Ray Allen	1.00	.30
❑ 53 David Robinson	1.00	.30
❑ 54 Elton Brand	1.00	.30
❑ 55 Jerry Stackhouse	1.00	.30
❑ 56 Brian Grant	.60	.18
❑ 57 Hakeem Olajuwon	1.00	.30
❑ 58 Jalen Rose	1.00	.30
❑ 59 Allen Iverson	2.00	.60
❑ 60 Darrell Armstrong	.30	.09
❑ 61 Joe Smith	.60	.18
❑ 62 Anthony Mason	.60	.18
❑ 63 Mike Bibby	1.00	.30
❑ 64 Gary Payton	1.00	.30
❑ 65 Glen Rice	.60	.18
❑ 66 Shandon Anderson	.30	.09
❑ 67 Antoine Walker	1.00	.30
❑ 68 Tim Thomas	.60	.18
❑ 69 Patrick Ewing	1.00	.30
❑ 70 Ben Wallace	1.00	.30
❑ 71 Corey Maggette	.60	.18
❑ 72 Larry Hughes	.60	.18
❑ 73 Scottie Pippen	1.50	.45
❑ 74 Michael Doleac	.30	.09
❑ 75 Clifford Robinson	.30	.09
❑ 76 Aaron McKie	.60	.18
❑ 77 Marc Jackson	.60	.18
❑ 78 Tom Gugliotta	.30	.09
❑ 79 James Posey	.60	.18
❑ 80 Moochie Norris	.30	.09
❑ 81 Speedy Claxton	.60	.18
❑ 82 Michael Redd	1.00	.30
❑ 83 Rasheed Wallace	1.00	.30
❑ 84 Juwan Howard	.60	.18
❑ 85 Nick Van Exel	1.00	.30
❑ 86 Toni Kukoc	.60	.18
❑ 87 Jamaal Magloire	.60	.18
❑ 88 Jermaine O'Neal	1.00	.30
❑ 89 Anthony Peeler	.30	.09
❑ 90 Marcus Fizer	.60	.18
❑ 91 Jumaine Jones	.60	.18
❑ 92 Kendall Gill	.30	.09
❑ 93 Antonio Daniels	.30	.09
❑ 94 DerMarr Johnson	.60	.18
❑ 95 Mitch Richmond	.60	.18
❑ 96 Antonio Davis	.30	.09
❑ 97 Ron Mercer	.60	.18
❑ 98 Keyon Dooling	.60	.18
❑ 99 Morris Peterson	.60	.18
❑ 100 Derek Anderson	.60	.18
❑ 101 Allen Iverson MO	1.50	.45
❑ 102 Glenn Robinson MO	.50	.15
❑ 103 Tim Duncan MO	1.50	.45
❑ 104 Shaquille O'Neal MO	2.00	.60
❑ 105 Vince Carter MO	2.00	.60
❑ 106 Tracy McGrady MO	2.00	.60
❑ 107 Jason Kidd MO	1.25	.35
❑ 108 Karl Malone MO	1.00	.30
❑ 109 Michael Jordan MO	15.00	4.50
❑ 110 Shareef Abdur-Rahim MO	.75	.23
❑ 111 Grant Hill MO	.75	.23
❑ 112 Stephon Marbury MO	.75	.23
❑ 113 Michael Finley MO	.75	.23
❑ 114 Antoine Walker MO	.75	.23
❑ 115 Kobe Bryant MO	3.00	.90
❑ 116 Dirk Nowitzki MO	1.25	.35
❑ 117 Alonzo Mourning MO	.50	.15
❑ 118 John Stockton MO	1.00	.30
❑ 119 Kevin Garnett MO	1.50	.45
❑ 120 Eddie Jones MO	.75	.23
❑ 121 Steven Hunter/500 RC	12.00	3.60
❑ 122 Tony Parker/500 RC	40.00	12.00
❑ 123 Zach Randolph/478 RC	25.00	7.50
❑ 124 R.Jefferson/500 RC	30.00	9.00
❑ 125 Kedrick Brown/433 RC	12.00	3.60
❑ 126 Kwame Brown/472 RC	25.00	7.50
❑ 127 B.Armstrong/500 RC	15.00	4.50
❑ 128 Pau Gasol/474 RC	50.00	15.00
❑ 129 Troy Murphy/500 RC	20.00	6.00
❑ 130 Rodney White/500 RC	15.00	4.50
❑ 131 Jamaal Tinsley/500 RC	15.00	4.50
❑ 132 Jeryl Sasser/500 RC	12.00	3.60
❑ 133 Eddie Griffin/500 RC	15.00	4.50
❑ 134 Michael Bradley/476 RC	12.00	3.60
❑ 135 V.Radmanovic/500 RC	15.00	4.50
❑ 136 J.Richardson/388 RC	40.00	12.00
❑ 137 Shane Battier/500 RC	15.00	4.50
❑ 138 Joe Johnson/300 RC	20.00	6.00
❑ 139 Andrei Kirilenko/500 RC	25.00	7.50
❑ 140 Kirk Haston/500 RC	12.00	3.60
❑ 141 Jason Collins/500 RC	12.00	3.60
❑ 142 Tyson Chandler/500 RC	25.00	7.50
❑ 143 DeSagana Diop/499 RC	12.00	3.60
❑ 144 Gerald Wallace/467 RC	20.00	6.00
❑ 145 Joseph Forte/450 RC	15.00	4.50
❑ 146 B.Haywood/500 RC	15.00	4.50
❑ 147 S.Dalembert/360 RC	12.00	3.60
❑ 148 Eddy Curry/500 RC	25.00	7.50
❑ 149 Primoz Brezec/500 RC	12.00	3.60

1999-00 Fleer Focus

	Nm-Mt	Ex-Mt
COMPLETE SET (150)	150.00	45.00
COMPLETE SET w/o RC (100)	20.00	6.00
COMMON CARD (1-100)	.25	.07
COMMON ROOKIE (101-150)	1.25	.35
❑ 1 Anfernee Hardaway	.75	.23
❑ 2 Derek Anderson	.50	.15
❑ 3 Jayson Williams	.25	.07
❑ 4 Ron Mercer	.50	.15
❑ 5 Jerry Stackhouse	.75	.23
❑ 6 Tariq Abdul-Wahad	.25	.07
❑ 7 Sean Elliott	.50	.15
❑ 8 Lindsey Hunter	.25	.07
❑ 9 Larry Johnson	.50	.15
❑ 10 Steve Smith	.50	.15
❑ 11 Raef LaFrentz	.50	.15
❑ 12 Jalen Rose	.75	.23
❑ 13 Stephon Marbury	.75	.23
❑ 14 Detlef Schrempf	.50	.15
❑ 15 Rod Strickland	.25	.07
❑ 16 Paul Pierce	.75	.23
❑ 17 Maurice Taylor	.50	.15
❑ 18 Allen Iverson	1.50	.45
❑ 19 Mitch Richmond	.50	.15
❑ 20 Gary Trent	.25	.07
❑ 21 Reggie Miller	.75	.23
❑ 22 Kerry Kittles	.25	.07
❑ 23 Rasheed Wallace	.75	.23
❑ 24 Steve Nash	.75	.23
❑ 25 Scottie Pippen	1.25	.35
❑ 26 Joe Smith	.50	.15
❑ 27 Jason Williams	.75	.23
❑ 28 Michael Finley	.75	.23
❑ 29 Hakeem Olajuwon	.75	.23

Card		
❑ 30 Kevin Garnett	1.50	.45
❑ 31 Darrell Armstrong	.25	.07
❑ 32 David Robinson	.75	.23
❑ 33 Anthony Mason	.50	.15
❑ 34 Jamal Mashburn	.50	.15
❑ 35 Gary Payton	.75	.23
❑ 36 Bryon Russell	.25	.07
❑ 37 Cedric Ceballos	.25	.07
❑ 38 Michael Dickerson	.50	.15
❑ 39 Robert Traylor	.25	.07
❑ 40 Vin Baker	.50	.15
❑ 41 Shawn Kemp	.50	.15
❑ 42 Charles Barkley	1.00	.30
❑ 43 Glenn Robinson	.75	.23
❑ 44 Vince Carter	2.00	.60
❑ 45 Zydrunas Ilgauskas	.50	.15
❑ 46 Sam Cassell	.75	.23
❑ 47 Tracy McGrady	2.00	.60
❑ 48 Chris Mills	.25	.07
❑ 49 Antawn Jamison	1.25	.35
❑ 50 Nick Anderson	.25	.07
❑ 51 Avery Johnson	.25	.07
❑ 52 Brent Barry	.50	.15
❑ 53 Alonzo Mourning	.50	.15
❑ 54 Karl Malone	.75	.23
❑ 55 Toni Kukoc	.50	.15
❑ 56 Ray Allen	.75	.23
❑ 57 Charles Oakley	.25	.07
❑ 58 Cuttino Mobley	.75	.23
❑ 59 Kenny Anderson	.50	.15
❑ 60 Tom Gugliotta	.25	.07
❑ 61 Antoine Walker	.75	.23
❑ 62 Kobe Bryant	3.00	.90
❑ 63 Larry Hughes	.75	.23
❑ 64 Vlade Divac	.50	.15
❑ 65 Juwan Howard	.50	.15
❑ 66 Isaiah Rider	.25	.07
❑ 67 Antonio McDyess	.50	.15
❑ 68 Rik Smits	.50	.15
❑ 69 Keith Van Horn	.75	.23
❑ 70 Doug Christie	.50	.15
❑ 71 Elden Campbell	.25	.07
❑ 72 Shaquille O'Neal	2.00	.60
❑ 73 Matt Geiger	.25	.07
❑ 74 Chris Webber	.75	.23
❑ 75 Troy Hudson	.25	.07
❑ 76 Eddie Jones	.75	.23
❑ 77 Tim Hardaway	.50	.15
❑ 78 Hersey Hawkins	.50	.15
❑ 79 Shareef Abdur-Rahim	.75	.23
❑ 80 Christian Laettner	.50	.15
❑ 81 Latrell Sprewell	.75	.23
❑ 82 Damon Stoudamire	.50	.15
❑ 83 Jason Caffey	.25	.07
❑ 84 Michael Olowokandi	.50	.15
❑ 85 Horace Grant	.50	.15
❑ 86 Grant Hill	.75	.23
❑ 87 Patrick Ewing	.75	.23
❑ 88 Clifford Robinson	.25	.07
❑ 89 Ricky Davis	.50	.15
❑ 90 Glen Rice	.50	.15
❑ 91 Matt Harpring	.75	.23
❑ 92 Mike Bibby	.75	.23
❑ 93 Dikembe Mutombo	.50	.15
❑ 94 Chris Mullin	.75	.23
❑ 95 Marcus Camby	.50	.15
❑ 96 Jason Kidd	1.25	.35
❑ 97 John Starks	.50	.15
❑ 98 Terrell Brandon	.50	.15
❑ 99 Tim Duncan	1.50	.45
❑ 100 John Stockton	.75	.23
❑ 101 Ron Artest RC	4.00	1.20
❑ 101A Ron Artest SP	8.00	2.40
❑ 102 William Avery RC	2.50	.75
❑ 102A William Avery SP	6.00	1.80
❑ 103 Jonathan Bender RC	6.00	1.80
❑ 103A Jonathan Bender SP	12.00	3.60
❑ 104 Cal Bowdler RC	2.00	.60
❑ 104A Cal Bowdler SP	5.00	1.50
❑ 105 Elton Brand RC	10.00	3.00
❑ 105A Elton Brand SP	20.00	6.00
❑ 106 Vonteego Cummings RC	2.50	.75
❑ 106A V.Cummings SP	4.00	1.20
❑ 107 Baron Davis RC	6.00	1.80
❑ 107A Baron Davis SP	12.00	3.60
❑ 108 Jeff Foster RC	2.00	.60
❑ 108A Jeff Foster SP	4.00	1.20
❑ 109 Steve Francis RC	12.00	3.60
❑ 109A Steve Francis SP	25.00	7.50
❑ 110 Devean George RC	3.00	.90
❑ 110A Devean George SP	6.00	1.80
❑ 111 Dion Glover RC	2.00	.60
❑ 111A Dion Glover SP	4.00	1.20
❑ 112 Richard Hamilton RC	6.00	1.80
❑ 112A Richard Hamilton SP	10.00	3.00
❑ 113 Tim James RC	2.00	.60
❑ 113A Tim James SP	5.00	1.50
❑ 114 Trajan Langdon RC	2.50	.75
❑ 114A Trajan Langdon SP	5.00	1.50
❑ 115 Quincy Lewis RC	2.00	.60
❑ 115A Quincy Lewis SP	4.00	1.20
❑ 116 Corey Maggette RC	6.00	1.80
❑ 116A Corey Maggette SP	12.00	3.60
❑ 117 Shawn Marion RC	10.00	3.00
❑ 117A Shawn Marion SP	20.00	6.00
❑ 118 Andre Miller RC	6.00	1.80
❑ 118A Andre Miller SP	12.00	3.60
❑ 119 Lamar Odom RC	8.00	2.40
❑ 119A Lamar Odom SP	15.00	4.50
❑ 120 Scott Padgett RC	2.00	.60
❑ 120A Scott Padgett SP	4.00	1.20
❑ 121 James Posey RC	4.00	1.20
❑ 121A James Posey SP	8.00	2.40
❑ 122 Aleksandar Radojevic RC	1.25	.35
❑ 122A A.Radojevic SP	2.50	.75
❑ 123 Wally Szczerbiak RC	6.00	1.80
❑ 123A Wally Szczerbiak SP	12.00	3.60
❑ 124 Jason Terry RC	4.00	1.20
❑ 124A Jason Terry SP	8.00	2.40
❑ 125 Kenny Thomas RC	2.50	.75
❑ 125A Kenny Thomas SP	4.00	1.20
❑ 126 Jumaine Jones RC	2.50	.75
❑ 126A Jumaine Jones SP	3.00	.90
❑ 127 Rick Hughes RC	1.25	.35
❑ 127A Rick Hughes SP	2.50	.75
❑ 128 John Celestand RC	2.00	.60
❑ 128A John Celestand SP	4.00	1.20
❑ 129 Adrian Griffin RC	2.00	.60
❑ 129A Adrian Griffin SP	3.00	.90
❑ 130 Michael Ruffin RC	1.50	.45
❑ 130A Michael Ruffin SP	3.00	.90
❑ 131 Chris Herren RC	1.25	.35
❑ 131A Chris Herren SP	2.50	.75
❑ 132 Evan Eschmeyer RC	1.25	.35
❑ 132A Evan Eschmeyer SP	2.50	.75
❑ 133 Tim Young RC	1.25	.35
❑ 133A Tim Young SP	2.50	.75
❑ 134 Obinna Ekezie RC	1.50	.45
❑ 134A Obinna Ekezie SP	3.00	.90
❑ 135 Laron Profit RC	2.00	.60
❑ 135A Laron Profit SP	4.00	1.20
❑ 136 A.J. Bramlett RC	1.25	.35
❑ 136A A.J. Bramlett SP	2.50	.75
❑ 137 Eddie Robinson RC	4.00	1.20
❑ 137A Eddie Robinson SP	8.00	2.40
❑ 138 Ryan Bowen RC	1.25	.35
❑ 138A Ryan Bowen SP	2.50	.75
❑ 139 Chucky Atkins RC	2.50	.75
❑ 139A Chucky Atkins SP	5.00	1.50
❑ 140 Ryan Robertson RC	1.50	.45
❑ 140A Ryan Robertson SP	3.00	.90
❑ 141 Derrick Dial RC	1.25	.35
❑ 141A Derrick Dial SP	2.50	.75
❑ 142 Todd MacCulloch RC	2.00	.60
❑ 142A Todd MacCulloch SP	4.00	1.20
❑ 143 DeMarco Johnson RC	1.50	.45
❑ 143A DeMarco Johnson SP	3.00	.90
❑ 144 Anthony Carter RC	4.00	1.20
❑ 144A Anthony Carter SP	10.00	3.00
❑ 145 Lazaro Borrell RC	1.25	.35
❑ 145A Lazaro Borrell SP	2.50	.75
❑ 146 Rafer Alston RC	2.50	.75
❑ 146A Rafer Alston SP	5.00	1.50
❑ 147 Nikita Morgunov RC	1.25	.35
❑ 147A Nikita Morgunov SP	2.50	.75
❑ 148 Rodney Buford RC	1.25	.35
❑ 148A Rodney Buford SP	2.50	.75
❑ 149 Milt Palacio RC	1.25	.35
❑ 149A Milt Palacio SP	2.50	.75
❑ 150 Jermaine Jackson RC	1.25	.35
❑ 150A Jermaine Jackson SP	2.50	.75

2000-01 Fleer Focus

	Nm-Mt	Ex-Mt
COMPLETE SET w/o RC (200)	40.00	12.00
COMMON CARD (1-180)	.25	.07
COMMON ROOKIE (181-216)	.50	.15
❑ 1 Vince Carter	2.00	.60
❑ 2 Shawn Marion	.75	.23
❑ 3 Muggsy Bogues	.50	.15
❑ 4 Dikembe Mutombo	.50	.15
❑ 5 Stephon Marbury	.75	.23
❑ 6 Michael Dickerson	.50	.15
❑ 7 Andre Miller	.50	.15
❑ 8 Toni Kukoc	.50	.15
❑ 9 Nick Van Exel	.75	.23
❑ 10 Aaron Williams	.25	.07
❑ 11 Derrick Coleman	.25	.07
❑ 12 Wally Szczerbiak	.50	.15
❑ 13 Rodney Rogers	.25	.07
❑ 14 Tom Gugliotta	.25	.07
❑ 15 Vonteego Cummings	.25	.07
❑ 16 Cedric Ceballos	.25	.07
❑ 17 Malik Rose	.25	.07
❑ 18 Shawn Bradley	.25	.07
❑ 19 Shandon Anderson	.25	.07
❑ 20 Jacque Vaughn	.25	.07
❑ 21 Jamie Feick	.25	.07
❑ 22 Shawn Kemp	.50	.15
❑ 23 Monty Williams	.25	.07
❑ 24 Allan Houston	.50	.15
❑ 25 Chauncey Billups	.50	.15
❑ 26 Vlade Divac	.50	.15
❑ 27 Othella Harrington	.25	.07
❑ 28 Dale Davis	.25	.07
❑ 29 Charlie Ward	.25	.07
❑ 30 Hakeem Olajuwon	.75	.23
❑ 31 Ray Allen	.75	.23
❑ 32 Lamar Odom	.75	.23
❑ 33 Shaquille O'Neal	2.00	.60
❑ 34 Chris Childs	.25	.07
❑ 35 Nick Anderson	.25	.07
❑ 36 Keon Clark	.50	.15
❑ 37 Danny Fortson	.25	.07
❑ 38 Sam Mitchell	.25	.07
❑ 39 Travis Best	.25	.07
❑ 40 Chris Webber	.75	.23
❑ 41 Brent Barry	.50	.15
❑ 42 Scottie Pippen	1.25	.35
❑ 43 Reggie Miller	.75	.23
❑ 44 Bryant Reeves	.25	.07
❑ 45 Bobby Jackson	.50	.15
❑ 46 Antonio McDyess	.50	.15
❑ 47 Elden Campbell	.25	.07
❑ 48 Kenny Anderson	.50	.15
❑ 49 Christian Laettner	.50	.15
❑ 50 Darrell Armstrong	.25	.07
❑ 51 Vinny Del Negro	.25	.07
❑ 52 Quincy Lewis	.25	.07
❑ 53 Peja Stojakovic	.75	.23

❑ 54 Matt Geiger .25 .07
❑ 55 Larry Hughes .50 .15
❑ 56 Tracy McGrady 2.00 .60
❑ 57 Tim Hardaway .50 .15
❑ 58 Brevin Knight .25 .07
❑ 59 Michael Finley .75 .23
❑ 60 Jason Kidd 1.25 .35
❑ 61 Matt Harpring .75 .23
❑ 62 Antawn Jamison .75 .23
❑ 63 Wesley Person .25 .07
❑ 64 Antonio Davis .25 .07
❑ 65 Roshown McLeod .25 .07
❑ 66 Anthony Peeler .25 .07
❑ 67 Grant Hill .75 .23
❑ 68 Michael Olowokandi .25 .07
❑ 69 Kerry Kittles .25 .07
❑ 70 Elton Brand .75 .23
❑ 71 Tariq Abdul-Wahad .25 .07
❑ 72 Aaron McKie .50 .15
❑ 73 Andrew DeClercq .25 .07
❑ 74 Anfernee Hardaway .75 .23
❑ 75 Bimbo Coles .25 .07
❑ 76 Terrell Brandon .50 .15
❑ 77 Jalen Rose .75 .23
❑ 78 Radoslav Nesterovic .50 .15
❑ 79 Howard Eisley .25 .07
❑ 80 Steve Smith .50 .15
❑ 81 Arvydas Sabonis .50 .15
❑ 82 Jim Jackson .25 .07
❑ 83 Corey Maggette .50 .15
❑ 84 James Posey .50 .15
❑ 85 LaPhonso Ellis .25 .07
❑ 86 Eric Snow .50 .15
❑ 87 Mikki Moore .25 .07
❑ 88 Baron Davis .75 .23
❑ 89 Jason Williams .50 .15
❑ 90 Mike Bibby .75 .23
❑ 91 Marcus Camby .50 .15
❑ 92 Bryon Russell .25 .07
❑ 93 Steve Francis .75 .23
❑ 94 Sam Cassell .75 .23
❑ 95 Rasheed Wallace .75 .23
❑ 96 Keith Van Horn .75 .23
❑ 97 Eddie Jones .75 .23
❑ 98 Corliss Williamson .50 .15
❑ 99 Ron Mercer .50 .15
❑ 100 Sean Elliott .50 .15
❑ 101 Shareef Abdur-Rahim .75 .23
❑ 102 Glen Rice .50 .15
❑ 103 Patrick Ewing .75 .23
❑ 104 Adrian Griffin .25 .07
❑ 105 David Robinson .75 .23
❑ 106 Isaac Austin .25 .07
❑ 107 Anthony Mason .50 .15
❑ 108 P.J. Brown .25 .07
❑ 109 Kendall Gill .25 .07
❑ 110 Tyrone Nesby .25 .07
❑ 111 Damon Stoudamire .50 .15
❑ 112 Latrell Sprewell .75 .23
❑ 113 Tim Duncan 1.50 .45
❑ 114 Glenn Robinson .75 .23
❑ 115 John Wallace .25 .07
❑ 116 Erick Strickland .25 .07
❑ 117 Doug Christie .50 .15
❑ 118 Juwan Howard .50 .15
❑ 119 Tim Thomas .50 .15
❑ 120 Tyrone Hill .25 .07
❑ 121 Avery Johnson .25 .07
❑ 122 Jerome Williams .25 .07
❑ 123 Mitch Richmond .50 .15
❑ 124 Hersey Hawkins .25 .07
❑ 125 Donyell Marshall .50 .15
❑ 126 Derek Anderson .50 .15
❑ 127 Jamal Mashburn .50 .15
❑ 128 Richard Hamilton .50 .15
❑ 129 Alonzo Mourning .50 .15
❑ 130 Kelvin Cato .25 .07
❑ 131 Lamond Murray .25 .07
❑ 132 Bo Outlaw .25 .07
❑ 133 Chris Carr .25 .07
❑ 134 Jonathan Bender .50 .15
❑ 135 Paul Pierce .75 .23
❑ 136 Dan Majerle .50 .15
❑ 137 Ron Artest .50 .15
❑ 138 Jermaine O'Neal .75 .23
❑ 139 Chris Whitney .25 .07
❑ 140 Anthony Carter .50 .15
❑ 141 Gary Payton .75 .23
❑ 142 Kevin Garnett 1.50 .45
❑ 143 Kevin Willis .25 .07
❑ 144 Charles Oakley .25 .07
❑ 145 Larry Johnson .50 .15
❑ 146 Bonzi Wells .50 .15
❑ 147 Clifford Robinson .25 .07
❑ 148 Chucky Atkins .25 .07
❑ 149 Brian Grant .50 .15
❑ 150 Voshon Lenard .25 .07
❑ 151 Antoine Walker .75 .23
❑ 152 Cuttino Mobley .50 .15
❑ 153 Robert Horry .50 .15
❑ 154 Tracy Murray .25 .07
❑ 155 Kobe Bryant 3.00 .90
❑ 156 Joe Smith .50 .15
❑ 157 Jaren Jackson .25 .07
❑ 158 Scott Williams .25 .07
❑ 159 Allen Iverson 1.50 .45
❑ 160 Rashard Lewis .50 .15
❑ 161 Chris Mills .25 .07
❑ 162 Karl Malone .75 .23
❑ 163 John Amaechi .25 .07
❑ 164 Jason Terry .75 .23
❑ 165 Ruben Patterson .50 .15
❑ 166 Austin Croshere .50 .15
❑ 167 Maurice Taylor .25 .07
❑ 168 Rod Strickland .25 .07
❑ 169 Clarence Weatherspoon .25 .07
❑ 170 Lindsey Hunter .25 .07
❑ 171 David Wesley .25 .07
❑ 172 Jerry Stackhouse .75 .23
❑ 173 Scott Burrell .25 .07
❑ 174 John Stockton .75 .23
❑ 175 Vitaly Potapenko .25 .07
❑ 176 Dirk Nowitzki 1.25 .35
❑ 177 Vin Baker .50 .15
❑ 178 Rick Fox .50 .15
❑ 179 Mookie Blaylock .25 .07
❑ 180 Felipe Lopez .25 .07
❑ 181 Chris Mihm A RC .50 .15
❑ 182 Mamadou N'Diaye A RC .50 .15
❑ 183 Joel Przybilla A RC .50 .15
❑ 184 Jamaal Magloire A RC .50 .15
❑ 185 Iakovos Tsakalidis A RC .50 .15
❑ 186 Etan Thomas A RC .50 .15
❑ 187 Mark Madsen B RC .50 .15
❑ 188 Hanno Mottola B RC .50 .15
❑ 189 Donnell Harvey B RC .50 .15
❑ 190 Jason Collier B RC .50 .15
❑ 191 Eduardo Najera B RC 1.50 .45
❑ 192 Jerome Moiso B RC .50 .15
❑ 193 Mateen Cleaves C RC .50 .15
❑ 194 Keyon Dooling C RC .50 .15
❑ 195 Speedy Claxton C RC .50 .15
❑ 196 Erick Barkley C RC .50 .15
❑ 197 A.J. Guyton C RC .50 .15
❑ 198 Jamal Crawford C RC .60 .18
❑ 199 Dan Langhi D RC .50 .15
❑ 200 Desmond Mason D RC .50 .15
❑ 201 Chris Porter D RC .50 .15
❑ 202 Corey Hightower D RC .50 .15
❑ 203 Morris Peterson D RC 4.00 1.20
❑ 204 Mark Karcher D RC .50 .15
❑ 205 Courtney Alexander E RC 1.00 .30
❑ 206 Quentin Richardson E RC 4.00 1.20
❑ 207 D.Stevenson E RC .50 .15
❑ 208 Michael Redd E RC 2.00 .60
❑ 209 Chris Carrawell E RC .50 .15
❑ 210 Hidayet Turkoglu E RC 6.00 1.80
❑ 211 Kenyon Martin F RC 10.00 3.00
❑ 212 Marcus Fizer F RC 4.00 1.20
❑ 213 Darius Miles F RC 8.00 2.40
❑ 214 Mike Miller F RC 6.00 1.80
❑ 215 DerMarr Johnson F RC .50 .15
❑ 216 Stromile Swift F RC 6.00 1.80
❑ 217 Shaquille O'Neal 20 .75 .23
❑ 218 Allen Iverson 20 .60 .18
❑ 219 Grant Hill 20 .75 .23
❑ 220 Vince Carter 20 .75 .23
❑ 221 Karl Malone 20 .75 .23
❑ 222 Chris Webber 20 .50 .15
❑ 223 Gary Payton 20 .50 .15
❑ 224 Jerry Stackhouse 20 .50 .15
❑ 225 Tim Duncan 20 .75 .23
❑ 226 Kevin Garnett 20 .60 .18
❑ 227 Michael Finley 20 .50 .15
❑ 228 Kobe Bryant 20 1.25 .35
❑ 229 Stephon Marbury 20 .50 .15
❑ 230 Ray Allen 20 .50 .15
❑ 231 Alonzo Mourning 20 .50 .15
❑ 232 Glenn Robinson 20 .25 .07
❑ 233 Antoine Walker 20 .50 .15
❑ 234 Shareef Abdur-Rahim 20 .50 .15
❑ 235 Elton Brand 20 .50 .15
❑ 236 Eddie Jones 20 .75 .23

2001-02 Fleer Focus

	Nm-Mt	Ex-Mt
COMP.SET w/o SP's (100)	40.00	12.00
COMMON CARD 1-100	.25	.07
COMMON ROOKIE (101-130)	2.50	.75

❑ 1 Vince Carter 2.00 .60
❑ 2 Steve Nash .75 .23
❑ 3 Anthony Mason .50 .15
❑ 4 Avery Johnson .25 .07
❑ 5 Peja Stojakovic .75 .23
❑ 6 Shaquille O'Neal 2.00 .60
❑ 7 Jason Kidd 1.25 .35
❑ 8 Steve Smith .50 .15
❑ 9 Kobe Bryant 3.00 .90
❑ 10 Eddie Robinson .50 .15
❑ 11 Allan Houston .50 .15
❑ 12 Larry Hughes .50 .15
❑ 13 Gary Payton .75 .23
❑ 14 Alonzo Mourning .50 .15
❑ 15 Baron Davis .75 .23
❑ 16 Speedy Claxton .50 .15
❑ 17 Hakeem Olajuwon .75 .23
❑ 18 Anthony Carter .50 .15
❑ 19 Raef LaFrentz .50 .15
❑ 20 Dikembe Mutombo .50 .15
❑ 21 Moochie Norris .25 .07
❑ 22 Karl Malone .75 .23
❑ 23 Darrell Armstrong .25 .07
❑ 24 Allen Iverson 1.50 .45
❑ 25 Danny Fortson .25 .07
❑ 26 Antonio Davis .25 .07
❑ 27 Eddie Jones .75 .23
❑ 28 Patrick Ewing .75 .23
❑ 29 Stephon Marbury .75 .23
❑ 30 Cuttino Mobley .50 .15
❑ 31 Morris Peterson .50 .15
❑ 32 Glenn Robinson .75 .23
❑ 33 Paul Pierce .75 .23
❑ 34 Shawn Marion .75 .23
❑ 35 Jermaine O'Neal .75 .23
❑ 36 Donyell Marshall .50 .15
❑ 37 Chauncey Billups .50 .15
❑ 38 Tracy McGrady 2.00 .60
❑ 39 Vlade Divac .50 .15
❑ 40 Lamar Odom .75 .23
❑ 41 Chris Mihm .50 .15
❑ 42 Kenyon Martin .75 .23
❑ 43 Antonio McDyess .50 .15
❑ 44 Mike Bibby .75 .23
❑ 45 Darius Miles .75 .23
❑ 46 Wesley Person .25 .07
❑ 47 Mark Jackson .50 .15
❑ 48 Nick Van Exel .75 .23
❑ 49 Tim Duncan 1.50 .45
❑ 50 Sam Cassell .75 .23
❑ 51 Jason Terry .75 .23

❑ 52 Bonzi Wells .50 .15
❑ 53 Al Harrington .50 .15
❑ 54 Richard Hamilton .50 .15
❑ 55 Wally Szczerbiak .50 .15
❑ 56 Toni Kukoc .50 .15
❑ 57 Rasheed Wallace .75 .23
❑ 58 Reggie Miller .75 .23
❑ 59 Courtney Alexander .50 .15
❑ 60 Terrell Brandon .50 .15
❑ 61 Dirk Nowitzki 1.25 .35
❑ 62 Chris Webber .75 .23
❑ 63 Lindsey Hunter .25 .07
❑ 64 Andre Miller .50 .15
❑ 65 Clifford Robinson .25 .07
❑ 66 David Robinson .75 .23
❑ 67 Stromile Swift .50 .15
❑ 68 Nazr Mohammed .25 .07
❑ 69 Kurt Thomas .50 .15
❑ 70 Corliss Williamson .50 .15
❑ 71 Rashard Lewis .50 .15
❑ 72 Lorenzen Wright .25 .07
❑ 73 David Wesley .25 .07
❑ 74 Derrick Coleman .25 .07
❑ 75 Jerry Stackhouse .75 .23
❑ 76 Antonio Daniels .25 .07
❑ 77 Mitch Richmond .50 .15
❑ 78 Ron Mercer .50 .15
❑ 79 Latrell Sprewell .75 .23
❑ 80 Antawn Jamison .75 .23
❑ 81 Desmond Mason .50 .15
❑ 82 Jason Williams .50 .15
❑ 83 Jamal Mashburn .50 .15
❑ 84 Grant Hill .75 .23
❑ 85 Elton Brand .75 .23
❑ 86 Brian Grant .50 .15
❑ 87 Antoine Walker .75 .23
❑ 88 Anfernee Hardaway .75 .23
❑ 89 Steve Francis .75 .23
❑ 90 John Stockton .75 .23
❑ 91 Ray Allen .75 .23
❑ 92 Tim Hardaway .50 .15
❑ 93 Derek Anderson .50 .15
❑ 94 Jalen Rose .75 .23
❑ 95 Michael Jordan 15.00 4.50
❑ 96 Kevin Garnett 1.50 .45
❑ 97 Shareef Abdur-Rahim .75 .23
❑ 98 Tony Delk .25 .07
❑ 99 Quentin Richardson .50 .15
❑ 100 Michael Finley .75 .23
❑ 101 Jamaal Tinsley RC 4.00 1.20
❑ 102 Zach Randolph RC 8.00 2.40
❑ 103 Kedrick Brown RC 2.50 .75
❑ 104 Kirk Haston RC 2.50 .75
❑ 105 Tyson Chandler RC 8.00 2.40
❑ 106 Shane Battier RC 4.00 1.20
❑ 107 Richard Jefferson RC 5.00 1.50
❑ 108 Gerald Wallace RC 5.00 1.50
❑ 109 DeSagana Diop RC 2.50 .75
❑ 110 R.Boumtje-Boumtje RC 2.50 .75
❑ 111 Rodney White RC 3.00 .90
❑ 112 Eddie Griffin RC 4.00 1.20
❑ 113 Pau Gasol RC 10.00 3.00
❑ 114 Tony Parker RC 10.00 3.00
❑ 115 Kwame Brown RC 6.00 1.80
❑ 116 Vladimir Radmanovic RC 3.00 .90
❑ 117 Troy Murphy RC 5.00 1.50
❑ 118 Loren Woods RC 2.50 .75
❑ 119 Joe Johnson RC 4.00 1.20
❑ 120 Brandon Armstrong RC 3.00 .90
❑ 121 Trenton Hassell RC 4.00 1.20
❑ 122 Andrei Kirilenko RC 8.00 2.40
❑ 123 Jason Richardson RC 10.00 3.00
❑ 124 Jason Collins RC 2.50 .75
❑ 125 Jeryl Sasser RC 2.50 .75
❑ 126 Michael Bradley RC 2.50 .75
❑ 127 Eddy Curry RC 8.00 2.40
❑ 128 Joseph Forte RC 6.00 1.80
❑ 129 Brendan Haywood RC 3.00 .90
❑ 130 Zeljko Rebraca RC 2.50 .75

2003-04 Fleer Focus

	MINT	NRMT
COMP.SET w/o SP's	30.00	13.50
COMMON ROOKIE (121-160)	8.00	3.60

❑ 1 Allan Houston .50 .23

❑ 2 Manu Ginobili .75 .35
❑ 3 Allen Iverson 1.50 .70
❑ 4 Kenyon Martin .75 .35
❑ 5 Rasho Nesterovic .50 .23
❑ 6 Tracy McGrady 2.00 .90
❑ 7 Drew Gooden .50 .23
❑ 8 Tony Parker .75 .35
❑ 9 Troy Murphy .75 .35
❑ 10 Alonzo Mourning .50 .23
❑ 11 Rasual Butler .50 .23
❑ 12 Alvin Williams .20 .09
❑ 13 Troy Hudson .20 .09
❑ 14 Gary Payton .75 .35
❑ 15 Tyson Chandler .75 .35
❑ 16 Ray Allen .75 .35
❑ 17 Amare Stoudemire 2.00 .90
❑ 18 Chauncey Billups .50 .23
❑ 19 Gilbert Arenas .50 .23
❑ 20 Eddie Jones .75 .35
❑ 21 Vince Carter 2.00 .90
❑ 22 Kobe Bryant 3.00 1.35
❑ 23 Reggie Miller .75 .35
❑ 24 Vincent Yarbrough .20 .09
❑ 25 Kevin Garnett 1.50 .70
❑ 26 Andre Miller .50 .23
❑ 27 Glenn Robinson .75 .35
❑ 28 Kurt Thomas .50 .23
❑ 29 Vladimir Radmanovic .20 .09
❑ 30 Richard Jefferson .50 .23
❑ 31 Andrei Kirilenko .75 .35
❑ 32 Wally Szczerbiak .50 .23
❑ 33 Gordan Giricek .50 .23
❑ 34 Kwame Brown .50 .23
❑ 35 Yao Ming 2.00 .90
❑ 36 Devean George .50 .23
❑ 37 Richard Hamilton .50 .23
❑ 38 Anfernee Hardaway .75 .35
❑ 39 Grant Hill .75 .35
❑ 40 Zach Randolph .75 .35
❑ 41 Dirk Nowitzki 1.25 .55
❑ 42 Zydrunas Ilgauskas .50 .23
❑ 43 Antawn Jamison .75 .35
❑ 44 J.R. Bremer .20 .09
❑ 45 Latrell Sprewell .75 .35
❑ 46 Ron Artest .50 .23
❑ 47 Antoine Walker .75 .35
❑ 48 Eddy Curry .50 .23
❑ 49 Larry Hughes .50 .23
❑ 50 Jalen Rose .75 .35
❑ 51 Matt Harpring .75 .35
❑ 52 Sam Cassell .75 .35
❑ 53 Antonio McDyess .50 .23
❑ 54 Jamaal Tinsley .75 .35
❑ 55 Mehmet Okur .20 .09
❑ 56 Scottie Pippen 1.25 .55
❑ 57 Antonio Davis .20 .09
❑ 58 Jamaal Magloire .20 .09
❑ 59 Michael Olowokandi .20 .09
❑ 60 Shane Battier .75 .35
❑ 61 Desmond Mason .50 .23
❑ 62 Baron Davis .75 .35
❑ 63 Jamal Mashburn .50 .23
❑ 64 Michael Redd .75 .35
❑ 65 Shaquille O'Neal 2.00 .90
❑ 66 Ben Wallace .75 .35
❑ 67 Jason Terry .75 .35
❑ 68 Michael Finley .75 .35
❑ 69 Shareef Abdur-Rahim .75 .35
❑ 70 Bobby Jackson .50 .23
❑ 71 Jason Williams .50 .23
❑ 72 Mike Bibby .75 .35
❑ 73 Shawn Marion .75 .35
❑ 74 Ricky Davis .75 .35
❑ 75 Bonzi Wells .50 .23
❑ 76 Jason Kidd 1.25 .55
❑ 77 Mike Miller .75 .35
❑ 78 Stephen Jackson .20 .09
❑ 79 Brad Miller .75 .35
❑ 80 Jason Richardson .75 .35
❑ 81 Mike Dunleavy Jr. .50 .23
❑ 82 Stephon Marbury .75 .35
❑ 83 Brian Grant .50 .23
❑ 84 Jay Williams .50 .23
❑ 85 Morris Peterson .50 .23
❑ 86 Steve Nash .75 .35
❑ 87 Carlos Boozer .75 .35
❑ 88 Jermaine O'Neal .75 .35
❑ 89 Nene .50 .23
❑ 90 Eric Snow .50 .23
❑ 91 Steve Francis .75 .35
❑ 92 Caron Butler .75 .35
❑ 93 Jerry Stackhouse .75 .35
❑ 94 Nick Van Exel .75 .35
❑ 95 Tayshaun Prince .50 .23
❑ 96 Calbert Cheaney .20 .09
❑ 97 Pau Gasol .75 .35
❑ 98 Theo Ratliff .50 .23
❑ 99 Chris Webber .75 .35
❑ 100 Juan Dixon .50 .23
❑ 101 Paul Pierce .75 .35
❑ 102 Tim Thomas .50 .23
❑ 103 Eddie Griffin .50 .23
❑ 104 Corey Maggette .50 .23
❑ 105 Juwan Howard .50 .23
❑ 106 Peja Stojakovic .75 .35
❑ 107 Tim Duncan 1.50 .70
❑ 108 Keith Van Horn .75 .35
❑ 109 Cuttino Mobley .50 .23
❑ 110 Kareem Rush .50 .23
❑ 111 Predrag Drobnjak .20 .09
❑ 112 Tony Delk .20 .09
❑ 113 Dajuan Wagner .50 .23
❑ 114 Karl Malone .75 .35
❑ 115 Rashard Lewis .75 .35
❑ 116 David Wesley .20 .09
❑ 117 Rasheed Wallace .75 .35
❑ 118 Derrick Coleman .20 .09
❑ 119 Donnell Harvey .20 .09
❑ 120 Elton Brand .75 .35
❑ 121 Carmelo Anthony RC 50.00 22.00
❑ 122 Keith Bogans RC 8.00 3.60
❑ 123 Leandro Barbosa RC 8.00 3.60
❑ 124 Troy Bell RC 8.00 3.60
❑ 125 Chris Bosh RC 20.00 9.00
❑ 126 Zarko Cabarkapa RC 8.00 3.60
❑ 127 Jason Kapono RC 8.00 3.60
❑ 128 Nick Collison RC 8.00 3.60
❑ 129 Boris Diaw-Riffiod RC 8.00 3.60
❑ 130 Marcus Banks RC 8.00 3.60
❑ 131 T.J. Ford RC 12.00 5.50
❑ 132 Reece Gaines RC 8.00 3.60
❑ 133 Travis Hansen RC 8.00 3.60
❑ 134 Jarvis Hayes RC 8.00 3.60
❑ 135 Kirk Hinrich RC 15.00 6.75
❑ 136 Josh Howard RC 10.00 4.50
❑ 137 LeBron James RC 120.00 55.00
❑ 138 Dahntay Jones RC 8.00 3.60
❑ 139 Chris Kaman RC 8.00 3.60
❑ 140 Maciej Lampe RC 8.00 3.60
❑ 141 Darko Milicic RC 15.00 6.75
❑ 142 Travis Outlaw RC 8.00 3.60
❑ 143 Mickael Pietrus RC 8.00 3.60
❑ 144 Rick Rickert RC 8.00 3.60
❑ 145 Luke Ridnour RC 12.00 5.50
❑ 146 Sofoklis Schortsanitis RC 8.00 3.60
❑ 147 Mike Sweetney RC 8.00 3.60
❑ 148 Dwyane Wade RC 25.00 11.00
❑ 149 Luke Walton RC 10.00 4.50
❑ 150 David West RC 8.00 3.60
❑ 151 Zoran Planinic RC 8.00 3.60
❑ 152 Ndudi Ebi RC 8.00 3.60
❑ 153 Aleksandar Pavlovic RC 8.00 3.60
❑ 154 Kendrick Perkins RC 8.00 3.60
❑ 155 Maurice Williams RC 8.00 3.60

	Card	Nm-Mt	Ex-Mt
❑	156 Jerome Beasley RC	8.00	3.60
❑	157 Slavko Vranes RC	8.00	3.60
❑	158 Zaur Pachulia RC	8.00	3.60
❑	159 Carlos Delfino RC	8.00	3.60
❑	160 Brian Cook RC	8.00	3.60

1999-00 Fleer Force

	Card	Nm-Mt	Ex-Mt
	COMPLETE SET (235)	250.00	75.00
	COMPLETE SET w/o RC (200)	30.00	9.00
	COMMON CARD (1-200)	.25	.07
	COMMON ROOKIE (201-235)	3.00	.90
❑	1 Vince Carter	2.00	.60
❑	2 Kobe Bryant	3.00	.90
❑	3 Keith Van Horn	.75	.23
❑	4 Tim Duncan	1.50	.45
❑	5 Grant Hill	.75	.23
❑	6 Kevin Garnett	1.50	.45
❑	7 Anfernee Hardaway	.75	.23
❑	8 Jason Williams	.75	.23
❑	9 Paul Pierce	.75	.23
❑	10 Mookie Blaylock	.25	.07
❑	11 Shawn Bradley	.25	.07
❑	12 Kenny Anderson	.50	.15
❑	13 Chauncey Billups	.50	.15
❑	14 Elden Campbell	.25	.07
❑	15 Jason Caffey	.25	.07
❑	16 Brent Barry	.50	.15
❑	17 Charles Barkley	1.00	.30
❑	18 Derek Anderson	.50	.15
❑	19 Darrick Martin	.25	.07
❑	20 Michael Curry	.25	.07
❑	21 Rick Fox	.50	.15
❑	22 Antonio Davis	.25	.07
❑	23 Terrell Brandon	.50	.15
❑	24 P.J. Brown	.25	.07
❑	25 Toby Bailey	.25	.07
❑	26 Ray Allen	.75	.23
❑	27 Brian Grant	.50	.15
❑	28 Scott Burrell	.25	.07
❑	29 Tariq Abdul-Wahad	.25	.07
❑	30 Marcus Camby	.50	.15
❑	31 John Stockton	.75	.23
❑	32 Nick Anderson	.25	.07
❑	33 Jamie Feick RC	3.00	.90
❑	34 Matt Geiger	.25	.07
❑	35 Vin Baker	.50	.15
❑	36 Dee Brown	.25	.07
❑	37 Shandon Anderson	.25	.07
❑	38 Vernon Maxwell	.25	.07
❑	39 Shareef Abdur-Rahim	.75	.23
❑	40 LaPhonso Ellis	.25	.07
❑	41 Cedric Ceballos	.25	.07
❑	42 Tony Battie	.25	.07
❑	43 Keon Clark	.50	.15
❑	44 Derrick Coleman	.50	.15
❑	45 Erick Dampier	.50	.15
❑	46 Corey Benjamin	.25	.07
❑	47 Michael Dickerson	.50	.15
❑	48 Cedric Henderson	.25	.07
❑	49 Lamond Murray	.25	.07
❑	50 Jerome Williams	.25	.07
❑	51 Shaquille O'Neal	2.00	.60
❑	52 Dale Davis	.25	.07
❑	53 Dean Garrett	.25	.07
❑	54 Tim Hardaway	.50	.15
❑	55 Dennis Rodman	.50	.15
❑	56 Sam Cassell	.75	.23
❑	57 Jim Jackson	.25	.07
❑	58 Kendall Gill	.25	.07
❑	59 Eric Williams	.25	.07
❑	60 Chris Childs	.25	.07
❑	61 Vlade Divac	.50	.15
❑	62 Darrell Armstrong	.25	.07
❑	63 Mario Elie	.25	.07
❑	64 Jaren Jackson	.25	.07
❑	65 Dale Ellis	.25	.07
❑	66 Doug Christie	.50	.15
❑	67 Howard Eisley	.25	.07
❑	68 Juwan Howard	.50	.15
❑	69 Mike Bibby	.75	.23
❑	70 Alan Henderson	.25	.07
❑	71 Michael Finley	.75	.23
❑	72 Dana Barros	.25	.07
❑	73 Troy Hudson	.25	.07
❑	74 Ricky Davis	.50	.15
❑	75 John Amaechi RC	.75	.23
❑	76 Erick Strickland	.25	.07
❑	77 Bryce Drew	.25	.07
❑	78 Shawn Kemp	.50	.15
❑	79 Tyrone Nesby RC	.25	.07
❑	80 Lindsey Hunter	.25	.07
❑	81 Ruben Patterson	.50	.15
❑	82 Al Harrington	.75	.23
❑	83 Bobby Jackson	.50	.15
❑	84 Dan Majerle	.50	.15
❑	85 Rex Chapman	.25	.07
❑	86 Dell Curry	.25	.07
❑	87 Robert Pack	.25	.07
❑	88 Kerry Kittles	.25	.07
❑	89 Isaiah Rider	.25	.07
❑	90 Patrick Ewing	.75	.23
❑	91 Lawrence Funderburke	.25	.07
❑	92 Isaac Austin	.25	.07
❑	93 Sean Elliott	.50	.15
❑	94 Larry Hughes	.75	.23
❑	95 Jelani McCoy	.25	.07
❑	96 Tracy McGrady	2.00	.60
❑	97 Jeff Hornacek	.50	.15
❑	98 Jahidi White	.25	.07
❑	99 Danny Manning	.25	.07
❑	100 Roshown McLeod	.25	.07
❑	101 Steve Nash	.75	.23
❑	102 Ron Mercer	.50	.15
❑	103 Raef LaFrentz	.50	.15
❑	104 Eddie Jones	.75	.23
❑	105 Antawn Jamison	1.25	.35
❑	106 Chucky Atkins RC	.50	.15
❑	107 Othella Harrington	.25	.07
❑	108 Brevin Knight	.25	.07
❑	109 Michael Olowokandi	.50	.15
❑	110 Christian Laettner	.50	.15
❑	111 J.R. Reid	.25	.07
❑	112 Reggie Miller	.75	.23
❑	113 Lazaro Borrell RC	3.00	.90
❑	114 Jamal Mashburn	.50	.15
❑	115 Glenn Robinson	.75	.23
❑	116 Pat Garrity	.25	.07
❑	117 Stephon Marbury	.75	.23
❑	118 Arvydas Sabonis	.50	.15
❑	119 Allan Houston	.50	.15
❑	120 Peja Stojakovic	1.00	.30
❑	121 Michael Doleac	.25	.07
❑	122 Avery Johnson	.25	.07
❑	123 Allen Iverson	1.50	.45
❑	124 Rashard Lewis	.75	.23
❑	125 Charles Oakley	.25	.07
❑	126 Karl Malone	.75	.23
❑	127 Tracy Murray	.25	.07
❑	128 Felipe Lopez	.25	.07
❑	129 Dikembe Mutombo	.50	.15
❑	130 Dirk Nowitzki	1.50	.45
❑	131 Vitaly Potapenko	.25	.07
❑	132 Antonio McDyess	.50	.15
❑	133 Anthony Mason	.50	.15
❑	134 Donyell Marshall	.50	.15
❑	135 Dickey Simpkins	.25	.07
❑	136 Cuttino Mobley	.75	.23
❑	137 Wesley Person	.25	.07
❑	138 Rodney Rogers	.25	.07
❑	139 Jerry Stackhouse	.75	.23
❑	140 Glen Rice	.50	.15
❑	141 Chris Mullin	.75	.23
❑	142 Anthony Peeler	.25	.07
❑	143 Alonzo Mourning	.50	.15
❑	144 Tom Gugliotta	.25	.07
❑	145 Tim Thomas	.50	.15
❑	146 Damon Stoudamire	.50	.15
❑	147 Jayson Williams	.25	.07
❑	148 Larry Johnson	.50	.15
❑	149 Chris Webber	.75	.23
❑	150 Matt Harpring	.75	.23
❑	151 David Robinson	.75	.23
❑	152 George Lynch	.25	.07
❑	153 Gary Payton	.75	.23
❑	154 John Wallace	.25	.07
❑	155 Greg Ostertag	.25	.07
❑	156 Mitch Richmond	.50	.15
❑	157 Cherokee Parks	.25	.07
❑	158 Steve Smith	.50	.15
❑	159 Gary Trent	.25	.07
❑	160 Antoine Walker	.75	.23
❑	161 Chris Herren RC	.25	.07
❑	162 Ron Harper	.50	.15
❑	163 Chris Mills	.25	.07
❑	164 Fred Hoiberg	.25	.07
❑	165 Hakeem Olajuwon	.75	.23
❑	166 Bob Sura	.25	.07
❑	167 Brian Skinner	.25	.07
❑	168 Loy Vaught	.25	.07
❑	169 A.C. Green	.50	.15
❑	170 Jalen Rose	.75	.23
❑	171 Joe Smith	.50	.15
❑	172 Clarence Weatherspoon	.25	.07
❑	173 Jason Kidd	1.25	.35
❑	174 Robert Traylor	.25	.07
❑	175 Rasheed Wallace	.75	.23
❑	176 Latrell Sprewell	.75	.23
❑	177 Corliss Williamson	.50	.15
❑	178 Bo Outlaw	.25	.07
❑	179 Malik Rose	.25	.07
❑	180 Nazr Mohammed	.25	.07
❑	181 Eric Murdock	.25	.07
❑	182 Kevin Willis	.25	.07
❑	183 Bryon Russell	.25	.07
❑	184 Bryant Reeves	.25	.07
❑	185 Rod Strickland	.25	.07
❑	186 Samaki Walker	.25	.07
❑	187 Nick Van Exel	.75	.23
❑	188 David Wesley	.25	.07
❑	189 John Starks	.50	.15
❑	190 Toni Kukoc	.50	.15
❑	191 Scottie Pippen	1.25	.35
❑	192 Johnny Newman	.25	.07
❑	193 Maurice Taylor	.50	.15
❑	194 Rik Smits	.50	.15
❑	195 Clifford Robinson	.25	.07
❑	196 Bonzi Wells	.75	.23
❑	197 Charlie Ward	.25	.07
❑	198 Detlef Schrempf	.50	.15
❑	199 Theo Ratliff	.50	.15
❑	200 Kelvin Cato	.25	.07
❑	201 Ron Artest RC	10.00	3.00
❑	202 William Avery RC	6.00	1.80
❑	203 Elton Brand RC	20.00	6.00
❑	204 Baron Davis RC	15.00	4.50
❑	205 Jumaine Jones RC	6.00	1.80
❑	206 Andre Miller RC	15.00	4.50
❑	207 Eddie Robinson RC	10.00	3.00
❑	208 James Posey RC	10.00	3.00
❑	209 Jason Terry RC	10.00	3.00
❑	210 Kenny Thomas RC	6.00	1.80
❑	211 Steve Francis RC	25.00	7.50
❑	212 Wally Szczerbiak RC	15.00	4.50
❑	213 Richard Hamilton RC	15.00	4.50
❑	214 Jonathan Bender RC	15.00	4.50
❑	215 Shawn Marion RC	20.00	6.00
❑	216 Aleksandar Radojevic RC	3.00	.90
❑	217 Tim James RC	5.00	1.50
❑	218 Trajan Langdon RC	6.00	1.80
❑	219 Lamar Odom RC	15.00	4.50
❑	220 Corey Maggette RC	15.00	4.50
❑	221 Dion Glover RC	5.00	1.50
❑	222 Cal Bowdler RC	5.00	1.50
❑	223 Vonteego Cummings RC	6.00	1.80
❑	224 Devean George RC	8.00	2.40
❑	225 Anthony Carter RC	10.00	3.00
❑	226 Laron Profit RC	6.00	1.80
❑	227 Quincy Lewis RC	5.00	1.50
❑	228 John Celestand RC	5.00	1.50

	Nm-Mt	Ex-Mt
❑ 229 Obinna Ekezie RC	4.00	1.20
❑ 230 Scott Padgett RC	5.00	1.50
❑ 231 Michael Ruffin RC	4.00	1.20
❑ 232 Jeff Foster RC	5.00	1.50
❑ 233 Jermaine Jackson RC	3.00	.90
❑ 234 Adrian Griffin RC	5.00	1.50
❑ 235 Todd MacCulloch RC	5.00	1.50
❑ NNO Vince Carter Sgt.Carter Jersey	20.00	6.00
❑ NNO Vince Carter Sgt.Carter Auto/300	100.00	30.00

2001-02 Fleer Force

	Nm-Mt	Ex-Mt
COMPLETE SET (180)	250.00	75.00
COMPLETE SET w/o SP's (150)	50.00	15.00
COMMON CARD (1-180)	.25	.07
COMMON ROOKIE (101-130)	4.00	1.20
❑ 1 Vince Carter	2.00	.60
❑ 2 Allan Houston	.50	.15
❑ 3 Steve Francis	.75	.23
❑ 4 Karl Malone	.75	.23
❑ 5 Joe Smith	.50	.15
❑ 6 Raef LaFrentz	.50	.15
❑ 7 David Robinson	.75	.23
❑ 8 Tim Thomas	.50	.15
❑ 9 Antonio McDyess	.50	.15
❑ 10 Steve Smith	.50	.15
❑ 11 Eddie Jones	.75	.23
❑ 12 Jumaine Jones	.50	.15
❑ 13 Derek Anderson	.50	.15
❑ 14 Shaquille O'Neal	2.00	.60
❑ 15 Eddie Robinson	.50	.15
❑ 16 Stephon Marbury	.75	.23
❑ 17 Darius Miles	.75	.23
❑ 18 Toni Kukoc	.50	.15
❑ 19 Latrell Sprewell	.75	.23
❑ 20 Wang Zhizhi	.75	.23
❑ 21 Tim Duncan	1.50	.45
❑ 22 Eddie House	.50	.15
❑ 23 Chris Mihm	.50	.15
❑ 24 Rasheed Wallace	.75	.23
❑ 25 Kobe Bryant	3.00	.90
❑ 26 Kenny Thomas	.25	.07
❑ 27 John Stockton	.75	.23
❑ 28 Mike Bibby	.75	.23
❑ 29 Larry Hughes	.50	.15
❑ 30 Antonio Davis	.25	.07
❑ 31 Ray Allen	.75	.23
❑ 32 Corliss Williamson	.50	.15
❑ 33 Desmond Mason	.50	.15
❑ 34 Sam Cassell	.75	.23
❑ 35 Dirk Nowitzki	1.25	.35
❑ 36 Chris Webber	.75	.23
❑ 37 Michael Dickerson	.50	.15
❑ 38 Ron Mercer	.50	.15
❑ 39 Iakovos Tsakalidis	.25	.07
❑ 40 Derek Fisher	.75	.23
❑ 41 Baron Davis	.75	.23
❑ 42 Allen Iverson	1.50	.45
❑ 43 Avery Johnson	.25	.07
❑ 44 Courtney Alexander	.50	.15
❑ 45 Alonzo Mourning	.50	.15
❑ 46 Steve Nash	.75	.23
❑ 47 Hidayet Turkoglu	.50	.15
❑ 48 Jason Williams	.50	.15
❑ 49 David Wesley	.25	.07
❑ 50 Dikembe Mutombo	.50	.15
❑ 51 LaPhonso Ellis	.25	.07
❑ 52 Trajan Langdon	.25	.07
❑ 53 Damon Stoudamire	.50	.15
❑ 54 Rick Fox	.50	.15
❑ 55 Paul Pierce	.75	.23
❑ 56 Tracy McGrady	2.00	.60
❑ 57 Lamar Odom	.75	.23
❑ 58 Antoine Walker	.75	.23
❑ 59 Mike Miller	.75	.23
❑ 60 Jermaine O'Neal	.75	.23
❑ 61 Michael Jordan	15.00	4.50
❑ 62 Jason Kidd	1.25	.35
❑ 63 Marc Jackson	.50	.15
❑ 64 Hakeem Olajuwon	.75	.23
❑ 65 Kevin Garnett	1.50	.45
❑ 66 Nick Van Exel	.75	.23
❑ 67 Rashard Lewis	.50	.15
❑ 68 Brian Grant	.50	.15
❑ 69 Keith Van Horn	.75	.23
❑ 70 Grant Hill	.75	.23
❑ 71 Reggie Miller	.75	.23
❑ 72 Richard Hamilton	.50	.15
❑ 73 Marcus Camby	.50	.15
❑ 74 Clifford Robinson	.25	.07
❑ 75 Gary Payton	.75	.23
❑ 76 Andre Miller	.50	.15
❑ 77 Bonzi Wells	.50	.15
❑ 78 Stromile Swift	.50	.15
❑ 79 Marcus Fizer	.50	.15
❑ 80 Shawn Marion	.75	.23
❑ 81 Elton Brand	.75	.23
❑ 82 Jamal Mashburn	.50	.15
❑ 83 Aaron McKie	.50	.15
❑ 84 Corey Maggette	.50	.15
❑ 85 Jason Terry	.75	.23
❑ 86 Anfernee Hardaway	.75	.23
❑ 87 Antawn Jamison	.75	.23
❑ 88 Morris Peterson	.50	.15
❑ 89 Wally Szczerbiak	.50	.15
❑ 90 Jerry Stackhouse	.75	.23
❑ 91 Shareef Abdur-Rahim	.75	.23
❑ 92 Glenn Robinson	.75	.23
❑ 93 Michael Finley	.75	.23
❑ 94 Peja Stojakovic	.75	.23
❑ 95 Jalen Rose	.75	.23
❑ 96 Theo Ratliff	.50	.15
❑ 97 Kurt Thomas	.50	.15
❑ 98 Cuttino Mobley	.50	.15
❑ 99 DeShawn Stevenson	.50	.15
❑ 100 Terrell Brandon	.50	.15
❑ 101 Kwame Brown RC	8.00	2.40
❑ 102 Tyson Chandler RC	10.00	3.00
❑ 103 Pau Gasol RC	15.00	4.50
❑ 104 Eddy Curry RC	10.00	3.00
❑ 105 Jason Richardson RC	12.00	3.60
❑ 106 Shane Battier RC	6.00	1.80
❑ 107 Eddie Griffin RC	6.00	1.80
❑ 108 DeSagana Diop RC	4.00	1.20
❑ 109 Rodney White RC	5.00	1.50
❑ 110 Joe Johnson RC	6.00	1.80
❑ 111 Kedrick Brown RC	4.00	1.20
❑ 112 Vladimir Radmanovic RC	5.00	1.50
❑ 113 Richard Jefferson RC	8.00	2.40
❑ 114 Troy Murphy RC	8.00	2.40
❑ 115 Steven Hunter RC	4.00	1.20
❑ 116 Kirk Haston RC	4.00	1.20
❑ 117 Michael Bradley RC	4.00	1.20
❑ 118 Jason Collins RC	4.00	1.20
❑ 119 Zach Randolph RC	12.00	3.60
❑ 120 Brendan Haywood RC	5.00	1.50
❑ 121 Joseph Forte RC	8.00	2.40
❑ 122 Jeryl Sasser RC	4.00	1.20
❑ 123 Brandon Armstrong RC	5.00	1.50
❑ 124 Andrei Kirilenko RC	10.00	3.00
❑ 125 Gerald Wallace RC	8.00	2.40
❑ 126 Samuel Dalembert RC	4.00	1.20
❑ 127 Jamaal Tinsley RC	6.00	1.80
❑ 128 Tony Parker RC	15.00	4.50
❑ 129 Loren Woods RC	4.00	1.20
❑ 130 Primoz Brezec RC	4.00	1.20
❑ 131 Dion Glover	.25	.07
❑ 132 Moochie Norris	.25	.07
❑ 133 Mark Jackson	.50	.15
❑ 134 Bryon Russell	.25	.07
❑ 135 Danny Fortson	.25	.07
❑ 136 Kenyon Martin	.75	.23
❑ 137 Alvin Williams	.25	.07
❑ 138 Erick Dampier	.50	.15
❑ 139 Clarence Weatherspoon	.25	.07
❑ 140 Brent Barry	.50	.15
❑ 141 Lamond Murray	.25	.07
❑ 142 Lindsey Hunter	.25	.07
❑ 143 Speedy Claxton	.50	.15
❑ 144 James Posey	.50	.15
❑ 145 Anthony Mason	.50	.15
❑ 146 Mateen Cleaves	.50	.15
❑ 147 Kenny Anderson	.50	.15
❑ 148 Travis Best	.25	.07
❑ 149 Patrick Ewing	.75	.23
❑ 150 Dana Barros	.25	.07
❑ 151 Lorenzen Wright	.25	.07
❑ 152 Rodney Rogers	.25	.07
❑ 153 Brad Miller	.75	.23
❑ 154 Anthony Peeler	.25	.07
❑ 155 Antonio Daniels	.25	.07
❑ 156 Tim Hardaway	.50	.15
❑ 157 Quentin Richardson	.50	.15
❑ 158 Darrell Armstrong	.25	.07
❑ 159 Nazr Mohammad	.25	.07
❑ 160 Todd MacCulloch	.25	.07
❑ 161 Ruben Patterson	.50	.15
❑ 162 Wesley Person	.25	.07
❑ 163 Jeff McInnis	.25	.07
❑ 164 Vin Baker	.50	.15
❑ 165 George McCloud	.25	.07
❑ 166 Chris Gatling	.25	.07
❑ 167 Derrick Coleman	.25	.07
❑ 168 Elden Campbell	.25	.07
❑ 169 Glen Rice	.50	.15
❑ 170 Donyell Marshall	.50	.15
❑ 171 Juwan Howard	.50	.15
❑ 172 Mitch Richmond	.50	.15
❑ 173 Tom Gugliotta	.25	.07
❑ 174 Chucky Atkins	.25	.07
❑ 175 Michael Redd	.75	.23
❑ 176 Malik Rose	.25	.07
❑ 177 Lee Nailon	.25	.07
❑ 178 Al Harrington	.50	.15
❑ 179 Matt Harpring	.75	.23
❑ 180 Tyronn Lue	.25	.07

2000-01 Fleer Futures

	Nm-Mt	Ex-Mt
COMPLETE SET (250)	80.00	24.00
COMPLETE SET w/o RCs (200)	25.00	7.50
COMMON CARD (1-200)	.20	.06
COMMON EVEN RC (201-250)	.25	.07
COMMON ODD RC (201-250)	.50	.15
❑ 1 Vince Carter	1.50	.45
❑ 2 Dan Majerle	.40	.12
❑ 3 George McCloud	.20	.06
❑ 4 Radoslav Nesterovic	.40	.12
❑ 5 Corey Maggette	.40	.12
❑ 6 Derek Anderson	.40	.12
❑ 7 Ray Allen	.60	.18
❑ 8 Greg Ostertag	.20	.06
❑ 9 Cedric Ceballos	.20	.06
❑ 10 Danny Fortson	.20	.06
❑ 11 Roshown McLeod	.20	.06
❑ 12 Christian Laettner	.40	.12
❑ 13 Avery Johnson	.20	.06
❑ 14 Clarence Weatherspoon	.20	.06
❑ 15 Michael Curry	.20	.06
❑ 16 Chris Whitney	.20	.06

	#	Player	Nm-Mt	Ex-Mt
❑	17	Anthony Mason	.40	.12
❑	18	Antonio McDyess	.40	.12
❑	19	Vitaly Potapenko	.20	.06
❑	20	Shaquille O'Neal	1.50	.45
❑	21	David Robinson	.60	.18
❑	22	Tyrone Hill	.20	.06
❑	23	Otis Thorpe	.20	.06
❑	24	Reggie Miller	.60	.18
❑	25	Kevin Garnett	1.25	.35
❑	26	Michael Dickerson	.40	.12
❑	27	John Amaechi	.20	.06
❑	28	Jason Kidd	1.00	.30
❑	29	Ron Artest	.40	.12
❑	30	Muggsy Bogues	.40	.12
❑	31	Antawn Jamison	.60	.18
❑	32	Brian Grant	.40	.12
❑	33	Stephon Marbury	.60	.18
❑	34	William Avery	.20	.06
❑	35	Paul Pierce	.60	.18
❑	36	Marcus Camby	.40	.12
❑	37	Kevin Willis	.20	.06
❑	38	Dikembe Mutombo	.40	.12
❑	39	Rashard Lewis	.40	.12
❑	40	Allan Houston	.40	.12
❑	41	Hakeem Olajuwon	.60	.18
❑	42	Rod Strickland	.20	.06
❑	43	Derrick Coleman	.20	.06
❑	44	Tariq Abdul-Wahad	.20	.06
❑	45	Terrell Brandon	.40	.12
❑	46	Michael Olowokandi	.20	.06
❑	47	Robert Horry	.40	.12
❑	48	Kelvin Cato	.20	.06
❑	49	Eric Williams	.20	.06
❑	50	Glen Rice	.40	.12
❑	51	Carlos Rogers	.20	.06
❑	52	Allen Iverson	1.25	.35
❑	53	P.J. Brown	.20	.06
❑	54	Jalen Rose	.60	.18
❑	55	Damon Stoudamire	.40	.12
❑	56	Damon Jones RC	.25	.07
❑	57	Darrell Armstrong	.20	.06
❑	58	Samaki Walker	.20	.06
❑	59	John Stockton	.60	.18
❑	60	Chucky Atkins	.20	.06
❑	61	Rasheed Wallace	.60	.18
❑	62	Jason Terry	.60	.18
❑	63	Aaron Williams	.20	.06
❑	64	Steve Nash	.60	.18
❑	65	Antoine Walker	.60	.18
❑	66	Patrick Ewing	.60	.18
❑	67	Cuttino Mobley	.40	.12
❑	68	Aaron McKie	.40	.12
❑	69	Jamal Mashburn	.40	.12
❑	70	Scottie Pippen	1.00	.30
❑	71	Bryant Reeves	.20	.06
❑	72	Isaiah Rider	.40	.12
❑	73	Jaren Jackson	.20	.06
❑	74	Lindsey Hunter	.20	.06
❑	75	Jacque Vaughn	.20	.06
❑	76	Travis Best	.20	.06
❑	77	Vinny Del Negro	.20	.06
❑	78	Othella Harrington	.20	.06
❑	79	Michael Finley	.60	.18
❑	80	Brent Barry	.40	.12
❑	81	Brevin Knight	.20	.06
❑	82	Kurt Thomas	.40	.12
❑	83	Mark Jackson	.20	.06
❑	84	Richard Hamilton	.40	.12
❑	85	Anthony Carter	.40	.12
❑	86	Matt Harpring	.60	.18
❑	87	Bobby Jackson	.40	.12
❑	88	Jerome Williams	.20	.06
❑	89	Jahidi White	.20	.06
❑	90	Lorenzen Wright	.20	.06
❑	91	Kerry Kittles	.20	.06
❑	92	Anthony Peeler	.20	.06
❑	93	Kenny Anderson	.40	.12
❑	94	Latrell Sprewell	.60	.18
❑	95	Maurice Taylor	.20	.06
❑	96	Toni Kukoc	.40	.12
❑	97	Eddie Robinson	.40	.12
❑	98	Voshon Lenard	.20	.06
❑	99	Sam Mitchell	.20	.06
❑	100	Isaac Austin	.20	.06
❑	101	Michael Doleac	.20	.06
❑	102	Andre Miller	.40	.12
❑	103	Jason Williams	.40	.12
❑	104	Charles Oakley	.20	.06
❑	105	Mitch Richmond	.40	.12
❑	106	Bruce Bowen	.20	.06
❑	107	Keith Van Horn	.60	.18
❑	108	Wally Szczerbiak	.40	.12
❑	109	Tony Battie	.20	.06
❑	110	Larry Johnson	.40	.12
❑	111	Shandon Anderson	.20	.06
❑	112	Sam Cassell	.60	.18
❑	113	David Wesley	.20	.06
❑	114	James Posey	.40	.12
❑	115	Bonzi Wells	.40	.12
❑	116	Mike Bibby	.60	.18
❑	117	Andrew DeClercq	.20	.06
❑	118	Clifford Robinson	.20	.06
❑	119	Corliss Williamson	.40	.12
❑	120	Antonio Davis	.20	.06
❑	121	Eddie Jones	.60	.18
❑	122	Jamie Feick	.20	.06
❑	123	Anfernee Hardaway	.60	.18
❑	124	Adrian Griffin	.20	.06
❑	125	Erick Strickland	.20	.06
❑	126	Doug Christie	.40	.12
❑	127	Scot Pollard	.20	.06
❑	128	Sam Perkins	.40	.12
❑	129	Raef LaFrentz	.40	.12
❑	130	Dale Davis	.20	.06
❑	131	Tyrone Nesby	.20	.06
❑	132	Rick Fox	.40	.12
❑	133	Tom Gugliotta	.20	.06
❑	134	Glenn Robinson	.60	.18
❑	135	Quincy Lewis	.20	.06
❑	136	Austin Croshere	.40	.12
❑	137	Shawn Kemp	.40	.12
❑	138	Lamar Odom	.60	.18
❑	139	Tim Duncan	1.25	.35
❑	140	Tim Thomas	.40	.12
❑	141	Bryon Russell	.20	.06
❑	142	Jermaine O'Neal	.60	.18
❑	143	Erick Dampier	.40	.12
❑	144	Shareef Abdur-Rahim	.60	.18
❑	145	Bo Outlaw	.20	.06
❑	146	Gary Payton	.60	.18
❑	147	Chris Gatling	.20	.06
❑	148	Vlade Divac	.40	.12
❑	149	Ben Wallace	.60	.18
❑	150	Larry Hughes	.40	.12
❑	151	Ron Mercer	.40	.12
❑	152	Karl Malone	.60	.18
❑	153	Jonathan Bender	.40	.12
❑	154	Mookie Blaylock	.20	.06
❑	155	Jim Jackson	.20	.06
❑	156	Chris Crawford	.20	.06
❑	157	Vin Baker	.40	.12
❑	158	Lamond Murray	.20	.06
❑	159	Charlie Ward	.20	.06
❑	160	Steve Francis	.60	.18
❑	161	Cherokee Parks	.20	.06
❑	162	Baron Davis	.60	.18
❑	163	Keon Clark	.40	.12
❑	164	Ruben Patterson	.40	.12
❑	165	Tracy McGrady	1.50	.45
❑	166	Antonio Daniels	.20	.06
❑	167	Scott Williams	.20	.06
❑	168	John Starks	.40	.12
❑	169	Jerry Stackhouse	.60	.18
❑	170	Vonteego Cummings	.20	.06
❑	171	LaPhonso Ellis	.20	.06
❑	172	Dirk Nowitzki	1.00	.30
❑	173	Horace Grant	.40	.12
❑	174	Wesley Person	.20	.06
❑	175	Peja Stojakovic	.60	.18
❑	176	Eric Snow	.40	.12
❑	177	Juwan Howard	.40	.12
❑	178	Tim Hardaway	.40	.12
❑	179	Kendall Gill	.20	.06
❑	180	Chauncey Billups	.40	.12
❑	181	Kobe Bryant	2.50	.75
❑	182	Sean Elliott	.40	.12
❑	183	Donyell Marshall	.40	.12
❑	184	Al Harrington	.40	.12
❑	185	Arvydas Sabonis	.40	.12
❑	186	Grant Hill	.60	.18
❑	187	Malik Rose	.20	.06
❑	188	Nazr Mohammed	.20	.06
❑	189	Elden Campbell	.20	.06
❑	190	Nick Van Exel	.60	.18
❑	191	Steve Smith	.40	.12
❑	192	Sean Rooks	.20	.06
❑	193	Monty Williams	.20	.06
❑	194	Elton Brand	.60	.18
❑	195	Chris Webber	.60	.18
❑	196	Mikki Moore	.20	.06
❑	197	Chris Mills	.20	.06
❑	198	Alan Henderson	.20	.06
❑	199	Shawn Bradley	.20	.06
❑	200	Shawn Marion	.60	.18
❑	201	Hidayet Turkoglu RC	4.00	1.20
❑	202	Iakovos Tsakalidis RC	.25	.07
❑	203	Kenyon Martin RC	5.00	1.50
❑	204	Mamadou N'Diaye RC	.25	.07
❑	205	Stromile Swift RC	3.00	.90
❑	206	Pepe Sanchez RC	.25	.07
❑	207	Chris Mihm RC	.50	.15
❑	208	Lavor Postell RC	.25	.07
❑	209	Marcus Fizer RC	.50	.15
❑	210	Ruben Garces RC	.25	.07
❑	211	Courtney Alexander RC	.50	.15
❑	212	A.J. Guyton RC	.25	.07
❑	213	Darius Miles RC	4.00	1.20
❑	214	Ademola Okulaja RC	.25	.07
❑	215	Jerome Moiso RC	.50	.15
❑	216	Khalid El-Amin RC	.25	.07
❑	217	Joel Przybilla RC	.50	.15
❑	218	Mike Smith RC	.25	.07
❑	219	DerMarr Johnson RC	.50	.15
❑	220	Soumaila Samake RC	.25	.07
❑	221	Mike Miller RC	4.00	1.20
❑	222	Eddie House RC	.25	.07
❑	223	Quentin Richardson RC	4.00	1.20
❑	224	Eduardo Najera RC	.60	.18
❑	225	Morris Peterson RC	3.00	.90
❑	226	Hanno Mottola RC	.25	.07
❑	227	Speedy Claxton RC	.50	.15
❑	228	Ruben Wolkowyski RC	.25	.07
❑	229	Keyon Dooling RC	.50	.15
❑	230	Olumide Oyedeji RC	.25	.07
❑	231	Mark Madsen RC	.50	.15
❑	232	Mike Penberthy RC	.25	.07
❑	233	Mateen Cleaves RC	.50	.15
❑	234	Brian Cardinal RC	.25	.07
❑	235	Etan Thomas RC	.50	.15
❑	236	Garth Joseph RC	.25	.07
❑	237	Jason Collier RC	.50	.15
❑	238	Paul McPherson RC	.25	.07
❑	239	Erick Barkley RC	.50	.15
❑	240	Stephen Jackson RC	.75	.23
❑	241	Desmond Mason RC	.50	.15
❑	242	Jason Hart RC	.25	.07
❑	243	Jamal Crawford RC	.60	.18
❑	244	Daniel Santiago RC	.25	.07
❑	245	DeShawn Stevenson RC	.50	.15
❑	246	S.Medvedenko RC	.25	.07
❑	247	Donnell Harvey RC	.50	.15
❑	248	Chris Porter RC	.25	.07
❑	249	Jamaal Magloire RC	.50	.15
❑	250	Dalibor Bagaric RC	.25	.07

2000-01 Fleer Game Time

	Nm-Mt	Ex-Mt
COMPLETE SET w/o RC (90)	25.00	7.50
COMMON CARD (1-90)	.25	.07

COMMON ROOKIE (91-120)	1.25	.35
❑ 1 Vince Carter	2.00	.60
❑ 2 Raef LaFrentz	.50	.15
❑ 3 Kobe Bryant	3.00	.90
❑ 4 Toni Kukoc	.50	.15
❑ 5 Bonzi Wells	.50	.15
❑ 6 Rashard Lewis	.50	.15
❑ 7 Karl Malone	.75	.23
❑ 8 Juwan Howard	.50	.15
❑ 9 Lindsey Hunter	.25	.07
❑ 10 Alonzo Mourning	.50	.15
❑ 11 Larry Hughes	.50	.15
❑ 12 Austin Croshere	.50	.15
❑ 13 Charles Oakley	.25	.07
❑ 14 Patrick Ewing	.75	.23
❑ 15 Vlade Divac	.50	.15
❑ 16 Michael Finley	.75	.23
❑ 17 Tim Hardaway	.50	.15
❑ 18 Jason Kidd	1.25	.35
❑ 19 Cal Bowdler	.25	.07
❑ 20 Dirk Nowitzki	1.25	.35
❑ 21 Terrell Brandon	.50	.15
❑ 22 Allan Houston	.50	.15
❑ 23 Theo Ratliff	.50	.15
❑ 24 Chris Webber	.75	.23
❑ 25 Shawn Kemp	.50	.15
❑ 26 Jalen Rose	.75	.23
❑ 27 Bryon Russell	.25	.07
❑ 28 Jahidi White	.25	.07
❑ 29 Trajan Langdon	.50	.15
❑ 30 Baron Davis	.75	.23
❑ 31 Cuttino Mobley	.50	.15
❑ 32 Wally Szczerbiak	.50	.15
❑ 33 Michael Dickerson	.50	.15
❑ 34 Andre Miller	.50	.15
❑ 35 Michael Olowokandi	.25	.07
❑ 36 Ray Allen	.75	.23
❑ 37 Latrell Sprewell	.75	.23
❑ 38 Jason Williams	.50	.15
❑ 39 Mikki Moore	.25	.07
❑ 40 Shawn Marion	.75	.23
❑ 41 Radoslav Nesterovic	.50	.15
❑ 42 Ron Artest	.50	.15
❑ 43 Vonteego Cummings	.25	.07
❑ 44 Anfernee Hardaway	.75	.23
❑ 45 Jerome Williams	.25	.07
❑ 46 John Stockton	.75	.23
❑ 47 Antawn Jamison	.75	.23
❑ 48 Grant Hill	.75	.23
❑ 49 Elden Campbell	.25	.07
❑ 50 Steve Francis	.75	.23
❑ 51 Jamie Feick	.25	.07
❑ 52 Gary Payton	.75	.23
❑ 53 Elton Brand	.75	.23
❑ 54 Eddie Jones	.75	.23
❑ 55 Tom Gugliotta	.25	.07
❑ 56 Richard Hamilton	.50	.15
❑ 57 Dion Glover	.25	.07
❑ 58 Shaquille O'Neal	2.00	.60
❑ 59 Kevin Garnett	1.50	.45
❑ 60 Paul Pierce	.75	.23
❑ 61 Brian Grant	.50	.15
❑ 62 Tim Thomas	.50	.15
❑ 63 Tracy McGrady	2.00	.60
❑ 64 Jonathan Bender	.50	.15
❑ 65 Adrian Griffin	.25	.07
❑ 66 Lamar Odom	.75	.23
❑ 67 Rasheed Wallace	.75	.23
❑ 68 Mike Bibby	.75	.23
❑ 69 Glenn Robinson	.75	.23
❑ 70 Eddie Robinson	.50	.15
❑ 71 Robert Horry	.50	.15
❑ 72 Jerry Stackhouse	.75	.23
❑ 73 Stephon Marbury	.75	.23
❑ 74 Marcus Camby	.50	.15
❑ 75 Scottie Pippen	1.25	.35
❑ 76 David Robinson	.75	.23
❑ 77 Jason Terry	.75	.23
❑ 78 Reggie Miller	.75	.23
❑ 79 Larry Johnson	.50	.15
❑ 80 Antonio Daniels	.25	.07
❑ 81 Shareef Abdur-Rahim	.75	.23
❑ 82 Ruben Patterson	.50	.15
❑ 83 Nick Van Exel	.75	.23
❑ 84 Keith Van Horn	.75	.23
❑ 85 Antonio Davis	.25	.07
❑ 86 Antoine Walker	.75	.23
❑ 87 Allen Iverson	1.50	.45
❑ 88 Antonio McDyess	.50	.15
❑ 89 Tim Duncan	1.50	.45
❑ 90 Hakeem Olajuwon	.75	.23
❑ 91 Jamaal Magloire RC	1.25	.35
❑ 92 DerMarr Johnson RC	1.25	.35
❑ 93 Jerome Moiso RC	1.25	.35
❑ 94 Marcus Fizer RC	1.25	.35
❑ 95 Jamal Crawford RC	1.50	.45
❑ 96 Chris Mihm RC	1.25	.35
❑ 97 Donnell Harvey RC	1.25	.35
❑ 98 Courtney Alexander RC	1.25	.35
❑ 99 Etan Thomas RC	1.25	.35
❑ 100 Mamadou N'diaye RC	1.25	.35
❑ 101 Mateen Cleaves RC	1.25	.35
❑ 102 Chris Porter RC	1.25	.35
❑ 103 Jason Collier RC	1.25	.35
❑ 104 Keyon Dooling RC	1.25	.35
❑ 105 Darius Miles RC	6.00	1.80
❑ 106 Mark Madsen RC	1.25	.35
❑ 107 Eddie House RC	1.25	.35
❑ 108 Joel Przybilla RC	1.25	.35
❑ 109 Kenyon Martin RC	8.00	2.40
❑ 110 Mike Miller RC	6.00	1.80
❑ 111 Speedy Claxton RC	1.25	.35
❑ 112 Iakovos Tsakalidis RC	1.25	.35
❑ 113 Erick Barkley RC	1.25	.35
❑ 114 Hidayet Turkoglu RC	6.00	1.80
❑ 115 Eduardo Najera RC	3.00	.90
❑ 116 Desmond Mason RC	1.25	.35
❑ 117 Morris Peterson RC	4.00	1.20
❑ 118 DeShawn Stevenson RC	1.25	.35
❑ 119 Stromile Swift RC	4.00	1.20
❑ 120 Mike Smith RC	1.25	.35

2000-01 Fleer Genuine

	Nm-Mt	Ex-Mt
COMPLETE SET w/o RC (100)	40.00	12.00
COMMON CARD (1-100)	.30	.09
COMMON ROOKIE (101-130)	4.00	1.20
❑ 1 Vince Carter	2.50	.75
❑ 2 Glenn Robinson	1.00	.30
❑ 3 Rasheed Wallace	1.00	.30
❑ 4 Michael Dickerson	.60	.18
❑ 5 Mikki Moore	.30	.09
❑ 6 Wally Szczerbiak	.60	.18
❑ 7 Shawn Marion	1.00	.30
❑ 8 Dan Majerle	.60	.18
❑ 9 Trajan Langdon	.60	.18
❑ 10 Chauncey Billups	.60	.18
❑ 11 Jason Kidd	1.50	.45
❑ 12 Derrick Coleman	.30	.09
❑ 13 Jason Terry	1.00	.30
❑ 14 Eddie Jones	1.00	.30
❑ 15 Scottie Pippen	1.50	.45
❑ 16 Mike Bibby	1.00	.30
❑ 17 Ron Mercer	.60	.18
❑ 18 Hakeem Olajuwon	1.00	.30
❑ 19 Patrick Ewing	1.00	.30
❑ 20 Ruben Patterson	.60	.18
❑ 21 Kenny Anderson	.60	.18
❑ 22 Alonzo Mourning	.60	.18
❑ 23 Steve Smith	.60	.18
❑ 24 Juwan Howard	.60	.18
❑ 25 Antoine Walker	1.00	.30
❑ 26 Kobe Bryant	4.00	1.20
❑ 27 Chris Webber	1.00	.30
❑ 28 Mitch Richmond	.60	.18
❑ 29 Paul Pierce	1.00	.30
❑ 30 Shaquille O'Neal	2.50	.75
❑ 31 Jason Williams	.60	.18
❑ 32 Richard Hamilton	.60	.18
❑ 33 Michael Finley	1.00	.30
❑ 34 Jalen Rose	1.00	.30
❑ 35 Grant Hill	1.00	.30
❑ 36 John Stockton	1.00	.30
❑ 37 Vitaly Potapenko	.30	.09
❑ 38 Glen Rice	.60	.18
❑ 39 Vlade Divac	.60	.18
❑ 40 Jahidi White	.30	.09
❑ 41 Baron Davis	1.00	.30
❑ 42 Michael Olowokandi	.30	.09
❑ 43 Tim Duncan	2.00	.60
❑ 44 Rod Strickland	.30	.09
❑ 45 Jamal Mashburn	.60	.18
❑ 46 Lamar Odom	1.00	.30
❑ 47 David Robinson	1.00	.30
❑ 48 Travis Best	.30	.09
❑ 49 Raef LaFrentz	.60	.18
❑ 50 Keith Van Horn	1.00	.30
❑ 51 Vonteego Cummings	.30	.09
❑ 52 Jerome Williams	.30	.09
❑ 53 Kevin Garnett	2.00	.60
❑ 54 Anfernee Hardaway	1.00	.30
❑ 55 Antonio McDyess	.60	.18
❑ 56 Reggie Miller	1.00	.30
❑ 57 Tracy McGrady	2.50	.75
❑ 58 Bryon Russell	.30	.09
❑ 59 Nick Van Exel	1.00	.30
❑ 60 Allen Iverson	2.00	.60
❑ 61 Karl Malone	1.00	.30
❑ 62 David Wesley	.30	.09
❑ 63 Bob Sura	.30	.09
❑ 64 Stephon Marbury	1.00	.30
❑ 65 Antonio Daniels	.30	.09
❑ 66 Shawn Kemp	.60	.18
❑ 67 Cuttino Mobley	.60	.18
❑ 68 Marcus Camby	.60	.18
❑ 69 Gary Payton	1.00	.30
❑ 70 Dikembe Mutombo	.60	.18
❑ 71 Tim Hardaway	.60	.18
❑ 72 Bonzi Wells	.60	.18
❑ 73 Shareef Abdur-Rahim	1.00	.30
❑ 74 Brevin Knight	.30	.09
❑ 75 Steve Francis	1.00	.30
❑ 76 Allan Houston	.60	.18
❑ 77 Dion Glover	.30	.09
❑ 78 Dirk Nowitzki	1.50	.45
❑ 79 Jonathan Bender	.60	.18
❑ 80 Darrell Armstrong	.30	.09
❑ 81 Antonio Davis	.30	.09
❑ 82 Jerry Stackhouse	1.00	.30
❑ 83 Terrell Brandon	.60	.18
❑ 84 Tom Gugliotta	.30	.09
❑ 85 Sean Elliott	.60	.18
❑ 86 Elton Brand	1.00	.30
❑ 87 Larry Hughes	.60	.18
❑ 88 Kerry Kittles	.30	.09
❑ 89 Vin Baker	.60	.18
❑ 90 Donyell Marshall	.60	.18
❑ 91 Tim Thomas	.60	.18
❑ 92 Toni Kukoc	.60	.18
❑ 93 Charles Oakley	.30	.09
❑ 94 Andre Miller	.60	.18
❑ 95 Austin Croshere	.60	.18
❑ 96 Latrell Sprewell	1.00	.30
❑ 97 Mark Jackson	.30	.09
❑ 98 Antawn Jamison	1.00	.30
❑ 99 Ray Allen	1.00	.30
❑ 100 Theo Ratliff	.60	.18
❑ 101 Chris Mihm RC	4.00	1.20
❑ 102 Mateen Cleaves RC	4.00	1.20
❑ 103 Etan Thomas RC	4.00	1.20
❑ 104 Morris Peterson RC	6.00	1.80
❑ 105 Jamal Crawford RC	5.00	1.50
❑ 106 Darius Miles RC	10.00	3.00
❑ 107 Desmond Mason RC	4.00	1.20
❑ 108 Joel Przybilla RC	4.00	1.20
❑ 109 Mike Miller RC	10.00	3.00
❑ 110 Quentin Richardson RC	8.00	2.40
❑ 111 Jason Collier RC	4.00	1.20
❑ 112 Keyon Dooling RC	4.00	1.20

Card	Nm-Mt	Ex-Mt
❑ 113 Courtney Alexander RC	5.00	1.50
❑ 114 Eddie House RC	4.00	1.20
❑ 115 DerMarr Johnson RC	4.00	1.20
❑ 116 Michael Redd RC	6.00	1.80
❑ 117 Mark Madsen RC	4.00	1.20
❑ 118 Stromile Swift RC	6.00	1.80
❑ 119 Mamadou N'Diaye RC	4.00	1.20
❑ 120 DeShawn Stevenson RC	4.00	1.20
❑ 121 Hidayet Turkoglu RC	10.00	3.00
❑ 122 Stephen Jackson RC	6.00	1.80
❑ 123 Marcus Fizer RC	4.00	1.20
❑ 124 Khalid El-Amin RC	4.00	1.20
❑ 125 Speedy Claxton RC	4.00	1.20
❑ 126 Hanno Mottola RC	4.00	1.20
❑ 127 Jerome Moiso RC	4.00	1.20
❑ 128 Jamaal Magloire RC	4.00	1.20
❑ 129 Donnell Harvey RC	4.00	1.20
❑ 130 Kenyon Martin RC	12.00	3.60
❑ NNO Vince Carter Main Man	80.00	24.00
❑ NNO Vince Carter Main Man Autograph	800.00	240.00

2001-02 Fleer Genuine

Card	Nm-Mt	Ex-Mt
COMMON CARD (1-120)	.30	.09
COMMON ROOKIE (121-150)	3.00	.90
❑ 1 Larry Hughes	.60	.18
❑ 2 Wally Szczerbiak	.60	.18
❑ 3 Jahidi White	.30	.09
❑ 4 Aaron McKie	.60	.18
❑ 5 Antonio McDyess	.60	.18
❑ 6 Tom Gugliotta	.30	.09
❑ 7 Elton Brand	1.00	.30
❑ 8 Lamar Odom	1.00	.30
❑ 9 Chris Webber	1.00	.30
❑ 10 Ron Artest	.60	.18
❑ 11 Gary Payton	1.00	.30
❑ 12 Brian Grant	.60	.18
❑ 13 Steve Nash	1.00	.30
❑ 14 DerMarr Johnson	.60	.18
❑ 15 Vince Carter	2.50	.75
❑ 16 Kurt Thomas	.60	.18
❑ 17 Cuttino Mobley	.60	.18
❑ 18 Marc Jackson	.60	.18
❑ 19 Stromile Swift	.60	.18
❑ 20 Grant Hill	1.00	.30
❑ 21 Raef LaFrentz	.60	.18
❑ 22 Marcus Fizer	.60	.18
❑ 23 Antonio Davis	.30	.09
❑ 24 John Starks	.60	.18
❑ 25 Trajan Langdon	.30	.09
❑ 26 Jason Williams	.60	.18
❑ 27 Toni Kukoc	.60	.18
❑ 28 Morris Peterson	.60	.18
❑ 29 Allen Iverson	2.00	.60
❑ 30 Andre Miller	.60	.18
❑ 31 Larry Johnson	.60	.18
❑ 32 Vitaly Potapenko	.30	.09
❑ 33 Tim Thomas	.60	.18
❑ 34 Eddie House	.60	.18
❑ 35 Juwan Howard	.60	.18
❑ 36 Joel Przybilla	.60	.18
❑ 37 John Stockton	1.00	.30
❑ 38 Michael Finley	1.00	.30
❑ 39 Hidayet Turkoglu	.60	.18
❑ 40 Keith Van Horn	1.00	.30
❑ 41 Shawn Marion	1.00	.30
❑ 42 Derek Fisher	1.00	.30
❑ 43 Terrell Brandon	.60	.18
❑ 44 Jamal Mashburn	.60	.18
❑ 45 Shareef Abdur-Rahim	1.00	.30
❑ 46 Brevin Knight	.30	.09
❑ 47 Antoine Walker	1.00	.30
❑ 48 Mateen Cleaves	.60	.18
❑ 49 Alonzo Mourning	.60	.18
❑ 50 Jermaine O'Neal	1.00	.30
❑ 51 Kenyon Martin	1.00	.30
❑ 52 Steve Smith	.60	.18
❑ 53 Jerry Stackhouse	1.00	.30
❑ 54 Mike Bibby	1.00	.30
❑ 55 Latrell Sprewell	1.00	.30
❑ 56 Iakovos Tsakalidis	.30	.09
❑ 57 Sam Cassell	1.00	.30
❑ 58 Michael Dickerson	.60	.18
❑ 59 Alan Henderson	.30	.09
❑ 60 Allan Houston	.60	.18
❑ 61 Patrick Ewing	1.00	.30
❑ 62 Joe Smith	.60	.18
❑ 63 Rick Fox	.60	.18
❑ 64 Tracy McGrady	2.50	.75
❑ 65 Scottie Pippen	1.50	.45
❑ 66 Chauncey Billups	.60	.18
❑ 67 Voshon Lenard	.30	.09
❑ 68 Jalen Rose	1.00	.30
❑ 69 Derrick Coleman	.30	.09
❑ 70 Shaquille O'Neal	2.50	.75
❑ 71 Anfernee Hardaway	1.00	.30
❑ 72 Derek Anderson	.60	.18
❑ 73 Travis Best	.30	.09
❑ 74 Darius Miles	1.00	.30
❑ 75 Glenn Robinson	1.00	.30
❑ 76 Darrell Armstrong	.30	.09
❑ 77 Dirk Nowitzki	1.50	.45
❑ 78 Stephon Marbury	1.00	.30
❑ 79 Tyronn Lue	.30	.09
❑ 80 Bonzi Wells	.60	.18
❑ 81 Mike Miller	1.00	.30
❑ 82 Tim Duncan	2.00	.60
❑ 83 Tim Hardaway	.60	.18
❑ 84 Desmond Mason	.60	.18
❑ 85 Ray Allen	1.00	.30
❑ 86 Sean Elliott	.60	.18
❑ 87 David Wesley	.30	.09
❑ 88 Rasheed Wallace	1.00	.30
❑ 89 Kevin Garnett	2.00	.60
❑ 90 Dikembe Mutombo	.60	.18
❑ 91 Baron Davis	1.00	.30
❑ 92 Donyell Marshall	.60	.18
❑ 93 Eddie Jones	1.00	.30
❑ 94 Vin Baker	.60	.18
❑ 95 Peja Stojakovic	1.00	.30
❑ 96 Antawn Jamison	1.00	.30
❑ 97 Maurice Taylor	.60	.18
❑ 98 Courtney Alexander	.60	.18
❑ 99 Steve Francis	1.00	.30
❑ 100 Chris Mihm	.60	.18
❑ 101 Kobe Bryant	4.00	1.20
❑ 102 Hakeem Olajuwon	1.00	.30
❑ 103 Richard Hamilton	.60	.18
❑ 104 Karl Malone	1.00	.30
❑ 105 Chucky Atkins	.30	.09
❑ 106 Eric Snow	.60	.18
❑ 107 Ruben Patterson	.60	.18
❑ 108 David Robinson	1.00	.30
❑ 109 Bryon Russell	.30	.09
❑ 110 Jason Terry	1.00	.30
❑ 111 Jason Kidd	1.50	.45
❑ 112 Charles Oakley	.30	.09
❑ 113 Wang Zhizhi	1.00	.30
❑ 114 Quentin Richardson	.60	.18
❑ 115 Clarence Weatherspoon	.30	.09
❑ 116 Nick Van Exel	1.00	.30
❑ 117 Reggie Miller	1.00	.30
❑ 118 Marcus Camby	.60	.18
❑ 119 Corey Maggette	.60	.18
❑ 120 Paul Pierce	1.00	.30
❑ 121 Kwame Brown RC	8.00	2.40
❑ 122 Eddie Griffin RC	6.00	1.80
❑ 123 Eddy Curry RC	12.00	3.60
❑ 124 Jamaal Tinsley RC	6.00	1.80
❑ 125 Jason Richardson RC	25.00	7.50
❑ 126 Shane Battier RC	6.00	1.80
❑ 127 Troy Murphy RC	6.00	1.80
❑ 128 Richard Jefferson RC	12.00	3.60
❑ 129 DeSagana Diop RC	3.00	.90
❑ 130 Tyson Chandler RC	12.00	3.60
❑ 131 Joe Johnson RC	5.00	1.50
❑ 132 Zach Randolph RC	12.00	3.60
❑ 133 Gerald Wallace RC	8.00	2.40
❑ 134 Loren Woods RC	3.00	.90
❑ 135 Jason Collins RC	3.00	.90
❑ 136 Rodney White RC	3.00	.90
❑ 137 Jeryl Sasser RC	4.00	1.20
❑ 138 Kirk Haston RC	3.00	.90
❑ 139 Pau Gasol RC	15.00	4.50
❑ 140 Kedrick Brown RC	3.00	.90
❑ 141 Steven Hunter RC	3.00	.90
❑ 142 Michael Bradley RC	3.00	.90
❑ 143 Joseph Forte RC	8.00	2.40
❑ 144 Brandon Armstrong RC	5.00	1.50
❑ 145 Samuel Dalembert RC	3.00	.90
❑ 146 Trenton Hassell RC	5.00	1.50
❑ 147 Gilbert Arenas RC	5.00	1.50
❑ 148 Omar Cook RC	3.00	.90
❑ 149 Tony Parker RC	15.00	4.50
❑ 150 Terence Morris RC	3.00	.90

2002-03 Fleer Genuine

Card	Nm-Mt	Ex-Mt
COMPLETE SET (135)	275.00	80.00
COMP.SET w/o SP's (100)	40.00	12.00
COMMON CARD (1-100)	.25	.07
COMMON ROOKIE (101-135)	3.00	.90
❑ 1 Shaquille O'Neal	2.00	.60
❑ 2 Allen Iverson	1.50	.45
❑ 3 Jerry Stackhouse	.75	.23
❑ 4 Kobe Bryant	3.00	.90
❑ 5 Jason Kidd	1.25	.35
❑ 6 Andre Miller	.50	.15
❑ 7 David Robinson	.75	.23
❑ 8 John Stockton	.75	.23
❑ 9 Glenn Robinson	.75	.23
❑ 10 Chauncey Billups	.50	.15
❑ 11 Chris Webber	.75	.23
❑ 12 Antawn Jamison	.75	.23
❑ 13 Sam Cassell	.75	.23
❑ 14 Vlade Divac	.50	.15
❑ 15 P.J. Brown	.25	.07
❑ 16 Robert Horry	.50	.15
❑ 17 Eric Snow	.50	.15
❑ 18 Popeye Jones	.25	.07
❑ 19 Paul Pierce	.75	.23
❑ 20 Eddie Griffin	.50	.15
❑ 21 Marcus Camby	.50	.15
❑ 22 Gary Payton	.75	.23
❑ 23 Michael Jordan	5.00	1.50
❑ 24 Shareef Abdur-Rahim	.75	.23
❑ 25 Anfernee Hardaway	.75	.23
❑ 26 Michael Finley	.75	.23
❑ 27 Steve Nash	.75	.23
❑ 28 Shane Battier	.75	.23
❑ 29 Stephon Marbury	.75	.23
❑ 30 Dirk Nowitzki	1.25	.35
❑ 31 Pau Gasol	.75	.23
❑ 32 Shawn Marion	.75	.23
❑ 33 Rodney Rogers	.25	.07
❑ 34 Steve Smith	.50	.15
❑ 35 Darrell Armstrong	.25	.07
❑ 36 Alvin Williams	.25	.07
❑ 37 Nick Van Exel	.75	.23
❑ 38 Jason Williams	.50	.15

❑ 39 Ruben Patterson	.50	.15
❑ 40 Juwan Howard	.50	.15
❑ 41 Brian Grant	.50	.15
❑ 42 Damon Stoudamire	.50	.15
❑ 43 Antonio McDyess	.50	.15
❑ 44 Eddie Jones	.75	.23
❑ 45 Rasheed Wallace	.75	.23
❑ 46 Larry Hughes	.50	.15
❑ 47 Wally Szczerbiak	.50	.15
❑ 48 Tony Parker	.75	.23
❑ 49 Ron Artest	.50	.15
❑ 50 Kevin Garnett	1.50	.45
❑ 51 Tim Duncan	1.50	.45
❑ 52 Marcus Fizer	.50	.15
❑ 53 Darius Miles	.75	.23
❑ 54 Grant Hill	.75	.23
❑ 55 Andrei Kirilenko	.75	.23
❑ 56 Jalen Rose	.75	.23
❑ 57 Lamar Odom	.75	.23
❑ 58 Tracy McGrady	2.00	.60
❑ 59 Karl Malone	.75	.23
❑ 60 Jason Terry	.75	.23
❑ 61 Steve Francis	.75	.23
❑ 62 Kenyon Martin	.75	.23
❑ 63 Brent Barry	.50	.15
❑ 64 Antoine Walker	.75	.23
❑ 65 Reggie Miller	.75	.23
❑ 66 Allan Houston	.50	.15
❑ 67 Vince Carter	2.00	.60
❑ 68 Toni Kukoc	.50	.15
❑ 69 Lamond Murray	.25	.07
❑ 70 Jason Richardson	.75	.23
❑ 71 Rick Fox	.50	.15
❑ 72 Kerry Kittles	.25	.07
❑ 73 Dikembe Mutombo	.50	.15
❑ 74 Tyson Chandler	.75	.23
❑ 75 Richard Hamilton	.50	.15
❑ 76 Elden Campbell	.25	.07
❑ 77 Jermaine O'Neal	.75	.23
❑ 78 Mike Miller	.75	.23
❑ 79 Morris Peterson	.75	.23
❑ 80 Jamal Mashburn	.50	.15
❑ 81 Elton Brand	.75	.23
❑ 82 Kurt Thomas	.50	.15
❑ 83 Antonio Davis	.25	.07
❑ 84 Ben Wallace	.75	.23
❑ 85 Anthony Mason	.50	.15
❑ 86 Peja Stojakovic	.75	.23
❑ 87 Kenny Anderson	.50	.15
❑ 88 Cuttino Mobley	.50	.15
❑ 89 Keith Van Horn	.75	.23
❑ 90 Rashard Lewis	.50	.15
❑ 91 Clifford Robinson	.25	.07
❑ 92 Ray Allen	.75	.23
❑ 93 Mike Bibby	.75	.23
❑ 94 Baron Davis	.75	.23
❑ 95 Jamaal Tinsley	.75	.23
❑ 96 Latrell Sprewell	.75	.23
❑ 97 Jon Barry	.25	.07
❑ 98 Desmond Mason	.50	.15
❑ 99 Alonzo Mourning	.50	.15
❑ 100 Bonzi Wells	.50	.15
❑ 101 Jay Williams RC	5.00	1.50
❑ 102 Mike Dunleavy RC	6.00	1.80
❑ 103 Amare Stoudemire RC	15.00	4.50
❑ 104 Caron Butler RC	10.00	3.00
❑ 105 Jared Jeffries RC	4.00	1.20
❑ 106 Fred Jones RC	4.00	1.20
❑ 107 Bostjan Nachbar RC	3.00	.90
❑ 108 Jiri Welsch RC	3.00	.90
❑ 109 Juan Dixon RC	6.00	1.80
❑ 110 Curtis Borchardt RC	3.00	.90
❑ 111 Kareem Rush RC	4.00	1.20
❑ 112 Qyntel Woods RC	4.00	1.20
❑ 113 Casey Jacobsen RC	3.00	.90
❑ 114 Frank Williams RC	3.00	.90
❑ 115 John Salmons RC	3.00	.90
❑ 116 Dan Dickau RC	3.00	.90
❑ 117 DaJuan Wagner RC	6.00	1.80
❑ 118 Drew Gooden EXCH	10.00	3.00
❑ 119 Nikoloz Tskitishvili EXCH	4.00	1.20
❑ 120 Yao Ming RC	25.00	7.50
❑ 120A Yao Ming EXCH		
❑ 121 Nene Hilario EXCH	5.00	1.50
❑ 122 Chris Wilcox EXCH	5.00	1.50
❑ 123 Melvin Ely EXCH	3.00	.90
❑ 124 Marcus Haislip EXCH	3.00	.90
❑ 125 Ryan Humphrey EXCH	3.00	.90
❑ 126 Tayshaun Prince EXCH	5.00	1.50
❑ 127 Tito Maddox EXCH	3.00	.90
❑ 128 Chris Jefferies EXCH	3.00	.90
❑ 129 Steve Logan EXCH	3.00	.90
❑ 130 Roger Mason EXCH	3.00	.90
❑ 131 Robert Archibald EXCH	3.00	.90
❑ 132 Vincent Yarbrough EXCH	3.00	.90
❑ 133 Dan Gadzuric EXCH	3.00	.90
❑ 134 Carlos Boozer EXCH	6.00	1.80
❑ 135 Rasual Butler EXCH	3.00	.90

2003-04 Fleer Genuine Insider

	Nm-Mt	Ex-Mt
COMP.SET w/o SP's (100)	30.00	9.00
COMMON ROOKIE (101-110)	6.00	1.80
COMMON ROOKIE (111-140)	4.00	1.20
COMMON ROOKIE (131-140)	6.00	1.80
❑ 1 Shareef Abdur-Rahim	.75	.23
❑ 2 Andre Miller	.50	.15
❑ 3 Reggie Miller	.75	.23
❑ 4 Michael Redd	.75	.23
❑ 5 Allan Houston	.50	.15
❑ 6 Mike Bibby	.75	.23
❑ 7 Kwame Brown	.75	.23
❑ 8 Earl Boykins	.50	.15
❑ 9 Ron Artest	.50	.15
❑ 10 Eddie Jones	.75	.23
❑ 11 Zach Randolph	.75	.23
❑ 12 Derek Anderson	.50	.15
❑ 13 Andrei Kirilenko	.75	.23
❑ 14 Carlos Boozer	.75	.23
❑ 15 Yao Ming	2.00	.60
❑ 16 Pau Gasol	.75	.23
❑ 17 Jamal Mashburn	.50	.15
❑ 18 Shawn Marion	.75	.23
❑ 19 Vince Carter	2.00	.60
❑ 20 Eddy Curry	.50	.15
❑ 21 Mike Dunleavy Jr.	.50	.15
❑ 22 Kobe Bryant	3.00	.90
❑ 23 Tim Thomas	.50	.15
❑ 24 Drew Gooden	.75	.23
❑ 25 Tim Duncan	1.50	.45
❑ 26 Dajuan Wagner	.50	.15
❑ 27 Speedy Claxton	.20	.06
❑ 28 Karl Malone	.75	.23
❑ 29 Jason Kidd	1.25	.35
❑ 30 Kenny Thomas	.20	.06
❑ 31 Vladimir Radmanovic	.20	.06
❑ 32 Tyson Chandler	.75	.23
❑ 33 Jason Richardson	.75	.23
❑ 34 Quentin Richardson	.50	.15
❑ 35 Kerry Kittles	.20	.06
❑ 36 Derrick Coleman	.20	.06
❑ 37 Manu Ginobili	.75	.23
❑ 38 Paul Pierce	.75	.23
❑ 39 Ben Wallace	.75	.23
❑ 40 Corey Maggette	.50	.15
❑ 41 Sam Cassell	.50	.15
❑ 42 Hidayet Turkoglu	.75	.23
❑ 43 Peja Stojakovic	.75	.23
❑ 44 Gilbert Arenas	.75	.23
❑ 45 Dirk Nowitzki	1.25	.35
❑ 46 Al Harrington	.50	.15
❑ 47 Caron Butler	.75	.23
❑ 48 Baron Davis	.75	.23
❑ 49 Rasheed Wallace	.75	.23
❑ 50 Morris Peterson	.50	.15
❑ 51 Steve Nash	.75	.23
❑ 52 Steve Francis	.75	.23
❑ 53 Lamar Odom	.75	.23
❑ 54 Jamaal Magloire	.20	.06
❑ 55 Amare Stoudemire	1.50	.45
❑ 56 Antonio Davis	.20	.06
❑ 57 Dan Dickau	.20	.06
❑ 58 Cuttino Mobley	.50	.15
❑ 59 Jason Williams	.50	.15
❑ 60 David Wesley	.20	.06
❑ 61 Stephon Marbury	.75	.23
❑ 62 Ray Allen	.75	.23
❑ 63 Scottie Pippen	1.25	.35
❑ 64 Nick Van Exel	.75	.23
❑ 65 Shaquille O'Neal	2.00	.60
❑ 66 Richard Jefferson	.50	.15
❑ 67 Allen Iverson	1.50	.45
❑ 68 Tony Parker	.75	.23
❑ 69 Jason Terry	.75	.23
❑ 70 Nenê	.50	.15
❑ 71 Marko Jaric	.50	.15
❑ 72 Troy Hudson	.20	.06
❑ 73 Malik Rose	.20	.06
❑ 74 Bobby Jackson	.50	.15
❑ 75 Jerry Stackhouse	.75	.23
❑ 76 Voshon Lenard	.20	.06
❑ 77 Richard Hamilton	.50	.15
❑ 78 Scot Pollard	.20	.06
❑ 79 Latrell Sprewell	.75	.23
❑ 80 Tracy McGrady	2.00	.60
❑ 81 Chris Webber	.75	.23
❑ 82 Raef LaFrentz	.50	.15
❑ 83 Tayshaun Prince	.50	.15
❑ 84 Elton Brand	.75	.23
❑ 85 Kevin Garnett	1.50	.45
❑ 86 Keon Clark	.50	.15
❑ 87 Brad Miller	.75	.23
❑ 88 Alvin Williams	.20	.06
❑ 89 Michael Finley	.75	.23
❑ 90 Jermaine O'Neal	.75	.23
❑ 91 Desmond Mason	.50	.15
❑ 92 Keith Van Horn	.75	.23
❑ 93 Bonzi Wells	.50	.15
❑ 94 Matt Harpring	.75	.23
❑ 95 Darius Miles	.75	.23
❑ 96 Eddie Griffin	.50	.15
❑ 97 Shane Battier	.75	.23
❑ 98 Kenyon Martin	.75	.23
❑ 99 Glenn Robinson	.75	.23
❑ 100 Rashard Lewis	.75	.23
❑ 101 Carmelo Anthony RC	40.00	12.00
❑ 102 Troy Bell RC	6.00	1.80
❑ 103 T.J. Ford RC	8.00	2.40
❑ 104 LeBron James RC	80.00	24.00
❑ 105 Mike Sweetney RC	6.00	1.80
❑ 106 Chris Bosh RC	12.00	3.60
❑ 107 Jarvis Hayes RC	6.00	1.80
❑ 108 Darko Milicic RC	10.00	3.00
❑ 109 Chris Kaman RC	6.00	1.80
❑ 110 Dwyane Wade RC	15.00	4.50
❑ 111 Udonis Haslem RC	4.00	1.20
❑ 112 Josh Howard RC	5.00	1.50
❑ 113 Mickael Pietrus RC	4.00	1.20
❑ 114 Reece Gaines RC	4.00	1.20
❑ 115 Nick Collison RC	4.00	1.20
❑ 116 Leandrinho Barbosa RC	4.00	1.20
❑ 117 Kendrick Perkins RC	4.00	1.20
❑ 118 Ndudi Ebi RC	4.00	1.20
❑ 119 Willie Green RC	4.00	1.20
❑ 120 Kirk Hinrich RC	6.00	1.80
❑ 121 Marcus Banks RC	4.00	1.20
❑ 122 Zarko Cabarkapa RC	4.00	1.20
❑ 123 Zoran Planinic RC	4.00	1.20
❑ 124 David West RC	4.00	1.20
❑ 125 Luke Ridnour RC	5.00	1.50
❑ 126 Brian Cook RC	4.00	1.20
❑ 127 Boris Diaw RC	4.00	1.20
❑ 128 Dahntay Jones RC	4.00	1.20
❑ 129 Maciej Lampe RC	4.00	1.20
❑ 130 Travis Outlaw RC	4.00	1.20
❑ 131 Ben Handlogten MM RC	6.00	1.80
❑ 132 Jerome Beasley MM RC	6.00	1.80
❑ 133 Marquis Daniels MM RC	12.00	3.60

Card	Nm-Mt	Ex-Mt
❑ 134 Luke Walton MM RC	8.00	2.40
❑ 135 Aleksandar Pavlovic MM RC	6.00	1.80
❑ 136 Matt Carroll MM RC	6.00	1.80
❑ 137 Curtis Borchardt MM RC	6.00	1.80
❑ 138 Jason Kapono MM RC	6.00	1.80
❑ 139 Steve Blake MM RC	6.00	1.80
❑ 140 Keith Bogans MM RC	6.00	1.80

2000-01 Fleer Glossy

	Nm-Mt	Ex-Mt
COMP.SET w/o SP's (200)	30.00	9.00
COMMON CARD (1-200)	.25	.07
COMMON ROOKIE (201-210)	4.00	1.20
COMMON ROOKIE (211-235)	3.00	.90
COMMON ROOKIE (236-245)	3.00	.90

Card	Nm-Mt	Ex-Mt
❑ 1 Lamar Odom	.75	.23
❑ 2 Christian Laettner	.50	.15
❑ 3 Michael Olowokandi	.25	.07
❑ 4 Anthony Carter	.50	.15
❑ 5 Steve Francis	.75	.23
❑ 6 Darvin Ham	.25	.07
❑ 7 Mitch Richmond	.50	.15
❑ 8 Corliss Williamson	.50	.15
❑ 9 Jason Terry	.75	.23
❑ 10 Brian Grant	.50	.15
❑ 11 Peja Stojakovic	.75	.23
❑ 12 Rick Fox	.50	.15
❑ 13 Tyrone Hill	.25	.07
❑ 14 Chauncey Billups	.50	.15
❑ 15 Otis Thorpe	.25	.07
❑ 16 Richard Hamilton	.50	.15
❑ 17 Ervin Johnson	.25	.07
❑ 18 Jim Jackson	.25	.07
❑ 19 Theo Ratliff	.50	.15
❑ 20 Doug Christie	.50	.15
❑ 21 Jalen Rose	.75	.23
❑ 22 John Wallace	.25	.07
❑ 23 Ruben Patterson	.50	.15
❑ 24 Steve Nash	.75	.23
❑ 25 Toni Kukoc	.50	.15
❑ 26 Anthony Peeler	.25	.07
❑ 27 Ray Allen	.75	.23
❑ 28 Adonal Foyle	.25	.07
❑ 29 Chris Whitney	.25	.07
❑ 30 Nick Van Exel	.75	.23
❑ 31 Sean Elliott	.50	.15
❑ 32 Erick Strickland	.25	.07
❑ 33 Jerry Stackhouse	.75	.23
❑ 34 Antawn Jamison	.75	.23
❑ 35 Grant Hill	.75	.23
❑ 36 Antonio Daniels	.25	.07
❑ 37 Karl Malone	.75	.23
❑ 38 Keith Van Horn	.75	.23
❑ 39 Ron Harper	.50	.15
❑ 40 Stephon Marbury	.75	.23
❑ 41 Bryon Russell	.25	.07
❑ 42 Corey Maggette	.50	.15
❑ 43 Hersey Hawkins	.25	.07
❑ 44 Vince Carter	2.00	.60
❑ 45 Paul Pierce	.75	.23
❑ 46 Mikki Moore	.25	.07
❑ 47 Othella Harrington	.25	.07
❑ 48 Erick Dampier	.50	.15
❑ 49 Jerome Williams	.25	.07
❑ 50 Nick Anderson	.25	.07
❑ 51 Tim Hardaway	.50	.15
❑ 52 Allan Houston	.50	.15
❑ 53 Tyrone Nesby	.25	.07
❑ 54 Brevin Knight	.25	.07
❑ 55 Chris Mills	.25	.07
❑ 56 Ron Artest	.50	.15
❑ 57 Walt Williams	.25	.07
❑ 58 Duane Causwell	.25	.07
❑ 59 Bonzi Wells	.50	.15
❑ 60 Rasheed Wallace	.75	.23
❑ 61 Dikembe Mutombo	.50	.15
❑ 62 Jahidi White	.25	.07
❑ 63 Chris Webber	.75	.23
❑ 64 Tony Battie	.25	.07
❑ 65 Mahmoud Abdul-Rauf	.25	.07
❑ 66 Monty Williams	.25	.07
❑ 67 Charlie Ward	.25	.07
❑ 68 David Robinson	.75	.23
❑ 69 Eric Snow	.50	.15
❑ 70 Jermaine O'Neal	.75	.23
❑ 71 Kurt Thomas	.50	.15
❑ 72 James Posey	.50	.15
❑ 73 Travis Best	.25	.07
❑ 74 Jonathan Bender	.50	.15
❑ 75 John Stockton	.75	.23
❑ 76 Jacque Vaughn	.25	.07
❑ 77 Ron Mercer	.50	.15
❑ 78 Shawn Marion	.75	.23
❑ 79 Larry Johnson	.50	.15
❑ 80 Maurice Taylor	.25	.07
❑ 81 Clifford Robinson	.25	.07
❑ 82 Scot Pollard	.25	.07
❑ 83 Patrick Ewing	.75	.23
❑ 84 Terrell Brandon	.50	.15
❑ 85 Horace Grant	.50	.15
❑ 86 Vin Baker	.50	.15
❑ 87 Al Harrington	.50	.15
❑ 88 Larry Hughes	.50	.15
❑ 89 David Wesley	.25	.07
❑ 90 Wally Szczerbiak	.50	.15
❑ 91 Charles Oakley	.25	.07
❑ 92 Tim Thomas	.50	.15
❑ 93 Mookie Blaylock	.25	.07
❑ 94 Jamal Mashburn	.50	.15
❑ 95 Roshown McLeod	.25	.07
❑ 96 John Starks	.50	.15
❑ 97 Rodney Rogers	.25	.07
❑ 98 Juwan Howard	.50	.15
❑ 99 Isaiah Rider	.50	.15
❑ 100 Rashard Lewis	.50	.15
❑ 101 Dion Glover	.25	.07
❑ 102 Johnny Newman	.25	.07
❑ 103 Avery Johnson	.25	.07
❑ 104 Darrell Armstrong	.25	.07
❑ 105 Eric Williams	.25	.07
❑ 106 Gary Payton	.75	.23
❑ 107 Antonio Davis	.25	.07
❑ 108 Dirk Nowitzki	1.25	.35
❑ 109 Trajan Langdon	.50	.15
❑ 110 Michael Dickerson	.50	.15
❑ 111 Joe Smith	.50	.15
❑ 112 Rod Strickland	.25	.07
❑ 113 Shawn Kemp	.50	.15
❑ 114 Voshon Lenard	.25	.07
❑ 115 Marcus Camby	.50	.15
❑ 116 Matt Harpring	.75	.23
❑ 117 Isaac Austin	.25	.07
❑ 118 Malik Rose	.25	.07
❑ 119 Pat Garrity	.25	.07
❑ 120 Kenny Thomas	.25	.07
❑ 121 LaPhonso Ellis	.25	.07
❑ 122 Danny Fortson	.25	.07
❑ 123 Elton Brand	.75	.23
❑ 124 Jason Williams	.50	.15
❑ 125 Kobe Bryant	3.00	.90
❑ 126 Tariq Abdul-Wahad	.25	.07
❑ 127 Tracy McGrady	2.00	.60
❑ 128 Matt Geiger	.25	.07
❑ 129 Antoine Walker	.75	.23
❑ 130 Michael Finley	.75	.23
❑ 131 Andre Miller	.50	.15
❑ 132 Robert Horry	.50	.15
❑ 133 Donyell Marshall	.50	.15
❑ 134 Shareef Abdur-Rahim	.75	.23
❑ 135 Vonteego Cummings	.25	.07
❑ 136 Anthony Mason	.50	.15
❑ 137 Mike Bibby	.75	.23
❑ 138 Raef LaFrentz	.50	.15
❑ 139 Glen Rice	.50	.15
❑ 140 Chris Gatling	.25	.07
❑ 141 Latrell Sprewell	.75	.23
❑ 142 Austin Croshere	.50	.15
❑ 143 Kenny Anderson	.50	.15
❑ 144 Elden Campbell	.25	.07
❑ 145 Jason Kidd	1.25	.35
❑ 146 Michael Doleac	.25	.07
❑ 147 Muggsy Bogues	.50	.15
❑ 148 Tim Duncan	1.50	.45
❑ 149 Samaki Walker	.25	.07
❑ 150 Gary Trent	.25	.07
❑ 151 Kevin Garnett	1.50	.45
❑ 152 Allen Iverson	1.50	.45
❑ 153 Anfernee Hardaway	.75	.23
❑ 154 Robert Traylor	.25	.07
❑ 155 Scottie Pippen	1.25	.35
❑ 156 Shaquille O'Neal	2.00	.60
❑ 157 Vlade Divac	.50	.15
❑ 158 Lucious Harris	.25	.07
❑ 159 Keon Clark	.50	.15
❑ 160 Bo Outlaw	.25	.07
❑ 161 P.J. Brown	.25	.07
❑ 162 Derrick Coleman	.25	.07
❑ 163 Mark Jackson	.25	.07
❑ 164 Lamond Murray	.25	.07
❑ 165 Dan Majerle	.50	.15
❑ 166 Eddie Jones	.75	.23
❑ 167 Cedric Ceballos	.25	.07
❑ 168 Kendall Gill	.25	.07
❑ 169 Tom Gugliotta	.25	.07
❑ 170 Jeff McInnis	.25	.07
❑ 171 Steve Smith	.50	.15
❑ 172 Kevin Willis	.25	.07
❑ 173 Lindsey Hunter	.25	.07
❑ 174 Derek Anderson	.50	.15
❑ 175 Shandon Anderson	.25	.07
❑ 176 Adrian Griffin	.25	.07
❑ 177 Baron Davis	.75	.23
❑ 178 Radoslav Nesterovic	.50	.15
❑ 179 Glenn Robinson	.75	.23
❑ 180 Sam Cassell	.75	.23
❑ 181 Chucky Atkins	.25	.07
❑ 182 Arvydas Sabonis	.50	.15
❑ 183 Damon Stoudamire	.50	.15
❑ 184 Antonio McDyess	.50	.15
❑ 185 Derek Fisher	.75	.23
❑ 186 Bryant Reeves	.25	.07
❑ 187 Hakeem Olajuwon	.75	.23
❑ 188 Kerry Kittles	.25	.07
❑ 189 Alan Henderson	.25	.07
❑ 190 Sam Perkins	.25	.07
❑ 191 Felipe Lopez	.50	.15
❑ 192 Tracy Murray	.25	.07
❑ 193 Shammond Williams	.25	.07
❑ 194 Vitaly Potapenko	.25	.07
❑ 195 John Amaechi	.25	.07
❑ 196 Quincy Lewis	.25	.07
❑ 197 Reggie Miller	.75	.23
❑ 198 Cuttino Mobley	.50	.15
❑ 199 Rex Chapman	.25	.07
❑ 200 Dale Davis	.25	.07
❑ 201 Stromile Swift RC	8.00	2.40
❑ 202 Stephen Jackson RC	6.00	1.80
❑ 203 Erick Barkley RC	4.00	1.20
❑ 204 Mike Miller RC	10.00	3.00
❑ 205 Kenyon Martin RC	12.00	3.60
❑ 206 Michael Redd RC	8.00	2.40
❑ 207 Darius Miles RC	10.00	3.00
❑ 208 Chris Mihm RC	4.00	1.20
❑ 209 Brian Cardinal RC	4.00	1.20
❑ 210 Khalid El-Amin RC	4.00	1.20
❑ 211 Hanno Mottola RC	3.00	.90
❑ 212 Jamaal Magloire RC	3.00	.90
❑ 213 Courtney Alexander RC	4.00	1.20
❑ 214 Mamadou N'Diaye RC	3.00	.90
❑ 215 Chris Porter RC	3.00	.90
❑ 216 Quentin Richardson RC	6.00	1.80
❑ 217 Eddie House RC	3.00	.90
❑ 218 Joel Przybilla RC	3.00	.90
❑ 219 Soumaila Samake RC	3.00	.90
❑ 220 Speedy Claxton RC	3.00	.90
❑ 221 Desmond Mason RC	3.00	.90
❑ 222 Mike Smith RC	3.00	.90
❑ 223 Lavor Postell RC	3.00	.90
❑ 224 Pepe Sanchez RC	3.00	.90
❑ 225 DeShawn Stevenson RC	3.00	.90

Card	Nm-Mt	Ex-Mt
❑ 226 Hidayet Turkoglu RC	6.00	1.80
❑ 227 Keyon Dooling RC	3.00	.90
❑ 228 Dan Langhi RC	3.00	.90
❑ 229 Mateen Cleaves RC	3.00	.90
❑ 230 Donnell Harvey RC	3.00	.90
❑ 231 DerMarr Johnson RC	3.00	.90
❑ 232 Jason Collier RC	3.00	.90
❑ 233 Jake Voskuhl RC	3.00	.90
❑ 234 Mark Madsen RC	3.00	.90
❑ 235 Jabari Smith RC	3.00	.90
❑ 236 Morris Peterson RC	6.00	1.80
❑ 237 Daniel Santiago RC	3.00	.90
❑ 238 Etan Thomas RC	3.00	.90
❑ 239 A.J. Guyton RC	3.00	.90
❑ 240 Marcus Fizer RC	3.00	.90
❑ 241 Jamal Crawford RC	4.00	1.20
❑ 242 Jerome Moiso RC	3.00	.90
❑ 243 Olumide Oyedeji RC	3.00	.90
❑ 244 Paul McPherson RC	3.00	.90
❑ 245 Eduardo Najera RC	4.00	1.20
❑ 246 M.Jackson EXCH AU RC	12.00	3.60
❑ 247 Mike Penberthy AU	12.00	3.60
❑ 248 Dragan Tarlac AU	12.00	3.60
❑ 249 Ruben Wolkowyski AU	12.00	3.60
❑ 250 Iakovos Tsakalidis AU	12.00	3.60
❑ 251 Ruben Garces AU	12.00	3.60
❑ NNO Rookie AU EXCH		

2002-03 Fleer Hot Shots

	Nm-Mt	Ex-Mt
COMP.SET w/o SP's (168)	40.00	12.00
COMMON CARD (1-168)	.20	.06
COMMON ROOKIE (169-195)	12.00	3.60
COMMON ROOKIE (196-201)	15.00	4.50
COMMON ROOKIE (202-207)	5.00	1.50
RC CARDS HAVE SHIRT UNLESS NOTED		
❑ 1 Shareef Abdur-Rahim	.75	.23
❑ 2 Kedrick Brown	.50	.15
❑ 3 Trenton Hassell	.50	.15
❑ 4 Raef LaFrentz	.50	.15
❑ 5 Donnell Harvey	.20	.06
❑ 6 Danny Fortson	.20	.06
❑ 7 Maurice Taylor	.20	.06
❑ 8 Wang Zhizhi	.75	.23
❑ 9 Malik Allen	.20	.06
❑ 10 Tim Thomas	.50	.15
❑ 11 Jason Kidd	1.25	.35
❑ 12 Jamaal Magloire	.20	.06
❑ 13 Grant Hill	.75	.23
❑ 14 Anfernee Hardaway	.75	.23
❑ 15 Bonzi Wells	.50	.15
❑ 16 Malik Rose	.20	.06
❑ 17 Antonio Davis	.20	.06
❑ 18 John Stockton	.75	.23
❑ 19 Theo Ratliff	.50	.15
❑ 20 Paul Pierce	.75	.23
❑ 21 Jalen Rose	.75	.23
❑ 22 Eduardo Najera	.50	.15
❑ 23 Chauncey Billups	.50	.15
❑ 24 Antawn Jamison	.75	.23
❑ 25 Jonathan Bender	.50	.15
❑ 26 Rick Fox	.50	.15
❑ 27 Brian Grant	.50	.15
❑ 28 Kevin Garnett	1.50	.45
❑ 29 Kenyon Martin	.75	.23
❑ 30 Allan Houston	.50	.15
❑ 31 Tracy McGrady	2.00	.60
❑ 32 Stephon Marbury	.75	.23
❑ 33 Mike Bibby	.75	.23
❑ 34 Predrag Drobnjak	.20	.06
❑ 35 Lamond Murray	.20	.06
❑ 36 Kwame Brown	.50	.15
❑ 37 Glenn Robinson	.75	.23
❑ 38 Antoine Walker	.75	.23
❑ 39 Zydrunas Ilgauskas	.50	.15
❑ 40 Clifford Robinson	.20	.06
❑ 41 Dirk Nowitzki	1.25	.35
❑ 42 Troy Murphy	.50	.15
❑ 43 Al Harrington	.50	.15
❑ 44 Shaquille O'Neal	2.00	.60
❑ 45 Eddie House	.20	.06
❑ 46 Troy Hudson	.20	.06
❑ 47 Rodney Rogers	.20	.06
❑ 48 Latrell Sprewell	.75	.23
❑ 49 Allen Iverson	1.50	.45
❑ 50 Derek Anderson	.20	.06
❑ 51 Vlade Divac	.50	.15
❑ 52 Rashard Lewis	.50	.15
❑ 53 Morris Peterson	.50	.15
❑ 54 Jerry Stackhouse	.75	.23
❑ 55 Jason Terry	.75	.23
❑ 56 Tyson Chandler	.75	.23
❑ 57 Jumaine Jones	.50	.15
❑ 58 Nick Van Exel	.75	.23
❑ 59 Ben Wallace	.75	.23
❑ 60 Jason Richardson	.75	.23
❑ 61 Ron Mercer	.50	.15
❑ 62 Shane Battier	.75	.23
❑ 63 Eddie Jones	.75	.23
❑ 64 Joe Smith	.50	.15
❑ 65 Courtney Alexander	.50	.15
❑ 66 Kurt Thomas	.50	.15
❑ 67 Todd MacCulloch	.20	.06
❑ 68 Ruben Patterson	.50	.15
❑ 69 Tim Duncan	1.50	.45
❑ 70 Gary Payton	.75	.23
❑ 71 Jarron Collins	.20	.06
❑ 72 Vin Baker	.50	.15
❑ 73 Eddy Curry	.75	.23
❑ 74 Michael Finley	.75	.23
❑ 75 Marcus Camby	.50	.15
❑ 76 Corliss Williamson	.50	.15
❑ 77 Steve Francis	.75	.23
❑ 78 Jermaine O'Neal	.75	.23
❑ 79 Michael Dickerson	.20	.06
❑ 80 Alonzo Mourning	.50	.15
❑ 81 Rod Strickland	.20	.06
❑ 82 Elden Campbell	.20	.06
❑ 83 Charlie Ward	.20	.06
❑ 84 Aaron McKie	.50	.15
❑ 85 Scottie Pippen	1.25	.35
❑ 86 Tony Parker	.75	.23
❑ 87 Vladimir Radmanovic	.50	.15
❑ 88 Matt Harpring	.75	.23
❑ 89 Eddie Griffin	.50	.15
❑ 90 Michael Olowokandi	.20	.06
❑ 91 Stromile Swift	.50	.15
❑ 92 Michael Redd	.75	.23
❑ 93 Richard Jefferson	.50	.15
❑ 94 Baron Davis	.75	.23
❑ 95 Pat Garrity	.20	.06
❑ 96 Tom Gugliotta	.20	.06
❑ 97 Arvydas Sabonis	.20	.06
❑ 98 David Robinson	.75	.23
❑ 99 Michael Bradley	.50	.15
❑ 100 Karl Malone	.75	.23
❑ 101 Jason Terry	.75	.23
Glenn Robinson		
❑ 102 Tony Delk	.50	.15
Paul Pierce		
❑ 103 Jalen Rose	.50	.15
Marcus Fizer		
❑ 104 Darius Miles	.75	.23
Ricky Davis		
❑ 105 Steve Nash	1.00	.30
Dirk Nowitzki		
❑ 106 Kenny Satterfield	.50	.15
Juwan Howard		
❑ 107 Richard Hamilton	.75	.23
Ben Wallace		
❑ 108 Gilbert Arenas	.75	.23
Antawn Jamison		
❑ 109 Moochie Norris	.50	.15
Cuttino Mobley		
❑ 110 Jamaal Tinsley	.75	.23
Reggie Miller		
❑ 111 Andre Miller	.50	.15
Lamar Odom		
❑ 112 Derek Fisher	1.50	.45
Kobe Bryant		
❑ 113 Jason Williams	.75	.23
Shane Battier		
❑ 114 Travis Best	.50	.15
Eddie Jones		
❑ 115 Sam Cassell	.75	.23
Ray Allen		
❑ 116 Terrell Brandon	.50	.15
Wally Szczerbiak		
❑ 117 Kerry Kittles	.50	.15
Richard Jefferson		
❑ 118 David Wesley	.50	.15
Jamal Mashburn		
❑ 119 Latrell Sprewell	.50	.15
Antonio McDyess		
❑ 120 Darrell Armstrong	.50	.15
Mike Miller		
❑ 121 Eric Snow	.50	.15
Keith Van Horn		
❑ 122 Stephon Marbury	.50	.15
Shawn Marion		
❑ 123 Damon Stoudamire	.50	.15
Rasheed Wallace		
❑ 124 Mike Bibby	.75	.23
Chris Webber		
❑ 125 Tony Parker	.75	.23
David Robinson		
❑ 126 Kenny Anderson	.50	.15
Rashard Lewis		
❑ 127 Alvin Williams	.75	.23
Vince Carter		
❑ 128 John Stockton	.75	.23
Karl Malone		
❑ 129 Larry Hughes	2.50	.75
Michael Jordan		
❑ 130 Joe Johnson AS	.50	.15
❑ 131 Andrei Kirilenko AS	.75	.23
❑ 132 Brendan Haywood AS	.50	.15
❑ 133 Zeljko Rebraca AS	.50	.15
❑ 134 Quentin Richardson AS	.75	.23
❑ 135 Chris Mihm AS	.20	.06
❑ 136 Darius Miles AS	.75	.23
❑ 137 Desmond Mason AS	.50	.15
❑ 138 Hidayet Turkoglu AS	.50	.15
❑ 139 Jason Richardson AS	.75	.23
❑ 140 Gerald Wallace AS	.75	.23
❑ 141 Steve Francis AS	.75	.23
❑ 142 Steve Nash AS	.75	.23
❑ 143 Peja Stojakovic AS	.75	.23
❑ 144 Ray Allen AS	.75	.23
❑ 145 Mike Miller AS	.75	.23
❑ 146 Pau Gasol AS	.75	.23
❑ 147 Steve Smith AS	.75	.23
❑ 148 Paul Pierce AS	.75	.23
❑ 149 Derek Fisher AS	.75	.23
❑ 150 Cuttino Mobley AS	.50	.15
❑ 151 Dikembe Mutombo AS	.50	.15
❑ 152 Vince Carter AS	2.00	.60
❑ 153 Antoine Walker AS	.75	.23
❑ 154 Allen Iverson AS	1.25	.35
❑ 155 Michael Jordan AS	6.00	1.80
❑ 156 Shaquille O'Neal AS	2.00	.60
❑ 157 Tim Duncan AS	1.50	.45
❑ 158 Kevin Garnett AS	1.50	.45
❑ 159 Kobe Bryant AS	3.00	.90
❑ 160 Shareef Abdur-Rahim AS	.75	.23
❑ 161 Baron Davis AS	.75	.23
❑ 162 Jason Kidd AS	1.25	.35
❑ 163 Tracy McGrady AS	2.00	.60
❑ 164 Jermaine O'Neal AS	.75	.23
❑ 165 Elton Brand AS	.75	.23
❑ 166 Gary Payton AS	.75	.23
❑ 167 Wally Szczerbiak AS	.50	.15
❑ 168 Chris Webber AS	.75	.23
❑ 169 Yao Ming Jsy RC	60.00	18.00
❑ 170 Fred Jones RC	12.00	3.60
❑ 171 Ryan Humphrey RC	12.00	3.60
❑ 172 D.Gooden Hat/300 RC	20.00	6.00
❑ 173 Nikoloz Tskitishvili RC	12.00	3.60
❑ 174 C.Butler Shorts/350 RC	15.00	4.50
❑ 175 Vincent Yarbrough RC	12.00	3.60

Card	Nm-Mt	Ex-Mt
❑ 176 DaJuan Wagner RC	12.00	3.60
❑ 177 Nene Hilario RC	12.00	3.60
❑ 178 Qyntel Woods/350 RC	12.00	3.60
❑ 179 Jared Jeffries RC	12.00	3.60
❑ 180 Casey Jacobsen RC	12.00	3.60
❑ 181 M.Haislip Hat/300 RC	12.00	3.60
❑ 182 Kareem Rush RC	15.00	4.50
❑ 183 Predrag Savovic RC	12.00	3.60
❑ 184 Melvin Ely RC	12.00	3.60
❑ 185 Amare Stoudmire RC	40.00	12.00
❑ 186 John Salmons RC	12.00	3.60
❑ 187 Chris Jefferies RC	12.00	3.60
❑ 188 Juan Dixon RC	20.00	6.00
❑ 189 Carlos Boozer RC	25.00	7.50
❑ 190 Roger Mason/350 RC	12.00	3.60
❑ 191 Ronald Murray/350 RC	15.00	4.50
❑ 192 Tayshaun Prince RC	15.00	4.50
❑ 193 Chris Wilcox/350 RC	12.00	3.60
❑ 194 Sam Clancy RC	12.00	3.60
❑ 195 Dan Gadzuric RC	12.00	3.60
❑ 196 D.Dickau RC/Carter Jsy	15.00	4.50
❑ 197 F.Williams RC/Carter Jsy	15.00	4.50
❑ 198 Dunleavy RC/VC Jsy/350	20.00	6.00
❑ 199 J.Will RC/Carter Jsy/350	10.00	3.00
❑ 200 Borchardt RC/VC Jsy/350	15.00	4.50
❑ 201 Giricek RC/Carter Jsy/350	15.00	4.50
❑ 202 Pat Burke RC	5.00	1.50
❑ 203 Reggie Evans RC	5.00	1.50
❑ 204 Rasual Butler RC	5.00	1.50
❑ 205 Jiri Welsch RC	5.00	1.50
❑ 206 Mehmet Okur RC	5.00	1.50
❑ 207 Jannero Pargo RC	5.00	1.50

2000-01 Fleer Legacy

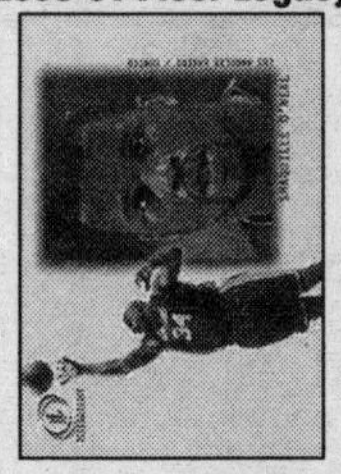

	Nm-Mt	Ex-Mt
COMP.SET w/o SP's (90)	50.00	15.00
COMMON CARD (1-90)	.30	.09
COMMON ROOKIE (91-115)	5.00	1.50
COMMON JSY RC (91-115)	10.00	3.00
❑ 1 Vince Carter	2.50	.75
❑ 2 Tim Duncan	2.00	.60
❑ 3 Darrell Armstrong	.30	.09
❑ 4 Chauncey Billups	.60	.18
❑ 5 Shawn Kemp	.60	.18
❑ 6 Stephon Marbury	1.00	.30
❑ 7 Dan Majerle	.60	.18
❑ 8 Antawn Jamison	1.00	.30
❑ 9 Hakeem Olajuwon	1.00	.30
❑ 10 Kobe Bryant	4.00	1.20
❑ 11 Paul Pierce	1.00	.30
❑ 12 Patrick Ewing	1.00	.30
❑ 13 Steve Francis	1.00	.30
❑ 14 Latrell Sprewell	1.00	.30
❑ 15 Andre Miller	.60	.18
❑ 16 Gary Payton	1.00	.30
❑ 17 Michael Finley	1.00	.30
❑ 18 Brian Grant	.60	.18
❑ 19 Scottie Pippen	1.50	.45
❑ 20 Antonio Davis	.30	.09
❑ 21 Jason Williams	.60	.18
❑ 22 Chris Gatling	.30	.09
❑ 23 David Robinson	1.00	.30
❑ 24 John Stockton	1.00	.30
❑ 25 Matt Harpring	1.00	.30
❑ 26 Rashard Lewis	.60	.18
❑ 27 Dirk Nowitzki	6.00	1.80
❑ 28 Alan Henderson	.30	.09
❑ 29 Rasheed Wallace	1.00	.30
❑ 30 Ben Wallace	1.00	.30
❑ 31 Chris Webber	1.00	.30
❑ 32 Elton Brand	1.00	.30
❑ 33 Anfernee Hardaway	1.00	.30
❑ 34 Isaiah Rider	.30	.09
❑ 35 Baron Davis	1.00	.30
❑ 36 Eric Snow	.60	.18
❑ 37 Tom Gugliotta	.30	.09
❑ 38 Grant Hill	1.00	.30
❑ 39 Lamar Odom	1.00	.30
❑ 40 Kevin Garnett	2.00	.60
❑ 41 Reggie Miller	1.00	.30
❑ 42 Karl Malone	1.00	.30
❑ 43 Ray Allen	1.00	.30
❑ 44 Derek Anderson	.60	.18
❑ 45 Glen Rice	.60	.18
❑ 46 Antonio McDyess	.60	.18
❑ 47 Eddie Jones	1.00	.30
❑ 48 Mitch Richmond	.60	.18
❑ 49 Mark Jackson	.60	.18
❑ 50 Larry Johnson	.60	.18
❑ 51 Ron Mercer	.60	.18
❑ 52 Jason Kidd	1.50	.45
❑ 53 Voshon Lenard	.30	.09
❑ 54 Rick Fox	.60	.18
❑ 55 Rod Strickland	.30	.09
❑ 56 Jalen Rose	1.00	.30
❑ 57 Tracy McGrady	2.50	.75
❑ 58 Dikembe Mutombo	.60	.18
❑ 59 Richard Hamilton	.60	.18
❑ 60 Jerry Stackhouse	1.00	.30
❑ 61 Peja Stojakovic	1.00	.30
❑ 62 Sam Cassell	1.00	.30
❑ 63 Sean Elliott	.60	.18
❑ 64 Keith Van Horn	1.00	.30
❑ 65 Mike Bibby	1.00	.30
❑ 66 Larry Hughes	.60	.18
❑ 67 Nick Van Exel	1.00	.30
❑ 68 Michael Dickerson	.30	.09
❑ 69 Terrell Brandon	.60	.18
❑ 70 Chucky Atkins	.30	.09
❑ 71 John Starks	.60	.18
❑ 72 Glenn Robinson	1.00	.30
❑ 73 Cuttino Mobley	.60	.18
❑ 74 Shaquille O'Neal	2.50	.75
❑ 75 Shareef Abdur-Rahim	1.00	.30
❑ 76 Danny Fortson	.30	.09
❑ 77 Austin Croshere	.60	.18
❑ 78 Jamal Mashburn	.60	.18
❑ 79 Kenny Anderson	.60	.18
❑ 80 Shawn Marion	1.00	.30
❑ 81 Travis Best	.30	.09
❑ 82 Derrick Coleman	.30	.09
❑ 83 Toni Kukoc	.60	.18
❑ 84 Allen Iverson	2.00	.60
❑ 85 Allan Houston	.60	.18
❑ 86 Antoine Walker	1.00	.30
❑ 87 Wally Szczerbiak	.60	.18
❑ 88 Raef LaFrentz	.60	.18
❑ 89 Tim Hardaway	.60	.18
❑ 90 Juwan Howard	.60	.18
❑ 91 Kenyon Martin JSY RC	20.00	6.00
❑ 92 Stromile Swift RC	6.00	1.80
❑ 93 Darius Miles JSY RC	15.00	4.50
❑ 94 Mike Miller JSY RC	12.00	3.60
❑ 95 Marcus Fizer RC	5.00	1.50
❑ 96 Jerome Moiso JSY RC	10.00	3.00
❑ 97 DerMarr Johnson JSY RC	10.00	3.00
❑ 98 Q.Richardson JSY RC	15.00	4.50
❑ 99 Morris Peterson JSY RC	12.00	3.60
❑ 100 Jamaal Magloire RC	5.00	1.50
❑ 101 Mateen Cleaves RC	5.00	1.50
❑ 102 Hidayet Turkoglu RC	8.00	2.40
❑ 103 Chris Mihm JSY RC	10.00	3.00
❑ 104 Courtney Alexander RC	5.00	1.50
❑ 105 Joel Przybilla RC	5.00	1.50
❑ 106 Speedy Claxton JSY RC	10.00	3.00
❑ 107 Keyon Dooling JSY RC	10.00	3.00
❑ 108 Desmond Mason JSY RC	10.00	3.00
❑ 109 Jamal Crawford RC	6.00	1.80
❑ 110 DeShawn Stevenson RC	5.00	1.50
❑ 111 Stephen Jackson RC	6.00	1.80
❑ 112 Marc Jackson RC	5.00	1.50
❑ 113 Hanno Mottola JSY RC	10.00	3.00
❑ 114 Eduardo Najera RC	6.00	1.80
❑ 115 Wang Zhizhi RC	12.00	3.60
❑ WUSA1 Vince Carter/600	100.00	30.00

2001-02 Fleer Marquee

	Nm-Mt	Ex-Mt
COMPLETE SET w/o SPs	40.00	12.00
COMMON ROOKIE (116-125)	4.00	1.20
❑ 1 DerMarr Johnson	.50	.15
❑ 2 Darius Miles	.75	.23
❑ 3 Michael Jordan	15.00	4.50
❑ 4 Speedy Claxton	.50	.15
❑ 5 Stromile Swift	.50	.15
❑ 6 Michael Finley	.75	.23
❑ 7 Kurt Thomas	.50	.15
❑ 8 Tim Duncan	1.50	.45
❑ 9 Kenyon Martin	.75	.23
❑ 10 Jermaine O'Neal	.75	.23
❑ 11 Elton Brand	.75	.23
❑ 12 Jamal Mashburn	.50	.15
❑ 13 Jumaine Jones	.50	.15
❑ 14 Stephon Marbury	.75	.23
❑ 15 Eddie Jones	.75	.23
❑ 16 Antonio McDyess	.50	.15
❑ 17 Tim Thomas	.50	.15
❑ 18 Gary Payton	.75	.23
❑ 19 Latrell Sprewell	.75	.23
❑ 20 Grant Hill	.75	.23
❑ 21 Jason Terry	.75	.23
❑ 22 Marcus Fizer	.50	.15
❑ 23 Anthony Mason	.50	.15
❑ 24 Bonzi Wells	.50	.15
❑ 25 Sam Cassell	.75	.23
❑ 26 Jerry Stackhouse	.75	.23
❑ 27 Hidayet Turkoglu	.50	.15
❑ 28 Morris Peterson	.50	.15
❑ 29 John Stockton	.75	.23
❑ 30 Dikembe Mutombo	.50	.15
❑ 31 Mitch Richmond	.50	.15
❑ 32 Andre Miller	.50	.15
❑ 33 Joe Smith	.50	.15
❑ 34 Mike Bibby	.75	.23
❑ 35 Wally Szczerbiak	.50	.15
❑ 36 Steve Francis	.75	.23
❑ 37 Nazr Mohammed	.25	.07
❑ 38 Antoine Walker	.75	.23
❑ 39 Courtney Alexander	.50	.15
❑ 40 Shawn Marion	.75	.23
❑ 41 Jason Williams	.50	.15
❑ 42 Steve Nash	.75	.23
❑ 43 Antonio Davis	.25	.07
❑ 44 Steve Smith	.50	.15
❑ 45 Jason Kidd	1.25	.35
❑ 46 Reggie Miller	.75	.23
❑ 47 Quentin Richardson	.50	.15
❑ 48 Baron Davis	.75	.23
❑ 49 Juwan Howard	.50	.15
❑ 50 Rasheed Wallace	.75	.23

Card	Nm-Mt	Ex-Mt
❑ 51 Brian Grant	.50	.15
❑ 52 Nick Van Exel	.75	.23
❑ 53 Donyell Marshall	.50	.15
❑ 54 Vin Baker	.50	.15
❑ 55 Allan Houston	.50	.15
❑ 56 Mike Miller	.75	.23
❑ 57 Shaquille O'Neal	2.00	.60
❑ 58 Ron Mercer	.50	.15
❑ 59 Lindsey Hunter	.25	.07
❑ 60 Peja Stojakovic	.75	.23
❑ 61 Ray Allen	.75	.23
❑ 62 Antawn Jamison	.75	.23
❑ 63 Theo Ratliff	.50	.15
❑ 64 Vince Carter	2.00	.60
❑ 65 DeShawn Stevenson	.50	.15
❑ 66 Allen Iverson	1.50	.45
❑ 67 Derek Fisher	.75	.23
❑ 68 Dirk Nowitzki	1.25	.35
❑ 69 Keith Van Horn	.75	.23
❑ 70 David Robinson	.75	.23
❑ 71 Terrell Brandon	.50	.15
❑ 72 Cuttino Mobley	.50	.15
❑ 73 Shareef Abdur-Rahim	.75	.23
❑ 74 Paul Pierce	.75	.23
❑ 75 Elden Campbell	.25	.07
❑ 76 Anfernee Hardaway	.75	.23
❑ 77 Alonzo Mourning	.50	.15
❑ 78 Raef LaFrentz	.50	.15
❑ 79 Richard Hamilton	.50	.15
❑ 80 Rashard Lewis	.50	.15
❑ 81 Marcus Camby	.50	.15
❑ 82 Jalen Rose	.75	.23
❑ 83 Lamar Odom	.75	.23
❑ 84 David Wesley	.25	.07
❑ 85 James Posey	.50	.15
❑ 86 Derek Anderson	.50	.15
❑ 87 Glenn Robinson	.50	.15
❑ 88 Clifford Robinson	.25	.07
❑ 89 Kerry Kittles	.25	.07
❑ 90 Hakeem Olajuwon	.75	.23
❑ 91 Patrick Ewing	.75	.23
❑ 92 Tracy McGrady	2.00	.60
❑ 93 Kobe Bryant	3.00	.90
❑ 94 Chris Mihm	.50	.15
❑ 95 Lorenzen Wright	.25	.07
❑ 96 Chris Webber	.75	.23
❑ 97 Kevin Garnett	1.50	.45
❑ 98 Larry Hughes	.50	.15
❑ 99 Keyon Dooling	.50	.15
❑ 100 Karl Malone	.75	.23
❑ 101 Joe Johnson RC	4.00	1.20
❑ 102 Tyson Chandler RC	8.00	2.40
❑ 103 Eddy Curry RC	6.00	1.80
❑ 104 Jason Richardson RC	8.00	2.40
❑ 105 Troy Murphy RC	5.00	1.50
❑ 106 Eddie Griffin RC	4.00	1.20
❑ 107 Jamaal Tinsley RC	4.00	1.20
❑ 108 Pau Gasol RC	10.00	3.00
❑ 109 Shane Battier RC	4.00	1.20
❑ 110 Richard Jefferson RC	5.00	1.50
❑ 111 Steven Hunter RC	2.50	.75
❑ 112 Tony Parker RC	10.00	3.00
❑ 113 Vladimir Radmanovic RC	3.00	.90
❑ 114 Andrei Kirilenko RC	8.00	2.40
❑ 115 Kwame Brown RC	5.00	1.50
❑ 116 Samuel Dalembert RC	4.00	1.20
Damone Brown RC		
❑ 117 Joseph Forte RC	4.00	1.20
Kedrick Brown RC		
❑ 118 Zach Randolph RC	8.00	2.40
Ruben Boumthe RC		
❑ 119 Oscar Torres RC	4.00	1.20
Terence Morris RC		
❑ 120 Alton Ford RC	5.00	1.50
Kenny Satterfield RC		
❑ 121 Rodney White RC	4.00	1.20
Zeljko Rebraca RC		
❑ 122 Trenton Hassell RC	4.00	1.20
Earl Watson RC		
❑ 123 DeSagana Diop RC	4.00	1.20
Primoz Brezec RC		
❑ 124 Ernest Brown RC	4.00	1.20
Gerald Wallace RC		
❑ 125 Loren Woods RC	4.00	1.20
Bendan Haywood RC		
❑ 126 Mengke Bateer RC	10.00	3.00
❑ NNO Vince Carter AU/113	120.00	36.00

2001-02 Fleer Maximum

	Nm-Mt	Ex-Mt
COMPLETE SET (220)	300.00	90.00
COMP.SET w/o SP's (180)	40.00	12.00
COMMON CARD (1-180)	.20	.06
COMMON ROOKIE (181-220)	3.00	.90
CARTER AU NOT INCLUDED IN SET PRICE		
❑ 1 Ray Allen	.60	.18
❑ 2 Elton Brand	.60	.18
❑ 3 Grant Hill	.60	.18
❑ 4 Tracy McGrady	1.50	.45
❑ 5 Chris Webber	.60	.18
❑ 6 Latrell Sprewell	.60	.18
❑ 7 Paul Pierce	.60	.18
❑ 8 Jason Kidd	.60	.18
❑ 9 Shaquille O'Neal	1.50	.45
❑ 10 Stephon Marbury	.60	.18
❑ 11 Steve Francis	.60	.18
❑ 12 Vince Carter	1.50	.45
❑ 13 Allen Iverson	1.25	.35
❑ 14 Kevin Garnett	1.25	.35
❑ 15 Eddie Jones	.60	.18
❑ 16 Antoine Walker	.60	.18
❑ 17 Kobe Bryant	2.50	.75
❑ 18 Avery Johnson	.20	.06
❑ 19 Damon Stoudamire	.40	.12
❑ 20 Kurt Thomas	.40	.12
❑ 21 Aaron McKie	.40	.12
❑ 22 Chris Whitney	.20	.06
❑ 23 David Robinson	.60	.18
❑ 24 Erick Dampier	.40	.12
❑ 25 Jumaine Jones	.40	.12
❑ 26 Radoslav Nesterovic	.40	.12
❑ 27 Robert Horry	.40	.12
❑ 28 Ben Wallace	.60	.18
❑ 29 Christian Laettner	.40	.12
❑ 30 Eddie Robinson	.40	.12
❑ 31 Alvin Williams	.20	.06
❑ 32 Matt Harpring	.60	.18
❑ 33 Terrell Brandon	.40	.12
❑ 34 Tim Duncan	1.25	.35
❑ 35 Bonzi Wells	.40	.12
❑ 36 Clarence Weatherspoon	.20	.06
❑ 37 George McCloud	.20	.06
❑ 38 Jermaine O'Neal	.60	.18
❑ 39 Al Harrington	.40	.12
❑ 40 Antawn Jamison	.60	.18
❑ 41 John Amaechi	.20	.06
❑ 42 Rod Strickland	.20	.06
❑ 43 Stacey Augmon	.20	.06
❑ 44 Dion Glover	.20	.06
❑ 45 Michael Dickerson	.40	.12
❑ 46 Anfernee Hardaway	.60	.18
❑ 47 Rashard Lewis	.40	.12
❑ 48 Shawn Bradley	.20	.06
❑ 49 Todd MacCulloch	.20	.06
❑ 50 Antonio McDyess	.40	.12
❑ 51 Darrell Armstrong	.20	.06
❑ 52 Jalen Rose	.60	.18
❑ 53 Mike Bibby	.60	.18
❑ 54 P.J. Brown	.20	.06
❑ 55 Quincy Lewis	.20	.06
❑ 56 Doug Christie	.40	.12
❑ 57 Elden Campbell	.20	.06
❑ 58 James Posey	.40	.12
❑ 59 Karl Malone	.60	.18
❑ 60 Patrick Ewing	.60	.18
❑ 61 Sam Cassell	.60	.18
❑ 62 Baron Davis	.60	.18
❑ 63 Corey Maggette	.40	.12
❑ 64 Donyell Marshall	.40	.12
❑ 65 Ervin Johnson	.20	.06
❑ 66 Horace Grant	.40	.12
❑ 67 Nick Van Exel	.60	.18
❑ 68 Vlade Divac	.40	.12
❑ 69 Allan Houston	.40	.12
❑ 70 Antonio Davis	.20	.06
❑ 71 Dale Davis	.40	.12
❑ 72 Eduardo Najera	.40	.12
❑ 73 Kenny Anderson	.40	.12
❑ 74 Kevin Willis	.20	.06
❑ 75 LaPhonso Ellis	.20	.06
❑ 76 Anthony Mason	.40	.12
❑ 77 Greg Ostertag	.20	.06
❑ 78 Jamal Mashburn	.40	.12
❑ 79 Jeff McInnis	.20	.06
❑ 80 Peja Stojakovic	.60	.18
❑ 81 Scott Williams	.20	.06
❑ 82 Bryon Russell	.20	.06
❑ 83 Chucky Atkins	.20	.06
❑ 84 Darius Miles	.60	.18
❑ 85 David Wesley	.20	.06
❑ 86 Hidayet Turkoglu	.40	.12
❑ 87 Mark Pope	.20	.06
❑ 88 Dana Barros	.20	.06
❑ 89 Glenn Robinson	.40	.12
❑ 90 John Stockton	.60	.18
❑ 91 Lamar Odom	.60	.18
❑ 92 Mike Miller	.60	.18
❑ 93 Ron Artest	.40	.12
❑ 94 Adonal Foyle	.20	.06
❑ 95 Andre Miller	.20	.06
❑ 96 Eric Snow	.40	.12
❑ 97 Stanislav Medvedenko	.20	.06
❑ 98 Steve Smith	.40	.12
❑ 99 Wally Szczerbiak	.40	.12
❑ 100 Chris Mihm	.40	.12
❑ 101 Danny Fortson	.20	.06
❑ 102 Dikembe Mutombo	.40	.12
❑ 103 Joe Smith	.40	.12
❑ 104 Lindsey Hunter	.20	.06
❑ 105 Malik Rose	.20	.06
❑ 106 Austin Croshere	.40	.12
❑ 107 Chris Gatling	.20	.06
❑ 108 Hakeem Olajuwon	.60	.18
❑ 109 Mark Jackson	.40	.12
❑ 110 Milt Palacio	.20	.06
❑ 111 Ruben Patterson	.40	.12
❑ 112 Steve Nash	.60	.18
❑ 113 Brian Grant	.40	.12
❑ 114 Dirk Nowitzki	1.00	.30
❑ 115 Jeff Foster	.20	.06
❑ 116 Morris Peterson	.40	.12
❑ 117 Scottie Pippen	1.50	.45
❑ 118 Lamond Murray	.20	.06
❑ 119 Larry Hughes	.40	.12
❑ 120 Shareef Abdur-Rahim	.60	.18
❑ 121 Tony Delk	.20	.06
❑ 122 Vin Baker	.40	.12
❑ 123 Art Long	.20	.06
❑ 124 Kenyon Martin	.60	.18
❑ 125 Michael Finley	.60	.18
❑ 126 Stromile Swift	.40	.12
❑ 127 Toni Kukoc	.40	.12
❑ 128 Alonzo Mourning	.40	.12
❑ 129 Charlie Ward	.20	.06
❑ 130 Eric Williams	.20	.06
❑ 131 Jerome Williams	.40	.12
❑ 132 Raef LaFrentz	.40	.12
❑ 133 Rasheed Wallace	.60	.18
❑ 134 Reggie Miller	.60	.18
❑ 135 Cuttino Mobley	.40	.12
❑ 136 Desmond Mason	.40	.12

❑ 137 Jason Williams .40 .12
❑ 138 Keith Van Horn .60 .18
❑ 139 Nazr Mohammed .20 .06
❑ 140 Shawn Marion .60 .18
❑ 141 Tim Hardaway .40 .12
❑ 142 Anthony Carter .40 .12
❑ 143 Danny Manning .20 .06
❑ 144 Derek Anderson .40 .12
❑ 145 Jason Terry .60 .18
❑ 146 Kenny Thomas .20 .06
❑ 147 Othella Harrington .20 .06
❑ 148 Corliss Williamson .40 .12
❑ 149 Derek Fisher .60 .18
❑ 150 Ricky Davis .40 .12
❑ 151 Stephen Jackson .40 .12
❑ 152 Tryone Nesby .20 .06
❑ 153 Calvin Booth .20 .06
❑ 154 Emanual Davis .20 .06
❑ 155 Kerry Kittles .20 .06
❑ 156 Marc Jackson .20 .06
❑ 157 Samaki Walker .20 .06
❑ 158 Tom Gugliotta .20 .06
❑ 159 Wesley Person .20 .06
❑ 160 Antonio Daniels .20 .06
❑ 161 Charles Oakley .20 .06
❑ 162 Chauncey Billups .40 .12
❑ 163 Derrick Coleman .20 .06
❑ 164 Jerry Stackhouse .60 .18
❑ 165 Michael Jordan 10.00 3.00
❑ 166 Quentin Richardson .40 .12
❑ 167 Gary Payton .60 .18
❑ 168 Iakovos Tsakalidis .20 .06
❑ 169 Juwan Howard .40 .12
❑ 170 Lorenzen Wright .20 .06
❑ 171 Marcus Camby .40 .12
❑ 172 Maurice Taylor .40 .12
❑ 173 Jacque Vaughn .20 .06
❑ 174 Bruce Bowen .20 .06
❑ 175 Clifford Robinson .20 .06
❑ 176 Michael Olowokandi .20 .06
❑ 177 Richard Hamilton .40 .12
❑ 178 Ron Mercer .40 .12
❑ 179 Speedy Claxton .40 .12
❑ 180 Tim Thomas .40 .12
❑ 181 Joe Johnson HW RC 5.00 1.50
❑ 182 Pau Gasol HW RC 12.00 3.60
❑ 183 Kwame Brown HW RC 6.00 1.80
❑ 184 Zach Randolph HW RC 10.00 3.00
❑ 185 J.Richardson HW RC 10.00 3.00
❑ 186 Jamaal Tinsley HW RC 5.00 1.50
❑ 187 Oscar Torres HW RC 4.00 1.20
❑ 188 Rodney White HW RC 4.00 1.20
❑ 189 Kedrick Brown HW RC 3.00 .90
❑ 190 Tony Parker HW RC 12.00 3.60
❑ 191 S.Dalembert HW RC 3.00 .90
❑ 192 Shane Battier HW RC 5.00 1.50
❑ 193 Loren Woods HW RC 3.00 .90
❑ 194 Richard Jefferson HW RC 6.00 1.80
❑ 195 Jeff Trepagnier HW RC 3.00 .90
❑ 196 Terence Morris HW RC 3.00 .90
❑ 197 Eddie Griffin TC RC 5.00 1.50
❑ 198 Primoz Brezec TC RC 3.00 .90
❑ 199 V.Radmanovic TC RC 4.00 1.20
❑ 200 Gerald Wallace TC RC 6.00 1.80
❑ 201 Alton Ford TC RC 4.00 1.20
❑ 202 Steven Hunter TC RC 3.00 .90
❑ 203 Michael Bradley TC RC 3.00 .90
❑ 204 B.Armstrong TC RC 4.00 1.20
❑ 205 Jamaal Tinsley TC RC 5.00 1.50
❑ 206 Bobby Simmons TC RC 3.00 .90
❑ 207 Zeljko Rebraca TC RC 3.00 .90
❑ 208 Tony Parker TC RC 12.00 3.60
❑ 209 Troy Murphy TC RC 6.00 1.80
❑ 210 Kwame Brown TC RC 6.00 1.80
❑ 211 Andrei Kirilenko TC RC 8.00 2.40
❑ 212 Trenton Hassell TC RC 5.00 1.50
❑ 213 Pau Gasol TC RC 12.00 3.60
❑ 214 Tang Hamilton TC RC 3.00 .90
❑ 215 Joseph Forte TC RC 8.00 2.40
❑ 216 Eddy Curry TC RC 8.00 2.40
❑ 217 DeSagana Diop TC RC 3.00 .90
❑ 218 Joe Johnson TC RC 5.00 1.50
❑ 219 Tyson Chandler TC RC 8.00 2.40
❑ 220 Jason Collins TC RC 3.00 .90
❑ NNO V.Carter AU/375 100.00 30.00

1999-00 Fleer Mystique

	Nm-Mt	Ex-Mt
COMPLETE SET (150)	150.00	45.00
COMPLETE SET w/o SP (100)	30.00	9.00
COMMON CARD (1-100)	.30	.09
COMMON ROOKIE (101-140)	1.25	.35
COMMON STAR (141-150)	2.00	.60

❑ 1 Allen Iverson 2.00 .60
❑ 2 Grant Hill 1.00 .30
❑ 3 Antawn Jamison 1.50 .45
❑ 4 Glenn Robinson 1.00 .30
❑ 5 Kenny Anderson .60 .18
❑ 6 Dikembe Mutombo .60 .18
❑ 7 Gary Trent .30 .09
❑ 8 Brevin Knight .30 .09
❑ 9 Chucky Brown .30 .09
❑ 10 Derek Anderson .60 .18
❑ 11 Ricky Davis .60 .18
❑ 12 Chris Webber 1.00 .30
❑ 13 Jalen Rose 1.00 .30
❑ 14 Antoine Walker 1.00 .30
❑ 15 Michael Dickerson .60 .18
❑ 16 Tim Hardaway .60 .18
❑ 17 Toni Kukoc .60 .18
❑ 18 Raef LaFrentz .60 .18
❑ 19 Anthony Mason .60 .18
❑ 20 John Stockton 1.00 .30
❑ 21 Hakeem Olajuwon 1.00 .30
❑ 22 Shaquille O'Neal 2.50 .75
❑ 23 Scottie Pippen 1.50 .45
❑ 24 Maurice Taylor .60 .18
❑ 25 Tariq Abdul-Wahad .30 .09
❑ 26 Tracy McGrady 2.50 .75
❑ 27 Joe Smith .60 .18
❑ 28 Rod Strickland .30 .09
❑ 29 Ruben Patterson .60 .18
❑ 30 Tom Gugliotta .30 .09
❑ 31 Ray Allen 1.00 .30
❑ 32 Elden Campbell .30 .09
❑ 33 Lindsey Hunter .30 .09
❑ 34 Larry Johnson .60 .18
❑ 35 Michael Olowokandi .60 .18
❑ 36 Mario Elie .30 .09
❑ 37 Anfernee Hardaway 1.00 .30
❑ 38 Juwan Howard .60 .18
❑ 39 Karl Malone 1.00 .30
❑ 40 Alonzo Mourning .60 .18
❑ 41 Billy Owens .30 .09
❑ 42 Mitch Richmond .60 .18
❑ 43 Darrell Armstrong .30 .09
❑ 44 Jason Williams 1.00 .30
❑ 45 Mookie Blaylock .30 .09
❑ 46 Gary Payton 1.00 .30
❑ 47 Brian Grant .60 .18
❑ 48 Paul Pierce 1.00 .30
❑ 49 Michael Finley 1.00 .30
❑ 50 Reggie Miller 1.00 .30
❑ 51 Corliss Williamson .60 .18
❑ 52 Shandon Anderson .30 .09
❑ 53 Stephon Marbury 1.00 .30
❑ 54 Sam Cassell 1.00 .30
❑ 55 Bryon Russell .30 .09
❑ 56 Rasheed Wallace 1.00 .30
❑ 57 Jayson Williams .30 .09
❑ 58 Damon Stoudamire .60 .18
❑ 59 Terrell Brandon .60 .18
❑ 60 Loy Vaught .30 .09
❑ 61 Kobe Bryant 4.00 1.20
❑ 62 Vlade Divac .60 .18
❑ 63 Derek Fisher 1.00 .30
❑ 64 Isaiah Rider .30 .09
❑ 65 Eddie Jones 1.00 .30
❑ 66 Kevin Garnett 2.00 .60
❑ 67 David Robinson 1.00 .30
❑ 68 Marcus Camby .60 .18
❑ 69 Glen Rice .60 .18
❑ 70 Mike Bibby 1.00 .30
❑ 71 Patrick Ewing 1.00 .30
❑ 72 Robert Traylor .30 .09
❑ 73 Tim Duncan 2.00 .60
❑ 74 Michael Doleac .30 .09
❑ 75 Steve Smith .60 .18
❑ 76 Allan Houston .60 .18
❑ 77 Jamal Mashburn .60 .18
❑ 78 Brent Barry .60 .18
❑ 79 Charles Barkley 1.25 .35
❑ 80 Ron Mercer .60 .18
❑ 81 Jerry Stackhouse 1.00 .30
❑ 82 Keith Van Horn 1.00 .30
❑ 83 Hersey Hawkins .60 .18
❑ 84 Avery Johnson .30 .09
❑ 85 Cedric Ceballos .30 .09
❑ 86 P.J. Brown .30 .09
❑ 87 Doug Christie .60 .18
❑ 88 Shawn Kemp .60 .18
❑ 89 Dirk Nowitzki 2.00 .60
❑ 90 Erick Dampier .60 .18
❑ 91 Antonio McDyess .60 .18
❑ 92 Mark Jackson .60 .18
❑ 93 Clifford Robinson .30 .09
❑ 94 Vince Carter 2.50 .75
❑ 95 Shareef Abdur-Rahim 1.00 .30
❑ 96 Vin Baker .60 .18
❑ 97 Larry Hughes 1.00 .30
❑ 98 Jason Kidd 1.50 .45
❑ 99 Kerry Kittles .30 .09
❑ 100 Latrell Sprewell 1.00 .30
❑ 101 Lamar Odom RC 6.00 1.80
❑ 102 Elton Brand RC 8.00 2.40
❑ 103 Baron Davis RC 6.00 1.80
❑ 104 Jason Terry RC 4.00 1.20
❑ 105 Corey Maggette RC 6.00 1.80
❑ 106 Wally Szczerbiak RC 6.00 1.80
❑ 107 Richard Hamilton RC 6.00 1.80
❑ 108 Milt Palacio RC 1.25 .35
❑ 109 Ron Artest RC 4.00 1.20
❑ 110 Eddie Robinson RC 4.00 1.20
❑ 111 Jumaine Jones RC 2.50 .75
❑ 112 Andre Miller RC 6.00 1.80
❑ 113 Chucky Atkins RC 2.50 .75
❑ 114 Kenny Thomas RC 2.50 .75
❑ 115 Scott Padgett RC 2.00 .60
❑ 116 Devean George RC 3.00 .90
❑ 117 Tim Young RC 1.25 .35
❑ 118 Tim James RC 2.00 .60
❑ 119 Quincy Lewis RC 2.00 .60
❑ 120 James Posey RC 4.00 1.20
❑ 121 Shawn Marion RC 8.00 2.40
❑ 122 Aleksandar Radojevic RC 1.25 .35
❑ 123 Trajan Langdon RC 2.50 .75
❑ 124 Laron Profit RC 2.00 .60
❑ 125 Jonathan Bender RC 6.00 1.80
❑ 126 William Avery RC 2.50 .75
❑ 127 Cal Bowdler RC 2.00 .60
❑ 128 Dion Glover RC 2.00 .60
❑ 129 Jeff Foster RC 2.00 .60
❑ 130 Steve Francis RC 10.00 3.00
❑ 131 Adrian Griffin RC 2.00 .60
❑ 132 Vonteego Cummings RC 2.50 .75
❑ 133 Rafer Alston RC 2.50 .75
❑ 134 Michael Ruffin RC 1.50 .45
❑ 135 Chris Herren RC 1.25 .35
❑ 136 Jermaine Jackson RC 1.25 .35
❑ 137 Lazaro Borrell RC 1.25 .35
❑ 138 Obinna Ekezie RC 1.50 .45
❑ 139 Rick Hughes RC 1.25 .35
❑ 140 Todd MacCulloch RC 2.00 .60
❑ 141 Kobe Bryant STAR 12.00 3.60
❑ 142 Vince Carter STAR 8.00 2.40
❑ 143 Tim Duncan STAR 6.00 1.80
❑ 144 Kevin Garnett STAR 6.00 1.80
❑ 145 Allen Iverson STAR 6.00 1.80
❑ 146 Keith Van Horn STAR - -

Card	Nm-Mt	Ex-Mt
❑ 147 Grant Hill STAR	2.00	.60
❑ 148 Stephon Marbury STAR	2.00	.60
❑ 149 Antoine Walker STAR	2.50	.75
❑ 150 Shaquille O'Neal STAR	8.00	2.40

2000-01 Fleer Mystique

	Nm-Mt	Ex-Mt
COMPLETE SET w/o RC (100)	30.00	9.00
COMMON CARD (1-100)	.25	.07
COMMON ROOKIE (101-106)	15.00	4.50
COMMON ROOKIE (107-112)	6.00	1.80
COMMON ROOKIE (113-117)	5.00	1.50
COMMON ROOKIE (118-124)	3.00	.90
COMMON ROOKIE (125-130)	1.50	.45
COMMON ROOKIE (131-136)	1.25	.35
❑ 1 Shaquille O'Neal	2.00	.60
❑ 2 Gary Payton	.75	.23
❑ 3 Nick Van Exel	.75	.23
❑ 4 Alonzo Mourning	.50	.15
❑ 5 Shawn Marion	.75	.23
❑ 6 Rod Strickland	.25	.07
❑ 7 Mookie Blaylock	.25	.07
❑ 8 Terrell Brandon	.50	.15
❑ 9 Bryon Russell	.25	.07
❑ 10 Jerry Stackhouse	.75	.23
❑ 11 Glenn Robinson	.75	.23
❑ 12 Rasheed Wallace	.75	.23
❑ 13 Tracy McGrady	2.00	.60
❑ 14 Raef LaFrentz	.50	.15
❑ 15 P.J. Brown	.25	.07
❑ 16 Anfernee Hardaway	.75	.23
❑ 17 Mike Bibby	.75	.23
❑ 18 Elden Campbell	.25	.07
❑ 19 Steve Francis	.75	.23
❑ 20 Keith Van Horn	.75	.23
❑ 21 Karl Malone	.75	.23
❑ 22 Dirk Nowitzki	1.25	.35
❑ 23 Glen Rice	.50	.15
❑ 24 Tom Gugliotta	.25	.07
❑ 25 Avery Johnson	.25	.07
❑ 26 Michael Finley	.75	.23
❑ 27 Theo Ratliff	.50	.15
❑ 28 Juwan Howard	.50	.15
❑ 29 Anthony Carter	.50	.15
❑ 30 Kobe Bryant	3.00	.90
❑ 31 Toni Kukoc	.50	.15
❑ 32 Jason Terry	.75	.23
❑ 33 Elton Brand	.75	.23
❑ 34 Reggie Miller	.75	.23
❑ 35 Latrell Sprewell	.75	.23
❑ 36 Adrian Griffin	.25	.07
❑ 37 Cuttino Mobley	.50	.15
❑ 38 Maurice Taylor	.25	.07
❑ 39 Allen Iverson	1.50	.45
❑ 40 Tim Duncan	1.50	.45
❑ 41 Andre Miller	.50	.15
❑ 42 Antonio Davis	.25	.07
❑ 43 Howard Eisley	.25	.07
❑ 44 Vlade Divac	.50	.15
❑ 45 Brevin Knight	.25	.07
❑ 46 Lamar Odom	.75	.23
❑ 47 Ron Mercer	.50	.15
❑ 48 Jason Williams	.50	.15
❑ 49 Antawn Jamison	.75	.23
❑ 50 Wally Szczerbiak	.50	.15
❑ 51 Chris Webber	.75	.23
❑ 52 Larry Hughes	.50	.15
❑ 53 Kevin Garnett	1.50	.45
❑ 54 Michael Dickerson	.50	.15
❑ 55 Chucky Atkins	.25	.07
❑ 56 Jalen Rose	.75	.23
❑ 57 John Amaechi	.25	.07
❑ 58 Shareef Abdur-Rahim	.75	.23
❑ 59 Shawn Kemp	.50	.15
❑ 60 Derek Anderson	.50	.15
❑ 61 Darrell Armstrong	.25	.07
❑ 62 Vin Baker	.50	.15
❑ 63 Paul Pierce	.75	.23
❑ 64 Donyell Marshall	.50	.15
❑ 65 Jamie Feick	.25	.07
❑ 66 Travis Best	.25	.07
❑ 67 Baron Davis	.75	.23
❑ 68 Hakeem Olajuwon	.75	.23
❑ 69 Joe Smith	.50	.15
❑ 70 Ruben Patterson	.50	.15
❑ 71 Antonio McDyess	.50	.15
❑ 72 Jamal Mashburn	.50	.15
❑ 73 Jason Kidd	1.25	.35
❑ 74 Eddie Jones	.75	.23
❑ 75 Kenny Thomas	.25	.07
❑ 76 Marcus Camby	.50	.15
❑ 77 Doug Christie	.50	.15
❑ 78 Ron Artest	.50	.15
❑ 79 Mark Jackson	.25	.07
❑ 80 Allan Houston	.50	.15
❑ 81 John Stockton	.75	.23
❑ 82 Jerome Williams	.25	.07
❑ 83 Tim Thomas	.50	.15
❑ 84 Alan Henderson	.25	.07
❑ 85 Antoine Walker	.75	.23
❑ 86 Robert Horry	.50	.15
❑ 87 Stephon Marbury	.75	.23
❑ 88 David Robinson	.75	.23
❑ 89 Lindsey Hunter	.25	.07
❑ 90 Richard Hamilton	.50	.15
❑ 91 Damon Stoudamire	.50	.15
❑ 92 Dikembe Mutombo	.50	.15
❑ 93 Anthony Mason	.50	.15
❑ 94 Austin Croshere	.50	.15
❑ 95 Patrick Ewing	.75	.23
❑ 96 Mitch Richmond	.50	.15
❑ 97 Grant Hill	.75	.23
❑ 98 Ray Allen	.75	.23
❑ 99 Scottie Pippen	1.25	.35
❑ 100 Vince Carter	2.00	.60
❑ 101 Kenyon Martin A RC	20.00	6.00
❑ 102 Stromile Swift A RC	12.00	3.60
❑ 103 Darius Miles A RC	15.00	4.50
❑ 104 Marcus Fizer A RC	15.00	4.50
❑ 105 Mike Miller A RC	15.00	4.50
❑ 106 DerMarr Johnson A RC	15.00	4.50
❑ 107 Chris Mihm B RC	6.00	1.80
❑ 108 Jamal Crawford B RC	8.00	2.40
❑ 109 Joel Przybilla B RC	6.00	1.80
❑ 110 Keyon Dooling B RC	6.00	1.80
❑ 111 Jerome Moiso B RC	6.00	1.80
❑ 112 Etan Thomas B RC	5.00	1.50
❑ 113 Courtney Alexander C RC	6.00	1.80
❑ 114 Mateen Cleaves C RC	5.00	1.50
❑ 115 Jason Collier C RC	5.00	1.50
❑ 116 Hidayet Turkoglu C RC	8.00	2.40
❑ 117 Desmond Mason C RC	5.00	1.50
❑ 118 Quentin Richardson C RC	8.00	2.40
❑ 119 Jamaal Magloire D RC	3.00	.90
❑ 120 Speedy Claxton D RC	3.00	.90
❑ 121 Morris Peterson D RC	5.00	1.50
❑ 122 Donnell Harvey D RC	3.00	.90
❑ 123 D.Stevenson D RC	3.00	.90
❑ 124 Mark Karcher D RC	3.00	.90
❑ 125 Mamadou N'diaye E RC	1.50	.45
❑ 126 Erick Barkley E RC	1.50	.45
❑ 127 Mark Madsen E RC	1.50	.45
❑ 128 Corey Hightower E RC	1.50	.45
❑ 129 Dan McClintock E RC	1.50	.45
❑ 130 Soumaila Samake E RC	1.50	.45
❑ 131 Hanno Mottola F RC	1.25	.35
❑ 132 Chris Carrawell F RC	1.25	.35
❑ 133 Olumide Oyedeji F RC	1.25	.35
❑ 134 Michael Redd F RC	2.00	.60
❑ 135 Chris Porter F RC	1.25	.35
❑ 136 Jabari Smith F RC	1.25	.35

2003-04 Fleer Mystique

	Nm-Mt	Ex-Mt
COMP.SET w/o SP's (80)	40.00	12.00
COMMON CARD (1-80)	.20	.06
COMMON ROOKIE (81-120)	6.00	1.80
❑ 1 Eric Williams	.20	.06
❑ 2 Dirk Nowitzki	1.25	.35
❑ 3 Jason Richardson	.75	.23
❑ 4 Corey Maggette	.50	.15
❑ 5 Troy Hudson	.20	.06
❑ 6 Tracy McGrady	2.00	.60
❑ 7 Zach Randolph	.75	.23
❑ 8 Bobby Jackson	.50	.15
❑ 9 Dan Gadzuric	.20	.06
❑ 10 Kevin Garnett	1.50	.45
❑ 11 Manu Ginobili	.75	.23
❑ 12 Andrei Kirilenko	.75	.23
❑ 13 Richard Hamilton	.50	.15
❑ 14 Mike Bibby	.75	.23
❑ 15 Vince Carter	2.00	.60
❑ 16 Jermaine O'Neal	.75	.23
❑ 17 Antoine Walker	.75	.23
❑ 18 Jalen Rose	.75	.23
❑ 19 Dajuan Wagner	.50	.15
❑ 20 Nene	.50	.15
❑ 21 Jamaal Tinsley	.75	.23
❑ 22 Kobe Bryant	3.00	.90
❑ 23 Shane Battier	.75	.23
❑ 24 Allan Houston	.50	.15
❑ 25 Jerry Stackhouse	.75	.23
❑ 26 Eddie Jones	.75	.23
❑ 27 Morris Peterson	.50	.15
❑ 28 Richard Jefferson	.50	.15
❑ 29 Tony Parker	.75	.23
❑ 30 Glenn Robinson	.75	.23
❑ 31 Ron Artest	.50	.15
❑ 32 Marcus Haislip	.20	.06
❑ 33 Drew Gooden	.50	.15
❑ 34 Keith Van Horn	.75	.23
❑ 35 Shareef Abdur-Rahim	.75	.23
❑ 36 Michael Redd	.75	.23
❑ 37 Stephon Marbury	.75	.23
❑ 38 Tim Duncan	1.50	.45
❑ 39 Eddie Griffin	.50	.15
❑ 40 Kwame Brown	.75	.23
❑ 41 Steve Francis	.75	.23
❑ 42 Vladimir Radmanovic	.20	.06
❑ 43 Kenyon Martin	.75	.23
❑ 44 Eddy Curry	.50	.15
❑ 45 Nikoloz Tskitishvili	.20	.06
❑ 46 Shaquille O'Neal	2.00	.60
❑ 47 Allen Iverson	1.50	.45
❑ 48 Jason Kidd	1.25	.35
❑ 49 Ben Wallace	.75	.23
❑ 50 Caron Butler	.75	.23
❑ 51 Dan Dickau	.20	.06

❑ 52	Baron Davis	.75	.23
❑ 53	Bruce Bowen	.20	.06
❑ 54	Amare Stoudemire	1.50	.45
❑ 55	Michael Finley	.75	.23
❑ 56	Jamal Mashburn	.50	.15
❑ 57	Pau Gasol	.75	.23
❑ 58	Shawn Marion	.75	.23
❑ 59	Rasheed Wallace	.75	.23
❑ 60	Chris Webber	.75	.23
❑ 61	Rodney White	.20	.06
❑ 62	Tayshaun Prince	.50	.15
❑ 63	Yao Ming	2.00	.60
❑ 64	Latrell Sprewell	.75	.23
❑ 65	Aaron McKie	.50	.15
❑ 66	Bonzi Wells	.75	.23
❑ 67	HedoTurkoglu	.75	.23
❑ 68	Ray Allen	.75	.23
❑ 69	Matt Harpring	.75	.23
❑ 70	Paul Pierce	.75	.23
❑ 71	Darius Miles	.75	.23
❑ 72	Chris Wilcox	.50	.15
❑ 73	Steve Nash	.75	.23
❑ 74	Antawn Jamison	.75	.23
❑ 75	Juan Dixon	.50	.15
❑ 76	Peja Stojakovic	.75	.23
❑ 77	Antonio Davis	.20	.06
❑ 78	Kenny Thomas	.20	.06
❑ 79	Elton Brand	.75	.23
❑ 80	Gilbert Arenas	.75	.23
❑ 81	Mickael Pietrus RC	6.00	1.80
❑ 82	Keith Bogans RC	6.00	1.80
❑ 83	Dahntay Jones RC	6.00	1.80
❑ 84	Darko Milicic RC	10.00	3.00
❑ 85	Torraye Braggs RC	6.00	1.80
❑ 86	Troy Bell RC	6.00	1.80
❑ 87	Maciej Lampe RC	6.00	1.80
❑ 88	Kendrick Perkins RC	6.00	1.80
❑ 89	Kirk Hinrich RC	10.00	3.00
❑ 90	Jason Kapono RC	6.00	1.80
❑ 91	Udonis Haslem RC	6.00	1.80
❑ 92	James Lang RC	6.00	1.80
❑ 93	Willie Green RC	6.00	1.80
❑ 94	Travis Outlaw RC	6.00	1.80
❑ 95	Nick Collison RC	6.00	1.80
❑ 96	Jarvis Hayes RC	6.00	1.80
❑ 97	Boris Diaw RC	6.00	1.80
❑ 98	Chris Bosh RC	12.00	3.60
❑ 99	LeBron James RC	80.00	24.00
❑ 100	Zarko Cabarkapa RC	6.00	1.80
❑ 101	Travis Hansen RC	6.00	1.80
❑ 102	James Jones RC	6.00	1.80
❑ 103	Aleksandar Pavlovic RC	6.00	1.80
❑ 104	Luke Walton RC	8.00	2.40
❑ 105	Maurice Williams RC	6.00	1.80
❑ 106	Linton Johnson RC	6.00	1.80
❑ 107	David West RC	6.00	1.80
❑ 108	Carmelo Anthony RC	40.00	12.00
❑ 109	T.J. Ford RC	8.00	2.40
❑ 110	Ndudi Ebi RC	6.00	1.80
❑ 111	Reece Gaines RC	6.00	1.80
❑ 112	Leandro Barbosa RC	6.00	1.80
❑ 113	Luke Ridnour RC	8.00	2.40
❑ 114	Brian Cook RC	6.00	1.80
❑ 115	Marcus Banks RC	6.00	1.80
❑ 116	Josh Howard RC	8.00	2.40
❑ 117	Chris Kaman RC	6.00	1.80
❑ 118	Zoran Planinic RC	6.00	1.80
❑ 119	Dwyane Wade RC	15.00	4.50
❑ 120	Mike Sweetney RC	6.00	1.80

2003-04 Fleer Patchworks

	Nm-Mt	Ex-Mt
COMP.SET w/o SP's (90)	30.00	9.00
COMMON CARD (1-90)	.20	.06
COMMON ROOKIE (91-120)	4.00	1.20

❑ 1	Shareef Abdur-Rahim	.75	.23
❑ 2	Theo Ratliff	.50	.15
❑ 3	Jason Terry	.75	.23
❑ 4	Carlos Boozer	.75	.23
❑ 5	Paul Pierce	.75	.23
❑ 6	Ricky Davis	.75	.23
❑ 7	Tyson Chandler	.75	.23
❑ 8	Jamal Crawford	.75	.23
❑ 9	Eddy Curry	.50	.15

❑ 10	Darius Miles	.75	.23
❑ 11	Dajuan Wagner	.50	.15
❑ 12	Michael Finley	.75	.23
❑ 13	Steve Nash	.75	.23
❑ 14	Dirk Nowitzki	1.25	.35
❑ 15	Earl Boykins	.50	.15
❑ 16	Andre Miller	.50	.15
❑ 17	Nene	.50	.15
❑ 18	Richard Hamilton	.50	.15
❑ 19	Tayshaun Prince	.50	.15
❑ 20	Ben Wallace	.75	.23
❑ 21	Mike Dunleavy	.50	.15
❑ 22	Troy Murphy	.75	.23
❑ 23	Jason Richardson	.75	.23
❑ 24	Steve Francis	.75	.23
❑ 25	Yao Ming	2.00	.60
❑ 26	Cuttino Mobley	.50	.15
❑ 27	Maurice Taylor	.20	.06
❑ 28	Ron Artest	.50	.15
❑ 29	Reggie Miller	.75	.23
❑ 30	Jermaine O'Neal	.75	.23
❑ 31	Jamaal Tinsley	.75	.23
❑ 32	Elton Brand	.75	.23
❑ 33	Marko Jaric	.50	.15
❑ 34	Corey Maggette	.50	.15
❑ 35	Kobe Bryant	3.00	.90
❑ 36	Karl Malone	.75	.23
❑ 37	Shaquille O'Neal	2.00	.60
❑ 38	Shane Battier	.75	.23
❑ 39	Pau Gasol	.75	.23
❑ 40	Jason Williams	.50	.15
❑ 41	Caron Butler	.75	.23
❑ 42	Lamar Odom	.75	.23
❑ 43	Desmond Mason	.50	.15
❑ 44	Michael Redd	.75	.23
❑ 45	Tim Thomas	.50	.15
❑ 46	Sam Cassell	.75	.23
❑ 47	Kevin Garnett	1.50	.45
❑ 48	Latrell Sprewell	.75	.23
❑ 49	Wally Szczerbiak	.50	.15
❑ 50	Richard Jefferson	.50	.15
❑ 51	Jason Kidd	1.25	.35
❑ 52	Kenyon Martin	.75	.23
❑ 53	Baron Davis	.75	.23
❑ 54	Jamal Mashburn	.50	.15
❑ 55	Jamaal Magloire	.20	.06
❑ 56	Allan Houston	.50	.15
❑ 57	Stephon Marbury	.75	.23
❑ 58	Kurt Thomas	.50	.15
❑ 59	Drew Gooden	.50	.15
❑ 60	Juwan Howard	.50	.15
❑ 61	Tracy McGrady	2.00	.60
❑ 62	Allen Iverson	1.50	.45
❑ 63	Aaron McKie	.50	.15
❑ 64	Glenn Robinson	.75	.23
❑ 65	Kenny Thomas	.20	.06
❑ 66	Shawn Marion	.75	.23
❑ 67	Antonio McDyess	.75	.23
❑ 68	Amare Stoudemire	1.50	.45
❑ 69	Zach Randolph	.75	.23
❑ 70	Damon Stoudamire	.50	.15
❑ 71	Rasheed Wallace	.75	.23
❑ 72	Qyntel Woods	.20	.06
❑ 73	Mike Bibby	.75	.23
❑ 74	Peja Stojakovic	.75	.23
❑ 75	Chris Webber	.75	.23
❑ 76	Tim Duncan	1.50	.45
❑ 77	Manu Ginobili	.75	.23
❑ 78	Tony Parker	.75	.23
❑ 79	Malik Rose	.20	.06
❑ 80	Ray Allen	.75	.23
❑ 81	Rashard Lewis	.75	.23
❑ 82	Vladimir Radmanovic	.20	.06
❑ 83	Vince Carter	2.00	.60
❑ 84	Donyell Marshall	.75	.23
❑ 85	Jalen Rose	.75	.23
❑ 86	Matt Harpring	.75	.23
❑ 87	Andrei Kirilenko	.75	.23
❑ 88	Gilbert Arenas	.75	.23
❑ 89	Larry Hughes	.50	.15
❑ 90	Jerry Stackhouse	.75	.23
❑ 91	Carmelo Anthony RC	20.00	6.00
❑ 92	Marcus Banks RC	4.00	1.20
❑ 93	Troy Bell RC	4.00	1.20
❑ 94	Chris Bosh RC	8.00	2.40
❑ 95	Zarko Cabarkapa RC	4.00	1.20
❑ 96	Nick Collison RC	4.00	1.20
❑ 97	Boris Diaw RC	4.00	1.20
❑ 98	Francisco Elson RC	4.00	1.20
❑ 99	T.J. Ford RC	5.00	1.50
❑ 100	Reece Gaines RC	4.00	1.20
❑ 101	Udonis Haslem RC	4.00	1.20
❑ 102	Jarvis Hayes RC	4.00	1.20
❑ 103	Kirk Hinrich RC	6.00	1.80
❑ 104	Josh Howard RC	5.00	1.50
❑ 105	LeBron James RC	50.00	15.00
❑ 106	Dahntay Jones RC	4.00	1.20
❑ 107	Chris Kaman RC	4.00	1.20
❑ 108	Jason Kapono RC	4.00	1.20
❑ 109	Raul Lopez	4.00	1.20
❑ 110	Darko Milicic RC	6.00	1.80
❑ 111	Zaur Pachulia RC	4.00	1.20
❑ 112	Mickael Pietrus RC	4.00	1.20
❑ 113	Zoran Planinic RC	4.00	1.20
❑ 114	Luke Ridnour RC	5.00	1.50
❑ 115	Darius Songaila RC	4.00	1.20
❑ 116	Mike Sweetney RC	4.00	1.20
❑ 117	Dwyane Wade RC	10.00	3.00
❑ 118	Luke Walton RC	5.00	1.50
❑ 119	David West RC	4.00	1.20
❑ 120	Maurice Williams RC	4.00	1.20

2001-02 Fleer Platinum

	Nm-Mt	Ex-Mt
COMPLETE SET (250)	300.00	90.00
COMP.SET w/o SP's (200)	20.00	6.00
COMMON CARD (1-200)	.20	.06
COMMON HL (201-220)	2.50	.75
COMMON ROOKIE (221-250)	3.00	.90

❑ 1	Tyrone Hill	.20	.06
❑ 2	Sam Cassell	.60	.18
❑ 3	Elton Brand	.60	.18
❑ 4	Andre Miller	.40	.12
❑ 5	Vitaly Potapenko	.20	.06
❑ 6	Lamar Odom	.60	.18
❑ 7	Mike Bibby	.60	.18
❑ 8	Alan Henderson	.20	.06
❑ 9	Dan Majerle	.40	.12
❑ 10	Donyell Marshall	.40	.12
❑ 11	Jason Williams	.40	.12
❑ 12	Glen Rice	.40	.12
❑ 13	Kobe Bryant	2.50	.75
❑ 14	Pat Garrity	.20	.06
❑ 15	Shawn Bradley	.20	.06
❑ 16	Aaron Williams	.20	.06
❑ 17	Antonio McDyess	.40	.12

Card	Nm-Mt	Ex-Mt
❑ 18 Jonathan Bender	.40	.12
❑ 19 Ben Wallace	.60	.18
❑ 20 Vince Carter	1.50	.45
❑ 21 Maurice Taylor	.40	.12
❑ 22 Antonio Daniels	.20	.06
❑ 23 Rodney Rogers	.20	.06
❑ 24 Patrick Ewing	.60	.18
❑ 25 Chauncey Billups	.40	.12
❑ 26 Steve Smith	.40	.12
❑ 27 Antawn Jamison	.60	.18
❑ 28 Mitch Richmond	.40	.12
❑ 29 Jumaine Jones	.40	.12
❑ 30 Glenn Robinson	.60	.18
❑ 31 Ron Mercer	.40	.12
❑ 32 Jelani McCoy	.20	.06
❑ 33 Paul Pierce	.60	.18
❑ 34 Jeff McInnis	.20	.06
❑ 35 Michael Dickerson	.40	.12
❑ 36 Toni Kukoc	.40	.12
❑ 37 Anthony Mason	.40	.12
❑ 38 Jamal Mashburn	.40	.12
❑ 39 John Stockton	.60	.18
❑ 40 Peja Stojakovic	.60	.18
❑ 41 Charlie Ward	.20	.06
❑ 42 Donnell Harvey	.40	.12
❑ 43 Darrell Armstrong	.20	.06
❑ 44 Michael Finley	.60	.18
❑ 45 Kerry Kittles	.20	.06
❑ 46 Voshon Lenard	.20	.06
❑ 47 Reggie Miller	.60	.18
❑ 48 Joe Smith	.40	.12
❑ 49 Antonio Davis	.20	.06
❑ 50 Hakeem Olajuwon	.60	.18
❑ 51 David Robinson	.60	.18
❑ 52 Tony Delk	.20	.06
❑ 53 Gary Payton	.60	.18
❑ 54 Kevin Garnett	1.25	.35
❑ 55 Arvydas Sabonis	.40	.12
❑ 56 Larry Hughes	.40	.12
❑ 57 Richard Hamilton	.40	.12
❑ 58 Aaron McKie	.40	.12
❑ 59 Tim Thomas	.40	.12
❑ 60 Ron Artest	.40	.12
❑ 61 Matt Harpring	.60	.18
❑ 62 Kenny Anderson	.40	.12
❑ 63 Quentin Richardson	.40	.12
❑ 64 Damon Jones	.40	.12
❑ 65 Theo Ratliff	.40	.12
❑ 66 Brian Grant	.40	.12
❑ 67 Eddie Robinson	.40	.12
❑ 68 Karl Malone	.60	.18
❑ 69 Bobby Jackson	.40	.12
❑ 70 Larry Johnson	.40	.12
❑ 71 Shareef Abdur-Rahim	.60	.18
❑ 72 Grant Hill	.60	.18
❑ 73 Eduardo Najera	.40	.12
❑ 74 Keith Van Horn	.60	.18
❑ 75 Nick Van Exel	.60	.18
❑ 76 Jalen Rose	.60	.18
❑ 77 Jerry Stackhouse	.60	.18
❑ 78 Jerome Williams	.20	.06
❑ 79 Cuttino Mobley	.40	.12
❑ 80 Derek Anderson	.40	.12
❑ 81 Anfernee Hardaway	.60	.18
❑ 82 Rashard Lewis	.40	.12
❑ 83 Terrell Brandon	.40	.12
❑ 84 Scottie Pippen	1.00	.30
❑ 85 Danny Fortson	.20	.06
❑ 86 Jahidi White	.20	.06
❑ 87 Eric Snow	.40	.12
❑ 88 Ervin Johnson	.20	.06
❑ 89 Marcus Fizer	.40	.12
❑ 90 Lamond Murray	.20	.06
❑ 91 Antoine Walker	.60	.18
❑ 92 Keyon Dooling	.40	.12
❑ 93 Bryant Reeves	.20	.06
❑ 94 Hanno Mottola	.40	.12
❑ 95 Tim Hardaway	.40	.12
❑ 96 David Wesley	.20	.06
❑ 97 John Starks	.40	.12
❑ 98 Hidayet Turkoglu	.40	.12
❑ 99 Allan Houston	.40	.12
❑ 100 Rick Fox	.40	.12
❑ 101 Bo Outlaw	.20	.06
❑ 102 Juwan Howard	.40	.12
❑ 103 Kendall Gill	.20	.06
❑ 104 Raef LaFrentz	.40	.12
❑ 105 Austin Croshere	.40	.12
❑ 106 Chucky Atkins	.20	.06
❑ 107 Morris Peterson	.40	.12
❑ 108 Shandon Anderson	.20	.06
❑ 109 Sean Elliott	.40	.12
❑ 110 Tom Gugliotta	.20	.06
❑ 111 Vin Baker	.40	.12
❑ 112 Wally Szczerbiak	.40	.12
❑ 113 Rasheed Wallace	.60	.18
❑ 114 Vonteego Cummings	.20	.06
❑ 115 Christian Laettner	.40	.12
❑ 116 Dikembe Mutombo	.40	.12
❑ 117 Lindsey Hunter	.20	.06
❑ 118 Jamal Crawford	.40	.12
❑ 119 Jim Jackson	.20	.06
❑ 120 Bryant Stith	.20	.06
❑ 121 Corey Maggette	.40	.12
❑ 122 Mahmoud Abdul-Rauf	.20	.06
❑ 123 Lorenzen Wright	.20	.06
❑ 124 Alonzo Mourning	.40	.12
❑ 125 Jamaal Magloire	.40	.12
❑ 126 Bryon Russell	.20	.06
❑ 127 Vlade Divac	.40	.12
❑ 128 Marcus Camby	.40	.12
❑ 129 Derek Fisher	.60	.18
❑ 130 Mike Miller	.60	.18
❑ 131 Steve Nash	.60	.18
❑ 132 Kenyon Martin	.60	.18
❑ 133 James Posey	.40	.12
❑ 134 Travis Best	.20	.06
❑ 135 Corliss Williamson	.40	.12
❑ 136 Alvin Williams	.20	.06
❑ 137 Walt Williams	.20	.06
❑ 138 Malik Rose	.20	.06
❑ 139 Clifford Robinson	.20	.06
❑ 140 Ruben Patterson	.40	.12
❑ 141 LaPhonso Ellis	.20	.06
❑ 142 Rod Strickland	.20	.06
❑ 143 Marc Jackson	.40	.12
❑ 144 Hubert Davis	.20	.06
❑ 145 Speedy Claxton	.40	.12
❑ 146 Scott Williams	.20	.06
❑ 147 Tyronn Lue	.20	.06
❑ 148 Chris Mihm	.40	.12
❑ 149 George Lynch	.20	.06
❑ 150 Michael Olowokandi	.20	.06
❑ 151 Nazr Mohammed	.20	.06
❑ 152 Eddie House	.40	.12
❑ 153 Elden Campbell	.20	.06
❑ 154 DeShawn Stevenson	.40	.12
❑ 155 Doug Christie	.40	.12
❑ 156 Kurt Thomas	.40	.12
❑ 157 Robert Horry	.40	.12
❑ 158 Radoslav Nesterovic	.40	.12
❑ 159 Wang Zhizhi	.60	.18
❑ 160 Stephen Jackson	.40	.12
❑ 161 George McCloud	.20	.06
❑ 162 Jermaine O'Neal	.60	.18
❑ 163 Mateen Cleaves	.40	.12
❑ 164 Charles Oakley	.20	.06
❑ 165 Kenny Thomas	.20	.06
❑ 166 Terry Porter	.20	.06
❑ 167 Iakovos Tsakalidis	.20	.06
❑ 168 Shammond Williams	.20	.06
❑ 169 Anthony Peeler	.20	.06
❑ 170 Damon Stoudamire	.40	.12
❑ 171 Chris Porter	.40	.12
❑ 172 Chris Whitney	.20	.06
❑ 173 Raja Bell RC	.75	.23
❑ 174 Darvin Ham	.20	.06
❑ 175 A.J. Guyton	.40	.12
❑ 176 Trajan Langdon	.20	.06
❑ 177 Jerome Moiso	.40	.12
❑ 178 Anthony Carter	.40	.12
❑ 179 P.J. Brown	.20	.06
❑ 180 Danny Manning	.20	.06
❑ 181 Scot Pollard	.20	.06
❑ 182 Mark Jackson	.40	.12
❑ 183 Mark Madsen	.40	.12
❑ 184 Michael Doleac	.20	.06
❑ 185 Calvin Booth	.20	.06
❑ 186 Kevin Willis	.20	.06
❑ 187 Al Harrington	.40	.12
❑ 188 Mikki Moore	.20	.06
❑ 189 Keon Clark	.40	.12
❑ 190 Moochie Norris	.20	.06
❑ 191 Ron Harper	.40	.12
❑ 192 Danny Ferry	.20	.06
❑ 193 Jacque Vaughn	.20	.06
❑ 194 Derrick Coleman	.20	.06
❑ 195 Brent Barry	.40	.12
❑ 196 Dion Glover	.20	.06
❑ 197 Felipe Lopez	.20	.06
❑ 198 Shawn Kemp	.40	.12
❑ 199 Mookie Blaylock	.20	.06
❑ 200 Bonzi Wells	.40	.12
❑ 201 Vince Carter HL	6.00	1.80
❑ 202 Ray Allen HL	2.50	.75
❑ 203 Darius Miles HL	.60	.18
❑ 204 Shaquille O'Neal HL	6.00	1.80
❑ 205 Stromile Swift HL	2.50	.75
❑ 206 DerMarr Johnson HL	2.50	.75
❑ 207 Eddie Jones HL	2.50	.75
❑ 208 Chris Webber HL	.60	.18
❑ 209 Latrell Sprewell HL	.60	.18
❑ 210 Tracy McGrady HL	6.00	1.80
❑ 211 Dirk Nowitzki HL	4.00	1.20
❑ 212 Stephon Marbury HL	2.50	.75
❑ 213 Steve Francis HL	.60	.18
❑ 214 Tim Duncan HL	5.00	1.50
❑ 215 Jason Kidd HL	4.00	1.20
❑ 216 Shawn Marion HL	.60	.18
❑ 217 Desmond Mason HL	2.50	.75
❑ 218 Courtney Alexander HL	2.50	.75
❑ 219 Baron Davis HL	2.50	.75
❑ 220 Allen Iverson HL	5.00	1.50
❑ 221 Joe Johnson RC	5.00	1.50
❑ 222 Kedrick Brown RC	3.00	.90
❑ 223 Joseph Forte RC	4.00	1.20
❑ 224 Kirk Haston RC	2.50	.75
❑ 225 Tyson Chandler RC	8.00	2.40
❑ 226 Eddy Curry RC	8.00	2.40
❑ 227 DeSagana Diop RC	3.00	.90
❑ 228 Jeff Trepagnier RC	3.00	.90
❑ 229 Oscar Torres RC	4.00	1.20
❑ 230 Rodney White RC	3.00	.90
❑ 231 Jason Richardson RC	10.00	3.00
❑ 232 Troy Murphy RC	6.00	1.80
❑ 233 Eddie Griffin RC	6.00	1.80
❑ 234 Jamaal Tinsley RC	5.00	1.50
❑ 235 Pau Gasol RC	12.00	3.60
❑ 236 Shane Battier RC	5.00	1.50
❑ 237 Richard Jefferson RC	10.00	3.00
❑ 238 Jason Collins RC	3.00	.90
❑ 239 Brendan Haywood RC	3.00	.90
❑ 240 Steven Hunter RC	3.00	.90
❑ 241 Zach Randolph RC	8.00	2.40
❑ 242 Gerald Wallace RC	6.00	1.80
❑ 243 Tony Parker RC	12.00	3.60
❑ 244 Vladimir Radmanovic RC	4.00	1.20
❑ 245 Michael Bradley RC	3.00	.90
❑ 246 Andrei Kirilenko RC	8.00	2.40
❑ 247 Kwame Brown RC	8.00	2.40
❑ 248 Alton Ford RC	2.50	.75
❑ 249 Zeljko Rebraca RC	3.00	.90
❑ 250 Trenton Hassell RC	5.00	1.50

2002-03 Fleer Platinum

	Nm-Mt	Ex-Mt
COMP.SET w/o SP's (160)	40.00	12.00
COMMON CARD (1-160)	.20	.06
COMMON ROOKIE (161-170)	3.00	.90
COMMON ROOKIE (171-180)	6.00	1.80

COMMON ROOKIE (181-190)	8.00	2.40
COMMON ROOKIE (191-200)	10.00	3.00
❑ 1 Vince Carter	2.00	.60
❑ 2 Lamar Odom	.75	.23
❑ 3 Darrell Armstrong	.20	.06
❑ 4 Kwame Brown	.50	.15
❑ 5 Ron Artest	.50	.15
❑ 6 Kurt Thomas	.50	.15
❑ 7 Jerry Stackhouse	.75	.23
❑ 8 Eddie Griffin	.50	.15
❑ 9 David Wesley	.20	.06
❑ 10 Morris Peterson	.50	.15
❑ 11 Jon Barry	.20	.06
❑ 12 Troy Hudson	.20	.06
❑ 13 Kenny Anderson	.50	.15
❑ 14 Corliss Williamson	.50	.15
❑ 15 Kevin Garnett	1.50	.45
❑ 16 Desmond Mason	.50	.15
❑ 17 Lucious Harris	.20	.06
❑ 18 Steve Smith	.50	.15
❑ 19 Nick Van Exel	.75	.23
❑ 20 Tyson Chandler	.75	.23
❑ 21 Shane Battier	.75	.23
❑ 22 Rasheed Wallace	.75	.23
❑ 23 Donyell Marshall	.75	.23
❑ 24 Anfernee Hardaway	.75	.23
❑ 25 Antoine Walker	.75	.23
❑ 26 Kobe Bryant	3.00	.90
❑ 27 Keith Van Horn	.75	.23
❑ 28 Elton Brand	.75	.23
❑ 29 Grant Hill	.75	.23
❑ 30 Elden Campbell	.20	.06
❑ 31 John Stockton	.75	.23
❑ 32 Wally Szczerbiak	.50	.15
❑ 33 Speedy Claxton	.20	.06
❑ 34 Voshon Lenard	.20	.06
❑ 35 Eddie Jones	.75	.23
❑ 36 Bonzi Wells	.50	.15
❑ 37 Jalen Rose	.75	.23
❑ 38 Jason Williams	.50	.15
❑ 39 Tom Gugliotta	.20	.06
❑ 40 Juwan Howard	.50	.15
❑ 41 Michael Redd	.75	.23
❑ 42 David Robinson	.75	.23
❑ 43 Steve Nash	.75	.23
❑ 44 Vlade Divac	.50	.15
❑ 45 Avery Johnson	.20	.06
❑ 46 Scottie Pippen	1.25	.35
❑ 47 Eric Williams	.20	.06
❑ 48 Derek Fisher	.75	.23
❑ 49 Tony Battie	.20	.06
❑ 50 Rick Fox	.50	.15
❑ 51 Theo Ratliff	.50	.15
❑ 52 Corey Maggette	.50	.15
❑ 53 Jermaine O'Neal	.75	.23
❑ 54 Bryon Russell	.20	.06
❑ 55 Steve Francis	.75	.23
❑ 56 Jamal Mashburn	.50	.15
❑ 57 Jerome Williams	.20	.06
❑ 58 Gilbert Arenas	.75	.23
❑ 59 Joe Smith	.50	.15
❑ 60 Brent Barry	.50	.15
❑ 61 Marcus Camby	.50	.15
❑ 62 Toni Kukoc	.50	.15
❑ 63 Tim Duncan	1.50	.45
❑ 64 Ira Newble	.20	.06
❑ 65 Brian Grant	.50	.15
❑ 66 Jason Terry	.75	.23
❑ 67 Andre Miller	.50	.15
❑ 68 Mike Miller	.75	.23
❑ 69 Troy Murphy	.75	.23
❑ 70 P.J. Brown	.20	.06
❑ 71 Jason Richardson	.75	.23
❑ 72 Glenn Robinson	.75	.23
❑ 73 Richard Jefferson	.75	.23
❑ 74 Richard Hamilton	.50	.15
❑ 75 Jason Kidd	1.25	.35
❑ 76 Rashard Lewis	.75	.23
❑ 77 Kenny Satterfield	.20	.06
❑ 78 Terrell Brandon	.50	.15
❑ 79 Dirk Nowitzki	1.25	.35
❑ 80 Chris Webber	.75	.23
❑ 81 Michael Finley	.75	.23
❑ 82 Malik Allen	.20	.06
❑ 83 Bobby Jackson	.50	.15
❑ 84 Darius Miles	.75	.23
❑ 85 Kendall Gill	.20	.06
❑ 86 Damon Stoudamire	.50	.15
❑ 87 Shammond Williams	.20	.06
❑ 88 Stephon Marbury	.75	.23
❑ 89 Shareef Abdur-Rahim	.75	.23
❑ 90 Charlie Ward	.20	.06
❑ 91 Michael Jordan	6.00	1.80
❑ 92 Jamaal Magloire	.20	.06
❑ 93 Karl Malone	.75	.23
❑ 94 Kerry Kittles	.20	.06
❑ 95 Lindsey Hunter	.20	.06
❑ 96 Gary Payton	.75	.23
❑ 97 Travis Best	.20	.06
❑ 98 Derek Anderson	.50	.15
❑ 99 Stromile Swift	.50	.15
❑ 100 Shaquille O'Neal	2.00	.60
❑ 101 Derrick Coleman	.20	.06
❑ 102 DeShawn Stevenson	.20	.06
❑ 103 Jamaal Tinsley	.75	.23
❑ 104 Latrell Sprewell	.75	.23
❑ 105 Larry Hughes	.50	.15
❑ 106 Eddy Curry	.75	.23
❑ 107 Shawn Marion	.75	.23
❑ 108 Paul Pierce	.75	.23
❑ 109 Samaki Walker	.20	.06
❑ 110 Allen Iverson	1.50	.45
❑ 111 Michael Olowokandi	.20	.06
❑ 112 Tracy McGrady	2.00	.60
❑ 113 Shawn Bradley	.20	.06
❑ 114 Reggie Miller	.75	.23
❑ 115 Antonio McDyess	.50	.15
❑ 116 Calbert Chaney	.20	.06
❑ 117 Al Harrington	.50	.15
❑ 118 Allan Houston	.50	.15
❑ 119 Andrei Kirilenko	.75	.23
❑ 120 Courtney Alexander	.50	.15
❑ 121 Alvin Williams	.20	.06
❑ 122 Antawn Jamison	.75	.23
❑ 123 Dikembe Mutombo	.50	.15
❑ 124 Tony Parker	.75	.23
❑ 125 Raef LaFrentz	.50	.15
❑ 126 Ray Allen	.75	.23
❑ 127 Peja Stojakovic	.75	.23
❑ 128 Zydrunas Ilgauskas	.50	.15
❑ 129 Gerald Wallace	.75	.23
❑ 130 Ruben Patterson	.50	.15
❑ 131 Pau Gasol	.75	.23
❑ 132 Joe Johnson	.75	.23
❑ 133 Aaron McKie	.50	.15
❑ 134 Walter McCarty	.20	.06
❑ 135 Baron Davis	.75	.23
❑ 136 Kenyon Martin	.75	.23
❑ 137 Antonio Davis	.20	.06
❑ 138 Ben Wallace	.75	.23
❑ 139 Sam Cassell	.75	.23
❑ 140 Mike Bibby	.75	.23
❑ 141 Cuttino Mobley	.50	.15
❑ 142 LaPhonso Ellis	.20	.06
❑ 143 Shandon Anderson	.20	.06
❑ 144 Hedo Turkoglu	.75	.23
❑ 145 Matt Harpring	.75	.23
❑ 146 Dion Glover	.20	.06
❑ 147 Tony Delk	.20	.06
❑ 148 Ricky Davis	.75	.23
❑ 149 James Posey	.50	.15
❑ 150 Chucky Atkins	.20	.06
❑ 151 Danny Fortson	.20	.06
❑ 152 Robert Horry	.50	.15
❑ 153 Radoslav Nesterovic	.50	.15
❑ 154 Pat Garrity	.20	.06
❑ 155 Todd MacCulloch	.20	.06
❑ 156 Eric Snow	.50	.15
❑ 157 Malik Rose	.20	.06
❑ 158 Vladimir Radmanovic	.50	.15
❑ 159 Trenton Hassell	.50	.15
❑ 160 Brad Miller	.75	.23
❑ 161 Kareem Rush RC	3.00	.90
❑ 162 Nikoloz Tskitishvili RC	3.00	.90
❑ 163 Nene Hilario RC	3.00	.90
❑ 164 Marcus Haislip RC	3.00	.90
❑ 165 Jiri Welsch RC	3.00	.90
❑ 166 Dan Dickau RC	3.00	.90
❑ 167 Vincent Yarbrough RC	3.00	.90
❑ 168 Tito Maddox RC	3.00	.90
❑ 169 Mike Dunleavy RC	4.00	1.20
❑ 170 Chris Wilcox RC	3.00	.90
❑ 171 Jared Jeffries RC	6.00	1.80
❑ 172 Bostjan Nachbar RC	6.00	1.80
❑ 173 Frank Williams RC	6.00	1.80
❑ 174 Reggie Evans RC	6.00	1.80
❑ 175 Casey Jacobsen RC	6.00	1.80
❑ 176 Tayshaun Prince RC	6.00	1.80
❑ 177 Mike Batiste RC	6.00	1.80
❑ 178 Drew Gooden RC	8.00	2.40
❑ 179 DaJuan Wagner RC	6.00	1.80
❑ 180 Tamar Slay RC	6.00	1.80
❑ 181 Melvin Ely RC	8.00	2.40
❑ 182 Rasual Butler RC	8.00	2.40
❑ 183 Dan Gadzuric RC	8.00	2.40
❑ 184 Ryan Humphrey RC	8.00	2.40
❑ 185 Gordan Giricek RC	8.00	2.40
❑ 186 Mehmet Okur RC	8.00	2.40
❑ 187 Jay Williams RC	8.00	2.40
❑ 188 Caron Butler RC	12.00	3.60
❑ 189 Qyntel Woods RC	8.00	2.40
❑ 190 Amare Stoudemire RC	25.00	7.50
❑ 191 Yao Ming RC	50.00	15.00
❑ 192 Carlos Boozer RC	15.00	4.50
❑ 193 John Salmons RC	10.00	3.00
❑ 194 Fred Jones RC	10.00	3.00
❑ 195 Juan Dixon RC	12.00	3.60
❑ 196 Manu Ginobili RC	20.00	6.00
❑ 197 Pat Burke RC	10.00	3.00
❑ 198 Smush Parker RC	10.00	3.00
❑ 199 Lonny Baxter RC	10.00	3.00
❑ 200 Ronald Murray RC	12.00	3.60

2003-04 Fleer Platinum

	Nm-Mt	Ex-Mt
COMMON CARD (1-170)	.20	.06
COMMON ROOKIE (171-180)	2.50	.75
COMMON ROOKIE (181-190)	4.00	1.20
COMMON ROOKIE (191-200)	5.00	1.50
❑ 1 Shane Battier	.60	.18
❑ 2 Brad Miller	.60	.18
❑ 3 Jason Kidd	1.00	.30
❑ 4 Nick Van Exel	.60	.18
❑ 5 David Wesley	.20	.06
❑ 6 Corey Maggette	.40	.12
❑ 7 Juan Dixon	.40	.12
❑ 8 Jamaal Tinsley	.60	.18
❑ 9 Stromile Swift	.40	.12
❑ 10 Dajuan Wagner	.40	.12
❑ 11 Joe Smith	.40	.12
❑ 12 Jermaine O'Neal	.60	.18
❑ 13 Steve Nash	.60	.18
❑ 14 Karl Malone	.60	.18
❑ 15 Vince Carter	1.50	.45
❑ 16 Antonio McDyess	.60	.18
❑ 17 Tim Thomas	.40	.12
❑ 18 Vladimir Radmanovic	.20	.06
❑ 19 Scottie Pippen	1.00	.30
❑ 20 Tracy McGrady	1.50	.45
❑ 21 Darius Miles	.60	.18
❑ 22 Toni Kukoc	.40	.12
❑ 23 Antonio Davis	.40	.12
❑ 24 Jamal Crawford	.40	.12
❑ 25 Rasho Nesterovic	.40	.12
❑ 26 Carlos Boozer	.60	.18
❑ 27 Cuttino Mobley	.40	.12
❑ 28 Larry Hughes	.40	.12
❑ 29 Alvin Williams	.20	.06
❑ 30 Andre Miller	.40	.12

#	Player	Nm-Mt	Ex-Mt
❑ 31	Amare Stoudemire	1.25	.35
❑ 32	Eric Williams	.20	.06
❑ 33	Pau Gasol	.60	.18
❑ 34	Kenyon Martin	.60	.18
❑ 35	Elton Brand	.60	.18
❑ 36	Charlie Ward	.20	.06
❑ 37	Andrei Kirilenko	.60	.18
❑ 38	Aaron McKie	.40	.12
❑ 39	Maurice Taylor	.20	.06
❑ 40	Baron Davis	.60	.18
❑ 41	Dirk Nowitzki	1.00	.30
❑ 42	Gary Payton	.60	.18
❑ 43	Grant Hill	.60	.18
❑ 44	Jalen Rose	.60	.18
❑ 45	Allan Houston	.40	.12
❑ 46	Erick Dampier	.20	.06
❑ 47	Brian Grant	.40	.12
❑ 48	Wally Szczerbiak	.40	.12
❑ 49	Greg Ostertag	.20	.06
❑ 50	Gilbert Arenas	.60	.18
❑ 51	Kenny Anderson	.40	.12
❑ 52	Juwan Howard	.40	.12
❑ 53	Jason Terry	.60	.18
❑ 54	Raef LaFrentz	.40	.12
❑ 55	Ricky Davis	.60	.18
❑ 56	Kobe Bryant	2.50	.75
❑ 57	Chris Webber	.60	.18
❑ 58	P.J. Brown	.20	.06
❑ 59	Nene	.40	.12
❑ 60	Kenny Thomas	.20	.06
❑ 61	Mike Bibby	.60	.18
❑ 62	Chris Wilcox	.40	.12
❑ 63	Anfernee Hardaway	.60	.18
❑ 64	Drew Gooden	.40	.12
❑ 65	Rodney White	.20	.06
❑ 66	Shareef Abdur-Rahim	.60	.18
❑ 67	Quentin Richardson	.40	.12
❑ 68	Ben Wallace	.60	.18
❑ 69	Latrell Sprewell	.60	.18
❑ 70	Shaquille O'Neal	1.50	.45
❑ 71	Vin Baker	.40	.12
❑ 72	Tony Parker	.60	.18
❑ 73	Stephen Jackson	.20	.06
❑ 74	Ray Allen	.60	.18
❑ 75	Eric Snow	.40	.12
❑ 76	Jason Richardson	.60	.18
❑ 77	Shammond Williams	.20	.06
❑ 78	Tayshaun Prince	.40	.12
❑ 79	Antawn Jamison	.60	.18
❑ 80	Derek Fisher	.60	.18
❑ 81	Jeff Foster	.20	.06
❑ 82	Kwame Brown	.60	.18
❑ 83	Yao Ming	1.50	.45
❑ 84	Rasheed Wallace	.60	.18
❑ 85	Tyson Chandler	.60	.18
❑ 86	Mike Dunleavy	.40	.12
❑ 87	Alan Henderson	.20	.06
❑ 88	Rashard Lewis	.60	.18
❑ 89	Jamaal Magloire	.20	.06
❑ 90	Stephon Marbury	.60	.18
❑ 91	DeShawn Stevenson	.20	.06
❑ 92	Damon Stoudamire	.40	.12
❑ 93	Eddy Curry	.40	.12
❑ 94	Peja Stojakovic	.60	.18
❑ 95	Glenn Robinson	.60	.18
❑ 96	Mike Miller	.60	.18
❑ 97	Richard Hamilton	.40	.12
❑ 98	Kevin Garnett	1.25	.35
❑ 99	Zach Randolph	.60	.18
❑ 100	Tony Delk	.20	.06
❑ 101	Clifford Robinson	.20	.06
❑ 102	Steve Francis	.60	.18
❑ 103	Curtis Borchardt	.20	.06
❑ 104	Jerry Stackhouse	.60	.18
❑ 105	Desmond Mason	.40	.12
❑ 106	Chauncey Billups	.40	.12
❑ 107	Sam Cassell	.40	.12
❑ 108	Michael Finley	.60	.18
❑ 109	Hedo Turkoglu	.60	.18
❑ 110	Ronald Murray	.40	.12
❑ 111	Allen Iverson	1.25	.35
❑ 112	Richard Jefferson	.40	.12
❑ 113	Theo Ratliff	.40	.12
❑ 114	Ron Artest	.40	.12
❑ 115	Doug Christie	.40	.12
❑ 116	Lamar Odom	.60	.18
❑ 117	Lamond Murray	.20	.06
❑ 118	Bonzi Wells	.40	.12
❑ 119	Caron Butler	.60	.18
❑ 120	Marcus Camby	.40	.12
❑ 121	Manu Ginobili	.60	.18
❑ 122	Paul Pierce	.60	.18
❑ 123	Troy Hudson	.20	.06
❑ 124	Jim Jackson	.20	.06
❑ 125	Keith Van Horn	.60	.18
❑ 126	Reggie Miller	.60	.18
❑ 127	Tim Duncan	1.25	.35
❑ 128	Shawn Marion	.60	.18
❑ 129	Eddie Jones	.60	.18
❑ 130	Matt Harpring	.60	.18
❑ 131	Elden Campbell	.20	.06
❑ 132	Marko Jaric	.40	.12
❑ 133	John Wallace	.20	.06
❑ 134	Erick Strickland	.20	.06
❑ 135	Voshon Lenard	.20	.06
❑ 136	Aaron Williams	.20	.06
❑ 137	Qyntel Woods	.40	.12
❑ 138	Kelvin Cato	.20	.06
❑ 139	Michael Curry	.20	.06
❑ 140	Vlade Divac	.40	.12
❑ 141	Jason Hart	.20	.06
❑ 142	Nazr Mohammed UH	.20	.06
❑ 143	Mike James UH	.20	.06
❑ 144	Jerome Williams UH	.20	.06
❑ 145	Zydrunas Ilgauskas UH	.40	.12
❑ 146	Antoine Walker UH	.60	.18
❑ 147	Earl Boykins UH	.40	.12
❑ 148	Mehmet Okur UH	.20	.06
❑ 149	Brian Cardinal UH	.20	.06
❑ 150	Bostjan Nachbar UH	.20	.06
❑ 151	Al Harrington UH	.40	.12
❑ 152	Eddie House UH	.20	.06
❑ 153	Devean George UH	.40	.12
❑ 154	Jason Williams UH	.40	.12
❑ 155	Rafer Alston UH	.20	.06
❑ 156	Michael Redd UH	.60	.18
❑ 157	Gary Trent UH	.20	.06
❑ 158	Kerry Kittles UH	.20	.06
❑ 159	Jamal Mashburn UH	.40	.12
❑ 160	Kurt Thomas UH	.40	.12
❑ 161	Tyronn Lue UH	.20	.06
❑ 162	Derrick Coleman UH	.20	.06
❑ 163	Joe Johnson UH	.40	.12
❑ 164	Dale Davis UH	.20	.06
❑ 165	Bobby Jackson UH	.40	.12
❑ 166	Malik Rose UH	.20	.06
❑ 167	Brent Barry UH	.40	.12
❑ 168	Donyell Marshall UH	.60	.18
❑ 169	Carlos Arroyo UH	.20	.06
❑ 170	Etan Thomas UH	.20	.06
❑ 171	Zoran Planinic RC	2.50	.75
❑ 172	Jason Kapono RC	2.50	.75
❑ 173	Zarko Cabarkapa RC	2.50	.75
❑ 174	Darko Milicic RC	4.00	1.20
❑ 175	Aleksandar Pavlovic RC	2.50	.75
❑ 176	Marcus Banks RC	2.50	.75
❑ 177	Willie Green RC	2.50	.75
❑ 178	Udonis Haslem RC	2.50	.75
❑ 179	Nick Collison RC	2.50	.75
❑ 180	Chris Kaman RC	2.50	.75
❑ 181	T.J. Ford RC	5.00	1.50
❑ 182	Travis Outlaw RC	4.00	1.20
❑ 183	LeBron James RC	40.00	12.00
❑ 184	Troy Bell RC	4.00	1.20
❑ 185	Reece Gaines RC	4.00	1.20
❑ 186	David West RC	4.00	1.20
❑ 187	Kirk Hinrich RC	6.00	1.80
❑ 188	Chris Bosh RC	6.00	1.80
❑ 189	Leandro Barbosa RC	4.00	1.20
❑ 190	Dwyane Wade RC	10.00	3.00
❑ 191	Mike Sweetney RC	5.00	1.50
❑ 192	Darius Songaila RC	5.00	1.50
❑ 193	Luke Ridnour RC	6.00	1.80
❑ 194	Carmelo Anthony RC	25.00	7.50
❑ 195	Jarvis Hayes RC	5.00	1.50
❑ 196	Mickael Pietrus RC	5.00	1.50
❑ 197	Dahntay Jones RC	5.00	1.50
❑ 198	Josh Howard RC	6.00	1.80
❑ 199	Maciej Lampe RC	5.00	1.50
❑ 200	Luke Walton RC	6.00	1.80

2000-01 Fleer Premium

		Nm-Mt	Ex-Mt
COMPLETE SET w/o RC (200)		40.00	12.00
COMMON CARD (1-200)		.25	.07
COMMON ROOKIE (201-241)		2.00	.60
❑ 1	Vince Carter	2.00	.60
❑ 2	Kobe Bryant	3.00	.90
❑ 3	Jermaine Jackson	.25	.07
❑ 4	Lamar Odom	.75	.23
❑ 5	Robert Traylor	.25	.07
❑ 6	Jason Kidd	1.25	.35
❑ 7	Rashard Lewis	.50	.15
❑ 8	Ron Artest	.50	.15
❑ 9	Grant Hill	.75	.23
❑ 10	Kenny Thomas	.25	.07
❑ 11	Anthony Carter	.50	.15
❑ 12	Kerry Kittles	.25	.07
❑ 13	Pat Garrity	.25	.07
❑ 14	David Robinson	.75	.23
❑ 15	Bryant Reeves	.25	.07
❑ 16	Fred Hoiberg	.25	.07
❑ 17	Jerry Stackhouse	.75	.23
❑ 18	Donyell Marshall	.50	.15
❑ 19	Ron Harper	.50	.15
❑ 20	Scott Burrell	.25	.07
❑ 21	Ron Mercer	.50	.15
❑ 22	Avery Johnson	.25	.07
❑ 23	Jacque Vaughn	.25	.07
❑ 24	Adrian Griffin	.25	.07
❑ 25	Antonio McDyess	.50	.15
❑ 26	Adonal Foyle	.25	.07
❑ 27	Derek Fisher	.75	.23
❑ 28	Terrell Brandon	.50	.15
❑ 29	Matt Harpring	.75	.23
❑ 30	Nazr Mohammed	.25	.07
❑ 31	Tom Gugliotta	.25	.07
❑ 32	Scott Padgett	.25	.07
❑ 33	Detlef Schrempf	.50	.15
❑ 34	Dirk Nowitzki	1.25	.35
❑ 35	Mookie Blaylock	.25	.07
❑ 36	James Posey	.50	.15
❑ 37	Latrell Sprewell	.75	.23
❑ 38	Michael Doleac	.25	.07
❑ 39	Damon Stoudamire	.50	.15
❑ 40	Tim Duncan	1.50	.45
❑ 41	John Stockton	.75	.23
❑ 42	Danny Fortson	.25	.07
❑ 43	Raef LaFrentz	.50	.15
❑ 44	Steve Francis	.75	.23
❑ 45	Travis Knight	.25	.07
❑ 46	Kevin Garnett	1.50	.45
❑ 47	Mitch Richmond	.50	.15
❑ 48	Olden Polynice	.25	.07
❑ 49	Derrick Coleman	.25	.07
❑ 50	Ervin Johnson	.25	.07
❑ 51	Shandon Anderson	.25	.07
❑ 52	Jamal Mashburn	.50	.15
❑ 53	Joe Smith	.50	.15
❑ 54	Bo Outlaw	.25	.07
❑ 55	Clifford Robinson	.25	.07
❑ 56	Scottie Pippen	1.25	.35
❑ 57	Chris Webber	.75	.23
❑ 58	Doug Christie	.50	.15
❑ 59	Michael Dickerson	.50	.15
❑ 60	Anthony Mason	.50	.15

❑ 61 Shawn Bradley .25 .07
❑ 62 Reggie Miller .75 .23
❑ 63 P.J. Brown .25 .07
❑ 64 Wally Szczerbiak .50 .15
❑ 65 Keon Clark .50 .15
❑ 66 Anthony Peeler .25 .07
❑ 67 Doug West .25 .07
❑ 68 Antoine Walker .75 .23
❑ 69 Trajan Langdon .50 .15
❑ 70 Mark Jackson .25 .07
❑ 71 Sam Cassell .75 .23
❑ 72 Kurt Thomas .50 .15
❑ 73 Ruben Patterson .50 .15
❑ 74 Alvin Williams .25 .07
❑ 75 Juwan Howard .50 .15
❑ 76 Baron Davis .75 .23
❑ 77 Otis Thorpe .25 .07
❑ 78 Austin Croshere .50 .15
❑ 79 Tony Delk .25 .07
❑ 80 William Avery .25 .07
❑ 81 Matt Geiger .25 .07
❑ 82 Richard Hamilton .50 .15
❑ 83 Ricky Davis .50 .15
❑ 84 Hubert Davis .25 .07
❑ 85 Jalen Rose .75 .23
❑ 86 Theo Ratliff .50 .15
❑ 87 Bobby Jackson .50 .15
❑ 88 Glenn Robinson .75 .23
❑ 89 Kendall Gill .25 .07
❑ 90 Laron Profit .25 .07
❑ 91 Brad Miller .75 .23
❑ 92 Cedric Ceballos .25 .07
❑ 93 Arvydas Sabonis .50 .15
❑ 94 Vitaly Potapenko .25 .07
❑ 95 Rod Strickland .25 .07
❑ 96 Erick Dampier .50 .15
❑ 97 Ryan Bowen .25 .07
❑ 98 Dale Davis .25 .07
❑ 99 Larry Johnson .50 .15
❑ 100 John Thomas .25 .07
❑ 101 Rodney Rogers .25 .07
❑ 102 Ray Allen .75 .23
❑ 103 Isaac Austin .25 .07
❑ 104 Radoslav Nesterovic .50 .15
❑ 105 Tariq Abdul-Wahad .25 .07
❑ 106 Jonathan Bender .50 .15
❑ 107 Tim Hardaway .50 .15
❑ 108 Jamie Feick .25 .07
❑ 109 Toni Kukoc .50 .15
❑ 110 Tyrone Corbin .25 .07
❑ 111 Aleksandar Radojevic .25 .07
❑ 112 Tony Battie .25 .07
❑ 113 Andre Miller .50 .15
❑ 114 Derek Anderson .50 .15
❑ 115 Tim Thomas .50 .15
❑ 116 Corey Maggette .50 .15
❑ 117 Rasheed Wallace .75 .23
❑ 118 Shammond Williams .25 .07
❑ 119 Charlie Ward .25 .07
❑ 120 Paul Pierce .75 .23
❑ 121 Shawn Kemp .50 .15
❑ 122 Darrell Armstrong .25 .07
❑ 123 Fred Vinson .25 .07
❑ 124 Jim Jackson .25 .07
❑ 125 Steve Nash .75 .23
❑ 126 Michael Stewart .25 .07
❑ 127 Maurice Taylor .25 .07
❑ 128 Michael Ruffin .25 .07
❑ 129 Vlade Divac .50 .15
❑ 130 LaPhonso Ellis .25 .07
❑ 131 Eddie Jones .75 .23
❑ 132 Hakeem Olajuwon .75 .23
❑ 133 Rick Fox .50 .15
❑ 134 Patrick Ewing .75 .23
❑ 135 Brian Grant .50 .15
❑ 136 Jaren Jackson .25 .07
❑ 137 Christian Laettner .50 .15
❑ 138 Greg Ostertag .25 .07
❑ 139 Anfernee Hardaway .75 .23
❑ 140 Nick Van Exel .75 .23
❑ 141 Jason Caffey .25 .07
❑ 142 Michael Olowokandi .25 .07
❑ 143 Darvin Ham .25 .07
❑ 144 Calbert Cheaney .25 .07
❑ 145 Steve Smith .50 .15
❑ 146 Jason Williams .50 .15
❑ 147 Jelani McCoy .25 .07
❑ 148 Karl Malone .75 .23
❑ 149 Dikembe Mutombo .50 .15
❑ 150 Wesley Person .25 .07
❑ 151 Kelvin Cato .25 .07
❑ 152 Alonzo Mourning .50 .15
❑ 153 Terry Mills .25 .07
❑ 154 Allen Iverson 1.50 .45
❑ 155 Bonzi Wells .50 .15
❑ 156 Antonio Daniels .25 .07
❑ 157 Shareef Abdur-Rahim .75 .23
❑ 158 Randy Brown .25 .07
❑ 159 Mike Bibby .50 .15
❑ 160 Travis Best .25 .07
❑ 161 Dan Majerle .50 .15
❑ 162 Aaron McKie .50 .15
❑ 163 Jason Terry .75 .23
❑ 164 Michael Finley .75 .23
❑ 165 Antonio Davis .25 .07
❑ 166 Lindsey Hunter .25 .07
❑ 167 Cuttino Mobley .50 .15
❑ 168 Glen Rice .50 .15
❑ 169 Stephon Marbury .75 .23
❑ 170 Sean Elliott .50 .15
❑ 171 Cedric Henderson .25 .07
❑ 172 Eric Snow .50 .15
❑ 173 Othella Harrington .25 .07
❑ 174 Vonteego Cummings .25 .07
❑ 175 John Amaechi .25 .07
❑ 176 Allan Houston .50 .15
❑ 177 Shawn Marion .75 .23
❑ 178 Scot Pollard .25 .07
❑ 179 Elton Brand .75 .23
❑ 180 Loy Vaught .25 .07
❑ 181 Larry Hughes .50 .15
❑ 182 Shaquille O'Neal 2.00 .60
❑ 183 Keith Van Horn .75 .23
❑ 184 Terry Porter .25 .07
❑ 185 Quincy Lewis .25 .07
❑ 186 Alan Henderson .25 .07
❑ 187 Brevin Knight .25 .07
❑ 188 Walt Williams .25 .07
❑ 189 Clarence Weatherspoon .25 .07
❑ 190 Marcus Camby .50 .15
❑ 191 Corliss Williamson .50 .15
❑ 192 Gary Payton .75 .23
❑ 193 Felipe Lopez .25 .07
❑ 194 Elden Campbell .25 .07
❑ 195 Jerome Williams .25 .07
❑ 196 Antawn Jamison .75 .23
❑ 197 Gerard King .25 .07
❑ 198 Andrae Patterson .25 .07
❑ 199 Vin Baker .50 .15
❑ 200 Tracy McGrady 2.00 .60
❑ 201 Chris Carrawell RC 2.00 .60
❑ 202 Eduardo Najera RC 5.00 1.50
❑ 203 Olumide Oyedeji RC 2.00 .60
❑ 204 Hanno Mottola RC 2.00 .60
❑ 205 Dan McClintock RC 2.00 .60
❑ 206 Jacquay Walls RC 2.00 .60
❑ 207 Corey Hightower RC 2.00 .60
❑ 208 Jamal Crawford RC 2.50 .75
❑ 209 Soumaila Samake RC 2.00 .60
❑ 210 Michael Redd RC 5.00 1.50
❑ 211 Jason Hart RC 2.00 .60
❑ 212 Mark Karcher RC 2.00 .60
❑ 213 Chris Porter RC 2.00 .60
❑ 214 Eddie House RC 2.00 .60
❑ 215 Jabari Smith RC 2.00 .60
❑ 216 Dan Langhi RC 2.00 .60
❑ 217 Desmond Mason RC 2.00 .60
❑ 218 Darius Miles RC 10.00 3.00
❑ 219 Donnell Harvey RC 2.00 .60
❑ 220 DeShawn Stevenson RC 2.00 .60
❑ 221 Kenyon Martin RC 12.00 3.60
❑ 222 Joel Przybilla RC 2.00 .60
❑ 223 Keyon Dooling RC 2.00 .60
❑ 224 Speedy Claxton RC 2.00 .60
❑ 225 Jerome Moiso RC 2.00 .60
❑ 226 Hidayet Turkoglu RC 8.00 2.40
❑ 227 Mark Madsen RC 2.00 .60
❑ 228 Morris Peterson RC 6.00 1.80
❑ 229 Courtney Alexander RC 4.00 1.20
❑ 230 Etan Thomas RC 2.00 .60
❑ 231 Mateen Cleaves RC 2.00 .60
❑ 232 Stromile Swift RC 6.00 1.80
❑ 233 Marcus Fizer RC 2.00 .60
❑ 234 Quentin Richardson RC 10.00 3.00
❑ 235 Jason Collier RC 2.00 .60
❑ 236 Jamaal Magloire RC 2.00 .60
❑ 237 Erick Barkley RC 2.00 .60
❑ 238 DerMarr Johnson RC 2.00 .60
❑ 239 Chris Mihm RC 2.00 .60
❑ 240 Mamadou N'diaye RC 2.00 .60
❑ 241 Mike Miller RC 10.00 3.00

2001-02 Fleer Premium

	Nm-Mt	Ex-Mt
COMPLETE SET (185)	350.00	105.00
COMP.SET w/o SP's (1-150)	40.00	12.00
COMMON CARD (1-150)	.25	.07
COMMON ROOKIE (151-185)	3.00	.90

❑ 1 Shareef Abdur-Rahim .75 .23
❑ 2 Charlie Ward .25 .07
❑ 3 Anfernee Hardaway .75 .23
❑ 4 Robert Horry .50 .15
❑ 5 Michael Jordan 15.00 4.50
❑ 6 Trajan Langdon .25 .07
❑ 7 Dan Majerle .50 .15
❑ 8 Tracy McGrady 2.00 .60
❑ 9 Alonzo Mourning .50 .15
❑ 10 Gary Payton .75 .23
❑ 11 Erick Barkley .50 .15
❑ 12 Jerry Stackhouse .75 .23
❑ 13 Vince Carter 2.00 .60
❑ 14 Speedy Claxton .50 .15
❑ 15 DerMarr Johnson .50 .15
❑ 16 Bryon Russell .25 .07
❑ 17 Derrick Coleman .25 .07
❑ 18 Kevin Willis .25 .07
❑ 19 Dirk Nowitzki 1.25 .35
❑ 20 Derek Anderson .50 .15
❑ 21 Tim Hardaway .50 .15
❑ 22 Avery Johnson .25 .07
❑ 23 Quincy Lewis .25 .07
❑ 24 Shawn Marion .75 .23
❑ 25 Joe Smith .50 .15
❑ 26 Tim Thomas .50 .15
❑ 27 Bonzi Wells .50 .15
❑ 28 Ron Artest .50 .15
❑ 29 Elton Brand .75 .23
❑ 30 Mateen Cleaves .50 .15
❑ 31 Marcus Fizer .50 .15
❑ 32 Ervin Johnson .25 .07
❑ 33 Mark Madsen .50 .15
❑ 34 Andre Miller .50 .15
❑ 35 Nazr Mohammed .25 .07
❑ 36 Dikembe Mutombo .50 .15
❑ 37 Ben Wallace .75 .23
❑ 38 Scottie Pippen 1.25 .35
❑ 39 Theo Ratliff .50 .15
❑ 40 Hidayet Turkoglu .50 .15
❑ 41 Alvin Williams .25 .07
❑ 42 Corey Maggette .50 .15
❑ 43 Steve Francis .75 .23
❑ 44 Dean Garrett .25 .07
❑ 45 Wally Szczerbiak .50 .15
❑ 46 Brent Barry .50 .15
❑ 47 Vlade Divac .50 .15
❑ 48 LaPhonso Ellis .25 .07
❑ 49 Tyrone Hill .25 .07
❑ 50 Toni Kukoc .50 .15
❑ 51 George Lynch .25 .07
❑ 52 Antonio McDyess .50 .15

Card		
❑ 53 Paul Pierce	.75	.23
❑ 54 Mitch Richmond	.50	.15
❑ 55 Latrell Sprewell	.75	.23
❑ 56 Otis Thorpe	.50	.15
❑ 57 Ray Allen	.75	.23
❑ 58 Mike Bibby	.75	.23
❑ 59 P.J. Brown	.25	.07
❑ 60 Allan Houston	.50	.15
❑ 61 Stephon Marbury	.75	.23
❑ 62 Aaron McKie	.50	.15
❑ 63 Reggie Miller	.75	.23
❑ 64 Eduardo Najera	.50	.15
❑ 65 Eddie Robinson	.50	.15
❑ 66 John Stockton	.75	.23
❑ 67 Chris Webber	.75	.23
❑ 68 Kenny Anderson	.50	.15
❑ 69 Alan Henderson	.25	.07
❑ 70 Dan Langhi	.50	.15
❑ 71 Rashard Lewis	.50	.15
❑ 72 Donyell Marshall	.50	.15
❑ 73 Charles Oakley	.25	.07
❑ 74 Stephen Jackson	.50	.15
❑ 75 Clarence Weatherspoon	.25	.07
❑ 76 David Wesley	.25	.07
❑ 77 Kobe Bryant	3.00	.90
❑ 78 Tom Gugliotta	.25	.07
❑ 79 Darius Miles	.75	.23
❑ 80 Cuttino Mobley	.50	.15
❑ 81 Jason Terry	.75	.23
❑ 82 Shandon Anderson	.25	.07
❑ 83 Antonio Daniels	.25	.07
❑ 84 Larry Hughes	.50	.15
❑ 85 Raef LaFrentz	.50	.15
❑ 86 Kenyon Martin	.75	.23
❑ 87 Lamar Odom	.75	.23
❑ 88 Jermaine O'Neal	.75	.23
❑ 89 Glenn Robinson	.75	.23
❑ 90 Damon Stoudamire	.50	.15
❑ 91 Eddie House	.50	.15
❑ 92 Antonio Davis	.25	.07
❑ 93 Rick Fox	.50	.15
❑ 94 Allen Iverson	1.50	.45
❑ 95 Chris Mihm	.50	.15
❑ 96 Hakeem Olajuwon	.75	.23
❑ 97 Clifford Robinson	.25	.07
❑ 98 Derek Fisher	.75	.23
❑ 99 Joel Przybilla	.50	.15
❑ 100 Sean Rooks	.25	.07
❑ 101 Jason Kidd	1.25	.35
❑ 102 Antoine Walker	.75	.23
❑ 103 Jason Williams	.50	.15
❑ 104 Jamal Mashburn	.50	.15
❑ 105 Courtney Alexander	.50	.15
❑ 106 Vin Baker	.50	.15
❑ 107 Chauncey Billups	.50	.15
❑ 108 Marcus Camby	.50	.15
❑ 109 Kevin Garnett	1.50	.45
❑ 110 Juwan Howard	.50	.15
❑ 111 Marc Jackson	.50	.15
❑ 112 Karl Malone	.75	.23
❑ 113 Ricky Davis	.50	.15
❑ 114 Desmond Mason	.50	.15
❑ 115 Jerome Moiso	.50	.15
❑ 116 Steve Nash	.75	.23
❑ 117 Quentin Richardson	.50	.15
❑ 118 Peja Stojakovic	.75	.23
❑ 119 Rasheed Wallace	.75	.23
❑ 120 Travis Best	.25	.07
❑ 121 Terrell Brandon	.50	.15
❑ 122 Austin Croshere	.50	.15
❑ 123 Tony Delk	.25	.07
❑ 124 Anthony Mason	.50	.15
❑ 125 Patrick Ewing	.75	.23
❑ 126 Brian Grant	.50	.15
❑ 127 Bobby Jackson	.50	.15
❑ 128 Eddie Jones	.75	.23
❑ 129 Popeye Jones	.25	.07
❑ 130 Brevin Knight	.25	.07
❑ 131 Mike Miller	.75	.23
❑ 132 Shaquille O'Neal	2.00	.60
❑ 133 Morris Peterson	.50	.15
❑ 134 Mookie Blaylock	.25	.07
❑ 135 David Robinson	.75	.23
❑ 136 John Starks	.50	.15
❑ 137 Stromile Swift	.50	.15
❑ 138 Nick Van Exel	.75	.23
❑ 139 Keith Van Horn	.75	.23
❑ 140 Antawn Jamison	.75	.23
❑ 141 Kurt Thomas	.50	.15
❑ 142 Sam Cassell	.75	.23
❑ 143 Tim Duncan	1.50	.45
❑ 144 Baron Davis	.75	.23
❑ 145 Jerome Williams	.25	.07
❑ 146 Michael Finley	.75	.23
❑ 147 Richard Hamilton	.50	.15
❑ 148 Grant Hill	.75	.23
❑ 149 Jalen Rose	.75	.23
❑ 150 Steve Smith	.50	.15
❑ 151 Kwame Brown RC	8.00	2.40
❑ 152 Jeryl Sasser RC	3.00	.90
❑ 153 Shane Battier RC	6.00	1.80
❑ 154 Gilbert Arenas RC	10.00	3.00
❑ 155 Jarron Collins RC	3.00	.90
❑ 156 Jamaal Tinsley RC	6.00	1.80
❑ 157 Brandon Armstrong RC	5.00	1.50
❑ 158 Michael Bradley RC	3.00	.90
❑ 159 Tyson Chandler RC	10.00	3.00
❑ 160 Joseph Forte RC	6.00	1.80
❑ 161 Brendan Haywood RC	5.00	1.50
❑ 162 Joe Johnson RC	6.00	1.80
❑ 163 Vladimir Radmanovic RC	5.00	1.50
❑ 164 Gerald Wallace RC	8.00	2.40
❑ 165 Steven Hunter RC	3.00	.90
❑ 166 Richard Jefferson RC	12.00	3.60
❑ 167 DeSagana Diop RC	3.00	.90
❑ 168 Terence Morris RC	3.00	.90
❑ 169 Jason Richardson RC	12.00	3.60
❑ 170 Jeff Trepagnier RC	3.00	.90
❑ 171 Kirk Haston RC	3.00	.90
❑ 172 Eddy Curry RC	10.00	3.00
❑ 173 Eddie Griffin RC	6.00	1.80
❑ 174 Omar Cook RC	3.00	.90
❑ 175 Pau Gasol RC	15.00	4.50
❑ 176 Troy Murphy RC	8.00	2.40
❑ 177 Trenton Hassell RC	6.00	1.80
❑ 178 Kedrick Brown RC	3.00	.90
❑ 179 Zeljko Rebraca RC	3.00	.90
❑ 180 Tony Parker RC	15.00	4.50
❑ 181 Rodney White RC	5.00	1.50
❑ 182 Jason Collins RC	3.00	.90
❑ 183 Samuel Dalembert RC	3.00	.90
❑ 184 Zach Randolph RC	12.00	3.60
❑ 185 Will Solomon RC	3.00	.90

2002-03 Fleer Premium

	Nm-Mt	Ex-Mt
COMP.SET w/o SP's (110)	40.00	12.00
COMMON ROOKIE (111-140)	4.00	1.20
❑ 1 Tracy McGrady	2.00	.60
❑ 2 Tim Duncan	1.50	.45
❑ 3 Shaquille O'Neal	2.00	.60
❑ 4 Jason Kidd	1.25	.35
❑ 5 Kobe Bryant	3.00	.90
❑ 6 Kevin Garnett	1.50	.45
❑ 7 Chris Webber	.75	.23
❑ 8 Dirk Nowitzki	1.25	.35
❑ 9 Gary Payton	.75	.23
❑ 10 Allen Iverson	1.50	.45
❑ 11 Ben Wallace	.75	.23
❑ 12 Jermaine O'Neal	.75	.23
❑ 13 Dikembe Mutombo	.50	.15
❑ 14 Paul Pierce	.75	.23
❑ 15 Steve Nash	.75	.23
❑ 16 Pau Gasol	.75	.23
❑ 17 Jason Richardson	.75	.23
❑ 18 Tony Parker	.75	.23
❑ 19 Andrei Kirilenko	.75	.23
❑ 20 Shane Battier	.75	.23
❑ 21 Jamaal Tinsley	.75	.23
❑ 22 Richard Jefferson	.50	.15
❑ 23 Joe Johnson	.75	.23
❑ 24 Eddie Griffin	.50	.15
❑ 25 Zeljko Rebraca	.50	.15
❑ 26 Vladimir Radmanovic	.50	.15
❑ 27 Damon Stoudamire	.50	.15
❑ 28 Eddie Jones	.75	.23
❑ 29 Tyson Chandler	.75	.23
❑ 30 Karl Malone	.75	.23
❑ 31 David Wesley	.25	.07
❑ 32 Steve Francis	.75	.23
❑ 33 Hakeem Olajuwon	.75	.23
❑ 34 Baron Davis	.75	.23
❑ 35 Antonio McDyess	.50	.15
❑ 36 Mike Bibby	.75	.23
❑ 37 Bonzi Wells	.50	.15
❑ 38 Ray Allen	.75	.23
❑ 39 Doug Christie	.50	.15
❑ 40 Richard Hamilton	.50	.15
❑ 41 Grant Hill	.75	.23
❑ 42 Elton Brand	.75	.23
❑ 43 Gilbert Arenas	.75	.23
❑ 44 Vlade Divac	.50	.15
❑ 45 Sam Cassell	.75	.23
❑ 46 Jalen Rose	.75	.23
❑ 47 PejaStojakovic	.75	.23
❑ 48 Glenn Robinson	.75	.23
❑ 49 Ricky Davis	.50	.15
❑ 50 Antonio Daniels	.25	.07
❑ 51 Tim Thomas	.50	.15
❑ 52 Andre Miller	.50	.15
❑ 53 Stephon Marbury	.75	.23
❑ 54 Robert Horry	.50	.15
❑ 55 Tony Delk	.25	.07
❑ 56 David Robinson	.75	.23
❑ 57 Radoslav Nesterovic	.50	.15
❑ 58 Lamond Murray	.25	.07
❑ 59 Brent Barry	.50	.15
❑ 60 Wally Szczerbiak	.50	.15
❑ 61 Lee Nailon	.25	.07
❑ 62 Rashard Lewis	.50	.15
❑ 63 Kenyon Martin	.75	.23
❑ 64 Michael Finley	.75	.23
❑ 65 John Stockton	.75	.23
❑ 66 Allan Houston	.50	.15
❑ 67 Terrell Brandon	.50	.15
❑ 68 Donyell Marshall	.50	.15
❑ 69 Marcus Camby	.50	.15
❑ 70 Cuttino Mobley	.50	.15
❑ 71 Shawn Marion	.75	.23
❑ 72 Jason Williams	.50	.15
❑ 73 Rodney Rogers	.25	.07
❑ 74 Scottie Pippen	1.25	.35
❑ 75 Brian Grant	.50	.15
❑ 76 Clifford Robinson	.25	.07
❑ 77 Antoine Walker	.75	.23
❑ 78 Michael Dickerson	.25	.07
❑ 79 Latrell Sprewell	.75	.23
❑ 80 Ron Artest	.50	.15
❑ 81 Shareef Abdur-Rahim	.75	.23
❑ 82 Michael Jordan	6.00	1.80
❑ 83 Mike Miller	.75	.23
❑ 84 Corey Maggette	.50	.15
❑ 85 Antawn Jamison	.75	.23
❑ 86 Rasheed Wallace	.75	.23
❑ 87 Alonzo Mourning	.50	.15
❑ 88 Eddy Curry	.75	.23
❑ 89 Derrick Coleman	.25	.07
❑ 90 Joe Smith	.50	.15
❑ 91 Darius Miles	.75	.23
❑ 92 Nick Van Exel	.75	.23
❑ 93 Derek Fisher	.75	.23
❑ 94 Nazr Mohammed	.25	.07
❑ 95 Morris Peterson	.50	.15
❑ 96 Jamal Mashburn	.50	.15
❑ 97 Jerry Stackhouse	.75	.23
❑ 98 Kwame Brown	.50	.15
❑ 99 Darrell Armstrong	.25	.07
❑ 100 Reggie Miller	.75	.23
❑ 101 Desmond Mason	.50	.15
❑ 102 Antonio Davis	.25	.07

❑ 103 Elden Campbell	.25	.07
❑ 104 Voshon Lenard	.25	.07
❑ 105 Eric Snow	.50	.15
❑ 106 Lamar Odom	.75	.23
❑ 107 Toni Kukoc	.50	.15
❑ 108 Vince Carter	2.00	.60
❑ 109 Keith Van Horn	.50	.15
❑ 110 Juwan Howard	.50	.15
❑ 111 Jay Williams RC	5.00	1.50
❑ 112 Rookie Exchange	20.00	6.00
❑ 113 Mike Dunleavy RC	6.00	1.80
❑ 114 Drew Gooden RC	10.00	3.00
❑ 115 Nikoloz Tskitishvili RC	4.00	1.20
❑ 116 DaJuan Wagner RC	6.00	1.80
❑ 117 Nene Hilario RC	4.00	1.20
❑ 118 Chris Wilcox RC	5.00	1.50
❑ 119 Amare Stoudemire RC	15.00	4.50
❑ 120 Caron Butler RC	8.00	2.40
❑ 121 Rookie Exchange	4.00	1.20
❑ 122 Marcus Haislip RC	4.00	1.20
❑ 123 Jared Jeffries RC	4.00	1.20
❑ 124 Fred Jones RC	4.00	1.20
❑ 125 Bostjan Nachbar RC	4.00	1.20
❑ 126 Jiri Welsch RC	4.00	1.20
❑ 127 Juan Dixon RC	6.00	1.80
❑ 128 Curtis Borchardt RC	4.00	1.20
❑ 129 Ryan Humphrey RC	4.00	1.20
❑ 130 Kareem Rush RC	5.00	1.50
❑ 131 Qyntel Woods RC	4.00	1.20
❑ 132 Casey Jacobsen RC	4.00	1.20
❑ 133 Tayshaun Prince RC	5.00	1.50
❑ 134 Carlos Boozer RC	15.00	4.50
❑ 135 Frank Williams RC	4.00	1.20
❑ 136 John Salmons RC	4.00	1.20
❑ 137 Rookie Exchange	4.00	1.20
❑ 138 Dan Dickau RC	4.00	1.20
❑ 139 Steve Logan RC	4.00	1.20
❑ 140 Roger Mason RC	4.00	1.20

2001-02 Fleer Shoebox

	Nm-Mt	Ex-Mt
COMP.SET w/o SP's (150)	40.00	12.00
COMMON CARD (1-150)	.25	.07
COMMON ROOKIE (151-180)	2.50	.75
❑ 1 Tariq Abdul-Wahad	.25	.07
❑ 2 Glen Rice	.50	.15
❑ 3 Derek Anderson	.50	.15
❑ 4 Desmond Mason	.50	.15
❑ 5 Al Harrington	.50	.15
❑ 6 Mitch Richmond	.50	.15
❑ 7 Felipe Lopez	.25	.07
❑ 8 Andre Miller	.50	.15
❑ 9 Jerry Stackhouse	.75	.23
❑ 10 Jalen Rose	.75	.23
❑ 11 Lindsey Hunter	.25	.07
❑ 12 Tim Thomas	.50	.15
❑ 13 Wally Szczerbiak	.50	.15
❑ 14 Vince Carter	2.00	.60
❑ 15 Nick Van Exel	.75	.23
❑ 16 Jon Barry	.25	.07
❑ 17 Aaron McKie	.50	.15
❑ 18 Iakovos Tsakalidis	.25	.07
❑ 19 Chris Webber	.75	.23
❑ 20 Karl Malone	.75	.23
❑ 21 Shareef Abdur-Rahim	.75	.23
❑ 22 Baron Davis	.75	.23
❑ 23 Michael Doleac	.25	.07
❑ 24 Jermaine O'Neal	.75	.23
❑ 25 Elton Brand	.75	.23
❑ 26 Glenn Robinson	.75	.23
❑ 27 Tracy McGrady	2.00	.60
❑ 28 Allen Iverson	1.50	.45
❑ 29 Anfernee Hardaway	.75	.23
❑ 30 Scot Pollard	.25	.07
❑ 31 David Robinson	.75	.23
❑ 32 John Stockton	.75	.23
❑ 33 Jason Williams	.50	.15
❑ 34 Voshon Lenard	.25	.07
❑ 35 Shaquille O'Neal	2.00	.60
❑ 36 Grant Hill	.75	.23
❑ 37 Shawn Marion	.75	.23
❑ 38 Vin Baker	.50	.15
❑ 39 Raef LaFrentz	.50	.15
❑ 40 Steve Francis	.75	.23
❑ 41 Michael Dickerson	.50	.15
❑ 42 Hidayet Turkoglu	.50	.15
❑ 43 Patrick Ewing	.75	.23
❑ 44 Dirk Nowitzki	1.25	.35
❑ 45 Keyon Dooling	.50	.15
❑ 46 Marcus Camby	.50	.15
❑ 47 Bonzi Wells	.50	.15
❑ 48 Tim Duncan	1.50	.45
❑ 49 Jamaal Magloire	.50	.15
❑ 50 Rick Fox	.50	.15
❑ 51 Kendall Gill	.25	.07
❑ 52 Michael Redd	.75	.23
❑ 53 Keith Van Horn	.75	.23
❑ 54 Eric Snow	.50	.15
❑ 55 Theo Ratliff	.50	.15
❑ 56 Clifford Robinson	.25	.07
❑ 57 Moochie Norris	.25	.07
❑ 58 Alonzo Mourning	.50	.15
❑ 59 Joe Smith	.50	.15
❑ 60 Brent Barry	.50	.15
❑ 61 Alvin Williams	.25	.07
❑ 62 Antoine Walker	.75	.23
❑ 63 Antonio McDyess	.50	.15
❑ 64 Derek Fisher	.75	.23
❑ 65 Ron Mercer	.50	.15
❑ 66 Hakeem Olajuwon	.75	.23
❑ 67 Jamal Crawford	.50	.15
❑ 68 Chris Mihm	.50	.15
❑ 69 Ben Wallace	.75	.23
❑ 70 Brian Grant	.50	.15
❑ 71 Kevin Garnett	1.50	.45
❑ 72 Shandon Anderson	.25	.07
❑ 73 Shawn Bradley	.25	.07
❑ 74 Danny Fortson	.25	.07
❑ 75 Jeff McInnis	.25	.07
❑ 76 LaPhonso Ellis	.25	.07
❑ 77 Sam Cassell	.75	.23
❑ 78 Rasheed Wallace	.75	.23
❑ 79 Malik Rose	.25	.07
❑ 80 Jahidi White	.25	.07
❑ 81 Milt Palacio	.25	.07
❑ 82 Tim Hardaway	.50	.15
❑ 83 Antonio Daniels	.25	.07
❑ 84 Tyronn Lue	.25	.07
❑ 85 Cuttino Mobley	.50	.15
❑ 86 DerMarr Johnson	.50	.15
❑ 87 Lamond Murray	.25	.07
❑ 88 Larry Hughes	.50	.15
❑ 89 Reggie Miller	.75	.23
❑ 90 Lorenzen Wright	.25	.07
❑ 91 Eddie Jones	.75	.23
❑ 92 Anthony Mason	.50	.15
❑ 93 Todd MacCulloch	.25	.07
❑ 94 Speedy Claxton	.50	.15
❑ 95 Mateen Cleaves	.50	.15
❑ 96 Gary Payton	.75	.23
❑ 97 Morris Peterson	.50	.15
❑ 98 Mike Miller	.75	.23
❑ 99 Hanno Mottola	.50	.15
❑ 100 Steve Nash	.75	.23
❑ 101 Stromile Swift	.50	.15
❑ 102 Ray Allen	.75	.23
❑ 103 Mark Jackson	.50	.15
❑ 104 Stephon Marbury	.75	.23
❑ 105 Mike Bibby	.75	.23
❑ 106 Rashard Lewis	.50	.15
❑ 107 Jason Kidd	1.25	.35
❑ 108 P.J. Brown	.25	.07
❑ 109 Kobe Bryant	3.00	.90
❑ 110 Tom Gugliotta	.25	.07
❑ 111 Richard Hamilton	.50	.15
❑ 112 Antawn Jamison	.75	.23
❑ 113 Lamar Odom	.75	.23
❑ 114 Kurt Thomas	.50	.15
❑ 115 Robert Horry	.50	.15
❑ 116 Dikembe Mutombo	.50	.15
❑ 117 Tony Delk	.25	.07
❑ 118 Peja Stojakovic	.75	.23
❑ 119 Donyell Marshall	.50	.15
❑ 120 Paul Pierce	.75	.23
❑ 121 Michael Finley	.75	.23
❑ 122 Quentin Richardson	.50	.15
❑ 123 Kenyon Martin	.75	.23
❑ 124 Allan Houston	.50	.15
❑ 125 Scottie Pippen	1.25	.35
❑ 126 Steve Smith	.50	.15
❑ 127 Bryon Russell	.25	.07
❑ 128 James Posey	.50	.15
❑ 129 Terrell Brandon	.50	.15
❑ 130 Toni Kukoc	.50	.15
❑ 131 Stephen Jackson	.50	.15
❑ 132 Marc Jackson	.50	.15
❑ 133 Kelvin Cato	.25	.07
❑ 134 Travis Best	.25	.07
❑ 135 David Wesley	.25	.07
❑ 136 Anthony Carter	.50	.15
❑ 137 Michael Jordan	12.00	3.60
❑ 138 Darrell Armstrong	.25	.07
❑ 139 Matt Harpring	.75	.23
❑ 140 Antonio Davis	.25	.07
❑ 141 Courtney Alexander	.50	.15
❑ 142 Jamal Mashburn	.50	.15
❑ 143 Jason Terry	.75	.23
❑ 144 Marcus Fizer	.50	.15
❑ 145 Juwan Howard	.50	.15
❑ 146 Darius Miles	.75	.23
❑ 147 Latrell Sprewell	.75	.23
❑ 148 Damon Stoudamire	.50	.15
❑ 149 John Starks	.50	.15
❑ 150 Jumaine Jones	.50	.15
❑ 151 Kedrick Brown RC	2.50	.75
❑ 152 Trenton Hassell RC	4.00	1.20
❑ 153 Kwame Brown RC	5.00	1.50
❑ 154 Terence Morris RC	2.50	.75
❑ 155 Richard Jefferson RC	5.00	1.50
❑ 156 Vladimir Radmanovic RC	3.00	.90
❑ 157 Brandon Armstrong RC	3.00	.90
❑ 158 Kirk Haston RC	2.50	.75
❑ 159 Eddie Griffin RC	4.00	1.20
❑ 160 Steven Hunter RC	2.50	.75
❑ 161 Troy Murphy RC	5.00	1.50
❑ 162 Andrei Kirilenko RC	6.00	1.80
❑ 163 Jeryl Sasser RC	2.50	.75
❑ 164 Michael Bradley RC	2.50	.75
❑ 165 Rodney White RC	3.00	.90
❑ 166 Loren Woods RC	2.50	.75
❑ 167 Zach Randolph RC	8.00	2.40
❑ 168 Joe Johnson RC	4.00	1.20
❑ 169 Eddy Curry RC	6.00	1.80
❑ 170 Jason Richardson RC	8.00	2.40
❑ 171 DeSagana Diop RC	2.50	.75
❑ 172 Jamaal Tinsley RC	4.00	1.20
❑ 173 Pau Gasol RC	10.00	3.00
❑ 174 Jason Collins RC	2.50	.75
❑ 175 Zeljko Rebraca RC	2.50	.75
❑ 176 Shane Battier RC	4.00	1.20
❑ 177 Gerald Wallace RC	5.00	1.50
❑ 178 Joseph Forte RC	6.00	1.80
❑ 179 Tyson Chandler RC	6.00	1.80
❑ 180 Tony Parker RC	10.00	3.00

2000-01 Fleer Showcase

	Nm-Mt	Ex-Mt
COMPLETE SET w/o RCs (90)	30.00	9.00
COMMON CARD (1-90)	.30	.09
COMMON ROOKIE (91-100)	12.00	3.60
COMMON ROOKIE (101-110)	5.00	1.50
COMMON ROOKIE (111-121)	4.00	1.20
❑ 1 Vince Carter	2.50	.75
❑ 2 Lamar Odom	1.00	.30
❑ 3 Larry Hughes	.60	.18
❑ 4 Brian Grant	.60	.18
❑ 5 Bryon Russell	.30	.09
❑ 6 Allan Houston	.60	.18

❑	7 Juwan Howard	.60	.18
❑	8 Cuttino Mobley	.60	.18
❑	9 Keith Van Horn	1.00	.30
❑	10 Mike Bibby	1.00	.30
❑	11 Jerome Williams	.30	.09
❑	12 Ray Allen	1.00	.30
❑	13 Antonio Davis	.30	.09
❑	14 Adrian Griffin	.30	.09
❑	15 Dan Majerle	.60	.18
❑	16 Rasheed Wallace	1.00	.30
❑	17 Antonio McDyess	.60	.18
❑	18 Tim Thomas	.60	.18
❑	19 Theo Ratliff	.60	.18
❑	20 Charles Oakley	.30	.09
❑	21 Nick Van Exel	1.00	.30
❑	22 Glenn Robinson	1.00	.30
❑	23 Cal Bowdler	.30	.09
❑	24 Raef LaFrentz	.60	.18
❑	25 Terrell Brandon	.60	.18
❑	26 Allen Iverson	2.00	.60
❑	27 Patrick Ewing	1.00	.30
❑	28 Ron Artest	.60	.18
❑	29 Michael Olowokandi	.30	.09
❑	30 Derek Anderson	.60	.18
❑	31 Dirk Nowitzki	1.50	.45
❑	32 Wally Szczerbiak	.60	.18
❑	33 Gary Payton	1.00	.30
❑	34 Michael Finley	1.00	.30
❑	35 Chauncey Billups	.60	.18
❑	36 Jason Kidd	1.50	.45
❑	37 Rashard Lewis	.60	.18
❑	38 Andre Miller	.60	.18
❑	39 Kevin Garnett	2.00	.60
❑	40 Tim Duncan	2.00	.60
❑	41 Jalen Rose	1.00	.30
❑	42 Marcus Camby	.60	.18
❑	43 Richard Hamilton	.60	.18
❑	44 Austin Croshere	.60	.18
❑	45 Latrell Sprewell	1.00	.30
❑	46 Shawn Marion	1.00	.30
❑	47 Jahidi White	.30	.09
❑	48 Elton Brand	1.00	.30
❑	49 Reggie Miller	1.00	.30
❑	50 David Robinson	1.00	.30
❑	51 Trajan Langdon	.30	.09
❑	52 Jonathan Bender	.60	.18
❑	53 Antonio Daniels	.30	.09
❑	54 Jason Terry	1.00	.30
❑	55 Eddie Jones	1.00	.30
❑	56 Mitch Richmond	.60	.18
❑	57 Antoine Walker	1.00	.30
❑	58 Robert Horry	.60	.18
❑	59 Tracy McGrady	2.50	.75
❑	60 Scottie Pippen	1.50	.45
❑	61 Jerry Stackhouse	1.00	.30
❑	62 Zydrunas Ilgauskas	.60	.18
❑	63 Toni Kukoc	.60	.18
❑	64 Karl Malone	1.00	.30
❑	65 Baron Davis	1.00	.30
❑	66 Shaquille O'Neal	2.50	.75
❑	67 Vlade Divac	.60	.18
❑	68 Eddie Robinson	.60	.18
❑	69 Dion Glover	.30	.09
❑	70 Jason Williams	.60	.18
❑	71 Steve Francis	1.00	.30
❑	72 Glen Rice	.60	.18
❑	73 Clifford Robinson	.30	.09
❑	74 Shareef Abdur-Rahim	1.00	.30
❑	75 Hakeem Olajuwon	1.00	.30
❑	76 Paul Pierce	1.00	.30
❑	77 Tim Hardaway	.60	.18
❑	78 Darrell Armstrong	.30	.09
❑	79 Bonzi Wells	.60	.18
❑	80 Antawn Jamison	1.00	.30
❑	81 Stephon Marbury	1.00	.30
❑	82 Tony Delk	.30	.09
❑	83 Michael Dickerson	.60	.18
❑	84 Jamal Mashburn	.60	.18
❑	85 Kobe Bryant	4.00	1.20
❑	86 Grant Hill	1.00	.30
❑	87 Chris Webber	1.00	.30
❑	88 Vonteego Cummings	.30	.09
❑	89 Jamie Feick	.30	.09
❑	90 John Stockton	1.00	.30
❑	91 Kenyon Martin RC	25.00	7.50
❑	92 Stromile Swift RC	15.00	4.50
❑	93 Darius Miles RC	20.00	6.00
❑	94 Marcus Fizer RC	12.00	3.60
❑	95 Mike Miller RC	20.00	6.00
❑	96 DerMarr Johnson RC	12.00	3.60
❑	97 Chris Mihm RC	12.00	3.60
❑	98 Jamal Crawford RC	15.00	4.50
❑	99 Joel Przybilla RC	12.00	3.60
❑	100 Keyon Dooling RC	12.00	3.60
❑	101 Jerome Moiso RC	5.00	1.50
❑	102 Etan Thomas RC	5.00	1.50
❑	103 Courtney Alexander RC	12.00	3.60
❑	104 Mateen Cleaves RC	5.00	1.50
❑	105 Jason Collier RC	5.00	1.50
❑	106 Hidayet Turkoglu RC	6.00	1.80
❑	107 Desmond Mason RC	5.00	1.50
❑	108 Quentin Richardson RC	6.00	1.80
❑	109 Jamaal Magloire RC	5.00	1.50
❑	110 Speedy Claxton RC	5.00	1.50
❑	111 Morris Peterson RC	6.00	1.80
❑	112 Donnell Harvey RC	4.00	1.20
❑	113 DeShawn Stevenson RC	4.00	1.20
❑	114 Dalibor Bagaric RC	4.00	1.20
❑	115 Mamadou N'Diaye RC	4.00	1.20
❑	116 Erick Barkley RC	4.00	1.20
❑	117 Mark Madsen RC	4.00	1.20
❑	118 Chris Porter RC	4.00	1.20
❑	119 Brian Cardinal RC	4.00	1.20
❑	120 Iakovos Tsakalidis RC	4.00	1.20
❑	121 Marc Jackson RC	12.00	3.60

2001-02 Fleer Showcase

	Nm-Mt	Ex-Mt
COMPLETE SET (123)	400.00	120.00
COMP.SET w/o SP's (86)	50.00	15.00
COMMON AVANT(87-91/123)	20.00	6.00
COMMON AVANT RC (92-97)	25.00	7.50
COMMON ROOKIE (98-112)	5.00	1.50
COMMON ROOKIE (113-122)	4.00	1.20

CARTER AU/150 NOT INCL.IN SET PRICE

❑	1 Grant Hill	1.00	.30
❑	2 Elton Brand	1.00	.30
❑	3 Sam Cassell	1.00	.30
❑	4 John Stockton	1.00	.30
❑	5 James Posey	.60	.18
❑	6 Eddie Jones	1.00	.30
❑	7 Damon Stoudamire	.60	.18
❑	8 Nick Van Exel	1.00	.30
❑	9 Brian Grant	.60	.18
❑	10 Mike Miller	1.00	.30
❑	11 Steve Smith	.60	.18
❑	12 Michael Finley	1.00	.30
❑	13 Peja Stojakovic	1.00	.30
❑	14 DerMarr Johnson	.60	.18
❑	15 Reggie Miller	1.00	.30
❑	16 Quentin Richardson	.60	.18
❑	17 Latrell Sprewell	1.00	.30
❑	18 Richard Hamilton	.60	.18
❑	19 Michael Doleac	.30	.09
❑	20 Derek Fisher	1.00	.30
❑	21 Marcus Camby	.60	.18
❑	22 Stephon Marbury	1.00	.30
❑	23 Bryon Russell	.30	.09
❑	24 Jumaine Jones	.60	.18
❑	25 Anfernee Hardaway	1.00	.30
❑	26 P.J. Brown	.30	.09
❑	27 Marc Jackson	.60	.18
❑	28 Dikembe Mutombo	.60	.18
❑	29 Andre Miller	.60	.18
❑	30 Robert Horry	.60	.18
❑	31 Tom Gugliotta	.30	.09
❑	32 David Robinson	1.00	.30
❑	33 Ron Mercer	.60	.18
❑	34 Shawn Marion	1.00	.30
❑	35 Ron Artest	.60	.18
❑	36 Jason Williams	.60	.18
❑	37 Scottie Pippen	1.50	.45
❑	38 Jerry Stackhouse	1.00	.30
❑	39 Stromile Swift	.60	.18
❑	40 Rasheed Wallace	1.00	.30
❑	41 Alonzo Mourning	.60	.18
❑	42 Eddie Robinson	.60	.18
❑	43 Shareef Abdur-Rahim	1.00	.30
❑	44 Wally Szczerbiak	.60	.18
❑	45 Antonio Davis	.30	.09
❑	46 Glen Rice	.60	.18
❑	47 Jason Kidd	1.50	.45
❑	48 Gary Payton	1.00	.30
❑	49 Steve Nash	1.00	.30
❑	50 Lamar Odom	1.00	.30
❑	51 Glenn Robinson	1.00	.30
❑	52 Mike Bibby	1.00	.30
❑	53 Hakeem Olajuwon	1.00	.30
❑	54 Theo Ratliff	.60	.18
❑	55 Kenyon Martin	1.00	.30
❑	56 Jamal Mashburn	.60	.18
❑	57 Larry Hughes	.60	.18
❑	58 Speedy Claxton	.60	.18
❑	59 Rashard Lewis	.60	.18
❑	60 Raef LaFrentz	.60	.18
❑	61 Antonio Daniels	.30	.09
❑	62 Jason Terry	1.00	.30
❑	63 Jalen Rose	1.00	.30
❑	64 Terrell Brandon	.60	.18
❑	65 Karl Malone	1.00	.30
❑	66 Antonio McDyess	.60	.18
❑	67 Anthony Carter	.60	.18
❑	68 Tim Hardaway	.60	.18
❑	69 Antoine Walker	1.00	.30
❑	70 Cuttino Mobley	.60	.18
❑	71 Allan Houston	.60	.18
❑	72 Desmond Mason	.60	.18
❑	73 Kurt Thomas	.60	.18
❑	74 Juwan Howard	.60	.18
❑	75 Tim Thomas	.60	.18
❑	76 Tracy McGrady	2.50	.75
❑	77 Dirk Nowitzki	1.50	.45
❑	78 Tim Duncan	2.00	.60
❑	79 Chris Webber	1.00	.30
❑	80 Steve Francis	1.00	.30
❑	81 Paul Pierce	1.00	.30
❑	82 Darius Miles	1.00	.30
❑	83 Ray Allen	1.00	.30
❑	84 Baron Davis	1.00	.30
❑	85 Antawn Jamison	1.00	.30
❑	86 Michael Jordan	15.00	4.50
❑	87 Vince Carter AVANT	20.00	6.00
❑	87A V.Carter AU/150	120.00	36.00
❑	88 Kobe Bryant AVANT	30.00	9.00
❑	89 Allen Iverson AVANT	20.00	6.00
❑	90 Kevin Garnett AVANT	20.00	6.00
❑	91 S.O'Neal AVANT	20.00	6.00
❑	92 K.Brown AVANT RC	25.00	7.50
❑	93 E.Griffin AVANT RC	25.00	7.50
❑	94 E.Curry AVANT RC	25.00	7.50
❑	95 S.Battier AVANT RC	25.00	7.50
❑	96 J.Johnson AVANT RC	25.00	7.50
❑	97 T.Chandler AVANT RC	25.00	7.50
❑	98 Jason Richardson RC	15.00	4.50
❑	99 Zach Randolph RC	15.00	4.50
❑	100 Rodney White RC	6.00	1.80
❑	101 Pau Gasol RC	15.00	4.50
❑	102 Jamaal Tinsley RC	8.00	2.40
❑	103 Troy Murphy RC	10.00	3.00

❑ 104 Richard Jefferson RC 10.00 3.00
❑ 105 DeSagana Diop RC 5.00 1.50
❑ 106 Joseph Forte RC 10.00 3.00
❑ 107 Gerald Wallace RC .. 10.00 3.00
❑ 108 Loren Woods RC 5.00 1.50
❑ 109 Jason Collins RC 5.00 1.50
❑ 110 Jeryl Sasser RC 5.00 1.50
❑ 111 Zeljko Rebraca RC 5.00 1.50
❑ 112 Kirk Haston RC 5.00 1.50
❑ 113 Kedrick Brown RC 4.00 1.20
❑ 114 Steven Hunter RC 5.00 1.50
❑ 115 Michael Bradley RC 4.00 1.20
❑ 116 Brandon Armstrong RC 5.00 1.50
❑ 117 Samuel Dalembert RC 5.00 1.50
❑ 118 Primoz Brezec RC 5.00 1.50
❑ 119 Andrei Kirilenko RC .. 10.00 3.00
❑ 120 Vladimir Radmanovic RC 5.00 1.50
❑ 121 Ratko Varda RC 5.00 1.50
❑ 122 Brendan Haywood RC 6.00 1.80
❑ 123 Wang Zhizhi AVANT 20.00 6.00

2002-03 Fleer Showcase

	Nm-Mt	Ex-Mt
COMP.SET w/o SP's (100)	30.00	9.00
COMMON CARD (1-148)	.25	.07
COMM.AVANT ROW 2 (101-112)	4.00	1.20
COMM.AVANT ROW 0 (113-118)	-	-
COMM.RC AVANT (119-124)	10.00	3.00
COMMON ROOKIE (125-148)	4.00	1.20

❑ 1 Michael Jordan 6.00 1.80
❑ 2 Shareef Abdur-Rahim .... 1.00 .30
❑ 3 Jalen Rose .... 1.00 .30
❑ 4 Antonio McDyess .... .60 .18
❑ 5 Malik Rose .... .25 .07
❑ 6 Juwan Howard .... .60 .18
❑ 7 Jason Williams .... .60 .18
❑ 8 Darrell Armstrong .... .25 .07
❑ 9 Karl Malone .... 1.00 .30
❑ 10 Jason Terry .... 1.00 .30
❑ 11 David Wesley .... .25 .07
❑ 12 David Robinson .... 1.00 .30
❑ 13 Gary Payton .... 1.00 .30
❑ 14 Quentin Richardson .... .60 .18
❑ 15 Allan Houston .... .60 .18
❑ 16 Alvin Williams .... .25 .07
❑ 17 Jamal Mashburn .... .60 .18
❑ 18 Theo Ratliff .... .60 .18
❑ 19 Tyson Chandler .... 1.00 .30
❑ 20 Gilbert Arenas .... 1.00 .30
❑ 21 Dikembe Mutombo .... .60 .18
❑ 22 Calbert Cheaney .... .25 .07
❑ 23 Rodney Rogers .... .25 .07
❑ 24 Shane Battier .... 1.00 .30
❑ 25 Mike Miller .... 1.00 .30
❑ 26 John Stockton .... 1.00 .30
❑ 27 Mengke Bateer .... 1.00 .30
❑ 28 Andre Miller .... .60 .18
❑ 29 Sam Cassell .... 1.00 .30
❑ 30 Anfernee Hardaway ...... 1.00 .30
❑ 31 Keith Van Horn .... 1.00 .30
❑ 32 Tony Battie .... .25 .07
❑ 33 Derek Fisher .... 1.00 .30
❑ 34 Grant Hill .... 1.00 .30
❑ 35 Andrei Kirilenko .... 1.00 .30
❑ 36 Toni Kukoc .... .60 .18
❑ 37 Jerry Stackhouse .... 1.00 .30
❑ 38 Latrell Sprewell .... 1.00 .30
❑ 39 Morris Peterson .... 1.00 .30
❑ 40 Darius Miles .... 1.00 .30
❑ 41 Eddie Jones .... 1.00 .30
❑ 42 Stephon Marbury .... 1.00 .30
❑ 43 Brent Barry .... .60 .18
❑ 44 DeShawn Stevenson ...... .25 .07
❑ 45 Brian Grant .... .60 .18
❑ 46 Derrick Coleman .... .25 .07
❑ 47 Richard Hamilton .... .60 .18
❑ 48 Jason Richardson .... 1.00 .30
❑ 49 Kerry Kittles .... .25 .07
❑ 50 Desmond Mason .... .60 .18
❑ 51 Stromile Swift .... .60 .18
❑ 52 Richard Jefferson .... .60 .18
❑ 53 Vladimir Radmanovic ...... .60 .18
❑ 54 Lamond Murray .... .25 .07
❑ 55 Troy Murphy .... .60 .18
❑ 56 Kenyon Martin .... 1.00 .30
❑ 57 Vlade Divac .... .60 .18
❑ 58 Chris Mihm .... .25 .07
❑ 59 Eddie Griffin .... .60 .18
❑ 60 Marc Jackson .... .60 .18
❑ 61 Peja Stojakovic .... 1.00 .30
❑ 62 Vin Baker .... .60 .18
❑ 63 Cuttino Mobley .... .60 .18
❑ 64 Joe Smith .... .60 .18
❑ 65 Damon Stoudamire .... .60 .18
❑ 66 Eddy Curry .... 1.00 .30
❑ 67 Alonzo Mourning .... .60 .18
❑ 68 Aaron McKie .... .60 .18
❑ 69 Kwame Brown .... .60 .18
❑ 70 Raef LaFrentz .... .60 .18
❑ 71 Jermaine O'Neal .... 1.00 .30
❑ 72 Terrell Brandon .... .60 .18
❑ 73 Bonzi Wells .... .60 .18
❑ 74 Steve Nash .... 1.00 .30
❑ 75 Jamaal Tinsley .... 1.00 .30
❑ 76 Wally Szczerbiak .... .60 .18
❑ 77 Scottie Pippen .... 1.50 .45
❑ 78 Michael Finley .... 1.00 .30
❑ 79 Reggie Miller .... 1.00 .30
❑ 80 Glenn Robinson .... 1.00 .30
❑ 81 Rasheed Wallace .... 1.00 .30
❑ 82 Antoine Walker .... 1.00 .30
❑ 83 Robert Horry .... .60 .18
❑ 84 Kurt Thomas .... .60 .18
❑ 85 Antonio Davis .... .25 .07
❑ 86 Nick Van Exel .... 1.00 .30
❑ 87 Al Harrington .... .60 .18
❑ 88 Tony Delk .... .25 .07
❑ 89 Joe Johnson .... 1.00 .30
❑ 90 Chauncey Billups .... .60 .18
❑ 91 P.J. Brown .... .25 .07
❑ 92 Tony Parker .... 1.00 .30
❑ 93 Antawn Jamison .... 1.00 .30
❑ 94 Courtney Alexander .... .60 .18
❑ 95 Kenny Anderson .... .60 .18
❑ 96 Clifford Robinson .... .25 .07
❑ 97 Lamar Odom .... 1.00 .30
❑ 98 Anthony Carter .... .60 .18
❑ 99 Shawn Marion .... 1.00 .30
❑ 100 Hidayet Turkoglu .... 1.00 .30
❑ 101 Paul Pierce AVANT 4.00 1.20
❑ 102 Dirk Nowitzki AVANT .. 4.00 1.20
❑ 103 Ben Wallace AVANT .. 4.00 1.20
❑ 104 Steve Francis AVANT 4.00 1.20
❑ 105 Pau Gasol AVANT 4.00 1.20
❑ 106 Ray Allen AVANT 4.00 1.20
❑ 107 Kevin Garnett AVANT 5.00 1.50
❑ 108 Jason Kidd AVANT 4.00 1.20
❑ 109 Baron Davis AVANT 4.00 1.20
❑ 110 Mike Bibby AVANT 4.00 1.20
❑ 111 Chris Webber AVANT 4.00 1.20
❑ 112 Tim Duncan AVANT 5.00 1.50
❑ 113 Kobe Bryant AVANT 15.00 4.50
❑ 114 Shaquille O'Neal AVANT 10.00 3.00
❑ 115 Tracy McGrady AVANT 10.00 3.00
❑ 116 Allen Iverson AVANT .. 8.00 2.40
❑ 117 Vince Carter AVANT 10.00 3.00
❑ 118 Elton Brand AVANT 5.00 1.50
❑ 119 J.Williams AVANT RC 4.00 1.20
❑ 120 Yao Ming AVANT RC 40.00 12.00
❑ 121 M.Dunleavy AVANT RC 4.00 1.20
❑ 122 D.Wagner AVANT RC 4.00 1.20
❑ 123 C.Butler AVANT RC .. 12.00 3.60
❑ 124 D.Gooden AVANT RC 15.00 4.50
❑ 125 Manu Ginobili RC 6.00 1.80
❑ 126 Mehmet Okur RC 4.00 1.20
❑ 127 Nene Hilario RC 5.00 1.50
❑ 128 Nikoloz Tskitishvili RC 5.00 1.50
❑ 129 Tayshaun Prince RC .. 6.00 1.80
❑ 130 Bostjan Nachbar RC .. 4.00 1.20
❑ 131 Fred Jones RC 4.00 1.20
❑ 132 Melvin Ely RC 4.00 1.20
❑ 133 Chris Wilcox RC 5.00 1.50
❑ 134 Kareem Rush RC 5.00 1.50
❑ 135 Marcus Haislip RC 4.00 1.20
❑ 136 Frank Williams RC 4.00 1.20
❑ 137 Ryan Humphrey RC 4.00 1.20
❑ 138 John Salmons RC 4.00 1.20
❑ 139 Casey Jacobsen RC .. 4.00 1.20
❑ 140 Amare Stoudemire RC 20.00 6.00
❑ 141 Qyntel Woods RC 5.00 1.50
❑ 142 Chris Jefferies RC 4.00 1.20
❑ 143 Juan Dixon RC 6.00 1.80
❑ 144 Jared Jeffries RC 4.00 1.20
❑ 145 Lonny Baxter RC 4.00 1.20
❑ 146 Dan Dickau RC 4.00 1.20
❑ 147 Carlos Boozer RC 8.00 2.40
❑ 148 Vincent Yarbrough RC 4.00 1.20

2003-04 Fleer Showcase

	Nm-Mt	Ex-Mt
COMP.SET w/o SP's (100)	40.00	12.00
COMMON SP (91-100)	5.00	1.50
COMMON ROOKIE (101-130)	6.00	1.80

❑ 1 Jason Richardson .... 1.00 .30
❑ 2 Andrei Kirilenko .... 1.00 .30
❑ 3 Steve Francis .... 1.00 .30
❑ 4 Shareef Abdur-Rahim .... 1.00 .30
❑ 5 Ben Wallace .... 1.00 .30
❑ 6 Predrag Drobnjak .... .25 .07
❑ 7 Jalen Rose .... 1.00 .30
❑ 8 Rashard Lewis .... 1.00 .30
❑ 9 Darius Miles .... 1.00 .30
❑ 10 Bobby Jackson .... .60 .18
❑ 11 Steve Nash .... 1.00 .30
❑ 12 Gilbert Arenas .... 1.00 .30
❑ 13 Aaron McKie .... .60 .18
❑ 14 Reggie Miller .... 1.00 .30
❑ 15 Elton Brand .... 1.00 .30
❑ 16 Allan Houston .... .60 .18
❑ 17 Pau Gasol .... 1.00 .30
❑ 18 Jamaal Magloire .... .25 .07
❑ 19 Eddie Jones .... 1.00 .30
❑ 20 Richard Jefferson .... .60 .18
❑ 21 Wally Szczerbiak .... .60 .18
❑ 22 Antonio McDyess .... .60 .18
❑ 23 Michael Redd .... 1.00 .30
❑ 24 Grant Hill .... 1.00 .30
❑ 25 Jason Williams .... .60 .18
❑ 26 Rasheed Wallace .... 1.00 .30
❑ 27 Andre Miller .... .60 .18
❑ 28 Peja Stojakovic .... 1.00 .30
❑ 29 Cuttino Mobley .... .60 .18
❑ 30 David Robinson .... 1.00 .30
❑ 31 Richard Hamilton .... .60 .18
❑ 32 Morris Peterson .... .60 .18
❑ 33 Karl Malone .... 1.00 .30
❑ 34 Zydrunas Ilgauskas .... .60 .18
❑ 35 Jerry Stackhouse .... 1.00 .30
❑ 36 Eddy Curry .... .60 .18
❑ 37 Sam Cassell .... 1.00 .30
❑ 38 Troy Hudson .... .25 .07
❑ 39 Jason Terry .... 1.00 .30
❑ 40 Kenyon Martin .... 1.00 .30
❑ 41 Bonzi Wells .... .60 .18
❑ 42 Donnell Harvey .... .25 .07
❑ 43 Tracy McGrady .... 2.50 .75
❑ 44 Allen Iverson .... 2.00 .60

Card	Nm-Mt	Ex-Mt
❑ 45 Jermaine O'Neal	1.00	.30
❑ 46 Larry Hughes	.60	.18
❑ 47 Scottie Pippen	1.50	.45
❑ 48 Antonio Davis	.25	.07
❑ 49 Chris Webber	1.00	.30
❑ 50 Vladimir Radmanovic	.25	.07
❑ 51 Glenn Robinson	1.00	.30
❑ 52 Antoine Walker	1.00	.30
❑ 53 Ricky Davis	1.00	.30
❑ 54 Michael Finley	1.00	.30
❑ 55 Nick Van Exel	1.00	.30
❑ 56 Tayshaun Prince	.60	.18
❑ 57 Antawn Jamison	1.00	.30
❑ 58 Jamal Mashburn	.60	.18
❑ 59 Jamaal Tinsley	1.00	.30
❑ 60 Kerry Kittles	.25	.07
❑ 61 Derek Fisher	1.00	.30
❑ 62 Radoslav Nesterovic	.60	.18
❑ 63 Mike Miller	1.00	.30
❑ 64 Gary Payton	1.00	.30
❑ 65 Brian Grant	.60	.18
❑ 66 Baron Davis	1.00	.30
❑ 67 Shane Battier	1.00	.30
❑ 68 Latrell Sprewell	1.00	.30
❑ 69 Keith Van Horn	1.00	.30
❑ 70 Eddie Griffin	.60	.18
❑ 71 Stephon Marbury	1.00	.30
❑ 72 Chauncey Billups	.60	.18
❑ 73 Shawn Marion	1.00	.30
❑ 74 Juwan Howard	.60	.18
❑ 75 Mike Bibby	1.00	.30
❑ 76 DaJuan Wagner	.60	.18
❑ 77 Tony Parker	1.00	.30
❑ 78 Tyson Chandler	1.00	.30
❑ 79 Ray Allen	1.00	.30
❑ 80 Matt Harpring	1.00	.30
❑ 81 Kwame Brown	.60	.18
❑ 82 Troy Murphy	1.00	.30
❑ 83 Ron Artest	.60	.18
❑ 84 Corey Maggette	.60	.18
❑ 85 Tony Delk	.25	.07
❑ 86 Jamal Crawford	.25	.07
❑ 87 Vince Carter	2.50	.75
❑ 88 Kevin Garnett	2.00	.60
❑ 89 Jason Kidd	1.50	.45
❑ 90 Paul Pierce	5.00	1.50
❑ 91 Nene SP	5.00	1.50
❑ 92 Drew Gooden SP	5.00	1.50
❑ 93 Caron Butler SP	5.00	1.50
❑ 94 Manu Ginobili SP	5.00	1.50
❑ 95 Dirk Nowitzki SP	5.00	1.50
❑ 96 Yao Ming SP	8.00	2.40
❑ 97 Amare Stoudemire SP	6.00	1.80
❑ 98 Kobe Bryant SP	12.00	3.60
❑ 99 Tim Duncan SP	6.00	1.80
❑ 100 Shaquille O'Neal SP	8.00	2.40
❑ 101 T.J. Ford RC	8.00	2.40
❑ 102 Chris Bosh RC	15.00	4.50
❑ 103 Boris Diaw RC	6.00	1.80
❑ 104 Luke Ridnour RC	8.00	2.40
❑ 105 Zoran Planinic RC	6.00	1.80
❑ 106 Josh Howard RC	8.00	2.40
❑ 107 Darko Milicic EXCH	10.00	3.00
❑ 108 Dahntay Jones RC	6.00	1.80
❑ 109 Mike Sweetney RC	5.00	1.50
❑ 110 Kirk Hinrich RC	10.00	3.00
❑ 111 Marcus Banks RC	5.00	1.50
❑ 112 Travis Outlaw RC	6.00	1.80
❑ 113 Brian Cook RC	6.00	1.80
❑ 114 Mario Austin RC	6.00	1.80
❑ 115 Dwyane Wade RC	15.00	4.50
❑ 116 Chris Kaman RC	6.00	1.80
❑ 117 Zarko Cabarkapa RC	6.00	1.80
❑ 118 Ndudi Ebi RC	6.00	1.80
❑ 119 Mickael Pietrus RC	6.00	1.80
❑ 120 Carmelo Anthony RC	40.00	12.00
❑ 121 Kendrick Perkins RC	6.00	1.80
❑ 122 Troy Bell RC	6.00	1.80
❑ 123 Maciej Lampe RC	6.00	1.80
❑ 124 Carlos Delfino RC	6.00	1.80
❑ 125 Leandro Barbosa RC	6.00	1.80
❑ 126 Sofoklis Schortsanitis RC	6.00	1.80
❑ 127 Reece Gaines RC	6.00	1.80
❑ 128 Nick Collison RC	6.00	1.80
❑ 129 David West RC	6.00	1.80
❑ 130 LeBron James RC	100.00	30.00

2002-03 Fleer Tradition

	Nm-Mt	Ex-Mt
COMPLETE SET (300)	80.00	24.00
COMMON CARD (1-270)	.20	.06
COMMON ROOKIE (271-300)	2.50	.75
❑ 1 Shareef Abdur-Rahim	.60	.18
❑ 2 Dion Glover	.20	.06
❑ 3 Theo Ratliff	.40	.12
❑ 4 Nazr Mohammed	.20	.06
❑ 5 Ira Newble	.20	.06
❑ 6 Alan Henderson	.20	.06
❑ 7 Vin Baker	.40	.12
❑ 8 Tony Battie	.20	.06
❑ 9 Eric Williams	.20	.06
❑ 10 Shammond Williams	.20	.06
❑ 11 Walter McCarty	.20	.06
❑ 12 Bruno Sundov	.20	.06
❑ 13 Donyell Marshall	.40	.12
❑ 14 Marcus Fizer	.40	.12
❑ 15 Eddie Robinson	.40	.12
❑ 16 Trenton Hassell	.40	.12
❑ 17 Ricky Davis	.40	.12
❑ 18 Jumaine Jones	.40	.12
❑ 19 Chris Mihm	.20	.06
❑ 20 Zydrunas Ilgauskas	.40	.12
❑ 21 Tyrone Hill	.20	.06
❑ 22 Adrian Griffin	.20	.06
❑ 23 Nick Van Exel	.60	.18
❑ 24 Raef LaFrentz	.40	.12
❑ 25 Eduardo Najera	.40	.12
❑ 26 Shawn Bradley	.20	.06
❑ 27 Evan Eschmeyer	.20	.06
❑ 28 Walt Williams	.20	.06
❑ 29 Raja Bell	.20	.06
❑ 30 Marcus Camby	.40	.12
❑ 31 Donnell Harvey	.20	.06
❑ 32 Kenny Satterfield	.20	.06
❑ 33 Rodney White	.40	.12
❑ 34 Chris Whitney	.20	.06
❑ 35 Clifford Robinson	.20	.06
❑ 36 Zeljko Rebraca	.40	.12
❑ 37 Corliss Williamson	.40	.12
❑ 38 Chucky Atkins	.20	.06
❑ 39 Jon Barry	.20	.06
❑ 40 Michael Curry	.20	.06
❑ 41 Erick Dampier	.40	.12
❑ 42 Danny Fortson	.20	.06
❑ 43 Adonal Foyle	.20	.06
❑ 44 Troy Murphy	.40	.12
❑ 45 Bob Sura	.20	.06
❑ 46 Moochie Norris	.20	.06
❑ 47 Kenny Thomas	.20	.06
❑ 48 Terence Morris	.20	.06
❑ 49 Glen Rice	.40	.12
❑ 50 Maurice Taylor	.20	.06
❑ 51 Erick Strickland	.20	.06
❑ 52 Al Harrington	.40	.12
❑ 53 Ron Artest	.40	.12
❑ 54 Austin Croshere	.20	.06
❑ 55 Ron Mercer	.40	.12
❑ 56 Brad Miller	.60	.18
❑ 57 Lamar Odom	.60	.18
❑ 58 Keyon Dooling	.20	.06
❑ 59 Corey Maggette	.40	.12
❑ 60 Michael Olowokandi	.20	.06
❑ 61 Stanislav Medvedenko	.20	.06
❑ 62 Rick Fox	.40	.12
❑ 63 Derek Fisher	.60	.18
❑ 64 Samaki Walker	.20	.06
❑ 65 Robert Horry	.40	.12
❑ 66 Mark Madsen	.20	.06
❑ 67 Wesley Person	.20	.06
❑ 68 Michael Dickerson	.20	.06
❑ 69 Lorenzen Wright	.20	.06
❑ 70 Brevin Knight	.20	.06
❑ 71 Travis Best	.20	.06
❑ 72 Brian Grant	.40	.12
❑ 73 Eddie Jones	.60	.18
❑ 74 LaPhonso Ellis	.20	.06
❑ 75 Anthony Carter	.40	.12
❑ 76 Tim Thomas	.40	.12
❑ 77 Toni Kukoc	.40	.12
❑ 78 Anthony Mason	.40	.12
❑ 79 Ervin Johnson	.20	.06
❑ 80 Joel Przybilla	.20	.06
❑ 81 Rod Strickland	.20	.06
❑ 82 Terrell Brandon	.40	.12
❑ 83 Anthony Peeler	.20	.06
❑ 84 Joe Smith	.40	.12
❑ 85 Gary Trent	.20	.06
❑ 86 Rasho Nesterovic	.40	.12
❑ 87 Loren Woods	.40	.12
❑ 88 Felipe Lopez	.20	.06
❑ 89 Dikembe Mutombo	.40	.12
❑ 90 Rodney Rogers	.20	.06
❑ 91 Jason Collins	.20	.06
❑ 92 Kerry Kittles	.20	.06
❑ 93 Lucious Harris	.20	.06
❑ 94 Aaron Williams	.20	.06
❑ 95 Jamal Mashburn	.40	.12
❑ 96 David Wesley	.20	.06
❑ 97 Elden Campbell	.20	.06
❑ 98 Jerome Moiso	.20	.06
❑ 99 P.J. Brown	.20	.06
❑ 100 George Lynch	.20	.06
❑ 101 Robert Traylor	.20	.06
❑ 102 Antonio McDyess	.40	.12
❑ 103 Kurt Thomas	.40	.12
❑ 104 Clarence Weatherspoon	.20	.06
❑ 105 Charlie Ward	.20	.06
❑ 106 Lavor Postell	.20	.06
❑ 107 Shandon Anderson	.20	.06
❑ 108 Michael Doleac	.20	.06
❑ 109 Othella Harrington	.20	.06
❑ 110 Darrell Armstrong	.20	.06
❑ 111 Steven Hunter	.20	.06
❑ 112 Pat Garrity	.20	.06
❑ 113 Horace Grant	.40	.12
❑ 114 Jacque Vaughn	.20	.06
❑ 115 Jeryl Sasser	.20	.06
❑ 116 Todd MacCulloch	.20	.06
❑ 117 Greg Buckner	.20	.06
❑ 118 Eric Snow	.40	.12
❑ 119 Samuel Dalembert	.20	.06
❑ 120 Monty Williams	.20	.06
❑ 121 Stephon Marbury	.60	.18
❑ 122 Anfernee Hardaway	.40	.12
❑ 123 Tom Gugliotta	.20	.06
❑ 124 Iakovos Tsakalidis	.20	.06
❑ 125 Bo Outlaw	.20	.06
❑ 126 Damon Stoudamire	.40	.12
❑ 127 Jeff McInnis	.20	.06
❑ 128 Derek Anderson	.40	.12
❑ 129 Antonio Daniels	.20	.06
❑ 130 Dale Davis	.20	.06
❑ 131 Zach Randolph	.60	.18
❑ 132 Bobby Jackson	.40	.12
❑ 133 Chris Webber	.60	.18
❑ 134 Vlade Divac	.40	.12
❑ 135 Keon Clark	.40	.12
❑ 136 Doug Christie	.40	.12
❑ 137 Scot Pollard	.20	.06
❑ 138 Mengke Bateer	.60	.18
❑ 139 David Robinson	.60	.18
❑ 140 Steve Smith	.40	.12
❑ 141 Malik Rose	.20	.06
❑ 142 Speedy Claxton	.20	.06
❑ 143 Danny Ferry	.20	.06
❑ 144 Brent Barry	.40	.12
❑ 145 Joseph Forte	.40	.12
❑ 146 Vladimir Radmanovic	.40	.12
❑ 147 Kenny Anderson	.40	.12
❑ 148 Predrag Drobnjak	.20	.06

❑ 149 Calvin Booth .20 .06
❑ 150 Ansu Sesay .20 .06
❑ 151 Voshon Lenard .20 .06
❑ 152 Lamond Murray .20 .06
❑ 153 Antonio Davis .20 .06
❑ 154 Lindsey Hunter .20 .06
❑ 155 Michael Bradley .40 .12
❑ 156 Jerome Williams .20 .06
❑ 157 Alvin Williams .20 .06
❑ 158 Mamadou N'diaye .20 .06
❑ 159 Raul Lopez .20 .06
❑ 160 John Stockton .60 .18
❑ 161 Mark Jackson .20 .06
❑ 162 DeShawn Stevenson .20 .06
❑ 163 Calbert Cheaney .20 .06
❑ 164 Matt Harpring .60 .18
❑ 165 Jarron Collins .20 .06
❑ 166 Tyronn Lue .20 .06
❑ 167 Bryon Russell .20 .06
❑ 168 Larry Hughes .40 .12
❑ 169 Brendan Haywood .40 .12
❑ 170 Christian Laettner .40 .12
❑ 171 Glenn Robinson .60 .18
❑ 172 Tony Delk .20 .06
❑ 173 Antoine Walker .60 .18
❑ 174 Jalen Rose .60 .18
❑ 175 Jamal Crawford .20 .06
❑ 176 DeSagana Diop .40 .12
❑ 177 Michael Finley .60 .18
❑ 178 Dirk Nowitzki 1.00 .30
❑ 179 Juwan Howard .40 .12
❑ 180 Chauncey Billups .40 .12
❑ 181 Richard Hamilton .40 .12
❑ 182 Antawn Jamison .60 .18
❑ 183 Steve Francis .60 .18
❑ 184 Eddie Griffin .40 .12
❑ 185 Jonathan Bender .40 .12
❑ 186 Reggie Miller .60 .18
❑ 187 Elton Brand .60 .18
❑ 188 Marco Jaric .20 .06
❑ 189 Kobe Bryant 2.50 .75
❑ 190 Shaquille O'Neal 1.50 .45
❑ 191 Jason Williams .40 .12
❑ 192 Stromile Swift .40 .12
❑ 193 Alonzo Mourning .40 .12
❑ 194 Malik Allen .20 .06
❑ 195 Sam Cassell .60 .18
❑ 196 Ray Allen .60 .18
❑ 197 Wally Szczerbiak .40 .12
❑ 197B Vince Carter Promo 2.50 .75
❑ 198 Jason Kidd 1.00 .30
❑ 199 Kenyon Martin .60 .18
❑ 200 Courtney Alexander .40 .12
❑ 201 Baron Davis .60 .18
❑ 202 Allan Houston .40 .12
❑ 203 Grant Hill .60 .18
❑ 204 Aaron McKie .40 .12
❑ 205 Keith Van Horn .60 .18
❑ 206 Shawn Marion .60 .18
❑ 207 Joe Johnson .40 .12
❑ 208 Scottie Pippen 1.00 .30
❑ 209 Rasheed Wallace .60 .18
❑ 210 Peja Stojakovic .60 .18
❑ 211 Hidayet Turkoglu .60 .18
❑ 212 Tony Parker .60 .18
❑ 213 Tim Duncan 1.25 .35
❑ 214 Gary Payton .60 .18
❑ 215 Desmond Mason .40 .12
❑ 216 Vince Carter 1.50 .45
❑ 217 Karl Malone .60 .18
❑ 218 Andrei Kirilenko .60 .18
❑ 219 Jerry Stackhouse .60 .18
❑ 220 Michael Jordan 5.00 1.50
❑ 221 DerMarr Johnson .20 .06
❑ 222 Kedrick Brown .40 .12
❑ 223 Eddy Curry .60 .18
❑ 224 Tyson Chandler .60 .18
❑ 225 Darius Miles .60 .18
❑ 226 Wang ZhiZhi .60 .18
❑ 227 James Posey .40 .12
❑ 228 Ben Wallace .60 .18
❑ 229 Jason Richardson .60 .18
❑ 230 Gilbert Arenas .60 .18
❑ 231 Eddie Griffin .40 .12
❑ 232 Jermaine O'Neal .60 .18
❑ 233 Quentin Richardson .40 .12
❑ 234 Devean George .40 .12
❑ 235 Shane Battier .60 .18
❑ 236 Pau Gasol .60 .18
❑ 237 Eddie House .20 .06
❑ 238 Michael Redd .60 .18
❑ 239 Troy Hudson .20 .06
❑ 240 Richard Jefferson .40 .12
❑ 241 Jamal Magloire .20 .06
❑ 242 Mike Miller .60 .18
❑ 243 Joe Johnson .40 .12
❑ 244 Ruben Patterson .40 .12
❑ 245 Gerald Wallace .40 .12
❑ 246 Tony Parker .60 .18
❑ 247 Rashard Lewis .40 .12
❑ 248 Morris Peterson .40 .12
❑ 249 Andrei Kirilenko .60 .18
❑ 250 Kwame Brown .40 .12
❑ 251 Jason Terry .60 .18
❑ 252 Paul Pierce .60 .18
❑ 253 Darius Miles .60 .18
❑ 254 Steve Nash .60 .18
❑ 255 Cuttino Mobley .40 .12
❑ 256 Jamaal Tinsley .60 .18
❑ 257 Andre Miller .40 .12
❑ 258 Shaquille O'Neal 1.50 .45
❑ 259 Kobe Bryant 2.50 .75
❑ 260 Kevin Garnett 1.50 .45
❑ 261 Kenyon Martin .60 .18
❑ 262 Latrell Sprewell .60 .18
❑ 263 Tracy McGrady 1.50 .45
❑ 264 Allen Iverson 1.25 .35
❑ 265 Shawn Marion .60 .18
❑ 266 Bonzi Wells .40 .12
❑ 267 Mike Bibby .60 .18
❑ 268 Tim Duncan 1.25 .35
❑ 269 Vince Carter 1.50 .45
❑ 270 Michael Jordan 5.00 1.50
❑ 271 Yao Ming 3.00 .90
Jay Williams
Mike Dunleavy
❑ 272 Manu Ginobili 4.00 1.20
Tayshaun Prince
Gordan Giricek
❑ 273 Jared Jeffries 2.50 .75
Frank Williams
Jannero Pargo
❑ 274 Chris Wilcox 2.50 .75
Juan Dixon
Lonny Baxter
❑ 275 DaJuan Wagner 2.50 .75
Dan Dickau
Manu Ginobili
❑ 276 Melvin Ely 2.50 .75
Chris Jefferies
Tito Maddox
❑ 277 Reggie Evans 4.00 1.20
J.R. Bremer
Frank Williams
❑ 278 Caron Butler 2.50 .75
Marcus Haislip
Ryan Humphrey
❑ 279 Robert Archibald 2.50 .75
Pat Burke
Nate Huffman
❑ 280 Andrew Gooden 4.00 1.20
Amare Stoudemire
Qyntel Woods
❑ 281 Bostjan Nachbar 2.50 .75
Jiri Welsch
Predrag Savovic
❑ 282 Curtis Borchardt 2.50 .75
Casey Jacobsen
Dan Gadzuric
❑ 283 Sam Clancy 2.50 .75
Mehmet Okur
Jamal Sampson
❑ 284 Tayshaun Prince 4.00 1.20
Kareem Rush
John Salmons
❑ 285 Yao Ming 6.00 1.80
Nikoloz Tskitishvili
Nene Hilario
❑ 286 DaJuan Wagner 1.50 .45
Qyntel Woods
Tamar Slay
❑ 287 Melvin Ely 2.50 .75
Macus Haislip
Fred Jones
❑ 288 Caron Butler 2.50 .75
Manu Ginobili
Marcus Haislip
❑ 289 Roger Mason Jr. 2.50 .75
Vincent Yarbrough
Dan Dickau
❑ 290 Ronald Murray 4.00 1.20
Chris Owens
Smush Parker
❑ 291 Rasual Butler 2.50 .75
Jannero Pargo
Gordan Giricek
❑ 292 Drew Gooden 1.25 .35
Nikoloz Tskitishvili
DaJuan Wagner
❑ 293 Nene Hilario 6.00 1.80
Chris Wilcox
Amare Stoudemire
❑ 294 Jay Williams 2.00 .60
Ryan Humphrey
Qyntel Woods
❑ 295 Yao Ming 12.00 3.60
Amare Stoudemire
Kareem Rush
❑ 296 Nikoloz Tskitshvil 2.50 .75
Caron Butler
Juan Dixon
❑ 297 Chris Wilcox 3.00 .90
Fred Jones
Bostjan Nachbar
❑ 298 Mike Dunleavy 2.50 .75
Nene Hilario
Casey Jacobsen
❑ 299 Jared Jeffries 2.00 .60
Juan Dixon
Drew Gooden
❑ 300 Carlos Boozer 2.50 .75
Jay Williams
Mike Dunleavy
❑ PROMO Caron Butler - -

2003-04 Fleer Tradition

	MINT	NRMT
COMP.SET w/o RC's (260)	50.00	22.00
COMMON CARD (1-260)	.20	.09
COMMON ROOKIE (261-290)	3.00	1.35
COMMON TRIPLE (291-300)	5.00	2.20

❑ 1 Shareef Abdur-Rahim .60 .25
❑ 2 Vince Carter 1.50 .70
❑ 3 Kevin Garnett 1.25 .55
❑ 4 Bobby Jackson .40 .18
❑ 5 Courtney Alexander .40 .18
❑ 6 Tracy McGrady 1.50 .70
❑ 7 Paul Pierce .60 .25
❑ 8 Sam Cassell .60 .25
❑ 9 Maurice Taylor .20 .09
❑ 10 Pat Garrity .20 .09
❑ 11 Casey Jacobsen .20 .09
❑ 12 Malik Allen .20 .09
❑ 13 Aaron McKie .40 .18
❑ 14 Tyson Chandler .60 .25
❑ 15 Scottie Pippen 1.00 .45
❑ 16 Jason Terry .60 .25
❑ 17 Pau Gasol .60 .25
❑ 18 Antawn Jamison .60 .25
❑ 19 Stanislav Medvedenko .20 .09

❑ 20 Ray Allen .60 .25
❑ 21 James Posey .40 .18
❑ 22 Calbert Cheaney .20 .09
❑ 23 Devean George .40 .18
❑ 24 Tim Thomas .40 .18
❑ 25 Marko Jaric .40 .18
❑ 26 Ron Mercer .20 .09
❑ 27 Rafer Alston .20 .09
❑ 28 Tayshaun Prince .40 .18
❑ 29 Doug Christie .40 .18
❑ 30 Kendall Gill .20 .09
❑ 31 Kurt Thomas .40 .18
❑ 32 Richard Jefferson .40 .18
❑ 33 Darius Miles .60 .25
❑ 34 Kenny Anderson .40 .18
❑ 35 Keon Clark .40 .18
❑ 36 Vladimir Radmanovic .20 .09
❑ 37 Kenny Thomas .20 .09
❑ 38 Manu Ginobili .60 .25
❑ 39 Jared Jeffries .20 .09
❑ 40 Brad Miller .60 .25
❑ 41 Derek Anderson .40 .18
❑ 42 Zach Randolph .60 .25
❑ 43 Speedy Claxton .20 .09
❑ 44 Jamaal Tinsley .60 .25
❑ 45 Gordan Giricek .40 .18
❑ 46 Joe Johnson .40 .18
❑ 47 Mike Miller .60 .25
❑ 48 Shandon Anderson .20 .09
❑ 49 Theo Ratliff .20 .09
❑ 50 Derrick Coleman .20 .09
❑ 51 Dion Glover .20 .09
❑ 52 Nikoloz Tskitishvili .20 .09
❑ 53 Jumaine Jones .40 .18
❑ 54 Gilbert Arenas .60 .25
❑ 55 Reggie Miller .60 .25
❑ 56 Michael Redd .60 .25
❑ 57 Jason Collins .20 .09
❑ 58 Drew Gooden .40 .18
❑ 59 Hidayet Turkoglu .60 .25
❑ 60 Eddie Jones .60 .25
❑ 61 Andre Miller .40 .18
❑ 62 Darrell Armstrong .20 .09
❑ 63 Glen Rice .40 .18
❑ 64 Jarron Collins .20 .09
❑ 65 Nick Van Exel .60 .25
❑ 66 Brian Grant .40 .18
❑ 67 Shawn Kemp .20 .09
❑ 68 Yao Ming 1.50 .70
❑ 69 Ron Artest .40 .18
❑ 70 Jamal Crawford .20 .09
❑ 71 Jason Richardson .60 .25
❑ 72 Eddie Griffin .40 .18
❑ 73 Keith Van Horn .60 .25
❑ 74 Jason Kidd 1.00 .45
❑ 75 Cuttino Mobley .40 .18
❑ 76 Brent Barry .40 .18
❑ 77 Eddy Curry .40 .18
❑ 78 Quentin Richardson .40 .18
❑ 79 Dajuan Wagner .40 .18
❑ 80 Tom Gugliotta .20 .09
❑ 81 Andrei Kirilenko .60 .25
❑ 82 Shane Battier .60 .25
❑ 83 Alonzo Mourning .40 .18
❑ 84 Clifford Robinson .20 .09
❑ 85 Erick Dampier .40 .18
❑ 86 Antoine Walker .60 .25
❑ 87 Marcus Haislip .20 .09
❑ 88 Kerry Kittles .20 .09
❑ 89 Lonny Baxter .20 .09
❑ 90 Troy Murphy .60 .25
❑ 91 Glenn Robinson .60 .25
❑ 92 Ricky Davis .60 .25
❑ 93 Richard Hamilton .40 .18
❑ 94 Ben Wallace .60 .25
❑ 95 Toni Kukoc .40 .18
❑ 96 Raja Bell .20 .09
❑ 97 Dikembe Mutombo .40 .18
❑ 98 Eddie Robinson .40 .18
❑ 99 Antonio Davis .20 .09
❑ 100 Anfernee Hardaway .60 .25
❑ 101 Rasheed Wallace .60 .25
❑ 102 Christian Laettner .40 .18
❑ 103 Eduardo Najera .40 .18
❑ 104 Jonathan Bender .40 .18
❑ 105 Rodney Rogers .20 .09
❑ 106 Baron Davis .60 .25
❑ 107 Chris Webber .60 .25
❑ 108 Matt Harpring .60 .25
❑ 109 Raef LaFrentz .40 .18
❑ 110 Steve Nash .60 .25
❑ 111 Travis Best .20 .09
❑ 112 Tony Delk .20 .09
❑ 113 Malik Rose .20 .09
❑ 114 Al Harrington .40 .18
❑ 115 Bonzi Wells .40 .18
❑ 116 Voshon Lenard .20 .09
❑ 117 Radoslav Nesterovic .40 .18
❑ 118 Mike Bibby .60 .25
❑ 119 Dan Dickau .20 .09
❑ 120 Jalen Rose .60 .25
❑ 121 Lucious Harris .20 .09
❑ 122 David Wesley .20 .09
❑ 123 Rashard Lewis .60 .25
❑ 124 Ira Newble .20 .09
❑ 125 Chauncey Billups .40 .18
❑ 126 Kareem Rush .40 .18
❑ 127 Michael Dickerson .20 .09
❑ 128 Walt Williams .20 .09
❑ 129 Donnell Harvey .20 .09
❑ 130 Tyronn Lue .20 .09
❑ 131 Carlos Boozer .60 .25
❑ 132 Moochie Norris .20 .09
❑ 133 John Salmons .20 .09
❑ 134 Vlade Divac .40 .18
❑ 135 Shammond Williams .20 .09
❑ 136 Brendan Haywood .20 .09
❑ 137 George Lynch .20 .09
❑ 138 Dirk Nowitzki 1.00 .45
❑ 139 Bruce Bowen .20 .09
❑ 140 Brian Skinner .20 .09
❑ 141 Juan Dixon .40 .18
❑ 142 Eric Williams .20 .09
❑ 143 Grant Hill .60 .25
❑ 144 Corey Maggette .40 .18
❑ 145 Earl Boykins .40 .18
❑ 146 Lamar Odom .60 .25
❑ 147 Keyon Dooling .20 .09
❑ 148 Joe Smith .40 .18
❑ 149 Corliss Williamson .40 .18
❑ 150 Robert Horry .40 .18
❑ 151 Jamaal Magloire .20 .09
❑ 152 Mehmet Okur .20 .09
❑ 153 Elton Brand .60 .25
❑ 154 Steve Smith .40 .18
❑ 155 Predrag Drobnjak .20 .09
❑ 156 Allan Houston .40 .18
❑ 157 Jerome Williams .20 .09
❑ 158 Karl Malone .60 .25
❑ 159 Michael Olowokandi .20 .09
❑ 160 Terrell Brandon .20 .09
❑ 161 Eric Snow .40 .18
❑ 162 Tim Duncan 1.25 .55
❑ 163 Juwan Howard .40 .18
❑ 164 Jason Williams .40 .18
❑ 165 Stephon Marbury .60 .25
❑ 166 J.R. Bremer .20 .09
❑ 167 Shaquille O'Neal 1.50 .70
❑ 168 Mike Dunleavy .40 .18
❑ 169 Latrell Sprewell .60 .25
❑ 170 Troy Hudson .20 .09
❑ 171 Alvin Williams .20 .09
❑ 172 Shawn Marion .60 .25
❑ 173 Jermaine O'Neal .60 .25
❑ 174 P.J. Brown .20 .09
❑ 175 Howard Eisley .20 .09
❑ 176 Jerry Stackhouse .60 .25
❑ 177 Qyntel Woods .20 .09
❑ 178 Larry Hughes .40 .18
❑ 179 Donyell Marshall .40 .18
❑ 180 Greg Ostertag .20 .09
❑ 181 Kwame Brown .40 .18
❑ 182 Reggie Evans .20 .09
❑ 183 DeShawn Stevenson .20 .09
❑ 184 Lorenzen Wright .20 .09
❑ 185 Lindsey Hunter .20 .09
❑ 186 Kenyon Martin .60 .25
❑ 187 Kobe Bryant 2.50 1.10
❑ 188 Scott Padgett .20 .09
❑ 189 Michael Finley .60 .25
❑ 190 Peja Stojakovic .60 .25
❑ 191 Zydrunas Ilgauskas .40 .18
❑ 192 Vincent Yarbrough .20 .09
❑ 193 Jamal Mashburn .40 .18
❑ 194 Smush Parker .20 .09
❑ 195 Caron Butler .60 .25
❑ 196 Derek Fisher .60 .25
❑ 197 Damon Stoudamire .40 .18
❑ 198 Nene Hilario .40 .18
❑ 199 Allen Iverson 1.25 .55
❑ 200 Anthony Mason .20 .09
❑ 201 Rasual Butler .40 .18
❑ 202 Tony Parker .60 .25
❑ 203 Marcus Fizer .40 .18
❑ 204 Amare Stoudemire 1.50 .70
❑ 205 Marc Jackson .40 .18
❑ 206 Desmond Mason .40 .18
❑ 207 Marcus Camby .40 .18
❑ 208 Ruben Patterson .40 .18
❑ 209 Bob Sura .20 .09
❑ 210 Rick Fox .40 .18
❑ 211 Jim Jackson .20 .09
❑ 212 Walter McCarty .20 .09
❑ 213 Gary Payton .60 .25
❑ 214 Elden Campbell .20 .09
❑ 215 Steve Francis .60 .25
❑ 216 Stromile Swift .40 .18
❑ 217 Stephen Jackson .20 .09
❑ 218 Antonio McDyess .40 .18
❑ 219 Morris Peterson .40 .18
❑ 220 Wally Szczerbiak .40 .18
❑ 221 Tim Duncan AW 1.25 .55
❑ 222 Amare Stoudemire AW 1.50 .70
❑ 223 Bobby Jackson AW .40 .18
❑ 224 Ben Wallace AW .60 .25
❑ 225 Gilbert Arenas AW .60 .25
❑ 226 Tracy McGrady AW 1.50 .70
❑ 227 Kobe Bryant AW 2.50 1.10
❑ 228 Kevin Garnett AW 1.25 .55
❑ 229 Shaquille O'Neal AW 1.50 .70
❑ 230 Yao Ming AW 1.50 .70
❑ 231 Stephon Marbury BS .60 .25
❑ 232 Ron Artest BS .40 .18
❑ 233 Troy Hudson BS .20 .09
❑ 234 Ray Allen BS .60 .25
❑ 235 Matt Harpring BS .60 .25
❑ 236 Jermaine O'Neal BS .60 .25
❑ 237 Jason Kidd BS 1.00 .45
❑ 238 Jason Williams BS .40 .18
❑ 239 Zydrunas Ilgauskas BS .40 .18
❑ 240 Jamal Mashburn BS .40 .18
❑ 241 Yao Ming BS 1.50 .70
❑ 242 Peja Stojakovic BS .60 .25
❑ 243 Tony Parker BS .60 .25
❑ 244 Caron Butler BS .60 .25
❑ 245 Amare Stoudemire BS 1.50 .70
❑ 246 Troy Murphy BS .60 .25
❑ 247 Nene Hilario BS .40 .18
❑ 248 Allen Iverson BS 1.25 .55
❑ 249 Kobe Bryant BS 2.50 1.10
❑ 250 Tim Duncan BS 1.25 .55
❑ 251 Tracy McGrady BS 1.50 .70
❑ 252 Kevin Garnett BS 1.25 .55
❑ 253 Drew Gooden BS .40 .18
❑ 254 Kenyon Martin BS .60 .25
❑ 255 Dirk Nowitzki BS 1.00 .45
❑ 256 Paul Pierce BS .60 .25
❑ 257 Steve Francis BS .60 .25
❑ 258 Steve Nash BS .60 .25
❑ 259 Gary Payton BS .60 .25
❑ 260 Chris Webber BS .40 .18
❑ 261 LeBron James RC 20.00 9.00
❑ 262 Darko Milicic RC 4.00 1.80
❑ 263 Carmelo Anthony RC 12.00 5.50
❑ 264 Chris Bosh RC 5.00 2.20
❑ 265 Dwyane Wade RC 6.00 2.70
❑ 266 Chris Kaman RC 3.00 1.35
❑ 267 Kirk Hinrich RC 5.00 2.20
❑ 268 T.J. Ford RC 4.00 1.80
❑ 269 Mike Sweetney RC 3.00 1.35
❑ 270 Mickael Pietrus RC 3.00 1.35
❑ 271 Jarvis Hayes RC 3.00 1.35
❑ 272 Nick Collison RC 3.00 1.35
❑ 273 Marcus Banks RC 4.00 1.80
❑ 274 Luke Ridnour RC 4.00 1.80
❑ 275 Reece Gaines RC 3.00 1.35
❑ 276 Troy Bell RC 3.00 1.35
❑ 277 Zarko Cabarkapa RC 3.00 1.35

☐ 278 David West RC	3.00	1.35
☐ 279 Luke Walton RC	4.00	1.80
☐ 280 Dahntay Jones RC	3.00	1.35
☐ 281 Boris Diaw RC	3.00	1.35
☐ 282 Zoran Planinic RC	3.00	1.35
☐ 283 Travis Outlaw RC	3.00	1.35
☐ 284 Brian Cook RC	3.00	1.35
☐ 285 Jason Kapono RC	3.00	1.35
☐ 286 Ndudi Ebi RC	3.00	1.35
☐ 287 Kendrick Perkins RC	3.00	1.35
☐ 288 Leandro Barbosa RC	3.00	1.35
☐ 289 Josh Howard RC	4.00	1.80
☐ 290 Maciej Lampe RC	3.00	1.35
☐ 291 LeBron James	30.00	13.50
Darko Milicic		
Carmelo Anthony		
☐ 292 Mike Sweetney	6.00	2.70
Chris Bosh		
Jarvis Hayes		
☐ 293 Kirk Hinrich	5.00	2.20
Nick Collison		
Chris Kaman		
☐ 294 Mike Sweetney	5.00	2.20
David West		
Brian Cook		
☐ 295 Chris Kaman	5.00	2.20
Chris Bosh		
Darko Milicic		
☐ 296 T.J. Ford	8.00	3.60
Dwyane Ford		
Kirk Hinrich		
☐ 297 Mickael Pietrus	5.00	2.20
Dahntay Jones		
Reece Gaines		
☐ 298 T.J. Ford	5.00	2.20
Marcus Banks		
Luke Ridnour		
☐ 299 Mickael Pietrus	5.00	2.20
Zarko Cabarkapa		
Jarvis Hayes		
☐ 300 LeBron James	30.00	13.50
Carmelo Anthony		
Dwyane Wade		

2000-01 Fleer Triple Crown

	Nm-Mt	Ex-Mt
COMPLETE SET w/o RC (200)	25.00	7.50
COMMON CARD (41-240)	.20	.06
COMMON ROOKIE (1-40/241)	.60	.18
☐ 1 Quentin Richardson RC	3.00	.90
☐ 2 Khalid El-Amin RC	.60	.18
☐ 3 Courtney Alexander RC	1.25	.35
☐ 4 Mike Penberthy RC	.60	.18
☐ 5 DerMarr Johnson RC	.60	.18
☐ 6 A.J. Guyton RC	.60	.18
☐ 7 Erick Barkley RC	.60	.18
☐ 8 Jamal Crawford RC	.75	.23
☐ 9 Hidayet Turkoglu RC	2.50	.75
☐ 10 Michael Redd RC	2.00	.60
☐ 11 Stromile Swift RC	2.50	.75
☐ 12 Eddie House RC	.60	.18
☐ 13 Keyon Dooling RC	.60	.18
☐ 14 Lavor Postell RC	.60	.18
☐ 15 Mateen Cleaves RC	.60	.18
☐ 16 Morris Peterson RC	2.50	.75
☐ 17 DeShawn Stevenson RC	.60	.18
☐ 18 Darius Miles RC	3.00	.90
☐ 19 Hanno Mottola RC	.60	.18
☐ 20 Jerome Moiso RC	.60	.18
☐ 21 Desmond Mason RC	.60	.18
☐ 22 Jason Collier RC	.60	.18
☐ 23 Ruben Wolkowyski RC	.60	.18
☐ 24 Eduardo Najera RC	1.50	.45
☐ 25 Kenyon Martin RC	4.00	1.20
☐ 26 Marcus Fizer RC	.60	.18
☐ 27 Etan Thomas RC	.60	.18
☐ 28 Mark Madsen RC	.60	.18
☐ 29 Pepe Sanchez RC	.60	.18
☐ 30 Brian Cardinal RC	.60	.18
☐ 31 Chris Porter RC	.60	.18
☐ 32 Dan Langhi RC	.60	.18
☐ 33 Mike Miller RC	3.00	.90
☐ 34 Chris Mihm RC	.60	.18
☐ 35 Mamadou N'Diaye RC	.60	.18
☐ 36 Dragan Tarlac RC	.60	.18
☐ 37 Iakovos Tsakalidis RC	.60	.18
☐ 38 Stephen Jackson RC	2.00	.60
☐ 39 Jamaal Magloire RC	.60	.18
☐ 40 Joel Przybilla RC	.60	.18
☐ 41 Adrian Griffin	.20	.06
☐ 42 Allan Houston	.40	.12
☐ 43 Mahmoud Abdul-Rauf	.20	.06
☐ 44 Avery Johnson	.20	.06
☐ 45 Damon Stoudamire	.40	.12
☐ 46 Jim Jackson	.20	.06
☐ 47 Jason Williams	.40	.12
☐ 48 Jason Kidd	1.00	.30
☐ 49 Ray Allen	.60	.18
☐ 50 Baron Davis	.60	.18
☐ 51 Mark Jackson	.20	.06
☐ 52 Darrick Martin	.20	.06
☐ 53 Derek Fisher	.60	.18
☐ 54 Anthony Peeler	.20	.06
☐ 55 Vince Carter	1.50	.45
☐ 56 Tim Hardaway	.40	.12
☐ 57 Richard Hamilton	.40	.12
☐ 58 Malik Rose	.20	.06
☐ 59 Antonio Daniels	.20	.06
☐ 60 Lindsey Hunter	.20	.06
☐ 61 William Avery	.20	.06
☐ 62 Reggie Miller	.60	.18
☐ 63 Shareef Abdur-Rahim	.60	.18
☐ 64 Travis Best	.20	.06
☐ 65 John Stockton	.60	.18
☐ 66 Kenny Anderson	.40	.12
☐ 67 Trajan Langdon	.20	.06
☐ 68 Sam Cassell	.60	.18
☐ 69 Chucky Atkins	.20	.06
☐ 70 Laron Profit	.20	.06
☐ 71 Andre Miller	.40	.12
☐ 72 Erick Strickland	.20	.06
☐ 73 Ron Artest	.40	.12
☐ 74 Kobe Bryant	2.50	.75
☐ 75 Ricky Davis	.40	.12
☐ 76 Allen Iverson	1.25	.35
☐ 77 Steve Smith	.40	.12
☐ 78 Alvin Williams	.20	.06
☐ 79 Randy Brown	.20	.06
☐ 80 Michael Dickerson	.40	.12
☐ 81 Tyronn Lue	.40	.12
☐ 82 Bonzi Wells	.40	.12
☐ 83 Felipe Lopez	.20	.06
☐ 84 Steve Francis	.60	.18
☐ 85 Jaren Jackson	.20	.06
☐ 86 Anthony Carter	.40	.12
☐ 87 Mitch Richmond	.40	.12
☐ 88 Sherman Douglas	.20	.06
☐ 89 Cuttino Mobley	.40	.12
☐ 90 Mario Elie	.20	.06
☐ 91 Tariq Abdul-Wahad	.20	.06
☐ 92 Ron Mercer	.40	.12
☐ 93 Jalen Rose	.60	.18
☐ 94 Mike Bibby	.60	.18
☐ 95 Voshon Lenard	.20	.06
☐ 96 Derek Anderson	.40	.12
☐ 97 Kendall Gill	.20	.06
☐ 98 Muggsy Bogues	.40	.12
☐ 99 Eddie Jones	.60	.18
☐ 100 Larry Hughes	.40	.12
☐ 101 Latrell Sprewell	.60	.18
☐ 102 Stephon Marbury	.60	.18
☐ 103 Eric Piatkowski	.40	.12
☐ 104 Brevin Knight	.20	.06
☐ 105 Isaiah Rider	.40	.12
☐ 106 Wesley Person	.20	.06
☐ 107 Nick Van Exel	.60	.18
☐ 108 Dell Curry	.20	.06
☐ 109 Tony Delk	.20	.06
☐ 110 Glen Rice	.40	.12
☐ 111 Bobby Jackson	.40	.12
☐ 112 Kerry Kittles	.20	.06
☐ 113 John Starks	.40	.12
☐ 114 Gary Payton	.60	.18
☐ 115 Mookie Blaylock	.20	.06
☐ 116 David Wesley	.20	.06
☐ 117 Rod Strickland	.20	.06
☐ 118 Terrell Brandon	.40	.12
☐ 119 Steve Nash	.60	.18
☐ 120 Moochie Norris	.20	.06
☐ 121 Eric Snow	.40	.12
☐ 122 Chauncey Billups	.40	.12
☐ 123 Darrell Armstrong	.20	.06
☐ 124 Ron Harper	.40	.12
☐ 125 Dion Glover	.20	.06
☐ 126 Vin Baker	.40	.12
☐ 127 Terry Mills	.20	.06
☐ 128 Joe Smith	.40	.12
☐ 129 Kurt Thomas	.40	.12
☐ 130 Dirk Nowitzki	1.00	.30
☐ 131 Sean Elliott	.40	.12
☐ 132 Jerome Williams	.20	.06
☐ 133 Larry Johnson	.40	.12
☐ 134 LaPhonso Ellis	.20	.06
☐ 135 Pat Garrity	.20	.06
☐ 136 Lawrence Funderburke	.20	.06
☐ 137 Elton Brand	.60	.18
☐ 138 Rashard Lewis	.40	.12
☐ 139 Shawn Kemp	.40	.12
☐ 140 Elden Campbell	.20	.06
☐ 141 Christian Laettner	.40	.12
☐ 142 Al Harrington	.40	.12
☐ 143 Billy Owens	.20	.06
☐ 144 Wally Szczerbiak	.40	.12
☐ 145 Jonathan Bender	.40	.12
☐ 146 Karl Malone	.60	.18
☐ 147 Andrew DeClercq	.20	.06
☐ 148 Danny Manning	.40	.12
☐ 149 Antoine Walker	.60	.18
☐ 150 Jason Caffey	.20	.06
☐ 151 P.J. Brown	.20	.06
☐ 152 Matt Harpring	.60	.18
☐ 153 Mark Strickland	.20	.06
☐ 154 Theo Ratliff	.40	.12
☐ 155 Ruben Patterson	.40	.12
☐ 156 Tom Gugliotta	.20	.06
☐ 157 Derrick Coleman	.20	.06
☐ 158 Lorenzen Wright	.20	.06
☐ 159 Tracy McGrady	1.50	.45
☐ 160 Quincy Lewis	.20	.06
☐ 161 Tony Battie	.20	.06
☐ 162 Keith Van Horn	.60	.18
☐ 163 Paul Pierce	.60	.18
☐ 164 Glenn Robinson	.60	.18
☐ 165 John Wallace	.20	.06
☐ 166 Popeye Jones	.20	.06
☐ 167 Kevin Garnett	1.25	.35
☐ 168 Donyell Marshall	.40	.12
☐ 169 Michael Finley	.60	.18
☐ 170 Nick Anderson	.20	.06
☐ 171 Danny Fortson	.20	.06
☐ 172 Keon Clark	.40	.12
☐ 173 Juwan Howard	.40	.12
☐ 174 Brian Grant	.40	.12
☐ 175 Marcus Camby	.40	.12
☐ 176 Scottie Pippen	1.00	.30
☐ 177 Shawn Marion	.60	.18
☐ 178 Lamar Odom	.60	.18
☐ 179 Charles Oakley	.20	.06
☐ 180 Tim James	.20	.06
☐ 181 Eric Williams	.20	.06
☐ 182 Tim Duncan	1.25	.35
☐ 183 Andrae Patterson	.20	.06
☐ 184 Toni Kukoc	.40	.12
☐ 185 Chris Mullin	.60	.18
☐ 186 Alan Henderson	.20	.06
☐ 187 Maurice Taylor	.20	.06
☐ 188 Chris Webber	.60	.18
☐ 189 Jamal Mashburn	.40	.12

❑ 190	Rodney Rogers	.20	.06
❑ 191	Loy Vaught	.20	.06
❑ 192	Carlos Rogers	.20	.06
❑ 193	Grant Hill	.60	.18
❑ 194	George Lynch	.20	.06
❑ 195	Antonio McDyess	.40	.12
❑ 196	Tim Thomas	.40	.12
❑ 197	Roshown McLeod	.20	.06
❑ 198	Antawn Jamison	.60	.18
❑ 199	Clifford Robinson	.20	.06
❑ 200	Corey Maggette	.40	.12
❑ 201	Horace Grant	.40	.12
❑ 202	David Benoit	.20	.06
❑ 203	Cedric Ceballos	.20	.06
❑ 204	Antonio Davis	.20	.06
❑ 205	Lamond Murray	.20	.06
❑ 206	Jerry Stackhouse	.60	.18
❑ 207	Jermaine O'Neal	.60	.18
❑ 208	Anthony Mason	.40	.12
❑ 209	Cedric Henderson	.20	.06
❑ 210	Corliss Williamson	.40	.12
❑ 211	Austin Croshere	.40	.12
❑ 212	Radoslav Nesterovic	.40	.12
❑ 213	Hakeem Olajuwon	.60	.18
❑ 214	Nazr Mohammed	.20	.06
❑ 215	David Robinson	.60	.18
❑ 216	Jeff McInnis	.20	.06
❑ 217	Brad Miller	.60	.18
❑ 218	Evan Eschmeyer	.20	.06
❑ 219	Jelani McCoy	.20	.06
❑ 220	Sean Rooks	.20	.06
❑ 221	Dikembe Mutombo	.40	.12
❑ 222	Othella Harrington	.20	.06
❑ 223	John Amaechi	.20	.06
❑ 224	Erick Dampier	.40	.12
❑ 225	Calvin Booth	.20	.06
❑ 226	Adonal Foyle	.20	.06
❑ 227	Michael Doleac	.20	.06
❑ 228	Michael Olowokandi	.20	.06
❑ 229	Matt Geiger	.20	.06
❑ 230	Vlade Divac	.40	.12
❑ 231	Bryant Reeves	.20	.06
❑ 232	Shaquille O'Neal	1.50	.45
❑ 233	Todd Fuller	.20	.06
❑ 234	Arvydas Sabonis	.40	.12
❑ 235	Jim McIlvaine	.20	.06
❑ 236	Isaac Austin	.20	.06
❑ 237	Raef LaFrentz	.40	.12
❑ 238	Rasheed Wallace	.60	.18
❑ 239	Kelvin Cato	.20	.06
❑ 240	Patrick Ewing	.60	.18
❑ 241	Marc Jackson RC	3.00	.90

1989-90 Hoops

	Nm-Mt	Ex-Mt
COMPLETE SET (352)	25.00	10.00
COMPLETE SERIES 1 (300)	20.00	8.00
COMPLETE SERIES 2 (52)	5.00	2.00
COMMON CARD (1-352)	.05	.02
COMMON SP	.15	.06

❑ 1	Joe Dumars	.25	.10
❑ 2	Tree Rollins	.05	.02
❑ 3	Kenny Walker	.05	.02
❑ 4	Mychal Thompson	.05	.02
❑ 5	Alvin Robertson SP	.15	.06
❑ 6	Vinny Del Negro RC	.25	.10
❑ 7	Greg Anderson SP	.15	.06
❑ 8	Rod Strickland RC	.75	.30
❑ 9	Ed Pinckney	.05	.02
❑ 10	Dale Ellis	.10	.04
❑ 11	Chuck Daly CO RC	.25	.10
❑ 12	Eric Leckner	.05	.02
❑ 13	Charles Davis	.05	.02
❑ 14	Cotton Fitzsimmons CO (No NBA logo on back in bottom right)	.05	.02
❑ 15	Byron Scott	.10	.04
❑ 16	Derrick Chievous	.05	.02
❑ 17	Reggie Lewis RC	.25	.10
❑ 18	Jim Paxson	.05	.02
❑ 19	Tony Campbell RC	.05	.02
❑ 20	Rolando Blackman	.05	.02
❑ 21	Michael Jordan AS	1.50	.60
❑ 22	Cliff Levingston	.05	.02
❑ 23	Roy Tarpley	.05	.02
❑ 24	Harold Pressley UER (Cinderella misspelled as cindarella)	.05	.02
❑ 25	Larry Nance	.10	.04
❑ 26	Chris Morris RC	.10	.04
❑ 27	Bob Hansen UER (Drafted in '84, should say '83)	.05	.02
❑ 28	Mark Price AS	.05	.02
❑ 29	Reggie Miller	.60	.24
❑ 30	Karl Malone	.40	.16
❑ 31	Sidney Lowe SP	.15	.06
❑ 32	Ron Anderson	.05	.02
❑ 33	Mike Gminski	.05	.02
❑ 34	Scott Brooks RC	.05	.02
❑ 35	Kevin Johnson RC	.50	.20
❑ 36	Mark Bryant RC	.05	.02
❑ 37	Rik Smits RC	.30	.12
❑ 38	Tim Perry RC	.05	.02
❑ 39	Ralph Sampson	.05	.02
❑ 40	Danny Manning RC UER (Missing 1988 in draft info)	.30	.12
❑ 41	Kevin Edwards RC	.05	.02
❑ 42	Paul Mokeski	.05	.02
❑ 43	Dale Ellis AS	.05	.02
❑ 44	Walter Berry	.05	.02
❑ 45	Chuck Person	.10	.04
❑ 46	Rick Mahorn SP	.15	.06
❑ 47	Joe Kleine	.05	.02
❑ 48	Brad Daugherty AS	.05	.02
❑ 49	Mike Woodson	.05	.02
❑ 50	Brad Daugherty	.05	.02
❑ 51	Shelton Jones SP	.15	.06
❑ 52	Michael Adams	.05	.02
❑ 53	Wes Unseld CO	.05	.02
❑ 54	Rex Chapman RC	.25	.10
❑ 55	Kelly Tripucka	.05	.02
❑ 56	Rickey Green	.05	.02
❑ 57	Frank Johnson SP	.15	.06
❑ 58	Johnny Newman RC	.05	.02
❑ 59	Billy Thompson	.05	.02
❑ 60	Stu Jackson CO	.05	.02
❑ 61	Walter Davis	.05	.02
❑ 62	Brian Shaw RC SP UER (Gary Grant led rookies in assists, not Shaw)	.25	.10
❑ 63	Gerald Wilkins	.05	.02
❑ 64	Armon Gilliam	.05	.02
❑ 65	Maurice Cheeks SP	.25	.10
❑ 66	Jack Sikma	.05	.02
❑ 67	Harvey Grant RC	.05	.02
❑ 68	Jim Lynam CO	.05	.02
❑ 69	Clyde Drexler AS	.10	.04
❑ 70	Xavier McDaniel	.05	.02
❑ 71	Danny Young	.05	.02
❑ 72	Fennis Dembo	.05	.02
❑ 73	Mark Acres SP	.15	.06
❑ 74	Brad Lohaus SP RC	.15	.06
❑ 75	Manute Bol	.05	.02
❑ 76	Purvis Short	.05	.02
❑ 77	Allen Leavell	.05	.02
❑ 78	Johnny Dawkins SP	.15	.06
❑ 79	Paul Pressey	.05	.02
❑ 80	Patrick Ewing	.25	.10
❑ 81	Bill Wennington RC	.25	.10
❑ 82	Danny Schayes	.05	.02
❑ 83	Derek Smith	.05	.02
❑ 84	Moses Malone AS	.10	.04
❑ 85	Jeff Malone	.05	.02
❑ 86	Otis Smith SP RC	.15	.06
❑ 87	Trent Tucker	.05	.02
❑ 88	Robert Reid	.05	.02
❑ 89	John Paxson	.05	.02
❑ 90	Chris Mullin	.25	.10
❑ 91	Tom Garrick	.05	.02
❑ 92	Willis Reed CO SP UER (Gambling, should be Grambling)	.25	.10
❑ 93	Dave Corzine SP	.15	.06
❑ 94	Mark Alarie	.05	.02
❑ 95	Mark Aguirre	.05	.02
❑ 96	Charles Barkley AS	.20	.08
❑ 97	Sidney Green SP	.15	.06
❑ 98	Kevin Willis	.10	.04
❑ 99	Dave Hoppen	.05	.02
❑ 100	Terry Cummings SP	.25	.10
❑ 101	Dwayne Washington SP	.15	.06
❑ 102	Larry Brown CO	.10	.04
❑ 103	Kevin Duckworth	.05	.02
❑ 104	Uwe Blab SP	.15	.06
❑ 105	Terry Porter	.05	.02
❑ 106	Craig Ehlo RC**	.05	.02
❑ 107	Don Casey CO	.05	.02
❑ 108	Pat Riley CO	.25	.10
❑ 109	John Salley	.05	.02
❑ 110	Charles Barkley	.40	.16
❑ 111	Sam Bowie SP	.15	.06
❑ 112	Earl Cureton	.05	.02
❑ 113	Craig Hodges UER (3-pointing shooting)	.05	.02
❑ 114	Benoit Benjamin	.05	.02
❑ 115A	Spud Webb ERR SP (Signed 9/27/89)	.25	.10
❑ 115B	Spud Webb COR (Second series; signed 9/26/85)	.10	.04
❑ 116	Karl Malone AS	.25	.10
❑ 117	Sleepy Floyd	.05	.02
❑ 118	John Williams	.05	.02
❑ 119	Michael Holton	.05	.02
❑ 120	Alex English	.05	.02
❑ 121	Dennis Johnson	.05	.02
❑ 122	Wayne Cooper SP	.15	.06
❑ 123A	Don Chaney CO (Line next to NBA coaching record)	.05	.02
❑ 123B	Don Chaney CO (No line)	.05	.02
❑ 124	A.C. Green	.10	.04
❑ 125	Adrian Dantley	.05	.02
❑ 126	Del Harris CO	.05	.02
❑ 127	Dick Harter CO	.05	.02
❑ 128	Reggie Williams RC	.05	.02
❑ 129	Bill Hanzlik	.05	.02
❑ 130	Dominique Wilkins	.25	.10
❑ 131	Herb Williams	.05	.02
❑ 132	Steve Johnson SP	.15	.06
❑ 133	Alex English AS	.05	.02
❑ 134	Darrell Walker	.05	.02
❑ 135	Bill Laimbeer	.10	.04
❑ 136	Fred Roberts RC**	.05	.02
❑ 137	Hersey Hawkins RC	.30	.12
❑ 138	David Robinson SP RC	10.00	4.00
❑ 139	Brad Sellers SP	.15	.06
❑ 140	John Stockton	.60	.24
❑ 141	Grant Long RC	.05	.02
❑ 142	Marc Iavaroni SP	.15	.06
❑ 143	Steve Alford SP RC	.25	.10
❑ 144	Jeff Lamp SP	.15	.06
❑ 145	Buck Williams SP UER (Won ROY in '81, should say '82)	.25	.10
❑ 146	Mark Jackson AS	.05	.02
❑ 147	Jim Petersen	.05	.02
❑ 148	Steve Stipanovich SP	.15	.06
❑ 149	Sam Vincent SP RC	.15	.06
❑ 150	Larry Bird	1.00	.40
❑ 151	Jon Koncak RC	.05	.02
❑ 152	Olden Polynice RC	.10	.04
❑ 153	Randy Breuer	.05	.02
❑ 154	John Battle RC	.05	.02
❑ 155	Mark Eaton	.05	.02
❑ 156	Kevin McHale AS UER (No TM on Celtics	.10	.04

logo on back)
❑ 157 Jerry Sichting SP .... .15 .06
❑ 158 Pat Cummings SP .... .15 .06
❑ 159 Patrick Ewing AS .... .10 .04
❑ 160 Mark Price .... .10 .04
❑ 161 Jerry Reynolds CO.......... .05 .02
❑ 162 Ken Norman RC.......... .05 .02
❑ 163 John Bagley SP UER .... .15 .06
(Picked in '83& should say '82)
❑ 164 Christian Welp SP .... .15 .06
❑ 165 Reggie Theus SP .... .25 .10
❑ 166 Magic Johnson AS .... .40 .16
❑ 167 John Long UER .... .05 .02
(Picked in '79, should say '78)
❑ 168 Larry Smith SP .... .15 .06
❑ 169 Charles Shackleford RC .05 .02
❑ 170 Tom Chambers .... .05 .02
❑ 171A John MacLeod CO SP .15 .06
ERR (NBA logo in wrong place)
❑ 171B John MacLeod CO...... .05 .02
COR (Second series)
❑ 172 Ron Rothstein CO .... .05 .02
❑ 173 Joe Wolf .... .05 .02
❑ 174 Mark Eaton AS .... .05 .02
❑ 175 Jon Sundvold .... .05 .02
❑ 176 Scott Hastings SP .... .15 .06
❑ 177 Isiah Thomas AS .... .10 .04
❑ 178 Hakeem Olajuwon AS .. .25 .10
❑ 179 Mike Fratello CO .... .10 .04
❑ 180 Hakeem Olajuwon .... .40 .16
❑ 181 Randolph Keys .... .05 .02
❑ 182 Richard Anderson UER .05 .02
(Trail Blazers on front should be all caps)
❑ 183 Dan Majerle RC .... .30 .12
❑ 184 Derek Harper .... .10 .04
❑ 185 Robert Parish .... .10 .04
❑ 186 Ricky Berry SP .... .15 .06
❑ 187 Michael Cooper .... .05 .02
❑ 188 Vinnie Johnson.......... .10 .04
❑ 189 James Donaldson .... .05 .02
❑ 190 Clyde Drexler UER.......... .25 .10
(4th pick, should be 14th)
❑ 191 Jay Vincent SP .... .15 .06
❑ 192 Nate McMillan .... .10 .04
❑ 193 Kevin Duckworth AS .... .05 .02
❑ 194 Ledell Eackles RC .... .05 .02
❑ 195 Eddie Johnson .... .10 .04
❑ 196 Terry Teagle.......... .05 .02
❑ 197 Tom Chambers AS.......... .05 .02
❑ 198 Joe Barry Carroll .... .05 .02
❑ 199 Dennis Hopson RC .... .05 .02
❑ 200 Michael Jordan.......... 3.00 1.20
❑ 201 Jerome Lane RC .... .05 .02
❑ 202 Greg Kite RC** .... .05 .02
❑ 203 David Rivers SP .... .15 .06
❑ 204 Sylvester Gray .... .05 .02
❑ 205 Ron Harper.......... .10 .04
❑ 206 Frank Brickowski .... .05 .02
❑ 207 Rory Sparrow .... .05 .02
❑ 208 Gerald Henderson .... .05 .02
❑ 209 Rod Higgins UER.......... .05 .02
('85-86 stats should also include San Antonio and Seattle)
❑ 210 James Worthy .... .25 .10
❑ 211 Dennis Rodman .... 1.00 .40
❑ 212 Ricky Pierce .... .05 .02
❑ 213 Charles Oakley.......... .10 .04
❑ 214 Steve Colter .... .05 .02
❑ 215 Danny Ainge.......... .10 .04
❑ 216 Lenny Wilkens CO UER .10 .04
(No NBA logo on back in bottom right)
❑ 217 Larry Nance AS .... .05 .02
❑ 218 Muggsy Bogues .... .10 .04
❑ 219 James Worthy AS .... .10 .04
❑ 220 Lafayette Lever .... .05 .02
❑ 221 Quintin Dailey SP.......... .15 .06
❑ 222 Lester Conner .... .05 .02
❑ 223 Jose Ortiz.......... .05 .02
❑ 224 Micheal Williams RC SP .25 .10

UER (Misspelled Michael on card)
❑ 225 Wayman Tisdale .... .05 .02
❑ 226 Mike Sanders SP .... .15 .06
❑ 227 Jim Farmer SP .... .15 .06
❑ 228 Mark West .... .05 .02
❑ 229 Jeff Hornacek RC.......... .30 .12
❑ 230 Chris Mullin AS.......... .10 .04
❑ 231 Vern Fleming .... .05 .02
❑ 232 Kenny Smith.......... .05 .02
❑ 233 Derrick McKey .... .05 .02
❑ 234 Dominique Wilkins AS .. .10 .04
❑ 235 Willie Anderson RC .... .05 .02
❑ 236 Keith Lee SP .... .15 .06
❑ 237 Buck Johnson RC .... .05 .02
❑ 238 Randy Wittman.......... .05 .02
❑ 239 Terry Catledge SP .... .15 .06
❑ 240 Bernard King .... .05 .02
❑ 241 Darrell Griffith.......... .05 .02
❑ 242 Horace Grant .... .10 .04
❑ 243 Rony Seikaly RC .... .25 .10
❑ 244 Scottie Pippen .... 1.50 .60
❑ 245 Michael Cage UER.......... .05 .02
(Picked in '85, should say '84)
❑ 246 Kurt Rambis .... .05 .02
❑ 247 Morlon Wiley SP RC .... .15 .06
❑ 248 Ronnie Grandison .... .05 .02
❑ 249 Scott Skiles SP RC .... .25 .10
❑ 250 Isiah Thomas .... .25 .10
❑ 251 Thurl Bailey .... .05 .02
❑ 252 Doc Rivers .... .10 .04
❑ 253 Stuart Gray SP .... .15 .06
❑ 254 John Williams.......... .05 .02
❑ 255 Bill Cartwright.......... .05 .02
❑ 256 Terry Cummings AS.......... .05 .02
❑ 257 Rodney McCray .... .05 .02
❑ 258 Larry Krystkowiak RC.... .05 .02
❑ 259 Will Perdue RC.......... .05 .02
❑ 260 Mitch Richmond RC .... 1.25 .50
❑ 261 Blair Rasmussen .... .05 .02
❑ 262 Charles Smith RC .... .25 .10
❑ 263 Tyrone Corbin SP RC .. .15 .06
❑ 264 Kelvin Upshaw .... .05 .02
❑ 265 Otis Thorpe .... .10 .04
❑ 266 Phil Jackson CO.......... .25 .10
❑ 267 Jerry Sloan CO.......... .10 .04
❑ 268 John Shasky.......... .05 .02
❑ 269A B. Bickerstaff CO SP .. .15 .06
ERR (Born 2/11/44)
❑ 269B B. Bickerstaff CO .... .05 .02
COR (Second series; Born 11/2/43)
❑ 270 Magic Johnson .... .75 .30
❑ 271 Vernon Maxwell RC .... .25 .10
❑ 272 Tim McCormick .... .05 .02
❑ 273 Don Nelson CO .... .10 .04
❑ 274 Gary Grant RC.......... .05 .02
❑ 275 Sidney Moncrief SP .... .15 .06
❑ 276 Roy Hinson.......... .05 .02
❑ 277 Jimmy Rodgers CO .... .05 .02
❑ 278 Antoine Carr.......... .05 .02
❑ 279A Orlando Woolridge SP .15 .06
ERR (No Trademark)
❑ 279B Orlando Woolridge...... .05 .02
COR (Second series)
❑ 280 Kevin McHale .... .25 .10
❑ 281 LaSalle Thompson .... .05 .02
❑ 282 Detlef Schrempf .... .10 .04
❑ 283 Doug Moe CO .... .05 .02
❑ 284A James Edwards .... .05 .02
(Small black line next to card number)
❑ 284B James Edwards .... .05 .02
(No small black line)
❑ 285 Jerome Kersey .... .05 .02
❑ 286 Sam Perkins.......... .10 .04
❑ 287 Sedale Threatt .... .05 .02
❑ 288 Tim Kempton SP .... .15 .06
❑ 289 Mark McNamara.......... .05 .02
❑ 290 Moses Malone .... .25 .10
❑ 291 Rick Adelman CO UER .05 .02
(Chemekata misspelled as Chemketa)
❑ 292 Dick Versace CO .... .05 .02
❑ 293 Alton Lister SP .... .15 .06

❑ 294 Winston Garland .... .05 .02
❑ 295 Kiki Vandeweghe .... .05 .02
❑ 296 Brad Davis .... .05 .02
❑ 297 John Stockton AS.......... .25 .10
❑ 298 Jay Humphries .... .05 .02
❑ 299 Dell Curry .... .05 .02
❑ 300 Mark Jackson.......... .10 .04
❑ 301 Morlon Wiley .... .05 .02
❑ 302 Reggie Theus.......... .10 .04
❑ 303 Otis Smith.......... .05 .02
❑ 304 Tod Murphy RC .... .05 .02
❑ 305 Sidney Green .... .05 .02
❑ 306 Shelton Jones .... .05 .02
❑ 307 Mark Acres.......... .05 .02
❑ 308 Terry Catledge .... .05 .02
❑ 309 Larry Smith .... .05 .02
❑ 310 David Robinson IA ...... 2.00 .80
❑ 311 Johnny Dawkins.......... .05 .02
❑ 312 Terry Cummings.......... .10 .04
❑ 313 Sidney Lowe.......... .05 .02
❑ 314 Bill Musselman CO.......... .05 .02
❑ 315 Buck Williams UER ...... .10 .04
(Won ROY in '81, should say '82)
❑ 316 Mel Turpin .... .05 .02
❑ 317 Scott Hastings .... .05 .02
❑ 318 Scott Skiles .... .10 .04
❑ 319 Tyrone Corbin .... .05 .02
❑ 320 Maurice Cheeks .... .05 .02
❑ 321 Matt Guokas CO .... .05 .02
❑ 322 Jeff Turner .... .05 .02
❑ 323 David Wingate .... .05 .02
❑ 324 Steve Johnson .... .05 .02
❑ 325 Alton Lister .... .05 .02
❑ 326 Ken Bannister.......... .05 .02
❑ 327 Bill Fitch CO UER.......... .05 .02
(Copyright missing on bottom of back)
❑ 328 Sam Vincent.......... .05 .02
❑ 329 Larry Drew .... .05 .02
❑ 330 Rick Mahorn .... .05 .02
❑ 331 Christian Welp .... .05 .02
❑ 332 Brad Lohaus.......... .05 .02
❑ 333 Frank Johnson .... .05 .02
❑ 334 Jim Farmer.......... .05 .02
❑ 335 Wayne Cooper .... .05 .02
❑ 336 Mike Brown RC .... .05 .02
❑ 337 Sam Bowie.......... .05 .02
❑ 338 Kevin Gamble RC .... .05 .02
❑ 339 Jerry Ice Reynolds RC .. .05 .02
❑ 340 Mike Sanders .... .05 .02
❑ 341 Bill Jones UER .... .05 .02
(Center on front, should be F)
❑ 342 Greg Anderson.......... .05 .02
❑ 343 Dave Corzine .... .05 .02
❑ 344 Micheal Williams UER .. .05 .02
(Misspelled Michael on card)
❑ 345 Jay Vincent.......... .05 .02
❑ 346 David Rivers.......... .05 .02
❑ 347 Caldwell Jones UER .... .05 .02
(He was not starting center on '83 Sixers)
❑ 348 Brad Sellers .... .05 .02
❑ 349 Scott Roth .... .05 .02
❑ 350 Alvin Robertson .... .05 .02
❑ 351 Steve Kerr RC .... .50 .20
❑ 352 Stuart Gray.......... .05 .02
❑ 353A World Champions SP 4.00 1.60
❑ 353B World Champions UER .50 .20
(George Blaha misspelled Blanha)

1990-91 Hoops

	Nm-Mt	Ex-Mt
COMPLETE SET (440)	15.00	4.50
COMPLETE SERIES 1 (336)	10.00	3.00
COMPLETE SERIES 2 (104) ..	5.00	1.50
COMMON CARD (1-440)	.05	.02
COMMON SP	.10	.03

❑ 1 Charles Barkley AS SP .... .25 .07
❑ 2 Larry Bird AS SP .... .60 .18
❑ 3 Joe Dumars AS SP .... .15 .04
❑ 4 Patrick Ewing AS SP .... .15 .04

(A-S blocks listed as 1, should be 5) UER
❑ 5 Michael Jordan AS SP .... 2.00 .60
(Won Slam Dunk in '87 and '88, not '86 and '88) UER
❑ 6 Kevin McHale AS SP .... .08 .02
❑ 7 Reggie Miller AS SP.......... .15 .04
❑ 8 Robert Parish AS SP .... .10 .03
❑ 9 Scottie Pippen AS SP ...... .60 .18
❑ 10 Dennis Rodman AS SP .. .40 .12
❑ 11 Isiah Thomas AS SP ...... .15 .04
❑ 12 Dominique Wilkins .... .15 .04
AS SP
❑ 13A All-Star Checklist SP .... .25 .07
ERR (No card number)
❑ 13B All-Star Checklist SP .... .10 .03
COR (Card number on back)
❑ 14 Rolando Blackman AS SP .10 .03
❑ 15 Tom Chambers AS SP.... .10 .03
❑ 16 Clyde Drexler AS SP ...... .08 .02
❑ 17 A.C. Green AS SP .... .10 .03
❑ 18 Magic Johnson AS SP .... .50 .15
❑ 19 Kevin Johnson AS SP .... .15 .04
❑ 20 Lafayette Lever AS SP.... .10 .03
❑ 21 Karl Malone AS SP .... .25 .07
❑ 22 Chris Mullin AS SP.......... .15 .04
❑ 23 Hakeem Olajuwon AS SP .25 .07
❑ 24 David Robinson AS SP .. .50 .15
❑ 25 John Stockton AS SP...... .20 .06
❑ 26 James Worthy AS SP...... .15 .04
❑ 27 John Battle .... .05 .02
❑ 28 Jon Koncak .... .05 .02
❑ 29 Cliff Levingston SP .... .10 .03
❑ 30 John Long SP.................. .10 .03
❑ 31 Moses Malone .... .15 .04
❑ 32 Doc Rivers .... .08 .02
❑ 33 Kenny Smith SP.............. .10 .03
❑ 34 Alexander Volkov .... .05 .02
❑ 35 Spud Webb .... .08 .02
❑ 36 Dominique Wilkins .... .15 .04
❑ 37 Kevin Willis...................... .08 .02
❑ 38 John Bagley .... .05 .02
❑ 39 Larry Bird .... .60 .18
❑ 40 Kevin Gamble.................. .05 .02
❑ 41 Dennis Johnson SP .... .05 .02
❑ 42 Joe Kleine .... .05 .02
❑ 43 Reggie Lewis .... .08 .02
❑ 44 Kevin McHale.................. .08 .02
❑ 45 Robert Parish .... .08 .02
❑ 46 Jim Paxson SP................ .08 .02
❑ 47 Ed Pinckney .... .05 .02
❑ 48 Brian Shaw...................... .15 .04
❑ 49 Richard Anderson SP...... .10 .03
❑ 50 Muggsy Bogues .... .08 .02
❑ 51 Rex Chapman .... .15 .04
❑ 52 Dell Curry .... .05 .02
❑ 53 Kenny Gattison RC .... .05 .02
❑ 54 Armon Gilliam.................. .05 .02
❑ 55 Dave Hoppen .... .05 .02
❑ 56 Randolph Keys................ .05 .02
❑ 57 J.R. Reid RC .... .05 .02
❑ 58 Robert Reid SP .... .10 .03
❑ 59 Kelly Tripucka.................. .05 .02
❑ 60 B.J. Armstrong RC .... .05 .02
❑ 61 Bill Cartwright.................. .05 .02
❑ 62 Charles Davis SP .... .10 .03
❑ 63 Horace Grant .... .08 .02
❑ 64 Craig Hodges .... .05 .02
❑ 65 Michael Jordan.............. 2.00 .60
❑ 66 Stacey King RC .... .05 .02
❑ 67 John Paxson .... .08 .02
❑ 68 Will Perdue...................... .05 .02
❑ 69 Scottie Pippen .... .60 .18
❑ 70 Winston Bennett.............. .05 .02
❑ 71 Chucky Brown RC .... .05 .02
❑ 72 Derrick Chievous .... .05 .02
❑ 73 Brad Daugherty .... .05 .02
❑ 74 Craig Ehlo .... .05 .02
❑ 75 Steve Kerr .... .15 .04
❑ 76 Paul Mokeski SP .... .10 .03
❑ 77 John Morton .... .05 .02
❑ 78 Larry Nance .... .05 .02
❑ 79 Mark Price .... .08 .02
❑ 80 Hot Rod Williams .... .05 .02
❑ 81 Steve Alford .... .05 .02
❑ 82 Rolando Blackman.......... .05 .02
❑ 83 Adrian Dantley SP .... .05 .02
❑ 84 Brad Davis .... .05 .02
❑ 85 James Donaldson .... .05 .02
❑ 86 Derek Harper .... .08 .02
❑ 87 Sam Perkins SP.............. .08 .02
❑ 88 Roy Tarpley .... .05 .02
❑ 89 Bill Wennington SP .... .10 .03
❑ 90 Herb Williams.................. .05 .02
❑ 91 Michael Adams................ .05 .02
❑ 92 Joe Barry Carroll SP ...... .10 .03
❑ 93 Walter Davis UER .... .05 .02
(Born NC, not PA)
❑ 94 Alex English SP .... .05 .02
❑ 95 Bill Hanzlik .... .05 .02
❑ 96 Jerome Lane .... .05 .02
❑ 97 Lafayette Lever SP.......... .10 .03
❑ 98 Todd Lichti RC .... .05 .02
❑ 99 Blair Rasmussen .... .05 .02
❑ 100 Danny Schayes SP ...... .10 .03
❑ 101 Mark Aguirre.................. .05 .02
❑ 102 William Bedford RC ...... .05 .02
❑ 103 Joe Dumars .... .15 .04
❑ 104 James Edwards .... .05 .02
❑ 105 Scott Hastings .... .05 .02
❑ 106 Gerald Henderson SP .. .10 .03
❑ 107 Vinnie Johnson.............. .05 .02
❑ 108 Bill Laimbeer .... .08 .02
❑ 109 Dennis Rodman .... .40 .12
❑ 110 John Salley.................... .05 .02
❑ 111 Isiah Thomas UER .... .15 .04
(No position listed on the card)
❑ 112 Manute Bol SP .... .10 .03
❑ 113 Tim Hardaway RC ...... 1.00 .30
❑ 114 Rod Higgins .... .05 .02
❑ 115 Sarunas Marciulionis RC .05 .02
❑ 116 Chris Mullin UER .... .15 .04
(Born Brooklyn, NY not New York, NY)
❑ 117 Jim Petersen .... .05 .02
❑ 118 Mitch Richmond .... .20 .06
❑ 119 Mike Smrek .... .05 .02
❑ 120 Terry Teagle SP .... .10 .03
❑ 121 Tom Tolbert RC .... .05 .02
❑ 122 Christian Welp SP .... .10 .03
❑ 123 Byron Dinkins SP .... .10 .03
❑ 124 Eric(Sleepy) Floyd .... .05 .02
❑ 125 Buck Johnson................ .05 .02
❑ 126 Vernon Maxwell .... .05 .02
❑ 127 Hakeem Olajuwon .... .25 .07
❑ 128 Larry Smith .... .05 .02
❑ 129 Otis Thorpe .... .08 .02
❑ 130 Mitchell Wiggins SP ...... .10 .03
❑ 131 Mike Woodson .... .05 .02
❑ 132 Greg Dreiling RC .... .05 .02
❑ 133 Vern Fleming .... .05 .02
❑ 134 Rickey Green SP .... .10 .03
❑ 135 Reggie Miller .... .20 .06
❑ 136 Chuck Person................ .08 .02
❑ 137 Mike Sanders................ .05 .02
❑ 138 Detlef Schrempf .... .08 .02
❑ 139 Rik Smits .... .15 .04
❑ 140 LaSalle Thompson .... .05 .02
❑ 141 Randy Wittman.............. .05 .02
❑ 142 Benoit Benjamin............ .05 .02
❑ 143 Winston Garland .... .05 .02
❑ 144 Tom Garrick .... .05 .02
❑ 145 Gary Grant .... .05 .02
❑ 146 Ron Harper.................... .08 .02
❑ 147 Danny Manning .... .08 .02
❑ 148 Jeff Martin .... .05 .02
❑ 149 Ken Norman.................. .05 .02
❑ 150 David Rivers SP .... .10 .03
❑ 151 Charles Smith................ .05 .02
❑ 152 Joe Wolf SP .... .10 .03
❑ 153 Michael Cooper SP ...... .10 .03
❑ 154 Vlade Divac RC UER.... .40 .12
(Height 6'11", should be 7'1")
❑ 155 Larry Drew .... .05 .02
❑ 156 A.C. Green .... .08 .02
❑ 157 Magic Johnson.............. .50 .15
❑ 158 Mark McNamara SP...... .10 .03
❑ 159 Byron Scott.................... .08 .02
❑ 160 Mychal Thompson .... .05 .02
❑ 161 Jay Vincent SP.............. .10 .03
❑ 162 Orlando Woolridge SP .. .10 .03
❑ 163 James Worthy .... .15 .04
❑ 164 Sherman Douglas RC .. .08 .02
❑ 165 Kevin Edwards.............. .05 .02
❑ 166 Tellis Frank SP.............. .10 .03
❑ 167 Grant Long .... .05 .02
❑ 168 Glen Rice RC .... .60 .18
❑ 169A Rony Seikaly .... .08 .02
(Athens)
❑ 169B Rony Seikaly .... .08 .02
(Beirut)
❑ 170 Rory Sparrow SP .... .10 .03
❑ 171A Jon Sundvold.............. .05 .02
(First series)
❑ 171B Billy Thompson .... .05 .02
(Second series)
❑ 172A Billy Thompson .... .05 .02
(First series)
❑ 172B Jon Sundvold.............. .05 .02
(Second series)
❑ 173 Greg Anderson.............. .05 .02
❑ 174 Jeff Grayer RC .... .05 .02
❑ 175 Jay Humphries .... .05 .02
❑ 176 Frank Kornet .... .05 .02
❑ 177 Larry Krystkowiak.......... .05 .02
❑ 178 Brad Lohaus.................. .05 .02
❑ 179 Ricky Pierce .... .05 .02
❑ 180 Paul Pressey SP .... .10 .03
❑ 181 Fred Roberts .... .05 .02
❑ 182 Alvin Robertson .... .05 .02
❑ 183 Jack Sikma.................... .05 .02
❑ 184 Randy Breuer................ .05 .02
❑ 185 Tony Campbell.............. .05 .02
❑ 186 Tyrone Corbin .... .05 .02
❑ 187 Sidney Lowe SP............ .10 .03
❑ 188 Sam Mitchell RC .... .05 .02
❑ 189 Tod Murphy .... .05 .02
❑ 190 Pooh Richardson RC .... .08 .02
❑ 191 Scott Roth SP................ .05 .02
❑ 192 Brad Sellers SP .... .10 .03
❑ 193 Mookie Blaylock RC...... .25 .07
❑ 194 Sam Bowie.................... .05 .02
❑ 195 Lester Conner .... .05 .02
❑ 196 Derrick Gervin .... .05 .02
❑ 197 Jack Haley RC .... .05 .02
❑ 198 Roy Hinson.................... .05 .02
❑ 199 Dennis Hopson SP........ .10 .03
❑ 200 Chris Morris .... .08 .02
❑ 201 Purvis Short SP .... .10 .03
❑ 202 Maurice Cheeks............ .05 .02
❑ 203 Patrick Ewing................ .15 .04
❑ 204 Stuart Gray.................... .05 .02
❑ 205 Mark Jackson................ .08 .02
❑ 206 Johnny Newman SP...... .10 .03
❑ 207 Charles Oakley.............. .08 .02
❑ 208 Trent Tucker.................. .05 .02
❑ 209 Kiki Vandeweghe .... .05 .02
❑ 210 Kenny Walker................ .05 .02
❑ 211 Eddie Lee Wilkins.......... .05 .02
❑ 212 Gerald Wilkins .... .05 .02
❑ 213 Mark Acres.................... .05 .02
❑ 214 Nick Anderson RC .... .25 .07
❑ 215 Michael Ansley UER .... .05 .02
(Ranked first, not third)
❑ 216 Terry Catledge .... .05 .02
❑ 217 Dave Corzine SP .... .10 .03
❑ 218 Sidney Green SP .... .10 .03

❑ 219 Jerry Reynolds .05 .02
❑ 220 Scott Skiles .05 .02
❑ 221 Otis Smith .05 .02
❑ 222 Reggie Theus SP .08 .02
❑ 223A Sam Vincent 1.50 .45
(Shows Michael Jordan)
❑ 223B Sam Vincent .05 .02
(Second series and shows
Sam dribbling)
❑ 224 Ron Anderson .05 .02
❑ 225 Charles Barkley .25 .07
❑ 226 Scott Brooks SP UER .10 .03
(Born French Camp,
not Lathron, Cal.)
❑ 227 Johnny Dawkins .05 .02
❑ 228 Mike Gminski .05 .02
❑ 229 Hersey Hawkins .08 .02
❑ 230 Rick Mahorn .05 .02
❑ 231 Derek Smith SP .10 .03
❑ 232 Bob Thornton .05 .02
❑ 233 Kenny Battle RC .05 .02
❑ 234A Tom Chambers .05 .02
(First series;
Forward on front)
❑ 234B Tom Chambers .05 .02
(Second series;
Guard on front)
❑ 235 Greg Grant SP RC .10 .03
❑ 236 Jeff Hornacek .08 .02
❑ 237 Eddie Johnson .08 .02
❑ 238A Kevin Johnson .15 .04
(First series;
Guard on front)
❑ 238B Kevin Johnson .15 .04
(Second series;
Forward on front)
❑ 239 Dan Majerle .15 .04
❑ 240 Tim Perry .05 .02
❑ 241 Kurt Rambis .05 .02
❑ 242 Mark West .05 .02
❑ 243 Mark Bryant .05 .02
❑ 244 Wayne Cooper .05 .02
❑ 245 Clyde Drexler .15 .04
❑ 246 Kevin Duckworth .05 .02
❑ 247 Jerome Kersey .05 .02
❑ 248 Drazen Petrovic RC .08 .02
❑ 249A Terry Porter ERR .50 .15
(No NBA symbol on back)
❑ 249B Terry Porter COR .05 .02
❑ 250 Clifford Robinson RC .25 .07
❑ 251 Buck Williams .05 .02
❑ 252 Danny Young .05 .02
❑ 253 Danny Ainge SP UER .08 .02
(Middle name Ray mis-
spelled as Rae on back)
❑ 254 Randy Allen SP .10 .03
❑ 255 Antoine Carr .05 .02
❑ 256 Vinny Del Negro SP .10 .03
❑ 257 Pervis Ellison SP RC .10 .03
❑ 258 Greg Kite SP .10 .03
❑ 259 Rodney McCray SP .10 .03
❑ 260 Harold Pressley SP .10 .03
❑ 261 Ralph Sampson .05 .02
❑ 262 Wayman Tisdale .05 .02
❑ 263 Willie Anderson .05 .02
❑ 264 Uwe Blab SP .10 .03
❑ 265 Frank Brickowski SP .10 .03
❑ 266 Terry Cummings .05 .02
❑ 267 Sean Elliott RC .30 .09
❑ 268 Caldwell Jones SP .10 .03
❑ 269 Johnny Moore SP .10 .03
❑ 270 David Robinson .50 .15
❑ 271 Rod Strickland .15 .04
❑ 272 Reggie Williams .05 .02
❑ 273 David Wingate SP .10 .03
❑ 274 Dana Barros RC UER .15 .04
(Born April, not March)
❑ 275 Michael Cage UER .05 .02
(Drafted '84, not '85)
❑ 276 Quintin Dailey .05 .02
❑ 277 Dale Ellis .08 .02
❑ 278 Steve Johnson SP .10 .03
❑ 279 Shawn Kemp RC 1.50 .45
❑ 280 Xavier McDaniel .05 .02
❑ 281 Derrick McKey .05 .02
❑ 282 Nate McMillan .08 .02

❑ 283 Olden Polynice .05 .02
❑ 284 Sedale Threatt .05 .02
❑ 285 Thurl Bailey .05 .02
❑ 286 Mike Brown .05 .02
❑ 287 Mark Eaton UER .05 .02
(72nd pick& not 82nd)
❑ 288 Blue Edwards RC .05 .02
❑ 289 Darrell Griffith .05 .02
❑ 290 Bobby Hansen SP .10 .03
❑ 291 Eric Leckner SP .10 .03
❑ 292 Karl Malone .25 .07
❑ 293 Delaney Rudd .05 .02
❑ 294 John Stockton .20 .06
❑ 295 Mark Alarie .05 .02
❑ 296 Ledell Eackles SP .10 .03
❑ 297 Harvey Grant .05 .02
❑ 298A Tom Hammonds RC .05 .02
(No rookie logo on front)
❑ 298B Tom Hammonds RC .05 .02
(Rookie logo on front)
❑ 299 Charles Jones .05 .02
❑ 300 Bernard King .05 .02
❑ 301 Jeff Malone SP .10 .03
❑ 302 Mel Turpin SP .10 .03
❑ 303 Darrell Walker .05 .02
❑ 304 John Williams .05 .02
❑ 305 Bob Weiss CO .05 .02
❑ 306 Chris Ford CO .05 .02
❑ 307 Gene Littles CO .05 .02
❑ 308 Phil Jackson CO .15 .04
❑ 309 Lenny Wilkens CO .08 .02
❑ 310 Richie Adubato CO .05 .02
❑ 311 Doug Moe CO SP .10 .03
❑ 312 Chuck Daly CO .08 .02
❑ 313 Don Nelson CO .08 .02
❑ 314 Don Chaney CO .05 .02
❑ 315 Dick Versace CO .05 .02
❑ 316 Mike Schuler CO .05 .02
❑ 317 Pat Riley CO SP .15 .04
❑ 318 Ron Rothstein CO .05 .02
❑ 319 Del Harris CO .05 .02
❑ 320 Bill Musselman CO .05 .02
❑ 321 Bill Fitch CO .05 .02
❑ 322 Stu Jackson CO .05 .02
❑ 323 Matt Guokas CO .05 .02
❑ 324 Jim Lynam CO .05 .02
❑ 325 Cotton Fitzsimmons CO .05 .02
❑ 326 Rick Adelman CO .05 .02
❑ 327 Dick Motta CO .05 .02
❑ 328 Larry Brown CO .08 .02
❑ 329 K.C. Jones CO .05 .02
❑ 330 Jerry Sloan CO .08 .02
❑ 331 Wes Unseld CO .05 .02
❑ 332 Checklist 1 SP .10 .03
❑ 333 Checklist 2 SP .10 .03
❑ 334 Checklist 3 SP .10 .03
❑ 335 Checklist 4 SP .10 .03
❑ 336 Danny Ferry SP RC .25 .07
❑ 337 Pistons Celebrate .15 .04
Dennis Rodman
❑ 338 Buck Williams FIN .15 .04
Dennis Rodman
❑ 339 Joe Dumars FIN .15 .04
❑ 340 Jerome Kersey FIN .08 .02
Isiah Thomas
❑ 341A V.Johnson FIN ERR .05 .02
No headline on back
❑ 341B Vinnie Johnson COR .05 .02
❑ 342 Pistons Celebrate UER .05 .02
James Edwards
Player named as Sidney
Green is really
David Greenwood
❑ 343 K.C. Jones CO .05 .02
❑ 344 Wes Unseld CO .05 .02
❑ 345 Don Nelson CO .08 .02
❑ 346 Bob Weiss CO .05 .02
❑ 347 Chris Ford CO .05 .02
❑ 348 Phil Jackson CO .15 .04
❑ 349 Lenny Wilkens CO .08 .02
❑ 350 Don Chaney CO .05 .02
❑ 351 Mike Dunleavy CO .05 .02
❑ 352 Matt Guokas CO .05 .02
❑ 353 Rick Adelman CO .05 .02
❑ 354 Jerry Sloan CO .08 .02
❑ 355 Dominique Wilkins TC .08 .02

❑ 356 Larry Bird TC .30 .09
❑ 357 Rex Chapman TC .05 .02
❑ 358 Michael Jordan TC 1.00 .30
❑ 359 Mark Price TC .05 .02
❑ 360 Rolando Blackman TC .05 .02
❑ 361 Michael Adams TC UER .05 .02
(Westhead should be
card 422, not 440)
❑ 362 Joe Dumars TC UER .08 .02
(Gerald Henderson's name
and number not listed)
❑ 363 Chris Mullin TC .08 .02
❑ 364 Hakeem Olajuwon TC .15 .04
❑ 365 Reggie Miller TC .15 .04
❑ 366 Danny Manning TC .05 .02
❑ 367 Magic Johnson TC UER .25 .07
(Dunleavy listed as 439,
should be 351)
❑ 368 Rony Seikaly TC .05 .02
❑ 369 Alvin Robertson TC .05 .02
❑ 370 Pooh Richardson TC .05 .02
❑ 371 Chris Morris TC .05 .02
❑ 372 Patrick Ewing TC .08 .02
❑ 373 Nick Anderson TC .15 .04
❑ 374 Charles Barkley TC .15 .04
❑ 375 Kevin Johnson TC .08 .02
❑ 376 Clyde Drexler TC .08 .02
❑ 377 Wayman Tisdale TC .05 .02
❑ 378 David Robinson TC .25 .07
(Basketball fully
visible)
❑ 378B David Robinson TC .30 .09
(Basketball partially
visible)
❑ 379 Xavier McDaniel TC .05 .02
❑ 380 Karl Malone TC .15 .04
❑ 381 Bernard King TC .05 .02
❑ 382 Michael Jordan 1.00 .30
Playground
❑ 383 Karl Malone horseback .15 .04
❑ 384 European Imports .05 .02
(Vlade Divac
Sarunas Marciulionis)
❑ 385 Super Streaks 1.00 .30
Stay In School
(Magic Johnson and
Michael Jordan)
❑ 386 Johnny Newman .05 .02
(Stay in School)
❑ 387 Dell Curry .05 .02
(Stay in School)
❑ 388 Patrick Ewing .08 .02
(Don't Foul Out)
❑ 389 Isiah Thomas .08 .02
(Don't Foul Out)
❑ 390 Derrick Coleman LS RC .30 .09
❑ 391 Gary Payton LS RC 1.50 .45
❑ 392 Chris Jackson LS RC .05 .02
❑ 393 Dennis Scott LS RC .20 .06
❑ 394 Kendall Gill LS RC .30 .09
❑ 395 Felton Spencer LS RC .08 .02
❑ 396 Lionel Simmons LS RC .08 .02
❑ 397 Bo Kimble LS RC .05 .02
❑ 398 Willie Burton LS RC .05 .02
❑ 399 Rumeal Robinson LS RC .05 .02
❑ 400 Tyrone Hill LS RC .05 .02
❑ 401 Tim McCormick .05 .02
❑ 402 Sidney Moncrief .05 .02
❑ 403 Johnny Newman .05 .02
❑ 404 Dennis Hopson .05 .02
❑ 405 Cliff Levingston .05 .02
❑ 406A Danny Ferry ERR .30 .09
(No position on
front of card)
❑ 406B Danny Ferry COR .15 .04
❑ 407 Alex English .05 .02
❑ 408 Lafayette Lever .05 .02
❑ 409 Rodney McCray .05 .02
❑ 410 Mike Dunleavy CO .05 .02
❑ 411 Orlando Woolridge .05 .02
❑ 412 Joe Wolf .05 .02
❑ 413 Tree Rollins .05 .02
❑ 414 Kenny Smith .05 .02
❑ 415 Sam Perkins .08 .02
❑ 416 Terry Teagle .05 .02
❑ 417 Frank Brickowski .05 .02

❑ 418 Danny Schayes .05 .02
❑ 419 Scott Brooks .05 .02
❑ 420 Reggie Theus .08 .02
❑ 421 Greg Grant .05 .02
❑ 422 Paul Westhead CO .05 .02
❑ 423 Greg Kite .05 .02
❑ 424 Manute Bol .05 .02
❑ 425 Rickey Green .05 .02
❑ 426 Ed Nealy .05 .02
❑ 427 Danny Ainge .08 .02
❑ 428 Bobby Hansen .05 .02
❑ 429 Eric Leckner .05 .02
❑ 430 Rory Sparrow .05 .02
❑ 431 Bill Wennington .05 .02
❑ 432 Paul Pressey .05 .02
❑ 433 David Greenwood .05 .02
❑ 434 Mark McNamara .05 .02
❑ 435 Sidney Green .05 .02
❑ 436 Dave Corzine .05 .02
❑ 437 Jeff Malone .05 .02
❑ 438 Pervis Ellison .08 .02
❑ 439 Checklist 5 .05 .02
❑ 440 Checklist 6 .05 .02
❑ NNO David Robinson and All-Rookie Team (No stats on back) 1.25 .35
❑ NNO David Robinson and All-Rookie Team (Stats on back) 5.00 1.50

1991-92 Hoops

	Nm-Mt	Ex-Mt
COMPLETE SET (590)	25.00	7.50
COMPLETE SERIES 1 (330)	10.00	3.00
COMPLETE SERIES 2 (260)	15.00	4.50

❑ 1 John Battle .05 .02
❑ 2 Moses Malone UER .25 .07
(119 rebounds 1982-83, should be 1194)
❑ 3 Sidney Moncrief .05 .02
❑ 4 Doc Rivers .10 .03
❑ 5 Rumeal Robinson UER .05 .02
(Back says 11th pick in 1990, should be 10th)
❑ 6 Spud Webb .10 .03
❑ 7 Dominique Wilkins .25 .07
❑ 8 Kevin Willis .05 .02
❑ 9 Larry Bird 1.00 .30
❑ 10 Dee Brown .05 .02
❑ 11 Kevin Gamble .05 .02
❑ 12 Joe Kleine .05 .02
❑ 13 Reggie Lewis .10 .03
❑ 14 Kevin McHale .10 .03
❑ 15 Robert Parish .10 .03
❑ 16 Ed Pinckney .05 .02
❑ 17 Brian Shaw .05 .02
❑ 18 Muggsy Bogues .10 .03
❑ 19 Rex Chapman .10 .03
❑ 20 Dell Curry .05 .02
❑ 21 Kendall Gill .10 .03
❑ 22 Mike Gminski .05 .02
❑ 23 Johnny Newman .05 .02
❑ 24 J.R. Reid .05 .02
❑ 25 Kelly Tripucka .05 .02
❑ 26 B.J. Armstrong .05 .02
(B.J. on front, Benjamin Roy on back)
❑ 27 Bill Cartwright .05 .02
❑ 28 Horace Grant .10 .03
❑ 29 Craig Hodges .05 .02
❑ 30 Michael Jordan 3.00 .90
❑ 31 Stacey King .05 .02
❑ 32 Cliff Levingston .05 .02
❑ 33 John Paxson .05 .02
❑ 34 Scottie Pippen .75 .23
❑ 35 Chucky Brown .05 .02
❑ 36 Brad Daugherty .05 .02
❑ 37 Craig Ehlo .05 .02
❑ 38 Danny Ferry .05 .02
❑ 39 Larry Nance .10 .03
❑ 40 Mark Price .05 .02
❑ 41 Darnell Valentine .05 .02
❑ 42 Hot Rod Williams .05 .02
❑ 43 Rolando Blackman .05 .02
❑ 44 Brad Davis .05 .02
❑ 45 James Donaldson .05 .02
❑ 46 Derek Harper .10 .03
❑ 47 Fat Lever .05 .02
❑ 48 Rodney McCray .05 .02
❑ 49 Roy Tarpley .05 .02
❑ 50 Herb Williams .05 .02
❑ 51 Michael Adams .05 .02
❑ 52 Chris Jackson UER .05 .02
(Born in Mississippi, not Michigan)
❑ 53 Jerome Lane .05 .02
❑ 54 Todd Lichti .05 .02
❑ 55 Blair Rasmussen .05 .02
❑ 56 Reggie Williams .05 .02
❑ 57 Joe Wolf .05 .02
❑ 58 Orlando Woolridge .05 .02
❑ 59 Mark Aguirre .05 .02
❑ 60 Joe Dumars .25 .07
❑ 61 James Edwards .05 .02
❑ 62 Vinnie Johnson .05 .02
❑ 63 Bill Laimbeer .10 .03
❑ 64 Dennis Rodman .50 .15
❑ 65 John Salley .05 .02
❑ 66 Isiah Thomas .25 .07
❑ 67 Tim Hardaway .40 .12
❑ 68 Rod Higgins .05 .02
❑ 69 Tyrone Hill .10 .03
❑ 70 Alton Lister .05 .02
❑ 71 Sarunas Marciulionis .05 .02
❑ 72 Chris Mullin .25 .07
❑ 73 Mitch Richmond .25 .07
❑ 74 Tom Tolbert .05 .02
❑ 75 Eric(Sleepy) Floyd .05 .02
❑ 76 Buck Johnson .05 .02
❑ 77 Vernon Maxwell .05 .02
❑ 78 Hakeem Olajuwon .40 .12
❑ 79 Kenny Smith .05 .02
❑ 80 Larry Smith .05 .02
❑ 81 Otis Thorpe .10 .03
❑ 82 David Wood RC .05 .02
❑ 83 Vern Fleming .05 .02
❑ 84 Reggie Miller .25 .07
❑ 85 Chuck Person .05 .02
❑ 86 Mike Sanders .05 .02
❑ 87 Detlef Schrempf .10 .03
❑ 88 Rik Smits .10 .03
❑ 89 LaSalle Thompson .05 .02
❑ 90 Micheal Williams .05 .02
❑ 91 Winston Garland .05 .02
❑ 92 Gary Grant .05 .02
❑ 93 Ron Harper .10 .03
❑ 94 Danny Manning .10 .03
❑ 95 Jeff Martin .05 .02
❑ 96 Ken Norman .05 .02
❑ 97 Olden Polynice .05 .02
❑ 98 Charles Smith .05 .02
❑ 99 Vlade Divac .10 .03
❑ 100 A.C. Green .10 .03
❑ 101 Magic Johnson .75 .23
❑ 102 Sam Perkins .10 .03
❑ 103 Byron Scott .10 .03
❑ 104 Terry Teagle .05 .02
❑ 105 Mychal Thompson .05 .02
❑ 106 James Worthy .25 .07
❑ 107 Willie Burton .05 .02
❑ 108 Bimbo Coles .05 .02
❑ 109 Terry Davis .05 .02
❑ 110 Sherman Douglas .05 .02
❑ 111 Kevin Edwards .05 .02
❑ 112 Alec Kessler .05 .02
❑ 113 Glen Rice .25 .07
❑ 114 Rony Seikaly .05 .02
❑ 115 Frank Brickowski .05 .02
❑ 116 Dale Ellis .10 .03
❑ 117 Jay Humphries .05 .02
❑ 118 Brad Lohaus .05 .02
❑ 119 Fred Roberts .05 .02
❑ 120 Alvin Robertson .05 .02
❑ 121 Danny Schayes .05 .02
❑ 122 Jack Sikma .05 .02
❑ 123 Randy Breuer .05 .02
❑ 124 Tony Campbell .05 .02
❑ 125 Tyrone Corbin .05 .02
❑ 126 Gerald Glass .05 .02
❑ 127 Sam Mitchell .05 .02
❑ 128 Tod Murphy .05 .02
❑ 129 Pooh Richardson .05 .02
❑ 130 Felton Spencer .05 .02
❑ 131 Mookie Blaylock .10 .03
❑ 132 Sam Bowie .05 .02
❑ 133 Jud Buechler .05 .02
❑ 134 Derrick Coleman .10 .03
❑ 135 Chris Dudley .05 .02
❑ 136 Chris Morris .05 .02
❑ 137 Drazen Petrovic .10 .03
❑ 138 Reggie Theus .10 .03
❑ 139 Maurice Cheeks .05 .02
❑ 140 Patrick Ewing .25 .07
❑ 141 Mark Jackson .10 .03
❑ 142 Charles Oakley .10 .03
❑ 143 Trent Tucker .05 .02
❑ 144 Kiki Vandeweghe .05 .02
❑ 145 Kenny Walker .05 .02
❑ 146 Gerald Wilkins .05 .02
❑ 147 Nick Anderson .10 .03
❑ 148 Michael Ansley .05 .02
❑ 149 Terry Catledge .05 .02
❑ 150 Jerry Reynolds .05 .02
❑ 151 Dennis Scott .10 .03
❑ 152 Scott Skiles .05 .02
❑ 153 Otis Smith .05 .02
❑ 154 Sam Vincent .05 .02
❑ 155 Ron Anderson .05 .02
❑ 156 Charles Barkley .40 .12
❑ 157 Manute Bol .05 .02
❑ 158 Johnny Dawkins .05 .02
❑ 159 Armon Gilliam .05 .02
❑ 160 Rickey Green .05 .02
❑ 161 Hersey Hawkins .10 .03
❑ 162 Rick Mahorn .05 .02
❑ 163 Tom Chambers .05 .02
❑ 164 Jeff Hornacek .10 .03
❑ 165 Kevin Johnson .25 .07
❑ 166 Andrew Lang .05 .02
❑ 167 Dan Majerle .10 .03
❑ 168 Xavier McDaniel .05 .02
❑ 169 Kurt Rambis .05 .02
❑ 170 Mark West .05 .02
❑ 171 Danny Ainge .10 .03
❑ 172 Mark Bryant .05 .02
❑ 173 Walter Davis .05 .02
❑ 174 Clyde Drexler .25 .07
❑ 175 Kevin Duckworth .05 .02
❑ 176 Jerome Kersey .05 .02
❑ 177 Terry Porter .05 .02
❑ 178 Clifford Robinson .10 .03
❑ 179 Buck Williams .05 .02
❑ 180 Anthony Bonner .05 .02
❑ 181 Antoine Carr .05 .02
❑ 182 Duane Causwell .05 .02
❑ 183 Bobby Hansen .05 .02
❑ 184 Travis Mays .05 .02
❑ 185 Lionel Simmons .05 .02
❑ 186 Rory Sparrow .05 .02
❑ 187 Wayman Tisdale .05 .02
❑ 188 Willie Anderson .05 .02
❑ 189 Terry Cummings .05 .02
❑ 190 Sean Elliott .10 .03
❑ 191 Sidney Green .05 .02
❑ 192 David Greenwood .05 .02
❑ 193 Paul Pressey .05 .02
❑ 194 David Robinson .50 .15
❑ 195 Dwayne Schintzius .05 .02
❑ 196 Rod Strickland .25 .07
❑ 197 Benoit Benjamin .05 .02

❑ 198 Michael Cage .05 .02
❑ 199 Eddie Johnson .10 .03
❑ 200 Shawn Kemp .60 .18
❑ 201 Derrick McKey .05 .02
❑ 202 Gary Payton .60 .18
❑ 203 Ricky Pierce .05 .02
❑ 204 Sedale Threatt .05 .02
❑ 205 Thurl Bailey .05 .02
❑ 206 Mike Brown .05 .02
❑ 207 Mark Eaton .05 .02
❑ 208 Blue Edwards UER .05 .02
(Forward/guard on front, guard on back)
❑ 209 Darrell Griffith .05 .02
❑ 210 Jeff Malone .05 .02
❑ 211 Karl Malone .40 .12
❑ 212 John Stockton .25 .07
❑ 213 Ledell Eackles .05 .02
❑ 214 Pervis Ellison .05 .02
❑ 215 A.J. English .05 .02
❑ 216 Harvey Grant .05 .02
(Shown boxing out twin brother Horace)
❑ 217 Charles Jones .05 .02
❑ 218 Bernard King .05 .02
❑ 219 Darrell Walker .05 .02
❑ 220 John Williams .05 .02
❑ 221 Bob Weiss CO .05 .02
❑ 222 Chris Ford CO .05 .02
❑ 223 Gene Littles CO .05 .02
❑ 224 Phil Jackson CO .10 .03
❑ 225 Lenny Wilkens CO .10 .03
❑ 226 Richie Adubato CO .05 .02
❑ 227 Paul Westhead CO .05 .02
❑ 228 Chuck Daly CO .10 .03
❑ 229 Don Nelson CO .10 .03
❑ 230 Don Chaney CO .05 .02
❑ 231 Bob Hill RC CO UER .05 .02
(Coached under Ted Owens, not Ted Owen)
❑ 232 Mike Schuler CO .05 .02
❑ 233 Mike Dunleavy CO .05 .02
❑ 234 Kevin Loughery CO .05 .02
❑ 235 Del Harris CO .05 .02
❑ 236 Jimmy Rodgers CO .05 .02
❑ 237 Bill Fitch CO .05 .02
❑ 238 Pat Riley CO .10 .03
❑ 239 Matt Guokas CO .05 .02
❑ 240 Jim Lynam CO .05 .02
❑ 241 Cotton Fitzsimmons CO .05 .02
❑ 242 Rick Adelman CO .05 .02
❑ 243 Dick Motta CO .05 .02
❑ 244 Larry Brown CO .05 .02
❑ 245 K.C. Jones CO .10 .03
❑ 246 Jerry Sloan CO .10 .03
❑ 247 Wes Unseld CO .10 .03
❑ 248 Charles Barkley AS .25 .07
❑ 249 Brad Daugherty AS .05 .02
❑ 250 Joe Dumars AS .10 .03
❑ 251 Patrick Ewing AS .10 .03
❑ 252 Hersey Hawkins AS .05 .02
❑ 253 Michael Jordan AS 1.50 .45
❑ 254 Bernard King AS .05 .02
❑ 255 Kevin McHale AS .05 .02
❑ 256 Robert Parish AS .05 .02
❑ 257 Ricky Pierce AS .05 .02
❑ 258 Alvin Robertson AS .05 .02
❑ 259 Dominique Wilkins AS .10 .03
❑ 260 Chris Ford CO AS .05 .02
❑ 261 Tom Chambers AS .05 .02
❑ 262 Clyde Drexler AS .10 .03
❑ 263 Kevin Duckworth AS .05 .02
❑ 264 Tim Hardaway AS .25 .07
❑ 265 Kevin Johnson AS .10 .03
❑ 266 Magic Johnson AS .40 .12
❑ 267 Karl Malone AS .25 .07
❑ 268 Chris Mullin AS .10 .03
❑ 269 Terry Porter AS .05 .02
❑ 270 David Robinson AS .25 .07
❑ 271 John Stockton AS .10 .03
❑ 272 James Worthy AS .10 .03
❑ 273 Rick Adelman CO AS .05 .02
❑ 274 Atlanta Hawks .05 .02
Team Card UER
(Actually began as Tri-Cities Blackhawks)
❑ 275 Boston Celtics .05 .02
Team Card UER
(No NBA Hoops logo on card front)
❑ 276 Charlotte Hornets .05 .02
Team Card
❑ 277 Chicago Bulls .05 .02
Team Card
❑ 278 Cleveland Cavaliers .05 .02
Team Card
❑ 279 Dallas Mavericks .05 .02
Team Card
❑ 280 Denver Nuggets .05 .02
Team Card
❑ 281 Detroit Pistons .05 .02
Team Card UER
(Pistons not NBA Finalists until 1988; Ft. Ft. Wayne Pistons in Finals in 1955 and 1956)
❑ 282 Golden State Warriors .05 .02
Team Card
❑ 283 Houston Rockets .05 .02
Team Card
❑ 284 Indiana Pacers .05 .02
Team Card
❑ 285 Los Angeles Clippers .05 .02
Team Card
❑ 286 Los Angeles Lakers .05 .02
Team Card
❑ 287 Miami Heat .05 .02
Team Card
❑ 288 Milwaukee Bucks .05 .02
Team Card
❑ 289 Minnesota Timberwolves .05 .02
Team Card
❑ 290 New Jersey Nets .05 .02
Team Card
❑ 291 New York Knicks .05 .02
Team Card UER
(Golden State not mentioned as an active charter member of NBA)
❑ 292 Orlando Magic .05 .02
Team Card
❑ 293 Philadelphia 76ers .05 .02
Team Card
❑ 294 Phoenix Suns .05 .02
Team Card
❑ 295 Portland Trail Blazers .05 .02
Team Card
❑ 296 Sacramento Kings .05 .02
Team Card
❑ 297 San Antonio Spurs .05 .02
Team Card
❑ 298 Seattle Supersonics .05 .02
Team Card
❑ 299 Utah Jazz .05 .02
Team Card
❑ 300 Washington Bullets .05 .02
Team Card
❑ 301 James Naismith .10 .03
Centennial Card
❑ 302 Kevin Johnson IS .10 .03
❑ 303 Reggie Miller IS .10 .03
❑ 304 Hakeem Olajuwon IS .25 .07
❑ 305 Robert Parish IS .05 .02
❑ 306 Scoring Leaders 1.00 .30
Michael Jordan
Karl Malone
❑ 307 3-Point FG Percent .05 .02
League Leaders
Jim Les
Trent Tucker
❑ 308 Free Throw Percent .10 .03
League Leaders
Reggie Miller
Jeff Malone
❑ 309 Blocks League Leaders .25 .07
Hakeem Olajuwon
David Robinson
❑ 310 Steals League Leaders .05 .02
Alvin Robertson
John Stockton
❑ 311 Rebounds LL UER .50 .15
David Robinson
Dennis Rodman
(Robinson credited as playing for Houston)
❑ 312 Assists League Leaders .10 .03
John Stockton
Magic Johnson
❑ 313 Field Goal Percent .10 .03
League Leaders
Buck Williams
Robert Parish
❑ 314 Larry Bird UER .50 .15
Milestone
(Should be card 315 to fit Milestone sequence)
❑ 315 Alex English .10 .03
Moses Malone
Milestone UER
(Should be card 314 and be a League Leader card)
❑ 316 Magic Johnson .40 .12
Milestone
❑ 317 Michael Jordan 1.50 .45
Milestone
❑ 318 Moses Malone .10 .03
Milestone
❑ 319 Larry Bird .50 .15
NBA Yearbook
Look Back
❑ 320 Maurice Cheeks .05 .02
NBA Yearbook
Look Back
❑ 321 Magic Johnson .40 .12
NBA Yearbook
Look Back
❑ 322 Bernard King .05 .02
NBA Yearbook
Look Back
❑ 323 Moses Malone .10 .03
NBA Yearbook
Look Back
❑ 324 Robert Parish .05 .02
NBA Yearbook
Look Back
❑ 325 All-Star Jam .10 .03
Jammin' With Will Smith
(Stay in School)
❑ 326 All-Star Jam .10 .03
Jammin' With The Boys and Will Smith
(Stay in School)
❑ 327 David Robinson .25 .07
Leave Alcohol Out
❑ 328 Checklist 1 .05 .02
❑ 329 Checklist 2 UER .05 .02
(Card front is from 330)
❑ 330 Checklist 3 UER .05 .02
(Card front is from 329; card 327 listed operation, should be celebration)
❑ 331 Maurice Cheeks .05 .02
❑ 332 Duane Ferrell .05 .02
❑ 333 Jon Koncak .05 .02
❑ 334 Gary Leonard .05 .02
❑ 335 Travis Mays .05 .02
❑ 336 Blair Rasmussen .05 .02
❑ 337 Alexander Volkov .05 .02
❑ 338 John Bagley .05 .02
❑ 339 Rickey Green UER .05 .02
(Ricky on front)
❑ 340 Derek Smith .05 .02
❑ 341 Stojko Vrankovic .05 .02
❑ 342 Anthony Frederick RC .05 .02
❑ 343 Kenny Gattison .05 .02
❑ 344 Eric Leckner .05 .02
❑ 345 Will Perdue .05 .02
❑ 346 Scott Williams RC .05 .02
❑ 347 John Battle .05 .02
❑ 348 Winston Bennett .05 .02
❑ 349 Henry James .05 .02
❑ 350 Steve Kerr .10 .03
❑ 351 John Morton .05 .02
❑ 352 Terry Davis .05 .02
❑ 353 Randy White .05 .02
❑ 354 Greg Anderson .05 .02
❑ 355 Anthony Cook .05 .02

❑ 356 Walter Davis .05 .02
❑ 357 Winston Garland .05 .02
❑ 358 Scott Hastings .05 .02
❑ 359 Marcus Liberty .05 .02
❑ 360 William Bedford .05 .02
❑ 361 Lance Blanks .05 .02
❑ 362 Brad Sellers .05 .02
❑ 363 Darrell Walker .05 .02
❑ 364 Orlando Woolridge .05 .02
❑ 365 Vincent Askew RC .05 .02
❑ 366 Mario Elie RC .25 .07
❑ 367 Jim Petersen .05 .02
❑ 368 Matt Bullard RC .05 .02
❑ 369 Gerald Henderson .05 .02
❑ 370 Dave Jamerson .05 .02
❑ 371 Tree Rollins .05 .02
❑ 372 Greg Dreiling .05 .02
❑ 373 George McCloud .05 .02
❑ 374 Kenny Williams .05 .02
❑ 375 Randy Wittman .05 .02
❑ 376 Tony Brown .05 .02
❑ 377 Lanard Copeland .05 .02
❑ 378 James Edwards .05 .02
❑ 379 Bo Kimble .05 .02
❑ 380 Doc Rivers .10 .03
❑ 381 Loy Vaught .05 .02
❑ 382 Elden Campbell .25 .07
❑ 383 Jack Haley .05 .02
❑ 384 Tony Smith .05 .02
❑ 385 Sedale Threatt .05 .02
❑ 386 Keith Askins RC .05 .02
❑ 387 Grant Long .05 .02
❑ 388 Alan Ogg .05 .02
❑ 389 Jon Sundvold .05 .02
❑ 390 Lester Conner .05 .02
❑ 391 Jeff Grayer .05 .02
❑ 392 Steve Henson .05 .02
❑ 393 Larry Krystkowiak .05 .02
❑ 394 Moses Malone .25 .07
❑ 395 Scott Brooks .05 .02
❑ 396 Tellis Frank .05 .02
❑ 397 Doug West .05 .02
❑ 398 Rafael Addison RC .05 .02
❑ 399 Dave Feitl RC .05 .02
❑ 400 Tate George .05 .02
❑ 401 Terry Mills RC .25 .07
❑ 402 Tim McCormick .05 .02
❑ 403 Xavier McDaniel .05 .02
❑ 404 Anthony Mason RC .50 .15
❑ 405 Brian Quinnett .05 .02
❑ 406 John Starks RC .25 .07
❑ 407 Mark Acres .05 .02
❑ 408 Greg Kite .05 .02
❑ 409 Jeff Turner .05 .02
❑ 410 Morlon Wiley .05 .02
❑ 411 Dave Hoppen .05 .02
❑ 412 Brian Oliver .05 .02
❑ 413 Kenny Payne .05 .02
❑ 414 Charles Shackleford .05 .02
❑ 415 Mitchell Wiggins .05 .02
❑ 416 Jayson Williams .25 .07
❑ 417 Cedric Ceballos .10 .03
❑ 418 Negele Knight .05 .02
❑ 419 Andrew Lang .05 .02
❑ 420 Jerrod Mustaf .05 .02
❑ 421 Ed Nealy .05 .02
❑ 422 Tim Perry .05 .02
❑ 423 Alaa Abdelnaby .05 .02
❑ 424 Wayne Cooper .05 .02
❑ 425 Danny Young .05 .02
❑ 426 Dennis Hopson .05 .02
❑ 427 Les Jepsen .05 .02
❑ 428 Jim Les RC .05 .02
❑ 429 Mitch Richmond .25 .07
❑ 430 Dwayne Schintzius .05 .02
❑ 431 Spud Webb .10 .03
❑ 432 Jud Buechler .05 .02
❑ 433 Antoine Carr .05 .02
❑ 434 Tom Garrick .05 .02
❑ 435 Sean Higgins RC .05 .02
❑ 436 Avery Johnson .10 .03
❑ 437 Tony Massenburg .05 .02
❑ 438 Dana Barros .05 .02
❑ 439 Quintin Dailey .05 .02
❑ 440 Bart Kofoed RC .05 .02
❑ 441 Nate McMillan .05 .02
❑ 442 Delaney Rudd .05 .02
❑ 443 Michael Adams .05 .02
❑ 444 Mark Alarie .05 .02
❑ 445 Greg Foster .05 .02
❑ 446 Tom Hammonds .05 .02
❑ 447 Andre Turner .05 .02
❑ 448 David Wingate .05 .02
❑ 449 Dominique Wilkins SC .10 .03
❑ 450 Kevin Willis SC .05 .02
❑ 451 Larry Bird SC .50 .15
❑ 452 Robert Parish SC .05 .02
❑ 453 Rex Chapman SC .05 .02
❑ 454 Kendall Gill SC .05 .02
❑ 455 Michael Jordan SC 1.50 .45
❑ 456 Scottie Pippen SC .40 .12
❑ 457 Brad Daugherty SC .05 .02
❑ 458 Larry Nance SC .05 .02
❑ 459 Rolando Blackman SC .05 .02
❑ 460 Derek Harper SC .05 .02
❑ 461 Chris Jackson SC .05 .02
❑ 462 Todd Lichti SC .05 .02
❑ 463 Joe Dumars SC .10 .03
❑ 464 Isiah Thomas SC .10 .03
❑ 465 Tim Hardaway SC .25 .07
❑ 466 Chris Mullin SC .10 .03
❑ 467 Hakeem Olajuwon SC .25 .07
❑ 468 Otis Thorpe SC .05 .02
❑ 469 Reggie Miller SC .10 .03
❑ 470 Detlef Schrempf SC .05 .02
❑ 471 Ron Harper SC .05 .02
❑ 472 Charles Smith SC .05 .02
❑ 473 Magic Johnson SC .40 .12
❑ 474 James Worthy SC .10 .03
❑ 475 Sherman Douglas SC .05 .02
❑ 476 Rony Seikaly SC .05 .02
❑ 477 Jay Humphries SC .05 .02
❑ 478 Alvin Robertson SC .05 .02
❑ 479 Tyrone Corbin SC .05 .02
❑ 480 Pooh Richardson SC .05 .02
❑ 481 Sam Bowie SC .05 .02
❑ 482 Derrick Coleman SC .05 .02
❑ 483 Patrick Ewing SC .10 .03
❑ 484 Charles Oakley SC .05 .02
❑ 485 Dennis Scott SC .05 .02
❑ 486 Scott Skiles SC .05 .02
❑ 487 Charles Barkley SC .25 .07
❑ 488 Hersey Hawkins SC .05 .02
❑ 489 Tom Chambers SC .05 .02
❑ 490 Kevin Johnson SC .10 .03
❑ 491 Clyde Drexler SC .10 .03
❑ 492 Terry Porter SC .05 .02
❑ 493 Lionel Simmons SC .05 .02
❑ 494 Wayman Tisdale SC .05 .02
❑ 495 Terry Cummings SC .05 .02
❑ 496 David Robinson SC .25 .07
❑ 497 Shawn Kemp SC .25 .07
❑ 498 Ricky Pierce SC .05 .02
❑ 499 Karl Malone SC .25 .07
❑ 500 John Stockton SC .10 .03
❑ 501 Harvey Grant SC .05 .02
❑ 502 Bernard King SC .05 .02
❑ 503 Travis Mays Art .05 .02
❑ 504 Kevin McHale Art .05 .02
❑ 505 Muggsy Bogues Art .05 .02
❑ 506 Scottie Pippen Art .40 .12
❑ 507 Brad Daugherty Art .05 .02
❑ 508 Derek Harper Art .05 .02
❑ 509 Chris Jackson Art .05 .02
❑ 510 Isiah Thomas Art .10 .03
❑ 511 Tim Hardaway Art .25 .07
❑ 512 Otis Thorpe Art .05 .02
❑ 513 Chuck Person Art .05 .02
❑ 514 Ron Harper Art .05 .02
❑ 515 James Worthy Art .10 .03
❑ 516 Sherman Douglas Art .05 .02
❑ 517 Dale Ellis Art .05 .02
❑ 518 Tony Campbell Art .05 .02
❑ 519 Derrick Coleman Art .05 .02
❑ 520 Gerald Wilkins Art .05 .02
❑ 521 Scott Skiles Art .05 .02
❑ 522 Manute Bol Art .05 .02
❑ 523 Tom Chambers Art .05 .02
❑ 524 Terry Porter Art .05 .02
❑ 525 Lionel Simmons Art .05 .02
❑ 526 Sean Elliott Art .05 .02
❑ 527 Shawn Kemp Art .25 .07
❑ 528 John Stockton Art .10 .03
❑ 529 Harvey Grant Art .05 .02
❑ 530 Michael Adams .05 .02
All-Time Active Leader
Three-Point Field Goals
❑ 531 Charles Barkley .25 .07
All-Time Active Leader
Field Goal Percentage
❑ 532 Larry Bird .50 .15
All-Time Active Leader
Free Throw Percentage
❑ 533 Maurice Cheeks .05 .02
All-Time Active Leader
Steals
❑ 534 Mark Eaton .05 .02
All-Time Active Leader
Blocks
❑ 535 Magic Johnson .40 .12
All-Time Active Leader
Assists
❑ 536 Michael Jordan 1.50 .45
All-Time Active Leader
Scoring Average
❑ 537 Moses Malone .10 .03
All-Time Active Leader
Rebounds
❑ 538 Sam Perkins FIN .05 .02
❑ 539 Scottie Pippen FIN .25 .07
James Worthy
❑ 540 Vlade Divac FIN .05 .02
❑ 541 John Paxson FIN .05 .02
❑ 542 Michael Jordan FIN 1.50 .45
Magic Johnson)
❑ 543 Michael Jordan FIN 1.50 .45
NBA Champs, kissing trophy)
❑ 544 Otis Smith .05 .02
Stay in School
❑ 545 Jeff Turner .05 .02
Stay in School
❑ 546 Larry Johnson RC 1.00 .30
❑ 547 Kenny Anderson RC .50 .15
❑ 548 Billy Owens RC .25 .07
❑ 549 Dikembe Mutombo RC 1.00 .30
❑ 550 Steve Smith RC 1.00 .30
❑ 551 Doug Smith RC .05 .02
❑ 552 Luc Longley RC .25 .07
❑ 553 Mark Macon RC .05 .02
❑ 554 Stacey Augmon RC .25 .07
❑ 555 Brian Williams RC .25 .07
❑ 556 Terrell Brandon RC .75 .23
❑ 557 Walter Davis .05 .02
Team USA 1976
❑ 558 Vern Fleming .05 .02
Team USA 1984
❑ 559 Joe Kleine .05 .02
Team USA 1984
❑ 560 Jon Koncak .05 .02
Team USA 1984
❑ 561 Sam Perkins .05 .02
Team USA 1984
❑ 562 Alvin Robertson .05 .02
Team USA 1984
❑ 563 Wayman Tisdale .05 .02
Team USA 1984
❑ 564 Jeff Turner .05 .02
Team USA 1984
❑ 565 Willie Anderson .05 .02
Team USA 1988
❑ 566 Stacey Augmon .25 .07
Team USA 1988
❑ 567 Bimbo Coles .05 .02
Team USA 1988
❑ 568 Jeff Grayer .05 .02
Team USA 1988
❑ 569 Hersey Hawkins .05 .02
Team USA 1988
❑ 570 Dan Majerle .05 .02
Team USA 1988
❑ 571 Danny Manning .05 .02
Team USA 1988
❑ 572 J.R. Reid .05 .02
Team USA 1988
❑ 573 Mitch Richmond .50 .15
Team USA 1988
❑ 574 Charles Smith .05 .02
Team USA 1988

❑ 575 Charles Barkley .75 .23
Team USA 1992
❑ 576 Larry Bird 2.00 .60
Team USA 1992
❑ 577 Patrick Ewing .50 .15
Team USA 1992
❑ 578 Magic Johnson 1.50 .45
Team USA 1992
❑ 579 Michael Jordan 6.00 1.80
Team USA 1992
❑ 580 Karl Malone .75 .23
Team USA 1992
❑ 581 Chris Mullin .25 .07
Team USA 1992
❑ 582 Scottie Pippen 1.50 .45
Team USA 1992
❑ 583 David Robinson 1.00 .30
Team USA 1992
❑ 584 John Stockton .50 .15
Team USA 1992
❑ 585 Chuck Daly CO .10 .03
Team USA 1992
❑ 586 Lenny Wilkens CO .10 .03
Team USA 1992
❑ 587 P.J. Carlesimo RC CO .05 .02
Team USA 1992
❑ 588 Mike Krzyzewski RC CO .40 .12
Team USA 1992
❑ 589 Checklist Card 1 .05 .02
❑ 590 Checklist Card 2 .05 .02
❑ CC1 Dr.James Naismith 1.00 .30
❑ XX Head of the Class 20.00 6.00
Kenny Anderson
Larry Johnson
Dikembe Mutombo
Billy Owens
Doug Smith
Steve Smith
❑ NNO Team USA SP .50 .15
Title Card
❑ NNO Centennial Card 1.00 .30
(Sendaway)

1992-93 Hoops

	Nm-Mt	Ex-Mt
COMPLETE SET (490)	35.00	10.50
COMPLETE SERIES 1 (350)	15.00	4.50
COMPLETE SERIES 2 (140)	20.00	6.00
COMMON CARD (1-350)	.05	.02
COMMON CARD (351-490)	.10	.03

BAR.PLASTIC PRICED UNDER SKYBOX USA

❑ 1 Stacey Augmon .10 .03
❑ 2 Maurice Cheeks .05 .02
❑ 3 Duane Ferrell .05 .02
❑ 4 Paul Graham .05 .02
❑ 5 Jon Koncak .05 .02
❑ 6 Blair Rasmussen .05 .02
❑ 7 Rumeal Robinson .05 .02
❑ 8 Dominique Wilkins .25 .07
❑ 9 Kevin Willis .05 .02
❑ 10 Larry Bird 1.00 .30
❑ 11 Dee Brown .05 .02
❑ 12 Sherman Douglas .05 .02
❑ 13 Rick Fox .10 .03
❑ 14 Kevin Gamble .05 .02
❑ 15 Reggie Lewis .10 .03
❑ 16 Kevin McHale .25 .07
❑ 17 Robert Parish .10 .03
❑ 18 Ed Pinckney UER .05 .02
(Wrong trade info,
Kleine to Sacramento
and Lohaus to Boston)
❑ 19 Muggsy Bogues .10 .03
❑ 20 Dell Curry .05 .02
❑ 21 Kenny Gattison .05 .02
❑ 22 Kendall Gill .10 .03
❑ 23 Mike Gminski .05 .02
❑ 24 Larry Johnson .30 .09
❑ 25 Johnny Newman .05 .02
❑ 26 J.R. Reid .05 .02
❑ 27 B.J. Armstrong .05 .02
❑ 28 Bill Cartwright .05 .02
❑ 29 Horace Grant .10 .03
❑ 30 Michael Jordan 3.00 .90
❑ 31 Stacey King .05 .02
❑ 32 John Paxson .05 .02
❑ 33 Will Perdue .05 .02
❑ 34 Scottie Pippen .75 .23
❑ 35 Scott Williams .05 .02
❑ 36 John Battle .05 .02
❑ 37 Terrell Brandon .25 .07
❑ 38 Brad Daugherty .05 .02
❑ 39 Craig Ehlo .05 .02
❑ 40 Danny Ferry .05 .02
❑ 41 Henry James .05 .02
❑ 42 Larry Nance .05 .02
❑ 43 Mark Price .05 .02
❑ 44 Hot Rod Williams .05 .02
❑ 45 Rolando Blackman .05 .02
❑ 46 Terry Davis .05 .02
❑ 47 Derek Harper .10 .03
❑ 48 Mike Iuzzolino .05 .02
❑ 49 Fat Lever .05 .02
❑ 50 Rodney McCray .05 .02
❑ 51 Doug Smith .05 .02
❑ 52 Randy White .05 .02
❑ 53 Herb Williams .05 .02
❑ 54 Greg Anderson .05 .02
❑ 55 Winston Garland .05 .02
❑ 56 Chris Jackson .05 .02
❑ 57 Marcus Liberty .05 .02
❑ 58 Todd Lichti .05 .02
❑ 59 Mark Macon .05 .02
❑ 60 Dikembe Mutombo .30 .09
❑ 61 Reggie Williams .05 .02
❑ 62 Mark Aguirre .05 .02
❑ 63 William Bedford .05 .02
❑ 64 Joe Dumars .25 .07
❑ 65 Bill Laimbeer .10 .03
❑ 66 Dennis Rodman .50 .15
❑ 67 John Salley .05 .02
❑ 68 Isiah Thomas .25 .07
❑ 69 Darrell Walker .05 .02
❑ 70 Orlando Woolridge .05 .02
❑ 71 Victor Alexander .05 .02
❑ 72 Mario Elie .10 .03
❑ 73 Chris Gatling .05 .02
❑ 74 Tim Hardaway .30 .09
❑ 75 Tyrone Hill .05 .02
❑ 76 Alton Lister .05 .02
❑ 77 Sarunas Marciulionis .05 .02
❑ 78 Chris Mullin .25 .07
❑ 79 Billy Owens .10 .03
❑ 80 Matt Bullard .05 .02
❑ 81 Sleepy Floyd .05 .02
❑ 82 Avery Johnson .05 .02
❑ 83 Buck Johnson .05 .02
❑ 84 Vernon Maxwell .05 .02
❑ 85 Hakeem Olajuwon .40 .12
❑ 86 Kenny Smith .05 .02
❑ 87 Larry Smith .05 .02
❑ 88 Otis Thorpe .10 .03
❑ 89 Dale Davis .05 .02
❑ 90 Vern Fleming .05 .02
❑ 91 George McCloud .05 .02
❑ 92 Reggie Miller .25 .07
❑ 93 Chuck Person .05 .02
❑ 94 Detlef Schrempf .10 .03
❑ 95 Rik Smits .10 .03
❑ 96 LaSalle Thompson .05 .02
❑ 97 Micheal Williams .05 .02
❑ 98 James Edwards .05 .02
❑ 99 Gary Grant .05 .02
❑ 100 Ron Harper .10 .03
❑ 101 Danny Manning .10 .03
❑ 102 Ken Norman .05 .02
❑ 103 Olden Polynice .05 .02
❑ 104 Doc Rivers .10 .03
❑ 105 Charles Smith .05 .02
❑ 106 Loy Vaught .05 .02
❑ 107 Elden Campbell .10 .03
❑ 108 Vlade Divac .10 .03
❑ 109 A.C. Green .10 .03
❑ 110 Sam Perkins .10 .03
❑ 111 Byron Scott .10 .03
❑ 112 Tony Smith .05 .02
❑ 113 Terry Teagle .05 .02
❑ 114 Sedale Threatt .05 .02
❑ 115 James Worthy .25 .07
❑ 116 Willie Burton .05 .02
❑ 117 Bimbo Coles .05 .02
❑ 118 Kevin Edwards .05 .02
❑ 119 Alec Kessler .05 .02
❑ 120 Grant Long .05 .02
❑ 121 Glen Rice .25 .07
❑ 122 Rony Seikaly .05 .02
❑ 123 Brian Shaw .05 .02
❑ 124 Steve Smith .30 .09
❑ 125 Frank Brickowski .05 .02
❑ 126 Dale Ellis .05 .02
❑ 127 Jeff Grayer .05 .02
❑ 128 Jay Humphries .05 .02
❑ 129 Larry Krystkowiak .05 .02
❑ 130 Moses Malone .25 .07
❑ 131 Fred Roberts .05 .02
❑ 132 Alvin Robertson .05 .02
❑ 133 Danny Schayes .05 .02
❑ 134 Thurl Bailey .05 .02
❑ 135 Scott Brooks .05 .02
❑ 136 Tony Campbell .05 .02
❑ 137 Gerald Glass .05 .02
❑ 138 Luc Longley .10 .03
❑ 139 Sam Mitchell .05 .02
❑ 140 Pooh Richardson .05 .02
❑ 141 Felton Spencer .05 .02
❑ 142 Doug West .05 .02
❑ 143 Rafael Addison .05 .02
❑ 144 Kenny Anderson .25 .07
❑ 145 Mookie Blaylock .10 .03
❑ 146 Sam Bowie .05 .02
❑ 147 Derrick Coleman .10 .03
❑ 148 Chris Dudley .05 .02
❑ 149 Terry Mills .05 .02
❑ 150 Chris Morris .05 .02
❑ 151 Drazen Petrovic .05 .02
❑ 152 Greg Anthony .05 .02
❑ 153 Patrick Ewing .25 .07
❑ 154 Mark Jackson .10 .03
❑ 155 Anthony Mason .25 .07
❑ 156 Xavier McDaniel .05 .02
❑ 157 Charles Oakley .10 .03
❑ 158 John Starks .10 .03
❑ 159 Gerald Wilkins .05 .02
❑ 160 Nick Anderson .10 .03
❑ 161 Terry Catledge .05 .02
❑ 162 Jerry Reynolds .05 .02
❑ 163 Stanley Roberts .05 .02
❑ 164 Dennis Scott .10 .03
❑ 165 Scott Skiles .05 .02
❑ 166 Jeff Turner .05 .02
❑ 167 Sam Vincent .05 .02
❑ 168 Brian Williams .05 .02
❑ 169 Ron Anderson .05 .02
❑ 170 Charles Barkley .40 .12
❑ 171 Manute Bol .05 .02
❑ 172 Johnny Dawkins .05 .02
❑ 173 Armon Gilliam .05 .02
❑ 174 Hersey Hawkins .10 .03
❑ 175 Brian Oliver .05 .02
❑ 176 Charles Shackleford .05 .02
❑ 177 Jayson Williams .10 .03
❑ 178 Cedric Ceballos .10 .03
❑ 179 Tom Chambers .05 .02
❑ 180 Jeff Hornacek .10 .03
❑ 181 Kevin Johnson .25 .07
❑ 182 Negele Knight .05 .02
❑ 183 Andrew Lang .05 .02
❑ 184 Dan Majerle .10 .03
❑ 185 Tim Perry .05 .02
❑ 186 Mark West .05 .02

❑ 187 Alaa Abdelnaby .05 .02
❑ 188 Danny Ainge .10 .03
❑ 189 Clyde Drexler .25 .07
❑ 190 Kevin Duckworth .05 .02
❑ 191 Jerome Kersey .05 .02
❑ 192 Robert Pack .05 .02
❑ 193 Terry Porter .05 .02
❑ 194 Clifford Robinson .10 .03
❑ 195 Buck Williams .10 .03
❑ 196 Anthony Bonner .05 .02
❑ 197 Duane Causwell .05 .02
❑ 198 Pete Chilcutt .05 .02
❑ 199 Dennis Hopson .05 .02
❑ 200 Mitch Richmond .25 .07
❑ 201 Lionel Simmons .05 .02
❑ 202 Wayman Tisdale .05 .02
❑ 203 Spud Webb .10 .03
❑ 204 Willie Anderson .05 .02
❑ 205 Antoine Carr .05 .02
❑ 206 Terry Cummings .10 .03
❑ 207 Sean Elliott .10 .03
❑ 208 Sidney Green .05 .02
❑ 209 David Robinson .40 .12
❑ 210 Rod Strickland .25 .07
❑ 211 Greg Sutton .05 .02
❑ 212 Dana Barros .05 .02
❑ 213 Benoit Benjamin .05 .02
❑ 214 Michael Cage .05 .02
❑ 215 Eddie Johnson .05 .02
❑ 216 Shawn Kemp .50 .15
❑ 217 Derrick McKey .05 .02
❑ 218 Nate McMillan .05 .02
❑ 219 Gary Payton .50 .15
❑ 220 Ricky Pierce .05 .02
❑ 221 David Benoit .05 .02
❑ 222 Mike Brown .05 .02
❑ 223 Tyrone Corbin .05 .02
❑ 224 Mark Eaton .05 .02
❑ 225 Blue Edwards .05 .02
❑ 226 Jeff Malone .05 .02
❑ 227 Karl Malone .40 .12
❑ 228 Eric Murdock .05 .02
❑ 229 John Stockton .25 .07
❑ 230 Michael Adams .05 .02
❑ 231 Rex Chapman .05 .02
❑ 232 Ledell Eackles .05 .02
❑ 233 Pervis Ellison .05 .02
❑ 234 A.J. English .05 .02
❑ 235 Harvey Grant .05 .02
❑ 236 Charles Jones .05 .02
❑ 237 LaBradford Smith .05 .02
❑ 238 Larry Stewart .05 .02
❑ 239 Bob Weiss CO .05 .02
❑ 240 Chris Ford CO .05 .02
❑ 241 Allan Bristow CO .05 .02
❑ 242 Phil Jackson CO .10 .03
❑ 243 Lenny Wilkens CO .10 .03
❑ 244 Richie Adubato CO .05 .02
❑ 245 Dan Issel CO .05 .02
❑ 246 Ron Rothstein CO .05 .02
❑ 247 Don Nelson CO .10 .03
❑ 248 Rudy Tomjanovich CO .10 .03
❑ 249 Bob Hill CO .05 .02
❑ 250 Larry Brown CO .10 .03
❑ 251 Randy Pfund CO RC .05 .02
❑ 252 Kevin Loughery CO .05 .02
❑ 253 Mike Dunleavy CO .05 .02
❑ 254 Jimmy Rodgers CO .05 .02
❑ 255 Chuck Daly CO .10 .03
❑ 256 Pat Riley CO .10 .03
❑ 257 Matt Guokas CO .05 .02
❑ 258 Doug Moe CO .05 .02
❑ 259 Paul Westphal CO .05 .02
❑ 260 Rick Adelman CO .05 .02
❑ 261 Garry St. Jean CO RC .05 .02
❑ 262 Jerry Tarkanian CO RC .05 .02
❑ 263 George Karl CO .10 .03
❑ 264 Jerry Sloan CO .10 .03
❑ 265 Wes Unseld CO .10 .03
❑ 266 Atlanta Hawks .05 .02
Team Card
❑ 267 Boston Celtics .05 .02
Team Card
❑ 268 Charlotte Hornets .05 .02
Team Card
❑ 269 Chicago Bulls .05 .02
Team Card
❑ 270 Cleveland Cavaliers .05 .02
Team Card
❑ 271 Dallas Mavericks .05 .02
Team Card
❑ 272 Denver Nuggets .05 .02
Team Card
❑ 273 Detroit Pistons .05 .02
Team Card
❑ 274 Golden State Warriors .05 .02
Team Card
❑ 275 Houston Rockets .05 .02
Team Card
❑ 276 Indiana Pacers .05 .02
Team Card
❑ 277 Los Angeles Clippers .05 .02
Team Card
❑ 278 Los Angeles Lakers .05 .02
Team Card
❑ 279 Miami Heat .05 .02
Team Card
❑ 280 Milwaukee Bucks .05 .02
Team Card
❑ 281 Minnesota Timberwolves .05 .02
Team Card
❑ 282 New Jersey Nets .05 .02
Team Card
❑ 283 New York Knicks .05 .02
Team Card
❑ 284 Orlando Magic .05 .02
Team Card
❑ 285 Philadelphia 76ers .05 .02
Team Card
❑ 286 Phoenix Suns .05 .02
Team Card
❑ 287 Portland Trail Blazers .05 .02
Team Card
❑ 288 Sacramento Kings .05 .02
Team Card
❑ 289 San Antonio Spurs .05 .02
Team Card
❑ 290 Seattle Supersonics .05 .02
Team Card
❑ 291 Utah Jazz .05 .02
Team Card
❑ 292 Washington Bullets .05 .02
Team Card
❑ 293 Michael Adams AS .05 .02
❑ 294 Charles Barkley AS .25 .07
❑ 295 Brad Daugherty AS .05 .02
❑ 296 Joe Dumars AS .10 .03
❑ 297 Patrick Ewing AS .10 .03
❑ 298 Michael Jordan AS 1.50 .45
❑ 299 Reggie Lewis AS .05 .02
❑ 300 Scottie Pippen AS .40 .12
❑ 301 Mark Price AS .05 .02
❑ 302 Dennis Rodman AS .25 .07
❑ 303 Isiah Thomas AS .10 .03
❑ 304 Kevin Willis AS .05 .02
❑ 305 Phil Jackson CO AS .10 .03
❑ 306 Clyde Drexler AS .10 .03
❑ 307 Tim Hardaway AS .25 .07
❑ 308 Jeff Hornacek AS .05 .02
❑ 309 Magic Johnson AS .40 .12
❑ 310 Dan Majerle AS .05 .02
❑ 311 Karl Malone AS .25 .07
❑ 312 Chris Mullin AS .10 .03
❑ 313 Dikembe Mutombo AS .25 .07
❑ 314 Hakeem Olajuwon AS .25 .07
❑ 315 David Robinson AS .25 .07
❑ 316 John Stockton AS .10 .03
❑ 317 Otis Thorpe AS .05 .02
❑ 318 James Worthy AS .10 .03
❑ 319 Don Nelson CO AS .10 .03
❑ 320 Scoring League Leaders 1.00 .30
Michael Jordan
Karl Malone
❑ 321 Three-Point Field .05 .02
Goal Percent
League Leaders
Dana Barros
Drazen Petrovic
❑ 322 Free Throw Percent .30 .09
League Leaders
Mark Price
Larry Bird
❑ 323 Blocks League Leaders .25 .07
David Robinson
Hakeem Olajuwon
❑ 324 Steals League Leaders .25 .07
John Stockton
Micheal Williams
❑ 325 Rebounds League .25 .07
Leaders
Dennis Rodman
Kevin Willis
❑ 326 Assists League Leaders .25 .07
John Stockton
Kevin Johnson
❑ 327 Field Goal Percent .05 .02
League Leaders
Buck Williams
Otis Thorpe
❑ 328 Magic Moments 1980 .25 .07
❑ 329 Magic Moments 1985 .25 .07
❑ 330 Magic Moments 87 and 88 .25 .07
❑ 331 Magic Numbers .25 .07
❑ 332 Drazen Petrovic .05 .02
Inside Stuff
❑ 333 Patrick Ewing .10 .03
Inside Stuff
❑ 334 David Robinson .25 .07
Stay in School
❑ 335 Kevin Johnson .10 .03
Stay in School
❑ 336 Charles Barkley .25 .07
Tournament of
The Americas
❑ 337 Larry Bird .50 .15
Tournament of
The Americas
❑ 338 Clyde Drexler .10 .03
Tournament of
The Americas
❑ 339 Patrick Ewing .10 .03
Tournament of
The Americas
❑ 340 Magic Johnson .40 .12
Tournament of
The Americas
❑ 341 Michael Jordan 1.50 .45
Tournament of
The Americas
❑ 342 Christian Laettner RC .50 .15
Tournament of
The Americas
❑ 343 Karl Malone .25 .07
Tournament of
The Americas
❑ 344 Chris Mullin .10 .03
Tournament of
The Americas
❑ 345 Scottie Pippen .40 .12
Tournament of
The Americas
❑ 346 David Robinson .25 .07
Tournament of
The Americas
❑ 347 John Stockton .10 .03
Tournament of
The Americas
❑ 348 Checklist 1 .05 .02
❑ 349 Checklist 2 .05 .02
❑ 350 Checklist 3 .05 .02
❑ 351 Mookie Blaylock .20 .06
❑ 352 Adam Keefe RC .10 .03
❑ 353 Travis Mays .10 .03
❑ 354 Morlon Wiley .10 .03
❑ 355 Joe Kleine .10 .03
❑ 356 Bart Kofoed .10 .03
❑ 357 Xavier McDaniel .10 .03
❑ 358 Tony Bennett RC .10 .03
❑ 359 Tom Hammonds .10 .03
❑ 360 Kevin Lynch .10 .03
❑ 361 Alonzo Mourning RC 2.50 .75
❑ 362 Rodney McCray .10 .03
❑ 363 Trent Tucker .10 .03
❑ 364 Corey Williams RC .10 .03
❑ 365 Steve Kerr .20 .06
Traded to Orlando
❑ 366 Jerome Lane .10 .03
❑ 367 Bobby Phills RC .40 .12

Card	Nm-Mt	Ex-Mt
368 Mike Sanders	.10	.03
369 Gerald Wilkins	.10	.03
370 Donald Hodge	.10	.03
371 Brian Howard RC	.10	.03
372 Tracy Moore RC	.10	.03
373 Sean Rooks RC	.10	.03
374 Kevin Brooks	.10	.03
375 LaPhonso Ellis RC	.40	.12
376 Scott Hastings	.10	.03
377 Robert Pack	.10	.03
378 Bryant Stith RC	.20	.06
379 Robert Werdann RC	.10	.03
380 Lance Blanks	.10	.03
Traded to Minnesota		
381 Terry Mills	.10	.03
382 Isaiah Morris RC	.10	.03
383 Olden Polynice	.10	.03
384 Brad Sellers	.10	.03
Traded to Minnesota		
385 Jud Buechler	.10	.03
386 Jeff Grayer	.10	.03
387 Byron Houston RC	.10	.03
388 Keith Jennings RC	.10	.03
389 Latrell Sprewell RC	3.00	.90
390 Scott Brooks	.10	.03
391 Carl Herrera	.10	.03
392 Robert Horry RC	.40	.12
393 Tree Rollins	.10	.03
394 Kennard Winchester	.10	.03
395 Greg Dreiling	.10	.03
396 Sean Green	.10	.03
397 Sam Mitchell	.10	.03
398 Pooh Richardson	.10	.03
399 Malik Sealy RC	.20	.06
400 Kenny Williams	.10	.03
401 Jaren Jackson RC	.20	.06
402 Mark Jackson	.20	.06
403 Stanley Roberts	.10	.03
404 Elmore Spencer RC	.10	.03
405 Kiki Vandeweghe	.10	.03
406 John Williams	.10	.03
407 Randy Woods RC	.10	.03
408 Alex Blackwell RC	.10	.03
409 Duane Cooper RC	.10	.03
410 Anthony Peeler RC	.20	.06
411 Keith Askins	.10	.03
412 Matt Geiger RC	.20	.06
413 Harold Miner RC	.20	.06
414 John Salley	.10	.03
415 Alaa Abdelnaby	.10	.03
Traded to Boston		
416 Todd Day RC	.20	.06
417 Blue Edwards	.10	.03
418 Brad Lohaus	.10	.03
419 Lee Mayberry RC	.10	.03
420 Eric Murdock	.10	.03
421 Christian Laettner	.75	.23
422 Bob McCann RC	.10	.03
423 Chuck Person	.10	.03
424 Chris Smith RC	.10	.03
425 Gundars Vetra RC	.10	.03
426 Micheal Williams	.10	.03
427 Chucky Brown	.10	.03
428 Tate George	.10	.03
429 Rick Mahorn	.10	.03
430 Rumeal Robinson	.10	.03
431 Jayson Williams	.20	.06
432 Eric Anderson RC	.10	.03
433 Rolando Blackman	.10	.03
434 Tony Campbell	.10	.03
435 Hubert Davis RC	.20	.06
436 Bo Kimble	.10	.03
437 Doc Rivers	.20	.06
438 Charles Smith	.10	.03
439 Anthony Bowie	.10	.03
440 Litterial Green RC	.10	.03
441 Greg Kite	.10	.03
442 Shaquille O'Neal RC	10.00	3.00
443 Donald Royal	.10	.03
444 Greg Grant	.10	.03
445 Jeff Hornacek	.20	.06
446 Andrew Lang	.10	.03
447 Kenny Payne	.10	.03
448 Tim Perry	.10	.03
449 C.Weatherspoon RC	.40	.12
450 Danny Ainge	.20	.06
451 Charles Barkley	.60	.18
452 Tim Kempton	.10	.03
453 Oliver Miller RC	.20	.06
454 Mark Bryant	.10	.03
455 Mario Elie	.20	.06
456 Dave Jamerson RC	.10	.03
457 Tracy Murray RC	.20	.06
458 Rod Strickland	.40	.12
459 Vincent Askew	.10	.03
Traded to Seattle		
460 Randy Brown	.10	.03
461 Marty Conlon	.10	.03
462 Jim Les	.10	.03
463 Walt Williams RC	.40	.12
464 William Bedford	.10	.03
465 Lloyd Daniels RC	.10	.03
466 Vinny Del Negro	.10	.03
467 Dale Ellis	.10	.03
468 Larry Smith	.10	.03
469 David Wood	.10	.03
470 Rich King	.10	.03
471 Isaac Austin RC	.20	.06
472 John Crotty RC	.10	.03
473 Stephen Howard RC	.10	.03
474 Jay Humphries	.10	.03
475 Larry Krystkowiak	.10	.03
476 Tom Gugliotta RC	1.25	.35
477 Buck Johnson	.10	.03
478 Don MacLean RC	.10	.03
479 Doug Overton	.10	.03
480 Brent Price RC	.20	.06
481 David Robinson TRIV	.40	.12
Blocks		
482 Magic Johnson TRIV	.60	.18
Assists		
483 John Stockton TRIV	.20	.06
Steals		
484 Patrick Ewing TRIV	.20	.06
Points		
485 Answer Card TRIV	.40	.12
Magic Johnson		
David Robinson		
Patrick Ewing		
John Stockton		
486 John Stockton	.20	.06
Stay in School		
487 Ahmad Rashad	.20	.06
Willow Bay		
Inside Stuff		
488 Rookie Checklist	.10	.03
489 Checklist 1	.10	.03
490 Checklist 2	.10	.03
AC1 Patrick Ewing Art	.50	.15
SU1 John Stockton AU	300.00	90.00
(Certified autograph)		
SU1 John Stockton Game	1.50	.45
His Ultimate Game		
TR1 NBA Championship	3.00	.90
Michael Jordan		
Clyde Drexler		
NNO M.Johnson Comm	1.00	.30
NNO M.Johnson AU	200.00	60.00
NNO Patrick Ewing Game	.50	.15
His Ultimate Game		
NNO Patrick Ewing AU	250.00	75.00
(Certified autograph)		

1993-94 Hoops

	Nm-Mt	Ex-Mt
COMPLETE SET (421)	20.00	6.00
COMPLETE SERIES 1 (300)	12.00	3.60
COMPLETE SERIES 2 (121)	8.00	2.40
BEWARE COUNTERFEIT BIRD/MAGIC AU		
1 Stacey Augmon	.05	.02
2 Mookie Blaylock	.10	.03
3 Duane Ferrell	.05	.02
4 Paul Graham	.05	.02
5 Adam Keefe	.05	.02
6 Blair Rasmussen	.05	.02
7 Dominique Wilkins	.25	.07
8 Kevin Willis	.05	.02
9 Alaa Abdelnaby	.05	.02
10 Dee Brown	.05	.02
11 Sherman Douglas	.05	.02
12 Rick Fox	.05	.02
13 Kevin Gamble	.05	.02
14 Joe Kleine	.05	.02
15 Xavier McDaniel	.05	.02
16 Robert Parish	.10	.03
17 Tony Bennett	.05	.02
18 Muggsy Bogues	.10	.03
19 Dell Curry	.05	.02
20 Kenny Gattison	.05	.02
21 Kendall Gill	.10	.03
22 Larry Johnson	.25	.07
23 Alonzo Mourning	.40	.12
24 Johnny Newman	.05	.02
25 B.J. Armstrong	.05	.02
26 Bill Cartwright	.05	.02
27 Horace Grant	.10	.03
28 Michael Jordan	3.00	.90
29 Stacey King	.05	.02
30 John Paxson	.05	.02
31 Will Perdue	.05	.02
32 Scottie Pippen	.75	.23
33 Scott Williams	.05	.02
34 Moses Malone	.25	.07
35 John Battle	.05	.02
36 Terrell Brandon	.10	.03
37 Brad Daugherty	.05	.02
38 Craig Ehlo	.05	.02
39 Danny Ferry	.05	.02
40 Larry Nance	.05	.02
41 Mark Price	.05	.02
42 Gerald Wilkins	.05	.02
43 John Williams	.05	.02
44 Terry Davis	.05	.02
45 Derek Harper	.10	.03
46 Donald Hodge	.05	.02
47 Mike Iuzzolino	.05	.02
48 Jim Jackson	.10	.03
49 Sean Rooks	.05	.02
50 Doug Smith	.05	.02
51 Randy White	.05	.02
52 Mahmoud Abdul-Rauf	.05	.02
53 LaPhonso Ellis	.05	.02
54 Marcus Liberty	.05	.02
55 Mark Macon	.05	.02
56 Dikembe Mutombo	.25	.07
57 Robert Pack	.05	.02
58 Bryant Stith	.05	.02
59 Reggie Williams	.05	.02
60 Mark Aguirre	.05	.02
61 Joe Dumars	.25	.07
62 Bill Laimbeer	.05	.02
63 Terry Mills	.05	.02
64 Olden Polynice	.05	.02
65 Alvin Robertson	.05	.02
66 Dennis Rodman	.50	.15
67 Isiah Thomas	.25	.07
68 Victor Alexander	.05	.02
69 Tim Hardaway	.25	.07
70 Tyrone Hill	.05	.02
71 Byron Houston	.05	.02
72 Sarunas Marciulionis	.05	.02
73 Chris Mullin	.25	.07
74 Billy Owens	.05	.02
75 Latrell Sprewell	.60	.18
76 Scott Brooks	.05	.02
77 Matt Bullard	.05	.02
78 Carl Herrera	.05	.02
79 Robert Horry	.10	.03
80 Vernon Maxwell	.05	.02

❑ 81 Hakeem Olajuwon .40 .12
❑ 82 Kenny Smith .05 .02
❑ 83 Otis Thorpe .10 .03
❑ 84 Dale Davis .05 .02
❑ 85 Vern Fleming .05 .02
❑ 86 George McCloud .05 .02
❑ 87 Reggie Miller .25 .07
❑ 88 Sam Mitchell .05 .02
❑ 89 Pooh Richardson .05 .02
❑ 90 Detlef Schrempf .10 .03
❑ 91 Malik Sealy .05 .02
❑ 92 Rik Smits .10 .03
❑ 93 Gary Grant .05 .02
❑ 94 Ron Harper .10 .03
❑ 95 Mark Jackson .10 .03
❑ 96 Danny Manning .10 .03
❑ 97 Ken Norman .05 .02
❑ 98 Stanley Roberts .05 .02
❑ 99 Elmore Spencer .05 .02
❑ 100 Loy Vaught .05 .02
❑ 101 John Williams .05 .02
❑ 102 Randy Woods .05 .02
❑ 103 Benoit Benjamin .05 .02
❑ 104 Elden Campbell .05 .02
❑ 105 Doug Christie UER .10 .03
(Has uniform number on front and 35 on back)
❑ 106 Vlade Divac .10 .03
❑ 107 Anthony Peeler .05 .02
❑ 108 Tony Smith .05 .02
❑ 109 Sedale Threatt .05 .02
❑ 110 James Worthy .25 .07
❑ 111 Bimbo Coles .05 .02
❑ 112 Grant Long .05 .02
❑ 113 Harold Miner .05 .02
❑ 114 Glen Rice .10 .03
❑ 115 John Salley .05 .02
❑ 116 Rony Seikaly .05 .02
❑ 117 Brian Shaw .05 .02
❑ 118 Steve Smith .25 .07
❑ 119 Anthony Avent .05 .02
❑ 120 Jon Barry .05 .02
❑ 121 Frank Brickowski .05 .02
❑ 122 Todd Day .05 .02
❑ 123 Blue Edwards .05 .02
❑ 124 Brad Lohaus .05 .02
❑ 125 Lee Mayberry .05 .02
❑ 126 Eric Murdock .05 .02
❑ 127 Derek Strong RC .05 .02
❑ 128 Thurl Bailey .05 .02
❑ 129 Christian Laettner .10 .03
❑ 130 Luc Longley .10 .03
❑ 131 Marlon Maxey .05 .02
❑ 132 Chuck Person .05 .02
❑ 133 Chris Smith .05 .02
❑ 134 Doug West .05 .02
❑ 135 Micheal Williams .05 .02
❑ 136 Rafael Addison .05 .02
❑ 137 Kenny Anderson .10 .03
❑ 138 Sam Bowie .05 .02
❑ 139 Chucky Brown .05 .02
❑ 140 Derrick Coleman .10 .03
❑ 141 Chris Morris .05 .02
❑ 142 Rumeal Robinson .05 .02
❑ 143 Greg Anthony .05 .02
❑ 144 Rolando Blackman .05 .02
❑ 145 Hubert Davis .05 .02
❑ 146 Patrick Ewing .25 .07
❑ 147 Anthony Mason .10 .03
❑ 148 Charles Oakley .10 .03
❑ 149 Doc Rivers .10 .03
❑ 150 Charles Smith .05 .02
❑ 151 John Starks .10 .03
❑ 152 Nick Anderson .10 .03
❑ 153 Anthony Bowie .05 .02
❑ 154 Litterial Green .05 .02
❑ 155 Shaquille O'Neal 1.25 .35
❑ 156 Donald Royal .05 .02
❑ 157 Dennis Scott .05 .02
❑ 158 Scott Skiles .05 .02
❑ 159 Tom Tolbert .05 .02
❑ 160 Jeff Turner .05 .02
❑ 161 Ron Anderson .05 .02
❑ 162 Johnny Dawkins .05 .02
❑ 163 Hersey Hawkins .10 .03
❑ 164 Jeff Hornacek .10 .03
❑ 165 Andrew Lang .05 .02
❑ 166 Tim Perry .05 .02
❑ 167 Clarence Weatherspoon .05 .02
❑ 168 Danny Ainge .10 .03
❑ 169 Charles Barkley .40 .12
❑ 170 Cedric Ceballos .10 .03
❑ 171 Richard Dumas .05 .02
❑ 172 Kevin Johnson .10 .03
❑ 173 Dan Majerle .10 .03
❑ 174 Oliver Miller .05 .02
❑ 175 Mark West .05 .02
❑ 176 Clyde Drexler .25 .07
❑ 177 Kevin Duckworth .05 .02
❑ 178 Mario Elie .05 .02
❑ 179 Dave Johnson .05 .02
❑ 180 Jerome Kersey .05 .02
❑ 181 Tracy Murray .05 .02
❑ 182 Terry Porter .05 .02
❑ 183 Clifford Robinson .10 .03
❑ 184 Rod Strickland .10 .03
❑ 185 Buck Williams .05 .02
❑ 186 Anthony Bonner .05 .02
❑ 187 Randy Brown .05 .02
❑ 188 Duane Causwell .05 .02
❑ 189 Pete Chilcutt .05 .02
❑ 190 Mitch Richmond .25 .07
❑ 191 Lionel Simmons .05 .02
❑ 192 Wayman Tisdale .05 .02
❑ 193 Spud Webb .10 .03
❑ 194 Walt Williams .05 .02
❑ 195 Willie Anderson .05 .02
❑ 196 Antoine Carr .05 .02
❑ 197 Terry Cummings .05 .02
❑ 198 Lloyd Daniels .05 .02
❑ 199 Sean Elliott .10 .03
❑ 200 Dale Ellis .05 .02
❑ 201 Avery Johnson .05 .02
❑ 202 J.R. Reid .05 .02
❑ 203 David Robinson .40 .12
❑ 204 Dana Barros .05 .02
❑ 205 Michael Cage .05 .02
❑ 206 Eddie Johnson .05 .02
❑ 207 Shawn Kemp .40 .12
❑ 208 Derrick McKey .05 .02
❑ 209 Nate McMillan .05 .02
❑ 210 Gary Payton .40 .12
❑ 211 Sam Perkins .10 .03
❑ 212 Ricky Pierce .05 .02
❑ 213 David Benoit .05 .02
❑ 214 Tyrone Corbin .05 .02
❑ 215 Mark Eaton .05 .02
❑ 216 Jay Humphries .05 .02
❑ 217 Jeff Malone .05 .02
❑ 218 Karl Malone .40 .12
❑ 219 John Stockton .25 .07
❑ 220 Michael Adams .05 .02
❑ 221 Rex Chapman .05 .02
❑ 222 Pervis Ellison .05 .02
❑ 223 Harvey Grant .05 .02
❑ 224 Tom Gugliotta .25 .07
❑ 225 Don MacLean .05 .02
❑ 226 Doug Overton .05 .02
❑ 227 Brent Price .05 .02
❑ 228 LaBradford Smith .05 .02
❑ 229 Larry Stewart .05 .02
❑ 230 Lenny Wilkens CO .10 .03
❑ 231 Chris Ford CO .05 .02
❑ 232 Allan Bristow CO .05 .02
❑ 233 Phil Jackson CO .10 .03
❑ 234 Mike Fratello CO .10 .03
❑ 235 Quinn Buckner CO .05 .02
❑ 236 Dan Issel CO .05 .02
❑ 237 Don Chaney CO .05 .02
❑ 238 Don Nelson CO .10 .03
❑ 239 Rudy Tomjanovich CO .10 .03
❑ 240 Larry Brown CO .10 .03
❑ 241 Bob Weiss CO .05 .02
❑ 242 Randy Pfund CO .05 .02
❑ 243 Kevin Loughery CO .05 .02
❑ 244 Mike Dunleavy CO .05 .02
❑ 245 Sidney Lowe CO .05 .02
❑ 246 Chuck Daly CO .10 .03
❑ 247 Pat Riley CO .10 .03
❑ 248 Brian Hill CO .05 .02
❑ 249 Fred Carter CO .05 .02
❑ 250 Paul Westphal CO .05 .02
❑ 251 Rick Adelman CO .05 .02
❑ 252 Garry St. Jean CO .05 .02
❑ 253 John Lucas CO .05 .02
❑ 254 George Karl CO .10 .03
❑ 255 Jerry Sloan CO .10 .03
❑ 256 Wes Unseld CO .10 .03
❑ 257 Michael Jordan AS 1.50 .45
❑ 258 Isiah Thomas AS .10 .03
❑ 259 Scottie Pippen AS .40 .12
❑ 260 Larry Johnson AS .10 .03
❑ 261 Dominique Wilkins AS .10 .03
❑ 262 Joe Dumars AS .10 .03
❑ 263 Mark Price AS .05 .02
❑ 264 Shaquille O'Neal AS .50 .15
❑ 265 Patrick Ewing AS .10 .03
❑ 266 Larry Nance AS .05 .02
❑ 267 Detlef Schrempf AS .05 .02
❑ 268 Brad Daugherty AS .05 .02
❑ 269 Charles Barkley AS .25 .07
❑ 270 Clyde Drexler AS .10 .03
❑ 271 Sean Elliott AS .05 .02
❑ 272 Tim Hardaway AS .10 .03
❑ 273 Shawn Kemp AS .25 .07
❑ 274 Dan Majerle AS .05 .02
❑ 275 Karl Malone AS .25 .07
❑ 276 Danny Manning AS .05 .02
❑ 277 Hakeem Olajuwon AS .25 .07
❑ 278 Terry Porter AS .05 .02
❑ 279 David Robinson AS .25 .07
❑ 280 John Stockton AS .10 .03
❑ 281 East Team Photo .05 .02
❑ 282 West Team Photo .05 .02
❑ 283 Michael Jordan .75 .23
Dominique Wilkins
Karl Malone LL
❑ 284 Dennis Rodman .50 .15
Shaquille O'Neal
Dikembe Mutombo LL
❑ 285 Cedric Ceballos .05 .02
Brad Daugherty
Dale Davis LL
❑ 286 John Stockton .10 .03
Tim Hardaway
Scott Skiles LL
❑ 287 Mark Price .05 .02
Mahmoud Abdul-Rauf
Eddie Johnson LL
❑ 288 B.J. Armstrong .05 .02
Chris Mullin
Kenny Smith LL
❑ 289 Michael Jordan .75 .23
Mookie Blaylock
John Stockton LL
❑ 290 Hakeem Olajuwon .40 .12
Shaquille O'Neal
Dikembe Mutombo LL
❑ 291 Boys and Girls Club .10 .03
David Robinson
❑ 292 B.J. Armstrong TRIB .05 .02
❑ 293 Scottie Pippen TRIB .40 .12
❑ 294 Kevin Johnson TRIB .05 .02
❑ 295 Charles Barkley TRIB .25 .07
❑ 296 Richard Dumas TRIB .05 .02
❑ 297 Horace Grant CL .05 .02
❑ 298 David Robinson CL .05 .02
❑ 299 David Robinson CL .05 .02
❑ 300 David Robinson CL .05 .02
❑ 301 Craig Ehlo .05 .02
❑ 302 Jon Koncak .05 .02
❑ 303 Andrew Lang .05 .02
❑ 304 Chris Corchiani .05 .02
❑ 305 Acie Earl RC .05 .02
❑ 306 Dino Radja RC .05 .02
❑ 307 Scott Burrell RC .25 .07
❑ 308 Hersey Hawkins .10 .03
❑ 309 Eddie Johnson .05 .02
❑ 310 David Wingate .05 .02
❑ 311 Corie Blount RC .05 .02
❑ 312 Steve Kerr .10 .03
❑ 313 Toni Kukoc RC 1.00 .30
❑ 314 Pete Myers .05 .02
❑ 315 Jay Guidinger .05 .02
❑ 316 Tyrone Hill .05 .02
❑ 317 Gerald Madkins RC .05 .02
❑ 318 Chris Mills RC .25 .07
❑ 319 Bobby Phills .05 .02

Card	Nm-Mt	Ex-Mt
❑ 320 Lucious Harris RC	.05	.02
❑ 321 Popeye Jones RC	.05	.02
❑ 322 Fat Lever	.05	.02
❑ 323 Jamal Mashburn RC	.60	.18
❑ 324 Darren Morningstar RC (See also 334)	.05	.02
❑ 325 Kevin Brooks	.05	.02
❑ 326 Tom Hammonds	.05	.02
❑ 327 Darnell Mee RC	.05	.02
❑ 328 Rodney Rogers RC	.25	.07
❑ 329 Brian Williams	.05	.02
❑ 330 Greg Anderson	.05	.02
❑ 331 Sean Elliott	.10	.03
❑ 332 Allan Houston RC	1.00	.30
❑ 333 Lindsey Hunter RC	.25	.07
❑ 334 David Wood UER (Card misnumbered 324)	.05	.02
❑ 335 Jud Buechler	.05	.02
❑ 336 Chris Gatling	.05	.02
❑ 337 Josh Grant RC	.05	.02
❑ 338 Jeff Grayer	.05	.02
❑ 339 Keith Jennings	.05	.02
❑ 340 Avery Johnson	.05	.02
❑ 341 Chris Webber RC	2.50	.75
❑ 342 Sam Cassell RC	1.00	.30
❑ 343 Mario Elie	.05	.02
❑ 344 Eric Riley RC	.05	.02
❑ 345 Antonio Davis RC	.30	.09
❑ 346 Scott Haskin RC	.05	.02
❑ 347 Gerald Paddio	.05	.02
❑ 348 LaSalle Thompson	.05	.02
❑ 349 Ken Williams	.05	.02
❑ 350 Mark Aguirre	.05	.02
❑ 351 Terry Dehere RC	.05	.02
❑ 352 Henry James	.05	.02
❑ 353 Sam Bowie	.05	.02
❑ 354 George Lynch RC	.05	.02
❑ 355 Kurt Rambis	.05	.02
• ❑ 356 Nick Van Exel RC	.75	.23
❑ 357 Trevor Wilson	.05	.02
❑ 358 Keith Askins	.05	.02
❑ 359 Manute Bol	.05	.02
❑ 360 Willie Burton	.05	.02
❑ 361 Matt Geiger	.05	.02
❑ 362 Alec Kessler	.05	.02
❑ 363 Vin Baker RC	.60	.18
❑ 364 Ken Norman	.05	.02
❑ 365 Danny Schayes	.05	.02
❑ 366 Mike Brown	.05	.02
❑ 367 Isaiah Rider RC	.50	.15
❑ 368 Benoit Benjamin	.05	.02
❑ 369 P.J. Brown RC	.25	.07
❑ 370 Kevin Edwards	.05	.02
❑ 371 Armon Gilliam	.05	.02
❑ 372 Rick Mahorn	.05	.02
❑ 373 Dwayne Schintzius	.05	.02
❑ 374 Rex Walters RC	.05	.02
❑ 375 Jayson Williams	.10	.03
❑ 376 Eric Anderson	.05	.02
❑ 377 Anthony Bonner	.05	.02
❑ 378 Tony Campbell	.05	.02
❑ 379 Herb Williams	.05	.02
❑ 380 Anfernee Hardaway RC	2.00	.60
❑ 381 Greg Kite	.05	.02
❑ 382 Larry Krystkowiak	.05	.02
❑ 383 Todd Lichti	.05	.02
❑ 384 Dana Barros	.05	.02
❑ 385 Shawn Bradley RC	.25	.07
❑ 386 Greg Graham RC	.05	.02
❑ 387 Warren Kidd RC	.05	.02
❑ 388 Eric Leckner	.05	.02
❑ 389 Moses Malone	.25	.07
❑ 390 A.C. Green	.10	.03
❑ 391 Frank Johnson	.05	.02
❑ 392 Joe Kleine	.05	.02
❑ 393 Malcolm Mackey RC	.05	.02
❑ 394 Jerrod Mustaf	.05	.02
❑ 395 Mark Bryant	.05	.02
❑ 396 Chris Dudley	.05	.02
❑ 397 Harvey Grant	.05	.02
❑ 398 James Robinson RC	.05	.02
❑ 399 Reggie Smith	.05	.02
❑ 400 Randy Brown	.05	.02
❑ 401 Bobby Hurley RC	.10	.03
❑ 402 Jim Les	.05	.02
❑ 403 Vinny Del Negro	.05	.02
❑ 404 Sleepy Floyd	.05	.02
❑ 405 Dennis Rodman	.50	.15
❑ 406 Chris Whitney RC	.05	.02
❑ 407 Vincent Askew	.05	.02
❑ 408 Kendall Gill	.10	.03
❑ 409 Ervin Johnson RC	.10	.03
❑ 410 Rich King	.05	.02
❑ 411 Detlef Schrempf	.10	.03
❑ 412 Tom Chambers	.05	.02
❑ 413 John Crotty	.05	.02
❑ 414 Felton Spencer	.05	.02
❑ 415 Luther Wright RC	.05	.02
❑ 416 Calbert Cheaney RC	.10	.03
❑ 417 Kevin Duckworth	.05	.02
❑ 418 Gheorghe Muresan RC	.25	.07
❑ 419 David Robinson CL	.05	.02
❑ 420 David Robinson CL	.05	.02
❑ 421 David Robinson CL	.05	.02
❑ DR1 David Robinson Commemorative 1989 Rookie Card	.40	.12
❑ MB1 Magic Johnson Larry Bird Commemorative	.50	.15
❑ MB1A Magic Johnson Larry Bird Autograph Card	400.00	120.00
❑ NNO David Robinson Autograph Card	80.00	24.00
❑ NNO David Robinson Expired Voucher	10.00	3.00
❑ NNO Magic Johnson Larry Bird Expired Voucher	30.00	9.00

1994-95 Hoops

	Nm-Mt	Ex-Mt
COMPLETE SET (450)	24.00	7.25
COMPLETE SERIES 1 (300)	12.00	3.60
COMPLETE SERIES 2 (150)	12.00	3.60
❑ 1 Stacey Augmon	.05	.02
❑ 2 Mookie Blaylock	.05	.02
❑ 3 Doug Edwards	.05	.02
❑ 4 Craig Ehlo	.05	.02
❑ 5 Jon Koncak	.05	.02
❑ 6 Danny Manning	.10	.03
❑ 7 Kevin Willis	.05	.02
❑ 8 Dee Brown	.05	.02
❑ 9 Sherman Douglas	.05	.02
❑ 10 Acie Earl	.05	.02
❑ 11 Kevin Gamble	.05	.02
❑ 12 Xavier McDaniel	.05	.02
❑ 13 Robert Parish	.10	.03
❑ 14 Dino Radja	.05	.02
❑ 15 Tony Bennett	.05	.02
❑ 16 Muggsy Bogues	.10	.03
❑ 17 Scott Burrell	.05	.02
❑ 18 Dell Curry	.05	.02
❑ 19 Hersey Hawkins	.10	.03
❑ 20 Eddie Johnson	.05	.02
❑ 21 Larry Johnson	.10	.03
❑ 22 Alonzo Mourning	.30	.09
❑ 23 B.J. Armstrong	.05	.02
❑ 24 Corie Blount	.05	.02
❑ 25 Bill Cartwright	.05	.02
❑ 26 Horace Grant	.10	.03
❑ 27 Toni Kukoc	.40	.12
❑ 28 Luc Longley	.05	.02
❑ 29 Pete Myers	.05	.02
❑ 30 Scottie Pippen	.75	.23
❑ 31 Scott Williams	.05	.02
❑ 32 Terrell Brandon	.10	.03
❑ 33 Brad Daugherty	.05	.02
❑ 34 Tyrone Hill	.05	.02
❑ 35 Chris Mills	.10	.03
❑ 36 Larry Nance	.05	.02
❑ 37 Bobby Phills	.05	.02
❑ 38 Mark Price	.05	.02
❑ 39 Gerald Wilkins	.05	.02
❑ 40 John Williams	.05	.02
❑ 41 Terry Davis	.05	.02
❑ 42 Lucious Harris	.05	.02
❑ 43 Jim Jackson	.10	.03
❑ 44 Popeye Jones	.05	.02
❑ 45 Tim Legler	.05	.02
❑ 46 Jamal Mashburn	.25	.07
❑ 47 Sean Rooks	.05	.02
❑ 48 Mahmoud Abdul-Rauf	.05	.02
❑ 49 LaPhonso Ellis	.05	.02
❑ 50 Dikembe Mutombo	.10	.03
❑ 51 Robert Pack	.05	.02
❑ 52 Rodney Rogers	.05	.02
❑ 53 Bryant Stith	.05	.02
❑ 54 Brian Williams	.05	.02
❑ 55 Reggie Williams	.05	.02
❑ 56 Greg Anderson	.05	.02
❑ 57 Joe Dumars	.25	.07
❑ 58 Sean Elliott	.10	.03
❑ 59 Allan Houston	.40	.12
❑ 60 Lindsey Hunter	.10	.03
❑ 61 Mark Macon	.05	.02
❑ 62 Terry Mills	.05	.02
❑ 63 Victor Alexander	.05	.02
❑ 64 Chris Gatling	.05	.02
❑ 65 Tim Hardaway	.25	.07
❑ 66 Avery Johnson	.05	.02
❑ 67 Sarunas Marciulionis	.05	.02
❑ 68 Chris Mullin	.25	.07
❑ 69 Billy Owens	.05	.02
❑ 70 Latrell Sprewell	.25	.07
❑ 71 Chris Webber	.60	.18
❑ 72 Matt Bullard	.05	.02
❑ 73 Sam Cassell	.25	.07
❑ 74 Mario Elie	.05	.02
❑ 75 Carl Herrera	.05	.02
❑ 76 Robert Horry	.10	.03
❑ 77 Vernon Maxwell	.05	.02
❑ 78 Hakeem Olajuwon	.40	.12
❑ 79 Kenny Smith	.05	.02
❑ 80 Otis Thorpe	.05	.02
❑ 81 Antonio Davis	.05	.02
❑ 82 Dale Davis	.05	.02
❑ 83 Vern Fleming	.05	.02
❑ 84 Scott Haskin	.05	.02
❑ 85 Derrick McKey	.05	.02
❑ 86 Reggie Miller	.25	.07
❑ 87 Byron Scott	.10	.03
❑ 88 Rik Smits	.05	.02
❑ 89 Haywoode Workman	.05	.02
❑ 90 Terry Dehere	.05	.02
❑ 91 Harold Ellis	.05	.02
❑ 92 Gary Grant	.05	.02
❑ 93 Ron Harper	.10	.03
❑ 94 Mark Jackson	.05	.02
❑ 95 Stanley Roberts	.05	.02
❑ 96 Loy Vaught	.05	.02
❑ 97 Dominique Wilkins	.25	.07
❑ 98 Elden Campbell	.05	.02
❑ 99 Doug Christie	.10	.03
❑ 100 Vlade Divac	.05	.02
❑ 101 Reggie Jordan	.05	.02
❑ 102 George Lynch	.05	.02
❑ 103 Anthony Peeler	.05	.02
❑ 104 Sedale Threatt	.05	.02
❑ 105 Nick Van Exel	.25	.07
❑ 106 James Worthy	.25	.07
❑ 107 Bimbo Coles	.05	.02
❑ 108 Matt Geiger	.05	.02
❑ 109 Grant Long	.05	.02
❑ 110 Harold Miner	.05	.02
❑ 111 Glen Rice	.10	.03
❑ 112 John Salley	.05	.02
❑ 113 Rony Seikaly	.05	.02
❑ 114 Brian Shaw	.05	.02

❑ 115 Steve Smith .10 .03
❑ 116 Vin Baker .25 .07
❑ 117 Jon Barry .05 .02
❑ 118 Todd Day .05 .02
❑ 119 Lee Mayberry .05 .02
❑ 120 Eric Murdock .05 .02
❑ 121 Ken Norman .05 .02
❑ 122 Mike Brown .05 .02
❑ 123 Stacey King .05 .02
❑ 124 Christian Laettner .10 .03
❑ 125 Chuck Person .05 .02
❑ 126 Isaiah Rider .10 .03
❑ 127 Chris Smith .05 .02
❑ 128 Doug West .05 .02
❑ 129 Micheal Williams .05 .02
❑ 130 Kenny Anderson .10 .03
❑ 131 Benoit Benjamin .05 .02
❑ 132 P.J. Brown .05 .02
❑ 133 Derrick Coleman .10 .03
❑ 134 Kevin Edwards .05 .02
❑ 135 Armon Gilliam .05 .02
❑ 136 Chris Morris .05 .02
❑ 137 Rex Walters .05 .02
❑ 138 David Wesley .05 .02
❑ 139 Greg Anthony .05 .02
❑ 140 Anthony Bonner .05 .02
❑ 141 Hubert Davis .05 .02
❑ 142 Patrick Ewing .25 .07
❑ 143 Derek Harper .05 .02
❑ 144 Anthony Mason .10 .03
❑ 145 Charles Oakley .05 .02
❑ 146 Charles Smith .05 .02
❑ 147 John Starks .05 .02
❑ 148 Nick Anderson .05 .02
❑ 149 Anthony Avent .05 .02
❑ 150 Anthony Bowie .05 .02
❑ 151 Anfernee Hardaway .60 .18
❑ 152 Shaquille O'Neal 1.25 .35
❑ 153 Donald Royal .05 .02
❑ 154 Dennis Scott .05 .02
❑ 155 Scott Skiles .05 .02
❑ 156 Jeff Turner .05 .02
❑ 157 Dana Barros .05 .02
❑ 158 Shawn Bradley .05 .02
❑ 159 Greg Graham .05 .02
❑ 160 Warren Kidd .05 .02
❑ 161 Eric Leckner .05 .02
❑ 162 Jeff Malone .05 .02
❑ 163 Tim Perry .05 .02
❑ 164 Clarence Weatherspoon .05 .02
❑ 165 Danny Ainge .05 .02
❑ 166 Charles Barkley .40 .12
❑ 167 Cedric Ceballos .05 .02
❑ 168 A.C. Green .10 .03
❑ 169 Kevin Johnson .10 .03
❑ 170 Malcolm Mackey .05 .02
❑ 171 Dan Majerle .10 .03
❑ 172 Oliver Miller .05 .02
❑ 173 Mark West .05 .02
❑ 174 Clyde Drexler .25 .07
❑ 175 Chris Dudley .05 .02
❑ 176 Harvey Grant .05 .02
❑ 177 Tracy Murray .05 .02
❑ 178 Terry Porter .05 .02
❑ 179 Clifford Robinson .10 .03
❑ 180 James Robinson .05 .02
❑ 181 Rod Strickland .10 .03
❑ 182 Buck Williams .05 .02
❑ 183 Duane Causwell .05 .02
❑ 184 Bobby Hurley .05 .02
❑ 185 Olden Polynice .05 .02
❑ 186 Mitch Richmond .25 .07
❑ 187 Lionel Simmons .05 .02
❑ 188 Wayman Tisdale .05 .02
❑ 189 Spud Webb .05 .02
❑ 190 Walt Williams .05 .02
❑ 191 Willie Anderson .05 .02
❑ 192 Lloyd Daniels .05 .02
❑ 193 Vinny Del Negro .05 .02
❑ 194 Dale Ellis .05 .02
❑ 195 J.R. Reid .05 .02
❑ 196 David Robinson .40 .12
❑ 197 Dennis Rodman .50 .15
❑ 198 Kendall Gill .10 .03
❑ 199 Ervin Johnson .05 .02
❑ 200 Shawn Kemp .40 .12
❑ 201 Chris King .05 .02
❑ 202 Nate McMillan .05 .02
❑ 203 Gary Payton .40 .12
❑ 204 Sam Perkins .10 .03
❑ 205 Ricky Pierce .05 .02
❑ 206 Detlef Schrempf .10 .03
❑ 207 David Benoit .05 .02
❑ 208 Tom Chambers .05 .02
❑ 209 Tyrone Corbin .05 .02
❑ 210 Jeff Hornacek .10 .03
❑ 211 Karl Malone .40 .12
❑ 212 Bryon Russell .05 .02
❑ 213 Felton Spencer .05 .02
❑ 214 John Stockton .25 .07
❑ 215 Luther Wright .05 .02
❑ 216 Michael Adams .05 .02
❑ 217 Mitchell Butler .05 .02
❑ 218 Rex Chapman .05 .02
❑ 219 Calbert Cheaney .05 .02
❑ 220 Pervis Ellison .05 .02
❑ 221 Tom Gugliotta .10 .03
❑ 222 Don MacLean .05 .02
❑ 223 Gheorghe Muresan .05 .02
❑ 224 Kenny Anderson AS .05 .02
❑ 225 B.J. Armstrong AS .05 .02
❑ 226 Mookie Blaylock AS .05 .02
❑ 227 Derrick Coleman AS .05 .02
❑ 228 Patrick Ewing AS .10 .03
❑ 229 Horace Grant AS .05 .02
❑ 230 Alonzo Mourning AS .25 .07
❑ 231 Shaquille O'Neal AS .50 .15
❑ 232 Charles Oakley AS .05 .02
❑ 233 Scottie Pippen AS .40 .12
❑ 234 Mark Price AS .05 .02
❑ 235 John Starks AS .05 .02
❑ 236 Dominique Wilkins AS .10 .03
❑ 237 East Team .05 .02
❑ 238 Charles Barkley AS .25 .07
❑ 239 Clyde Drexler AS .10 .03
❑ 240 Kevin Johnson AS .05 .02
❑ 241 Shawn Kemp AS .25 .07
❑ 242 Karl Malone AS .25 .07
❑ 243 Danny Manning AS .05 .02
❑ 244 Hakeem Olajuwon AS .25 .07
❑ 245 Gary Payton AS .25 .07
❑ 246 Mitch Richmond AS .10 .03
❑ 247 Clifford Robinson AS .05 .02
❑ 248 David Robinson AS .25 .07
❑ 249 Latrell Sprewell AS .25 .07
❑ 250 John Stockton AS .10 .03
❑ 251 West Team .05 .02
❑ 252 Tracy Murray LL .05 .02
B.J. Armstrong
Reggie Miller
❑ 253 John Stockton LL .10 .03
Muggsy Bogues
Mookie Blaylock
❑ 254 Dikembe Mutombo LL .25 .07
Hakeem Olajuwon
Houston Rockets
David Robinson
❑ 255 Mahmoud Abdul-Rauf LL .05 .02
Reggie Miller
Indiana Pacers
Ricky Pierce
❑ 256 Dennis Rodman LL .40 .12
Shaquille O'Neal
Kevin Willis
❑ 257 David Robinson LL .40 .12
Shaquille O'Neal
Hakeem Olajuwon
❑ 258 Nate McMillan LL .25 .07
Scottie Pippen
Mookie Blaylock
❑ 259 Chris Webber AW .30 .09
❑ 260 Hakeem Olajuwon AW .25 .07
❑ 261 Hakeem Olajuwon AW .25 .07
❑ 262 Dell Curry AW .05 .02
❑ 263 Scottie Pippen AW .40 .12
❑ 264 Anfernee Hardaway AW .30 .09
❑ 265 Don MacLean AW .05 .02
❑ 266 Hakeem Olajuwon FIN .25 .07
❑ 267 Derek Harper FIN .05 .02
❑ 268 Sam Cassell FIN .25 .07
❑ 269 Hakeem Olajuwon .25 .07
Tribute
❑ 270 Patrick Ewing FIN .10 .03
Hakeem Olajuwon
❑ 271 Carl Herrera FIN .05 .02
❑ 272 Vernon Maxwell FIN .05 .02
❑ 273 Hakeem Olajuwon FIN .25 .07
❑ 274 Lenny Wilkens CO .10 .03
❑ 275 Chris Ford CO .05 .02
❑ 276 Allan Bristow CO .05 .02
❑ 277 Phil Jackson CO .10 .03
❑ 278 Mike Fratello CO .10 .03
❑ 279 Dick Motta CO .05 .02
❑ 280 Dan Issel CO .10 .03
❑ 281 Don Chaney CO .05 .02
❑ 282 Don Nelson CO .10 .03
❑ 283 Rudy Tomjanovich CO .10 .03
❑ 284 Larry Brown CO .10 .03
❑ 285 Del Harris CO UER .05 .02
(Back refers to Ralph Sampson and Akeem Olajuwon as part of '80-'81 Rockets)
❑ 286 Kevin Loughery CO .05 .02
❑ 287 Mike Dunleavy CO .05 .02
❑ 288 Sidney Lowe CO .05 .02
❑ 289 Pat Riley CO .10 .03
❑ 290 Brian Hill CO .05 .02
❑ 291 John Lucas CO .10 .03
❑ 292 Paul Westphal CO .05 .02
❑ 293 Garry St. Jean CO .05 .02
❑ 294 George Karl CO .10 .03
❑ 295 Jerry Sloan CO .10 .03
❑ 296 Magic Johnson .75 .23
Commemorative
❑ 297 Denzel Washington .10 .03
❑ 298 Checklist .05 .02
❑ 299 Checklist .05 .02
❑ 300 Checklist .05 .02
❑ 301 Sergei Bazarevich .05 .02
❑ 302 Tyrone Corbin .05 .02
❑ 303 Grant Long .05 .02
❑ 304 Ken Norman .05 .02
❑ 305 Steve Smith .10 .03
❑ 306 Blue Edwards .05 .02
❑ 307 Greg Minor RC .05 .02
❑ 308 Eric Montross RC .05 .02
❑ 309 Dominique Wilkins .25 .07
❑ 310 Michael Adams .05 .02
❑ 311 Darrin Hancock RC .05 .02
❑ 312 Robert Parish .10 .03
❑ 313 Ron Harper .10 .03
❑ 314 Dickey Simpkins RC .05 .02
❑ 315 Michael Cage .05 .02
❑ 316 Tony Dumas RC .05 .02
❑ 317 Jason Kidd RC 3.00 .90
❑ 318 Roy Tarpley .05 .02
❑ 319 Dale Ellis .05 .02
❑ 320 Jalen Rose RC 1.00 .30
❑ 321 Bill Curley RC .05 .02
❑ 322 Grant Hill RC 1.25 .35
❑ 323 Oliver Miller .05 .02
❑ 324 Mark West .05 .02
❑ 325 Tom Gugliotta .10 .03
❑ 326 Ricky Pierce .05 .02
❑ 327 Carlos Rogers RC .05 .02
❑ 328 Clifford Rozier RC .05 .02
❑ 329 Rony Seikaly .05 .02
❑ 330 Tim Breaux .05 .02
❑ 331 Duane Ferrell .05 .02
❑ 332 Mark Jackson .05 .02
❑ 333 Lamond Murray RC .10 .03
❑ 334 Bo Outlaw RC .05 .02
❑ 335 Eric Piatkowski RC .05 .02
❑ 336 Pooh Richardson .05 .02
❑ 337 Malik Sealy .05 .02
❑ 338 Cedric Ceballos .05 .02
❑ 339 Eddie Jones RC 1.25 .35
❑ 340 Anthony Miller RC .05 .02
❑ 341 Kevin Gamble .05 .02
❑ 342 Brad Lohaus .05 .02
❑ 343 Billy Owens .05 .02
❑ 344 Khalid Reeves RC .05 .02
❑ 345 Kevin Willis .05 .02
❑ 346 Eric Mobley RC .05 .02
❑ 347 Johnny Newman .05 .02
❑ 348 Ed Pinckney .05 .02
❑ 349 Glenn Robinson RC .75 .23
❑ 350 Howard Eisley RC .05 .02

	Card	Nm-Mt	Ex-Mt
❑ 351	Donyell Marshall RC	.25	.07
❑ 352	Yinka Dare RC	.05	.02
❑ 353	Charlie Ward RC	.25	.07
❑ 354	Monty Williams RC	.05	.02
❑ 355	Horace Grant	.10	.03
❑ 356	Brian Shaw	.05	.02
❑ 357	Brooks Thompson RC	.05	.02
❑ 358	Derrick Alston RC	.05	.02
❑ 359	B.J. Tyler RC	.05	.02
❑ 360	Scott Williams	.05	.02
❑ 361	Sharone Wright RC	.05	.02
❑ 362	Antonio Lang RC	.05	.02
❑ 363	Danny Manning	.10	.03
❑ 364	Wesley Person RC	.25	.07
❑ 365	Wayman Tisdale	.05	.02
❑ 366	Trevor Ruffin RC	.05	.02
❑ 367	Aaron McKie RC	.50	.15
❑ 368	Brian Grant RC	.60	.18
❑ 369	Michael Smith RC	.05	.02
❑ 370	Sean Elliott	.10	.03
❑ 371	Avery Johnson	.05	.02
❑ 372	Chuck Person	.05	.02
❑ 373	Bill Cartwright	.05	.02
❑ 374	Sarunas Marciulionis	.05	.02
❑ 375	Dontonio Wingfield RC	.05	.02
❑ 376	Antoine Carr	.05	.02
❑ 377	Jamie Watson RC	.05	.02
❑ 378	Juwan Howard RC	.60	.18
❑ 379	Jim McIlvaine RC	.05	.02
❑ 380	Scott Skiles	.05	.02
❑ 381	Anthony Tucker RC	.05	.02
❑ 382	Chris Webber	.60	.18
❑ 383	Bill Fitch CO	.05	.02
❑ 384	Bill Blair CO	.05	.02
❑ 385	Butch Beard CO	.05	.02
❑ 386	P.J. Carlesimo CO	.05	.02
❑ 387	Bob Hill CO	.05	.02
❑ 388	Jim Lynam CO	.05	.02
❑ 389	Checklist 4	.05	.02
❑ 390	Checklist 5	.05	.02
❑ 391	Atlanta Hawks TC	.05	.02
❑ 392	Boston Celtics TC	.05	.02
❑ 393	Charlotte Hornets TC	.05	.02
❑ 394	Chicago Bulls TC	.05	.02
❑ 395	Cleveland Cavaliers TC	.05	.02
❑ 396	Dallas Mavericks TC	.05	.02
❑ 397	Denver Nuggets TC	.05	.02
❑ 398	Detroit Pistons TC	.05	.02
❑ 399	Golden State Warriors TC	.05	.02
❑ 400	Houston Rockets TC	.05	.02
❑ 401	Indiana Pacers TC	.05	.02
❑ 402	Los Angeles Clippers TC	.05	.02
❑ 403	Los Angeles Lakers TC	.05	.02
❑ 404	Miami Heat TC	.05	.02
❑ 405	Milwaukee Bucks TC	.05	.02
❑ 406	Minnesota Timberwolves TC	.05	.02
❑ 407	New Jersey Nets TC	.05	.02
❑ 408	New York Knicks TC	.05	.02
❑ 409	Orlando Magic TC	.05	.02
❑ 410	Philadelphia 76ers TC	.05	.02
❑ 411	Phoenix Suns TC	.05	.02
❑ 412	Portland Trail Blazers TC	.05	.02
❑ 413	Sacramento Kings TC	.05	.02
❑ 414	San Antonio Spurs TC	.05	.02
❑ 415	Seattle Supersonics TC	.05	.02
❑ 416	Utah Jazz TC	.05	.02
❑ 417	Washington Bullets TC	.05	.02
❑ 418	Toronto Raptors TC	.05	.02
❑ 419	Vancouver Grizzlies TC	.05	.02
❑ 420	NBA Logo Card	.05	.02
❑ 421	Glenn Robinson TOP Chris Webber	.25	.07
❑ 422	Jason Kidd TOP Shawn Bradley	.50	.15
❑ 423	Grant Hill TOP Anfernee Hardaway	.50	.15
❑ 424	Donyell Marshall TOP Jamal Mashburn	.25	.07
❑ 425	Juwan Howard TOP Isaiah Rider	.25	.07
❑ 426	Sharone Wright TOP Calbert Cheaney	.05	.02
❑ 427	Lamond Murray TOP Bobby Hurley	.05	.02
❑ 428	Brian Grant TOP Vin Baker	.25	.07
❑ 429	Eric Montross TOP Rodney Rogers	.05	.02
❑ 430	Eddie Jones TOP Lindsey Hunter	.30	.09
❑ 431	Craig Ehlo GM	.05	.02
❑ 432	Dino Radja GM	.05	.02
❑ 433	Toni Kukoc GM	.25	.07
❑ 434	Mark Price GM	.05	.02
❑ 435	Latrell Sprewell GM	.25	.07
❑ 436	Sam Cassell GM	.25	.07
❑ 437	Vernon Maxwell GM	.05	.02
❑ 438	Haywoode Workman GM	.05	.02
❑ 439	Harold Ellis GM	.05	.02
❑ 440	Cedric Ceballos GM	.05	.02
❑ 441	Vlade Divac GM	.05	.02
❑ 442	Nick Van Exel GM	.10	.03
❑ 443	John Starks GM	.05	.02
❑ 444	Scott Williams GM	.05	.02
❑ 445	Clifford Robinson GM	.05	.02
❑ 446	Spud Webb GM	.05	.02
❑ 447	Avery Johnson GM	.05	.02
❑ 448	Dennis Rodman GM	.25	.07
❑ 449	Sarunas Marciulionis GM	.05	.02
❑ 450	Nate McMillan GM	.05	.02
❑ NNO	Shaq Sheet Wrapper Exchange Autograph	400.00	120.00
❑ NNO	G.Hill Wrapper Exch.	4.00	1.20
❑ NNO	Shaq Sheet Wrap.Exch.	30.00	9.00

1995-96 Hoops

	Nm-Mt	Ex-Mt
COMPLETE SET (400)	35.00	10.50
COMPLETE SERIES 1 (250)	20.00	6.00
COMPLETE SERIES 2 (150)	15.00	4.50

	Card	Nm-Mt	Ex-Mt
❑ 1	Stacey Augmon	.15	.04
❑ 2	Mookie Blaylock	.15	.04
❑ 3	Craig Ehlo	.15	.04
❑ 4	Andrew Lang	.15	.04
❑ 5	Grant Long	.15	.04
❑ 6	Ken Norman	.15	.04
❑ 7	Steve Smith	.30	.09
❑ 8	Dee Brown	.15	.04
❑ 9	Sherman Douglas	.15	.04
❑ 10	Pervis Ellison	.15	.04
❑ 11	Eric Montross	.15	.04
❑ 12	Dino Radja	.15	.04
❑ 13	Dominique Wilkins	.50	.15
❑ 14	Muggsy Bogues	.30	.09
❑ 15	Scott Burrell	.15	.04
❑ 16	Dell Curry	.15	.04
❑ 17	Hersey Hawkins	.15	.04
❑ 18	Larry Johnson	.30	.09
❑ 19	Alonzo Mourning	.30	.09
❑ 20	B.J. Armstrong	.15	.04
❑ 21	Michael Jordan	3.00	.90
❑ 22	Toni Kukoc	.30	.09
❑ 23	Will Perdue	.15	.04
❑ 24	Scottie Pippen	.75	.23
❑ 25	Dickey Simpkins	.15	.04
❑ 26	Terrell Brandon	.30	.09
❑ 27	Tyrone Hill	.15	.04
❑ 28	Chris Mills	.15	.04
❑ 29	Bobby Phills	.15	.04
❑ 30	Mark Price	.30	.09
❑ 31	John Williams	.15	.04
❑ 32	Tony Dumas	.15	.04
❑ 33	Jim Jackson	.15	.04
❑ 34	Popeye Jones	.15	.04
❑ 35	Jason Kidd	1.50	.45
❑ 36	Jamal Mashburn	.30	.09
❑ 37	Roy Tarpley	.15	.04
❑ 38	Mahmoud Abdul-Rauf	.15	.04
❑ 39	LaPhonso Ellis	.15	.04
❑ 40	Dikembe Mutombo	.30	.09
❑ 41	Robert Pack	.15	.04
❑ 42	Rodney Rogers	.15	.04
❑ 43	Jalen Rose	.60	.18
❑ 44	Bryant Stith	.15	.04
❑ 45	Joe Dumars	.50	.15
❑ 46	Grant Hill	.60	.18
❑ 47	Allan Houston	.30	.09
❑ 48	Lindsey Hunter	.15	.04
❑ 49	Oliver Miller	.15	.04
❑ 50	Terry Mills	.15	.04
❑ 51	Chris Gatling	.15	.04
❑ 52	Tim Hardaway	.30	.09
❑ 53	Donyell Marshall	.30	.09
❑ 54	Chris Mullin	.50	.15
❑ 55	Carlos Rogers	.15	.04
❑ 56	Clifford Rozier	.15	.04
❑ 57	Rony Seikaly	.15	.04
❑ 58	Latrell Sprewell	.50	.15
❑ 59	Sam Cassell	.50	.15
❑ 60	Clyde Drexler	.50	.15
❑ 61	Robert Horry	.30	.09
❑ 62	Vernon Maxwell	.15	.04
❑ 63	Hakeem Olajuwon	.50	.15
❑ 64	Kenny Smith	.15	.04
❑ 65	Dale Davis	.15	.04
❑ 66	Mark Jackson	.30	.09
❑ 67	Derrick McKey	.15	.04
❑ 68	Reggie Miller	.50	.15
❑ 69	Byron Scott	.15	.04
❑ 70	Rik Smits	.30	.09
❑ 71	Terry Dehere	.15	.04
❑ 72	Lamond Murray	.15	.04
❑ 73	Eric Piatkowski	.30	.09
❑ 74	Pooh Richardson	.15	.04
❑ 75	Malik Sealy	.15	.04
❑ 76	Loy Vaught	.15	.04
❑ 77	Elden Campbell	.15	.04
❑ 78	Cedric Ceballos	.15	.04
❑ 79	Vlade Divac	.30	.09
❑ 80	Eddie Jones	.60	.18
❑ 81	Sedale Threatt	.15	.04
❑ 82	Nick Van Exel	.50	.15
❑ 83	Bimbo Coles	.15	.04
❑ 84	Harold Miner	.15	.04
❑ 85	Billy Owens	.15	.04
❑ 86	Khalid Reeves	.15	.04
❑ 87	Glen Rice	.30	.09
❑ 88	Kevin Willis	.30	.09
❑ 89	Vin Baker	.30	.09
❑ 90	Marty Conlon	.15	.04
❑ 91	Todd Day	.15	.04
❑ 92	Eric Mobley	.15	.04
❑ 93	Eric Murdock	.15	.04
❑ 94	Glenn Robinson	.50	.15
❑ 95	Winston Garland	.15	.04
❑ 96	Tom Gugliotta	.15	.04
❑ 97	Christian Laettner	.30	.09
❑ 98	Isaiah Rider	.15	.04
❑ 99	Sean Rooks	.15	.04
❑ 100	Doug West	.15	.04
❑ 101	Kenny Anderson	.30	.09
❑ 102	Benoit Benjamin	.15	.04
❑ 103	Derrick Coleman	.15	.04
❑ 104	Kevin Edwards	.15	.04
❑ 105	Armon Gilliam	.15	.04
❑ 106	Chris Morris	.15	.04
❑ 107	Patrick Ewing	.50	.15
❑ 108	Derek Harper	.30	.09
❑ 109	Anthony Mason	.30	.09
❑ 110	Charles Oakley	.15	.04
❑ 111	Charles Smith	.15	.04
❑ 112	John Starks	.30	.09
❑ 113	Monty Williams	.15	.04
❑ 114	Nick Anderson	.15	.04
❑ 115	Horace Grant	.30	.09
❑ 116	Anfernee Hardaway	.50	.15
❑ 117	Shaquille O'Neal	1.25	.35

- ❑ 118 Dennis Scott .15 .04
- ❑ 119 Brian Shaw .15 .04
- ❑ 120 Dana Barros .15 .04
- ❑ 121 Shawn Bradley .15 .04
- ❑ 122 Willie Burton .15 .04
- ❑ 123 Jeff Malone .15 .04
- ❑ 124 Clarence Weatherspoon .15 .04
- ❑ 125 Sharone Wright .15 .04
- ❑ 126 Charles Barkley .26 .08
- ❑ 127 A.C. Green .30 .09
- ❑ 128 Kevin Johnson .30 .09
- ❑ 129 Dan Majerle .30 .09
- ❑ 130 Danny Manning .30 .09
- ❑ 131 Elliot Perry .15 .04
- ❑ 132 Wesley Person .15 .04
- ❑ 133 Chris Dudley .15 .04
- ❑ 134 Clifford Robinson .15 .04
- ❑ 135 James Robinson .15 .04
- ❑ 136 Rod Strickland .15 .04
- ❑ 137 Otis Thorpe .15 .04
- ❑ 138 Buck Williams .15 .04
- ❑ 139 Brian Grant .50 .15
- ❑ 140 Olden Polynice .15 .04
- ❑ 141 Mitch Richmond .30 .09
- ❑ 142 Michael Smith .15 .04
- ❑ 143 Spud Webb .30 .09
- ❑ 144 Walt Williams .15 .04
- ❑ 145 Vinny Del Negro .15 .04
- ❑ 146 Sean Elliott .30 .09
- ❑ 147 Avery Johnson .15 .04
- ❑ 148 Chuck Person .15 .04
- ❑ 149 David Robinson .50 .15
- ❑ 150 Dennis Rodman .30 .09
- ❑ 151 Kendall Gill .15 .04
- ❑ 152 Ervin Johnson .15 .04
- ❑ 153 Shawn Kemp .30 .09
- ❑ 154 Nate McMillan .15 .04
- ❑ 155 Gary Payton .50 .15
- ❑ 156 Detlef Schrempf .30 .09
- ❑ 157 Dontonio Wingfield .15 .04
- ❑ 158 David Benoit .15 .04
- ❑ 159 Jeff Hornacek .30 .09
- ❑ 160 Karl Malone .60 .18
- ❑ 161 Felton Spencer .15 .04
- ❑ 162 John Stockton .60 .18
- ❑ 163 Jamie Watson .15 .04
- ❑ 164 Rex Chapman .15 .04
- ❑ 165 Calbert Cheaney .15 .04
- ❑ 166 Juwan Howard .50 .15
- ❑ 167 Don MacLean .15 .04
- ❑ 168 Gheorghe Muresan .15 .04
- ❑ 169 Scott Skiles .15 .04
- ❑ 170 Chris Webber .60 .18
- ❑ 171 Lenny Wilkens CO .30 .09
- ❑ 172 Allan Bristow CO .15 .04
- ❑ 173 Phil Jackson CO .30 .09
- ❑ 174 Mike Fratello CO .30 .09
- ❑ 175 Dick Motta CO .15 .04
- ❑ 176 Bernie Bickerstaff CO .15 .04
- ❑ 177 Doug Collins CO .15 .04
- ❑ 178 Rick Adelman CO .15 .04
- ❑ 179 Rudy Tomjanovich CO .30 .09
- ❑ 180 Larry Brown CO .30 .09
- ❑ 181 Bill Fitch CO .15 .04
- ❑ 182 Del Harris CO .15 .04
- ❑ 183 Mike Dunleavy CO .15 .04
- ❑ 184 Bill Blair CO .15 .04
- ❑ 185 Butch Beard CO .15 .04
- ❑ 186 Pat Riley CO .30 .09
- ❑ 187 Brian Hill CO .15 .04
- ❑ 188 John Lucas CO .30 .09
- ❑ 189 Paul Westphal CO .15 .04
- ❑ 190 P.J. Carlesimo CO .15 .04
- ❑ 191 Garry St. Jean CO .15 .04
- ❑ 192 Bob Hill CO .15 .04
- ❑ 193 George Karl CO .30 .09
- ❑ 194 Brendan Malone CO .15 .04
- ❑ 195 Jerry Sloan CO .30 .09
- ❑ 196 Kevin Pritchard .15 .04
- ❑ 197 Jim Lynam CO .15 .04
- ❑ 198 Brian Grant SS .30 .09
- ❑ 199 Grant Hill SS .30 .09
- ❑ 200 Juwan Howard SS .30 .09
- ❑ 201 Eddie Jones SS .50 .15
- ❑ 202 Jason Kidd SS .75 .23
- ❑ 203 Donyell Marshall SS .30 .09
- ❑ 204 Eric Montross SS .15 .04
- ❑ 205 Glenn Robinson SS .30 .09
- ❑ 206 Jalen Rose SS .50 .15
- ❑ 207 Sharone Wright SS .15 .04
- ❑ 208 Dana Barros MS .15 .04
- ❑ 209 Joe Dumars MS .30 .09
- ❑ 210 A.C. Green MS .15 .04
- ❑ 211 Grant Hill MS .50 .15
- ❑ 212 Karl Malone MS .50 .15
- ❑ 213 Reggie Miller MS .30 .09
- ❑ 214 Glen Rice MS .15 .04
- ❑ 215 John Stockton MS .50 .15
- ❑ 216 Lenny Wilkens MS .30 .09
- ❑ 217 Dominique Wilkins MS .30 .09
- ❑ 218 Kenny Anderson BB .15 .04
- ❑ 219 Mookie Blaylock BB .15 .04
- ❑ 220 Larry Johnson BB .15 .04
- ❑ 221 Shawn Kemp BB .15 .04
- ❑ 222 Toni Kukoc BB .15 .04
- ❑ 223 Jamal Mashburn BB .15 .04
- ❑ 224 Glen Rice BB .15 .04
- ❑ 225 Mitch Richmond BB .15 .04
- ❑ 226 Latrell Sprewell BB .50 .15
- ❑ 227 Rod Strickland BB .15 .04
- ❑ 228 Michael Adams PL .15 .04
Darrick Martin
- ❑ 229 Craig Ehlo PL .15 .04
Jerome Harmon
- ❑ 230 Mario Elie PL .15 .04
George McCloud
- ❑ 231 Anthony Mason PL .15 .04
Chucky Brown
- ❑ 232 John Starks PL .15 .04
Tim Legler
- ❑ 233 Muggsy Bogues CA .15 .04
- ❑ 234 Joe Dumars CA .30 .09
- ❑ 235 LaPhonso Ellis CA .15 .04
- ❑ 236 Patrick Ewing CA .30 .09
- ❑ 237 Grant Hill CA .50 .15
- ❑ 238 Kevin Johnson CA .15 .04
- ❑ 239 Dan Majerle CA .15 .04
- ❑ 240 Karl Malone CA .50 .15
- ❑ 241 Hakeem Olajuwon CA .30 .09
- ❑ 242 David Robinson CA .30 .09
- ❑ 243 Dana Barros TT .15 .04
- ❑ 244 Scott Burrell TT .15 .04
- ❑ 245 Reggie Miller TT .30 .09
- ❑ 246 Glen Rice TT .15 .04
- ❑ 247 John Stockton TT .50 .15
- ❑ 248 Checklist #1 .15 .04
- ❑ 249 Checklist #2 .15 .04
- ❑ 250 Checklist #3 .15 .04
- ❑ 251 Alan Henderson RC .50 .15
- ❑ 252 Junior Burrough RC .15 .04
- ❑ 253 Eric Williams RC .30 .09
- ❑ 254 George Zidek RC .15 .04
- ❑ 255 Jason Caffey RC .30 .09
- ❑ 256 Donny Marshall RC .15 .04
- ❑ 257 Bob Sura RC .30 .09
- ❑ 258 Loren Meyer RC .15 .04
- ❑ 259 Cherokee Parks RC .15 .04
- ❑ 260 Antonio McDyess RC 1.00 .30
- ❑ 261 Theo Ratliff RC .60 .18
- ❑ 262 Lou Roe RC .15 .04
- ❑ 263 Andrew DeClercq RC .15 .04
- ❑ 264 Joe Smith RC .75 .23
- ❑ 265 Travis Best RC .15 .04
- ❑ 266 Brent Barry RC .50 .15
- ❑ 267 Frankie King RC .15 .04
- ❑ 268 Sasha Danilovic RC .15 .04
- ❑ 269 Kurt Thomas RC .30 .09
- ❑ 270 Shawn Respert RC .15 .04
- ❑ 271 Jerome Allen RC .15 .04
- ❑ 272 Kevin Garnett RC 2.50 .75
- ❑ 273 Ed O'Bannon RC .15 .04
- ❑ 274 David Vaughn RC .15 .04
- ❑ 275 Jerry Stackhouse RC 1.50 .45
- ❑ 276 Mario Bennett RC .15 .04
- ❑ 277 Michael Finley RC 1.25 .35
- ❑ 278 Randolph Childress RC .15 .04
- ❑ 279 Arvydas Sabonis RC .60 .18
- ❑ 280 Gary Trent RC .15 .04
- ❑ 281 Tyus Edney RC .15 .04
- ❑ 282 Corliss Williamson RC .50 .15
- ❑ 283 Cory Alexander RC .15 .04
- ❑ 284 Sherrell Ford RC .15 .04
- ❑ 285 Jimmy King RC .15 .04
- ❑ 286 Damon Stoudamire RC 1.00 .30
- ❑ 287 Greg Ostertag RC .15 .04
- ❑ 288 Lawrence Moten RC .15 .04
- ❑ 289 Bryant Reeves RC .50 .15
- ❑ 290 Rasheed Wallace RC 1.25 .35
- ❑ 291 Spud Webb .30 .09
- ❑ 292 Dana Barros .15 .04
- ❑ 293 Rick Fox .30 .09
- ❑ 294 Kendall Gill .15 .04
- ❑ 295 Khalid Reeves .15 .04
- ❑ 296 Glen Rice .30 .09
- ❑ 297 Luc Longley .15 .04
- ❑ 298 Dennis Rodman .30 .09
- ❑ 299 Dan Majerle .30 .09
- ❑ 300 Lorenzo Williams .15 .04
- ❑ 301 Dale Ellis .15 .04
- ❑ 302 Reggie Williams .15 .04
- ❑ 303 Otis Thorpe .15 .04
- ❑ 304 B.J. Armstrong .15 .04
- ❑ 305 Pete Chilcutt .15 .04
- ❑ 306 Mario Elie .15 .04
- ❑ 307 Antonio Davis .15 .04
- ❑ 308 Ricky Pierce .15 .04
- ❑ 309 Rodney Rogers .15 .04
- ❑ 310 Brian Williams .15 .04
- ❑ 311 Corie Blount .15 .04
- ❑ 312 George Lynch .15 .04
- ❑ 313 Alonzo Mourning .30 .09
- ❑ 314 Lee Mayberry .15 .04
- ❑ 315 Terry Porter .15 .04
- ❑ 316 P.J. Brown .15 .04
- ❑ 317 Hubert Davis .15 .04
- ❑ 318 Charlie Ward .15 .04
- ❑ 319 Jon Koncak .15 .04
- ❑ 320 Derrick Coleman .15 .04
- ❑ 321 Richard Dumas .15 .04
- ❑ 322 Vernon Maxwell .15 .04
- ❑ 323 Wayman Tisdale .15 .04
- ❑ 324 Dontonio Wingfield .15 .04
- ❑ 325 Tyrone Corbin .15 .04
- ❑ 326 Bobby Hurley .15 .04
- ❑ 327 Will Perdue .15 .04
- ❑ 328 J.R. Reid .15 .04
- ❑ 329 Hersey Hawkins .15 .04
- ❑ 330 Sam Perkins .30 .09
- ❑ 331 Adam Keefe .15 .04
- ❑ 332 Chris Morris .15 .04
- ❑ 333 Robert Pack .15 .04
- ❑ 334 M.L. Carr CO .15 .04
- ❑ 335 Pat Riley CO .30 .09
- ❑ 336 Don Nelson CO .30 .09
- ❑ 337 Brian Winters CO .15 .04
- ❑ 338 Willie Anderson ET .15 .04
- ❑ 339 Acie Earl ET .15 .04
- ❑ 340 Jimmy King ET .15 .04
- ❑ 341 Oliver Miller ET .15 .04
- ❑ 342 Tracy Murray ET .15 .04
- ❑ 343 Ed Pinckney ET .15 .04
- ❑ 344 Alvin Robertson ET .15 .04
- ❑ 345 Carlos Rogers ET .15 .04
- ❑ 346 John Salley ET .15 .04
- ❑ 347 Damon Stoudamire ET .60 .18
- ❑ 348 Zan Tabak ET .15 .04
- ❑ 349 Greg Anthony ET .15 .04
- ❑ 350 Blue Edwards ET .15 .04
- ❑ 351 Kenny Gattison ET .15 .04
- ❑ 352 Antonio Harvey ET .15 .04
- ❑ 353 Chris King ET .15 .04
- ❑ 354 Darrick Martin ET .15 .04
- ❑ 355 Lawrence Moten ET .15 .04
- ❑ 356 Bryant Reeves ET .30 .09
- ❑ 357 Byron Scott ET .15 .04
- ❑ 358 Michael Jordan ES 1.50 .45
- ❑ 359 Dikembe Mutombo ES .15 .04
- ❑ 360 Grant Hill ES .30 .09
- ❑ 361 Robert Horry ES .15 .04
- ❑ 362 Alonzo Mourning ES .15 .04
- ❑ 363 Vin Baker ES .15 .04
- ❑ 364 Isaiah Rider ES .15 .04
- ❑ 365 Charles Oakley ES .15 .04
- ❑ 366 Shaquille O'Neal ES .50 .15
- ❑ 367 Jerry Stackhouse ES .75 .23
- ❑ 368 C. Weatherspoon ES .15 .04
- ❑ 369 Charles Barkley ES .50 .15
- ❑ 370 Sean Elliott ES .15 .04

❑ 371 Shawn Kemp ES	.15	.04
❑ 372 Chris Webber ES	.30	.09
❑ 373 Spud Webb RH	.15	.04
❑ 374 Muggsy Bogues RH	.15	.04
❑ 375 Toni Kukoc RH	.15	.04
❑ 376 Dennis Rodman RH	.15	.04
❑ 377 Jamal Mashburn RH	.15	.04
❑ 378 Jalen Rose RH	.50	.15
❑ 379 Clyde Drexler RH	.30	.09
❑ 380 Mark Jackson RH	.15	.04
❑ 381 Cedric Ceballos RH	.15	.04
❑ 382 Nick Van Exel RH	.15	.04
❑ 383 John Starks RH	.15	.04
❑ 384 Vernon Maxwell RH	.15	.04
❑ 385 Shawn Kemp RH	.15	.04
❑ 386 Gary Payton RH	.30	.09
❑ 387 Karl Malone RH	.50	.15
❑ 388 Mookie Blaylock WD	.15	.04
❑ 389 Muggsy Bogues WD	.15	.04
❑ 390 Jason Kidd WD	.75	.23
❑ 391 Tim Hardaway WD	.15	.04
❑ 392 Nick Van Exel WD	.15	.04
❑ 393 Kenny Anderson WD	.15	.04
❑ 394 Anfernee Hardaway WD	.30	.09
❑ 395 Rod Strickland WD	.15	.04
❑ 396 Avery Johnson WD	.15	.04
❑ 397 John Stockton WD	.50	.15
❑ 398 Grant Hill SPEC	.50	.15
❑ 399 Checklist (251-367)	.15	.04
❑ 400 Checklist (368-400/Ins.)	.15	.04
❑ NNO Grant Hill Co-ROY Exchange	12.00	3.60
❑ NNO Grant Hill Sweepstakes	.60	.18
❑ NNO Grant Hill Tribute	25.00	7.50

1996-97 Hoops

	Nm-Mt	Ex-Mt
COMPLETE SET (350)	30.00	9.00
COMPLETE SERIES 1 (200)	15.00	4.50
COMPLETE SERIES 2 (150)	15.00	4.50
❑ 1 Stacey Augmon	.15	.04
❑ 2 Mookie Blaylock	.15	.04
❑ 3 Alan Henderson	.15	.04
❑ 4 Christian Laettner	.30	.09
❑ 5 Grant Long	.15	.04
❑ 6 Steve Smith	.30	.09
❑ 7 Dana Barros	.15	.04
❑ 8 Todd Day	.15	.04
❑ 9 Rick Fox	.15	.04
❑ 10 Eric Montross	.15	.04
❑ 11 Dino Radja	.15	.04
❑ 12 Eric Williams	.15	.04
❑ 13 Kenny Anderson	.15	.04
❑ 14 Scott Burrell	.15	.04
❑ 15 Dell Curry	.15	.04
❑ 16 Matt Geiger	.15	.04
❑ 17 Larry Johnson	.30	.09
❑ 18 Glen Rice	.30	.09
❑ 19 Ron Harper	.30	.09
❑ 20 Michael Jordan	3.00	.90
❑ 21 Steve Kerr	.30	.09
❑ 22 Toni Kukoc	.30	.09
❑ 23 Luc Longley	.15	.04
❑ 24 Scottie Pippen	.75	.23
❑ 25 Dennis Rodman	.30	.09
❑ 26 Terrell Brandon	.30	.09
❑ 27 Danny Ferry	.15	.04
❑ 28 Tyrone Hill	.15	.04
❑ 29 Chris Mills	.15	.04
❑ 30 Bobby Phills	.15	.04
❑ 31 Bob Sura	.15	.04
❑ 32 Tony Dumas	.15	.04
❑ 33 Jim Jackson	.15	.04
❑ 34 Popeye Jones	.15	.04
❑ 35 Jason Kidd	.75	.23
❑ 36 Jamal Mashburn	.30	.09
❑ 37 George McCloud	.15	.04
❑ 38 Cherokee Parks	.15	.04
❑ 39 Mahmoud Abdul-Rauf	.15	.04
❑ 40 LaPhonso Ellis	.15	.04
❑ 41 Antonio McDyess	.30	.09
❑ 42 Dikembe Mutombo	.30	.09
❑ 43 Jalen Rose	.50	.15
❑ 44 Bryant Stith	.15	.04
❑ 45 Joe Dumars	.50	.15
❑ 46 Grant Hill	.50	.15
❑ 47 Allan Houston	.30	.09
❑ 48 Lindsey Hunter	.15	.04
❑ 49 Terry Mills	.15	.04
❑ 50 Theo Ratliff	.30	.09
❑ 51 Otis Thorpe	.15	.04
❑ 52 B.J. Armstrong	.15	.04
❑ 53 Donyell Marshall	.30	.09
❑ 54 Chris Mullin	.50	.15
❑ 55 Joe Smith	.30	.09
❑ 56 Rony Seikaly	.15	.04
❑ 57 Latrell Sprewell	.50	.15
❑ 58 Mark Bryant	.15	.04
❑ 59 Sam Cassell	.50	.15
❑ 60 Clyde Drexler	.50	.15
❑ 61 Mario Elie	.15	.04
❑ 62 Robert Horry	.30	.09
❑ 63 Hakeem Olajuwon	.50	.15
❑ 64 Travis Best	.15	.04
❑ 65 Antonio Davis	.15	.04
❑ 66 Mark Jackson	.15	.04
❑ 67 Derrick McKey	.15	.04
❑ 68 Reggie Miller	.50	.15
❑ 69 Rik Smits	.30	.09
❑ 70 Brent Barry	.15	.04
❑ 71 Terry Dehere	.15	.04
❑ 72 Pooh Richardson	.15	.04
❑ 73 Rodney Rogers	.15	.04
❑ 74 Loy Vaught	.15	.04
❑ 75 Brian Williams	.15	.04
❑ 76 Elden Campbell	.15	.04
❑ 77 Cedric Ceballos	.15	.04
❑ 78 Vlade Divac	.15	.04
❑ 79 Eddie Jones	.50	.15
❑ 80 Anthony Peeler	.15	.04
❑ 81 Nick Van Exel	.50	.15
❑ 82 Sasha Danilovic	.15	.04
❑ 83 Tim Hardaway	.30	.09
❑ 84 Alonzo Mourning	.30	.09
❑ 85 Kurt Thomas	.30	.09
❑ 86 Walt Williams	.15	.04
❑ 87 Vin Baker	.30	.09
❑ 88 Sherman Douglas	.15	.04
❑ 89 Johnny Newman	.15	.04
❑ 90 Shawn Respert	.15	.04
❑ 91 Glenn Robinson	.50	.15
❑ 92 Kevin Garnett	1.00	.30
❑ 93 Tom Gugliotta	.15	.04
❑ 94 Andrew Lang	.15	.04
❑ 95 Sam Mitchell	.15	.04
❑ 96 Isaiah Rider	.30	.09
❑ 97 Shawn Bradley	.15	.04
❑ 98 P.J. Brown	.15	.04
❑ 99 Chris Childs	.15	.04
❑ 100 Armon Gilliam	.15	.04
❑ 101 Ed O'Bannon	.15	.04
❑ 102 Jayson Williams	.30	.09
❑ 103 Hubert Davis	.15	.04
❑ 104 Patrick Ewing	.50	.15
❑ 105 Anthony Mason	.30	.09
❑ 106 Charles Oakley	.15	.04
❑ 107 John Starks	.30	.09
❑ 108 Charlie Ward	.15	.04
❑ 109 Nick Anderson	.15	.04
❑ 110 Horace Grant	.30	.09
❑ 111 Anfernee Hardaway	.50	.15
❑ 112 Shaquille O'Neal	1.25	.35
❑ 113 Dennis Scott	.15	.04
❑ 114 Brian Shaw	.15	.04
❑ 115 Derrick Coleman	.30	.09
❑ 116 Vernon Maxwell	.15	.04
❑ 117 Trevor Ruffin	.15	.04
❑ 118 Jerry Stackhouse	.60	.18
❑ 119 Clarence Weatherspoon	.15	.04
❑ 120 Charles Barkley	.60	.18
❑ 121 Michael Finley	.60	.18
❑ 122 A.C. Green	.30	.09
❑ 123 Kevin Johnson	.30	.09
❑ 124 Danny Manning	.30	.09
❑ 125 Wesley Person	.15	.04
❑ 126 John Williams	.15	.04
❑ 127 Harvey Grant	.15	.04
❑ 128 Aaron McKie	.30	.09
❑ 129 Clifford Robinson	.15	.04
❑ 130 Arvydas Sabonis	.30	.09
❑ 131 Rod Strickland	.15	.04
❑ 132 Gary Trent	.15	.04
❑ 133 Tyus Edney	.15	.04
❑ 134 Brian Grant	.50	.15
❑ 135 Billy Owens	.15	.04
❑ 136 Olden Polynice	.15	.04
❑ 137 Mitch Richmond	.30	.09
❑ 138 Corliss Williamson	.30	.09
❑ 139 Vinny Del Negro	.15	.04
❑ 140 Sean Elliott	.30	.09
❑ 141 Avery Johnson	.15	.04
❑ 142 Chuck Person	.15	.04
❑ 143 David Robinson	.50	.15
❑ 144 Charles Smith	.15	.04
❑ 145 Sherrell Ford	.15	.04
❑ 146 Hersey Hawkins	.30	.09
❑ 147 Shawn Kemp	.30	.09
❑ 148 Nate McMillan	.15	.04
❑ 149 Gary Payton	.50	.15
❑ 150 Detlef Schrempf	.30	.09
❑ 151 Oliver Miller	.15	.04
❑ 152 Tracy Murray	.15	.04
❑ 153 Carlos Rogers	.15	.04
❑ 154 Damon Stoudamire	.50	.15
❑ 155 Zan Tabak	.15	.04
❑ 156 Sharone Wright	.15	.04
❑ 157 Antoine Carr	.15	.04
❑ 158 Jeff Hornacek	.30	.09
❑ 159 Adam Keefe	.15	.04
❑ 160 Karl Malone	.50	.15
❑ 161 Chris Morris	.15	.04
❑ 162 John Stockton	.50	.15
❑ 163 Greg Anthony	.15	.04
❑ 164 Blue Edwards	.15	.04
❑ 165 Chris King	.15	.04
❑ 166 Lawrence Moten	.15	.04
❑ 167 Bryant Reeves	.15	.04
❑ 168 Byron Scott	.15	.04
❑ 169 Calbert Cheaney	.15	.04
❑ 170 Juwan Howard	.30	.09
❑ 171 Tim Legler	.15	.04
❑ 172 Gheorghe Muresan	.15	.04
❑ 173 Rasheed Wallace	.60	.18
❑ 174 Chris Webber	.50	.15
❑ 175 Steve Smith BF	.15	.04
❑ 176 Michael Jordan BF	1.50	.45
❑ 177 Scottie Pippen BF	.30	.09
❑ 178 Dennis Rodman BF	.15	.04
❑ 179 Allan Houston BF	.15	.04
❑ 180 Hakeem Olajuwon BF	.30	.09
❑ 181 Patrick Ewing BF	.30	.09
❑ 182 Anfernee Hardaway BF	.30	.09
❑ 183 Shaquille O'Neal BF	.50	.15
❑ 184 Charles Barkley BF	.50	.15
❑ 185 Arvydas Sabonis BF	.15	.04
❑ 186 David Robinson BF	.30	.09
❑ 187 Shawn Kemp BF	.15	.04
❑ 188 Gary Payton BF	.30	.09
❑ 189 Karl Malone BF	.50	.15
❑ 190 Kenny Anderson PLA	.15	.04
❑ 191 Toni Kukoc PLA	.15	.04
❑ 192 Brent Barry PLA	.15	.04
❑ 193 Cedric Ceballos PLA	.15	.04
❑ 194 Shawn Bradley PLA	.15	.04
❑ 195 Charles Oakley PLA	.15	.04
❑ 196 Dennis Scott PLA	.15	.04
❑ 197 Clifford Robinson PLA	.15	.04
❑ 198 Mitch Richmond PLA	.15	.04
❑ 199 Checklist	.15	.04

❑ 200 Checklist .15 .04
❑ 201 Dikembe Mutombo .30 .09
❑ 202 Dee Brown .15 .04
❑ 203 David Wesley .15 .04
❑ 204 Vlade Divac .15 .04
❑ 205 Anthony Mason .30 .09
❑ 206 Chris Gatling .15 .04
❑ 207 Eric Montross .15 .04
❑ 208 Ervin Johnson .15 .04
❑ 209 Stacey Augmon .15 .04
❑ 210 Joe Dumars .50 .15
❑ 211 Grant Hill .50 .15
❑ 212 Charles Barkley .60 .18
❑ 213 Jalen Rose .50 .15
❑ 214 Lamond Murray .15 .04
❑ 215 Shaquille O'Neal 1.25 .35
❑ 216 P.J. Brown .15 .04
❑ 217 Dan Majerle .30 .09
❑ 218 Armon Gilliam .15 .04
❑ 219 Andrew Lang .15 .04
❑ 220 Kevin Garnett 1.00 .30
❑ 221 Tom Gugliotta .15 .04
❑ 222 Cherokee Parks .15 .04
❑ 223 Doug West .15 .04
❑ 224 Kendall Gill .15 .04
❑ 225 Robert Pack .15 .04
❑ 226 Allan Houston .30 .09
❑ 227 Larry Johnson .30 .09
❑ 228 Rony Seikaly .15 .04
❑ 229 Gerald Wilkins .15 .04
❑ 230 Michael Cage .15 .04
❑ 231 Lucious Harris .15 .04
❑ 232 Sam Cassell .50 .15
❑ 233 Robert Horry .30 .09
❑ 234 Kenny Anderson .15 .04
❑ 235 Isaiah Rider .30 .09
❑ 236 Rasheed Wallace .60 .18
❑ 237 Mahmoud Abdul-Rauf .15 .04
❑ 238 Vernon Maxwell .15 .04
❑ 239 Dominique Wilkins .50 .15
❑ 240 Jim McIlvaine .15 .04
❑ 241 Hubert Davis .15 .04
❑ 242 Popeye Jones .15 .04
❑ 243 Walt Williams .15 .04
❑ 244 Karl Malone .50 .15
❑ 245 John Stockton .50 .15
❑ 246 Anthony Peeler .15 .04
❑ 247 Tracy Murray .15 .04
❑ 248 Rod Strickland .15 .04
❑ 249 Lenny Wilkens CO .30 .09
❑ 250 M.L. Carr CO .15 .04
❑ 251 Dave Cowens CO .15 .04
❑ 252 Phil Jackson CO .30 .09
❑ 253 Mike Fratello CO .30 .09
❑ 254 Jim Cleamons CO .15 .04
❑ 255 Dick Motta CO .15 .04
❑ 256 Doug Collins CO .15 .04
❑ 257 Rick Adelman CO .15 .04
❑ 258 Rudy Tomjanovich CO .30 .09
❑ 259 Larry Brown CO .30 .09
❑ 260 Bill Fitch CO .15 .04
❑ 261 Del Harris CO .15 .04
❑ 262 Pat Riley CO .30 .09
❑ 263 Chris Ford CO .15 .04
❑ 264 Flip Saunders CO .15 .04
❑ 265 John Calipari CO .30 .09
❑ 266 Jeff Van Gundy CO .15 .04
❑ 267 Brian Hill CO .15 .04
❑ 268 Johnny Davis CO .15 .04
❑ 269 Danny Ainge CO .30 .09
❑ 270 P.J. Carlesimo CO .15 .04
❑ 271 Garry St. Jean CO .15 .04
❑ 272 Bob Hill CO .15 .04
❑ 273 George Karl CO .30 .09
❑ 274 Darrell Walker CO .15 .04
❑ 275 Jerry Sloan CO .30 .09
❑ 276 Brian Winters CO .15 .04
❑ 277 Jim Lynam CO .15 .04
❑ 278 Shareef Abdur-Rahim RC 1.50 .45
❑ 279 Ray Allen RC 1.50 .45
❑ 280 Shandon Anderson RC .30 .09
❑ 281 Kobe Bryant RC 8.00 2.40
❑ 282 Marcus Camby RC .60 .18
❑ 283 Erick Dampier RC .50 .15
❑ 284 Emanual Davis RC .15 .04
❑ 285 Tony Delk RC .50 .15
❑ 286 Brian Evans RC .15 .04
❑ 287 Derek Fisher RC .75 .23
❑ 288 Todd Fuller RC .15 .04
❑ 289 Dean Garrett RC .15 .04
❑ 290 Reggie Geary RC .15 .04
❑ 291 Darvin Ham RC .15 .04
❑ 292 Othella Harrington RC .50 .15
❑ 293 Shane Heal RC .15 .04
❑ 294 Mark Hendrickson RC .15 .04
❑ 295 Allen Iverson RC 2.50 .75
❑ 296 Dontae' Jones RC .15 .04
❑ 297 Kerry Kittles RC .50 .15
❑ 298 Priest Lauderdale RC .15 .04
❑ 299 Matt Maloney RC .30 .09
❑ 300 Stephon Marbury RC 1.50 .45
❑ 301 Walter McCarty RC .15 .04
❑ 302 Jeff McInnis RC .15 .04
❑ 303 Martin Muursepp RC .15 .04
❑ 304 Steve Nash RC 1.50 .45
❑ 305 Moochie Norris RC .30 .09
❑ 306 Jermaine O'Neal RC 1.50 .45
❑ 307 Vitaly Potapenko RC .15 .04
❑ 308 Virginius Praskevicius RC .15 .04
❑ 309 Roy Rogers RC .15 .04
❑ 310 Malik Rose RC .30 .09
❑ 311 James Scott RC .15 .04
❑ 312 Antoine Walker RC 1.50 .45
❑ 313 Samaki Walker RC .15 .04
❑ 314 Ben Wallace RC 3.00 .90
❑ 315 John Wallace RC .50 .15
❑ 316 Jerome Williams RC .50 .15
❑ 317 Lorenzen Wright RC .30 .09
❑ 318 Charles Barkley ST .50 .15
❑ 319 Derrick Coleman ST .15 .04
❑ 320 Michael Finley ST .50 .15
❑ 321 Stephon Marbury ST 1.00 .30
❑ 322 Reggie Miller ST .30 .09
❑ 323 Alonzo Mourning ST .15 .04
❑ 324 Shaquille O'Neal ST .50 .15
❑ 325 Gary Payton ST .30 .09
❑ 326 Dennis Rodman ST .15 .04
❑ 327 Damon Stoudamire ST .30 .09
❑ 328 Vin Baker CBG .15 .04
❑ 329 Clyde Drexler CBG .30 .09
❑ 330 Patrick Ewing CBG .30 .09
❑ 331 Anfernee Hardaway CBG .30 .09
❑ 332 Grant Hill CBG .30 .09
❑ 333 Juwan Howard CBG .15 .04
❑ 334 Larry Johnson CBG .15 .04
❑ 335 Michael Jordan CBG 1.50 .45
❑ 336 Shawn Kemp CBG .15 .04
❑ 337 Jason Kidd CBG .30 .09
❑ 338 Karl Malone CBG .50 .15
❑ 339 Reggie Miller CBG .30 .09
❑ 340 Hakeem Olajuwon CBG .30 .09
❑ 341 Scottie Pippen CBG .30 .09
❑ 342 Mitch Richmond CBG .15 .04
❑ 343 David Robinson CBG .30 .09
UER back David Robininson
❑ 344 Dennis Rodman CBG .15 .04
❑ 345 Joe Smith CBG .15 .04
❑ 346 Jerry Stackhouse CBG .50 .15
❑ 347 John Stockton CBG .50 .15
❑ 348 Jerry Stackhouse BG .50 .15
❑ 349 Checklist .15 .04
201-350/inserts
❑ 350 Checklist (inserts) .15 .04
❑ NNO Grant Hill 2.00 .60
Jerry Stackhouse Promo
❑ NNO G.Hill Z-Force Preview 10.00 3.00

1997-98 Hoops

	Nm-Mt	Ex-Mt
COMPLETE SET (330)	30.00	9.00
COMPLETE SERIES 1 (165)	12.00	3.60
COMPLETE SERIES 2 (165)	18.00	5.50

❑ 1 Michael Jordan LL 1.50 .45
❑ 2 Dennis Rodman LL .15 .04
❑ 3 Mark Jackson LL .30 .09
❑ 4 Shawn Bradley LL .15 .04
❑ 5 Glen Rice LL .15 .04
❑ 6 Mookie Blaylock LL .15 .04
❑ 7 Gheorghe Muresan LL .15 .04
❑ 8 Mark Price LL .30 .09
❑ 9 Tyrone Corbin .15 .04

❑ 10 Christian Laettner .30 .09
❑ 11 Priest Lauderdale .15 .04
❑ 12 Dikembe Mutombo .30 .09
❑ 13 Steve Smith .30 .09
❑ 14 Todd Day .15 .04
❑ 15 Rick Fox .30 .09
❑ 16 Brett Szabo .15 .04
❑ 17 Antoine Walker .60 .18
❑ 18 David Wesley .15 .04
❑ 19 Muggsy Bogues .30 .09
❑ 20 Dell Curry .15 .04
❑ 21 Tony Delk .15 .04
❑ 22 Anthony Mason .30 .09
❑ 23 Glen Rice .30 .09
❑ 24 Malik Rose .15 .04
❑ 25 Steve Kerr .30 .09
❑ 26 Toni Kukoc .30 .09
❑ 27 Luc Longley .15 .04
❑ 28 Robert Parish .30 .09
❑ 29 Scottie Pippen .75 .23
❑ 30 Dennis Rodman .30 .09
❑ 31 Terrell Brandon .30 .09
❑ 32 Danny Ferry .15 .04
❑ 33 Tyrone Hill .15 .04
❑ 34 Bobby Phills .15 .04
❑ 35 Vitaly Potapenko .15 .04
❑ 36 Shawn Bradley .15 .04
❑ 37 Sasha Danilovic .15 .04
❑ 38 Derek Harper .30 .09
❑ 39 Martin Muursepp .15 .04
❑ 40 Robert Pack .15 .04
❑ 41 Khalid Reeves .15 .04
❑ 42 Vincent Askew .15 .04
❑ 43 Dale Ellis .15 .04
❑ 44 LaPhonso Ellis .15 .04
❑ 45 Antonio McDyess .30 .09
❑ 46 Bryant Stith .15 .04
❑ 47 Joe Dumars .50 .15
❑ 48 Grant Hill .50 .15
❑ 49 Lindsey Hunter .15 .04
❑ 50 Aaron McKie .30 .09
❑ 51 Theo Ratliff .15 .04
❑ 52 Scott Burrell .15 .04
❑ 53 Todd Fuller .15 .04
❑ 54 Chris Mullin .50 .15
❑ 55 Mark Price .30 .09
❑ 56 Joe Smith .30 .09
❑ 57 Latrell Sprewell .50 .15
❑ 58 Clyde Drexler .50 .15
❑ 59 Mario Elie .15 .04
❑ 60 Othella Harrington .15 .04
❑ 61 Matt Maloney .15 .04
❑ 62 Hakeem Olajuwon .50 .15
❑ 63 Kevin Willis .30 .09
❑ 64 Travis Best .15 .04
❑ 65 Erick Dampier .30 .09
❑ 66 Antonio Davis .15 .04
❑ 67 Dale Davis .15 .04
❑ 68 Mark Jackson .30 .09
❑ 69 Reggie Miller .50 .15
❑ 70 Brent Barry .30 .09
❑ 71 Darrick Martin .15 .04
❑ 72 Bo Outlaw .15 .04
❑ 73 Loy Vaught .15 .04
❑ 74 Lorenzen Wright .15 .04
❑ 75 Kobe Bryant 2.00 .60
❑ 76 Derek Fisher .50 .15
❑ 77 Robert Horry .30 .09

#	Player		
❑ 78	Eddie Jones	.50	.15
❑ 79	Travis Knight	.15	.04
❑ 80	George McCloud	.15	.04
❑ 81	Shaquille O'Neal	1.25	.35
❑ 82	P.J. Brown	.15	.04
❑ 83	Tim Hardaway	.30	.09
❑ 84	Voshon Lenard	.15	.04
❑ 85	Jamal Mashburn	.30	.09
❑ 86	Alonzo Mourning	.30	.09
❑ 87	Ray Allen	.50	.15
❑ 88	Vin Baker	.30	.09
❑ 89	Sherman Douglas	.15	.04
❑ 90	Armon Gilliam	.15	.04
❑ 91	Glenn Robinson	.50	.15
❑ 92	Kevin Garnett	1.00	.30
❑ 93	Dean Garrett	.15	.04
❑ 94	Tom Gugliotta	.30	.09
❑ 95	Stephon Marbury	.60	.18
❑ 96	Doug West	.15	.04
❑ 97	Chris Gatling	.15	.04
❑ 98	Kendall Gill	.15	.04
❑ 99	Kerry Kittles	.50	.15
❑ 100	Jayson Williams	.15	.04
❑ 101	Chris Childs	.15	.04
❑ 102	Patrick Ewing	.50	.15
❑ 103	Allan Houston	.30	.09
❑ 104	Larry Johnson	.30	.09
❑ 105	Charles Oakley	.30	.09
❑ 106	John Starks	.30	.09
❑ 107	John Wallace	.15	.04
❑ 108	Nick Anderson	.15	.04
❑ 109	Horace Grant	.30	.09
❑ 110	Anfernee Hardaway	.50	.15
❑ 111	Rony Seikaly	.15	.04
❑ 112	Derek Strong	.15	.04
❑ 113	Derrick Coleman	.15	.04
❑ 114	Allen Iverson	1.25	.35
❑ 115	Doug Overton	.15	.04
❑ 116	Jerry Stackhouse	.50	.15
❑ 117	Rex Walters	.15	.04
❑ 118	Cedric Ceballos	.15	.04
❑ 119	Kevin Johnson	.30	.09
❑ 120	Jason Kidd	.75	.23
❑ 121	Steve Nash	.50	.15
❑ 122	Wesley Person	.15	.04
❑ 123	Kenny Anderson	.30	.09
❑ 124	Jermaine O'Neal	.75	.23
❑ 125	Isaiah Rider	.30	.09
❑ 126	Arvydas Sabonis	.30	.09
❑ 127	Gary Trent	.15	.04
❑ 128	Tyus Edney	.15	.04
❑ 129	Brian Grant	.30	.09
❑ 130	Olden Polynice	.15	.04
❑ 131	Mitch Richmond	.30	.09
❑ 132	Corliss Williamson	.30	.09
❑ 133	Vinny Del Negro	.15	.04
❑ 134	Sean Elliott	.30	.09
❑ 135	Avery Johnson	.15	.04
❑ 136	Will Perdue	.15	.04
❑ 137	Dominique Wilkins	.50	.15
❑ 138	Craig Ehlo	.15	.04
❑ 139	Hersey Hawkins	.15	.04
❑ 140	Shawn Kemp	.30	.09
❑ 141	Jim McIlvaine	.15	.04
❑ 142	Sam Perkins	.30	.09
❑ 143	Detlef Schrempf	.30	.09
❑ 144	Marcus Camby	.50	.15
❑ 145	Doug Christie	.30	.09
❑ 146	Popeye Jones	.15	.04
❑ 147	Damon Stoudamire	.30	.09
❑ 148	Walt Williams	.15	.04
❑ 149	Jeff Hornacek	.30	.09
❑ 150	Karl Malone	.50	.15
❑ 151	Greg Ostertag	.15	.04
❑ 152	Bryon Russell	.15	.04
❑ 153	John Stockton	.50	.15
❑ 154	Shareef Abdur-Rahim	.75	.23
❑ 155	Greg Anthony	.15	.04
❑ 156	Anthony Peeler	.15	.04
❑ 157	Bryant Reeves	.15	.04
❑ 158	Roy Rogers	.15	.04
❑ 159	Calbert Cheaney	.15	.04
❑ 160	Juwan Howard	.30	.09
❑ 161	Gheorghe Muresan	.15	.04
❑ 162	Rod Strickland	.15	.04
❑ 163	Chris Webber	.50	.15
❑ 164	Checklist	.15	.04
❑ 165	Checklist	.15	.04
❑ 166	Tim Duncan RC	2.00	.60
❑ 167	Chauncey Billups RC	.50	.15
❑ 168	Keith Van Horn RC	.75	.23
❑ 169	Tracy McGrady RC	2.50	.75
❑ 170	John Thomas RC	.15	.04
❑ 171	Tim Thomas RC	.75	.23
❑ 172	Ron Mercer RC	.60	.18
❑ 173	Scot Pollard RC	.30	.09
❑ 174	Jason Lawson RC	.15	.04
❑ 175	Keith Booth RC	.15	.04
❑ 176	Adonal Foyle RC	.30	.09
❑ 177	Bubba Wells RC	.15	.04
❑ 178	Derek Anderson RC	1.00	.30
❑ 179	Rodrick Rhodes RC	.15	.04
❑ 180	Kelvin Cato RC	.50	.15
❑ 181	Serge Zwikker RC	.15	.04
❑ 182	Ed Gray RC	.15	.04
❑ 183	Brevin Knight RC	.30	.09
❑ 184	Alvin Williams RC	.15	.04
❑ 185	Paul Grant RC	.15	.04
❑ 186	Austin Croshere RC	.50	.15
❑ 187	Chris Crawford RC	.15	.04
❑ 188	Anthony Johnson RC	.15	.04
❑ 189	James Cotton RC	.15	.04
❑ 190	James Collins RC	.15	.04
❑ 191	Tony Battie RC	.50	.15
❑ 192	Tariq Abdul-Wahad RC	.30	.09
❑ 193	Danny Fortson RC	.30	.09
❑ 194	Maurice Taylor RC	.50	.15
❑ 195	Bobby Jackson RC	.75	.23
❑ 196	Charles Smith RC	.15	.04
❑ 197	Johnny Taylor RC	.15	.04
❑ 198	Jerald Honeycutt RC	.15	.04
❑ 199	Marko Milic RC	.15	.04
❑ 200	Anthony Parker RC	.15	.04
❑ 201	Jacque Vaughn RC	.30	.09
❑ 202	Antonio Daniels RC	.50	.15
❑ 203	Charles O'Bannon RC	.15	.04
❑ 204	God Shammgod RC	.15	.04
❑ 205	Kebu Stewart RC	.15	.04
❑ 206	Mookie Blaylock	.15	.04
❑ 207	Chucky Brown	.15	.04
❑ 208	Alan Henderson	.15	.04
❑ 209	Dana Barros	.15	.04
❑ 210	Tyus Edney	.15	.04
❑ 211	Travis Knight	.15	.04
❑ 212	Walter McCarty	.15	.04
❑ 213	Vlade Divac	.30	.09
❑ 214	Matt Geiger	.15	.04
❑ 215	Bobby Phills	.15	.04
❑ 216	J.R. Reid	.15	.04
❑ 217	David Wesley	.15	.04
❑ 218	Scott Burrell	.15	.04
❑ 219	Ron Harper	.30	.09
❑ 220	Michael Jordan	3.00	.90
❑ 221	Bill Wennington	.15	.04
❑ 222	Mitchell Butler	.15	.04
❑ 223	Zydrunas Ilgauskas	.30	.09
❑ 224	Shawn Kemp	.30	.09
❑ 225	Wesley Person	.15	.04
❑ 226	Shawnelle Scott RC	.15	.04
❑ 227	Bob Sura	.15	.04
❑ 228	Hubert Davis	.15	.04
❑ 229	Michael Finley	.50	.15
❑ 230	Dennis Scott	.15	.04
❑ 231	Erick Strickland RC	.30	.09
❑ 232	Samaki Walker	.15	.04
❑ 233	Dean Garrett	.15	.04
❑ 234	Priest Lauderdale	.15	.04
❑ 235	Eric Williams	.15	.04
❑ 236	Grant Long	.15	.04
❑ 237	Malik Sealy	.15	.04
❑ 238	Brian Williams	.15	.04
❑ 239	Muggsy Bogues	.30	.09
❑ 240	Bimbo Coles	.15	.04
❑ 241	Brian Shaw	.15	.04
❑ 242	Joe Smith	.30	.09
❑ 243	Latrell Sprewell	.50	.15
❑ 244	Charles Barkley	.60	.18
❑ 245	Emanual Davis	.15	.04
❑ 246	Brent Price	.15	.04
❑ 247	Reggie Miller	.50	.15
❑ 248	Chris Mullin	.50	.15
❑ 249	Jalen Rose	.50	.15
❑ 250	Rik Smits	.30	.09
❑ 251	Mark West	.15	.04
❑ 252	Lamond Murray	.15	.04
❑ 253	Pooh Richardson	.15	.04
❑ 254	Rodney Rogers	.15	.04
❑ 255	Stojko Vrankovic	.15	.04
❑ 256	Jon Barry	.15	.04
❑ 257	Corie Blount	.15	.04
❑ 258	Elden Campbell	.15	.04
❑ 259	Rick Fox	.30	.09
❑ 260	Nick Van Exel	.50	.15
❑ 261	Isaac Austin	.15	.04
❑ 262	Dan Majerle	.30	.09
❑ 263	Terry Mills	.15	.04
❑ 264	Mark Strickland RC	.15	.04
❑ 265	Terrell Brandon	.30	.09
❑ 266	Tyrone Hill	.15	.04
❑ 267	Ervin Johnson	.15	.04
❑ 268	Andrew Lang	.15	.04
❑ 269	Elliot Perry	.15	.04
❑ 270	Chris Carr	.15	.04
❑ 271	Reggie Jordan	.15	.04
❑ 272	Sam Mitchell	.15	.04
❑ 273	Stanley Roberts	.15	.04
❑ 274	Michael Cage	.15	.04
❑ 275	Sam Cassell	.50	.15
❑ 276	Lucious Harris	.15	.04
❑ 277	Kerry Kittles	.50	.15
❑ 278	Don MacLean	.15	.04
❑ 279	Chris Dudley	.15	.04
❑ 280	Chris Mills	.15	.04
❑ 281	Charlie Ward	.15	.04
❑ 282	Buck Williams	.15	.04
❑ 283	Herb Williams	.15	.04
❑ 284	Derek Harper	.30	.09
❑ 285	Mark Price	.30	.09
❑ 286	Gerald Wilkins	.15	.04
❑ 287	Allen Iverson	1.25	.35
❑ 288	Jim Jackson	.15	.04
❑ 289	Eric Montross	.15	.04
❑ 290	Jerry Stackhouse	.50	.15
❑ 291	Clarence Weatherspoon	.15	.04
❑ 292	Tom Chambers	.15	.04
❑ 293	Rex Chapman	.15	.04
❑ 294	Danny Manning	.30	.09
❑ 295	Antonio McDyess	.30	.09
❑ 296	Clifford Robinson	.15	.04
❑ 297	Stacey Augmon	.15	.04
❑ 298	Brian Grant	.30	.09
❑ 299	Rasheed Wallace	.50	.15
❑ 300	Mahmoud Abdul-Rauf	.15	.04
❑ 301	Terry Dehere	.15	.04
❑ 302	Billy Owens	.15	.04
❑ 303	Michael Smith	.15	.04
❑ 304	Cory Alexander	.15	.04
❑ 305	Chuck Person	.15	.04
❑ 306	David Robinson	.50	.15
❑ 307	Charles Smith	.15	.04
❑ 308	Monty Williams	.15	.04
❑ 309	Vin Baker	.30	.09
❑ 310	Jerome Kersey	.15	.04
❑ 311	Nate McMillan	.15	.04
❑ 312	Gary Payton	.50	.15
❑ 313	Eric Snow	.30	.09
❑ 314	Carlos Rogers	.15	.04
❑ 315	Zan Tabak	.15	.04
❑ 316	John Wallace	.15	.04
❑ 317	Sharone Wright	.15	.04
❑ 318	Shandon Anderson	.15	.04
❑ 319	Antoine Carr	.15	.04
❑ 320	Howard Eisley	.15	.04
❑ 321	Chris Morris	.15	.04
❑ 322	Pete Chilcutt	.15	.04
❑ 323	George Lynch	.15	.04
❑ 324	Chris Robinson	.15	.04
❑ 325	Otis Thorpe	.15	.04
❑ 326	Harvey Grant	.15	.04
❑ 327	Darvin Ham	.15	.04

Card	Nm-Mt	Ex-Mt
❑ 328 Juwan Howard	.30	.09
❑ 329 Ben Wallace	.50	.15
❑ 330 Chris Webber	.50	.15
❑ NNO Grant Hill Promo	.50	.15

1998-99 Hoops

	Nm-Mt	Ex-Mt
COMPLETE SET (167)	20.00	6.00
❑ 1 Kobe Bryant	2.00	.60
❑ 2 Glenn Robinson	.30	.09
❑ 3 Derek Anderson	.50	.15
❑ 4 Terry Dehere	.15	.04
❑ 5 Jalen Rose	.50	.15
❑ 6 Zydrunas Ilgauskas	.30	.09
❑ 7 Scott Williams	.15	.04
❑ 8 Toni Kukoc	.30	.09
❑ 9 John Stockton	.50	.15
❑ 10 Kevin Garnett	1.00	.30
❑ 11 Jerome Williams	.15	.04
❑ 12 Anthony Mason	.30	.09
❑ 13 Harvey Grant	.15	.04
❑ 14 Mookie Blaylock	.15	.04
❑ 15 Tyrone Hill	.15	.04
❑ 16 Dale Davis	.30	.09
❑ 17 Eric Washington	.15	.04
❑ 18 Aaron McKie	.30	.09
❑ 19 Jermaine O'Neal	.50	.15
❑ 20 Anfernee Hardaway	.50	.15
❑ 21 Derrick Coleman	.15	.04
❑ 22 Allan Houston	.30	.09
❑ 23 Michael Jordan	3.00	.90
❑ 24 Jason Kidd	.75	.23
❑ 25 Tyrone Corbin	.15	.04
❑ 26 Jacque Vaughn	.15	.04
❑ 27 Bobby Jackson	.30	.09
❑ 28 Chris Anstey	.15	.04
❑ 29 Brent Barry	.30	.09
❑ 30 Shareef Abdur-Rahim	.50	.15
❑ 31 Jeff Hornacek	.30	.09
❑ 32 Ed Gray	.15	.04
❑ 33 Grant Hill	.50	.15
❑ 34 Steve Smith	.30	.09
❑ 35 Rony Seikaly	.15	.04
❑ 36 Mark Jackson	.30	.09
❑ 37 Shawn Bradley	.15	.04
❑ 38 Corie Blount	.15	.04
❑ 39 Erick Dampier	.30	.09
❑ 40 Kerry Kittles	.15	.04
❑ 41 David Wesley	.15	.04
❑ 42 Horace Grant	.30	.09
❑ 43 Bobby Hurley	.15	.04
❑ 44 Tariq Abdul-Wahad	.15	.04
❑ 45 Brian Williams	.15	.04
❑ 46 Ray Allen	.50	.15
❑ 47 Kenny Anderson	.30	.09
❑ 48 Rodrick Rhodes	.15	.04
❑ 49 Greg Foster	.15	.04
❑ 50 Tim Duncan	.75	.23
❑ 51 Steve Nash	.50	.15
❑ 52 Kelvin Cato	.15	.04
❑ 53 Donyell Marshall	.30	.09
❑ 54 Marcus Camby	.30	.09
❑ 55 Kevin Willis	.15	.04
❑ 56 Michael Finley	.50	.15
❑ 57 Muggsy Bogues	.30	.09
❑ 58 Mark Price	.30	.09
❑ 59 Larry Johnson	.30	.09
❑ 60 Karl Malone	.50	.15
❑ 61 Greg Ostertag	.15	.04
❑ 62 Sean Elliott	.30	.09
❑ 63 Johnny Taylor	.15	.04
❑ 64 Howard Eisley	.15	.04
❑ 65 Chris Childs	.15	.04
❑ 66 Walt Williams	.15	.04
❑ 67 Tracy Murray	.15	.04
❑ 68 Patrick Ewing	.50	.15
❑ 69 Olden Polynice	.15	.04
❑ 70 Allen Iverson	1.00	.30
❑ 71 David Robinson	.50	.15
❑ 72 Calbert Cheaney	.15	.04
❑ 73 Lamond Murray	.15	.04
❑ 74 Scot Pollard	.15	.04
❑ 75 Alonzo Mourning	.30	.09
❑ 76 Tracy McGrady	1.25	.35
❑ 77 Jim McIlvaine	.15	.04
❑ 78 Bob Sura	.15	.04
❑ 79 Anthony Peeler	.15	.04
❑ 80 Keith Van Horn	.50	.15
❑ 81 Maurice Taylor	.30	.09
❑ 82 Charles Smith	.15	.04
❑ 83 Dikembe Mutombo	.30	.09
❑ 84 Nick Anderson	.15	.04
❑ 85 Austin Croshere	.50	.15
❑ 86 Armon Gilliam	.15	.04
❑ 87 Eddie Jones	.50	.15
❑ 88 Glen Rice	.30	.09
❑ 89 Sam Cassell	.50	.15
❑ 90 Stephon Marbury	.50	.15
❑ 91 Elliot Perry UER Back spelled Elliott	.15	.04
❑ 92 Jamal Mashburn	.30	.09
❑ 93 Adonal Foyle	.15	.04
❑ 94 Avery Johnson	.15	.04
❑ 95 Micheal Williams	.15	.04
❑ 96 Danny Fortson	.15	.04
❑ 97 Brevin Knight	.15	.04
❑ 98 Ron Harper	.30	.09
❑ 99 Chauncey Billups	.30	.09
❑ 100 Shaquille O'Neal	1.25	.35
❑ 101 Brent Price	.15	.04
❑ 102 Tim Thomas	.30	.09
❑ 103 Khalid Reeves	.15	.04
❑ 104 Chris Gatling	.15	.04
❑ 105 Terry Cummings	.15	.04
❑ 106 Vin Baker	.30	.09
❑ 107 Bryant Reeves	.15	.04
❑ 108 John Starks	.30	.09
❑ 109 Juwan Howard	.30	.09
❑ 110 Antoine Walker	.50	.15
❑ 111 Rodney Rogers	.15	.04
❑ 112 Nick Van Exel	.50	.15
❑ 113 Chris Whitney	.15	.04
❑ 114 Bobby Phills	.15	.04
❑ 115 Travis Knight	.15	.04
❑ 116 Robert Horry	.30	.09
❑ 117 Erick Strickland	.15	.04
❑ 118 Dontae Jones	.15	.04
❑ 119 Tony Battie	.15	.04
❑ 120 Lindsey Hunter	.15	.04
❑ 121 Reggie Miller	.50	.15
❑ 122 John Wallace	.15	.04
❑ 123 Ron Mercer	.30	.09
❑ 124 Antonio Daniels	.15	.04
❑ 125 Paul Grant	.15	.04
❑ 126 Voshon Lenard	.15	.04
❑ 127 Shawn Kemp	.30	.09
❑ 128 Antonio Davis	.15	.04
❑ 129 Hakeem Olajuwon	.50	.15
❑ 130 Danny Manning	.15	.04
❑ 131 Bimbo Coles	.15	.04
❑ 132 Tim Hardaway	.30	.09
❑ 133 Lorenzo Williams	.15	.04
❑ 134 Dan Majerle	.30	.09
❑ 135 Bryant Stith	.15	.04
❑ 136 Randy Brown	.15	.04
❑ 137 Hubert Davis	.15	.04
❑ 138 Gary Payton	.50	.15
❑ 139 Rasheed Wallace	.50	.15
❑ 140 Chris Robinson	.15	.04
❑ 141 Doug Christie	.30	.09
❑ 142 Brian Grant	.30	.09
❑ 143 Isaiah Rider	.15	.04
❑ 144 Kendall Gill	.15	.04
❑ 145 Lorenzen Wright	.15	.04
❑ 146 Ervin Johnson	.15	.04
❑ 147 Monty Williams	.15	.04
❑ 148 Keith Closs	.15	.04
❑ 149 Tony Delk	.15	.04
❑ 150 Hersey Hawkins	.15	.04
❑ 151 Dean Garrett	.15	.04
❑ 152 Cedric Henderson	.15	.04
❑ 153 Detlef Schrempf	.30	.09
❑ 154 Dana Barros	.15	.04
❑ 155 Dee Brown	.15	.04
❑ 156 Jayson Williams SO	.15	.04
❑ 157 Charles Barkley SO	.50	.15
❑ 158 Damon Stoudamire SO	.15	.04
❑ 159 Scottie Pippen SO	.50	.15
❑ 160 Joe Smith SO	.15	.04
❑ 161 Antonio McDyess SO	.30	.09
❑ 162 Jerry Stackhouse SO	.30	.09
❑ 163 Dennis Rodman SO	.15	.04
❑ 164 Shaquille O'Neal SO	.50	.15
❑ 165 Grant Hill SO	.30	.09
❑ 166 Checklist	.15	.04
❑ 167 Checklist	.15	.04

1999-00 Hoops

	Nm-Mt	Ex-Mt
COMPLETE SET (185)	30.00	9.00
COMMON CARD (1-165)	.15	.04
COMMON ROOKIE (166-185)	.25	.07
❑ 1 Paul Pierce	.50	.15
❑ 2 Ray Allen	.50	.15
❑ 3 Jason Williams	.50	.15
❑ 4 Sean Elliott	.30	.09
❑ 5 Al Harrington	.50	.15
❑ 6 Bobby Phills	.15	.04
❑ 7 Tyronn Lue	.30	.09
❑ 8 James Cotton	.15	.04
❑ 9 Anthony Peeler	.15	.04
❑ 10 LaPhonso Ellis	.15	.04
❑ 11 Voshon Lenard	.15	.04
❑ 12 Kornel David RC	.15	.04
❑ 13 Michael Finley	.50	.15
❑ 14 Danny Fortson	.15	.04
❑ 15 Antawn Jamison	.75	.23
❑ 16 Reggie Miller	.50	.15
❑ 17 Shaquille O'Neal	1.25	.35
❑ 18 P.J. Brown	.15	.04
❑ 19 Roshown McLeod	.15	.04
❑ 20 Larry Johnson	.30	.09
❑ 21 Rashard Lewis	.50	.15
❑ 22 Tracy McGrady	1.25	.35
❑ 23 Peja Stojakovic	.60	.18
❑ 24 Tracy Murray	.15	.04
❑ 25 Gary Payton	.50	.15
❑ 26 Ricky Davis	.30	.09
❑ 27 Kobe Bryant	2.00	.60
❑ 28 Avery Johnson	.15	.04
❑ 29 Kevin Garnett	1.00	.30
❑ 30 Charles Jones	.15	.04
❑ 31 Brevin Knight	.15	.04
❑ 32 Lindsey Hunter	.15	.04
❑ 33 Felipe Lopez	.15	.04
❑ 34 Rik Smits	.30	.09
❑ 35 Maurice Taylor	.30	.09
❑ 36 Corey Benjamin	.15	.04
❑ 37 Ervin Johnson	.15	.04
❑ 38 Steve Smith	.30	.09
❑ 39 Austin Croshere	.30	.09
❑ 40 Matt Geiger	.15	.04

❑ 41 Tom Gugliotta	.15	.04
❑ 42 Radoslav Nesterovic RC	.50	.15
❑ 43 Juwan Howard	.30	.09
❑ 44 Keon Clark	.30	.09
❑ 45 Latrell Sprewell	.50	.15
❑ 46 George Lynch	.15	.04
❑ 47 Greg Ostertag	.15	.04
❑ 48 J.R. Henderson	.15	.04
❑ 49 Kerry Kittles	.15	.04
❑ 50 Matt Harpring	.50	.15
❑ 51 Duane Causwell	.15	.04
❑ 52 Andrae Patterson	.15	.04
❑ 53 Jerry Stackhouse	.50	.15
❑ 54 Adonal Foyle	.15	.04
❑ 55 Bryce Drew	.15	.04
❑ 56 Chris Childs	.15	.04
❑ 57 Charles Smith	.15	.04
❑ 58 Rony Seikaly	.15	.04
❑ 59 Chauncey Billups	.30	.09
❑ 60 Grant Hill	.50	.15
❑ 61 Marlon Garnett RC	.15	.04
❑ 62 Tim Hardaway	.30	.09
❑ 63 Vlade Divac	.30	.09
❑ 64 Chris Gatling	.15	.04
❑ 65 Glenn Robinson	.50	.15
❑ 66 Michael Olowokandi	.30	.09
❑ 67 Elliot Perry	.15	.04
❑ 68 Howard Eisley	.15	.04
❑ 69 Glen Rice	.30	.09
❑ 70 Marcus Camby	.30	.09
❑ 71 Theo Ratliff	.30	.09
❑ 72 Brian Skinner	.15	.04
❑ 73 Kenny Anderson	.30	.09
❑ 74 Jamal Mashburn	.30	.09
❑ 75 Vladimir Stepania	.15	.04
❑ 76 Jayson Williams	.15	.04
❑ 77 Brian Grant	.30	.09
❑ 78 Raef LaFrentz	.30	.09
❑ 79 John Starks	.30	.09
❑ 80 Mike Bibby	.50	.15
❑ 81 Stephon Marbury	.50	.15
❑ 82 Armon Gilliam	.15	.04
❑ 83 Sam Jacobson	.15	.04
❑ 84 Derrick Coleman	.30	.09
❑ 85 Allan Houston	.30	.09
❑ 86 Miles Simon	.15	.04
❑ 87 Allen Iverson	1.00	.30
❑ 88 Derek Anderson	.30	.09
❑ 89 Chris Anstey	.15	.04
❑ 90 Larry Hughes	.50	.15
❑ 91 Vitaly Potapenko	.15	.04
❑ 92 Cherokee Parks	.15	.04
❑ 93 Donyell Marshall	.30	.09
❑ 94 Danny Manning	.15	.04
❑ 95 Bryon Russell	.15	.04
❑ 96 Randell Jackson	.15	.04
❑ 97 Antoine Walker	.50	.15
❑ 98 Dirk Nowitzki	1.00	.30
❑ 99 Karl Malone	.50	.15
❑ 100 Vince Carter	1.25	.35
❑ 101 Eddie Jones	.50	.15
❑ 102 Bryant Stith	.15	.04
❑ 103 Korleone Young	.15	.04
❑ 104 Tim Duncan	1.00	.30
❑ 105 Jerome Kersey	.15	.04
❑ 106 Bonzi Wells	.50	.15
❑ 107 Wesley Person	.15	.04
❑ 108 Steve Nash	.50	.15
❑ 109 Tyrone Nesby RC	.15	.04
❑ 110 Doug Christie	.30	.09
❑ 111 David Robinson	.50	.15
❑ 112 Ruben Patterson	.30	.09
❑ 113 Dikembe Mutombo	.30	.09
❑ 114 Ron Mercer	.30	.09
❑ 115 Elden Campbell	.15	.04
❑ 116 Kevin Willis	.15	.04
❑ 117 Hakeem Olajuwon	.50	.15
❑ 118 Shawn Kemp	.30	.09
❑ 119 Eric Montross	.15	.04
❑ 120 Shareef Abdur-Rahim	.50	.15
❑ 121 Bob Sura	.15	.04
❑ 122 James Robinson	.15	.04
❑ 123 Shawn Bradley	.15	.04
❑ 124 Robert Traylor	.15	.04
❑ 125 Dean Garrett	.15	.04
❑ 126 Keith Van Horn	.50	.15
❑ 127 Patrick Ewing	.50	.15
❑ 128 Isaac Austin	.15	.04
❑ 129 Jason Kidd	.75	.23
❑ 130 Isaiah Rider	.15	.04
❑ 131 Jerome James RC	.15	.04
❑ 132 John Stockton	.50	.15
❑ 133 Jason Caffey	.15	.04
❑ 134 Bryant Reeves	.15	.04
❑ 135 Michael Dickerson	.30	.09
❑ 136 Chris Mullin	.50	.15
❑ 137 Rasheed Wallace	.50	.15
❑ 138 Cuttino Mobley	.50	.15
❑ 139 Antonio McDyess	.30	.09
❑ 140 Chris Webber	.50	.15
❑ 141 Jelani McCoy	.15	.04
❑ 142 Damon Stoudamire	.30	.09
❑ 143 Gerald Brown	.15	.04
❑ 144 Cory Carr	.15	.04
❑ 145 Brent Barry	.30	.09
❑ 146 Alan Henderson	.15	.04
❑ 147 Nazr Mohammed	.15	.04
❑ 148 Bison Dele	.15	.04
❑ 149 Scottie Pippen	.75	.23
❑ 150 Michael Doleac	.15	.04
❑ 151 Nick Anderson	.15	.04
❑ 152 Alonzo Mourning	.30	.09
❑ 153 Jahidi White	.15	.04
❑ 154 Jalen Rose	.50	.15
❑ 155 Brad Miller	.50	.15
❑ 156 Andrew DeClercq	.15	.04
❑ 157 Erick Strickland	.15	.04
❑ 158 Toni Kukoc	.30	.09
❑ 159 Pat Garrity	.15	.04
❑ 160 Bobby Jackson	.30	.09
❑ 161 Steve Kerr	.30	.09
❑ 162 Toby Bailey	.15	.04
❑ 163 Charles Oakley	.15	.04
❑ 164 Rod Strickland	.15	.04
❑ 165 Rodrick Rhodes	.15	.04
❑ 166 Ron Artest RC	.75	.23
❑ 167 William Avery RC	.50	.15
❑ 168 Elton Brand RC	1.50	.45
❑ 169 Baron Davis RC	1.25	.35
❑ 170 John Celestand RC	.40	.12
❑ 171 Jumaine Jones RC	.50	.15
❑ 172 Andre Miller RC	1.25	.35
❑ 173 Lee Nailon RC	.25	.07
❑ 174 James Posey RC	.75	.23
❑ 175 Jason Terry RC	.75	.23
❑ 176 Kenny Thomas RC	.50	.15
❑ 177 Steve Francis RC	2.00	.60
❑ 178 Wally Szczerbiak RC	1.25	.35
❑ 179 Richard Hamilton RC	1.25	.35
❑ 180 Jonathan Bender RC	1.25	.35
❑ 181 Shawn Marion RC	1.50	.45
❑ 182 Aleksandar Radojevic RC	.25	.07
❑ 183 Tim James RC	.40	.12
❑ 184 Trajan Langdon RC	.50	.15
❑ 185 Corey Maggette RC	1.25	.35

2000-01 Hoops Hot Prospects

	Nm-Mt	Ex-Mt
COMPLETE SET w/o RC (120)	40.00	12.00
COMMON CARD (1-120)	.30	.09
COMMON ROOKIE (121-145)	10.00	3.00
❑ 1 Vince Carter	2.50	.75
❑ 2 Wesley Person	.30	.09
❑ 3 Juwan Howard	.60	.18
❑ 4 Rodney Rogers	.30	.09
❑ 5 Tim Duncan	2.00	.60
❑ 6 Rasheed Wallace	1.00	.30
❑ 7 Anthony Peeler	.30	.09
❑ 8 John Amaechi	.30	.09
❑ 9 Tim Hardaway	.60	.18
❑ 10 Mark Jackson	.30	.09
❑ 11 Latrell Sprewell	1.00	.30
❑ 12 Kevin Garnett	2.00	.60
❑ 13 Alonzo Mourning	.60	.18
❑ 14 Jerome Williams	.30	.09
❑ 15 Anfernee Hardaway	1.00	.30
❑ 16 Clifford Robinson	.30	.09
❑ 17 Mike Bibby	1.00	.30
❑ 18 Allen Iverson	2.00	.60
❑ 19 Terrell Brandon	.60	.18
❑ 20 Jerry Stackhouse	1.00	.30
❑ 21 Brian Grant	.60	.18
❑ 22 Lamond Murray	.30	.09
❑ 23 Nick Anderson	.30	.09
❑ 24 Alan Henderson	.30	.09
❑ 25 Bryon Russell	.30	.09
❑ 26 Elton Brand	1.00	.30
❑ 27 Antawn Jamison	1.00	.30
❑ 28 Mitch Richmond	.60	.18
❑ 29 Marcus Camby	.60	.18
❑ 30 Raef LaFrentz	.60	.18
❑ 31 Damon Stoudamire	.60	.18
❑ 32 Vin Baker	.60	.18
❑ 33 Allan Houston	.60	.18
❑ 34 Doug Christie	.60	.18
❑ 35 Stephon Marbury	1.00	.30
❑ 36 Tim Thomas	.60	.18
❑ 37 Tracy McGrady	2.50	.75
❑ 38 Shareef Abdur-Rahim	1.00	.30
❑ 39 Eddie Jones	1.00	.30
❑ 40 Glenn Robinson	1.00	.30
❑ 41 Sam Cassell	1.00	.30
❑ 42 Dan Majerle	.60	.18
❑ 43 Maurice Taylor	.30	.09
❑ 44 Anthony Mason	.60	.18
❑ 45 Dirk Nowitzki	1.50	.45
❑ 46 Kobe Bryant	4.00	1.20
❑ 47 Kerry Kittles	.30	.09
❑ 48 Derrick Coleman	.30	.09
❑ 49 Cuttino Mobley	.60	.18
❑ 50 Nick Van Exel	1.00	.30
❑ 51 LaPhonso Ellis	.30	.09
❑ 52 Kendall Gill	.30	.09
❑ 53 Hakeem Olajuwon	1.00	.30
❑ 54 Rashard Lewis	.60	.18
❑ 55 Dale Davis	.30	.09
❑ 56 Keith Van Horn	1.00	.30
❑ 57 Michael Finley	1.00	.30
❑ 58 Othella Harrington	.30	.09
❑ 59 Gary Payton	1.00	.30
❑ 60 Michael Dickerson	.60	.18
❑ 61 Voshon Lenard	.30	.09
❑ 62 Patrick Ewing	1.00	.30
❑ 63 Ron Mercer	.60	.18
❑ 64 Kenny Anderson	.60	.18
❑ 65 Shaquille O'Neal	2.50	.75
❑ 66 Tariq Abdul-Wahad	.30	.09
❑ 67 Antonio Davis	.30	.09
❑ 68 Rick Fox	.60	.18
❑ 69 Lamar Odom	1.00	.30
❑ 70 Derek Anderson	.60	.18
❑ 71 Vitaly Potapenko	.30	.09
❑ 72 Karl Malone	1.00	.30
❑ 73 Wally Szczerbiak	.60	.18
❑ 74 Jason Williams	.60	.18
❑ 75 Steve Francis	1.00	.30
❑ 76 John Starks	.60	.18
❑ 77 Ron Artest	.60	.18
❑ 78 Grant Hill	1.00	.30
❑ 79 Theo Ratliff	.60	.18
❑ 80 Antonio McDyess	.60	.18
❑ 81 Antoine Walker	1.00	.30
❑ 82 Sean Elliott	.60	.18
❑ 83 Ruben Patterson	.60	.18
❑ 84 Ray Allen	1.00	.30
❑ 85 Tom Gugliotta	.30	.09
❑ 86 Scottie Pippen	1.50	.45
❑ 87 Jim Jackson	.30	.09

❑ 88 Joe Smith .60 .18
❑ 89 Reggie Miller 1.00 .30
❑ 90 Richard Hamilton .60 .18
❑ 91 Paul Pierce 1.00 .30
❑ 92 Mookie Blaylock .30 .09
❑ 93 Glen Rice .60 .18
❑ 94 P.J. Brown .30 .09
❑ 95 Avery Johnson .30 .09
❑ 96 John Stockton 1.00 .30
❑ 97 Tyrone Hill .30 .09
❑ 98 Tracy Murray .30 .09
❑ 99 Darrell Armstrong .30 .09
❑ 100 Steve Smith .60 .18
❑ 101 Shawn Kemp .60 .18
❑ 102 Jalen Rose 1.00 .30
❑ 103 Vonteego Cummings .30 .09
❑ 104 Larry Hughes .60 .18
❑ 105 Charles Oakley .30 .09
❑ 106 Rod Strickland .30 .09
❑ 107 Christian Laettner .60 .18
❑ 108 Baron Davis 1.00 .30
❑ 109 Jamal Mashburn .60 .18
❑ 110 Lindsey Hunter .30 .09
❑ 111 Toni Kukoc .60 .18
❑ 112 Austin Croshere .60 .18
❑ 113 Chris Webber 1.00 .30
❑ 114 Vlade Divac .60 .18
❑ 115 Andre Miller .60 .18
❑ 116 Larry Johnson .60 .18
❑ 117 Jason Kidd 1.50 .45
❑ 118 David Robinson 1.00 .30
❑ 119 Donyell Marshall .60 .18
❑ 120 Jason Terry 1.00 .30
❑ 121 Kenyon Martin RC 25.00 7.50
❑ 122 Stromile Swift RC 15.00 4.50
❑ 123 Chris Mihm RC 10.00 3.00
❑ 124 Marcus Fizer RC 10.00 3.00
❑ 125 Courtney Alexander RC 15.00 4.50
❑ 126 Darius Miles RC 25.00 7.50
❑ 127 Jerome Moiso RC 10.00 3.00
❑ 128 Joel Przybilla RC 10.00 3.00
❑ 129 DerMarr Johnson RC 10.00 3.00
❑ 130 Mike Miller RC 15.00 4.50
❑ 131 Quentin Richardson RC 15.00 4.50
❑ 132 Morris Peterson RC 15.00 4.50
❑ 133 Speedy Claxton RC 10.00 3.00
❑ 134 Keyon Dooling RC 10.00 3.00
❑ 135 Mark Madsen RC 10.00 3.00
❑ 136 Mateen Cleaves RC 10.00 3.00
❑ 137 Etan Thomas RC 10.00 3.00
❑ 138 Jason Collier RC 10.00 3.00
❑ 139 Erick Barkley RC 10.00 3.00
❑ 140 Desmond Mason RC 10.00 3.00
❑ 141 Mamadou N'diaye RC 10.00 3.00
❑ 142 DeShawn Stevenson RC 10.00 3.00
❑ 143 Donnell Harvey RC 10.00 3.00
❑ 144 Jamaal Magloire RC 10.00 3.00
❑ 145 Hidayet Turkoglu RC 15.00 4.50

2001-02 Hoops Hot Prospects

	Nm-Mt	Ex-Mt
COMP.SET w/o SP's (80)	40.00	12.00
COMMON CARD (1-80)	.30	.09
COMMON ROOKIE (81-108)	12.00	3.60

❑ 1 Vince Carter 2.50 .75
❑ 2 John Stockton 1.00 .30
❑ 3 Steve Smith .60 .18
❑ 4 Kevin Garnett 2.00 .60
❑ 5 Larry Hughes .60 .18
❑ 6 Ron Mercer .60 .18
❑ 7 Marcus Fizer .60 .18
❑ 8 Rashard Lewis .60 .18
❑ 9 Mike Miller 1.00 .30
❑ 10 Darius Miles 1.00 .30
❑ 11 Michael Finley 1.00 .30
❑ 12 Marcus Camby .60 .18
❑ 13 Morris Peterson .60 .18
❑ 14 Shawn Marion 1.00 .30
❑ 15 Alonzo Mourning .60 .18
❑ 16 Jamal Mashburn .60 .18
❑ 17 Michael Jordan 15.00 4.50
❑ 18 Jason Williams .60 .18
❑ 19 Latrell Sprewell 1.00 .30
❑ 20 Reggie Miller 1.00 .30
❑ 21 Glenn Robinson 1.00 .30
❑ 22 Steve Francis 1.00 .30
❑ 23 Antoine Walker 1.00 .30
❑ 24 Stromile Swift .60 .18
❑ 25 Damon Stoudamire .60 .18
❑ 26 Allan Houston .60 .18
❑ 27 Kobe Bryant 4.00 1.20
❑ 28 Dirk Nowitzki 1.50 .45
❑ 29 Iakovos Tsakalidis .30 .09
❑ 30 Gary Payton 1.00 .30
❑ 31 Allen Iverson 2.00 .60
❑ 32 Eddie Jones 1.00 .30
❑ 33 Mateen Cleaves .60 .18
❑ 34 Nick Van Exel 1.00 .30
❑ 35 Terrell Brandon .60 .18
❑ 36 Wally Szczerbiak .60 .18
❑ 37 Jalen Rose 1.00 .30
❑ 38 Elton Brand 1.00 .30
❑ 39 DerMarr Johnson .60 .18
❑ 40 Peja Stojakovic 1.00 .30
❑ 41 Jason Kidd 1.50 .45
❑ 42 Sam Cassell 1.00 .30
❑ 43 Cuttino Mobley .60 .18
❑ 44 Toni Kukoc .60 .18
❑ 45 DeShawn Stevenson .60 .18
❑ 46 David Robinson 1.00 .30
❑ 47 Grant Hill 1.00 .30
❑ 48 Shaquille O'Neal 2.50 .75
❑ 49 Andre Miller .60 .18
❑ 50 Corey Maggette .60 .18
❑ 51 Jason Terry 1.00 .30
❑ 52 Aaron McKie .60 .18
❑ 53 Eddie House .60 .18
❑ 54 Steve Nash 1.00 .30
❑ 55 Clifford Robinson .30 .09
❑ 56 Chris Webber 1.00 .30
❑ 57 Kenyon Martin 1.00 .30
❑ 58 Jermaine O'Neal 1.00 .30
❑ 59 Baron Davis 1.00 .30
❑ 60 Mitch Richmond .60 .18
❑ 61 Antawn Jamison 1.00 .30
❑ 62 Paul Pierce 1.00 .30
❑ 63 Shareef Abdur-Rahim 1.00 .30
❑ 64 Rasheed Wallace 1.00 .30
❑ 65 Ray Allen 1.00 .30
❑ 66 Lamar Odom 1.00 .30
❑ 67 Chris Mihm .60 .18
❑ 68 Raef LaFrentz .60 .18
❑ 69 Patrick Ewing 1.00 .30
❑ 70 Tracy McGrady 2.50 .75
❑ 71 Derek Fisher 1.00 .30
❑ 72 Jerry Stackhouse 1.00 .30
❑ 73 Antonio McDyess .60 .18
❑ 74 Karl Malone 1.00 .30
❑ 75 Dikembe Mutombo .60 .18
❑ 76 Hakeem Olajuwon 1.00 .30
❑ 77 David Wesley .30 .09
❑ 78 Courtney Alexander .60 .18
❑ 79 Tim Duncan 2.00 .60
❑ 80 Stephon Marbury 1.00 .30
❑ 81 Kwame Brown JSY RC 25.00 7.50
❑ 82 Tyson Chandler JSY RC 20.00 6.00
❑ 83 Pau Gasol JSY RC 40.00 12.00
❑ 84 Eddy Curry JSY RC 20.00 6.00
❑ 85 J.Richardson JSY/300 RC 40.00 12.00
❑ 86 Shane Battier JSY RC 15.00 4.50
❑ 87 E.Griffin JSY/300 RC 15.00 4.50
❑ 88 DeSagana Diop JSY RC 12.00 3.60
❑ 89 Rodney White JSY RC 15.00 4.50
❑ 90 J.Johnson JSY/300 RC 20.00 6.00
❑ 91 Ke.Brown JSY/300 RC 12.00 3.60
❑ 92 V.Radmanovic JSY RC 12.00 3.60
❑ 93 Richard Jefferson JSY RC 30.00 9.00
❑ 94 Troy Murphy JSY RC 20.00 6.00
❑ 95 Steven Hunter JSY RC 12.00 3.60
❑ 96 Kirk Haston JSY RC 12.00 3.60
❑ 97 Michael Bradley JSY RC 12.00 3.60
❑ 98 Jason Collins JSY RC 12.00 3.60
❑ 99 Zach Randolph JSY RC 30.00 9.00
❑ 100 Brendan Haywood JSY RC 15.00 4.50
❑ 101 Joseph Forte JSY RC 20.00 6.00
❑ 102 Jeryl Sasser JSY RC 12.00 3.60
❑ 103 B.Armstrong JSY/300 RC 12.00 3.60
❑ 104 Andrei Kirilenko JSY RC 20.00 6.00
❑ 105 Primos Brezec JSY RC 12.00 3.60
❑ 106 S.Dalembert JSY/300 RC 12.00 3.60
❑ 107 Jamaal Tinsley JSY RC 15.00 4.50
❑ 108 Tony Parker JSY RC 40.00 12.00

2002-03 Hoops Hot Prospects

	Nm-Mt	Ex-Mt
COMP.SET w/o SP's (80)	50.00	15.00
COMMON JSY RC (81-108)	20.00	6.00
COMMON ROOKIE (109-120)	10.00	3.00

❑ 1 Vince Carter 3.00 .90
❑ 2 Chris Webber 1.00 .30
❑ 3 Latrell Sprewell 1.00 .30
❑ 4 Brian Grant .60 .18
❑ 5 Jerry Stackhouse 1.00 .30
❑ 6 Joe Smith .60 .18
❑ 7 Jason Terry 1.00 .30
❑ 8 Shawn Marion 1.00 .30
❑ 9 Wally Szczerbiak .60 .18
❑ 10 Reggie Miller 1.00 .30
❑ 11 Steve Nash 1.00 .30
❑ 12 Karl Malone 1.00 .30
❑ 13 Damon Stoudamire .60 .18
❑ 14 Jamal Mashburn .60 .18
❑ 15 Kobe Bryant 4.00 1.20
❑ 16 Paul Pierce 1.00 .30
❑ 17 Tony Parker 1.00 .30
❑ 18 Mike Miller 1.00 .30
❑ 19 Sam Cassell 1.00 .30
❑ 20 Eddie Griffin .60 .18
❑ 21 Jason Williams .60 .18
❑ 22 Jason Richardson 1.00 .30
❑ 23 Antoine Walker 1.00 .30
❑ 24 Tim Duncan 2.00 .60
❑ 25 Baron Davis 1.00 .30
❑ 26 Glenn Robinson 1.00 .30
❑ 27 Darius Miles 1.00 .30
❑ 28 Dirk Nowitzki 1.50 .45
❑ 29 John Stockton 1.00 .30
❑ 30 Allen Iverson 2.00 .60
❑ 31 Richard Jefferson .60 .18
❑ 32 Rick Fox .60 .18
❑ 33 Ben Wallace 1.00 .30
❑ 34 Michael Jordan 8.00 2.40
❑ 35 Rasheed Wallace 1.00 .30
❑ 36 Alonzo Mourning .60 .18
❑ 37 Steve Francis 1.00 .30
❑ 38 Jalen Rose 1.00 .30
❑ 39 Rashard Lewis .60 .18
❑ 40 Tracy McGrady 2.50 .75

Card		
❑ 41 David Wesley	.25	.07
❑ 42 Pau Gasol	1.00	.30
❑ 43 Antawn Jamison	1.00	.30
❑ 44 Shareef Abdur-Rahim	1.00	.30
❑ 45 Mike Bibby	1.00	.30
❑ 46 Dikembe Mutombo	.60	.18
❑ 47 Kevin Garnett	2.00	.60
❑ 48 Elton Brand	1.00	.30
❑ 49 Lamond Murray	.25	.07
❑ 50 Morris Peterson	.60	.18
❑ 51 Joe Johnson	.60	.18
❑ 52 Kenyon Martin	1.00	.30
❑ 53 Shaquille O'Neal	2.50	.75
❑ 54 Antonio McDyess	.60	.18
❑ 55 Vin Baker	.60	.18
❑ 56 Marcus Camby	.60	.18
❑ 57 Ray Allen	1.00	.30
❑ 58 Jermain O'Neal	1.00	.30
❑ 59 Eddy Curry	1.00	.30
❑ 60 David Robinson	1.00	.30
❑ 61 Clifford Robinson	.25	.07
❑ 62 Rodney Rogers	.25	.07
❑ 63 Peja Stojakovic	1.00	.30
❑ 64 Allan Houston	.60	.18
❑ 65 Shane Battier	1.00	.30
❑ 66 Jamaal Tinsley	1.00	.30
❑ 67 Michael Finley	1.00	.30
❑ 68 Kenny Anderson	.60	.18
❑ 69 Stephon Marbury	1.00	.30
❑ 70 Terrell Brandon	.60	.18
❑ 71 Lamar Odom	1.00	.30
❑ 72 Raef LaFrentz	.60	.18
❑ 73 Jamaal Magloire	.25	.07
❑ 74 Bonzi Wells	.60	.18
❑ 75 Jason Kidd	1.50	.45
❑ 76 Cuttino Mobley	.60	.18
❑ 77 Tyson Chandler	1.00	.30
❑ 78 Gary Payton	1.00	.30
❑ 79 Grant Hill	1.00	.30
❑ 80 Eddie Jones	1.00	.30
❑ 81 Yao Ming JSY RC	80.00	24.00
❑ 82 Fred Jones JSY RC	20.00	6.00
❑ 83 R.Humphrey JSY RC	20.00	6.00
❑ 84 Drew Gooden JSY RC	40.00	12.00
❑ 85 N.Tskitishvili JSY RC	20.00	6.00
❑ 86 Caron Butler JSY RC	30.00	9.00
❑ 87 V.Yarbrough JSY RC	20.00	6.00
❑ 88 DaJ.Wagner JSY RC	25.00	7.50
❑ 89 Nene Hilario JSY RC	30.00	9.00
❑ 90 Qyntel Woods JSY RC	20.00	6.00
❑ 91 Jared Jeffries JSY RC	20.00	6.00
❑ 92 C.Jacobsen JSY RC	20.00	6.00
❑ 93 Marcus Haislip JSY RC	20.00	6.00
❑ 94 Kareem Rush JSY RC	20.00	6.00
❑ 95 P.Savovic JSY RC	20.00	6.00
❑ 96 Melvin Ely JSY RC	20.00	6.00
❑ 97 Steve Logan JSY RC	20.00	6.00
❑ 98 A.Stoudemire JSY RC	80.00	24.00
❑ 99 John Salmons JSY RC	20.00	6.00
❑ 100 Chris Jefferies JSY RC	25.00	7.50
❑ 101 Juan Dixon JSY RC	25.00	7.50
❑ 102 Carlos Boozer JSY RC	30.00	9.00
❑ 103 Roger Mason JSY RC	20.00	6.00
❑ 104 Rod Grizzard JSY RC	20.00	6.00
❑ 105 T.Prince JSY RC	25.00	7.50
❑ 106 Chris Wilcox JSY RC	25.00	7.50
❑ 107 Sam Clancy JSY RC	25.00	7.50
❑ 108 Dan Gadzuric JSY RC	20.00	6.00
❑ 109 Dan Dickau/900 RC	10.00	3.00
❑ 110 Jay Williams/900 RC	12.00	3.60
❑ 111 Mike Dunleavy/900 RC	10.00	3.00
❑ 112 Robert Archibald/900 RC	10.00	3.00
❑ 113 Curtis Borchardt/900 RC	10.00	3.00
❑ 114 Bostjan Nachbar/900 RC	10.00	3.00
❑ 115 Jiri Welsch/1500 RC	10.00	3.00
❑ 116 Frank Williams/1500 RC	10.00	3.00
❑ 117 Rasual Butler/1500 RC	10.00	3.00
❑ 118 Tamar Slay/1500 RC	10.00	3.00
❑ 119 Ronald Murray/1500 RC	12.00	3.60
❑ 120 Corsley Edwards/1500 RC	10.00	3.00

2003-04 Hoops Hot Prospects

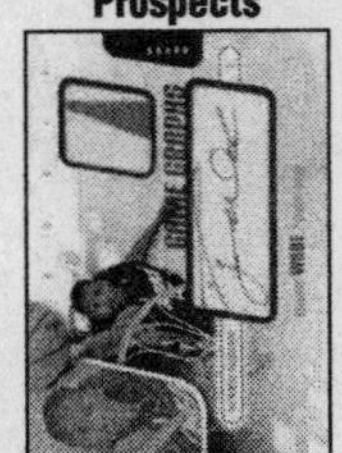

	MINT	NRMT
COMP.SET w/o SP's	40.00	18.00
COMMON CARD (1-80)	.25	.11
COMMON AU RC (81-87)	12.00	5.50
COMMON JSY RC (88-94)	20.00	9.00
COMMON JSY AU RC (95-111)	30.00	13.50
COMMON ROOKIE (112-117)	8.00	3.60
WHITE HOT ONE OF ONE's EXIST		-
WHITE HOT UNPRICED DUE TO SCARCITY		
❑ 1 Shareef Abdur-Rahim	1.00	.45
❑ 2 Mike Bibby	1.00	.45
❑ 3 Allan Houston	.60	.25
❑ 4 Pau Gasol	1.00	.45
❑ 5 Tayshaun Prince	.60	.25
❑ 6 Darius Miles	1.00	.45
❑ 7 Ray Allen	1.00	.45
❑ 8 Amare Stoudemire	2.00	.90
❑ 9 Latrell Sprewell	1.00	.45
❑ 10 Jamaal Tinsley	1.00	.45
❑ 11 Nene	.60	.25
❑ 12 Matt Harpring	1.00	.45
❑ 13 Bonzi Wells	.60	.25
❑ 14 Alonzo Mourning	.60	.25
❑ 15 Elton Brand	1.00	.45
❑ 16 Paul Pierce	1.00	.45
❑ 17 Tony Parker	1.00	.45
❑ 18 Glenn Robinson	1.00	.45
❑ 19 Marcus Haislip	.25	.11
❑ 20 Eddie Griffin	.60	.25
❑ 21 Jamaal Magloire	.25	.11
❑ 22 Gilbert Arenas	1.00	.45
❑ 23 Antoine Walker	1.00	.45
❑ 24 Manu Ginobili	1.00	.45
❑ 25 Jamal Mashburn	.60	.25
❑ 26 Michael Redd	1.00	.45
❑ 27 Ron Artest	.60	.25
❑ 28 Steve Nash	1.00	.45
❑ 29 Andrei Kirilenko	1.00	.45
❑ 30 Stephon Marbury	1.00	.45
❑ 31 Richard Jefferson	.60	.25
❑ 32 Kobe Bryant	4.00	1.80
❑ 33 Cuttino Mobley	.60	.25
❑ 34 Juan Dixon	.60	.25
❑ 35 Rasheed Wallace	1.00	.45
❑ 36 Eddie Jones	1.00	.45
❑ 37 Steve Francis	1.00	.45
❑ 38 Dajuan Wagner	.60	.25
❑ 39 Vladimir Radmanovic	.25	.11
❑ 40 Drew Gooden	.60	.25
❑ 41 Baron Davis	1.00	.45
❑ 42 Mike Miller	1.00	.45
❑ 43 Jason Richardson	1.00	.45
❑ 44 Dan Dickau	.25	.11
❑ 45 Chris Webber	1.00	.45
❑ 46 Kenny Thomas	.25	.11
❑ 47 Kevin Garnett	2.00	.90
❑ 48 Reggie Miller	1.00	.45
❑ 49 Dirk Nowitzki	1.50	.70
❑ 50 Vince Carter	2.50	1.10
❑ 51 Zach Randolph	1.00	.45
❑ 52 Jason Kidd	1.50	.70
❑ 53 Shaquille O'Neal	2.50	1.10
❑ 54 Nikoloz Tskitishvili	.25	.11
❑ 55 Jerry Stackhouse	1.00	.45
❑ 56 Tracy McGrady	2.50	1.10
❑ 57 Desmond Mason	.60	.25
❑ 58 Yao Ming	2.50	1.10
❑ 59 Jalen Rose	1.00	.45
❑ 60 Tim Duncan	2.00	.90
❑ 61 Ben Wallace	1.00	.45
❑ 62 Mike Dunleavy	.60	.25
❑ 63 Peja Stojakovic	1.00	.45
❑ 64 Keith Van Horn	1.00	.45
❑ 65 Karl Malone	1.00	.45
❑ 66 Jermaine O'Neal	1.00	.45
❑ 67 Michael Finley	1.00	.45
❑ 68 Morris Peterson	.60	.25
❑ 69 Shawn Marion	1.00	.45
❑ 70 John Salmons	.25	.11
❑ 71 Chris Wilcox	.60	.25
❑ 72 Rodney White	.25	.11
❑ 73 Kwame Brown	.60	.25
❑ 74 Bobby Jackson	.60	.25
❑ 75 Kenyon Martin	1.00	.45
❑ 76 Antawn Jamison	1.00	.45
❑ 77 Eddy Curry	.60	.25
❑ 78 Bruce Bowen	.25	.11
❑ 79 Allen Iverson	2.00	.90
❑ 80 Caron Butler	1.00	.45
❑ 81 Boris Diaw AU RC	12.00	5.50
❑ 82 Quinton Ross AU RC	12.00	5.50
❑ 83 Matt Carroll AU RC	12.00	5.50
❑ 84 Travis Hansen AU RC	12.00	5.50
❑ 85 Zaur Pachulia AU RC	12.00	5.50
❑ 86 Zarko Cabarkapa AU RC	12.00	5.50
❑ 87 Maciej Lampe AU RC	12.00	5.50
❑ 88 Ndudi Ebi JSY RC	20.00	9.00
❑ 89 Jarvis Hayes JSY RC	25.00	11.00
❑ 90 Steve Blake JSY RC	20.00	9.00
❑ 91 Keith Bogans JSY RC	20.00	9.00
❑ 92 Reece Gaines JSY RC	20.00	9.00
❑ 93 Chris Kaman JSY RC	20.00	9.00
❑ 94 Slavko Vranes JSY RC	20.00	9.00
❑ 95 C.Anthony JSY AU RC	300.00	135.00
❑ 96 Troy Bell JSY AU RC	30.00	13.50
❑ 97 Travis Outlaw JSY AU RC	30.00	13.50
❑ 98 M.Sweetney JSY AU RC	30.00	13.50
❑ 99 Dahntay Jones JSY AU RC	30.00	13.50
❑ 100 Chris Bosh JSY AU RC	100.00	45.00
❑ 101 Brian Cook JSY AU RC	30.00	13.50
❑ 102 Luke Ridnour JSY AU RC	40.00	18.00
❑ 103 David West JSY AU RC	30.00	13.50
❑ 104 Banks JSY AU RC EXCH	30.00	13.50
❑ 105 Ken.Perkins JSY AU RC	30.00	13.50
❑ 106 Barbosa JSY AU RC EXCH	30.00	13.50
❑ 107 M.Pietrus JSY AU RC	30.00	13.50
❑ 108 D.Wade JSY AU RC	120.00	55.00
❑ 109 Howard JSY AU RC EXCH	40.00	18.00
❑ 110 J.Kapono JSY AU RC	30.00	13.50
❑ 111 Luke Walton JSY AU RC	40.00	18.00
❑ 112 LeBron James RC	60.00	27.00
❑ 113 T.J. Ford RC	8.00	3.60
❑ 114 Zoran Planinic RC	8.00	3.60
❑ 115 Darko Milicic RC	10.00	4.50
❑ 116 Kirk Hinrich RC	10.00	4.50
❑ 117 Nick Collison RC	8.00	3.60

2002-03 Hoops Stars

	Nm-Mt	Ex-Mt
COMP.SET w/o RC's (170)	30.00	9.00
COMMON CARD (1-170)	.20	.06
COMMON ROOKIE (171-200)	2.50	.75
❑ 1 Tracy McGrady	2.00	.60

❑ 2 Kevin Garnett 1.50 .45
❑ 3 Allen Iverson 1.50 .45
❑ 4 Keith Van Horn .75 .23
❑ 5 Kwame Brown .50 .15
❑ 6 Alan Henderson .20 .06
❑ 7 Kenny Anderson .50 .15
❑ 8 Antoine Walker .75 .23
❑ 9 Tony Delk .20 .06
❑ 10 Tony Battie .20 .06
❑ 11 Wally Szczerbiak .50 .15
❑ 12 Paul Pierce .75 .23
❑ 13 Glenn Robinson .75 .23
❑ 14 Tim Thomas .50 .15
❑ 15 Vince Carter 2.00 .60
❑ 16 Pau Gasol .75 .23
❑ 17 Eddy Curry .75 .23
❑ 18 Darrell Armstrong .20 .06
❑ 19 Sam Cassell .75 .23
❑ 20 Darius Miles .75 .23
❑ 21 Jason Richardson .75 .23
❑ 22 Elton Brand .75 .23
❑ 23 Michael Jordan 6.00 1.80
❑ 24 Andre Miller .50 .15
❑ 25 Anfernee Hardaway .75 .23
❑ 26 Steve Nash .75 .23
❑ 27 Ron Artest .50 .15
❑ 28 Raef LaFrentz .50 .15
❑ 29 Troy Hudson .20 .06
❑ 30 Rasheed Wallace .75 .23
❑ 31 Ricky Davis .75 .23
❑ 32 Juwan Howard .50 .15
❑ 33 Steve Francis .75 .23
❑ 34 Shaquille O'Neal .75 .23
❑ 35 James Posey .50 .15
❑ 36 DeShawn Stevenson .20 .06
❑ 37 Clifford Robinson .20 .06
❑ 38 Jerry Stackhouse .75 .23
❑ 39 Chauncey Billups .50 .15
❑ 40 Mike Bibby .75 .23
❑ 41 Dirk Nowitzki 1.25 .35
❑ 42 Corliss Williamson .50 .15
❑ 43 Antawn Jamison .75 .23
❑ 44 Jamal Mashburn .50 .15
❑ 45 Danny Fortson .20 .06
❑ 46 Reggie Miller .75 .23
❑ 47 Scottie Pippen 1.25 .35
❑ 48 Donnell Harvey .20 .06
❑ 49 Moochie Norris .20 .06
❑ 50 Corey Maggette .50 .15
❑ 51 Eddie Griffin .50 .15
❑ 52 Karl Malone .75 .23
❑ 53 Maurice Taylor .20 .06
❑ 54 Al Harrington .50 .15
❑ 55 Kenyon Martin .75 .23
❑ 56 Nick Van Exel .75 .23
❑ 57 Jermaine O'Neal .75 .23
❑ 58 Anthony Mason .50 .15
❑ 59 Jamaal Tinsley .75 .23
❑ 60 Chris Mihm .20 .06
❑ 61 Lamar Odom .75 .23
❑ 62 Cuttino Mobley .50 .15
❑ 63 Michael Olowokandi .20 .06
❑ 64 Michael Finley .75 .23
❑ 65 Anthony Peeler .20 .06
❑ 66 Mengke Bateer .75 .23
❑ 67 Rick Fox .50 .15
❑ 68 Steve Smith .50 .15
❑ 69 Robert Horry .50 .15
❑ 70 Devean George .50 .15
❑ 71 Jason Williams .75 .23
❑ 72 Stromile Swift .50 .15
❑ 73 Marcus Fizer .50 .15
❑ 74 Michael Dickerson .20 .06
❑ 75 Shane Battier .75 .23
❑ 76 Larry Hughes .75 .23
❑ 77 Brian Skinner .20 .06
❑ 78 Eddie Jones .75 .23
❑ 79 Malik Allen .20 .06
❑ 80 Ray Allen .75 .23
❑ 81 Jumaine Jones .50 .15
❑ 82 Donyell Marshall .50 .15
❑ 83 Toni Kukoc .50 .15
❑ 84 Michael Redd .75 .23
❑ 85 Ron Mercer .50 .15
❑ 86 Terrell Brandon .50 .15
❑ 87 Latrell Sprewell .75 .23
❑ 88 Kobe Bryant 3.00 .90
❑ 89 Kurt Thomas .50 .15
❑ 90 Rasho Nesterovic .20 .06
❑ 91 Shareef Abdur-Rahim .75 .23
❑ 92 Eduardo Najera .50 .15
❑ 93 Jamaal Magloire .20 .06
❑ 94 Antonio Davis .20 .06
❑ 95 Rodney Rogers .20 .06
❑ 96 Jason Collins .20 .06
❑ 97 Marcus Camby .50 .15
❑ 98 Joe Smith .50 .15
❑ 99 Richard Jefferson .50 .15
❑ 100 Gilbert Arenas .75 .23
❑ 101 Courtney Alexander .50 .15
❑ 102 David Wesley .20 .06
❑ 103 Baron Davis .75 .23
❑ 104 Elden Campbell .20 .06
❑ 105 Jason Kidd 1.25 .35
❑ 106 P.J. Brown .20 .06
❑ 107 Rashard Lewis .50 .15
❑ 108 Alvin Williams .20 .06
❑ 109 Kerry Kittles .20 .06
❑ 110 Charlie Ward .20 .06
❑ 111 Kedrick Brown .50 .15
❑ 112 Shandon Anderson .20 .06
❑ 113 Grant Hill .75 .23
❑ 114 Tyson Chandler .75 .23
❑ 115 Brent Barry .50 .15
❑ 116 Travis Best .20 .06
❑ 117 Mike Miller .75 .23
❑ 118 Aaron McKie .50 .15
❑ 119 Theo Ratliff .50 .15
❑ 120 Todd MacCulloch .20 .06
❑ 121 Trenton Hassell .50 .15
❑ 122 Vin Baker .50 .15
❑ 123 Dion Glover .20 .06
❑ 124 Stephon Marbury .75 .23
❑ 125 Ben Wallace .75 .23
❑ 126 Glen Rice .50 .15
❑ 127 Joe Johnson .50 .15
❑ 128 Chris Webber .75 .23
❑ 129 Damon Stoudamire .50 .15
❑ 130 Voshon Lenard .20 .06
❑ 131 Troy Murphy .50 .15
❑ 132 Desmond Mason .50 .15
❑ 133 Ruben Patterson .50 .15
❑ 134 John Stockton .75 .23
❑ 135 Bobby Jackson .50 .15
❑ 136 Shawn Marion .75 .23
❑ 137 Jarron Collins .20 .06
❑ 138 Tom Gugliotta .20 .06
❑ 139 Doug Christie .50 .15
❑ 140 Zeljko Rebraca .50 .15
❑ 141 Tim Duncan 1.50 .45
❑ 142 David Robinson .75 .23
❑ 143 Tony Parker .75 .23
❑ 144 Derek Fisher .75 .23
❑ 145 Speedy Claxton .50 .15
❑ 146 Eric Snow .50 .15
❑ 147 Gary Payton .75 .23
❑ 148 Pat Garrity .20 .06
❑ 149 Joseph Forte .50 .15
❑ 150 Derek Anderson .50 .15
❑ 151 Vladimir Radmanovic .50 .15
❑ 152 Samuel Dalembert .20 .06
❑ 153 Allan Houston .50 .15
❑ 154 Jalen Rose .75 .23
❑ 155 Dikembe Mutombo .50 .15
❑ 156 Jerome Williams .20 .06
❑ 157 Antonio McDyess .50 .15
❑ 158 Morris Peterson .50 .15
❑ 159 Bonzi Wells .50 .15
❑ 160 Hedo Turkoglu .75 .23
❑ 161 Gerald Wallace .75 .23
❑ 162 Andrei Kirilenko .75 .23
❑ 163 Matt Harpring .75 .23
❑ 164 Peja Stojakovic .75 .23
❑ 165 Zydrunas Ilgauskas .50 .15
❑ 166 Richard Hamilton .50 .15
❑ 167 Brian Grant .50 .15
❑ 168 Christian Laettner .50 .15
❑ 169 Jason Terry .75 .23
❑ 170 Alonzo Mourning .50 .15
❑ 171 Yao Ming RC 15.00 4.50
❑ 172 Jay Williams RC 3.00 .90
❑ 173 Mike Dunleavy RC 4.00 1.20
❑ 174 Chris Wilcox RC 3.00 .90
❑ 175 Amare Stoudemire RC 12.00 3.60
❑ 176 Fred Jones RC 2.50 .75
❑ 177 Caron Butler RC 5.00 1.50
❑ 178 Melvin Ely RC 2.50 .75
❑ 179 Drew Gooden RC 6.00 1.80
❑ 180 DaJuan Wagner RC 4.00 1.20
❑ 181 Jared Jeffries RC 2.50 .75
❑ 182 Nikoloz Tskitishvili RC 2.50 .75
❑ 183 Nene Hilario RC 2.50 .75
❑ 184 Dan Dickau RC 2.50 .75
❑ 185 Marcus Haislip RC 2.50 .75
❑ 186 Gordan Giricek RC 3.00 .90
❑ 187 Jiri Welsch RC 2.50 .75
❑ 188 Juan Dixon RC 4.00 1.20
❑ 189 Curtis Borchardt RC 2.50 .75
❑ 190 Ryan Humphrey RC 2.50 .75
❑ 191 Kareem Rush RC 3.00 .90
❑ 192 Qyntel Woods RC 2.50 .75
❑ 193 Casey Jacobsen RC 2.50 .75
❑ 194 Tayshaun Prince RC 3.00 .90
❑ 195 Frank Williams RC 2.50 .75
❑ 196 Pat Burke RC 2.50 .75
❑ 197 Chris Jefferies RC 2.50 .75
❑ 198 Carlos Boozer RC 5.00 1.50
❑ 199 Manu Ginobili RC 6.00 1.80
❑ 200 Vincent Yarbrough RC 2.50 .75

1995-96 Metal

	Nm-Mt	Ex-Mt
COMPLETE SET (220)	40.00	12.00
COMPLETE SERIES 1 (120)	20.00	6.00
COMPLETE SERIES 2 (100)	20.00	6.00

❑ 1 Stacey Augmon .25 .07
❑ 2 Mookie Blaylock .25 .07
❑ 3 Grant Long .25 .07
❑ 4 Steve Smith .50 .15
❑ 5 Dee Brown .25 .07
❑ 6 Sherman Douglas .25 .07
❑ 7 Eric Montross .25 .07
❑ 8 Dino Radja .25 .07
❑ 9 Muggsy Bogues .50 .15
❑ 10 Scott Burrell .25 .07
❑ 11 Larry Johnson .50 .15
❑ 12 Alonzo Mourning .50 .15
❑ 13 Michael Jordan 5.00 1.50
❑ 14 Toni Kukoc .50 .15
❑ 15 Scottie Pippen 1.25 .35
❑ 16 Terrell Brandon .50 .15
❑ 17 Tyrone Hill .25 .07
❑ 18 Mark Price .50 .15
❑ 19 John Williams .25 .07
❑ 20 Jim Jackson .25 .07
❑ 21 Popeye Jones .25 .07
❑ 22 Jason Kidd 2.50 .75
❑ 23 Jamal Mashburn .50 .15
❑ 24 Mahmoud Abdul-Rauf .25 .07
❑ 25 Dikembe Mutombo .50 .15
❑ 26 Robert Pack .25 .07
❑ 27 Jalen Rose 1.25 .35
❑ 28 Joe Dumars .75 .23
❑ 29 Grant Hill 1.00 .30
❑ 30 Lindsey Hunter .25 .07
❑ 31 Terry Mills .25 .07
❑ 32 Tim Hardaway .50 .15
❑ 33 Donyell Marshall .50 .15
❑ 34 Chris Mullin .75 .23
❑ 35 Clifford Rozier .25 .07

	No.	Player	Nm-Mt	Ex-Mt
❑	36	Latrell Sprewell	.75	.23
❑	37	Sam Cassell	.75	.23
❑	38	Clyde Drexler	.75	.23
❑	39	Robert Horry	.50	.15
❑	40	Hakeem Olajuwon	.75	.23
❑	41	Kenny Smith	.25	.07
❑	42	Dale Davis	.25	.07
❑	43	Mark Jackson	.50	.15
❑	44	Derrick McKey	.25	.07
❑	45	Reggie Miller	.75	.23
❑	46	Rik Smits	.50	.15
❑	47	Lamond Murray	.25	.07
❑	48	Pooh Richardson	.25	.07
❑	49	Malik Sealy	.25	.07
❑	50	Loy Vaught	.25	.07
❑	51	Elden Campbell	.25	.07
❑	52	Cedric Ceballos	.25	.07
❑	53	Vlade Divac	.50	.15
❑	54	Eddie Jones	1.00	.30
❑	55	Nick Van Exel	.75	.23
❑	56	Bimbo Coles	.25	.07
❑	57	Billy Owens	.25	.07
❑	58	Khalid Reeves	.25	.07
❑	59	Glen Rice	.50	.15
❑	60	Kevin Willis	.50	.15
❑	61	Vin Baker	.50	.15
❑	62	Todd Day	.25	.07
❑	63	Eric Murdock	.25	.07
❑	64	Glenn Robinson	.75	.23
❑	65	Tom Gugliotta	.25	.07
❑	66	Christian Laettner	.50	.15
❑	67	Isaiah Rider	.25	.07
❑	68	Kenny Anderson	.50	.15
❑	69	P.J. Brown	.25	.07
❑	70	Derrick Coleman	.25	.07
❑	71	Patrick Ewing	.75	.23
❑	72	Anthony Mason	.50	.15
❑	73	Charles Oakley	.25	.07
❑	74	John Starks	.50	.15
❑	75	Nick Anderson	.25	.07
❑	76	Horace Grant	.50	.15
❑	77	Anfernee Hardaway	.75	.23
❑	78	Shaquille O'Neal	2.00	.60
❑	79	Dennis Scott	.25	.07
❑	80	Dana Barros	.25	.07
❑	81	Shawn Bradley	.25	.07
❑	82	Clarence Weatherspoon	.25	.07
❑	83	Sharone Wright	.25	.07
❑	84	Charles Barkley	1.00	.30
❑	85	Kevin Johnson	.50	.15
❑	86	Dan Majerle	.50	.15
❑	87	Danny Manning	.50	.15
❑	88	Wesley Person	.25	.07
❑	89	Clifford Robinson	.25	.07
❑	90	Rod Strickland	.25	.07
❑	91	Otis Thorpe	.25	.07
❑	92	Buck Williams	.25	.07
❑	93	Brian Grant	.75	.23
❑	94	Olden Polynice	.25	.07
❑	95	Mitch Richmond	.50	.15
❑	96	Walt Williams	.25	.07
❑	97	Sean Elliott	.50	.15
❑	98	Avery Johnson	.25	.07
❑	99	David Robinson	.75	.23
❑	100	Dennis Rodman	.50	.15
❑	101	Shawn Kemp	.50	.15
❑	102	Nate McMillan	.25	.07
❑	103	Gary Payton	.75	.23
❑	104	Detlef Schrempf	.50	.15
❑	105	B.J. Armstrong	.25	.07
❑	106	Oliver Miller	.25	.07
❑	107	John Salley	.25	.07
❑	108	David Benoit	.25	.07
❑	109	Jeff Hornacek	.50	.15
❑	110	Karl Malone	1.00	.30
❑	111	John Stockton	1.00	.30
❑	112	Greg Anthony	.25	.07
❑	113	Benoit Benjamin	.25	.07
❑	114	Byron Scott	.25	.07
❑	115	Calbert Cheaney	.25	.07
❑	116	Juwan Howard	.75	.23
❑	117	Gheorghe Muresan	.25	.07
❑	118	Chris Webber	1.00	.30
❑	119	Checklist	.25	.07
❑	120	Checklist	.25	.07
❑	121	Stacey Augmon	.25	.07
❑	122	Mookie Blaylock	.25	.07
❑	123	Alan Henderson RC	.75	.23
❑	124	Andrew Lang	.25	.07
❑	125	Ken Norman	.25	.07
❑	126	Steve Smith	.50	.15
❑	127	Dana Barros	.25	.07
❑	128	Rick Fox	.50	.15
❑	129	Eric Williams RC	.50	.15
❑	130	Kendall Gill	.25	.07
❑	131	Khalid Reeves	.25	.07
❑	132	Glen Rice	.50	.15
❑	133	George Zidek RC	.25	.07
❑	134	Dennis Rodman	.50	.15
❑	135	Danny Ferry	.25	.07
❑	136	Dan Majerle	.50	.15
❑	137	Chris Mills	.25	.07
❑	138	Bobby Phills	.25	.07
❑	139	Bob Sura RC	.50	.15
❑	140	Tony Dumas	.25	.07
❑	141	Dale Ellis	.25	.07
❑	142	Don MacLean	.25	.07
❑	143	Antonio McDyess RC	1.50	.45
❑	144	Bryant Stith	.25	.07
❑	145	Allan Houston	.50	.15
❑	146	Theo Ratliff RC	1.00	.30
❑	147	Otis Thorpe	.25	.07
❑	148	B.J. Armstrong	.25	.07
❑	149	Rony Seikaly	.25	.07
❑	150	Joe Smith RC	1.25	.35
❑	151	Sam Cassell	.75	.23
❑	152	Clyde Drexler	.75	.23
❑	153	Robert Horry	.50	.15
❑	154	Hakeem Olajuwon	.75	.23
❑	155	Antonio Davis	.25	.07
❑	156	Ricky Pierce	.25	.07
❑	157	Brent Barry RC	.75	.23
❑	158	Terry Dehere	.25	.07
❑	159	Rodney Rogers	.25	.07
❑	160	Brian Williams	.25	.07
❑	161	Magic Johnson	1.25	.35
❑	162	Sasha Danilovic RC	.25	.07
❑	163	Alonzo Mourning	.50	.15
❑	164	Kurt Thomas RC	.50	.15
❑	165	Sherman Douglas	.25	.07
❑	166	Shawn Respert RC	.25	.07
❑	167	Kevin Garnett RC	4.00	1.20
❑	168	Terry Porter	.25	.07
❑	169	Shawn Bradley	.25	.07
❑	170	Kevin Edwards	.25	.07
❑	171	Ed O'Bannon RC	.25	.07
❑	172	Jayson Williams	.25	.07
❑	173	Derek Harper	.50	.15
❑	174	Charles Smith	.25	.07
❑	175	Brian Shaw	.25	.07
❑	176	Derrick Coleman	.25	.07
❑	177	Vernon Maxwell	.25	.07
❑	178	Trevor Ruffin	.25	.07
❑	179	Jerry Stackhouse RC	2.50	.75
❑	180	Michael Finley RC	2.00	.60
❑	181	A.C. Green	.50	.15
❑	182	John Williams	.25	.07
❑	183	Aaron McKie	.50	.15
❑	184	Arvydas Sabonis RC	1.00	.30
❑	185	Gary Trent RC	.25	.07
❑	186	Tyus Edney RC	.25	.07
❑	187	Sarunas Marciulionis	.25	.07
❑	188	Michael Smith	.25	.07
❑	189	Corliss Williamson RC	.75	.23
❑	190	Vinny Del Negro	.25	.07
❑	191	Hersey Hawkins	.25	.07
❑	192	Shawn Kemp	.50	.15
❑	193	Gary Payton	.75	.23
❑	194	Sam Perkins	.50	.15
❑	195	Detlef Schrempf	.50	.15
❑	196	Willie Anderson	.25	.07
❑	197	Oliver Miller	.25	.07
❑	198	Tracy Murray	.25	.07
❑	199	Alvin Robertson	.25	.07
❑	200	Damon Stoudamire RC	1.50	.45
❑	201	Chris Morris	.25	.07
❑	202	Greg Anthony	.25	.07
❑	203	Blue Edwards	.25	.07
❑	204	Eric Murdock	.25	.07
❑	205	Bryant Reeves RC	.75	.23
❑	206	Byron Scott	.25	.07
❑	207	Robert Pack	.25	.07
❑	208	Rasheed Wallace RC	2.00	.60
❑	209	Anfernee Hardaway NB	.50	.15
❑	210	Grant Hill NB	.75	.23
❑	211	Larry Johnson NB	.25	.07
❑	212	Michael Jordan NB	2.50	.75
❑	213	Jason Kidd NB	1.25	.35
❑	214	Karl Malone NB	.75	.23
❑	215	Shaquille O'Neal NB	.75	.23
❑	216	Scottie Pippen NB	.75	.23
❑	217	David Robinson NB	.50	.15
❑	218	Glenn Robinson NB	.50	.15
❑	219	Checklist	.25	.07
❑	220	Checklist	.25	.07

1996-97 Metal

	Nm-Mt	Ex-Mt
COMPLETE SET (250)	45.00	13.50
COMPLETE SERIES 1 (150)	25.00	7.50
COMPLETE SERIES 2 (100)	20.00	6.00

	No.	Player	Nm-Mt	Ex-Mt
❑	1	Mookie Blaylock	.25	.07
❑	2	Christian Laettner	.50	.15
❑	3	Steve Smith	.50	.15
❑	4	Dana Barros	.25	.07
❑	5	Rick Fox	.25	.07
❑	6	Dino Radja	.25	.07
❑	7	Eric Williams	.25	.07
❑	8	Dell Curry	.25	.07
❑	9	Matt Geiger	.25	.07
❑	10	Glen Rice	.50	.15
❑	11	Michael Jordan	5.00	1.50
❑	12	Toni Kukoc	.50	.15
❑	13	Luc Longley	.25	.07
❑	14	Scottie Pippen	1.25	.35
❑	15	Dennis Rodman	.50	.15
❑	16	Terrell Brandon	.50	.15
❑	17	Danny Ferry	.25	.07
❑	18	Chris Mills	.25	.07
❑	19	Bobby Phills	.25	.07
❑	20	Bob Sura	.25	.07
❑	21	Jim Jackson	.25	.07
❑	22	Jason Kidd	1.25	.35
❑	23	Jamal Mashburn	.50	.15
❑	24	George McCloud	.25	.07
❑	25	LaPhonso Ellis	.25	.07
❑	26	Antonio McDyess	.50	.15
❑	27	Bryant Stith	.25	.07
❑	28	Joe Dumars	.75	.23
❑	29	Grant Hill	.75	.23
❑	30	Theo Ratliff	.50	.15
❑	31	Otis Thorpe	.25	.07
❑	32	Chris Mullin	.75	.23
❑	33	Joe Smith	.50	.15
❑	34	Latrell Sprewell	.75	.23
❑	35	Sam Cassell	.75	.23
❑	36	Clyde Drexler	.75	.23
❑	37	Robert Horry	.50	.15
❑	38	Hakeem Olajuwon	.75	.23
❑	39	Antonio Davis	.25	.07
❑	40	Dale Davis	.25	.07
❑	41	Derrick McKey	.25	.07
❑	42	Reggie Miller	.75	.23
❑	43	Rik Smits	.50	.15
❑	44	Brent Barry	.25	.07
❑	45	Malik Sealy	.25	.07
❑	46	Loy Vaught	.25	.07
❑	47	Elden Campbell	.25	.07
❑	48	Cedric Ceballos	.25	.07
❑	49	Eddie Jones	.75	.23

❑ 50 Nick Van Exel .75 .23
❑ 51 Sasha Danilovic .25 .07
❑ 52 Tim Hardaway .50 .15
❑ 53 Alonzo Mourning .50 .15
❑ 54 Kurt Thomas .50 .15
❑ 55 Vin Baker .50 .15
❑ 56 Sherman Douglas .25 .07
❑ 57 Glenn Robinson .75 .23
❑ 58 Kevin Garnett 1.50 .45
❑ 59 Tom Gugliotta .25 .07
❑ 60 Doug West .25 .07
❑ 61 Shawn Bradley .25 .07
❑ 62 Ed O'Bannon .25 .07
❑ 63 Jayson Williams .50 .15
❑ 64 Patrick Ewing .75 .23
❑ 65 Charles Oakley .25 .07
❑ 66 John Starks .50 .15
❑ 67 Nick Anderson .25 .07
❑ 68 Horace Grant .50 .15
❑ 69 Anfernee Hardaway .75 .23
❑ 70 Dennis Scott .25 .07
❑ 71 Brian Shaw .25 .07
❑ 72 Derrick Coleman .50 .15
❑ 73 Jerry Stackhouse .60 .18
❑ 74 Clarence Weatherspoon .25 .07
❑ 75 Charles Barkley 1.00 .30
❑ 76 Michael Finley 1.00 .30
❑ 77 Kevin Johnson .50 .15
❑ 78 Wesley Person .25 .07
❑ 79 Aaron McKie .50 .15
❑ 80 Clifford Robinson .25 .07
❑ 81 Arvydas Sabonis .50 .15
❑ 82 Gary Trent .25 .07
❑ 83 Tyus Edney .25 .07
❑ 84 Brian Grant .75 .23
❑ 85 Billy Owens .25 .07
❑ 86 Olden Polynice .25 .07
❑ 87 Mitch Richmond .50 .15
❑ 88 Vinny Del Negro .25 .07
❑ 89 Sean Elliott .50 .15
❑ 90 Avery Johnson .25 .07
❑ 91 David Robinson .75 .23
❑ 92 Hersey Hawkins .50 .15
❑ 93 Shawn Kemp .50 .15
❑ 94 Gary Payton .75 .23
❑ 95 Sam Perkins .50 .15
❑ 96 Detlef Schrempf .50 .15
❑ 97 Doug Christie .50 .15
❑ 98 Damon Stoudamire .75 .23
❑ 99 Sharone Wright .25 .07
❑ 100 Jeff Hornacek .50 .15
❑ 101 Karl Malone .75 .23
❑ 102 John Stockton .75 .23
❑ 103 Greg Anthony .25 .07
❑ 104 Blue Edwards .25 .07
❑ 105 Bryant Reeves .25 .07
❑ 106 Juwan Howard .50 .15
❑ 107 Gheorghe Muresan .25 .07
❑ 108 Chris Webber .75 .23
❑ 109 Kenny Anderson OTM .25 .07
❑ 110 Stacey Augmon OTM .25 .07
❑ 111 Chris Childs OTM .25 .07
❑ 112 Vlade Divac OTM .25 .07
❑ 113 Allan Houston OTM .25 .07
❑ 114 Mark Jackson OTM .25 .07
❑ 115 Larry Johnson OTM .25 .07
❑ 116 Grant Long OTM .25 .07
❑ 117 Anthony Mason OTM .25 .07
❑ 118 Dikembe Mutombo OTM .25 .07
❑ 119 Shaquille O'Neal OTM .75 .23
❑ 120 Isaiah Rider OTM .25 .07
❑ 121 Rod Strickland OTM .25 .07
❑ 122 Rasheed Wallace OTM .75 .23
❑ 123 Jalen Rose OTM .50 .15
❑ 124 Anfernee Hardaway MET .50 .15
❑ 125 Tim Hardaway MET .25 .07
❑ 126 Allan Houston MET .25 .07
❑ 127 Eddie Jones MET .50 .15
❑ 128 Michael Jordan MET 2.50 .75
❑ 129 Reggie Miller MET .50 .15
❑ 130 Glen Rice MET .25 .07
❑ 131 Mitch Richmond MET .25 .07
❑ 132 Steve Smith MET .25 .07
❑ 133 John Stockton MET .75 .23
❑ 134 Stephon Marbury FF RC 2.00 .60
❑ 135 S.Abdur-Rahim FF RC 2.50 .75
❑ 136 Ray Allen FF RC 2.50 .75
❑ 137 Kobe Bryant FF RC 10.00 3.00
❑ 138 Steve Nash FF RC 2.00 .60
❑ 139 Grant Hill MS .50 .15
❑ 140 Jason Kidd MS .60 .18
❑ 141 Karl Malone MS .75 .23
❑ 142 Hakeem Olajuwon MS .50 .15
❑ 143 Shaquille O'Neal MS .75 .23
❑ 144 Gary Payton MS .50 .15
❑ 145 Scottie Pippen MS .60 .18
❑ 146 Jerry Stackhouse MS .75 .23
❑ 147 Damon Stoudamire MS .50 .15
❑ 148 Rod Strickland MS .25 .07
❑ 149 Checklist (1-102) .25 .07
❑ 150 Checklist 103-150/inserts .25 .07
❑ 151 Tyrone Corbin .25 .07
❑ 152 Dikembe Mutombo .50 .15
❑ 153 Antoine Walker RC 2.00 .60
❑ 154 David Wesley .25 .07
❑ 155 Vlade Divac .25 .07
❑ 156 Anthony Mason .50 .15
❑ 157 Ron Harper .50 .15
❑ 158 Steve Kerr .50 .15
❑ 159 Robert Parish .50 .15
❑ 160 Tyrone Hill .25 .07
❑ 161 Vitaly Potapenko RC .25 .07
❑ 162 Sam Cassell .75 .23
❑ 163 Chris Gatling .25 .07
❑ 164 Samaki Walker RC .25 .07
❑ 165 Dale Ellis .25 .07
❑ 166 Mark Jackson .25 .07
❑ 167 Ervin Johnson .25 .07
❑ 168 Grant Hill .75 .23
❑ 169 Lindsey Hunter .25 .07
❑ 170 Todd Fuller RC .25 .07
❑ 171 Mark Price .50 .15
❑ 172 Charles Barkley 1.00 .30
❑ 173 Othella Harrington RC .75 .23
❑ 174 Matt Maloney RC .50 .15
❑ 175 Kevin Willis .25 .07
❑ 176 Travis Best .25 .07
❑ 177 Erick Dampier RC .75 .23
❑ 178 Jalen Rose .75 .23
❑ 179 Rodney Rogers .25 .07
❑ 180 Lorenzen Wright RC .50 .15
❑ 181 Kobe Bryant 6.00 1.80
❑ 182 Robert Horry .50 .15
❑ 183 Shaquille O'Neal 2.00 .60
❑ 184 P.J. Brown .25 .07
❑ 185 Dan Majerle .50 .15
❑ 186 Ray Allen 1.25 .35
❑ 187 Armon Gilliam .25 .07
❑ 188 Andrew Lang .25 .07
❑ 189 Stephon Marbury 1.00 .30
❑ 190 Stojko Vrankovic .25 .07
❑ 191 Kendall Gill .25 .07
❑ 192 Kerry Kittles RC .75 .23
❑ 193 Robert Pack .25 .07
❑ 194 Chris Childs .25 .07
❑ 195 Allan Houston .50 .15
❑ 196 Larry Johnson .50 .15
❑ 197 John Wallace RC .75 .23
❑ 198 Rony Seikaly .25 .07
❑ 199 Gerald Wilkins .25 .07
❑ 200 Lucious Harris .25 .07
❑ 201 Allen Iverson RC 5.00 1.50
❑ 202 Cedric Ceballos .25 .07
❑ 203 Jason Kidd 1.25 .35
❑ 204 Danny Manning .50 .15
❑ 205 Steve Nash .75 .23
❑ 206 Kenny Anderson .25 .07
❑ 207 Isaiah Rider .50 .15
❑ 208 Rasheed Wallace 1.00 .30
❑ 209 Mahmoud Abdul-Rauf .25 .07
❑ 210 Corliss Williamson .50 .15
❑ 211 Vernon Maxwell .25 .07
❑ 212 Dominique Wilkins .75 .23
❑ 213 Craig Ehlo .25 .07
❑ 214 Jim McIlvaine .25 .07
❑ 215 Marcus Camby RC 1.00 .30
❑ 216 Hubert Davis .25 .07
❑ 217 Walt Williams .25 .07
❑ 218 Shandon Anderson RC .50 .15
❑ 219 Bryon Russell .25 .07
❑ 220 Shareef Abdur-Rahim 1.25 .35
❑ 221 Roy Rogers RC .25 .07
❑ 222 Tracy Murray .25 .07
❑ 223 Rod Strickland .25 .07
❑ 224 Kevin Garnett MET .75 .23
❑ 225 Karl Malone MET .75 .23
❑ 226 Alonzo Mourning MET .25 .07
❑ 227 Hakeem Olajuwon MET .50 .15
❑ 228 Gary Payton MET .50 .15
❑ 229 Scottie Pippen MET .60 .18
❑ 230 David Robinson MET .50 .15
❑ 231 Dennis Rodman MET .25 .07
❑ 232 Latrell Sprewell MET .75 .23
❑ 233 Jerry Stackhouse MET .75 .23
❑ 234 Marcus Camby FF .75 .23
❑ 235 Todd Fuller FF .25 .07
❑ 236 Allen Iverson FF 2.00 .60
❑ 237 Kerry Kittles FF .75 .23
❑ 238 Roy Rogers FF .25 .07
❑ 239 Anfernee Hardaway MS .50 .15
❑ 240 Juwan Howard MS .25 .07
❑ 241 Michael Jordan MS 2.50 .75
❑ 242 Shawn Kemp MS .25 .07
❑ 243 Gary Payton MS .50 .15
❑ 244 Mitch Richmond MS .25 .07
❑ 245 Glenn Robinson MS .50 .15
❑ 246 John Stockton MS .75 .23
❑ 247 Damon Stoudamire MS .50 .15
❑ 248 Chris Webber MS .50 .15
❑ 249 Checklist .25 .07
❑ 250 Checklist .25 .07

1999-00 Metal

	Nm-Mt	Ex-Mt
COMPLETE SET (180)	50.00	15.00
COMMON CARD (1-150)	.15	.04
COMMON ROOKIE (151-180)	.50	.15

❑ 1 Vince Carter 1.25 .35
❑ 2 Stephon Marbury .50 .15
❑ 3 David Robinson .50 .15
❑ 4 Ray Allen .50 .15
❑ 5 P.J. Brown .15 .04
❑ 6 Shawn Kemp .30 .09
❑ 7 Cedric Ceballos .15 .04
❑ 8 Dale Davis .15 .04
❑ 9 Rodney Rogers .15 .04
❑ 10 Chris Gatling .15 .04
❑ 11 Bryant Reeves .15 .04
❑ 12 Al Harrington .50 .15
❑ 13 Brent Barry .30 .09
❑ 14 Brevin Knight .15 .04
❑ 15 Radoslav Nesterovic RC 1.00 .30
❑ 16 Tom Gugliotta .15 .04
❑ 17 Charles Barkley .60 .18
❑ 18 Cuttino Mobley .50 .15
❑ 19 Corliss Williamson .30 .09
❑ 20 Hersey Hawkins .30 .09
❑ 21 Mike Bibby .50 .15
❑ 22 Pat Garrity .15 .04
❑ 23 Kelvin Cato .15 .04
❑ 24 Alan Henderson .15 .04
❑ 25 Alvin Williams .15 .04
❑ 26 Antonio McDyess .30 .09
❑ 27 Damon Stoudamire .30 .09
❑ 28 Kerry Kittles .15 .04
❑ 29 Michael Olowokandi .30 .09
❑ 30 Brent Price .15 .04
❑ 31 Fred Hoiberg .15 .04
❑ 32 Glenn Robinson .50 .15
❑ 33 Hakeem Olajuwon .50 .15

	Player		
❑ 34	Monty Williams	.15	.04
❑ 35	Terry Porter	.15	.04
❑ 36	Allen Iverson	1.00	.30
❑ 37	Juwan Howard	.30	.09
❑ 38	Mario Elie	.15	.04
❑ 39	Mookie Blaylock	.15	.04
❑ 40	Sam Cassell	.50	.15
❑ 41	Toni Kukoc	.30	.09
❑ 42	Anthony Mason	.30	.09
❑ 43	George Lynch	.15	.04
❑ 44	John Starks	.30	.09
❑ 45	Malik Rose	.15	.04
❑ 46	Rod Strickland	.15	.04
❑ 47	Tim Thomas	.30	.09
❑ 48	Howard Eisley	.15	.04
❑ 49	Kenny Anderson	.30	.09
❑ 50	Kurt Thomas	.30	.09
❑ 51	Lindsey Hunter	.15	.04
❑ 52	Rick Fox	.30	.09
❑ 53	Vlade Divac	.30	.09
❑ 54	Avery Johnson	.15	.04
❑ 55	Dale Ellis	.15	.04
❑ 56	Donyell Marshall	.30	.09
❑ 57	Elden Campbell	.15	.04
❑ 58	Larry Hughes	.50	.15
❑ 59	Mitch Richmond	.30	.09
❑ 60	Chris Mills	.15	.04
❑ 61	David Wesley	.15	.04
❑ 62	Gary Payton	.50	.15
❑ 63	Isaac Austin	.15	.04
❑ 64	Robert Traylor	.15	.04
❑ 65	Theo Ratliff	.30	.09
❑ 66	Antawn Jamison	.75	.23
❑ 67	Eddie Jones	.50	.15
❑ 68	Kevin Garnett	1.00	.30
❑ 69	Matt Geiger	.15	.04
❑ 70	Vernon Maxwell	.15	.04
❑ 71	Antonio Davis	.15	.04
❑ 72	Dirk Nowitzki	1.00	.30
❑ 73	Johnny Newman	.15	.04
❑ 74	Maurice Taylor	.30	.09
❑ 75	Steve Smith	.30	.09
❑ 76	Derek Anderson	.30	.09
❑ 77	Doug Christie	.30	.09
❑ 78	Erick Strickland	.15	.04
❑ 79	Keith Van Horn	.50	.15
❑ 80	Luc Longley	.15	.04
❑ 81	Alonzo Mourning	.30	.09
❑ 82	Christian Laettner	.30	.09
❑ 83	Jamal Mashburn	.30	.09
❑ 84	Jon Barry	.15	.04
❑ 85	Patrick Ewing	.50	.15
❑ 86	Shareef Abdur-Rahim	.50	.15
❑ 87	Vitaly Potapenko	.15	.04
❑ 88	Darrell Armstrong	.15	.04
❑ 89	Eric Williams	.15	.04
❑ 90	Jerome Williams	.15	.04
❑ 91	Nick Anderson	.15	.04
❑ 92	Othella Harrington	.15	.04
❑ 93	Tim Hardaway	.30	.09
❑ 94	Eric Piatkowski	.30	.09
❑ 95	Isaiah Rider	.15	.04
❑ 96	Kendall Gill	.15	.04
❑ 97	Rasheed Wallace	.50	.15
❑ 98	Robert Pack	.15	.04
❑ 99	Tracy McGrady	1.25	.35
❑ 100	Allan Houston	.30	.09
❑ 101	Brian Grant	.30	.09
❑ 102	Dikembe Mutombo	.30	.09
❑ 103	Karl Malone	.50	.15
❑ 104	Nick Van Exel	.50	.15
❑ 105	Shaquille O'Neal	1.25	.35
❑ 106	Chris Anstey	.15	.04
❑ 107	Michael Dickerson	.30	.09
❑ 108	Shandon Anderson	.15	.04
❑ 109	Tariq Adbul-Wahad	.15	.04
❑ 110	Tim Duncan	1.00	.30
❑ 111	Voshon Lenard	.15	.04
❑ 112	Bimbo Coles	.15	.04
❑ 113	Detlef Schrempf	.30	.09
❑ 114	John Stockton	.50	.15
❑ 115	Kobe Bryant	2.00	.60
❑ 116	Latrell Sprewell	.50	.15
❑ 117	Raef LaFrentz	.30	.09
❑ 118	Antoine Walker	.50	.15
❑ 119	Bryon Russell	.15	.04
❑ 120	Derek Fisher	.50	.15
❑ 121	Jason Williams	.50	.15
❑ 122	Jerry Stackhouse	.50	.15
❑ 123	Larry Johnson	.30	.09
❑ 124	Clifford Robinson	.15	.04
❑ 125	Horace Grant	.30	.09
❑ 126	Malik Sealy	.15	.04
❑ 127	Michael Finley	.50	.15
❑ 128	Rik Smits	.30	.09
❑ 129	Dell Curry	.15	.04
❑ 130	Jim Jackson	.15	.04
❑ 131	Ron Mercer	.30	.09
❑ 132	Scott Burrell	.15	.04
❑ 133	Scottie Pippen	.75	.23
❑ 134	Troy Hudson	.15	.04
❑ 135	Anfernee Hardaway	.50	.15
❑ 136	Anthony Peeler	.15	.04
❑ 137	Jalen Rose	.50	.15
❑ 138	Lamond Murray	.15	.04
❑ 139	Ruben Patterson	.30	.09
❑ 140	Chris Webber	.50	.15
❑ 141	Glen Rice	.30	.09
❑ 142	Grant Hill	.50	.15
❑ 143	Jeff Hornacek	.30	.09
❑ 144	Marcus Camby	.30	.09
❑ 145	Paul Pierce	.50	.15
❑ 146	Bob Sura	.15	.04
❑ 147	Jason Kidd	.75	.23
❑ 148	Reggie Miller	.50	.15
❑ 149	Terrell Brandon	.30	.09
❑ 150	Vin Baker	.30	.09
❑ 151	Lamar Odom RC	2.50	.75
❑ 152	Steve Francis RC	4.00	1.20
❑ 153	Elton Brand RC	3.00	.90
❑ 154	Wally Szczerbiak RC	2.50	.75
❑ 155	Adrian Griffin RC	.75	.23
❑ 156	Andre Miller RC	2.50	.75
❑ 157	Jason Terry RC	1.50	.45
❑ 158	Richard Hamilton RC	2.50	.75
❑ 159	Ron Artest RC	1.50	.45
❑ 160	Shawn Marion RC	3.00	.90
❑ 161	James Posey RC	1.50	.45
❑ 162	Greg Buckner RC	.50	.15
❑ 163	Chucky Atkins RC	1.00	.30
❑ 164	Corey Maggette RC	2.50	.75
❑ 165	Todd MacCulloch RC	.75	.23
❑ 166	Baron Davis RC	2.50	.75
❑ 167	Trajan Langdon RC	1.00	.30
❑ 168	Bruno Sundov RC	.50	.15
❑ 169	Scott Padgett RC	.75	.23
❑ 170	Vonteego Cummings RC	1.00	.30
❑ 171	Ryan Bowen RC	.50	.15
❑ 172	Jonathan Bender RC	2.50	.75
❑ 173	Jermaine Jackson RC	.50	.15
❑ 174	Devean George RC	1.25	.35
❑ 175	Chris Herren RC	.50	.15
❑ 176	Rodney Buford RC	.50	.15
❑ 177	Laron Profit RC	.75	.23
❑ 178	Mirsad Turkcan RC	.50	.15
❑ 179	Eddie Robinson RC	1.50	.45
❑ 180	Anthony Carter RC	1.50	.45

1997-98 Metal Universe

		Nm-Mt	Ex-Mt
COMPLETE SET (125)		25.00	7.50
❑ 1	Charles Barkley	1.00	.30
❑ 2	Dell Curry	.25	.07
❑ 3	Derek Fisher	.75	.23
❑ 4	Derek Harper	.50	.15
❑ 5	Avery Johnson	.25	.07
❑ 6	Steve Smith	.50	.15
❑ 7	Alonzo Mourning	.50	.15
❑ 8	Rod Strickland	.25	.07
❑ 9	Chris Mullin	.75	.23
❑ 10	Rony Seikaly	.25	.07
❑ 11	Vin Baker	.50	.15
❑ 12	Austin Croshere RC	.75	.23
❑ 13	Vinny Del Negro	.25	.07
❑ 14	Sherman Douglas	.25	.07
❑ 15	Priest Lauderdale	.25	.07
❑ 16	Cedric Ceballos	.25	.07
❑ 17	LaPhonso Ellis	.25	.07
❑ 18	Luc Longley	.25	.07
❑ 19	Brian Grant	.50	.15
❑ 20	Allen Iverson	2.00	.60
❑ 21	Anthony Mason	.50	.15
❑ 22	Bryant Reeves	.25	.07
❑ 23	Michael Jordan	5.00	1.50
❑ 24	Dale Ellis	.25	.07
❑ 25	Terrell Brandon	.50	.15
❑ 26	Patrick Ewing	.75	.23
❑ 27	Allan Houston	.50	.15
❑ 28	Damon Stoudamire	.50	.15
❑ 29	Loy Vaught	.25	.07
❑ 30	Walt Williams	.25	.07
❑ 31	Shareef Abdur-Rahim	1.25	.35
❑ 32	Mario Elie	.25	.07
❑ 33	Juwan Howard	.50	.15
❑ 34	Tom Gugliotta	.50	.15
❑ 35	Glen Rice	.50	.15
❑ 36	Isaiah Rider	.50	.15
❑ 37	Arvydas Sabonis	.50	.15
❑ 38	Derrick Coleman	.25	.07
❑ 39	Kevin Willis	.50	.15
❑ 40	Kendall Gill	.25	.07
❑ 41	John Wallace	.25	.07
❑ 42	Tracy McGrady RC	4.00	1.20
❑ 43	Travis Best	.25	.07
❑ 44	Malik Rose	.25	.07
❑ 45	Anfernee Hardaway	.75	.23
❑ 46	Roy Rogers	.25	.07
❑ 47	Kerry Kittles	.75	.23
❑ 48	Matt Maloney	.25	.07
❑ 49	Antonio McDyess	.50	.15
❑ 50	Shaquille O'Neal	2.00	.60
❑ 51	George McCloud	.25	.07
❑ 52	Wesley Person	.25	.07
❑ 53	Shawn Bradley	.25	.07
❑ 54	Antonio Davis	.25	.07
❑ 55	P.J. Brown	.25	.07
❑ 56	Joe Dumars	.75	.23
❑ 57	Horace Grant	.50	.15
❑ 58	Steve Kerr	.50	.15
❑ 59	Hakeem Olajuwon	.75	.23
❑ 60	Tim Hardaway	.50	.15
❑ 61	Toni Kukoc	.50	.15
❑ 62	Ron Mercer RC	1.00	.30
❑ 63	Gary Payton	.75	.23
❑ 64	Grant Hill	.75	.23
❑ 65	Detlef Schrempf	.50	.15
❑ 66	Tim Duncan RC	3.00	.90
❑ 67	Shawn Kemp	.50	.15
❑ 68	Voshon Lenard	.25	.07
❑ 69	Othella Harrington	.25	.07
❑ 70	Hersey Hawkins	.25	.07
❑ 71	Lindsey Hunter	.25	.07
❑ 72	Antoine Walker	1.00	.30
❑ 73	Jamal Mashburn	.50	.15
❑ 74	Kenny Anderson	.50	.15
❑ 75	Todd Day	.25	.07
❑ 76	Todd Fuller	.25	.07
❑ 77	Jermaine O'Neal	1.25	.35
❑ 78	David Robinson	.75	.23
❑ 79	Erick Dampier	.50	.15
❑ 80	Keith Van Horn RC	1.25	.35
❑ 81	Kobe Bryant	3.00	.90
❑ 82	Chris Childs	.25	.07
❑ 83	Scottie Pippen	1.25	.35
❑ 84	Marcus Camby	.75	.23
❑ 85	Danny Ferry	.25	.07
❑ 86	Jeff Hornacek	.50	.15
❑ 87	Bo Outlaw	.25	.07
❑ 88	Larry Johnson	.50	.15
❑ 89	Tony Delk	.25	.07

Card	Nm-Mt	Ex-Mt
❑ 90 Stephon Marbury	1.00	.30
❑ 91 Robert Pack	.25	.07
❑ 92 Chris Webber	.75	.23
❑ 93 Clyde Drexler	.75	.23
❑ 94 Eddie Jones	.75	.23
❑ 95 Jerry Stackhouse	.75	.23
❑ 96 Tyrone Hill	.25	.07
❑ 97 Karl Malone	.75	.23
❑ 98 Reggie Miller	.75	.23
❑ 99 Bryon Russell	.25	.07
❑ 100 Dale Davis	.25	.07
❑ 101 Steve Nash	.75	.23
❑ 102 Vitaly Potapenko	.25	.07
❑ 103 Nick Anderson	.25	.07
❑ 104 Ray Allen	.75	.23
❑ 105 Sean Elliott	.50	.15
❑ 106 Dikembe Mutombo	.50	.15
❑ 107 Dennis Rodman	.50	.15
❑ 108 Lorenzen Wright	.25	.07
❑ 109 Kevin Garnett	1.50	.45
❑ 110 Christian Laettner	.50	.15
❑ 111 Mitch Richmond	.50	.15
❑ 112 Joe Smith	.50	.15
❑ 113 Jason Kidd	1.25	.35
❑ 114 Glenn Robinson	.75	.23
❑ 115 Mark Price	.50	.15
❑ 116 Mark Jackson	.50	.15
❑ 117 Bobby Phills	.25	.07
❑ 118 John Starks	.50	.15
❑ 119 John Stockton	.75	.23
❑ 120 Mookie Blaylock	.25	.07
❑ 121 Dean Garrett	.25	.07
❑ 122 Olden Polynice	.25	.07
❑ 123 Latrell Sprewell	.75	.23
❑ 124 Checklist	.25	.07
❑ 125 Checklist	.25	.07

1998-99 Metal Universe

	Nm-Mt	Ex-Mt
COMPLETE SET (125)	25.00	7.50
❑ 1 Michael Jordan	5.00	1.50
❑ 2 Mario Elie	.25	.07
❑ 3 Voshon Lenard	.25	.07
❑ 4 John Starks	.50	.15
❑ 5 Juwan Howard	.50	.15
❑ 6 Michael Finley	.75	.23
❑ 7 Bobby Jackson	.50	.15
❑ 8 Glenn Robinson	.50	.15
❑ 9 Antonio McDyess	.50	.15
❑ 10 Marcus Camby	.50	.15
❑ 11 Zydrunas Ilgauskas	.50	.15
❑ 12 LaPhonso Ellis	.25	.07
❑ 13 Terrell Brandon	.50	.15
❑ 14 Rex Chapman	.25	.07
❑ 15 Rod Strickland	.25	.07
❑ 16 Dennis Rodman	.50	.15
❑ 17 Clarence Weatherspoon	.25	.07
❑ 18 P.J. Brown	.25	.07
❑ 19 Anfernee Hardaway	.75	.23
❑ 20 Dikembe Mutombo	.50	.15
❑ 21 Gary Trent	.25	.07
❑ 22 Patrick Ewing	.75	.23
❑ 23 Sam Mack	.25	.07
❑ 24 Scottie Pippen	1.25	.35
❑ 25 Shaquille O'Neal	2.00	.60
❑ 26 Donyell Marshall	.50	.15
❑ 27 Bo Outlaw	.25	.07
❑ 28 Isaiah Rider	.25	.07
❑ 29 Detlef Schrempf	.50	.15
❑ 30 Mark Price	.50	.15
❑ 31 Jim Jackson	.25	.07
❑ 32 Eddie Jones	.75	.23
❑ 33 Allen Iverson	1.50	.45
❑ 34 Corliss Williamson	.50	.15
❑ 35 Tim Duncan	1.25	.35
❑ 36 Ron Harper	.50	.15
❑ 37 Tony Delk	.25	.07
❑ 38 Derek Fisher	.75	.23
❑ 39 Kendall Gill	.25	.07
❑ 40 Theo Ratliff	.50	.15
❑ 41 Kelvin Cato	.25	.07
❑ 42 Antoine Walker	.75	.23
❑ 43 Lamond Murray	.25	.07
❑ 44 Avery Johnson	.25	.07
❑ 45 John Stockton	.75	.23
❑ 46 David Wesley	.25	.07
❑ 47 Brian Williams	.25	.07
❑ 48 Elden Campbell	.25	.07
❑ 49 Sam Cassell	.75	.23
❑ 50 Grant Hill	.75	.23
❑ 51 Tracy McGrady	2.00	.60
❑ 52 Glen Rice	.50	.15
❑ 53 Kobe Bryant	3.00	.90
❑ 54 Cherokee Parks	.25	.07
❑ 55 John Wallace	.25	.07
❑ 56 Bobby Phills	.25	.07
❑ 57 Jerry Stackhouse	.75	.23
❑ 58 Lorenzen Wright	.25	.07
❑ 59 Stephon Marbury	.75	.23
❑ 60 Shandon Anderson	.25	.07
❑ 61 Jeff Hornacek	.50	.15
❑ 62 Joe Dumars	.75	.23
❑ 63 Tom Gugliotta	.25	.07
❑ 64 Johnny Newman	.25	.07
❑ 65 Kevin Garnett	1.50	.45
❑ 66 Clifford Robinson	.25	.07
❑ 67 Dennis Scott	.25	.07
❑ 68 Anthony Mason	.50	.15
❑ 69 Rodney Rogers	.25	.07
❑ 70 Bryon Russell	.25	.07
❑ 71 Maurice Taylor	.50	.15
❑ 72 Mookie Blaylock	.25	.07
❑ 73 Shawn Bradley	.25	.07
❑ 74 Matt Maloney	.25	.07
❑ 75 Karl Malone	.75	.23
❑ 76 Larry Johnson	.50	.15
❑ 77 Calbert Cheaney	.25	.07
❑ 78 Steve Smith	.50	.15
❑ 79 Toni Kukoc	.50	.15
❑ 80 Reggie Miller	.75	.23
❑ 81 Jayson Williams	.25	.07
❑ 82 Gary Payton	.75	.23
❑ 83 George Lynch	.25	.07
❑ 84 Wesley Person	.25	.07
❑ 85 Charles Barkley	1.00	.30
❑ 86 Tim Hardaway	.50	.15
❑ 87 Darrell Armstrong	.25	.07
❑ 88 Rasheed Wallace	.75	.23
❑ 89 Tariq Abdul-Wahad	.25	.07
❑ 90 Kenny Anderson	.50	.15
❑ 91 Chris Mullin	.75	.23
❑ 92 Keith Van Horn	.75	.23
❑ 93 Hersey Hawkins	.25	.07
❑ 94 Billy Owens	.25	.07
❑ 95 Ron Mercer	.50	.15
❑ 96 Rik Smits	.50	.15
❑ 97 David Robinson	.75	.23
❑ 98 Derek Anderson	.75	.23
❑ 99 Danny Fortson	.25	.07
❑ 100 Jason Kidd	1.25	.35
❑ 101 Sean Elliott	.50	.15
❑ 102 Chauncey Billups	.50	.15
❑ 103 Tyrone Hill	.25	.07
❑ 104 Alan Henderson	.25	.07
❑ 105 Chris Anstey	.25	.07
❑ 106 Hakeem Olajuwon	.75	.23
❑ 107 Allan Houston	.50	.15
❑ 108 Bryant Reeves	.25	.07
❑ 109 Anthony Johnson	.25	.07
❑ 110 Shawn Kemp	.50	.15
❑ 111 Brevin Knight	.25	.07
❑ 112 A.C. Green	.50	.15
❑ 113 Ray Allen	.75	.23
❑ 114 Tim Thomas	.50	.15
❑ 115 Walter McCarty	.25	.07
❑ 116 Jalen Rose	.75	.23
❑ 117 Kerry Kittles	.25	.07
❑ 118 Vin Baker	.50	.15
❑ 119 Shareef Abdur-Rahim	.75	.23
❑ 120 Alonzo Mourning	.50	.15
❑ 121 Joe Smith	.50	.15
❑ 122 Tracy Murray	.25	.07
❑ 123 Damon Stoudamire	.50	.15
❑ 124 Checklist	.25	.07
❑ 125 Checklist	.25	.07
❑ NNO Grant Hill SAMPLE	1.50	.45

1990-91 SkyBox

	Nm-Mt	Ex-Mt
COMPLETE SET (423)	20.00	6.00
COMPLETE SERIES 1 (300)	12.00	3.60
COMPLETE SERIES 2 (123)	8.00	2.40
COMMON CARD (1-300)	.05	.02
COMMON CARD (301-423)	.10	.03
COMMON SP	.10	.03
❑ 1 John Battle	.05	.02
❑ 2 Duane Ferrell SP RC	.10	.03
❑ 3 Jon Koncak	.05	.02
❑ 4 Cliff Levingston SP	.10	.03
❑ 5 John Long SP	.10	.03
❑ 6 Moses Malone	.25	.07
❑ 7 Doc Rivers	.10	.03
❑ 8 Kenny Smith SP	.10	.03
❑ 9 Alexander Volkov	.05	.02
❑ 10 Spud Webb	.10	.03
❑ 11 Dominique Wilkins	.25	.07
❑ 12 Kevin Willis	.10	.03
❑ 13 John Bagley	.05	.02
❑ 14 Larry Bird	1.00	.30
❑ 15 Kevin Gamble	.05	.02
❑ 16 Dennis Johnson SP	.05	.02
❑ 17 Joe Kleine	.05	.02
❑ 18 Reggie Lewis	.10	.03
❑ 19 Kevin McHale	.10	.03
❑ 20 Robert Parish	.10	.03
❑ 21 Jim Paxson SP	.10	.03
❑ 22 Ed Pinckney	.05	.02
❑ 23 Brian Shaw	.25	.07
❑ 24 Michael Smith	.05	.02
❑ 25 Richard Anderson SP	.10	.03
❑ 26 Muggsy Bogues	.10	.03
❑ 27 Rex Chapman	.25	.07
❑ 28 Dell Curry	.05	.02
❑ 29 Armon Gilliam	.05	.02
❑ 30 Michael Holton SP	.10	.03
❑ 31 Dave Hoppen	.05	.02
❑ 32 J.R. Reid RC	.05	.02
❑ 33 Robert Reid SP	.10	.03
❑ 34 Brian Rowsom SP	.10	.03
❑ 35 Kelly Tripucka	.05	.02
❑ 36 Micheal Williams SP UER (Misspelled Michael on card)	.10	.03
❑ 37 B.J. Armstrong RC	.05	.02
❑ 38 Bill Cartwright	.05	.02
❑ 39 Horace Grant	.10	.03
❑ 40 Craig Hodges	.05	.02
❑ 41 Michael Jordan	3.00	.90
❑ 42 Stacey King RC	.05	.02
❑ 43 Ed Nealy SP	.10	.03
❑ 44 John Paxson	.10	.03
❑ 45 Will Perdue	.05	.02

❑ 46 Scottie Pippen 1.00 .30
❑ 47 Jeff Sanders SP RC .10 .03
❑ 48 Winston Bennett .05 .02
❑ 49 Chucky Brown RC .05 .02
❑ 50 Brad Daugherty .05 .02
❑ 51 Craig Ehlo .05 .02
❑ 52 Steve Kerr .25 .07
❑ 53 Paul Mokeski SP .10 .03
❑ 54 John Morton .05 .02
❑ 55 Larry Nance .05 .02
❑ 56 Mark Price .10 .03
❑ 57 Tree Rollins SP .10 .03
❑ 58 Hot Rod Williams .05 .02
❑ 59 Steve Alford .05 .02
❑ 60 Rolando Blackman .05 .02
❑ 61 Adrian Dantley SP .05 .02
❑ 62 Brad Davis .05 .02
❑ 63 James Donaldson .05 .02
❑ 64 Derek Harper .10 .03
❑ 65 Anthony Jones SP .10 .03
❑ 66 Sam Perkins SP .10 .03
❑ 67 Roy Tarpley .05 .02
❑ 68 Bill Wennington SP .10 .03
❑ 69 Randy White RC .05 .02
❑ 70 Herb Williams .05 .02
❑ 71 Michael Adams .05 .02
❑ 72 Joe Barry Carroll SP .10 .03
❑ 73 Walter Davis .05 .02
❑ 74 Alex English SP .05 .02
❑ 75 Bill Hanzlik .05 .02
❑ 76 Tim Kempton SP .05 .02
❑ 77 Jerome Lane .05 .02
❑ 78 Lafayette Lever SP .10 .03
❑ 79 Todd Lichti RC .05 .02
❑ 80 Blair Rasmussen .05 .02
❑ 81 Danny Schayes SP .10 .03
❑ 82 Mark Aguirre .05 .02
❑ 83 William Bedford RC .05 .02
❑ 84 Joe Dumars .25 .07
❑ 85 James Edwards .05 .02
❑ 86 David Greenwood SP .10 .03
❑ 87 Scott Hastings .05 .02
❑ 88 Gerald Henderson SP .10 .03
❑ 89 Vinnie Johnson .05 .02
❑ 90 Bill Laimbeer .10 .03
❑ 91 Dennis Rodman .60 .18
(SkyBox logo in upper right or left)
❑ 91B Dennis Rodman 1.00 .30
(SkyBox logo in upper left corner)
❑ 92 John Salley .05 .02
❑ 93 Isiah Thomas .25 .07
❑ 94 Manute Bol SP .10 .03
❑ 95 Tim Hardaway RC 1.50 .45
❑ 96 Rod Higgins .05 .02
❑ 97 Sarunas Marciulionis RC .05 .02
❑ 98 Chris Mullin .25 .07
❑ 99 Jim Petersen .05 .02
❑ 100 Mitch Richmond .30 .09
❑ 101 Mike Smrek .05 .02
❑ 102 Terry Teagle SP .10 .03
❑ 103 Tom Tolbert RC .05 .02
❑ 104 Kelvin Upshaw SP .10 .03
❑ 105 Anthony Bowie SP RC .10 .03
❑ 106 Adrian Caldwell .05 .02
❑ 107 Eric(Sleepy) Floyd .05 .02
❑ 108 Buck Johnson .05 .02
❑ 109 Vernon Maxwell .05 .02
❑ 110 Hakeem Olajuwon .40 .12
❑ 111 Larry Smith .05 .02
❑ 112A Otis Thorpe ERR 1.50 .45
(Front photo actually Mitchell Wiggins)
❑ 112B Otis Thorpe COR .10 .03
❑ 113A M. Wiggins SP ERR 1.50 .45
(Front photo actually Otis Thorpe)
❑ 113B M. Wiggins SP COR .10 .03
❑ 114 Vern Fleming .05 .02
❑ 115 Rickey Green SP .10 .03
❑ 116 George McCloud RC .25 .07
❑ 117 Reggie Miller .30 .09
❑ 118A Dyron Nix SP ERR 1.50 .45
(Back photo actually Wayman Tisdale)
❑ 118B Dyron Nix SP COR .10 .03
❑ 119 Chuck Person .10 .03
❑ 120 Mike Sanders .05 .02
❑ 121 Detlef Schrempf .10 .03
❑ 122 Rik Smits .25 .07
❑ 123 LaSalle Thompson .05 .02
❑ 124 Benoit Benjamin .05 .02
❑ 125 Winston Garland .05 .02
❑ 126 Tom Garrick .05 .02
❑ 127 Gary Grant .05 .02
❑ 128 Ron Harper .10 .03
❑ 129 Danny Manning .10 .03
❑ 130 Jeff Martin .05 .02
❑ 131 Ken Norman .05 .02
❑ 132 Charles Smith .05 .02
❑ 133 Joe Wolf SP .10 .03
❑ 134 Michael Cooper SP .10 .03
❑ 135 Vlade Divac RC .60 .18
❑ 136 Larry Drew .05 .02
❑ 137 A.C. Green .10 .03
❑ 138 Magic Johnson .75 .23
❑ 139 Mark McNamara SP .10 .03
❑ 140 Byron Scott .10 .03
❑ 141 Mychal Thompson .05 .02
❑ 142 Orlando Woolridge SP .10 .03
❑ 143 James Worthy .25 .07
❑ 144 Terry Davis RC .05 .02
❑ 145 Sherman Douglas RC .10 .03
❑ 146 Kevin Edwards .05 .02
❑ 147 Tellis Frank SP .10 .03
❑ 148 Scott Haffner SP .10 .03
❑ 149 Grant Long .05 .02
❑ 150 Glen Rice RC 1.00 .30
❑ 151 Rony Seikaly .10 .03
❑ 152 Rory Sparrow SP .10 .03
❑ 153 Jon Sundvold .05 .02
❑ 154 Billy Thompson .05 .02
❑ 155 Greg Anderson .05 .02
❑ 156 Ben Coleman SP .10 .03
❑ 157 Jeff Grayer RC .05 .02
❑ 158 Jay Humphries .05 .02
❑ 159 Frank Kornet .05 .02
❑ 160 Larry Krystkowiak .05 .02
❑ 161 Brad Lohaus .05 .02
❑ 162 Ricky Pierce .05 .02
❑ 163 Paul Pressey SP .10 .03
❑ 164 Fred Roberts .05 .02
❑ 165 Alvin Robertson .05 .02
❑ 166 Jack Sikma .05 .02
❑ 167 Randy Breuer .05 .02
❑ 168 Tony Campbell .05 .02
❑ 169 Tyrone Corbin .05 .02
❑ 170 Sidney Lowe SP .10 .03
❑ 171 Sam Mitchell RC .05 .02
❑ 172 Tod Murphy .05 .02
❑ 173 Pooh Richardson RC .10 .03
❑ 174 Donald Royal SP RC .10 .03
❑ 175 Brad Sellers SP .10 .03
❑ 176 Mookie Blaylock RC .40 .12
❑ 177 Sam Bowie .05 .02
❑ 178 Lester Conner .05 .02
❑ 179 Derrick Gervin .05 .02
❑ 180 Jack Haley RC .05 .02
❑ 181 Roy Hinson .05 .02
❑ 182 Dennis Hopson SP .10 .03
❑ 183 Chris Morris .10 .03
❑ 184 Pete Myers SP RC .10 .03
❑ 185 Purvis Short SP .10 .03
❑ 186 Maurice Cheeks .05 .02
❑ 187 Patrick Ewing .25 .07
❑ 188 Stuart Gray .05 .02
❑ 189 Mark Jackson .10 .03
❑ 190 Johnny Newman SP .10 .03
❑ 191 Charles Oakley .10 .03
❑ 192 Brian Quinnett .05 .02
❑ 193 Trent Tucker .05 .02
❑ 194 Kiki Vandeweghe .05 .02
❑ 195 Kenny Walker .05 .02
❑ 196 Eddie Lee Wilkins .05 .02
❑ 197 Gerald Wilkins .05 .02
❑ 198 Mark Acres .05 .02
❑ 199 Nick Anderson RC .40 .12
❑ 200 Michael Ansley .05 .02
❑ 201 Terry Catledge .05 .02
❑ 202 Dave Corzine SP .10 .03
❑ 203 Sidney Green SP .10 .03
❑ 204 Jerry Reynolds .05 .02
❑ 205 Scott Skiles .05 .02
❑ 206 Otis Smith .05 .02
❑ 207 Reggie Theus SP .10 .03
❑ 208 Jeff Turner .05 .02
❑ 209 Sam Vincent .05 .02
❑ 210 Ron Anderson .05 .02
❑ 211 Charles Barkley .40 .12
❑ 212 Scott Brooks SP .10 .03
❑ 213 Lanard Copeland SP .10 .03
❑ 214 Johnny Dawkins .05 .02
❑ 215 Mike Gminski .05 .02
❑ 216 Hersey Hawkins .10 .03
❑ 217 Rick Mahorn .05 .02
❑ 218 Derek Smith SP .10 .03
❑ 219 Bob Thornton .05 .02
❑ 220 Tom Chambers .05 .02
❑ 221 Greg Grant SP RC .10 .03
❑ 222 Jeff Hornacek .10 .03
❑ 223 Eddie Johnson .10 .03
❑ 224A Kevin Johnson .25 .07
(SkyBox logo in lower right corner)
❑ 224B Kevin Johnson .25 .07
(SkyBox logo in upper right corner)
❑ 225 Andrew Lang RC .25 .07
❑ 226 Dan Majerle .25 .07
❑ 227 Mike McGee SP .10 .03
❑ 228 Tim Perry .05 .02
❑ 229 Kurt Rambis .05 .02
❑ 230 Mark West .05 .02
❑ 231 Mark Bryant .05 .02
❑ 232 Wayne Cooper .05 .02
❑ 233 Clyde Drexler .25 .07
❑ 234 Kevin Duckworth .05 .02
❑ 235 Byron Irvin SP .10 .03
❑ 236 Jerome Kersey .05 .02
❑ 237 Drazen Petrovic RC .30 .09
❑ 238 Terry Porter .05 .02
❑ 239 Clifford Robinson RC .40 .12
❑ 240 Buck Williams .05 .02
❑ 241 Danny Young .05 .02
❑ 242 Danny Ainge SP .10 .03
❑ 243 Randy Allen SP .10 .03
❑ 244A Antoine Carr SP .15 .04
(Wearing Atlanta jersey on back)
❑ 244B Antoine Carr .05 .02
(Wearing Sacramento jersey on back)
❑ 245 Vinny Del Negro SP .10 .03
❑ 246 Pervis Ellison SP RC .10 .03
❑ 247 Greg Kite SP .10 .03
❑ 248 Rodney McCray SP .10 .03
❑ 249 Harold Pressley SP .10 .03
❑ 250 Ralph Sampson .05 .02
❑ 251 Wayman Tisdale .05 .02
❑ 252 Willie Anderson .05 .02
❑ 253 Uwe Blab SP .10 .03
❑ 254 Frank Brickowski SP .10 .03
❑ 255 Terry Cummings .05 .02
❑ 256 Sean Elliott RC .50 .15
❑ 257 Caldwell Jones SP .10 .03
❑ 258 Johnny Moore SP .10 .03
❑ 259 Zarko Paspalj SP .10 .03
❑ 260 David Robinson .75 .23
❑ 261 Rod Strickland .25 .07
❑ 262 David Wingate SP .10 .03
❑ 263 Dana Barros RC .25 .07
❑ 264 Michael Cage .05 .02
❑ 265 Quintin Dailey .05 .02
❑ 266 Dale Ellis .10 .03
❑ 267 Steve Johnson SP .10 .03
❑ 268 Shawn Kemp RC 2.50 .75
❑ 269 Xavier McDaniel .05 .02
❑ 270 Derrick McKey .05 .02
❑ 271A Nate McMillan SP ERR .20 .06
(Back photo actually Olden Polynice; first series)
❑ 271B Nate McMillan COR .10 .03
(second series)
❑ 272 Olden Polynice .05 .02
❑ 273 Sedale Threatt .05 .02
❑ 274 Thurl Bailey .05 .02

Card		
☐ 275 Mike Brown	.05	.02
☐ 276 Mark Eaton	.05	.02
☐ 277 Blue Edwards RC	.05	.02
☐ 278 Darrell Griffith	.05	.02
☐ 279 Bobby Hansen SP	.10	.03
☐ 280 Eric Johnson	.05	.02
☐ 281 Eric Leckner SP	.10	.03
☐ 282 Karl Malone	.40	.12
☐ 283 Delaney Rudd	.05	.02
☐ 284 John Stockton	.30	.09
☐ 285 Mark Alarie	.05	.02
☐ 286 Steve Colter SP	.10	.03
☐ 287 Ledell Eackles SP	.10	.03
☐ 288 Harvey Grant	.05	.02
☐ 289 Tom Hammonds RC	.05	.02
☐ 290 Charles Jones	.05	.02
☐ 291 Bernard King	.05	.02
☐ 292 Jeff Malone SP	.10	.03
☐ 293 Darrell Walker	.05	.02
☐ 294 John Williams	.05	.02
☐ 295 Checklist 1 SP	.10	.03
☐ 296 Checklist 2 SP	.10	.03
☐ 297 Checklist 3 SP	.10	.03
☐ 298 Checklist 4 SP	.10	.03
☐ 299 Checklist 5 SP	.10	.03
☐ 300 Danny Ferry SP RC	.50	.15
☐ 301 Bob Weiss CO	.10	.03
☐ 302 Chris Ford CO	.10	.03
☐ 303 Gene Littles CO	.10	.03
☐ 304 Phil Jackson CO	.30	.09
☐ 305 Lenny Wilkens CO	.30	.09
☐ 306 Richie Adubato CO	.10	.03
☐ 307 Paul Westhead CO	.10	.03
☐ 308 Chuck Daly CO	.30	.09
☐ 309 Don Nelson CO	.30	.09
☐ 310 Don Chaney CO	.10	.03
☐ 311 Dick Versace CO	.10	.03
☐ 312 Mike Schuler CO	.10	.03
☐ 313 Mike Dunleavy CO	.10	.03
☐ 314 Ron Rothstein CO	.10	.03
☐ 315 Del Harris CO	.10	.03
☐ 316 Bill Musselman CO	.10	.03
☐ 317 Bill Fitch CO	.10	.03
☐ 318 Stu Jackson CO	.10	.03
☐ 319 Matt Guokas CO	.10	.03
☐ 320 Jim Lynam CO	.10	.03
☐ 321 Cotton Fitzsimmons CO	.10	.03
☐ 322 Rick Adelman CO	.10	.03
☐ 323 Dick Motta CO	.10	.03
☐ 324 Larry Brown CO	.10	.03
☐ 325 K.C. Jones CO	.30	.09
☐ 326 Jerry Sloan CO	.30	.09
☐ 327 Wes Unseld CO	.10	.03
☐ 328 Atlanta Hawks TC	.10	.03
☐ 329 Boston Celtics TC	.10	.03
☐ 330 Charlotte Hornets TC	.10	.03
☐ 331 Chicago Bulls TC	.30	.09
☐ 332 Cleveland Cavaliers TC	.10	.03
☐ 333 Dallas Mavericks TC	.10	.03
☐ 334 Denver Nuggets TC	.10	.03
☐ 335 Detroit Pistons TC	.10	.03
☐ 336 Golden State Warriors TC	.10	.03
☐ 337 Houston Rockets TC	.10	.03
☐ 338 Indiana Pacers TC	.10	.03
☐ 339 Los Angeles Clippers TC	.10	.03
☐ 340 Los Angeles Lakers TC	.10	.03
☐ 341 Miami Heat TC	.10	.03
☐ 342 Milwaukee Bucks TC	.10	.03
☐ 343 Minn. Timberwolves TC	.10	.03
☐ 344 New Jersey Nets TC	.10	.03
☐ 345 New York Knicks TC	.10	.03
☐ 346 Orlando Magic TC	.10	.03
☐ 347 Philadelphia 76ers TC	.10	.03
☐ 348 Phoenix Suns TC	.10	.03
☐ 349 Portland Trail Blazers TC	.10	.03
☐ 350 Sacramento Kings TC	.10	.03
☐ 351 San Antonio Spurs TC	.10	.03
☐ 352 Seattle SuperSonics TC	.10	.03
☐ 353 Utah Jazz TC	.10	.03
☐ 354 Washington Bullets TC	.10	.03
☐ 355 Rumeal Robinson RC	.10	.03
☐ 356 Kendall Gill RC	1.25	.35
☐ 357 Chris Jackson RC	.60	.18
☐ 358 Tyrone Hill RC	.50	.15
☐ 359 Bo Kimble RC	.10	.03
☐ 360 Willie Burton RC	.10	.03
☐ 361 Felton Spencer RC	.30	.09
☐ 362 Derrick Coleman RC	1.25	.35
☐ 363 Dennis Scott RC	.75	.23
☐ 364 Lionel Simmons RC	.30	.09
☐ 365 Gary Payton RC	5.00	1.50
☐ 366 Tim McCormick	.10	.03
☐ 367 Sidney Moncrief	.10	.03
☐ 368 Kenny Gattison RC	.10	.03
☐ 369 Randolph Keys	.10	.03
☐ 370 Johnny Newman	.10	.03
☐ 371 Dennis Hopson	.10	.03
☐ 372 Cliff Levingston	.10	.03
☐ 373 Derrick Chievous	.10	.03
☐ 374 Danny Ferry	.30	.09
☐ 375 Alex English	.10	.03
☐ 376 Lafayette Lever	.10	.03
☐ 377 Rodney McCray	.10	.03
☐ 378 T.R. Dunn	.10	.03
☐ 379 Corey Gaines	.10	.03
☐ 380 Avery Johnson RC	.75	.23
☐ 381 Joe Wolf	.10	.03
☐ 382 Orlando Woolridge	.10	.03
☐ 383 Tree Rollins	.10	.03
☐ 384 Steve Johnson	.10	.03
☐ 385 Kenny Smith	.10	.03
☐ 386 Mike Woodson	.10	.03
☐ 387 Greg Dreiling RC	.10	.03
☐ 388 Micheal Williams	.30	.09
☐ 389 Randy Wittman	.10	.03
☐ 390 Ken Bannister	.10	.03
☐ 391 Sam Perkins	.30	.09
☐ 392 Terry Teagle	.10	.03
☐ 393 Milt Wagner	.10	.03
☐ 394 Frank Brickowski	.10	.03
☐ 395 Danny Schayes	.10	.03
☐ 396 Scott Brooks	.10	.03
☐ 397 Doug West RC	.30	.09
☐ 398 Chris Dudley RC	.10	.03
☐ 399 Reggie Theus	.30	.09
☐ 400 Greg Grant	.10	.03
☐ 401 Greg Kite	.10	.03
☐ 402 Mark McNamara	.10	.03
☐ 403 Manute Bol	.10	.03
☐ 404 Rickey Green	.10	.03
☐ 405 Kenny Battle RC	.10	.03
☐ 406 Ed Nealy	.10	.03
☐ 407 Danny Ainge	.30	.09
☐ 408 Steve Colter	.10	.03
☐ 409 Bobby Hansen	.10	.03
☐ 410 Eric Leckner	.10	.03
☐ 411 Rory Sparrow	.10	.03
☐ 412 Bill Wennington	.10	.03
☐ 413 Sidney Green	.10	.03
☐ 414 David Greenwood	.10	.03
☐ 415 Paul Pressey	.10	.03
☐ 416 Reggie Williams	.10	.03
☐ 417 Dave Corzine	.10	.03
☐ 418 Jeff Malone	.10	.03
☐ 419 Pervis Ellison	.10	.03
☐ 420 Byron Irvin	.10	.03
☐ 421 Checklist 1	.10	.03
☐ 422 Checklist 2	.10	.03
☐ 423 Checklist 3	.10	.03
☐ NNO SkyBox Salutes the NBA	5.00	1.50

1991-92 SkyBox

	Nm-Mt	Ex-Mt
COMPLETE SET (659)	60.00	18.00
COMPLETE SERIES 1 (350)	20.00	6.00
COMPLETE SERIES 2 (309)	40.00	12.00
☐ 1 John Battle	.05	.02
☐ 2 Duane Ferrell	.05	.02
☐ 3 Jon Koncak	.05	.02
☐ 4 Moses Malone	.40	.12
☐ 5 Tim McCormick	.05	.02
☐ 6 Sidney Moncrief	.05	.02
☐ 7 Doc Rivers	.20	.06
☐ 8 Rumeal Robinson UER (Drafted 11th & should say 10th)	.05	.02
☐ 9 Spud Webb	.20	.06
☐ 10 Dominique Wilkins	.40	.12
☐ 11 Kevin Willis	.05	.02
☐ 12 Larry Bird	1.50	.45
☐ 13 Dee Brown	.05	.02
☐ 14 Kevin Gamble	.05	.02
☐ 15 Joe Kleine	.05	.02
☐ 16 Reggie Lewis	.20	.06
☐ 17 Kevin McHale	.20	.06
☐ 18 Robert Parish	.20	.06
☐ 19 Ed Pinckney	.05	.02
☐ 20 Brian Shaw	.05	.02
☐ 21 Michael Smith	.05	.02
☐ 22 Stojko Vrankovic	.05	.02
☐ 23 Muggsy Bogues	.20	.06
☐ 24 Rex Chapman	.20	.06
☐ 25 Dell Curry	.05	.02
☐ 26 Kenny Gattison	.05	.02
☐ 27 Kendall Gill	.20	.06
☐ 28 Mike Gminski	.05	.02
☐ 29 Randolph Keys	.05	.02
☐ 30 Eric Leckner	.05	.02
☐ 31 Johnny Newman	.05	.02
☐ 32 J.R. Reid	.05	.02
☐ 33 Kelly Tripucka	.05	.02
☐ 34 B.J. Armstrong	.05	.02
☐ 35 Bill Cartwright	.05	.02
☐ 36 Horace Grant	.20	.06
☐ 37 Craig Hodges	.05	.02
☐ 38 Dennis Hopson	.05	.02
☐ 39 Michael Jordan	5.00	1.50
☐ 40 Stacey King	.05	.02
☐ 41 Cliff Levingston	.05	.02
☐ 42 John Paxson	.05	.02
☐ 43 Will Perdue	.05	.02
☐ 44 Scottie Pippen	1.25	.35
☐ 45 Winston Bennett	.05	.02
☐ 46 Chucky Brown	.05	.02
☐ 47 Brad Daugherty	.05	.02
☐ 48 Craig Ehlo	.05	.02
☐ 49 Danny Ferry	.05	.02
☐ 50 Steve Kerr	.20	.06
☐ 51 John Morton	.05	.02
☐ 52 Larry Nance	.20	.06
☐ 53 Mark Price	.05	.02
☐ 54 Darnell Valentine	.05	.02
☐ 55 John Williams	.05	.02
☐ 56 Steve Alford	.05	.02
☐ 57 Rolando Blackman	.05	.02
☐ 58 Brad Davis	.05	.02
☐ 59 James Donaldson	.05	.02
☐ 60 Derek Harper	.20	.06
☐ 61 Fat Lever	.05	.02
☐ 62 Rodney McCray	.05	.02
☐ 63 Roy Tarpley	.05	.02
☐ 64 Kelvin Upshaw	.05	.02
☐ 65 Randy White	.05	.02
☐ 66 Herb Williams	.05	.02
☐ 67 Michael Adams	.05	.02
☐ 68 Greg Anderson	.05	.02
☐ 69 Anthony Cook	.05	.02
☐ 70 Chris Jackson	.05	.02
☐ 71 Jerome Lane	.05	.02
☐ 72 Marcus Liberty	.05	.02
☐ 73 Todd Lichti	.05	.02
☐ 74 Blair Rasmussen	.05	.02
☐ 75 Reggie Williams	.05	.02
☐ 76 Joe Wolf	.05	.02
☐ 77 Orlando Woolridge	.05	.02
☐ 78 Mark Aguirre	.05	.02
☐ 79 William Bedford	.05	.02

❑ 80 Lance Blanks .05 .02
❑ 81 Joe Dumars .40 .12
❑ 82 James Edwards .05 .02
❑ 83 Scott Hastings .05 .02
❑ 84 Vinnie Johnson .05 .02
❑ 85 Bill Laimbeer .20 .06
❑ 86 Dennis Rodman .75 .23
❑ 87 John Salley .05 .02
❑ 88 Isiah Thomas .40 .12
❑ 89 Mario Elie RC .40 .12
❑ 90 Tim Hardaway .60 .18
❑ 91 Rod Higgins .05 .02
❑ 92 Tyrone Hill .20 .06
❑ 93 Les Jepsen .05 .02
❑ 94 Alton Lister .05 .02
❑ 95 Sarunas Marciulionis .05 .02
❑ 96 Chris Mullin .40 .12
❑ 97 Jim Petersen .05 .02
❑ 98 Mitch Richmond .40 .12
❑ 99 Tom Tolbert .05 .02
❑ 100 Adrian Caldwell .05 .02
❑ 101 Eric(Sleepy) Floyd .05 .02
❑ 102 Dave Jamerson .05 .02
❑ 103 Buck Johnson .05 .02
❑ 104 Vernon Maxwell .05 .02
❑ 105 Hakeem Olajuwon .60 .18
❑ 106 Kenny Smith .05 .02
❑ 107 Larry Smith .05 .02
❑ 108 Otis Thorpe .20 .06
❑ 109 Kennard Winchester RC .05 .02
❑ 110 David Wood RC .05 .02
❑ 111 Greg Dreiling .05 .02
❑ 112 Vern Fleming .05 .02
❑ 113 George McCloud .05 .02
❑ 114 Reggie Miller .40 .12
❑ 115 Chuck Person .05 .02
❑ 116 Mike Sanders .05 .02
❑ 117 Detlef Schrempf .20 .06
❑ 118 Rik Smits .20 .06
❑ 119 LaSalle Thompson .05 .02
❑ 120 Kenny Williams .05 .02
❑ 121 Micheal Williams .05 .02
❑ 122 Ken Bannister .05 .02
❑ 123 Winston Garland .05 .02
❑ 124 Gary Grant .05 .02
❑ 125 Ron Harper .20 .06
❑ 126 Bo Kimble .05 .02
❑ 127 Danny Manning .20 .06
❑ 128 Jeff Martin .05 .02
❑ 129 Ken Norman .05 .02
❑ 130 Olden Polynice .05 .02
❑ 131 Charles Smith .05 .02
❑ 132 Loy Vaught .05 .02
❑ 133 Elden Campbell .20 .06
❑ 134 Vlade Divac .20 .06
❑ 135 Larry Drew .05 .02
❑ 136 A.C. Green .20 .06
❑ 137 Magic Johnson 1.25 .35
❑ 138 Sam Perkins .20 .06
❑ 139 Byron Scott .20 .06
❑ 140 Tony Smith .05 .02
❑ 141 Terry Teagle .05 .02
❑ 142 Mychal Thompson .05 .02
❑ 143 James Worthy .40 .12
❑ 144 Willie Burton .05 .02
❑ 145 Bimbo Coles .05 .02
❑ 146 Terry Davis .05 .02
❑ 147 Sherman Douglas .05 .02
❑ 148 Kevin Edwards .05 .02
❑ 149 Alec Kessler .05 .02
❑ 150 Grant Long .05 .02
❑ 151 Glen Rice .40 .12
❑ 152 Rony Seikaly .05 .02
❑ 153 Jon Sundvold .05 .02
❑ 154 Billy Thompson .05 .02
❑ 155 Frank Brickowski .05 .02
❑ 156 Lester Conner .05 .02
❑ 157 Jeff Grayer .05 .02
❑ 158 Jay Humphries .05 .02
❑ 159 Larry Krystkowiak .05 .02
❑ 160 Brad Lohaus .05 .02
❑ 161 Dale Ellis .20 .06
❑ 162 Fred Roberts .05 .02
❑ 163 Alvin Robertson .05 .02
❑ 164 Danny Schayes .05 .02
❑ 165 Jack Sikma .05 .02
❑ 166 Randy Breuer .05 .02
❑ 167 Scott Brooks .05 .02
❑ 168 Tony Campbell .05 .02
❑ 169 Tyrone Corbin .05 .02
❑ 170 Gerald Glass .05 .02
❑ 171 Sam Mitchell .05 .02
❑ 172 Tod Murphy .05 .02
❑ 173 Pooh Richardson .05 .02
❑ 174 Felton Spencer .05 .02
❑ 175 Bob Thornton .05 .02
❑ 176 Doug West .05 .02
❑ 177 Mookie Blaylock .20 .06
❑ 178 Sam Bowie .05 .02
❑ 179 Jud Buechler .05 .02
❑ 180 Derrick Coleman .20 .06
❑ 181 Chris Dudley .05 .02
❑ 182 Tate George .05 .02
❑ 183 Jack Haley .05 .02
❑ 184 Terry Mills RC .40 .12
❑ 185 Chris Morris .05 .02
❑ 186 Drazen Petrovic .20 .06
❑ 187 Reggie Theus .20 .06
❑ 188 Maurice Cheeks .05 .02
❑ 189 Patrick Ewing .40 .12
❑ 190 Mark Jackson .20 .06
❑ 191 Jerrod Mustaf .05 .02
❑ 192 Charles Oakley .20 .06
❑ 193 Brian Quinnett .05 .02
❑ 194 John Starks RC .40 .12
❑ 195 Trent Tucker .05 .02
❑ 196 Kiki Vandeweghe .05 .02
❑ 197 Kenny Walker .05 .02
❑ 198 Gerald Wilkins .05 .02
❑ 199 Mark Acres .05 .02
❑ 200 Nick Anderson .20 .06
❑ 201 Michael Ansley .05 .02
❑ 202 Terry Catledge .05 .02
❑ 203 Greg Kite .05 .02
❑ 204 Jerry Reynolds .05 .02
❑ 205 Dennis Scott .20 .06
❑ 206 Scott Skiles .05 .02
❑ 207 Otis Smith .05 .02
❑ 208 Jeff Turner .05 .02
❑ 209 Sam Vincent .05 .02
❑ 210 Ron Anderson .05 .02
❑ 211 Charles Barkley .60 .18
❑ 212 Manute Bol .05 .02
❑ 213 Johnny Dawkins .05 .02
❑ 214 Armon Gilliam .05 .02
❑ 215 Rickey Green .05 .02
❑ 216 Hersey Hawkins .20 .06
❑ 217 Rick Mahorn .05 .02
❑ 218 Brian Oliver .05 .02
❑ 219 Andre Turner .05 .02
❑ 220 Jayson Williams .40 .12
❑ 221 Joe Barry Carroll .05 .02
❑ 222 Cedric Ceballos .20 .06
❑ 223 Tom Chambers .05 .02
❑ 224 Jeff Hornacek .20 .06
❑ 225 Kevin Johnson .40 .12
❑ 226 Negele Knight .05 .02
❑ 227 Andrew Lang .05 .02
❑ 228 Dan Majerle .20 .06
❑ 229 Xavier McDaniel .05 .02
❑ 230 Kurt Rambis .05 .02
❑ 231 Mark West .05 .02
❑ 232 Alaa Abdelnaby .05 .02
❑ 233 Danny Ainge .20 .06
❑ 234 Mark Bryant .05 .02
❑ 235 Wayne Cooper .05 .02
❑ 236 Walter Davis .05 .02
❑ 237 Clyde Drexler .40 .12
❑ 238 Kevin Duckworth .05 .02
❑ 239 Jerome Kersey .05 .02
❑ 240 Terry Porter .05 .02
❑ 241 Clifford Robinson .20 .06
❑ 242 Buck Williams .05 .02
❑ 243 Anthony Bonner .05 .02
❑ 244 Antoine Carr .05 .02
❑ 245 Duane Causwell .05 .02
❑ 246 Bobby Hansen .05 .02
❑ 247 Jim Les RC .05 .02
❑ 248 Travis Mays .05 .02
❑ 249 Ralph Sampson .05 .02
❑ 250 Lionel Simmons .05 .02
❑ 251 Rory Sparrow .05 .02
❑ 252 Wayman Tisdale .05 .02
❑ 253 Bill Wennington .05 .02
❑ 254 Willie Anderson .05 .02
❑ 255 Terry Cummings .05 .02
❑ 256 Sean Elliott .20 .06
❑ 257 Sidney Green .05 .02
❑ 258 David Greenwood .05 .02
❑ 259 Avery Johnson .20 .06
❑ 260 Paul Pressey .05 .02
❑ 261 David Robinson .75 .23
❑ 262 Dwayne Schintzius .05 .02
❑ 263 Rod Strickland .40 .12
❑ 264 David Wingate .05 .02
❑ 265 Dana Barros .05 .02
❑ 266 Benoit Benjamin .05 .02
❑ 267 Michael Cage .05 .02
❑ 268 Quintin Dailey .05 .02
❑ 269 Ricky Pierce .05 .02
❑ 270 Eddie Johnson .20 .06
❑ 271 Shawn Kemp 1.00 .30
❑ 272 Derrick McKey .05 .02
❑ 273 Nate McMillan .05 .02
❑ 274 Gary Payton 1.00 .30
❑ 275 Sedale Threatt .05 .02
❑ 276 Thurl Bailey .05 .02
❑ 277 Mike Brown .05 .02
❑ 278 Tony Brown .05 .02
❑ 279 Mark Eaton .05 .02
❑ 280 Blue Edwards .05 .02
❑ 281 Darrell Griffith .05 .02
❑ 282 Jeff Malone .05 .02
❑ 283 Karl Malone .60 .18
❑ 284 Delaney Rudd .05 .02
❑ 285 John Stockton .40 .12
❑ 286 Andy Toolson .05 .02
❑ 287 Mark Alarie .05 .02
❑ 288 Ledell Eackles .05 .02
❑ 289 Pervis Ellison .05 .02
❑ 290 A.J. English .05 .02
❑ 291 Harvey Grant .05 .02
❑ 292 Tom Hammonds .05 .02
❑ 293 Charles Jones .05 .02
❑ 294 Bernard King .05 .02
❑ 295 Darrell Walker .05 .02
❑ 296 John Williams .05 .02
❑ 297 Haywoode Workman RC .20 .06
❑ 298 Muggsy Bogues .05 .02
Assist-to-Turnover
Ratio Leader
❑ 299 Lester Conner .05 .02
Steal-to Turnover
Ratio Leader
❑ 300 Michael Adams .05 .02
Largest One-Year
Scoring Improvement
❑ 301 Chris Mullin .20 .06
Most Minutes Per Game
❑ 302 Otis Thorpe .05 .02
Most Consecutive
Games Played
❑ 303 Mitch Richmond .40 .12
Chris Mullin
Tim Hardaway
Highest Scoring Trio
❑ 304 Darrell Walker .05 .02
Top Rebounding Guard
❑ 305 Jerome Lane .05 .02
Rebounds Per 48 Minutes
❑ 306 John Stockton .20 .06
Assists Per 48 Minutes
❑ 307 Michael Jordan 2.50 .75
Points Per 48 Minutes
❑ 308 Michael Adams .05 .02
Best Single Game
Performance: Points
❑ 309 Larry Smith .05 .02
Jerome Lane
Best Single Game
Performance: Rebounds
❑ 310 Scott Skiles .05 .02
Best Single Game
Performance: Assists
❑ 311 Hakeem Olajuwon .40 .12
David Robinson
Best Single Game
Performance: Blocks

❑ 312 Alvin Robertson .05 .02
Best Single Game
Performance: Steals
❑ 313 Stay In School Jam .05 .02
❑ 314 Craig Hodges .05 .02
Three-Point Shootout
❑ 315 Dee Brown .05 .02
Slam-Dunk Championship
❑ 316 Charles Barkley .40 .12
All-Star Game MVP
❑ 317 Behind the Scenes .40 .12
Charles Barkley
Joe Dumars
Kevin McHale
❑ 318 Derrick Coleman ART .05 .02
❑ 319 Lionel Simmons ART .05 .02
❑ 320 Dennis Scott ART .05 .02
❑ 321 Kendall Gill ART .05 .02
❑ 322 Dee Brown ART .05 .02
❑ 323 Magic Johnson .60 .18
GQ All-Star Style Team
❑ 324 Hakeem Olajuwon .40 .12
GQ All-Star Style Team
❑ 325 Kevin Willis .20 .06
Dominique Wilkins
GQ All-Star Style Team
❑ 326 Kevin Willis .20 .06
Dominique Wilkins
GQ All-Star Style Team
❑ 327 Gerald Wilkins .05 .02
GQ All-Star Style Team
❑ 328 1891-1991 Basketball .05 .02
Centennial Logo
❑ 329 Old-Fashioned Ball .05 .02
❑ 330 Women Take the Court .05 .02
❑ 331 The Peach Basket .05 .02
❑ 332 James A. Naismith .20 .06
Founder of Basketball
❑ 333 Magic Johnson FIN 2.00 .60
Michael Jordan FIN
❑ 334 Michael Jordan FIN 2.50 .75
❑ 335 Vlade Divac FIN .05 .02
❑ 336 John Paxson FIN .05 .02
❑ 337 Bulls Starting Five 1.25 .35
Great Moments from
the NBA Finals
❑ 338 Language Arts .05 .02
Stay in School
❑ 339 Mathematics .05 .02
Stay in School
❑ 340 Vocational Education .05 .02
Stay in School
❑ 341 Social Studies .05 .02
Stay in School
❑ 342 Physical Education .05 .02
Stay in School
❑ 343 Art .05 .02
Stay in School
❑ 344 Science .05 .02
Stay in School
❑ 345 Checklist 1 (1-60) .05 .02
❑ 346 Checklist 2 (61-120) .05 .02
❑ 347 Checklist 3 (121-180) .05 .02
❑ 348 Checklist 4 (181-244) .05 .02
❑ 349 Checklist 5 (245-305) .05 .02
❑ 350 Checklist 6 (306-350) .05 .02
❑ 351 Atlanta Hawks .05 .02
Team Logo
❑ 352 Boston Celtics .05 .02
Team Logo
❑ 353 Charlotte Hornets .05 .02
Team Logo
❑ 354 Chicago Bulls .05 .02
Team Logo
❑ 355 Cleveland Cavaliers .05 .02
Team Logo
❑ 356 Dallas Mavericks .05 .02
Team Logo
❑ 357 Denver Nuggets .05 .02
Team Logo
❑ 358 Detroit Pistons .05 .02
Team Logo
❑ 359 Golden State Warriors .05 .02
Team Logo
❑ 360 Houston Rockets .05 .02
Team Logo
❑ 361 Indiana Pacers .05 .02
Team Logo
❑ 362 Los Angeles Clippers .05 .02
Team Logo
❑ 363 Los Angeles Lakers .05 .02
Team Logo
❑ 364 Miami Heat .05 .02
Team Logo
❑ 365 Milwaukee Bucks .05 .02
Team Logo
❑ 366 Minnesota Timberwolves .05 .02
Team Logo
❑ 367 New Jersey Nets .05 .02
Team Logo
❑ 368 New York Knicks .05 .02
Team Logo
❑ 369 Orlando Magic .05 .02
Team Logo
❑ 370 Philadelphia 76ers .05 .02
Team Logo
❑ 371 Phoenix Suns .05 .02
Team Logo
❑ 372 Portland Trail Blazers .05 .02
Team Logo
❑ 373 Sacramento Kings .05 .02
Team Logo
❑ 374 San Antonio Spurs .05 .02
Team Logo
❑ 375 Seattle Supersonics .05 .02
Team Logo
❑ 376 Utah Jazz .05 .02
Team Logo
❑ 377 Washington Bullets .05 .02
Team Logo
❑ 378 Bob Weiss CO .05 .02
❑ 379 Chris Ford CO .05 .02
❑ 380 Allan Bristow CO .05 .02
❑ 381 Phil Jackson CO .20 .06
❑ 382 Lenny Wilkens CO .20 .06
❑ 383 Richie Adubato CO .05 .02
❑ 384 Paul Westhead CO .05 .02
❑ 385 Chuck Daly CO .20 .06
❑ 386 Don Nelson CO .20 .06
❑ 387 Don Chaney CO .05 .02
❑ 388 Bob Hill CO RC .05 .02
❑ 389 Mike Schuler CO .05 .02
❑ 390 Mike Dunleavy CO .05 .02
❑ 391 Kevin Loughery CO .05 .02
❑ 392 Del Harris CO .05 .02
❑ 393 Jimmy Rodgers CO .05 .02
❑ 394 Bill Fitch CO .05 .02
❑ 395 Pat Riley CO .20 .06
❑ 396 Matt Guokas CO .05 .02
❑ 397 Jim Lynam CO .05 .02
❑ 398 Cotton Fitzsimmons CO .05 .02
❑ 399 Rick Adelman CO .05 .02
❑ 400 Dick Motta CO .05 .02
❑ 401 Larry Brown CO .05 .02
❑ 402 K.C. Jones CO .20 .06
❑ 403 Jerry Sloan CO .20 .06
❑ 404 Wes Unseld CO .20 .06
❑ 405 Mo Cheeks GF .05 .02
❑ 406 Dee Brown GF .05 .02
❑ 407 Rex Chapman GF .05 .02
❑ 408 Michael Jordan GF 2.50 .75
❑ 409 John Williams GF .05 .02
❑ 410 James Donaldson GF .05 .02
❑ 411 Dikembe Mutombo GF .40 .12
❑ 412 Isiah Thomas GF .20 .06
❑ 413 Tim Hardaway GF .40 .12
❑ 414 Hakeem Olajuwon GF .40 .12
❑ 415 Detlef Schrempf GF .05 .02
❑ 416 Danny Manning GF .05 .02
❑ 417 Magic Johnson GF .60 .18
❑ 418 Bimbo Coles GF .05 .02
❑ 419 Alvin Robertson GF .05 .02
❑ 420 Sam Mitchell GF .05 .02
❑ 421 Sam Bowie GF .05 .02
❑ 422 Mark Jackson GF .05 .02
❑ 423 Orlando Magic .05 .02
Game Frame
❑ 424 Charles Barkley GF .40 .12
❑ 425 Dan Majerle GF .05 .02
❑ 426 Robert Pack GF .05 .02
❑ 427 Wayman Tisdale GF .05 .02
❑ 428 David Robinson GF .40 .12
❑ 429 Nate McMillan GF .05 .02
Seattle Supersonics)
❑ 430 Karl Malone GF .40 .12
❑ 431 Michael Adams GF .05 .02
❑ 432 Duane Ferrell SM .05 .02
❑ 433 Kevin McHale SM .05 .02
❑ 434 Dell Curry SM .05 .02
❑ 435 B.J. Armstrong SM .05 .02
❑ 436 John Williams SM .05 .02
❑ 437 Brad Davis SM .05 .02
❑ 438 Marcus Liberty SM .05 .02
❑ 439 Mark Aguirre SM .05 .02
❑ 440 Rod Higgins SM .05 .02
❑ 441 Eric(Sleepy) Floyd SM .05 .02
❑ 442 Detlef Schrempf SM .05 .02
❑ 443 Loy Vaught SM .05 .02
❑ 444 Terry Teagle SM .05 .02
❑ 445 Kevin Edwards SM .05 .02
❑ 446 Dale Ellis SM .05 .02
❑ 447 Tod Murphy SM .05 .02
❑ 448 Chris Dudley SM .05 .02
❑ 449 Mark Jackson SM .05 .02
❑ 450 Jerry Reynolds SM .05 .02
❑ 451 Ron Anderson SM .05 .02
❑ 452 Dan Majerle SM .05 .02
❑ 453 Danny Ainge SM .05 .02
❑ 454 Jim Les SM .05 .02
❑ 455 Paul Pressey SM .05 .02
❑ 456 Ricky Pierce SM .05 .02
❑ 457 Mike Brown SM .05 .02
❑ 458 Ledell Eackles SM .05 .02
❑ 459 Atlanta Hawks .20 .06
Teamwork
(Dominique Wilkins
and Kevin Willis)
❑ 460 Boston Celtics .40 .12
Teamwork
(Larry Bird and
Robert Parish)
❑ 461 Charlotte Hornets .05 .02
Teamwork
(Rex Chapman and
Kendall Gill)
❑ 462 Chicago Bulls 1.50 .45
Teamwork
(Michael Jordan and
Scottie Pippen)
❑ 463 Cleveland Cavaliers .05 .02
Teamwork
(Craig Ehlo and
Mark Price)
❑ 464 Dallas Mavericks .05 .02
Teamwork
(Derek Harper and
Rolando Blackman)
❑ 465 Denver Nuggets .05 .02
Teamwork
(Reggie Williams and
Chris Jackson)
❑ 466 Detroit Pistons .20 .06
Teamwork
(Isiah Thomas and
Bill Laimbeer)
❑ 467 Golden State Warriors .20 .06
Teamwork
(Tim Hardaway and
Chris Mullin)
❑ 468 Houston Rockets .05 .02
Teamwork
(Vernon Maxwell and
Kenny Smith)
❑ 469 Indiana Pacers .20 .06
Teamwork
(Detlef Schrempf and
Reggie Miller)
❑ 470 Los Angeles Clippers .05 .02
Teamwork
(Charles Smith and
Danny Manning)
❑ 471 Los Angeles Lakers .40 .12
Teamwork
(Magic Johnson and
James Worthy)
❑ 472 Miami Heat .40 .12
Teamwork
(Glen Rice and

Rony Seikaly)
❑ 473 Milwaukee Bucks .05 .02
Teamwork
(Jay Humphries and
Alvin Robertson)
❑ 474 Minnesota Timberwolves .05 .02
Teamwork
(Tony Campbell and
Pooh Richardson)
❑ 475 New Jersey Nets .05 .02
Teamwork
(Derrick Coleman and
Sam Bowie)
❑ 476 New York Knicks .20 .06
Teamwork
(Patrick Ewing and
Charles Oakley)
❑ 477 Orlando Magic .05 .02
Teamwork
(Dennis Scott and
Scott Skiles)
❑ 478 Philadelphia 76ers .40 .12
Teamwork
(Charles Barkley and
Hersey Hawkins)
❑ 479 Phoenix Suns .20 .06
Teamwork
(Kevin Johnson and
Tom Chambers)
❑ 480 Portland Trail Blazers .40 .12
Teamwork
(Clyde Drexler and
Terry Porter)
❑ 481 Sacramento Kings .05 .02
Teamwork
(Lionel Simmons and
Wayman Tisdale)
❑ 482 San Antonio Spurs .05 .02
Teamwork
(Terry Cummings and
Sean Elliott)
❑ 483 Seattle Supersonics .05 .02
Teamwork
(Eddie Johnson and
Ricky Pierce)
❑ 484 Utah Jazz .40 .12
Teamwork
(Karl Malone and
John Stockton)
❑ 485 Washington Bullets .05 .02
Teamwork
(Harvey Grant and
Bernard King)
❑ 486 Rumeal Robinson RS .05 .02
❑ 487 Dee Brown RS .05 .02
❑ 488 Kendall Gill RS .05 .02
❑ 489 B.J. Armstrong RS .05 .02
❑ 490 Danny Ferry RS .05 .02
❑ 491 Randy White RS .05 .02
❑ 492 Chris Jackson RS .05 .02
❑ 493 Lance Blanks RS .05 .02
❑ 494 Tim Hardaway RS .40 .12
❑ 495 Vernon Maxwell RS .05 .02
❑ 496 Micheal Williams RS .05 .02
❑ 497 Charles Smith RS .05 .02
❑ 498 Vlade Divac RS .05 .02
❑ 499 Willie Burton RS .05 .02
❑ 500 Jeff Grayer RS .05 .02
❑ 501 Pooh Richardson RS .05 .02
❑ 502 Derrick Coleman RS .05 .02
❑ 503 John Starks RS .20 .06
❑ 504 Dennis Scott RS .05 .02
❑ 505 Hersey Hawkins RS .05 .02
❑ 506 Negele Knight RS .05 .02
❑ 507 Clifford Robinson RS .05 .02
❑ 508 Lionel Simmons RS .05 .02
❑ 509 David Robinson RS .40 .12
❑ 510 Gary Payton RS .50 .15
❑ 511 Blue Edwards RS .05 .02
❑ 512 Harvey Grant RS .05 .02
❑ 513 Larry Johnson RC 1.50 .45
❑ 514 Kenny Anderson RC .75 .23
❑ 515 Billy Owens RC .40 .12
❑ 516 Dikembe Mutombo RC 1.50 .45
❑ 517 Steve Smith RC 1.50 .45
❑ 518 Doug Smith RC .05 .02
❑ 519 Luc Longley RC .40 .12
❑ 520 Mark Macon RC .05 .02
❑ 521 Stacey Augmon RC .40 .12
❑ 522 Brian Williams RC .40 .12
❑ 523 Terrell Brandon RC 1.25 .35
❑ 524 The Ball .05 .02
❑ 525 The Basket .05 .02
❑ 526 The 24-second Shot .05 .02
Clock
❑ 527 The Game Program .05 .02
❑ 528 The Championship Gift .05 .02
❑ 529 Championship Trophy .05 .02
❑ 530 Charles Barkley USA 1.25 .35
❑ 531 Larry Bird USA 3.00 .90
❑ 532 Patrick Ewing USA .75 .23
❑ 533 Magic Johnson USA 2.50 .75
❑ 534 Michael Jordan USA 8.00 2.40
❑ 535 Karl Malone USA 1.25 .35
❑ 536 Chris Mullin USA .40 .12
❑ 537 Scottie Pippen USA 2.50 .75
❑ 538 David Robinson USA 1.50 .45
❑ 539 John Stockton USA .75 .23
❑ 540 Chuck Daly CO USA .20 .06
❑ 541 P.J.Carlesimo CO USA RC .05 .02
❑ 542 M.Krzyzewski CO USA RC .60 .18
❑ 543 Lenny Wilkens CO USA .20 .06
❑ 544 Team USA Card 1 2.50 .75
❑ 545 Team USA Card 2 2.50 .75
❑ 546 Team USA Card 3 2.50 .75
❑ 547 Willie Anderson USA .05 .02
❑ 548 Stacey Augmon USA .40 .12
❑ 549 Bimbo Coles USA .05 .02
❑ 550 Jeff Grayer USA .05 .02
❑ 551 Hersey Hawkins USA .05 .02
❑ 552 Dan Majerle USA .05 .02
❑ 553 Danny Manning USA .05 .02
❑ 554 J.R. Reid USA .05 .02
❑ 555 Mitch Richmond USA .75 .23
❑ 556 Charles Smith USA .05 .02
❑ 557 Vern Fleming USA .05 .02
❑ 558 Joe Kleine USA .05 .02
❑ 559 Jon Koncak USA .05 .02
❑ 560 Sam Perkins USA .05 .02
❑ 561 Alvin Robertson USA .05 .02
❑ 562 Wayman Tisdale USA .05 .02
❑ 563 Jeff Turner USA .05 .02
❑ 564 Tony Campbell .05 .02
Magic of SkyBox
❑ 565 Joe Dumars .20 .06
Magic of SkyBox
❑ 566 Horace Grant .05 .02
Magic of SkyBox
❑ 567 Reggie Lewis .05 .02
Magic of SkyBox
❑ 568 Hakeem Olajuwon .40 .12
Magic of SkyBox
❑ 569 Sam Perkins .05 .02
Magic of SkyBox
❑ 570 Chuck Person .05 .02
Magic of SkyBox
❑ 571 Buck Williams .05 .02
Magic of SkyBox
❑ 572 Michael Jordan 2.50 .75
SkyBox Salutes
❑ 573 Bernard King .05 .02
NBA All-Star
SkyBox Salutes
❑ 574 Moses Malone .20 .06
SkyBox Salutes
❑ 575 Robert Parish .05 .02
SkyBox Salutes
❑ 576 Pat Riley CO .20 .06
SkyBox Salutes
❑ 577 Dee Brown .05 .02
SkyMaster
❑ 578 Rex Chapman .05 .02
SkyMaster
❑ 579 Clyde Drexler .20 .06
SkyMaster
❑ 580 Blue Edwards .05 .02
SkyMaster
❑ 581 Ron Harper .05 .02
SkyMaster
❑ 582 Kevin Johnson .20 .06
SkyMaster
❑ 583 Michael Jordan 2.50 .75
SkyMaster
❑ 584 Shawn Kemp .75 .23
SkyMaster
❑ 585 Xavier McDaniel .05 .02
SkyMaster
❑ 586 Scottie Pippen .60 .18
SkyMaster
❑ 587 Kenny Smith .05 .02
SkyMaster
❑ 588 Dominique Wilkins .20 .06
SkyMaster
❑ 589 Michael Adams .05 .02
Shooting Star
❑ 590 Danny Ainge .05 .02
Shooting Star
❑ 591 Larry Bird .75 .23
Shooting Star
❑ 592 Dale Ellis .05 .02
Shooting Star
❑ 593 Hersey Hawkins .05 .02
Shooting Star
❑ 594 Jeff Hornacek .05 .02
Shooting Star
❑ 595 Jeff Malone .05 .02
Shooting Star
❑ 596 Reggie Miller .20 .06
Shooting Star
❑ 597 Chris Mullin .20 .06
Shooting Star
❑ 598 John Paxson .05 .02
Shooting Star
❑ 599 Drazen Petrovic .05 .02
Shooting Star
❑ 600 Ricky Pierce .05 .02
Shooting Star
❑ 601 Mark Price .05 .02
Shooting Star
❑ 602 Dennis Scott .05 .02
Shooting Star
❑ 603 Manute Bol .05 .02
Small School Sensation
❑ 604 Jerome Kersey .05 .02
Small School Sensation
❑ 605 Charles Oakley .05 .02
Small School Sensation
❑ 606 Scottie Pippen .60 .18
Small School Sensation
❑ 607 Terry Porter .05 .02
Small School Sensation
❑ 608 Dennis Rodman .40 .12
Small School Sensation
❑ 609 Sedale Threatt .05 .02
Small School Sensation
❑ 610 Business .05 .02
Stay in School
❑ 611 Engineering .05 .02
Stay in School
❑ 612 Law .05 .02
Stay in School
❑ 613 Liberal Arts .05 .02
Stay in School
❑ 614 Medicine .05 .02
Stay in School
❑ 615 Maurice Cheeks .05 .02
❑ 616 Travis Mays .05 .02
❑ 617 Blair Rasmussen .05 .02
❑ 618 Alexander Volkov .05 .02
❑ 619 Rickey Green .05 .02
❑ 620 Bobby Hansen .05 .02
❑ 621 John Battle .05 .02
❑ 622 Terry Davis .05 .02
❑ 623 Walter Davis .05 .02
❑ 624 Winston Garland .05 .02
❑ 625 Scott Hastings .05 .02
❑ 626 Brad Sellers .05 .02
❑ 627 Darrell Walker .05 .02
❑ 628 Orlando Woolridge .05 .02
❑ 629 Tony Brown .05 .02
❑ 630 James Edwards .05 .02
❑ 631 Doc Rivers .20 .06
❑ 632 Jack Haley .05 .02
❑ 633 Sedale Threatt .05 .02
❑ 634 Moses Malone .40 .12
❑ 635 Thurl Bailey .05 .02
❑ 636 Rafael Addison RC .05 .02
❑ 637 Tim McCormick .05 .02

❑ 638 Xavier McDaniel	.05	.02
❑ 639 Charles Shackleford	.05	.02
❑ 640 Mitchell Wiggins	.05	.02
❑ 641 Jerrod Mustaf	.05	.02
❑ 642 Dennis Hopson	.05	.02
❑ 643 Les Jepsen	.05	.02
❑ 644 Mitch Richmond	.40	.12
❑ 645 Dwayne Schintzius	.05	.02
❑ 646 Spud Webb	.20	.06
❑ 647 Jud Buechler	.05	.02
❑ 648 Antoine Carr	.05	.02
❑ 649 Tyrone Corbin	.05	.02
❑ 650 Michael Adams	.05	.02
❑ 651 Ralph Sampson	.05	.02
❑ 652 Andre Turner	.05	.02
❑ 653 David Wingate	.05	.02
❑ 654 Checklist "S" (351-404)	.05	.02
❑ 655 Checklist "K" (405-458)	.05	.02
❑ 656 Checklist "Y" (459-512)	.05	.02
❑ 657 Checklist "B" (513-563)	.05	.02
❑ 658 Checklist "O" (564-614)	.05	.02
❑ 659 Checklist "X" (615-659)	.05	.02
❑ NNO Clyde Drexler USA (Send-away)	75.00	22.00
❑ NNO Team USA Card	12.00	3.60

1992-93 SkyBox

	Nm-Mt	Ex-Mt
COMPLETE SET (413)	50.00	15.00
COMPLETE SERIES 1 (327)	30.00	9.00
COMPLETE SERIES 2 (86)	20.00	6.00
❑ 1 Stacey Augmon	.25	.07
❑ 2 Maurice Cheeks	.10	.03
❑ 3 Duane Ferrell	.10	.03
❑ 4 Paul Graham	.10	.03
❑ 5 Jon Koncak	.10	.03
❑ 6 Blair Rasmussen	.10	.03
❑ 7 Rumeal Robinson	.10	.03
❑ 8 Dominique Wilkins	.50	.15
❑ 9 Kevin Willis	.10	.03
❑ 10 Larry Bird	2.00	.60
❑ 11 Dee Brown	.10	.03
❑ 12 Sherman Douglas	.10	.03
❑ 13 Rick Fox	.25	.07
❑ 14 Kevin Gamble	.10	.03
❑ 15 Reggie Lewis	.25	.07
❑ 16 Kevin McHale	.50	.15
❑ 17 Robert Parish	.25	.07
❑ 18 Ed Pinckney	.10	.03
❑ 19 Muggsy Bogues	.25	.07
❑ 20 Dell Curry	.10	.03
❑ 21 Kenny Gattison	.10	.03
❑ 22 Kendall Gill	.25	.07
❑ 23 Mike Gminski	.10	.03
❑ 24 Tom Hammonds	.10	.03
❑ 25 Larry Johnson	.60	.18
❑ 26 Johnny Newman	.10	.03
❑ 27 J.R. Reid	.10	.03
❑ 28 B.J. Armstrong	.10	.03
❑ 29 Bill Cartwright	.10	.03
❑ 30 Horace Grant	.25	.07
❑ 31 Michael Jordan	6.00	1.80
❑ 32 Stacey King	.10	.03
❑ 33 John Paxson	.10	.03
❑ 34 Will Perdue	.10	.03
❑ 35 Scottie Pippen	1.50	.45
❑ 36 Scott Williams	.10	.03
❑ 37 John Battle	.10	.03
❑ 38 Terrell Brandon	.50	.15
❑ 39 Brad Daugherty	.10	.03
❑ 40 Craig Ehlo	.10	.03
❑ 41 Danny Ferry	.10	.03
❑ 42 Henry James	.10	.03
❑ 43 Larry Nance	.10	.03
❑ 44 Mark Price	.10	.03
❑ 45 Mike Sanders	.10	.03
❑ 46 Hot Rod Williams	.10	.03
❑ 47 Rolando Blackman	.10	.03
❑ 48 Terry Davis	.10	.03
❑ 49 Derek Harper	.25	.07
❑ 50 Donald Hodge	.10	.03
❑ 51 Mike Iuzzolino	.10	.03
❑ 52 Fat Lever	.10	.03
❑ 53 Rodney McCray	.10	.03
❑ 54 Doug Smith	.10	.03
❑ 55 Randy White	.10	.03
❑ 56 Herb Williams	.10	.03
❑ 57 Greg Anderson	.10	.03
❑ 58 Walter Davis	.10	.03
❑ 59 Winston Garland	.10	.03
❑ 60 Chris Jackson	.10	.03
❑ 61 Marcus Liberty	.10	.03
❑ 62 Todd Lichti	.10	.03
❑ 63 Mark Macon	.10	.03
❑ 64 Dikembe Mutombo	.60	.18
❑ 65 Reggie Williams	.10	.03
❑ 66 Mark Aguirre	.10	.03
❑ 67 William Bedford	.10	.03
❑ 68 Lance Blanks	.10	.03
❑ 69 Joe Dumars	.50	.15
❑ 70 Bill Laimbeer	.25	.07
❑ 71 Dennis Rodman	1.00	.30
❑ 72 John Salley	.10	.03
❑ 73 Isiah Thomas	.50	.15
❑ 74 Darrell Walker	.10	.03
❑ 75 Orlando Woolridge	.10	.03
❑ 76 Victor Alexander	.10	.03
❑ 77 Mario Elie	.25	.07
❑ 78 Chris Gatling	.10	.03
❑ 79 Tim Hardaway	.60	.18
❑ 80 Tyrone Hill	.10	.03
❑ 81 Alton Lister	.10	.03
❑ 82 Sarunas Marciulionis	.10	.03
❑ 83 Chris Mullin	.50	.15
❑ 84 Billy Owens	.25	.07
❑ 85 Matt Bullard	.10	.03
❑ 86 Sleepy Floyd	.10	.03
❑ 87 Avery Johnson	.10	.03
❑ 88 Buck Johnson	.10	.03
❑ 89 Vernon Maxwell	.10	.03
❑ 90 Hakeem Olajuwon	.75	.23
❑ 91 Kenny Smith	.10	.03
❑ 92 Larry Smith	.10	.03
❑ 93 Otis Thorpe	.25	.07
❑ 94 Dale Davis	.10	.03
❑ 95 Vern Fleming	.10	.03
❑ 96 George McCloud	.10	.03
❑ 97 Reggie Miller	.50	.15
❑ 98 Chuck Person	.10	.03
❑ 99 Detlef Schrempf	.25	.07
❑ 100 Rik Smits	.25	.07
❑ 101 LaSalle Thompson	.10	.03
❑ 102 Micheal Williams	.10	.03
❑ 103 James Edwards	.10	.03
❑ 104 Gary Grant	.10	.03
❑ 105 Ron Harper	.25	.07
❑ 106 Bo Kimble	.10	.03
❑ 107 Danny Manning	.25	.07
❑ 108 Ken Norman	.10	.03
❑ 109 Olden Polynice	.10	.03
❑ 110 Doc Rivers	.25	.07
❑ 111 Charles Smith	.10	.03
❑ 112 Loy Vaught	.10	.03
❑ 113 Elden Campbell	.25	.07
❑ 114 Vlade Divac	.25	.07
❑ 115 A.C. Green	.25	.07
❑ 116 Jack Haley	.10	.03
❑ 117 Sam Perkins	.25	.07
❑ 118 Byron Scott	.25	.07
❑ 119 Tony Smith	.10	.03
❑ 120 Sedale Threatt	.10	.03
❑ 121 James Worthy	.50	.15
❑ 122 Keith Askins	.10	.03
❑ 123 Willie Burton	.10	.03
❑ 124 Bimbo Coles	.10	.03
❑ 125 Kevin Edwards	.10	.03
❑ 126 Alec Kessler	.10	.03
❑ 127 Grant Long	.10	.03
❑ 128 Glen Rice	.50	.15
❑ 129 Rony Seikaly	.10	.03
❑ 130 Brian Shaw	.10	.03
❑ 131 Steve Smith	.60	.18
❑ 132 Frank Brickowski	.10	.03
❑ 133 Dale Ellis	.10	.03
❑ 134 Jeff Grayer	.10	.03
❑ 135 Jay Humphries	.10	.03
❑ 136 Larry Krystkowiak	.10	.03
❑ 137 Moses Malone	.50	.15
❑ 138 Fred Roberts	.10	.03
❑ 139 Alvin Robertson	.10	.03
❑ 140 Danny Schayes	.10	.03
❑ 141 Thurl Bailey	.10	.03
❑ 142 Scott Brooks	.10	.03
❑ 143 Tony Campbell	.10	.03
❑ 144 Gerald Glass	.10	.03
❑ 145 Luc Longley	.25	.07
❑ 146 Sam Mitchell	.10	.03
❑ 147 Pooh Richardson	.10	.03
❑ 148 Felton Spencer	.10	.03
❑ 149 Doug West	.10	.03
❑ 150 Rafael Addison	.10	.03
❑ 151 Kenny Anderson	.50	.15
❑ 152 Mookie Blaylock	.25	.07
❑ 153 Sam Bowie	.10	.03
❑ 154 Derrick Coleman	.25	.07
❑ 155 Chris Dudley	.10	.03
❑ 156 Tate George	.10	.03
❑ 157 Terry Mills	.10	.03
❑ 158 Chris Morris	.10	.03
❑ 159 Drazen Petrovic	.10	.03
❑ 160 Greg Anthony	.10	.03
❑ 161 Patrick Ewing	.50	.15
❑ 162 Mark Jackson	.25	.07
❑ 163 Anthony Mason	.50	.15
❑ 164 Tim McCormick	.10	.03
❑ 165 Xavier McDaniel	.10	.03
❑ 166 Charles Oakley	.25	.07
❑ 167 John Starks	.25	.07
❑ 168 Gerald Wilkins	.10	.03
❑ 169 Nick Anderson	.25	.07
❑ 170 Terry Catledge	.10	.03
❑ 171 Jerry Reynolds	.10	.03
❑ 172 Stanley Roberts	.10	.03
❑ 173 Dennis Scott	.25	.07
❑ 174 Scott Skiles	.10	.03
❑ 175 Jeff Turner	.10	.03
❑ 176 Sam Vincent	.10	.03
❑ 177 Brian Williams	.10	.03
❑ 178 Ron Anderson	.10	.03
❑ 179 Charles Barkley	.75	.23
❑ 180 Manute Bol	.10	.03
❑ 181 Johnny Dawkins	.10	.03
❑ 182 Armon Gilliam	.10	.03
❑ 183 Greg Grant	.10	.03
❑ 184 Hersey Hawkins	.25	.07
❑ 185 Brian Oliver	.10	.03
❑ 186 Charles Shackleford	.10	.03
❑ 187 Jayson Williams	.25	.07
❑ 188 Cedric Ceballos	.25	.07
❑ 189 Tom Chambers	.10	.03
❑ 190 Jeff Hornacek	.25	.07
❑ 191 Kevin Johnson	.50	.15
❑ 192 Negele Knight	.10	.03
❑ 193 Andrew Lang	.10	.03
❑ 194 Dan Majerle	.25	.07
❑ 195 Jerrod Mustaf	.10	.03
❑ 196 Tim Perry	.10	.03
❑ 197 Mark West	.10	.03
❑ 198 Alaa Abdelnaby	.10	.03
❑ 199 Danny Ainge	.25	.07
❑ 200 Mark Bryant	.10	.03
❑ 201 Clyde Drexler	.50	.15
❑ 202 Kevin Duckworth	.10	.03
❑ 203 Jerome Kersey	.10	.03

❑ 204 Robert Pack .10 .03
❑ 205 Terry Porter .10 .03
❑ 206 Clifford Robinson .25 .07
❑ 207 Buck Williams .25 .07
❑ 208 Anthony Bonner .10 .03
❑ 209 Randy Brown .10 .03
❑ 210 Duane Causwell .10 .03
❑ 211 Pete Chilcutt .10 .03
❑ 212 Dennis Hopson .10 .03
❑ 213 Jim Les .10 .03
❑ 214 Mitch Richmond .50 .15
❑ 215 Lionel Simmons .10 .03
❑ 216 Wayman Tisdale .10 .03
❑ 217 Spud Webb .25 .07
❑ 218 Willie Anderson .10 .03
❑ 219 Antoine Carr .10 .03
❑ 220 Terry Cummings .25 .07
❑ 221 Sean Elliott .25 .07
❑ 222 Sidney Green .10 .03
❑ 223 Vinnie Johnson .10 .03
❑ 224 David Robinson .75 .23
❑ 225 Rod Strickland .50 .15
❑ 226 Greg Sutton .10 .03
❑ 227 Dana Barros .10 .03
❑ 228 Benoit Benjamin .10 .03
❑ 229 Michael Cage .10 .03
❑ 230 Eddie Johnson .10 .03
❑ 231 Shawn Kemp 1.00 .30
❑ 232 Derrick McKey .10 .03
❑ 233 Nate McMillan .10 .03
❑ 234 Gary Payton 1.00 .30
❑ 235 Ricky Pierce .10 .03
❑ 236 David Benoit .10 .03
❑ 237 Mike Brown .10 .03
❑ 238 Tyrone Corbin .10 .03
❑ 239 Mark Eaton .10 .03
❑ 240 Blue Edwards .10 .03
❑ 241 Jeff Malone .10 .03
❑ 242 Karl Malone .75 .23
❑ 243 Eric Murdock .10 .03
❑ 244 John Stockton .50 .15
❑ 245 Michael Adams .10 .03
❑ 246 Rex Chapman .10 .03
❑ 247 Ledell Eackles .10 .03
❑ 248 Pervis Ellison .10 .03
❑ 249 A.J. English .10 .03
❑ 250 Harvey Grant .10 .03
❑ 251 Charles Jones .10 .03
❑ 252 Bernard King .10 .03
❑ 253 LaBradford Smith .10 .03
❑ 254 Larry Stewart .10 .03
❑ 255 Bob Weiss CO .10 .03
❑ 256 Chris Ford CO .10 .03
❑ 257 Allan Bristow CO .10 .03
❑ 258 Phil Jackson CO .25 .07
❑ 259 Lenny Wilkens CO .25 .07
❑ 260 Richie Adubato CO .10 .03
❑ 261 Dan Issel CO .10 .03
❑ 262 Ron Rothstein CO .10 .03
❑ 263 Don Nelson CO .25 .07
❑ 264 Rudy Tomjanovich CO .25 .07
❑ 265 Bob Hill CO .10 .03
❑ 266 Larry Brown CO .25 .07
❑ 267 Randy Pfund CO RC .10 .03
❑ 268 Kevin Loughery CO .10 .03
❑ 269 Mike Dunleavy CO .10 .03
❑ 270 Jimmy Rodgers CO .10 .03
❑ 271 Chuck Daly CO .25 .07
❑ 272 Pat Riley CO .25 .07
❑ 273 Matt Guokas CO .10 .03
❑ 274 Doug Moe CO .10 .03
❑ 275 Paul Westphal CO .10 .03
❑ 276 Rick Adelman CO .10 .03
❑ 277 Garry St. Jean CO RC .10 .03
❑ 278 Jerry Tarkanian CO RC .10 .03
❑ 279 George Karl CO .25 .07
❑ 280 Jerry Sloan CO .25 .07
❑ 281 Wes Unseld CO .25 .07
❑ 282 Dominique Wilkins TT .25 .07
❑ 283 Reggie Lewis TT .10 .03
❑ 284 Kendall Gill TT .10 .03
❑ 285 Horace Grant TT .10 .03
❑ 286 Brad Daugherty TT .10 .03
❑ 287 Derek Harper TT .10 .03
❑ 288 Chris Jackson TT .10 .03
❑ 289 Isiah Thomas TT .25 .07
❑ 290 Chris Mullin TT .25 .07
❑ 291 Kenny Smith TT .10 .03
❑ 292 Reggie Miller TT .25 .07
❑ 293 Ron Harper TT .10 .03
❑ 294 Vlade Divac TT .10 .03
❑ 295 Glen Rice TT .25 .07
❑ 296 Moses Malone TT .25 .07
❑ 297 Doug West TT .10 .03
❑ 298 Derrick Coleman TT .10 .03
❑ 299 Patrick Ewing TT .25 .07
(See also card 305)
❑ 300 Scott Skiles TT .10 .03
❑ 301 Hersey Hawkins TT .10 .03
❑ 302 Kevin Johnson TT .25 .07
❑ 303 Clifford Robinson TT .10 .03
❑ 304 Spud Webb TT .10 .03
❑ 305 David Robinson TT COR .50 .15
❑ 305A D.Robinson TT ERR .50 .15
(Card misnumbered as 299)
❑ 306 Shawn Kemp TT .50 .15
❑ 307 John Stockton TT .25 .07
❑ 308 Pervis Ellison TT .10 .03
❑ 309 Craig Hodges AS .10 .03
❑ 310 Magic Johnson A-S MVP .75 .23
❑ 311 Cedric Ceballos .10 .03
Slam Dunk Champ
❑ 312 Karl Malone ASG .50 .15
❑ 313 Dennis Rodman ASG .50 .15
❑ 314 Michael Jordan MVP 3.00 .90
❑ 315 Clyde Drexler FIN .25 .07
❑ 316 Danny Ainge PO .25 .07
❑ 317 Scottie Pippen PO .75 .23
❑ 318 NBA Champs .10 .03
❑ 319 Larry Johnson ART .50 .15
Dikembe Mutombo
❑ 320 NBA Stay in School .10 .03
❑ 321 Boys and Girls .10 .03
Clubs of America
❑ 322 Checklist 1 .10 .03
❑ 323 Checklist 2 .10 .03
❑ 324 Checklist 3 .10 .03
❑ 325 Checklist 4 .10 .03
❑ 326 Checklist 5 .10 .03
❑ 327 Checklist 6 .10 .03
❑ 328 Adam Keefe RC .10 .03
❑ 329 Sean Rooks RC .10 .03
❑ 330 Xavier McDaniel .10 .03
❑ 331 Kiki Vandeweghe .10 .03
❑ 332 Alonzo Mourning RC 3.00 .90
❑ 333 Rodney McCray .10 .03
❑ 334 Gerald Wilkins .10 .03
❑ 335 Tony Bennett RC .10 .03
❑ 336 LaPhonso Ellis RC .50 .15
❑ 337 Bryant Stith RC .25 .07
❑ 338 Isaiah Morris RC .10 .03
❑ 339 Olden Polynice .10 .03
❑ 340 Jeff Grayer .10 .03
❑ 341 Byron Houston RC .10 .03
❑ 342 Latrell Sprewell RC 4.00 1.20
❑ 343 Scott Brooks .10 .03
❑ 344 Frank Johnson .10 .03
❑ 345 Robert Horry RC .50 .15
❑ 346 David Wood .10 .03
❑ 347 Sam Mitchell .10 .03
❑ 348 Pooh Richardson .10 .03
❑ 349 Malik Sealy RC .25 .07
❑ 350 Morlon Wiley .10 .03
❑ 351 Mark Jackson .25 .07
❑ 352 Stanley Roberts .10 .03
❑ 353 Elmore Spencer RC .10 .03
❑ 354 John Williams .10 .03
❑ 355 Randy Woods RC .10 .03
❑ 356 James Edwards .10 .03
❑ 357 Jeff Sanders .10 .03
❑ 358 Magic Johnson 1.50 .45
❑ 359 Anthony Peeler RC .25 .07
❑ 360 Harold Miner RC .25 .07
❑ 361 John Salley .10 .03
❑ 362 Alaa Abdelnaby .10 .03
❑ 363 Todd Day RC .25 .07
❑ 364 Blue Edwards .10 .03
❑ 365 Lee Mayberry RC .10 .03
❑ 366 Eric Murdock .10 .03
❑ 367 Mookie Blaylock .25 .07
❑ 368 Anthony Avent RC .10 .03
❑ 369 Christian Laettner RC 1.00 .30
❑ 370 Chuck Person .10 .03
❑ 371 Chris Smith RC .10 .03
❑ 372 Micheal Williams .10 .03
❑ 373 Rolando Blackman .10 .03
❑ 374 Tony Campbell UER .10 .03
(Back photo actually
Alvin Robertson)
❑ 375 Hubert Davis RC .25 .07
❑ 376 Travis Mays .10 .03
❑ 377 Doc Rivers .25 .07
❑ 378 Charles Smith .10 .03
❑ 379 Rumeal Robinson .10 .03
❑ 380 Vinny Del Negro .10 .03
❑ 381 Steve Kerr .25 .07
❑ 382 Shaquille O'Neal RC 12.00 3.60
❑ 383 Donald Royal .10 .03
❑ 384 Jeff Hornacek .25 .07
❑ 385 Andrew Lang .10 .03
❑ 386 Tim Perry UER .10 .03
(Alvin Robertson pictured on back)
❑ 387 C.Weatherspoon RC .50 .15
❑ 388 Danny Ainge .25 .07
❑ 389 Charles Barkley .75 .23
❑ 390 Tim Kempton .10 .03
❑ 391 Oliver Miller RC .25 .07
❑ 392 Dave Johnson RC .10 .03
❑ 393 Tracy Murray RC .25 .07
❑ 394 Rod Strickland .50 .15
❑ 395 Marty Conlon .10 .03
❑ 396 Walt Williams RC .50 .15
❑ 397 Lloyd Daniels RC .10 .03
❑ 398 Dale Ellis .10 .03
❑ 399 Dave Hoppen .10 .03
❑ 400 Larry Smith .10 .03
❑ 401 Doug Overton .10 .03
❑ 402 Isaac Austin RC .25 .07
❑ 403 Jay Humphries .10 .03
❑ 404 Larry Krystkowiak .10 .03
❑ 405 Tom Gugliotta RC 1.50 .45
❑ 406 Buck Johnson .10 .03
❑ 407 Don MacLean RC .10 .03
❑ 408 Marlon Maxey RC .10 .03
❑ 409 Corey Williams RC .10 .03
❑ 410 Special Olympics .25 .07
Dan Majerle
❑ 411 Checklist 1 .10 .03
❑ 412 Checklist 2 .10 .03
❑ 413 Checklist 3 .10 .03
❑ NNO David Robinson AU 100.00 30.00
❑ NNO David Robinson 4.00 1.20
The Admiral Comes
Prepared
❑ NNO Magic Johnson AU 200.00 60.00
❑ NNO Head of the Class 30.00 9.00
LaPhonso Ellis
Tom Gugliotta
Christian Laettner
Alonzo Mourning
Shaquille O'Neal
Walt Williams
❑ NNO Magic Johnson 6.00 1.80
The Magic Never Ends

1993-94 SkyBox Premium

	Nm-Mt	Ex-Mt
COMPLETE SET (341)	30.00	9.00
COMPLETE SERIES 1 (191)	15.00	4.50

Card	Player	Price	Price
	COMPLETE SERIES 2 (150)	15.00	4.50
❑ 1	Checklist	.05	.02
❑ 2	Checklist	.05	.02
❑ 3	Checklist	.05	.02
❑ 4	Larry Johnson PO	.15	.04
❑ 5	Alonzo Mourning PO	.30	.09
❑ 6	Hakeem Olajuwon PO	.30	.09
❑ 7	Brad Daugherty PO	.05	.02
❑ 8	Oliver Miller PO	.05	.02
❑ 9	David Robinson PO	.30	.09
❑ 10	Patrick Ewing PO	.15	.04
❑ 11	Ricky Pierce PO	.05	.02
❑ 12	Sam Perkins PO	.05	.02
❑ 13	John Starks PO	.05	.02
❑ 14	Michael Jordan PO	2.00	.60
❑ 15	Dan Majerle PO	.05	.02
❑ 16	Scottie Pippen PO	.50	.15
❑ 17	Shawn Kemp PO	.30	.09
❑ 18	Charles Barkley PO	.30	.09
❑ 19	Horace Grant PO	.05	.02
❑ 20	Kevin Johnson PO	.05	.02
❑ 21	John Paxson PO	.05	.02
❑ 22	David Robinson IS	.30	.09
❑ 23	NBA On NBC	.05	.02
❑ 24	Stacey Augmon	.05	.02
❑ 25	Mookie Blaylock	.15	.04
❑ 26	Craig Ehlo	.05	.02
❑ 27	Adam Keefe	.05	.02
❑ 28	Dominique Wilkins	.30	.09
❑ 29	Kevin Willis	.05	.02
❑ 30	Dee Brown	.05	.02
❑ 31	Sherman Douglas	.05	.02
❑ 32	Rick Fox	.05	.02
❑ 33	Kevin Gamble	.05	.02
❑ 34	Xavier McDaniel	.05	.02
❑ 35	Robert Parish	.15	.04
❑ 36	Muggsy Bogues	.15	.04
❑ 37	Dell Curry	.05	.02
❑ 38	Kendall Gill	.15	.04
❑ 39	Larry Johnson	.30	.09
❑ 40	Alonzo Mourning	.50	.15
❑ 41	Johnny Newman	.05	.02
❑ 42	B.J. Armstrong	.05	.02
❑ 43	Bill Cartwright	.05	.02
❑ 44	Horace Grant	.15	.04
❑ 45	Michael Jordan	4.00	1.20
❑ 46	John Paxson	.05	.02
❑ 47	Scottie Pippen	1.00	.30
❑ 48	Scott Williams	.05	.02
❑ 49	Terrell Brandon	.15	.04
❑ 50	Brad Daugherty	.05	.02
❑ 51	Larry Nance	.05	.02
❑ 52	Mark Price	.05	.02
❑ 53	Gerald Wilkins	.05	.02
❑ 54	John Williams	.05	.02
❑ 55	Terry Davis	.05	.02
❑ 56	Derek Harper	.15	.04
❑ 57	Jim Jackson	.15	.04
❑ 58	Sean Rooks	.05	.02
❑ 59	Doug Smith	.05	.02
❑ 60	Mahmoud Abdul-Rauf	.05	.02
❑ 61	LaPhonso Ellis	.05	.02
❑ 62	Mark Macon	.05	.02
❑ 63	Dikembe Mutombo	.30	.09
❑ 64	Bryant Stith	.05	.02
❑ 65	Reggie Williams	.05	.02
❑ 66	Joe Dumars	.30	.09
❑ 67	Bill Laimbeer	.05	.02
❑ 68	Terry Mills	.05	.02
❑ 69	Alvin Robertson	.05	.02
❑ 70	Dennis Rodman	.60	.18
❑ 71	Isiah Thomas	.30	.09
❑ 72	Victor Alexander	.05	.02
❑ 73	Tim Hardaway	.30	.09
❑ 74	Tyrone Hill	.05	.02
❑ 75	Sarunas Marciulionis	.05	.02
❑ 76	Chris Mullin	.30	.09
❑ 77	Billy Owens	.05	.02
❑ 78	Latrell Sprewell	.75	.23
❑ 79	Robert Horry	.15	.04
❑ 80	Vernon Maxwell	.05	.02
❑ 81	Hakeem Olajuwon	.50	.15
❑ 82	Kenny Smith	.05	.02
❑ 83	Otis Thorpe	.15	.04
❑ 84	Dale Davis	.05	.02
❑ 85	Reggie Miller	.30	.09
❑ 86	Pooh Richardson	.05	.02
❑ 87	Detlef Schrempf	.15	.04
❑ 88	Malik Sealy	.05	.02
❑ 89	Rik Smits	.15	.04
❑ 90	Ron Harper	.15	.04
❑ 91	Mark Jackson	.15	.04
❑ 92	Danny Manning	.15	.04
❑ 93	Stanley Roberts	.05	.02
❑ 94	Loy Vaught	.05	.02
❑ 95	Randy Woods	.05	.02
❑ 96	Sam Bowie	.05	.02
❑ 97	Doug Christie	.15	.04
❑ 98	Vlade Divac	.15	.04
❑ 99	Anthony Peeler	.05	.02
❑ 100	Sedale Threatt	.05	.02
❑ 101	James Worthy	.30	.09
❑ 102	Grant Long	.05	.02
❑ 103	Harold Miner	.05	.02
❑ 104	Glen Rice	.15	.04
❑ 105	John Salley	.05	.02
❑ 106	Rony Seikaly	.05	.02
❑ 107	Steve Smith	.30	.09
❑ 108	Anthony Avent	.05	.02
❑ 109	Jon Barry	.05	.02
❑ 110	Frank Brickowski	.05	.02
❑ 111	Blue Edwards	.05	.02
❑ 112	Todd Day	.05	.02
❑ 113	Lee Mayberry	.05	.02
❑ 114	Eric Murdock	.05	.02
❑ 115	Thurl Bailey	.05	.02
❑ 116	Christian Laettner	.15	.04
❑ 117	Chuck Person	.05	.02
❑ 118	Doug West	.05	.02
❑ 119	Micheal Williams	.05	.02
❑ 120	Kenny Anderson	.15	.04
❑ 121	Benoit Benjamin	.05	.02
❑ 122	Derrick Coleman	.15	.04
❑ 123	Chris Morris	.05	.02
❑ 124	Rumeal Robinson	.05	.02
❑ 125	Rolando Blackman	.05	.02
❑ 126	Patrick Ewing	.30	.09
❑ 127	Anthony Mason	.15	.04
❑ 128	Charles Oakley	.15	.04
❑ 129	Doc Rivers	.15	.04
❑ 130	Charles Smith	.05	.02
❑ 131	John Starks	.15	.04
❑ 132	Nick Anderson	.15	.04
❑ 133	Shaquille O'Neal	1.50	.45
❑ 134	Donald Royal	.05	.02
❑ 135	Dennis Scott	.05	.02
❑ 136	Scott Skiles	.05	.02
❑ 137	Brian Williams	.05	.02
❑ 138	Johnny Dawkins	.05	.02
❑ 139	Hersey Hawkins	.15	.04
❑ 140	Jeff Hornacek	.15	.04
❑ 141	Andrew Lang	.05	.02
❑ 142	Tim Perry	.05	.02
❑ 143	Clarence Weatherspoon	.05	.02
❑ 144	Danny Ainge	.15	.04
❑ 145	Charles Barkley	.50	.15
❑ 146	Cedric Ceballos	.15	.04
❑ 147	Kevin Johnson	.15	.04
❑ 148	Oliver Miller	.05	.02
❑ 149	Dan Majerle	.15	.04
❑ 150	Clyde Drexler	.30	.09
❑ 151	Harvey Grant	.05	.02
❑ 152	Jerome Kersey	.05	.02
❑ 153	Terry Porter	.05	.02
❑ 154	Clifford Robinson	.15	.04
❑ 155	Rod Strickland	.15	.04
❑ 156	Buck Williams	.05	.02
❑ 157	Mitch Richmond	.30	.09
❑ 158	Lionel Simmons	.05	.02
❑ 159	Wayman Tisdale	.05	.02
❑ 160	Spud Webb	.15	.04
❑ 161	Walt Williams	.05	.02
❑ 162	Antoine Carr	.05	.02
❑ 163	Lloyd Daniels	.05	.02
❑ 164	Sean Elliott	.15	.04
❑ 165	Dale Ellis	.05	.02
❑ 166	Avery Johnson	.05	.02
❑ 167	J.R. Reid	.05	.02
❑ 168	David Robinson	.50	.15
❑ 169	Shawn Kemp	.50	.15
❑ 170	Derrick McKey	.05	.02
❑ 171	Nate McMillan	.05	.02
❑ 172	Gary Payton	.50	.15
❑ 173	Sam Perkins	.15	.04
❑ 174	Ricky Pierce	.05	.02
❑ 175	Tyrone Corbin	.05	.02
❑ 176	Jay Humphries	.05	.02
❑ 177	Jeff Malone	.05	.02
❑ 178	Karl Malone	.50	.15
❑ 179	John Stockton	.30	.09
❑ 180	Michael Adams	.05	.02
❑ 181	Kevin Duckworth	.05	.02
❑ 182	Pervis Ellison	.05	.02
❑ 183	Tom Gugliotta	.30	.09
❑ 184	Don MacLean	.05	.02
❑ 185	Brent Price	.05	.02
❑ 186	George Lynch RC	.05	.02
❑ 187	Rex Walters RC	.05	.02
❑ 188	Shawn Bradley RC	.30	.09
❑ 189	Ervin Johnson RC	.15	.04
❑ 190	Luther Wright RC	.05	.02
❑ 191	Calbert Cheaney RC	.15	.04
❑ 192	Craig Ehlo	.05	.02
❑ 193	Duane Ferrell	.05	.02
❑ 194	Paul Graham	.05	.02
❑ 195	Andrew Lang	.05	.02
❑ 196	Chris Corchiani	.05	.02
❑ 197	Acie Earl RC	.05	.02
❑ 198	Dino Radja RC	.05	.02
❑ 199	Ed Pinckney	.05	.02
❑ 200	Tony Bennett	.05	.02
❑ 201	Scott Burrell RC	.30	.09
❑ 202	Kenny Gattison	.05	.02
❑ 203	Hersey Hawkins	.15	.04
❑ 204	Eddie Johnson	.05	.02
❑ 205	Corie Blount RC	.05	.02
❑ 206	Steve Kerr	.15	.04
❑ 207	Toni Kukoc RC	1.25	.35
❑ 208	Pete Myers	.05	.02
❑ 209	Danny Ferry	.05	.02
❑ 210	Tyrone Hill	.05	.02
❑ 211	Gerald Madkins RC	.05	.02
❑ 212	Chris Mills RC	.30	.09
❑ 213	Lucious Harris RC	.05	.02
❑ 214	Popeye Jones RC	.05	.02
❑ 215	Jamal Mashburn RC	.75	.23
❑ 216	Darnell Mee RC	.05	.02
❑ 217	Rodney Rogers RC	.30	.09
❑ 218	Brian Williams	.05	.02
❑ 219	Greg Anderson	.05	.02
❑ 220	Sean Elliott	.15	.04
❑ 221	Allan Houston RC	1.25	.35
❑ 222	Lindsey Hunter RC	.30	.09
❑ 223	Chris Gatling	.05	.02
❑ 224	Josh Grant RC	.05	.02
❑ 225	Keith Jennings	.05	.02
❑ 226	Avery Johnson	.05	.02
❑ 227	Chris Webber RC	3.00	.90
❑ 228	Sam Cassell RC	1.25	.35
❑ 229	Mario Elie	.05	.02
❑ 230	Richard Petruska RC	.05	.02
❑ 231	Eric Riley RC	.05	.02
❑ 232	Antonio Davis RC	.40	.12
❑ 233	Scott Haskin RC	.05	.02
❑ 234	Derrick McKey	.05	.02
❑ 235	Mark Aguirre	.05	.02
❑ 236	Terry Dehere RC	.05	.02
❑ 237	Gary Grant	.05	.02
❑ 238	Randy Woods	.05	.02
❑ 239	Sam Bowie	.05	.02
❑ 240	Elden Campbell	.05	.02
❑ 241	Nick Van Exel RC	1.00	.30
❑ 242	Manute Bol	.05	.02
❑ 243	Brian Shaw	.05	.02
❑ 244	Vin Baker RC	.75	.23
❑ 245	Brad Lohaus	.05	.02
❑ 246	Ken Norman	.05	.02
❑ 247	Derek Strong RC	.05	.02
❑ 248	Danny Schayes	.05	.02
❑ 249	Mike Brown	.05	.02
❑ 250	Luc Longley	.15	.04
❑ 251	Isaiah Rider RC	.60	.18
❑ 252	Kevin Edwards	.05	.02
❑ 253	Armon Gilliam	.05	.02
❑ 254	Greg Anthony	.05	.02
❑ 255	Anthony Bonner	.05	.02
❑ 256	Tony Campbell	.05	.02

❑ 257	Hubert Davis	.05	.02
❑ 258	Litterial Green	.05	.02
❑ 259	Anfernee Hardaway RC	2.50	.75
❑ 260	Larry Krystkowiak	.05	.02
❑ 261	Todd Lichti	.05	.02
❑ 262	Dana Barros	.05	.02
❑ 263	Greg Graham RC	.05	.02
❑ 264	Warren Kidd RC	.05	.02
❑ 265	Moses Malone	.30	.09
❑ 266	A.C. Green	.15	.04
❑ 267	Joe Kleine	.05	.02
❑ 268	Malcolm Mackey RC	.05	.02
❑ 269	Mark Bryant	.05	.02
❑ 270	Chris Dudley	.05	.02
❑ 271	Harvey Grant	.05	.02
❑ 272	James Robinson RC	.05	.02
❑ 273	Duane Causwell	.05	.02
❑ 274	Bobby Hurley RC	.15	.04
❑ 275	Jim Les	.05	.02
❑ 276	Willie Anderson	.05	.02
❑ 277	Terry Cummings	.05	.02
❑ 278	Vinny Del Negro	.05	.02
❑ 279	Sleepy Floyd	.05	.02
❑ 280	Dennis Rodman	.60	.18
❑ 281	Vincent Askew	.05	.02
❑ 282	Kendall Gill	.15	.04
❑ 283	Steve Scheffler	.05	.02
❑ 284	Detlef Schrempf	.15	.04
❑ 285	David Benoit	.05	.02
❑ 286	Tom Chambers	.05	.02
❑ 287	Felton Spencer	.05	.02
❑ 288	Rex Chapman	.05	.02
❑ 289	Kevin Duckworth	.05	.02
❑ 290	Gheorghe Muresan RC	.30	.09
❑ 291	Kenny Walker	.05	.02
❑ 292	Andrew Lang CF	.05	.02
	Craig Ehlo		
❑ 293	Dino Radja CF	.05	.02
	Acie Earl		
❑ 294	Eddie Johnson CF	.05	.02
	Hersey Hawkins		
❑ 295	Toni Kukoc CF	.30	.09
	Corie Blount		
❑ 296	Tyrone Hill CF	.05	.02
	Chris Mills		
❑ 297	Jamal Mashburn CF	.30	.09
	Popeye Jones		
❑ 298	Darnell Mee CF	.05	.02
	Rodney Rogers		
❑ 299	Lindsey Hunter CF	.15	.04
	Allan Houston		
❑ 300	Chris Webber CF	.60	.18
	Avery Johnson		
❑ 301	Sam Cassell CF	.30	.09
	Mario Elie		
❑ 302	Derrick McKey CF	.05	.02
	Antonio Davis		
❑ 303	Terry Dehere CF	.05	.02
	Mark Aguirre		
❑ 304	Nick Van Exel CF	.30	.09
	George Lynch		
❑ 305	Harold Miner CF	.05	.02
	Steve Smith		
❑ 306	Ken Norman CF	.15	.04
	Vin Baker		
❑ 307	Mike Brown CF	.15	.04
	Isaiah Rider		
❑ 308	Kevin Edwards CF	.05	.02
	Rex Walters		
❑ 309	Hubert Davis CF	.05	.02
	Anthony Bonner		
❑ 310	Anfernee Hardaway CF	1.00	.30
	Larry Krystkowiak		
❑ 311	Moses Malone CF	.30	.09
	Shawn Bradley		
❑ 312	Joe Kleine CF	.05	.02
	A.C. Green		
❑ 313	Harvey Grant CF	.05	.02
	Chris Dudley		
❑ 314	Bobby Hurley CF	.30	.09
	Mitch Richmond		
❑ 315	Sleepy Floyd CF	.30	.09
	Dennis Rodman		
❑ 316	Kendall Gill CF	.05	.02
	Detlef Schrempf		
❑ 317	Felton Spencer CF	.05	.02
	Luther Wright		
❑ 318	Calbert Cheaney CF	.05	.02
	Kevin Duckworth		
❑ 319	Karl Malone PC	.30	.09
❑ 320	Alonzo Mourning PC	.30	.09
❑ 321	Scottie Pippen PC	.50	.15
❑ 322	Mark Price PC	.05	.02
❑ 323	LaPhonso Ellis PC	.05	.02
❑ 324	Joe Dumars PC	.15	.04
❑ 325	Chris Mullin PC	.15	.04
❑ 326	Ron Harper PC	.05	.02
❑ 327	Glen Rice PC	.05	.02
❑ 328	Christian Laettner PC	.05	.02
❑ 329	Kenny Anderson PC	.05	.02
❑ 330	John Starks PC	.05	.02
❑ 331	Shaquille O'Neal PC	.60	.18
❑ 332	Charles Barkley PC	.30	.09
❑ 333	Clifford Robinson PC	.05	.02
❑ 334	Clyde Drexler PC	.15	.04
❑ 335	Mitch Richmond PC	.15	.04
❑ 336	David Robinson PC	.30	.09
❑ 337	Shawn Kemp PC	.30	.09
❑ 338	John Stockton PC	.15	.04
❑ 339	Checklist 4	.05	.02
❑ 340	Checklist 5	.05	.02
❑ 341	Checklist 6	.05	.02
❑ DP4	Jim Jackson	1.50	.45
❑ DP17	Doug Christie	.40	.12
❑ NNO	Head of the Class	1.50	.45
	Expired Exchange		
❑ NNO	HOC Card	30.00	9.00
	Shawn Bradley		
	Calbert Cheaney		
	Anfernee Hardaway		
	Jamal Mashburn		
	Isaiah Rider		
	Chris Webber		

1994-95 SkyBox Premium

	Nm-Mt	Ex-Mt
COMPLETE SET (350)	30.00	9.00
COMPLETE SERIES 1 (200)	15.00	4.50
COMPLETE SERIES 2 (150)	15.00	4.50
COMMON CARD (1-200)	.10	.03
COMMON CARD (201-350)	.05	.02

❑ 1	Stacey Augmon	.10	.03
❑ 2	Mookie Blaylock	.10	.03
❑ 3	Doug Edwards	.10	.03
❑ 4	Craig Ehlo	.10	.03
❑ 5	Adam Keefe	.10	.03
❑ 6	Danny Manning	.20	.06
❑ 7	Kevin Willis	.10	.03
❑ 8	Dee Brown	.10	.03
❑ 9	Sherman Douglas	.10	.03
❑ 10	Acie Earl	.10	.03
❑ 11	Kevin Gamble	.10	.03
❑ 12	Xavier McDaniel	.10	.03
❑ 13	Dino Radja	.10	.03
❑ 14	Muggsy Bogues	.20	.06
❑ 15	Scott Burrell	.10	.03
❑ 16	Dell Curry	.10	.03
❑ 17	LeRon Ellis	.10	.03
❑ 18	Hersey Hawkins	.20	.06
❑ 19	Larry Johnson	.20	.06
❑ 20	Alonzo Mourning	.50	.15
❑ 21	B.J. Armstrong	.10	.03
❑ 22	Corie Blount	.10	.03
❑ 23	Horace Grant	.20	.06
❑ 24	Toni Kukoc	.60	.18
❑ 25	Luc Longley	.10	.03
❑ 26	Scottie Pippen	1.25	.35
❑ 27	Scott Williams	.10	.03
❑ 28	Terrell Brandon	.20	.06
❑ 29	Brad Daugherty	.10	.03
❑ 30	Tyrone Hill	.10	.03
❑ 31	Chris Mills	.20	.06
❑ 32	Bobby Phills	.10	.03
❑ 33	Mark Price	.10	.03
❑ 34	Gerald Wilkins	.10	.03
❑ 35	Lucious Harris	.10	.03
❑ 36	Jim Jackson	.20	.06
❑ 37	Popeye Jones	.10	.03
❑ 38	Jamal Mashburn	.40	.12
❑ 39	Sean Rooks	.10	.03
❑ 40	Mahmoud Abdul-Rauf	.10	.03
❑ 41	LaPhonso Ellis	.10	.03
❑ 42	Dikembe Mutombo	.20	.06
❑ 43	Robert Pack	.10	.03
❑ 44	Rodney Rogers	.10	.03
❑ 45	Bryant Stith	.10	.03
❑ 46	Reggie Williams	.10	.03
❑ 47	Joe Dumars	.40	.12
❑ 48	Sean Elliott	.20	.06
❑ 49	Allan Houston	.60	.18
❑ 50	Lindsey Hunter	.20	.06
❑ 51	Terry Mills	.10	.03
❑ 52	Victor Alexander	.10	.03
❑ 53	Tim Hardaway	.40	.12
❑ 54	Chris Mullin	.40	.12
❑ 55	Billy Owens	.10	.03
❑ 56	Latrell Sprewell	.40	.12
❑ 57	Chris Webber	1.00	.30
❑ 58	Sam Cassell	.40	.12
❑ 59	Carl Herrera	.10	.03
❑ 60	Robert Horry	.20	.06
❑ 61	Vernon Maxwell	.10	.03
❑ 62	Hakeem Olajuwon	.60	.18
❑ 63	Kenny Smith	.10	.03
❑ 64	Otis Thorpe	.10	.03
❑ 65	Antonio Davis	.10	.03
❑ 66	Dale Davis	.10	.03
❑ 67	Derrick McKey	.10	.03
❑ 68	Reggie Miller	.40	.12
❑ 69	Pooh Richardson	.10	.03
❑ 70	Rik Smits	.10	.03
❑ 71	Haywoode Workman	.10	.03
❑ 72	Terry Dehere	.10	.03
❑ 73	Harold Ellis	.10	.03
❑ 74	Ron Harper	.20	.06
❑ 75	Mark Jackson	.10	.03
❑ 76	Loy Vaught	.10	.03
❑ 77	Dominique Wilkins	.40	.12
❑ 78	Elden Campbell	.10	.03
❑ 79	Doug Christie	.20	.06
❑ 80	Vlade Divac	.10	.03
❑ 81	George Lynch	.10	.03
❑ 82	Anthony Peeler	.10	.03
❑ 83	Sedale Threatt	.10	.03
❑ 84	Nick Van Exel	.40	.12
❑ 85	Harold Miner	.10	.03
❑ 86	Glen Rice	.20	.06
❑ 87	John Salley	.10	.03
❑ 88	Rony Seikaly	.10	.03
❑ 89	Brian Shaw	.10	.03
❑ 90	Steve Smith	.20	.06
❑ 91	Vin Baker	.40	.12
❑ 92	Jon Barry	.10	.03
❑ 93	Todd Day	.10	.03
❑ 94	Blue Edwards	.10	.03
❑ 95	Lee Mayberry	.10	.03
❑ 96	Eric Murdock	.10	.03
❑ 97	Mike Brown	.10	.03
❑ 98	Stacey King	.10	.03
❑ 99	Christian Laettner	.20	.06
❑ 100	Isaiah Rider	.20	.06
❑ 101	Doug West	.10	.03
❑ 102	Micheal Williams	.10	.03
❑ 103	Kenny Anderson	.20	.06
❑ 104	P.J. Brown	.10	.03
❑ 105	Derrick Coleman	.20	.06
❑ 106	Kevin Edwards	.10	.03
❑ 107	Chris Morris	.10	.03

No.	Card		
❑ 108	Rex Walters	.10	.03
❑ 109	Hubert Davis	.10	.03
❑ 110	Patrick Ewing	.40	.12
❑ 111	Derek Harper	.10	.03
❑ 112	Anthony Mason	.20	.06
❑ 113	Charles Oakley	.10	.03
❑ 114	Charles Smith	.10	.03
❑ 115	John Starks	.10	.03
❑ 116	Nick Anderson	.10	.03
❑ 117	Anfernee Hardaway	1.00	.30
❑ 118	Shaquille O'Neal	2.00	.60
❑ 119	Donald Royal	.10	.03
❑ 120	Dennis Scott	.10	.03
❑ 121	Scott Skiles	.10	.03
❑ 122	Dana Barros	.10	.03
❑ 123	Shawn Bradley	.10	.03
❑ 124	Johnny Dawkins	.10	.03
❑ 125	Greg Graham	.10	.03
❑ 126	Clarence Weatherspoon	.10	.03
❑ 127	Danny Ainge	.10	.03
❑ 128	Charles Barkley	.60	.18
❑ 129	Cedric Ceballos	.10	.03
❑ 130	A.C. Green	.20	.06
❑ 131	Kevin Johnson	.20	.06
❑ 132	Dan Majerle	.20	.06
❑ 133	Oliver Miller	.10	.03
❑ 134	Clyde Drexler	.40	.12
❑ 135	Harvey Grant	.10	.03
❑ 136	Tracy Murray	.10	.03
❑ 137	Terry Porter	.10	.03
❑ 138	Clifford Robinson	.20	.06
❑ 139	James Robinson	.10	.03
❑ 140	Rod Strickland	.20	.06
❑ 141	Bobby Hurley	.10	.03
❑ 142	Olden Polynice	.10	.03
❑ 143	Mitch Richmond	.40	.12
❑ 144	Lionel Simmons	.10	.03
❑ 145	Wayman Tisdale	.10	.03
❑ 146	Spud Webb	.10	.03
❑ 147	Walt Williams	.10	.03
❑ 148	Willie Anderson	.10	.03
❑ 149	Vinny Del Negro	.10	.03
❑ 150	Dale Ellis	.10	.03
❑ 151	J.R. Reid	.10	.03
❑ 152	David Robinson	.60	.18
❑ 153	Dennis Rodman	.75	.23
❑ 154	Kendall Gill	.20	.06
❑ 155	Shawn Kemp	.60	.18
❑ 156	Nate McMillan	.10	.03
❑ 157	Gary Payton	.60	.18
❑ 158	Sam Perkins	.20	.06
❑ 159	Ricky Pierce	.10	.03
❑ 160	Detlef Schrempf	.20	.06
❑ 161	David Benoit	.10	.03
❑ 162	Tyrone Corbin	.10	.03
❑ 163	Jeff Hornacek	.20	.06
❑ 164	Jay Humphries	.10	.03
❑ 165	Karl Malone	.60	.18
❑ 166	Bryon Russell	.10	.03
❑ 167	Felton Spencer	.10	.03
❑ 168	John Stockton	.40	.12
❑ 169	Michael Adams	.10	.03
❑ 170	Rex Chapman	.10	.03
❑ 171	Calbert Cheaney	.10	.03
❑ 172	Pervis Ellison	.10	.03
❑ 173	Tom Gugliotta	.20	.06
❑ 174	Don MacLean	.10	.03
❑ 175	Gheorghe Muresan	.10	.03
❑ 176	Charles Barkley NBC	.40	.12
❑ 177	Charles Oakley NBC	.10	.03
❑ 178	Hakeem Olajuwon NBC	.40	.12
❑ 179	Dikembe Mutombo NBC	.10	.03
❑ 180	Scottie Pippen NBC	.60	.18
❑ 181	Sam Cassell NBC	.40	.12
❑ 182	Karl Malone NBC	.40	.12
❑ 183	Reggie Miller PO	.20	.06
❑ 184	Patrick Ewing NBC	.20	.06
❑ 185	Vernon Maxwell NBC	.10	.03
❑ 186	Anfernee Hardaway DD Steve Smith	.40	.12
❑ 187	Chris Webber DD Shaquille O'Neal	.40	.12
❑ 188	Jamal Mashburn DD Rodney Rogers	.10	.03
❑ 189	Toni Kukoc DD Dino Radja	.20	.06
❑ 190	Lindsey Hunter DD Kenny Anderson	.10	.03
❑ 191	Latrell Sprewell DD Jimmy Jackson	.20	.06
❑ 192	Clarence Weatherspoon Vin Baker DD	.20	.06
❑ 193	Calbert Cheaney DD Chris Mills	.10	.03
❑ 194	Isaiah Rider DD Robert Horry	.20	.06
❑ 195	Sam Cassell DD Nick Van Exel	.10	.03
❑ 196	Gheorghe Muresan DD Shawn Bradley	.10	.03
❑ 197	LaPhonso Ellis DD Tom Gugliotta	.10	.03
❑ 198	USA Basketball Card	.10	.03
❑ 199	Checklist	.10	.03
❑ 200	Checklist	.10	.03
❑ 201	Sergei Bazarevich	.05	.02
❑ 202	Tyrone Corbin	.05	.02
❑ 203	Grant Long	.05	.02
❑ 204	Ken Norman	.05	.02
❑ 205	Steve Smith	.10	.03
❑ 206	Blue Edwards	.05	.02
❑ 207	Greg Minor RC	.05	.02
❑ 208	Eric Montross RC	.05	.02
❑ 209	Dominique Wilkins	.25	.07
❑ 210	Michael Adams	.05	.02
❑ 211	Kenny Gattison	.05	.02
❑ 212	Darrin Hancock	.05	.02
❑ 213	Robert Parish	.10	.03
❑ 214	Ron Harper	.10	.03
❑ 215	Steve Kerr	.05	.02
❑ 216	Will Perdue	.05	.02
❑ 217	Dickey Simpkins RC	.05	.02
❑ 218	John Battle	.05	.02
❑ 219	Michael Cage	.05	.02
❑ 220	Tony Dumas RC	.05	.02
❑ 221	Jason Kidd RC	2.50	.75
❑ 222	Roy Tarpley	.05	.02
❑ 223	Dale Ellis	.05	.02
❑ 224	Jalen Rose RC	1.00	.30
❑ 225	Bill Curley RC	.05	.02
❑ 226	Grant Hill RC	1.25	.35
❑ 227	Oliver Miller	.05	.02
❑ 228	Mark West	.05	.02
❑ 229	Tom Gugliotta	.10	.03
❑ 230	Ricky Pierce	.05	.02
❑ 231	Carlos Rogers RC	.05	.02
❑ 232	Clifford Rozier RC	.05	.02
❑ 233	Rony Seikaly	.05	.02
❑ 234	Tim Breaux	.05	.02
❑ 235	Duane Ferrell	.05	.02
❑ 236	Mark Jackson	.05	.02
❑ 237	Byron Scott	.10	.03
❑ 238	John Williams	.05	.02
❑ 239	Lamond Murray RC	.10	.03
❑ 240	Eric Piatkowski RC	.05	.02
❑ 241	Pooh Richardson	.05	.02
❑ 242	Malik Sealy	.05	.02
❑ 243	Cedric Ceballos	.05	.02
❑ 244	Eddie Jones RC	1.25	.35
❑ 245	Anthony Miller RC	.05	.02
❑ 246	Tony Smith	.05	.02
❑ 247	Kevin Gamble	.05	.02
❑ 248	Brad Lohaus	.05	.02
❑ 249	Billy Owens	.05	.02
❑ 250	Khalid Reeves RC	.05	.02
❑ 251	Kevin Willis	.05	.02
❑ 252	Eric Mobley RC	.05	.02
❑ 253	Johnny Newman	.05	.02
❑ 254	Ed Pinckney	.05	.02
❑ 255	Glenn Robinson RC	.75	.23
❑ 256	Howard Eisley	.05	.02
❑ 257	Donyell Marshall RC	.25	.07
❑ 258	Yinka Dare RC	.05	.02
❑ 259	Sean Higgins	.05	.02
❑ 260	Jayson Williams	.10	.03
❑ 261	Charlie Ward RC	.25	.07
❑ 262	Monty Williams RC	.05	.02
❑ 263	Horace Grant	.10	.03
❑ 264	Brian Shaw	.05	.02
❑ 265	Brooks Thompson RC	.05	.02
❑ 266	Derrick Alston RC	.05	.02
❑ 267	B.J. Tyler RC	.05	.02
❑ 268	Scott Williams	.05	.02
❑ 269	Sharone Wright RC	.05	.02
❑ 270	Antonio Lang RC	.05	.02
❑ 271	Danny Manning	.10	.03
❑ 272	Wesley Person RC	.25	.07
❑ 273	Trevor Ruffin RC	.05	.02
❑ 274	Wayman Tisdale	.05	.02
❑ 275	Jerome Kersey	.05	.02
❑ 276	Aaron McKie RC	.50	.15
❑ 277	Frank Brickowski	.05	.02
❑ 278	Brian Grant RC	.60	.18
❑ 279	Michael Smith RC	.05	.02
❑ 280	Terry Cummings	.05	.02
❑ 281	Sean Elliott	.10	.03
❑ 282	Avery Johnson	.05	.02
❑ 283	Moses Malone	.25	.07
❑ 284	Chuck Person	.05	.02
❑ 285	Vincent Askew	.05	.02
❑ 286	Bill Cartwright	.05	.02
❑ 287	Sarunas Marciulionis	.05	.02
❑ 288	Dontonio Wingfield RC	.05	.02
❑ 289	Jay Humphries	.05	.02
❑ 290	Adam Keefe	.05	.02
❑ 291	Jamie Watson RC	.05	.02
❑ 292	Kevin Duckworth	.05	.02
❑ 293	Juwan Howard RC	.60	.18
❑ 294	Jim McIlvaine	.05	.02
❑ 295	Scott Skiles	.05	.02
❑ 296	Anthony Tucker RC	.05	.02
❑ 297	Chris Webber	.60	.18
❑ 298	Checklist 201-265	.05	.02
❑ 299	Checklist 266-345	.05	.02
❑ 300	Checklist 346-350/Inserts	.05	.02
❑ 301	Vin Baker SSL	.10	.03
❑ 302	Charles Barkley SSL	.25	.07
❑ 303	Derrick Coleman SSL	.05	.02
❑ 304	Clyde Drexler SSL	.10	.03
❑ 305	LaPhonso Ellis SSL	.05	.02
❑ 306	Larry Johnson SSL	.05	.02
❑ 307	Shawn Kemp SSL	.25	.07
❑ 308	Karl Malone SSL	.25	.07
❑ 309	Jamal Mashburn SSL	.10	.03
❑ 310	Scottie Pippen SSL	.40	.12
❑ 311	Dominique Wilkins SSL	.10	.03
❑ 312	Walt Williams SSL	.05	.02
❑ 313	Sharone Wright SSL	.05	.02
❑ 314	B.J. Armstrong SSH	.05	.02
❑ 315	Joe Dumars SSH	.10	.03
❑ 316	Tony Dumas SSH	.05	.02
❑ 317	Tim Hardaway SSH	.10	.03
❑ 318	Toni Kukoc SSH	.25	.07
❑ 319	Danny Manning SSH	.05	.02
❑ 320	Reggie Miller SSH	.10	.03
❑ 321	Chris Mullin SSH	.10	.03
❑ 322	Wesley Person SSH	.10	.03
❑ 323	John Starks SSH	.05	.02
❑ 324	John Stockton SSH	.10	.03
❑ 325	C. Weatherspoon SSH	.05	.02
❑ 326	Shawn Bradley SSW	.05	.02
❑ 327	Vlade Divac SSW	.05	.02
❑ 328	Patrick Ewing SSW	.10	.03
❑ 329	Christian Laettner SSW	.05	.02
❑ 330	Eric Montross SSW	.05	.02
❑ 331	Gheorghe Muresan SSW	.05	.02
❑ 332	Dikembe Mutombo SSW	.05	.02
❑ 333	Hakeem Olajuwon SSW	.25	.07
❑ 334	Robert Parish SSW	.05	.02
❑ 335	David Robinson SSW	.25	.07
❑ 336	Dennis Rodman SSW	.25	.07
❑ 337	Rony Seikaly SSW	.05	.02
❑ 338	Rik Smits SSW	.10	.03
❑ 339	Kenny Anderson SPI	.05	.02
❑ 340	Dee Brown SPI	.05	.02
❑ 341	Bobby Hurley SPI	.05	.02
❑ 342	Kevin Johnson SPI	.05	.02
❑ 343	Jason Kidd SPI	1.00	.30
❑ 344	Gary Payton SPI	.25	.07
❑ 345	Mark Price SPI	.05	.02
❑ 346	Khalid Reeves SPI	.05	.02
❑ 347	Jalen Rose SPI	.10	.03
❑ 348	Latrell Sprewell SPI	.25	.07
❑ 349	B.J. Tyler SPI	.05	.02
❑ 350	Charlie Ward SPI	.10	.03
❑ GHO	Grant Hill Gold	12.00	3.60
❑ NNO	Grant Hill	6.00	1.80

Hoops Jumbo		
❑ NNO Grant Hill	6.00	1.80
SkyBox Jumbo		
❑ NNO Grant Hill	6.00	1.80
Slammin' Universe		
Jumbo Card		
❑ NNO Hakeem Olajuwon	10.00	3.00
Gold		
❑ NNO Emotion Sheet A	30.00	9.00
❑ NNO Emotion Sheet B	30.00	9.00
❑ NNO Emotion Exchange A	1.00	.30
Expired		
❑ NNO Emotion Exchange B	1.00	.30
Expired		
❑ NNO Emotion Exchange C	1.00	.30
Expired		
❑ NNO 3rd Prize Game Card	.25	.07
Expired		
❑ NNO Hakeem Olajuwon	300.00	90.00
David Robinson AU		
❑ NNO Magic Johnson	5.00	1.50
Exchange Card		
❑ NNO 3 Card Panel Exchange	4.00	1.20
Magic Johnson		
Hakeem Olajuwon		
David Robinson		

1995-96 SkyBox Premium

	Nm-Mt	Ex-Mt
COMPLETE SET (301)	35.00	10.50
COMPLETE SERIES 1 (150)	15.00	4.50
COMPLETE SERIES 2 (151)	20.00	6.00
❑ 1 Stacey Augmon	.20	.06
❑ 2 Mookie Blaylock	.20	.06
❑ 3 Grant Long	.20	.06
❑ 4 Steve Smith	.40	.12
❑ 5 Dee Brown	.20	.06
❑ 6 Sherman Douglas	.20	.06
❑ 7 Eric Montross	.20	.06
❑ 8 Dino Radja	.20	.06
❑ 9 Dominique Wilkins	.60	.18
❑ 10 Muggsy Bogues	.40	.12
❑ 11 Scott Burrell	.20	.06
❑ 12 Dell Curry	.20	.06
❑ 13 Larry Johnson	.40	.12
❑ 14 Alonzo Mourning	.40	.12
❑ 15 Michael Jordan UER	4.00	1.20
Career block total is wrong		
❑ 16 Steve Kerr	.40	.12
❑ 17 Toni Kukoc	.40	.12
❑ 18 Scottie Pippen	1.00	.30
❑ 19 Terrell Brandon	.40	.12
❑ 20 Tyrone Hill	.20	.06
❑ 21 Chris Mills	.20	.06
❑ 22 Mark Price	.40	.12
❑ 23 John Williams	.20	.06
❑ 24 Tony Dumas	.20	.06
❑ 25 Jim Jackson	.20	.06
❑ 26 Popeye Jones	.20	.06
❑ 27 Jason Kidd	2.00	.60
❑ 28 Jamal Mashburn	.40	.12
❑ 29 LaPhonso Ellis	.20	.06
❑ 30 Dikembe Mutombo	.40	.12
❑ 31 Robert Pack	.20	.06
❑ 32 Jalen Rose	.75	.23
❑ 33 Bryant Stith	.20	.06
❑ 34 Joe Dumars	.60	.18
❑ 35 Grant Hill	.75	.23
❑ 36 Allan Houston	.40	.12
❑ 37 Lindsey Hunter	.20	.06
❑ 38 Chris Gatling	.20	.06
❑ 39 Tim Hardaway	.40	.12
❑ 40 Donyell Marshall	.40	.12
❑ 41 Chris Mullin	.60	.18
❑ 42 Carlos Rogers	.20	.06
❑ 43 Latrell Sprewell	.60	.18
❑ 44 Sam Cassell	.60	.18
❑ 45 Clyde Drexler	.60	.18
❑ 46 Robert Horry	.40	.12
❑ 47 Hakeem Olajuwon	.60	.18
❑ 48 Kenny Smith	.20	.06
❑ 49 Dale Davis	.20	.06
❑ 50 Mark Jackson	.40	.12
❑ 51 Reggie Miller	.60	.18
❑ 52 Rik Smits	.40	.12
❑ 53 Lamond Murray	.20	.06
❑ 54 Eric Piatkowski	.40	.12
❑ 55 Pooh Richardson	.20	.06
❑ 56 Rodney Rogers	.20	.06
❑ 57 Loy Vaught	.20	.06
❑ 58 Elden Campbell	.20	.06
❑ 59 Cedric Ceballos	.20	.06
❑ 60 Vlade Divac	.40	.12
❑ 61 Eddie Jones	.75	.23
❑ 62 Anthony Peeler	.20	.06
❑ 63 Nick Van Exel	.60	.18
❑ 64 Bimbo Coles	.20	.06
❑ 65 Billy Owens	.20	.06
❑ 66 Khalid Reeves	.20	.06
❑ 67 Glen Rice	.40	.12
❑ 68 Kevin Willis	.40	.12
❑ 69 Vin Baker	.40	.12
❑ 70 Todd Day	.20	.06
❑ 71 Eric Murdock	.20	.06
❑ 72 Glenn Robinson	.60	.18
❑ 73 Tom Gugliotta	.20	.06
❑ 74 Christian Laettner	.40	.12
❑ 75 Isaiah Rider	.20	.06
❑ 76 Doug West	.20	.06
❑ 77 Kenny Anderson	.40	.12
❑ 78 P.J. Brown	.20	.06
❑ 79 Derrick Coleman	.20	.06
❑ 80 Armon Gilliam	.20	.06
❑ 81 Patrick Ewing	.60	.18
❑ 82 Derek Harper	.40	.12
❑ 83 Anthony Mason	.40	.12
❑ 84 Charles Oakley	.20	.06
❑ 85 John Starks	.40	.12
❑ 86 Nick Anderson	.20	.06
❑ 87 Horace Grant	.40	.12
❑ 88 Anfernee Hardaway	.60	.18
❑ 89 Shaquille O'Neal	1.50	.45
❑ 90 Dana Barros	.20	.06
❑ 91 Shawn Bradley	.20	.06
❑ 92 Clarence Weatherspoon	.20	.06
❑ 93 Sharone Wright	.20	.06
❑ 94 Charles Barkley	.75	.23
❑ 95 Kevin Johnson	.40	.12
❑ 96 Dan Majerle	.40	.12
❑ 97 Danny Manning	.40	.12
❑ 98 Wesley Person	.20	.06
❑ 99 Clifford Robinson	.20	.06
❑ 100 Rod Strickland	.20	.06
❑ 101 Otis Thorpe	.20	.06
❑ 102 Buck Williams	.20	.06
❑ 103 Brian Grant	.60	.18
❑ 104 Olden Polynice	.20	.06
❑ 105 Mitch Richmond	.40	.12
❑ 106 Walt Williams	.20	.06
❑ 107 Vinny Del Negro	.20	.06
❑ 108 Sean Elliott	.40	.12
❑ 109 Avery Johnson	.20	.06
❑ 110 David Robinson	.60	.18
❑ 111 Dennis Rodman	.40	.12
❑ 112 Shawn Kemp	.40	.12
❑ 113 Gary Payton	.60	.18
❑ 114 Sam Perkins	.40	.12
❑ 115 Detlef Schrempf	.40	.12
❑ 116 David Benoit	.20	.06
❑ 117 Jeff Hornacek	.40	.12
❑ 118 Karl Malone	.75	.23
❑ 119 John Stockton	.75	.23
❑ 120 Calbert Cheaney	.20	.06
❑ 121 Juwan Howard	.60	.18
❑ 122 Don MacLean	.20	.06
❑ 123 Gheorghe Muresan	.20	.06
❑ 124 Chris Webber	.75	.23
❑ 125 Robert Horry FC	.20	.06
❑ 126 Mark Jackson FC	.20	.06
❑ 127 Steve Smith FC	.20	.06
❑ 128 Lamond Murray FC	.20	.06
❑ 129 Christian Laettner FC	.20	.06
❑ 130 Kenny Anderson FC	.20	.06
❑ 131 Anthony Mason FC	.20	.06
❑ 132 Kevin Johnson FC	.20	.06
❑ 133 Jeff Hornacek FC	.20	.06
❑ 134 Larry Johnson TP	.20	.06
❑ 135 Popeye Jones TP	.20	.06
❑ 136 Allan Houston TP	.20	.06
❑ 137 Chris Gatling TP	.20	.06
❑ 138 Sam Cassell TP	.20	.06
❑ 139 Anthony Peeler TP	.20	.06
❑ 140 Vin Baker TP	.20	.06
❑ 141 Dana Barros TP	.20	.06
❑ 142 Gheorghe Muresan TP	.20	.06
❑ 143 Toronto Raptors	.20	.06
❑ 144 Vancouver Grizzlies	.20	.06
❑ 145 Glen Rice EXP	.40	.12
Muggsy Bogues EXP		
❑ 146 Nick Anderson EXP	.20	.06
Christian Laettner EXP		
❑ 147 John Salley TF	.20	.06
❑ 148 Greg Anthony TF	.20	.06
❑ 149 Checklist #1	.20	.06
❑ 150 Checklist #2	.20	.06
❑ 151 Craig Ehlo	.20	.06
❑ 152 Spud Webb	.40	.12
❑ 153 Dana Barros	.20	.06
❑ 155 Kendall Gill	.20	.06
❑ 156 Khalid Reeves	.20	.06
❑ 157 Glen Rice	.40	.12
❑ 158 Luc Longley	.20	.06
❑ 159 Dennis Rodman	.40	.12
❑ 160 Dickey Simpkins	.20	.06
❑ 161 Danny Ferry	.20	.06
❑ 162 Dan Majerle	.40	.12
❑ 163 Bobby Phills	.20	.06
❑ 164 Lucious Harris	.20	.06
❑ 165 George McCloud	.20	.06
❑ 166 Mahmoud Abdul-Rauf	.20	.06
❑ 167 Don MacLean	.20	.06
❑ 168 Reggie Williams	.20	.06
❑ 169 Terry Mills	.20	.06
❑ 170 Otis Thorpe	.20	.06
❑ 171 B.J. Armstrong	.20	.06
❑ 172 Rony Seikaly	.20	.06
❑ 173 Chucky Brown	.20	.06
❑ 174 Mario Elie	.20	.06
❑ 175 Antonio Davis	.20	.06
❑ 176 Ricky Pierce	.20	.06
❑ 177 Terry Dehere	.20	.06
❑ 178 Rodney Rogers	.20	.06
❑ 179 Malik Sealy	.20	.06
❑ 180 Brian Williams	.20	.06
❑ 181 Sedale Threatt	.20	.06
❑ 182 Alonzo Mourning	.40	.12
❑ 183 Lee Mayberry	.20	.06
❑ 184 Sean Rooks	.20	.06
❑ 185 Shawn Bradley	.20	.06
❑ 186 Kevin Edwards	.20	.06
❑ 187 Hubert Davis	.20	.06
❑ 188 Charles Smith	.20	.06
❑ 189 Charlie Ward	.20	.06
❑ 190 Dennis Scott	.20	.06
❑ 191 Brian Shaw	.20	.06
❑ 192 Derrick Coleman	.20	.06
❑ 193 Richard Dumas	.20	.06
❑ 194 Vernon Maxwell	.20	.06
❑ 195 A.C. Green	.40	.12
❑ 196 Elliot Perry	.20	.06
❑ 197 John Williams	.20	.06
❑ 198 Aaron McKie	.40	.12
❑ 199 Bobby Hurley	.20	.06
❑ 200 Michael Smith	.20	.06
❑ 201 J.R. Reid	.20	.06
❑ 202 Hersey Hawkins	.20	.06
❑ 203 Willie Anderson	.20	.06
❑ 204 Oliver Miller	.20	.06

❑ 205	Tracy Murray	.20	.06
❑ 206	Alvin Robertson	.20	.06
❑ 207	Carlos Rogers UER Card says Rodney Rogers on front with picture	.20	.06
❑ 208	John Salley	.20	.06
❑ 209	Zan Tabak	.20	.06
❑ 210	Adam Keefe	.20	.06
❑ 211	Chris Morris	.20	.06
❑ 212	Greg Anthony	.20	.06
❑ 213	Blue Edwards	.20	.06
❑ 214	Kenny Gattison	.20	.06
❑ 215	Antonio Harvey	.20	.06
❑ 216	Chris King	.20	.06
❑ 217	Byron Scott	.20	.06
❑ 218	Robert Pack	.20	.06
❑ 219	Alan Henderson RC	.60	.18
❑ 220	Eric Williams RC	.40	.12
❑ 221	George Zidek RC	.20	.06
❑ 222	Jason Caffey RC	.40	.12
❑ 223	Bob Sura RC	.40	.12
❑ 224	Cherokee Parks RC	.20	.06
❑ 225	Antonio McDyess RC	1.25	.35
❑ 226	Theo Ratliff RC	.75	.23
❑ 227	Joe Smith RC	1.00	.30
❑ 228	Travis Best RC	.20	.06
❑ 229	Brent Barry RC	.60	.18
❑ 230	Sasha Danilovic RC	.20	.06
❑ 231	Kurt Thomas RC	.40	.12
❑ 232	Shawn Respert RC	.20	.06
❑ 233	Kevin Garnett RC	3.00	.90
❑ 234	Ed O'Bannon RC	.20	.06
❑ 235	Jerry Stackhouse RC	2.00	.60
❑ 236	Michael Finley RC	1.50	.45
❑ 237	Mario Bennett RC	.20	.06
❑ 238	Randolph Childress RC	.20	.06
❑ 239	Arvydas Sabonis RC	.75	.23
❑ 240	Gary Trent RC	.20	.06
❑ 241	Tyus Edney RC	.20	.06
❑ 242	Corliss Williamson RC	.60	.18
❑ 243	Cory Alexander RC	.20	.06
❑ 244	Damon Stoudamire RC	1.25	.35
❑ 245	Greg Ostertag RC	.20	.06
❑ 246	Lawrence Moten RC	.20	.06
❑ 247	Bryant Reeves RC	.60	.18
❑ 248	Rasheed Wallace RC	1.50	.45
❑ 249	Muggsy Bogues HR	.20	.06
❑ 250	Dell Curry HR	.20	.06
❑ 251	Scottie Pippen HR	.40	.12
❑ 252	Danny Ferry HR	.20	.06
❑ 253	Mahmoud Abdul-Rauf HR	.20	.06
❑ 254	Joe Dumars HR	.40	.12
❑ 255	Tim Hardaway HR	.20	.06
❑ 256	Chris Mullin HR	.40	.12
❑ 257	Hakeem Olajuwon HR	.40	.12
❑ 258	Kenny Smith HR	.20	.06
❑ 259	Reggie Miller HR	.40	.12
❑ 260	Rik Smits HR	.20	.06
❑ 261	Vlade Divac HR	.20	.06
❑ 262	Doug West HR	.20	.06
❑ 263	Patrick Ewing HR	.40	.12
❑ 264	Charles Oakley HR	.20	.06
❑ 265	Nick Anderson HR	.20	.06
❑ 266	Dennis Scott HR	.20	.06
❑ 267	Jeff Turner HR	.20	.06
❑ 268	Charles Barkley HR	.60	.18
❑ 269	Kevin Johnson HR	.20	.06
❑ 270	Clifford Robinson HR	.20	.06
❑ 271	Buck Williams HR	.20	.06
❑ 272	Lionel Simmons HR	.20	.06
❑ 273	David Robinson HR	.40	.12
❑ 274	Gary Payton HR	.40	.12
❑ 275	Karl Malone HR	.60	.18
❑ 276	John Stockton HR	.60	.18
❑ 277	Steve Smith ELE	.20	.06
❑ 278	Michael Jordan ELE	2.00	.60
❑ 279	Jim Jackson ELE	.20	.06
❑ 280	Jason Kidd ELE	1.00	.30
❑ 281	Jamal Mashburn ELE	.20	.06
❑ 282	Dikembe Mutombo ELE	.20	.06
❑ 283	Grant Hill ELE	.60	.18
❑ 284	Tim Hardaway ELE	.20	.06
❑ 285	Clyde Drexler ELE	.40	.12
❑ 286	Cedric Ceballos ELE	.20	.06
❑ 287	Gary Payton ELE	.40	.12
❑ 288	Billy Owens ELE	.20	.06
❑ 289	Vin Baker ELE	.20	.06
❑ 290	Glenn Robinson ELE	.40	.12
❑ 291	Kenny Anderson ELE	.20	.06
❑ 292	Anfernee Hardaway ELE	.40	.12
❑ 293	Shaquille O'Neal ELE	.60	.18
❑ 294	Charles Barkley ELE	.60	.18
❑ 295	Rod Strickland ELE	.20	.06
❑ 296	Mitch Richmond ELE	.20	.06
❑ 297	Juwan Howard ELE	.40	.12
❑ 298	Chris Webber ELE	.60	.18
❑ 299	Checklist #1	.20	.06
❑ 300	Checklist #2	.20	.06
❑ 301	Magic Johnson	1.00	.30
❑ PR	Grant Hill JUMBO	6.00	1.80
❑ NNO	Grant Hill Meltdown Exchange	25.00	7.50
❑ NNO	Jerry Stackhouse Meltdown Exchange	30.00	9.00

1996-97 SkyBox Premium

	Nm-Mt	Ex-Mt
COMPLETE SET (281)	35.00	10.50
COMPLETE SERIES 1 (131)	25.00	7.50
COMPLETE SERIES 2 (150)	15.00	4.50

❑ 1	Mookie Blaylock	.20	.06
❑ 2	Alan Henderson	.20	.06
❑ 3	Christian Laettner	.40	.12
❑ 4	Dikembe Mutombo	.40	.12
❑ 5	Steve Smith	.40	.12
❑ 6	Dana Barros	.20	.06
❑ 7	Rick Fox	.20	.06
❑ 8	Dino Radja	.20	.06
❑ 9	Antoine Walker RC	2.00	.60
❑ 10	Eric Williams	.20	.06
❑ 11	Dell Curry	.20	.06
❑ 12	Tony Delk RC	.60	.18
❑ 13	Matt Geiger	.20	.06
❑ 14	Glen Rice	.40	.12
❑ 15	Ron Harper	.40	.12
❑ 16	Michael Jordan	4.00	1.20
❑ 17	Toni Kukoc	.40	.12
❑ 18	Scottie Pippen	1.00	.30
❑ 19	Dennis Rodman	.40	.12
❑ 20	Terrell Brandon	.40	.12
❑ 21	Danny Ferry	.20	.06
❑ 22	Chris Mills	.20	.06
❑ 23	Bobby Phills	.20	.06
❑ 24	Vitaly Potapenko RC	.20	.06
❑ 25	Jim Jackson	.20	.06
❑ 26	Jason Kidd	1.00	.30
❑ 27	Jamal Mashburn	.40	.12
❑ 28	George McCloud	.20	.06
❑ 29	Samaki Walker RC	.20	.06
❑ 30	LaPhonso Ellis	.20	.06
❑ 31	Antonio McDyess	.40	.12
❑ 32	Bryant Stith	.20	.06
❑ 33	Joe Dumars	.60	.18
❑ 34	Grant Hill	.60	.18
❑ 35	Lindsey Hunter	.20	.06
❑ 36	Theo Ratliff	.40	.12
❑ 37	Otis Thorpe	.20	.06
❑ 38	Todd Fuller RC	.20	.06
❑ 39	Chris Mullin	.60	.18
❑ 40	Joe Smith	.40	.12
❑ 41	Latrell Sprewell	.60	.18
❑ 42	Charles Barkley	.75	.23
❑ 43	Clyde Drexler	.60	.18
❑ 44	Mario Elie	.20	.06
❑ 45	Hakeem Olajuwon	.60	.18
❑ 46	Erick Dampier RC	.60	.18
❑ 47	Dale Davis	.20	.06
❑ 48	Derrick McKey	.20	.06
❑ 49	Reggie Miller	.60	.18
❑ 50	Rik Smits	.40	.12
❑ 51	Brent Barry	.20	.06
❑ 52	Rodney Rogers	.20	.06
❑ 53	Loy Vaught	.20	.06
❑ 54	Lorenzen Wright RC	.40	.12
❑ 55	Kobe Bryant RC	10.00	3.00
❑ 56	Cedric Ceballos	.20	.06
❑ 57	Eddie Jones	.60	.18
❑ 58	Shaquille O'Neal	1.50	.45
❑ 59	Nick Van Exel	.60	.18
❑ 60	Tim Hardaway	.40	.12
❑ 61	Alonzo Mourning	.40	.12
❑ 62	Kurt Thomas	.40	.12
❑ 63	Ray Allen RC	2.50	.75
❑ 64	Vin Baker	.40	.12
❑ 65	Shawn Respert	.20	.06
❑ 66	Glenn Robinson	.60	.18
❑ 67	Kevin Garnett	1.25	.35
❑ 68	Tom Gugliotta	.20	.06
❑ 69	Stephon Marbury RC	2.00	.60
❑ 70	Sam Mitchell	.20	.06
❑ 71	Shawn Bradley	.20	.06
❑ 72	Kendall Gill	.20	.06
❑ 73	Kerry Kittles RC	.60	.18
❑ 74	Ed O'Bannon	.20	.06
❑ 75	Patrick Ewing	.60	.18
❑ 76	Larry Johnson	.40	.12
❑ 77	Charles Oakley	.20	.06
❑ 78	John Starks	.40	.12
❑ 79	John Wallace RC	.60	.18
❑ 80	Nick Anderson	.20	.06
❑ 81	Horace Grant	.40	.12
❑ 82	Anfernee Hardaway	.60	.18
❑ 83	Dennis Scott	.20	.06
❑ 84	Derrick Coleman	.40	.12
❑ 85	Allen Iverson RC	4.00	1.20
❑ 86	Jerry Stackhouse	.75	.23
❑ 87	Clarence Weatherspoon	.20	.06
❑ 88	Michael Finley	.75	.23
❑ 89	Robert Horry	.40	.12
❑ 90	Kevin Johnson	.40	.12
❑ 91	Steve Nash RC	2.00	.60
❑ 92	Wesley Person	.20	.06
❑ 93	Aaron McKie	.40	.12
❑ 94	Jermaine O'Neal RC	2.00	.60
❑ 95	Clifford Robinson	.20	.06
❑ 96	Arvydas Sabonis	.40	.12
❑ 97	Gary Trent	.20	.06
❑ 98	Tyus Edney	.20	.06
❑ 99	Brian Grant	.60	.18
❑ 100	Mitch Richmond	.40	.12
❑ 101	Billy Owens	.20	.06
❑ 102	Corliss Williamson	.40	.12
❑ 103	Vinny Del Negro	.20	.06
❑ 104	Sean Elliott	.40	.12
❑ 105	Avery Johnson	.20	.06
❑ 106	Chuck Person	.20	.06
❑ 107	David Robinson	.60	.18
❑ 108	Hersey Hawkins	.40	.12
❑ 109	Shawn Kemp	.40	.12
❑ 110	Gary Payton	.60	.18
❑ 111	Sam Perkins	.40	.12
❑ 112	Detlef Schrempf	.40	.12
❑ 113	Marcus Camby RC	.75	.23
❑ 114	Carlos Rogers	.20	.06
❑ 115	Damon Stoudamire	.60	.18
❑ 116	Zan Tabak	.20	.06
❑ 117	Antoine Carr	.20	.06
❑ 118	Jeff Hornacek	.40	.12
❑ 119	Karl Malone	.60	.18
❑ 120	Chris Morris	.20	.06
❑ 121	John Stockton	.60	.18
❑ 122	Shareef Abdur-Rahim RC	2.00	.60
❑ 123	Greg Anthony	.20	.06
❑ 124	Bryant Reeves	.20	.06
❑ 125	Roy Rogers RC	.20	.06
❑ 126	Calbert Cheaney	.20	.06
❑ 127	Juwan Howard	.40	.12
❑ 128	Gheorghe Muresan	.20	.06

#	Player	Nm-Mt	Ex-Mt
❑ 129	Chris Webber	.60	.18
❑ 130	Checklist	.20	.06
❑ 131	Checklist	.20	.06
❑ 132	Jon Barry	.20	.06
❑ 133	Christian Laettner	.40	.12
❑ 134	Dikembe Mutombo	.40	.12
❑ 135	Dee Brown	.20	.06
❑ 136	Todd Day	.20	.06
❑ 137	David Wesley	.20	.06
❑ 138	Vlade Divac	.20	.06
❑ 139	Anthony Goldwire	.20	.06
❑ 140	Anthony Mason	.40	.12
❑ 141	Jason Caffey	.20	.06
❑ 142	Luc Longley	.20	.06
❑ 143	Tyrone Hill	.20	.06
❑ 144	Antonio Lang	.20	.06
❑ 145	Sam Cassell	.60	.18
❑ 146	Chris Gatling	.20	.06
❑ 147	Eric Montross	.20	.06
❑ 148	Ervin Johnson	.20	.06
❑ 149	Sarunas Marciulionis	.20	.06
❑ 150	Stacey Augmon	.20	.06
❑ 151	Grant Long	.20	.06
❑ 152	Terry Mills	.20	.06
❑ 153	Kenny Smith	.20	.06
❑ 154	B.J. Armstrong	.20	.06
❑ 155	Bimbo Coles	.20	.06
❑ 156	Charles Barkley	.75	.23
❑ 157	Brent Price	.20	.06
❑ 158	Duane Ferrell	.20	.06
❑ 159	Jalen Rose	.60	.18
❑ 160	Terry Dehere	.20	.06
❑ 161	Bo Outlaw	.20	.06
❑ 162	Corie Blount	.20	.06
❑ 163	Shaquille O'Neal	1.50	.45
❑ 164	Rumeal Robinson	.20	.06
❑ 165	P.J. Brown	.20	.06
❑ 166	Ronnie Grandison	.20	.06
❑ 167	Sherman Douglas	.20	.06
❑ 168	Johnny Newman	.20	.06
❑ 169	James Robinson	.20	.06
❑ 170	Doug West	.20	.06
❑ 171	Robert Pack	.20	.06
❑ 172	Khalid Reeves	.20	.06
❑ 173	Chris Childs	.20	.06
❑ 174	Allan Houston	.40	.12
❑ 175	Charlie Ward	.20	.06
❑ 176	Darrell Armstrong RC	2.00	.60
❑ 177	Gerald Wilkins	.20	.06
❑ 178	Lucious Harris	.20	.06
❑ 179	Robert Horry	.40	.12
❑ 180	Danny Manning	.40	.12
❑ 181	Kenny Anderson	.20	.06
❑ 182	Isaiah Rider	.40	.12
❑ 183	Rasheed Wallace	.75	.23
❑ 184	Mahmoud Abdul-Rauf	.20	.06
❑ 185	Cory Alexander	.20	.06
❑ 186	Vernon Maxwell	.20	.06
❑ 187	Dominique Wilkins	.60	.18
❑ 188	Nate McMillan	.20	.06
❑ 189	Larry Stewart	.20	.06
❑ 190	Doug Christie	.40	.12
❑ 191	Hubert Davis	.20	.06
❑ 192	Walt Williams	.20	.06
❑ 193	Adam Keefe	.20	.06
❑ 194	Greg Ostertag	.20	.06
❑ 195	John Stockton	.60	.18
❑ 196	George Lynch	.20	.06
❑ 197	Lee Mayberry	.20	.06
❑ 198	Tracy Murray	.20	.06
❑ 199	Rod Strickland	.20	.06
❑ 200	S. Abdur-Rahim ROO	1.00	.30
❑ 201	Ray Allen ROO	1.00	.30
❑ 202	S.Anderson ROO RC	.40	.12
❑ 203	Kobe Bryant ROO	3.00	.90
❑ 204	Marcus Camby ROO	.40	.12
❑ 205	Erick Dampier ROO	.20	.06
❑ 206	Emanual Davis ROO RC	.20	.06
❑ 207	Tony Delk ROO	.40	.12
❑ 208	Brian Evans ROO RC	.20	.06
❑ 209	Derek Fisher ROO RC	1.00	.30
❑ 210	Todd Fuller ROO	.20	.06
❑ 211	Dean Garrett ROO RC	.20	.06
❑ 212	Reggie Geary ROO RC	.20	.06
❑ 213	Darvin Ham ROO RC	.20	.06
❑ 214	O.Harrington ROO RC	.40	.12
❑ 215	Shane Heal ROO RC	.20	.06
❑ 216	Allen Iverson ROO	1.50	.45
❑ 217	Dontae' Jones ROO RC	.20	.06
❑ 218	Kerry Kittles ROO	.60	.18
❑ 219	P.Lauderdale ROO RC	.20	.06
❑ 220	R.Livingston ROO RC	.20	.06
❑ 221	Matt Maloney ROO RC	.20	.06
❑ 222	Stephon Marbury ROO	1.25	.35
❑ 223	Walter McCarty ROO RC	.20	.06
❑ 224	Amal McCaskill ROO RC	.20	.06
❑ 225	Jeff McInnis ROO RC	.20	.06
❑ 226	M.Muursepp ROO RC	.20	.06
❑ 227	Steve Nash ROO	.60	.18
❑ 228	R.Nembhard ROO RC	.20	.06
❑ 229	Jermaine O'Neal ROO	.75	.23
❑ 230	Vitaly Potapenko ROO	.20	.06
❑ 231	V. Praskevicius ROO RC	.20	.06
❑ 232	Roy Rogers ROO	.20	.06
❑ 233	Malik Rose ROO RC	.40	.12
❑ 234	Antoine Walker ROO	1.50	.45
❑ 235	Samaki Walker ROO	.20	.06
❑ 236	Ben Wallace ROO RC	4.00	1.20
❑ 237	John Wallace ROO	.40	.12
❑ 238	J.Williams ROO RC	.60	.18
❑ 239	Lorenzen Wright ROO	.20	.06
❑ 240	Sam Cassell PM	.20	.06
❑ 241	Anfernee Hardaway PM	.40	.12
❑ 242	Tim Hardaway PM	.20	.06
❑ 243	Grant Hill PM	.40	.12
❑ 244	Allan Houston PM	.20	.06
❑ 245	Juwan Howard PM	.20	.06
❑ 246	Kevin Johnson PM	.40	.12
❑ 247	Michael Jordan PM	2.00	.60
❑ 248	Jason Kidd PM	.50	.15
❑ 249	Karl Malone PM	.60	.18
❑ 250	Reggie Miller PM	.40	.12
❑ 251	Gary Payton PM	.40	.12
❑ 252	Wesley Person PM	.20	.06
❑ 253	Glen Rice PM	.20	.06
❑ 254	David Robinson PM	.40	.12
❑ 255	Steve Smith PM	.20	.06
❑ 256	Latrell Sprewell PM	.60	.18
❑ 257	Jerry Stackhouse PM	.60	.18
❑ 258	Rod Strickland PM	.20	.06
❑ 259	Nick Van Exel PM	.20	.06
❑ 260	Charles Barkley DT	.60	.18
❑ 261	Dale Davis DT	.20	.06
❑ 262	Patrick Ewing DT	.40	.12
❑ 263	Michael Finley DT	.60	.18
❑ 264	Chris Gatling DT	.20	.06
❑ 265	Armon Gilliam DT	.20	.06
❑ 266	Tyrone Hill DT	.20	.06
❑ 267	Robert Horry DT	.20	.06
❑ 268	Mark Jackson DT	.20	.06
❑ 269	Shawn Kemp DT	.20	.06
❑ 270	Jamal Mashburn DT	.20	.06
❑ 271	Anthony Mason DT	.20	.06
❑ 272	Alonzo Mourning DT	.20	.06
❑ 273	Dikembe Mutombo DT	.20	.06
❑ 274	Shaquille O'Neal DT	.60	.18
❑ 275	Isaiah Rider DT	.20	.06
❑ 276	Dennis Rodman DT	.20	.06
❑ 277	Damon Stoudamire DT	.40	.12
❑ 278	Chris Webber DT	.40	.12
❑ 279	Jayson Williams DT	.20	.06
❑ 280	Checklist (132-239)	.20	.06
❑ 281	Checklist (240-281/inserts)	.20	.06
❑ NNO	Jerry Stackhouse Promo	2.00	.60

1997-98 SkyBox Premium

	Nm-Mt	Ex-Mt
COMPLETE SET (250)	90.00	27.00
COMPLETE SERIES 1 (125)	25.00	7.50
COMPLETE SERIES 2 (125)	70.00	21.00

#	Player	Nm-Mt	Ex-Mt
❑ 1	Grant Hill	.75	.23
❑ 2	Matt Maloney	.25	.07
❑ 3	Vinny Del Negro	.25	.07
❑ 4	Kevin Willis	.50	.15
❑ 5	Mark Jackson	.50	.15
❑ 6	Ray Allen	.75	.23
❑ 7	Derrick Coleman	.25	.07
❑ 8	Isaiah Rider	.50	.15
❑ 9	Rod Strickland	.25	.07
❑ 10	Danny Ferry	.25	.07
❑ 11	Antonio Davis	.25	.07
❑ 12	Glenn Robinson	.75	.23
❑ 13	Cedric Ceballos	.25	.07
❑ 14	Sean Elliott	.50	.15
❑ 15	Walt Williams	.25	.07
❑ 16	Glen Rice	.50	.15
❑ 17	Clyde Drexler	.75	.23
❑ 18	Sherman Douglas	.25	.07
❑ 19	Othella Harrington	.25	.07
❑ 20	John Stockton	.75	.23
❑ 21	Priest Lauderdale	.25	.07
❑ 22	Khalid Reeves	.25	.07
❑ 23	Kobe Bryant	3.00	.90
❑ 24	Vin Baker UER G.Robinson photo on back	.50	.15
❑ 25	Steve Nash	.75	.23
❑ 26	Jeff Hornacek	.50	.15
❑ 27	Tyrone Corbin	.25	.07
❑ 28	Charles Barkley	1.00	.30
❑ 29	Michael Jordan	5.00	1.50
❑ 30	Latrell Sprewell	.75	.23
❑ 31	Anfernee Hardaway	.75	.23
❑ 32	Steve Kerr	.50	.15
❑ 33	Joe Smith	.50	.15
❑ 34	Jermaine O'Neal	1.25	.35
❑ 35	Ron Mercer RC	.75	.23
❑ 36	Antonio McDyess	.50	.15
❑ 37	Patrick Ewing	.75	.23
❑ 38	Avery Johnson	.25	.07
❑ 39	Toni Kukoc	.50	.15
❑ 40	Sam Perkins	.50	.15
❑ 41	Voshon Lenard	.25	.07
❑ 42	Detlef Schrempf	.50	.15
❑ 43	Horace Grant	.50	.15
❑ 44	Luc Longley	.25	.07
❑ 45	Todd Fuller	.25	.07
❑ 46	Tim Hardaway	.50	.15
❑ 47	Nick Anderson	.25	.07
❑ 48	Scottie Pippen	1.25	.35
❑ 49	Lindsey Hunter	.25	.07
❑ 50	Shawn Kemp	.50	.15
❑ 51	Larry Johnson	.50	.15
❑ 52	Shawn Bradley	.25	.07
❑ 53	Martin Muursepp	.25	.07
❑ 54	Jamal Mashburn	.50	.15
❑ 55	John Starks	.50	.15
❑ 56	Rony Seikaly	.25	.07
❑ 57	Gary Payton	.75	.23
❑ 58	Juwan Howard	.50	.15
❑ 59	Vitaly Potapenko	.25	.07
❑ 60	Reggie Miller	.75	.23
❑ 61	Alonzo Mourning	.50	.15
❑ 62	Roy Rogers	.25	.07
❑ 63	Antoine Walker	1.00	.30
❑ 64	Joe Dumars	.75	.23
❑ 65	Allan Houston	.50	.15
❑ 66	Hersey Hawkins	.25	.07
❑ 67	Dell Curry	.25	.07
❑ 68	Tony Delk	.25	.07
❑ 69	Mookie Blaylock	.25	.07
❑ 70	Derek Harper	.50	.15
❑ 71	Loy Vaught	.25	.07
❑ 72	Tom Gugliotta	.50	.15
❑ 73	Mitch Richmond	.50	.15
❑ 74	Dikembe Mutombo	.50	.15
❑ 75	Tony Battie RC	.75	.23

Card	Player	Nm-Mt	Ex-Mt
❑ 76	Derek Fisher	.75	.23
❑ 77	Jason Kidd	1.25	.35
❑ 78	Shareef Abdur-Rahim	1.25	.35
❑ 79	Tracy McGrady RC	5.00	1.50
❑ 80	Anthony Mason	.50	.15
❑ 81	Mario Elie	.25	.07
❑ 82	Karl Malone	.75	.23
❑ 83	Mark Price	.50	.15
❑ 84	Steve Smith	.50	.15
❑ 85	LaPhonso Ellis	.25	.07
❑ 86	Robert Horry	.50	.15
❑ 87	Wesley Person	.25	.07
❑ 88	Marcus Camby	.75	.23
❑ 89	Antonio Daniels RC	.75	.23
❑ 90	Eddie Jones	.75	.23
❑ 91	Gary Trent	.25	.07
❑ 92	Danny Fortson RC	.75	.23
❑ 93	Chris Childs	.25	.07
❑ 94	David Robinson	.75	.23
❑ 95	Bryant Reeves	.25	.07
❑ 96	Chris Webber	.75	.23
❑ 97	P.J. Brown	.25	.07
❑ 98	Tyrone Hill	.25	.07
❑ 99	Dale Davis	.25	.07
❑ 100	Allen Iverson	2.00	.60
❑ 101	Jerry Stackhouse	.75	.23
❑ 102	Arvydas Sabonis	.50	.15
❑ 103	Damon Stoudamire	.50	.15
❑ 104	Tim Thomas RC	1.50	.45
❑ 105	Christian Laettner	.50	.15
❑ 106	Robert Pack	.25	.07
❑ 107	Lorenzen Wright	.25	.07
❑ 108	Olden Polynice	.25	.07
❑ 109	Terrell Brandon	.50	.15
❑ 110	Theo Ratliff	.25	.07
❑ 111	Kevin Garnett	1.50	.45
❑ 112	Tim Duncan RC	4.00	1.20
❑ 113	Bryon Russell	.25	.07
❑ 114	Chauncey Billups RC	1.25	.35
❑ 115	Dale Ellis	.25	.07
❑ 116	Shaquille O'Neal	2.00	.60
❑ 117	Keith Van Horn RC	1.50	.45
❑ 118	Kenny Anderson	.50	.15
❑ 119	Dennis Rodman	.50	.15
❑ 120	Hakeem Olajuwon	.75	.23
❑ 121	Stephon Marbury	1.00	.30
❑ 122	Kendall Gill	.25	.07
❑ 123	Kerry Kittles	.75	.23
❑ 124	Checklist	.25	.07
❑ 125	Checklist	.25	.07
❑ 126	Anthony Johnson RC	.25	.07
❑ 127	Chris Anstey RC	.25	.07
❑ 128	Dean Garrett	.25	.07
❑ 129	Rik Smits	.50	.15
❑ 130	Tracy Murray	.25	.07
❑ 131	Charles O'Bannon RC	.25	.07
❑ 132	Eldridge Recasner	.25	.07
❑ 133	Johnny Taylor RC	.25	.07
❑ 134	Priest Lauderdale	.25	.07
❑ 135	Rod Strickland	.25	.07
❑ 136	Alan Henderson	.25	.07
❑ 137	Austin Croshere RC	.75	.23
❑ 138	Buck Williams	.25	.07
❑ 139	Clifford Robinson	.25	.07
❑ 140	Darrell Armstrong	.25	.07
❑ 141	Dennis Scott	.25	.07
❑ 142	Carl Herrera	.25	.07
❑ 143	Maurice Taylor RC	.75	.23
❑ 144	Chris Gatling	.25	.07
❑ 145	Alvin Williams RC	.25	.07
❑ 146	Antonio McDyess	.50	.15
❑ 147	Chauncey Billups	.50	.15
❑ 148	George McCloud	.25	.07
❑ 149	George Lynch	.25	.07
❑ 150	John Thomas RC	.25	.07
❑ 151	Jayson Williams	.25	.07
❑ 152	Otis Thorpe	.25	.07
❑ 153	Serge Zwikker RC	.25	.07
❑ 154	Chris Crawford RC	.25	.07
❑ 155	Muggsy Bogues	.50	.15
❑ 156	Mark Jackson	.50	.15
❑ 157	Dontonio Wingfield	.25	.07
❑ 158	Rodrick Rhodes RC	.25	.07
❑ 159	Sam Cassell	.75	.23
❑ 160	Hubert Davis	.25	.07
❑ 161	Clarence Weatherspoon	.25	.07
❑ 162	Eddie Johnson	.25	.07
❑ 163	Jacque Vaughn RC	.50	.15
❑ 164	Mark Price	.50	.15
❑ 165	Terry Dehere	.25	.07
❑ 166	Travis Knight	.25	.07
❑ 167	Charles Smith RC	.25	.07
❑ 168	David Wesley	.25	.07
❑ 169	David Wingate	.25	.07
❑ 170	Todd Day	.25	.07
❑ 171	Adonal Foyle RC	.50	.15
❑ 172	Chris Mills	.25	.07
❑ 173	Paul Grant RC	.25	.07
❑ 174	Adam Keefe	.25	.07
❑ 175	Erick Dampier UER back Eric	.50	.15
❑ 176	Ervin Johnson	.25	.07
❑ 177	Lamond Murray	.25	.07
❑ 178	Vlade Divac	.50	.15
❑ 179	Bobby Phills	.25	.07
❑ 180	Brian Williams	.25	.07
❑ 181	Chris Dudley	.25	.07
❑ 182	Tyrone Hill	.25	.07
❑ 183	Donyell Marshall	.50	.15
❑ 184	Kevin Gamble	.25	.07
❑ 185	Scot Pollard RC	.50	.15
❑ 186	Cherokee Parks	.25	.07
❑ 187	Terry Mills	.25	.07
❑ 188	Glen Rice	.50	.15
❑ 189	Shawn Respert	.25	.07
❑ 190	Terrell Brandon	.50	.15
❑ 191	Keith Closs RC	.25	.07
❑ 192	Tariq Abdul-Wahad RC	.50	.15
❑ 193	Wesley Person	.25	.07
❑ 194	Chuck Person	.25	.07
❑ 195	Derek Anderson RC	1.50	.45
❑ 196	Jon Barry	.25	.07
❑ 197	Chris Mullin	.75	.23
❑ 198	Ed Gray RC	.25	.07
❑ 199	Charlie Ward	.25	.07
❑ 200	Kelvin Cato RC	.75	.23
❑ 201	Michael Finley	.75	.23
❑ 202	Rick Fox	.50	.15
❑ 203	Scott Burrell	.25	.07
❑ 204	Vin Baker	.50	.15
❑ 205	Eric Snow	.50	.15
❑ 206	Isaac Austin	.25	.07
❑ 207	Keith Booth RC	.25	.07
❑ 208	Brian Grant	.50	.15
❑ 209	Chris Webber	.75	.23
❑ 210	Eric Williams	.25	.07
❑ 211	Jim Jackson	.25	.07
❑ 212	Anthony Parker RC	.25	.07
❑ 213	Brevin Knight RC	.75	.23
❑ 214	Cory Alexander	.25	.07
❑ 215	James Robinson	.25	.07
❑ 216	Bobby Jackson RC	1.25	.35
❑ 217	Bo Outlaw	.25	.07
❑ 218	God Shammgod RC	.25	.07
❑ 219	James Cotton RC	.25	.07
❑ 220	Jud Buechler	.25	.07
❑ 221	Shandon Anderson	.25	.07
❑ 222	Kevin Johnson	.50	.15
❑ 223	Chris Morris	.25	.07
❑ 224	Shareef Abdur-Rahim TS	2.50	.75
❑ 225	Ray Allen TS	.75	.23
❑ 226	Kobe Bryant TS	6.00	1.80
❑ 227	Marcus Camby TS	.75	.23
❑ 228	Antonio Daniels TS	1.00	.30
❑ 229	Tim Duncan TS	3.00	.90
❑ 230	Kevin Garnett TS	3.00	.90
❑ 231	Anfernee Hardaway TS	2.00	.60
❑ 232	Grant Hill TS	1.50	.45
❑ 233	Allen Iverson TS	4.00	1.20
❑ 234	Bobby Jackson TS	.75	.23
❑ 235	Michael Jordan TS	10.00	3.00
❑ 236	Shawn Kemp TS	1.50	.45
❑ 237	Karl Malone TS	.75	.23
❑ 238	Stephon Marbury TS	2.50	.75
❑ 239	Hakeem Olajuwon TS	1.50	.45
❑ 240	Shaquille O'Neal TS	4.00	1.20
❑ 241	Gary Payton TS	1.25	.35
❑ 242	Scottie Pippen TS	2.50	.75
❑ 243	David Robinson TS	1.50	.45
❑ 244	Dennis Rodman TS	2.50	.75
❑ 245	Jerry Stackhouse TS	1.00	.30
❑ 246	Damon Stoudamire TS	1.00	.30
❑ 247	Keith Van Horn TS	2.50	.75
❑ 248	Antoine Walker TS	4.00	1.20
❑ 249	Grant Hill CL	.50	.15
❑ 250	Hakeem Olajuwon CL	.50	.15
❑ NNO	Allen Iverson Bronze Shoe	1.25	.35
❑ NNO	Allen Iverson Ruby Shoe	12.00	3.60
❑ NNO	Allen Iverson Gold Shoe	4.00	1.20
❑ NNO	Allen Iverson Silver Shoe	2.00	.60
❑ NNO	Allen Iverson Emerald Shoe	30.00	9.00

1998-99 SkyBox Premium

	Nm-Mt	Ex-Mt
COMPLETE SET (265)	120.00	36.00
COMPLETE SET w/o SP (225)	40.00	12.00
COMPLETE SERIES 1 (125)	25.00	7.50
COMPLETE SERIES 2 (140)	100.00	30.00
COMMON CARD (1-225)	.25	.07
COMMON ROOKIE (226-265)	.75	.23

Card	Player	Nm-Mt	Ex-Mt
❑ 1	Tim Duncan	1.25	.35
❑ 2	Voshon Lenard	.25	.07
❑ 3	John Starks	.50	.15
❑ 4	Juwan Howard	.50	.15
❑ 5	Michael Finley	.75	.23
❑ 6	Bobby Jackson	.50	.15
❑ 7	Glenn Robinson	.50	.15
❑ 8	Antonio McDyess	.50	.15
❑ 9	Eric Williams	.25	.07
❑ 10	Zydrunas Ilgauskas	.50	.15
❑ 11	Terrell Brandon	.50	.15
❑ 12	Shandon Anderson	.25	.07
❑ 13	Rod Strickland	.25	.07
❑ 14	Dennis Rodman	.50	.15
❑ 15	Clarence Weatherspoon	.25	.07
❑ 16	P.J. Brown	.25	.07
❑ 17	Anfernee Hardaway	.75	.23
❑ 18	Dikembe Mutombo	.50	.15
❑ 19	Patrick Ewing	.75	.23
❑ 20	Scottie Pippen	1.25	.35
❑ 21	Shaquille O'Neal	2.00	.60
❑ 22	Donyell Marshall	.50	.15
❑ 23	Michael Jordan	5.00	1.50
❑ 24	Mark Price	.50	.15
❑ 25	Jim Jackson	.25	.07
❑ 26	Isaiah Rider	.25	.07
❑ 27	Eddie Jones	.75	.23
❑ 28	Detlef Schrempf	.50	.15
❑ 29	Corliss Williamson	.50	.15
❑ 30	Bo Outlaw	.25	.07
❑ 31	Allen Iverson	1.50	.45
❑ 32	Luc Longley	.25	.07
❑ 33	Theo Ratliff	.50	.15
❑ 34	Antoine Walker	.75	.23
❑ 35	Lamond Murray	.25	.07
❑ 36	Avery Johnson	.25	.07
❑ 37	John Stockton	.75	.23
❑ 38	David Wesley	.25	.07
❑ 39	Elden Campbell	.25	.07
❑ 40	Grant Hill	.75	.23
❑ 41	Sam Cassell	.75	.23
❑ 42	Tracy McGrady	2.00	.60
❑ 43	Glen Rice	.50	.15

❑ 44 Kobe Bryant 3.00 .90
❑ 45 John Wallace .25 .07
❑ 46 Bobby Phills .25 .07
❑ 47 Jerry Stackhouse .75 .23
❑ 48 Stephon Marbury .75 .23
❑ 49 Jeff Hornacek .50 .15
❑ 50 Tom Gugliotta .25 .07
❑ 51 Joe Dumars .75 .23
❑ 52 Johnny Newman .25 .07
❑ 53 Kevin Garnett 1.50 .45
❑ 54 Dennis Scott .25 .07
❑ 55 Anthony Mason .50 .15
❑ 56 Rodney Rogers .25 .07
❑ 57 Bryon Russell .25 .07
❑ 58 Maurice Taylor .50 .15
❑ 59 Mookie Blaylock .25 .07
❑ 60 Shawn Bradley .25 .07
❑ 61 Matt Maloney .25 .07
❑ 62 Karl Malone .75 .23
❑ 63 Larry Johnson .50 .15
❑ 64 Calbert Cheaney .25 .07
❑ 65 Steve Smith .50 .15
❑ 66 Toni Kukoc .50 .15
❑ 67 Reggie Miller .75 .23
❑ 68 Jayson Williams .25 .07
❑ 69 Gary Payton .75 .23
❑ 70 Sean Elliott .50 .15
❑ 71 Charles Barkley 1.00 .30
❑ 72 Tim Hardaway .50 .15
❑ 73 Rasheed Wallace .75 .23
❑ 74 Tariq Abdul-Wahad .25 .07
❑ 75 Kenny Anderson .50 .15
❑ 76 Chris Mullin .75 .23
❑ 77 Keith Van Horn .75 .23
❑ 78 Hersey Hawkins .25 .07
❑ 79 Ron Mercer .50 .15
❑ 80 Rik Smits .50 .15
❑ 81 David Robinson .75 .23
❑ 82 Derek Anderson .75 .23
❑ 83 Danny Fortson .25 .07
❑ 84 Jason Kidd 1.25 .35
❑ 85 Chauncey Billups .50 .15
❑ 86 Chris Anstey .25 .07
❑ 87 Hakeem Olajuwon .75 .23
❑ 88 Bryant Reeves .25 .07
❑ 89 Anthony Johnson .25 .07
❑ 90 Shawn Kemp .50 .15
❑ 91 Brevin Knight .25 .07
❑ 92 Ray Allen .75 .23
❑ 93 Tim Thomas .50 .15
❑ 94 Jalen Rose .75 .23
❑ 95 Kerry Kittles .25 .07
❑ 96 Vin Baker .50 .15
❑ 97 Shareef Abdur-Rahim .75 .23
❑ 98 Alonzo Mourning .50 .15
❑ 99 Joe Smith .50 .15
❑ 100 Damon Stoudamire .50 .15
❑ 101 Alan Henderson .25 .07
❑ 102 Walter McCarty .25 .07
❑ 103 Vlade Divac .50 .15
❑ 104 Wesley Person .25 .07
❑ 105 A.C. Green .50 .15
❑ 106 Malik Sealy .25 .07
❑ 107 Carl Thomas .25 .07
❑ 108 Brent Price .25 .07
❑ 109 Mark Jackson .50 .15
❑ 110 Lorenzen Wright .25 .07
❑ 111 Derek Fisher .75 .23
❑ 112 Michael Smith .25 .07
❑ 113 Tyrone Hill .25 .07
❑ 114 Cherokee Parks .25 .07
❑ 115 Kendall Gill .25 .07
❑ 116 Darrell Armstrong .25 .07
❑ 117 Derrick Coleman .25 .07
❑ 118 Rex Chapman .25 .07
❑ 119 Arvydas Sabonis .50 .15
❑ 120 Billy Owens .25 .07
❑ 121 Sam Perkins .25 .07
❑ 122 Gary Trent .25 .07
❑ 123 Sam Mack .25 .07
❑ 124 Tracy Murray .25 .07
❑ 125 Allan Houston .50 .15
❑ 126 Mitch Richmond .50 .15
❑ 127 Carl Herrera .25 .07
❑ 128 Ron Harper .50 .15
❑ 129 Gary Trent .25 .07
❑ 130 Chris Webber .75 .23
❑ 131 Antonio Daniels .25 .07
❑ 132 Charles Oakley .25 .07
❑ 133 Marcus Camby .50 .15
❑ 134 Tony Battie .25 .07
❑ 135 Otis Thorpe .25 .07
❑ 136 Dale Davis .50 .15
❑ 137 Chuck Person .25 .07
❑ 138 Ervin Johnson .25 .07
❑ 139 Jamal Mashburn .50 .15
❑ 140 Brian Grant .50 .15
❑ 141 Chris Mills .25 .07
❑ 142 Doug Christie .50 .15
❑ 143 George McCloud .25 .07
❑ 144 Todd Fuller .25 .07
❑ 145 Jerome Williams .25 .07
❑ 146 Chauncey Billups .50 .15
❑ 147 Dean Garrett .25 .07
❑ 148 Robert Pack .25 .07
❑ 149 Clarence Weatherspoon .25 .07
❑ 150 Tim Legler .25 .07
❑ 151 Bob Sura .25 .07
❑ 152 B.J. Armstrong .25 .07
❑ 153 Charlie Ward .25 .07
❑ 154 Rony Seikaly .25 .07
❑ 155 Chris Carr .25 .07
❑ 156 Eldridge Recasner .25 .07
❑ 157 Michael Stewart .25 .07
❑ 158 Jim McIlvaine .25 .07
❑ 159 Adam Keefe .25 .07
❑ 160 Antonio Davis .25 .07
❑ 161 Lawrence Funderburke .25 .07
❑ 162 Greg Ostertag .25 .07
❑ 163 Dan Majerle .50 .15
❑ 164 Dale Ellis .25 .07
❑ 165 Greg Anthony .25 .07
❑ 166 Chris Whitney .25 .07
❑ 167 Eric Piatkowski .50 .15
❑ 168 Tom Gugliotta .25 .07
❑ 169 Luc Longley .25 .07
❑ 170 Antonio McDyess .50 .15
❑ 171 George Lynch .25 .07
❑ 172 Dell Curry .25 .07
❑ 173 Johnny Newman .25 .07
❑ 174 Christian Laettner .50 .15
❑ 175 Steve Kerr .50 .15
❑ 176 Popeye Jones .25 .07
❑ 177 Brent Barry .50 .15
❑ 178 Billy Owens .25 .07
❑ 179 Cherokee Parks .25 .07
❑ 180 Derek Harper .25 .07
❑ 181 Howard Eisley .25 .07
❑ 182 Matt Geiger .25 .07
❑ 183 Darrick Martin .25 .07
❑ 184 Isaac Austin .25 .07
❑ 185 Dennis Scott .25 .07
❑ 186 Derrick Coleman .25 .07
❑ 187 Sam Perkins .25 .07
❑ 188 Latrell Sprewell .75 .23
❑ 189 Jud Buechler .25 .07
❑ 190 Jason Caffey .25 .07
❑ 191 Vlade Divac .50 .15
❑ 192 Travis Best .25 .07
❑ 193 Loy Vaught .25 .07
❑ 194 Mario Elie .25 .07
❑ 195 Ed Gray .25 .07
❑ 196 Joe Smith .50 .15
❑ 197 John Starks .50 .15
❑ 198 Anthony Johnson .25 .07
❑ 199 Kurt Thomas .50 .15
❑ 200 Chris Dudley .25 .07
❑ 201 Shareef Abdur-Rahim NF .25 .07
❑ 202 Ray Allen NF .25 .07
❑ 203 Vin Baker NF .25 .07
❑ 204 Charles Barkley NF .25 .07
❑ 205 Kobe Bryant NF 1.50 .45
❑ 206 Tim Duncan NF .75 .23
❑ 207 Anfernee Hardaway NF .25 .07
❑ 208 Grant Hill NF .75 .23
❑ 209 Allen Iverson NF 1.25 .35
❑ 210 Jason Kidd NF .75 .23
❑ 211 Shawn Kemp NF .25 .07
❑ 212 Shaquille O'Neal NF 1.00 .30
❑ 213 Kerry Kittles NF .25 .07
❑ 214 Karl Malone NF .25 .07
❑ 215 Stephon Marbury NF .25 .07
❑ 216 Ron Mercer NF .25 .07
❑ 217 Reggie Miller NF .25 .07
❑ 218 Kevin Garnett NF .75 .23
❑ 219 Gary Payton NF .25 .07
❑ 220 Scottie Pippen NF .75 .23
❑ 221 David Robinson NF .25 .07
❑ 222 Hakeem Olajuwon NF .25 .07
❑ 223 Damon Stoudamire NF .25 .07
❑ 224 Keith Van Horn NF .25 .07
❑ 225 Antoine Walker NF .25 .07
❑ 226 Cory Carr RC .75 .23
❑ 227 Cuttino Mobley RC 6.00 1.80
❑ 228 Miles Simon RC .75 .23
❑ 229 J.R. Henderson RC .75 .23
❑ 230 Jason Williams RC 5.00 1.50
❑ 231 Felipe Lopez RC 1.50 .45
❑ 232 Shammond Williams RC 3.00 .90
❑ 233 Ricky Davis RC 5.00 1.50
❑ 234 Vince Carter RC 15.00 4.50
❑ 235 Antawn Jamison RC 6.00 1.80
❑ 236 Ryan Stack RC .75 .23
❑ 237 Nazr Mohammed RC 1.00 .30
❑ 238 Sam Jacobson RC .75 .23
❑ 239 Larry Hughes RC 4.00 1.20
❑ 240 Ruben Patterson RC 2.50 .75
❑ 241 Al Harrington RC 3.00 .90
❑ 242 Ansu Sesay RC .75 .23
❑ 243 Vladimir Stepania RC .75 .23
❑ 244 Matt Harpring RC 2.00 .60
❑ 245 Andrae Patterson RC .75 .23
❑ 246 Pat Garrity RC 1.00 .30
❑ 247 Bonzi Wells RC 5.00 1.50
❑ 248 Bryce Drew RC 1.50 .45
❑ 249 Toby Bailey RC .75 .23
❑ 250 Michael Doleac RC 1.50 .45
❑ 251 Michael Dickerson RC 2.50 .75
❑ 252 Peja Stojakovic RC 5.00 1.50
❑ 253 Robert Traylor RC 1.50 .45
❑ 254 Tyronn Lue RC 2.00 .60
❑ 255 Dirk Nowitzki RC 12.00 3.60
❑ 256 Raef LaFrentz RC 2.00 .60
❑ 257 Jelani McCoy RC .75 .23
❑ 258 Michael Olowokandi RC 2.00 .60
❑ 259 Brian Skinner RC 1.50 .45
❑ 260 Keon Clark RC 2.00 .60
❑ 261 Roshown McLeod RC 1.00 .30
❑ 262 Mike Bibby RC 6.00 1.80
❑ 263 Paul Pierce RC 6.00 1.80
❑ 264 Tyson Wheeler RC .75 .23
❑ 265 Corey Benjamin RC 1.50 .45

1999-00 SkyBox Premium

	Nm-Mt	Ex-Mt
COMPLETE SET (150)	120.00	36.00
COMPLETE SET w/o SP (125)	40.00	12.00
COMMON CARD (1-100)	.25	.07
COMMON ROOKIE (101-125)	.30	.09
COMMON SP (101-125)	1.25	.35

❑ 1 Vince Carter 2.00 .60
❑ 2 Nick Anderson .25 .07
❑ 3 Isaiah Rider .25 .07
❑ 4 Mitch Richmond .50 .15
❑ 5 Danny Fortson .25 .07
❑ 6 Kenny Anderson .50 .15
❑ 7 Reggie Miller .75 .23
❑ 8 Tracy McGrady 2.00 .60

Card	Nm-Mt	Ex-Mt
❑ 9 Steve Nash	.75	.23
❑ 10 Robert Traylor	.25	.07
❑ 11 Tom Gugliotta	.25	.07
❑ 12 Steve Smith	.50	.15
❑ 13 Jalen Rose	.75	.23
❑ 14 Kerry Kittles	.25	.07
❑ 15 Nick Van Exel	.75	.23
❑ 16 Raef LaFrentz	.50	.15
❑ 17 Damon Stoudamire	.50	.15
❑ 18 Gary Trent	.25	.07
❑ 19 Jayson Williams	.25	.07
❑ 20 Brian Grant	.50	.15
❑ 21 Rod Strickland	.25	.07
❑ 22 Larry Hughes	.75	.23
❑ 23 Derek Anderson	.50	.15
❑ 24 Hakeem Olajuwon	.75	.23
❑ 25 Ray Allen	.75	.23
❑ 26 Gary Payton	.75	.23
❑ 27 Michael Finley	.75	.23
❑ 28 Keith Van Horn	.75	.23
❑ 29 Clifford Robinson	.25	.07
❑ 30 Shawn Kemp	.50	.15
❑ 31 Glenn Robinson	.75	.23
❑ 32 Theo Ratliff	.50	.15
❑ 33 Lindsey Hunter	.25	.07
❑ 34 Chris Webber	.75	.23
❑ 35 Grant Hill	.75	.23
❑ 36 Vlade Divac	.50	.15
❑ 37 Paul Pierce	.75	.23
❑ 38 Tyrone Nesby RC	.25	.07
❑ 39 Larry Johnson	.50	.15
❑ 40 Bryon Russell	.25	.07
❑ 41 Antoine Walker	.75	.23
❑ 42 Michael Olowokandi	.50	.15
❑ 43 John Stockton	.75	.23
❑ 44 Elden Campbell	.25	.07
❑ 45 Christian Laettner	.50	.15
❑ 46 Maurice Taylor	.50	.15
❑ 47 Shareef Abdur-Rahim	.75	.23
❑ 48 Ricky Davis	.50	.15
❑ 49 Jerry Stackhouse	.75	.23
❑ 50 Kobe Bryant	3.00	.90
❑ 51 Jason Williams	.75	.23
❑ 52 Mike Bibby	.75	.23
❑ 53 Eddie Jones	.75	.23
❑ 54 Antawn Jamison	1.25	.35
❑ 55 Shaquille O'Neal	2.00	.60
❑ 56 Tim Duncan	1.50	.45
❑ 57 Cherokee Parks	.25	.07
❑ 58 Antonio McDyess	.50	.15
❑ 59 Rasheed Wallace	.75	.23
❑ 60 Anthony Mason	.50	.15
❑ 61 Chris Mills	.25	.07
❑ 62 Glen Rice	.50	.15
❑ 63 Latrell Sprewell	.75	.23
❑ 64 Darrell Armstrong	.25	.07
❑ 65 Sean Elliott	.50	.15
❑ 66 Juwan Howard	.50	.15
❑ 67 Brent Barry	.50	.15
❑ 68 John Starks	.50	.15
❑ 69 Tim Hardaway	.50	.15
❑ 70 Marcus Camby	.50	.15
❑ 71 Anfernee Hardaway	.75	.23
❑ 72 Avery Johnson	.25	.07
❑ 73 Tariq Abdul-Wahad	.25	.07
❑ 74 Charles Barkley	1.00	.30
❑ 75 Stephon Marbury	.75	.23
❑ 76 Jamal Mashburn	.50	.15
❑ 77 Matt Harpring	.75	.23
❑ 78 David Robinson	.75	.23
❑ 79 Cedric Ceballos	.25	.07
❑ 80 Terrell Brandon	.50	.15
❑ 81 Jason Kidd	1.25	.35
❑ 82 Toni Kukoc	.50	.15
❑ 83 Michael Dickerson	.50	.15
❑ 84 Alonzo Mourning	.50	.15
❑ 85 Kevin Garnett	1.50	.45
❑ 86 Matt Geiger	.25	.07
❑ 87 Vin Baker	.50	.15
❑ 88 Dikembe Mutombo	.50	.15
❑ 89 Hersey Hawkins	.50	.15
❑ 90 Joe Smith	.50	.15
❑ 91 Charles Oakley	.25	.07
❑ 92 Ron Mercer	.50	.15
❑ 93 Rik Smits	.50	.15
❑ 94 Patrick Ewing	.75	.23
❑ 95 Karl Malone	.75	.23
❑ 96 Scottie Pippen	1.25	.35
❑ 97 Zydrunas Ilgauskas	.50	.15
❑ 98 Sam Cassell	.75	.23
❑ 99 Detlef Schrempf	.50	.15
❑ 100 Allen Iverson	1.50	.45
❑ 101 Elton Brand RC	2.00	.60
❑ 101A Elton Brand SP	8.00	2.40
❑ 102 Steve Francis RC	2.50	.75
❑ 102A Steve Francis SP	10.00	3.00
❑ 103 Baron Davis RC	1.50	.45
❑ 103A Baron Davis SP	6.00	1.80
❑ 104 Lamar Odom RC	1.50	.45
❑ 104A Lamar Odom SP	6.00	1.80
❑ 105 Jonathan Bender RC	1.50	.45
❑ 105A Jonathan Bender SP	6.00	1.80
❑ 106 Wally Szczerbiak RC	1.50	.45
❑ 106A Wally Szczerbiak SP	6.00	1.80
❑ 107 Richard Hamilton RC	1.50	.45
❑ 107A Richard Hamilton SP	5.00	1.50
❑ 108 Andre Miller RC	1.50	.45
❑ 108A Andre Miller SP	6.00	1.80
❑ 109 Shawn Marion RC	2.00	.60
❑ 109A Shawn Marion SP	8.00	2.40
❑ 110 Jason Terry RC	1.00	.30
❑ 110A Jason Terry SP	4.00	1.20
❑ 111 Trajan Langdon RC	.60	.18
❑ 111A Trajan Langdon SP	2.50	.75
❑ 112 Aleksandar Radojevic RC	.30	.09
❑ 112A Alekandar Radojevic SP	1.25	.35
❑ 113 Corey Maggette RC	1.50	.45
❑ 113A Corey Maggette SP	6.00	1.80
❑ 114 William Avery RC	.60	.18
❑ 114A William Avery SP	2.50	.75
❑ 115 Vonteego Cummings RC	.60	.18
❑ 115A V.Cummings SP	2.50	.75
❑ 116 Ron Artest RC	1.00	.30
❑ 116A Ron Artest SP	4.00	1.20
❑ 117 Cal Bowdler RC	.50	.15
❑ 117A Cal Bowdler SP	1.50	.45
❑ 118 James Posey RC	1.00	.30
❑ 118A James Posey SP	4.00	1.20
❑ 119 Quincy Lewis RC	.50	.15
❑ 119A Quincy Lewis SP	1.50	.45
❑ 120 Dion Glover RC	.50	.15
❑ 120A Dion Glover SP	1.50	.45
❑ 121 Jeff Foster RC	.50	.15
❑ 121A Jeff Foster SP	1.50	.45
❑ 122 Kenny Thomas RC	.60	.18
❑ 122A Kenny Thomas SP	2.50	.75
❑ 123 Devean George RC	.75	.23
❑ 123A Devean George SP	3.00	.90
❑ 124 Scott Padgett RC	.50	.15
❑ 124A Scott Padgett SP	1.50	.45
❑ 125 Tim James RC	.50	.15
❑ 125A Tim James SP	2.00	.60

2003-04 Skybox Autographics

	Nm-Mt	Ex-Mt
COMP.SET w/o SP's (45)	30.00	9.00
COMMON CARD (1-45)	.25	.07
COMMON ROOKIE (46-90)	5.00	1.50
❑ 1 Vince Carter	2.50	.75
❑ 2 Kobe Bryant	4.00	1.20
❑ 3 Tony Parker	1.00	.30
❑ 4 Richard Hamilton	.60	.18
❑ 5 Jamal Mashburn	.60	.18
❑ 6 Paul Pierce	1.00	.30
❑ 7 Allan Houston	.60	.18
❑ 8 Carlos Boozer	.60	.18
❑ 9 Michael Redd	1.00	.30
❑ 10 Chris Webber	1.00	.30
❑ 11 Yao Ming	2.50	.75
❑ 12 Tracy McGrady	2.50	.75
❑ 13 Zach Randolph	1.00	.30
❑ 14 Ben Wallace	1.00	.30
❑ 15 Kenyon Martin	1.00	.30
❑ 16 Ray Allen	1.00	.30
❑ 17 Jermaine O'Neal	1.00	.30
❑ 18 Bonzi Wells	.60	.18
❑ 19 Ron Artest	.60	.18
❑ 20 Peja Stojakovic	1.00	.30
❑ 21 Dirk Nowitzki	1.50	.45
❑ 22 Desmond Mason	.60	.18
❑ 23 Morris Peterson	.60	.18
❑ 24 Eddy Curry	.60	.18
❑ 25 Kevin Garnett	2.00	.60
❑ 26 Rashard Lewis	1.00	.30
❑ 27 Jason Richardson	1.00	.30
❑ 28 Amare Stoudemire	2.00	.60
❑ 29 Steve Francis	1.00	.30
❑ 30 Allen Iverson	2.00	.60
❑ 31 Jason Terry	1.00	.30
❑ 32 Pau Gasol	1.00	.30
❑ 33 Manu Ginobili	1.00	.30
❑ 34 Reggie Miller	1.00	.30
❑ 35 Cuttino Mobley	.60	.18
❑ 36 Mike Bibby	1.00	.30
❑ 37 Mike Dunleavy	.60	.18
❑ 38 Jason Kidd	1.50	.45
❑ 39 Shareef Abdur-Rahim	1.00	.30
❑ 40 Elton Brand	1.00	.30
❑ 41 Kwame Brown	1.00	.30
❑ 42 Shaquille O'Neal	2.50	.75
❑ 43 Tim Duncan	2.00	.60
❑ 44 Nene	.60	.18
❑ 45 Baron Davis	1.00	.30
❑ 46 Boris Diaw RC	5.00	1.50
❑ 47 Luke Walton RC	6.00	1.80
❑ 48 Willie Green RC	5.00	1.50
❑ 49 Marcus Banks RC	5.00	1.50
❑ 50 Dahntay Jones RC	5.00	1.50
❑ 51 Leandro Barbosa RC	5.00	1.50
❑ 52 Josh Howard RC	6.00	1.80
❑ 53 Ndudi Ebi RC	5.00	1.50
❑ 54 Chris Bosh RC	10.00	3.00
❑ 55 Carmelo Anthony RC	25.00	7.50
❑ 56 Zoran Planinic RC	5.00	1.50
❑ 57 Aleksandar Pavlovic RC	5.00	1.50
❑ 58 Marquis Daniels RC	10.00	3.00
❑ 59 Keith McLeod RC	5.00	1.50
❑ 60 Ben Handlogten RC	5.00	1.50
❑ 61 Francisco Elson RC	5.00	1.50
❑ 62 David West RC	5.00	1.50
❑ 63 Maurice Williams RC	5.00	1.50
❑ 64 Brian Cook RC	5.00	1.50
❑ 65 Keith Bogans RC	5.00	1.50
❑ 66 Kendrick Perkins RC	5.00	1.50
❑ 67 Troy Bell RC	5.00	1.50
❑ 68 Kyle Korver RC	6.00	1.80
❑ 69 Mickael Pietrus RC	5.00	1.50
❑ 70 Maciej Lampe RC	5.00	1.50
❑ 71 Steve Blake RC	5.00	1.50
❑ 72 Chris Kaman RC	5.00	1.50
❑ 73 Curtis Borchardt RC	5.00	1.50
❑ 74 Kirk Hinrich RC	8.00	2.40
❑ 75 Dwyane Wade RC	12.00	3.60
❑ 76 Zarko Cabarkapa RC	5.00	1.50
❑ 77 LeBron James RC	50.00	15.00
❑ 78 Jerome Beasley RC	5.00	1.50
❑ 79 Nick Collison RC	5.00	1.50
❑ 80 Linton Johnson RC	5.00	1.50
❑ 81 Udonis Haslem RC	5.00	1.50
❑ 82 Travis Outlaw RC	5.00	1.50
❑ 83 Jason Kapono RC	5.00	1.50
❑ 84 T.J. Ford RC	6.00	1.80
❑ 85 Luke Ridnour RC	6.00	1.80
❑ 86 Darko Milicic RC	8.00	2.40
❑ 87 Mike Sweetney RC	5.00	1.50
❑ 88 Jarvis Hayes RC	5.00	1.50
❑ 89 Josh Moore RC	5.00	1.50
❑ 90 Reece Gaines RC	5.00	1.50

2003-04 Skybox LE

	Nm-Mt	Ex-Mt
COMP.SET w/o SP's (110)	30.00	9.00
COMMON CARD (1-110)	.20	.06
COMMON ROOKIE (111-160)	6.00	1.80
❑ 1 Jason Terry	.75	.23
❑ 2 Antoine Walker	.75	.23
❑ 3 Paul Pierce	.75	.23
❑ 4 Eddy Curry	.50	.15
❑ 5 Ricky Davis	.75	.23
❑ 6 Jamal Crawford	.50	.15
❑ 7 Raef LaFrentz	.50	.15
❑ 8 Darius Miles	.75	.23
❑ 9 Ray Allen	.75	.23
❑ 10 Sam Cassell	.75	.23
❑ 11 Andre Miller	.50	.15
❑ 12 Dirk Nowitzki	1.25	.35
❑ 13 Zach Randolph	.75	.23
❑ 14 Tim Duncan	1.50	.45
❑ 15 Gary Payton	.75	.23
❑ 16 Ben Wallace	.75	.23
❑ 17 Michael Finley	.75	.23
❑ 18 David Wesley	.20	.06
❑ 19 Nick Van Exel	.75	.23
❑ 20 Marcus Camby	.50	.15
❑ 21 Gilbert Arenas	.75	.23
❑ 22 Marcus Haislip	.20	.06
❑ 23 Cuttino Mobley	.50	.15
❑ 24 Tayshaun Prince	.50	.15
❑ 25 Chris Webber	.75	.23
❑ 26 Reggie Miller	.75	.23
❑ 27 Chauncey Billups	.50	.15
❑ 28 Quentin Richardson	.50	.15
❑ 29 Mike Dunleavy	.50	.15
❑ 30 Karl Malone	.75	.23
❑ 31 Yao Ming	2.00	.60
❑ 32 Tyson Chandler	.75	.23
❑ 33 Jason Williams	.50	.15
❑ 34 Eddie Griffin	.50	.15
❑ 35 Eddie Jones	.75	.23
❑ 36 Jamaal Tinsley	.75	.23
❑ 37 Michael Redd	.75	.23
❑ 38 Elton Brand	.75	.23
❑ 39 Rashard Lewis	.75	.23
❑ 40 Vince Carter	2.00	.60
❑ 41 Wally Szczerbiak	.50	.15
❑ 42 Chris Wilcox	.50	.15
❑ 43 Kenyon Martin	.75	.23
❑ 44 Shaquille O'Neal	2.00	.60
❑ 45 Baron Davis	.75	.23
❑ 46 Pau Gasol	.75	.23
❑ 47 Dikembe Mutombo	.50	.15
❑ 48 Shane Battier	.75	.23
❑ 49 Drew Gooden	.75	.23
❑ 50 Lamar Odom	.75	.23
❑ 51 Glenn Robinson	.75	.23
❑ 52 Tim Thomas	.50	.15
❑ 53 Shawn Marion	.75	.23
❑ 54 Kevin Garnett	1.50	.45
❑ 55 Stephon Marbury	.75	.23
❑ 56 Rasheed Wallace	.75	.23
❑ 57 Troy Hudson	.20	.06
❑ 58 Mike Bibby	.75	.23
❑ 59 Jason Kidd	1.25	.35
❑ 60 Tony Parker	.75	.23
❑ 61 Andrei Kirilenko	.75	.23
❑ 62 Manu Ginobili	.75	.23
❑ 63 Kerry Kittles	.20	.06
❑ 64 Brent Barry	.50	.15
❑ 65 Allan Houston	.50	.15
❑ 66 Morris Peterson	.50	.15
❑ 67 Tracy McGrady	2.00	.60
❑ 68 Matt Harpring	.75	.23
❑ 69 Erick Dampier	.20	.06
❑ 70 Jerry Stackhouse	.50	.15
❑ 71 John Salmons	.20	.06
❑ 72 Stephen Jackson	.20	.06
❑ 73 Scottie Pippen	1.25	.35
❑ 74 Dajuan Wagner	.50	.15
❑ 75 Keon Clark	.20	.06
❑ 76 Carlos Boozer	.75	.23
❑ 77 Steve Nash	.75	.23
❑ 78 Nene	.50	.15
❑ 79 Keith Van Horn	.75	.23
❑ 80 Earl Boykins	.50	.15
❑ 81 Richard Hamilton	.50	.15
❑ 82 Jason Richardson	.75	.23
❑ 83 Steve Francis	.75	.23
❑ 84 Jermaine O'Neal	.75	.23
❑ 85 Ron Artest	.50	.15
❑ 86 Corey Maggette	.50	.15
❑ 87 Kwame Brown	.75	.23
❑ 88 Kobe Bryant	3.00	.90
❑ 89 Mike Miller	.75	.23
❑ 90 Caron Butler	.75	.23
❑ 91 Desmond Mason	.50	.15
❑ 92 Latrell Sprewell	.75	.23
❑ 93 Richard Jefferson	.50	.15
❑ 94 Jamal Mashburn	.50	.15
❑ 95 Troy Murphy	.75	.23
❑ 96 Peja Stojakovic	.75	.23
❑ 97 Allen Iverson	1.50	.45
❑ 98 Amare Stoudemire	1.50	.45
❑ 99 Rasho Nesterovic	.50	.15
❑ 100 Bonzi Wells	.50	.15
❑ 101 Bobby Jackson	.50	.15
❑ 102 Anfernee Hardaway	.75	.23
❑ 103 Larry Hughes	.50	.15
❑ 104 Shareef Abdur-Rahim	.75	.23
❑ 105 Hedo Turkoglu	.75	.23
❑ 106 Alvin Williams	.20	.06
❑ 107 Qyntel Woods	.20	.06
❑ 108 Brad Miller	.75	.23
❑ 109 Jalen Rose	.75	.23
❑ 110 Antonio Davis	.20	.06
❑ 111 David West RC	6.00	1.80
❑ 112 Boris Diaw RC	6.00	1.80
❑ 113 Travis Hansen RC	6.00	1.80
❑ 114 Marcus Banks RC	6.00	1.80
❑ 115 Kendrick Perkins RC	6.00	1.80
❑ 116 Darius Songaila RC	6.00	1.80
❑ 117 Kirk Hinrich /99 RC	50.00	15.00
❑ 118 LeBron James /99 RC	350.00	105.00
❑ 119 Jason Kapono RC	6.00	1.80
❑ 120 Josh Howard RC	8.00	2.40
❑ 121 Marquis Daniels RC	12.00	3.60
❑ 122 Carmelo Anthony /99 RC	200.00	60.00
❑ 123 Darko Milicic /99 RC	50.00	15.00
❑ 124 Zaur Pachulia RC	6.00	1.80
❑ 125 Mickael Pietrus RC	6.00	1.80
❑ 126 Ben Handlogten RC	6.00	1.80
❑ 127 James Jones RC	6.00	1.80
❑ 128 Chris Kaman RC	6.00	1.80
❑ 129 Josh Moore RC	6.00	1.80
❑ 130 Brian Cook RC	6.00	1.80
❑ 131 Luke Walton RC	10.00	3.00
❑ 132 Troy Bell RC	6.00	1.80
❑ 133 Dahntay Jones RC	6.00	1.80
❑ 134 Dwyane Wade /99 RC	80.00	24.00
❑ 135 Udonis Haslem RC	6.00	1.80
❑ 136 T.J. Ford /99 RC	40.00	12.00
❑ 137 Ndudi Ebi RC	6.00	1.80
❑ 138 Zoran Planinic RC	6.00	1.80
❑ 139 Raul Lopez RC	6.00	1.80
❑ 140 Francisco Elson RC	6.00	1.80
❑ 141 Mike Sweetney RC	6.00	1.80
❑ 142 Maciej Lampe RC	6.00	1.80
❑ 143 Slavko Vranes RC	6.00	1.80
❑ 144 Keith Bogans /99 RC	20.00	6.00
❑ 145 Reece Gaines RC	6.00	1.80
❑ 146 Willie Green RC	6.00	1.80
❑ 147 Kyle Korver RC	8.00	2.40
❑ 148 Zarko Cabarkapa RC	6.00	1.80
❑ 149 Leandro Barbosa RC	6.00	1.80
❑ 150 Travis Outlaw RC	6.00	1.80
❑ 151 Curtis Borchardt RC	6.00	1.80
❑ 152 Alex Garcia RC	6.00	1.80
❑ 153 Richie Frahm RC	6.00	1.80
❑ 154 Nick Collison RC	6.00	1.80
❑ 155 Luke Ridnour /99 RC	40.00	12.00
❑ 156 Chris Bosh /99 RC	60.00	18.00
❑ 157 Aleksandar Pavlovic RC	6.00	1.80
❑ 158 Maurice Williams RC	6.00	1.80
❑ 159 Jarvis Hayes /99 RC	20.00	6.00
❑ 160 Steve Blake RC	6.00	1.80

1998-99 SkyBox Molten Metal

	Nm-Mt	Ex-Mt
COMPLETE SET (150)	80.00	24.00
COMMON CARD (1-100)	.10	.03
COMMON ROOKIE	.60	.18
COMMON CARD (101-130)	.15	.04
COMMON CARD (131-150)	.50	.15
❑ 1 Maurice Taylor	.15	.04
❑ 2 Bison Dele	.10	.03
❑ 3 Anthony Mason	.15	.04
❑ 4 John Starks	.15	.04
❑ 5 Anthony Johnson	.10	.03
❑ 6 Calbert Cheaney	.10	.03
❑ 7 Roshown McLeod RC	.60	.18
❑ 8 Jalen Rose	.25	.07
❑ 9 Kelvin Cato	.10	.03
❑ 10 Walter McCarty	.10	.03
❑ 11 Isaac Austin	.10	.03
❑ 12 Arvydas Sabonis	.15	.04
❑ 13 David Wesley	.10	.03
❑ 14 Jim Jackson	.10	.03
❑ 15 Elden Campbell	.10	.03
❑ 16 Michael Doleac RC	1.25	.35
❑ 17 Chris Webber	.25	.07
❑ 18 Mitch Richmond	.15	.04
❑ 19 Johnny Newman	.10	.03
❑ 20 Jayson Williams	.10	.03
❑ 21 George Lynch	.10	.03
❑ 22 Ron Harper	.15	.04
❑ 23 Donyell Marshall	.15	.04
❑ 24 Derek Fisher	.25	.07
❑ 25 Matt Harpring RC	2.00	.60
❑ 26 Jason Williams RC	5.00	1.50
❑ 27 Toni Kukoc	.15	.04
❑ 28 Clarence Weatherspoon	.10	.03
❑ 29 Eddie Jones	.25	.07
❑ 30 Bo Outlaw	.10	.03
❑ 31 Zydrunas Ilgauskas	.15	.04
❑ 32 Michael Dickerson RC	2.50	.75

❑ 33 Tyronn Lue RC	1.50	.45
❑ 34 Theo Ratliff	.15	.04
❑ 35 Dirk Nowitzki RC	12.00	3.60
❑ 36 Robert Traylor RC	1.25	.35
❑ 37 Gary Trent	.10	.03
❑ 38 Wesley Person	.10	.03
❑ 39 Bryce Drew RC	1.25	.35
❑ 40 P.J. Brown	.10	.03
❑ 41 Joe Smith	.15	.04
❑ 42 Avery Johnson	.10	.03
❑ 43 Chris Anstey	.10	.03
❑ 44 Mario Elie	.10	.03
❑ 45 Voshon Lenard	.10	.03
❑ 46 Rex Chapman	.10	.03
❑ 47 Hersey Hawkins	.10	.03
❑ 48 Shawn Bradley	.10	.03
❑ 49 Matt Maloney	.10	.03
❑ 50 Dan Majerle	.15	.04
❑ 51 Pat Garrity RC	.75	.23
❑ 52 Sam Perkins	.10	.03
❑ 53 Mookie Blaylock	.10	.03
❑ 54 Al Harrington RC	3.00	.90
❑ 55 Clifford Robinson	.10	.03
❑ 56 Alan Henderson	.10	.03
❑ 57 Chris Mullin	.25	.07
❑ 58 Dennis Scott	.10	.03
❑ 59 A.C. Green	.15	.04
❑ 60 Tyrone Hill	.10	.03
❑ 61 Chauncey Billups	.15	.04
❑ 62 Michael Finley	.25	.07
❑ 63 Terrell Brandon	.15	.04
❑ 64 Detlef Schrempf	.15	.04
❑ 65 Bonzi Wells RC	5.00	1.50
❑ 66 Larry Johnson	.15	.04
❑ 67 Bryant Reeves	.10	.03
❑ 68 Raef LaFrentz RC	2.00	.60
❑ 69 Kendall Gill	.10	.03
❑ 70 Bryon Russell	.10	.03
❑ 71 Bobby Phills	.10	.03
❑ 72 Tony Delk	.10	.03
❑ 73 Lorenzen Wright	.10	.03
❑ 74 Keon Clark RC	2.00	.60
❑ 75 Billy Owens	.10	.03
❑ 76 Tracy Murray	.10	.03
❑ 77 Bobby Jackson	.15	.04
❑ 78 Sam Cassell	.25	.07
❑ 79 Corliss Williamson	.15	.04
❑ 80 Jeff Hornacek	.15	.04
❑ 81 LaPhonso Ellis	.10	.03
❑ 82 Sam Mitchell	.10	.03
❑ 83 Sean Elliott	.15	.04
❑ 84 John Wallace	.10	.03
❑ 85 Dikembe Mutombo	.15	.04
❑ 86 Rik Smits	.15	.04
❑ 87 Isaiah Rider	.10	.03
❑ 88 Joe Dumars	.25	.07
❑ 89 Allan Houston	.15	.04
❑ 90 Sam Mack	.10	.03
❑ 91 Paul Pierce RC	6.00	1.80
❑ 92 Lamond Murray	.10	.03
❑ 93 Rasheed Wallace	.25	.07
❑ 94 Danny Fortson	.10	.03
❑ 95 Cherokee Parks	.10	.03
❑ 96 Antonio Daniels	.10	.03
❑ 97 Shandon Anderson	.10	.03
❑ 98 Ricky Davis RC	4.00	1.20
❑ 99 Rodney Rogers	.10	.03
❑ 100 Tariq Abdul-Wahad	.15	.04
❑ 101 Glenn Robinson	.20	.06
❑ 102 Ron Mercer	.20	.06
❑ 103 Alonzo Mourning	.20	.06
❑ 104 Marcus Camby	.20	.06
❑ 105 Steve Smith	.20	.06
❑ 106 Tim Hardaway	.20	.06
❑ 107 Rod Strickland	.15	.04
❑ 108 Reggie Miller	.40	.12
❑ 109 Juwan Howard	.20	.06
❑ 110 Hakeem Olajuwon	.40	.12
❑ 111 John Stockton	.25	.07
❑ 112 Antonio McDyess	.20	.06
❑ 113 Charles Barkley	1.00	.30
❑ 114 Karl Malone	.25	.07
❑ 115 Jerry Stackhouse	.40	.12
❑ 116 Tracy McGrady	2.00	.60
❑ 117 Brevin Knight	.15	.04
❑ 118 Gary Payton	.40	.12
❑ 119 Derek Anderson	.40	.12
❑ 120 Glen Rice	.20	.06
❑ 121 David Robinson	.40	.12
❑ 122 Vin Baker	.20	.06
❑ 123 Tom Gugliotta	.15	.04
❑ 124 Patrick Ewing	.40	.12
❑ 125 Ray Allen	.40	.12
❑ 126 Anfernee Hardaway	.40	.12
❑ 127 Jason Kidd	1.25	.35
❑ 128 Kenny Anderson	.20	.06
❑ 129 Kerry Kittles	.15	.04
❑ 130 Tim Thomas	.20	.06
❑ 131 Shareef Abdur-Rahim	1.50	.45
❑ 132 Mike Bibby RC	8.00	2.40
❑ 133 Kobe Bryant	6.00	1.80
❑ 134 Vince Carter RC	15.00	4.50
❑ 135 Tim Duncan	2.50	.75
❑ 136 Kevin Garnett	3.00	.90
❑ 137 Grant Hill	.25	.07
❑ 138 Larry Hughes RC	5.00	1.50
❑ 139 Allen Iverson	3.00	.90
❑ 140 Antawn Jamison RC	8.00	2.40
❑ 141 Michael Jordan	10.00	3.00
❑ 142 Shawn Kemp	1.00	.30
❑ 143 Stephon Marbury	1.50	.45
❑ 144 Michael Olowokandi RC	2.50	.75
❑ 145 Shaquille O'Neal	4.00	1.20
❑ 146 Scottie Pippen	2.50	.75
❑ 147 Dennis Rodman	1.00	.30
❑ 148 Damon Stoudamire	1.00	.30
❑ 149 Keith Van Horn	1.50	.45
❑ 150 Antoine Walker	1.50	.45

1994-95 SP

	Nm-Mt	Ex-Mt
COMPLETE SET (165)	30.00	9.00
COMMON FOIL RC (1-30)	.50	.15
COMMON CARD (31-165)	.15	.04
❑ 1 Glenn Robinson FOIL RC	2.50	.75
❑ 2 Jason Kidd FOIL RC	8.00	2.40
❑ 3 Grant Hill FOIL RC	5.00	1.50
❑ 4 Donyell Marshall FOIL RC	.75	.23
❑ 5 Juwan Howard FOIL RC	1.50	.45
❑ 6 Sharone Wright FOIL RC	.50	.15
❑ 7 Lamond Murray FOIL RC	.50	.15
❑ 8 Brian Grant FOIL RC	2.00	.60
❑ 9 Eric Montross FOIL RC	.50	.15
❑ 10 Eddie Jones FOIL RC	3.00	.90
❑ 11 Carlos Rogers FOIL RC	.50	.15
❑ 12 Khalid Reeves FOIL RC	.50	.15
❑ 13 Jalen Rose FOIL RC	3.00	.90
❑ 14 Eric Piatkowski FOIL RC	.50	.15
❑ 15 Clifford Rozier FOIL RC	.50	.15
❑ 16 Aaron McKie FOIL RC	1.50	.45
❑ 17 Eric Mobley FOIL RC	.50	.15
❑ 18 Tony Dumas FOIL RC	.50	.15
❑ 19 B.J. Tyler FOIL RC	.50	.15
❑ 20 Dickey Simpkins FOIL RC	.50	.15
❑ 21 Bill Curley FOIL RC	.50	.15
❑ 22 Wesley Person FOIL RC	.75	.23
❑ 23 Monty Williams FOIL RC	.50	.15
❑ 24 Greg Minor FOIL RC	.50	.15
❑ 25 Charlie Ward FOIL RC	.50	.15
❑ 26 B.Thompson FOIL RC	.50	.15
❑ 27 Trevor Ruffin FOIL RC	.50	.15
❑ 28 Derrick Alston FOIL RC	.50	.15
❑ 29 Michael Smith FOIL RC	.50	.15
❑ 30 D.Wingfield FOIL RC	.50	.15
❑ 31 Stacey Augmon	.15	.04
❑ 32 Steve Smith	.25	.07
❑ 33 Mookie Blaylock	.15	.04
❑ 34 Grant Long	.15	.04
❑ 35 Ken Norman	.15	.04
❑ 36 Dominique Wilkins	.50	.15
❑ 37 Dino Radja	.15	.04
❑ 38 Dee Brown	.15	.04
❑ 39 David Wesley	.15	.04
❑ 40 Rick Fox	.15	.04
❑ 41 Alonzo Mourning	.60	.18
❑ 42 Larry Johnson	.25	.07
❑ 43 Hersey Hawkins	.25	.07
❑ 44 Scott Burrell	.15	.04
❑ 45 Muggsy Bogues	.25	.07
❑ 46 Scottie Pippen	1.50	.45
❑ 47 Toni Kukoc	.75	.23
❑ 48 B.J. Armstrong	.15	.04
❑ 49 Will Perdue	.15	.04
❑ 50 Ron Harper	.25	.07
❑ 51 Mark Price	.15	.04
❑ 52 Tyrone Hill	.15	.04
❑ 53 Chris Mills	.25	.07
❑ 54 John Williams	.15	.04
❑ 55 Bobby Phills	.15	.04
❑ 56 Jim Jackson	.25	.07
❑ 57 Jamal Mashburn	.50	.15
❑ 58 Popeye Jones	.15	.04
❑ 59 Roy Tarpley	.15	.04
❑ 60 Lorenzo Williams	.15	.04
❑ 61 Mahmoud Abdul-Rauf	.15	.04
❑ 62 Rodney Rogers	.15	.04
❑ 63 Bryant Stith	.15	.04
❑ 64 Dikembe Mutombo	.25	.07
❑ 65 Robert Pack	.15	.04
❑ 66 Joe Dumars	.50	.15
❑ 67 Terry Mills	.15	.04
❑ 68 Oliver Miller	.15	.04
❑ 69 Lindsey Hunter	.25	.07
❑ 70 Mark West	.15	.04
❑ 71 Latrell Sprewell	.50	.15
❑ 72 Tim Hardaway	.50	.15
❑ 73 Ricky Pierce	.15	.04
❑ 74 Rony Seikaly	.15	.04
❑ 75 Tom Gugliotta	.25	.07
❑ 76 Hakeem Olajuwon	.75	.23
❑ 77 Clyde Drexler	.50	.15
❑ 78 Vernon Maxwell	.15	.04
❑ 79 Robert Horry	.25	.07
❑ 80 Sam Cassell	.50	.15
❑ 81 Reggie Miller	.50	.15
❑ 82 Rik Smits	.15	.04
❑ 83 Derrick McKey	.15	.04
❑ 84 Mark Jackson	.15	.04
❑ 85 Dale Davis	.15	.04
❑ 86 Loy Vaught	.15	.04
❑ 87 Terry Dehere	.15	.04
❑ 88 Malik Sealy	.15	.04
❑ 89 Pooh Richardson	.15	.04
❑ 90 Tony Massenburg	.15	.04
❑ 91 Cedric Ceballos	.15	.04
❑ 92 Nick Van Exel	.50	.15
❑ 93 George Lynch	.15	.04
❑ 94 Vlade Divac	.15	.04
❑ 95 Elden Campbell	.15	.04
❑ 96 Glen Rice	.25	.07
❑ 97 Kevin Willis	.15	.04
❑ 98 Billy Owens	.15	.04
❑ 99 Bimbo Coles	.15	.04
❑ 100 Harold Miner	.15	.04
❑ 101 Vin Baker	.50	.15
❑ 102 Todd Day	.15	.04
❑ 103 Marty Conlon	.15	.04
❑ 104 Lee Mayberry	.15	.04
❑ 105 Eric Murdock	.15	.04
❑ 106 Isaiah Rider	.25	.07
❑ 107 Doug West	.15	.04
❑ 108 Christian Laettner	.25	.07
❑ 109 Sean Rooks	.15	.04
❑ 110 Stacey King	.15	.04
❑ 111 Derrick Coleman	.25	.07
❑ 112 Kenny Anderson	.25	.07
❑ 113 Chris Morris	.15	.04
❑ 114 Armon Gilliam	.15	.04
❑ 115 Benoit Benjamin	.15	.04
❑ 116 Patrick Ewing	.50	.15

	Card	Player	Nm-Mt	Ex-Mt
❑	117	Charles Oakley	.15	.04
❑	118	John Starks	.15	.04
❑	119	Derek Harper	.15	.04
❑	120	Charles Smith	.15	.04
❑	121	Shaquille O'Neal	2.50	.75
❑	122	Anfernee Hardaway	1.25	.35
❑	123	Nick Anderson	.15	.04
❑	124	Horace Grant	.25	.07
❑	125	Donald Royal	.15	.04
❑	126	Clarence Weatherspoon	.15	.04
❑	127	Dana Barros	.15	.04
❑	128	Jeff Malone	.15	.04
❑	129	Willie Burton	.15	.04
❑	130	Shawn Bradley	.15	.04
❑	131	Charles Barkley	.75	.23
❑	132	Kevin Johnson	.25	.07
❑	133	Danny Manning	.25	.07
❑	134	Dan Majerle	.25	.07
❑	135	A.C. Green	.25	.07
❑	136	Otis Thorpe	.15	.04
❑	137	Clifford Robinson	.25	.07
❑	138	Rod Strickland	.25	.07
❑	139	Buck Williams	.15	.04
❑	140	James Robinson	.15	.04
❑	141	Mitch Richmond	.50	.15
❑	142	Walt Williams	.15	.04
❑	143	Olden Polynice	.15	.04
❑	144	Spud Webb	.15	.04
❑	145	Duane Causwell	.15	.04
❑	146	David Robinson	.75	.23
❑	147	Dennis Rodman	1.00	.30
❑	148	Sean Elliott	.25	.07
❑	149	Avery Johnson	.15	.04
❑	150	J.R. Reid	.15	.04
❑	151	Shawn Kemp	.75	.23
❑	152	Gary Payton	.75	.23
❑	153	Detlef Schrempf	.25	.07
❑	154	Nate McMillan	.15	.04
❑	155	Kendall Gill	.25	.07
❑	156	Karl Malone	.75	.23
❑	157	John Stockton	.50	.15
❑	158	Jeff Hornacek	.25	.07
❑	159	Felton Spencer	.15	.04
❑	160	David Benoit	.15	.04
❑	161	Chris Webber	1.25	.35
❑	162	Rex Chapman	.15	.04
❑	163	Don MacLean	.15	.04
❑	164	Calbert Cheaney	.15	.04
❑	165	Scott Skiles	.15	.04
❑	P23	Michael Jordan Promo	10.00	3.00
❑	MJ1R	Michael Jordan Red	5.00	1.50
❑	MJ1S	Michael Jordan Silver	15.00	4.50

1995-96 SP

	Card	Player	Nm-Mt	Ex-Mt
		COMPLETE SET (167)	30.00	9.00
❑	1	Stacey Augmon	.25	.07
❑	2	Mookie Blaylock	.25	.07
❑	3	Andrew Lang	.25	.07
❑	4	Steve Smith	.50	.15
❑	5	Spud Webb	.50	.15
❑	6	Dana Barros	.25	.07
❑	7	Dee Brown	.25	.07
❑	8	Todd Day	.25	.07
❑	9	Rick Fox	.50	.15
❑	10	Eric Montross	.25	.07
❑	11	Dino Radja	.25	.07
❑	12	Kenny Anderson	.50	.15
❑	13	Scott Burrell	.25	.07
❑	14	Dell Curry	.25	.07
❑	15	Matt Geiger	.25	.07
❑	16	Larry Johnson	.50	.15
❑	17	Glen Rice	.50	.15
❑	18	Steve Kerr	.50	.15
❑	19	Toni Kukoc	.50	.15
❑	20	Luc Longley	.25	.07
❑	21	Scottie Pippen	1.25	.35
❑	22	Dennis Rodman	.50	.15
❑	23	Michael Jordan	5.00	1.50
❑	24	Terrell Brandon	.50	.15
❑	25	Michael Cage	.25	.07
❑	26	Danny Ferry	.25	.07
❑	27	Chris Mills	.25	.07
❑	28	Bobby Phills	.25	.07
❑	29	Tony Dumas	.25	.07
❑	30	Jim Jackson	.25	.07
❑	31	Popeye Jones	.25	.07
❑	32	Jason Kidd	2.50	.75
❑	33	Jamal Mashburn	.50	.15
❑	34	Mahmoud Abdul-Rauf	.25	.07
❑	35	LaPhonso Ellis	.25	.07
❑	36	Dikembe Mutombo	.50	.15
❑	37	Jalen Rose	1.00	.30
❑	38	Bryant Stith	.25	.07
❑	39	Joe Dumars	.75	.23
❑	40	Grant Hill	1.00	.30
❑	41	Lindsey Hunter	.25	.07
❑	42	Allan Houston	.50	.15
❑	43	Otis Thorpe	.25	.07
❑	44	B.J. Armstrong	.25	.07
❑	45	Tim Hardaway	.50	.15
❑	46	Chris Mullin	.75	.23
❑	47	Latrell Sprewell	.75	.23
❑	48	Rony Seikaly	.25	.07
❑	49	Sam Cassell	.75	.23
❑	50	Clyde Drexler	.75	.23
❑	51	Robert Horry	.50	.15
❑	52	Hakeem Olajuwon	.75	.23
❑	53	Kenny Smith	.25	.07
❑	54	Dale Davis	.25	.07
❑	55	Derrick McKey	.25	.07
❑	56	Reggie Miller	.75	.23
❑	57	Ricky Pierce	.25	.07
❑	58	Rik Smits	.50	.15
❑	59	Lamond Murray	.25	.07
❑	60	Rodney Rogers	.25	.07
❑	61	Malik Sealy	.25	.07
❑	62	Loy Vaught	.25	.07
❑	63	Brian Williams	.25	.07
❑	64	Elden Campbell	.25	.07
❑	65	Cedric Ceballos	.25	.07
❑	66	Magic Johnson	1.25	.35
❑	67	Eddie Jones	1.00	.30
❑	68	Nick Van Exel	.75	.23
❑	69	Bimbo Coles	.25	.07
❑	70	Alonzo Mourning	.50	.15
❑	71	Billy Owens	.25	.07
❑	72	Kevin Willis	.50	.15
❑	73	Vin Baker	.50	.15
❑	74	Benoit Benjamin	.25	.07
❑	75	Sherman Douglas	.25	.07
❑	76	Lee Mayberry	.25	.07
❑	77	Glenn Robinson	.75	.23
❑	78	Tom Gugliotta	.25	.07
❑	79	Christian Laettner	.50	.15
❑	80	Sam Mitchell	.25	.07
❑	81	Terry Porter	.25	.07
❑	82	Isaiah Rider	.25	.07
❑	83	Shawn Bradley	.25	.07
❑	84	P.J. Brown	.25	.07
❑	85	Kendall Gill	.25	.07
❑	86	Armon Gilliam	.25	.07
❑	87	Jayson Williams	.25	.07
❑	88	Patrick Ewing	.75	.23
❑	89	Derek Harper	.50	.15
❑	90	Anthony Mason	.50	.15
❑	91	Charles Oakley	.25	.07
❑	92	John Starks	.50	.15
❑	93	Nick Anderson	.25	.07
❑	94	Horace Grant	.50	.15
❑	95	Anfernee Hardaway	.75	.23
❑	96	Shaquille O'Neal	2.00	.60
❑	97	Dennis Scott	.25	.07
❑	98	Derrick Coleman	.25	.07
❑	99	Vernon Maxwell	.25	.07
❑	100	Trevor Ruffin	.25	.07
❑	101	Clarence Weatherspoon	.25	.07
❑	102	Sharone Wright	.25	.07
❑	103	Charles Barkley	1.00	.30
❑	104	A.C. Green	.50	.15
❑	105	Kevin Johnson	.50	.15
❑	106	Wesley Person	.25	.07
❑	107	John Williams	.25	.07
❑	108	Chris Dudley	.25	.07
❑	109	Harvey Grant	.25	.07
❑	110	Aaron McKie	.50	.15
❑	111	Clifford Robinson	.25	.07
❑	112	Rod Strickland	.25	.07
❑	113	Brian Grant	.75	.23
❑	114	Sarunas Marciulionis	.25	.07
❑	115	Olden Polynice	.25	.07
❑	116	Mitch Richmond	.50	.15
❑	117	Walt Williams	.25	.07
❑	118	Vinny Del Negro	.25	.07
❑	119	Sean Elliott	.50	.15
❑	120	Avery Johnson	.25	.07
❑	121	Chuck Person	.25	.07
❑	122	David Robinson	.75	.23
❑	123	Hersey Hawkins	.25	.07
❑	124	Shawn Kemp	.50	.15
❑	125	Gary Payton	.75	.23
❑	126	Sam Perkins	.50	.15
❑	127	Detlef Schrempf	.50	.15
❑	128	Oliver Miller	.25	.07
❑	129	Tracy Murray	.25	.07
❑	130	Ed Pinckney	.25	.07
❑	131	Alvin Robertson	.25	.07
❑	132	Zan Tabak	.25	.07
❑	133	Jeff Hornacek	.50	.15
❑	134	Adam Keefe	.25	.07
❑	135	Karl Malone	1.00	.30
❑	136	Chris Morris	.25	.07
❑	137	John Stockton	1.00	.30
❑	138	Greg Anthony	.25	.07
❑	139	Blue Edwards	.25	.07
❑	140	Kenny Gattison	.25	.07
❑	141	Chris King	.25	.07
❑	142	Byron Scott	.25	.07
❑	143	Calbert Cheaney	.25	.07
❑	144	Juwan Howard	.75	.23
❑	145	Gheorghe Muresan	.25	.07
❑	146	Robert Pack	.25	.07
❑	147	Chris Webber	1.00	.30
❑	148	Alan Henderson RC	.75	.23
❑	149	Eric Williams RC	.50	.15
❑	150	George Zidek RC	.25	.07
❑	151	Bob Sura RC	.50	.15
❑	152	Antonio McDyess RC	1.50	.45
❑	153	Theo Ratliff RC	1.00	.30
❑	154	Joe Smith RC	1.25	.35
❑	155	Brent Barry RC	.75	.23
❑	156	Sasha Danilovic RC	.25	.07
❑	157	Kurt Thomas RC	.50	.15
❑	158	Shawn Respert RC	.25	.07
❑	159	Kevin Garnett RC	12.00	3.60
❑	160	Ed O'Bannon RC	.25	.07
❑	161	Jerry Stackhouse RC	5.00	1.50
❑	162	Michael Finley RC	2.50	.75
❑	163	Arvydas Sabonis RC	1.00	.30
❑	164	Cory Alexander RC	.25	.07
❑	165	Damon Stoudamire RC	1.50	.45
❑	166	Bryant Reeves RC	.75	.23
❑	167	Rasheed Wallace RC	2.50	.75
❑	C1	Hakeem Olajuwon Commemorative	12.00	3.60
❑	P23	Michael Jordan Promo	10.00	3.00

1996-97 SP

	Card	Player	Nm-Mt	Ex-Mt
		COMPLETE SET (146)	35.00	10.50
		COMMON CARD (1-126)	.25	.07
		COMMON ROOKIE (127-146)	.75	.23
❑	1	Mookie Blaylock	.25	.07
❑	2	Christian Laettner	.50	.15
❑	3	Dikembe Mutombo	.50	.15
❑	4	Steve Smith	.50	.15

❑ 5 Dana Barros .25 .07
❑ 6 Rick Fox .25 .07
❑ 7 Dino Radja .25 .07
❑ 8 Eric Williams .25 .07
❑ 9 Dell Curry .25 .07
❑ 10 Vlade Divac .25 .07
❑ 11 Anthony Mason .50 .15
❑ 12 Glen Rice .50 .15
❑ 13 Scottie Pippen 1.25 .35
❑ 14 Toni Kukoc .50 .15
❑ 15 Luc Longley .25 .07
❑ 16 Michael Jordan 5.00 1.50
❑ 17 Dennis Rodman .50 .15
❑ 18 Terrell Brandon .50 .15
❑ 19 Tyrone Hill .25 .07
❑ 20 Bobby Phills .25 .07
❑ 21 Bob Sura .25 .07
❑ 22 Chris Gatling .25 .07
❑ 23 Jim Jackson .25 .07
❑ 24 Sam Cassell .75 .23
❑ 25 Jamal Mashburn .50 .15
❑ 26 Dale Ellis .25 .07
❑ 27 LaPhonso Ellis .25 .07
❑ 28 Mark Jackson .25 .07
❑ 29 Antonio McDyess .50 .15
❑ 30 Bryant Stith .25 .07
❑ 31 Joe Dumars .75 .23
❑ 32 Grant Hill .75 .23
❑ 33 Lindsey Hunter .25 .07
❑ 34 Otis Thorpe .25 .07
❑ 35 Chris Mullin .75 .23
❑ 36 Mark Price .50 .15
❑ 37 Joe Smith .50 .15
❑ 38 Latrell Sprewell .75 .23
❑ 39 Charles Barkley 1.00 .30
❑ 40 Clyde Drexler .75 .23
❑ 41 Mario Elie .25 .07
❑ 42 Hakeem Olajuwon .75 .23
❑ 43 Travis Best .25 .07
❑ 44 Dale Davis .25 .07
❑ 45 Reggie Miller .75 .23
❑ 46 Rik Smits .50 .15
❑ 47 Pooh Richardson .25 .07
❑ 48 Rodney Rogers .25 .07
❑ 49 Malik Sealy .25 .07
❑ 50 Loy Vaught .25 .07
❑ 51 Elden Campbell .25 .07
❑ 52 Robert Horry .50 .15
❑ 53 Eddie Jones .75 .23
❑ 54 Shaquille O'Neal 2.00 .60
❑ 55 Nick Van Exel .75 .23
❑ 56 Sasha Danilovic .25 .07
❑ 57 Tim Hardaway .50 .15
❑ 58 Dan Majerle .50 .15
❑ 59 Alonzo Mourning .50 .15
❑ 60 Vin Baker .50 .15
❑ 61 Sherman Douglas .25 .07
❑ 62 Armon Gilliam .25 .07
❑ 63 Glenn Robinson .75 .23
❑ 64 Kevin Garnett 1.50 .45
❑ 65 Tom Gugliotta .25 .07
❑ 66 Terry Porter .25 .07
❑ 67 Doug West .25 .07
❑ 68 Shawn Bradley .25 .07
❑ 69 Kendall Gill .25 .07
❑ 70 Robert Pack .25 .07
❑ 71 Jayson Williams .50 .15
❑ 72 Chris Childs .25 .07
❑ 73 Patrick Ewing .75 .23
❑ 74 Allan Houston .50 .15
❑ 75 Larry Johnson .50 .15
❑ 76 John Starks .50 .15
❑ 77 Nick Anderson .25 .07
❑ 78 Horace Grant .50 .15
❑ 79 Anfernee Hardaway .75 .23
❑ 80 Dennis Scott .25 .07
❑ 81 Derrick Coleman .50 .15
❑ 82 Mark Davis .25 .07
❑ 83 Jerry Stackhouse 1.00 .30
❑ 84 Clarence Weatherspoon .25 .07
❑ 85 Cedric Ceballos .25 .07
❑ 86 Kevin Johnson .50 .15
❑ 87 Jason Kidd 1.25 .35
❑ 88 Danny Manning .50 .15
❑ 89 Wesley Person .25 .07
❑ 90 Kenny Anderson .25 .07
❑ 91 Isaiah Rider .50 .15
❑ 92 Clifford Robinson .25 .07
❑ 93 Arvydas Sabonis .50 .15
❑ 94 Rasheed Wallace 1.00 .30
❑ 95 Mahmoud Abdul-Rauf .25 .07
❑ 96 Brian Grant .75 .23
❑ 97 Olden Polynice .25 .07
❑ 98 Mitch Richmond .50 .15
❑ 99 Corliss Williamson .50 .15
❑ 100 Sean Elliott .50 .15
❑ 101 Avery Johnson .25 .07
❑ 102 David Robinson .75 .23
❑ 103 Dominique Wilkins .75 .23
❑ 104 Hersey Hawkins .50 .15
❑ 105 Jim McIlvaine .25 .07
❑ 106 Shawn Kemp .50 .15
❑ 107 Gary Payton .75 .23
❑ 108 Detlef Schrempf .50 .15
❑ 109 Doug Christie .50 .15
❑ 110 Popeye Jones .25 .07
❑ 111 Damon Stoudamire .75 .23
❑ 112 Walt Williams .25 .07
❑ 113 Jeff Hornacek .50 .15
❑ 114 Karl Malone .75 .23
❑ 115 Greg Ostertag .25 .07
❑ 116 Bryon Russell .25 .07
❑ 117 John Stockton .75 .23
❑ 118 Greg Anthony .25 .07
❑ 119 Blue Edwards .25 .07
❑ 120 Anthony Peeler .25 .07
❑ 121 Bryant Reeves .25 .07
❑ 122 Calbert Cheaney .25 .07
❑ 123 Juwan Howard .50 .15
❑ 124 Gheorghe Muresan .25 .07
❑ 125 Rod Strickland .25 .07
❑ 126 Chris Webber .75 .23
❑ 127 Antoine Walker RC 4.00 1.20
❑ 128 Tony Delk RC .75 .23
❑ 129 Vitaly Potapenko RC .75 .23
❑ 130 Samaki Walker RC .75 .23
❑ 131 Todd Fuller RC .75 .23
❑ 132 Erick Dampier RC .75 .23
❑ 133 Lorenzen Wright RC .75 .23
❑ 134 Kobe Bryant RC 15.00 4.50
❑ 135 Derek Fisher RC 1.50 .45
❑ 136 Ray Allen RC 5.00 1.50
❑ 137 Stephon Marbury RC 3.00 .90
❑ 138 Kerry Kittles RC .75 .23
❑ 139 Walter McCarty RC .75 .23
❑ 140 John Wallace RC .75 .23
❑ 141 Allen Iverson RC 10.00 3.00
❑ 142 Steve Nash RC 5.00 1.50
❑ 143 Jermaine O'Neal RC 5.00 1.50
❑ 144 Marcus Camby RC 1.50 .45
❑ 145 Shareef Abdur-Rahim RC 4.00 1.20
❑ 146 Roy Rogers RC .75 .23
❑ S16 M.Jordan Sample 5.00 1.50

1997-98 SP Authentic

	Nm-Mt	Ex-Mt
COMPLETE SET (176)	120.00	36.00
COMMON CARD (1-176)	.40	.12
COMMON ROOKIE	.75	.23

❑ 1 Steve Smith .75 .23
❑ 2 Dikembe Mutombo .75 .23
❑ 3 Christian Laettner .75 .23
❑ 4 Mookie Blaylock .40 .12

❑ 5 Alan Henderson .40 .12
❑ 6 Antoine Walker 1.50 .45
❑ 7 Ron Mercer RC 4.00 1.20
❑ 8 Walter McCarty .40 .12
❑ 9 Kenny Anderson .75 .23
❑ 10 Travis Knight .40 .12
❑ 11 Dana Barros .40 .12
❑ 12 Glen Rice .75 .23
❑ 13 Vlade Divac .75 .23
❑ 14 Dell Curry .40 .12
❑ 15 David Wesley .40 .12
❑ 16 Bobby Phills .40 .12
❑ 17 Anthony Mason .75 .23
❑ 18 Toni Kukoc .75 .23
❑ 19 Dennis Rodman .75 .23
❑ 20 Ron Harper .75 .23
❑ 21 Steve Kerr .75 .23
❑ 22 Scottie Pippen 2.00 .60
❑ 23 Michael Jordan 8.00 2.40
❑ 24 Shawn Kemp .75 .23
❑ 25 Wesley Person .40 .12
❑ 26 Derek Anderson RC 8.00 2.40
❑ 27 Zydrunas Ilgauskas .75 .23
❑ 28 Brevin Knight RC 1.50 .45
❑ 29 Michael Finley 1.25 .35
❑ 30 Shawn Bradley .40 .12
❑ 31 A.C. Green .75 .23
❑ 32 Hubert Davis .40 .12
❑ 33 Dennis Scott .40 .12
❑ 34 Tony Battie RC 1.50 .45
❑ 35 Bobby Jackson RC 8.00 2.40
❑ 36 LaPhonso Ellis .40 .12
❑ 37 Bryant Stith .40 .12
❑ 38 Dean Garrett .40 .12
❑ 39 Danny Fortson RC 4.00 1.20
❑ 40 Grant Hill 1.25 .35
❑ 41 Brian Williams .40 .12
❑ 42 Lindsey Hunter .40 .12
❑ 43 Malik Sealy .40 .12
❑ 44 Jerry Stackhouse 1.25 .35
❑ 45 Muggsy Bogues .75 .23
❑ 46 Joe Smith .75 .23
❑ 47 Donyell Marshall .75 .23
❑ 48 Erick Dampier .75 .23
❑ 49 Bimbo Coles .40 .12
❑ 50 Charles Barkley 1.50 .45
❑ 51 Hakeem Olajuwon 1.25 .35
❑ 52 Clyde Drexler 1.25 .35
❑ 53 Kevin Willis .75 .23
❑ 54 Mario Elie .40 .12
❑ 55 Reggie Miller 1.25 .35
❑ 56 Rik Smits .75 .23
❑ 57 Chris Mullin 1.25 .35
❑ 58 Antonio Davis .40 .12
❑ 59 Dale Davis .40 .12
❑ 60 Mark Jackson .75 .23
❑ 61 Brent Barry .75 .23
❑ 62 Loy Vaught .40 .12
❑ 63 Rodney Rogers .40 .12
❑ 64 Lamond Murray .40 .12
❑ 65 Maurice Taylor RC 4.00 1.20
❑ 66 Shaquille O'Neal 3.00 .90
❑ 67 Eddie Jones 1.25 .35
❑ 68 Kobe Bryant 5.00 1.50
❑ 69 Nick Van Exel 1.25 .35
❑ 70 Robert Horry .75 .23
❑ 71 Tim Hardaway .75 .23
❑ 72 Jamal Mashburn .75 .23

Card	Nm-Mt	Ex-Mt
❑ 73 Alonzo Mourning	.75	.23
❑ 74 Isaac Austin	.40	.12
❑ 75 P.J. Brown	.40	.12
❑ 76 Ray Allen	1.25	.35
❑ 77 Glenn Robinson	1.25	.35
❑ 78 Ervin Johnson	.40	.12
❑ 79 Terrell Brandon	.75	.23
❑ 80 Tyrone Hill	.40	.12
❑ 81 Stephon Marbury	1.50	.45
❑ 82 Kevin Garnett	2.50	.75
❑ 83 Tom Gugliotta	.75	.23
❑ 84 Chris Carr	.40	.12
❑ 85 Cherokee Parks	.40	.12
❑ 86 Sam Cassell	1.25	.35
❑ 87 Chris Gatling	.40	.12
❑ 88 Kendall Gill	.40	.12
❑ 89 Keith Van Horn RC	5.00	1.50
❑ 90 Jayson Williams	.40	.12
❑ 91 Kerry Kittles	1.25	.35
❑ 92 Patrick Ewing	1.25	.35
❑ 93 Larry Johnson	.75	.23
❑ 94 Chris Childs	.40	.12
❑ 95 John Starks	.75	.23
❑ 96 Charles Oakley	.75	.23
❑ 97 Allan Houston	.75	.23
❑ 98 Mark Price	.75	.23
❑ 99 Anfernee Hardaway	1.25	.35
❑ 100 Rony Seikaly	.40	.12
❑ 101 Horace Grant	.75	.23
❑ 102 Bo Outlaw	.40	.12
❑ 103 Clarence Weatherspoon	.40	.12
❑ 104 Allen Iverson	3.00	.90
❑ 105 Jim Jackson	.40	.12
❑ 106 Theo Ratliff	.40	.12
❑ 107 Tim Thomas RC	8.00	2.40
❑ 108 Danny Manning	.75	.23
❑ 109 Jason Kidd	2.00	.60
❑ 110 Kevin Johnson	.75	.23
❑ 111 Rex Chapman	.40	.12
❑ 112 Clifford Robinson	.40	.12
❑ 113 Antonio McDyess	.75	.23
❑ 114 Damon Stoudamire	.75	.23
❑ 115 Isaiah Rider	.75	.23
❑ 116 Arvydas Sabonis	.75	.23
❑ 117 Rasheed Wallace	1.25	.35
❑ 118 Brian Grant	.75	.23
❑ 119 Gary Trent	.40	.12
❑ 120 Mitch Richmond	.75	.23
❑ 121 Corliss Williamson	.75	.23
❑ 122 L.Funderburke RC	1.00	.30
❑ 123 Olden Polynice	.40	.12
❑ 124 Billy Owens	.40	.12
❑ 125 Avery Johnson	.40	.12
❑ 126 Sean Elliott	.75	.23
❑ 127 David Robinson	1.25	.35
❑ 128 Tim Duncan RC	25.00	7.50
❑ 129 Jaren Jackson	.40	.12
❑ 130 Detlef Schrempf	.75	.23
❑ 131 Gary Payton	1.25	.35
❑ 132 Vin Baker	.75	.23
❑ 133 Hersey Hawkins	.40	.12
❑ 134 Dale Ellis	.40	.12
❑ 135 Sam Perkins	.75	.23
❑ 136 Marcus Camby	1.25	.35
❑ 137 John Wallace	.40	.12
❑ 138 Doug Christie	.75	.23
❑ 139 Chauncey Billups RC	2.50	.75
❑ 140 Walt Williams	.40	.12
❑ 141 Karl Malone	1.25	.35
❑ 142 Bryon Russell	.40	.12
❑ 143 Jeff Hornacek	.75	.23
❑ 144 Greg Ostertag	.40	.12
❑ 145 John Stockton	1.25	.35
❑ 146 Shandon Anderson	.40	.12
❑ 147 Shareef Abdur-Rahim	2.00	.60
❑ 148 Bryant Reeves	.40	.12
❑ 149 Antonio Daniels RC	1.50	.45
❑ 150 Otis Thorpe	.40	.12
❑ 151 Blue Edwards	.40	.12
❑ 152 Chris Webber	1.25	.35
❑ 153 Juwan Howard	.75	.23
❑ 154 Rod Strickland	.40	.12
❑ 155 Calbert Cheaney	.40	.12
❑ 156 Tracy Murray	.40	.12
❑ 157 Chauncey Billups	.75	.23
❑ 158 Ed Gray RC	.75	.23
❑ 159 Tony Battie FW	1.00	.30
❑ 160 Keith Van Horn FW	2.00	.60
❑ 161 Cedric Henderson RC	1.00	.30
❑ 162 Kelvin Cato RC	1.50	.45
❑ 163 Tariq Abdul-Wahad RC	1.00	.30
❑ 164 Derek Anderson FW	1.50	.45
❑ 165 Tim Duncan FW	5.00	1.50
❑ 166 Tracy McGrady RC	50.00	15.00
❑ 167 Ron Mercer FW	1.50	.45
❑ 168 Bobby Jackson FW	.75	.23
❑ 169 Antonio Daniels FW	1.00	.30
❑ 170 Zydrunas Ilgauskas FW	.75	.23
❑ 171 Maurice Taylor FW	1.25	.35
❑ 172 Tim Thomas FW	2.00	.60
❑ 173 Brevin Knight FW	.75	.23
❑ 174 L. Funderburke FW	.75	.23
❑ 175 Jacque Vaughn RC	1.00	.30
❑ 176 Danny Fortson FW	1.00	.30
❑ SPA23 M.Jordan Promo	6.00	1.80

1998-99 SP Authentic

	Nm-Mt	Ex-Mt
COMPLETE SET w/o RC (90)	40.00	12.00
COMMON MJ (1-10)	3.00	.90
COMMON CARD (11-90)	.30	.09
COMMON ROOKIE (91-120)	5.00	1.50
❑ 1 Michael Jordan	3.00	.90
❑ 2 Michael Jordan	3.00	.90
❑ 3 Michael Jordan	3.00	.90
❑ 4 Michael Jordan	3.00	.90
❑ 5 Michael Jordan	3.00	.90
❑ 6 Michael Jordan	3.00	.90
❑ 7 Michael Jordan	3.00	.90
❑ 8 Michael Jordan	3.00	.90
❑ 9 Michael Jordan	3.00	.90
❑ 10 Michael Jordan	3.00	.90
❑ 11 Steve Smith	.60	.18
❑ 12 Dikembe Mutombo	.60	.18
❑ 13 Alan Henderson	.30	.09
❑ 14 Antoine Walker	1.00	.30
❑ 15 Ron Mercer	.60	.18
❑ 16 Kenny Anderson	.60	.18
❑ 17 Derrick Coleman	.30	.09
❑ 18 David Wesley	.30	.09
❑ 19 Glen Rice	.60	.18
❑ 20 Toni Kukoc	.60	.18
❑ 21 Ron Harper	.60	.18
❑ 22 Brent Barry	.60	.18
❑ 23 Shawn Kemp	.60	.18
❑ 24 Zydrunas Ilgauskas	.60	.18
❑ 25 Brevin Knight	.30	.09
❑ 26 Michael Finley	1.00	.30
❑ 27 Steve Nash	1.00	.30
❑ 28 Cedric Ceballos	.30	.09
❑ 29 Antonio McDyess	.60	.18
❑ 30 Nick Van Exel	1.00	.30
❑ 31 Grant Hill	1.00	.30
❑ 32 Jerry Stackhouse	1.00	.30
❑ 33 Bison Dele	.30	.09
❑ 34 John Starks	.60	.18
❑ 35 Chris Mills	.30	.09
❑ 36 Hakeem Olajuwon	1.00	.30
❑ 37 Charles Barkley	1.25	.35
❑ 38 Scottie Pippen	1.50	.45
❑ 39 Reggie Miller	1.00	.30
❑ 40 Chris Mullin	1.00	.30
❑ 41 Rik Smits	.60	.18
❑ 42 Lamond Murray	.30	.09
❑ 43 Maurice Taylor	.60	.18
❑ 44 Kobe Bryant	4.00	1.20
❑ 45 Dennis Rodman	.60	.18
❑ 46 Shaquille O'Neal	2.50	.75
❑ 47 Alonzo Mourning	.60	.18
❑ 48 Tim Hardaway	.60	.18
❑ 49 Jamal Mashburn	.60	.18
❑ 50 Ray Allen	1.00	.30
❑ 51 Glenn Robinson	.60	.18
❑ 52 Terrell Brandon	.60	.18
❑ 53 Kevin Garnett	2.00	.60
❑ 54 Stephon Marbury	1.00	.30
❑ 55 Joe Smith	.60	.18
❑ 56 Keith Van Horn	1.00	.30
❑ 57 Kendall Gill	.30	.09
❑ 58 Jayson Williams	.30	.09
❑ 59 Patrick Ewing	1.00	.30
❑ 60 Allan Houston	.60	.18
❑ 61 Larry Johnson	.60	.18
❑ 62 Anfernee Hardaway	1.00	.30
❑ 63 Horace Grant	.60	.18
❑ 64 Allen Iverson	2.00	.60
❑ 65 Tim Thomas	.60	.18
❑ 66 Jason Kidd	1.50	.45
❑ 67 Tom Gugliotta	.30	.09
❑ 68 Rex Chapman	.30	.09
❑ 69 Damon Stoudamire	.60	.18
❑ 70 Isaiah Rider	.30	.09
❑ 71 Rasheed Wallace	1.00	.30
❑ 72 Chris Webber	1.00	.30
❑ 73 Vlade Divac	.60	.18
❑ 74 Corliss Williamson	.60	.18
❑ 75 Tim Duncan	1.50	.45
❑ 76 David Robinson	1.00	.30
❑ 77 Sean Elliott	.60	.18
❑ 78 Detlef Schrempf	.60	.18
❑ 79 Vin Baker	.60	.18
❑ 80 Gary Payton	1.00	.30
❑ 81 Doug Christie	.60	.18
❑ 82 Tracy McGrady	2.50	.75
❑ 83 Karl Malone	1.00	.30
❑ 84 John Stockton	1.00	.30
❑ 85 Jeff Hornacek	.60	.18
❑ 86 Shareef Abdur-Rahim	1.00	.30
❑ 87 Bryant Reeves	.30	.09
❑ 88 Juwan Howard	.60	.18
❑ 89 Mitch Richmond	.60	.18
❑ 90 Rod Strickland	.30	.09
❑ 91 Michael Olowokandi RC	8.00	2.40
❑ 92 Mike Bibby RC	40.00	12.00
❑ 93 Raef LaFrentz RC	15.00	4.50
❑ 94 Antawn Jamison RC	50.00	15.00
❑ 95 Vince Carter RC	200.00	60.00
❑ 96 Robert Traylor RC	6.00	1.80
❑ 97 Jason Williams RC	40.00	12.00
❑ 98 Larry Hughes RC	30.00	9.00
❑ 99 Dirk Nowitzki RC	80.00	24.00
❑ 100 Paul Pierce RC	60.00	18.00
❑ 101 Bonzi Wells RC	40.00	12.00
❑ 102 Michael Doleac RC	6.00	1.80
❑ 103 Keon Clark RC	20.00	6.00
❑ 104 Michael Dickerson RC	15.00	4.50
❑ 105 Matt Harpring RC	8.00	2.40
❑ 106 Bryce Drew RC	6.00	1.80
❑ 107 Pat Garrity RC	8.00	2.40
❑ 108 Roshown McLeod RC	8.00	2.40
❑ 109 Ricky Davis RC	25.00	7.50
❑ 110 Brian Skinner RC	6.00	1.80

	Nm-Mt	Ex-Mt
❑ 111 Tyronn Lue RC	8.00	2.40
❑ 112 Felipe Lopez RC	8.00	2.40
❑ 113 Al Harrington RC	30.00	9.00
❑ 114 Sam Jacobson RC	5.00	1.50
❑ 115 Cory Carr RC	5.00	1.50
❑ 116 Corey Benjamin RC	8.00	2.40
❑ 117 Nazr Mohammed RC	8.00	2.40
❑ 118 Rashard Lewis RC	50.00	15.00
❑ 119 Peja Stojakovic RC	60.00	18.00
❑ 120 Andrae Patterson RC	5.00	1.50

1999-00 SP Authentic

	Nm-Mt	Ex-Mt
COMPLETE SET w/o RC (90)	30.00	9.00
COMMON CARD (1-90)	.30	.09
COMMON ROOKIE (91-135)	10.00	3.00
❑ 1 Dikembe Mutombo	.60	.18
❑ 2 Jim Jackson	.30	.09
❑ 3 Alan Henderson	.30	.09
❑ 4 Antoine Walker	1.00	.30
❑ 5 Paul Pierce	1.00	.30
❑ 6 Kenny Anderson	.60	.18
❑ 7 Eddie Jones	1.00	.30
❑ 8 Derrick Coleman	.60	.18
❑ 9 Anthony Mason	.60	.18
❑ 10 Chris Carr	.30	.09
❑ 11 Hersey Hawkins	.60	.18
❑ 12 B.J. Armstrong	.30	.09
❑ 13 Shawn Kemp	.60	.18
❑ 14 Bob Sura	.30	.09
❑ 15 Lamond Murray	.30	.09
❑ 16 Michael Finley	1.00	.30
❑ 17 Cedric Ceballos	.30	.09
❑ 18 Dirk Nowitzki	2.00	.60
❑ 19 Erick Strickland	.30	.09
❑ 20 Antonio McDyess	.60	.18
❑ 21 Nick Van Exel	1.00	.30
❑ 22 Grant Hill	1.00	.30
❑ 23 Jerry Stackhouse	1.00	.30
❑ 24 Lindsey Hunter	.30	.09
❑ 25 Christian Laettner	.60	.18
❑ 26 Antawn Jamison	1.50	.45
❑ 27 Chris Mills	.30	.09
❑ 28 Larry Hughes	1.00	.30
❑ 29 Charles Barkley	1.25	.35
❑ 30 Hakeem Olajuwon	1.00	.30
❑ 31 Cuttino Mobley	1.00	.30
❑ 32 Reggie Miller	1.00	.30
❑ 33 Jalen Rose	1.00	.30
❑ 34 Rik Smits	.60	.18
❑ 35 Maurice Taylor	.60	.18
❑ 36 Derek Anderson	.60	.18
❑ 37 Tyrone Nesby RC	.30	.09
❑ 38 Kobe Bryant	4.00	1.20
❑ 39 Shaquille O'Neal	2.50	.75
❑ 40 Glen Rice	.60	.18
❑ 41 Tim Hardaway	.60	.18
❑ 42 Alonzo Mourning	.60	.18
❑ 43 Jamal Mashburn	.60	.18
❑ 44 Ray Allen	1.00	.30
❑ 45 Sam Cassell	1.00	.30
❑ 46 Glenn Robinson	1.00	.30
❑ 47 Kevin Garnett	2.00	.60
❑ 48 Terrell Brandon	.60	.18
❑ 49 Joe Smith	.60	.18
❑ 50 Stephon Marbury	1.00	.30
❑ 51 Keith Van Horn	1.00	.30
❑ 52 Jamie Feick RC	1.00	.30
❑ 53 Kerry Kittles	.30	.09
❑ 54 Allan Houston	.60	.18
❑ 55 Latrell Sprewell	1.00	.30
❑ 56 Patrick Ewing	1.00	.30
❑ 57 Darrell Armstrong	.30	.09
❑ 58 Ron Mercer	.60	.18
❑ 59 Michael Doleac	.30	.09
❑ 60 Allen Iverson	2.00	.60
❑ 61 Toni Kukoc	.60	.18
❑ 62 Eric Snow	.60	.18
❑ 63 Anfernee Hardaway	1.00	.30
❑ 64 Jason Kidd	1.50	.45
❑ 65 Tom Gugliotta	.30	.09
❑ 66 Scottie Pippen	1.50	.45
❑ 67 Steve Smith	.60	.18
❑ 68 Damon Stoudamire	.60	.18
❑ 69 Jason Williams	1.00	.30
❑ 70 Peja Stojakovic	1.25	.35
❑ 71 Chris Webber	1.00	.30
❑ 72 Vlade Divac	.60	.18
❑ 73 Tim Duncan	2.00	.60
❑ 74 David Robinson	1.00	.30
❑ 75 Avery Johnson	.30	.09
❑ 76 Gary Payton	1.00	.30
❑ 77 Vin Baker	.60	.18
❑ 78 Vernon Maxwell	.30	.09
❑ 79 Vince Carter	2.50	.75
❑ 80 Tracy McGrady	2.50	.75
❑ 81 Doug Christie	.60	.18
❑ 82 Karl Malone	1.00	.30
❑ 83 John Stockton	1.00	.30
❑ 84 Jeff Hornacek	.60	.18
❑ 85 Mike Bibby	1.00	.30
❑ 86 Shareef Abdur-Rahim	1.00	.30
❑ 87 Othella Harrington	.30	.09
❑ 88 Mitch Richmond	.60	.18
❑ 89 Juwan Howard	.60	.18
❑ 90 Rod Strickland	.30	.09
❑ 91 Elton Brand RC	30.00	9.00
❑ 92 Steve Francis RC	50.00	15.00
❑ 93 Baron Davis RC	50.00	15.00
❑ 94 Lamar Odom RC	40.00	12.00
❑ 95 Jonathan Bender RC	25.00	7.50
❑ 96 Wally Szczerbiak RC	30.00	9.00
❑ 97 Richard Hamilton RC	50.00	15.00
❑ 98 Andre Miller RC	30.00	9.00
❑ 99 Shawn Marion RC	50.00	15.00
❑ 100 Jason Terry RC	25.00	7.50
❑ 101 Trajan Langdon RC	15.00	4.50
❑ 102 Aleksandar Radojevic RC	10.00	3.00
❑ 103 Corey Maggette RC	30.00	9.00
❑ 104 William Avery RC	15.00	4.50
❑ 105 Ron Artest RC	15.00	4.50
❑ 106 James Posey RC	15.00	4.50
❑ 107 Quincy Lewis RC	15.00	4.50
❑ 108 Dion Glover RC	10.00	3.00
❑ 109 Kenny Thomas RC	15.00	4.50
❑ 110 Devean George RC	15.00	4.50
❑ 111 Tim James RC	10.00	3.00
❑ 112 Vonteego Cummings RC	15.00	4.50
❑ 113 Jumaine Jones RC	15.00	4.50
❑ 114 Scott Padgett RC	10.00	3.00
❑ 115 Adrian Griffin RC	10.00	3.00
❑ 116 Anthony Carter RC	15.00	4.50
❑ 117 Todd MacCulloch RC	10.00	3.00
❑ 118 Chucky Atkins RC	10.00	3.00
❑ 119 Obinna Ekezie RC	10.00	3.00
❑ 120 Eddie Robinson RC	15.00	4.50
❑ 121 Michael Ruffin RC	10.00	3.00
❑ 122 Laron Profit RC	10.00	3.00
❑ 123 Cal Bowdler RC	10.00	3.00
❑ 124 Chris Herren RC	10.00	3.00
❑ 125 Milt Palacio RC	10.00	3.00
❑ 126 Jeff Foster RC	10.00	3.00
❑ 127 Ryan Bowen RC	10.00	3.00
❑ 128 Tim Young RC	10.00	3.00
❑ 129 Derrick Dial RC	10.00	3.00
❑ 130 Greg Buckner RC	10.00	3.00
❑ 131 Rodney Buford RC	10.00	3.00
❑ 132 Evan Eschmeyer RC	10.00	3.00
❑ 133 Jermaine Jackson RC	10.00	3.00
❑ 134 John Celestand RC	10.00	3.00
❑ 135 Ryan Robertson RC	10.00	3.00
❑ KG Kevin Garnett PROMO	2.00	.60

2000-01 SP Authentic

	Nm-Mt	Ex-Mt
COMP.SET w/o SP's (90)	25.00	7.50
COMMON CARD (1-90)	.30	.09
COMMON RC/500 (91-136)	40.00	12.00
COMMON RC/1250 (91-136)	12.00	3.60
COMMON RC/2000 (91-136)	8.00	2.40
❑ 1 Jason Terry	1.00	.30
❑ 2 Alan Henderson	.30	.09
❑ 3 Lorenzen Wright	.30	.09
❑ 4 Paul Pierce	1.00	.30
❑ 5 Antoine Walker	1.00	.30
❑ 6 Bryant Stith	.30	.09
❑ 7 Jamal Mashburn	.60	.18
❑ 8 Baron Davis	1.00	.30
❑ 9 David Wesley	.30	.09
❑ 10 Elton Brand	1.00	.30
❑ 11 Ron Artest	.60	.18
❑ 12 Ron Mercer	.60	.18
❑ 13 Andre Miller	.60	.18
❑ 14 Lamond Murray	.30	.09
❑ 15 Jim Jackson	.30	.09
❑ 16 Michael Finley	1.00	.30
❑ 17 Dirk Nowitzki	2.00	.60
❑ 18 Steve Nash	1.00	.30
❑ 19 Antonio McDyess	.60	.18
❑ 20 Nick Van Exel	1.00	.30
❑ 21 Raef LaFrentz	.60	.18
❑ 22 Jerry Stackhouse	1.00	.30
❑ 23 Chucky Atkins	.30	.09
❑ 24 Joe Smith	.60	.18
❑ 25 Antawn Jamison	1.00	.30
❑ 26 Larry Hughes	.60	.18
❑ 27 Mookie Blaylock	.30	.09
❑ 28 Steve Francis	1.00	.30
❑ 29 Hakeem Olajuwon	1.00	.30
❑ 30 Cuttino Mobley	.60	.18
❑ 31 Reggie Miller	1.00	.30
❑ 32 Jermaine O'Neal	1.00	.30
❑ 33 Jalen Rose	1.00	.30
❑ 34 Travis Best	.30	.09
❑ 35 Lamar Odom	1.00	.30
❑ 36 Corey Maggette	.60	.18
❑ 37 Eric Piatkowski	.60	.18
❑ 38 Shaquille O'Neal	2.50	.75
❑ 39 Kobe Bryant	4.00	1.20
❑ 40 Isaiah Rider	.30	.09
❑ 41 Horace Grant	.60	.18
❑ 42 Eddie Jones	1.00	.30
❑ 43 Brian Grant	.60	.18
❑ 44 Tim Hardaway	.60	.18
❑ 45 Ray Allen	1.00	.30
❑ 46 Glenn Robinson	1.00	.30
❑ 47 Sam Cassell	1.00	.30
❑ 48 Kevin Garnett	2.00	.60
❑ 49 Terrell Brandon	.60	.18
❑ 50 Chauncey Billups	.60	.18
❑ 51 Wally Szczerbiak	.60	.18
❑ 52 Stephon Marbury	1.00	.30
❑ 53 Keith Van Horn	1.00	.30
❑ 54 Aaron Williams	.30	.09
❑ 55 Latrell Sprewell	1.00	.30
❑ 56 Allan Houston	.60	.18
❑ 57 Glen Rice	.60	.18
❑ 58 Tracy McGrady	2.50	.75
❑ 59 Grant Hill	1.00	.30
❑ 60 Darrell Armstrong	.30	.09

❑ 61 Allen Iverson	2.00	.60
❑ 62 Dikembe Mutombo	.60	.18
❑ 63 Aaron McKie	.60	.18
❑ 64 Jason Kidd	1.50	.45
❑ 65 Clifford Robinson	.30	.09
❑ 66 Shawn Marion	1.00	.30
❑ 67 Damon Stoudamire	.60	.18
❑ 68 Steve Smith	.60	.18
❑ 69 Rasheed Wallace	1.00	.30
❑ 70 Chris Webber	1.00	.30
❑ 71 Jason Williams	.60	.18
❑ 72 Peja Stojakovic	1.00	.30
❑ 73 Tim Duncan	2.00	.60
❑ 74 David Robinson	1.00	.30
❑ 75 Derek Anderson	.60	.18
❑ 76 Gary Payton	1.00	.30
❑ 77 Rashard Lewis	.60	.18
❑ 78 Patrick Ewing	1.00	.30
❑ 79 Vince Carter	2.50	.75
❑ 80 Charles Oakley	.30	.09
❑ 81 Antonio Davis	.30	.09
❑ 82 Karl Malone	1.00	.30
❑ 83 John Stockton	1.00	.30
❑ 84 John Starks	.60	.18
❑ 85 Shareef Abdur-Rahim	1.00	.30
❑ 86 Mike Bibby	1.00	.30
❑ 87 Michael Dickerson	.60	.18
❑ 88 Richard Hamilton	.60	.18
❑ 89 Mitch Richmond	.60	.18
❑ 90 Christian Laettner	.60	.18
❑ 91 K.Martin AU/500 RC	80.00	24.00
❑ 92 S.Swift AU/500 RC	50.00	15.00
❑ 93 Darius Miles AU/500 RC	80.00	24.00
❑ 94 Marcus Fizer/1250 RC	12.00	3.60
❑ 95 Mike Miller AU/500 RC	50.00	15.00
❑ 96 D.Johnson AU/500 RC	40.00	12.00
❑ 97 Chris Mihm/1250 RC	12.00	3.60
❑ 98 Jamal Crawford/1250 RC	15.00	4.50
❑ 99 Joel Przybilla/2000 RC	8.00	2.40
❑ 100 Keyon Dooling/1250 RC	12.00	3.60
❑ 101 Jerome Moiso/1250 RC	12.00	3.60
❑ 102 Etan Thomas/2000 RC	8.00	2.40
❑ 103 C.Alexander/1250 RC	15.00	4.50
❑ 104 Mateen Cleaves/1250 RC	12.00	3.60
❑ 105 Jason Collier/2000 RC	8.00	2.40
❑ 106 H.Turkoglu/1250 RC	20.00	6.00
❑ 107 D.Mason/1250 RC	12.00	3.60
❑ 108 Q.Richardson/1250 RC	25.00	7.50
❑ 109 Jamaal Magloire/1250 RC	12.00	3.60
❑ 110 Speedy Claxton/2000 RC	8.00	2.40
❑ 111 M.Peterson AU/500 RC	25.00	7.50
❑ 112 Donnell Harvey/2000 RC	8.00	2.40
❑ 113 D.Stevenson/1250 RC	12.00	3.60
❑ 114 I.Tsakalidis/2000 RC	8.00	2.40
❑ 115 S.Samake/2000 RC	8.00	2.40
❑ 116 Erick Barkley/2000 RC	8.00	2.40
❑ 117 Mark Madsen/2000 RC	8.00	2.40
❑ 118 A.J. Guyton/1250 RC	8.00	2.40
❑ 119 O.Oyedeji/2000 RC	8.00	2.40
❑ 120 Eddie House/1250 RC	12.00	3.60
❑ 121 Eduardo Najera/2000 RC	12.00	3.60
❑ 122 Lavor Postell/2000 RC	8.00	2.40
❑ 123 Hanno Mottola/1250 RC	12.00	3.60
❑ 124 Ira Newble/2000 RC	8.00	2.40
❑ 125 Chris Porter/1250 RC	12.00	3.60
❑ 126 R.Wolkowyski/2000 RC	8.00	2.40
❑ 127 Pepe Sanchez/2000 RC	8.00	2.40
❑ 128 S.Jackson/1250 RC	15.00	4.50
❑ 129 Marc Jackson/1250 RC	12.00	3.60
❑ 130 Dragan Tarlac/2000 RC	8.00	2.40
❑ 131 Lee Nailon/2000 RC	8.00	2.40
❑ 132 Mike Penberthy/1250 RC	12.00	3.60
❑ 133 Mark Blount/2000 RC	8.00	2.40
❑ 134 Dan Langhi/2000 RC	8.00	2.40
❑ 135 Daniel Santiago/2000 RC	8.00	2.40
❑ 136 Wang Zhizhi AU/500 RC	40.00	12.00

2001-02 SP Authentic

	Nm-Mt	Ex-Mt
COMP.SET w/o SP's (90)	40.00	12.00
COMMON CARD (1-165)	.30	.09
COMMON ROOKIE (91-106)	6.00	1.80
COMMON ROOKIE (107-115)	12.00	3.60
COMMON ROOKIE (116-131)	12.00	3.60
COMMON ROOKIE (132-140)	25.00	7.50
❑ 1 Shareef Abdur-Rahim	1.00	.30
❑ 2 Jason Terry	1.00	.30
❑ 3 Dion Glover	.30	.09
❑ 4 Paul Pierce	1.00	.30
❑ 5 Antoine Walker	1.00	.30
❑ 6 Kenny Anderson	.60	.18
❑ 7 Baron Davis	1.00	.30
❑ 8 David Wesley	.30	.09
❑ 9 Jamal Mashburn	.60	.18
❑ 10 Jalen Rose	1.00	.30
❑ 11 Fred Hoiberg	.30	.09
❑ 12 Marcus Fizer	.60	.18
❑ 13 Andre Miller	.60	.18
❑ 14 Lamond Murray	.30	.09
❑ 15 Chris Mihm	.60	.18
❑ 16 Dirk Nowitzki	1.50	.45
❑ 17 Steve Nash	1.00	.30
❑ 18 Michael Finley	1.00	.30
❑ 19 Nick Van Exel	1.00	.30
❑ 20 Antonio McDyess	.60	.18
❑ 21 Juwan Howard	.60	.18
❑ 22 James Posey	.60	.18
❑ 23 Jerry Stackhouse	1.00	.30
❑ 24 Clifford Robinson	.30	.09
❑ 25 Ben Wallace	1.00	.30
❑ 26 Antawn Jamison	1.00	.30
❑ 27 Larry Hughes	.60	.18
❑ 28 Danny Fortson	.30	.09
❑ 29 Steve Francis	1.00	.30
❑ 30 Cuttino Mobley	.60	.18
❑ 31 Reggie Miller	1.00	.30
❑ 32 Al Harrington	.60	.18
❑ 33 Jermaine O'Neal	1.00	.30
❑ 34 Darius Miles	1.00	.30
❑ 35 Elton Brand	1.00	.30
❑ 36 Lamar Odom	1.00	.30
❑ 37 Corey Maggette	.60	.18
❑ 38 Kobe Bryant	4.00	1.20
❑ 39 Shaquille O'Neal	2.50	.75
❑ 40 Rick Fox	.60	.18
❑ 41 Lindsey Hunter	.30	.09
❑ 42 Stromile Swift	.60	.18
❑ 43 Michael Dickerson	.60	.18
❑ 44 Jason Williams	.60	.18
❑ 45 Alonzo Mourning	.60	.18
❑ 46 Eddie Jones	1.00	.30
❑ 47 Anthony Carter	.60	.18
❑ 48 Ray Allen	1.00	.30
❑ 49 Glenn Robinson	1.00	.30
❑ 50 Sam Cassell	1.00	.30
❑ 51 Kevin Garnett	2.00	.60
❑ 52 Terrell Brandon	.60	.18
❑ 53 Wally Szczerbiak	.60	.18
❑ 54 Joe Smith	.60	.18
❑ 55 Jason Kidd	1.50	.45
❑ 56 Kenyon Martin	1.00	.30
❑ 57 Mark Jackson	.60	.18
❑ 58 Allan Houston	.60	.18
❑ 59 Latrell Sprewell	1.00	.30
❑ 60 Marcus Camby	.60	.18
❑ 61 Tracy McGrady	2.50	.75
❑ 62 Grant Hill	1.00	.30
❑ 63 Mike Miller	1.00	.30
❑ 64 Allen Iverson	2.00	.60
❑ 65 Dikembe Mutombo	.60	.18
❑ 66 Aaron McKie	.60	.18
❑ 67 Stephon Marbury	1.00	.30
❑ 68 Shawn Marion	1.00	.30
❑ 69 Anfernee Hardaway	1.00	.30
❑ 70 Rasheed Wallace	1.00	.30
❑ 71 Bonzi Wells	.60	.18
❑ 72 Derek Anderson	.60	.18
❑ 73 Chris Webber	1.00	.30
❑ 74 Mike Bibby	1.00	.30
❑ 75 Peja Stojakovic	1.00	.30
❑ 76 Tim Duncan	2.00	.60
❑ 77 David Robinson	1.00	.30
❑ 78 Antonio Daniels	.30	.09
❑ 79 Gary Payton	1.00	.30
❑ 80 Rashard Lewis	.60	.18
❑ 81 Desmond Mason	.60	.18
❑ 82 Vince Carter	2.50	.75
❑ 83 Morris Peterson	.60	.18
❑ 84 Antonio Davis	.30	.09
❑ 85 Karl Malone	1.00	.30
❑ 86 John Stockton	1.00	.30
❑ 87 Donyell Marshall	.60	.18
❑ 88 Richard Hamilton	.60	.18
❑ 89 Courtney Alexander	.60	.18
❑ 90 Michael Jordan	15.00	4.50
❑ 91 Tierre Brown RC	6.00	1.80
❑ 92 Damone Brown RC	6.00	1.80
❑ 93 Michael Bradley RC	6.00	1.80
❑ 94 Kedrick Brown RC	6.00	1.80
❑ 95 Alton Ford RC	6.00	1.80
❑ 96 Jason Collins RC	6.00	1.80
❑ 97 Antonis Fotsis RC	6.00	1.80
❑ 98 Mengke Bateer RC	15.00	4.50
❑ 99 Trenton Hassell RC	10.00	3.00
❑ 100 Jamison Brewer RC	6.00	1.80
❑ 101 Bobby Simmons RC	6.00	1.80
❑ 102 Mike James RC	6.00	1.80
❑ 103 Oscar Torres RC	6.00	1.80
❑ 104 Brandon Armstrong RC	6.00	1.80
❑ 105 Will Solomon RC	6.00	1.80
❑ 106 Vladimir Radmanovic RC	8.00	2.40
❑ 107 Kirk Haston RC	12.00	3.60
❑ 108 Gerald Wallace RC	12.00	3.60
❑ 109 Andrei Kirilenko RC	30.00	9.00
❑ 110 Joseph Forte RC	20.00	6.00
❑ 111 Brendan Haywood RC	15.00	4.50
❑ 112 Zach Randolph RC	25.00	7.50
❑ 113 DeSagana Diop RC	6.00	1.80
❑ 114 Shane Battier RC	12.00	3.60
❑ 115 Pau Gasol RC	40.00	12.00
❑ 116 Alvin Jones AU RC	12.00	3.60
❑ 117 Zeljko Rebraca AU RC	12.00	3.60
❑ 118 Kenny Satterfield AU RC	12.00	3.60
❑ 119 Jarron Collins AU RC	12.00	3.60
❑ 120 R.Boumtje-Boumtje AU RC	12.00	3.60
❑ 121 Loren Woods AU RC	12.00	3.60
❑ 122 Earl Watson AU RC	12.00	3.60
❑ 123 Jeff Trepagnier AU RC	12.00	3.60
❑ 124 Brian Scalabrine AU RC	12.00	3.60
❑ 125 Terence Morris AU RC	12.00	3.60
❑ 126 Gilbert Arenas AU RC	50.00	15.00
❑ 127 S.Dalembert AU RC	12.00	3.60
❑ 128 Jeryl Sasser AU RC	12.00	3.60
❑ 129 Rodney White AU RC	20.00	6.00
❑ 130 Eddie Griffin AU RC	25.00	7.50
❑ 131 Tyson Chandler AU RC	60.00	18.00
❑ 132 Steven Hunter AU RC	20.00	6.00
❑ 133 Troy Murphy AU RC	20.00	6.00
❑ 134 R.Jefferson AU RC EXCH	60.00	18.00
❑ 135 J.Johnson AU RC EXCH	25.00	7.50
❑ 136 Eddy Curry AU RC	50.00	15.00
❑ 137 J.Richardson AU RC	120.00	36.00
❑ 138 Tony Parker AU RC	60.00	18.00
❑ 139 Jamaal Tinsley AU RC	30.00	9.00
❑ 140 Kwame Brown AU RC	50.00	15.00
❑ 141 Paul Pierce SPEC	6.00	1.80
❑ 142 Tim Duncan SPEC	10.00	3.00
❑ 143 Stephon Marbury SPEC	6.00	1.80

❑ 144 S.Abdur-Rahim SPEC	6.00	1.80
❑ 145 Ray Allen SPEC	6.00	1.80
❑ 146 Bonzi Wells SPEC	5.00	1.50
❑ 147 Kenyon Martin SPEC	6.00	1.80
❑ 148 Darius Miles SPEC	6.00	1.80
❑ 149 Baron Davis SPEC	6.00	1.80
❑ 150 Dirk Nowitzki SPEC	8.00	2.40
❑ 151 Antoine Walker SPEC	6.00	1.80
❑ 152 Mike Miller SPEC	6.00	1.80
❑ 153 Shawn Marion SPEC	6.00	1.80
❑ 154 Jason Kidd SPEC	8.00	2.40
❑ 155 Elton Brand SPEC	4.00	1.20
❑ 156 Antawn Jamison SPEC	6.00	1.80
❑ 157 Rashard Lewis SPEC	6.00	1.80
❑ 158 Steve Francis SPEC	6.00	1.80
❑ 159 Tracy McGrady SPEC	12.00	3.60
❑ 160 Kobe Bryant SPECT	25.00	7.50
❑ 161 Allen Iverson SPECT	12.00	3.60
❑ 162 Vince Carter SPECT	15.00	4.50
❑ 163 Shaquille O'Neal SPECT	15.00	4.50
❑ 164 Kevin Garnett SPECT	12.00	3.60
❑ 165 Michael Jordan SPECT	40.00	12.00
❑ PROMO Michael Jordan	10.00	3.00

2002-03 SP Authentic

	Nm-Mt	Ex-Mt
COMP.SET w/o SP's (100)	40.00	12.00
COMMON CARD (1-100)	.25	.07
COMMON SPEC (101-142)	5.00	1.50
COMMON AU RC (143-174)	15.00	4.50
COMMON ROOKIE (175-203)	6.00	1.80
❑ 1 Glenn Robinson	1.00	.30
❑ 2 Shareef Abdur-Rahim	1.00	.30
❑ 3 Jason Terry	1.00	.30
❑ 4 Theo Ratliff	.60	.18
❑ 5 Paul Pierce	1.00	.30
❑ 5A Paul Pierce AU	30.00	9.00
❑ 6 Antoine Walker	1.00	.30
❑ 6A Antoine Walker AU	25.00	7.50
❑ 7 Tony Delk	.25	.07
❑ 8 Vin Baker	.60	.18
❑ 9 Jalen Rose	1.00	.30
❑ 10 Eddy Curry	1.00	.30
❑ 11 Tyson Chandler	1.00	.30
❑ 11A Tyson Chandler AU	20.00	6.00
❑ 12 Marcus Fizer	.60	.18
❑ 12A M.Fizer AU EXCH	15.00	4.50
❑ 13 Darius Miles	1.00	.30
❑ 14 Zydrunas Ilgauskas	.60	.18
❑ 15 Dirk Nowitzki	1.50	.45
❑ 16 Michael Finley	1.00	.30
❑ 17 Steve Nash	1.00	.30
❑ 18 Raef LaFrentz	.60	.18
❑ 19 Juwan Howard	.60	.18
❑ 20 Rodney White	.60	.18
❑ 21 Ben Wallace	1.00	.30
❑ 22 Richard Hamilton	.60	.18
❑ 23 Chauncey Billups	.60	.18
❑ 24 Chucky Atkins	.25	.07
❑ 25 Jason Richardson	1.00	.30
❑ 26 Antawn Jamison	1.00	.30
❑ 27 Gilbert Arenas	1.00	.30
❑ 28 Steve Francis	1.00	.30
❑ 29 Cuttino Mobley	.60	.18
❑ 30 Jermaine O'Neal	1.00	.30
❑ 30A Jermaine O'Neal AU	25.00	7.50
❑ 31 Jamaal Tinsley	1.00	.30
❑ 32 Reggie Miller	1.00	.30
❑ 33 Ron Artest	.60	.18
❑ 34 Elton Brand	1.00	.30
❑ 35 Andre Miller	.60	.18
❑ 36 Michael Olowokandi	.25	.07
❑ 37 Kobe Bryant	4.00	1.20
❑ 38 Shaquille O'Neal	2.50	.75
❑ 39 Robert Horry	.60	.18
❑ 40 Derek Fisher	1.00	.30
❑ 41 Pau Gasol	1.00	.30
❑ 42 Shane Battier	1.00	.30
❑ 43 Eddie Jones	1.00	.30
❑ 44 Brian Grant	.60	.18
❑ 45 Malik Allen	.25	.07
❑ 46 Gary Payton	1.00	.30
❑ 47 Sam Cassell	1.00	.30
❑ 48 Kevin Garnett	2.00	.60
❑ 49 Wally Szczerbiak	.60	.18
❑ 50 Troy Hudson	.25	.07
❑ 51 Radoslav Nesterovic	.60	.18
❑ 52 Jason Kidd	1.50	.45
❑ 53 Richard Jefferson	.60	.18
❑ 54 Kenyon Martin	1.00	.30
❑ 54A K.Martin AU EXCH	20.00	6.00
❑ 55 Kerry Kittles	.25	.07
❑ 56 Baron Davis	1.00	.30
❑ 57 Jamal Mashburn	.60	.18
❑ 58 David Wesley	.25	.07
❑ 59 P.J. Brown	.25	.07
❑ 60 Jamaal Magloire	.25	.07
❑ 60A Jamaal Magloire AU	12.00	3.60
❑ 61 Allan Houston	.60	.18
❑ 62 Kurt Thomas	.60	.18
❑ 63 Latrell Sprewell	1.00	.30
❑ 64 Clarence Weatherspoon	.25	.07
❑ 65 Tracy McGrady	2.50	.75
❑ 66 Grant Hill	1.00	.30
❑ 67 Mike Miller	1.00	.30
❑ 67A Mike Miller AU	20.00	6.00
❑ 68 Allen Iverson	2.00	.60
❑ 69 Keith Van Horn	1.00	.30
❑ 70 Stephon Marbury	1.00	.30
❑ 71 Shawn Marion	1.00	.30
❑ 72 Anfernee Hardaway	1.00	.30
❑ 73 Rasheed Wallace	1.00	.30
❑ 74 Derek Anderson	.60	.18
❑ 75 Scottie Pippen	1.50	.45
❑ 76 Bonzi Wells	.60	.18
❑ 77 Chris Webber	1.00	.30
❑ 78 Mike Bibby	1.00	.30
❑ 78A Mike Bibby AU	25.00	7.50
❑ 79 Peja Stojakovic	1.00	.30
❑ 80 Hedo Turkoglu	1.00	.30
❑ 81 Vlade Divac	.60	.18
❑ 82 Tim Duncan	2.00	.60
❑ 83 David Robinson	1.00	.30
❑ 84 Tony Parker	1.00	.30
❑ 85 Steve Smith	.60	.18
❑ 86 Ray Allen	1.00	.30
❑ 87 Rashard Lewis	1.00	.30
❑ 88 Brent Barry	.60	.18
❑ 89 Elden Campbell	.25	.07
❑ 90 Vince Carter	2.50	.75
❑ 91 Morris Peterson	.60	.18
❑ 92 Antonio Davis	.25	.07
❑ 93 Alvin Williams	.25	.07
❑ 94 Karl Malone	1.00	.30
❑ 95 John Stockton	1.00	.30
❑ 96 Andrei Kirilenko	1.00	.30
❑ 97 DeShawn Stevenson	.25	.07
❑ 97A DeShawn Stevenson AU	12.00	3.60
❑ 98 Jerry Stackhouse	1.00	.30
❑ 99 Michael Jordan	8.00	2.40
❑ 100 Kwame Brown	.60	.18
❑ 101 Kobe Bryant SPEC	8.00	2.40
❑ 102 Allen Iverson SPEC	6.00	1.80
❑ 103 Pau Gasol SPEC	5.00	1.50
❑ 104 Antoine Walker SPEC	5.00	1.50
❑ 105 J.O'Neal SPEC	5.00	1.50
❑ 106 Ray Allen SPEC	5.00	1.50
❑ 107 Baron Davis SPEC	5.00	1.50
❑ 108 Tim Duncan SPEC	6.00	1.80
❑ 109 Rashard Lewis SPEC	5.00	1.50
❑ 110 Michael Jordan SPEC	20.00	6.00
❑ 111 S.Marbury SPEC	5.00	1.50
❑ 112 S.Abdur-Rahim SPEC	5.00	1.50
❑ 113 Vince Carter SPEC	8.00	2.40
❑ 114 Allan Houston SPEC	5.00	1.50
❑ 115 Dirk Nowitzki SPEC	6.00	1.80
❑ 116 Grant Hill SPEC	5.00	1.50
❑ 117 Mike Bibby SPEC	5.00	1.50
❑ 118 Der.Anderson SPEC	5.00	1.50
❑ 119 S.O'Neal SPEC	8.00	2.40
❑ 120 Steve Francis SPEC	5.00	1.50
❑ 121 R.Jefferson SPEC	5.00	1.50
❑ 122 Ben Wallace SPEC	5.00	1.50
❑ 123 Jason Kidd SPEC	6.00	1.80
❑ 124 Jalen Rose SPEC	5.00	1.50
❑ 125 Paul Pierce SPEC	5.00	1.50
❑ 126 Michael Finley SPEC	5.00	1.50
❑ 127 J.Mashburn SPEC	5.00	1.50
❑ 128 Elton Brand SPEC	5.00	1.50
❑ 129 R.Wallace SPEC	5.00	1.50
❑ 130 Gary Payton SPEC	5.00	1.50
❑ 131 Tracy McGrady SPEC	8.00	2.40
❑ 132 Rich.Hamilton SPEC	5.00	1.50
❑ 133 Chris Webber SPEC	5.00	1.50
❑ 134 Karl Malone SPEC	5.00	1.50
❑ 135 Darius Miles SPEC	5.00	1.50
❑ 136 Shawn Marion SPEC	5.00	1.50
❑ 137 Kevin Garnett SPEC	6.00	1.80
❑ 138 Eddie Jones SPEC	5.00	1.50
❑ 139 J.Richardson SPEC	5.00	1.50
❑ 140 Glenn Robinson SPEC	5.00	1.50
❑ 141 J.Stackhouse SPEC	5.00	1.50
❑ 142 Shane Battier SPEC	5.00	1.50
❑ 143 Yao Ming AU RC	120.00	36.00
❑ 144 Jay Williams AU RC	25.00	7.50
❑ 145 Drew Gooden AU RC	40.00	12.00
❑ 146 N.Tskitishvili AU RC	20.00	6.00
❑ 147 D.Wagner AU RC	30.00	9.00
❑ 148 Nene Hilario AU RC	25.00	7.50
❑ 149 Chris Wilcox AU RC	25.00	7.50
❑ 150 A.Stoudemire AU RC	100.00	30.00
❑ 151 Caron Butler AU RC	40.00	12.00
❑ 152 Jared Jeffries AU RC	20.00	6.00
❑ 153 Melvin Ely AU RC	15.00	4.50
❑ 154 Marcus Haislip AU RC	15.00	4.50
❑ 155 Fred Jones AU RC	15.00	4.50
❑ 156 B.Nachbar AU RC	15.00	4.50
❑ 157 Jiri Welsch AU RC	15.00	4.50
❑ 158 Juan Dixon AU RC	30.00	9.00
❑ 159 C.Borchardt AU RC	15.00	4.50
❑ 160 R.Humphrey AU RC	15.00	4.50
❑ 161 Kareem Rush AU RC	25.00	7.50
❑ 162 Qyntel Woods AU RC	20.00	6.00
❑ 163 C.Jacobsen AU RC	15.00	4.50
❑ 164 T.Prince AU RC	25.00	7.50
❑ 165 Frank Williams AU RC	15.00	4.50
❑ 166 John Salmons AU RC	15.00	4.50
❑ 167 Chris Jefferies AU RC	15.00	4.50
❑ 168 Dan Dickau AU RC	15.00	4.50
❑ 169 Carlos Boozer AU RC	40.00	12.00
❑ 170 Marko Jaric AU RC	15.00	4.50
❑ 171 Sam Clancy AU RC	15.00	4.50
❑ 172 M.Ginobili AU RC	50.00	15.00
❑ 173 V.Yarbrough AU RC	15.00	4.50
❑ 174 Gordan Giricek AU RC	25.00	7.50
❑ 175 Predrag Savovic RC	6.00	1.80
❑ 176 Mike Dunleavy RC	12.00	3.60
❑ 177 Tamar Slay RC	6.00	1.80
❑ 178 Rasual Butler RC	6.00	1.80
❑ 179 Reggie Evans RC	6.00	1.80
❑ 180 Igor Rakocevic RC	6.00	1.80

Card	Nm-Mt	Ex-Mt
❑ 181 Juaquin Hawkins RC	6.00	1.80
❑ 182 J.R. Bremer RC	6.00	1.80
❑ 183 Cezary Trybanski RC	6.00	1.80
❑ 184 Junior Harrington RC	6.00	1.80
❑ 185 Efthimios Rentzias RC	6.00	1.80
❑ 186 Smush Parker RC	6.00	1.80
❑ 187 Jamal Sampson RC	6.00	1.80
❑ 188 Roger Mason RC	6.00	1.80
❑ 189 Robert Archibald RC	6.00	1.80
❑ 190 Mehmet Okur RC	8.00	2.40
❑ 191 Dan Gadzuric RC	6.00	1.80
❑ 192 Pat Burke RC	6.00	1.80
❑ 193 Lonny Baxter RC	6.00	1.80
❑ 194 Tito Maddox RC	6.00	1.80
❑ 195 Jannero Pargo RC	8.00	2.40
❑ 196 Ronald Murray RC	20.00	6.00
❑ 197 Mike Wilks RC	6.00	1.80
❑ 198 Mike Batiste RC	6.00	1.80
❑ 199 Chris Owens RC	6.00	1.80
❑ 200 Raul Lopez RC	6.00	1.80
❑ 201 Antoine Rigaudeau RC	6.00	1.80
❑ 202 Ken Johnson RC	6.00	1.80
❑ 203 Maceo Baston RC	6.00	1.80

2003-04 SP Authentic

	Nm-Mt	Ex-Mt
COMP.SET w/o SP's (90)	40.00	12.00
COMMON CARD (1-90)	.25	.07
COMMON SPEC (91-132 & 144)	4.00	1.20
COMMON ROOKIE (133-147)	6.00	1.80
COMMON AU RC (148-153)	20.00	6.00
COMMON AU RC (154-189)	15.00	4.50
❑ 1 Shareef Abdur-Rahim	1.00	.30
❑ 2 Theo Ratliff	.60	.18
❑ 3 Jason Terry	1.00	.30
❑ 4 Raef LaFrentz	.60	.18
❑ 5 Vin Baker	.60	.18
❑ 6 Paul Pierce	1.00	.30
❑ 7 Antonio Davis	.25	.07
❑ 8 Scottie Pippen	1.50	.45
❑ 9 Tyson Chandler	1.00	.30
❑ 10 Dajuan Wagner	.60	.18
❑ 11 Carlos Boozer	1.00	.30
❑ 12 Zydrunas Ilgauskas	.60	.18
❑ 13 Dirk Nowitzki	1.50	.45
❑ 14 Antoine Walker	1.00	.30
❑ 15 Steve Nash	1.00	.30
❑ 16 Michael Finley	1.00	.30
❑ 17 Earl Boykins	.60	.18
❑ 18 Andre Miller	.60	.18
❑ 19 Nene	.60	.18
❑ 20 Chauncey Billups	.60	.18
❑ 21 Richard Hamilton	.60	.18
❑ 22 Ben Wallace	1.00	.30
❑ 23 Clifford Robinson	.25	.07
❑ 24 Jason Richardson	1.00	.30
❑ 25 Nick Van Exel	1.00	.30
❑ 26 Yao Ming	2.50	.75
❑ 27 Cuttino Mobley	.60	.18
❑ 28 Steve Francis	1.00	.30
❑ 29 Jermaine O'Neal	1.00	.30
❑ 30 Reggie Miller	1.00	.30
❑ 31 Ron Artest	.60	.18
❑ 32 Elton Brand	1.00	.30
❑ 33 Corey Maggette	.60	.18
❑ 34 Quentin Richardson	.60	.18
❑ 35 Kobe Bryant	4.00	1.20
❑ 36 Karl Malone	1.00	.30
❑ 37 Gary Payton	1.00	.30
❑ 38 Shaquille O'Neal	2.50	.75
❑ 39 Pau Gasol	1.00	.30
❑ 40 Bonzi Wells	.60	.18
❑ 41 Mike Miller	1.00	.30
❑ 42 Lamar Odom	1.00	.30
❑ 43 Eddie Jones	1.00	.30
❑ 44 Caron Butler	1.00	.30
❑ 45 Toni Kukoc	.60	.18
❑ 46 Desmond Mason	.60	.18
❑ 47 Michael Redd	.60	.18
❑ 48 Latrell Sprewell	1.00	.30
❑ 49 Kevin Garnett	2.00	.60
❑ 50 Sam Cassell	1.00	.30
❑ 51 Richard Jefferson	.60	.18
❑ 52 Kenyon Martin	1.00	.30
❑ 53 Jason Kidd	1.50	.45
❑ 54 Jamal Mashburn	.60	.18
❑ 55 Baron Davis	1.00	.30
❑ 56 David Wesley	.25	.07
❑ 57 Allan Houston	.60	.18
❑ 58 Stephon Marbury	1.00	.30
❑ 59 Keith Van Horn	1.00	.30
❑ 60 Gordan Giricek	.60	.18
❑ 61 Drew Gooden	.60	.18
❑ 62 Tracy McGrady	2.50	.75
❑ 63 Glenn Robinson	1.00	.30
❑ 64 Allen Iverson	2.00	.60
❑ 65 Eric Snow	.60	.18
❑ 66 Amare Stoudemire	2.00	.60
❑ 67 Antonio McDyess	1.00	.30
❑ 68 Shawn Marion	1.00	.30
❑ 69 Zach Randolph	1.00	.30
❑ 70 Damon Stoudamire	.60	.18
❑ 71 Rasheed Wallace	1.00	.30
❑ 72 Peja Stojakovic	1.00	.30
❑ 73 Chris Webber	1.00	.30
❑ 74 Mike Bibby	1.00	.30
❑ 75 Brad Miller	1.00	.30
❑ 76 Tony Parker	1.00	.30
❑ 77 Tim Duncan	2.00	.60
❑ 78 Manu Ginobili	1.00	.30
❑ 79 Vladimir Radmanovic	.25	.07
❑ 80 Ray Allen	1.00	.30
❑ 81 Rashard Lewis	1.00	.30
❑ 82 Morris Peterson	.60	.18
❑ 83 Vince Carter	2.50	.75
❑ 84 Jalen Rose	1.00	.30
❑ 85 Andrei Kirilenko	1.00	.30
❑ 86 Matt Harpring	1.00	.30
❑ 87 Carlos Arroyo	4.00	1.20
❑ 88 Gilbert Arenas	1.00	.30
❑ 89 Larry Hughes	.60	.18
❑ 90 Jerry Stackhouse	1.00	.30
❑ 91 Kobe Bryant SPEC	10.00	3.00
❑ 92 Jason Kidd SPEC	4.00	1.20
❑ 93 Rasheed Wallace SPEC	4.00	1.20
❑ 94 Jalen Rose SPEC	4.00	1.20
❑ 95 Tim Duncan SPEC	5.00	1.50
❑ 96 S.Abdur-Rahim SPEC	4.00	1.20
❑ 97 Baron Davis SPEC	4.00	1.20
❑ 98 Pau Gasol SPEC	4.00	1.20
❑ 99 Allen Iverson SPEC	5.00	1.50
❑ 100 Yao Ming SPEC	6.00	1.80
❑ 101 Gary Payton SPEC	4.00	1.20
❑ 102 Ray Allen SPEC	4.00	1.20
❑ 103 Tracy McGrady SPEC	6.00	1.80
❑ 104 Amare Stoudemire SPEC	5.00	1.50
❑ 105 Tony Parker SPEC	4.00	1.20
❑ 106 Stephon Marbury SPEC	4.00	1.20
❑ 107 Richard Hamilton SPEC	4.00	1.20
❑ 108 Chris Webber SPEC	4.00	1.20
❑ 109 Elton Brand SPEC	4.00	1.20
❑ 110 Jerry Stackhouse SPEC	4.00	1.20
❑ 111 Andre Miller SPEC	4.00	1.20
❑ 112 Kevin Garnett SPEC	5.00	1.50
❑ 113 Jason Richardson SPEC	4.00	1.20
❑ 114 Allan Houston SPEC	4.00	1.20
❑ 115 Dajuan Wagner SPEC	4.00	1.20
❑ 116 Richard Jefferson SPEC	4.00	1.20
❑ 117 Shaquille O'Neal SPEC	6.00	1.80
❑ 118 Latrell Sprewell SPEC	4.00	1.20
❑ 119 Rashard Lewis SPEC	4.00	1.20
❑ 120 Steve Nash SPEC	4.00	1.20
❑ 121 Desmond Mason SPEC	4.00	1.20
❑ 122 Mike Bibby SPEC	4.00	1.20
❑ 123 Shawn Marion SPEC	4.00	1.20
❑ 124 Vince Carter SPEC	6.00	1.80
❑ 125 Caron Butler SPEC	4.00	1.20
❑ 126 Gilbert Arenas SPEC	4.00	1.20
❑ 127 Dirk Nowitzki SPEC	4.00	1.20
❑ 128 Paul Pierce SPEC	4.00	1.20
❑ 129 Jermaine O'Neal SPEC	4.00	1.20
❑ 130 Andrei Kirilenko SPEC	4.00	1.20
❑ 131 Michael Jordan SPEC	12.00	3.60
❑ 132 Steve Francis SPEC	4.00	1.20
❑ 133 T.J. Ford RC	8.00	2.40
❑ 134 Kirk Hinrich RC	10.00	3.00
❑ 135 Nick Collison RC	6.00	1.80
❑ 136 Maurice Carter RC	6.00	1.80
❑ 137 Francisco Elson RC	6.00	1.80
❑ 138 Udonis Haslem	6.00	1.80
❑ 139 Jon Stefansson RC	6.00	1.80
❑ 140 Richie Frahm RC	6.00	1.80
❑ 141 Ronald Dupree RC	6.00	1.80
❑ 142 Josh Moore RC	6.00	1.80
❑ 143 Alex Garcia RC	6.00	1.80
❑ 144 Zach Randolph SPEC	4.00	1.20
❑ 145 Ben Handlogten RC	6.00	1.80
❑ 146 Devin Brown RC	6.00	1.80
❑ 147 Marquis Daniels RC	12.00	3.60
❑ 148 LeBron James AU RC	700.00	210.00
❑ 149 Darko Milicic AU RC	80.00	24.00
❑ 150 Carmelo Anthony AU RC	300.00	90.00
❑ 151 Chris Bosh AU RC	80.00	24.00
❑ 152 Dwyane Wade AU RC	100.00	30.00
❑ 153 Jarvis Hayes AU RC	20.00	6.00
❑ 154 Mickael Pietrus AU RC	15.00	4.50
❑ 155 Chris Kaman AU RC	15.00	4.50
❑ 156 Dahntay Jones AU RC	15.00	4.50
❑ 157 Marcus Banks AU RC	15.00	4.50
❑ 158 Luke Ridnour AU RC	25.00	7.50
❑ 159 Reece Gaines AU RC	15.00	4.50
❑ 160 Troy Bell AU RC	15.00	4.50
❑ 161 Mike Sweetney AU RC	15.00	4.50
❑ 162 David West AU RC	15.00	4.50
❑ 163 Aleksandar Pavlovic AU RC	15.00	4.50
❑ 164 Steve Blake AU RC	15.00	4.50
❑ 165 Boris Diaw AU RC	15.00	4.50
❑ 166 Zoran Planinic AU RC	15.00	4.50
❑ 167 Travis Outlaw AU RC	15.00	4.50
❑ 168 Brian Cook AU RC EXCH*	15.00	4.50
❑ 169 Jerome Beasley AU RC	15.00	4.50
❑ 170 Ndudi Ebi AU RC	15.00	4.50
❑ 171 Kendrick Perkins AU RC	15.00	4.50
❑ 172 Leandro Barbosa AU RC	15.00	4.50
❑ 173 Josh Howard AU RC	20.00	6.00
❑ 174 Maciej Lampe AU RC	15.00	4.50
❑ 175 Jason Kapono AU RC	15.00	4.50
❑ 176 Luke Walton AU RC	20.00	6.00
❑ 177 Slavko Vranes AU RC	15.00	4.50
❑ 178 Zarko Cabarkapa AU RC	15.00	4.50
❑ 179 Zaur Pachulia AU RC	15.00	4.50
❑ 180 Maurice Williams AU RC	15.00	4.50
❑ 181 Brandon Hunter AU RC	15.00	4.50
❑ 182 Keith Bogans AU RC	15.00	4.50
❑ 183 Travis Hansen AU RC	15.00	4.50
❑ 184 Theron Smith AU RC	15.00	4.50
❑ 185 Willie Green AU RC	15.00	4.50
❑ 186 James Jones AU RC	15.00	4.50
❑ 187 Kyle Korver AU RC	20.00	6.00

❑ 188 Udonis Haslem AU RC	15.00	4.50
❑ 189 James Lang AU RC	15.00	4.50

1995-96 SP Championship

	Nm-Mt	Ex-Mt
COMPLETE SET (146)	40.00	12.00
❑ 1 Stacey Augmon	.25	.07
❑ 2 Mookie Blaylock	.25	.07
❑ 3 Alan Henderson RC	.75	.23
❑ 4 Steve Smith	.50	.15
❑ 5 Dana Barros	.25	.07
❑ 6 Dee Brown	.25	.07
❑ 7 Eric Montross	.25	.07
❑ 8 Dino Radja	.25	.07
❑ 9 Eric Williams RC	.50	.15
❑ 10 Kenny Anderson	.50	.15
❑ 11 Larry Johnson	.50	.15
❑ 12 Glen Rice	.50	.15
❑ 13 George Zidek RC	.25	.07
❑ 14 Toni Kukoc	.50	.15
❑ 15 Scottie Pippen	1.25	.35
❑ 16 Dennis Rodman	.50	.15
❑ 17 Michael Jordan	5.00	1.50
❑ 18 Terrell Brandon	.50	.15
❑ 19 Danny Ferry	.25	.07
❑ 20 Chris Mills	.25	.07
❑ 21 Bobby Phills	.25	.07
❑ 22 Jim Jackson	.25	.07
❑ 23 Popeye Jones	.25	.07
❑ 24 Jason Kidd	2.50	.75
❑ 25 Jamal Mashburn	.50	.15
❑ 26 Mahmoud Abdul-Rauf	.25	.07
❑ 27 Dale Ellis	.25	.07
❑ 28 Antonio McDyess RC	1.50	.45
❑ 29 Dikembe Mutombo	.50	.15
❑ 30 Joe Dumars	.75	.23
❑ 31 Grant Hill	1.00	.30
❑ 32 Allan Houston	.50	.15
❑ 33 Otis Thorpe	.25	.07
❑ 34 Tim Hardaway	.50	.15
❑ 35 Chris Mullin	.75	.23
❑ 36 Latrell Sprewell	.75	.23
❑ 37 Joe Smith RC	1.25	.35
❑ 38 Sam Cassell	.75	.23
❑ 39 Clyde Drexler	.75	.23
❑ 40 Robert Horry	.50	.15
❑ 41 Hakeem Olajuwon	.75	.23
❑ 42 Dale Davis	.25	.07
❑ 43 Derrick McKey	.25	.07
❑ 44 Reggie Miller	.75	.23
❑ 45 Rik Smits	.50	.15
❑ 46 Brent Barry RC	.75	.23
❑ 47 Lamond Murray	.25	.07
❑ 48 Loy Vaught	.25	.07
❑ 49 Brian Williams	.25	.07
❑ 50 Cedric Ceballos	.25	.07
❑ 51 Magic Johnson	1.25	.35
❑ 52 Eddie Jones	1.00	.30
❑ 53 Nick Van Exel	.75	.23
❑ 54 Sasha Danilovic RC	.25	.07
❑ 55 Alonzo Mourning	.50	.15
❑ 56 Billy Owens	.25	.07
❑ 57 Kevin Willis	.50	.15
❑ 58 Vin Baker	.50	.15
❑ 59 Sherman Douglas	.25	.07
❑ 60 Lee Mayberry	.25	.07
❑ 61 Glenn Robinson	.75	.23
❑ 62 Kevin Garnett RC	6.00	1.80
❑ 63 Tom Gugliotta	.25	.07
❑ 64 Christian Laettner	.50	.15
❑ 65 Isaiah Rider	.25	.07
❑ 66 Chris Childs	.25	.07
❑ 67 Kendall Gill	.25	.07
❑ 68 Armon Gilliam	.25	.07
❑ 69 Ed O'Bannon RC	.25	.07
❑ 70 Patrick Ewing	.75	.23
❑ 71 Derek Harper	.50	.15
❑ 72 Charles Oakley	.25	.07
❑ 73 John Starks	.50	.15
❑ 74 Horace Grant	.50	.15
❑ 75 Anfernee Hardaway	.75	.23
❑ 76 Shaquille O'Neal	2.00	.60
❑ 77 Dennis Scott	.25	.07
❑ 78 Derrick Coleman	.25	.07
❑ 79 Trevor Ruffin	.25	.07
❑ 80 Jerry Stackhouse RC	2.50	.75
❑ 81 Clarence Weatherspoon	.25	.07
❑ 82 Charles Barkley	1.00	.30
❑ 83 Michael Finley RC	2.00	.60
❑ 84 Kevin Johnson	.50	.15
❑ 85 Danny Manning	.50	.15
❑ 86 Randolph Childress RC	.25	.07
❑ 87 Clifford Robinson	.25	.07
❑ 88 Arvydas Sabonis RC	1.00	.30
❑ 89 Rod Strickland	.25	.07
❑ 90 Tyus Edney RC	.25	.07
❑ 91 Brian Grant	.75	.23
❑ 92 Mitch Richmond	.50	.15
❑ 93 Walt Williams	.25	.07
❑ 94 Sean Elliott	.50	.15
❑ 95 Avery Johnson	.25	.07
❑ 96 Chuck Person	.25	.07
❑ 97 David Robinson	.75	.23
❑ 98 Shawn Kemp	.50	.15
❑ 99 Gary Payton	.75	.23
❑ 100 Sam Perkins	.50	.15
❑ 101 Detlef Schrempf	.50	.15
❑ 102 Ed Pinckney	.25	.07
❑ 103 Tracy Murray	.25	.07
❑ 104 Alvin Robertson	.25	.07
❑ 105 Damon Stoudamire RC	1.50	.45
❑ 106 Jeff Hornacek	.50	.15
❑ 107 Karl Malone	1.00	.30
❑ 108 Chris Morris	.25	.07
❑ 109 John Stockton	1.00	.30
❑ 110 Greg Anthony	.25	.07
❑ 111 Blue Edwards	.25	.07
❑ 112 Bryant Reeves RC	.75	.23
❑ 113 Byron Scott	.25	.07
❑ 114 Juwan Howard	.75	.23
❑ 115 Gheorghe Muresan	.25	.07
❑ 116 Rasheed Wallace RC	2.00	.60
❑ 117 Chris Webber	1.00	.30
❑ 118 Mookie Blaylock RP	.25	.07
❑ 119 Dana Barros RP	.25	.07
❑ 120 Larry Johnson RP	.25	.07
❑ 121 Michael Jordan RP	2.50	.75
❑ 122 Terrell Brandon RP	.25	.07
❑ 123 Jason Kidd RP	1.25	.35
❑ 124 Mahmoud Abdul-Rauf RP	.25	.07
❑ 125 Grant Hill RP	.75	.23
❑ 126 Latrell Sprewell RP	.75	.23
❑ 127 Hakeem Olajuwon RP	.50	.15
❑ 128 Reggie Miller RP	.50	.15
❑ 129 Loy Vaught RP	.25	.07
❑ 130 Magic Johnson RP	.75	.23
❑ 131 Alonzo Mourning RP	.25	.07
❑ 132 Vin Baker RP	.25	.07
❑ 133 Tom Gugliotta RP	.25	.07
❑ 134 Ed O'Bannon RP	.25	.07
❑ 135 Patrick Ewing RP	.50	.15
❑ 136 Anfernee Hardaway RP	.50	.15
❑ 137 Jerry Stackhouse RP	1.25	.35
❑ 138 Charles Barkley RP	.75	.23
❑ 139 Clifford Robinson RP	.25	.07
❑ 140 Mitch Richmond RP	.25	.07
❑ 141 David Robinson RP	.50	.15
❑ 142 Shawn Kemp RP	.25	.07
❑ 143 Damon Stoudamire RP	1.00	.30
❑ 144 John Stockton RP	.75	.23
❑ 145 Bryant Reeves RP	.50	.15
❑ 146 Juwan Howard RP	.50	.15

2000-01 SP Game Floor

	Nm-Mt	Ex-Mt
COMMON CARD (1-60)	.75	.23
COMMON ROOKIE (61-100)	10.00	3.00
❑ 1 Jason Terry	2.50	.75
❑ 2 Toni Kukoc	1.50	.45
❑ 3 Antoine Walker	2.50	.75
❑ 4 Paul Pierce	2.50	.75
❑ 5 Jamal Mashburn	1.50	.45
❑ 6 Baron Davis	2.50	.75
❑ 7 Elton Brand	2.50	.75
❑ 8 Ron Mercer	1.50	.45
❑ 9 Andre Miller	1.50	.45
❑ 10 Lamond Murray	.75	.23
❑ 11 Michael Finley	2.50	.75
❑ 12 Dirk Nowitzki	4.00	1.20
❑ 13 Antonio McDyess	1.50	.45
❑ 14 Nick Van Exel	2.50	.75
❑ 15 Jerry Stackhouse	2.50	.75
❑ 16 Joe Smith	1.50	.45
❑ 17 Antawn Jamison	2.50	.75
❑ 18 Larry Hughes	1.50	.45
❑ 19 Steve Francis	2.50	.75
❑ 20 Maurice Taylor	1.50	.45
❑ 21 Jalen Rose	2.50	.75
❑ 22 Reggie Miller	2.50	.75
❑ 23 Lamar Odom	2.50	.75
❑ 24 Corey Maggette	1.50	.45
❑ 25 Kobe Bryant	10.00	3.00
❑ 26 Shaquille O'Neal	6.00	1.80
❑ 27 Horace Grant	1.50	.45
❑ 28 Eddie Jones	2.50	.75
❑ 29 Tim Hardaway	1.50	.45
❑ 30 Glenn Robinson	2.50	.75
❑ 31 Ray Allen	2.50	.75
❑ 32 Kevin Garnett	5.00	1.50
❑ 33 Terrell Brandon	1.50	.45
❑ 34 Wally Szczerbiak	1.50	.45
❑ 35 Stephon Marbury	2.50	.75
❑ 36 Keith Van Horn	2.50	.75
❑ 37 Latrell Sprewell	2.50	.75
❑ 38 Allan Houston	1.50	.45
❑ 39 Tracy McGrady	6.00	1.80
❑ 40 Darrell Armstrong	.75	.23
❑ 41 Allen Iverson	5.00	1.50
❑ 42 Dikembe Mutombo	1.50	.45
❑ 43 Jason Kidd	4.00	1.20
❑ 44 Shawn Marion	3.00	.90
❑ 45 Rasheed Wallace	2.50	.75
❑ 46 Damon Stoudamire	1.50	.45
❑ 47 Chris Webber	2.50	.75
❑ 48 Jason Williams	1.50	.45
❑ 49 Tim Duncan	5.00	1.50
❑ 50 David Robinson	2.50	.75
❑ 51 Gary Payton	2.50	.75
❑ 52 Rashard Lewis	1.50	.45
❑ 53 Vince Carter	6.00	1.80
❑ 54 Charles Oakley	.75	.23
❑ 55 Karl Malone	2.50	.75
❑ 56 John Stockton	2.50	.75
❑ 57 Shareef Abdur-Rahim	2.50	.75
❑ 58 Mike Bibby	2.50	.75
❑ 59 Richard Hamilton	1.50	.45
❑ 60 Mitch Richmond	1.50	.45
❑ 61 Kenyon Martin RC	30.00	9.00
❑ 62 Marc Jackson RC	10.00	3.00
❑ 63 Darius Miles RC	25.00	7.50

Card	Nm-Mt	Ex-Mt
❑ 64 Morris Peterson RC	15.00	4.50
❑ 65 Mike Miller RC	20.00	6.00
❑ 66 Quentin Richardson RC	25.00	7.50
❑ 67 DerMarr Johnson RC	10.00	3.00
❑ 68 Chris Mihm RC	10.00	3.00
❑ 69 Jamal Crawford RC	12.00	3.60
❑ 70 Joel Przybilla RC	10.00	3.00
❑ 71 Keyon Dooling RC	10.00	3.00
❑ 72 Jerome Moiso RC	10.00	3.00
❑ 73 Mike Penberthy RC	10.00	3.00
❑ 74 Courtney Alexander RC	15.00	4.50
❑ 75 Mateen Cleaves RC	10.00	3.00
❑ 76 Wang Zhizhi RC	20.00	6.00
❑ 77 Hidayet Turkoglu RC	15.00	4.50
❑ 78 Desmond Mason RC	10.00	3.00
❑ 79 Marcus Fizer RC	10.00	3.00
❑ 80 Jamaal Magloire RC	10.00	3.00
❑ 81 Stromile Swift RC	15.00	4.50
❑ 82 DeShawn Stevenson RC	10.00	3.00
❑ 83 Stephen Jackson RC	15.00	4.50
❑ 84 Erick Barkley RC	10.00	3.00
❑ 85 Mark Madsen RC	10.00	3.00
❑ 86 Dan Langhi RC	10.00	3.00
❑ 87 Hanno Mottola RC	10.00	3.00
❑ 88 Paul McPherson RC	10.00	3.00
❑ 89 Eddie House RC	10.00	3.00
❑ 90 Chris Porter RC	10.00	3.00
❑ 91 Jason Collier RC	10.00	3.00
❑ 92 Speedy Claxton RC	10.00	3.00
❑ 93 Ruben Wolkowyski RC	10.00	3.00
❑ 94 A.J. Guyton RC	10.00	3.00
❑ 95 Donnell Harvey RC	10.00	3.00
❑ 96 Ira Newble RC	10.00	3.00
❑ 97 Lee Nailon RC	10.00	3.00
❑ 98 Pepe Sanchez RC	10.00	3.00
❑ 99 Eduardo Najera RC	12.00	3.60
❑ 100 David Vanterpool RC	10.00	3.00

2002-03 SP Game Used

	Nm-Mt	Ex-Mt
COMMON CARD (1-102)	2.50	.75
COMMON JSY	12.00	3.60
COMMON ROOKIE (103-144)	10.00	3.00
❑ 1 S.Abdur-Rahim JSY	15.00	4.50
❑ 2 DerMarr Johnson JSY	12.00	3.60
❑ 3 Jason Terry JSY	15.00	4.50
❑ 4 Antoine Walker JSY	15.00	4.50
❑ 5 Paul Pierce SP JSY	40.00	12.00
❑ 6 Kedrick Brown JSY	12.00	3.60
❑ 7 Tony Battie	2.50	.75
❑ 8 Jamal Mashburn JSY	12.00	3.60
❑ 9 Baron Davis	5.00	1.50
❑ 10 David Wesley	2.50	.75
❑ 11 Jalen Rose	5.00	1.50
❑ 12 Eddy Curry JSY	15.00	4.50
❑ 13 Tyson Chandler JSY	15.00	4.50
❑ 14 Marcus Fizer JSY	12.00	3.60
❑ 15 Lamond Murray	2.50	.75
❑ 16 Andre Miller JSY	12.00	3.60
❑ 17 Chris Mihm JSY	12.00	3.60
❑ 18 Ricky Davis	3.00	.90
❑ 19 Dirk Nowitzki	8.00	2.40
❑ 20 Michael Finley	5.00	1.50
❑ 21 Steve Nash	5.00	1.50
❑ 22 Nick Van Exel	5.00	1.50
❑ 23 Antonio McDyess JSY	12.00	3.60
❑ 24 Juwan Howard	3.00	.90
❑ 25 James Posey	3.00	.90
❑ 26 Jerry Stackhouse	5.00	1.50
❑ 27 Clifford Robinson	2.50	.75
❑ 28 Ben Wallace	5.00	1.50
❑ 29 Antawn Jamison	6.00	1.80
❑ 30 J.Richardson SP JSY	15.00	4.50
❑ 31 Gilbert Arenas	5.00	1.50
❑ 32 Steve Francis	5.00	1.50
❑ 33 Cuttino Mobley	3.00	.90
❑ 34 Eddie Griffin JSY	12.00	3.60
❑ 35 Reggie Miller JSY	15.00	4.50
❑ 36 Jermaine O'Neal	5.00	1.50
❑ 37 Jamaal Tinsley JSY	15.00	4.50
❑ 38 Elton Brand	5.00	1.50
❑ 39 Darius Miles JSY	15.00	4.50
❑ 40 Lamar Odom JSY	15.00	4.50
❑ 41 Corey Maggette JSY	15.00	4.50
❑ 42 Kobe Bryant SP JSY	80.00	24.00
❑ 43 Shaquille O'Neal	12.00	3.60
❑ 44 Derek Fisher	5.00	1.50
❑ 45 Devean George	3.00	.90
❑ 46 Pau Gasol	5.00	1.50
❑ 47 Jason Williams	3.00	.90
❑ 48 Shane Battier	5.00	1.50
❑ 49 Stromile Swift	3.00	.90
❑ 50 Alonzo Mourning	3.00	.90
❑ 51 Eddie Jones	5.00	1.50
❑ 52 Brian Grant	3.00	.90
❑ 53 Ray Allen	5.00	1.50
❑ 54 Glenn Robinson	5.00	1.50
❑ 55 Sam Cassell	5.00	1.50
❑ 56 Kevin Garnett SP JSY	40.00	12.00
❑ 57 Wally Szczerbiak JSY	15.00	4.50
❑ 58 Terrell Brandon JSY	12.00	3.60
❑ 59 Chauncey Billups JSY	12.00	3.60
❑ 60 Jason Kidd SP JSY	40.00	12.00
❑ 61 Richard Jefferson	3.00	.90
❑ 62 Kenyon Martin JSY	12.00	3.60
❑ 63 B.Armstrong JSY	12.00	3.60
❑ 64 Keith Van Horn	5.00	1.50
❑ 65 Allan Houston	3.00	.90
❑ 66 Latrell Sprewell	5.00	1.50
❑ 67 Kurt Thomas	3.00	.90
❑ 68 Tracy McGrady	12.00	3.60
❑ 69 Mike Miller JSY	15.00	4.50
❑ 70 Darrell Armstrong JSY	12.00	3.60
❑ 71 Allen Iverson JSY	25.00	7.50
❑ 72 D.Mutombo JSY	15.00	4.50
❑ 73 Aaron McKie	3.00	.90
❑ 74 Stephon Marbury	5.00	1.50
❑ 75 Shawn Marion	5.00	1.50
❑ 76 Joe Johnson JSY	12.00	3.60
❑ 77 Anfernee Hardaway	5.00	1.50
❑ 78 Rasheed Wallace	5.00	1.50
❑ 79 Damon Stoudamire	3.00	.90
❑ 80 Scottie Pippen	8.00	2.40
❑ 81 Chris Webber	5.00	1.50
❑ 82 Peja Stojakovic	5.00	1.50
❑ 83 Mike Bibby JSY	15.00	4.50
❑ 84 Gerald Wallace JSY	12.00	3.60
❑ 85 Tim Duncan	10.00	3.00
❑ 86 David Robinson	5.00	1.50
❑ 87 Tony Parker JSY	20.00	6.00
❑ 88 Gary Payton	5.00	1.50
❑ 89 Rashard Lewis	3.00	.90
❑ 90 Desmond Mason	3.00	.90
❑ 91 V.Radmanovic JSY	12.00	3.60
❑ 92 Morris Peterson	3.00	.90
❑ 93 Antonio Davis	2.50	.75
❑ 94 Vince Carter	12.00	3.60
❑ 95 Karl Malone	5.00	1.50
❑ 96 John Stockton JSY	20.00	6.00
❑ 97 Donyell Marshall	3.00	.90
❑ 98 Andrei Kirilenko	5.00	1.50
❑ 99 Richard Hamilton	3.00	.90
❑ 100 Michael Jordan SP JSY	300.00	90.00
❑ 101 C.Alexander JSY	12.00	3.60
❑ 102 Kwame Brown JSY	12.00	3.60
❑ 103 Jay Williams RC	20.00	6.00
❑ 104 Yao Ming RC	150.00	45.00
❑ 105 Drew Gooden RC	40.00	12.00
❑ 106 Dajuan Wagner RC	25.00	7.50
❑ 107 Curtis Borchardt RC	12.00	3.60
❑ 108 Amare Stoudemire RC	80.00	24.00
❑ 109 Caron Butler RC	30.00	9.00
❑ 110 Jared Jeffries RC	12.00	3.60
❑ 111 Chris Wilcox RC	20.00	6.00
❑ 112 Qyntel Woods RC	15.00	4.50
❑ 113 Casey Jacobsen RC	15.00	4.50
❑ 114 Melvin Ely RC	12.00	3.60
❑ 115 Kareem Rush RC	15.00	4.50
❑ 116 Mike Dunleavy RC	25.00	7.50
❑ 117 Dan Dickau RC	10.00	3.00
❑ 118 Juan Dixon RC	20.00	6.00
❑ 119 Sam Clancy RC	12.00	3.60
❑ 120 Tayshaun Prince RC	20.00	6.00
❑ 121 Dan Gadzuric RC	12.00	3.60
❑ 122 Chris Jefferies RC	12.00	3.60
❑ 123 Steve Logan RC	15.00	4.50
❑ 124 Vincent Yarbrough RC	12.00	3.60
❑ 125 Fred Jones RC	15.00	4.50
❑ 126 Efthimios Rentzias RC	12.00	3.60
❑ 127 Nene Hilario RC	20.00	6.00
❑ 128 Rod Grizzard RC	12.00	3.60
❑ 129 Matt Barnes RC	12.00	3.60
❑ 130 Nikoloz Tskitishvili RC	15.00	4.50
❑ 131 Bostjan Nachbar RC	12.00	3.60
❑ 132 Marcus Haislip RC	12.00	3.60
❑ 133 Jamal Sampson RC	12.00	3.60
❑ 134 Frank Williams RC	10.00	3.00
❑ 135 Tito Maddox RC	12.00	3.60
❑ 136 Carlos Boozer RC	25.00	7.50
❑ 137 Jiri Welsch RC	12.00	3.60
❑ 138 John Salmons RC	12.00	3.60
❑ 139 Predrag Savovic RC	12.00	3.60
❑ 140 Marko Jaric RC	12.00	3.60
❑ 141 Robert Archibald RC	12.00	3.60
❑ 142 Manu Ginobili RC	30.00	9.00
❑ 143 Chris Owens RC	12.00	3.60
❑ 144 Ryan Humphrey RC	12.00	3.60

2003-04 SP Game Used

	Nm-Mt	Ex-Mt
COMMON CARD (1-94)	1.50	.45
COMMON JSY (1-94)	10.00	3.00
COMMON MJ TRIB (95-106)	25.00	7.50
COMMON ROOKIE (107-148)	12.00	3.60
❑ 1 Shareef Abdur-Rahim	5.00	1.50
❑ 2 Glenn Robinson	5.00	1.50
❑ 3 Jason Terry JSY	10.00	3.00
❑ 4 Paul Pierce	5.00	1.50
❑ 5 Antoine Walker	5.00	1.50
❑ 6 Eddy Curry	5.00	1.50
❑ 7 Tyson Chandler JSY	10.00	3.00
❑ 8 Jalen Rose JSY	10.00	3.00
❑ 9 Jay Williams JSY	10.00	3.00
❑ 10 DaJuan Wagner JSY	10.00	3.00
❑ 11 Darius Miles JSY	10.00	3.00
❑ 12 Carlos Boozer JSY	10.00	3.00
❑ 13 Steve Nash	5.00	1.50
❑ 14 Michael Finley	5.00	1.50
❑ 15 Nick Van Exel	5.00	1.50
❑ 16 Dirk Nowitzki JSY	15.00	4.50
❑ 17 Rodney White	1.50	.45
❑ 18 Marcus Camby	3.00	.90
❑ 19 Nikoloz Tskitishvili	3.00	.90
❑ 20 Nene Hilario JSY	10.00	3.00
❑ 21 Richard Hamilton	3.00	.90
❑ 22 Chauncey Billups	3.00	.90
❑ 23 Ben Wallace	5.00	1.50
❑ 24 Gilbert Arenas	5.00	1.50
❑ 25 Troy Murphy	5.00	1.50
❑ 26 Jason Richardson JSY	10.00	3.00
❑ 27 Antawn Jamison JSY	10.00	3.00
❑ 28 Cuttino Mobley	3.00	.90

❑ 29 Steve Francis 5.00 1.50
❑ 30 Eddie Griffin 3.00 .90
❑ 31 Jermaine O'Neal 5.00 1.50
❑ 32 Reggie Miller 5.00 1.50
❑ 33 Jamaal Tinsley JSY 10.00 3.00
❑ 34 Lamar Odom 5.00 1.50
❑ 35 Chris Wilcox 3.00 .90
❑ 36 Marko Jaric 3.00 .90
❑ 37 Elton Brand JSY 10.00 3.00
❑ 38 Andre Miller JSY 10.00 3.00
❑ 39 Kobe Bryant 15.00 4.50
❑ 40 Shaquille O'Neal 12.00 3.60
❑ 41 Gary Payton 5.00 1.50
❑ 42 Kareem Rush JSY 10.00 3.00
❑ 43 Mike Miller 5.00 1.50
❑ 44 Shane Battier JSY 10.00 3.00
❑ 45 Pau Gasol JSY 10.00 3.00
❑ 46 Eddie Jones 5.00 1.50
❑ 47 Brian Grant 3.00 .90
❑ 48 Caron Butler JSY 10.00 3.00
❑ 49 Joe Smith 3.00 .90
❑ 50 Desmond Mason 3.00 .90
❑ 51 Toni Kukoc 3.00 .90
❑ 52 Wally Szczerbiak 3.00 .90
❑ 53 Kevin Garnett JSY 20.00 6.00
❑ 54 Alonzo Mourning 3.00 .90
❑ 55 Kenyon Martin 5.00 1.50
❑ 56 Jason Kidd JSY 15.00 4.50
❑ 57 Richard Jefferson JSY 10.00 3.00
❑ 58 Baron Davis 5.00 1.50
❑ 59 Jamal Mashburn JSY 10.00 3.00
❑ 60 Latrell Sprewell 5.00 1.50
❑ 61 Allan Houston 3.00 .90
❑ 62 Antonio McDyess 3.00 .90
❑ 63 Juwan Howard 3.00 .90
❑ 64 Drew Gooden JSY 10.00 3.00
❑ 65 Tracy McGrady JSY 25.00 7.50
❑ 66 Keith Van Horn 5.00 1.50
❑ 67 Aaron McKie 3.00 .90
❑ 68 Allen Iverson JSY 20.00 6.00
❑ 69 Stephon Marbury 5.00 1.50
❑ 70 Shawn Marion 5.00 1.50
❑ 71 Anfernee Hardaway 5.00 1.50
❑ 72 Joe Johnson 3.00 .90
❑ 73 Amare Stoudemire JSY 15.00 4.50
❑ 74 Rasheed Wallace 5.00 1.50
❑ 75 Scottie Pippen 8.00 2.40
❑ 76 Mike Bibby 5.00 1.50
❑ 77 Peja Stojakovic 5.00 1.50
❑ 78 Gerald Wallace 3.00 .90
❑ 79 Chris Webber JSY 10.00 3.00
❑ 80 Tim Duncan 10.00 3.00
❑ 81 Manu Ginobili 5.00 1.50
❑ 82 Tony Parker JSY 10.00 3.00
❑ 83 Ray Allen 5.00 1.50
❑ 84 Rashard Lewis JSY 10.00 3.00
❑ 85 Morris Peterson 3.00 .90
❑ 86 Antonio Davis 1.50 .45
❑ 87 Vince Carter 12.00 3.60
❑ 88 John Stockton JSY 10.00 3.00
❑ 89 Karl Malone JSY 10.00 3.00
❑ 90 Jerry Stackhouse 3.00 .90
❑ 91 Michael Jordan 20.00 6.00
❑ 92 Michael Jordan JSY 150.00 45.00
❑ 93 Kobe Bryant JSY 40.00 12.00
❑ 94 Yao Ming JSY 25.00 7.50
❑ 95 M.Jordan Tribute 25.00 7.50
❑ 96 M.Jordan Tribute 25.00 7.50
❑ 97 M.Jordan Tribute 25.00 7.50
❑ 98 M.Jordan Tribute 25.00 7.50
❑ 99 M.Jordan Tribute 25.00 7.50
❑ 100 M.Jordan Tribute 25.00 7.50
❑ 101 M.Jordan Tribute 25.00 7.50
❑ 102 M.Jordan Tribute 25.00 7.50
❑ 103 M.Jordan Tribute 25.00 7.50
❑ 104 M.Jordan Tribute 25.00 7.50
❑ 105 M.Jordan Tribute 25.00 7.50
❑ 106 Michael Jordan Tribute 25.00 7.50
❑ 107 Lebron James RC 150.00 45.00
❑ 108 Darko Milicic RC 20.00 6.00
❑ 109 Carmelo Anthony RC 80.00 24.00
❑ 110 Chris Bosh RC 30.00 9.00
❑ 111 Dwyane Wade RC 30.00 9.00
❑ 112 Chris Kaman RC 12.00 3.60
❑ 113 Kirk Hinrich RC 20.00 6.00
❑ 114 T.J. Ford RC 15.00 4.50
❑ 115 Mike Sweetney RC 12.00 3.60
❑ 116 Jarvis Hayes RC 10.00 3.00
❑ 117 Mickael Pietrus RC 12.00 3.60
❑ 118 Nick Collison RC 12.00 3.60
❑ 119 Marcus Banks RC 12.00 3.60
❑ 120 Luke Ridnour RC 15.00 4.50
❑ 121 Reece Gaines RC 12.00 3.60
❑ 122 Troy Bell RC 10.00 3.00
❑ 123 Zarko Cabarkapa RC 10.00 3.00
❑ 124 David West RC 10.00 3.00
❑ 125 Aleksandar Pavlovic RC 10.00 3.00
❑ 126 Dahntay Jones RC 12.00 3.60
❑ 127 Boris Diaw RC 12.00 3.60
❑ 128 Zoran Planinic RC 12.00 3.60
❑ 129 Travis Outlaw RC 12.00 3.60
❑ 130 Brian Cook RC 12.00 3.60
❑ 131 Carlos Delfino RC 12.00 3.60
❑ 132 Ndudi Ebi RC 12.00 3.60
❑ 133 Kendrick Perkins RC 12.00 3.60
❑ 134 Leandro Barbosa RC 12.00 3.60
❑ 135 Josh Howard RC 12.00 3.60
❑ 136 Maciej Lampe RC 12.00 3.60
❑ 137 Jason Kapono RC 12.00 3.60
❑ 138 Luke Walton RC 12.00 3.60
❑ 139 Jerome Beasley RC 12.00 3.60
❑ 140 Sofoklis Schortsanitis RC 12.00 3.60
❑ 141 Mario Austin RC 12.00 3.60
❑ 142 Travis Hansen RC 12.00 3.60
❑ 143 Steve Blake RC 12.00 3.60
❑ 144 Slavko Vranes RC 12.00 3.60
❑ 145 Zaur Pachulia RC 12.00 3.60
❑ 146 Keith Bogans RC 12.00 3.60
❑ 147 Matt Bonner RC 12.00 3.60
❑ 148 Maurice Williams RC 12.00 3.60

2003-04 SP Signature Edition

	Nm-Mt	Ex-Mt
COMP.SET w/o SP's (100)	80.00	24.00
COMMON CARD (1-100)	.50	.15
COMMON ROOKIE (101-142)	10.00	3.00
MOST UNPRICED DUE TO SCARCITY		-

❑ 1 Shareef Abdur-Rahim 1.50 .45
❑ 2 Jason Terry 1.50 .45
❑ 3 Theo Ratliff 1.00 .30
❑ 4 Raef LaFrentz 1.00 .30
❑ 5 Paul Pierce 1.50 .45
❑ 6 Larry Bird 6.00 1.80
❑ 7 Jalen Rose 1.50 .45
❑ 8 Scottie Pippen 2.00 .60
❑ 9 Michael Jordan 10.00 3.00
❑ 10 Dennis Rodman 2.00 .60
❑ 11 Dajuan Wagner 1.00 .30
❑ 12 Darius Miles 1.50 .45
❑ 13 Carlos Boozer 1.50 .45
❑ 14 Zydrunas Ilgauskas 1.00 .30
❑ 15 Dirk Nowitzki 2.00 .60
❑ 16 Steve Nash 1.50 .45
❑ 17 Antoine Walker 1.50 .45
❑ 18 Antawn Jamison 1.50 .45
❑ 19 Andre Miller 1.00 .30
❑ 20 Nene 1.00 .30
❑ 21 Nikoloz Tskitishvili .50 .15
❑ 22 Ben Wallace 1.50 .45
❑ 23 Richard Hamilton 1.00 .30
❑ 24 Chauncey Billups 1.00 .30
❑ 25 Nick Van Exel 1.50 .45
❑ 26 Jason Richardson 1.50 .45
❑ 27 Mike Dunleavy 1.00 .30
❑ 28 Yao Ming 4.00 1.20
❑ 29 Steve Francis 1.50 .45
❑ 30 Cuttino Mobley 1.00 .30
❑ 31 Reggie Miller 1.50 .45
❑ 32 Jermaine O'Neal 1.50 .45
❑ 33 Jamaal Tinsley 1.50 .45
❑ 34 Chris Wilcox .50 .15
❑ 35 Elton Brand 1.50 .45
❑ 36 Wang Zhizhi 1.50 .45
❑ 37 Corey Maggette 1.00 .30
❑ 38 Kobe Bryant 6.00 1.80
❑ 39 Shaquille O'Neal 4.00 1.20
❑ 40 Gary Payton 1.50 .45
❑ 41 Karl Malone 1.50 .45
❑ 42 Pau Gasol 1.50 .45
❑ 43 Shane Battier 1.50 .45
❑ 44 Mike Miller 1.50 .45
❑ 45 Caron Butler 1.50 .45
❑ 46 Eddie Jones 1.50 .45
❑ 47 Lamar Odom 1.50 .45
❑ 48 Brian Grant 1.00 .30
❑ 49 Desmond Mason 1.00 .30
❑ 50 Michael Redd 1.50 .45
❑ 51 Tim Thomas 1.00 .30
❑ 52 Wally Szczerbiak 1.00 .30
❑ 53 Kevin Garnett 3.00 .90
❑ 54 Latrell Sprewell 1.50 .45
❑ 55 Sam Cassell 1.50 .45
❑ 56 Richard Jefferson 1.00 .30
❑ 57 Kenyon Martin 1.50 .45
❑ 58 Jason Kidd 2.00 .60
❑ 59 Alonzo Mourning 1.00 .30
❑ 60 Jamal Mashburn 1.00 .30
❑ 61 Baron Davis 1.50 .45
❑ 62 David Wesley .50 .15
❑ 63 Allan Houston 1.00 .30
❑ 64 Keith Van Horn 1.50 .45
❑ 65 Antonio McDyess 1.50 .45
❑ 66 Gordan Giricek 1.00 .30
❑ 67 Tracy McGrady 4.00 1.20
❑ 68 Drew Gooden 1.50 .45
❑ 69 Grant Hill 1.50 .45
❑ 70 Glenn Robinson 1.50 .45
❑ 71 Allen Iverson 3.00 .90
❑ 72 Julius Erving 4.00 1.20
❑ 73 Eric Snow 1.00 .30
❑ 74 Shawn Marion 1.50 .45
❑ 75 Amare Stoudemire 3.00 .90
❑ 76 Stephon Marbury 1.50 .45
❑ 77 Damon Stoudamire 1.00 .30
❑ 78 Rasheed Wallace 1.50 .45
❑ 79 Derek Anderson 1.00 .30
❑ 80 Zach Randolph 1.50 .45
❑ 81 Mike Bibby 1.50 .45
❑ 82 Chris Webber 1.50 .45
❑ 83 Peja Stojakovic 1.50 .45
❑ 84 Brad Miller 1.50 .45
❑ 85 Tony Parker 1.50 .45
❑ 86 Tim Duncan 3.00 .90
❑ 87 Manu Ginobili 1.50 .45
❑ 88 David Robinson 1.50 .45
❑ 89 Rashard Lewis 1.50 .45
❑ 90 Ray Allen 1.50 .45
❑ 91 Vladimir Radmanovic .50 .15
❑ 92 Morris Peterson 1.00 .30
❑ 93 Vince Carter 4.00 1.20
❑ 94 Antonio Davis .50 .15
❑ 95 Andrei Kirilenko 1.50 .45
❑ 96 Matt Harpring 1.50 .45
❑ 97 Jarron Collins .50 .15
❑ 98 Gilbert Arenas 1.50 .45
❑ 99 Jerry Stackhouse 1.00 .30
❑ 100 Kwame Brown 1.50 .45
❑ 101 LeBron James RC 160.00 47.50
❑ 102 Darko Milicic RC 20.00 6.00
❑ 103 Carmelo Anthony RC 80.00 24.00
❑ 104 Chris Bosh RC 25.00 7.50
❑ 105 Dwyane Wade RC 30.00 9.00
❑ 106 Chris Kaman RC 10.00 3.00
❑ 107 Kirk Hinrich RC 20.00 6.00
❑ 108 T.J. Ford RC 15.00 4.50
❑ 109 Mike Sweetney RC 10.00 3.00
❑ 110 Jarvis Hayes RC 10.00 3.00

❑ 111 Mickael Pietrus RC 10.00 3.00
❑ 112 Nick Collison RC 10.00 3.00
❑ 113 Marcus Banks RC 10.00 3.00
❑ 114 Luke Ridnour RC 15.00 4.50
❑ 115 Reece Gaines RC 10.00 3.00
❑ 116 Troy Bell RC 10.00 3.00
❑ 117 Zarko Cabarkapa RC 10.00 3.00
❑ 118 David West RC 10.00 3.00
❑ 119 Aleksandar Pavlovic RC 10.00 3.00
❑ 120 Dahntay Jones RC 10.00 3.00
❑ 121 Boris Diaw RC 10.00 3.00
❑ 122 Zoran Planinic RC 10.00 3.00
❑ 123 Travis Outlaw RC 10.00 3.00
❑ 124 Brian Cook RC 10.00 3.00
❑ 125 James Lang RC 10.00 3.00
❑ 126 Ndudi Ebi RC 10.00 3.00
❑ 127 Kendrick Perkins RC 10.00 3.00
❑ 128 Leandro Barbosa RC 10.00 3.00
❑ 129 Josh Howard RC 15.00 4.50
❑ 130 Maciej Lampe RC 10.00 3.00
❑ 131 Jason Kapono RC 10.00 3.00
❑ 132 Luke Walton RC 15.00 4.50
❑ 133 Jerome Beasley RC .. 10.00 3.00
❑ 134 Willie Green RC 10.00 3.00
❑ 135 James Jones RC 10.00 3.00
❑ 136 Travis Hansen RC 10.00 3.00
❑ 137 Steve Blake RC 10.00 3.00
❑ 138 Slavko Vranes RC 10.00 3.00
❑ 139 Zaur Pachulia RC 10.00 3.00
❑ 140 Keith Bogans RC 10.00 3.00
❑ 141 Kyle Korver RC 15.00 4.50
❑ 142 Brandon Hunter RC .. 10.00 3.00
❑ 143 Kobe Bryant/8 .... -
❑ 144 LeBron James/23 .... -
❑ 145 Michael Jordan/23 .... -
❑ 146 Darius Miles/21 .... -
❑ 147 Yao Ming/11 .... -
❑ 148 Gary Payton/20 .... -
❑ 149 Tim Thomas/5 .... -
❑ 150 Allan Houston/20 .... -
❑ 151 Stephon Marbury/3 ...... -
❑ 152 Ray Allen/34 .... 50.00 15.00
❑ 153 Paul Pierce/34 .... 50.00 15.00
❑ 154 Carmelo Anthony/15 .... -
❑ 155 Jamaal Tinsley/11 .... -
❑ 156 Kirk Hinrich/12 .... -
❑ 157 Jason Kidd/5 .... -
❑ 158 Julius Erving/6 .... -
❑ 159 Mike Bibby/10 .... -
❑ 160 Andrei Kirilenko/47 .... 25.00 7.50
❑ 161 T.J. Ford/11 .... -
❑ 162 Nene/31 .... 20.00 6.00
❑ 163 Elton Brand/42 .... 25.00 7.50
❑ 164 Caron Butler/4 .... -
❑ 165 Richard Jefferson/24 .... -
❑ 166 Allen Iverson/3 .... -
❑ 167 Peja Stojakovic/16 ...... -
❑ 168 Jerry Stackhouse/42 25.00 7.50
❑ 169 Jalen Rose/5 .... -
❑ 170 Ben Wallace/3 .... -
❑ 171 Darko Milicic/31 .... 50.00 15.00
❑ 172 Lamar Odom/7 .... -
❑ 173 Kenyon Martin/6 .... -
❑ 174 Glenn Robinson/31 .. 20.00 6.00
❑ 175 Tim Duncan/21 .... -
❑ 176 Gilbert Arenas/10 .... -
❑ 177 Scottie Pippen/33 .... 100.00 30.00
❑ 178 Richard Hamilton/32 .. 25.00 7.50
❑ 179 Corey Maggette/50 .... 20.00 6.00
❑ 180 Dwyane Wade/3 .... -
❑ 181 Baron Davis/1 .... -
❑ 182 Amare Stoudemire/32 40.00 12.00
❑ 183 Tony Parker/9 .... -
❑ 184 Shareef Abdur-Rahim/3 -
❑ 185 Dirk Nowitzki/41 .... 30.00 9.00
❑ 186 Steve Francis/3 .... -
❑ 187 Magic Johnson/32 .... 60.00 18.00
❑ 188 Michael Redd/22 .... -
❑ 189 Keith Van Horn/2 .... -
❑ 190 Rasheed Wallace/30 30.00 9.00
❑ 191 Nick Collison/4 .... -
❑ 192 Jason Terry/31 .... 25.00 7.50
❑ 193 Steve Nash/13 .... -
❑ 194 Cuttino Mobley/5 .... -
❑ 195 Karl Malone/11 .... -
❑ 196 Kevin Garnett/21 .... -
❑ 197 Tracy McGrady/1 .... -
❑ 198 Bonzi Wells/6 .... -
❑ 199 Rashard Lewis/7 .... -
❑ 200 Antoine Walker/8 .... -
❑ 201 Michael Finley/4 .... -
❑ 202 Jermaine O'Neal/7 ...... -
❑ 203 Mike Miller/33 .... 20.00 6.00
❑ 204 Wally Szczerbiak/10 .... -
❑ 205 Gordan Giricek/7 .... -
❑ 206 Chris Webber/4 .... -
❑ 207 Morris Peterson/24 ...... -
❑ 208 Dajuan Wagner/2 .... -
❑ 209 Jason Richardson/23 .. -
❑ 210 Shaquille O'Neal/34 .. 60.00 18.00
❑ 211 Desmond Mason/24 .... -
❑ 212 Jamal Mashburn/24 .... -
❑ 213 Shawn Marion/31 ...... 25.00 7.50
❑ 214 Manu Ginobili/20 .... -
❑ 215 Larry Bird/33 .... 150.00 45.00
❑ 216 Antawn Jamison/33 .. 25.00 7.50
❑ 217 Reggie Miller/31 .... 40.00 12.00
❑ 218 Pau Gasol/16 .... -
❑ 219 Latrell Sprewell/8 .... -
❑ 220 Drew Gooden/10 .... -
❑ 221 Damon Stoudamire/3 .. -
❑ 222 Vince Carter/15 .... -
❑ 223 Spike Lee 4.00 1.20
❑ 224 Summer Sanders .... 3.00 .90
❑ 225 Cheryl Miller .... 2.00 .60

1997 SPx

	Nm-Mt	Ex-Mt
COMPLETE SET (50)	100.00	30.00
❑ 1 Mookie Blaylock	1.00	.30
❑ 2 Antoine Walker	4.00	1.20
❑ 3 Eric Williams	1.00	.30
❑ 4 Tony Delk	1.00	.30
❑ 5 Michael Jordan	20.00	6.00
❑ 6 Dennis Rodman	2.00	.60
❑ 7 Vitaly Potapenko	1.00	.30
❑ 8 Bob Sura	1.00	.30
❑ 9 Jamal Mashburn	2.00	.60
❑ 10 Samaki Walker	1.00	.30
❑ 11 Antonio McDyess	2.00	.60
❑ 12 Joe Dumars	3.00	.90
❑ 13 Grant Hill	3.00	.90
❑ 14 Joe Smith	2.00	.60
❑ 15 Latrell Sprewell	3.00	.90
❑ 16 Charles Barkley	4.00	1.20
❑ 17 Hakeem Olajuwon	3.00	.90
❑ 18 Erick Dampier	2.00	.60
❑ 19 Reggie Miller	3.00	.90
❑ 20 Brent Barry	2.00	.60
❑ 21 Lorenzen Wright	1.00	.30
❑ 22 Kobe Bryant	20.00	6.00
❑ 23 Eddie Jones	3.00	.90
❑ 24 Shaquille O'Neal	8.00	2.40
❑ 25 Alonzo Mourning	2.00	.60
❑ 26 Kurt Thomas	2.00	.60
❑ 27 Vin Baker	2.00	.60
❑ 28 Glenn Robinson	3.00	.90
❑ 29 Kevin Garnett	6.00	1.80
❑ 30 Stephon Marbury	4.00	1.20
❑ 31 Kerry Kittles	3.00	.90
❑ 32 Patrick Ewing	3.00	.90
❑ 33 Larry Johnson	2.00	.60
❑ 34 Anfernee Hardaway	3.00	.90
❑ 35 Allen Iverson	10.00	3.00
❑ 36 Jerry Stackhouse	3.00	.90
❑ 37 Kevin Johnson	2.00	.60
❑ 38 Steve Nash	3.00	.90
❑ 39 Jermaine O'Neal	5.00	1.50
❑ 40 Mitch Richmond	2.00	.60
❑ 41 David Robinson	3.00	.90
❑ 42 Shawn Kemp	2.00	.60
❑ 43 Gary Payton	3.00	.90
❑ 44 Marcus Camby	3.00	.90
❑ 45 Damon Stoudamire	2.00	.60
❑ 46 Karl Malone	3.00	.90
❑ 47 John Stockton	3.00	.90
❑ 48 Shareef Abdur-Rahim	5.00	1.50
❑ 49 Bryant Reeves	1.00	.30
❑ 50 Juwan Howard	2.00	.60
❑ SPX5 Michael Jordan Promo	15.00	4.50

1997-98 SPx

	Nm-Mt	Ex-Mt
COMPLETE SET (50)	75.00	22.00
❑ 1 Mookie Blaylock	.60	.18
❑ 2 Dikembe Mutombo	1.50	.45
❑ 3 Chauncey Billups RC	2.50	.75
❑ 4 Antoine Walker	2.50	.75
❑ 5 Glen Rice	1.50	.45
❑ 6 Michael Jordan	12.00	3.60
❑ 7 Scottie Pippen	3.00	.90
❑ 8 Dennis Rodman	1.50	.45
❑ 9 Shawn Kemp	1.50	.45
❑ 10 Michael Finley	2.00	.60
❑ 11 Tony Battie RC	2.00	.60
❑ 12 LaPhonso Ellis	.60	.18
❑ 13 Grant Hill	2.00	.60
❑ 14 Joe Dumars	2.00	.60
❑ 15 Joe Smith	1.50	.45
❑ 16 Clyde Drexler	2.00	.60
❑ 17 Charles Barkley	2.50	.75
❑ 18 Hakeem Olajuwon	2.00	.60
❑ 19 Reggie Miller	2.00	.60
❑ 20 Brent Barry	1.50	.45
❑ 21 Kobe Bryant	8.00	2.40
❑ 22 Shaquille O'Neal	5.00	1.50
❑ 23 Alonzo Mourning	1.50	.45
❑ 24 Glenn Robinson	2.00	.60
❑ 25 Kevin Garnett	4.00	1.20
❑ 26 Stephon Marbury	2.50	.75
❑ 27 Keith Van Horn RC	4.00	1.20
❑ 28 Patrick Ewing	2.00	.60
❑ 29 Anfernee Hardaway	2.00	.60
❑ 30 Allen Iverson	5.00	1.50
❑ 31 Kevin Johnson	1.50	.45
❑ 32 Antonio McDyess	1.50	.45
❑ 33 Jason Kidd	3.00	.90
❑ 34 Kenny Anderson	1.50	.45
❑ 35 Rasheed Wallace	2.00	.60
❑ 36 Mitch Richmond	1.50	.45
❑ 37 Tim Duncan RC	10.00	3.00
❑ 38 David Robinson	2.00	.60
❑ 39 Vin Baker	1.50	.45
❑ 40 Gary Payton	2.00	.60
❑ 41 Marcus Camby	2.00	.60
❑ 42 Tracy McGrady RC	20.00	6.00
❑ 43 Damon Stoudamire	1.50	.45
❑ 44 Karl Malone	2.00	.60
❑ 45 John Stockton	2.00	.60
❑ 46 Shareef Abdur-Rahim	3.00	.90
❑ 47 Antonio Daniels RC	2.00	.60

Card	Nm-Mt	Ex-Mt
❑ 48 Bryant Reeves	.60	.18
❑ 49 Juwan Howard	1.50	.45
❑ 50 Chris Webber	2.00	.60
❑ T1 Piece of History Trade	200.00	60.00

1998-99 SPx Finite

	Nm-Mt	Ex-Mt
COMPLETE SET w/o RC (90)	100.00	30.00
COMP.ST.POWER SET (60)	125.00	38.00
COMMON ST.POWER (91-150)	1.25	.35
COMP.SPx 2000 SET (30)	125.00	38.00
COMMON SPx 2000 (151-180)	2.00	.60
COMP.TP.FLIGHT SET (20)	100.00	30.00
COMMON TP.FLIGHT (181-200)	2.50	.75
COMP.FIN.EXC.SET (10)	125.00	38.00
COMMON FIN.EXC. (201-210)	4.00	1.20
COMP.ROOKIE SET (28)	400.00	120.00
COMMON ROOKIE (211-240)	5.00	1.50
❑ 1 Michael Jordan	15.00	4.50
❑ 2 Hakeem Olajuwon	2.50	.75
❑ 3 Keith Van Horn	2.50	.75
❑ 4 Rasheed Wallace	2.50	.75
❑ 5 Mookie Blaylock	.75	.23
❑ 6 Bobby Jackson	1.50	.45
❑ 7 Detlef Schrempf	1.50	.45
❑ 8 Antonio McDyess	1.50	.45
❑ 9 Lamond Murray	.75	.23
❑ 10 Chris Mullin	2.50	.75
❑ 11 Zydrunas Ilgauskas	1.50	.45
❑ 12 Tracy Murray	.75	.23
❑ 13 Jerry Stackhouse	2.50	.75
❑ 14 Avery Johnson	.75	.23
❑ 15 Larry Johnson	1.50	.45
❑ 16 Alan Henderson	.75	.23
❑ 17 David Wesley	.75	.23
❑ 18 Kevin Willis	.75	.23
❑ 19 Eddie Jones	2.50	.75
❑ 20 Horace Grant	1.50	.45
❑ 21 Ray Allen	2.50	.75
❑ 22 Derrick Coleman	.75	.23
❑ 23 Derek Anderson	2.50	.75
❑ 24 Tim Hardaway	1.50	.45
❑ 25 Danny Fortson	.75	.23
❑ 26 Tariq Abdul-Wahad	.75	.23
❑ 27 Charles Barkley	3.00	.90
❑ 28 Sam Cassell	2.50	.75
❑ 29 Kevin Garnett	5.00	1.50
❑ 30 Jeff Hornacek	1.50	.45
❑ 31 Isaac Austin	.75	.23
❑ 32 Allan Houston	2.50	.75
❑ 33 David Robinson	2.50	.75
❑ 34 Tracy McGrady	6.00	1.80
❑ 35 LaPhonso Ellis	.75	.23
❑ 36 Shawn Kemp	1.50	.45
❑ 37 Glenn Robinson	1.50	.45
❑ 38 Shareef Abdur-Rahim	2.50	.75
❑ 39 Vin Baker	1.50	.45
❑ 40 Rik Smits	1.50	.45
❑ 41 Jason Kidd	4.00	1.20
❑ 42 Erick Dampier	1.50	.45
❑ 43 Shawn Bradley	.75	.23
❑ 44 Anfernee Hardaway	2.50	.75
❑ 45 John Stockton	2.50	.75
❑ 46 Calbert Cheaney	.75	.23
❑ 47 Terrell Brandon	1.50	.45
❑ 48 Hubert Davis	.75	.23
❑ 49 Patrick Ewing	2.50	.75
❑ 50 Kobe Bryant	10.00	3.00
❑ 51 Gary Payton	2.50	.75
❑ 52 Marcus Camby	1.50	.45
❑ 53 Bryant Reeves	.75	.23
❑ 54 Reggie Miller	2.50	.75
❑ 55 Antoine Walker	2.50	.75
❑ 56 Scottie Pippen	4.00	1.20
❑ 57 Hersey Hawkins	.75	.23
❑ 58 John Starks	1.50	.45
❑ 59 Dikembe Mutombo	1.50	.45
❑ 60 Damon Stoudamire	1.50	.45
❑ 61 Rodney Rogers	.75	.23
❑ 62 Nick Anderson	.75	.23
❑ 63 Brian Williams	.75	.23
❑ 64 Ron Mercer	1.50	.45
❑ 65 Donyell Marshall	1.50	.45
❑ 66 Glen Rice	1.50	.45
❑ 67 Michael Finley	2.50	.75
❑ 68 Tim Duncan	4.00	1.20
❑ 69 Stephon Marbury	2.50	.75
❑ 70 Antonio Daniels	.75	.23
❑ 71 Chauncey Billups	1.50	.45
❑ 72 Kerry Kittles	.75	.23
❑ 73 Brian Grant	1.50	.45
❑ 74 Anthony Mason	1.50	.45
❑ 75 Allen Iverson	5.00	1.50
❑ 76 Juwan Howard	1.50	.45
❑ 77 Grant Hill	2.50	.75
❑ 78 Tony Delk	.75	.23
❑ 79 Olden Polynice	.75	.23
❑ 80 Alonzo Mourning	1.50	.45
❑ 81 Karl Malone	2.50	.75
❑ 82 Isaiah Rider	.75	.23
❑ 83 Shaquille O'Neal	6.00	1.80
❑ 84 Steve Smith	1.50	.45
❑ 85 Kenny Anderson	1.50	.45
❑ 86 Toni Kukoc	1.50	.45
❑ 87 Anthony Peeler	.75	.23
❑ 88 Tim Thomas	1.50	.45
❑ 89 Nick Van Exel	2.50	.75
❑ 90 Jamal Mashburn	1.50	.45
❑ 91 Reggie Miller SP	4.00	1.20
❑ 92 Juwan Howard SP	2.50	.75
❑ 93 Glen Rice SP	2.50	.75
❑ 94 Grant Hill SP	4.00	1.20
❑ 95 Maurice Taylor SP	2.50	.75
❑ 96 Vin Baker SP	2.50	.75
❑ 97 Tim Thomas SP	2.50	.75
❑ 98 Bobby Jackson SP	1.25	.35
❑ 99 Damon Stoudamire SP	2.50	.75
❑ 100 Michael Jordan SP	30.00	9.00
❑ 101 Eddie Jones SP	4.00	1.20
❑ 102 Keith Van Horn SP	4.00	1.20
❑ 103 Dikembe Mutombo SP	2.50	.75
❑ 104 Brevin Knight SP	1.25	.35
❑ 105 Shawn Bradley SP	1.25	.35
❑ 106 Lamond Murray SP	1.25	.35
❑ 107 Tim Duncan SP	6.00	1.80
❑ 108 Bryant Reeves SP	1.25	.35
❑ 109 Antoine Walker SP	4.00	1.20
❑ 110 John Stockton SP	4.00	1.20
❑ 111 Nick Anderson SP	1.25	.35
❑ 112 Chris Mullin SP	4.00	1.20
❑ 113 Glenn Robinson SP	2.50	.75
❑ 114 Kevin Garnett SP	8.00	2.40
❑ 115 Michael Stewart SP	1.25	.35
❑ 116 Antonio McDyess SP	2.50	.75
❑ 117 Jim Jackson SP	1.25	.35
❑ 118 Chauncey Billups SP	1.25	.35
❑ 119 Sam Cassell SP	4.00	1.20
❑ 120 Dennis Rodman SP	2.50	.75
❑ 121 Rasheed Wallace SP	4.00	1.20
❑ 122 Brian Williams SP	1.25	.35
❑ 123 Anfernee Hardaway SP	4.00	1.20
❑ 124 Scottie Pippen SP	6.00	1.80
❑ 125 Terrell Brandon SP	2.50	.75
❑ 126 Michael Finley SP	4.00	1.20
❑ 127 Kerry Kittles SP	1.25	.35
❑ 128 Toni Kukoc SP	2.50	.75
❑ 129 Hakeem Olajuwon SP	4.00	1.20
❑ 130 Tim Hardaway SP	2.50	.75
❑ 131 Shareef Abdur-Rahim SP	4.00	1.20
❑ 132 Donyell Marshall SP	1.25	.35
❑ 133 David Robinson SP	4.00	1.20
❑ 134 LaPhonso Ellis SP	1.25	.35
❑ 135 Ray Allen SP	4.00	1.20
❑ 136 Nick Van Exel SP	4.00	1.20
❑ 137 Patrick Ewing SP	4.00	1.20
❑ 138 Anthony Mason SP	2.50	.75
❑ 139 Shaquille O'Neal SP	10.00	3.00
❑ 140 Shawn Kemp SP	2.50	.75
❑ 141 Stephon Marbury SP	4.00	1.20
❑ 142 Karl Malone SP	4.00	1.20
❑ 143 Allen Iverson SP	8.00	2.40
❑ 144 Kenny Anderson SP	2.50	.75
❑ 145 Marcus Camby SP	4.00	1.20
❑ 146 Steve Smith SP	2.50	.75
❑ 147 Gary Payton SP	4.00	1.20
❑ 148 Jason Kidd SP	6.00	1.80
❑ 149 Alonzo Mourning SP	4.00	1.20
❑ 150 Charles Barkley SP	5.00	1.50
❑ 151 Kobe Bryant SPx	25.00	7.50
❑ 152 Ron Mercer SPx	6.00	1.80
❑ 153 Maurice Taylor SPx	4.00	1.20
❑ 154 Tim Duncan SPx	6.00	1.80
❑ 155 S. Abdur-Rahim SPx	6.00	1.80
❑ 156 Eddie Jones SPx	6.00	1.80
❑ 157 Chauncey Billups SPx	2.00	.60
❑ 158 Derek Anderson SPx	6.00	1.80
❑ 159 Bobby Jackson SPx	2.00	.60
❑ 160 Stephon Marbury SPx	6.00	1.80
❑ 161 Anfernee Hardaway SPx	6.00	1.80
❑ 162 Zydrunas Ilgauskas SPx	4.00	1.20
❑ 163 Allen Iverson SPx	12.00	3.60
❑ 164 Antoine Walker SPx	6.00	1.80
❑ 165 Tracy McGrady SPx	15.00	4.50
❑ 166 Rasheed Wallace SPx	6.00	1.80
❑ 167 Jason Kidd SPx	10.00	3.00
❑ 168 Kevin Garnett SPx	12.00	3.60
❑ 169 Damon Stoudamire SPx	4.00	1.20
❑ 170 Brevin Knight SPx	2.00	.60
❑ 171 Tim Thomas SPx	4.00	1.20
❑ 172 Danny Fortson SPx	2.00	.60
❑ 173 Jermaine O'Neal SPx	6.00	1.80
❑ 174 Keith Van Horn SPx	6.00	1.80
❑ 175 Ray Allen SPx	6.00	1.80
❑ 176 Kerry Kittles SPx	2.00	.60
❑ 177 Vin Baker SPx	4.00	1.20
❑ 178 Allan Houston SPx	6.00	1.80
❑ 179 Alan Henderson SPx	2.00	.60
❑ 180 Bryon Russell SPx	2.00	.60
❑ 181 Michael Jordan TF	50.00	15.00
❑ 182 Maurice Taylor TF	5.00	1.50
❑ 183 Isaiah Rider TF	2.50	.75
❑ 184 Antonio McDyess TF	5.00	1.50
❑ 185 Anfernee Hardaway TF	8.00	2.40
❑ 186 Glenn Robinson TF	5.00	1.50
❑ 187 Dikembe Mutombo TF	5.00	1.50
❑ 188 Shawn Kemp TF	5.00	1.50
❑ 189 Tracy McGrady TF	20.00	6.00
❑ 190 Reggie Miller TF	8.00	2.40
❑ 191 Derek Anderson TF	8.00	2.40
❑ 192 Allan Houston TF	8.00	2.40
❑ 193 Michael Finley TF	8.00	2.40
❑ 194 Nick Van Exel TF	8.00	2.40
❑ 195 Juwan Howard TF	5.00	1.50
❑ 196 LaPhonso Ellis TF	2.50	.75
❑ 197 Ron Mercer TF	5.00	1.50
❑ 198 Glen Rice TF	5.00	1.50
❑ 199 Joe Smith TF	5.00	1.50
❑ 200 Kobe Bryant TF	30.00	9.00
❑ 201 Michael Jordan FE	80.00	24.00
❑ 202 Karl Malone FE	4.00	1.20
❑ 203 Hakeem Olajuwon FE	12.00	3.60
❑ 204 David Robinson FE	12.00	3.60
❑ 205 Shaquille O'Neal FE	30.00	9.00
❑ 206 John Stockton FE	12.00	3.60
❑ 207 Grant Hill FE	12.00	3.60
❑ 208 Tim Hardaway FE	8.00	2.40
❑ 209 Scottie Pippen FE	20.00	6.00
❑ 210 Gary Payton FE	12.00	3.60
❑ 211 Michael Olowokandi RC	6.00	1.80
❑ 212 Mike Bibby RC	25.00	7.50
❑ 213 Raef LaFrentz RC	8.00	2.40
❑ 214 Antawn Jamison RC	25.00	7.50
❑ 215 Vince Carter RC	120.00	36.00
❑ 216 Robert Traylor RC	5.00	1.50
❑ 217 Jason Williams RC	20.00	6.00
❑ 218 Larry Hughes RC	15.00	4.50
❑ 219 Dirk Nowitzki RC	50.00	15.00
❑ 220 Paul Pierce RC	30.00	9.00
❑ 221 Bonzi Wells RC	20.00	6.00
❑ 222 Michael Doleac RC	5.00	1.50

Card		
❑ 223 Keon Clark RC	10.00	3.00
❑ 224 Michael Dickerson RC	12.00	3.60
❑ 225 Matt Harpring RC	8.00	2.40
❑ 226 Bryce Drew RC	5.00	1.50
❑ 227 Does not exist	-	-
❑ 228 Does not exist	-	-
❑ 229 Pat Garrity RC	5.00	1.50
❑ 230 Roshown McLeod RC	5.00	1.50
❑ 231 Ricky Davis RC	10.00	3.00
❑ 232 Brian Skinner RC	5.00	1.50
❑ 233 Tyronn Lue RC	8.00	2.40
❑ 234 Felipe Lopez RC	5.00	1.50
❑ 235 Al Harrington RC	15.00	4.50
❑ 236 Ruben Patterson RC	8.00	2.40
❑ 237 Jelani McCoy RC	5.00	1.50
❑ 238 Corey Benjamin RC	5.00	1.50
❑ 239 Nazr Mohammed RC	5.00	1.50
❑ 240 Rashard Lewis RC	25.00	7.50

1999-00 SPx

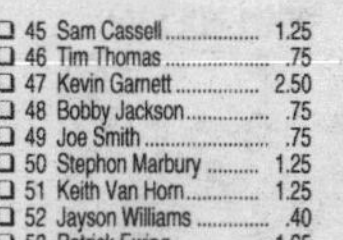
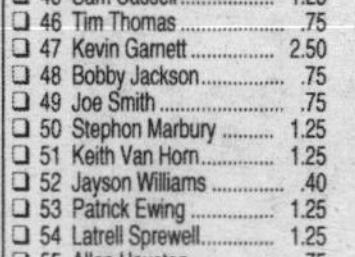

	Nm-Mt	Ex-Mt
COMPLETE SET w/o RC (90)	30.00	9.00
COMMON CARD (1-90)	.40	.12
COMMON ROOKIE (91-120)	3.00	.90
❑ 1 Dikembe Mutombo	.75	.23
❑ 2 Alan Henderson	.40	.12
❑ 3 Antoine Walker	1.25	.35
❑ 4 Paul Pierce	1.25	.35
❑ 5 Kenny Anderson	.75	.23
❑ 6 Eddie Jones	1.25	.35
❑ 7 David Wesley	.40	.12
❑ 8 Elden Campbell	.40	.12
❑ 9 Toni Kukoc	.75	.23
❑ 10 Dickey Simpkins	.40	.12
❑ 11 Shawn Kemp	.75	.23
❑ 12 Brevin Knight	.40	.12
❑ 13 Michael Finley	1.25	.35
❑ 14 Cedric Ceballos	.40	.12
❑ 15 Dirk Nowitzki	2.50	.75
❑ 16 Antonio McDyess	.75	.23
❑ 17 Nick Van Exel	1.25	.35
❑ 18 Chauncey Billups	.75	.23
❑ 19 Grant Hill	1.25	.35
❑ 20 Jerry Stackhouse	1.25	.35
❑ 21 Bison Dele	.40	.12
❑ 22 Lindsey Hunter	.40	.12
❑ 23 Antawn Jamison	2.00	.60
❑ 24 Donyell Marshall	.75	.23
❑ 25 John Starks	.75	.23
❑ 26 Chris Mills	.40	.12
❑ 27 Hakeem Olajuwon	1.25	.35
❑ 28 Scottie Pippen	2.00	.60
❑ 29 Charles Barkley	1.50	.45
❑ 30 Reggie Miller	1.25	.35
❑ 31 Rik Smits	.75	.23
❑ 32 Jalen Rose	1.25	.35
❑ 33 Chris Mullin	1.25	.35
❑ 34 Maurice Taylor	.75	.23
❑ 35 Michael Olowokandi	.75	.23
❑ 36 Shaquille O'Neal	3.00	.90
❑ 37 Kobe Bryant	5.00	1.50
❑ 38 Glen Rice	.75	.23
❑ 39 Tim Hardaway	.75	.23
❑ 40 Alonzo Mourning	.75	.23
❑ 41 Dan Majerle	.75	.23
❑ 42 P.J. Brown	.40	.12
❑ 43 Glenn Robinson	1.25	.35
❑ 44 Ray Allen	1.25	.35
❑ 45 Sam Cassell	1.25	.35
❑ 46 Tim Thomas	.75	.23
❑ 47 Kevin Garnett	2.50	.75
❑ 48 Bobby Jackson	.75	.23
❑ 49 Joe Smith	.75	.23
❑ 50 Stephon Marbury	1.25	.35
❑ 51 Keith Van Horn	1.25	.35
❑ 52 Jayson Williams	.40	.12
❑ 53 Patrick Ewing	1.25	.35
❑ 54 Latrell Sprewell	1.25	.35
❑ 55 Allan Houston	.75	.23
❑ 56 Marcus Camby	.75	.23
❑ 57 Bo Outlaw	.40	.12
❑ 58 Darrell Armstrong	.40	.12
❑ 59 Allen Iverson	2.50	.75
❑ 60 Theo Ratliff	.75	.23
❑ 61 Larry Hughes	1.25	.35
❑ 62 Jason Kidd	2.00	.60
❑ 63 Tom Gugliotta	.40	.12
❑ 64 Clifford Robinson	.40	.12
❑ 65 Brian Grant	.75	.23
❑ 66 Jermaine O'Neal	1.25	.35
❑ 67 Rasheed Wallace	1.25	.35
❑ 68 Damon Stoudamire	.75	.23
❑ 69 Jason Williams	1.25	.35
❑ 70 Chris Webber	1.25	.35
❑ 71 Vlade Divac	.75	.23
❑ 72 Avery Johnson	.40	.12
❑ 73 Tim Duncan	2.50	.75
❑ 74 David Robinson	1.25	.35
❑ 75 Sean Elliott	.75	.23
❑ 76 Gary Payton	1.25	.35
❑ 77 Vin Baker	.75	.23
❑ 78 Jelani McCoy	.40	.12
❑ 79 Charles Oakley	.40	.12
❑ 80 Vince Carter	3.00	.90
❑ 81 Tracy McGrady	3.00	.90
❑ 82 Doug Christie	.75	.23
❑ 83 Karl Malone	1.25	.35
❑ 84 John Stockton	1.25	.35
❑ 85 Shareef Abdur-Rahim	1.25	.35
❑ 86 Bryant Reeves	.40	.12
❑ 87 Mike Bibby	1.25	.35
❑ 88 Juwan Howard	.75	.23
❑ 89 Mitch Richmond	.75	.23
❑ 90 Rod Strickland	.40	.12
❑ 91 Elton Brand RC	25.00	7.50
❑ 92 Steve Francis AU RC	250.00	75.00
❑ 93 Baron Davis AU RC	200.00	60.00
❑ 94 Lamar Odom RC	20.00	6.00
❑ 95 Jonathan Bender RC	15.00	4.50
❑ 96 Wally Szczerbiak AU RC	150.00	45.00
❑ 97 Richard Hamilton AU RC	50.00	15.00
❑ 98 Andre Miller AU RC	150.00	45.00
❑ 99 Shawn Marion AU RC	50.00	15.00
❑ 100 Jason Terry AU RC	30.00	9.00
❑ 101 Trajan Langdon AU RC	12.00	3.60
❑ 102 Venson Hamilton RC	3.00	.90
❑ 103 Corey Maggette AU RC	150.00	45.00
❑ 104 William Avery AU RC	12.00	3.60
❑ 105 Dion Glover RC	4.00	1.20
❑ 106 Ron Artest AU RC	20.00	6.00
❑ 107 Cal Bowdler RC	4.00	1.20
❑ 108 James Posey AU RC	15.00	4.50
❑ 109 Quincy Lewis AU RC	8.00	2.40
❑ 110 Devean George AU RC	15.00	4.50
❑ 111 Tim James AU RC	10.00	3.00
❑ 112 Vonteego Cummings RC	5.00	1.50
❑ 113 Jumaine Jones AU RC	15.00	4.50
❑ 114 Scott Padgett AU RC	8.00	2.40
❑ 115 Kenny Thomas RC	5.00	1.50
❑ 116 Jeff Foster RC	4.00	1.20
❑ 117 Ryan Robertson RC	4.00	1.20
❑ 118 Chris Herren AU RC	8.00	2.40
❑ 119 Evan Eschmeyer AU RC	8.00	2.40
❑ 120 A.J. Bramlett AU RC	8.00	2.40
❑ P32 Karl Malone	1.25	.35

2000-01 SPx

	Nm-Mt	Ex-Mt
COMPLETE SET w/o RC (90)	40.00	12.00
COMMON CARD (1-90)	.40	.12
COMM.RC (91/93-98/138)	2.00	.60
COMMON RC (99-104)	4.00	1.20
COMMON RC (105-110)	20.00	6.00
COMM.RC (92/111-130/136-137)	10.00	3.00
COMMON RC (131-135)	15.00	4.50
❑ 1 Dikembe Mutombo	.75	.23
❑ 2 Jim Jackson	.40	.12
❑ 3 Jason Terry	1.25	.35
❑ 4 Paul Pierce	1.25	.35
❑ 5 Kenny Anderson	.75	.23
❑ 6 Antoine Walker	1.25	.35
❑ 7 Derrick Coleman	.40	.12
❑ 8 Baron Davis	1.25	.35
❑ 9 David Wesley	.40	.12
❑ 10 Elton Brand	1.25	.35
❑ 11 Ron Artest	.75	.23
❑ 12 Corey Benjamin	.40	.12
❑ 13 Trajan Langdon	.75	.23
❑ 14 Lamond Murray	.40	.12
❑ 15 Andre Miller	.75	.23
❑ 16 Michael Finley	1.25	.35
❑ 17 Gary Trent	.40	.12
❑ 18 Dirk Nowitzki	2.00	.60
❑ 19 Antonio McDyess	.75	.23
❑ 20 Nick Van Exel	1.25	.35
❑ 21 Raef LaFrentz	.75	.23
❑ 22 Jerry Stackhouse	1.25	.35
❑ 23 Michael Curry	.40	.12
❑ 24 Jerome Williams	.40	.12
❑ 25 Larry Hughes	.75	.23
❑ 26 Antawn Jamison	1.25	.35
❑ 27 Mookie Blaylock	.40	.12
❑ 28 Hakeem Olajuwon	1.25	.35
❑ 29 Steve Francis	1.25	.35
❑ 30 Shandon Anderson	.40	.12
❑ 31 Reggie Miller	1.25	.35
❑ 32 Jalen Rose	1.25	.35
❑ 33 Austin Croshere	.75	.23
❑ 34 Lamar Odom	1.25	.35
❑ 35 Michael Olowokandi	.40	.12
❑ 36 Tyrone Nesby	.40	.12
❑ 37 Shaquille O'Neal	3.00	.90
❑ 38 Kobe Bryant	5.00	1.50
❑ 39 Robert Horry	.75	.23
❑ 40 Ron Harper	.75	.23
❑ 41 Alonzo Mourning	.75	.23
❑ 42 Eddie Jones	1.25	.35
❑ 43 Tim Hardaway	.75	.23
❑ 44 Glenn Robinson	1.25	.35
❑ 45 Sam Cassell	1.25	.35
❑ 46 Ray Allen	1.25	.35
❑ 47 Tim Thomas	.75	.23
❑ 48 Kevin Garnett	2.50	.75
❑ 49 Terrell Brandon	.75	.23
❑ 50 Wally Szczerbiak	.75	.23
❑ 51 Keith Van Horn	1.25	.35
❑ 52 Stephon Marbury	1.25	.35
❑ 53 Jamie Feick	.40	.12
❑ 54 Latrell Sprewell	1.25	.35
❑ 55 Marcus Camby	.75	.23
❑ 56 Allan Houston	.75	.23
❑ 57 Grant Hill	1.25	.35
❑ 58 Tracy McGrady	3.00	.90
❑ 59 Darrell Armstrong	.40	.12
❑ 60 Allen Iverson	2.50	.75
❑ 61 Toni Kukoc	.75	.23

❑ 62 Theo Ratliff .75 .23
❑ 63 Anfernee Hardaway 1.25 .35
❑ 64 Jason Kidd 2.00 .60
❑ 65 Shawn Marion 1.25 .35
❑ 66 Steve Smith .75 .23
❑ 67 Rasheed Wallace 1.25 .35
❑ 68 Scottie Pippen 2.00 .60
❑ 69 Bonzi Wells .75 .23
❑ 70 Jason Williams .75 .23
❑ 71 Vlade Divac .75 .23
❑ 72 Chris Webber 1.25 .35
❑ 73 David Robinson 1.25 .35
❑ 74 Sean Elliott .75 .23
❑ 75 Tim Duncan 2.50 .75
❑ 76 Gary Payton 1.25 .35
❑ 77 Rashard Lewis .75 .23
❑ 78 Vin Baker .75 .23
❑ 79 Vince Carter 3.00 .90
❑ 80 Muggsy Bogues .75 .23
❑ 81 Antonio Davis .40 .12
❑ 82 Karl Malone 1.25 .35
❑ 83 John Stockton 1.25 .35
❑ 84 Bryon Russell .40 .12
❑ 85 Shareef Abdur-Rahim 1.25 .35
❑ 86 Michael Dickerson .75 .23
❑ 87 Mike Bibby 1.25 .35
❑ 88 Mitch Richmond .75 .23
❑ 89 Richard Hamilton .75 .23
❑ 90 Juwan Howard .75 .23
❑ 91 Lavor Postell RC 2.00 .60
❑ 92 Mark Madsen JSY RC 10.00 3.00
❑ 93 Soumaila Samake RC 2.00 .60
❑ 94 Michael Redd RC 15.00 4.50
❑ 95 Paul McPherson RC 2.00 .60
❑ 96 Ruben Wolkowyski RC 2.00 .60
❑ 97 Daniel Santiago RC 2.00 .60
❑ 98 Pepe Sanchez RC 2.00 .60
❑ 99 Marc Jackson RC 4.00 1.20
❑ 100 Khalid El-Amin RC 4.00 1.20
❑ 101 Iakovos Tsakalidis RC 4.00 1.20
❑ 102 Jabari Smith RC 4.00 1.20
❑ 103 Jason Hart RC 4.00 1.20
❑ 104 Stephen Jackson RC 5.00 1.50
❑ 105 Eduardo Najera RC 25.00 7.50
❑ 106 Hanno Mottola RC 20.00 6.00
❑ 107 Eddie House RC 20.00 6.00
❑ 108 Dan Langhi RC 20.00 6.00
❑ 109 A.J. Guyton RC 20.00 6.00
❑ 110 Chris Porter RC 20.00 6.00
❑ 111 Mike Miller JSY RC 25.00 7.50
❑ 112 Keyon Dooling JSY RC 10.00 3.00
❑ 113 C.Alexander GJ RC 20.00 6.00
❑ 114 Desmond Mason GJ RC 10.00 3.00
❑ 115 Jamaal Magloire GJ RC 10.00 3.00
❑ 116 DeShawn Stevenson GJ RC 10.00 3.00
❑ 117 Dermarr Johnson JSY RC 10.00 3.00
❑ 117A D.Johnson GJ RC 10.00 3.00
❑ 118 M.Cleaves JSY RC EXCH 10.00 3.00
❑ 119 Morris Peterson JSY RC 25.00 7.50
❑ 120 Jerome Moiso JSY RC 10.00 3.00
❑ 121 Donnell Harvey JSY RC 10.00 3.00
❑ 122 Q.Richardson GJ RC 25.00 7.50
❑ 123 J.Crawford JSY RC 25.00 7.50
❑ 124 Erick Barkley JSY RC 10.00 3.00
❑ 125 Hidayet Turkoglu GJ RC 25.00 7.50
❑ 126 Etan Thomas JSY RC 10.00 3.00
❑ 127 Mamadou N'Diaye GJ RC 10.00 3.00
❑ 128 Joel Przybilla JSY RC 10.00 3.00
❑ 129 Jason Collier JSY RC 10.00 3.00
❑ 130 Speedy Claxton JSY RC 10.00 3.00
❑ 131 Kenyon Martin JSY RC 100.00 30.00
❑ 132 Stromile Swift JSY RC 60.00 18.00
❑ 133 Darius Miles JSY RC 100.00 30.00
❑ 134 Marcus Fizer JSY RC 15.00 4.50
❑ 135 Chris Mihm JSY RC 15.00 4.50
❑ 136 J.Voskuhl JSY RC EXCH 10.00 3.00
❑ 137 P.Mickeal JSY RC EXCH 10.00 3.00
❑ 138 Dalibor Bagaric RC 2.00 .60

2001-02 SPx

	Nm-Mt	Ex-Mt
COMPLETE SET (173)	3,500.00	1,050.00
COMP.SET w/o SP's (90)	60.00	18.00
COMMON CARD (1-90)	.40	.12
COMMON ROOKIE (91-105)	20.00	6.00
COMMON ROOKIE (106-111)	80.00	24.00
COMMON ROOKIE (121-140)	10.00	3.00

❑ 1 Jason Terry 1.25 .35
❑ 2 Shareef Abdur-Rahim 1.25 .35
❑ 3 DerMarr Johnson .75 .23
❑ 4 Paul Pierce 1.25 .35
❑ 5 Antoine Walker 1.25 .35
❑ 6 Kenny Anderson .75 .23
❑ 7 Baron Davis 1.25 .35
❑ 8 Jamal Mashburn .75 .23
❑ 9 David Wesley .40 .12
❑ 10 Ron Mercer .75 .23
❑ 11 Ron Artest .75 .23
❑ 12 Marcus Fizer .75 .23
❑ 13 Andre Miller .75 .23
❑ 14 Lamond Murray .40 .12
❑ 15 Chris Mihm .75 .23
❑ 16 Michael Finley 1.25 .35
❑ 17 Dirk Nowitzki 2.00 .60
❑ 18 Steve Nash 1.25 .35
❑ 19 Antonio McDyess .75 .23
❑ 20 Nick Van Exel 1.25 .35
❑ 21 Raef LaFrentz .75 .23
❑ 22 Jerry Stackhouse 1.25 .35
❑ 23 Chucky Atkins .40 .12
❑ 24 Corliss Williamson .75 .23
❑ 25 Antawn Jamison 1.25 .35
❑ 26 Larry Hughes .75 .23
❑ 27 Chris Porter .75 .23
❑ 28 Steve Francis 1.25 .35
❑ 29 Cuttino Mobley .75 .23
❑ 30 Maurice Taylor .75 .23
❑ 31 Reggie Miller 1.25 .35
❑ 32 Jalen Rose 1.25 .35
❑ 33 Jermaine O'Neal 1.25 .35
❑ 34 Darius Miles 1.25 .35
❑ 35 Elton Brand 1.25 .35
❑ 36 Lamar Odom 1.25 .35
❑ 37 Quentin Richardson .75 .23
❑ 38 Kobe Bryant 5.00 1.50
❑ 39 Shaquille O'Neal 3.00 .90
❑ 40 Rick Fox .75 .23
❑ 41 Derek Fisher 1.25 .35
❑ 42 Stromile Swift .75 .23
❑ 43 Jason Williams .75 .23
❑ 44 Michael Dickerson .75 .23
❑ 45 Alonzo Mourning .75 .23
❑ 46 Eddie Jones 1.25 .35
❑ 47 Anthony Carter .40 .12
❑ 48 Glenn Robinson 1.25 .35
❑ 49 Ray Allen 1.25 .35
❑ 50 Sam Cassell 1.25 .35
❑ 51 Kevin Garnett 2.50 .75
❑ 52 Wally Szczerbiak .75 .23
❑ 53 Terrell Brandon .75 .23
❑ 54 Chauncey Billups .75 .23
❑ 55 Kenyon Martin 1.25 .35
❑ 56 Keith Van Horn 1.25 .35
❑ 57 Jason Kidd 2.00 .60
❑ 58 Latrell Sprewell 1.25 .35
❑ 59 Allan Houston .75 .23
❑ 60 Marcus Camby .75 .23
❑ 61 Tracy McGrady 3.00 .90
❑ 62 Mike Miller 1.25 .35
❑ 63 Grant Hill 1.25 .35
❑ 64 Allen Iverson 2.50 .75
❑ 65 Dikembe Mutombo .75 .23
❑ 66 Aaron McKie .75 .23
❑ 67 Stephon Marbury 1.25 .35
❑ 68 Shawn Marion 1.25 .35
❑ 69 Tom Gugliotta .40 .12
❑ 70 Rasheed Wallace 1.25 .35
❑ 71 Damon Stoudamire .75 .23
❑ 72 Bonzi Wells .75 .23
❑ 73 Chris Webber 1.25 .35
❑ 74 Peja Stojakovic 1.25 .35
❑ 75 Mike Bibby 1.25 .35
❑ 76 Tim Duncan 2.50 .75
❑ 77 David Robinson 1.25 .35
❑ 78 Antonio Daniels .40 .12
❑ 79 Gary Payton 1.25 .35
❑ 80 Rashard Lewis .75 .23
❑ 81 Desmond Mason .75 .23
❑ 82 Vince Carter 3.00 .90
❑ 83 Morris Peterson .75 .23
❑ 84 Antonio Davis .40 .12
❑ 85 Karl Malone 1.25 .35
❑ 86 John Stockton 1.25 .35
❑ 87 Donyell Marshall .75 .23
❑ 88 Richard Hamilton .75 .23
❑ 89 Courtney Alexander .75 .23
❑ 90 Michael Jordan 25.00 7.50
❑ 91A Tony Parker 80.00 24.00
❑ 91B Tony Parker JSY AU RC 80.00 24.00
❑ 91C Tony Parker JSY AU RC 80.00 24.00
❑ 92A J.Tinsley JSY AU RC 40.00 12.00
❑ 92B J.Tinsley JSY AU RC 40.00 12.00
❑ 92C J.Tinsley JSY AU RC 40.00 12.00
❑ 93A S.Dalembert JSY AU RC 20.00 6.00
❑ 93B S.Dalembert JSY AU RC 20.00 6.00
❑ 93C S.Dalembert JSY AU RC 20.00 6.00
❑ 94A G.Wallace JSY AU RC 30.00 9.00
❑ 94B G.Wallace JSY AU RC 30.00 9.00
❑ 94C G.Wallace JSY AU RC 30.00 9.00
❑ 95A B.Armstrong JSY AU RC 25.00 7.50
❑ 95B B.Armstrong JSY AU RC 25.00 7.50
❑ 95C B.Armstrong JSY AU RC 25.00 7.50
❑ 96A Jeryl Sasser JSY AU RC 20.00 6.00
❑ 96B Jeryl Sasser JSY AU RC 20.00 6.00
❑ 96C Jeryl Sasser JSY AU RC 20.00 6.00
❑ 97A Jas.Collins JSY AU RC 20.00 6.00
❑ 97B Jas.Collins JSY AU RC 20.00 6.00
❑ 97C Jas.Collins JSY AU RC 20.00 6.00
❑ 98A M.Bradley JSY AU RC 20.00 6.00
❑ 98B M.Bradley JSY AU RC 20.00 6.00
❑ 98C M.Bradley JSY AU RC 20.00 6.00
❑ 99A S.Hunter JSY AU RC 20.00 6.00
❑ 99B S.Hunter JSY AU RC 20.00 6.00
❑ 99C S.Hunter JSY AU RC 20.00 6.00
❑ 100A T.Murphy JSY AU RC 30.00 9.00
❑ 100B T.Murphy JSY AU RC 30.00 9.00
❑ 100C T.Murphy JSY AU RC 30.00 9.00
❑ 101A R.Jefferson JSY AU RC 60.00 18.00
❑ 101B R.Jefferson JSY AU RC 50.00 15.00
❑ 101C R.Jefferson JSY AU RC 50.00 15.00
❑ 102A V.Radmanov JSY AU RC 25.00 7.50
❑ 102B V.Radmanov JSY AU RC 25.00 7.50
❑ 102C V.Radmanov JSY AU RC 25.00 7.50
❑ 103A Ke.Brown JSY AU RC 20.00 6.00
❑ 103B Ke.Brown JSY AU RC 20.00 6.00
❑ 103C Ke.Brown JSY AU RC 20.00 6.00
❑ 104A J.Johnson JSY AU RC 25.00 7.50
❑ 104B J.Johnson JSY AU RC ERR 25.00 7.50
Photo of Joseph Forte
❑ 104C J.Johnson JSY AU RC 25.00 7.50
❑ 104D J.Johnson JSY AU RC COR
❑ 104E J.Johnson JSY AU RC COR -
❑ 104F J.Johnson JSY AU RC COR -
❑ 105A Kirk Haston JSY AU RC 20.00 6.00
❑ 105B Kirk Haston JSY AU RC 20.00 6.00
❑ 105C Kirk Haston JSY AU RC 20.00 6.00
❑ 106A R.White JSY AU RC 80.00 24.00
❑ 106B R.White JSY AU RC 80.00 24.00
❑ 106C R.White JSY AU RC 80.00 24.00
❑ 107A Eddie Griffin JSY AU RC 80.00 24.00
❑ 107B Eddie Griffin JSY AU RC 80.00 24.00
❑ 107C Eddie Griffin JSY AU RC 80.00 24.00

❑ 108A J.Richardson JSY AU RC 150.00 45.00
❑ 108B J.Richardson JSY AU RC 150.00 45.00
❑ 108C J.Richardson JSY AU RC 150.00 45.00
❑ 109A Eddy Curry JSY AU RC 100.00 30.00
❑ 109B Eddy Curry JSY AU RC 100.00 30.00
❑ 109C Eddy Curry JSY AU RC 100.00 30.00
❑ 110A T.Chandler JSY AU RC 100.00 30.00
❑ 110B T.Chandler JSY AU RC 100.00 30.00
❑ 110C T.Chandler JSY AU RC 100.00 30.00
❑ 111A Kw.Brown JSY AU RC 100.00 30.00
❑ 111B Kw.Brown JSY AU RC 100.00 30.00
❑ 111C Kw.Brown JSY AU RC 100.00 30.00
❑ 121 Shane Battier RC 12.00 3.60
❑ 122 Brendan Haywood RC 12.00 3.60
❑ 123 Joseph Forte RC 12.00 3.60
❑ 124 Zach Randolph RC.... 25.00 7.50
❑ 125 DeSagana Diop RC .. 10.00 3.00
❑ 126 Damone Brown RC .. 10.00 3.00
❑ 127 Andrei Kirilenko RC .. 20.00 6.00
❑ 128 Trenton Hassell RC .. 12.00 3.60
❑ 129 Gilbert Arenas RC 25.00 7.50
❑ 130 Earl Watson RC 10.00 3.00
❑ 131 Kenny Satterfield RC 10.00 3.00
❑ 132 Will Solomon RC 10.00 3.00
❑ 133 Bobby Simmons RC.. 10.00 3.00
❑ 134 Brian Scalabrine RC.. 10.00 3.00
❑ 135 Charlie Bell RC.......... 10.00 3.00
❑ 136 Zeljko Rebraca RC.... 10.00 3.00
❑ 137 Loren Woods RC 10.00 3.00
❑ 138 Terence Morris RC.... 10.00 3.00
❑ 139 Jamison Brewer RC .. 10.00 3.00
❑ 140 Pau Gasol RC 30.00 9.00
❑ NNO Kobe Bryant Promo .. 5.00 1.50

2002-03 SPx

	Nm-Mt	Ex-Mt
COMP.SET w/o SP's (90)	60.00	18.00
COMMON CARD (1-90)	.40	.12
COMMON JSY AU (91-110) ..	25.00	7.50
COM. JSY AU RC (111-	20.00	6.00
COMMON ROOKIE (133-138)	6.00	1.80
COMMON ROOKIE (139-147)	6.00	1.80
COMMON ROOKIE (148-162)	5.00	1.50

❑ 1 Shareef Abdur-Rahim .... 1.25 .35
❑ 2 Jason Terry .... 1.25 .35
❑ 3 Glenn Robinson .... 1.25 .35
❑ 4 Paul Pierce.................... 1.25 .35
❑ 5 Antoine Walker............... 1.25 .35
❑ 6 Kedrick Brown .... .75 .23
❑ 7 Vin Baker .... .75 .23
❑ 8 Jalen Rose .... 1.25 .35
❑ 9 Tyson Chandler .... 1.25 .35
❑ 10 Eddy Curry .... 1.25 .35
❑ 11 Ricky Davis .... .75 .23
❑ 12 Chris Mihm .... .40 .12
❑ 13 Darius Miles .... 1.25 .35
❑ 14 Dirk Nowitzki .... 2.00 .60
❑ 15 Michael Finley .... 1.25 .35
❑ 16 Steve Nash.................... 1.25 .35
❑ 17 Raef LaFrentz .... .75 .23
❑ 18 James Posey .... .40 .12
❑ 19 Juwan Howard .... .75 .23
❑ 20 Richard Hamilton .... .75 .23
❑ 21 Ben Wallace.................. 1.25 .35
❑ 22 Chauncey Billups .... .75 .23
❑ 23 Antawn Jamison........... 1.25 .35
❑ 24 Jason Richardson .... 1.25 .35
❑ 25 Steve Francis .... 1.25 .35
❑ 26 Eddie Griffin .... .75 .23
❑ 27 Cuttino Mobley .... .75 .23
❑ 28 Reggie Miller .... 1.25 .35
❑ 29 Jamaal Tinsley .... 1.25 .35
❑ 30 Jermaine O'Neal.......... 1.25 .35
❑ 31 Elton Brand .... 1.25 .35
❑ 32 Andre Miller .... .75 .23
❑ 33 Lamar Odom .... 1.25 .35
❑ 34 Kobe Bryant 5.00 1.50
❑ 35 Shaquille O'Neal.......... 3.00 .90
❑ 36 Robert Horry.................... .75 .23
❑ 37 Devean George .... .75 .23
❑ 38 Pau Gasol .... 1.25 .35
❑ 39 Shane Battier .... 1.25 .35
❑ 40 Jason Williams .... .75 .23
❑ 41 Alonzo Mourning .... .75 .23
❑ 42 Eddie Jones .... 1.25 .35
❑ 43 Brian Grant...................... .75 .23
❑ 44 Ray Allen .... 1.25 .35
❑ 45 Tim Thomas .... .75 .23
❑ 46 Kevin Garnett .... 2.50 .75
❑ 47 Terrell Brandon .... .75 .23
❑ 48 Wally Szczerbiak .... .75 .23
❑ 49 Jason Kidd .... 2.00 .60
❑ 50 Richard Jefferson........... .75 .23
❑ 51 Kenyon Martin .... 1.25 .35
❑ 52 Baron Davis .... 1.25 .35
❑ 53 Jamal Mashburn............. .75 .23
❑ 54 David Wesley .... .40 .12
❑ 55 P.J. Brown .... .40 .12
❑ 56 Allan Houston.................. .75 .23
❑ 57 Antonio McDyess .... .75 .23
❑ 58 Latrell Sprewell............ 1.25 .35
❑ 59 Tracy McGrady............. 4.00 1.20
❑ 60 Mike Miller .... 1.25 .35
❑ 61 Darrell Armstrong........... .40 .12
❑ 62 Allen Iverson .... 2.50 .75
❑ 63 Keith Van Horn............. 1.25 .35
❑ 64 Stephon Marbury .... 1.25 .35
❑ 65 Shawn Marion .... 1.25 .35
❑ 66 Anfernee Hardaway ..... 1.25 .35
❑ 67 Rasheed Wallace......... 1.25 .35
❑ 68 Damon Stoudamire .... .75 .23
❑ 69 Scottie Pippen .... 2.00 .60
❑ 70 Chris Webber .... 1.25 .35
❑ 71 Mike Bibby .... 1.25 .35
❑ 72 Peja Stojakovic............ 1.25 .35
❑ 73 Hidayet Turkoglu .... 1.25 .35
❑ 74 Tim Duncan .... 3.00 .90
❑ 75 David Robinson .... 1.25 .35
❑ 76 Tony Parker .... 1.25 .35
❑ 77 Steve Smith .... .75 .23
❑ 78 Gary Payton .... 1.25 .35
❑ 79 Rashard Lewis .... .75 .23
❑ 80 Brent Barry...................... .75 .23
❑ 81 Desmond Mason .... .75 .23
❑ 82 Vince Carter 4.00 1.20
❑ 83 Morris Peterson .... .75 .23
❑ 84 Antonio Davis.................. .40 .12
❑ 85 Karl Malone .... 1.25 .35
❑ 86 John Stockton .... 1.25 .35
❑ 87 Andrei Kirilenko .... 1.25 .35
❑ 88 Jerry Stackhouse .... 1.25 .35
❑ 89 Michael Jordan........... 10.00 3.00
❑ 90 Kwame Brown .... .75 .23
❑ 91 J.Richardson JSY AU.... 1.25 .35
❑ 92 Tyson Chandler JSY AU 25.00 7.50
❑ 93 Kenyon Martin JSY AU 50.00 15.00
❑ 94 G.Wallace JSY AU SP 25.00 7.50
❑ 95 K.Abdul-Jbbr JSY AU SP 200.00 60.00
❑ 96 Mo.Peterson JSY AU SP 25.00 7.50
❑ 97 Andre Miller JSY AU .. 25.00 7.50
❑ 98 Q.Richardson JSY AU 25.00 7.50
❑ 99 Mike Miller JSY AU 25.00 7.50
❑ 100 J.O'Neal JSY AU SP 50.00 15.00
❑ 101 Marcus Fizer JSY AU 25.00 7.50
❑ 102 Mike Bibby JSY AU 100.00 30.00
❑ 103 C.Billups JSY AU SP .. - -
❑ 104 Lamar Odom JSY AU SP 50.00 15.00
❑ 105 Antoine Walker JSY AU 50.00 15.00
❑ 106 Paul Pierce JSY AU .. 60.00 18.00
❑ 107 Jason Kidd JSY AU SP 80.00 24.00
❑ 108 K.Garnett JSY AU SP .. - -
❑ 109 K.Bryant JSY AU SP.... - -
❑ 110 M.Jordan JSY AU SP .. - -
❑ 111 Chris Jefferies JSY AU RC 20.00 6.00
❑ 112 John Salmons JSY AU RC 20.00 6.00
❑ 113 T.Prince JSY AU RC 30.00 9.00
❑ 114 C.Jacobsen JSY AU RC 20.00 6.00
❑ 115 Qyntel Woods JSY AU RC 25.00 7.50
❑ 116 Kareem Rush JSY AU RC 30.00 9.00
❑ 117 R.Humphrey JSY AU RC 20.00 6.00
❑ 118 Carlos Boozer JSY AU RC 60.00 18.00
❑ 119 Sam Clancy JSY AU RC 20.00 6.00
❑ 120 Fred Jones JSY AU RC 25.00 7.50
❑ 121 Marcus Haislip JSY AU RC 20.00 6.00
❑ 122 Melvin Ely JSY AU RC 20.00 6.00
❑ 123 Jared Jeffries JSY AU RC 25.00 7.50
❑ 124 Dan Gadzuric JSY AU RC 20.00 6.00
❑ 125 A.Stoudemire JSY AU RC 150.00 45.00
❑ 126 Caron Butler JSY AU RC 60.00 18.00
❑ 127 Nene Hilario JSY AU RC 50.00 15.00
❑ 128 D.Wagner JSY AU RC 50.00 15.00
❑ 129 N.Tskitishvili JSY AU RC 25.00 7.50
❑ 130 Drew Gooden JSY AU RC 60.00 18.00
❑ 131 Jay Williams JSY AU RC 40.00 12.00
❑ 132 Yao Ming JSY AU RC 250.00 75.00
❑ 133 Mike Dunleavy RC 12.00 3.60
❑ 134 Frank Williams RC 6.00 1.80
❑ 135 Jiri Welsch RC 6.00 1.80
❑ 136 Dan Dickau RC 6.00 1.80
❑ 137 Efthimios Rentzias RC 6.00 1.80
❑ 138 Chris Wilcox RC 10.00 3.00
❑ 139 Curtis Borchardt RC 6.00 1.80
❑ 140 Predrag Savovic RC.... 6.00 1.80
❑ 141 Tito Maddox RC 6.00 1.80
❑ 142 Roger Mason RC 6.00 1.80
❑ 143 Juan Dixon RC 6.00 1.80
❑ 144 Pat Burke RC 6.00 1.80
❑ 145 Marko Jaric RC 6.00 1.80
❑ 146 Gordan Giricek RC...... 8.00 2.40
❑ 147 Juaquin Hawkins RC .. 6.00 1.80
❑ 148 Vincent Yarbrough RC 5.00 1.50
❑ 149 Robert Archibald RC .. 5.00 1.50
❑ 150 Bostjan Nachbar RC .. 5.00 1.50
❑ 151 Jamal Sampson RC 5.00 1.50
❑ 152 Lonny Baxter RC 5.00 1.50
❑ 153 J.R. Bremer RC 5.00 1.50
❑ 154 Cezary Trybanski RC .. 5.00 1.50
❑ 155 Manu Ginobili RC 12.00 3.60
❑ 156 Raul Lopez RC............ 5.00 1.50
❑ 157 Rasual Butler RC 5.00 1.50
❑ 158 Tamar Slay RC............ 5.00 1.50
❑ 159 Ronald Murray RC 20.00 6.00
❑ 160 Igor Rakocevic RC 5.00 1.50
❑ 161 Reggie Evans RC........ 5.00 1.50
❑ 162 Jannero Pargo RC 5.00 1.50

2003-04 SPx

	MINT	NRMT
COMP.SET w/o SP's (90)	60.00	27.00
COMMON SPXCCL (91-	3.00	1.35
COMMON ROOKIE (133-150)	8.00	3.60
COMMON JSY AU RC (151-156)	40.00	18.00
COMMON JSY AU RC (163-185)	20.00	9.00
COMMON JSY AU (186-206)	30.00	13.50
SOME UNPRICED DUE TO SCARCITY		-

❑ 1 Shareef Abdur-Rahim .... 1.25 .55
❑ 2 Jason Terry .... 1.25 .55
❑ 3 Theo Ratliff.................... .75 .35
❑ 4 Paul Pierce.................. 1.25 .55
❑ 5 Raef LaFrentz .... .75 .35
❑ 6 Vin Baker .... .75 .35
❑ 7 Jalen Rose .... 1.25 .55

❑ 8 Tyson Chandler 1.25 .55
❑ 9 Michael Jordan 8.00 3.60
❑ 10 Dajuan Wagner .75 .35
❑ 11 Darius Miles 1.25 .55
❑ 12 Carlos Boozer 1.25 .55
❑ 13 Dirk Nowitzki 2.00 .90
❑ 14 Antoine Walker 1.25 .55
❑ 15 Steve Nash 1.25 .55
❑ 16 Nene .75 .35
❑ 17 Marcus Camby .75 .35
❑ 18 Andre Miller .75 .35
❑ 19 Richard Hamilton .75 .35
❑ 20 Ben Wallace 1.25 .55
❑ 21 Chauncey Billups .75 .35
❑ 22 Nick Van Exel 1.25 .55
❑ 23 Jason Richardson 1.25 .55
❑ 24 Speedy Claxton .40 .18
❑ 25 Steve Francis 1.25 .55
❑ 26 Yao Ming 3.00 1.35
❑ 27 Cuttino Mobley .75 .35
❑ 28 Reggie Miller 1.25 .55
❑ 29 Jamaal Tinsley 1.25 .55
❑ 30 Jermaine O'Neal 1.25 .55
❑ 31 Elton Brand 1.25 .55
❑ 32 Corey Maggette .75 .35
❑ 33 Quentin Richardson .75 .35
❑ 34 Kobe Bryant 5.00 2.20
❑ 35 Karl Malone 1.25 .55
❑ 36 Shaquille O'Neal 3.00 1.35
❑ 37 Gary Payton 1.25 .55
❑ 38 Pau Gasol 1.25 .55
❑ 39 Shane Battier 1.25 .55
❑ 40 Mike Miller 1.25 .55
❑ 41 Eddie Jones 1.25 .55
❑ 42 Lamar Odom 1.25 .55
❑ 43 Caron Butler 1.25 .55
❑ 44 Michael Redd 1.25 .55
❑ 45 Joe Smith .75 .35
❑ 46 Desmond Mason .75 .35
❑ 47 Kevin Garnett 2.50 1.10
❑ 48 Latrell Sprewell 1.25 .55
❑ 49 Michael Olowokandi .40 .18
❑ 50 Jason Kidd 2.00 .90
❑ 51 Richard Jefferson .75 .35
❑ 52 Kenyon Martin 1.25 .55
❑ 53 Baron Davis 1.25 .55
❑ 54 Jamal Mashburn .75 .35
❑ 55 David Wesley .40 .18
❑ 56 Allan Houston .75 .35
❑ 57 Antonio McDyess .75 .35
❑ 58 Keith Van Horn 1.25 .55
❑ 59 Tracy McGrady 3.00 1.35
❑ 60 Grant Hill 1.25 .55
❑ 61 Drew Gooden .75 .35
❑ 62 Juwan Howard .75 .35
❑ 63 Allen Iverson 2.50 1.10
❑ 64 Glenn Robinson 1.25 .55
❑ 65 Eric Snow .75 .35
❑ 66 Stephon Marbury 1.25 .55
❑ 67 Shawn Marion 1.25 .55
❑ 68 Amare Stoudemire 2.50 1.10
❑ 69 Rasheed Wallace 1.25 .55
❑ 70 Bonzi Wells .75 .35
❑ 71 Damon Stoudamire .75 .35
❑ 72 Chris Webber 1.25 .55
❑ 73 Mike Bibby 1.25 .55
❑ 74 Peja Stojakovic 1.25 .55
❑ 75 Brad Miller 1.25 .55
❑ 76 Tim Duncan 2.50 1.10
❑ 77 Tony Parker 1.25 .55
❑ 78 Manu Ginobili 1.25 .55
❑ 79 Ray Allen 1.25 .55
❑ 80 Rashard Lewis 1.25 .55
❑ 81 Vladimir Radmanovic .40 .18
❑ 82 Vince Carter 3.00 1.35
❑ 83 Morris Peterson .75 .35
❑ 84 Antonio Davis .40 .18
❑ 85 Raul Lopez .40 .18
❑ 86 Matt Harpring 1.25 .55
❑ 87 Andrei Kirilenko 1.25 .55
❑ 88 Jerry Stackhouse 1.25 .55
❑ 89 Gilbert Arenas 1.25 .55
❑ 90 Larry Hughes .75 .35
❑ 91 Allen Iverson 5.00 2.20
❑ 92 Dirk Nowitzki 4.00 1.80
❑ 93 Kobe Bryant 10.00 4.50
❑ 94 Michael Jordan 15.00 6.75
❑ 95 Vince Carter 6.00 2.70
❑ 96 Shaquille O'Neal 6.00 2.70
❑ 97 Yao Ming 6.00 2.70
❑ 98 Amare Stoudemire 5.00 2.20
❑ 99 Paul Pierce 3.00 1.35
❑ 100 Jason Richardson 3.00 1.35
❑ 101 Steve Francis 1.25 .55
❑ 102 Jermaine O'Neal 3.00 1.35
❑ 103 Karl Malone 3.00 1.35
❑ 104 Tracy McGrady 6.00 2.70
❑ 105 Stephon Marbury 3.00 1.35
❑ 106 Chris Webber 3.00 1.35
❑ 107 Tim Duncan 5.00 2.20
❑ 108 Ray Allen 3.00 1.35
❑ 109 Antoine Walker 3.00 1.35
❑ 110 Steve Nash 3.00 1.35
❑ 111 Elton Brand 3.00 1.35
❑ 112 Rashard Lewis 3.00 1.35
❑ 113 Jerry Stackhouse 3.00 1.35
❑ 114 Shawn Marion 3.00 1.35
❑ 115 Mike Bibby 3.00 1.35
❑ 116 Tony Parker 3.00 1.35
❑ 117 Michael Finley 3.00 1.35
❑ 118 Allan Houston 3.00 1.35
❑ 119 Richard Hamilton 3.00 1.35
❑ 120 Ben Wallace 3.00 1.35
❑ 121 Reggie Miller 3.00 1.35
❑ 122 Richard Jefferson 3.00 1.35
❑ 123 Glenn Robinson 3.00 1.35
❑ 124 Rasheed Wallace 3.00 1.35
❑ 125 Gilbert Arenas 3.00 1.35
❑ 126 Jason Kidd 4.00 1.80
❑ 127 Latrell Sprewell 3.00 1.35
❑ 128 Kevin Garnett 5.00 2.20
❑ 129 Caron Butler 3.00 1.35
❑ 130 Pau Gasol 3.00 1.35
❑ 131 Alonzo Mourning 3.00 1.35
❑ 132 Gary Payton 3.00 1.35
❑ 133 Kirk Hinrich RC 12.00 5.50
❑ 134 T.J. Ford RC 10.00 4.50
❑ 135 Nick Collison RC 8.00 3.60
❑ 136 Keith McLeod RC 8.00 3.60
❑ 137 Jon Stefansson RC 8.00 3.60
❑ 138 Britton Johnsen RC 8.00 3.60
❑ 139 Matt Carroll RC 8.00 3.60
❑ 140 Linton Johnson RC 8.00 3.60
❑ 141 Francisco Elson RC 8.00 3.60
❑ 142 Willie Green RC 8.00 3.60
❑ 143 Kyle Korver RC 10.00 4.50
❑ 144 Theron Smith RC 8.00 3.60
❑ 145 Brandon Hunter RC 8.00 3.60
❑ 146 Josh Moore RC 8.00 3.60
❑ 147 Marquis Daniels RC 15.00 6.75
❑ 148 James Lang RC 8.00 3.60
❑ 149 Udonis Haslem RC 8.00 3.60
❑ 150 Alex Garcia RC 8.00 3.60
❑ 151 L.James JSY AU RC 800.00 350.00
❑ 152 D.Milicic JSY AU RC 80.00 36.00
❑ 153 C.Anthony JSY AU RC 400.00 180.00
❑ 154 Chris Bosh JSY AU RC 100.00 45.00
❑ 155 D.Wade JSY AU RC 120.00 55.00
❑ 156 Chris Kaman JSY AU RC 40.00 18.00
❑ 157 Jarvis Hayes JSY AU RC 40.00 18.00
❑ 158 M.Pietrus JSY AU RC 25.00 11.00
❑ 159 D.Jones JSY AU RC 25.00 11.00
❑ 160 M.Banks JSY AU RC 25.00 11.00
❑ 161 Luke Ridnour JSY AU RC 40.00 18.00
❑ 162 R.Gaines JSY AU RC 20.00 9.00
❑ 163 Troy Bell JSY AU RC 20.00 9.00
❑ 164 M.Sweetney JSY AU RC 20.00 9.00
❑ 165 David West JSY AU RC 20.00 9.00
❑ 166 A.Pavlovic JSY AU RC 20.00 9.00
❑ 167 M.Williams JSY AU RC 20.00 9.00
❑ 168 Boris Diaw JSY AU RC 20.00 9.00
❑ 169 Z.Planinic JSY AU RC 20.00 9.00
❑ 170 Travis Outlaw JSY AU RC 20.00 9.00
❑ 171 Brian Cook JSY AU RC 20.00 9.00
❑ 172 J.Beasley JSY AU RC 20.00 9.00
❑ 173 Ndudi Ebi JSY AU RC 20.00 9.00
❑ 174 K.Perkins JSY AU RC 20.00 9.00
❑ 175 L.Barbosa JSY AU RC 20.00 9.00
❑ 176 J.Howard JSY AU RC 25.00 11.00
❑ 177 Maciej Lampe JSY AU RC 20.00 9.00
❑ 178 J.Kapono JSY AU RC 20.00 9.00
❑ 179 Luke Walton JSY AU RC 30.00 13.50
❑ 180 S.Vranes JSY AU RC 20.00 9.00
❑ 181 Z.Cabarkapa JSY AU RC 20.00 9.00
❑ 182 T.Hansen JSY AU RC 20.00 9.00
❑ 183 Steve Blake JSY AU RC 20.00 9.00
❑ 184 Zaur Pachulia JSY AU RC 20.00 9.00
❑ 185 Keith Bogans JSY AU RC 20.00 9.00
❑ 186 M.Jordan JSY AU/23 -
❑ 187 Kobe Bryant JSY AU/25 -
❑ 188 K.Garnett JSY AU/150 120.00 55.00
❑ 189 R.Jefferson JSY AU/215 30.00 13.50
❑ 190 G.Arenas JSY AU/215 30.00 13.50
❑ 191 A.Jamison JSY AU/215 30.00 13.50
❑ 192 T.McGrady JSY AU/50 160.00 70.00
❑ 193 S.Francis JSY AU/100 50.00 22.00
❑ 194 Ming JSY AU/100 EXCH 80.00 36.00
❑ 195 A.Stoudemire JSY AU/215 60.00 27.00
❑ 196 Abdur-Rahim JSY AU/342 30.00 13.50
❑ 197 Shane Battier JSY AU/280 30.00 13.50
❑ 198 Tony Parker JSY AU/200 30.00 13.50
❑ 199 Andre Miller JSY AU/215 30.00 13.50
❑ 200 Shawn Marion JSY AU/265 30.00 13.50
❑ 201 R.Hamilton JSY AU/215 30.00 13.50
❑ 202 Lamar Odom JSY AU/215 30.00 13.50
❑ 203 J.Stackhouse JSY AU/215 30.00 13.50
❑ 204 A.McDyess JSY AU/230 -
❑ 205 Manu Ginobili JSY AU/215 40.00 18.00
❑ 206 Drew Gooden JSY AU/215 30.00 13.50

1992-93 Stadium Club

	Nm-Mt	Ex-Mt
COMPLETE SET (400)	50.00	15.00
COMPLETE SERIES 1 (200)	20.00	6.00
COMPLETE SERIES 2 (200)	30.00	9.00

❑ 1 Michael Jordan 8.00 2.40
❑ 2 Greg Anthony .10 .03
❑ 3 Otis Thorpe .30 .09
❑ 4 Jim Les .10 .03
❑ 5 Kevin Willis .10 .03
❑ 6 Derek Harper .30 .09
❑ 7 Elden Campbell .30 .09
❑ 8 A.J. English .10 .03
❑ 9 Kenny Gattison .10 .03
❑ 10 Drazen Petrovic .10 .03
❑ 11 Chris Mullin .60 .18
❑ 12 Mark Price .10 .03
❑ 13 Karl Malone 1.00 .30
❑ 14 Gerald Glass .10 .03
❑ 15 Negele Knight .10 .03
❑ 16 Mark Macon .10 .03
❑ 17 Michael Cage .10 .03
❑ 18 Kevin Edwards .10 .03
❑ 19 Sherman Douglas .10 .03
❑ 20 Ron Harper .30 .09
❑ 21 Clifford Robinson .30 .09
❑ 22 Byron Scott .30 .09
❑ 23 Antoine Carr .10 .03
❑ 24 Greg Dreiling .10 .03
❑ 25 Bill Laimbeer .30 .09
❑ 26 Hersey Hawkins .30 .09
❑ 27 Will Perdue .10 .03
❑ 28 Todd Lichti .10 .03
❑ 29 Gary Grant .10 .03
❑ 30 Sam Perkins .30 .09
❑ 31 Jayson Williams .30 .09
❑ 32 Magic Johnson 2.00 .60
❑ 33 Larry Bird 2.50 .75
❑ 34 Chris Morris .10 .03

❑ 35 Nick Anderson .30 .09
❑ 36 Scott Hastings .10 .03
❑ 37 Ledell Eackles .10 .03
❑ 38 Robert Pack .10 .03
❑ 39 Dana Barros .10 .03
❑ 40 Anthony Bonner .10 .03
❑ 41 J.R. Reid .10 .03
❑ 42 Tyrone Hill .10 .03
❑ 43 Rik Smits .30 .09
❑ 44 Kevin Duckworth .10 .03
❑ 45 LaSalle Thompson .10 .03
❑ 46 Brian Williams .10 .03
❑ 47 Willie Anderson .10 .03
❑ 48 Ken Norman .10 .03
❑ 49 Mike Iuzzolino .10 .03
❑ 50 Isiah Thomas .60 .18
❑ 51 Alec Kessler .10 .03
❑ 52 Johnny Dawkins .10 .03
❑ 53 Avery Johnson .10 .03
❑ 54 Stacey Augmon .30 .09
❑ 55 Charles Oakley .30 .09
❑ 56 Rex Chapman .10 .03
❑ 57 Charles Shackleford .10 .03
❑ 58 Jeff Ruland .10 .03
❑ 59 Craig Ehlo .10 .03
❑ 60 Jon Koncak .10 .03
❑ 61 Danny Schayes .10 .03
❑ 62 David Benoit .10 .03
❑ 63 Robert Parish .30 .09
❑ 64 Mookie Blaylock .30 .09
❑ 65 Sean Elliott .30 .09
❑ 66 Mark Aguirre .10 .03
❑ 67 Scott Williams .10 .03
❑ 68 Doug West .10 .03
❑ 69 Kenny Anderson .60 .18
❑ 70 Randy Brown .10 .03
❑ 71 Muggsy Bogues .30 .09
❑ 72 Spud Webb .30 .09
❑ 73 Sedale Threatt .10 .03
❑ 74 Chris Gatling .10 .03
❑ 75 Derrick McKey .10 .03
❑ 76 Sleepy Floyd .10 .03
❑ 77 Chris Jackson .10 .03
❑ 78 Thurl Bailey .10 .03
❑ 79 Steve Smith .75 .23
❑ 80 Jerrod Mustaf .10 .03
❑ 81 Anthony Bowie .10 .03
❑ 82 John Williams .10 .03
❑ 83 Paul Graham .10 .03
❑ 84 Willie Burton .10 .03
❑ 85 Vernon Maxwell .10 .03
❑ 86 Stacey King .10 .03
❑ 87 B.J. Armstrong .10 .03
❑ 88 Kevin Gamble .10 .03
❑ 89 Terry Catledge .10 .03
❑ 90 Jeff Malone .10 .03
❑ 91 Sam Bowie .10 .03
❑ 92 Orlando Woolridge .10 .03
❑ 93 Steve Kerr .30 .09
❑ 94 Eric Leckner .10 .03
❑ 95 Loy Vaught .10 .03
❑ 96 Jud Buechler .10 .03
❑ 97 Doug Smith .10 .03
❑ 98 Sidney Green .10 .03
❑ 99 Jerome Kersey .10 .03
❑ 100 Patrick Ewing .60 .18
❑ 101 Ed Nealy .10 .03
❑ 102 Shawn Kemp 1.25 .35
❑ 103 Luc Longley .30 .09
❑ 104 George McCloud .10 .03
❑ 105 Ron Anderson .10 .03
❑ 106 Moses Malone UER .60 .18
(Rookie Card is 1975-76, not 1976-77)
❑ 107 Tony Smith .10 .03
❑ 108 Terry Porter .10 .03
❑ 109 Blair Rasmussen .10 .03
❑ 110 Bimbo Coles .10 .03
❑ 111 Grant Long .10 .03
❑ 112 John Battle .10 .03
❑ 113 Brian Oliver .10 .03
❑ 114 Tyrone Corbin .10 .03
❑ 115 Benoit Benjamin .10 .03
❑ 116 Rick Fox .30 .09
❑ 117 Rafael Addison .10 .03
❑ 118 Danny Young .10 .03
❑ 119 Fat Lever .10 .03
❑ 120 Terry Cummings .30 .09
❑ 121 Felton Spencer .10 .03
❑ 122 Joe Kleine .10 .03
❑ 123 Johnny Newman .10 .03
❑ 124 Gary Payton 1.25 .35
❑ 125 Kurt Rambis .10 .03
❑ 126 Vlade Divac .30 .09
❑ 127 John Paxson .10 .03
❑ 128 Lionel Simmons .10 .03
❑ 129 Randy Wittman .10 .03
❑ 130 Winston Garland .10 .03
❑ 131 Jerry Reynolds .10 .03
❑ 132 Dell Curry .10 .03
❑ 133 Fred Roberts .10 .03
❑ 134 Michael Adams .10 .03
❑ 135 Charles Jones .10 .03
❑ 136 Frank Brickowski .10 .03
❑ 137 Alton Lister .10 .03
❑ 138 Horace Grant .30 .09
❑ 139 Greg Sutton .10 .03
❑ 140 John Starks .30 .09
❑ 141 Detlef Schrempf .30 .09
❑ 142 Rodney Monroe .10 .03
❑ 143 Pete Chilcutt .10 .03
❑ 144 Mike Brown .10 .03
❑ 145 Rony Seikaly .10 .03
❑ 146 Donald Hodge .10 .03
❑ 147 Kevin McHale .60 .18
❑ 148 Ricky Pierce .10 .03
❑ 149 Brian Shaw .10 .03
❑ 150 Reggie Williams .10 .03
❑ 151 Kendall Gill .30 .09
❑ 152 Tom Chambers .10 .03
❑ 153 Jack Haley .10 .03
❑ 154 Terrell Brandon .60 .18
❑ 155 Dennis Scott .30 .09
❑ 156 Mark Randall .10 .03
❑ 157 Kenny Payne .10 .03
❑ 158 Bernard King .10 .03
❑ 159 Tate George .10 .03
❑ 160 Scott Skiles .10 .03
❑ 161 Pervis Ellison .10 .03
❑ 162 Marcus Liberty .10 .03
❑ 163 Rumeal Robinson .10 .03
❑ 164 Anthony Mason .60 .18
❑ 165 Les Jepsen .10 .03
❑ 166 Kenny Smith .10 .03
❑ 167 Randy White .10 .03
❑ 168 Dee Brown .10 .03
❑ 169 Chris Dudley .10 .03
❑ 170 Armon Gilliam .10 .03
❑ 171 Eddie Johnson .10 .03
❑ 172 A.C. Green .30 .09
❑ 173 Darrell Walker .10 .03
❑ 174 Bill Cartwright .10 .03
❑ 175 Mike Gminski .10 .03
❑ 176 Tom Tolbert .10 .03
❑ 177 Buck Williams .30 .09
❑ 178 Mark Eaton .10 .03
❑ 179 Danny Manning .30 .09
❑ 180 Glen Rice .60 .18
❑ 181 Sarunas Marciulionis .10 .03
❑ 182 Danny Ferry .10 .03
❑ 183 Chris Corchiani .10 .03
❑ 184 Dan Majerle .30 .09
❑ 185 Alvin Robertson .10 .03
❑ 186 Vern Fleming .10 .03
❑ 187 Kevin Lynch .10 .03
❑ 188 John Williams .10 .03
❑ 189 Checklist 1-100 .10 .03
❑ 190 Checklist 101-200 .10 .03
❑ 191 David Robinson MC .60 .18
❑ 192 Larry Johnson MC .60 .18
❑ 193 Derrick Coleman MC .10 .03
❑ 194 Larry Bird MC 1.25 .35
❑ 195 Billy Owens MC .10 .03
❑ 196 Dikembe Mutombo MC .60 .18
❑ 197 Charles Barkley MC .60 .18
❑ 198 Scottie Pippen MC 1.00 .30
❑ 199 Clyde Drexler MC .30 .09
❑ 200 John Stockton MC .30 .09
❑ 201 Shaquille O'Neal MC 8.00 2.40
❑ 202 Chris Mullin MC .30 .09
❑ 203 Glen Rice MC .30 .09
❑ 204 Isiah Thomas MC .30 .09
❑ 205 Karl Malone MC .60 .18
❑ 206 Christian Laettner MC .60 .18
❑ 207 Patrick Ewing MC .30 .09
❑ 208 Dominique Wilkins MC .30 .09
❑ 209 Alonzo Mourning MC 1.25 .35
❑ 210 Michael Jordan MC 4.00 1.20
❑ 211 Tim Hardaway .75 .23
❑ 212 Rodney McCray .10 .03
❑ 213 Larry Johnson .75 .23
❑ 214 Charles Smith .10 .03
❑ 215 Kevin Brooks .10 .03
❑ 216 Kevin Johnson .60 .18
❑ 217 Duane Cooper RC .10 .03
❑ 218 C.Laettner RC UER 1.25 .35
(Missing '92 Draft Pick logo)
❑ 219 Tim Perry .10 .03
❑ 220 Hakeem Olajuwon 1.00 .30
❑ 221 Lee Mayberry RC .10 .03
❑ 222 Mark Bryant .10 .03
❑ 223 Robert Horry RC .60 .18
❑ 224 Tracy Murray RC UER .30 .09
(Missing '92 Draft Pick logo)
❑ 225 Greg Grant .10 .03
❑ 226 Rolando Blackman .10 .03
❑ 227 James Edwards UER .10 .03
(Rookie Card is 1978-79, not 1980-81)
❑ 228 Sean Green .10 .03
❑ 229 Buck Johnson .10 .03
❑ 230 Andrew Lang .10 .03
❑ 231 Tracy Moore RC .10 .03
❑ 232 Adam Keefe RC UER .10 .03
(Missing '92 Draft Pick logo)
❑ 233 Tony Campbell .10 .03
❑ 234 Rod Strickland .60 .18
❑ 235 Terry Mills .10 .03
❑ 236 Billy Owens .30 .09
❑ 237 Bryant Stith RC UER .30 .09
(Missing '92 Draft Pick logo)
❑ 238 Tony Bennett RC UER .10 .03
(Missing '92 Draft Pick logo)
❑ 239 David Wood .10 .03
❑ 240 Jay Humphries .10 .03
❑ 241 Doc Rivers .30 .09
❑ 242 Wayman Tisdale .10 .03
❑ 243 Litterial Green RC .10 .03
❑ 244 Jon Barry .30 .09
❑ 245 Brad Daugherty .10 .03
❑ 246 Nate McMillan .10 .03
❑ 247 Shaquille O'Neal RC 15.00 4.50
❑ 248 Chris Smith RC .10 .03
❑ 249 Duane Ferrell .10 .03
❑ 250 Anthony Peeler RC .30 .09
❑ 251 Gundars Vetra RC .10 .03
❑ 252 Danny Ainge .30 .09
❑ 253 Mitch Richmond .60 .18
❑ 254 Malik Sealy RC .30 .09
❑ 255 Brent Price RC .30 .09
❑ 256 Xavier McDaniel .10 .03
❑ 257 Bobby Phills RC .60 .18
❑ 258 Donald Royal .10 .03
❑ 259 Olden Polynice .10 .03
❑ 260 Dominique Wilkins UER .60 .18
(Scoring 10,000th point&

should be 20,000th)
❑ 261 Larry Krystkowiak .10 .03
❑ 262 Duane Causwell .10 .03
❑ 263 Todd Day RC .30 .09
❑ 264 Sam Mack RC .30 .09
❑ 265 John Stockton .60 .18
❑ 266 Eddie Lee Wilkins .10 .03
❑ 267 Gerald Glass .10 .03
❑ 268 Robert Pack .10 .03
❑ 269 Gerald Wilkins .10 .03
❑ 270 Reggie Lewis .30 .09
❑ 271 Scott Brooks .10 .03
❑ 272 Randy Woods RC UER .10 .03
(Missing '92 Draft
Pick logo)
❑ 273 Dikembe Mutombo .75 .23
❑ 274 Kiki Vandeweghe .10 .03
❑ 275 Rich King .10 .03
❑ 276 Jeff Turner .10 .03
❑ 277 Vinny Del Negro .10 .03
❑ 278 Marlon Maxey RC .10 .03
❑ 279 Elmore Spencer RC UER .10 .03
(Missing '92 Draft
Pick logo)
❑ 280 Cedric Ceballos .30 .09
❑ 281 Alex Blackwell RC .10 .03
❑ 282 Terry Davis .10 .03
❑ 283 Morlon Wiley .10 .03
❑ 284 Trent Tucker .10 .03
❑ 285 Carl Herrera .10 .03
❑ 286 Eric Anderson RC .10 .03
❑ 287 Clyde Drexler .60 .18
❑ 288 Tom Gugliotta RC 2.00 .60
❑ 289 Dale Ellis .10 .03
❑ 290 Lance Blanks .10 .03
❑ 291 Tom Hammonds .10 .03
❑ 292 Eric Murdock .10 .03
❑ 293 Walt Williams RC .60 .18
❑ 294 Gerald Paddio .10 .03
❑ 295 Brian Howard RC .10 .03
❑ 296 Ken Williams .10 .03
❑ 297 Alonzo Mourning RC 4.00 1.20
❑ 298 Larry Nance .10 .03
❑ 299 Jeff Grayer .10 .03
❑ 300 Dave Johnson RC .10 .03
❑ 301 Bob McCann RC .10 .03
❑ 302 Bart Kofoed .10 .03
❑ 303 Anthony Cook .10 .03
❑ 304 Radisav Curcic RC .10 .03
❑ 305 John Crotty RC .10 .03
❑ 306 Brad Sellers .10 .03
❑ 307 Marcus Webb RC .10 .03
❑ 308 Winston Garland .10 .03
❑ 309 Walter Palmer .10 .03
❑ 310 Rod Higgins .10 .03
❑ 311 Travis Mays .10 .03
❑ 312 Alex Stivrins RC .10 .03
❑ 313 Greg Kite .10 .03
❑ 314 Dennis Rodman 1.25 .35
❑ 315 Mike Sanders .10 .03
❑ 316 Ed Pinckney .10 .03
❑ 317 Harold Miner RC .30 .09
❑ 318 Pooh Richardson .10 .03
❑ 319 Oliver Miller RC .30 .09
❑ 320 Latrell Sprewell RC 5.00 1.50
❑ 321 Anthony Pullard RC .10 .03
❑ 322 Mark Randall .10 .03
❑ 323 Jeff Hornacek .30 .09
❑ 324 Rick Mahorn UER .10 .03
(Rookie Card is 1981-82,
not 1992-93)
❑ 325 Sean Rooks RC .10 .03
❑ 326 Paul Pressey .10 .03
❑ 327 James Worthy .60 .18
❑ 328 Matt Bullard .10 .03
❑ 329 Reggie Smith RC .10 .03
❑ 330 Don MacLean RC UER .10 .03
(Missing '92 Draft
Pick logo)
❑ 331 John Williams UER .10 .03
(Rookie Card erroneously
shows Hot Rod)
❑ 332 Frank Johnson .10 .03
❑ 333 Hubert Davis RC UER .30 .09
(Missing '92 Draft
Pick logo)
❑ 334 Lloyd Daniels RC .10 .03
❑ 335 Steve Bardo RC .10 .03
❑ 336 Jeff Sanders .10 .03
❑ 337 Tree Rollins .10 .03
❑ 338 Micheal Williams .10 .03
❑ 339 Lorenzo Williams RC .10 .03
❑ 340 Harvey Grant .10 .03
❑ 341 Avery Johnson .10 .03
❑ 342 Bo Kimble .10 .03
❑ 343 LaPhonso Ellis RC UER .60 .18
(Missing '92 Draft
Pick logo)
❑ 344 Mookie Blaylock .30 .09
❑ 345 Isaiah Morris RC UER .10 .03
(Missing '92 Draft
Pick logo)
❑ 346 C.Weatherspoon RC .60 .18
❑ 347 Manute Bol .10 .03
❑ 348 Victor Alexander .10 .03
❑ 349 Corey Williams RC .10 .03
❑ 350 Byron Houston RC .10 .03
❑ 351 Stanley Roberts .10 .03
❑ 352 Anthony Avent RC .10 .03
❑ 353 Vincent Askew .10 .03
❑ 354 Herb Williams .10 .03
❑ 355 J.R. Reid .10 .03
❑ 356 Brad Lohaus .10 .03
❑ 357 Reggie Miller .60 .18
❑ 358 Blue Edwards .10 .03
❑ 359 Tom Tolbert .10 .03
❑ 360 Charles Barkley 1.00 .30
❑ 361 David Robinson 1.00 .30
❑ 362 Dale Davis .10 .03
❑ 363 Robert Werdann RC UER .10 .03
(Missing '92 Draft
Pick logo)
❑ 364 Chuck Person .10 .03
❑ 365 Alaa Abdelnaby .10 .03
❑ 366 Dave Jamerson .10 .03
❑ 367 Scottie Pippen 2.00 .60
❑ 368 Mark Jackson .30 .09
❑ 369 Keith Askins .10 .03
❑ 370 Marty Conlon .10 .03
❑ 371 Chucky Brown .10 .03
❑ 372 LaBradford Smith .10 .03
❑ 373 Tim Kempton .10 .03
❑ 374 Sam Mitchell .10 .03
❑ 375 John Salley .10 .03
❑ 376 Mario Elie .30 .09
❑ 377 Mark West .10 .03
❑ 378 David Wingate .10 .03
❑ 379 Jaren Jackson RC .30 .09
❑ 380 Rumeal Robinson .10 .03
❑ 381 Kennard Winchester .10 .03
❑ 382 Walter Bond RC .10 .03
❑ 383 Isaac Austin RC .30 .09
❑ 384 Derrick Coleman .30 .09
❑ 385 Larry Smith .10 .03
❑ 386 Joe Dumars .60 .18
❑ 387 Matt Geiger RC UER .30 .09
(Missing '92 Draft
Pick logo)
❑ 388 Stephen Howard RC .10 .03
❑ 389 William Bedford .10 .03
❑ 390 Jayson Williams .30 .09
❑ 391 Kurt Rambis .10 .03
❑ 392 Keith Jennings RC .10 .03
❑ 393 Steve Kerr UER .30 .09
(The words key stat
are repeated on back)
❑ 394 Larry Stewart .10 .03
❑ 395 Danny Young .10 .03
❑ 396 Doug Overton .10 .03
❑ 397 Mark Acres .10 .03
❑ 398 John Bagley .10 .03
❑ 399 Checklist 201-300 .10 .03
❑ 400 Checklist 301-400 .10 .03

1993-94 Stadium Club

	Nm-Mt	Ex-Mt
COMPLETE SET (360)	40.00	12.00
COMPLETE SERIES 1 (180)	20.00	6.00
COMPLETE SERIES 2 (180)	20.00	6.00
COMMON CARD (1-180)	.10	.03
COMMON CARD (181-360)	.05	.02

❑ 1 Michael Jordan TD 2.50 .75
❑ 2 Kenny Anderson TD .10 .03
❑ 3 Steve Smith TD .20 .06
❑ 4 Kevin Gamble TD .10 .03
❑ 5 Detlef Schrempf TD .10 .03
❑ 6 Larry Johnson TD .20 .06
❑ 7 Brad Daugherty TD .10 .03
❑ 8 Rumeal Robinson TD .10 .03
❑ 9 Micheal Williams TD .10 .03
❑ 10 David Robinson TD .40 .12
❑ 11 Sam Perkins TD .10 .03
❑ 12 Thurl Bailey .10 .03
❑ 13 Sherman Douglas .10 .03
❑ 14 Larry Stewart .10 .03
❑ 15 Kevin Johnson .20 .06
❑ 16 Bill Cartwright .10 .03
❑ 17 Larry Nance .10 .03
❑ 18 P.J. Brown RC .40 .12
❑ 19 Tony Bennett .10 .03
❑ 20 Robert Parish .20 .06
❑ 21 David Benoit .10 .03
❑ 22 Detlef Schrempf .20 .06
❑ 23 Hubert Davis .10 .03
❑ 24 Donald Hodge .10 .03
❑ 25 Hersey Hawkins .20 .06
❑ 26 Mark Jackson .20 .06
❑ 27 Reggie Williams .10 .03
❑ 28 Lionel Simmons .10 .03
❑ 29 Ron Harper .20 .06
❑ 30 Chris Mills RC .40 .12
❑ 31 Danny Schayes .10 .03
❑ 32 J.R. Reid .10 .03
❑ 33 Willie Burton .10 .03
❑ 34 Greg Anthony .10 .03
❑ 35 Elden Campbell .10 .03
❑ 36 Ervin Johnson RC .20 .06
❑ 37 Scott Brooks .10 .03
❑ 38 Johnny Newman .10 .03
❑ 39 Rex Chapman .10 .03
❑ 40 Chuck Person .10 .03
❑ 41 John Williams .10 .03
❑ 42 Anthony Bowie .10 .03
❑ 43 Negele Knight .10 .03
❑ 44 Tyrone Corbin .10 .03
❑ 45 Jud Buechler .10 .03
❑ 46 Adam Keefe .10 .03
❑ 47 Glen Rice .20 .06
❑ 48 Tracy Murray .10 .03
❑ 49 Rick Mahorn .10 .03

Card		
❑ 50 Vlade Divac	.20	.06
❑ 51 Eric Murdock	.10	.03
❑ 52 Isaiah Morris	.10	.03
❑ 53 Bobby Hurley RC	.20	.06
❑ 54 Mitch Richmond	.40	.12
❑ 55 Danny Ainge	.20	.06
❑ 56 Dikembe Mutombo	.40	.12
❑ 57 Jeff Hornacek	.20	.06
❑ 58 Tony Campbell	.10	.03
❑ 59 Vinny Del Negro	.10	.03
❑ 60 Xavier McDaniel HC	.10	.03
❑ 61 Scottie Pippen HC	.60	.18
❑ 62 Larry Nance HC	.10	.03
❑ 63 Dikembe Mutombo HC	.20	.06
❑ 64 Hakeem Olajuwon HC	.40	.12
❑ 65 Dominique Wilkins HC	.20	.06
❑ 66 C.Weatherspoon HC	.10	.03
❑ 67 Chris Morris HC	.10	.03
❑ 68 Patrick Ewing HC	.20	.06
❑ 69 Kevin Willis HC	.10	.03
❑ 70 Jon Barry	.10	.03
❑ 71 Jerry Reynolds	.10	.03
❑ 72 Sarunas Marciulionis	.10	.03
❑ 73 Mark West	.10	.03
❑ 74 B.J. Armstrong	.10	.03
❑ 75 Greg Kite	.10	.03
❑ 76 LaSalle Thompson	.10	.03
❑ 77 Randy White	.10	.03
❑ 78 Alaa Abdelnaby	.10	.03
❑ 79 Kevin Brooks	.10	.03
❑ 80 Vern Fleming	.10	.03
❑ 81 Doc Rivers	.20	.06
❑ 82 Shawn Bradley RC	.40	.12
❑ 83 Wayman Tisdale	.10	.03
❑ 84 Olden Polynice	.10	.03
❑ 85 Michael Cage	.10	.03
❑ 86 Harold Miner	.10	.03
❑ 87 Doug Smith	.10	.03
❑ 88 Tom Gugliotta	.40	.12
❑ 89 Hakeem Olajuwon	.60	.18
❑ 90 Loy Vaught	.10	.03
❑ 91 James Worthy	.40	.12
❑ 92 John Paxson	.10	.03
❑ 93 Jon Koncak	.10	.03
❑ 94 Lee Mayberry	.10	.03
❑ 95 Clarence Weatherspoon	.10	.03
❑ 96 Mark Eaton	.10	.03
❑ 97 Rex Walters RC	.10	.03
❑ 98 Alvin Robertson	.10	.03
❑ 99 Dan Majerle	.20	.06
❑ 100 Shaquille O'Neal	2.00	.60
❑ 101 Derrick Coleman TD	.10	.03
❑ 102 Hersey Hawkins TD	.10	.03
❑ 103 Scottie Pippen TD	.60	.18
❑ 104 Scott Skiles TD	.10	.03
❑ 105 Rod Strickland TD	.10	.03
❑ 106 Pooh Richardson TD	.10	.03
❑ 107 Tom Gugliotta TD	.20	.06
❑ 108 Mark Jackson TD	.10	.03
❑ 109 Dikembe Mutombo TD	.20	.06
❑ 110 Charles Barkley TD	.40	.12
❑ 111 Otis Thorpe TD	.10	.03
❑ 112 Malik Sealy	.10	.03
❑ 113 Mark Macon	.10	.03
❑ 114 Dee Brown	.10	.03
❑ 115 Nate McMillan	.10	.03
❑ 116 John Starks	.20	.06
❑ 117 Clyde Drexler	.40	.12
❑ 118 Antoine Carr	.10	.03
❑ 119 Doug West	.10	.03
❑ 120 Victor Alexander	.10	.03
❑ 121 Kenny Gattison	.10	.03
❑ 122 Spud Webb	.20	.06
❑ 123 Rumeal Robinson	.10	.03
❑ 124 Tim Kempton	.10	.03
❑ 125 Karl Malone	.60	.18
❑ 126 Randy Woods	.10	.03
❑ 127 Calbert Cheaney RC	.20	.06
❑ 128 Johnny Dawkins	.10	.03
❑ 129 Dominique Wilkins	.40	.12
❑ 130 Horace Grant	.20	.06
❑ 131 Bill Laimbeer	.10	.03
❑ 132 Kenny Smith	.10	.03
❑ 133 Sedale Threatt	.10	.03
❑ 134 Brian Shaw	.10	.03
❑ 135 Dennis Scott	.10	.03
❑ 136 Mark Bryant	.10	.03
❑ 137 Xavier McDaniel	.10	.03
❑ 138 David Wood	.10	.03
❑ 139 Luther Wright RC	.10	.03
❑ 140 Lloyd Daniels	.10	.03
❑ 141 Marlon Maxey UER	.10	.03
(Name spelled Maxley on the front)		
❑ 142 Pooh Richardson	.10	.03
❑ 143 Jeff Grayer	.10	.03
❑ 144 LaPhonso Ellis	.10	.03
❑ 145 Gerald Wilkins	.10	.03
❑ 146 Dell Curry	.10	.03
❑ 147 Duane Causwell	.10	.03
❑ 148 Tim Hardaway	.40	.12
❑ 149 Isiah Thomas	.40	.12
❑ 150 Doug Edwards RC	.10	.03
❑ 151 Anthony Peeler	.10	.03
❑ 152 Tate George	.10	.03
❑ 153 Terry Davis	.10	.03
❑ 154 Sam Perkins	.20	.06
❑ 155 John Salley	.10	.03
❑ 156 Vernon Maxwell	.10	.03
❑ 157 Anthony Avent	.10	.03
❑ 158 Clifford Robinson	.20	.06
❑ 159 Corie Blount RC	.10	.03
❑ 160 Gerald Paddio	.10	.03
❑ 161 Blair Rasmussen	.10	.03
❑ 162 Carl Herrera	.10	.03
❑ 163 Chris Smith	.10	.03
❑ 164 Pervis Ellison	.10	.03
❑ 165 Rod Strickland	.20	.06
❑ 166 Jeff Malone	.10	.03
❑ 167 Danny Ferry	.10	.03
❑ 168 Kevin Lynch	.10	.03
❑ 169 Michael Jordan	5.00	1.50
❑ 170 Derrick Coleman HC	.10	.03
❑ 171 Jerome Kersey HC	.10	.03
❑ 172 David Robinson HC	.40	.12
❑ 173 Shawn Kemp HC	.40	.12
❑ 174 Karl Malone HC	.40	.12
❑ 175 Shaquille O'Neal HC	.75	.23
❑ 176 Alonzo Mourning HC	.40	.12
❑ 177 Charles Barkley HC	.40	.12
❑ 178 Larry Johnson HC	.20	.06
❑ 179 Checklist 1-90	.10	.03
❑ 180 Checklist 91-180	.10	.03
❑ 181 Michael Jordan FF	2.00	.60
❑ 182 Dominique Wilkins FF	.15	.04
❑ 183 Dennis Rodman FF	.30	.09
❑ 184 Scottie Pippen FF	.50	.15
❑ 185 Larry Johnson FF	.20	.06
❑ 186 Karl Malone FF	.30	.09
❑ 187 C.Weatherspoon FF	.05	.02
❑ 188 Charles Barkley FF	.30	.09
❑ 189 Patrick Ewing FF	.20	.06
❑ 190 Derrick Coleman FF	.05	.02
❑ 191 LaBradford Smith	.05	.02
❑ 192 Derek Harper	.15	.04
❑ 193 Ken Norman	.05	.02
❑ 194 Rodney Rogers RC	.30	.09
❑ 195 Chris Dudley	.05	.02
❑ 196 Gary Payton	.50	.15
❑ 197 Andrew Lang	.05	.02
❑ 198 Billy Owens	.05	.02
❑ 199 Bryon Russell RC	.30	.09
❑ 200 Patrick Ewing	.30	.09
❑ 201 Stacey King	.05	.02
❑ 202 Grant Long	.05	.02
❑ 203 Sean Elliott	.15	.04
❑ 204 Muggsy Bogues	.15	.04
❑ 205 Kevin Edwards	.05	.02
❑ 206 Dale Davis	.05	.02
❑ 207 Dale Ellis	.05	.02
❑ 208 Terrell Brandon	.15	.04
❑ 209 Kevin Gamble	.05	.02
❑ 210 Robert Horry	.15	.04
❑ 211 Moses Malone UER	.40	.12
Birthdate on back is 1993		
❑ 212 Gary Grant	.05	.02
❑ 213 Bobby Hurley	.15	.04
❑ 214 Larry Krystkowiak	.05	.02
❑ 215 A.C. Green	.15	.04
❑ 216 Christian Laettner	.15	.04
❑ 217 Orlando Woolridge	.05	.02
❑ 218 Craig Ehlo	.05	.02
❑ 219 Terry Porter	.05	.02
❑ 220 Jamal Mashburn RC	1.00	.30
❑ 221 Kevin Duckworth	.05	.02
❑ 222 Shawn Kemp	.50	.15
❑ 223 Frank Brickowski	.05	.02
❑ 224 Chris Webber RC	3.00	.90
❑ 225 Charles Oakley	.15	.04
❑ 226 Jay Humphries	.05	.02
❑ 227 Steve Kerr	.15	.04
❑ 228 Tim Perry	.05	.02
❑ 229 Sleepy Floyd	.05	.02
❑ 230 Bimbo Coles	.05	.02
❑ 231 Eddie Johnson	.05	.02
❑ 232 Terry Mills	.05	.02
❑ 233 Danny Manning	.15	.04
❑ 234 Isaiah Rider RC	.75	.23
❑ 235 Darnell Mee RC	.05	.02
❑ 236 Haywoode Workman	.05	.02
❑ 237 Scott Skiles	.05	.02
❑ 238 Otis Thorpe	.15	.04
❑ 239 Mike Peplowski RC	.05	.02
❑ 240 Eric Leckner	.05	.02
❑ 241 Johnny Newman	.05	.02
❑ 242 Benoit Benjamin	.05	.02
❑ 243 Doug Christie	.15	.04
❑ 244 Acie Earl RC	.05	.02
❑ 245 Luc Longley	.15	.04
❑ 246 Tyrone Hill	.05	.02
❑ 247 Allan Houston RC	1.25	.35
❑ 248 Joe Kleine	.05	.02
❑ 249 Mookie Blaylock	.15	.04
❑ 250 Anthony Bonner	.05	.02
❑ 251 Luther Wright	.05	.02
❑ 252 Todd Day	.05	.02
❑ 253 Kendall Gill	.15	.04
❑ 254 Mario Elie	.05	.02
❑ 255 Pete Myers UER	.05	.02
Card has born in 1993		
❑ 256 Jim Les	.05	.02
❑ 257 Stanley Roberts	.05	.02
❑ 258 Michael Adams	.05	.02
❑ 259 Hersey Hawkins	.15	.04
❑ 260 Shawn Bradley	.20	.06
❑ 261 Scott Haskin RC	.05	.02
❑ 262 Corie Blount	.05	.02
❑ 263 Charles Smith	.05	.02
❑ 264 Armon Gilliam	.05	.02
❑ 265 Jamal Mashburn NW	.30	.09
❑ 266 Anfernee Hardaway NW	1.25	.35
❑ 267 Shawn Bradley NW	.20	.06
❑ 268 Chris Webber NW	1.50	.45
❑ 269 Bobby Hurley NW	.05	.02
❑ 270 Isaiah Rider NW	.30	.09
❑ 271 Dino Radja NW	.05	.02
❑ 272 Chris Mills NW	.15	.04
❑ 273 Nick Van Exel NW	.30	.09
❑ 274 Lindsey Hunter NW	.20	.06
❑ 275 Toni Kukoc NW	.30	.09
❑ 276 Popeye Jones NW	.05	.02
❑ 277 Chris Mills	.40	.12
❑ 278 Ricky Pierce	.05	.02
❑ 279 Negele Knight	.05	.02
❑ 280 Kenny Walker	.05	.02
❑ 281 Nick Van Exel RC	1.00	.30
❑ 282 Derrick Coleman UER	.15	.04

(Career stats listed under '92-93)

Card	Nm-Mt	Ex-Mt
❑ 283 Popeye Jones RC	.05	.02
❑ 284 Derrick McKey	.05	.02
❑ 285 Rick Fox	.05	.02
❑ 286 Jerome Kersey	.05	.02
❑ 287 Steve Smith	.30	.09
❑ 288 Brian Williams	.05	.02
❑ 289 Chris Mullin	.30	.09
❑ 290 Terry Cummings	.05	.02
❑ 291 Donald Royal	.05	.02
❑ 292 Alonzo Mourning	.50	.15
❑ 293 Mike Brown	.05	.02
❑ 294 Latrell Sprewell	.75	.23
❑ 295 Oliver Miller	.05	.02
❑ 296 Terry Dehere RC	.05	.02
❑ 297 Detlef Schrempf	.15	.04
❑ 298 Sam Bowie UER	.05	.02
(Last name Bowe on front)		
❑ 299 Chris Morris	.05	.02
❑ 300 Scottie Pippen	1.00	.30
❑ 301 Warren Kidd RC	.05	.02
❑ 302 Don MacLean	.05	.02
❑ 303 Sean Rooks	.05	.02
❑ 304 Matt Geiger	.05	.02
❑ 305 Dennis Rodman	.60	.18
❑ 306 Reggie Miller	.30	.09
❑ 307 Vin Baker RC	.75	.23
❑ 308 Anfernee Hardaway RC	2.50	.75
❑ 309 Lindsey Hunter RC	.30	.09
❑ 310 Stacey Augmon	.05	.02
❑ 311 Randy Brown	.05	.02
❑ 312 Anthony Mason	.15	.04
❑ 313 John Stockton	.30	.09
❑ 314 Sam Cassell RC	1.25	.35
❑ 315 Buck Williams	.05	.02
❑ 316 Bryant Stith	.05	.02
❑ 317 Brad Daugherty	.05	.02
❑ 318 Dino Radja RC	.05	.02
❑ 319 Rony Seikaly	.05	.02
❑ 320 Charles Barkley	.60	.18
❑ 321 Avery Johnson	.05	.02
❑ 322 Mahmoud Abdul-Rauf	.05	.02
❑ 323 Larry Johnson	.30	.09
❑ 324 Micheal Williams	.05	.02
❑ 325 Mark Aguirre	.05	.02
❑ 326 Jim Jackson	.15	.04
❑ 327 Antonio Harvey RC	.05	.02
❑ 328 David Robinson	.50	.15
❑ 329 Calbert Cheaney	.10	.03
❑ 330 Kenny Anderson	.20	.06
❑ 331 Walt Williams	.10	.03
❑ 332 Kevin Willis	.05	.02
❑ 333 Nick Anderson	.15	.04
❑ 334 Rik Smits	.15	.04
❑ 335 Joe Dumars	.40	.12
❑ 336 Toni Kukoc RC	1.25	.35
❑ 337 Harvey Grant	.05	.02
❑ 338 Tom Chambers	.05	.02
❑ 339 Blue Edwards	.05	.02
❑ 340 Mark Price	.05	.02
❑ 341 Ervin Johnson	.15	.04
❑ 342 Rolando Blackman	.05	.02
❑ 343 Scott Burrell RC	.30	.09
❑ 344 Gheorghe Muresan RC	.30	.09
❑ 345 Chris Corchiani UER 336	.05	.02
❑ 346 Richard Petruska RC	.05	.02
❑ 347 Dana Barros	.05	.02
❑ 348 Hakeem Olajuwon FF	.30	.09
❑ 349 Dee Brown FF	.05	.02
❑ 350 John Starks FF	.05	.02
❑ 351 Ron Harper FF	.05	.02
❑ 352 Chris Webber FF	1.50	.45
❑ 353 Dan Majerle FF	.05	.02
❑ 354 Clyde Drexler FF	.15	.04
❑ 355 Shawn Kemp FF	.30	.09
❑ 356 David Robinson FF	.30	.09
❑ 357 Chris Morris FF	.05	.02
❑ 358 Shaquille O'Neal FF	.60	.18
❑ 359 Checklist	.05	.02
❑ 360 Checklist	.05	.02

1994-95 Stadium Club

	Nm-Mt	Ex-Mt
COMPLETE SET (362)	40.00	12.00
COMPLETE SERIES 1 (182)	20.00	6.00
COMPLETE SERIES 2 (180)	20.00	6.00
❑ 1 Patrick Ewing	.40	.12
❑ 2 Patrick Ewing TTG	.15	.04
❑ 3 Bimbo Coles	.10	.03
❑ 4 Elden Campbell	.10	.03
❑ 5 Brent Price	.10	.03
❑ 6 Hubert Davis	.10	.03
❑ 7 Donald Royal	.10	.03
❑ 8 Tim Perry	.10	.03
❑ 9 Chris Webber	1.00	.30
❑ 10 Chris Webber TTG	.50	.15
❑ 11 Brad Daugherty	.10	.03
❑ 12 P.J. Brown	.10	.03
❑ 13 Charles Barkley	.60	.18
❑ 14 Mario Elie	.10	.03
❑ 15 Tyrone Hill	.10	.03
❑ 16 Anfernee Hardaway	1.00	.30
❑ 17 Anfernee Hardaway TTG	.50	.15
❑ 18 Toni Kukoc	.60	.18
❑ 19 Chris Morris	.10	.03
❑ 20 Gerald Wilkins	.10	.03
❑ 21 David Benoit	.10	.03
❑ 22 Kevin Duckworth	.10	.03
❑ 23 Derrick Coleman	.15	.04
❑ 24 Adam Keefe	.10	.03
❑ 25 Marlon Maxey	.10	.03
❑ 26 Vern Fleming	.10	.03
❑ 27 Jeff Malone	.10	.03
❑ 28 Rodney Rogers	.10	.03
❑ 29 Terry Mills	.10	.03
❑ 30 Doug West	.10	.03
❑ 31 Doug West TTG	.10	.03
❑ 32 Shaquille O'Neal	2.00	.60
❑ 33 Scottie Pippen	1.25	.35
❑ 34 Lee Mayberry	.10	.03
❑ 35 Dale Ellis	.10	.03
❑ 36 Cedric Ceballos	.10	.03
❑ 37 Lionel Simmons	.10	.03
❑ 38 Kenny Gattison	.10	.03
❑ 39 Popeye Jones	.10	.03
❑ 40 Jerome Kersey	.10	.03
❑ 41 Jerome Kersey TTG	.10	.03
❑ 42 Larry Stewart	.10	.03
❑ 43 Rod Strickland	.15	.04
❑ 44 Chris Mills	.15	.04
❑ 45 Latrell Sprewell	.40	.12
❑ 46 Haywoode Workman	.10	.03
❑ 47 Charles Smith	.10	.03
❑ 48 Detlef Schrempf	.15	.04
❑ 49 Gary Grant	.10	.03
❑ 50 Gary Grant TTG	.10	.03
❑ 51 Tom Chambers	.10	.03
❑ 52 J.R. Reid	.10	.03
❑ 53 Mookie Blaylock	.10	.03
❑ 54 Mookie Blaylock TTG	.10	.03
❑ 55 Rony Seikaly	.10	.03
❑ 56 Isaiah Rider	.15	.04
❑ 57 Isaiah Rider TTG	.10	.03
❑ 58 Nick Anderson	.10	.03
❑ 59 Victor Alexander	.10	.03
❑ 60 Lucious Harris	.10	.03
❑ 61 Mark Macon	.10	.03
❑ 62 Otis Thorpe	.10	.03
❑ 63 Randy Woods	.10	.03
❑ 64 Clyde Drexler	.40	.12
❑ 65 Dikembe Mutombo	.15	.04
❑ 66 Todd Day	.10	.03
❑ 67 Greg Anthony	.10	.03
❑ 68 Sherman Douglas	.10	.03
❑ 69 Chris Mullin	.40	.12
❑ 70 Kevin Johnson	.15	.04
❑ 71 Kendall Gill	.15	.04
❑ 72 Dennis Rodman	.75	.23
❑ 73 Dennis Rodman TG	.40	.12
❑ 74 Jeff Turner	.10	.03
❑ 75 John Stockton	.40	.12
❑ 76 John Stockton TTG	.15	.04
❑ 77 Doug Edwards	.10	.03
❑ 78 Jim Jackson	.15	.04
❑ 79 Hakeem Olajuwon	.60	.18
❑ 80 Glen Rice	.15	.04
❑ 81 Christian Laettner	.15	.04
❑ 82 Terry Porter	.10	.03
❑ 83 Joe Dumars	.40	.12
❑ 84 David Wingate	.10	.03
❑ 85 B.J. Armstrong	.10	.03
❑ 86 Derrick McKey	.10	.03
❑ 87 Elmore Spencer	.10	.03
❑ 88 Walt Williams	.10	.03
❑ 89 Shawn Bradley	.10	.03
❑ 90 Acie Earl	.10	.03
❑ 91 Acie Earl TTG	.10	.03
❑ 92 Randy Brown	.10	.03
❑ 93 Grant Long	.10	.03
❑ 94 Terry Dehere	.10	.03
❑ 95 Spud Webb	.10	.03
❑ 96 Lindsey Hunter	.15	.04
❑ 97 Blair Rasmussen	.10	.03
❑ 98 Tim Hardaway	.40	.12
❑ 99 Kevin Edwards	.10	.03
❑ 100 Patrick Ewing CT	.15	.04
Reggie Williams CT		
❑ 101 Chuck Person CT	.40	.12
Charles Barkley CT		
❑ 102 Mahmoud Abdul-Rauf CT	.40	.12
Shaquille O'Neal CT		
❑ 103 Rony Seikaly CT	.10	.03
Derrick Coleman CT		
❑ 104 Hakeem Olajuwon CT	.40	.12
Clyde Drexler CT		
❑ 105 Chris Mullin CT	.15	.04
Mark Jackson CT		
❑ 106 Robert Horry CT	.40	.12
Latrell Sprewell CT		
❑ 107 Pooh Richardson CT	.15	.04
Reggie Miller CT		
❑ 108 Dennis Scott CT	.10	.03
Kenny Anderson CT		
❑ 109 Kendall Gill CT	.10	.03
Ken Norman CT		
❑ 110 Scott Skiles CT	.10	.03
Kevin Willis CT		
❑ 111 Terry Mills CT	.15	.04
Glen Rice CT		
❑ 112 Christian Laettner CT	.10	.03
Bobby Hurley CT		
❑ 113 Stacey Augmon CT	.10	.03
Larry Johnson CT		
❑ 114 Sam Perkins CT	.15	.04
James Worthy CT		
❑ 115 Carl Herrera	.10	.03
❑ 116 Sam Bowie	.10	.03
❑ 117 Gary Payton	.60	.18
❑ 118 Danny Ainge	.10	.03

❑ 119 Danny Ainge TTG .10 .03
❑ 120 Luc Longley .10 .03
❑ 121 Antonio Davis .10 .03
❑ 122 Terry Cummings .10 .03
❑ 123 Terry Cummings TTG .10 .03
❑ 124 Mark Price .10 .03
❑ 125 Jamal Mashburn .40 .12
❑ 126 Mahmoud Abdul-Rauf .10 .03
❑ 127 Charles Oakley .10 .03
❑ 128 Steve Smith .15 .04
❑ 129 Vin Baker .40 .12
❑ 130 Robert Horry .15 .04
❑ 131 Doug Christie .15 .04
❑ 132 Wayman Tisdale .10 .03
❑ 133 Wayman Tisdale TTG .10 .03
❑ 134 Muggsy Bogues .15 .04
❑ 135 Dino Radja .10 .03
❑ 136 Jeff Hornacek .15 .04
❑ 137 Gheorghe Muresan .10 .03
❑ 138 Loy Vaught .10 .03
❑ 139 Loy Vaught TTG .10 .03
❑ 140 Benoit Benjamin .10 .03
❑ 141 Johnny Dawkins .10 .03
❑ 142 Allan Houston .60 .18
❑ 143 Jon Barry .10 .03
❑ 144 Reggie Miller .40 .12
❑ 145 Kevin Willis .10 .03
❑ 146 James Worthy .40 .12
❑ 147 James Worthy TTG .15 .04
❑ 148 Scott Burrell .10 .03
❑ 149 Tom Gugliotta .15 .04
❑ 150 LaPhonso Ellis .10 .03
❑ 151 Doug Smith .10 .03
❑ 152 A.C. Green .15 .04
❑ 153 A.C. Green TTG .10 .03
❑ 154 George Lynch .10 .03
❑ 155 Sam Perkins .15 .04
❑ 156 Corie Blount .10 .03
❑ 157 Xavier McDaniel .10 .03
❑ 158 Xavier McDaniel TTG .10 .03
❑ 159 Eric Murdock .10 .03
❑ 160 David Robinson .60 .18
❑ 161 Karl Malone .60 .18
❑ 162 Karl Malone TTG .40 .12
❑ 163 Clarence Weatherspoon .10 .03
❑ 164 Calbert Cheaney .10 .03
❑ 165 Tom Hammonds .10 .03
❑ 166 Tom Hammonds TTG .10 .03
❑ 167 Alonzo Mourning .50 .15
❑ 168 Clifford Robinson .15 .04
❑ 169 Micheal Williams .10 .03
❑ 170 Ervin Johnson .10 .03
❑ 171 Mike Gminski .10 .03
❑ 172 Jason Kidd RC 4.00 1.20
❑ 173 Anthony Bonner .10 .03
❑ 174 Stacey King .10 .03
❑ 175 Rex Chapman .10 .03
❑ 176 Greg Graham .10 .03
❑ 177 Stanley Roberts .10 .03
❑ 178 Mitch Richmond .40 .12
❑ 179 Eric Montross RC .10 .03
❑ 180 Eddie Jones RC 2.00 .60
❑ 181 Grant Hill RC 2.00 .60
❑ 182 Donyell Marshall RC .40 .12
❑ 183 Glenn Robinson RC 1.25 .35
❑ 184 Dominique Wilkins .40 .12
❑ 185 Mark Price .10 .03
❑ 186 Anthony Mason .15 .04
❑ 187 Tyrone Corbin .10 .03
❑ 188 Dale Davis .10 .03
❑ 189 Nate McMillan .10 .03
❑ 190 Jason Kidd 2.00 .60
❑ 191 John Salley .10 .03
❑ 192 Keith Jennings .10 .03
❑ 193 Mark Bryant .10 .03
❑ 194 Sleepy Floyd .10 .03
❑ 195 Grant Hill 1.00 .30
❑ 196 Joe Kleine .10 .03
❑ 197 Anthony Peeler .10 .03
❑ 198 Malik Sealy .10 .03
❑ 199 Kenny Walker .10 .03
❑ 200 Donyell Marshall .40 .12
❑ 201 Vlade Divac AI .10 .03
❑ 202 Dino Radja AI .10 .03
❑ 203 Carl Herrera AI .10 .03
❑ 204 Olden Polynice AI .10 .03
❑ 205 Patrick Ewing AI .15 .04
❑ 206 Willie Anderson .10 .03
❑ 207 Mitch Richmond .40 .12
❑ 208 John Crotty .10 .03
❑ 209 Tracy Murray .10 .03
❑ 210 Juwan Howard RC 1.00 .30
❑ 211 Robert Parish .15 .04
❑ 212 Steve Kerr .10 .03
❑ 213 Anthony Bowie .10 .03
❑ 214 Tim Breaux .10 .03
❑ 215 Sharone Wright RC .10 .03
❑ 216 Brian Williams .10 .03
❑ 217 Rick Fox .10 .03
❑ 218 Harold Miner .10 .03
❑ 219 Duane Ferrell .10 .03
❑ 220 Lamond Murray RC .15 .04
❑ 221 Blue Edwards .10 .03
❑ 222 Bill Cartwright .10 .03
❑ 223 Sergei Bazarevich .10 .03
❑ 224 Herb Williams .10 .03
❑ 225 Brian Grant RC 1.00 .30
❑ 226 Derek Harper BCT .10 .03
John Starks
❑ 227 Rod Strickland BCT .40 .12
Clyde Drexler
❑ 228 Kevin Johnson BCT .10 .03
Dan Majerle
❑ 229 Lindsey Hunter BCT .10 .03
Joe Dumars
❑ 230 Tim Hardaway BCT .15 .04
Latrell Sprewell
❑ 231 Bill Wennington .10 .03
❑ 232 Brian Shaw .10 .03
❑ 233 Jamie Watson RC .10 .03
❑ 234 Chris Whitney .10 .03
❑ 235 Eric Montross .10 .03
❑ 236 Kenny Smith .10 .03
❑ 237 Andrew Lang .10 .03
❑ 238 Lorenzo Williams .10 .03
❑ 239 Dana Barros .10 .03
❑ 240 Eddie Jones 1.00 .30
❑ 241 Harold Ellis .10 .03
❑ 242 James Edwards .10 .03
❑ 243 Don MacLean .10 .03
❑ 244 Ed Pinckney .10 .03
❑ 245 Carlos Rogers RC .10 .03
❑ 246 Michael Adams .10 .03
❑ 247 Rex Walters .10 .03
❑ 248 John Starks .10 .03
❑ 249 Terrell Brandon .15 .04
❑ 250 Khalid Reeves RC .10 .03
❑ 251 Dominique Wilkins AI .15 .04
❑ 252 Toni Kukoc AI .40 .12
❑ 253 Rick Fox AI .10 .03
❑ 254 Detlef Schrempf AI .10 .03
❑ 255 Rik Smits AI .10 .03
❑ 256 Johnny Dawkins .10 .03
❑ 257 Dan Majerle .15 .04
❑ 258 Mike Brown .10 .03
❑ 259 Byron Scott .15 .04
❑ 260 Jalen Rose RC 1.50 .45
❑ 261 Byron Houston .10 .03
❑ 262 Frank Brickowski .10 .03
❑ 263 Vernon Maxwell .10 .03
❑ 264 Craig Ehlo .10 .03
❑ 265 Yinka Dare RC .10 .03
❑ 266 Dee Brown .10 .03
❑ 267 Felton Spencer .10 .03
❑ 268 Harvey Grant .10 .03
❑ 269 Nick Van Exel .40 .12
❑ 270 Bob Martin .10 .03
❑ 271 Hersey Hawkins .15 .04
❑ 272 Scott Williams .10 .03
❑ 273 Sarunas Marciulionis .10 .03
❑ 274 Kevin Gamble .10 .03
❑ 275 Clifford Rozier RC .10 .03
❑ 276 B.J. Armstrong BCT .10 .03
Ron Harper
❑ 277 John Stockton BCT .15 .04
Jeff Hornacek
❑ 278 Bobby Hurley BCT .15 .04
Mitch Richmond
❑ 279 Anfernee Hardaway BCT .30 .09
Dennis Scott
❑ 280 Jason Kidd BCT .40 .12
Jim Jackson
❑ 281 Ron Harper .15 .04
❑ 282 Chuck Person .10 .03
❑ 283 John Williams .10 .03
❑ 284 Robert Pack .10 .03
❑ 285 Aaron McKie RC .75 .23
❑ 286 Chris Smith .10 .03
❑ 287 Horace Grant .15 .04
❑ 288 Oliver Miller .10 .03
❑ 289 Derek Harper .10 .03
❑ 290 Eric Mobley RC .10 .03
❑ 291 Scott Skiles .10 .03
❑ 292 Olden Polynice .10 .03
❑ 293 Mark Jackson .10 .03
❑ 294 Wayman Tisdale .10 .03
❑ 295 Tony Dumas RC .10 .03
❑ 296 Bryon Russell .10 .03
❑ 297 Vlade Divac .10 .03
❑ 298 David Wesley .10 .03
❑ 299 Askia Jones RC .10 .03
❑ 300 B.J. Tyler RC .10 .03
❑ 301 Hakeem Olajuwon AI .40 .12
❑ 302 Luc Longley AI .10 .03
❑ 303 Rony Seikaly AI .10 .03
❑ 304 Sarunas Marciulionis AI .10 .03
❑ 305 Dikembe Mutombo AI .10 .03
❑ 306 Ken Norman .10 .03
❑ 307 Dell Curry .10 .03
❑ 308 Danny Ferry .10 .03
❑ 309 Shawn Kemp .60 .18
❑ 310 Dickey Simpkins RC .10 .03
❑ 311 Johnny Newman .10 .03
❑ 312 Dwayne Schintzius .10 .03
❑ 313 Sean Elliott .15 .04
❑ 314 Sean Rooks .10 .03
❑ 315 Bill Curley RC .10 .03
❑ 316 Bryant Stith .10 .03
❑ 317 Pooh Richardson .10 .03
❑ 318 Jim McIlvaine .10 .03
❑ 319 Dennis Scott .10 .03
❑ 320 Wesley Person RC .40 .12
❑ 321 Bobby Hurley .10 .03
❑ 322 Armon Gilliam .10 .03
❑ 323 Rik Smits .10 .03
❑ 324 Tony Smith .10 .03
❑ 325 Monty Williams RC .10 .03
❑ 326 Gary Payton BCT .40 .12
Kendall Gill
❑ 327 Mookie Blaylock BCT .10 .03
Stacey Augmon
❑ 328 Mark Jackson BCT .15 .04
Reggie Miller
❑ 329 Sam Cassell BCT .40 .12
Vernon Maxwell
❑ 330 Harold Miner BCT .10 .03
Khalid Reeves
❑ 331 Vinny Del Negro .10 .03
❑ 332 Billy Owens .10 .03
❑ 333 Mark West .10 .03
❑ 334 Matt Geiger .10 .03

Card	Nm-Mt	Ex-Mt
❑ 335 Greg Minor RC	.10	.03
❑ 336 Larry Johnson	.15	.04
❑ 337 Donald Hodge	.10	.03
❑ 338 Aaron Williams RC	.10	.03
❑ 339 Jay Humphries	.10	.03
❑ 340 Charlie Ward RC	.40	.12
❑ 341 Scott Brooks	.10	.03
❑ 342 Stacey Augmon	.10	.03
❑ 343 Will Perdue	.10	.03
❑ 344 Dale Ellis	.10	.03
❑ 345 Brooks Thompson RC	.10	.03
❑ 346 Manute Bol	.10	.03
❑ 347 Kenny Anderson	.15	.04
❑ 348 Willie Burton	.10	.03
❑ 349 Michael Cage	.10	.03
❑ 350 Danny Manning	.15	.04
❑ 351 Ricky Pierce	.10	.03
❑ 352 Sam Cassell	.40	.12
❑ 353 Reggie Miller FG	.15	.04
❑ 354 David Robinson FG	.40	.12
❑ 355 Shaquille O'Neal FG	.75	.23
❑ 356 Scottie Pippen FG	.60	.18
❑ 357 Alonzo Mourning FG	.40	.12
❑ 358 C. Weatherspoon FG	.10	.03
❑ 359 Derrick Coleman FG	.10	.03
❑ 360 Charles Barkley FG	.40	.12
❑ 361 Karl Malone FG	.40	.12
❑ 362 Chris Webber FG	.50	.15

1995-96 Stadium Club

	Nm-Mt	Ex-Mt
COMPLETE SET (361)	50.00	15.00
COMPLETE SERIES 1 (180)	25.00	7.50
COMPLETE SERIES 2 (181)	25.00	7.50
❑ 1 Michael Jordan	5.00	1.50
❑ 2 Glenn Robinson	.75	.23
❑ 3 Jason Kidd	2.50	.75
❑ 4 Clyde Drexler	.75	.23
❑ 5 Horace Grant	.50	.15
❑ 6 Allan Houston	.50	.15
❑ 7 Xavier McDaniel	.25	.07
❑ 8 Jeff Hornacek	.50	.15
❑ 9 Vlade Divac	.50	.15
❑ 10 Juwan Howard	.75	.23
❑ 11 Keith Jennings EXP	.25	.07
❑ 12 Grant Long	.25	.07
❑ 13 Jalen Rose	1.00	.30
❑ 14 Malik Sealy	.25	.07
❑ 15 Gary Payton	.75	.23
❑ 16 Danny Ferry	.25	.07
❑ 17 Glen Rice	.50	.15
❑ 18 Randy Brown	.25	.07
❑ 19 Greg Graham	.25	.07
❑ 20 Kenny Anderson UER Name is spelled Kenney	.50	.15
❑ 21 Aaron McKie	.50	.15
❑ 22 John Salley EXP	.25	.07
❑ 23 Darrin Hancock	.25	.07
❑ 24 Carlos Rogers	.25	.07
❑ 25 Vin Baker	.50	.15
❑ 26 Bill Wennington	.25	.07
❑ 27 Kenny Smith	.25	.07
❑ 28 Sherman Douglas	.25	.07
❑ 29 Terry Davis	.25	.07
❑ 30 Grant Hill	1.00	.30
❑ 31 Reggie Miller	.75	.23
❑ 32 Anfernee Hardaway	.75	.23
❑ 33 Patrick Ewing	.75	.23
❑ 34 Charles Barkley	1.00	.30
❑ 35 Eddie Jones	1.00	.30
❑ 36 Kevin Duckworth	.25	.07
❑ 37 Tom Hammonds	.25	.07
❑ 38 Craig Ehlo	.25	.07
❑ 39 Micheal Williams	.25	.07
❑ 40 Alonzo Mourning	.50	.15
❑ 41 John Williams	.25	.07
❑ 42 Felton Spencer	.25	.07
❑ 43 Lamond Murray	.25	.07
❑ 44 Dontonio Wingfield EXP	.25	.07
❑ 45 Rik Smits	.50	.15
❑ 46 Donyell Marshall	.50	.15
❑ 47 Clarence Weatherspoon	.25	.07
❑ 48 Kevin Edwards	.25	.07
❑ 49 Charlie Ward	.25	.07
❑ 50 David Robinson	.75	.23
❑ 51 James Robinson	.25	.07
❑ 52 Bill Cartwright	.25	.07
❑ 53 Bobby Hurley	.25	.07
❑ 54 Kevin Gamble	.25	.07
❑ 55 B.J. Tyler EXP	.25	.07
❑ 56 Chris Smith	.25	.07
❑ 57 Wesley Person	.25	.07
❑ 58 Tim Breaux	.25	.07
❑ 59 Mitchell Butler	.25	.07
❑ 60 Toni Kukoc	.50	.15
❑ 61 Roy Tarpley	.25	.07
❑ 62 Todd Day	.25	.07
❑ 63 Anthony Peeler	.25	.07
❑ 64 Brian Williams	.25	.07
❑ 65 Muggsy Bogues	.50	.15
❑ 66 Jerome Kersey EXP	.25	.07
❑ 67 Eric Piatkowski	.50	.15
❑ 68 Tim Perry	.25	.07
❑ 69 Chris Gatling	.25	.07
❑ 70 Mark Price	.50	.15
❑ 71 Terry Mills	.25	.07
❑ 72 Anthony Avent	.25	.07
❑ 73 Matt Geiger	.25	.07
❑ 74 Walt Williams	.25	.07
❑ 75 Sean Elliott	.50	.15
❑ 76 Ken Norman	.25	.07
❑ 77 Kendall Gill TA	.25	.07
❑ 78 Byron Houston	.25	.07
❑ 79 Rick Fox	.50	.15
❑ 80 Derek Harper	.50	.15
❑ 81 Rod Strickland	.25	.07
❑ 82 Bryon Russell	.25	.07
❑ 83 Antonio Davis	.25	.07
❑ 84 Isaiah Rider	.25	.07
❑ 85 Kevin Johnson	.50	.15
❑ 86 Derrick Coleman	.25	.07
❑ 87 Doug Overton	.25	.07
❑ 88 Hersey Hawkins TA	.25	.07
❑ 89 Popeye Jones	.25	.07
❑ 90 Dickey Simpkins	.25	.07
❑ 91 Rodney Rogers TA	.25	.07
❑ 92 Rex Chapman TA	.25	.07
❑ 93 Spud Webb TA	.25	.07
❑ 94 Lee Mayberry	.25	.07
❑ 95 Cedric Ceballos	.25	.07
❑ 96 Tyrone Hill	.25	.07
❑ 97 Bill Curley	.25	.07
❑ 98 Jeff Turner	.25	.07
❑ 99 Tyrone Corbin TA	.25	.07
❑ 100 John Stockton	1.00	.30
❑ 101 Mookie Blaylock EC	.25	.07
❑ 102 Dino Radja EC	.25	.07
❑ 103 Alonzo Mourning EC	.50	.15
❑ 104 Scottie Pippen EC	1.25	.35
❑ 105 Terrell Brandon EC	.50	.15
❑ 106 Jim Jackson EC	.25	.07
❑ 107 Mahmoud Abdul-Rauf EC	.25	.07
❑ 108 Grant Hill EC	1.00	.30
❑ 109 Tim Hardaway EC	.25	.07
❑ 110 Hakeem Olajuwon EC	.50	.15
❑ 111 Rik Smits EC	.25	.07
❑ 112 Loy Vaught EC	.25	.07
❑ 113 Vlade Divac EC	.25	.07
❑ 114 Kevin Willis EC	.25	.07
❑ 115 Glenn Robinson EC	.75	.23
❑ 116 Christian Laettner EC	.50	.15
❑ 117 Derrick Coleman EC	.25	.07
❑ 118 Patrick Ewing EC	.75	.23
❑ 119 Shaquille O'Neal EC	2.00	.60
❑ 120 Dana Barros EC	.25	.07
❑ 121 Charles Barkley EC	.75	.23
❑ 122 Rod Strickland EC	.25	.07
❑ 123 Brian Grant EC	.75	.23
❑ 124 David Robinson EC	.50	.15
❑ 125 Shawn Kemp EC	.25	.07
❑ 126 Oliver Miller EC	.25	.07
❑ 127 Karl Malone EC	.75	.23
❑ 128 Benoit Benjamin EC	.25	.07
❑ 129 Chris Webber EC	.75	.23
❑ 130 Dan Majerle	.50	.15
❑ 131 Calbert Cheaney	.25	.07
❑ 132 Mark Jackson	.50	.15
❑ 133 Greg Anthony EXP	.25	.07
❑ 134 Scott Burrell	.25	.07
❑ 135 Detlef Schrempf	.50	.15
❑ 136 Marty Conlon	.25	.07
❑ 137 Rony Seikaly	.25	.07
❑ 138 Olden Polynice	.25	.07
❑ 139 Terry Cummings	.25	.07
❑ 140 Stacey Augmon	.25	.07
❑ 141 Bryant Stith	.25	.07
❑ 142 Sean Higgins	.25	.07
❑ 143 Antoine Carr	.25	.07
❑ 144 Blue Edwards EXP	.25	.07
❑ 145 A.C. Green	.50	.15
❑ 146 Bobby Phills	.25	.07
❑ 147 Terry Dehere	.25	.07
❑ 148 Sharone Wright	.25	.07
❑ 149 Nick Anderson	.25	.07
❑ 150 Jim Jackson	.25	.07
❑ 151 Eric Montross	.25	.07
❑ 152 Doug West	.25	.07
❑ 153 Charles Smith	.25	.07
❑ 154 Will Perdue	.25	.07
❑ 155 Gerald Wilkins EXP	.25	.07
❑ 156 Robert Horry	.50	.15
❑ 157 Robert Parish	.50	.15
❑ 158 Lindsey Hunter	.25	.07
❑ 159 Harvey Grant	.25	.07
❑ 160 Tim Hardaway	.50	.15
❑ 161 Sarunas Marciulionis	.25	.07
❑ 162 Khalid Reeves	.25	.07
❑ 163 Bo Outlaw	.25	.07
❑ 164 Dale Davis	.25	.07
❑ 165 Nick Van Exel	.75	.23
❑ 166 Byron Scott EXP	.25	.07
❑ 167 Steve Smith	.50	.15
❑ 168 Brian Grant	.75	.23
❑ 169 Avery Johnson	.25	.07
❑ 170 Dikembe Mutombo	.50	.15
❑ 171 Tom Gugliotta	.25	.07
❑ 172 Armon Gilliam	.25	.07
❑ 173 Shawn Bradley	.25	.07
❑ 174 Herb Williams	.25	.07
❑ 175 Dino Radja	.25	.07
❑ 176 Billy Owens	.25	.07
❑ 177 Kenny Gattison EXP	.25	.07
❑ 178 J.R. Reid	.25	.07
❑ 179 Otis Thorpe	.25	.07
❑ 180 Sam Cassell	.75	.23
❑ 181 Sam Cassell	.75	.23
❑ 182 Pooh Richardson	.25	.07
❑ 183 Johnny Newman	.25	.07
❑ 184 Dennis Scott	.25	.07
❑ 185 Will Perdue	.25	.07
❑ 186 Andrew Lang	.25	.07
❑ 187 Karl Malone	1.00	.30
❑ 188 Buck Williams	.25	.07
❑ 189 P.J. Brown	.25	.07
❑ 190 Khalid Reeves	.25	.07
❑ 191 Kevin Willis	.50	.15
❑ 192 Robert Pack	.25	.07
❑ 193 Joe Dumars	.75	.23
❑ 194 Sam Perkins	.50	.15

	Card	Nm-Mt	Ex-Mt
❑	195 Dan Majerle	.50	.15
❑	196 John Williams	.25	.07
❑	197 Reggie Williams	.25	.07
❑	198 Greg Anthony	.25	.07
❑	199 Steve Kerr	.50	.15
❑	200 Richard Dumas	.25	.07
❑	201 Dee Brown	.25	.07
❑	202 Zan Tabak	.25	.07
❑	203 David Wood	.25	.07
❑	204 Duane Causwell	.25	.07
❑	205 Sedale Threatt	.25	.07
❑	206 Hubert Davis	.25	.07
❑	207 Donald Hodge	.25	.07
❑	208 Duane Ferrell	.25	.07
❑	209 Sam Mitchell	.25	.07
❑	210 Adam Keefe	.25	.07
❑	211 Clifford Robinson	.25	.07
❑	212 Rodney Rogers	.25	.07
❑	213 Jayson Williams	.25	.07
❑	214 Brian Shaw	.25	.07
❑	215 Luc Longley	.25	.07
❑	216 Don MacLean	.25	.07
❑	217 Rex Chapman	.25	.07
❑	218 Wayman Tisdale	.25	.07
❑	219 Shawn Kemp	.50	.15
❑	220 Chris Webber	1.00	.30
❑	221 Antonio Harvey	.25	.07
❑	222 Sarunas Marciulionis	.25	.07
❑	223 Jeff Malone	.25	.07
❑	224 Chucky Brown	.25	.07
❑	225 Greg Minor	.25	.07
❑	226 Clifford Rozier	.25	.07
❑	227 Derrick McKey	.25	.07
❑	228 Tony Dumas	.25	.07
❑	229 Oliver Miller	.25	.07
❑	230 Charles Oakley	.25	.07
❑	231 Fred Roberts	.25	.07
❑	232 Glen Rice	.50	.15
❑	233 Terry Porter	.25	.07
❑	234 Mark Macon	.25	.07
❑	235 Michael Cage	.25	.07
❑	236 Eric Murdock	.25	.07
❑	237 Vinny Del Negro	.25	.07
❑	238 Spud Webb	.50	.15
❑	239 Mario Elie	.25	.07
❑	240 Blue Edwards	.25	.07
❑	241 Dontonio Wingfield	.25	.07
❑	242 Brooks Thompson	.25	.07
❑	243 Alonzo Mourning	.50	.15
❑	244 Dennis Rodman	.50	.15
❑	245 Lorenzo Williams	.25	.07
❑	246 Haywoode Workman	.25	.07
❑	247 Loy Vaught	.25	.07
❑	248 Vernon Maxwell	.25	.07
❑	249 Lionel Simmons	.25	.07
❑	250 Chris Childs	.25	.07
❑	251 Mahmoud Abdul-Rauf	.25	.07
❑	252 Vincent Askew	.25	.07
❑	253 Chris Morris	.25	.07
❑	254 Elliot Perry	.25	.07
❑	255 Dell Curry	.25	.07
❑	256 Dana Barros	.25	.07
❑	257 Terrell Brandon	.50	.15
❑	258 Monty Williams	.25	.07
❑	259 Corie Blount	.25	.07
❑	260 B.J. Armstrong	.25	.07
❑	261 Jim McIlvaine	.25	.07
❑	262 Otis Thorpe	.25	.07
❑	263 Sean Rooks	.25	.07
❑	264 Tony Massenburg	.25	.07
❑	265 Steve Smith	.50	.15
❑	266 Ron Harper	.50	.15
❑	267 Dale Ellis	.25	.07
❑	268 Clyde Drexler	.75	.23
❑	269 Jamie Watson	.25	.07
❑	270 Doc Rivers	.50	.15
❑	271 Derrick Alston	.25	.07
❑	272 Eric Mobley	.25	.07
❑	273 Ricky Pierce	.25	.07
❑	274 David Wesley	.25	.07
❑	275 John Starks	.50	.15
❑	276 Chris Mullin	.75	.23
❑	277 Ervin Johnson	.25	.07
❑	278 Jamal Mashburn	.50	.15
❑	279 Joe Kleine	.25	.07
❑	280 Mitch Richmond	.50	.15
❑	281 Chris Mills	.25	.07
❑	282 Bimbo Coles	.25	.07
❑	283 Larry Johnson	.50	.15
❑	284 Stanley Roberts	.25	.07
❑	285 Rex Walters	.25	.07
❑	286 Donald Royal	.25	.07
❑	287 Benoit Benjamin	.25	.07
❑	288 Chris Dudley	.25	.07
❑	289 Elden Campbell	.25	.07
❑	290 Mookie Blaylock	.25	.07
❑	291 Hersey Hawkins	.25	.07
❑	292 Anthony Mason	.50	.15
❑	293 Latrell Sprewell	.75	.23
❑	294 Harold Miner	.25	.07
❑	295 Scott Williams	.25	.07
❑	296 David Benoit	.25	.07
❑	297 Christian Laettner	.50	.15
❑	298 LaPhonso Ellis	.25	.07
❑	299 Gheorghe Muresan	.25	.07
❑	300 Kendall Gill	.25	.07
❑	301 Eddie Johnson	.25	.07
❑	302 Terry Cummings	.25	.07
❑	303 Chuck Person	.25	.07
❑	304 Michael Smith	.25	.07
❑	305 Mark West	.25	.07
❑	306 Willie Anderson	.25	.07
❑	307 Pervis Ellison	.25	.07
❑	308 Brian Williams	.25	.07
❑	309 Danny Manning	.50	.15
❑	310 Hakeem Olajuwon	.75	.23
❑	311 Scottie Pippen	1.25	.35
❑	312 Jon Koncak	.25	.07
❑	313 Sasha Danilovic RC	.25	.07
❑	314 Lucious Harris	.25	.07
❑	315 Yinka Dare	.25	.07
❑	316 Eric Williams RC	.50	.15
❑	317 Gary Trent RC	.25	.07
❑	318 Theo Ratliff RC	1.00	.30
❑	319 Lawrence Moten RC	.25	.07
❑	320 Jerome Allen RC	.25	.07
❑	321 Tyus Edney RC	.25	.07
❑	322 Loren Meyer RC	.25	.07
❑	323 Michael Finley RC	2.00	.60
❑	324 Alan Henderson RC	.75	.23
❑	325 Bob Sura RC	.50	.15
❑	326 Joe Smith RC	1.25	.35
❑	327 Damon Stoudamire RC	1.50	.45
❑	328 Sherrell Ford RC	.25	.07
❑	329 Jerry Stackhouse RC	2.50	.75
❑	330 George Zidek RC	.25	.07
❑	331 Brent Barry RC	.75	.23
❑	332 Shawn Respert RC	.25	.07
❑	333 Rasheed Wallace RC	2.00	.60
❑	334 Antonio McDyess RC	1.50	.45
❑	335 David Vaughn RC	.25	.07
❑	336 Cory Alexander RC	.25	.07
❑	337 Jason Caffey RC	.50	.15
❑	338 Frankie King RC	.25	.07
❑	339 Travis Best RC	.25	.07
❑	340 Greg Ostertag RC	.25	.07
❑	341 Ed O'Bannon RC	.25	.07
❑	342 Kurt Thomas RC	.50	.15
❑	343 Kevin Garnett RC	4.00	1.20
❑	344 Bryant Reeves RC	.75	.23
❑	345 Corliss Williamson RC	.75	.23
❑	346 Cherokee Parks RC	.25	.07
❑	347 Junior Burrough RC	.25	.07
❑	348 Randolph Childress RC	.25	.07
❑	349 Lou Roe RC	.25	.07
❑	350 Mario Bennett RC	.25	.07
❑	351 Dikembe Mutombo XP	.25	.07
❑	352 Larry Johnson XP	.50	.15
❑	353 Vlade Divac XP	.25	.07
❑	354 Karl Malone XP	.75	.23
❑	355 John Stockton XP	.75	.23
❑	356 Alonzo Mourning TA	.25	.07
❑	357 Glen Rice TA	.25	.07
❑	358 Dan Majerle TA	.25	.07
❑	359 John Williams TA	.25	.07
❑	360 Mark Price TA	.25	.07
❑	361 Magic Johnson	1.25	.35

1996-97 Stadium Club

		Nm-Mt	Ex-Mt
	COMPLETE SET (180)	25.00	7.50
	COMPLETE SERIES 1 (90)	10.00	3.00
	COMPLETE SERIES 2 (90)	15.00	4.50
❑	1 Scottie Pippen	1.25	.35
❑	2 Dale Davis	.25	.07
❑	3 Horace Grant	.50	.15
❑	4 Gheorghe Muresan	.25	.07
❑	5 Elliot Perry	.25	.07
❑	6 Carlos Rogers	.25	.07
❑	7 Glenn Robinson	.75	.23
❑	8 Avery Johnson	.25	.07
❑	9 Dee Brown	.25	.07
❑	10 Grant Hill	.75	.23
❑	11 Tyus Edney	.25	.07
❑	12 Patrick Ewing	.75	.23
❑	13 Jason Kidd	1.25	.35
❑	14 Clifford Robinson	.25	.07
❑	15 Robert Horry	.50	.15
❑	16 Dell Curry	.25	.07
❑	17 Terry Porter	.25	.07
❑	18 Shaquille O'Neal	2.00	.60
❑	19 Bryant Stith	.25	.07
❑	20 Shawn Kemp	.50	.15
❑	21 Kurt Thomas	.50	.15
❑	22 Pooh Richardson	.25	.07
❑	23 Bob Sura	.25	.07
❑	24 Olden Polynice	.25	.07
❑	25 Lawrence Moten	.25	.07
❑	26 Kendall Gill	.25	.07
❑	27 Cedric Ceballos	.25	.07
❑	28 Latrell Sprewell	.75	.23
❑	29 Christian Laettner	.50	.15
❑	30 Jamal Mashburn	.50	.15
❑	31 Jerry Stackhouse	1.00	.30
❑	32 John Stockton	.75	.23
❑	33 Arvydas Sabonis	.50	.15
❑	34 Detlef Schrempf	.50	.15
❑	35 Toni Kukoc	.50	.15
❑	36 Sasha Danilovic	.25	.07
❑	37 Dana Barros	.25	.07
❑	38 Loy Vaught	.25	.07
❑	39 John Starks	.50	.15
❑	40 Marty Conlon	.25	.07
❑	41 Antonio McDyess	.50	.15
❑	42 Michael Finley	1.00	.30
❑	43 Tom Gugliotta	.25	.07
❑	44 Terrell Brandon	.50	.15
❑	45 Derrick McKey	.25	.07
❑	46 Damon Stoudamire	.75	.23

❑ 47 Elden Campbell .25 .07
❑ 48 Luc Longley .25 .07
❑ 49 B.J. Armstrong .25 .07
❑ 50 Lindsey Hunter .25 .07
❑ 51 Glen Rice .50 .15
❑ 52 Shawn Respert .25 .07
❑ 53 Cory Alexander .25 .07
❑ 54 Tim Legler .25 .07
❑ 55 Bryant Reeves .25 .07
❑ 56 Anfernee Hardaway .75 .23
❑ 57 Charles Barkley 1.00 .30
❑ 58 Mookie Blaylock .25 .07
❑ 59 Kevin Garnett 1.50 .45
❑ 60 Hersey Hawkins .50 .15
❑ 61 Ed O'Bannon .25 .07
❑ 62 George Zidek .25 .07
❑ 63 Mitch Richmond .50 .15
❑ 64 Derrick Coleman .50 .15
❑ 65 Chris Webber .75 .23
❑ 66 Bobby Phills .25 .07
❑ 67 Rik Smits .50 .15
❑ 68 Jeff Hornacek .50 .15
❑ 69 Sam Cassell .75 .23
❑ 70 Gary Trent .25 .07
❑ 71 LaPhonso Ellis .25 .07
❑ 72 Oliver Miller .25 .07
❑ 73 Rex Chapman .25 .07
❑ 74 Jim Jackson .25 .07
❑ 75 Eric Williams .25 .07
❑ 76 Brent Barry .25 .07
❑ 77 Nick Anderson .25 .07
❑ 78 David Robinson .75 .23
❑ 79 Calbert Cheaney .25 .07
❑ 80 Joe Smith .50 .15
❑ 81 Steve Kerr .50 .15
❑ 82 Wayman Tisdale .25 .07
❑ 83 Steve Smith .50 .15
❑ 84 Clyde Drexler .75 .23
❑ 85 Theo Ratliff .50 .15
❑ 86 Charlie Ward .25 .07
❑ 87 Karl Malone .75 .23
❑ 88 Clarence Weatherspoon .25 .07
❑ 89 Greg Anthony .25 .07
❑ 90 Shawn Bradley .25 .07
❑ 91 Otis Thorpe .25 .07
❑ 92 Larry Johnson .50 .15
❑ 93 Sharone Wright .25 .07
❑ 94 Charles Barkley 1.00 .30
❑ 95 Wesley Person .25 .07
❑ 96 Dikembe Mutombo .50 .15
❑ 97 Eddie Jones .75 .23
❑ 98 Juwan Howard .50 .15
❑ 99 Grant Hill .75 .23
❑ 100 Chris Carr RC .25 .07
❑ 101 Michael Jordan 5.00 1.50
❑ 102 Vincent Askew .25 .07
❑ 103 Gary Payton .75 .23
❑ 104 Chris Mills .25 .07
❑ 105 Reggie Miller .75 .23
❑ 106 Don MacLean .25 .07
❑ 107 John Stockton .75 .23
❑ 108 Mahmoud Abdul-Rauf .25 .07
❑ 109 P.J. Brown .25 .07
❑ 110 Kenny Anderson .25 .07
❑ 111 Mark Price .50 .15
❑ 112 Derek Harper .25 .07
❑ 113 Dino Radja .25 .07
❑ 114 Terry Dehere .25 .07
❑ 115 Mark Jackson .25 .07
❑ 116 Vin Baker .50 .15
❑ 117 Dennis Scott .25 .07
❑ 118 Sean Elliott .50 .15
❑ 119 Lee Mayberry .25 .07
❑ 120 Vlade Divac .25 .07
❑ 121 Joe Dumars .75 .23
❑ 122 Isaiah Rider .50 .15
❑ 123 Hakeem Olajuwon .75 .23
❑ 124 Robert Pack .25 .07
❑ 125 Jalen Rose .75 .23
❑ 126 Allan Houston .50 .15
❑ 127 Nate McMillan .25 .07
❑ 128 Rod Strickland .25 .07
❑ 129 Sean Rooks .25 .07
❑ 130 Dennis Rodman .50 .15
❑ 131 Alonzo Mourning .50 .15
❑ 132 Danny Ferry .25 .07
❑ 133 Sam Cassell .75 .23
❑ 134 Brian Grant .75 .23
❑ 135 Karl Malone .75 .23
❑ 136 Chris Gatling .25 .07
❑ 137 Tom Gugliotta .25 .07
❑ 138 Hubert Davis .25 .07
❑ 139 Lucious Harris .25 .07
❑ 140 Rony Seikaly .25 .07
❑ 141 Alan Henderson .25 .07
❑ 142 Mario Elie .25 .07
❑ 143 Vinny Del Negro .25 .07
❑ 144 Harvey Grant .25 .07
❑ 145 Muggsy Bogues .25 .07
❑ 146 Rodney Rogers .25 .07
❑ 147 Kevin Johnson .50 .15
❑ 148 Anthony Peeler .25 .07
❑ 149 Jon Koncak .25 .07
❑ 150 Ricky Pierce .25 .07
❑ 151 Todd Day .25 .07
❑ 152 Tyrone Hill .25 .07
❑ 153 Nick Van Exel .75 .23
❑ 154 Rasheed Wallace 1.00 .30
❑ 155 Jayson Williams .50 .15
❑ 156 Sherman Douglas .25 .07
❑ 157 Bryon Russell .25 .07
❑ 158 Ron Harper .50 .15
❑ 159 Stacey Augmon .25 .07
❑ 160 Antonio Davis .25 .07
❑ 161 Tim Hardaway .50 .15
❑ 162 Charles Oakley .25 .07
❑ 163 Billy Owens .25 .07
❑ 164 Sam Perkins .50 .15
❑ 165 Chris Whitney .25 .07
❑ 166 Matt Geiger .25 .07
❑ 167 Andrew Lang .25 .07
❑ 168 Danny Manning .50 .15
❑ 169 Doug Christie .50 .15
❑ 170 George Lynch .25 .07
❑ 171 Malik Sealy .25 .07
❑ 172 Eric Montross .25 .07
❑ 173 Rick Fox .25 .07
❑ 174 Chris Mullin .75 .23
❑ 175 Ken Norman .25 .07
❑ 176 Sarunas Marciulionis .25 .07
❑ 177 Kevin Garnett 1.50 .45
❑ 178 Brian Shaw .25 .07
❑ 179 Will Perdue .25 .07
❑ 180 Scott Williams .25 .07
❑ NNO Checklist .25 .07

1997-98 Stadium Club

	Nm-Mt	Ex-Mt
COMPLETE SET (240)	45.00	13.50
COMPLETE SERIES 1 (120)	25.00	7.50
COMPLETE SERIES 2 (120)	20.00	6.00

❑ 1 Scottie Pippen 1.25 .35
❑ 2 Bryon Russell .25 .07
❑ 3 Muggsy Bogues .50 .15
❑ 4 Gary Payton .75 .23
❑ 5 Ron Harper 5.00 1.50
Michael Jordan
Scottie Pippen
Dennis Rodman
❑ 6 Corliss Williamson .50 .15
❑ 7 Samaki Walker .25 .07
❑ 8 Allan Houston .50 .15
❑ 9 Ray Allen .75 .23
❑ 10 Nick Van Exel .75 .23
❑ 11 Chris Mullin .75 .23
❑ 12 Popeye Jones .25 .07
❑ 13 Horace Grant .50 .15
❑ 14 Rik Smits .50 .15
❑ 15 Wayman Tisdale .25 .07
❑ 16 Donny Marshall .25 .07
❑ 17 Rod Strickland .25 .07
❑ 18 Rod Strickland .25 .07
❑ 19 Greg Anthony .25 .07
❑ 20 Lindsey Hunter .25 .07
❑ 21 Glen Rice .50 .15
❑ 22 Anthony Goldwire .25 .07
❑ 23 Mahmoud Abdul-Rauf .25 .07
❑ 24 Sean Elliott .50 .15
❑ 25 Cory Alexander .25 .07
❑ 26 Tyrone Corbin .25 .07
❑ 27 Sam Perkins .50 .15
❑ 28 Brian Shaw .25 .07
❑ 29 Doug Christie .50 .15
❑ 30 Mark Jackson .50 .15
❑ 31 Christian Laettner .50 .15
❑ 32 Damon Stoudamire .50 .15
❑ 33 Eric Williams .25 .07
❑ 34 Glenn Robinson .75 .23
❑ 35 Brooks Thompson .25 .07
❑ 36 Derrick Coleman .25 .07
❑ 37 Theo Ratliff .25 .07
❑ 38 Ron Harper .50 .15
❑ 39 Hakeem Olajuwon .75 .23
❑ 40 Mitch Richmond .50 .15
❑ 41 Reggie Miller .75 .23
❑ 42 Reggie Miller .75 .23
❑ 43 Shaquille O'Neal 2.00 .60
❑ 44 Zydrunas Ilgauskas .50 .15
❑ 45 Jamal Mashburn .50 .15
❑ 46 Isaiah Rider .50 .15
❑ 47 Tom Gugliotta .50 .15
❑ 48 Rex Chapman .25 .07
❑ 49 Lorenzen Wright .25 .07
❑ 50 Pooh Richardson .25 .07
❑ 51 Armon Gilliam .25 .07
❑ 52 Kevin Johnson .50 .15
❑ 53 Kerry Kittles .75 .23
❑ 54 Kerry Kittles .75 .23
❑ 55 Charles Oakley .50 .15
❑ 56 Dennis Rodman .50 .15
❑ 57 Greg Ostertag .25 .07
❑ 58 Todd Fuller .25 .07
❑ 59 Mark Davis .25 .07
❑ 60 Erick Strickland RC .50 .15
❑ 61 Clifford Robinson .25 .07
❑ 62 Nate McMillan .25 .07
❑ 63 Steve Kerr .50 .15
❑ 64 Bob Sura .25 .07
❑ 65 Danny Ferry .25 .07
❑ 66 Loy Vaught .25 .07
❑ 67 A.C. Green .50 .15
❑ 68 John Stockton .75 .23
❑ 69 Terry Mills .25 .07
❑ 70 Voshon Lenard .25 .07
❑ 71 Matt Maloney .25 .07
❑ 72 Charlie Ward .25 .07
❑ 73 Brent Barry .50 .15
❑ 74 Chris Webber .75 .23
❑ 75 Stephon Marbury 1.00 .30
❑ 76 Bryant Stith .25 .07
❑ 77 Shareef Abdur-Rahim 1.25 .35
❑ 78 Sean Rooks .25 .07
❑ 79 Rony Seikaly .25 .07
❑ 80 Brent Price .25 .07
❑ 81 Wesley Person .25 .07
❑ 82 Michael Smith .25 .07
❑ 83 Gary Trent .25 .07
❑ 84 Dan Majerle .50 .15
❑ 85 Rex Walters .25 .07
❑ 86 Clarence Weatherspoon .25 .07
❑ 87 Patrick Ewing .75 .23
❑ 88 B.J. Armstrong .25 .07
❑ 89 Travis Best .25 .07
❑ 90 Steve Smith .50 .15
❑ 91 Vitaly Potapenko .25 .07
❑ 92 Derek Strong .25 .07
❑ 93 Michael Finley .75 .23
❑ 94 Will Perdue .25 .07
❑ 95 Antoine Walker 1.00 .30
❑ 96 Chuck Person .25 .07

Card		
❑ 97 Mookie Blaylock	.25	.07
❑ 98 Eric Snow	.50	.15
❑ 99 Tony Delk	.25	.07
❑ 100 Mario Elie	.25	.07
❑ 101 Terrell Brandon	.50	.15
❑ 102 Shawn Bradley	.25	.07
❑ 103 Latrell Sprewell	.75	.23
❑ 104 Latrell Sprewell	.75	.23
❑ 105 Tim Hardaway	.50	.15
❑ 106 Terry Porter	.25	.07
❑ 107 Darrell Armstrong	.25	.07
❑ 108 Rasheed Wallace	.75	.23
❑ 109 Vinny Del Negro	.25	.07
❑ 110 Tracy Murray	.25	.07
❑ 111 Lawrence Moten	.25	.07
❑ 112 Lamond Murray	.25	.07
❑ 113 Juwan Howard	.50	.15
❑ 114 Juwan Howard	.50	.15
❑ 115 Karl Malone	.75	.23
❑ 116 Aaron McKie	.50	.15
❑ 117 Shawn Respert	.25	.07
❑ 118 Michael Jordan	5.00	1.50
❑ 119 Shawn Kemp	.50	.15
❑ 120 Arvydas Sabonis	.50	.15
❑ 121 Tyus Edney	.25	.07
❑ 122 Bryant Reeves	.25	.07
❑ 123 Jason Kidd	1.25	.35
❑ 124 Dikembe Mutombo	.50	.15
❑ 125 Allen Iverson	2.00	.60
❑ 126 Allen Iverson	2.00	.60
❑ 127 Larry Johnson	.50	.15
❑ 128 Jerry Stackhouse	.75	.23
❑ 129 Kendall Gill	.25	.07
❑ 130 Kendall Gill	.25	.07
❑ 131 Vin Baker	.50	.15
❑ 132 Joe Dumars	.75	.23
❑ 133 Calbert Cheaney	.25	.07
❑ 134 Alonzo Mourning	.50	.15
❑ 135 Isaac Austin	.25	.07
❑ 136 Joe Smith	.50	.15
❑ 137 Elden Campbell	.25	.07
❑ 138 Kevin Garnett	1.50	.45
❑ 139 Malik Sealy	.25	.07
❑ 140 John Starks	.50	.15
❑ 141 Clyde Drexler	.75	.23
❑ 142 Matt Geiger	.25	.07
❑ 143 Mark Price	.50	.15
❑ 144 Buck Williams	.25	.07
❑ 145 Grant Hill	.75	.23
❑ 146 Kobe Bryant	3.00	.90
❑ 147 Dale Ellis	.25	.07
❑ 148 Jason Caffey	.25	.07
❑ 149 Toni Kukoc	.50	.15
❑ 150 Avery Johnson	.25	.07
❑ 151 Alan Henderson	.25	.07
❑ 152 Walt Williams	.25	.07
❑ 153 Greg Minor	.25	.07
❑ 154 Calbert Cheaney	.25	.07
❑ 155 Vlade Divac	.50	.15
❑ 156 Greg Foster	.25	.07
❑ 157 LaPhonso Ellis	.25	.07
❑ 158 Charles Barkley	1.00	.30
❑ 159 Antonio Davis	.25	.07
❑ 160 Roy Rogers	.25	.07
❑ 161 Robert Horry	.50	.15
❑ 162 Sam Cassell	.75	.23
❑ 163 Chris Carr	.25	.07
❑ 164 Robert Pack	.25	.07
❑ 165 Sam Cassell	.75	.23
❑ 166 Rodney Rogers	.25	.07
❑ 167 Chris Childs	.25	.07
❑ 168 Shandon Anderson	.25	.07
❑ 169 Kenny Anderson	.50	.15
❑ 170 Anthony Mason	.50	.15
❑ 171 Olden Polynice	.25	.07
❑ 172 David Wingate	.25	.07
❑ 173 David Robinson	.75	.23
❑ 174 Billy Owens	.25	.07
❑ 175 Detlef Schrempf	.50	.15
❑ 176 Carlos Rogers	.25	.07
❑ 177 Marcus Camby	.75	.23
❑ 178 Dana Barros	.25	.07
❑ 179 Shandon Anderson	.25	.07
❑ 180 Jayson Williams	.25	.07
❑ 181 Eldridge Recasner	.25	.07
❑ 182 Doug West	.25	.07
❑ 183 Kevin Willis	.50	.15
❑ 184 Eddie Johnson	.25	.07
❑ 185 Derek Fisher	.75	.23
❑ 186 Eddie Jones	.75	.23
❑ 187 Sherman Douglas	.25	.07
❑ 188 Anthony Peeler	.25	.07
❑ 189 Danny Manning	.50	.15
❑ 190 Stacey Augmon	.25	.07
❑ 191 Hersey Hawkins	.25	.07
❑ 192 Micheal Williams	.25	.07
❑ 193 Jeff Hornacek	.50	.15
❑ 194 Anfernee Hardaway	.75	.23
❑ 195 Harvey Grant	.25	.07
❑ 196 Nick Anderson	.25	.07
❑ 197 Luc Longley	.25	.07
❑ 198 Andrew Lang	.25	.07
❑ 199 P.J. Brown	.25	.07
❑ 200 Cedric Ceballos	.25	.07
❑ 201 Tim Duncan RC	3.00	.90
❑ 202 Ervin Johnson TRAN	.25	.07
❑ 203 Keith Van Horn RC	1.25	.35
❑ 204 David Wesley TRAN	.25	.07
❑ 205 Chauncey Billups RC	.75	.23
❑ 206 Jim Jackson TRAN	.25	.07
❑ 207 Antonio Daniels RC	.75	.23
❑ 208 Travis Knight TRAN	.25	.07
❑ 209 Tony Battie RC	.75	.23
❑ 210 Bobby Phills TRAN	.25	.07
❑ 211 Bobby Jackson RC	1.00	.30
❑ 212 Otis Thorpe TRAN	.25	.07
❑ 213 Tim Thomas RC	1.25	.35
❑ 214 Chris Mullin TRAN	.50	.15
❑ 215 Adonal Foyle RC	.50	.15
❑ 216 Brian Williams TRAN	.25	.07
❑ 217 Tracy McGrady RC	4.00	1.20
❑ 218 Tyus Edney TRAN	.25	.07
❑ 219 Danny Fortson RC	.50	.15
❑ 220 Clifford Robinson TRAN	.25	.07
❑ 221 Olivier Saint-Jean RC	.25	.07
❑ 222 Vin Baker TRAN	.25	.07
❑ 223 Austin Croshere RC	.75	.23
❑ 224 John Wallace TRAN	.25	.07
❑ 225 Derek Anderson RC	1.50	.45
❑ 226 Kelvin Cato RC	.75	.23
❑ 227 Maurice Taylor RC	.75	.23
❑ 228 Scot Pollard RC	.50	.15
❑ 229 John Thomas RC	.25	.07
❑ 230 Dean Garrett TRAN	.25	.07
❑ 231 Brevin Knight RC	.50	.15
❑ 232 Ron Mercer RC	1.00	.30
❑ 233 Johnny Taylor RC	.25	.07
❑ 234 Antonio McDyess TRAN	.50	.15
❑ 235 Ed Gray RC	.25	.07
❑ 236 Terrell Brandon TRAN	.25	.07
❑ 237 Anthony Parker RC	.25	.07
❑ 238 Shawn Kemp TRAN	.25	.07
❑ 239 Paul Grant RC	.25	.07
❑ 240 Dennis Scott TRAN	.25	.07

1998-99 Stadium Club

	Nm-Mt	Ex-Mt
COMPLETE SET (240)	250.00	75.00
COMPLETE SERIES 1 (120)	200.00	60.00
COMP.SERIES 1 w/o RC (100)	15.00	4.50
COMPLETE SERIES 2 (120)	30.00	9.00
COMMON CARD (1-240)	.25	.07
COMMON CARD (101-120)	2.50	.75
❑ 1 Eddie Jones	.75	.23
❑ 2 Matt Geiger	.25	.07
❑ 3 Ray Allen	.75	.23
❑ 4 Billy Owens	.25	.07
❑ 5 Larry Johnson	.50	.15
❑ 6 Jerry Stackhouse	.75	.23
❑ 7 Travis Best	.25	.07
❑ 8 Sam Cassell	.75	.23
❑ 9 Isaiah Rider	.25	.07
❑ 10 Walter McCarty	.25	.07
❑ 11 Hakeem Olajuwon	.75	.23
❑ 12 Detlef Schrempf	.50	.15
❑ 13 Chris Garner	.25	.07
❑ 14 Voshon Lenard	.25	.07
❑ 15 Kevin Garnett	1.50	.45
❑ 16 Doug Christie	.50	.15
❑ 17 Dikembe Mutombo	.50	.15
❑ 18 Terrell Brandon	.50	.15
❑ 19 Brevin Knight	.25	.07
❑ 20 Dan Majerle	.50	.15
❑ 21 Keith Van Horn	.75	.23
❑ 22 Jim Jackson	.25	.07
❑ 23 Theo Ratliff	.50	.15
❑ 24 Anthony Peeler	.25	.07
❑ 25 Tim Hardaway	.50	.15
❑ 26 Bo Outlaw	.25	.07
❑ 27 Blue Edwards	.25	.07
❑ 28 Khalid Reeves	.25	.07
❑ 29 David Wesley	.25	.07
❑ 30 Toni Kukoc	.50	.15
❑ 31 Jaren Jackson	.25	.07
❑ 32 Mario Elie	.25	.07
❑ 33 Nick Anderson	.25	.07
❑ 34 Derek Anderson	.75	.23
❑ 35 Rodney Rogers	.25	.07
❑ 36 Jalen Rose	.75	.23
❑ 37 Corliss Williamson	.50	.15
❑ 38 Tyrone Corbin	.25	.07
❑ 39 Antonio Davis	.25	.07
❑ 40 Chris Mills	.25	.07
❑ 41 Clarence Weatherspoon	.25	.07
❑ 42 George Lynch	.25	.07
❑ 43 Kelvin Cato	.25	.07
❑ 44 Anthony Mason	.50	.15
❑ 45 Tracy McGrady	2.00	.60
❑ 46 Lamond Murray	.25	.07
❑ 47 Mookie Blaylock	.25	.07
❑ 48 Tracy Murray	.25	.07
❑ 49 Ron Harper	.50	.15
❑ 50 Tom Gugliotta	.25	.07
❑ 51 Allan Houston	.50	.15
❑ 52 Arvydas Sabonis	.50	.15
❑ 53 Brian Williams	.25	.07
❑ 54 Brian Shaw	.25	.07
❑ 55 John Stockton	.75	.23
❑ 56 Rick Fox	.50	.15
❑ 57 Hersey Hawkins	.25	.07
❑ 58 Danny Manning	.25	.07
❑ 59 Chris Carr	.25	.07
❑ 60 Lindsey Hunter	.25	.07
❑ 61 Donyell Marshall	.50	.15
❑ 62 Michael Jordan	5.00	1.50
❑ 63 Mark Strickland	.25	.07
❑ 64 LaPhonso Ellis	.25	.07
❑ 65 Rod Strickland	.25	.07
❑ 66 David Robinson	.75	.23
❑ 67 Cedric Ceballos	.25	.07
❑ 68 Christian Laettner	.50	.15
❑ 69 Anthony Goldwire	.25	.07
❑ 70 Armon Gilliam	.25	.07
❑ 71 Shaquille O'Neal	2.00	.60
❑ 72 Sherman Douglas	.25	.07
❑ 73 Kendall Gill	.25	.07
❑ 74 Charlie Ward	.25	.07
❑ 75 Allen Iverson	1.50	.45
❑ 76 Shawn Kemp	.50	.15
❑ 77 Travis Knight	.25	.07
❑ 78 Gary Payton	.75	.23
❑ 79 Cedric Henderson	.25	.07

Card	Player	Nm-Mt	Ex-Mt
❑ 80	Matt Bullard	.25	.07
❑ 81	Steve Kerr	.50	.15
❑ 82	Shawn Bradley	.25	.07
❑ 83	Antonio McDyess	.50	.15
❑ 84	Robert Horry	.50	.15
❑ 85	Darrick Martin	.25	.07
❑ 86	Derek Strong	.25	.07
❑ 87	Shandon Anderson	.25	.07
❑ 88	Lawrence Funderburke	.25	.07
❑ 89	Brent Price	.25	.07
❑ 90	Reggie Miller	.75	.23
❑ 91	Shareef Abdur-Rahim	.75	.23
❑ 92	Jeff Hornacek	.50	.15
❑ 93	Antoine Carr	.25	.07
❑ 94	Greg Anthony	.25	.07
❑ 95	Rex Chapman	.25	.07
❑ 96	Antoine Walker	.75	.23
❑ 97	Bobby Jackson	.50	.15
❑ 98	Calbert Cheaney	.25	.07
❑ 99	Avery Johnson	.25	.07
❑ 100	Jason Kidd	1.25	.35
❑ 101	Michael Olowokandi RC	5.00	1.50
❑ 102	Mike Bibby RC	12.00	3.60
❑ 103	Raef LaFrentz RC	5.00	1.50
❑ 104	Antawn Jamison RC	30.00	9.00
❑ 105	Vince Carter RC	60.00	18.00
❑ 106	Robert Traylor RC	5.00	1.50
❑ 107	Jason Williams RC	12.00	3.60
❑ 108	Larry Hughes RC	6.00	1.80
❑ 109	Dirk Nowitzki RC	50.00	15.00
❑ 110	Paul Pierce RC	20.00	6.00
❑ 111	Bonzi Wells RC	10.00	3.00
❑ 112	Michael Doleac RC	5.00	1.50
❑ 113	Keon Clark RC	5.00	1.50
❑ 114	Michael Dickerson RC	6.00	1.80
❑ 115	Matt Harpring RC	5.00	1.50
❑ 116	Bryce Drew RC	5.00	1.50
❑ 117	Pat Garrity RC	3.00	.90
❑ 118	Roshown McLeod RC	2.50	.75
❑ 119	Ricky Davis RC	10.00	3.00
❑ 120	Brian Skinner RC	5.00	1.50
❑ 121	Dee Brown	.25	.07
❑ 122	Hubert Davis	.25	.07
❑ 123	Vitaly Potapenko	.25	.07
❑ 124	Ervin Johnson	.25	.07
❑ 125	Chris Gatling	.25	.07
❑ 126	Darrell Armstrong	.25	.07
❑ 127	Glen Rice	.50	.15
❑ 128	Ben Wallace	.75	.23
❑ 129	Sam Mitchell	.25	.07
❑ 130	Joe Dumars	.75	.23
❑ 131	Terry Davis	.25	.07
❑ 132	A.C. Green	.50	.15
❑ 133	Alan Henderson	.25	.07
❑ 134	Ron Mercer	.50	.15
❑ 135	Brian Grant	.50	.15
❑ 136	Chris Childs	.25	.07
❑ 137	Rony Seikaly	.25	.07
❑ 138	Pete Chilcutt	.25	.07
❑ 139	Anfernee Hardaway	.75	.23
❑ 140	Bryon Russell	.25	.07
❑ 141	Tim Thomas	.50	.15
❑ 142	Erick Dampier	.50	.15
❑ 143	Charles Barkley	1.00	.30
❑ 144	Mark Jackson	.50	.15
❑ 145	Bryant Reeves	.25	.07
❑ 146	Tyrone Hill	.25	.07
❑ 147	Rasheed Wallace	.75	.23
❑ 148	Tim Duncan	1.25	.35
❑ 149	Steve Smith	.50	.15
❑ 150	Alonzo Mourning	.50	.15
❑ 151	Danny Fortson	.25	.07
❑ 152	Aaron Williams	.25	.07
❑ 153	Andrew DeClercq	.25	.07
❑ 154	Elden Campbell	.25	.07
❑ 155	Don Reid	.25	.07
❑ 156	Rik Smits	.50	.15
❑ 157	Adonal Foyle	.25	.07
❑ 158	Muggsy Bogues	.50	.15
❑ 159	Chris Mullin	.75	.23
❑ 160	Randy Brown	.25	.07
❑ 161	Kenny Anderson	.50	.15
❑ 162	Tariq Abdul-Wahad	.25	.07
❑ 163	P.J. Brown	.25	.07
❑ 164	Jayson Williams	.25	.07
❑ 165	Grant Hill	.75	.23
❑ 166	Clifford Robinson	.25	.07
❑ 167	Damon Stoudamire	.50	.15
❑ 168	Aaron McKie	.50	.15
❑ 169	Erick Strickland	.25	.07
❑ 170	Kobe Bryant	3.00	.90
❑ 171	Karl Malone	.75	.23
❑ 172	Eric Piatkowski	.50	.15
❑ 173	Rodrick Rhodes	.25	.07
❑ 174	Sean Elliott	.50	.15
❑ 175	John Wallace	.25	.07
❑ 176	Derek Fisher	.75	.23
❑ 177	Maurice Taylor	.50	.15
❑ 178	Wesley Person	.25	.07
❑ 179	Jamal Mashburn	.50	.15
❑ 180	Patrick Ewing	.75	.23
❑ 181	Howard Eisley	.25	.07
❑ 182	Michael Finley	.75	.23
❑ 183	Juwan Howard	.50	.15
❑ 184	Matt Maloney	.25	.07
❑ 185	Glenn Robinson	.50	.15
❑ 186	Zydrunas Ilgauskas	.50	.15
❑ 187	Dana Barros	.25	.07
❑ 188	Stacey Augmon	.25	.07
❑ 189	Bobby Phills	.25	.07
❑ 190	Kerry Kittles	.25	.07
❑ 191	Vin Baker	.50	.15
❑ 192	Stephon Marbury	.75	.23
❑ 193	Peja Stojakovic RC	1.50	.45
❑ 194	Michael Olowokandi	.60	.18
❑ 195	Mike Bibby	2.00	.60
❑ 196	Raef LaFrentz	.60	.18
❑ 197	Antawn Jamison	2.00	.60
❑ 198	Vince Carter	5.00	1.50
❑ 199	Robert Traylor	.25	.07
❑ 200	Jason Williams	1.50	.45
❑ 201	Larry Hughes	1.25	.35
❑ 202	Dirk Nowitzki	4.00	1.20
❑ 203	Paul Pierce	2.00	.60
❑ 204	Bonzi Wells	1.50	.45
❑ 205	Michael Doleac	.50	.15
❑ 206	Keon Clark	.75	.23
❑ 207	Michael Dickerson	.75	.23
❑ 208	Matt Harpring	.75	.23
❑ 209	Bryce Drew	.50	.15
❑ 210	Pat Garrity	.25	.07
❑ 211	Roshown McLeod	.50	.15
❑ 212	Ricky Davis	.75	.23
❑ 213	Brian Skinner	.50	.15
❑ 214	Tyronn Lue RC	.50	.15
❑ 215	Felipe Lopez RC	.50	.15
❑ 216	Al Harrington RC	1.00	.30
❑ 217	Sam Jacobson RC	.25	.07
❑ 218	Vladimir Stepania RC	.25	.07
❑ 219	Corey Benjamin RC	.75	.23
❑ 220	Nazr Mohammed RC	.50	.15
❑ 221	Tom Gugliotta TRAN	.25	.07
❑ 222	Derrick Coleman TRAN	.25	.07
❑ 223	Mitch Richmond TRAN	.50	.15
❑ 224	John Starks TRAN	.25	.07
❑ 225	Antonio McDyess TRAN	.50	.15
❑ 226	Joe Smith TRAN	.25	.07
❑ 227	Bobby Jackson TRAN	.25	.07
❑ 228	Luc Longley TRAN	.25	.07
❑ 229	Isaac Austin TRAN	.25	.07
❑ 230	Chris Webber TRAN	.50	.15
❑ 231	Chauncey Billups TRAN	.50	.15
❑ 232	Sam Perkins TRAN	.25	.07
❑ 233	Loy Vaught TRAN	.25	.07
❑ 234	Antonio Daniels TRAN	.25	.07
❑ 235	Brent Barry TRAN	.25	.07
❑ 236	Latrell Sprewell TRAN	.75	.23
❑ 237	Vlade Divac TRAN	.25	.07
❑ 238	Marcus Camby TRAN	.50	.15
❑ 239	Charles Oakley TRAN	.25	.07
❑ 240	Scottie Pippen TRAN	.60	.18

1999-00 Stadium Club

	Nm-Mt	Ex-Mt
COMPLETE SET (201)	80.00	24.00
COMPLETE SET w/o RC (175)	40.00	12.00
COMMON CARD (1-175)	.20	.06
COMMON ROOKIE (176-201)	.60	.18

Card	Player	Nm-Mt	Ex-Mt
❑ 1	Allen Iverson	1.25	.35
❑ 2	Chris Crawford	.20	.06
❑ 3	Chris Webber	.60	.18
❑ 4	Antawn Jamison	1.00	.30
❑ 5	Karl Malone	.60	.18
❑ 6	Sam Cassell	.60	.18
❑ 7	Kerry Kittles	.20	.06
❑ 8	Tim Thomas	.40	.12
❑ 9	Chauncey Billups	.40	.12
❑ 10	Shawn Bradley	.20	.06
❑ 11	Alan Henderson	.20	.06
❑ 12	David Wesley	.20	.06
❑ 13	Glenn Robinson	.60	.18
❑ 14	Mitch Richmond	.40	.12
❑ 15	Luc Longley	.20	.06
❑ 16	Shareef Abdur-Rahim	.60	.18
❑ 17	Christian Laettner	.40	.12
❑ 18	Anthony Mason	.40	.12
❑ 19	Randy Brown	.20	.06
❑ 20	Charles Barkley	.75	.23
❑ 21	Bob Sura	.20	.06
❑ 22	Bobby Jackson	.40	.12
❑ 23	Arvydas Sabonis	.40	.12
❑ 24	Tracy Murray	.20	.06
❑ 25	Matt Harpring	.60	.18
❑ 26	Shawn Kemp	.40	.12
❑ 27	Travis Best	.20	.06
❑ 28	Ruben Patterson	.40	.12
❑ 29	Mike Bibby	.60	.18
❑ 30	Vlade Divac	.40	.12
❑ 31	Tyrone Hill	.20	.06
❑ 32	David Robinson	.60	.18
❑ 33	Keith Van Horn	.60	.18
❑ 34	Alvin Williams	.20	.06
❑ 35	Juwan Howard	.40	.12
❑ 36	Shaquille O'Neal	1.50	.45
❑ 37	Dale Davis	.20	.06
❑ 38	Alonzo Mourning	.40	.12
❑ 39	Michael Olowokandi	.40	.12
❑ 40	Jason Caffey	.20	.06
❑ 41	Andrew DeClercq	.20	.06
❑ 42	Jud Buechler	.20	.06
❑ 43	Toni Kukoc	.40	.12
❑ 44	Dikembe Mutombo	.40	.12
❑ 45	Steve Nash	.60	.18
❑ 46	Eddie Jones	.60	.18
❑ 47	Reggie Miller	.60	.18
❑ 48	Rick Fox	.40	.12
❑ 49	Larry Hughes	.60	.18
❑ 50	Tim Duncan	1.25	.35
❑ 51	Jerome Williams	.20	.06
❑ 52	Rod Strickland	.20	.06
❑ 53	Anthony Peeler	.20	.06
❑ 54	Greg Ostertag	.20	.06
❑ 55	Patrick Ewing	.60	.18
❑ 56	Grant Hill	.60	.18

Card	Nm-Mt	Ex-Mt
❑ 57 Derrick Coleman	.40	.12
❑ 58 Raef LaFrentz	.40	.12
❑ 59 Mark Bryant	.20	.06
❑ 60 Rik Smits	.40	.12
❑ 61 Latrell Sprewell	.60	.18
❑ 62 John Starks	.40	.12
❑ 63 Brevin Knight	.20	.06
❑ 64 Cuttino Mobley	.60	.18
❑ 65 Clarence Weatherspoon	.20	.06
❑ 66 Marcus Camby	.40	.12
❑ 67 Stephon Marbury	.60	.18
❑ 68 Tom Gugliotta	.20	.06
❑ 69 Vince Carter	1.50	.45
❑ 70 Vladimir Stepania	.20	.06
❑ 71 Chris Mullin	.60	.18
❑ 72 Tyrone Nesby RC	.20	.06
❑ 73 Kornel David RC	.20	.06
❑ 74 Elden Campbell	.20	.06
❑ 75 Lindsey Hunter	.20	.06
❑ 76 Chris Childs	.20	.06
❑ 77 Ervin Johnson	.20	.06
❑ 78 Rasheed Wallace	.60	.18
❑ 79 Jeff Hornacek	.40	.12
❑ 80 Matt Geiger	.20	.06
❑ 81 Antoine Walker	.60	.18
❑ 82 Jason Williams	.60	.18
❑ 83 Robert Horry	.40	.12
❑ 84 Jaren Jackson	.20	.06
❑ 85 Kendall Gill	.20	.06
❑ 86 Dan Majerle	.40	.12
❑ 87 Bobby Phills	.20	.06
❑ 88 Eric Piatkowski	.40	.12
❑ 89 Robert Traylor	.20	.06
❑ 90 Cory Carr	.20	.06
❑ 91 P.J. Brown	.20	.06
❑ 92 Terrell Brandon	.40	.12
❑ 93 Corliss Williamson	.40	.12
❑ 94 Bryant Reeves	.20	.06
❑ 95 Larry Johnson	.40	.12
❑ 96 Keith Closs	.20	.06
❑ 97 Gary Trent	.20	.06
❑ 98 Walter McCarty	.20	.06
❑ 99 Wesley Person	.20	.06
❑ 100 Chris Mills	.20	.06
❑ 101 Glen Rice	.40	.12
❑ 102 Peja Stojakovic	.75	.23
❑ 103 Jason Kidd	1.00	.30
❑ 104 Dirk Nowitzki	1.25	.35
❑ 105 Bryon Russell	.20	.06
❑ 106 Vin Baker	.40	.12
❑ 107 Darrell Armstrong	.20	.06
❑ 108 Eric Snow	.40	.12
❑ 109 Hakeem Olajuwon	.60	.18
❑ 110 Tracy McGrady	1.50	.45
❑ 111 Kenny Anderson	.40	.12
❑ 112 Jalen Rose	.60	.18
❑ 113 Greg Anthony	.20	.06
❑ 114 Tim Hardaway	.40	.12
❑ 115 Doug Christie	.40	.12
❑ 116 Allan Houston	.40	.12
❑ 117 Kobe Bryant	2.50	.75
❑ 118 Kevin Garnett	1.25	.35
❑ 119 Vitaly Potapenko	.20	.06
❑ 120 Steve Kerr	.40	.12
❑ 121 Nick Van Exel	.60	.18
❑ 122 Jerry Stackhouse	.60	.18
❑ 123 Derek Fisher	.60	.18
❑ 124 Donyell Marshall	.40	.12
❑ 125 Mark Jackson	.40	.12
❑ 126 Ray Allen	.60	.18
❑ 127 Avery Johnson	.20	.06
❑ 128 Michael Doleac	.20	.06
❑ 129 Charles Oakley	.20	.06
❑ 130 Gary Payton	.60	.18
❑ 131 Theo Ratliff	.40	.12
❑ 132 Cedric Ceballos	.20	.06
❑ 133 Paul Pierce	.60	.18
❑ 134 Michael Finley	.60	.18
❑ 135 Malik Sealy	.20	.06
❑ 136 Brian Grant	.40	.12
❑ 137 John Stockton	.60	.18
❑ 138 Chris Whitney	.20	.06
❑ 139 Maurice Taylor	.40	.12
❑ 140 Antonio McDyess	.40	.12
❑ 141 Adrian Griffin RC	1.00	.30
❑ 142 Vernon Maxwell	.20	.06
❑ 143 Jamal Mashburn	.40	.12
❑ 144 Jayson Williams	.20	.06
❑ 145 Joe Smith	.40	.12
❑ 146 Clifford Robinson	.20	.06
❑ 147 Mario Elie	.20	.06
❑ 148 Damon Stoudamire	.40	.12
❑ 149 Felipe Lopez	.20	.06
❑ 150 Rex Chapman	.20	.06
❑ 151 Antonio Davis TRAN	.20	.06
❑ 152 Mookie Blaylock TRAN	.20	.06
❑ 153 Ron Mercer TRAN	.40	.12
❑ 154 Horace Grant TRAN	.40	.12
❑ 155 Steve Smith TRAN	.40	.12
❑ 156 Isaiah Rider TRAN	.20	.06
❑ 157 T.Abdul-Wahad TRAN	.20	.06
❑ 158 Michael Dickerson TRAN	.40	.12
❑ 159 Nick Anderson TRAN	.20	.06
❑ 160 Jim Jackson TRAN	.20	.06
❑ 161 Hersey Hawkins TRAN	.40	.12
❑ 162 Brent Barry TRAN	.20	.06
❑ 163 Shandon Anderson TRAN	.20	.06
❑ 164 Scottie Pippen TRAN	1.00	.30
❑ 165 Isaac Austin TRAN	.20	.06
❑ 166 A.Hardaway TRAN	.60	.18
❑ 167 Natalie Williams USA	2.50	.75
❑ 168 Teresa Edwards USA	2.00	.60
❑ 169 Yolanda Griffith USA	2.50	.75
❑ 170 Nikki McCray USA	1.25	.35
❑ 171 Katie Smith USA	1.50	.45
❑ 172 C.Holdsclaw USA	8.00	2.40
❑ 173 Dawn Staley USA	2.00	.60
❑ 174 R.Bolton-Holifield USA	1.25	.35
❑ 175 Lisa Leslie USA	2.00	.60
❑ 176 Elton Brand RC	4.00	1.20
❑ 177 Steve Francis RC	5.00	1.50
❑ 178 Baron Davis RC	3.00	.90
❑ 179 Lamar Odom RC	3.00	.90
❑ 180 Jonathan Bender RC	3.00	.90
❑ 181 Wally Szczerbiak RC	3.00	.90
❑ 182 Richard Hamilton RC	3.00	.90
❑ 183 Andre Miller RC	3.00	.90
❑ 184 Shawn Marion RC	4.00	1.20
❑ 185 Jason Terry RC	2.00	.60
❑ 186 Trajan Langdon RC	1.25	.35
❑ 187 Aleksandar Radojevic RC	.60	.18
❑ 188 Corey Maggette RC	3.00	.90
❑ 189 William Avery RC	1.25	.35
❑ 190 DeMarco Johnson RC	.75	.23
❑ 191 Ron Artest RC	2.00	.60
❑ 192 Cal Bowdler RC	1.00	.30
❑ 193 James Posey RC	2.00	.60
❑ 194 Quincy Lewis RC	1.00	.30
❑ 195 Scott Padgett RC	1.00	.30
❑ 196 Jeff Foster RC	1.00	.30
❑ 197 Kenny Thomas RC	1.25	.35
❑ 198 Devean George RC	1.50	.45
❑ 199 Tim James RC	1.00	.30
❑ 200 Vonteego Cummings RC	1.25	.35
❑ 201 Jumaine Jones RC	1.25	.35

2000-01 Stadium Club

	Nm-Mt	Ex-Mt
COMPLETE SET (175)	60.00	18.00
COMPLETE SET w/o RC (150)	25.00	7.50
COMMON CARD (1-150)	.20	.06
COMMON ROOKIE (151-175)	1.00	.30
❑ 1 Baron Davis	.60	.18
❑ 2 Adrian Griffin	.20	.06
❑ 3 Dikembe Mutombo	.40	.12
❑ 4 Andre Miller	.40	.12
❑ 5 Kenny Anderson	.40	.12
❑ 6 Keon Clark	.40	.12
❑ 7 Larry Hughes	.40	.12
❑ 8 Ruben Patterson	.40	.12
❑ 9 Shandon Anderson	.20	.06
❑ 10 Reggie Miller	.60	.18
❑ 11 Lamar Odom	.60	.18
❑ 12 John Stockton	.60	.18
❑ 13 Rod Strickland	.20	.06
❑ 14 Michael Dickerson	.40	.12
❑ 15 Quincy Lewis	.20	.06
❑ 16 Vin Baker	.40	.12
❑ 17 Vince Carter	1.50	.45
❑ 18 Avery Johnson	.20	.06
❑ 19 Michael Finley	.60	.18
❑ 20 Eric Snow	.40	.12
❑ 21 Kevin Garnett	1.25	.35
❑ 22 Rodney Rogers	.20	.06
❑ 23 Bonzi Wells	.40	.12
❑ 24 Jason Kidd	1.00	.30
❑ 25 Toni Kukoc	.40	.12
❑ 26 Darrell Armstrong	.20	.06
❑ 27 Larry Johnson	.40	.12
❑ 28 Kendall Gill	.20	.06
❑ 29 Wally Szczerbiak	.40	.12
❑ 30 Tim Thomas	.40	.12
❑ 31 Dan Majerle	.40	.12
❑ 32 Karl Malone	.60	.18
❑ 33 Juwan Howard	.40	.12
❑ 34 Kobe Bryant	2.50	.75
❑ 35 Bryant Reeves	.20	.06
❑ 36 Cuttino Mobley	.40	.12
❑ 37 Mookie Blaylock	.20	.06
❑ 38 Jerome Williams	.20	.06
❑ 39 James Posey	.40	.12
❑ 40 Shawn Bradley	.20	.06
❑ 41 Tim Hardaway	.40	.12
❑ 42 Theo Ratliff	.40	.12
❑ 43 Damon Stoudamire	.40	.12
❑ 44 Derrick Coleman	.20	.06
❑ 45 Ron Artest	.40	.12
❑ 46 Antoine Walker	.60	.18
❑ 47 Jason Terry	.60	.18
❑ 48 Antonio McDyess	.40	.12
❑ 49 Jonathan Bender	.40	.12
❑ 50 Shaquille O'Neal	1.50	.45
❑ 51 Anthony Carter	.40	.12
❑ 52 Ray Allen	.60	.18
❑ 53 Joe Smith	.40	.12
❑ 54 Marcus Camby	.40	.12
❑ 55 Keith Van Horn	.60	.18
❑ 56 Charlie Ward	.20	.06
❑ 57 John Amaechi	.20	.06
❑ 58 Tom Gugliotta	.20	.06
❑ 59 Allan Houston	.40	.12
❑ 60 Anfernee Hardaway	.60	.18
❑ 61 Scottie Pippen	1.00	.30
❑ 62 Jason Williams	.40	.12
❑ 63 Steve Smith	.40	.12
❑ 64 David Robinson	.60	.18
❑ 65 Gary Payton	.60	.18
❑ 66 Robert Horry	.40	.12
❑ 67 Greg Ostertag	.20	.06
❑ 68 Mike Bibby	.60	.18
❑ 69 Tim Duncan	1.25	.35
❑ 70 Richard Hamilton	.40	.12
❑ 71 Bryon Russell	.20	.06
❑ 72 Charles Oakley	.20	.06
❑ 73 Rashard Lewis	.40	.12
❑ 74 Chris Webber	.60	.18
❑ 75 Arvydas Sabonis	.40	.12
❑ 76 Allen Iverson	1.25	.35
❑ 77 Bo Outlaw	.20	.06
❑ 78 Elden Campbell	.20	.06
❑ 79 Dirk Nowitzki	1.00	.30
❑ 80 Elton Brand	.60	.18
❑ 81 Brevin Knight	.20	.06
❑ 82 David Wesley	.20	.06
❑ 83 Raef LaFrentz	.40	.12
❑ 84 Antawn Jamison	.60	.18
❑ 85 Hakeem Olajuwon	.60	.18
❑ 86 Jamie Feick	.20	.06
❑ 87 Jalen Rose	.60	.18
❑ 88 Michael Olowokandi	.20	.06

❑ 89 Rick Fox .40 .12
❑ 90 Austin Croshere .40 .12
❑ 91 Glenn Robinson .60 .18
❑ 92 Stephon Marbury .60 .18
❑ 93 Clifford Robinson .20 .06
❑ 94 Derek Fisher .60 .18
❑ 95 Vlade Divac .40 .12
❑ 96 Jim Jackson .20 .06
❑ 97 Paul Pierce .60 .18
❑ 98 Corey Benjamin .20 .06
❑ 99 Lamond Murray .20 .06
❑ 100 Steve Francis .60 .18
❑ 101 Mitch Richmond .40 .12
❑ 102 Othella Harrington .20 .06
❑ 103 Nick Anderson .20 .06
❑ 104 Antonio Davis .20 .06
❑ 105 Ervin Johnson .20 .06
❑ 106 Rasheed Wallace .60 .18
❑ 107 Shawn Marion .60 .18
❑ 108 Latrell Sprewell .60 .18
❑ 109 Terrell Brandon .40 .12
❑ 110 Sam Cassell .60 .18
❑ 111 Shareef Abdur-Rahim .60 .18
❑ 112 Travis Best .20 .06
❑ 113 Tyrone Nesby .20 .06
❑ 114 Alan Henderson .20 .06
❑ 115 Vonteego Cummings .20 .06
❑ 116 Kelvin Cato .20 .06
❑ 117 Jerry Stackhouse .60 .18
❑ 118 Nick Van Exel .60 .18
❑ 119 Corliss Williamson TRAN .20 .06
❑ 120 Doug Christie TRAN .20 .06
❑ 121 Horace Grant TRAN .40 .12
❑ 122 Glen Rice TRAN .40 .12
❑ 123 Patrick Ewing TRAN .60 .18
❑ 124 Dale Davis TRAN .20 .06
❑ 125 Brian Grant TRAN .40 .12
❑ 126 Shawn Kemp TRAN .20 .06
❑ 127 Cedric Ceballos TRAN .20 .06
❑ 128 Christian Laettner TRAN .40 .12
❑ 129 Lindsey Hunter TRAN .20 .06
❑ 130 Donyell Marshall TRAN .40 .12
❑ 131 Robert Pack TRAN .20 .06
❑ 132 Danny Fortson TRAN .20 .06
❑ 133 Howard Eisley TRAN .20 .06
❑ 134 Andrew DeClercq TRAN .20 .06
❑ 135 Mark Jackson TRAN .20 .06
❑ 136 Grant Hill TRAN .40 .12
❑ 137 Tracy McGrady TRAN 1.50 .45
❑ 138 Maurice Taylor TRAN .20 .06
❑ 139 Derek Anderson TRAN .20 .06
❑ 140 Corey Maggette TRAN .40 .12
❑ 141 Jermaine O'Neal TRAN .60 .18
❑ 142 Ben Wallace TRAN .60 .18
❑ 143 Ron Mercer TRAN .20 .06
❑ 144 John Starks TRAN .60 .18
❑ 145 Erick Strickland TRAN .20 .06
❑ 146 Isaiah Rider TRAN .40 .12
❑ 147 Eddie Jones TRAN .40 .12
❑ 148 Anthony Mason TRAN .20 .06
❑ 149 P.J. Brown TRAN .20 .06
❑ 150 Jamal Mashburn TRAN .40 .12
❑ 151 Kenyon Martin RC 4.00 1.20
❑ 152 Stromile Swift RC 2.00 .60
❑ 153 Darius Miles RC 3.00 .90
❑ 154 Marcus Fizer RC 1.00 .30
❑ 155 Mike Miller RC 3.00 .90
❑ 156 DerMarr Johnson RC 1.00 .30
❑ 157 Chris Mihm RC 1.00 .30
❑ 158 Jamal Crawford RC 1.25 .35
❑ 159 Joel Przybilla RC 1.00 .30
❑ 160 Keyon Dooling RC 1.00 .30
❑ 161 Jerome Moiso RC 1.00 .30
❑ 162 Etan Thomas RC 1.00 .30
❑ 163 Courtney Alexander RC 1.25 .35
❑ 164 Mateen Cleaves RC 1.00 .30
❑ 165 Jason Collier RC 1.00 .30
❑ 166 Desmond Mason RC 1.00 .30
❑ 167 Quentin Richardson RC 3.00 .90
❑ 168 Jamaal Magloire RC 1.00 .30
❑ 169 Speedy Claxton RC 1.00 .30
❑ 170 Morris Peterson RC 2.00 .60
❑ 171 Donnell Harvey RC 1.00 .30
❑ 172 DeShawn Stevenson RC 1.00 .30
❑ 173 Mamadou N'Diaye RC 1.00 .30
❑ 174 Erick Barkley RC 1.00 .30
❑ 175 Mark Madsen RC 1.00 .30

2001-02 Stadium Club

	Nm-Mt	Ex-Mt
COMP.SET w/o SP's (101)	25.00	7.50
COMMON CARD (1-134)	.20	.06
COMMON ROOKIE (101-133)	2.00	.60

❑ 1 Dikembe Mutombo .40 .12
❑ 2 Clifford Robinson .20 .06
❑ 3 Bonzi Wells .40 .12
❑ 4 Peja Stojakovic .60 .18
❑ 5 Gary Payton .60 .18
❑ 6 Morris Peterson .40 .12
❑ 7 Patrick Ewing .60 .18
❑ 8 Terrell Brandon .40 .12
❑ 9 Tim Thomas .40 .12
❑ 10 Kobe Bryant 2.50 .75
❑ 11 Hakeem Olajuwon .60 .18
❑ 12 Marc Jackson .40 .12
❑ 13 Wang Zhizhi .60 .18
❑ 14 Andre Miller .40 .12
❑ 15 Elton Brand .60 .18
❑ 16 Eddie Robinson .40 .12
❑ 17 Jason Terry .60 .18
❑ 18 Allan Houston .40 .12
❑ 19 Grant Hill .60 .18
❑ 20 Tim Duncan 1.25 .35
❑ 21 Kevin Garnett 1.25 .35
❑ 22 Jahidi White .20 .06
❑ 23 Michael Dickerson .40 .12
❑ 24 Karl Malone .60 .18
❑ 25 Chris Webber .60 .18
❑ 26 Scottie Pippen 1.00 .30
❑ 27 Latrell Sprewell .60 .18
❑ 28 Keith Van Horn .60 .18
❑ 29 Ray Allen .60 .18
❑ 30 Alonzo Mourning .40 .12
❑ 31 Lamar Odom .60 .18
❑ 32 Jalen Rose .60 .18
❑ 33 Ben Wallace .60 .18
❑ 34 Shaquille O'Neal 1.50 .45
❑ 35 Antonio McDyess .40 .12
❑ 36 Dirk Nowitzki 1.00 .30
❑ 37 Marcus Fizer .40 .12
❑ 38 Jamal Mashburn .40 .12
❑ 39 Paul Pierce .60 .18
❑ 40 DerMarr Johnson .40 .12
❑ 41 Steve Nash .60 .18
❑ 42 Jerry Stackhouse .60 .18
❑ 43 Larry Hughes .40 .12
❑ 44 Cuttino Mobley .40 .12
❑ 45 Horace Grant .40 .12
❑ 46 Eddie Jones .60 .18
❑ 47 Wally Szczerbiak .40 .12
❑ 48 Marcus Camby .40 .12
❑ 49 Jamal Crawford .40 .12
❑ 50 Vince Carter 1.50 .45
❑ 51 Donyell Marshall .40 .12
❑ 52 Shareef Abdur-Rahim .60 .18
❑ 53 Courtney Alexander .40 .12
❑ 54 Kenny Anderson .40 .12
❑ 55 Ron Mercer .40 .12
❑ 56 Lamond Murray .20 .06
❑ 57 Michael Finley .60 .18
❑ 58 Raef LaFrentz .40 .12
❑ 59 Reggie Miller .60 .18
❑ 60 Steve Francis .60 .18
❑ 61 Rick Fox .40 .12
❑ 62 Tim Hardaway .40 .12
❑ 63 Glenn Robinson .60 .18
❑ 64 LaPhonso Ellis .20 .06
❑ 65 Kenyon Martin .60 .18
❑ 66 Jason Williams .40 .12
❑ 67 Derek Anderson .40 .12
❑ 68 Eric Snow .40 .12
❑ 69 Darius Miles .60 .18
❑ 70 Antawn Jamison .60 .18
❑ 71 Mateen Cleaves .40 .12
❑ 72 Jason Kidd 1.00 .30
❑ 73 Rasheed Wallace .60 .18
❑ 74 Chris Porter .40 .12
❑ 75 Tracy McGrady 1.50 .45
❑ 76 Aaron McKie .40 .12
❑ 77 Baron Davis .60 .18
❑ 78 Toni Kukoc .40 .12
❑ 79 Antoine Walker .60 .18
❑ 80 Shawn Marion .60 .18
❑ 81 Mike Miller .60 .18
❑ 82 Stephon Marbury .60 .18
❑ 83 Glen Rice .40 .12
❑ 84 David Robinson .60 .18
❑ 85 Rashard Lewis .40 .12
❑ 86 John Stockton .60 .18
❑ 87 Stromile Swift .40 .12
❑ 88 Richard Hamilton .40 .12
❑ 89 Desmond Mason .40 .12
❑ 90 Brian Grant .40 .12
❑ 91 Keyon Dooling .40 .12
❑ 92 Jermaine O'Neal .60 .18
❑ 93 Nick Van Exel .60 .18
❑ 94 Tom Gugliotta .20 .06
❑ 95 Darrell Armstrong .20 .06
❑ 96 Sam Cassell .60 .18
❑ 97 Mike Bibby .60 .18
❑ 98 DeShawn Stevenson .40 .12
❑ 99 Antonio Davis .20 .06
❑ 100 Allen Iverson 1.25 .35
❑ 101 Kwame Brown RC 6.00 1.80
❑ 102 Tyson Chandler RC 6.00 1.80
❑ 103 Pau Gasol RC 6.00 1.80
❑ 104 Eddy Curry RC 6.00 1.80
❑ 105 Jason Richardson RC 10.00 3.00
❑ 106 Shane Battier RC 3.00 .90
❑ 107 Eddie Griffin RC 3.00 .90
❑ 108 DeSagana Diop RC 2.00 .60
❑ 109 Rodney White RC 2.50 .75
❑ 110 Joe Johnson RC 4.00 1.20
❑ 111 Kedrick Brown RC 2.00 .60
❑ 112 Vladimir Radmanovic RC 2.50 .75
❑ 113 Richard Jefferson RC 8.00 2.40
❑ 114 Troy Murphy RC 4.00 1.20
❑ 115 Steven Hunter RC 2.00 .60
❑ 116 Kirk Haston RC 2.00 .60
❑ 117 Michael Bradley RC 2.00 .60
❑ 118 Jason Collins RC 2.50 .75
❑ 119 Zach Randolph RC 6.00 1.80
❑ 120 Brendan Haywood RC 2.50 .75
❑ 121 Joseph Forte RC 2.50 .75
❑ 122 Jeryl Sasser RC 2.00 .60
❑ 123 Brandon Armstrong RC 2.50 .75
❑ 124 Gerald Wallace RC 4.00 1.20
❑ 125 Samuel Dalembert RC 2.00 .60
❑ 126 Jamaal Tinsley RC 3.00 .90

❑ 127 Tony Parker RC	8.00	2.40
❑ 128 Trenton Hassell RC	4.00	1.20
❑ 129 Gilbert Arenas RC	5.00	1.50
❑ 130 Omar Cook RC	2.00	.60
❑ 131 Jeff Trepagnier RC	2.00	.60
❑ 132 Loren Woods RC	2.00	.60
❑ 133 Terence Morris RC	2.00	.60
❑ 134 Michael Jordan	15.00	4.50

2002-03 Stadium Club

	Nm-Mt	Ex-Mt
COMPLETE SET (133)	100.00	30.00
COMP.SET w/o SP's (100)	25.00	7.50
COMMON CARD (1-100)	.20	.06
COMMON ROOKIE (101-133)	2.00	.60
❑ 1 Shaquille O'Neal	1.50	.45
❑ 2 Pau Gasol	.60	.18
❑ 3 Allen Iverson	1.25	.35
❑ 4 Bonzi Wells	.40	.12
❑ 5 Mike Bibby	.60	.18
❑ 6 Rashard Lewis	.40	.12
❑ 7 Aaron McKie	.40	.12
❑ 8 Shane Battier	.60	.18
❑ 9 Kenyon Martin	.60	.18
❑ 10 Tim Duncan	1.25	.35
❑ 11 Richard Jefferson	.40	.12
❑ 12 Jalen Rose	.60	.18
❑ 13 Antoine Walker	.60	.18
❑ 14 Michael Finley	.60	.18
❑ 15 Clifford Robinson	.20	.06
❑ 16 Antawn Jamison	.60	.18
❑ 17 Reggie Miller	.60	.18
❑ 18 Elton Brand	.60	.18
❑ 19 Robert Horry	.40	.12
❑ 20 Kevin Garnett	1.25	.35
❑ 21 Baron Davis	.60	.18
❑ 22 Latrell Sprewell	.60	.18
❑ 23 Glenn Robinson	.60	.18
❑ 24 Wally Szczerbiak	.40	.12
❑ 25 Tracy McGrady	1.50	.45
❑ 26 Stephon Marbury	.60	.18
❑ 27 Rasheed Wallace	.60	.18
❑ 28 Doug Christie	.40	.12
❑ 29 Desmond Mason	.40	.12
❑ 30 Vince Carter	1.50	.45
❑ 31 Andrei Kirilenko	.60	.18
❑ 32 Richard Hamilton	.40	.12
❑ 33 Jamaal Tinsley	.60	.18
❑ 34 Steve Francis	.60	.18
❑ 35 Ben Wallace	.60	.18
❑ 36 Juwan Howard	.40	.12
❑ 37 Dirk Nowitzki	1.00	.30
❑ 38 Andre Miller	.40	.12
❑ 39 Elden Campbell	.20	.06
❑ 40 Paul Pierce	.60	.18
❑ 41 Shareef Abdur-Rahim	.60	.18
❑ 42 John Stockton	.60	.18
❑ 43 Gary Payton	.60	.18
❑ 44 David Robinson	.60	.18
❑ 45 Scottie Pippen	1.00	.30
❑ 46 Morris Peterson	.40	.12
❑ 47 Mike Miller	.60	.18
❑ 48 Marcus Camby	.40	.12
❑ 49 Joe Smith	.40	.12
❑ 50 Kobe Bryant	2.50	.75
❑ 51 Alonzo Mourning	.40	.12
❑ 52 Ray Allen	.60	.18
❑ 53 Keith Van Horn	.60	.18
❑ 54 Grant Hill	.60	.18
❑ 55 Dikembe Mutombo	.40	.12
❑ 56 Shawn Marion	.60	.18
❑ 57 Peja Stojakovic	.60	.18
❑ 58 Tony Parker	.60	.18
❑ 59 Keon Clark	.40	.12
❑ 60 Brendan Haywood	.40	.12
❑ 61 Derek Anderson	.40	.12
❑ 62 Allan Houston	.40	.12
❑ 63 Brian Grant	.40	.12
❑ 64 Lamar Odom	.60	.18
❑ 65 Jermaine O'Neal	.60	.18
❑ 66 Kenny Anderson	.40	.12
❑ 67 Dermarr Johnson	.20	.06
❑ 68 Lamond Murray	.20	.06
❑ 69 Jason Richardson	.60	.18
❑ 70 Rodney Rogers	.20	.06
❑ 71 Rick Fox	.40	.12
❑ 72 Tim Thomas	.40	.12
❑ 73 Darrell Armstrong	.20	.06
❑ 74 Anfernee Hardaway	.60	.18
❑ 75 Chris Webber	.60	.18
❑ 76 Derrick Coleman	.20	.06
❑ 77 Karl Malone	.60	.18
❑ 78 Antonio Davis	.20	.06
❑ 79 Jason Terry	.60	.18
❑ 80 Wang Zhizhi	.60	.18
❑ 81 Steve Nash	.60	.18
❑ 82 Eddy Curry UER Jamal Crawford pic on front	.60	.18
❑ 83 Tim Hardaway	.40	.12
❑ 84 Corliss Williamson	.40	.12
❑ 85 Eddie Griffin	.40	.12
❑ 86 Darius Miles	.60	.18
❑ 87 Jason Williams	.40	.12
❑ 88 Sam Cassell	.60	.18
❑ 89 Kwame Brown	.40	.12
❑ 90 Jason Kidd	1.00	.30
❑ 91 Jamal Mashburn	.40	.12
❑ 92 Jamaal Magloire	.20	.06
❑ 93 Tyson Chandler	.60	.18
❑ 94 Jumaine Jones	.40	.12
❑ 95 Antonio McDyess	.40	.12
❑ 96 Jerry Stackhouse	.60	.18
❑ 97 Gilbert Arenas	.60	.18
❑ 98 Cuttino Mobley	.40	.12
❑ 99 Eddie Jones	.60	.18
❑ 100 Michael Jordan	6.00	1.80
❑ 101 Yao Ming RC	10.00	3.00
❑ 102 Jay Williams RC	2.50	.75
❑ 103 Mike Dunleavy RC	4.00	1.20
❑ 104 Drew Gooden RC	4.00	1.20
❑ 105 Nikoloz Tskitishvili RC	2.00	.60
❑ 106 DaJuan Wagner RC	3.00	.90
❑ 107 Nene Hilario RC	2.50	.75
❑ 108 Chris Wilcox RC	2.50	.75
❑ 109 Amare Stoudemire RC	10.00	3.00
❑ 110 Caron Butler RC	4.00	1.20
❑ 111 Jared Jeffries RC	2.00	.60
❑ 112 Melvin Ely RC	2.00	.60
❑ 113 Marcus Haislip RC	2.00	.60
❑ 114 Fred Jones RC	2.00	.60
❑ 115 Bostjan Nachbar RC	2.00	.60
❑ 116 Dan Dickau RC	2.00	.60
❑ 117 Juan Dixon RC	3.00	.90
❑ 118 Dan Gadzuric RC	2.00	.60
❑ 119 Ryan Humphrey RC	2.00	.60
❑ 120 Kareem Rush RC	3.00	.90
❑ 121 Qyntel Woods RC	2.00	.60
❑ 122 Casey Jacobsen RC	2.00	.60
❑ 123 Tayshaun Prince RC	2.50	.75
❑ 124 Frank Williams RC	2.00	.60
❑ 125 John Salmons RC	2.00	.60
❑ 126 Chris Jefferies RC	2.00	.60
❑ 127 Sam Clancy RC	2.00	.60
❑ 128 Ronald Murray RC	3.00	.90
❑ 129 Roger Mason RC	2.00	.60
❑ 130 Robert Archibald RC	2.00	.60
❑ 131 Vincent Yarbrough RC	2.00	.60
❑ 132 Darius Songaila RC	2.00	.60
❑ 133 Carlos Boozer RC	4.00	1.20

1999-00 Stadium Club Chrome

	Nm-Mt	Ex-Mt
COMPLETE SET (150)	80.00	24.00
COMMON CARD (1-150)	.25	.07
COMMON ROOKIE	.75	.23
❑ 1 Allen Iverson	1.50	.45
❑ 2 Chris Webber	.75	.23
❑ 3 Antawn Jamison	1.25	.35
❑ 4 Karl Malone	.75	.23
❑ 5 Sam Cassell	.75	.23
❑ 6 Kerry Kittles	.25	.07
❑ 7 Tim Thomas	.50	.15
❑ 8 Shawn Bradley	.25	.07
❑ 9 David Wesley	.25	.07
❑ 10 Glenn Robinson	.75	.23
❑ 11 Mitch Richmond	.50	.15
❑ 12 Shareef Abdur-Rahim	.75	.23
❑ 13 Christian Laettner	.50	.15
❑ 14 Anthony Mason	.50	.15
❑ 15 Randy Brown	.25	.07
❑ 16 Charles Barkley	1.00	.30
❑ 17 Bobby Jackson	.50	.15
❑ 18 Matt Harpring	.75	.23
❑ 19 Shawn Kemp	.50	.15
❑ 20 Ruben Patterson	.50	.15
❑ 21 Mike Bibby	.75	.23
❑ 22 Vlade Divac	.50	.15
❑ 23 David Robinson	.75	.23
❑ 24 Keith Van Horn	.75	.23
❑ 25 Juwan Howard	.50	.15
❑ 26 Shaquille O'Neal	2.00	.60
❑ 27 Alonzo Mourning	.50	.15
❑ 28 Michael Olowokandi	.50	.15
❑ 29 Andrew DeClercq	.25	.07
❑ 30 Toni Kukoc	.50	.15
❑ 31 Dikembe Mutombo	.50	.15
❑ 32 Steve Nash	.75	.23
❑ 33 Eddie Jones	.75	.23
❑ 34 Reggie Miller	.75	.23
❑ 35 Larry Hughes	.75	.23
❑ 36 Tim Duncan	1.50	.45
❑ 37 Jerome Williams	.25	.07
❑ 38 Rod Strickland	.25	.07
❑ 39 Patrick Ewing	.75	.23
❑ 40 Grant Hill	.75	.23
❑ 41 Derrick Coleman	.50	.15
❑ 42 Raef LaFrentz	.50	.15
❑ 43 Rik Smits	.50	.15
❑ 44 Latrell Sprewell	.75	.23
❑ 45 John Starks	.50	.15
❑ 46 Cuttino Mobley	.75	.23
❑ 47 Marcus Camby	.50	.15
❑ 48 Stephon Marbury	.75	.23
❑ 49 Tom Gugliotta	.25	.07
❑ 50 Vince Carter	2.00	.60
❑ 51 Chris Mullin	.75	.23
❑ 52 Tyrone Nesby RC	.25	.07

53 Elden Campbell	.25	.07
54 Lindsey Hunter	.25	.07
55 Rasheed Wallace	.75	.23
56 Jeff Hornacek	.50	.15
57 Matt Geiger	.25	.07
58 Antoine Walker	.75	.23
59 Jason Williams	.75	.23
60 Robert Horry	.50	.15
61 Kendall Gill	.25	.07
62 Dan Majerle	.50	.15
63 Robert Traylor	.25	.07
64 P.J. Brown	.25	.07
65 Terrell Brandon	.50	.15
66 Corliss Williamson	.50	.15
67 Bryant Reeves	.25	.07
68 Larry Johnson	.50	.15
69 Keith Closs	.25	.07
70 Walter McCarty	.25	.07
71 Wesley Person	.25	.07
72 Chris Mills	.25	.07
73 Glen Rice	.50	.15
74 Jason Kidd	1.25	.35
75 Dirk Nowitzki	1.50	.45
76 Bryon Russell	.25	.07
77 Vin Baker	.50	.15
78 Darrell Armstrong	.25	.07
79 Eric Snow	.50	.15
80 Hakeem Olajuwon	.75	.23
81 Tracy McGrady	2.00	.60
82 Kenny Anderson	.50	.15
83 Jalen Rose	.75	.23
84 Tim Hardaway	.50	.15
85 Doug Christie	.50	.15
86 Allan Houston	.50	.15
87 Kobe Bryant	3.00	.90
88 Kevin Garnett	1.50	.45
89 Steve Kerr	.50	.15
90 Nick Van Exel	.75	.23
91 Jerry Stackhouse	.75	.23
92 Derek Fisher	.75	.23
93 Donyell Marshall	.50	.15
94 Mark Jackson	.50	.15
95 Ray Allen	.75	.23
96 Avery Johnson	.25	.07
97 Michael Doleac	.25	.07
98 Charles Oakley	.25	.07
99 Gary Payton	.75	.23
100 Theo Ratliff	.50	.15
101 Cedric Ceballos	.25	.07
102 Paul Pierce	.75	.23
103 Michael Finley	.75	.23
104 Brian Grant	.50	.15
105 John Stockton	.75	.23
106 Maurice Taylor	.50	.15
107 Antonio McDyess	.50	.15
108 Adrian Griffin RC	1.25	.35
109 Jamal Mashburn	.50	.15
110 Jayson Williams	.25	.07
111 Joe Smith	.50	.15
112 Clifford Robinson	.25	.07
113 Mario Elie	.25	.07
114 Damon Stoudamire	.50	.15
115 Felipe Lopez	.25	.07
116 Antonio Davis TRAN	.25	.07
117 Mookie Blaylock TRAN	.25	.07
118 Ron Mercer TRAN	.50	.15
119 Horace Grant TRAN	.50	.15
120 Steve Smith TRAN	.50	.15
121 Isaiah Rider TRAN	.25	.07
122 T.Abdul-Wahad TRAN	.25	.07
123 Michael Dickerson TRAN	.50	.15
124 Nick Anderson TRAN	.25	.07
125 Jim Jackson TRAN	.25	.07
126 Hersey Hawkins TRAN	.50	.15
127 Brent Barry TRAN	.25	.07
128 Shandon Anderson TRAN	.25	.07
129 Scottie Pippen TRAN	1.25	.35
130 Isaac Austin TRAN	.25	.07
131 A.Hardaway TRAN	1.25	.35
132 Elton Brand RC	5.00	1.50
133 Steve Francis RC	6.00	1.80
134 Baron Davis RC	4.00	1.20
135 Lamar Odom RC	4.00	1.20
136 Jonathan Bender RC	4.00	1.20
137 Wally Szczerbiak RC	4.00	1.20
138 Richard Hamilton RC	4.00	1.20
139 Andre Miller RC	4.00	1.20
140 Shawn Marion RC	5.00	1.50
141 Jason Terry RC	3.00	.90
142 Trajan Langdon RC	1.50	.45
143 Aleksandar Radojevic RC	.75	.23
144 Corey Maggette RC	4.00	1.20
145 William Avery RC	1.50	.45
146 Ron Artest RC	2.50	.75
147 Cal Bowdler RC	1.25	.35
148 James Posey RC	2.50	.75
149 Quincy Lewis RC	1.25	.35
150 Scott Padgett RC	1.25	.35

1957-58 Topps

	Ex-Mt	VG
COMPLETE SET (80)	5,500.00	2,800.00
COMMON CARD (1-80)	40.00	20.00
COMMON DP	25.00	12.50
1 Nat Clifton DP RC	250.00	75.00
2 George Yardley DP RC	70.00	35.00
3 Neil Johnston DP RC	55.00	28.00
4 Carl Braun DP	50.00	25.00
5 Bill Sharman DP RC	125.00	60.00
6 George King DP RC	35.00	17.50
7 Kenny Sears DP RC	35.00	17.50
8 Dick Ricketts DP RC	35.00	17.50
9 Jack Nichols DP	25.00	12.50
10 Paul Arizin DP RC	100.00	50.00
11 Chuck Noble DP	25.00	12.50
12 Slater Martin DP RC	70.00	35.00
13 Dolph Schayes DP RC	70.00	35.00
14 Dick Atha DP	25.00	12.50
15 Frank Ramsey DP RC	90.00	45.00
16 Dick McGuire DP RC	55.00	28.00
17 Bob Cousy DP RC	400.00	200.00
18 Larry Foust DP RC	35.00	17.50
19 Tom Heinsohn RC	250.00	125.00
20 Bill Thieben DP	25.00	12.50
21 Don Meineke DP RC	35.00	17.50
22 Tom Marshall	40.00	20.00
23 Dick Garmaker	40.00	20.00
24 Bob Pettit QP RC	150.00	75.00
25 Jim Krebs DP RC	35.00	17.50
26 Gene Shue DP RC	60.00	30.00
27 Ed Macauley DP RC	70.00	35.00
28 Vern Mikkelsen RC	100.00	50.00
29 Willie Naulls RC	60.00	30.00
30 Walter Dukes DP RC	45.00	22.00
31 Dave Piontek DP	25.00	12.50
32 John Kerr RC	100.00	50.00
33 Larry Costello DP RC	50.00	25.00
34 Woody Sauldsberry DP RC	35.00	17.50
35 Ray Felix RC	45.00	22.00
36 Ernie Beck	40.00	20.00
37 Cliff Hagan RC	100.00	50.00
38 Guy Sparrow DP	25.00	12.50
39 Jim Loscutoff RC	60.00	30.00
40 Arnie Risen DP	45.00	22.00
41 Joe Graboski	40.00	20.00
42 M.Stokes DP RC UER Text refers to N.F.L. Record	100.00	50.00
43 Rod Hundley DP RC	100.00	50.00
44 Tom Gola DP RC	80.00	40.00
45 Med Park RC	45.00	22.00
46 Mel Hutchins DP	25.00	12.50
47 Larry Friend DP	25.00	12.50
48 Lennie Rosenbluth DP RC	50.00	25.00
49 Walt Davis	40.00	20.00
50 Richie Regan RC	45.00	22.00
51 Frank Selvy DP RC	50.00	25.00
52 Art Spoelstra DP	25.00	12.50
53 Bob Hopkins RC	45.00	22.00
54 Earl Lloyd RC	50.00	25.00
55 Phil Jordan DP	25.00	12.50
56 Bob Houbregs DP RC	40.00	20.00
57 Lou Tsioropoulos DP	25.00	12.50
58 Ed Conlin RC	45.00	22.00
59 Al Bianchi RC	80.00	40.00
60 George Dempsey RC	45.00	22.00
61 Chuck Share	40.00	20.00
62 Harry Gallatin DP RC	50.00	25.00
63 Bob Harrison	40.00	20.00
64 Bob Burrow DP	25.00	12.50
65 Win Wilfong DP	25.00	12.50
66 Jack McMahon DP RC	35.00	17.50
67 Jack George	40.00	20.00
68 Charlie Tyra DP	25.00	12.50
69 Ron Sobie	40.00	20.00
70 Jack Coleman	40.00	20.00
71 Jack Twyman DP RC	110.00	55.00
72 Paul Seymour RC	45.00	22.00
73 Jim Paxson DP RC	55.00	28.00
74 Bob Leonard RC	50.00	25.00
75 Andy Phillip	60.00	30.00
76 Joe Holup	40.00	20.00
77 Bill Russell RC	1,000.00	500.00
78 Clyde Lovellette DP RC	100.00	50.00
79 Ed Fleming DP	25.00	12.50
80 Dick Schnittker RC	120.00	36.00

1969-70 Topps

	NM	Ex
COMPLETE SET (99)	1,800.00	700.00
1 Wilt Chamberlain	175.00	52.50
2 Gail Goodrich RC	50.00	20.00
3 Cazzie Russell RC	15.00	6.00
4 Darrall Imhoff RC	6.00	2.40
5 Bailey Howell	8.00	3.20
6 Lucius Allen RC	10.00	4.00
7 Tom Boerwinkle RC	6.00	2.40
8 Jimmy Walker RC	8.00	3.20
9 John Block RC	6.00	2.40
10 Nate Thurmond RC	35.00	14.00
11 Gary Gregor	4.00	1.60
12 Gus Johnson RC	20.00	8.00
13 Luther Rackley	4.00	1.60
14 Jon McGlocklin RC	6.00	2.40

❑ 15 Connie Hawkins RC	45.00	18.00
❑ 16 Johnny Egan	4.00	1.60
❑ 17 Jim Washington	4.00	1.60
❑ 18 Dick Barnett RC	8.00	3.20
❑ 19 Tom Meschery	8.00	3.20
❑ 20 John Havlicek RC	150.00	60.00
❑ 21 Eddie Miles	4.00	1.60
❑ 22 Walt Wesley	6.00	2.40
❑ 23 Rick Adelman RC	8.00	3.20
❑ 24 Al Attles	8.00	3.20
❑ 25 Lew Alcindor RC	400.00	160.00
❑ 26 Jack Marin RC	8.00	3.20
❑ 27 Walt Hazzard RC	12.00	4.80
❑ 28 Connie Dierking	4.00	1.60
❑ 29 Keith Erickson RC	12.00	4.80
❑ 30 Bob Rule RC	10.00	4.00
❑ 31 Dick Van Arsdale RC	12.00	4.80
❑ 32 Archie Clark RC	12.00	4.80
❑ 33 Terry Dischinger RC	4.00	1.60
❑ 34 Henry Finkel RC	4.00	1.60
❑ 35 Elgin Baylor	50.00	20.00
❑ 36 Ron Williams	4.00	1.60
❑ 37 Loy Petersen	4.00	1.60
❑ 38 Guy Rodgers	8.00	3.20
❑ 39 Toby Kimball	4.00	1.60
❑ 40 Billy Cunningham RC	50.00	20.00
❑ 41 Joe Caldwell RC	8.00	3.20
❑ 42 Leroy Ellis RC	6.00	2.40
❑ 43 Bill Bradley RC	125.00	50.00
❑ 44 Len Wilkens UER (Misspelled Wilkins on card back)	30.00	12.00
❑ 45 Jerry Lucas RC	40.00	16.00
❑ 46 Neal Walk RC	6.00	2.40
❑ 47 Emmette Bryant RC	6.00	2.40
❑ 48 Bob Kauffman RC	4.00	1.60
❑ 49 Mel Counts RC	6.00	2.40
❑ 50 Oscar Robertson	60.00	24.00
❑ 51 Jim Barnett RC	8.00	3.20
❑ 52 Don Smith	4.00	1.60
❑ 53 Jim Davis	4.00	1.60
❑ 54 Wally Jones RC	6.00	2.40
❑ 55 Dave Bing RC	35.00	14.00
❑ 56 Wes Unseld RC	50.00	20.00
❑ 57 Joe Ellis	4.00	1.60
❑ 58 John Tresvant	4.00	1.60
❑ 59 Larry Siegfried RC	6.00	2.40
❑ 60 Willis Reed RC	50.00	20.00
❑ 61 Paul Silas RC	20.00	8.00
❑ 62 Bob Weiss RC	8.00	3.20
❑ 63 Willie McCarter	4.00	1.60
❑ 64 Don Kojis RC	4.00	1.60
❑ 65 Lou Hudson RC	20.00	8.00
❑ 66 Jim King	4.00	1.60
❑ 67 Luke Jackson RC	6.00	2.40
❑ 68 Len Chappell RC	4.00	1.60
❑ 69 Ray Scott	4.00	1.60
❑ 70 Jeff Mullins RC	8.00	3.20
❑ 71 Howie Komives	4.00	1.60
❑ 72 Tom Sanders RC	10.00	4.00
❑ 73 Dick Snyder	4.00	1.60
❑ 74 Dave Stallworth RC	6.00	2.40
❑ 75 Elvin Hayes RC	70.00	28.00
❑ 76 Art Harris	4.00	1.60
❑ 77 Don Ohl	6.00	2.40
❑ 78 Bob Love RC	50.00	20.00
❑ 79 Tom Van Arsdale RC	10.00	4.00
❑ 80 Earl Monroe RC	40.00	16.00
❑ 81 Greg Smith	4.00	1.60
❑ 82 Don Nelson RC	35.00	14.00
❑ 83 Happy Hairston RC	8.00	3.20
❑ 84 Hal Greer	12.00	4.80
❑ 85 Dave DeBusschere RC	40.00	16.00
❑ 86 Bill Bridges RC	8.00	3.20
❑ 87 Herm Gilliam RC	6.00	2.40
❑ 88 Jim Fox	4.00	1.60
❑ 89 Bob Boozer	6.00	2.40
❑ 90 Jerry West	100.00	40.00
❑ 91 Chet Walker RC	15.00	6.00
❑ 92 Flynn Robinson RC	6.00	2.40
❑ 93 Clyde Lee	4.00	1.60
❑ 94 Kevin Loughery RC	10.00	4.00
❑ 95 Walt Bellamy	10.00	4.00
❑ 96 Art Williams	4.00	1.60
❑ 97 Adrian Smith RC	6.00	2.40
❑ 98 Walt Frazier RC	70.00	28.00
❑ 99 Checklist 1-99	300.00	90.00

1970-71 Topps

	NM	Ex
COMPLETE SET (175)	1,200.00	475.00
COMMON CARD (1-110)	2.50	1.00
COMMON CARD (111-175)	3.00	1.20
❑ 1 Lew Alcindor / Jerry West / Elvin Hayes LL	35.00	10.50
❑ 2 Jerry West / Lew Alcindor / Elvin Hayes LL SP	35.00	14.00
❑ 3 Johnny Green / Darrall Imhoff / Lou Hudson LL	5.00	2.00
❑ 4 Flynn Robinson / Chet Walker / Jeff Mullins LL SP	10.00	4.00
❑ 5 Elvin Hayes / Wes Unseld / Lew Alcindor LL	25.00	10.00
❑ 6 Len Wilkens / Walt Frazier / Clem Haskins LL SP	12.00	4.80
❑ 7 Bill Bradley	50.00	20.00
❑ 8 Ron Williams	2.50	1.00
❑ 9 Otto Moore	2.50	1.00
❑ 10 John Havlicek SP	75.00	30.00
❑ 11 George Wilson RC	2.50	1.00
❑ 12 John Trapp	2.50	1.00
❑ 13 Pat Riley RC	60.00	24.00
❑ 14 Jim Washington	2.50	1.00
❑ 15 Bob Rule	4.00	1.60
❑ 16 Bob Weiss	4.00	1.60
❑ 17 Neil Johnson	2.50	1.00
❑ 18 Walt Bellamy	6.00	2.40
❑ 19 McCoy McLemore	2.50	1.00
❑ 20 Earl Monroe	15.00	6.00
❑ 21 Wally Anderzunas	2.50	1.00
❑ 22 Guy Rodgers	4.00	1.60
❑ 23 Rick Roberson	2.50	1.00
❑ 24 Checklist 1-110	40.00	12.00
❑ 25 Jimmy Walker	4.00	1.60
❑ 26 Mike Riordan RC	6.00	2.40
❑ 27 Henry Finkel	2.50	1.00
❑ 28 Joe Ellis	2.50	1.00
❑ 29 Mike Davis	2.50	1.00
❑ 30 Lou Hudson	6.00	2.40
❑ 31 Lucius Allen SP	8.00	3.20
❑ 32 Toby Kimball SP	6.00	2.40
❑ 33 Luke Jackson SP	6.00	2.40
❑ 34 Johnny Egan	2.50	1.00
❑ 35 Leroy Ellis SP	6.00	2.40
❑ 36 Jack Marin SP	8.00	3.20
❑ 37 Joe Caldwell SP	8.00	3.20
❑ 38 Keith Erickson	6.00	2.40
❑ 39 Don Smith	2.50	1.00
❑ 40 Flynn Robinson	4.00	1.60
❑ 41 Bob Boozer	2.50	1.00
❑ 42 Howie Komives	2.50	1.00
❑ 43 Dick Barnett	4.00	1.60
❑ 44 Stu Lantz RC	3.00	1.20
❑ 45 Dick Van Arsdale	6.00	2.40
❑ 46 Jerry Lucas	10.00	4.00
❑ 47 Don Chaney RC	10.00	4.00
❑ 48 Ray Scott	2.50	1.00
❑ 49 Dick Cunningham SP	8.00	3.20
❑ 50 Wilt Chamberlain	80.00	32.00
❑ 51 Kevin Loughery	4.00	1.60
❑ 52 Stan McKenzie	2.50	1.00
❑ 53 Fred Foster	2.50	1.00
❑ 54 Jim Davis	2.50	1.00
❑ 55 Walt Wesley	2.50	1.00
❑ 56 Bill Hewitt	2.50	1.00
❑ 57 Darrall Imhoff	2.50	1.00
❑ 58 John Block	2.50	1.00
❑ 59 Al Attles SP	8.00	3.20
❑ 60 Chet Walker	6.00	2.40
❑ 61 Luther Rackley	2.50	1.00
❑ 62 Jerry Chambers SP RC	8.00	3.20
❑ 63 Bob Dandridge RC	8.00	3.20
❑ 64 Dick Snyder	2.50	1.00
❑ 65 Elgin Baylor	30.00	12.00
❑ 66 Connie Dierking	2.50	1.00
❑ 67 Steve Kuberski RC	2.50	1.00
❑ 68 Tom Boerwinkle	2.50	1.00
❑ 69 Paul Silas	6.00	2.40
❑ 70 Elvin Hayes	30.00	12.00
❑ 71 Bill Bridges	4.00	1.60
❑ 72 Wes Unseld	15.00	6.00
❑ 73 Herm Gilliam	2.50	1.00
❑ 74 Bobby Smith SP RC	8.00	3.20
❑ 75 Lew Alcindor	80.00	32.00
❑ 76 Jeff Mullins	4.00	1.60
❑ 77 Happy Hairston	4.00	1.60
❑ 78 Dave Stallworth SP	6.00	2.40
❑ 79 Fred Hetzel	2.50	1.00
❑ 80 Len Wilkens SP	20.00	8.00
❑ 81 Johnny Green RC	6.00	2.40
❑ 82 Erwin Mueller	2.50	1.00
❑ 83 Wally Jones	4.00	1.60
❑ 84 Bob Love	8.00	3.20
❑ 85 Dick Garrett RC	2.50	1.00
❑ 86 Don Nelson SP	20.00	8.00
❑ 87 Neal Walk SP	6.00	2.40
❑ 88 Larry Siegfried	2.50	1.00
❑ 89 Gary Gregor	2.50	1.00
❑ 90 Nate Thurmond	8.00	3.20
❑ 91 John Warren	2.50	1.00
❑ 92 Gus Johnson	6.00	2.40
❑ 93 Gail Goodrich	15.00	6.00
❑ 94 Dorie Murrey	2.50	1.00
❑ 95 Cazzie Russell SP	10.00	4.00
❑ 96 Terry Dischinger	2.50	1.00
❑ 97 Norm Van Lier SP RC	15.00	6.00
❑ 98 Jim Fox	2.50	1.00
❑ 99 Tom Meschery	2.50	1.00
❑ 100 Oscar Robertson	35.00	14.00
❑ 101A Checklist 111-175 (1970-71 in black)	30.00	9.00
❑ 101B Checklist 111-175 (1970-71 in white)	30.00	9.00
❑ 102 Rich Johnson	2.50	1.00
❑ 103 Mel Counts	4.00	1.60
❑ 104 Bill Hosket SP RC	6.00	2.40
❑ 105 Archie Clark	4.00	1.60
❑ 106 Walt Frazier AS	10.00	4.00
❑ 107 Jerry West AS	25.00	10.00
❑ 108 Bill Cunningham AS	10.00	4.00
❑ 109 Connie Hawkins AS	8.00	3.20
❑ 110 Willis Reed AS	8.00	3.20
❑ 111 Nate Thurmond AS	5.00	2.00
❑ 112 John Havlicek AS	30.00	12.00
❑ 113 Elgin Baylor AS	18.00	7.25
❑ 114 Oscar Robertson AS	20.00	8.00
❑ 115 Lou Hudson AS	4.00	1.60
❑ 116 Emmette Bryant	3.00	1.20
❑ 117 Greg Howard	3.00	1.20
❑ 118 Rick Adelman	5.00	2.00
❑ 119 Barry Clemens	3.00	1.20
❑ 120 Walt Frazier	30.00	12.00
❑ 121 Jim Barnes RC	3.00	1.20
❑ 122 Bernie Williams	3.00	1.20
❑ 123 Pete Maravich RC	250.00	100.00

Card	NM	Ex
❑ 124 Matt Guokas RC	8.00	3.20
❑ 125 Dave Bing	12.00	4.80
❑ 126 John Tresvant	3.00	1.20
❑ 127 Shaler Halimon	3.00	1.20
❑ 128 Don Ohl	3.00	1.20
❑ 129 Fred Carter RC	6.00	2.40
❑ 130 Connie Hawkins	18.00	7.25
❑ 131 Jim King	3.00	1.20
❑ 132 Ed Manning RC	6.00	2.40
❑ 133 Adrian Smith	3.00	1.20
❑ 134 Walt Hazzard	6.00	2.40
❑ 135 Dave DeBusschere	15.00	6.00
❑ 136 Don Kojis	3.00	1.20
❑ 137 Calvin Murphy RC	35.00	14.00
❑ 138 Nate Bowman	3.00	1.20
❑ 139 Jon McGlocklin	5.00	2.00
❑ 140 Billy Cunningham	18.00	7.25
❑ 141 Willie McCarter	3.00	1.20
❑ 142 Jim Barnett	3.00	1.20
❑ 143 JoJo White RC	20.00	8.00
❑ 144 Clyde Lee	3.00	1.20
❑ 145 Tom Van Arsdale	6.00	2.40
❑ 146 Len Chappell	3.00	1.20
❑ 147 Lee Winfield	3.00	1.20
❑ 148 Jerry Sloan RC	20.00	8.00
❑ 149 Art Harris	3.00	1.20
❑ 150 Willis Reed	20.00	8.00
❑ 151 Art Williams	3.00	1.20
❑ 152 Don May	3.00	1.20
❑ 153 Loy Petersen	3.00	1.20
❑ 154 Dave Gambee	3.00	1.20
❑ 155 Hal Greer	6.00	2.40
❑ 156 Dave Newmark	3.00	1.20
❑ 157 Jimmy Collins	3.00	1.20
❑ 158 Bill Turner	3.00	1.20
❑ 159 Eddie Miles	3.00	1.20
❑ 160 Jerry West	50.00	20.00
❑ 161 Bob Quick	3.00	1.20
❑ 162 Fred Crawford	3.00	1.20
❑ 163 Tom Sanders	6.00	2.40
❑ 164 Dale Schlueter	3.00	1.20
❑ 165 Clem Haskins RC	12.00	4.80
❑ 166 Greg Smith	3.00	1.20
❑ 167 Rod Thorn RC	8.00	3.20
❑ 168 Willis Reed PO	10.00	4.00
❑ 169 Dick Garrett PO	5.00	2.00
❑ 170 Dave DeBusschere PO	10.00	4.00
❑ 171 Jerry West PO	18.00	7.25
❑ 172 Bill Bradley PO	18.00	7.25
❑ 173 Wilt Chamberlain PO	18.00	7.25
❑ 174 Walt Frazier PO	12.00	4.80
❑ 175 Knicks Celebrate	20.00	6.00
(New York Knicks, World Champs)		

1971-72 Topps

	NM	Ex
COMPLETE SET (233)	750.00	300.00
COM. NBA CARD (1-144)	1.50	.60
COM. ABA CARD (145-233)	2.00	.80
❑ 1 Oscar Robertson	40.00	12.00
❑ 2 Bill Bradley	30.00	12.00
❑ 3 Jim Fox	1.50	.60
❑ 4 John Johnson RC	2.00	.80
❑ 5 Luke Jackson	2.00	.80
❑ 6 Don May DP	1.50	.60
❑ 7 Kevin Loughery	2.00	.80
❑ 8 Terry Dischinger	1.50	.60
❑ 9 Neal Walk	2.00	.80
❑ 10 Elgin Baylor	25.00	10.00
❑ 11 Rick Adelman	2.00	.80
❑ 12 Clyde Lee	1.50	.60
❑ 13 Jerry Chambers	1.50	.60
❑ 14 Fred Carter	2.00	.80
❑ 15 Tom Boerwinkle DP	1.50	.60
❑ 16 John Block	1.50	.60
❑ 17 Dick Barnett	2.00	.80
❑ 18 Henry Finkel	1.50	.60
❑ 19 Norm Van Lier	4.00	1.60
❑ 20 Spencer Haywood RC	15.00	6.00
❑ 21 George Johnson	1.50	.60
❑ 22 Bobby Lewis	1.50	.60
❑ 23 Bill Hewitt	1.50	.60
❑ 24 Walt Hazzard DP	4.00	1.60
❑ 25 Happy Hairston	2.00	.80
❑ 26 George Wilson	1.50	.60
❑ 27 Lucius Allen	2.00	.80
❑ 28 Jim Washington	1.50	.60
❑ 29 Nate Archibald RC	25.00	10.00
❑ 30 Willis Reed	10.00	4.00
❑ 31 Erwin Mueller	1.50	.60
❑ 32 Art Harris	1.50	.60
❑ 33 Pete Cross	1.50	.60
❑ 34 Geoff Petrie RC	4.00	1.60
❑ 35 John Havlicek	30.00	12.00
❑ 36 Larry Siegfried	1.50	.60
❑ 37 John Tresvant DP	1.50	.60
❑ 38 Ron Williams	1.50	.60
❑ 39 Lamar Green DP	1.50	.60
❑ 40 Bob Rule DP	2.00	.80
❑ 41 Jim McMillian RC	2.00	.80
❑ 42 Wally Jones	2.00	.80
❑ 43 Bob Boozer	1.50	.60
❑ 44 Eddie Miles	1.50	.60
❑ 45 Bob Love DP	5.00	2.00
❑ 46 Claude English	1.50	.60
❑ 47 Dave Cowens RC	40.00	16.00
❑ 48 Emmette Bryant	1.50	.60
❑ 49 Dave Stallworth	2.00	.80
❑ 50 Jerry West	40.00	16.00
❑ 51 Joe Ellis	1.50	.60
❑ 52 Walt Wesley DP	1.50	.60
❑ 53 Howie Komives	1.50	.60
❑ 54 Paul Silas	4.00	1.60
❑ 55 Pete Maravich DP	40.00	16.00
❑ 56 Gary Gregor	1.50	.60
❑ 57 Sam Lacey RC	4.00	1.60
❑ 58 Calvin Murphy DP	6.00	2.40
❑ 59 Bob Dandridge	2.00	.80
❑ 60 Hal Greer	4.00	1.60
❑ 61 Keith Erickson	4.00	1.60
❑ 62 Joe Cooke	1.50	.60
❑ 63 Bob Lanier RC	40.00	16.00
❑ 64 Don Kojis	1.50	.60
❑ 65 Walt Frazier	20.00	8.00
❑ 66 Chet Walker DP	4.00	1.60
❑ 67 Dick Garrett	1.50	.60
❑ 68 John Trapp	2.00	.80
❑ 69 JoJo White	8.00	3.20
❑ 70 Wilt Chamberlain	50.00	20.00
❑ 71 Dave Sorenson	1.50	.60
❑ 72 Jim King	1.50	.60
❑ 73 Cazzie Russell	4.00	1.60
❑ 74 Jon McGlocklin	2.00	.80
❑ 75 Tom Van Arsdale	2.00	.80
❑ 76 Dale Schlueter	1.50	.60
❑ 77 Gus Johnson DP	4.00	1.60
❑ 78 Dave Bing	8.00	3.20
❑ 79 Billy Cunningham	10.00	4.00
❑ 80 Len Wilkens	10.00	4.00
❑ 81 Jerry Lucas DP	5.00	2.00
❑ 82 Don Chaney	4.00	1.60
❑ 83 McCoy McLemore	1.50	.60
❑ 84 Bob Kauffman DP	1.50	.60
❑ 85 Dick Van Arsdale	4.00	1.60
❑ 86 Johnny Green	2.00	.80
❑ 87 Jerry Sloan	5.00	2.00
❑ 88 Luther Rackley DP	1.50	.60
❑ 89 Shaler Halimon	1.50	.60
❑ 90 Jimmy Walker	2.00	.80
❑ 91 Rudy Tomjanovich RC	25.00	10.00
❑ 92 Levi Fontaine	1.50	.60
❑ 93 Bobby Smith	2.00	.80
❑ 94 Bob Arnzen	1.50	.60
❑ 95 Wes Unseld DP	6.00	2.40
❑ 96 Clem Haskins DP	4.00	1.60
❑ 97 Jim Davis	1.50	.60
❑ 98 Steve Kuberski	1.50	.60
❑ 99 Mike Davis DP	1.50	.60
❑ 100 Lew Alcindor	50.00	20.00
❑ 101 Willie McCarter	1.50	.60
❑ 102 Charlie Paulk	1.50	.60
❑ 103 Lee Winfield	1.50	.60
❑ 104 Jim Barnett	1.50	.60
❑ 105 Connie Hawkins DP	8.00	3.20
❑ 106 Archie Clark DP	2.00	.80
❑ 107 Dave DeBusschere	8.00	3.20
❑ 108 Stu Lantz DP	2.00	.80
❑ 109 Don Smith	1.50	.60
❑ 110 Lou Hudson	4.00	1.60
❑ 111 Leroy Ellis	1.50	.60
❑ 112 Jack Marin	2.00	.80
❑ 113 Matt Guokas	2.00	.80
❑ 114 Don Nelson	6.00	2.40
❑ 115 Jeff Mullins DP	2.00	.80
❑ 116 Walt Bellamy	6.00	2.40
❑ 117 Bob Quick	1.50	.60
❑ 118 John Warren	1.50	.60
❑ 119 Barry Clemens	1.50	.60
❑ 120 Elvin Hayes DP	10.00	4.00
❑ 121 Gail Goodrich	8.00	3.20
❑ 122 Ed Manning	2.00	.80
❑ 123 Herm Gilliam DP	1.50	.60
❑ 124 Dennis Awtrey RC	2.00	.80
❑ 125 John Hummer DP	1.50	.60
❑ 126 Mike Riordan	2.00	.80
❑ 127 Mel Counts	1.50	.60
❑ 128 Bob Weiss DP	1.50	.60
❑ 129 Greg Smith DP	1.50	.60
❑ 130 Earl Monroe	10.00	4.00
❑ 131 Nate Thurmond DP	4.00	1.60
❑ 132 Bill Bridges DP	2.00	.80
❑ 133 Lew Alcindor PO	12.00	4.80
❑ 134 NBA Playoffs G2 Bucks make it Two Straight	3.00	1.20
❑ 135 Bob Dandridge PO	3.00	1.20
❑ 136 Oscar Robertson PO	8.00	3.20
❑ 137 Oscar Robertson PO	15.00	6.00
❑ 138 Lew Alcindor Elvin Hayes John Havlicek LL	20.00	8.00
❑ 139 Lew Alcindor John Havlicek Elvin Hayes LL	20.00	8.00
❑ 140 Johnny Green Lew Alcindor Wilt Chamberlain LL	15.00	6.00
❑ 141 Chet Walker Oscar Robertson Ron Williams LL	5.00	2.00
❑ 142 Wilt Chamberlain Elvin Hayes Lew Alcindor LL	25.00	10.00
❑ 143 Norm Van Lier Oscar Robertson Jerry West LL	12.00	4.80
❑ 144A NBA Checklist 1-144 (Copyright notation extends up to card 110)	18.00	5.50
❑ 144B NBA Checklist 1-144 (Copyright notation extends up to card 108)	18.00	5.50
❑ 145 ABA Checklist 145-233	18.00	5.50
❑ 146 Dan Issel John Brisker Charlie Scott LL	8.00	3.20
❑ 147 Dan Issel Rick Barry John Brisker LL	12.00	4.80
❑ 148 Zelmo Beaty Bill Paultz Roger Brown LL	4.00	1.60
❑ 149 Rick Barry Darrell Carrier Billy Keller LL	10.00	4.00
❑ 150 Mel Daniels Julius Keye Mike Lewis LL	4.00	1.60

Card	NM	Ex
❑ 151 Bill Melchionni Mack Calvin Charlie Scott LL	4.00	1.60
❑ 152 Larry Brown RC	20.00	8.00
❑ 153 Bob Bedell	2.00	.80
❑ 154 Merv Jackson	2.00	.80
❑ 155 Joe Caldwell	2.50	1.00
❑ 156 Billy Paultz RC	5.00	2.00
❑ 157 Les Hunter	2.50	1.00
❑ 158 Charlie Williams	2.00	.80
❑ 159 Stew Johnson	2.00	.80
❑ 160 Mack Calvin RC	5.00	2.00
❑ 161 Don Sidle	2.00	.80
❑ 162 Mike Barrett	2.00	.80
❑ 163 Tom Workman	2.00	.80
❑ 164 Joe Hamilton	2.50	1.00
❑ 165 Zelmo Beaty RC	8.00	3.20
❑ 166 Dan Hester	2.00	.80
❑ 167 Bob Verga	2.00	.80
❑ 168 Wilbert Jones	2.00	.80
❑ 169 Skeeter Swift	2.00	.80
❑ 170 Rick Barry RC	50.00	20.00
❑ 171 Billy Keller RC	4.00	1.60
❑ 172 Ron Franz	2.00	.80
❑ 173 Roland Taylor RC	2.50	1.00
❑ 174 Julian Hammond	2.00	.80
❑ 175 Steve Jones RC	6.00	2.40
❑ 176 Gerald Govan	2.50	1.00
❑ 177 Darrell Carrier RC	2.50	1.00
❑ 178 Ron Boone RC	5.00	2.00
❑ 179 George Peeples	2.00	.80
❑ 180 John Brisker	2.50	1.00
❑ 181 Doug Moe RC	6.00	2.40
❑ 182 Ollie Taylor	2.00	.80
❑ 183 Bob Netolicky RC	2.50	1.00
❑ 184 Sam Robinson	2.00	.80
❑ 185 James Jones	2.50	1.00
❑ 186 Julius Keye	2.50	1.00
❑ 187 Wayne Hightower	2.00	.80
❑ 188 Warren Armstrong RC	2.50	1.00
❑ 189 Mike Lewis	2.00	.80
❑ 190 Charlie Scott RC	8.00	3.20
❑ 191 Jim Ard	2.00	.80
❑ 192 George Lehmann	2.00	.80
❑ 193 Ira Harge	2.00	.80
❑ 194 Willie Wise RC	5.00	2.00
❑ 195 Mel Daniels RC	8.00	3.20
❑ 196 Larry Cannon	2.00	.80
❑ 197 Jim Eakins	2.50	1.00
❑ 198 Rich Jones	2.50	1.00
❑ 199 Bill Melchionni RC	4.00	1.60
❑ 200 Dan Issel RC	30.00	12.00
❑ 201 George Stone	2.00	.80
❑ 202 George Thompson	2.00	.80
❑ 203 Craig Raymond	2.00	.80
❑ 204 Freddie Lewis RC	2.50	1.00
❑ 205 George Carter	2.50	1.00
❑ 206 Lonnie Wright	2.00	.80
❑ 207 Cincy Powell	2.50	1.00
❑ 208 Larry Miller	2.50	1.00
❑ 209 Sonny Dove	2.00	.80
❑ 210 Byron Beck RC	2.50	1.00
❑ 211 John Beasley	2.00	.80
❑ 212 Lee Davis	2.00	.80
❑ 213 Rick Mount RC	6.00	2.40
❑ 214 Walt Simon	2.00	.80
❑ 215 Glen Combs	2.00	.80
❑ 216 Neil Johnson	2.00	.80
❑ 217 Manny Leaks	2.00	.80
❑ 218 Chuck Williams	2.50	1.00
❑ 219 Warren Davis	2.00	.80
❑ 220 Donnie Freeman RC	2.50	1.00
❑ 221 Randy Mahaffey	2.00	.80
❑ 222 John Barnhill	2.00	.80
❑ 223 Al Cueto	2.00	.80
❑ 224 Louie Dampier RC	8.00	3.20
❑ 225 Roger Brown RC	5.00	2.00
❑ 226 Joe DePre	2.00	.80
❑ 227 Ray Scott	2.00	.80
❑ 228 Arvesta Kelly	2.00	.80
❑ 229 Vann Williford	2.00	.80
❑ 230 Larry Jones	2.50	1.00
❑ 231 Gene Moore	2.00	.80
❑ 232 Ralph Simpson RC	2.50	1.00
❑ 233 Red Robbins RC	5.00	1.50

1972-73 Topps

	NM	Ex
COMPLETE SET (264)	800.00	325.00
COM. NBA CARD (1-176)	1.00	.40
COM. ABA CARD (177-264)	1.50	.60
❑ 1 Wilt Chamberlain	60.00	18.00
❑ 2 Stan Love	1.00	.40
❑ 3 Geoff Petrie	1.50	.60
❑ 4 Curtis Perry RC	1.00	.40
❑ 5 Pete Maravich	35.00	14.00
❑ 6 Gus Johnson	3.00	1.20
❑ 7 Dave Cowens	15.00	6.00
❑ 8 Randy Smith RC	4.00	1.60
❑ 9 Matt Guokas	1.50	.60
❑ 10 Spencer Haywood	4.00	1.60
❑ 11 Jerry Sloan	3.00	1.20
❑ 12 Dave Sorenson	1.00	.40
❑ 13 Howie Komives	1.00	.40
❑ 14 Joe Ellis	1.00	.40
❑ 15 Jerry Lucas	5.00	2.00
❑ 16 Stu Lantz	1.50	.60
❑ 17 Bill Bridges	1.50	.60
❑ 18 Leroy Ellis	1.00	.40
❑ 19 Art Williams	1.00	.40
❑ 20 Sidney Wicks RC	8.00	3.20
❑ 21 Wes Unseld	6.00	2.40
❑ 22 Jim Washington	1.00	.40
❑ 23 Fred Hilton	1.00	.40
❑ 24 Curtis Rowe RC	1.50	.60
❑ 25 Oscar Robertson	20.00	8.00
❑ 26 Larry Steele RC	1.50	.60
❑ 27 Charlie Davis	1.00	.40
❑ 28 Nate Thurmond	5.00	2.00
❑ 29 Fred Carter	1.50	.60
❑ 30 Connie Hawkins	7.00	2.80
❑ 31 Calvin Murphy	5.00	2.00
❑ 32 Phil Jackson RC	40.00	16.00
❑ 33 Lee Winfield	1.00	.40
❑ 34 Jim Fox	1.00	.40
❑ 35 Dave Bing	6.00	2.40
❑ 36 Gary Gregor	1.00	.40
❑ 37 Mike Riordan	1.50	.60
❑ 38 George Trapp	1.00	.40
❑ 39 Mike Davis	1.00	.40
❑ 40 Bob Rule	1.50	.60
❑ 41 John Block	1.00	.40
❑ 42 Bob Dandridge	1.50	.60
❑ 43 John Johnson	1.50	.60
❑ 44 Rick Barry	18.00	7.25
❑ 45 JoJo White	4.00	1.60
❑ 46 Cliff Meely	1.00	.40
❑ 47 Charlie Scott	3.00	1.20
❑ 48 Johnny Green	1.50	.60
❑ 49 Pete Cross	1.00	.40
❑ 50 Gail Goodrich	6.00	2.40
❑ 51 Jim Davis	1.00	.40
❑ 52 Dick Barnett	1.50	.60
❑ 53 Bob Christian	1.00	.40
❑ 54 Jon McGlocklin	1.50	.60
❑ 55 Paul Silas	3.00	1.20
❑ 56 Hal Greer	3.00	1.20
❑ 57 Barry Clemens	1.00	.40
❑ 58 Nick Jones	1.00	.40
❑ 59 Cornell Warner	1.00	.40
❑ 60 Walt Frazier	10.00	4.00
❑ 61 Dorie Murrey	1.00	.40
❑ 62 Dick Cunningham	1.00	.40
❑ 63 Sam Lacey	1.50	.60
❑ 64 John Warren	1.00	.40
❑ 65 Tom Boerwinkle	1.00	.40
❑ 66 Fred Foster	1.00	.40
❑ 67 Mel Counts	1.00	.40
❑ 68 Toby Kimball	1.00	.40
❑ 69 Dale Schlueter	1.00	.40
❑ 70 Jack Marin	1.50	.60
❑ 71 Jim Barnett	1.00	.40
❑ 72 Clem Haskins	3.00	1.20
❑ 73 Earl Monroe	6.00	2.40
❑ 74 Tom Sanders	1.50	.60
❑ 75 Jerry West	25.00	10.00
❑ 76 Elmore Smith RC	1.50	.60
❑ 77 Don Adams	1.00	.40
❑ 78 Wally Jones	1.50	.60
❑ 79 Tom Van Arsdale	1.50	.60
❑ 80 Bob Lanier	20.00	8.00
❑ 81 Len Wilkens	8.00	3.20
❑ 82 Neal Walk	1.50	.60
❑ 83 Kevin Loughery	1.50	.60
❑ 84 Stan McKenzie	1.00	.40
❑ 85 Jeff Mullins	1.50	.60
❑ 86 Otto Moore	1.00	.40
❑ 87 John Tresvant	1.00	.40
❑ 88 Dean Meminger RC	1.00	.40
❑ 89 Jim McMillian	1.50	.60
❑ 90 Austin Carr RC	7.00	2.80
❑ 91 Clifford Ray RC	1.50	.60
❑ 92 Don Nelson	4.00	1.60
❑ 93 Mahdi Abdul-Rahman (formerly Walt Hazzard)	1.50	.60
❑ 94 Willie Norwood	1.00	.40
❑ 95 Dick Van Arsdale	1.50	.60
❑ 96 Don May	1.00	.40
❑ 97 Walt Bellamy	4.00	1.60
❑ 98 Garfield Heard RC	4.00	1.60
❑ 99 Dave Wohl	1.00	.40
❑ 100 Kareem Abdul-Jabbar	30.00	12.00
❑ 101 Ron Knight	1.00	.40
❑ 102 Phil Chenier RC	4.00	1.60
❑ 103 Rudy Tomjanovich	8.00	3.20
❑ 104 Flynn Robinson	1.00	.40
❑ 105 Dave DeBusschere	6.00	2.40
❑ 106 Dennis Layton	1.00	.40
❑ 107 Bill Hewitt	1.00	.40
❑ 108 Dick Garrett	1.00	.40
❑ 109 Walt Wesley	1.00	.40
❑ 110 John Havlicek	25.00	10.00
❑ 111 Norm Van Lier	1.50	.60
❑ 112 Cazzie Russell	3.00	1.20
❑ 113 Herm Gilliam	1.00	.40
❑ 114 Greg Smith	1.00	.40
❑ 115 Nate Archibald	6.00	2.40
❑ 116 Don Kojis	1.00	.40
❑ 117 Rick Adelman	1.50	.60
❑ 118 Luke Jackson	1.50	.60
❑ 119 Lamar Green	1.00	.40
❑ 120 Archie Clark	1.50	.60
❑ 121 Happy Hairston	1.50	.60
❑ 122 Bill Bradley	20.00	8.00
❑ 123 Ron Williams	1.00	.40
❑ 124 Jimmy Walker	1.50	.60
❑ 125 Bob Kauffman	1.00	.40
❑ 126 Rick Roberson	1.00	.40
❑ 127 Howard Porter RC	1.50	.60
❑ 128 Mike Newlin RC	1.50	.60
❑ 129 Willis Reed	8.00	3.20
❑ 130 Lou Hudson	3.00	1.20
❑ 131 Don Chaney	3.00	1.20
❑ 132 Dave Stallworth	1.00	.40
❑ 133 Charlie Yelverton	1.00	.40
❑ 134 Ken Durrett	1.00	.40
❑ 135 John Brisker	1.50	.60
❑ 136 Dick Snyder	1.00	.40
❑ 137 Jim McDaniels	1.00	.40
❑ 138 Clyde Lee	1.00	.40
❑ 139 Dennis Awtrey UER (Misspelled Awtry on card front)	1.50	.60
❑ 140 Keith Erickson	1.50	.60
❑ 141 Bob Weiss	1.50	.60
❑ 142 Butch Beard RC	3.00	1.20
❑ 143 Terry Dischinger	1.00	.40
❑ 144 Pat Riley	18.00	7.25
❑ 145 Lucius Allen	1.50	.60

No.	Card	NM	Ex
❑ 146	John Mengelt RC	1.00	.40
❑ 147	John Hummer	1.00	.40
❑ 148	Bob Love	5.00	2.00
❑ 149	Bobby Smith	1.50	.60
❑ 150	Elvin Hayes	10.00	4.00
❑ 151	Nate Williams	1.00	.40
❑ 152	Chet Walker	3.00	1.20
❑ 153	Steve Kuberski	1.00	.40
❑ 154	Earl Monroe PO	3.00	1.20
❑ 155	NBA Playoffs G2	2.50	1.00
	Lakers Come Back		
	(under the basket)		
❑ 156	NBA Playoffs G3	2.50	1.00
	Two in a Row		
	(under the basket)		
❑ 157	Leroy Ellis PO	2.50	1.00
❑ 158	Jerry West PO	8.00	3.20
❑ 159	Wilt Chamberlain PO	10.00	4.00
❑ 160	NBA Checklist 1-176	16.00	4.80
	UER (135 Jim King)		
❑ 161	John Havlicek AS	10.00	4.00
❑ 162	Spencer Haywood AS	2.00	.80
❑ 163	Kareem Abdul-Jabbar AS	25.00	10.00
❑ 164	Jerry West AS	18.00	7.25
❑ 165	Walt Frazier AS	5.00	2.00
❑ 166	Bob Love AS	2.00	.80
❑ 167	Billy Cunningham AS	4.00	1.60
❑ 168	Wilt Chamberlain AS	20.00	8.00
❑ 169	Nate Archibald AS	4.00	1.60
❑ 170	Archie Clark AS	2.00	.80
❑ 171	Kareem Abdul-Jabbar	14.00	5.50
	John Havlicek		
	Nate Archibald LL		
❑ 172	Kareem Abdul-Jabbar	14.00	5.50
	Nate Archibald		
	John Havlicek LL		
❑ 173	Wilt Chamberlain	16.00	6.50
	Kareem Abdul-Jabbar		
	Walt Bellamy LL		
❑ 174	Jack Marin	3.00	1.20
	Calvin Murphy		
	Gail Goodrich LL		
❑ 175	Wilt Chamberlain	16.00	6.50
	Kareem Abdul-Jabbar		
	Wes Unseld LL		
❑ 176	Len Wilkens	12.00	4.80
	Jerry West		
	Nate Archibald LL		
❑ 177	Roland Taylor	1.50	.60
❑ 178	Art Becker	1.50	.60
❑ 179	Mack Calvin	2.00	.80
❑ 180	Artis Gilmore RC	20.00	8.00
❑ 181	Collis Jones	1.50	.60
❑ 182	John Roche RC	2.00	.80
❑ 183	George McGinnis RC	14.00	5.50
❑ 184	Johnny Neumann	2.00	.80
❑ 185	Willie Wise	2.00	.80
❑ 186	Bernie Williams	1.50	.60
❑ 187	Byron Beck	2.00	.80
❑ 188	Larry Miller	2.00	.80
❑ 189	Cincy Powell	1.50	.60
❑ 190	Donnie Freeman	2.00	.80
❑ 191	John Baum	1.50	.60
❑ 192	Billy Keller	2.00	.80
❑ 193	Wilbert Jones	1.50	.60
❑ 194	Glen Combs	1.50	.60
❑ 195	Julius Erving RC	200.00	80.00
	(Forward on front,		
	but Center on back)		
❑ 196	Al Smith	1.50	.60
❑ 197	George Carter	1.50	.60
❑ 198	Louie Dampier	3.00	1.20
❑ 199	Rich Jones	1.50	.60
❑ 200	Mel Daniels	3.00	1.20
❑ 201	Gene Moore	1.50	.60
❑ 202	Randy Denton	1.50	.60
❑ 203	Larry Jones	1.50	.60

No.	Card	NM	Ex
❑ 204	Jim Ligon	1.50	.60
❑ 205	Warren Jabali	2.00	.80
❑ 206	Joe Caldwell	2.00	.80
❑ 207	Darrell Carrier	2.00	.80
❑ 208	Gene Kennedy	1.50	.60
❑ 209	Ollie Taylor	1.50	.60
❑ 210	Roger Brown	2.00	.80
❑ 211	George Lehmann	1.50	.60
❑ 212	Red Robbins	2.00	.80
❑ 213	Jim Eakins	2.00	.80
❑ 214	Willie Long	1.50	.60
❑ 215	Billy Cunningham	8.00	3.20
❑ 216	Steve Jones	2.00	.80
❑ 217	Les Hunter	1.50	.60
❑ 218	Billy Paultz	2.00	.80
❑ 219	Freddie Lewis	2.00	.80
❑ 220	Zelmo Beaty	2.00	.80
❑ 221	George Thompson	1.50	.60
❑ 222	Neil Johnson	1.50	.60
❑ 223	Dave Robisch RC	2.00	.80
❑ 224	Walt Simon	1.50	.60
❑ 225	Bill Melchionni	2.00	.80
❑ 226	Wendell Ladner RC	2.00	.80
❑ 227	Joe Hamilton	1.50	.60
❑ 228	Bob Netolicky	2.00	.80
❑ 229	James Jones	2.00	.80
❑ 230	Dan Issel	10.00	4.00
❑ 231	Charlie Williams	1.50	.60
❑ 232	Willie Sojourner	1.50	.60
❑ 233	Merv Jackson	1.50	.60
❑ 234	Mike Lewis	1.50	.60
❑ 235	Ralph Simpson	2.00	.80
❑ 236	Darnell Hillman	2.00	.80
❑ 237	Rick Mount	3.00	1.20
❑ 238	Gerald Govan	1.50	.60
❑ 239	Ron Boone	2.00	.80
❑ 240	Tom Washington	1.50	.60
❑ 241	ABA Playoffs G1	2.50	1.00
	Pacers take lead		
	(under the basket)		
❑ 242	Rick Barry PO	5.00	2.00
❑ 243	George McGinnis PO	4.00	1.60
❑ 244	Rick Barry PO	5.00	2.00
❑ 245	Billy Keller PO	2.50	1.00
❑ 246	ABA Playoffs G6	2.50	1.00
	Tight Defense		
❑ 247	ABA Champs: Pacers	3.00	1.20
❑ 248	ABA Checklist 177-264	16.00	4.80
	UER (236 John Brisker)		
❑ 249	Dan Issel AS	6.00	2.40
❑ 250	Rick Barry AS	8.00	3.20
❑ 251	Artis Gilmore AS	6.00	2.40
❑ 252	Donnie Freeman AS	2.50	1.00
❑ 253	Bill Melchionni AS	2.50	1.00
❑ 254	Willie Wise AS	2.50	1.00
❑ 255	Julius Erving AS	50.00	20.00
❑ 256	Zelmo Beaty AS	2.50	1.00
❑ 257	Ralph Simpson AS	2.50	1.00
❑ 258	Charlie Scott AS	2.50	1.00
❑ 259	Charlie Scott	8.00	3.20
	Rick Barry		
	Dan Issel LL		
❑ 260	Artis Gilmore	4.00	1.60
	Tom Washington		
	Larry Jones LL		
❑ 261	Glen Combs	2.50	1.00
	Louie Dampier		
	Warren Jabali LL		
❑ 262	Rick Barry	4.00	1.60
	Mack Calvin		
	Steve Jones LL		
❑ 263	Artis Gilmore	20.00	8.00
	Julius Erving		
	Mel Daniels LL		
❑ 264	Bill Melchionni	6.00	1.80
	Larry Brown		
	Louie Dampier LL		

1973-74 Topps

	NM	Ex
COMPLETE SET (264)	325.00	130.00
COM. NBA CARD (1-176)	.50	.20
COM. ABA CARD (177-264)	1.00	.40
❑ 1 Nate Archibald AS1	10.00	3.00
❑ 2 Steve Kuberski	.50	.20
❑ 3 John Mengelt	.50	.20
❑ 4 Jim McMillian	1.00	.40
❑ 5 Nate Thurmond	4.00	1.60
❑ 6 Dave Wohl	.50	.20
❑ 7 John Brisker	.50	.20
❑ 8 Charlie Davis	.50	.20
❑ 9 Lamar Green	.50	.20
❑ 10 Walt Frazier AS2	6.00	2.40
❑ 11 Bob Christian	.50	.20
❑ 12 Cornell Warner	.50	.20
❑ 13 Calvin Murphy	4.00	1.60
❑ 14 Dave Sorenson	.50	.20
❑ 15 Archie Clark	1.00	.40
❑ 16 Clifford Ray	1.00	.40
❑ 17 Terry Driscoll	.50	.20
❑ 18 Matt Guokas	1.00	.40
❑ 19 Elmore Smith	1.00	.40
❑ 20 John Havlicek AS1	15.00	6.00
❑ 21 Pat Riley	8.00	3.20
❑ 22 George Trapp	.50	.20
❑ 23 Ron Williams	.50	.20
❑ 24 Jim Fox	.50	.20
❑ 25 Dick Van Arsdale	1.00	.40
❑ 26 John Tresvant	.50	.20
❑ 27 Rick Adelman	1.00	.40
❑ 28 Eddie Mast	.50	.20
❑ 29 Jim Cleamons	1.00	.40
❑ 30 Dave DeBusschere AS2	5.00	2.00
❑ 31 Norm Van Lier	1.00	.40
❑ 32 Stan McKenzie	.50	.20
❑ 33 Bob Dandridge	1.00	.40
❑ 34 Leroy Ellis	1.00	.40
❑ 35 Mike Riordan	1.00	.40
❑ 36 Fred Hilton	.50	.20
❑ 37 Toby Kimball	.50	.20
❑ 38 Jim Price	.50	.20
❑ 39 Willie Norwood	.50	.20
❑ 40 Dave Cowens AS2	10.00	4.00
❑ 41 Cazzie Russell	1.00	.40
❑ 42 Lee Winfield	.50	.20
❑ 43 Connie Hawkins	5.00	2.00
❑ 44 Mike Newlin	1.00	.40
❑ 45 Chet Walker	1.00	.40
❑ 46 Walt Bellamy	4.00	1.60
❑ 47 John Johnson	1.00	.40
❑ 48 Henry Bibby RC	5.00	2.00
❑ 49 Bobby Smith	1.00	.40
❑ 50 K.Abdul-Jabbar AS1	25.00	10.00
❑ 51 Mike Price	.50	.20
❑ 52 John Hummer	.50	.20
❑ 53 Kevin Porter RC	5.00	2.00
❑ 54 Nate Williams	.50	.20
❑ 55 Gail Goodrich	4.00	1.60
❑ 56 Fred Foster	.50	.20
❑ 57 Don Chaney	1.00	.40
❑ 58 Bud Stallworth	.50	.20
❑ 59 Clem Haskins	1.00	.40
❑ 60 Bob Love AS2	3.00	1.20
❑ 61 Jimmy Walker	1.00	.40
❑ 62 NBA Eastern Semis	1.00	.40

Knicks shoot down
Bullets in 5
❑ 63 NBA Eastern Semis ...... 1.00 .40
Celts oust Hawks
2nd Straight Year
❑ 64 Wilt Chamberlain PO 8.00 3.20
❑ 65 NBA Western Semis .... 1.00 .40
Warriors over-
whelm Milwaukee
❑ 66 Willis Reed PO 3.00 1.20
Henry Finkel
❑ 67 NBA Western Finals...... 1.00 .40
Lakers Breeze Past
Golden State
❑ 68 NBA Championship 4.00 1.60
Knicks Do It
Repeat '70 Miracle
(Walt Frazier
Keith Erickson)
❑ 69 Larry Steele .... 1.00 .40
❑ 70 Oscar Robertson 15.00 6.00
❑ 71 Phil Jackson 15.00 6.00
❑ 72 John Wetzel .... .50 .20
❑ 73 Steve Patterson RC ...... 1.00 .40
❑ 74 Manny Leaks .... .50 .20
❑ 75 Jeff Mullins .... 1.00 .40
❑ 76 Stan Love .... .50 .20
❑ 77 Dick Garrett .... .50 .20
❑ 78 Don Nelson 4.00 1.60
❑ 79 Chris Ford RC 3.00 1.20
❑ 80 Wilt Chamberlain 25.00 10.00
❑ 81 Dennis Layton .... .50 .20
❑ 82 Bill Bradley 15.00 6.00
❑ 83 Jerry Sloan .... 1.00 .40
❑ 84 Cliff Meely .... .50 .20
❑ 85 Sam Lacey .... .50 .20
❑ 86 Dick Snyder .... .50 .20
❑ 87 Jim Washington .... .50 .20
❑ 88 Lucius Allen .... 1.00 .40
❑ 89 LaRue Martin .... .50 .20
❑ 90 Rick Barry 8.00 3.20
❑ 91 Fred Boyd .... .50 .20
❑ 92 Barry Clemens .... .50 .20
❑ 93 Dean Meminger .... .50 .20
❑ 94 Henry Finkel .... .50 .20
❑ 95 Elvin Hayes 6.00 2.40
❑ 96 Stu Lantz .... 1.00 .40
❑ 97 Bill Hewitt .... .50 .20
❑ 98 Neal Walk .... .50 .20
❑ 99 Garfield Heard .... 1.00 .40
❑ 100 Jerry West AS1 .... 20.00 8.00
❑ 101 Otto Moore .... .50 .20
❑ 102 Don Kojis .... .50 .20
❑ 103 Fred Brown RC 6.00 2.40
❑ 104 Dwight Davis .... .50 .20
❑ 105 Willis Reed 6.00 2.40
❑ 106 Herm Gilliam .... .50 .20
❑ 107 Mickey Davis .... .50 .20
❑ 108 Jim Barnett .... .50 .20
❑ 109 Ollie Johnson .... .50 .20
❑ 110 Bob Lanier 6.00 2.40
❑ 111 Fred Carter .... 1.00 .40
❑ 112 Paul Silas 3.00 1.20
❑ 113 Phil Chenier .... 1.00 .40
❑ 114 Dennis Awtrey .... .50 .20
❑ 115 Austin Carr .... 1.00 .40
❑ 116 Bob Kauffman .... .50 .20
❑ 117 Keith Erickson .... 1.00 .40
❑ 118 Walt Wesley .... .50 .20
❑ 119 Steve Bracey .... .50 .20
❑ 120 Spencer Haywood AS1 3.00 1.20
❑ 121 NBA Checklist 1-176 12.00 3.60
❑ 122 Jack Marin .... 1.00 .40
❑ 123 Jon McGlocklin .... .50 .20
❑ 124 Johnny Green .... 1.00 .40
❑ 125 Jerry Lucas 3.00 1.20
❑ 126 Paul Westphal RC 20.00 8.00
❑ 127 Curtis Rowe .... 1.00 .40
❑ 128 Mahdi Abdul-Rahman 1.00 .40
(formerly Walt Hazzard)
❑ 129 Lloyd Neal RC .... .50 .20
❑ 130 Pete Maravich AS1 .. 30.00 12.00
❑ 131 Don May .... .50 .20
❑ 132 Bob Weiss .... 1.00 .40
❑ 133 Dave Stallworth .... .50 .20
❑ 134 Dick Cunningham .... .50 .20
❑ 135 Bob McAdoo RC 20.00 8.00
❑ 136 Butch Beard .... 1.00 .40
❑ 137 Happy Hairston .... 1.00 .40
❑ 138 Bob Rule .... 1.00 .40
❑ 139 Don Adams .... .50 .20
❑ 140 Charlie Scott .... 1.00 .40
❑ 141 Ron Riley .... .50 .20
❑ 142 Earl Monroe 4.00 1.60
❑ 143 Clyde Lee .... .50 .20
❑ 144 Rick Roberson .... .50 .20
❑ 145 Rudy Tomjanovich 6.00 2.40
(Printed without
Houston on basket)
❑ 146 Tom Van Arsdale .... 1.00 .40
❑ 147 Art Williams .... .50 .20
❑ 148 Curtis Perry .... .50 .20
❑ 149 Rich Rinaldi .... .50 .20
❑ 150 Lou Hudson .... 1.00 .40
❑ 151 Mel Counts .... .50 .20
❑ 152 Jim McDaniels .... .50 .20
❑ 153 Nate Archibald 8.00 3.20
Kareem Abdul-Jabbar
Spencer Haywood LL
❑ 154 Nate Archibald 8.00 3.20
Kareem Abdul-Jabbar
Spencer Haywood LL
❑ 155 Wilt Chamberlain 12.00 4.80
Matt Guokas
Kareem Abdul-Jabbar LL
❑ 156 Rick Barry 4.00 1.60
Calvin Murphy
Mike Newlin LL
❑ 157 Wilt Chamberlain 8.00 3.20
Nate Thurmond
Dave Cowens LL
❑ 158 Nate Archibald 4.00 1.60
Len Wilkens
Dave Bing LL
❑ 159 Don Smith .... .50 .20
❑ 160 Sidney Wicks 3.00 1.20
❑ 161 Howie Komives .... .50 .20
❑ 162 John Gianelli .... .50 .20
❑ 163 Jeff Halliburton .... .50 .20
❑ 164 Kennedy McIntosh .... .50 .20
❑ 165 Len Wilkens 6.00 2.40
❑ 166 Corky Calhoun .... .50 .20
❑ 167 Howard Porter .... 1.00 .40
❑ 168 JoJo White 3.00 1.20
❑ 169 John Block .... .50 .20
❑ 170 Dave Bing 4.00 1.60
❑ 171 Joe Ellis .... .50 .20
❑ 172 Chuck Terry .... .50 .20
❑ 173 Randy Smith .... 1.00 .40
❑ 174 Bill Bridges .... 1.00 .40
❑ 175 Geoff Petrie .... 1.00 .40
❑ 176 Wes Unseld 4.00 1.60
❑ 177 Skeeter Swift .... 1.00 .40
❑ 178 Jim Eakins .... 1.50 .60
❑ 179 Steve Jones .... 1.50 .60
❑ 180 George McGinnis AS1 3.00 1.20
❑ 181 Al Smith .... 1.00 .40
❑ 182 Tom Washington .... 1.00 .40
❑ 183 Louie Dampier .... 1.50 .60
❑ 184 Simmie Hill .... 1.00 .40
❑ 185 George Thompson ...... 1.00 .40
❑ 186 Cincy Powell .... 1.50 .60
❑ 187 Larry Jones .... 1.00 .40
❑ 188 Neil Johnson .... 1.00 .40
❑ 189 Tom Owens .... 1.00 .40
❑ 190 Ralph Simpson AS2 .... 1.50 .60
❑ 191 George Carter .... 1.50 .60
❑ 192 Rick Mount .... 1.50 .60
❑ 193 Red Robbins .... 1.50 .60
❑ 194 George Lehmann .... 1.00 .40
❑ 195 Mel Daniels AS2 .... 1.50 .60
❑ 196 Bob Warren .... 1.00 .40
❑ 197 Gene Kennedy .... 1.00 .40
❑ 198 Mike Barr .... 1.00 .40
❑ 199 Dave Robisch .... 1.00 .40
❑ 200 Billy Cunningham AS1 5.00 2.00
❑ 201 John Roche .... 1.50 .60
❑ 202 ABA Western Semis.... 2.00 .80
Pacers Oust
Injured Rockets
❑ 203 ABA Western Semis.... 2.00 .80
Stars sweep Q's
in Four Straight
❑ 204 Dan Issel PO .... 2.00 .80
❑ 205 ABA Eastern Semis .... 2.00 .80
Cougars in strong
finish over Nets
❑ 206 ABA Western Finals.... 2.00 .80
Pacers nip bitter
rival& Stars
❑ 207 Artis Gilmore PO 3.00 1.20
❑ 208 George McGinnis PO .. 2.00 .80
❑ 209 Glen Combs .... 1.00 .40
❑ 210 Dan Issel AS2 .... 6.00 2.40
❑ 211 Randy Denton .... 1.00 .40
❑ 212 Freddie Lewis .... 1.50 .60
❑ 213 Stew Johnson .... 1.00 .40
❑ 214 Roland Taylor .... 1.00 .40
❑ 215 Rich Jones .... 1.00 .40
❑ 216 Billy Paultz .... 1.50 .60
❑ 217 Ron Boone .... 1.50 .60
❑ 218 Walt Simon .... 1.00 .40
❑ 219 Mike Lewis .... 1.00 .40
❑ 220 Warren Jabali AS1 ...... 1.50 .60
❑ 221 Wilbert Jones .... 1.00 .40
❑ 222 Don Buse RC .... 1.50 .60
❑ 223 Gene Moore .... 1.00 .40
❑ 224 Joe Hamilton .... 1.50 .60
❑ 225 Zelmo Beaty .... 1.50 .60
❑ 226 Brian Taylor RC .... 1.50 .60
❑ 227 Julius Keye .... 1.00 .40
❑ 228 Mike Gale RC .... 1.50 .60
❑ 229 Warren Davis .... 1.00 .40
❑ 230 Mack Calvin AS2 .... 1.50 .60
❑ 231 Roger Brown .... 1.50 .60
❑ 232 Chuck Williams .... 1.50 .60
❑ 233 Gerald Govan .... 1.50 .60
❑ 234 Julius Erving 10.00 4.00
George McGinnis
Dan Issel LL
❑ 235 Artis Gilmore .... 2.00 .80
Gene Kennedy
Tom Owens LL
❑ 236 Glen Combs .... 2.00 .80
Roger Brown
Louie Dampier LL
❑ 237 Billy Keller .... 2.00 .80
Ron Boone
Bob Warren LL
❑ 238 Artis Gilmore 3.00 1.20
Mel Daniels
Bill Paultz LL
❑ 239 Bill Melchionni .... 2.00 .80
Chuck Williams
Warren Jabali LL
❑ 240 Julius Erving AS2 ...... 50.00 20.00
❑ 241 Jimmy O'Brien .... 1.00 .40
❑ 242 ABA Checklist 177-264 12.00 3.60
❑ 243 Johnny Neumann .... 1.00 .40
❑ 244 Darnell Hillman .... 1.50 .60
❑ 245 Willie Wise .... 1.50 .60
❑ 246 Collis Jones .... 1.00 .40
❑ 247 Ted McClain .... 1.00 .40
❑ 248 George Irvine RC .... 1.00 .40

Card	NM	Ex
❑ 249 Bill Melchionni	1.50	.60
❑ 250 Artis Gilmore AS1	6.00	2.40
❑ 251 Willie Long	1.00	.40
❑ 252 Larry Miller	1.00	.40
❑ 253 Lee Davis	1.00	.40
❑ 254 Donnie Freeman	1.50	.60
❑ 255 Joe Caldwell	1.50	.60
❑ 256 Bob Netolicky	1.50	.60
❑ 257 Bernie Williams	1.00	.40
❑ 258 Byron Beck	1.50	.60
❑ 259 Jim Chones RC	3.00	1.20
❑ 260 James Jones AS1	1.50	.60
❑ 261 Wendell Ladner	1.00	.40
❑ 262 Ollie Taylor	1.00	.40
❑ 263 Les Hunter	1.00	.40
❑ 264 Billy Keller	3.00	.90

1974-75 Topps

	NM	Ex
COMPLETE SET (264)	325.00	130.00
COM. NBA CARD (1-176)	.50	.20
COM. ABA CARD (177-264)	1.00	.40
❑ 1 K.Abdul-Jabbar AS1	30.00	9.00
❑ 2 Don May	.50	.20
❑ 3 Bernie Fryer RC	1.00	.40
❑ 4 Don Adams	.50	.20
❑ 5 Herm Gilliam	.50	.20
❑ 6 Jim Chones	1.00	.40
❑ 7 Rick Adelman	1.00	.40
❑ 8 Randy Smith	1.00	.40
❑ 9 Paul Silas	3.00	1.20
❑ 10 Pete Maravich	25.00	10.00
❑ 11 Ron Behagen	.50	.20
❑ 12 Kevin Porter	1.00	.40
❑ 13 Bill Bridges	1.00	.40
(On back team shown as		
Los And.& should		
be Los Ang.)		
❑ 14 Charles Johnson RC	.50	.20
❑ 15 Bob Love	1.00	.40
❑ 16 Henry Bibby	1.00	.40
❑ 17 Neal Walk	.50	.20
❑ 18 John Brisker	.50	.20
❑ 19 Lucius Allen	.50	.20
❑ 20 Tom Van Arsdale	1.00	.40
❑ 21 Larry Steele	.50	.20
❑ 22 Curtis Rowe	1.00	.40
❑ 23 Dean Meminger	.50	.20
❑ 24 Steve Patterson	.50	.20
❑ 25 Earl Monroe	3.00	1.20
❑ 26 Jack Marin	.50	.20
❑ 27 JoJo White	3.00	1.20
❑ 28 Rudy Tomjanovich	6.00	2.40
❑ 29 Otto Moore	.50	.20
❑ 30 Elvin Hayes AS2	5.00	2.00
❑ 31 Pat Riley	8.00	3.20
❑ 32 Clyde Lee	.50	.20
❑ 33 Bob Weiss	.50	.20
❑ 34 Jim Fox	.50	.20
❑ 35 Charlie Scott	1.00	.40
❑ 36 Cliff Meely	.50	.20
❑ 37 Jon McGlocklin	.50	.20
❑ 38 Jim McMillian	1.00	.40
❑ 39 Bill Walton RC	50.00	20.00
❑ 40 Dave Bing AS2	3.00	1.20
❑ 41 Jim Washington	.50	.20
❑ 42 Jim Cleamons	1.00	.40
❑ 43 Mel Davis	.50	.20
❑ 44 Garfield Heard	1.00	.40
❑ 45 Jimmy Walker	1.00	.40
❑ 46 Don Nelson	1.00	.40
❑ 47 Jim Barnett	.50	.20
❑ 48 Manny Leaks	.50	.20
❑ 49 Elmore Smith	1.00	.40
❑ 50 Rick Barry AS1	6.00	2.40
❑ 51 Jerry Sloan	1.00	.40
❑ 52 John Hummer	.50	.20
❑ 53 Keith Erickson	1.00	.40
❑ 54 George E. Johnson	.50	.20
❑ 55 Oscar Robertson	12.00	4.80
❑ 56 Steve Mix RC	1.00	.40
❑ 57 Rick Roberson	.50	.20
❑ 58 John Mengelt	.50	.20
❑ 59 Dwight Jones RC	1.00	.40
❑ 60 Austin Carr	1.00	.40
❑ 61 Nick Weatherspoon RC	1.00	.40
❑ 62 Clem Haskins	1.00	.40
❑ 63 Don Kojis	.50	.20
❑ 64 Paul Westphal	3.00	1.20
❑ 65 Walt Bellamy	4.00	1.60
❑ 66 John Johnson	1.00	.40
❑ 67 Butch Beard	1.00	.40
❑ 68 Happy Hairston	1.00	.40
❑ 69 Tom Boerwinkle	.50	.20
❑ 70 Spencer Haywood AS2	3.00	1.20
❑ 71 Gary Melchionni	.50	.20
❑ 72 Ed Ratleff RC	1.00	.40
❑ 73 Mickey Davis	.50	.20
❑ 74 Dennis Awtrey	.50	.20
❑ 75 Fred Carter	1.00	.40
❑ 76 George Trapp	.50	.20
❑ 77 John Wetzel	.50	.20
❑ 78 Bobby Smith	1.00	.40
❑ 79 John Gianelli	.50	.20
❑ 80 Bob McAdoo AS2	6.00	2.40
❑ 81 Pete Maravich	6.00	2.40
Lou Hudson		
Walt Bellamy		
Pete Maravich TL		
❑ 82 John Havlicek	5.00	2.00
JoJo White		
Dave Cowens		
JoJo White TL		
❑ 83 Bob McAdoo	1.00	.40
Ernie DiGregorio		
Bob McAdoo		
Ernie DiGregorio TL		
❑ 84 Bob Love	3.00	1.20
Chet Walker		
Clifford Ray		
Norm Van Lier TL		
❑ 85 Austin Carr	1.00	.40
Austin Carr		
Dwight Davis		
Len Wilkens TL		
❑ 86 Bob Lanier	1.00	.40
Stu Lantz		
Bob Lanier		
Dave Bing TL		
❑ 87 Rick Barry	3.00	1.20
Rick Barry		
Nate Thurmond		
Rick Barry TL		
❑ 88 Rudy Tomjanovich	1.00	.40
Calvin Murphy		
Don Smith		
Calvin Murphy TL		
❑ 89 Jimmy Walker	1.00	.40
Jimmy Walker		
Sam Lacey		
Jimmy Walker TL		
❑ 90 Gail Goodrich	1.00	.40
Gail Goodrich		
Happy Hairston		
Gail Goodrich TL		
❑ 91 Kareem Abdul-Jabbar	12.00	4.80
Oscar Robertson		
Kareem Abdul-Jabbar		
Oscar Robertson TL		
❑ 92 New Orleans Jazz	1.00	.40
Emblem; Expansion		
Draft Picks on Back		
❑ 93 Walt Frazier	5.00	2.00
Bill Bradley		
Dave DeBusschere		
Walt Frazier TL		
❑ 94 Fred Carter	1.00	.40
Tom Van Arsdale		
Leroy Ellis		
Fred Carter TL		
❑ 95 Charlie Scott	1.00	.40
Dick Van Arsdale		
Neal Walk		
Neal Walk TL		
❑ 96 Geoff Petrie	1.00	.40
Geoff Petrie		
Rick Roberson		
Sidney Wicks TL		
❑ 97 Spencer Haywood	1.00	.40
Dick Snyder		
Spencer Haywood		
Fred Brown TL		
❑ 98 Phil Chenier	1.00	.40
Phil Chenier		
Elvin Hayes		
Kevin Porter TL		
❑ 99 Sam Lacey	.50	.20
❑ 100 John Havlicek AS1	10.00	4.00
❑ 101 Stu Lantz	1.00	.40
❑ 102 Mike Riordan	.50	.20
❑ 103 Larry Jones	.50	.20
❑ 104 Connie Hawkins	4.00	1.60
❑ 105 Nate Thurmond	3.00	1.20
❑ 106 Dick Gibbs	.50	.20
❑ 107 Corky Calhoun	.50	.20
❑ 108 Dave Wohl	.50	.20
❑ 109 Cornell Warner	.50	.20
❑ 110 Geoff Petrie UER	1.00	.40
(Misspelled Patrie		
on card front)		
❑ 111 Leroy Ellis	1.00	.40
❑ 112 Chris Ford	1.00	.40
❑ 113 Bill Bradley	10.00	4.00
❑ 114 Clifford Ray	1.00	.40
❑ 115 Dick Snyder	.50	.20
❑ 116 Nate Williams	.50	.20
❑ 117 Matt Guokas	1.00	.40
❑ 118 Henry Finkel	.50	.20
❑ 119 Curtis Perry	.50	.20
❑ 120 Gail Goodrich AS1	3.00	1.20
❑ 121 Wes Unseld	3.00	1.20
❑ 122 Howard Porter	1.00	.40
❑ 123 Jeff Mullins	.50	.20
❑ 124 Mike Bantom RC	1.00	.40
❑ 125 Fred Brown	1.00	.40
❑ 126 Bob Dandridge	1.00	.40
❑ 127 Mike Newlin	1.00	.40
❑ 128 Greg Smith	.50	.20
❑ 129 Doug Collins RC	16.00	6.50
❑ 130 Lou Hudson	1.00	.40
❑ 131 Bob Lanier	5.00	2.00
❑ 132 Phil Jackson	10.00	4.00
❑ 133 Don Chaney	1.00	.40
❑ 134 Jim Brewer RC	1.00	.40
❑ 135 Ernie DiGregorio RC	3.00	1.20
❑ 136 Steve Kuberski	.50	.20
❑ 137 Jim Price	.50	.20
❑ 138 Mike D'Antoni	.50	.20
❑ 139 John Brown	.50	.20
❑ 140 Norm Van Lier AS2	1.00	.40
❑ 141 NBA Checklist 1-176	10.00	3.00
❑ 142 Don Slick Watts RC	1.00	.40
❑ 143 Walt Wesley	.50	.20
❑ 144 Bob McAdoo	12.00	4.80
Kareem Abdul-Jabbar		
Pete Maravich LL		
❑ 145 Bob McAdoo	12.00	4.80
Pete Maravich		
Kareem Abdul-Jabbar LL		
❑ 146 Bob McAdoo	10.00	4.00
Kareem Abdul-Jabbar		
Rudy Tomjanovich LL		
❑ 147 Ernie DiGregorio	1.00	.40
Rick Barry		
Jeff Mullins LL		
❑ 148 Elvin Hayes	4.00	1.60
Dave Cowens		
Bob McAdoo LL		
❑ 149 Ernie DiGregorio	1.00	.40

Calvin Murphy
Len Wilkens LL
❑ 150 Walt Frazier AS1 5.00 2.00
❑ 151 Cazzie Russell 1.00 .40
❑ 152 Calvin Murphy 3.00 1.20
❑ 153 Bob Kauffman .50 .20
❑ 154 Fred Boyd .50 .20
❑ 155 Dave Cowens 6.00 2.40
❑ 156 Willie Norwood .50 .20
❑ 157 Lee Winfield .50 .20
❑ 158 Dwight Davis .50 .20
❑ 159 George T. Johnson .50 .20
❑ 160 Dick Van Arsdale 1.00 .40
❑ 161 NBA Eastern Semis 1.00 .40
Celts over Braves
Knicks edge Bullets
❑ 162 NBA Western Semis 1.00 .40
Bucks over Lakers
Bulls edge Pistons
❑ 163 NBA Div. Finals 1.00 .40
Celts over Knicks
Bucks sweep Bulls
❑ 164 NBA Championship 1.50 .60
Celtics over Bucks
❑ 165 Phil Chenier 1.00 .40
❑ 166 Kermit Washington RC 1.00 .40
❑ 167 Dale Schlueter .50 .20
❑ 168 John Block .50 .20
❑ 169 Don Smith .50 .20
❑ 170 Nate Archibald 4.00 1.60
❑ 171 Chet Walker 1.00 .40
❑ 172 Archie Clark 1.00 .40
❑ 173 Kennedy McIntosh .50 .20
❑ 174 George Thompson .50 .20
❑ 175 Sidney Wicks 3.00 1.20
❑ 176 Jerry West 20.00 8.00
❑ 177 Dwight Lamar 1.00 .40
❑ 178 George Carter 1.50 .60
❑ 179 Wil Robinson 1.00 .40
❑ 180 Artis Gilmore AS1 4.00 1.60
❑ 181 Brian Taylor 1.50 .60
❑ 182 Darnell Hillman 1.50 .60
❑ 183 Dave Robisch 1.50 .60
❑ 184 Gene Littles RC 1.50 .60
❑ 185 Willie Wise AS2 1.50 .60
❑ 186 James Silas RC 3.00 1.20
❑ 187 Caldwell Jones RC 3.00 1.20
❑ 188 Roland Taylor 1.00 .40
❑ 189 Randy Denton 1.00 .40
❑ 190 Dan Issel AS2 5.00 2.00
❑ 191 Mike Gale 1.00 .40
❑ 192 Mel Daniels 1.50 .60
❑ 193 Steve Jones 1.50 .60
❑ 194 Marv Roberts 1.00 .40
❑ 195 Ron Boone AS2 1.50 .60
❑ 196 George Gervin RC 40.00 16.00
❑ 197 Flynn Robinson 1.00 .40
❑ 198 Cincy Powell 1.50 .60
❑ 199 Glen Combs 1.00 .40
❑ 200 Julius Erving AS1 UER 40.00 16.00
(Misspelled Irving
on card back)
❑ 201 Billy Keller 1.50 .60
❑ 202 Willie Long 1.00 .40
❑ 203 ABA Checklist 177-264 10.00 3.00
❑ 204 Joe Caldwell 1.50 .60
❑ 205 Swen Nater AS2 RC 1.50 .60
❑ 206 Rick Mount 1.50 .60
❑ 207 Julius Erving 10.00 4.00
George McGinnis
Dan Issel LL
❑ 208 Swen Nater 2.00 .80
James Jones
Tom Owens LL
❑ 209 Louie Dampier 2.00 .80
Billy Keller
Roger Brown LL
❑ 210 James Jones 2.00 .80
Mack Calvin
Ron Boone LL
❑ 211 Artis Gilmore 2.00 .80
George McGinnis
Caldwell Jones LL
❑ 212 Al Smith 2.00 .80
Chuck Williams
Louie Dampier LL
❑ 213 Larry Miller 1.00 .40
❑ 214 Stew Johnson 1.00 .40
❑ 215 Larry Finch RC 1.50 .60
❑ 216 Larry Kenon RC 3.00 1.20
❑ 217 Joe Hamilton 1.50 .60
❑ 218 Gerald Govan 1.50 .60
❑ 219 Ralph Simpson 1.50 .60
❑ 220 George McGinnis AS1 3.00 1.20
❑ 221 Billy Cunningham 2.00 .80
Mack Calvin
Tom Owens
Joe Caldwell TL
❑ 222 Ralph Simpson 2.00 .80
Byron Beck
Dave Robisch
Al Smith TL
❑ 223 George McGinnis 2.00 .80
Billy Keller
George McGinnis
Freddie Lewis TL
❑ 224 Dan Issel 3.00 1.20
Louie Dampier
Artis Gilmore
Louie Dampier TL
❑ 225 George Thompson 2.00 .80
Larry Finch
Randy Denton
George Thompson TL
❑ 226 Julius Erving 10.00 4.00
John Roche
Larry Kenon
Julius Erving TL
❑ 227 George Gervin 6.00 2.40
George Gervin
Swen Nater
James Silas TL
❑ 228 Dwight Lamar 2.00 .80
Stew Johnson
Caldwell Jones
Chuck Williams TL
❑ 229 Willie Wise 2.00 .80
James Jones
Gerald Govan
James Jones TL
❑ 230 George Carter 2.00 .80
George Irvine
Jim Eakins
Roland Taylor TL
❑ 231 Bird Averitt 1.00 .40
❑ 232 John Roche 1.00 .40
❑ 233 George Irvine 1.00 .40
❑ 234 John Williamson RC 1.50 .60
❑ 235 Billy Cunningham 4.00 1.60
❑ 236 Jimmy O'Brien 1.00 .40
❑ 237 Wilbert Jones 1.00 .40
❑ 238 Johnny Neumann 1.00 .40
❑ 239 Al Smith 1.00 .40
❑ 240 Roger Brown 1.50 .60
❑ 241 Chuck Williams 1.50 .60
❑ 242 Rich Jones 1.00 .40
❑ 243 Dave Twardzik RC 1.50 .60
❑ 244 Wendell Ladner 1.50 .60
❑ 245 Mack Calvin AS1 1.50 .60
❑ 246 ABA Eastern Semis 2.00 .80
Nets over Squires
Colonels sweep Cougars
❑ 247 ABA Western Semis 2.00 .80
Stars over Conquistadors
Pacers over Spurs
❑ 248 ABA Div. Finals 2.00 .80
Nets sweep Colonels
Stars edge Pacers
❑ 249 Julius Erving PO 12.00 4.80
❑ 250 Wilt Chamberlain CO 35.00 14.00
❑ 251 Ron Robinson 1.00 .40
❑ 252 Zelmo Beaty 1.50 .60
❑ 253 Donnie Freeman 1.50 .60
❑ 254 Mike Green 1.00 .40
❑ 255 Louie Dampier AS2 1.50 .60
❑ 256 Tom Owens 1.00 .40
❑ 257 George Karl RC 10.00 4.00
❑ 258 Jim Eakins 1.50 .60
❑ 259 Travis Grant 1.50 .60
❑ 260 James Jones AS1 1.50 .60
❑ 261 Mike Jackson 1.00 .40
❑ 262 Billy Paultz 1.50 .60
❑ 263 Freddie Lewis 1.50 .60
❑ 264 Byron Beck 3.00 .90
(Back refers to ANA, should be ABA)

1975-76 Topps

	NM	Ex
COMPLETE SET (330)	450.00	180.00
COM. NBA CARD (1-220)	.75	.30
COM. ABA CARD (221-330)	1.50	.60

❑ 1 Bob McAdoo 12.00 3.60
Rick Barry
Kareem Abdul-Jabbar LL
❑ 2 Don Nelson 4.00 1.60
Butch Beard
Rudy Tomjanovich LL
❑ 3 Rick Barry 5.00 2.00
Calvin Murphy
Bill Bradley LL
❑ 4 Wes Unseld 1.50 .60
Dave Cowens
Sam Lacey LL
❑ 5 Kevin Porter 1.50 .60
Dave Bing
Nate Archibald LL
❑ 6 Rick Barry 4.00 1.60
Walt Frazier
Larry Steele LL
❑ 7 Tom Van Arsdale 1.25 .50
❑ 8 Paul Silas 1.25 .50
❑ 9 Jerry Sloan 1.25 .50
❑ 10 Bob McAdoo AS1 6.00 2.40
❑ 11 Dwight Davis .75 .30
❑ 12 John Mengelt .75 .30
❑ 13 George Johnson .75 .30
❑ 14 Ed Ratleff .75 .30
❑ 15 Nate Archibald AS1 4.00 1.60
❑ 16 Elmore Smith .75 .30
❑ 17 Bob Dandridge 1.25 .50
❑ 18 Louie Nelson RC .75 .30
❑ 19 Neal Walk .75 .30
❑ 20 Billy Cunningham 4.00 1.60
❑ 21 Gary Melchionni .75 .30
❑ 22 Barry Clemens .75 .30
❑ 23 Jimmy Jones .75 .30
❑ 24 Tom Burleson RC 1.25 .50
❑ 25 Lou Hudson 1.25 .50
❑ 26 Henry Finkel .75 .30
❑ 27 Jim McMillian 1.25 .50
❑ 28 Matt Guokas 1.25 .50
❑ 29 Fred Foster DP .75 .30
❑ 30 Bob Lanier 5.00 2.00
❑ 31 Jimmy Walker 1.25 .50
❑ 32 Cliff Meely .75 .30
❑ 33 Butch Beard 1.25 .50
❑ 34 Cazzie Russell 1.25 .50
❑ 35 Jon McGlocklin .75 .30
❑ 36 Bernie Fryer .75 .30
❑ 37 Bill Bradley 10.00 4.00
❑ 38 Fred Carter 1.25 .50
❑ 39 Dennis Awtrey DP .75 .30
❑ 40 Sidney Wicks 1.25 .50
❑ 41 Fred Brown 1.25 .50
❑ 42 Rowland Garrett .75 .30
❑ 43 Herm Gilliam .75 .30
❑ 44 Don Nelson 1.25 .50
❑ 45 Ernie DiGregorio 1.25 .50
❑ 46 Jim Brewer .75 .30
❑ 47 Chris Ford 1.25 .50

❑ 48 Nick Weatherspoon .... .75 .30
❑ 49 Zaid Abdul-Aziz .... .75 .30
(formerly Don Smith)
❑ 50 Keith Wilkes RC 10.00 4.00
❑ 51 Ollie Johnson DP .... .75 .30
❑ 52 Lucius Allen .... 1.25 .50
❑ 53 Mickey Davis .... .75 .30
❑ 54 Otto Moore .... .75 .30
❑ 55 Walt Frazier AS1 .... 5.00 2.00
❑ 56 Steve Mix .... 1.25 .50
❑ 57 Nate Hawthorne .... .75 .30
❑ 58 Lloyd Neal .... .75 .30
❑ 59 Don Slick Watts .... 1.25 .50
❑ 60 Elvin Hayes 5.00 2.00
❑ 61 Checklist 1-110 .... 8.00 2.40
❑ 62 Mike Sojourner .... .75 .30
❑ 63 Randy Smith .... 1.25 .50
❑ 64 John Block DP .... .75 .30
❑ 65 Charlie Scott .... 1.25 .50
❑ 66 Jim Chones .... 1.25 .50
❑ 67 Rick Adelman .... 1.25 .50
❑ 68 Curtis Rowe .... .75 .30
❑ 69 Derrek Dickey RC .... 1.25 .50
❑ 70 Rudy Tomjanovich 5.00 2.00
❑ 71 Pat Riley 6.00 2.40
❑ 72 Cornell Warner .... .75 .30
❑ 73 Earl Monroe 3.00 1.20
❑ 74 Allan Bristow RC 3.00 1.20
❑ 75 Pete Maravich DP 20.00 8.00
❑ 76 Curtis Perry .... .75 .30
❑ 77 Bill Walton 20.00 8.00
❑ 78 Leonard Gray .... .75 .30
❑ 79 Kevin Porter .... 1.25 .50
❑ 80 John Havlicek AS2...... 10.00 4.00
❑ 81 Dwight Jones .... .75 .30
❑ 82 Jack Marin .... .75 .30
❑ 83 Dick Snyder .... .75 .30
❑ 84 George Trapp .... .75 .30
❑ 85 Nate Thurmond 3.00 1.20
❑ 86 Charles Johnson .... .75 .30
❑ 87 Ron Riley .... .75 .30
❑ 88 Stu Lantz .... 1.25 .50
❑ 89 Scott Wedman RC .... 1.25 .50
❑ 90 Kareem Abdul-Jabbar 20.00 8.00
❑ 91 Aaron James .... .75 .30
❑ 92 Jim Barnett .... .75 .30
❑ 93 Clyde Lee .... .75 .30
❑ 94 Larry Steele .... 1.25 .50
❑ 95 Mike Riordan .... .75 .30
❑ 96 Archie Clark .... 1.25 .50
❑ 97 Mike Bantom .... .75 .30
❑ 98 Bob Kauffman .... .75 .30
❑ 99 Kevin Stacom RC .... .75 .30
❑ 100 Rick Barry AS1 .... 6.00 2.40
❑ 101 Ken Charles .... .75 .30
❑ 102 Tom Boerwinkle .... .75 .30
❑ 103 Mike Newlin .... 1.25 .50
❑ 104 Leroy Ellis .... 1.25 .50
❑ 105 Austin Carr .... 1.25 .50
❑ 106 Ron Behagen .... .75 .30
❑ 107 Jim Price .... .75 .30
❑ 108 Bud Stallworth .... .75 .30
❑ 109 Earl Williams .... .75 .30
❑ 110 Gail Goodrich 3.00 1.20
❑ 111 Phil Jackson 7.00 2.80
❑ 112 Rod Derline .... .75 .30
❑ 113 Keith Erickson .... .75 .30
❑ 114 Phil Lumpkin .... .75 .30
❑ 115 Wes Unseld 3.00 1.20
❑ 116 Lou Hudson .... 1.50 .60
Lou Hudson
John Drew
Dean Meminger TL
❑ 117 Dave Cowens 3.00 1.20
Kevin Stacom
Paul Silas
JoJo White TL
❑ 118 Bob McAdoo 3.00 1.20
Jack Marin
Bob McAdoo
Randy Smith TL
❑ 119 Bob Love 3.00 1.20
Chet Walker
Nate Thurmond
Norm Van Lier TL
❑ 120 Bobby Smith .... 1.50 .60
Dick Snyder
Jim Chones
Jim Cleamons TL
❑ 121 Bob Lanier 3.00 1.20
John Mengelt
Bob Lanier
Dave Bing TL
❑ 122 Rick Barry 3.00 1.20
Rick Barry
Clifford Ray
Rick Barry TL
❑ 123 Rudy Tomjanovich ..... 2.00 .80
Calvin Murphy
Kevin Kunnert
Mike Newlin TL
❑ 124 Nate Archibald .... 2.00 .80
Ollie Johnson
Sam Lacey UER
(Lacy on front)
Nate Archibald TL
❑ 125 Gail Goodrich .... 1.50 .60
Cazzie Russell
Happy Hairston
Gail Goodrich TL
❑ 126 Kareem Abdul-Jabbar 8.00 3.20
Mickey Davis
Kareem Abdul-Jabbar
Kareem Abdul-Jabbar TL
❑ 127 Pete Maravich 10.00 4.00
Stu Lantz
E.C. Coleman
Pete Maravich TL
❑ 128 Walt Frazier 3.00 1.20
Bill Bradley
John Gianelli
Walt Frazier TL DP
❑ 129 Fred Carter .... 2.00 .80
Doug Collins
Billy Cunningham
Billy Cunningham TL DP
❑ 130 Charlie Scott .... 1.50 .60
Keith Erickson
Curtis Perry
Dennis Awtrey TL DP
❑ 131 Sidney Wicks .... 1.50 .60
Geoff Petrie
Sidney Wicks
Geoff Petrie TL DP
❑ 132 Spencer Haywood ...... 2.00 .80
Archie Clark
Spencer Haywood
Don Watts TL
❑ 133 Elvin Hayes 3.00 1.20
Clem Haskins
Wes Unseld
Kevin Porter TL
❑ 134 John Drew RC .... 1.25 .50
❑ 135 JoJo White AS2 .... 2.00 .80
❑ 136 Garfield Heard .... 1.25 .50
❑ 137 Jim Cleamons .... .75 .30
❑ 138 Howard Porter .... 1.25 .50
❑ 139 Phil Smith RC .... 1.25 .50
❑ 140 Bob Love .... 1.25 .50
❑ 141 John Gianelli DP .... .75 .30
❑ 142 Larry McNeill RC .... .75 .30
❑ 143 Brian Winters RC 3.00 1.20
❑ 144 George Thompson .... .75 .30
❑ 145 Kevin Kunnert .... .75 .30
❑ 146 Henry Bibby .... 1.25 .50
❑ 147 John Johnson .... .75 .30
❑ 148 Doug Collins 4.00 1.60
❑ 149 John Brisker .... .75 .30
❑ 150 Dick Van Arsdale .... 1.25 .50
❑ 151 Leonard Robinson RC 3.00 1.20
❑ 152 Dean Meminger .... .75 .30
❑ 153 Phil Hankinson .... .75 .30
❑ 154 Dale Schlueter .... .75 .30
❑ 155 Norm Van Lier .... 1.25 .50
❑ 156 Campy Russell RC...... 3.00 1.20
❑ 157 Jeff Mullins .... 1.25 .50
❑ 158 Sam Lacey .... .75 .30
❑ 159 Happy Hairston .... 1.25 .50
❑ 160 Dave Bing DP 3.00 1.20
❑ 161 Kevin Restani RC .... .75 .30
❑ 162 Dave Wohl .... .75 .30
❑ 163 E.C. Coleman .... .75 .30
❑ 164 Jim Fox .... .75 .30
❑ 165 Geoff Petrie .... 1.25 .50
❑ 166 H.Wingo DP UER .... .75 .30
Misspelled Harthorne
on card front
❑ 167 Fred Boyd .... .75 .30
❑ 168 Willie Norwood .... .75 .30
❑ 169 Bob Wilson .... .75 .30
❑ 170 Dave Cowens 6.00 2.40
❑ 171 Tom Henderson RC ...... .75 .30
❑ 172 Jim Washington .... .75 .30
❑ 173 Clem Haskins .... 1.25 .50
❑ 174 Jim Davis .... .75 .30
❑ 175 Bobby Smith DP .... .75 .30
❑ 176 Mike D'Antoni .... .75 .30
❑ 177 Zelmo Beaty .... 1.25 .50
❑ 178 Gary Brokaw RC .... .75 .30
❑ 179 Mel Davis .... .75 .30
❑ 180 Calvin Murphy 3.00 1.20
❑ 181 Checklist 111-220 DP 8.00 2.40
❑ 182 Nate Williams .... .75 .30
❑ 183 LaRue Martin .... .75 .30
❑ 184 George McGinnis 3.00 1.20
❑ 185 Clifford Ray .... .75 .30
❑ 186 Paul Westphal 4.00 1.60
❑ 187 Talvin Skinner .... .75 .30
❑ 188 NBA Playoff Semis DP 1.50 .60
Warriors edge Bulls
Bullets over Celts
❑ 189 Clifford Ray PO .... 1.50 .60
❑ 190 Phil Chenier AS2 DP .. 1.25 .50
❑ 191 John Brown .... .75 .30
❑ 192 Lee Winfield .... .75 .30
❑ 193 Steve Patterson .... .75 .30
❑ 194 Charles Dudley .... .75 .30
❑ 195 Connie Hawkins DP 3.00 1.20
❑ 196 Leon Benbow .... .75 .30
❑ 197 Don Kojis .... .75 .30
❑ 198 Ron Williams .... .75 .30
❑ 199 Mel Counts .... .75 .30
❑ 200 Spencer Haywood AS2 3.00 1.20
❑ 201 Greg Jackson .... .75 .30
❑ 202 Tom Kozelko DP .... .75 .30
❑ 203 Atlanta Hawks CL .... 1.50 .60
❑ 204 Boston Celtics CL 3.00 1.20
❑ 205 Buffalo Braves CL ...... 1.50 .60
❑ 206 Chicago Bulls CL 3.00 1.20
❑ 207 Cleveland Cavs CL .... 1.50 .60
❑ 208 Detroit Pistons CL ...... 1.50 .60
❑ 209 Golden State CL .... 1.50 .60
❑ 210 Houston Rockets CL .. 1.50 .60
❑ 211 Kansas City Kings CL DP 1.50 .60
❑ 212 Los Angeles Lakers CL DP 1.50
.60
❑ 213 Milwaukee Bucks CL .. 1.50 .60
❑ 214 New Orleans Jazz CL 1.50 .60
❑ 215 New York Knicks CL .. 1.50 .60
❑ 216 Philadelphia 76ers CL 1.50 .60
❑ 217 Phoenix Suns CL DP .. 1.50 .60
❑ 218 Portland Blazers CL .... 1.50 .60
❑ 219 Seattle Sonics CL DP 10.00 4.00
❑ 220 Washington Bullets CL 1.50 .60
❑ 221 George McGinnis 8.00 3.20
Julius Erving
Ron Boone LL
❑ 222 Bobby Jones 8.00 3.20
Artis Gilmore
Moses Malone LL
❑ 223 Billy Shepherd .... 2.00 .80
Louie Dampier
Al Smith LL
❑ 224 Mack Calvin .... 2.00 .80
James Silas
Dave Robisch LL
❑ 225 Swen Nater .... 2.00 .80
Artis Gilmore
Marvin Barnes LL
❑ 226 Mack Calvin .... 2.00 .80
Chuck Williams
George McGinnis LL
❑ 227 Mack Calvin AS1 .... 2.00 .80
❑ 228 Billy Knight AS1 RC 3.00 1.20
❑ 229 Bird Averitt .... 1.50 .60
❑ 230 George Carter .... 1.50 .60
❑ 231 Swen Nater AS2 .... 2.00 .80
❑ 232 Steve Jones .... 2.00 .80

	NM	Ex
❑ 233 George Gervin	20.00	8.00
❑ 234 Lee Davis	1.50	.60
❑ 235 Ron Boone AS1	2.00	.80
❑ 236 Mike Jackson	1.50	.60
❑ 237 Kevin Joyce RC	1.50	.60
❑ 238 Marv Roberts	1.50	.60
❑ 239 Tom Owens	1.50	.60
❑ 240 Ralph Simpson	2.00	.80
❑ 241 Gus Gerard	1.50	.60
❑ 242 Brian Taylor AS2	2.00	.80
❑ 243 Rich Jones	1.50	.60
❑ 244 John Roche	1.50	.60
❑ 245 Travis Grant	2.00	.80
❑ 246 Dave Twardzik	2.00	.80
❑ 247 Mike Green	1.50	.60
❑ 248 Billy Keller	2.00	.80
❑ 249 Stew Johnson	1.50	.60
❑ 250 Artis Gilmore AS1	4.00	1.60
❑ 251 John Williamson	2.00	.80
❑ 252 Marvin Barnes AS2 RC	4.00	1.60
❑ 253 James Silas AS2	2.00	.80
❑ 254 Moses Malone RC	35.00	14.00
❑ 255 Willie Wise	2.00	.80
❑ 256 Dwight Lamar	1.50	.60
❑ 257 Checklist 221-330	8.00	2.40
❑ 258 Byron Beck	2.00	.80
❑ 259 Len Elmore RC	3.00	1.20
❑ 260 Dan Issel	5.00	2.00
❑ 261 Rick Mount	1.50	.60
❑ 262 Billy Paultz	2.00	.80
❑ 263 Donnie Freeman	1.50	.60
❑ 264 George Adams	1.50	.60
❑ 265 Don Chaney	2.00	.80
❑ 266 Randy Denton	1.50	.60
❑ 267 Don Washington	1.50	.60
❑ 268 Roland Taylor	1.50	.60
❑ 269 Charlie Edge	1.50	.60
❑ 270 Louie Dampier	2.00	.80
❑ 271 Collis Jones	1.50	.60
❑ 272 Al Skinner RC	1.50	.60
❑ 273 Coby Dietrick	1.50	.60
❑ 274 Tim Bassett	1.50	.60
❑ 275 Freddie Lewis	2.00	.80
❑ 276 Gerald Govan	1.50	.60
❑ 277 Ron Thomas	1.50	.60
❑ 278 Ralph Simpson Mack Calvin Mike Green Mack Calvin TL	2.00	.80
❑ 279 George McGinnis Billy Keller George McGinnis George McGinnis TL	2.50	1.00
❑ 280 Artis Gilmore Louie Dampier Artis Gilmore Louie Dampier TL	2.50	1.00
❑ 281 George Carter Larry Finch Tom Owens Chuck Williams TL	2.00	.80
❑ 282 Julius Erving John Williamson Julius Erving Julius Erving TL	15.00	6.00
❑ 283 Marvin Barnes Freddie Lewis Marvin Barnes Freddie Lewis TL	2.50	1.00
❑ 284 George Gervin James Silas Swen Nater James Silas TL	5.00	2.00
❑ 285 Travis Grant Jimmy O'Brien Caldwell Jones Jimmy O'Brien TL	2.00	.80
❑ 286 Ron Boone Ron Boone Moses Malone Al Smith TL	8.00	3.20
❑ 287 Willie Wise Red Robbins Dave Vaughn Dave Twardzik TL	2.00	.80
❑ 288 Claude Terry	1.50	.60
❑ 289 Wilbert Jones	1.50	.60
❑ 290 Darnell Hillman	2.00	.80
❑ 291 Bill Melchionni	2.00	.80
❑ 292 Mel Daniels	2.00	.80
❑ 293 Fly Williams RC	2.00	.80
❑ 294 Larry Kenon	2.00	.80
❑ 295 Red Robbins	2.00	.80
❑ 296 Warren Jabali	2.00	.80
❑ 297 Jim Eakins	2.00	.80
❑ 298 Bobby Jones RC	12.00	4.80
❑ 299 Don Buse	2.00	.80
❑ 300 Julius Erving AS1	35.00	14.00
❑ 301 Billy Shepherd	1.50	.60
❑ 302 Maurice Lucas RC	6.00	2.40
❑ 303 George Karl	5.00	2.00
❑ 304 Jim Bradley	1.50	.60
❑ 305 Caldwell Jones	2.00	.80
❑ 306 Al Smith	1.50	.60
❑ 307 Jan Van Breda Kolff RC	2.00	.80
❑ 308 Darrell Elston	1.50	.60
❑ 309 ABA Playoff Semifinals Colonels over Spirits; Pacers edge Nuggets	2.00	.80
❑ 310 Artis Gilmore PO	2.50	1.00
❑ 311 Ted McClain	1.50	.60
❑ 312 Willie Sojourner	1.50	.60
❑ 313 Bob Warren	1.50	.60
❑ 314 Bob Netolicky	2.00	.80
❑ 315 Chuck Williams	1.50	.60
❑ 316 Gene Kennedy	1.50	.60
❑ 317 Jimmy O'Brien	1.50	.60
❑ 318 Dave Robisch	1.50	.60
❑ 319 Wali Jones	1.50	.60
❑ 320 George Irvine	1.50	.60
❑ 321 Denver Nuggets CL	2.00	.80
❑ 322 Indiana Pacers CL	2.00	.80
❑ 323 Kentucky Colonels CL	2.00	.80
❑ 324 Memphis Sounds CL	2.00	.80
❑ 325 New York Nets CL	2.00	.80
❑ 326 St. Louis Spirits CL (Spirits of St. Louis on card back)	2.00	.80
❑ 327 San Antonio Spurs CL	2.00	.80
❑ 328 San Diego Sails CL	2.00	.80
❑ 329 Utah Stars CL	2.00	.80
❑ 330 Virginia Squires CL	4.00	1.20

1976-77 Topps

	NM	Ex
COMPLETE SET (144)	375.00	150.00
❑ 1 Julius Erving	60.00	18.00
❑ 2 Dick Snyder	1.75	.70
❑ 3 Paul Silas	2.50	1.00
❑ 4 Keith Erickson	1.75	.70
❑ 5 Wes Unseld	5.00	2.00
❑ 6 Butch Beard	2.50	1.00
❑ 7 Lloyd Neal	1.75	.70
❑ 8 Tom Henderson	1.75	.70
❑ 9 Jim McMillian	2.50	1.00
❑ 10 Bob Lanier	6.00	2.40
❑ 11 Junior Bridgeman RC	2.50	1.00
❑ 12 Corky Calhoun	1.75	.70
❑ 13 Billy Keller	2.50	1.00
❑ 14 Mickey Johnson RC	1.75	.70
❑ 15 Fred Brown	2.50	1.00
❑ 16 Jamaal Wilkes	2.50	1.00
❑ 17 Louie Nelson	1.75	.70
❑ 18 Ed Ratleff	1.75	.70
❑ 19 Billy Paultz	2.50	1.00
❑ 20 Nate Archibald	5.00	2.00
❑ 21 Steve Mix	2.50	1.00
❑ 22 Ralph Simpson	1.75	.70
❑ 23 Campy Russell	2.50	1.00
❑ 24 Charlie Scott	2.50	1.00
❑ 25 Artis Gilmore	5.00	2.00
❑ 26 Dick Van Arsdale	2.50	1.00
❑ 27 Phil Chenier	2.50	1.00
❑ 28 Spencer Haywood	5.00	2.00
❑ 29 Chris Ford	2.50	1.00
❑ 30 Dave Cowens	10.00	4.00
❑ 31 Sidney Wicks	2.50	1.00
❑ 32 Jim Price	1.75	.70
❑ 33 Dwight Jones	1.75	.70
❑ 34 Lucius Allen	1.75	.70
❑ 35 Marvin Barnes	2.50	1.00
❑ 36 Henry Bibby	2.50	1.00
❑ 37 Joe Meriweather RC	1.75	.70
❑ 38 Doug Collins	6.00	2.40
❑ 39 Garfield Heard	2.50	1.00
❑ 40 Randy Smith	2.50	1.00
❑ 41 Tom Burleson	2.50	1.00
❑ 42 Dave Twardzik	2.50	1.00
❑ 43 Bill Bradley	12.00	4.80
❑ 44 Calvin Murphy	5.00	2.00
❑ 45 Bob Love	2.50	1.00
❑ 46 Brian Winters	2.50	1.00
❑ 47 Glenn McDonald	1.75	.70
❑ 48 Checklist 1-144	30.00	9.00
❑ 49 Bird Averitt	1.75	.70
❑ 50 Rick Barry	10.00	4.00
❑ 51 Ticky Burden	1.75	.70
❑ 52 Rich Jones	1.75	.70
❑ 53 Austin Carr	2.50	1.00
❑ 54 Steve Kuberski	1.75	.70
❑ 55 Paul Westphal	2.50	1.00
❑ 56 Mike Riordan	1.75	.70
❑ 57 Bill Walton	25.00	10.00
❑ 58 Eric Money RC	1.75	.70
❑ 59 John Drew	2.50	1.00
❑ 60 Pete Maravich	45.00	18.00
❑ 61 John Shumate RC	2.50	1.00
❑ 62 Mack Calvin	2.50	1.00
❑ 63 Bruce Seals	1.75	.70
❑ 64 Walt Frazier	6.00	2.40
❑ 65 Elmore Smith	1.75	.70
❑ 66 Rudy Tomjanovich	6.00	2.40
❑ 67 Sam Lacey	1.75	.70
❑ 68 George Gervin	25.00	10.00
❑ 69 Gus Williams RC	5.00	2.00
❑ 70 George McGinnis	2.50	1.00
❑ 71 Len Elmore	1.75	.70
❑ 72 Jack Marin	1.75	.70
❑ 73 Brian Taylor	1.75	.70
❑ 74 Jim Brewer	1.75	.70
❑ 75 Alvan Adams RC	6.00	2.40
❑ 76 Dave Bing	5.00	2.00
❑ 77 Phil Jackson	10.00	4.00
❑ 78 Geoff Petrie	2.50	1.00
❑ 79 Mike Sojourner	1.75	.70
❑ 80 James Silas	2.50	1.00
❑ 81 Bob Dandridge	2.50	1.00
❑ 82 Ernie DiGregorio	2.50	1.00
❑ 83 Cazzie Russell	2.50	1.00
❑ 84 Kevin Porter	2.50	1.00
❑ 85 Tom Boerwinkle	1.75	.70
❑ 86 Darnell Hillman	2.50	1.00
❑ 87 Herm Gilliam	1.75	.70
❑ 88 Nate Williams	1.75	.70
❑ 89 Phil Smith	2.50	1.00
❑ 90 John Havlicek	15.00	6.00
❑ 91 Kevin Kunnert	1.75	.70
❑ 92 Jimmy Walker	2.50	1.00
❑ 93 Billy Cunningham	5.00	2.00
❑ 94 Dan Issel	6.00	2.40
❑ 95 Ron Boone	2.50	1.00
❑ 96 Lou Hudson	2.50	1.00
❑ 97 Jim Chones	2.50	1.00
❑ 98 Earl Monroe	5.00	2.00
❑ 99 Tom Van Arsdale	2.50	1.00
❑ 100 Kareem Abdul-Jabbar	40.00	16.00
❑ 101 Moses Malone	25.00	10.00
❑ 102 Ricky Sobers RC	1.75	.70
❑ 103 Swen Nater	2.50	1.00
❑ 104 Leonard Robinson	2.50	1.00

Card	Nm-Mt	Ex-Mt
❑ 105 Don Slick Watts	2.50	1.00
❑ 106 Otto Moore	1.75	.70
❑ 107 Maurice Lucas	2.50	1.00
❑ 108 Norm Van Lier	2.50	1.00
❑ 109 Clifford Ray	1.75	.70
❑ 110 David Thompson RC	40.00	16.00
❑ 111 Fred Carter	2.50	1.00
❑ 112 Caldwell Jones	2.50	1.00
❑ 113 John Williamson	2.50	1.00
❑ 114 Bobby Smith	2.50	1.00
❑ 115 JoJo White	2.50	1.00
❑ 116 Curtis Perry	1.75	.70
❑ 117 John Gianelli	1.75	.70
❑ 118 Curtis Rowe	1.75	.70
❑ 119 Lionel Hollins RC	2.50	1.00
❑ 120 Elvin Hayes	6.00	2.40
❑ 121 Ken Charles	1.75	.70
❑ 122 Dave Meyers RC	2.50	1.00
❑ 123 Jerry Sloan	2.50	1.00
❑ 124 Billy Knight	2.50	1.00
❑ 125 Gail Goodrich	2.50	1.00
❑ 126 Kareem Abdul-Jabbar AS	20.00	8.00
❑ 127 Julius Erving AS	25.00	10.00
❑ 128 George McGinnis AS	2.50	1.00
❑ 129 Nate Archibald AS	2.50	1.00
❑ 130 Pete Maravich AS	25.00	10.00
❑ 131 Dave Cowens AS	5.00	2.00
❑ 132 Rick Barry AS	5.00	2.00
❑ 133 Elvin Hayes AS	5.00	2.00
❑ 134 James Silas AS	2.00	.80
❑ 135 Randy Smith AS	2.00	.80
❑ 136 Leonard Gray	1.75	.70
❑ 137 Charles Johnson	1.75	.70
❑ 138 Ron Behagen	1.75	.70
❑ 139 Mike Newlin	2.50	1.00
❑ 140 Bob McAdoo	6.00	2.40
❑ 141 Mike Gale	1.75	.70
❑ 142 Scott Wedman	2.50	1.00
❑ 143 Lloyd Free RC	6.00	2.40
❑ 144 Bobby Jones	8.00	2.40

1977-78 Topps

	Nm-Mt	Ex-Mt
COMPLETE SET (132)	100.00	40.00
❑ 1 Kareem Abdul-Jabbar	15.00	4.50
❑ 2 Henry Bibby	.40	.16
❑ 3 Curtis Rowe	.30	.12
❑ 4 Norm Van Lier	.40	.16
❑ 5 Darnell Hillman	.40	.16
❑ 6 Earl Monroe	1.50	.60
❑ 7 Leonard Gray	.30	.12
❑ 8 Bird Averitt	.30	.12
❑ 9 Jim Brewer	.30	.12
❑ 10 Paul Westphal	1.00	.40
❑ 11 Bob Gross RC	.40	.16
❑ 12 Phil Smith	.30	.12
❑ 13 Dan Roundfield RC	.60	.24
❑ 14 Brian Taylor	.30	.12
❑ 15 Rudy Tomjanovich	2.00	.80
❑ 16 Kevin Porter	.40	.16
❑ 17 Scott Wedman	.40	.16
❑ 18 Lloyd Free	.60	.24
❑ 19 Tom Boswell RC	.30	.12
❑ 20 Pete Maravich	15.00	6.00
❑ 21 Cliff Poindexter	.30	.12
❑ 22 Bubbles Hawkins	.40	.16
❑ 23 Kevin Grevey RC	1.25	.50
❑ 24 Ken Charles	.30	.12
❑ 25 Bob Dandridge	.40	.16
❑ 26 Lonnie Shelton RC	.40	.16
❑ 27 Don Chaney	.40	.16
❑ 28 Larry Kenon	.40	.16
❑ 29 Checklist 1-132	-	-
❑ 30 Fred Brown	.40	.16
❑ 31 John Gianelli UER (Listed as Cavaliers, should be Buffalo Braves)	.30	.12
❑ 32 Austin Carr	.40	.16
❑ 33 Jamaal Wilkes	.60	.24
❑ 34 Caldwell Jones	.40	.16
❑ 35 JoJo White	.60	.24
❑ 36 Scott May RC	1.25	.50
❑ 37 Mike Newlin	.30	.12
❑ 38 Mel Davis	.30	.12
❑ 39 Lionel Hollins	.60	.24
❑ 40 Elvin Hayes	2.50	1.00
❑ 41 Dan Issel	2.00	.80
❑ 42 Ricky Sobers	.30	.12
❑ 43 Don Ford	.30	.12
❑ 44 John Williamson	.30	.12
❑ 45 Bob McAdoo	2.00	.80
❑ 46 Geoff Petrie	.40	.16
❑ 47 M.L. Carr RC	2.00	.80
❑ 48 Brian Winters	.60	.24
❑ 49 Sam Lacey	.30	.12
❑ 50 George McGinnis	.60	.24
❑ 51 Don Slick Watts	.40	.16
❑ 52 Sidney Wicks	.60	.24
❑ 53 Wilbur Holland	.30	.12
❑ 54 Tim Bassett	.30	.12
❑ 55 Phil Chenier	.40	.16
❑ 56 Adrian Dantley RC	8.00	3.20
❑ 57 Jim Chones	.40	.16
❑ 58 John Lucas RC	2.50	1.00
❑ 59 Cazzie Russell	.40	.16
❑ 60 David Thompson	5.00	2.00
❑ 61 Bob Lanier	2.00	.80
❑ 62 Dave Twardzik	.40	.16
❑ 63 Wilbert Jones	.30	.12
❑ 64 Clifford Ray	.30	.12
❑ 65 Doug Collins	1.50	.60
❑ 66 Tom McMillen RC	2.50	1.00
❑ 67 Rich Kelley RC	.30	.12
❑ 68 Mike Bantom	.30	.12
❑ 69 Tom Boerwinkle	.30	.12
❑ 70 John Havlicek	6.00	2.40
❑ 71 Marvin Webster RC	.40	.16
❑ 72 Curtis Perry	.30	.12
❑ 73 George Gervin	8.00	3.20
❑ 74 Leonard Robinson	.60	.24
❑ 75 Wes Unseld	1.50	.60
❑ 76 Dave Meyers	.40	.16
❑ 77 Gail Goodrich	.60	.24
❑ 78 Richard Washington RC	.60	.24
❑ 79 Mike Gale	.30	.12
❑ 80 Maurice Lucas	.60	.24
❑ 81 Harvey Catchings RC	.40	.16
❑ 82 Randy Smith	.30	.12
❑ 83 Campy Russell	.40	.16
❑ 84 Kevin Kunnert	.30	.12
❑ 85 Lou Hudson	.40	.16
❑ 86 Mickey Johnson	.30	.12
❑ 87 Lucius Allen	.30	.12
❑ 88 Spencer Haywood	1.00	.40
❑ 89 Gus Williams	.60	.24
❑ 90 Dave Cowens	3.00	1.20
❑ 91 Al Skinner	.30	.12
❑ 92 Swen Nater	.30	.12
❑ 93 Tom Henderson	.30	.12
❑ 94 Don Buse	.40	.16
❑ 95 Alvan Adams	.60	.24
❑ 96 Mack Calvin	.40	.16
❑ 97 Tom Burleson	.30	.12
❑ 98 John Drew	.40	.16
❑ 99 Mike Green	.30	.12
❑ 100 Julius Erving	15.00	6.00
❑ 101 John Mengelt	.30	.12
❑ 102 Howard Porter	.40	.16
❑ 103 Billy Paultz	.40	.16
❑ 104 John Shumate	.40	.16
❑ 105 Calvin Murphy	1.50	.60
❑ 106 Elmore Smith	.30	.12
❑ 107 Jim McMillian	.30	.12
❑ 108 Kevin Stacom	.30	.12
❑ 109 Jan Van Breda Kolff	.30	.12
❑ 110 Billy Knight	.40	.16
❑ 111 Robert Parish RC	25.00	10.00
❑ 112 Larry Wright	.30	.12
❑ 113 Bruce Seals	.30	.12
❑ 114 Junior Bridgeman	.40	.16
❑ 115 Artis Gilmore	1.50	.60
❑ 116 Steve Mix	.40	.16
❑ 117 Ron Lee	.30	.12
❑ 118 Bobby Jones	.60	.24
❑ 119 Ron Boone	.40	.16
❑ 120 Bill Walton	8.00	3.20
❑ 121 Chris Ford	.40	.16
❑ 122 Earl Tatum	.30	.12
❑ 123 E.C. Coleman	.30	.12
❑ 124 Moses Malone	6.00	2.40
❑ 125 Charlie Scott	.40	.16
❑ 126 Bobby Smith	.30	.12
❑ 127 Nate Archibald	1.50	.60
❑ 128 Mitch Kupchak RC	1.25	.50
❑ 129 Walt Frazier	2.50	1.00
❑ 130 Rick Barry	3.00	1.20
❑ 131 Ernie DiGregorio	.40	.16
❑ 132 Darryl Dawkins RC	10.00	3.00

1978-79 Topps

	Nm-Mt	Ex-Mt
❑ 1 Bill Walton	10.00	3.00
❑ 2 Doug Collins	1.50	.60
❑ 3 Jamaal Wilkes	.75	.30
❑ 4 Wilbur Holland	.30	.12
❑ 5 Bob McAdoo	1.25	.50
❑ 6 Lucius Allen	.30	.12
❑ 7 Wes Unseld	1.25	.50
❑ 8 Dave Meyers	.50	.20
❑ 9 Austin Carr	.50	.20
❑ 10 Walter Davis RC	7.00	2.80
❑ 11 John Williamson	.30	.12
❑ 12 E.C. Coleman	.30	.12
❑ 13 Calvin Murphy	1.00	.40
❑ 14 Bobby Jones	.75	.30
❑ 15 Chris Ford	.50	.20
❑ 16 Kermit Washington	.50	.20
❑ 17 Butch Beard	.50	.20
❑ 18 Steve Mix	.30	.12
❑ 19 Marvin Webster	.50	.20
❑ 20 George Gervin	6.00	2.40
❑ 21 Steve Hawes	.30	.12
❑ 22 Johnny Davis RC	.50	.20
❑ 23 Swen Nater	.30	.12
❑ 24 Lou Hudson	.50	.20
❑ 25 Elvin Hayes	1.50	.60
❑ 26 Nate Archibald	1.00	.40
❑ 27 James Edwards RC	3.00	1.20
❑ 28 Howard Porter	.50	.20
❑ 29 Quinn Buckner RC	1.25	.50
❑ 30 Leonard Robinson	.50	.20
❑ 31 Jim Cleamons	.30	.12
❑ 32 Campy Russell	.50	.20
❑ 33 Phil Smith	.30	.12
❑ 34 Darryl Dawkins	2.00	.80
❑ 35 Don Buse	.50	.20
❑ 36 Mickey Johnson	.30	.12
❑ 37 Mike Gale	.30	.12
❑ 38 Moses Malone	4.00	1.60
❑ 39 Gus Williams	.75	.30
❑ 40 Dave Cowens	2.00	.80
❑ 41 Bobby Wilkerson RC	.50	.20

Card	Nm-Mt	Ex-Mt
❑ 42 Wilbert Jones	.30	.12
❑ 43 Charlie Scott	.50	.20
❑ 44 John Drew	.50	.20
❑ 45 Earl Monroe	1.25	.50
❑ 46 John Shumate	.50	.20
❑ 47 Earl Tatum	.30	.12
❑ 48 Mitch Kupchak	.50	.20
❑ 49 Ron Boone	.50	.20
❑ 50 Maurice Lucas	.75	.30
❑ 51 Louie Dampier	.50	.20
❑ 52 Aaron James	.30	.12
❑ 53 John Mengelt	.30	.12
❑ 54 Garfield Heard	.50	.20
❑ 55 George Johnson	.30	.12
❑ 56 Junior Bridgeman	.30	.12
❑ 57 Elmore Smith	.30	.12
❑ 58 Rudy Tomjanovich	1.50	.60
❑ 59 Fred Brown	.50	.20
❑ 60 Rick Barry UER (reversed negative)	2.00	.80
❑ 61 Dave Bing	1.25	.50
❑ 62 Anthony Roberts	.30	.12
❑ 63 Norm Nixon RC	2.00	.80
❑ 64 Leon Douglas RC	.50	.20
❑ 65 Henry Bibby	.50	.20
❑ 66 Lonnie Shelton	.30	.12
❑ 67 Checklist 1-132	2.00	.60
❑ 68 Tom Henderson	.30	.12
❑ 69 Dan Roundfield	.50	.20
❑ 70 Armond Hill RC	.50	.20
❑ 71 Larry Kenon	.50	.20
❑ 72 Billy Knight	.50	.20
❑ 73 Artis Gilmore	1.00	.40
❑ 74 Lionel Hollins	.50	.20
❑ 75 Bernard King RC	7.00	2.80
❑ 76 Brian Winters	.75	.30
❑ 77 Alvan Adams	.75	.30
❑ 78 Dennis Johnson RC	8.00	3.20
❑ 79 Scott Wedman	.30	.12
❑ 80 Pete Maravich	10.00	4.00
❑ 81 Dan Issel	1.50	.60
❑ 82 M.L. Carr	.75	.30
❑ 83 Walt Frazier	1.50	.60
❑ 84 Dwight Jones	.30	.12
❑ 85 JoJo White	.75	.30
❑ 86 Robert Parish	5.00	2.00
❑ 87 Charlie Criss RC	.50	.20
❑ 88 Jim McMillian	.30	.12
❑ 89 Chuck Williams	.30	.12
❑ 90 George McGinnis	.75	.30
❑ 91 Billy Paultz	.50	.20
❑ 92 Bob Dandridge	.50	.20
❑ 93 Ricky Sobers	.30	.12
❑ 94 Paul Silas	.50	.20
❑ 95 Gail Goodrich	.75	.30
❑ 96 Tim Bassett	.30	.12
❑ 97 Ron Lee	.30	.12
❑ 98 Bob Gross	.50	.20
❑ 99 Sam Lacey	.30	.12
❑ 100 David Thompson (College North Carolina, should be NC State)	3.00	1.20
❑ 101 John Gianelli	.30	.12
❑ 102 Norm Van Lier	.50	.20
❑ 103 Caldwell Jones	.50	.20
❑ 104 Eric Money	.30	.12
❑ 105 Jim Chones	.50	.20
❑ 106 John Lucas	1.00	.40
❑ 107 Spencer Haywood	.75	.30
❑ 108 Eddie Johnson RC	.30	.12
❑ 109 Sidney Wicks	.75	.30
❑ 110 Kareem Abdul-Jabbar	8.00	3.20
❑ 111 Sonny Parker RC	.50	.20
❑ 112 Randy Smith	.30	.12
❑ 113 Kevin Grevey	.50	.20
❑ 114 Rich Kelley	.30	.12
❑ 115 Scott May	.50	.20
❑ 116 Lloyd Free	.75	.30
❑ 117 Jack Sikma RC	2.00	.80
❑ 118 Kevin Porter	.50	.20
❑ 119 Darnell Hillman	.50	.20
❑ 120 Paul Westphal	1.00	.40
❑ 121 Richard Washington	.30	.12
❑ 122 Dave Twardzik	.50	.20
❑ 123 Mike Bantom	.30	.12
❑ 124 Mike Newlin	.30	.12
❑ 125 Bob Lanier	1.50	.60
❑ 126 Marques Johnson RC	4.00	1.60
❑ 127 Foots Walker RC	.50	.20
❑ 128 Cedric Maxwell RC	1.25	.50
❑ 129 Ray Williams RC	.50	.20
❑ 130 Julius Erving	10.00	4.00
❑ 131 Clifford Ray	.30	.12
❑ 132 Adrian Dantley	3.00	.90

1979-80 Topps

	Nm-Mt	Ex-Mt
COMPLETE SET (132)	80.00	32.00
❑ 1 George Gervin	6.00	2.40
❑ 2 Mitch Kupchak	.40	.16
❑ 3 Henry Bibby	.40	.16
❑ 4 Bob Gross	.40	.16
❑ 5 Dave Cowens	2.00	.80
❑ 6 Dennis Johnson	1.50	.60
❑ 7 Scott Wedman	.30	.12
❑ 8 Earl Monroe	1.25	.50
❑ 9 Mike Bantom	.30	.12
❑ 10 Kareem Abdul-Jabbar AS	8.00	3.20
❑ 11 JoJo White	.60	.24
❑ 12 Spencer Haywood	.60	.24
❑ 13 Kevin Porter	.40	.16
❑ 14 Bernard King	1.50	.60
❑ 15 Mike Newlin	.30	.12
❑ 16 Sidney Wicks	.60	.24
❑ 17 Dan Issel	1.25	.50
❑ 18 Tom Henderson	.30	.12
❑ 19 Jim Chones	.40	.16
❑ 20 Julius Erving	10.00	4.00
❑ 21 Brian Winters	.60	.24
❑ 22 Billy Paultz	.40	.16
❑ 23 Cedric Maxwell	.40	.16
❑ 24 Eddie Johnson	.30	.12
❑ 25 Artis Gilmore	.75	.30
❑ 26 Maurice Lucas	.60	.24
❑ 27 Gus Williams	.60	.24
❑ 28 Sam Lacey	.30	.12
❑ 29 Toby Knight	.30	.12
❑ 30 Paul Westphal AS1	.60	.24
❑ 31 Alex English RC	8.00	3.20
❑ 32 Gail Goodrich	.60	.24
❑ 33 Caldwell Jones	.40	.16
❑ 34 Kevin Grevey	.40	.16
❑ 35 Jamaal Wilkes	.60	.24
❑ 36 Sonny Parker	.30	.12
❑ 37 John Gianelli	.30	.12
❑ 38 John Long RC	.40	.16
❑ 39 George Johnson	.30	.12
❑ 40 Lloyd Free AS2	.60	.24
❑ 41 Rudy Tomjanovich	1.25	.50
❑ 42 Foots Walker	.40	.16
❑ 43 Dan Roundfield	.40	.16
❑ 44 Reggie Theus RC	3.00	1.20
❑ 45 Bill Walton	3.00	1.20
❑ 46 Fred Brown	.40	.16
❑ 47 Darnell Hillman	.40	.16
❑ 48 Ray Williams	.30	.12
❑ 49 Larry Kenon	.40	.16
❑ 50 David Thompson	2.00	.80
❑ 51 Billy Knight	.40	.16
❑ 52 Alvan Adams	.60	.24
❑ 53 Phil Smith	.30	.12
❑ 54 Adrian Dantley	1.25	.50
❑ 55 John Williamson	.30	.12
❑ 56 Campy Russell	.40	.16
❑ 57 Armond Hill	.40	.16
❑ 58 Bob Lanier	1.25	.50
❑ 59 Mickey Johnson	.30	.12
❑ 60 Pete Maravich	10.00	4.00
❑ 61 Nick Weatherspoon	.30	.12
❑ 62 Robert Reid RC	.60	.24
❑ 63 Mychal Thompson RC	1.50	.60
❑ 64 Doug Collins	1.00	.40
❑ 65 Wes Unseld	1.25	.50
❑ 66 Jack Sikma	.60	.24
❑ 67 Bobby Wilkerson	.30	.12
❑ 68 Bill Robinzine	.30	.12
❑ 69 Joe Meriweather	.30	.12
❑ 70 Marques Johnson AS1	.40	.16
❑ 71 Ricky Sobers	.30	.12
❑ 72 Clifford Ray	.30	.12
❑ 73 Tim Bassett	.30	.12
❑ 74 James Silas	.40	.16
❑ 75 Bob McAdoo	.75	.30
❑ 76 Austin Carr	.40	.16
❑ 77 Don Ford	.30	.12
❑ 78 Steve Hawes	.30	.12
❑ 79 Ron Brewer RC	.30	.12
❑ 80 Walter Davis	1.00	.40
❑ 81 Calvin Murphy	.75	.30
❑ 82 Tom Boswell	.30	.12
❑ 83 Lonnie Shelton	.30	.12
❑ 84 Terry Tyler RC	.40	.16
❑ 85 Randy Smith	.30	.12
❑ 86 Rich Kelley	.30	.12
❑ 87 Otis Birdsong RC	.60	.24
❑ 88 Marvin Webster	.30	.12
❑ 89 Eric Money	.30	.12
❑ 90 Elvin Hayes AS1	1.50	.60
❑ 91 Junior Bridgeman	.30	.12
❑ 92 Johnny Davis	.30	.12
❑ 93 Robert Parish	3.00	1.20
❑ 94 Eddie Jordan	.40	.16
❑ 95 Leonard Robinson	.40	.16
❑ 96 Rick Robey RC	.40	.16
❑ 97 Norm Nixon	.60	.24
❑ 98 Mark Olberding	.30	.12
❑ 99 Wilbur Holland	.30	.12
❑ 100 Moses Malone AS1	3.00	1.20
❑ 101 Checklist 1-132	2.00	.60
❑ 102 Tom Owens	.30	.12
❑ 103 Phil Chenier	.40	.16
❑ 104 John Johnson	.30	.12
❑ 105 Darryl Dawkins	1.00	.40
❑ 106 Charlie Scott	.40	.16
❑ 107 M.L. Carr	.60	.24
❑ 108 Phil Ford RC	2.50	1.00
❑ 109 Swen Nater	.30	.12
❑ 110 Nate Archibald	1.25	.50
❑ 111 Aaron James	.30	.12
❑ 112 Jim Cleamons	.30	.12
❑ 113 James Edwards	.60	.24
❑ 114 Don Buse	.40	.16
❑ 115 Steve Mix	.30	.12
❑ 116 Charles Johnson	.30	.12
❑ 117 Elmore Smith	.30	.12
❑ 118 John Drew	.30	.12
❑ 119 Lou Hudson	.40	.16
❑ 120 Rick Barry	2.00	.80
❑ 121 Kent Benson RC	.40	.16
❑ 122 Mike Gale	.30	.12
❑ 123 Jan Van Breda Kolff	.30	.12
❑ 124 Chris Ford	.40	.16
❑ 125 George McGinnis	.60	.24
❑ 126 Leon Douglas	.30	.12
❑ 127 John Lucas	.60	.24
❑ 128 Kermit Washington	.40	.16
❑ 129 Lionel Hollins	.40	.16

	Card	Nm-Mt	Ex-Mt
❑	130 Bob Dandridge AS2	.40	.16
❑	131 James McElroy	.30	.12
❑	132 Bobby Jones	1.50	.60

1980-81 Topps

	Cards	Nm-Mt	Ex-Mt
	COMPLETE SET (176)	500.00	200.00
❑ 1	3 Dan Roundfield AS 181 Julius Erving 258 Ron Brewer SD	5.00	2.00
❑ 2	7 Moses Malone AS 185 Steve Mix 92 Robert Parish TL	1.50	.60
❑ 3	12 Gus Williams AS 67 Geoff Huston 5 John Drew AS	.60	.24
❑ 4	24 Steve Hawes 32 Nate Archibald TL 248 Elvin Hayes	1.00	.40
❑ 5	29 Dan Roundfield 73 Dan Issel TL 152 Brian Winters	.60	.24
❑ 6	34 Larry Bird 174 Julius Erving TL 139 Magic Johnson	300.00	120.00
❑ 7	36 Dave Cowens 186 Paul Westphal TL 142 Jamaal Wilkes	1.00	.40
❑ 8	38 Pete Maravich 264 Lloyd Free SD 194 Dennis Johnson	6.00	2.40
❑ 9	40 Rick Robey 234 Ad.Dantley TL 26 Eddie Johnson	.60	.24
❑ 10	47 Scott May 196 K.Washington TL 177 Henry Bibby	.30	.12
❑ 11	55 Don Ford 145 Quinn Buckner TL 138 Brad Holland	.30	.12
❑ 12	58 Campy Russell 247 Kevin Grevey 52 Dave Robisch TL	.30	.12
❑ 13	60 Foots Walker 113 Mick.Johnson TL 130 Bill Robinzine	.30	.12
❑ 14	61 Austin Carr 8 Kareem Abdul-Jabbar AS 200 Calvin Natt	3.00	1.20
❑ 15	63 Jim Cleamons 256 Robert Reid SD 22 Charlie Criss	.30	.12
❑ 16	69 Tom LaGarde 215 Swen Nater TL 213 James Silas	.30	.12
❑ 17	71 Jerome Whitehead 259 Artis Gilmore SD 184 Caldwell Jones	.60	.24
❑ 18	74 John Roche TL 99 Clifford Ray 235 Ben Poquette TL	.30	.12
❑ 19	75 Alex English 2 Marques Johnson AS 68 Jeff Judkins	1.25	.50
❑ 20	82 Terry Tyler TL 21 Armond Hill TL 171 M.R. Richardson	.30	.12
❑ 21	84 Kent Benson 212 John Shumate 229 Paul Westphal	.60	.24
❑ 22	86 Phil Hubbard 93 Robert Parish TL 126 Tom Burleson	1.50	.60
❑ 23	88 John Long 1 Julius Erving AS 49 Ricky Sobers	3.00	1.20
❑ 24	90 Eric Money 57 Dave Robisch 254 Rick Robey SD	.30	.12
❑ 25	95 Wayne Cooper 226 John Johnson TL 45 David Greenwood	.30	.12
❑ 26	97 Robert Parish 187 Leon.Robinson TL 46 Dwight Jones	2.00	.80
❑ 27	98 Sonny Parker 197 Dave Twardzik TL 39 Cedric Maxwell	.30	.12
❑ 28	105 Rick Barry 122 Otis Birdsong TL 48 John Mengelt	1.00	.40
❑ 29	106 Allen Leavell 53 Foots Walker TL 223 Freeman Williams	.30	.12
❑ 30	108 Calvin Murphy 176 Maur.Cheeks TL 87 Greg Kelser	.60	.24
❑ 31	110 Robert Reid 243 Wes Unseld TL 50 Reggie Theus	.60	.24
❑ 32	111 Rudy Tomjanovich 13 Eddie Johnson AS 179 Doug Collins	.60	.24
❑ 33	112 Mickey Johnson TL 28 Wayne Rollins 15 M.R.Richardson AS	.30	.12
❑ 34	115 Mike Bantom 6 Adrian Dantley AS 227 James Bailey	.60	.24
❑ 35	116 Dudley Bradley 155 Eddie Jordan TL 239 Allan Bristow	.30	.12
❑ 36	118 James Edwards 153 Mike Newlin TL 182 Lionel Hollins	.30	.12
❑ 37	119 Mickey Johnson 154 Geo.Johnson TL 193 Leonard Robinson	.30	.12
❑ 38	120 Billy Knight 16 Paul Westphal AS 59 Randy Smith	.60	.24
❑ 39	121 George McGinnis 83 Eric Money TL 65 Mike Bratz	.60	.24
❑ 40	124 Phil Ford TL 101 Phil Smith 224 Gus Williams TL	.30	.12
❑ 41	127 Phil Ford 19 John Drew TL 209 Larry Kenon	.30	.12
❑ 42	131 Scott Wedman 164 B.Cartwright TL 23 John Drew	.60	.24
❑ 43	132 K.Abdul-Jabbar TL 56 Mike Mitchell 81 Terry Tyler TL	3.00	1.20
❑ 44	135 K.Abdul-Jabbar 79 David Thompson 216 Brian Taylor TL	5.00	2.00
❑ 45	137 Michael Cooper 103 Moses Malone TL 148 George Johnson	1.50	.60
❑ 46	140 Mark Landsberger 10 Bob Lanier AS 222 Bill Walton	1.50	.60
❑ 47	141 Norm Nixon 123 Sam Lacey TL 54 Kenny Carr	.60	.24
❑ 48	143 Marq.Johnson TL 30 Larry Bird TL 232 Jack Sikma	20.00	8.00
❑ 49	146 Junior Bridgeman 31 Larry Bird TL 198 Ron Brewer	15.00	6.00
❑ 50	147 Quinn Buckner 133 K.Abdul-Jabbar TL 207 Mike Gale	3.00	1.20
❑ 51	149 Marques Johnson 262 Julius Erving SD 62 Abdul Jeelani	3.00	1.20
❑ 52	151 Sidney Moncrief 260 Lonnie Shelton SD 220 Paul Silas	3.00	1.20
❑ 53	156 George Johnson 9 Bill Cartwright AS 199 Bob Gross	.60	.24
❑ 54	158 Maurice Lucas 261 James Edwards SD 157 Eddie Jordan	.60	.24
❑ 55	159 Mike Newlin 134 Norm Nixon TL 180 Darryl Dawkins	.30	.12
❑ 56	160 Roger Phegley 206 James Silas TL 91 Terry Tyler UER (First name spelled Jams)	.30	.12
❑ 57	161 Cliff Robinson 51 Mike Mitchell TL 80 Bobby Wilkerson	.30	.12
❑ 58	162 Jan V.Breda Kolff 204 George Gervin TL 117 Johnny Davis	.60	.24
❑ 59	165 M.R.Richardson TL 214 Lloyd Free TL 44 Artis Gilmore	.30	.12
❑ 60	166 Bill Cartwright 244 Kevin Porter TL 25 Armond Hill	1.50	.60
❑ 61	168 Toby Knight 14 Lloyd Free AS 240 Adrian Dantley	.30	.12
❑ 62	169 Joe Meriweather 218 Lloyd Free 42 D.Greenwood TL	.60	.24
❑ 63	170 Earl Monroe 27 James McElroy 85 Leon Douglas	.60	.24
❑ 64	172 Marvin Webster 175 Caldwell Jones TL 129 Sam Lacey	.60	.24
❑ 65	173 Ray Williams 94 John Lucas TL 202 Dave Twardzik	.30	.12
❑ 66	178 Maurice Cheeks 18 Magic Johnson AS 237 Ron Boone	12.00	4.80
❑ 67	183 Bobby Jones 37 Chris Ford 66 Joe Hassett	1.00	.40
❑ 68	189 Alvan Adams 163 B.Cartwright TL 76 Dan Issel	1.00	.40
❑ 69	190 Don Buse 242 Elvin Hayes TL 35 M.L. Carr	.60	.24
❑ 70	191 Walter Davis 11 George Gervin AS 136 Jim Chones	1.00	.40
❑ 71	192 Rich Kelley 102 Moses Malone TL 64 Winford Boynes	1.00	.40
❑ 72	201 Tom Owens 225 Jack Sikma TL 100 Purvis Short	.30	.12
❑ 73	208 George Gervin 72 Dan Issel TL 249 Mitch Kupchak	1.50	.60
❑ 74	217 Joe Bryant 263 Bobby Jones SD 107 Moses Malone	1.50	.60
❑ 75	219 Swen Nater 17 Calvin Murphy AS 70 Rich.Washington	.60	.24
❑ 76	221 Brian Taylor 253 John Shumate SD 167 Larry Demic	.30	.12
❑ 77	228 Fred Brown 205 Larry Kenon TL 203 Kerm.Washington	.30	.12
❑ 78	230 John Johnson	1.00	.40

4 Walter Davis AS
33 Nate Archibald

❑ 79 231 Lonnie Shelton .... .60 .24
104 Allen Leavell TL
96 John Lucas

❑ 80 233 Gus Williams .... .30 .12
20 Dan Roundfield TL
211 Kevin Restani

❑ 81 236 Allan Bristow TL ...... .30 .12
210 Mark Olberding
255 James Bailey SD

❑ 82 238 Tom Boswell .... 1.00 .40
109 Billy Paultz
150 Bob Lanier

❑ 83 241 Ben Poquette .... 1.00 .40
188 Paul Westphal TL
77 Charlie Scott

❑ 84 245 Greg Ballard .... .30 .12
43 Reggie Theus TL
252 John Williamson

❑ 85 246 Bob Dandridge .... .60 .24
41 Reggie Theus TL
128 Reggie King

❑ 86 250 Kevin Porter .... .30 .12
114 Johnny Davis TL
125 Otis Birdsong

❑ 87 251 Wes Unseld .... .60 .24
195 Tom Owens TL
78 John Roche

❑ 88 257 Elvin Hayes SD .... .60 .24
144 Marq.Johnson TL
89 Bob McAdoo

❑ 89 3 Dan Roundfield .... .60 .24
218 Lloyd Free
42 D.Greenwood TL

❑ 90 7 Moses Malone .... 1.00 .40
247 Kevin Grevey
52 Dave Robisch TL

❑ 91 12 Gus Williams .... .30 .12
210 Mark Olberding
255 James Bailey SD

❑ 92 24 Steve Hawes .... .30 .12
226 John Johnson TL
45 David Greenwood

❑ 93 29 Dan Roundfield .... .30 .12
113 Mick.Johnson TL
130 Bill Robinzine

❑ 94 34 Larry Bird 40.00 16.00
164 B.Cartwright TL
23 John Drew

❑ 95 36 Dave Cowens .... 1.00 .40
16 Paul Westphal AS
59 Randy Smith

❑ 96 38 Pete Maravich 5.00 2.00
187 Leon.Robinson TL
46 Dwight Jones

❑ 97 40 Rick Robey .... .60 .24
37 Chris Ford
66 Joe Hassett

❑ 98 47 Scott May 15.00 6.00
30 Larry Bird TL
232 Jack Sikma

❑ 99 55 Don Ford .... 1.00 .40
144 Marq.Johnson TL
89 Bob McAdoo

❑ 100 58 Campy Russell .... .60 .24
21 Armond Hill TL
171 M.R.Richardson

❑ 101 60 Foots Walker .... .30 .12
122 Otis Birdsong TL
48 John Mengelt

❑ 102 61 Austin Carr .... .30 .12
56 Mike Mitchell
81 Terry Tyler TL

❑ 103 63 Jim Cleamons .... .30 .12
261 James Edwards SD
157 Eddie Jordan

❑ 104 69 Tom LaGarde .... 1.00 .40
109 Billy Paultz
150 Bob Lanier

❑ 105 71 Jerome Whitehead .. .60 .24
17 Calvin Murphy AS
70 Rich.Washington

❑ 106 74 John Roche TL .... .30 .12
28 Wayne Rollins
15 M.R.Richardson AS

❑ 107 75 Alex English .... 1.50 .60
102 Moses Malone TL
64 Winford Boynes

❑ 108 82 Terry Tyler TL .... .30 .12
79 David Thompson
216 Brian Taylor TL

❑ 109 84 Kent Benson .... .60 .24
259 Artis Gilmore SD
184 Caldwell Jones

❑ 110 86 Phil Hubbard .... .30 .12
195 Tom Owens TL
78 John Roche

❑ 111 88 John Long 10.00 4.00
18 Magic Johnson AS
237 Ron Boone

❑ 112 90 Eric Money .... .30 .12
215 Swen Nater TL
213 James Silas

❑ 113 95 Wayne Cooper .... .30 .12
154 Geo.Johnson TL
193 Leon.Robinson

❑ 114 97 Robert Parish .... 2.00 .80
103 Moses Malone TL
148 George Johnson

❑ 115 98 Sonny Parker .... .60 .24
94 John Lucas TL
202 Dave Twardzik

❑ 116 105 Rick Barry .... 1.00 .40
123 Sam Lacey TL
54 Kenny Carr

❑ 117 106 Allen Leavell .... .30 .12
197 Dave Twardzik TL
39 Cedric Maxwell

❑ 118 108 Calvin Murphy .... .60 .24
51 Mike Mitchell TL
80 Bobby Wilkerson

❑ 119 110 Robert Reid .... .60 .24
153 Mike Newlin TL
182 Lionel Hollins

❑ 120 111 Rudy Tomjanovich 1.00 .40
73 Dan Issel TL
152 Brian Winters

❑ 121 112 Mick.Johnson TL .. 1.00 .40
264 Lloyd Free SD
194 Dennis Johnson

❑ 122 115 Mike Bantom .... .60 .24
204 George Gervin TL
117 Johnny Davis

❑ 123 116 Dudley Bradley .... 1.00 .40
186 Paul Westphal TL
142 Jamaal Wilkes

❑ 124 118 James Edwards.... 1.25 .50
32 Nate Archibald TL
248 Elvin Hayes

❑ 125 119 Mickey Johnson .. 1.00 .40
72 Dan Issel TL
249 Mitch Kupchak

❑ 126 120 Billy Knight .... .30 .12
104 Allen Leavell TL
96 John Lucas

❑ 127 121 George McGinnis 1.50 .60
10 Bob Lanier AS
222 Bill Walton

❑ 128 124 Phil Ford TL............ .60 .24
234 Adr.Dantley TL
26 Eddie Johnson

❑ 129 127 Phil Ford .... .60 .24
43 Reggie Theus TL
252 John Williamson

❑ 130 131 Scott Wedman........ .30 .12
244 Kevin Porter TL
25 Armond Hill

❑ 131 132 K.Abdul-Jabbar TL 4.00 1.60
93 Robert Parish TL
126 Tom Burleson

❑ 132 135 K.Abdul-Jabbar 5.00 2.00
253 John Shumate SD
167 Larry Demic

❑ 133 137 Michael Cooper.... 1.00 .40
212 John Shumate
229 Paul Westphal

❑ 134 140 Mark Landsberger .. .60 .24
214 Lloyd Free TL
44 Artis Gilmore

❑ 135 141 Norm Nixon .... .60 .24
242 Elvin Hayes TL
35 M.L. Carr

❑ 136 143 Marq.Johnson TL .. .30 .12
57 Dave Robisch
254 Rick Robey SD

❑ 137 146 Junior Bridgeman 3.00 1.20
1 Julius Erving AS
49 Ricky Sobers

❑ 138 147 Quinn Buckner ...... .60 .24
2 Marques Johnson AS
68 Jeff Judkins

❑ 139 149 Marques Johnson .. .30 .12
83 Eric Money TL
65 Mike Bratz

❑ 140 151 Sidney Moncrief .. 4.00 1.60
133 K.Abdul-Jabbar TL
207 Mike Gale

❑ 141 156 George Johnson .... .30 .12
175 Caldw.Jones TL
129 Sam Lacey

❑ 142 158 Maurice Lucas...... 3.00 1.20
262 Julius Erving SD
62 Abdul Jeelani

❑ 143 159 Mike Newlin............ .60 .24
243 Wes Unseld TL
50 Reggie Theus

❑ 144 160 Roger Phegley ...... .30 .12
145 Quinn Buckner TL
138 Brad Holland

❑ 145 161 Cliff Robinson .... .30 .12
114 Johnny Davis TL
125 Otis Birdsong

❑ 146 162 Jan V.Breda Kolff 35.00 14.00
174 Julius Erving TL
139 Magic Johnson

❑ 147 165 M.R.Richardson TL 1.00 .40
185 Steve Mix
92 Robert Parish TL

❑ 148 166 Bill Cartwright ...... 1.00 .40
13 Eddie Johnson AS
179 Doug Collins

❑ 149 168 Toby Knight............ .60 .24
188 Paul Westphal TL
77 Charlie Scott

❑ 150 169 Joe Meriweather .... .30 .12
196 K.Washington TL
177 Henry Bibby

❑ 151 170 Earl Monroe............ .30 .12
206 James Silas TL
91 Terry Tyler

❑ 152 172 Marvin Webster...... .60 .24
155 Eddie Jordan TL
239 Allan Bristow

❑ 153 173 Ray Williams .... .30 .12
225 Jack Sikma TL
100 Purvis Short

❑ 154 178 Maurice Cheeks .. 4.00 1.60
11 George Gervin AS
136 Jim Chones

❑ 155 183 Bobby Jones .... .60 .24
99 Clifford Ray
235 Ben Poquette TL

❑ 156 189 Alvan Adams.......... .60 .24
14 Lloyd Free AS
240 Adrian Dantley

❑ 157 190 Don Buse .... .60 .24
6 Adrian Dantley AS
227 James Bailey

❑ 158 191 Walter Davis .... .60 .24
9 Bill Cartwright AS
199 Bob Gross

❑ 159 192 Rich Kelley .... 1.50 .60
263 Bobby Jones SD
107 Moses Malone

❑ 160 201 Tom Owens............ .60 .24
134 Norm Nixon TL
180 Darryl Dawkins

❑ 161 208 George Gervin...... 1.50 .60
53 Foots Walker TL
223 Freeman Williams

❑ 162 217 Joe Bryant............ 3.00 1.20
8 K.Abdul-Jabbar AS
200 Calvin Natt

❑ 163 219 Swen Nater .... .30 .12
101 Phil Smith
224 Gus Williams TL

❑ 164 221 Brian Taylor........... .30 .12

256 Robert Reid SD
22 Charlie Criss
❑ 165 228 Fred Brown 15.00 6.00
31 Larry Bird TL
198 Ron Brewer
❑ 166 230 John Johnson ...... 1.00 .40
163 B.Cartwright TL
76 Dan Issel
❑ 167 231 Lonnie Shelton ...... .30 .12
205 Larry Kenon TL
203 Kermit Washington
❑ 168 233 Gus Williams .... .60 .24
41 Reggie Theus TL
128 Reggie King
❑ 169 236 Allan Bristow TL .... .30 .12
260 Lonnie Shelton SD
220 Paul Silas
❑ 170 238 Tom Boswell .... .30 .12
27 James McElroy
85 Leon Douglas
❑ 171 241 Ben Poquette ...... 1.00 .40
176 Maurice Cheeks TL
87 Greg Kelser
❑ 172 245 Greg Ballard .... 1.00 .40
4 Walter Davis AS
33 Nate Archibald
❑ 173 246 Bob Dandridge ...... .30 .12
19 John Drew TL
209 Larry Kenon
❑ 174 250 Kevin Porter .... .30 .12
20 Dan Roundfield TL
211 Kevin Restani
❑ 175 251 Wes Unseld.......... 1.00 .40
67 Geoff Huston
5 John Drew AS
❑ 176 257 Elvin Hayes SD 5.00 2.00
181 Julius Erving
258 Ron Brewer SD

1981-82 Topps

	Nm-Mt	Ex-Mt
COMPLETE SET (198)	80.00	32.00
COMMON CARD (1-66)	.10	.04
COMMON CARD (E67-E110)	.15	.06
COMMON CARD (MW67-MW110)..	.15	.06
COMMON CARD (W67-W110) ..	.15	.06
TL (44-66)	.15	.06

❑ 1 John Drew .... .20 .08
❑ 2 Dan Roundfield .... .20 .08
❑ 3 Nate Archibald .... .60 .24
❑ 4 Larry Bird 15.00 6.00
❑ 5 Cedric Maxwell .... .20 .08
❑ 6 Robert Parish .... 1.50 .60
❑ 7 Artis Gilmore .... .60 .24
❑ 8 Ricky Sobers .... .10 .04
❑ 9 Mike Mitchell .... .20 .08
❑ 10 Tom LaGarde .... .10 .04
❑ 11 Dan Issel .... .75 .30
❑ 12 David Thompson .... .75 .30
❑ 13 Lloyd Free .... .25 .10
❑ 14 Moses Malone .... 1.50 .60
❑ 15 Calvin Murphy .... .25 .10
❑ 16 Johnny Davis .... .10 .04
❑ 17 Otis Birdsong .... .25 .10
❑ 18 Phil Ford .... .20 .08
❑ 19 Scott Wedman .... .10 .04
❑ 20 Kareem Abdul-Jabbar .. 4.00 1.60
❑ 21 Magic Johnson 10.00 4.00
❑ 22 Norm Nixon .... .25 .10
❑ 23 Jamaal Wilkes .... .25 .10
❑ 24 Marques Johnson.......... .25 .10
❑ 25 Bob Lanier .... .75 .30
❑ 26 Bill Cartwright .... .50 .20
❑ 27 Michael Ray Richardson .20 .08
❑ 28 Ray Williams .... .20 .08
❑ 29 Darryl Dawkins .... .25 .10
❑ 30 Julius Erving 4.00 1.60
❑ 31 Lionel Hollins .... .10 .04
❑ 32 Bobby Jones .... .25 .10
❑ 33 Walter Davis .... .50 .20
❑ 34 Dennis Johnson .... .50 .20
❑ 35 Leonard Robinson .... .25 .10
❑ 36 Mychal Thompson .... .25 .10
❑ 37 George Gervin .... 2.00 .80
❑ 38 Swen Nater .... .10 .04
❑ 39 Jack Sikma .... .25 .10
❑ 40 Adrian Dantley .... .60 .24
❑ 41 Darrell Griffith RC.......... 1.00 .40
❑ 42 Elvin Hayes .... .75 .30
❑ 43 Fred Brown.......... .25 .10
❑ 44 John Drew .... .15 .06
Dan Roundfield
Eddie Johnson TL
❑ 45 Larry Bird .... 2.00 .80
Larry Bird
Nate Archibald TL
❑ 46 Reggie Theus.......... .25 .10
Artis Gilmore
Reggie Theus TL
❑ 47 Mike Mitchell .... .15 .06
Kenny Carr
Mike Bratz TL
❑ 48 Jim Spanarkel .... .15 .06
Tom LaGarde
Brad Davis TL
❑ 49 David Thompson .... .25 .10
Dan Issel
Kenny Higgs TL
❑ 50 John Long .... .15 .06
Phil Hubbard
Ron Lee TL
❑ 51 Lloyd Free .... .25 .10
Larry Smith
John Lucas TL
❑ 52 Moses Malone .... .40 .16
Moses Malone
Allen Leavell TL
❑ 53 Billy Knight .... .25 .10
James Edwards
Johnny Davis TL
❑ 54 Otis Birdsong .... .15 .06
Reggie King
Phil Ford TL
❑ 55 Kareem Abdul-Jabbar .. 1.25 .50
Kareem Abdul-Jabbar
Norm Nixon TL
❑ 56 Marques Johnson.......... .25 .10
Mickey Johnson
Quinn Buckner TL
❑ 57 Mike Newlin .... .15 .06
Maurice Lucas
Mike Newlin TL
❑ 58 Bill Cartwright.......... .25 .10
Bill Cartwright
Micheal Ray Richardson TL
❑ 59 Julius Erving.......... 1.25 .50
Caldwell Jones
Maurice Cheeks TL
❑ 60 Truck Robinson .... .25 .10
Truck Robinson
Alvan Adams TL
❑ 61 Jim Paxson.......... .15 .06
Mychal Thompson
Kermit Washington
Kelvin Ransey TL
❑ 62 George Gervin .... .25 .10
Dave Corzine
Johnny Moore TL
❑ 63 Freeman Williams .... .15 .06
Swen Nater
Brian Taylor TL
❑ 64 Jack Sikma.......... .25 .10
Jack Sikma
Vinnie Johnson TL
❑ 65 Adrian Dantley .... .25 .10
Ben Poquette
Allan Bristow TL
❑ 66 Elvin Hayes .... .25 .10
Elvin Hayes
Kevin Porter TL
❑ E67 Charlie Criss .... .25 .10
❑ E68 Eddie Johnson .... .15 .06
❑ E69 Wes Matthews .... .15 .06
❑ E70 Tom McMillen .... .40 .16
❑ E71 Tree Rollins .... .40 .16
❑ E72 M.L. Carr .... .25 .10
❑ E73 Chris Ford .... .25 .10
❑ E74 Gerald Henderson RC .. .40 .16
❑ E75 Kevin McHale RC 20.00 8.00
❑ E76 Rick Robey .... .25 .10
❑ E77 Darwin Cook RC .... .15 .06
❑ E78 Mike Gminski RC .... .75 .30
❑ E79 Maurice Lucas .... .25 .10
❑ E80 Mike Newlin .... .25 .10
❑ E81 Mike O'Koren RC.......... .25 .10
❑ E82 Steve Hawes .... .15 .06
❑ E83 Foots Walker .... .25 .10
❑ E84 Campy Russell.......... .25 .10
❑ E85 DeWayne Scales .... .15 .06
❑ E86 Randy Smith .... .25 .10
❑ E87 Marvin Webster .... .25 .10
❑ E88 Sly Williams .... .15 .06
❑ E89 Mike Woodson RC.......... .25 .10
❑ E90 Maurice Cheeks.......... 1.50 .60
❑ E91 Caldwell Jones.......... .25 .10
❑ E92 Steve Mix.......... .25 .10
❑ E93A Checklist 1-110 ERR 2.00 .60
(WEST above card number)
❑ E93B Checklist 1-110 COR - -
❑ E94 Greg Ballard.......... .15 .06
❑ E95 Don Collins .... .15 .06
❑ E96 Kevin Grevey .... .25 .10
❑ E97 Mitch Kupchak .... .25 .10
❑ E98 Rick Mahorn RC .... .75 .30
❑ E99 Kevin Porter.......... .25 .10
❑ E100 Nate Archibald SA .... .25 .10
❑ E101 Larry Bird SA 12.00 4.80
❑ E102 Bill Cartwright SA.......... .15 .06
❑ E103 Darryl Dawkins SA.......... .25 .10
❑ E104 Julius Erving SA.......... 2.00 .80
❑ E105 Kevin Porter SA .... .25 .10
❑ E106 Bobby Jones SA .... .25 .10
❑ E107 Cedric Maxwell SA.......... .25 .10
❑ E108 Robert Parish SA.......... 1.00 .40
❑ E109 M.R.Richardson SA .... .25 .10
❑ E110 Dan Roundfield SA .... .25 .10
❑ W67 T.R. Dunn RC .... .15 .06
❑ W68 Alex English .... 1.50 .60
❑ W69 Billy McKinney RC .... .25 .10
❑ W70 Dave Robisch .... .25 .10
❑ W71 Joe Barry Carroll RC.... .40 .16
❑ W72 Bernard King.......... 1.00 .40
❑ W73 Sonny Parker .... .15 .06
❑ W74 Purvis Short .... .25 .10
❑ W75 Larry Smith RC .... .40 .16
❑ W76 Jim Chones.......... .25 .10
❑ W77 Michael Cooper.......... .75 .30
❑ W78 Mark Landsberger.......... .15 .06
❑ W79 Alvan Adams.......... .25 .10
❑ W80 Jeff Cook.......... .15 .06
❑ W81 Rich Kelley .... .15 .06
❑ W82 Kyle Macy RC.......... .40 .16
❑ W83 Billy Ray Bates RC .... .40 .16
❑ W84 Bob Gross.......... .25 .10
❑ W85 Calvin Natt .... .25 .10
❑ W86 Lonnie Shelton .... .25 .10
❑ W87 Jim Paxson RC .... .75 .30
❑ W88 Kelvin Ransey.......... .15 .06
❑ W89 Kermit Washington .... .25 .10
❑ W90 Henry Bibby .... .25 .10
❑ W91 Michael Brooks RC.......... .15 .06
❑ W92 Joe Bryant.......... .15 .06
❑ W93 Phil Smith .... .15 .06
❑ W94 Brian Taylor .... .15 .06
❑ W95 Freeman Williams .... .25 .10
❑ W96 James Bailey .... .15 .06
❑ W97 Checklist 1-110 .... - -
❑ W98 John Johnson .... .15 .06
❑ W99 Vinnie Johnson RC.... 1.50 .60

❑ W100 Wally Walker RC .25 .10
❑ W101 Paul Westphal .25 .10
❑ W102 Allan Bristow .25 .10
❑ W103 Wayne Cooper .15 .06
❑ W104 Carl Nicks .15 .06
❑ W105 Ben Poquette .15 .06
❑ W106 K. Abdul-Jabbar SA 2.00 .80
❑ W107 Dan Issel SA .50 .20
❑ W108 Dennis Johnson SA .25 .10
❑ W109 Magic Johnson SA 8.00 3.20
❑ W110 Jack Sikma SA .25 .10
❑ MW67 David Greenwood .25 .10
❑ MW68 Dwight Jones .15 .06
❑ MW69 Reggie Theus .25 .10
❑ MW70 Bobby Wilkerson .15 .06
❑ MW71 Mike Bratz .15 .06
❑ MW72 Kenny Carr .15 .06
❑ MW73 Geoff Huston .15 .06
❑ MW74 Bill Laimbeer RC 3.00 1.20
❑ MW75 Roger Phegley .15 .06
❑ MW76 Checklist 1-110 - -
❑ MW77 Abdul Jeelani .15 .06
❑ MW78 Bill Robinzine .15 .06
❑ MW79 Jim Spanarkel .15 .06
❑ MW80 Kent Benson .25 .10
❑ MW81 Keith Herron .15 .06
❑ MW82 Phil Hubbard .15 .06
❑ MW83 John Long .15 .06
❑ MW84 Terry Tyler .15 .06
❑ MW85 Mike Dunleavy RC .75 .30
❑ MW86 Tom Henderson .15 .06
❑ MW87 Billy Paultz .25 .10
❑ MW88 Robert Reid .15 .06
❑ MW89 Mike Bantom .15 .06
❑ MW90 James Edwards .25 .10
❑ MW91 Billy Knight .25 .10
❑ MW92 George McGinnis .25 .10
❑ MW93 Louis Orr .15 .06
❑ MW94 Ernie Grunfeld RC .40 .16
❑ MW95 Reggie King .15 .06
❑ MW96 Sam Lacey .15 .06
❑ MW97 Junior Bridgeman .25 .10
❑ MW98 Mickey Johnson .25 .10
❑ MW99 Sidney Moncrief .75 .30
❑ MW100 Brian Winters .25 .10
❑ MW101 Dave Corzine RC .15 .06
❑ MW102 Paul Griffin .15 .06
❑ MW103 Johnny Moore RC .25 .10
❑ MW104 Mark Olberding .15 .06
❑ MW105 James Silas .25 .10
❑ MW106 George Gervin SA .75 .30
❑ MW107 Artis Gilmore SA .25 .10
❑ MW108 Marques Johnson SA .25 .10
❑ MW109 Bob Lanier SA .50 .20
❑ MW110 Moses Malone SA 1.00 .40

1992-93 Topps

	Nm-Mt	Ex-Mt
COMPLETE SET (396)	15.00	4.50
COMPLETE FACT. SET (408)	20.00	6.00
COMPLETE SERIES 1 (198)	4.00	1.20
COMPLETE SERIES 2 (198)	12.00	3.60

❑ 1 Larry Bird .60 .18
❑ 2 Magic Johnson HL .25 .07
Earvin's Magical Moment 2/9/92
❑ 3 Michael Jordan HL 1.00 .30
Michael Lights It Up 6/3/92
❑ 4 David Robinson HL .15 .04
Admiral Ranks High In Five 4/19/92
❑ 5 Johnny Newman .05 .02
❑ 6 Mike Iuzzolino .05 .02
❑ 7 Ken Norman .05 .02
❑ 8 Chris Jackson .05 .02
❑ 9 Duane Ferrell .05 .02
❑ 10 Sean Elliott .08 .02
❑ 11 Bernard King .05 .02
❑ 12 Armon Gilliam .05 .02
❑ 13 Reggie Williams .05 .02
❑ 14 Steve Kerr .08 .02
❑ 15 Anthony Bowie .05 .02
❑ 16 Alton Lister .05 .02
❑ 17 Dee Brown .05 .02
❑ 18 Tom Chambers .05 .02
❑ 19 Otis Thorpe .08 .02
❑ 20 Karl Malone .25 .07
❑ 21 Kenny Gattison .05 .02
❑ 22 Lionel Simmons UER .05 .02
(Misspelled Lionell on card front)
❑ 23 Vern Fleming .05 .02
❑ 24 John Paxson .05 .02
❑ 25 Mitch Richmond .15 .04
❑ 26 Danny Schayes .05 .02
❑ 27 Derrick McKey .05 .02
❑ 28 Mark Randall .05 .02
❑ 29 Bill Laimbeer .08 .02
❑ 30 Chris Morris .05 .02
❑ 31 Alec Kessler .05 .02
❑ 32 Vlade Divac .08 .02
❑ 33 Rick Fox .08 .02
❑ 34 Charles Shackleford .05 .02
❑ 35 Dominique Wilkins .15 .04
❑ 36 Sleepy Floyd .05 .02
❑ 37 Doug West .05 .02
❑ 38 Pete Chilcutt .05 .02
❑ 39 Orlando Woolridge .05 .02
❑ 40 Eric Leckner .05 .02
❑ 41 Joe Kleine .05 .02
❑ 42 Scott Skiles .05 .02
❑ 43 Jerrod Mustaf .05 .02
❑ 44 John Starks .08 .02
❑ 45 Sedale Threatt .05 .02
❑ 46 Doug Smith .05 .02
❑ 47 Byron Scott .08 .02
❑ 48 Willie Anderson .05 .02
❑ 49 David Benoit .05 .02
❑ 50 Scott Hastings .05 .02
❑ 51 Terry Porter .05 .02
❑ 52 Sidney Green .05 .02
❑ 53 Danny Young .05 .02
❑ 54 Magic Johnson .50 .15
❑ 55 Brian Williams .05 .02
❑ 56 Randy Wittman .05 .02
❑ 57 Kevin McHale .15 .04
❑ 58 Dana Barros .05 .02
❑ 59 Thurl Bailey .05 .02
❑ 60 Kevin Duckworth .05 .02
❑ 61 John Williams .05 .02
❑ 62 Willie Burton .05 .02
❑ 63 Spud Webb .08 .02
❑ 64 Detlef Schrempf .08 .02
❑ 65 Sherman Douglas .05 .02
❑ 66 Patrick Ewing .15 .04
❑ 67 Michael Adams .05 .02
❑ 68 Vernon Maxwell .05 .02
❑ 69 Terrell Brandon .15 .04
❑ 70 Terry Catledge .05 .02
❑ 71 Mark Eaton .05 .02
❑ 72 Tony Smith .05 .02
❑ 73 B.J. Armstrong .05 .02
❑ 74 Moses Malone .15 .04
❑ 75 Anthony Bonner .05 .02
❑ 76 George McCloud .05 .02
❑ 77 Glen Rice .15 .04
❑ 78 Jon Koncak .05 .02
❑ 79 Michael Cage .05 .02
❑ 80 Ron Harper .08 .02
❑ 81 Tom Tolbert .05 .02
❑ 82 Brad Sellers .05 .02
❑ 83 Winston Garland .05 .02
❑ 84 Negele Knight .05 .02
❑ 85 Ricky Pierce .05 .02
❑ 86 Mark Aguirre .05 .02
❑ 87 Ron Anderson .05 .02
❑ 88 Loy Vaught .05 .02
❑ 89 Luc Longley .08 .02
❑ 90 Jerry Reynolds .05 .02
❑ 91 Terry Cummings .08 .02
❑ 92 Rony Seikaly .05 .02
❑ 93 Derek Harper .08 .02
❑ 94 Clifford Robinson .08 .02
❑ 95 Kenny Anderson .15 .04
❑ 96 Chris Gatling .05 .02
❑ 97 Stacey Augmon .08 .02
❑ 98 Chris Corchiani .05 .02
❑ 99 Pervis Ellison .05 .02
❑ 100 Larry Bird AS .30 .09
❑ 101 John Stockton AS UER .08 .02
(Listed as Center on card back)
❑ 102 Clyde Drexler AS .08 .02
❑ 103 Scottie Pippen AS .25 .07
❑ 104 Reggie Lewis AS .05 .02
❑ 105 Hakeem Olajuwon AS .15 .04
❑ 106 David Robinson AS .15 .04
❑ 107 Charles Barkley AS .15 .04
❑ 108 James Worthy AS .08 .02
❑ 109 Kevin Willis AS .05 .02
❑ 110 Dikembe Mutombo AS .15 .04
❑ 111 Joe Dumars AS .08 .02
❑ 112 Jeff Hornacek AS UER .05 .02
(5 or 7 shots should be 5 of 7 shots)
❑ 113 Mark Price AS .05 .02
❑ 114 Michael Adams AS .05 .02
❑ 115 Michael Jordan AS 1.00 .30
❑ 116 Brad Daugherty AS .05 .02
❑ 117 Dennis Rodman AS .15 .04
❑ 118 Isiah Thomas AS .08 .02
❑ 119 Tim Hardaway AS .15 .04
❑ 120 Chris Mullin AS .08 .02
❑ 121 Patrick Ewing AS .08 .02
❑ 122 Dan Majerle AS .05 .02
❑ 123 Karl Malone AS .15 .04
❑ 124 Otis Thorpe AS .05 .02
❑ 125 Dominique Wilkins AS .08 .02
❑ 126 Magic Johnson AS .25 .07
❑ 127 Charles Oakley .08 .02
❑ 128 Robert Pack .05 .02
❑ 129 Billy Owens .08 .02
❑ 130 Jeff Malone .05 .02
❑ 131 Danny Ferry .05 .02
❑ 132 Sam Bowie .05 .02
❑ 133 Avery Johnson .05 .02
❑ 134 Jayson Williams .08 .02
❑ 135 Fred Roberts .05 .02
❑ 136 Greg Sutton .05 .02
❑ 137 Dennis Rodman .30 .09
❑ 138 John Williams .05 .02
❑ 139 Greg Dreiling .05 .02
❑ 140 Rik Smits .08 .02
❑ 141 Michael Jordan 2.00 .60
❑ 142 Nick Anderson .08 .02
❑ 143 Jerome Kersey .05 .02
❑ 144 Fat Lever .05 .02
❑ 145 Tyrone Corbin .05 .02
❑ 146 Robert Parish .08 .02
❑ 147 Steve Smith .20 .06
❑ 148 Chris Dudley .05 .02
❑ 149 Antoine Carr .05 .02
❑ 150 Elden Campbell .08 .02
❑ 151 Randy White .05 .02
❑ 152 Felton Spencer .05 .02
❑ 153 Cedric Ceballos .08 .02
❑ 154 Mark Macon .05 .02
❑ 155 Jack Haley .05 .02
❑ 156 Bimbo Coles .05 .02
❑ 157 A.J. English .05 .02
❑ 158 Kendall Gill .08 .02
❑ 159 A.C. Green .08 .02
❑ 160 Mark West .05 .02
❑ 161 Benoit Benjamin .05 .02
❑ 162 Tyrone Hill .05 .02
❑ 163 Larry Nance .05 .02
❑ 164 Gary Grant .05 .02
❑ 165 Bill Cartwright .05 .02
❑ 166 Greg Anthony .05 .02

❑ 167 Jim Les	.05	.02
❑ 168 Johnny Dawkins	.05	.02
❑ 169 Alvin Robertson	.05	.02
❑ 170 Kenny Smith	.05	.02
❑ 171 Gerald Glass	.05	.02
❑ 172 Harvey Grant	.05	.02
❑ 173 Paul Graham	.05	.02
❑ 174 Sam Perkins	.08	.02
❑ 175 Manute Bol	.05	.02
❑ 176 Muggsy Bogues	.08	.02
❑ 177 Mike Brown	.05	.02
❑ 178 Donald Hodge	.05	.02
❑ 179 Dave Jamerson	.05	.02
❑ 180 Mookie Blaylock	.08	.02
❑ 181 Randy Brown	.05	.02
❑ 182 Todd Lichti	.05	.02
❑ 183 Kevin Gamble	.05	.02
❑ 184 Gary Payton	.30	.09
❑ 185 Brian Shaw	.05	.02
❑ 186 Grant Long	.05	.02
❑ 187 Frank Brickowski	.05	.02
❑ 188 Tim Hardaway	.20	.06
❑ 189 Danny Manning	.08	.02
❑ 190 Kevin Johnson	.15	.04
❑ 191 Craig Ehlo	.05	.02
❑ 192 Dennis Scott	.08	.02
❑ 193 Reggie Miller	.15	.04
❑ 194 Darrell Walker	.05	.02
❑ 195 Anthony Mason	.15	.04
❑ 196 Buck Williams	.08	.02
❑ 197 Checklist 1-99	.05	.02
❑ 198 Checklist 100-198	.05	.02
❑ 199 Karl Malone 50P	.15	.04
❑ 200 Dominique Wilkins 50P	.08	.02
❑ 201 Tom Chambers 50P	.05	.02
❑ 202 Bernard King 50P	.05	.02
❑ 203 Kiki Vandeweghe 50P	.05	.02
❑ 204 Dale Ellis 50P	.05	.02
❑ 205 Michael Jordan 50P	1.00	.30
❑ 206 Michael Adams 50P	.05	.02
❑ 207 Charles Smith 50P	.05	.02
❑ 208 Moses Malone 50P	.08	.02
❑ 209 Terry Cummings 50P	.05	.02
❑ 210 Vernon Maxwell 50P	.05	.02
❑ 211 Patrick Ewing 50P	.08	.02
❑ 212 Clyde Drexler 50P	.08	.02
❑ 213 Kevin McHale 50P	.08	.02
❑ 214 Hakeem Olajuwon 50P	.15	.04
❑ 215 Reggie Miller 50P	.08	.02
❑ 216 Gary Grant 20A	.05	.02
❑ 217 Doc Rivers 20A	.05	.02
❑ 218 Mark Price 20A	.05	.02
❑ 219 Isiah Thomas 20A	.08	.02
❑ 220 Nate McMillan 20A	.05	.02
❑ 221 Fat Lever 20A	.05	.02
❑ 222 Kevin Johnson 20A	.08	.02
❑ 223 John Stockton 20A	.08	.02
❑ 224 Scott Skiles 20A	.05	.02
❑ 225 Kevin Brooks	.05	.02
❑ 226 Bobby Phills RC	.15	.04
❑ 227 Oliver Miller RC	.08	.02
❑ 228 John Williams	.05	.02
❑ 229 Brad Lohaus	.05	.02
❑ 230 Derrick Coleman	.08	.02
❑ 231 Ed Pinckney	.05	.02
❑ 232 Trent Tucker	.05	.02
❑ 233 Lance Blanks	.05	.02
❑ 234 Drazen Petrovic	.05	.02
❑ 235 Mark Bryant	.05	.02
❑ 236 Lloyd Daniels RC	.05	.02
❑ 237 Dale Davis	.05	.02
❑ 238 Jayson Williams	.08	.02
❑ 239 Mike Sanders	.05	.02
❑ 240 Mike Gminski	.05	.02
❑ 241 William Bedford	.05	.02
❑ 242 Dell Curry	.05	.02
❑ 243 Gerald Paddio	.05	.02
❑ 244 Chris Smith RC	.05	.02
❑ 245 Jud Buechler	.05	.02
❑ 246 Walter Palmer	.05	.02
❑ 247 Larry Krystkowiak	.05	.02
❑ 248 Marcus Liberty	.05	.02
❑ 249 Sam Mitchell	.05	.02
❑ 250 Kiki Vandeweghe	.05	.02
❑ 251 Vincent Askew	.05	.02
❑ 252 Travis Mays	.05	.02
❑ 253 Charles Smith	.05	.02
❑ 254 John Bagley	.05	.02
❑ 255 James Worthy	.15	.04
❑ 256 Paul Pressey P/CO	.05	.02
❑ 257 Rumeal Robinson	.05	.02
❑ 258 Tom Gugliotta RC	.50	.15
❑ 259 Eric Anderson RC	.05	.02
❑ 260 Hersey Hawkins	.08	.02
❑ 261 Terry Davis	.05	.02
❑ 262 Rex Chapman	.05	.02
❑ 263 Chucky Brown	.05	.02
❑ 264 Danny Young	.05	.02
❑ 265 Olden Polynice	.05	.02
❑ 266 Kevin Willis	.05	.02
❑ 267 Shawn Kemp	.30	.09
❑ 268 Mookie Blaylock	.08	.02
❑ 269 Malik Sealy RC	.08	.02
❑ 270 Charles Barkley	.25	.07
❑ 271 Corey Williams RC	.05	.02
❑ 272 Stephen Howard RC	.05	.02
(See also card 286)		
❑ 273 Keith Askins	.05	.02
❑ 274 Matt Bullard	.05	.02
❑ 275 John Battle	.05	.02
❑ 276 Andrew Lang	.05	.02
❑ 277 David Robinson	.25	.07
❑ 278 Harold Miner RC	.08	.02
❑ 279 Tracy Murray RC	.08	.02
❑ 280 Pooh Richardson	.05	.02
❑ 281 Dikembe Mutombo	.20	.06
❑ 282 Wayman Tisdale	.05	.02
❑ 283 Larry Johnson	.20	.06
❑ 284 Todd Day RC	.08	.02
❑ 285 Stanley Roberts	.05	.02
❑ 286 Randy Woods RC UER	.05	.02
(Card misnumbered 272; run he show should be run the show)		
❑ 287 Avery Johnson	.05	.02
❑ 288 Anthony Peeler RC	.08	.02
❑ 289 Mario Elie	.08	.02
❑ 290 Doc Rivers	.08	.02
❑ 291 Blue Edwards	.05	.02
❑ 292 Sean Rooks RC	.05	.02
❑ 293 Xavier McDaniel	.05	.02
❑ 294 C.Weatherspoon RC	.15	.04
❑ 295 Morlon Wiley	.05	.02
❑ 296 LaBradford Smith	.05	.02
❑ 297 Reggie Lewis	.08	.02
❑ 298 Chris Mullin	.15	.04
❑ 299 Litterial Green RC	.05	.02
❑ 300 Elmore Spencer RC	.05	.02
❑ 301 John Stockton	.15	.04
❑ 302 Walt Williams RC	.15	.04
❑ 303 Anthony Pullard RC	.05	.02
❑ 304 Gundars Vetra RC	.05	.02
❑ 305 LaSalle Thompson	.05	.02
❑ 306 Nate McMillan	.05	.02
❑ 307 Steve Bardo RC	.05	.02
❑ 308 Robert Horry RC	.15	.04
❑ 309 Scott Williams	.05	.02
❑ 310 Bo Kimble	.05	.02
❑ 311 Tree Rollins	.05	.02
❑ 312 Tim Perry	.05	.02
❑ 313 Isaac Austin RC	.08	.02
❑ 314 Tate George	.05	.02
❑ 315 Kevin Lynch	.05	.02
❑ 316 Victor Alexander	.05	.02
❑ 317 Doug Overton	.05	.02
❑ 318 Tom Hammonds	.05	.02
❑ 319 LaPhonso Ellis RC	.15	.04
❑ 320 Scott Brooks	.05	.02
❑ 321 Anthony Avent RC UER	.05	.02
(Front photo actually Blue Edwards)		
❑ 322 Matt Geiger RC	.08	.02
❑ 323 Duane Causwell	.05	.02
❑ 324 Horace Grant	.08	.02
❑ 325 Mark Jackson	.08	.02
❑ 326 Dan Majerle	.08	.02
❑ 327 Chuck Person	.05	.02
❑ 328 Buck Johnson	.05	.02
❑ 329 Duane Cooper RC	.05	.02
❑ 330 Rod Strickland	.15	.04
❑ 331 Isiah Thomas	.15	.04
❑ 332 Greg Kite	.05	.02
(See also card 387)		
❑ 333 Don MacLean RC	.05	.02
❑ 334 Christian Laettner RC	.30	.09
❑ 335 John Crotty RC	.05	.02
❑ 336 Tracy Moore RC	.05	.02
❑ 337 Hakeem Olajuwon	.25	.07
❑ 338 Byron Houston RC	.05	.02
❑ 339 Walter Bond RC	.05	.02
❑ 340 Brent Price RC	.08	.02
❑ 341 Bryant Stith RC	.08	.02
❑ 342 Will Perdue	.05	.02
❑ 343 Jeff Hornacek	.08	.02
❑ 344 Adam Keefe RC	.05	.02
❑ 345 Rafael Addison	.05	.02
❑ 346 Marlon Maxey RC	.05	.02
❑ 347 Joe Dumars	.15	.04
❑ 348 Jon Barry RC	.08	.02
❑ 349 Marty Conlon	.05	.02
❑ 350 Alaa Abdelnaby	.05	.02
❑ 351 Micheal Williams	.05	.02
❑ 352 Brad Daugherty	.05	.02
❑ 353 Tony Bennett RC	.05	.02
❑ 354 Clyde Drexler	.15	.04
❑ 355 Rolando Blackman	.05	.02
❑ 356 Tom Tolbert	.05	.02
❑ 357 Sarunas Marciulionis	.05	.02
❑ 358 Jaren Jackson RC	.08	.02
❑ 359 Stacey King	.05	.02
❑ 360 Danny Ainge	.08	.02
❑ 361 Dale Ellis	.05	.02
❑ 362 Shaquille O'Neal RC	10.00	3.00
❑ 363 Bob McCann RC	.05	.02
❑ 364 Reggie Smith RC	.05	.02
❑ 365 Vinny Del Negro	.05	.02
❑ 366 Robert Pack	.05	.02
❑ 367 David Wood	.05	.02
❑ 368 Rodney McCray	.05	.02
❑ 369 Terry Mills	.05	.02
❑ 370 Eric Murdock UER	.05	.02
(Jazz on back spelled Jass)		
❑ 371 Alex Blackwell RC	.05	.02
❑ 372 Jay Humphries	.05	.02
❑ 373 Eddie Lee Wilkins	.05	.02
❑ 374 James Edwards	.05	.02
❑ 375 Tim Kempton	.05	.02
❑ 376 J.R. Reid	.05	.02
❑ 377 Sam Mack RC	.08	.02
❑ 378 Donald Royal	.05	.02
❑ 379 Mark Price	.05	.02
❑ 380 Mark Acres	.05	.02
❑ 381 Hubert Davis RC	.08	.02
❑ 382 Dave Johnson RC	.05	.02
❑ 383 John Salley	.05	.02
❑ 384 Eddie Johnson	.05	.02
❑ 385 Brian Howard RC	.05	.02
❑ 386 Isaiah Morris RC	.05	.02
❑ 387 Frank Johnson	.05	.02
(Card misnumbered 332)		
❑ 388 Rick Mahorn	.05	.02
❑ 389 Scottie Pippen	.50	.15
❑ 390 Lee Mayberry RC	.05	.02
❑ 391 Tony Campbell	.05	.02

Card		
❑ 392 Latrell Sprewell RC	1.25	.35
❑ 393 Alonzo Mourning RC	1.00	.30
❑ 394 Robert Werdann RC	.05	.02
❑ 395 Checklist 199-297 UER (286 Kennard Winchester; should be Randy Woods)	.05	.02
❑ 396 Checklist 298-396	.05	.02

1993-94 Topps

	Nm-Mt	Ex-Mt
COMPLETE SET (396)	20.00	6.00
COMPLETE FACT.SET (410)	25.00	7.50
COMPLETE SERIES 1 (198)	10.00	3.00
COMPLETE SERIES 2 (198)	10.00	3.00
❑ 1 Charles Barkley HL	.25	.07
❑ 2 Hakeem Olajuwon HL	.25	.07
❑ 3 Shaquille O'Neal HL	.50	.15
❑ 4 Chris Jackson HL	.05	.02
❑ 5 Clifford Robinson HL	.05	.02
❑ 6 Donald Hodge	.05	.02
❑ 7 Victor Alexander	.05	.02
❑ 8 Chris Morris	.05	.02
❑ 9 Muggsy Bogues	.10	.03
❑ 10 Steve Smith UER (Listed with Kings in '90-91; was not in NBA that year)	.25	.07
❑ 11 Dave Johnson	.05	.02
❑ 12 Tom Gugliotta	.25	.07
❑ 13 Doug Edwards RC	.05	.02
❑ 14 Vlade Divac	.10	.03
❑ 15 Corie Blount RC	.05	.02
❑ 16 Derek Harper	.10	.03
❑ 17 Matt Bullard	.05	.02
❑ 18 Terry Catledge	.05	.02
❑ 19 Mark Eaton	.05	.02
❑ 20 Mark Jackson	.10	.03
❑ 21 Terry Mills	.05	.02
❑ 22 Johnny Dawkins	.05	.02
❑ 23 Michael Jordan UER (Listed as a forward with birthdate of 1968; he is a guard with bithdate of 1963)	3.00	.90
❑ 24 Rick Fox UER (Listed with Kings in '91-92)	.05	.02
❑ 25 Charles Oakley	.10	.03
❑ 26 Derrick McKey	.05	.02
❑ 27 Christian Laettner	.10	.03
❑ 28 Todd Day	.05	.02
❑ 29 Danny Ferry	.05	.02
❑ 30 Kevin Johnson	.10	.03
❑ 31 Vinny Del Negro	.05	.02
❑ 32 Kevin Brooks	.05	.02
❑ 33 Pete Chilcutt	.05	.02
❑ 34 Larry Stewart	.05	.02
❑ 35 Dave Jamerson	.05	.02
❑ 36 Sidney Green	.05	.02
❑ 37 J.R. Reid	.05	.02
❑ 38 Jim Jackson	.10	.03
❑ 39 Micheal Williams UER (350.2 minutes per game)	.05	.02
❑ 40 Rex Walters RC	.05	.02
❑ 41 Shawn Bradley RC	.25	.07
❑ 42 Jon Koncak	.05	.02
❑ 43 Byron Houston	.05	.02
❑ 44 Brian Shaw	.05	.02
❑ 45 Bill Cartwright	.05	.02
❑ 46 Jerome Kersey	.05	.02
❑ 47 Danny Schayes	.05	.02
❑ 48 Olden Polynice	.05	.02
❑ 49 Anthony Peeler	.05	.02
❑ 50 Nick Anderson 50	.05	.02
❑ 51 David Benoit	.05	.02
❑ 52 David Robinson	.25	.07
❑ 53 Greg Kite	.05	.02
❑ 54 Gerald Paddio	.05	.02
❑ 55 Don MacLean	.05	.02
❑ 56 Randy Woods	.05	.02
❑ 57 Reggie Miller 50	.10	.03
❑ 58 Kevin Gamble	.05	.02
❑ 59 Sean Green	.05	.02
❑ 60 Jeff Hornacek	.10	.03
❑ 61 John Starks	.10	.03
❑ 62 Gerald Wilkins	.05	.02
❑ 63 Jim Les	.05	.02
❑ 64 Michael Jordan 50	1.50	.45
❑ 65 Alvin Robertson	.05	.02
❑ 66 Tim Kempton	.05	.02
❑ 67 Bryant Stith	.05	.02
❑ 68 Jeff Turner	.05	.02
❑ 69 Malik Sealy	.05	.02
❑ 70 Dell Curry	.05	.02
❑ 71 Brent Price	.05	.02
❑ 72 Kevin Lynch	.05	.02
❑ 73 Bimbo Coles	.05	.02
❑ 74 Larry Nance	.05	.02
❑ 75 Luther Wright RC	.05	.02
❑ 76 Willie Anderson	.05	.02
❑ 77 Dennis Rodman	.50	.15
❑ 78 Anthony Mason	.10	.03
❑ 79 Chris Gatling	.05	.02
❑ 80 Antoine Carr	.05	.02
❑ 81 Kevin Willis	.05	.02
❑ 82 Thurl Bailey	.05	.02
❑ 83 Reggie Williams	.05	.02
❑ 84 Rod Strickland	.10	.03
❑ 85 Rolando Blackman	.05	.02
❑ 86 Bobby Hurley RC	.10	.03
❑ 87 Jeff Malone	.05	.02
❑ 88 James Worthy	.25	.07
❑ 89 Alaa Abdelnaby	.05	.02
❑ 90 Duane Ferrell	.05	.02
❑ 91 Anthony Avent	.05	.02
❑ 92 Scottie Pippen	.75	.23
❑ 93 Ricky Pierce	.05	.02
❑ 94 P.J. Brown RC	.25	.07
❑ 95 Jeff Grayer	.05	.02
❑ 96 Jerrod Mustaf	.05	.02
❑ 97 Elmore Spencer	.05	.02
❑ 98 Walt Williams	.05	.02
❑ 99 Otis Thorpe	.10	.03
❑ 100 Patrick Ewing AS	.10	.03
❑ 101 Michael Jordan AS	1.50	.45
❑ 102 John Stockton AS	.10	.03
❑ 103 Dominique Wilkins AS	.10	.03
❑ 104 Charles Barkley AS	.25	.07
❑ 105 Lee Mayberry	.05	.02
❑ 106 James Edwards	.05	.02
❑ 107 Scott Brooks	.05	.02
❑ 108 John Battle	.05	.02
❑ 109 Kenny Gattison	.05	.02
❑ 110 Pooh Richardson	.05	.02
❑ 111 Rony Seikaly	.05	.02
❑ 112 Mahmoud Abdul-Rauf	.05	.02
❑ 113 Nick Anderson	.10	.03
❑ 114 Gundars Vetra	.05	.02
❑ 115 Joe Dumars AS	.10	.03
❑ 116 Hakeem Olajuwon AS	.25	.07
❑ 117 Scottie Pippen AS	.40	.12
❑ 118 Mark Price AS	.05	.02
❑ 119 Karl Malone AS	.25	.07
❑ 120 Michael Cage	.05	.02
❑ 121 Ed Pinckney	.05	.02
❑ 122 Jay Humphries	.05	.02
❑ 123 Dale Davis	.05	.02
❑ 124 Sean Rooks	.05	.02
❑ 125 Mookie Blaylock	.10	.03
❑ 126 Buck Williams	.05	.02
❑ 127 John Williams	.05	.02
❑ 128 Stacey King	.05	.02
❑ 129 Tim Perry	.05	.02
❑ 130 Tim Hardaway AS	.10	.03
❑ 131 Larry Johnson AS	.10	.03
❑ 132 Detlef Schrempf AS	.05	.02
❑ 133 Reggie Miller AS	.10	.03
❑ 134 Shaquille O'Neal	.50	.15
❑ 135 Dale Ellis	.05	.02
❑ 136 Duane Causwell	.05	.02
❑ 137 Rumeal Robinson	.05	.02
❑ 138 Billy Owens	.05	.02
❑ 139 Malcolm Mackey RC	.05	.02
❑ 140 Vernon Maxwell	.05	.02
❑ 141 LaPhonso Ellis	.05	.02
❑ 142 Robert Parish	.10	.03
❑ 143 LaBradford Smith	.05	.02
❑ 144 Charles Smith	.05	.02
❑ 145 Terry Porter	.05	.02
❑ 146 Elden Campbell	.05	.02
❑ 147 Bill Laimbeer	.05	.02
❑ 148 Chris Mills RC	.25	.07
❑ 149 Brad Lohaus	.05	.02
❑ 150 Jimmy Jackson ART	.05	.02
❑ 151 Tom Gugliotta ART	.10	.03
❑ 152 Shaquille O'Neal ART	.50	.15
❑ 153 Latrell Sprewell ART	.25	.07
❑ 154 Walt Williams ART	.05	.02
❑ 155 Gary Payton	.40	.12
❑ 156 Orlando Woolridge	.05	.02
❑ 157 Adam Keefe	.05	.02
❑ 158 Calbert Cheaney RC	.10	.03
❑ 159 Rick Mahorn	.05	.02
❑ 160 Robert Horry	.10	.03
❑ 161 John Salley	.05	.02
❑ 162 Sam Mitchell	.05	.02
❑ 163 Stanley Roberts	.05	.02
❑ 164 Clarence Weatherspoon	.05	.02
❑ 165 Anthony Bowie	.05	.02
❑ 166 Derrick Coleman	.10	.03
❑ 167 Negele Knight	.05	.02
❑ 168 Marlon Maxey	.05	.02
❑ 169 Spud Webb UER (Listed as center instead of guard)	.10	.03
❑ 170 Alonzo Mourning	.40	.12
❑ 171 Ervin Johnson RC	.10	.03
❑ 172 Sedale Threatt	.05	.02
❑ 173 Mark Macon	.05	.02
❑ 174 B.J. Armstrong	.05	.02
❑ 175 Harold Miner ART	.05	.02
❑ 176 Anthony Peeler ART	.05	.02
❑ 177 Alonzo Mourning ART	.25	.07
❑ 178 Christian Laettner ART	.05	.02
❑ 179 Clarence Weatherspoon ART	.05	.02
❑ 180 Dee Brown	.05	.02
❑ 181 Shaquille O'Neal	1.25	.35
❑ 182 Lov Vaught	.05	.02
❑ 183 Terrell Brandon	.10	.03
❑ 184 Lionel Simmons	.05	.02
❑ 185 Mark Aguirre	.05	.02
❑ 186 Danny Ainge	.10	.03
❑ 187 Reggie Miller	.25	.07
❑ 188 Terry Davis	.05	.02
❑ 189 Mark Bryant	.05	.02
❑ 190 Tyrone Corbin	.05	.02
❑ 191 Chris Mullin	.25	.07
❑ 192 Johnny Newman	.05	.02
❑ 193 Doug West	.05	.02
❑ 194 Keith Askins	.05	.02
❑ 195 Bo Kimble	.05	.02
❑ 196 Sean Elliott	.10	.03
❑ 197 Checklist 1-99 UER (No. 18 listed as Terry Mills instead of Terry Cummings and No. 23 listed as Sam Mitchell instead of Michael Jordan)	.05	.02
❑ 198 Checklist 100-198	.05	.02
❑ 199 Michael Jordan FPM	1.50	.45
❑ 200 Patrick Ewing FPM	.10	.03
❑ 201 John Stockton FPM	.10	.03
❑ 202 Shawn Kemp FPM	.25	.07
❑ 203 Mark Price FPM	.05	.02
❑ 204 Charles Barkley FPM	.25	.07
❑ 205 Hakeem Olajuwon FPM	.25	.07
❑ 206 Clyde Drexler FPM	.10	.03
❑ 207 Kevin Johnson FPM	.05	.02
❑ 208 John Starks FPM	.05	.02
❑ 209 Chris Mullin FPM	.10	.03
❑ 210 Doc Rivers	.10	.03
❑ 211 Kenny Walker	.05	.02
❑ 212 Doug Christie	.10	.03

Card	Player	Nm-Mt	Ex-Mt
❑ 213	James Robinson RC	.05	.02
❑ 214	Larry Krystkowiak	.05	.02
❑ 215	Manute Bol	.05	.02
❑ 216	Carl Herrera	.05	.02
❑ 217	Paul Graham	.05	.02
❑ 218	Jud Buechler	.05	.02
❑ 219	Mike Brown	.05	.02
❑ 220	Tom Chambers	.05	.02
❑ 221	Kendall Gill	.10	.03
❑ 222	Kenny Anderson	.10	.03
❑ 223	Larry Johnson	.25	.07
❑ 224	Chris Webber RC	2.50	.75
❑ 225	Randy White	.05	.02
❑ 226	Rik Smits	.10	.03
❑ 227	A.C. Green	.10	.03
❑ 228	David Robinson	.40	.12
❑ 229	Sean Elliott	.10	.03
❑ 230	Gary Grant	.05	.02
❑ 231	Dana Barros	.05	.02
❑ 232	Bobby Hurley	.10	.03
❑ 233	Blue Edwards	.05	.02
❑ 234	Tom Hammonds	.05	.02
❑ 235	Pete Myers UER Card says born in 1993	.05	.02
❑ 236	Acie Earl RC	.05	.02
❑ 237	Tony Smith	.05	.02
❑ 238	Bill Wennington	.05	.02
❑ 239	Andrew Lang	.05	.02
❑ 240	Ervin Johnson	.10	.03
❑ 241	Byron Scott	.10	.03
❑ 242	Eddie Johnson	.05	.02
❑ 243	Anthony Bonner	.05	.02
❑ 244	Luther Wright	.05	.02
❑ 245	LaSalle Thompson	.05	.02
❑ 246	Harold Miner	.05	.02
❑ 247	Chris Smith	.05	.02
❑ 248	John Williams	.05	.02
❑ 249	Clyde Drexler	.25	.07
❑ 250	Calbert Cheaney	.10	.03
❑ 251	Avery Johnson	.05	.02
❑ 252	Steve Kerr	.10	.03
❑ 253	Warren Kidd RC	.05	.02
❑ 254	Wayman Tisdale	.05	.02
❑ 255	Bob Martin RC	.05	.02
❑ 256	Popeye Jones RC	.05	.02
❑ 257	Jimmy Oliver	.05	.02
❑ 258	Kevin Edwards	.05	.02
❑ 259	Dan Majerle	.10	.03
❑ 260	Jon Barry	.05	.02
❑ 261	Allan Houston RC	1.00	.30
❑ 262	Dikembe Mutombo	.25	.07
❑ 263	Sleepy Floyd	.05	.02
❑ 264	George Lynch RC	.05	.02
❑ 265	Stacey Augmon UER (Listed with Heat in stats)	.05	.02
❑ 266	Hakeem Olajuwon	.40	.12
❑ 267	Scott Skiles	.05	.02
❑ 268	Detlef Schrempf	.10	.03
❑ 269	Brian Davis RC	.05	.02
❑ 270	Tracy Murray	.05	.02
❑ 271	Gheorghe Muresan RC	.25	.07
❑ 272	Terry Dehere RC	.05	.02
❑ 273	Terry Cummings	.05	.02
❑ 274	Keith Jennings	.05	.02
❑ 275	Tyrone Hill	.05	.02
❑ 276	Hersey Hawkins	.10	.03
❑ 277	Grant Long	.05	.02
❑ 278	Herb Williams	.05	.02
❑ 279	Karl Malone	.40	.12
❑ 280	Mitch Richmond	.25	.07
❑ 281	Derek Strong RC	.05	.02
❑ 282	Dino Radja RC	.05	.02
❑ 283	Jack Haley	.05	.02
❑ 284	Derek Harper	.10	.03
❑ 285	Dwayne Schintzius	.05	.02
❑ 286	Michael Curry RC	.05	.02
❑ 287	Rodney Rogers RC	.25	.07
❑ 288	Horace Grant	.10	.03
❑ 289	Oliver Miller	.05	.02
❑ 290	Luc Longley	.10	.03
❑ 291	Walter Bond	.05	.02
❑ 292	Dominique Wilkins	.25	.07
❑ 293	Vern Fleming	.05	.02
❑ 294	Mark Price	.05	.02
❑ 295	Mark Aguirre	.05	.02
❑ 296	Shawn Kemp	.40	.12
❑ 297	Pervis Ellison	.05	.02
❑ 298	Josh Grant RC	.05	.02
❑ 299	Scott Burrell RC	.25	.07
❑ 300	Patrick Ewing	.25	.07
❑ 301	Sam Cassell RC	1.00	.30
❑ 302	Nick Van Exel RC	.75	.23
❑ 303	Clifford Robinson	.10	.03
❑ 304	Frank Johnson	.05	.02
❑ 305	Matt Geiger	.05	.02
❑ 306	Vin Baker RC	.60	.18
❑ 307	Benoit Benjamin	.05	.02
❑ 308	Shawn Bradley	.25	.07
❑ 309	Chris Whitney RC	.05	.02
❑ 310	Eric Riley RC	.05	.02
❑ 311	Isiah Thomas	.25	.07
❑ 312	Jamal Mashburn RC	.60	.18
❑ 313	Xavier McDaniel	.05	.02
❑ 314	Mike Peplowski RC	.05	.02
❑ 315	Darnell Mee RC	.05	.02
❑ 316	Toni Kukoc RC	1.00	.30
❑ 317	Felton Spencer	.05	.02
❑ 318	Sam Bowie	.05	.02
❑ 319	Mario Elie	.05	.02
❑ 320	Tim Hardaway	.25	.07
❑ 321	Ken Norman	.05	.02
❑ 322	Isaiah Rider RC	.50	.15
❑ 323	Rex Chapman	.05	.02
❑ 324	Dennis Rodman	.50	.15
❑ 325	Derrick McKey	.05	.02
❑ 326	Corie Blount	.05	.02
❑ 327	Fat Lever	.05	.02
❑ 328	Ron Harper	.10	.03
❑ 329	Eric Anderson	.05	.02
❑ 330	Armon Gilliam	.05	.02
❑ 331	Lindsey Hunter RC	.25	.07
❑ 332	Eric Leckner	.05	.02
❑ 333	Chris Corchiani	.05	.02
❑ 334	Anfernee Hardaway RC	2.00	.60
❑ 335	Randy Brown	.05	.02
❑ 336	Sam Perkins	.10	.03
❑ 337	Glen Rice	.10	.03
❑ 338	Orlando Woolridge	.05	.02
❑ 339	Mike Gminski	.05	.02
❑ 340	Latrell Sprewell	.60	.18
❑ 341	Harvey Grant	.05	.02
❑ 342	Doug Smith	.05	.02
❑ 343	Kevin Duckworth	.05	.02
❑ 344	Cedric Ceballos	.10	.03
❑ 345	Chuck Person	.05	.02
❑ 346	Scott Haskin RC	.05	.02
❑ 347	Frank Brickowski	.05	.02
❑ 348	Scott Williams	.05	.02
❑ 349	Brad Daugherty	.05	.02
❑ 350	Willie Burton	.05	.02
❑ 351	Joe Dumars	.25	.07
❑ 352	Craig Ehlo	.05	.02
❑ 353	Lucious Harris RC	.05	.02
❑ 354	Danny Manning	.10	.03
❑ 355	Litterial Green	.05	.02
❑ 356	John Stockton	.25	.07
❑ 357	Nate McMillan	.05	.02
❑ 358	Greg Graham RC	.05	.02
❑ 359	Rex Walters	.05	.02
❑ 360	Lloyd Daniels	.05	.02
❑ 361	Antonio Harvey RC	.05	.02
❑ 362	Brian Williams	.05	.02
❑ 363	LeRon Ellis	.05	.02
❑ 364	Chris Dudley	.05	.02
❑ 365	Hubert Davis	.05	.02
❑ 366	Evers Burns RC	.05	.02
❑ 367	Sherman Douglas	.05	.02
❑ 368	Sarunas Marciulionis	.05	.02
❑ 369	Tom Tolbert	.05	.02
❑ 370	Robert Pack	.05	.02
❑ 371	Michael Adams	.05	.02
❑ 372	Negele Knight	.05	.02
❑ 373	Charles Barkley	.40	.12
❑ 374	Bryon Russell RC	.25	.07
❑ 375	Greg Anthony	.05	.02
❑ 376	Ken Williams	.05	.02
❑ 377	John Paxson	.05	.02
❑ 378	Corey Gaines	.05	.02
❑ 379	Eric Murdock	.05	.02
❑ 380	Kevin Thompson RC	.05	.02
❑ 381	Moses Malone	.25	.07
❑ 382	Kenny Smith	.05	.02
❑ 383	Dennis Scott	.05	.02
❑ 384	Michael Jordan FSL	1.50	.45
❑ 385	Hakeem Olajuwon FSL	.25	.07
❑ 386	Shaquille O'Neal FSL	.50	.15
❑ 387	David Robinson FSL	.25	.07
❑ 388	Derrick Coleman FSL	.05	.02
❑ 389	Karl Malone FSL	.25	.07
❑ 390	Patrick Ewing FSL	.10	.03
❑ 391	Scottie Pippen FSL	.40	.12
❑ 392	Dominique Wilkins FSL	.10	.03
❑ 393	Charles Barkley FSL	.25	.07
❑ 394	Larry Johnson FSL	.10	.03
❑ 395	Checklist	.05	.02
❑ 396	Checklist	.05	.02
❑ NNO	Expired Finest Redemption Card	1.00	.30

1994-95 Topps

	Nm-Mt	Ex-Mt
COMPLETE SET (396)	25.00	7.50
COMPLETE SERIES 1 (198)	10.00	3.00
COMPLETE SERIES 2 (198)	15.00	4.50

Card	Player	Nm-Mt	Ex-Mt
❑ 1	Patrick Ewing AS	.10	.03
❑ 2	Mookie Blaylock AS	.05	.02
❑ 3	Charles Oakley AS	.05	.02
❑ 4	Mark Price AS	.05	.02
❑ 5	John Starks AS	.05	.02
❑ 6	Dominique Wilkins AS	.10	.03
❑ 7	Horace Grant AS	.05	.02
❑ 8	Alonzo Mourning AS	.25	.07
❑ 9	B.J. Armstrong AS	.05	.02
❑ 10	Kenny Anderson AS	.05	.02
❑ 11	Scottie Pippen AS	.40	.12
❑ 12	Derrick Coleman AS	.05	.02
❑ 13	Shaquille O'Neal AS	.50	.15
❑ 14	Anfernee Hardaway SPEC	.40	.12
❑ 15	Isaiah Rider SPEC	.05	.02
❑ 16	John Williams	.05	.02
❑ 17	Todd Day	.05	.02
❑ 18	Dale Davis	.05	.02
❑ 19	Sean Rooks	.05	.02
❑ 20	George Lynch	.05	.02
❑ 21	Mitchell Butler	.05	.02
❑ 22	Stacey King	.05	.02
❑ 23	Sherman Douglas	.05	.02
❑ 24	Derrick McKey	.05	.02
❑ 25	Joe Dumars	.25	.07
❑ 26	Scott Brooks	.05	.02
❑ 27	Clarence Weatherspoon	.05	.02
❑ 28	Jayson Williams	.10	.03
❑ 29	Scottie Pippen	.75	.23
❑ 30	John Starks	.05	.02
❑ 31	Robert Pack	.05	.02
❑ 32	Donald Royal	.05	.02
❑ 33	Haywoode Workman	.05	.02
❑ 34	Greg Graham	.05	.02
❑ 35	Terry Cummings	.05	.02
❑ 36	Andrew Lang	.05	.02
❑ 37	Jason Kidd RC	2.50	.75
❑ 38	Terry Mills	.05	.02
❑ 39	Alonzo Mourning	.30	.09
❑ 40	Shawn Kemp	.40	.12
❑ 41	Kevin Willis FTR	.05	.02
❑ 42	Kevin Willis	.05	.02
❑ 43	Armon Gilliam	.05	.02
❑ 44	Bobby Hurley	.05	.02
❑ 45	Jerome Kersey	.05	.02
❑ 46	Xavier McDaniel	.05	.02

❑ 47 Chris Webber .60 .18
❑ 48 Chris Webber FTR .30 .09
❑ 49 Jeff Malone .05 .02
❑ 50 Dikembe Mutombo SPEC .05 .02
❑ 51 Dan Majerle SPEC .05 .02
❑ 52 Dee Brown SPEC .05 .02
❑ 53 John Stockton SPEC .10 .03
❑ 54 Dennis Rodman SPEC .25 .07
❑ 55 Eric Murdock SPEC .05 .02
❑ 56 Glen Rice .10 .03
❑ 57 Glen Rice FTR .05 .02
❑ 58 Dino Radja .05 .02
❑ 59 Billy Owens .05 .02
❑ 60 Doc Rivers .10 .03
❑ 61 Don MacLean .05 .02
❑ 62 Lindsey Hunter .10 .03
❑ 63 Sam Cassell .25 .07
❑ 64 James Worthy .25 .07
❑ 65 Christian Laettner .10 .03
❑ 66 Wesley Person RC .25 .07
❑ 67 Rich King .05 .02
❑ 68 Jon Koncak .05 .02
❑ 69 Muggsy Bogues .10 .03
❑ 70 Jamal Mashburn .25 .07
❑ 71 Gary Grant .05 .02
❑ 72 Eric Murdock .05 .02
❑ 73 Scott Burrell .05 .02
❑ 74 Scott Burrell FTR .05 .02
❑ 75 Anfernee Hardaway .60 .18
❑ 76 Anfernee Hardaway FTR .30 .09
❑ 77 Yinka Dare RC .05 .02
❑ 78 Anthony Avent .05 .02
❑ 79 Jon Barry .05 .02
❑ 80 Rodney Rogers .05 .02
❑ 81 Chris Mills .10 .03
❑ 82 Antonio Davis .05 .02
❑ 83 Steve Smith .10 .03
❑ 84 Buck Williams .05 .02
❑ 85 Spud Webb .05 .02
❑ 86 Stacey Augmon .05 .02
❑ 87 Allan Houston .40 .12
❑ 88 Will Perdue .05 .02
❑ 89 Chris Gatling .05 .02
❑ 90 Danny Ainge .05 .02
❑ 91 Rick Mahorn .05 .02
❑ 92 Elmore Spencer .05 .02
❑ 93 Vin Baker .25 .07
❑ 94 Rex Chapman .05 .02
❑ 95 Dale Ellis .05 .02
❑ 96 Doug Smith .05 .02
❑ 97 Tim Perry .05 .02
❑ 98 Toni Kukoc .40 .12
❑ 99 Terry Dehere .05 .02
❑ 100 Shaquille O'Neal PP .50 .15
❑ 101 Shawn Kemp PP .25 .07
❑ 102 Hakeem Olajuwon PP .25 .07
❑ 103 Derrick Coleman PP .05 .02
❑ 104 Alonzo Mourning PP .25 .07
❑ 105 Dikembe Mutombo PP .05 .02
❑ 106 Chris Webber PP .30 .09
❑ 107 Dennis Rodman PP .25 .07
❑ 108 David Robinson PP .25 .07
❑ 109 Charles Barkley PP .25 .07
❑ 110 Brad Daugherty .05 .02
❑ 111 Derek Harper .05 .02
❑ 112 Detlef Schrempf .10 .03
❑ 113 Harvey Grant .05 .02
❑ 114 Vlade Divac .05 .02
❑ 115 Isaiah Rider .10 .03
❑ 116 Mitch Richmond .25 .07
❑ 117 Tom Chambers .05 .02
❑ 118 Kenny Gattison .05 .02
❑ 119 Kenny Gattison FTR .05 .02
❑ 120 Vernon Maxwell .05 .02
❑ 121 Reggie Williams .05 .02
❑ 122 Chris Mullin .25 .07
❑ 123 Harold Miner .05 .02
❑ 124 Harold Miner FTR .05 .02
❑ 125 Calbert Cheaney .05 .02
❑ 126 Randy Woods .05 .02
❑ 127 Mike Gminski .05 .02
❑ 128 Willie Anderson .05 .02
❑ 129 Mark Macon .05 .02
❑ 130 Avery Johnson .05 .02
❑ 131 Bimbo Coles .05 .02
❑ 132 Kenny Smith .05 .02
❑ 133 Dennis Scott .05 .02
❑ 134 Lionel Simmons .05 .02
❑ 135 Nate McMillan .05 .02
❑ 136 Eric Montross RC .05 .02
❑ 137 Sedale Threatt .05 .02
❑ 138 Kenny Anderson .10 .03
❑ 139 Micheal Williams .05 .02
❑ 140 Grant Long .05 .02
❑ 141 Grant Long FTR .05 .02
❑ 142 Tyrone Corbin .05 .02
❑ 143 Craig Ehlo .05 .02
❑ 144 Gerald Wilkins .05 .02
❑ 145 LaPhonso Ellis .05 .02
❑ 146 Reggie Miller .25 .07
❑ 147 Tracy Murray .05 .02
❑ 148 Victor Alexander .05 .02
❑ 149 Victor Alexander FTR .05 .02
❑ 150 Clifford Robinson .10 .03
❑ 151 Anthony Mason FTR .05 .02
❑ 152 Anthony Mason .10 .03
❑ 153 Jim Jackson .10 .03
❑ 154 Jeff Hornacek .10 .03
❑ 155 Nick Anderson .05 .02
❑ 156 Mike Brown .05 .02
❑ 157 Kevin Johnson .10 .03
❑ 158 John Paxson .05 .02
❑ 159 Loy Vaught .05 .02
❑ 160 Carl Herrera .05 .02
❑ 161 Shawn Bradley .05 .02
❑ 162 Hubert Davis .05 .02
❑ 163 David Benoit .05 .02
❑ 164 Dell Curry .05 .02
❑ 165 Dee Brown .05 .02
❑ 166 LaSalle Thompson .05 .02
❑ 167 Eddie Jones RC 1.25 .35
❑ 168 Walt Williams .05 .02
❑ 169 A.C. Green .10 .03
❑ 170 Kendall Gill .10 .03
❑ 171 Kendall Gill FTR .05 .02
❑ 172 Danny Ferry .05 .02
❑ 173 Bryant Stith .05 .02
❑ 174 John Salley .05 .02
❑ 175 Cedric Ceballos .05 .02
❑ 176 Derrick Coleman .10 .03
❑ 177 Tony Bennett .05 .02
❑ 178 Kevin Duckworth .05 .02
❑ 179 Jay Humphries .05 .02
❑ 180 Sean Elliott .10 .03
❑ 181 Sam Perkins .10 .03
❑ 182 Luc Longley .05 .02
❑ 183 Mitch Richmond AS .10 .03
❑ 184 Clyde Drexler AS .10 .03
❑ 185 Karl Malone AS .25 .07
❑ 186 Shawn Kemp AS .25 .07
❑ 187 Hakeem Olajuwon AS .25 .07
❑ 188 Danny Manning AS .05 .02
❑ 189 Kevin Johnson AS .05 .02
❑ 190 John Stockton AS .10 .03
❑ 191 Latrell Sprewell AS .25 .07
❑ 192 Gary Payton AS .25 .07
❑ 193 Clifford Robinson AS .05 .02
❑ 194 David Robinson AS .25 .07
❑ 195 Charles Barkley AS .25 .07
❑ 196 Mark Price SPEC .05 .02
❑ 197 Checklist 1-99 .05 .02
❑ 198 Checklist 100-198 .05 .02
❑ 199 Patrick Ewing .25 .07
❑ 200 Patrick Ewing FTR .10 .03
❑ 201 Tracy Murray PP .05 .02
❑ 202 Craig Ehlo PP .05 .02
❑ 203 Nick Anderson PP .05 .02
❑ 204 John Starks PP .05 .02
❑ 205 Rex Chapman PP .05 .02
❑ 206 Hersey Hawkins PP .05 .02
❑ 207 Glen Rice PP .05 .02
❑ 208 Jeff Malone PP .05 .02
❑ 209 Dan Majerle PP .05 .02
❑ 210 Chris Mullin PP .10 .03
❑ 211 Grant Hill RC 1.25 .35
❑ 212 Bobby Phills .05 .02
❑ 213 Dennis Rodman .50 .15
❑ 214 Doug West .05 .02
❑ 215 Harold Ellis .05 .02
❑ 216 Kevin Edwards .05 .02
❑ 217 Lorenzo Williams .05 .02
❑ 218 Rick Fox .05 .02
❑ 219 Mookie Blaylock .05 .02
❑ 220 Mookie Blaylock FTR .05 .02
❑ 221 John Williams .05 .02
❑ 222 Keith Jennings .05 .02
❑ 223 Nick Van Exel .25 .07
❑ 224 Gary Payton .40 .12
❑ 225 John Stockton .25 .07
❑ 226 Ron Harper .10 .03
❑ 227 Monty Williams RC .05 .02
❑ 228 Marty Conlon .05 .02
❑ 229 Hersey Hawkins .10 .03
❑ 230 Rik Smits .05 .02
❑ 231 James Robinson .05 .02
❑ 232 Malik Sealy .05 .02
❑ 233 Sergei Bazarevich .05 .02
❑ 234 Brad Lohaus .05 .02
❑ 235 Olden Polynice .05 .02
❑ 236 Brian Williams .05 .02
❑ 237 Tyrone Hill .05 .02
❑ 238 Jim McIlvaine RC .05 .02
❑ 239 Latrell Sprewell .25 .07
❑ 240 Latrell Sprewell FTR .25 .07
❑ 241 Popeye Jones .05 .02
❑ 242 Scott Williams .05 .02
❑ 243 Eddie Jones .60 .18
❑ 244 Moses Malone .25 .07
❑ 245 B.J. Armstrong .05 .02
❑ 246 Jim Les .05 .02
❑ 247 Greg Grant .05 .02
❑ 248 Lee Mayberry .05 .02
❑ 249 Mark Jackson .05 .02
❑ 250 Larry Johnson .10 .03
❑ 251 Terrell Brandon .10 .03
❑ 252 Ledell Eackles .05 .02
❑ 253 Yinka Dare .05 .02
❑ 254 Dontonio Wingfield RC .05 .02
❑ 255 Clyde Drexler .25 .07
❑ 256 Andres Guibert .05 .02
❑ 257 Gheorghe Muresan .05 .02
❑ 258 Tom Hammonds .05 .02
❑ 259 Charles Barkley .40 .12
❑ 260 Charles Barkley FTR .25 .07
❑ 261 Acie Earl .05 .02
❑ 262 Lamond Murray RC .10 .03
❑ 263 Dana Barros .05 .02
❑ 264 Greg Anthony .05 .02
❑ 265 Dan Majerle .10 .03
❑ 266 Zan Tabak .05 .02
❑ 267 Ricky Pierce .05 .02
❑ 268 Eric Leckner .05 .02
❑ 269 Duane Ferrell .05 .02
❑ 270 Mark Price .05 .02
❑ 271 Anthony Peeler .05 .02
❑ 272 Adam Keefe .05 .02
❑ 273 Rex Walters .05 .02
❑ 274 Scott Skiles .05 .02
❑ 275 Glenn Robinson RC .75 .23
❑ 276 Tony Dumas RC .05 .02
❑ 277 Elliot Perry .05 .02
❑ 278 Bo Outlaw RC .05 .02
❑ 279 Karl Malone .40 .12
❑ 280 Karl Malone FTR .25 .07
❑ 281 Herb Williams .05 .02
❑ 282 Vincent Askew .05 .02
❑ 283 Askia Jones RC .05 .02
❑ 284 Shawn Bradley .05 .02
❑ 285 Tim Hardaway .25 .07
❑ 286 Mark West .05 .02
❑ 287 Chuck Person .05 .02
❑ 288 James Edwards .05 .02
❑ 289 Antonio Lang RC .05 .02
❑ 290 Dominique Wilkins .25 .07
❑ 291 Khalid Reeves RC .05 .02
❑ 292 Jamie Watson RC .05 .02
❑ 293 Darnell Mee .05 .02
❑ 294 Brian Grant RC .60 .18
❑ 295 Hakeem Olajuwon .40 .12
❑ 296 Dickey Simpkins RC .05 .02
❑ 297 Tyrone Corbin .05 .02
❑ 298 David Wingate .05 .02
❑ 299 Shaquille O'Neal 1.25 .35
❑ 300 Shaquille O'Neal FR .50 .15
❑ 301 B.J. Armstrong PP .05 .02
❑ 302 Mitch Richmond PP .10 .03
❑ 303 Jim Jackson PP .05 .02
❑ 304 Jeff Hornacek PP .05 .02

❑ 305 Mark Price PP	.05	.02
❑ 306 Kendall Gill PP	.05	.02
❑ 307 Dale Ellis PP	.05	.02
❑ 308 Vernon Maxwell PP	.05	.02
❑ 309 Joe Dumars PP	.10	.03
❑ 310 Reggie Miller PP	.10	.03
❑ 311 Geert Hammink	.05	.02
❑ 312 Charles Smith	.05	.02
❑ 313 Bill Cartwright	.05	.02
❑ 314 Aaron McKie RC	.75	.23
❑ 315 Tom Gugliotta	.10	.03
❑ 316 P.J. Brown	.05	.02
❑ 317 David Wesley	.05	.02
❑ 318 Felton Spencer	.05	.02
❑ 319 Robert Horry	.10	.03
❑ 320 Robert Horry FR	.05	.02
❑ 321 Larry Krystkowiak	.05	.02
❑ 322 Eric Piatkowski RC	.05	.02
❑ 323 Anthony Bonner	.05	.02
❑ 324 Keith Askins	.05	.02
❑ 325 Mahmoud Abdul-Rauf	.05	.02
❑ 326 Darrin Hancock RC	.05	.02
❑ 327 Vern Fleming	.05	.02
❑ 328 Wayman Tisdale	.05	.02
❑ 329 Sam Bowie	.05	.02
❑ 330 Billy Owens	.05	.02
❑ 331 Donald Hodge	.05	.02
❑ 332 Derrick Alston RC	.05	.02
❑ 333 Doug Edwards	.05	.02
❑ 334 Johnny Newman	.05	.02
❑ 335 Otis Thorpe	.05	.02
❑ 336 Bill Curley RC	.05	.02
❑ 337 Michael Cage	.05	.02
❑ 338 Chris Smith	.05	.02
❑ 339 Dikembe Mutombo	.10	.03
❑ 340 Dikembe Mutombo FTR	.05	.02
❑ 341 Duane Causwell	.05	.02
❑ 342 Sean Higgins	.05	.02
❑ 343 Steve Kerr	.05	.02
❑ 344 Eric Montross	.05	.02
❑ 345 Charles Oakley	.05	.02
❑ 346 Brooks Thompson RC	.05	.02
❑ 347 Rony Seikaly	.05	.02
❑ 348 Chris Dudley	.05	.02
❑ 349 Sharone Wright RC	.05	.02
❑ 350 Sarunas Marciulionis	.05	.02
❑ 351 Anthony Miller RC	.05	.02
❑ 352 Pooh Richardson	.05	.02
❑ 353 Byron Scott	.10	.03
❑ 354 Michael Adams	.05	.02
❑ 355 Ken Norman	.05	.02
❑ 356 Clifford Rozier RC	.05	.02
❑ 357 Tim Breaux	.05	.02
❑ 358 Derek Strong	.05	.02
❑ 359 David Robinson	.40	.12
❑ 360 David Robinson FR	.25	.07
❑ 361 Benoit Benjamin	.05	.02
❑ 362 Terry Porter	.05	.02
❑ 363 Ervin Johnson	.05	.02
❑ 364 Alaa Abdelnaby	.05	.02
❑ 365 Robert Parish	.10	.03
❑ 366 Mario Elie	.05	.02
❑ 367 Antonio Harvey	.05	.02
❑ 368 Charlie Ward RC	.25	.07
❑ 369 Kevin Gamble	.05	.02
❑ 370 Rod Strickland	.10	.03
❑ 371 Jason Kidd	1.25	.35
❑ 372 Oliver Miller	.05	.02
❑ 373 Eric Mobley RC	.05	.02
❑ 374 Brian Shaw	.05	.02
❑ 375 Horace Grant	.10	.03
❑ 376 Corie Blount	.05	.02
❑ 377 Sam Mitchell	.05	.02
❑ 378 Jalen Rose RC	1.00	.30
❑ 379 Elden Campbell	.05	.02
❑ 380 Elden Campbell FTR	.05	.02
❑ 381 Donyell Marshall RC	.25	.07
❑ 382 Frank Brickowski	.05	.02
❑ 383 B.J. Tyler RC	.05	.02
❑ 384 Bryon Russell	.05	.02
❑ 385 Danny Manning	.10	.03
❑ 386 Manute Bol	.05	.02
❑ 387 Brent Price	.05	.02
❑ 388 J.R. Reid	.05	.02
❑ 389 Byron Houston	.05	.02
❑ 390 Blue Edwards	.05	.02
❑ 391 Adrian Caldwell	.05	.02
❑ 392 Wesley Person	.10	.03
❑ 393 Juwan Howard RC	.60	.18
❑ 394 Chris Morris	.05	.02
❑ 395 Checklist 199-296	.05	.02
❑ 396 Checklist 297-396	.05	.02

1995-96 Topps

	Nm-Mt	Ex-Mt
COMPLETE SET (291)	30.00	9.00
COMPLETE SERIES 1 (181)	15.00	4.50
COMPLETE SERIES 2 (110)	15.00	4.50
❑ 1 Michael Jordan AL	1.50	.45
❑ 2 Dennis Rodman AL	.15	.04
❑ 3 John Stockton AL	.50	.15
❑ 4 Michael Jordan AL	1.50	.45
❑ 5 David Robinson AL	.30	.09
❑ 6 Shaquille O'Neal LL	.50	.15
❑ 7 Hakeem Olajuwon LL	.30	.09
❑ 8 David Robinson LL	.30	.09
❑ 9 Karl Malone LL	.50	.15
❑ 10 Jamal Mashburn LL	.15	.04
❑ 11 Dennis Rodman LL	.15	.04
❑ 12 Dikembe Mutombo LL	.15	.04
❑ 13 Shaquille O'Neal LL	.50	.15
❑ 14 Patrick Ewing LL	.30	.09
❑ 15 Tyrone Hill LL	.15	.04
❑ 16 John Stockton LL	.50	.15
❑ 17 Kenny Anderson LL	.15	.04
❑ 18 Tim Hardaway LL	.15	.04
❑ 19 Rod Strickland LL	.15	.04
❑ 20 Muggsy Bogues LL	.15	.04
❑ 21 Scottie Pippen LL	.30	.09
❑ 22 Mookie Blaylock LL	.15	.04
❑ 23 Gary Payton LL	.30	.09
❑ 24 John Stockton LL	.50	.15
❑ 25 Nate McMillan LL	.15	.04
❑ 26 Dikembe Mutombo LL	.15	.04
❑ 27 Hakeem Olajuwon LL	.30	.09
❑ 28 Shawn Bradley LL	.15	.04
❑ 29 David Robinson LL	.30	.09
❑ 30 Alonzo Mourning LL	.15	.04
❑ 31 Reggie Miller	.50	.15
❑ 32 Karl Malone	.60	.18
❑ 33 Grant Hill	.60	.18
❑ 34 Charles Barkley	.60	.18
❑ 35 Cedric Ceballos	.15	.04
❑ 36 Gheorghe Muresan	.15	.04
❑ 37 Doug West	.15	.04
❑ 38 Tony Dumas	.15	.04
❑ 39 Kenny Gattison	.15	.04
❑ 40 Chris Mullin	.50	.15
❑ 41 Pervis Ellison	.15	.04
❑ 42 Vinny Del Negro	.15	.04
❑ 43 Mario Elie	.15	.04
❑ 44 Todd Day	.15	.04
❑ 45 Scottie Pippen	.75	.23
❑ 46 Buck Williams	.15	.04
❑ 47 P.J. Brown	.15	.04
❑ 48 Bimbo Coles	.15	.04
❑ 49 Terrell Brandon	.30	.09
❑ 50 Charles Oakley	.15	.04
❑ 51 Sam Perkins	.30	.09
❑ 52 Dale Ellis	.15	.04
❑ 53 Andrew Lang	.15	.04
❑ 54 Harold Ellis	.15	.04
❑ 55 Clarence Weatherspoon	.15	.04
❑ 56 Bill Curley	.15	.04
❑ 57 Robert Parish	.30	.09
❑ 58 David Benoit	.15	.04
❑ 59 Anthony Avent	.15	.04
❑ 60 Jamal Mashburn	.30	.09
❑ 61 Duane Ferrell	.15	.04
❑ 62 Elden Campbell	.15	.04
❑ 63 Rex Chapman	.15	.04
❑ 64 Wesley Person	.15	.04
❑ 65 Mitch Richmond	.30	.09
❑ 66 Micheal Williams	.15	.04
❑ 67 Clifford Rozier	.15	.04
❑ 68 Eric Montross	.15	.04
❑ 69 Dennis Rodman	.30	.09
❑ 70 Vin Baker	.30	.09
❑ 71 Tyrone Hill	.15	.04
❑ 72 Tyrone Corbin	.15	.04
❑ 73 Chris Dudley	.15	.04
❑ 74 Nate McMillan	.15	.04
❑ 75 Kenny Anderson	.30	.09
❑ 76 Monty Williams	.15	.04
❑ 77 Kenny Smith	.15	.04
❑ 78 Rodney Rogers	.15	.04
❑ 79 Corie Blount	.15	.04
❑ 80 Glen Rice	.30	.09
❑ 81 Walt Williams	.15	.04
❑ 82 Scott Williams	.15	.04
❑ 83 Michael Adams	.15	.04
❑ 84 Terry Mills	.15	.04
❑ 85 Horace Grant	.30	.09
❑ 86 Chuck Person	.15	.04
❑ 87 Adam Keefe	.15	.04
❑ 88 Scott Brooks	.15	.04
❑ 89 George Lynch	.15	.04
❑ 90 Kevin Johnson	.30	.09
❑ 91 Armon Gilliam	.15	.04
❑ 92 Greg Minor	.15	.04
❑ 93 Derrick McKey	.15	.04
❑ 94 Victor Alexander	.15	.04
❑ 95 B.J. Armstrong	.15	.04
❑ 96 Terry Dehere	.15	.04
❑ 97 Christian Laettner	.30	.09
❑ 98 Hubert Davis	.15	.04
❑ 99 Aaron McKie	.30	.09
❑ 100 Hakeem Olajuwon	.50	.15
❑ 101 Michael Cage	.15	.04
❑ 102 Grant Long	.15	.04
❑ 103 Calbert Cheaney	.15	.04
❑ 104 Olden Polynice	.15	.04
❑ 105 Sharone Wright	.15	.04
❑ 106 Lee Mayberry	.15	.04
❑ 107 Robert Pack	.15	.04
❑ 108 Loy Vaught	.15	.04
❑ 109 Khalid Reeves	.15	.04
❑ 110 Shawn Kemp	.30	.09
❑ 111 Lindsey Hunter	.15	.04
❑ 112 Dell Curry	.15	.04
❑ 113 Dan Majerle	.30	.09
❑ 114 Bryon Russell	.15	.04
❑ 115 John Starks	.30	.09
❑ 116 Roy Tarpley	.15	.04
❑ 117 Dale Davis	.15	.04
❑ 118 Nick Anderson	.15	.04
❑ 119 Rex Walters	.15	.04
❑ 120 Dominique Wilkins	.50	.15
❑ 121 Sam Cassell	.50	.15
❑ 122 Sean Elliott	.30	.09
❑ 123 B.J. Tyler	.15	.04
❑ 124 Eric Mobley	.15	.04
❑ 125 Toni Kukoc	.30	.09
❑ 126 Pooh Richardson	.15	.04
❑ 127 Isaiah Rider	.15	.04
❑ 128 Steve Smith	.30	.09
❑ 129 Chris Mills	.15	.04
❑ 130 Detlef Schrempf	.30	.09
❑ 131 Donyell Marshall	.30	.09
❑ 132 Eddie Jones	.60	.18
❑ 133 Otis Thorpe	.15	.04
❑ 134 Lionel Simmons	.15	.04
❑ 135 Jeff Hornacek	.30	.09
❑ 136 Jalen Rose	.60	.18
❑ 137 Kevin Willis	.30	.09
❑ 138 Don MacLean	.15	.04
❑ 139 Dee Brown	.15	.04
❑ 140 Glenn Robinson	.50	.15
❑ 141 Joe Kleine	.15	.04
❑ 142 Ron Harper	.30	.09

#	Card	Nm-Mt	Ex-Mt
143	Antonio Davis	.15	.04
144	Jeff Malone	.15	.04
145	Joe Dumars	.50	.15
146	Jason Kidd	1.50	.45
147	J.R. Reid	.15	.04
148	Lamond Murray	.15	.04
149	Derrick Coleman	.15	.04
150	Alonzo Mourning	.30	.09
151	Clifford Robinson	.15	.04
152	Kendall Gill	.15	.04
153	Doug Christie	.30	.09
154	Stacey Augmon	.15	.04
155	Anfernee Hardaway	.50	.15
156	Mahmoud Abdul-Rauf	.15	.04
157	Latrell Sprewell	.50	.15
158	Mark Price	.30	.09
159	Brian Grant	.50	.15
160	Clyde Drexler	.50	.15
161	Juwan Howard	.50	.15
162	Tom Gugliotta	.15	.04
163	Nick Van Exel	.50	.15
164	Billy Owens	.15	.04
165	Brooks Thompson	.15	.04
166	Acie Earl	.15	.04
167	Ed Pinckney	.15	.04
168	Oliver Miller	.15	.04
169	John Salley	.15	.04
170	Jerome Kersey	.15	.04
171	Willie Anderson	.15	.04
172	Keith Jennings	.15	.04
173	Doug Smith	.15	.04
174	Gerald Wilkins	.15	.04
175	Byron Scott	.15	.04
176	Benoit Benjamin	.15	.04
177	Blue Edwards	.15	.04
178	Greg Anthony	.15	.04
179	Trevor Ruffin	.15	.04
180	Kenny Gattison	.15	.04
181	Checklist 1-181	.15	.04
182	Cherokee Parks RC	.15	.04
183	Kurt Thomas RC	.30	.09
184	Ervin Johnson	.15	.04
185	Chucky Brown	.15	.04
186	Luc Longley	.15	.04
187	Anthony Miller	.15	.04
188	Ed O'Bannon RC	.15	.04
189	Bobby Hurley	.15	.04
190	Dikembe Mutombo	.30	.09
191	Robert Horry	.30	.09
192	George Zidek RC	.15	.04
193	Rasheed Wallace RC	1.25	.35
194	Marty Conlon	.15	.04
195	A.C. Green	.30	.09
196	Mike Brown	.15	.04
197	Oliver Miller	.15	.04
198	Charles Smith	.15	.04
199	Eric Williams RC	.30	.09
200	Rik Smits	.30	.09
201	Donald Royal	.15	.04
202	Bryant Reeves RC	.50	.15
203	Danny Ferry	.15	.04
204	Brian Williams	.15	.04
205	Joe Smith RC	.75	.23
206	Gary Trent RC	.15	.04
207	Greg Ostertag RC	.15	.04
208	Ken Norman	.15	.04
209	Avery Johnson	.15	.04
210	Theo Ratliff RC UER Card has no draft pick logo	.60	.18
211	Corie Blount	.15	.04
212	Hersey Hawkins	.15	.04
213	Loren Meyer RC	.15	.04
214	Mario Bennett RC	.15	.04
215	Randolph Childress RC	.15	.04
216	Spud Webb	.30	.09
217	Popeye Jones	.15	.04
218	Shawn Respert RC	.15	.04
219	Malik Sealy	.15	.04
220	Dino Radja	.15	.04
221	James Robinson	.15	.04
222	David Vaughn	.15	.04
223	Michael Smith	.15	.04
224	Jamie Watson	.15	.04
225	LaPhonso Ellis	.15	.04
226	Kevin Gamble	.15	.04
227	Dennis Rodman	.30	.09
228	B.J. Armstrong	.15	.04
229	Jerry Stackhouse RC	1.50	.45
230	Muggsy Bogues	.30	.09
231	Lawrence Moten RC	.15	.04
232	Cory Alexander RC	.15	.04
233	Carlos Rogers	.15	.04
234	Tyus Edney RC	.15	.04
235	Doc Rivers	.30	.09
236	Antonio Harvey	.15	.04
237	Kevin Garnett RC	2.50	.75
238	Derek Harper	.30	.09
239	Kevin Edwards	.15	.04
240	Chris Smith	.15	.04
241	Haywoode Workman	.15	.04
242	Bobby Phills	.15	.04
243	Sherrell Ford RC	.15	.04
244	Corliss Williamson RC	.50	.15
245	Shawn Bradley	.15	.04
246	Jason Caffey RC	.30	.09
247	Bryant Stith	.15	.04
248	Mark West	.15	.04
249	Dennis Scott	.15	.04
250	Jim Jackson	.15	.04
251	Travis Best RC	.15	.04
252	Sean Rooks	.15	.04
253	Yinka Dare	.15	.04
254	Felton Spencer	.15	.04
255	Vlade Divac	.30	.09
256	Michael Finley RC	1.25	.35
257	Damon Stoudamire RC	1.00	.30
258	Mark Bryant	.15	.04
259	Brent Barry RC	.50	.15
260	Rony Seikaly	.15	.04
261	Alan Henderson RC	.50	.15
262	Kendall Gill	.15	.04
263	Rex Chapman	.15	.04
264	Eric Murdock	.15	.04
265	Rodney Rogers	.15	.04
266	Greg Graham	.15	.04
267	Jayson Williams	.15	.04
268	Antonio McDyess RC	1.00	.30
269	Sedale Threatt	.15	.04
270	Danny Manning	.30	.09
271	Pete Chilcutt	.15	.04
272	Bob Sura RC	.30	.09
273	Dana Barros	.15	.04
274	Allan Houston	.30	.09
275	Tracy Murray	.15	.04
276	Anthony Mason	.30	.09
277	Michael Jordan	3.00	.90
278	Patrick Ewing	.50	.15
279	Shaquille O'Neal	1.25	.35
280	Larry Johnson	.30	.09
281	Mark Jackson	.30	.09
282	Chris Webber	.60	.18
283	David Robinson	.50	.15
284	John Stockton	.60	.18
285	Mookie Blaylock	.15	.04
286	Mark Price	.30	.09
287	Tim Hardaway	.30	.09
288	Rod Strickland	.15	.04
289	Sherman Douglas	.15	.04
290	Gary Payton	.50	.15
291	Checklist (182-291)	.15	.04

1996-97 Topps

	Nm-Mt	Ex-Mt
COMPLETE SET (221)	30.00	9.00
COMP.FACT.HOB.SET (227)	35.00	10.50
COMPLETE SERIES 1 (110)	12.00	3.60
COMPLETE SERIES 2 (111)	20.00	6.00

#	Card	Nm-Mt	Ex-Mt
1	Patrick Ewing	.50	.15
2	Christian Laettner	.30	.09
3	Mahmoud Abdul-Rauf	.15	.04
4	Chris Webber	.50	.15
5	Jason Kidd	.75	.23
6	Clifford Rozier	.15	.04
7	Elden Campbell	.15	.04
8	Chuck Person	.15	.04
9	Jeff Hornacek	.30	.09
10	Rik Smits	.30	.09
11	Kurt Thomas	.30	.09
12	Rod Strickland	.15	.04
13	Kendall Gill	.15	.04
14	Brian Williams	.15	.04
15	Tom Gugliotta	.15	.04
16	Ron Harper	.30	.09
17	Eric Williams	.15	.04
18	A.C. Green	.30	.09
19	Scott Williams	.15	.04
20	Damon Stoudamire	.50	.15
21	Bryant Reeves	.15	.04
22	Bob Sura	.15	.04
23	Mitch Richmond	.30	.09
24	Larry Johnson	.30	.09
25	Vin Baker	.30	.09
26	Mark Bryant	.15	.04
27	Horace Grant	.30	.09
28	Allan Houston	.30	.09
29	Sam Perkins	.30	.09
30	Antonio McDyess	.30	.09
31	Rasheed Wallace	.60	.18
32	Malik Sealy	.15	.04
33	Scottie Pippen	.75	.23
34	Charles Barkley	.60	.18
35	Hakeem Olajuwon	.50	.15
36	John Starks	.30	.09
37	Byron Scott	.15	.04
38	Arvydas Sabonis	.30	.09
39	Vlade Divac	.15	.04
40	Joe Dumars	.50	.15
41	Danny Ferry	.15	.04
42	Jerry Stackhouse	.60	.18
43	B.J. Armstrong	.15	.04
44	Shawn Bradley	.15	.04
45	Kevin Garnett	1.00	.30
46	Dee Brown	.15	.04
47	Michael Smith	.15	.04
48	Doug Christie	.30	.09
49	Mark Jackson	.15	.04
50	Shawn Kemp	.30	.09
51	Sasha Danilovic	.15	.04
52	Nick Anderson	.15	.04
53	Matt Geiger	.15	.04
54	Charles Smith	.15	.04
55	Mookie Blaylock	.15	.04
56	Johnny Newman	.15	.04
57	George McCloud	.15	.04
58	Greg Ostertag	.15	.04
59	Reggie Williams	.15	.04
60	Brent Barry	.15	.04
61	Doug West	.15	.04
62	Donald Royal	.15	.04
63	Randy Brown	.15	.04
64	Vincent Askew	.15	.04
65	John Stockton	.50	.15
66	Joe Kleine	.15	.04
67	Keith Askins	.15	.04
68	Bobby Phills	.15	.04
69	Chris Mullin	.50	.15
70	Nick Van Exel	.50	.15
71	Rick Fox	.15	.04
72	Chicago Bulls - 72 Wins	1.50	.45
73	Shawn Respert	.15	.04
74	Hubert Davis	.15	.04
75	Jim Jackson	.15	.04
76	Olden Polynice	.15	.04
77	Gheorghe Muresan	.15	.04
78	Theo Ratliff	.30	.09
79	Khalid Reeves	.15	.04
80	David Robinson	.50	.15
81	Lawrence Moten	.15	.04
82	Sam Cassell	.50	.15

❑ 83 George Zidek .15 .04
❑ 84 Sharone Wright .15 .04
❑ 85 Clarence Weatherspoon .15 .04
❑ 86 Alan Henderson .15 .04
❑ 87 Chris Dudley .15 .04
❑ 88 Ed O'Bannon .15 .04
❑ 89 Calbert Cheaney .15 .04
❑ 90 Cedric Ceballos .15 .04
❑ 91 Michael Cage .15 .04
❑ 92 Ervin Johnson .15 .04
❑ 93 Gary Trent .15 .04
❑ 94 Sherman Douglas .15 .04
❑ 95 Joe Smith .30 .09
❑ 96 Dale Davis .15 .04
❑ 97 Tony Dumas .15 .04
❑ 98 Muggsy Bogues .15 .04
❑ 99 Toni Kukoc .30 .09
❑ 100 Grant Hill .50 .15
❑ 101 Michael Finley .60 .18
❑ 102 Isaiah Rider .30 .09
❑ 103 Bryant Stith .15 .04
❑ 104 Pooh Richardson .15 .04
❑ 105 Karl Malone .50 .15
❑ 106 Brian Grant .50 .15
❑ 107 Sean Elliott .30 .09
❑ 108 Charles Oakley .15 .04
❑ 109 Pervis Ellison .15 .04
❑ 110 Anfernee Hardaway .50 .15
❑ 111 Checklist SP .50 .15
❑ 112 Dikembe Mutombo .30 .09
❑ 113 Alonzo Mourning .30 .09
❑ 114 Hubert Davis .15 .04
❑ 115 Rony Seikaly .15 .04
❑ 116 Danny Manning .30 .09
❑ 117 Donyell Marshall .30 .09
❑ 118 Gerald Wilkins .15 .04
❑ 119 Ervin Johnson .15 .04
❑ 120 Jalen Rose .50 .15
❑ 121 Dino Radja .15 .04
❑ 122 Glenn Robinson .50 .15
❑ 123 John Stockton .50 .15
❑ 124 Matt Maloney RC .30 .09
❑ 125 Clifford Robinson .15 .04
❑ 126 Steve Kerr .30 .09
❑ 127 Nate McMillan .15 .04
❑ 128 Shareef Abdur-Rahim RC 1.50 .45
❑ 129 Loy Vaught .15 .04
❑ 130 Anthony Mason .30 .09
❑ 131 Kevin Garnett 1.00 .30
❑ 132 Roy Rogers RC .15 .04
❑ 133 Erick Dampier RC .50 .15
❑ 134 Tyus Edney .15 .04
❑ 135 Chris Mills .15 .04
❑ 136 Cory Alexander .15 .04
❑ 137 Juwan Howard .30 .09
❑ 138 Kobe Bryant RC 10.00 3.00
❑ 139 Michael Jordan 3.00 .90
❑ 140 Jayson Williams .30 .09
❑ 141 Rod Strickland .15 .04
❑ 142 Lorenzen Wright RC .30 .09
❑ 143 Will Perdue .15 .04
❑ 144 Derek Harper .15 .04
❑ 145 Billy Owens .15 .04
❑ 146 Antoine Walker RC 1.50 .45
❑ 147 P.J. Brown .15 .04
❑ 148 Terrell Brandon .30 .09
❑ 149 Larry Johnson .30 .09
❑ 150 Steve Smith .30 .09
❑ 151 Eddie Jones .50 .15
❑ 152 Detlef Schrempf .30 .09
❑ 153 Dale Ellis .15 .04
❑ 154 Isaiah Rider .30 .09
❑ 155 Tony Delk RC .50 .15
❑ 156 Adrian Caldwell .15 .04
❑ 157 Jamal Mashburn .30 .09
❑ 158 Dennis Scott .15 .04
❑ 159 Dana Barros .15 .04
❑ 160 Martin Muursepp RC .15 .04
❑ 161 Marcus Camby RC .60 .18
❑ 162 Jerome Williams RC .50 .15
❑ 163 Wesley Person .15 .04
❑ 164 Luc Longley .15 .04
❑ 165 Charlie Ward .15 .04
❑ 166 Mark Jackson .15 .04
❑ 167 Derrick Coleman .30 .09
❑ 168 Dell Curry .15 .04
❑ 169 Armon Gilliam .15 .04
❑ 170 Vlade Divac .15 .04
❑ 171 Allen Iverson RC 4.00 1.20
❑ 172 Vitaly Potapenko RC .15 .04
❑ 173 Jon Koncak .15 .04
❑ 174 Lindsey Hunter .15 .04
❑ 175 Kevin Johnson .30 .09
❑ 176 Dennis Rodman .30 .09
❑ 177 Stephon Marbury RC 1.25 .35
❑ 178 Karl Malone .50 .15
❑ 179 Charles Barkley .60 .18
❑ 180 Popeye Jones .15 .04
❑ 181 Samaki Walker RC .15 .04
❑ 182 Steve Nash RC 1.50 .45
❑ 183 Latrell Sprewell .50 .15
❑ 184 Kenny Anderson .15 .04
❑ 185 Tyrone Hill .15 .04
❑ 186 Robert Pack .15 .04
❑ 187 Greg Anthony .15 .04
❑ 188 Derrick McKey .15 .04
❑ 189 John Wallace RC .50 .15
❑ 190 Bryon Russell .15 .04
❑ 191 Jermaine O'Neal RC 1.50 .45
❑ 192 Clyde Drexler .50 .15
❑ 193 Mahmoud Abdul-Rauf .15 .04
❑ 194 Eric Montross .15 .04
❑ 195 Allan Houston .30 .09
❑ 196 Harvey Grant .15 .04
❑ 197 Rodney Rogers .15 .04
❑ 198 Kerry Kittles RC .50 .15
❑ 199 Grant Hill .50 .15
❑ 200 Lionel Simmons .15 .04
❑ 201 Reggie Miller .50 .15
❑ 202 Avery Johnson .15 .04
❑ 203 LaPhonso Ellis .15 .04
❑ 204 Brian Shaw .15 .04
❑ 205 Priest Lauderdale RC .15 .04
❑ 206 Derek Fisher RC 1.25 .35
❑ 207 Terry Porter .15 .04
❑ 208 Todd Fuller RC .15 .04
❑ 209 Hersey Hawkins .30 .09
❑ 210 Tim Legler .15 .04
❑ 211 Terry Dehere .15 .04
❑ 212 Gary Payton .50 .15
❑ 213 Joe Dumars .50 .15
❑ 214 Don MacLean .15 .04
❑ 215 Greg Minor .15 .04
❑ 216 Tim Hardaway .30 .09
❑ 217 Ray Allen RC 1.25 .35
❑ 218 Mario Elie .15 .04
❑ 219 Brooks Thompson .15 .04
❑ 220 Shaquille O'Neal 1.25 .35

1997-98 Topps

	Nm-Mt	Ex-Mt
COMPLETE SET (220)	30.00	9.00
COMPLETE SERIES 1 (110)	10.00	3.00
COMPLETE SERIES 2 (110)	20.00	6.00

❑ 1 Scottie Pippen .75 .23
❑ 2 Nate McMillan .15 .04
❑ 3 Byron Scott .15 .04
❑ 4 Mark Davis .15 .04
❑ 5 Rod Strickland .15 .04
❑ 6 Brian Grant .30 .09
❑ 7 Damon Stoudamire .30 .09
❑ 8 John Stockton .50 .15
❑ 9 Grant Long .15 .04
❑ 10 Darrell Armstrong .15 .04
❑ 11 Anthony Mason .30 .09
❑ 12 Travis Best .15 .04
❑ 13 Stephon Marbury .60 .18
❑ 14 Jamal Mashburn .30 .09
❑ 15 Detlef Schrempf .30 .09
❑ 16 Terrell Brandon .30 .09
❑ 17 Charles Barkley .60 .18
❑ 18 Vin Baker .30 .09
❑ 19 Gary Trent .15 .04
❑ 20 Vinny Del Negro .15 .04
❑ 21 Todd Day .15 .04
❑ 22 Malik Sealy .15 .04
❑ 23 Wesley Person .15 .04
❑ 24 Reggie Miller .50 .15
❑ 25 Dan Majerle .30 .09
❑ 26 Todd Fuller .15 .04
❑ 27 Juwan Howard .30 .09
❑ 28 Clarence Weatherspoon .15 .04
❑ 29 Grant Hill .50 .15
❑ 30 John Williams .30 .09
❑ 31 Ken Norman .15 .04
❑ 32 Patrick Ewing .50 .15
❑ 33 Bryon Russell .15 .04
❑ 34 Tony Smith .15 .04
❑ 35 Andrew Lang .15 .04
❑ 36 Rony Seikaly .15 .04
❑ 37 Billy Owens .15 .04
❑ 38 Dino Radja .15 .04
❑ 39 Chris Gatling .15 .04
❑ 40 Dale Davis .15 .04
❑ 41 Arvydas Sabonis .30 .09
❑ 42 Chris Mills .15 .04
❑ 43 A.C. Green .30 .09
❑ 44 Tyrone Hill .15 .04
❑ 45 Tracy Murray .15 .04
❑ 46 David Robinson .50 .15
❑ 47 Lee Mayberry .15 .04
❑ 48 Jayson Williams .15 .04
❑ 49 Jason Kidd .75 .23
❑ 50 Bryant Stith .15 .04
❑ 51 Latrell Sprewell .50 .15
❑ 52 Brent Barry .30 .09
❑ 53 Henry James .15 .04
❑ 54 Allen Iverson 1.25 .35
❑ 55 Shandon Anderson .15 .04
❑ 56 Mitch Richmond .30 .09
❑ 57 Allan Houston .30 .09
❑ 58 Ron Harper .30 .09
❑ 59 Gheorghe Muresan .15 .04
❑ 60 Vincent Askew .15 .04
❑ 61 Ray Allen .50 .15
❑ 62 Kenny Anderson .30 .09
❑ 63 Dikembe Mutombo .30 .09
❑ 64 Sam Perkins .30 .09
❑ 65 Walt Williams .15 .04
❑ 66 Chris Carr .15 .04
❑ 67 Vlade Divac .30 .09
❑ 68 LaPhonso Ellis .15 .04
❑ 69 B.J. Armstrong .15 .04
❑ 70 Jim Jackson .15 .04
❑ 71 Clyde Drexler .50 .15
❑ 72 Lindsey Hunter .15 .04
❑ 73 Sasha Danilovic .15 .04
❑ 74 Elden Campbell .15 .04
❑ 75 Robert Pack .15 .04
❑ 76 Dennis Scott .15 .04
❑ 77 Will Perdue .15 .04
❑ 78 Anthony Peeler .15 .04
❑ 79 Steve Smith .30 .09
❑ 80 Steve Kerr .30 .09
❑ 81 Buck Williams .15 .04
❑ 82 Terry Mills .15 .04
❑ 83 Michael Smith .15 .04
❑ 84 Adam Keefe .15 .04
❑ 85 Kevin Willis .30 .09
❑ 86 David Wesley .15 .04
❑ 87 Muggsy Bogues .30 .09
❑ 88 Bimbo Coles .15 .04
❑ 89 Tom Gugliotta .30 .09
❑ 90 Jermaine O'Neal .75 .23
❑ 91 Cedric Ceballos .15 .04
❑ 92 Shawn Kemp .30 .09
❑ 93 Horace Grant .30 .09
❑ 94 Shareef Abdur-Rahim .75 .23
❑ 95 Robert Horry .30 .09
❑ 96 Vitaly Potapenko .15 .04

❑ 97 Pooh Richardson	.15	.04
❑ 98 Doug Christie	.30	.09
❑ 99 Voshon Lenard	.15	.04
❑ 100 Dominique Wilkins	.50	.15
❑ 101 Alonzo Mourning	.30	.09
❑ 102 Sam Cassell	.50	.15
❑ 103 Sherman Douglas	.15	.04
❑ 104 Shawn Bradley	.15	.04
❑ 105 Mark Jackson	.30	.09
❑ 106 Dennis Rodman	.30	.09
❑ 107 Charles Oakley	.30	.09
❑ 108 Matt Maloney	.15	.04
❑ 109 Shaquille O'Neal	1.25	.35
❑ 110 Checklist	.15	.04
❑ 111 Antonio McDyess	.30	.09
❑ 112 Bob Sura	.15	.04
❑ 113 Terrell Brandon	.30	.09
❑ 114 Tim Thomas RC	.75	.23
❑ 115 Tim Duncan RC	2.00	.60
❑ 116 Antonio Daniels RC	.50	.15
❑ 117 Bryant Reeves	.15	.04
❑ 118 Keith Van Horn RC	.75	.23
❑ 119 Loy Vaught	.15	.04
❑ 120 Rasheed Wallace	.50	.15
❑ 121 Bobby Jackson RC	.75	.23
❑ 122 Kevin Johnson	.30	.09
❑ 123 Michael Jordan	3.00	.90
❑ 124 Ron Mercer RC	.60	.18
❑ 125 Tracy McGrady RC	3.00	.90
❑ 126 Antoine Walker	.60	.18
❑ 127 Carlos Rogers	.15	.04
❑ 128 Isaac Austin	.15	.04
❑ 129 Mookie Blaylock	.15	.04
❑ 130 Rodrick Rhodes RC	.15	.04
❑ 131 Dennis Scott	.15	.04
❑ 132 Chris Mullin	.50	.15
❑ 133 P.J. Brown	.15	.04
❑ 134 Rex Chapman	.15	.04
❑ 135 Sean Elliott	.30	.09
❑ 136 Alan Henderson	.15	.04
❑ 137 Austin Croshere RC	.50	.15
❑ 138 Nick Van Exel	.50	.15
❑ 139 Derek Strong	.15	.04
❑ 140 Glenn Robinson	.50	.15
❑ 141 Avery Johnson	.15	.04
❑ 142 Calbert Cheaney	.15	.04
❑ 143 Mahmoud Abdul-Rauf	.15	.04
❑ 144 Stojko Vrankovic	.15	.04
❑ 145 Chris Childs	.15	.04
❑ 146 Danny Manning	.30	.09
❑ 147 Jeff Hornacek	.30	.09
❑ 148 Kevin Garnett	1.00	.30
❑ 149 Joe Dumars	.50	.15
❑ 150 Johnny Taylor RC	.15	.04
❑ 151 Mark Price	.30	.09
❑ 152 Toni Kukoc	.30	.09
❑ 153 Erick Dampier	.30	.09
❑ 154 Lorenzen Wright	.15	.04
❑ 155 Matt Geiger	.15	.04
❑ 156 Tim Hardaway	.30	.09
❑ 157 Charles Smith RC	.15	.04
❑ 158 Hersey Hawkins	.15	.04
❑ 159 Michael Finley	.50	.15
❑ 160 Tyus Edney	.15	.04
❑ 161 Christian Laettner	.30	.09
❑ 162 Doug West	.15	.04
❑ 163 Jim Jackson	.15	.04
❑ 164 Larry Johnson	.30	.09
❑ 165 Vin Baker	.30	.09
❑ 166 Karl Malone	.50	.15
❑ 167 Kelvin Cato RC	.50	.15
❑ 168 Luc Longley	.15	.04
❑ 169 Dale Davis	.15	.04
❑ 170 Joe Smith	.30	.09
❑ 171 Kobe Bryant	2.00	.60
❑ 172 Scot Pollard RC	.30	.09
❑ 173 Derek Anderson RC	1.00	.30
❑ 174 Erick Strickland RC	.30	.09
❑ 175 Olden Polynice	.15	.04
❑ 176 Chris Whitney	.15	.04
❑ 177 Anthony Parker RC	.15	.04
❑ 178 Armon Gilliam	.15	.04
❑ 179 Gary Payton	.50	.15
❑ 180 Glen Rice	.30	.09
❑ 181 Chauncey Billups RC	.50	.15
❑ 182 Derek Fisher	.50	.15
❑ 183 John Starks	.30	.09
❑ 184 Mario Elie	.15	.04
❑ 185 Chris Webber	.50	.15
❑ 186 Shawn Kemp	.30	.09
❑ 187 Greg Ostertag	.15	.04
❑ 188 Olivier Saint-Jean RC	.15	.04
❑ 189 Eric Snow	.30	.09
❑ 190 Isaiah Rider	.30	.09
❑ 191 Paul Grant RC	.15	.04
❑ 192 Samaki Walker	.15	.04
❑ 193 Cory Alexander	.15	.04
❑ 194 Eddie Jones	.50	.15
❑ 195 John Thomas RC	.15	.04
❑ 196 Otis Thorpe	.15	.04
❑ 197 Rod Strickland	.15	.04
❑ 198 David Wesley	.15	.04
❑ 199 Jacque Vaughn RC	.30	.09
❑ 200 Rik Smits	.30	.09
❑ 201 Brevin Knight RC	.30	.09
❑ 202 Clifford Robinson	.15	.04
❑ 203 Hakeem Olajuwon	.50	.15
❑ 204 Jerry Stackhouse	.50	.15
❑ 205 Tyrone Hill	.15	.04
❑ 206 Kendall Gill	.15	.04
❑ 207 Marcus Camby	.50	.15
❑ 208 Tony Battie RC	.50	.15
❑ 209 Brent Price	.15	.04
❑ 210 Danny Fortson RC	.30	.09
❑ 211 Jerome Williams	.30	.09
❑ 212 Maurice Taylor RC	.50	.15
❑ 213 Brian Williams	.15	.04
❑ 214 Keith Booth RC	.15	.04
❑ 215 Nick Anderson	.15	.04
❑ 216 Travis Knight	.15	.04
❑ 217 Adonal Foyle RC	.30	.09
❑ 218 Anfernee Hardaway	.50	.15
❑ 219 Kerry Kittles	.50	.15
❑ 220 Checklist	.15	.04

1998-99 Topps

	Nm-Mt	Ex-Mt
COMPLETE SET (220)	30.00	9.00
COMPLETE SERIES 1 (110)	10.00	3.00
COMPLETE SERIES 2 (110)	20.00	6.00
❑ 1 Scottie Pippen	.75	.23
❑ 2 Shareef Abdur-Rahim	.50	.15
❑ 3 Rod Strickland	.15	.04
❑ 4 Keith Van Horn	.50	.15
❑ 5 Ray Allen	.50	.15
❑ 6 Chris Mullin	.50	.15
❑ 7 Anthony Parker	.15	.04
❑ 8 Lindsey Hunter	.15	.04
❑ 9 Mario Elie	.15	.04
❑ 10 Jerry Stackhouse	.50	.15
❑ 11 Eldridge Recasner	.15	.04
❑ 12 Jeff Hornacek	.30	.09
❑ 13 Chris Webber	.50	.15
❑ 14 Lee Mayberry	.15	.04
❑ 15 Erick Strickland	.15	.04
❑ 16 Arvydas Sabonis	.30	.09
❑ 17 Tim Thomas	.30	.09
❑ 18 Luc Longley	.15	.04
❑ 19 Detlef Schrempf	.30	.09
❑ 20 Alonzo Mourning	.30	.09
❑ 21 Adonal Foyle	.15	.04
❑ 22 Tony Battie	.15	.04
❑ 23 Robert Horry	.30	.09
❑ 24 Derek Harper	.15	.04
❑ 25 Jamal Mashburn	.30	.09
❑ 26 Elliot Perry	.15	.04
❑ 27 Jalen Rose	.50	.15
❑ 28 Joe Smith	.30	.09
❑ 29 Henry James	.15	.04
❑ 30 Travis Knight	.15	.04
❑ 31 Tom Gugliotta	.15	.04
❑ 32 Chris Anstey	.15	.04
❑ 33 Antonio Daniels	.15	.04
❑ 34 Elden Campbell	.15	.04
❑ 35 Charlie Ward	.15	.04
❑ 36 Eddie Johnson	.15	.04
❑ 37 John Wallace	.15	.04
❑ 38 Antonio Davis	.15	.04
❑ 39 Antoine Walker	.50	.15
❑ 40 Patrick Ewing	.50	.15
❑ 41 Doug Christie	.30	.09
❑ 42 Andrew Lang	.15	.04
❑ 43 Joe Dumars	.50	.15
❑ 44 Jaren Jackson	.15	.04
❑ 45 Loy Vaught	.15	.04
❑ 46 Allan Houston	.30	.09
❑ 47 Mark Jackson	.30	.09
❑ 48 Tracy Murray	.15	.04
❑ 49 Tim Duncan	.75	.23
❑ 50 Micheal Williams	.15	.04
❑ 51 Steve Nash	.50	.15
❑ 52 Matt Maloney	.15	.04
❑ 53 Sam Cassell	.50	.15
❑ 54 Voshon Lenard	.15	.04
❑ 55 Dikembe Mutombo	.30	.09
❑ 56 Malik Sealy	.15	.04
❑ 57 Dell Curry	.15	.04
❑ 58 Stephon Marbury	.50	.15
❑ 59 Tariq Abdul-Wahad	.15	.04
❑ 60 Isaiah Rider	.15	.04
❑ 61 Kelvin Cato	.15	.04
❑ 62 LaPhonso Ellis	.15	.04
❑ 63 Jim Jackson	.15	.04
❑ 64 Greg Ostertag	.15	.04
❑ 65 Glenn Robinson	.30	.09
❑ 66 Chris Carr	.15	.04
❑ 67 Marcus Camby	.30	.09
❑ 68 Kobe Bryant	2.00	.60
❑ 69 Bobby Jackson	.30	.09
❑ 70 B.J. Armstrong	.15	.04
❑ 71 Alan Henderson	.15	.04
❑ 72 Terry Davis	.15	.04
❑ 73 John Stockton	.50	.15
❑ 74 Lamond Murray	.15	.04
❑ 75 Mark Price	.30	.09
❑ 76 Rex Chapman	.15	.04
❑ 77 Michael Jordan	3.00	.90
❑ 78 Terry Cummings	.15	.04
❑ 79 Dan Majerle	.30	.09
❑ 80 Bo Outlaw	.15	.04
❑ 81 Michael Finley	.50	.15
❑ 82 Vin Baker	.30	.09
❑ 83 Clifford Robinson	.15	.04
❑ 84 Greg Anthony	.15	.04
❑ 85 Brevin Knight	.15	.04
❑ 86 Jacque Vaughn	.15	.04
❑ 87 Bobby Phills	.15	.04
❑ 88 Sherman Douglas	.15	.04
❑ 89 Kevin Johnson	.30	.09
❑ 90 Mahmoud Abdul-Rauf	.15	.04
❑ 91 Lorenzen Wright	.15	.04
❑ 92 Eric Williams	.15	.04
❑ 93 Will Perdue	.15	.04
❑ 94 Charles Barkley	.60	.18
❑ 95 Kendall Gill	.15	.04
❑ 96 Wesley Person	.15	.04
❑ 97 Buck Williams	.15	.04
❑ 98 Erick Dampier	.30	.09
❑ 99 Nate McMillan	.15	.04
❑ 100 Sean Elliott	.30	.09
❑ 101 Rasheed Wallace	.50	.15
❑ 102 Zydrunas Ilgauskas	.30	.09
❑ 103 Eddie Jones	.50	.15
❑ 104 Ron Mercer	.30	.09
❑ 105 Horace Grant	.30	.09
❑ 106 Corliss Williamson	.30	.09
❑ 107 Anthony Mason	.30	.09
❑ 108 Mookie Blaylock	.15	.04
❑ 109 Dennis Rodman	.30	.09
❑ 110 Checklist	.15	.04

❑ 111 Steve Smith .30 .09
❑ 112 Cedric Henderson .15 .04
❑ 113 Raef LaFrentz RC .50 .15
❑ 114 Calbert Cheaney .15 .04
❑ 115 Rik Smits .30 .09
❑ 116 Rony Seikaly .15 .04
❑ 117 Lawrence Funderburke .15 .04
❑ 118 Ricky Davis RC 1.50 .45
❑ 119 Howard Eisley .15 .04
❑ 120 Kenny Anderson .30 .09
❑ 121 Corey Benjamin RC .30 .09
❑ 122 Maurice Taylor .30 .09
❑ 123 Eric Murdock .15 .04
❑ 124 Derek Fisher .50 .15
❑ 125 Kevin Garnett 1.00 .30
❑ 126 Walt Williams .15 .04
❑ 127 Bryce Drew RC .30 .09
❑ 128 A.C. Green .30 .09
❑ 129 Ervin Johnson .15 .04
❑ 130 Christian Laettner .30 .09
❑ 131 Chauncey Billups .30 .09
❑ 132 Hakeem Olajuwon .50 .15
❑ 133 Al Harrington RC .75 .23
❑ 134 Danny Manning .15 .04
❑ 135 Paul Pierce RC 2.50 .75
❑ 136 Terrell Brandon .30 .09
❑ 137 Bob Sura .15 .04
❑ 138 Chris Gatling .15 .04
❑ 139 Donyell Marshall .30 .09
❑ 140 Marcus Camby .30 .09
❑ 141 Brian Skinner RC .30 .09
❑ 142 Charles Oakley .15 .04
❑ 143 Antawn Jamison RC 1.50 .45
❑ 144 Nazr Mohammed RC .20 .06
❑ 145 Karl Malone .50 .15
❑ 146 Chris Mills .15 .04
❑ 147 Bison Dele .15 .04
❑ 148 Gary Payton .50 .15
❑ 149 Terry Porter .15 .04
❑ 150 Tim Hardaway .30 .09
❑ 151 Larry Hughes RC 1.00 .30
❑ 152 Derek Anderson .50 .15
❑ 153 Jason Williams RC 1.25 .35
❑ 154 Dirk Nowitzki RC 4.00 1.20
❑ 155 Juwan Howard .30 .09
❑ 156 Avery Johnson .15 .04
❑ 157 Matt Harpring RC .60 .18
❑ 158 Reggie Miller .50 .15
❑ 159 Walter McCarty .15 .04
❑ 160 Allen Iverson 1.00 .30
❑ 161 Felipe Lopez RC .40 .12
❑ 162 Tracy McGrady 1.25 .35
❑ 163 Damon Stoudamire .30 .09
❑ 164 Antonio McDyess .30 .09
❑ 165 Grant Hill .50 .15
❑ 166 Tyronn Lue RC .40 .12
❑ 167 P.J. Brown .15 .04
❑ 168 Antonio Daniels .15 .04
❑ 169 Mitch Richmond .30 .09
❑ 170 David Robinson .50 .15
❑ 171 Shawn Bradley .15 .04
❑ 172 Shandon Anderson .15 .04
❑ 173 Chris Childs .15 .04
❑ 174 Shawn Kemp .30 .09
❑ 175 Shaquille O'Neal 1.25 .35
❑ 176 John Starks .30 .09
❑ 177 Tyrone Hill .15 .04
❑ 178 Jayson Williams .15 .04
❑ 179 Anfernee Hardaway .50 .15
❑ 180 Chris Webber .50 .15
❑ 181 Don Reid .15 .04
❑ 182 Stacey Augmon .15 .04
❑ 183 Hersey Hawkins .15 .04
❑ 184 Sam Mitchell .15 .04
❑ 185 Jason Kidd .75 .23
❑ 186 Nick Van Exel .50 .15
❑ 187 Larry Johnson .30 .09
❑ 188 Bryant Reeves .15 .04
❑ 189 Glen Rice .30 .09
❑ 190 Kerry Kittles .15 .04
❑ 191 Toni Kukoc .30 .09
❑ 192 Ron Harper .30 .09
❑ 193 Bryon Russell .15 .04
❑ 194 Vladimir Stepania RC .15 .04
❑ 195 Michael Olowokandi RC .50 .15
❑ 196 Mike Bibby RC 2.00 .60
❑ 197 Dale Ellis .15 .04
❑ 198 Muggsy Bogues .30 .09
❑ 199 Vince Carter RC 6.00 1.80
❑ 200 Robert Traylor RC .30 .09
❑ 201 Peja Stojakovic RC 3.00 .90
❑ 202 Aaron McKie .30 .09
❑ 203 Hubert Davis .15 .04
❑ 204 Dana Barros .15 .04
❑ 205 Bonzi Wells RC 1.25 .35
❑ 206 Michael Doleac RC .30 .09
❑ 207 Keon Clark RC .50 .15
❑ 208 Michael Dickerson RC .60 .18
❑ 209 Nick Anderson .15 .04
❑ 210 Brent Price .15 .04
❑ 211 Cherokee Parks .15 .04
❑ 212 Sam Jacobson RC .15 .04
❑ 213 Pat Garrity RC .20 .06
❑ 214 Tyrone Corbin .15 .04
❑ 215 David Wesley .15 .04
❑ 216 Rodney Rogers .15 .04
❑ 217 Dean Garrett .15 .04
❑ 218 Roshown McLeod RC .20 .06
❑ 219 Dale Davis .30 .09
❑ 220 Checklist .15 .04

1999-00 Topps

	Nm-Mt	Ex-Mt
COMPLETE SET (257)	60.00	18.00
COMPLETE SERIES 1 (120)	25.00	7.50
COMPLETE SERIES 2 (137)	35.00	10.50
COMP.SERIES 1 w/o SP (110)	12.00	3.60
COMP.SERIES 2 w/o SP (110)	10.00	3.00
COMMON CARD (1-257)	.15	.04
COMMON RC(111-120/231-248)	.50	.15
COMMON USA (249-257)	.30	.09

❑ 1 Steve Smith .30 .09
❑ 2 Ron Harper .30 .09
❑ 3 Michael Dickerson .30 .09
❑ 4 LaPhonso Ellis .15 .04
❑ 5 Chris Webber .50 .15
❑ 6 Jason Caffey .15 .04
❑ 7 Bryon Russell .15 .04
❑ 8 Bison Dele .15 .04
❑ 9 Isaiah Rider .15 .04
❑ 10 Dean Garrett .15 .04
❑ 11 Eric Murdock .15 .04
❑ 12 Juwan Howard .30 .09
❑ 13 Latrell Sprewell .50 .15
❑ 14 Jalen Rose .50 .15
❑ 15 Larry Johnson .30 .09
❑ 16 Eric Williams .15 .04
❑ 17 Bryant Reeves .15 .04
❑ 18 Tony Battie .15 .04
❑ 19 Luc Longley .15 .04
❑ 20 Gary Payton .50 .15
❑ 21 Tariq Abdul-Wahad .15 .04
❑ 22 Armen Gilliam UER .15 .04
should be Armon
❑ 23 Shaquille O'Neal 1.25 .35
❑ 24 Gary Trent .15 .04
❑ 25 John Stockton .50 .15
❑ 26 Mark Jackson .30 .09
❑ 27 Cherokee Parks .15 .04
❑ 28 Michael Olowokandi .30 .09
❑ 29 Raef LaFrentz .30 .09
❑ 30 Dell Curry .15 .04
❑ 31 Travis Best .15 .04
❑ 32 Shawn Kemp .30 .09
❑ 33 Voshon Lenard .15 .04
❑ 34 Brian Grant .30 .09
❑ 35 Alvin Williams .15 .04
❑ 36 Derek Fisher .50 .15
❑ 37 Allan Houston .30 .09
❑ 38 Arvydas Sabonis .30 .09
❑ 39 Terry Cummings .15 .04
❑ 40 Dale Ellis .15 .04
❑ 41 Maurice Taylor .30 .09
❑ 42 Grant Hill .50 .15
❑ 43 Anthony Mason .30 .09
❑ 44 John Wallace .15 .04
❑ 45 David Wesley .15 .04
❑ 46 Nick Van Exel .50 .15
❑ 47 Cuttino Mobley .50 .15
❑ 48 Anfernee Hardaway .50 .15
❑ 49 Terry Porter .15 .04
❑ 50 Brent Barry .30 .09
❑ 51 Derek Harper .30 .09
❑ 52 Antoine Walker .50 .15
❑ 53 Karl Malone .50 .15
❑ 54 Ben Wallace .50 .15
❑ 55 Vlade Divac .30 .09
❑ 56 Sam Mitchell .15 .04
❑ 57 Joe Smith .30 .09
❑ 58 Shawn Bradley .15 .04
❑ 59 Darrell Armstrong .15 .04
❑ 60 Kenny Anderson .30 .09
❑ 61 Jason Williams .50 .15
❑ 62 Alonzo Mourning .30 .09
❑ 63 Matt Harpring .50 .15
❑ 64 Antonio Davis .15 .04
❑ 65 Lindsey Hunter .15 .04
❑ 66 Allen Iverson 1.00 .30
❑ 67 Mookie Blaylock .15 .04
❑ 68 Wesley Person .15 .04
❑ 69 Bobby Phills .15 .04
❑ 70 Theo Ratliff .30 .09
❑ 71 Antonio Daniels .15 .04
❑ 72 P.J. Brown .15 .04
❑ 73 David Robinson .50 .15
❑ 74 Sean Elliott .30 .09
❑ 75 Zydrunas Ilgauskas .30 .09
❑ 76 Kerry Kittles .15 .04
❑ 77 Otis Thorpe .30 .09
❑ 78 John Starks .30 .09
❑ 79 Jaren Jackson .15 .04
❑ 80 Hersey Hawkins .30 .09
❑ 81 Glenn Robinson .50 .15
❑ 82 Paul Pierce .50 .15
❑ 83 Glen Rice .30 .09
❑ 84 Charlie Ward .15 .04
❑ 85 Dee Brown .15 .04
❑ 86 Danny Fortson .15 .04
❑ 87 Billy Owens .15 .04
❑ 88 Jason Kidd .75 .23
❑ 89 Brent Price .15 .04
❑ 90 Don Reid .15 .04
❑ 91 Mark Bryant .15 .04
❑ 92 Vinny Del Negro .15 .04
❑ 93 Stephon Marbury .50 .15
❑ 94 Donyell Marshall .30 .09
❑ 95 Jim Jackson .15 .04
❑ 96 Horace Grant .30 .09
❑ 97 Calbert Cheaney .15 .04
❑ 98 Vince Carter 1.25 .35
❑ 99 Bobby Jackson .30 .09
❑ 100 Alan Henderson .15 .04
❑ 101 Mike Bibby .50 .15
❑ 102 Cedric Henderson .15 .04
❑ 103 Lamond Murray .15 .04
❑ 104 A.C. Green .30 .09
❑ 105 Hakeem Olajuwon .50 .15
❑ 106 George Lynch .15 .04
❑ 107 Kendall Gill .15 .04

❑ 108 Rex Chapman .15 .04
❑ 109 Eddie Jones .50 .15
❑ 110 Kornel David RC .15 .04
❑ 111 Jason Terry RC 2.00 .60
❑ 112 Corey Maggette RC 2.50 .75
❑ 113 Ron Artest RC 1.50 .45
❑ 114 Richard Hamilton RC 2.50 .75
❑ 115 Elton Brand RC 3.00 .90
❑ 116 Baron Davis RC 2.50 .75
❑ 117 Wally Szczerbiak RC 2.50 .75
❑ 118 Steve Francis RC 4.00 1.20
❑ 119 James Posey RC 1.50 .45
❑ 120 Shawn Marion RC 3.00 .90
❑ 121 Tim Duncan 1.00 .30
❑ 122 Danny Manning .15 .04
❑ 123 Chris Mullin .50 .15
❑ 124 Antawn Jamison .75 .23
❑ 125 Kobe Bryant 2.00 .60
❑ 126 Matt Geiger .15 .04
❑ 127 Rod Strickland .15 .04
❑ 128 Howard Eisley .15 .04
❑ 129 Steve Nash .50 .15
❑ 130 Felipe Lopez .15 .04
❑ 131 Ron Mercer .30 .09
❑ 132 Ruben Patterson .30 .09
❑ 133 Dana Barros .15 .04
❑ 134 Dale Davis .15 .04
❑ 135 Bo Outlaw .15 .04
❑ 136 Shandon Anderson .15 .04
❑ 137 Mitch Richmond .30 .09
❑ 138 Doug Christie .30 .09
❑ 139 Rasheed Wallace .50 .15
❑ 140 Chris Childs .15 .04
❑ 141 Jamal Mashburn .30 .09
❑ 142 Terrell Brandon .30 .09
❑ 143 Jamie Feick RC .50 .15
❑ 144 Robert Traylor .15 .04
❑ 145 Rick Fox .30 .09
❑ 146 Charles Barkley .60 .18
❑ 147 Tyrone Nesby RC .15 .04
❑ 148 Jerry Stackhouse .50 .15
❑ 149 Cedric Ceballos .15 .04
❑ 150 Dikembe Mutombo .30 .09
❑ 151 Anthony Peeler .15 .04
❑ 152 Larry Hughes .50 .15
❑ 153 Clifford Robinson .15 .04
❑ 154 Corliss Williamson .30 .09
❑ 155 Olden Polynice .15 .04
❑ 156 Avery Johnson .15 .04
❑ 157 Tracy Murray .15 .04
❑ 158 Tom Gugliotta .15 .04
❑ 159 Tim Thomas .30 .09
❑ 160 Reggie Miller .50 .15
❑ 161 Tim Hardaway .30 .09
❑ 162 Dan Majerle .30 .09
❑ 163 Will Perdue .15 .04
❑ 164 Brevin Knight .15 .04
❑ 165 Elden Campbell .15 .04
❑ 166 Chris Gatling .15 .04
❑ 167 Walter McCarty .15 .04
❑ 168 Chauncey Billups .30 .09
❑ 169 Chris Mills .15 .04
❑ 170 Christian Laettner .30 .09
❑ 171 Robert Pack .15 .04
❑ 172 Rik Smits .30 .09
❑ 173 Tyrone Hill .15 .04
❑ 174 Damon Stoudamire .30 .09
❑ 175 Nick Anderson .15 .04
❑ 176 Peja Stojakovic .60 .18
❑ 177 Vladimir Stepania .15 .04
❑ 178 Tracy McGrady 1.25 .35
❑ 179 Adam Keefe .15 .04
❑ 180 Shareef Abdur-Rahim .50 .15
❑ 181 Isaac Austin .15 .04
❑ 182 Mario Elie .15 .04
❑ 183 Rashard Lewis .50 .15
❑ 184 Scott Burrell .15 .04
❑ 185 Othella Harrington .15 .04
❑ 186 Eric Piatkowski .30 .09
❑ 187 Bryant Stith .15 .04
❑ 188 Michael Finley .50 .15
❑ 189 Chris Crawford .15 .04
❑ 190 Toni Kukoc .30 .09
❑ 191 Danny Ferry .15 .04
❑ 192 Erick Dampier .30 .09
❑ 193 Clarence Weatherspoon .15 .04
❑ 194 Bob Sura .15 .04
❑ 195 Jayson Williams .15 .04
❑ 196 Kurt Thomas .30 .09
❑ 197 Greg Anthony .15 .04
❑ 198 Rodney Rogers .15 .04
❑ 199 Detlef Schrempf .30 .09
❑ 200 Keith Van Horn .50 .15
❑ 201 Robert Horry .30 .09
❑ 202 Sam Cassell .50 .15
❑ 203 Malik Sealy .15 .04
❑ 204 Kelvin Cato .15 .04
❑ 205 Antonio McDyess .30 .09
❑ 206 Andrew DeClercq .15 .04
❑ 207 Ricky Davis .30 .09
❑ 208 Vitaly Potapenko .15 .04
❑ 209 Loy Vaught .15 .04
❑ 210 Kevin Garnett 1.00 .30
❑ 211 Eric Snow .30 .09
❑ 212 Anfernee Hardaway .50 .15
❑ 213 Vin Baker .30 .09
❑ 214 Lawrence Funderburke .15 .04
❑ 215 Jeff Hornacek .30 .09
❑ 216 Doug West .15 .04
❑ 217 Michael Doleac .15 .04
❑ 218 Ray Allen .50 .15
❑ 219 Derek Anderson .30 .09
❑ 220 Jerome Williams .15 .04
❑ 221 Derrick Coleman .30 .09
❑ 222 Randy Brown .15 .04
❑ 223 Patrick Ewing .50 .15
❑ 224 Walt Williams .15 .04
❑ 225 Charles Oakley .15 .04
❑ 226 Steve Kerr .30 .09
❑ 227 Muggsy Bogues .30 .09
❑ 228 Kevin Willis .15 .04
❑ 229 Marcus Camby .30 .09
❑ 230 Scottie Pippen .75 .23
❑ 231 Lamar Odom RC 2.50 .75
❑ 232 Jonathan Bender RC 2.50 .75
❑ 233 Andre Miller RC 2.50 .75
❑ 234 Trajan Langdon RC 1.00 .30
❑ 235 Aleksandar Radojevic RC .50 .15
❑ 236 William Avery RC 1.00 .30
❑ 237 Cal Bowdler RC .75 .23
❑ 238 Quincy Lewis RC .75 .23
❑ 239 Dion Glover RC .75 .23
❑ 240 Jeff Foster RC .75 .23
❑ 241 Kenny Thomas RC 1.00 .30
❑ 242 Devean George RC 1.25 .35
❑ 243 Tim James RC .75 .23
❑ 244 Vonteego Cummings RC 1.00 .30
❑ 245 Jumaine Jones RC 1.00 .30
❑ 246 Scott Padgett RC .75 .23
❑ 247 Adrian Griffin RC .75 .23
❑ 248 Chris Herren RC .50 .15
❑ 249 Allan Houston USA .50 .15
❑ 250 Kevin Garnett USA 2.00 .60
❑ 251 Gary Payton USA .50 .15
❑ 252 Steve Smith USA .30 .09
❑ 253 Tim Hardaway USA .50 .15
❑ 254 Tim Duncan USA 2.00 .60
❑ 255 Jason Kidd USA 1.50 .45
❑ 256 Tom Gugliotta USA .30 .09
❑ 257 Vin Baker USA .30 .09

2000-01 Topps

	Nm-Mt	Ex-Mt
COMPLETE SET (295)	80.00	24.00
COMPLETE SERIES 1 (155)	60.00	18.00
COMP.SERIES 1 w/o RC (130)	15.00	4.50
COMPLETE SERIES 2 (140)	25.00	7.50
COMP.SERIES 2 w/o RC (120)	15.00	4.50
COMMON CARD (1-124)	.15	.04
COMMON ROOKIE	1.00	.30

❑ 1 Elton Brand .50 .15
❑ 2 Marcus Camby .30 .09
❑ 3 Jalen Rose .50 .15
❑ 4 Jamie Feick .15 .04
❑ 5 Toni Kukoc .30 .09
❑ 6 Todd MacCulloch .15 .04
❑ 7 Mario Elie .15 .04
❑ 8 Doug Christie .30 .09
❑ 9 Sam Cassell .50 .15
❑ 10 Shaquille O'Neal 1.25 .35
❑ 11 Larry Hughes .30 .09
❑ 12 Jerry Stackhouse .50 .15
❑ 13 Rick Fox .30 .09
❑ 14 Clifford Robinson .15 .04
❑ 15 Felipe Lopez .15 .04
❑ 16 Dirk Nowitzki .75 .23
❑ 17 Cuttino Mobley .30 .09
❑ 18 Latrell Sprewell .50 .15
❑ 19 Nick Anderson .15 .04
❑ 20 Kevin Garnett 1.00 .30
❑ 21 Rik Smits .30 .09
❑ 22 Jerome Williams .15 .04
❑ 23 Chris Webber .50 .15
❑ 24 Jason Terry .50 .15
❑ 25 Elden Campbell .15 .04
❑ 26 Kelvin Cato .15 .04
❑ 27 Tyrone Nesby .15 .04
❑ 28 Jonathan Bender .30 .09
❑ 29 Otis Thorpe .15 .04
❑ 30 Scottie Pippen .75 .23
❑ 31 Radoslav Nesterovic .30 .09
❑ 32 P.J. Brown .15 .04
❑ 33 Reggie Miller .50 .15
❑ 34 Andre Miller .30 .09
❑ 35 Tariq Abdul-Wahad .15 .04
❑ 36 Michael Doleac .15 .04
❑ 37 Rashard Lewis .30 .09
❑ 38 Jacque Vaughn .15 .04
❑ 39 Larry Johnson .30 .09
❑ 40 Steve Francis .50 .15
❑ 41 Arvydas Sabonis .30 .09
❑ 42 Jaren Jackson .15 .04
❑ 43 Howard Eisley .15 .04
❑ 44 Rod Strickland .15 .04
❑ 45 Tim Thomas .30 .09
❑ 46 Robert Horry .30 .09
❑ 47 Kenny Thomas .15 .04
❑ 48 Anthony Peeler .15 .04
❑ 49 Darrell Armstrong .15 .04
❑ 50 Vince Carter 1.25 .35
❑ 51 Othella Harrington .15 .04
❑ 52 Derek Anderson .30 .09
❑ 53 Anthony Carter .30 .09
❑ 54 Scott Burrell .15 .04
❑ 55 Ray Allen .50 .15
❑ 56 Jason Kidd .75 .23
❑ 57 Sean Elliott .30 .09
❑ 58 Muggsy Bogues .30 .09
❑ 59 LaPhonso Ellis .15 .04
❑ 60 Tim Duncan 1.00 .30
❑ 61 Adrian Griffin .15 .04
❑ 62 Wally Szczerbiak .30 .09
❑ 63 Austin Croshere .30 .09
❑ 64 Wesley Person .15 .04
❑ 65 James Posey .30 .09
❑ 66 Alan Henderson .15 .04
❑ 67 Ruben Patterson .30 .09
❑ 68 Jahidi White .15 .04
❑ 69 Shawn Marion .50 .15
❑ 70 Lamar Odom .50 .15
❑ 71 Lindsey Hunter .15 .04
❑ 72 Keon Clark .30 .09
❑ 73 Gary Trent .15 .04
❑ 74 Lamond Murray .15 .04
❑ 75 Paul Pierce .50 .15
❑ 76 Charlie Ward .15 .04
❑ 77 Matt Geiger .15 .04

❑ 78 Greg Anthony .15 .04
❑ 79 Horace Grant .30 .09
❑ 80 John Stockton .50 .15
❑ 81 Peja Stojakovic .50 .15
❑ 82 William Avery .15 .04
❑ 83 Dan Majerle .30 .09
❑ 84 Christian Laettner .30 .09
❑ 85 Dana Barros .15 .04
❑ 86 Corey Benjamin .15 .04
❑ 87 Keith Van Horn .50 .15
❑ 88 Patrick Ewing .50 .15
❑ 89 Steve Smith .30 .09
❑ 90 Antonio Davis .15 .04
❑ 91 Samaki Walker .15 .04
❑ 92 Mitch Richmond .30 .09
❑ 93 Michael Olowokandi .15 .04
❑ 94 Baron Davis .50 .15
❑ 95 Dikembe Mutombo .30 .09
❑ 96 Andrew DeClercq .15 .04
❑ 97 Raef LaFrentz .30 .09
❑ 98 Trajan Langdon .30 .09
❑ 99 Ervin Johnson .15 .04
❑ 100 Alonzo Mourning .30 .09
❑ 101 Kendall Gill .15 .04
❑ 102 George Lynch .15 .04
❑ 103 Detlef Schrempf .30 .09
❑ 104 Donyell Marshall .30 .09
❑ 105 Bo Outlaw .15 .04
❑ 106 Kenny Anderson .30 .09
❑ 107 Eddie Robinson .30 .09
❑ 108 Jermaine O'Neal .50 .15
❑ 109 John Amaechi .15 .04
❑ 110 Glen Rice .30 .09
❑ 111 Vlade Divac .30 .09
❑ 112 Vin Baker .30 .09
❑ 113 Mike Bibby .50 .15
❑ 114 Richard Hamilton .30 .09
❑ 115 Mookie Blaylock .15 .04
❑ 116 Vitaly Potapenko .15 .04
❑ 117 Anthony Mason .30 .09
❑ 118 Robert Pack .15 .04
❑ 119 Vonteego Cummings .15 .04
❑ 120 Michael Finley .50 .15
❑ 121 Ron Artest .30 .09
❑ 122 Tyrone Hill .15 .04
❑ 123 Rodney Rogers .15 .04
❑ 124 Quincy Lewis .15 .04
❑ 125 Kenyon Martin RC 4.00 1.20
❑ 126 Stromile Swift RC 2.00 .60
❑ 127 Darius Miles RC 3.00 .90
❑ 128 Marcus Fizer EXCH RC 1.00 .30
❑ 129 Mike Miller RC 3.00 .90
❑ 130 DerMarr Johnson RC 1.00 .30
❑ 131 Chris Mihm RC 1.00 .30
❑ 132 J.Crawford RC EXCH 1.25 .35
❑ 133 Joel Przybilla RC 1.00 .30
❑ 134 Keyon Dooling RC 1.00 .30
❑ 135 Jerome Moiso EXCH RC 1.00 .30
❑ 136 Etan Thomas RC 1.00 .30
❑ 137 Courtney Alexander RC 1.00 .30
❑ 138 M.Cleaves RC EXCH 1.00 .30
❑ 139 Jason Collier RC 1.00 .30
❑ 140 Desmond Mason RC 1.00 .30
❑ 141 Quentin Richardson RC 3.00 .90
❑ 142 Jamaal Magloire RC 1.00 .30
❑ 143 Speedy Claxton RC 1.00 .30
❑ 144 M.Peterson RC EXCH 2.00 .60
❑ 145 D.Harvey RC EXCH 1.00 .30
❑ 146 DeShawn Stevenson RC 1.00 .30
❑ 147 Mamadou N'diaye RC 1.00 .30
❑ 148 Erick Barkley EXCH RC 1.00 .30
❑ 149 Mark Madsen RC 1.00 .30
❑ 150 Shaquille O'Neal .40 .12
Allen Iverson
Grant Hill SL
❑ 151 Jason Kidd .50 .15
Sam Cassell
Nick Van Exel SL
❑ 152 Dikembe Mutombo .60 .18
Shaquille O'Neal
Tim Duncan SL
❑ 153 Eddie Jones .30 .09
Paul Pierce
Darrell Armstrong SL
❑ 154 Alonzo Mourning .50 .15
Dikembe Mutombo
Shaquille O'Neal SL
❑ 155 Team Championship SL .75 .23
❑ 156 Jason Williams .30 .09
❑ 157 David Robinson .50 .15
❑ 158 Shammond Williams .15 .04
❑ 159 Charles Oakley .15 .04
❑ 160 Greg Ostertag .15 .04
❑ 161 Juwan Howard .30 .09
❑ 162 Antoine Walker .50 .15
❑ 163 Alan Henderson .15 .04
❑ 164 Eddie Jones .50 .15
❑ 165 Allen Iverson 1.00 .30
❑ 166 Grant Hill .50 .15
❑ 167 Terrell Brandon .30 .09
❑ 168 Stephon Marbury .50 .15
❑ 169 Jason Caffey .15 .04
❑ 170 Sam Mitchell .15 .04
❑ 171 Jamal Mashburn .30 .09
❑ 172 Ron Harper .30 .09
❑ 173 Eric Piatkowski .30 .09
❑ 174 Sam Perkins .30 .09
❑ 175 Walt Williams .15 .04
❑ 176 Bob Sura .15 .04
❑ 177 Michael Curry .15 .04
❑ 178 Nick Van Exel .50 .15
❑ 179 Danny Ferry .15 .04
❑ 180 Randy Brown .15 .04
❑ 181 Danny Fortson .15 .04
❑ 182 Jim Jackson .15 .04
❑ 183 Brad Miller .50 .15
❑ 184 Shawn Bradley .15 .04
❑ 185 Voshon Lenard .15 .04
❑ 186 Erick Dampier .30 .09
❑ 187 Mark Jackson .15 .04
❑ 188 Maurice Taylor .15 .04
❑ 189 Kobe Bryant 2.00 .60
❑ 190 Clarence Weatherspoon .15 .04
❑ 191 Bobby Jackson .30 .09
❑ 192 Eric Snow .30 .09
❑ 193 Allan Houston .30 .09
❑ 194 Kurt Thomas .30 .09
❑ 195 Chauncey Billups .30 .09
❑ 196 Tom Gugliotta .15 .04
❑ 197 Theo Ratliff .30 .09
❑ 198 Rasheed Wallace .50 .15
❑ 199 Jon Barry .15 .04
❑ 200 Malik Rose .15 .04
❑ 201 Vernon Maxwell .15 .04
❑ 202 Dee Brown .15 .04
❑ 203 Bryon Russell .15 .04
❑ 204 Brent Barry .30 .09
❑ 205 Tracy McGrady 1.25 .35
❑ 206 Bryant Reeves .15 .04
❑ 207 Isaac Austin .15 .04
❑ 208 Damon Stoudamire .30 .09
❑ 209 Anfernee Hardaway .50 .15
❑ 210 Aaron McKie .30 .09
❑ 211 Johnny Newman .15 .04
❑ 212 Scott Williams .15 .04
❑ 213 Brian Shaw .15 .04
❑ 214 Corey Maggette .30 .09
❑ 215 Travis Best .15 .04
❑ 216 Hakeem Olajuwon .50 .15
❑ 217 Antawn Jamison .50 .15
❑ 218 John Starks .30 .09
❑ 219 Antonio McDyess .30 .09
❑ 220 Cedric Ceballos .15 .04
❑ 221 Chris Carr .15 .04
❑ 222 Roshown McLeod .15 .04
❑ 223 Calbert Cheaney .15 .04
❑ 224 Gary Payton .50 .15
❑ 225 Karl Malone .50 .15
❑ 226 Michael Dickerson .30 .09
❑ 227 Tracy Murray .15 .04
❑ 228 Chris Childs .15 .04
❑ 229 Pat Garrity .15 .04
❑ 230 Rex Chapman .15 .04
❑ 231 Jumaine Jones .30 .09
❑ 232 Fred Hoiberg .15 .04
❑ 233 Bimbo Coles .15 .04
❑ 234 Shawn Kemp .30 .09
❑ 235 David Wesley .15 .04
❑ 236 Tony Battie .15 .04
❑ 237 Ron Mercer .30 .09
❑ 238 John Wallace .15 .04
❑ 239 Robert Traylor .15 .04
❑ 240 Derrick Coleman .15 .04
❑ 241 Steve Nash .50 .15
❑ 242 Ben Wallace .50 .15
❑ 243 Brian Skinner .15 .04
❑ 244 Chris Gatling .15 .04
❑ 245 Dale Davis .15 .04
❑ 246 Joe Smith .30 .09
❑ 247 Glenn Robinson .50 .15
❑ 248 Kerry Kittles .15 .04
❑ 249 Erick Strickland .15 .04
❑ 250 Sam Cassell .50 .15
❑ 251 Chucky Atkins .15 .04
❑ 252 Brian Grant .30 .09
❑ 253 Bonzi Wells .30 .09
❑ 254 Corliss Williamson .30 .09
❑ 255 Shareef Abdur-Rahim .50 .15
❑ 256 Kevin Willis .15 .04
❑ 257 Scott Padgett .15 .04
❑ 258 Terry Porter .15 .04
❑ 259 Tony Delk .15 .04
❑ 260 Avery Johnson .15 .04
❑ 261 Tim Hardaway .30 .09
❑ 262 Derek Fisher .50 .15
❑ 263 Isaiah Rider .30 .09
❑ 264 Shandon Anderson .15 .04
❑ 265 Adonal Foyle .15 .04
❑ 266 Hidayet Turkoglu RC 2.50 .75
❑ 267 Brian Cardinal RC 1.00 .30
❑ 268 Iakovos Tsakalidis RC 1.00 .30
❑ 269 Dalibor Bagaric RC 1.00 .30
❑ 270 Marko Jaric RC 1.00 .30
❑ 271 Dan Langhi RC 1.00 .30
❑ 272 A.J. Guyton RC 1.00 .30
❑ 273 Jake Voskuhl RC 1.00 .30
❑ 274 Khalid El-Amin RC 1.00 .30
❑ 275 Mike Smith RC 1.00 .30
❑ 276 Soumaila Samake RC 1.00 .30
❑ 277 Eddie House RC 1.00 .30
❑ 278 Eduardo Najera RC 1.50 .45
❑ 279 Lavor Postell RC 1.00 .30
❑ 280 Hanno Mottola RC 1.00 .30
❑ 281 Chris Carrawell RC 1.00 .30
❑ 282 Olumide Oyedeji RC 1.00 .30
❑ 283 Michael Redd RC 2.00 .60
❑ 284 Chris Porter RC 1.00 .30
❑ 285 Mark Karcher RC 1.00 .30
❑ 286 Steve Francis .50 .15
Gary Payton SC
❑ 287 Darius Miles .30 .09
Kevin Garnett SC
❑ 288 Lamar Odom .50 .15
Shareef Abdur-Rahim SC
❑ 289 Tim Duncan .60 .18
Alonzo Mourning SC
❑ 290 Elton Brand .50 .15
Karl Malone SC
❑ 291 Larry Hughes .50 .15
Allen Iverson SC
❑ 292 Kobe Bryant 1.25 .35
Reggie Miller SC
❑ 293 Vince Carter .60 .18
Grant Hill SC
❑ 294 Tracy McGrady 1.00 .30
Scottie Pippen SC
❑ 295 Kenyon Martin 2.00 .60
Marcus Camby SC

2001-02 Topps

	Nm-Mt	Ex-Mt
COMPLETE SET (257)	80.00	24.00
COMP.SET w/o RC (220)	30.00	9.00
COMMON CARD (1-220)	.15	.04
COMMON ROOKIE (221-256)	1.25	.35
❑ 1 Shaquille O'Neal	1.25	.35
❑ 2 Travis Best	.15	.04
❑ 3 Allen Iverson	1.00	.30
❑ 4 Shawn Marion	.50	.15
❑ 5 Rasheed Wallace	.50	.15
❑ 6 Antonio Daniels	.15	.04
❑ 7 Rashard Lewis	.30	.09
❑ 8 John Starks	.30	.09
❑ 9 Stromile Swift	.30	.09
❑ 10 Vince Carter	1.25	.35
❑ 11 George Lynch	.15	.04
❑ 12 Kendall Gill	.15	.04
❑ 13 Glen Rice	.30	.09
❑ 14 Glenn Robinson	.50	.15
❑ 15 Wally Szczerbiak	.30	.09
❑ 16 Rick Fox	.30	.09
❑ 17 Darius Miles	.50	.15
❑ 18 Jermaine O'Neal	.50	.15
❑ 19 Erick Dampier	.30	.09
❑ 20 Tracy McGrady	1.25	.35
❑ 21 Kevin Garnett	1.00	.30
❑ 22 Tim Thomas	.30	.09
❑ 23 Larry Hughes	.30	.09
❑ 24 Jerry Stackhouse	.50	.15
❑ 25 Voshon Lenard	.15	.04
❑ 26 Howard Eisley	.15	.04
❑ 27 Clarence Weatherspoon	.15	.04
❑ 28 Marcus Fizer	.30	.09
❑ 29 Elden Campbell	.15	.04
❑ 30 Tim Duncan	1.00	.30
❑ 31 Doug Christie	.30	.09
❑ 32 Keon Clark	.30	.09
❑ 33 Patrick Ewing	.50	.15
❑ 34 Hakeem Olajuwon	.50	.15
❑ 35 Stephen Jackson	.30	.09
❑ 36 Larry Johnson	.30	.09
❑ 37 Eric Snow	.30	.09
❑ 38 Tom Gugliotta	.15	.04
❑ 39 Scottie Pippen	.75	.23
❑ 40 Chris Webber	.50	.15
❑ 41 David Robinson	.50	.15
❑ 42 Elton Brand	.50	.15
❑ 43 Theo Ratliff	.30	.09
❑ 44 Paul Pierce	.50	.15
❑ 45 Jamal Mashburn	.30	.09
❑ 46 Eric Williams	.15	.04
❑ 47 DerMarr Johnson	.30	.09
❑ 48 Andre Miller	.30	.09
❑ 49 Dirk Nowitzki	.75	.23
❑ 50 Kobe Bryant	2.00	.60
❑ 51 Keyon Dooling	.30	.09
❑ 52 Brian Grant	.30	.09
❑ 53 Ervin Johnson	.15	.04
❑ 54 Anthony Peeler	.15	.04
❑ 55 Dikembe Mutombo	.30	.09
❑ 56 Steve Smith	.30	.09
❑ 57 Hidayet Turkoglu	.30	.09
❑ 58 Terry Porter	.15	.04
❑ 59 Lorenzen Wright	.15	.04
❑ 60 Jason Terry	.50	.15
❑ 61 Vitaly Potapenko	.15	.04
❑ 62 Derrick Coleman	.15	.04
❑ 63 Ron Artest	.30	.09
❑ 64 Chris Gatling	.15	.04
❑ 65 Chris Mihm	.15	.04
❑ 66 Reggie Miller	.50	.15
❑ 67 Lamar Odom	.50	.15
❑ 68 Ron Harper	.30	.09
❑ 69 Baron Davis	.50	.15
❑ 70 Brad Miller	.50	.15
❑ 71 Shawn Bradley	.15	.04
❑ 72 James Posey	.30	.09
❑ 73 Ben Wallace	.50	.15
❑ 74 Marc Jackson	.30	.09
❑ 75 Maurice Taylor	.30	.09
❑ 76 Aaron McKie	.30	.09
❑ 77 Grant Hill	.50	.15
❑ 78 Arvydas Sabonis	.30	.09
❑ 79 Peja Stojakovic	.50	.15
❑ 80 Jason Kidd	.75	.23
❑ 81 Vin Baker	.30	.09
❑ 82 Morris Peterson	.30	.09
❑ 83 Bryon Russell	.15	.04
❑ 84 Michael Dickerson	.30	.09
❑ 85 Christian Laettner	.30	.09
❑ 86 Jerome Williams	.15	.04
❑ 87 Desmond Mason	.30	.09
❑ 88 Sean Elliott	.30	.09
❑ 89 Marcus Camby	.30	.09
❑ 90 Stephon Marbury	.50	.15
❑ 91 Joel Przybilla	.30	.09
❑ 92 Alonzo Mourning	.30	.09
❑ 93 Brian Shaw	.15	.04
❑ 94 Austin Croshere	.30	.09
❑ 95 Mookie Blaylock	.15	.04
❑ 96 Mateen Cleaves	.30	.09
❑ 97 Nick Van Exel	.50	.15
❑ 98 Michael Finley	.50	.15
❑ 99 Jamal Crawford	.30	.09
❑ 100 Steve Francis	.50	.15
❑ 101 Tim Hardaway	.30	.09
❑ 102 Sam Cassell	.50	.15
❑ 103 Shammond Williams	.15	.04
❑ 104 DeShawn Stevenson	.30	.09
❑ 105 Bryant Reeves	.15	.04
❑ 106 Richard Hamilton	.30	.09
❑ 107 Antonio Davis	.15	.04
❑ 108 Brent Barry	.30	.09
❑ 109 Derek Anderson	.30	.09
❑ 110 Kenny Anderson	.30	.09
❑ 111 Brevin Knight	.15	.04
❑ 112 Tyrone Nesby	.15	.04
❑ 113 Erick Strickland	.15	.04
❑ 114 Jacque Vaughn	.15	.04
❑ 115 John Stockton	.50	.15
❑ 116 Alvin Williams	.15	.04
❑ 117 Speedy Claxton	.30	.09
❑ 118 Bo Outlaw	.15	.04
❑ 119 Jahidi White	.15	.04
❑ 120 Karl Malone	.50	.15
❑ 121 Charles Oakley	.15	.04
❑ 122 Malik Rose	.15	.04
❑ 123 Avery Johnson	.15	.04
❑ 124 Toni Kukoc	.30	.09
❑ 125 Bryant Stith	.15	.04
❑ 126 P.J. Brown	.15	.04
❑ 127 Ron Mercer	.30	.09
❑ 128 Lamond Murray	.15	.04
❑ 129 Steve Nash	.50	.15
❑ 130 Raef LaFrentz	.30	.09
❑ 131 Corliss Williamson	.30	.09
❑ 132 Danny Fortson	.15	.04
❑ 133 Chris Porter	.30	.09
❑ 134 Shandon Anderson	.15	.04
❑ 135 Jalen Rose	.50	.15
❑ 136 Corey Maggette	.30	.09
❑ 137 Horace Grant	.30	.09
❑ 138 Eddie Jones	.50	.15
❑ 139 Chauncey Billups	.30	.09
❑ 140 Ray Allen	.50	.15
❑ 141 Terrell Brandon	.30	.09
❑ 142 Keith Van Horn	.50	.15
❑ 143 Allan Houston	.30	.09
❑ 144 Mark Jackson	.30	.09
❑ 145 Pat Garrity	.15	.04
❑ 146 Anfernee Hardaway	.50	.15
❑ 147 Iakovos Tsakalidis	.15	.04
❑ 148 Damon Stoudamire	.30	.09
❑ 149 Bobby Jackson	.30	.09
❑ 150 Antawn Jamison	.50	.15
❑ 151 Kenny Thomas	.15	.04
❑ 152 Jonathan Bender	.30	.09
❑ 153 Jeff McInnis	.15	.04
❑ 154 Robert Horry	.30	.09
❑ 155 Anthony Mason	.30	.09
❑ 156 Lindsey Hunter	.15	.04
❑ 157 LaPhonso Ellis	.15	.04
❑ 158 Jamie Feick	.15	.04
❑ 159 Kurt Thomas	.30	.09
❑ 160 Gary Payton	.50	.15
❑ 161 Rod Strickland	.15	.04
❑ 162 Bonzi Wells	.30	.09
❑ 163 Scot Pollard	.15	.04
❑ 164 Raja Bell RC	1.25	.35
❑ 165 Rodney Rogers	.15	.04
❑ 166 John Amaechi	.15	.04
❑ 167 Darrell Armstrong	.15	.04
❑ 168 Aaron Williams	.15	.04
❑ 169 Latrell Sprewell	.50	.15
❑ 170 Radoslav Nesterovic	.30	.09
❑ 171 Anthony Carter	.30	.09
❑ 172 Quentin Richardson	.30	.09
❑ 173 Primoz Brezec RC	1.25	.35
❑ 174 Michael Olowokandi	.15	.04
❑ 175 Jason Williams	.30	.09
❑ 176 Ruben Patterson	.30	.09
❑ 177 Chris Childs	.15	.04
❑ 178 Greg Ostertag	.15	.04
❑ 179 Mike Bibby	.50	.15
❑ 180 Mitch Richmond	.30	.09
❑ 181 Donyell Marshall	.30	.09
❑ 182 Dale Davis	.30	.09
❑ 183 Tony Delk	.15	.04
❑ 184 Mike Miller	.50	.15
❑ 185 Charlie Ward	.15	.04
❑ 186 Kenyon Martin	.50	.15
❑ 187 Walt Williams	.15	.04
❑ 188 Al Harrington	.30	.09
❑ 189 Chucky Atkins	.15	.04
❑ 190 Kevin Willis	.15	.04
❑ 191 Juwan Howard	.30	.09
❑ 192 Jim Jackson	.15	.04
❑ 193 Antonio McDyess	.30	.09
❑ 194 Jamaal Magloire	.30	.09
❑ 195 Mark Blount	.15	.04
❑ 196 Fred Hoiberg	.15	.04
❑ 197 Nazr Mohammed	.15	.04
❑ 198 Antoine Walker	.50	.15
❑ 199 Wang Zhizhi	.50	.15
❑ 200 Shareef Abdur-Rahim	.50	.15
❑ 201 Chris Whitney	.15	.04
❑ 202 David Wesley	.15	.04
❑ 203 Matt Harpring	.50	.15
❑ 204 George McCloud	.15	.04
❑ 205 Joe Smith	.30	.09
❑ 206 Cuttino Mobley	.30	.09
❑ 207 Tyrone Hill	.15	.04
❑ 208 Clifford Robinson	.15	.04
❑ 209 Vlade Divac	.30	.09
❑ 210 Eddie Robinson	.30	.09
❑ 211 Michael Curry	.15	.04
❑ 212 Courtney Alexander	.30	.09
❑ 213 Grant Long	.15	.04
❑ 214 Dan Majerle	.30	.09
❑ 215 Points Leaders	.75	.23
Shaquille O'Neal		
Kobe Bryant		
Chris Webber		
Allen Iverson		
Jerry Stackhouse		
Vince Carter		
❑ 216 Rebound Leaders	.30	.09
Shaquille O'Neal		
Tim Duncan		
Antonio McDyess		
Dikembe Mutombo		

Ben Wallace
Antonio Davis
❑ 217 Assist Leaders .50 .15
Jason Kidd
John Stockton
Nick Van Exel
Andre Miller
Mark Jackson
Sam Cassell
❑ 218 Steals Leaders .30 .09
Mookie Blaylock
Doug Christie
Jason Kidd
Allen Iverson
Baron Davis
Ron Artest
❑ 219 Block Leaders .30 .09
Shawn Bradley
Shaquille O'Neal
Adonal Foyle
Theo Ratliff
Jermaine O'Neal
Dikembe Mutombo
❑ 220 Team Championship .. 1.00 .30
Los Angeles Lakers
❑ 221 Kwame Brown RC 4.00 1.20
❑ 222 Tyson Chandler RC 4.00 1.20
❑ 223 Pau Gasol RC 5.00 1.50
❑ 224 Eddy Curry RC 5.00 1.50
❑ 225 Jason Richardson RC 6.00 1.80
❑ 226 Shane Battier RC 2.50 .75
❑ 227 Eddie Griffin RC 2.50 .75
❑ 228 DeSagana Diop RC 1.25 .35
❑ 229 Rodney White RC 1.50 .45
❑ 230 Joe Johnson RC 2.50 .75
❑ 231 Kedrick Brown RC 1.25 .35
❑ 232 Vladimir Radmanovic RC 1.25 .35
❑ 233 Richard Jefferson RC .. 5.00 1.50
❑ 234 Troy Murphy RC 2.50 .75
❑ 235 Steven Hunter RC 1.25 .35
❑ 236 Kirk Haston RC 1.25 .35
❑ 237 Michael Bradley RC 1.25 .35
❑ 238 Jason Collins RC 1.25 .35
❑ 239 Zach Randolph RC 5.00 1.50
❑ 240 Brendan Haywood RC 1.50 .45
❑ 241 Joseph Forte RC 2.00 .60
❑ 242 Jeryl Sasser RC 1.25 .35
❑ 243 Brandon Armstrong RC 1.25 .35
❑ 244 Gerald Wallace RC 5.00 1.50
❑ 245 Samuel Dalembert RC 1.25 .35
❑ 246 Jamaal Tinsley RC 2.50 .75
❑ 247 Tony Parker RC 6.00 1.80
❑ 248 Trenton Hassell RC 2.00 .60
❑ 249 Gilbert Arenas RC 8.00 2.40
❑ 250 Jeff Trepagnier RC 1.25 .35
❑ 251 Damone Brown RC 1.25 .35
❑ 252 Loren Woods RC 1.25 .35
❑ 253 Ousmane Cisse RC 1.25 .35
❑ 254 Ken Johnson RC 1.25 .35
❑ 255 Kenny Satterfield RC .. 1.25 .35
❑ 256 Alvin Jones RC 1.25 .35
❑ 257 Pau Gasol Preseason 12.00 3.60
❑ TR-SC Shaquille O'Neal 250.00 75.00
Kareem Abdul-Jabbar
❑ NNO G.Arenas SPEC AU .. - -

2002-03 Topps

	Nm-Mt	Ex-Mt
COMPLETE SET (220)	80.00	24.00
COMMON CARD (1-184)	.15	.04
COMMON ROOKIE (185-220)	1.25	.35

❑ 1 Shaquille O'Neal 1.25 .35
❑ 2 Pau Gasol .50 .15
❑ 3 Allen Iverson 1.00 .30
❑ 4 Tom Gugliotta .15 .04
❑ 5 Rasheed Wallace .50 .15
❑ 6 Peja Stojakovic .50 .15
❑ 7 Jason Richardson .50 .15
❑ 8 Rashard Lewis .30 .09
❑ 9 Morris Peterson .30 .09
❑ 10 Michael Jordan 4.00 1.20
❑ 11 Matt Harpring .50 .15
❑ 12 Shareef Abdur-Rahim .50 .15
❑ 13 Antoine Walker .50 .15
❑ 14 Stephon Marbury .50 .15
❑ 15 Jamal Mashburn .30 .09
❑ 16 Eddy Curry .50 .15
❑ 17 Jumaine Jones .30 .09
❑ 18 Wang Zhizhi .50 .15
❑ 19 James Posey .30 .09
❑ 20 Jason Kidd .75 .23
❑ 21 Jerry Stackhouse .50 .15
❑ 22 Kenny Thomas .15 .04
❑ 23 Ron Mercer .30 .09
❑ 24 Jeff Mcinnis .15 .04
❑ 25 Kobe Bryant 2.00 .60
❑ 26 Jason Williams .30 .09
❑ 27 Eddie Jones .50 .15
❑ 28 Anthony Mason .30 .09
❑ 29 Kenyon Martin .50 .15
❑ 30 Kevin Garnett 1.00 .30
❑ 31 Kurt Thomas .30 .09
❑ 32 Karl Malone .50 .15
❑ 33 Patrick Ewing .50 .15
❑ 34 Antonio McDyess .30 .09
❑ 35 Dirk Nowitzki .75 .23
❑ 36 Wesley Person .15 .04
❑ 37 Theo Ratliff .30 .09
❑ 38 Jarron Collins .15 .04
❑ 39 Horace Grant .30 .09
❑ 40 Vince Carter 1.25 .35
❑ 41 Desmond Mason .30 .09
❑ 42 Todd MacCulloch .15 .04
❑ 43 Bobby Jackson .30 .09
❑ 44 Vlade Divac .30 .09
❑ 45 Keith Van Horn .50 .15
❑ 46 Bo Outlaw .15 .04
❑ 47 Eric Snow .30 .09
❑ 48 Grant Hill .50 .15
❑ 49 Terrell Brandon .30 .09
❑ 50 Tracy Mcgrady 1.25 .35
❑ 51 Tim Thomas .30 .09
❑ 52 Loren Woods .30 .09
❑ 53 Michael Redd .50 .15
❑ 54 Stromile Swift .30 .09
❑ 55 Dikembe Mutombo .30 .09
❑ 56 Richard Jefferson .30 .09
❑ 57 Glenn Robinson .50 .15
❑ 58 Samaki Walker .15 .04
❑ 59 Quentin Richardson .30 .09
❑ 60 Elton Brand .50 .15
❑ 61 Reggie Miller .50 .15
❑ 62 Eddie Griffin .30 .09
❑ 63 Gilbert Arenas .50 .15
❑ 64 Zeljko Rebraca .30 .09
❑ 65 Donnell Harvey .15 .04
❑ 66 Juwan Howard .30 .09
❑ 67 Nick Van Exel .50 .15
❑ 68 Donyell Marshall .30 .09
❑ 69 Tyson Chandler .50 .15
❑ 70 Baron Davis .50 .15
❑ 71 Nazr Mohammed .15 .04
❑ 72 Marcus Camby .30 .09
❑ 73 Jamaal Magloire .15 .04
❑ 74 Marcus Fizer .30 .09
❑ 75 Steve Francis .50 .15
❑ 76 Aaron Mckie .30 .09
❑ 77 Anfernee Hardaway .50 .15
❑ 78 Scottie Pippen .75 .23
❑ 79 Mike Bibby .50 .15
❑ 80 Paul Pierce .50 .15
❑ 81 Tony Delk .15 .04
❑ 82 Kwame Brown .30 .09
❑ 83 Andrei Kirilenko .50 .15
❑ 84 Keon Clark .30 .09
❑ 85 Alvin Williams .15 .04
❑ 86 Brent Barry .30 .09
❑ 87 David Robinson .50 .15
❑ 88 Doug Christie .30 .09
❑ 89 Derek Anderson .30 .09
❑ 90 Chris Webber .50 .15
❑ 91 Speedy Claxton .30 .09
❑ 92 Robert Horry .30 .09
❑ 93 Allan Houston .30 .09
❑ 94 Kerry Kittles .15 .04
❑ 95 Wally Szczerbiak .30 .09
❑ 96 Jonathan Bender .30 .09
❑ 97 Sam Cassell .50 .15
❑ 98 Rod Strickland .15 .04
❑ 99 Shane Battier .50 .15
❑ 100 Tim Duncan 1.00 .30
❑ 101 Jermaine O'Neal .50 .15
❑ 102 Cuttino Mobley .30 .09
❑ 103 Danny Fortson .15 .04
❑ 104 Clifford Robinson .15 .04
❑ 105 Tim Hardaway .30 .09
❑ 106 Steve Nash .50 .15
❑ 107 Zydrunas Ilgauskas .30 .09
❑ 108 Travis Best .15 .04
❑ 109 Eddie Robinson .30 .09
❑ 110 David Wesley .15 .04
❑ 111 Kenny Anderson .30 .09
❑ 112 DerMarr Johnson .15 .04
❑ 113 Courtney Alexander .30 .09
❑ 114 Brian Grant .30 .09
❑ 115 Lorenzen Wright .15 .04
❑ 116 Corliss Williamson .30 .09
❑ 117 Malik Rose .15 .04
❑ 118 Tony Parker .50 .15
❑ 119 Vladimir Radmanovic .30 .09
❑ 120 Hidayet Turkoglu .50 .15
❑ 121 Damon Stoudamire .30 .09
❑ 122 Brendan Haywood .30 .09
❑ 123 Jalen Rose .50 .15
❑ 124 Mike Miller .50 .15
❑ 125 Derrick Coleman .15 .04
❑ 126 Mark Jackson .15 .04
❑ 127 Raef Lafrentz .30 .09
❑ 128 Ben Wallace .50 .15
❑ 129 Larry Hughes .30 .09
❑ 130 Ray Allen .50 .15
❑ 131 Gary Payton .50 .15
❑ 132 P.J. Brown .15 .04
❑ 133 Derek Fisher .50 .15
❑ 134 Michael Olowokandi .15 .04
❑ 135 Jamaal Tinsley .50 .15
❑ 136 Moochie Norris .15 .04
❑ 137 Chris Mihm .15 .04
❑ 138 Antawn Jamison .50 .15
❑ 139 Chucky Atkins .15 .04
❑ 140 Mengke Bateer .50 .15
❑ 141 Brad Miller .50 .15
❑ 142 Michael Finley .50 .15

Card	Nm-Mt	Ex-Mt
❑ 143 Andre Miller	.30	.09
❑ 144 Michael Dickerson	.15	.04
❑ 145 Elden Campbell	.15	.04
❑ 146 Kedrick Brown	.30	.09
❑ 147 Jason Terry	.50	.15
❑ 148 Chris Whitney	.15	.04
❑ 149 Bryon Russell	.15	.04
❑ 150 Darius Miles	.50	.15
❑ 151 Latrell Sprewell	.50	.15
❑ 152 Darrell Armstrong	.15	.04
❑ 153 Joe Johnson	.50	.15
❑ 154 Bonzi Wells	.30	.09
❑ 155 Jim Jackson	.15	.04
❑ 156 Steve Smith	.30	.09
❑ 157 Vin Baker	.30	.09
❑ 158 Antonio Davis	.15	.04
❑ 159 John Stockton	.50	.15
❑ 160 Shawn Marion	.50	.15
❑ 161 Devean George	.30	.09
❑ 162 Clarence Weatherspoon	.15	.04
❑ 163 Rick Fox	.30	.09
❑ 164 Chauncey Billups	.30	.09
❑ 165 Joe Smith	.30	.09
❑ 166 Laphonso Ellis	.15	.04
❑ 167 Maurice Taylor	.15	.04
❑ 168 Lamond Murray	.15	.04
❑ 169 Lamar Odom	.50	.15
❑ 170 Toni Kukoc	.30	.09
❑ 171 Alonzo Mourning	.30	.09
❑ 172 Antonio Daniels	.15	.04
❑ 173 Troy Murphy	.30	.09
❑ 174 Hakeem Olajuwon	.50	.15
❑ 175 Richard Hamilton	.30	.09
❑ 176 Rodney Rogers	.15	.04
❑ 177 Ruben Patterson	.30	.09
❑ 178 Dale Davis	.30	.09
❑ 179 Shaquille O'Neal Tim Duncan Kobe Bryant Allen Iverson Paul Pierce Tracy McGrady	1.25	.35
❑ 180 Tim Duncan Kevin Garnett Danny Fortson Ben Wallace Dikembe Mutombo Jermaine O'Neal	.50	.15
❑ 181 Gary Payton John Stockton Stephon Marbury Andre Miller Jason Kidd Baron Davis	.50	.15
❑ 182 Doug Christie Karl Malone John Stockton Allen Iverson Ron Artest Jason Kidd	.50	.15
❑ 183 Raef LaFrentz Tim Duncan Erick Dampier Ben Wallace Alonzo Mourning Dikembe Mutombo	.50	.15
❑ 184 Team Championship Card	1.50	.45
❑ 185 Yao Ming RC	12.00	3.60
❑ 186 Jay Williams RC	2.50	.75
❑ 187 Mike Dunleavy RC	3.00	.90
❑ 188 Drew Gooden RC	5.00	1.50
❑ 189 Nikoloz Tskitishvili RC	2.00	.60
❑ 190 DaJuan Wagner RC	3.00	.90
❑ 191 Nene Hilario RC	2.50	.75
❑ 192 Chris Wilcox RC	2.50	.75
❑ 193 Amare Stoudemire RC	10.00	3.00
❑ 194 Caron Butler RC	4.00	1.20
❑ 195 Jared Jeffries RC	1.25	.35
❑ 196 Melvin Ely RC	1.50	.45
❑ 197 Marcus Haislip RC	1.25	.35
❑ 198 Fred Jones RC	2.00	.60
❑ 199 Bostjan Nachbar RC	1.50	.45
❑ 200 Jiri Welsch RC	1.25	.35
❑ 201 Juan Dixon RC	3.00	.90
❑ 202 Curtis Borchardt RC	1.25	.35
❑ 203 Ryan Humphrey RC	1.25	.35
❑ 204 Kareem Rush RC	2.00	.60
❑ 205 Qyntel Woods RC	2.00	.60
❑ 206 Casey Jacobsen RC	1.25	.35
❑ 207 Tayshaun Prince RC	2.50	.75
❑ 208 Frank Williams RC	1.25	.35
❑ 209 John Salmons RC	1.25	.35
❑ 210 Chris Jefferies ERR RC Photo of Kareem Rush	1.50	.45
❑ 211 Sam Clancy RC	1.25	.35
❑ 212 Dan Gadzuric RC	1.25	.35
❑ 213 Matt Barnes RC	1.25	.35
❑ 214 Robert Archibald RC	1.25	.35
❑ 215 Vincent Yarbrough RC	1.25	.35
❑ 216 Dan Dickau RC	3.00	.90
❑ 217 Carlos Boozer RC	4.00	1.20
❑ 218 Tito Maddox RC	1.25	.35
❑ 219 Chris Owens RC	1.25	.35
❑ 220 Ronald Murray RC	2.50	.75

2003-04 Topps

	Nm-Mt	Ex-Mt
COMPLETE SET (249)	60.00	18.00
COMMON CARD (1-220)	.15	.04
COMMON ROOKIE (221-249)	1.50	.45
❑ 1 Tracy McGrady	1.25	.35
❑ 2 DaJuan Wagner	.25	.07
❑ 3 Allen Iverson	1.00	.30
❑ 4 Chris Webber	.50	.15
❑ 5 Jason Kidd	.75	.23
❑ 6 Stephon Marbury	.50	.15
❑ 7 Jermaine O'Neal	.50	.15
❑ 8 Antoine Walker	.50	.15
❑ 9 Tony Parker	.50	.15
❑ 10 Mike Bibby	.50	.15
❑ 11 Yao Ming	1.50	.45
❑ 12 Walter McCarty	.15	.04
❑ 13 Steve Nash	.50	.15
❑ 14 Paul Pierce	.50	.15
❑ 15 Vince Carter	1.25	.35
❑ 16 Peja Stojakovic	.50	.15
❑ 17 Kenny Anderson	.25	.07
❑ 18 Kenyon Martin	.50	.15
❑ 19 Pau Gasol	.50	.15
❑ 20 Gary Payton	.50	.15
❑ 21 Tim Duncan	1.00	.30
❑ 22 Jay Williams	.25	.07
❑ 23 Jason Richardson	.50	.15
❑ 24 Andre Miller	.25	.07
❑ 25 Latrell Sprewell	.50	.15
❑ 26 Darius Miles	.50	.15
❑ 27 Richard Jefferson	.25	.07
❑ 28 Shawn Marion	.50	.15
❑ 29 Baron Davis	.50	.15
❑ 30 Ben Wallace	.50	.15
❑ 31 Reggie Miller	.50	.15
❑ 32 Karl Malone	.50	.15
❑ 33 Grant Hill	.50	.15
❑ 34 Shaquille O'Neal	1.25	.35
❑ 35 Steve Francis	.50	.15
❑ 36 Kobe Bryant	2.00	.60
❑ 37 Mike Dunleavy	.25	.07
❑ 38 Glenn Robinson	.50	.15
❑ 39 Allan Houston	.25	.07
❑ 40 Kevin Ollie	.15	.04
❑ 41 Dirk Nowitzki	.75	.23
❑ 42 Elton Brand	.50	.15
❑ 43 Juan Dixon	.25	.07
❑ 44 Brian Grant	.25	.07
❑ 45 Jason Terry	.50	.15
❑ 46 Richard Hamilton	.25	.07
❑ 47 Morris Peterson	.25	.07
❑ 48 Ray Allen	.50	.15
❑ 49 Scottie Pippen	.75	.23
❑ 50 David Robinson	.50	.15
❑ 51 Cuttino Mobley	.25	.07
❑ 52 Jerry Stackhouse	.50	.15
❑ 53 Marcus Camby	.25	.07
❑ 54 Jalen Rose	.50	.15
❑ 55 Dikembe Mutombo	.25	.07
❑ 56 P.J. Brown	.15	.04
❑ 57 Jumaine Jones	.25	.07
❑ 58 Shawn Bradley	.15	.04
❑ 59 Juwan Howard	.25	.07
❑ 60 Clifford Robinson	.15	.04
❑ 61 Antawn Jamison	.50	.15
❑ 62 Raef LaFrentz	.25	.07
❑ 63 Kareem Rush	.25	.07
❑ 64 LaPhonso Ellis	.15	.04
❑ 65 Toni Kukoc	.15	.04
❑ 66 Mike Miller	.25	.07
❑ 67 Aaron McKie	.25	.07
❑ 68 Tom Gugliotta	.15	.04
❑ 69 Dale Davis	.25	.07
❑ 70 Jared Jeffries	.15	.04
❑ 71 Alvin Williams	.15	.04
❑ 72 DeShawn Stevenson	.15	.04
❑ 73 Doug Christie	.25	.07
❑ 74 Troy Hudson	.15	.04
❑ 75 Jason Collins	.15	.04
❑ 76 Eddie Griffin	.25	.07
❑ 77 Vladimir Radmanovic	.15	.04
❑ 78 Michael Olowokandi	.15	.04
❑ 79 Michael Redd	.50	.15
❑ 80 Tim Thomas	.25	.07
❑ 81 Ron Mercer	.15	.04
❑ 82 Shareef Abdur-Rahim	.50	.15
❑ 83 Eduardo Najera	.25	.07
❑ 84 Jon Barry	.15	.04
❑ 85 Erick Dampier	.25	.07
❑ 86 Derek Fisher	.50	.15
❑ 87 Drew Gooden	.25	.07
❑ 88 Dan Gadzuric	.15	.04
❑ 89 Antonio McDyess	.25	.07
❑ 90 Derrick Coleman	.50	.15
❑ 91 Carlos Boozer	.50	.15
❑ 92 Rasheed Wallace	.50	.15
❑ 93 Antonio Davis	.15	.04
❑ 94 Kwame Brown	.25	.07
❑ 95 Manu Ginobili	.50	.15
❑ 96 Eric Williams	.15	.04
❑ 97 Trenton Hassell	.15	.04
❑ 98 Chris Whitney	.15	.04
❑ 99 Chauncey Billups	.25	.07
❑ 100 Kevin Garnett	1.00	.30
❑ 101 Marko Jaric	.25	.07
❑ 102 Rasual Butler	.25	.07
❑ 103 Gilbert Arenas	.50	.15
❑ 104 Keith Van Horn	.50	.15
❑ 105 Iakovos Tsakalidis	.15	.04
❑ 106 Ruben Patterson	.25	.07
❑ 107 Jarron Collins	.15	.04
❑ 108 Rodney White	.15	.04
❑ 109 Rashard Lewis	.50	.15
❑ 110 Malik Rose	.15	.04
❑ 111 Bobby Jackson	.25	.07
❑ 112 Brendan Haywood	.15	.04
❑ 113 Charlie Ward	.15	.04
❑ 114 Courtney Alexander	.25	.07
❑ 115 Kerry Kittles	.15	.04
❑ 116 Wally Szczerbiak	.25	.07
❑ 117 Darrell Armstrong	.15	.04
❑ 118 Anfernee Hardaway	.50	.15
❑ 119 Qyntel Woods	.15	.04
❑ 120 Quentin Richardson	.25	.07
❑ 121 Jonathan Bender	.25	.07
❑ 122 Robert Horry	.25	.07
❑ 123 Lorenzen Wright	.15	.04
❑ 124 Malik Allen	.15	.04
❑ 125 Sam Cassell	.50	.15
❑ 126 Joe Smith	.25	.07

❑ 127 Dion Glover .15 .04
❑ 128 Jamal Crawford .15 .04
❑ 129 Ricky Davis .50 .15
❑ 130 Nikoloz Tskitishvili .15 .04
❑ 131 Tyronn Lue .15 .04
❑ 132 Scott Padgett .15 .04
❑ 133 Jerome James .15 .04
❑ 134 Hedo Turkoglu .50 .15
❑ 135 Jamal Mashburn .25 .07
❑ 136 Pat Burke .15 .04
❑ 137 Joe Johnson .25 .07
❑ 138 Anthony Peeler .15 .04
❑ 139 Ron Artest .25 .07
❑ 140 Theo Ratliff .25 .07
❑ 141 Caron Butler .50 .15
❑ 142 Anthony Mason .25 .07
❑ 143 Vin Baker .25 .07
❑ 144 Donyell Marshall .50 .15
❑ 145 Nene .25 .07
❑ 146 Chucky Atkins .15 .04
❑ 147 Tyson Chandler .50 .15
❑ 148 Jason Williams .25 .07
❑ 149 Larry Hughes .25 .07
❑ 150 Stephen Jackson .15 .04
❑ 151 Kurt Thomas .25 .07
❑ 152 Mehmet Okur .15 .04
❑ 153 Amare Stoudemire 1.00 .30
❑ 154 Elden Campbell .15 .04
❑ 155 Jamaal Tinsley .50 .15
❑ 156 Chris Wilcox .25 .07
❑ 157 Rick Fox .25 .07
❑ 158 Gordan Giricek .25 .07
❑ 159 Voshon Lenard .15 .04
❑ 160 Brent Barry .25 .07
❑ 161 Dan Dickau .15 .04
❑ 162 Junior Harrington .15 .04
❑ 163 Jiri Welsch .25 .07
❑ 164 Vladimir Stepania .15 .04
❑ 165 Brad Miller .50 .15
❑ 166 Moochie Norris .15 .04
❑ 167 Wesley Person .15 .04
❑ 168 Greg Buckner .15 .04
❑ 169 Bonzi Wells .25 .07
❑ 170 Predrag Drobnjak .15 .04
❑ 171 Andrei Kirilenko .50 .15
❑ 172 Vlade Divac .25 .07
❑ 173 Rodney Rogers .15 .04
❑ 174 Kendall Gill .15 .04
❑ 175 Kenny Thomas .15 .04
❑ 176 Derek Anderson .25 .07
❑ 177 Steve Smith .25 .07
❑ 178 Christian Laettner .25 .07
❑ 179 Tony Delk .15 .04
❑ 180 Zydrunas Ilgauskas .25 .07
❑ 181 James Posey .25 .07
❑ 182 Tayshaun Prince .25 .07
❑ 183 Devean George .25 .07
❑ 184 Eddie Jones .50 .15
❑ 185 Corey Maggette .25 .07
❑ 186 Ira Newble .15 .04
❑ 187 Shane Battier .50 .15
❑ 188 Clarence Weatherspoon .15 .04
❑ 189 Eric Snow .25 .07
❑ 190 Damon Stoudamire .25 .07
❑ 191 Keon Clark .25 .07
❑ 192 Desmond Mason .25 .07
❑ 193 Matt Harpring .50 .15
❑ 194 Radoslav Nesterovic .25 .07
❑ 195 Jamaal Magloire .15 .04
❑ 196 Pat Garrity .15 .04
❑ 197 Fred Jones .15 .04
❑ 198 Tony Battie .15 .04
❑ 199 Tyrone Hill .15 .04
❑ 200 Adrian Griffin .15 .04
❑ 201 Nick Van Exel .50 .15
❑ 202 Shammond Williams .15 .04
❑ 203 Corliss Williamson .25 .07
❑ 204 Lamar Odom .50 .15
❑ 205 Travis Best .15 .04
❑ 206 Howard Eisley .15 .04
❑ 207 Jerome Williams .15 .04
❑ 208 David Wesley .15 .04
❑ 209 Bostjan Nachbar .15 .04
❑ 210 Marcus Fizer .25 .07
❑ 211 Michael Finley .50 .15
❑ 212 Troy Murphy .50 .15
❑ 213 Adonal Foyle .15 .04
❑ 214 Samaki Walker .15 .04
❑ 215 Lucious Harris .15 .04
❑ 216 Lindsey Hunter .15 .04
❑ 217 Stromile Swift .25 .07
❑ 218 Eddy Curry .25 .07
❑ 219 Kelvin Cato .15 .04
❑ 220 Chris Anderson .15 .04
❑ 221 LeBron James RC 20.00 6.00
❑ 222 Darko Milicic EXCH 3.00 .90
❑ 223 Carmelo Anthony RC 15.00 4.50
❑ 224 Chris Bosh RC 5.00 1.50
❑ 225 Dwyane Wade RC 5.00 1.50
❑ 226 Chris Kaman RC 1.50 .45
❑ 227 Kirk Hinrich RC 3.00 .90
❑ 228 T.J. Ford RC 2.50 .75
❑ 229 Mike Sweetney RC 1.50 .45
❑ 230 Jarvis Hayes RC 1.50 .45
❑ 231 Mickael Pietrus RC 1.50 .45
❑ 232 Nick Collison RC 1.50 .45
❑ 233 Marcus Banks RC 1.50 .45
❑ 234 Luke Ridnour RC 2.50 .75
❑ 235 Reece Gaines RC 1.50 .45
❑ 236 Troy Bell RC 2.00 .60
❑ 237 Zarko Cabarkapa RC 2.00 .60
❑ 238 David West RC 2.00 .60
❑ 239 Aleksandar Pavlovic RC 2.00 .60
❑ 240 Dahntay Jones RC 1.50 .45
❑ 241 Boris Diaw RC 1.50 .45
❑ 242 Zoran Planinic RC 1.50 .45
❑ 243 Travis Outlaw RC 1.50 .45
❑ 244 Brian Cook RC 1.50 .45
❑ 245 Carlos Delfino RC 1.50 .45
❑ 246 Ndudi Ebi RC 1.50 .45
❑ 247 Kendrick Perkins RC 1.50 .45
❑ 248 Leandro Barbosa RC 1.50 .45
❑ 249 Josh Howard RC 2.00 .60

2003-04 Topps Bazooka

	Nm-Mt	Ex-Mt
COMP.SET w/o RC's (220)	30.00	9.00
COMMON CARD (1-220)	.20	.06
COMMON ROOKIE (221-275)	1.50	.45
COMMON BAZ.JOE (276-288)	1.50	.45
CARDS 1, 3, 31,	-	
240, 243, 245, 250, 252, 260 ..	-	
AND 275 HAVE HOME & AWAY VERSIONS		
B VERSION AWAY SAME VALUE AS A	-	

❑ 1A Tracy McGady 1.50 .45
❑ 1B Tracy McGrady 1.50 .45
❑ 2 DaJuan Wagner .40 .12
❑ 3A Allen Iverson 1.25 .35
❑ 3B Allen Iverson 1.25 .35
❑ 4 Stromile Swift .40 .12
❑ 5 Jalen Rose .60 .18
❑ 6 Morris Peterson .40 .12
❑ 7 Lamar Odom .60 .18
❑ 8 Kobe Bryant 2.50 .75
❑ 9 Chauncey Billups .40 .12
❑ 10 Jason Kidd 1.00 .30
❑ 11 Yao Ming 1.50 .45
❑ 12 Stephon Marbury .60 .18
❑ 13 Ricky Davis .60 .18
❑ 14 Andrei Kirilenko .60 .18
❑ 15 Courtney Alexander .40 .12
❑ 16 Brad Miller .60 .18
❑ 17 Bobby Jackson .40 .12
❑ 18 Rashard Lewis .60 .18
❑ 19 Juwan Howard .40 .12
❑ 20 Allan Houston .40 .12
❑ 21 Kevin Garnett 1.25 .35
❑ 22 Jason Terry .60 .18
❑ 23A Jason Richardson .60 .18
❑ 23B Jason Richardson -
❑ 24 Jerry Stackhouse .60 .18
❑ 25 Tyson Chandler .60 .18
❑ 26 Drew Gooden .40 .12
❑ 27 Jason Williams .40 .12
❑ 28 Eddie Jones .60 .18
❑ 29 Quentin Richardson .40 .12
❑ 30 Rasheed Wallace .60 .18
❑ 31A Shawn Marion .60 .18
❑ 31B Shawn Marion .60 .18
❑ 32 Malik Rose .20 .06
❑ 33 Ben Wallace .60 .18
❑ 34 Paul Pierce .60 .18
❑ 35 Matt Harpring .60 .18
❑ 36 Eddie Griffin .40 .12
❑ 37 Toni Kukoc .40 .12
❑ 38 Mike Bibby .60 .18
❑ 39 Kwame Brown .40 .12
❑ 40 Kurt Thomas .40 .12
❑ 41 Dirk Nowitzki 1.00 .30
❑ 42 Theo Ratliff .40 .12
❑ 43 Ray Allen .60 .18
❑ 44 Michael Finley .60 .18
❑ 45 Lucious Harris .20 .06
❑ 46 Anfernee Hardaway .60 .18
❑ 47 Christian Laettner .40 .12
❑ 48 Manu Ginobili .60 .18
❑ 49 Tayshaun Prince .40 .12
❑ 50 Shaquille O'Neal 1.50 .45
❑ 51 Vladimir Radmanovic .20 .06
❑ 52 Calbert Cheaney .20 .06
❑ 53 Eric Snow .40 .12
❑ 54 Pau Gasol .60 .18
❑ 55 Dikembe Mutombo .40 .12
❑ 56 Alvin Williams .20 .06
❑ 57 Corliss Williamson .40 .12
❑ 58 Kedrick Brown .20 .06
❑ 59 Jamaal Tinsley .60 .18
❑ 60 Chris Webber .60 .18
❑ 61 Donyell Marshall .60 .18
❑ 62 Darrell Armstrong .20 .06
❑ 63 Kenny Thomas .20 .06
❑ 64 Mehmet Okur .20 .06
❑ 65 Carlos Boozer .60 .18
❑ 66A Kenyon Martin .60 .18
❑ 66B Kenyon Martin -
❑ 67 Speedy Claxton .20 .06
❑ 68 Brent Barry .40 .12
❑ 69 Ron Artest .40 .12
❑ 70 Elton Brand .60 .18
❑ 71 Troy Hudson .20 .06
❑ 72A Steve Nash .60 .18
❑ 72B Steve Nash .60 .18
❑ 73 Tony Parker .60 .18
❑ 74 Earl Boykins .40 .12
❑ 75 Kerry Kittles .20 .06
❑ 76 Shawn Bradley .20 .06
❑ 77 Tony Delk .20 .06
❑ 78 Zydrunas Ilgauskas .40 .12
❑ 79 Doug Christie .40 .12
❑ 80 Amare Stoudemire 1.25 .35
❑ 81 Rick Fox .40 .12
❑ 82 Brian Skinner .20 .06
❑ 83 Jamal Mashburn .40 .12
❑ 84 Qyntel Woods .20 .06
❑ 85 Rafer Alston .20 .06
❑ 86 Derek Anderson .40 .12
❑ 87 Andre Miller .40 .12

Card		
❑ 88 Antoine Walker	.60	.18
❑ 89 Frank Williams	.20	.06
❑ 90A Vince Carter	1.50	.45
❑ 90B Vince Carter	1.50	.45
❑ 91 Donnell Harvey	.20	.06
❑ 92 Raef Lafrentz	.40	.12
❑ 93 Desmond Mason	.40	.12
❑ 94 Rodney Rogers	.20	.06
❑ 95 Juan Dixon	.40	.12
❑ 96 Kareem Rush	.40	.12
❑ 97 Bryon Russell	.20	.06
❑ 98 Shandon Anderson	.20	.06
❑ 99 Gordan Giricek	.40	.12
❑ 100 Tim Duncan	1.25	.35
❑ 101 Zach Randolph	.60	.18
❑ 102 Malik Allen	.20	.06
❑ 103 Richard Hamilton	.40	.12
❑ 104 Maurice Taylor	.20	.06
❑ 105 Marko Jaric	.40	.12
❑ 106 Joe Smith	.40	.12
❑ 107 Peja Stojakovic	.60	.18
❑ 108 Othella Harrington	.20	.06
❑ 109 Anthony Carter	.40	.12
❑ 110 Wally Szczerbiak	.40	.12
❑ 111 Troy Murphy	.60	.18
❑ 112 Shareef Abdur-Rahim	.60	.18
❑ 113 Reggie Miller	.60	.18
❑ 114 Vin Baker	.20	.06
❑ 115 Brian Scalabrine	.20	.06
❑ 116 Eric Piatkowski	.40	.12
❑ 117 Cuttino Mobley	.40	.12
❑ 118 Erick Dampier	.40	.12
❑ 119 Walter Mccarty	.20	.06
❑ 120 Caron Butler	.60	.18
❑ 121 Keyon Dooling	.20	.06
❑ 122 Michael Redd	.60	.18
❑ 123 Kenny Anderson	.40	.12
❑ 124 P.J. Brown	.20	.06
❑ 125 Devean George	.40	.12
❑ 126 Joe Johnson	.40	.12
❑ 127 Adrian Griffin	.20	.06
❑ 128 Bonzi Wells	.40	.12
❑ 129 Rasual Butler	.40	.12
❑ 130 Baron Davis	.60	.18
❑ 131 Wesley Person	.20	.06
❑ 132 Shammond Williams	.20	.06
❑ 133 Tyronn Lue	.20	.06
❑ 134 Brian Grant	.40	.12
❑ 135 Elden Campbell	.20	.06
❑ 136 Glen Rice	.40	.12
❑ 137 Michael Olowokandi	.20	.06
❑ 138 Anthony Peeler	.20	.06
❑ 139 Steven Hunter	.20	.06
❑ 140 Eddy Curry	.40	.12
❑ 141 Jerome James	.20	.06
❑ 142 Travis Best	.20	.06
❑ 143 Nazr Mohammed	.20	.06
❑ 144 Tony Battie	.20	.06
❑ 145 Scot Pollard	.20	.06
❑ 146 Stanislav Medvedenko	.20	.06
❑ 147 Jim Jackson	.20	.06
❑ 148 Marcus Camby	.40	.12
❑ 149 Marcus Haislip	.20	.06
❑ 150 Glenn Robinson	.60	.18
❑ 151 Jerome Williams	.20	.06
❑ 152 Greg Ostertag	.20	.06
❑ 153 Stephen Jackson	.20	.06
❑ 154 David Wesley	.20	.06
❑ 155 Sam Cassell	.60	.18
❑ 156 Hedo Turkoglu	.60	.18
❑ 157 Al Harrington	.40	.12
❑ 158 John Salmons	.20	.06
❑ 159 Nikoloz Tskitishvili	.20	.06
❑ 160 Samaki Walker	.20	.06
❑ 161 Jake Tsakalidis	.20	.06
❑ 162 Tim Thomas	.40	.12
❑ 163 Ronald Murray	.20	.06
❑ 164 Alonzo Mourning	.40	.12
❑ 165 Chris Jefferies	.20	.06
❑ 166 Darius Miles	.60	.18
❑ 167 Kendall Gill	.20	.06
❑ 168 Lonny Baxter	.20	.06
❑ 169 Jonathan Bender	.40	.12
❑ 170 Antawn Jamison	.60	.18
❑ 171 Keon Clark	.40	.12
❑ 172 Chris Wilcox	.40	.12
❑ 173 Brendan Haywood	.20	.06
❑ 174 Predrag Drobnjak	.20	.06
❑ 175 Nene	.40	.12
❑ 176 Casey Jacobsen	.20	.06
❑ 177 Marcus Fizer	.40	.12
❑ 178 Howard Eisley	.20	.06
❑ 179 Damon Stoudamire	.40	.12
❑ 180 Gary Payton	.60	.18
❑ 181 Shane Battier	.60	.18
❑ 182 Desagana Diop	.20	.06
❑ 183 Antonio Davis	.20	.06
❑ 184 Keith Van Horn	.60	.18
❑ 185 Corey Maggette	.40	.12
❑ 186 Jarron Collins	.20	.06
❑ 187 James Posey	.40	.12
❑ 188 Latrell Sprewell	.60	.18
❑ 189 Aaron McKie	.40	.12
❑ 190 Vlade Divac	.40	.12
❑ 191 Pat Garrity	.20	.06
❑ 192 Eric Williams	.20	.06
❑ 193 Radoslav Nesterovic	.40	.12
❑ 194 Dan Gadzuric	.20	.06
❑ 195 Moochie Norris	.20	.06
❑ 196 Clifford Robinson	.20	.06
❑ 197 Richard Jefferson	.40	.12
❑ 198 Lorenzen Wright	.20	.06
❑ 199 Nick Van Exel	.60	.18
❑ 200 Gilbert Arenas	.60	.18
❑ 201 Robert Horry	.40	.12
❑ 202 Scottie Pippen	1.00	.30
❑ 203 Jon Barry	.20	.06
❑ 204 Derrick Coleman	.20	.06
❑ 205 Ron Mercer	.20	.06
❑ 206 DeShawn Stevenson	.20	.06
❑ 207 Ruben Patterson	.40	.12
❑ 208 Rodney White	.20	.06
❑ 209 Jamal Crawford	.40	.12
❑ 210 Jermaine O'Neal	.60	.18
❑ 211 Eduardo Najera	.40	.12
❑ 212 Dan Dickau	.20	.06
❑ 213 Antonio McDyess	.60	.18
❑ 214 J.R. Bremer	.20	.06
❑ 215 Dion Glover	.20	.06
❑ 216 Lamond Murray	.20	.06
❑ 217 Larry Hughes	.40	.12
❑ 218 Mike Miller	.60	.18
❑ 219 Mike Dunleavy	.40	.12
❑ 220 Karl Malone	.60	.18
❑ 221 David West RC	1.50	.45
❑ 222 Steve Blake RC	1.50	.45
❑ 223A LeBron James RC	15.00	4.50
❑ 223B LeBron James RC	15.00	4.50
❑ 224 Keith Bogans RC	1.50	.45
❑ 225 Josh Howard RC	2.00	.60
❑ 226A Chris Kaman RC	1.50	.45
❑ 226B Chris Kaman RC	1.50	.45
❑ 227A Marcus Banks RC	1.50	.45
❑ 227B Marcus Banks RC	1.50	.45
❑ 228A Chris Bosh RC	3.00	.90
❑ 228B Chris Bosh RC	3.00	.90
❑ 229 Troy Bell RC	1.50	.45
❑ 230 Luke Walton RC	2.00	.60
❑ 231 Francisco Elson RC	1.50	.45
❑ 232 Ndudi Ebi RC	1.50	.45
❑ 233 Maurice Williams RC	1.50	.45
❑ 234 Kendrick Perkins RC	1.50	.45
❑ 235 Dahntay Jones RC	1.50	.45
❑ 236 Jason Kapono RC	1.50	.45
❑ 237 Kyle Korver RC	2.00	.60
❑ 238 Josh Moore RC	1.50	.45
❑ 239 Travis Hansen RC	1.50	.45
❑ 240A Carmelo Anthony RC	10.00	3.00
❑ 240B Carmelo Anthony RC	10.00	3.00
❑ 241 Keith McLeod RC	1.50	.45
❑ 242 Zoran Planinic RC	1.50	.45
❑ 243A Jarvis Hayes RC	1.50	.45
❑ 243B Jarvis Hayes RC	1.50	.45
❑ 244A Mickael Pietrus RC	1.50	.45
❑ 244B Mickael Pietrus RC	1.50	.45
❑ 245A Mike Sweetney RC	1.50	.45
❑ 245B Mike Sweetney RC	1.50	.45
❑ 246 Jerome Beasley RC	1.50	.45
❑ 247 Zaza Pachulia RC	1.50	.45
❑ 248 Ben Handlogten RC	1.50	.45
❑ 249 Torraye Braggs RC	1.50	.45
❑ 250A Nick Collison RC	1.50	.45
❑ 250B Nick Collison RC	1.50	.45
❑ 251 Reece Gaines RC	1.50	.45
❑ 252A Dwyane Wade RC	4.00	1.20
❑ 252B Dwyane Wade RC	4.00	1.20
❑ 253 Devin Brown RC	1.50	.45
❑ 254 Leandro Barbosa RC	1.50	.45
❑ 255 Boris Diaw RC	1.50	.45
❑ 256 Aleksandar Pavlovic RC	1.50	.45
❑ 257 Udonis Haslem RC	1.50	.45
❑ 258 Brian Cook RC	1.50	.45
❑ 259 Maciej Lampe RC	1.50	.45
❑ 260A T.J. Ford RC	2.00	.60
❑ 260B T.J. Ford RC	2.00	.60
❑ 261 Matt Carroll RC	1.50	.45
❑ 262 James Jones RC	1.50	.45
❑ 263 Brandon Hunter RC	1.50	.45
❑ 264 Luke Ridnour RC	2.00	.60
❑ 265 Theron Smith RC	1.50	.45
❑ 266 Jon Stefansson RC	1.50	.45
❑ 267 Zarko Cabarkapa RC	1.50	.45
❑ 268 Marquis Daniels RC	3.00	.90
❑ 269 Willie Green RC	1.50	.45
❑ 270A Kirk Hinrich RC	2.50	.75
❑ 270B Kirk Hinrich RC	2.50	.75
❑ 271 Linton Johnson RC	1.50	.45
❑ 272 Travis Outlaw RC	1.50	.45
❑ 273 James Lang RC	1.50	.45
❑ 274 Slavko Vranes RC	1.50	.45
❑ 275A Darko Milicic RC	2.50	.75
❑ 275B Darko Milicic RC	2.50	.75
❑ 276 LeBron James BAZ	12.00	3.60
❑ 277 Darko Milicic BAZ	2.00	.60
❑ 278 Carmelo Anthony BAZ	8.00	2.40
❑ 279 Chris Bosh BAZ	2.50	.75
❑ 280 Dwyane Wade BAZ	3.00	.90
❑ 281 Chris Kaman BAZ	1.50	.45
❑ 282 Kirk Hinrich BAZ	2.00	.60
❑ 283 T.J. Ford BAZ	2.00	.60
❑ 284 Mike Sweetney BAZ	1.50	.45
❑ 285 Jarvis Hayes BAZ	1.50	.45
❑ 286 Mickael Pietrus BAZ	1.50	.45
❑ 287 Nick Collison BAZ	1.50	.45
❑ 288 Marcus Banks BAZ	1.50	.45

1996-97 Topps Chrome

	Nm-Mt	Ex-Mt
COMPLETE SET (220)	700.00	210.00
COMMON CARD (1-220)	.50	.15
COMMON RC	2.50	.75
❑ 1 Patrick Ewing	1.50	.45
❑ 2 Christian Laettner	1.00	.30
❑ 3 Mahmoud Abdul-Rauf	.50	.15
❑ 4 Chris Webber	1.50	.45
❑ 5 Jason Kidd	2.50	.75
❑ 6 Clifford Rozier	.50	.15

#	Player	Nm-Mt	Ex-Mt
❑ 7	Elden Campbell	.50	.15
❑ 8	Chuck Person	.50	.15
❑ 9	Jeff Hornacek	1.00	.30
❑ 10	Rik Smits	1.00	.30
❑ 11	Kurt Thomas	1.00	.30
❑ 12	Rod Strickland	.50	.15
❑ 13	Kendall Gill	.50	.15
❑ 14	Brian Williams	.50	.15
❑ 15	Tom Gugliotta	.50	.15
❑ 16	Ron Harper	1.00	.30
❑ 17	Eric Williams	.50	.15
❑ 18	A.C. Green	1.00	.30
❑ 19	Scott Williams	.50	.15
❑ 20	Damon Stoudamire	1.50	.45
❑ 21	Bryant Reeves	.50	.15
❑ 22	Bob Sura	.50	.15
❑ 23	Mitch Richmond	1.00	.30
❑ 24	Larry Johnson	1.00	.30
❑ 25	Vin Baker	1.00	.30
❑ 26	Mark Bryant	.50	.15
❑ 27	Horace Grant	1.00	.30
❑ 28	Allan Houston	1.00	.30
❑ 29	Sam Perkins	1.00	.30
❑ 30	Antonio McDyess	1.00	.30
❑ 31	Rasheed Wallace	2.00	.60
❑ 32	Malik Sealy	.50	.15
❑ 33	Scottie Pippen	2.50	.75
❑ 34	Charles Barkley	2.00	.60
❑ 35	Hakeem Olajuwon	1.50	.45
❑ 36	John Starks	1.00	.30
❑ 37	Byron Scott	.50	.15
❑ 38	Arvydas Sabonis	1.00	.30
❑ 39	Vlade Divac	.50	.15
❑ 40	Joe Dumars	1.50	.45
❑ 41	Danny Ferry	.50	.15
❑ 42	Jerry Stackhouse	2.00	.60
❑ 43	B.J. Armstrong	.50	.15
❑ 44	Shawn Bradley	.50	.15
❑ 45	Kevin Garnett	4.00	1.20
❑ 46	Dee Brown	.50	.15
❑ 47	Michael Smith	.50	.15
❑ 48	Doug Christie	1.00	.30
❑ 49	Mark Jackson	.50	.15
❑ 50	Shawn Kemp	1.00	.30
❑ 51	Sasha Danilovic	.50	.15
❑ 52	Nick Anderson	.50	.15
❑ 53	Matt Geiger	.50	.15
❑ 54	Charles Smith	.50	.15
❑ 55	Mookie Blaylock	.50	.15
❑ 56	Johnny Newman	.50	.15
❑ 57	George McCloud	.50	.15
❑ 58	Greg Ostertag	.50	.15
❑ 59	Reggie Williams	.50	.15
❑ 60	Brent Barry	.50	.15
❑ 61	Doug West	.50	.15
❑ 62	Donald Royal	.50	.15
❑ 63	Randy Brown	.50	.15
❑ 64	Vincent Askew	.50	.15
❑ 65	John Stockton	1.50	.45
❑ 66	Joe Kleine	.50	.15
❑ 67	Keith Askins	.50	.15
❑ 68	Bobby Phills	.50	.15
❑ 69	Chris Mullin	1.50	.45
❑ 70	Nick Van Exel	1.50	.45
❑ 71	Rick Fox	.50	.15
❑ 72	Chicago Bulls - 72 Wins	4.00	1.20
❑ 73	Shawn Respert	.50	.15
❑ 74	Hubert Davis	.50	.15
❑ 75	Jim Jackson	.50	.15
❑ 76	Olden Polynice	.50	.15
❑ 77	Gheorghe Muresan	.50	.15
❑ 78	Theo Ratliff	1.00	.30
❑ 79	Khalid Reeves	.50	.15
❑ 80	David Robinson	1.50	.45
❑ 81	Lawrence Moten	.50	.15
❑ 82	Sam Cassell	1.50	.45
❑ 83	George Zidek	.50	.15
❑ 84	Sharone Wright	.50	.15
❑ 85	Clarence Weatherspoon	.50	.15
❑ 86	Alan Henderson	.50	.15
❑ 87	Chris Dudley	.50	.15
❑ 88	Ed O'Bannon	.50	.15
❑ 89	Calbert Cheaney	.50	.15
❑ 90	Cedric Ceballos	.50	.15
❑ 91	Michael Cage	.50	.15
❑ 92	Ervin Johnson	.50	.15
❑ 93	Gary Trent	.50	.15
❑ 94	Sherman Douglas	.50	.15
❑ 95	Joe Smith	1.00	.30
❑ 96	Dale Davis	.50	.15
❑ 97	Tony Dumas	.50	.15
❑ 98	Muggsy Bogues	.50	.15
❑ 99	Toni Kukoc	1.00	.30
❑ 100	Grant Hill	1.50	.45
❑ 101	Michael Finley	2.00	.60
❑ 102	Isaiah Rider	1.00	.30
❑ 103	Bryant Stith	.50	.15
❑ 104	Pooh Richardson	.50	.15
❑ 105	Karl Malone	1.50	.45
❑ 106	Brian Grant	1.50	.45
❑ 107	Sean Elliott	1.00	.30
❑ 108	Charles Oakley	.50	.15
❑ 109	Pervis Ellison	.50	.15
❑ 110	Anfernee Hardaway	1.50	.45
❑ 111	Checklist (1-220)	.50	.15
❑ 112	Dikembe Mutombo	1.00	.30
❑ 113	Alonzo Mourning	1.00	.30
❑ 114	Hubert Davis	.50	.15
❑ 115	Rony Seikaly	.50	.15
❑ 116	Danny Manning	1.00	.30
❑ 117	Donyell Marshall	1.00	.30
❑ 118	Gerald Wilkins	.50	.15
❑ 119	Ervin Johnson	.50	.15
❑ 120	Jalen Rose	1.50	.45
❑ 121	Dino Radja	.50	.15
❑ 122	Glenn Robinson	1.50	.45
❑ 123	John Stockton	1.50	.45
❑ 124	Matt Maloney RC	2.50	.75
❑ 125	Clifford Robinson	.50	.15
❑ 126	Steve Kerr	1.00	.30
❑ 127	Nate McMillan	.50	.15
❑ 128	Shareef Abdur-Rahim RC	30.00	9.00
❑ 129	Loy Vaught	.50	.15
❑ 130	Anthony Mason	1.00	.30
❑ 131	Kevin Garnett	4.00	1.20
❑ 132	Roy Rogers RC	2.50	.75
❑ 133	Erick Dampier RC	5.00	1.50
❑ 134	Tyus Edney	.50	.15
❑ 135	Chris Mills	.50	.15
❑ 136	Cory Alexander	.50	.15
❑ 137	Juwan Howard	1.00	.30
❑ 138	Kobe Bryant RC	200.00	60.00
❑ 139	Michael Jordan	20.00	6.00
❑ 140	Jayson Williams	1.00	.30
❑ 141	Rod Strickland	.50	.15
❑ 142	Lorenzen Wright RC	3.00	.90
❑ 143	Will Perdue	.50	.15
❑ 144	Derek Harper	.50	.15
❑ 145	Billy Owens	.50	.15
❑ 146	Antoine Walker RC	30.00	9.00
❑ 147	P.J. Brown	.50	.15
❑ 148	Terrell Brandon	1.00	.30
❑ 149	Larry Johnson	1.00	.30
❑ 150	Steve Smith	1.00	.30
❑ 151	Eddie Jones	1.50	.45
❑ 152	Detlef Schrempf	1.00	.30
❑ 153	Dale Ellis	.50	.15
❑ 154	Isaiah Rider	1.00	.30
❑ 155	Tony Delk RC	6.00	1.80
❑ 156	Adrian Caldwell	.50	.15
❑ 157	Jamal Mashburn	1.00	.30
❑ 158	Dennis Scott	.50	.15
❑ 159	Dana Barros	.50	.15
❑ 160	Martin Muursepp RC	2.50	.75
❑ 161	Marcus Camby RC	12.00	3.60
❑ 162	Jerome Williams RC	8.00	2.40
❑ 163	Wesley Person	.50	.15
❑ 164	Luc Longley	.50	.15
❑ 165	Charlie Ward	.50	.15
❑ 166	Mark Jackson	.50	.15
❑ 167	Derrick Coleman	1.00	.30
❑ 168	Dell Curry	.50	.15
❑ 169	Armon Gilliam	.50	.15
❑ 170	Vlade Divac	.50	.15
❑ 171	Allen Iverson RC	60.00	18.00
❑ 172	Vitaly Potapenko RC	2.50	.75
❑ 173	Jon Koncak	.50	.15
❑ 174	Lindsey Hunter	.50	.15
❑ 175	Kevin Johnson	1.00	.30
❑ 176	Dennis Rodman	1.00	.30
❑ 177	Stephon Marbury RC	30.00	9.00
❑ 178	Karl Malone	1.50	.45
❑ 179	Charles Barkley	2.00	.60
❑ 180	Popeye Jones	.50	.15
❑ 181	Samaki Walker RC	2.50	.75
❑ 182	Steve Nash RC	30.00	9.00
❑ 183	Latrell Sprewell	1.50	.45
❑ 184	Kenny Anderson	.50	.15
❑ 185	Tyrone Hill	.50	.15
❑ 186	Robert Pack	.50	.15
❑ 187	Greg Anthony	.50	.15
❑ 188	Derrick McKey	.50	.15
❑ 189	John Wallace RC	5.00	1.50
❑ 190	Bryon Russell	.50	.15
❑ 191	Jermaine O'Neal RC	40.00	12.00
❑ 192	Clyde Drexler	1.50	.45
❑ 193	Mahmoud Abdul-Rauf	.50	.15
❑ 194	Eric Montross	.50	.15
❑ 195	Allan Houston	1.00	.30
❑ 196	Harvey Grant	.50	.15
❑ 197	Rodney Rogers	.50	.15
❑ 198	Kerry Kittles RC	5.00	1.50
❑ 199	Grant Hill	1.50	.45
❑ 200	Lionel Simmons	.50	.15
❑ 201	Reggie Miller	1.50	.45
❑ 202	Avery Johnson	.50	.15
❑ 203	LaPhonso Ellis	.50	.15
❑ 204	Brian Shaw	.50	.15
❑ 205	Priest Lauderdale RC	2.50	.75
❑ 206	Derek Fisher RC	20.00	6.00
❑ 207	Terry Porter	.50	.15
❑ 208	Todd Fuller RC	2.50	.75
❑ 209	Hersey Hawkins	1.00	.30
❑ 210	Tim Legler	.50	.15
❑ 211	Terry Dehere	.50	.15
❑ 212	Gary Payton	1.50	.45
❑ 213	Joe Dumars	1.50	.45
❑ 214	Don MacLean	.50	.15
❑ 215	Greg Minor	.50	.15
❑ 216	Tim Hardaway	1.00	.30
❑ 217	Ray Allen RC	40.00	12.00
❑ 218	Mario Elie	.50	.15
❑ 219	Brooks Thompson	.50	.15
❑ 220	Shaquille O'Neal	4.00	1.20

1997-98 Topps Chrome

	Nm-Mt	Ex-Mt
COMPLETE SET (220)	120.00	36.00
COMMON CARD (1-220)	.50	.15

COMMON ROOKIE .... 1.50 .45
❑ 1 Scottie Pippen .... 2.50 .75
❑ 2 Nate McMillan .... .50 .15
❑ 3 Byron Scott .... .50 .15
❑ 4 Mark Davis .... .50 .15
❑ 5 Rod Strickland .... .50 .15
❑ 6 Brian Grant .... 1.00 .30
❑ 7 Damon Stoudamire .... 1.00 .30
❑ 8 John Stockton .... 1.50 .45
❑ 9 Grant Long .... .50 .15
❑ 10 Darrell Armstrong .... .50 .15
❑ 11 Anthony Mason .... 1.00 .30
❑ 12 Travis Best .... .50 .15
❑ 13 Stephon Marbury .... 2.00 .60
❑ 14 Jamal Mashburn .... 1.00 .30
❑ 15 Detlef Schrempf .... 1.00 .30
❑ 16 Terrell Brandon .... 1.00 .30
❑ 17 Charles Barkley .... 2.00 .60
❑ 18 Vin Baker .... 1.00 .30
❑ 19 Gary Trent .... .50 .15
❑ 20 Vinny Del Negro .... .50 .15
❑ 21 Todd Day .... .50 .15
❑ 22 Malik Sealy .... .50 .15
❑ 23 Wesley Person .... .50 .15
❑ 24 Reggie Miller .... 1.50 .45
❑ 25 Dan Majerle .... 1.00 .30
❑ 26 Todd Fuller .... .50 .15
❑ 27 Juwan Howard .... 1.00 .30
❑ 28 Clarence Weatherspoon .50 .15
❑ 29 Grant Hill .... 1.50 .45
❑ 30 John Williams .... .50 .15
❑ 31 Ken Norman .... .50 .15
❑ 32 Patrick Ewing .... 1.50 .45
❑ 33 Bryon Russell .... .50 .15
❑ 34 Tony Smith .... .50 .15
❑ 35 Andrew Lang .... .50 .15
❑ 36 Rony Seikaly .... .50 .15
❑ 37 Billy Owens .... .50 .15
❑ 38 Dino Radja .... .50 .15
❑ 39 Chris Gatling .... .50 .15
❑ 40 Dale Davis .... .50 .15
❑ 41 Arvydas Sabonis .... 1.00 .30
❑ 42 Chris Mills .... .50 .15
❑ 43 A.C. Green .... 1.00 .30
❑ 44 Tyrone Hill .... .50 .15
❑ 45 Tracy Murray .... .50 .15
❑ 46 David Robinson .... 1.50 .45
❑ 47 Lee Mayberry .... .50 .15
❑ 48 Jayson Williams .... .50 .15
❑ 49 Jason Kidd .... 2.50 .75
❑ 50 Bryant Stith .... .50 .15
❑ 51 Checklist 4.00 1.20
Bulls - Team of the 90s
Michael Jordan
Scottie Pippen
Dennis Rodman
Ron Harper
❑ 52 Brent Barry .... 1.00 .30
❑ 53 Henry James .... .50 .15
❑ 54 Allen Iverson 4.00 1.20
❑ 55 Shandon Anderson .... .50 .15
❑ 56 Mitch Richmond .... 1.00 .30
❑ 57 Allan Houston .... 1.00 .30
❑ 58 Ron Harper .... 1.00 .30
❑ 59 Gheorghe Muresan .... .50 .15
❑ 60 Vincent Askew .... .50 .15
❑ 61 Ray Allen .... 1.50 .45
❑ 62 Kenny Anderson .... 1.00 .30
❑ 63 Dikembe Mutombo .... 1.00 .30
❑ 64 Sam Perkins .... 1.00 .30
❑ 65 Walt Williams .... .50 .15
❑ 66 Chris Carr .... .50 .15
❑ 67 Vlade Divac .... 1.00 .30
❑ 68 LaPhonso Ellis .... .50 .15
❑ 69 B.J. Armstrong .... .50 .15
❑ 70 Jim Jackson .... .50 .15
❑ 71 Clyde Drexler .... 1.50 .45
❑ 72 Lindsey Hunter .... .50 .15
❑ 73 Sasha Danilovic .... .50 .15
❑ 74 Elden Campbell .... .50 .15
❑ 75 Robert Pack .... .50 .15
❑ 76 Dennis Scott .... .50 .15
❑ 77 Will Perdue .... .50 .15
❑ 78 Anthony Peeler .... .50 .15
❑ 79 Steve Smith .... 1.00 .30
❑ 80 Steve Kerr .... 1.00 .30
❑ 81 Buck Williams .... .50 .15
❑ 82 Terry Mills .... .50 .15
❑ 83 Michael Smith .... .50 .15
❑ 84 Adam Keefe .... .50 .15
❑ 85 Kevin Willis .... 1.00 .30
❑ 86 David Wesley .... .50 .15
❑ 87 Muggsy Bogues .... 1.00 .30
❑ 88 Bimbo Coles .... .50 .15
❑ 89 Tom Gugliotta .... 1.00 .30
❑ 90 Jermaine O'Neal .... 2.50 .75
❑ 91 Cedric Ceballos .... .50 .15
❑ 92 Shawn Kemp .... 1.00 .30
❑ 93 Horace Grant .... 1.00 .30
❑ 94 Shareef Abdur-Rahim .. 2.50 .75
❑ 95 Robert Horry .... 1.00 .30
❑ 96 Vitaly Potapenko .... .50 .15
❑ 97 Pooh Richardson .... .50 .15
❑ 98 Doug Christie .... 1.00 .30
❑ 99 Voshon Lenard .... .50 .15
❑ 100 Dominique Wilkins .... 1.50 .45
❑ 101 Alonzo Mourning .... 1.00 .30
❑ 102 Sam Cassell .... 1.50 .45
❑ 103 Sherman Douglas .... .50 .15
❑ 104 Shawn Bradley .... .50 .15
❑ 105 Mark Jackson .... 1.00 .30
❑ 106 Dennis Rodman .... 1.00 .30
❑ 107 Charles Oakley .... 1.00 .30
❑ 108 Matt Maloney .... .50 .15
❑ 109 Shaquille O'Neal 4.00 1.20
❑ 110 Checklist .... 1.50 .45
Karl Malone MVP
❑ 111 Antonio McDyess .... 1.00 .30
❑ 112 Bob Sura .... .50 .15
❑ 113 Terrell Brandon .... 1.00 .30
❑ 114 Tim Thomas RC 8.00 2.40
❑ 115 Tim Duncan RC 40.00 12.00
❑ 116 Antonio Daniels RC .... 2.00 .60
❑ 117 Bryant Reeves .... .50 .15
❑ 118 Keith Van Horn RC 8.00 2.40
❑ 119 Loy Vaught .... .50 .15
❑ 120 Rasheed Wallace .... 1.50 .45
❑ 121 Bobby Jackson RC 5.00 1.50
❑ 122 Kevin Johnson .... 1.00 .30
❑ 123 Michael Jordan 12.00 3.60
❑ 124 Ron Mercer RC 5.00 1.50
❑ 125 Tracy McGrady RC .. 30.00 9.00
❑ 126 Antoine Walker .... 2.00 .60
❑ 127 Carlos Rogers .... .50 .15
❑ 128 Isaac Austin .... .50 .15
❑ 129 Mookie Blaylock .... .50 .15
❑ 130 Rodrick Rhodes RC .... 1.50 .45
❑ 131 Dennis Scott .... .50 .15
❑ 132 Chris Mullin .... 1.50 .45
❑ 133 P.J. Brown .... .50 .15
❑ 134 Rex Chapman .... .50 .15
❑ 135 Sean Elliott .... 1.00 .30
❑ 136 Alan Henderson .... .50 .15
❑ 137 Austin Croshere RC 5.00 1.50
❑ 138 Nick Van Exel .... 1.50 .45
❑ 139 Derek Strong .... .50 .15
❑ 140 Glenn Robinson .... 1.50 .45
❑ 141 Avery Johnson .... .50 .15
❑ 142 Calbert Cheaney .... .50 .15
❑ 143 Mahmoud Abdul-Rauf .. .50 .15
❑ 144 Stojko Vrankovic .... .50 .15
❑ 145 Chris Childs .... .50 .15
❑ 146 Danny Manning .... 1.00 .30
❑ 147 Jeff Hornacek .... 1.00 .30
❑ 148 Kevin Garnett .... 3.00 .90
❑ 149 Joe Dumars .... 1.50 .45
❑ 150 Johnny Taylor RC .... 1.50 .45
❑ 151 Mark Price .... 1.00 .30
❑ 152 Toni Kukoc .... 1.00 .30
❑ 153 Erick Dampier .... 1.00 .30
❑ 154 Lorenzen Wright .... .50 .15
❑ 155 Matt Geiger .... .50 .15
❑ 156 Tim Hardaway .... 1.00 .30
❑ 157 Charles Smith RC .... 1.50 .45
❑ 158 Hersey Hawkins .... .50 .15
❑ 159 Michael Finley .... 1.50 .45
❑ 160 Tyus Edney .... .50 .15
❑ 161 Christian Laettner .... 1.00 .30
❑ 162 Doug West .... .50 .15
❑ 163 Jim Jackson .... .50 .15
❑ 164 Larry Johnson .... 1.00 .30
❑ 165 Vin Baker .... 1.00 .30
❑ 166 Karl Malone .... 1.50 .45
❑ 167 Kelvin Cato RC .... 2.00 .60
❑ 168 Luc Longley .... .50 .15
❑ 169 Dale Davis .... .50 .15
❑ 170 Joe Smith .... 1.00 .30
❑ 171 Kobe Bryant 8.00 2.40
❑ 172 Scot Pollard RC .... 2.00 .60
❑ 173 Derek Anderson RC 8.00 2.40
❑ 174 Erick Strickland RC .... 2.00 .60
❑ 175 Olden Polynice .... .50 .15
❑ 176 Chris Whitney .... .50 .15
❑ 177 Anthony Parker RC .... 1.50 .45
❑ 178 Armon Gilliam .... .50 .15
❑ 179 Gary Payton .... 1.50 .45
❑ 180 Glen Rice .... 1.00 .30
❑ 181 Chauncey Billups RC .. 4.00 1.20
❑ 182 Derek Fisher .... 1.50 .45
❑ 183 John Starks .... 1.00 .30
❑ 184 Mario Elie .... .50 .15
❑ 185 Chris Webber .... 1.50 .45
❑ 186 Shawn Kemp .... 1.00 .30
❑ 187 Greg Ostertag .... .50 .15
❑ 188 Olivier Saint-Jean RC .. 1.50 .45
❑ 189 Eric Snow .... 1.00 .30
❑ 190 Isaiah Rider .... 1.00 .30
❑ 191 Paul Grant RC .... 1.50 .45
❑ 192 Samaki Walker .... .50 .15
❑ 193 Cory Alexander .... .50 .15
❑ 194 Eddie Jones .... 1.50 .45
❑ 195 John Thomas RC .... 1.50 .45
❑ 196 Otis Thorpe .... .50 .15
❑ 197 Rod Strickland .... .50 .15
❑ 198 David Wesley .... .50 .15
❑ 199 Jacque Vaughn RC .... 2.00 .60
❑ 200 Rik Smits .... 1.00 .30
❑ 201 Brevin Knight RC .... 2.50 .75
❑ 202 Clifford Robinson .... .50 .15
❑ 203 Hakeem Olajuwon .... 1.50 .45
❑ 204 Jerry Stackhouse .... 1.50 .45
❑ 205 Tyrone Hill .... .50 .15
❑ 206 Kendall Gill .... .50 .15
❑ 207 Marcus Camby .... 1.50 .45
❑ 208 Tony Battie RC .... 2.00 .60
❑ 209 Brent Price .... .50 .15
❑ 210 Danny Fortson RC 5.00 1.50
❑ 211 Jerome Williams .... 1.00 .30
❑ 212 Maurice Taylor RC 6.00 1.80
❑ 213 Brian Williams .... .50 .15
❑ 214 Keith Booth RC .... 1.50 .45
❑ 215 Nick Anderson .... .50 .15
❑ 216 Travis Knight .... .50 .15
❑ 217 Adonal Foyle RC .... 2.00 .60
❑ 218 Anfernee Hardaway .... 1.50 .45
❑ 219 Kerry Kittles .... 1.50 .45
❑ 220 Checklist .... .50 .15
Dikembe Mutombo
Defensive POY

1998-99 Topps Chrome

	Nm-Mt	Ex-Mt
COMPLETE SET (220)	150.00	45.00
COMP.SET W/PREV (230) ..	200.00	60.00
COMMON CARD (1-235)	.40	.12
COMMON ROOKIE	1.00	.30
❑ 1 Scottie Pippen	2.00	.60
❑ 2 Shareef Abdur-Rahim	1.25	.35
❑ 3 Rod Strickland	.40	.12

❑ 4 Keith Van Horn 1.25 .35
❑ 5 Ray Allen 1.25 .35
❑ 6 Does not exist - -
❑ 7 Anthony Parker .40 .12
❑ 8 Lindsey Hunter .40 .12
❑ 9 Mario Elie .40 .12
❑ 10 Does not exist - -
❑ 11 Eldridge Recasner .40 .12
❑ 12 Jeff Hornacek .75 .23
❑ 13 Chris Webber 1.25 .35
❑ 14 Lee Mayberry .40 .12
❑ 15 Erick Strickland .40 .12
❑ 16 Arvydas Sabonis .75 .23
❑ 17 Tim Thomas .75 .23
❑ 18 Luc Longley .40 .12
❑ 19 Does not exist - -
❑ 20 Alonzo Mourning .75 .23
❑ 21 Adonal Foyle .40 .12
❑ 22 Tony Battie .40 .12
❑ 23 Robert Horry .75 .23
❑ 24 Derek Harper .40 .12
❑ 25 Jamal Mashburn .75 .23
❑ 26 Elliott Perry .40 .12
❑ 27 Jalen Rose 1.25 .35
❑ 28 Joe Smith .75 .23
❑ 29 Henry James .40 .12
❑ 30 Travis Knight .40 .12
❑ 31 Tom Gugliotta .40 .12
❑ 32 Chris Anstey .40 .12
❑ 33 Antonio Daniels .40 .12
❑ 34 Elden Campbell .40 .12
❑ 35 Charlie Ward .40 .12
❑ 36 Eddie Johnson .40 .12
❑ 37 John Wallace .40 .12
❑ 38 Antonio Davis .40 .12
❑ 39 Antoine Walker 1.25 .35
❑ 40 Does not exist - -
❑ 41 Doug Christie .75 .23
❑ 42 Andrew Lang .40 .12
❑ 43 Does not exist - -
❑ 44 Jaren Jackson .40 .12
❑ 45 Loy Vaught .40 .12
❑ 46 Allan Houston .75 .23
❑ 47 Mark Jackson .75 .23
❑ 48 Tracy Murray .40 .12
❑ 49 Tim Duncan 2.00 .60
❑ 50 Micheal Williams .40 .12
❑ 51 Steve Nash 1.25 .35
❑ 52 Matt Maloney .40 .12
❑ 53 Sam Cassell 1.25 .35
❑ 54 Voshon Lenard .40 .12
❑ 55 Dikembe Mutombo .75 .23
❑ 56 Malik Sealy .40 .12
❑ 57 Dell Curry .40 .12
❑ 58 Stephon Marbury 1.25 .35
❑ 59 Tariq Abdul-Wahad .40 .12
❑ 60 Does not exist - -
❑ 61 Kelvin Cato .40 .12
❑ 62 LaPhonso Ellis .40 .12
❑ 63 Jim Jackson .40 .12
❑ 64 Greg Ostertag .40 .12
❑ 65 Glenn Robinson .75 .23
❑ 66 Chris Carr .40 .12
❑ 67 Marcus Camby .75 .23
❑ 68 Kobe Bryant 5.00 1.50
❑ 69 Bobby Jackson .75 .23
❑ 70 B.J. Armstrong .40 .12
❑ 71 Alan Henderson .40 .12
❑ 72 Terry Davis .40 .12
❑ 73 Does not exist - -
❑ 74 Lamond Murray .40 .12
❑ 75 Does not exist - -
❑ 76 Rex Chapman .40 .12
❑ 77 Does not exist - -
❑ 78 Terry Cummings .40 .12
❑ 79 Dan Majerle .75 .23
❑ 80 Bo Outlaw .40 .12
❑ 81 Does not exist - -
❑ 82 Vin Baker .75 .23
❑ 83 Clifford Robinson .40 .12
❑ 84 Greg Anthony .40 .12
❑ 85 Brevin Knight .40 .12
❑ 86 Jacque Vaughn .40 .12
❑ 87 Bobby Phills .40 .12
❑ 88 Sherman Douglas .40 .12
❑ 89 Does not exist - -
❑ 90 Does not exist - -
❑ 91 Lorenzen Wright .40 .12
❑ 92 Eric Williams .40 .12
❑ 93 Will Perdue .40 .12
❑ 94 Charles Barkley 1.50 .45
❑ 95 Kendall Gill .40 .12
❑ 96 Wesley Person .40 .12
❑ 97 Does not exist - -
❑ 98 Erick Dampier .75 .23
❑ 99 Does not exist - -
❑ 100 Does not exist - -
❑ 101 Rasheed Wallace 1.25 .35
❑ 102 Zydrunas Ilgauskas .75 .23
❑ 103 Eddie Jones 1.25 .35
❑ 104 Ron Mercer .75 .23
❑ 105 Horace Grant .75 .23
❑ 106 Corliss Williamson .75 .23
❑ 107 Anthony Mason .75 .23
❑ 108 Mookie Blaylock .40 .12
❑ 109 Dennis Rodman .75 .23
❑ 110 Checklist .40 .12
❑ 111 Steve Smith .75 .23
❑ 112 Cedric Henderson .40 .12
❑ 113 Raef LaFrentz RC 4.00 1.20
❑ 114 Calbert Cheaney .40 .12
❑ 115 Rik Smits .75 .23
❑ 116 Rony Seikaly .40 .12
❑ 117 Lawrence Funderburke .40 .12
❑ 118 Ricky Davis RC 6.00 1.80
❑ 119 Howard Eisley .40 .12
❑ 120 Kenny Anderson .75 .23
❑ 121 Corey Benjamin RC 2.00 .60
❑ 122 Maurice Taylor .75 .23
❑ 123 Eric Murdock .40 .12
❑ 124 Derek Fisher 1.25 .35
❑ 125 Kevin Garnett 2.50 .75
❑ 126 Walt Williams .40 .12
❑ 127 Bryce Drew RC 2.00 .60
❑ 128 A.C. Green .75 .23
❑ 129 Ervin Johnson .40 .12
❑ 130 Christian Laettner .75 .23
❑ 131 Chauncey Billups .75 .23
❑ 132 Hakeem Olajuwon 1.25 .35
❑ 133 Al Harrington RC 5.00 1.50
❑ 134 Danny Manning .40 .12
❑ 135 Paul Pierce RC 10.00 3.00
❑ 136 Terrell Brandon .75 .23
❑ 137 Bob Sura .40 .12
❑ 138 Chris Gatling .40 .12
❑ 139 Donyell Marshall .75 .23
❑ 140 Marcus Camby .75 .23
❑ 141 Brian Skinner RC 2.00 .60
❑ 142 Charles Oakley .40 .12
❑ 143 Antawn Jamison RC 6.00 1.80
❑ 144 Nazr Mohammed RC 1.00 .30
❑ 145 Karl Malone 1.25 .35
❑ 146 Chris Mills .40 .12
❑ 147 Bison Dele .40 .12
❑ 148 Gary Payton 1.25 .35
❑ 149 Terry Porter .40 .12
❑ 150 Tim Hardaway .75 .23
❑ 151 Larry Hughes RC 5.00 1.50
❑ 152 Derek Anderson 1.25 .35
❑ 153 Jason Williams RC 6.00 1.80
❑ 154 Dirk Nowitzki RC 15.00 4.50
❑ 155 Juwan Howard .75 .23
❑ 156 Avery Johnson .40 .12
❑ 157 Matt Harpring RC 2.50 .75
❑ 158 Reggie Miller 1.25 .35
❑ 159 Walter McCarty .40 .12
❑ 160 Allen Iverson 2.50 .75
❑ 161 Felipe Lopez RC 2.00 .60
❑ 162 Tracy McGrady 3.00 .90
❑ 163 Damon Stoudamire .75 .23
❑ 164 Antonio McDyess .75 .23
❑ 165 Grant Hill 1.25 .35
❑ 166 Tyronn Lue RC 2.00 .60
❑ 167 P.J. Brown .40 .12
❑ 168 Antonio Daniels .40 .12
❑ 169 Mitch Richmond .75 .23
❑ 170 David Robinson 1.25 .35
❑ 171 Shawn Bradley .40 .12
❑ 172 Shandon Anderson .40 .12
❑ 173 Chris Childs .40 .12
❑ 174 Shawn Kemp .75 .23
❑ 175 Shaquille O'Neal 3.00 .90
❑ 176 John Starks .75 .23
❑ 177 Tyrone Hill .40 .12
❑ 178 Jayson Williams .40 .12
❑ 179 Anfernee Hardaway 1.25 .35
❑ 180 Chris Webber 1.25 .35
❑ 181 Don Reid .40 .12
❑ 182 Stacey Augmon .40 .12
❑ 183 Hersey Hawkins .40 .12
❑ 184 Sam Mitchell .40 .12
❑ 185 Jason Kidd 2.00 .60
❑ 186 Nick Van Exel 1.25 .35
❑ 187 Larry Johnson .75 .23
❑ 188 Bryant Reeves .40 .12
❑ 189 Glen Rice .75 .23
❑ 190 Kerry Kittles .40 .12
❑ 191 Toni Kukoc .75 .23
❑ 192 Ron Harper .75 .23
❑ 193 Bryon Russell .40 .12
❑ 194 Vladimir Stepania RC 1.00 .30
❑ 195 Michael Olowokandi RC 2.50 .75
❑ 196 Mike Bibby RC 12.00 3.60
❑ 197 Dale Ellis .40 .12
❑ 198 Muggsy Bogues .75 .23
❑ 199 Vince Carter RC 30.00 9.00
❑ 200 Robert Traylor RC 2.00 .60
❑ 201 Peja Stojakovic RC 6.00 1.80
❑ 202 Aaron McKie .75 .23
❑ 203 Hubert Davis .40 .12
❑ 204 Dana Barros .40 .12
❑ 205 Bonzi Wells RC 6.00 1.80
❑ 206 Michael Doleac RC 2.00 .60
❑ 207 Keon Clark RC 2.50 .75
❑ 208 Michael Dickerson RC 3.00 .90
❑ 209 Nick Anderson .40 .12
❑ 210 Brent Price .40 .12
❑ 211 Cherokee Parks .40 .12
❑ 212 Sam Jacobson RC 1.00 .30
❑ 213 Pat Garrity RC 1.25 .35
❑ 214 Tyrone Corbin .40 .12
❑ 215 David Wesley .40 .12
❑ 216 Rodney Rogers .40 .12
❑ 217 Dean Garrett .40 .12
❑ 218 Roshown McLeod RC 1.25 .35
❑ 219 Dale Davis .75 .23
❑ 220 Checklist .40 .12
❑ 221 Scottie Pippen MO 1.25 .35
❑ 222 Antonio McDyess MO .75 .23
❑ 223 Stephon Marbury MO 1.25 .35
❑ 224 Tom Gugliotta MO .40 .12
❑ 225 Chris Webber MO .75 .23
❑ 226 Latrell Sprewell MO 1.25 .35
❑ 227 Mitch Richmond MO .75 .23
❑ 228 Joe Smith MO .40 .12
❑ 229 John Starks MO .40 .12
❑ 230 Charles Oakley MO .40 .12
❑ 231 Dennis Rodman MO .40 .12
❑ 232 Eddie Jones MO 1.25 .35
❑ 233 Nick Van Exel MO .40 .12
❑ 234 Bobby Jackson MO .75 .23
❑ 235 Glen Rice MO .40 .12

1999-00 Topps Chrome

	Nm-Mt	Ex-Mt
COMMON CARD (1-257)	.30	.09
COMMON USA (249-257)	.50	.15
COMMON ROOKIE	1.25	.35

❑ 1 Steve Smith .60 .18
❑ 2 Ron Harper .60 .18

❑ 3 Michael Dickerson .60 .18
❑ 4 LaPhonso Ellis .30 .09
❑ 5 Chris Webber 1.00 .30
❑ 6 Jason Caffey .30 .09
❑ 7 Bryon Russell .30 .09
❑ 8 Bison Dele .30 .09
❑ 9 Isaiah Rider .30 .09
❑ 10 Dean Garrett .30 .09
❑ 11 Eric Murdock .30 .09
❑ 12 Juwan Howard .60 .18
❑ 13 Latrell Sprewell 1.00 .30
❑ 14 Jalen Rose 1.00 .30
❑ 15 Larry Johnson .60 .18
❑ 16 Eric Williams .30 .09
❑ 17 Bryant Reeves .30 .09
❑ 18 Tony Battie .30 .09
❑ 19 Luc Longley .30 .09
❑ 20 Gary Payton 1.00 .30
❑ 21 Tariq Abdul-Wahad .30 .09
❑ 22 Armon Gilliam UER .30 .09
mispelled Armen
❑ 23 Shaquille O'Neal 2.50 .75
❑ 24 Gary Trent .30 .09
❑ 25 John Stockton 1.00 .30
❑ 26 Mark Jackson .60 .18
❑ 27 Cherokee Parks .30 .09
❑ 28 Michael Olowokandi .60 .18
❑ 29 Raef LaFrentz .60 .18
❑ 30 Dell Curry .30 .09
❑ 31 Travis Best .30 .09
❑ 32 Shawn Kemp .60 .18
❑ 33 Voshon Lenard .30 .09
❑ 34 Brian Grant .60 .18
❑ 35 Alvin Williams .30 .09
❑ 36 Derek Fisher 1.00 .30
❑ 37 Allan Houston .60 .18
❑ 38 Arvydas Sabonis .60 .18
❑ 39 Terry Cummings .30 .09
❑ 40 Dale Ellis .30 .09
❑ 41 Maurice Taylor .60 .18
❑ 42 Grant Hill 1.00 .30
❑ 43 Anthony Mason .60 .18
❑ 44 John Wallace .30 .09
❑ 45 David Wesley .30 .09
❑ 46 Nick Van Exel 1.00 .30
❑ 47 Cuttino Mobley 1.00 .30
❑ 48 Anfernee Hardaway 1.00 .30
❑ 49 Terry Porter .30 .09
❑ 50 Brent Barry .60 .18
❑ 51 Derek Harper .60 .18
❑ 52 Antoine Walker 1.00 .30
❑ 53 Karl Malone 1.00 .30
❑ 54 Ben Wallace 1.00 .30
❑ 55 Vlade Divac .60 .18
❑ 56 Sam Mitchell .30 .09
❑ 57 Joe Smith .60 .18
❑ 58 Shawn Bradley .30 .09
❑ 59 Darrell Armstrong .30 .09
❑ 60 Kenny Anderson .60 .18
❑ 61 Jason Williams 1.00 .30
❑ 62 Alonzo Mourning .60 .18
❑ 63 Matt Harpring 1.00 .30
❑ 64 Antonio Davis .30 .09
❑ 65 Lindsey Hunter .30 .09
❑ 66 Allen Iverson 2.00 .60
❑ 67 Mookie Blaylock .30 .09
❑ 68 Wesley Person .30 .09
❑ 69 Bobby Phills .30 .09
❑ 70 Theo Ratliff .60 .18
❑ 71 Antonio Daniels .30 .09
❑ 72 P.J. Brown .30 .09
❑ 73 David Robinson 1.00 .30
❑ 74 Sean Elliott .60 .18
❑ 75 Zydrunas Ilgauskas .60 .18
❑ 76 Kerry Kittles .30 .09
❑ 77 Otis Thorpe .60 .18
❑ 78 John Starks .60 .18
❑ 79 Jaren Jackson .30 .09
❑ 80 Hersey Hawkins .60 .18
❑ 81 Glenn Robinson 1.00 .30
❑ 82 Paul Pierce 1.00 .30
❑ 83 Glen Rice .60 .18
❑ 84 Charlie Ward .30 .09
❑ 85 Dee Brown .30 .09
❑ 86 Danny Fortson .30 .09
❑ 87 Billy Owens .30 .09
❑ 88 Jason Kidd 1.50 .45
❑ 89 Brent Price .30 .09
❑ 90 Don Reid .30 .09
❑ 91 Mark Bryant .30 .09
❑ 92 Vinny Del Negro .30 .09
❑ 93 Stephon Marbury 1.00 .30
❑ 94 Donyell Marshall .60 .18
❑ 95 Jim Jackson .30 .09
❑ 96 Horace Grant .60 .18
❑ 97 Calbert Cheaney .30 .09
❑ 98 Vince Carter 2.50 .75
❑ 99 Bobby Jackson .60 .18
❑ 100 Alan Henderson .30 .09
❑ 101 Mike Bibby 1.00 .30
❑ 102 Cedric Henderson .30 .09
❑ 103 Lamond Murray .30 .09
❑ 104 A.C. Green .60 .18
❑ 105 Hakeem Olajuwon 1.00 .30
❑ 106 George Lynch .30 .09
❑ 107 Kendall Gill .30 .09
❑ 108 Rex Chapman .30 .09
❑ 109 Eddie Jones 1.00 .30
❑ 110 Kornel David RC .30 .09
❑ 111 Jason Terry RC 5.00 1.50
❑ 112 Corey Maggette RC 6.00 1.80
❑ 113 Ron Artest RC 4.00 1.20
❑ 114 Richard Hamilton RC 10.00 3.00
❑ 115 Elton Brand RC 8.00 2.40
❑ 116 Baron Davis RC 6.00 1.80
❑ 117 Wally Szczerbiak RC 6.00 1.80
❑ 118 Steve Francis RC 10.00 3.00
❑ 119 James Posey RC 4.00 1.20
❑ 120 Shawn Marion RC 8.00 2.40
❑ 121 Tim Duncan 2.00 .60
❑ 122 Danny Manning .30 .09
❑ 123 Chris Mullin 1.00 .30
❑ 124 Antawn Jamison 1.50 .45
❑ 125 Kobe Bryant 4.00 1.20
❑ 126 Matt Geiger .30 .09
❑ 127 Rod Strickland .30 .09
❑ 128 Howard Eisley .30 .09
❑ 129 Steve Nash 1.00 .30
❑ 130 Felipe Lopez .30 .09
❑ 131 Ron Mercer .60 .18
❑ 132 Ruben Patterson .60 .18
❑ 133 Dana Barros .30 .09
❑ 134 Dale Davis .30 .09
❑ 135 Bo Outlaw .30 .09
❑ 136 Shandon Anderson .30 .09
❑ 137 Mitch Richmond .60 .18
❑ 138 Doug Christie .60 .18
❑ 139 Rasheed Wallace 1.00 .30
❑ 140 Chris Childs .30 .09
❑ 141 Jamal Mashburn .60 .18
❑ 142 Terrell Brandon .60 .18
❑ 143 Jamie Feick RC 1.25 .35
❑ 144 Robert Traylor .30 .09
❑ 145 Rick Fox .60 .18
❑ 146 Charles Barkley 1.25 .35
❑ 147 Tyrone Nesby RC 1.25 .35
❑ 148 Jerry Stackhouse 1.00 .30
❑ 149 Cedric Ceballos .30 .09
❑ 150 Dikembe Mutombo .60 .18
❑ 151 Anthony Peeler .30 .09
❑ 152 Larry Hughes 1.00 .30
❑ 153 Clifford Robinson .30 .09
❑ 154 Corliss Williamson .60 .18
❑ 155 Olden Polynice .30 .09
❑ 156 Avery Johnson .30 .09
❑ 157 Tracy Murray .30 .09
❑ 158 Tom Gugliotta .30 .09
❑ 159 Tim Thomas .60 .18
❑ 160 Reggie Miller 1.00 .30
❑ 161 Tim Hardaway .60 .18
❑ 162 Dan Majerle .60 .18
❑ 163 Will Perdue .30 .09
❑ 164 Brevin Knight .30 .09
❑ 165 Elden Campbell .30 .09
❑ 166 Chris Gatling .30 .09
❑ 167 Walter McCarty .30 .09
❑ 168 Chauncey Billups .60 .18
❑ 169 Chris Mills .30 .09
❑ 170 Christian Laettner .60 .18
❑ 171 Robert Pack .30 .09
❑ 172 Rik Smits .60 .18
❑ 173 Tyrone Hill .30 .09
❑ 174 Damon Stoudamire .60 .18
❑ 175 Nick Anderson .30 .09
❑ 176 Peja Stojakovic 1.25 .35
❑ 177 Vladimir Stepania .30 .09
❑ 178 Tracy McGrady 2.50 .75
❑ 179 Adam Keefe .30 .09
❑ 180 Shareef Abdur-Rahim 1.00 .30
❑ 181 Isaac Austin .30 .09
❑ 182 Mario Elie .30 .09
❑ 183 Rashard Lewis 1.00 .30
❑ 184 Scott Burrell .30 .09
❑ 185 Othella Harrington .30 .09
❑ 186 Eric Piatkowski .60 .18
❑ 187 Bryant Stith .30 .09
❑ 188 Michael Finley 1.00 .30
❑ 189 Chris Crawford .30 .09
❑ 190 Toni Kukoc .60 .18
❑ 191 Danny Ferry .30 .09
❑ 192 Erick Dampier .60 .18
❑ 193 Clarence Weatherspoon .30 .09
❑ 194 Bob Sura .30 .09
❑ 195 Jayson Williams .30 .09
❑ 196 Kurt Thomas .60 .18
❑ 197 Greg Anthony .30 .09
❑ 198 Rodney Rogers .30 .09
❑ 199 Detlef Schrempf .60 .18
❑ 200 Keith Van Horn 1.00 .30
❑ 201 Robert Horry .60 .18
❑ 202 Sam Cassell 1.00 .30
❑ 203 Malik Sealy .30 .09
❑ 204 Kelvin Cato .30 .09
❑ 205 Antonio McDyess .60 .18
❑ 206 Andrew DeClercq .30 .09
❑ 207 Ricky Davis .60 .18
❑ 208 Vitaly Potapenko .30 .09
❑ 209 Loy Vaught .30 .09
❑ 210 Kevin Garnett 2.00 .60
❑ 211 Eric Snow .60 .18
❑ 212 Anfernee Hardaway 1.00 .30
❑ 213 Vin Baker .60 .18
❑ 214 Lawrence Funderburke .30 .09
❑ 215 Jeff Hornacek .60 .18
❑ 216 Doug West .30 .09
❑ 217 Michael Doleac .30 .09
❑ 218 Ray Allen 1.00 .30
❑ 219 Derek Anderson .60 .18
❑ 220 Jerome Williams .30 .09
❑ 221 Derrick Coleman .60 .18
❑ 222 Randy Brown .30 .09
❑ 223 Patrick Ewing 1.00 .30
❑ 224 Walt Williams .30 .09
❑ 225 Charles Oakley .30 .09
❑ 226 Steve Kerr .60 .18
❑ 227 Muggsy Bogues .60 .18
❑ 228 Kevin Willis .30 .09
❑ 229 Marcus Camby .60 .18
❑ 230 Scottie Pippen 1.50 .45
❑ 231 Lamar Odom RC 6.00 1.80
❑ 232 Jonathan Bender RC 6.00 1.80
❑ 233 Andre Miller RC 6.00 1.80
❑ 234 Trajan Langdon RC 2.50 .75
❑ 235 Aleksandar Radojevic RC 1.25 .35

Card	Nm-Mt	Ex-Mt
❑ 236 William Avery RC	2.50	.75
❑ 237 Cal Bowdler RC	2.00	.60
❑ 238 Quincy Lewis RC	2.00	.60
❑ 239 Dion Glover RC	2.00	.60
❑ 240 Jeff Foster RC	2.00	.60
❑ 241 Kenny Thomas RC	2.50	.75
❑ 242 Devean George RC	3.00	.90
❑ 243 Tim James RC	2.00	.60
❑ 244 Vonteego Cummings RC	2.50	.75
❑ 245 Jumaine Jones RC	2.50	.75
❑ 246 Scott Padgett RC	2.00	.60
❑ 247 Adrian Griffin RC	2.00	.60
❑ 248 Chris Herren RC	1.25	.35
❑ 249 Allan Houston USA	1.00	.30
❑ 250 Kevin Garnett USA	3.00	.90
❑ 251 Gary Payton USA	1.00	.30
❑ 252 Steve Smith USA	.50	.15
❑ 253 Tim Hardaway USA	1.00	.30
❑ 254 Tim Duncan USA	3.00	.90
❑ 255 Jason Kidd USA	2.50	.75
❑ 256 Tom Gugliotta USA	.50	.15
❑ 257 Vin Baker USA	.50	.15

2000-01 Topps Chrome

	Nm-Mt	Ex-Mt
COMPLETE SET (200)	300.00	90.00
COMPLETE SET w/o SP's (150)	40.00	12.00
COMMON CARD (1-150)	.30	.09
COMMON ROOKIE (151-200)	5.00	1.50
❑ 1 Elton Brand	1.00	.30
❑ 2 Marcus Camby	.60	.18
❑ 3 Jalen Rose	1.00	.30
❑ 4 Jamie Feick	.30	.09
❑ 5 Toni Kukoc	.60	.18
❑ 6 Doug Christie	.60	.18
❑ 7 Sam Cassell	1.00	.30
❑ 8 Shaquille O'Neal	2.50	.75
❑ 9 Larry Hughes	.60	.18
❑ 10 Jerry Stackhouse	1.00	.30
❑ 11 Rick Fox	.60	.18
❑ 12 Clifford Robinson	.30	.09
❑ 13 Dirk Nowitzki	1.50	.45
❑ 14 Cuttino Mobley	.60	.18
❑ 15 Latrell Sprewell	1.00	.30
❑ 16 Kevin Garnett	2.00	.60
❑ 17 Jerome Williams	.30	.09
❑ 18 Chris Webber	1.00	.30
❑ 19 Jason Terry	1.00	.30
❑ 20 Elden Campbell	.30	.09
❑ 21 Jonathan Bender	.60	.18
❑ 22 Scottie Pippen	1.50	.45
❑ 23 Radoslav Nesterovic	.60	.18
❑ 24 Reggie Miller	1.00	.30
❑ 25 Andre Miller	.60	.18
❑ 26 Rashard Lewis	.60	.18
❑ 27 Larry Johnson	.60	.18
❑ 28 Steve Francis	1.00	.30
❑ 29 Rod Strickland	.30	.09
❑ 30 Tim Thomas	.60	.18
❑ 31 Robert Horry	.60	.18
❑ 32 Darrell Armstrong	.30	.09
❑ 33 Vince Carter	2.50	.75
❑ 34 Othella Harrington	.30	.09
❑ 35 Derek Anderson	.60	.18
❑ 36 Anthony Carter	.60	.18
❑ 37 Ray Allen	1.00	.30
❑ 38 Jason Kidd	1.50	.45
❑ 39 Sean Elliott	.60	.18
❑ 40 Tim Duncan	2.00	.60
❑ 41 Adrian Griffin	.30	.09
❑ 42 Wally Szczerbiak	.60	.18
❑ 43 Austin Croshere	.60	.18
❑ 44 James Posey	.60	.18
❑ 45 Alan Henderson	.30	.09
❑ 46 Jahidi White	.30	.09
❑ 47 Shawn Marion	1.00	.30
❑ 48 Lamar Odom	1.00	.30
❑ 49 Keon Clark	.60	.18
❑ 50 Lamond Murray	.30	.09
❑ 51 Paul Pierce	1.00	.30
❑ 52 Charlie Ward	.30	.09
❑ 53 Horace Grant	.60	.18
❑ 54 John Stockton	1.00	.30
❑ 55 Peja Stojakovic	1.00	.30
❑ 56 Christian Laettner	.60	.18
❑ 57 Keith Van Horn	1.00	.30
❑ 58 Patrick Ewing	1.00	.30
❑ 59 Steve Smith	.60	.18
❑ 60 Antonio Davis	.30	.09
❑ 61 Mitch Richmond	.60	.18
❑ 62 Michael Olowokandi	.30	.09
❑ 63 Baron Davis	1.00	.30
❑ 64 Dikembe Mutombo	.60	.18
❑ 65 Raef LaFrentz	.60	.18
❑ 66 Ervin Johnson	.30	.09
❑ 67 Alonzo Mourning	.60	.18
❑ 68 Kendall Gill	.30	.09
❑ 69 George Lynch	.30	.09
❑ 70 Donyell Marshall	.60	.18
❑ 71 Bo Outlaw	.30	.09
❑ 72 Kenny Anderson	.60	.18
❑ 73 John Amaechi	.30	.09
❑ 74 Vlade Divac	.60	.18
❑ 75 Vin Baker	.60	.18
❑ 76 Mike Bibby	1.00	.30
❑ 77 Richard Hamilton	.60	.18
❑ 78 Mookie Blaylock	.30	.09
❑ 79 Vitaly Potapenko	.30	.09
❑ 80 Anthony Mason	.60	.18
❑ 81 Vonteego Cummings	.30	.09
❑ 82 Michael Finley	1.00	.30
❑ 83 Ron Artest	.60	.18
❑ 84 Rodney Rogers	.30	.09
❑ 85 Team Championship	2.00	.60
❑ 86 Jason Williams	.60	.18
❑ 87 David Robinson	1.00	.30
❑ 88 Charles Oakley	.30	.09
❑ 89 Juwan Howard	.60	.18
❑ 90 Antoine Walker	1.00	.30
❑ 91 Roshown McLeod	.30	.09
❑ 92 Eddie Jones	1.00	.30
❑ 93 Allen Iverson	2.00	.60
❑ 94 Grant Hill	1.00	.30
❑ 95 Terrell Brandon	.60	.18
❑ 96 Stephon Marbury	1.00	.30
❑ 97 Jamal Mashburn	.60	.18
❑ 98 Ron Harper	.60	.18
❑ 99 Jermaine O'Neal	1.00	.30
❑ 100 Nick Van Exel	1.00	.30
❑ 101 Danny Fortson	.30	.09
❑ 102 Jim Jackson	.30	.09
❑ 103 Brad Miller	1.00	.30
❑ 104 Shawn Bradley	.30	.09
❑ 105 Mark Jackson	.30	.09
❑ 106 Maurice Taylor	.30	.09
❑ 107 Kobe Bryant	4.00	1.20
❑ 108 Clarence Weatherspoon	.30	.09
❑ 109 Eric Snow	.60	.18
❑ 110 Allan Houston	.60	.18
❑ 111 Chauncey Billups	.60	.18
❑ 112 Tom Gugliotta	.30	.09
❑ 113 Theo Ratliff	.60	.18
❑ 114 Rasheed Wallace	1.00	.30
❑ 115 Glen Rice	.60	.18
❑ 116 Bryon Russell	.30	.09
❑ 117 Tracy McGrady	2.50	.75
❑ 118 Bryant Reeves	.30	.09
❑ 119 Damon Stoudamire	.60	.18
❑ 120 Anfernee Hardaway	1.00	.30
❑ 121 Johnny Newman	.30	.09
❑ 122 Corey Maggette	.60	.18
❑ 123 Travis Best	.30	.09
❑ 124 Hakeem Olajuwon	1.00	.30
❑ 125 Antawn Jamison	1.00	.30
❑ 126 John Starks	.60	.18
❑ 127 Antonio McDyess	.60	.18
❑ 128 Gary Payton	1.00	.30
❑ 129 Karl Malone	1.00	.30
❑ 130 Michael Dickerson	.60	.18
❑ 131 Shawn Kemp	.60	.18
❑ 132 J.Crawford RC EXCH	.30	.09
❑ 133 P.J. Brown	.30	.09
❑ 134 Ron Mercer	.60	.18
❑ 135 Robert Traylor	.30	.09
❑ 136 Derrick Coleman	.30	.09
❑ 137 Steve Nash	1.00	.30
❑ 138 M.Cleaves RC EXCH	1.00	.30
❑ 139 Brian Skinner	.30	.09
❑ 140 Chris Gatling	.30	.09
❑ 141 Dale Davis	.30	.09
❑ 142 Glenn Robinson	1.00	.30
❑ 143 Chucky Atkins	.30	.09
❑ 144 M.Peterson RC EXCH	.60	.18
❑ 145 D.Harvey RC EXCH	.60	.18
❑ 146 Shareef Abdur-Rahim	1.00	.30
❑ 147 Avery Johnson	.30	.09
❑ 148 Tim Hardaway	.60	.18
❑ 149 Isaiah Rider	.60	.18
❑ 150 Shaquille O'Neal / Allen Iverson / Grant Hill SL	.30	.09
❑ 151 Jason Kidd / Sam Cassell / Nick Van Exel SL	12.00	3.60
❑ 152 Dikembe Mutombo / Shaquille O'Neal / Tim Duncan SL	8.00	2.40
❑ 153 Eddie Jones / Paul Pierce / Darrell Armstrong SL	15.00	4.50
❑ 154 Alonzo Mourning / Dikembe Mutombo / Shaquille O'Neal SL	5.00	1.50
❑ 155 Mike Miller RC	15.00	4.50
❑ 156 DerMarr Johnson RC	5.00	1.50
❑ 157 Chris Mihm RC	5.00	1.50
❑ 158 Jamal Crawford RC	6.00	1.80
❑ 159 Joel Przybilla RC	5.00	1.50
❑ 160 Keyon Dooling RC	5.00	1.50
❑ 161 Jerome Moiso RC	5.00	1.50
❑ 162 Etan Thomas RC	5.00	1.50
❑ 163 Courtney Alexander RC	8.00	2.40
❑ 164 Mateen Cleaves RC	5.00	1.50
❑ 165 Jason Collier RC	5.00	1.50
❑ 166 Desmond Mason RC	5.00	1.50
❑ 167 Quentin Richardson RC	6.00	1.80
❑ 168 Jamaal Magloire RC	5.00	1.50
❑ 169 Speedy Claxton RC	5.00	1.50
❑ 170 Morris Peterson RC	8.00	2.40
❑ 171 Donnell Harvey RC	5.00	1.50
❑ 172 DeShawn Stevenson RC	5.00	1.50
❑ 173 Mamadou N'Diaye RC	5.00	1.50
❑ 174 Erick Barkley RC	5.00	1.50
❑ 175 Mark Madsen RC	5.00	1.50
❑ 176 Hidayet Turkoglu RC	8.00	2.40
❑ 177 Brian Cardinal RC	5.00	1.50
❑ 178 Iakovos Tsakalidis RC	5.00	1.50
❑ 179 Dalibor Bagaric RC	5.00	1.50
❑ 180 Dragan Tarlac RC	5.00	1.50
❑ 181 Dan Langhi RC	5.00	1.50
❑ 182 A.J. Guyton RC	5.00	1.50
❑ 183 Jake Voskuhl RC	5.00	1.50
❑ 184 Khalid El-Amin RC	5.00	1.50
❑ 185 Mike Smith RC	5.00	1.50
❑ 186 Soumaila Samake RC	5.00	1.50
❑ 187 Eddie House RC	5.00	1.50
❑ 188 Eduardo Najera RC	6.00	1.80

Card		
❑ 189 Lavor Postell RC	5.00	1.50
❑ 190 Hanno Mottola RC	5.00	1.50
❑ 191 Olumide Oyedeji RC	5.00	1.50
❑ 192 Michael Redd RC	12.00	3.60
❑ 193 Chris Porter RC	5.00	1.50
❑ 194 Jabari Smith RC	5.00	1.50
❑ 195 Marc Jackson RC	5.00	1.50
❑ 196 Stephen Jackson RC	6.00	1.80
❑ 197 Pepe Sanchez RC	5.00	1.50
❑ 198 Daniel Santiago RC	5.00	1.50
❑ 199 Paul McPherson RC	5.00	1.50
❑ 200 Mike Penberthy RC	5.00	1.50

2001-02 Topps Chrome

	Nm-Mt	Ex-Mt
COMP.SET w/o RC's (129)	60.00	18.00
COMMON CARD (1-129)	.30	.09
COMMON ROOKIE (130-165)	2.50	.75
❑ 1 Shaquille O'Neal	2.50	.75
❑ 2 Steve Nash	1.00	.30
❑ 3 Allen Iverson	2.00	.60
❑ 4 Shawn Marion	1.00	.30
❑ 5 Rasheed Wallace	1.00	.30
❑ 6 Antonio Daniels	.30	.09
❑ 7 Rashard Lewis	.60	.18
❑ 8 Raef LaFrentz	.60	.18
❑ 9 Stromile Swift	.60	.18
❑ 10 Vince Carter	2.50	.75
❑ 11 Danny Fortson	.30	.09
❑ 12 Jalen Rose	1.00	.30
❑ 13 Glen Rice	.60	.18
❑ 14 Glenn Robinson	1.00	.30
❑ 15 Wally Szczerbiak	.60	.18
❑ 16 Rick Fox	.60	.18
❑ 17 Darius Miles	1.00	.30
❑ 18 Jermaine O'Neal	1.00	.30
❑ 19 Eddie Jones	1.00	.30
❑ 20 Tracy McGrady	2.50	.75
❑ 21 Kevin Garnett	2.00	.60
❑ 22 Tim Thomas	.60	.18
❑ 23 Larry Hughes	.60	.18
❑ 24 Jerry Stackhouse	1.00	.30
❑ 25 Ray Allen	1.00	.30
❑ 26 Terrell Brandon	.60	.18
❑ 27 Keith Van Horn	1.00	.30
❑ 28 Marcus Fizer	.60	.18
❑ 29 Elden Campbell	.30	.09
❑ 30 Tim Duncan	2.00	.60
❑ 31 Doug Christie	.60	.18
❑ 32 Allan Houston	.60	.18
❑ 33 Patrick Ewing	1.00	.30
❑ 34 Hakeem Olajuwon	.60	.18
❑ 35 Anfernee Hardaway	1.00	.30
❑ 36 Larry Johnson	.60	.18
❑ 37 Eric Snow	.60	.18
❑ 38 Tom Gugliotta	.30	.09
❑ 39 Scottie Pippen	1.50	.45
❑ 40 Chris Webber	1.00	.30
❑ 41 David Robinson	1.00	.30
❑ 42 Elton Brand	1.00	.30
❑ 43 Theo Ratliff	.60	.18
❑ 44 Paul Pierce	1.00	.30
❑ 45 Jamal Mashburn	.60	.18
❑ 46 Damon Stoudamire	.60	.18
❑ 47 DerMarr Johnson	.60	.18
❑ 48 Andre Miller	.60	.18
❑ 49 Dirk Nowitzki	1.50	.45
❑ 50 Kobe Bryant	4.00	1.20
❑ 51 Keyon Dooling	.60	.18
❑ 52 Brian Grant	.60	.18
❑ 53 Antawn Jamison	1.00	.30
❑ 54 Jonathan Bender	.60	.18
❑ 55 Dikembe Mutombo	.60	.18
❑ 56 Steve Smith	.60	.18
❑ 57 Hidayet Turkoglu	.60	.18
❑ 58 Robert Horry	.60	.18
❑ 59 Kurt Thomas	.60	.18
❑ 60 Jason Terry	1.00	.30
❑ 61 Vitaly Potapenko	.30	.09
❑ 62 Gary Payton	1.00	.30
❑ 63 Bonzi Wells	.60	.18
❑ 64 Raja Bell RC	5.00	1.50
❑ 65 Chris Mihm	.60	.18
❑ 66 Reggie Miller	1.00	.30
❑ 67 Lamar Odom	1.00	.30
❑ 68 Darrell Armstrong	.30	.09
❑ 69 Baron Davis	1.00	.30
❑ 70 Aaron Williams	.30	.09
❑ 71 Latrell Sprewell	1.00	.30
❑ 72 James Posey	.60	.18
❑ 73 Ben Wallace	1.00	.30
❑ 74 Marc Jackson	.60	.18
❑ 75 Maurice Taylor	.60	.18
❑ 76 Aaron McKie	.60	.18
❑ 77 Grant Hill	1.00	.30
❑ 78 Anthony Carter	.60	.18
❑ 79 Peja Stojakovic	1.00	.30
❑ 80 Jason Kidd	1.50	.45
❑ 81 Vin Baker	.60	.18
❑ 82 Morris Peterson	.60	.18
❑ 83 Bryon Russell	.30	.09
❑ 84 Michael Dickerson	.60	.18
❑ 85 Quentin Richardson	.60	.18
❑ 86 Primoz Brezec RC	2.50	.75
❑ 87 Desmond Mason	.60	.18
❑ 88 Jason Williams	.60	.18
❑ 89 Marcus Camby	.60	.18
❑ 90 Stephon Marbury	1.00	.30
❑ 91 Mike Bibby	1.00	.30
❑ 92 Alonzo Mourning	.60	.18
❑ 93 Mitch Richmond	.60	.18
❑ 94 Donyell Marshall	.60	.18
❑ 95 Michael Jordan	20.00	6.00
❑ 96 Mike Miller	1.00	.30
❑ 97 Nick Van Exel	1.00	.30
❑ 98 Michael Finley	1.00	.30
❑ 99 Jamal Crawford	.60	.18
❑ 100 Steve Francis	1.00	.30
❑ 101 Kenyon Martin	1.00	.30
❑ 102 Sam Cassell	1.00	.30
❑ 103 Chucky Atkins	.30	.09
❑ 104 Juwan Howard	.60	.18
❑ 105 Bryant Reeves	.30	.09
❑ 106 Richard Hamilton	.60	.18
❑ 107 Antonio Davis	.30	.09
❑ 108 Antonio McDyess	.60	.18
❑ 109 Derek Anderson	.60	.18
❑ 110 Kenny Anderson	.60	.18
❑ 111 Antoine Walker	1.00	.30
❑ 112 Wang ZhiZhi	1.00	.30
❑ 113 Shareef Abdur-Rahim	1.00	.30
❑ 114 Chris Whitney	.30	.09
❑ 115 John Stockton	1.00	.30
❑ 116 Alvin Williams	.30	.09
❑ 117 David Wesley	.30	.09
❑ 118 Joe Smith	.60	.18
❑ 119 Jahidi White	.30	.09
❑ 120 Karl Malone	1.00	.30
❑ 121 Cuttino Mobley	.60	.18
❑ 122 Tyrone Hill	.30	.09
❑ 123 Clifford Robinson	.60	.18
❑ 124 Toni Kukoc	.60	.18
❑ 125 Eddie Robinson	.60	.18
❑ 126 Courtney Alexander	.60	.18
❑ 127 Ron Mercer	.60	.18
❑ 128 Lamond Murray	.30	.09
❑ 129 Rodney Rogers	.30	.09
❑ 130 Tyson Chandler RC	6.00	1.80
❑ 131 Pau Gasol RC	8.00	2.40
❑ 132 Eddy Curry RC	6.00	1.80
❑ 133 Jason Richardson RC	8.00	2.40
❑ 134 Shane Battier RC	4.00	1.20
❑ 135 Eddie Griffin RC	4.00	1.20
❑ 136 DeSagana Diop RC	2.50	.75
❑ 137 Rodney White RC	3.00	.90
❑ 138 Joe Johnson RC	4.00	1.20
❑ 139 Kedrick Brown RC	2.50	.75
❑ 140 Vladimir Radmanovic RC	3.00	.90
❑ 141 Richard Jefferson RC	8.00	2.40
❑ 142 Troy Murphy RC	5.00	1.50
❑ 143 Steven Hunter RC	2.50	.75
❑ 144 Kirk Haston RC	2.50	.75
❑ 145 Michael Bradley RC	2.50	.75
❑ 146 Jason Collins RC	2.50	.75
❑ 147 Zach Randolph RC	8.00	2.40
❑ 148 Brendan Haywood RC	3.00	.90
❑ 149 Joseph Forte RC	6.00	1.80
❑ 150 Jeryl Sasser RC	2.50	.75
❑ 151 Brandon Armstrong RC	3.00	.90
❑ 152 Gerald Wallace RC	6.00	1.80
❑ 153 Samuel Dalembert RC	2.50	.75
❑ 154 Jamaal Tinsley RC	4.00	1.20
❑ 155 Tony Parker RC	10.00	3.00
❑ 156 Trenton Hassell RC	4.00	1.20
❑ 157 Gilbert Arenas RC	6.00	1.80
❑ 158 Jeff Trepagnier RC	2.50	.75
❑ 159 Damone Brown RC	2.50	.75
❑ 160 Loren Woods RC	2.50	.75
❑ 161 Andrei Kirilenko RC	6.00	1.80
❑ 162 Zeljko Rebraca RC	2.50	.75
❑ 163 Kenny Satterfield RC	2.50	.75
❑ 164 Alvin Jones RC	2.50	.75
❑ 165 Kwame Brown RC	5.00	1.50

2002-03 Topps Chrome

	Nm-Mt	Ex-Mt
COMPLETE SET (175)	180.00	55.00
COMMON CARD (1-165)	.25	.07
COMMON ROOKIE	5.00	1.50
❑ 1 Shaquille O'Neal	2.50	.75
❑ 2 Pau Gasol	1.00	.30
❑ 3 Allen Iverson	2.00	.60
❑ 4 Tom Gugliotta	.25	.07
❑ 5 Rasheed Wallace	1.00	.30
❑ 6 Peja Stojakovic	1.00	.30
❑ 7 Jason Richardson	1.00	.30
❑ 8 Rashard Lewis	.60	.18
❑ 9 Morris Peterson	.60	.18
❑ 10 Michael Jordan	8.00	2.40
❑ 11 Matt Harpring	1.00	.30
❑ 12 Shareef Abdur-Rahim	1.00	.30
❑ 13 Antoine Walker	1.00	.30
❑ 14 Stephon Marbury	1.00	.30
❑ 15 Jamal Mashburn	.60	.18
❑ 16 Eddy Curry	1.00	.30
❑ 17 Jumaine Jones	.60	.18
❑ 18 Jason Kidd	1.50	.45
❑ 19 Jerry Stackhouse	1.00	.30
❑ 20 Kenny Thomas	.25	.07
❑ 21 Kobe Bryant	4.00	1.20
❑ 22 Jason Williams	.60	.18
❑ 23 Eddie Jones	1.00	.30
❑ 24 Kenyon Martin	1.00	.30
❑ 25 Kevin Garnett	1.50	.45

Card		
❑ 26 Kurt Thomas	.60	.18
❑ 27 Karl Malone	1.00	.30
❑ 28 Reggie Evans RC	5.00	1.50
❑ 29 Dirk Nowitzki	1.50	.45
❑ 30 Vince Carter	2.50	.75
❑ 31 Desmond Mason	.60	.18
❑ 32 Todd MacCulloch	.25	.07
❑ 33 Grant Hill	1.00	.30
❑ 34 Terrell Brandon	.60	.18
❑ 35 Tracy McGrady	2.50	.75
❑ 36 Tim Thomas	.60	.18
❑ 37 Loren Woods	.60	.18
❑ 38 Michael Redd	1.00	.30
❑ 39 Stromile Swift	.60	.18
❑ 40 Dikembe Mutombo	.60	.18
❑ 41 Richard Jefferson	.60	.18
❑ 42 Glenn Robinson	1.00	.30
❑ 43 Quentin Richardson	.60	.18
❑ 44 Elton Brand	1.00	.30
❑ 45 Reggie Miller	1.00	.30
❑ 46 Eddie Griffin	.60	.18
❑ 47 Gilbert Arenas	1.00	.30
❑ 48 Zeljko Rebraca	.60	.18
❑ 49 Mark Jackson	.25	.07
❑ 50 Juwan Howard	.60	.18
❑ 51 Nick Van Exel	1.00	.30
❑ 52 Donyell Marshall	.60	.18
❑ 53 Tyson Chandler	1.00	.30
❑ 54 Baron Davis	1.00	.30
❑ 55 Nate Huffman RC	.25	.07
❑ 56 Jamaal Magloire	.25	.07
❑ 57 Marcus Fizer	.60	.18
❑ 58 Steve Francis	1.00	.30
❑ 59 Aaron McKie	.60	.18
❑ 60 Scottie Pippen	1.50	.45
❑ 61 Mike Bibby	1.00	.30
❑ 62 Paul Pierce	1.00	.30
❑ 63 Kwame Brown	.60	.18
❑ 64 Andrei Kirilenko	1.00	.30
❑ 65 Keon Clark	.60	.18
❑ 66 Alvin Williams	.25	.07
❑ 67 Brent Barry	.60	.18
❑ 68 Doug Christie	.60	.18
❑ 69 Chris Webber	1.00	.30
❑ 70 Robert Horry	.60	.18
❑ 71 Allan Houston	.60	.18
❑ 72 Kerry Kittles	.25	.07
❑ 73 Wally Szczerbiak	.60	.18
❑ 74 Jonathan Bender	.60	.18
❑ 75 Sam Cassell	1.00	.30
❑ 76 Rod Strickland	.25	.07
❑ 77 Shane Battier	1.00	.30
❑ 78 Tim Duncan	2.00	.60
❑ 79 Jermaine O'Neal	1.00	.30
❑ 80 Cuttino Mobley	.60	.18
❑ 81 Clifford Robinson	.25	.07
❑ 82 Steve Nash	1.00	.30
❑ 83 Dermarr Johnson	.25	.07
❑ 84 Courtney Alexander	.60	.18
❑ 85 Corliss Williamson	.60	.18
❑ 86 Tony Parker	1.00	.30
❑ 87 Damon Stoudamire	.60	.18
❑ 88 Jalen Rose	1.00	.30
❑ 89 Mike Miller	1.00	.30
❑ 90 Raef Lafrentz	.60	.18
❑ 91 Ben Wallace	1.00	.30
❑ 92 Ray Allen	1.00	.30
❑ 93 Gary Payton	1.00	.30
❑ 94 Derek Fisher	1.00	.30
❑ 95 Michael Olowokandi	.25	.07
❑ 96 Jamaal Tinsley	1.00	.30
❑ 97 Chris Mihm	.25	.07
❑ 98 Antawn Jamison	1.00	.30
❑ 99 Mengke Bateer	1.00	.30
❑ 100 Michael Finley	1.00	.30
❑ 101 Andre Miller	.60	.18
❑ 102 Elden Campbell	.25	.07
❑ 103 Kedrick Brown	.60	.18
❑ 104 Jason Terry	1.00	.30
❑ 105 Kenny Anderson	.60	.18
❑ 106 Darius Miles	1.00	.30
❑ 107 Latrell Sprewell	1.00	.30
❑ 108 Darrell Armstrong	.25	.07
❑ 109 Joe Johnson	1.00	.30
❑ 110 Bonzi Wells	.60	.18
❑ 111 LaPhonso Ellis	.25	.07
❑ 112 Steve Smith	.60	.18
❑ 113 Vin Baker	.60	.18
❑ 114 Antonio Davis	.25	.07
❑ 115 John Stockton	1.00	.30
❑ 116 Shawn Marion	1.00	.30
❑ 117 Devean George	.60	.18
❑ 118 Joe Smith	.60	.18
❑ 119 Sean Lampley	.25	.07
❑ 120 Lamar Odom	1.00	.30
❑ 121 Alonzo Mourning	.60	.18
❑ 122 Antonio Daniels	.25	.07
❑ 123 Troy Murphy	1.00	.30
❑ 124A Manu Ginobili RC	12.00	3.60
❑ 124B Manu Ginobili	8.00	2.40
Spanish		
❑ 125 Richard Hamilton	.60	.18
❑ 126 Amare Stoudemire RC	25.00	7.50
❑ 127 Carlos Boozer RC	10.00	3.00
❑ 128 Casey Jacobsen RC	5.00	1.50
❑ 129 Juaquin Hawkins RC	5.00	1.50
❑ 130 Pat Burke RC	5.00	1.50
❑ 131 Dan Dickau RC	5.00	1.50
❑ 132 Drew Gooden RC	10.00	3.00
❑ 133 Fred Jones RC	5.00	1.50
❑ 134 Jared Jeffries RC	5.00	1.50
❑ 135A Jiri Welsch RC	5.00	1.50
❑ 135B Jiri Welsch	5.00	1.50
Czech		
❑ 136 Juan Dixon RC	8.00	2.40
❑ 137 Marcus Haislip RC	5.00	1.50
❑ 138 Melvin Ely RC	5.00	1.50
❑ 139A Nene Hilario RC	6.00	1.80
❑ 139B Nene Hilario	6.00	1.80
Spanish		
❑ 140 Qyntel Woods RC	5.00	1.50
❑ 141 Lonny Baxter RC	5.00	1.50
❑ 142 Ryan Humphrey RC	5.00	1.50
❑ 143 Smush Parker RC	5.00	1.50
❑ 144 Tayshaun Prince RC	6.00	1.80
❑ 145 Vincent Yarbrough RC	5.00	1.50
❑ 146A Yao Ming RC	30.00	9.00
❑ 146B Yao Ming	30.00	9.00
Chinese		
❑ 147 Pete Mickeal	.25	.07
❑ 148 Tamar Slay RC	5.00	1.50
❑ 149A Efthimios Rentzias RC	5.00	1.50
❑ 149B Efthimios Rentzias	5.00	1.50
Greek		
❑ 150A Igor Rakocevic RC	5.00	1.50
❑ 150B Igor Rakocevic	5.00	1.50
Yugoslavian		
❑ 151A Gordan Giricek RC	6.00	1.80
❑ 151B Gordan Giricek	6.00	1.80
Croatian		
❑ 152A Nikoloz Tskitishvili RC	5.00	1.50
❑ 152B Nikoloz Tskitishvili	5.00	1.50
Russian		
❑ 153 Mike Dunleavy RC	8.00	2.40
❑ 154A Marko Jaric RC	5.00	1.50
❑ 154B Marko Jaric	5.00	1.50
Yugoslavian		
❑ 155 Kareem Rush RC	6.00	1.80
❑ 156 John Salmons RC	5.00	1.50
❑ 157 Jay Williams RC	6.00	1.80
❑ 158 J.R. Bremer RC	5.00	1.50
❑ 159 Frank Williams RC	5.00	1.50
❑ 160 Adam Harrington RC	5.00	1.50
❑ 161 DaJuan Wagner RC	8.00	2.40
❑ 162 Chris Wilcox RC	6.00	1.80
❑ 163 Chris Jefferies RC	5.00	1.50
❑ 164 Caron Butler RC	10.00	3.00
❑ 165A Bostjan Nachbar RC	5.00	1.50
❑ 165B Bostjan Nachbar	5.00	1.50
Slovenian		

2003-04 Topps Chrome

	Nm-Mt	Ex-Mt
COMP.SET w/o RC's (110)	50.00	15.00
COMMON CARD (1-110)	.25	.07
COMMON ROOKIE (111-165)	5.00	1.50
RC B VER. FOR 112, 129, 131, 132, 138, 140, 146, 147, 149, 154	-	
CARD B VERSION NOT IN ENGLISH		-
❑ 1 Tracy McGrady	2.50	.75
❑ 2 Dajuan Wagner	.60	.18
❑ 3 Allen Iverson	2.00	.60
❑ 4 Chris Webber	1.00	.30
❑ 5 Jason Kidd	1.50	.45
❑ 6 Stephon Marbury	1.00	.30
❑ 7 Jermaine O'Neal	1.00	.30
❑ 8 Antoine Walker	1.00	.30
❑ 9 Tony Parker	1.00	.30
❑ 10 Mike Bibby	1.00	.30
❑ 11 Yao Ming	2.50	.75
❑ 12 Bobby Jackson	.60	.18
❑ 13 Steve Nash	1.00	.30
❑ 14 Paul Pierce	1.00	.30
❑ 15 Vince Carter	2.50	.75
❑ 16 Peja Stojakovic	1.00	.30
❑ 17 Wally Szczerbiak	.60	.18
❑ 18 Kenyon Martin	1.00	.30
❑ 19 Pau Gasol	1.00	.30
❑ 20 Gary Payton	1.00	.30
❑ 21 Tim Duncan	2.00	.60
❑ 22 Anfernee Hardaway	1.00	.30
❑ 23 Jason Richardson	1.00	.30
❑ 24 Andre Miller	.60	.18
❑ 25 Latrell Sprewell	1.00	.30
❑ 26 Darius Miles	1.00	.30
❑ 27 Richard Jefferson	.60	.18
❑ 28 Shawn Marion	1.00	.30
❑ 29 Baron Davis	1.00	.30
❑ 30 Ben Wallace	1.00	.30
❑ 31 Reggie Miller	1.00	.30
❑ 32 Karl Malone	1.00	.30
❑ 33 Jonathan Bender	.60	.18
❑ 34 Shaquille O'Neal	2.50	.75
❑ 35 Steve Francis	1.00	.30
❑ 36 Kobe Bryant	4.00	1.20
❑ 37 Mike Dunleavy	.60	.18
❑ 38 Glenn Robinson	1.00	.30
❑ 39 Allan Houston	.60	.18
❑ 40 Sam Cassell	1.00	.30
❑ 41 Dirk Nowitzki	1.50	.45
❑ 42 Elton Brand	1.00	.30
❑ 43 Joe Smith	.60	.18
❑ 44 Brian Grant	.60	.18
❑ 45 Jason Terry	1.00	.30
❑ 46 Richard Hamilton	.60	.18
❑ 47 Morris Peterson	.60	.18
❑ 48 Ray Allen	1.00	.30
❑ 49 Scottie Pippen	1.50	.45
❑ 50 Jamal Crawford	.60	.18
❑ 51 Cuttino Mobley	.60	.18
❑ 52 Jerry Stackhouse	1.00	.30

❑ 53 Marcus Camby	.60	.18
❑ 54 Jalen Rose	1.00	.30
❑ 55 Ricky Davis	1.00	.30
❑ 56 Jamal Mashburn	.60	.18
❑ 57 Ron Artest	.60	.18
❑ 58 Theo Ratliff	.60	.18
❑ 59 Juwan Howard	.60	.18
❑ 60 Caron Butler	1.00	.30
❑ 61 Antawn Jamison	1.00	.30
❑ 62 Nene	.60	.18
❑ 63 Tyson Chandler	1.00	.30
❑ 64 Jason Williams	.60	.18
❑ 65 Kurt Thomas	.60	.18
❑ 66 Mike Miller	1.00	.30
❑ 67 Amare Stoudemire	2.50	.75
❑ 68 Jamaal Tinsley	1.00	.30
❑ 69 Brent Barry	.60	.18
❑ 70 Brad Miller	1.00	.30
❑ 71 Bonzi Wells	.60	.18
❑ 72 Andrei Kirilenko	1.00	.30
❑ 73 Kenny Thomas	.25	.07
❑ 74 Derek Anderson	.60	.18
❑ 75 Zydrunas Ilgauskas	.60	.18
❑ 76 Eddie Griffin	.60	.18
❑ 77 Tayshaun Prince	.60	.18
❑ 78 Michael Olowokandi	.25	.07
❑ 79 Michael Redd	1.00	.30
❑ 80 Tim Thomas	.60	.18
❑ 81 Eddie Jones	1.00	.30
❑ 82 Shareef Abdur-Rahim	1.00	.30
❑ 83 Corey Maggette	.60	.18
❑ 84 Eric Snow	.60	.18
❑ 85 Keon Clark	.60	.18
❑ 86 Desmond Mason	.60	.18
❑ 87 Drew Gooden	.60	.18
❑ 88 Matt Harpring	1.00	.30
❑ 89 Antonio McDyess	1.00	.30
❑ 90 Radoslav Nesterovic	.60	.18
❑ 91 Jamaal Magloire	.25	.07
❑ 92 Rasheed Wallace	1.00	.30
❑ 93 Antonio Davis	.25	.07
❑ 94 Kwame Brown	1.00	.30
❑ 95 Manu Ginobili	1.00	.30
❑ 96 Eric Williams	.25	.07
❑ 97 Nick Van Exel	1.00	.30
❑ 98 Lamar Odom	1.00	.30
❑ 99 Chauncey Billups	.60	.18
❑ 100 Kevin Garnett	2.00	.60
❑ 101 Marko Jaric	.60	.18
❑ 102 David Wesley	.25	.07
❑ 103 Gilbert Arenas	1.00	.30
❑ 104 Keith Van Horn	1.00	.30
❑ 105 Bostjan Nachbar	.25	.07
❑ 106 Michael Finley	1.00	.30
❑ 107 Troy Murphy	1.00	.30
❑ 108 Eddy Curry	.60	.18
❑ 109 Rashard Lewis	1.00	.30
❑ 110 Tony Battie	.25	.07
❑ 111 Lebron James RC	60.00	18.00
❑ 112A Darko Milicic RC	10.00	3.00
❑ 112B Darko Milicic	10.00	3.00
❑ 113 Carmelo Anthony RC	40.00	12.00
❑ 114 Chris Bosh RC	12.00	3.60
❑ 115 Dwyane Wade RC	15.00	4.50
❑ 116 Chris Kaman RC	5.00	1.50
❑ 117 Kirk Hinrich RC	10.00	3.00
❑ 118 T.J. Ford RC	8.00	2.40
❑ 119 Mike Sweetney RC	5.00	1.50
❑ 120 Jarvis Hayes RC	5.00	1.50
❑ 121A Mickael Pietrus RC	5.00	1.50
❑ 121B Mickael Pietrus	5.00	1.50
❑ 122 Nick Collison RC	5.00	1.50
❑ 123 Marcus Banks RC	5.00	1.50
❑ 124 Luke Ridnour RC	8.00	2.40
❑ 125 Reece Gaines RC	5.00	1.50
❑ 126 Troy Bell RC	5.00	1.50
❑ 127A Zarko Cabarkapa RC	5.00	1.50
❑ 127B Zarko Cabarkapa	5.00	1.50
❑ 128 David West RC	5.00	1.50
❑ 129A Aleksandar Pavlovic RC	5.00	1.50
❑ 129B Aleksandar Pavlovic	5.00	1.50
❑ 130 Dahntay Jones RC	5.00	1.50
❑ 131A Boris Diaw RC	5.00	1.50
❑ 131B Boris Diaw RC	5.00	1.50
❑ 132A Zoran Planinic RC	5.00	1.50
❑ 132B Zoran Planinic	5.00	1.50
❑ 133 Travis Outlaw RC	5.00	1.50
❑ 134 Brian Cook RC	5.00	1.50
❑ 135 Matt Carroll RC	5.00	1.50
❑ 136 Ndudi Ebi RC	5.00	1.50
❑ 137 Kendrick Perkins RC	5.00	1.50
❑ 138A Leandro Barbosa RC	5.00	1.50
❑ 138B Leandro Barbosa	5.00	1.50
❑ 139 Josh Howard RC	8.00	2.40
❑ 140A Maciej Lampe RC	5.00	1.50
❑ 140B Maciej Lampe	5.00	1.50
❑ 141 Jason Kapono RC	5.00	1.50
❑ 142 Luke Walton RC	8.00	2.40
❑ 143 Jerome Beasley RC	5.00	1.50
❑ 144 Travis Hansen RC	5.00	1.50
❑ 145 Steve Blake RC	5.00	1.50
❑ 146A Slavko Vranes RC	5.00	1.50
❑ 146B Slavko Vranes	5.00	1.50
❑ 147A Francisco Elson RC	5.00	1.50
❑ 147B Francisco Elson RC	5.00	1.50
❑ 148 Willie Green RC	5.00	1.50
❑ 149A Zaur Pachulia RC	5.00	1.50
❑ 149B Zaur Pachulia	5.00	1.50
❑ 150 Keith Bogans RC	5.00	1.50
❑ 151 Maurice Williams RC	5.00	1.50
❑ 152 James Jones RC	5.00	1.50
❑ 153 Kyle Korver RC	8.00	2.40
❑ 154A Jon Stefansson RC	5.00	1.50
❑ 154B Jon Stefansson	5.00	1.50
❑ 155 Brandon Hunter RC	5.00	1.50
❑ 156 Josh Moore RC	5.00	1.50
❑ 157 Torraye Braggs RC	5.00	1.50
❑ 158 Devin Brown RC	5.00	1.50
❑ 159 James Lang RC	5.00	1.50
❑ 160 Theron Smith RC	5.00	1.50
❑ 161 Linton Johnson RC	5.00	1.50
❑ 162 Marquis Daniels RC	12.00	3.60
❑ 163 Keith Mcleod RC	5.00	1.50
❑ 164 Udonis Haslem RC	5.00	1.50
❑ 165 Ben Handlogten RC	5.00	1.50

2003-04 Topps Contemporary Collection

	Nm-Mt	Ex-Mt
COMMON ROOKIE (1-20)	8.00	2.40
COMMON AU RC (21-30)	15.00	4.50
COMMON CARD (31-130)	.75	.23
COMMON AU (131-140)	15.00	4.50
❑ 1 LeBron James RC	60.00	18.00
❑ 2 Darko Milicic RC	12.00	3.60
❑ 3 Chris Bosh RC	15.00	4.50
❑ 4 Dwyane Wade RC	20.00	6.00
❑ 5 Chris Kaman RC	8.00	2.40
❑ 6 Kirk Hinrich RC	12.00	3.60
❑ 7 Jarvis Hayes RC	8.00	2.40
❑ 8 Mickael Pietrus RC	8.00	2.40
❑ 9 Luke Ridnour RC	10.00	3.00
❑ 10 David West RC	8.00	2.40
❑ 11 Aleksandar Pavlovic RC	8.00	2.40
❑ 12 Boris Diaw RC	8.00	2.40
❑ 13 Zoran Planinic RC	8.00	2.40
❑ 14 Francisco Elson RC	8.00	2.40
❑ 15 Leandro Barbosa RC	8.00	2.40
❑ 16 Josh Howard RC	10.00	3.00
❑ 17 Luke Walton RC	10.00	3.00
❑ 18 Willie Green RC	8.00	2.40
❑ 19 Maurice Williams RC	8.00	2.40
❑ 20 Udonis Haslem RC	8.00	2.40
❑ 21 Reece Gaines AU RC	15.00	4.50
❑ 22 Carmelo Anthony AU RC	150.00	45.00
❑ 23 Zarko Cabarkapa AU RC	15.00	4.50
❑ 24 Troy Bell AU RC	15.00	4.50
❑ 25 Travis Outlaw AU RC	15.00	4.50
❑ 26 Marcus Banks AU RC	15.00	4.50
❑ 27 Kendrick Perkins AU RC	15.00	4.50
❑ 28 Dahntay Jones AU RC	15.00	4.50
❑ 29 T.J. Ford AU RC	20.00	6.00
❑ 30 Mike Sweetney AU RC	15.00	4.50
❑ 31 Jason Terry	2.50	.75
❑ 32 Theo Ratliff	1.50	.45
❑ 33 Raef LaFrentz	1.50	.45
❑ 34 Eddy Curry	1.50	.45
❑ 35 Ricky Davis	2.50	.75
❑ 36 Zydrunas Ilgauskas	1.50	.45
❑ 37 Darius Miles	2.50	.75
❑ 38 Dirk Nowitzki	4.00	1.20
❑ 39 Steve Nash	2.50	.75
❑ 40 Antawn Jamison	2.50	.75
❑ 41 Antoine Walker	2.50	.75
❑ 42 Andre Miller	1.50	.45
❑ 43 Nene	1.50	.45
❑ 44 Richard Hamilton	1.50	.45
❑ 45 Ben Wallace	2.50	.75
❑ 46 Jason Richardson	2.50	.75
❑ 47 Nick Van Exel	2.50	.75
❑ 48 Troy Murphy	2.50	.75
❑ 49 Yao Ming	6.00	1.80
❑ 50 Steve Francis	2.50	.75
❑ 51 Ron Artest	1.50	.45
❑ 52 Jermaine O'Neal	2.50	.75
❑ 53 Al Harrington	1.50	.45
❑ 54 Marko Jaric	1.50	.45
❑ 55 Corey Maggette	1.50	.45
❑ 56 Kobe Bryant	10.00	3.00
❑ 57 Shaquille O'Neal	6.00	1.80
❑ 58 Devean George	1.50	.45
❑ 59 Gary Payton	2.50	.75
❑ 60 Pau Gasol	2.50	.75
❑ 61 Stromile Swift	1.50	.45
❑ 62 Mike Miller	2.50	.75
❑ 63 Lamar Odom	2.50	.75
❑ 64 Caron Butler	2.50	.75
❑ 65 Eddie Jones	2.50	.75
❑ 66 Brian Grant	1.50	.45
❑ 67 Desmond Mason	1.50	.45
❑ 68 Tim Thomas	1.50	.45
❑ 69 Michael Redd	1.50	.45
❑ 70 Sam Cassell	2.50	.75
❑ 71 Kevin Garnett	5.00	1.50
❑ 72 Latrell Sprewell	2.50	.75
❑ 73 Michael Olowokandi	.75	.23
❑ 74 Wally Szczerbiak	1.50	.45
❑ 75 Richard Jefferson	1.50	.45
❑ 76 Kenyon Martin	2.50	.75
❑ 77 Alonzo Mourning	1.50	.45
❑ 78 Baron Davis	2.50	.75
❑ 79 Jamal Mashburn	1.50	.45
❑ 80 Allan Houston	1.50	.45
❑ 81 Keith Van Horn	2.50	.75
❑ 82 Kurt Thomas	1.50	.45
❑ 83 Tracy McGrady	6.00	1.80
❑ 84 Juwan Howard	1.50	.45
❑ 85 Drew Gooden	1.50	.45
❑ 86 Allen Iverson	5.00	1.50
❑ 87 Glenn Robinson	2.50	.75
❑ 88 Derrick Coleman	.75	.23
❑ 89 Stephon Marbury	2.50	.75
❑ 90 Shawn Marion	2.50	.75
❑ 91 Amare Stoudemire	5.00	1.50
❑ 92 Zach Randolph	2.50	.75
❑ 93 Rasheed Wallace	2.50	.75
❑ 94 Bonzi Wells	1.50	.45
❑ 95 Mike Bibby	2.50	.75
❑ 96 Chris Webber	2.50	.75
❑ 97 Brad Miller	2.50	.75
❑ 98 Tim Duncan	5.00	1.50
❑ 99 Rasho Nesterovic	1.50	.45
❑ 100 Tony Parker	2.50	.75
❑ 101 Manu Ginobili	2.50	.75
❑ 102 Brent Barry	1.50	.45
❑ 103 Rashard Lewis	2.50	.75
❑ 104 Ray Allen	2.50	.75
❑ 105 Vince Carter	6.00	1.80
❑ 106 Jerome Williams	.75	.23
❑ 107 Carlos Arroyo	2.50	.75
❑ 108 Matt Harpring	2.50	.75
❑ 109 Andrei Kirilenko	2.50	.75
❑ 110 Gilbert Arenas	2.50	.75
❑ 111 Kwame Brown	1.50	.45

❑ 112 Jerry Stackhouse	2.50	.75
❑ 113 Darrell Armstrong	.75	.23
❑ 114 Alvin Williams	.75	.23
❑ 115 Kelvin Cato	.75	.23
❑ 116 Stephen Jackson	.75	.23
❑ 117 Shareef Abdur-Rahim	2.50	.75
❑ 118 Eric Williams	.75	.23
❑ 119 Tony Battie	.75	.23
❑ 120 Tyson Chandler	2.50	.75
❑ 121 Scottie Pippen	4.00	1.20
❑ 122 Nikoloz Tskitishvili	.75	.23
❑ 123 Chauncey Billups	1.50	.45
❑ 124 Quentin Richardson	1.50	.45
❑ 125 Dikembe Mutombo	1.50	.45
❑ 126 Joe Smith	1.50	.45
❑ 127 Qyntel Woods	.75	.23
❑ 128 Dajuan Wagner	1.50	.45
❑ 129 Robert Horry	1.50	.45
❑ 130 Cuttino Mobley	1.50	.45
❑ 131 Bobby Jackson AU	15.00	4.50
❑ 132 Elton Brand AU	15.00	4.50
❑ 133 Peja Stojakovic AU	20.00	6.00
❑ 134 Jamal Crawford AU	15.00	4.50
❑ 135 Jalen Rose AU	15.00	4.50
❑ 136 Paul Pierce AU	30.00	9.00
❑ 137 Jason Kidd AU	30.00	9.00
❑ 138 Tayshaun Prince AU	20.00	6.00
❑ 139 Morris Peterson AU	15.00	4.50
❑ 140 Speedy Claxton AU	15.00	4.50

1999-00 Topps Gallery

	Nm-Mt	Ex-Mt
COMPLETE SET (150)	60.00	18.00
COMMON CARD (1-124)	.25	.07
COMMON ROOKIE (125-150)	.50	.15
❑ 1 Gary Payton	.75	.23
❑ 2 Derek Anderson	.50	.15
❑ 3 Jalen Rose	.75	.23
❑ 4 Tim Hardaway	.50	.15
❑ 5 Jerry Stackhouse	.75	.23
❑ 6 Antonio McDyess	.50	.15
❑ 7 Paul Pierce	.75	.23
❑ 8 Reggie Miller	.75	.23
❑ 9 Maurice Taylor	.50	.15
❑ 10 Stephon Marbury	.75	.23
❑ 11 Terrell Brandon	.50	.15
❑ 12 Marcus Camby	.50	.15
❑ 13 Michael Doleac	.25	.07
❑ 14 Doug Christie	.50	.15
❑ 15 Brent Barry	.50	.15
❑ 16 John Stockton	.75	.23
❑ 17 Rod Strickland	.25	.07
❑ 18 Shareef Abdur-Rahim	.75	.23
❑ 19 Vin Baker	.50	.15
❑ 20 Jason Kidd	1.25	.35
❑ 21 Nick Anderson	.25	.07
❑ 22 Brian Grant	.50	.15
❑ 23 Chris Webber	.75	.23
❑ 24 Tariq Abdul-Wahad	.25	.07
❑ 25 Jason Williams	.75	.23
❑ 26 Joe Smith	.50	.15
❑ 27 Ray Allen	.75	.23
❑ 28 Glenn Robinson	.75	.23
❑ 29 Alonzo Mourning	.50	.15
❑ 30 Scottie Pippen	1.25	.35
❑ 31 Mookie Blaylock	.25	.07
❑ 32 Christian Laettner	.50	.15
❑ 33 Mark Jackson	.50	.15
❑ 34 Shawn Kemp	.50	.15
❑ 35 Anfernee Hardaway	.75	.23
❑ 36 Chris Mullin	.75	.23
❑ 37 Dennis Rodman	.50	.15
❑ 38 Lamond Murray	.25	.07
❑ 39 Jim Jackson	.25	.07
❑ 40 Shaquille O'Neal	2.00	.60
❑ 41 Randy Brown	.25	.07
❑ 42 Nick Van Exel	.75	.23
❑ 43 Robert Traylor	.25	.07
❑ 44 Vlade Divac	.50	.15
❑ 45 Karl Malone	.75	.23
❑ 46 Avery Johnson	.25	.07
❑ 47 Jayson Williams	.25	.07
❑ 48 Darrell Armstrong	.25	.07
❑ 49 Michael Olowokandi	.50	.15
❑ 50 Kevin Garnett	1.50	.45
❑ 51 Dirk Nowitzki	1.50	.45
❑ 52 Antawn Jamison	1.25	.35
❑ 53 Latrell Sprewell	.75	.23
❑ 54 Ruben Patterson	.50	.15
❑ 55 Vince Carter	2.00	.60
❑ 56 Michael Dickerson	.50	.15
❑ 57 Raef LaFrentz	.50	.15
❑ 58 Keith Van Horn	.75	.23
❑ 59 Tom Gugliotta	.25	.07
❑ 60 Allen Iverson	1.50	.45
❑ 61 Eric Snow	.50	.15
❑ 62 Kerry Kittles	.25	.07
❑ 63 Sam Cassell	.75	.23
❑ 64 Rik Smits	.50	.15
❑ 65 Isaiah Rider	.25	.07
❑ 66 Anthony Mason	.50	.15
❑ 67 Hersey Hawkins	.50	.15
❑ 68 Cuttino Mobley	.75	.23
❑ 69 Allan Houston	.50	.15
❑ 70 Kobe Bryant	3.00	.90
❑ 71 Damon Stoudamire	.50	.15
❑ 72 Charles Oakley	.25	.07
❑ 73 Mike Bibby	.75	.23
❑ 74 David Robinson	.75	.23
❑ 75 Eddie Jones	.75	.23
❑ 76 Juwan Howard	.50	.15
❑ 77 Antoine Walker	.75	.23
❑ 78 Michael Finley	.75	.23
❑ 79 Larry Hughes	.75	.23
❑ 80 Charles Barkley	1.00	.30
❑ 81 Tracy McGrady	2.00	.60
❑ 82 Dikembe Mutombo	.50	.15
❑ 83 Rasheed Wallace	.75	.23
❑ 84 Jeff Hornacek	.50	.15
❑ 85 Patrick Ewing	.75	.23
❑ 86 P.J. Brown	.25	.07
❑ 87 Brevin Knight	.25	.07
❑ 88 Elden Campbell	.25	.07
❑ 89 Kenny Anderson	.50	.15
❑ 90 Grant Hill	.75	.23
❑ 91 Mitch Richmond	.50	.15
❑ 92 Steve Smith	.50	.15
❑ 93 Jamal Mashburn	.50	.15
❑ 94 Toni Kukoc	.50	.15
❑ 95 Hakeem Olajuwon	.75	.23
❑ 96 Ron Mercer	.50	.15
❑ 97 John Starks	.50	.15
❑ 98 Glen Rice	.50	.15
❑ 99 Cedric Ceballos	.25	.07
❑ 100 Tim Duncan	1.50	.45
❑ 101 Karl Malone MAS	.75	.23
❑ 102 Alonzo Mourning MAS	.50	.15
❑ 103 Gary Payton MAS	.50	.15
❑ 104 Scottie Pippen MAS	.75	.23
❑ 105 Shaquille O'Neal MAS	1.00	.30
❑ 106 Charles Barkley MAS	.75	.23
❑ 107 Grant Hill MAS	.50	.15
❑ 108 John Stockton MAS	.75	.23
❑ 109 Jason Kidd MAS	.75	.23
❑ 110 Reggie Miller MAS	.50	.15
❑ 111 Shawn Kemp MAS	.25	.07
❑ 112 Patrick Ewing MAS	.50	.15
❑ 113 Kevin Garnett ART	.75	.23
❑ 114 Vince Carter ART	1.00	.30
❑ 115 Kobe Bryant ART	1.50	.45
❑ 116 Chris Webber ART	.50	.15
❑ 117 Tracy McGrady ART	1.00	.30
❑ 118 S.Abdur-Rahim ART	.50	.15
❑ 119 Paul Pierce ART	.75	.23
❑ 120 Jason Williams ART	.50	.15
❑ 121 Tim Duncan ART	.75	.23
❑ 122 Eddie Jones ART	.50	.15
❑ 123 Allen Iverson ART	.75	.23
❑ 124 Stephon Marbury ART	.50	.15
❑ 125 Elton Brand RC	3.00	.90
❑ 126 Lamar Odom RC	2.50	.75
❑ 127 Steve Francis RC	4.00	1.20
❑ 128 Adrian Griffin RC	.75	.23
❑ 129 Wally Szczerbiak RC	2.50	.75
❑ 130 Baron Davis RC	2.50	.75
❑ 131 Richard Hamilton RC	2.50	.75
❑ 132 Jonathan Bender RC	2.50	.75
❑ 133 Andre Miller RC	2.50	.75
❑ 134 Shawn Marion RC	3.00	.90
❑ 135 Jason Terry RC	2.00	.60
❑ 136 Trajan Langdon RC	1.00	.30
❑ 137 Corey Maggette RC	2.50	.75
❑ 138 William Avery RC	1.00	.30
❑ 139 Ron Artest RC	1.50	.45
❑ 140 Cal Bowdler RC	.75	.23
❑ 141 James Posey RC	1.50	.45
❑ 142 Quincy Lewis RC	.75	.23
❑ 143 Kenny Thomas RC	1.00	.30
❑ 144 Vonteego Cummings RC	1.00	.30
❑ 145 Todd MacCulloch RC	.75	.23
❑ 146 Anthony Carter RC	1.50	.45
❑ 147 Aleksandar Radojevic RC	.50	.15
❑ 148 Devean George RC	1.25	.35
❑ 149 Scott Padgett RC	.75	.23
❑ 150 Jumaine Jones RC	1.00	.30

2000-01 Topps Gallery

	Nm-Mt	Ex-Mt
COMP.SET w/o RC's (125)	40.00	12.00
COMMON CARD (1-125)	.20	.06
COMMON ROOKIE (126-150)	3.00	.90
❑ 1 Allen Iverson	1.25	.35
❑ 2 Terrell Brandon	.40	.12
❑ 3 Tracy McGrady	1.50	.45
❑ 4 Shawn Marion	.60	.18
❑ 5 Steve Smith	.40	.12
❑ 6 Avery Johnson	.20	.06
❑ 7 Gary Payton	.60	.18
❑ 8 Mark Jackson	.40	.12
❑ 9 Mike Bibby	.60	.18
❑ 10 Karl Malone	.60	.18
❑ 11 Kevin Garnett	1.25	.35
❑ 12 Tim Hardaway	.40	.12
❑ 13 Isaiah Rider	.20	.06
❑ 14 Corey Maggette	.40	.12
❑ 15 Vince Carter	1.50	.45
❑ 16 Vin Baker	.40	.12
❑ 17 Paul Pierce	.60	.18
❑ 18 Matt Harpring	.60	.18
❑ 19 Ron Artest	.40	.12
❑ 20 Kenny Anderson	.40	.12
❑ 21 Larry Hughes	.40	.12
❑ 22 Antonio McDyess	.40	.12
❑ 23 Shandon Anderson	.20	.06
❑ 24 Joe Smith	.40	.12
❑ 25 Jermaine O'Neal	.60	.18
❑ 26 Horace Grant	.40	.12
❑ 27 Ray Allen	.60	.18
❑ 28 Keith Van Horn	.60	.18
❑ 29 Darrell Armstrong	.20	.06
❑ 30 Shaquille O'Neal	1.50	.45

❑ 31 Reggie Miller .60 .18
❑ 32 Allan Houston .40 .12
❑ 33 Grant Hill .60 .18
❑ 34 David Robinson .60 .18
❑ 35 Clifford Robinson .20 .06
❑ 36 Theo Ratliff .40 .12
❑ 37 Rashard Lewis .40 .12
❑ 38 Peja Stojakovic .60 .18
❑ 39 Jason Kidd 1.00 .30
❑ 40 Latrell Sprewell .60 .18
❑ 41 Stephon Marbury .60 .18
❑ 42 Sam Cassell .60 .18
❑ 43 Brian Grant .40 .12
❑ 44 Jalen Rose .60 .18
❑ 45 Antawn Jamison .60 .18
❑ 46 Raef LaFrentz .40 .12
❑ 47 Dirk Nowitzki 1.00 .30
❑ 48 Lamond Murray .20 .06
❑ 49 Derrick Coleman .20 .06
❑ 50 Steve Francis .60 .18
❑ 51 Dikembe Mutombo .40 .12
❑ 52 Elton Brand .60 .18
❑ 53 Christian Laettner .40 .12
❑ 54 Ben Wallace .60 .18
❑ 55 Jim Jackson .20 .06
❑ 56 Cuttino Mobley .40 .12
❑ 57 Jonathan Bender .40 .12
❑ 58 Anthony Mason .20 .06
❑ 59 Tim Thomas .40 .12
❑ 60 Lamar Odom .60 .18
❑ 61 Glenn Robinson .60 .18
❑ 62 Kendall Gill .20 .06
❑ 63 Glen Rice .40 .12
❑ 64 Anfernee Hardaway .60 .18
❑ 65 Jason Williams .40 .12
❑ 66 Shawn Kemp .40 .12
❑ 67 Derek Anderson .40 .12
❑ 68 Patrick Ewing .60 .18
❑ 69 Shareef Abdur-Rahim .60 .18
❑ 70 Tim Duncan 1.25 .35
❑ 71 Rod Strickland .20 .06
❑ 72 Bryon Russell .20 .06
❑ 73 Antonio Davis .20 .06
❑ 74 Rasheed Wallace .60 .18
❑ 75 Wally Szczerbiak .40 .12
❑ 76 Eric Snow .40 .12
❑ 77 Toni Kukoc .40 .12
❑ 78 Michael Olowokandi .20 .06
❑ 79 Hakeem Olajuwon .60 .18
❑ 80 Kobe Bryant 2.50 .75
❑ 81 Mookie Blaylock .20 .06
❑ 82 Michael Finley .60 .18
❑ 83 Jerry Stackhouse .60 .18
❑ 84 Baron Davis .60 .18
❑ 85 Jason Terry .60 .18
❑ 86 Andre Miller .40 .12
❑ 87 Antoine Walker .60 .18
❑ 88 Jamal Mashburn .40 .12
❑ 89 Nick Van Exel .60 .18
❑ 90 Eddie Jones .60 .18
❑ 91 Marcus Camby .40 .12
❑ 92 Scottie Pippen 1.00 .30
❑ 93 John Stockton .60 .18
❑ 94 Richard Hamilton .40 .12
❑ 95 John Starks .40 .12
❑ 96 Juwan Howard .40 .12
❑ 97 Michael Dickerson .40 .12
❑ 98 Ron Mercer .40 .12
❑ 99 Chris Webber .60 .18
❑ 100 Magic Johnson 3.00 .90
❑ 101 Shaquille O'Neal MAS 1.50 .45
❑ 102 Tim Duncan MAS 1.25 .35
❑ 103 Chris Webber MAS .40 .12
❑ 104 Grant Hill MAS .60 .18
❑ 105 Kevin Garnett MAS 1.25 .35
❑ 106 Vince Carter MAS 1.50 .45
❑ 107 Gary Payton MAS .60 .18
❑ 108 Jason Kidd MAS 1.00 .30
❑ 109 Kobe Bryant MAS 2.50 .75
❑ 110 Karl Malone MAS .60 .18
❑ 111 Scottie Pippen MAS 1.00 .30
❑ 112 Reggie Miller MAS .60 .18
❑ 113 John Stockton MAS .60 .18
❑ 114 Elton Brand ART .60 .18
❑ 115 Tracy McGrady ART 1.50 .45
❑ 116 Steve Francis ART .60 .18
❑ 117 Lamar Odom ART .60 .18
❑ 118 Baron Davis ART .60 .18
❑ 119 Andre Miller ART .40 .12
❑ 120 Jonathan Bender ART .40 .12
❑ 121 Paul Pierce ART .60 .18
❑ 122 Jason Williams ART .40 .12
❑ 123 Rashard Lewis ART .40 .12
❑ 124 Larry Hughes ART .40 .12
❑ 125 Shawn Marion ART .60 .18
❑ 126 Kenyon Martin RC 10.00 3.00
❑ 127 Stromile Swift RC 5.00 1.50
❑ 128 Darius Miles RC 8.00 2.40
❑ 129 Marcus Fizer RC 3.00 .90
❑ 130 Mike Miller RC 8.00 2.40
❑ 131 DerMarr Johnson RC 3.00 .90
❑ 132 Chris Mihm RC 3.00 .90
❑ 133 Jamal Crawford RC 4.00 1.20
❑ 134 Joel Przybilla RC 3.00 .90
❑ 135 Keyon Dooling RC 4.00 1.20
❑ 136 Jerome Moiso RC 3.00 .90
❑ 137 Etan Thomas RC 3.00 .90
❑ 138 Courtney Alexander RC 3.00 .90
❑ 139 Mateen Cleaves RC 3.00 .90
❑ 140 Jason Collier RC 3.00 .90
❑ 141 Hidayet Turkoglu RC 6.00 1.80
❑ 142 Desmond Mason RC 3.00 .90
❑ 143 Quentin Richardson RC 6.00 1.80
❑ 144 Jamaal Magloire RC 3.00 .90
❑ 145 Speedy Claxton RC 3.00 .90
❑ 146 Morris Peterson RC 5.00 1.50
❑ 147 Donnell Harvey RC 3.00 .90
❑ 148 DeShawn Stevenson RC 3.00 .90
❑ 149 Stephen Jackson RC 5.00 1.50
❑ 150 Marc Jackson RC 3.00 .90

1999-00 Topps Gold Label Class 1

	Nm-Mt	Ex-Mt
COMPLETE SET (100)	60.00	18.00
COMMON CARD (1-85)	.30	.09
COMMON ROOKIE (86-100)	.60	.18

❑ 1 Tim Duncan 2.00 .60
❑ 2 Steve Smith .60 .18
❑ 3 Jeff Hornacek .60 .18
❑ 4 Kevin Garnett 2.00 .60
❑ 5 Paul Pierce 1.00 .30
❑ 6 Doug Christie .60 .18
❑ 7 Charles Barkley 1.25 .35
❑ 8 Nick Van Exel 1.00 .30
❑ 9 Shareef Abdur-Rahim 1.00 .30
❑ 10 Rod Strickland .30 .09
❑ 11 Keith Van Horn 1.00 .30
❑ 12 Matt Harpring 1.00 .30
❑ 13 Randy Brown .30 .09
❑ 14 Vin Baker .60 .18
❑ 15 Mark Jackson .60 .18
❑ 16 Latrell Sprewell 1.00 .30
❑ 17 Anthony Mason .60 .18
❑ 18 Brian Grant .60 .18
❑ 19 Brevin Knight .30 .09
❑ 20 Elden Campbell .30 .09
❑ 21 Allen Iverson 2.00 .60
❑ 22 Kobe Bryant 4.00 1.20
❑ 23 Antawn Jamison 1.50 .45
❑ 24 Lindsey Hunter .30 .09
❑ 25 Eddie Jones 1.00 .30
❑ 26 Michael Finley 1.00 .30
❑ 27 Juwan Howard .60 .18
❑ 28 Antonio McDyess .60 .18
❑ 29 David Robinson 1.00 .30
❑ 30 Karl Malone 1.00 .30
❑ 31 Jason Kidd 1.50 .45
❑ 32 Zydrunas Ilgauskas .60 .18
❑ 33 Vince Carter 2.50 .75
❑ 34 Maurice Taylor .60 .18
❑ 35 Alonzo Mourning .60 .18
❑ 36 Tim Thomas .60 .18
❑ 37 Dikembe Mutombo .60 .18
❑ 38 Grant Hill 1.00 .30
❑ 39 Jason Williams 1.00 .30
❑ 40 Scottie Pippen 1.50 .45
❑ 41 Stephon Marbury 1.00 .30
❑ 42 Reggie Miller 1.00 .30
❑ 43 Tyrone Nesby RC .30 .09
❑ 44 Ron Mercer .60 .18
❑ 45 Terrell Brandon .60 .18
❑ 46 Darrell Armstrong .30 .09
❑ 47 Larry Hughes 1.00 .30
❑ 48 Alan Henderson .30 .09
❑ 49 Ray Allen 1.00 .30
❑ 50 Rasheed Wallace 1.00 .30
❑ 51 Toni Kukoc .60 .18
❑ 52 Patrick Ewing 1.00 .30
❑ 53 Tom Gugliotta .30 .09
❑ 54 Chris Mills .30 .09
❑ 55 Gary Payton 1.00 .30
❑ 56 Michael Olowokandi .60 .18
❑ 57 Chris Mullin 1.00 .30
❑ 58 Shawn Kemp .60 .18
❑ 59 Joe Smith .60 .18
❑ 60 Steve Nash 1.00 .30
❑ 61 Gary Trent .30 .09
❑ 62 Shaquille O'Neal 2.50 .75
❑ 63 Kerry Kittles .30 .09
❑ 64 Tim Hardaway .60 .18
❑ 65 Glenn Robinson 1.00 .30
❑ 66 Damon Stoudamire .60 .18
❑ 67 Anfernee Hardaway 1.00 .30
❑ 68 Vlade Divac .60 .18
❑ 69 John Starks .60 .18
❑ 70 Allan Houston .60 .18
❑ 71 Jerry Stackhouse 1.00 .30
❑ 72 Avery Johnson .30 .09
❑ 73 Glen Rice .60 .18
❑ 74 Felipe Lopez .30 .09
❑ 75 Clifford Robinson .30 .09
❑ 76 Jamal Mashburn .60 .18
❑ 77 Hakeem Olajuwon 1.00 .30
❑ 78 Matt Geiger .30 .09
❑ 79 John Stockton 1.00 .30
❑ 80 Chauncey Billups .60 .18
❑ 81 Chris Webber 1.00 .30
❑ 82 Antoine Walker 1.00 .30
❑ 83 Mike Bibby 1.00 .30
❑ 84 Tracy McGrady 2.50 .75
❑ 85 Mitch Richmond .60 .18
❑ 86 Elton Brand RC 4.00 1.20
❑ 87 Steve Francis RC 5.00 1.50
❑ 88 Baron Davis RC 3.00 .90
❑ 89 Lamar Odom RC 3.00 .90
❑ 90 Jonathan Bender RC 3.00 .90
❑ 91 Wally Szczerbiak RC 3.00 .90
❑ 92 Richard Hamilton RC 3.00 .90
❑ 93 Andre Miller RC 3.00 .90
❑ 94 Shawn Marion RC 4.00 1.20
❑ 95 Jason Terry RC 2.50 .75

❑ 96 Trajan Langdon RC	1.25	.35
❑ 97 Aleksandar Radojevic RC	.60	.18
❑ 98 Corey Maggette RC	3.00	.90
❑ 99 William Avery RC	1.25	.35
❑ 100 Cal Bowdler RC	1.00	.30

2000-01 Topps Gold Label Class 1

	Nm-Mt	Ex-Mt
COMPLETE SET w/o RC (80)	30.00	9.00
COMMON CARD (1-80)	.30	.09
COMMON ROOKIE (81-100)	4.00	1.20
❑ 1 Steve Francis	1.00	.30
❑ 2 Jalen Rose	1.00	.30
❑ 3 Allen Iverson	2.00	.60
❑ 4 Damon Stoudamire	.60	.18
❑ 5 David Robinson	1.00	.30
❑ 6 Bryon Russell	.30	.09
❑ 7 Toni Kukoc	.60	.18
❑ 8 Tracy McGrady	2.50	.75
❑ 9 John Stockton	1.00	.30
❑ 10 Tim Duncan	2.00	.60
❑ 11 Hakeem Olajuwon	1.00	.30
❑ 12 Antoine Walker	1.00	.30
❑ 13 Dikembe Mutombo	.60	.18
❑ 14 Shawn Kemp	.60	.18
❑ 15 Ron Artest	.60	.18
❑ 16 Eddie Jones	1.00	.30
❑ 17 Dirk Nowitzki	1.50	.45
❑ 18 Nick Van Exel	1.00	.30
❑ 19 Grant Hill	1.00	.30
❑ 20 Antawn Jamison	1.00	.30
❑ 21 Cuttino Mobley	.60	.18
❑ 22 Jonathan Bender	.60	.18
❑ 23 Maurice Taylor	.30	.09
❑ 24 Kobe Bryant	4.00	1.20
❑ 25 Tim Hardaway	.60	.18
❑ 26 Tim Thomas	.60	.18
❑ 27 Terrell Brandon	.60	.18
❑ 28 Marcus Camby	.60	.18
❑ 29 Keith Van Horn	1.00	.30
❑ 30 Shawn Marion	1.00	.30
❑ 31 Rasheed Wallace	1.00	.30
❑ 32 Corey Maggette	.60	.18
❑ 33 Jason Kidd	1.50	.45
❑ 34 Shaquille O'Neal	2.50	.75
❑ 35 Rashard Lewis	.60	.18
❑ 36 Karl Malone	1.00	.30
❑ 37 Michael Dickerson	.60	.18
❑ 38 Richard Hamilton	.60	.18
❑ 39 Darrell Armstrong	.30	.09
❑ 40 Wally Szczerbiak	.60	.18
❑ 41 Glen Rice	.60	.18
❑ 42 Glenn Robinson	1.00	.30
❑ 43 Reggie Miller	1.00	.30
❑ 44 Alonzo Mourning	.60	.18
❑ 45 Larry Hughes	.60	.18
❑ 46 Antonio McDyess	.60	.18
❑ 47 Derrick Coleman	.30	.09
❑ 48 Brevin Knight	.30	.09
❑ 49 Jason Terry	1.00	.30
❑ 50 Elton Brand	1.00	.30
❑ 51 Latrell Sprewell	1.00	.30
❑ 52 Theo Ratliff	.60	.18
❑ 53 Scottie Pippen	1.50	.45
❑ 54 Jason Williams	.60	.18
❑ 55 Gary Payton	1.00	.30
❑ 56 Mitch Richmond	.60	.18
❑ 57 Vin Baker	.60	.18
❑ 58 Raef LaFrentz	.60	.18
❑ 59 Anfernee Hardaway	1.00	.30
❑ 60 Steve Smith	.60	.18
❑ 61 Stephon Marbury	1.00	.30
❑ 62 Vlade Divac	.60	.18
❑ 63 Jamal Mashburn	.60	.18
❑ 64 Jerome Williams	.30	.09
❑ 65 Patrick Ewing	1.00	.30
❑ 66 Lamar Odom	1.00	.30
❑ 67 Jerry Stackhouse	1.00	.30
❑ 68 Michael Finley	1.00	.30
❑ 69 Vince Carter	2.50	.75
❑ 70 Andre Miller	.60	.18
❑ 71 Paul Pierce	1.00	.30
❑ 72 Baron Davis	1.00	.30
❑ 73 Derek Anderson	.60	.18
❑ 74 Chris Webber	1.00	.30
❑ 75 Ray Allen	1.00	.30
❑ 76 Kevin Garnett	2.00	.60
❑ 77 Allan Houston	.60	.18
❑ 78 Mike Bibby	1.00	.30
❑ 79 Shareef Abdur-Rahim	1.00	.30
❑ 80 Juwan Howard	.60	.18
❑ 81 Kenyon Martin RC	12.00	3.60
❑ 82 Stromile Swift RC	6.00	1.80
❑ 83 Darius Miles RC	10.00	3.00
❑ 84 Marcus Fizer RC	4.00	1.20
❑ 85 Mike Miller RC	10.00	3.00
❑ 86 DerMarr Johnson RC	4.00	1.20
❑ 87 Chris Mihm RC	4.00	1.20
❑ 88 Jamal Crawford RC	5.00	1.50
❑ 89 Joel Przybilla RC	4.00	1.20
❑ 90 Keyon Dooling RC	4.00	1.20
❑ 91 Jerome Moiso RC	4.00	1.20
❑ 92 Etan Thomas RC	4.00	1.20
❑ 93 Courtney Alexander RC	4.00	1.20
❑ 94 Mateen Cleaves RC	4.00	1.20
❑ 95 Jason Collier RC	4.00	1.20
❑ 96 Desmond Mason RC	4.00	1.20
❑ 97 Quentin Richardson RC	10.00	3.00
❑ 98 Jamaal Magloire RC	4.00	1.20
❑ 99 Speedy Claxton RC	4.00	1.20
❑ 100 Morris Peterson RC	6.00	1.80

2003-04 Topps Collection

	MINT	NRMT
COMP.FACT.SET (265)	65.00	29.00
COL.SINGLES: .4X TO 1X BASE TOPPS HI	-	
COMMON ROOKIE (250-265)	1.50	.70
❑ 250 Maciej Lampe RC	-	
❑ 251 Luke Walton RC	2.50	1.10
❑ 252 Maurice Williams RC	1.50	.70
❑ 253 Jason Kapono RC	1.50	.70
❑ 254 Travis Hansen RC	1.50	.70
❑ 255 Zaur Pachulia RC	1.50	.70
❑ 256 Willie Green RC	1.50	.70
❑ 257 James Jones RC	1.50	.70
❑ 258 Slavko Vranes RC	1.50	.70
❑ 259 Keith Bogans RC	1.50	.70
❑ 260 Steve Blake RC	1.50	.70
❑ 261 Carl English RC	1.50	.70
❑ 262 James Lang RC	1.50	.70
❑ 263 Brandon Hunter RC	1.50	.70
❑ 264 Kyle Korver RC	2.00	.90
❑ 265 Devin Brown RC	1.50	.70

2000-01 Topps Heritage

	Nm-Mt	Ex-Mt
COMPLETE SET w/o RC (197)	60.00	18.00
COMMON CARD (1-233)	.30	.09
COMMON ROOKIE (25-60)	5.00	1.50
❑ 1 Jason Kidd	1.50	.45
❑ 2 Allen Iverson	2.00	.60
❑ 3 Tracy McGrady	2.50	.75
❑ 4 Tim Duncan	2.00	.60
❑ 5 Michael Finley	1.00	.30
❑ 6 Jason Williams	.60	.18
❑ 7 Kobe Bryant	4.00	1.20
❑ 8 Gary Payton	1.00	.30
❑ 9 Latrell Sprewell	1.00	.30
❑ 10 Antonio McDyess	.60	.18
❑ 11 Antoine Walker	1.00	.30
❑ 12 Steve Francis	1.00	.30
❑ 13 Elton Brand	1.00	.30
❑ 14 Larry Hughes	.60	.18
❑ 15 Shaquille O'Neal	2.50	.75
❑ 16 Lamar Odom	1.00	.30
❑ 17 Kevin Garnett	2.00	.60
❑ 18 Vince Carter	2.50	.75
❑ 19 Ray Allen	1.00	.30
❑ 20 Grant Hill	1.00	.30
❑ 21 Chris Webber	1.00	.30
❑ 22 Paul Pierce	1.00	.30
❑ 23 Shareef Abdur-Rahim	1.00	.30
❑ 24 Eddie Jones	1.00	.30
❑ 25 Kenyon Martin RC	20.00	6.00
❑ 26 Stromile Swift RC	10.00	3.00
❑ 27 Darius Miles RC	12.00	3.60
❑ 28 Marcus Fizer RC	5.00	1.50
❑ 29 Mike Miller RC	15.00	4.50
❑ 30 DerMarr Johnson RC	5.00	1.50
❑ 31 Chris Mihm RC	5.00	1.50
❑ 32 Jamal Crawford RC	6.00	1.80
❑ 33 Joel Przybilla RC	5.00	1.50
❑ 34 Keyon Dooling RC	5.00	1.50
❑ 35 Jerome Moiso RC	5.00	1.50
❑ 36 Etan Thomas RC	5.00	1.50
❑ 37 Courtney Alexander RC	8.00	2.40
❑ 38 Mateen Cleaves RC	5.00	1.50
❑ 39 Jason Collier RC	5.00	1.50
❑ 40 Hidayet Turkoglu RC	12.00	3.60
❑ 41 Desmond Mason RC	5.00	1.50
❑ 42 Quentin Richardson RC	12.00	3.60
❑ 43 Jamaal Magloire RC	5.00	1.50
❑ 44 Speedy Claxton RC	5.00	1.50
❑ 45 Morris Peterson RC	10.00	3.00
❑ 46 Donnell Harvey RC	5.00	1.50
❑ 47 DeShawn Stevenson RC	5.00	1.50
❑ 48 Dalibor Bagaric RC	5.00	1.50
❑ 49 Iakovos Tsakalidis RC	5.00	1.50
❑ 50 Mamadou N'Diaye RC	5.00	1.50
❑ 51 Erick Barkley RC	5.00	1.50
❑ 52 Mark Madsen RC	5.00	1.50
❑ 53 Dan Langhi RC	5.00	1.50
❑ 54 A.J. Guyton RC	5.00	1.50
❑ 55 Jake Voskuhl RC	5.00	1.50
❑ 56 Khalid El-Amin RC	5.00	1.50
❑ 57 Lavor Postell RC	5.00	1.50
❑ 58 Eduardo Najera RC	8.00	2.40
❑ 59 Michael Redd RC	12.00	3.60
❑ 60 Stephen Jackson RC	10.00	3.00

❑ 61 Andrew DeClercq .30 .09
❑ 62 Darrell Armstrong .30 .09
❑ 63 Al Harrington .60 .18
❑ 64 Johnny Newman .30 .09
❑ 65 Baron Davis 1.00 .30
❑ 66 Adrian Griffin .30 .09
❑ 67 Anthony Mason .60 .18
❑ 68 Ron Harper .60 .18
❑ 69 Michael Olowokandi .30 .09
❑ 70 Maurice Taylor .30 .09
❑ 71 Travis Best .30 .09
❑ 72 Chucky Atkins .30 .09
❑ 73 Bob Sura .30 .09
❑ 74 Jason Terry 1.00 .30
❑ 75 Ervin Johnson .30 .09
❑ 76 Eric Snow .60 .18
❑ 77 Shawn Bradley .30 .09
❑ 78 Christian Laettner .60 .18
❑ 79 Keith Van Horn 1.00 .30
❑ 80 Damon Stoudamire .60 .18
❑ 81 Peja Stojakovic 1.00 .30
❑ 82 Clifford Robinson .30 .09
❑ 83 Elden Campbell .30 .09
❑ 84 Kenny Anderson .60 .18
❑ 85 Patrick Ewing 1.00 .30
❑ 86 Mookie Blaylock .30 .09
❑ 87 Brian Skinner .30 .09
❑ 88 Rick Fox .60 .18
❑ 89 Tim Hardaway .60 .18
❑ 90 Brian Grant .60 .18
❑ 91 Joe Smith .60 .18
❑ 92 Kerry Kittles .30 .09
❑ 93 Scottie Pippen 1.50 .45
❑ 94 Steve Smith .60 .18
❑ 95 Sean Elliott .60 .18
❑ 96 Rashard Lewis .60 .18
❑ 97 Michael Dickerson .60 .18
❑ 98 Rod Strickland .30 .09
❑ 99 Sam Cassell 1.00 .30
❑ 100 Kareem Abdul-Jabbar 3.00 .90
❑ 101 John Amaechi .30 .09
❑ 102 Kendall Gill .30 .09
❑ 103 Terrell Brandon .60 .18
❑ 104 Dan Majerle .60 .18
❑ 105 Mark Jackson .30 .09
❑ 106 Hakeem Olajuwon 1.00 .30
❑ 107 Antawn Jamison 1.00 .30
❑ 108 Cedric Ceballos .30 .09
❑ 109 Shandon Anderson .30 .09
❑ 110 Gary Trent .30 .09
❑ 111 Wesley Person .30 .09
❑ 112 James Posey .60 .18
❑ 113 David Wesley .30 .09
❑ 114 Vitaly Potapenko .30 .09
❑ 115 P.J. Brown .30 .09
❑ 116 Alan Henderson .30 .09
❑ 117 Terry Porter .30 .09
❑ 118 Lindsey Hunter .30 .09
❑ 119 Chauncey Billups .60 .18
❑ 120 Doug Christie .60 .18
❑ 121 Glen Rice .60 .18
❑ 122 Jamie Feick .30 .09
❑ 123 Tom Gugliotta .30 .09
❑ 124 Arvydas Sabonis .60 .18
❑ 125 Toni Kukoc .60 .18
❑ 126 Shawn Marion 1.00 .30
❑ 127 Dale Davis .30 .09
❑ 128 Corliss Williamson .60 .18
❑ 129 Brent Barry .60 .18
❑ 130 Shammond Williams .30 .09
❑ 131 Nick Anderson .30 .09
❑ 132 Charles Oakley .30 .09
❑ 133 Shaquille O'Neal CHAMP 1.25 .35
❑ 134 Ron Harper CHAMP .30 .09
❑ 135 Kobe Bryant CHAMP 2.00 .60
❑ 136 Shaquille O'Neal CHAMP 1.25 .35
❑ 137 L.A. Lakers CHAMP 1.00 .30
❑ 138 Vince Carter 1.25 .35
Allen Iverson
Jerry Stackhouse
❑ 139 Allen Iverson 1.00 .30
Grant Hill
Vince Carter
❑ 140 Dikembe Mutombo 1.00 .30
Alonzo Mourning
Dale Davis
❑ 141 Reggie Miller 1.00 .30
Darrell Armstrong
Ray Allen
❑ 142 Dikembe Mutombo 1.00 .30
Elton Brand
Jerome Williams
❑ 143 Sam Cassell 1.00 .30
Mark Jackson
Eric Snow
❑ 144 Checklist .30 .09
❑ 145 Checklist .30 .09
❑ 146 Shaquille O'Neal 2.00 .60
Karl Malone
Gary Payton
❑ 147 Shaquille O'Neal 1.50 .45
Karl Malone
Chris Webber
❑ 148 Shaquille O'Neal 1.50 .45
Ruben Patterson
Rasheed Wallace
❑ 149 Jeff Hornacek .30 .09
Terrell Brandon
Peja Stojakovic
❑ 150 Shaquille O'Neal 1.50 .45
Kevin Garnett
Tim Duncan
❑ 151 Gary Payton 1.00 .30
Nick Van Exel
John Stockton
❑ 152 Chris Whitney .30 .09
❑ 153 Isaac Austin .30 .09
❑ 154 Kevin Willis .30 .09
❑ 155 Vin Baker .60 .18
❑ 156 Avery Johnson .30 .09
❑ 157 Rodney Rogers .30 .09
❑ 158 Allan Houston .60 .18
❑ 159 Austin Croshere .60 .18
❑ 160 George Lynch .30 .09
❑ 161 Howard Eisley .30 .09
❑ 162 Jerome Williams .30 .09
❑ 163 LaPhonso Ellis .30 .09
❑ 164 Ron Mercer .60 .18
❑ 165 Andre Miller .60 .18
❑ 166 Tariq Abdul-Wahad .30 .09
❑ 167 Donyell Marshall .60 .18
❑ 168 Quincy Lewis .30 .09
❑ 169 Mitch Richmond .60 .18
❑ 170 Richard Hamilton .60 .18
❑ 171 Bryant Reeves .30 .09
❑ 172 Jim Jackson .30 .09
❑ 173 David Robinson 1.00 .30
❑ 174 Derrick Coleman .30 .09
❑ 175 Anthony Peeler .30 .09
❑ 176 Theo Ratliff .60 .18
❑ 177 Roshown McLeod .30 .09
❑ 178 Ron Artest .60 .18
❑ 179 Bryon Russell .30 .09
❑ 180 Othella Harrington .30 .09
❑ 181 Juwan Howard .60 .18
❑ 182 Antonio Davis .30 .09
❑ 183 Ruben Patterson .60 .18
❑ 184 Shawn Kemp .60 .18
❑ 185 Larry Johnson .60 .18
❑ 186 Marcus Camby .60 .18
❑ 187 Eric Piatkowski .60 .18
❑ 188 Reggie Miller 1.00 .30
❑ 189 Anfernee Hardaway 1.00 .30
❑ 190 Kelvin Cato .30 .09
❑ 191 Erick Dampier .60 .18
❑ 192 Keon Clark .60 .18
❑ 193 Dirk Nowitzki 1.50 .45
❑ 194 Robert Traylor .30 .09
❑ 195 Lamond Murray .30 .09
❑ 196 John Wallace .30 .09
❑ 197 Robert Horry .60 .18
❑ 198 Robert Pack .30 .09
❑ 199 Jamal Mashburn .60 .18
❑ 200 Corey Benjamin .30 .09
❑ 201 Matt Harpring 1.00 .30
❑ 202 Nick Van Exel 1.00 .30
❑ 203 Vonteego Cummings .30 .09
❑ 204 Ben Wallace 1.00 .30
❑ 205 Karl Malone 1.00 .30
❑ 206 Jonathan Bender .60 .18
❑ 207 Cuttino Mobley .60 .18
❑ 208 Isaiah Rider .60 .18
❑ 209 Tyrone Nesby .30 .09
❑ 210 Jermaine O'Neal 1.00 .30
❑ 211 Corey Maggette .60 .18
❑ 212 Anthony Carter .60 .18
❑ 213 Horace Grant .60 .18
❑ 214 Tim Thomas .60 .18
❑ 215 Wally Szczerbiak .60 .18
❑ 216 Stephon Marbury 1.00 .30
❑ 217 Charlie Ward .30 .09
❑ 218 Bo Outlaw .30 .09
❑ 219 Matt Geiger .30 .09
❑ 220 Vlade Divac .60 .18
❑ 221 Rasheed Wallace 1.00 .30
❑ 222 Derek Anderson .60 .18
❑ 223 John Stockton 1.00 .30
❑ 224 Dikembe Mutombo .60 .18
❑ 225 John Starks .60 .18
❑ 226 Mike Bibby .60 .18
❑ 227 Jahidi White .30 .09
❑ 228 Jalen Rose 1.00 .30
❑ 229 Glenn Robinson 1.00 .30
❑ 230 Brevin Knight .30 .09
❑ 231 Jerry Stackhouse 1.00 .30
❑ 232 Raef LaFrentz .60 .18
❑ 233 Brad Miller 1.00 .30

2001-02 Topps Heritage

	Nm-Mt	Ex-Mt
COMPLETE SET (264)	300.00	90.00
COMMON CARD (1-264)	.30	.09
COMMON ROOKIE	2.50	.75

❑ 1 Shaquille O'Neal 2.50 .75
❑ 2 Jalen Rose 1.00 .30
❑ 3 Kwame Brown RC 6.00 1.80
❑ 4 Bryon Russell .30 .09
❑ 5 Hakeem Olajuwon .60 .18
❑ 6 Shammond Williams .30 .09
❑ 7 Aaron Mckie .60 .18
❑ 8 Anfernee Hardaway 1.00 .30
❑ 9 Dale Davis .60 .18
❑ 10 Tracy McGrady 2.50 .75
❑ 11 Speedy Claxton .60 .18
❑ 12 Kurt Thomas .60 .18
❑ 13 Keith Van Horn 1.00 .30
❑ 14 Tyson Chandler RC 8.00 2.40
❑ 15 Andre Miller .60 .18
❑ 16 Dirk Nowitzki 1.50 .45
❑ 17 Raef Lafrentz .60 .18
❑ 18 Mateen Cleaves .60 .18
❑ 19 Danny Fortson .30 .09
❑ 20 Steve Francis 1.00 .30
❑ 21 Al Harrington .60 .18
❑ 22 Keyon Dooling .60 .18
❑ 23 Rick Fox .60 .18
❑ 24 Michael Dickerson .60 .18
❑ 25 Alonzo Mourning .60 .18
❑ 26 Glenn Robinson 1.00 .30
❑ 27 Wally Szczerbiak .60 .18
❑ 28 Todd MacCulloch .30 .09
❑ 29 Shandon Anderson .30 .09
❑ 30 Kobe Bryant 4.00 1.20
❑ 31 Tyrone Hill .30 .09
❑ 32 Grant Hill 1.00 .30
❑ 33 Shawn Marion 1.00 .30
❑ 34 Derek Anderson .60 .18
❑ 35 Hidayet Turkoglu .60 .18
❑ 36 David Robinson 1.00 .30
❑ 37 Gary Payton 1.00 .30

❑ 38 Alvin Williams .30 .09
❑ 39 Pau Gasol RC 8.00 2.40
❑ 40 Tim Duncan 2.00 .60
❑ 41 Rashard Lewis .60 .18
❑ 42 Antonio Davis .30 .09
❑ 43 Donyell Marshall .60 .18
❑ 44 Jahidi White .30 .09
❑ 45 Shareef Abdur-Rahim 1.00 .30
❑ 46 Antoine Walker 1.00 .30
❑ 47 P.J. Brown .30 .09
❑ 48 Eddie Robinson .60 .18
❑ 49 Chris Mihm .60 .18
❑ 50 Kevin Garnett 2.00 .60
❑ 51 Marcus Camby .60 .18
❑ 52 Mike Miller 1.00 .30
❑ 53 Tony Delk .30 .09
❑ 54 Mike Bibby 1.00 .30
❑ 55 Dikembe Mutombo .60 .18
❑ 56 Eddy Curry RC 8.00 2.40
❑ 57 Shawn Bradley .30 .09
❑ 58 James Posey .60 .18
❑ 59 Jason Richardson RC 10.00 3.00
❑ 60 Jason Kidd 1.50 .45
❑ 61 Eddie Griffin RC 4.00 1.20
❑ 62 Larry Hughes .60 .18
❑ 63 Ben Wallace 1.00 .30
❑ 64 Antonio McDyess .60 .18
❑ 65 Tim Hardaway .60 .18
❑ 66 Shawn Kemp .60 .18
❑ 67 Bobby Jackson .60 .18
❑ 68 Tom Gugliotta .30 .09
❑ 69 Antawn Jamison 1.00 .30
❑ 70 Lamar Odom 1.00 .30
❑ 71 Jamaal Tinsley RC 4.00 1.20
❑ 72 Moochie Norris .30 .09
❑ 73 Marc Jackson .60 .18
❑ 74 Andrei Kirilenko RC 8.00 2.40
❑ 75 Wang Zhizhi 1.00 .30
❑ 76 Eric Snow .60 .18
❑ 77 Rasheed Wallace 1.00 .30
❑ 78 Antonio Daniels .30 .09
❑ 79 Vladimir Radmanovic RC 2.50 .75
❑ 80 Morris Peterson .60 .18
❑ 81 Jason Terry 1.00 .30
Jason Terry
Dikembe Mutombo
Jason Terry
❑ 82 Paul Pierce .60 .18
Milt Pallacio
Antoine Walker
Antoine Walker
❑ 83 Jamal Mashburn .60 .18
Hersey Hawkins
P.J.Brown
Baron Davis
❑ 84 Elton Brand 1.00 .30
Fred Hoiberg
Elton Brnad
Fred Hoiberg
❑ 85 Andre Miller .60 .18
Trajan Langdon
Clarence Weatherspoon
Andre Miller
❑ 86 Dirk Nowitzki 1.00 .30
Steve Nash
Dirk Nowitzki
Steve Nash
❑ 87 Antonio McDyess .60 .18
George McCloud
Antonio McDyess
Nick Van Exel
❑ 88 Jerry Stackhouse 1.00 .30
Dana Barros
Ben Wallace
Jerry Stackhouse
❑ 89 Antawn Jamison 1.00 .30
Marc Jackson
Antawn Jamison
Mookie Blaylock
❑ 90 Steve Francis .30 .09
Cuttino Mobley
Steve Francis
Steve Francis
❑ 91 Jalen Rose 1.00 .30
Reggie Miller
Jermaine O'Neal
Travis Best
❑ 92 Lamar Odom 1.00 .30
Eric Piatkowski
Lamar Odom
Jeff McInnis
❑ 93 Shaquille O'Neal 1.50 .45
Mike Penberthy
Shaquille O'Neal
Kobe Bryant
❑ 94 Shareef Abdur-Rahim 1.00 .30
Shareef Abdur-Rahim
Shareff Abdur-Rahim
Mike Bibby
❑ 95 Eddie Jones .60 .18
Eddie Jones
Anthony Mason
Tim Hardaway
❑ 96 Glenn Robinson 1.00 .30
Ray Allen
Ervin Johnson
Sam Cassell
❑ 97 Kevin Garnett 1.25 .35
Terrell Brandon
Kevin Garnett
Terrell Brandon
❑ 98 Stephon Marbury .60 .18
Johnny Newman
Aaron Williams
Stephon Marbury
❑ 99 Deshawn Stevenson .60 .18
❑ 100 Allen Iverson 2.00 .60
❑ 101 Jeryl Sasser RC 2.50 .75
❑ 102 Jason Terry 1.00 .30
❑ 103 Vitaly Potapenko .30 .09
❑ 104 Elden Campbell .30 .09
❑ 105 Jamal Crawford .60 .18
❑ 106 Michael Finley 1:00 .30
❑ 107 Earl Watson RC 2.50 .75
❑ 108 Clifford Robinson .30 .09
❑ 109 Chucky Atkins .30 .09
❑ 110 Glen Rice .60 .18
❑ 111 Jermaine O'Neal 1.00 .30
❑ 112 Jonathan Bender .60 .18
❑ 113 Michael Olowokandi .30 .09
❑ 114 Derek Fisher 1.00 .30
❑ 115 Stromile Swift .60 .18
❑ 116 Toni Kukoc .60 .18
❑ 117 Samuel Dalembert RC 2.50 .75
❑ 118 Paul Pierce 1.00 .30
❑ 119 Jamal Mashburn .60 .18
❑ 120 Ron Mercer .60 .18
❑ 121 Lamond Murray .30 .09
❑ 122 Steve Nash 1.00 .30
❑ 123 Nick Van Exel 1.00 .30
❑ 124 Desagana Diop RC 2.50 .75
❑ 125 Ron Artest .60 .18
❑ 126 Marcus Fizer .60 .18
❑ 127 Jumaine Jones .60 .18
❑ 128 Corliss Williamson .60 .18
❑ 129 Rodney White RC 3.00 .90
❑ 130 Cuttino Mobley .60 .18
❑ 131 Reggie Miller 1.00 .30
❑ 132 Austin Croshere .30 .09
❑ 133 Jeff Mcinnis .30 .09
❑ 134 Joe Johnson RC 4.00 1.20
❑ 135 Kedrick Brown RC 2.50 .75
❑ 136 Theo Ratliff .60 .18
❑ 137 Laphonso Ellis .30 .09
❑ 138 Ervin Johnson .30 .09
❑ 139 Terrell Brandon .60 .18
❑ 140 Chauncey Billups .60 .18
❑ 141 Kenyon Martin 1.00 .30
❑ 142 Richard Jefferson RC 5.00 1.50
❑ 143 Howard Eisley .30 .09
❑ 144 Jerry Stackhouse 1.25 .35
Allen Iverson
Shaquille O'Neal
❑ 145 Allen Iverson 1.50 .45
Jerry Stackhouse
Shaquille O'Neal
❑ 146 Shaquille O'Neal 1.00 .30
Bonzi Wells
Marcus Camby
❑ 147 Reggie Miller .60 .18
Allan Houston
Doug Christie
❑ 148 Dikembe Mutombo 1.00 .30
Ben Wallace
Shaquille O'Neal
❑ 149 Jason Kidd 1.00 .30
John Stockton
Nick Van Exel
❑ 150 Vince Carter 2.50 .75
❑ 151 Calvin Booth .30 .09
❑ 152 Chris Whitney .30 .09
❑ 153 John Amaechi .30 .09
❑ 154 Keon Clark .60 .18
❑ 155 Terry Porter .30 .09
❑ 156 Doug Christie .60 .18
❑ 157 Gerald Wallace RC 6.00 1.80
❑ 158 Zach Randolph RC 5.00 1.50
❑ 159 Iakovos Tsakalidis .30 .09
❑ 160 Damone Brown RC 2.50 .75
❑ 161 Allen Iverson 1.25 .35
Reggie Miller
Kevin Garnett
Tim Duncan
❑ 162 Ray Allen 2.50 .75
Tracy McGrady
Shaquille O'Neal
Steve Smith
❑ 163 Alonzo Mourning 1.00 .30
Baron Davis
Chris Webber
Anfernee Hardaway
❑ 164 Allan Houston 1.50 .45
Vince Carter
Dirk Nowitzki
Karl Malone
❑ 165 Christian Laettner .60 .18
❑ 166 John Starks .60 .18
❑ 167 Jerome Williams .30 .09
❑ 168 Brent Barry .60 .18
❑ 169 Malik Rose .30 .09
❑ 170 Vlade Divac .60 .18
❑ 171 Damon Stoudamire .60 .18
❑ 172 Rodney Rogers .30 .09
❑ 173 Alvin Jones RC 2.50 .75
❑ 174 Darrell Armstrong .30 .09
❑ 175 Mark Jackson .60 .18
❑ 176 Kerry Kittles ERR .30 .09
Has Heritage Rookie Logo
❑ 177 Radoslav Nesterovic .60 .18
❑ 178 Brandon Armstrong RC 2.50 .75
❑ 179 Joe Smith .60 .18
❑ 180 Ray Allen 1.00 .30
❑ 181 Anthony Mason .60 .18
❑ 182 Bryant Reeves .30 .09
❑ 183 Jason Williams .60 .18
❑ 184 Terence Morris RC 2.50 .75
❑ 185 Travis Best .30 .09
❑ 186 Troy Murphy RC 5.00 1.50
❑ 187 Gilbert Arenas RC 6.00 1.80
❑ 188 Avery Johnson .30 .09
❑ 189 Juwan Howard .60 .18
❑ 190 Checklist .30 .09
❑ 191 Courtney Alexander .60 .18
❑ 192 John Stockton 1.00 .30
❑ 193 Vin Baker .60 .18
❑ 194 Desmond Mason .60 .18
❑ 195 Steve Smith .60 .18
❑ 196 Steven Hunter RC 2.50 .75
❑ 197 Stephon Marbury 1.00 .30
❑ 198 Patrick Ewing 1.00 .30
❑ 199 Allan Houston .60 .18
❑ 200 Karl Malone 1.00 .30
❑ 201 Peja Stojakovic 1.00 .30
❑ 202 Bonzi Wells .60 .18
❑ 203 Latrell Sprewell 1.00 .30
❑ 204 Rafer Alston .30 .09
❑ 205 Tony Parker RC 10.00 3.00
❑ 206 Michael Bradley RC 2.50 .75
❑ 207 Richard Hamilton .60 .18
❑ 208 Zeljko Rebraca RC 2.50 .75
❑ 209 Joel Przybilla .60 .18
❑ 210 Tim Thomas .60 .18
❑ 211 Eddie House .60 .18
❑ 212 Brian Grant .60 .18
❑ 213 Lindsey Hunter .30 .09
❑ 214 Corey Maggette .60 .18
❑ 215 Shane Battier RC 4.00 1.20
❑ 216 Will Solomon .30 .09

❑ 217 Mitch Richmond .60 .18
❑ 218 Eddie Jones 1.00 .30
❑ 219 Elton Brand 1.00 .30
❑ 220 Quentin Richardson .60 .18
❑ 221 Allan Houston .60 .18
Allan Houston
Marcus Camby
Charlie Ward
❑ 222 Tracy McGrady 1.00 .30
Darrell Armstrong
Bo Outlaw
Darrell Armstrong
❑ 223 Allen Iverson 1.50 .45
Allen Iverson
Tyrone Hill
Aaron McKie
❑ 224 Shawn Marion 1.00 .30
Jason Kidd
Shawn Marion
Jason Kidd
❑ 225 Rasheed Wallace .60 .18
Steve Smith
Dale Davis
Damon Stoudamire
❑ 226 Chris Webber 1.00 .30
Doug Christie
Chris Webber
Jason Williams
❑ 227 Tim Duncan 1.00 .30
Derek Anderson
Tim Duncan
Antonio Daniels
❑ 228 Gary Payton .60 .18
Shammond Williams
Patrick Ewing
Gary Payton
❑ 229 Vince Carter 1.00 .30
Dell Curry
Antonio Davis
Mark Jackson
❑ 230 Karl Malone 1.00 .30
John Stockton
Karl Malone
John Stockton
❑ 231 Juwan Howard .60 .18
Chris Whitney
Jahidi White
Chris Whitney
❑ 232 Brendan Haywood RC 3.00 .90
❑ 233 Scottie Pippen 1.50 .45
❑ 234 Loren Woods RC 2.50 .75
❑ 235 Sam Cassell 1.00 .30
❑ 236 Anthony Carter .60 .18
❑ 237 Raja Bell RC 2.50 .75
❑ 238 Robert Horry .60 .18
❑ 239 Maurice Taylor .60 .18
❑ 240 Zydrunas Ilgauskas .60 .18
❑ 241 Derrick Coleman .30 .09
❑ 242 Kenny Anderson .60 .18
❑ 243 Joseph Forte RC 5.00 1.50
❑ 244 Baron Davis 1.00 .30
❑ 245 Nazr Mohammed .30 .09
❑ 246 Allen Iverson 1.25 .35
Vince Carter
Tim Duncan
Shawn Bradley
❑ 247 Ray Allen 2.00 .60
Baron Davis
Kobe Bryant
Vlade Divac
❑ 248 Dikembe Mutombo 1.00 .30
Glenn Robinson
David Robinson
Tyrone Lue
❑ 249 Kobe Bryant 1.25 .35
Allen Iverson
❑ 250 Darius Miles 1.00 .30
❑ 251 Samaki Walker .30 .09
❑ 252 Dermarr Johnson .60 .18
❑ 253 David Wesley .30 .09
❑ 254 Trenton Hassell RC 4.00 1.20
❑ 255 Jeff Trepagnier RC 2.50 .75
❑ 256 Jacque Vaughn .30 .09
❑ 257 Kirk Haston RC 2.50 .75
❑ 258 Jamaal Magloire .60 .18
❑ 259 Jason Collins RC 2.50 .75
❑ 260 Chris Webber 1.00 .30
❑ 261 Kenny Satterfield RC 2.50 .75
❑ 262 Horace Grant .60 .18
❑ 263 Jerry Stackhouse 1.00 .30
❑ 264 Michael Jordan 15.00 4.50

2001-02 Topps High Topps

	Nm-Mt	Ex-Mt
COMPLETE SET (164)	800.00	240.00
COMP.SET w/o SP's (105)	60.00	18.00
COMMON CARD (1-105)	.30	.09
COMMON AU (106-113)	12.00	3.60
COMMON JSY (114-129)	15.00	4.50
COMMON AU RC (130-140)	12.00	3.60
COMMON JSY RC (141-153)	15.00	4.50
COMMON ROOKIE (154-164)	5.00	1.50

❑ 1 Shaquille O'Neal 2.50 .75
❑ 2 Reggie Miller 1.00 .30
❑ 3 Steve Francis 1.00 .30
❑ 4 Jerry Stackhouse 1.00 .30
❑ 5 Nick Van Exel 1.00 .30
❑ 6 Dirk Nowitzki 1.50 .45
❑ 7 Dikembe Mutombo .60 .18
❑ 8 Terrell Brandon .60 .18
❑ 9 Allan Houston .60 .18
❑ 10 Kevin Garnett 2.00 .60
❑ 11 Eric Snow .60 .18
❑ 12 Stephon Marbury 1.00 .30
❑ 13 Jalen Rose 1.00 .30
❑ 14 Rick Fox .60 .18
❑ 15 Alonzo Mourning .60 .18
❑ 16 Tim Thomas .60 .18
❑ 17 Keith Van Horn 1.00 .30
❑ 18 Glen Rice .60 .18
❑ 19 Mike Miller 1.00 .30
❑ 20 Chris Webber 1.00 .30
❑ 21 Larry Hughes .60 .18
❑ 22 Joe Smith 1.00 .30
❑ 23 Ron Mercer .60 .18
❑ 24 Jamal Mashburn .60 .18
❑ 25 Shareef Abdur-Rahim 1.00 .30
❑ 26 P.J. Brown .30 .09
❑ 27 Ben Wallace 1.00 .30
❑ 28 Wang Zhizhi 1.00 .30
❑ 29 Jermaine O'Neal 1.00 .30
❑ 30 Lamar Odom 1.00 .30
❑ 31 Stromile Swift .60 .18
❑ 32 Theo Ratliff .60 .18
❑ 33 Patrick Ewing 1.00 .30
❑ 34 Antonio Davis .30 .09
❑ 35 John Stockton 1.00 .30
❑ 36 Courtney Alexander .60 .18
❑ 37 Alvin Williams .30 .09
❑ 38 Rashard Lewis .60 .18
❑ 39 Mike Bibby 1.00 .30
❑ 40 Scottie Pippen 1.50 .45
❑ 41 Anfernee Hardaway 1.00 .30
❑ 42 Marcus Camby .60 .18
❑ 43 Glenn Robinson .60 .18
❑ 44 Jason Williams .60 .18
❑ 45 Horace Grant .60 .18
❑ 46 Chris Mihm .60 .18
❑ 47 Paul Pierce 1.00 .30
❑ 48 DerMarr Johnson .60 .18
❑ 49 Steve Nash 1.00 .30
❑ 50 Vince Carter 2.50 .75
❑ 51 Michael Jordan 15.00 4.50
❑ 52 Donyell Marshall .60 .18
❑ 53 Desmond Mason .60 .18
❑ 54 Tom Gugliotta .30 .09
❑ 55 Hidayet Turkoglu .60 .18
❑ 56 Grant Hill 1.00 .30
❑ 57 Kenyon Martin 1.00 .30
❑ 58 Wally Szczerbiak .60 .18
❑ 59 Eddie Jones 1.00 .30
❑ 60 Kobe Bryant 4.00 1.20
❑ 61 Cuttino Mobley .60 .18
❑ 62 Michael Dickerson .60 .18
❑ 63 Clifford Robinson .30 .09
❑ 64 Raef LaFrentz .60 .18
❑ 65 Lamond Murray .30 .09
❑ 66 Kenny Anderson .60 .18
❑ 67 Antonio Daniels .30 .09
❑ 68 Hakeem Olajuwon .60 .18
❑ 69 Eddie Robinson .60 .18
❑ 70 Karl Malone 1.00 .30
❑ 71 Richard Hamilton .60 .18
❑ 72 Derek Anderson .60 .18
❑ 73 Bonzi Wells .60 .18
❑ 74 Darrell Armstrong .30 .09
❑ 75 Gary Payton 1.00 .30
❑ 76 Bryon Russell .30 .09
❑ 77 Steve Smith .60 .18
❑ 78 Sam Cassell 1.00 .30
❑ 79 Brian Grant .60 .18
❑ 80 Antoine Walker 1.00 .30
❑ 81 Marcus Fizer .60 .18
❑ 82 Tim Duncan AN 2.00 .60
❑ 83 Chris Webber AN .60 .18
❑ 84 Shaquille O'Neal AN 2.50 .75
❑ 85 Allen Iverson AN 2.00 .60
❑ 86 Jason Kidd AN 1.50 .45
❑ 87 Kevin Garnett AN 2.00 .60
❑ 88 Vince Carter AN 2.50 .75
❑ 89 Dikembe Mutombo AN .60 .18
❑ 90 Kobe Bryant AN 4.00 1.20
❑ 91 Tracy McGrady AN 2.50 .75
❑ 92 Allen Iverson SL 1.25 .35
❑ 93 Dikembe Mutombo SL .30 .09
❑ 94 Jason Kidd SL 1.00 .30
❑ 95 Allen Iverson SL 1.25 .35
❑ 96 Theo Ratliff SL .30 .09
❑ 97 Shaquille O'Neal SL 1.50 .45
❑ 98 Reggie Miller SL .60 .18
❑ 99 Antoine Walker SL .60 .18
❑ 100 Michael Finley SL .60 .18
❑ 101 Jason Kidd SL 1.00 .30
❑ 102 Shaquille O'Neal RTC 1.50 .45
❑ 103 Kobe Bryant RTC 2.50 .75
❑ 104 Derek Fisher RTC 1.00 .30
❑ 105 Shaquille O'Neal RTC 1.50 .45
❑ 106 Shawn Marion AU 20.00 6.00
❑ 107 Antawn Jamison AU 25.00 7.50
❑ 108 Peja Stojakovic AU 50.00 15.00
❑ 109 Jason Terry AU 15.00 4.50
❑ 110 Aaron McKie AU 12.00 3.60
❑ 111 Keyon Dooling AU 12.00 3.60
❑ 112 Al Harrington AU 12.00 3.60
❑ 113 Chauncey Billups AU 12.00 3.60
❑ 114 Tim Duncan JSY 30.00 9.00
❑ 115 Tracy McGrady JSY 30.00 9.00
❑ 116 Jason Kidd JSY 25.00 7.50
❑ 117 Latrell Sprewell JSY 25.00 7.50
❑ 118 David Robinson JSY 30.00 9.00
❑ 119 Baron Davis JSY 15.00 4.50
❑ 120 Allen Iverson JSY 30.00 9.00
❑ 121 Ray Allen JSY 20.00 6.00
❑ 122 Rasheed Wallace JSY 15.00 4.50
❑ 123 Morris Peterson JSY 15.00 4.50
❑ 124 Darius Miles JSY 25.00 7.50
❑ 125 Marc Jackson JSY 15.00 4.50
❑ 126 Michael Finley JSY 15.00 4.50
❑ 127 Elton Brand JSY 25.00 7.50
❑ 128 Antonio McDyess JSY - -
❑ 129 Andre Miller JSY 15.00 4.50
❑ 130 Kwame Brown AU RC 25.00 7.50
❑ 131 Eddy Curry AU RC 25.00 7.50
❑ 132 Loren Woods AU RC 12.00 3.60
❑ 133 Joe Johnson AU RC 20.00 6.00
❑ 134 R.Jefferson AU RC 30.00 9.00
❑ 135 Z.Randolph AU RC 30.00 9.00
❑ 136 B.Haywood AU RC 15.00 4.50

❑ 137 Gilbert Arenas AU RC 40.00 12.00
❑ 138 Damone Brown AU RC 12.00 3.60
❑ 139 K.Satterfield AU RC .. 12.00 3.60
❑ 140 V.Radmanovic AU RC 12.00 3.60
❑ 141 Eddie Griffin JSY RC 15.00 4.50
❑ 142 Shane Battier JSY RC 20.00 6.00
❑ 143 M.Bradley JSY RC 15.00 4.50
❑ 144 Gerald Wallace JSY RC 25.00 7.50
❑ 145 S.Dalembert JSY RC 15.00 4.50
❑ 146 Tyson Chandler JSY RC 20.00 6.00
❑ 147 Pau Gasol JSY RC.... 30.00 9.00
❑ 148 Steven Hunter JSY RC 15.00 4.50
❑ 149 Rodney White JSY RC 15.00 4.50
❑ 150 Jeryl Sasser JSY RC 15.00 4.50
❑ 151 B.Armstrong JSY RC 20.00 6.00
❑ 152 Jamaal Tinsley JSY RC 15.00 4.50
❑ 153 DeSagana Diop JSY RC 15.00 4.50
❑ 154 Jason Richardson RC 12.00 3.60
❑ 155 Kirk Haston RC 5.00 1.50
❑ 156 Joseph Forte RC 6.00 1.80
❑ 157 Jason Collins RC 5.00 1.50
❑ 158 Kedrick Brown RC 5.00 1.50
❑ 159 Troy Murphy RC.......... 8.00 2.40
❑ 160 Tony Parker RC 15.00 4.50
❑ 161 Raja Bell RC................ 5.00 1.50
❑ 162 Jeff Trepagnier RC...... 5.00 1.50
❑ 163 Terence Morris RC...... 5.00 1.50
❑ 164 Zeljko Rebraca RC...... 5.00 1.50

2002-03 Topps Jersey Edition

Nm-Mt Ex-Mt

ASTERISKS PERCIEVED AS SP VERSION -

❑ JEAD Antonio Davis R UER 12.00 3.60
❑ JEAFM Aaron McKie R UER 12.00 3.60
❑ JEAHO Allan Houston H .. 12.00 3.60
❑ JEAI Allen Iverson R *...... 20.00 6.00
❑ JEAIV Allen Iverson H...... 15.00 4.50
❑ JEAJ Antawn Jamison R.. 12.00 3.60
❑ JEAK Andrei Kirilenko R .. 12.00 3.60
❑ JEALM Andre Miller R...... 12.00 3.60
❑ JEAMG Drew Gooden R .. 20.00 6.00
❑ JEAMI Andre Miller H 12.00 3.60
❑ JEAS A.Stoudemire R RC 40.00 12.00
❑ JEAST Amare Stoudemire H 40.00 12.00
❑ JEBD Baron Davis R........ 12.00 3.60
❑ JEBDA Baron Davis H 12.00 3.60
❑ JEBG Brian Grant R 12.00 3.60
❑ JEBW Ben Wallace R 12.00 3.60
❑ JEBWA Ben Wallace H.... 12.00 3.60
❑ JECA Courtney Alexander R UER 12.00 3.60
❑ JECB Carlos Boozer H RC 25.00 7.50
❑ JECBU Caron Butler H RC 20.00 6.00
❑ JECJ Chris Jefferies H RC 12.00 3.60
❑ JECM Cuttino Mobley R .. 12.00 3.60
❑ JECW C.Wilcox R UER RC 15.00 4.50
❑ JEDAS Damon Stoudamire H 12.00 3.60
❑ JEDD Dan Dickau R RC .. 12.00 3.60
❑ JEDDI Dan Dickau H UER 12.00 3.60
❑ JEDF Derek Fisher R 12.00 3.60
❑ JEDGO Drew Gooden H .. 20.00 6.00
❑ JEDJG Devean George R 12.00 3.60
❑ JEDLM Darius Miles R 12.00 3.60
❑ JEDMA Donyell Marshall R UER 12.00 3.60
❑ JEDN Dirk Nowitzki R 15.00 4.50
❑ JEDNO Dirk Nowitzki H.... 15.00 4.50
❑ JEDW DaJuan Wagner R 15.00 4.50
❑ JEDWA DaJuan Wagner H RC 15.00 4.50
❑ JEEB Elton Brand R 12.00 3.60
❑ JEEBR Elton Brand H 12.00 3.60
❑ JEEC Eddy Curry R 12.00 3.60
❑ JEECU Eddy Curry H 12.00 3.60
❑ JEEG Eddie Griffin R UER 12.00 3.60
❑ JEEJ Eddie Jones R 12.00 3.60
❑ JEEJC Elden Campbell R UER 12.00 3.60
❑ JEFJ Fred Jones R RC 12.00 3.60
❑ JEGA Gilbert Arenas R UER 12.00 3.60
❑ JEGDW Bonzi Wells R 12.00 3.60
❑ JEGG Gordan Giricek R RC 15.00 4.50
❑ JEGRO Glenn Robinson H 12.00 3.60
❑ JEJAR Jason Richardson R 12.00 3.60
❑ JEJAT Jason Terry R 12.00 3.60
❑ JEJCB Caron Butler R 20.00 6.00
❑ JEJDM Jamaal Magloire R UER 12.00 3.60
❑ JEJH Juwan Howard R 12.00 3.60
❑ JEJHS John Stockton R .. 12.00 3.60
❑ JEJKI Jason Kidd H 15.00 4.50
❑ JEJM Jamal Mashburn R 12.00 3.60
❑ JEJMJ Joe Johnson R 12.00 3.60
❑ JEJO Jermaine O'Neal R 12.00 3.60
❑ JEJON Jermaine O'Neal H 12.00 3.60
❑ JEJOS John Stockton H .. 12.00 3.60
❑ JEJR Jalen Rose R 12.00 3.60
❑ JEJRI Jason Richardson H 12.00 3.60
❑ JEJRO Jalen Rose H 12.00 3.60
❑ JEJRS John Salmons R RC 12.00 3.60
❑ JEJS Joe Smith R 12.00 3.60
❑ JEJT Jamaal Tinsley R 12.00 3.60
❑ JEJWL Jerome Williams H 12.00 3.60
❑ JEKAM Karl Malone R 12.00 3.60
❑ JEKG Kevin Garnett R .. 20.00 6.00
❑ JEKGA Kevin Garnett H .. 20.00 6.00
❑ JEKMA Karl Malone H 12.00 3.60
❑ JEKR Kareem Rush R RC 15.00 4.50
❑ JEKRU Kareem Rush H .. 15.00 4.50
❑ JEKS Kenny Satterfield R 12.00 3.60
❑ JEKV Keith Van Horn R .. 12.00 3.60
❑ JEKVH Keith Van Horn H 12.00 3.60
❑ JELSP Latrell Sprewell H 12.00 3.60
❑ JEMAF Marcus Fizer R 12.00 3.60
❑ JEMD Mike Dunleavy H RC 20.00 6.00
❑ JEMF Michael Finley R 12.00 3.60
❑ JEMO Mehmet Okur R 12.00 3.60
❑ JEMOK Mehmet Okur H RC 12.00 3.60
❑ JEMP Morris Peterson R UER 12.00 3.60
❑ JENT N.Tskitishvili R RC.. 12.00 3.60
❑ JENTS Nikoloz Tskitishvili H 12.00 3.60
❑ JEPG Pau Gasol R 12.00 3.60
❑ JEPGA Pau Gasol H 12.00 3.60
❑ JEPP Paul Pierce R 12.00 3.60
❑ JEQR Quentin Richardson R 12.00 3.60
❑ JEQRI Quentin Richardson H 12.00 3.60
❑ JEQW Qyntel Woods R RC 12.00 3.60
❑ JEQWO Qyntel Woods H 12.00 3.60
❑ JERAO Ron Artest R........ 12.00 3.60
❑ JERAW Rasheed Wallace R 12.00 3.60
❑ JERB Rasual Butler R RC 12.00 3.60
❑ JERBU Rasual Butler H .. 12.00 3.60
❑ JERCH Richard Hamilton R 12.00 3.60
❑ JERHO Robert Horry R 12.00 3.60
❑ JERIH Richard Hamilton H 12.00 3.60
❑ JERM Reggie Miller R...... 12.00 3.60
❑ JERWA Rasheed Wallace H 12.00 3.60
❑ JESA Shareef Abdur-Rahim R 12.00 3.60
❑ JESCB Shane Battier R .. 12.00 3.60
❑ JESDM Shawn Marion R 12.00 3.60
❑ JESFR Steve Francis H .. 12.00 3.60
❑ JESM Stephon Marbury R 12.00 3.60
❑ JESMA Shawn Marion H.. 12.00 3.60
❑ JESN Steve Nash R 12.00 3.60
❑ JESNA Steve Nash H * 15.00 4.50
❑ JESO Shaquille O'Neal R 25.00 7.50
❑ JESON Shaquille O'Neal H 25.00 7.50
❑ JETC Tyson Chandler R .. 12.00 3.60
❑ JETCH Tyson Chandler H 12.00 3.60
❑ JETDU Tim Duncan H...... 25.00 7.50
❑ JETDU Tim Duncan R...... 20.00 6.00
❑ JETH Troy Hudson R 12.00 3.60
❑ JETML Tracy McGrady R 25.00 7.50
❑ JETPA Tony Parker H...... 12.00 3.60
❑ JETPR Tayshaun Prince R RC 15.00 4.50
❑ JEWS Wally Szczerbiak R 12.00 3.60
❑ JEWSZ Wally Szczerbiak H 12.00 3.60
❑ JEYM Yao Ming R RC...... 60.00 18.00
❑ NNO Jason Kidd
Tony Parker EXCH
❑ NNO Antoine Walker........ 20.00 6.00
Chris Webber EXCH
❑ NNO Paul Pierce............ Null
Ray Allen EXCH
❑ NNO Gary Payton 20.00 6.00
Juan Dixon EXCH
❑ NNO Tracy McGrady
Mike Dunleavy EXCH
❑ NNO Manu Ginobili 20.00 6.00
Peja Stojakovic EXCH

2003-04 Topps Jersey Edition

Nm-Mt Ex-Mt

COMMON CARD..................... 8.00 2.40
COMMON ROOKIE.................. 8.00 2.40
COMMON SS RC 10.00 3.00

❑ AD Antonio Davis 8.00 2.40
❑ AH Allan Houston 8.00 2.40
❑ AI Allen Iverson............... 12.00 3.60
❑ AJ Antawn Jamison........... 8.00 2.40
❑ AK Andrei Kirilenko 8.00 2.40
❑ AM Andre Miller.................. 8.00 2.40
❑ AP Aleksandar Pavlovic RC 8.00 2.40
❑ AS Amare Stoudemire 12.00 3.60
❑ BB Brent Barry 8.00 2.40
❑ BC Brian Cook RC EXCH .. 8.00 2.40
❑ BD Baron Davis.................. 8.00 2.40
❑ BH Brandon Hunter RC...... 8.00 2.40
❑ BJ Bobby Jackson............. 8.00 2.40
❑ BM Brad Miller................... 8.00 2.40
❑ BW Ben Wallace 8.00 2.40
❑ CA Carmelo Anthony SS RC 50.00 15.00
❑ CB Caron Butler 8.00 2.40
❑ CK Chris Kaman RC 8.00 2.40
❑ CM Corey Maggette 8.00 2.40
❑ CW Chris Webber EXCH .. 8.00 2.40
❑ DC Derrick Coleman EXCH 8.00 2.40
❑ DG Drew Gooden 8.00 2.40
❑ DJ Dahntay Jones RC........ 8.00 2.40
❑ DM Desmond Mason EXCH 8.00 2.40
❑ DN Dirk Nowitzki 10.00 3.00
❑ DW Dwyane Wade SS RC 20.00 6.00
❑ EB Elton Brand AU 20.00 6.00
❑ EC Eddy Curry 8.00 2.40
❑ EG Manu Ginobili 8.00 2.40
❑ GA Gilbert Arenas............. 8.00 2.40
❑ GP Gary Payton EXCH...... 8.00 2.40
❑ GR Glenn Robinson 8.00 2.40
❑ HT Hedo Turkoglu............. 8.00 2.40
❑ JB Jerome Beasley RC...... 8.00 2.40
❑ JC Jamal Crawford 8.00 2.40
❑ JH Juwan Howard............. 8.00 2.40
❑ JJ James Jones RC 8.00 2.40
❑ JK Jason Kidd 10.00 3.00
❑ JM Jamal Mashburn 8.00 2.40
❑ JO Jermaine O'Neal 8.00 2.40
❑ JR Jalen Rose.................... 8.00 2.40
❑ JS Jerry Stackhouse 8.00 2.40
❑ JT Jason Terry 8.00 2.40
❑ JW Jason Williams 8.00 2.40
❑ KB Kwame Brown.............. 8.00 2.40
❑ KC Keon Clark 8.00 2.40
❑ KG Kevin Garnett 12.00 3.60

Card	Nm-Mt	Ex-Mt
❑ KH Kirk Hinrich AU RC	50.00	15.00
❑ KM Karl Malone EXCH	8.00	2.40
❑ KP Kendrick Perkins RC	8.00	2.40
❑ KR Kareem Rush EXCH	8.00	2.40
❑ KT Kurt Thomas	8.00	2.40
❑ LB Leandro Barbosa SS RC	10.00	3.00
❑ LJ Lebron James SS RC	80.00	24.00
❑ LO Lamar Odom	8.00	2.40
❑ LR Luke Ridnour AU RC	25.00	7.50
❑ LS Latrell Sprewell	8.00	2.40
❑ LW Luke Walton SS RC	12.00	3.60
❑ MB Mike Bibby	8.00	2.40
❑ MC Marcus Camby	8.00	2.40
❑ MD Mike Dunleavy	8.00	2.40
❑ MJ Marko Jaric	8.00	2.40
❑ MM Mike Miller	8.00	2.40
❑ MO Michael Olowokandi	8.00	2.40
❑ MP Morris Peterson	8.00	2.40
❑ MR Michael Redd EXCH	8.00	2.40
❑ MS Mike Sweetney SS RC	10.00	3.00
❑ MT Maurice Taylor	8.00	2.40
❑ MW Maurice Williams RC	8.00	2.40
❑ NE Ndudi Ebi RC	8.00	2.40
❑ NH Nene	8.00	2.40
❑ PG Pau Gasol	8.00	2.40
❑ PP Paul Pierce	8.00	2.40
❑ PS Peja Stojakovic	8.00	2.40
❑ QR Quentin Richardson	8.00	2.40
❑ QW Qyntel Woods	8.00	2.40
❑ RA Ray Allen	8.00	2.40
❑ RD Ricky Davis	8.00	2.40
❑ RG Reece Gaines SS RC	10.00	3.00
❑ RH Richard Hamilton	8.00	2.40
❑ RJ Richard Jefferson	8.00	2.40
❑ RL Raef LaFrentz	8.00	2.40
❑ RL Rashard Lewis	8.00	2.40
❑ RM Ron Mercer	8.00	2.40
❑ RN Radoslav Nesterovic	8.00	2.40
❑ RW Rasheed Wallace	8.00	2.40
❑ SB Steve Blake RC	8.00	2.40
❑ SC Sam Cassell	8.00	2.40
❑ SF Steve Francis	8.00	2.40
❑ SM Shawn Marion	8.00	2.40
❑ SN Steve Nash	8.00	2.40
❑ SO Shaquille O'Neal AU	80.00	24.00
❑ SP Scottie Pippen	10.00	3.00
❑ TB Troy Bell RC	8.00	2.40
❑ TC Tyson Chandler EXCH	8.00	2.40
❑ TD Tim Duncan	12.00	3.60
❑ TF T.J. Ford AU RC EXCH	25.00	7.50
❑ TM Tracy McGrady	15.00	4.50
❑ TO Travis Outlaw RC	8.00	2.40
❑ TP Tony Parker	8.00	2.40
❑ TR Theo Ratliff	8.00	2.40
❑ TS Theron Smith RC	8.00	2.40
❑ TT Tim Thomas	8.00	2.40
❑ WG Willie Green RC	8.00	2.40
❑ YM Yao Ming	15.00	4.50
❑ ZC Zarko Cabarkapa RC	8.00	2.40
❑ ZI Zydrunas Ilgauskas	8.00	2.40
❑ ZP Zoran Planinic RC	8.00	2.40
❑ ZR Zach Randolph	8.00	2.40
❑ AHA Al Harrington	8.00	2.40
❑ BDR Boris Diaw RC	8.00	2.40
❑ CBI Chauncey Billups	8.00	2.40
❑ CBO Chris Bosh RC	15.00	4.50
❑ CBO Carlos Boozer	8.00	2.40
❑ CMO Cuttino Mobley	8.00	2.40
❑ CWI Corliss Williamson	8.00	2.40
❑ DAM Darko Milicic SS RC	20.00	6.00
❑ DCH Doug Christie	8.00	2.40
❑ DGE Devean George	8.00	2.40
❑ DMI Darius Miles	8.00	2.40
❑ DWA DaJuan Wagner EXCH	8.00	2.40
❑ DWE David West SS RC	10.00	3.00
❑ JHA Jarvis Hayes RC	8.00	2.40
❑ JHO Josh Howard RC	10.00	3.00
❑ JKA Jason Kapono SS RC	10.00	3.00
❑ JMA Jamaal Magloire	8.00	2.40
❑ JRI Jason Richardson	8.00	2.40
❑ JSM Joe Smith EXCH	8.00	2.40
❑ JWI Jerome Williams	8.00	2.40
❑ KMA Kenyon Martin	8.00	2.40
❑ KVH Keith Van Horn	8.00	2.40
❑ MBA Marcus Banks RC	8.00	2.40
❑ MJA Marc Jackson	8.00	2.40
❑ MPI Mickael Pietrus RC	8.00	2.40
❑ NVE Nick Van Exel	8.00	2.40
❑ RAR Ron Artest	8.00	2.40
❑ RHO Robert Horry	8.00	2.40
❑ RLO Raul Lopez	8.00	2.40
❑ RMI Reggie Miller	8.00	2.40
❑ SAR Shareef Abdur-Rahim	8.00	2.40
❑ SBA Shane Battier	8.00	2.40
❑ SCL Speedy Claxton	8.00	2.40
❑ SMA Stephon Marbury	8.00	2.40
❑ TMU Troy Murphy	8.00	2.40
❑ TPR Tayshaun Prince	8.00	2.40
❑ ZPA Zaur Pachulia RC	8.00	2.40

2001-02 Topps Pristine

	Nm-Mt	Ex-Mt
COMPLETE SET (110)	500.00	150.00
COMP.SET w/o SP's (50)	120.00	36.00
COMMON CARD (1-50)	1.50	.45
COMMON ROOKIE (51-110)	4.00	1.20
❑ 1 Allen Iverson	5.00	1.50
❑ 2 Shawn Marion	2.50	.75
❑ 3 Baron Davis	2.50	.75
❑ 4 Peja Stojakovic	2.50	.75
❑ 5 Dirk Nowitzki	4.00	1.20
❑ 6 Michael Jordan	25.00	7.50
❑ 7 Dikembe Mutombo	1.50	.45
❑ 8 Antoine Walker	2.50	.75
❑ 9 David Robinson	2.50	.75
❑ 10 Tracy McGrady	6.00	1.80
❑ 11 Rasheed Wallace	2.50	.75
❑ 12 Kenyon Martin	2.50	.75
❑ 13 Glenn Robinson	1.50	.45
❑ 14 Shareef Abdur-Rahim	2.50	.75
❑ 15 Lamar Odom	2.50	.75
❑ 16 Alonzo Mourning	1.50	.45
❑ 17 Latrell Sprewell	2.50	.75
❑ 18 Stephon Marbury	2.50	.75
❑ 19 Chris Webber	2.50	.75
❑ 20 Darius Miles	2.50	.75
❑ 21 Tim Duncan	5.00	1.50
❑ 22 Antawn Jamison	2.50	.75
❑ 23 Jason Kidd	4.00	1.20
❑ 24 John Stockton	2.50	.75
❑ 25 Michael Finley	2.50	.75
❑ 26 Eddie Jones	2.50	.75
❑ 27 Jamal Mashburn	1.50	.45
❑ 28 Paul Pierce	2.50	.75
❑ 29 Jason Terry	2.50	.75
❑ 30 Kobe Bryant	10.00	3.00
❑ 31 Reggie Miller	2.50	.75
❑ 32 Elton Brand	2.50	.75
❑ 33 Antonio McDyess	1.50	.45
❑ 34 Ray Allen	2.50	.75
❑ 35 Kevin Garnett	5.00	1.50
❑ 36 Allan Houston	1.50	.45
❑ 37 Grant Hill	2.50	.75
❑ 38 Jalen Rose	2.50	.75
❑ 39 Gary Payton	2.50	.75
❑ 40 Vince Carter	6.00	1.80
❑ 41 Jerry Stackhouse	2.50	.75
❑ 42 Karl Malone	2.50	.75
❑ 43 Wang Zhizhi	2.50	.75
❑ 44 Marcus Fizer	1.50	.45
❑ 45 Marcus Camby	1.50	.45
❑ 46 Andre Miller	1.50	.45
❑ 47 Jason Williams	1.50	.45
❑ 48 Hakeem Olajuwon	2.50	.75
❑ 49 Shaquille O'Neal	6.00	1.80
❑ 50 Steve Francis	2.50	.75
❑ 51 Eddie Griffin C RC	4.00	1.20
❑ 52 Eddie Griffin U	5.00	1.50
❑ 53 Eddie Griffin R	6.00	1.80
❑ 54 Kwame Brown C RC	5.00	1.50
❑ 55 Kwame Brown U	6.00	1.80
❑ 56 Kwame Brown R	8.00	2.40
❑ 57 Shane Battier C RC	4.00	1.20
❑ 58 Shane Battier U	5.00	1.50
❑ 59 Shane Battier R	6.00	1.80
❑ 60 Eddy Curry C RC	6.00	1.80
❑ 61 Eddy Curry U	8.00	2.40
❑ 62 Eddy Curry R	10.00	3.00
❑ 63 Tyson Chandler C RC	6.00	1.80
❑ 64 Tyson Chandler U	8.00	2.40
❑ 65 Tyson Chandler R	10.00	3.00
❑ 66 Rodney White C RC	4.00	1.20
❑ 67 Rodney White U	6.00	1.80
❑ 68 Rodney White R	8.00	2.40
❑ 69 J.Richardson C RC	8.00	2.40
❑ 70 Jason Richardson U	10.00	3.00
❑ 71 Jason Richardson R	12.00	3.60
❑ 72 Joe Johnson C RC	4.00	1.20
❑ 73 Joe Johnson U	5.00	1.50
❑ 74 Joe Johnson R	6.00	1.80
❑ 75 Pau Gasol C RC	8.00	2.40
❑ 76 Pau Gasol U	10.00	3.00
❑ 77 Pau Gasol R	12.00	3.60
❑ 78 Desagana Diop C RC	4.00	1.20
❑ 79 Desagana Diop U	5.00	1.50
❑ 80 Desagana Diop R	6.00	1.80
❑ 81 V.Radmanovic C RC	3.00	.90
❑ 82 V.Radmanovic U	4.00	1.20
❑ 83 V.Radmanovic R	5.00	1.50
❑ 84 Troy Murphy C RC	4.00	1.20
❑ 85 Troy Murphy U	6.00	1.80
❑ 86 Troy Murphy R	8.00	2.40
❑ 87 Zach Randolph C RC	8.00	2.40
❑ 88 Zach Randolph U	10.00	3.00
❑ 89 Zach Randolph R	12.00	3.60
❑ 90 Jamaal Tinsley C RC	4.00	1.20
❑ 91 Jamaal Tinsley U	5.00	1.50
❑ 92 Jamaal Tinsley R	6.00	1.80
❑ 93 Richard Jefferson C RC	5.00	1.50
❑ 94 Richard Jefferson U	6.00	1.80
❑ 95 Richard Jefferson R	8.00	2.40
❑ 96 Loren Woods C RC	4.00	1.20
❑ 97 Loren Woods U	5.00	1.50
❑ 98 Loren Woods R	6.00	1.80
❑ 99 Joseph Forte C RC	6.00	1.80
❑ 100 Joseph Forte U	8.00	2.40
❑ 101 Joseph Forte R	10.00	3.00
❑ 102 Gerald Wallace C RC	6.00	1.80
❑ 103 Gerald Wallace U	8.00	2.40
❑ 104 Gerald Wallace R	10.00	3.00
❑ 105 Andrei Kirilenko C RC	6.00	1.80
❑ 106 Andrei Kirilenko U	8.00	2.40
❑ 107 Andrei Kirilenko R	10.00	3.00
❑ 108 Tony Parker C RC	10.00	3.00
❑ 109 Tony Parker U	12.00	3.60
❑ 110 Tony Parker R	15.00	4.50

2002-03 Topps Pristine

	Nm-Mt	Ex-Mt
COMMON CARD (1-50)	.50	.15
COMMON ROOKIE (51-125)	4.00	1.20
❑ 1 Shaquille O'Neal	4.00	1.20

❑ 2 Steve Nash	1.50	.45
❑ 3 Vince Carter	4.00	1.20
❑ 4 Michael Jordan	12.00	3.60
❑ 5 Chris Webber	1.50	.45
❑ 6 Tim Duncan	3.00	.90
❑ 7 Vladimir Radmanovic	1.00	.30
❑ 8 Kobe Bryant	6.00	1.80
❑ 9 Allan Houston	1.00	.30
❑ 10 Tracy McGrady	4.00	1.20
❑ 11 Allen Iverson	3.00	.90
❑ 12 Scottie Pippen	2.50	.75
❑ 13 Steve Francis	1.50	.45
❑ 14 Reggie Miller	1.50	.45
❑ 15 Antoine Walker	1.50	.45
❑ 16 Shawn Marion	1.50	.45
❑ 17 Wally Szczerbiak	1.00	.30
❑ 18 Elton Brand	1.50	.45
❑ 19 Jerry Stackhouse	1.50	.45
❑ 20 Andre Miller	1.00	.30
❑ 21 Gary Payton	1.50	.45
❑ 22 Richard Hamilton	1.00	.30
❑ 23 Pau Gasol	1.50	.45
❑ 24 Juwan Howard	1.00	.30
❑ 25 Jalen Rose	1.50	.45
❑ 26 Eddie Jones	1.50	.45
❑ 27 Baron Davis	1.50	.45
❑ 28 Darrell Armstrong	.50	.15
❑ 29 John Stockton	1.50	.45
❑ 30 Mike Bibby	1.50	.45
❑ 31 Eddy Curry	1.50	.45
❑ 32 Kevin Garnett	4.00	1.20
❑ 33 Dikembe Mutombo	1.00	.30
❑ 34 Jason Kidd	2.50	.75
❑ 35 Clifford Robinson	.50	.15
❑ 36 Ray Allen	1.50	.45
❑ 37 Paul Pierce	1.50	.45
❑ 38 Shane Battier	1.50	.45
❑ 39 Kenyon Martin	1.50	.45
❑ 40 Rasheed Wallace	1.50	.45
❑ 41 Latrell Sprewell	1.50	.45
❑ 42 Cuttino Mobley	1.00	.30
❑ 43 Karl Malone	1.50	.45
❑ 44 Dirk Nowitzki	2.50	.75
❑ 45 Antawn Jamison	1.50	.45
❑ 46 Elden Campbell	.50	.15
❑ 47 Lamar Odom	1.50	.45
❑ 48 Jason Richardson	1.50	.45
❑ 49 Jermaine O'Neal	1.50	.45
❑ 50 Shareef Abdur-Rahim	1.50	.45
❑ 51 Yao Ming C RC	30.00	9.00
❑ 52 Yao Ming U	40.00	12.00
❑ 53 Yao Ming R	80.00	24.00
❑ 54 Jay Williams C RC	6.00	1.80
❑ 55 Jay Williams U	8.00	2.40
❑ 56 Jay Williams R	15.00	4.50
❑ 57 Mike Dunleavy C RC	8.00	2.40
❑ 58 Mike Dunleavy U	10.00	3.00
❑ 59 Mike Dunleavy R	20.00	6.00
❑ 60 Drew Gooden C RC	12.00	3.60
❑ 61 Drew Gooden U	15.00	4.50
❑ 62 Drew Gooden R	30.00	9.00
❑ 63 Nikoloz Tskitishvili C RC	6.00	1.80
❑ 64 Nikoloz Tskitishvili U	8.00	2.40
❑ 65 Nikoloz Tskitishvili R	15.00	4.50
❑ 66 DaJuan Wagner C RC	8.00	2.40
❑ 67 DaJuan Wagner U	10.00	3.00
❑ 68 DaJuan Wagner R	20.00	6.00
❑ 69 Nene Hilario C RC	6.00	1.80
❑ 70 Nene Hilario U	8.00	2.40
❑ 71 Nene Hilario R	15.00	4.50
❑ 72 Chris Wilcox C RC	6.00	1.80
❑ 73 Chris Wilcox U	8.00	2.40
❑ 74 Chris Wilcox R	15.00	4.50
❑ 75 Amare Stoudemire C RC	25.00	7.50
❑ 75A A.Stoudemire ERR	-	-
Gold Refractor appears on back		
❑ 76 Amare Stoudemire U	30.00	9.00
❑ 77 Amare Stoudemire R	60.00	18.00
❑ 78 Caron Butler C RC	8.00	2.40
❑ 79 Caron Butler U	10.00	3.00
❑ 80 Caron Butler R	20.00	6.00
❑ 81 Jared Jeffries C RC	4.00	1.20
❑ 82 Jared Jeffries U	5.00	1.50
❑ 83 Jared Jeffries R	10.00	3.00
❑ 84 Melvin Ely C RC	4.00	1.20
❑ 85 Melvin Ely U	5.00	1.50
❑ 86 Melvin Ely R	10.00	3.00
❑ 87 Marcus Haislip C RC	4.00	1.20
❑ 88 Marcus Haislip U	5.00	1.50
❑ 89 Marcus Haislip R	10.00	3.00
❑ 90 Fred Jones C RC	4.00	1.20
❑ 91 Fred Jones U	5.00	1.50
❑ 92 Fred Jones R	10.00	3.00
❑ 93 Casey Jacobsen C RC	4.00	1.20
❑ 94 Casey Jacobsen U	4.00	1.20
❑ 95 Casey Jacobsen R	8.00	2.40
❑ 96 John Salmons C RC	4.00	1.20
❑ 97 John Salmons U	5.00	1.50
❑ 98 John Salmons R	10.00	3.00
❑ 99 Juan Dixon C RC	6.00	1.80
❑ 100 Juan Dixon U	8.00	2.40
❑ 101 Juan Dixon R	15.00	4.50
❑ 102 Chris Jefferies C RC	4.00	1.20
❑ 103 Chris Jefferies U	5.00	1.50
❑ 104 Chris Jefferies R	10.00	3.00
❑ 105 Ryan Humphrey C RC	4.00	1.20
❑ 106 Ryan Humphrey U	5.00	1.50
❑ 107 Ryan Humphrey R	10.00	3.00
❑ 108 Kareem Rush C RC	5.00	1.50
❑ 109 Kareem Rush U	6.00	1.80
❑ 110 Kareem Rush R	12.00	3.60
❑ 111 Qyntel Woods C RC	4.00	1.20
❑ 112 Qyntel Woods U	5.00	1.50
❑ 113 Qyntel Woods R	10.00	3.00
❑ 114 Frank Williams C RC	4.00	1.20
❑ 115 Frank Williams U	5.00	1.50
❑ 116 Frank Williams R	10.00	3.00
❑ 117 Tayshaun Prince C RC	5.00	1.50
❑ 118 Tayshaun Prince U	6.00	1.80
❑ 119 Tayshaun Prince R	12.00	3.60
❑ 120 Carlos Boozer C RC	8.00	2.40
❑ 121 Carlos Boozer U	10.00	3.00
❑ 122 Carlos Boozer R	20.00	6.00
❑ 123 Dan Dickau C RC	4.00	1.20
❑ 124 Dan Dickau U	4.00	1.20
❑ 125 Dan Dickau R	8.00	2.40

2003-04 Topps Pristine

	MINT	NRMT
COMP.SET w/o RC's (100)	60.00	27.00
COMMON CARD (1-100)	.40	.18
COMMON ROOKIE (101-197)	5.00	2.20
❑ 1 Tracy McGrady	3.00	1.35
❑ 2 DaJuan Wagner	.75	.35
❑ 3 Allen Iverson	2.50	1.10
❑ 4 Chris Webber	1.25	.55
❑ 5 Jason Kidd	2.00	.90
❑ 6 Eddie Jones	1.25	.55
❑ 7 Jermaine O'Neal	1.25	.55
❑ 8 Kobe Bryant	5.00	2.20
❑ 9 Tony Parker	1.25	.55
❑ 10 Wally Szczerbiak	.75	.35
❑ 11 Yao Ming	3.00	1.35
❑ 12 Amare Stoudemire	2.50	1.10
❑ 13 Steve Nash	1.25	.55
❑ 14 Baron Davis	1.25	.55
❑ 15 Vince Carter	3.00	1.35
❑ 16 Peja Stojakovic	1.25	.55
❑ 17 Desmond Mason	.75	.35
❑ 18 Antoine Walker	1.25	.55
❑ 19 Steve Francis	1.25	.55
❑ 20 Gary Payton	1.25	.55
❑ 21 Tim Duncan	2.50	1.10
❑ 22 Jalen Rose	1.25	.55
❑ 23 Jason Richardson	1.25	.55
❑ 24 Andre Miller	.75	.35
❑ 25 Allan Houston	.75	.35
❑ 26 Ron Artest	.75	.35
❑ 27 Andrei Kirilenko	1.25	.55
❑ 28 Kenyon Martin	1.25	.55
❑ 29 Kevin Garnett	2.50	1.10
❑ 30 Rasheed Wallace	1.25	.55
❑ 31 Shawn Marion	1.25	.55
❑ 32 Karl Malone	1.25	.55
❑ 33 Antawn Jamison	1.25	.55
❑ 34 Shaquille O'Neal	3.00	1.35
❑ 35 Paul Pierce	1.25	.55
❑ 36 Nene	.75	.35
❑ 37 Ray Allen	1.25	.55
❑ 38 Bonzi Wells	.75	.35
❑ 39 Ben Wallace	1.25	.55
❑ 40 Jerry Stackhouse	1.25	.55
❑ 41 Dirk Nowitzki	2.00	.90
❑ 42 Elton Brand	1.25	.55
❑ 43 Pau Gasol	1.25	.55
❑ 44 Richard Hamilton	.75	.35
❑ 45 Shareef Abdur-Rahim	1.25	.55
❑ 46 Jason Terry	1.25	.55
❑ 47 Jamal Mashburn	.75	.35
❑ 48 Latrell Sprewell	1.25	.55
❑ 49 Keith Van Horn	1.25	.55
❑ 50 Mike Miller	1.25	.55
❑ 51 Theo Ratliff	.75	.35
❑ 52 Scottie Pippen	2.00	.90
❑ 53 Nick Van Exel	1.25	.55
❑ 54 Chauncey Billups	.75	.35
❑ 55 Al Harrington	.75	.35
❑ 56 Corey Maggette	.75	.35
❑ 57 Shane Battier	1.25	.55
❑ 58 Tim Thomas	.75	.35
❑ 59 Darius Miles	1.25	.55
❑ 60 Alonzo Mourning	.75	.35
❑ 61 Jamaal Magloire	.40	.18
❑ 62 Antonio McDyess	.75	.35
❑ 63 Juwan Howard	.75	.35
❑ 64 Eric Snow	.75	.35
❑ 65 Anfernee Hardaway	1.25	.55
❑ 66 Tayshaun Prince	.75	.35
❑ 67 Derek Anderson	.75	.35
❑ 68 Mike Bibby	1.25	.55
❑ 69 Deshawn Stevenson	.40	.18
❑ 70 Kwame Brown	1.25	.55
❑ 71 Jerome Williams	.40	.18
❑ 72 Radoslav Nesterovic	.75	.35
❑ 73 Stephon Marbury	1.25	.55
❑ 74 P.J. Brown	.40	.18
❑ 75 Sam Cassell	1.25	.55
❑ 76 Kenny Thomas	.40	.18
❑ 77 Jason Williams	.75	.35
❑ 78 Jamaal Tinsley	1.25	.55
❑ 79 Nikoloz Tskitishvili	.40	.18
❑ 80 Michael Finley	1.25	.55
❑ 81 Jamal Crawford	.40	.18
❑ 82 Brent Barry	.75	.35
❑ 83 Gilbert Arenas	1.25	.55
❑ 84 Morris Peterson	.75	.35
❑ 85 Manu Ginobili	1.25	.55
❑ 86 Dale Davis	.75	.35
❑ 87 Aaron McKie	.75	.35
❑ 88 Richard Jefferson	.75	.35
❑ 89 Michael Redd	1.25	.55
❑ 90 Reggie Miller	1.25	.55
❑ 91 Cuttino Mobley	.75	.35
❑ 92 Marcus Camby	.75	.35
❑ 93 Tony Delk	.40	.18
❑ 94 Tyson Chandler	1.25	.55
❑ 95 Caron Butler	1.25	.55
❑ 96 Kurt Thomas	.75	.35
❑ 97 Glenn Robinson	1.25	.55
❑ 98 Brad Miller	1.25	.55
❑ 99 Matt Harpring	1.25	.55
❑ 100 Alvin Williams	.40	.18
❑ 101 LeBron James C RC	50.00	22.00
❑ 102 LeBron James U	75.00	34.00
❑ 103 LeBron James R	100.00	45.00
❑ 104 Darko Milicic C RC	6.00	2.70
❑ 105 Darko Milicic U	10.00	4.50
❑ 106 Darko Milicic R	12.00	5.50
❑ 107 Carmelo Anthony C RC	30.00	13.50
❑ 108 Carmelo Anthony U	45.00	20.00

❑ 109 Carmelo Anthony R .. 60.00 27.00
❑ 110 Chris Bosh C RC 8.00 3.60
❑ 111 Chris Bosh U 12.00 5.50
❑ 112 Chris Bosh R 15.00 6.75
❑ 113 Dwyane Wade C RC 10.00 4.50
❑ 114 Dwyane Wade U 15.00 6.75
❑ 115 Dwyane Wade R 20.00 9.00
❑ 116 Chris Kaman C RC..... 5.00 2.20
❑ 117 Chris Kaman U.......... 5.00 2.20
❑ 118 Chris Kaman R.......... 5.00 2.20
❑ 119 Kirk Hinrich C RC....... 6.00 2.70
❑ 120 Kirk Hinrich U 10.00 4.50
❑ 121 Kirk Hinrich R 12.00 5.50
❑ 122 T.J. Ford C RC........... 5.00 2.20
❑ 123 T.J. Ford U 8.00 3.60
❑ 124 T.J. Ford R 10.00 4.50
❑ 125 Mike Sweetney C RC .. 5.00 2.20
❑ 126 Mike Sweetney U 8.00 3.60
❑ 127 Mike Sweetney R 10.00 4.50
❑ 128 Jarvis Hayes C RC...... 5.00 2.20
❑ 129 Jarvis Hayes U........... 8.00 3.60
❑ 130 Jarvis Hayes R.......... 10.00 4.50
❑ 131 Mickael Pietrus C RC .. 5.00 2.20
❑ 132 Mickael Pietrus U 8.00 3.60
❑ 133 Mickael Pietrus R 10.00 4.50
❑ 134 Nick Collison C RC...... 5.00 2.20
❑ 135 Nick Collison U........... 6.00 2.70
❑ 136 Nick Collison R........... 8.00 3.60
❑ 137 Marcus Banks C RC.... 5.00 2.20
❑ 138 Marcus Banks U.......... 8.00 3.60
❑ 139 Marcus Banks R........ 10.00 4.50
❑ 140 Luke Ridnour C RC 5.00 2.20
❑ 141 Luke Ridnour U 8.00 3.60
❑ 142 Luke Ridnour R 10.00 4.50
❑ 143 Reece Gaines C RC.... 5.00 2.20
❑ 144 Reece Gaines U.......... 8.00 3.60
❑ 145 Reece Gaines R........ 10.00 4.50
❑ 146 Troy Bell C RC 5.00 2.20
❑ 147 Troy Bell U 8.00 3.60
❑ 148 Troy Bell R 10.00 4.50
❑ 149 Zarko Cabarkapa C RC 5.00 2.20
❑ 150 Zarko Cabarkapa U 8.00 3.60
❑ 151 Zarko Cabarkapa R .. 10.00 4.50
❑ 152 David West C RC 5.00 2.20
❑ 153 David West U 8.00 3.60
❑ 154 David West R 10.00 4.50
❑ 155 Aleksandar Pavlovic C RC 5.00 2.20
❑ 156 Aleksandar Pavlovic U 8.00 3.60
❑ 157 Aleksandar Pavlovic R 10.00 4.50
❑ 158 Dahntay Jones C RC .. 5.00 2.20
❑ 159 Dahntay Jones U 8.00 3.60
❑ 160 Dahntay Jones R 10.00 4.50
❑ 161 Boris Diaw C RC 5.00 2.20
❑ 162 Boris Diaw U 8.00 3.60
❑ 163 Boris Diaw R 10.00 4.50
❑ 164 Zoran Planinic C RC .. 5.00 2.20
❑ 165 Zoran Planinic U.......... 8.00 3.60
❑ 166 Zoran Planinic R........ 10.00 4.50
❑ 167 Travis Outlaw C RC 5.00 2.20
❑ 168 Travis Outlaw U 8.00 3.60
❑ 169 Travis Outlaw R 10.00 4.50
❑ 170 Brian Cook C RC 5.00 2.20
❑ 171 Brian Cook U 8.00 3.60
❑ 172 Brian Cook R 10.00 4.50
❑ 173 Travis Hansen C RC .. 5.00 2.20
❑ 174 Travis Hansen U 8.00 3.60
❑ 175 Travis Hansen R 10.00 4.50
❑ 176 Ndudi Ebi C RC 5.00 2.20
❑ 177 Ndudi Ebi U 8.00 3.60
❑ 178 Ndudi Ebi R 10.00 4.50
❑ 179 Kendrick Perkins C RC 5.00 2.20
❑ 180 Kendrick Perkins U...... 8.00 3.60
❑ 181 Kendrick Perkins R..... 10.00 4.50
❑ 182 Leandro Barbosa C RC 5.00 2.20
❑ 183 Leandro Barbosa U 8.00 3.60
❑ 184 Leandro Barbosa R .. 10.00 4.50
❑ 185 Josh Howard C RC 6.00 2.70
❑ 186 Josh Howard U.......... 10.00 4.50
❑ 187 Josh Howard R.......... 12.00 5.50
❑ 188 Maciej Lampe C RC 5.00 2.20
❑ 189 Maciej Lampe U 8.00 3.60
❑ 190 Maciej Lampe R 10.00- 4.50
❑ 191 Jason Kapono C RC .. 5.00 2.20
❑ 192 Jason Kapono U.......... 8.00 3.60
❑ 193 Jason Kapono R........ 10.00 4.50
❑ 194 Luke Walton C RC 5.00 2.20
❑ 195 Luke Walton U 8.00 3.60
❑ 196 Luke Walton R 10.00 4.50
❑ 197 Jerome Beasley C RC 5.00 2.20
❑ 198 Jerome Beasley U 8.00 3.60
❑ 199 Jerome Beasley R 10.00 4.50

2000-01 Topps Reserve

	Nm-Mt	Ex-Mt
COMPLETE SET (134)	300.00	90.00
COMP.SET w/o SP's (100)	80.00	24.00
COMMON CARD (1-100)	.40	.12
COMMON ROOKIE/499	3.00	.90
COMMON ROOKIE/999	8.00	2.40
COMMON ROOKIE/1499	4.00	1.20

❑ 1 Tim Duncan .... 2.50 .75
❑ 2 Clifford Robinson .... .40 .12
❑ 3 Allen Iverson .... 2.50 .75
❑ 4 Marcus Camby .... .75 .23
❑ 5 Chauncey Billups .... .75 .23
❑ 6 Anthony Mason .... .40 .12
❑ 7 Toni Kukoc .... .75 .23
❑ 8 Tim Thomas .... .75 .23
❑ 9 Corey Maggette .... .75 .23
❑ 10 Steve Francis .... 1.25 .35
❑ 11 Larry Hughes .... .75 .23
❑ 12 Jerome Williams............. .40 .12
❑ 13 Reggie Miller .... 1.25 .35
❑ 14 Chris Gatling .... .40 .12
❑ 15 Ron Artest .... .75 .23
❑ 16 Derrick Coleman .... .40 .12
❑ 17 Paul Pierce................... 1.25 .35
❑ 18 Dikembe Mutombo .... .75 .23
❑ 19 Andre Miller .... .75 .23
❑ 20 Gary Payton .... 1.25 .35
❑ 21 Kevin Garnett .... 2.50 .75
❑ 22 Allan Houston .... .75 .23
❑ 23 Rasheed Wallace .... 1.25 .35
❑ 24 Derek Anderson .... .75 .23
❑ 25 Vin Baker .... .75 .23
❑ 26 John Stockton .... 1.25 .35
❑ 27 Richard Hamilton .... .75 .23
❑ 28 Mike Bibby .... 1.25 .35
❑ 29 Dale Davis .... .40 .12
❑ 30 Vince Carter .... 3.00 .90
❑ 31 Shawn Marion .... 1.25 .35
❑ 32 Karl Malone .... 1.25 .35
❑ 33 Patrick Ewing .... 1.25 .35
❑ 34 Shaquille O'Neal........... 3.00 .90
❑ 35 Jermaine O'Neal........... 1.25 .35
❑ 36 Danny Fortson .... .40 .12
❑ 37 Steve Nash................... 1.25 .35
❑ 38 Antoine Walker............. 1.25 .35
❑ 39 Jason Terry .... 1.25 .35
❑ 40 Vlade Divac .... .75 .23
❑ 41 Avery Johnson .... .40 .12
❑ 42 Elton Brand .... 1.25 .35
❑ 43 Mitch Richmond .... .75 .23
❑ 44 Antonio Davis .... .40 .12
❑ 45 Shawn Kemp .... .75 .23
❑ 46 Anfernee Hardaway ...... 1.25 .35
❑ 47 Kendall Gill...................... .40 .12
❑ 48 Glen Rice .... .75 .23
❑ 49 Tim Hardaway .... .75 .23
❑ 50 Tracy McGrady............. 3.00 .90
❑ 51 Horace Grant .... .75 .23
❑ 52 Hakeem Olajuwon .... 1.25 .35
❑ 53 Antawn Jamison........... 1.25 .35
❑ 54 Dirk Nowitzki .... 2.00 .60
❑ 55 Antonio McDyess .... .75 .23
❑ 56 Michael Dickerson .... .75 .23
❑ 57 Baron Davis .... 1.25 .35
❑ 58 Nick Van Exel............... 1.25 .35
❑ 59 Joe Smith .... .75 .23
❑ 60 Kobe Bryant 5.00 1.50
❑ 61 Ray Allen .... 1.25 .35
❑ 62 Keith Van Horn............. 1.25 .35
❑ 63 Latrell Sprewell............. 1.25 .35
❑ 64 Jason Kidd .... 2.00 .60
❑ 65 Chris Webber .... 1.25 .35
❑ 66 David Robinson .... 1.25 .35
❑ 67 Mark Jackson .... .75 .23
❑ 68 Bryon Russell .... .40 .12
❑ 69 Lamar Odom .... 1.25 .35
❑ 70 Maurice Taylor .... .75 .23
❑ 71 Jonathan Bender .... .75 .23
❑ 72 Raef LaFrentz .... .75 .23
❑ 73 Sam Cassell................. 1.25 .35
❑ 74 Wally Szczerbiak .... .75 .23
❑ 75 Grant Hill .... 1.25 .35
❑ 76 Theo Ratliff...................... .75 .23
❑ 77 Rashard Lewis .... .75 .23
❑ 78 Darrell Armstrong............ .40 .12
❑ 79 Glenn Robinson .... 1.25 .35
❑ 80 Stephon Marbury .... 1.25 .35
❑ 81 Michael Olowokandi........ .40 .12
❑ 82 Isaiah Rider .... .40 .12
❑ 83 Jalen Rose .... 1.25 .35
❑ 84 Cuttino Mobley .... .75 .23
❑ 85 Jerry Stackhouse .... 1.25 .35
❑ 86 Jamal Mashburn.............. .75 .23
❑ 87 Kenny Anderson.............. .75 .23
❑ 88 Michael Finley .... 1.25 .35
❑ 89 Lamond Murray .... .40 .12
❑ 90 Eddie Jones .... 1.25 .35
❑ 91 Eric Snow .... .75 .23
❑ 92 Terrell Brandon .... .75 .23
❑ 93 Jason Williams .... .75 .23
❑ 94 Scottie Pippen .... 2.00 .60
❑ 95 Rod Strickland .... .40 .12
❑ 96 Jim Jackson .... .40 .12
❑ 97 Ron Mercer .... .75 .23
❑ 98 Juwan Howard .... .75 .23
❑ 99 Brian Grant...................... .75 .23
❑ 100 Shareef Abdur-Rahim 1.25 .35
❑ 101 Kenyon Martin/499 RC 25.00 7.50
❑ 102 Stromile Swift/999 RC 10.00 3.00
❑ 103 Darius Miles/1499 RC 12.00 3.60
❑ 104 Marcus Fizer/499 RC .. 3.00 .90
❑ 105 Mike Miller/999 RC.... 15.00 4.50
❑ 106 D.Johnson/1499 RC.... 4.00 1.20
❑ 107 Chris Mihm/499 RC .... 3.00 .90
❑ 108 Jamal Crawford/999 RC 10.00 3.00
❑ 109 Joel Przybilla/1499 RC 4.00 1.20
❑ 110 Keyon Dooling/499 RC 3.00 .90
❑ 111 Jerome Moiso/999 RC 8.00 2.40
❑ 112 Etan Thomas/1499 RC 4.00 1.20
❑ 113 C.Alexander/499 RC 10.00 3.00
❑ 114 Mateen Cleaves/999 RC 8.00 2.40
❑ 115 Jason Collier/1499 RC 4.00 1.20
❑ 116 Hidayet Turkoglu/499 RC 15.00 4.50
❑ 117 Desmond Mason/999 RC 8.00 2.40
❑ 118 Q.Richardson/1499 RC 12.00 3.60
❑ 119 Jamaal Magloire/499 RC 3.00 .90
❑ 120 Speedy Claxton/999 RC 8.00 2.40
❑ 121 Morris Peterson/1499 RC 10.00 3.00
❑ 122 Donnell Harvey/499 RC 3.00 .90
❑ 123 D.Stevenson/999 RC .. 8.00 2.40
❑ 124 Dalibor Bagaric/1499 RC 4.00 1.20
❑ 125 I.Tsakalidis/499 RC .... 3.00 .90
❑ 126 M.N'Diaye/999 RC 8.00 2.40
❑ 127 Erick Barkley/1499 RC 4.00 1.20

❑ 128 Mark Madsen/499 RC 3.00 .90
❑ 129 A.J. Guyton/999 RC 8.00 2.40
❑ 130 Khalid El-Amin/1499 RC 4.00 1.20
❑ 131 Lavor Postell/499 RC .. 3.00 .90
❑ 132 Marc Jackson/999 RC 8.00 2.40
❑ 133 S.Jackson/1499 RC 8.00 2.40
❑ 134 Wang Zhizhi/1499 RC 20.00 6.00

2003-04 Topps Rookie Matrix

	Nm-Mt	Ex-Mt
COMP.SET w/o RC's (110)	30.00	9.00
COMMON CARD (1-110)	.20	.06
COMMON TRI-RC..................	3.00	.90

❑ 1 Allen Iverson .... 1.50 .45
❑ 2 Anfernee Hardaway .... .75 .23
❑ 3 Bonzi Wells .... .50 .15
❑ 4 Bobby Jackson................ .50 .15
❑ 5 Manu Ginobili .... .75 .23
❑ 6 Andrei Kirilenko .... .75 .23
❑ 7 Ray Allen .... .75 .23
❑ 8 Kwame Brown .... .50 .15
❑ 9 Jason Terry .... .75 .23
❑ 10 Paul Pierce.................... .75 .23
❑ 11 Tyson Chandler .... .75 .23
❑ 12 Darius Miles .... .75 .23
❑ 13 Antoine Walker............... .75 .23
❑ 14 Antawn Jamison.............. .75 .23
❑ 15 Steve Nash.................... .75 .23
❑ 16 Marcus Camby................ .50 .15
❑ 17 Chauncey Billups............. .50 .15
❑ 18 Jason Richardson .... .75 .23
❑ 19 Cuttino Mobley................ .50 .15
❑ 20 Yao Ming .... 2.00 .60
❑ 21 Ron Artest .... .50 .15
❑ 22 Gary Payton.................... .75 .23
❑ 23 Jason Williams................ .50 .15
❑ 24 Eddie Jones .... .75 .23
❑ 25 Kevin Garnett.................. 1.50 .45
❑ 26 Wally Szczerbiak .... .50 .15
❑ 27 Kenyon Martin .... .75 .23
❑ 28 Jamaal Magloire.............. .20 .06
❑ 29 Keith Van Horn................ .75 .23
❑ 30 Tracy McGrady............... 2.00 .60
❑ 31 Glenn Robinson .... .75 .23
❑ 32 Derek Anderson............... .50 .15
❑ 33 Chris Webber.................. .75 .23
❑ 34 Tony Parker .... .75 .23
❑ 35 Morris Peterson .... .50 .15
❑ 36 Jerry Stackhouse .... .75 .23
❑ 37 Theo Ratliff..................... .50 .15
❑ 38 Jalen Rose .... .75 .23
❑ 39 Dajuan Wagner .... .50 .15
❑ 40 Dirk Nowitzki .... 1.25 .35
❑ 41 Nikoloz Tskitishvili .... .20 .06
❑ 42 Ben Wallace.................... .75 .23
❑ 43 Tayshaun Prince .... .50 .15
❑ 44 Troy Murphy.................... .75 .23
❑ 45 Jamaal Tinsley................ .75 .23
❑ 46 Corey Maggette .... .50 .15
❑ 47 Karl Malone .... .75 .23
❑ 48 Mike Miller .... .75 .23
❑ 49 Lamar Odom .... .75 .23
❑ 50 Shaquille O'Neal............. 2.00 .60
❑ 51 Michael Redd .... .75 .23
❑ 52 Sam Cassell.................... .75 .23
❑ 53 Raef LaFrentz .... .50 .15
❑ 54 Baron Davis .... .75 .23
❑ 55 Allan Houston.................. .50 .15
❑ 56 Drew Gooden.................. .50 .15
❑ 57 Eric Snow........................ .50 .15
❑ 58 Stephon Marbury .... .75 .23
❑ 59 Zach Randolph................ .75 .23
❑ 60 Peja Stojakovic............... .75 .23
❑ 61 Brent Barry..................... .50 .15
❑ 62 Radoslav Nesterovic ...... .50 .15
❑ 63 Antonio Davis.................. .20 .06
❑ 64 Gilbert Arenas .... .75 .23
❑ 65 Shareef Abdur-Rahim .... .75 .23
❑ 66 Scottie Pippen .... 1.25 .35
❑ 67 Ronald Murray .... .50 .15
❑ 68 Zydrunas Ilgauskas .... .50 .15
❑ 69 Nene............................... .50 .15
❑ 70 Steve Francis .... .75 .23
❑ 71 Mike Dunleavy .... .50 .15
❑ 72 Jermaine O'Neal............. .75 .23
❑ 73 Elton Brand .... .75 .23
❑ 74 Caron Butler................... .75 .23
❑ 75 Kobe Bryant .... 3.00 .90
❑ 76 Kenny Thomas................ .20 .06
❑ 77 Joe Smith .... .50 .15
❑ 78 Jason Kidd .... 1.25 .35
❑ 79 Antonio McDyess .... .75 .23
❑ 80 Shawn Marion .... .75 .23
❑ 81 Rasheed Wallace .... .75 .23
❑ 82 Mike Bibby .... .75 .23
❑ 83 Tim Thomas .... .50 .15
❑ 84 Rashard Lewis .... .75 .23
❑ 85 Vince Carter .... 2.00 .60
❑ 86 Matt Harpring .... .75 .23
❑ 87 Ricky Davis .... .75 .23
❑ 88 Michael Finley .... .75 .23
❑ 89 Andre Miller .... .50 .15
❑ 90 Pau Gasol .... .75 .23
❑ 91 Dion Glover .... .20 .06
❑ 92 Jamal Crawford .... .50 .15
❑ 93 Richard Hamilton .... .50 .15
❑ 94 Nick Van Exel................. .75 .23
❑ 95 Maurice Taylor .... .20 .06
❑ 96 Reggie Miller .... .75 .23
❑ 97 Marko Jaric..................... .50 .15
❑ 98 Brian Grant..................... .50 .15
❑ 99 Desmond Mason .... .50 .15
❑ 100 Tim Duncan .... 1.50 .45
❑ 101 Latrell Sprewell.............. .75 .23
❑ 102 Richard Jefferson.......... .50 .15
❑ 103 David Wesley................ .20 .06
❑ 104 Kurt Thomas.................. .50 .15
❑ 105 Juwan Howard .... .50 .15
❑ 106 Amare Stoudemire ...... 1.50 .45
❑ 107 Brad Miller .... .75 .23
❑ 108 Keon Clark .... .50 .15
❑ 109 Pat Garrity .... .20 .06
❑ 110 Jamal Mashburn............ .50 .15
❑ AJF Carmelo Anthony 113 12.00 3.60
LeBron James 111
T.J. Ford 118
❑ AKM Carmelo Anthony 113 5.00 1.50
Chris Kaman 116
Darko Milicic 112
❑ AMB Carmelo Anthony 113 6.00 1.80
Darko Milicic 112
Chris Bosh 114
❑ AWB Carmelo Anthony 113 6.00 1.80
Dwyane Wade 115
Chris Bosh 114
❑ BAH Chris Bosh 114 .... 5.00 1.50
Carmelo Anthony 113
Kirk Hinrich 117
❑ BAJ Chris Bosh 114 .... 15.00 4.50
Carmelo Anthony 113
LeBron James 111
❑ BBG Leandro Barbosa 137 3.00 .90
Troy Bell 126
Reece Gaines 125
❑ BBR Marcus Banks 125 .... 3.00 .90
Troy Bell 126
Luke Ridnour 124
❑ BCC Troy Bell 126 .... 3.00 .90
Zarko Cabarkapa 127
Nick Collison 122
❑ BCG Troy Bell 126 .... 3.00 .90
Nick Collison 122
Reece Gaines 125
❑ BCP Leandro Barbosa 137 3.00 .90
Zarko Cabarkapa 127
Aleksandar Pavlovic 129
❑ BCP Marcus Banks 125 .... 3.00 .90
Nick Collison 122
Mickael Pietrus 121
❑ BHJ Chris Bosh 114 .... 8.00 2.40
Kirk Hinrich 117
LeBron James 111
❑ BJP Troy Bell 126 .... 3.00 .90
Dahntay Jones 130
Zoran Planinic 132
❑ BKC Jerome Beasley 142 .. 3.00 .90
Jason Kapono 140
Brian Cook 134
❑ BKS Marcus Banks 123 .... 3.00 .90
Chris Kaman 116
Mike Sweetney 119
❑ BKW Chris Bosh 114 .... 4.00 1.20
Chris Kaman 116
Dwyane Wade 115
❑ BPH Marcus Banks 123 .... 3.00 .90
Mickael Pietrus 121
Jarvis Hayes 120
❑ BPW Leandro Barbosa 137 3.00 .90
Aleksandar Pavlovic 129
Maurice Williams 143
❑ BRG Marcus Banks 123 .... 3.00 .90
Luke Ridnour 124
Reece Gaines 125
❑ BWM Chris Bosh 114 .... 5.00 1.50
Dwyane Wade 115
Darko Milicic 112
❑ CEK Brian Cook 134 .... 3.00 .90
Ndudi Ebi 135
Jason Kapono 140
❑ CHB Nick Collison 122 ...... 3.00 .90
Jarvis Hayes 120
Marcus Banks 123
❑ CHC Brian Cook 134......... 3.00 .90
Josh Howard 138
Zarko Cabarkapa 127
❑ CPD Zarko Cabarkapa 127 3.00 .90
Mickael Pietrus 121
Boris Diaw 131
❑ CPS Nick Collison 122 ...... 3.00 .90
Mickael Pietrus 121
Mike Sweetney 119
❑ CSH Nick Collison 122 ...... 3.00 .90
Mike Sweetney 119
Jarvis Hayes 120
❑ CWC Brian Cook 134 .... 3.00 .90
David West 128
Nick Collison 122
❑ DPP Boris Diaw 131 .... 3.00 .90
Aleksandar Pavlovic 129
Zoran Planinic 132
❑ DPW Boris Diaw 131.......... 3.00 .90
Aleksandar Pavlovic 129
David West 128
❑ EPW Ndudi Ebi 135 .... 3.00 .90
Kendrick Perkins 136
David West 128
❑ EWC Ndudi Ebi 135 .... 3.00 .90
David West 128
Brian Cook 134
❑ FAH T.J. Ford 118............. 5.00 1.50
Carmelo Anthony 113
Kirk Hinrich 117
❑ FBH T.J. Ford 118............. 4.00 1.20
Marcus Banks 123
Kirk Hinrich 117
❑ FBJ T.J. Ford 118 .... 8.00 2.40
Chris Bosh 114
LeBron James 111
❑ FBR T.J. Ford 118............. 4.00 1.20
Marcus Banks 123
Luke Ridnour 124
❑ FBW T.J. Ford 118 .... 5.00 1.50
Chris Bosh 114
Dwyane Wade 115
❑ FCH T.J. Ford 118 .... 4.00 1.20
Nick Collison 122
Kirk Hinrich 117
❑ FGB T.J. Ford 118 .... 3.00 .90

Reece Gaines 125
Marcus Banks 123
❑ FKW T.J. Ford 118 .... 4.00 1.20
Chris Kaman 116
Dwyane Wade 115
❑ GBB Reece Gaines 125 .... 3.00 .90
Marcus Banks 123
Troy Bell 126
❑ GBR Reece Gaines 125 .... 3.00 .90
Troy Bell 126
Luke Ridnour 124
❑ HAM Kirk Hinrich 117 .... 6.00 1.80
Carmelo Anthony 113
Darko Milicic 112
❑ HBM Kirk Hinrich 117 .... 5.00 1.50
Chris Bosh 114
Darko Milicic 112
❑ HBS Jarvis Hayes 120 ...... 3.00 .90
Marcus Banks 123
Mike Sweetney 119
❑ HCJ Josh Howard 138 ...... 3.00 .90
Brian Cook 134
Dahntay Jones 130
❑ HGP Jarvis Hayes 120 ...... 3.00 .90
Reece Gaines 125
Mickael Pietrus 121
❑ HJM Kirk Hinrich 117 .... 8.00 2.40
LeBron James 111
Darko Milicic 112
❑ HKC Jarvis Hayes 120 ...... 3.00 .90
Chris Kaman 116
Nick Collison 122
❑ HLC Josh Howard 138 ...... 3.00 .90
Maciej Lampe 139
Brian Cook 134
❑ HLK Josh Howard 138 ...... 3.00 .90
Maciej Lampe 139
Jason Kapono 140
❑ HPR Jarvis Hayes 120 ...... 3.00 .90
Mickael Pietrus 121
Luke Ridnour 124
❑ HSL Jarvis Hayes 120........ 3.00 .90
Mike Sweetney 119
Maciej Lampe 139
❑ HSP Jarvis Hayes 120 ...... 3.00 .90
Mike Sweetney 119
Mickael Pietrus 121
❑ HWS Kirk Hinrich 117 .... 4.00 1.20
Dwyane Wade 115
Mike Sweetney 119
❑ JAW LeBron James 111 .. 15.00 4.50
Carmelo Anthony 113
Dwyane Wade 115
❑ JBM LeBron James 111 .... 8.00 2.40
Chris Bosh 114
Darko Milicic 112
❑ JHA LeBron James 111 .. 12.00 3.60
Kirk Hinrich 117
Carmelo Anthony 113
❑ JKA LeBron James 111 .. 10.00 3.00
Chris Kaman 116
Carmelo Anthony 113
❑ JMA LeBron James 111 .. 15.00 4.50
Darko Milicic 112
Carmelo Anthony 113
❑ JMK LeBron James 111 .... 8.00 2.40
Darko Milicic 112
Chris Kaman 116
❑ JOB Dahntay Jones 130..... 3.00 .90
Travis Outlaw 133
Leandro Barbosa 137
❑ JWE Dahntay Jones 130..... 3.00 .90
Luke Walton 141
Ndudi Ebi 135
❑ KCP Chris Kaman 116 ...... 3.00 .90
Zarko Cabarkapa 127
Kendrick Perkins 136
❑ KEW Jason Kapono 140..... 3.00 .90
Ndudi Ebi 135
Maurice Williams 143
❑ KHW Chris Kaman 116...... 4.00 1.20
Kirk Hinrich 117
Dwyane Wade 115
❑ KPH Chris Kaman 116 ...... 3.00 .90
Mickael Pietrus 121
Jarvis Hayes 120
❑ KSC Chris Kaman 22+ ...... 3.00 .90
Mike Sweetney 119
Nick Collison 122
❑ LBB Maciej Lampe 139...... 3.00 .90
Leandro Barbosa 137
Jerome Beasley 142
❑ LHC Maciej Lampe 139...... 3.00 .90
Josh Howard 138
Zarko Cabarkapa 127
❑ LSP Maciej Lampe 139...... 3.00 .90
Mike Sweetney 119
Zoran Planinic 132
❑ MAF Darko Milicic 112 ...... 5.00 1.50
Carmelo Anthony 113
T.J. Ford 118
❑ MBF Darko Milicic 112 ...... 4.00 1.20
Chris Bosh 114
T.J. Ford 118
❑ MFJ Darko Milicic 112........ 8.00 2.40
T.J. Ford 118
LeBron James 111
❑ MJW Darko Milicic 112 .... 10.00 3.00
LeBron James 111
Dwyane Wade 115
❑ OBD Travis Outlaw 133 .... 3.00 .90
Leandro Barbosa 137
Boris Diaw 131
❑ OCB Travis Outlaw 133 .... 3.00 .90
Brian Cook 134
Jerome Beasley 142
❑ OEJ Travis Outlaw 133...... 3.00 .90
Ndudi Ebi 135
Dahntay Jones 130
❑ OPE Travis Outlaw 133...... 3.00 .90
Kendrick Perkins 136
Ndudi Ebi 135
❑ PBE Kendrick Perkins 136 3.00 .90
Jerome Beasley 142
Ndudi Ebi 135
❑ PBG Kendrick Perkins 136 3.00 .90
Marcus Banks 123
Reece Gaines 125
❑ PBH Mickael Pietrus 121 .. 3.00 .90
Troy Bell 126
Jarvis Hayes 120
❑ PCH Mickael Pietrus 121 .. 3.00 .90
Nick Collison 122
Jarvis Hayes 120
❑ PCR Mickael Pietrus 121 .. 3.00 .90
Nick Collison 122
Luke Ridnour 124
❑ PCW Kendrick Perkins 136 3.00 .90
Zarko Cabarkapa 127
David West 128
❑ PDB Zoran Planinic 132 .... 3.00 .90
Boris Diaw 131
Leandro Barbosa 137
❑ PJD Aleksandar Pavlovic 129 3.00 .90
Dahntay Jones 130
Boris Diaw 131
❑ PLH Kendrick Perkins 136 3.00 .90
Maciej Lampe 139
Josh Howard 138
❑ POP Aleksandar Pavlovic 129 3.00 .90
Travis Outlaw 133
Zoran Planinic 132
❑ PPC Mickael Pietrus 121 .. 3.00 .90
Aleksandar Pavlovic 129
Zarko Cabarkapa 127
❑ PSK Mickael Pietrus 121..... 3.00 .90
Aleksandar Pavlovic 119
Chris Kaman 116
❑ PWO Zoran Planinic 132..... 3.00 .90
David West 128
Travis Outlaw 133
❑ RFH Luke Ridnour 124 ...... 4.00 1.20
T.J. Ford 118
Kirk Hinrich 117
❑ RHC Luke Ridnour 124...... 3.00 .90
Jarvis Hayes 120
Nick Collison 122
❑ SBC Mike Sweetney 119 .. 3.00 .90
Marcus Banks 123
Nick Collison 122
❑ SHK Mike Sweetney 119 .. 3.00 .90
Jarvis Hayes 120
Chris Kaman 116
❑ SPB Mike Sweetney 119..... 3.00 .90
Mickael Pietrus 121
Marcus Banks 123
❑ WBH Dwyane Wade 115 .. 4.00 1.20
Chris Bosh 114
Kirk Hinrich 117
❑ WBP Maurice Williams 143 3.00 .90
Leandro Barbosa 137
Zoran Planinic 2
❑ WDJ David West 128 .... 3.00 .90
Boris Diaw 131
Dahntay Jones 130
❑ WDP Maurice Williams 143 3.00 .90
Boris Diaw 131
Dahntay Jones 130
❑ WFH Dwyane Wade 115..... 4.00 1.20
T.J. Ford 118
Kirk Hinrich 117
❑ WHL Luke Walton 141 ...... 3.00 .90
Josh Howard 138
Maciej Lampe 139
❑ WHO Luke Walton 141 ...... 3.00 .90
Travis Outlaw 133
Josh Howard 138
❑ WJB Dwyane Wade 115 .. 10.00 3.00
LeBron James 111
Chris Bosh 114
❑ WKP Luke Walton 141 ...... 3.00 .90
Jason Kapono 140
Kendrick Perkins 136
❑ WKS Dwyane Wade 115..... 4.00 1.20
Chris Kaman 116
Mike Sweetney 119
❑ WMA Dwyane Wade 115 .. 8.00 2.40
Darko Milicic 112
Carmelo Anthony 113
❑ WPJ David West 128 .... 3.00 .90
Aleksandar Pavlovic 129
Dahntay Jones 130
❑ WWB Luke Walton 141...... 3.00 .90
Maurice Williams 143
Jerome Beasley 142

2000-01 Topps Stars

	Nm-Mt	Ex-Mt
COMPLETE SET (150)	60.00	18.00
COMMON CARD (1-150)	.20	.06
COMMON ROOKIE (101-125) ..	.60	.18
❑ 1 Elton Brand	.60	.18
❑ 2 Paul Pierce....................	.60	.18
❑ 3 Baron Davis	.60	.18
❑ 4 Corey Benjamin	.20	.06
❑ 5 Jason Kidd	1.00	.30

❑ 6 Stephon Marbury .60 .18
❑ 7 Eric Snow .40 .12
❑ 8 Joe Smith .40 .12
❑ 9 Larry Hughes .40 .12
❑ 10 Tim Duncan 1.25 .35
❑ 11 Theo Ratliff .40 .12
❑ 12 Dikembe Mutombo .40 .12
❑ 13 Tim Hardaway .40 .12
❑ 14 Glenn Robinson .60 .18
❑ 15 Grant Hill .60 .18
❑ 16 Patrick Ewing .60 .18
❑ 17 Ron Mercer .40 .12
❑ 18 Ron Artest .40 .12
❑ 19 Tom Gugliotta .20 .06
❑ 20 Steve Smith .40 .12
❑ 21 Vlade Divac .40 .12
❑ 22 Rashard Lewis .40 .12
❑ 23 Tracy McGrady 1.50 .45
❑ 24 Bryon Russell .20 .06
❑ 25 Michael Dickerson .40 .12
❑ 26 Juwan Howard .40 .12
❑ 27 Damon Stoudamire .40 .12
❑ 28 Hakeem Olajuwon .60 .18
❑ 29 Antonio McDyess .40 .12
❑ 30 Kobe Bryant 2.50 .75
❑ 31 Lindsey Hunter .20 .06
❑ 32 Magic Johnson 2.50 .75
❑ 33 Alonzo Mourning .40 .12
❑ 34 Kenny Anderson .40 .12
❑ 35 Allan Houston .40 .12
❑ 36 Keith Van Horn .60 .18
❑ 37 Shawn Marion .60 .18
❑ 38 David Robinson .60 .18
❑ 39 Mitch Richmond .40 .12
❑ 40 Shaquille O'Neal 1.50 .45
❑ 41 Gary Payton .60 .18
❑ 42 Sean Elliott .40 .12
❑ 43 Sam Cassell .60 .18
❑ 44 dale .20 .06
❑ 45 Derek Anderson .40 .12
❑ 46 Jonathan Bender .40 .12
❑ 47 Shandon Anderson .20 .06
❑ 48 Raef LaFrentz .40 .12
❑ 49 Michael Finley .60 .18
❑ 50 Toni Kukoc .40 .12
❑ 51 Anthony Mason .40 .12
❑ 52 Jim Jackson .20 .06
❑ 53 Glen Rice .40 .12
❑ 54 Jalen Rose .60 .18
❑ 55 Keon Clark .40 .12
❑ 56 Anfernee Hardaway .60 .18
❑ 57 Vin Baker .40 .12
❑ 58 Shawn Kemp .40 .12
❑ 59 John Stockton .60 .18
❑ 60 Shareef Abdur-Rahim .60 .18
❑ 61 Doug Christie .40 .12
❑ 62 Lamond Murray .20 .06
❑ 63 Scottie Pippen 1.00 .30
❑ 64 Darrell Armstrong .20 .06
❑ 65 Marcus Camby .40 .12
❑ 66 Wally Szczerbiak .40 .12
❑ 67 Jamal Mashburn .40 .12
❑ 68 Antonio Davis .20 .06
❑ 69 Kevin Garnett 1.25 .35
❑ 70 Cuttino Mobley .40 .12
❑ 71 Jerry Stackhouse .60 .18
❑ 72 Cedric Ceballos .20 .06
❑ 73 Nick Van Exel .60 .18
❑ 74 Latrell Sprewell .60 .18
❑ 75 Antoine Walker .60 .18
❑ 76 Allen Iverson 1.25 .35
❑ 77 Antawn Jamison .60 .18
❑ 78 Derrick Coleman .20 .06
❑ 79 Jason Terry .60 .18
❑ 80 Steve Francis .60 .18
❑ 81 Reggie Miller .60 .18
❑ 82 Rasheed Wallace .60 .18
❑ 83 Chris Webber .60 .18
❑ 84 Donyell Marshall .40 .12
❑ 85 Ruben Patterson .40 .12
❑ 86 Terrell Brandon .40 .12
❑ 87 Mike Bibby .60 .18
❑ 88 Richard Hamilton .40 .12
❑ 89 Jason Williams .40 .12
❑ 90 Corey Maggette .40 .12
❑ 91 Kerry Kittles .20 .06
❑ 92 Karl Malone .60 .18
❑ 93 Rod Strickland .20 .06
❑ 94 Eddie Jones .60 .18
❑ 95 Maurice Taylor .20 .06
❑ 96 Dirk Nowitzki 1.00 .30
❑ 97 Andre Miller .40 .12
❑ 98 Lamar Odom .60 .18
❑ 99 Ray Allen .60 .18
❑ 100 Vince Carter 1.50 .45
❑ 101 Chris Mihm RC .60 .18
❑ 102 Kenyon Martin RC 2.50 .75
❑ 103 Stromile Swift RC 1.25 .35
❑ 104 Joel Przybilla RC .60 .18
❑ 105 Marcus Fizer RC .60 .18
❑ 106 Mike Miller RC 2.00 .60
❑ 107 Darius Miles RC 2.00 .60
❑ 108 Mark Madsen RC .60 .18
❑ 109 Courtney Alexander RC .60 .18
❑ 110 DeShawn Stevenson RC .60 .18
❑ 111 DerMarr Johnson RC .60 .18
❑ 112 Mamadou N'diaye RC .60 .18
❑ 113 Mateen Cleaves RC .60 .18
❑ 114 Morris Peterson RC 1.25 .35
❑ 115 Etan Thomas RC .60 .18
❑ 116 Erick Barkley RC .60 .18
❑ 117 Quentin Richardson RC 2.00 .60
❑ 118 Keyon Dooling RC .60 .18
❑ 119 Jerome Moiso RC .60 .18
❑ 120 Desmond Mason RC .60 .18
❑ 121 Speedy Claxton RC .60 .18
❑ 122 Jamaal Magloire RC .60 .18
❑ 123 Donnell Harvey RC .60 .18
❑ 124 Jamal Crawford RC .75 .23
❑ 125 Jason Collier RC .60 .18
❑ 126 Tim Duncan SPOT .60 .18
❑ 127 Shaquille O'Neal SPOT .60 .18
❑ 128 Vince Carter SPOT .75 .23
❑ 129 Allen Iverson SPOT .60 .18
❑ 130 Jason Kidd SPOT .60 .18
❑ 131 Kevin Garnett SPOT .60 .18
❑ 132 Gary Payton SPOT .60 .18
❑ 133 Tracy McGrady SPOT .60 .18
❑ 134 Jason Williams SPOT .20 .06
❑ 135 Kobe Bryant SPOT 1.25 .35
❑ 136 Elton Brand SPOT .40 .12
❑ 137 Ray Allen SPOT .40 .12
❑ 138 Grant Hill SPOT .60 .18
❑ 139 Chris Webber SPOT .40 .12
❑ 140 Latrell Sprewell SPOT .60 .18
❑ 141 Alonzo Mourning SPOT .60 .18
❑ 142 Lamar Odom SPOT .40 .12
❑ 143 S.Abdur-Rahim SPOT .40 .12
❑ 144 Steve Francis SPOT .60 .18
❑ 145 Magic Johnson SPOT 1.25 .35
❑ 146 Darius Miles SPOT 1.00 .30
❑ 147 Kenyon Martin SPOT 1.25 .35
❑ 148 Marcus Fizer SPOT .60 .18
❑ 149 Mateen Cleaves SPOT .60 .18
❑ 150 Stromile Swift SPOT .60 .18

2001-02 Topps TCC

	Nm-Mt	Ex-Mt
COMPLETE SET (150)	80.00	24.00
COMMON CARD	.20	.06
COMMON ROOKIE (118-150)	1.00	.30

❑ 1 Shaquille O'Neal 1.50 .45
❑ 2 Jason Williams .40 .12
❑ 3 Eddie Jones .60 .18
❑ 4 Anthony Mason .40 .12
❑ 5 Joe Smith .40 .12
❑ 6 Kenyon Martin .60 .18
❑ 7 Tracy McGrady 1.50 .45
❑ 8 Horace Grant .40 .12
❑ 9 Andre Miller .40 .12
❑ 10 Allen Iverson 1.25 .35
❑ 11 Shawn Marion .60 .18
❑ 12 Derek Anderson .40 .12
❑ 13 Chris Webber .60 .18
❑ 14 Bruce Bowen .20 .06
❑ 15 Alvin Williams .20 .06
❑ 16 Brent Barry .40 .12
❑ 17 Donyell Marshall .40 .12
❑ 18 Richard Hamilton .40 .12
❑ 19 Vlade Divac .40 .12
❑ 20 Vince Carter 1.50 .45
❑ 21 Kevin Garnett 1.25 .35
❑ 22 Jason Terry .60 .18
❑ 23 Antoine Walker .60 .18
❑ 24 P.J. Brown .20 .06
❑ 25 Baron Davis .60 .18
❑ 26 Eddie Robinson .40 .12
❑ 27 Chris Mihm .40 .12
❑ 28 Michael Finley .60 .18
❑ 29 Nick Van Exel .60 .18
❑ 30 Steve Francis .60 .18
❑ 31 Chucky Atkins .20 .06
❑ 32 Raef LaFrentz .40 .12
❑ 33 Antawn Jamison .60 .18
❑ 34 Jalen Rose .60 .18
❑ 35 Lamar Odom .60 .18
❑ 36 Elton Brand .60 .18
❑ 37 Derek Fisher .60 .18
❑ 38 Alonzo Mourning .40 .12
❑ 39 Ervin Johnson .20 .06
❑ 40 Tim Duncan 1.25 .35
❑ 41 Kurt Thomas .40 .12
❑ 42 Latrell Sprewell .60 .18
❑ 43 Darrell Armstrong .20 .06
❑ 44 Tom Gugliotta .20 .06
❑ 45 Derrick Coleman .20 .06
❑ 46 Dale Davis .40 .12
❑ 47 David Robinson .60 .18
❑ 48 Scottie Pippen 1.00 .30
❑ 49 Hakeem Olajuwon .60 .18
❑ 50 Darius Miles .60 .18
❑ 51 Greg Ostertag .20 .06
❑ 52 Karl Malone .60 .18
❑ 53 Morris Peterson .40 .12
❑ 54 Shareef Abdur-Rahim .60 .18
❑ 55 Dikembe Mutombo .40 .12
❑ 56 Elden Campbell .20 .06
❑ 57 Ron Mercer .40 .12

❑ 58 Jumaine Jones	.40	.12
❑ 59 Wang ZhiZhi	.60	.18
❑ 60 Ray Allen	.60	.18
❑ 61 Marcus Camby	.40	.12
❑ 62 Jermaine O'Neal	.60	.18
❑ 63 Kenny Thomas	.20	.06
❑ 64 Danny Fortson	.20	.06
❑ 65 Ben Wallace	.60	.18
❑ 66 DeShawn Stevenson	.40	.12
❑ 67 Antonio Davis	.20	.06
❑ 68 Doug Christie	.40	.12
❑ 69 Rasheed Wallace	.60	.18
❑ 70 Stephon Marbury	.60	.18
❑ 71 Allan Houston	.40	.12
❑ 72 Kerry Kittles	.20	.06
❑ 73 Todd MacCulloch	.20	.06
❑ 74 Sam Cassell	.60	.18
❑ 75 Kobe Bryant	2.50	.75
❑ 76 Aaron McKie	.40	.12
❑ 77 Terrell Brandon	.40	.12
❑ 78 Brian Grant	.40	.12
❑ 79 Michael Dickerson	.40	.12
❑ 80 Jerry Stackhouse	.60	.18
❑ 81 Antonio McDyess	.40	.12
❑ 82 Steve Nash	.60	.18
❑ 83 Paul Pierce	.60	.18
❑ 84 Jamal Mashburn	.40	.12
❑ 85 Toni Kukoc	.40	.12
❑ 86 James Posey	.40	.12
❑ 87 Larry Hughes	.40	.12
❑ 88 Cuttino Mobley	.40	.12
❑ 89 Jeff Foster	.20	.06
❑ 90 Jason Kidd	1.00	.30
❑ 91 Keith Van Horn	.60	.18
❑ 92 Mike Miller	.60	.18
❑ 93 Anfernee Hardaway	.60	.18
❑ 94 Bonzi Wells	.40	.12
❑ 95 Mike Bibby	.60	.18
❑ 96 Steve Smith	.40	.12
❑ 97 Gary Payton	.60	.18
❑ 98 John Stockton	.60	.18
❑ 99 Peja Stojakovic	.60	.18
❑ 100 Michael Jordan	12.00	3.60
❑ 101 Iakovos Tsakalidis	.20	.06
❑ 102 Mark Jackson	.40	.12
❑ 103 Wally Szczerbiak	.40	.12
❑ 104 Rod Strickland	.20	.06
❑ 105 Rick Fox	.40	.12
❑ 106 Glenn Robinson	.60	.18
❑ 107 Michael Olowokandi	.20	.06
❑ 108 Reggie Miller	.60	.18
❑ 109 Kelvin Cato	.20	.06
❑ 110 Clifford Robinson	.20	.06
❑ 111 Dirk Nowitzki	1.00	.30
❑ 112 Brad Miller	.60	.18
❑ 113 David Wesley	.20	.06
❑ 114 Kenny Anderson	.40	.12
❑ 115 Theo Ratliff	.40	.12
❑ 116 Rashard Lewis	.40	.12
❑ 117 Matt Harpring	.60	.18
❑ 118 Eddie Griffin RC	1.50	.45
❑ 119 Brendan Haywood RC	1.25	.35
❑ 120 Steven Hunter RC	1.00	.30
❑ 121 Jamaal Tinsley RC	1.50	.45
❑ 122 Jason Richardson RC	3.00	.90
❑ 123 Tony Parker RC	4.00	1.20
❑ 124 Pau Gasol RC	3.00	.90
❑ 125 Shane Battier RC	2.00	.60
❑ 126 Joe Johnson RC	1.50	.45
❑ 127 Leon Smith RC	1.00	.30
❑ 128 Mengke Bateer RC	2.50	.75
❑ 129 Loren Woods RC	1.00	.30
❑ 130 Kwame Brown RC	2.00	.60
❑ 131 Tyson Chandler RC	2.50	.75
❑ 132 Eddy Curry RC	2.50	.75
❑ 133 Kedrick Brown RC	1.00	.30
❑ 134 Joseph Forte RC	2.50	.75
❑ 135 Troy Murphy RC	2.00	.60
❑ 136 Richard Jefferson RC	2.00	.60
❑ 137 DeSagana Diop RC	1.00	.30
❑ 138 Vladimir Radmanovic RC	1.25	.35
❑ 139 Zach Randolph RC	3.00	.90
❑ 140 Gerald Wallace RC	2.50	.75
❑ 141 Brandon Armstrong RC	1.25	.35
❑ 142 Jeryl Sasser RC	1.00	.30
❑ 143 Rodney White RC	1.25	.35
❑ 144 Samuel Dalembert RC	1.00	.30
❑ 145 Jason Collins RC	1.00	.30
❑ 146 Michael Bradley RC	1.00	.30
❑ 147 Oscar Torres RC	1.00	.30
❑ 148 Zeljko Rebraca RC	1.00	.30
❑ 149 Andrei Kirilenko RC	2.50	.75
❑ 150 Trenton Hassell RC	1.50	.45

2002-03 Topps Ten

	Nm-Mt	Ex-Mt
COMPLETE SET (150)	50.00	15.00
COMMON CARD (1-121)	.20	.06
COMMON ROOKIE (121-150)	2.00	.60
❑ 1 Allen Iverson	1.25	.35
❑ 2 Shaquille O'Neal	1.50	.45
❑ 3 Paul Pierce	.60	.18
❑ 4 Tracy McGrady	1.50	.45
❑ 5 Tim Duncan	1.25	.35
❑ 6 Kobe Bryant	2.50	.75
❑ 7 Dirk Nowitzki	1.00	.30
❑ 8 Karl Malone	.60	.18
❑ 9 Antoine Walker	.60	.18
❑ 10 Gary Payton	.60	.18
❑ 11 Shaquille O'Neal	1.50	.45
❑ 12 Allen Iverson	1.25	.35
❑ 13 Tracy McGrady	1.50	.45
❑ 14 Kobe Bryant	2.50	.75
❑ 15 Michael Jordan	5.00	1.50
❑ 16 Paul Pierce	.60	.18
❑ 17 Chris Webber	.60	.18
❑ 18 Tim Duncan	1.25	.35
❑ 19 Corliss Williamson	.40	.12
❑ 20 Dirk Nowitzki	1.00	.30
❑ 21 Ben Wallace	.60	.18
❑ 22 Tim Duncan	1.25	.35
❑ 23 Kevin Garnett	1.25	.35
❑ 24 Danny Fortson	.20	.06
❑ 25 Elton Brand	.60	.18
❑ 26 Dikembe Mutombo	.40	.12
❑ 27 Jermaine O'Neal	.60	.18
❑ 28 Dirk Nowitzki	1.00	.30
❑ 29 Shawn Marion	.60	.18
❑ 30 P.J. Brown	.20	.06
❑ 31 Andre Miller	.40	.12
❑ 32 Jason Kidd	1.00	.30
❑ 33 Gary Payton	.60	.18
❑ 34 Baron Davis	.60	.18
❑ 35 John Stockton	.60	.18
❑ 36 Stephon Marbury	.60	.18
❑ 37 Jamaal Tinsley	.60	.18
❑ 38 Jason Williams	.40	.12
❑ 39 Steve Nash	.60	.18
❑ 40 Mark Jackson	.20	.06
❑ 41 Ben Wallace	.60	.18
❑ 42 Raef LaFrentz	.40	.12
❑ 43 Alonzo Mourning	.40	.12
❑ 44 Tim Duncan	1.25	.35
❑ 45 Dikembe Mutombo	.40	.12
❑ 46 Jermaine O'Neal	.60	.18
❑ 47 Erick Dampier	.40	.12
❑ 48 Adonal Foyle	.20	.06
❑ 49 Pau Gasol	.60	.18
❑ 50 Shaquille O'Neal	1.50	.45
❑ 51 Allen Iverson	1.25	.35
❑ 52 Ron Artest	.40	.12
❑ 53 Jason Kidd	1.00	.30
❑ 54 Baron Davis	.60	.18
❑ 55 Doug Christie	.40	.12
❑ 56 Darrell Armstrong	.20	.06
❑ 57 Karl Malone	.60	.18
❑ 58 Paul Pierce	.60	.18
❑ 59 Kenny Anderson	.40	.12
❑ 60 John Stockton	.60	.18
❑ 61 Shaquille O'Neal	1.50	.45
❑ 62 Elton Brand	.60	.18
❑ 63 Donyell Marshall	.40	.12
❑ 64 Pau Gasol	.60	.18
❑ 65 John Stockton	.60	.18
❑ 66 Alonzo Mourning	.40	.12
❑ 67 Ruben Patterson	.40	.12
❑ 68 Corliss Williamson	.40	.12
❑ 69 Tim Duncan	1.25	.35
❑ 70 Brent Barry	.40	.12
❑ 71 Steve Smith	.40	.12
❑ 72 Jon Barry	.20	.06
❑ 73 Eric Piatkowski	.40	.12
❑ 74 Wally Szczerbiak	.40	.12
❑ 75 Steve Nash	.60	.18
❑ 76 Hubert Davis	.20	.06
❑ 77 Tyronn Lue	.20	.06
❑ 78 Michael Redd	.60	.18
❑ 79 Wesley Person	.20	.06
❑ 80 Ray Allen	.60	.18
❑ 81 Reggie Miller	.60	.18
❑ 82 Richard Hamilton	.40	.12
❑ 83 Darrell Armstrong	.20	.06
❑ 84 Damon Stoudamire	.40	.12
❑ 85 Steve Nash	.60	.18
❑ 86 Chauncey Billups	.40	.12
❑ 87 Chris Whitney	.20	.06
❑ 88 Steve Smith	.40	.12
❑ 89 Peja Stojakovic	.60	.18
❑ 90 Troy Hudson	.20	.06
❑ 91 Allen Iverson	1.25	.35
❑ 92 Cuttino Mobley	.40	.12
❑ 93 Antoine Walker	.60	.18
❑ 94 Steve Francis	.60	.18
❑ 95 Latrell Sprewell	.60	.18
❑ 96 Tim Duncan	1.25	.35
❑ 97 Baron Davis	.60	.18
❑ 98 Paul Pierce	.60	.18
❑ 99 Gary Payton	.60	.18
❑ 100 Michael Finley	.60	.18
❑ 101 Tim Duncan	1.25	.35
❑ 102 Kevin Garnett	1.25	.35
❑ 103 Elton Brand	.60	.18
❑ 104 Jason Kidd	1.00	.30
❑ 105 Shawn Marion	.60	.18
❑ 106 Andre Miller	.40	.12
❑ 107 Shaquille O'Neal	1.50	.45
❑ 108 Jermaine O'Neal	.60	.18
❑ 109 Dirk Nowitzki	1.00	.30
❑ 110 Pau Gasol	.60	.18
❑ 111 Pau Gasol	.60	.18
❑ 112 Shane Battier	.60	.18
❑ 113 Jason Richardson	.60	.18
❑ 114 Gilbert Arenas	.60	.18
❑ 115 Andrei Kirilenko	.60	.18
❑ 116 Richard Jefferson	.40	.12
❑ 117 Jamaal Tinsley	.60	.18
❑ 118 Tony Parker	.60	.18
❑ 119 Eddie Griffin	.40	.12
❑ 120 Trenton Hassell	.40	.12
❑ 121 Jay Williams RC	3.00	.90
❑ 122 DaJuan Wagner RC	4.00	1.20
❑ 123 Fred Jones RC	2.50	.75
❑ 124 Jiri Welsch RC	2.00	.60
❑ 125 Juan Dixon RC	4.00	1.20
❑ 126 Kareem Rush RC	3.00	.90
❑ 127 Casey Jacobsen RC	2.00	.60
❑ 128 Frank Williams RC	2.00	.60
❑ 129 John Salmons RC	2.00	.60
❑ 130 Dan Dickau RC	2.00	.60
❑ 131 Mike Dunleavy RC	4.00	1.20
❑ 132 Nikoloz Tskitishvili RC	2.50	.75

	Nm-Mt	Ex-Mt
❑ 133 Caron Butler RC	5.00	1.50
❑ 134 Jared Jeffries RC	2.00	.60
❑ 135 Bostjan Nachbar RC	2.00	.60
❑ 136 Ryan Humphrey RC	2.00	.60
❑ 137 Qyntel Woods RC	2.50	.75
❑ 138 Tayshaun Prince RC	4.00	1.20
❑ 139 Chris Jefferies RC	2.00	.60
❑ 140 Vincent Yarbrough RC	2.00	.60
❑ 141 Yao Ming RC	15.00	4.50
❑ 142 Drew Gooden RC	6.00	1.80
❑ 143 Nene Hilario RC	3.00	.90
❑ 144 Chris Wilcox RC	3.00	.90
❑ 145 Amare Stoudemire RC	12.00	3.60
❑ 146 Melvin Ely RC	2.00	.60
❑ 147 Marcus Haislip RC	2.00	.60
❑ 148 Curtis Borchardt RC	2.00	.60
❑ 149 Robert Archibald RC	2.00	.60
❑ 150 Dan Gadzuric RC	2.00	.60

1999-00 Topps Tip-Off

	Nm-Mt	Ex-Mt
COMPLETE SET (132)	30.00	9.00
❑ 1 Steve Smith	.30	.09
❑ 2 Ron Harper	.30	.09
❑ 3 Michael Dickerson	.30	.09
❑ 4 LaPhonso Ellis	.15	.04
❑ 5 Chris Webber	.50	.15
❑ 6 Jason Caffey	.15	.04
❑ 7 Bryon Russell	.15	.04
❑ 8 Bison Dele	.15	.04
❑ 9 Isaiah Rider	.15	.04
❑ 10 Dean Garrett	.15	.04
❑ 11 Eric Murdock	.15	.04
❑ 12 Juwan Howard	.30	.09
❑ 13 Latrell Sprewell	.50	.15
❑ 14 Jalen Rose	.50	.15
❑ 15 Larry Johnson	.30	.09
❑ 16 Eric Williams	.15	.04
❑ 17 Bryant Reeves	.15	.04
❑ 18 Tony Battie	.15	.04
❑ 19 Luc Longley	.15	.04
❑ 20 Gary Payton	.50	.15
❑ 21 Tariq Abdul-Wahad	.15	.04
❑ 22 Armen Gilliam	.15	.04
❑ 23 Shaquille O'Neal	1.25	.35
❑ 24 Gary Trent	.15	.04
❑ 25 John Stockton	.50	.15
❑ 26 Mark Jackson	.30	.09
❑ 27 Cherokee Parks	.15	.04
❑ 28 Michael Olowokandi	.30	.09
❑ 29 Raef LaFrentz	.30	.09
❑ 30 Dell Curry	.15	.04
❑ 31 Travis Best	.15	.04
❑ 32 Shawn Kemp	.30	.09
❑ 33 Voshon Lenard	.15	.04
❑ 34 Brian Grant	.30	.09
❑ 35 Alvin Williams	.15	.04
❑ 36 Derek Fisher	.50	.15
❑ 37 Allan Houston	.30	.09
❑ 38 Arvydas Sabonis	.30	.09
❑ 39 Terry Cummings	.15	.04
❑ 40 Dale Ellis	.15	.04
❑ 41 Maurice Taylor	.30	.09
❑ 42 Grant Hill	.50	.15
❑ 43 Anthony Mason	.30	.09
❑ 44 John Wallace	.15	.04
❑ 45 David Wesley	.15	.04
❑ 46 Nick Van Exel	.50	.15
❑ 47 Cuttino Mobley	.50	.15
❑ 48 Anfernee Hardaway	.50	.15
❑ 49 Terry Porter	.15	.04
❑ 50 Brent Barry	.30	.09
❑ 51 Derek Harper	.30	.09
❑ 52 Antoine Walker	.50	.15
❑ 53 Karl Malone	.50	.15
❑ 54 Ben Wallace	.50	.15
❑ 55 Vlade Divac	.30	.09
❑ 56 Sam Mitchell	.15	.04
❑ 57 Joe Smith	.30	.09
❑ 58 Shawn Bradley	.15	.04
❑ 59 Darrell Armstrong	.15	.04
❑ 60 Kenny Anderson	.30	.09
❑ 61 Jason Williams	.50	.15
❑ 62 Alonzo Mourning	.30	.09
❑ 63 Matt Harpring	.50	.15
❑ 64 Antonio Davis	.15	.04
❑ 65 Lindsey Hunter	.15	.04
❑ 66 Allen Iverson	1.00	.30
❑ 67 Mookie Blaylock	.15	.04
❑ 68 Wesley Person	.15	.04
❑ 69 Bobby Phills	.15	.04
❑ 70 Theo Ratliff	.30	.09
❑ 71 Antonio Daniels	.15	.04
❑ 72 P.J. Brown	.15	.04
❑ 73 David Robinson	.50	.15
❑ 74 Sean Elliott	.30	.09
❑ 75 Zydrunas Ilgauskas	.30	.09
❑ 76 Kerry Kittles	.15	.04
❑ 77 Otis Thorpe	.30	.09
❑ 78 John Starks	.30	.09
❑ 79 Jaren Jackson	.15	.04
❑ 80 Hersey Hawkins	.30	.09
❑ 81 Glenn Robinson	.50	.15
❑ 82 Paul Pierce	.50	.15
❑ 83 Glen Rice	.30	.09
❑ 84 Charlie Ward	.15	.04
❑ 85 Dee Brown	.15	.04
❑ 86 Danny Fortson	.15	.04
❑ 87 Billy Owens	.15	.04
❑ 88 Jason Kidd	.75	.23
❑ 89 Brent Price	.15	.04
❑ 90 Don Reid	.15	.04
❑ 91 Mark Bryant	.15	.04
❑ 92 Vinny Del Negro	.15	.04
❑ 93 Stephon Marbury	.50	.15
❑ 94 Donyell Marshall	.30	.09
❑ 95 Jim Jackson	.15	.04
❑ 96 Horace Grant	.30	.09
❑ 97 Calbert Cheaney	.15	.04
❑ 98 Vince Carter	1.25	.35
❑ 99 Bobby Jackson	.30	.09
❑ 100 Alan Henderson	.15	.04
❑ 101 Mike Bibby	.50	.15
❑ 102 Cedric Henderson	.15	.04
❑ 103 Lamond Murray	.15	.04
❑ 104 A.C. Green	.30	.09
❑ 105 Hakeem Olajuwon	.50	.15
❑ 106 George Lynch	.15	.04
❑ 107 Kendall Gill	.15	.04
❑ 108 Rex Chapman	.15	.04
❑ 109 Eddie Jones	.50	.15
❑ 110 Kornel David RC	.15	.04
❑ 111 Jason Terry RC	2.00	.60
❑ 112 Corey Maggette RC	2.50	.75
❑ 113 Ron Artest RC	1.50	.45
❑ 114 Richard Hamilton RC	2.50	.75
❑ 115 Elton Brand RC	3.00	.90
❑ 116 Baron Davis RC	2.50	.75
❑ 117 Wally Szczerbiak RC	2.50	.75
❑ 118 Steve Francis RC	4.00	1.20
❑ 119 James Posey RC	1.50	.45
❑ 120 Shawn Marion RC	3.00	.90
❑ 121 Tim Duncan	1.00	.30
❑ 122 Danny Manning	.15	.04
❑ 123 Chris Mullin	.50	.15
❑ 124 Antawn Jamison	.75	.23
❑ 125 Kobe Bryant	2.00	.60
❑ 126 Matt Geiger	.15	.04
❑ 127 Rod Strickland	.15	.04
❑ 128 Howard Eisley	.15	.04
❑ 129 Steve Nash	.50	.15
❑ 130 Felipe Lopez	.15	.04
❑ 131 Ron Mercer	.30	.09
❑ 132 Checklist	.15	.04

2001-02 Topps Xpectations

	Nm-Mt	Ex-Mt
COMP.SET w/o SP's (145)	120.00	36.00
COMMON CARD (1-151)	.25	.07
COMMON ROOKIE (101-150)	2.00	.60
❑ 1 Baron Davis	.75	.23
❑ 2 Jason Terry	.75	.23
❑ 3 Paul Pierce	.75	.23
❑ 4 Ron Mercer	.50	.15
❑ 5 Dirk Nowitzki	1.25	.35
❑ 6 Marc Jackson	.50	.15
❑ 7 Cuttino Mobley	.50	.15
❑ 8 Al Harrington	.50	.15
❑ 9 Keyon Dooling	.50	.15
❑ 10 Mark Madsen	.50	.15
❑ 11 Jumaine Jones	.50	.15
❑ 12 Shawn Marion	.75	.23
❑ 13 Mike Bibby	.75	.23
❑ 14 Antonio Daniels	.25	.07
❑ 15 Vince Carter	2.00	.60
❑ 16 Stromile Swift	.50	.15
❑ 17 Courtney Alexander	.50	.15
❑ 18 Desmond Mason	.50	.15
❑ 19 Hidayet Turkoglu	.50	.15
❑ 20 Speedy Claxton	.50	.15
❑ 21 Lavor Postell	.50	.15
❑ 22 Chauncey Billups	.50	.15
❑ 23 Eddie House	.50	.15
❑ 24 Maurice Taylor	.25	.07
❑ 25 Lamar Odom	.75	.23
❑ 26 Antawn Jamison	.75	.23
❑ 27 Raef LaFrentz	.50	.15
❑ 28 Marcus Fizer	.50	.15
❑ 29 Chris Mihm	.50	.15
❑ 30 Eddie Robinson	.50	.15
❑ 31 Mark Blount	.25	.07
❑ 32 DerMarr Johnson	.50	.15
❑ 33 Wang Zhizhi	.75	.23
❑ 34 Danny Fortson	.25	.07
❑ 35 Elton Brand	.75	.23
❑ 36 Anthony Carter	.50	.15
❑ 37 Wally Szczerbiak	.50	.15
❑ 38 Mike Miller	.75	.23
❑ 39 Bonzi Wells	.50	.15
❑ 40 Tim Duncan	1.50	.45
❑ 41 Ruben Patterson	.50	.15
❑ 42 Keon Clark	.50	.15
❑ 43 Jason Williams	.50	.15
❑ 44 Richard Hamilton	.50	.15
❑ 45 Scott Padgett	.25	.07
❑ 46 Derek Anderson	.50	.15
❑ 47 Keith Van Horn	.75	.23
❑ 48 Tim Thomas	.50	.15
❑ 49 Jonathan Bender	.50	.15
❑ 50 Tracy McGrady	2.00	.60
❑ 51 Tyronn Lue	.25	.07
❑ 52 Austin Croshere	.50	.15
❑ 53 James Posey	.50	.15
❑ 54 Mateen Cleaves	.50	.15
❑ 55 Matt Harpring	.75	.23
❑ 56 Calvin Booth	.25	.07
❑ 57 Quentin Richardson	.50	.15
❑ 58 Joel Przybilla	.50	.15
❑ 59 Kenyon Martin	.75	.23
❑ 60 Iakovos Tsakalidis	.25	.07
❑ 61 Peja Stojakovic	.75	.23

❑ 62 Shammond Williams .25 .07
❑ 63 Alvin Williams .25 .07
❑ 64 Jahidi White .50 .15
❑ 65 Morris Peterson .50 .15
❑ 66 Larry Hughes .50 .15
❑ 67 Andre Miller .50 .15
❑ 68 Jamaal Magloire .50 .15
❑ 69 Steve Francis .75 .23
❑ 70 Todd MacCulloch .25 .07
❑ 71 Rashard Lewis .50 .15
❑ 72 Michael Dickerson .50 .15
❑ 73 Nazr Mohammed .25 .07
❑ 74 Jamal Crawford .50 .15
❑ 75 Darius Miles .75 .23
❑ 76 Allen Iverson 1.50 .45
❑ 77 Shaquille O'Neal 2.00 .60
❑ 78 Michael Finley .75 .23
❑ 79 Antonio McDyess .50 .15
❑ 80 Jerry Stackhouse .75 .23
❑ 81 Chris Webber .75 .23
❑ 82 Eddie Jones .75 .23
❑ 83 Reggie Miller .75 .23
❑ 84 Antoine Walker .75 .23
❑ 85 Latrell Sprewell .75 .23
❑ 86 Alonzo Mourning .50 .15
❑ 87 Jalen Rose .75 .23
❑ 88 Ray Allen .75 .23
❑ 89 Gary Payton .75 .23
❑ 90 Jason Kidd 1.25 .35
❑ 91 Stephon Marbury .75 .23
❑ 92 Kobe Bryant 3.00 .90
❑ 93 Grant Hill .75 .23
❑ 94 Karl Malone .75 .23
❑ 95 John Stockton .75 .23
❑ 96 Anfernee Hardaway .50 .15
❑ 97 Rasheed Wallace .75 .23
❑ 98 Hakeem Olajuwon .75 .23
❑ 99 Shareef Abdur-Rahim .75 .23
❑ 100 Kevin Garnett 1.50 .45
❑ 101 Kwame Brown/250 RC 25.00 7.50
❑ 102 Tyson Chandler RC 5.00 1.50
❑ 103 Pau Gasol RC 6.00 1.80
❑ 104 Eddy Curry RC 5.00 1.50
❑ 105 J.Richardson/250 RC 40.00 12.00
❑ 106 Shane Battier/250 RC 25.00 7.50
❑ 107 Eddie Griffin RC 3.00 .90
❑ 108 DeSagana Diop RC 2.00 .60
❑ 109 Rodney White RC 2.50 .75
❑ 110 Joe Johnson/250 RC 20.00 6.00
❑ 111 Kedrick Brown RC 2.00 .60
❑ 112 Vladimir Radmanovic RC 2.50 .75
❑ 113 Richard Jefferson RC 6.00 1.80
❑ 114 Troy Murphy/250 RC 30.00 9.00
❑ 115 Steven Hunter RC 2.00 .60
❑ 116 Kirk Haston RC 2.00 .60
❑ 117 Michael Bradley RC 2.00 .60
❑ 118 Jason Collins RC 2.00 .60
❑ 119 Zach Randolph/250 RC 40.00 12.00
❑ 120 Brendan Haywood RC 2.50 .75
❑ 121 Joseph Forte RC 4.00 1.20
❑ 122 Jeryl Sasser RC 2.00 .60
❑ 123 Brandon Armstrong RC 2.50 .75
❑ 124 Gerald Wallace RC 5.00 1.50
❑ 125 Samuel Dalembert RC 2.00 .60
❑ 126 Jamaal Tinsley RC 3.00 .90
❑ 127 Tony Parker RC 8.00 2.40
❑ 128 Trenton Hassell RC 3.00 .90
❑ 129 Gilbert Arenas RC 5.00 1.50
❑ 130 Raja Bell RC 2.50 .75
❑ 131 Will Solomon RC 2.00 .60
❑ 132 Terence Morris RC 2.00 .60
❑ 133 Brian Scalabrine RC 2.00 .60
❑ 134 Jeff Trepagnier RC 2.00 .60
❑ 135 Damone Brown RC 2.00 .60
❑ 136 Carlos Arroyo RC 15.00 4.50
❑ 137 Earl Watson RC 2.50 .75
❑ 138 Jamison Brewer RC 2.00 .60
❑ 139 Bobby Simmons RC 2.00 .60
❑ 140 Andrei Kirilenko RC 5.00 1.50
❑ 141 Zeljko Rebraca RC 2.00 .60
❑ 142 Sean Lampley RC 2.00 .60
❑ 143 Loren Woods RC 2.00 .60
❑ 144 Alton Ford RC 2.50 .75
❑ 145 Antonis Fotsis RC 2.00 .60
❑ 146 Charlie Bell RC 3.00 .90
❑ 147 R.Boumtje-Boumtje RC 2.00 .60
❑ 148 Jarron Collins RC 2.00 .60
❑ 149 Kenny Satterfield RC 2.00 .60
❑ 150 Alvin Jones RC 2.00 .60
❑ 151 Michael Jordan 12.00 3.60

2002-03 Topps Xpectations

	Nm-Mt	Ex-Mt
COMPLETE SET (178)	300.00	90.00
COMP.SET w/o SP's (100)	25.00	7.50
COMMON CARD (1-100)	.20	.06
COMMON ROOKIE (101-133)	2.50	.75
COMMON ROOKIE (134-153)	6.00	1.80
COMMON CARD (154-178)	2.50	.75

❑ 1 Darius Miles .60 .18
❑ 2 Jason Williams .40 .12
❑ 3 Speedy Claxton .40 .12
❑ 4 Eduardo Najera .40 .12
❑ 5 Chris Mihm .20 .06
❑ 6 Eddie Robinson .40 .12
❑ 7 Lee Nailon .20 .06
❑ 8 Joseph Forte .40 .12
❑ 9 Jason Terry .60 .18
❑ 10 Vince Carter 1.50 .45
❑ 11 Matt Harpring .60 .18
❑ 12 Bonzi Wells .40 .12
❑ 13 Mike Bibby .60 .18
❑ 14 Jerome James .20 .06
❑ 15 Morris Peterson .40 .12
❑ 16 Jarron Collins .20 .06
❑ 17 Brendan Haywood .40 .12
❑ 18 Dermarr Johnson .20 .06
❑ 19 Kirk Haston .40 .12
❑ 20 Paul Pierce .60 .18
❑ 21 Eddy Curry .60 .18
❑ 22 Ricky Davis .40 .12
❑ 23 James Posey .40 .12
❑ 24 Zeljko Rebraca .40 .12
❑ 25 Jason Richardson .60 .18
❑ 26 Ron Artest .20 .06
❑ 27 Jonathan Bender .40 .12
❑ 28 Elton Brand .60 .18
❑ 29 Stromile Swift .40 .12
❑ 30 Steve Francis .60 .18
❑ 31 Devean George .40 .12
❑ 32 Eddie House .20 .06
❑ 33 Loren Woods .40 .12
❑ 34 Richard Jefferson .40 .12
❑ 35 Mike Miller .60 .18
❑ 36 Joe Johnson .60 .18
❑ 37 Zach Randolph .60 .18
❑ 38 Peja Stojakovic .60 .18
❑ 39 Predrag Drobnjak .20 .06
❑ 40 Kwame Brown .40 .12
❑ 41 DeShawn Stevenson .20 .06
❑ 42 Desmond Mason .40 .12
❑ 43 Stephen Jackson .20 .06
❑ 44 Ruben Patterson .40 .12
❑ 45 Samuel Dalembert .20 .06
❑ 46 Pat Garrity .20 .06
❑ 47 Jason Collins .20 .06
❑ 48 Marc Jackson .40 .12
❑ 49 Rafer Alston .20 .06
❑ 50 Shawn Marion .60 .18
❑ 51 Joel Przybilla .20 .06
❑ 52 Shane Battier .60 .18
❑ 53 Quentin Richardson .40 .12
❑ 54 Jamaal Tinsley .60 .18
❑ 55 Cuttino Mobley .40 .12
❑ 56 Antawn Jamison .60 .18
❑ 57 Chucky Atkins .20 .06
❑ 58 Raef Lafrentz .40 .12
❑ 59 Jumaine Jones .40 .12
❑ 60 Dirk Nowitzki 1.00 .30
❑ 61 Marcus Fizer .40 .12
❑ 62 Kedrick Brown .40 .12
❑ 63 Nazr Mohammed .20 .06
❑ 64 Jamaal Magloire .20 .06
❑ 65 Tyson Chandler .60 .18
❑ 66 Andre Miller .40 .12
❑ 67 Wang Zhizhi .60 .18
❑ 68 Mengke Bateer .60 .18
❑ 69 Gilbert Arenas .60 .18
❑ 70 Baron Davis .60 .18
❑ 71 Lamar Odom .60 .18
❑ 72 Mark Madsen .20 .06
❑ 73 Pau Gasol .60 .18
❑ 74 Anthony Carter .40 .12
❑ 75 Wally Szczerbiak .40 .12
❑ 76 Todd MacCulloch .20 .06
❑ 77 Steven Hunter .20 .06
❑ 78 Iakovos Tsakalidis .20 .06
❑ 79 Ruben Boumtje-Boumtje .20 .06
❑ 80 Gerald Wallace .60 .18
❑ 81 Vladimir Radmanovic .40 .12
❑ 82 Keon Clark .40 .12
❑ 83 Andrei Kirilenko .60 .18
❑ 84 Richard Hamilton .40 .12
❑ 85 Trenton Hassell .40 .12
❑ 86 Donnell Harvey .20 .06
❑ 87 Rodney White .40 .12
❑ 88 Troy Murphy .40 .12
❑ 89 Terence Morris .20 .06
❑ 90 Al Harrington .40 .12
❑ 91 Michael Redd .60 .18
❑ 92 Kenyon Martin .60 .18
❑ 93 Lavor Postell .20 .06
❑ 94 Jeryl Sasser .20 .06
❑ 95 Hidayet Turkoglu .60 .18
❑ 96 Tony Parker .60 .18
❑ 97 Rashard Lewis .40 .12
❑ 98 Michael Bradley .40 .12
❑ 99 Courtney Alexander .40 .12
❑ 100 Eddie Griffin .40 .12
❑ 101 Yao Ming RC 12.00 3.60
❑ 102 Dan Gadzuric RC 2.50 .75
❑ 103 Mike Dunleavy RC 4.00 1.20
❑ 104 Drew Gooden RC 6.00 1.80
❑ 105 Nikoloz Tskitishvili RC 2.50 .75
❑ 106 Roger Mason RC 2.50 .75
❑ 107 Nene Hilario RC 3.00 .90
❑ 108 Chris Wilcox RC 3.00 .90
❑ 109 Rod Grizzard RC 2.50 .75
❑ 110 Chris Owens RC 2.50 .75
❑ 111 Jared Jeffries RC 2.50 .75
❑ 112 Efthimios Rentzias RC 2.50 .75
❑ 113 Marcus Haislip RC 2.50 .75
❑ 114 Fred Jones RC 2.50 .75
❑ 115 Bostjan Nachbar RC 2.50 .75
❑ 116 Jiri Welsch RC 2.50 .75
❑ 117 Jannero Pargo RC 2.50 .75
❑ 118 Curtis Borchardt RC 2.50 .75
❑ 119 Ryan Humphrey RC 2.50 .75
❑ 120 Raul Lopez RC 3.00 .90
❑ 121 Cezary Trybanski RC 2.50 .75
❑ 122 Predrag Savovic RC 2.50 .75
❑ 123 Tayshaun Prince RC 3.00 .90
❑ 124 Frank Williams RC 2.50 .75
❑ 125 John Salmons RC 2.50 .75
❑ 126 Chris Jefferies RC 2.50 .75
❑ 127 Luke Recker RC 3.00 .90
❑ 128 Tamar Slay RC 2.50 .75
❑ 129 Matt Barnes RC 2.50 .75
❑ 130 Rasual Butler RC 2.50 .75

❑ 131 Vincent Yarbrough RC 2.50 .75
❑ 132 Junior Harrington RC .. 2.50 .75
❑ 133 Carlos Boozer RC 5.00 1.50
❑ 134 DaJuan Wagner/500 RC 10.00 3.00
❑ 135 Jay Williams/500 RC .. 8.00 2.40
❑ 136 Amare Stoudemire/500 RC 30.00 9.00
❑ 137 Caron Butler/500 RC 15.00 4.50
❑ 138 Melvin Ely/500 RC 6.00 1.80
❑ 139 Juan Dixon/500 RC .. 10.00 3.00
❑ 140 Kareem Rush/500 RC 8.00 2.40
❑ 141 Qyntel Woods/500 RC 2.50 .75
❑ 142 Casey Jacobsen/500 RC 6.00 1.80
❑ 143 Robert Archibald/500 RC 6.00 1.80
❑ 144 Tito Maddox/500 RC .. 6.00 1.80
❑ 145 Ronald Murray/500 RC 8.00 2.40
❑ 146 Sam Clancy/500 RC.... 6.00 1.80
❑ 147 Dan Dickau/500 RC .... 2.50 .75
❑ 148 Mehmet Okur/500 RC 8.00 2.40
❑ 149 Marko Jaric/500 RC 6.00 1.80
❑ 150 Gordan Giricek/500 RC 10.00 3.00
❑ 151 Manu Ginobili/500 RC 20.00 6.00
❑ 152 J.R. Bremer/500 RC 6.00 1.80
❑ 153 Corsley Edwards/500 RC 6.00 1.80
❑ 154 Michael Jordan XX 25.00 7.50
❑ 155 Allen Iverson XX.......... 5.00 1.50
❑ 156 Shaquille O'Neal XX.... 6.00 1.80
❑ 157 Tim Duncan XX 5.00 1.50
❑ 158 Tracy McGrady XX...... 6.00 1.80
❑ 159 Kevin Garnett XX 5.00 1.50
❑ 160 Chris Webber XX .... 2.50 .75
❑ 161 Alonzo Mourning XX .. 2.50 .75
❑ 162 Antoine Walker XX...... 2.50 .75
❑ 163 Latrell Sprewell XX...... 2.50 .75
❑ 164 Eddie Jones XX .... 2.50 .75
❑ 165 Kobe Bryant XX 10.00 3.00
❑ 166 Allan Houston XX........ 2.50 .75
❑ 167 Ray Allen XX .... 2.50 .75
❑ 168 Gary Payton XX .... 2.50 .75
❑ 169 Antonio McDyess XX .. 6.00 1.80
❑ 170 Jason Kidd XX 4.00 1.20
❑ 171 Jerry Stackhouse XX .. 2.50 .75
❑ 172 Stephon Marbury XX .. 2.50 .75
❑ 173 Karl Malone XX .... 2.50 .75
❑ 174 Reggie Miller XX .... 2.50 .75
❑ 175 S.Abdur-Rahim XX...... 2.50 .75
❑ 176 Rasheed Wallace XX .. 2.50 .75
❑ 177 John Stockton XX........ 2.50 .75
❑ 178 Grant Hill XX .... 2.50 .75

2002-03 UD Authentics

	Nm-Mt	Ex-Mt
COMPLETE SET (132)	350.00	105.00
COMP.SET w/o SP's (90)	40.00	12.00
COMMON CARD (1-90)	.20	.06
COMMON ROOKIE (91-	6.00	1.80
COMMON ROOKIE (124-132)	15.00	4.50

❑ 1 Shareef Abdur-Rahim ...... .75 .23
❑ 2 Jason Terry .... .75 .23
❑ 3 Glenn Robinson .... .75 .23
❑ 4 Paul Pierce....................... .75 .23
❑ 5 Antoine Walker.................. .75 .23
❑ 6 Eric Williams..................... .20 .06
❑ 7 Kedrick Brown .... .50 .15
❑ 8 Jalen Rose .... .75 .23
❑ 9 Tyson Chandler .... .75 .23
❑ 10 Eddy Curry........................ .75 .23
❑ 11 Darius Miles .... .75 .23
❑ 12 Lamond Murray .... .20 .06
❑ 13 Chris Mihm....................... .20 .06
❑ 14 Dirk Nowitzki .... 1.25 .35
❑ 15 Steve Nash...................... .75 .23
❑ 16 Michael Finley .... .75 .23
❑ 17 Raef LaFrentz .... .50 .15
❑ 18 James Posey .... .50 .15
❑ 19 Juwan Howard .... .50 .15
❑ 20 Jerry Stackhouse .... .75 .23
❑ 21 Ben Wallace .... .75 .23
❑ 22 Clifford Robinson .... .50 .15
❑ 23 Jason Richardson .... .75 .23
❑ 24 Antawn Jamison.............. .75 .23
❑ 25 Gilbert Arenas .... .75 .23
❑ 26 Steve Francis .... .75 .23
❑ 27 Eddie Griffin .... .50 .15
❑ 28 Cuttino Mobley .... .50 .15
❑ 29 Reggie Miller .... .75 .23
❑ 30 Jamaal Tinsley .... .75 .23
❑ 31 Jermaine O'Neal.............. .75 .23
❑ 32 Elton Brand .... .75 .23
❑ 33 Lamar Odom .... .75 .23
❑ 34 Andre Miller .... .50 .15
❑ 35 Kobe Bryant .... 3.00 .90
❑ 36 Shaquille O'Neal............ 2.00 .60
❑ 37 Derek Fisher.................... .75 .23
❑ 38 Devean George .... .50 .15
❑ 39 Pau Gasol .... .75 .23
❑ 40 Shane Battier .... .75 .23
❑ 41 Alonzo Mourning .... .50 .15
❑ 42 Brian Grant...................... .50 .15
❑ 43 Eddie Jones .... .75 .23
❑ 44 Ray Allen .... .75 .23
❑ 45 Tim Thomas .... .50 .15
❑ 46 Kevin Garnett .... 1.50 .45
❑ 47 Wally Szczerbiak .... .50 .15
❑ 48 Terrell Brandon .... .50 .15
❑ 49 Jason Kidd .... 1.25 .35
❑ 50 Dikembe Mutombo .... .50 .15
❑ 51 Richard Jefferson............. .50 .15
❑ 52 Baron Davis .... .75 .23
❑ 53 Jamal Mashburn.............. .50 .15
❑ 54 David Wesley .... .20 .06
❑ 55 P.J. Brown .... .20 .06
❑ 56 Latrell Sprewell................ .75 .23
❑ 57 Allan Houston.................. .50 .15
❑ 58 Antonio McDyess .... .50 .15
❑ 59 Tracy McGrady.............. 2.00 .60
❑ 60 Mike Miller .... .75 .23
❑ 61 Darrell Armstrong .... .20 .06
❑ 62 Allen Iverson .... 1.50 .45
❑ 63 Keith Van Horn................ .75 .23
❑ 64 Stephon Marbury .... .75 .23
❑ 65 Shawn Marion .... .75 .23
❑ 66 Anfernee Hardaway .... .75 .23
❑ 67 Rasheed Wallace .... .75 .23
❑ 68 Bonzi Wells .... .50 .15
❑ 69 Scottie Pippen .... 1.25 .35
❑ 70 Chris Webber................... .75 .23
❑ 71 Peja Stojakovic................ .75 .23
❑ 72 Mike Bibby....................... .75 .23
❑ 73 Hidayet Turkoglu .... .75 .23
❑ 74 Tim Duncan .... 1.50 .45
❑ 75 David Robinson .... .75 .23
❑ 76 Tony Parker .... .75 .23
❑ 77 Malik Rose .... .20 .06
❑ 78 Gary Payton .... .75 .23
❑ 79 Rashard Lewis .... .50 .15
❑ 80 Desmond Mason .... .50 .15
❑ 81 Brent Barry...................... .50 .15
❑ 82 Vince Carter .... 2.00 .60
❑ 83 Morris Peterson .... .50 .15
❑ 84 Antonio Davis .... .20 .06
❑ 85 Karl Malone .... .75 .23
❑ 86 John Stockton .... .75 .23
❑ 87 Andrei Kirilenko .... .75 .23
❑ 88 Michael Jordan.............. 6.00 1.80
❑ 89 Richard Hamilton .... .50 .15
❑ 90 Kwame Brown .... .50 .15
❑ 91 Efthimios Rentzias RC .. 6.00 1.80
❑ 92 Darius Songaila RC 6.00 1.80
❑ 93 Matt Barnes RC 6.00 1.80
❑ 94 Sam Clancy RC 6.00 1.80
❑ 95 Lonny Baxter RC 6.00 1.80
❑ 96 Manu Ginobili RC 15.00 4.50
❑ 97 Rod Grizzard RC 6.00 1.80
❑ 98 Tito Maddox RC 6.00 1.80
❑ 99 Predrag Savovic RC...... 6.00 1.80
❑ 100 Carlos Boozer RC 10.00 3.00
❑ 101 Dan Gadzuric RC........ 6.00 1.80
❑ 102 Vincent Yarbrough RC 6.00 1.80
❑ 103 Robert Archibald RC .. 6.00 1.80
❑ 104 Roger Mason RC 6.00 1.80
❑ 105 Steve Logan RC.......... 6.00 1.80
❑ 106 Dan Dickau RC 6.00 1.80
❑ 107 Chris Jefferies RC 6.00 1.80
❑ 108 John Salmons RC 6.00 1.80
❑ 109 Frank Williams RC 6.00 1.80
❑ 110 Tayshaun Prince RC .. 8.00 2.40
❑ 111 Casey Jacobsen RC .. 6.00 1.80
❑ 112 Qyntel Woods RC 6.00 1.80
❑ 113 Kareem Rush RC 6.00 1.80
❑ 114 Ryan Humphrey RC.... 6.00 1.80
❑ 115 Curtis Borchardt RC.... 6.00 1.80
❑ 116 Juan Dixon RC.......... 15.00 4.50
❑ 117 Jiri Welsch RC 6.00 1.80
❑ 118 Bostjan Nachbar RC .. 6.00 1.80
❑ 119 Fred Jones RC............ 6.00 1.80
❑ 120 Marcus Haislip RC 6.00 1.80
❑ 121 Melvin Ely RC............ 6.00 1.80
❑ 122 Jared Jeffries RC 6.00 1.80
❑ 123 Caron Butler RC........ 12.00 3.60
❑ 124 Amare Stoudemire RC 40.00 12.00
❑ 125 Chris Wilcox RC 15.00 4.50
❑ 126 Nene Hilario RC 15.00 4.50
❑ 127 DaJuan Wagner RC .. 15.00 4.50
❑ 128 Nikoloz Tskitishvili RC 15.00 4.50
❑ 129 Drew Gooden RC...... 25.00 7.50
❑ 130 Mike Dunleavy RC 15.00 4.50
❑ 131 Jay Williams RC 12.00 3.60
❑ 132 Yao Ming RC 50.00 15.00

2003-04 UD Exquisite Collection

	Nm-Mt	Ex-Mt
COMMON CARD (1-42)	8.00	1.80
COMMON ROOKIE (44-73) ..	30.00	9.00

❑ 1 Jason Terry 10.00 3.00
❑ 2 Paul Pierce.................. 10.00 3.00
❑ 3 Michael Jordan............ 60.00 15.00
❑ 4 Kirk Hinrich RC............ 30.00 9.00
❑ 5 Dajuan Wagner 6.00 1.80
❑ 6 Dirk Nowitzki 15.00 3.60
❑ 7 Steve Nash.................. 10.00 3.00
❑ 8 Andre Miller 6.00 1.80
❑ 9 Ben Wallace................ 10.00 3.00
❑ 10 Jason Richardson 10.00 3.00
❑ 11 Steve Francis 10.00 3.00
❑ 12 Yao Ming 25.00 6.00
❑ 13 Jermaine O'Neal......... 10.00 3.00
❑ 14 Elton Brand 10.00 3.00
❑ 15 Kobe Bryant 40.00 9.00
❑ 16 Gary Payton 10.00 3.00
❑ 17 Shaquille O'Neal......... 25.00 6.00
❑ 18 Pau Gasol 10.00 3.00
❑ 19 Lamar Odom 10.00 3.00
❑ 20 T.J. Ford RC............... 30.00 9.00
❑ 21 Kevin Garnett 20.00 4.50
❑ 22 Latrell Sprewell........... 10.00 3.00
❑ 23 Jason Kidd 15.00 3.60
❑ 24 Richard Jefferson 6.00 1.80
❑ 25 Baron Davis 10.00 3.00
❑ 26 Allan Houston............... 6.00 1.80
❑ 27 Stephon Marbury 10.00 3.00
❑ 28 Tracy McGrady........... 25.00 6.00
❑ 29 Allen Iverson 20.00 4.50
❑ 30 Shawn Marion 10.00 3.00
❑ 31 Amare Stoudemire....... 20.00 4.50
❑ 32 Shareef Abdur-Rahim .. 10.00 3.00
❑ 33 Mike Bibby 10.00 3.00

❑ 34 Chris Webber 10.00 3.00
❑ 35 Tim Duncan 20.00 4.50
❑ 36 Manu Ginobili 10.00 3.00
❑ 37 Ray Allen 10.00 3.00
❑ 38 Nick Collison RC 20.00 6.00
❑ 39 Vince Carter 25.00 6.00
❑ 40 Andrei Kirilenko 10.00 3.00
❑ 41 Gilbert Arenas 10.00 3.00
❑ 42 Jerry Stackhouse 6.00 1.80
❑ 43 U.Haslem JSY AU RC 60.00 18.00
❑ 44 M.Williams JSY AU RC 30.00 9.00
❑ 45 Keith Bogans JSY AU RC 40.00 12.00
❑ 46 T.Hansen JSY AU RC 30.00 9.00
❑ 47 J.Kapono JSY AU RC 40.00 12.00
❑ 48 Z.Pachulia JSY AU RC 30.00 9.00
❑ 49 Z.Cabarkapa JSY AU RC 40.00 12.00
❑ 50 Kyle Korver JSY AU RC 40.00 12.00
❑ 51 Luke Walton JSY AU RC 100.00 30.00
❑ 52 Maciej Lampe JSY AU RC 50.00 15.00
❑ 53 Josh Howard JSY AU RC 80.00 24.00
❑ 54 L.Barbosa JSY AU RC 50.00 15.00
❑ 55 K.Perkins JSY AU RC 40.00 12.00
❑ 56 Ndudi Ebi JSY AU RC 60.00 18.00
❑ 57 J.Beasley JSY AU RC 30.00 9.00
❑ 58 Brian Cook JSY AU RC 40.00 12.00
❑ 59 Travis Outlaw JSY AU RC 60.00 18.00
❑ 60 Z.Planinic JSY AU RC 40.00 12.00
❑ 61 Boris Diaw JSY AU RC 40.00 12.00
❑ 62 Steve Blake JSY AU RC 40.00 12.00
❑ 63 A.Pavlovic JSY AU RC 40.00 12.00
❑ 64 David West JSY AU RC 40.00 12.00
❑ 65 M.Sweetney JSY AU RC 40.00 12.00
❑ 66 Troy Bell JSY AU RC .. 40.00 12.00
❑ 67 R.Gaines JSY AU RC 30.00 9.00
❑ 68 Luke Ridnour JSY AU RC 80.00 24.00
❑ 69 Marcus Banks JSY AU RC 40.00 12.00
❑ 70 Dahntay Jones JSY AU RC 40.00 12.00
❑ 71 M.Pietrus JSY AU RC 50.00 15.00
❑ 72 Chris Kaman JSY AU RC 50.00 15.00
❑ 73 Jarvis Hayes JSY AU RC 50.00 15.00
❑ 74 D.Wade JSY AU RC 600.00 180.00
❑ 75 Chris Bosh JSY AU RC 350.00 105.00
❑ 76 C.Anthony JSY AU RC 800.00 240.00
❑ 77 Darko Milicic JSY AU RC 250.00 75.00
❑ 78 L.James JSY AU RC 2,500.00 750.00

2002-03 UD Glass

	Nm-Mt	Ex-Mt
COMP.SET w/o SP's (90)	40.00	12.00
COMMON CARD (1-90)	.25	.07
COMMON CW (91-110)	12.00	3.60
COMMON ROOKIE (111-120)	20.00	6.00
COMMON ROOKIE (121-130)	12.00	3.60
COMMON ROOKIE (131-150)	10.00	3.00

❑ 1 Shareef Abdur-Rahim .... 1.00 .30
❑ 2 Glenn Robinson .... 1.00 .30
❑ 3 Jason Terry .... 1.00 .30
❑ 4 Paul Pierce .... 1.00 .30
❑ 5 Antoine Walker .... 1.00 .30
❑ 6 Vin Baker .... .60 .18
❑ 7 Jalen Rose .... 1.00 .30
❑ 8 Eddy Curry .... 1.00 .30
❑ 9 Tyson Chandler .... 1.00 .30
❑ 10 Darius Miles .... 1.00 .30
❑ 11 Ricky Davis .... 1.00 .30
❑ 12 Zydrunas Ilgauskas .... .60 .18
❑ 13 Dirk Nowitzki .... 1.50 .45
❑ 14 Michael Finley .... 1.00 .30
❑ 15 Steve Nash .... 1.00 .30
❑ 16 Raef LaFrentz .... .60 .18
❑ 17 Rodney White .... .60 .18
❑ 18 Marcus Camby .... .60 .18
❑ 19 Juwan Howard .... .60 .18
❑ 20 Richard Hamilton .... .60 .18
❑ 21 Ben Wallace .... 1.00 .30
❑ 22 Chauncey Billups .... .60 .18
❑ 23 Jason Richardson .... 1.00 .30
❑ 24 Antawn Jamison .... 1.00 .30
❑ 25 Steve Francis .... 1.00 .30
❑ 26 Cuttino Mobley .... .60 .18
❑ 27 Eddie Griffin .... .60 .18
❑ 28 Jermaine O'Neal .... 1.00 .30
❑ 29 Reggie Miller .... 1.00 .30
❑ 30 Jamaal Tinsley .... 1.00 .30
❑ 31 Andre Miller .... .60 .18
❑ 32 Elton Brand .... 1.00 .30
❑ 33 Quentin Richardson .... .60 .18
❑ 34 Kobe Bryant 4.00 1.20
❑ 35 Shaquille O'Neal .... 2.50 .75
❑ 36 Robert Horry .... .60 .18
❑ 37 Pau Gasol .... 1.00 .30
❑ 38 Shane Battier .... 1.00 .30
❑ 39 Jason Williams .... .60 .18
❑ 40 Eddie Jones .... 1.00 .30
❑ 41 Brian Grant .... .60 .18
❑ 42 Malik Allen .... .25 .07
❑ 43 Ray Allen .... 1.00 .30
❑ 44 Tim Thomas .... .60 .18
❑ 45 Sam Cassell .... 1.00 .30
❑ 46 Kevin Garnett .... 2.00 .60
❑ 47 Wally Szczerbiak .... .60 .18
❑ 48 Troy Hudson .... .25 .07
❑ 49 Loren Woods .... .60 .18
❑ 50 Jason Kidd .... 1.50 .45
❑ 51 Richard Jefferson .... .60 .18
❑ 52 Kenyon Martin .... 1.00 .30
❑ 53 Baron Davis .... 1.00 .30
❑ 54 Jamal Mashburn .... .60 .18
❑ 55 David Wesley .... .25 .07
❑ 56 P.J. Brown .... .25 .07
❑ 57 Allan Houston .... .60 .18
❑ 58 Kurt Thomas .... .60 .18
❑ 59 Latrell Sprewell .... 1.00 .30
❑ 60 Tracy McGrady .... 2.50 .75
❑ 61 Mike Miller .... 1.00 .30
❑ 62 Grant Hill .... 1.00 .30
❑ 63 Allen Iverson .... 2.00 .60
❑ 64 Keith Van Horn .... 1.00 .30
❑ 65 Aaron McKie .... .60 .18
❑ 66 Stephon Marbury .... 1.00 .30
❑ 67 Shawn Marion .... 1.00 .30
❑ 68 Anfernee Hardaway .... 1.00 .30
❑ 69 Rasheed Wallace .... 1.00 .30
❑ 70 Damon Stoudamire .... .60 .18
❑ 71 Bonzi Wells .... .60 .18
❑ 72 Chris Webber .... 1.00 .30
❑ 73 Mike Bibby .... 1.00 .30
❑ 74 Peja Stojakovic .... 1.00 .30
❑ 75 Hedo Turkoglu .... 1.00 .30
❑ 76 Tim Duncan .... 2.00 .60
❑ 77 David Robinson .... 1.00 .30
❑ 78 Tony Parker .... 1.00 .30
❑ 79 Gary Payton .... 1.00 .30
❑ 80 Rashard Lewis .... .60 .18
❑ 81 Desmond Mason .... .60 .18
❑ 82 Vince Carter .... 2.50 .75
❑ 83 Antonio Davis .... .25 .07
❑ 84 Morris Peterson .... .60 .18
❑ 85 John Stockton .... 1.00 .30
❑ 86 Karl Malone .... 1.00 .30
❑ 87 Andrei Kirilenko .... 1.00 .30
❑ 88 Jerry Stackhouse .... 1.00 .30
❑ 89 Larry Hughes .... .60 .18
❑ 90 Michael Jordan 8.00 2.40
❑ 91 Kobe Bryant CW 20.00 6.00
❑ 92 Paul Pierce CW 12.00 3.60
❑ 93 Chris Webber CW 12.00 3.60
❑ 94 Vince Carter CW 15.00 4.50
❑ 95 Tracy McGrady CW 15.00 4.50
❑ 96 Allen Iverson CW 15.00 4.50
❑ 97 Pau Gasol CW 12.00 3.60
❑ 98 Steve Francis CW 12.00 3.60
❑ 99 Jason Kidd CW 12.00 3.60
❑ 100 Dirk Nowitzki CW 12.00 3.60
❑ 101 Antoine Walker CW .. 12.00 3.60
❑ 102 Jason Richardson CW 12.00 3.60
❑ 103 Baron Davis CW 12.00 3.60
❑ 104 Elton Brand CW 12.00 3.60
❑ 105 Stephon Marbury CW 12.00 3.60
❑ 106 Ray Allen CW 12.00 3.60
❑ 107 Shaquille O'Neal CW 15.00 4.50
❑ 108 Kevin Garnett CW 15.00 4.50
❑ 109 Tim Duncan CW 15.00 4.50
❑ 110 Mike Bibby CW 12.00 3.60
❑ 111 Jay Williams RC 20.00 6.00
❑ 112 Yao Ming RC 120.00 36.00
❑ 113 Mike Dunleavy RC 30.00 9.00
❑ 114 Drew Gooden RC 40.00 12.00
❑ 115 Nikoloz Tskitishvili RC 20.00 6.00
❑ 116 DaJuan Wagner RC .. 25.00 7.50
❑ 117 Nene Hilario RC 25.00 7.50
❑ 118 Amare Stoudemire RC 100.00 30.00
❑ 119 Caron Butler RC 40.00 12.00
❑ 120 Manu Ginobili RC 50.00 15.00
❑ 121 Juaquin Hawkins RC 12.00 3.60
❑ 122 Kareem Rush RC 20.00 6.00
❑ 123 Jiri Welsch RC 12.00 3.60
❑ 124 Chris Wilcox RC 20.00 6.00
❑ 125 Tayshaun Prince RC 15.00 4.50
❑ 126 Qyntel Woods RC 12.00 3.60
❑ 127 Jared Jeffries RC 12.00 3.60
❑ 128 Gordan Giricek RC 20.00 6.00
❑ 129 Ryan Humphrey RC .. 12.00 3.60
❑ 130 Marko Jaric RC 12.00 3.60
❑ 131 Casey Jacobsen RC 10.00 3.00
❑ 132 Dan Dickau RC 10.00 3.00
❑ 133 Juan Dixon RC 12.00 3.60
❑ 134 Melvin Ely RC 10.00 3.00
❑ 135 Fred Jones RC 10.00 3.00
❑ 136 John Salmons RC 10.00 3.00
❑ 137 Marcus Haislip RC 10.00 3.00
❑ 138 Carlos Boozer RC 20.00 6.00
❑ 139 Chris Jefferies RC 10.00 3.00
❑ 140 Smush Parker RC 10.00 3.00
❑ 141 Vincent Yarbrough RC 10.00 3.00
❑ 142 Pat Burke RC 10.00 3.00
❑ 143 Lonny Baxter RC 10.00 3.00
❑ 144 Bostjan Nachbar RC 10.00 3.00
❑ 145 Rasual Butler RC 10.00 3.00
❑ 146 Ronald Murray RC 20.00 6.00
❑ 147 J.R. Bremer RC 10.00 3.00
❑ 148 Reggie Evans RC 10.00 3.00
❑ 149 Sam Clancy RC 10.00 3.00
❑ 150 Tamar Slay RC 10.00 3.00
❑ NNO K.Bryant AF Promo 12.00 3.60

2003-04 UD Glass

	Nm-Mt	Ex-Mt
COMP.SET w/o SP's (60)	35.00	10.50
COMMON CARD (1-60)	.40	.12
COMMON LEV.3 RC (61-80)	8.00	2.40
COMMON LEV.2 RC (81-90)	10.00	3.00
COMMON LEV.1 RC (91-100)	20.00	6.00

❑ 1 Shareef Abdur-Rahim .... 1.25 .35
❑ 2 Jason Terry .... 1.25 .35
❑ 3 Paul Pierce .... 1.25 .35
❑ 4 Antoine Walker .... 1.25 .35
❑ 5 Scottie Pippen .... 2.00 .60
❑ 6 Jalen Rose .... 1.25 .35
❑ 7 Darius Miles .... 1.25 .35
❑ 8 Dajuan Wagner .... .75 .23
❑ 9 Dirk Nowitzki .... 2.00 .60
❑ 10 Steve Nash .... 1.25 .35
❑ 11 Michael Finley .... 1.25 .35
❑ 12 Andre Miller .... .75 .23
❑ 13 Nene .... .75 .23
❑ 14 Richard Hamilton .... .75 .23
❑ 15 Ben Wallace .... 1.25 .35
❑ 16 Jason Richardson .... 1.25 .35

Card		
❑ 17 Nick Van Exel	1.25	.35
❑ 18 Steve Francis	1.25	.35
❑ 19 Yao Ming	3.00	.90
❑ 20 Jermaine O'Neal	1.25	.35
❑ 21 Reggie Miller	1.25	.35
❑ 22 Elton Brand	1.25	.35
❑ 23 Corey Maggette	.75	.23
❑ 24 Kobe Bryant	5.00	1.50
❑ 25 Shaquille O'Neal	3.00	.90
❑ 26 Gary Payton	1.25	.35
❑ 27 Pau Gasol	1.25	.35
❑ 28 Shane Battier	1.25	.35
❑ 29 Caron Butler	1.25	.35
❑ 30 Eddie Jones	1.25	.35
❑ 31 Desmond Mason	.75	.23
❑ 32 Michael Redd	1.25	.35
❑ 33 Kevin Garnett	2.50	.75
❑ 34 Latrell Sprewell	1.25	.35
❑ 35 Jason Kidd	2.00	.60
❑ 36 Richard Jefferson	.75	.23
❑ 37 Baron Davis	1.25	.35
❑ 38 Jamal Mashburn	.75	.23
❑ 39 Allan Houston	.75	.23
❑ 40 Keith Van Horn	1.25	.35
❑ 41 Tracy McGrady	3.00	.90
❑ 42 Juwan Howard	.75	.23
❑ 43 Allen Iverson	2.50	.75
❑ 44 Glenn Robinson	1.25	.35
❑ 45 Amare Stoudemire	2.50	.75
❑ 46 Stephon Marbury	1.25	.35
❑ 47 Rasheed Wallace	1.25	.35
❑ 48 Bonzi Wells	.75	.23
❑ 49 Chris Webber	1.25	.35
❑ 50 Mike Bibby	1.25	.35
❑ 51 Tim Duncan	2.50	.75
❑ 52 Tony Parker	1.25	.35
❑ 53 Ray Allen	1.25	.35
❑ 54 Rashard Lewis	1.25	.35
❑ 55 Vince Carter	3.00	.90
❑ 56 Antonio Davis	.40	.12
❑ 57 Andrei Kirilenko	1.25	.35
❑ 58 Jarron Collins	.40	.12
❑ 59 Gilbert Arenas	1.25	.35
❑ 60 Jerry Stackhouse	1.25	.35
❑ 61 Kyle Korver RC	10.00	3.00
❑ 62 Travis Hansen RC	8.00	2.40
❑ 63 Willie Green RC	8.00	2.40
❑ 64 Keith Bogans RC	8.00	2.40
❑ 65 Theron Smith RC	8.00	2.40
❑ 66 Zaur Pachulia RC	8.00	2.40
❑ 67 Derrick Zimmerman RC	8.00	2.40
❑ 68 Jason Kapono RC	8.00	2.40
❑ 69 Steve Blake RC	8.00	2.40
❑ 70 Slavko Vranes RC	8.00	2.40
❑ 71 Jerome Beasley RC	8.00	2.40
❑ 72 Aleksandar Pavlovic RC	8.00	2.40
❑ 73 Boris Diaw RC	8.00	2.40
❑ 74 Kendrick Perkins RC	8.00	2.40
❑ 75 Leandro Barbosa RC	8.00	2.40
❑ 76 Josh Howard RC	10.00	3.00
❑ 77 Luke Walton RC	10.00	3.00
❑ 78 Maciej Lampe RC	8.00	2.40
❑ 79 Brian Cook RC	8.00	2.40
❑ 80 Zarko Cabarkapa RC	8.00	2.40
❑ 81 Travis Outlaw RC	10.00	3.00
❑ 82 Ndudi Ebi RC	10.00	3.00
❑ 83 David West RC	10.00	3.00
❑ 84 Reece Gaines RC	10.00	3.00
❑ 85 Dahntay Jones RC	10.00	3.00
❑ 86 Marcus Banks RC	10.00	3.00
❑ 87 Troy Bell RC	10.00	3.00
❑ 88 Luke Ridnour RC	12.00	3.60
❑ 89 Mickael Pietrus RC	10.00	3.00
❑ 90 Chris Kaman RC	10.00	3.00
❑ 91 Nick Collison RC	20.00	6.00
❑ 92 Mike Sweetney RC	20.00	6.00
❑ 93 Jarvis Hayes RC	20.00	6.00
❑ 94 T.J. Ford RC	25.00	7.50
❑ 95 Kirk Hinrich RC	30.00	9.00
❑ 96 Chris Bosh RC	40.00	12.00
❑ 97 Dwyane Wade RC	50.00	15.00
❑ 98 Carmelo Anthony RC	200.00	60.00
❑ 99 Darko Milicic RC	60.00	18.00
❑ 100 LeBron James RC	350.00	105.00

1999-00 UD Ionix

	Nm-Mt	Ex-Mt
COMPLETE SET (90)	100.00	30.00
COMPLETE SET w/o SP (60)	20.00	6.00
COMMON CARD (1-60)	.25	.07
COMMON ROOKIE (61-90)	1.25	.35
❑ 1 Dikembe Mutombo	.50	.15
❑ 2 Isaiah Rider	.25	.07
❑ 3 Antoine Walker	.75	.23
❑ 4 Paul Pierce	.75	.23
❑ 5 Eddie Jones	.75	.23
❑ 6 Anthony Mason	.50	.15
❑ 7 Toni Kukoc	.50	.15
❑ 8 Hersey Hawkins	.50	.15
❑ 9 Shawn Kemp	.50	.15
❑ 10 Lamond Murray	.25	.07
❑ 11 Michael Finley	.75	.23
❑ 12 Cedric Ceballos	.25	.07
❑ 13 Antonio McDyess	.50	.15
❑ 14 Ron Mercer	.50	.15
❑ 15 Grant Hill	.75	.23
❑ 16 Jerry Stackhouse	.75	.23
❑ 17 Antawn Jamison	1.25	.35
❑ 18 Mookie Blaylock	.25	.07
❑ 19 Charles Barkley	1.00	.30
❑ 20 Hakeem Olajuwon	.75	.23
❑ 21 Reggie Miller	.75	.23
❑ 22 Rik Smits	.50	.15
❑ 23 Maurice Taylor	.50	.15
❑ 24 Derek Anderson	.50	.15
❑ 25 Kobe Bryant	3.00	.90
❑ 26 Shaquille O'Neal	2.00	.60
❑ 27 Tim Hardaway	.50	.15
❑ 28 Alonzo Mourning	.50	.15
❑ 29 Ray Allen	.75	.23
❑ 30 Glenn Robinson	.75	.23
❑ 31 Kevin Garnett	1.50	.45
❑ 32 Terrell Brandon	.50	.15
❑ 33 Stephon Marbury	.75	.23
❑ 34 Keith Van Horn	.75	.23
❑ 35 Allan Houston	.50	.15
❑ 36 Latrell Sprewell	.75	.23
❑ 37 Darrell Armstrong	.25	.07
❑ 38 Tariq Abdul-Wahad	.25	.07
❑ 39 Allen Iverson	1.50	.45
❑ 40 Larry Hughes	.75	.23
❑ 41 Anfernee Hardaway	.75	.23
❑ 42 Jason Kidd	1.25	.35
❑ 43 Tom Gugliotta	.25	.07
❑ 44 Scottie Pippen	1.25	.35
❑ 45 Damon Stoudamire	.50	.15
❑ 46 Rasheed Wallace	.75	.23
❑ 47 Jason Williams	.75	.23
❑ 48 Chris Webber	.75	.23
❑ 49 Tim Duncan	1.50	.45
❑ 50 David Robinson	.75	.23
❑ 51 Gary Payton	.75	.23
❑ 52 Vin Baker	.50	.15
❑ 53 Vince Carter	2.00	.60
❑ 54 Tracy McGrady	2.00	.60
❑ 55 Karl Malone	.75	.23
❑ 56 John Stockton	.75	.23
❑ 57 Mike Bibby	.75	.23
❑ 58 Shareef Abdur-Rahim	.75	.23
❑ 59 Mitch Richmond	.50	.15
❑ 60 Juwan Howard	.50	.15
❑ 61 Elton Brand RC	8.00	2.40
❑ 62 Steve Francis RC	10.00	3.00
❑ 63 Baron Davis RC	6.00	1.80
❑ 64 Lamar Odom RC	6.00	1.80
❑ 65 Jonathan Bender RC	6.00	1.80
❑ 66 Wally Szczerbiak RC	6.00	1.80
❑ 67 Richard Hamilton RC	6.00	1.80
❑ 68 Andre Miller RC	6.00	1.80
❑ 69 Shawn Marion RC	8.00	2.40
❑ 70 Jason Terry RC	5.00	1.50
❑ 71 Trajan Langdon RC	2.50	.75
❑ 72 Aleksandar Radojevic RC	1.25	.35
❑ 73 Corey Maggette RC	6.00	1.80
❑ 74 William Avery RC	2.50	.75
❑ 75 Ron Artest RC	4.00	1.20
❑ 76 Cal Bowdler RC	2.00	.60
❑ 77 James Posey RC	4.00	1.20
❑ 78 Quincy Lewis RC	2.00	.60
❑ 79 Dion Glover RC	2.00	.60
❑ 80 Jeff Foster RC	2.00	.60
❑ 81 Kenny Thomas RC	2.50	.75
❑ 82 Devean George RC	3.00	.90
❑ 83 Tim James RC	2.00	.60
❑ 84 Vonteego Cummings RC	2.50	.75
❑ 85 Jumaine Jones RC	2.50	.75
❑ 86 Scott Padgett RC	2.00	.60
❑ 87 Chucky Atkins RC	2.50	.75
❑ 88 Adrian Griffin RC	2.00	.60
❑ 89 Todd MacCulloch RC	2.00	.60
❑ 90 Anthony Carter RC	4.00	1.20

2000-01 UD Reserve

	Nm-Mt	Ex-Mt
COMP.SET w/o SP's (90)	25.00	7.50
COMMON CARD (1-90)	.25	.07
COMMON ROOKIE (91-120)	1.00	.30
❑ 1 Dikembe Mutombo	.50	.15
❑ 2 Jason Terry	.75	.23
❑ 3 Alan Henderson	.25	.07
❑ 4 Paul Pierce	.75	.23
❑ 5 Antoine Walker	.75	.23
❑ 6 Kenny Anderson	.50	.15
❑ 7 Derrick Coleman	.25	.07
❑ 8 Baron Davis	.75	.23
❑ 9 Jamal Mashburn	.50	.15
❑ 10 Elton Brand	.75	.23
❑ 11 Ron Mercer	.50	.15
❑ 12 Ron Artest	.50	.15
❑ 13 Lamond Murray	.25	.07
❑ 14 Andre Miller	.50	.15
❑ 15 Matt Harpring	.75	.23
❑ 16 Michael Finley	.75	.23
❑ 17 Dirk Nowitzki	1.25	.35
❑ 18 Steve Nash	.75	.23
❑ 19 Antonio McDyess	.50	.15
❑ 20 James Posey	.50	.15
❑ 21 Nick Van Exel	.25	.07
❑ 22 Jerry Stackhouse	.75	.23
❑ 23 Jerome Williams	.25	.07
❑ 24 Chucky Atkins	.25	.07
❑ 25 Antawn Jamison	.75	.23
❑ 26 Larry Hughes	.50	.15
❑ 27 Chris Mills	.25	.07
❑ 28 Steve Francis	.75	.23
❑ 29 Hakeem Olajuwon	.75	.23
❑ 30 Cuttino Mobley	.50	.15
❑ 31 Reggie Miller	.75	.23
❑ 32 Jalen Rose	.75	.23
❑ 33 Austin Croshere	.75	.23
❑ 34 Lamar Odom	.75	.23

❑ 35 Jeff McInnis	.25	.07
❑ 36 Corey Maggette	.50	.15
❑ 37 Shaquille O'Neal	2.00	.60
❑ 38 Kobe Bryant	3.00	.90
❑ 39 Isaiah Rider	.50	.15
❑ 40 Horace Grant	.50	.15
❑ 41 Eddie Jones	.75	.23
❑ 42 Tim Hardaway	.50	.15
❑ 43 Brian Grant	.50	.15
❑ 44 Ray Allen	.75	.23
❑ 45 Tim Thomas	.50	.15
❑ 46 Glenn Robinson	.75	.23
❑ 47 Sam Cassell	.75	.23
❑ 48 Kevin Garnett	1.50	.45
❑ 49 Wally Szczerbiak	.50	.15
❑ 50 Terrell Brandon	.50	.15
❑ 51 Chauncey Billups	.50	.15
❑ 52 Stephon Marbury	.75	.23
❑ 53 Keith Van Horn	.75	.23
❑ 54 Kendall Gill	.25	.07
❑ 55 Latrell Sprewell	.75	.23
❑ 56 Marcus Camby	.50	.15
❑ 57 Allan Houston	.50	.15
❑ 58 Grant Hill	.75	.23
❑ 59 Tracy McGrady	2.00	.60
❑ 60 Darrell Armstrong	.25	.07
❑ 61 Allen Iverson	1.50	.45
❑ 62 Theo Ratliff	.50	.15
❑ 63 Toni Kukoc	.50	.15
❑ 64 Jason Kidd	1.25	.35
❑ 65 Clifford Robinson	.25	.07
❑ 66 Shawn Marion	.75	.23
❑ 67 Rasheed Wallace	.75	.23
❑ 68 Scottie Pippen	1.25	.35
❑ 69 Damon Stoudamire	.50	.15
❑ 70 Chris Webber	.75	.23
❑ 71 Jason Williams	.50	.15
❑ 72 Vlade Divac	.50	.15
❑ 73 Tim Duncan	1.50	.45
❑ 74 David Robinson	.75	.23
❑ 75 Derek Anderson	.50	.15
❑ 76 Gary Payton	.75	.23
❑ 77 Patrick Ewing	.75	.23
❑ 78 Rashard Lewis	.50	.15
❑ 79 Vince Carter	2.00	.60
❑ 80 Mark Jackson	.25	.07
❑ 81 Antonio Davis	.25	.07
❑ 82 Karl Malone	.75	.23
❑ 83 John Stockton	.75	.23
❑ 84 John Starks	.50	.15
❑ 85 Shareef Abdur-Rahim	.75	.23
❑ 86 Mike Bibby	.75	.23
❑ 87 Michael Dickerson	.50	.15
❑ 88 Mitch Richmond	.50	.15
❑ 89 Richard Hamilton	.50	.15
❑ 90 Juwan Howard	.50	.15
❑ 91 Kenyon Martin RC	3.00	.90
❑ 92 Stromile Swift RC	2.00	.60
❑ 93 Darius Miles RC	2.50	.75
❑ 94 Marcus Fizer RC	1.00	.30
❑ 95 Mike Miller RC	2.50	.75
❑ 96 DerMarr Johnson RC	1.00	.30
❑ 97 Chris Mihm RC	1.00	.30
❑ 98 Jamal Crawford RC	1.25	.35
❑ 99 Joel Przybilla RC	1.00	.30
❑ 100 Keyon Dooling RC	1.00	.30
❑ 101 Jerome Moiso RC	1.00	.30
❑ 102 Etan Thomas RC	1.00	.30
❑ 103 Courtney Alexander RC	1.00	.30
❑ 104 Mateen Cleaves RC	1.00	.30
❑ 105 Hidayet Turkoglu RC	2.00	.60
❑ 106 Desmond Mason RC	1.00	.30
❑ 107 Quentin Richardson RC	2.50	.75
❑ 108 Jamaal Magloire RC	1.00	.30
❑ 109 Speedy Claxton RC	1.00	.30
❑ 110 Morris Peterson RC	2.00	.60
❑ 111 Donnell Harvey RC	1.00	.30
❑ 112 DeShawn Stevenson RC	1.00	.30
❑ 113 Mamadou N'diaye RC	1.00	.30
❑ 114 Erick Barkley RC	1.00	.30
❑ 115 Mark Madsen RC	1.00	.30
❑ 116 Eduardo Najera RC	1.25	.35
❑ 117 Lavor Postell RC	1.00	.30
❑ 118 Hanno Mottola RC	1.00	.30
❑ 119 Stephen Jackson RC	1.50	.45
❑ 120 Marc Jackson RC	1.00	.30

2000-01 Ultimate Collection

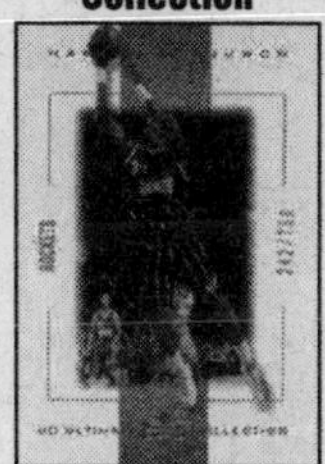

	Nm-Mt	Ex-Mt
COMMON CARD (1-60)	2.50	.75
COMMON ROOKIE	12.00	3.60
❑ 1 Dikembe Mutombo	4.00	1.20
❑ 2 Hanno Mottola RC	12.00	3.60
❑ 3 Paul Pierce	6.00	1.80
❑ 4 Antoine Walker	6.00	1.80
❑ 5 Derrick Coleman	2.50	.75
❑ 6 Baron Davis	6.00	1.80
❑ 7 Elton Brand	6.00	1.80
❑ 8 Michael Jordan	50.00	15.00
❑ 9 Andre Miller	4.00	1.20
❑ 10 Chris Mihm RC	12.00	3.60
❑ 11 Michael Finley	6.00	1.80
❑ 12 Donnell Harvey RC	12.00	3.60
❑ 13 Antonio McDyess	4.00	1.20
❑ 14 Nick Van Exel	6.00	1.80
❑ 15 Jerry Stackhouse	6.00	1.80
❑ 16 Jerome Williams	2.50	.75
❑ 17 Larry Hughes	4.00	1.20
❑ 18 Antawn Jamison	6.00	1.80
❑ 19 Steve Francis	6.00	1.80
❑ 20 Hakeem Olajuwon	6.00	1.80
❑ 21 Reggie Miller	6.00	1.80
❑ 22 Jalen Rose	6.00	1.80
❑ 23 Lamar Odom	6.00	1.80
❑ 24 Michael Olowokandi	2.50	.75
❑ 25 Shaquille O'Neal	15.00	4.50
❑ 26 Kobe Bryant	25.00	7.50
❑ 27 Ron Harper	4.00	1.20
❑ 28 Alonzo Mourning	4.00	1.20
❑ 29 Eddie House RC	12.00	3.60
❑ 30 Glenn Robinson	6.00	1.80
❑ 31 Ray Allen	6.00	1.80
❑ 32 Kevin Garnett	12.00	3.60
❑ 33 Wally Szczerbiak	4.00	1.20
❑ 34 Terrell Brandon	4.00	1.20
❑ 35 Stephon Marbury	6.00	1.80
❑ 36 Keith Van Horn	6.00	1.80
❑ 37 Allan Houston	4.00	1.20
❑ 38 Latrell Sprewell	6.00	1.80
❑ 39 Grant Hill	6.00	1.80
❑ 40 Tracy McGrady	12.00	3.60
❑ 41 Allen Iverson	12.00	3.60
❑ 42 Toni Kukoc	4.00	1.20
❑ 43 Jason Kidd	10.00	3.00
❑ 44 Anfernee Hardaway	6.00	1.80
❑ 45 Scottie Pippen	10.00	3.00
❑ 46 Rasheed Wallace	6.00	1.80
❑ 47 Chris Webber	6.00	1.80
❑ 48 Jason Williams	4.00	1.20
❑ 49 Tim Duncan	12.00	3.60
❑ 50 David Robinson	6.00	1.80
❑ 51 Gary Payton	6.00	1.80
❑ 52 Rashard Lewis	4.00	1.20
❑ 53 Vince Carter	12.00	3.60
❑ 54 Morris Peterson RC	30.00	9.00
❑ 55 Karl Malone	6.00	1.80
❑ 56 John Stockton	6.00	1.80
❑ 57 Shareef Abdur-Rahim	6.00	1.80
❑ 58 Mike Bibby	6.00	1.80
❑ 59 Mike Smith RC	12.00	3.60
❑ 60 Richard Hamilton	4.00	1.20
❑ P1 Kenyon Martin SAMPLE	-	-

2001-02 Ultimate Collection

	Nm-Mt	Ex-Mt
COMPLETE SET (90)	2,500.00	750.00
COMP.SET w/o SP's (60)	500.00	150.00
COMMON CARD (1-60)	2.50	.75
COMMON ROOKIE (61-70)	20.00	6.00
COMMON ROOKIE (71-84)	40.00	12.00
❑ 1 Jason Terry	8.00	2.40
❑ 2 Shareef Abdur-Rahim	8.00	2.40
❑ 3 Paul Pierce	8.00	2.40
❑ 4 Antoine Walker	8.00	2.40
❑ 5 Baron Davis	8.00	2.40
❑ 6 Jamal Mashburn	5.00	1.50
❑ 7 Ron Mercer	5.00	1.50
❑ 8 Marcus Fizer	5.00	1.50
❑ 9 Andre Miller	5.00	1.50
❑ 10 Lamond Murray	2.50	.75
❑ 11 Dirk Nowitzki	12.00	3.60
❑ 12 Michael Finley	8.00	2.40
❑ 13 Antonio McDyess	5.00	1.50
❑ 14 Nick Van Exel	8.00	2.40
❑ 15 Jerry Stackhouse	8.00	2.40
❑ 16 Zeljko Rebraca RC	40.00	12.00
❑ 17 Antawn Jamison	8.00	2.40
❑ 18 Larry Hughes	5.00	1.50
❑ 19 Steve Francis	8.00	2.40
❑ 20 Cuttino Mobley	5.00	1.50
❑ 21 Reggie Miller	8.00	2.40
❑ 22 Jalen Rose	8.00	2.40
❑ 23 Darius Miles	8.00	2.40
❑ 24 Quentin Richardson	5.00	1.50
❑ 25 Kobe Bryant	30.00	9.00
❑ 26 Shaquille O'Neal	20.00	6.00
❑ 27 Mitch Richmond	5.00	1.50
❑ 28 Stromile Swift	5.00	1.50
❑ 29 Jason Williams	5.00	1.50
❑ 30 Alonzo Mourning	5.00	1.50
❑ 31 Eddie Jones	8.00	2.40
❑ 32 Ray Allen	8.00	2.40
❑ 33 Glenn Robinson	8.00	2.40
❑ 34 Kevin Garnett	15.00	4.50
❑ 35 Terrell Brandon	5.00	1.50
❑ 36 Wally Szczerbiak	5.00	1.50
❑ 37 Jason Kidd	12.00	3.60
❑ 38 Kenyon Martin	8.00	2.40
❑ 39 Latrell Sprewell	8.00	2.40
❑ 40 Allan Houston	5.00	1.50
❑ 41 Tracy McGrady	20.00	6.00
❑ 42 Grant Hill	8.00	2.40
❑ 43 Allen Iverson	15.00	4.50
❑ 44 Dikembe Mutombo	5.00	1.50
❑ 45 Stephon Marbury	8.00	2.40
❑ 46 Anfernee Hardaway	8.00	2.40
❑ 47 Rasheed Wallace	8.00	2.40
❑ 48 Derek Anderson	5.00	1.50
❑ 49 Chris Webber	8.00	2.40
❑ 50 Peja Stojakovic	8.00	2.40
❑ 51 Tim Duncan	15.00	4.50
❑ 52 David Robinson	8.00	2.40
❑ 53 Rashard Lewis	5.00	1.50
❑ 54 Desmond Mason	5.00	1.50
❑ 55 Vince Carter	20.00	6.00
❑ 56 Morris Peterson	5.00	1.50
❑ 57 Karl Malone	8.00	2.40
❑ 58 John Stockton	8.00	2.40
❑ 59 Richard Hamilton	5.00	1.50

	Nm-Mt	Ex-Mt
❑ 60 Michael Jordan	80.00	24.00
❑ 61 Andrei Kirilenko RC	40.00	12.00
❑ 62 Gilbert Arenas RC	50.00	15.00
❑ 63 Trenton Hassell RC	20.00	6.00
❑ 64 Tony Parker RC	50.00	15.00
❑ 65 Jamaal Tinsley RC	20.00	6.00
❑ 66 Samuel Dalembert RC	20.00	6.00
❑ 67 Gerald Wallace RC	40.00	12.00
❑ 68 Brandon Armstrong RC	20.00	6.00
❑ 69 Jeryl Sasser RC	20.00	6.00
❑ 70 Joseph Forte RC	25.00	7.50
❑ 71 Pau Gasol RC	120.00	36.00
❑ 72 Brendan Haywood RC	50.00	15.00
❑ 73 Zach Randolph RC	60.00	18.00
❑ 74 Jason Collins RC	40.00	12.00
❑ 75 Michael Bradley RC	40.00	12.00
❑ 76 Kirk Haston RC	40.00	12.00
❑ 77 Steven Hunter RC	40.00	12.00
❑ 78 Troy Murphy RC	40.00	12.00
❑ 79 Richard Jefferson RC	60.00	18.00
❑ 80 Vladimir Radmanovic RC	40.00	12.00
❑ 81 Kedrick Brown RC	40.00	12.00
❑ 82 Joe Johnson RC	30.00	9.00
❑ 83 DeSagana Diop RC	40.00	12.00
❑ 84 Shane Battier RC	40.00	12.00
❑ 85 Rodney White AU RC	50.00	15.00
❑ 86 Eddie Griffin AU RC	100.00	30.00
❑ 87 Jason Richardson AU RC	300.00	90.00
❑ 88 Eddy Curry AU RC	100.00	30.00
❑ 89 Tyson Chandler AU RC	120.00	36.00
❑ 90 Kwame Brown AU RC	120.00	36.00

2002-03 Ultimate Collection

	Nm-Mt	Ex-Mt
COMP.SET w/o SP's (67)	350.00	105.00
COMMON CARD (1-67)	2.00	.60
COMMON AU RC (68-79)	50.00	15.00
COMMON ROOKIE (80-103)	25.00	7.50
COMMON ROOKIE (104-120)	12.00	3.60
❑ 1 Shareef Abdur-Rahim	6.00	1.80
❑ 2 Glenn Robinson	6.00	1.80
❑ 3 Jason Terry	6.00	1.80
❑ 4 Paul Pierce	6.00	1.80
❑ 5 Antoine Walker	6.00	1.80
❑ 6 Vin Baker	4.00	1.20
❑ 7 Jalen Rose	6.00	1.80
❑ 8 Darius Miles	6.00	1.80
❑ 9 Dirk Nowitzki	10.00	3.00
❑ 10 Michael Finley	6.00	1.80
❑ 11 Steve Nash	6.00	1.80
❑ 12 Raef LaFrentz	4.00	1.20
❑ 13 Juwan Howard	4.00	1.20
❑ 14 Richard Hamilton	4.00	1.20
❑ 15 Chauncey Billups	4.00	1.20
❑ 16 Ben Wallace	6.00	1.80
❑ 17 Jason Richardson	6.00	1.80
❑ 18 Gilbert Arenas	6.00	1.80
❑ 19 Antawn Jamison	6.00	1.80
❑ 20 Steve Francis	6.00	1.80
❑ 21 Reggie Miller	6.00	1.80
❑ 22 Jamaal Tinsley	6.00	1.80
❑ 23 Jermaine O'Neal	6.00	1.80
❑ 24 Elton Brand	6.00	1.80
❑ 25 Andre Miller	4.00	1.20
❑ 26 Kobe Bryant	25.00	7.50
❑ 27 Shaquille O'Neal	15.00	4.50
❑ 28 Pau Gasol	6.00	1.80
❑ 29 Shane Battier	6.00	1.80
❑ 30 Eddie Jones	6.00	1.80
❑ 31 Brian Grant	4.00	1.20
❑ 32 Ray Allen	6.00	1.80
❑ 33 Kevin Garnett	12.00	3.60
❑ 34 Wally Szczerbiak	4.00	1.20
❑ 35 Troy Hudson	2.00	.60
❑ 36 Jason Kidd	10.00	3.00
❑ 37 Richard Jefferson	4.00	1.20
❑ 38 Kenyon Martin	6.00	1.80
❑ 39 Baron Davis	6.00	1.80
❑ 40 Jamal Mashburn	4.00	1.20
❑ 41 David Wesley	2.00	.60
❑ 42 P.J. Brown	2.00	.60
❑ 43 Allan Houston	4.00	1.20
❑ 44 Latrell Sprewell	6.00	1.80
❑ 45 Kurt Thomas	4.00	1.20
❑ 46 Tracy McGrady	15.00	4.50
❑ 47 Grant Hill	6.00	1.80
❑ 48 Allen Iverson	12.00	3.60
❑ 49 Stephon Marbury	6.00	1.80
❑ 50 Shawn Marion	6.00	1.80
❑ 51 Rasheed Wallace	6.00	1.80
❑ 52 Derek Anderson	4.00	1.20
❑ 53 Bonzi Wells	4.00	1.20
❑ 54 Chris Webber	6.00	1.80
❑ 55 Mike Bibby	6.00	1.80
❑ 56 Peja Stojakovic	6.00	1.80
❑ 57 Tim Duncan	12.00	3.60
❑ 58 David Robinson	6.00	1.80
❑ 59 Tony Parker	6.00	1.80
❑ 60 Gary Payton	6.00	1.80
❑ 61 Rashard Lewis	4.00	1.20
❑ 62 Desmond Mason	4.00	1.20
❑ 63 Vince Carter	15.00	4.50
❑ 64 Morris Peterson	4.00	1.20
❑ 65 Karl Malone	6.00	1.80
❑ 66 John Stockton	6.00	1.80
❑ 67 Michael Jordan	40.00	12.00
❑ 68 Chris Wilcox AU RC	60.00	18.00
❑ 69 Drew Gooden AU RC	160.00	47.50
❑ 70 M.Haislip AU RC EXCH	50.00	15.00
❑ 71 Melvin Ely AU RC	50.00	15.00
❑ 72 Jared Jeffries AU RC	50.00	15.00
❑ 73 Caron Butler AU RC	150.00	45.00
❑ 74 A.Stoudemire AU RC	350.00	105.00
❑ 75 Nene Hilario AU RC	100.00	30.00
❑ 76 DaJuan Wagner AU RC	120.00	36.00
❑ 77 N.Tskitishvili AU RC	60.00	18.00
❑ 78 Jay Williams AU RC	100.00	30.00
❑ 79 Yao Ming AU RC	500.00	150.00
❑ 80 Predrag Savovic RC	25.00	7.50
❑ 81 Igor Rakocevic RC	25.00	7.50
❑ 82 Sam Clancy RC	25.00	7.50
❑ 83 Ronald Murray RC	50.00	15.00
❑ 84 Tito Maddox RC	25.00	7.50
❑ 85 Carlos Boozer RC	50.00	15.00
❑ 86 Dan Gadzuric RC	25.00	7.50
❑ 87 Vincent Yarbrough RC	25.00	7.50
❑ 88 Robert Archibald RC	25.00	7.50
❑ 89 Roger Mason RC	25.00	7.50
❑ 90 Juaquin Hawkins RC	25.00	7.50
❑ 91 Chris Jefferies RC	25.00	7.50
❑ 92 John Salmons RC	25.00	7.50
❑ 93 Manu Ginobili RC	60.00	18.00
❑ 94 Tayshaun Prince RC	30.00	9.00
❑ 95 Casey Jacobsen RC	25.00	7.50
❑ 96 Qyntel Woods RC	25.00	7.50
❑ 97 Kareem Rush RC	25.00	7.50
❑ 98 Ryan Humphrey RC	25.00	7.50
❑ 99 Juan Dixon RC	30.00	9.00
❑ 100 Fred Jones RC	25.00	7.50
❑ 101 Jiri Welsch RC	25.00	7.50
❑ 102 Bostjan Nachbar RC	25.00	7.50
❑ 103 Marko Jaric RC	25.00	7.50
❑ 104 Gordan Giricek RC	15.00	4.50
❑ 105 Frank Williams RC	12.00	3.60
❑ 106 Pat Burke RC	12.00	3.60
❑ 107 Junior Harrington RC	12.00	3.60
❑ 108 Rasual Butler RC	12.00	3.60
❑ 109 Raul Lopez RC	12.00	3.60
❑ 110 Cezary Trybanski RC	12.00	3.60
❑ 111 Dan Dickau RC	12.00	3.60
❑ 112 Efthimios Rentzias RC	12.00	3.60
❑ 113 Mehmet Okur RC	12.00	3.60
❑ 114 Curtis Borchardt RC	12.00	3.60
❑ 115 J.R. Bremer RC	12.00	3.60
❑ 116 Lonny Baxter RC	12.00	3.60
❑ 117 Jamal Sampson RC	12.00	3.60
❑ 118 Tamar Slay RC	12.00	3.60
❑ 119 Jannero Pargo RC	12.00	3.60
❑ 120 Smush Parker RC	12.00	3.60

2003-04 Ultimate Collection

	Nm-Mt	Ex-Mt
COMMON CARD (1-116)	2.00	.60
COMMON ROOKIE (117-126)	12.00	3.60
COMMON AU RC (127-164)	40.00	12.00
COMMON US (165-190)	8.00	2.40
LIMITED PRINT RUN 25 SER.#'d SETS	-	
LIMITED NOT PRICED DUE TO SCARCITY	-	
LIM.BLACK SER.#'D TO ONE EXIST	-	
❑ 1 Dominique Wilkins	10.00	3.00
❑ 2 Jason Terry	6.00	1.80
❑ 3 Dion Glover	2.00	.60
❑ 4 Stephen Jackson	2.00	.60
❑ 5 Bill Russell	10.00	3.00
❑ 6 Paul Pierce	6.00	1.80
❑ 7 Larry Bird	12.00	3.60
❑ 8 Ricky Davis	6.00	1.80
❑ 9 Antonio Davis	4.00	1.20
❑ 10 Michael Jordan	25.00	7.50
❑ 11 Scottie Pippen	10.00	3.00
❑ 12 Tyson Chandler	6.00	1.80
❑ 13 Jeff McInnis	2.00	.60
❑ 14 Dajuan Wagner	4.00	1.20
❑ 15 Carlos Boozer	6.00	1.80
❑ 16 Zydrunas Ilgauskas	4.00	1.20
❑ 17 Dirk Nowitzki	10.00	3.00
❑ 18 Steve Nash	6.00	1.80
❑ 19 Antoine Walker	6.00	1.80
❑ 20 Michael Finley	6.00	1.80
❑ 21 Andre Miller	4.00	1.20
❑ 22 Nene	4.00	1.20
❑ 23 Nikoloz Tskitishvili	2.00	.60
❑ 24 Marcus Camby	4.00	1.20
❑ 25 Richard Hamilton	4.00	1.20
❑ 26 Ben Wallace	6.00	1.80
❑ 27 Chauncey Billups	4.00	1.20
❑ 28 Rasheed Wallace	6.00	1.80
❑ 29 Jason Richardson	6.00	1.80
❑ 30 Nick Van Exel	6.00	1.80
❑ 31 Speedy Claxton	2.00	.60
❑ 32 Mike Dunleavy	4.00	1.20
❑ 33 Yao Ming	15.00	4.50
❑ 34 Steve Francis	6.00	1.80
❑ 35 Cuttino Mobley	4.00	1.20
❑ 36 Jim Jackson	2.00	.60
❑ 37 Reggie Miller	6.00	1.80
❑ 38 Jermaine O'Neal	6.00	1.80
❑ 39 Ron Artest	4.00	1.20
❑ 40 Al Harrington	4.00	1.20
❑ 41 Elton Brand	6.00	1.80
❑ 42 Corey Maggette	4.00	1.20
❑ 43 Quentin Richardson	4.00	1.20
❑ 44 Chris Wilcox	4.00	1.20
❑ 45 Kobe Bryant	20.00	6.00
❑ 46 Shaquille O'Neal	15.00	4.50
❑ 47 Gary Payton	6.00	1.80
❑ 48 Karl Malone	6.00	1.80
❑ 49 Pau Gasol	6.00	1.80
❑ 50 Bonzi Wells	4.00	1.20
❑ 51 Mike Miller	6.00	1.80
❑ 52 Jason Williams	4.00	1.20
❑ 53 Caron Butler	6.00	1.80
❑ 54 Lamar Odom	6.00	1.80
❑ 55 Eddie Jones	6.00	1.80
❑ 56 Brian Grant	4.00	1.20
❑ 57 Desmond Mason	4.00	1.20
❑ 58 Oscar Robertson	10.00	3.00
❑ 59 Michael Redd	6.00	1.80
❑ 60 Toni Kukoc	4.00	1.20
❑ 61 Latrell Sprewell	6.00	1.80
❑ 62 Kevin Garnett	12.00	3.60
❑ 63 Wally Szczerbiak	4.00	1.20

❑ 64 Sam Cassell	6.00	1.80
❑ 65 Kenyon Martin	6.00	1.80
❑ 66 Jason Kidd	10.00	3.00
❑ 67 Richard Jefferson	4.00	1.20
❑ 68 Alonzo Mourning	4.00	1.20
❑ 69 Jamal Mashburn	4.00	1.20
❑ 70 David Wesley	2.00	.60
❑ 71 Baron Davis	6.00	1.80
❑ 72 Jamaal Magloire	2.00	.60
❑ 73 Allan Houston	4.00	1.20
❑ 74 Patrick Ewing	6.00	1.80
❑ 75 Stephon Marbury	6.00	1.80
❑ 76 Dikembe Mutombo	4.00	1.20
❑ 77 Tracy McGrady	15.00	4.50
❑ 78 Drew Gooden	4.00	1.20
❑ 79 Juwan Howard	4.00	1.20
❑ 80 DeShawn Stevenson	2.00	.60
❑ 81 Julius Erving	10.00	3.00
❑ 82 Allen Iverson	12.00	3.60
❑ 83 Glenn Robinson	6.00	1.80
❑ 84 Eric Snow	4.00	1.20
❑ 85 Amare Stoudemire	15.00	4.50
❑ 86 Shawn Marion	6.00	1.80
❑ 87 Antonio McDyess	6.00	1.80
❑ 88 Joe Johnson	4.00	1.20
❑ 89 Shareef Abdur-Rahim	6.00	1.80
❑ 90 Derek Anderson	4.00	1.20
❑ 91 Damon Stoudamire	4.00	1.20
❑ 92 Zach Randolph	6.00	1.80
❑ 93 Mike Bibby	6.00	1.80
❑ 94 Chris Webber	6.00	1.80
❑ 95 Peja Stojakovic	6.00	1.80
❑ 96 Bobby Jackson	6.00	1.80
❑ 97 Manu Ginobili	6.00	1.80
❑ 98 Tim Duncan	12.00	3.60
❑ 99 Tony Parker	6.00	1.80
❑ 100 Radoslav Nesterovic	4.00	1.20
❑ 101 Rashard Lewis	6.00	1.80
❑ 102 Ray Allen	6.00	1.80
❑ 103 Vladimir Radmanovic	-	
❑ 104 Brent Barry	4.00	1.20
❑ 105 Vince Carter	15.00	4.50
❑ 106 Morris Peterson	4.00	1.20
❑ 107 Jalen Rose	6.00	1.80
❑ 108 Donyell Marshall	6.00	1.80
❑ 109 John Stockton	6.00	1.80
❑ 110 Andrei Kirilenko	6.00	1.80
❑ 111 Matt Harpring	6.00	1.80
❑ 112 Carlos Arroyo	6.00	1.80
❑ 113 Gilbert Arenas	6.00	1.80
❑ 114 Jerry Stackhouse	6.00	1.80
❑ 115 Kwame Brown	6.00	1.80
❑ 116 Larry Hughes	4.00	1.20
❑ 117 T.J. Ford RC	15.00	4.50
❑ 118 Kirk Hinrich RC	20.00	6.00
❑ 119 Nick Collison RC	12.00	3.60
❑ 120 James Jones RC	12.00	3.60
❑ 121 Travis Hansen RC	12.00	3.60
❑ 122 Alex Garcia RC	12.00	3.60
❑ 123 Theron Smith RC	12.00	3.60
❑ 124 Francisco Elson RC	12.00	3.60
❑ 125 Jon Stefansson RC	12.00	3.60
❑ 126 Ronald Dupree RC	12.00	3.60
❑ 127 LeBron James AU RC	1,200.00	350.00
❑ 128 Darko Milicic AU RC	150.00	45.00
❑ 129 Carmelo Anthony AU RC	600.00	180.00
❑ 130 Chris Bosh AU RC	150.00	45.00
❑ 131 Dwyane Wade AU RC	250.00	75.00
❑ 132 Chris Kaman AU RC	40.00	12.00
❑ 133 Jarvis Hayes AU RC	40.00	12.00
❑ 134 Mickael Pietrus AU RC	40.00	12.00
❑ 135 Dahntay Jones AU RC	40.00	12.00
❑ 136 Marcus Banks AU RC	40.00	12.00
❑ 137 Luke Ridnour AU RC	60.00	18.00
❑ 138 Reece Gaines AU RC	40.00	12.00
❑ 139 Troy Bell AU RC	40.00	12.00
❑ 140 Mike Sweetney AU RC	40.00	12.00
❑ 141 David West AU RC	40.00	12.00
❑ 142 Aleksandar Pavlovic AU RC	40.00	12.00
❑ 143 Steve Blake AU RC	40.00	12.00
❑ 144 Boris Diaw AU RC	40.00	12.00
❑ 145 Zoran Planinic AU RC	40.00	12.00
❑ 146 Travis Outlaw AU RC	40.00	12.00
❑ 147 Brian Cook AU RC	40.00	12.00
❑ 148 Jerome Beasley AU RC	40.00	12.00
❑ 149 Ndudi Ebi AU RC	40.00	12.00
❑ 150 Kendrick Perkins AU RC	40.00	12.00
❑ 151 Leandro Barbosa AU RC	40.00	12.00
❑ 152 Josh Howard AU RC	60.00	18.00
❑ 153 Maciej Lampe AU RC	40.00	12.00
❑ 154 Jason Kapono AU RC	40.00	12.00
❑ 155 Luke Walton AU RC	50.00	15.00
❑ 156 Kyle Korver AU RC	50.00	15.00
❑ 157 Zarko Cabarkapa AU RC	40.00	12.00
❑ 158 Zaur Pachulia AU RC	40.00	12.00
❑ 159 Maurice Williams AU RC	40.00	12.00
❑ 160 Brandon Hunter AU RC	40.00	12.00
❑ 161 Keith Bogans AU RC	40.00	12.00
❑ 162 Marquis Daniels AU RC	120.00	36.00
❑ 163 Willie Green AU RC	40.00	12.00
❑ 164 Udonis Haslem AU RC	40.00	12.00
❑ 165 Larry Bird US	15.00	4.50
❑ 166 Bill Russell US	12.00	3.60
❑ 167 Michael Jordan US	30.00	9.00
❑ 168 Steve Nash US	8.00	2.40
❑ 169 Michael Finley US	8.00	2.40
❑ 170 Ben Wallace US	8.00	2.40
❑ 171 Jason Richardson US	8.00	2.40
❑ 172 Yao Ming US	20.00	6.00
❑ 173 Reggie Miller US	8.00	2.40
❑ 174 Kobe Bryant US	25.00	7.50
❑ 175 Shaquille O'Neal US	20.00	6.00
❑ 176 Gary Payton US	8.00	2.40
❑ 177 Magic Johnson US	10.00	3.00
❑ 178 Pau Gasol US	8.00	2.40
❑ 179 Lamar Odom US	8.00	2.40
❑ 180 Oscar Robertson US	12.00	3.60
❑ 181 Kenyon Martin US	8.00	2.40
❑ 182 Baron Davis US	8.00	2.40
❑ 183 Julius Erving US	12.00	3.60
❑ 184 Amare Stoudemire US	20.00	6.00
❑ 185 Mike Bibby US	8.00	2.40
❑ 186 Tony Parker US	8.00	2.40
❑ 187 Rashard Lewis US	8.00	2.40
❑ 188 Vince Carter US	20.00	6.00
❑ 189 Andrei Kirilenko US	8.00	2.40
❑ 190 Gilbert Arenas US	8.00	2.40

1992-93 Ultra

	Nm-Mt	Ex-Mt
COMPLETE SET (375)	30.00	9.00
COMPLETE SERIES 1 (200)	15.00	4.50
COMPLETE SERIES 2 (175)	15.00	4.50
COMMON CARD (1-200)	.10	.03
COMMON CARD (201-375)	.05	.02
❑ 1 Stacey Augmon	.25	.07
❑ 2 Duane Ferrell	.10	.03
❑ 3 Paul Graham	.10	.03
❑ 4 Blair Rasmussen	.10	.03
❑ 5 Rumeal Robinson	.10	.03
❑ 6 Dominique Wilkins	.50	.15
❑ 7 Kevin Willis	.10	.03
❑ 8 John Bagley	.10	.03
❑ 9 Dee Brown	.10	.03
❑ 10 Rick Fox	.25	.07
❑ 11 Kevin Gamble	.10	.03
❑ 12 Joe Kleine	.10	.03
❑ 13 Reggie Lewis	.25	.07
❑ 14 Kevin McHale	.50	.15
❑ 15 Robert Parish	.25	.07
❑ 16 Ed Pinckney	.10	.03
❑ 17 Muggsy Bogues	.25	.07
❑ 18 Dell Curry	.10	.03
❑ 19 Kenny Gattison	.10	.03
❑ 20 Kendall Gill	.25	.07
❑ 21 Larry Johnson	.60	.18
❑ 22 Johnny Newman	.10	.03
❑ 23 J.R. Reid	.10	.03
❑ 24 B.J. Armstrong	.10	.03
❑ 25 Bill Cartwright	.10	.03
❑ 26 Horace Grant	.25	.07
❑ 27 Michael Jordan	6.00	1.80
❑ 28 Stacey King	.10	.03
❑ 29 John Paxson	.10	.03
❑ 30 Will Perdue	.10	.03
❑ 31 Scottie Pippen	1.50	.45
❑ 32 Scott Williams	.10	.03
❑ 33 John Battle	.10	.03
❑ 34 Terrell Brandon	.50	.15
❑ 35 Brad Daugherty	.10	.03
❑ 36 Craig Ehlo	.10	.03
❑ 37 Larry Nance	.10	.03
❑ 38 Mark Price	.10	.03
❑ 39 Mike Sanders	.10	.03
❑ 40 John Williams	.10	.03
❑ 41 Terry Davis	.10	.03
❑ 42 Derek Harper	.25	.07
❑ 43 Donald Hodge	.10	.03
❑ 44 Mike Iuzzolino	.10	.03
❑ 45 Fat Lever	.10	.03
❑ 46 Doug Smith	.10	.03
❑ 47 Randy White	.10	.03
❑ 48 Winston Garland	.10	.03
❑ 49 Chris Jackson	.10	.03
❑ 50 Marcus Liberty	.10	.03
❑ 51 Todd Lichti	.10	.03
❑ 52 Mark Macon	.10	.03
❑ 53 Dikembe Mutombo	.60	.18
❑ 54 Reggie Williams	.10	.03
❑ 55 Mark Aguirre	.10	.03
❑ 56 Joe Dumars	.50	.15
❑ 57 Bill Laimbeer	.25	.07
❑ 58 Dennis Rodman	1.00	.30
❑ 59 Isiah Thomas	.50	.15
❑ 60 Darrell Walker	.10	.03
❑ 61 Orlando Woolridge	.10	.03
❑ 62 Victor Alexander	.10	.03
❑ 63 Chris Gatling	.10	.03
❑ 64 Tim Hardaway	.60	.18
❑ 65 Tyrone Hill	.10	.03
❑ 66 Sarunas Marciulionis	.10	.03
❑ 67 Chris Mullin	.50	.15
❑ 68 Billy Owens	.25	.07
❑ 69 Sleepy Floyd	.10	.03
❑ 70 Avery Johnson	.10	.03
❑ 71 Vernon Maxwell	.10	.03
❑ 72 Hakeem Olajuwon	.75	.23
❑ 73 Kenny Smith	.10	.03
❑ 74 Otis Thorpe	.25	.07
❑ 75 Dale Davis	.10	.03
❑ 76 Vern Fleming	.10	.03
❑ 77 George McCloud	.10	.03
❑ 78 Reggie Miller	.50	.15
❑ 79 Detlef Schrempf	.25	.07
❑ 80 Rik Smits	.25	.07
❑ 81 LaSalle Thompson	.10	.03
❑ 82 Gary Grant	.10	.03
❑ 83 Ron Harper	.25	.07
❑ 84 Mark Jackson	.25	.07
❑ 85 Danny Manning	.25	.07
❑ 86 Ken Norman	.10	.03
❑ 87 Stanley Roberts	.10	.03
❑ 88 Loy Vaught	.10	.03
❑ 89 Elden Campbell	.25	.07
❑ 90 Vlade Divac	.25	.07
❑ 91 A.C. Green	.25	.07
❑ 92 Sam Perkins	.25	.07
❑ 93 Byron Scott	.25	.07
❑ 94 Tony Smith	.10	.03
❑ 95 Sedale Threatt	.10	.03
❑ 96 James Worthy	.50	.15
❑ 97 Willie Burton	.10	.03
❑ 98 Bimbo Coles	.10	.03
❑ 99 Kevin Edwards	.10	.03
❑ 100 Grant Long	.10	.03
❑ 101 Glen Rice	.50	.15
❑ 102 Rony Seikaly	.10	.03
❑ 103 Brian Shaw	.10	.03
❑ 104 Steve Smith	.60	.18
❑ 105 Frank Brickowski	.10	.03

❑ 106	Moses Malone	.50	.15
❑ 107	Fred Roberts	.10	.03
❑ 108	Alvin Robertson	.10	.03
❑ 109	Thurl Bailey	.10	.03
❑ 110	Gerald Glass	.10	.03
❑ 111	Luc Longley	.25	.07
❑ 112	Felton Spencer	.10	.03
❑ 113	Doug West	.10	.03
❑ 114	Kenny Anderson	.50	.15
❑ 115	Mookie Blaylock	.25	.07
❑ 116	Sam Bowie	.10	.03
❑ 117	Derrick Coleman	.25	.07
❑ 118	Chris Dudley	.10	.03
❑ 119	Chris Morris	.10	.03
❑ 120	Drazen Petrovic	.10	.03
❑ 121	Greg Anthony	.10	.03
❑ 122	Patrick Ewing	.50	.15
❑ 123	Anthony Mason	.50	.15
❑ 124	Charles Oakley	.25	.07
❑ 125	Doc Rivers	.25	.07
❑ 126	Charles Smith	.10	.03
❑ 127	John Starks	.25	.07
❑ 128	Nick Anderson	.25	.07
❑ 129	Anthony Bowie	.10	.03
❑ 130	Terry Catledge	.10	.03
❑ 131	Jerry Reynolds	.10	.03
❑ 132	Dennis Scott	.25	.07
❑ 133	Scott Skiles	.10	.03
❑ 134	Brian Williams	.10	.03
❑ 135	Ron Anderson	.10	.03
❑ 136	Manute Bol	.10	.03
❑ 137	Johnny Dawkins	.10	.03
❑ 138	Armon Gilliam	.10	.03
❑ 139	Hersey Hawkins	.25	.07
❑ 140	Jeff Ruland	.10	.03
❑ 141	Charles Shackleford	.10	.03
❑ 142	Cedric Ceballos	.25	.07
❑ 143	Tom Chambers	.10	.03
❑ 144	Kevin Johnson	.50	.15
❑ 145	Negele Knight	.10	.03
❑ 146	Dan Majerle	.25	.07
❑ 147	Mark West	.10	.03
❑ 148	Mark Bryant	.10	.03
❑ 149	Clyde Drexler	.50	.15
❑ 150	Kevin Duckworth	.10	.03
❑ 151	Jerome Kersey	.10	.03
❑ 152	Robert Pack	.10	.03
❑ 153	Terry Porter	.10	.03
❑ 154	Clifford Robinson	.25	.07
❑ 155	Buck Williams	.25	.07
❑ 156	Anthony Bonner	.10	.03
❑ 157	Duane Causwell	.10	.03
❑ 158	Mitch Richmond	.50	.15
❑ 159	Lionel Simmons	.10	.03
❑ 160	Wayman Tisdale	.10	.03
❑ 161	Spud Webb	.25	.07
❑ 162	Willie Anderson	.10	.03
❑ 163	Antoine Carr	.10	.03
❑ 164	Terry Cummings	.25	.07
❑ 165	Sean Elliott	.25	.07
❑ 166	Sidney Green	.10	.03
❑ 167	David Robinson	.75	.23
❑ 168	Dana Barros	.10	.03
❑ 169	Benoit Benjamin	.10	.03
❑ 170	Michael Cage	.10	.03
❑ 171	Eddie Johnson	.10	.03
❑ 172	Shawn Kemp	1.00	.30
❑ 173	Derrick McKey	.10	.03
❑ 174	Nate McMillan	.10	.03
❑ 175	Gary Payton	1.00	.30
❑ 176	Ricky Pierce	.10	.03
❑ 177	David Benoit	.10	.03
❑ 178	Mike Brown	.10	.03
❑ 179	Tyrone Corbin	.10	.03
❑ 180	Mark Eaton	.10	.03
❑ 181	Jeff Malone	.10	.03
❑ 182	Karl Malone	.75	.23
❑ 183	John Stockton	.50	.15
❑ 184	Michael Adams	.10	.03
❑ 185	Ledell Eackles	.10	.03
❑ 186	Pervis Ellison	.10	.03
❑ 187	A.J. English	.10	.03
❑ 188	Harvey Grant	.10	.03
❑ 189	Buck Johnson	.10	.03
❑ 190	LaBradford Smith	.10	.03
❑ 191	Larry Stewart	.10	.03
❑ 192	David Wingate	.10	.03
❑ 193	Alonzo Mourning RC	2.00	.60
❑ 194	Adam Keefe RC	.10	.03
❑ 195	Robert Horry RC	.50	.15
❑ 196	Anthony Peeler RC	.25	.07
❑ 197	Tracy Murray RC	.25	.07
❑ 198	Dave Johnson RC	.10	.03
❑ 199	Checklist 1-104	.10	.03
❑ 200	Checklist 105-200	.10	.03
❑ 201	David Robinson JS	.30	.09
❑ 202	Dikembe Mutombo JS	.30	.09
❑ 203	Otis Thorpe JS	.05	.02
❑ 204	Hakeem Olajuwon JS	.30	.09
❑ 205	Shawn Kemp JS	.50	.15
❑ 206	Charles Barkley JS	.30	.09
❑ 207	Pervis Ellison JS	.05	.02
❑ 208	Chris Morris JS	.05	.02
❑ 209	Brad Daugherty JS	.05	.02
❑ 210	Derrick Coleman JS	.05	.02
❑ 211	Tim Perry JS	.05	.02
❑ 212	Duane Causwell JS	.05	.02
❑ 213	Scottie Pippen JS	.50	.15
❑ 214	Robert Parish JS	.05	.02
❑ 215	Stacey Augmon JS	.05	.02
❑ 216	Michael Jordan JS	2.00	.60
❑ 217	Karl Malone JS	.30	.09
❑ 218	John Williams JS	.05	.02
❑ 219	Horace Grant JS	.05	.02
❑ 220	Orlando Woolridge JS	.05	.02
❑ 221	Mookie Blaylock	.15	.04
❑ 222	Greg Foster	.05	.02
❑ 223	Steve Henson	.05	.02
❑ 224	Adam Keefe	.05	.02
❑ 225	Jon Koncak	.05	.02
❑ 226	Travis Mays	.05	.02
❑ 227	Alaa Abdelnaby	.05	.02
❑ 228	Sherman Douglas	.05	.02
❑ 229	Xavier McDaniel	.05	.02
❑ 230	Marcus Webb RC	.05	.02
❑ 231	Tony Bennett RC	.05	.02
❑ 232	Mike Gminski	.05	.02
❑ 233	Kevin Lynch	.05	.02
❑ 234	Alonzo Mourning	.75	.23
❑ 235	David Wingate	.05	.02
❑ 236	Rodney McCray	.05	.02
❑ 237	Trent Tucker	.05	.02
❑ 238	Corey Williams RC	.05	.02
❑ 239	Danny Ferry	.05	.02
❑ 240	Jay Guidinger RC	.05	.02
❑ 241	Jerome Lane	.05	.02
❑ 242	Bobby Phills RC	.30	.09
❑ 243	Gerald Wilkins	.05	.02
❑ 244	Walter Bond RC	.05	.02
❑ 245	Dexter Cambridge RC	.05	.02
❑ 246	Radisav Curcic RC UER (Misspelled Radislav on card front)	.05	.02
❑ 247	Brian Howard RC	.05	.02
❑ 248	Tracy Moore RC	.05	.02
❑ 249	Sean Rooks RC	.05	.02
❑ 250	Kevin Brooks	.05	.02
❑ 251	LaPhonso Ellis RC	.30	.09
❑ 252	Scott Hastings	.05	.02
❑ 253	Robert Pack	.05	.02
❑ 254	Gary Plummer RC	.05	.02
❑ 255	Bryant Stith RC	.15	.04
❑ 256	Robert Werdann RC	.05	.02
❑ 257	Gerald Glass	.05	.02
❑ 258	Terry Mills	.05	.02
❑ 259	Olden Polynice	.05	.02
❑ 260	Danny Young	.05	.02
❑ 261	Jud Buechler	.05	.02
❑ 262	Jeff Grayer	.05	.02
❑ 263	Bryon Houston RC	.05	.02
❑ 264	Keith Jennings RC	.05	.02
❑ 265	Ed Nealy	.05	.02
❑ 266	Latrell Sprewell RC	2.50	.75
❑ 267	Scott Brooks	.05	.02
❑ 268	Matt Bullard	.05	.02
❑ 269	Winston Garland	.05	.02
❑ 270	Carl Herrera	.05	.02
❑ 271	Robert Horry	.30	.09
❑ 272	Tree Rollins	.05	.02
❑ 273	Greg Dreiling	.05	.02
❑ 274	Sean Green	.05	.02
❑ 275	Sam Mitchell	.05	.02
❑ 276	Pooh Richardson	.05	.02
❑ 277	Malik Sealy RC	.15	.04
❑ 278	Kenny Williams	.05	.02
❑ 279	Mark Jackson	.15	.04
❑ 280	Stanley Roberts	.05	.02
❑ 281	Elmore Spencer RC	.05	.02
❑ 282	Kiki Vandeweghe	.05	.02
❑ 283	John S. Williams	.05	.02
❑ 284	Randy Woods RC	.05	.02
❑ 285	Alex Blackwell RC	.05	.02
❑ 286	Duane Cooper RC	.05	.02
❑ 287	James Edwards	.05	.02
❑ 288	Jack Haley	.05	.02
❑ 289	Anthony Peeler	.15	.04
❑ 290	Keith Askins	.05	.02
❑ 291	Matt Geiger RC	.15	.04
❑ 292	Alec Kessler	.05	.02
❑ 293	Harold Miner RC	.15	.04
❑ 294	John Salley	.05	.02
❑ 295	Anthony Avent RC	.05	.02
❑ 296	Jon Barry RC	.15	.04
❑ 297	Todd Day RC	.15	.04
❑ 298	Blue Edwards	.05	.02
❑ 299	Brad Lohaus	.05	.02
❑ 300	Lee Mayberry RC	.05	.02
❑ 301	Eric Murdock	.05	.02
❑ 302	Danny Schayes	.05	.02
❑ 303	Lance Blanks	.05	.02
❑ 304	Christian Laettner RC	.60	.18
❑ 305	Marlon Maxey RC	.05	.02
❑ 306	Bob McCann RC	.05	.02
❑ 307	Chuck Person	.05	.02
❑ 308	Brad Sellers	.05	.02
❑ 309	Chris Smith RC	.05	.02
❑ 310	Gundars Vetra RC	.05	.02
❑ 311	Micheal Williams	.05	.02
❑ 312	Rafael Addison	.05	.02
❑ 313	Chucky Brown	.05	.02
❑ 314	Maurice Cheeks	.05	.02
❑ 315	Tate George	.05	.02
❑ 316	Rick Mahorn	.05	.02
❑ 317	Rumeal Robinson	.05	.02
❑ 318	Eric Anderson RC	.05	.02
❑ 319	Rolando Blackman	.05	.02
❑ 320	Tony Campbell	.05	.02
❑ 321	Hubert Davis RC	.15	.04
❑ 322	Doc Rivers	.15	.04
❑ 323	Charles Smith	.05	.02
❑ 324	Herb Williams	.05	.02
❑ 325	Litterial Green RC	.05	.02
❑ 326	Steve Kerr	.15	.04
❑ 327	Greg Kite	.05	.02
❑ 328	Shaquille O'Neal RC	10.00	3.00
❑ 329	Tom Tolbert	.05	.02
❑ 330	Jeff Turner	.05	.02
❑ 331	Greg Grant	.05	.02
❑ 332	Jeff Hornacek	.15	.04
❑ 333	Andrew Lang	.05	.02
❑ 334	Tim Perry	.05	.02
❑ 335	C.Weatherspoon RC	.30	.09
❑ 336	Danny Ainge	.15	.04
❑ 337	Charles Barkley	.50	.15
❑ 338	Richard Dumas RC	.05	.02
❑ 339	Frank Johnson	.05	.02
❑ 340	Tim Kempton	.05	.02
❑ 341	Oliver Miller RC	.15	.04
❑ 342	Jerrod Mustaf	.05	.02
❑ 343	Mario Elie	.15	.04
❑ 344	Dave Johnson	.05	.02
❑ 345	Tracy Murray	.15	.04
❑ 346	Rod Strickland	.30	.09
❑ 347	Randy Brown	.05	.02
❑ 348	Pete Chilcutt	.05	.02
❑ 349	Marty Conlon	.05	.02
❑ 350	Jim Les	.05	.02
❑ 351	Kurt Rambis	.05	.02
❑ 352	Walt Williams RC	.30	.09
❑ 353	Lloyd Daniels RC	.05	.02
❑ 354	Vinny Del Negro	.05	.02
❑ 355	Dale Ellis	.05	.02
❑ 356	Avery Johnson	.05	.02
❑ 357	Sam Mack RC	.15	.04
❑ 358	J.R. Reid	.05	.02
❑ 359	David Wood	.05	.02
❑ 360	Vincent Askew	.05	.02
❑ 361	Isaac Austin RC	.15	.04

❑ 362 John Crotty RC	.05	.02
❑ 363 Stephen Howard RC	.05	.02
❑ 364 Jay Humphries	.05	.02
❑ 365 Larry Krystkowiak	.05	.02
❑ 366 Rex Chapman	.05	.02
❑ 367 Tom Gugliotta RC	1.00	.30
❑ 368 Buck Johnson	.05	.02
❑ 369 Charles Jones	.05	.02
❑ 370 Don MacLean RC	.05	.02
❑ 371 Doug Overton	.05	.02
❑ 372 Brent Price RC	.15	.04
❑ 373 Checklist 201-266	.05	.02
❑ 374 Checklist 267-330	.05	.02
❑ 375 Checklist 331-375	.05	.02
❑ JS207 Pervis Ellison AU (Certified Autograph)	20.00	6.00
❑ JS212 Duane Causwell AU (Certified Autograph)	15.00	4.50
❑ JS215 Stacey Augmon AU (Certified Autograph)	30.00	9.00
❑ NNO Jam Session Rank 1-10: David Robinson, Dikembe Mutombo, Otis Thorpe, Hakeem Olajuwon, Shawn Kemp, Charles Barkley, Pervis Ellison, Chris Morris, Brad Daugherty, Derrick Coleman	2.50	.75
❑ NNO Jam Session 11-20: Tim Perry, Duane Causwell, Scottie Pippen, Robert Parish, Stacey Augmon, Michael Jordan, Karl Malone, John Williams, Horace Grant, Orlando Woolridge	2.50	.75

1993-94 Ultra

	Nm-Mt	Ex-Mt
COMPLETE SET (375)	30.00	9.00
COMPLETE SERIES 1 (200)	15.00	4.50
COMPLETE SERIES 2 (175)	15.00	4.50
❑ 1 Stacey Augmon	.05	.02
❑ 2 Mookie Blaylock	.15	.04
❑ 3 Doug Edwards RC	.05	.02
❑ 4 Duane Ferrell	.05	.02
❑ 5 Paul Graham	.05	.02
❑ 6 Adam Keefe	.05	.02
❑ 7 Dominique Wilkins	.30	.09
❑ 8 Kevin Willis	.05	.02
❑ 9 Alaa Abdelnaby	.05	.02
❑ 10 Dee Brown	.05	.02
❑ 11 Sherman Douglas	.05	.02
❑ 12 Rick Fox	.05	.02
❑ 13 Kevin Gamble	.05	.02
❑ 14 Xavier McDaniel	.05	.02
❑ 15 Robert Parish	.15	.04
❑ 16 Muggsy Bogues	.15	.04
❑ 17 Scott Burrell RC	.30	.09
❑ 18 Dell Curry	.05	.02
❑ 19 Kenny Gattison	.05	.02
❑ 20 Hersey Hawkins	.15	.04
❑ 21 Eddie Johnson	.05	.02
❑ 22 Larry Johnson	.30	.09
❑ 23 Alonzo Mourning	.50	.15
❑ 24 Johnny Newman	.05	.02
❑ 25 David Wingate	.05	.02
❑ 26 B.J. Armstrong	.05	.02
❑ 27 Corie Blount RC	.05	.02
❑ 28 Bill Cartwright	.05	.02
❑ 29 Horace Grant	.15	.04
❑ 30 Michael Jordan	4.00	1.20
❑ 31 Stacey King	.05	.02
❑ 32 John Paxson	.05	.02
❑ 33 Will Perdue	.05	.02
❑ 34 Scottie Pippen	1.00	.30
❑ 35 Terrell Brandon	.15	.04
❑ 36 Brad Daugherty	.05	.02
❑ 37 Danny Ferry	.05	.02
❑ 38 Chris Mills RC	.30	.09
❑ 39 Larry Nance	.05	.02
❑ 40 Mark Price	.05	.02
❑ 41 Gerald Wilkins	.05	.02
❑ 42 John Williams	.05	.02
❑ 43 Terry Davis	.05	.02
❑ 44 Derek Harper	.15	.04
❑ 45 Donald Hodge	.05	.02
❑ 46 Jim Jackson	.15	.04
❑ 47 Sean Rooks	.05	.02
❑ 48 Doug Smith	.05	.02
❑ 49 Mahmoud Abdul-Rauf	.05	.02
❑ 50 LaPhonso Ellis	.05	.02
❑ 51 Mark Macon	.05	.02
❑ 52 Dikembe Mutombo	.30	.09
❑ 53 Bryant Stith	.05	.02
❑ 54 Reggie Williams	.05	.02
❑ 55 Mark Aguirre	.05	.02
❑ 56 Joe Dumars	.30	.09
❑ 57 Bill Laimbeer	.05	.02
❑ 58 Terry Mills	.05	.02
❑ 59 Olden Polynice	.05	.02
❑ 60 Alvin Robertson	.05	.02
❑ 61 Sean Elliott	.15	.04
❑ 62 Isiah Thomas	.30	.09
❑ 63 Victor Alexander	.05	.02
❑ 64 Chris Gatling	.05	.02
❑ 65 Tim Hardaway	.30	.09
❑ 66 Byron Houston	.05	.02
❑ 67 Sarunas Marciulionis	.05	.02
❑ 68 Chris Mullin	.30	.09
❑ 69 Billy Owens	.05	.02
❑ 70 Latrell Sprewell	.75	.23
❑ 71 Matt Bullard	.05	.02
❑ 72 Sam Cassell RC	1.25	.35
❑ 73 Carl Herrera	.05	.02
❑ 74 Robert Horry	.15	.04
❑ 75 Vernon Maxwell	.05	.02
❑ 76 Hakeem Olajuwon	.50	.15
❑ 77 Kenny Smith	.05	.02
❑ 78 Otis Thorpe	.15	.04
❑ 79 Dale Davis	.05	.02
❑ 80 Vern Fleming	.05	.02
❑ 81 Reggie Miller	.30	.09
❑ 82 Sam Mitchell	.05	.02
❑ 83 Pooh Richardson	.05	.02
❑ 84 Detlef Schrempf	.15	.04
❑ 85 Rik Smits	.15	.04
❑ 86 Ron Harper	.15	.04
❑ 87 Mark Jackson	.15	.04
❑ 88 Danny Manning	.15	.04
❑ 89 Stanley Roberts	.05	.02
❑ 90 Loy Vaught	.05	.02
❑ 91 John Williams	.05	.02
❑ 92 Sam Bowie	.05	.02
❑ 93 Doug Christie	.15	.04
❑ 94 Vlade Divac	.15	.04
❑ 95 George Lynch RC	.05	.02
❑ 96 Anthony Peeler	.05	.02
❑ 97 James Worthy	.30	.09
❑ 98 Bimbo Coles	.05	.02
❑ 99 Grant Long	.05	.02
❑ 100 Harold Miner	.05	.02
❑ 101 Glen Rice	.15	.04
❑ 102 Rony Seikaly	.05	.02
❑ 103 Brian Shaw	.05	.02
❑ 104 Steve Smith	.30	.09
❑ 105 Anthony Avent	.05	.02
❑ 106 Vin Baker RC	.75	.23
❑ 107 Frank Brickowski	.05	.02
❑ 108 Todd Day	.05	.02
❑ 109 Blue Edwards	.05	.02
❑ 110 Lee Mayberry	.05	.02
❑ 111 Eric Murdock	.05	.02
❑ 112 Orlando Woolridge	.05	.02
❑ 113 Thurl Bailey	.05	.02
❑ 114 Christian Laettner	.15	.04
❑ 115 Chuck Person	.05	.02
❑ 116 Doug West	.05	.02
❑ 117 Micheal Williams	.05	.02
❑ 118 Kenny Anderson	.15	.04
❑ 119 Derrick Coleman	.15	.04
❑ 120 Rick Mahorn	.05	.02
❑ 121 Chris Morris	.05	.02
❑ 122 Rumeal Robinson	.05	.02
❑ 123 Rex Walters RC	.05	.02
❑ 124 Greg Anthony	.05	.02
❑ 125 Rolando Blackman	.05	.02
❑ 126 Hubert Davis	.05	.02
❑ 127 Patrick Ewing	.30	.09
❑ 128 Anthony Mason	.15	.04
❑ 129 Charles Oakley	.15	.04
❑ 130 Doc Rivers	.15	.04
❑ 131 Charles Smith	.05	.02
❑ 132 John Starks	.15	.04
❑ 133 Nick Anderson	.15	.04
❑ 134 Anthony Bowie	.05	.02
❑ 135 Shaquille O'Neal	1.50	.45
❑ 136 Dennis Scott	.05	.02
❑ 137 Scott Skiles	.05	.02
❑ 138 Jeff Turner	.05	.02
❑ 139 Shawn Bradley RC	.30	.09
❑ 140 Johnny Dawkins	.05	.02
❑ 141 Jeff Hornacek	.15	.04
❑ 142 Tim Perry	.05	.02
❑ 143 Clarence Weatherspoon	.05	.02
❑ 144 Danny Ainge	.15	.04
❑ 145 Charles Barkley	.50	.15
❑ 146 Cedric Ceballos	.15	.04
❑ 147 Kevin Johnson	.15	.04
❑ 148 Negele Knight	.05	.02
❑ 149 Malcolm Mackey RC	.05	.02
❑ 150 Dan Majerle	.15	.04
❑ 151 Oliver Miller	.05	.02
❑ 152 Mark West	.05	.02
❑ 153 Mark Bryant	.05	.02
❑ 154 Clyde Drexler	.30	.09
❑ 155 Jerome Kersey	.05	.02
❑ 156 Terry Porter	.05	.02
❑ 157 Clifford Robinson	.15	.04
❑ 158 Rod Strickland	.15	.04
❑ 159 Buck Williams	.05	.02
❑ 160 Duane Causwell	.05	.02
❑ 161 Bobby Hurley RC	.15	.04
❑ 162 Mitch Richmond	.30	.09
❑ 163 Lionel Simmons	.05	.02
❑ 164 Wayman Tisdale	.05	.02
❑ 165 Spud Webb	.15	.04
❑ 166 Walt Williams	.05	.02
❑ 167 Willie Anderson	.05	.02
❑ 168 Antoine Carr	.05	.02
❑ 169 Lloyd Daniels	.05	.02
❑ 170 Dennis Rodman	.60	.18
❑ 171 Dale Ellis	.05	.02
❑ 172 Avery Johnson	.05	.02
❑ 173 J.R. Reid	.05	.02
❑ 174 David Robinson	.50	.15
❑ 175 Michael Cage	.05	.02
❑ 176 Kendall Gill	.15	.04
❑ 177 Ervin Johnson RC	.15	.04
❑ 178 Shawn Kemp	.50	.15
❑ 179 Derrick McKey	.05	.02
❑ 180 Nate McMillan	.05	.02
❑ 181 Gary Payton	.50	.15
❑ 182 Sam Perkins	.15	.04
❑ 183 Ricky Pierce	.05	.02
❑ 184 David Benoit	.05	.02
❑ 185 Tyrone Corbin	.05	.02
❑ 186 Mark Eaton	.05	.02
❑ 187 Jay Humphries	.05	.02
❑ 188 Jeff Malone	.05	.02
❑ 189 Karl Malone	.50	.15
❑ 190 John Stockton	.30	.09
❑ 191 Luther Wright RC	.05	.02
❑ 192 Michael Adams	.05	.02

❑ 193	Calbert Cheaney RC	.15	.04
❑ 194	Pervis Ellison	.05	.02
❑ 195	Tom Gugliotta	.30	.09
❑ 196	Buck Johnson	.05	.02
❑ 197	LaBradford Smith	.05	.02
❑ 198	Larry Stewart	.05	.02
❑ 199	Checklist	.05	.02
❑ 200	Checklist	.05	.02
❑ 201	Doug Edwards	.05	.02
❑ 202	Craig Ehlo	.05	.02
❑ 203	Jon Koncak	.05	.02
❑ 204	Andrew Lang	.05	.02
❑ 205	Ennis Whatley	.05	.02
❑ 206	Chris Corchiani	.05	.02
❑ 207	Acie Earl RC	.05	.02
❑ 208	Jimmy Oliver	.05	.02
❑ 209	Ed Pinckney	.05	.02
❑ 210	Dino Radja RC	.05	.02
❑ 211	Matt Wenstrom RC	.05	.02
❑ 212	Tony Bennett	.05	.02
❑ 213	Scott Burrell	.30	.09
❑ 214	LeRon Ellis	.05	.02
❑ 215	Hersey Hawkins	.15	.04
❑ 216	Eddie Johnson	.05	.02
❑ 217	Rumeal Robinson	.05	.02
❑ 218	Corie Blount	.05	.02
❑ 219	Dave Johnson	.05	.02
❑ 220	Steve Kerr	.15	.04
❑ 221	Toni Kukoc RC	1.25	.35
❑ 222	Pete Myers	.05	.02
❑ 223	Bill Wennington	.05	.02
❑ 224	Scott Williams	.05	.02
❑ 225	John Battle	.05	.02
❑ 226	Tyrone Hill	.05	.02
❑ 227	Gerald Madkins RC	.05	.02
❑ 228	Chris Mills	.30	.09
❑ 229	Bobby Phills	.05	.02
❑ 230	Greg Dreiling	.05	.02
❑ 231	Lucious Harris RC	.05	.02
❑ 232	Popeye Jones RC	.05	.02
❑ 233	Tim Legler RC	.05	.02
❑ 234	Fat Lever	.05	.02
❑ 235	Jamal Mashburn RC	.75	.23
❑ 236	Tom Hammonds	.05	.02
❑ 237	Darnell Mee RC	.05	.02
❑ 238	Robert Pack	.05	.02
❑ 239	Rodney Rogers RC	.30	.09
❑ 240	Brian Williams	.05	.02
❑ 241	Greg Anderson	.05	.02
❑ 242	Sean Elliott	.15	.04
❑ 243	Allan Houston RC	1.25	.35
❑ 244	Lindsey Hunter RC	.30	.09
❑ 245	Mark Macon	.05	.02
❑ 246	David Wood	.05	.02
❑ 247	Jud Buechler	.05	.02
❑ 248	Josh Grant RC	.05	.02
❑ 249	Jeff Grayer	.05	.02
❑ 250	Keith Jennings	.05	.02
❑ 251	Avery Johnson	.05	.02
❑ 252	Chris Webber RC	3.00	.90
❑ 253	Scott Brooks	.05	.02
❑ 254	Sam Cassell	.30	.09
❑ 255	Mario Elie	.05	.02
❑ 256	Richard Petruska RC	.05	.02
❑ 257	Eric Riley RC	.05	.02
❑ 258	Antonio Davis RC	.40	.12
❑ 259	Scott Haskin RC	.05	.02
❑ 260	Derrick McKey	.05	.02
❑ 261	Byron Scott	.15	.04
❑ 262	Malik Sealy	.05	.02
❑ 263	Kenny Williams	.05	.02
❑ 264	Haywoode Workman	.05	.02
❑ 265	Mark Aguirre	.05	.02
❑ 266	Terry Dehere RC	.05	.02
❑ 267	Harold Ellis RC	.05	.02
❑ 268	Gary Grant	.05	.02
❑ 269	Bob Martin RC	.05	.02
❑ 270	Elmore Spencer	.05	.02
❑ 271	Tom Tolbert	.05	.02
❑ 272	Sam Bowie	.05	.02
❑ 273	Elden Campbell	.05	.02
❑ 274	Antonio Harvey RC	.05	.02
❑ 275	George Lynch	.05	.02
❑ 276	Tony Smith	.05	.02
❑ 277	Sedale Threatt	.05	.02
❑ 278	Nick Van Exel RC	1.00	.30
❑ 279	Willie Burton	.05	.02
❑ 280	Matt Geiger	.05	.02
❑ 281	John Salley	.05	.02
❑ 282	Vin Baker	.40	.12
❑ 283	Jon Barry	.05	.02
❑ 284	Brad Lohaus	.05	.02
❑ 285	Ken Norman	.05	.02
❑ 286	Derek Strong RC	.05	.02
❑ 287	Mike Brown	.05	.02
❑ 288	Brian Davis RC	.05	.02
❑ 289	Tellis Frank	.05	.02
❑ 290	Luc Longley	.15	.04
❑ 291	Marlon Maxey	.05	.02
❑ 292	Isaiah Rider RC	.60	.18
❑ 293	Chris Smith	.05	.02
❑ 294	P.J. Brown RC	.30	.09
❑ 295	Kevin Edwards	.05	.02
❑ 296	Armon Gilliam	.05	.02
❑ 297	Johnny Newman	.05	.02
❑ 298	Rex Walters	.05	.02
❑ 299	David Wesley RC	.30	.09
❑ 300	Jayson Williams	.15	.04
❑ 301	Anthony Bonner	.05	.02
❑ 302	Derek Harper	.15	.04
❑ 303	Herb Williams	.05	.02
❑ 304	Litterial Green	.05	.02
❑ 305	Anfernee Hardaway RC	2.50	.75
❑ 306	Greg Kite	.05	.02
❑ 307	Larry Krystkowiak	.05	.02
❑ 308	Keith Tower RC	.05	.02
❑ 309	Dana Barros	.05	.02
❑ 310	Shawn Bradley	.30	.09
❑ 311	Greg Graham RC	.05	.02
❑ 312	Sean Green	.05	.02
❑ 313	Warren Kidd RC	.05	.02
❑ 314	Eric Leckner	.05	.02
❑ 315	Moses Malone	.30	.09
❑ 316	Orlando Woolridge	.05	.02
❑ 317	Duane Cooper	.05	.02
❑ 318	Joe Courtney RC	.05	.02
❑ 319	A.C. Green	.15	.04
❑ 320	Frank Johnson	.05	.02
❑ 321	Joe Kleine	.05	.02
❑ 322	Chris Dudley	.05	.02
❑ 323	Harvey Grant	.05	.02
❑ 324	Jaren Jackson	.05	.02
❑ 325	Tracy Murray	.05	.02
❑ 326	James Robinson RC	.05	.02
❑ 327	Reggie Smith	.05	.02
❑ 328	Kevin Thompson RC	.05	.02
❑ 329	Randy Brown	.05	.02
❑ 330	Evers Burns RC	.05	.02
❑ 331	Pete Chilcutt	.05	.02
❑ 332	Bobby Hurley	.15	.04
❑ 333	Mike Peplowski RC	.05	.02
❑ 334	LaBradford Smith	.05	.02
❑ 335	Trevor Wilson	.05	.02
❑ 336	Terry Cummings	.05	.02
❑ 337	Vinny Del Negro	.05	.02
❑ 338	Sleepy Floyd	.05	.02
❑ 339	Negele Knight	.05	.02
❑ 340	Dennis Rodman	.60	.18
❑ 341	Chris Whitney RC	.05	.02
❑ 342	Vincent Askew	.05	.02
❑ 343	Kendall Gill	.15	.04
❑ 344	Ervin Johnson	.15	.04
❑ 345	Chris King RC	.05	.02
❑ 346	Detlef Schrempf	.15	.04
❑ 347	Walter Bond	.05	.02
❑ 348	Tom Chambers	.05	.02
❑ 349	John Crotty	.05	.02
❑ 350	Bryon Russell RC	.30	.09
❑ 351	Felton Spencer	.05	.02
❑ 352	Mitchell Butler RC	.05	.02
❑ 353	Rex Chapman	.05	.02
❑ 354	Calbert Cheaney	.15	.04
❑ 355	Kevin Duckworth	.05	.02
❑ 356	Don MacLean	.05	.02
❑ 357	Gheorghe Muresan RC	.30	.09
❑ 358	Doug Overton	.05	.02
❑ 359	Brent Price	.05	.02
❑ 360	Kenny Walker	.05	.02
❑ 361	Derrick Coleman USA	.05	.02
❑ 362	Joe Dumars USA	.15	.04
❑ 363	Tim Hardaway USA	.15	.04
❑ 364	Larry Johnson USA	.15	.04
❑ 365	Shawn Kemp USA	.40	.12
❑ 366	Dan Majerle USA	.05	.02
❑ 367	Alonzo Mourning USA	.30	.09
❑ 368	Mark Price USA	.05	.02
❑ 369	Steve Smith USA	.15	.04
❑ 370	Isiah Thomas USA	.15	.04
❑ 371	Dominique Wilkins USA	.15	.04
❑ 372	Don Nelson Don Chaney	.15	.04
❑ 373	Jamal Mashburn CL	.30	.09
❑ 374	Checklist	.05	.02
❑ 375	Checklist	.05	.02
❑ M1	Reggie Miller USA	.75	.23
❑ M2	Shaquille O'Neal USA	6.00	1.80
❑ M3	Team Checklist USA	2.00	.60

1994-95 Ultra

		Nm-Mt	Ex-Mt
COMPLETE SET (350)		35.00	10.50
COMPLETE SERIES 1 (200)		20.00	6.00
COMPLETE SERIES 2 (150)		15.00	4.50
❑ 1	Stacey Augmon	.10	.03
❑ 2	Mookie Blaylock	.10	.03
❑ 3	Craig Ehlo	.10	.03
❑ 4	Adam Keefe	.10	.03
❑ 5	Andrew Lang	.10	.03
❑ 6	Ken Norman	.10	.03
❑ 7	Kevin Willis	.10	.03
❑ 8	Dee Brown	.10	.03
❑ 9	Sherman Douglas	.10	.03
❑ 10	Acie Earl	.10	.03
❑ 11	Pervis Ellison	.10	.03
❑ 12	Rick Fox	.10	.03
❑ 13	Xavier McDaniel	.10	.03
❑ 14	Eric Montross RC	.10	.03
❑ 15	Dino Radja	.10	.03
❑ 16	Dominique Wilkins	.40	.12
❑ 17	Michael Adams	.10	.03
❑ 18	Muggsy Bogues	.15	.04
❑ 19	Dell Curry	.10	.03
❑ 20	Kenny Gattison	.10	.03
❑ 21	Hersey Hawkins	.15	.04
❑ 22	Larry Johnson	.15	.04
❑ 23	Alonzo Mourning	.50	.15
❑ 24	Robert Parish	.15	.04
❑ 25	B.J. Armstrong	.10	.03
❑ 26	Steve Kerr	.10	.03
❑ 27	Toni Kukoc	.60	.18
❑ 28	Luc Longley	.10	.03
❑ 29	Pete Myers	.10	.03
❑ 30	Will Perdue	.10	.03
❑ 31	Scottie Pippen	1.25	.35
❑ 32	Terrell Brandon	.15	.04
❑ 33	Brad Daugherty	.10	.03
❑ 34	Tyrone Hill	.10	.03
❑ 35	Chris Mills	.15	.04
❑ 36	Bobby Phills	.10	.03
❑ 37	Mark Price	.10	.03
❑ 38	Gerald Wilkins	.10	.03
❑ 39	John Williams	.10	.03
❑ 40	Terry Davis	.10	.03
❑ 41	Jim Jackson	.15	.04
❑ 42	Popeye Jones	.10	.03
❑ 43	Jason Kidd RC	4.00	1.20
❑ 44	Jamal Mashburn	.40	.12
❑ 45	Sean Rooks	.10	.03
❑ 46	Doug Smith	.10	.03
❑ 47	Mahmoud Abdul-Rauf	.10	.03

❑ 48 LaPhonso Ellis .10 .03
❑ 49 Dikembe Mutombo .15 .04
❑ 50 Robert Pack .10 .03
❑ 51 Rodney Rogers .10 .03
❑ 52 Bryant Stith .10 .03
❑ 53 Brian Williams .10 .03
❑ 54 Reggie Williams .10 .03
❑ 55 Greg Anderson .10 .03
❑ 56 Joe Dumars .40 .12
❑ 57 Allan Houston .60 .18
❑ 58 Lindsey Hunter .15 .04
❑ 59 Terry Mills .10 .03
❑ 60 Tim Hardaway .40 .12
❑ 61 Chris Mullin .40 .12
❑ 62 Billy Owens .10 .03
❑ 63 Latrell Sprewell .40 .12
❑ 64 Chris Webber 1.00 .30
❑ 65 Sam Cassell .40 .12
❑ 66 Carl Herrera .10 .03
❑ 67 Robert Horry .15 .04
❑ 68 Vernon Maxwell .10 .03
❑ 69 Hakeem Olajuwon .60 .18
❑ 70 Kenny Smith .10 .03
❑ 71 Otis Thorpe .10 .03
❑ 72 Antonio Davis .10 .03
❑ 73 Dale Davis .10 .03
❑ 74 Mark Jackson .10 .03
❑ 75 Derrick McKey .10 .03
❑ 76 Reggie Miller .40 .12
❑ 77 Byron Scott .15 .04
❑ 78 Rik Smits .10 .03
❑ 79 Haywoode Workman .10 .03
❑ 80 Gary Grant .10 .03
❑ 81 Ron Harper .15 .04
❑ 82 Elmore Spencer .10 .03
❑ 83 Loy Vaught .10 .03
❑ 84 Elden Campbell .10 .03
❑ 85 Doug Christie .15 .04
❑ 86 Vlade Divac .10 .03
❑ 87 Eddie Jones RC 2.00 .60
❑ 88 George Lynch .10 .03
❑ 89 Anthony Peeler .10 .03
❑ 90 Sedale Threatt .10 .03
❑ 91 Nick Van Exel .40 .12
❑ 92 James Worthy .40 .12
❑ 93 Bimbo Coles .10 .03
❑ 94 Matt Geiger .10 .03
❑ 95 Grant Long .10 .03
❑ 96 Harold Miner .10 .03
❑ 97 Glen Rice .15 .04
❑ 98 John Salley .10 .03
❑ 99 Rony Seikaly .10 .03
❑ 100 Brian Shaw .10 .03
❑ 101 Steve Smith .15 .04
❑ 102 Vin Baker .40 .12
❑ 103 Jon Barry .10 .03
❑ 104 Todd Day .10 .03
❑ 105 Lee Mayberry .10 .03
❑ 106 Eric Murdock .10 .03
❑ 107 Thurl Bailey .10 .03
❑ 108 Stacey King .10 .03
❑ 109 Christian Laettner .15 .04
❑ 110 Isaiah Rider .15 .04
❑ 111 Chris Smith .10 .03
❑ 112 Doug West .10 .03
❑ 113 Micheal Williams .10 .03
❑ 114 Kenny Anderson .15 .04
❑ 115 Benoit Benjamin .10 .03
❑ 116 P.J. Brown .10 .03
❑ 117 Derrick Coleman .15 .04
❑ 118 Yinka Dare RC .10 .03
❑ 119 Kevin Edwards .10 .03
❑ 120 Armon Gilliam .10 .03
❑ 121 Chris Morris .10 .03
❑ 122 Greg Anthony .10 .03
❑ 123 Anthony Bonner .10 .03
❑ 124 Hubert Davis .10 .03
❑ 125 Patrick Ewing .40 .12
❑ 126 Derek Harper .10 .03
❑ 127 Anthony Mason .15 .04
❑ 128 Charles Oakley .10 .03
❑ 129 Doc Rivers .15 .04
❑ 130 John Starks .10 .03
❑ 131 Nick Anderson .10 .03
❑ 132 Anthony Avent .10 .03
❑ 133 Anthony Bowie .10 .03
❑ 134 Anfernee Hardaway 1.00 .30
❑ 135 Shaquille O'Neal 2.00 .60
❑ 136 Dennis Scott .10 .03
❑ 137 Jeff Turner .10 .03
❑ 138 Dana Barros .10 .03
❑ 139 Shawn Bradley .10 .03
❑ 140 Greg Graham .10 .03
❑ 141 Jeff Malone .10 .03
❑ 142 Tim Perry .10 .03
❑ 143 Clarence Weatherspoon .10 .03
❑ 144 Scott Williams .10 .03
❑ 145 Danny Ainge .10 .03
❑ 146 Charles Barkley .60 .18
❑ 147 Cedric Ceballos .10 .03
❑ 148 A.C. Green .15 .04
❑ 149 Frank Johnson .10 .03
❑ 150 Kevin Johnson .15 .04
❑ 151 Dan Majerle .15 .04
❑ 152 Oliver Miller .10 .03
❑ 153 Wesley Person RC .40 .12
❑ 154 Mark Bryant .10 .03
❑ 155 Clyde Drexler .40 .12
❑ 156 Harvey Grant .10 .03
❑ 157 Jerome Kersey .10 .03
❑ 158 Tracy Murray .10 .03
❑ 159 Terry Porter .10 .03
❑ 160 Clifford Robinson .15 .04
❑ 161 James Robinson .10 .03
❑ 162 Rod Strickland .15 .04
❑ 163 Buck Williams .10 .03
❑ 164 Duane Causwell .10 .03
❑ 165 Olden Polynice .10 .03
❑ 166 Mitch Richmond .40 .12
❑ 167 Lionel Simmons .10 .03
❑ 168 Walt Williams .10 .03
❑ 169 Willie Anderson .10 .03
❑ 170 Terry Cummings .10 .03
❑ 171 Sean Elliott .15 .04
❑ 172 Avery Johnson .10 .03
❑ 173 J.R. Reid .10 .03
❑ 174 David Robinson .60 .18
❑ 175 Dennis Rodman .75 .23
❑ 176 Kendall Gill .15 .04
❑ 177 Shawn Kemp .60 .18
❑ 178 Nate McMillan .10 .03
❑ 179 Gary Payton .60 .18
❑ 180 Sam Perkins .15 .04
❑ 181 Detlef Schrempf .15 .04
❑ 182 David Benoit .10 .03
❑ 183 Tyrone Corbin .10 .03
❑ 184 Jeff Hornacek .15 .04
❑ 185 Jay Humphries .10 .03
❑ 186 Karl Malone .60 .18
❑ 187 Bryon Russell .10 .03
❑ 188 Felton Spencer .10 .03
❑ 189 John Stockton .40 .12
❑ 190 Mitchell Butler .10 .03
❑ 191 Rex Chapman .10 .03
❑ 192 Calbert Cheaney .10 .03
❑ 193 Kevin Duckworth .10 .03
❑ 194 Tom Gugliotta .15 .04
❑ 195 Don MacLean .10 .03
❑ 196 Gheorghe Muresan .10 .03
❑ 197 Scott Skiles .10 .03
❑ 198 Checklist .10 .03
❑ 199 Checklist .10 .03
❑ 200 Checklist .10 .03
❑ 201 Tyrone Corbin .10 .03
❑ 202 Doug Edwards .10 .03
❑ 203 Jim Les .10 .03
❑ 204 Grant Long .10 .03
❑ 205 Ken Norman .10 .03
❑ 206 Steve Smith .15 .04
❑ 207 Blue Edwards .10 .03
❑ 208 Greg Minor RC .10 .03
❑ 209 Eric Montross .10 .03
❑ 210 Derek Strong .10 .03
❑ 211 David Wesley .10 .03
❑ 212 Tony Bennett .10 .03
❑ 213 Scott Burrell .10 .03
❑ 214 Darrin Hancock .10 .03
❑ 215 Greg Sutton .10 .03
❑ 216 Corie Blount .10 .03
❑ 217 Jud Buechler .10 .03
❑ 218 Ron Harper .15 .04
❑ 219 Larry Krystkowiak .10 .03
❑ 220 Dickey Simpkins RC .10 .03
❑ 221 Bill Wennington .10 .03
❑ 222 Michael Cage .10 .03
❑ 223 Tony Campbell .10 .03
❑ 224 Steve Colter .10 .03
❑ 225 Greg Dreiling .10 .03
❑ 226 Danny Ferry .10 .03
❑ 227 Tony Dumas RC .10 .03
❑ 228 Lucious Harris .10 .03
❑ 229 Donald Hodge .10 .03
❑ 230 Jason Kidd 2.00 .60
❑ 231 Lorenzo Williams .10 .03
❑ 232 Dale Ellis .10 .03
❑ 233 Tom Hammonds .10 .03
❑ 234 Jalen Rose RC 1.50 .45
❑ 235 Reggie Slater .10 .03
❑ 236 Rafael Addison .10 .03
❑ 237 Bill Curley RC .10 .03
❑ 238 Johnny Dawkins .10 .03
❑ 239 Grant Hill RC 2.00 .60
❑ 240 Eric Leckner .10 .03
❑ 241 Mark Macon .10 .03
❑ 242 Oliver Miller .10 .03
❑ 243 Mark West .10 .03
❑ 244 Victor Alexander .10 .03
❑ 245 Chris Gatling .10 .03
❑ 246 Tom Gugliotta .15 .04
❑ 247 Keith Jennings .10 .03
❑ 248 Ricky Pierce .10 .03
❑ 249 Carlos Rogers RC .10 .03
❑ 250 Clifford Rozier RC .10 .03
❑ 251 Rony Seikaly .10 .03
❑ 252 David Wood .10 .03
❑ 253 Tim Breaux .10 .03
❑ 254 Scott Brooks .10 .03
❑ 255 Zan Tabak .10 .03
❑ 256 Duane Ferrell .10 .03
❑ 257 Mark Jackson .10 .03
❑ 258 Sam Mitchell .10 .03
❑ 259 John Williams .10 .03
❑ 260 Terry Dehere .10 .03
❑ 261 Harold Ellis .10 .03
❑ 262 Matt Fish .10 .03
❑ 263 Tony Massenburg .10 .03
❑ 264 Lamond Murray RC .15 .04
❑ 265 Bo Outlaw RC .10 .03
❑ 266 Eric Piatkowski RC .10 .03
❑ 267 Pooh Richardson .10 .03
❑ 268 Malik Sealy .10 .03
❑ 269 Randy Woods .10 .03
❑ 270 Sam Bowie .10 .03
❑ 271 Cedric Ceballos .10 .03
❑ 272 Antonio Harvey .10 .03
❑ 273 Eddie Jones 1.00 .30
❑ 274 Anthony Miller RC .10 .03
❑ 275 Tony Smith .10 .03
❑ 276 Ledell Eackles .10 .03
❑ 277 Kevin Gamble .10 .03
❑ 278 Brad Lohaus .10 .03
❑ 279 Billy Owens .10 .03
❑ 280 Khalid Reeves RC .10 .03
❑ 281 Kevin Willis .10 .03
❑ 282 Marty Conlon .10 .03
❑ 283 Alton Lister .10 .03
❑ 284 Eric Mobley RC .10 .03
❑ 285 Johnny Newman .10 .03
❑ 286 Ed Pinckney .10 .03
❑ 287 Glenn Robinson RC 1.25 .35
❑ 288 Howard Eisley .10 .03
❑ 289 Winston Garland .10 .03
❑ 290 Andres Guibert .10 .03
❑ 291 Donyell Marshall RC .40 .12
❑ 292 Sean Rooks .10 .03
❑ 293 Yinka Dare .10 .03
❑ 294 Sleepy Floyd .10 .03
❑ 295 Sean Higgins .10 .03
❑ 296 Rex Walters .10 .03
❑ 297 Jayson Williams .15 .04
❑ 298 Charles Smith .10 .03
❑ 299 Charlie Ward RC .40 .12
❑ 300 Herb Williams .10 .03
❑ 301 Monty Williams RC .10 .03
❑ 302 Horace Grant .15 .04
❑ 303 Geert Hammink .10 .03
❑ 304 Tree Rollins .10 .03
❑ 305 Donald Royal .10 .03

Card	Nm-Mt	Ex-Mt
❑ 306 Brian Shaw	.10	.03
❑ 307 Brooks Thompson RC	.10	.03
❑ 308 Derrick Alston RC	.10	.03
❑ 309 Willie Burton	.10	.03
❑ 310 Jaren Jackson	.10	.03
❑ 311 B.J. Tyler RC	.10	.03
❑ 312 Scott Williams	.10	.03
❑ 313 Sharone Wright RC	.10	.03
❑ 314 Joe Kleine	.10	.03
❑ 315 Danny Manning	.15	.04
❑ 316 Elliot Perry	.10	.03
❑ 317 Wesley Person	.15	.04
❑ 318 Trevor Ruffin RC	.10	.03
❑ 319 Danny Schayes	.10	.03
❑ 320 Wayman Tisdale	.10	.03
❑ 321 Chris Dudley	.10	.03
❑ 322 James Edwards	.10	.03
❑ 323 Alaa Abdelnaby	.10	.03
❑ 324 Randy Brown	.10	.03
❑ 325 Brian Grant RC	1.00	.30
❑ 326 Bobby Hurley	.10	.03
❑ 327 Michael Smith RC	.10	.03
❑ 328 Henry Turner	.10	.03
❑ 329 Trevor Wilson	.10	.03
❑ 330 Vinny Del Negro	.10	.03
❑ 331 Moses Malone	.40	.12
❑ 332 Julius Nwosu	.10	.03
❑ 333 Chuck Person	.10	.03
❑ 334 Chris Whitney	.10	.03
❑ 335 Vincent Askew	.10	.03
❑ 336 Bill Cartwright	.10	.03
❑ 337 Ervin Johnson	.10	.03
❑ 338 Sarunas Marciulionis	.10	.03
❑ 339 Antoine Carr	.10	.03
❑ 340 Tom Chambers	.10	.03
❑ 341 John Crotty	.10	.03
❑ 342 Jamie Watson RC	.10	.03
❑ 343 Juwan Howard RC	1.00	.30
❑ 344 Jim McIlvaine	.10	.03
❑ 345 Doug Overton	.10	.03
❑ 346 Scott Skiles	.10	.03
❑ 347 Anthony Tucker RC	.10	.03
❑ 348 Chris Webber	1.00	.30
❑ 349 Checklist	.10	.03
❑ 350 Checklist	.10	.03

1995-96 Ultra

	Nm-Mt	Ex-Mt
COMPLETE SET (350)	40.00	12.00
COMPLETE SERIES 1 (200)	20.00	6.00
COMPLETE SERIES 2 (150)	20.00	6.00
❑ 1 Stacey Augmon	.25	.07
❑ 2 Mookie Blaylock	.25	.07
❑ 3 Craig Ehlo	.25	.07
❑ 4 Andrew Lang	.25	.07
❑ 5 Grant Long	.25	.07
❑ 6 Ken Norman	.25	.07
❑ 7 Steve Smith	.50	.15
❑ 8 Spud Webb	.50	.15
❑ 9 Dee Brown	.25	.07
❑ 10 Sherman Douglas	.25	.07
❑ 11 Pervis Ellison	.25	.07
❑ 12 Rick Fox	.50	.15
❑ 13 Eric Montross	.25	.07
❑ 14 Dino Radja	.25	.07
❑ 15 David Wesley	.25	.07
❑ 16 Dominique Wilkins	.75	.23
❑ 17 Muggsy Bogues	.50	.15
❑ 18 Scott Burrell	.25	.07
❑ 19 Dell Curry	.25	.07
❑ 20 Kendall Gill	.25	.07
❑ 21 Larry Johnson	.50	.15
❑ 22 Alonzo Mourning	.50	.15
❑ 23 Robert Parish	.50	.15
❑ 24 Ron Harper	.50	.15
❑ 25 Michael Jordan	5.00	1.50
❑ 26 Toni Kukoc	.50	.15
❑ 27 Will Perdue	.25	.07
❑ 28 Scottie Pippen	1.25	.35
❑ 29 Terrell Brandon	.50	.15
❑ 30 Michael Cage	.25	.07
❑ 31 Tyrone Hill	.25	.07
❑ 32 Chris Mills	.25	.07
❑ 33 Bobby Phills	.25	.07
❑ 34 Mark Price	.50	.15
❑ 35 John Williams	.25	.07
❑ 36 Lucious Harris	.25	.07
❑ 37 Jim Jackson	.25	.07
❑ 38 Popeye Jones	.25	.07
❑ 39 Jason Kidd	2.50	.75
❑ 40 Jamal Mashburn	.50	.15
❑ 41 George McCloud	.25	.07
❑ 42 Roy Tarpley	.25	.07
❑ 43 Lorenzo Williams	.25	.07
❑ 44 Mahmoud Abdul-Rauf	.25	.07
❑ 45 Dikembe Mutombo	.50	.15
❑ 46 Robert Pack	.25	.07
❑ 47 Jalen Rose	1.00	.30
❑ 48 Bryant Stith	.25	.07
❑ 49 Brian Williams	.25	.07
❑ 50 Reggie Williams	.25	.07
❑ 51 Joe Dumars	.75	.23
❑ 52 Grant Hill	1.00	.30
❑ 53 Allan Houston	.50	.15
❑ 54 Lindsey Hunter	.25	.07
❑ 55 Terry Mills	.25	.07
❑ 56 Mark West	.25	.07
❑ 57 Chris Gatling	.25	.07
❑ 58 Tim Hardaway	.50	.15
❑ 59 Donyell Marshall	.50	.15
❑ 60 Chris Mullin	.75	.23
❑ 61 Carlos Rogers	.25	.07
❑ 62 Clifford Rozier	.25	.07
❑ 63 Rony Seikaly	.25	.07
❑ 64 Latrell Sprewell	.75	.23
❑ 65 Sam Cassell	.75	.23
❑ 66 Clyde Drexler	.75	.23
❑ 67 Mario Elie	.25	.07
❑ 68 Carl Herrera	.25	.07
❑ 69 Robert Horry	.50	.15
❑ 70 Hakeem Olajuwon	.75	.23
❑ 71 Kenny Smith	.25	.07
❑ 72 Antonio Davis	.25	.07
❑ 73 Dale Davis	.25	.07
❑ 74 Mark Jackson	.50	.15
❑ 75 Derrick McKey	.25	.07
❑ 76 Reggie Miller	.75	.23
❑ 77 Rik Smits	.50	.15
❑ 78 Terry Dehere	.25	.07
❑ 79 Lamond Murray	.25	.07
❑ 80 Bo Outlaw	.25	.07
❑ 81 Pooh Richardson	.25	.07
❑ 82 Rodney Rogers	.25	.07
❑ 83 Malik Sealy	.25	.07
❑ 84 Loy Vaught	.25	.07
❑ 85 Sam Bowie	.25	.07
❑ 86 Elden Campbell	.25	.07
❑ 87 Cedric Ceballos	.25	.07
❑ 88 Vlade Divac	.50	.15
❑ 89 Eddie Jones	1.00	.30
❑ 90 Anthony Peeler	.25	.07
❑ 91 Sedale Threatt	.25	.07
❑ 92 Nick Van Exel	.75	.23
❑ 93 Rex Chapman	.25	.07
❑ 94 Bimbo Coles	.25	.07
❑ 95 Matt Geiger	.25	.07
❑ 96 Billy Owens	.25	.07
❑ 97 Khalid Reeves	.25	.07
❑ 98 Glen Rice	.50	.15
❑ 99 Kevin Willis	.50	.15
❑ 100 Vin Baker	.50	.15
❑ 101 Marty Conlon	.25	.07
❑ 102 Todd Day	.25	.07
❑ 103 Eric Murdock	.25	.07
❑ 104 Glenn Robinson	.75	.23
❑ 105 Winston Garland	.25	.07
❑ 106 Tom Gugliotta	.25	.07
❑ 107 Christian Laettner	.50	.15
❑ 108 Isaiah Rider	.25	.07
❑ 109 Sean Rooks	.25	.07
❑ 110 Doug West	.25	.07
❑ 111 Kenny Anderson	.50	.15
❑ 112 P.J. Brown	.25	.07
❑ 113 Derrick Coleman	.25	.07
❑ 114 Armon Gilliam	.25	.07
❑ 115 Chris Morris	.25	.07
❑ 116 Anthony Bonner	.25	.07
❑ 117 Patrick Ewing	.75	.23
❑ 118 Derek Harper	.50	.15
❑ 119 Anthony Mason	.50	.15
❑ 120 Charles Oakley	.25	.07
❑ 121 Charles Smith	.25	.07
❑ 122 John Starks	.50	.15
❑ 123 Nick Anderson	.25	.07
❑ 124 Horace Grant	.50	.15
❑ 125 Anfernee Hardaway	.75	.23
❑ 126 Shaquille O'Neal	2.00	.60
❑ 127 Donald Royal	.25	.07
❑ 128 Dennis Scott	.25	.07
❑ 129 Brian Shaw	.25	.07
❑ 130 Derrick Alston	.25	.07
❑ 131 Dana Barros	.25	.07
❑ 132 Shawn Bradley	.25	.07
❑ 133 Willie Burton	.25	.07
❑ 134 Jeff Malone	.25	.07
❑ 135 Clarence Weatherspoon	.25	.07
❑ 136 Scott Williams	.25	.07
❑ 137 Sharone Wright	.25	.07
❑ 138 Danny Ainge	.25	.07
❑ 139 Charles Barkley	1.00	.30
❑ 140 A.C. Green	.50	.15
❑ 141 Kevin Johnson	.50	.15
❑ 142 Dan Majerle	.50	.15
❑ 143 Danny Manning	.50	.15
❑ 144 Elliot Perry	.25	.07
❑ 145 Wesley Person	.25	.07
❑ 146 Wayman Tisdale	.25	.07
❑ 147 Chris Dudley	.25	.07
❑ 148 Harvey Grant	.25	.07
❑ 149 Aaron McKie	.50	.15
❑ 150 Terry Porter	.25	.07
❑ 151 Clifford Robinson	.25	.07
❑ 152 Rod Strickland	.25	.07
❑ 153 Otis Thorpe	.25	.07
❑ 154 Buck Williams	.25	.07
❑ 155 Brian Grant	.75	.23
❑ 156 Bobby Hurley	.25	.07
❑ 157 Olden Polynice	.25	.07
❑ 158 Mitch Richmond	.50	.15
❑ 159 Michael Smith	.25	.07
❑ 160 Walt Williams	.25	.07
❑ 161 Vinny Del Negro	.25	.07
❑ 162 Sean Elliott	.50	.15
❑ 163 Avery Johnson	.25	.07
❑ 164 Chuck Person	.25	.07
❑ 165 J.R. Reid	.25	.07
❑ 166 Doc Rivers	.50	.15
❑ 167 David Robinson	.75	.23
❑ 168 Dennis Rodman	.50	.15
❑ 169 Vincent Askew	.25	.07
❑ 170 Hersey Hawkins	.25	.07
❑ 171 Shawn Kemp	.50	.15
❑ 172 Sarunas Marciulionis	.25	.07
❑ 173 Nate McMillan	.25	.07
❑ 174 Gary Payton	.75	.23
❑ 175 Sam Perkins	.50	.15
❑ 176 Detlef Schrempf	.50	.15
❑ 177 B.J. Armstrong	.25	.07
❑ 178 Jerome Kersey	.25	.07
❑ 179 Tony Massenburg	.25	.07
❑ 180 Oliver Miller	.25	.07
❑ 181 John Salley	.25	.07
❑ 182 David Benoit	.25	.07
❑ 183 Antoine Carr	.25	.07
❑ 184 Jeff Hornacek	.50	.15
❑ 185 Karl Malone	1.00	.30
❑ 186 Felton Spencer	.25	.07
❑ 187 John Stockton	1.00	.30
❑ 188 Greg Anthony	.25	.07
❑ 189 Benoit Benjamin	.25	.07

Card	Nm-Mt	Ex-Mt
❑ 190 Byron Scott	.25	.07
❑ 191 Calbert Cheaney	.25	.07
❑ 192 Juwan Howard	.75	.23
❑ 193 Don MacLean	.25	.07
❑ 194 Gheorghe Muresan	.25	.07
❑ 195 Doug Overton	.25	.07
❑ 196 Scott Skiles	.25	.07
❑ 197 Chris Webber	1.00	.30
❑ 198 Checklist (1-94)	.25	.07
❑ 199 Checklist (95-190)	.25	.07
❑ 200 Checklist (191-200)	.25	.07
❑ 201 Stacey Augmon	.25	.07
❑ 202 Mookie Blaylock	.25	.07
❑ 203 Grant Long	.25	.07
❑ 204 Steve Smith	.50	.15
❑ 205 Dana Barros	.25	.07
❑ 206 Kendall Gill	.25	.07
❑ 207 Khalid Reeves	.25	.07
❑ 208 Glen Rice	.50	.15
❑ 209 Luc Longley	.25	.07
❑ 210 Dennis Rodman	.50	.15
❑ 211 Dan Majerle	.50	.15
❑ 212 Tony Dumas	.25	.07
❑ 213 Elmore Spencer	.25	.07
❑ 214 Otis Thorpe	.25	.07
❑ 215 B.J. Armstrong	.25	.07
❑ 216 Sam Cassell	.75	.23
❑ 217 Clyde Drexler	.75	.23
❑ 218 Robert Horry	.50	.15
❑ 219 Hakeem Olajuwon	.75	.23
❑ 220 Eddie Johnson	.25	.07
❑ 221 Ricky Pierce	.25	.07
❑ 222 Eric Piatkowski	.50	.15
❑ 223 Rodney Rogers	.25	.07
❑ 224 Brian Williams	.25	.07
❑ 225 George Lynch	.25	.07
❑ 226 Alonzo Mourning	.50	.15
❑ 227 Benoit Benjamin	.25	.07
❑ 228 Terry Porter	.25	.07
❑ 229 Shawn Bradley	.25	.07
❑ 230 Kevin Edwards	.25	.07
❑ 231 Jayson Williams	.25	.07
❑ 232 Charlie Ward	.25	.07
❑ 233 Jon Koncak	.25	.07
❑ 234 Derrick Coleman	.25	.07
❑ 235 Richard Dumas	.25	.07
❑ 236 Vernon Maxwell	.25	.07
❑ 237 John Williams	.25	.07
❑ 238 Dontonio Wingfield	.25	.07
❑ 239 Tyrone Corbin	.25	.07
❑ 240 Will Perdue	.25	.07
❑ 241 Shawn Kemp	.50	.15
❑ 242 Gary Payton	.75	.23
❑ 243 Sam Perkins	.50	.15
❑ 244 Detlef Schrempf	.50	.15
❑ 245 Chris Morris	.25	.07
❑ 246 Robert Pack	.25	.07
❑ 247 Willie Anderson EXP	.25	.07
❑ 248 Oliver Miller EXP	.25	.07
❑ 249 Tracy Murray EXP	.25	.07
❑ 250 Alvin Robertson EXP	.25	.07
❑ 251 Carlos Rogers EXP	.25	.07
❑ 252 John Salley EXP	.25	.07
❑ 253 Damon Stoudamire EXP	1.00	.30
❑ 254 Zan Tabak EXP	.25	.07
❑ 255 Greg Anthony EXP	.25	.07
❑ 256 Blue Edwards EXP	.25	.07
❑ 257 Kenny Gattison EXP	.25	.07
❑ 258 Chris King EXP	.25	.07
❑ 259 Lawrence Moten EXP	.25	.07
❑ 260 Eric Murdock EXP	.25	.07
❑ 261 Bryant Reeves EXP	.50	.15
❑ 262 Byron Scott EXP	.25	.07
❑ 263 Cory Alexander RC	.25	.07
❑ 264 Brent Barry RC	.75	.23
❑ 265 Mario Bennett RC	.25	.07
❑ 266 Travis Best RC	.25	.07
❑ 267 Junior Burrough RC	.25	.07
❑ 268 Jason Caffey RC	.50	.15
❑ 269 Randolph Childress RC	.25	.07
❑ 270 Sasha Danilovic RC	.25	.07
❑ 271 Tyus Edney RC	.25	.07
❑ 272 Michael Finley RC	3.00	.90
❑ 273 Sherrell Ford RC	.25	.07
❑ 274 Kevin Garnett RC	4.00	1.20
❑ 275 Alan Henderson RC	.75	.23
❑ 276 Donny Marshall RC	.25	.07
❑ 277 Antonio McDyess RC	1.50	.45
❑ 278 Loren Meyer RC	.25	.07
❑ 279 Lawrence Moten RC	.25	.07
❑ 280 Ed O'Bannon RC	.25	.07
❑ 281 Greg Ostertag RC	.25	.07
❑ 282 Cherokee Parks RC	.25	.07
❑ 283 Theo Ratliff RC	1.00	.30
❑ 284 Bryant Reeves RC	.75	.23
❑ 285 Shawn Respert RC	.25	.07
❑ 286 Lou Roe RC	.25	.07
❑ 287 Arvydas Sabonis RC	1.00	.30
❑ 288 Joe Smith RC	1.25	.35
❑ 289 Jerry Stackhouse RC	2.50	.75
❑ 290 Damon Stoudamire RC	1.50	.45
❑ 291 Bob Sura RC	.50	.15
❑ 292 Kurt Thomas RC	.50	.15
❑ 293 Gary Trent RC	.25	.07
❑ 294 David Vaughn RC	.25	.07
❑ 295 Rasheed Wallace RC	2.00	.60
❑ 296 Eric Williams RC	.50	.15
❑ 297 Corliss Williamson RC	.75	.23
❑ 298 George Zidek RC	.25	.07
❑ 299 M. Abdul-Rauf ENC	.25	.07
❑ 300 Kenny Anderson ENC	.25	.07
❑ 301 Vin Baker ENC	.25	.07
❑ 302 Charles Barkley ENC	.75	.23
❑ 303 Mookie Blaylock ENC	.25	.07
❑ 304 Cedric Ceballos ENC	.25	.07
❑ 305 Vlade Divac ENC	.25	.07
❑ 306 Clyde Drexler ENC	.50	.15
❑ 307 Joe Dumars ENC	.50	.15
❑ 308 Sean Elliott ENC	.25	.07
❑ 309 Patrick Ewing ENC	.50	.15
❑ 310 Anfernee Hardaway ENC	.50	.15
❑ 311 Tim Hardaway ENC	.25	.07
❑ 312 Grant Hill ENC	.75	.23
❑ 313 Tyrone Hill ENC	.25	.07
❑ 314 Robert Horry ENC	.25	.07
❑ 315 Juwan Howard ENC	.50	.15
❑ 316 Jim Jackson ENC	.25	.07
❑ 317 Kevin Johnson ENC	.25	.07
❑ 318 Larry Johnson ENC	.25	.07
❑ 319 Eddie Jones ENC	.75	.23
❑ 320 Shawn Kemp ENC	.25	.07
❑ 321 Jason Kidd ENC	1.25	.35
❑ 322 Christian Laettner ENC	.25	.07
❑ 323 Karl Malone ENC	.75	.23
❑ 324 Jamal Mashburn ENC	.25	.07
❑ 325 Reggie Miller ENC	.50	.15
❑ 326 Alonzo Mourning ENC	.25	.07
❑ 327 Dikembe Mutombo ENC	.25	.07
❑ 328 Hakeem Olajuwon ENC	.50	.15
❑ 329 Gary Payton ENC	.50	.15
❑ 330 Scottie Pippen ENC	.50	.15
❑ 331 Dino Radja ENC	.25	.07
❑ 332 Glen Rice ENC	.25	.07
❑ 333 Mitch Richmond ENC	.25	.07
❑ 334 Clifford Robinson ENC	.25	.07
❑ 335 David Robinson ENC	.50	.15
❑ 336 Glenn Robinson ENC	.50	.15
❑ 337 Dennis Rodman ENC	.25	.07
❑ 338 Carlos Rogers ENC	.25	.07
❑ 339 Detlef Schrempf ENC	.25	.07
❑ 340 Byron Scott ENC	.25	.07
❑ 341 Rik Smits ENC	.25	.07
❑ 342 Latrell Sprewell ENC	.75	.23
❑ 343 John Stockton ENC	.75	.23
❑ 344 Nick Van Exel ENC	.25	.07
❑ 345 Loy Vaught ENC	.25	.07
❑ 346 C. Weatherspoon ENC	.25	.07
❑ 347 Chris Webber ENC	.75	.23
❑ 348 Kevin Willis ENC	.25	.07
❑ 349 Checklist (201-298)	.25	.07
❑ 350 Checklist (299-350/ins.)	.25	.07

1996-97 Ultra

	Nm-Mt	Ex-Mt
COMPLETE SET (300)	50.00	15.00
COMPLETE SERIES 1 (150)	35.00	10.50
COMPLETE SERIES 2 (150)	15.00	4.50
❑ 1 Mookie Blaylock	.25	.07
❑ 2 Alan Henderson	.25	.07
❑ 3 Christian Laettner	.50	.15
❑ 4 Dikembe Mutombo	.50	.15

Card	Nm-Mt	Ex-Mt
❑ 5 Steve Smith	.50	.15
❑ 6 Dana Barros	.25	.07
❑ 7 Rick Fox	.25	.07
❑ 8 Dino Radja	.25	.07
❑ 9 Antoine Walker RC	2.00	.60
❑ 10 Eric Williams	.25	.07
❑ 11 Dell Curry	.25	.07
❑ 12 Tony Delk RC	.75	.23
❑ 13 Matt Geiger	.25	.07
❑ 14 Glen Rice	.50	.15
❑ 15 Ron Harper	.50	.15
❑ 16 Michael Jordan	5.00	1.50
❑ 17 Toni Kukoc	.50	.15
❑ 18 Scottie Pippen	1.25	.35
❑ 19 Dennis Rodman	.50	.15
❑ 20 Terrell Brandon	.50	.15
❑ 21 Chris Mills	.25	.07
❑ 22 Bobby Phills	.25	.07
❑ 23 Bob Sura	.25	.07
❑ 24 Jim Jackson	.25	.07
❑ 25 Jason Kidd	1.25	.35
❑ 26 Jamal Mashburn	.50	.15
❑ 27 George McCloud	.25	.07
❑ 28 Samaki Walker RC	.25	.07
❑ 29 LaPhonso Ellis	.25	.07
❑ 30 Antonio McDyess	.50	.15
❑ 31 Bryant Stith	.25	.07
❑ 32 Joe Dumars	.75	.23
❑ 33 Grant Hill	.75	.23
❑ 34 Theo Ratliff	.50	.15
❑ 35 Otis Thorpe	.25	.07
❑ 36 Chris Mullin	.75	.23
❑ 37 Joe Smith	.50	.15
❑ 38 Latrell Sprewell	.75	.23
❑ 39 Charles Barkley	1.00	.30
❑ 40 Clyde Drexler	.75	.23
❑ 41 Mario Elie	.25	.07
❑ 42 Hakeem Olajuwon	.75	.23
❑ 43 Erick Dampier RC	.75	.23
❑ 44 Dale Davis	.25	.07
❑ 45 Derrick McKey	.25	.07
❑ 46 Reggie Miller	.75	.23
❑ 47 Rik Smits	.50	.15
❑ 48 Brent Barry	.25	.07
❑ 49 Malik Sealy	.25	.07
❑ 50 Loy Vaught	.25	.07
❑ 51 Lorenzen Wright RC	.50	.15
❑ 52 Kobe Bryant RC	12.00	3.60
❑ 53 Cedric Ceballos	.25	.07
❑ 54 Eddie Jones	.75	.23
❑ 55 Shaquille O'Neal	2.00	.60
❑ 56 Nick Van Exel	.75	.23
❑ 57 Tim Hardaway	.50	.15
❑ 58 Alonzo Mourning	.50	.15
❑ 59 Kurt Thomas	.50	.15
❑ 60 Ray Allen RC	2.50	.75
❑ 61 Vin Baker	.50	.15
❑ 62 Sherman Douglas	.25	.07
❑ 63 Glenn Robinson	.75	.23
❑ 64 Kevin Garnett	1.50	.45
❑ 65 Tom Gugliotta	[illegible]	.07
❑ 66 Stephon Marbury RC	[illegible]	[illegible]
❑ 67 Doug West	[illegible]	[illegible]
❑ 68 Shawn Bradley	[illegible]	[illegible]
❑ 69 Kendall Gill	[illegible]	[illegible]
❑ 70 Kerry Kittles RC	[illegible]	[illegible]
❑ 71 Ed O'Bannon	[illegible]	[illegible]
❑ 72 Patrick Ewing	[illegible]	[illegible]

Card	Nm-Mt	Ex-Mt
❑ 73 Larry Johnson	.50	.15
❑ 74 Charles Oakley	.25	.07
❑ 75 John Starks	.50	.15
❑ 76 John Wallace RC	.75	.23
❑ 77 Nick Anderson	.25	.07
❑ 78 Horace Grant	.50	.15
❑ 79 Anfernee Hardaway	.75	.23
❑ 80 Dennis Scott	.25	.07
❑ 81 Derrick Coleman	.50	.15
❑ 82 Allen Iverson RC	8.00	2.40
❑ 83 Jerry Stackhouse	1.00	.30
❑ 84 Clarence Weatherspoon	.25	.07
❑ 85 Michael Finley	1.00	.30
❑ 86 Kevin Johnson	.50	.15
❑ 87 Steve Nash RC	2.00	.60
❑ 88 Wesley Person	.25	.07
❑ 89 Jermaine O'Neal RC	2.50	.75
❑ 90 Clifford Robinson	.25	.07
❑ 91 Arvydas Sabonis	.50	.15
❑ 92 Gary Trent	.25	.07
❑ 93 Tyus Edney	.25	.07
❑ 94 Brian Grant	.75	.23
❑ 95 Olden Polynice	.25	.07
❑ 96 Mitch Richmond	.50	.15
❑ 97 Corliss Williamson	.50	.15
❑ 98 Vinny Del Negro	.25	.07
❑ 99 Sean Elliott	.50	.15
❑ 100 Avery Johnson	.25	.07
❑ 101 David Robinson	.75	.23
❑ 102 Hersey Hawkins	.50	.15
❑ 103 Shawn Kemp	.50	.15
❑ 104 Gary Payton	.75	.23
❑ 105 Sam Perkins	.50	.15
❑ 106 Detlef Schrempf	.50	.15
❑ 107 Marcus Camby RC	1.00	.30
❑ 108 Doug Christie	.50	.15
❑ 109 Damon Stoudamire	.75	.23
❑ 110 Sharone Wright	.25	.07
❑ 111 Jeff Hornacek	.50	.15
❑ 112 Karl Malone	.75	.23
❑ 113 Chris Morris	.25	.07
❑ 114 Bryon Russell	.25	.07
❑ 115 John Stockton	.75	.23
❑ 116 Shareef Abdur-Rahim RC	2.50	.75
❑ 117 Greg Anthony	.25	.07
❑ 118 Blue Edwards	.25	.07
❑ 119 Bryant Reeves	.25	.07
❑ 120 Calbert Cheaney	.25	.07
❑ 121 Juwan Howard	.50	.15
❑ 122 Gheorghe Muresan	.25	.07
❑ 123 Chris Webber	.75	.23
❑ 124 Vin Baker OTB	.25	.07
❑ 125 Charles Barkley OTB	.75	.23
❑ 126 Kevin Garnett OTB	.75	.23
❑ 127 Juwan Howard OTB	.25	.07
❑ 128 Larry Johnson OTB	.25	.07
❑ 129 Shawn Kemp OTB	.25	.07
❑ 130 Karl Malone OTB	.75	.23
❑ 131 Anthony Mason OTB	.25	.07
❑ 132 Antonio McDyess OTB	.50	.15
❑ 133 Alonzo Mourning OTB	.25	.07
❑ 134 Hakeem Olajuwon OTB	.50	.15
❑ 135 Shaquille O'Neal OTB	.75	.23
❑ 136 David Robinson OTB	.50	.15
❑ 137 Dennis Rodman OTB	.25	.07
❑ 138 Joe Smith OTB	.25	.07
❑ 139 Mookie Blaylock UE	.25	.07
❑ 140 Terrell Brandon UE	.25	.07
❑ 141 Anfernee Hardaway UE	.50	.15
❑ 142 Grant Hill UE	.50	.15
❑ 143 Michael Jordan UE	2.50	.75
❑ 144 Jason Kidd UE	.50	.15
❑ 145 Gary Payton UE	.50	.15
❑ 146 Jerry Stackhouse UE	.75	.23
❑ 147 Damon Stoudamire UE	.50	.15
❑ 148 Hakeem Olajuwon David Robinson Robert Horry Oliver Miller Clarence Weatherspoon	.75	.23
❑ 149 Checklist	.25	.07
❑ 150 Checklist	.25	.07
❑ 151 Tyrone Corbin	.25	.07
❑ 152 Priest Lauderdale RC	.25	.07
153 Dikembe Mutombo	.50	.15
Eldridge Recasner RC	.25	.07
❑ 155 Todd Day	.25	.07
❑ 156 Greg Minor	.25	.07
❑ 157 David Wesley	.25	.07
❑ 158 Vlade Divac	.25	.07
❑ 159 Anthony Mason	.50	.15
❑ 160 Malik Rose RC	.50	.15
❑ 161 Jason Caffey	.25	.07
❑ 162 Steve Kerr	.50	.15
❑ 163 Luc Longley	.25	.07
❑ 164 Danny Ferry	.25	.07
❑ 165 Tyrone Hill	.25	.07
❑ 166 Vitaly Potapenko RC	.25	.07
❑ 167 Sam Cassell	.75	.23
❑ 168 Michael Finley	1.00	.30
❑ 169 Chris Gatling	.25	.07
❑ 170 A.C. Green	.50	.15
❑ 171 Oliver Miller	.25	.07
❑ 172 Eric Montross	.25	.07
❑ 173 Dale Ellis	.25	.07
❑ 174 Mark Jackson	.25	.07
❑ 175 Ervin Johnson	.25	.07
❑ 176 Sarunas Marciulionis	.25	.07
❑ 177 Stacey Augmon	.25	.07
❑ 178 Joe Dumars	.75	.23
❑ 179 Grant Hill	.75	.23
❑ 180 Lindsey Hunter	.25	.07
❑ 181 Grant Long	.25	.07
❑ 182 Terry Mills	.25	.07
❑ 183 Otis Thorpe	.25	.07
❑ 184 Jerome Williams RC	.75	.23
❑ 185 Todd Fuller RC	.25	.07
❑ 186 Ray Owes RC	.25	.07
❑ 187 Mark Price	.50	.15
❑ 188 Felton Spencer	.25	.07
❑ 189 Charles Barkley	1.00	.30
❑ 190 Emanual Davis RC	.25	.07
❑ 191 Othella Harrington RC	.75	.23
❑ 192 Matt Maloney RC	.50	.15
❑ 193 Brent Price	.25	.07
❑ 194 Kevin Willis	.25	.07
❑ 195 Travis Best	.25	.07
❑ 196 Antonio Davis	.25	.07
❑ 197 Jalen Rose	.75	.23
❑ 198 Pooh Richardson	.25	.07
❑ 199 Stanley Roberts	.25	.07
❑ 200 Rodney Rogers	.25	.07
❑ 201 Elden Campbell	.25	.07
❑ 202 Derek Fisher RC	1.25	.35
❑ 203 Travis Knight RC	.25	.07
❑ 204 Shaquille O'Neal	2.00	.60
❑ 205 Byron Scott	.25	.07
❑ 206 Sasha Danilovic	.25	.07
❑ 207 Dan Majerle	.50	.15
❑ 208 Martin Muursepp RC	.25	.07
❑ 209 Armon Gilliam	.25	.07
❑ 210 Andrew Lang	.25	.07
❑ 211 Johnny Newman	.25	.07
❑ 212 Kevin Garnett	1.50	.45
❑ 213 Tom Gugliotta	.25	.07
❑ 214 Shane Heal RC	.25	.07
❑ 215 Stojko Vrankovic	.25	.07
❑ 216 Robert Pack	.25	.07
❑ 217 Khalid Reeves	.25	.07
❑ 218 Jayson Williams	.50	.15
❑ 219 Chris Childs	.25	.07
❑ 220 Allan Houston	.50	.15
❑ 221 Larry Johnson	.50	.15
❑ 222 Walter McCarty RC	.25	.07
❑ 223 Charlie Ward	.25	.07
❑ 224 Brian Evans RC	.25	.07
❑ 225 Amal McCaskill RC	.25	.07
❑ 226 Rony Seikaly	.25	.07
❑ 227 Gerald Wilkins	.25	.07
❑ 228 Mark Davis	.25	.07
❑ 229 Lucious Harris	.25	.07
❑ 230 Don MacLean	.25	.07
❑ 231 Cedric Ceballos	.25	.07
❑ 232 Rex Chapman	.25	.07
❑ 233 Jason Kidd	1.25	.35
❑ 234 Danny Manning	.50	.15
❑ 235 Kenny Anderson	.25	.07
❑ 236 Aaron McKie	.50	.15
❑ 237 Isaiah Rider	.50	.15
❑ 238 Rasheed Wallace	1.00	.30
❑ 239 Mahmoud Abdul-Rauf	.25	.07
❑ 240 Billy Owens	.25	.07
❑ 241 Michael Smith	.25	.07
❑ 242 Vernon Maxwell	.25	.07
❑ 243 Charles Smith	.25	.07
❑ 244 Dominique Wilkins	.75	.23
❑ 245 Craig Ehlo	.25	.07
❑ 246 Jim McIlvaine	.25	.07
❑ 247 Nate McMillan	.25	.07
❑ 248 Hubert Davis	.25	.07
❑ 249 Carlos Rogers	.25	.07
❑ 250 Zan Tabak	.25	.07
❑ 251 Walt Williams	.25	.07
❑ 252 Jeff Hornacek	.50	.15
❑ 253 Karl Malone	.75	.23
❑ 254 Greg Ostertag	.25	.07
❑ 255 Bryon Russell	.25	.07
❑ 256 John Stockton	.75	.23
❑ 257 George Lynch	.25	.07
❑ 258 Lawrence Moten	.25	.07
❑ 259 Anthony Peeler	.25	.07
❑ 260 Roy Rogers RC	.25	.07
❑ 261 Tracy Murray	.25	.07
❑ 262 Rod Strickland	.25	.07
❑ 263 Ben Wallace RC	5.00	1.50
❑ 264 Shareef Abdur-Rahim RE	1.25	.35
❑ 265 Ray Allen RE	1.50	.45
❑ 266 Kobe Bryant RE	6.00	1.80
❑ 267 Marcus Camby RE	.50	.15
❑ 268 Erick Dampier RE	.25	.07
❑ 269 Tony Delk RE	.50	.15
❑ 270 Allen Iverson RE	2.00	.60
❑ 271 Kerry Kittles RE	.75	.23
❑ 272 Stephon Marbury RE	1.50	.45
❑ 273 Steve Nash RE	.75	.23
❑ 274 Jermaine O'Neal RE	2.00	.60
❑ 275 Antoine Walker RE	1.50	.45
❑ 276 Samaki Walker RE	.25	.07
❑ 277 John Wallace RE	.50	.15
❑ 278 Lorenzen Wright RE	.25	.07
❑ 279 Anfernee Hardaway SU	.50	.15
❑ 280 Michael Jordan SU	2.50	.75
❑ 281 Jason Kidd SU	.50	.15
❑ 282 Hakeem Olajuwon SU	.50	.15
❑ 283 Gary Payton SU	.50	.15
❑ 284 Mitch Richmond SU	.25	.07
❑ 285 David Robinson SU	.50	.15
❑ 286 John Stockton SU	.75	.23
❑ 287 Damon Stoudamire SU	.50	.15
❑ 288 Chris Webber SU	.75	.23
❑ 289 Clyde Drexler PG	.50	.15
❑ 290 Kevin Garnett PG	.75	.23
❑ 291 Grant Hill PG	.50	.15
❑ 292 Shawn Kemp PG	.25	.07
❑ 293 Karl Malone PG	.75	.23
❑ 294 Antonio McDyess PG	.50	.15
❑ 295 Alonzo Mourning PG	.25	.07
❑ 296 Shaquille O'Neal PG	.75	.23
❑ 297 Scottie Pippen PG	.75	.23
❑ 298 Jerry Stackhouse PG	.75	.23
❑ 299 Checklist (151-263)	.25	.07
❑ 300 Checklist 264-300/inserts	.25	.07
❑ NNO J.Stackhouse Promo	3.00	.90

1997-98 Ultra

	Nm-Mt	Ex-Mt
COMPLETE SET (275)	100.00	30.00
COMPLETE SERIES 1 (150)	50.00	15.00
COMPLETE SERIES 2 (125)	50.00	15.00

COMMON CARD (1-275) .25 .07
COMMON ROOKIE (124-148) 1.00 .30
❑ 1 Kobe Bryant 3.00 .90
❑ 2 Charles Barkley 1.00 .30
❑ 3 Joe Dumars .75 .23
❑ 4 Wesley Person .25 .07
❑ 5 Walt Williams .25 .07
❑ 6 Vlade Divac .50 .15
❑ 7 Mookie Blaylock .25 .07
❑ 8 Jason Kidd 1.25 .35
❑ 9 Ron Harper .50 .15
❑ 10 Sherman Douglas .25 .07
❑ 11 Cedric Ceballos .25 .07
❑ 12 Karl Malone .75 .23
❑ 13 Antonio McDyess .50 .15
❑ 14 Steve Kerr .50 .15
❑ 15 Matt Maloney .25 .07
❑ 16 Glenn Robinson .75 .23
❑ 17 Rony Seikaly .25 .07
❑ 18 Derrick Coleman .25 .07
❑ 19 Jermaine O'Neal 1.25 .35
❑ 20 Scott Burrell .25 .07
❑ 21 Glen Rice .50 .15
❑ 22 Dale Ellis .25 .07
❑ 23 Michael Jordan 5.00 1.50
❑ 24 Anfernee Hardaway .75 .23
❑ 25 Bryon Russell .25 .07
❑ 26 Toni Kukoc .50 .15
❑ 27 Theo Ratliff .25 .07
❑ 28 Tom Gugliotta .50 .15
❑ 29 Dennis Rodman .50 .15
❑ 30 John Stockton .75 .23
❑ 31 Priest Lauderdale .25 .07
❑ 32 Luc Longley .25 .07
❑ 33 Grant Hill .75 .23
❑ 34 Antonio Davis .25 .07
❑ 35 Eddie Jones .75 .23
❑ 36 Nick Anderson .25 .07
❑ 37 Shareef Abdur-Rahim 1.25 .35
❑ 38 Stephon Marbury 1.00 .30
❑ 39 Todd Day .25 .07
❑ 40 Tim Hardaway .50 .15
❑ 41 Larry Johnson .50 .15
❑ 42 Sam Perkins .50 .15
❑ 43 Dikembe Mutombo .50 .15
❑ 44 Bo Outlaw .25 .07
❑ 45 Mitch Richmond .50 .15
❑ 46 Bryant Reeves .25 .07
❑ 47 P.J. Brown .25 .07
❑ 48 Steve Smith .50 .15
❑ 49 Martin Muursepp .25 .07
❑ 50 Jamal Mashburn .50 .15
❑ 51 Kendall Gill .25 .07
❑ 52 Vinny Del Negro .25 .07
❑ 53 Roy Rogers .25 .07
❑ 54 Khalid Reeves .25 .07
❑ 55 Scottie Pippen 1.25 .35
❑ 56 Joe Smith .50 .15
❑ 57 Mark Jackson .50 .15
❑ 58 Voshon Lenard .25 .07
❑ 59 Dan Majerle .50 .15
❑ 60 Alonzo Mourning .50 .15
❑ 61 Kerry Kittles .75 .23
❑ 62 Chris Childs .25 .07
❑ 63 Patrick Ewing .75 .23
❑ 64 Allan Houston .50 .15
❑ 65 Marcus Camby .75 .23
❑ 66 Christian Laettner .50 .15
❑ 67 Loy Vaught .25 .07
❑ 68 Jayson Williams .25 .07
❑ 69 Avery Johnson .25 .07
❑ 70 Damon Stoudamire .50 .15
❑ 71 Kevin Johnson .50 .15
❑ 72 Gheorghe Muresan .25 .07
❑ 73 Reggie Miller .75 .23
❑ 74 John Wallace .25 .07
❑ 75 Terrell Brandon .50 .15
❑ 76 Dale Davis .25 .07
❑ 77 Latrell Sprewell .75 .23
❑ 78 Lorenzen Wright .25 .07
❑ 79 Rod Strickland .25 .07
❑ 80 Kenny Anderson .50 .15
❑ 81 Anthony Mason .50 .15
❑ 82 Hakeem Olajuwon .75 .23
❑ 83 Kevin Garnett 1.50 .45
❑ 84 Isaiah Rider .50 .15
❑ 85 Mark Price .50 .15
❑ 86 Shawn Bradley .25 .07
❑ 87 Vin Baker .50 .15
❑ 88 Steve Nash .75 .23
❑ 89 Jeff Hornacek .50 .15
❑ 90 Tony Delk .25 .07
❑ 91 Horace Grant .50 .15
❑ 92 Othella Harrington .25 .07
❑ 93 Arvydas Sabonis .50 .15
❑ 94 Antoine Walker 1.00 .30
❑ 95 Todd Fuller .25 .07
❑ 96 John Starks .50 .15
❑ 97 Olden Polynice .25 .07
❑ 98 Sean Elliott .50 .15
❑ 99 Travis Best .25 .07
❑ 100 Chris Gatling .25 .07
❑ 101 Derek Harper .50 .15
❑ 102 LaPhonso Ellis .25 .07
❑ 103 Dean Garrett .25 .07
❑ 104 Hersey Hawkins .25 .07
❑ 105 Jerry Stackhouse .75 .23
❑ 106 Ray Allen .75 .23
❑ 107 Allen Iverson 2.00 .60
❑ 108 Chris Webber .75 .23
❑ 109 Robert Pack .25 .07
❑ 110 Gary Payton .75 .23
❑ 111 Mario Elie .25 .07
❑ 112 Dell Curry .25 .07
❑ 113 Lindsey Hunter .25 .07
❑ 114 Robert Horry .50 .15
❑ 115 David Robinson .75 .23
❑ 116 Kevin Willis .50 .15
❑ 117 Tyrone Hill .25 .07
❑ 118 Vitaly Potapenko .25 .07
❑ 119 Clyde Drexler .75 .23
❑ 120 Derek Fisher .75 .23
❑ 121 Detlef Schrempf .50 .15
❑ 122 Gary Trent .25 .07
❑ 123 Danny Ferry .25 .07
❑ 124 Derek Anderson RC 8.00 2.40
❑ 125 Chris Anstey RC 1.00 .30
❑ 126 Tony Battie RC 2.00 .60
❑ 127 Chauncey Billups RC 4.00 1.20
❑ 128 Kelvin Cato RC 2.00 .60
❑ 129 Austin Croshere RC 4.00 1.20
❑ 130 Antonio Daniels RC 2.00 .60
❑ 131 Tim Duncan RC ! 15.00 4.50
❑ 132 Danny Fortson RC 2.50 .75
❑ 133 Adonal Foyle RC 1.50 .45
❑ 134 Paul Grant RC 1.00 .30
❑ 135 Ed Gray RC 1.00 .30
❑ 136 Bobby Jackson RC 3.00 .90
❑ 137 Brevin Knight RC 2.50 .75
❑ 138 Tracy McGrady RC 20.00 6.00
❑ 139 Ron Mercer RC 5.00 1.50
❑ 140 Anthony Parker RC 1.00 .30
❑ 141 Scot Pollard RC 1.50 .45
❑ 142 Rodrick Rhodes RC 1.00 .30
❑ 143 Olivier Saint-Jean RC 1.00 .30
❑ 144 Maurice Taylor RC 4.00 1.20
❑ 145 Johnny Taylor RC 1.00 .30
❑ 146 Tim Thomas RC 6.00 1.80
❑ 147 Keith Van Horn RC 6.00 1.80
❑ 148 Jacque Vaughn RC 1.50 .45
❑ 149 Checklist .25 .07
❑ 150 Checklist .25 .07
❑ 151 Scott Burrell .25 .07
❑ 152 Brian Williams .25 .07
❑ 153 Terry Mills .25 .07
❑ 154 Jim Jackson .25 .07
❑ 155 Michael Finley .75 .23
❑ 156 Jeff Nordgaard RC .25 .07
❑ 157 Carl Herrera .25 .07
❑ 158 Otis Thorpe .25 .07
❑ 159 Wesley Person .25 .07
❑ 160 Tyrone Hill .25 .07
❑ 161 Charles O'Bannon RC .25 .07
❑ 162 Greg Anthony .25 .07
❑ 163 Rusty LaRue RC .25 .07
❑ 164 David Wesley .25 .07
❑ 165 Chris Garner RC .25 .07
❑ 166 George McCloud .25 .07
❑ 167 Mark Price .50 .15
❑ 168 God Shammgod RC .25 .07
❑ 169 Isaac Austin .25 .07
❑ 170 Alan Henderson .25 .07
❑ 171 Eric Washington RC .75 .23
❑ 172 Darrell Armstrong .25 .07
❑ 173 Calbert Cheaney .25 .07
❑ 174 Cedric Henderson RC .25 .07
❑ 175 Bryant Stith .25 .07
❑ 176 Sean Rooks .25 .07
❑ 177 Chris Mills .25 .07
❑ 178 Eldridge Recasner .25 .07
❑ 179 Priest Lauderdale .25 .07
❑ 180 Rick Fox .50 .15
❑ 181 Keith Closs RC .25 .07
❑ 182 Chris Dudley .25 .07
❑ 183 L.Funderburke RC .50 .15
❑ 184 Michael Stewart RC .25 .07
❑ 185 Alvin Williams RC 1.00 .30
❑ 186 Adam Keefe .25 .07
❑ 187 Chauncey Billups .50 .15
❑ 188 Jon Barry .25 .07
❑ 189 Bobby Jackson .50 .15
❑ 190 Sam Cassell .75 .23
❑ 191 Dee Brown .25 .07
❑ 192 Travis Knight .25 .07
❑ 193 Dean Garrett .25 .07
❑ 194 David Benoit .25 .07
❑ 195 Chris Morris .25 .07
❑ 196 Bubba Wells RC .25 .07
❑ 197 James Robinson .25 .07
❑ 198 Anthony Johnson RC .25 .07
❑ 199 Dennis Scott .25 .07
❑ 200 DeJuan Wheat RC .25 .07
❑ 201 Rodney Rogers .25 .07
❑ 202 Tariq Abdul-Wahad .25 .07
❑ 203 Cherokee Parks .25 .07
❑ 204 Jacque Vaughn .25 .07
❑ 205 Cory Alexander .25 .07
❑ 206 Kevin Ollie RC .25 .07
❑ 207 George Lynch .25 .07
❑ 208 Lamond Murray .25 .07
❑ 209 Jud Buechler .25 .07
❑ 210 Erick Dampier .50 .15
❑ 211 Malcolm Huckaby RC .25 .07
❑ 212 Chris Webber .75 .23
❑ 213 Chris Crawford RC .25 .07
❑ 214 J.R. Reid .25 .07
❑ 215 Eddie Johnson .25 .07
❑ 216 Nick Van Exel .75 .23
❑ 217 Antonio McDyess .50 .15
❑ 218 David Wingate .25 .07
❑ 219 Malik Sealy .25 .07
❑ 220 Bo Outlaw .25 .07
❑ 221 Serge Zwikker RC .25 .07
❑ 222 Bobby Phills .25 .07
❑ 223 Shea Seals RC .25 .07
❑ 224 Clifford Robinson .25 .07
❑ 225 Zydrunas Ilgauskas .50 .15
❑ 226 John Thomas RC .25 .07
❑ 227 Rik Smits .50 .15
❑ 228 Rasheed Wallace .75 .23
❑ 229 John Wallace .25 .07
❑ 230 Bob Sura .25 .07
❑ 231 Ervin Johnson .25 .07
❑ 232 Keith Booth RC .25 .07
❑ 233 Chuck Person .25 .07
❑ 234 Brian Shaw .25 .07
❑ 235 Todd Day .25 .07
❑ 236 Clarence Weatherspoon .25 .07
❑ 237 Charlie Ward .25 .07
❑ 238 Rod Strickland .25 .07
❑ 239 Shawn Kemp .50 .15
❑ 240 Terrell Brandon .50 .15
❑ 241 Corey Beck RC .25 .07
❑ 242 Vin Baker .50 .15
❑ 243 Fred Hoiberg .25 .07
❑ 244 Chris Mullin .75 .23
❑ 245 Brian Grant .50 .15
❑ 246 Derek Anderson 2.00 .60
❑ 247 Zan Tabak .25 .07
❑ 248 Charles Smith RC .25 .07
❑ 249 S. Abdur-Rahim GRE 2.50 .75
❑ 250 Ray Allen GRE 1.50 .45
❑ 251 Charles Barkley GRE 2.00 .60
❑ 252 Kobe Bryant GRE 6.00 1.80
❑ 253 Marcus Camby GRE 1.50 .45
❑ 254 Kevin Garnett GRE 3.00 .90
❑ 255 Anfernee Hardaway GRE 1.50 .45

Card		
❑ 256 Grant Hill GRE	1.50	.45
❑ 257 Juwan Howard GRE	.75	.23
❑ 258 Allen Iverson GRE	4.00	1.20
❑ 259 Michael Jordan GRE	10.00	3.00
❑ 260 Shawn Kemp GRE	1.00	.30
❑ 261 Kerry Kittles GRE	1.50	.45
❑ 262 Karl Malone GRE	1.50	.45
❑ 263 Stephon Marbury GRE	2.00	.60
❑ 264 Hakeem Olajuwon GRE	1.50	.45
❑ 265 Shaquille O'Neal GRE	3.00	.90
❑ 266 Gary Payton GRE	1.50	.45
❑ 267 Scottie Pippen GRE	2.50	.75
❑ 268 David Robinson GRE	1.50	.45
❑ 269 Dennis Rodman GRE	1.00	.30
❑ 270 Joe Smith GRE	1.00	.30
❑ 271 Jerry Stackhouse GRE	1.50	.45
❑ 272 Damon Stoudamire GRE	1.00	.30
❑ 273 Antoine Walker GRE	2.00	.60
❑ 274 Checklist	.25	.07
❑ 275 Checklist	.25	.07
❑ NNO J.Stackhouse Promo	2.00	.60

1998-99 Ultra

	Nm-Mt	Ex-Mt
COMPLETE SET (125)	100.00	30.00
COMPLETE SET w/o SP (100)	25.00	7.50
COMMON CARD (1-100)	.25	.07
COMMON ROOKIE (101-125)	.50	.15
❑ 1 Keith Van Horn	.75	.23
❑ 1B K.Van Horn Promo	.75	.23
❑ 2 Antonio Daniels	.25	.07
❑ 3 Patrick Ewing	.75	.23
❑ 4 Alonzo Mourning	.50	.15
❑ 5 Isaac Austin	.25	.07
❑ 6 Bryant Reeves	.25	.07
❑ 7 Dennis Scott	.25	.07
❑ 8 Damon Stoudamire	.50	.15
❑ 9 Kenny Anderson	.50	.15
❑ 10 Mookie Blaylock	.25	.07
❑ 11 Mitch Richmond	.50	.15
❑ 12 Jalen Rose	.75	.23
❑ 13 Vin Baker	.50	.15
❑ 14 Donyell Marshall	.50	.15
❑ 15 Bryon Russell	.25	.07
❑ 16 Rasheed Wallace	.75	.23
❑ 17 Allan Houston	.50	.15
❑ 18 Shawn Kemp	.50	.15
❑ 19 Nick Van Exel	.75	.23
❑ 20 Theo Ratliff	.50	.15
❑ 21 Jayson Williams	.25	.07
❑ 22 Chauncey Billups	.50	.15
❑ 23 Brent Barry	.50	.15
❑ 24 David Wesley	.25	.07
❑ 25 Joe Dumars	.75	.23
❑ 26 Marcus Camby	.50	.15
❑ 27 Juwan Howard	.50	.15
❑ 28 Brevin Knight	.25	.07
❑ 29 Reggie Miller	.75	.23
❑ 30 Ray Allen	.75	.23
❑ 31 Michael Finley	.75	.23
❑ 32 Tom Gugliotta	.25	.07
❑ 33 Allen Iverson	1.50	.45
❑ 34 Toni Kukoc	.50	.15
❑ 35 Tim Thomas	.50	.15
❑ 36 Jeff Hornacek	.50	.15
❑ 37 Bobby Jackson	.50	.15
❑ 38 Bo Outlaw	.25	.07
❑ 39 Steve Smith	.50	.15
❑ 40 Terrell Brandon	.50	.15
❑ 41 Glen Rice	.50	.15
❑ 42 Rik Smits	.50	.15
❑ 43 Calbert Cheaney	.25	.07
❑ 44 Stephon Marbury	.75	.23
❑ 45 Glenn Robinson	.50	.15
❑ 46 Corliss Williamson	.50	.15
❑ 47 Larry Johnson	.50	.15
❑ 48 Antonio McDyess	.50	.15
❑ 49 Detlef Schrempf	.50	.15
❑ 50 Jerry Stackhouse	.75	.23
❑ 51 Doug Christie	.50	.15
❑ 52 Eddie Jones	.75	.23
❑ 53 Karl Malone	.75	.23
❑ 54 Anthony Mason	.50	.15
❑ 55 Tim Duncan	1.25	.35
❑ 56 Christian Laettner	.50	.15
❑ 57 Isaiah Rider	.25	.07
❑ 58 Shawn Bradley	.25	.07
❑ 59 Jim Jackson	.25	.07
❑ 60 Mark Jackson	.50	.15
❑ 61 Kobe Bryant	3.00	.90
❑ 62 Zydrunas Ilgauskas	.50	.15
❑ 63 Ron Mercer	.50	.15
❑ 64 Hersey Hawkins	.25	.07
❑ 65 John Wallace	.25	.07
❑ 66 Avery Johnson	.25	.07
❑ 67 Dikembe Mutombo	.50	.15
❑ 68 Hakeem Olajuwon	.75	.23
❑ 69 Tony Battie	.25	.07
❑ 70 Jason Kidd	1.25	.35
❑ 71 Latrell Sprewell	.75	.23
❑ 72 Kevin Garnett	1.50	.45
❑ 73 Voshon Lenard	.25	.07
❑ 74 Gary Payton	.75	.23
❑ 75 Cherokee Parks	.25	.07
❑ 76 Antoine Walker	.75	.23
❑ 77 Anthony Johnson	.25	.07
❑ 78 Danny Fortson	.25	.07
❑ 79 Grant Hill	.75	.23
❑ 80 Dennis Rodman	.50	.15
❑ 81 Arvydas Sabonis	.50	.15
❑ 82 Tracy McGrady	2.00	.60
❑ 83 David Robinson	.75	.23
❑ 84 Tariq Abdul-Wahad	.25	.07
❑ 85 Michael Jordan	5.00	1.50
❑ 86 Kerry Kittles	.25	.07
❑ 87 Maurice Taylor	.50	.15
❑ 88 Cedric Ceballos	.25	.07
❑ 89 Anfernee Hardaway	.75	.23
❑ 90 John Stockton	.75	.23
❑ 91 Shareef Abdur-Rahim	.75	.23
❑ 92 Tim Hardaway	.50	.15
❑ 93 Shaquille O'Neal	2.00	.60
❑ 94 Rodney Rogers	.25	.07
❑ 95 Derek Anderson	.75	.23
❑ 96 Kendall Gill	.25	.07
❑ 97 Rod Strickland	.25	.07
❑ 98 Charles Barkley	1.00	.30
❑ 99 Chris Webber	.75	.23
❑ 100 Scottie Pippen	1.25	.35
❑ 101 Raef LaFrentz RC	2.00	.60
❑ 102 Ricky Davis RC	4.00	1.20
❑ 103 Robert Traylor RC	1.25	.35
❑ 104 Roshown McLeod RC	.60	.18
❑ 105 Tyronn Lue RC	1.50	.45
❑ 106 Vince Carter RC	12.00	3.60
❑ 107 Miles Simon RC	.50	.15
❑ 108 Paul Pierce RC	6.00	1.80
❑ 109 Pat Garrity RC	.60	.18
❑ 110 Nazr Mohammed RC	.60	.18
❑ 111 Mike Bibby RC	6.00	1.80
❑ 112 Michael Dickerson RC	2.50	.75
❑ 113 Michael Doleac RC	1.25	.35
❑ 114 Matt Harpring RC	2.00	.60
❑ 115 Larry Hughes RC	4.00	1.20
❑ 116 Keon Clark RC	2.00	.60
❑ 117 Felipe Lopez RC	1.50	.45
❑ 118 Dirk Nowitzki RC	12.00	3.60
❑ 119 Corey Benjamin RC	1.25	.35
❑ 120 Bryce Drew RC	1.25	.35
❑ 121 Brian Skinner RC	1.25	.35
❑ 122 Bonzi Wells RC	5.00	1.50
❑ 123 Antawn Jamison RC	6.00	1.80
❑ 124 Al Harrington RC	3.00	.90
❑ 125 Michael Olowokandi RC	2.00	.60

1999-00 Ultra

	Nm-Mt	Ex-Mt
COMPLETE SET (150)	100.00	30.00
COMPLETE SET w/o RC (125)	25.00	7.50
COMMON CARD (1-125)	.25	.07
COMMON ROOKIE (126-150)	1.00	.30
❑ 1 Vince Carter	2.00	.60
❑ 2 Randell Jackson	.25	.07
❑ 3 Ray Allen	.75	.23
❑ 4 Corliss Williamson	.50	.15
❑ 5 Darrell Armstrong	.25	.07
❑ 6 Charles Oakley	.25	.07
❑ 7 Tyrone Nesby RC	.25	.07
❑ 8 Eddie Jones	.75	.23
❑ 9 Kerry Kittles	.25	.07
❑ 10 Jason Williams	.75	.23
❑ 11 Elden Campbell	.25	.07
❑ 12 Mookie Blaylock	.25	.07
❑ 13 Brent Barry	.50	.15
❑ 14 Mark Jackson	.50	.15
❑ 15 Tim Hardaway	.50	.15
❑ 16 Kendall Gill	.25	.07
❑ 17 Larry Johnson	.50	.15
❑ 18 Eric Snow	.50	.15
❑ 19 Raef LaFrentz	.50	.15
❑ 20 Allen Iverson	1.50	.45
❑ 21 Kenny Anderson	.50	.15
❑ 22 John Starks	.50	.15
❑ 23 Isaiah Rider	.25	.07
❑ 24 Tariq Abdul-Wahad	.25	.07
❑ 25 Vitaly Potapenko	.25	.07
❑ 26 Patrick Ewing	.75	.23
❑ 27 Mitch Richmond	.50	.15
❑ 28 Steve Nash	.75	.23
❑ 29 Dickey Simpkins	.25	.07
❑ 30 Grant Hill	.75	.23
❑ 31 Matt Geiger	.25	.07
❑ 32 John Stockton	.75	.23
❑ 33 Jayson Williams	.25	.07
❑ 34 Reggie Miller	.75	.23
❑ 35 Eric Piatkowski	.50	.15
❑ 36 Jason Kidd	1.25	.35
❑ 37 Allan Houston	.50	.15
❑ 38 Christian Laettner	.50	.15
❑ 39 Marcus Camby	.50	.15
❑ 40 Shaquille O'Neal	2.00	.60
❑ 41 Derek Anderson	.50	.15
❑ 42 Gary Trent	.25	.07
❑ 43 Vin Baker	.50	.15
❑ 44 Alonzo Mourning	.50	.15
❑ 45 Latrell Sprewell	.75	.23
❑ 46 Rod Strickland	.25	.07
❑ 47 Bobby Jackson	.50	.15
❑ 48 Karl Malone	.75	.23
❑ 49 Mario Elie	.25	.07
❑ 50 Kobe Bryant	3.00	.90
❑ 51 Clifford Robinson	.25	.07
❑ 52 Jamal Mashburn	.50	.15
❑ 53 Dirk Nowitzki	1.50	.45
❑ 54 Rik Smits	.50	.15
❑ 55 Doug Christie	.50	.15
❑ 56 Ricky Davis	.50	.15
❑ 57 Jalen Rose	.75	.23
❑ 58 Michael Olowokandi	.50	.15
❑ 59 Cedric Ceballos	.25	.07
❑ 60 Ron Mercer	.50	.15
❑ 61 Brevin Knight	.25	.07

Card		
❑ 62 Rashard Lewis	.75	.23
❑ 63 Detlef Schrempf	.50	.15
❑ 64 Keith Van Horn	.75	.23
❑ 64B K.Van Horn Promo	.75	.23
❑ 65 Nick Anderson	.25	.07
❑ 66 Larry Hughes	.75	.23
❑ 67 Antonio McDyess	.50	.15
❑ 68 Terrell Brandon	.50	.15
❑ 69 Felipe Lopez	.25	.07
❑ 70 Scottie Pippen	1.25	.35
❑ 71 Erick Dampier	.50	.15
❑ 72 Arvydas Sabonis	.50	.15
❑ 73 Brian Grant	.50	.15
❑ 74 Nick Van Exel	.75	.23
❑ 75 Bryon Russell	.25	.07
❑ 76 Danny Fortson	.25	.07
❑ 77 Avery Johnson	.25	.07
❑ 78 Jerry Stackhouse	.75	.23
❑ 79 Robert Traylor	.25	.07
❑ 80 Tim Duncan	1.50	.45
❑ 81 Lindsey Hunter	.25	.07
❑ 82 Tyronn Lue	.50	.15
❑ 83 Michael Finley	.75	.23
❑ 84 Dikembe Mutombo	.50	.15
❑ 85 Zydrunas Ilgauskas	.50	.15
❑ 86 Pat Garrity	.25	.07
❑ 87 Damon Stoudamire	.50	.15
❑ 88 Shareef Abdur-Rahim	.75	.23
❑ 89 Matt Harpring	.75	.23
❑ 90 Michael Dickerson	.50	.15
❑ 91 Steve Smith	.50	.15
❑ 92 Bison Dele	.25	.07
❑ 93 Glenn Robinson	.75	.23
❑ 94 Antawn Jamison	1.25	.35
❑ 95 Glen Rice	.50	.15
❑ 96 Vlade Divac	.50	.15
❑ 97 Vladimir Stepania	.25	.07
❑ 98 Kornel David RC	.25	.07
❑ 99 Shawn Kemp	.50	.15
❑ 100 Kevin Garnett	1.50	.45
❑ 101 Tim Thomas	.50	.15
❑ 102 Mike Bibby	.75	.23
❑ 103 Maurice Taylor	.50	.15
❑ 104 Gary Payton	.75	.23
❑ 105 Voshon Lenard	.25	.07
❑ 106 Theo Ratliff	.50	.15
❑ 107 Hakeem Olajuwon	.75	.23
❑ 108 Joe Smith	.50	.15
❑ 109 Toni Kukoc	.50	.15
❑ 110 Stephon Marbury	.75	.23
❑ 111 Anthony Mason	.50	.15
❑ 112 Anfernee Hardaway	.75	.23
❑ 113 Juwan Howard	.50	.15
❑ 114 Charles Barkley	1.00	.30
❑ 115 Antoine Walker	.75	.23
❑ 116 Donyell Marshall	.50	.15
❑ 117 Tom Gugliotta	.25	.07
❑ 118 Rasheed Wallace	.75	.23
❑ 119 Tracy McGrady	2.00	.60
❑ 120 Paul Pierce	.75	.23
❑ 121 Sean Elliott	.50	.15
❑ 122 Bryant Reeves	.25	.07
❑ 123 Michael Doleac	.25	.07
❑ 124 Chris Webber	.75	.23
❑ 125 David Robinson	.75	.23
❑ 126 Steve Francis RC	8.00	2.40
❑ 127 Elton Brand RC	6.00	1.80
❑ 128 Wally Szczerbiak RC	5.00	1.50
❑ 129 Richard Hamilton RC	5.00	1.50
❑ 130 Shawn Marion RC	6.00	1.80
❑ 131 Trajan Langdon RC	2.00	.60
❑ 132 Corey Maggette RC	5.00	1.50
❑ 133 Dion Glover RC	1.50	.45
❑ 134 James Posey RC	3.00	.90
❑ 135 Lamar Odom RC	5.00	1.50
❑ 136 Aleksandar Radojevic RC	1.00	.30
❑ 137 Cal Bowdler RC	1.50	.45
❑ 138 Scott Padgett RC	1.50	.45
❑ 139 Jumaine Jones RC	2.00	.60
❑ 140 Jonathan Bender RC	5.00	1.50
❑ 141 Tim James RC	1.50	.45
❑ 142 Jason Terry RC	4.00	1.20
❑ 143 Quincy Lewis RC	1.50	.45
❑ 144 William Avery RC	2.00	.60
❑ 145 Galen Young RC	1.00	.30
❑ 146 Ron Artest RC	3.00	.90
❑ 147 Kenny Thomas RC	2.00	.60
❑ 148 Devean George RC	2.50	.75
❑ 149 Andre Miller RC	5.00	1.50
❑ 150 Baron Davis RC	5.00	1.50

2000-01 Ultra

	Nm-Mt	Ex-Mt
COMPLETE SET w/o RC (200)	40.00	12.00
COMMON CARD (1-200)	.25	.07
COMMON ROOKIE (201-225)	2.00	.60
❑ 1 Vince Carter	2.00	.60
❑ 2 Antawn Jamison	.75	.23
❑ 3 Shaquille O'Neal	2.00	.60
❑ 4 Paul Pierce	.75	.23
❑ 5 Antonio McDyess	.50	.15
❑ 6 Scott Burrell	.25	.07
❑ 7 Elton Brand	.75	.23
❑ 8 Lamar Odom	.75	.23
❑ 9 Nick Van Exel	.75	.23
❑ 10 Kobe Bryant	3.00	.90
❑ 11 Reggie Miller	.75	.23
❑ 12 Sam Cassell	.75	.23
❑ 13 Darrell Armstrong	.25	.07
❑ 14 Rasheed Wallace	.75	.23
❑ 15 Charles Oakley	.25	.07
❑ 16 David Wesley	.25	.07
❑ 17 Al Harrington	.50	.15
❑ 18 Latrell Sprewell	.75	.23
❑ 19 Rick Brunson	.50	.15
❑ 20 Steve Smith	.50	.15
❑ 21 Antonio Davis	.25	.07
❑ 22 Michael Finley	.75	.23
❑ 23 Shandon Anderson	.25	.07
❑ 24 Danny Fortson	.25	.07
❑ 25 Kerry Kittles	.25	.07
❑ 26 Anfernee Hardaway	.75	.23
❑ 27 Vin Baker	.50	.15
❑ 28 Calvin Booth	.25	.07
❑ 29 Haywoode Workman	.25	.07
❑ 30 Dickey Simpkins	.25	.07
❑ 31 Jerome Williams	.25	.07
❑ 32 Ron Artest	.50	.15
❑ 33 Dennis Scott	.25	.07
❑ 34 Ron Mercer	.50	.15
❑ 35 Chris Webber	.75	.23
❑ 36 Bryon Russell	.25	.07
❑ 37 Dale Davis	.25	.07
❑ 38 Dirk Nowitzki	1.25	.35
❑ 39 Steve Francis	.75	.23
❑ 40 Glen Rice	.50	.15
❑ 41 Stephon Marbury	.75	.23
❑ 42 Jason Kidd	1.25	.35
❑ 43 Brent Barry	.50	.15
❑ 44 Richard Hamilton	.50	.15
❑ 45 Antoine Walker	.75	.23
❑ 46 Gary Trent	.25	.07
❑ 47 Cuttino Mobley	.50	.15
❑ 48 P.J. Brown	.25	.07
❑ 49 Elliot Perry	.25	.07
❑ 50 Shawn Marion	.75	.23
❑ 51 Horace Grant	.50	.15
❑ 52 Juwan Howard	.50	.15
❑ 53 Elden Campbell	.25	.07
❑ 54 Erick Strickland	.25	.07
❑ 55 Hakeem Olajuwon	.75	.23
❑ 56 Anthony Carter	.50	.15
❑ 57 Keith Van Horn	.75	.23
❑ 58 Clifford Robinson	.25	.07
❑ 59 Ruben Patterson	.50	.15
❑ 60 Mitch Richmond	.50	.15
❑ 61 Jason Terry	.75	.23
❑ 62 Andre Miller	.50	.15
❑ 63 Vonteego Cummings	.25	.07
❑ 64 Joe Smith	.50	.15
❑ 65 Toni Kukoc	.50	.15
❑ 66 Sean Elliott	.50	.15
❑ 67 Michael Dickerson	.50	.15
❑ 68 Derrick Coleman	.25	.07
❑ 69 Shawn Bradley	.25	.07
❑ 70 Kenny Thomas	.25	.07
❑ 71 Tim Hardaway	.50	.15
❑ 72 Rex Chapman	.25	.07
❑ 73 Gary Payton	.75	.23
❑ 74 Jahidi White	.25	.07
❑ 75 Baron Davis	.75	.23
❑ 76 Chauncey Billups	.50	.15
❑ 77 Moochie Norris	.25	.07
❑ 78 Dan Majerle	.50	.15
❑ 79 Marcus Camby	.50	.15
❑ 80 Rodney Rogers	.25	.07
❑ 81 Rashard Lewis	.50	.15
❑ 82 Laron Profit	.25	.07
❑ 83 Ricky Davis	.50	.15
❑ 84 Keon Clark	.50	.15
❑ 85 Anthony Miller	.50	.15
❑ 86 Jamal Mashburn	.50	.15
❑ 87 Chris Childs	.25	.07
❑ 88 Brian Grant	.50	.15
❑ 89 Muggsy Bogues	.50	.15
❑ 90 Randy Brown	.25	.07
❑ 91 Tariq Abdul-Wahad	.25	.07
❑ 92 Lindsey Hunter	.25	.07
❑ 93 Rik Smits	.50	.15
❑ 94 Glenn Robinson	.75	.23
❑ 95 Michael Doleac	.25	.07
❑ 96 Quincy Lewis	.25	.07
❑ 97 Grant Hill	.75	.23
❑ 98 Jalen Rose	.75	.23
❑ 99 Ervin Johnson	.25	.07
❑ 100 Chucky Atkins	.25	.07
❑ 101 Jermaine O'Neal	.75	.23
❑ 102 Howard Eisley	.25	.07
❑ 103 Kenny Anderson	.50	.15
❑ 104 Lamond Murray	.25	.07
❑ 105 Adonal Foyle	.25	.07
❑ 106 Derek Fisher	.75	.23
❑ 107 Wally Szczerbiak	.50	.15
❑ 108 Todd MacCulloch	.25	.07
❑ 109 Avery Johnson	.25	.07
❑ 110 Othella Harrington	.25	.07
❑ 111 Tony Battie	.25	.07
❑ 112 Bob Sura	.25	.07
❑ 113 Larry Hughes	.50	.15
❑ 114 Rick Fox	.50	.15
❑ 115 Travis Best	.25	.07
❑ 116 Theo Ratliff	.50	.15
❑ 117 David Robinson	.75	.23
❑ 118 Felipe Lopez	.25	.07
❑ 119 John Amaechi	.25	.07
❑ 120 George Lynch	.25	.07
❑ 121 Christian Laettner	.50	.15
❑ 122 Derek Anderson	.50	.15
❑ 123 Tim Thomas	.50	.15
❑ 124 Matt Harpring	.75	.23
❑ 125 Nick Anderson	.25	.07
❑ 126 Karl Malone	.75	.23
❑ 127 Dion Glover	.25	.07
❑ 128 Wesley Person	.25	.07
❑ 129 Mikki Moore	.25	.07
❑ 130 Michael Olowokandi	.25	.07
❑ 131 William Avery	.25	.07
❑ 132 Bo Outlaw	.25	.07
❑ 133 Jason Williams	.50	.15
❑ 134 John Stockton	.75	.23
❑ 135 Adrian Griffin	.25	.07
❑ 136 Hubert Davis	.25	.07
❑ 137 Donyell Marshall	.50	.15
❑ 138 Travis Knight	.25	.07
❑ 139 Kendall Gill	.25	.07
❑ 140 Tom Gugliotta	.25	.07
❑ 141 Malik Rose	.25	.07
❑ 142 Isaac Austin	.25	.07
❑ 143 Alan Henderson	.25	.07
❑ 144 Shawn Kemp	.50	.15

Card	Nm-Mt	Ex-Mt
❑ 145 Terry Mills	.25	.07
❑ 146 Maurice Taylor	.25	.07
❑ 147 Terrell Brandon	.50	.15
❑ 148 Matt Geiger	.25	.07
❑ 149 Corliss Williamson	.50	.15
❑ 150 Jacque Vaughn	.25	.07
❑ 151 Dikembe Mutombo	.50	.15
❑ 152 Trajan Langdon	.50	.15
❑ 153 Jason Caffey	.25	.07
❑ 154 Tyrone Nesby	.25	.07
❑ 155 Bobby Jackson	.50	.15
❑ 156 Allen Iverson	1.50	.45
❑ 157 Mario Elie	.25	.07
❑ 158 Mike Bibby	.75	.23
❑ 159 Robert Horry	.50	.15
❑ 160 James Posey	.50	.15
❑ 161 Mark Jackson	.25	.07
❑ 162 Ray Allen	.75	.23
❑ 163 Charlie Ward	.25	.07
❑ 164 Damon Stoudamire	.50	.15
❑ 165 Tracy McGrady	2.00	.60
❑ 166 Bimbo Coles	.25	.07
❑ 167 Chucky Brown	.25	.07
❑ 168 Jerry Stackhouse	.75	.23
❑ 169 Greg Ostertag	.25	.07
❑ 170 Radoslav Nesterovic	.50	.15
❑ 171 Corey Maggette	.50	.15
❑ 172 Vlade Divac	.50	.15
❑ 173 Scott Padgett	.25	.07
❑ 174 Anthony Mason	.50	.15
❑ 175 Raef LaFrentz	.50	.15
❑ 176 Austin Croshere	.50	.15
❑ 177 Mark Strickland	.25	.07
❑ 178 Allan Houston	.50	.15
❑ 179 Arvydas Sabonis	.50	.15
❑ 180 Doug Christie	.50	.15
❑ 181 Jim Jackson	.25	.07
❑ 182 Brevin Knight	.25	.07
❑ 183 Mookie Blaylock	.25	.07
❑ 184 Chris Herren	.25	.07
❑ 185 Kevin Garnett	1.50	.45
❑ 186 Tyrone Hill	.25	.07
❑ 187 Tim Duncan	1.50	.45
❑ 188 Shareef Abdur-Rahim	.75	.23
❑ 189 Eddie Jones	.75	.23
❑ 190 Jonathan Bender	.50	.15
❑ 191 Alonzo Mourning	.50	.15
❑ 192 Patrick Ewing	.75	.23
❑ 193 Scottie Pippen	1.25	.35
❑ 194 Scot Pollard	.25	.07
❑ 195 Cedric Ceballos	.25	.07
❑ 196 Clarence Weatherspoon	.25	.07
❑ 197 Jamie Feick	.25	.07
❑ 198 Eric Snow	.50	.15
❑ 199 Ron Harper	.50	.15
❑ 200 Bryant Reeves	.25	.07
❑ 201 Chris Mihm RC	2.00	.60
❑ 202 Joel Przybilla RC	2.00	.60
❑ 203 Kenyon Martin RC	8.00	2.40
❑ 204 Stromile Swift RC	4.00	1.20
❑ 205 Etan Thomas RC	2.00	.60
❑ 206 Jason Collier RC	2.00	.60
❑ 207 Marcus Fizer RC	2.00	.60
❑ 208 Mateen Cleaves RC	2.00	.60
❑ 209 Dan Langhi RC	2.00	.60
❑ 210 Mike Miller RC	6.00	1.80
❑ 211 Jabari Smith RC	2.00	.60
❑ 212 Hanno Mottola RC	2.00	.60
❑ 213 Chris Porter RC	2.00	.60
❑ 214 Desmond Mason RC	2.00	.60
❑ 215 Erick Barkley RC	2.00	.60
❑ 216 Donnell Harvey RC	2.00	.60
❑ 217 DerMarr Johnson RC	2.00	.60
❑ 218 Jerome Moiso RC	2.00	.60
❑ 219 Quentin Richardson RC	6.00	1.80
❑ 220 Courtney Alexander RC	2.00	.60
❑ 221 Michael Redd RC	4.00	1.20
❑ 222 Morris Peterson RC	4.00	1.20
❑ 223 Darius Miles RC	6.00	1.80
❑ 224 Jamal Crawford RC	2.50	.75
❑ 225 Keyon Dooling RC	2.50	.75

2001-02 Ultra

	Nm-Mt	Ex-Mt
COMP.SET w/o SP's (150)	40.00	12.00
COMP.UPDATE SET (6)	40.00	12.00
COMMON CARD (1-150)	.25	.07
COMMON ROOKIE (151-175)	3.00	.90
151-175 PRINT RUN 2222 SERIAL #'d SETS		
COMMON UPDATE (1U-6U)	3.00	.90

Card	Nm-Mt	Ex-Mt
❑ 1 Vince Carter	2.00	.60
❑ 2 Allen Iverson	1.50	.45
❑ 3 Jerry Stackhouse	.75	.23
❑ 4 Travis Best	.25	.07
❑ 5 Eddie Jones	.75	.23
❑ 6 Felipe Lopez	.25	.07
❑ 7 Antonio Daniels	.25	.07
❑ 8 A.J. Guyton	.50	.15
❑ 9 Quentin Richardson	.50	.15
❑ 10 Charlie Ward	.25	.07
❑ 11 Ron Mercer	.50	.15
❑ 12 Shandon Anderson	.25	.07
❑ 13 Antawn Jamison	.75	.23
❑ 14 Darius Miles	.75	.23
❑ 15 Anthony Mason	.50	.15
❑ 16 Latrell Sprewell	.75	.23
❑ 17 Scottie Pippen	1.25	.35
❑ 18 Shammond Williams	.25	.07
❑ 19 P.J. Brown	.25	.07
❑ 20 Dirk Nowitzki	1.25	.35
❑ 21 Mateen Cleaves	.50	.15
❑ 22 Tim Hardaway	.50	.15
❑ 23 Christian Laettner	.50	.15
❑ 24 Toni Kukoc	.50	.15
❑ 25 Bob Sura	.25	.07
❑ 26 Kobe Bryant	3.00	.90
❑ 27 Wally Szczerbiak	.50	.15
❑ 28 Darrell Armstrong	.25	.07
❑ 29 Chris Webber	.75	.23
❑ 30 David Wesley	.25	.07
❑ 31 Michael Finley	.75	.23
❑ 32 Jermaine O'Neal	.75	.23
❑ 33 Jason Kidd	1.25	.35
❑ 34 Tony Delk	.25	.07
❑ 35 Avery Johnson	.25	.07
❑ 36 Elden Campbell	.25	.07
❑ 37 Lamond Murray	.25	.07
❑ 38 Ben Wallace	.75	.23
❑ 39 Jalen Rose	.75	.23
❑ 40 Michael Dickerson	.50	.15
❑ 41 Shawn Marion	.75	.23
❑ 42 Jahidi White	.50	.15
❑ 43 Jamal Mashburn	.50	.15
❑ 44 Trajan Langdon	.25	.07
❑ 45 Reggie Miller	.75	.23
❑ 46 Stromile Swift	.50	.15
❑ 47 Keith Van Horn	.75	.23
❑ 48 Tom Gugliotta	.25	.07
❑ 49 Brent Barry	.50	.15
❑ 50 Courtney Alexander	.50	.15
❑ 51 Antonio McDyess	.50	.15
❑ 52 Robert Horry	.50	.15
❑ 53 Ervin Johnson	.25	.07
❑ 54 Speedy Claxton	.50	.15
❑ 55 Bryon Russell	.25	.07
❑ 56 Baron Davis	.75	.23
❑ 57 Robert Traylor	.25	.07
❑ 58 Chucky Atkins	.25	.07
❑ 59 Stephon Marbury	.75	.23
❑ 60 Desmond Mason	.50	.15
❑ 61 Tyrone Nesby	.25	.07
❑ 62 Brevin Knight	.25	.07
❑ 63 Kenyon Martin	.75	.23
❑ 64 Jumaine Jones	.50	.15
❑ 65 Rashard Lewis	.50	.15
❑ 66 Kenny Anderson	.50	.15
❑ 67 Andre Miller	.50	.15
❑ 68 Joe Smith	.50	.15
❑ 69 Kelvin Cato	.25	.07
❑ 70 Jason Williams	.50	.15
❑ 71 Marcus Camby	.50	.15
❑ 72 Eric Snow	.50	.15
❑ 73 Gary Payton	.75	.23
❑ 74 Robert Pack	.25	.07
❑ 75 Brian Cardinal	.50	.15
❑ 76 Sam Cassell	.75	.23
❑ 77 Allan Houston	.50	.15
❑ 78 Anfernee Hardaway	.50	.15
❑ 79 Morris Peterson	.50	.15
❑ 80 Chris Mihm	.50	.15
❑ 81 Elton Brand	.75	.23
❑ 82 Glenn Robinson	.75	.23
❑ 83 Damon Stoudamire	.50	.15
❑ 84 Alvin Williams	.25	.07
❑ 85 Paul Pierce	.75	.23
❑ 86 James Posey	.50	.15
❑ 87 Cuttino Mobley	.50	.15
❑ 88 Tim Thomas	.50	.15
❑ 89 Dikembe Mutombo	.50	.15
❑ 90 Tim Duncan	1.50	.45
❑ 91 John Starks	.50	.15
❑ 92 Antoine Walker	.75	.23
❑ 93 Moochie Norris	.25	.07
❑ 94 Dalibor Bagaric	.25	.07
❑ 95 Ray Allen	.75	.23
❑ 96 David Robinson	.75	.23
❑ 97 Shareef Abdur-Rahim	.75	.23
❑ 98 Wang Zhizhi	.75	.23
❑ 99 Chris Porter	.50	.15
❑ 100 Chauncey Billups	.50	.15
❑ 101 Tracy McGrady	2.00	.60
❑ 102 Michael Jordan	12.00	3.60
❑ 103 Jerome Williams	.25	.07
❑ 104 Jason Terry	.75	.23
❑ 105 Calvin Booth	.25	.07
❑ 106 Shaquille O'Neal	2.00	.60
❑ 107 Kevin Garnett	1.50	.45
❑ 108 Doug Christie	.50	.15
❑ 109 Karl Malone	.75	.23
❑ 110 Steve Nash	.75	.23
❑ 111 Austin Croshere	.50	.15
❑ 112 Alonzo Mourning	.50	.15
❑ 113 Dan Majerle	.50	.15
❑ 114 Malik Rose	.25	.07
❑ 115 Richard Hamilton	.50	.15
❑ 116 DerMarr Johnson	.50	.15
❑ 117 Raef LaFrentz	.50	.15
❑ 118 Derek Fisher	.75	.23
❑ 119 Vlade Divac	.50	.15
❑ 120 John Stockton	.75	.23
❑ 121 Dion Glover	.25	.07
❑ 122 Voshon Lenard	.25	.07
❑ 123 Steve Francis	.75	.23
❑ 124 Darvin Ham	.25	.07
❑ 125 Aaron McKie	.50	.15
❑ 126 Peja Stojakovic	.75	.23
❑ 127 Ron Artest	.50	.15
❑ 128 Keyon Dooling	.50	.15
❑ 129 Anthony Carter	.50	.15
❑ 130 Kurt Thomas	.50	.15
❑ 131 Rasheed Wallace	.75	.23
❑ 132 Theo Ratliff	.50	.15
❑ 133 Eric Piatkowski	.50	.15
❑ 134 Terrell Brandon	.50	.15
❑ 135 Mike Miller	.75	.23
❑ 136 Mike Bibby	.75	.23
❑ 137 Antonio Davis	.25	.07
❑ 138 Lamar Odom	.75	.23
❑ 139 Eddie House	.50	.15
❑ 140 Nick Van Exel	.75	.23
❑ 141 Rick Fox	.50	.15
❑ 142 Juwan Howard	.50	.15
❑ 143 Hidayet Turkoglu	.50	.15
❑ 144 Donyell Marshall	.50	.15
❑ 145 Marcus Fizer	.50	.15
❑ 146 Larry Hughes	.50	.15
❑ 147 Steve Smith	.50	.15
❑ 148 Brian Grant	.50	.15
❑ 149 Grant Hill	.75	.23
❑ 150 Derek Anderson	.50	.15

Card	Nm-Mt	Ex-Mt
❑ 151 Kwame Brown RC	5.00	1.50
❑ 152 Eddie Griffin RC	4.00	1.20
❑ 153 Eddy Curry RC	6.00	1.80
❑ 154 Jamaal Tinsley RC	5.00	1.50
❑ 155 Jason Richardson RC	8.00	2.40
❑ 156 Shane Battier RC	5.00	1.50
❑ 157 Troy Murphy RC	5.00	1.50
❑ 158 Richard Jefferson RC	8.00	2.40
❑ 159 DeSagana Diop RC	3.00	.90
❑ 160 Tyson Chandler RC	6.00	1.80
❑ 161 Joe Johnson RC	4.00	1.20
❑ 162 Zach Randolph RC	8.00	2.40
❑ 163 Andrei Kirilenko RC	6.00	1.80
❑ 164 Loren Woods RC	3.00	.90
❑ 165 Jason Collins RC	3.00	.90
❑ 166 Rodney White RC	4.00	1.20
❑ 167 Jeryl Sasser RC	3.00	.90
❑ 168 Kirk Haston RC	3.00	.90
❑ 169 Pau Gasol RC	8.00	2.40
❑ 170 Kedrick Brown RC	3.00	.90
❑ 171 Steven Hunter RC	3.00	.90
❑ 172 Michael Bradley RC	3.00	.90
❑ 173 Joseph Forte RC	5.00	1.50
❑ 174 Brandon Armstrong RC	4.00	1.20
❑ 175 Primoz Brezec RC	3.00	.90
❑ 1U Gerald Wallace RC	6.00	1.80
❑ 2U Tony Parker RC	10.00	3.00
❑ 3U Vladimir Radmanovic RC	3.00	.90
❑ 4U Trenton Hassell RC	4.00	1.20
❑ 5U Zeljko Rebraca RC	3.00	.90
❑ 6U Oscar Torres RC	3.00	.90

2002-03 Ultra

	Nm-Mt	Ex-Mt
COMPLETET SET (210)	250.00	75.00
COMP.SET w/o RC's (180)	50.00	15.00
COMMON CARD (1-180)	.25	.07
COMMON ROOKIE (181-210)	3.00	.90
❑ 1 Vince Carter	2.00	.60
❑ 2 Ben Wallace	.75	.23
❑ 3 Tim Thomas	.50	.15
❑ 4 Eric Snow	.50	.15
❑ 5 Peja Stojakovic	.75	.23
❑ 6 Andrei Kirilenko	.75	.23
❑ 7 Dion Glover	.25	.07
❑ 8 James Posey	.50	.15
❑ 9 Kenny Thomas	.25	.07
❑ 10 Michael Dickerson	.25	.07
❑ 11 Charlie Ward	.25	.07
❑ 12 Gary Payton	.75	.23
❑ 13 Eddy Curry	.75	.23
❑ 14 Rick Fox	.50	.15
❑ 15 Joel Przybilla	.25	.07
❑ 16 Aaron McKie	.50	.15
❑ 17 Hidayet Turkoglu	.75	.23
❑ 18 Jarron Collins	.25	.07
❑ 19 Jason Collins	.25	.07
❑ 20 Nick Van Exel	.75	.23
❑ 21 Reggie Miller	.75	.23
❑ 22 Devean George	.50	.15
❑ 23 Michael Jordan	6.00	1.80
❑ 24 Tony Parker	.75	.23
❑ 25 Robert Horry	.50	.15
❑ 26 Wally Szczerbiak	.50	.15
❑ 27 Dikembe Mutombo	.50	.15
❑ 28 Scot Pollard	.25	.07
❑ 29 Darrell Armstrong	.25	.07
❑ 30 Jalen Rose	.75	.23
❑ 31 Antawn Jamison	1.00	.30
❑ 32 Anfernee Hardaway	.75	.23
❑ 33 Paul Pierce	.75	.23
❑ 34 Juwan Howard	.50	.15
❑ 35 Eddie Griffin	.50	.15
❑ 36 Shane Battier	.75	.23
❑ 37 Shandon Anderson	.25	.07
❑ 38 Vladimir Radmanovic	.50	.15
❑ 39 DerMarr Johnson	.25	.07
❑ 40 Antonio McDyess	.50	.15
❑ 41 Cuttino Mobley	.50	.15
❑ 42 Stromile Swift	.50	.15
❑ 43 Tracy McGrady	2.00	.60
❑ 44 Charles Smith	.25	.07
❑ 45 Shawn Marion	.75	.23
❑ 46 P.J. Brown	.25	.07
❑ 47 Wang Zhizhi	.75	.23
❑ 48 Austin Croshere	.25	.07
❑ 49 Ervin Johnson	.25	.07
❑ 50 Jason Kidd	1.25	.35
❑ 51 Tom Gugliotta	.25	.07
❑ 52 Jamal Crawford	.25	.07
❑ 53 Toni Kukoc	.50	.15
❑ 54 Mengke Bateer	.75	.23
❑ 55 Moochie Norris	.25	.07
❑ 56 Jason Williams	.50	.15
❑ 57 Mike Miller	.75	.23
❑ 58 Steve Smith	.50	.15
❑ 59 Shareef Abdur-Rahim	.75	.23
❑ 60 Michael Finley	.75	.23
❑ 61 Jermaine O'Neal	.75	.23
❑ 62 Mark Madsen	.25	.07
❑ 63 Troy Hudson	.25	.07
❑ 64 David Robinson	.75	.23
❑ 65 Corliss Williamson	.50	.15
❑ 66 Rodney Rogers	.25	.07
❑ 67 Derek Fisher	.75	.23
❑ 68 Anthony Carter	.50	.15
❑ 69 Allan Houston	.50	.15
❑ 70 Desmond Mason	.50	.15
❑ 71 Brendan Haywood	.50	.15
❑ 72 Tony Delk	.25	.07
❑ 73 Ryan Bowen	.25	.07
❑ 74 Danny Fortson	.25	.07
❑ 75 Alonzo Mourning	.50	.15
❑ 76 Latrell Sprewell	.75	.23
❑ 77 Rashard Lewis	.50	.15
❑ 78 Courtney Alexander	.50	.15
❑ 79 Marcus Fizer	.50	.15
❑ 80 Jason Richardson	.75	.23
❑ 81 Terrell Brandon	.50	.15
❑ 82 Allen Iverson	1.50	.45
❑ 83 Vlade Divac	.50	.15
❑ 84 Jahidi White	.25	.07
❑ 85 Eric Piatkowski	.50	.15
❑ 86 Marc Jackson	.50	.15
❑ 87 Pat Garrity	.25	.07
❑ 88 Tim Duncan	1.50	.45
❑ 89 Kwame Brown	.50	.15
❑ 90 Andre Miller	.50	.15
❑ 91 Troy Murphy	.50	.15
❑ 92 John Stockton	.75	.23
❑ 93 Kenny Anderson	.50	.15
❑ 94 Chris Mihm	.25	.07
❑ 95 Larry Hughes	.50	.15
❑ 96 Lamar Odom	.75	.23
❑ 97 Brian Grant	.50	.15
❑ 98 Marcus Camby	.50	.15
❑ 99 Mike Bibby	.75	.23
❑ 100 Joseph Forte	.50	.15
❑ 101 Lamond Murray	.25	.07
❑ 102 Darius Miles	.75	.23
❑ 103 Eddie Jones	.75	.23
❑ 104 Aaron Williams	.25	.07
❑ 105 Derek Anderson	.50	.15
❑ 106 Karl Malone	.75	.23
❑ 107 Jon Barry	.25	.07
❑ 108 Tony Battie	.25	.07
❑ 109 Jumaine Jones	.50	.15
❑ 110 Corey Maggette	.50	.15
❑ 111 Eddie House	.25	.07
❑ 112 Theo Ratliff	.50	.15
❑ 113 Scottie Pippen	1.25	.35
❑ 114 Hakeem Olajuwon	.75	.23
❑ 115 Antoine Walker	.75	.23
❑ 116 Tim Hardaway	.75	.23
❑ 117 Steve Francis	.75	.23
❑ 118 Lorenzen Wright	.25	.07
❑ 119 Howard Eisley	.25	.07
❑ 120 Brent Barry	.50	.15
❑ 121 Baron Davis	.75	.23
❑ 122 Michael Doleac	.25	.07
❑ 123 Quentin Richardson	.50	.15
❑ 124 LaPhonso Ellis	.25	.07
❑ 125 Richard Jefferson	.50	.15
❑ 126 Damon Stoudamire	.50	.15
❑ 127 Alvin Williams	.25	.07
❑ 128 Chucky Atkins	.25	.07
❑ 129 Jamal Mashburn	.50	.15
❑ 130 Wesley Person	.25	.07
❑ 131 Elton Brand	.75	.23
❑ 132 Ray Allen	.75	.23
❑ 133 Kerry Kittles	.25	.07
❑ 134 Rasheed Wallace	.75	.23
❑ 135 Antonio Davis	.25	.07
❑ 136 David Wesley	.25	.07
❑ 137 Dirk Nowitzki	1.25	.35
❑ 138 Rodney White	.50	.15
❑ 139 Jamaal Tinsley	.75	.23
❑ 140 Sam Cassell	.75	.23
❑ 141 Keith Van Horn	.75	.23
❑ 142 Ruben Patterson	.50	.15
❑ 143 Jerome Williams	.25	.07
❑ 144 Jason Terry	.75	.23
❑ 145 Eduardo Najera	.50	.15
❑ 146 Maurice Taylor	.25	.07
❑ 147 Pau Gasol	.75	.23
❑ 148 Grant Hill	.75	.23
❑ 149 Antonio Daniels	.25	.07
❑ 150 George Lynch	.25	.07
❑ 151 Steve Nash	.75	.23
❑ 152 Al Harrington	.50	.15
❑ 153 Anthony Mason	.50	.15
❑ 154 Kenyon Martin	.50	.15
❑ 155 Bonzi Wells	.50	.15
❑ 156 Morris Peterson	.50	.15
❑ 157 Eddie Robinson	.50	.15
❑ 158 Kevin Garnett	1.50	.45
❑ 159 Chris Webber	.75	.23
❑ 160 John Amaechi	.25	.07
❑ 161 Kobe Bryant	3.00	.90
❑ 162 Joe Smith	.75	.23
❑ 163 Speedy Claxton	.50	.15
❑ 164 Doug Christie	.50	.15
❑ 165 Richard Hamilton	.50	.15
❑ 166 Tyson Chandler	.75	.23
❑ 167 Gilbert Arenas	.75	.23
❑ 168 Stephon Marbury	.75	.23
❑ 169 Jamaal Magloire	.25	.07
❑ 170 Raef LaFrentz	.50	.15
❑ 171 Ron Mercer	.50	.15
❑ 172 Glenn Robinson	.75	.23
❑ 173 Chauncey Billups	.50	.15
❑ 174 Iakovos Tsakalidis	.25	.07
❑ 175 Vin Baker	.50	.15
❑ 176 Joe Johnson	.75	.23
❑ 177 Jerry Stackhouse	.75	.23
❑ 178 Shaquille O'Neal	2.00	.60
❑ 179 Derrick Coleman	.25	.07
❑ 180 Bryon Russell	.25	.07
❑ 181 Yao Ming RC	20.00	6.00
❑ 181B Rookie Exchange	Null	
❑ 182 Jay Williams RC	5.00	1.50
❑ 183 Drew Gooden RC	8.00	2.40
❑ 184 DaJuan Wagner RC	6.00	1.80
❑ 185 Qyntel Woods RC	3.00	.90
❑ 186 Rookie Exchange	4.00	1.20
❑ 187 Curtis Borchardt RC	3.00	.90
❑ 188 Rookie Exchange	3.00	.90
❑ 189 Caron Butler RC	8.00	2.40
❑ 190 Nene Hilario RC	5.00	1.50
❑ 191 Jared Jeffries RC	4.00	1.20
❑ 192 Mike Dunleavy RC	6.00	1.80
❑ 193 Kareem Rush RC	4.00	1.20
❑ 194 Amare Stoudemire RC	15.00	4.50
❑ 194B Rookie Exchange	Null	
❑ 195 Rookie Exchange	3.00	.90
❑ 196 Rookie Exchange	4.00	1.20
❑ 197 Jiri Welsch RC	3.00	.90
❑ 198 Frank Williams RC	3.00	.90
❑ 199 John Salmons RC	3.00	.90
❑ 200 Gordan Giricek RC	5.00	1.50

- ❑ 200B Rookie Exchange Null
- ❑ 201 Ryan Humphrey RC 3.00 .90
- ❑ 201B Rookie Exchange Null
- ❑ 202 Casey Jacobsen RC 3.00 .90
- ❑ 203 Carlos Boozer RC 8.00 2.40
- ❑ 203B Rookie Exchange Null
- ❑ 204 Manu Ginobili RC 8.00 2.40
- ❑ 204B Rookie Exchange Null
- ❑ 205 Bostjan Nachbar RC 3.00 .90
- ❑ 206 Fred Jones RC 4.00 1.20
- ❑ 207 Dan Dickau RC 3.00 .90
- ❑ 208 Tayshaun Prince RC 5.00 1.50
- ❑ 208B Rookie Exchange Null
- ❑ 209 Rookie Exchange 5.00 1.50
- ❑ 210 Juan Dixon RC 6.00 1.80

2003-04 Ultra

	Nm-Mt	Ex-Mt
COMP. SET w/o SP's	30.00	9.00
COMMON CARD (1-170)	.20	.06
COMMON L13 RC (171-	10.00	3.00
COMMON ROOKIE (184-195)	4.00	1.20

- ❑ 1 Yao Ming 2.00 .60
- ❑ 2 DeShawn Stevenson .20 .06
- ❑ 3 Malik Rose .20 .06
- ❑ 4 DaJuan Wagner .50 .15
- ❑ 5 Troy Murphy .75 .23
- ❑ 6 Caron Butler .75 .23
- ❑ 7 Radoslav Nesterovic .50 .15
- ❑ 8 Joe Johnson .50 .15
- ❑ 9 Al Harrington .50 .15
- ❑ 10 Carlos Boozer .75 .23
- ❑ 11 Morris Peterson .50 .15
- ❑ 12 Malik Allen .20 .06
- ❑ 13 Kurt Thomas .50 .15
- ❑ 14 Derek Anderson .50 .15
- ❑ 15 Zydrunas Ilgauskas .50 .15
- ❑ 16 Jason Richardson .75 .23
- ❑ 17 Brian Grant .50 .15
- ❑ 18 Allan Houston .50 .15
- ❑ 19 Bonzi Wells .50 .15
- ❑ 20 Stephen Jackson .20 .06
- ❑ 21 Eddy Curry .75 .23
- ❑ 22 Tayshaun Prince .50 .15
- ❑ 23 Brad Miller .75 .23
- ❑ 24 Stromile Swift .50 .15
- ❑ 25 Kendall Gill .20 .06
- ❑ 26 Vladimir Radmanovic .20 .06
- ❑ 27 Theo Ratliff .50 .15
- ❑ 28 Nick Van Exel .75 .23
- ❑ 29 Marko Jaric .20 .06
- ❑ 30 Jason Collins .20 .06
- ❑ 31 Darrell Armstrong .20 .06
- ❑ 32 Vlade Divac .50 .15
- ❑ 33 Juan Dixon .50 .15
- ❑ 34 Calbert Cheaney .20 .06
- ❑ 35 Tyson Chandler .75 .23
- ❑ 36 Chauncey Billups .50 .15
- ❑ 37 Reggie Miller .75 .23
- ❑ 38 Mike Miller .75 .23
- ❑ 39 Marc Jackson .50 .15
- ❑ 40 Casey Jacobsen .20 .06
- ❑ 41 Ray Allen .75 .23
- ❑ 42 Mehmet Okur .20 .06
- ❑ 43 Jermaine O'Neal .75 .23
- ❑ 44 Lorenzen Wright .20 .06
- ❑ 45 Wally Szczerbiak .50 .15
- ❑ 46 Anfernee Hardaway .75 .23
- ❑ 47 Matt Harpring .75 .23
- ❑ 48 Jay Williams .50 .15
- ❑ 49 Corliss Williamson .50 .15
- ❑ 50 Jamaal Tinsley .75 .23
- ❑ 51 Shane Battier .75 .23
- ❑ 52 Kevin Garnett 1.50 .45
- ❑ 53 Shawn Marion .75 .23
- ❑ 54 Alvin Williams .20 .06
- ❑ 55 Juwan Howard .50 .15
- ❑ 56 Shaquille O'Neal 2.00 .60
- ❑ 57 Jamal Mashburn .50 .15
- ❑ 58 Kenny Thomas .20 .06
- ❑ 59 Tim Duncan 1.50 .45
- ❑ 60 Predrag Drobnjak .20 .06
- ❑ 61 Jalen Rose .75 .23
- ❑ 62 Ben Wallace .75 .23
- ❑ 63 James Posey .50 .15
- ❑ 64 Pau Gasol .75 .23
- ❑ 65 Michael Redd .75 .23
- ❑ 66 Amare Stoudemire 1.50 .45
- ❑ 67 Karl Malone .75 .23
- ❑ 68 Richard Hamilton .50 .15
- ❑ 69 Eddie Griffin .50 .15
- ❑ 70 Robert Horry .50 .15
- ❑ 71 Tim Thomas .50 .15
- ❑ 72 Eric Snow .50 .15
- ❑ 73 Brent Barry .50 .15
- ❑ 74 Jamal Crawford .20 .06
- ❑ 75 Nikoloz Tskitishvili .20 .06
- ❑ 76 Bostjan Nachbar .20 .06
- ❑ 77 Devean George .50 .15
- ❑ 78 Dan Gadzuric .20 .06
- ❑ 79 Brian Skinner .20 .06
- ❑ 80 Cuttino Mobley .50 .15
- ❑ 81 Desmond Mason .50 .15
- ❑ 82 Othella Harrington .20 .06
- ❑ 83 Chris Webber .75 .23
- ❑ 84 Dirk Nowitzki 1.25 .35
- ❑ 85 Steve Francis .75 .23
- ❑ 86 Gary Payton .75 .23
- ❑ 87 Howard Eisley .20 .06
- ❑ 88 Zach Randolph .75 .23
- ❑ 89 Sam Cassell .75 .23
- ❑ 90 Tony Battie .20 .06
- ❑ 91 Shammond Williams .20 .06
- ❑ 92 Rick Fox .50 .15
- ❑ 93 David Wesley .20 .06
- ❑ 94 Frank Williams .20 .06
- ❑ 95 Tony Delk .20 .06
- ❑ 96 Troy Hudson .20 .06
- ❑ 97 Donnell Harvey .20 .06
- ❑ 98 Derek Fisher .75 .23
- ❑ 99 Jamaal Magloire .20 .06
- ❑ 100 Keith Van Horn .75 .23
- ❑ 101 Tony Parker .75 .23
- ❑ 102 Rashard Lewis .75 .23
- ❑ 103 Shareef Abdur-Rahim .75 .23
- ❑ 104 Michael Finley .75 .23
- ❑ 105 Jason Kidd 1.25 .35
- ❑ 106 Drew Gooden .50 .15
- ❑ 107 Mike Bibby .75 .23
- ❑ 108 Jerry Stackhouse .75 .23
- ❑ 109 Chris Jefferies .20 .06
- ❑ 110 Glenn Robinson .75 .23
- ❑ 111 Shawn Bradley .20 .06
- ❑ 112 Corey Maggette .50 .15
- ❑ 113 Richard Jefferson .50 .15
- ❑ 114 Gordan Giricek .50 .15
- ❑ 115 Bobby Jackson .50 .15
- ❑ 116 Larry Hughes .50 .15
- ❑ 117 Scott Padgett .20 .06
- ❑ 118 Gilbert Arenas .75 .23
- ❑ 119 Ron Artest .50 .15
- ❑ 120 Jason Williams .50 .15
- ❑ 121 Eric Williams .20 .06
- ❑ 122 Stephon Marbury .75 .23
- ❑ 123 Vince Carter 2.00 .60
- ❑ 124 Jason Terry .75 .23
- ❑ 125 Raef LaFrentz .50 .15
- ❑ 126 Michael Olowokandi .20 .06
- ❑ 127 Kerry Kittles .20 .06
- ❑ 128 Pat Garrity .20 .06
- ❑ 129 Peja Stojakovic .75 .23
- ❑ 130 Jared Jeffries .20 .06
- ❑ 131 Antonio Davis .20 .06
- ❑ 132 Rodney White .20 .06
- ❑ 133 Kobe Bryant 3.00 .90
- ❑ 134 Baron Davis .75 .23
- ❑ 135 Derrick Coleman .20 .06
- ❑ 136 Walter McCarty .20 .06
- ❑ 137 Bruce Bowen .20 .06
- ❑ 138 Mike Dunleavy .50 .15
- ❑ 139 Rasual Butler .50 .15
- ❑ 140 Latrell Sprewell .75 .23
- ❑ 141 Rasheed Wallace .75 .23
- ❑ 142 Andrei Kirilenko .75 .23
- ❑ 143 Dan Dickau .20 .06
- ❑ 144 Steve Nash .75 .23
- ❑ 145 Elton Brand .75 .23
- ❑ 146 Kenyon Martin .75 .23
- ❑ 147 Jeryl Sasser .20 .06
- ❑ 148 Doug Christie .50 .15
- ❑ 149 Kwame Brown .50 .15
- ❑ 150 Ricky Davis .75 .23
- ❑ 151 Antawn Jamison .75 .23
- ❑ 152 Travis Best .20 .06
- ❑ 153 Courtney Alexander .50 .15
- ❑ 154 Scottie Pippen 1.25 .35
- ❑ 155 Jerome Williams .20 .06
- ❑ 156 Quentin Richardson .50 .15
- ❑ 157 Lucious Harris .20 .06
- ❑ 158 Allen Iverson 1.50 .45
- ❑ 159 Manu Ginobili .75 .23
- ❑ 160 Bryon Russell .20 .06
- ❑ 161 Paul Pierce .75 .23
- ❑ 162 Nene .50 .15
- ❑ 163 Darius Miles .75 .23
- ❑ 164 Earl Boykins .50 .15
- ❑ 165 Eddie Jones .75 .23
- ❑ 166 P.J. Brown .20 .06
- ❑ 167 Qyntel Woods .20 .06
- ❑ 168 Andre Miller .50 .15
- ❑ 169 Tracy McGrady 2.00 .60
- ❑ 170 Antoine Walker .75 .23
- ❑ 171 LeBron James L13 RC 175.00 52.50
- ❑ 172 Lucky 13 Exchange 30.00 9.00
- ❑ 173 Carmelo Anthony L13 RC 80.00 24.00
- ❑ 174 Chris Bosh L13 RC 25.00 7.50
- ❑ 175 Dwyane Wade L13 RC 25.00 7.50
- ❑ 176 Chris Kaman L13 RC 10.00 3.00
- ❑ 177 Lucky 13 Exchange 25.00 7.50
- ❑ 178 T.J. Ford L13 RC 12.00 3.60
- ❑ 179 Mike Sweetney L13 RC 10.00 3.00
- ❑ 180 Lucky 13 Exchange 10.00 3.00
- ❑ 181 Mickael Pietrus L13 RC 12.00 3.60
- ❑ 182 Nick Collison L13 RC 10.00 3.00
- ❑ 183 Marcus Banks L13 RC 10.00 3.00
- ❑ 184 Luke Ridnour RC 5.00 1.50
- ❑ 185 Troy Bell RC 4.00 1.20
- ❑ 186 Zarko Cabarkapa RC 4.00 1.20
- ❑ 187 David West RC 4.00 1.20
- ❑ 188 Sofoklis Schortsanitis RC 4.00 1.20
- ❑ 189 Travis Outlaw RC 4.00 1.20
- ❑ 190 Leandro Barbosa RC 4.00 1.20
- ❑ 191 Josh Howard RC 5.00 1.50
- ❑ 192 Maciej Lampe RC 4.00 1.20
- ❑ 193 Luke Walton RC 5.00 1.50
- ❑ 194 Travis Hansen RC 4.00 1.20
- ❑ 195 Rick Rickert RC 4.00 1.20

1991-92 Upper Deck

	Nm-Mt	Ex-Mt
COMPLETE SET (500)	20.00	6.00
COMPLETE FACT.SET (500)	20.00	6.00

Card		
COMPLETE SERIES 1 (400)	12.00	3.60
COMMON CARD (1-400)	.05	.02
COMPLETE SERIES 2 (100)	8.00	2.40
COMMON CARD (401-500)	.10	.03
❑ 1 Stacey Augmon CL Rodney Monroe	.05	.02
❑ 2 Larry Johnson RC UER (Career FG Percentage is .643 not .648)	1.00	.30
❑ 3 Dikembe Mutombo RC	1.00	.30
❑ 4 Steve Smith RC	1.00	.30
❑ 5 Stacey Augmon RC	.25	.07
❑ 6 Terrell Brandon RC	.75	.23
❑ 7 Greg Anthony RC	.25	.07
❑ 8 Rich King RC	.05	.02
❑ 9 Chris Gatling RC	.25	.07
❑ 10 Victor Alexander RC	.05	.02
❑ 11 John Turner	.05	.02
❑ 12 Eric Murdock RC	.05	.02
❑ 13 Mark Randall RC	.05	.02
❑ 14 Rodney Monroe RC	.05	.02
❑ 15 Myron Brown	.05	.02
❑ 16 Mike Iuzzolino RC	.05	.02
❑ 17 Chris Corchiani RC	.05	.02
❑ 18 Elliot Perry RC	.10	.03
❑ 19 Jimmy Oliver RC	.05	.02
❑ 20 Doug Overton RC	.05	.02
❑ 21 Steve Hood UER (Card has NBA record, but he's a rookie)	.05	.02
❑ 22 Michael Jordan Stay In School	.75	.23
❑ 23 Kevin Johnson Stay In School	.10	.03
❑ 24 Kurk Lee	.05	.02
❑ 25 Sean Higgins RC	.05	.02
❑ 26 Morlon Wiley	.05	.02
❑ 27 Derek Smith	.05	.02
❑ 28 Kenny Payne	.05	.02
❑ 29 Magic Johnson Assist Record	.40	.12
❑ 30 Larry Bird CC and Chuck Person	.25	.07
❑ 31 Karl Malone CC and Charles Barkley	.25	.07
❑ 32 Kevin Johnson CC and John Stockton	.10	.03
❑ 33 Hakeem Olajuwon CC and Patrick Ewing	.25	.07
❑ 34 Magic Johnson CC and Michael Jordan	1.00	.30
❑ 35 Derrick Coleman ART	.05	.02
❑ 36 Lionel Simmons ART	.05	.02
❑ 37 Dee Brown ART	.05	.02
❑ 38 Dennis Scott ART	.05	.02
❑ 39 Kendall Gill ART	.05	.02
❑ 40 Winston Garland	.05	.02
❑ 41 Danny Young	.05	.02
❑ 42 Rick Mahorn	.05	.02
❑ 43 Michael Adams	.05	.02
❑ 44 Michael Jordan	3.00	.90
❑ 45 Magic Johnson	.75	.23
❑ 46 Doc Rivers	.10	.03
❑ 47 Moses Malone	.25	.07
❑ 48 Michael Jordan AS CL	1.50	.45
❑ 49 James Worthy AS	.10	.03
❑ 50 Tim Hardaway AS	.25	.07
❑ 51 Karl Malone AS	.25	.07
❑ 52 John Stockton AS	.10	.03
❑ 53 Clyde Drexler AS	.10	.03
❑ 54 Terry Porter AS	.05	.02
❑ 55 Kevin Duckworth AS	.05	.02
❑ 56 Tom Chambers AS	.05	.02
❑ 57 Magic Johnson AS	.40	.12
❑ 58 David Robinson AS	.25	.07
❑ 59 Kevin Johnson AS	.10	.03
❑ 60 Chris Mullin AS	.10	.03
❑ 61 Joe Dumars AS	.10	.03
❑ 62 Kevin McHale AS	.05	.02
❑ 63 Brad Daugherty AS	.05	.02
❑ 64 Alvin Robertson AS	.05	.02
❑ 65 Bernard King AS	.05	.02
❑ 66 Dominique Wilkins AS	.10	.03
❑ 67 Ricky Pierce AS	.05	.02
❑ 68 Patrick Ewing AS	.10	.03
❑ 69 Michael Jordan AS	1.50	.45
❑ 70 Charles Barkley AS	.25	.07
❑ 71 Hersey Hawkins AS	.05	.02
❑ 72 Robert Parish AS	.05	.02
❑ 73 Alvin Robertson TC	.05	.02
❑ 74 Bernard King TC	.05	.02
❑ 75 Michael Jordan TC	1.50	.45
❑ 76 Brad Daugherty TC	.05	.02
❑ 77 Larry Bird TC	.50	.15
❑ 78 Ron Harper TC	.05	.02
❑ 79 Dominique Wilkins TC	.10	.03
❑ 80 Rony Seikaly TC	.05	.02
❑ 81 Rex Chapman TC	.05	.02
❑ 82 Mark Eaton TC	.05	.02
❑ 83 Lionel Simmons TC	.05	.02
❑ 84 Gerald Wilkins TC	.05	.02
❑ 85 James Worthy TC	.10	.03
❑ 86 Scott Skiles TC	.05	.02
❑ 87 Rolando Blackman TC	.05	.02
❑ 88 Derrick Coleman TC	.05	.02
❑ 89 Chris Jackson TC	.05	.02
❑ 90 Reggie Miller TC	.10	.03
❑ 91 Isiah Thomas TC	.10	.03
❑ 92 Hakeem Olajuwon TC	.25	.07
❑ 93 Hersey Hawkins TC	.05	.02
❑ 94 David Robinson TC	.25	.07
❑ 95 Tom Chambers TC	.05	.02
❑ 96 Shawn Kemp TC	.25	.07
❑ 97 Pooh Richardson TC	.05	.02
❑ 98 Clyde Drexler TC	.10	.03
❑ 99 Chris Mullin TC	.10	.03
❑ 100 Checklist 1-100	.05	.02
❑ 101 John Shasky	.05	.02
❑ 102 Dana Barros	.05	.02
❑ 103 Stojko Vrankovic	.05	.02
❑ 104 Larry Drew	.05	.02
❑ 105 Randy White	.05	.02
❑ 106 Dave Corzine	.05	.02
❑ 107 Joe Kleine	.05	.02
❑ 108 Lance Blanks	.05	.02
❑ 109 Rodney McCray	.05	.02
❑ 110 Sedale Threatt	.05	.02
❑ 111 Ken Norman	.05	.02
❑ 112 Rickey Green	.05	.02
❑ 113 Andy Toolson	.05	.02
❑ 114 Bo Kimble	.05	.02
❑ 115 Mark West	.05	.02
❑ 116 Mark Eaton	.05	.02
❑ 117 John Paxson	.05	.02
❑ 118 Mike Brown	.05	.02
❑ 119 Brian Oliver	.05	.02
❑ 120 Will Perdue	.05	.02
❑ 121 Michael Smith	.05	.02
❑ 122 Sherman Douglas	.05	.02
❑ 123 Reggie Lewis	.10	.03
❑ 124 James Donaldson	.05	.02
❑ 125 Scottie Pippen	.75	.23
❑ 126 Elden Campbell	.10	.03
❑ 127 Michael Cage	.05	.02
❑ 128 Tony Smith	.05	.02
❑ 129 Ed Pinckney	.05	.02
❑ 130 Keith Askins RC	.05	.02
❑ 131 Darrell Griffith	.05	.02
❑ 132 Vinnie Johnson	.05	.02
❑ 133 Ron Harper	.10	.03
❑ 134 Andre Turner	.05	.02
❑ 135 Jeff Hornacek	.10	.03
❑ 136 John Stockton	.25	.07
❑ 137 Derek Harper	.10	.03
❑ 138 Loy Vaught	.05	.02
❑ 139 Thurl Bailey	.05	.02
❑ 140 Olden Polynice	.05	.02
❑ 141 Kevin Edwards	.05	.02
❑ 142 Byron Scott	.10	.03
❑ 143 Dee Brown	.05	.02
❑ 144 Sam Perkins	.10	.03
❑ 145 Rony Seikaly	.05	.02
❑ 146 James Worthy	.25	.07
❑ 147 Glen Rice	.25	.07
❑ 148 Craig Hodges	.05	.02
❑ 149 Bimbo Coles	.05	.02
❑ 150 Mychal Thompson	.05	.02
❑ 151 Xavier McDaniel	.05	.02
❑ 152 Roy Tarpley	.05	.02
❑ 153 Gary Payton	.60	.18
❑ 154 Rolando Blackman	.05	.02
❑ 155 Hersey Hawkins	.10	.03
❑ 156 Ricky Pierce	.05	.02
❑ 157 Fat Lever	.05	.02
❑ 158 Andrew Lang	.05	.02
❑ 159 Benoit Benjamin	.05	.02
❑ 160 Cedric Ceballos	.10	.03
❑ 161 Charles Smith	.05	.02
❑ 162 Jeff Martin	.05	.02
❑ 163 Robert Parish	.10	.03
❑ 164 Danny Manning	.10	.03
❑ 165 Mark Aguirre	.05	.02
❑ 166 Jeff Malone	.05	.02
❑ 167 Bill Laimbeer	.10	.03
❑ 168 Willie Burton	.05	.02
❑ 169 Dennis Hopson	.05	.02
❑ 170 Kevin Gamble	.05	.02
❑ 171 Terry Teagle	.05	.02
❑ 172 Dan Majerle	.10	.03
❑ 173 Shawn Kemp	.60	.18
❑ 174 Tom Chambers	.05	.02
❑ 175 Vlade Divac	.10	.03
❑ 176 Johnny Dawkins	.05	.02
❑ 177 A.C. Green	.10	.03
❑ 178 Manute Bol	.05	.02
❑ 179 Terry Davis	.05	.02
❑ 180 Ron Anderson	.05	.02
❑ 181 Horace Grant	.10	.03
❑ 182 Stacey King	.05	.02
❑ 183 William Bedford	.05	.02
❑ 184 B.J. Armstrong	.05	.02
❑ 185 Dennis Rodman	.50	.15
❑ 186 Nate McMillan	.05	.02
❑ 187 Cliff Levingston	.05	.02
❑ 188 Quintin Dailey	.05	.02
❑ 189 Bill Cartwright	.05	.02
❑ 190 John Salley	.05	.02
❑ 191 Jayson Williams	.25	.07
❑ 192 Grant Long	.05	.02
❑ 193 Negele Knight	.05	.02
❑ 194 Alec Kessler	.05	.02
❑ 195 Gary Grant	.05	.02
❑ 196 Billy Thompson	.05	.02
❑ 197 Delaney Rudd	.05	.02
❑ 198 Alan Ogg	.05	.02
❑ 199 Blue Edwards	.05	.02
❑ 200 Checklist 101-200	.05	.02
❑ 201 Mark Acres	.05	.02
❑ 202 Craig Ehlo	.05	.02
❑ 203 Anthony Cook	.05	.02
❑ 204 Eric Leckner	.05	.02
❑ 205 Terry Catledge	.05	.02
❑ 206 Reggie Williams	.05	.02
❑ 207 Greg Kite	.05	.02
❑ 208 Steve Kerr	.10	.03
❑ 209 Kenny Battle	.05	.02
❑ 210 John Morton	.05	.02
❑ 211 Kenny Williams	.05	.02
❑ 212 Mark Jackson	.10	.03
❑ 213 Alaa Abdelnaby	.05	.02
❑ 214 Rod Strickland	.25	.07
❑ 215 Micheal Williams	.05	.02
❑ 216 Kevin Duckworth	.05	.02
❑ 217 David Wingate	.05	.02
❑ 218 LaSalle Thompson	.05	.02
❑ 219 John Starks RC	.25	.07
❑ 220 Clifford Robinson	.10	.03
❑ 221 Jeff Grayer	.05	.02
❑ 222 Marcus Liberty	.05	.02
❑ 223 Larry Nance	.10	.03
❑ 224 Michael Ansley	.05	.02
❑ 225 Kevin McHale	.10	.03
❑ 226 Scott Skiles	.05	.02
❑ 227 Darnell Valentine	.05	.02
❑ 228 Nick Anderson	.10	.03
❑ 229 Brad Davis	.05	.02
❑ 230 Gerald Paddio	.05	.02
❑ 231 Sam Bowie	.05	.02
❑ 232 Sam Vincent	.05	.02
❑ 233 George McCloud	.05	.02
❑ 234 Gerald Wilkins	.05	.02
❑ 235 Mookie Blaylock	.10	.03
❑ 236 Jon Koncak	.05	.02
❑ 237 Danny Ferry	.05	.02
❑ 238 Vern Fleming	.05	.02
❑ 239 Mark Price	.05	.02
❑ 240 Sidney Moncrief	.05	.02

❑ 241 Jay Humphries .05 .02
❑ 242 Muggsy Bogues .10 .03
❑ 243 Tim Hardaway .40 .12
❑ 244 Alvin Robertson .05 .02
❑ 245 Chris Mullin .25 .07
❑ 246 Pooh Richardson .05 .02
❑ 247 Winston Bennett .05 .02
❑ 248 Kelvin Upshaw .05 .02
❑ 249 John Williams .05 .02
❑ 250 Steve Alford .05 .02
❑ 251 Spud Webb .10 .03
❑ 252 Sleepy Floyd .05 .02
❑ 253 Chuck Person .05 .02
❑ 254 Hakeem Olajuwon .40 .12
❑ 255 Dominique Wilkins .25 .07
❑ 256 Reggie Miller .25 .07
❑ 257 Dennis Scott .10 .03
❑ 258 Charles Oakley .10 .03
❑ 259 Sidney Green .05 .02
❑ 260 Detlef Schrempf .10 .03
❑ 261 Rod Higgins .05 .02
❑ 262 J.R. Reid .05 .02
❑ 263 Tyrone Hill .10 .03
❑ 264 Reggie Theus .10 .03
❑ 265 Mitch Richmond .25 .07
❑ 266 Dale Ellis .10 .03
❑ 267 Terry Cummings .05 .02
❑ 268 Johnny Newman .05 .02
❑ 269 Doug West .05 .02
❑ 270 Jim Petersen .05 .02
❑ 271 Otis Thorpe .10 .03
❑ 272 John Williams .05 .02
❑ 273 Kennard Winchester RC .05 .02
❑ 274 Duane Ferrell .05 .02
❑ 275 Vernon Maxwell .05 .02
❑ 276 Kenny Smith .05 .02
❑ 277 Jerome Kersey .05 .02
❑ 278 Kevin Willis .05 .02
❑ 279 Danny Ainge .10 .03
❑ 280 Larry Smith .05 .02
❑ 281 Maurice Cheeks .05 .02
❑ 282 Willie Anderson .05 .02
❑ 283 Tom Tolbert .05 .02
❑ 284 Jerrod Mustaf .05 .02
❑ 285 Randolph Keys .05 .02
❑ 286 Jerry Reynolds .05 .02
❑ 287 Sean Elliott .10 .03
❑ 288 Otis Smith .05 .02
❑ 289 Terry Mills RC .25 .07
❑ 290 Kelly Tripucka .05 .02
❑ 291 Jon Sundvold .05 .02
❑ 292 Rumeal Robinson .05 .02
❑ 293 Fred Roberts .05 .02
❑ 294 Rik Smits .10 .03
❑ 295 Jerome Lane .05 .02
❑ 296 Dave Jamerson .05 .02
❑ 297 Joe Wolf .05 .02
❑ 298 David Wood RC .05 .02
❑ 299 Todd Lichti .05 .02
❑ 300 Checklist 201-300 .05 .02
❑ 301 Randy Breuer .05 .02
❑ 302 Buck Johnson .05 .02
❑ 303 Scott Brooks .05 .02
❑ 304 Jeff Turner .05 .02
❑ 305 Felton Spencer .05 .02
❑ 306 Greg Dreiling .05 .02
❑ 307 Gerald Glass .05 .02
❑ 308 Tony Brown .05 .02
❑ 309 Sam Mitchell .05 .02
❑ 310 Adrian Caldwell .05 .02
❑ 311 Chris Dudley .05 .02
❑ 312 Blair Rasmussen .05 .02
❑ 313 Antoine Carr .05 .02
❑ 314 Greg Anderson .05 .02
❑ 315 Drazen Petrovic .10 .03
❑ 316 Alton Lister .05 .02
❑ 317 Jack Haley .05 .02
❑ 318 Bobby Hansen .05 .02
❑ 319 Chris Jackson .05 .02
❑ 320 Herb Williams .05 .02
❑ 321 Kendall Gill .10 .03
❑ 322 Tyrone Corbin .05 .02
❑ 323 Kiki Vandeweghe .05 .02
❑ 324 David Robinson .50 .15
❑ 325 Rex Chapman .10 .03
❑ 326 Tony Campbell .05 .02
❑ 327 Dell Curry .05 .02
❑ 328 Charles Jones .05 .02
❑ 329 Kenny Gattison .05 .02
❑ 330 Haywoode Workman RC .10 .03
❑ 331 Travis Mays .05 .02
❑ 332 Derrick Coleman .10 .03
❑ 333 Isiah Thomas .25 .07
❑ 334 Jud Buechler .05 .02
❑ 335 Joe Dumars .25 .07
❑ 336 Tate George .05 .02
❑ 337 Mike Sanders .05 .02
❑ 338 James Edwards .05 .02
❑ 339 Chris Morris .05 .02
❑ 340 Scott Hastings .05 .02
❑ 341 Trent Tucker .05 .02
❑ 342 Harvey Grant .05 .02
❑ 343 Patrick Ewing .25 .07
❑ 344 Larry Bird 1.00 .30
❑ 345 Charles Barkley .40 .12
❑ 346 Brian Shaw .05 .02
❑ 347 Kenny Walker .05 .02
❑ 348 Danny Schayes .05 .02
❑ 349 Tom Hammonds .05 .02
❑ 350 Frank Brickowski .05 .02
❑ 351 Terry Porter .05 .02
❑ 352 Orlando Woolridge .05 .02
❑ 353 Buck Williams .05 .02
❑ 354 Sarunas Marciulionis .05 .02
❑ 355 Karl Malone .40 .12
❑ 356 Kevin Johnson .25 .07
❑ 357 Clyde Drexler .25 .07
❑ 358 Duane Causwell .05 .02
❑ 359 Paul Pressey .05 .02
❑ 360 Jim Les RC .05 .02
❑ 361 Derrick McKey .05 .02
❑ 362 Scott Williams RC .05 .02
❑ 363 Mark Alarie .05 .02
❑ 364 Brad Daugherty .05 .02
❑ 365 Bernard King .05 .02
❑ 366 Steve Henson .05 .02
❑ 367 Darrell Walker .05 .02
❑ 368 Larry Krystkowiak .05 .02
❑ 369 Henry James UER .05 .02
(Scored 20 points vs. Pistons, not Jazz)
❑ 370 Jack Sikma .05 .02
❑ 371 Eddie Johnson .10 .03
❑ 372 Wayman Tisdale .05 .02
❑ 373 Joe Barry Carroll .05 .02
❑ 374 David Greenwood .05 .02
❑ 375 Lionel Simmons .05 .02
❑ 376 Dwayne Schintzius .05 .02
❑ 377 Tod Murphy .05 .02
❑ 378 Wayne Cooper .05 .02
❑ 379 Anthony Bonner .05 .02
❑ 380 Walter Davis .05 .02
❑ 381 Lester Conner .05 .02
❑ 382 Ledell Eackles .05 .02
❑ 383 Brad Lohaus .05 .02
❑ 384 Derrick Gervin .05 .02
❑ 385 Pervis Ellison .05 .02
❑ 386 Tim McCormick .05 .02
❑ 387 A.J. English .05 .02
❑ 388 John Battle .05 .02
❑ 389 Roy Hinson .05 .02
❑ 390 Armon Gilliam .05 .02
❑ 391 Kurt Rambis .05 .02
❑ 392 Mark Bryant .05 .02
❑ 393 Chucky Brown .05 .02
❑ 394 Avery Johnson .10 .03
❑ 395 Rory Sparrow .05 .02
❑ 396 Mario Elie RC .25 .07
❑ 397 Ralph Sampson .05 .02
❑ 398 Mike Gminski .05 .02
❑ 399 Bill Wennington .05 .02
❑ 400 Checklist 301-400 .05 .02
❑ 401 David Wingate .10 .03
❑ 402 Moses Malone .50 .15
❑ 403 Darrell Walker .10 .03
❑ 404 Antoine Carr .10 .03
❑ 405 Charles Shackleford .10 .03
❑ 406 Orlando Woolridge .10 .03
❑ 407 Robert Pack RC .25 .07
❑ 408 Bobby Hansen .10 .03
❑ 409 Dale Davis RC .50 .15
❑ 410 Vincent Askew RC .10 .03
❑ 411 Alexander Volkov .10 .03
❑ 412 Dwayne Schintzius .10 .03
❑ 413 Tim Perry .10 .03
❑ 414 Tyrone Corbin .10 .03
❑ 415 Pete Chilcutt RC .10 .03
❑ 416 James Edwards .10 .03
❑ 417 Jerrod Mustaf .10 .03
❑ 418 Thurl Bailey .10 .03
❑ 419 Spud Webb .25 .07
❑ 420 Doc Rivers .25 .07
❑ 421 Sean Green RC .10 .03
❑ 422 Walter Davis .10 .03
❑ 423 Terry Davis .10 .03
❑ 424 John Battle .10 .03
❑ 425 Vinnie Johnson .10 .03
❑ 426 Sherman Douglas .10 .03
❑ 427 Kevin Brooks RC .10 .03
❑ 428 Greg Sutton .10 .03
❑ 429 Rafael Addison RC .10 .03
❑ 430 Anthony Mason RC 1.00 .30
❑ 431 Paul Graham RC .10 .03
❑ 432 Anthony Frederick RC .10 .03
❑ 433 Dennis Hopson .10 .03
❑ 434 Rory Sparrow .10 .03
❑ 435 Michael Adams .10 .03
❑ 436 Kevin Lynch RC .10 .03
❑ 437 Randy Brown RC .10 .03
❑ 438 Larry Johnson CL .25 .07
Billy Owens
❑ 439 Stacey Augmon TP .10 .03
❑ 440 Larry Stewart TP RC .10 .03
❑ 441 Terrell Brandon TP .50 .15
❑ 442 Billy Owens TP RC .10 .03
❑ 443 Rick Fox TP RC .25 .07
❑ 444 Kenny Anderson TP RC 1.00 .30
❑ 445 Larry Johnson TP .50 .15
❑ 446 Dikembe Mutombo TP .50 .15
❑ 447 Steve Smith TP .50 .15
❑ 448 Greg Anthony TP .25 .07
❑ 449 East All-Star .25 .07
Checklist
❑ 450 West All-Star .25 .07
Checklist
❑ 451 Isiah Thomas AS .50 .15
(Magic Johnson also shown)
❑ 452 Michael Jordan AS 3.00 .90
❑ 453 Scottie Pippen AS .75 .23
❑ 454 Charles Barkley AS .50 .15
❑ 455 Patrick Ewing AS .25 .07
❑ 456 Michael Adams AS .10 .03
❑ 457 Dennis Rodman AS .50 .15
❑ 458 Reggie Lewis AS .10 .03
❑ 459 Joe Dumars AS .25 .07
❑ 460 Mark Price AS .10 .03
❑ 461 Brad Daugherty AS .10 .03
❑ 462 Kevin Willis AS .10 .03
❑ 463 Clyde Drexler AS .25 .07
❑ 464 Magic Johnson AS .75 .23
❑ 465 Chris Mullin AS .25 .07
❑ 466 Karl Malone AS .50 .15
❑ 467 David Robinson AS .50 .15
❑ 468 Tim Hardaway AS .50 .15
❑ 469 Jeff Hornacek AS .10 .03
❑ 470 John Stockton AS .25 .07
❑ 471 D. Mutombo AS UER .25 .07
Drafted in 1992 should be 1991
❑ 472 Hakeem Olajuwon AS .50 .15
❑ 473 James Worthy AS .25 .07
❑ 474 Otis Thorpe AS .10 .03
❑ 475 Dan Majerle AS .10 .03
❑ 476 Cedric Ceballos CL .10 .03
All-Star Skills
❑ 477 Nick Anderson SD .10 .03
❑ 478 Stacey Augmon SD .25 .07
❑ 479 Cedric Ceballos SD .10 .03
❑ 480 Larry Johnson SD .50 .15
❑ 481 Shawn Kemp SD .60 .18
❑ 482 John Starks SD .25 .07
❑ 483 Doug West SD .10 .03
❑ 484 Craig Hodges .10 .03
Long Distance Shoot Out
❑ 485 LaBradford Smith RC .10 .03
❑ 486 Winston Garland .10 .03
❑ 487 David Benoit RC .25 .07

❑ 488 John Bagley .10 .03
❑ 489 Mark Macon RC .10 .03
❑ 490 Mitch Richmond .25 .07
❑ 491 Luc Longley RC .25 .07
❑ 492 Sedale Threatt .10 .03
❑ 493 Doug Smith RC .10 .03
❑ 494 Travis Mays .10 .03
❑ 495 Xavier McDaniel .10 .03
❑ 496 Brian Shaw .10 .03
❑ 497 Stanley Roberts RC .10 .03
❑ 498 Blair Rasmussen .10 .03
❑ 499 Brian Williams RC .50 .15
❑ 500 Checklist Card .10 .03

1992-93 Upper Deck

	Nm-Mt	Ex-Mt
COMPLETE SET (514)	80.00	24.00
COMPLETE LO SERIES (311)	20.00	6.00
COMPLETE HI SERIES (203)	60.00	18.00

❑ 1 Shaquille O'Neal RC SP 40.00 12.00
NBA First Draft Pick
❑ 1A 1992 NBA Draft Trade .30 .09
Card SP
❑ 1B Shaquille O'Neal TRADE 15.00 4.50
❑ 1AX 1992 NBA Draft Trade .30 .09
Card (Stamped)
❑ 2 Alonzo Mourning RC 2.00 .60
❑ 3 Christian Laettner RC .60 .18
❑ 4 LaPhonso Ellis RC .30 .09
❑ 5 Clarence Weatherspoon RC .30 .09
❑ 6 Adam Keefe RC .05 .02
❑ 7 Robert Horry RC .30 .09
❑ 8 Harold Miner RC .15 .04
❑ 9 Bryant Stith RC .15 .04
❑ 10 Malik Sealy RC .15 .04
❑ 11 Anthony Peeler RC .15 .04
❑ 12 Randy Woods RC .05 .02
❑ 13 Tracy Murray RC .15 .04
❑ 14 Tom Gugliotta RC 1.00 .30
❑ 15 Hubert Davis RC .15 .04
❑ 16 Don MacLean RC .05 .02
❑ 17 Lee Mayberry RC .05 .02
❑ 18 Corey Williams RC .05 .02
❑ 19 Sean Rooks RC .05 .02
❑ 20 Todd Day RC .15 .04
❑ 21 Bryant Stith CL .30 .09
LaPhonso Ellis
❑ 22 Jeff Hornacek .15 .04
❑ 23 Michael Jordan 4.00 1.20
❑ 24 John Salley .05 .02
❑ 25 Andre Turner .05 .02
❑ 26 Charles Barkley .50 .15
❑ 27 Anthony Frederick .05 .02
❑ 28 Mario Elie .15 .04
❑ 29 Olden Polynice .05 .02
❑ 30 Rodney Monroe .05 .02
❑ 31 Tim Perry .05 .02
❑ 32 Doug Christie SP RC 1.00 .30
❑ 32A Magic Johnson SP 2.00 .60
❑ 33 Jim Jackson SP RC 2.50 .75
❑ 33A Larry Bird SP 2.50 .75
❑ 34 Randy White .05 .02
❑ 35 Frank Brickowski TC .05 .02
❑ 36 Michael Adams TC .05 .02
❑ 37 Scottie Pippen TC .50 .15
❑ 38 Mark Price TC .05 .02
❑ 39 Robert Parish TC .05 .02
❑ 40 Danny Manning TC .05 .02
❑ 41 Kevin Willis TC .05 .02
❑ 42 Glen Rice TC .15 .04
❑ 43 Kendall Gill TC .05 .02
❑ 44 Karl Malone TC .30 .09
❑ 45 Mitch Richmond TC .30 .09
❑ 46 Patrick Ewing TC .30 .09
❑ 47 Sam Perkins TC .05 .02
❑ 48 Dennis Scott TC .05 .02
❑ 49 Derek Harper TC .05 .02
❑ 50 Drazen Petrovic TC .05 .02
❑ 51 Reggie Williams TC .05 .02
❑ 52 Rik Smits TC .05 .02
❑ 53 Joe Dumars TC .15 .04
❑ 54 Otis Thorpe TC .05 .02
❑ 55 Johnny Dawkins TC .05 .02
❑ 56 Sean Elliott TC .05 .02
❑ 57 Kevin Johnson TC .15 .04
❑ 58 Ricky Pierce TC .05 .02
❑ 59 Doug West TC .05 .02
❑ 60 Terry Porter TC .05 .02
❑ 61 Tim Hardaway TC .30 .09
❑ 62 Michael Jordan ST 1.00 .30
Scottie Pippen
❑ 63 Kendall Gill ST .30 .09
Larry Johnson
❑ 64 Tom Chambers ST .15 .04
Kevin Johnson
❑ 65 Tim Hardaway ST .15 .04
Chris Mullin
❑ 66 Karl Malone ST .30 .09
John Stockton
❑ 67 Michael Jordan MVP 2.00 .60
❑ 68 Stacey Augmon .05 .02
Six Million Point Man
❑ 69 Bob Lanier .15 .04
Stay in School
❑ 70 Alaa Abdelnaby .05 .02
❑ 71 Andrew Lang .05 .02
❑ 72 Larry Krystkowiak .05 .02
❑ 73 Gerald Wilkins .05 .02
❑ 74 Rod Strickland .30 .09
❑ 75 Danny Ainge .15 .04
❑ 76 Chris Corchiani .05 .02
❑ 77 Jeff Grayer .05 .02
❑ 78 Eric Murdock .05 .02
❑ 79 Rex Chapman .05 .02
❑ 80 LaBradford Smith .05 .02
❑ 81 Jay Humphries .05 .02
❑ 82 David Robinson .50 .15
❑ 83 William Bedford .05 .02
❑ 84 James Edwards .05 .02
❑ 85 Danny Schayes .05 .02
❑ 86 Lloyd Daniels RC .05 .02
❑ 87 Blue Edwards .05 .02
❑ 88 Dale Ellis .05 .02
❑ 89 Rolando Blackman .05 .02
❑ 90 Michael Jordan CL .30 .09
❑ 91 Rik Smits .15 .04
❑ 92 Terry Davis .05 .02
❑ 93 Bill Cartwright .05 .02
❑ 94 Avery Johnson .05 .02
❑ 95 Micheal Williams .05 .02
❑ 96 Spud Webb .15 .04
❑ 97 Benoit Benjamin .05 .02
❑ 98 Derek Harper .15 .04
❑ 99 Matt Bullard .05 .02
❑ 100A Tyrone Corbin ERR 1.00 .30
(Heat on front)
❑ 100B Tyrone Corbin COR .05 .02
❑ 101 Doc Rivers .15 .04
❑ 102 Tony Smith .05 .02
❑ 103 Doug West .05 .02
❑ 104 Kevin Duckworth .05 .02
❑ 105 Luc Longley .15 .04
❑ 106 Antoine Carr .05 .02
❑ 107 Clifford Robinson .15 .04
❑ 108 Grant Long .05 .02
❑ 109 Terry Porter .05 .02
❑ 110A Steve Smith ERR 4.00 1.20
(Jazz on front)
❑ 110B Steve Smith COR .40 .12
❑ 111 Brian Williams .05 .02
❑ 112 Karl Malone .50 .15
❑ 113 Reggie Williams .05 .02
❑ 114 Tom Chambers .05 .02
❑ 115 Winston Garland .05 .02
❑ 116 John Stockton .30 .09
❑ 117 Chris Jackson .05 .02
❑ 118 Mike Brown .05 .02
❑ 119 Kevin Johnson .30 .09
❑ 120 Reggie Lewis .15 .04
❑ 121 Bimbo Coles .05 .02
❑ 122 Drazen Petrovic .05 .02
❑ 123 Reggie Miller .30 .09
❑ 124 Derrick Coleman .15 .04
❑ 125 Chuck Person .05 .02
❑ 126 Glen Rice .30 .09
❑ 127 Kenny Anderson .30 .09
❑ 128 Willie Burton .05 .02
❑ 129 Chris Morris .05 .02
❑ 130 Patrick Ewing .30 .09
❑ 131 Sean Elliott .15 .04
❑ 132 Clyde Drexler .30 .09
❑ 133 Scottie Pippen 1.00 .30
❑ 134 Pooh Richardson .05 .02
❑ 135 Horace Grant .15 .04
❑ 136 Hakeem Olajuwon .50 .15
❑ 137 John Paxson .05 .02
❑ 138 Kendall Gill .15 .04
❑ 139 Michael Adams .05 .02
❑ 140 Otis Thorpe .15 .04
❑ 141 Dennis Scott .15 .04
❑ 142 Stacey Augmon .15 .04
❑ 143 Robert Pack .05 .02
❑ 144 Kevin Willis .05 .02
❑ 145 Jerome Kersey .05 .02
❑ 146 Paul Graham .05 .02
❑ 147 Stanley Roberts .05 .02
❑ 148 Dominique Wilkins .30 .09
❑ 149 Scott Skiles .05 .02
❑ 150 Rumeal Robinson .05 .02
❑ 151 Mookie Blaylock .15 .04
❑ 152 Elden Campbell .15 .04
❑ 153 Chris Dudley .05 .02
❑ 154 Sedale Threatt .05 .02
❑ 155 Tate George .05 .02
❑ 156 James Worthy .30 .09
❑ 157 B.J. Armstrong .05 .02
❑ 158 Gary Payton .60 .18
❑ 159 Ledell Eackles .05 .02
❑ 160 Sam Perkins .15 .04
❑ 161 Nick Anderson .15 .04
❑ 162 Mitch Richmond .30 .09
❑ 163 Buck Williams .15 .04
❑ 164 Blair Rasmussen .05 .02
❑ 165 Vern Fleming .05 .02
❑ 166 Duane Ferrell .05 .02
❑ 167 George McCloud .05 .02
❑ 168 Terry Cummings .15 .04
❑ 169 Detlef Schrempf .15 .04
❑ 170 Willie Anderson .05 .02
❑ 171 Scott Williams .05 .02
❑ 172 Vernon Maxwell .05 .02
❑ 173 Todd Lichti .05 .02
❑ 174 David Benoit .05 .02
❑ 175 Marcus Liberty .05 .02
❑ 176 Kenny Smith .05 .02
❑ 177 Dan Majerle .15 .04
❑ 178 Jeff Malone .05 .02
❑ 179 Robert Parish .15 .04
❑ 180 Mark Eaton .05 .02
❑ 181 Rony Seikaly .05 .02
❑ 182 Tony Campbell .05 .02
❑ 183 Kevin McHale .30 .09
❑ 184 Thurl Bailey .05 .02
❑ 185 Kevin Edwards .05 .02
❑ 186 Gerald Glass .05 .02
❑ 187 Hersey Hawkins .15 .04
❑ 188 Sam Mitchell .05 .02
❑ 189 Brian Shaw .05 .02
❑ 190 Felton Spencer .05 .02
❑ 191 Mark Macon .05 .02
❑ 192 Jerry Reynolds .05 .02
❑ 193 Dale Davis .05 .02
❑ 194 Sleepy Floyd .05 .02
❑ 195 A.C. Green .15 .04
❑ 196 Terry Catledge .05 .02
❑ 197 Byron Scott .15 .04
❑ 198 Sam Bowie .05 .02
❑ 199 Vlade Divac .15 .04
❑ 200 Michael Jordan CL .30 .09
❑ 201 Brad Lohaus .05 .02

202 Johnny Newman .05 .02
203 Gary Grant .05 .02
204 Sidney Green .05 .02
205 Frank Brickowski .05 .02
206 Anthony Bowie .05 .02
207 Duane Causwell .05 .02
208 A.J. English .05 .02
209 Mark Aguirre .05 .02
210 Jon Koncak .05 .02
211 Kevin Gamble .05 .02
212 Craig Ehlo .05 .02
213 Herb Williams .15 .04
214 Cedric Ceballos .15 .04
215 Mark Jackson .15 .04
216 John Bagley .05 .02
217 Ron Anderson .05 .02
218 John Battle .05 .02
219 Kevin Lynch .05 .02
220 Donald Hodge .05 .02
221 Chris Gatling .05 .02
222 Muggsy Bogues .15 .04
223 Bill Laimbeer .15 .04
224 Anthony Bonner .05 .02
225 Fred Roberts .05 .02
226 Larry Stewart .05 .02
227 Darrell Walker .05 .02
228 Larry Smith .05 .02
229 Billy Owens .15 .04
230 Vinnie Johnson .05 .02
231 Johnny Dawkins .05 .02
232 Rick Fox .15 .04
233 Travis Mays .05 .02
234 Mark Price .05 .02
235 Derrick McKey .05 .02
236 Greg Anthony .05 .02
237 Doug Smith .05 .02
238 Alec Kessler .05 .02
239 Anthony Mason .30 .09
240 Shawn Kemp .60 .18
241 Jim Les .05 .02
242 Dennis Rodman .60 .18
243 Lionel Simmons .05 .02
244 Pervis Ellison .05 .02
245 Terrell Brandon .30 .09
246 Mark Bryant .05 .02
247 Brad Daugherty .05 .02
248 Scott Brooks .05 .02
249 Sarunas Marciulionis .05 .02
250 Danny Ferry .05 .02
251 Loy Vaught .05 .02
252 Dee Brown .05 .02
253 Alvin Robertson .05 .02
254 Charles Smith .05 .02
255 Dikembe Mutombo .40 .12
256 Greg Kite .05 .02
257 Ed Pinckney .05 .02
258 Ron Harper .15 .04
259 Elliot Perry .05 .02
260 Rafael Addison .05 .02
261 Tim Hardaway .40 .12
262 Randy Brown .05 .02
263 Isiah Thomas .30 .09
264 Victor Alexander .05 .02
265 Wayman Tisdale .05 .02
266 Harvey Grant .05 .02
267 Mike Iuzzolino .05 .02
268 Joe Dumars .30 .09
269 Xavier McDaniel .05 .02
270 Jeff Sanders .05 .02
271 Danny Manning .15 .04
272 Jayson Williams .15 .04
273 Ricky Pierce .05 .02
274 Will Perdue .05 .02
275 Dana Barros .05 .02
276 Randy Breuer .05 .02
277 Manute Bol .05 .02
278 Negele Knight .05 .02
279 Rodney McCray .05 .02
280 Greg Sutton .05 .02
281 Larry Nance .05 .02
282 John Starks .15 .04
283 Pete Chilcutt .05 .02
284 Kenny Gattison .05 .02
285 Stacey King .05 .02
286 Bernard King .05 .02
287 Larry Johnson .40 .12
288 John Williams .05 .02
289 Dell Curry .05 .02
290 Orlando Woolridge .05 .02
291 Nate McMillan .05 .02
292 Terry Mills .05 .02
293 Sherman Douglas .05 .02
294 Charles Shackleford .05 .02
295 Ken Norman .05 .02
296 LaSalle Thompson .05 .02
297 Chris Mullin .30 .09
298 Eddie Johnson .05 .02
299 Armon Gilliam .05 .02
300 Michael Cage .05 .02
301 Moses Malone .30 .09
302 Charles Oakley .15 .04
303 David Wingate .05 .02
304 Steve Kerr .15 .04
305 Tyrone Hill .05 .02
306 Mark West .05 .02
307 Fat Lever .05 .02
308 J.R. Reid .05 .02
309 Ed Nealy .05 .02
310 Michael Jordan CL .30 .09
311 Alaa Abdelnaby .05 .02
312 Stacey Augmon .15 .04
313 Anthony Avent RC .05 .02
314 Walter Bond RC .05 .02
315 Byron Houston RC .05 .02
316 Rick Mahorn .05 .02
317 Sam Mitchell .05 .02
318 Mookie Blaylock .15 .04
319 Lance Blanks .05 .02
320 John Williams .05 .02
321 Rolando Blackman .05 .02
322 Danny Ainge .15 .04
323 Gerald Glass .05 .02
324 Robert Pack .05 .02
325 Oliver Miller RC .15 .04
326 Charles Smith .05 .02
327 Duane Ferrell .05 .02
328 Pooh Richardson .05 .02
329 Scott Brooks .05 .02
330 Walt Williams RC .30 .09
331 Andrew Lang .05 .02
332 Eric Murdock .05 .02
333 Vinny Del Negro .05 .02
334 Charles Barkley .50 .15
335 James Edwards .05 .02
336 Xavier McDaniel .05 .02
337 Paul Graham .05 .02
338 David Wingate .05 .02
339 Richard Dumas RC .05 .02
340 Jay Humphries .05 .02
341 Mark Jackson .15 .04
342 John Salley .05 .02
343 Jon Koncak .05 .02
344 Rodney McCray .05 .02
345 Chuck Person .05 .02
346 Mario Elie .15 .04
347 Frank Johnson .05 .02
348 Rumeal Robinson .05 .02
349 Terry Mills .05 .02
350 Kevin Willis TFC .05 .02
351 Dee Brown TFC .05 .02
352 Muggsy Bogues TFC .05 .02
353 B.J. Armstrong TFC .05 .02
354 Larry Nance TFC .05 .02
355 Doug Smith TFC .05 .02
356 Robert Pack TFC .05 .02
357 Joe Dumars TFC .15 .04
358 Sarunas Marciulionis TFC .05 .02
359 Kenny Smith TFC .05 .02
360 Pooh Richardson TFC .05 .02
361 Mark Jackson TFC .05 .02
362 Sedale Threatt TFC .05 .02
363 Grant Long TFC .05 .02
364 Eric Murdock TFC .05 .02
365 Doug West TFC .05 .02
366 Kenny Anderson TFC .15 .04
367 Anthony Mason TFC .15 .04
368 Nick Anderson TFC .05 .02
369 Jeff Hornacek TFC .05 .02
370 Dan Majerle TFC .05 .02
371 Clifford Robinson TFC .05 .02
372 Lionel Simmons TFC .05 .02
373 Dale Ellis TFC .05 .02
374 Gary Payton TFC .30 .09
375 David Benoit TFC .05 .02
376 Harvey Grant TFC .05 .02
377 Buck Johnson .05 .02
378 Brian Howard RC .05 .02
379 Travis Mays .05 .02
380 Jud Buechler .05 .02
381 Matt Geiger RC .15 .04
382 Bob McCann RC .05 .02
383 Cedric Ceballos .15 .04
384 Rod Strickland .30 .09
385 Kiki Vandeweghe .05 .02
386 Latrell Sprewell RC 2.50 .75
387 Larry Krystkowiak .05 .02
388 Dale Ellis .05 .02
389 Trent Tucker .05 .02
390 Negele Knight .05 .02
391 Stanley Roberts .05 .02
392 Tony Campbell .05 .02
393 Tim Perry .05 .02
394 Doug Overton .05 .02
395 Dan Majerle .15 .04
396 Duane Cooper RC .05 .02
397 Kevin Willis .05 .02
398 Micheal Williams .05 .02
399 Avery Johnson .05 .02
400 Dominique Wilkins .30 .09
401 Chris Smith RC .05 .02
402 Blair Rasmussen .05 .02
403 Jeff Hornacek .15 .04
404 Blue Edwards .05 .02
405 Olden Polynice .05 .02
406 Jeff Grayer .05 .02
407 Tony Bennett RC .05 .02
408 Don MacLean .05 .02
409 Tom Chambers .05 .02
410 Keith Jennings RC .05 .02
411 Gerald Wilkins .05 .02
412 Kennard Winchester .05 .02
413 Doc Rivers .15 .04
414 Brent Price RC .15 .04
415 Mark West .05 .02
416 J.R. Reid .05 .02
417 Jon Barry RC .15 .04
418 Kevin Johnson .30 .09
419 Michael Jordan CL .30 .09
420 Michael Jordan CL .30 .09
421 Brad Daugherty CL .05 .02
Mark Price
Larry Nance
422 Scottie Pippen AS .50 .15
423 Larry Johnson AS .30 .09
424 Shaquille O'Neal AS 2.50 .75
425 Michael Jordan AS 2.00 .60
426 Isiah Thomas AS .15 .04
427 Brad Daugherty AS .05 .02
428 Joe Dumars AS .15 .04
429 Patrick Ewing AS .15 .04
430 Larry Nance AS .05 .02
431 Mark Price AS .05 .02
432 Detlef Schrempf AS .05 .02
433 Dominique Wilkins AS .15 .04
434 Karl Malone AS .30 .09
435 Charles Barkley AS .30 .09
436 David Robinson AS .30 .09
437 John Stockton AS .15 .04
438 Clyde Drexler AS .15 .04
439 Sean Elliott AS .05 .02
440 Tim Hardaway AS .30 .09
441 Shawn Kemp AS .30 .09
442 Dan Majerle AS .05 .02
443 Danny Manning AS .05 .02
444 Hakeem Olajuwon AS .30 .09
445 Terry Porter AS .05 .02
446 Harold Miner FACE .15 .04
447 David Benoit FACE .05 .02
448 Cedric Ceballos FACE .05 .02
449 Chris Jackson FACE .05 .02
450 Tim Perry FACE .05 .02
451 Kenny Smith FACE .05 .02
452 Clarence Weatherspoon FACE .30 .09
453A Michael Jordan FACE ERR (Slam Dunk Champ in 1985 and 1990) 15.00 4.50
453B Michael Jordan 2.00 .60

No.	Card	Nm-Mt	Ex-Mt
	FACE COR (Slam Dunk Champ in 1987 and 1988)		
❑ 454A	Dominique Wilkins	2.00	.60
	FACE ERR (Slam Dunk Champ in 1987 and 1988)		
❑ 454B	Dominique Wilkins	.30	.09
	FACE COR (Slam Dunk Champ in 1985 and 1990)		
❑ 455	Anthony Peeler	.05	.02
	Duane Cooper CL		
❑ 456	Adam Keefe TP	.05	.02
❑ 457	Alonzo Mourning TP	.50	.15
❑ 458	Jim Jackson TP	.30	.09
❑ 459	Sean Rooks TP	.05	.02
❑ 460	LaPhonso Ellis TP	.15	.04
❑ 461	Bryant Stith TP	.05	.02
❑ 462	Byron Houston TP	.05	.02
❑ 463	Latrell Sprewell TP	.30	.09
❑ 464	Robert Horry TP	.15	.04
❑ 465	Malik Sealy TP	.05	.02
❑ 466	Doug Christie TP	.30	.09
❑ 467	Duane Cooper TP	.05	.02
❑ 468	Anthony Peeler TP	.05	.02
❑ 469	Harold Miner TP	.05	.02
❑ 470	Todd Day TP	.05	.02
❑ 471	Lee Mayberry TP	.05	.02
❑ 472	Christian Laettner TP	.30	.09
❑ 473	Hubert Davis TP	.05	.02
❑ 474	Shaquille O'Neal TP	2.50	.75
❑ 475	C. Weatherspoon TP	.30	.09
❑ 476	Richard Dumas TP	.05	.02
❑ 477	Oliver Miller TP	.05	.02
❑ 478	Tracy Murray TP	.05	.02
❑ 479	Walt Williams TP	.15	.04
❑ 480	Lloyd Daniels TP	.05	.02
❑ 481	Tom Gugliotta TP	.30	.09
❑ 482	Brent Price TP	.05	.02
❑ 483	Mark Aguirre GF	.05	.02
❑ 484	Frank Brickowski GF	.05	.02
❑ 485	Derrick Coleman GF	.05	.02
❑ 486	Clyde Drexler GF	.15	.04
❑ 487	Harvey Grant GF	.05	.02
❑ 488	Michael Jordan GF	2.00	.60
❑ 489	Karl Malone GF	.30	.09
❑ 490	Xavier McDaniel GF	.05	.02
❑ 491	Drazen Petrovic GF	.05	.02
❑ 492	John Starks GF	.05	.02
❑ 493	Robert Parish GF	.05	.02
❑ 494	Christian Laettner GF	.30	.09
❑ 495	Ron Harper GF	.05	.02
❑ 496	David Robinson GF	.30	.09
❑ 497	John Salley GF	.05	.02
❑ 498	Brad Daugherty ST	.05	.02
	Mark Price		
❑ 499	Dikembe Mutombo ST	.30	.09
	Chris Jackson		
❑ 500	Isiah Thomas ST	.30	.09
	Joe Dumars		
❑ 501	Hakeem Olajuwon	.30	.09
	Otis Thorpe ST		
❑ 502	Derrick Coleman ST	.15	.04
	Drazen Petrovic		
❑ 503	Terry Porter ST	.30	.09
	Clyde Drexler		
❑ 504	Lionel Simmons ST	.15	.04
	Mitch Richmond		
❑ 505	David Robinson ST	.30	.09
	Sean Elliott		
❑ 506	Michael Jordan FAN	2.00	.60
❑ 507	Larry Bird FAN	.60	.18
❑ 508	Karl Malone FAN	.30	.09
❑ 509	Dikembe Mutombo FAN	.30	.09
❑ 510	Larry Bird FAN	1.00	.30
	Michael Jordan		
❑ SP1	Larry Bird	3.00	.90
	Magic Johnson		
	Retirement		
❑ SP2	20,000 Points	6.00	1.80
	Dominique Wilkins		
	Nov. 6, 1992		
	Michael Jordan		
	Jan. 8, 1993		

1993-94 Upper Deck

No.	Card	Nm-Mt	Ex-Mt
	COMPLETE SET (510)	30.00	9.00
	COMPLETE SERIES 1 (255)	15.00	4.50
	COMPLETE SERIES 2 (255)	15.00	4.50
❑ 1	Muggsy Bogues	.15	.04
❑ 2	Kenny Anderson	.15	.04
❑ 3	Dell Curry	.05	.02
❑ 4	Charles Smith	.05	.02
❑ 5	Chuck Person	.05	.02
❑ 6	Chucky Brown	.05	.02
❑ 7	Kevin Johnson	.15	.04
❑ 8	Winston Garland	.05	.02
❑ 9	John Salley	.05	.02
❑ 10	Dale Ellis	.05	.02
❑ 11	Otis Thorpe	.15	.04
❑ 12	John Stockton	.30	.09
❑ 13	Kendall Gill	.15	.04
❑ 14	Randy White	.05	.02
❑ 15	Mark Jackson	.15	.04
❑ 16	Vlade Divac	.15	.04
❑ 17	Scott Skiles	.05	.02
❑ 18	Xavier McDaniel	.05	.02
❑ 19	Jeff Hornacek	.15	.04
❑ 20	Stanley Roberts	.05	.02
❑ 21	Harold Miner	.05	.02
❑ 22	Terrell Brandon	.15	.04
❑ 23	Michael Jordan	4.00	1.20
❑ 24	Jim Jackson	.15	.04
❑ 25	Keith Askins	.05	.02
❑ 26	Corey Williams	.05	.02
❑ 27	David Benoit	.05	.02
❑ 28	Charles Oakley	.15	.04
❑ 29	Michael Adams	.05	.02
❑ 30	Clarence Weatherspoon	.05	.02
❑ 31	Jon Koncak	.05	.02
❑ 32	Gerald Wilkins	.05	.02
❑ 33	Anthony Bowie	.05	.02
❑ 34	Willie Burton	.05	.02
❑ 35	Stacey Augmon	.05	.02
❑ 36	Doc Rivers	.15	.04
❑ 37	Luc Longley	.15	.04
❑ 38	Dee Brown	.05	.02
❑ 39	Litterial Green	.05	.02
❑ 40	Dan Majerle	.15	.04
❑ 41	Doug West	.05	.02
❑ 42	Joe Dumars	.30	.09
❑ 43	Dennis Scott	.05	.02
❑ 44	Mahmoud Abdul-Rauf	.05	.02
❑ 45	Mark Eaton	.05	.02
❑ 46	Danny Ferry	.05	.02
❑ 47	Kenny Smith	.05	.02
❑ 48	Ron Harper	.15	.04
❑ 49	Adam Keefe	.05	.02
❑ 50	David Robinson	.50	.15
❑ 51	John Starks	.15	.04
❑ 52	Jeff Malone	.05	.02
❑ 53	Vern Fleming	.05	.02
❑ 54	Olden Polynice	.05	.02
❑ 55	Dikembe Mutombo	.30	.09
❑ 56	Chris Morris	.05	.02
❑ 57	Paul Graham	.05	.02
❑ 58	Richard Dumas	.05	.02
❑ 59	J.R. Reid	.05	.02
❑ 60	Brad Daugherty	.05	.02
❑ 61	Blue Edwards	.05	.02
❑ 62	Mark Macon	.05	.02
❑ 63	Latrell Sprewell	.75	.23
❑ 64	Mitch Richmond	.30	.09
❑ 65	David Wingate	.05	.02
❑ 66	LaSalle Thompson	.05	.02
❑ 67	Sedale Threatt	.05	.02
❑ 68	Larry Krystkowiak	.05	.02
❑ 69	John Paxson	.05	.02
❑ 70	Frank Brickowski	.05	.02
❑ 71	Duane Causwell	.05	.02
❑ 72	Fred Roberts	.05	.02
❑ 73	Rod Strickland	.15	.04
❑ 74	Willie Anderson	.05	.02
❑ 75	Thurl Bailey	.05	.02
❑ 76	Ricky Pierce	.05	.02
❑ 77	Todd Day	.05	.02
❑ 78	Hot Rod Williams	.05	.02
❑ 79	Danny Ainge	.15	.04
❑ 80	Mark West	.05	.02
❑ 81	Marcus Liberty	.05	.02
❑ 82	Keith Jennings	.05	.02
❑ 83	Derrick Coleman	.15	.04
❑ 84	Larry Stewart	.05	.02
❑ 85	Tracy Murray	.05	.02
❑ 86	Robert Horry	.15	.04
❑ 87	Derek Harper	.15	.04
❑ 88	Scott Hastings	.05	.02
❑ 89	Sam Perkins	.15	.04
❑ 90	Clyde Drexler	.30	.09
❑ 91	Brent Price	.05	.02
❑ 92	Chris Mullin	.30	.09
❑ 93	Rafael Addison	.05	.02
❑ 94	Tyrone Corbin	.05	.02
❑ 95	Sarunas Marciulionis	.05	.02
❑ 96	Antoine Carr	.05	.02
❑ 97	Tony Bennett	.05	.02
❑ 98	Sam Mitchell	.05	.02
❑ 99	Lionel Simmons	.05	.02
❑ 100	Tim Perry	.05	.02
❑ 101	Horace Grant	.15	.04
❑ 102	Tom Hammonds	.05	.02
❑ 103	Walter Bond	.05	.02
❑ 104	Detlef Schrempf	.15	.04
❑ 105	Terry Porter	.05	.02
❑ 106	Danny Schayes	.05	.02
❑ 107	Rumeal Robinson	.05	.02
❑ 108	Gerald Glass	.05	.02
❑ 109	Mike Gminski	.05	.02
❑ 110	Terry Mills	.05	.02
❑ 111	Loy Vaught	.05	.02
❑ 112	Jim Les	.05	.02
❑ 113	Byron Houston	.05	.02
❑ 114	Randy Brown	.05	.02
❑ 115	Anthony Avent	.05	.02
❑ 116	Donald Hodge	.05	.02
❑ 117	Kevin Willis	.05	.02
❑ 118	Robert Pack	.05	.02
❑ 119	Dale Davis	.05	.02
❑ 120	Grant Long	.05	.02
❑ 121	Anthony Bonner	.05	.02
❑ 122	Chris Smith	.05	.02
❑ 123	Elden Campbell	.05	.02
❑ 124	Clifford Robinson	.15	.04
❑ 125	Sherman Douglas	.05	.02
❑ 126	Alvin Robertson	.05	.02
❑ 127	Rolando Blackman	.05	.02
❑ 128	Malik Sealy	.05	.02
❑ 129	Ed Pinckney	.05	.02
❑ 130	Anthony Peeler	.05	.02
❑ 131	Scott Brooks	.05	.02
❑ 132	Rik Smits	.15	.04
❑ 133	Derrick McKey	.05	.02
❑ 134	Alaa Abdelnaby	.05	.02
❑ 135	Rex Chapman	.05	.02
❑ 136	Tony Campbell	.05	.02
❑ 137	John Williams	.05	.02
❑ 138	Vincent Askew	.05	.02
❑ 139	LaBradford Smith	.05	.02
❑ 140	Vinny Del Negro	.05	.02
❑ 141	Darrell Walker	.05	.02
❑ 142	James Worthy	.30	.09
❑ 143	Jeff Turner	.05	.02
❑ 144	Duane Ferrell	.05	.02
❑ 145	Larry Smith	.05	.02
❑ 146	Eddie Johnson	.05	.02
❑ 147	Chris Gatling	.05	.02
❑ 148	Buck Williams	.05	.02
❑ 149	Donald Royal	.05	.02
❑ 150	Dino Radja RC	.05	.02
❑ 151	Johnny Dawkins	.05	.02
❑ 152	Tim Legler RC	.05	.02

❑ 153 Bill Laimbeer .05 .02
❑ 154 Glen Rice .15 .04
❑ 155 Bill Cartwright .05 .02
❑ 156 Luther Wright RC .05 .02
❑ 157 Rex Walters RC .05 .02
❑ 158 Doug Edwards RC .05 .02
❑ 159 George Lynch RC .05 .02
❑ 160 Chris Mills RC .30 .09
❑ 161 Sam Cassell RC 1.25 .35
❑ 162 Nick Van Exel RC 1.00 .30
❑ 163 Shawn Bradley RC .30 .09
❑ 164 Calbert Cheaney RC .15 .04
❑ 165 Corie Blount RC .05 .02
❑ 166 Michael Jordan SL 2.00 .60
Scoring
❑ 167 Dennis Rodman SL .30 .09
Rebounds
❑ 168 John Stockton SL .15 .04
Assists
❑ 169 B.J. Armstrong SL .05 .02
3-pt. field goals
❑ 170 Hakeem Olajuwon SL .30 .09
Blocked shots
❑ 171 Michael Jordan SL 2.00 .60
Steals
❑ 172 Cedric Ceballos SL .05 .02
Field goal percentage
❑ 173 Mark Price SL .05 .02
Free-throw percentage
❑ 174 Charles Barkley SL .30 .09
MVP
❑ 175 Clifford Robinson SL .05 .02
Sixth man
❑ 176 Hakeem Olajuwon SL .30 .09
Defensive player
❑ 177 Shaquille O'Neal SL .60 .18
ROY
❑ 178 Reggie Miller .15 .04
Charles Oakley PO
❑ 179 Rick Fox .05 .02
Kenny Gattison PO
❑ 180 Michael Jordan 1.00 .30
Stackey Augmon PO
❑ 181 Brad Daugherty PO .05 .02
❑ 182 Oliver Miller .05 .02
Byron Scott PO
❑ 183 David Robinson .30 .09
Sean Elliott PO
❑ 184 Kenny Smith .05 .02
Mark Jackson PO
❑ 185 Eddie Johnson PO .05 .02
❑ 186 Anthony Mason .30 .09
Patrick Ewing
A Mourning PO
❑ 187 Michael Jordan 1.00 .30
Gerald Wilkins PO
❑ 188 Oliver Miller PO .05 .02
❑ 189 Sam Perkins .30 .09
Hakeem Olajuwon PO
❑ 190 Bill Cartwright PO .05 .02
❑ 191 Kevin Johnson PO .15 .04
❑ 192 Dan Majerle PO .05 .02
❑ 193 Michael Jordan PO 2.00 .60
❑ 194 Larry Johnson .05 .02
Muggsy Bogues PO
❑ 195 Reggie Miller PO .15 .04
❑ 196 John Starks .30 .09
Scottie Pippen PO
❑ 197 Charles Barkley PO .30 .09
❑ 198 Michael Jordan FIN 2.00 .60
❑ 199 Scottie Pippen FIN .50 .15
❑ 200 Kevin Johnson FIN .05 .02
❑ 201 Michael Jordan FIN 2.00 .60
❑ 202 Richard Dumas FIN .05 .02
❑ 203 Horace Grant FIN .05 .02
❑ 204 Michael Jordan FIN 2.00 .60
1993 Finals MVP
❑ 205 Scottie Pippen FIN .30 .09
Charles Barkley
❑ 206 John Paxson FIN .05 .02
Hits 3 for title
❑ 207 B.J. Armstrong FIN .05 .02
Finals records
❑ 208 1992-93 Bulls FIN .05 .02
Road to 1993 Finals
❑ 209 1992-93 Suns FIN .05 .02
Road to 1993 Finals
❑ 210 Atlanta Hawks Sked .05 .02
Kevin Willis
❑ 211 Boston Celtics Sked .05 .02
Brian Shaw
❑ 212 Charlotte Hornets Sked .05 .02
❑ 213 Chicago Bulls Sked 1.00 .30
Michael Jordan
❑ 214 Cleveland Cavaliers .05 .02
Sked (Mark Price)
❑ 215 Dallas Mavericks Sked .05 .02
(Jim Jackson
Sean Rooks)
❑ 216 Denver Nuggets Sked .15 .04
Dikembe Mutumbo
❑ 217 Detroit Pistons Sked .15 .04
Isiah Thomas
Bill Laimbeer
Terry Mills
❑ 218 Golden State Warriors .05 .02
Sked
❑ 219 Houston Rockets Sked .30 .09
(Hakeem Olajuwon)
❑ 220 Indiana Pacers Sked .05 .02
Rik Smits
Detlef Schrempf
❑ 221 L.A. Clippers Sked .05 .02
Ron Harper
Danny Manning
Mark Jackson
❑ 222 L.A. Lakers Sked .05 .02
❑ 223 Miami Heat Sked .15 .04
Steve Smith
Harold Miner
Rony Seikaly
❑ 224 Milwaukee Bucks Sked .05 .02
❑ 225 Minnesota Timberwolves .05 .02
Sked
❑ 226 New Jersey Nets Sked .05 .02
Kenny Anderson
❑ 227 New York Knicks Sked .05 .02
Rolando Blackmon
❑ 228 Orlando Magic Sked .40 .12
(Shaquille O'Neal)
❑ 229 Philadelphia 76ers .05 .02
Sked
Hersey Hawkins
Jeff Hornacek
❑ 230 Phoenix Suns Sked .30 .09
(Charles Barkley)
❑ 231 Portland Trail Blazers .05 .02
Sked
Buck Williams
Jerome Kersey
Terry Porter)
❑ 232 Sacramento Kings Sked .05 .02
❑ 233 San Antonio Spurs Sked .30 .09
David Robinson
Avery Johnson
Sean Elliott
❑ 234 Seattle Supersonics Sked .15 .04
Gary Payton
Shawn Kemp
❑ 235 Utah Jazz Sked .05 .02
❑ 236 Washington Bullets .15 .04
Sked
Tom Gugliotta
Michael Adams
❑ 237 Michael Jordan SM 2.00 .60
❑ 238 Clyde Drexler SM .15 .04
❑ 239 Tim Hardaway SM .15 .04
❑ 240 Dominique Wilkins SM .15 .04
❑ 241 Brad Daugherty SM .05 .02
❑ 242 Chris Mullin SM .15 .04
❑ 243 Kenny Anderson SM .05 .02
❑ 244 Patrick Ewing SM .15 .04
❑ 245 Isiah Thomas SM .15 .04
❑ 246 Dikembe Mutombo SM .15 .04
❑ 247 Danny Manning SM .05 .02
❑ 248 David Robinson SM .30 .09
❑ 249 Karl Malone SM .30 .09
❑ 250 James Worthy SM .15 .04
❑ 251 Shawn Kemp SM .30 .09
❑ 252 Checklist 1-64 .05 .02
❑ 253 Checklist 65-128 .05 .02
❑ 254 Checklist 129-192 .05 .02
❑ 255 Checklist 193-255 .05 .02
❑ 256 Patrick Ewing .30 .09
❑ 257 B.J. Armstrong .05 .02
❑ 258 Oliver Miller .05 .02
❑ 259 Jud Buechler .05 .02
❑ 260 Pooh Richardson .05 .02
❑ 261 Victor Alexander .05 .02
❑ 262 Kevin Gamble .05 .02
❑ 263 Doug Smith .05 .02
❑ 264 Isiah Thomas .30 .09
❑ 265 Doug Christie .15 .04
❑ 266 Mark Bryant .05 .02
❑ 267 Lloyd Daniels .05 .02
❑ 268 Micheal Williams .05 .02
❑ 269 Nick Anderson .15 .04
❑ 270 Tom Gugliotta .30 .09
❑ 271 Kenny Gattison .05 .02
❑ 272 Vernon Maxwell .05 .02
❑ 273 Terry Cummings .05 .02
❑ 274 Karl Malone .50 .15
❑ 275 Rick Fox .05 .02
❑ 276 Matt Bullard .05 .02
❑ 277 Johnny Newman .05 .02
❑ 278 Mark Price .05 .02
❑ 279 Mookie Blaylock .15 .04
❑ 280 Charles Barkley .50 .15
❑ 281 Larry Nance .05 .02
❑ 282 Walt Williams .05 .02
❑ 283 Brian Shaw .05 .02
❑ 284 Robert Parish .15 .04
❑ 285 Pervis Ellison .05 .02
❑ 286 Spud Webb .15 .04
❑ 287 Hakeem Olajuwon .50 .15
❑ 288 Jerome Kersey .05 .02
❑ 289 Carl Herrera .05 .02
❑ 290 Dominique Wilkins .30 .09
❑ 291 Billy Owens .05 .02
❑ 292 Greg Anthony .05 .02
❑ 293 Nate McMillan .05 .02
❑ 294 Christian Laettner .15 .04
❑ 295 Gary Payton .50 .15
❑ 296 Steve Smith .30 .09
❑ 297 Anthony Mason .15 .04
❑ 298 Sean Rooks .05 .02
❑ 299 Toni Kukoc RC 1.25 .35
❑ 300 Shaquille O'Neal 1.50 .45
❑ 301 Jay Humphries .05 .02
❑ 302 Sleepy Floyd .05 .02
❑ 303 Bimbo Coles .05 .02
❑ 304 John Battle .05 .02
❑ 305 Shawn Kemp .50 .15
❑ 306 Scott Williams .05 .02
❑ 307 Wayman Tisdale .05 .02
❑ 308 Rony Seikaly .05 .02
❑ 309 Reggie Miller .30 .09
❑ 310 Scottie Pippen 1.00 .30
❑ 311 Chris Webber RC 3.00 .90
❑ 312 Trevor Wilson .05 .02
❑ 313 Derek Strong RC .05 .02
❑ 314 Bobby Hurley RC .15 .04
❑ 315 Herb Williams .05 .02
❑ 316 Rex Walters .05 .02
❑ 317 Doug Edwards .05 .02
❑ 318 Ken Williams .05 .02
❑ 319 Jon Barry .05 .02
❑ 320 Joe Courtney RC .05 .02
❑ 321 Ervin Johnson RC .15 .04
❑ 322 Sam Cassell .30 .09
❑ 323 Tim Hardaway .30 .09
❑ 324 Ed Stokes .05 .02
❑ 325 Steve Kerr .15 .04
❑ 326 Doug Overton .05 .02
❑ 327 Reggie Williams .05 .02
❑ 328 Avery Johnson .05 .02
❑ 329 Stacey King .05 .02
❑ 330 Vin Baker RC .75 .23
❑ 331 Greg Kite .05 .02
❑ 332 Michael Cage .05 .02
❑ 333 Alonzo Mourning .50 .15
❑ 334 Acie Earl RC .05 .02
❑ 335 Terry Dehere RC .05 .02
❑ 336 Negele Knight .05 .02
❑ 337 Gerald Madkins RC .05 .02
❑ 338 Lindsey Hunter RC .30 .09
❑ 339 Luther Wright .05 .02
❑ 340 Mike Peplowski RC .05 .02

❑ 341 Dino Radja	.05	.02
❑ 342 Danny Manning	.15	.04
❑ 343 Chris Mills	.30	.09
❑ 344 Kevin Lynch	.05	.02
❑ 345 Shawn Bradley	.30	.09
❑ 346 Evers Burns RC	.05	.02
❑ 347 Rodney Rogers RC	.30	.09
❑ 348 Cedric Ceballos	.15	.04
❑ 349 Warren Kidd RC	.05	.02
❑ 350 Darnell Mee RC	.05	.02
❑ 351 Matt Geiger	.05	.02
❑ 352 Jamal Mashburn RC	.75	.23
❑ 353 Antonio Davis RC	.40	.12
❑ 354 Calbert Cheaney	.15	.04
❑ 355 George Lynch	.05	.02
❑ 356 Derrick McKey	.05	.02
❑ 357 Jerry Reynolds	.05	.02
❑ 358 Don MacLean	.05	.02
❑ 359 Scott Haskin RC	.05	.02
❑ 360 Malcolm Mackey RC	.05	.02
❑ 361 Isaiah Rider RC	.60	.18
❑ 362 Detlef Schrempf	.15	.04
❑ 363 Josh Grant RC	.05	.02
❑ 364 Richard Petruska	.05	.02
❑ 365 Larry Johnson	.30	.09
❑ 366 Felton Spencer RC	.05	.02
❑ 367 Ken Norman	.05	.02
❑ 368 Anthony Cook	.05	.02
❑ 369 James Robinson RC	.05	.02
❑ 370 Kevin Duckworth	.05	.02
❑ 371 Chris Whitney RC	.05	.02
❑ 372 Moses Malone	.30	.09
❑ 373 Nick Van Exel	.50	.15
❑ 374 Scott Burrell RC	.30	.09
❑ 375 Harvey Grant	.05	.02
❑ 376 Benoit Benjamin	.05	.02
❑ 377 Henry James	.05	.02
❑ 378 Craig Ehlo	.05	.02
❑ 379 Ennis Whatley	.05	.02
❑ 380 Sean Green	.05	.02
❑ 381 Eric Murdock	.05	.02
❑ 382 Anfernee Hardaway RC	2.50	.75
❑ 383 Gheorghe Muresan RC	.30	.09
❑ 384 Kendall Gill	.15	.04
❑ 385 David Wood	.05	.02
❑ 386 Mario Elie	.05	.02
❑ 387 Chris Corchiani	.05	.02
❑ 388 Greg Graham RC	.05	.02
❑ 389 Hersey Hawkins	.15	.04
❑ 390 Mark Aguirre	.05	.02
❑ 391 LaPhonso Ellis	.05	.02
❑ 392 Anthony Bonner	.05	.02
❑ 393 Lucious Harris RC	.05	.02
❑ 394 Andrew Lang	.05	.02
❑ 395 Chris Dudley	.05	.02
❑ 396 Dennis Rodman	.60	.18
❑ 397 Larry Krystkowiak	.05	.02
❑ 398 A.C. Green	.15	.04
❑ 399 Eddie Johnson	.05	.02
❑ 400 Kevin Edwards	.05	.02
❑ 401 Tyrone Hill	.05	.02
❑ 402 Greg Anderson	.05	.02
❑ 403 P.J. Brown RC	.30	.09
❑ 404 Dana Barros	.05	.02
❑ 405 Allan Houston RC	1.25	.35
❑ 406 Mike Brown	.05	.02
❑ 407 Lee Mayberry	.05	.02
❑ 408 Fat Lever	.05	.02
❑ 409 Tony Smith	.05	.02
❑ 410 Tom Chambers	.05	.02
❑ 411 Manute Bol	.05	.02
❑ 412 Joe Kleine	.05	.02
❑ 413 Bryant Stith	.05	.02
❑ 414 Eric Riley RC	.05	.02
❑ 415 Jo Jo English RC	.05	.02
❑ 416 Sean Elliott	.15	.04
❑ 417 Sam Bowie	.05	.02
❑ 418 Armon Gilliam	.05	.02
❑ 419 Brian Williams	.05	.02
❑ 420 Popeye Jones RC	.05	.02
❑ 421 Dennis Rodman EB	.30	.09
❑ 422 Karl Malone EB	.30	.09
❑ 423 Tom Gugliotta EB	.15	.04
❑ 424 Kevin Willis EB	.05	.02
❑ 425 Hakeem Olajuwon EB	.30	.09
❑ 426 Charles Oakley EB	.05	.02

❑ 427 C. Weatherspoon EB	.05	.02
❑ 428 Derrick Coleman EB	.05	.02
❑ 429 Buck Williams EB	.05	.02
❑ 430 Christian Laettner EB	.05	.02
❑ 431 Dikembe Mutombo EB	.15	.04
❑ 432 Rony Seikaly EB	.05	.02
❑ 433 Brad Daugherty EB	.05	.02
❑ 434 Horace Grant EB	.05	.02
❑ 435 Larry Johnson EB	.15	.04
❑ 436 Dee Brown BT	.05	.02
❑ 437 Muggsy Bogues BT	.05	.02
❑ 438 Michael Jordan BT	2.00	.60
❑ 439 Tim Hardaway BT	.15	.04
❑ 440 Micheal Williams BT	.05	.02
❑ 441 Gary Payton BT	.30	.09
❑ 442 Mookie Blaylock BT	.05	.02
❑ 443 Doc Rivers BT	.05	.02
❑ 444 Kenny Smith BT	.05	.02
❑ 445 John Stockton BT	.15	.04
❑ 446 Alvin Robertson BT	.05	.02
❑ 447 Mark Jackson BT	.05	.02
❑ 448 Kenny Anderson BT	.05	.02
❑ 449 Scottie Pippen BT	.50	.15
❑ 450 Isiah Thomas BT	.15	.04
❑ 451 Mark Price BT	.05	.02
❑ 452 Latrell Sprewell BT	.30	.09
❑ 453 Sedale Threatt BT	.05	.02
❑ 454 Nick Anderson BT	.05	.02
❑ 455 Rod Strickland BT	.05	.02
❑ 456 Oliver Miller GI	.05	.02
❑ 457 James Worthy Vlade Divac GI	.05	.02
❑ 458 Robert Horry GI	.05	.02
❑ 459 Rockets Shoot-Around GI	.05	.02
❑ 460 Sean Rooks Jim Jackson Tim Legler GI	.05	.02
❑ 461 Mitch Richmond GI	.15	.04
❑ 462 Chris Morris GI	.05	.02
❑ 463 Mark Jackson Gary Grant GI	.05	.02
❑ 464 David Robinson GI	.30	.09
❑ 465 Danny Ainge GI	.05	.02
❑ 466 Michael Jordan SL	2.00	.60
❑ 467 Dominique Wilkins SL	.15	.04
❑ 468 Alonzo Mourning SL	.30	.09
❑ 469 Shaquille O'Neal SL	.60	.18
❑ 470 Tim Hardaway SL	.15	.04
❑ 471 Patrick Ewing SL	.15	.04
❑ 472 Kevin Johnson SL	.05	.02
❑ 473 Clyde Drexler SL	.15	.04
❑ 474 David Robinson SL	.30	.09
❑ 475 Shawn Kemp SL	.30	.09
❑ 476 Dee Brown SL	.05	.02
❑ 477 Jim Jackson SL	.05	.02
❑ 478 John Stockton SL	.15	.04
❑ 479 Robert Horry SL	.05	.02
❑ 480 Glen Rice SL	.05	.02
❑ 481 Micheal Williams SIS	.05	.02
❑ 482 George Lynch Terry Dehere CL	.05	.02
❑ 483 Chris Webber TP	1.50	.45
❑ 484 Anfernee Hardaway TP	1.25	.35
❑ 485 Shawn Bradley TP	.15	.04
❑ 486 Jamal Mashburn TP	.30	.09
❑ 487 Calbert Cheaney TP	.05	.02
❑ 488 Isaiah Rider TP	.30	.09
❑ 489 Bobby Hurley TP	.05	.02
❑ 490 Vin Baker TP	.30	.09
❑ 491 Rodney Rogers TP	.15	.04
❑ 492 Lindsey Hunter TP	.15	.04
❑ 493 Allan Houston TP	.30	.09
❑ 494 Terry Dehere TP	.05	.02
❑ 495 George Lynch TP	.05	.02
❑ 496 Toni Kukoc TP	.30	.09
❑ 497 Nick Van Exel TP	.30	.09
❑ 498 Charles Barkley MO	.30	.09
❑ 499 A.C. Green MO	.05	.02
❑ 500 Dan Majerle MO	.05	.02
❑ 501 Jerrod Mustaf MO	.05	.02
❑ 502 Kevin Johnson MO	.05	.02
❑ 503 Negele Knight MO	.05	.02
❑ 504 Danny Ainge MO	.05	.02
❑ 505 Oliver Miller MO	.05	.02
❑ 506 Joe Courtney MO	.05	.02
❑ 507 Checklist	.05	.02

❑ 508 Checklist	.05	.02
❑ 509 Checklist	.05	.02
❑ 510 Checklist	.05	.02
❑ SP3 Michael Jordan Wilt Chamberlain	8.00	2.40
❑ SP4 Chicago Bulls' Third NBA Championship	8.00	2.40

1994-95 Upper Deck

	Nm-Mt	Ex-Mt
COMPLETE SET (360)	45.00	13.50
COMPLETE SERIES 1 (180)	25.00	7.50
COMPLETE SERIES 2 (180)	20.00	6.00
❑ 1 Chris Webber ART	.50	.15
❑ 2 Anfernee Hardaway ART	.50	.15
❑ 3 Vin Baker ART	.15	.04
❑ 4 Jamal Mashburn ART	.15	.04
❑ 5 Isaiah Rider ART	.10	.03
❑ 6 Dino Radja ART	.10	.03
❑ 7 Nick Van Exel ART	.15	.04
❑ 8 Shawn Bradley ART	.10	.03
❑ 9 Toni Kukoc ART	.40	.12
❑ 10 Lindsey Hunter ART	.10	.03
❑ 11 Scottie Pippen AN	.60	.18
❑ 12 Karl Malone AN	.40	.12
❑ 13 Hakeem Olajuwon AN	.40	.12
❑ 14 John Stockton AN	.15	.04
❑ 15 Latrell Sprewell AN	.40	.12
❑ 16 Shawn Kemp AN	.40	.12
❑ 17 Charles Barkley AN	.40	.12
❑ 18 David Robinson AN	.40	.12
❑ 19 Mitch Richmond AN	.15	.04
❑ 20 Kevin Johnson AN	.10	.03
❑ 21 Derrick Coleman AN	.10	.03
❑ 22 Dominique Wilkins AN	.15	.04
❑ 23 Shaquille O'Neal AN	.75	.23
❑ 24 Mark Price AN	.10	.03
❑ 25 Gary Payton AN	.40	.12
❑ 26 Dan Majerle	.15	.04
❑ 27 Vernon Maxwell	.10	.03
❑ 28 Matt Geiger	.10	.03
❑ 29 Jeff Turner	.10	.03
❑ 30 Vinny Del Negro	.10	.03
❑ 31 B.J. Armstrong	.10	.03
❑ 32 Chris Gatling	.10	.03
❑ 33 Tony Smith	.10	.03
❑ 34 Doug West	.10	.03
❑ 35 Clyde Drexler	.40	.12
❑ 36 Keith Jennings	.10	.03
❑ 37 Steve Smith	.15	.04
❑ 38 Kendall Gill	.15	.04
❑ 39 Bob Martin	.10	.03
❑ 40 Calbert Cheaney	.10	.03
❑ 41 Terrell Brandon	.15	.04
❑ 42 Pete Chilcutt	.10	.03
❑ 43 Avery Johnson	.10	.03
❑ 44 Tom Gugliotta	.15	.04
❑ 45 LaBradford Smith	.10	.03
❑ 46 Sedale Threatt	.10	.03
❑ 47 Chris Smith	.10	.03
❑ 48 Kevin Edwards	.10	.03
❑ 49 Lucious Harris	.10	.03
❑ 50 Tim Perry	.10	.03
❑ 51 Lloyd Daniels	.10	.03
❑ 52 Dee Brown	.10	.03
❑ 53 Sean Elliott	.15	.04
❑ 54 Tim Hardaway	.40	.12
❑ 55 Christian Laettner	.15	.04

❑ 56 Bo Outlaw RC .10 .03
❑ 57 Kevin Johnson .15 .04
❑ 58 Duane Ferrell .10 .03
❑ 59 Jo Jo English .10 .03
❑ 60 Stanley Roberts .10 .03
❑ 61 Kevin Willis .10 .03
❑ 62 Dana Barros .10 .03
❑ 63 Gheorghe Muresan .10 .03
❑ 64 Vern Fleming .10 .03
❑ 65 Anthony Peeler .10 .03
❑ 66 Negele Knight .10 .03
❑ 67 Harold Ellis .10 .03
❑ 68 Vincent Askew .10 .03
❑ 69 Ennis Whatley .10 .03
❑ 70 Elden Campbell .10 .03
❑ 71 Sherman Douglas .10 .03
❑ 72 Luc Longley .10 .03
❑ 73 Lorenzo Williams .10 .03
❑ 74 Jay Humphries .10 .03
❑ 75 Chris King .10 .03
❑ 76 Tyrone Corbin .10 .03
❑ 77 Bobby Hurley .10 .03
❑ 78 Dell Curry .10 .03
❑ 79 Dino Radja .10 .03
❑ 80 A.C. Green .15 .04
❑ 81 Craig Ehlo .10 .03
❑ 82 Gary Payton .60 .18
❑ 83 Sleepy Floyd .10 .03
❑ 84 Rodney Rogers .10 .03
❑ 85 Brian Shaw .10 .03
❑ 86 Kevin Gamble .10 .03
❑ 87 John Stockton .40 .12
❑ 88 Hersey Hawkins .15 .04
❑ 89 Johnny Newman .10 .03
❑ 90 Larry Johnson .15 .04
❑ 91 Robert Pack .10 .03
❑ 92 Willie Burton .10 .03
❑ 93 Bobby Phills .10 .03
❑ 94 David Benoit .10 .03
❑ 95 Harold Miner .10 .03
❑ 96 David Robinson .60 .18
❑ 97 Nate McMillan .10 .03
❑ 98 Chris Mills .15 .04
❑ 99 Hubert Davis .10 .03
❑ 100 Shaquille O'Neal 2.00 .60
❑ 101 Loy Vaught .10 .03
❑ 102 Kenny Smith .10 .03
❑ 103 Terry Dehere .10 .03
❑ 104 Carl Herrera .10 .03
❑ 105 LaPhonso Ellis .10 .03
❑ 106 Armon Gilliam .10 .03
❑ 107 Greg Graham .10 .03
❑ 108 Eric Murdock .10 .03
❑ 109 Ron Harper .15 .04
❑ 110 Andrew Lang .10 .03
❑ 111 Johnny Dawkins .10 .03
❑ 112 David Wingate .10 .03
❑ 113 Tom Hammonds .10 .03
❑ 114 Brad Daugherty .10 .03
❑ 115 Charles Smith .10 .03
❑ 116 Dale Ellis .10 .03
❑ 117 Bryant Stith .10 .03
❑ 118 Lindsey Hunter .15 .04
❑ 119 Patrick Ewing .40 .12
❑ 120 Kenny Anderson .15 .04
❑ 121 Charles Barkley .60 .18
❑ 122 Harvey Grant .10 .03
❑ 123 Anthony Bowie .10 .03
❑ 124 Shawn Kemp .60 .18
❑ 125 Lee Mayberry .10 .03
❑ 126 Reggie Miller .40 .12
❑ 127 Scottie Pippen 1.25 .35
❑ 128 Spud Webb .10 .03
❑ 129 Antonio Davis .10 .03
❑ 130 Greg Anderson .10 .03
❑ 131 Jim Jackson .15 .04
❑ 132 Dikembe Mutombo .15 .04
❑ 133 Terry Porter .10 .03
❑ 134 Mario Elie .10 .03
❑ 135 Vlade Divac .10 .03
❑ 136 Robert Horry .15 .04
❑ 137 Popeye Jones .10 .03
❑ 138 Brad Lohaus .10 .03
❑ 139 Anthony Bonner .10 .03
❑ 140 Doug Christie .15 .04
❑ 141 Rony Seikaly .10 .03
❑ 142 Allan Houston .60 .18
❑ 143 Tyrone Hill .10 .03
❑ 144 Latrell Sprewell .40 .12
❑ 145 Andres Guibert .10 .03
❑ 146 Dominique Wilkins .40 .12
❑ 147 Jon Barry .10 .03
❑ 148 Tracy Murray .10 .03
❑ 149 Mike Peplowski .10 .03
❑ 150 Mike Brown .10 .03
❑ 151 Cedric Ceballos .10 .03
❑ 152 Stacey King .10 .03
❑ 153 Trevor Wilson .10 .03
❑ 154 Anthony Avent .10 .03
❑ 155 Horace Grant .15 .04
❑ 156 Bill Curley RC .10 .03
❑ 157 Grant Hill RC 2.00 .60
❑ 158 Charlie Ward RC .40 .12
❑ 159 Jalen Rose RC 1.50 .45
❑ 160 Jason Kidd RC 4.00 1.20
❑ 161 Yinka Dare RC .10 .03
❑ 162 Eric Montross RC .10 .03
❑ 163 Donyell Marshall RC .40 .12
❑ 164 Tony Dumas RC .10 .03
❑ 165 Wesley Person RC .40 .12
❑ 166 Eddie Jones RC 2.00 .60
❑ 167 Tim Hardaway USA .15 .04
❑ 168 Isiah Thomas USA .15 .04
❑ 169 Joe Dumars USA .15 .04
❑ 170 Mark Price USA .10 .03
❑ 171 Derrick Coleman USA .10 .03
❑ 172 Shawn Kemp USA .40 .12
❑ 173 Steve Smith USA .10 .03
❑ 174 Dan Majerle USA .10 .03
❑ 175 Reggie Miller USA .15 .04
❑ 176 Kevin Johnson USA .10 .03
❑ 177 Dominique Wilkins USA .15 .04
❑ 178 Shaquille O'Neal USA .75 .23
❑ 179 Alonzo Mourning USA .40 .12
❑ 180 Larry Johnson USA .10 .03
❑ 181 Brian Grant DA .15 .04
❑ 182 Darrin Hancock DA .10 .03
❑ 183 Grant Hill DA .75 .23
❑ 184 Jalen Rose DA .15 .04
❑ 185 Lamond Murray DA .10 .03
❑ 186 Jason Kidd DA 1.50 .45
❑ 187 Donyell Marshall DA .15 .04
❑ 188 Eddie Jones DA 1.00 .30
❑ 189 Eric Montross DA .10 .03
❑ 190 Khalid Reeves DA .10 .03
❑ 191 Sharone Wright DA .10 .03
❑ 192 Wesley Person DA .15 .04
❑ 193 Glenn Robinson DA .60 .18
❑ 194 Carlos Rogers DA .10 .03
❑ 195 Aaron McKie DA .15 .04
❑ 196 Juwan Howard DA .75 .23
❑ 197 Charlie Ward DA .15 .04
❑ 198 Brooks Thompson DA .10 .03
❑ 199 Tony Massenburg .10 .03
❑ 200 James Robinson .10 .03
❑ 201 Dickey Simpkins RC .10 .03
❑ 202 Johnny Dawkins .10 .03
❑ 203 Joe Kleine .10 .03
❑ 204 Bill Wennington .10 .03
❑ 205 Sean Higgins .10 .03
❑ 206 Larry Krystkowiak .10 .03
❑ 207 Winston Garland .10 .03
❑ 208 Muggsy Bogues .15 .04
❑ 209 Charles Oakley .10 .03
❑ 210 Vin Baker .40 .12
❑ 211 Malik Sealy .10 .03
❑ 212 Willie Anderson .10 .03
❑ 213 Dale Davis .10 .03
❑ 214 Grant Long .10 .03
❑ 215 Danny Ainge .10 .03
❑ 216 Toni Kukoc .60 .18
❑ 217 Doug Smith .10 .03
❑ 218 Danny Manning .15 .04
❑ 219 Otis Thorpe .10 .03
❑ 220 Mark Price .10 .03
❑ 221 Victor Alexander .10 .03
❑ 222 Brent Price .10 .03
❑ 223 Howard Eisley RC .10 .03
❑ 224 Chris Mullin .40 .12
❑ 225 Nick Van Exel .40 .12
❑ 226 Xavier McDaniel .10 .03
❑ 227 Khalid Reeves RC .10 .03
❑ 228 Anfernee Hardaway 1.00 .30
❑ 229 B.J. Tyler RC .10 .03
❑ 230 Elmore Spencer .10 .03
❑ 231 Rick Fox .10 .03
❑ 232 Alonzo Mourning .50 .15
❑ 233 Hakeem Olajuwon .60 .18
❑ 234 Blue Edwards .10 .03
❑ 235 P.J. Brown .10 .03
❑ 236 Ron Harper .15 .04
❑ 237 Isaiah Rider .15 .04
❑ 238 Eric Mobley RC .10 .03
❑ 239 Brian Williams .10 .03
❑ 240 Eric Piatkowski RC .10 .03
❑ 241 Karl Malone .60 .18
❑ 242 Wayman Tisdale .10 .03
❑ 243 Sarunas Marciulionis .10 .03
❑ 244 Sean Rooks .10 .03
❑ 245 Ricky Pierce .10 .03
❑ 246 Don MacLean .10 .03
❑ 247 Aaron McKie RC .75 .23
❑ 248 Kenny Gattison .10 .03
❑ 249 Derek Harper .10 .03
❑ 250 Michael Smith RC .10 .03
❑ 251 John Williams .10 .03
❑ 252 Pooh Richardson .10 .03
❑ 253 Sergei Bazarevich .10 .03
❑ 254 Brian Grant RC 1.00 .30
❑ 255 Ed Pinckney .10 .03
❑ 256 Ken Norman .10 .03
❑ 257 Marty Conlon .10 .03
❑ 258 Matt Fish .10 .03
❑ 259 Darrin Hancock RC .10 .03
❑ 260 Mahmoud Abdul-Rauf .10 .03
❑ 261 Roy Tarpley .10 .03
❑ 262 Chris Morris .10 .03
❑ 263 Sharone Wright RC .10 .03
❑ 264 Jamal Mashburn .40 .12
❑ 265 John Starks .10 .03
❑ 266 Rod Strickland .15 .04
❑ 267 Adam Keefe .10 .03
❑ 268 Scott Burrell .10 .03
❑ 269 Eric Riley .10 .03
❑ 270 Sam Perkins .15 .04
❑ 271 Stacey Augmon .10 .03
❑ 272 Kevin Willis .10 .03
❑ 273 Lamond Murray RC .15 .04
❑ 274 Derrick Coleman .15 .04
❑ 275 Scott Skiles .10 .03
❑ 276 Buck Williams .10 .03
❑ 277 Sam Cassell .40 .12
❑ 278 Rik Smits .10 .03
❑ 279 Dennis Rodman .75 .23
❑ 280 Olden Polynice .10 .03
❑ 281 Glenn Robinson RC 1.25 .35
❑ 282 Clarence Weatherspoon .10 .03
❑ 283 Monty Williams RC .10 .03
❑ 284 Terry Mills .10 .03
❑ 285 Oliver Miller .10 .03
❑ 286 Dennis Scott .10 .03
❑ 287 Micheal Williams .10 .03
❑ 288 Moses Malone .40 .12
❑ 289 Donald Royal .10 .03
❑ 290 Mark Jackson .10 .03
❑ 291 Walt Williams .10 .03
❑ 292 Bimbo Coles .10 .03
❑ 293 Derrick Alston RC .10 .03
❑ 294 Scott Williams .10 .03
❑ 295 Acie Earl .10 .03
❑ 296 Jeff Hornacek .15 .04
❑ 297 Kevin Duckworth .10 .03
❑ 298 Dontonio Wingfield RC .10 .03
❑ 299 Danny Ferry .10 .03
❑ 300 Mark West .10 .03
❑ 301 Jayson Williams .15 .04
❑ 302 David Wesley .10 .03
❑ 303 Jim McIlvaine RC .10 .03
❑ 304 Michael Adams .10 .03
❑ 305 Greg Minor RC .10 .03
❑ 306 Jeff Malone .10 .03
❑ 307 Pervis Ellison .10 .03
❑ 308 Clifford Rozier RC .10 .03
❑ 309 Billy Owens .10 .03
❑ 310 Duane Causwell .10 .03
❑ 311 Rex Chapman .10 .03
❑ 312 Detlef Schrempf .15 .04
❑ 313 Mitch Richmond .40 .12

❑ 314 Carlos Rogers RC .10 .03
❑ 315 Byron Scott .15 .04
❑ 316 Dwayne Morton .10 .03
❑ 317 Bill Cartwright .10 .03
❑ 318 J.R. Reid .10 .03
❑ 319 Derrick McKey .10 .03
❑ 320 Jamie Watson RC .10 .03
❑ 321 Mookie Blaylock .10 .03
❑ 322 Chris Webber 1.00 .30
❑ 323 Joe Dumars .40 .12
❑ 324 Shawn Bradley .10 .03
❑ 325 Chuck Person .10 .03
❑ 326 Haywoode Workman .10 .03
❑ 327 Benoit Benjamin .10 .03
❑ 328 Will Perdue .10 .03
❑ 329 Sam Mitchell .10 .03
❑ 330 George Lynch .10 .03
❑ 331 Juwan Howard RC 1.00 .30
❑ 332 Robert Parish .15 .04
❑ 333 Glen Rice .15 .04
❑ 334 Michael Cage .10 .03
❑ 335 Brooks Thompson RC .10 .03
❑ 336 Rony Seikaly .10 .03
❑ 337 Steve Kerr .10 .03
❑ 338 Anthony Miller RC .10 .03
❑ 339 Nick Anderson .10 .03
❑ 340 Clifford Robinson .15 .04
❑ 341 Todd Day .10 .03
❑ 342 Jon Koncak .10 .03
❑ 343 Felton Spencer .10 .03
❑ 344 Willie Burton .10 .03
❑ 345 Ledell Eackles .10 .03
❑ 346 Anthony Mason .15 .04
❑ 347 Derek Strong .10 .03
❑ 348 Reggie Williams .10 .03
❑ 349 Johnny Newman .10 .03
❑ 350 Terry Cummings .10 .03
❑ 351 Anthony Tucker RC .10 .03
❑ 352 Junior Bridgeman TN .10 .03
❑ 353 Jerry West TN .40 .12
❑ 354 Harvey Catchings TN .10 .03
❑ 355 John Lucas TN .15 .04
❑ 356 Bill Bradley TN .15 .04
❑ 357 Bill Walton TN .15 .04
❑ 358 Don Nelson TN .15 .04
❑ 359 Michael Jordan TN 2.50 .75
❑ 360 Tom(Satch) Sanders TN .10 .03

1995-96 Upper Deck

	Nm-Mt	Ex-Mt
COMPLETE SET (360)	50.00	15.00
COMPLETE SERIES 1 (180)	20.00	6.00
COMPLETE SERIES 2 (180)	30.00	9.00

❑ 1 Eddie Jones 1.00 .30
❑ 2 Hubert Davis .25 .07
❑ 3 Latrell Sprewell .75 .23
❑ 4 Stacey Augmon .25 .07
❑ 5 Mario Elie .25 .07
❑ 6 Tyrone Hill .25 .07
❑ 7 Dikembe Mutombo .50 .15
❑ 8 Antonio Davis .25 .07
❑ 9 Horace Grant .50 .15
❑ 10 Ken Norman .25 .07
❑ 11 Aaron McKie .50 .15
❑ 12 Vinny Del Negro .25 .07
❑ 13 Glenn Robinson .75 .23
❑ 14 Allan Houston .50 .15
❑ 15 Bryon Russell .25 .07
❑ 16 Tony Dumas .25 .07
❑ 17 Gary Payton .75 .23
❑ 18 Rik Smits .50 .15
❑ 19 Dino Radja .25 .07
❑ 20 Robert Pack .25 .07
❑ 21 Calbert Cheaney .25 .07
❑ 22 Clarence Weatherspoon .25 .07
❑ 23 Michael Jordan 5.00 1.50
❑ 24 Felton Spencer .25 .07
❑ 25 J.R. Reid .25 .07
❑ 26 Cedric Ceballos .25 .07
❑ 27 Dan Majerle .50 .15
❑ 28 Donald Hodge .25 .07
❑ 29 Nate McMillan .25 .07
❑ 30 Bimbo Coles .25 .07
❑ 31 Mitch Richmond .50 .15
❑ 32 Scott Brooks .25 .07
❑ 33 Patrick Ewing .75 .23
❑ 34 Carl Herrera .25 .07
❑ 35 Rick Fox .50 .15
❑ 36 James Robinson .25 .07
❑ 37 Donald Royal .25 .07
❑ 38 Joe Dumars .75 .23
❑ 39 Rony Seikaly .25 .07
❑ 40 Dennis Rodman .50 .15
❑ 41 Muggsy Bogues .50 .15
❑ 42 Gheorghe Muresan .25 .07
❑ 43 Ervin Johnson .25 .07
❑ 44 Todd Day .25 .07
❑ 45 Rex Walters .25 .07
❑ 46 Terrell Brandon .50 .15
❑ 47 Wesley Person .25 .07
❑ 48 Terry Dehere .25 .07
❑ 49 Steve Smith .50 .15
❑ 50 Brian Grant .75 .23
❑ 51 Eric Piatkowski .50 .15
❑ 52 Lindsey Hunter .25 .07
❑ 53 Chris Webber .75 .23
❑ 54 Antoine Carr .25 .07
❑ 55 Chris Dudley .25 .07
❑ 56 Clyde Drexler .75 .23
❑ 57 P.J. Brown .25 .07
❑ 58 Kevin Willis .50 .15
❑ 59 Jeff Turner .25 .07
❑ 60 Sean Elliott .50 .15
❑ 61 Kevin Johnson .50 .15
❑ 62 Scott Skiles .25 .07
❑ 63 Charles Smith .25 .07
❑ 64 Derrick McKey .25 .07
❑ 65 Danny Ferry .25 .07
❑ 66 Detlef Schrempf .50 .15
❑ 67 Shawn Bradley .25 .07
❑ 68 Isaiah Rider .25 .07
❑ 69 Karl Malone 1.00 .30
❑ 70 Will Perdue .25 .07
❑ 71 Terry Mills .25 .07
❑ 72 Glen Rice .50 .15
❑ 73 Tim Breaux .25 .07
❑ 74 Malik Sealy .25 .07
❑ 75 Walt Williams .25 .07
❑ 76 Bobby Phills .25 .07
❑ 77 Anthony Avent .25 .07
❑ 78 Jamal Mashburn UER .50 .15
Career FG percentage is wrong
❑ 79 Vlade Divac .50 .15
❑ 80 Reggie Williams .25 .07
❑ 81 Xavier McDaniel .25 .07
❑ 82 Avery Johnson .25 .07
❑ 83 Derek Harper .50 .15
❑ 84 Don MacLean .25 .07
❑ 85 Tom Gugliotta .25 .07
❑ 86 Craig Ehlo .25 .07
❑ 87 Robert Horry .50 .15
❑ 88 Kevin Edwards .25 .07
❑ 89 Chuck Person .25 .07
❑ 90 Sharone Wright .25 .07
❑ 91 Steve Kerr .50 .15
❑ 92 Marty Conlon .25 .07
❑ 93 Jalen Rose 1.00 .30
❑ 94 Bryant Reeves RC .75 .23
❑ 95 Shaquille O'Neal 2.00 .60
❑ 96 David Wesley .25 .07
❑ 97 Chris Mills .25 .07
❑ 98 Rod Strickland .25 .07
❑ 99 Pooh Richardson .25 .07
❑ 100 Sam Perkins .50 .15
❑ 101 Dell Curry .25 .07
❑ 102 David Benoit .25 .07
❑ 103 Christian Laettner .50 .15
❑ 104 Duane Causwell .25 .07
❑ 105 Jason Kidd 2.50 .75
❑ 106 Mark West .25 .07
❑ 107 Lee Mayberry .25 .07
❑ 108 John Salley .25 .07
❑ 109 Jeff Malone .25 .07
❑ 110 George Zidek RC .25 .07
❑ 111 Kenny Smith .25 .07
❑ 112 George Lynch .25 .07
❑ 113 Toni Kukoc .50 .15
❑ 114 A.C. Green .50 .15
❑ 115 Kenny Anderson .50 .15
❑ 116 Robert Parish .50 .15
❑ 117 Chris Mullin .75 .23
❑ 118 Loy Vaught .25 .07
❑ 119 Olden Polynice .25 .07
❑ 120 Clifford Robinson .25 .07
❑ 121 Eric Mobley .25 .07
❑ 122 Doug West .25 .07
❑ 123 Sam Cassell .75 .23
❑ 124 Nick Anderson .25 .07
❑ 125 Matt Geiger .25 .07
❑ 126 Elden Campbell .25 .07
❑ 127 Alonzo Mourning .50 .15
❑ 128 Bryant Stith .25 .07
❑ 129 Mark Jackson .50 .15
❑ 130 Cherokee Parks RC .25 .07
❑ 131 Shawn Respert RC .25 .07
❑ 132 Alan Henderson RC .75 .23
❑ 133 Jerry Stackhouse RC 2.50 .75
❑ 134 Rasheed Wallace RC 2.00 .60
❑ 135 Antonio McDyess RC 1.50 .45
❑ 136 Charles Barkley ROO .75 .23
❑ 137 Michael Jordan ROO 2.50 .75
❑ 138 Hakeem Olajuwon ROO .50 .15
❑ 139 Joe Dumars ROO .50 .15
❑ 140 Patrick Ewing ROO .50 .15
❑ 141 A.C. Green ROO .25 .07
❑ 142 Karl Malone ROO .75 .23
❑ 143 Detlef Schrempf ROO .25 .07
❑ 144 Chuck Person ROO .25 .07
❑ 145 Muggsy Bogues ROO .25 .07
❑ 146 Horace Grant ROO .25 .07
❑ 147 Mark Jackson ROO .25 .07
❑ 148 Kevin Johnson ROO .25 .07
❑ 149 Mitch Richmond ROO .25 .07
❑ 150 Rik Smits ROO .25 .07
❑ 151 Nick Anderson ROO .25 .07
❑ 152 Tim Hardaway ROO .25 .07
❑ 153 Shawn Kemp ROO .25 .07
❑ 154 David Robinson ROO .50 .15
❑ 155 Jason Kidd ART 1.25 .35
❑ 156 Grant Hill ART .75 .23
❑ 157 Glenn Robinson ART .50 .15
❑ 158 Eddie Jones ART .75 .23
❑ 159 Brian Grant ART .50 .15
❑ 160 Juwan Howard ART .50 .15
❑ 161 Eric Montross ART .25 .07
❑ 162 Wesley Person ART .25 .07
❑ 163 Jalen Rose ART .75 .23
❑ 164 Donyell Marshall ART .50 .15
❑ 165 Sharone Wright ART .25 .07
❑ 166 Karl Malone AN .75 .23
❑ 167 Scottie Pippen AN .50 .15
❑ 168 David Robinson AN .50 .15
❑ 169 John Stockton AN .75 .23
❑ 170 Anfernee Hardaway AN .50 .15
❑ 171 Charles Barkley AN .75 .23
❑ 172 Shawn Kemp AN .25 .07
❑ 173 Shaquille O'Neal AN .75 .23
❑ 174 Gary Payton AN .50 .15
❑ 175 Mitch Richmond AN .25 .07
❑ 176 Dennis Rodman AN .25 .07
❑ 177 Detlef Schrempf AN .25 .07
❑ 178 Hakeem Olajuwon AN .50 .15
❑ 179 Reggie Miller AN .50 .15
❑ 180 Clyde Drexler AN .50 .15
❑ 181 Hakeem Olajuwon .75 .23
❑ 182 Vin Baker .50 .15
❑ 183 Jeff Hornacek .50 .15
❑ 184 Popeye Jones .25 .07
❑ 185 Sedale Threatt .25 .07
❑ 186 Scottie Pippen 1.25 .35

❑	Card	Nm-Mt	Ex-Mt
❑	187 Terry Porter	.25	.07
❑	188 Dan Majerle	.50	.15
❑	189 Clifford Rozier	.25	.07
❑	190 Greg Minor	.25	.07
❑	191 Dennis Scott	.25	.07
❑	192 Hersey Hawkins	.25	.07
❑	193 Chris Gatling	.25	.07
❑	194 Charles Oakley	.25	.07
❑	195 Dale Davis	.25	.07
❑	196 Robert Pack	.25	.07
❑	197 Lamond Murray	.25	.07
❑	198 Mookie Blaylock	.25	.07
❑	199 Dickey Simpkins	.25	.07
❑	200 Kevin Gamble	.25	.07
❑	201 Lorenzo Williams	.25	.07
❑	202 Scott Burrell	.25	.07
❑	203 Armon Gilliam	.25	.07
❑	204 Doc Rivers	.50	.15
❑	205 Blue Edwards	.25	.07
❑	206 Billy Owens	.25	.07
❑	207 Juwan Howard	.75	.23
❑	208 Harvey Grant	.25	.07
❑	209 Richard Dumas	.25	.07
❑	210 Anthony Peeler	.25	.07
❑	211 Matt Geiger	.25	.07
❑	212 Lucious Harris	.25	.07
❑	213 Grant Long	.25	.07
❑	214 Sasha Danilovic RC	.25	.07
❑	215 Chris Morris	.25	.07
❑	216 Donyell Marshall	.50	.15
❑	217 Alonzo Mourning	.50	.15
❑	218 John Stockton	1.00	.30
❑	219 Khalid Reeves	.25	.07
❑	220 Mahmoud Abdul-Rauf	.25	.07
❑	221 Sean Rooks	.25	.07
❑	222 Shawn Kemp	.50	.15
❑	223 John Williams	.25	.07
❑	224 Dee Brown	.25	.07
❑	225 Jim Jackson	.25	.07
❑	226 Harold Miner	.25	.07
❑	227 B.J. Armstrong	.25	.07
❑	228 Elliot Perry	.25	.07
❑	229 Anthony Miller	.25	.07
❑	230 Donny Marshall RC	.25	.07
❑	231 Tyrone Corbin	.25	.07
❑	232 Anthony Mason	.50	.15
❑	233 Grant Hill	1.00	.30
❑	234 Buck Williams	.25	.07
❑	235 Brian Shaw	.25	.07
❑	236 Dale Ellis	.25	.07
❑	237 Magic Johnson	1.25	.35
❑	238 Eric Montross	.25	.07
❑	239 Rex Chapman	.25	.07
❑	240 Otis Thorpe	.25	.07
❑	241 Tracy Murray	.25	.07
❑	242 Sarunas Marciulionis	.25	.07
❑	243 Luc Longley	.25	.07
❑	244 Elmore Spencer	.25	.07
❑	245 Terry Cummings	.25	.07
❑	246 Sam Mitchell	.25	.07
❑	247 Terrence Rencher RC	.25	.07
❑	248 Byron Houston	.25	.07
❑	249 Pervis Ellison	.25	.07
❑	250 Carlos Rogers	.25	.07
❑	251 Kendall Gill	.25	.07
❑	252 Sherrell Ford RC	.25	.07
❑	253 Michael Finley RC	3.00	.90
❑	254 Kurt Thomas RC	.50	.15
❑	255 Joe Smith RC	1.25	.35
❑	256 Bobby Hurley	.25	.07
❑	257 Greg Anthony	.25	.07
❑	258 Willie Anderson	.25	.07
❑	259 Theo Ratliff RC	1.00	.30
❑	260 Duane Ferrell	.25	.07
❑	261 Antonio Harvey	.25	.07
❑	262 Gary Grant	.25	.07
❑	263 Brian Williams	.25	.07
❑	264 Danny Manning	.50	.15
❑	265 Micheal Williams	.25	.07
❑	266 Dennis Rodman	.50	.15
❑	267 Arvydas Sabonis RC	1.00	.30
❑	268 Don MacLean	.25	.07
❑	269 Keith Askins	.25	.07
❑	270 Reggie Miller	.75	.23
❑	271 Ed Pinckney	.25	.07
❑	272 Bob Sura RC	.50	.15
❑	273 Kevin Garnett RC	5.00	1.50
❑	274 Byron Scott	.25	.07
❑	275 Mario Bennett RC	.25	.07
❑	276 Junior Burrough RC	.25	.07
❑	277 Anfernee Hardaway	.75	.23
❑	278 George McCloud	.25	.07
❑	279 Loren Meyer RC	.25	.07
❑	280 Ed O'Bannon RC	.25	.07
❑	281 Lawrence Moten RC	.25	.07
❑	282 Dana Barros	.25	.07
❑	283 Damon Stoudamire RC	1.50	.45
❑	284 Eric Williams RC	.50	.15
❑	285 Wayman Tisdale	.25	.07
❑	286 Rodney Rogers	.25	.07
❑	287 Sherman Douglas	.25	.07
❑	288 Greg Ostertag RC	.25	.07
❑	289 Alvin Robertson	.25	.07
❑	290 Tim Legler	.25	.07
❑	291 Zan Tabak	.25	.07
❑	292 Gary Trent RC	.25	.07
❑	293 Haywoode Workman	.25	.07
❑	294 Charles Barkley	1.00	.30
❑	295 Derrick Coleman	.25	.07
❑	296 Ricky Pierce	.25	.07
❑	297 Benoit Benjamin	.25	.07
❑	298 Larry Johnson	.50	.15
❑	299 Travis Best RC	.25	.07
❑	300 Jason Caffey RC	.50	.15
❑	301 Cory Alexander RC	.25	.07
❑	302 Nick Van Exel	.75	.23
❑	303 Corliss Williamson RC	.75	.23
❑	304 Eric Murdock	.25	.07
❑	305 Tyus Edney RC	.25	.07
❑	306 Lou Roe RC	.25	.07
❑	307 John Salley	.25	.07
❑	308 Spud Webb	.50	.15
❑	309 Brent Barry RC	.75	.23
❑	310 David Robinson	.75	.23
❑	311 Glen Rice	.50	.15
❑	312 Chris King	.25	.07
❑	313 David Vaughn RC	.25	.07
❑	314 Kenny Gattison	.25	.07
❑	315 Randolph Childress RC	.25	.07
❑	316 Anfernee Hardaway USA	.50	.15
❑	317 Grant Hill USA	.75	.23
❑	318 Karl Malone USA	.75	.23
❑	319 Reggie Miller USA	.50	.15
❑	320 Hakeem Olajuwon USA	.50	.15
❑	321 Shaquille O'Neal USA	.75	.23
❑	322 Scottie Pippen USA	.50	.15
❑	323 David Robinson USA	.50	.15
❑	324 Glenn Robinson USA	.50	.15
❑	325 John Stockton USA	.75	.23
❑	326 Cedric Ceballos I95	.25	.07
❑	327 Shaquille O'Neal I95	.75	.23
❑	328 Glenn Robinson I95	.50	.15
❑	329 Shawn Kemp I95	.25	.07
❑	330 Nick Anderson I95	.25	.07
❑	331 Shawn Bradley I95	.25	.07
❑	332 Horace Grant I95	.25	.07
	Brooks Thompson		
❑	333 Robert Horry I95	.50	.15
❑	334 NBA Expansion I95	.25	.07
	Grizzlies/Raptors		
❑	335 Michael Jordan I95	2.50	.75
❑	336 Nick Van Exel	.25	.07
	Dyan Cannon MA		
❑	337 Michael Jordan	1.25	.35
	David Hanson MA		
❑	338 Scottie Pippen	.75	.23
	Jenna Von Oy MA		
❑	339 Michael Jordan	1.25	.35
	Charlie Sheen MA		
❑	340 Jason Kidd	.75	.23
	Christopher "Kid" Reid MA		
❑	341 Michael Jordan	1.25	.35
	Queen Latifah MA		
❑	342 Charles Barkley	.75	.23
	Don Johnson MA		
❑	343 Hakeem Olajuwon	.75	.23
	Corbin Bernsen MA		
❑	344 Ahmad Rashad MA	.25	.07
❑	345 Willow Bay MA	.25	.07
❑	346 Gary Payton	.75	.23
	Mark Curry MA		
❑	347 Horace Grant SJ	.25	.07
❑	348 Juwan Howard SJ	.50	.15
❑	349 David Robinson SJ	.50	.15
❑	350 Reggie Miller SJ	.50	.15
❑	351 Brian Grant SJ	.50	.15
❑	352 Michael Jordan SJ	2.50	.75
❑	353 Cedric Ceballos SJ	.25	.07
❑	354 Blue Edwards SJ	.25	.07
❑	355 Acie Earl SJ	.25	.07
❑	356 Dennis Rodman SJ	.25	.07
❑	357 Shawn Kemp SJ	.25	.07
❑	358 Jerry Stackhouse SJ	1.25	.35
❑	359 Jamal Mashburn SJ	.25	.07
❑	360 Antonio McDyess SJ	.75	.23

1996-97 Upper Deck

	Nm-Mt	Ex-Mt
COMPLETE SET (360)	50.00	15.00
COMPLETE SERIES 1 (180)	30.00	9.00
COMPLETE SERIES 2 (180)	20.00	6.00

❑	Card	Nm-Mt	Ex-Mt
❑	1 Mookie Blaylock	.25	.07
❑	2 Alan Henderson	.25	.07
❑	3 Christian Laettner	.50	.15
❑	4 Ken Norman	.25	.07
❑	5 Dee Brown	.25	.07
❑	6 Todd Day	.25	.07
❑	7 Rick Fox	.25	.07
❑	8 Dino Radja	.25	.07
❑	9 Dana Barros	.25	.07
❑	10 Eric Williams	.25	.07
❑	11 Scott Burrell	.25	.07
❑	12 Dell Curry	.25	.07
❑	13 Matt Geiger	.25	.07
❑	14 Glen Rice	.50	.15
❑	15 Ron Harper	.50	.15
❑	16 Michael Jordan	5.00	1.50
❑	17 Luc Longley	.25	.07
❑	18 Toni Kukoc	.50	.15
❑	19 Dennis Rodman	.50	.15
❑	20 Danny Ferry	.25	.07
❑	21 Tyrone Hill	.25	.07
❑	22 Bobby Phills	.25	.07
❑	23 Bob Sura	.25	.07
❑	24 Tony Dumas	.25	.07
❑	25 George McCloud	.25	.07
❑	26 Jim Jackson	.25	.07
❑	27 Jamal Mashburn	.50	.15
❑	28 Loren Meyer	.25	.07
❑	29 Dale Ellis	.25	.07
❑	30 LaPhonso Ellis	.25	.07
❑	31 Tom Hammonds	.25	.07
❑	32 Antonio McDyess	.50	.15
❑	33 Joe Dumars	.75	.23
❑	34 Grant Hill	.75	.23
❑	35 Lindsey Hunter	.25	.07
❑	36 Terry Mills	.25	.07
❑	37 Theo Ratliff	.50	.15
❑	38 B.J. Armstrong	.25	.07
❑	39 Donyell Marshall	.50	.15
❑	40 Chris Mullin	.75	.23
❑	41 Rony Seikaly	.25	.07
❑	42 Joe Smith	.50	.15
❑	43 Sam Cassell	.75	.23
❑	44 Clyde Drexler	.75	.23
❑	45 Mario Elie	.25	.07
❑	46 Robert Horry	.50	.15
❑	47 Travis Best	.25	.07
❑	48 Antonio Davis	.25	.07
❑	49 Dale Davis	.25	.07

❑ 50 Eddie Johnson .25 .07
❑ 51 Derrick McKey .25 .07
❑ 52 Reggie Miller .75 .23
❑ 53 Brent Barry .25 .07
❑ 54 Lamond Murray .25 .07
❑ 55 Eric Piatkowski .50 .15
❑ 56 Rodney Rogers .25 .07
❑ 57 Loy Vaught .25 .07
❑ 58 Kobe Bryant RC 10.00 3.00
❑ 59 Eddie Jones .75 .23
❑ 60 Elden Campbell .25 .07
❑ 61 Shaquille O'Neal 2.00 .60
❑ 62 Nick Van Exel .75 .23
❑ 63 Keith Askins .25 .07
❑ 64 Rex Chapman .25 .07
❑ 65 Sasha Danilovic .25 .07
❑ 66 Alonzo Mourning .50 .15
❑ 67 Kurt Thomas .50 .15
❑ 68 Tim Hardaway .50 .15
❑ 69 Ray Allen RC 2.50 .75
❑ 70 Johnny Newman .25 .07
❑ 71 Shawn Respert .25 .07
❑ 72 Glenn Robinson .75 .23
❑ 73 Tom Gugliotta .25 .07
❑ 74 Stephon Marbury RC 2.00 .60
❑ 75 Terry Porter .25 .07
❑ 76 Doug West .25 .07
❑ 77 Shawn Bradley .25 .07
❑ 78 Kevin Edwards .25 .07
❑ 79 Vern Fleming .25 .07
❑ 80 Ed O'Bannon .25 .07
❑ 81 Jayson Williams .50 .15
❑ 82 John Starks .50 .15
❑ 83 Patrick Ewing .75 .23
❑ 84 Charlie Ward .25 .07
❑ 85 Nick Anderson .25 .07
❑ 86 Anfernee Hardaway .75 .23
❑ 87 Jon Koncak .25 .07
❑ 88 Donald Royal .25 .07
❑ 89 Brian Shaw .25 .07
❑ 90 Derrick Coleman .50 .15
❑ 91 Allen Iverson RC 5.00 1.50
❑ 92 Jerry Stackhouse 1.00 .30
❑ 93 Clarence Weatherspoon .25 .07
❑ 94 Charles Barkley 1.00 .30
❑ 95 Kevin Johnson .50 .15
❑ 96 Danny Manning .50 .15
❑ 97 Elliot Perry .25 .07
❑ 98 Wayman Tisdale .25 .07
❑ 99 Randolph Childress .25 .07
❑ 100 Aaron McKie .50 .15
❑ 101 Arvydas Sabonis .50 .15
❑ 102 Gary Trent .25 .07
❑ 103 Chris Dudley .25 .07
❑ 104 Tyus Edney .25 .07
❑ 105 Brian Grant .75 .23
❑ 106 Bobby Hurley .25 .07
❑ 107 Olden Polynice .25 .07
❑ 108 Corliss Williamson .50 .15
❑ 109 Vinny Del Negro .25 .07
❑ 110 Avery Johnson .25 .07
❑ 111 Will Perdue .25 .07
❑ 112 David Robinson .75 .23
❑ 113 Hersey Hawkins .50 .15
❑ 114 Shawn Kemp .50 .15
❑ 115 Nate McMillan .25 .07
❑ 116 Detlef Schrempf .50 .15
❑ 117 Gary Payton .75 .23
❑ 118 Marcus Camby RC 1.00 .30
❑ 119 Zan Tabak .25 .07
❑ 120 Damon Stoudamire .75 .23
❑ 121 Carlos Rogers .25 .07
❑ 122 Sharone Wright .25 .07
❑ 123 Antoine Carr .25 .07
❑ 124 Jeff Hornacek .50 .15
❑ 125 Adam Keefe .25 .07
❑ 126 Chris Morris .25 .07
❑ 127 John Stockton .75 .23
❑ 128 Blue Edwards .25 .07
❑ 129 Shareef Abdur-Rahim RC 2.50 .75
❑ 130 Bryant Reeves .25 .07
❑ 131 Roy Rogers RC .25 .07
❑ 132 Calbert Cheaney .25 .07
❑ 133 Tim Legler .25 .07
❑ 134 Gheorghe Muresan .25 .07
❑ 135 Chris Webber .75 .23
❑ 136 Dikembe Mutombo .75 .23
    Mookie Blaylock
    Steve Smith
    Christian Laettner
    Alan Henderson
❑ 137 Dana Barros .25 .07
    Dino Radja
    Eric Williams
    Dee Brown
    Pervis Ellison
❑ 138 Glen Rice .75 .23
    Matt Geiger
    Vlade Divac
    Scott Burrell
    George Zidek
❑ 139 Michael Jordan 2.00 .60
    Scottie Pippen
    Dennis Rodman
    Toni Kukoc
    Ron Harper
❑ 140 Terrell Brandon .50 .15
    Danny Ferry
    Tyrone Hill
    Bobby Phills
    Bobby Sura
❑ 141 Jason Kidd .50 .15
    Jamal Mashburn
    Jim Jackson
    Tony Dumas
    Loren Meyer
❑ 142 LaPhonso Ellis .25 .07
    Antonio McDyess
    Mark Jackson
    Dale Ellis
    Bryant Stith
❑ 143 Joe Dumars .75 .23
    Grant Hill
    Stacey Augmon
    Lindsey Hunter
    Theo Ratliff
❑ 144 Joe Smith .75 .23
    Latrell Sprewell
    Chris Mullin
    Rony Seikaly
    BJ Armstrong
❑ 145 Hakeem Olajuwon .75 .23
    Clyde Drexler
    Charles Barkley
    Brent Price
    Mario Elie
❑ 146 Reggie Miller .50 .15
    Travis Best
    Rik Smits
    Dale Davis
    Antonio Davis
❑ 147 Brent Barry .25 .07
    Lamond Murray
    Rodney Rogers
    Terry Dehere
    Eric Piatkowski
❑ 148 Shaquille O'Neal 1.50 .45
    Eddie Jones
    Kobe Bryant
    Cedric Ceballos
    Nick Van Exel
❑ 149 Alonzo Mourning .75 .23
    Tim Hardaway
    Sasha Danilovic
    Kurt Thomas
    Keith Askins
❑ 150 Vin Baker .75 .23
    Glenn Robinson
    Sherman Douglas
    Shawn Respert
    Johnnie Newman
❑ 151 Kevin Garnett .75 .23
    Tom Gugliotta
    Cherokee Parks
    Terry Porter
    Doug West
❑ 152 Shawn Bradley .50 .15
    Kendall Gill
    Ed O'Bannon
    Jayson Williams
    Robert Pack
❑ 153 Patrick Ewing .75 .23
    Allan Houston
    Larry Johnson
    Charles Oakley
    John Starks
❑ 154 Anfernee Hardaway .50 .15
    Dennis Scott
    Horace Grant
    Nick Anderson
    Brian Shaw
❑ 155 Jerry Stackhouse .50 .15
    Clarence Weatherspoon
    Derrick Coleman
    Scott Williams
    Rex Walters
❑ 156 Kevin Johnson .50 .15
    Danny Manning
    Michael Finley
    Wesley Person
    A.C. Green
❑ 157 Clifford Robinson .50 .15
    Isaiah Rider
    Arvydas Sabonis
    Rasheed Wallace
    Kenny Anderson
❑ 158 Mitch Richmond .50 .15
    Brian Grant
    Billy Owens
    Tyus Edney
    Michael Smith
❑ 159 David Robinson .75 .23
    Sean Elliott
    Avery Johnson
    Vinny Del Negro
    Chuck Person
❑ 160 Shawn Kemp .50 .15
    Gary Payton
    Detlef Schrempf
    Hersey Hawkins
    Sam Perkins
❑ 161 Damon Stoudamire .75 .23
    Zan Tabak
    Sharone Wright
    Doug Christie
    Carlos Rogers
❑ 162 John Stockton .75 .23
    Karl Malone
    Jeff Hornacek
    Bryon Russell
    Antoine Carr
❑ 163 Bryant Reeves .75 .23
    Shareef Abdur-Rahim
    Greg Anthony
    Blue Edwards
    Lawrence Moten
❑ 164 Juwan Howard .75 .23
    Gheorge Muresan
    Chris Webber
    Calbert Cheaney
    Tim Legler
❑ 165 Michael Jordan GP 2.50 .75
❑ 166 Corliss Williamson GP .25 .07
❑ 167 Dell Curry GP .25 .07
❑ 168 John Starks GP .25 .07
❑ 169 Dennis Rodman GP .25 .07
❑ 170 Chris Webber .75 .23
    Latrell Sprewell
❑ 171 Cedric Ceballos GP .25 .07
❑ 172 Theo Ratliff GP .25 .07
❑ 173 Anfernee Hardaway GP .50 .15
❑ 174 Grant Hill GP .75 .23
❑ 175 Alonzo Mourning GP .25 .07
❑ 176 Shawn Kemp GP .25 .07
❑ 177 Jason Kidd GP .75 .23
❑ 178 Avery Johnson GP .25 .07
❑ 179 Gary Payton GP .50 .15
❑ 180 Checklist .25 .07
❑ 181 Priest Lauderdale RC .25 .07
❑ 182 Dikembe Mutombo .50 .15
❑ 183 Eldridge Recasner RC .25 .07
❑ 184 Steve Smith .50 .15
❑ 185 Pervis Ellison .25 .07
❑ 186 Greg Minor .25 .07
❑ 187 Antoine Walker RC 2.50 .75
❑ 188 David Wesley .25 .07
❑ 189 Muggsy Bogues .25 .07
❑ 190 Tony Delk RC .75 .23

		Nm-Mt	Ex-Mt
❑ 191	Vlade Divac	.25	.07
❑ 192	Anthony Mason	.50	.15
❑ 193	George Zidek	.25	.07
❑ 194	Jason Caffey	.25	.07
❑ 195	Steve Kerr	.50	.15
❑ 196	Robert Parish	.50	.15
❑ 197	Scottie Pippen	1.25	.35
❑ 198	Terrell Brandon	.50	.15
❑ 199	Antonio Lang	.25	.07
❑ 200	Chris Mills	.25	.07
❑ 201	Vitaly Potapenko RC	.25	.07
❑ 202	Mark West	.25	.07
❑ 203	Chris Gatling	.25	.07
❑ 204	Derek Harper	.25	.07
❑ 205	Sam Cassell	.75	.23
❑ 206	Eric Montross	.25	.07
❑ 207	Samaki Walker RC	.25	.07
❑ 208	Mark Jackson	.25	.07
❑ 209	Ervin Johnson	.25	.07
❑ 210	Sarunas Marciulionis	.25	.07
❑ 211	Ricky Pierce	.25	.07
❑ 212	Bryant Stith	.25	.07
❑ 213	Stacey Augmon	.25	.07
❑ 214	Grant Long	.25	.07
❑ 215	Rick Mahorn	.25	.07
❑ 216	Otis Thorpe	.25	.07
❑ 217	Jerome Williams RC	.75	.23
❑ 218	Bimbo Coles	.25	.07
❑ 219	Todd Fuller RC	.25	.07
❑ 220	Mark Price	.50	.15
❑ 221	Felton Spencer	.25	.07
❑ 222	Latrell Sprewell	.75	.23
❑ 223	Charles Barkley	1.00	.30
❑ 224	Othella Harrington RC	.75	.23
❑ 225	Hakeem Olajuwon	.75	.23
❑ 226	Matt Maloney RC	.50	.15
❑ 227	Kevin Willis	.25	.07
❑ 228	Erick Dampier RC	.75	.23
❑ 229	Duane Ferrell	.25	.07
❑ 230	Jalen Rose	.75	.23
❑ 231	Rik Smits	.50	.15
❑ 232	Terry Dehere	.25	.07
❑ 233	Bo Outlaw	.25	.07
❑ 234	Pooh Richardson	.25	.07
❑ 235	Malik Sealy	.25	.07
❑ 236	Lorenzen Wright RC	.50	.15
❑ 237	Cedric Ceballos	.25	.07
❑ 238	Derek Fisher RC	1.25	.35
❑ 239	Travis Knight RC	.25	.07
❑ 240	Sean Rooks	.25	.07
❑ 241	Byron Scott	.25	.07
❑ 242	P.J. Brown	.25	.07
❑ 243	Voshon Lenard RC	.50	.15
❑ 244	Dan Majerle	.50	.15
❑ 245	Martin Muursepp RC	.25	.07
❑ 246	Gary Grant	.25	.07
❑ 247	Vin Baker	.50	.15
❑ 248	Armon Gilliam	.25	.07
❑ 249	Andrew Lang	.25	.07
❑ 250	Elliot Perry	.25	.07
❑ 251	Kevin Garnett	1.50	.45
❑ 252	Shane Heal RC	.25	.07
❑ 253	Cherokee Parks	.25	.07
❑ 254	Stojko Vrankovic	.25	.07
❑ 255	Kendall Gill	.25	.07
❑ 256	Kerry Kittles RC	.75	.23
❑ 257	Xavier McDaniel	.25	.07
❑ 258	Robert Pack	.25	.07
❑ 259	Chris Childs	.25	.07
❑ 260	Allan Houston	.50	.15
❑ 261	Larry Johnson	.50	.15
❑ 262	Dontae' Jones RC	.25	.07
❑ 263	Walter McCarty RC	.25	.07
❑ 264	Charles Oakley	.25	.07
❑ 265	John Wallace RC	.75	.23
❑ 266	Buck Williams	.25	.07
❑ 267	Brian Evans RC	.25	.07
❑ 268	Horace Grant	.50	.15
❑ 269	Dennis Scott	.25	.07
❑ 270	Rony Seikaly	.25	.07
❑ 271	David Vaughn	.25	.07
❑ 272	Michael Cage	.25	.07
❑ 273	Lucious Harris	.25	.07
❑ 274	Don MacLean	.25	.07
❑ 275	Mark Davis	.25	.07
❑ 276	Jason Kidd	1.25	.35

		Nm-Mt	Ex-Mt
❑ 277	Michael Finley	1.00	.30
❑ 278	A.C. Green	.50	.15
❑ 279	Robert Horry	.50	.15
❑ 280	Steve Nash RC	2.00	.60
❑ 281	Wesley Person	.25	.07
❑ 282	Kenny Anderson	.25	.07
❑ 283	Aleksandar Djordjevic RC	.25	.07
❑ 284	Jermaine O'Neal RC	2.50	.75
❑ 285	Isaiah Rider	.50	.15
❑ 286	Clifford Robinson	.25	.07
❑ 287	Rasheed Wallace	1.00	.30
❑ 288	Mahmoud Abdul-Rauf	.25	.07
❑ 289	Billy Owens	.25	.07
❑ 290	Mitch Richmond	.50	.15
❑ 291	Michael Smith	.25	.07
❑ 292	Cory Alexander	.25	.07
❑ 293	Sean Elliott	.50	.15
❑ 294	Vernon Maxwell	.25	.07
❑ 295	Dominique Wilkins	.75	.23
❑ 296	Craig Ehlo	.25	.07
❑ 297	Jim McIlvaine	.25	.07
❑ 298	Sam Perkins	.50	.15
❑ 299	Steve Scheffler RC	.25	.07
❑ 300	Hubert Davis	.25	.07
❑ 301	Popeye Jones	.25	.07
❑ 302	Donald Whiteside RC	.25	.07
❑ 303	Walt Williams	.25	.07
❑ 304	Karl Malone	.75	.23
❑ 305	Greg Ostertag	.25	.07
❑ 306	Bryon Russell	.25	.07
❑ 307	Jamie Watson	.25	.07
❑ 308	Greg Anthony	.25	.07
❑ 309	George Lynch	.25	.07
❑ 310	Lawrence Moten	.25	.07
❑ 311	Anthony Peeler	.25	.07
❑ 312	Juwan Howard	.50	.15
❑ 313	Tracy Murray	.25	.07
❑ 314	Rod Strickland	.25	.07
❑ 315	Harvey Grant	.25	.07
❑ 316	Charles Barkley DN	.75	.23
❑ 317	Clyde Drexler DN	.50	.15
❑ 318	Dikembe Mutombo DN	.25	.07
❑ 319	Larry Johnson DN	.25	.07
❑ 320	Shaquille O'Neal DN	.75	.23
❑ 321	Mookie Blaylock DN	.25	.07
❑ 322	Tim Hardaway DN	.25	.07
❑ 323	Dennis Rodman DN	.25	.07
❑ 324	Dan Majerle DN	.25	.07
❑ 325	Stacey Augmon DN	.25	.07
❑ 326	Anthony Mason DN	.25	.07
❑ 327	Kenny Anderson DN	.25	.07
❑ 328	Mahmoud Abdul-Rauf DN	.25	.07
❑ 329	Chris Webber DN	.75	.23
❑ 330	Dominique Wilkins DN	.50	.15
❑ 331	Dikembe Mutombo WD	.25	.07
❑ 332	Dana Barros WD	.25	.07
❑ 333	Glen Rice WD	.25	.07
❑ 334	Dennis Rodman WD	.25	.07
❑ 335	Terrell Brandon WD	.25	.07
❑ 336	Jason Kidd WD	.75	.23
❑ 337	Antonio McDyess WD	.50	.15
❑ 338	Grant Hill WD	.75	.23
❑ 339	Joe Smith WD	.25	.07
❑ 340	Charles Barkley WD	.75	.23
❑ 341	Reggie Miller WD	.50	.15
❑ 342	Brent Barry WD	.25	.07
❑ 343	Shaquille O'Neal WD	.75	.23
❑ 344	Alonzo Mourning WD	.25	.07
❑ 345	Glenn Robinson WD	.50	.15
❑ 346	Stephon Marbury WD	1.50	.45
❑ 347	Kerry Kittles WD	.75	.23
❑ 348	Patrick Ewing WD	.50	.15
❑ 349	Anfernee Hardaway WD	.50	.15
❑ 350	Allen Iverson WD	2.00	.60
❑ 351	Danny Manning WD	.25	.07
❑ 352	Arvydas Sabonis WD	.25	.07
❑ 353	Mitch Richmond WD	.25	.07
❑ 354	David Robinson WD	.50	.15
❑ 355	Shawn Kemp WD	.25	.07
❑ 356	Marcus Camby WD	.50	.15
❑ 357	Karl Malone WD	.75	.23
❑ 358	S.Abdur-Rahim WD	1.25	.35
❑ 359	Gheorghe Muresan WD	.25	.07
❑ 360	Checklist 181-360	.25	.07

1997-98 Upper Deck

		Nm-Mt	Ex-Mt
COMPLETE SET (360)		50.00	15.00
COMPLETE SERIES 1 (180)		25.00	7.50
COMPLETE SERIES 2 (180)		25.00	7.50
❑ 1	Steve Smith	.50	.15
❑ 2	Christian Laettner	.50	.15
❑ 3	Alan Henderson	.25	.07
❑ 4	Dikembe Mutombo	.50	.15
❑ 5	Dana Barros	.25	.07
❑ 6	Antoine Walker	1.00	.30
❑ 7	Dee Brown	.25	.07
❑ 8	Eric Williams	.25	.07
❑ 9	Muggsy Bogues	.50	.15
❑ 10	Dell Curry	.25	.07
❑ 11	Vlade Divac	.50	.15
❑ 12	Anthony Mason	.50	.15
❑ 13	Glen Rice	.50	.15
❑ 14	Jason Caffey	.25	.07
❑ 15	Steve Kerr	.50	.15
❑ 16	Toni Kukoc	.50	.15
❑ 17	Luc Longley	.25	.07
❑ 18	Michael Jordan	5.00	1.50
❑ 19	Terrell Brandon	.50	.15
❑ 20	Danny Ferry	.25	.07
❑ 21	Tyrone Hill	.25	.07
❑ 22	Derek Anderson RC	1.50	.45
❑ 23	Bob Sura	.25	.07
❑ 24	Eric Williams	.25	.07
❑ 25	Michael Finley	.75	.23
❑ 26	Ed O'Bannon	.25	.07
❑ 27	Robert Pack	.25	.07
❑ 28	Samaki Walker	.25	.07
❑ 29	LaPhonso Ellis	.25	.07
❑ 30	Tony Battie RC	.75	.23
❑ 31	Antonio McDyess	.50	.15
❑ 32	Bryant Stith	.25	.07
❑ 33	Randolph Childress	.25	.07
❑ 34	Grant Hill	.75	.23
❑ 35	Lindsey Hunter	.25	.07
❑ 36	Grant Long	.25	.07
❑ 37	Theo Ratliff	.25	.07
❑ 38	B.J. Armstrong	.25	.07
❑ 39	Adonal Foyle RC	.50	.15
❑ 40	Mark Price	.50	.15
❑ 41	Felton Spencer	.25	.07
❑ 42	Latrell Sprewell	.75	.23
❑ 43	Clyde Drexler	.75	.23
❑ 44	Mario Elie	.25	.07
❑ 45	Hakeem Olajuwon	.75	.23
❑ 46	Brent Price	.25	.07
❑ 47	Kevin Willis	.50	.15
❑ 48	Erick Dampier	.50	.15
❑ 49	Antonio Davis	.25	.07
❑ 50	Dale Davis	.25	.07
❑ 51	Mark Jackson	.50	.15
❑ 52	Rik Smits	.50	.15
❑ 53	Brent Barry	.50	.15
❑ 54	Lamond Murray	.25	.07
❑ 55	Eric Piatkowski	.50	.15
❑ 56	Loy Vaught	.25	.07
❑ 57	Lorenzen Wright	.25	.07
❑ 58	Kobe Bryant	3.00	.90
❑ 59	Elden Campbell	.25	.07
❑ 60	Derek Fisher	.75	.23
❑ 61	Eddie Jones	.75	.23
❑ 62	Nick Van Exel	.75	.23

❑ 63 Keith Askins .25 .07
❑ 64 Isaac Austin .25 .07
❑ 65 P.J. Brown .25 .07
❑ 66 Tim Hardaway .50 .15
❑ 67 Alonzo Mourning .50 .15
❑ 68 Ray Allen .75 .23
❑ 69 Vin Baker .50 .15
❑ 70 Sherman Douglas .25 .07
❑ 71 Armon Gilliam .25 .07
❑ 72 Elliot Perry .25 .07
❑ 73 Chris Carr .25 .07
❑ 74 Tom Gugliotta .50 .15
❑ 75 Kevin Garnett 1.50 .45
❑ 76 Doug West .25 .07
❑ 77 Keith Van Horn RC 1.25 .35
❑ 78 Chris Gatling .25 .07
❑ 79 Kendall Gill .25 .07
❑ 80 Kerry Kittles .75 .23
❑ 81 Jayson Williams .25 .07
❑ 82 Chris Childs .25 .07
❑ 83 Allan Houston .50 .15
❑ 84 Larry Johnson .50 .15
❑ 85 Charles Oakley .50 .15
❑ 86 John Starks .50 .15
❑ 87 Horace Grant .50 .15
❑ 88 Anfernee Hardaway .75 .23
❑ 89 Dennis Scott .25 .07
❑ 90 Rony Seikaly .25 .07
❑ 91 Brian Shaw .25 .07
❑ 92 Derrick Coleman .25 .07
❑ 93 Allen Iverson 2.00 .60
❑ 94 Tim Thomas RC 1.25 .35
❑ 95 Scott Williams .25 .07
❑ 96 Cedric Ceballos .25 .07
❑ 97 Kevin Johnson .50 .15
❑ 98 Loren Meyer .25 .07
❑ 99 Steve Nash .75 .23
❑ 100 Wesley Person .25 .07
❑ 101 Kenny Anderson .50 .15
❑ 102 Jermaine O'Neal 1.25 .35
❑ 103 Isaiah Rider .50 .15
❑ 104 Arvydas Sabonis .50 .15
❑ 105 Gary Trent .25 .07
❑ 106 Mahmoud Abdul-Rauf .25 .07
❑ 107 Billy Owens .25 .07
❑ 108 Olden Polynice .25 .07
❑ 109 Mitch Richmond .50 .15
❑ 110 Michael Smith .25 .07
❑ 111 Cory Alexander .25 .07
❑ 112 Vinny Del Negro .25 .07
❑ 113 Carl Herrera .25 .07
❑ 114 Tim Duncan RC 4.00 1.20
❑ 115 Hersey Hawkins .25 .07
❑ 116 Shawn Kemp .50 .15
❑ 117 Nate McMillan .25 .07
❑ 118 Sam Perkins .50 .15
❑ 119 Detlef Schrempf .50 .15
❑ 120 Doug Christie .50 .15
❑ 121 Popeye Jones .25 .07
❑ 122 Carlos Rogers .25 .07
❑ 123 Damon Stoudamire .50 .15
❑ 124 Adam Keefe .25 .07
❑ 125 Chris Morris .25 .07
❑ 126 Greg Ostertag .25 .07
❑ 127 John Stockton .75 .23
❑ 128 Shareef Abdur-Rahim 1.25 .35
❑ 129 George Lynch .25 .07
❑ 130 Lee Mayberry .25 .07
❑ 131 Anthony Peeler .25 .07
❑ 132 Calbert Cheaney .25 .07
❑ 133 Tracy Murray .25 .07
❑ 134 Rod Strickland .25 .07
❑ 135 Chris Webber .75 .23
❑ 136 Christian Laettner JAM .25 .07
❑ 137 Eric Williams JAM .25 .07
❑ 138 Vlade Divac JAM .25 .07
❑ 139 Michael Jordan JAM 2.50 .75
❑ 140 Tyrone Hill JAM .25 .07
❑ 141 Michael Finley JAM .50 .15
❑ 142 Tom Hammonds JAM .25 .07
❑ 143 Theo Ratliff JAM .25 .07
❑ 144 Latrell Sprewell JAM .75 .23
❑ 145 Hakeem Olajuwon JAM .50 .15
❑ 146 Reggie Miller JAM .50 .15
❑ 147 Rodney Rogers JAM .25 .07
❑ 148 Eddie Jones JAM .50 .15
❑ 149 Jamal Mashburn JAM .50 .15
❑ 150 Glenn Robinson JAM .50 .15
❑ 151 Chris Carr JAM .25 .07
❑ 152 Kendall Gill JAM .25 .07
❑ 153 John Starks JAM .25 .07
❑ 154 Anfernee Hardaway JAM .50 .15
❑ 155 Derrick Coleman JAM .25 .07
❑ 156 Cedric Ceballos JAM .25 .07
❑ 157 Rasheed Wallace JAM .50 .15
❑ 158 Corliss Williamson JAM .25 .07
❑ 159 Sean Elliott JAM .50 .15
❑ 160 Shawn Kemp JAM .25 .07
❑ 161 Doug Christie JAM .50 .15
❑ 162 Karl Malone JAM .75 .23
❑ 163 Bryant Reeves JAM .25 .07
❑ 164 Gheorghe Muresan JAM .25 .07
❑ 165 Michael Jordan CP 2.50 .75
❑ 166 Dikembe Mutombo CP .25 .07
❑ 167 Glen Rice CP .25 .07
❑ 168 Mitch Richmond CP .25 .07
❑ 169 Juwan Howard CP .25 .07
❑ 170 Clyde Drexler CP .50 .15
❑ 171 Terrell Brandon CP .25 .07
❑ 172 Jerry Stackhouse CP .50 .15
❑ 173 Damon Stoudamire CP .25 .07
❑ 174 Jayson Williams CP .25 .07
❑ 175 P.J. Brown CP .25 .07
❑ 176 Anfernee Hardaway CP .50 .15
❑ 177 Vin Baker CP .25 .07
❑ 178 LaPhonso Ellis CP .25 .07
❑ 179 Shawn Kemp CP .25 .07
❑ 180 Checklist .25 .07
❑ 181 Mookie Blaylock .25 .07
❑ 182 Tyrone Corbin .25 .07
❑ 183 Chucky Brown .25 .07
❑ 184 Ed Gray RC .25 .07
❑ 185 Chauncey Billups RC .75 .23
❑ 186 Tyus Edney .25 .07
❑ 187 Travis Knight .25 .07
❑ 188 Ron Mercer RC 1.00 .30
❑ 189 Walter McCarty .25 .07
❑ 190 B.J. Armstrong .25 .07
❑ 191 Matt Geiger .25 .07
❑ 192 Bobby Phills .25 .07
❑ 193 David Wesley .25 .07
❑ 194 Keith Booth RC .25 .07
❑ 195 Randy Brown .25 .07
❑ 196 Ron Harper .50 .15
❑ 197 Scottie Pippen 1.25 .35
❑ 198 Dennis Rodman .50 .15
❑ 199 Zydrunas Ilgauskas .50 .15
❑ 200 Brevin Knight RC .50 .15
❑ 201 Shawn Kemp .50 .15
❑ 202 Vitaly Potapenko .25 .07
❑ 203 Wesley Person .25 .07
❑ 204 Erick Strickland RC .50 .15
❑ 205 A.C. Green .50 .15
❑ 206 Khalid Reeves .25 .07
❑ 207 Hubert Davis .25 .07
❑ 208 Dennis Scott .25 .07
❑ 209 Danny Fortson RC .50 .15
❑ 210 Bobby Jackson RC 1.25 .35
❑ 211 Eric Williams .25 .07
❑ 212 Dean Garrett .25 .07
❑ 213 Priest Lauderdale .25 .07
❑ 214 Joe Dumars .75 .23
❑ 215 Aaron McKie .50 .15
❑ 216 Scot Pollard RC .50 .15
❑ 217 Brian Williams .25 .07
❑ 218 Malik Sealy .25 .07
❑ 219 Duane Ferrell .25 .07
❑ 220 Erick Dampier .50 .15
❑ 221 Todd Fuller .25 .07
❑ 222 Donyell Marshall .50 .15
❑ 223 Joe Smith .50 .15
❑ 224 Charles Barkley 1.00 .30
❑ 225 Matt Bullard .25 .07
❑ 226 Othella Harrington .25 .07
❑ 227 Rodrick Rhodes RC .25 .07
❑ 228 Eddie Johnson .25 .07
❑ 229 Matt Maloney .25 .07
❑ 230 Travis Best .25 .07
❑ 231 Reggie Miller .75 .23
❑ 232 Chris Mullin .75 .23
❑ 233 Fred Hoiberg .25 .07
❑ 234 Austin Croshere RC .75 .23
❑ 235 Keith Closs RC .25 .07
❑ 236 Darrick Martin .25 .07
❑ 237 Pooh Richardson .25 .07
❑ 238 Rodney Rogers .25 .07
❑ 239 Maurice Taylor RC .75 .23
❑ 240 Robert Horry .50 .15
❑ 241 Rick Fox .50 .15
❑ 242 Shaquille O'Neal 2.00 .60
❑ 243 Corie Blount .25 .07
❑ 244 Charles Smith RC .25 .07
❑ 245 Voshon Lenard .25 .07
❑ 246 Eric Murdock .25 .07
❑ 247 Dan Majerle .50 .15
❑ 248 Terry Mills .25 .07
❑ 249 Terrell Brandon .50 .15
❑ 250 Tyrone Hill .25 .07
❑ 251 Ervin Johnson .25 .07
❑ 252 Glenn Robinson .75 .23
❑ 253 Terry Porter .25 .07
❑ 254 Paul Grant RC .25 .07
❑ 255 Stephon Marbury 1.00 .30
❑ 256 Sam Mitchell .25 .07
❑ 257 Cherokee Parks .25 .07
❑ 258 Sam Cassell .75 .23
❑ 259 David Benoit .25 .07
❑ 260 Kevin Edwards .25 .07
❑ 261 Don MacLean .25 .07
❑ 262 Patrick Ewing .75 .23
❑ 263 Herb Williams .25 .07
❑ 264 John Starks .50 .15
❑ 265 Chris Mills .25 .07
❑ 266 Chris Dudley .25 .07
❑ 267 Darrell Armstrong .25 .07
❑ 268 Nick Anderson .25 .07
❑ 269 Derek Harper .50 .15
❑ 270 Johnny Taylor RC .25 .07
❑ 271 Mark Price .50 .15
❑ 272 Clarence Weatherspoon .25 .07
❑ 273 Jerry Stackhouse .75 .23
❑ 274 Eric Montross .25 .07
❑ 275 Anthony Parker RC .25 .07
❑ 276 Antonio McDyess .50 .15
❑ 277 Clifford Robinson .25 .07
❑ 278 Jason Kidd 1.25 .35
❑ 279 Danny Manning .50 .15
❑ 280 Rex Chapman .25 .07
❑ 281 Stacey Augmon .25 .07
❑ 282 Kelvin Cato RC .75 .23
❑ 283 Brian Grant .50 .15
❑ 284 Rasheed Wallace .75 .23
❑ 285 L.Funderburke RC .50 .15
❑ 286 Anthony Johnson .25 .07
❑ 287 Tariq Abdul-Wahad RC .50 .15
❑ 288 Corliss Williamson .50 .15
❑ 289 Sean Elliott .50 .15
❑ 290 Avery Johnson .25 .07
❑ 291 David Robinson .75 .23
❑ 292 Will Perdue .25 .07
❑ 293 Greg Anthony .25 .07
❑ 294 Jim McIlvaine .25 .07
❑ 295 Dale Ellis .25 .07
❑ 296 Gary Payton .75 .23
❑ 297 Aaron Williams .25 .07
❑ 298 Marcus Camby .75 .23
❑ 299 John Wallace .25 .07
❑ 300 Tracy McGrady RC 4.00 1.20
❑ 301 Walt Williams .25 .07
❑ 302 Shandon Anderson .25 .07
❑ 303 Antoine Carr .25 .07
❑ 304 Jeff Hornacek .50 .15
❑ 305 Karl Malone .75 .23
❑ 306 Bryon Russell .25 .07
❑ 307 Jacque Vaughn RC .50 .15
❑ 308 Antonio Daniels RC .75 .23
❑ 309 Blue Edwards .25 .07
❑ 310 Bryant Reeves .25 .07
❑ 311 Otis Thorpe .25 .07
❑ 312 Harvey Grant .25 .07
❑ 313 Terry Davis .25 .07
❑ 314 Juwan Howard .50 .15
❑ 315 Gheorghe Muresan .25 .07
❑ 316 Michael Jordan OT 2.50 .75
❑ 317 Allen Iverson OT .75 .23
❑ 318 Karl Malone OT .75 .23
❑ 319 Glen Rice OT .25 .07
❑ 320 Dikembe Mutombo OT .25 .07

❑ 321 Grant Hill OT	.50	.15
❑ 322 Hakeem Olajuwon OT	.50	.15
❑ 323 Stephon Marbury OT	.75	.23
❑ 324 Anfernee Hardaway OT	.50	.15
❑ 325 Eddie Jones OT	.50	.15
❑ 326 Mitch Richmond OT	.25	.07
❑ 327 Kevin Johnson OT	.25	.07
❑ 328 Kevin Garnett OT	.75	.23
❑ 329 Shareef Abdur-Rahim OT	.60	.18
❑ 330 Damon Stoudamire OT	.25	.07
❑ 331 Dikembe Mutombo	.25	.07
Christian Laettner		
Mookie Blaylock		
Steve Smith		
❑ 332 Antoine Walker	.50	.15
Ron Mercer		
Chauncey Billups		
Dana Barros		
❑ 333 Glen Rice	.50	.15
Larry Johnson		
Alonzo Mourning		
Vlade Divac		
Anthony Mason		
❑ 334 Michael Jordan	1.00	.30
Scottie Pippen		
Dennis Rodman		
Toni Kukoc		
❑ 335 Shawn Kemp	.50	.15
Brevin Knight		
Terrell Brandon		
Mark Price		
❑ 336 A.C. Green	.50	.15
Michael Finley		
Derek Harper		
Detlef Schrempf		
❑ 337 Bobby Jackson	.75	.23
Tony Battie		
Dikembe Mutombo		
LaPhonso Ellis		
❑ 338 Joe Dumars	.75	.23
Grant Hill		
Dennis Rodman		
Lindsey Hunter		
❑ 339 Joe Smith	.75	.23
Chris Mullin		
Chris Webber		
Tim Hardaway		
❑ 340 Hakeem Olajuwon	.75	.23
Charles Barkley		
Clyde Drexler		
Sam Cassell		
Otis Thorpe		
❑ 341 Chris Mullin	.50	.15
Reggie Miller		
Antonio Davis		
Dale Davis		
Rik Smits		
❑ 342 Brent Barry	.25	.07
Loy Vaught		
Danny Manning		
Ron Harper		
❑ 343 Shaquille O'Neal	.60	.18
Kobe Bryant		
Eddie Jones		
Nick Van Exel		
❑ 344 Tim Hardaway	.75	.23
Alonzo Mourning		
P.J. Brown		
Rony Seikaly		
Glen Rice		
❑ 345 Terrell Brandon	.50	.15
Glenn Robinson		
Vin Baker		
Terry Cummings		
❑ 346 Kevin Garnett	.30	.09
Stephon Marbury		
Tom Gugliotta		
Sam Mitchell		
Isaiah Rider		
❑ 347 Keith Van Horn	.50	.15
Jayson Williams		
Buck Williams		
Kenny Anderson		
❑ 348 Patrick Ewing	.50	.15
Larry Johnson		
John Starks		
Charles Oakley		
❑ 349 Anfernee Hardaway	.75	.23
Rony Seikaly		
Shaquille O'Neal		
Nick Anderson		
❑ 350 Allen Iverson	.30	.09
Jerry Stackhouse		
Charles Barkley		
Clarence Weatherspoon		
❑ 351 Antonio McDyess	.50	.15
Jason Kidd		
Charles Barkley		
Kevin Johnson		
❑ 352 Kenny Anderson	.25	.07
Isaiah Rider		
Clyde Drexler		
Terry Porter		
❑ 353 Mitch Richmond	.50	.15
Corliss Williamson		
Lionel Simmons		
Billy Owens		
❑ 354 Tim Duncan	.40	.12
David Robinson		
Sean Elliott		
Dennis Rodman		
❑ 355 Gary Payton	.75	.23
Vin Baker		
Nate McMillan		
Shawn Kemp		
❑ 356 Damon Stoudamire	.50	.15
Tracy McGrady		
Marcus Camby		
Walt Williams		
❑ 357 John Stockton	.50	.15
Karl Malone		
Jeff Hornacek		
❑ 358 Bryant Reeves	.25	.07
Shareef Abdur-Rahim		
Antonio Daniels		
Greg Anthony		
❑ 359 Chris Webber	.75	.23
Juwan Howard		
Gheorghe Muresan		
Rod Strickland		
❑ 360 Checklist	.25	.07
❑ NNO M.Jordan Red Audio	25.00	7.50
❑ NNO M.Jordan Black Audio	10.00	3.00

1998-99 Upper Deck

	Nm-Mt	Ex-Mt
COMPLETE SET (355)	180.00	55.00
COMPLETE SERIES 1 (175)	100.00	30.00
COMPLETE SERIES 2 (180)	80.00	24.00
COMMON CARD (1-311)	.25	.07
COMMON ROOKIE (312-333)	.60	.18
COMMON JORDAN (230A-W)	3.00	.90
COMMON HS SUBSET	.75	.23
COMMON TN SUBSET	1.00	.30
❑ 1 Mookie Blaylock	.25	.07
❑ 2 Ed Gray	.25	.07
❑ 3 Dikembe Mutombo	.50	.15
❑ 4 Steve Smith	.50	.15
❑ 5 Dikembe Mutombo	.75	.23
Steve Smith HS		
❑ 6 Kenny Anderson	.50	.15
❑ 7 Dana Barros	.25	.07
❑ 8 Travis Knight	.25	.07
❑ 9 Walter McCarty	.25	.07
❑ 10 Ron Mercer	.50	.15
❑ 11 Greg Minor	.25	.07
❑ 12 Antoine Walker	.75	.23
Ron Mercer HS		
❑ 13 B.J. Armstrong	.25	.07
❑ 14 David Wesley	.25	.07
❑ 15 Anthony Mason	.50	.15
❑ 16 Glen Rice	.50	.15
❑ 17 J.R. Reid	.25	.07
❑ 18 Bobby Phills	.25	.07
❑ 19 Glen Rice	.75	.23
Anthony Mason HS		
❑ 20 Ron Harper	.50	.15
❑ 21 Toni Kukoc	.50	.15
❑ 22 Scottie Pippen	1.25	.35
❑ 23 Michael Jordan	5.00	1.50
❑ 24 Dennis Rodman	.50	.15
❑ 25 Michael Jordan	10.00	3.00
Scottie Pippen HS		
❑ 26 Michael Jordan	12.00	3.60
Michael Jordan HS		
❑ 27 Shawn Kemp	.50	.15
❑ 28 Zydrunas Ilgauskas	.50	.15
❑ 29 Cedric Henderson	.25	.07
❑ 30 Vitaly Potapenko	.25	.07
❑ 31 Derek Anderson	.75	.23
❑ 32 Shawn Kemp	1.25	.35
Zydrunas Ilgauskas HS		
❑ 33 Shawn Bradley	.25	.07
❑ 34 Khalid Reeves	.25	.07
❑ 35 Robert Pack	.25	.07
❑ 36 Michael Finley	.75	.23
❑ 37 Erick Strickland	.25	.07
❑ 38 Michael Finley	1.00	.30
Shawn Bradley HS		
❑ 39 Bryant Stith	.25	.07
❑ 40 Dean Garrett	.25	.07
❑ 41 Eric Williams	.25	.07
❑ 42 Bobby Jackson	.50	.15
❑ 43 Danny Fortson	.25	.07
❑ 44 LaPhonso Ellis	.75	.23
Bryant Stith HS		
❑ 45 Grant Hill	.75	.23
❑ 46 Lindsey Hunter	.25	.07
❑ 47 Brian Williams	.25	.07
❑ 48 Scot Pollard	.25	.07
❑ 49 Grant Hill	.75	.23
Brian Williams HS		
❑ 50 Donyell Marshall	.50	.15
❑ 51 Tony Delk	.25	.07
❑ 52 Erick Dampier	.50	.15
❑ 53 Felton Spencer	.25	.07
❑ 54 Bimbo Coles	.25	.07
❑ 55 Muggsy Bogues	.50	.15
❑ 56 Donyell Marshall	.75	.23
Muggsy Bogues HS		
❑ 57 Charles Barkley	1.00	.30
❑ 58 Brent Price	.25	.07
❑ 59 Hakeem Olajuwon	.75	.23
❑ 60 Rodrick Rhodes	.25	.07
❑ 61 Charles Barkley	2.00	.60
Hakeem Olajuwon HS		
❑ 62 Dale Davis	.50	.15
❑ 63 Antonio Davis	.25	.07
❑ 64 Chris Mullin	.75	.23
❑ 65 Jalen Rose	.75	.23
❑ 66 Reggie Miller	.75	.23
❑ 67 Mark Jackson	.50	.15
❑ 68 Reggie Miller	1.25	.35
Mark Jackson HS		
❑ 69 Rodney Rogers	.25	.07
❑ 70 Lamond Murray	.25	.07
❑ 71 Eric Piatkowski	.50	.15
❑ 72 Lorenzen Wright	.25	.07
❑ 73 Maurice Taylor	.50	.15
❑ 74 Maurice Taylor	.75	.23
Lamond Murray HS		
❑ 75 Kobe Bryant	3.00	.90
❑ 76 Shaquille O'Neal	2.00	.60
❑ 77 Derek Fisher	.75	.23
❑ 78 Elden Campbell	.25	.07
❑ 79 Corie Blount	.25	.07
❑ 80 Shaquille O'Neal	8.00	2.40
Kobe Bryant HS		
❑ 81 Jamal Mashburn	.50	.15
❑ 82 Alonzo Mourning	.50	.15

No.	Card	Price	Price
❑ 83	Tim Hardaway	.50	.15
❑ 84	Voshon Lenard	.25	.07
❑ 85	Alonzo Mourning	1.25	.35
	Tim Hardaway HS		
❑ 86	Ray Allen	.75	.23
❑ 87	Terrell Brandon	.50	.15
❑ 88	Elliot Perry	.25	.07
❑ 89	Ervin Johnson	.25	.07
❑ 90	Ray Allen	.75	.23
	Glenn Robinson HS		
❑ 91	Micheal Williams	.25	.07
❑ 92	Anthony Peeler	.25	.07
❑ 93	Chris Carr	.25	.07
❑ 94	Kevin Garnett	1.50	.45
❑ 95	Kevin Garnett	3.00	.90
	Stephon Marbury HS		
❑ 96	Keith Van Horn	.75	.23
❑ 97	Kerry Kittles	.25	.07
❑ 98	Kendall Gill	.25	.07
❑ 99	Sam Cassell	.75	.23
❑ 100	Chris Gatling	.25	.07
❑ 101	Keith Van Horn	1.00	.30
	Sam Cassell HS		
❑ 102	Patrick Ewing	.75	.23
❑ 103	John Starks	.50	.15
❑ 104	Allan Houston	.50	.15
❑ 105	Chris Mills	.25	.07
❑ 106	Chris Childs	.25	.07
❑ 107	Charlie Ward	.25	.07
❑ 108	Patrick Ewing	1.25	.35
	John Starks HS		
❑ 109	Anfernee Hardaway	.75	.23
❑ 110	Horace Grant	.50	.15
❑ 111	Nick Anderson	.25	.07
❑ 112	Johnny Taylor	.25	.07
❑ 113	Anfernee Hardaway	2.00	.60
	Horace Grant HS		
❑ 114	Allen Iverson	1.50	.45
❑ 115	Scott Williams	.25	.07
❑ 116	Tim Thomas	.50	.15
❑ 117	Brian Shaw	.25	.07
❑ 118	Anthony Parker	.25	.07
❑ 119	Allen Iverson	2.00	.60
	Tim Thomas HS		
❑ 120	Jason Kidd	1.25	.35
❑ 121	Rex Chapman	.25	.07
❑ 122	Danny Manning	.25	.07
❑ 123	Jason Kidd	2.50	.75
	Danny Manning HS		
❑ 124	Rasheed Wallace	.75	.23
❑ 125	Walt Williams	.25	.07
❑ 126	Kelvin Cato	.25	.07
❑ 127	Arvydas Sabonis	.50	.15
❑ 128	Brian Grant	.50	.15
❑ 129	Rasheed Wallace	.75	.23
	Isaiah Rider HS		
❑ 130	Tariq Abdul-Wahad	.25	.07
❑ 131	Corliss Williamson	.50	.15
❑ 132	Olden Polynice	.25	.07
❑ 133	Chris Robinson	.25	.07
❑ 134	Tariq Abdul-Wahad	.75	.23
	Olden Polynice HS		
❑ 135	Tim Duncan	1.25	.35
❑ 136	Avery Johnson	.25	.07
❑ 137	David Robinson	.75	.23
❑ 138	Monty Williams	.25	.07
❑ 139	Tim Duncan	2.50	.75
	David Robinson HS		
❑ 140	Vin Baker	.50	.15
❑ 141	Hersey Hawkins	.25	.07
❑ 142	Detlef Schrempf	.50	.15
❑ 143	Jim McIlvaine	.25	.07
❑ 144	Gary Payton	1.00	.30
	Vin Baker HS		
❑ 145	Chauncey Billups	.50	.15
❑ 146	Tracy McGrady	2.00	.60
❑ 147	John Wallace	.25	.07
❑ 148	Doug Christie	.50	.15
❑ 149	Dee Brown	.25	.07
❑ 150	Tracy McGrady	1.50	.45
	Chauncey Billups HS		
❑ 151	Karl Malone	.75	.23
❑ 152	John Stockton	.75	.23
❑ 153	Adam Keefe	.25	.07
❑ 154	Howard Eisley	.25	.07
❑ 155	Karl Malone	.75	.23
	John Stockton HS		
❑ 156	Bryant Reeves	.25	.07
❑ 157	Lee Mayberry	.25	.07
❑ 158	Michael Smith	.25	.07
❑ 159	Shareef Abdur-Rahim	2.00	.60
	Bryant Reeves HS		
❑ 160	Juwan Howard	.50	.15
❑ 161	Calbert Cheaney	.25	.07
❑ 162	Tracy Murray	.25	.07
❑ 163	Juwan Howard	.75	.23
	Calbert Cheaney HS		
❑ 164	Shaquille O'Neal TN	4.00	1.20
❑ 165	Maurice Taylor TN	1.00	.30
❑ 166	Stephon Marbury TN	.75	.23
❑ 167	Tracy McGrady TN	4.00	1.20
❑ 168	Antoine Walker TN	1.25	.35
❑ 169	Michael Jordan TN	10.00	3.00
❑ 170	Keith Van Horn TN	.75	.23
❑ 171	Shareef Abdur-Rahim TN	2.00	.60
❑ 172	Kobe Bryant TN	6.00	1.80
❑ 173	Gary Payton TN	1.50	.45
❑ 174	Michael Jordan CL	1.00	.30
❑ 175	Michael Jordan CL	1.00	.30
❑ 176	Kevin Johnson	.50	.15
❑ 177	Glenn Robinson	.50	.15
❑ 178	Antoine Walker	.75	.23
❑ 179	Jerry Stackhouse	.75	.23
❑ 180	Mark Price	.50	.15
❑ 181	Stephon Marbury	.75	.23
❑ 182	Shareef Abdur-Rahim	.75	.23
❑ 183	Wesley Person	.25	.07
❑ 184	Keith Booth	.25	.07
❑ 185	Sean Elliott	.50	.15
❑ 186	Alan Henderson	.25	.07
❑ 187	Bryon Russell	.25	.07
❑ 188	Jermaine O'Neal	.75	.23
❑ 189	Steve Nash	.75	.23
❑ 190	Eldridge Recasner	.25	.07
❑ 191	Damon Stoudamire	.50	.15
❑ 192	Dell Curry	.25	.07
❑ 193	Michael Stewart	.25	.07
❑ 194	Bruce Bowen	.25	.07
❑ 195	Steve Kerr	.50	.15
❑ 196	Dale Ellis	.25	.07
❑ 197	Shandon Anderson	.25	.07
❑ 198	Larry Johnson	.50	.15
❑ 199	Chris Webber	.75	.23
❑ 200	Matt Geiger	.25	.07
❑ 201	Chris Anstey	.25	.07
❑ 202	Loy Vaught	.25	.07
❑ 203	Aaron McKie	.50	.15
❑ 204	A.C. Green	.50	.15
❑ 205	Bo Outlaw	.25	.07
❑ 206	Antonio McDyess	.50	.15
❑ 207	Priest Lauderdale	.25	.07
❑ 208	Greg Ostertag	.25	.07
❑ 209	Dan Majerle	.50	.15
❑ 210	Johnny Newman	.25	.07
❑ 211	Tyrone Corbin	.25	.07
❑ 212	Pervis Ellison	.25	.07
❑ 213	Shawnelle Scott	.25	.07
❑ 214	Travis Best	.25	.07
❑ 215	Stacey Augmon	.25	.07
❑ 216	Brevin Knight	.25	.07
❑ 217	Jerome Williams	.25	.07
❑ 218	Terry Mills	.25	.07
❑ 219	Matt Maloney	.25	.07
❑ 220	Dennis Scott	.25	.07
❑ 221	John Thomas	.25	.07
❑ 222	Nick Van Exel	.75	.23
❑ 223	Duane Ferrell	.25	.07
❑ 224	Chris Whitney	.25	.07
❑ 225	Luc Longley	.25	.07
❑ 226	Robert Horry	.50	.15
❑ 227	Clifford Robinson	.25	.07
❑ 228	Samaki Walker	.25	.07
❑ 229	Derrick McKey	.25	.07
❑ 230A	Michael Jordan	3.00	.90
❑ 230B	Michael Jordan	3.00	.90
❑ 230C	Michael Jordan	3.00	.90
❑ 230D	Michael Jordan	3.00	.90
❑ 230E	Michael Jordan	3.00	.90
❑ 230F	Michael Jordan	3.00	.90
❑ 230G	Michael Jordan	3.00	.90
❑ 230H	Michael Jordan	3.00	.90
❑ 230I	Michael Jordan	3.00	.90
❑ 230J	Michael Jordan	3.00	.90
❑ 230K	Michael Jordan	3.00	.90
❑ 230L	Michael Jordan	3.00	.90
❑ 230M	Michael Jordan	3.00	.90
❑ 230N	Michael Jordan	3.00	.90
❑ 230O	Michael Jordan	3.00	.90
❑ 230P	Michael Jordan	3.00	.90
❑ 230Q	Michael Jordan	3.00	.90
❑ 230R	Michael Jordan	3.00	.90
❑ 230S	Michael Jordan	3.00	.90
❑ 230T	Michael Jordan	3.00	.90
❑ 230U	Michael Jordan	3.00	.90
❑ 230V	Michael Jordan	3.00	.90
❑ 230W	Michael Jordan	3.00	.90
❑ 231	Armon Gilliam	.25	.07
❑ 232	Andrew DeClercq	.25	.07
❑ 233	Stojko Vrankovic	.25	.07
❑ 234	Jayson Williams	.25	.07
❑ 235	Vinny Del Negro	.25	.07
❑ 236	Theo Ratliff	.50	.15
❑ 237	Othella Harrington	.25	.07
❑ 238	Mitch Richmond	.50	.15
❑ 239	Vlade Divac	.50	.15
❑ 240	Duane Causwell	.25	.07
❑ 241	Todd Fuller	.25	.07
❑ 242	Tom Gugliotta	.25	.07
❑ 243	LaPhonso Ellis	.25	.07
❑ 244	Brian Evans	.25	.07
❑ 245	Jason Caffey	.25	.07
❑ 246	Pooh Richardson	.25	.07
❑ 247	George Lynch	.25	.07
❑ 248	Bill Wennington	.25	.07
❑ 249	Rik Smits	.50	.15
❑ 250	Kevin Willis	.25	.07
❑ 251	Mario Elie	.25	.07
❑ 252	Austin Croshere	.75	.23
❑ 253	Sharone Wright	.25	.07
❑ 254	Danny Ferry	.25	.07
❑ 255	Jacque Vaughn	.25	.07
❑ 256	Adonal Foyle	.25	.07
❑ 257	Billy Owens	.25	.07
❑ 258	Randy Brown	.25	.07
❑ 259	Joe Smith	.50	.15
❑ 260	Joe Dumars	.75	.23
❑ 261	Sean Rooks	.25	.07
❑ 262	Eric Montross	.25	.07
❑ 263	Hubert Davis	.25	.07
❑ 264	Gary Payton	.75	.23
❑ 265	Tyrone Hill	.25	.07
❑ 266	John Crotty	.25	.07
❑ 267	P.J. Brown	.25	.07
❑ 268	Michael Cage	.25	.07
❑ 269	Scott Burrell	.25	.07
❑ 270	Marcus Camby	.50	.15
❑ 271	Rod Strickland	.25	.07
❑ 272	Jim Jackson	.25	.07
❑ 273	Corey Beck	.25	.07
❑ 274	James Robinson	.25	.07
❑ 275	Cedric Ceballos	.25	.07
❑ 276	Charles Oakley	.25	.07
❑ 277	Anthony Johnson	.25	.07
❑ 278	Bob Sura	.25	.07
❑ 279	Isaiah Rider	.25	.07
❑ 280	Jeff Hornacek	.50	.15
❑ 281	Rony Seikaly	.25	.07
❑ 282	Charles Smith	.25	.07
❑ 283	Eddie Jones	.75	.23
❑ 284	Lucious Harris	.25	.07
❑ 285	Andrew Lang	.25	.07
❑ 286	Terry Cummings	.25	.07
❑ 287	Keith Closs	.25	.07
❑ 288	Chris Anstey	.25	.07
❑ 289	Clarence Weatherspoon	.25	.07
❑ 290	Michael Jordan H99	2.50	.75
❑ 291	Shawn Kemp H99	.50	.15
❑ 292	Tracy McGrady H99	1.00	.30
❑ 293	Glen Rice H99	.25	.07
❑ 294	David Robinson H99	.75	.23
❑ 295	Antonio McDyess H99	.50	.15
❑ 296	Vin Baker H99	.25	.07
❑ 297	Juwan Howard H99	.25	.07
❑ 298	Ron Mercer H99	.50	.15
❑ 299	Michael Finley H99	.50	.15
❑ 300	Scottie Pippen H99	.60	.18
❑ 301	Tim Thomas H99	.50	.15
❑ 302	Rasheed Wallace H99	.50	.15

❑ 303 Alonzo Mourning H99 .... .50 .15
❑ 304 Dikembe Mutombo H99 .25 .07
❑ 305 Derek Anderson H99 .... .50 .15
❑ 306 Ray Allen H99 .... .75 .23
❑ 307 Patrick Ewing H99 .... .50 .15
❑ 308 Sean Elliott H99 .... .25 .07
❑ 309 Shaquille O'Neal H99 .. 1.00 .30
❑ 310 Michael Jordan........... 1.00 .30
Checklist
❑ 311 Michael Jordan........... 1.00 .30
Checklist
❑ 312 Michael Olowokandi RC 2.50 .75
❑ 313 Mike Bibby RC 8.00 2.40
❑ 314 Raef LaFrentz RC ...... 2.50 .75
❑ 315 Antawn Jamison RC.... 8.00 2.40
❑ 316 Vince Carter RC 15.00 4.50
❑ 317 Robert Traylor RC ...... 1.50 .45
❑ 318 Jason Williams RC...... 6.00 1.80
❑ 319 Larry Hughes RC 5.00 1.50
❑ 320 Dirk Nowitzki RC 15.00 4.50
❑ 321 Paul Pierce RC............ 8.00 2.40
❑ 322 Bonzi Wells RC 6.00 1.80
❑ 323 Michael Doleac RC .... 1.50 .45
❑ 324 Keon Clark RC............ 2.50 .75
❑ 325 Michael Dickerson RC 3.00 .90
❑ 326 Matt Harpring RC .... 2.50 .75
❑ 327 Bryce Drew RC .... 1.50 .45
❑ 328 Pat Garrity RC .... .75 .23
❑ 329 Roshown McLeod RC .. .60 .18
❑ 330 Ricky Davis RC 5.00 1.50
❑ 331 Peja Stojakovic RC 6.00 1.80
❑ 332 Felipe Lopez RC .... 2.00 .60
❑ 333 Al Harrington RC 4.00 1.20
❑ UDX Michael Jordan .... 3.00 .90
Retires

1999-00 Upper Deck

	Nm-Mt	Ex-Mt
COMPLETE SET (360)	180.00	55.00
COMPLETE SERIES 1 (180)	120.00	36.00
COMPLETE SERIES 2 (180)	60.00	18.00
COMP.SERIES 1 w/o RC (155)	50.00	15.00
COMP.SERIES 2 w/o SP (133)	10.00	3.00
COMMON CARD (1-133/181-315)	.25	.07
COMMON RC (156-180/316-360)	1.00	.30
COMMON MJ (134-153)	2.50	.75

❑ 1 Roshown McLeod .... .25 .07
❑ 2 Dikembe Mutombo .... .50 .15
❑ 3 Alan Henderson .... .25 .07
❑ 4 LaPhonso Ellis .... .25 .07
❑ 5 Chris Crawford .... .25 .07
❑ 6 Kenny Anderson .... .50 .15
❑ 7 Antoine Walker .... .75 .23
❑ 8 Paul Pierce....................... .75 .23
❑ 9 Vitaly Potapenko .... .25 .07
❑ 10 Dana Barros .... .25 .07
❑ 11 Elden Campbell .... .25 .07
❑ 12 Eddie Jones .... .75 .23
❑ 13 David Wesley .... .25 .07
❑ 14 Derrick Coleman .... .50 .15
❑ 15 Ricky Davis .... .50 .15
❑ 16 Corey Benjamin .... .25 .07
❑ 17 Randy Brown .... .25 .07
❑ 18 Kornel David RC .... .25 .07
❑ 19 Toni Kukoc .... .50 .15
❑ 20 Keith Booth .... .25 .07
❑ 21 Shawn Kemp .... .50 .15
❑ 22 Wesley Person .... .25 .07
❑ 23 Brevin Knight .... .25 .07
❑ 24 Bob Sura .... .25 .07
❑ 25 Zydrunas Ilgauskas .... .50 .15
❑ 26 Michael Finley .... .75 .23
❑ 27 Shawn Bradley .... .25 .07
❑ 28 Dirk Nowitzki .... 1.50 .45
❑ 29 Steve Nash .... .75 .23
❑ 30 Antonio McDyess .... .50 .15
❑ 31 Nick Van Exel .... .75 .23
❑ 32 Chauncey Billups .... .50 .15
❑ 33 Bryant Stith .... .25 .07
❑ 34 Raef LaFrentz .... .50 .15
❑ 35 Grant Hill .... .75 .23
❑ 36 Lindsey Hunter .... .25 .07
❑ 37 Bison Dele .... .25 .07
❑ 38 Jerry Stackhouse .... .75 .23
❑ 39 John Starks .... .50 .15
❑ 40 Antawn Jamison .... 1.25 .35
❑ 41 Erick Dampier .... .50 .15
❑ 42 Jason Caffey .... .25 .07
❑ 43 Hakeem Olajuwon .... .75 .23
❑ 44 Scottie Pippen .... 1.25 .35
❑ 45 Cuttino Mobley .... .75 .23
❑ 46 Charles Barkley .... 1.00 .30
❑ 47 Bryce Drew .... .25 .07
❑ 48 Reggie Miller .... .75 .23
❑ 49 Jalen Rose .... .75 .23
❑ 50 Mark Jackson .... .50 .15
❑ 51 Dale Davis .... .25 .07
❑ 52 Chris Mullin .... .75 .23
❑ 53 Maurice Taylor .... .50 .15
❑ 54 Tyrone Nesby RC .... .25 .07
❑ 55 Michael Olowokandi .... .50 .15
❑ 56 Eric Piatkowski .... .50 .15
❑ 57 Troy Hudson RC .... .25 .07
❑ 58 Kobe Bryant .... 3.00 .90
❑ 59 Shaquille O'Neal .... 2.00 .60
❑ 60 Glen Rice .... .50 .15
❑ 61 Robert Horry .... .50 .15
❑ 62 Tim Hardaway .... .50 .15
❑ 63 Alonzo Mourning .... .50 .15
❑ 64 P.J. Brown .... .25 .07
❑ 65 Dan Majerle .... .50 .15
❑ 66 Ray Allen .... .75 .23
❑ 67 Glenn Robinson .... .75 .23
❑ 68 Sam Cassell .... .75 .23
❑ 69 Robert Traylor .... .25 .07
❑ 70 Kevin Garnett .... 1.50 .45
❑ 71 Sam Mitchell .... .25 .07
❑ 72 Dean Garrett .... .25 .07
❑ 73 Bobby Jackson .... .50 .15
❑ 74 Radoslav Nesterovic RC 1.00 .30
❑ 75 Keith Van Horn .... .75 .23
❑ 76 Stephon Marbury .... .75 .23
❑ 77 Kendall Gill .... .25 .07
❑ 78 Scott Burrell .... .25 .07
❑ 79 Patrick Ewing .... .75 .23
❑ 80 Allan Houston .... .50 .15
❑ 81 Latrell Sprewell .... .75 .23
❑ 82 Larry Johnson .... .50 .15
❑ 83 Marcus Camby .... .50 .15
❑ 84 Darrell Armstrong .... .25 .07
❑ 85 Derek Strong .... .25 .07
❑ 86 Matt Harpring .... .75 .23
❑ 87 Michael Doleac .... .25 .07
❑ 88 Bo Outlaw .... .25 .07
❑ 89 Allen Iverson .... 1.50 .45
❑ 90 Theo Ratliff .... .50 .15
❑ 91 Larry Hughes .... .75 .23
❑ 92 Eric Snow .... .50 .15
❑ 93 Jason Kidd .... 1.25 .35
❑ 94 Clifford Robinson .... .25 .07
❑ 95 Tom Gugliotta .... .25 .07
❑ 96 Luc Longley .... .25 .07
❑ 97 Rasheed Wallace .... .75 .23
❑ 98 Arvydas Sabonis .... .50 .15
❑ 99 Damon Stoudamire .... .50 .15
❑ 100 Brian Grant .... .50 .15
❑ 101 Jason Williams .... .75 .23
❑ 102 Vlade Divac .... .50 .15
❑ 103 Peja Stojakovic .... 1.00 .30
❑ 104 Lawrence Funderburke .25 .07
❑ 105 Tim Duncan .... 1.50 .45
❑ 106 Sean Elliott .... .50 .15
❑ 107 David Robinson .... .75 .23
❑ 108 Mario Elie .... .25 .07
❑ 109 Avery Johnson .... .25 .07
❑ 110 Gary Payton .... .75 .23
❑ 111 Vin Baker .... .50 .15
❑ 112 Rashard Lewis .... .75 .23
❑ 113 Jelani McCoy .... .25 .07
❑ 114 Vladimir Stepania .... .25 .07
❑ 115 Vince Carter .... 2.00 .60
❑ 116 Doug Christie .... .50 .15
❑ 117 Kevin Willis .... .25 .07
❑ 118 Dee Brown .... .25 .07
❑ 119 John Thomas .... .25 .07
❑ 120 Karl Malone .... .75 .23
❑ 121 John Stockton .... .75 .23
❑ 122 Howard Eisley .... .25 .07
❑ 123 Bryon Russell .... .25 .07
❑ 124 Greg Ostertag .... .25 .07
❑ 125 Shareef Abdur-Rahim .. .75 .23
❑ 126 Mike Bibby .... .75 .23
❑ 127 Felipe Lopez .... .25 .07
❑ 128 Cherokee Parks .... .25 .07
❑ 129 Juwan Howard .... .50 .15
❑ 130 Rod Strickland .... .25 .07
❑ 131 Chris Whitney .... .25 .07
❑ 132 Tracy Murray .... .25 .07
❑ 133 Jahidi White .... .25 .07
❑ 134 Michael Jordan AIR .... 2.50 .75
❑ 135 Michael Jordan AIR .... 2.50 .75
❑ 136 Michael Jordan AIR .... 2.50 .75
❑ 137 Michael Jordan AIR .... 2.50 .75
❑ 138 Michael Jordan AIR .... 2.50 .75
❑ 139 Michael Jordan AIR .... 2.50 .75
❑ 140 Michael Jordan AIR .... 2.50 .75
❑ 141 Michael Jordan AIR .... 2.50 .75
❑ 142 Michael Jordan AIR .... 2.50 .75
❑ 143 Michael Jordan AIR .... 2.50 .75
❑ 144 Michael Jordan AIR .... 2.50 .75
❑ 145 Michael Jordan AIR .... 2.50 .75
❑ 146 Michael Jordan AIR .... 2.50 .75
❑ 147 Michael Jordan AIR .... 2.50 .75
❑ 148 Michael Jordan AIR .... 2.50 .75
❑ 149 Michael Jordan AIR .... 2.50 .75
❑ 150 Michael Jordan AIR .... 2.50 .75
❑ 151 Michael Jordan AIR .... 2.50 .75
❑ 152 Michael Jordan AIR .... 2.50 .75
❑ 153 Michael Jordan AIR .... 2.50 .75
❑ 154 Michael Jordan CL ...... 1.00 .30
❑ 155 Michael Jordan CL ...... 1.00 .30
❑ 156 Elton Brand RC 6.00 1.80
❑ 157 Steve Francis RC 8.00 2.40
❑ 158 Baron Davis RC 5.00 1.50
❑ 159 Lamar Odom RC 5.00 1.50
❑ 160 Jonathan Bender RC .. 5.00 1.50
❑ 161 Wally Szczerbiak RC .. 5.00 1.50
❑ 162 Richard Hamilton RC .. 5.00 1.50
❑ 163 Andre Miller RC 5.00 1.50
❑ 164 Shawn Marion RC 6.00 1.80
❑ 165 Jason Terry RC 4.00 1.20
❑ 166 Trajan Langdon RC .... 2.00 .60
❑ 167 Kenny Thomas RC ...... 2.00 .60
❑ 168 Corey Maggette RC 5.00 1.50
❑ 169 William Avery RC .... 2.00 .60
❑ 170 Jumaine Jones RC ...... 1.25 .35
❑ 171 Ron Artest RC .... 3.00 .90
❑ 172 Cal Bowdler RC .... 1.50 .45
❑ 173 James Posey RC .... 3.00 .90
❑ 174 Quincy Lewis RC .... 1.50 .45
❑ 175 Vonteego Cummings RC 2.00 .60
❑ 176 Jeff Foster RC .... 1.50 .45
❑ 177 Dion Glover RC .... 1.50 .45
❑ 178 Devean George RC .... 2.50 .75
❑ 179 Evan Eschmeyer RC .. 1.00 .30
❑ 180 Tim James RC .... 1.50 .45
❑ 181 Jim Jackson .... .25 .07
❑ 182 Isaiah Rider .... .25 .07
❑ 183 Lorenzen Wright .... .25 .07
❑ 184 Bimbo Coles .... .25 .07
❑ 185 Anthony Johnson .... .25 .07
❑ 186 Calbert Cheaney .... .25 .07
❑ 187 Pervis Ellison .... .25 .07
❑ 188 Walter McCarty .... .25 .07
❑ 189 Eric Williams .... .25 .07
❑ 190 Tony Battie .... .25 .07
❑ 191 Anthony Mason .... .50 .15
❑ 192 Bobby Phills .... .25 .07
❑ 193 Todd Fuller .... .25 .07
❑ 194 Brad Miller .... .75 .23

Card		
❑ 195 Eldridge Recasner	.25	.07
❑ 196 Chris Anstey	.25	.07
❑ 197 Fred Hoiberg	.25	.07
❑ 198 Hersey Hawkins	.50	.15
❑ 199 Will Perdue	.25	.07
❑ 200 Mark Bryant	.25	.07
❑ 201 Lamond Murray	.25	.07
❑ 202 Cedric Henderson	.25	.07
❑ 203 Andrew DeClercq	.25	.07
❑ 204 Danny Ferry	.25	.07
❑ 205 Erick Strickland	.25	.07
❑ 206 Cedric Ceballos	.25	.07
❑ 207 Hubert Davis	.25	.07
❑ 208 Robert Pack	.25	.07
❑ 209 Gary Trent	.25	.07
❑ 210 Ron Mercer	.50	.15
❑ 211 George McCloud	.25	.07
❑ 212 Roy Rogers	.25	.07
❑ 213 Keon Clark	.50	.15
❑ 214 Terry Mills	.25	.07
❑ 215 Michael Curry	.25	.07
❑ 216 Christian Laettner	.50	.15
❑ 217 Jerome Williams	.25	.07
❑ 218 Loy Vaught	.25	.07
❑ 219 Jud Buechler	.25	.07
❑ 220 Mookie Blaylock	.25	.07
❑ 221 Terry Cummings	.25	.07
❑ 222 Donyell Marshall	.50	.15
❑ 223 Chris Mills	.25	.07
❑ 224 Adonal Foyle	.25	.07
❑ 225 Shandon Anderson	.25	.07
❑ 226 Kelvin Cato	.25	.07
❑ 227 Walt Williams	.25	.07
❑ 228 Al Harrington	.75	.23
❑ 229 Rik Smits	.50	.15
❑ 230 Derrick McKey	.25	.07
❑ 231 Sam Perkins	.25	.07
❑ 232 Austin Croshere	.50	.15
❑ 233 Derek Anderson	.50	.15
❑ 234 Keith Closs	.25	.07
❑ 235 Eric Murdock	.25	.07
❑ 236 Brian Skinner	.25	.07
❑ 237 Charles Jones	.25	.07
❑ 238 Ron Harper	.50	.15
❑ 239 Derek Fisher	.75	.23
❑ 240 Rick Fox	.50	.15
❑ 241 A.C. Green	.50	.15
❑ 242 Jamal Mashburn	.50	.15
❑ 243 Mark Strickland	.25	.07
❑ 244 Rex Walters	.25	.07
❑ 245 Clarence Weatherspoon	.25	.07
❑ 246 Ervin Johnson	.25	.07
❑ 247 J.R. Reid	.25	.07
❑ 248 Dale Ellis	.25	.07
❑ 249 Danny Manning	.25	.07
❑ 250 Tim Thomas	.50	.15
❑ 251 Terrell Brandon	.50	.15
❑ 252 Malik Sealy	.25	.07
❑ 253 Joe Smith	.50	.15
❑ 254 Anthony Peeler	.25	.07
❑ 255 Jayson Williams	.25	.07
❑ 256 Jamie Feick RC	1.00	.30
❑ 257 Kerry Kittles	.25	.07
❑ 258 Johnny Newman	.25	.07
❑ 259 Chris Childs	.25	.07
❑ 260 Kurt Thomas	.50	.15
❑ 261 Charlie Ward	.25	.07
❑ 262 Chris Dudley	.25	.07
❑ 263 John Wallace	.25	.07
❑ 264 Tariq Abdul-Wahad	.25	.07
❑ 265 John Amaechi RC	1.00	.30
❑ 266 Chris Gatling	.25	.07
❑ 267 Monty Williams	.25	.07
❑ 268 Ben Wallace	.75	.23
❑ 269 George Lynch	.25	.07
❑ 270 Tyrone Hill	.25	.07
❑ 271 Billy Owens	.25	.07
❑ 272 Anfernee Hardaway	.75	.23
❑ 273 Rex Chapman	.25	.07
❑ 274 Oliver Miller	.25	.07
❑ 275 Rodney Rogers	.25	.07
❑ 276 Randy Livingston	.25	.07
❑ 277 Scottie Pippen	1.25	.35
❑ 278 Detlef Schrempf	.50	.15
❑ 279 Steve Smith	.50	.15
❑ 280 Jermaine O'Neal	.75	.23
❑ 281 Bonzi Wells	.75	.23
❑ 282 Chris Webber	.75	.23
❑ 283 Nick Anderson	.25	.07
❑ 284 Darrick Martin	.25	.07
❑ 285 Corliss Williamson	.50	.15
❑ 286 Samaki Walker	.25	.07
❑ 287 Terry Porter	.25	.07
❑ 288 Malik Rose	.25	.07
❑ 289 Jaren Jackson	.25	.07
❑ 290 Antonio Daniels	.25	.07
❑ 291 Steve Kerr	.50	.15
❑ 292 Brent Barry	.50	.15
❑ 293 Horace Grant	.50	.15
❑ 294 Vernon Maxwell	.25	.07
❑ 295 Ruben Patterson	.50	.15
❑ 296 Shammond Williams	.25	.07
❑ 297 Antonio Davis	.25	.07
❑ 298 Tracy McGrady	2.00	.60
❑ 299 Dell Curry	.25	.07
❑ 300 Charles Oakley	.25	.07
❑ 301 Muggsy Bogues	.50	.15
❑ 302 Jeff Hornacek	.50	.15
❑ 303 Adam Keefe	.25	.07
❑ 304 Olden Polynice	.25	.07
❑ 305 Doug West	.25	.07
❑ 306 Michael Dickerson	.50	.15
❑ 307 Othella Harrington	.25	.07
❑ 308 Bryant Reeves	.25	.07
❑ 309 Brent Price	.25	.07
❑ 310 Mitch Richmond	.50	.15
❑ 311 Aaron Williams	.25	.07
❑ 312 Isaac Austin	.25	.07
❑ 313 Michael Smith	.25	.07
❑ 314 Michael Jordan CL	1.00	.30
❑ 315 Kevin Garnett CL	.50	.15
❑ 316 Elton Brand	3.00	.90
❑ 317 Steve Francis	4.00	1.20
❑ 318 Baron Davis	2.50	.75
❑ 319 Lamar Odom	2.50	.75
❑ 320 Jonathan Bender	2.50	.75
❑ 321 Wally Szczerbiak	2.50	.75
❑ 322 Richard Hamilton	2.00	.60
❑ 323 Andre Miller	2.50	.75
❑ 324 Shawn Marion	3.00	.90
❑ 325 Jason Terry	.75	.23
❑ 326 Trajan Langdon	1.25	.35
❑ 327 Aleksandar Radojevic RC	1.00	.30
❑ 328 Corey Maggette	2.50	.75
❑ 329 William Avery	1.25	.35
❑ 330 Ron Artest	1.25	.35
❑ 331 Cal Bowdler	1.25	.35
❑ 332 James Posey	1.25	.35
❑ 333 Quincy Lewis	1.25	.35
❑ 334 Dion Glover	1.25	.35
❑ 335 Jeff Foster	1.00	.30
❑ 336 Kenny Thomas	1.25	.35
❑ 337 Devean George	.75	.23
❑ 338 Tim James	1.25	.35
❑ 339 Vonteego Cummings	1.25	.35
❑ 340 Jumaine Jones	2.00	.60
❑ 341 Scott Padgett RC	1.50	.45
❑ 342 John Celestand RC	1.50	.45
❑ 343 Adrian Griffin RC	1.50	.45
❑ 344 Michael Ruffin RC	1.25	.35
❑ 345 Chris Herren RC	1.00	.30
❑ 346 Evan Eschmeyer	.75	.23
❑ 347 Eddie Robinson RC	3.00	.90
❑ 348 Obinna Ekezie RC	1.25	.35
❑ 349 Laron Profit RC	1.50	.45
❑ 350 Jermaine Jackson RC	1.00	.30
❑ 351 Lazaro Borrell RC	1.00	.30
❑ 352 Chucky Atkins RC	2.00	.60
❑ 353 Ryan Robertson RC	1.25	.35
❑ 354 Todd MacCulloch RC	1.50	.45
❑ 355 Rafer Alston RC	2.00	.60
❑ 356 Mirsad Turkcan RC	1.00	.30
❑ 357 Anthony Carter RC	3.00	.90
❑ 358 Ryan Bowen RC	1.00	.30
❑ 359 Rodney Buford RC	1.00	.30
❑ 360 Tim Young RC	1.00	.30

2000-01 Upper Deck

	Nm-Mt	Ex-Mt
COMPLETE SET (445)	200.00	60.00
COMPLETE SERIES 1 (245)	120.00	36.00
COMPLETE SER.1 w/o RC (200)	40.00	12.00
COMPLETE SERIES 2 (200)	80.00	24.00
COMMON CARD (1-445)	.25	.07
COMMON ROOKIE (201-245/	.75	.23
❑ 1 Dikembe Mutombo	.50	.15
❑ 2 Jim Jackson	.25	.07
❑ 3 Alan Henderson	.25	.07
❑ 4 Jason Terry	.75	.23
❑ 5 Roshown McLeod	.25	.07
❑ 6 Lorenzen Wright	.25	.07
❑ 7 Paul Pierce	.75	.23
❑ 8 Antoine Walker	.75	.23
❑ 9 Vitaly Potapenko	.25	.07
❑ 10 Kenny Anderson	.50	.15
❑ 11 Tony Battie	.25	.07
❑ 12 Adrian Griffin	.25	.07
❑ 13 Eric Williams	.25	.07
❑ 14 Derrick Coleman	.25	.07
❑ 15 David Wesley	.25	.07
❑ 16 Baron Davis	.75	.23
❑ 17 Elden Campbell	.25	.07
❑ 18 Jamal Mashburn	.50	.15
❑ 19 Eddie Robinson	.50	.15
❑ 20 Elton Brand	.75	.23
❑ 21 Chris Carr	.25	.07
❑ 22 Ron Artest	.50	.15
❑ 23 Michael Ruffin	.25	.07
❑ 24 Fred Hoiberg	.25	.07
❑ 25 Corey Benjamin	.25	.07
❑ 26 Shawn Kemp	.50	.15
❑ 27 Lamond Murray	.25	.07
❑ 28 Andre Miller	.50	.15
❑ 29 Cedric Henderson	.25	.07
❑ 30 Wesley Person	.25	.07
❑ 31 Brevin Knight	.25	.07
❑ 32 Mark Bryant	.25	.07
❑ 33 Michael Finley	.75	.23
❑ 34 Cedric Ceballos	.25	.07
❑ 35 Dirk Nowitzki	1.25	.35
❑ 36 Hubert Davis	.25	.07
❑ 37 Steve Nash	.75	.23
❑ 38 Gary Trent	.25	.07
❑ 39 Antonio McDyess	.50	.15
❑ 40 James Posey	.50	.15
❑ 41 Nick Van Exel	.75	.23
❑ 42 Raef LaFrentz	.50	.15
❑ 43 George McCloud	.25	.07
❑ 44 Keon Clark	.50	.15
❑ 45 Jerry Stackhouse	.75	.23
❑ 46 Christian Laettner	.50	.15
❑ 47 Loy Vaught	.25	.07
❑ 48 Jerome Williams	.25	.07
❑ 49 Michael Curry	.25	.07
❑ 50 Lindsey Hunter	.25	.07
❑ 51 Antawn Jamison	.75	.23
❑ 52 Larry Hughes	.50	.15
❑ 53 Chris Mills	.25	.07
❑ 54 Donyell Marshall	.50	.15
❑ 55 Mookie Blaylock	.25	.07
❑ 56 Vonteego Cummings	.25	.07
❑ 57 Erick Dampier	.50	.15
❑ 58 Steve Francis	.75	.23
❑ 59 Shandon Anderson	.25	.07
❑ 60 Hakeem Olajuwon	.75	.23
❑ 61 Walt Williams	.25	.07
❑ 62 Kenny Thomas	.25	.07
❑ 63 Kelvin Cato	.25	.07
❑ 64 Cuttino Mobley	.50	.15
❑ 65 Reggie Miller	.75	.23

	#	Player		
❑	66	Jalen Rose	.75	.23
❑	67	Austin Croshere	.50	.15
❑	68	Dale Davis	.25	.07
❑	69	Travis Best	.25	.07
❑	70	Jonathan Bender	.50	.15
❑	71	Al Harrington	.50	.15
❑	72	Lamar Odom	.75	.23
❑	73	Tyrone Nesby	.25	.07
❑	74	Michael Olowokandi	.25	.07
❑	75	Brian Skinner	.25	.07
❑	76	Eric Piatkowski	.50	.15
❑	77	Keith Closs	.25	.07
❑	78	Shaquille O'Neal	2.00	.60
❑	79	Ron Harper	.50	.15
❑	80	Kobe Bryant	3.00	.90
❑	81	Rick Fox	.50	.15
❑	82	Robert Horry	.50	.15
❑	83	Derek Fisher	.75	.23
❑	84	Devean George	.50	.15
❑	85	Alonzo Mourning	.50	.15
❑	86	Eddie Jones	.75	.23
❑	87	Anthony Carter	.50	.15
❑	88	Bruce Bowen	.25	.07
❑	89	Clarence Weatherspoon	.25	.07
❑	90	Tim Hardaway	.50	.15
❑	91	Ray Allen	.75	.23
❑	92	Tim Thomas	.50	.15
❑	93	Glenn Robinson	.75	.23
❑	94	Scott Williams	.25	.07
❑	95	Sam Cassell	.75	.23
❑	96	Ervin Johnson	.25	.07
❑	97	Darvin Ham	.25	.07
❑	98	Kevin Garnett	1.50	.45
❑	99	Wally Szczerbiak	.50	.15
❑	100	Terrell Brandon	.50	.15
❑	101	Joe Smith	.50	.15
❑	102	Radoslav Nesterovic	.50	.15
❑	103	William Avery	.25	.07
❑	104	Stephon Marbury	.75	.23
❑	105	Kerry Kittles	.25	.07
❑	106	Keith Van Horn	.75	.23
❑	107	Lucious Harris	.25	.07
❑	108	Jamie Feick	.25	.07
❑	109	Johnny Newman	.25	.07
❑	110	Patrick Ewing	.75	.23
❑	111	Latrell Sprewell	.75	.23
❑	112	Marcus Camby	.50	.15
❑	113	Larry Johnson	.50	.15
❑	114	Charlie Ward	.25	.07
❑	115	Allan Houston	.50	.15
❑	116	Chris Childs	.25	.07
❑	117	Grant Hill	.75	.23
❑	118	John Amaechi	.25	.07
❑	119	Tracy McGrady	2.00	.60
❑	120	Michael Doleac	.25	.07
❑	121	Darrell Armstrong	.25	.07
❑	122	Bo Outlaw	.25	.07
❑	123	Allen Iverson	1.50	.45
❑	124	Theo Ratliff	.50	.15
❑	125	Matt Geiger	.25	.07
❑	126	Tyrone Hill	.25	.07
❑	127	George Lynch	.25	.07
❑	128	Toni Kukoc	.50	.15
❑	129	Jason Kidd	1.25	.35
❑	130	Rodney Rogers	.25	.07
❑	131	Anfernee Hardaway	.75	.23
❑	132	Clifford Robinson	.25	.07
❑	133	Tom Gugliotta	.25	.07
❑	134	Shawn Marion	.75	.23
❑	135	Luc Longley	.25	.07
❑	136	Rasheed Wallace	.75	.23
❑	137	Scottie Pippen	1.25	.35
❑	138	Arvydas Sabonis	.50	.15
❑	139	Steve Smith	.50	.15
❑	140	Damon Stoudamire	.50	.15
❑	141	Bonzi Wells	.50	.15
❑	142	Jermaine O'Neal	.75	.23
❑	143	Chris Webber	.75	.23
❑	144	Jason Williams	.50	.15
❑	145	Nick Anderson	.25	.07
❑	146	Vlade Divac	.50	.15
❑	147	Peja Stojakovic	.75	.23
❑	148	Jon Barry	.25	.07
❑	149	Corliss Williamson	.50	.15
❑	150	Tim Duncan	1.50	.45
❑	151	David Robinson	.75	.23
❑	152	Terry Porter	.25	.07
❑	153	Malik Rose	.25	.07
❑	154	Steve Kerr	.50	.15
❑	155	Avery Johnson	.25	.07
❑	156	Gary Payton	.75	.23
❑	157	Brent Barry	.50	.15
❑	158	Vin Baker	.50	.15
❑	159	Rashard Lewis	.50	.15
❑	160	Ruben Patterson	.50	.15
❑	161	Shammond Williams	.25	.07
❑	162	Vince Carter	2.00	.60
❑	163	Dell Curry	.25	.07
❑	164	Doug Christie	.50	.15
❑	165	Antonio Davis	.25	.07
❑	166	Kevin Willis	.25	.07
❑	167	Charles Oakley	.25	.07
❑	168	Karl Malone	.75	.23
❑	169	John Stockton	.75	.23
❑	170	Bryon Russell	.25	.07
❑	171	Olden Polynice	.25	.07
❑	172	Quincy Lewis	.25	.07
❑	173	Scott Padgett	.25	.07
❑	174	Shareef Abdur-Rahim	.75	.23
❑	175	Mike Bibby	.75	.23
❑	176	Michael Dickerson	.50	.15
❑	177	Bryant Reeves	.25	.07
❑	178	Othella Harrington	.25	.07
❑	179	Grant Long	.25	.07
❑	180	Mitch Richmond	.50	.15
❑	181	Richard Hamilton	.50	.15
❑	182	Juwan Howard	.50	.15
❑	183	Rod Strickland	.25	.07
❑	184	Tracy Murray	.25	.07
❑	185	Chris Whitney	.25	.07
❑	186	Kobe Bryant Y3K	.75	.23
❑	187	Kobe Bryant Y3K	.75	.23
❑	188	Kobe Bryant Y3K	.75	.23
❑	189	Kobe Bryant Y3K	.75	.23
❑	190	Kobe Bryant Y3K	.75	.23
❑	191	Kevin Garnett Y3K	.75	.23
❑	192	Kevin Garnett Y3K	.75	.23
❑	193	Kevin Garnett Y3K	.75	.23
❑	194	Kevin Garnett Y3K	.75	.23
❑	195	Kevin Garnett Y3K	.75	.23
❑	196	Kenyon Martin Y3K	.75	.23
❑	197	Kenyon Martin Y3K	.75	.23
❑	198	Kenyon Martin Y3K	.75	.23
❑	199	Kenyon Martin Y3K	.75	.23
❑	200	Kenyon Martin Y3K	.75	.23
❑	201	Kenyon Martin RC	5.00	1.50
❑	202	Stromile Swift RC	2.50	.75
❑	203	Chris Mihm RC	.75	.23
❑	204	Marcus Fizer RC	.75	.23
❑	205	Darius Miles RC	4.00	1.20
❑	206	Joel Przybilla RC	.75	.23
❑	207	Mike Miller RC	4.00	1.20
❑	208	Courtney Alexander RC	.75	.23
❑	209	DerMarr Johnson RC	.75	.23
❑	210	Iakovos Tsakalidis RC	.75	.23
❑	211	Jerome Moiso RC	.75	.23
❑	212	Keyon Dooling RC	.75	.23
❑	213	Erick Barkley RC	.75	.23
❑	214	Jason Collier RC	.75	.23
❑	215	Jamaal Magloire RC	.75	.23
❑	216	DeShawn Stevenson RC	.75	.23
❑	217	Hidayet Turkoglu RC	3.00	.90
❑	218	Morris Peterson RC	2.50	.75
❑	219	Jamal Crawford RC	1.00	.30
❑	220	Etan Thomas RC	.75	.23
❑	221	Quentin Richardson RC	3.00	.90
❑	222	Mateen Cleaves RC	.75	.23
❑	223	Chris Carrawell RC	.75	.23
❑	224	Corey Hightower RC	.75	.23
❑	225	Donnell Harvey RC	.75	.23
❑	226	Mark Madsen RC	.75	.23
❑	227	Jake Voskuhl RC	.75	.23
❑	228	Soumaila Samake RC	.75	.23
❑	229	Mamadou N'diaye RC	.75	.23
❑	230	Dan Langhi RC	.75	.23
❑	231	Hanno Mottola RC	.75	.23
❑	232	Olumide Oyedeji RC	.75	.23
❑	233	Jason Hart RC	.75	.23
❑	234	Mike Smith RC	.75	.23
❑	235	Chris Porter RC	.75	.23
❑	236	Jabari Smith RC	.75	.23
❑	237	Desmond Mason RC	.75	.23
❑	238	Eddie House RC	.75	.23
❑	239	A.J. Guyton RC	.75	.23
❑	240	Speedy Claxton RC	.75	.23
❑	241	Lavor Postell RC	.75	.23
❑	242	Khalid El-Amin RC	.75	.23
❑	243	Pepe Sanchez RC	.75	.23
❑	244	Eduardo Najera RC	2.00	.60
❑	245	Michael Redd RC	2.00	.60
❑	246	DerMarr Johnson	1.25	.35
❑	247	Hanno Mottola	.75	.23
❑	248	Dion Glover	.25	.07
❑	249	Matt Maloney	.25	.07
❑	250	Jason Terry	.75	.23
❑	251	Jerome Moiso	.75	.23
❑	252	Bryant Stith	.25	.07
❑	253	Randy Brown	.25	.07
❑	254	Mark Blount	.25	.07
❑	255	Chris Herren	.25	.07
❑	256	Jamal Mashburn	.50	.15
❑	257	P.J. Brown	.25	.07
❑	258	Lee Nailon	.25	.07
❑	259	Jamaal Magloire	1.00	.30
❑	260	Otis Thorpe	.25	.07
❑	261	Ron Mercer	.50	.15
❑	262	Marcus Fizer	1.50	.45
❑	263	Jamal Crawford	.75	.23
❑	264	A.J. Guyton	1.00	.30
❑	265	Dalibor Bagaric RC	.75	.23
❑	266	Chris Mihm	.50	.15
❑	267	Robert Traylor	.25	.07
❑	268	Matt Harpring	.75	.23
❑	269	Clarence Weatherspoon	.25	.07
❑	270	Bimbo Coles	.25	.07
❑	271	Etan Thomas	.75	.23
❑	272	Courtney Alexander	1.25	.35
❑	273	Donnell Harvey	.25	.07
❑	274	Eduardo Najera	1.00	.30
❑	275	Christian Laettner	.50	.15
❑	276	Mamadou N'Diaye	.50	.15
❑	277	Tariq Abdul-Wahad	.25	.07
❑	278	Voshon Lenard	.25	.07
❑	279	Robert Pack	.25	.07
❑	280	Tracy Murray	.25	.07
❑	281	Mateen Cleaves	.75	.23
❑	282	Ben Wallace	.75	.23
❑	283	Chucky Atkins	.25	.07
❑	284	Billy Owens	.25	.07
❑	285	Brian Cardinal RC	.75	.23
❑	286	Chris Porter	1.50	.45
❑	287	Bob Sura	.25	.07
❑	288	Vinny Del Negro	.25	.07
❑	289	Marc Jackson RC	4.00	1.20
❑	290	Danny Fortson	.25	.07
❑	291	Jason Collier	.75	.23
❑	292	Maurice Taylor	.25	.07
❑	293	Dan Langhi	.75	.23
❑	294	Carlos Rogers	.25	.07
❑	295	Moochie Norris	.25	.07
❑	296	Jermaine O'Neal	.75	.23
❑	297	Derrick McKey	.25	.07
❑	298	Sam Perkins	.50	.15
❑	299	Zan Tabak	.25	.07
❑	300	Jeff Foster	.25	.07
❑	301	Corey Maggette	.50	.15
❑	302	Darius Miles	2.00	.60
❑	303	Keyon Dooling	.75	.23
❑	304	Quentin Richardson	1.50	.45
❑	305	Jeff McInnis	.25	.07
❑	306	Isaiah Rider	.50	.15
❑	307	Mark Madsen	.75	.23
❑	308	Mike Penberthy RC	3.00	.90
❑	309	Brian Shaw	.25	.07
❑	310	Horace Grant	.50	.15
❑	311	Eddie Jones	.75	.23
❑	312	Brian Grant	.50	.15
❑	313	Anthony Mason	.50	.15
❑	314	Duane Causwell	.25	.07
❑	315	Eddie House	1.25	.35
❑	316	Lindsey Hunter	.25	.07
❑	317	Jason Caffey	.25	.07
❑	318	Joel Przybilla	.75	.23
❑	319	Michael Redd	1.50	.45
❑	320	Rafer Alston	.25	.07
❑	321	Chauncey Billups	.50	.15
❑	322	LaPhonso Ellis	.25	.07
❑	323	Sam Mitchell	.25	.07

❑ 324 Dean Garrett .25 .07
❑ 325 Tom Hammonds .25 .07
❑ 326 Kenyon Martin 2.50 .75
❑ 327 Soumaila Samake .50 .15
❑ 328 Aaron Williams .25 .07
❑ 329 Kendall Gill .25 .07
❑ 330 Stephen Jackson RC .. 2.50 .75
❑ 331 Lavor Postell .75 .23
❑ 332 Pete Mickeal RC .75 .23
❑ 333 Kurt Thomas .50 .15
❑ 334 Erick Strickland .25 .07
❑ 335 Glen Rice .50 .15
❑ 336 Grant Hill .75 .23
❑ 337 Tracy McGrady 2.00 .60
❑ 338 Pat Garrity .25 .07
❑ 339 Troy Hudson .25 .07
❑ 340 Mike Miller 2.00 .60
❑ 341 Speedy Claxton .75 .23
❑ 342 Eric Snow .50 .15
❑ 343 Pepe Sanchez .75 .23
❑ 344 Aaron McKie .50 .15
❑ 345 Nazr Mohammed .25 .07
❑ 346 Ruben Garces RC .75 .23
❑ 347 Daniel Santiago RC .... 2.00 .60
❑ 348 Tony Delk .25 .07
❑ 349 Paul McPherson RC.... 2.00 .60
❑ 350 Iakovos Tsakalidis .50 .15
❑ 351 Dale Davis .25 .07
❑ 352 Shawn Kemp .50 .15
❑ 353 Erick Barkley 1.00 .30
❑ 354 Greg Anthony .25 .07
❑ 355 Stacey Augmon .25 .07
❑ 356 Bobby Jackson .50 .15
❑ 357 Hidayet Turkoglu 1.50 .45
❑ 358 Jabari Smith .50 .15
❑ 359 Doug Christie .50 .15
❑ 360 Darrick Martin .25 .07
❑ 361 Sean Elliott .50 .15
❑ 362 Jaren Jackson .25 .07
❑ 363 Samaki Walker .25 .07
❑ 364 Derek Anderson .50 .15
❑ 365 Antonio Daniels .25 .07
❑ 366 Patrick Ewing .75 .23
❑ 367 Desmond Mason .75 .23
❑ 368 Jelani McCoy .25 .07
❑ 369 Ruben Wolkowyski RC 1.00 .30
❑ 370 Emanual Davis .25 .07
❑ 371 Mark Jackson .25 .07
❑ 372 Morris Peterson 1.50 .45
❑ 373 Muggsy Bogues .50 .15
❑ 374 Alvin Williams .25 .07
❑ 375 Corliss Williamson .50 .15
❑ 376 John Starks .50 .15
❑ 377 Danny Manning .50 .15
❑ 378 DeShawn Stevenson .... .75 .23
❑ 379 Donyell Marshall .50 .15
❑ 380 David Benoit .25 .07
❑ 381 Isaac Austin .25 .07
❑ 382 Mahmoud Abdul-Rauf .. .25 .07
❑ 383 Stromile Swift .75 .23
❑ 384 Kevin Edwards .25 .07
❑ 385 Brent Price .25 .07
❑ 386 Popeye Jones .25 .07
❑ 387 Mike Smith RC 1.00 .30
❑ 388 Jahidi White .25 .07
❑ 389 Laron Profit .25 .07
❑ 390 Felipe Lopez .25 .07
❑ 391 Dikembe Mutombo MVP .25 .07
❑ 392 Paul Pierce MVP .50 .15
❑ 393 Derrick Coleman MVP .. .25 .07
❑ 394 Elton Brand MVP .75 .23
❑ 395 Andre Miller MVP .50 .15
❑ 396 Michael Finley MVP .50 .15
❑ 397 Antonio McDyess MVP .50 .15
❑ 398 Jerry Stackhouse MVP.. .50 .15
❑ 399 Larry Hughes MVP .25 .07
❑ 400 Steve Francis MVP .75 .23
❑ 401 Reggie Miller MVP .50 .15
❑ 402 Lamar Odom MVP .50 .15
❑ 403 Shaquille O'Neal MVP 1.00 .30
❑ 404 Tim Hardaway MVP .25 .07
❑ 405 Ray Allen MVP .50 .15
❑ 406 Kevin Garnett MVP .75 .23
❑ 407 Stephon Marbury MVP.. .50 .15
❑ 408 Allan Houston MVP .50 .15
❑ 409 Grant Hill MVP .50 .15
❑ 410 Allen Iverson MVP .75 .23
❑ 411 Jason Kidd MVP .75 .23
❑ 412 Rasheed Wallace MVP .50 .15
❑ 413 Chris Webber MVP .50 .15
❑ 414 Tim Duncan MVP .75 .23
❑ 415 Gary Payton MVP .75 .23
❑ 416 Vince Carter MVP 1.00 .30
❑ 417 Karl Malone MVP .75 .23
❑ 418 S.Abdur-Rahim MVP .50 .15
❑ 419 Mitch Richmond MVP .25 .07
❑ 420 Kobe Bryant MVP 1.50 .45
❑ 421 Mateen Cleaves ROC .. .75 .23
❑ 422 Speedy Claxton ROC .75 .23
❑ 423 Courtney Alexander ROC .60 .18
❑ 424 Desmond Mason ROC .. .75 .23
❑ 425 Mike Miller ROC .75 .23
❑ 426 DerMarr Johnson ROC .75 .23
❑ 427 Chris Mihm ROC .50 .15
❑ 428 Jamal Crawford ROC .75 .23
❑ 429 Joel Przybilla ROC .50 .15
❑ 430 Keyon Dooling ROC .75 .23
❑ 431 Kobe Bryant PR .75 .23
❑ 432 Kobe Bryant PR .75 .23
❑ 433 Kobe Bryant PR .75 .23
❑ 434 Kobe Bryant PR .75 .23
❑ 435 Kobe Bryant PR .75 .23
❑ 436 Kobe Bryant PR .75 .23
❑ 437 Kobe Bryant PR .75 .23
❑ 438 Kobe Bryant PR .75 .23
❑ 439 Kobe Bryant PR .75 .23
❑ 440 Kobe Bryant PR .75 .23
❑ 441 Kobe Bryant PR .75 .23
❑ 442 Kobe Bryant PR .75 .23
❑ 443 Kobe Bryant PR .75 .23
❑ 444 Kobe Bryant PR .75 .23
❑ 445 Kobe Bryant PR .75 .23
❑ CL1 Checklist .25 .07
❑ CL1 Checklist .25 .07
❑ CL2 Checklist .25 .07
❑ CL2 Checklist .25 .07
❑ CL3 Checklist .25 .07
❑ CL3 Checklist .25 .07

2001-02 Upper Deck

	Nm-Mt	Ex-Mt
COMP.SET w/o SP's (360) ..	120.00	36.00
COMPLETE SER.1 (225)	200.00	60.00
COMP.SER 1 w/o SP's (180)	40.00	12.00
COMPLETE SER.2 (225)	200.00	60.00
COMP.SER 2 w/o SP's (180)	80.00	24.00
COMMON CARD (1-405)	.25	.07
COMMON ROOKIE (181-225)	2.00	.60
COMMON CARD (406A-450B) ..	.50	.15
SEMISTARS 406-450	1.00	.30
UNLISTED STARS 406-450	1.50	.45
COMMON ROOKIE (406A-	3.00	.90
406B-NOT INCLUDED IN SET PRICES		-
-		

❑ 1 Jason Terry .75 .23
❑ 2 Toni Kukoc .50 .15
❑ 3 Alan Henderson .25 .07
❑ 4 Theo Ratliff .50 .15
❑ 5 Shareef Abdur-Rahim .75 .23
❑ 6 DerMarr Johnson .50 .15
❑ 7 Paul Pierce .75 .23
❑ 8 Antoine Walker .75 .23
❑ 9 Kenny Anderson .50 .15
❑ 10 Vitaly Potapenko .25 .07
❑ 11 Eric Williams .25 .07
❑ 12 Jamal Mashburn .50 .15
❑ 13 Baron Davis .75 .23
❑ 14 David Wesley .25 .07
❑ 15 P.J. Brown .25 .07
❑ 16 Elden Campbell .25 .07
❑ 17 Jamaal Magloire .50 .15
❑ 18 Lee Nailon .25 .07
❑ 19 A.J. Guyton .50 .15
❑ 20 Ron Mercer .50 .15
❑ 21 Jamal Crawford .50 .15
❑ 22 Fred Hoiberg .25 .07
❑ 23 Marcus Fizer .50 .15
❑ 24 Ron Artest .50 .15
❑ 25 Lamond Murray .25 .07
❑ 26 Andre Miller .50 .15
❑ 27 Jim Jackson .25 .07
❑ 28 Chris Mihm .50 .15
❑ 29 Trajan Langdon .25 .07
❑ 30 Chris Gatling .25 .07
❑ 31 Michael Finley .75 .23
❑ 32 Dirk Nowitzki 1.25 .35
❑ 33 Steve Nash .75 .23
❑ 34 Juwan Howard .50 .15
❑ 35 Wang Zhizhi .75 .23
❑ 36 Eduardo Najera .50 .15
❑ 37 Shawn Bradley .25 .07
❑ 38 Antonio McDyess .50 .15
❑ 39 Nick Van Exel .75 .23
❑ 40 Raef LaFrentz .50 .15
❑ 41 James Posey .50 .15
❑ 42 Voshon Lenard .25 .07
❑ 43 Ben Wallace .75 .23
❑ 44 Jerry Stackhouse .75 .23
❑ 45 Corliss Williamson .50 .15
❑ 46 Chucky Atkins .25 .07
❑ 47 Michael Curry .25 .07
❑ 48 Dana Barros .25 .07
❑ 49 Antawn Jamison .75 .23
❑ 50 Larry Hughes .50 .15
❑ 51 Bob Sura .25 .07
❑ 52 Marc Jackson .50 .15
❑ 53 Chris Porter .50 .15
❑ 54 Vonteego Cummings .25 .07
❑ 55 Steve Francis .75 .23
❑ 56 Cuttino Mobley .50 .15
❑ 57 Maurice Taylor .50 .15
❑ 58 Kenny Thomas .25 .07
❑ 59 Moochie Norris .25 .07
❑ 60 Walt Williams .25 .07
❑ 61 Reggie Miller .75 .23
❑ 62 Jalen Rose .75 .23
❑ 63 Jermaine O'Neal .75 .23
❑ 64 Austin Croshere .25 .07
❑ 65 Travis Best .25 .07
❑ 66 Jonathan Bender .50 .15
❑ 67 Eric Piatkowski .50 .15
❑ 68 Darius Miles .75 .23
❑ 69 Lamar Odom .75 .23
❑ 70 Quentin Richardson .50 .15
❑ 71 Corey Maggette .50 .15
❑ 72 Elton Brand .75 .23
❑ 73 Jeff McInnis .25 .07
❑ 74 Kobe Bryant 3.00 .90
❑ 75 Shaquille O'Neal 2.00 .60
❑ 76 Derek Fisher .75 .23
❑ 77 Rick Fox .50 .15
❑ 78 Mitch Richmond .50 .15
❑ 79 Ron Harper .50 .15
❑ 80 Brian Shaw .25 .07
❑ 81 Stromile Swift .50 .15
❑ 82 Michael Dickerson .50 .15
❑ 83 Jason Williams .50 .15
❑ 84 Grant Long .25 .07
❑ 85 Bryant Reeves .25 .07
❑ 86 Alonzo Mourning .50 .15
❑ 87 Eddie Jones .75 .23
❑ 88 Brian Grant .50 .15
❑ 89 Anthony Mason .50 .15
❑ 90 LaPhonso Ellis .25 .07
❑ 91 Anthony Carter .50 .15
❑ 92 Jason Caffey .25 .07
❑ 93 Ray Allen .75 .23
❑ 94 Glenn Robinson .75 .23
❑ 95 Sam Cassell .75 .23
❑ 96 Tim Thomas .50 .15

❑ 97 Ervin Johnson .25 .07
❑ 98 Joel Przybilla .50 .15
❑ 99 Kevin Garnett 1.50 .45
❑ 100 Terrell Brandon .50 .15
❑ 101 Wally Szczerbiak .50 .15
❑ 102 Felipe Lopez .25 .07
❑ 103 Chauncey Billups .50 .15
❑ 104 Anthony Peeler .25 .07
❑ 105 Kenyon Martin .75 .23
❑ 106 Keith Van Horn .75 .23
❑ 107 Jamie Feick .25 .07
❑ 108 Aaron Williams .25 .07
❑ 109 Lucious Harris .25 .07
❑ 110 Jason Kidd 1.25 .35
❑ 111 Latrell Sprewell .75 .23
❑ 112 Allan Houston .50 .15
❑ 113 Marcus Camby .50 .15
❑ 114 Mark Jackson .25 .07
❑ 115 Othella Harrington .25 .07
❑ 116 Kurt Thomas .50 .15
❑ 117 Tracy McGrady 2.00 .60
❑ 118 Mike Miller .75 .23
❑ 119 Darrell Armstrong .25 .07
❑ 120 Grant Hill .75 .23
❑ 121 Pat Garrity .25 .07
❑ 122 Bo Outlaw .25 .07
❑ 123 Allen Iverson 1.50 .45
❑ 124 Dikembe Mutombo .50 .15
❑ 125 Aaron McKie .50 .15
❑ 126 Matt Geiger .25 .07
❑ 127 Eric Snow .50 .15
❑ 128 George Lynch .25 .07
❑ 129 Raja Bell RC 2.00 .60
❑ 130 Shawn Marion .75 .23
❑ 131 Tom Gugliotta .25 .07
❑ 132 Rodney Rogers .25 .07
❑ 133 Anfernee Hardaway .75 .23
❑ 134 Tony Delk .25 .07
❑ 135 Stephon Marbury .75 .23
❑ 136 Rasheed Wallace .75 .23
❑ 137 Damon Stoudamire .50 .15
❑ 138 Rod Strickland .25 .07
❑ 139 Dale Davis .50 .15
❑ 140 Scottie Pippen 1.25 .35
❑ 141 Bonzi Wells .50 .15
❑ 142 Peja Stojakovic .75 .23
❑ 143 Chris Webber .75 .23
❑ 144 Doug Christie .50 .15
❑ 145 Mike Bibby .75 .23
❑ 146 Hidayet Turkoglu .50 .15
❑ 147 Scot Pollard .25 .07
❑ 148 Vlade Divac .50 .15
❑ 149 Tim Duncan 1.50 .45
❑ 150 David Robinson .75 .23
❑ 151 Antonio Daniels .25 .07
❑ 152 Danny Ferry .25 .07
❑ 153 Malik Rose .25 .07
❑ 154 Terry Porter .25 .07
❑ 155 Rashard Lewis .25 .07
❑ 156 Gary Payton .75 .23
❑ 157 Brent Barry .50 .15
❑ 158 Vin Baker .50 .15
❑ 159 Desmond Mason .50 .15
❑ 160 Shammond Williams .25 .07
❑ 161 Vince Carter 2.00 .60
❑ 162 Antonio Davis .25 .07
❑ 163 Morris Peterson .50 .15
❑ 164 Keon Clark .50 .15
❑ 165 Chris Childs .25 .07
❑ 166 Alvin Williams .25 .07
❑ 167 Karl Malone .75 .23
❑ 168 John Stockton .75 .23
❑ 169 Donyell Marshall .50 .15
❑ 170 John Starks .50 .15
❑ 171 Bryon Russell .25 .07
❑ 172 David Benoit .25 .07
❑ 173 DeShawn Stevenson .50 .15
❑ 174 Richard Hamilton .50 .15
❑ 175 Jahidi White .25 .07
❑ 176 Courtney Alexander .50 .15
❑ 177 Chris Whitney .25 .07
❑ 178 Michael Jordan 10.00 3.00
❑ 179 Kobe Bryant CL .50 .15
❑ 180 Kevin Garnett CL .75 .23
❑ 181 Sean Lampley RC 2.00 .60
❑ 182 Andrei Kirilenko RC 6.00 1.80
❑ 183 Brandon Armstrong RC 2.50 .75
❑ 184 Gerald Wallace RC 6.00 1.80
❑ 185 Tony Parker RC 10.00 3.00
❑ 186 Jeryl Sasser RC 2.00 .60
❑ 187 Alton Ford RC 3.00 .90
❑ 188 Kenny Satterfield RC 2.00 .60
❑ 189 Will Solomon RC 2.00 .60
❑ 190 Earl Watson RC 3.00 .90
❑ 191 Michael Wright RC 2.00 .60
❑ 192 Samuel Dalembert RC 2.00 .60
❑ 193 Ousmane Cisse RC 2.00 .60
❑ 194 Ruben Boumtje-Boumtje RC 2.00 .60
❑ 195 Damone Brown RC 2.00 .60
❑ 196 Jarron Collins RC 2.00 .60
❑ 197 Terence Morris RC 2.00 .60
❑ 198 Pau Gasol RC 8.00 2.40
❑ 199 Trenton Hassell RC 4.00 1.20
❑ 200 Kirk Haston RC 2.00 .60
❑ 201 Brian Scalabrine RC 2.00 .60
❑ 202 Gilbert Arenas RC 5.00 1.50
❑ 203 Jeff Trepagnier RC 2.00 .60
❑ 204 Joseph Forte RC 5.00 1.50
❑ 205 Steven Hunter RC 2.00 .60
❑ 206 Omar Cook RC 2.00 .60
❑ 207 Jason Collins RC 2.00 .60
❑ 208 Kedrick Brown RC 2.00 .60
❑ 209 Michael Bradley RC 2.00 .60
❑ 210 Zach Randolph RC 8.00 2.40
❑ 211 Richard Jefferson RC 8.00 2.40
❑ 212 Jamaal Tinsley RC 4.00 1.20
❑ 213 Vladimir Radmanovic RC 3.00 .90
❑ 214 Brendan Haywood RC 3.00 .90
❑ 215 Troy Murphy RC 5.00 1.50
❑ 216 DeSagana Diop RC 2.00 .60
❑ 217 Jason Richardson RC 8.00 2.40
❑ 218 Joe Johnson RC 4.00 1.20
❑ 219 Rodney White RC 3.00 .90
❑ 220 Loren Woods RC 2.00 .60
❑ 221 Tyson Chandler RC 6.00 1.80
❑ 222 Eddy Curry RC 6.00 1.80
❑ 223 Shane Battier RC 4.00 1.20
❑ 224 Eddie Griffin RC 4.00 1.20
❑ 225 Kwame Brown RC 5.00 1.50
❑ 226 Shareef Abdur-Rahim .75 .23
❑ 227 Nazr Mohammed .25 .07
❑ 228 Hanno Mottola .50 .15
❑ 229 Emanual Davis .25 .07
❑ 230 Dion Glover .25 .07
❑ 231 Chris Crawford .25 .07
❑ 232 Mark Blount .25 .07
❑ 233 Joe Johnson 4.00 1.20
❑ 234 Milt Palacio .25 .07
❑ 235 Kedrick Brown .75 .23
❑ 236 Tony Battie .25 .07
❑ 237 Erick Strickland .25 .07
❑ 238 Kirk Haston 1.00 .30
❑ 239 Stacey Augmon .25 .07
❑ 240 Matt Bullard .25 .07
❑ 241 Bryce Drew .25 .07
❑ 242 Jerome Moiso .50 .15
❑ 243 Robert Traylor .25 .07
❑ 244 Tyson Chandler 3.00 .90
❑ 245 Eddy Curry 3.00 .90
❑ 246 Charles Oakley .25 .07
❑ 247 Brad Miller .75 .23
❑ 248 Kevin Ollie .25 .07
❑ 249 Trenton Hassell 2.00 .60
❑ 250 Ricky Davis .50 .15
❑ 251 Jumaine Jones .50 .15
❑ 252 DeSagana Diop 1.00 .30
❑ 253 Bryant Stith .25 .07
❑ 254 Jeff Trepagnier 1.00 .30
❑ 255 Michael Doleac .25 .07
❑ 256 Tim Hardaway .75 .23
❑ 257 Danny Manning .25 .07
❑ 258 Johnny Newman .25 .07
❑ 259 Adrian Griffin .25 .07
❑ 260 Greg Buckner .25 .07
❑ 261 Donnell Harvey .25 .07
❑ 262 Evan Eschmeyer .25 .07
❑ 263 Avery Johnson .25 .07
❑ 264 Kenny Satterfield 1.00 .30
❑ 265 Scott Williams .25 .07
❑ 266 Tariq Abdul-Wahad .25 .07
❑ 267 George McCloud .25 .07
❑ 268 Clifford Robinson .25 .07
❑ 269 Jon Barry .25 .07
❑ 270 Brian Cardinal .25 .07
❑ 271 Rodney White 1.50 .45
❑ 272 Mikki Moore .25 .07
❑ 273 Victor Alexander .25 .07
❑ 274 Jason Richardson 4.00 1.20
❑ 275 Adonal Foyle .25 .07
❑ 276 Troy Murphy 2.50 .75
❑ 277 Chris Mills .25 .07
❑ 278 Gilbert Arenas 2.00 .60
❑ 279 Erick Dampier .50 .15
❑ 280 Glen Rice .50 .15
❑ 281 Eddie Griffin 2.00 .60
❑ 282 Kevin Willis .25 .07
❑ 283 Terence Morris 1.00 .30
❑ 284 Kelvin Cato .25 .07
❑ 285 Dan Langhi .50 .15
❑ 286 Jason Collier .25 .07
❑ 287 Jamaal Tinsley 2.00 .60
❑ 288 Carlos Rogers .25 .07
❑ 289 Jeff Foster .25 .07
❑ 290 Al Harrington .50 .15
❑ 291 Bruno Sundov .25 .07
❑ 292 Elton Brand .75 .23
❑ 293 Keyon Dooling .50 .15
❑ 294 Michael Olowokandi .50 .15
❑ 295 Obinna Ekezie .25 .07
❑ 296 Earl Boykins .50 .15
❑ 297 Harold Jamison .25 .07
❑ 298 Sean Rooks .25 .07
❑ 299 Lindsey Hunter .25 .07
❑ 300 Samaki Walker .25 .07
❑ 301 Mitch Richmond .50 .15
❑ 302 Stanislav Medvedenko .25 .07
❑ 303 Devean George .50 .15
❑ 304 Robert Horry .50 .15
❑ 305 Jelani McCoy .25 .07
❑ 306 Pau Gasol 4.00 1.20
❑ 307 Shane Battier 2.50 .75
❑ 308 Jason Williams .50 .15
❑ 309 Isaac Austin .25 .07
❑ 310 Will Solomon .25 .07
❑ 311 Lorenzen Wright .25 .07
❑ 312 Kendall Gill .25 .07
❑ 313 LaPhonso Ellis .25 .07
❑ 314 Sean Marks .25 .07
❑ 315 Rod Strickland .25 .07
❑ 316 Jim Jackson .25 .07
❑ 317 Eddie House .50 .15
❑ 318 Jason Caffey .25 .07
❑ 319 Rafer Alston .25 .07
❑ 320 Anthony Mason .50 .15
❑ 321 Mark Pope .25 .07
❑ 322 Michael Redd .75 .23
❑ 323 Darvin Ham .25 .07
❑ 324 Joe Smith .50 .15
❑ 325 William Avery .25 .07
❑ 326 Sam Mitchell .25 .07
❑ 327 Loren Woods 1.00 .30
❑ 328 Dean Garrett .25 .07
❑ 329 Gary Trent .25 .07
❑ 330 Jason Kidd 1.25 .35
❑ 331 Todd MacCulloch .25 .07
❑ 332 Richard Jefferson 4.00 1.20
❑ 333 Brandon Armstrong 1.25 .35
❑ 334 Jason Collins 1.00 .30
❑ 335 Kerry Kittles .50 .15
❑ 336 Shandon Anderson .25 .07
❑ 337 Howard Eisley .25 .07
❑ 338 Charlie Ward .25 .07
❑ 339 Lavor Postell .50 .15
❑ 340 Clarence Weatherspoon .25 .07
❑ 341 Travis Knight .25 .07
❑ 342 Horace Grant .50 .15
❑ 343 Steven Hunter 1.00 .30
❑ 344 Patrick Ewing .75 .23
❑ 345 Jeryl Sasser 1.00 .30
❑ 346 Don Reid .25 .07
❑ 347 Troy Hudson .25 .07
❑ 348 Speedy Claxton .50 .15
❑ 349 Derrick Coleman .25 .07
❑ 350 Damone Brown 1.00 .30
❑ 351 Samuel Dalembert .75 .23
❑ 352 Vonteego Cummings .25 .07
❑ 353 Matt Harpring .75 .23

Card	Player	Nm-Mt	Ex-Mt
❑ 354	Corie Blount	.25	.07
❑ 355	Stephon Marbury	.75	.23
❑ 356	Dan Majerle	.50	.15
❑ 357	Jake Voskuhl	.50	.15
❑ 358	Alton Ford	1.50	.45
❑ 359	Iakovos Tsakalidis	.25	.07
❑ 360	John Wallace	.25	.07
❑ 361	Derek Anderson	.50	.15
❑ 362	Erick Barkley	.50	.15
❑ 363	R.Boumtje-Boumtje	2.00	.60
❑ 364	Zach Randolph	4.00	1.20
❑ 365	Steve Kerr	.50	.15
❑ 366	Shawn Kemp	.50	.15
❑ 367	Mateen Cleaves	.50	.15
❑ 368	Bobby Jackson	.25	.07
❑ 369	Mike Bibby	.75	.23
❑ 370	Gerald Wallace	3.00	.90
❑ 371	Jabari Smith	.50	.15
❑ 372	Lawrence Funderburke	.25	.07
❑ 373	Brent Price	.25	.07
❑ 374	Bruce Bowen	.25	.07
❑ 375	Stephen Jackson	.50	.15
❑ 376	Tony Parker	5.00	1.50
❑ 377	Steve Smith	.50	.15
❑ 378	Cherokee Parks	.25	.07
❑ 379	Mark Bryant	.25	.07
❑ 380	Jerome James	.25	.07
❑ 381	Earl Watson	1.50	.45
❑ 382	Vladimir Radmanovic	1.50	.45
❑ 383	Art Long	.25	.07
❑ 384	Calvin Booth	.25	.07
❑ 385	Olumide Oyedeji	.25	.07
❑ 386	Jerome Williams	.25	.07
❑ 387	Hakeem Olajuwon	.75	.23
❑ 388	Dell Curry	.25	.07
❑ 389	Michael Bradley	1.00	.30
❑ 390	Tracy Murray	.25	.07
❑ 391	Eric Montross	.25	.07
❑ 392	John Amaechi	.25	.07
❑ 393	John Crotty	.25	.07
❑ 394	Scott Padgett	.25	.07
❑ 395	Andrei Kirilenko	3.00	.90
❑ 396	Jarron Collins	1.00	.30
❑ 397	Quincy Lewis	.25	.07
❑ 398	Kwame Brown	2.50	.75
❑ 399	Christian Laettner	.50	.15
❑ 400	Tyrone Nesby	.25	.07
❑ 401	Brendan Haywood	2.00	.60
❑ 402	Tyronn Lue	.25	.07
❑ 403	Michael Jordan	10.00	3.00
❑ 404	Kobe Bryant CL	.50	.15
❑ 405	Michael Jordan CL	4.00	1.20
❑ 406A	Zeljko Rebraca RC	3.00	.90
❑ 406B	Zeljko Rebraca RC	3.00	.90
❑ 407A	Jamison Brewer RC	3.00	.90
❑ 407B	Jamison Brewer RC	3.00	.90
❑ 408A	Shawn Marion	1.50	.45
❑ 408B	Shawn Marion	1.50	.45
❑ 409A	Primoz Brezec RC	3.00	.90
❑ 409B	Primoz Brezec RC	3.00	.90
❑ 410A	Antonis Fotsis RC	3.00	.90
❑ 410B	Antonis Fotsis RC	3.00	.90
❑ 411A	Bobby Simmons RC	3.00	.90
❑ 411B	Bobby Simmons RC	3.00	.90
❑ 412A	Malik Allen RC	3.00	.90
❑ 412B	Malik Allen RC	3.00	.90
❑ 413A	Ratko Varda RC	3.00	.90
❑ 413B	Ratko Varda RC	3.00	.90
❑ 414A	Tierre Brown RC	3.00	.90
❑ 414B	Tierre Brown RC	3.00	.90
❑ 415A	Norm Richardson RC	3.00	.90
❑ 415B	Norm Richardson RC	3.00	.90
❑ 416A	Oscar Torres RC	3.00	.90
❑ 416B	Oscar Torres RC	3.00	.90
❑ 417A	Chris Anderson RC	3.00	.90
❑ 417B	Chris Anderson RC	3.00	.90
❑ 418A	Peja Stojakovic	1.50	.45
❑ 418B	Peja Stojakovic	1.50	.45
❑ 419A	Dirk Nowitzki	2.50	.75
❑ 419B	Dirk Nowitzki	2.50	.75
❑ 420A	Shareef Abdur-Rahim	1.50	.45
❑ 420B	Shareef Abdur-Rahim	1.50	.45
❑ 421A	Kenny Anderson	.50	.15
❑ 421B	Kenny Anderson	.50	.15
❑ 422A	Jamal Mashburn	1.00	.30
❑ 422B	Jamal Mashburn	1.00	.30
❑ 423A	Charles Oakley	.50	.15
❑ 423B	Charles Oakley	.50	.15
❑ 424A	Andre Miller	1.00	.30
❑ 424B	Andre Miller	1.00	.30
❑ 425A	Michael Finley	1.50	.45
❑ 425B	Michael Finley	1.50	.45
❑ 426A	Tim Hardaway	1.50	.45
❑ 426B	Tim Hardaway	1.50	.45
❑ 427A	Nick Van Exel	1.50	.45
❑ 427B	Nick Van Exel	1.50	.45
❑ 428A	Jerry Stackhouse	1.50	.45
❑ 428B	Jerry Stackhouse	1.50	.45
❑ 429A	Mookie Blaylock	.50	.15
❑ 429B	Mookie Blaylock	.50	.15
❑ 430A	Glen Rice	1.00	.30
❑ 430B	Glen Rice	1.00	.30
❑ 431A	Reggie Miller	1.50	.45
❑ 431B	Reggie Miller	1.50	.45
❑ 432A	Elton Brand	1.50	.45
❑ 432B	Elton Brand	1.50	.45
❑ 433A	Kobe Bryant	6.00	1.80
❑ 433B	Kobe Bryant	6.00	1.80
❑ 434A	Jason Williams	1.00	.30
❑ 434B	Jason Williams	1.00	.30
❑ 435A	Eddie Jones	1.50	.45
❑ 435B	Eddie Jones	1.50	.45
❑ 436A	Alonzo Mourning	1.00	.30
❑ 436B	Alonzo Mourning	1.00	.30
❑ 437A	Glenn Robinson	1.00	.30
❑ 437B	Glenn Robinson	1.00	.30
❑ 438A	Kevin Garnett	3.00	.90
❑ 438B	Kevin Garnett	3.00	.90
❑ 439A	Jason Kidd	2.50	.75
❑ 439B	Jason Kidd	2.50	.75
❑ 440A	Latrell Sprewell	.75	.23
❑ 440B	Latrell Sprewell	.75	.23
❑ 441A	Grant Hill	1.50	.45
❑ 441B	Grant Hill	1.50	.45
❑ 442A	Dikembe Mutombo	1.50	.45
❑ 442B	Dikembe Mutombo	1.50	.45
❑ 443A	Anfernee Hardaway	1.50	.45
❑ 443B	Anfernee Hardaway	1.50	.45
❑ 444A	Scottie Pippen	2.50	.75
❑ 444B	Scottie Pippen	2.50	.75
❑ 445A	Mike Bibby	1.50	.45
❑ 445B	Mike Bibby	1.50	.45
❑ 446A	David Robinson	1.50	.45
❑ 446B	David Robinson	1.50	.45
❑ 447A	Gary Payton	1.50	.45
❑ 447B	Gary Payton	1.50	.45
❑ 448A	Vince Carter	4.00	1.20
❑ 448B	Vince Carter	4.00	1.20
❑ 449A	John Stockton	.75	.23
❑ 449B	John Stockton	.75	.23
❑ 450A	Michael Jordan Bulls	20.00	6.00
❑ 450B	Michael Jordan Wizards	20.00	6.00
❑ NNO	M.Jordan Buyback EXCH		-

2002-03 Upper Deck

	Nm-Mt	Ex-Mt
COMPLETE SER.1 (210)	160.00	47.50
COMPLETE SER. 2 (220)	40.00	12.00
COMP.SER.1 w/o SP's (180)	40.00	12.00
COMMON CARD (1-420)	.20	.06
COMMON ROOKIE	3.00	.90

Card	Player	Nm-Mt	Ex-Mt
❑ 1	Shareef Abdur-Rahim	.75	.23
❑ 2	Jason Terry	.75	.23
❑ 3	Glenn Robinson	.75	.23
❑ 4	Nazr Mohammed	.20	.06
❑ 5	DerMarr Johnson	.20	.06
❑ 6	Dion Glover	.20	.06
❑ 7	Paul Pierce	.75	.23
❑ 8	Antoine Walker	.75	.23
❑ 9	Vin Baker	.50	.15
❑ 10	Eric Williams	.20	.06
❑ 11	Tony Delk	.20	.06
❑ 12	Kedrick Brown	.50	.15
❑ 13	Jalen Rose	.75	.23
❑ 14	Eddy Curry	.75	.23
❑ 15	Tyson Chandler	.75	.23
❑ 16	Jamal Crawford	.20	.06
❑ 17	Marcus Fizer	.50	.15
❑ 18	Trenton Hassell	.50	.15
❑ 19	Zydrunas Ilgauskas	.50	.15
❑ 20	Tyrone Hill	.20	.06
❑ 21	Darius Miles	.75	.23
❑ 22	Chris Mihm	.20	.06
❑ 23	Ricky Davis	.50	.15
❑ 24	Jumaine Jones	.50	.15
❑ 25	Dirk Nowitzki	1.25	.35
❑ 26	Michael Finley	.75	.23
❑ 27	Steve Nash	.75	.23
❑ 28	Raef LaFrentz	.50	.15
❑ 29	Nick Van Exel	.75	.23
❑ 30	Adrian Griffin	.20	.06
❑ 31	Wang Zhizhi	.75	.23
❑ 32	Marcus Camby	.50	.15
❑ 33	Juwan Howard	.50	.15
❑ 34	James Posey	.50	.15
❑ 35	Donnell Harvey	.20	.06
❑ 36	Ryan Bowen	.20	.06
❑ 37	Zeljko Rebraca	.50	.15
❑ 38	Ben Wallace	.75	.23
❑ 39	Clifford Robinson	.20	.06
❑ 40	Corliss Williamson	.50	.15
❑ 41	Chucky Atkins	.20	.06
❑ 42	Michael Curry	.20	.06
❑ 43	Jason Richardson	.75	.23
❑ 44	Antawn Jamison	.75	.23
❑ 45	Troy Murphy	.50	.15
❑ 46	Gilbert Arenas	.75	.23
❑ 47	Danny Fortson	.20	.06
❑ 48	Steve Francis	.75	.23
❑ 49	Eddie Griffin	.50	.15
❑ 50	Cuttino Mobley	.50	.15
❑ 51	Kenny Thomas	.20	.06
❑ 52	Moochie Norris	.20	.06
❑ 53	Kelvin Cato	.20	.06
❑ 54	Reggie Miller	.75	.23
❑ 55	Jermaine O'Neal	.75	.23
❑ 56	Ron Mercer	.50	.15
❑ 57	Austin Croshere	.20	.06
❑ 58	Ron Artest	.50	.15
❑ 59	Jamaal Tinsley	.75	.23
❑ 60	Elton Brand	.75	.23
❑ 61	Andre Miller	.50	.15
❑ 62	Lamar Odom	.75	.23
❑ 63	Michael Olowokandi	.20	.06
❑ 64	Quentin Richardson	.50	.15
❑ 65	Corey Maggette	.50	.15
❑ 66	Kobe Bryant	3.00	.90
❑ 67	Shaquille O'Neal	2.00	.60
❑ 68	Rick Fox	.50	.15
❑ 69	Robert Horry	.50	.15
❑ 70	Devean George	.50	.15
❑ 71	Samaki Walker	.20	.06
❑ 72	Brian Shaw	.20	.06
❑ 73	Pau Gasol	.75	.23
❑ 74	Jason Williams	.50	.15
❑ 75	Shane Battier	.75	.23
❑ 76	Stromile Swift	.50	.15
❑ 77	Lorenzen Wright	.20	.06
❑ 78	LaPhonso Ellis	.20	.06
❑ 79	Eddie Jones	.75	.23
❑ 80	Brian Grant	.50	.15
❑ 81	Vladimir Stepania	.20	.06
❑ 82	Eddie House	.20	.06
❑ 83	Anthony Carter	.50	.15
❑ 84	Ray Allen	.75	.23
❑ 85	Sam Cassell	.75	.23
❑ 86	Tim Thomas	.50	.15

Card	Player	Price 1	Price 2
❑ 87	Toni Kukoc	.50	.15
❑ 88	Jason Caffey	.20	.06
❑ 89	Anthony Mason	.50	.15
❑ 90	Joel Przybilla	.20	.06
❑ 91	Kevin Garnett	1.50	.45
❑ 92	Wally Szczerbiak	.50	.15
❑ 93	Terrell Brandon	.50	.15
❑ 94	Joe Smith	.50	.15
❑ 95	Felipe Lopez	.20	.06
❑ 96	Anthony Peeler	.20	.06
❑ 97	Radoslav Nesterovic	.50	.15
❑ 98	Jason Kidd	1.25	.35
❑ 99	Kenyon Martin	.75	.23
❑ 100	Dikembe Mutombo	.50	.15
❑ 101	Richard Jefferson	.50	.15
❑ 102	Kerry Kittles	.20	.06
❑ 103	Lucious Harris	.20	.06
❑ 104	Jason Collins	.20	.06
❑ 105	Baron Davis	.75	.23
❑ 106	Jamal Mashburn	.50	.15
❑ 107	Elden Campbell	.20	.06
❑ 108	David Wesley	.20	.06
❑ 109	P.J. Brown	.20	.06
❑ 110	Lee Nailon	.20	.06
❑ 111	Latrell Sprewell	.75	.23
❑ 112	Allan Houston	.50	.15
❑ 113	Kurt Thomas	.50	.15
❑ 114	Antonio McDyess	.50	.15
❑ 115	Othella Harrington	.20	.06
❑ 116	Clarence Weatherspoon	.20	.06
❑ 117	Tracy McGrady	2.00	.60
❑ 118	Mike Miller	.75	.23
❑ 119	Darrell Armstrong	.20	.06
❑ 120	Grant Hill	.75	.23
❑ 121	Pat Garrity	.20	.06
❑ 122	Steven Hunter	.20	.06
❑ 123	Allen Iverson	1.50	.45
❑ 124	Keith Van Horn	.75	.23
❑ 125	Aaron McKie	.50	.15
❑ 126	Eric Snow	.50	.15
❑ 127	Derrick Coleman	.20	.06
❑ 128	Samuel Dalembert	.20	.06
❑ 129	Stephon Marbury	.75	.23
❑ 130	Shawn Marion	.75	.23
❑ 131	Joe Johnson	.50	.15
❑ 132	Tom Gugliotta	.20	.06
❑ 133	Anfernee Hardaway	.75	.23
❑ 134	Iakovos Tsakalidis	.20	.06
❑ 135	Rasheed Wallace	.75	.23
❑ 136	Bonzi Wells	.50	.15
❑ 137	Damon Stoudamire	.50	.15
❑ 138	Scottie Pippen	1.25	.35
❑ 139	Derek Anderson	.50	.15
❑ 140	Ruben Patterson	.20	.06
❑ 141	Dale Davis	.50	.15
❑ 142	Mike Bibby	.75	.23
❑ 143	Chris Webber	.75	.23
❑ 144	Peja Stojakovic	.75	.23
❑ 145	Doug Christie	.50	.15
❑ 146	Hidayet Turkoglu	.75	.23
❑ 147	Vlade Divac	.50	.15
❑ 148	Scot Pollard	.20	.06
❑ 149	Tim Duncan	1.50	.45
❑ 150	David Robinson	.75	.23
❑ 151	Tony Parker	.75	.23
❑ 152	Malik Rose	.20	.06
❑ 153	Steve Smith	.50	.15
❑ 154	Bruce Bowen	.20	.06
❑ 155	Danny Ferry	.20	.06
❑ 156	Gary Payton	.75	.23
❑ 157	Rashard Lewis	.50	.15
❑ 158	Brent Barry	.50	.15
❑ 159	Kenny Anderson	.50	.15
❑ 160	Desmond Mason	.50	.15
❑ 161	Predrag Drobnjak	.20	.06
❑ 162	Vince Carter	2.00	.60
❑ 163	Morris Peterson	.50	.15
❑ 164	Antonio Davis	.20	.06
❑ 165	Alvin Williams	.20	.06
❑ 166	Jerome Williams	.20	.06
❑ 167	Michael Bradley	.50	.15
❑ 168	Karl Malone	.75	.23
❑ 169	John Stockton	.75	.23
❑ 170	John Amaechi	.20	.06
❑ 171	Andrei Kirilenko	.75	.23
❑ 172	Greg Ostertag	.20	.06
❑ 173	Jarron Collins	.20	.06
❑ 174	DeShawn Stevenson	.20	.06
❑ 175	Christian Laettner	.50	.15
❑ 176	Brendan Haywood	.50	.15
❑ 177	Chris Whitney	.20	.06
❑ 178	Tyronn Lue	.20	.06
❑ 179	Kwame Brown	.50	.15
❑ 180	Michael Jordan	6.00	1.80
❑ 181	Jay Williams RC	4.00	1.20
❑ 182	Juan Dixon RC	5.00	1.50
❑ 183	Vincent Yarbrough RC	3.00	.90
❑ 184	Casey Jacobsen RC	3.00	.90
❑ 185	Chris Wilcox RC	4.00	1.20
❑ 186	John Salmons RC	3.00	.90
❑ 187	Marcus Haislip RC	3.00	.90
❑ 188	Robert Archibald RC	3.00	.90
❑ 189	Jared Jeffries RC	3.00	.90
❑ 190	Nikoloz Tskitishvili RC	4.00	1.20
❑ 191	Kareem Rush RC	4.00	1.20
❑ 192	Fred Jones RC	4.00	1.20
❑ 193	Caron Butler RC	6.00	1.80
❑ 194	Chris Jefferies RC	3.00	.90
❑ 195	Ryan Humphrey RC	3.00	.90
❑ 196	Frank Williams RC	3.00	.90
❑ 197	DaJuan Wagner RC	5.00	1.50
❑ 198	Bostjan Nachbar RC	3.00	.90
❑ 199	Mike Dunleavy RC	5.00	1.50
❑ 200	Roger Mason RC	3.00	.90
❑ 201	Nene Hilario RC	4.00	1.20
❑ 202	Melvin Ely RC	3.00	.90
❑ 203	Tayshaun Prince RC	5.00	1.50
❑ 204	Jiri Welsch RC	3.00	.90
❑ 205	Dan Dickau RC	3.00	.90
❑ 206	Qyntel Woods RC	4.00	1.20
❑ 207	Curtis Borchardt RC	3.00	.90
❑ 208	Amare Stoudemire RC	12.00	3.60
❑ 209	Drew Gooden RC	8.00	2.40
❑ 210	Yao Ming RC	15.00	4.50
❑ 211	Glenn Robinson	.75	.23
❑ 212	Theo Ratliff	.50	.15
❑ 213	Emanual Davis	.20	.06
❑ 214	Dan Dickau	2.00	.60
❑ 215	Alan Henderson	.20	.06
❑ 216	Chris Crawford	.20	.06
❑ 217	Darvin Ham	.20	.06
❑ 218	Ira Newble	.20	.06
❑ 219	Vin Baker	.50	.15
❑ 220	Shammond Williams	.20	.06
❑ 221	Tony Battie	.20	.06
❑ 222	Walter McCarty	.20	.06
❑ 223	Bruno Sundov	.20	.06
❑ 224	Ruben Wolkowyski	.20	.06
❑ 225	Eddie Robinson	.50	.15
❑ 226	Jay Williams	3.00	.90
❑ 227	Fred Hoiberg	.20	.06
❑ 228	Donyell Marshall	.50	.15
❑ 229	Roger Mason	1.50	.45
❑ 230	Darius Miles	.75	.23
❑ 231	Michael Stewart	.20	.06
❑ 232	Tyrone Hill	.20	.06
❑ 233	DaJuan Wagner	3.00	.90
❑ 234	DeSagana Diop	.50	.15
❑ 235	Bimbo Coles	.20	.06
❑ 236	Milt Palacio	.20	.06
❑ 237	Avery Johnson	.20	.06
❑ 238	Evan Eschmeyer	.20	.06
❑ 239	Raja Bell	.20	.06
❑ 240	Shawn Bradley	.20	.06
❑ 241	Walt Williams	.20	.06
❑ 242	Eduardo Najera	.50	.15
❑ 243	Marcus Camby	.50	.15
❑ 244	Chris Whitney	.20	.06
❑ 245	Nikoloz Tskitishvili	2.00	.60
❑ 246	Kenny Satterfield	.20	.06
❑ 247	Nene Hilario	2.00	.60
❑ 248	Mark Blount	.20	.06
❑ 249	Richard Hamilton	.50	.15
❑ 250	Chauncey Billups	.50	.15
❑ 251	Tayshaun Prince	2.50	.75
❑ 252	Don Reid	.20	.06
❑ 253	Jon Barry	.20	.06
❑ 254	Hubert Davis	.20	.06
❑ 255	Pepe Sanchez	.20	.06
❑ 256	Chris Mills	.20	.06
❑ 257	Bob Sura	.20	.06
❑ 258	Mike Dunleavy	2.50	.75
❑ 259	Jiri Welsch	1.50	.45
❑ 260	Adonal Foyle	.20	.06
❑ 261	Erick Dampier	.50	.15
❑ 262	Maurice Taylor	.20	.06
❑ 263	Glen Rice	.50	.15
❑ 264	Yao Ming	8.00	2.40
❑ 265	Bostjan Nachbar	1.50	.45
❑ 266	Jason Collier	.20	.06
❑ 267	Terence Morris	.20	.06
❑ 268	Jonathan Bender	.50	.15
❑ 269	Jeff Foster	.20	.06
❑ 270	Fred Jones	2.00	.60
❑ 271	Al Harrington	.50	.15
❑ 272	Brad Miller	.75	.23
❑ 273	Jamison Brewer	.20	.06
❑ 274	Erick Strickland	.20	.06
❑ 275	Andre Miller	.50	.15
❑ 276	Melvin Ely	1.50	.45
❑ 277	Keyon Dooling	.20	.06
❑ 278	Chris Wilcox	2.00	.60
❑ 279	Eric Piatkowski	.50	.15
❑ 280	Sean Rooks	.20	.06
❑ 281	Wang Zhi Zhi	.75	.23
❑ 282	Mark Madsen	.20	.06
❑ 283	Kareem Rush	2.00	.60
❑ 284	Stanislav Medvedenko	.20	.06
❑ 285	Derek Fisher	.75	.23
❑ 286	Tracy Murray	.20	.06
❑ 287	Michael Dickerson	.20	.06
❑ 288	Wesley Person	.20	.06
❑ 289	Drew Gooden	4.00	1.20
❑ 290	Robert Archibald	.20	.06
❑ 291	Brevin Knight	.20	.06
❑ 292	Mike James	.20	.06
❑ 293	LaPhonso Ellis	.20	.06
❑ 294	Caron Butler	3.00	.90
❑ 295	Malik Allen	.20	.06
❑ 296	Travis Best	.20	.06
❑ 297	Alonzo Mourning	.50	.15
❑ 298	Toni Kukoc	.50	.15
❑ 299	Michael Redd	.75	.23
❑ 300	Marcus Haislip	1.50	.45
❑ 301	Ervin Johnson	.20	.06
❑ 302	Kevin Ollie	.20	.06
❑ 303	Troy Hudson	.20	.06
❑ 304	Marc Jackson	.50	.15
❑ 305	Gary Trent	.20	.06
❑ 306	Kendall Gill	.20	.06
❑ 307	Loren Woods	.50	.15
❑ 308	Dikembe Mutombo	.50	.15
❑ 309	Anthony Johnson	.20	.06
❑ 310	Rodney Rogers	.20	.06
❑ 311	Brandon Armstrong	.50	.15
❑ 312	Brian Scalabrine	.20	.06
❑ 313	Aaron Williams	.20	.06
❑ 314	Courtney Alexander	.50	.15
❑ 315	Kirk Haston	.50	.15
❑ 316	George Lynch	.20	.06
❑ 317	Stacey Augmon	.20	.06
❑ 318	Robert Traylor	.20	.06
❑ 319	Jamaal Magloire	.20	.06
❑ 320	Lee Nailon	.20	.06
❑ 321	Frank Williams	1.50	.45
❑ 322	Michael Doleac	.20	.06
❑ 323	Shandon Anderson	.20	.06
❑ 324	Howard Eisley	.20	.06
❑ 325	Travis Knight	.20	.06
❑ 326	Lavor Postell	.20	.06
❑ 327	Charlie Ward	.20	.06
❑ 328	Mark Pope	.20	.06
❑ 329	Olumide Oyedeji	.20	.06
❑ 330	Shawn Kemp	.20	.06
❑ 331	Jacque Vaughn	.20	.06
❑ 332	Ryan Humphrey	1.50	.45
❑ 333	Andrew DeClercq	.20	.06
❑ 334	Jeryl Sasser	.20	.06
❑ 335	Keith Van Horn	.75	.23
❑ 336	Todd MacCulloch	.20	.06
❑ 337	Monty Williams	.20	.06
❑ 338	John Salmons	.20	.06
❑ 339	Brian Skinner	.20	.06
❑ 340	Mark Bryant	.20	.06
❑ 341	Greg Buckner	.20	.06
❑ 342	Bo Outlaw	.20	.06
❑ 343	Amare Stoudemire	6.00	1.80
❑ 344	Casey Jacobsen	1.25	.35

❑ 345 Alton Ford .50 .15
❑ 346 Scott Williams .20 .06
❑ 347 Dan Langhi .20 .06
❑ 348 Arvydas Sabonis .20 .06
❑ 349 Antonio Daniels .20 .06
❑ 350 Jeff McInnis .20 .06
❑ 351 Qyntel Woods 2.00 .60
❑ 352 Zach Randolph .75 .23
❑ 353 Ruben Boumtje-Boumtje .20 .06
❑ 354 Chris Dudley .20 .06
❑ 355 Charles Smith .20 .06
❑ 356 Keon Clark .50 .15
❑ 357 Bobby Jackson .50 .15
❑ 358 Mateen Cleaves .20 .06
❑ 359 Gerald Wallace .50 .15
❑ 360 Lawrence Funderburke .20 .06
❑ 361 Speedy Claxton .20 .06
❑ 362 Stephen Jackson .20 .06
❑ 363 Kevin Willis .20 .06
❑ 364 Steve Kerr .20 .06
❑ 365 Mengke Bateer .50 .15
❑ 366 Kenny Anderson .50 .15
❑ 367 Vladimir Radmanovic .50 .15
❑ 368 Joseph Forte .50 .15
❑ 369 Jerome James .20 .06
❑ 370 Vitaly Potapenko .20 .06
❑ 371 Calvin Booth .20 .06
❑ 372 Ansu Sesay .20 .06
❑ 373 Voshon Lenard .20 .06
❑ 374 Lindsey Hunter .20 .06
❑ 375 Mamadou N'diaye .20 .06
❑ 376 Chris Jefferies .20 .06
❑ 377 Jelani McCoy .20 .06
❑ 378 Lamond Murray .20 .06
❑ 379 Eric Montross .20 .06
❑ 380 Matt Harpring .75 .23
❑ 381 Calbert Cheaney .20 .06
❑ 382 Curtis Borchardt 1.50 .45
❑ 383 Mark Jackson .20 .06
❑ 384 Scott Padgett .20 .06
❑ 385 Jerry Stackhouse .50 .15
❑ 386 Jared Jeffries 1.50 .45
❑ 387 Larry Hughes .50 .15
❑ 388 Juan Dixon 2.50 .75
❑ 389 Bryon Russell .20 .06
❑ 390 Etan Thomas .20 .06
❑ 391 Efthimios Rentzias RC 3.00 .90
❑ 392 Manu Ginobili RC 8.00 2.40
❑ 393 Juaquin Hawkins RC 3.00 .90
❑ 394 Rasual Butler RC 3.00 .90
❑ 395 Ronald Murray RC 5.00 1.50
❑ 396 Igor Rakocevic RC 3.00 .90
❑ 397 Tito Maddox RC 3.00 .90
❑ 398 Mike Batiste RC 3.00 .90
❑ 399 Sam Clancy RC 3.00 .90
❑ 400 Tamar Slay RC 3.00 .90
❑ 401 Lonny Baxter RC 3.00 .90
❑ 402 Marko Jaric RC 3.00 .90
❑ 403 Dan Gadzuric RC 3.00 .90
❑ 404 Jannero Pargo RC 3.00 .90
❑ 405 Pat Burke RC 3.00 .90
❑ 406 Smush Parker RC 3.00 .90
❑ 407 Reggie Evans RC 3.00 .90
❑ 408 Gordan Giricek RC 3.00 .90
❑ 409 Mehmet Okur RC 3.00 .90
❑ 410 Jamal Sampson RC 3.00 .90
❑ 411 Raul Lopez RC 3.00 .90
❑ 412 Predrag Savovic RC 3.00 .90
❑ 413 Carlos Boozer RC 6.00 1.80
❑ 414 Ken Johnson RC 3.00 .90
❑ 415 Cezary Trybanski RC 3.00 .90
❑ 416 Mike Wilks RC 3.00 .90
❑ 417 J.R. Bremer RC 3.00 .90
❑ 418 Junior Harrington RC 3.00 .90
❑ 419 Nate Huffman RC 3.00 .90
❑ 420 Michael Jordan 6.00 1.80

2003-04 Upper Deck

	MINT	NRMT
COMP.SER.1 w/o SP's (300)	40.00	18.00
COMMON CARD (1-300)	.20	.09
COMMON ROOKIE (301-342)	3.00	1.35

❑ 1 Shareef Abdur-Rahim .75 .35
❑ 2 Alan Henderson .20 .09
❑ 3 Dan Dickau .20 .09
❑ 4 Theo Ratliff .50 .23

❑ 5 Terrell Brandon .20 .09
❑ 6 Darvin Ham .20 .09
❑ 7 Nazr Mohammed .20 .09
❑ 8 Jason Terry .75 .35
❑ 9 Dion Glover .20 .09
❑ 10 Chris Crawford .20 .09
❑ 11 Paul Pierce .75 .35
❑ 12 Antoine Walker .75 .35
❑ 13 Eric Williams .20 .09
❑ 14 Kedrick Brown .20 .09
❑ 15 Tony Battie .20 .09
❑ 16 Vin Baker .50 .23
❑ 17 Mark Blount .20 .09
❑ 18 Tony Delk .20 .09
❑ 19 Walter McCarty .20 .09
❑ 20 Jumaine Jones .50 .23
❑ 21 Jalen Rose .75 .35
❑ 22 Marcus Fizer .50 .23
❑ 23 Jamal Crawford .20 .09
❑ 24 Donyell Marshall .50 .23
❑ 25 Eddy Curry .50 .23
❑ 26 Trenton Hassell .20 .09
❑ 27 Michael Jordan 5.00 2.20
❑ 28 Tyson Chandler .75 .35
❑ 29 Jay Williams .50 .23
❑ 30 Scottie Pippen 1.25 .55
❑ 31 Eddie Robinson .50 .23
❑ 32 Lonny Baxter .20 .09
❑ 33 Darius Miles .75 .35
❑ 34 DeSagana Diop .20 .09
❑ 35 Ricky Davis .75 .35
❑ 36 Chris Mihm .20 .09
❑ 37 Carlos Boozer .75 .35
❑ 38 Michael Stewart .20 .09
❑ 39 Zydrunas Ilgauskas .50 .23
❑ 40 Dajuan Wagner .50 .23
❑ 41 J.R. Bremer .20 .09
❑ 42 Kevin Ollie .20 .09
❑ 43 Dirk Nowitzki 1.25 .55
❑ 44 Antawn Jamison .75 .35
❑ 45 Shawn Bradley .20 .09
❑ 46 Raef LaFrentz .50 .23
❑ 47 Eduardo Najera .50 .23
❑ 48 Travis Best .20 .09
❑ 49 Danny Fortson .20 .09
❑ 50 Michael Finley .75 .35
❑ 51 Jiri Welsch .50 .23
❑ 52 Steve Nash .75 .35
❑ 53 Marcus Camby .50 .23
❑ 54 Chris Anderson .20 .09
❑ 55 Rodney White .20 .09
❑ 56 Vincent Yarbrough .20 .09
❑ 57 Nikoloz Tskitishvili .20 .09
❑ 58 Nene .50 .23
❑ 59 Andre Miller .50 .23
❑ 60 Earl Boykins .50 .23
❑ 61 Ryan Bowen .20 .09
❑ 62 Ben Wallace .75 .35
❑ 63 Tayshaun Prince .50 .23
❑ 64 Richard Hamilton .50 .23
❑ 65 Mehmet Okur .20 .09
❑ 66 Bob Sura .20 .09
❑ 67 Chucky Atkins .20 .09
❑ 68 Chauncey Billups .50 .23
❑ 69 Elden Campbell .20 .09
❑ 70 Corliss Williamson .50 .23
❑ 71 Zeljko Rebraca .20 .09
❑ 72 Jason Richardson .75 .35
❑ 73 Popeye Jones .20 .09
❑ 74 Clifford Robinson .20 .09
❑ 75 Mike Dunleavy .50 .23
❑ 76 Troy Murphy .75 .35
❑ 77 Speedy Claxton .20 .09
❑ 78 Erick Dampier .50 .23
❑ 79 Nick Van Exel .75 .35
❑ 80 Avery Johnson .20 .09
❑ 81 Adonal Foyle .20 .09
❑ 82 Pepe Sanchez .20 .09
❑ 83 Steve Francis .75 .35
❑ 84 Glen Rice .50 .23
❑ 85 Eddie Griffin .50 .23
❑ 86 Moochie Norris .20 .09
❑ 87 Maurice Taylor .20 .09
❑ 88 Kelvin Cato .20 .09
❑ 89 Jason Collier .20 .09
❑ 90 Cuttino Mobley .50 .23
❑ 91 Yao Ming 2.00 .90
❑ 92 Eric Piatkowski .50 .23
❑ 93 Bostjan Nachbar .20 .09
❑ 94 Adrian Griffin .20 .09
❑ 95 Reggie Miller .75 .35
❑ 96 Fred Jones .20 .09
❑ 97 Scot Pollard .20 .09
❑ 98 Jamaal Tinsley .75 .35
❑ 99 Al Harrington .50 .23
❑ 100 Jonathan Bender .50 .23
❑ 101 Primoz Brezec .20 .09
❑ 102 Ron Artest .50 .23
❑ 103 Jermaine O'Neal .75 .35
❑ 104 Kenny Anderson .50 .23
❑ 105 Jeff Foster .20 .09
❑ 106 Austin Croshere .20 .09
❑ 107 Elton Brand .75 .35
❑ 108 Tremaine Fowlkes .20 .09
❑ 109 Quentin Richardson .50 .23
❑ 110 Melvin Ely .20 .09
❑ 111 Marko Jaric .50 .23
❑ 112 Chris Wilcox .20 .09
❑ 113 Wang Zhizhi .75 .35
❑ 114 Corey Maggette .50 .23
❑ 115 Keyon Dooling .20 .09
❑ 116 Kobe Bryant 3.00 1.35
❑ 117 Shaquille O'Neal 2.00 .90
❑ 118 Slava Medvedenko .20 .09
❑ 119 Gary Payton .75 .35
❑ 120 Jannero Pargo .20 .09
❑ 121 Kareem Rush .50 .23
❑ 122 Karl Malone .75 .35
❑ 123 Derek Fisher .75 .35
❑ 124 Rick Fox .50 .23
❑ 125 Devean George .50 .23
❑ 126 Pau Gasol .75 .35
❑ 127 Jason Williams .50 .23
❑ 128 Stromile Swift .50 .23
❑ 129 Wesley Person .20 .09
❑ 130 Michael Dickerson .20 .09
❑ 131 Lorenzen Wright .20 .09
❑ 132 Earl Watson .20 .09
❑ 133 Mike Miller .75 .35
❑ 134 Shane Battier .75 .35
❑ 135 Eddie Jones .75 .35
❑ 136 Rasual Butler .20 .09
❑ 137 Caron Butler .75 .35
❑ 138 Brian Grant .50 .23
❑ 139 Lamar Odom .75 .35
❑ 140 Malik Allen .20 .09
❑ 141 Ken Johnson .20 .09
❑ 142 Samaki Walker .20 .09
❑ 143 Sean Lampley .20 .09
❑ 144 Vladimir Stepania .20 .09
❑ 145 Erick Strickland .20 .09
❑ 146 Toni Kukoc .50 .23
❑ 147 Joel Przybilla .20 .09
❑ 148 Tim Thomas .50 .23
❑ 149 Dan Gadzuric .20 .09
❑ 150 Joe Smith .50 .23
❑ 151 Michael Redd .75 .35
❑ 152 Desmond Mason .50 .23
❑ 153 Brian Skinner .20 .09
❑ 154 Kevin Garnett 1.50 .70
❑ 155 Michael Olowokandi .20 .09
❑ 156 Troy Hudson .20 .09
❑ 157 Latrell Sprewell .75 .35
❑ 158 Wally Szczerbiak .50 .23

- ❑ 159 Sam Cassell .75 .35
- ❑ 160 Fred Hoiberg .20 .09
- ❑ 161 Ervin Johnson .20 .09
- ❑ 162 Mark Madsen .20 .09
- ❑ 163 Gary Trent .20 .09
- ❑ 164 Jason Kidd 1.25 .55
- ❑ 165 Dikembe Mutombo .50 .23
- ❑ 166 Lucious Harris .20 .09
- ❑ 167 Kerry Kittles .20 .09
- ❑ 168 Brandon Armstrong .20 .09
- ❑ 169 Jason Collins .20 .09
- ❑ 170 Alonzo Mourning .50 .23
- ❑ 171 Kenyon Martin .75 .35
- ❑ 172 Richard Jefferson .50 .23
- ❑ 173 Rodney Rogers .20 .09
- ❑ 174 Aaron Williams .20 .09
- ❑ 175 Jamal Mashburn .50 .23
- ❑ 176 David Wesley .20 .09
- ❑ 177 Kirk Haston .20 .09
- ❑ 178 Courtney Alexander .50 .23
- ❑ 179 Darrell Armstrong .20 .09
- ❑ 180 Robert Traylor .20 .09
- ❑ 181 George Lynch .20 .09
- ❑ 182 Jamaal Magloire .20 .09
- ❑ 183 Baron Davis .75 .35
- ❑ 184 P.J. Brown .20 .09
- ❑ 185 Sean Rooks .20 .09
- ❑ 186 Stacey Augmon .20 .09
- ❑ 187 Allan Houston .50 .23
- ❑ 188 Antonio McDyess .50 .23
- ❑ 189 Clarence Weatherspoon .20 .09
- ❑ 190 Kurt Thomas .50 .23
- ❑ 191 Shandon Anderson .20 .09
- ❑ 192 Keith Van Horn .75 .35
- ❑ 193 Michael Doleac .20 .09
- ❑ 194 Othella Harrington .20 .09
- ❑ 195 Charlie Ward .20 .09
- ❑ 196 Lee Nailon .20 .09
- ❑ 197 Tracy McGrady 2.00 .90
- ❑ 198 Pat Garrity .20 .09
- ❑ 199 Grant Hill .75 .35
- ❑ 200 Gordan Giricek .50 .23
- ❑ 201 Steven Hunter .20 .09
- ❑ 202 Jeryl Sasser .20 .09
- ❑ 203 Andrew DeClercq .20 .09
- ❑ 204 Juwan Howard .50 .23
- ❑ 205 Tyronn Lue .20 .09
- ❑ 206 Drew Gooden .50 .23
- ❑ 207 Marc Jackson .50 .23
- ❑ 208 Aaron McKie .50 .23
- ❑ 209 Derrick Coleman .20 .09
- ❑ 210 Eric Snow .50 .23
- ❑ 211 Glenn Robinson .75 .35
- ❑ 212 Greg Buckner .20 .09
- ❑ 213 Allen Iverson 1.50 .70
- ❑ 214 Kenny Thomas .20 .09
- ❑ 215 Sam Clancy .20 .09
- ❑ 216 Monty Williams .20 .09
- ❑ 217 Stephon Marbury .75 .35
- ❑ 218 Shawn Marion .75 .35
- ❑ 219 Joe Johnson .50 .23
- ❑ 220 Bo Outlaw .20 .09
- ❑ 221 Amare Stoudemire 1.50 .70
- ❑ 222 Casey Jacobsen .20 .09
- ❑ 223 Tom Gugliotta .20 .09
- ❑ 224 Scott Williams .20 .09
- ❑ 225 Jake Tsakalidis .20 .09
- ❑ 226 Damon Stoudamire .50 .23
- ❑ 227 Arvydas Sabonis .20 .09
- ❑ 228 Zach Randolph .75 .35
- ❑ 229 Ruben Patterson .50 .23
- ❑ 230 Derek Anderson .50 .23
- ❑ 231 Dale Davis .50 .23
- ❑ 232 Bonzi Wells .50 .23
- ❑ 233 Rasheed Wallace .75 .35
- ❑ 234 Jeff McInnis .20 .09
- ❑ 235 Qyntel Woods .20 .09
- ❑ 236 Chris Webber .75 .35
- ❑ 237 Doug Christie .50 .23
- ❑ 238 Vlade Divac .50 .23
- ❑ 239 Bobby Jackson .50 .23
- ❑ 240 Lawrence Funderburke .20 .09
- ❑ 241 Peja Stojakovic .75 .35
- ❑ 242 Gerald Wallace .50 .23
- ❑ 243 Brad Miller .75 .35
- ❑ 244 Mike Bibby .75 .35
- ❑ 245 Anthony Peeler .20 .09
- ❑ 246 Jim Jackson .20 .09
- ❑ 247 David Robinson .75 .35
- ❑ 248 Ron Mercer .20 .09
- ❑ 249 Tony Parker .75 .35
- ❑ 250 Malik Rose .20 .09
- ❑ 251 Kevin Willis .20 .09
- ❑ 252 Manu Ginobili .75 .35
- ❑ 253 Bruce Bowen .20 .09
- ❑ 254 Hedo Turkoglu .75 .35
- ❑ 255 Tim Duncan 1.50 .70
- ❑ 256 Robert Horry .50 .23
- ❑ 257 Radoslav Nesterovic .50 .23
- ❑ 258 Ray Allen .75 .35
- ❑ 259 Rashard Lewis .75 .35
- ❑ 260 Reggie Evans .20 .09
- ❑ 261 Brent Barry .50 .23
- ❑ 262 Ronald Murray .20 .09
- ❑ 263 Vladimir Radmanovic .20 .09
- ❑ 264 Predrag Drobnjak .20 .09
- ❑ 265 Antonio Daniels .20 .09
- ❑ 266 Vitaly Potapenko .20 .09
- ❑ 267 Calvin Booth .20 .09
- ❑ 268 Vince Carter 2.00 .90
- ❑ 269 Chris Jefferies .20 .09
- ❑ 270 Mengke Bateer .20 .09
- ❑ 271 Alvin Williams .20 .09
- ❑ 272 Jerome Williams .20 .09
- ❑ 273 Michael Bradley .20 .09
- ❑ 274 Lamond Murray .20 .09
- ❑ 275 Antonio Davis .20 .09
- ❑ 276 Morris Peterson .50 .23
- ❑ 277 Jerome Moiso .20 .09
- ❑ 278 Carlos Arroyo .20 .09
- ❑ 279 Matt Harpring .75 .35
- ❑ 280 Andrei Kirilenko .75 .35
- ❑ 281 Jarron Collins .20 .09
- ❑ 282 Greg Ostertag .20 .09
- ❑ 283 Curtis Borchardt .20 .09
- ❑ 284 DeShawn Stevenson .20 .09
- ❑ 285 Keon Clark .50 .23
- ❑ 286 John Amaechi .20 .09
- ❑ 287 Raul Lopez .20 .09
- ❑ 288 Jerry Stackhouse .75 .35
- ❑ 289 Kwame Brown .75 .35
- ❑ 290 Larry Hughes .50 .23
- ❑ 291 Brendan Haywood .20 .09
- ❑ 292 Juan Dixon .50 .23
- ❑ 293 Bryon Russell .20 .09
- ❑ 294 Christian Laettner .50 .23
- ❑ 295 Jahidi White .20 .09
- ❑ 296 Jared Jeffries .20 .09
- ❑ 297 Gilbert Arenas .75 .35
- ❑ 298 Kobe Bryant CL 1.50 .70
- ❑ 299 Michael Jordan CL 2.50 1.10
- ❑ 300 Michael Jordan CL 2.50 1.10
- ❑ 301 LeBron James RC 40.00 18.00
- ❑ 302 Darko Milicic RC 6.00 2.70
- ❑ 303 Carmelo Anthony RC 20.00 9.00
- ❑ 304 Chris Bosh RC 6.00 2.70
- ❑ 305 Dwyane Wade RC 8.00 3.60
- ❑ 306 Chris Kaman RC 3.00 1.35
- ❑ 307 Kirk Hinrich RC 5.00 2.20
- ❑ 308 T.J. Ford RC 4.00 1.80
- ❑ 309 Mike Sweetney RC 3.00 1.35
- ❑ 310 Jarvis Hayes RC 3.00 1.35
- ❑ 311 Mickael Pietrus RC 3.00 1.35
- ❑ 312 Nick Collison RC 3.00 1.35
- ❑ 313 Marcus Banks RC 3.00 1.35
- ❑ 314 Luke Ridnour RC 4.00 1.80
- ❑ 315 Reece Gaines RC 3.00 1.35
- ❑ 316 Troy Bell RC 3.00 1.35
- ❑ 317 Zarko Cabarkapa RC 3.00 1.35
- ❑ 318 David West RC 3.00 1.35
- ❑ 319 Aleksandar Pavlovic RC 3.00 1.35
- ❑ 320 Dahntay Jones RC 3.00 1.35
- ❑ 321 Boris Diaw RC 3.00 1.35
- ❑ 322 Zoran Planinic RC 3.00 1.35
- ❑ 323 Travis Outlaw RC 3.00 1.35
- ❑ 324 Brian Cook RC 3.00 1.35
- ❑ 325 Kirk Penney RC 3.00 1.35
- ❑ 326 Ndudi Ebi RC 3.00 1.35
- ❑ 327 Kendrick Perkins RC 3.00 1.35
- ❑ 328 Leandro Barbosa RC 3.00 1.35
- ❑ 329 Josh Howard RC 4.00 1.80
- ❑ 330 Maciej Lampe RC 3.00 1.35
- ❑ 331 Jason Kapono RC 3.00 1.35
- ❑ 332 Luke Walton RC 4.00 1.80
- ❑ 333 Jerome Beasley RC 3.00 1.35
- ❑ 334 Brandon Hunter RC 3.00 1.35
- ❑ 335 Kyle Korver RC 4.00 1.80
- ❑ 336 Travis Hansen RC 3.00 1.35
- ❑ 337 Steve Blake RC 3.00 1.35
- ❑ 338 Slavko Vranes RC 3.00 1.35
- ❑ 339 Zaur Pachulia RC 3.00 1.35
- ❑ 340 Keith Bogans RC 3.00 1.35
- ❑ 341 Willie Green RC 3.00 1.35
- ❑ 342 Maurice Williams RC 3.00 1.35

2002-03 Upper Deck Championship Drive

	Nm-Mt	Ex-Mt
COMP.SET w/o SP's (100)	40.00	12.00
COMMON CARD (1-100)	.25	.07
COMMON JSY RC (101-130)	10.00	3.00
COMMON ROOKIE (131-155)	5.00	1.50

- ❑ 1 Shareef Abdur-Rahim 1.00 .30
- ❑ 2 Glenn Robinson 1.00 .30
- ❑ 3 Jason Terry 1.00 .30
- ❑ 4 Dion Glover .25 .07
- ❑ 5 Antoine Walker 1.00 .30
- ❑ 6 Paul Pierce 1.00 .30
- ❑ 7 Vin Baker .60 .18
- ❑ 8 Kedrick Brown .60 .18
- ❑ 9 Jalen Rose 1.00 .30
- ❑ 10 Tyson Chandler 1.00 .30
- ❑ 11 Eddy Curry 1.00 .30
- ❑ 12 Darius Miles 1.00 .30
- ❑ 13 Ricky Davis 1.00 .30
- ❑ 14 Zydrunas Ilgauskas .60 .18
- ❑ 15 Dirk Nowitzki 1.50 .45
- ❑ 16 Michael Finley 1.00 .30
- ❑ 17 Steve Nash 1.00 .30
- ❑ 18 Raef LaFrentz .60 .18
- ❑ 19 Nick Van Exel 1.00 .30
- ❑ 20 James Posey .60 .18
- ❑ 21 Juwan Howard .60 .18
- ❑ 22 Chauncey Billups .60 .18
- ❑ 23 Ben Wallace 1.00 .30
- ❑ 24 Richard Hamilton .60 .18
- ❑ 25 Jason Richardson 1.00 .30
- ❑ 26 Antawn Jamison 1.00 .30
- ❑ 27 Gilbert Arenas 1.00 .30
- ❑ 28 Steve Francis 1.00 .30
- ❑ 29 Cuttino Mobley .60 .18
- ❑ 30 Eddie Griffin .60 .18
- ❑ 31 Reggie Miller 1.00 .30
- ❑ 32 Jermaine O'Neal 1.00 .30
- ❑ 33 Jamaal Tinsley 1.00 .30
- ❑ 34 Ron Mercer .60 .18
- ❑ 35 Elton Brand 1.00 .30
- ❑ 36 Andre Miller .60 .18
- ❑ 37 Kobe Bryant 4.00 1.20
- ❑ 38 Shaquille O'Neal 2.50 .75
- ❑ 39 Rick Fox .60 .18
- ❑ 40 Devean George .60 .18
- ❑ 41 Pau Gasol 1.00 .30
- ❑ 42 Shane Battier 1.00 .30
- ❑ 43 Jason Williams .60 .18
- ❑ 44 Eddie Jones 1.00 .30
- ❑ 45 Brian Grant .60 .18
- ❑ 46 Anthony Carter .60 .18
- ❑ 47 Ray Allen 1.00 .30

Card		
❑ 48 Tim Thomas	.60	.18
❑ 49 Kevin Garnett	2.00	.60
❑ 50 Terrell Brandon	.60	.18
❑ 51 Wally Szczerbiak	.60	.18
❑ 52 Joe Smith	.60	.18
❑ 53 Jason Kidd	1.50	.45
❑ 54 Richard Jefferson	.60	.18
❑ 55 Dikembe Mutombo	.60	.18
❑ 56 Kenyon Martin	1.00	.30
❑ 57 Baron Davis	1.00	.30
❑ 58 Jamal Mashburn	.60	.18
❑ 59 David Wesley	.25	.07
❑ 60 P.J. Brown	.25	.07
❑ 61 Courtney Alexander	.60	.18
❑ 62 Latrell Sprewell	1.00	.30
❑ 63 Allan Houston	.60	.18
❑ 64 Kurt Thomas	.60	.18
❑ 65 Antonio McDyess	.60	.18
❑ 66 Tracy McGrady	2.50	.75
❑ 67 Mike Miller	1.00	.30
❑ 68 Grant Hill	1.00	.30
❑ 69 Allen Iverson	2.00	.60
❑ 70 Keith Van Horn	1.00	.30
❑ 71 Shawn Marion	1.00	.30
❑ 72 Stephon Marbury	1.00	.30
❑ 73 Anfernee Hardaway	1.00	.30
❑ 74 Rasheed Wallace	1.00	.30
❑ 75 Bonzi Wells	.60	.18
❑ 76 Scottie Pippen	1.50	.45
❑ 77 Mike Bibby	1.00	.30
❑ 78 Peja Stojakovic	1.00	.30
❑ 79 Chris Webber	1.00	.30
❑ 80 Hidayet Turkoglu	1.00	.30
❑ 81 Vlade Divac	.60	.18
❑ 82 Tim Duncan	2.00	.60
❑ 83 David Robinson	1.00	.30
❑ 84 Tony Parker	1.00	.30
❑ 85 Malik Rose	.25	.07
❑ 86 Gary Payton	1.00	.30
❑ 87 Rashard Lewis	.60	.18
❑ 88 Brent Barry	.60	.18
❑ 89 Desmond Mason	.60	.18
❑ 90 Vladimir Radmanovic	.60	.18
❑ 91 Vince Carter	2.50	.75
❑ 92 Morris Peterson	.60	.18
❑ 93 Antonio Davis	.25	.07
❑ 94 Karl Malone	1.00	.30
❑ 95 John Stockton	1.00	.30
❑ 96 Andrei Kirilenko	1.00	.30
❑ 97 Matt Harpring	1.00	.30
❑ 98 Jerry Stackhouse	1.00	.30
❑ 99 Larry Hughes	.60	.18
❑ 100 Michael Jordan	6.00	1.80
❑ 101 Juan Dixon JSY RC	15.00	4.50
❑ 102 Carlos Boozer JSY RC	20.00	6.00
❑ 103 Dan Gadzuric JSY RC	10.00	3.00
❑ 104 V.Yarbrough JSY RC	10.00	3.00
❑ 105 R.Archibald JSY RC	10.00	3.00
❑ 106 Roger Mason JSY RC	10.00	3.00
❑ 107 Ronald Murray JSY RC	15.00	4.50
❑ 108 Chris Jefferies JSY RC	10.00	3.00
❑ 109 John Salmons JSY RC	10.00	3.00
❑ 110 P.Savovic JSY RC	10.00	3.00
❑ 111 Tayshaun Prince JSY RC	12.00	3.60
❑ 112 Casey Jacobsen JSY RC	10.00	3.00
❑ 113 Qyntel Woods JSY RC	10.00	3.00
❑ 114 Kareem Rush JSY RC	12.00	3.60
❑ 115 Ryan Humphrey JSY RC	10.00	3.00
❑ 116 Sam Clancy JSY RC	10.00	3.00
❑ 117 Lonny Baxter JSY RC	10.00	3.00
❑ 118 Fred Jones JSY RC	10.00	3.00
❑ 119 Marcus Haislip JSY RC	10.00	3.00
❑ 120 Melvin Ely JSY RC	10.00	3.00
❑ 121 Jared Jeffries JSY RC	10.00	3.00
❑ 122 Caron Butler JSY RC	20.00	6.00
❑ 123 A.Stoudemire JSY RC	50.00	15.00
❑ 124 Chris Wilcox JSY RC	12.00	3.60
❑ 125 Nene Hilario JSY RC	12.00	3.60
❑ 126 DaJuan Wagner JSY RC	15.00	4.50
❑ 127 N.Tskitishvili JSY RC	10.00	3.00
❑ 128 Drew Gooden JSY RC	25.00	7.50
❑ 129 Jay Williams JSY RC	12.00	3.60
❑ 130 Yao Ming JSY RC	60.00	18.00
❑ 131 Manu Ginobili RC	12.00	3.60
❑ 132 Efthimios Rentzias RC	5.00	1.50
❑ 133 Juaquin Hawkins RC	5.00	1.50
❑ 134 Marko Jaric RC	5.00	1.50
❑ 135 Dan Dickau RC	5.00	1.50
❑ 136 Frank Williams RC	5.00	1.50
❑ 137 Curtis Borchardt RC	5.00	1.50
❑ 138 Mike Dunleavy RC	8.00	2.40
❑ 139 Smush Parker RC	5.00	1.50
❑ 140 Tito Maddox RC	5.00	1.50
❑ 141 Jannero Pargo RC	5.00	1.50
❑ 142 Jiri Welsch RC	5.00	1.50
❑ 143 Bostjan Nachbar RC	5.00	1.50
❑ 144 Rasual Butler RC	5.00	1.50
❑ 145 Gordan Giricek RC	6.00	1.80
❑ 146 Igor Rakocevic RC	5.00	1.50
❑ 147 Tamar Slay RC	5.00	1.50
❑ 148 Junior Harrington RC	5.00	1.50
❑ 149 Nate Huffman RC	5.00	1.50
❑ 150 Jamal Sampson RC	5.00	1.50
❑ 151 Reggie Evans RC	5.00	1.50
❑ 152 Cezary Trybanski RC	5.00	1.50
❑ 153 Pat Burke RC	5.00	1.50
❑ 154 J.R. Bremer RC	5.00	1.50
❑ 155 Mehmet Okur RC	5.00	1.50

1998-99 Upper Deck Encore

	Nm-Mt	Ex-Mt
COMPLETE SET (150)	120.00	36.00
COMMON CARD (1-90)	.25	.07
COMMON MJ (91-113)	3.00	.90
COMMON ROOKIE (114-143)	.60	.18
COMMON BONUS (144-150)	1.25	.35
❑ 1 Mookie Blaylock	.25	.07
❑ 2 Dikembe Mutombo	.50	.15
❑ 3 Steve Smith	.50	.15
❑ 4 Kenny Anderson	.50	.15
❑ 5 Antoine Walker	.75	.23
❑ 6 Ron Mercer	.50	.15
❑ 7 David Wesley	.25	.07
❑ 8 Elden Campbell	.25	.07
❑ 9 Eddie Jones	.75	.23
❑ 10 Ron Harper	.50	.15
❑ 11 Toni Kukoc	.50	.15
❑ 12 Brent Barry	.50	.15
❑ 13 Shawn Kemp	.50	.15
❑ 14 Brevin Knight	.25	.07
❑ 15 Derek Anderson	.75	.23
❑ 16 Shawn Bradley	.25	.07
❑ 17 Robert Pack	.25	.07
❑ 18 Michael Finley	.75	.23
❑ 19 Antonio McDyess	.50	.15
❑ 20 Nick Van Exel	.75	.23
❑ 21 Danny Fortson	.25	.07
❑ 22 Grant Hill	.75	.23
❑ 23 Jerry Stackhouse	.75	.23
❑ 24 Bison Dele	.25	.07
❑ 25 Donyell Marshall	.50	.15
❑ 26 Tony Delk	.25	.07
❑ 27 Erick Dampier	.50	.15
❑ 28 John Starks	.50	.15
❑ 29 Charles Barkley	1.00	.30
❑ 30 Hakeem Olajuwon	.75	.23
❑ 31 Othella Harrington	.25	.07
❑ 32 Scottie Pippen	1.25	.35
❑ 33 Rik Smits	.50	.15
❑ 34 Reggie Miller	.75	.23
❑ 35 Mark Jackson	.50	.15
❑ 36 Rodney Rogers	.25	.07
❑ 37 Lamond Murray	.25	.07
❑ 38 Maurice Taylor	.50	.15
❑ 39 Kobe Bryant	3.00	.90
❑ 40 Shaquille O'Neal	2.00	.60
❑ 41 Derek Fisher	.75	.23
❑ 42 Glen Rice	.50	.15
❑ 43 Jamal Mashburn	.50	.15
❑ 44 Alonzo Mourning	.50	.15
❑ 45 Tim Hardaway	.50	.15
❑ 46 Ray Allen	.75	.23
❑ 47 Vinny Del Negro	.25	.07
❑ 48 Glenn Robinson	.50	.15
❑ 49 Joe Smith	.50	.15
❑ 50 Terrell Brandon	.50	.15
❑ 51 Kevin Garnett	1.50	.45
❑ 52 Keith Van Horn	.75	.23
❑ 53 Stephon Marbury	.75	.23
❑ 54 Jayson Williams	.25	.07
❑ 55 Patrick Ewing	.75	.23
❑ 56 Allan Houston	.50	.15
❑ 57 Latrell Sprewell	.75	.23
❑ 58 Anfernee Hardaway	.75	.23
❑ 59 Horace Grant	.50	.15
❑ 60 Nick Anderson	.25	.07
❑ 61 Allen Iverson	1.50	.45
❑ 62 Matt Geiger	.25	.07
❑ 63 Theo Ratliff	.50	.15
❑ 64 Jason Kidd	1.25	.35
❑ 65 Rex Chapman	.25	.07
❑ 66 Tom Gugliotta	.25	.07
❑ 67 Rasheed Wallace	.75	.23
❑ 68 Arvydas Sabonis	.50	.15
❑ 69 Damon Stoudamire	.50	.15
❑ 70 Vlade Divac	.50	.15
❑ 71 Corliss Williamson	.50	.15
❑ 72 Chris Webber	.75	.23
❑ 73 Tim Duncan	1.25	.35
❑ 74 Sean Elliott	.50	.15
❑ 75 David Robinson	.75	.23
❑ 76 Vin Baker	.50	.15
❑ 77 Gary Payton	.75	.23
❑ 78 Detlef Schrempf	.50	.15
❑ 79 Tracy McGrady	2.00	.60
❑ 80 John Wallace	.25	.07
❑ 81 Doug Christie	.50	.15
❑ 82 Karl Malone	.75	.23
❑ 83 John Stockton	.75	.23
❑ 84 Jeff Hornacek	.50	.15
❑ 85 Bryant Reeves	.25	.07
❑ 86 Michael Smith	.25	.07
❑ 87 Shareef Abdur-Rahim	.75	.23
❑ 88 Juwan Howard	.50	.15
❑ 89 Rod Strickland	.25	.07
❑ 90 Mitch Richmond	.50	.15
❑ 91 Michael Jordan	3.00	.90
❑ 92 Michael Jordan	3.00	.90
❑ 93 Michael Jordan	3.00	.90
❑ 94 Michael Jordan	3.00	.90
❑ 95 Michael Jordan	3.00	.90
❑ 96 Michael Jordan	3.00	.90
❑ 97 Michael Jordan	3.00	.90
❑ 98 Michael Jordan	3.00	.90
❑ 99 Michael Jordan	3.00	.90
❑ 100 Michael Jordan	3.00	.90
❑ 101 Michael Jordan	3.00	.90
❑ 102 Michael Jordan	3.00	.90
❑ 103 Michael Jordan	3.00	.90
❑ 104 Michael Jordan	3.00	.90
❑ 105 Michael Jordan	3.00	.90
❑ 106 Michael Jordan	3.00	.90
❑ 107 Michael Jordan	3.00	.90
❑ 108 Michael Jordan	3.00	.90
❑ 109 Michael Jordan	3.00	.90
❑ 110 Michael Jordan	3.00	.90
❑ 111 Michael Jordan	3.00	.90
❑ 112 Michael Jordan	3.00	.90
❑ 113 Michael Jordan	3.00	.90
❑ 114 Michael Olowokandi RC	2.50	.75
❑ 115 Mike Bibby RC	8.00	2.40
❑ 116 Raef LaFrentz RC	2.50	.75
❑ 117 Antawn Jamison RC	6.00	1.80
❑ 118 Vince Carter RC	15.00	4.50
❑ 119 Robert Traylor RC	1.50	.45
❑ 120 Jason Williams RC	6.00	1.80
❑ 121 Larry Hughes RC	5.00	1.50
❑ 122 Dirk Nowitzki RC	15.00	4.50

❑ 123 Paul Pierce RC 10.00 3.00
❑ 124 Michael Doleac RC 1.50 .45
❑ 125 Keon Clark RC 2.50 .75
❑ 126 Michael Dickerson RC 3.00 .90
❑ 127 Matt Harpring RC 2.50 .75
❑ 128 Bryce Drew RC 1.50 .45
❑ 129 Pat Garrity RC .75 .23
❑ 130 Roshown McLeod RC .75 .23
❑ 131 Ricky Davis RC 5.00 1.50
❑ 132 Peja Stojakovic RC 6.00 1.80
❑ 133 Felipe Lopez RC 2.00 .60
❑ 134 Al Harrington RC 4.00 1.20
❑ 135 Ruben Patterson RC 3.00 .90
❑ 136 Cuttino Mobley RC 8.00 2.40
❑ 137 Tyronn Lue RC 1.00 .30
❑ 138 Brian Skinner RC 1.50 .45
❑ 139 Nazr Mohammed RC .75 .23
❑ 140 Toby Bailey RC .60 .18
❑ 141 Casey Shaw RC .60 .18
❑ 142 Corey Benjamin RC 1.50 .45
❑ 143 Rashard Lewis RC 6.00 1.80
❑ 144 Jason Williams BON 3.00 .90
❑ 145 Paul Pierce BON 4.00 1.20
❑ 146 Vince Carter BON 10.00 3.00
❑ 147 Antawn Jamison BON 4.00 1.20
❑ 148 Raef LaFrentz BON - -
❑ 149 Mike Bibby BON 4.00 1.20
❑ 150 Michael Olowokandi BON 1.25 .35
❑ MJ Michael Jordan AU 2,000.00 600.00

1999-00 Upper Deck Encore

	Nm-Mt	Ex-Mt
COMPLETE SET (120)	150.00	45.00
COMPLETE SET w/o RC (90)	25.00	7.50
COMMON CARD (1-90)	.25	.07
COMMON ROOKIE (91-120)	1.50	.45

❑ 1 Dikembe Mutombo .50 .15
❑ 2 Alan Henderson .25 .07
❑ 3 Isaiah Rider .25 .07
❑ 4 Kenny Anderson .50 .15
❑ 5 Antoine Walker .75 .23
❑ 6 Paul Pierce .75 .23
❑ 7 Elden Campbell .25 .07
❑ 8 Eddie Jones .75 .23
❑ 9 David Wesley .25 .07
❑ 10 Hersey Hawkins .50 .15
❑ 11 Randy Brown .25 .07
❑ 12 Toni Kukoc .50 .15
❑ 13 Shawn Kemp .50 .15
❑ 14 Bob Sura .25 .07
❑ 15 Michael Finley .75 .23
❑ 16 Dirk Nowitzki 1.50 .45
❑ 17 Gary Trent .25 .07
❑ 18 Antonio McDyess .50 .15
❑ 19 Nick Van Exel .75 .23
❑ 20 Raef LaFrentz .50 .15
❑ 21 Christian Laettner .50 .15
❑ 22 Grant Hill .75 .23
❑ 23 Lindsey Hunter .25 .07
❑ 24 Jerry Stackhouse .75 .23
❑ 25 John Starks .50 .15
❑ 26 Antawn Jamison 1.25 .35
❑ 27 Tony Farmer .25 .07
❑ 28 Hakeem Olajuwon .75 .23
❑ 29 Cuttino Mobley .75 .23
❑ 30 Charles Barkley 1.00 .30
❑ 31 Reggie Miller .75 .23
❑ 32 Jalen Rose .75 .23
❑ 33 Mark Jackson .50 .15
❑ 34 Maurice Taylor .50 .15
❑ 35 Derek Anderson .50 .15
❑ 36 Michael Olowokandi .50 .15
❑ 37 Kobe Bryant 3.00 .90
❑ 38 Shaquille O'Neal 2.00 .60
❑ 39 Glen Rice .50 .15
❑ 40 Tim Hardaway .50 .15
❑ 41 Alonzo Mourning .50 .15
❑ 42 Ray Allen .75 .23
❑ 43 Glenn Robinson .75 .23
❑ 44 Sam Cassell .75 .23
❑ 45 Tim Thomas .50 .15
❑ 46 Kevin Garnett 1.50 .45
❑ 47 Terrell Brandon .50 .15
❑ 48 Keith Van Horn .75 .23
❑ 49 Stephon Marbury .75 .23
❑ 50 Kendall Gill .25 .07
❑ 51 Patrick Ewing .75 .23
❑ 52 Allan Houston .50 .15
❑ 53 Latrell Sprewell .75 .23
❑ 54 Darrell Armstrong .25 .07
❑ 55 John Amaechi RC .75 .23
❑ 56 Michael Doleac .25 .07
❑ 57 Allen Iverson 1.50 .45
❑ 58 Theo Ratliff .50 .15
❑ 59 Larry Hughes .75 .23
❑ 60 Jason Kidd 1.25 .35
❑ 61 Tom Gugliotta .25 .07
❑ 62 Anfernee Hardaway .75 .23
❑ 63 Rasheed Wallace .75 .23
❑ 64 Steve Smith .50 .15
❑ 65 Damon Stoudamire .50 .15
❑ 66 Scottie Pippen 1.25 .35
❑ 67 Corliss Williamson .50 .15
❑ 68 Jason Williams .75 .23
❑ 69 Vlade Divac .50 .15
❑ 70 Chris Webber .75 .23
❑ 71 Tim Duncan 1.50 .45
❑ 72 David Robinson .75 .23
❑ 73 Avery Johnson .25 .07
❑ 74 Mario Elie .25 .07
❑ 75 Gary Payton .75 .23
❑ 76 Vin Baker .50 .15
❑ 77 Ruben Patterson .50 .15
❑ 78 Brent Barry .50 .15
❑ 79 Vince Carter 2.00 .60
❑ 80 Antonio Davis .25 .07
❑ 81 Tracy McGrady 2.00 .60
❑ 82 Karl Malone .75 .23
❑ 83 John Stockton .75 .23
❑ 84 Bryon Russell .25 .07
❑ 85 Shareef Abdur-Rahim .75 .23
❑ 86 Mike Bibby .75 .23
❑ 87 Othella Harrington .25 .07
❑ 88 Juwan Howard .50 .15
❑ 89 Rod Strickland .25 .07
❑ 90 Mitch Richmond .50 .15
❑ 91 Elton Brand RC 10.00 3.00
❑ 92 Steve Francis RC 15.00 4.50
❑ 93 Baron Davis RC 8.00 2.40
❑ 94 Lamar Odom RC 8.00 2.40
❑ 95 Jonathan Bender RC 8.00 2.40
❑ 96 Wally Szczerbiak RC 8.00 2.40
❑ 97 Richard Hamilton RC 8.00 2.40
❑ 98 Andre Miller RC 8.00 2.40
❑ 99 Shawn Marion RC 10.00 3.00
❑ 100 Jason Terry RC 6.00 1.80
❑ 101 Trajan Langdon RC 3.00 .90
❑ 102 Kenny Thomas RC 3.00 .90
❑ 103 Corey Maggette RC 8.00 2.40
❑ 104 William Avery RC 3.00 .90
❑ 105 Ron Artest RC 5.00 1.50
❑ 106 Aleksandar Radojevic RC 1.50 .45
❑ 107 James Posey RC 5.00 1.50
❑ 108 Quincy Lewis RC 2.50 .75
❑ 109 Vonteego Cummings RC 3.00 .90
❑ 110 Jeff Foster RC 2.50 .75
❑ 111 Dion Glover RC 2.50 .75
❑ 112 Devean George RC 4.00 1.20
❑ 113 Evan Eschmeyer RC 1.50 .45
❑ 114 Tim James RC 2.50 .75
❑ 115 Adrian Griffin RC 2.50 .75
❑ 116 Anthony Carter RC 5.00 1.50
❑ 117 Obinna Ekezie RC 2.00 .60
❑ 118 Todd MacCulloch RC 2.50 .75
❑ 119 Chucky Atkins RC 3.00 .90
❑ 120 Lazaro Borrell RC 1.50 .45

2000-01 Upper Deck Encore

	Nm-Mt	Ex-Mt
COMPLETE SET w/o RC's	25.00	7.50
COMMON CARD (1-139)	.25	.07
COMMON ROOKIE (136-165)	3.00	.90

❑ 1 Brevin Knight .25 .07
❑ 2 Lorenzen Wright .25 .07
❑ 3 Alan Henderson .25 .07
❑ 4 Jason Terry .75 .23
❑ 5 Paul Pierce .75 .23
❑ 6 Antoine Walker .75 .23
❑ 7 Kenny Anderson .50 .15
❑ 8 Tony Battie .25 .07
❑ 9 Adrian Griffin .25 .07
❑ 10 Derrick Coleman .25 .07
❑ 11 David Wesley .25 .07
❑ 12 Baron Davis .75 .23
❑ 13 Elden Campbell .25 .07
❑ 14 Jamal Mashburn .50 .15
❑ 15 Elton Brand .75 .23
❑ 16 Ron Mercer .50 .15
❑ 17 Ron Artest .50 .15
❑ 18 Michael Ruffin .50 .15
❑ 19 Lamond Murray .25 .07
❑ 20 Andre Miller .50 .15
❑ 21 Matt Harpring .75 .23
❑ 22 Jim Jackson .25 .07
❑ 23 Michael Finley .75 .23
❑ 24 Dirk Nowitzki 1.25 .35
❑ 25 Steve Nash .75 .23
❑ 26 Howard Eisley .25 .07
❑ 27 Antonio McDyess .50 .15
❑ 28 James Posey .50 .15
❑ 29 Nick Van Exel .25 .07
❑ 30 Raef LaFrentz .50 .15
❑ 31 Voshon Lenard .25 .07
❑ 32 Jerry Stackhouse .75 .23
❑ 33 Ben Wallace .75 .23
❑ 34 Michael Curry .25 .07
❑ 35 Joe Smith .50 .15
❑ 36 Chucky Atkins .25 .07
❑ 37 Antawn Jamison .75 .23
❑ 38 Larry Hughes .50 .15
❑ 39 Chris Mills .25 .07
❑ 40 Mookie Blaylock .25 .07
❑ 41 Vonteego Cummings .25 .07
❑ 42 Steve Francis .75 .23
❑ 43 Maurice Taylor .25 .07
❑ 44 Hakeem Olajuwon .75 .23
❑ 45 Walt Williams .25 .07
❑ 46 Cuttino Mobley .50 .15
❑ 47 Reggie Miller .75 .23
❑ 48 Jalen Rose .75 .23
❑ 49 Austin Croshere .50 .15
❑ 50 Travis Best .25 .07
❑ 51 Jermaine O'Neal .75 .23
❑ 52 Lamar Odom .75 .23
❑ 53 Jeff McInnis .25 .07
❑ 54 Michael Olowokandi .25 .07
❑ 55 Brian Skinner .25 .07
❑ 56 Corey Maggette .50 .15

❑ 57 Shaquille O'Neal 2.00 .60
❑ 58 Ron Harper .50 .15
❑ 59 Kobe Bryant 4.00 1.20
❑ 60 Robert Horry .50 .15
❑ 61 Isaiah Rider .50 .15
❑ 62 Eddie Jones .75 .23
❑ 63 Anthony Carter .50 .15
❑ 64 Tim Hardaway .50 .15
❑ 65 Brian Grant .50 .15
❑ 66 Anthony Mason .50 .15
❑ 67 Ray Allen .75 .23
❑ 68 Tim Thomas .50 .15
❑ 69 Glenn Robinson .75 .23
❑ 70 Sam Cassell .75 .23
❑ 71 Lindsey Hunter .25 .07
❑ 72 Kevin Garnett 1.50 .45
❑ 73 Wally Szczerbiak .50 .15
❑ 74 Terrell Brandon .50 .15
❑ 75 Chauncey Billups .50 .15
❑ 76 Stephon Marbury .75 .23
❑ 77 Keith Van Horn .75 .23
❑ 78 Lucious Harris .25 .07
❑ 79 Kendall Gill .25 .07
❑ 80 Latrell Sprewell .75 .23
❑ 81 Marcus Camby .50 .15
❑ 82 Larry Johnson .50 .15
❑ 83 Allan Houston .50 .15
❑ 84 Glen Rice .50 .15
❑ 85 Grant Hill .75 .23
❑ 86 Tracy McGrady 2.00 .60
❑ 87 John Amaechi .25 .07
❑ 88 Darrell Armstrong .25 .07
❑ 89 Allen Iverson 1.50 .45
❑ 90 Dikembe Mutombo .50 .15
❑ 91 George Lynch .25 .07
❑ 92 Aaron McKie .50 .15
❑ 93 Eric Snow .50 .15
❑ 94 Jason Kidd 1.25 .35
❑ 95 Tony Delk .25 .07
❑ 96 Clifford Robinson .25 .07
❑ 97 Tom Gugliotta .25 .07
❑ 98 Shawn Marion .75 .23
❑ 99 Rasheed Wallace .75 .23
❑ 100 Scottie Pippen 1.25 .35
❑ 101 Steve Smith .50 .15
❑ 102 Damon Stoudamire .50 .15
❑ 103 Bonzi Wells .50 .15
❑ 104 Chris Webber .75 .23
❑ 105 Jason Williams .50 .15
❑ 106 Peja Stojakovic .75 .23
❑ 107 Vlade Divac .50 .15
❑ 108 Doug Christie .50 .15
❑ 109 Tim Duncan 1.50 .45
❑ 110 David Robinson .75 .23
❑ 111 Derek Anderson .50 .15
❑ 112 Antonio Daniels .25 .07
❑ 113 Sean Elliott .50 .15
❑ 114 Gary Payton .75 .23
❑ 115 Patrick Ewing .75 .23
❑ 116 Vin Baker .50 .15
❑ 117 Rashard Lewis .50 .15
❑ 118 Vince Carter 2.00 .60
❑ 119 Alvin Williams .25 .07
❑ 120 Antonio Davis .25 .07
❑ 121 Charles Oakley .25 .07
❑ 122 Karl Malone .75 .23
❑ 123 John Stockton .75 .23
❑ 124 Bryon Russell .25 .07
❑ 125 John Starks .50 .15
❑ 126 Shareef Abdur-Rahim .75 .23
❑ 127 Mike Bibby .75 .23
❑ 128 Michael Dickerson .50 .15
❑ 129 Grant Long .25 .07
❑ 130 Mitch Richmond .50 .15
❑ 131 Richard Hamilton .50 .15
❑ 132 Chris Whitney .25 .07
❑ 133 Jahidi White .25 .07
❑ 134 Checklist 1 .25 .07
❑ 135 Checklist 2 .25 .07
❑ 136 Kenyon Martin RC 10.00 3.00
❑ 137 Stromile Swift RC 6.00 1.80
❑ 138 Chris Mihm RC 3.00 .90
❑ 139 Marcus Fizer RC 3.00 .90
❑ 140 Darius Miles RC 8.00 2.40
❑ 141 Joel Przybilla RC 3.00 .90
❑ 142 Mike Miller RC 8.00 2.40
❑ 143 Courtney Alexander RC 3.00 .90
❑ 144 DerMarr Johnson RC 3.00 .90
❑ 145 Stephen Jackson RC 5.00 1.50
❑ 146 Jerome Moiso RC 3.00 .90
❑ 147 Keyon Dooling RC 3.00 .90
❑ 148 Erick Barkley RC 3.00 .90
❑ 149 Jason Collier RC 3.00 .90
❑ 150 Jamaal Magloire RC 3.00 .90
❑ 151 DeShawn Stevenson RC 3.00 .90
❑ 152 Hidayet Turkoglu RC 6.00 1.80
❑ 153 Morris Peterson RC 6.00 1.80
❑ 154 Jamal Crawford RC 4.00 1.20
❑ 155 Etan Thomas RC 3.00 .90
❑ 156 Quentin Richardson RC 8.00 2.40
❑ 157 Mateen Cleaves RC 3.00 .90
❑ 158 Donnell Harvey RC 3.00 .90
❑ 159 Mark Madsen RC 3.00 .90
❑ 160 Desmond Mason RC 3.00 .90
❑ 161 Speedy Claxton RC 3.00 .90
❑ 162 Hanno Mottola RC 3.00 .90
❑ 163 Mamadou N'diaye RC 3.00 .90
❑ 164 Eduardo Najera RC 4.00 1.20
❑ 165 Khalid El-Amin RC 3.00 .90

2002-03 Upper Deck Finite

	Nm-Mt	Ex-Mt
COMP.SET w/o SP's (100)	40.00	12.00
COMMON CARD (1-100)	.40	.12
181-200 NOT PRICED DUE TO SCARCITY		-
COMMON ROOKIE (201-221)	8.00	2.40
COMMON ROOKIE (222-233)	8.00	2.40
COMMON ROOKIE (234-242)	30.00	9.00

❑ 1 Shareef Abdur-Rahim 1.25 .35
❑ 2 Theo Ratliff .75 .23
❑ 3 Glenn Robinson 1.25 .35
❑ 4 Jason Terry 1.25 .35
❑ 5 Vin Baker .75 .23
❑ 6 Kedrick Brown .75 .23
❑ 7 Paul Pierce 1.25 .35
❑ 8 Antoine Walker 1.25 .35
❑ 9 Tyson Chandler 1.25 .35
❑ 10 Eddy Curry 1.25 .35
❑ 11 Jalen Rose 1.25 .35
❑ 12 Chris Mihm .40 .12
❑ 13 Darius Miles 1.25 .35
❑ 14 Ricky Davis .75 .23
❑ 15 Michael Finley 1.25 .35
❑ 16 Raef LaFrentz .75 .23
❑ 17 Steve Nash 1.25 .35
❑ 18 Dirk Nowitzki 2.00 .60
❑ 19 Nick Van Exel 1.25 .35
❑ 20 Marcus Camby .75 .23
❑ 21 Juwan Howard .75 .23
❑ 22 James Posey .75 .23
❑ 23 Chauncey Billups .75 .23
❑ 24 Richard Hamilton .75 .23
❑ 25 Ben Wallace 1.25 .35
❑ 26 Clifford Robinson .40 .12
❑ 27 Gilbert Arenas 1.25 .35
❑ 28 Antawn Jamison 1.25 .35
❑ 29 Jason Richardson 1.25 .35
❑ 30 Eddie Griffin .75 .23
❑ 31 Steve Francis 1.25 .35
❑ 32 Cuttino Mobley .75 .23
❑ 33 Reggie Miller 1.25 .35
❑ 34 Jermaine O'Neal 1.25 .35
❑ 35 Jamaal Tinsley 1.25 .35
❑ 36 Ron Mercer .75 .23
❑ 37 Elton Brand 1.25 .35
❑ 38 Andre Miller .75 .23
❑ 39 Lamar Odom 1.25 .35
❑ 40 Kobe Bryant 6.00 1.80
❑ 41 Rick Fox .75 .23
❑ 42 Devean George .75 .23
❑ 43 Shaquille O'Neal 3.00 .90
❑ 44 Shane Battier 1.25 .35
❑ 45 Pau Gasol 1.25 .35
❑ 46 Jason Williams .75 .23
❑ 47 LaPhonso Ellis .40 .12
❑ 48 Eddie Jones 1.25 .35
❑ 49 Brian Grant .75 .23
❑ 50 Ray Allen 1.25 .35
❑ 51 Tim Thomas .75 .23
❑ 52 Sam Cassell 1.25 .35
❑ 53 Terrell Brandon .75 .23
❑ 54 Kevin Garnett 3.00 .90
❑ 55 Wally Szczerbiak .75 .23
❑ 56 Marc Jackson .75 .23
❑ 57 Richard Jefferson .75 .23
❑ 58 Jason Kidd 1.50 .45
❑ 59 Kenyon Martin 1.25 .35
❑ 60 Kerry Kittles .40 .12
❑ 61 Baron Davis 1.25 .35
❑ 62 Jamal Mashburn .75 .23
❑ 63 David Wesley .40 .12
❑ 64 P.J. Brown .40 .12
❑ 65 Latrell Sprewell 1.25 .35
❑ 66 Antonio McDyess .75 .23
❑ 67 Allan Houston .75 .23
❑ 68 Tracy McGrady 4.00 1.20
❑ 69 Mike Miller 1.25 .35
❑ 70 Darrell Armstrong .40 .12
❑ 71 Allen Iverson 2.50 .75
❑ 72 Aaron McKie .75 .23
❑ 73 Keith Van Horn 1.25 .35
❑ 74 Stephon Marbury 1.25 .35
❑ 75 Shawn Marion 1.25 .35
❑ 76 Anfernee Hardaway 1.25 .35
❑ 77 Rasheed Wallace 1.25 .35
❑ 78 Bonzi Wells .75 .23
❑ 79 Scottie Pippen 2.00 .60
❑ 80 Mike Bibby 1.25 .35
❑ 81 Peja Stojakovic 1.25 .35
❑ 82 Chris Webber 1.25 .35
❑ 83 Hidayet Turkoglu 1.25 .35
❑ 84 Tim Duncan 3.00 .90
❑ 85 David Robinson 1.25 .35
❑ 86 Tony Parker 1.25 .35
❑ 87 Malik Rose .40 .12
❑ 88 Gary Payton 1.25 .35
❑ 89 Rashard Lewis .75 .23
❑ 90 Brent Barry .75 .23
❑ 91 Desmond Mason .75 .23
❑ 92 Vince Carter 3.00 .90
❑ 93 Morris Peterson .75 .23
❑ 94 Antonio Davis .40 .12
❑ 95 Karl Malone 1.25 .35
❑ 96 John Stockton 1.25 .35
❑ 97 Andrei Kirilenko 1.25 .35
❑ 98 Kwame Brown .75 .23
❑ 99 Jerry Stackhouse 1.25 .35
❑ 100 Michael Jordan 12.00 3.60
❑ 101 Kobe Bryant MF 12.00 3.60
❑ 102 Eddie Griffin MF .75 .23
❑ 103 Shawn Marion MF 2.50 .75
❑ 104 Richard Jefferson MF 1.50 .45
❑ 105 Jermaine O'Neal MF 2.50 .75
❑ 106 Allan Houston MF 1.50 .45
❑ 107 Shane Battier MF 3.00 .90
❑ 108 Hidayet Turkoglu MF 2.50 .75
❑ 109 Michael Finley MF 2.50 .75
❑ 110 Jamal Mashburn MF 1.50 .45
❑ 111 Rashard Lewis MF 1.50 .45
❑ 112 Tyson Chandler MF 2.50 .75
❑ 113 Terrell Brandon MF 1.50 .45
❑ 114 Antonio Davis MF 1.00 .30
❑ 115 Jamaal Tinsley MF 2.50 .75
❑ 116 Tony Parker MF 3.00 .90
❑ 117 Ray Allen MF 2.00 .60
❑ 118 Rasheed Wallace MF 2.00 .60
❑ 119 Cuttino Mobley MF 1.50 .45
❑ 120 Jason Terry MF 1.50 .45
❑ 121 Mike Miller MF 2.50 .75
❑ 122 Jalen Rose MF 2.50 .75

❑ 123 Morris Peterson MF 1.25 .35
❑ 124 Ricky Davis MF 1.50 .45
❑ 125 Peja Stojakovic MF 2.50 .75
❑ 126 Gary Payton MF 2.50 .75
❑ 127 Andrei Kirilenko MF 2.00 .60
❑ 128 Tim Duncan MF 6.00 1.80
❑ 129 Anfernee Hardaway MF 2.50 .75
❑ 130 Shaquille O'Neal MF 6.00 1.80
❑ 131 Latrell Sprewell MF 1.25 .35
❑ 132 Shareef Abdur-Rahim MF 2.50 .75
❑ 133 Steve Nash MF 2.50 .75
❑ 134 Lamar Odom MF 2.50 .75
❑ 135 Antawn Jamison MF 2.50 .75
❑ 136 Reggie Miller MF 2.00 .60
❑ 137 Tim Thomas MF 1.50 .45
❑ 138 Eddy Curry MF 2.00 .60
❑ 139 Jason Williams MF 1.50 .45
❑ 140 John Stockton MF 2.50 .75
❑ 141 Ben Wallace MF 1.50 .45
❑ 142 Bonzi Wells MF 1.50 .45
❑ 143 David Robinson MF 2.50 .75
❑ 144 Stephon Marbury MF 2.50 .75
❑ 145 Vince Carter MF 6.00 1.80
❑ 146 James Posey MF 1.50 .45
❑ 147 Wally Szczerbiak MF 1.50 .45
❑ 148 Eddie Jones MF 2.50 .75
❑ 149 Scottie Pippen MF 10.00 3.00
❑ 150 Michael Jordan MF 25.00 7.50
❑ 151 Kobe Bryant PP 30.00 9.00
❑ 152 Pau Gasol PP 5.00 1.50
❑ 153 Tim Duncan PP 15.00 4.50
❑ 154 Karl Malone PP 6.00 1.80
❑ 155 Allan Houston PP 4.00 1.20
❑ 156 Steve Nash PP 6.00 1.80
❑ 157 Shawn Marion PP 6.00 1.80
❑ 158 Jamal Mashburn PP 4.00 1.20
❑ 159 Shaquille O'Neal PP 15.00 4.50
❑ 160 Reggie Miller PP 6.00 1.80
❑ 161 Latrell Sprewell PP 1.25 .35
❑ 162 Peja Stojakovic PP 6.00 1.80
❑ 163 Jalen Rose PP 6.00 1.80
❑ 164 Kenyon Martin PP 6.00 1.80
❑ 165 Baron Davis PP 6.00 1.80
❑ 166 Ray Allen PP 6.00 1.80
❑ 167 Vince Carter PP 15.00 4.50
❑ 168 Rashard Lewis PP 4.00 1.20
❑ 169 Steve Francis PP - -
❑ 170 Jermaine O'Neal PP 6.00 1.80
❑ 171 Shane Battier PP 8.00 2.40
❑ 172 Shareef Abdur-Rahim PP 6.00 1.80
❑ 173 Michael Finley PP 6.00 1.80
❑ 174 John Stockton PP 6.00 1.80
❑ 175 Jamaal Tinsley PP 4.00 1.20
❑ 176 Wally Szczerbiak PP 4.00 1.20
❑ 177 Antawn Jamison PP 6.00 1.80
❑ 178 Richard Jefferson PP 4.00 1.20
❑ 179 Rasheed Wallace PP 6.00 1.80
❑ 180 Michael Jordan PP 60.00 18.00
❑ 181 Kobe Bryant FC - -
❑ 182 Paul Pierce FC - -
❑ 183 Nikoloz Tskitishvili FC - -
❑ 184 Kareem Rush FC - -
❑ 185 Jason Kidd FC - -
❑ 186 Dominique Wilkins FC - -
❑ 187 Kevin Garnett FC - -
❑ 188 Antoine Walker FC - -
❑ 189 Jay Williams FC - -
❑ 190 DaJuan Wagner FC - -
❑ 191 Caron Butler FC - -
❑ 192 Mike Bibby FC - -
❑ 193 Mike Miller FC - -
❑ 194 Tyson Chandler FC - -
❑ 195 Drew Gooden FC - -
❑ 196 Kenyon Martin FC - -
❑ 197 Marcus Fizer FC - -
❑ 198 Nene Hilario FC - -
❑ 199 Yao Ming FC - -
❑ 200 Michael Jordan FC - -
❑ 201 Marko Jaric RC 8.00 2.40
❑ 202 Dan Dickau RC 8.00 2.40
❑ 203 Tito Maddox RC 8.00 2.40
❑ 204 Predrag Savovic RC 8.00 2.40
❑ 205 Robert Archibald RC 8.00 2.40
❑ 206 Frank Williams RC 8.00 2.40
❑ 207 Ronald Murray RC 12.00 3.60
❑ 208 Lonny Baxter RC 8.00 2.40
❑ 209 Efthimios Rentzias RC 8.00 2.40
❑ 210 Vincent Yarbrough RC 8.00 2.40
❑ 211 Gordan Giricek RC 12.00 3.60
❑ 212 Carlos Boozer RC 20.00 6.00
❑ 213 John Salmons RC 8.00 2.40
❑ 214 Manu Ginobili RC 25.00 7.50
❑ 215 Roger Mason Jr. RC 8.00 2.40
❑ 216 Chris Jefferies RC 8.00 2.40
❑ 217 Sam Clancy RC 8.00 2.40
❑ 218 Rasual Butler RC 8.00 2.40
❑ 219 Dan Gadzuric RC 8.00 2.40
❑ 220 Tayshaun Prince RC 12.00 3.60
❑ 221 Casey Jacobsen RC 8.00 2.40
❑ 222 Qyntel Woods RC 10.00 3.00
❑ 223 Jiri Welsch RC 8.00 2.40
❑ 224 Curtis Borchardt RC 8.00 2.40
❑ 225 Marcus Haislip RC 8.00 2.40
❑ 226 Kareem Rush RC 12.00 3.60
❑ 227 Fred Jones RC 10.00 3.00
❑ 228 Caron Butler RC 20.00 6.00
❑ 229 Juan Dixon RC 15.00 4.50
❑ 230 Ryan Humphrey RC 8.00 2.40
❑ 231 Melvin Ely RC 8.00 2.40
❑ 232 Bostjan Nachbar RC 8.00 2.40
❑ 233 Jared Jeffries RC 10.00 3.00
❑ 234 Jay Williams RC 30.00 9.00
❑ 235 Nikoloz Tskitishvili RC 8.00 2.40
❑ 236 Chris Wilcox RC 8.00 2.40
❑ 237 Drew Gooden RC 60.00 18.00
❑ 238 Amare Stoudemire RC 150.00 45.00
❑ 239 DaJuan Wagner RC 40.00 12.00
❑ 240 Nene Hilario RC 8.00 2.40
❑ 241 Mike Dunleavy RC 40.00 12.00
❑ 242 Yao Ming RC 150.00 45.00

2003-04 Upper Deck Finite

	Nm-Mt	Ex-Mt
COMMON ODD (1-200)	.40	.12
COMMON EVEN (1-200)	.60	.18
COMMON ROOKIE (201-228)	5.00	1.50
COMMON ROOKIE (229-236)	6.00	1.80
COMMON ROOKIE (237-242)	20.00	6.00
COMMON MAJ.FACT.(243-292)	3.00	.90
COMMON PROM.POW.(293-322)	5.00	1.50
COMMON FIRST CLS.(323-342)	20.00	6.00

❑ 1 Shareef Abdur-Rahim 1.25 .35
❑ 2 Dominique Wilkins 2.00 .60
❑ 3 Theo Ratliff .75 .23
❑ 4 Dan Dickau .60 .18
❑ 5 Jason Terry 1.25 .35
❑ 6 Dion Glover .60 .18
❑ 7 Alan Henderson .40 .12
❑ 8 Paul Pierce 2.00 .60
❑ 9 Larry Bird 10.00 3.00
❑ 10 Raef LaFrentz 1.25 .35
❑ 11 Robert Parish 2.50 .75
❑ 12 Jiri Welsch 1.25 .35
❑ 13 John Havlicek 2.50 .75
❑ 14 Vin Baker 1.25 .35
❑ 15 Jamal Crawford .40 .12
❑ 16 Michael Jordan 12.00 3.60
❑ 17 Scottie Pippen 2.00 .60
❑ 18 Reggie Theus 2.00 .60
❑ 19 Jalen Rose 1.25 .35
❑ 20 Tyson Chandler 2.00 .60
❑ 21 Eddy Curry 1.25 .35
❑ 22 Dajuan Wagner 1.25 .35
❑ 23 Lenny Wilkens 2.00 .60
❑ 24 Carlos Boozer 2.00 .60
❑ 25 World B. Free 1.50 .45
❑ 26 Darius Miles 2.00 .60
❑ 27 Craig Ehlo 1.25 .35
❑ 28 Ricky Davis 2.00 .60
❑ 29 Dirk Nowitzki 2.00 .60
❑ 30 Rolando Blackman 2.00 .60
❑ 31 Steve Nash 1.25 .35
❑ 32 Tony Delk .60 .18
❑ 33 Antawn Jamison 1.25 .35
❑ 34 Antoine Walker 2.00 .60
❑ 35 Michael Finley 1.25 .35
❑ 36 Andre Miller 1.25 .35
❑ 37 David Thompson 1.25 .35
❑ 38 Nene 1.25 .35
❑ 39 Dan Issel 1.25 .35
❑ 40 Nikoloz Tskitishvili .60 .18
❑ 41 Alex English 1.50 .45
❑ 42 Earl Boykins 1.25 .35
❑ 43 Richard Hamilton .75 .23
❑ 44 Mehmet Okur .60 .18
❑ 45 Ben Wallace 1.25 .35
❑ 46 Bob Lanier 2.50 .75
❑ 47 Chauncey Billups .75 .23
❑ 48 Dave Bing 2.00 .60
❑ 49 Tayshaun Prince .75 .23
❑ 50 Nick Van Exel 2.00 .60
❑ 51 Erick Dampier .75 .23
❑ 52 Jason Richardson 2.00 .60
❑ 53 Joe Barry Carroll 1.25 .35
❑ 54 Mike Dunleavy 1.25 .35
❑ 55 Wilt Chamberlain 5.00 1.50
❑ 56 Troy Murphy 2.00 .60
❑ 57 Steve Francis 1.25 .35
❑ 58 Maurice Taylor 2.00 .60
❑ 59 Yao Ming 3.00 .90
❑ 60 Robert Reid 2.00 .60
❑ 61 Cuttino Mobley .75 .23
❑ 62 Moses Malone 2.00 .60
❑ 63 Eddie Griffin .75 .23
❑ 64 Jermaine O'Neal 2.00 .60
❑ 65 George McGinnis 1.25 .35
❑ 66 Reggie Miller 2.00 .60
❑ 67 Clark Kellogg 1.25 .35
❑ 68 Jamaal Tinsley 2.00 .60
❑ 69 Al Harrington .75 .23
❑ 70 Ron Artest 2.00 .60
❑ 71 Elton Brand 1.25 .35
❑ 72 Corey Maggette 1.25 .35
❑ 73 Chris Wilcox .40 .12
❑ 74 Quentin Richardson 1.25 .35
❑ 75 Bill Walton 2.50 .75
❑ 76 Marko Jaric .60 .18
❑ 77 Kobe Bryant 5.00 1.50
❑ 78 Kareem Abdul-Jabbar 4.00 1.20
❑ 79 Shaquille O'Neal 3.00 .90
❑ 80 Michael Cooper 2.00 .60
❑ 81 Gary Payton 1.25 .35
❑ 82 James Worthy 2.50 .75
❑ 83 Karl Malone 1.25 .35
❑ 84 Pau Gasol 2.00 .60
❑ 85 Michael Dickerson .40 .12
❑ 86 Mike Miller 2.00 .60
❑ 87 Brevin Knight .40 .12
❑ 88 Shane Battier 2.00 .60
❑ 89 Stromile Swift .40 .12
❑ 90 Jason Williams 1.25 .35
❑ 91 Caron Butler 1.25 .35
❑ 92 Samaki Walker .60 .18
❑ 93 Eddie Jones 1.25 .35
❑ 94 Rasual Butler 1.25 .35
❑ 95 Brian Grant .75 .23
❑ 96 Loren Woods .60 .18
❑ 97 Lamar Odom 1.25 .35
❑ 98 Desmond Mason 1.25 .35
❑ 99 Sidney Moncrief 1.25 .35
❑ 100 Toni Kukoc 1.25 .35
❑ 101 Oscar Robertson 3.00 .90
❑ 102 Michael Redd 2.00 .60
❑ 103 Terry Cummings 1.25 .35
❑ 104 Tim Thomas 1.25 .35
❑ 105 Kevin Garnett 2.50 .75
❑ 106 Troy Hudson .60 .18
❑ 107 Sam Cassell 1.25 .35
❑ 108 Latrell Sprewell 2.00 .60
❑ 109 Michael Olowokandi .40 .12
❑ 110 Wally Szczerbiak 1.25 .35
❑ 111 Jason Kidd 2.00 .60

❑ 112 Otis Birdsong 2.00 .60
❑ 113 Kenyon Martin 1.25 .35
❑ 114 Albert King 2.00 .60
❑ 115 Richard Jefferson .75 .23
❑ 116 Kerry Kittles .60 .18
❑ 117 Alonzo Mourning .75 .23
❑ 118 Baron Davis 2.00 .60
❑ 119 Darrell Armstrong .40 .12
❑ 120 Jamal Mashburn 1.25 .35
❑ 121 P.J. Brown .40 .12
❑ 122 David Wesley .60 .18
❑ 123 Courtney Alexander .75 .23
❑ 124 Jamaal Magloire .60 .18
❑ 125 Allan Houston .75 .23
❑ 126 Willis Reed 2.50 .75
❑ 127 Keith Van Horn 1.25 .35
❑ 128 Walt Frazier 2.50 .75
❑ 129 Antonio McDyess .75 .23
❑ 130 Earl Monroe 2.50 .75
❑ 131 Kurt Thomas .75 .23
❑ 132 Tracy McGrady 5.00 1.50
❑ 133 Pat Garrity .40 .12
❑ 134 Grant Hill 2.00 .60
❑ 135 Tyronn Lue .40 .12
❑ 136 Drew Gooden 1.25 .35
❑ 137 Juwan Howard .75 .23
❑ 138 Gordan Giricek 1.25 .35
❑ 139 Allen Iverson 3.00 .90
❑ 140 Julius Erving 5.00 1.50
❑ 141 Glenn Robinson .75 .23
❑ 142 Maurice Cheeks 2.50 .75
❑ 143 Aaron McKie .75 .23
❑ 144 Billy Cunningham 2.00 .60
❑ 145 Eric Snow .75 .23
❑ 146 Stephon Marbury 2.00 .60
❑ 147 Kevin Johnson 1.25 .35
❑ 148 Amare Stoudemire 4.00 1.20
❑ 149 Larry Nance 1.25 .35
❑ 150 Shawn Marion 2.00 .60
❑ 151 Walter Davis 1.25 .35
❑ 152 Anfernee Hardaway 2.00 .60
❑ 153 Rasheed Wallace 1.25 .35
❑ 154 Zach Randolph 2.00 .60
❑ 155 Derek Anderson .75 .23
❑ 156 Dale Davis .60 .18
❑ 157 Bonzi Wells .75 .23
❑ 158 Jim Paxson 2.00 .60
❑ 159 Damon Stoudamire .75 .23
❑ 160 Chris Webber 2.00 .60
❑ 161 Vlade Divac .75 .23
❑ 162 Mike Bibby 2.00 .60
❑ 163 Bobby Jackson .75 .23
❑ 164 Peja Stojakovic 2.00 .60
❑ 165 Doug Christie .75 .23
❑ 166 Brad Miller 2.00 .60
❑ 167 Tim Duncan 2.50 .75
❑ 168 Radoslav Nesterovic 1.25 .35
❑ 169 Tony Parker 1.25 .35
❑ 170 George Gervin 2.50 .75
❑ 171 Manu Ginobili 1.25 .35
❑ 172 Artis Gilmore 2.00 .60
❑ 173 Ron Mercer .40 .12
❑ 174 Ray Allen 2.00 .60
❑ 175 Spencer Haywood 1.25 .35
❑ 176 Rashard Lewis 2.00 .60
❑ 177 Fred Brown 1.25 .35
❑ 178 Vladimir Radmanovic .60 .18
❑ 179 Jack Sikma 1.25 .35
❑ 180 Brent Barry 2.00 .60
❑ 181 Vince Carter 3.00 .90
❑ 182 Antonio Davis .60 .18
❑ 183 Morris Peterson .75 .23
❑ 184 Alvin Williams .60 .18
❑ 185 Chris Jefferies .40 .12
❑ 186 Jerome Williams .60 .18
❑ 187 Andrei Kirilenko 1.25 .35
❑ 188 Pete Maravich 12.00 3.60
❑ 189 Matt Harpring 1.25 .35
❑ 190 Mark Eaton 2.00 .60
❑ 191 Jarron Collins .40 .12
❑ 192 Greg Ostertag .60 .18
❑ 193 Carlos Arroyo 15.00 4.50
❑ 194 Jerry Stackhouse 2.00 .60
❑ 195 Wes Unseld 1.25 .35
❑ 196 Gilbert Arenas 2.00 .60
❑ 197 Larry Hughes .75 .23
❑ 198 Kwame Brown 1.25 .35
❑ 199 Jeff Malone 1.25 .35
❑ 200 Jared Jeffries .60 .18
❑ 201 Aleksandar Pavlovic RC 5.00 1.50
❑ 202 James Lang RC 5.00 1.50
❑ 203 Jason Kapono RC 5.00 1.50
❑ 204 Luke Walton RC 6.00 1.80
❑ 205 Jerome Beasley RC 5.00 1.50
❑ 206 Willie Green RC 5.00 1.50
❑ 207 Steve Blake RC 5.00 1.50
❑ 208 Slavko Vranes RC 5.00 1.50
❑ 209 Zaur Pachulia RC 5.00 1.50
❑ 210 Travis Hansen RC 5.00 1.50
❑ 211 Keith Bogans RC 5.00 1.50
❑ 212 Kyle Korver RC 6.00 1.80
❑ 213 Brandon Hunter RC 5.00 1.50
❑ 214 James Jones RC 5.00 1.50
❑ 215 Josh Howard RC 6.00 1.80
❑ 216 Leandro Barbosa RC 5.00 1.50
❑ 217 Kendrick Perkins RC 5.00 1.50
❑ 218 Ndudi Ebi RC 5.00 1.50
❑ 219 Brian Cook RC 5.00 1.50
❑ 220 Travis Outlaw RC 5.00 1.50
❑ 221 Zoran Planinic RC 5.00 1.50
❑ 222 Dahntay Jones RC 5.00 1.50
❑ 223 Boris Diaw RC 5.00 1.50
❑ 224 Zarko Cabarkapa RC 5.00 1.50
❑ 225 Troy Bell RC 5.00 1.50
❑ 226 Reece Gaines RC 5.00 1.50
❑ 227 Luke Ridnour RC 6.00 1.80
❑ 228 Chris Kaman RC 5.00 1.50
❑ 229 Marcus Banks RC 6.00 1.80
❑ 230 Maciej Lampe RC 6.00 1.80
❑ 231 David West RC 6.00 1.80
❑ 232 Mickael Pietrus RC 6.00 1.80
❑ 233 Jarvis Hayes RC .60 .18
❑ 234 Mike Sweetney RC 6.00 1.80
❑ 235 Kirk Hinrich RC 10.00 3.00
❑ 236 Chris Bosh RC 12.00 3.60
❑ 237 Nick Collison RC 20.00 6.00
❑ 238 T.J. Ford RC 25.00 7.50
❑ 239 Dwyane Wade RC 50.00 15.00
❑ 240 Carmelo Anthony RC 160.00 47.50
❑ 241 Darko Milicic RC 30.00 9.00
❑ 242 LeBron James RC 300.00 90.00
❑ 243 Michael Jordan MF 15.00 4.50
❑ 244 Kobe Bryant MF 10.00 3.00
❑ 245 Michael Finley MF 3.00 .90
❑ 246 Andrei Kirilenko MF 3.00 .90
❑ 247 Desmond Mason MF 3.00 .90
❑ 248 Kenyon Martin MF 3.00 .90
❑ 249 Shaquille O'Neal MF 6.00 1.80
❑ 250 Jamal Mashburn MF 3.00 .90
❑ 251 Jason Terry MF 3.00 .90
❑ 252 Andre Miller MF 3.00 .90
❑ 253 Keith Van Horn MF 3.00 .90
❑ 254 Derek Anderson MF 3.00 .90
❑ 255 Stephon Marbury MF 3.00 .90
❑ 256 Glenn Robinson MF 3.00 .90
❑ 257 Richard Hamilton MF 3.00 .90
❑ 258 Lamar Odom MF 3.00 .90
❑ 259 Bonzi Wells MF 3.00 .90
❑ 260 Wally Szczerbiak MF 3.00 .90
❑ 261 Alonzo Mourning MF 3.00 .90
❑ 262 Gilbert Arenas MF 3.00 .90
❑ 263 Mike Bibby MF 3.00 .90
❑ 264 Antawn Jamison MF 3.00 .90
❑ 265 Tony Parker MF 3.00 .90
❑ 266 Reggie Miller MF 3.00 .90
❑ 267 Vince Carter MF 6.00 1.80
❑ 268 Richard Jefferson MF 3.00 .90
❑ 269 Nene MF 3.00 .90
❑ 270 Grant Hill MF 3.00 .90
❑ 271 Rashard Lewis MF 3.00 .90
❑ 272 Shawn Marion MF 3.00 .90
❑ 273 Morris Peterson MF 3.00 .90
❑ 274 Chauncey Billups MF 3.00 .90
❑ 275 Eddie Jones MF 3.00 .90
❑ 276 Raef LaFrentz MF 3.00 .90
❑ 277 Jerry Stackhouse MF 3.00 .90
❑ 278 Pau Gasol MF 3.00 .90
❑ 279 Darius Miles MF 3.00 .90
❑ 280 Nick Van Exel MF 3.00 .90
❑ 281 Gary Payton MF 3.00 .90
❑ 282 Peja Stojakovic MF 3.00 .90
❑ 283 Karl Malone MF 3.00 .90
❑ 284 Mike Miller MF 3.00 .90
❑ 285 Caron Butler MF 3.00 .90
❑ 286 Cuttino Mobley MF 3.00 .90
❑ 287 Zach Randolph MF 3.00 .90
❑ 288 Scottie Pippen MF 4.00 1.20
❑ 289 Gordan Giricek MF 3.00 .90
❑ 290 Ben Wallace MF 3.00 .90
❑ 291 Manu Ginobili MF 3.00 .90
❑ 292 Vladimir Radmanovic MF 3.00 .90
❑ 293 Michael Jordan PP 25.00 7.50
❑ 294 Kobe Bryant PP 15.00 4.50
❑ 295 Vince Carter PP 10.00 3.00
❑ 296 Steve Nash PP 5.00 1.50
❑ 297 Shaquille O'Neal PP 10.00 3.00
❑ 298 Amare Stoudemire PP 8.00 2.40
❑ 299 Tracy McGrady PP 10.00 3.00
❑ 300 Gary Payton PP 5.00 1.50
❑ 301 Chris Bosh PP 8.00 2.40
❑ 302 Michael Finley PP 5.00 1.50
❑ 303 Caron Butler PP 5.00 1.50
❑ 304 Jarvis Hayes PP 6.00 1.80
❑ 305 Ben Wallace PP 5.00 1.50
❑ 306 Allan Houston PP 5.00 1.50
❑ 307 Mike Bibby PP 5.00 1.50
❑ 308 Antoine Walker PP 5.00 1.50
❑ 309 Dajuan Wagner PP 5.00 1.50
❑ 310 Kevin Garnett PP 8.00 2.40
❑ 311 Mickael Pietrus PP 5.00 1.50
❑ 312 Baron Davis PP 5.00 1.50
❑ 313 Paul Pierce PP 5.00 1.50
❑ 314 Rasheed Wallace PP 5.00 1.50
❑ 315 Chris Webber PP 5.00 1.50
❑ 316 Jermaine O'Neal PP 5.00 1.50
❑ 317 Shareef Abdur-Rahim PP 5.00 1.50
❑ 318 Ray Allen PP 5.00 1.50
❑ 319 Peja Stojakovic PP 5.00 1.50
❑ 320 Tim Duncan PP 8.00 2.40
❑ 321 Gilbert Arenas PP 5.00 1.50
❑ 322 Jason Richardson PP 5.00 1.50
❑ 323 Dwyane Wade FC 30.00 9.00
❑ 324 Gary Payton FC 20.00 6.00
❑ 325 Karl Malone FC 20.00 6.00
❑ 326 Jason Kidd FC 25.00 7.50
❑ 327 Darko Milicic FC 30.00 9.00
❑ 328 Steve Francis FC 20.00 6.00
❑ 329 Vince Carter FC 40.00 12.00
❑ 330 Elton Brand FC 20.00 6.00
❑ 331 Amare Stoudemire FC 40.00 12.00
❑ 332 Shaquille O'Neal FC 40.00 12.00
❑ 333 Carmelo Anthony FC 150.00 45.00
❑ 334 Tracy McGrady FC 40.00 12.00
❑ 335 Tim Duncan FC 40.00 12.00
❑ 336 Chris Webber FC 20.00 6.00
❑ 337 Allen Iverson FC 40.00 12.00
❑ 338 Dirk Nowitzki FC 30.00 9.00
❑ 339 Kevin Garnett FC 40.00 12.00
❑ 340 Kobe Bryant FC 50.00 15.00
❑ 341 LeBron James FC 300.00 90.00
❑ 342 Michael Jordan FC 100.00 30.00

2001-02 Upper Deck Flight Team

	Nm-Mt	Ex-Mt
COMPLETE SET (240)	600.00	180.00
COMP.SET w/o SP's (90)	40.00	12.00
COMMON CARD (1-90)	.25	.07
COMMON ROOKIE (91-120)	2.50	.75
COMMON ROOKIE (121-134)	3.00	.90
COMMON ROOKIE (135-140)	8.00	2.40

❑ 1 Michael Jordan 12.00 3.60
❑ 2 Dirk Nowitzki 1.25 .35

❑ 3 Antawn Jamison .75 .23
❑ 4 Latrell Sprewell .75 .23
❑ 5 Peja Stojakovic .75 .23
❑ 6 Dikembe Mutombo .50 .15
❑ 7 Jason Williams .50 .15
❑ 8 Kobe Bryant 3.00 .90
❑ 9 Baron Davis .75 .23
❑ 10 Wally Szczerbiak .50 .15
❑ 11 Reggie Miller .75 .23
❑ 12 Marcus Fizer .50 .15
❑ 13 Desmond Mason .50 .15
❑ 14 Glenn Robinson .75 .23
❑ 15 Vince Carter 2.00 .60
❑ 16 James Posey .50 .15
❑ 17 Darius Miles .75 .23
❑ 18 Jason Kidd 1.25 .35
❑ 19 Anfernee Hardaway .75 .23
❑ 20 Karl Malone .75 .23
❑ 21 Kevin Garnett 1.50 .45
❑ 22 Shareef Abdur-Rahim .75 .23
❑ 23 Steve Francis .75 .23
❑ 24 Paul Pierce .75 .23
❑ 25 Mike Miller .75 .23
❑ 26 Tim Duncan 1.50 .45
❑ 27 Derek Anderson .50 .15
❑ 28 Eddie Jones .75 .23
❑ 29 Keith Van Horn .75 .23
❑ 30 Chris Mihm .50 .15
❑ 31 Clifford Robinson .25 .07
❑ 32 Gary Payton .75 .23
❑ 33 Courtney Alexander .50 .15
❑ 34 Shaquille O'Neal 2.00 .60
❑ 35 Tim Thomas .50 .15
❑ 36 Raef LaFrentz .50 .15
❑ 37 Stromile Swift .50 .15
❑ 38 Stephon Marbury .75 .23
❑ 39 Morris Peterson .50 .15
❑ 40 Donyell Marshall .50 .15
❑ 41 Kenny Thomas .25 .07
❑ 42 Juwan Howard .50 .15
❑ 43 Tracy McGrady 2.00 .60
❑ 44 Kenny Anderson .50 .15
❑ 45 Larry Hughes .50 .15
❑ 46 Allan Houston .50 .15
❑ 47 Chris Webber .75 .23
❑ 48 Andre Miller .50 .15
❑ 49 Corey Maggette .50 .15
❑ 50 Sam Cassell .75 .23
❑ 51 Steve Smith .50 .15
❑ 52 Jamal Mashburn .50 .15
❑ 53 Al Harrington .50 .15
❑ 54 Brian Grant .50 .15
❑ 55 Rasheed Wallace .75 .23
❑ 56 Rick Fox .50 .15
❑ 57 Jason Terry .75 .23
❑ 58 Rashard Lewis .50 .15
❑ 59 Joe Smith .50 .15
❑ 60 Michael Dickerson .50 .15
❑ 61 Michael Finley .75 .23
❑ 62 Danny Fortson .25 .07
❑ 63 Allen Iverson 1.50 .45
❑ 64 Richard Hamilton .50 .15
❑ 65 Antonio McDyess .50 .15
❑ 66 David Wesley .25 .07
❑ 67 Ben Wallace .75 .23
❑ 68 Mike Bibby .75 .23
❑ 69 Antonio Davis .25 .07
❑ 70 Cuttino Mobley .50 .15
❑ 71 Lamond Murray .25 .07
❑ 72 Antoine Walker .75 .23
❑ 73 Jermaine O'Neal .75 .23
❑ 74 Alonzo Mourning .50 .15
❑ 75 Shawn Marion .75 .23
❑ 76 John Stockton .75 .23
❑ 77 Marcus Camby .50 .15
❑ 78 Derek Fisher .75 .23
❑ 79 DerMarr Johnson .50 .15
❑ 80 Aaron McKie .50 .15
❑ 81 David Robinson .75 .23
❑ 82 Steve Nash .75 .23
❑ 83 Ray Allen .75 .23
❑ 84 Elton Brand .75 .23
❑ 85 Kenyon Martin .75 .23
❑ 86 Bonzi Wells .50 .15
❑ 87 Grant Hill .75 .23
❑ 88 Terrell Brandon .50 .15
❑ 89 Toni Kukoc .50 .15
❑ 90 Jerry Stackhouse .75 .23
❑ 91A Tierre Brown RC 2.50 .75
❑ 91B Tierre Brown RC 2.50 .75
❑ 91C Tierre Brown RC 2.50 .75
❑ 92A Jamison Brewer RC 2.50 .75
❑ 92B Jamison Brewer RC 2.50 .75
❑ 92C Jamison Brewer RC 2.50 .75
❑ 93A Antonis Fotsis RC 2.50 .75
❑ 93B Antonis Fotsis RC 2.50 .75
❑ 93C Antonis Fotsis RC 2.50 .75
❑ 94A Mike James RC 2.50 .75
❑ 94B Mike James RC 2.50 .75
❑ 94C Mike James RC 2.50 .75
❑ 95A Primoz Brezec RC 2.50 .75
❑ 95B Primoz Brezec RC 2.50 .75
❑ 95C Primoz Brezec RC 2.50 .75
❑ 96A Jeryl Sasser RC 2.50 .75
❑ 96B Jeryl Sasser RC - -
❑ 96C Jeryl Sasser RC 2.50 .75
❑ 97A DeSagana Diop RC 2.50 .75
❑ 97B DeSagana Diop RC 2.50 .75
❑ 97C DeSagana Diop RC 2.50 .75
❑ 98A Mengke Bateer RC 2.50 .75
❑ 98B Mengke Bateer RC 2.50 .75
❑ 98C Mengke Bateer RC 2.50 .75
❑ 99A Gerald Wallace RC 5.00 1.50
❑ 99B Gerald Wallace RC 5.00 1.50
❑ 99C Gerald Wallace RC 5.00 1.50
❑ 100A Kenny Satterfield RC 2.50 .75
❑ 100B Kenny Satterfield RC 2.50 .75
❑ 100C Kenny Satterfield RC 2.50 .75
❑ 101A R.Boumtje-Boumtje RC 2.50 .75
❑ 101B R.Boumtje-Boumtje RC 2.50 .75
❑ 101C R.Boumtje-Boumtje RC 2.50 .75
❑ 102A Brian Scalabrine RC 2.50 .75
❑ 102B Brian Scalabrine RC 2.50 .75
❑ 102C Brian Scalabrine RC 2.50 .75
❑ 103A Oscar Torres RC 2.50 .75
❑ 103B Oscar Torres RC 2.50 .75
❑ 103C Oscar Torres RC 2.50 .75
❑ 104A Jarron Collins RC 2.50 .75
❑ 104B Jarron Collins RC 2.50 .75
❑ 104C Jarron Collins RC 2.50 .75
❑ 105A Jeff Trepagnier RC 2.50 .75
❑ 105B Jeff Trepagnier RC 2.50 .75
❑ 105C Jeff Trepagnier RC 2.50 .75
❑ 106A Brendan Haywood RC 3.00 .90
❑ 106B Brendan Haywood RC 3.00 .90
❑ 106C Brendan Haywood RC 3.00 .90
❑ 107A Vladimir Radmanovic RC 3.00 .90
❑ 107B Vladimir Radmanovic RC 3.00 .90
❑ 107C Vladimir Radmanovic RC 3.00 .90
❑ 108A Loren Woods RC 2.50 .75
❑ 108B Loren Woods RC 2.50 .75
❑ 108C Loren Woods RC 2.50 .75
❑ 109A Terence Morris RC 2.50 .75
❑ 109B Terence Morris RC 2.50 .75
❑ 109C Terence Morris RC 2.50 .75
❑ 110A Kirk Haston RC 2.50 .75
❑ 110B Kirk Haston RC 2.50 .75
❑ 110C Kirk Haston RC 2.50 .75
❑ 111A Earl Watson RC 2.50 .75
❑ 111B Earl Watson RC 2.50 .75
❑ 111C Earl Watson RC 2.50 .75
❑ 112A Brandon Armstrong RC 3.00 .90
❑ 112B Brandon Armstrong RC 3.00 .90
❑ 112C Brandon Armstrong RC 3.00 .90
❑ 113A Zach Randolph RC 8.00 2.40
❑ 113B Zach Randolph RC 8.00 2.40
❑ 113C Zach Randolph RC 8.00 2.40
❑ 114A Bobby Simmons RC 2.50 .75
❑ 114B Bobby Simmons RC 2.50 .75
❑ 114C Bobby Simmons RC 2.50 .75
❑ 115A Alton Ford RC 2.50 .75
❑ 115B Alton Ford RC 2.50 .75
❑ 115C Alton Ford RC 2.50 .75
❑ 116A Predrag Drobnjak RC 3.00 .90
❑ 116B Predrag Drobnjak RC 3.00 .90
❑ 116C Predrag Drobnjak RC 3.00 .90
❑ 117A Michael Bradley RC 2.50 .75
❑ 117B Michael Bradley RC 2.50 .75
❑ 117C Michael Bradley RC 2.50 .75
❑ 118A Samuel Dalembert RC 2.50 .75
❑ 118B Samuel Dalembert RC 2.50 .75
❑ 118C Samuel Dalembert RC 2.50 .75
❑ 119A Gilbert Arenas RC 4.00 1.20
❑ 119B Gilbert Arenas RC 4.00 1.20
❑ 119C Gilbert Arenas RC 4.00 1.20
❑ 120A Kedrick Brown RC 2.50 .75
❑ 120B Kedrick Brown RC 2.50 .75
❑ 120C Kedrick Brown RC 2.50 .75
❑ 121A Trenton Hassell RC 5.00 1.50
❑ 121B Trenton Hassell RC 5.00 1.50
❑ 121C Trenton Hassell RC 5.00 1.50
❑ 122A Zeljko Rebraca RC 3.00 .90
❑ 122B Zeljko Rebraca RC 3.00 .90
❑ 122C Zeljko Rebraca RC 3.00 .90
❑ 123A Jason Collins RC 3.00 .90
❑ 123B Jason Collins RC 3.00 .90
❑ 123C Jason Collins RC 3.00 .90
❑ 124A Will Solomon RC 3.00 .90
❑ 124B Will Solomon RC 3.00 .90
❑ 124C Will Solomon RC 3.00 .90
❑ 125A Joseph Forte RC 8.00 2.40
❑ 125B Joseph Forte RC 8.00 2.40
❑ 125C Joseph Forte RC 8.00 2.40
❑ 126A Steven Hunter RC 3.00 .90
❑ 126B Steven Hunter RC 3.00 .90
❑ 126C Steven Hunter RC 3.00 .90
❑ 127A Eddy Curry RC 8.00 2.40
❑ 127B Eddy Curry RC 8.00 2.40
❑ 127C Eddy Curry RC 8.00 2.40
❑ 128A Troy Murphy RC 6.00 1.80
❑ 128B Troy Murphy RC 6.00 1.80
❑ 128C Troy Murphy RC 6.00 1.80
❑ 129A Shane Battier RC 5.00 1.50
❑ 129B Shane Battier RC 5.00 1.50
❑ 129C Shane Battier RC 5.00 1.50
❑ 130A Tyson Chandler RC 10.00 3.00
❑ 130B Tyson Chandler RC 10.00 3.00
❑ 130C Tyson Chandler RC 10.00 3.00
❑ 131A Joe Johnson RC 5.00 1.50
❑ 131B Joe Johnson RC 5.00 1.50
❑ 131C Joe Johnson RC 5.00 1.50
❑ 132A Richard Jefferson RC 6.00 1.80
❑ 132B Richard Jefferson RC 6.00 1.80
❑ 132C Richard Jefferson RC 6.00 1.80
❑ 133A Eddie Griffin RC 5.00 1.50
❑ 133A Eddie Griffin RC 5.00 1.50
❑ 133B Eddie Griffin RC 5.00 1.50
❑ 134B Rodney White RC 4.00 1.20
❑ 134C Rodney White RC 4.00 1.20
❑ 134C Rodney White RC 4.00 1.20
❑ 135A Andrei Kirilenko RC 8.00 2.40
❑ 135B Andrei Kirilenko RC 10.00 3.00
❑ 135C Andrei Kirilenko RC 10.00 3.00
❑ 136A Tony Parker RC 15.00 4.50
❑ 136B Tony Parker RC 15.00 4.50
❑ 136C Tony Parker RC 15.00 4.50
❑ 137A Jamaal Tinsley RC 8.00 2.40
❑ 137B Jamaal Tinsley RC 8.00 2.40
❑ 137C Jamaal Tinsley RC 8.00 2.40
❑ 138A Pau Gasol RC 12.00 3.60
❑ 138B Pau Gasol RC 12.00 3.60
❑ 138C Pau Gasol RC 12.00 3.60
❑ 139A Jason Richardson RC 12.00 3.60
❑ 139B Jason Richardson RC 12.00 3.60
❑ 139C Jason Richardson RC 12.00 3.60
❑ 140A Kwame Brown RC 8.00 2.40
❑ 140B Kwame Brown RC 8.00 2.40
❑ 140C Kwame Brown RC 8.00 2.40

2002-03 Upper Deck Generations

	Nm-Mt	Ex-Mt
COMP.SET w/o SP's (150)	60.00	18.00

Card	Price	Price
COMMON CARD (1-50)	.20	.06
COMMON ROOKIE (51-92)	4.00	1.20
COMMON CARD (93-192)	.75	.23
COMMON CARD (193-234)	4.00	1.20
❑ 1 Shareef Abdur-Rahim	.75	.23
❑ 2 Paul Pierce	.75	.23
❑ 3 Antoine Walker	.75	.23
❑ 4 Jalen Rose	.75	.23
❑ 5 Tyson Chandler	.75	.23
❑ 6 Darius Miles	.75	.23
❑ 7 Dirk Nowitzki	1.25	.35
❑ 8 Steve Nash	.75	.23
❑ 9 James Posey	.50	.15
❑ 10 Richard Hamilton	.50	.15
❑ 11 Ben Wallace	.75	.23
❑ 12 Antawn Jamison	.75	.23
❑ 13 Jason Richardson	.75	.23
❑ 14 Steve Francis	.75	.23
❑ 15 Eddie Griffin	.50	.15
❑ 16 Reggie Miller	.75	.23
❑ 17 Jamaal Tinsley	.75	.23
❑ 18 Elton Brand	.75	.23
❑ 19 Andre Miller	.50	.15
❑ 20 Kobe Bryant	3.00	.90
❑ 21 Shaquille O'Neal	2.00	.60
❑ 22 Pau Gasol	.75	.23
❑ 23 Shane Battier	.75	.23
❑ 24 Alonzo Mourning	.50	.15
❑ 25 Ray Allen	.75	.23
❑ 26 Kevin Garnett	1.50	.45
❑ 27 Wally Szczerbiak	.50	.15
❑ 28 Jason Kidd	1.25	.35
❑ 29 Kenyon Martin	.75	.23
❑ 30 Jamal Mashburn	.50	.15
❑ 31 Baron Davis	.75	.23
❑ 32 Latrell Sprewell	.75	.23
❑ 33 Tracy McGrady	2.00	.60
❑ 34 Allen Iverson	1.50	.45
❑ 35 Stephon Marbury	.75	.23
❑ 36 Shawn Marion	.75	.23
❑ 37 Rasheed Wallace	.75	.23
❑ 38 Bonzi Wells	.50	.15
❑ 39 Chris Webber	.75	.23
❑ 40 Mike Bibby	.75	.23
❑ 41 Tim Duncan	1.50	.45
❑ 42 Tony Parker	.75	.23
❑ 43 Gary Payton	.75	.23
❑ 44 Rashard Lewis	.50	.15
❑ 45 Vince Carter	2.00	.60
❑ 46 Morris Peterson	.50	.15
❑ 47 Karl Malone	.75	.23
❑ 48 John Stockton	.75	.23
❑ 49 Michael Jordan	8.00	2.40
❑ 50 Jerry Stackhouse	.75	.23
❑ 51 Yao Ming RC	20.00	6.00
❑ 52 Jay Williams RC	5.00	1.50
❑ 53 Mike Dunleavy RC	6.00	1.80
❑ 54 Drew Gooden RC	10.00	3.00
❑ 55 Nikoloz Tskitishvili RC	4.00	1.20
❑ 56 DaJuan Wagner RC	6.00	1.80
❑ 57 Nene Hilario RC	5.00	1.50
❑ 58 Chris Wilcox RC	5.00	1.50
❑ 59 Amare Stoudemire RC	15.00	4.50
❑ 60 Caron Butler RC	8.00	2.40
❑ 61 Jared Jeffries RC	4.00	1.20
❑ 62 Melvin Ely RC	4.00	1.20
❑ 63 Marcus Haislip RC	4.00	1.20
❑ 64 Fred Jones RC	4.00	1.20
❑ 65 Bostjan Nachbar RC	4.00	1.20
❑ 66 Jiri Welsch RC	4.00	1.20
❑ 67 Juan Dixon RC	6.00	1.80
❑ 68 Curtis Borchardt RC	4.00	1.20
❑ 69 Ryan Humphrey RC	4.00	1.20
❑ 70 Kareem Rush RC	5.00	1.50
❑ 71 Qyntel Woods RC	4.00	1.20
❑ 72 Casey Jacobsen RC	4.00	1.20
❑ 73 Tayshaun Prince RC	5.00	1.50
❑ 74 Predrag Savovic RC	4.00	1.20
❑ 75 Frank Williams RC	4.00	1.20
❑ 76 John Salmons RC	4.00	1.20
❑ 77 Chris Jefferies RC	4.00	1.20
❑ 78 Dan Dickau RC	4.00	1.20
❑ 79 Marcus Taylor RC	5.00	1.50
❑ 80 Roger Mason RC	4.00	1.20
❑ 81 Robert Archibald RC	4.00	1.20
❑ 82 Vincent Yarbrough RC	4.00	1.20
❑ 83 Dan Gadzuric RC	4.00	1.20
❑ 84 Carlos Boozer RC	8.00	2.40
❑ 85 Tito Maddox RC	4.00	1.20
❑ 86 Rod Grizzard RC	4.00	1.20
❑ 87 Ronald Murray RC	6.00	1.80
❑ 88 Marko Jaric RC	4.00	1.20
❑ 89 Lonny Baxter RC	4.00	1.20
❑ 90 Sam Clancy RC	4.00	1.20
❑ 91 Matt Barnes RC	4.00	1.20
❑ 92 Jamal Sampson RC	4.00	1.20
❑ 93 Oscar Robertson	2.00	.60
❑ 94 Moses Malone	1.25	.35
❑ 95 Earl Monroe	.75	.23
❑ 96 Pete Maravich	3.00	.90
❑ 97 Artis Gilmore	.75	.23
❑ 98 Julius Erving	3.00	.90
❑ 99 Nate Archibald	.75	.23
❑ 100 Wes Unseld	.75	.23
❑ 101 Willis Reed	.75	.23
❑ 102 Jo Jo White	.75	.23
❑ 103 Isiah Thomas	1.25	.35
❑ 104 Bill Sharman	.75	.23
❑ 105 Wilt Chamberlain	2.00	.60
❑ 106 Bob Cousy	1.25	.35
❑ 107 Tom Heinsohn	.75	.23
❑ 108 Terry Cummings	.75	.23
❑ 109 John Havlicek	1.50	.45
❑ 110 Bob Pettit	.75	.23
❑ 111 Drazen Petrovic	.75	.23
❑ 112 Dan Roundfield	.75	.23
❑ 113 David Thompson	.75	.23
❑ 114 Bobby Jones	.75	.23
❑ 115 Clyde Lovellette	.75	.23
❑ 116 Rick Barry	1.25	.35
❑ 117 K.C. Jones	.75	.23
❑ 118 Lionel Hollins	.75	.23
❑ 119 Bob Lanier	.75	.23
❑ 120 Al Attles	.75	.23
❑ 121 Jack Sikma	.75	.23
❑ 122 George McGinnis	.75	.23
❑ 123 Quinn Buckner	.75	.23
❑ 124 Magic Johnson	3.00	.90
❑ 125 Larry Bird	4.00	1.20
❑ 126 Cliff Hagan	.75	.23
❑ 127 Jerry Lucas	.75	.23
❑ 128 Ricky Pierce	.75	.23
❑ 129 Walter Davis	.75	.23
❑ 130 Danny Ainge	.75	.23
❑ 131 Reggie Theus	.75	.23
❑ 132 Darryl Dawkins	1.25	.35
❑ 133 Tom Chambers	.75	.23
❑ 134 M.L. Carr	.75	.23
❑ 135 Kelly Tripucka	.75	.23
❑ 136 George Gervin	1.25	.35
❑ 137 Robert Parish	1.25	.35
❑ 138 Mitch Kupchak	.75	.23
❑ 139 Lou Hudson	.75	.23
❑ 140 Bill Cartwright	.75	.23
❑ 141 Lafayette Lever	.75	.23
❑ 142 Kevin Loughery	.75	.23
❑ 143 Hal Greer	.75	.23
❑ 144 Jamaal Wilkes	.75	.23
❑ 145 Alvan Adams	.75	.23
❑ 146 Thomas Sanders	.75	.23
❑ 147 Cazzie Russell	1.25	.35
❑ 148 Austin Carr	.75	.23
❑ 149 Gail Goodrich	.75	.23
❑ 150 Billy Knight	.75	.23
❑ 151 Dave Bing	.75	.23
❑ 152 Bill Walton	2.00	.60
❑ 153 Sam Jones	.75	.23
❑ 154 Swen Nater	.75	.23
❑ 155 Bobby Dandridge	.75	.23
❑ 156 Junior Bridgeman	.75	.23
❑ 157 Paul Silas	1.25	.35
❑ 158 John Kerr	.75	.23
❑ 159 Phil Chenier	.75	.23
❑ 160 Alex English	.75	.23
❑ 161 Geoff Petrie	.75	.23
❑ 162 Walt Bellamy	.75	.23
❑ 163 Don Nelson	.75	.23
❑ 164 Byron Scott	.75	.23
❑ 165 Harvey Catchings	.75	.23
❑ 166 Edward Macauley	.75	.23
❑ 167 John Drew	.75	.23
❑ 168 Detlef Schrempf	.75	.23
❑ 169 Rolando Blackman	.75	.23
❑ 170 Dave DeBusschere	1.25	.35
❑ 171 Marvin Barnes	.75	.23
❑ 172 Elgin Baylor	1.25	.35
❑ 173 Cedric Maxwell	.75	.23
❑ 174 Vern Mikkelsen	.75	.23
❑ 175 Larry Brown	.75	.23
❑ 176 Rick Mahorn	.75	.23
❑ 177 Dolph Schayes	.75	.23
❑ 178 Kevin McHale	1.50	.45
❑ 179 Clark Kellogg	.75	.23
❑ 180 Otis Birdsong	.75	.23
❑ 181 Michael Cooper	.75	.23
❑ 182 Mike Dunleavy	.75	.23
❑ 183 Spencer Haywood	.75	.23
❑ 184 Larry Nance	.75	.23
❑ 185 Maurice Lucas	.75	.23
❑ 186 Fred Brown	.75	.23
❑ 187 Jerry West	1.50	.45
❑ 188 Joe Barry Carroll	.75	.23
❑ 189 Dave Cowens	.75	.23
❑ 190 Sidney Moncrief	1.25	.35
❑ 191 Kiki Vandeweghe	.75	.23
❑ 192 Walt Frazier	1.25	.35
❑ 193 Yao Ming	15.00	4.50
Wilt Chamberlain		
❑ 194 Jay Williams	6.00	1.80
Julius Erving		
❑ 196 Drew Gooden	10.00	3.00
John Havlicek		
❑ 197 Nikoloz Tskitishvili	4.00	1.20
Kevin McHale		
❑ 198 DaJuan Wagner	4.00	1.20
Oscar Robertson		
❑ 199 Nene Hilario	6.00	1.80
Kiki Vandeweghe		
❑ 200 Chris Wilcox	5.00	1.50
❑ 201 Amare Stoudemire	15.00	4.50
George McGinnis		
❑ 202 Caron Butler	8.00	2.40
Willis Reed		
❑ 203 Jared Jeffries	6.00	1.80
Larry Bird		
❑ 204 Melvin Ely	4.00	1.20
Elgin Baylor		
❑ 205 Marcus Haislip	4.00	1.20
Kareem Abdul-Jabbar		
❑ 206 Fred Jones	4.00	1.20
K.C. Jones		
❑ 207 Bostjan Nachbar	4.00	1.20
❑ 208 Jiri Welsch	4.00	1.20
❑ 209 Juan Dixon	6.00	1.80
❑ 210 Curtis Borchardt	4.00	1.20
❑ 211 Ryan Humphrey	4.00	1.20
Bob Lanier		
❑ 212 Kareem Rush	5.00	1.50
Walt Frazier		
❑ 213 Qyntel Woods	4.00	1.20
Jamaal Wilkes		
❑ 214 Casey Jacobsen	4.00	1.20
Tom Chambers		
❑ 215 Tayshaun Prince	5.00	1.50
Byron Scott		
❑ 216 Predrag Savovic	4.00	1.20
Drazen Petrovic		
❑ 217 Frank Williams	4.00	1.20
❑ 218 John Salmons	4.00	1.20
Elgin Baylor		
❑ 219 Chris Jefferies	4.00	1.20
Walter Davis		
❑ 220 Dan Dickau	4.00	1.20
❑ 221 Marcus Taylor	4.00	1.20
Oscar Robertson		
❑ 222 Roger Mason	4.00	1.20
Jo Jo White		
❑ 223 Robert Archibald	4.00	1.20
Sidney Moncrief		
❑ 224 Vincent Yarbrough	4.00	1.20
Earl Monroe		
❑ 225 Dan Gadzuric	4.00	1.20
Bill Walton		
❑ 226 Carlos Boozer	8.00	2.40
Robert Parish		
❑ 227 Tito Maddox	4.00	1.20
❑ 228 Rod Grizzard	4.00	1.20
George Gervin		
❑ 229 Ronald Murray	4.00	1.20
Lafayette Lever		
❑ 230 Marko Jaric	4.00	1.20

231 Lonny Baxter	4.00	1.20
232 Sam Clancy Wes Unseld	4.00	1.20
233 Matt Barnes	4.00	1.20
234 Jamal Sampson	4.00	1.20
195 Mike Dunleavy Jr. Mike Dunleavy Sr.	8.00	2.40

1998 Upper Deck Hardcourt

	Nm-Mt	Ex-Mt
COMPLETE SET (90)	75.00	22.00
1 Kobe Bryant	8.00	2.40
2 Donyell Marshall	1.50	.45
3 Bryant Reeves	.60	.18
4 Keith Van Horn	2.00	.60
5 David Robinson	2.00	.60
6 Nick Anderson	.60	.18
7 Nick Van Exel	2.00	.60
8 David Wesley	.60	.18
9 Alonzo Mourning	1.50	.45
10 Shawn Kemp	1.50	.45
11 Maurice Taylor	1.50	.45
12 Kenny Anderson	1.50	.45
13 Jason Kidd	3.00	.90
14 Marcus Camby	1.50	.45
15 Tim Hardaway	1.50	.45
16 Damon Stoudamire	1.50	.45
17 Detlef Schrempf	1.50	.45
18 Dikembe Mutombo	1.50	.45
19 Charles Barkley	2.50	.75
20 Ray Allen	2.00	.60
21 Ron Mercer	1.50	.45
22 Shawn Bradley	.60	.18
23 Michael Jordan	10.00	3.00
23A Michael Jordan Spec.	20.00	6.00
24 Antonio McDyess	1.50	.45
25 Stephon Marbury	2.00	.60
26 Rik Smits	1.50	.45
27 Michael Stewart	.60	.18
28 Steve Smith	1.50	.45
29 Glenn Robinson	1.50	.45
30 Chris Webber	2.00	.60
31 Antoine Walker	2.00	.60
32 Eddie Jones	2.00	.60
33 Mitch Richmond	1.50	.45
34 Kevin Garnett	4.00	1.20
35 Grant Hill	2.00	.60
36 John Stockton	2.00	.60
37 Allan Houston	1.50	.45
38 Bobby Jackson	1.50	.45
39 Sam Cassell	2.00	.60
40 Allen Iverson	4.00	1.20
41 LaPhonso Ellis	.60	.18
42 Lorenzen Wright	.60	.18
43 Gary Payton	2.00	.60
44 Patrick Ewing	2.00	.60
45 Scottie Pippen	3.00	.90
46 Hakeem Olajuwon	2.00	.60
47 Glen Rice	1.50	.45
48 Antonio Daniels	.60	.18
49 Jayson Williams	.60	.18
50 Juwan Howard	1.50	.45
51 Reggie Miller	2.00	.60
52 Joe Smith	1.50	.45
53 Shaquille O'Neal	5.00	1.50
54 Dennis Rodman	1.50	.45
55 Vin Baker	1.50	.45
56 Rod Strickland	.60	.18
57 Anfernee Hardaway	2.00	.60
58 Zydrunas Ilgauskas	1.50	.45
59 Chris Mullin	2.00	.60
60 Rasheed Wallace	2.00	.60
61 Shareef Abdur-Rahim	2.00	.60
62 Tom Gugliotta	.60	.18
63 Tim Duncan	3.00	.90
64 Michael Finley	2.00	.60
65 Jim Jackson	.60	.18
66 Chauncey Billups	1.50	.45
67 Jerry Stackhouse	2.00	.60
68 Jeff Hornacek	1.50	.45
69 Clyde Drexler	2.00	.60
70 Karl Malone	2.00	.60
71 Tim Duncan RE	1.50	.45
72 Keith Van Horn RE	1.50	.45
73 Chauncey Billups RE	1.50	.45
74 Antonio Daniels RE	.60	.18
75 Tony Battie RE	.60	.18
76 Ron Mercer RE	1.50	.45
77 Tim Thomas RE	1.50	.45
78 Tracy McGrady RE	5.00	1.50
79 Danny Fortson RE	.60	.18
80 Derek Anderson RE	2.00	.60
81 Maurice Taylor RE	1.50	.45
82 Kelvin Cato RE	.60	.18
83 Brevin Knight RE	.60	.18
84 Bobby Jackson RE	.60	.18
85 Rodrick Rhodes RE	.60	.18
86 Anthony Johnson RE	.60	.18
87 Cedric Henderson RE	.60	.18
88 Chris Anstey RE	.60	.18
89 Michael Stewart RE	.60	.18
90 Zydrunas Ilgauskas RE	.60	.18
NNO Michael Jordan Jumbo	10.00	3.00

1999-00 Upper Deck Hardcourt

	Nm-Mt	Ex-Mt
COMPLETE SET (90)	100.00	30.00
COMPLETE SET w/o RC (60)	25.00	7.50
COMMON CARD (1-60)	.30	.09
COMMON ROOKIE 61-90	1.00	.30
1 Dikembe Mutombo	.60	.18
2 Alan Henderson	.30	.09
3 Antoine Walker	1.00	.30
4 Paul Pierce	1.00	.30
5 Eddie Jones	1.00	.30
6 Elden Campbell	.30	.09
7 Toni Kukoc	.60	.18
8 Randy Brown	.30	.09
9 Shawn Kemp	.60	.18
10 Brevin Knight	.30	.09
11 Michael Finley	1.00	.30
12 Dirk Nowitzki	2.00	.60
13 Antonio McDyess	.60	.18
14 Nick Van Exel	1.00	.30
15 Grant Hill	1.00	.30
16 Jerry Stackhouse	1.00	.30
17 Antawn Jamison	1.50	.45
18 John Starks	.60	.18
19 Hakeem Olajuwon	1.00	.30
20 Scottie Pippen	1.50	.45
21 Reggie Miller	1.00	.30
22 Jalen Rose	1.00	.30
23 Maurice Taylor	.60	.18
24 Michael Olowokandi	.60	.18
25 Shaquille O'Neal	2.50	.75
26 Kobe Bryant	4.00	1.20
27 Tim Hardaway	.60	.18
28 Alonzo Mourning	.60	.18
29 Glenn Robinson	1.00	.30
30 Ray Allen	1.00	.30
31 Kevin Garnett	2.00	.60
32 Terrell Brandon	.60	.18
33 Stephon Marbury	1.00	.30
34 Keith Van Horn	1.00	.30
35 Latrell Sprewell	1.00	.30
36 Allan Houston	.60	.18
37 Patrick Ewing	1.00	.30
38 Darrell Armstrong	.30	.09
39 Bo Outlaw	.30	.09
40 Allen Iverson	2.00	.60
41 Larry Hughes	1.00	.30
42 Jason Kidd	1.50	.45
43 Tom Gugliotta	.30	.09
44 Brian Grant	.60	.18
45 Damon Stoudamire	.60	.18
46 Jason Williams	1.00	.30
47 Vlade Divac	.60	.18
48 Tim Duncan	2.00	.60
49 David Robinson	1.00	.30
50 Avery Johnson	.30	.09
51 Gary Payton	1.00	.30
52 Vin Baker	.60	.18
53 Vince Carter	2.50	.75
54 Tracy McGrady	2.50	.75
55 Karl Malone	1.00	.30
56 John Stockton	1.00	.30
57 Shareef Abdur-Rahim	1.00	.30
58 Mike Bibby	1.00	.30
59 Juwan Howard	.60	.18
60 Mitch Richmond	.60	.18
61 Elton Brand RC	6.00	1.80
62 Jason Terry RC	4.00	1.20
63 Kenny Thomas RC	2.00	.60
64 Jonathan Bender RC	5.00	1.50
65 Aleksandar Radojevic RC	1.00	.30
66 Galen Young RC	1.00	.30
67 Baron Davis RC	5.00	1.50
68 Corey Maggette RC	5.00	1.50
69 Dion Glover RC	1.50	.45
70 Scott Padgett RC	1.50	.45
71 Steve Francis RC	8.00	2.40
72 Richard Hamilton RC	5.00	1.50
73 James Posey RC	3.00	.90
74 Jumaine Jones RC	2.00	.60
75 Chris Herren RC	1.00	.30
76 Andre Miller RC	5.00	1.50
77 Lamar Odom RC	5.00	1.50
78 Wally Szczerbiak RC	5.00	1.50
79 William Avery RC	2.00	.60
80 Devean George RC	2.50	.75
81 Trajan Langdon RC	2.00	.60
82 Cal Bowdler RC	1.50	.45
83 Kris Clack RC	1.00	.30
84 Tim James RC	1.50	.45
85 Shawn Marion RC	6.00	1.80
86 Ryan Robertson RC	1.25	.35
87 Quincy Lewis RC	1.50	.45
88 Vonteego Cummings RC	2.00	.60
89 Obinna Ekezie RC	1.25	.35
90 Jeff Foster RC	1.50	.45
GF1 Michael Jordan Floor	1,200.00	350.00
GF6 Wilt Chamberlain Floor	200.00	60.00

2000-01 Upper Deck Hardcourt

	Nm-Mt	Ex-Mt
COMPLETE SET w/o RC (60)	25.00	7.50
COMMON CARD (1-60)	.25	.07

COMMON ROOKIE (61-102) ..	4.00	1.20
❑ 1 Dikembe Mutombo	.50	.15
❑ 2 Jason Terry	.75	.23
❑ 3 Antoine Walker	.75	.23
❑ 4 Paul Pierce	.75	.23
❑ 5 Eddie Jones	.75	.23
❑ 6 Baron Davis	.75	.23
❑ 7 Elton Brand	.75	.23
❑ 8 Ron Artest	.50	.15
❑ 9 Andre Miller	.50	.15
❑ 10 Shawn Kemp	.50	.15
❑ 11 Dirk Nowitzki	1.25	.35
❑ 12 Michael Finley	.75	.23
❑ 13 Antonio McDyess	.50	.15
❑ 14 Nick Van Exel	.75	.23
❑ 15 Grant Hill	.75	.23
❑ 16 Jerry Stackhouse	.75	.23
❑ 17 Antawn Jamison	.75	.23
❑ 18 Larry Hughes	.50	.15
❑ 19 Steve Francis	.75	.23
❑ 20 Hakeem Olajuwon	.75	.23
❑ 21 Reggie Miller	.75	.23
❑ 22 Jalen Rose	.75	.23
❑ 23 Lamar Odom	.75	.23
❑ 24 Eric Piatkowski	.50	.15
❑ 25 Shaquille O'Neal	2.00	.60
❑ 26 Kobe Bryant	3.00	.90
❑ 27 Alonzo Mourning	.50	.15
❑ 28 Jamal Mashburn	.50	.15
❑ 29 Ray Allen	.75	.23
❑ 30 Glenn Robinson	.75	.23
❑ 31 Kevin Garnett	1.50	.45
❑ 32 Wally Szczerbiak	.50	.15
❑ 33 Keith Van Horn	.75	.23
❑ 34 Stephon Marbury	.75	.23
❑ 35 Allan Houston	.50	.15
❑ 36 Latrell Sprewell	.75	.23
❑ 37 Darrell Armstrong	.25	.07
❑ 38 Ron Mercer	.50	.15
❑ 39 Allen Iverson	1.50	.45
❑ 40 Toni Kukoc	.50	.15
❑ 41 Jason Kidd	1.25	.35
❑ 42 Anfernee Hardaway	.75	.23
❑ 43 Shawn Marion	.75	.23
❑ 44 Scottie Pippen	1.25	.35
❑ 45 Damon Stoudamire	.50	.15
❑ 46 Chris Webber	.75	.23
❑ 47 Jason Williams	.50	.15
❑ 48 Tim Duncan	1.50	.45
❑ 49 David Robinson	.75	.23
❑ 50 Gary Payton	.75	.23
❑ 51 Vin Baker	.50	.15
❑ 52 Rashard Lewis	.50	.15
❑ 53 Tracy McGrady	2.00	.60
❑ 54 Vince Carter	2.00	.60
❑ 55 Karl Malone	.75	.23
❑ 56 John Stockton	.75	.23
❑ 57 Shareef Abdur-Rahim	.75	.23
❑ 58 Mike Bibby	.75	.23
❑ 59 Mitch Richmond	.50	.15
❑ 60 Richard Hamilton	.50	.15
❑ 61 Kenyon Martin RC	20.00	6.00
❑ 62 Marcus Fizer RC	4.00	1.20
❑ 63 Chris Mihm RC	4.00	1.20
❑ 64 Chris Porter RC	4.00	1.20
❑ 65 Stromile Swift RC	8.00	2.40
❑ 66 Morris Peterson RC	8.00	2.40
❑ 67 Quentin Richardson RC	10.00	3.00
❑ 68 Courtney Alexander RC	5.00	1.50
❑ 69 Scoonie Penn RC	4.00	1.20
❑ 70 Mateen Cleaves RC	4.00	1.20
❑ 71 Erick Barkley RC	4.00	1.20
❑ 72 A.J. Guyton RC	4.00	1.20
❑ 73 Darius Miles RC	15.00	4.50
❑ 74 DerMarr Johnson RC	4.00	1.20
❑ 75 Hidayet Turkoglu RC	8.00	2.40
❑ 76 Hanno Mottola RC	4.00	1.20
❑ 77 Mike Miller RC	8.00	2.40
❑ 78 Desmond Mason RC	4.00	1.20
❑ 79 Mark Madsen RC	4.00	1.20
❑ 80 Eduardo Najera RC	6.00	1.80
❑ 81 Speedy Claxton RC	4.00	1.20
❑ 82 Joel Przybilla RC	4.00	1.20
❑ 83 Brian Cardinal RC	4.00	1.20
❑ 84 Khalid El-Amin RC	4.00	1.20
❑ 85 Etan Thomas RC	4.00	1.20
❑ 86 Corey Hightower RC	4.00	1.20
❑ 87 Dan Langhi RC	4.00	1.20
❑ 88 Michael Redd RC	6.00	1.80
❑ 89 Pete Mickeal RC	4.00	1.20
❑ 90 Mamadou N'diaye RC ..	4.00	1.20
❑ 91 Jerome Moiso RC	4.00	1.20
❑ 92 Chris Carrawell RC	4.00	1.20
❑ 93 Jason Collier RC	4.00	1.20
❑ 94 Keyon Dooling RC	4.00	1.20
❑ 95 Mark Karcher RC	4.00	1.20
❑ 96 Jamaal Magloire RC	4.00	1.20
❑ 97 Jason Hart RC	4.00	1.20
❑ 98 Jabari Smith RC	4.00	1.20
❑ 99 Donnell Harvey RC	4.00	1.20
❑ 100 Lavor Postell RC	4.00	1.20
❑ 101 Eddie House RC	4.00	1.20
❑ 102 Dan McClintock RC	4.00	1.20

2001-02 Upper Deck Hardcourt

	Nm-Mt	Ex-Mt
COMP.SET w/o SP's (90)	50.00	15.00
COMMON CARD (1-121)	.30	.09
COMMON ROOKIE (101-110)	5.00	1.50
COMMON ROOKIE (111-120)	12.00	3.60
❑ 1 Jason Terry	1.00	.30
❑ 2 DerMarr Johnson	.60	.18
❑ 3 Toni Kukoc	.60	.18
❑ 4 Antoine Walker	1.00	.30
❑ 5 Paul Pierce	1.00	.30
❑ 6 Kenny Anderson	.60	.18
❑ 7 Jamal Mashburn	.60	.18
❑ 8 Baron Davis	1.00	.30
❑ 9 David Wesley	.30	.09
❑ 10 Ron Artest	.60	.18
❑ 11 Jamal Crawford	.60	.18
❑ 12 Ron Mercer	.60	.18
❑ 13 Andre Miller	.60	.18
❑ 14 Lamond Murray	.30	.09
❑ 15 Matt Harpring	1.00	.30
❑ 16 Michael Finley	1.00	.30
❑ 17 Dirk Nowitzki	1.50	.45
❑ 18 Steve Nash	1.00	.30
❑ 19 Antonio McDyess	.60	.18
❑ 20 Nick Van Exel	1.00	.30
❑ 21 James Posey	.60	.18
❑ 22 Jerry Stackhouse	1.00	.30
❑ 23 Chucky Atkins	.30	.09
❑ 24 Mateen Cleaves	.60	.18
❑ 25 Antawn Jamison	1.00	.30
❑ 26 Larry Hughes	.60	.18
❑ 27 Marc Jackson	.60	.18
❑ 28 Steve Francis	1.00	.30
❑ 29 Maurice Taylor	.60	.18
❑ 30 Cuttino Mobley	.60	.18
❑ 31 Reggie Miller	1.00	.30
❑ 32 Jalen Rose	1.00	.30
❑ 33 Jermaine O'Neal	1.00	.30
❑ 34 Darius Miles	1.00	.30
❑ 35 Lamar Odom	1.00	.30
❑ 36 Elton Brand	1.00	.30
❑ 37 Kobe Bryant	4.00	1.20
❑ 38 Shaquille O'Neal	2.50	.75
❑ 39 Derek Fisher	1.00	.30
❑ 40 Robert Horry	.60	.18
❑ 41 Alonzo Mourning	.60	.18
❑ 42 Eddie Jones	1.00	.30
❑ 43 Brian Grant	.60	.18
❑ 44 Anthony Mason	.60	.18
❑ 45 Ray Allen	1.00	.30
❑ 46 Glenn Robinson	1.00	.30
❑ 47 Tim Thomas	.60	.18
❑ 48 Kevin Garnett	2.00	.60
❑ 49 Wally Szczerbiak	.60	.18
❑ 50 Terrell Brandon	.60	.18
❑ 51 Anthony Peeler	.30	.09
❑ 52 Jason Kidd	1.50	.45
❑ 53 Kenyon Martin	1.00	.30
❑ 54 Stephen Jackson	.60	.18
❑ 55 Latrell Sprewell	1.00	.30
❑ 56 Allan Houston	.60	.18
❑ 57 Glen Rice	.60	.18
❑ 58 Tracy McGrady	2.50	.75
❑ 59 Darrell Armstrong	.30	.09
❑ 60 Mike Miller	1.00	.30
❑ 61 Allen Iverson	2.00	.60
❑ 62 Dikembe Mutombo	.60	.18
❑ 63 Aaron McKie	.60	.18
❑ 64 Stephon Marbury	1.00	.30
❑ 65 Shawn Marion	1.00	.30
❑ 66 Tom Gugliotta	.30	.09
❑ 67 Rasheed Wallace	1.00	.30
❑ 68 Scottie Pippen	1.50	.45
❑ 69 Damon Stoudamire	.60	.18
❑ 70 Chris Webber	1.00	.30
❑ 71 Mike Bibby	1.00	.30
❑ 72 Peja Stojakovic	1.00	.30
❑ 73 Tim Duncan	2.00	.60
❑ 74 David Robinson	1.00	.30
❑ 75 Derek Anderson	.60	.18
❑ 76 Gary Payton	1.00	.30
❑ 77 Rashard Lewis	.60	.18
❑ 78 Desmond Mason	.60	.18
❑ 79 Vince Carter	2.50	.75
❑ 80 Morris Peterson	.60	.18
❑ 81 Antonio Davis	.30	.09
❑ 82 Karl Malone	1.00	.30
❑ 83 John Stockton	1.00	.30
❑ 84 Donyell Marshall	.60	.18
❑ 85 Bryant Reeves	.30	.09
❑ 86 Jason Williams	.60	.18
❑ 87 Stromile Swift	.60	.18
❑ 88 Richard Hamilton	.60	.18
❑ 89 Courtney Alexander	.60	.18
❑ 90 Chris Whitney	.30	.09
❑ 91A Kenny Satterfield ON RC	4.00	1.20
❑ 92A Jeff Trepagnier ON RC	4.00	1.20
❑ 93A Michael Wright ON RC	4.00	1.20
❑ 94A Terence Morris ON RC	4.00	1.20
❑ 95A Omar Cook ON RC	4.00	1.20
❑ 96A Gilbert Arenas ON RC	10.00	3.00
❑ 97A Joseph Forte ON RC	5.00	1.50
❑ 98A Jamaal Tinsley ON RC	6.00	1.80
❑ 99A Samuel Dalembert ON RC	4.00	1.20
❑ 100A Gerald Wallace ON RC	8.00	2.40
❑ 101A Brendan Haywood ON RC	6.00	1.80
❑ 102A Richard Jefferson ON RC	15.00	4.50
❑ 103A Michael Bradley ON RC	5.00	1.50
❑ 104A Loren Woods ON RC	5.00	1.50
❑ 105A Jeryl Sasser ON RC	5.00	1.50
❑ 106A Jason Collins ON RC	5.00	1.50
❑ 107A Kirk Haston ON RC	4.00	1.20
❑ 108A Steven Hunter ON RC	5.00	1.50
❑ 109A Troy Murphy ON RC	5.00	1.50
❑ 110A Vladimir Radmanovic ON RC	5.00	1.50
❑ 111A Rodney White ON RC	12.00	3.60
❑ 112A Kedrick Brown ON RC	12.00	3.60
❑ 113A Joe Johnson ON RC	12.00	3.60
❑ 114A Eddie Griffin ON RC	12.00	3.60
❑ 115A Shane Battier ON RC	12.00	3.60
❑ 116A Eddy Curry ON RC	20.00	6.00
❑ 117A Jason Richardson ON RC	25.00	7.50
❑ 118A DeSagana Diop ON RC	12.00	3.60
❑ 119A Tyson Chandler ON RC	20.00	6.00
❑ 120A Kwame Brown ON RC	15.00	4.50
❑ 121 Michael Jordan	15.00	4.50

2002-03 Upper Deck Hardcourt

	Nm-Mt	Ex-Mt
COMP.SET w/o SP's (90)	50.00	15.00
COMMON CARD (1-90)	.30	.09
COMMON ROOKIE (91-120)	5.00	1.50
COMMON ROOKIE (121-129)	6.00	1.80
❑ 1 Shareef Abdur-Rahim	1.00	.30
❑ 2 Glenn Robinson	1.00	.30
❑ 3 Jason Terry	1.00	.30
❑ 4 Antoine Walker	1.00	.30
❑ 5 Paul Pierce	1.00	.30

❑ 6 Kedrick Brown	.60	.18
❑ 7 Jalen Rose	1.00	.30
❑ 8 Eddy Curry	1.00	.30
❑ 9 Tyson Chandler	1.00	.30
❑ 10 Marcus Fizer	.60	.18
❑ 11 Lamond Murray	.30	.09
❑ 12 Darius Miles	1.00	.30
❑ 13 Chris Mihm	.30	.09
❑ 14 Dirk Nowitzki	1.50	.45
❑ 15 Michael Finley	.60	.18
❑ 16 Steve Nash	1.00	.30
❑ 17 James Posey	.60	.18
❑ 18 Juwan Howard	.60	.18
❑ 19 Kenny Satterfield	.30	.09
❑ 20 Jerry Stackhouse	1.00	.30
❑ 21 Clifford Robinson	.30	.09
❑ 22 Ben Wallace	1.00	.30
❑ 23 Antawn Jamison	1.00	.30
❑ 24 Jason Richardson	1.00	.30
❑ 25 Gilbert Arenas	1.00	.30
❑ 26 Steve Francis	1.00	.30
❑ 27 Cuttino Mobley	.60	.18
❑ 28 Eddie Griffin	.60	.18
❑ 29 Reggie Miller	1.00	.30
❑ 30 Jermaine O'Neal	1.00	.30
❑ 31 Jamaal Tinsley	1.00	.30
❑ 32 Elton Brand	1.00	.30
❑ 33 Andre Miller	.60	.18
❑ 34 Lamar Odom	1.00	.30
❑ 35 Kobe Bryant	4.00	1.20
❑ 36 Shaquille O' Neal	2.50	.75
❑ 37 Derek Fisher	1.00	.30
❑ 38 Devean George	.60	.18
❑ 39 Pau Gasol	1.00	.30
❑ 40 Jason Williams	.60	.18
❑ 41 Shane Battier	1.00	.30
❑ 42 Alonzo Mourning	.60	.18
❑ 43 Eddie Jones	1.00	.30
❑ 44 Brian Grant	.60	.18
❑ 45 Ray Allen	1.00	.30
❑ 46 Tim Thomas	.60	.18
❑ 47 Sam Cassell	1.00	.30
❑ 48 Kevin Garnett	2.00	.60
❑ 49 Wally Szczerbiak	.60	.18
❑ 50 Terrell Brandon	.60	.18
❑ 51 Jason Kidd	1.50	.45
❑ 52 Richard Jefferson	.60	.18
❑ 53 Dikembe Mutombo	.60	.18
❑ 54 Jamal Mashburn	.60	.18
❑ 55 Baron Davis	1.00	.30
❑ 56 David Wesley	.30	.09
❑ 57 Allan Houston	.60	.18
❑ 58 Latrell Sprewell	1.00	.30
❑ 59 Antonio McDyess	.60	.18
❑ 60 Tracy McGrady	2.50	.75
❑ 61 Mike Miller	1.00	.30
❑ 62 Darrell Armstrong	.30	.09
❑ 63 Allen Iverson	2.00	.60
❑ 64 Keith Van Horn	1.00	.30
❑ 65 Aaron McKie	.60	.18
❑ 66 Stephon Marbury	1.00	.30
❑ 67 Shawn Marion	1.00	.30
❑ 68 Anfernee Hardaway	1.00	.30
❑ 69 Rasheed Wallace	1.00	.30
❑ 70 Damon Stoudamire	.60	.18
❑ 71 Scottie Pippen	1.50	.45
❑ 72 Chris Webber	1.00	.30
❑ 73 Mike Bibby	1.00	.30
❑ 74 Peja Stojakovic	1.00	.30
❑ 75 Tim Duncan	2.00	.60
❑ 76 David Robinson	1.00	.30
❑ 77 Tony Parker	1.00	.30
❑ 78 Gary Payton	1.00	.30
❑ 79 Rashard Lewis	.60	.18
❑ 80 Desmond Mason	.60	.18
❑ 81 Vince Carter	2.50	.75
❑ 82 Morris Peterson	.60	.18
❑ 83 Antonio Davis	.30	.09
❑ 84 Karl Malone	1.00	.30
❑ 85 John Stockton	1.00	.30
❑ 86 Andrei Kirilenko	1.00	.30
❑ 87 Richard Hamilton	.60	.18
❑ 88 Michael Jordan	8.00	2.40
❑ 89 Chris Whitney	.30	.09
❑ 90 Kwame Brown	.60	.18
❑ 91 Efthimios Rentzias RC	5.00	1.50
❑ 92 Marko Jaric RC	5.00	1.50
❑ 93 Jiri Welsch RC	5.00	1.50
❑ 94 Carlos Boozer RC	12.00	3.60
❑ 95 Fred Jones RC	6.00	1.80
❑ 96 Sam Clancy RC	5.00	1.50
❑ 97 Predrag Savovic RC	5.00	1.50
❑ 98 Frank Williams RC	5.00	1.50
❑ 99 Rod Grizzard RC	5.00	1.50
❑ 100 Casey Jacobsen RC	5.00	1.50
❑ 101 Jamal Sampson RC	5.00	1.50
❑ 102 Lonny Baxter RC	5.00	1.50
❑ 103 Darius Songaila RC	5.00	1.50
❑ 104 Tito Maddox RC	5.00	1.50
❑ 105 Chris Owens RC	5.00	1.50
❑ 106 Juan Dixon RC	10.00	3.00
❑ 107 Chris Jefferies RC	5.00	1.50
❑ 108 Dan Dickau RC	5.00	1.50
❑ 109 Manu Ginobili RC	15.00	4.50
❑ 110 Tamar Slay RC	6.00	1.80
❑ 111 Matt Barnes RC	5.00	1.50
❑ 112 Vincent Yarbrough RC	5.00	1.50
❑ 113 Bostjan Nachbar RC	5.00	1.50
❑ 114 Dan Gadzuric RC	5.00	1.50
❑ 115 Robert Archibald RC	5.00	1.50
❑ 116 Ryan Humphrey RC	5.00	1.50
❑ 117 Tayshaun Prince RC	8.00	2.40
❑ 118 John Salmons RC	5.00	1.50
❑ 119 Steve Logan RC	5.00	1.50
❑ 120 Melvin Ely RC	5.00	1.50
❑ 121 Nikoloz Tskitishvili RC	8.00	2.40
❑ 122 Qyntel Woods RC	8.00	2.40
❑ 123 Marcus Haislip RC	6.00	1.80
❑ 124 Nene Hilario RC	10.00	3.00
❑ 125 Amare Stoudemire RC	30.00	9.00
❑ 126 Jared Jeffries RC	8.00	2.40
❑ 127 Kareem Rush RC	10.00	3.00
❑ 128 Chris Wilcox RC	10.00	3.00
❑ 129 Curtis Borchardt RC	6.00	1.80
❑ 130 Drew Gooden RC	25.00	7.50
❑ 131 Mike Dunleavy RC	15.00	4.50
❑ 132 DaJuan Wagner RC	15.00	4.50
❑ 133 Caron Butler RC	20.00	6.00
❑ 134 Yao Ming RC	60.00	18.00
❑ 135 Jay Williams RC	12.00	3.60

2003-04 Upper Deck Hardcourt

	MINT	NRMT
COMP.SET w/o SP's (100)	40.00	18.00
COMMON CARD (1-90)	.20	.09
COMMON ROOKIE (91-126)	6.00	2.70
COMMON ROOKIE (127-132)	15.00	6.75
❑ 1 Shareef Abdur-Rahim	.75	.35
❑ 2 Jason Terry	.75	.35
❑ 3 Glenn Robinson	.75	.35
❑ 4 Paul Pierce	.75	.35
❑ 5 Antoine Walker	.75	.35
❑ 6 Vin Baker	.50	.23
❑ 7 Jalen Rose	.75	.35
❑ 8 Tyson Chandler	.75	.35
❑ 9 Michael Jordan	5.00	2.20
❑ 10 DaJuan Wagner	.50	.23
❑ 11 Ricky Davis	.75	.35
❑ 12 Darius Miles	.75	.35
❑ 13 Dirk Nowitzki	1.25	.55
❑ 14 Michael Finley	.75	.35
❑ 15 Steve Nash	.75	.35
❑ 16 Nene	.50	.23
❑ 17 Marcus Camby	.50	.23
❑ 18 Nikoloz Tskitishvili	.20	.09
❑ 19 Richard Hamilton	.50	.23
❑ 20 Ben Wallace	.75	.35
❑ 21 Tayshaun Prince	.50	.23
❑ 22 Antawn Jamison	.75	.35
❑ 23 Jason Richardson	.75	.35
❑ 24 Gilbert Arenas	.75	.35
❑ 25 Steve Francis	.75	.35
❑ 26 Yao Ming	2.00	.90
❑ 27 Eddie Griffin	.50	.23
❑ 28 Reggie Miller	.75	.35
❑ 29 Jamaal Tinsley	.75	.35
❑ 30 Jermaine O'Neal	.75	.35
❑ 31 Elton Brand	.75	.35
❑ 32 Andre Miller	.50	.23
❑ 33 Lamar Odom	.75	.35
❑ 34 Kobe Bryant	3.00	1.35
❑ 35 Gary Payton	.75	.35
❑ 36 Shaquille O'Neal	2.00	.90
❑ 37 Karl Malone	.75	.35
❑ 38 Pau Gasol	.75	.35
❑ 39 Shane Battier	.75	.35
❑ 40 Mike Miller	.75	.35
❑ 41 Eddie Jones	.75	.35
❑ 42 Rasual Butler	.50	.23
❑ 43 Caron Butler	.75	.35
❑ 44 Michael Redd	.75	.35
❑ 45 Joe Smith	.50	.23
❑ 46 Desmond Mason	.50	.23
❑ 47 Kevin Garnett	1.50	.70
❑ 48 Wally Szczerbiak	.50	.23
❑ 49 Sam Cassell	.75	.35
❑ 50 Jason Kidd	1.25	.55
❑ 51 Richard Jefferson	.50	.23
❑ 52 Alonzo Mourning	.50	.23
❑ 53 Baron Davis	.75	.35
❑ 54 Jamal Mashburn	.50	.23
❑ 55 Jamaal Magloire	.20	.09
❑ 56 Allan Houston	.50	.23
❑ 57 Antonio McDyess	.50	.23
❑ 58 Latrell Sprewell	.75	.35
❑ 59 Tracy McGrady	2.00	.90
❑ 60 Grant Hill	.75	.35
❑ 61 Drew Gooden	.50	.23
❑ 62 Allen Iverson	1.50	.70
❑ 63 Keith Van Horn	.75	.35
❑ 64 Kenny Thomas	.20	.09
❑ 65 Stephon Marbury	.75	.35
❑ 66 Shawn Marion	.75	.35
❑ 67 Amare Stoudemire	1.50	.70
❑ 68 Rasheed Wallace	.75	.35
❑ 69 Bonzi Wells	.50	.23
❑ 70 Damon Stoudamire	.50	.23
❑ 71 Chris Webber	.75	.35
❑ 72 Mike Bibby	.75	.35
❑ 73 Peja Stojakovic	.75	.35
❑ 74 Bobby Jackson	.50	.23
❑ 75 Tim Duncan	1.50	.70
❑ 76 David Robinson	.75	.35
❑ 77 Tony Parker	.75	.35
❑ 78 Manu Ginobili	.75	.35
❑ 79 Ray Allen	.75	.35
❑ 80 Rashard Lewis	.75	.35
❑ 81 Reggie Evans	.20	.09
❑ 82 Vince Carter	2.00	.90
❑ 83 Morris Peterson	.50	.23

Card	Nm-Mt	Ex-Mt
❑ 84 Antonio Davis	.20	.09
❑ 85 Matt Harpring	.75	.35
❑ 86 John Stockton	.75	.35
❑ 87 Andrei Kirilenko	.75	.35
❑ 88 Jerry Stackhouse	.75	.35
❑ 89 Kwame Brown	.50	.23
❑ 90 Larry Hughes	.50	.23
❑ 91 Kirk Hinrich RC	10.00	4.50
❑ 92 T.J. Ford RC	8.00	3.60
❑ 93 Mike Sweetney RC	6.00	2.70
❑ 94 Jarvis Hayes RC	6.00	2.70
❑ 95 Mickael Pietrus RC	6.00	2.70
❑ 96 Nick Collison RC	6.00	2.70
❑ 97 Marcus Banks RC	6.00	2.70
❑ 98 Luke Ridnour RC	8.00	3.60
❑ 99 Reece Gaines RC	6.00	2.70
❑ 100 Troy Bell RC	6.00	2.70
❑ 101 Zarko Cabarkapa RC	6.00	2.70
❑ 102 David West RC	6.00	2.70
❑ 103 Aleksandar Pavlovic RC	6.00	2.70
❑ 104 Dahntay Jones RC	6.00	2.70
❑ 105 Boris Diaw RC	6.00	2.70
❑ 106 Zoran Planinic RC	6.00	2.70
❑ 107 Travis Outlaw RC	6.00	2.70
❑ 108 Brian Cook RC	6.00	2.70
❑ 109 Carlos Delfino RC	6.00	2.70
❑ 110 Ndudi Ebi RC	6.00	2.70
❑ 111 Kendrick Perkins RC	6.00	2.70
❑ 112 Leandro Barbosa RC	6.00	2.70
❑ 113 Josh Howard RC	8.00	3.60
❑ 114 Maciej Lampe RC	6.00	2.70
❑ 115 Jason Kapono RC	6.00	2.70
❑ 116 Luke Walton RC	8.00	3.60
❑ 117 Jerome Beasley RC	6.00	2.70
❑ 118 Sofoklis Schortsanitis RC	6.00	2.70
❑ 119 Kyle Korver RC	8.00	3.60
❑ 120 Travis Hansen RC	6.00	2.70
❑ 121 Steve Blake RC	6.00	2.70
❑ 122 Slavko Vranes RC	6.00	2.70
❑ 123 Zaur Pachulia RC	6.00	2.70
❑ 124 Keith Bogans RC	6.00	2.70
❑ 125 Matt Bonner RC	6.00	2.70
❑ 126 Maurice Williams RC	6.00	2.70
❑ 127 Chris Kaman RC	15.00	6.75
❑ 128 Dwyane Wade RC	15.00	6.75
❑ 129 Chris Bosh RC	20.00	9.00
❑ 130 Carmelo Anthony RC	60.00	27.00
❑ 131 Darko Milicic RC	15.00	6.75
❑ 132 LeBron James RC	120.00	55.00

2001-02 Upper Deck Honor Roll

	Nm-Mt	Ex-Mt
COMPLETE SET (130)	350.00	105.00
COMP.SET w/o SP's (90)	40.00	12.00
COMMON CARD (1-90)	.25	.07
COMMON ROOKIE (91-120)	3.00	.90
COMMON JSY RC (121-130)	12.00	3.60
❑ 1 Shareef Abdur-Rahim	.75	.23
❑ 2 Jason Terry	.75	.23
❑ 3 Dion Glover	.25	.07
❑ 4 Paul Pierce	.75	.23
❑ 5 Antoine Walker	.75	.23
❑ 6 Kenny Anderson	.50	.15
❑ 7 Baron Davis	.75	.23
❑ 8 Jamal Mashburn	.50	.15
❑ 9 David Wesley	.25	.07
❑ 10 Ron Mercer	.50	.15
❑ 11 Brad Miller	.75	.23
❑ 12 Andre Miller	.50	.15
❑ 13 Lamond Murray	.25	.07
❑ 14 Chris Mihm	.50	.15
❑ 15 Michael Finley	.75	.23
❑ 16 Dirk Nowitzki	1.25	.35
❑ 17 Steve Nash	.75	.23
❑ 18 Juwan Howard	.50	.15
❑ 19 Nick Van Exel	.75	.23
❑ 20 Raef LaFrentz	.50	.15
❑ 21 Antonio McDyess	.50	.15
❑ 22 James Posey	.50	.15
❑ 23 Jerry Stackhouse	.75	.23
❑ 24 Clifford Robinson	.25	.07
❑ 25 Ben Wallace	.75	.23
❑ 26 Antawn Jamison	.75	.23
❑ 27 Larry Hughes	.50	.15
❑ 28 Steve Francis	.75	.23
❑ 29 Cuttino Mobley	.50	.15
❑ 30 Glen Rice	.50	.15
❑ 31 Reggie Miller	.75	.23
❑ 32 Jalen Rose	.75	.23
❑ 33 Jermaine O'Neal	.75	.23
❑ 34 Darius Miles	.75	.23
❑ 35 Elton Brand	.75	.23
❑ 36 Lamar Odom	.75	.23
❑ 37 Corey Maggette	.50	.15
❑ 38 Kobe Bryant	3.00	.90
❑ 39 Shaquille O'Neal	2.00	.60
❑ 40 Rick Fox	.50	.15
❑ 41 Lindsey Hunter	.25	.07
❑ 42 Stromile Swift	.50	.15
❑ 43 Jason Williams	.50	.15
❑ 44 Alonzo Mourning	.50	.15
❑ 45 Eddie Jones	.75	.23
❑ 46 Anthony Carter	.50	.15
❑ 47 Brian Grant	.50	.15
❑ 48 Ray Allen	.75	.23
❑ 49 Glenn Robinson	.75	.23
❑ 50 Sam Cassell	.75	.23
❑ 51 Kevin Garnett	1.50	.45
❑ 52 Terrell Brandon	.50	.15
❑ 53 Wally Szczerbiak	.50	.15
❑ 54 Joe Smith	.50	.15
❑ 55 Jason Kidd	1.25	.35
❑ 56 Kenyon Martin	.75	.23
❑ 57 Allan Houston	.50	.15
❑ 58 Latrell Sprewell	.75	.23
❑ 59 Marcus Camby	.50	.15
❑ 60 Mark Jackson	.50	.15
❑ 61 Tracy McGrady	2.00	.60
❑ 62 Grant Hill	.75	.23
❑ 63 Mike Miller	.75	.23
❑ 64 Allen Iverson	1.50	.45
❑ 65 Dikembe Mutombo	.50	.15
❑ 66 Aaron McKie	.50	.15
❑ 67 Stephon Marbury	.75	.23
❑ 68 Shawn Marion	.75	.23
❑ 69 Anfernee Hardaway	.75	.23
❑ 70 Tom Gugliotta	.25	.07
❑ 71 Rasheed Wallace	.75	.23
❑ 72 Damon Stoudamire	.50	.15
❑ 73 Derek Anderson	.50	.15
❑ 74 Chris Webber	.75	.23
❑ 75 Mike Bibby	.75	.23
❑ 76 Peja Stojakovic	.75	.23
❑ 77 Tim Duncan	1.50	.45
❑ 78 David Robinson	.75	.23
❑ 79 Steve Smith	.50	.15
❑ 80 Gary Payton	.75	.23
❑ 81 Rashard Lewis	.50	.15
❑ 82 Desmond Mason	.50	.15
❑ 83 Vince Carter	2.00	.60
❑ 84 Morris Peterson	.50	.15
❑ 85 Antonio Davis	.25	.07
❑ 86 Karl Malone	.75	.23
❑ 87 John Stockton	.75	.23
❑ 88 Donyell Marshall	.50	.15
❑ 89 Richard Hamilton	.50	.15
❑ 90 Michael Jordan	12.00	3.60
❑ 91 Andrei Kirilenko RC	6.00	1.80
❑ 92 Gilbert Arenas RC	8.00	2.40
❑ 93 Earl Watson RC	3.00	.90
❑ 94 Terence Morris RC	3.00	.90
❑ 95 Kedrick Brown RC	3.00	.90
❑ 96 Zach Randolph RC	8.00	2.40
❑ 97 Joe Johnson RC	4.00	1.20
❑ 98 Brandon Armstrong RC	3.00	.90
❑ 99 DeSagana Diop RC	3.00	.90
❑ 100 Joseph Forte RC	6.00	1.80
❑ 101 Brendan Haywood RC	4.00	1.20
❑ 102 Samuel Dalembert RC	3.00	.90
❑ 103 Jason Collins RC	3.00	.90
❑ 104 Michael Bradley RC	3.00	.90
❑ 105 Gerald Wallace RC	6.00	1.80
❑ 106 Tierre Brown RC	3.00	.90
❑ 107 Troy Murphy RC	5.00	1.50
❑ 108 Alton Ford RC	3.00	.90
❑ 109 Vladimir Radmanovic RC	3.00	.90
❑ 110 Ruben Boumtje-Boumtje RC	3.00	.90
❑ 111 Bobby Simmons RC	3.00	.90
❑ 112 Oscar Torres RC	3.00	.90
❑ 113 Jeryl Sasser RC	3.00	.90
❑ 114 Loren Woods RC	3.00	.90
❑ 115 Shane Battier RC	4.00	1.20
❑ 116 Jamison Brewer RC	3.00	.90
❑ 117 Richard Jefferson RC	5.00	1.50
❑ 118 Pau Gasol RC	8.00	2.40
❑ 119 Damone Brown RC	3.00	.90
❑ 120 Rodney White RC	4.00	1.20
❑ 121 Kwame Brown JSY RC Kevin Garnett JSY	20.00	6.00
❑ 122 Tyson Chandler JSY RC Darius Miles JSY	12.00	3.60
❑ 123 Eddy Curry JSY RC Karl Malone JSY	25.00	7.50
❑ 124 Jason Richardson JSY RC Kobe Bryant JSY	40.00	12.00
❑ 125 Tony Parker JSY RC Jason Kidd JSY	40.00	12.00
❑ 126 Eddie Griffin JSY RC Anfernee Hardaway JSY	12.00	3.60
❑ 127 Kirk Haston JSY RC Jamal Mashburn JSY	12.00	3.60
❑ 128 Jamaal Tinsley JSY RC Andre Miller JSY	8.00	2.40
❑ 129 Trenton Hassell JSY RC Marcus Fizer JSY	8.00	2.40
❑ 130 Steven Hunter JSY RC Tracy McGrady JSY	20.00	6.00

2002-03 Upper Deck Honor Roll

	Nm-Mt	Ex-Mt
COMP.SET w/o SP's (90)	30.00	9.00
COMMON CARD (1-90)	.20	.06
COMMON JSY RC (91-105)	10.00	3.00
COMMON ROOKIE (106-135)	6.00	1.80
❑ 1 Glenn Robinson	.75	.23
❑ 2 Shareef Abdur-Rahim	.75	.23
❑ 3 Jason Terry	.75	.23
❑ 4 Paul Pierce	.75	.23
❑ 5 Antoine Walker	.75	.23
❑ 6 Tony Delk	.20	.06
❑ 7 Jalen Rose	.75	.23
❑ 8 Tyson Chandler	.75	.23
❑ 9 Eddy Curry	.75	.23
❑ 10 Darius Miles	.75	.23
❑ 11 Zydrunas Ilgauskas	.50	.15
❑ 12 Ricky Davis	.75	.23
❑ 13 Dirk Nowitzki	1.25	.35
❑ 14 Michael Finley	.75	.23
❑ 15 Steve Nash	.75	.23

❑ 16 Raef LaFrentz .50 .15
❑ 17 Eduardo Najera .50 .15
❑ 18 Rodney White .50 .15
❑ 19 Juwan Howard .50 .15
❑ 20 Chris Whitney .20 .06
❑ 21 Ben Wallace .75 .23
❑ 22 Richard Hamilton .50 .15
❑ 23 Chauncey Billups .50 .15
❑ 24 Chucky Atkins .20 .06
❑ 25 Jason Richardson .75 .23
❑ 26 Antawn Jamison .75 .23
❑ 27 Gilbert Arenas .75 .23
❑ 28 Steve Francis .75 .23
❑ 29 Cuttino Mobley .50 .15
❑ 30 Jermaine O'Neal .75 .23
❑ 31 Reggie Miller .75 .23
❑ 32 Jamaal Tinsley .75 .23
❑ 33 Andre Miller .50 .15
❑ 34 Elton Brand .75 .23
❑ 35 Quentin Richardson .50 .15
❑ 36 Shaquille O'Neal 2.00 .60
❑ 37 Kobe Bryant 3.00 .90
❑ 38 Robert Horry .50 .15
❑ 39 Shane Battier .75 .23
❑ 40 Pau Gasol .75 .23
❑ 41 Stromile Swift .50 .15
❑ 42 Eddie Jones .75 .23
❑ 43 Brian Grant .50 .15
❑ 44 Malik Allen .20 .06
❑ 45 Ray Allen .75 .23
❑ 46 Tim Thomas .50 .15
❑ 47 Kevin Garnett 1.50 .45
❑ 48 Wally Szczerbiak .50 .15
❑ 49 Jason Kidd 1.25 .35
❑ 50 Kenyon Martin .75 .23
❑ 51 Richard Jefferson .50 .15
❑ 52 Baron Davis .75 .23
❑ 53 Jamal Mashburn .50 .15
❑ 54 David Wesley .20 .06
❑ 55 P.J. Brown .20 .06
❑ 56 Allan Houston .50 .15
❑ 57 Latrell Sprewell .75 .23
❑ 58 Kurt Thomas .50 .15
❑ 59 Tracy McGrady 2.00 .60
❑ 60 Grant Hill .75 .23
❑ 61 Mike Miller .75 .23
❑ 62 Allen Iverson 1.50 .45
❑ 63 Keith Van Horn .75 .23
❑ 64 Aaron McKie .50 .15
❑ 65 Shawn Marion .75 .23
❑ 66 Stephon Marbury .75 .23
❑ 67 Rasheed Wallace .75 .23
❑ 68 Derek Anderson .50 .15
❑ 69 Bonzi Wells .50 .15
❑ 70 Mike Bibby .75 .23
❑ 71 Chris Webber .75 .23
❑ 72 Peja Stojakovic .75 .23
❑ 73 Hedo Turkoglu .75 .23
❑ 74 Tim Duncan 1.50 .45
❑ 75 David Robinson .75 .23
❑ 76 Tony Parker .75 .23
❑ 77 Gary Payton .75 .23
❑ 78 Rashard Lewis .50 .15
❑ 79 Brent Barry .50 .15
❑ 80 Desmond Mason .50 .15
❑ 81 Vince Carter 2.00 .60
❑ 82 Antonio Davis .20 .06
❑ 83 Morris Peterson .50 .15
❑ 84 John Stockton .75 .23
❑ 85 Karl Malone .75 .23
❑ 86 Andrei Kirilenko .75 .23
❑ 87 Matt Harpring .75 .23
❑ 88 Jerry Stackhouse .75 .23
❑ 89 Kwame Brown .50 .15
❑ 90 Michael Jordan 6.00 1.80
❑ 91 R.Humphrey JSY RC 10.00 3.00
❑ 92 Juan Dixon JSY RC 15.00 4.50
❑ 93 Fred Jones JSY RC 10.00 3.00
❑ 94 Marcus Haislip JSY RC 10.00 3.00
❑ 95 Melvin Ely JSY RC 10.00 3.00
❑ 96 Jared Jeffries JSY RC 12.00 3.60
❑ 97 Caron Butler JSY RC 20.00 6.00
❑ 98 A.Stoudemire JSY RC 50.00 15.00
❑ 99 Chris Wilcox JSY RC 12.00 3.60
❑ 100 Nene Hilario JSY RC 10.00 3.00
❑ 101 Dajuan Wagner JSY RC 12.00 3.60
❑ 102 N.Tskitishvili JSY RC 10.00 3.00
❑ 103 Drew Gooden JSY RC 20.00 6.00
❑ 104 Jay Williams JSY RC 12.00 3.60
❑ 105 Yao Ming JSY RC 60.00 18.00
❑ 106 Mike Dunleavy RC 10.00 3.00
❑ 107 Bostjan Nachbar RC 6.00 1.80
❑ 108 Jiri Welsch RC 6.00 1.80
❑ 109 Rasual Butler RC 6.00 1.80
❑ 110 Kareem Rush RC 8.00 2.40
❑ 111 Qyntel Woods RC 6.00 1.80
❑ 112 Casey Jacobsen RC 6.00 1.80
❑ 113 Tayshaun Prince RC 8.00 2.40
❑ 114 Frank Williams RC 6.00 1.80
❑ 115 John Salmons RC 6.00 1.80
❑ 116 Chris Jefferies RC 6.00 1.80
❑ 117 Dan Dickau RC 6.00 1.80
❑ 118 Juaquin Hawkins RC 6.00 1.80
❑ 119 Roger Mason RC 6.00 1.80
❑ 120 Robert Archibald RC 6.00 1.80
❑ 121 Vincent Yarbrough RC 6.00 1.80
❑ 122 Dan Gadzuric RC 6.00 1.80
❑ 123 Carlos Boozer RC 12.00 3.60
❑ 124 Tito Maddox RC 6.00 1.80
❑ 125 Gordan Giricek RC 8.00 2.40
❑ 126 Ronald Murray RC 10.00 3.00
❑ 127 Lonny Baxter RC 6.00 1.80
❑ 128 Pat Burke RC 6.00 1.80
❑ 129 Manu Ginobili RC 15.00 4.50
❑ 130 Predrag Savovic RC 6.00 1.80
❑ 131 Marko Jaric RC 6.00 1.80
❑ 132 Efthimios Rentzias RC 6.00 1.80
❑ 133 J.R. Bremer RC 6.00 1.80
❑ 134 Igor Rakocevic RC 6.00 1.80
❑ 135 Tamar Slay RC 6.00 1.80

2003-04 Upper Deck Honor Roll

	Nm-Mt	Ex-Mt
COMP.SET w/o SP's (90)	40.00	12.00
COMMON ROOKIE (91-	4.00	1.20
COMMON JSY RC (106-130)	10.00	3.00

JSY RC SWATCHES ARE EVENT WORN

❑ 8 Scottie Pippen 1.25 .35
❑ 9 Jamal Crawford .50 .15
❑ 10 Dajuan Wagner .50 .15
❑ 11 Ricky Davis .75 .23
❑ 12 Darius Miles .75 .23
❑ 13 Dirk Nowitzki 1.25 .35
❑ 14 Antoine Walker .75 .23
❑ 15 Steve Nash .75 .23
❑ 16 Michael Finley .75 .23
❑ 17 Nikoloz Tskitishvili .20 .06
❑ 18 Andre Miller .50 .15
❑ 19 Nene .50 .15
❑ 20 Chauncey Billups .50 .15
❑ 21 Richard Hamilton .50 .15
❑ 22 Ben Wallace .75 .23
❑ 23 Clifford Robinson .20 .06
❑ 24 Jason Richardson .75 .23
❑ 25 Mike Dunleavy .50 .15
❑ 26 Yao Ming 2.00 .60
❑ 27 Cuttino Mobley .50 .15
❑ 28 Steve Francis .75 .23
❑ 29 Jermaine O'Neal .75 .23
❑ 30 Reggie Miller .75 .23
❑ 31 Al Harrington .50 .15
❑ 32 Elton Brand .75 .23
❑ 33 Corey Maggette .50 .15
❑ 34 Quentin Richardson .50 .15
❑ 35 Kobe Bryant 3.00 .90
❑ 36 Karl Malone .75 .23
❑ 37 Gary Payton .75 .23
❑ 38 Shaquille O'Neal 2.00 .60
❑ 39 Pau Gasol .75 .23
❑ 40 Jason Williams .50 .15
❑ 41 Mike Miller .75 .23
❑ 42 Lamar Odom .75 .23
❑ 43 Eddie Jones .75 .23
❑ 44 Caron Butler .75 .23
❑ 45 Michael Redd .75 .23
❑ 46 Desmond Mason .50 .15
❑ 47 Tim Thomas .50 .15
❑ 48 Latrell Sprewell .75 .23
❑ 49 Kevin Garnett 1.50 .45
❑ 50 Wally Szczerbiak .50 .15
❑ 51 Richard Jefferson .50 .15
❑ 52 Kenyon Martin .75 .23
❑ 53 Jason Kidd 1.25 .35
❑ 54 Jamal Mashburn .50 .15
❑ 55 Baron Davis .75 .23
❑ 56 Jamaal Magloire .20 .06
❑ 57 Allan Houston .50 .15
❑ 58 Antonio McDyess .75 .23
❑ 59 Keith Van Horn .75 .23
❑ 60 Grant Hill .75 .23
❑ 61 Drew Gooden .50 .15
❑ 62 Tracy McGrady 2.00 .60
❑ 63 Glenn Robinson .75 .23
❑ 64 Allen Iverson 1.50 .45
❑ 65 Eric Snow .50 .15
❑ 66 Amare Stoudemire 1.50 .45
❑ 67 Stephon Marbury .75 .23
❑ 68 Shawn Marion .75 .23
❑ 69 Derek Anderson .50 .15
❑ 70 Damon Stoudamire .50 .15
❑ 71 Rasheed Wallace .75 .23
❑ 72 Peja Stojakovic .75 .23
❑ 73 Chris Webber .75 .23
❑ 74 Mike Bibby .75 .23
❑ 75 Bobby Jackson .50 .15
❑ 76 Tony Parker .75 .23
❑ 77 Tim Duncan 1.50 .45
❑ 78 Manu Ginobili .75 .23
❑ 79 Vladimir Radmanovic .20 .06
❑ 80 Ray Allen .75 .23
❑ 81 Rashard Lewis .75 .23
❑ 82 Morris Peterson .50 .15
❑ 83 Vince Carter 2.00 .60
❑ 84 Jalen Rose .75 .23
❑ 85 Andrei Kirilenko .75 .23
❑ 86 Matt Harpring .75 .23
❑ 87 Greg Ostertag .20 .06
❑ 88 Gilbert Arenas .75 .23
❑ 89 Larry Hughes .50 .15
❑ 90 Jerry Stackhouse .75 .23
❑ 91 Kirk Hinrich RC 6.00 1.80
❑ 92 T.J. Ford RC 5.00 1.50
❑ 93 Nick Collison RC 4.00 1.20
❑ 94 Kendrick Perkins RC 4.00 1.20
❑ 95 Leandro Barbosa RC 4.00 1.20
❑ 96 Josh Howard RC 5.00 1.50
❑ 97 Jason Kapono RC 4.00 1.20
❑ 98 Jerome Beasley RC 4.00 1.20
❑ 99 Travis Hansen RC 4.00 1.20
❑ 100 Steve Blake RC 4.00 1.20
❑ 101 Willie Green RC 4.00 1.20
❑ 102 Zaur Pachulia RC 4.00 1.20
❑ 103 Keith Bogans RC 4.00 1.20
❑ 104 Kyle Korver RC 5.00 1.50
❑ 105 Brandon Hunter RC 4.00 1.20
❑ 106 LeBron James JSY RC 120.00 36.00
❑ 107 Darko Milicic JSY RC 15.00 4.50
❑ 108 Carmelo Anthony JSY RC 60.00 18.00
❑ 109 Chris Bosh JSY RC 20.00 6.00
❑ 110 Dwyane Wade JSY RC 25.00 7.50
❑ 111 Chris Kaman JSY RC 10.00 3.00
❑ 112 Mike Sweetney JSY RC 10.00 3.00
❑ 113 Jarvis Hayes JSY RC 10.00 3.00
❑ 114 Mickael Pietrus JSY RC 10.00 3.00
❑ 115 Marcus Banks JSY RC 10.00 3.00
❑ 116 Luke Ridnour JSY RC 12.00 3.60
❑ 117 Reece Gaines JSY RC 10.00 3.00
❑ 118 Troy Bell JSY RC 10.00 3.00
❑ 119 Z.Cabarkapa JSY RC 10.00 3.00
❑ 120 David West JSY RC 10.00 3.00
❑ 121 A.Pavlovic JSY RC 10.00 3.00
❑ 122 Dahntay Jones JSY RC 10.00 3.00
❑ 123 Boris Diaw JSY RC 10.00 3.00
❑ 124 Zoran Planinic JSY RC 10.00 3.00
❑ 125 Travis Outlaw JSY RC 10.00 3.00
❑ 126 Brian Cook JSY RC 10.00 3.00
❑ 127 Ndudi Ebi JSY RC 10.00 3.00

❑ 128 Maciej Lampe JSY RC 10.00 3.00
❑ 129 Slavko Vranes JSY RC 10.00 3.00
❑ 130 Luke Walton JSY RC 12.00 3.60

2001-02 Upper Deck Inspirations

	Nm-Mt	Ex-Mt
COMP.SET w/o SP's (90)	40.00	12.00
COMMON CARD (1-90)	.25	.07
COMMON ROOKIE (91-103)	6.00	1.80
COMMON ROOKIE (104-109)	80.00	24.00
COMMON ROOKIE (110-116)	20.00	6.00
COMMON ROOKIE (117-124)	12.00	3.60
COMMON ROOKIE (125-134)	15.00	4.50
COMMON ROOKIE (135-140)	20.00	6.00
COMMON XRC (141-152)	5.00	1.50
COMMON XRC (153-164)	6.00	1.80
COMMON XRC (165-176)	8.00	2.40
COMMON XRC (177-182)	-	-

❑ 1 Shareef Abdur-Rahim .75 .23
❑ 2 Jason Terry .75 .23
❑ 3 Dion Glover .25 .07
❑ 4 Antoine Walker .75 .23
❑ 5 Paul Pierce .75 .23
❑ 6 Larry Bird 2.50 .75
❑ 7 Baron Davis .75 .23
❑ 8 Jamal Mashburn .50 .15
❑ 9 David Wesley .25 .07
❑ 10 Elden Campbell .25 .07
❑ 11 Jalen Rose .75 .23
❑ 12 Marcus Fizer .50 .15
❑ 13 Andre Miller .50 .15
❑ 14 Lamond Murray .25 .07
❑ 15 Chris Mihm .50 .15
❑ 16 Dirk Nowitzki 1.25 .35
❑ 17 Steve Nash .75 .23
❑ 18 Michael Finley .75 .23
❑ 19 Nick Van Exel .75 .23
❑ 20 Raef LaFrentz .50 .15
❑ 21 Antonio McDyess .50 .15
❑ 22 Juwan Howard .50 .15
❑ 23 Tim Hardaway .50 .15
❑ 24 James Posey .50 .15
❑ 25 Jerry Stackhouse .75 .23
❑ 26 Ben Wallace .75 .23
❑ 27 Isiah Thomas 1.25 .35
❑ 28 Antawn Jamison .75 .23
❑ 29 Larry Hughes .50 .15
❑ 30 Steve Francis .75 .23
❑ 31 Moses Malone 1.00 .30
❑ 32 Reggie Miller .75 .23
❑ 33 Jermaine O'Neal .75 .23
❑ 34 Elton Brand .75 .23
❑ 35 Darius Miles .75 .23
❑ 36 Lamar Odom .75 .23
❑ 37 Quentin Richardson .50 .15
❑ 38 Kobe Bryant 3.00 .90
❑ 39 Shaquille O'Neal 2.00 .60
❑ 40 Derek Fisher .75 .23
❑ 41 Devean George .50 .15
❑ 42 Stromile Swift .50 .15
❑ 43 Jason Williams .50 .15
❑ 44 Alonzo Mourning .50 .15
❑ 45 Eddie Jones .75 .23
❑ 46 Anthony Carter .50 .15
❑ 47 Ray Allen .75 .23
❑ 48 Sam Cassell .75 .23
❑ 49 Glenn Robinson .75 .23
❑ 50 Tim Thomas .50 .15
❑ 51 Oscar Robertson 1.00 .30
❑ 52 Kevin Garnett 1.50 .45
❑ 53 Wally Szczerbiak .50 .15
❑ 54 Terrell Brandon .50 .15
❑ 55 Chauncey Billups .50 .15
❑ 56 Jason Kidd 1.25 .35
❑ 57 Kenyon Martin .75 .23
❑ 58 Latrell Sprewell .75 .23
❑ 59 Allan Houston .50 .15
❑ 60 Marcus Camby .50 .15
❑ 61 Kurt Thomas .50 .15
❑ 62 Grant Hill .75 .23
❑ 63 Mike Miller .75 .23
❑ 64 Tracy McGrady 2.00 .60
❑ 65 Allen Iverson 1.50 .45
❑ 66 Julius Erving 2.00 .60
❑ 67 Bobby Jones .25 .07
❑ 68 Stephon Marbury .75 .23
❑ 69 Shawn Marion .75 .23
❑ 70 Anfernee Hardaway .75 .23
❑ 71 Rasheed Wallace .75 .23
❑ 72 Bill Walton 1.00 .30
❑ 73 Chris Webber .75 .23
❑ 74 Peja Stojakovic .75 .23
❑ 75 Mike Bibby .75 .23
❑ 76 Tim Duncan 1.50 .45
❑ 77 David Robinson .75 .23
❑ 78 George Gervin 1.00 .30
❑ 79 Gary Payton .75 .23
❑ 80 Rashard Lewis .50 .15
❑ 81 Desmond Mason .50 .15
❑ 82 Vince Carter 2.00 .60
❑ 83 Morris Peterson .75 .23
❑ 84 Antonio Davis .25 .07
❑ 85 Hakeem Olajuwon .75 .23
❑ 86 Karl Malone .75 .23
❑ 87 John Stockton .75 .23
❑ 88 Donyell Marshall .50 .15
❑ 89 Richard Hamilton .50 .15
❑ 90 Michael Jordan 10.00 3.00
❑ 91 Zeljko Rebraca RC 6.00 1.80
Shaquille O'Neal
❑ 92 Oscar Robertson 6.00 1.80
Oscar Torres RC
❑ 93 Reggie Miller 6.00 1.80
Jamison Brewer RC
❑ 94 Peja Stojakovic 6.00 1.80
Predrag Drobnjak RC
❑ 95 Mengke Bateer RC 5.00 1.50
Wang Zhi-Zhi
❑ 96 Jerry West 6.00 1.80
Willie Solomon RC
❑ 97 Tim Duncan 6.00 1.80
Malik Allen RC
❑ 98 Walt Frazier 6.00 1.80
Damone Brown RC
❑ 99 Shawn Marion 6.00 1.80
Alton Ford RC
❑ 100 Toni Kukoc 6.00 1.80
Antonis Fotsis RC
❑ 101 Bill Walton 15.00 4.50
Zach Randolph RC
❑ 102 Stephon Marbury 6.00 1.80
Joe Crispin RC
❑ 103 Wes Unseld 6.00 1.80
Bobby Simmons RC
❑ 104 Jason Kidd AU 30.00 9.00
Jamaal Tinsley RC
❑ 105 Kevin Garnett AU 60.00 18.00
Pau Gasol RC
❑ 106 Kobe Bryant AU 120.00 36.00
Shane Battier RC
❑ 107 Vince Carter 25.00 7.50
Jeff Trepagnier AU RC
❑ 108 Julius Erving 50.00 15.00
Kwame Brown AU RC
❑ 109 Tim Duncan 80.00 24.00
Eddy Curry AU RC
❑ 110 Lamar Odom AU 40.00 12.00
Eddie Griffin AU RC
❑ 111 Courtney Alexander AU 20.00 6.00
Earl Watson AU RC
❑ 112 Morris Peterson AU 40.00 12.00
Gilbert Arenas AU RC
❑ 113 Kenyon Martin AU 30.00 9.00
Brian Scalabrine AU RC
❑ 114 Tyson Chandler AU RC 40.00 12.00
Marcus Fizer AU
❑ 115 Corey Maggette AU 20.00 6.00
Ruben Boumtje-Boumtje AU RC
❑ 116 Jarron Collins AU RC 20.00 6.00
Mark Madsen AU
❑ 117 Vince Carter 15.00 4.50
Joseph Forte JSY RC
❑ 118 Antawn Jamison 25.00 7.50
Troy Murphy JSY SP RC
❑ 119 Kenyon Martin 12.00 3.60
Brandon Armstrong JSY RC
❑ 120 Steve Francis 15.00 4.50
Terence Morris JSY RC
❑ 121 Grant Hill 12.00 3.60
Steven Hunter JSY RC
❑ 122 Alonzo Mourning 12.00 3.60
Vladimir Radmanovic JSY RC
❑ 123 Brendan Haywood JSY RC 20.00 6.00
Shaquille O'Neal
❑ 124 Samuel Dalembert JSY RC 12.00 3.60
Moses Malone
❑ 125 Wally Szczerbiak JSY 15.00 4.50
Primoz Brezec JSY RC
❑ 126 Peja Stojakovic JSY 15.00 4.50
Michael Bradley JSY RC
❑ 127 Anfernee Hardaway JSY 10.00 3.00
Joe Johnson JSY RC
❑ 128 Loren Woods JSY RC 15.00 4.50
Theo Ratliff JSY
❑ 129 Chris Webbe JSY 12.00 3.60
Gerald Wallace JSY RC
❑ 130 Antoine Walker JSY 15.00 4.50
Kedrick Brown JSY RC
❑ 131 Baron Davis JSY 15.00 4.50
Jamison Brewer JSY RC
❑ 132 Dirk Nowitzki JSY 25.00 7.50
Andrei Kirilenko JSY RC
❑ 133 Joe Smith JSY 15.00 4.50
Alton Ford JSY RC
❑ 134 John Stockton JSY 15.00 4.50
Joseph Crispin JSY RC
❑ 135 Karl Malone JSY 20.00 6.00
Rodney White JSY RC
❑ 136 Tracy McGrady JSY 40.00 12.00
Jeryl Sasser JSY RC
❑ 137 Elton Brand JSY 20.00 6.00
Jason Collins JSY RC
❑ 138 Kobe Bryant JSY 100.00 30.00
Richard Jefferson JSY RC
❑ 139 Allen Iverson JSY 50.00 15.00
Tony Parke JSY RC
❑ 140 Michael Jordan JSY 160.00 47.50
Jason Richardson JSY RC
❑ 141 Ronald Murray XRC 8.00 2.40
❑ 141T Draft Pick #42 EXCH - -
❑ 142 Pat Burke XRC 5.00 1.50
❑ 142T Draft Pick #41 EXCH - -
❑ 143 Manu Ginobili XRC 8.00 2.40
❑ 143T Draft Pick #40 EXCH - -
❑ 144 Gordan Giricek XRC 8.00 2.40
❑ 144T Draft Pick #39 EXCH - -
❑ 145 Tito Maddox XRC 5.00 1.50
❑ 145T Draft Pick #38 EXCH - -
❑ 146 Tamar Slay XRC 5.00 1.50
❑ 146T Draft Pick #37 EXCH - -
❑ 147 Rasual Butler XRC 5.00 1.50
❑ 147T Draft Pick #36 EXCH - -
❑ 148 Carlos Boozer XRC 12.00 3.60
❑ 148T Draft Pick #35 EXCH - -
❑ 149 Dan Gadzuric XRC 5.00 1.50
❑ 149T Draft Pick #34 EXCH - -
❑ 150 Vincent Yarbrough XRC 5.00 1.50
❑ 150T Draft Pick #33 EXCH - -
❑ 151 Robert Archibald XRC 5.00 1.50
❑ 151T Draft Pick #32 EXCH - -
❑ 152 Roger Mason XRC 5.00 1.50
❑ 152T Draft Pick #31 EXCH - -
❑ 153 Jamal Sampson XRC 6.00 1.80
❑ 153T Draft Pick #30 EXCH - -
❑ 154 Sam Clancy XRC 6.00 1.80
❑ 154T Draft Pick #29 EXCH - -
❑ 155 Dan Dickau XRC 6.00 1.80
❑ 155T Draft Pick #28 EXCH - -
❑ 156 Chris Jefferies XRC 6.00 1.80
❑ 156T Draft Pick #27 EXCH - -
❑ 157 John Salmons XRC 6.00 1.80
❑ 157T Draft Pick #26 EXCH - -
❑ 158 Frank Williams XRC 6.00 1.80
❑ 158T Draft Pick #25 EXCH - -
❑ 159 Lonny Baxter XRC 6.00 1.80
❑ 159T Draft Pick #24 EXCH - -

❑ 160 Tayshaun Prince XRC	6.00	1.80
❑ 160T Draft Pick #23 EXCH	-	-
❑ 161 Casey Jacobsen XRC	6.00	1.80
❑ 161T Draft Pick #22 EXCH	-	-
❑ 162 Qyntel Woods XRC	6.00	1.80
❑ 162T Draft Pick #21 EXCH	-	-
❑ 163 Kareem Rush XRC......	6.00	1.80
❑ 163T Draft Pick #20 EXCH	-	-
❑ 164 Ryan Humphrey XRC..	6.00	1.80
❑ 164T Draft Pick #19 EXCH	-	-
❑ 165 Curtis Borchardt XRC..	8.00	2.40
❑ 165T Draft Pick #18 EXCH	-	-
❑ 166 Juan Dixon XRC........	15.00	4.50
❑ 166T Draft Pick #17 EXCH	-	-
❑ 167 Jiri Welsch XRC	8.00	2.40
❑ 167T Draft Pick #16 EXCH	-	-
❑ 168 Bostjan Nachbar XRC..	-	-
❑ 168T Draft Pick #15 EXCH	-	-
❑ 169 Fred Jones XRC..........	8.00	2.40
❑ 169T Draft Pick #14 EXCH	-	-
❑ 170 Marcus Haislip XRC....	8.00	2.40
❑ 170T Draft Pick #13 EXCH	-	-
❑ 171 Melvin Ely XRC	8.00	2.40
❑ 171T Draft Pick #12 EXCH	-	-
❑ 172 Jared Jeffries XRC	-	-
❑ 172T Draft Pick #11 EXCH	-	-
❑ 173 Caron Butler XRC	15.00	4.50
❑ 173T Draft Pick #10 EXCH	-	-
❑ 174 Amare Stoudemire XRC	25.00	7.50
❑ 174T Draft Pick #9 EXCH ..	-	-
❑ 175 Chris Wilcox XRC......	10.00	3.00
❑ 175T Draft Pick #8 EXCH ..	-	-
❑ 176 Nene Hilario XRC......	10.00	3.00
❑ 176T Draft Pick #7 EXCH ..	-	-
❑ 177 Dajuan Wagner XRC	30.00	9.00
❑ 177T Draft Pick #6 EXCH ..	-	-
❑ 178 Nikoloz Tskitishvili XRC	-	-
❑ 178T Draft Pick #5 EXCH ..	-	-
❑ 179 Drew Gooden XRC......	-	-
❑ 179T Draft Pick #4 EXCH ..	-	-
❑ 180 Mike Dunleavy XRC..	25.00	7.50
❑ 180T Draft Pick #3 EXCH ..	-	-
❑ 181 Jay Williams XRC......	30.00	9.00
❑ 181T Draft Pick #2 EXCH ..	-	-
❑ 182 Yao Ming XRC	80.00	24.00
❑ 182T Draft Pick #1 EXCH ..	-	-

2002-03 Upper Deck Inspirations

	Nm-Mt	Ex-Mt
COMP.SET w/o SP's (90)	30.00	9.00
COMMON CARD (1-90)...........	.20	.06
COMMON ROOKIE (91-104) ..	5.00	1.50
COMMON ROOKIE (105-110)	20.00	6.00
COMMON ROOKIE (111-127)	12.00	3.60
111-127 PRINT RUN 1500 SER.#'d SETS		-
111-127 DUAL JERSEY CARDS	-	-
COMMON ROOKIE (128-133)	30.00	9.00
128-133 PRINT RUN 275 SER.#'d SETS		-
128-133 DUAL AUTOGRAPH CARDS		-
COMMON ROOKIE (134-139)	20.00	6.00
134-139 PRINT RUN 1600 SER.#'d SETS		-
134-139 DUAL AUTOGRAPH CARDS		-
COMMON ROOKIE (140-149)	12.00	3.60
140-149 PRINT RUN 1600 SER.#'d SETS		-
140-149 ROOKIE AUTOGRAPH ONLY		-
COMMON DRAFT (156-161)	20.00	6.00
156-161 PRINT RUN 499 SER.#'d SETS		-
COMMON DRAFT (162-167)	12.00	3.60
162-167 PRINT RUN 799 SER.#'d SETS		-
COMMON DRAFT (168-175) ..	8.00	2.40
168-175 PRINT RUN 1499 SER.#'d SETS		-
COMMON DRAFT (176-197) ..	6.00	1.80
176-197 PRINT RUN 2999 SER.#'d SETS		-

❑ 1 Shareef Abdur-Rahim	.75	.23
❑ 2 Jason Terry	.75	.23
❑ 3 Glenn Robinson	.75	.23
❑ 4 Paul Pierce........................	.75	.23
❑ 5 Antoine Walker..................	.75	.23
❑ 6 Bill Russell	1.50	.45
❑ 7 Vin Baker	.50	.15
❑ 8 Jalen Rose	.75	.23
❑ 9 Tyson Chandler	.75	.23
❑ 10 Eddy Curry	.75	.23
❑ 11 Ricky Davis	.75	.23
❑ 12 Zydrunas Ilgauskas	.50	.15
❑ 13 Darius Miles	.75	.23
❑ 14 Dirk Nowitzki	1.25	.35
❑ 15 Michael Finley	.75	.23
❑ 16 Steve Nash........................	.75	.23
❑ 17 Nick Van Exel..................	.75	.23
❑ 18 Rodney White..................	.50	.15
❑ 19 Juwan Howard	.50	.15
❑ 20 Richard Hamilton	.50	.15
❑ 21 Ben Wallace......................	.75	.23
❑ 22 Isiah Thomas	1.50	.45
❑ 23 Antawn Jamison..............	.75	.23
❑ 24 Jason Richardson	.75	.23
❑ 25 Gilbert Arenas	.75	.23
❑ 26 Steve Francis	.75	.23
❑ 27 Eddie Griffin	.50	.15
❑ 28 Cuttino Mobley	.50	.15
❑ 29 Reggie Miller	.75	.23
❑ 30 Jamaal Tinsley	.75	.23
❑ 31 Jermaine O'Neal	.75	.23
❑ 32 Elton Brand	.75	.23
❑ 33 Andre Miller	.50	.15
❑ 34 Lamar Odom	.75	.23
❑ 35 Kobe Bryant	3.00	.90
❑ 36 Shaquille O'Neal	2.00	.60
❑ 37 Wilt Chamberlain	2.50	.75
❑ 38 Derek Fisher....................	.75	.23
❑ 39 Pau Gasol	.75	.23
❑ 40 Shane Battier	.75	.23
❑ 41 Stromile Swift	.50	.15
❑ 42 Eddie Jones	.75	.23
❑ 43 Alonzo Mourning	.50	.15
❑ 44 Travis Best	.20	.06
❑ 45 Gary Payton	.75	.23
❑ 46 Sam Cassell......................	.75	.23
❑ 47 Desmond Mason	.50	.15
❑ 48 Kevin Garnett................	1.50	.45
❑ 49 Wally Szczerbiak	.50	.15
❑ 50 Joe Smith..........................	.50	.15
❑ 51 Jason Kidd	1.25	.35
❑ 52 Richard Jefferson............	.50	.15
❑ 53 Kenyon Martin	.75	.23
❑ 54 Baron Davis	.75	.23
❑ 55 Jamal Mashburn..............	.50	.15
❑ 56 David Wesley	.20	.06
❑ 57 Allan Houston..................	.50	.15
❑ 58 Antonio McDyess	.50	.15
❑ 59 Latrell Sprewell................	.75	.23
❑ 60 Tracy McGrady..............	2.00	.60
❑ 61 Grant Hill	.75	.23
❑ 62 Pat Garrity	.20	.06
❑ 63 Allen Iverson	1.50	.45
❑ 64 Julius Erving..................	2.00	.60
❑ 65 Stephon Marbury	.75	.23
❑ 66 Shawn Marion	.75	.23
❑ 67 Anfernee Hardaway	.75	.23
❑ 68 Rasheed Wallace............	.75	.23
❑ 69 Derek Anderson	.50	.15
❑ 70 Scottie Pippen	1.25	.35
❑ 71 Chris Webber....................	.75	.23
❑ 72 Mike Bibby	.75	.23
❑ 73 Peja Stojakovic..................	.75	.23
❑ 74 Hedo Turkoglu	.75	.23
❑ 75 Tim Duncan	1.50	.45
❑ 76 David Robinson	.75	.23
❑ 77 Tony Parker	.75	.23
❑ 78 Ray Allen	.75	.23
❑ 79 Rashard Lewis	.75	.23
❑ 80 Brent Barry........................	.50	.15
❑ 81 Voshon Lenard..................	.20	.06
❑ 82 Vince Carter	2.00	.60
❑ 83 Morris Peterson	.50	.15
❑ 84 Antonio Davis..................	.20	.06
❑ 85 Karl Malone	.75	.23
❑ 86 John Stockton	.75	.23
❑ 87 Andrei Kirilenko	.75	.23
❑ 88 Jerry Stackhouse	.75	.23
❑ 89 Michael Jordan..............	6.00	1.80
❑ 90 Kwame Brown	.50	.15
❑ 91 Roger Mason / Michael Jordan	6.00	1.80
❑ 92 Junior Harrington .... / Alex English	5.00	1.50
❑ 93 Mike Dunleavy Jr........... / Rick Barry	6.00	1.80
❑ 94 Robert Archibald .... / Stromile Swift	5.00	1.50
❑ 95 Tito Maddox .... / Steve Francis	5.00	1.50
❑ 96 Juaquin Hawkins .... / Moses Malone	5.00	1.50
❑ 97 Mike Batiste .... / Jason Williams	5.00	1.50
❑ 98 Ken Johnson .... / Alonzo Mourning	5.00	1.50
❑ 99 Smush Parker .... / Darius Miles	5.00	1.50
❑ 100 Pat Burke .... / Shaquille O'Neal	5.00	1.50
❑ 101 Raul Lopez.................... / John Stockton	5.00	1.50
❑ 102 Chris Owens.................. / Shane Battier	5.00	1.50
❑ 103 Mike Wilks .... / Earl Boykins	5.00	1.50
❑ 104 Antoine Rigadeau........ / Dirk Nowitzki	5.00	1.50
❑ 105 Caron Butler.............. / Kevin Garnett	30.00	9.00
❑ 106 Dajuan Wagner .... / Allen Iverson	30.00	9.00
❑ 107 Kareem Rush .... / Kobe Bryant	40.00	12.00
❑ 108 Nene Hilario .... / Tim Duncan	30.00	9.00
❑ 109 Melvin Ely.................. / Elton Brand	20.00	6.00
❑ 110 Ryan Humphrey........ / Tracy McGrady	25.00	7.50
❑ 111 Marco Jaric................ / Andre Miller	12.00	3.60
❑ 112 Fred Jones.................. / Reggie Miller	12.00	3.60
❑ 113 Lonny Baxter .... / Joe Smith	12.00	3.60
❑ 114 J.R. Bremer .... / Paul Pierce	12.00	3.60
❑ 115 Carlos Boozer .... / Grant Hill	25.00	7.50
❑ 116 Predrag Savovic........ / Vlade Divac	12.00	3.60
❑ 117 Mehmet Okur............ / Hedo Turkoglu	12.00	3.60
❑ 118 Jannero Pargo .... / Derek Fisher	12.00	3.60
❑ 119 Cezary Trybanski ...... / Stromile Swift	12.00	3.60
❑ 120 Ronald Murray .... / Rashard Lewis	20.00	6.00
❑ 121 Reggie Evans............ / Ray Allen	12.00	3.60
❑ 122 Rasual Butler .... / Eddie Jones	12.00	3.60
❑ 123 Jamal Sampson .... / Shareef Abdur Rahim	12.00	3.60
❑ 124 Igor Rakocevic .... / Terrell Brandon	12.00	3.60
❑ 125 Tamar Slay................ / Richard Jefferson	12.00	3.60
❑ 126 Efthimios Rentzias .... / Keith Van Horn	12.00	3.60
❑ 127 Vincent Yarbrough .... / Juwan Howard	12.00	3.60
❑ 128A Jay Williams..........	200.00	60.00

Kobe Bryant
❑ 128B JayWill AU RC/Jordan AU 600.00 180.00
❑ 129 Drew Gooden 100.00 30.00
Kevin Garnett
❑ 130 Amare Stoudemire 100.00 30.00
Shawn Marion
❑ 131 Nikoloz Tskitishvili 30.00 9.00
Peja Stojakovic
❑ 132 Yao Ming 160.00 47.50
Wang Zhi Zhi
❑ 133 Juan Dixon 60.00 18.00
Jason Kidd
❑ 134 Jared Jeffries 25.00 7.50
Jerry Stackhouse
❑ 135 Marcus Haislip 25.00 7.50
Kenyon Martin
❑ 136 Jiri Welsch 25.00 7.50
Jason Richardson
❑ 137 John Salmons 20.00 6.00
Gerald Wallace
❑ 138 Manu Ginobili 50.00 15.00
Tony Parker
❑ 139 Dan Dickau 30.00 9.00
Mike Bibby
❑ 140 Sam Clancy 12.00 3.60
Julius Erving
❑ 141 Qyntel Woods 12.00 3.60
Rasheed Wallace
❑ 142 Frank Williams 12.00 3.60
Allan Houston
❑ 143 Casey Jacobsen 12.00 3.60
Anfernee Hardaway
❑ 144 Bostjan Nachbar 12.00 3.60
Tim Duncan
❑ 145 Dan Gadzuric 12.00 3.60
Shaquille O'Neal
❑ 146 Gordon Giricek 15.00 4.50
Tracy McGrady
❑ 147 Curtis Borchardt 12.00 3.60
Karl Malone
❑ 148 Tayshaun Prince 15.00 4.50
Antoine Walker
❑ 149 Chris Wilcox 12.00 3.60
Vince Carter
❑ 150 Wilt Chamberlain - -
Yao Ming
❑ 151 Bill Russell - -
Amare Stoudemire
❑ 152 Julius Erving - -
Jay Williams
❑ 153 Larry Bird - -
Manu Ginobili
❑ 154 Michael Jordan - -
Dajuan Wagner
❑ 155 Kobe Bryant - -
Caron Butler
❑ 156A LeBron James XRC 200.00 60.00
❑ 156B Draft Pick #1 90.00
❑ 157A Darko Milicic XRC 20.00 6.00
❑ 157B Draft Pick #2 24.00
❑ 158A Carmelo Anthony XRC 100.00 30.00
❑ 158B Draft Pick #3 36.00
❑ 159A Chris Bosh XRC 30.00 9.00
❑ 159B Draft Pick #4 12.00
❑ 160A Dwyane Wade XRC 30.00 9.00
❑ 160B Draft Pick #5 12.00
❑ 161A Chris Kaman XRC 20.00 6.00
❑ 161B Draft Pick #6 6.00
❑ 162A Kirk Hinrich XRC 20.00 6.00
❑ 162B Draft Pick #7 9.00
❑ 163A T.J. Ford XRC 20.00 6.00
❑ 163B Draft Pick #8 9.00
❑ 164A Michael Sweetney XRC 12.00 3.60
❑ 164B Draft Pick #9 6.00
❑ 165A Jarvis Hayes XRC 12.00 3.60
❑ 165B Draft Pick #10 6.00
❑ 166A Mickael Pietrus XRC 12.00 3.60
❑ 166B Draft Pick #11 4.50
❑ 167A Nick Collison XRC 12.00 3.60
❑ 167B Draft Pick #12 9.00
❑ 168A Marcus Banks XRC 8.00 2.40
❑ 168B Draft Pick #13 4.50
❑ 169A Luke Ridnour XRC 10.00 3.00
❑ 169B Draft Pick #14 6.00
❑ 170A Reece Gaines XRC 8.00 2.40
❑ 170B Draft Pick #15 4.50
❑ 171A Troy Bell XRC 8.00 2.40
❑ 171B Draft Pick #16 3.00
❑ 172A Zarko Cabarkapa XRC 8.00 2.40
❑ 172B Draft Pick #17 3.00
❑ 173A David West XRC 8.00 2.40
❑ 173B Draft Pick #18 3.00
❑ 174A Aleksandar Pavlovic XRC 8.00 2.40
❑ 174B Draft Pick #19 3.00
❑ 175A Dahntay Jones XRC 8.00 2.40
❑ 175B Draft Pick #20 3.60
❑ 176A Boris Diaw XRC 6.00 1.80
❑ 176B Draft Pick #21 3.00
❑ 177A Zoran Planinic XRC 6.00 1.80
❑ 177B Draft Pick #22 2.40
❑ 178A Travis Outlaw XRC 6.00 1.80
❑ 178B Draft Pick #23 3.00
❑ 179A Brian Cook XRC 6.00 1.80
❑ 179B Draft Pick #24 4.50
❑ 180A Carlos Delfino XRC 6.00 1.80
❑ 180B Draft Pick #25 2.40
❑ 181A Ndudi Ebi XRC 6.00 1.80
❑ 181B Draft Pick #26 2.40
❑ 182A Kendrick Perkins XRC 6.00 1.80
❑ 182B Draft Pick #27 2.40
❑ 183A Leandro Barbosa XRC 6.00 1.80
❑ 183B Draft Pick #28 2.40
❑ 184A Josh Howard XRC 8.00 2.40
❑ 184B Draft Pick #29 3.00
❑ 185A Maciej Lampe XRC 6.00 1.80
❑ 185B Draft Pick #30 3.00
❑ 186A Jason Kapono XRC 6.00 1.80
❑ 186B Draft Pick #31 1.80
❑ 187A Null -
❑ 187B Draft Pick #32 6.00 1.80
❑ 188A Null -
❑ 188B Draft Pick #33 6.00 1.80
❑ 189A Null -
❑ 189B Draft Pick #34 6.00 1.80
❑ 190A Luke Walton XRC 8.00 2.40
❑ 190B Draft Pick #35 1.80
❑ 191A Jerome Beasley XRC 6.00 1.80
❑ 191B Draft Pick #36 1.80
❑ 192A Travis Hanson XRC 6.00 1.80
❑ 192B Draft Pick #37 1.80
❑ 193A Steve Blake XRC 6.00 1.80
❑ 193B Draft Pick #38 2.40
❑ 194A Slavko Vranes XRC 6.00 1.80
❑ 194B Draft Pick #39 1.80
❑ 195A Keith Bogans XRC 6.00 1.80
❑ 195B Draft Pick #40 1.80
❑ 196A Willie Green XRC 6.00 1.80
❑ 196B Draft Pick #41 1.80
❑ 197A Zaur Pachulia XRC 6.00 1.80
❑ 197B Draft Pick #42 1.80

2001-02 Upper Deck Legends

	Nm-Mt	Ex-Mt
COMP.SET w/o SP's (90)	25.00	7.50
COMMON CARD	.20	.06
SEMISTARS	.40	.12
COMMON ROOKIE (91-110)	5.00	1.50
COMMON ROOKIE (111-125)	12.00	3.60
NOTE CARDS READ 2000-01..	-	-

❑ 1 Michael Jordan 4.00 1.20
❑ 2 Wilt Chamberlain 1.00 .30
❑ 3 Karl Malone .60 .18
❑ 4 Steve Francis .60 .18
❑ 5 George McGinnis .40 .12
❑ 6 Julius Erving 1.00 .30
❑ 7 Alonzo Mourning .40 .12
❑ 8 Kobe Bryant 2.50 .75
❑ 9 Glen Rice .40 .12
❑ 10 Mitch Kupchak .20 .06
❑ 11 Isiah Thomas .60 .18
❑ 12 Rick Barry .60 .18
❑ 13 Moses Malone .60 .18
❑ 14 Larry Bird 2.50 .75
❑ 15 Vince Carter 1.50 .45
❑ 16 Jamaal Wilkes .40 .12
❑ 17 John Havlicek .75 .23
❑ 18 Elgin Baylor .60 .18
❑ 19 Dave Bing .40 .12
❑ 20 Steve Smith .20 .06
❑ 21 Kevin Garnett 1.25 .35
❑ 22 Hakeem Olajuwon .60 .18
❑ 23 Walt Bellamy .20 .06
❑ 24 Kevin McHale .60 .18
❑ 25 Kareem Abdul-Jabbar 1.00 .30
❑ 26 Chris Webber .60 .18
❑ 27 Tom Heinsohn .20 .06
❑ 28 Walt Frazier .60 .18
❑ 29 Ron Boone .40 .12
❑ 30 Gary Payton .60 .18
❑ 31 Wes Unseld .20 .06
❑ 32 Magic Johnson 2.00 .60
❑ 33 David Thompson .20 .06
❑ 34 Maurice Lucas .20 .06
❑ 35 Paul Pierce .60 .18
❑ 36 Dikembe Mutombo .40 .12
❑ 37 Gail Goodrich .40 .12
❑ 38 Bob Lanier .20 .06
❑ 39 Chris Mullin .20 .06
❑ 40 Allen Iverson 1.25 .35
❑ 41 Sam Jones .20 .06
❑ 42 James Worthy .60 .18
❑ 43 Cedric Maxwell .20 .06
❑ 44 George Gervin .60 .18
❑ 45 Earl Monroe .60 .18
❑ 46 Lenny Wilkens .40 .12
❑ 47 Tracy McGrady 1.50 .45
❑ 48 Walter Davis .20 .06
❑ 49 Stephon Marbury .60 .18
❑ 50 Bob Cousy .60 .18
❑ 51 Spencer Haywood .20 .06
❑ 52 Dave Cowens .40 .12
❑ 53 Scottie Pippen 1.00 .30
❑ 54 Hal Greer .20 .06
❑ 55 Kiki Vandeweghe .40 .12
❑ 56 Paul Silas .40 .12
❑ 57 Elton Brand .40 .12
❑ 58 John Stockton .60 .18
❑ 59 Shareef Abdur-Rahim .60 .18
❑ 60 Reggie Miller .60 .18
❑ 61 Nate Thurmond .20 .06
❑ 62 Billy Cunningham .20 .06
❑ 63 Patrick Ewing .60 .18
❑ 64 Nate Archibald .60 .18
❑ 65 Tim Duncan 1.25 .35
❑ 66 Lafayette Lever .40 .12
❑ 67 Willis Reed .40 .12
❑ 68 Ray Allen .60 .18
❑ 69 Jo Jo White .20 .06
❑ 70 Pete Maravich .75 .23
❑ 71 Grant Hill .60 .18
❑ 72 Jerry West .60 .18
❑ 73 George Karl .40 .12
❑ 74 Bill Sharman .20 .06
❑ 75 Dave DeBusschere .20 .06
❑ 76 Tim Hardaway .40 .12
❑ 77 Bill Walton .60 .18
❑ 78 Jerry Lucas .20 .06
❑ 79 Antonio McDyess .40 .12
❑ 80 Robert Parish .60 .18
❑ 81 Shaquille O'Neal 1.50 .45
❑ 82 Bill Russell 1.00 .30
❑ 83 Clyde Drexler .60 .18
❑ 84 Dolph Schayes .40 .12
❑ 85 K.C. Jones .20 .06
❑ 86 Bob Pettit .40 .12
❑ 87 Jason Kidd 1.00 .30
❑ 88 Mitch Richmond .40 .12

Card	Nm-Mt	Ex-Mt
❑ 89 Oscar Robertson	.75	.23
❑ 90 David Robinson	.60	.18
❑ 91 Bobby Simmons RC	5.00	1.50
❑ 92 Jamison Brewer RC	5.00	1.50
❑ 93 Earl Watson RC	5.00	1.50
❑ 94 Kenny Satterfield RC	5.00	1.50
❑ 95 Zeljko Rebraca RC	5.00	1.50
❑ 96 Damone Brown RC	5.00	1.50
❑ 97 R.Boumtje-Boumtje RC	5.00	1.50
❑ 98 Brian Scalabrine RC	5.00	1.50
❑ 99 Terence Morris RC	5.00	1.50
❑ 100 Willie Solomon RC	5.00	1.50
❑ 101 Primoz Brezec RC	5.00	1.50
❑ 102 Gilbert Arenas RC	15.00	4.50
❑ 103 Trenton Hassell RC	8.00	2.40
❑ 104 Loren Woods RC	5.00	1.50
❑ 105 Tony Parker RC	20.00	6.00
❑ 106 Jamaal Tinsley RC	8.00	2.40
❑ 107 Samuel Dalembert RC	5.00	1.50
❑ 108 Gerald Wallace RC	12.00	3.60
❑ 109 Andrei Kirilenko RC	15.00	4.50
❑ 110 Brandon Armstrong RC	8.00	2.40
❑ 111 Jeryl Sasser RC	12.00	3.60
❑ 112 Joseph Forte RC	15.00	4.50
❑ 113 Brendan Haywood RC	15.00	4.50
❑ 114 Zach Randolph RC	25.00	7.50
❑ 115 Jason Collins RC	12.00	3.60
❑ 116 Michael Bradley RC	12.00	3.60
❑ 117 Kirk Haston RC	12.00	3.60
❑ 118 Steven Hunter RC	12.00	3.60
❑ 119 Troy Murphy RC	20.00	6.00
❑ 120 Richard Jefferson RC	20.00	6.00
❑ 121 Vladimir Radmanovic RC	12.00	3.60
❑ 122 Kedrick Brown RC	12.00	3.60
❑ 123 Joe Johnson RC	15.00	4.50
❑ 124 Rodney White RC	15.00	4.50
❑ 125 DeSagana Diop RC	12.00	3.60
❑ 126 Eddie Griffin RC	20.00	6.00
❑ 127 Shane Battier RC	25.00	7.50
❑ 128 Jason Richardson RC	30.00	9.00
❑ 129 Eddy Curry RC	30.00	9.00
❑ 130 Pau Gasol RC	40.00	12.00
❑ 131 Tyson Chandler RC	25.00	7.50
❑ 132 Kwame Brown RC	20.00	6.00

2003-04 Upper Deck Legends

	Nm-Mt	Ex-Mt
COMP.SET w/o SP's (90)	30.00	9.00
COMMON CARD (1-90)	.20	.06
COMMON ROOKIE (91-125)	5.00	1.50
COMMON ROOKIE (126-135)	6.00	1.80
COMMON DRAFT (136-150)	10.00	3.00

Card	Nm-Mt	Ex-Mt
❑ 1 Bob Sura	.20	.06
❑ 2 Stephen Jackson	.20	.06
❑ 3 Jason Terry	.75	.23
❑ 4 Ricky Davis	.75	.23
❑ 5 Jiri Welsch	.50	.15
❑ 6 Paul Pierce	.75	.23
❑ 7 Eddy Curry	.50	.15
❑ 8 Jamal Crawford	.50	.15
❑ 9 Tyson Chandler	.75	.23
❑ 10 Dajuan Wagner	.50	.15
❑ 11 Carlos Boozer	.75	.23
❑ 12 Zydrunas Ilgauskas	.50	.15
❑ 13 Dirk Nowitzki	1.25	.35
❑ 14 Antoine Walker	.75	.23
❑ 15 Steve Nash	.75	.23
❑ 16 Michael Finley	.75	.23
❑ 17 Jon Barry	.20	.06
❑ 18 Andre Miller	.50	.15
❑ 19 Nene	.50	.15
❑ 20 Rasheed Wallace	.75	.23
❑ 21 Richard Hamilton	.50	.15
❑ 22 Ben Wallace	.75	.23
❑ 23 Erick Dampier	.50	.15
❑ 24 Jason Richardson	.75	.23
❑ 25 Nick Van Exel	.75	.23
❑ 26 Yao Ming	2.00	.60
❑ 27 Cuttino Mobley	.50	.15
❑ 28 Steve Francis	.75	.23
❑ 29 Jermaine O'Neal	.75	.23
❑ 30 Reggie Miller	.75	.23
❑ 31 Ron Artest	.50	.15
❑ 32 Elton Brand	.75	.23
❑ 33 Corey Maggette	.50	.15
❑ 34 Quentin Richardson	.50	.15
❑ 35 Kobe Bryant	3.00	.90
❑ 36 Karl Malone	.75	.23
❑ 37 Gary Payton	.75	.23
❑ 38 Shaquille O'Neal	2.00	.60
❑ 39 Pau Gasol	.75	.23
❑ 40 Bonzi Wells	.50	.15
❑ 41 Mike Miller	.75	.23
❑ 42 Lamar Odom	.75	.23
❑ 43 Eddie Jones	.75	.23
❑ 44 Caron Butler	.75	.23
❑ 45 Keith Van Horn	.75	.23
❑ 46 Desmond Mason	.50	.15
❑ 47 Michael Redd	.50	.15
❑ 48 Latrell Sprewell	.75	.23
❑ 49 Kevin Garnett	1.50	.45
❑ 50 Sam Cassell	.75	.23
❑ 51 Richard Jefferson	.50	.15
❑ 52 Kenyon Martin	.75	.23
❑ 53 Jason Kidd	1.25	.35
❑ 54 Jamal Mashburn	.50	.15
❑ 55 Baron Davis	.75	.23
❑ 56 David Wesley	.20	.06
❑ 57 Allan Houston	.50	.15
❑ 58 Stephon Marbury	.75	.23
❑ 59 Kurt Thomas	.50	.15
❑ 60 Juwan Howard	.50	.15
❑ 61 Drew Gooden	.50	.15
❑ 62 Tracy McGrady	2.00	.60
❑ 63 Zendon Hamilton RC	1.00	.30
❑ 64 Allen Iverson	1.50	.45
❑ 65 Eric Snow	.50	.15
❑ 66 Amare Stoudemire	1.50	.45
❑ 67 Joe Johnson	.50	.15
❑ 68 Shawn Marion	.75	.23
❑ 69 Zach Randolph	.75	.23
❑ 70 Darius Miles	.75	.23
❑ 71 Shareef Abdur-Rahim	.75	.23
❑ 72 Peja Stojakovic	.75	.23
❑ 73 Chris Webber	.75	.23
❑ 74 Mike Bibby	.75	.23
❑ 75 Brad Miller	.75	.23
❑ 76 Tony Parker	.75	.23
❑ 77 Tim Duncan	1.50	.45
❑ 78 Manu Ginobili	.75	.23
❑ 79 Ronald Murray	.20	.06
❑ 80 Ray Allen	.75	.23
❑ 81 Rashard Lewis	.75	.23
❑ 82 Donyell Marshall	.75	.23
❑ 83 Vince Carter	2.00	.60
❑ 84 Jalen Rose	.75	.23
❑ 85 Andrei Kirilenko	.75	.23
❑ 86 Matt Harpring	.75	.23
❑ 87 Carlos Arroyo	1.00	.30
❑ 88 Gilbert Arenas	.75	.23
❑ 89 Larry Hughes	.50	.15
❑ 90 Jerry Stackhouse	.75	.23
❑ 91 Devin Brown RC	5.00	1.50
❑ 92 Ronald Dupree RC	5.00	1.50
❑ 93 Alex Garcia RC	5.00	1.50
❑ 94 Udonis Haslem RC	5.00	1.50
❑ 95 Maurice Williams RC	5.00	1.50
❑ 96 Brandon Hunter RC	5.00	1.50
❑ 97 Keith Bogans RC	5.00	1.50
❑ 98 Willie Green RC	5.00	1.50
❑ 99 Zaza Pachulia RC	5.00	1.50
❑ 100 Zarko Cabarkapa RC	5.00	1.50
❑ 101 Kyle Korver RC	6.00	1.80
❑ 102 Luke Walton RC	6.00	1.80
❑ 103 Maciej Lampe RC	5.00	1.50
❑ 104 Josh Howard RC	6.00	1.80
❑ 105 Kendrick Perkins RC	5.00	1.50
❑ 106 Ndudi Ebi RC	5.00	1.50
❑ 107 Jerome Beasley RC	5.00	1.50
❑ 108 Brian Cook RC	5.00	1.50
❑ 109 Travis Outlaw RC	5.00	1.50
❑ 110 Zoran Planinic RC	5.00	1.50
❑ 111 Boris Diaw RC	5.00	1.50
❑ 112 Steve Blake RC	5.00	1.50
❑ 113 Aleksandar Pavlovic RC	5.00	1.50
❑ 114 David West RC	5.00	1.50
❑ 115 Mike Sweetney RC	5.00	1.50
❑ 116 Troy Bell RC	5.00	1.50
❑ 117 Reece Gaines RC	5.00	1.50
❑ 118 Marcus Banks RC	5.00	1.50
❑ 119 Dahntay Jones RC	5.00	1.50
❑ 120 Chris Kaman RC	5.00	1.50
❑ 121 Mickael Pietrus RC	5.00	1.50
❑ 122 Luke Ridnour RC	6.00	1.80
❑ 123 Jason Kapono RC	5.00	1.50
❑ 124 Marquis Daniels RC	8.00	2.40
❑ 125 Travis Hansen RC	5.00	1.50
❑ 126 Leandro Barbosa RC	6.00	1.80
❑ 127 Nick Collison RC	6.00	1.80
❑ 128 Kirk Hinrich RC	12.00	3.60
❑ 129 T.J. Ford RC	10.00	3.00
❑ 130 Jarvis Hayes RC	6.00	1.80
❑ 131 Dwyane Wade RC	15.00	4.50
❑ 132 Chris Bosh RC	12.00	3.60
❑ 133 Carmelo Anthony RC	30.00	9.00
❑ 134 Darko Milicic RC	12.00	3.60
❑ 135 LeBron James RC	60.00	18.00
❑ 136 Draft Pick #1 EXCH	60.00	18.00
❑ 137 Draft Pick #2 EXCH	60.00	18.00
❑ 138 Draft Pick #3 EXCH	30.00	9.00
❑ 139 Draft Pick #4 EXCH	30.00	9.00
❑ 140 Draft Pick #5 EXCH	20.00	6.00
❑ 141 Draft Pick #6 EXCH	12.00	3.60
❑ 142 Draft Pick #7 EXCH	15.00	4.50
❑ 143 Draft Pick #8 EXCH	12.00	3.60
❑ 144 Draft Pick #9 EXCH	12.00	3.60
❑ 145 Draft Pick #10 EXCH	15.00	4.50
❑ 146 Draft Pick #11 EXCH	10.00	3.00
❑ 147 Draft Pick #12 EXCH	10.00	3.00
❑ 148 Draft Pick #13 EXCH	20.00	6.00
❑ 149 Draft Pick #14 EXCH	12.00	3.60
❑ 150 Draft Pick #15 EXCH	12.00	3.60

1999-00 Upper Deck MVP

	Nm-Mt	Ex-Mt
COMPLETE SET (220)	40.00	12.00
COMMON CARD (1-178)	.15	.04
COMMON ROOKIE (209-218)	.75	.23
COMMON MJ (179-208)	1.50	.45

Card	Nm-Mt	Ex-Mt
❑ 1 Dikembe Mutombo	.30	.09
❑ 2 Steve Smith	.30	.09
❑ 3 Mookie Blaylock	.15	.04
❑ 4 Alan Henderson	.15	.04
❑ 5 LaPhonso Ellis	.15	.04
❑ 6 Grant Long	.15	.04
❑ 7 Kenny Anderson	.30	.09
❑ 8 Antoine Walker	.50	.15
❑ 9 Ron Mercer	.30	.09

Card	Nm-Mt	Ex-Mt
❑ 10 Paul Pierce	.50	.15
❑ 11 Vitaly Potapenko	.15	.04
❑ 12 Dana Barros	.15	.04
❑ 13 Elden Campbell	.15	.04
❑ 14 Eddie Jones	.50	.15
❑ 15 David Wesley	.15	.04
❑ 16 Bobby Phills	.15	.04
❑ 17 Derrick Coleman	.30	.09
❑ 18 Ricky Davis	.30	.09
❑ 19 Toni Kukoc	.30	.09
❑ 20 Brent Barry	.30	.09
❑ 21 Ron Harper	.30	.09
❑ 22 Kornel David RC	.15	.04
❑ 23 Mark Bryant	.15	.04
❑ 24 Dickey Simpkins	.15	.04
❑ 25 Shawn Kemp	.30	.09
❑ 26 Derek Anderson	.30	.09
❑ 27 Brevin Knight	.15	.04
❑ 28 Andrew DeClercq	.15	.04
❑ 29 Zydrunas Ilgauskas	.30	.09
❑ 30 Cedric Henderson	.15	.04
❑ 31 Shawn Bradley	.15	.04
❑ 32 A.C. Green	.30	.09
❑ 33 Gary Trent	.15	.04
❑ 34 Michael Finley	.50	.15
❑ 35 Dirk Nowitzki	1.00	.30
❑ 36 Steve Nash	.50	.15
❑ 37 Antonio McDyess	.30	.09
❑ 38 Nick Van Exel	.50	.15
❑ 39 Chauncey Billups	.30	.09
❑ 40 Danny Fortson	.15	.04
❑ 41 Eric Washington	.15	.04
❑ 42 Raef LaFrentz	.30	.09
❑ 43 Grant Hill	.50	.15
❑ 44 Bison Dele	.15	.04
❑ 45 Lindsey Hunter	.15	.04
❑ 46 Jerry Stackhouse	.50	.15
❑ 47 Don Reid	.15	.04
❑ 48 Christian Laettner	.30	.09
❑ 49 John Starks	.30	.09
❑ 50 Antawn Jamison	.75	.23
❑ 51 Erick Dampier	.30	.09
❑ 52 Donyell Marshall	.30	.09
❑ 53 Chris Mills	.15	.04
❑ 54 Bimbo Coles	.15	.04
❑ 55 Charles Barkley	.75	.23
❑ 56 Hakeem Olajuwon	.50	.15
❑ 57 Scottie Pippen	.75	.23
❑ 58 Othella Harrington	.15	.04
❑ 59 Bryce Drew	.15	.04
❑ 60 Michael Dickerson	.30	.09
❑ 61 Rik Smits	.30	.09
❑ 62 Reggie Miller	.50	.15
❑ 63 Mark Jackson	.30	.09
❑ 64 Antonio Davis	.15	.04
❑ 65 Jalen Rose	.50	.15
❑ 66 Dale Davis	.15	.04
❑ 67 Chris Mullin	.50	.15
❑ 68 Maurice Taylor	.30	.09
❑ 69 Lamond Murray	.15	.04
❑ 70 Rodney Rogers	.15	.04
❑ 71 Darrick Martin	.15	.04
❑ 72 Michael Olowokandi	.30	.09
❑ 73 Tyrone Nesby RC	.15	.04
❑ 74 Kobe Bryant	2.00	.60
❑ 75 Shaquille O'Neal	1.25	.35
❑ 76 Robert Horry	.30	.09
❑ 77 Glen Rice	.30	.09
❑ 78 J.R. Reid	.15	.04
❑ 79 Rick Fox	.30	.09
❑ 80 Derek Fisher	.50	.15
❑ 81 Tim Hardaway	.30	.09
❑ 82 Alonzo Mourning	.30	.09
❑ 83 Jamal Mashburn	.30	.09
❑ 84 P.J. Brown	.15	.04
❑ 85 Terry Porter	.15	.04
❑ 86 Dan Majerle	.30	.09
❑ 87 Ray Allen	.50	.15
❑ 88 Vinny Del Negro	.15	.04
❑ 89 Glenn Robinson	.50	.15
❑ 90 Dell Curry	.15	.04
❑ 91 Sam Cassell	.50	.15
❑ 92 Robert Traylor	.15	.04
❑ 93 Kevin Garnett	1.00	.30
❑ 94 Terrell Brandon	.30	.09
❑ 95 Joe Smith	.30	.09
❑ 96 Sam Mitchell	.15	.04
❑ 97 Anthony Peeler	.15	.04
❑ 98 Bobby Jackson	.30	.09
❑ 99 Keith Van Horn	.50	.15
❑ 100 Stephon Marbury	.50	.15
❑ 101 Jayson Williams	.15	.04
❑ 102 Kendall Gill	.15	.04
❑ 103 Kerry Kittles	.15	.04
❑ 104 Scott Burrell	.15	.04
❑ 105 Patrick Ewing	.50	.15
❑ 106 Allan Houston	.30	.09
❑ 107 Latrell Sprewell	.50	.15
❑ 108 Larry Johnson	.30	.09
❑ 109 Marcus Camby	.30	.09
❑ 110 Charlie Ward	.15	.04
❑ 111 Anfernee Hardaway	.50	.15
❑ 112 Darrell Armstrong	.15	.04
❑ 113 Nick Anderson	.15	.04
❑ 114 Horace Grant	.30	.09
❑ 115 Isaac Austin	.15	.04
❑ 116 Matt Harpring	.50	.15
❑ 117 Michael Doleac	.15	.04
❑ 118 Allen Iverson	1.00	.30
❑ 119 Theo Ratliff	.30	.09
❑ 120 Matt Geiger	.15	.04
❑ 121 Larry Hughes	.50	.15
❑ 122 Tyrone Hill	.15	.04
❑ 123 George Lynch	.15	.04
❑ 124 Jason Kidd	.75	.23
❑ 125 Tom Gugliotta	.15	.04
❑ 126 Rex Chapman	.15	.04
❑ 127 Clifford Robinson	.15	.04
❑ 128 Luc Longley	.15	.04
❑ 129 Danny Manning	.15	.04
❑ 130 Rasheed Wallace	.50	.15
❑ 131 Arvydas Sabonis	.30	.09
❑ 132 Damon Stoudamire	.30	.09
❑ 133 Brian Grant	.30	.09
❑ 134 Isaiah Rider	.15	.04
❑ 135 Walt Williams	.15	.04
❑ 136 Jim Jackson	.15	.04
❑ 137 Jason Williams	.50	.15
❑ 138 Vlade Divac	.30	.09
❑ 139 Chris Webber	.50	.15
❑ 140 Corliss Williamson	.30	.09
❑ 141 Peja Stojakovic	.60	.18
❑ 142 Tariq Abdul-Wahad	.15	.04
❑ 143 Tim Duncan	1.00	.30
❑ 144 Sean Elliott	.30	.09
❑ 145 David Robinson	.50	.15
❑ 146 Mario Elie	.15	.04
❑ 147 Avery Johnson	.15	.04
❑ 148 Steve Kerr	.30	.09
❑ 149 Gary Payton	.50	.15
❑ 150 Vin Baker	.30	.09
❑ 151 Detlef Schrempf	.30	.09
❑ 152 Hersey Hawkins	.30	.09
❑ 153 Dale Ellis	.15	.04
❑ 154 Olden Polynice	.15	.04
❑ 155 Vince Carter	1.25	.35
❑ 156 John Wallace	.15	.04
❑ 157 Doug Christie	.30	.09
❑ 158 Tracy McGrady	1.25	.35
❑ 159 Kevin Willis	.15	.04
❑ 160 Charles Oakley	.15	.04
❑ 161 Karl Malone	.50	.15
❑ 162 John Stockton	.50	.15
❑ 163 Jeff Hornacek	.30	.09
❑ 164 Bryon Russell	.15	.04
❑ 165 Howard Eisley	.15	.04
❑ 166 Shandon Anderson	.15	.04
❑ 167 Shareef Abdur-Rahim	.50	.15
❑ 168 Mike Bibby	.50	.15
❑ 169 Bryant Reeves	.15	.04
❑ 170 Felipe Lopez	.15	.04
❑ 171 Cherokee Parks	.15	.04
❑ 172 Michael Smith	.15	.04
❑ 173 Juwan Howard	.30	.09
❑ 174 Rod Strickland	.15	.04
❑ 175 Mitch Richmond	.30	.09
❑ 176 Otis Thorpe	.30	.09
❑ 177 Calbert Cheaney	.15	.04
❑ 178 Tracy Murray	.15	.04
❑ 179 Michael Jordan	1.50	.45
❑ 180 Michael Jordan	1.50	.45
❑ 181 Michael Jordan	1.50	.45
❑ 182 Michael Jordan	1.50	.45
❑ 183 Michael Jordan	1.50	.45
❑ 184 Michael Jordan	1.50	.45
❑ 185 Michael Jordan	1.50	.45
❑ 186 Michael Jordan	1.50	.45
❑ 187 Michael Jordan	1.50	.45
❑ 188 Michael Jordan	1.50	.45
❑ 189 Michael Jordan	1.50	.45
❑ 190 Michael Jordan	1.50	.45
❑ 191 Michael Jordan	1.50	.45
❑ 192 Michael Jordan	1.50	.45
❑ 193 Michael Jordan	1.50	.45
❑ 194 Michael Jordan	1.50	.45
❑ 195 Michael Jordan	1.50	.45
❑ 196 Michael Jordan	1.50	.45
❑ 197 Michael Jordan	1.50	.45
❑ 198 Michael Jordan	1.50	.45
❑ 199 Michael Jordan	1.50	.45
❑ 200 Michael Jordan	1.50	.45
❑ 201 Michael Jordan	1.50	.45
❑ 202 Michael Jordan	1.50	.45
❑ 203 Michael Jordan	1.50	.45
❑ 204 Michael Jordan	1.50	.45
❑ 205 Michael Jordan	1.50	.45
❑ 206 Michael Jordan	1.50	.45
❑ 207 Michael Jordan	1.50	.45
❑ 208 Michael Jordan	1.50	.45
❑ 209 Elton Brand RC	1.50	.45
❑ 210 Steve Francis RC	2.00	.60
❑ 211 Baron Davis RC	1.25	.35
❑ 212 Wally Szczerbiak RC	1.25	.35
❑ 213 Richard Hamilton RC	1.25	.35
❑ 214 Andre Miller RC	1.25	.35
❑ 215 Jason Terry RC	1.00	.30
❑ 216 Corey Maggette RC	1.25	.35
❑ 217 Shawn Marion RC	1.50	.45
❑ 218 Lamar Odom RC	1.25	.35
❑ 219 Michael Jordan Checklist	1.00	.30
❑ 220 Michael Jordan Checklist	1.00	.30

2000-01 Upper Deck MVP

	Nm-Mt	Ex-Mt
COMPLETE SET (220)	40.00	12.00
COMMON CARD (1-190)	.15	.04
COMMON ROOKIE (191-220)	.40	.12

Card	Nm-Mt	Ex-Mt
❑ 1 Dikembe Mutombo	.30	.09
❑ 2 Jason Terry	.50	.15
❑ 3 Jim Jackson	.15	.04
❑ 4 Alan Henderson	.15	.04
❑ 5 Roshown McLeod	.15	.04
❑ 6 Bimbo Coles	.15	.04
❑ 7 Lorenzen Wright	.15	.04
❑ 8 Antoine Walker	.50	.15
❑ 9 Paul Pierce	.50	.15
❑ 10 Kenny Anderson	.30	.09
❑ 11 Adrian Griffin	.15	.04
❑ 12 Vitaly Potapenko	.15	.04
❑ 13 Dana Barros	.15	.04
❑ 14 Eric Williams	.15	.04
❑ 15 Eddie Jones	.50	.15
❑ 16 Eddie Robinson	.30	.09
❑ 17 Ricky Davis	.30	.09
❑ 18 Elden Campbell	.15	.04
❑ 19 Derrick Coleman	.15	.04

❑ 20 David Wesley .15 .04
❑ 21 Baron Davis .50 .15
❑ 22 Elton Brand .50 .15
❑ 23 Ron Artest .30 .09
❑ 24 Hersey Hawkins .15 .04
❑ 25 Chris Carr .15 .04
❑ 26 Corey Benjamin .15 .04
❑ 27 Will Perdue .15 .04
❑ 28 Andre Miller .30 .09
❑ 29 Shawn Kemp .30 .09
❑ 30 Wesley Person .15 .04
❑ 31 Lamond Murray .15 .04
❑ 32 Bob Sura .15 .04
❑ 33 Andrew DeClercq .15 .04
❑ 34 Dirk Nowitzki .75 .23
❑ 35 Michael Finley .50 .15
❑ 36 Cedric Ceballos .15 .04
❑ 37 Shawn Bradley .15 .04
❑ 38 Erick Strickland .15 .04
❑ 39 Hubert Davis .15 .04
❑ 40 Antonio McDyess .30 .09
❑ 41 Raef LaFrentz .30 .09
❑ 42 Keon Clark .30 .09
❑ 43 Nick Van Exel .50 .15
❑ 44 James Posey .30 .09
❑ 45 Chris Gatling .15 .04
❑ 46 George McCloud .15 .04
❑ 47 Grant Hill .50 .15
❑ 48 Jerry Stackhouse .50 .15
❑ 49 Lindsey Hunter .15 .04
❑ 50 Christian Laettner .30 .09
❑ 51 Jerome Williams .15 .04
❑ 52 Terry Mills .15 .04
❑ 53 Antawn Jamison .50 .15
❑ 54 Donyell Marshall .30 .09
❑ 55 Chris Mills .15 .04
❑ 56 Larry Hughes .30 .09
❑ 57 Mookie Blaylock .15 .04
❑ 58 Vonteego Cummings .15 .04
❑ 59 Steve Francis .50 .15
❑ 60 Shandon Anderson .15 .04
❑ 61 Cuttino Mobley .30 .09
❑ 62 Hakeem Olajuwon .50 .15
❑ 63 Walt Williams .15 .04
❑ 64 Kelvin Cato .15 .04
❑ 65 Reggie Miller .50 .15
❑ 66 Austin Croshere .30 .09
❑ 67 Rik Smits .30 .09
❑ 68 Jalen Rose .50 .15
❑ 69 Dale Davis .15 .04
❑ 70 Jonathan Bender .30 .09
❑ 71 Michael Olowokandi .15 .04
❑ 72 Lamar Odom .50 .15
❑ 73 Tyrone Nesby .15 .04
❑ 74 Etdrick Bohannon RC .15 .04
❑ 75 Eric Piatkowski .30 .09
❑ 76 Shaquille O'Neal 1.25 .35
❑ 77 Kobe Bryant 2.00 .60
❑ 78 Robert Horry .30 .09
❑ 79 Ron Harper .30 .09
❑ 80 Rick Fox .30 .09
❑ 81 Derek Fisher .50 .15
❑ 82 Devean George .30 .09
❑ 83 Alonzo Mourning .30 .09
❑ 84 Clarence Weatherspoon .15 .04
❑ 85 Anthony Carter .30 .09
❑ 86 P.J. Brown .15 .04
❑ 87 Tim Hardaway .30 .09
❑ 88 Jamal Mashburn .30 .09
❑ 89 Voshon Lenard .15 .04
❑ 90 Ray Allen .50 .15
❑ 91 Glenn Robinson .50 .15
❑ 92 Tim Thomas .30 .09
❑ 93 Sam Cassell .50 .15
❑ 94 Robert Traylor .15 .04
❑ 95 Ervin Johnson .15 .04
❑ 96 Danny Manning .30 .09
❑ 97 Kevin Garnett 1.00 .30
❑ 98 Wally Szczerbiak .30 .09
❑ 99 Terrell Brandon .30 .09
❑ 100 William Avery .15 .04
❑ 101 Anthony Peeler .15 .04
❑ 102 Radoslav Nesterovic .30 .09
❑ 103 Dean Garrett .15 .04
❑ 104 Keith Van Horn .50 .15
❑ 105 Kerry Kittles .15 .04
❑ 106 Stephon Marbury .50 .15
❑ 107 Evan Eschmeyer .15 .04
❑ 108 Jim McIlvaine .15 .04
❑ 109 Lucious Harris .15 .04
❑ 110 Jamie Feick .15 .04
❑ 111 Allan Houston .30 .09
❑ 112 Latrell Sprewell .50 .15
❑ 113 Patrick Ewing .50 .15
❑ 114 Chris Childs .15 .04
❑ 115 Marcus Camby .30 .09
❑ 116 Charlie Ward .15 .04
❑ 117 Larry Johnson .30 .09
❑ 118 Darrell Armstrong .15 .04
❑ 119 Corey Maggette .30 .09
❑ 120 Ron Mercer .30 .09
❑ 121 Pat Garrity .15 .04
❑ 122 Chucky Atkins .15 .04
❑ 123 Ben Wallace .50 .15
❑ 124 Michael Doleac .15 .04
❑ 125 Allen Iverson 1.00 .30
❑ 126 Matt Geiger .15 .04
❑ 127 Eric Snow .30 .09
❑ 128 Toni Kukoc .30 .09
❑ 129 Theo Ratliff .30 .09
❑ 130 George Lynch .15 .04
❑ 131 Jason Kidd .75 .23
❑ 132 Tom Gugliotta .15 .04
❑ 133 Rodney Rogers .15 .04
❑ 134 Shawn Marion .50 .15
❑ 135 Clifford Robinson .15 .04
❑ 136 Kevin Johnson .30 .09
❑ 137 Anfernee Hardaway .50 .15
❑ 138 Scottie Pippen .75 .23
❑ 139 Damon Stoudamire .30 .09
❑ 140 Arvydas Sabonis .30 .09
❑ 141 Jermaine O'Neal .50 .15
❑ 142 Bonzi Wells .30 .09
❑ 143 Rasheed Wallace .50 .15
❑ 144 Detlef Schrempf .30 .09
❑ 145 Chris Webber .50 .15
❑ 146 Vlade Divac .30 .09
❑ 147 Peja Stojakovic .50 .15
❑ 148 Jason Williams .30 .09
❑ 149 Corliss Williamson .30 .09
❑ 150 Nick Anderson .15 .04
❑ 151 Jon Barry .15 .04
❑ 152 Tim Duncan 1.00 .30
❑ 153 David Robinson .50 .15
❑ 154 Avery Johnson .15 .04
❑ 155 Terry Porter .15 .04
❑ 156 Mario Elie .15 .04
❑ 157 Jaren Jackson .15 .04
❑ 158 Steve Kerr .30 .09
❑ 159 Gary Payton .50 .15
❑ 160 Vin Baker .30 .09
❑ 161 Brent Barry .30 .09
❑ 162 Horace Grant .30 .09
❑ 163 Ruben Patterson .30 .09
❑ 164 Rashard Lewis .30 .09
❑ 165 Tracy McGrady 1.50 .45
❑ 166 Charles Oakley .15 .04
❑ 167 Doug Christie .30 .09
❑ 168 Antonio Davis .15 .04
❑ 169 Vince Carter 1.25 .35
❑ 170 Kevin Willis .15 .04
❑ 171 Karl Malone .50 .15
❑ 172 John Stockton .50 .15
❑ 173 Bryon Russell .15 .04
❑ 174 Quincy Lewis .15 .04
❑ 175 Olden Polynice .15 .04
❑ 176 Jacque Vaughn .15 .04
❑ 177 Shareef Abdur-Rahim .50 .15
❑ 178 Michael Dickerson .30 .09
❑ 179 Bryant Reeves .15 .04
❑ 180 Mike Bibby .50 .15
❑ 181 Othella Harrington .15 .04
❑ 182 Felipe Lopez .15 .04
❑ 183 Mitch Richmond .30 .09
❑ 184 Richard Hamilton .30 .09
❑ 185 Jahidi White .15 .04
❑ 186 Aaron Williams .15 .04
❑ 187 Juwan Howard .30 .09
❑ 188 Rod Strickland .15 .04
❑ 189 Kobe Bryant CL 1.00 .30
❑ 190 Kevin Garnett CL .50 .15
❑ 191 Kenyon Martin RC 1.50 .45
❑ 192 Marcus Fizer RC .40 .12
❑ 193 Chris Mihm RC .40 .12
❑ 194 Stromile Swift RC .75 .23
❑ 195 Morris Peterson RC .75 .23
❑ 196 Quentin Richardson RC 1.25 .35
❑ 197 Courtney Alexander RC .40 .12
❑ 198 Scoonie Penn RC .40 .12
❑ 199 Mateen Cleaves RC .40 .12
❑ 200 Erick Barkley RC .40 .12
❑ 201 A.J. Guyton RC .40 .12
❑ 202 Darius Miles RC 1.25 .35
❑ 203 DerMarr Johnson RC .40 .12
❑ 204 Jerome Moiso RC .40 .12
❑ 205 Jamaal Magloire RC .40 .12
❑ 206 Hanno Mottola RC .40 .12
❑ 207 Mike Miller RC 1.25 .35
❑ 208 Desmond Mason RC .40 .12
❑ 209 Chris Carrawell RC .40 .12
❑ 210 Eduardo Najera RC .60 .18
❑ 211 Speedy Claxton RC .40 .12
❑ 212 Joel Przybilla RC .40 .12
❑ 213 Mark Madsen RC .40 .12
❑ 214 Khalid El-Amin RC .40 .12
❑ 215 Etan Thomas RC .40 .12
❑ 216 Jason Collier RC .40 .12
❑ 217 Jason Hart RC .40 .12
❑ 218 Michael Redd RC 1.25 .35
❑ 219 Keyon Dooling RC .40 .12
❑ 220 Mamadou N'diaye RC .40 .12

2002-03 Upper Deck MVP

	Nm-Mt	Ex-Mt
COMPLETE SET (220)	50.00	15.00
COMMON ROOKIE (191-220)	1.25	.35

❑ 1 Shareef Abdur-Rahim .50 .15
❑ 2 Jason Terry .50 .15
❑ 3 Toni Kukoc .30 .09
❑ 4 DerMarr Johnson .15 .04
❑ 5 Nazr Mohammed .15 .04
❑ 6 Theo Ratliff .30 .09
❑ 7 Dion Glover .15 .04
❑ 8 Paul Pierce .50 .15
❑ 9 Antoine Walker .50 .15
❑ 10 Kenny Anderson .30 .09
❑ 11 Tony Delk .15 .04
❑ 12 Eric Williams .15 .04
❑ 13 Rodney Rogers .15 .04
❑ 14 Jamal Mashburn .30 .09
❑ 15 Baron Davis .50 .15
❑ 16 David Wesley .15 .04
❑ 17 Elden Campbell .15 .04
❑ 18 P.J. Brown .15 .04
❑ 19 Jamaal Magloire .15 .04
❑ 20 Stacey Augmon .15 .04
❑ 21 Jalen Rose .50 .15
❑ 22 Marcus Fizer .30 .09
❑ 23 Tyson Chandler .50 .15
❑ 24 Trenton Hassell .30 .09
❑ 25 Eddy Curry .50 .15
❑ 26 Travis Best .15 .04
❑ 27 Andre Miller .30 .09
❑ 28 Lamond Murray .15 .04
❑ 29 Ricky Davis .30 .09
❑ 30 Zydrunas Ilgauskas .30 .09
❑ 31 Jumaine Jones .30 .09
❑ 32 Chris Mihm .15 .04

	Card	Mint	NrMt
❑	33 Dirk Nowitzki	.75	.23
❑	34 Michael Finley	.50	.15
❑	35 Steve Nash	.50	.15
❑	36 Nick Van Exel	.50	.15
❑	37 Raef LaFrentz	.30	.09
❑	38 Adrian Griffin	.15	.04
❑	39 Avery Johnson	.15	.04
❑	40 Marcus Camby	.30	.09
❑	41 Juwan Howard	.30	.09
❑	42 James Posey	.30	.09
❑	43 Ryan Bowen	.15	.04
❑	44 Donnell Harvey	.15	.04
❑	45 Voshon Lenard	.15	.04
❑	46 Jerry Stackhouse	.50	.15
❑	47 Clifford Robinson	.15	.04
❑	48 Chucky Atkins	.15	.04
❑	49 Ben Wallace	.50	.15
❑	50 Jon Barry	.15	.04
❑	51 Corliss Williamson	.30	.09
❑	52 Antawn Jamison	.50	.15
❑	53 Jason Richardson	.50	.15
❑	54 Danny Fortson	.15	.04
❑	55 Gilbert Arenas	.50	.15
❑	56 Bob Sura	.15	.04
❑	57 Troy Murphy	.30	.09
❑	58 Steve Francis	.50	.15
❑	59 Cuttino Mobley	.30	.09
❑	60 Eddie Griffin	.30	.09
❑	61 Kenny Thomas	.15	.04
❑	62 Moochie Norris	.15	.04
❑	63 Kelvin Cato	.15	.04
❑	64 Glen Rice	.30	.09
❑	65 Reggie Miller	.50	.15
❑	66 Jermaine O'Neal	.50	.15
❑	67 Ron Mercer	.30	.09
❑	68 Jamaal Tinsley	.50	.15
❑	69 Al Harrington	.30	.09
❑	70 Ron Artest	.30	.09
❑	71 Austin Croshere	.15	.04
❑	72 Elton Brand	.50	.15
❑	73 Darius Miles	.50	.15
❑	74 Lamar Odom	.50	.15
❑	75 Quentin Richardson	.30	.09
❑	76 Corey Maggette	.30	.09
❑	77 Jeff McInnis	.15	.04
❑	78 Michael Olowokandi	.15	.04
❑	79 Kobe Bryant	2.00	.60
❑	80 Shaquille O'Neal	1.25	.35
❑	81 Derek Fisher	.50	.15
❑	82 Rick Fox	.30	.09
❑	83 Robert Horry	.30	.09
❑	84 Devean George	.30	.09
❑	85 Samaki Walker	.15	.04
❑	86 Pau Gasol	.50	.15
❑	87 Jason Williams	.30	.09
❑	88 Shane Battier	.50	.15
❑	89 Stromile Swift	.30	.09
❑	90 Lorenzen Wright	.15	.04
❑	91 Tony Massenburg	.15	.04
❑	92 Eddie Jones	.50	.15
❑	93 Alonzo Mourning	.30	.09
❑	94 Brian Grant	.30	.09
❑	95 Anthony Carter	.30	.09
❑	96 LaPhonso Ellis	.15	.04
❑	97 Jim Jackson	.15	.04
❑	98 Ray Allen	.50	.15
❑	99 Glenn Robinson	.50	.15
❑	100 Sam Cassell	.50	.15
❑	101 Tim Thomas	.30	.09
❑	102 Anthony Mason	.30	.09
❑	103 Joel Przybilla	.15	.04
❑	104 Ervin Johnson	.15	.04
❑	105 Kevin Garnett	1.00	.30
❑	106 Wally Szczerbiak	.50	.15
❑	107 Chauncey Billups	.30	.09
❑	108 Terrell Brandon	.30	.09
❑	109 Marc Jackson	.30	.09
❑	110 Joe Smith	.30	.09
❑	111 Jason Kidd	.75	.23
❑	112 Keith Van Horn	.50	.15
❑	113 Kenyon Martin	.50	.15
❑	114 Kerry Kittles	.15	.04
❑	115 Richard Jefferson	.30	.09
❑	116 Jason Collins	.15	.04
❑	117 Todd MacCulloch	.15	.04
❑	118 Allan Houston	.30	.09
❑	119 Latrell Sprewell	.50	.15
❑	120 Kurt Thomas	.30	.09
❑	121 Antonio McDyess	.30	.09
❑	122 Othella Harrington	.15	.04
❑	123 Clarence Weatherspoon	.15	.04
❑	124 Tracy McGrady	1.25	.35
❑	125 Mike Miller	.50	.15
❑	126 Darrell Armstrong	.15	.04
❑	127 Grant Hill	.50	.15
❑	128 Horace Grant	.30	.09
❑	129 Steven Hunter	.15	.04
❑	130 Allen Iverson	1.00	.30
❑	131 Dikembe Mutombo	.30	.09
❑	132 Aaron McKie	.30	.09
❑	133 Derrick Coleman	.15	.04
❑	134 Eric Snow	.30	.09
❑	135 Matt Harpring	.50	.15
❑	136 Stephon Marbury	.50	.15
❑	137 Shawn Marion	.50	.15
❑	138 Joe Johnson	.50	.15
❑	139 Anfernee Hardaway	.50	.15
❑	140 Iakovos Tsakalidis	.15	.04
❑	141 Tom Gugliotta	.15	.04
❑	142 Bo Outlaw	.15	.04
❑	143 Rasheed Wallace	.50	.15
❑	144 Damon Stoudamire	.30	.09
❑	145 Scottie Pippen	.75	.23
❑	146 Ruben Patterson	.30	.09
❑	147 Derek Anderson	.30	.09
❑	148 Dale Davis	.30	.09
❑	149 Bonzi Wells	.30	.09
❑	150 Chris Webber	.50	.15
❑	151 Peja Stojakovic	.50	.15
❑	152 Mike Bibby	.50	.15
❑	153 Doug Christie	.30	.09
❑	154 Vlade Divac	.30	.09
❑	155 Bobby Jackson	.30	.09
❑	156 Hidayet Turkoglu	.50	.15
❑	157 Tim Duncan	1.00	.30
❑	158 David Robinson	.50	.15
❑	159 Steve Smith	.30	.09
❑	160 Tony Parker	.50	.15
❑	161 Antonio Daniels	.15	.04
❑	162 Charles Smith	.15	.04
❑	163 Bruce Bowen	.15	.04
❑	164 Gary Payton	.50	.15
❑	165 Rashard Lewis	.30	.09
❑	166 Vin Baker	.30	.09
❑	167 Brent Barry	.30	.09
❑	168 Desmond Mason	.30	.09
❑	169 Vladimir Radmanovic	.30	.09
❑	170 Vince Carter	1.25	.35
❑	171 Morris Peterson	.30	.09
❑	172 Antonio Davis	.15	.04
❑	173 Hakeem Olajuwon	.50	.15
❑	174 Alvin Williams	.15	.04
❑	175 Jerome Williams	.15	.04
❑	176 Keon Clark	.30	.09
❑	177 Karl Malone	.50	.15
❑	178 John Stockton	.50	.15
❑	179 Donyell Marshall	.30	.09
❑	180 Andrei Kirilenko	.50	.15
❑	181 Bryon Russell	.15	.04
❑	182 Jarron Collins	.15	.04
❑	183 DeShawn Stevenson	.15	.04
❑	184 Michael Jordan	4.00	1.20
❑	185 Richard Hamilton	.30	.09
❑	186 Kwame Brown	.30	.09
❑	187 Chris Whitney	.15	.04
❑	188 Tyronn Lue	.15	.04
❑	189 Brendan Haywood	.30	.09
❑	190 Jahidi White	.15	.04
❑	191 DaJuan Wagner RC	2.00	.60
❑	192 Jay Williams RC	1.50	.45
❑	193 Yao Ming RC	8.00	2.40
❑	194 Drew Gooden RC	4.00	1.20
❑	195 Chris Jefferies RC	1.25	.35
❑	196 Casey Jacobsen RC	1.25	.35
❑	197 Juan Dixon RC	2.00	.60
❑	198 Melvin Ely RC	1.25	.35
❑	199 Curtis Borchardt RC	1.25	.35
❑	200 John Salmons RC	1.25	.35
❑	201 Carlos Boozer RC	2.50	.75
❑	202 Fred Jones RC	1.25	.35
❑	203 Frank Williams RC	1.25	.35
❑	204 Jamal Sampson RC	1.25	.35
❑	205 Dan Dickau RC	1.25	.35
❑	206 Marcus Haislip RC	1.25	.35
❑	207 Jared Jeffries RC	1.25	.35
❑	208 Amare Stoudemire RC	6.00	1.80
❑	209 Caron Butler RC	2.50	.75
❑	210 Qyntel Woods RC	1.25	.35
❑	211 Kareem Rush RC	1.50	.45
❑	212 Ryan Humphrey RC	1.25	.35
❑	213 Jiri Welsch RC	1.25	.35
❑	214 Mike Dunleavy RC	5.00	1.50
❑	215 Tayshaun Prince RC	1.50	.45
❑	216 Nene Hilario RC	2.00	.60
❑	217 Nikoloz Tskitishvili RC	1.25	.35
❑	218 Bostjan Nachbar RC	1.25	.35
❑	219 Efthimios Rentzias RC	1.25	.35
❑	220 Rod Grizzard RC	1.25	.35

2003-04 Upper Deck MVP

	MINT	NRMT
COMP.SET w/o SP's	-	
COMMON ROOKIE (201-230)	1.50	.70
BLACK NOT PRICED DUE TO SCARCITY	-	
*GOLD SINGLES: 8X TO 20X BASE CARD HI		
*GOLD RC's: 4X TO 10X BASE CARD HI	-	
*SILVER SINGLES: .75X TO 2X BASE CARD HI		

	Card	Mint	NrMt
❑	1 Shareef Abdur-Rahim	.50	.23
❑	2 Jason Terry	.50	.23
❑	3 Terrell Brandon	.15	.07
❑	4 Alan Henderson	.15	.07
❑	5 Dan Dickau	.15	.07
❑	6 Theo Ratliff	.25	.11
❑	7 Dion Glover	.15	.07
❑	8 Paul Pierce	.50	.23
❑	9 Antoine Walker	.50	.23
❑	10 Eric Williams	.15	.07
❑	11 Tony Delk	.15	.07
❑	12 J.R. Bremer	.15	.07
❑	13 Vin Baker	.25	.11
❑	14 Jalen Rose	.50	.23
❑	15 Marcus Fizer	.15	.07
❑	16 Tyson Chandler	.50	.23
❑	17 Jamal Crawford	.15	.07
❑	18 Eddy Curry	.25	.11
❑	19 Scottie Pippen	.75	.35
❑	20 Darius Miles	.50	.23
❑	21 Dajuan Wagner	.25	.11
❑	22 Ricky Davis	.50	.23
❑	23 Zydrunas Ilgauskas	.25	.11
❑	24 Carlos Boozer	.50	.23
❑	25 Chris Mihm	.15	.07
❑	26 Dirk Nowitzki	.75	.35
❑	27 Michael Finley	.50	.23
❑	28 Steve Nash	.50	.23
❑	29 Nick Van Exel	.50	.23
❑	30 Raef LaFrentz	.25	.11
❑	31 Eduardo Najera	.25	.11
❑	32 Shawn Bradley	.15	.07
❑	33 Marcus Camby	.25	.11
❑	34 Vincent Yarbrough	.15	.07
❑	35 Rodney White	.15	.07
❑	36 Nene Hilario	.25	.11
❑	37 Nikoloz Tskitishvili	.15	.07
❑	38 Shammond Williams	.15	.07
❑	39 Richard Hamilton	.25	.11

❑ 40 Clifford Robinson .15 .07
❑ 41 Chauncey Billups .25 .11
❑ 42 Ben Wallace .50 .23
❑ 43 Elden Campbell .15 .07
❑ 44 Corliss Williamson .25 .11
❑ 45 Antawn Jamison .50 .23
❑ 46 Jason Richardson .50 .23
❑ 47 Danny Fortson .15 .07
❑ 48 Speedy Claxton .15 .07
❑ 49 Mike Dunleavy .25 .11
❑ 50 Troy Murphy .50 .23
❑ 51 Steve Francis .50 .23
❑ 52 Cuttino Mobley .25 .11
❑ 53 Eddie Griffin .25 .11
❑ 54 Yao Ming 1.25 .55
❑ 55 Maurice Taylor .15 .07
❑ 56 Kelvin Cato .15 .07
❑ 57 Glen Rice .25 .11
❑ 58 Reggie Miller .50 .23
❑ 59 Jermaine O'Neal .50 .23
❑ 60 Scot Pollard .15 .07
❑ 61 Jamaal Tinsley .50 .23
❑ 62 Al Harrington .25 .11
❑ 63 Ron Artest .25 .11
❑ 64 Danny Ferry .15 .07
❑ 65 Elton Brand .50 .23
❑ 66 Andre Miller .25 .11
❑ 67 Lamar Odom .50 .23
❑ 68 Quentin Richardson .25 .11
❑ 69 Corey Maggette .25 .11
❑ 70 Chris Wilcox .25 .11
❑ 71 Marko Jaric .25 .11
❑ 72 Kobe Bryant 2.00 .90
❑ 73 Shaquille O'Neal 1.25 .55
❑ 74 Derek Fisher .50 .23
❑ 75 Karl Malone .50 .23
❑ 76 Gary Payton .50 .23
❑ 77 Devean George .25 .11
❑ 78 Kareem Rush .25 .11
❑ 79 Pau Gasol .50 .23
❑ 80 Jason Williams .25 .11
❑ 81 Shane Battier .50 .23
❑ 82 Stromile Swift .25 .11
❑ 83 Lorenzen Wright .15 .07
❑ 84 Mike Miller .50 .23
❑ 85 Eddie Jones .50 .23
❑ 86 Ken Johnson .15 .07
❑ 87 Brian Grant .25 .11
❑ 88 Anthony Carter .25 .11
❑ 89 Rasual Butler .25 .11
❑ 90 Caron Butler .50 .23
❑ 91 Marcus Haislip .15 .07
❑ 92 Toni Kukoc .25 .11
❑ 93 Joe Smith .25 .11
❑ 94 Tim Thomas .25 .11
❑ 95 Anthony Mason .25 .11
❑ 96 Joel Przybilla .15 .07
❑ 97 Desmond Mason .25 .11
❑ 98 Kevin Garnett 1.00 .45
❑ 99 Wally Szczerbiak .25 .11
❑ 100 Troy Hudson .15 .07
❑ 101 Michael Olowokandi .15 .07
❑ 102 Kendall Gill .15 .07
❑ 103 Sam Cassell .50 .23
❑ 104 Jason Kidd .75 .35
❑ 105 Kenyon Martin .50 .23
❑ 106 Alonzo Mourning .25 .11
❑ 107 Kerry Kittles .15 .07
❑ 108 Richard Jefferson .25 .11
❑ 109 Jason Collins .15 .07
❑ 110 Dikembe Mutombo .25 .11
❑ 111 Jamal Mashburn .25 .11
❑ 112 Baron Davis .50 .23
❑ 113 David Wesley .15 .07
❑ 114 Kenny Anderson .25 .11
❑ 115 P.J. Brown .15 .07
❑ 116 Jamaal Magloire .15 .07
❑ 117 George Lynch .15 .07
❑ 118 Courtney Alexander .25 .11
❑ 119 Allan Houston .25 .11
❑ 120 Keith Van Horn .50 .23
❑ 121 Kurt Thomas .25 .11
❑ 122 Antonio McDyess .25 .11
❑ 123 Othella Harrington .15 .07
❑ 124 Clarence Weatherspoon .15 .07
❑ 125 Tracy McGrady 1.25 .55
❑ 126 Drew Gooden .25 .11
❑ 127 Tyronn Lue .15 .07
❑ 128 Pat Garrity .15 .07
❑ 129 Grant Hill .50 .23
❑ 130 Gordan Giricek .25 .11
❑ 131 Juwan Howard .25 .11
❑ 132 Allen Iverson 1.00 .45
❑ 133 Glenn Robinson .25 .11
❑ 134 Aaron McKie .25 .11
❑ 135 Derrick Coleman .15 .07
❑ 136 Eric Snow .25 .11
❑ 137 Kenny Thomas .15 .07
❑ 138 Stephon Marbury .50 .23
❑ 139 Shawn Marion .50 .23
❑ 140 Joe Johnson .25 .11
❑ 141 Anfernee Hardaway .50 .23
❑ 142 Amare Stoudemire 1.00 .45
❑ 143 Casey Jacobsen .15 .07
❑ 144 Tom Gugliotta .15 .07
❑ 145 Bo Outlaw .15 .07
❑ 146 Rasheed Wallace .50 .23
❑ 147 Damon Stoudamire .25 .11
❑ 148 Jeff McInnis .15 .07
❑ 149 Ruben Patterson .25 .11
❑ 150 Derek Anderson .25 .11
❑ 151 Dale Davis .25 .11
❑ 152 Bonzi Wells .25 .11
❑ 153 Chris Webber .50 .23
❑ 154 Peja Stojakovic .50 .23
❑ 155 Mike Bibby .50 .23
❑ 156 Doug Christie .25 .11
❑ 157 Vlade Divac .25 .11
❑ 158 Bobby Jackson .25 .11
❑ 159 Brad Miller .50 .23
❑ 160 Keon Clark .25 .11
❑ 161 Tim Duncan 1.00 .45
❑ 162 David Robinson .50 .23
❑ 163 Steve Smith .25 .11
❑ 164 Tony Parker .50 .23
❑ 165 Hedo Turkoglu .50 .23
❑ 166 Radoslav Nesterovic .25 .11
❑ 167 Manu Ginobili .50 .23
❑ 168 Ron Mercer .15 .07
❑ 169 Ray Allen .50 .23
❑ 170 Rashard Lewis .50 .23
❑ 171 Antonio Daniels .15 .07
❑ 172 Brent Barry .25 .11
❑ 173 Predrag Drobnjak .15 .07
❑ 174 Vladimir Radmanovic .15 .07
❑ 175 Vince Carter 1.00 .45
❑ 176 Morris Peterson .25 .11
❑ 177 Antonio Davis .15 .07
❑ 178 Chris Jefferies .15 .07
❑ 179 Lindsey Hunter .15 .07
❑ 180 Alvin Williams .15 .07
❑ 181 Jerome Williams .15 .07
❑ 182 Jerome Moiso .15 .07
❑ 183 Greg Ostertag .15 .07
❑ 184 John Stockton .50 .23
❑ 185 Matt Harpring .50 .23
❑ 186 Andrei Kirilenko .50 .23
❑ 187 Calbert Cheaney .15 .07
❑ 188 Jarron Collins .15 .07
❑ 189 DeShawn Stevenson .15 .07
❑ 190 Michael Jordan 3.00 1.35
❑ 191 Jerry Stackhouse .50 .23
❑ 192 Kwame Brown .25 .11
❑ 193 Larry Hughes .25 .11
❑ 194 Gilbert Arenas .50 .23
❑ 195 Brendan Haywood .15 .07
❑ 196 Juan Dixon .25 .11
❑ 197 Jahidi White .15 .07
❑ 198 Etan Thomas .15 .07
❑ 199 Michael Jordan - Checklist 2.00 .90
❑ 200 Michael Jordan - Checklist 2.00 .90
❑ 201 LeBron James RC 15.00 6.75
❑ 202 Darko Milicic RC 2.50 1.10
❑ 203 Carmelo Anthony RC 10.00 4.50
❑ 204 Chris Bosh RC 2.50 1.10
❑ 205 Dwyane Wade RC 4.00 1.80
❑ 206 Chris Kaman RC 1.50 .70
❑ 207 Kirk Hinrich RC 2.50 1.10
❑ 208 T.J. Ford RC 2.00 .90
❑ 209 Mike Sweetney RC 1.50 .70
❑ 210 Jarvis Hayes RC 1.50 .70
❑ 211 Mickael Pietrus RC 1.50 .70
❑ 212 Nick Collison RC 1.50 .70
❑ 213 Marcus Banks RC 1.50 .70
❑ 214 Luke Ridnour RC 2.00 .90
❑ 215 Reece Gaines RC 1.50 .70
❑ 216 Troy Bell RC 1.50 .70
❑ 217 Zarko Cabarkapa RC 1.50 .70
❑ 218 David West RC 1.50 .70
❑ 219 Aleksandar Pavlovic RC 1.50 .70
❑ 220 Dahntay Jones RC 1.50 .70
❑ 221 Boris Diaw-Riffiod RC 1.50 .70
❑ 222 Zoran Planinic RC 1.50 .70
❑ 223 Travis Outlaw RC 1.50 .70
❑ 224 Brian Cook RC 1.50 .70
❑ 225 Carlos Delfino RC 1.50 .70
❑ 226 Ndudi Ebi RC 1.50 .70
❑ 227 Kendrick Perkins RC 1.50 .70
❑ 228 Leandro Barbosa RC 1.50 .70
❑ 229 Josh Howard RC 2.00 .90
❑ 230 Maciej Lampe RC 1.50 .70

1998-99 Upper Deck Ovation

	Nm-Mt	Ex-Mt
COMPLETE SET (80)	120.00	36.00
COMPLETE SET w/o RC (70)	40.00	12.00
COMMON CARD (1-70)	.40	.12
COMMON ROOKIE (71-80)	2.00	.60

❑ 1 Steve Smith .75 .23
❑ 2 Dikembe Mutombo .75 .23
❑ 3 Antoine Walker 1.25 .35
❑ 4 Ron Mercer .75 .23
❑ 5 Glen Rice .75 .23
❑ 6 Bobby Phills .40 .12
❑ 7 Michael Jordan 8.00 2.40
❑ 8 Toni Kukoc .75 .23
❑ 9 Dennis Rodman .75 .23
❑ 10 Scottie Pippen 2.00 .60
❑ 11 Shawn Kemp .75 .23
❑ 12 Derek Anderson 1.25 .35
❑ 13 Brevin Knight .40 .12
❑ 14 Michael Finley 1.25 .35
❑ 15 Shawn Bradley .40 .12
❑ 16 LaPhonso Ellis .40 .12
❑ 17 Bobby Jackson .75 .23
❑ 18 Grant Hill 1.25 .35
❑ 19 Jerry Stackhouse 1.25 .35
❑ 20 Donyell Marshall .75 .23
❑ 21 Erick Dampier .75 .23
❑ 22 Hakeem Olajuwon 1.25 .35
❑ 23 Charles Barkley 1.50 .45
❑ 24 Reggie Miller 1.25 .35
❑ 25 Chris Mullin 1.25 .35
❑ 26 Rik Smits .75 .23
❑ 27 Maurice Taylor .75 .23
❑ 28 Lorenzen Wright .40 .12
❑ 29 Kobe Bryant 5.00 1.50
❑ 30 Eddie Jones 1.25 .35
❑ 31 Shaquille O'Neal 3.00 .90
❑ 32 Alonzo Mourning .75 .23
❑ 33 Tim Hardaway .75 .23
❑ 34 Jamal Mashburn .75 .23
❑ 35 Ray Allen 1.25 .35
❑ 36 Terrell Brandon .75 .23
❑ 37 Glenn Robinson .75 .23
❑ 38 Kevin Garnett 4.00 1.20
❑ 39 Tom Gugliotta .40 .12
❑ 40 Stephon Marbury 1.25 .35

	Nm-Mt	Ex-Mt
❑ 41 Keith Van Horn	1.25	.35
❑ 42 Kerry Kittles	.40	.12
❑ 43 Jayson Williams	.40	.12
❑ 44 Patrick Ewing	1.25	.35
❑ 45 Allan Houston	.75	.23
❑ 46 Larry Johnson	.75	.23
❑ 47 Anfernee Hardaway	1.25	.35
❑ 48 Nick Anderson	.40	.12
❑ 49 Allen Iverson	2.50	.75
❑ 50 Joe Smith	.75	.23
❑ 51 Tim Thomas	.75	.23
❑ 52 Jason Kidd	2.00	.60
❑ 53 Antonio McDyess	.75	.23
❑ 54 Damon Stoudamire	.75	.23
❑ 55 Isaiah Rider	.40	.12
❑ 56 Rasheed Wallace	1.25	.35
❑ 57 Tariq Abdul-Wahad	.40	.12
❑ 58 Corliss Williamson	.75	.23
❑ 59 Tim Duncan	2.00	.60
❑ 60 David Robinson	1.25	.35
❑ 61 Vin Baker	.75	.23
❑ 62 Gary Payton	1.25	.35
❑ 63 Chauncey Billups	.75	.23
❑ 64 Tracy McGrady	3.00	.90
❑ 65 Karl Malone	1.25	.35
❑ 66 John Stockton	1.25	.35
❑ 67 Shareef Abdur-Rahim	1.25	.35
❑ 68 Bryant Reeves	.40	.12
❑ 69 Juwan Howard	.75	.23
❑ 70 Rod Strickland	.40	.12
❑ 71 Michael Olowokandi RC	2.00	.60
❑ 72 Mike Bibby RC	8.00	2.40
❑ 73 Raef LaFrentz RC	2.50	.75
❑ 74 Antawn Jamison RC	6.00	1.80
❑ 75 Vince Carter RC	20.00	6.00
❑ 76 Robert Traylor RC	2.00	.60
❑ 77 Jason Williams RC	5.00	1.50
❑ 78 Larry Hughes RC	5.00	1.50
❑ 79 Dirk Nowitzki RC	15.00	4.50
❑ 80 Paul Pierce RC	8.00	2.40
❑ BK1 Michael Jordan Game Used Basketball Card Serial #'d to 90	1,500.00	450.00

1999-00 Upper Deck Ovation

	Nm-Mt	Ex-Mt
COMPLETE SET (90)	100.00	30.00
COMPLETE SET w/o RC (60)	25.00	7.50
COMMON CARD (1-60)	.30	.09
COMMON ROOKIE (61-90)	1.00	.30
❑ 1 Dikembe Mutombo	.60	.18
❑ 2 Alan Henderson	.30	.09
❑ 3 Antoine Walker	1.00	.30
❑ 4 Paul Pierce	1.00	.30
❑ 5 David Wesley	.30	.09
❑ 6 Eddie Jones	1.00	.30
❑ 7 Toni Kukoc	.60	.18
❑ 8 Randy Brown	.30	.09
❑ 9 Shawn Kemp	.60	.18
❑ 10 Zydrunas Ilgauskas	.60	.18
❑ 11 Michael Finley	1.00	.30
❑ 12 Dirk Nowitzki	2.00	.60
❑ 13 Nick Van Exel	1.00	.30
❑ 14 Antonio McDyess	.60	.18
❑ 15 Grant Hill	1.00	.30
❑ 16 Jerry Stackhouse	1.00	.30
❑ 17 Antawn Jamison	1.50	.45
❑ 18 John Starks	.60	.18
❑ 19 Hakeem Olajuwon	1.00	.30
❑ 20 Charles Barkley	1.25	.35
❑ 21 Cuttino Mobley	1.00	.30
❑ 22 Reggie Miller	1.00	.30
❑ 23 Rik Smits	.60	.18
❑ 24 Maurice Taylor	.60	.18
❑ 25 Michael Olowokandi	.60	.18
❑ 26 Kobe Bryant	4.00	1.20
❑ 27 Shaquille O'Neal	2.50	.75
❑ 28 Tim Hardaway	.60	.18
❑ 29 Alonzo Mourning	.60	.18
❑ 30 Glenn Robinson	1.00	.30
❑ 31 Ray Allen	1.00	.30
❑ 32 Kevin Garnett	2.00	.60
❑ 33 Joe Smith	.60	.18
❑ 34 Stephon Marbury	1.00	.30
❑ 35 Keith Van Horn	1.00	.30
❑ 36 Patrick Ewing	1.00	.30
❑ 37 Latrell Sprewell	1.00	.30
❑ 38 Darrell Armstrong	.30	.09
❑ 39 Bo Outlaw	.30	.09
❑ 40 Allen Iverson	2.00	.60
❑ 41 Larry Hughes	1.00	.30
❑ 42 Jason Kidd	1.50	.45
❑ 43 Anfernee Hardaway	1.00	.30
❑ 44 Brian Grant	.60	.18
❑ 45 Damon Stoudamire	.60	.18
❑ 46 Jason Williams	1.00	.30
❑ 47 Chris Webber	1.00	.30
❑ 48 Tim Duncan	2.00	.60
❑ 49 David Robinson	1.00	.30
❑ 50 Sean Elliott	.60	.18
❑ 51 Gary Payton	1.00	.30
❑ 52 Vin Baker	.60	.18
❑ 53 Vince Carter	2.50	.75
❑ 54 Tracy McGrady	2.50	.75
❑ 55 Karl Malone	1.00	.30
❑ 56 John Stockton	1.00	.30
❑ 57 Shareef Abdur-Rahim	1.00	.30
❑ 58 Mike Bibby	1.00	.30
❑ 59 Juwan Howard	.60	.18
❑ 60 Mitch Richmond	.60	.18
❑ 61 Elton Brand RC	6.00	1.80
❑ 62 Steve Francis RC	8.00	2.40
❑ 63 Baron Davis RC	5.00	1.50
❑ 64 Lamar Odom RC	5.00	1.50
❑ 65 Jonathan Bender RC	3.00	.90
❑ 66 Wally Szczerbiak RC	5.00	1.50
❑ 67 Richard Hamilton RC	5.00	1.50
❑ 68 Andre Miller RC	5.00	1.50
❑ 69 Shawn Marion RC	6.00	1.80
❑ 70 Jason Terry RC	4.00	1.20
❑ 71 Trajan Langdon RC	2.00	.60
❑ 72 Aleksandar Radojevic RC	1.00	.30
❑ 73 Corey Maggette RC	5.00	1.50
❑ 74 William Avery RC	2.00	.60
❑ 75 Galen Young RC	1.00	.30
❑ 76 Chris Herren RC	1.00	.30
❑ 77 Cal Bowdler RC	1.50	.45
❑ 78 James Posey RC	3.00	.90
❑ 79 Quincy Lewis RC	1.50	.45
❑ 80 Dion Glover RC	1.50	.45
❑ 81 Jeff Foster RC	1.50	.45
❑ 82 Kenny Thomas RC	2.00	.60
❑ 83 Devean George RC	2.50	.75
❑ 84 Tim James RC	1.50	.45
❑ 85 Vonteego Cummings RC	2.00	.60
❑ 86 Jumaine Jones RC	2.00	.60
❑ 87 Scott Padgett RC	2.00	.60
❑ 88 Obinna Ekezie RC	1.25	.35
❑ 89 Ryan Robertson RC	1.25	.35
❑ 90 Evan Eschmeyer RC	1.00	.30
❑ MJ-S M.Jordan AU/23	-	-

2000-01 Upper Deck Ovation

	Nm-Mt	Ex-Mt
COMPLETE SET w/o RC (60)	25.00	7.50
COMMON CARD (1-60)	.25	.07
COMMON ROOKIE (61-90)	3.00	.90
❑ 1 Dikembe Mutombo	.50	.15
❑ 2 Jim Jackson	.25	.07
❑ 3 Paul Pierce	.75	.23

	Nm-Mt	Ex-Mt
❑ 4 Antoine Walker	.75	.23
❑ 5 Derrick Coleman	.25	.07
❑ 6 Baron Davis	.75	.23
❑ 7 Elton Brand	.75	.23
❑ 8 Ron Artest	.50	.15
❑ 9 Lamond Murray	.25	.07
❑ 10 Andre Miller	.50	.15
❑ 11 Michael Finley	.75	.23
❑ 12 Dirk Nowitzki	1.25	.35
❑ 13 Antonio McDyess	.50	.15
❑ 14 Nick Van Exel	.75	.23
❑ 15 Jerry Stackhouse	.75	.23
❑ 16 Jerome Williams	.25	.07
❑ 17 Larry Hughes	.50	.15
❑ 18 Antawn Jamison	.75	.23
❑ 19 Steve Francis	.75	.23
❑ 20 Hakeem Olajuwon	.75	.23
❑ 21 Reggie Miller	.75	.23
❑ 22 Jalen Rose	.75	.23
❑ 23 Lamar Odom	.75	.23
❑ 24 Michael Olowokandi	.25	.07
❑ 25 Shaquille O'Neal	2.00	.60
❑ 26 Kobe Bryant	3.00	.90
❑ 27 Alonzo Mourning	.50	.15
❑ 28 Anthony Carter	.50	.15
❑ 29 Ray Allen	.75	.23
❑ 30 Tim Thomas	.50	.15
❑ 31 Kevin Garnett	1.50	.45
❑ 32 Wally Szczerbiak	.50	.15
❑ 33 Stephon Marbury	.75	.23
❑ 34 Keith Van Horn	.75	.23
❑ 35 Allan Houston	.50	.15
❑ 36 Latrell Sprewell	.75	.23
❑ 37 Grant Hill	.75	.23
❑ 38 Tracy McGrady	2.00	.60
❑ 39 Allen Iverson	1.50	.45
❑ 40 Toni Kukoc	.50	.15
❑ 41 Jason Kidd	1.25	.35
❑ 42 Anfernee Hardaway	.75	.23
❑ 43 Rasheed Wallace	.75	.23
❑ 44 Scottie Pippen	1.25	.35
❑ 45 Damon Stoudamire	.50	.15
❑ 46 Chris Webber	.75	.23
❑ 47 Jason Williams	.50	.15
❑ 48 Tim Duncan	1.50	.45
❑ 49 David Robinson	.75	.23
❑ 50 Gary Payton	.75	.23
❑ 51 Brent Barry	.50	.15
❑ 52 Rashard Lewis	.50	.15
❑ 53 Vince Carter	2.00	.60
❑ 54 Antonio Davis	.25	.07
❑ 55 Karl Malone	.75	.23
❑ 56 John Stockton	.75	.23
❑ 57 Shareef Abdur-Rahim	.75	.23
❑ 58 Mike Bibby	.75	.23
❑ 59 Mitch Richmond	.50	.15
❑ 60 Richard Hamilton	.50	.15
❑ 61 Kenyon Martin RC	12.00	3.60
❑ 62 Stromile Swift RC	6.00	1.80
❑ 63 Darius Miles RC	10.00	3.00
❑ 64 Marcus Fizer RC	3.00	.90
❑ 65 Mike Miller RC	10.00	3.00
❑ 66 DerMarr Johnson RC	3.00	.90
❑ 67 Chris Mihm RC	3.00	.90
❑ 68 Jamal Crawford RC	4.00	1.20
❑ 69 Joel Przybilla RC	3.00	.90
❑ 70 Keyon Dooling RC	3.00	.90
❑ 71 Jerome Moiso RC	3.00	.90

Card		
❑ 72 Etan Thomas RC	3.00	.90
❑ 73 Courtney Alexander RC	4.00	1.20
❑ 74 Mateen Cleaves RC	3.00	.90
❑ 75 Jason Collier RC	3.00	.90
❑ 76 Hidayet Turkoglu RC	8.00	2.40
❑ 77 Desmond Mason RC	3.00	.90
❑ 78 Quentin Richardson RC	8.00	2.40
❑ 79 Jamaal Magloire RC	3.00	.90
❑ 80 Speedy Claxton RC	3.00	.90
❑ 81 Morris Peterson RC	6.00	1.80
❑ 82 Donnell Harvey RC	3.00	.90
❑ 83 DeShawn Stevenson RC	3.00	.90
❑ 84 Mamadou N'Diaye RC	3.00	.90
❑ 85 Erick Barkley RC	3.00	.90
❑ 86 Mark Madsen RC	3.00	.90
❑ 87 A.J. Guyton RC	3.00	.90
❑ 88 Khalid El-Amin RC	3.00	.90
❑ 89 Eddie House RC	3.00	.90
❑ 90 Chris Porter RC	3.00	.90

2001-02 Upper Deck Ovation

	Nm-Mt	Ex-Mt
COMP.SET w/o SP's (90)	40.00	12.00
COMMON CARD (1-90)	.25	.07
COMMON ROOKIE (91-110)	2.50	.75
COMMON ROOKIE (111-120)	6.00	1.80
❑ 1 Jason Terry	.75	.23
❑ 2 DerMarr Johnson	.50	.15
❑ 3 Shareef Abdur-Rahim	.75	.23
❑ 4 Paul Pierce	.75	.23
❑ 5 Antoine Walker	.75	.23
❑ 6 Kenny Anderson	.50	.15
❑ 7 Jamal Mashburn	.50	.15
❑ 8 David Wesley	.25	.07
❑ 9 Baron Davis	.75	.23
❑ 10 Ron Mercer	.50	.15
❑ 11 Marcus Fizer	.50	.15
❑ 12 Ron Artest	.50	.15
❑ 13 Andre Miller	.50	.15
❑ 14 Lamond Murray	.25	.07
❑ 15 Chris Mihm	.50	.15
❑ 16 Michael Finley	.75	.23
❑ 17 Steve Nash	.75	.23
❑ 18 Dirk Nowitzki	1.25	.35
❑ 19 Antonio McDyess	.50	.15
❑ 20 Nick Van Exel	.75	.23
❑ 21 Raef LaFrentz	.50	.15
❑ 22 Jerry Stackhouse	.75	.23
❑ 23 Chucky Atkins	.25	.07
❑ 24 Corliss Williamson	.50	.15
❑ 25 Antawn Jamison	.75	.23
❑ 26 Chris Porter	.50	.15
❑ 27 Larry Hughes	.50	.15
❑ 28 Steve Francis	.75	.23
❑ 29 Cuttino Mobley	.50	.15
❑ 30 Maurice Taylor	.50	.15
❑ 31 Reggie Miller	.75	.23
❑ 32 Jalen Rose	.75	.23
❑ 33 Jermaine O'Neal	.75	.23
❑ 34 Darius Miles	.75	.23
❑ 35 Corey Maggette	.50	.15
❑ 36 Lamar Odom	.75	.23
❑ 37 Elton Brand	.75	.23
❑ 38 Kobe Bryant	3.00	.90
❑ 39 Shaquille O'Neal	2.00	.60
❑ 40 Rick Fox	.50	.15
❑ 41 Derek Fisher	.75	.23
❑ 42 Stromile Swift	.50	.15
❑ 43 Michael Dickerson	.50	.15
❑ 44 Jason Williams	.50	.15
❑ 45 Alonzo Mourning	.50	.15
❑ 46 Eddie Jones	.75	.23
❑ 47 Anthony Carter	.50	.15
❑ 48 Ray Allen	.75	.23
❑ 49 Glenn Robinson	.75	.23
❑ 50 Sam Cassell	.75	.23
❑ 51 Kevin Garnett	1.50	.45
❑ 52 Terrell Brandon	.50	.15
❑ 53 Wally Szczerbiak	.50	.15
❑ 54 Joe Smith	.50	.15
❑ 55 Kenyon Martin	.75	.23
❑ 56 Keith Van Horn	.75	.23
❑ 57 Jason Kidd	1.25	.35
❑ 58 Latrell Sprewell	.75	.23
❑ 59 Allan Houston	.50	.15
❑ 60 Marcus Camby	.50	.15
❑ 61 Tracy McGrady	2.00	.60
❑ 62 Mike Miller	.75	.23
❑ 63 Grant Hill	.75	.23
❑ 64 Allen Iverson	1.50	.45
❑ 65 Dikembe Mutombo	.50	.15
❑ 66 Aaron McKie	.50	.15
❑ 67 Stephon Marbury	.75	.23
❑ 68 Shawn Marion	.75	.23
❑ 69 Tom Gugliotta	.25	.07
❑ 70 Rasheed Wallace	.75	.23
❑ 71 Damon Stoudamire	.50	.15
❑ 72 Bonzi Wells	.50	.15
❑ 73 Chris Webber	.75	.23
❑ 74 Peja Stojakovic	.75	.23
❑ 75 Mike Bibby	.75	.23
❑ 76 Tim Duncan	1.50	.45
❑ 77 David Robinson	.75	.23
❑ 78 Antonio Daniels	.25	.07
❑ 79 Gary Payton	.75	.23
❑ 80 Rashard Lewis	.50	.15
❑ 81 Desmond Mason	.50	.15
❑ 82 Vince Carter	2.00	.60
❑ 83 Morris Peterson	.50	.15
❑ 84 Antonio Davis	.25	.07
❑ 85 Karl Malone	.75	.23
❑ 86 John Stockton	.75	.23
❑ 87 Donyell Marshall	.50	.15
❑ 88 Richard Hamilton	.50	.15
❑ 89 Courtney Alexander	.50	.15
❑ 90 Michael Jordan	15.00	4.50
❑ 91A Jeff Trepagnier P RC	2.50	.75
❑ 91B Jeff Trepagnier S RC	2.50	.75
❑ 91C Jeff Trepagnier SR RC	2.50	.75
❑ 92A Pau Gasol P RC	10.00	3.00
❑ 92B Pau Gasol S RC	10.00	3.00
❑ 92C Pau Gasol SR RC	10.00	3.00
❑ 93A Will Solomon P RC	2.50	.75
❑ 93B Will Solomon S RC	2.50	.75
❑ 93C Will Solomon SP RC	2.50	.75
❑ 94A Gilbert Arenas P RC	6.00	1.80
❑ 94B Gilbert Arenas S RC	6.00	1.80
❑ 94C Gilbert Arenas SR RC	6.00	1.80
❑ 95A Andrei Kirilenko P RC	10.00	3.00
❑ 95B Andrei Kirilenko S RC	10.00	3.00
❑ 95C Andrei Kirilenko SR RC	10.00	3.00
❑ 96A Jamaal Tinsley P RC	5.00	1.50
❑ 96B Jamaal Tinsley S RC	5.00	1.50
❑ 96C Jamaal Tinsley SR RC	5.00	1.50
❑ 97A Samuel Dalembert P RC	2.50	.75
❑ 97B Samuel Dalembert S RC	2.50	.75
❑ 97C Samuel Dalembert SR RC	2.50	.75
❑ 98A Gerald Wallace P RC	8.00	2.40
❑ 98B Gerald Wallace S RC	8.00	2.40
❑ 98C Gerald Wallace SR RC	8.00	2.40
❑ 99A B.Armstrong P RC	3.00	.90
❑ 99B B.Armstrong S RC	3.00	.90
❑ 99C B.Armstrong SR RC	3.00	.90
❑ 100A Jeryl Sasser P RC	2.50	.75
❑ 100B Jeryl Sasser S RC	2.50	.75
❑ 100C Jeryl Sasser SR RC	2.50	.75
❑ 101A Joseph Forte P RC	6.00	1.80
❑ 101B Joseph Forte S RC	6.00	1.80
❑ 101C Joseph Forte SR RC	6.00	1.80
❑ 102A B.Haywood P RC	3.00	.90
❑ 102B B.Haywood S RC	3.00	.90
❑ 102C B.Haywood SR RC	3.00	.90
❑ 103A Z.Randolph P RC	10.00	3.00
❑ 103B Z.Randolph S RC	10.00	3.00
❑ 103C Z.Randolph SR RC	10.00	3.00
❑ 104A Jason Collins P RC	2.50	.75
❑ 104B Jason Collins S RC	2.50	.75
❑ 104C Jason Collins SR RC	2.50	.75
❑ 105A Michael Bradley P RC	2.50	.75
❑ 105B Michael Bradley S RC	2.50	.75
❑ 105C Michael Bradley SR RC	2.50	.75
❑ 106A Kirk Haston P RC	2.50	.75
❑ 106B Kirk Haston S RC	2.50	.75
❑ 106C Kirk Haston SR RC	2.50	.75
❑ 107A Steven Hunter P RC	2.50	.75
❑ 107B Steven Hunter S RC	2.50	.75
❑ 107C Steven Hunter SR RC	2.50	.75
❑ 108A Troy Murphy P RC	6.00	1.80
❑ 108B Troy Murphy S RC	6.00	1.80
❑ 108C Troy Murphy SR RC	6.00	1.80
❑ 109A R.Jefferson P RC	10.00	3.00
❑ 109B R.Jefferson S RC	10.00	3.00
❑ 109C R.Jefferson SR RC	10.00	3.00
❑ 110A V.Radmanovic P RC	4.00	1.20
❑ 110B V.Radmanovic S RC	4.00	1.20
❑ 110C V.Radmanovic SR RC	4.00	1.20
❑ 111A Kedrick Brown P RC	6.00	1.80
❑ 111B Kedrick Brown S RC	6.00	1.80
❑ 111C Kedrick Brown SR RC	6.00	1.80
❑ 112A Joe Johnson P RC	8.00	2.40
❑ 112B Joe Johnson S RC	8.00	2.40
❑ 112C Joe Johnson SR RC	8.00	2.40
❑ 113A Rodney White P RC	8.00	2.40
❑ 113B Rodney White S RC	8.00	2.40
❑ 113C Rodney White SR RC	8.00	2.40
❑ 114A DeSagana Diop P RC	6.00	1.80
❑ 114B DeSagana Diop S RC	6.00	1.80
❑ 114C DeSagana Diop SR RC	6.00	1.80
❑ 115A Eddie Griffin P RC	8.00	2.40
❑ 115B Eddie Griffin S RC	8.00	2.40
❑ 115C Eddie Griffin SR RC	8.00	2.40
❑ 116A Shane Battier P RC	8.00	2.40
❑ 116B Shane Battier S RC	8.00	2.40
❑ 116C Shane Battier SR RC	8.00	2.40
❑ 117A J.Richardson P RC	15.00	4.50
❑ 117B J.Richardson S RC	15.00	4.50
❑ 117C J.Richardson SR RC	15.00	4.50
❑ 118A Eddy Curry P RC	12.00	3.60
❑ 118B Eddy Curry S RC	12.00	3.60
❑ 118C Eddy Curry SR RC	12.00	3.60
❑ 119A Tyson Chandler P RC	10.00	3.00
❑ 119B Tyson Chandler S RC	10.00	3.00
❑ 119C Tyson Chandler SR RC	10.00	3.00
❑ 120A Kwame Brown P RC	10.00	3.00
❑ 120B Kwame Brown S RC	10.00	3.00
❑ 120C Kwame Brown SR RC	10.00	3.00

2002-03 Upper Deck Ovation

	Nm-Mt	Ex-Mt
COMP.SET w/o SP's (90)	50.00	15.00
COMMON CARD (1-90)	.25	.07
COMMON ROOKIE (100-119)	6.00	1.80
COMMON ROOKIE (120-134)	8.00	2.40
❑ 1 Shareef Abdur-Rahim	.75	.23
❑ 2 Jason Terry	.75	.23
❑ 3 Glenn Robinson	.75	.23
❑ 4 Paul Pierce	.75	.23
❑ 5 Antoine Walker	.75	.23

Card	Nm-Mt	Ex-Mt
❑ 6 Vin Baker	.50	.15
❑ 7 Jalen Rose	.75	.23
❑ 8 Tyson Chandler	.75	.23
❑ 9 Eddy Curry	.75	.23
❑ 10 Marcus Fizer	.50	.15
❑ 11 Darius Miles	.75	.23
❑ 12 Lamond Murray	.25	.07
❑ 13 Chris Mihm	.25	.07
❑ 14 Dirk Nowitzki	1.25	.35
❑ 15 Michael Finley	.75	.23
❑ 16 Steve Nash	.75	.23
❑ 17 Marcus Camby	.50	.15
❑ 18 Juwan Howard	.50	.15
❑ 19 James Posey	.50	.15
❑ 20 Jerry Stackhouse	.75	.23
❑ 21 Ben Wallace	.75	.23
❑ 22 Clifford Robinson	.25	.07
❑ 23 Antawn Jamison	.75	.23
❑ 24 Jason Richardson	.75	.23
❑ 25 Gilbert Arenas	.75	.23
❑ 26 Steve Francis	.75	.23
❑ 27 Eddie Griffin	.50	.15
❑ 28 Cuttino Mobley	.50	.15
❑ 29 Jermaine O'Neal	.75	.23
❑ 30 Reggie Miller	.75	.23
❑ 31 Jamaal Tinsley	.75	.23
❑ 32 Elton Brand	.75	.23
❑ 33 Andre Miller	.50	.15
❑ 34 Lamar Odom	.75	.23
❑ 35 Kobe Bryant	3.00	.90
❑ 36 Shaquille O'Neal	2.00	.60
❑ 37 Derek Fisher	.75	.23
❑ 38 Devean George	.50	.15
❑ 39 Pau Gasol	.75	.23
❑ 40 Shane Battier	.75	.23
❑ 41 Jason Williams	.50	.15
❑ 42 Alonzo Mourning	.50	.15
❑ 43 Eddie Jones	.75	.23
❑ 44 Brian Grant	.50	.15
❑ 45 Ray Allen	.75	.23
❑ 46 Tim Thomas	.50	.15
❑ 47 Sam Cassell	.75	.23
❑ 48 Kevin Garnett	1.50	.45
❑ 49 Wally Szczerbiak	.50	.15
❑ 50 Terrell Brandon	.50	.15
❑ 51 Jason Kidd	1.25	.35
❑ 52 Kenyon Martin	.75	.23
❑ 53 Richard Jefferson	.50	.15
❑ 54 Jamal Mashburn	.50	.15
❑ 55 Baron Davis	.75	.23
❑ 56 David Wesley	.25	.07
❑ 57 Latrell Sprewell	.75	.23
❑ 58 Allan Houston	.50	.15
❑ 59 Antonio McDyess	.50	.15
❑ 60 Tracy McGrady	2.00	.60
❑ 61 Mike Miller	.75	.23
❑ 62 Darrell Armstrong	.25	.07
❑ 63 Allen Iverson	1.50	.45
❑ 64 Eric Snow	.50	.15
❑ 65 Aaron McKie	.50	.15
❑ 66 Stephon Marbury	.75	.23
❑ 67 Shawn Marion	.75	.23
❑ 68 Anfernee Hardaway	.75	.23
❑ 69 Rasheed Wallace	.75	.23
❑ 70 Bonzi Wells	.50	.15
❑ 71 Scottie Pippen	1.25	.35
❑ 72 Chris Webber	.75	.23
❑ 73 Mike Bibby	.75	.23
❑ 74 Peja Stojakovic	.75	.23
❑ 75 Tim Duncan	1.50	.45
❑ 76 David Robinson	.75	.23
❑ 77 Tony Parker	.75	.23
❑ 78 Gary Payton	.75	.23
❑ 79 Rashard Lewis	.50	.15
❑ 80 Desmond Mason	.50	.15
❑ 81 Vince Carter	2.00	.60
❑ 82 Morris Peterson	.50	.15
❑ 83 Antonio Davis	.25	.07
❑ 84 Karl Malone	.75	.23
❑ 85 John Stockton	.75	.23
❑ 86 Andrei Kirilenko	.75	.23
❑ 87 Michael Jordan	8.00	2.40
❑ 88 Richard Hamilton	.50	.15
❑ 89 Chris Whitney	.25	.07
❑ 90 Kwame Brown	.50	.15
❑ 91 Kevin Garnett/2999	8.00	2.40
❑ 92 Kevin Garnett/2999	8.00	2.40
❑ 93 Kevin Garnett/2999	8.00	2.40
❑ 94 Kobe Bryant/1999	10.00	3.00
❑ 95 Kobe Bryant/1999	10.00	3.00
❑ 96 Kobe Bryant/1999	10.00	3.00
❑ 97 Michael Jordan/499	50.00	15.00
❑ 98 Michael Jordan/499	50.00	15.00
❑ 99 Michael Jordan/499	50.00	15.00
❑ 100 Fred Jones RC	8.00	2.40
❑ 101 Jamal Sampson RC	6.00	1.80
❑ 102 John Salmons RC	6.00	1.80
❑ 103 Jiri Welsch RC	6.00	1.80
❑ 104 Dan Gadzuric RC	6.00	1.80
❑ 105 Vincent Yarbrough RC	6.00	1.80
❑ 106 Juan Dixon RC	12.00	3.60
❑ 107 Efthimios Rentzias RC	6.00	1.80
❑ 108 Predrag Savovic RC	6.00	1.80
❑ 109 Rod Grizzard RC	6.00	1.80
❑ 110 Bostjan Nachbar RC	6.00	1.80
❑ 111 Marko Jaric RC	6.00	1.80
❑ 112 Tayshaun Prince RC	10.00	3.00
❑ 113 Chris Jefferies RC	6.00	1.80
❑ 114 Casey Jacobsen RC	6.00	1.80
❑ 115 Carlos Boozer RC	15.00	4.50
❑ 116 Frank Williams RC	8.00	2.40
❑ 117 Dan Dickau RC	8.00	2.40
❑ 118 Ryan Humphrey RC	6.00	1.80
❑ 119 Melvin Ely RC	6.00	1.80
❑ 120 Nene Hilario RC	8.00	2.40
❑ 121 Nikoloz Tskitishvili RC	8.00	2.40
❑ 122 Marcus Haislip RC	8.00	2.40
❑ 123 Qyntel Woods RC	8.00	2.40
❑ 124 Caron Butler RC	20.00	6.00
❑ 125 Amare Stoudemire RC	40.00	12.00
❑ 126 Curtis Borchardt RC	8.00	2.40
❑ 127 Chris Wilcox RC	12.00	3.60
❑ 128 Drew Gooden RC	20.00	6.00
❑ 129 Jared Jeffries RC	10.00	3.00
❑ 130 Kareem Rush RC	12.00	3.60
❑ 131 Mike Dunleavy RC	10.00	3.00
❑ 132 Yao Ming RC	50.00	15.00
❑ 133 DaJuan Wagner RC	15.00	4.50
❑ 134 Jay Williams RC	12.00	3.60

2001-02 Upper Deck Playmakers

	Nm-Mt	Ex-Mt
COMPLETE SET (145)	200.00	60.00
COMP.SET w/o SP's (100)	40.00	12.00
COMMON CARD (1-100)	.25	.07
COMMON ROOKIE (101-130)	3.00	.90
COMMON ROOKIE (131-145)	6.00	1.80
❑ 1 Shareef Abdur-Rahim	.75	.23
❑ 2 Dion Glover	.25	.07
❑ 3 Jason Terry	.75	.23
❑ 4 Toni Kukoc	.50	.15
❑ 5 Theo Ratliff	.50	.15
❑ 6 Paul Pierce	.75	.23
❑ 7 Antoine Walker	.75	.23
❑ 8 Baron Davis	.75	.23
❑ 9 Jamal Mashburn	.50	.15
❑ 10 Ron Mercer	.50	.15
❑ 11 Brad Miller	.75	.23
❑ 12 Marcus Fizer	.50	.15
❑ 13 Andre Miller	.50	.15
❑ 14 Chris Mihm	.50	.15
❑ 15 Lamond Murray	.25	.07
❑ 16 Michael Finley	.75	.23
❑ 17 Dirk Nowitzki	1.25	.35
❑ 18 Steve Nash	.75	.23
❑ 19 Tim Hardaway	.50	.15
❑ 20 Antonio McDyess	.50	.15
❑ 21 Nick Van Exel	.75	.23
❑ 22 Raef LaFrentz	.50	.15
❑ 23 Jerry Stackhouse	.75	.23
❑ 24 Clifford Robinson	.25	.07
❑ 25 Ben Wallace	.75	.23
❑ 26 Antawn Jamison	.75	.23
❑ 27 Larry Hughes	.50	.15
❑ 28 Danny Fortson	.25	.07
❑ 29 Steve Francis	.75	.23
❑ 30 Cuttino Mobley	.50	.15
❑ 31 Kenny Thomas	.25	.07
❑ 32 Jalen Rose	.75	.23
❑ 33 Reggie Miller	.75	.23
❑ 34 Jermaine O'Neal	.75	.23
❑ 35 Darius Miles	.75	.23
❑ 36 Elton Brand	.75	.23
❑ 37 Corey Maggette	.50	.15
❑ 38 Quentin Richardson	.50	.15
❑ 39 Kobe Bryant	3.00	.90
❑ 40 Shaquille O'Neal	2.00	.60
❑ 41 Mitch Richmond	.50	.15
❑ 42 Derek Fisher	.75	.23
❑ 43 Lindsey Hunter	.25	.07
❑ 44 Stromile Swift	.50	.15
❑ 45 Jason Williams	.50	.15
❑ 46 Michael Dickerson	.50	.15
❑ 47 Eddie Jones	.75	.23
❑ 48 Alonzo Mourning	.50	.15
❑ 49 Anthony Carter	.50	.15
❑ 50 Brian Grant	.50	.15
❑ 51 Glenn Robinson	.75	.23
❑ 52 Ray Allen	.75	.23
❑ 53 Sam Cassell	.75	.23
❑ 54 Tim Thomas	.50	.15
❑ 55 Anthony Mason	.50	.15
❑ 56 Kevin Garnett	1.50	.45
❑ 57 Wally Szczerbiak	.50	.15
❑ 58 Terrell Brandon	.50	.15
❑ 59 Joe Smith	.50	.15
❑ 60 Jason Kidd	1.25	.35
❑ 61 Kenyon Martin	.75	.23
❑ 62 Allan Houston	.50	.15
❑ 63 Latrell Sprewell	.75	.23
❑ 64 Marcus Camby	.50	.15
❑ 65 Mark Jackson	.50	.15
❑ 66 Kurt Thomas	.50	.15
❑ 67 Tracy McGrady	2.00	.60
❑ 68 Grant Hill	.75	.23
❑ 69 Mike Miller	.75	.23
❑ 70 Allen Iverson	1.50	.45
❑ 71 Dikembe Mutombo	.50	.15
❑ 72 Aaron McKie	.50	.15
❑ 73 Stephon Marbury	.75	.23
❑ 74 Shawn Marion	.75	.23
❑ 75 Anfernee Hardaway	.75	.23
❑ 76 Tom Gugliotta	.25	.07
❑ 77 Rasheed Wallace	.75	.23
❑ 78 Derek Anderson	.50	.15
❑ 79 Bonzi Wells	.50	.15
❑ 80 Chris Webber	.75	.23
❑ 81 Peja Stojakovic	.75	.23
❑ 82 Mike Bibby	.75	.23
❑ 83 Doug Christie	.50	.15
❑ 84 Tim Duncan	1.50	.45
❑ 85 David Robinson	.75	.23
❑ 86 Antonio Daniels	.25	.07
❑ 87 Steve Smith	.50	.15
❑ 88 Gary Payton	.75	.23
❑ 89 Rashard Lewis	.50	.15
❑ 90 Desmond Mason	.50	.15
❑ 91 Vince Carter	2.00	.60
❑ 92 Morris Peterson	.50	.15
❑ 93 Antonio Davis	.25	.07
❑ 94 Hakeem Olajuwon	.75	.23
❑ 95 Karl Malone	.75	.23
❑ 96 John Stockton	.75	.23
❑ 97 Donyell Marshall	.50	.15
❑ 98 Michael Jordan	12.00	3.60
❑ 99 Courtney Alexander	.50	.15
❑ 100 Richard Hamilton	.50	.15
❑ 101 Jeryl Sasser RC	3.00	.90

	Nm-Mt	Ex-Mt
❑ 102 DeSagana Diop RC	3.00	.90
❑ 103 Alvin Jones RC	3.00	.90
❑ 104 Gerald Wallace RC	6.00	1.80
❑ 105 Kenny Satterfield RC	3.00	.90
❑ 106 Ruben Boumtje-Boumtje RC	3.00	.90
❑ 107 Brian Scalabrine RC	3.00	.90
❑ 108 Oscar Torres RC	3.00	.90
❑ 109 Jarron Collins RC	3.00	.90
❑ 110 Jeff Trepagnier RC	3.00	.90
❑ 111 Brendan Haywood RC	4.00	1.20
❑ 112 Vladimir Radmanovic RC	3.00	.90
❑ 113 Loren Woods RC	3.00	.90
❑ 114 Terence Morris RC	3.00	.90
❑ 115 Kirk Haston RC	3.00	.90
❑ 116 Earl Watson RC	3.00	.90
❑ 117 Brandon Armstrong RC	3.00	.90
❑ 118 Zach Randolph RC	8.00	2.40
❑ 119 Bobby Simmons RC	3.00	.90
❑ 120 Alton Ford RC	3.00	.90
❑ 121 Trenton Hassell RC	4.00	1.20
❑ 122 Damone Brown RC	3.00	.90
❑ 123 Michael Bradley RC	3.00	.90
❑ 124 Zeljko Rebraca RC	3.00	.90
❑ 125 Jason Collins RC	3.00	.90
❑ 126 Samuel Dalembert RC	3.00	.90
❑ 127 Gilbert Arenas RC	8.00	2.40
❑ 128 Willie Solomon RC	3.00	.90
❑ 129 Joseph Forte RC	6.00	1.80
❑ 130 Steven Hunter RC	3.00	.90
❑ 131 Andrei Kirilenko RC	10.00	3.00
❑ 132 Eddy Curry RC	10.00	3.00
❑ 133 Tony Parker RC	15.00	4.50
❑ 134 Troy Murphy RC	6.00	1.80
❑ 135 Shane Battier RC	6.00	1.80
❑ 136 Kedrick Brown RC	6.00	1.80
❑ 137 Tyson Chandler RC	10.00	3.00
❑ 138 Jamaal Tinsley RC	6.00	1.80
❑ 139 Pau Gasol RC	12.00	3.60
❑ 140 Joe Johnson RC	12.00	3.60
❑ 141 Jason Richardson RC	12.00	3.60
❑ 142 Richard Jefferson RC	6.00	1.80
❑ 143 Eddie Griffin RC	6.00	1.80
❑ 144 Rodney White RC	6.00	1.80
❑ 145 Kwame Brown RC	8.00	2.40

2000-01 Upper Deck Pros and Prospects

	Nm-Mt	Ex-Mt
COMPLETE SET (120)	250.00	75.00
COMP.SET w/o RC (90)	25.00	7.50
COMMON CARD (1-90)	.25	.07
COMMON ROOKIE (91-120)	6.00	1.80
❑ 1 Dikembe Mutombo	.50	.15
❑ 2 Alan Henderson	.25	.07
❑ 3 Jim Jackson	.25	.07
❑ 4 Paul Pierce	.75	.23
❑ 5 Kenny Anderson	.50	.15
❑ 6 Antoine Walker	.75	.23
❑ 7 Baron Davis	.75	.23
❑ 8 Derrick Coleman	.25	.07
❑ 9 David Wesley	.25	.07
❑ 10 Elton Brand	.75	.23
❑ 11 Ron Artest	.50	.15
❑ 12 Hersey Hawkins	.25	.07
❑ 13 Andre Miller	.50	.15
❑ 14 Lamond Murray	.25	.07
❑ 15 Shawn Kemp	.50	.15
❑ 16 Michael Finley	.75	.23
❑ 17 Dirk Nowitzki	1.25	.35
❑ 18 Cedric Ceballos	.25	.07
❑ 19 Antonio McDyess	.50	.15
❑ 20 Nick Van Exel	.75	.23
❑ 21 Raef LaFrentz	.50	.15
❑ 22 Christian Laettner	.50	.15
❑ 23 Jerry Stackhouse	.75	.23
❑ 24 Lindsey Hunter	.25	.07
❑ 25 Antawn Jamison	.75	.23
❑ 26 Larry Hughes	.50	.15
❑ 27 Chris Mills	.25	.07
❑ 28 Steve Francis	.75	.23
❑ 29 Hakeem Olajuwon	.75	.23
❑ 30 Shandon Anderson	.25	.07
❑ 31 Reggie Miller	.75	.23
❑ 32 Jonathan Bender	.50	.15
❑ 33 Jalen Rose	.75	.23
❑ 34 Lamar Odom	.75	.23
❑ 35 Michael Olowokandi	.25	.07
❑ 36 Tyrone Nesby	.25	.07
❑ 37 Kobe Bryant	3.00	.90
❑ 38 Shaquille O'Neal	2.00	.60
❑ 39 Ron Harper	.50	.15
❑ 40 Robert Horry	.50	.15
❑ 41 Alonzo Mourning	.50	.15
❑ 42 P.J. Brown	.25	.07
❑ 43 Jamal Mashburn	.50	.15
❑ 44 Ray Allen	.75	.23
❑ 45 Glenn Robinson	.75	.23
❑ 46 Sam Cassell	.75	.23
❑ 47 Kevin Garnett	1.50	.45
❑ 48 Wally Szczerbiak	.50	.15
❑ 49 Terrell Brandon	.50	.15
❑ 50 William Avery	.25	.07
❑ 51 Stephon Marbury	.75	.23
❑ 52 Keith Van Horn	.75	.23
❑ 53 Kerry Kittles	.25	.07
❑ 54 Latrell Sprewell	.75	.23
❑ 55 Allan Houston	.50	.15
❑ 56 Patrick Ewing	.75	.23
❑ 57 Darrell Armstrong	.25	.07
❑ 58 Pat Garrity	.25	.07
❑ 59 Michael Doleac	.25	.07
❑ 60 Allen Iverson	1.50	.45
❑ 61 Theo Ratliff	.50	.15
❑ 62 Tyrone Hill	.25	.07
❑ 63 Jason Kidd	1.25	.35
❑ 64 Anfernee Hardaway	.75	.23
❑ 65 Shawn Marion	.75	.23
❑ 66 Scottie Pippen	1.25	.35
❑ 67 Rasheed Wallace	.75	.23
❑ 68 Damon Stoudamire	.50	.15
❑ 69 Bonzi Wells	.50	.15
❑ 70 Chris Webber	.75	.23
❑ 71 Peja Stojakovic	.75	.23
❑ 72 Jason Williams	.50	.15
❑ 73 Tim Duncan	1.50	.45
❑ 74 David Robinson	.75	.23
❑ 75 Terry Porter	.25	.07
❑ 76 Gary Payton	.75	.23
❑ 77 Rashard Lewis	.50	.15
❑ 78 Vin Baker	.50	.15
❑ 79 Vince Carter	2.00	.60
❑ 80 Doug Christie	.50	.15
❑ 81 Antonio Davis	.25	.07
❑ 82 Karl Malone	.75	.23
❑ 83 John Stockton	.75	.23
❑ 84 Bryon Russell	.25	.07
❑ 85 Shareef Abdur-Rahim	.75	.23
❑ 86 Mike Bibby	.75	.23
❑ 87 Michael Dickerson	.50	.15
❑ 88 Mitch Richmond	.50	.15
❑ 89 Richard Hamilton	.50	.15
❑ 90 Juwan Howard	.50	.15
❑ 91 Kenyon Martin JSY RC	40.00	12.00
❑ 92 Stromile Swift RC	10.00	3.00
❑ 93 Darius Miles RC	15.00	4.50
❑ 94 Marcus Fizer JSY RC	6.00	1.80
❑ 95 Mike Miller RC	15.00	4.50
❑ 96 DerMarr Johnson RC	6.00	1.80
❑ 97 Chris Mihm RC	6.00	1.80
❑ 98 Chris Porter RC	6.00	1.80
❑ 99 Joel Przybilla RC	6.00	1.80
❑ 100 Keyon Dooling RC	6.00	1.80
❑ 101 Jerome Moiso RC	6.00	1.80
❑ 102 Etan Thomas RC	6.00	1.80
❑ 103 Courtney Alexander RC	8.00	2.40
❑ 104 Mateen Cleaves RC	6.00	1.80
❑ 105 Jason Collier RC	6.00	1.80
❑ 106 Dan Langhi RC	6.00	1.80
❑ 107 Desmond Mason RC	6.00	1.80
❑ 108 Quentin Richardson RC	12.00	3.60
❑ 109 Jamaal Magloire RC	6.00	1.80
❑ 110 Speedy Claxton RC	6.00	1.80
❑ 111 Morris Peterson RC	10.00	3.00
❑ 112 Donnell Harvey RC	6.00	1.80
❑ 113 Hanno Mottola RC	6.00	1.80
❑ 114 Mamadou N'diaye RC	6.00	1.80
❑ 115 Erick Barkley RC	6.00	1.80
❑ 116 Mark Madsen RC	6.00	1.80
❑ 117 A.J. Guyton RC	6.00	1.80
❑ 118 Khalid El-Amin RC	6.00	1.80
❑ 119 Lavor Postell RC	6.00	1.80
❑ 120 Eddie House RC	6.00	1.80

2001-02 Upper Deck Pros and Prospects

	Nm-Mt	Ex-Mt
COMP.SET w/o SP's (90)	25.00	7.50
COMMON CARD (1-90)	.25	.07
COMMON ROOKIE (91-125)	6.00	1.80
COMMON ROOKIE (126-131)	30.00	9.00
❑ 1 Jason Terry	.75	.23
❑ 2 Toni Kukoc	.50	.15
❑ 3 DerMarr Johnson	.50	.15
❑ 4 Paul Pierce	.75	.23
❑ 5 Antoine Walker	.75	.23
❑ 6 Kenny Anderson	.50	.15
❑ 7 Jamal Mashburn	.50	.15
❑ 8 Baron Davis	.75	.23
❑ 9 David Wesley	.25	.07
❑ 10 Elton Brand	.75	.23
❑ 11 Ron Mercer	.50	.15
❑ 12 Jamal Crawford	.50	.15
❑ 13 Andre Miller	.50	.15
❑ 14 Lamond Murray	.25	.07
❑ 15 Chris Mihm	.50	.15
❑ 16 Michael Finley	.75	.23
❑ 17 Wang ZhiZHi	.75	.23
❑ 18 Dirk Nowitzki	1.25	.35
❑ 19 Antonio McDyess	.50	.15
❑ 20 Nick Van Exel	.75	.23
❑ 21 Raef LaFrentz	.50	.15
❑ 22 Jerry Stackhouse	.75	.23
❑ 23 Joe Smith	.50	.15
❑ 24 Mateen Cleaves	.50	.15
❑ 25 Antawn Jamison	.75	.23
❑ 26 Marc Jackson	.50	.15
❑ 27 Larry Hughes	.50	.15
❑ 28 Steve Francis	.75	.23
❑ 29 Maurice Taylor	.50	.15
❑ 30 Hakeem Olajuwon	.75	.23
❑ 31 Reggie Miller	.75	.23
❑ 32 Jermaine O'Neal	.75	.23
❑ 33 Jalen Rose	.75	.23
❑ 34 Lamar Odom	.75	.23
❑ 35 Darius Miles	.75	.23
❑ 36 Quentin Richardson	.50	.15
❑ 37 Kobe Bryant	3.00	.90
❑ 38 Shaquille O'Neal	2.00	.60
❑ 39 Derek Fisher	.75	.23
❑ 40 Rick Fox	.50	.15

- 41 Alonzo Mourning .50 .15
- 42 Eddie Jones .75 .23
- 43 Tim Hardaway .50 .15
- 44 Brian Grant .50 .15
- 45 Ray Allen .75 .23
- 46 Glenn Robinson .75 .23
- 47 Tim Thomas .50 .15
- 48 Kevin Garnett 1.50 .45
- 49 Terrell Brandon .50 .15
- 50 Wally Szczerbiak .50 .15
- 51 Chauncey Billups .50 .15
- 52 Stephon Marbury .75 .23
- 53 Kenyon Martin .75 .23
- 54 Keith Van Horn .75 .23
- 55 Allan Houston .50 .15
- 56 Latrell Sprewell .75 .23
- 57 Glen Rice .50 .15
- 58 Tracy McGrady 2.00 .60
- 59 Mike Miller .75 .23
- 60 Darrell Armstrong .25 .07
- 61 Allen Iverson 1.50 .45
- 62 Dikembe Mutombo .50 .15
- 63 Aaron McKie .50 .15
- 64 Jason Kidd 1.25 .35
- 65 Shawn Marion .75 .23
- 66 Tom Gugliotta .25 .07
- 67 Rasheed Wallace .75 .23
- 68 Damon Stoudamire .50 .15
- 69 Scottie Pippen 1.25 .35
- 70 Peja Stojakovic .75 .23
- 71 Jason Williams .50 .15
- 72 Chris Webber .75 .23
- 73 Tim Duncan 1.50 .45
- 74 Derek Anderson .50 .15
- 75 David Robinson .75 .23
- 76 Gary Payton .75 .23
- 77 Rashard Lewis .50 .15
- 78 Desmond Mason .50 .15
- 79 Vince Carter 2.00 .60
- 80 Morris Peterson .50 .15
- 81 Antonio Davis .25 .07
- 82 Karl Malone .75 .23
- 83 John Stockton .75 .23
- 84 Donyell Marshall .50 .15
- 85 Shareef Abdur-Rahim .75 .23
- 86 Mike Bibby .75 .23
- 87 Stromile Swift .50 .15
- 88 Richard Hamilton .50 .15
- 89 Courtney Alexander .50 .15
- 90 Chris Whitney .25 .07
- 91 Ruben Boumtje-Boumtje RC 6.00 1.80
- 92 Sean Lampley RC 6.00 1.80
- 93 Ken Johnson RC 8.00 2.40
- 94 Earl Watson RC 8.00 2.40
- 95 Jamaal Tinsley RC 15.00 4.50
- 96 Damone Brown RC 8.00 2.40
- 97 Michael Wright RC 8.00 2.40
- 98 Alvin Jones RC 6.00 1.80
- 99 Omar Cook RC 8.00 2.40
- 100 Jarron Collins RC 10.00 3.00
- 101 Brian Scalabrine RC 8.00 2.40
- 102 Jeryl Sasser RC 12.00 3.60
- 103 Samuel Dalembert RC 6.00 1.80
- 104 Terence Morris RC 8.00 2.40
- 105 Will Solomon RC 8.00 2.40
- 106 Kirk Haston RC 12.00 3.60
- 107 Richard Jefferson RC 40.00 12.00
- 108 Jason Collins RC 10.00 3.00
- 109 Troy Murphy RC 20.00 6.00
- 110 Gerald Wallace RC 20.00 6.00
- 111 Shane Battier RC 15.00 4.50
- 112 Jeff Trepagnier RC 12.00 3.60
- 113 Brandon Armstrong RC 10.00 3.00
- 114 Loren Woods RC 6.00 1.80
- 115 Joseph Forte RC 12.00 3.60
- 116 Michael Bradley RC 6.00 1.80
- 117 Joe Johnson RC 15.00 4.50
- 118 Gilbert Arenas RC 60.00 18.00
- 119 Ousmane Cisse RC 8.00 2.40
- 120 Kenny Satterfield RC 6.00 1.80
- 121 Vladimir Radmanovic RC 10.00 3.00
- 122 DeSagana Diop RC 6.00 1.80
- 123 Kedrick Brown RC 6.00 1.80
- 124 Trenton Hassell RC 15.00 4.50
- 125 Steven Hunter RC 8.00 2.40
- 126 Rodney White RC 30.00 9.00
- 127 Eddy Curry RC 50.00 15.00
- 128 Jason Richardson RC 60.00 18.00
- 129 Tyson Chandler RC 30.00 9.00
- 130 Eddie Griffin RC 30.00 9.00
- 131 Kwame Brown RC 30.00 9.00

1999-00 Upper Deck Retro

	Nm-Mt	Ex-Mt
COMPLETE SET (110)	40.00	12.00
COMMON CARD (1-95)	.20	.06
COMMON ROOKIE (96-110)	.50	.15

- 1 Michael Jordan 4.00 1.20
- 2 John Havlicek .75 .23
- 3 Antawn Jamison 1.00 .30
- 4 Chris Webber .60 .18
- 5 Maurice Taylor .40 .12
- 6 Kevin Garnett 1.25 .35
- 7 Walter Davis .20 .06
- 8 Kobe Bryant 2.50 .75
- 9 Tim Duncan 1.25 .35
- 10 Karl Malone .60 .18
- 11 Larry Bird 2.00 .60
- 12 Juwan Howard .40 .12
- 13 Bill Walton .60 .18
- 14 Bob Cousy .60 .18
- 15 Dave DeBusschere .20 .06
- 16 Toni Kukoc .40 .12
- 17 Allan Houston .40 .12
- 18 Grant Hill .60 .18
- 19 Rik Smits .40 .12
- 20 Glenn Robinson .60 .18
- 21 Dave Cowens .40 .12
- 22 Isaac Austin .20 .06
- 23 Derek Anderson .40 .12
- 24 Tracy McGrady 1.50 .45
- 25 Nate Thurmond .20 .06
- 26 Dikembe Mutombo .40 .12
- 27 Oscar Robertson .75 .23
- 28 Antonio McDyess .40 .12
- 29 Jamaal Wilkes .20 .06
- 30 Eddie Jones .60 .18
- 31 Nick Van Exel .60 .18
- 32 Reggie Miller .60 .18
- 33 David Thompson .20 .06
- 34 Ray Allen .60 .18
- 35 Anfernee Hardaway .60 .18
- 36 Brian Grant .40 .12
- 37 Allen Iverson 1.25 .35
- 38 Vince Carter 1.50 .45
- 39 Mitch Richmond .40 .12
- 40 Kareem Abdul-Jabbar 1.00 .30
- 41 Alonzo Mourning .40 .12
- 42 Jonathan Bender RC .75 .23
- 43 Scottie Pippen 1.00 .30
- 44 George Gervin .60 .18
- 45 Shawn Kemp .40 .12
- 46 Dave Bing .20 .06
- 47 John Starks .40 .12
- 48 Earl Monroe .60 .18
- 49 Stephon Marbury .60 .18
- 50 Cedric Maxwell .20 .06
- 51 Tom Gugliotta .20 .06
- 52 David Robinson .60 .18
- 53 Shareef Abdur-Rahim .60 .18
- 54 Elvin Hayes .40 .12
- 55 Wilt Chamberlain 1.00 .30
- 56 Willis Reed .40 .12
- 57 Kevin McHale .60 .18
- 58 Elden Campbell .20 .06
- 59 Steve Smith .40 .12
- 60 Brent Barry .40 .12
- 61 Jerry Stackhouse .60 .18
- 62 Otis Birdsong .20 .06
- 63 Michael Olowokandi .40 .12
- 64 Joe Smith .40 .12
- 65 Tim Thomas .40 .12
- 66 Rick Barry .40 .12
- 67 Jason Williams .60 .18
- 68 Julius Erving 1.00 .30
- 69 John Stockton .60 .18
- 70 Cal Bowdler RC .60 .18
- 71 Nate Archibald .60 .18
- 72 Elgin Baylor .60 .18
- 73 Ron Mercer .40 .12
- 74 Damon Stoudamire .40 .12
- 75 Jerry West .60 .18
- 76 Michael Finley .60 .18
- 77 Charles Barkley .75 .23
- 78 Shaquille O'Neal 1.50 .45
- 79 Paul Pierce .60 .18
- 80 Keith Van Horn .60 .18
- 81 Jason Kidd 1.00 .30
- 82 Gary Payton .60 .18
- 83 James Worthy .60 .18
- 84 Mike Bibby .60 .18
- 85 Bill Russell 1.00 .30
- 86 Wes Unseld .20 .06
- 87 Robert Parish .60 .18
- 88 Walt Frazier .60 .18
- 89 Antoine Walker .60 .18
- 90 Steve Nash .60 .18
- 91 Moses Malone .60 .18
- 92 Hakeem Olajuwon .60 .18
- 93 Tim Hardaway .40 .12
- 94 Patrick Ewing .60 .18
- 95 Vin Baker .40 .12
- 96 Trajan Langdon RC .60 .18
- 97 Ron Artest RC 1.00 .30
- 98 James Posey RC 1.00 .30
- 99 Shawn Marion RC 2.00 .60
- 100 Jumaine Jones RC .75 .23
- 101 William Avery RC .60 .18
- 102 Corey Maggette RC 1.50 .45
- 103 Andre Miller RC 1.50 .45
- 104 Jason Terry RC 1.25 .35
- 105 Wally Szczerbiak RC 1.50 .45
- 106 Richard Hamilton RC 1.50 .45
- 107 Elton Brand RC 2.00 .60
- 108 Baron Davis RC 1.50 .45
- 109 Steve Francis RC 2.50 .75
- 110 Lamar Odom RC 1.50 .45

2003-04 Upper Deck Rookie Exclusives

	Nm-Mt	Ex-Mt
COMPLETE SET (60)	30.00	9.00
COMMON ROOKIE (1-30)	1.00	.30
COMMON CARD (31-60)	.20	.06

- 1 LeBron James RC 10.00 3.00
- 2 Darko Milicic RC 1.50 .45
- 3 Carmelo Anthony RC 5.00 1.50
- 4 Chris Bosh RC 2.00 .60
- 5 Dwyane Wade RC 2.50 .75

Card		
❑ 6 Chris Kaman RC	1.00	.30
❑ 7 Jarvis Hayes RC	1.00	.30
❑ 8 Mickael Pietrus RC	1.00	.30
❑ 9 Marcus Banks RC	1.00	.30
❑ 10 Luke Ridnour RC	1.25	.35
❑ 11 Reece Gaines RC	1.00	.30
❑ 12 Troy Bell RC	1.00	.30
❑ 13 Zarko Cabarkapa RC	1.00	.30
❑ 14 David West RC	1.00	.30
❑ 15 Aleksandar Pavlovic RC	1.00	.30
❑ 16 Dahntay Jones RC	1.00	.30
❑ 17 Boris Diaw RC	1.00	.30
❑ 18 Zoran Planinic RC	1.00	.30
❑ 19 Travis Outlaw RC	1.00	.30
❑ 20 Brian Cook RC	1.00	.30
❑ 21 Ndudi Ebi RC	1.00	.30
❑ 22 Kendrick Perkins RC	1.00	.30
❑ 23 Leandro Barbosa RC	1.00	.30
❑ 24 Josh Howard RC	1.25	.35
❑ 25 Maciej Lampe RC	1.00	.30
❑ 26 Jason Kapono RC	1.00	.30
❑ 27 Luke Walton RC	1.25	.35
❑ 28 Travis Hansen RC	1.00	.30
❑ 29 Steve Blake RC	1.00	.30
❑ 30 Slavko Vranes RC	1.00	.30
❑ 31 Darius Miles	1.00	.30
❑ 32 Tony Parker	1.00	.30
❑ 33 Chauncey Billups	1.00	.30
❑ 34 Carlos Boozer	1.00	.30
❑ 35 Richard Hamilton	1.00	.30
❑ 36 Jamaal Tinsley	1.00	.30
❑ 37 Tracy McGrady	1.50	.45
❑ 38 Manu Ginobili	1.00	.30
❑ 39 Andre Miller	1.00	.30
❑ 40 Richard Jefferson	1.00	.30
❑ 41 Paul Pierce	1.00	.30
❑ 42 Peja Stojakovic	1.00	.30
❑ 43 Jason Richardson	1.00	.30
❑ 44 Shawn Marion	1.00	.30
❑ 45 Antawn Jamison	1.00	.30
❑ 46 Reggie Evans	1.00	.30
❑ 47 Earl Boykins	1.00	.30
❑ 48 Corey Maggette	1.00	.30
❑ 49 Cuttino Mobley	1.00	.30
❑ 50 Shane Battier	1.00	.30
❑ 51 Shareef Abdur-Rahim	1.00	.30
❑ 52 Chris Wilcox	1.00	.30
❑ 53 Steve Francis	1.00	.30
❑ 54 Mike Bibby	1.00	.30
❑ 55 Morris Peterson	1.00	.30
❑ 56 Nene	1.00	.30
❑ 57 Juan Dixon	1.00	.30
❑ 58 Yao Ming	1.50	.45
❑ 59 Kobe Bryant	2.50	.75
❑ 60 Michael Jordan	5.00	1.50

2000-01 Upper Deck Slam

	Nm-Mt	Ex-Mt
COMPLETE SET w/o RC (60)	20.00	6.00
COMMON CARD (1-60)	.25	.07
COMMON RC/2500 (61-100)	1.25	.35
❑ 1 Dikembe Mutombo	.50	.15
❑ 2 Jim Jackson	.25	.07
❑ 3 Paul Pierce	.75	.23
❑ 4 Antoine Walker	.75	.23
❑ 5 Eddie Jones	.75	.23
❑ 6 Baron Davis	.75	.23
❑ 7 Derrick Coleman	.25	.07
❑ 8 Elton Brand	.75	.23
❑ 9 Ron Artest	.50	.15
❑ 10 Andre Miller	.50	.15
❑ 11 Shawn Kemp	.50	.15
❑ 12 Michael Finley	.75	.23
❑ 13 Dirk Nowitzki	1.25	.35
❑ 14 Antonio McDyess	.50	.15
❑ 15 James Posey	.50	.15
❑ 16 Jerry Stackhouse	.75	.23
❑ 17 Jerome Williams	.25	.07
❑ 18 Larry Hughes	.50	.15
❑ 19 Antawn Jamison	.75	.23
❑ 20 Steve Francis	.75	.23
❑ 21 Hakeem Olajuwon	.75	.23
❑ 22 Reggie Miller	.75	.23
❑ 23 Jalen Rose	.75	.23
❑ 24 Lamar Odom	.75	.23
❑ 25 Michael Olowokandi	.25	.07
❑ 26 Shaquille O'Neal	2.00	.60
❑ 27 Kobe Bryant	3.00	.90
❑ 28 Alonzo Mourning	.50	.15
❑ 29 Jamal Mashburn	.50	.15
❑ 30 Ray Allen	.75	.23
❑ 31 Glenn Robinson	.75	.23
❑ 32 Kevin Garnett	1.50	.45
❑ 33 Wally Szczerbiak	.50	.15
❑ 34 Stephon Marbury	.75	.23
❑ 35 Keith Van Horn	.75	.23
❑ 36 Latrell Sprewell	.75	.23
❑ 37 Allan Houston	.50	.15
❑ 38 Darrell Armstrong	.25	.07
❑ 39 Ron Mercer	.50	.15
❑ 40 Allen Iverson	1.50	.45
❑ 41 Toni Kukoc	.50	.15
❑ 42 Jason Kidd	1.25	.35
❑ 43 Anfernee Hardaway	.75	.23
❑ 44 Shawn Marion	.75	.23
❑ 45 Scottie Pippen	1.25	.35
❑ 46 Rasheed Wallace	.75	.23
❑ 47 Chris Webber	.75	.23
❑ 48 Vlade Divac	.50	.15
❑ 49 Tim Duncan	1.50	.45
❑ 50 David Robinson	.75	.23
❑ 51 Gary Payton	.75	.23
❑ 52 Rashard Lewis	.50	.15
❑ 53 Vince Carter	2.00	.60
❑ 54 Doug Christie	.50	.15
❑ 55 Karl Malone	.75	.23
❑ 56 Bryon Russell	.25	.07
❑ 57 Shareef Abdur-Rahim	.75	.23
❑ 58 Michael Dickerson	.50	.15
❑ 59 Juwan Howard	.50	.15
❑ 60 Richard Hamilton	.50	.15
❑ 61 Jerome Moiso RC	1.25	.35
❑ 62 Etan Thomas RC	1.25	.35
❑ 63 Courtney Alexander RC	1.25	.35
❑ 64 Mateen Cleaves RC	1.25	.35
❑ 65 Jason Collier RC	1.25	.35
❑ 66 Hidayet Turkoglu RC	15.00	4.50
❑ 67 Desmond Mason RC	1.25	.35
❑ 68 Quentin Richardson RC	6.00	1.80
❑ 69 Jamaal Magloire RC	1.25	.35
❑ 70 Speedy Claxton RC	1.25	.35
❑ 71 Morris Peterson RC	4.00	1.20
❑ 72 Donnell Harvey RC	1.25	.35
❑ 73 Ira Newble RC	1.25	.35
❑ 74 Mamadou N'diaye RC	1.25	.35
❑ 75 Erick Barkley RC	1.25	.35
❑ 76 Mark Madsen RC	1.25	.35
❑ 77 Dan Langhi RC	1.25	.35
❑ 78 A.J. Guyton RC	1.25	.35
❑ 79 Olumide Oyedeji RC	6.00	1.80
❑ 80 Eddie House RC	6.00	1.80
❑ 81 Eduardo Najera RC	10.00	3.00
❑ 82 Lavor Postell RC	6.00	1.80
❑ 83 Hanno Mottola RC	1.25	.35
❑ 84 Chris Carrawell RC	1.25	.35
❑ 85 Michael Redd RC	12.00	3.60
❑ 86 Jabari Smith RC	6.00	1.80
❑ 87 Jason Hart RC	6.00	1.80
❑ 88 Corey Hightower RC	1.25	.35
❑ 89 Chris Porter RC	1.25	.35
❑ 90 Justin Love RC	6.00	1.80
❑ 91 Kenyon Martin RC	8.00	2.40
❑ 92 Stromile Swift RC	4.00	1.20
❑ 93 Darius Miles RC	6.00	1.80
❑ 94 Marcus Fizer RC	1.25	.35
❑ 95 Mike Miller RC	6.00	1.80
❑ 96 DerMarr Johnson RC	1.25	.35
❑ 97 Chris Mihm RC	1.25	.35
❑ 98 Jamal Crawford RC	1.50	.45
❑ 99 Joel Przybilla RC	1.25	.35
❑ 100 Keyon Dooling RC	1.25	.35
❑ P21 Kevin Garnett	2.50	.75

2003-04 Upper Deck Standing O

	MINT	NRMT
COMP.SET w/o SP's	40.00	18.00
COMMON ROOKIE (85-126)	4.00	1.80
*DIECUT SINGLES: .75X TO 2X BASE HI	-	
*EMBOSS RC's: .6X TO 1.5X BASE HI	-	
❑ 1 Shareef Abdur-Rahim	.75	.35
❑ 2 Jason Terry	.75	.35
❑ 3 Theo Ratliff	.50	.23
❑ 4 Paul Pierce	.75	.35
❑ 5 Antoine Walker	.75	.35
❑ 6 Vin Baker	.50	.23
❑ 7 Jalen Rose	.75	.35
❑ 8 Tyson Chandler	.75	.35
❑ 9 Michael Jordan	5.00	2.20
❑ 10 Dajuan Wagner	.50	.23
❑ 11 Zydrunas Ilgauskas	.50	.23
❑ 12 Darius Miles	.75	.35
❑ 13 Dirk Nowitzki	1.25	.55
❑ 14 Michael Finley	.75	.35
❑ 15 Steve Nash	.75	.35
❑ 16 Nene	.50	.23
❑ 17 Rodney White	.20	.09
❑ 18 Richard Hamilton	.50	.23
❑ 19 Ben Wallace	.75	.35
❑ 20 Chauncey Billups	.50	.23
❑ 21 Nick Van Exel	.75	.35
❑ 22 Jason Richardson	.75	.35
❑ 23 Mike Dunleavy	.50	.23
❑ 24 Steve Francis	.75	.35
❑ 25 Yao Ming	2.00	.90
❑ 26 Cuttino Mobley	.50	.23
❑ 27 Reggie Miller	.75	.35
❑ 28 Jamaal Tinsley	.75	.35
❑ 29 Jermaine O'Neal	.75	.35
❑ 30 Elton Brand	.75	.35
❑ 31 Corey Maggette	.50	.23
❑ 32 Quentin Richardson	.50	.23
❑ 33 Kobe Bryant	3.00	1.35
❑ 34 Shaquille O'Neal	2.00	.90
❑ 35 Gary Payton	.75	.35
❑ 36 Karl Malone	.75	.35
❑ 37 Pau Gasol	.75	.35
❑ 38 Mike Miller	.75	.35
❑ 39 Eddie Jones	.75	.35
❑ 40 Brian Grant	.50	.23
❑ 41 Caron Butler	.75	.35
❑ 42 Michael Redd	.75	.35
❑ 43 Joe Smith	.50	.23
❑ 44 Desmond Mason	.50	.23
❑ 45 Kevin Garnett	1.50	.70
❑ 46 Latrell Sprewell	.75	.35
❑ 47 Sam Cassell	.75	.35
❑ 48 Jason Kidd	1.25	.55
❑ 49 Richard Jefferson	.50	.23

Card	Nm-Mt	Ex-Mt
❑ 50 Alonzo Mourning	.50	.23
❑ 51 Baron Davis	.75	.35
❑ 52 Jamal Mashburn	.50	.23
❑ 53 Jamaal Magloire	.20	.09
❑ 54 Allan Houston	.50	.23
❑ 55 Antonio McDyess	.50	.23
❑ 56 Keith Van Horn	.75	.35
❑ 57 Tracy McGrady	2.00	.90
❑ 58 Juwan Howard	.50	.23
❑ 59 Drew Gooden	.50	.23
❑ 60 Allen Iverson	1.50	.70
❑ 61 Glenn Robinson	.50	.23
❑ 62 Stephon Marbury	.75	.35
❑ 63 Shawn Marion	.75	.35
❑ 64 Amare Stoudemire	1.50	.70
❑ 65 Rasheed Wallace	.75	.35
❑ 66 Bonzi Wells	.50	.23
❑ 67 Chris Webber	.75	.35
❑ 68 Mike Bibby	.75	.35
❑ 69 Peja Stojakovic	.75	.35
❑ 70 Tim Duncan	1.50	.70
❑ 71 David Robinson	.75	.35
❑ 72 Tony Parker	.75	.35
❑ 73 Ray Allen	.75	.35
❑ 74 Rashard Lewis	.75	.35
❑ 75 Reggie Evans	.20	.09
❑ 76 Vince Carter	2.00	.90
❑ 77 Morris Peterson	.50	.23
❑ 78 Antonio Davis	.20	.09
❑ 79 Jarron Collins	.20	.09
❑ 80 John Stockton	.75	.35
❑ 81 Andrei Kirilenko	.75	.35
❑ 82 Jerry Stackhouse	.75	.35
❑ 83 Gilbert Arenas	.75	.35
❑ 84 Larry Hughes	.50	.23
❑ 85 LeBron James RC	50.00	22.00
❑ 86 Darko Milicic RC	6.00	2.70
❑ 87 Carmelo Anthony RC	25.00	11.00
❑ 88 Chris Bosh RC	8.00	3.60
❑ 89 Dwyane Wade RC	10.00	4.50
❑ 90 Chris Kaman RC	4.00	1.80
❑ 91 Kirk Hinrich RC	6.00	2.70
❑ 92 T.J. Ford RC	5.00	2.20
❑ 93 Mike Sweetney RC	4.00	1.80
❑ 94 Jarvis Hayes RC	4.00	1.80
❑ 95 Mickael Pietrus RC	4.00	1.80
❑ 96 Nick Collison RC	4.00	1.80
❑ 97 Marcus Banks RC	4.00	1.80
❑ 98 Luke Ridnour RC	5.00	2.20
❑ 99 Reece Gaines RC	4.00	1.80
❑ 100 Troy Bell RC	4.00	1.80
❑ 101 Zarko Cabarkapa RC	4.00	1.80
❑ 102 David West RC	4.00	1.80
❑ 103 Aleksandar Pavlovic RC	4.00	1.80
❑ 104 Dahntay Jones RC	4.00	1.80
❑ 105 Boris Diaw RC	4.00	1.80
❑ 106 Zoran Planinic RC	4.00	1.80
❑ 107 Travis Outlaw RC	4.00	1.80
❑ 108 Brian Cook RC	4.00	1.80
❑ 109 Carlos Delfino RC	4.00	1.80
❑ 110 Ndudi Ebi RC	4.00	1.80
❑ 111 Kendrick Perkins RC	4.00	1.80
❑ 112 Leandro Barbosa RC	4.00	1.80
❑ 113 Josh Howard RC	5.00	2.20
❑ 114 Maciej Lampe RC	4.00	1.80
❑ 115 Jason Kapono RC	4.00	1.80
❑ 116 Luke Walton RC	5.00	2.20
❑ 117 Jerome Beasley RC	4.00	1.80
❑ 118 Willie Green RC	4.00	1.80
❑ 119 Kyle Korver RC	5.00	2.20
❑ 120 Travis Hansen RC	4.00	1.80
❑ 121 Steve Blake RC	4.00	1.80
❑ 122 Slavko Vranes RC	4.00	1.80
❑ 123 Zaur Pachulia RC	4.00	1.80
❑ 124 Keith Bogans RC	4.00	1.80
❑ 125 Theron Smith RC	4.00	1.80
❑ 126 Brandon Hunter RC	4.00	1.80

2001-02 Upper Deck Sweet Shot

	Nm-Mt	Ex-Mt
COMP.SET w/o SP's	40.00	12.00
COMMON CARD (1-90)	.25	.07
COMMON ROOKIE (91-110)	5.00	1.50
COMMON ROOKIE (110-120)	6.00	1.80
❑ 1 Jason Terry	.75	.23
❑ 2 Shareef Abdur-Rahim	.75	.23
❑ 3 Toni Kukoc	.50	.15
❑ 4 Paul Pierce	.75	.23
❑ 5 Antoine Walker	.75	.23
❑ 6 Kenny Anderson	.50	.15
❑ 7 Baron Davis	.75	.23
❑ 8 Jamal Mashburn	.50	.15
❑ 9 David Wesley	.25	.07
❑ 10 Ron Mercer	.50	.15
❑ 11 Ron Artest	.50	.15
❑ 12 A.J. Guyton	.50	.15
❑ 13 Andre Miller	.50	.15
❑ 14 Lamond Murray	.25	.07
❑ 15 Chris Mihm	.50	.15
❑ 16 Michael Finley	.75	.23
❑ 17 Dirk Nowitzki	1.25	.35
❑ 18 Steve Nash	.75	.23
❑ 19 Antonio McDyess	.50	.15
❑ 20 Nick Van Exel	.75	.23
❑ 21 Raef LaFrentz	.50	.15
❑ 22 Jerry Stackhouse	.75	.23
❑ 23 Chucky Atkins	.25	.07
❑ 24 Corliss Williamson	.50	.15
❑ 25 Antawn Jamison	.75	.23
❑ 26 Marc Jackson	.50	.15
❑ 27 Larry Hughes	.50	.15
❑ 28 Steve Francis	.75	.23
❑ 29 Cuttino Mobley	.50	.15
❑ 30 Maurice Taylor	.50	.15
❑ 31 Reggie Miller	.75	.23
❑ 32 Jalen Rose	.75	.23
❑ 33 Jermaine O'Neal	.75	.23
❑ 34 Darius Miles	.75	.23
❑ 35 Elton Brand	.75	.23
❑ 36 Corey Maggette	.50	.15
❑ 37 Quentin Richardson	.50	.15
❑ 38 Kobe Bryant	3.00	.90
❑ 39 Shaquille O'Neal	2.00	.60
❑ 40 Rick Fox	.50	.15
❑ 41 Derek Fisher	.75	.23
❑ 42 Stromile Swift	.50	.15
❑ 43 Jason Williams	.50	.15
❑ 44 Michael Dickerson	.50	.15
❑ 45 Alonzo Mourning	.50	.15
❑ 46 Eddie Jones	.75	.23
❑ 47 Anthony Carter	.50	.15
❑ 48 Glenn Robinson	.75	.23
❑ 49 Ray Allen	.75	.23
❑ 50 Sam Cassell	.75	.23
❑ 51 Kevin Garnett	1.50	.45
❑ 52 Chauncey Billups	.50	.15
❑ 53 Terrell Brandon	.50	.15
❑ 54 Joe Smith	.50	.15
❑ 55 Kenyon Martin	.75	.23
❑ 56 Keith Van Horn	.50	.15
❑ 57 Jason Kidd	1.25	.35
❑ 58 Latrell Sprewell	.75	.23
❑ 59 Allan Houston	.50	.15
❑ 60 Marcus Camby	.50	.15
❑ 61 Tracy McGrady	2.00	.60
❑ 62 Mike Miller	.75	.23
❑ 63 Grant Hill	.75	.23
❑ 64 Allen Iverson	1.50	.45
❑ 65 Dikembe Mutombo	.50	.15
❑ 66 Aaron McKie	.50	.15
❑ 67 Stephon Marbury	.75	.23
❑ 68 Shawn Marion	.75	.23
❑ 69 Tom Gugliotta	.25	.07
❑ 70 Rasheed Wallace	.75	.23
❑ 71 Damon Stoudamire	.50	.15
❑ 72 Bonzi Wells	.50	.15
❑ 73 Chris Webber	.75	.23
❑ 74 Peja Stojakovic	.75	.23
❑ 75 Mike Bibby	.75	.23
❑ 76 Tim Duncan	1.50	.45
❑ 77 David Robinson	.75	.23
❑ 78 Antonio Daniels	.25	.07
❑ 79 Gary Payton	.75	.23
❑ 80 Rashard Lewis	.50	.15
❑ 81 Desmond Mason	.50	.15
❑ 82 Vince Carter	2.00	.60
❑ 83 Morris Peterson	.50	.15
❑ 84 Antonio Davis	.25	.07
❑ 85 Karl Malone	.75	.23
❑ 86 John Stockton	.75	.23
❑ 87 Donyell Marshall	.50	.15
❑ 88 Richard Hamilton	.50	.15
❑ 89 Courtney Alexander	.50	.15
❑ 90 Michael Jordan	15.00	4.50
❑ 91 Zach Randolph RC	12.00	3.60
❑ 92 Troy Murphy RC	10.00	3.00
❑ 93 Michael Bradley RC	5.00	1.50
❑ 94 Vladimir Radmanovic RC	6.00	1.80
❑ 95 Kirk Haston RC	5.00	1.50
❑ 96 Joseph Forte RC	10.00	3.00
❑ 97 Jamaal Tinsley RC	8.00	2.40
❑ 98 Jason Collins RC	5.00	1.50
❑ 99 Brendan Haywood RC	6.00	1.80
❑ 100 Richard Jefferson RC	15.00	4.50
❑ 101 Gerald Wallace RC	12.00	3.60
❑ 102 Jeryl Sasser RC	5.00	1.50
❑ 103 Samuel Dalembert RC	5.00	1.50
❑ 104 Tony Parker RC	20.00	6.00
❑ 105 Kedrick Brown RC	5.00	1.50
❑ 106 Brandon Armstrong RC	6.00	1.80
❑ 107 Steven Hunter RC	5.00	1.50
❑ 108 Andrei Kirilenko RC	15.00	4.50
❑ 109 Primoz Brezec RC	5.00	1.50
❑ 110 Terence Morris RC	5.00	1.50
❑ 111 Eddie Griffin RC	10.00	3.00
❑ 112 DeSagana Diop RC	6.00	1.80
❑ 113 Tyson Chandler RC	15.00	4.50
❑ 114 Joe Johnson RC	10.00	3.00
❑ 115 Rodney White RC	10.00	3.00
❑ 116 Eddy Curry RC	20.00	6.00
❑ 117 Shane Battier RC	10.00	3.00
❑ 118 Jason Richardson RC	25.00	7.50
❑ 119 Kwame Brown RC	15.00	4.50
❑ 120 Pau Gasol RC	20.00	6.00

2002-03 Upper Deck Sweet Shot

	Nm-Mt	Ex-Mt
COMP.SET w/o SP's (90)	40.00	12.00
COMMON ROOKIE (91-123)	8.00	2.40
COMMON ROOKIE (124-132)	20.00	6.00

	#	Player	MINT	NRMT
❑	1	Shareef Abdur-Rahim	.75	.23
❑	2	Jason Terry	.75	.23
❑	3	Glenn Robinson	.75	.23
❑	4	Paul Pierce	.75	.23
❑	5	Antoine Walker	.75	.23
❑	6	Kedrick Brown	.50	.15
❑	7	Vin Baker	.50	.15
❑	8	Jalen Rose	.75	.23
❑	9	Eddy Curry	.75	.23
❑	10	Tyson Chandler	.75	.23
❑	11	Zydrunas Ilgauskas	.50	.15
❑	12	Chris Mihm	.20	.06
❑	13	Darius Miles	.75	.23
❑	14	Dirk Nowitzki	1.25	.35
❑	15	Michael Finley	.75	.23
❑	16	Steve Nash	.75	.23
❑	17	Raef LaFrentz	.50	.15
❑	18	James Posey	.50	.15
❑	19	Juwan Howard	.50	.15
❑	20	Richard Hamilton	.50	.15
❑	21	Ben Wallace	.75	.23
❑	22	Chauncey Billups	.50	.15
❑	23	Jason Richardson	.75	.23
❑	24	Antawn Jamison	.75	.23
❑	25	Steve Francis	.75	.23
❑	26	Eddie Griffin	.50	.15
❑	27	Cuttino Mobley	.50	.15
❑	28	Reggie Miller	.75	.23
❑	29	Jamaal Tinsley	.75	.23
❑	30	Jermaine O'Neal	.75	.23
❑	31	Elton Brand	.75	.23
❑	32	Lamar Odom	.75	.23
❑	33	Andre Miller	.50	.15
❑	34	Kobe Bryant	3.00	.90
❑	35	Shaquille O'Neal	2.00	.60
❑	36	Devean George	.50	.15
❑	37	Pau Gasol	.75	.23
❑	38	Shane Battier	.75	.23
❑	39	Jason Williams	.50	.15
❑	40	Eddie House	.20	.06
❑	41	Eddie Jones	.75	.23
❑	42	Brian Grant	.50	.15
❑	43	Ray Allen	.75	.23
❑	44	Tim Thomas	.50	.15
❑	45	Kevin Garnett	2.00	.60
❑	46	Terrell Brandon	.50	.15
❑	47	Wally Szczerbiak	.50	.15
❑	48	Joe Smith	.50	.15
❑	49	Jason Kidd	1.25	.35
❑	50	Richard Jefferson	.50	.15
❑	51	Kenyon Martin	.75	.23
❑	52	Dikembe Mutombo	.50	.15
❑	53	Jamal Mashburn	.50	.15
❑	54	Baron Davis	.75	.23
❑	55	David Wesley	.20	.06
❑	56	Allan Houston	.50	.15
❑	57	Antonio McDyess	.50	.15
❑	58	Latrell Sprewell	.75	.23
❑	59	Tracy McGrady	2.00	.60
❑	60	Mike Miller	.75	.23
❑	61	Darrell Armstrong	.20	.06
❑	62	Allen Iverson	1.50	.45
❑	63	Keith Van Horn	.75	.23
❑	64	Stephon Marbury	.75	.23
❑	65	Shawn Marion	.75	.23
❑	66	Anfernee Hardaway	.75	.23
❑	67	Rasheed Wallace	.75	.23
❑	68	Bonzi Wells	.50	.15
❑	69	Scottie Pippen	1.25	.35
❑	70	Chris Webber	.75	.23
❑	71	Mike Bibby	.75	.23
❑	72	Peja Stojakovic	.75	.23
❑	73	Hidayet Turkoglu	.50	.15
❑	74	Tim Duncan	1.50	.45
❑	75	David Robinson	.75	.23
❑	76	Tony Parker	.75	.23
❑	77	Steve Smith	.50	.15
❑	78	Gary Payton	.75	.23
❑	79	Rashard Lewis	.50	.15
❑	80	Desmond Mason	.50	.15
❑	81	Brent Barry	.50	.15
❑	82	Vince Carter	2.00	.60
❑	83	Morris Peterson	.50	.15
❑	84	Antonio Davis	.20	.06
❑	85	Karl Malone	.75	.23
❑	86	John Stockton	.75	.23
❑	87	Andrei Kirilenko	.75	.23
❑	88	Jerry Stackhouse	.75	.23
❑	89	Michael Jordan	6.00	1.80
❑	90	Kwame Brown	.50	.15
❑	91	Efthimios Rentzias RC	8.00	2.40
❑	92	Marko Jaric RC	8.00	2.40
❑	93	Rasual Butler RC	8.00	2.40
❑	94	Predrag Savovic RC	10.00	3.00
❑	95	Sam Clancy RC	8.00	2.40
❑	96	Lonny Baxter RC	8.00	2.40
❑	97	Raul Lopez RC	8.00	2.40
❑	98	Rod Grizzard RC	8.00	2.40
❑	99	Tito Maddox RC	8.00	2.40
❑	100	Carlos Boozer RC	25.00	7.50
❑	101	Dan Gadzuric RC	8.00	2.40
❑	102	Vincent Yarbrough RC	8.00	2.40
❑	103	Robert Archibald RC	8.00	2.40
❑	104	Roger Mason RC	8.00	2.40
❑	105	Ronald Murray RC	12.00	3.60
❑	106	Dan Dickau RC	8.00	2.40
❑	107	Chris Jefferies RC	10.00	3.00
❑	108	John Salmons RC	8.00	2.40
❑	109	Frank Williams RC	10.00	3.00
❑	110	Tayshaun Prince RC	15.00	4.50
❑	111	Casey Jacobsen RC	8.00	2.40
❑	112	Qyntel Woods RC	12.00	3.60
❑	113	Kareem Rush RC	15.00	4.50
❑	114	Ryan Humphrey RC	8.00	2.40
❑	115	Curtis Borchardt RC	8.00	2.40
❑	116	Juan Dixon RC	20.00	6.00
❑	117	Jiri Welsch RC	8.00	2.40
❑	118	Bostjan Nachbar RC	10.00	3.00
❑	119	Fred Jones RC	12.00	3.60
❑	120	Marcus Haislip RC	8.00	2.40
❑	121	Melvin Ely RC	10.00	3.00
❑	122	Jared Jeffries RC	10.00	3.00
❑	123	Caron Butler RC	30.00	9.00
❑	124	Amare Stoudemire RC	60.00	18.00
❑	125	Chris Wilcox RC	20.00	6.00
❑	126	Nene Hilario RC	20.00	6.00
❑	127	DaJuan Wagner RC	25.00	7.50
❑	128	Nikoloz Tskitishvili RC	20.00	6.00
❑	129	Drew Gooden RC	40.00	12.00
❑	130	Mike Dunleavy RC	25.00	7.50
❑	131	Jay Williams RC	20.00	6.00
❑	132	Yao Ming RC	100.00	30.00

2003-04 Upper Deck Sweet Shot

	MINT	NRMT
COMP.SET w/o SP's (90)	40.00	18.00
COMMON CARD (1-90)	.20	.09
COMMON ROOKIE (91-96)	20.00	9.00
COMMON ROOKIE (97-132)	10.00	4.50
COMMON JORDAN (133-144)	25.00	11.00

	#	Player	MINT	NRMT
❑	1	Shareef Abdur-Rahim	.75	.35
❑	2	Jason Terry	.75	.35
❑	3	Theo Ratliff	.50	.23
❑	4	Paul Pierce	.75	.35
❑	5	Antoine Walker	.75	.35
❑	6	Vin Baker	.50	.23
❑	7	Jalen Rose	.75	.35
❑	8	Tyson Chandler	.75	.35
❑	9	Jay Williams	.50	.23
❑	10	Dajuan Wagner	.50	.23
❑	11	Zydrunas Ilgauskas	.50	.23
❑	12	Darius Miles	.75	.35
❑	13	Dirk Nowitzki	1.25	.55
❑	14	Antawn Jamison	.75	.35
❑	15	Steve Nash	.75	.35
❑	16	Nene Hilario	.50	.23
❑	17	Marcus Camby	.50	.23
❑	18	Andre Miller	.50	.23
❑	19	Richard Hamilton	.50	.23
❑	20	Ben Wallace	.75	.35
❑	21	Chauncey Billups	.50	.23
❑	22	Nick Van Exel	.75	.35
❑	23	Jason Richardson	.75	.35
❑	24	Erick Dampier	.50	.23
❑	25	Steve Francis	.75	.35
❑	26	Yao Ming	2.00	.90
❑	27	Cuttino Mobley	.50	.23
❑	28	Reggie Miller	.75	.35
❑	29	Jamaal Tinsley	.75	.35
❑	30	Jermaine O'Neal	.75	.35
❑	31	Elton Brand	.75	.35
❑	32	Corey Maggette	.50	.23
❑	33	Marko Jaric	.50	.23
❑	34	Kobe Bryant	3.00	1.35
❑	35	Gary Payton	.75	.35
❑	36	Shaquille O'Neal	2.00	.90
❑	37	Karl Malone	.75	.35
❑	38	Pau Gasol	.75	.35
❑	39	Shane Battier	.75	.35
❑	40	Mike Miller	.75	.35
❑	41	Eddie Jones	.75	.35
❑	42	Lamar Odom	.75	.35
❑	43	Caron Butler	.75	.35
❑	44	Michael Redd	.75	.35
❑	45	Joe Smith	.50	.23
❑	46	Desmond Mason	.50	.23
❑	47	Kevin Garnett	1.50	.70
❑	48	Wally Szczerbiak	.50	.23
❑	49	Latrell Sprewell	.75	.35
❑	50	Jason Kidd	1.25	.55
❑	51	Richard Jefferson	.50	.23
❑	52	Kenyon Martin	.75	.35
❑	53	Baron Davis	.75	.35
❑	54	Jamal Mashburn	.50	.23
❑	55	David Wesley	.20	.09
❑	56	Allan Houston	.50	.23
❑	57	Antonio McDyess	.50	.23
❑	58	Keith Van Horn	.75	.35
❑	59	Tracy McGrady	2.00	.90
❑	60	Grant Hill	.75	.35
❑	61	Drew Gooden	.50	.23
❑	62	Allen Iverson	1.50	.70
❑	63	Does Not Exist	-	
❑	64	Eric Snow	.50	.23
❑	64A	Glenn Robinson	.75	.35
❑	65	Stephon Marbury	.75	.35
❑	66	Shawn Marion	.75	.35
❑	67	Amare Stoudemire	1.50	.70
❑	68	Rasheed Wallace	.75	.35
❑	69	Bonzi Wells	.50	.23
❑	70	Damon Stoudamire	.50	.23
❑	71	Chris Webber	.75	.35
❑	72	Mike Bibby	.75	.35
❑	73	Peja Stojakovic	.75	.35
❑	74	Vlade Divac	.50	.23
❑	75	Tim Duncan	1.50	.70
❑	76	David Robinson	.75	.35
❑	77	Tony Parker	.75	.35
❑	78	Manu Ginobili	.75	.35
❑	79	Ray Allen	.75	.35
❑	80	Rashard Lewis	.75	.35
❑	81	Vladimir Radmanovic	.20	.09
❑	82	Vince Carter	2.00	.90
❑	83	Morris Peterson	.50	.23
❑	84	Antonio Davis	.20	.09
❑	85	Keon Clark	.50	.23
❑	86	John Stockton	.75	.35
❑	87	Andrei Kirilenko	.75	.35
❑	88	Jerry Stackhouse	.75	.35
❑	89	Kwame Brown	.50	.23
❑	90	Larry Hughes	.50	.23
❑	91	LeBron James RC	150.00	70.00
❑	92	Darko Milicic RC	25.00	11.00
❑	93	Carmelo Anthony RC	80.00	36.00
❑	94	Chris Bosh RC	30.00	13.50
❑	95	Dwyane Wade RC	20.00	9.00
❑	96	Chris Kaman RC	20.00	9.00
❑	97	Kirk Hinrich RC	20.00	9.00

Card	Nm-Mt	Ex-Mt
❑ 98 T.J. Ford RC	12.00	5.50
❑ 99 Mike Sweetney RC	10.00	4.50
❑ 100 Jarvis Hayes RC	20.00	9.00
❑ 101 Mickael Pietrus RC	10.00	4.50
❑ 102 Nick Collison RC	10.00	4.50
❑ 103 Marcus Banks RC	10.00	4.50
❑ 104 Luke Ridnour RC	15.00	6.75
❑ 105 Reece Gaines RC	10.00	4.50
❑ 106 Troy Bell RC	10.00	4.50
❑ 107 Zarko Cabarkapa RC	10.00	4.50
❑ 108 David West RC	10.00	4.50
❑ 109 Aleksandar Pavlovic RC	10.00	4.50
❑ 110 Dahntay Jones RC	10.00	4.50
❑ 111 Boris Diaw RC	10.00	4.50
❑ 112 Zoran Planinic RC	10.00	4.50
❑ 113 Travis Outlaw RC	10.00	4.50
❑ 114 Brian Cook RC	10.00	4.50
❑ 115 Carlos Delfino RC	10.00	4.50
❑ 116 Ndudi Ebi RC	10.00	4.50
❑ 117 Kendrick Perkins RC	10.00	4.50
❑ 118 Leandro Barbosa RC	10.00	4.50
❑ 119 Josh Howard RC	12.00	5.50
❑ 120 Jason Kapono RC	10.00	4.50
❑ 121 Luke Walton RC	15.00	6.75
❑ 122 Jerome Beasley RC	10.00	4.50
❑ 123 Kyle Korver RC	12.00	5.50
❑ 124 Maciej Lampe RC	10.00	4.50
❑ 125 Travis Hansen RC	10.00	4.50
❑ 126 Steve Blake RC	10.00	4.50
❑ 127 Willie Green RC	10.00	4.50
❑ 128 Slavko Vranes RC	10.00	4.50
❑ 129 Keith Bogans RC	10.00	4.50
❑ 130 Maurice Williams RC	10.00	4.50
❑ 131 Matt Bonner RC	10.00	4.50
❑ 132 Zaur Pachulia RC	10.00	4.50

2003-04 Upper Deck Triple Dimensions

	Nm-Mt	Ex-Mt
COMP.SET w/o SP's (90)	30.00	9.00
COMMON CARD (1-90)	.20	.06
COMMON ROOKIE (91-126)	5.00	1.50
❑ 1 Jason Terry	.75	.23
❑ 2 Theo Ratliff	.50	.15
❑ 3 Shareef Abdur-Rahim	.75	.23
❑ 4 Raef LaFrentz	.50	.15
❑ 5 Vin Baker	.50	.15
❑ 6 Paul Pierce	.75	.23
❑ 7 Eddy Curry	.50	.15
❑ 8 Tyson Chandler	.75	.23
❑ 9 Antonio Davis	.20	.06
❑ 10 Dajuan Wagner	.50	.15
❑ 11 Zydrunas Ilgauskas	.50	.15
❑ 12 Carlos Boozer	.75	.23
❑ 13 Steve Nash	.75	.23
❑ 14 Antoine Walker	.75	.23
❑ 15 Dirk Nowitzki	1.25	.35
❑ 16 Michael Finley	.75	.23
❑ 17 Andre Miller	.50	.15
❑ 18 Nene	.50	.15
❑ 19 Earl Boykins	.50	.15
❑ 20 Ben Wallace	.75	.23
❑ 21 Chauncey Billups	.50	.15
❑ 22 Richard Hamilton	.50	.15
❑ 23 Mike Dunleavy	.50	.15
❑ 24 Jason Richardson	.75	.23
❑ 25 Nick Van Exel	.75	.23
❑ 26 Cuttino Mobley	.50	.15
❑ 27 Yao Ming	2.00	.60
❑ 28 Steve Francis	.75	.23
❑ 29 Reggie Miller	.75	.23
❑ 30 Jamaal Tinsley	.75	.23
❑ 31 Jermaine O'Neal	.75	.23
❑ 32 Corey Maggette	.50	.15
❑ 33 Elton Brand	.75	.23
❑ 34 Quentin Richardson	.50	.15
❑ 35 Shaquille O'Neal	2.00	.60
❑ 36 Kobe Bryant	3.00	.90
❑ 37 Karl Malone	.75	.23
❑ 38 Gary Payton	.75	.23
❑ 39 Mike Miller	.75	.23
❑ 40 Pau Gasol	.75	.23
❑ 41 Shane Battier	.75	.23
❑ 42 Eddie Jones	.75	.23
❑ 43 Caron Butler	.75	.23
❑ 44 Lamar Odom	.75	.23
❑ 45 Desmond Mason	.50	.15
❑ 46 Tim Thomas	.50	.15
❑ 47 Michael Redd	.75	.23
❑ 48 Latrell Sprewell	.75	.23
❑ 49 Kevin Garnett	1.50	.45
❑ 50 Wally Szczerbiak	.50	.15
❑ 51 Kenyon Martin	.75	.23
❑ 52 Jason Kidd	1.25	.35
❑ 53 Richard Jefferson	.50	.15
❑ 54 Jamal Mashburn	.50	.15
❑ 55 Baron Davis	.75	.23
❑ 56 Jamaal Magloire	.20	.06
❑ 57 Stephon Marbury	.75	.23
❑ 58 Allan Houston	.50	.15
❑ 59 Keith Van Horn	.75	.23
❑ 60 Drew Gooden	.50	.15
❑ 61 Tracy McGrady	2.00	.60
❑ 62 Gordan Giricek	.50	.15
❑ 63 Glenn Robinson	.75	.23
❑ 64 Allen Iverson	1.50	.45
❑ 65 Eric Snow	.50	.15
❑ 66 Antonio McDyess	.50	.15
❑ 67 Amare Stoudemire	2.00	.60
❑ 68 Shawn Marion	.75	.23
❑ 69 Zach Randolph	.75	.23
❑ 70 Rasheed Wallace	.75	.23
❑ 71 Damon Stoudamire	.50	.15
❑ 72 Mike Bibby	.75	.23
❑ 73 Chris Webber	.75	.23
❑ 74 Peja Stojakovic	.75	.23
❑ 75 Brad Miller	.75	.23
❑ 76 Tony Parker	.75	.23
❑ 77 Tim Duncan	1.50	.45
❑ 78 Manu Ginobili	.75	.23
❑ 79 Rashard Lewis	.75	.23
❑ 80 Ray Allen	.75	.23
❑ 81 Vladimir Radmanovic	.20	.06
❑ 82 Morris Peterson	.50	.15
❑ 83 Vince Carter	2.00	.60
❑ 84 Jalen Rose	.75	.23
❑ 85 Andrei Kirilenko	.75	.23
❑ 86 Matt Harpring	.75	.23
❑ 87 Carlos Arroyo	1.00	.30
❑ 88 Jerry Stackhouse	.75	.23
❑ 89 Gilbert Arenas	.75	.23
❑ 90 Larry Hughes	.50	.15
❑ 91 Udonis Haslem RC	5.00	1.50
❑ 92 Brandon Hunter RC	5.00	1.50
❑ 93 Maurice Williams RC	5.00	1.50
❑ 94 Keith Bogans RC	5.00	1.50
❑ 95 Zaur Pachulia RC	5.00	1.50
❑ 96 Willie Green RC	5.00	1.50
❑ 97 Kyle Korver RC	6.00	1.80
❑ 98 James Jones RC	5.00	1.50
❑ 99 Steve Blake RC	5.00	1.50
❑ 100 Travis Hansen RC	5.00	1.50
❑ 101 Jerome Beasley RC	5.00	1.50
❑ 102 Luke Walton RC	6.00	1.80
❑ 103 Jason Kapono RC	5.00	1.50
❑ 104 Maciej Lampe RC	5.00	1.50
❑ 105 Josh Howard RC	6.00	1.80
❑ 106 Leandro Barbosa RC	5.00	1.50
❑ 107 Kendrick Perkins RC	5.00	1.50
❑ 108 Ndudi Ebi RC	5.00	1.50
❑ 109 Brian Cook RC	5.00	1.50
❑ 110 Travis Outlaw RC	5.00	1.50
❑ 111 Zoran Planinic RC	5.00	1.50
❑ 112 Boris Diaw RC	5.00	1.50
❑ 113 Dahntay Jones RC	5.00	1.50
❑ 114 Aleksandar Pavlovic RC	5.00	1.50
❑ 115 David West RC	5.00	1.50
❑ 116 Zarko Cabarkapa RC	5.00	1.50
❑ 117 Troy Bell RC	5.00	1.50
❑ 118 Reece Gaines RC	5.00	1.50
❑ 119 Luke Ridnour RC	6.00	1.80
❑ 120 Marcus Banks RC	5.00	1.50
❑ 121 Nick Collison RC	5.00	1.50
❑ 122 Mickael Pietrus RC	5.00	1.50
❑ 123 Mike Sweetney RC	5.00	1.50
❑ 124 Chris Kaman RC	5.00	1.50
❑ 125 T.J. Ford RC	6.00	1.80
❑ 126 Kirk Hinrich RC	8.00	2.40
❑ 127 Jarvis Hayes RC	5.00	1.50
❑ 128 Dwyane Wade RC	15.00	4.50
❑ 129 Chris Bosh RC	12.00	3.60
❑ 130 Carmelo Anthony RC	40.00	12.00
❑ 131 Darko Milicic RC	12.00	3.60
❑ 132 LeBron James RC	80.00	24.00

1999-00 Upper Deck Ultimate Victory

	Nm-Mt	Ex-Mt
COMPLETE SET (150)	100.00	30.00
COMP. SET w/o RC (120)	60.00	18.00
COMMON CARD (1-90)	.30	.09
COMMON ROOKIE (121-150)	1.00	.30
COMMON MJ GH (91-120)	1.50	.45
❑ 1 Dikembe Mutombo	.60	.18
❑ 2 Alan Henderson	.30	.09
❑ 3 LaPhonso Ellis	.30	.09
❑ 4 Kenny Anderson	.60	.18
❑ 5 Antoine Walker	1.00	.30
❑ 6 Paul Pierce	1.00	.30
❑ 7 Elden Campbell	.30	.09
❑ 8 Eddie Jones	1.00	.30
❑ 9 David Wesley	.30	.09
❑ 10 Michael Jordan	5.00	1.50
❑ 11 Kornel David RC	.30	.09
❑ 12 Toni Kukoc	.60	.18
❑ 13 Shawn Kemp	.60	.18
❑ 14 Brevin Knight	.30	.09
❑ 15 Zydrunas Ilgauskas	.60	.18
❑ 16 Michael Finley	1.00	.30
❑ 17 Shawn Bradley	.30	.09
❑ 18 Dirk Nowitzki	2.00	.60
❑ 19 Antonio McDyess	.60	.18
❑ 20 Nick Van Exel	1.00	.30
❑ 21 Ron Mercer	.60	.18
❑ 22 Grant Hill	1.00	.30
❑ 23 Lindsey Hunter	.30	.09
❑ 24 Jerry Stackhouse	1.00	.30
❑ 25 John Starks	.60	.18
❑ 26 Antawn Jamison	1.50	.45
❑ 27 Mookie Blaylock	.30	.09
❑ 28 Hakeem Olajuwon	1.00	.30
❑ 29 Cuttino Mobley	1.00	.30
❑ 30 Charles Barkley	1.25	.35
❑ 31 Reggie Miller	1.00	.30
❑ 32 Rik Smits	.60	.18
❑ 33 Jalen Rose	1.00	.30
❑ 34 Maurice Taylor	.60	.18
❑ 35 Tyrone Nesby RC	.30	.09
❑ 36 Michael Olowokandi	.60	.18
❑ 37 Kobe Bryant	4.00	1.20

- ❑ 38 Shaquille O'Neal 2.50 .75
- ❑ 39 Glen Rice .60 .18
- ❑ 40 Robert Horry .60 .18
- ❑ 41 Tim Hardaway .60 .18
- ❑ 42 Alonzo Mourning .60 .18
- ❑ 43 Jamal Mashburn .60 .18
- ❑ 44 Ray Allen 1.00 .30
- ❑ 45 Glenn Robinson 1.00 .30
- ❑ 46 Robert Traylor .30 .09
- ❑ 47 Kevin Garnett 2.00 .60
- ❑ 48 Joe Smith .60 .18
- ❑ 49 Bobby Jackson .60 .18
- ❑ 50 Keith Van Horn 1.00 .30
- ❑ 51 Stephon Marbury 1.00 .30
- ❑ 52 Jayson Williams .30 .09
- ❑ 53 Patrick Ewing 1.00 .30
- ❑ 54 Allan Houston .60 .18
- ❑ 55 Latrell Sprewell 1.00 .30
- ❑ 56 Marcus Camby .60 .18
- ❑ 57 Darrell Armstrong .30 .09
- ❑ 58 Matt Harpring 1.00 .30
- ❑ 59 Bo Outlaw .30 .09
- ❑ 60 Allen Iverson 2.00 .60
- ❑ 61 Theo Ratliff .60 .18
- ❑ 62 Larry Hughes 1.00 .30
- ❑ 63 Jason Kidd 1.50 .45
- ❑ 64 Tom Gugliotta .30 .09
- ❑ 65 Anfernee Hardaway 1.00 .30
- ❑ 66 Scottie Pippen 1.50 .45
- ❑ 67 Damon Stoudamire .60 .18
- ❑ 68 Brian Grant .60 .18
- ❑ 69 Jason Williams 1.00 .30
- ❑ 70 Vlade Divac .60 .18
- ❑ 71 Chris Webber 1.00 .30
- ❑ 72 Tim Duncan 2.00 .60
- ❑ 73 Sean Elliott .60 .18
- ❑ 74 David Robinson 1.00 .30
- ❑ 75 Avery Johnson .30 .09
- ❑ 76 Gary Payton 1.00 .30
- ❑ 77 Vin Baker .60 .18
- ❑ 78 Brent Barry .60 .18
- ❑ 79 Vince Carter 2.50 .75
- ❑ 80 Doug Christie .60 .18
- ❑ 81 Tracy McGrady 2.50 .75
- ❑ 82 Karl Malone 1.00 .30
- ❑ 83 John Stockton 1.00 .30
- ❑ 84 Bryon Russell .30 .09
- ❑ 85 Shareef Abdur-Rahim 1.00 .30
- ❑ 86 Mike Bibby 1.00 .30
- ❑ 87 Felipe Lopez .30 .09
- ❑ 88 Juwan Howard .60 .18
- ❑ 89 Rod Strickland .30 .09
- ❑ 90 Mitch Richmond .60 .18
- ❑ 91 Michael Jordan GH 1.50 .45
- ❑ 92 Michael Jordan GH 1.50 .45
- ❑ 93 Michael Jordan GH 1.50 .45
- ❑ 94 Michael Jordan GH 1.50 .45
- ❑ 95 Michael Jordan GH 1.50 .45
- ❑ 96 Michael Jordan GH 1.50 .45
- ❑ 97 Michael Jordan GH 1.50 .45
- ❑ 98 Michael Jordan GH 1.50 .45
- ❑ 99 Michael Jordan GH 1.50 .45
- ❑ 100 Michael Jordan GH 1.50 .45
- ❑ 101 Michael Jordan GH 1.50 .45
- ❑ 102 Michael Jordan GH 1.50 .45
- ❑ 103 Michael Jordan GH 1.50 .45
- ❑ 104 Michael Jordan GH 1.50 .45
- ❑ 105 Michael Jordan GH 1.50 .45
- ❑ 106 Michael Jordan GH 1.50 .45
- ❑ 107 Michael Jordan GH 1.50 .45
- ❑ 108 Michael Jordan GH 1.50 .45
- ❑ 109 Michael Jordan GH 1.50 .45
- ❑ 110 Michael Jordan GH 1.50 .45
- ❑ 111 Michael Jordan GH 1.50 .45
- ❑ 112 Michael Jordan GH 1.50 .45
- ❑ 113 Michael Jordan GH 1.50 .45
- ❑ 114 Michael Jordan GH 1.50 .45
- ❑ 115 Michael Jordan GH 1.50 .45
- ❑ 116 Michael Jordan GH 1.50 .45
- ❑ 117 Michael Jordan GH 1.50 .45
- ❑ 118 Michael Jordan GH 1.50 .45
- ❑ 119 Michael Jordan GH 1.50 .45
- ❑ 120 Michael Jordan GH 1.50 .45
- ❑ 121 Elton Brand RC 6.00 1.80
- ❑ 122 Steve Francis RC 8.00 2.40
- ❑ 123 Baron Davis RC 5.00 1.50
- ❑ 124 Lamar Odom RC 5.00 1.50
- ❑ 125 Jonathan Bender RC 3.00 .90
- ❑ 126 Wally Szczerbiak RC 5.00 1.50
- ❑ 127 Richard Hamilton RC 5.00 1.50
- ❑ 128 Andre Miller RC 5.00 1.50
- ❑ 129 Shawn Marion RC 6.00 1.80
- ❑ 130 Jason Terry RC 4.00 1.20
- ❑ 131 Trajan Langdon RC 2.00 .60
- ❑ 132 Aleksandar Radojevic RC 1.00 .30
- ❑ 133 Corey Maggette RC 5.00 1.50
- ❑ 134 William Avery RC 2.00 .60
- ❑ 135 Ron Artest RC 3.00 .90
- ❑ 136 Cal Bowdler RC 1.50 .45
- ❑ 137 James Posey RC 3.00 .90
- ❑ 138 Quincy Lewis RC 1.50 .45
- ❑ 139 Dion Glover RC 1.50 .45
- ❑ 140 Jeff Foster RC 1.50 .45
- ❑ 141 Kenny Thomas RC 2.00 .60
- ❑ 142 Devean George RC 2.50 .75
- ❑ 143 Tim James RC 1.50 .45
- ❑ 144 Vonteego Cummings RC 2.00 .60
- ❑ 145 Jumaine Jones RC 2.00 .60
- ❑ 146 Scott Padgett RC 1.50 .45
- ❑ 147 John Celestand RC 1.50 .45
- ❑ 148 Adrian Griffin RC 1.50 .45
- ❑ 149 Chris Herren RC 1.00 .30
- ❑ 150 Anthony Carter RC 3.00 .90

2000-01 Upper Deck Ultimate Victory

	Nm-Mt	Ex-Mt
COMP.SET w/o SP (60)	25.00	7.50
COMMON CARD (1-60)	.25	.07
COMMON KOBE (61-75)	3.00	.90
COMMON KG (76-90)	3.00	.90
COMMON ROOKIE (91-120)	3.00	.90

- ❑ 1 Dikembe Mutombo .50 .15
- ❑ 2 Jim Jackson .25 .07
- ❑ 3 Paul Pierce .75 .23
- ❑ 4 Antoine Walker .75 .23
- ❑ 5 Jamal Mashburn .50 .15
- ❑ 6 Baron Davis .75 .23
- ❑ 7 Elton Brand .75 .23
- ❑ 8 Ron Artest .50 .15
- ❑ 9 Lamond Murray .25 .07
- ❑ 10 Andre Miller .50 .15
- ❑ 11 Michael Finley .75 .23
- ❑ 12 Dirk Nowitzki 1.25 .35
- ❑ 13 Antonio McDyess .50 .15
- ❑ 14 Nick Van Exel .75 .23
- ❑ 15 Jerry Stackhouse .75 .23
- ❑ 16 Chucky Atkins .25 .07
- ❑ 17 Antawn Jamison .75 .23
- ❑ 18 Larry Hughes .50 .15
- ❑ 19 Steve Francis .75 .23
- ❑ 20 Hakeem Olajuwon .75 .23
- ❑ 21 Reggie Miller .75 .23
- ❑ 22 Jalen Rose .75 .23
- ❑ 23 Lamar Odom .75 .23
- ❑ 24 Corey Maggette .50 .15
- ❑ 25 Shaquille O'Neal 2.00 .60
- ❑ 26 Kobe Bryant 3.00 .90
- ❑ 27 Ron Harper .50 .15
- ❑ 28 Tim Hardaway .50 .15
- ❑ 29 Eddie Jones .75 .23
- ❑ 30 Ray Allen .75 .23
- ❑ 31 Tim Thomas .50 .15
- ❑ 32 Kevin Garnett 1.50 .45
- ❑ 33 Wally Szczerbiak .50 .15
- ❑ 34 Terrell Brandon .50 .15
- ❑ 35 Stephon Marbury .75 .23
- ❑ 36 Keith Van Horn .75 .23
- ❑ 37 Allan Houston .50 .15
- ❑ 38 Latrell Sprewell .75 .23
- ❑ 39 Grant Hill .75 .23
- ❑ 40 Tracy McGrady 2.00 .60
- ❑ 41 Allen Iverson 1.50 .45
- ❑ 42 Toni Kukoc .50 .15
- ❑ 43 Jason Kidd 1.25 .35
- ❑ 44 Anfernee Hardaway .75 .23
- ❑ 45 Scottie Pippen 1.25 .35
- ❑ 46 Rasheed Wallace .75 .23
- ❑ 47 Jason Williams .50 .15
- ❑ 48 Chris Webber .75 .23
- ❑ 49 Tim Duncan 1.50 .45
- ❑ 50 David Robinson .75 .23
- ❑ 51 Gary Payton .75 .23
- ❑ 52 Rashard Lewis .50 .15
- ❑ 53 Vince Carter 2.00 .60
- ❑ 54 Mark Jackson .25 .07
- ❑ 55 Karl Malone .75 .23
- ❑ 56 John Stockton .75 .23
- ❑ 57 Shareef Abdur-Rahim .75 .23
- ❑ 58 Mike Bibby .75 .23
- ❑ 59 Mitch Richmond .50 .15
- ❑ 60 Richard Hamilton .50 .15
- ❑ 61 Kobe Bryant FLY 3.00 .90
- ❑ 62 Kobe Bryant FLY 3.00 .90
- ❑ 63 Kobe Bryant FLY 3.00 .90
- ❑ 64 Kobe Bryant FLY 3.00 .90
- ❑ 65 Kobe Bryant FLY 3.00 .90
- ❑ 66 Kobe Bryant FLY 3.00 .90
- ❑ 67 Kobe Bryant FLY 3.00 .90
- ❑ 68 Kobe Bryant FLY 3.00 .90
- ❑ 69 Kobe Bryant FLY 3.00 .90
- ❑ 70 Kobe Bryant FLY 3.00 .90
- ❑ 71 Kobe Bryant FLY 3.00 .90
- ❑ 72 Kobe Bryant FLY 3.00 .90
- ❑ 73 Kobe Bryant FLY 3.00 .90
- ❑ 74 Kobe Bryant FLY 3.00 .90
- ❑ 75 Kobe Bryant FLY 3.00 .90
- ❑ 76 Kevin Garnett FLY 3.00 .90
- ❑ 77 Kevin Garnett FLY 3.00 .90
- ❑ 78 Kevin Garnett FLY 3.00 .90
- ❑ 79 Kevin Garnett FLY 3.00 .90
- ❑ 80 Kevin Garnett FLY 3.00 .90
- ❑ 81 Kevin Garnett FLY 3.00 .90
- ❑ 82 Kevin Garnett FLY 3.00 .90
- ❑ 83 Kevin Garnett FLY 3.00 .90
- ❑ 84 Kevin Garnett FLY 3.00 .90
- ❑ 85 Kevin Garnett FLY 3.00 .90
- ❑ 86 Kevin Garnett FLY 3.00 .90
- ❑ 87 Kevin Garnett FLY 3.00 .90
- ❑ 88 Kevin Garnett FLY 3.00 .90
- ❑ 89 Kevin Garnett FLY 3.00 .90
- ❑ 90 Kevin Garnett FLY 3.00 .90
- ❑ 91 Kenyon Martin RC 12.00 3.60
- ❑ 92 Stromile Swift RC 6.00 1.80
- ❑ 93 Darius Miles RC 12.00 3.60
- ❑ 94 Marcus Fizer RC 3.00 .90
- ❑ 95 Mike Miller RC 10.00 3.00
- ❑ 96 DerMarr Johnson RC 3.00 .90
- ❑ 97 Chris Mihm RC 3.00 .90
- ❑ 98 Jamal Crawford RC 4.00 1.20
- ❑ 99 Joel Przybilla RC 3.00 .90
- ❑ 100 Keyon Dooling RC 3.00 .90
- ❑ 101 Jerome Moiso RC 3.00 .90
- ❑ 102 Etan Thomas RC 3.00 .90
- ❑ 103 Courtney Alexander RC 4.00 1.20
- ❑ 104 Mateen Cleaves RC 3.00 .90
- ❑ 105 Jason Collier RC 3.00 .90
- ❑ 106 Hidayet Turkoglu RC 8.00 2.40
- ❑ 107 Desmond Mason RC 3.00 .90
- ❑ 108 Quentin Richardson RC 8.00 2.40
- ❑ 109 Jamaal Magloire RC 3.00 .90
- ❑ 110 Speedy Claxton RC 3.00 .90
- ❑ 111 Morris Peterson RC 6.00 1.80
- ❑ 112 Donnell Harvey RC 3.00 .90
- ❑ 113 DeShawn Stevenson RC 3.00 .90
- ❑ 114 Mamadou N'Diaye RC 3.00 .90
- ❑ 115 Erick Barkley RC 3.00 .90
- ❑ 116 Mike Smith RC 3.00 .90
- ❑ 117 Eddie House RC 3.00 .90

Card	Nm-Mt	Ex-Mt
118 Eduardo Najera RC	5.00	1.50
119 Jason Hart RC	3.00	.90
120 Chris Porter RC	3.00	.90

1999-00 Upper Deck Victory

	Nm-Mt	Ex-Mt
COMPLETE SET (440)	60.00	18.00
COMMON CARD (1-380)	.15	.04
COMMON ROOKIE (431-440)	1.00	.30
COMMON MJ HITS (381-430)	1.00	.30
1 Dikembe Mutombo CL	.15	.04
2 Steve Smith	.25	.07
3 Dikembe Mutombo	.25	.07
4 Ed Gray	.15	.04
5 Alan Henderson	.15	.04
6 LaPhonso Ellis	.15	.04
7 Roshown McLeod	.15	.04
8 Bimbo Coles	.15	.04
9 Chris Crawford	.15	.04
10 Anthony Johnson	.15	.04
11 Antoine Walker CL	.25	.07
12 Kenny Anderson	.25	.07
13 Antoine Walker	.40	.12
14 Greg Minor	.15	.04
15 Tony Battie	.15	.04
16 Ron Mercer	.25	.07
17 Paul Pierce	.40	.12
18 Vitaly Potapenko	.15	.04
19 Dana Barros	.15	.04
20 Walter McCarty	.15	.04
21 Elden Campbell CL	.15	.04
22 Elden Campbell	.15	.04
23 Eddie Jones	.40	.12
24 David Wesley	.15	.04
25 Bobby Phills	.15	.04
26 Derrick Coleman	.25	.07
27 Anthony Mason	.25	.07
28 Brad Miller	.40	.12
29 Eldridge Recasner	.15	.04
30 Ricky Davis	.25	.07
31 Toni Kukoc CL	.15	.04
32 Michael Jordan	2.50	.75
33 Brent Barry	.25	.07
34 Randy Brown	.15	.04
35 Keith Booth	.15	.04
36 Kornel David RC	.15	.04
37 Mark Bryant	.15	.04
38 Toni Kukoc	.25	.07
39 Rusty LaRue	.15	.04
40 Brevin Knight CL	.15	.04
41 Shawn Kemp	.25	.07
42 Wesley Person	.15	.04
43 Johnny Newman	.15	.04
44 Derek Anderson	.25	.07
45 Brevin Knight	.15	.04
46 Bob Sura	.15	.04
47 Andrew DeClercq	.15	.04
48 Zydrunas Ilgauskas	.25	.07
49 Danny Ferry	.15	.04
50 Steve Nash CL	.25	.07
51 Michael Finley	.40	.12
52 Robert Pack	.15	.04
53 Shawn Bradley	.15	.04
54 John Williams	.15	.04
55 Hubert Davis	.15	.04
56 Dirk Nowitzki	.75	.23
57 Steve Nash	.40	.12
58 Chris Anstey	.15	.04
59 Erick Strickland	.15	.04
60 Nick Van Exel CL	.15	.04
61 Antonio McDyess	.25	.07
62 Nick Van Exel	.40	.12
63 Bryant Stith	.15	.04
64 Chauncey Billups	.25	.07
65 Danny Fortson	.15	.04
66 Eric Williams	.15	.04
67 Eric Washington	.15	.04
68 Raef LaFrentz	.25	.07
69 Johnny Taylor	.15	.04
70 Jerry Stackhouse CL	.25	.07
71 Grant Hill	.40	.12
72 Lindsey Hunter	.15	.04
73 Bison Dele	.15	.04
74 Loy Vaught	.15	.04
75 Jerome Williams	.15	.04
76 Jerry Stackhouse	.40	.12
77 Christian Laettner	.25	.07
78 Jud Buechler	.15	.04
79 Don Reid	.15	.04
80 Antawn Jamison CL	.40	.12
81 John Starks	.25	.07
82 Antawn Jamison	.60	.18
83 Adonal Foyle	.15	.04
84 Jason Caffey	.15	.04
85 Donyell Marshall	.25	.07
86 Chris Mills	.15	.04
87 Tony Delk	.15	.04
88 Mookie Blaylock	.15	.04
89 Charles Barkley CL	.40	.12
90 Hakeem Olajuwon	.40	.12
91 Scottie Pippen	.60	.18
92 Charles Barkley	.50	.15
93 Bryce Drew	.15	.04
94 Cuttino Mobley	.40	.12
95 Othella Harrington	.15	.04
96 Matt Maloney	.15	.04
97 Michael Dickerson	.25	.07
98 Matt Bullard	.15	.04
99 Jalen Rose CL	.25	.07
100 Reggie Miller	.40	.12
101 Rik Smits	.25	.07
102 Jalen Rose	.40	.12
103 Antonio Davis	.15	.04
104 Mark Jackson	.25	.07
105 Sam Perkins	.15	.04
106 Travis Best	.15	.04
107 Dale Davis	.15	.04
108 Chris Mullin	.40	.12
109 Michael Olowokandi CL	.15	.04
110 Maurice Taylor	.25	.07
111 Tyrone Nesby RC	.15	.04
112 Lamond Murray	.15	.04
113 Darrick Martin	.15	.04
114 Michael Olowokandi	.25	.07
115 Rodney Rogers	.15	.04
116 Eric Piatkowski	.25	.07
117 Lorenzen Wright	.15	.04
118 Brian Skinner	.15	.04
119 Kobe Bryant CL	.75	.23
120 Kobe Bryant	1.50	.45
121 Shaquille O'Neal	1.00	.30
122 Derek Fisher	.40	.12
123 Tyronn Lue	.25	.07
124 Travis Knight	.15	.04
125 Glen Rice	.25	.07
126 Derek Harper	.25	.07
127 Robert Horry	.25	.07
128 Rick Fox	.25	.07
129 Tim Hardaway CL	.15	.04
130 Tim Hardaway	.25	.07
131 Alonzo Mourning	.25	.07
132 Keith Askins	.15	.04
133 Jamal Mashburn	.25	.07
134 P.J. Brown	.15	.04
135 Clarence Weatherspoon	.15	.04
136 Terry Porter	.15	.04
137 Dan Majerle	.25	.07
138 Voshon Lenard	.15	.04
139 Ray Allen CL	.25	.07
140 Ray Allen	.40	.12
141 Vinny Del Negro	.15	.04
142 Glenn Robinson	.40	.12
143 Dell Curry	.15	.04
144 Sam Cassell	.40	.12
145 Haywoode Workman	.15	.04
146 Armon Gilliam	.15	.04
147 Robert Traylor	.15	.04
148 Chris Gatling	.15	.04
149 Kevin Garnett CL	.40	.12
150 Kevin Garnett	.75	.23
151 Malik Sealy	.15	.04
152 Radoslav Nesterovic	.25	.07
153 Joe Smith	.25	.07
154 Sam Mitchell	.15	.04
155 Dean Garrett	.15	.04
156 Anthony Peeler	.15	.04
157 Tom Hammonds	.15	.04
158 Bobby Jackson	.25	.07
159 Jayson Williams CL	.15	.04
160 Keith Van Horn	.40	.12
161 Stephon Marbury	.40	.12
162 Jayson Williams	.15	.04
163 Kendall Gill	.15	.04
164 Kerry Kittles	.15	.04
165 Jamie Feick RC	.15	.04
166 Scott Burrell	.15	.04
167 Lucious Harris	.15	.04
168 Marcus Camby CL	.15	.04
169 Patrick Ewing	.40	.12
170 Allan Houston	.25	.07
171 Latrell Sprewell	.40	.12
172 Kurt Thomas	.25	.07
173 Larry Johnson	.25	.07
174 Chris Childs	.15	.04
175 Marcus Camby	.25	.07
176 Charlie Ward	.15	.04
177 Chris Dudley	.15	.04
178 Bo Outlaw CL	.15	.04
179 Anfernee Hardaway	.40	.12
180 Darrell Armstrong	.15	.04
181 Nick Anderson	.15	.04
182 Horace Grant	.25	.07
183 Isaac Austin	.15	.04
184 Matt Harpring	.40	.12
185 Michael Doleac	.15	.04
186 Bo Outlaw	.15	.04
187 Allen Iverson CL	.40	.12
188 Allen Iverson	.75	.23
189 Theo Ratliff	.25	.07
190 Matt Geiger	.15	.04
191 Larry Hughes	.40	.12
192 Tyrone Hill	.15	.04
193 George Lynch	.15	.04
194 Eric Snow	.25	.07
195 Aaron McKie	.25	.07
196 Harvey Grant	.15	.04
197 Jason Kidd CL	.25	.07
198 Jason Kidd	.60	.18
199 Tom Gugliotta	.15	.04
200 Rex Chapman	.15	.04
201 Clifford Robinson	.15	.04
202 Luc Longley	.15	.04
203 Danny Manning	.15	.04
204 Pat Garrity	.15	.04
205 George McCloud	.15	.04
206 Toby Bailey	.15	.04
207 Brian Grant CL	.15	.04
208 Rasheed Wallace	.40	.12
209 Arvydas Sabonis	.25	.07
210 Damon Stoudamire	.25	.07
211 Brian Grant	.25	.07
212 Isaiah Rider	.15	.04
213 Walt Williams	.15	.04
214 Jim Jackson	.15	.04
215 Greg Anthony	.15	.04
216 Stacey Augmon	.15	.04
217 Vlade Divac CL	.15	.04
218 Jason Williams	.40	.12
219 Vlade Divac	.25	.07
220 Chris Webber	.40	.12
221 Nick Anderson	.15	.04
222 Peja Stojakovic	.50	.15
223 Tariq Abdul-Wahad	.15	.04
224 Vernon Maxwell	.15	.04
225 Lawrence Funderburke	.15	.04
226 Jon Barry	.15	.04
227 David Robinson CL	.25	.07
228 Tim Duncan	.75	.23

❑ 229 Sean Elliott .25 .07
❑ 230 David Robinson .40 .12
❑ 231 Mario Elie .15 .04
❑ 232 Avery Johnson .15 .04
❑ 233 Steve Kerr .25 .07
❑ 234 Malik Rose .15 .04
❑ 235 Jaren Jackson .15 .04
❑ 236 Vin Baker CL .15 .04
❑ 237 Gary Payton .40 .12
❑ 238 Vin Baker .25 .07
❑ 239 Detlef Schrempf .25 .07
❑ 240 Hersey Hawkins .25 .07
❑ 241 Dale Ellis .15 .04
❑ 242 Rashard Lewis .40 .12
❑ 243 Billy Owens .15 .04
❑ 244 Aaron Williams .15 .04
❑ 245 Vince Carter CL .50 .15
❑ 246 Vince Carter 1.00 .30
❑ 247 John Wallace .15 .04
❑ 248 Doug Christie .25 .07
❑ 249 Tracy McGrady 1.00 .30
❑ 250 Kevin Willis .15 .04
❑ 251 Michael Stewart .15 .04
❑ 252 Dee Brown .15 .04
❑ 253 John Thomas .15 .04
❑ 254 Alvin Williams .15 .04
❑ 255 Karl Malone CL .40 .12
❑ 256 Karl Malone .40 .12
❑ 257 John Stockton .40 .12
❑ 258 Jacque Vaughn .15 .04
❑ 259 Bryon Russell .15 .04
❑ 260 Howard Eisley .15 .04
❑ 261 Greg Ostertag .15 .04
❑ 262 Adam Keefe .15 .04
❑ 263 Todd Fuller .15 .04
❑ 264 Mike Bibby CL .25 .07
❑ 265 Shareef Abdur-Rahim .40 .12
❑ 266 Mike Bibby .40 .12
❑ 267 Bryant Reeves .15 .04
❑ 268 Felipe Lopez .15 .04
❑ 269 Cherokee Parks .15 .04
❑ 270 Michael Smith .15 .04
❑ 271 Tony Massenburg .15 .04
❑ 272 Rodrick Rhodes .15 .04
❑ 273 Juwan Howard CL .15 .04
❑ 274 Juwan Howard .25 .07
❑ 275 Rod Strickland .15 .04
❑ 276 Mitch Richmond .25 .07
❑ 277 Otis Thorpe .25 .07
❑ 278 Calbert Cheaney .15 .04
❑ 279 Tracy Murray .15 .04
❑ 280 Ben Wallace .40 .12
❑ 281 Terry Davis .15 .04
❑ 282 Michael Jordan RF 1.25 .35
❑ 283 Reggie Miller RF .25 .07
❑ 284 Dikembe Mutombo RF .15 .04
❑ 285 Patrick Ewing RF .25 .07
❑ 286 Allan Houston RF .25 .07
❑ 287 Danny Manning RF .15 .04
❑ 288 Jalen Rose RF .25 .07
❑ 289 Rasheed Wallace RF .25 .07
❑ 290 Jerry Stackhouse RF .25 .07
❑ 291 Damon Stoudamire RF .15 .04
❑ 292 Kenny Anderson RF .15 .04
❑ 293 Shawn Kemp RF .15 .04
❑ 294 Vlade Divac RF .15 .04
❑ 295 Larry Johnson RF .15 .04
❑ 296 Jamal Mashburn RF .15 .04
❑ 297 Ron Harper RF .15 .04
❑ 298 Steve Smith RF .15 .04
❑ 299 Kendall Gill RF .15 .04
❑ 300 Chris Mullin RF .25 .07
❑ 301 Robert Horry RF .15 .04
❑ 302 Dikembe Mutombo DD .15 .04
❑ 303 Ron Mercer DD .15 .04
❑ 304 Eddie Jones DD .25 .07
❑ 305 Toni Kukoc DD .15 .04
❑ 306 Derek Anderson DD .15 .04
❑ 307 Shawn Bradley DD .15 .04
❑ 308 Danny Fortson DD .15 .04
❑ 309 Bison Dele DD .15 .04
❑ 310 Antawn Jamison DD .40 .12
❑ 311 Scottie Pippen DD .25 .07
❑ 312 Reggie Miller DD .25 .07
❑ 313 Maurice Taylor DD .15 .04
❑ 314 Glen Rice DD .15 .04
❑ 315 Alonzo Mourning DD .25 .07
❑ 316 Glenn Robinson DD .25 .07
❑ 317 Anthony Peeler DD .15 .04
❑ 318 Kerry Kittles DD .15 .04
❑ 319 Latrell Sprewell DD .40 .12
❑ 320 Darrell Armstrong DD .15 .04
❑ 321 Larry Hughes DD .25 .07
❑ 322 Tom Gugliotta DD .15 .04
❑ 323 Brian Grant DD .15 .04
❑ 324 Chris Webber DD .25 .07
❑ 325 David Robinson DD .25 .07
❑ 326 Vin Baker DD .15 .04
❑ 327 Vince Carter DD .50 .15
❑ 328 Bryon Russell DD .15 .04
❑ 329 Felipe Lopez DD .15 .04
❑ 330 Juwan Howard DD .15 .04
❑ 331 Michael Jordan DD 1.25 .35
❑ 332 Jason Kidd CC .25 .07
❑ 333 Rod Strickland CC .15 .04
❑ 334 Stephon Marbury CC .25 .07
❑ 335 Gary Payton CC .25 .07
❑ 336 Mark Jackson CC .15 .04
❑ 337 John Stockton CC .25 .07
❑ 338 Brevin Knight CC .15 .04
❑ 339 Bobby Jackson CC .15 .04
❑ 340 Nick Van Exel CC .15 .04
❑ 341 Tim Hardaway CC .15 .04
❑ 342 Darrell Armstrong CC .15 .04
❑ 343 Avery Johnson CC .15 .04
❑ 344 Mike Bibby CC .25 .07
❑ 345 Damon Stoudamire CC .15 .04
❑ 346 Jason Williams CC .25 .07
❑ 347 Allen Iverson PC .40 .12
❑ 348 Kobe Bryant PC .75 .23
❑ 349 Karl Malone PC .40 .12
❑ 350 Keith Van Horn PC .40 .12
❑ 351 Kevin Garnett PC .40 .12
❑ 352 Antoine Walker PC .25 .07
❑ 353 Tim Duncan PC .50 .15
❑ 354 Scottie Pippen PC .25 .07
❑ 355 Paul Pierce PC .40 .12
❑ 356 Michael Finley PC .25 .07
❑ 357 Shaquille O'Neal PC .50 .15
❑ 358 Grant Hill PC .25 .07
❑ 359 Jason Williams PC .25 .07
❑ 360 Antonio McDyess PC .25 .07
❑ 361 Shareef Abdur-Rahim PC .25 .07
❑ 362 Allen Iverson SC .40 .12
❑ 363 Shaquille O'Neal SC .50 .15
❑ 364 Karl Malone SC .40 .12
❑ 365 Shareef Abdur-Rahim SC .25 .07
❑ 366 Keith Van Horn SC .40 .12
❑ 367 Tim Duncan SC .50 .15
❑ 368 Gary Payton SC .25 .07
❑ 369 Stephon Marbury SC .25 .07
❑ 370 Antonio McDyess SC .25 .07
❑ 371 Grant Hill SC .25 .07
❑ 372 Kevin Garnett SC .40 .12
❑ 373 Shawn Kemp SC .15 .04
❑ 374 Kobe Bryant SC .75 .23
❑ 375 Michael Finley SC .25 .07
❑ 376 Vince Carter SC .50 .15
❑ 377 Checklist .15 .04
❑ 378 Checklist .15 .04
❑ 379 Checklist .15 .04
❑ 380 Checklist .15 .04
❑ 381 Michael Jordan GH 1.00 .30
❑ 382 Michael Jordan GH 1.00 .30
❑ 383 Michael Jordan GH 1.00 .30
❑ 384 Michael Jordan GH 1.00 .30
❑ 385 Michael Jordan GH 1.00 .30
❑ 386 Michael Jordan GH 1.00 .30
❑ 387 Michael Jordan GH 1.00 .30
❑ 388 Michael Jordan GH 1.00 .30
❑ 389 Michael Jordan GH 1.00 .30
❑ 390 Michael Jordan GH 1.00 .30
❑ 391 Michael Jordan GH 1.00 .30
❑ 392 Michael Jordan GH 1.00 .30
❑ 393 Michael Jordan GH 1.00 .30
❑ 394 Michael Jordan GH 1.00 .30
❑ 395 Michael Jordan GH 1.00 .30
❑ 396 Michael Jordan GH 1.00 .30
❑ 397 Michael Jordan GH 1.00 .30
❑ 398 Michael Jordan GH 1.00 .30
❑ 399 Michael Jordan GH 1.00 .30
❑ 400 Michael Jordan GH 1.00 .30
❑ 401 Michael Jordan GH 1.00 .30
❑ 402 Michael Jordan GH 1.00 .30
❑ 403 Michael Jordan GH 1.00 .30
❑ 404 Michael Jordan GH 1.00 .30
❑ 405 Michael Jordan GH 1.00 .30
❑ 406 Michael Jordan GH 1.00 .30
❑ 407 Michael Jordan GH 1.00 .30
❑ 408 Michael Jordan GH 1.00 .30
❑ 409 Michael Jordan GH 1.00 .30
❑ 410 Michael Jordan GH 1.00 .30
❑ 411 Michael Jordan GH 1.00 .30
❑ 412 Michael Jordan GH 1.00 .30
❑ 413 Michael Jordan GH 1.00 .30
❑ 414 Michael Jordan GH 1.00 .30
❑ 415 Michael Jordan GH 1.00 .30
❑ 416 Michael Jordan GH 1.00 .30
❑ 417 Michael Jordan GH 1.00 .30
❑ 418 Michael Jordan GH 1.00 .30
❑ 419 Michael Jordan GH 1.00 .30
❑ 420 Michael Jordan GH 1.00 .30
❑ 421 Michael Jordan GH 1.00 .30
❑ 422 Michael Jordan GH 1.00 .30
❑ 423 Michael Jordan GH 1.00 .30
❑ 424 Michael Jordan GH 1.00 .30
❑ 425 Michael Jordan GH 1.00 .30
❑ 426 Michael Jordan GH 1.00 .30
❑ 427 Michael Jordan GH 1.00 .30
❑ 428 Michael Jordan GH 1.00 .30
❑ 429 Michael Jordan GH 1.00 .30
❑ 430 Michael Jordan GH 1.00 .30
❑ 431 Elton Brand RC 2.00 .60
❑ 432 Steve Francis RC 2.50 .75
❑ 433 Baron Davis RC 1.50 .45
❑ 434 Lamar Odom RC 1.50 .45
❑ 435 Wally Szczerbiak RC 1.50 .45
❑ 436 Richard Hamilton RC 1.50 .45
❑ 437 Andre Miller RC 1.50 .45
❑ 438 Shawn Marion RC 2.00 .60
❑ 439 Jason Terry RC 1.25 .35
❑ 440 Corey Maggette RC 1.50 .45

2000-01 Upper Deck Victory

	Nm-Mt	Ex-Mt
COMPLETE SET (330)	60.00	18.00
COMMON CARD (1-260)	.15	.04
COMMON KOBE (281-305)	.60	.18
COMMON KG (306-330)	.50	.15
COMMON ROOKIE (261-280)	.60	.18

❑ 1 Dikembe Mutombo .25 .07
❑ 2 Jim Jackson .15 .04
❑ 3 Jason Terry .40 .12
❑ 4 Roshown McLeod .15 .04
❑ 5 Alan Henderson .15 .04
❑ 6 Bimbo Coles .15 .04
❑ 7 Dion Glover .15 .04
❑ 8 Lorenzen Wright .15 .04
❑ 9 Paul Pierce .40 .12
❑ 10 Kenny Anderson .25 .07
❑ 11 Antoine Walker .40 .12
❑ 12 Adrian Griffin .15 .04
❑ 13 Vitaly Potapenko .15 .04
❑ 14 Dana Barros .15 .04
❑ 15 Eric Williams .15 .04
❑ 16 Calbert Cheaney .15 .04
❑ 17 Derrick Coleman .15 .04
❑ 18 Eddie Jones .40 .12

❑ 19 Anthony Mason .25 .07
❑ 20 Elden Campbell .15 .04
❑ 21 Eddie Robinson .25 .07
❑ 22 David Wesley .15 .04
❑ 23 Baron Davis .40 .12
❑ 24 Ricky Davis .25 .07
❑ 25 Elton Brand .40 .12
❑ 26 Ron Artest .25 .07
❑ 27 Chris Carr .15 .04
❑ 28 Fred Hoiberg .15 .04
❑ 29 Hersey Hawkins .15 .04
❑ 30 Dickey Simpkins .15 .04
❑ 31 Corey Benjamin .15 .04
❑ 32 Matt Maloney .15 .04
❑ 33 Shawn Kemp .25 .07
❑ 34 Lamond Murray .15 .04
❑ 35 Wesley Person .15 .04
❑ 36 Andre Miller .25 .07
❑ 37 Bob Sura .15 .04
❑ 38 Andrew DeClercq .15 .04
❑ 39 Brevin Knight .15 .04
❑ 40 Earl Boykins RC 2.00 .60
❑ 41 Michael Finley .40 .12
❑ 42 Dirk Nowitzki .60 .18
❑ 43 Cedric Ceballos .15 .04
❑ 44 Robert Pack .15 .04
❑ 45 Erick Strickland .15 .04
❑ 46 Sean Rooks .15 .04
❑ 47 Shawn Bradley .15 .04
❑ 48 Steve Nash .40 .12
❑ 49 Antonio McDyess .25 .07
❑ 50 Nick Van Exel .40 .12
❑ 51 Keon Clark .25 .07
❑ 52 Raef LaFrentz .25 .07
❑ 53 James Posey .25 .07
❑ 54 Chris Gatling .15 .04
❑ 55 George McCloud .15 .04
❑ 56 Bryant Stith .15 .04
❑ 57 Jerry Stackhouse .40 .12
❑ 58 Lindsey Hunter .15 .04
❑ 59 Christian Laettner .25 .07
❑ 60 Jerome Williams .15 .04
❑ 61 Michael Curry .15 .04
❑ 62 Loy Vaught .15 .04
❑ 63 Eric Montross .15 .04
❑ 64 Grant Hill .40 .12
❑ 65 Antawn Jamison .40 .12
❑ 66 Chris Mills .15 .04
❑ 67 Vonteego Cummings .15 .04
❑ 68 Larry Hughes .25 .07
❑ 69 Donyell Marshall .25 .07
❑ 70 Mookie Blaylock .15 .04
❑ 71 Erick Dampier .25 .07
❑ 72 Jason Caffey .15 .04
❑ 73 Steve Francis .40 .12
❑ 74 Shandon Anderson .15 .04
❑ 75 Hakeem Olajuwon .40 .12
❑ 76 Walt Williams .15 .04
❑ 77 Kenny Thomas .15 .04
❑ 78 Carlos Rogers .15 .04
❑ 79 Bryce Drew .15 .04
❑ 80 Kelvin Cato .15 .04
❑ 81 Reggie Miller .40 .12
❑ 82 Austin Croshere .25 .07
❑ 83 Rik Smits .25 .07
❑ 84 Jalen Rose .40 .12
❑ 85 Dale Davis .15 .04
❑ 86 Jonathan Bender .25 .07
❑ 87 Travis Best .15 .04
❑ 88 Chris Mullin .40 .12
❑ 89 Lamar Odom .40 .12
❑ 90 Tyrone Nesby .15 .04
❑ 91 Michael Olowokandi .15 .04
❑ 92 Eric Piatkowski .25 .07
❑ 93 Jeff McInnis .15 .04
❑ 94 Brian Skinner .15 .04
❑ 95 Pete Chilcutt .15 .04
❑ 96 Eric Murdock .15 .04
❑ 97 Shaquille O'Neal 1.00 .30
❑ 98 Kobe Bryant 1.50 .45
❑ 99 Ron Harper .25 .07
❑ 100 Robert Horry .25 .07
❑ 101 Rick Fox .25 .07
❑ 102 Derek Fisher .40 .12
❑ 103 Tyronn Lue .25 .07
❑ 104 Devean George .25 .07
❑ 105 Alonzo Mourning .25 .07
❑ 106 Jamal Mashburn .25 .07
❑ 107 Anthony Carter .25 .07
❑ 108 P.J. Brown .15 .04
❑ 109 Clarence Weatherspoon .15 .04
❑ 110 Otis Thorpe .15 .04
❑ 111 Voshon Lenard .15 .04
❑ 112 Tim Hardaway .25 .07
❑ 113 Ray Allen .40 .12
❑ 114 Glenn Robinson .40 .12
❑ 115 Sam Cassell .40 .12
❑ 116 Robert Traylor .15 .04
❑ 117 Ervin Johnson .15 .04
❑ 118 Scott Williams .15 .04
❑ 119 Tim Thomas .25 .07
❑ 120 Vinny Del Negro .15 .04
❑ 121 Kevin Garnett .75 .23
❑ 122 Wally Szczerbiak .25 .07
❑ 123 Terrell Brandon .25 .07
❑ 124 Dean Garrett .15 .04
❑ 125 William Avery .15 .04
❑ 126 Sam Mitchell .15 .04
❑ 127 Radoslav Nesterovic .25 .07
❑ 128 Anthony Peeler .15 .04
❑ 129 Stephon Marbury .40 .12
❑ 130 Keith Van Horn .40 .12
❑ 131 Kerry Kittles .15 .04
❑ 132 Lucious Harris .15 .04
❑ 133 Evan Eschmeyer .15 .04
❑ 134 Jamie Feick .15 .04
❑ 135 Jim McIlvaine .15 .04
❑ 136 Kendall Gill .15 .04
❑ 137 Allan Houston .25 .07
❑ 138 Marcus Camby .25 .07
❑ 139 Latrell Sprewell .40 .12
❑ 140 Patrick Ewing .40 .12
❑ 141 Larry Johnson .25 .07
❑ 142 Charlie Ward .15 .04
❑ 143 Chris Childs .15 .04
❑ 144 John Wallace .15 .04
❑ 145 Darrell Armstrong .15 .04
❑ 146 Corey Maggette .25 .07
❑ 147 Pat Garrity .15 .04
❑ 148 John Amaechi .15 .04
❑ 149 Matt Harpring .40 .12
❑ 150 Michael Doleac .15 .04
❑ 151 Ron Mercer .25 .07
❑ 152 Chucky Atkins .15 .04
❑ 153 Allen Iverson .75 .23
❑ 154 Matt Geiger .15 .04
❑ 155 Eric Snow .25 .07
❑ 156 Tyrone Hill .15 .04
❑ 157 Theo Ratliff .25 .07
❑ 158 George Lynch .15 .04
❑ 159 Kevin Ollie .15 .04
❑ 160 Toni Kukoc .25 .07
❑ 161 Jason Kidd .60 .18
❑ 162 Anfernee Hardaway .40 .12
❑ 163 Rodney Rogers .15 .04
❑ 164 Shawn Marion .40 .12
❑ 165 Clifford Robinson .15 .04
❑ 166 Tom Gugliotta .15 .04
❑ 167 Luc Longley .15 .04
❑ 168 Randy Livingston .15 .04
❑ 169 Scottie Pippen .60 .18
❑ 170 Steve Smith .25 .07
❑ 171 Damon Stoudamire .25 .07
❑ 172 Bonzi Wells .25 .07
❑ 173 Jermaine O'Neal .40 .12
❑ 174 Arvydas Sabonis .25 .07
❑ 175 Rasheed Wallace .40 .12
❑ 176 Detlef Schrempf .25 .07
❑ 177 Jason Williams .25 .07
❑ 178 Chris Webber .40 .12
❑ 179 Peja Stojakovic .40 .12
❑ 180 Vlade Divac .25 .07
❑ 181 Lawrence Funderburke .15 .04
❑ 182 Tony Delk .15 .04
❑ 183 Jon Barry .15 .04
❑ 184 Tim Duncan .75 .23
❑ 185 Sean Elliott .25 .07
❑ 186 Terry Porter .15 .04
❑ 187 David Robinson .40 .12
❑ 188 Samaki Walker .15 .04
❑ 189 Malik Rose .15 .04
❑ 190 Jaren Jackson .15 .04
❑ 191 Steve Kerr .25 .07
❑ 192 Gary Payton .40 .12
❑ 193 Brent Barry .25 .07
❑ 194 Vin Baker .25 .07
❑ 195 Horace Grant .25 .07
❑ 196 Ruben Patterson .25 .07
❑ 197 Vernon Maxwell .15 .04
❑ 198 Shammond Williams .15 .04
❑ 199 Rashard Lewis .25 .07
❑ 200 Tracy McGrady 1.00 .30
❑ 201 Charles Oakley .15 .04
❑ 202 Doug Christie .25 .07
❑ 203 Antonio Davis .15 .04
❑ 204 Vince Carter 1.00 .30
❑ 205 Kevin Willis .15 .04
❑ 206 Dell Curry .15 .04
❑ 207 Dee Brown .15 .04
❑ 208 Karl Malone .40 .12
❑ 209 John Stockton .40 .12
❑ 210 Bryon Russell .15 .04
❑ 211 Olden Polynice .15 .04
❑ 212 Jacque Vaughn .15 .04
❑ 213 Greg Ostertag .15 .04
❑ 214 Quincy Lewis .15 .04
❑ 215 Armon Gilliam .15 .04
❑ 216 Shareef Abdur-Rahim .40 .12
❑ 217 Michael Dickerson .25 .07
❑ 218 Mike Bibby .40 .12
❑ 219 Bryant Reeves .15 .04
❑ 220 Othella Harrington .15 .04
❑ 221 Grant Long .15 .04
❑ 222 Felipe Lopez .15 .04
❑ 223 Obinna Ekezie .15 .04
❑ 224 Mitch Richmond .25 .07
❑ 225 Richard Hamilton .25 .07
❑ 226 Tracy Murray .15 .04
❑ 227 Jahidi White .15 .04
❑ 228 Aaron Williams .15 .04
❑ 229 Juwan Howard .25 .07
❑ 230 Rod Strickland .15 .04
❑ 231 Isaac Austin .15 .04
❑ 232 Dikembe Mutombo VL .15 .04
❑ 233 Antoine Walker VL .25 .07
❑ 234 Derrick Coleman VL .15 .04
❑ 235 Elton Brand VL .25 .07
❑ 236 Shawn Kemp VL .15 .04
❑ 237 Michael Finley VL .25 .07
❑ 238 Antonio McDyess VL .25 .07
❑ 239 Grant Hill VL .25 .07
❑ 240 Antawn Jamison VL .40 .12
❑ 241 Steve Francis VL .25 .07
❑ 242 Jalen Rose VL .25 .07
❑ 243 Lamar Odom VL .25 .07
❑ 244 Shaquille O'Neal VL .50 .15
❑ 245 Alonzo Mourning VL .25 .07
❑ 246 Ray Allen VL .25 .07
❑ 247 Kevin Garnett VL .40 .12
❑ 248 Stephon Marbury VL .25 .07
❑ 249 Allan Houston VL .25 .07
❑ 250 Darrell Armstrong VL .15 .04
❑ 251 Allen Iverson VL .40 .12
❑ 252 Jason Kidd VL .40 .12
❑ 253 Rasheed Wallace VL .25 .07
❑ 254 Chris Webber VL .25 .07
❑ 255 Tim Duncan VL .40 .12
❑ 256 Gary Payton VL .40 .12
❑ 257 Vince Carter VL .50 .15
❑ 258 Karl Malone VL .40 .12
❑ 259 Shareef Abdur-Rahim VL .25 .07
❑ 260 Mitch Richmond VL .15 .04
❑ 261 Kenyon Martin RC 2.50 .75
❑ 262 Marcus Fizer RC .60 .18
❑ 263 Chris Mihm RC .60 .18
❑ 264 Stromile Swift RC 1.25 .35
❑ 265 Keyon Dooling RC .60 .18
❑ 266 Morris Peterson RC 1.25 .35
❑ 267 Quentin Richardson RC 2.00 .60
❑ 268 Courtney Alexander RC .60 .18
❑ 269 Desmond Mason RC .60 .18
❑ 270 Mateen Cleaves RC .60 .18
❑ 271 Erick Barkley RC .60 .18
❑ 272 A.J. Guyton RC .60 .18
❑ 273 Darius Miles RC 2.00 .60
❑ 274 DerMarr Johnson RC .60 .18
❑ 275 Joel Przybilla RC .60 .18
❑ 276 Hanno Mottola RC .60 .18

❑ 277 Mike Miller RC	2.00	.60
❑ 278 Donnell Harvey RC	.60	.18
❑ 279 Speedy Claxton RC	.60	.18
❑ 280 Khalid El-Amin RC	.60	.18
❑ 281 Kobe Bryant FLY	.60	.18
❑ 282 Kobe Bryant FLY	.60	.18
❑ 283 Kobe Bryant FLY	.60	.18
❑ 284 Kobe Bryant FLY	.60	.18
❑ 285 Kobe Bryant FLY	.60	.18
❑ 286 Kobe Bryant FLY	.60	.18
❑ 287 Kobe Bryant FLY	.60	.18
❑ 288 Kobe Bryant FLY	.60	.18
❑ 289 Kobe Bryant FLY	.60	.18
❑ 290 Kobe Bryant FLY	.60	.18
❑ 291 Kobe Bryant FLY	.60	.18
❑ 292 Kobe Bryant FLY	.60	.18
❑ 293 Kobe Bryant FLY	.60	.18
❑ 294 Kobe Bryant FLY	.60	.18
❑ 295 Kobe Bryant FLY	.60	.18
❑ 296 Kobe Bryant FLY	.60	.18
❑ 297 Kobe Bryant FLY	.60	.18
❑ 298 Kobe Bryant FLY	.60	.18
❑ 299 Kobe Bryant FLY	.60	.18
❑ 300 Kobe Bryant FLY	.60	.18
❑ 301 Kobe Bryant FLY	.60	.18
❑ 302 Kobe Bryant FLY	.60	.18
❑ 303 Kobe Bryant FLY	.60	.18
❑ 304 Kobe Bryant FLY	.60	.18
❑ 305 Kobe Bryant FLY	.60	.18
❑ 306 Kevin Garnett FLY	.50	.15
❑ 307 Kevin Garnett FLY	.50	.15
❑ 308 Kevin Garnett FLY	.50	.15
❑ 309 Kevin Garnett FLY	.50	.15
❑ 310 Kevin Garnett FLY	.50	.15
❑ 311 Kevin Garnett FLY	.50	.15
❑ 312 Kevin Garnett FLY	.50	.15
❑ 313 Kevin Garnett FLY	.50	.15
❑ 314 Kevin Garnett FLY	.50	.15
❑ 315 Kevin Garnett FLY	.50	.15
❑ 316 Kevin Garnett FLY	.50	.15
❑ 317 Kevin Garnett FLY	.50	.15
❑ 318 Kevin Garnett FLY	.50	.15
❑ 319 Kevin Garnett FLY	.50	.15
❑ 320 Kevin Garnett FLY	.50	.15
❑ 321 Kevin Garnett FLY	.50	.15
❑ 322 Kevin Garnett FLY	.50	.15
❑ 323 Kevin Garnett FLY	.50	.15
❑ 324 Kevin Garnett FLY	.50	.15
❑ 325 Kevin Garnett FLY	.50	.15
❑ 326 Kevin Garnett FLY	.50	.15
❑ 327 Kevin Garnett FLY	.50	.15
❑ 328 Kevin Garnett FLY	.50	.15
❑ 329 Kevin Garnett FLY	.50	.15
❑ 330 Kevin Garnett FLY	.50	.15

2003-04 Upper Deck Victory

	Nm-Mt	Ex-Mt
COMP.SET w/o SP's (100)	15.00	4.50
COMMON ROOKIE (101-130)	1.50	.45
COMMON POD (182-201)	1.00	.30
❑ 1 Shareef Abdur-Rahim	.25	.07
❑ 2 Jason Terry	.25	.07
❑ 3 Glenn Robinson	.25	.07
❑ 4 Paul Pierce	.25	.07
❑ 5 Antoine Walker	.25	.07
❑ 6 J.R.Bremer	.10	.03
❑ 7 Vin Baker	.20	.06
❑ 8 Jalen Rose	.25	.07
❑ 9 Tyson Chandler	.25	.07
❑ 10 Eddy Curry	.25	.07
❑ 11 Jay Williams	.20	.06
❑ 12 DaJuan Wagner	.20	.06
❑ 13 Ricky Davis	.25	.07
❑ 14 Zydrunas Ilgauskas	.20	.06
❑ 15 Darius Miles	.25	.07
❑ 16 Dirk Nowitzki	.50	.15
❑ 17A Michael Finley	.25	.07
❑ 17B Jermaine O'Neal	.25	.07
❑ 18 Steve Nash	.25	.07
❑ 19 Nick Van Exel	.25	.07
❑ 20 Rodney White	.10	.03
❑ 21 Juwan Howard	.20	.06
❑ 22 Marcus Camby	.20	.06
❑ 23 Nene Hilario	.20	.06
❑ 24 Richard Hamilton	.20	.06
❑ 25 Ben Wallace	.25	.07
❑ 26 Cliff Robinson	.10	.03
❑ 27 Antawn Jamison	.25	.07
❑ 28 Jason Richardson	.25	.07
❑ 29 Gilbert Arenas	.25	.07
❑ 30 Mike Dunleavy	.20	.06
❑ 31 Steve Francis	.25	.07
❑ 32 Eddie Griffin	.20	.06
❑ 33 Cuttino Mobley	.20	.06
❑ 34 Yao Ming	1.50	.45
❑ 35 Reggie Miller	.25	.07
❑ 36 Jamaal Tinsley	.25	.07
❑ 37 Does Not Exist	-	-
❑ 38 Elton Brand	.25	.07
❑ 39 Andre Miller	.20	.06
❑ 40 Lamar Odom	.25	.07
❑ 41 Kobe Bryant	1.25	.35
❑ 42 Shaquille O'Neal	.75	.23
❑ 43 Derek Fisher	.25	.07
❑ 44 Pau Gasol	.25	.07
❑ 45 Shane Battier	.25	.07
❑ 46 Mike Miller	.25	.07
❑ 47 Eddie Jones	.25	.07
❑ 48 Alonzo Mourning	.20	.06
❑ 49 Caron Butler	.25	.07
❑ 50 Gary Payton	.25	.07
❑ 51 Desmond Mason	.20	.06
❑ 52 Sam Cassell	.25	.07
❑ 53 Toni Kukoc	.20	.06
❑ 54 Kevin Garnett	.60	.18
❑ 55 Wally Szczerbiak	.20	.06
❑ 56 Joe Smith	.20	.06
❑ 57 Jason Kidd	.50	.15
❑ 58 Richard Jefferson	.20	.06
❑ 59 Kenyon Martin	.25	.07
❑ 60 Baron Davis	.25	.07
❑ 61 Jamal Mashburn	.20	.06
❑ 62 Jamaal Magloire	.10	.03
❑ 63 Allan Houston	.20	.06
❑ 64 Antonio McDyess	.20	.06
❑ 65 Latrell Sprewell	.25	.07
❑ 66 Tracy McGrady	1.00	.30
❑ 67 Grant Hill	.25	.07
❑ 68 Drew Gooden	.20	.06
❑ 69 Gordan Giricek	.20	.06
❑ 70 Allen Iverson	.60	.18
❑ 71 Keith Van Horn	.25	.07
❑ 72 Aaron McKie	.20	.06
❑ 73 Stephon Marbury	.25	.07
❑ 74 Shawn Marion	.25	.07
❑ 75 Anfernee Hardaway	.25	.07
❑ 76 Amare Stoudemire	.60	.18
❑ 77 Rasheed Wallace	.25	.07
❑ 78 Derek Anderson	.20	.06
❑ 79 Scottie Pippen	.50	.15
❑ 80 Chris Webber	.25	.07
❑ 81 Mike Bibby	.25	.07
❑ 82 Peja Stojakovic	.25	.07
❑ 83 Hedo Turkoglu	.25	.07
❑ 84 Tim Duncan	.60	.18
❑ 85 David Robinson	.25	.07
❑ 86 Tony Parker	.25	.07
❑ 87 Manu Ginobili	.25	.07
❑ 88 Ray Allen	.25	.07
❑ 89 Rashard Lewis	.25	.07
❑ 90 Reggie Evans	.10	.03
❑ 91 Alvin Williams	.10	.03
❑ 92 Vince Carter	.75	.23
❑ 93 Morris Peterson	.20	.06
❑ 94 Antonio Davis	.10	.03
❑ 95 Karl Malone	.25	.07
❑ 96 John Stockton	.25	.07
❑ 97 Andrei Kirilenko	.25	.07
❑ 98 Jerry Stackhouse	.25	.07
❑ 99 Kwame Brown	.20	.06
❑ 100 Michael Jordan	3.00	.90
❑ 101 Lebron James SP RC	15.00	4.50
❑ 102 Darko Milicic RC	2.00	.60
❑ 103 Carmelo Anthony RC	8.00	2.40
❑ 104 Chris Bosh RC	4.00	1.20
❑ 105 Dwyane Wade RC	4.00	1.20
❑ 106 Chris Kaman RC	1.50	.45
❑ 107 Kirk Hinrich RC	2.50	.75
❑ 108 T.J. Ford RC	2.00	.60
❑ 109 Mike Sweetney RC	1.50	.45
❑ 110 Jarvis Hayes RC	1.50	.45
❑ 111 Mickael Pietrus RC	1.50	.45
❑ 112 Nick Collison RC	1.50	.45
❑ 113 Marcus Banks RC	1.50	.45
❑ 114 Luke Ridnour RC	2.00	.60
❑ 115 Reece Gaines RC	1.50	.45
❑ 116 Troy Bell RC	1.50	.45
❑ 117 Zarko Cabarkapa RC	1.50	.45
❑ 118 David West RC	1.50	.45
❑ 119 Aleksandar Pavlovic RC	1.50	.45
❑ 120 Dahntay Jones RC	1.50	.45
❑ 121 Boris Diaw RC	1.50	.45
❑ 122 Zoran Planinic RC	1.50	.45
❑ 123 Travis Outlaw RC	1.50	.45
❑ 124 Brian Cook RC	1.50	.45
❑ 125 Carlos Delfino RC	1.50	.45
❑ 126 Ndudi Ebi RC	1.50	.45
❑ 127 Kendrick Perkins RC	1.50	.45
❑ 128 Leandro Barbosa RC	1.50	.45
❑ 129 Josh Howard RC	2.00	.60
❑ 130 Maciej Lampe RC	2.00	.60
❑ 134 Michael Jordan AS	10.00	3.00
❑ 135 Kobe Bryant AS	5.00	1.50
❑ 136 Kevin Garnett AS	2.50	.75
❑ 137 Yao Ming AS	3.00	.90
❑ 138 Vince Carter AS	3.00	.90
❑ 139 Dirk Nowitzki AS	2.00	.60
❑ 140 Antoine Walker AS	1.00	.30
❑ 141 Chris Webber AS	-	-
❑ 142 Ben Wallace AS	1.00	.30
❑ 143 Tracy McGrady AS	3.00	.90
❑ 144 Jason Kidd AS	2.00	.60
❑ 145 Steve Francis AS	-	-
❑ 146 Gary Payton AS	1.00	.30
❑ 147 Peja Stojakovic AS	1.00	.30
❑ 148 Brad Miller AS	1.25	.35
❑ 149 Shawn Marion AS	1.00	.30
❑ 150 Zydrunas Ilgauskas AS	.75	.23
❑ 151 Stephon Marbury AS	1.00	.30
❑ 152 Jermaine O'Neal AS	1.00	.30
❑ 153 Desmond Mason AS	.75	.23
❑ 154 Jeson Richardson AS	-	-
❑ 155 Tony Parker AS	1.00	.30
❑ 156 Tim Duncan AS	2.50	.75
❑ 157 Jamal Mashburn AS	1.00	.30
❑ 158 Allen Iverson AS	2.50	.75
❑ 159 Shaquille O'Neal AS	3.00	.90
❑ 160 Paul Pierce AS	1.00	.30
❑ 161 Steve Nash AS	1.00	.30
❑ 162 Michael Jordan CS	10.00	3.00
❑ 163 Mike Bibby CS	1.00	.30
❑ 164 Jay Williams CS	.75	.23
❑ 165 Richard Hamilton CS	.75	.23
❑ 166 Jerry Stackhouse CS	1.00	.30
❑ 167 Peja Stojakovic CS	1.00	.30
❑ 168 Reggie Miller CS	1.00	.30
❑ 169 Robert Horry CS	1.00	.30
❑ 170 Tim Duncan CS	2.50	.75
❑ 171 Jalen Rose CS	1.00	.30
❑ 172 Jason Richardson CS	2.00	.60
❑ 173 Allen Iverson CS	2.50	.75
❑ 174 Tracy McGrady CS	3.00	.90
❑ 175 Paul Pierce CS	1.00	.30
❑ 176 Dirk Nowitzki CS	2.00	.60
❑ 177 Baron Davis CS	1.00	.30
❑ 178 Latrell Sprewell CS	1.00	.30
❑ 179 John Stockton CS	1.00	.30
❑ 180 Ray Allen CS	1.00	.30

Card	Nm-Mt	Ex-Mt
❑ 181 Kobe Bryant CS	5.00	1.50
❑ 182 Mike Bibby POD	1.00	.30
❑ 183 Earl Boykins POD	1.00	.30
❑ 184 John Stockton POD	1.00	.30
❑ 185 Alvin Williams POD	1.00	.30
❑ 186 Darrell Armstrong POD	1.00	.30
❑ 187 Tony Parker POD	1.00	.30
❑ 188 Gary Payton POD	1.00	.30
❑ 189 Jalen Rose POD	1.00	.30
❑ 190 Jason Williams POD	1.00	.30
❑ 191 Derek Fisher POD	1.00	.30
❑ 192 Steve Nash POD	1.00	.30
❑ 193 Jamaal Tinsley POD	1.00	.30
❑ 194 Andre Miller POD	1.00	.30
❑ 195 Baron Davis POD	1.00	.30
❑ 196 Steve Francis POD	1.00	.30
❑ 197 DaJuan Wagner POD	1.00	.30
❑ 198 Stephon Marbury POD	1.00	.30
❑ 199 Jason Kidd POD	2.00	.60
❑ 200 Chauncey Billups POD	1.00	.30
❑ 201 Jay Williams POD	1.00	.30
❑ 202 Allen Iverson AKA	4.00	1.20
❑ 203 Steve Francis AKA	3.00	.90
❑ 204 Kenyon Martin AKA	1.50	.45
❑ 205 Vince Carter AKA	3.00	.90
❑ 206 Lebron James AKA	10.00	3.00
❑ 207 Julius Erving AKA	4.00	1.20
❑ 208 Tracy McGrady AKA	5.00	1.50
❑ 209 Jason Richardson AKA	3.00	.90
❑ 210 Earvin Johnson AKA	4.00	1.20
❑ 211 Michael Jordan AKA	15.00	4.50
❑ 212 Michael Jordan MJ	15.00	4.50
❑ 213 Kobe Bryant MJ	8.00	2.40
❑ 214 Richard Jefferson MJ	1.25	.35
❑ 215 Desmond Mason MJ	1.25	.35
❑ 216 Vince Carter MJ	5.00	1.50
❑ 217 Amare Stoudemire MJ	4.00	1.20
❑ 218 Yao Ming MJ	5.00	1.50
❑ 219 Elton Brand MJ	1.50	.45
❑ 220 Kevin Garnett MJ	4.00	1.20
❑ 221 Shaquille O'Neal MJ	5.00	1.50
❑ 222 Lebron James HR	15.00	4.50
❑ 223 Kobe Bryant HR	10.00	3.00
❑ 224 Richard Jefferson HR	1.50	.45
❑ 225 Yao Ming HR	6.00	1.80
❑ 226 Amare Stoudemire HR	5.00	1.50
❑ 227 Michael Jordan HR	12.00	3.60
❑ 228 Michael Jordan FL	12.00	3.60
❑ 229 Michael Jordan FL	12.00	3.60
❑ 230 Michael Jordan FL	12.00	3.60
❑ 231 Michael Jordan FL	12.00	3.60
❑ 232 Michael Jordan FL	12.00	3.60
❑ 233 Michael Jordan FL	12.00	3.60

1996-97 Z-Force

	Nm-Mt	Ex-Mt
COMPLETE SET (200)	40.00	12.00
COMPLETE SERIES 1 (100)	20.00	6.00
COMPLETE SERIES 2 (100)	20.00	6.00
❑ 1 Mookie Blaylock	.20	.06
❑ 2 Alan Henderson	.20	.06
❑ 3 Christian Laettner	.40	.12
❑ 4 Steve Smith	.40	.12
❑ 5 Rick Fox	.20	.06
❑ 6 Dino Radja	.20	.06
❑ 7 Eric Williams	.20	.06
❑ 8 Muggsy Bogues	.20	.06
❑ 9 Larry Johnson	.40	.12
❑ 10 Glen Rice	.40	.12
❑ 11 Michael Jordan	4.00	1.20
❑ 12 Toni Kukoc	.40	.12
❑ 13 Scottie Pippen	1.00	.30
❑ 14 Dennis Rodman	.40	.12
❑ 15 Terrell Brandon	.40	.12
❑ 16 Bobby Phills	.20	.06
❑ 17 Bob Sura	.20	.06
❑ 18 Jim Jackson	.20	.06
❑ 19 Jason Kidd	1.00	.30
❑ 20 Jamal Mashburn	.40	.12
❑ 21 George McCloud	.20	.06
❑ 22 Mahmoud Abdul-Rauf	.20	.06
❑ 23 Antonio McDyess	.40	.12
❑ 24 Dikembe Mutombo	.40	.12
❑ 25 Joe Dumars	.60	.18
❑ 26 Grant Hill	.60	.18
❑ 27 Allan Houston	.40	.12
❑ 28 Otis Thorpe	.20	.06
❑ 29 Chris Mullin	.60	.18
❑ 30 Joe Smith	.40	.12
❑ 31 Latrell Sprewell	.60	.18
❑ 32 Sam Cassell	.60	.18
❑ 33 Clyde Drexler	.60	.18
❑ 34 Robert Horry	.40	.12
❑ 35 Hakeem Olajuwon	.60	.18
❑ 36 Travis Best	.20	.06
❑ 37 Dale Davis	.20	.06
❑ 38 Reggie Miller	.60	.18
❑ 39 Rik Smits	.40	.12
❑ 40 Brent Barry	.20	.06
❑ 41 Loy Vaught	.20	.06
❑ 42 Brian Williams	.20	.06
❑ 43 Cedric Ceballos	.20	.06
❑ 44 Eddie Jones	.60	.18
❑ 45 Nick Van Exel	.60	.18
❑ 46 Tim Hardaway	.40	.12
❑ 47 Alonzo Mourning	.40	.12
❑ 48 Kurt Thomas	.40	.12
❑ 49 Walt Williams	.20	.06
❑ 50 Vin Baker	.40	.12
❑ 51 Glenn Robinson	.60	.18
❑ 52 Kevin Garnett	1.25	.35
❑ 53 Tom Gugliotta	.20	.06
❑ 54 Isaiah Rider	.40	.12
❑ 55 Shawn Bradley	.20	.06
❑ 56 Chris Childs	.20	.06
❑ 57 Jayson Williams	.40	.12
❑ 58 Patrick Ewing	.60	.18
❑ 59 Anthony Mason	.40	.12
❑ 60 Charles Oakley	.20	.06
❑ 61 Nick Anderson	.20	.06
❑ 62 Horace Grant	.40	.12
❑ 63 Anfernee Hardaway	.60	.18
❑ 64 Shaquille O'Neal	1.50	.45
❑ 65 Dennis Scott	.20	.06
❑ 66 Jerry Stackhouse	.75	.23
❑ 67 Clarence Weatherspoon	.20	.06
❑ 68 Charles Barkley	.75	.23
❑ 69 Michael Finley	.75	.23
❑ 70 Kevin Johnson	.40	.12
❑ 71 Clifford Robinson	.20	.06
❑ 72 Arvydas Sabonis	.40	.12
❑ 73 Rod Strickland	.20	.06
❑ 74 Tyus Edney	.20	.06
❑ 75 Brian Grant	.60	.18
❑ 76 Billy Owens	.20	.06
❑ 77 Mitch Richmond	.40	.12
❑ 78 Vinny Del Negro	.20	.06
❑ 79 Sean Elliott	.40	.12
❑ 80 Avery Johnson	.20	.06
❑ 81 David Robinson	.60	.18
❑ 82 Hersey Hawkins	.40	.12
❑ 83 Shawn Kemp	.40	.12
❑ 84 Gary Payton	.60	.18
❑ 85 Detlef Schrempf	.40	.12
❑ 86 Doug Christie	.40	.12
❑ 87 Damon Stoudamire	.60	.18
❑ 88 Sharone Wright	.20	.06
❑ 89 Jeff Hornacek	.40	.12
❑ 90 Karl Malone	.60	.18
❑ 91 John Stockton	.60	.18
❑ 92 Greg Anthony	.20	.06
❑ 93 Bryant Reeves	.20	.06
❑ 94 Byron Scott	.20	.06
❑ 95 Juwan Howard	.40	.12
❑ 96 Gheorghe Muresan	.20	.06
❑ 97 Rasheed Wallace	.75	.23
❑ 98 Chris Webber	.60	.18
❑ 99 Checklist	.20	.06
❑ 100 Checklist	.20	.06
❑ 101 Dikembe Mutombo	.40	.12
❑ 102 Dee Brown	.20	.06
❑ 103 Dell Curry	.20	.06
❑ 104 Vlade Divac	.20	.06
❑ 105 Anthony Mason	.40	.12
❑ 106 Robert Parish	.40	.12
❑ 107 Oliver Miller	.20	.06
❑ 108 Eric Montross	.20	.06
❑ 109 Ervin Johnson	.20	.06
❑ 110 Stacey Augmon	.20	.06
❑ 111 Charles Barkley	.75	.23
❑ 112 Jalen Rose	.60	.18
❑ 113 Rodney Rogers	.20	.06
❑ 114 Shaquille O'Neal	1.50	.45
❑ 115 Dan Majerle	.40	.12
❑ 116 Kendall Gill	.20	.06
❑ 117 Khalid Reeves	.20	.06
❑ 118 Allan Houston	.40	.12
❑ 119 Larry Johnson	.40	.12
❑ 120 John Starks	.40	.12
❑ 121 Rony Seikaly	.20	.06
❑ 122 Gerald Wilkins	.20	.06
❑ 123 Michael Cage	.20	.06
❑ 124 Derrick Coleman	.40	.12
❑ 125 Sam Cassell	.60	.18
❑ 126 Danny Manning	.40	.12
❑ 127 Robert Horry	.40	.12
❑ 128 Kenny Anderson	.20	.06
❑ 129 Isaiah Rider	.40	.12
❑ 130 Rasheed Wallace	.75	.23
❑ 131 Mahmoud Abdul-Rauf	.20	.06
❑ 132 Vernon Maxwell	.20	.06
❑ 133 Dominique Wilkins	.60	.18
❑ 134 Hubert Davis	.20	.06
❑ 135 Popeye Jones	.20	.06
❑ 136 Anthony Peeler	.20	.06
❑ 137 Tracy Murray	.20	.06
❑ 138 Rod Strickland	.20	.06
❑ 139 Shareef Abdur-Rahim RC	2.00	.60
❑ 140 Ray Allen RC	2.00	.60
❑ 141 Shandon Anderson RC	.40	.12
❑ 142 Kobe Bryant RC	8.00	2.40
❑ 143 Marcus Camby RC	.75	.23
❑ 144 Erick Dampier RC	.60	.18
❑ 145 Emanual Davis RC	.20	.06
❑ 146 Tony Delk RC	.60	.18
❑ 147 Todd Fuller RC	.20	.06
❑ 148 Darvin Ham RC	.20	.06
❑ 149 Othella Harrington RC	.60	.18
❑ 150 Shane Heal RC	.20	.06
❑ 151 Allen Iverson RC	3.00	.90
❑ 152 Dontae' Jones RC	.20	.06
❑ 153 Kerry Kittles RC	.60	.18
❑ 154 Priest Lauderdale RC	.20	.06
❑ 155 Matt Maloney RC	.40	.12
❑ 156 Stephon Marbury RC	1.50	.45
❑ 157 Walter McCarty RC	.20	.06
❑ 158 Steve Nash RC	2.00	.60
❑ 159 Jermaine O'Neal RC	2.00	.60
❑ 160 Ray Owes RC	.20	.06
❑ 161 Vitaly Potapenko RC	.20	.06
❑ 162 Roy Rogers RC	.20	.06
❑ 163 Antoine Walker RC	2.00	.60
❑ 164 Samaki Walker RC	.20	.06
❑ 165 Ben Wallace RC	4.00	1.20
❑ 166 John Wallace RC	.60	.18
❑ 167 Jerome Williams RC	.60	.18
❑ 168 Lorenzen Wright RC	.40	.12
❑ 169 Vin Baker ZUP	.20	.06
❑ 170 Charles Barkley ZUP	.60	.18
❑ 171 Patrick Ewing ZUP	.40	.12
❑ 172 Michael Finley ZUP	.60	.18
❑ 173 Kevin Garnett ZUP	.60	.18
❑ 174 Anfernee Hardaway ZUP	.40	.12
❑ 175 Grant Hill ZUP	.60	.18
❑ 176 Juwan Howard ZUP	.20	.06
❑ 177 Jim Jackson ZUP	.20	.06
❑ 178 Eddie Jones ZUP	.40	.12
❑ 179 Michael Jordan ZUP	2.00	.60
❑ 180 Shawn Kemp ZUP	.20	.06
❑ 181 Jason Kidd ZUP	.60	.18

	Nm-Mt	Ex-Mt
❑ 182 Karl Malone ZUP	.60	.18
❑ 183 Antonio McDyess ZUP	.60	.18
❑ 184 Reggie Miller ZUP	.40	.12
❑ 185 Alonzo Mourning ZUP	.20	.06
❑ 186 Hakeem Olajuwon ZUP	.40	.12
❑ 187 Shaquille O'Neal ZUP	.60	.18
❑ 188 Gary Payton ZUP	.40	.12
❑ 189 Mitch Richmond ZUP	.20	.06
❑ 190 Clifford Robinson ZUP	.20	.06
❑ 191 David Robinson ZUP	.40	.12
❑ 192 Glenn Robinson ZUP	.40	.12
❑ 193 Dennis Rodman ZUP	.20	.06
❑ 194 Joe Smith ZUP	.20	.06
❑ 195 Jerry Stackhouse ZUP	.60	.18
❑ 196 John Stockton ZUP	.40	.12
❑ 197 Damon Stoudamire ZUP	.40	.12
❑ 198 Chris Webber ZUP	.60	.18
❑ 199 Checklist (101-157)	.20	.06
❑ 200 Checklist (158-200/ins.)	.20	.06
❑ NNO Grant Hill Promo	2.00	.60
❑ NNO Grant Hill Total Z	12.00	3.60
❑ NNO Grant Hill Jerry Stackhouse Promo	2.00	.60

1997-98 Z-Force

	Nm-Mt	Ex-Mt
COMPLETE SET (210)	25.00	7.50
COMPLETE SERIES 1 (110)	10.00	3.00
COMPLETE SERIES 2 (100)	15.00	4.50
❑ 1 Anfernee Hardaway	.50	.15
❑ 2 Mitch Richmond	.30	.09
❑ 3 Stephon Marbury	.60	.18
❑ 4 Charles Barkley	.60	.18
❑ 5 Juwan Howard	.30	.09
❑ 6 Avery Johnson	.15	.04
❑ 7 Rex Chapman	.15	.04
❑ 8 Antoine Walker	.60	.18
❑ 9 Nick Van Exel	.50	.15
❑ 10 Tim Hardaway	.30	.09
❑ 11 Clarence Weatherspoon	.15	.04
❑ 12 John Stockton	.50	.15
❑ 13 Glenn Robinson	.50	.15
❑ 14 Anthony Mason	.30	.09
❑ 15 Latrell Sprewell	.50	.15
❑ 16 Kendall Gill	.15	.04
❑ 17 Terry Mills	.15	.04
❑ 18 Mookie Blaylock	.15	.04
❑ 19 Michael Finley	.50	.15
❑ 20 Gary Payton	.50	.15
❑ 21 Kevin Garnett	1.00	.30
❑ 22 Clyde Drexler	.50	.15
❑ 23 Michael Jordan	3.00	.90
❑ 24 Antonio McDyess	.30	.09
❑ 25 Nick Anderson	.15	.04
❑ 26 Patrick Ewing	.50	.15
❑ 27 Anthony Peeler	.15	.04
❑ 28 Doug Christie	.30	.09
❑ 29 Bobby Phills	.15	.04
❑ 30 Kerry Kittles	.50	.15
❑ 31 Reggie Miller	.50	.15
❑ 32 Karl Malone	.50	.15
❑ 33 Grant Hill	.50	.15
❑ 34 Shaquille O'Neal	1.25	.35
❑ 35 Loy Vaught	.15	.04
❑ 36 Kenny Anderson	.30	.09
❑ 37 Wesley Person	.15	.04
❑ 38 Jamal Mashburn	.30	.09
❑ 39 Christian Laettner	.30	.09
❑ 40 Shawn Kemp	.30	.09
❑ 41 Glen Rice	.30	.09
❑ 42 Vin Baker	.30	.09
❑ 43 Popeye Jones	.15	.04
❑ 44 Derrick Coleman	.15	.04
❑ 45 Rik Smits	.30	.09
❑ 46 Dale Ellis	.15	.04
❑ 47 Rod Strickland	.15	.04
❑ 48 Mark Price	.30	.09
❑ 49 Toni Kukoc	.30	.09
❑ 50 David Robinson	.50	.15
❑ 51 John Wallace	.15	.04
❑ 52 Samaki Walker	.15	.04
❑ 53 Shareef Abdur-Rahim	.75	.23
❑ 54 Rodney Rogers	.15	.04
❑ 55 Dikembe Mutombo	.30	.09
❑ 56 Rony Seikaly	.15	.04
❑ 57 Matt Maloney	.15	.04
❑ 58 Chris Webber	.50	.15
❑ 59 Robert Horry	.30	.09
❑ 60 Rasheed Wallace	.50	.15
❑ 61 Jeff Hornacek	.30	.09
❑ 62 Walt Williams	.15	.04
❑ 63 Detlef Schrempf	.30	.09
❑ 64 Dan Majerle	.30	.09
❑ 65 Dell Curry	.15	.04
❑ 66 Scottie Pippen	.75	.23
❑ 67 Greg Anthony	.15	.04
❑ 68 Mahmoud Abdul-Rauf	.15	.04
❑ 69 Cedric Ceballos	.15	.04
❑ 70 Terrell Brandon	.30	.09
❑ 71 Arvydas Sabonis	.30	.09
❑ 72 Malik Sealy	.15	.04
❑ 73 Dean Garrett	.15	.04
❑ 74 Joe Dumars	.50	.15
❑ 75 Joe Smith	.30	.09
❑ 76 Shawn Bradley	.15	.04
❑ 77 Gheorghe Muresan	.15	.04
❑ 78 Dale Davis	.15	.04
❑ 79 Bryant Stith	.15	.04
❑ 80 Lorenzen Wright	.15	.04
❑ 81 Chris Childs	.15	.04
❑ 82 Bryon Russell	.15	.04
❑ 83 Steve Smith	.30	.09
❑ 84 Jerry Stackhouse	.50	.15
❑ 85 Hersey Hawkins	.15	.04
❑ 86 Ray Allen	.50	.15
❑ 87 Dominique Wilkins	.50	.15
❑ 88 Kobe Bryant	2.00	.60
❑ 89 Tom Gugliotta	.30	.09
❑ 90 Dennis Scott	.15	.04
❑ 91 Dennis Rodman	.30	.09
❑ 92 Bryant Reeves	.15	.04
❑ 93 Vlade Divac	.30	.09
❑ 94 Jason Kidd	.75	.23
❑ 95 Mario Elie	.15	.04
❑ 96 Lindsey Hunter	.15	.04
❑ 97 Olden Polynice	.15	.04
❑ 98 Allan Houston	.30	.09
❑ 99 Alonzo Mourning	.30	.09
❑ 100 Allen Iverson	1.25	.35
❑ 101 LaPhonso Ellis	.15	.04
❑ 102 Bob Sura	.15	.04
❑ 103 Chris Mullin	.50	.15
❑ 104 Sam Cassell	.50	.15
❑ 105 Eric Williams	.15	.04
❑ 106 Antonio Davis	.15	.04
❑ 107 Marcus Camby	.50	.15
❑ 108 Isaiah Rider	.30	.09
❑ 109 Checklist (Atlanta Hawks-Phoenix Suns)	.15	.04
❑ 110 Checklist (Portland-inserts)	.15	.04
❑ 111 Tim Duncan RC	2.00	.60
❑ 112 Joe Smith	.30	.09
❑ 113 Shawn Kemp	.30	.09
❑ 114 Terry Mills	.15	.04
❑ 115 Jacque Vaughn RC	.30	.09
❑ 116 Ron Mercer RC	.60	.18
❑ 117 Brian Williams	.15	.04
❑ 118 Rik Smits	.30	.09
❑ 119 Eric Williams	.15	.04
❑ 120 Tim Thomas RC	.75	.23
❑ 121 Damon Stoudamire	.30	.09
❑ 122 God Shammgod RC	.15	.04
❑ 123 Tyrone Hill	.15	.04
❑ 124 Elden Campbell	.15	.04
❑ 125 Keith Van Horn RC	.75	.23
❑ 126 Brian Grant	.30	.09
❑ 127 Antonio McDyess	.30	.09
❑ 128 Darrell Armstrong	.15	.04
❑ 129 Sam Perkins	.30	.09
❑ 130 Chris Mills	.15	.04
❑ 131 Reggie Miller	.50	.15
❑ 132 Chris Gatling	.15	.04
❑ 133 Ed Gray RC	.15	.04
❑ 134 Hakeem Olajuwon	.50	.15
❑ 135 Chris Webber	.50	.15
❑ 136 Kendall Gill	.15	.04
❑ 137 Wesley Person	.15	.04
❑ 138 Derrick Coleman	.15	.04
❑ 139 Dana Barros	.15	.04
❑ 140 Dennis Scott	.15	.04
❑ 141 Paul Grant RC	.15	.04
❑ 142 Scott Burrell	.15	.04
❑ 143 Does not Exist	-	-
❑ 144 Austin Croshere RC	.50	.15
❑ 145 Maurice Taylor RC	.50	.15
❑ 146 Kevin Johnson	.30	.09
❑ 147 Tony Battie RC	.50	.15
❑ 148 Tariq Abdul-Wahad RC	.30	.09
❑ 149 Johnny Taylor RC	.15	.04
❑ 150 Allen Iverson	1.25	.35
❑ 151 Terrell Brandon	.30	.09
❑ 152 Derek Anderson RC	1.00	.30
❑ 153 Calbert Cheaney	.15	.04
❑ 154 Jayson Williams	.15	.04
❑ 155 Rick Fox	.30	.09
❑ 156 John Thomas RC	.15	.04
❑ 157 David Wesley	.15	.04
❑ 158 Bobby Jackson RC	1.00	.30
❑ 159 Kelvin Cato RC	.50	.15
❑ 160 Vinny Del Negro	.15	.04
❑ 161 Adonal Foyle RC	.30	.09
❑ 162 Larry Johnson	.30	.09
❑ 163 Brevin Knight RC	.30	.09
❑ 164 Rod Strickland	.15	.04
❑ 165 Rodrick Rhodes RC	.15	.04
❑ 166 Scot Pollard RC	.30	.09
❑ 167 Sam Cassell	.50	.15
❑ 168 Jerry Stackhouse	.50	.15
❑ 169 Mark Jackson	.30	.09
❑ 170 John Wallace	.15	.04
❑ 171 Horace Grant	.30	.09
❑ 172A Vin Baker	.30	.09
❑ 172B T.McGrady RC ERR	2.50	.75
❑ 173 Eddie Jones	.50	.15
❑ 174 Kerry Kittles	.50	.15
❑ 175 Antonio Daniels RC	.50	.15
❑ 176 Alan Henderson	.15	.04
❑ 177 Sean Elliott	.30	.09
❑ 178 John Starks	.30	.09
❑ 179 Chauncey Billups RC	.50	.15
❑ 180 Juwan Howard	.30	.09
❑ 181 Bobby Phills	.15	.04
❑ 182 Latrell Sprewell	.50	.15
❑ 183 Jim Jackson	.15	.04
❑ 184 Danny Fortson RC	.30	.09
❑ 185 Zydrunas Ilgauskas	.30	.09
❑ 186 Clifford Robinson	.15	.04
❑ 187 Chris Mullin	.50	.15
❑ 188 Greg Ostertag	.15	.04
❑ 189 Antoine Walker ZUP	.50	.15
❑ 190 Michael Jordan ZUP	1.50	.45
❑ 191 Scottie Pippen ZUP	.40	.12
❑ 192 Dennis Rodman ZUP	.15	.04
❑ 193 Grant Hill ZUP	.30	.09
❑ 194 Clyde Drexler ZUP	.30	.09
❑ 195 Kobe Bryant ZUP	1.00	.30
❑ 196 Shaquille O'Neal ZUP	.50	.15
❑ 197 Alonzo Mourning ZUP	.30	.09
❑ 198 Ray Allen ZUP	.50	.15
❑ 199 Kevin Garnett ZUP	.50	.15
❑ 200 Stephon Marbury ZUP	.50	.15
❑ 201 Anfernee Hardaway ZUP	.30	.09
❑ 202 Jason Kidd ZUP	.40	.12
❑ 203 David Robinson ZUP	.30	.09
❑ 204 Gary Payton ZUP	.30	.09
❑ 205 Marcus Camby ZUP	.30	.09
❑ 206 Karl Malone ZUP	.50	.15
❑ 207 John Stockton ZUP	.50	.15
❑ 208 S. Abdur-Rahim ZUP	.40	.12
❑ 209 Charles Barkley CL	.50	.15
❑ 210 Gary Payton CL	.30	.09

Acknowledgments

Each year we refine the process of developing the most accurate and up-to-date information for this book. We believe this year's price guide is our best yet. Thanks again to all the contributors nationwide (listed below) as well as our staff here in Dallas.

Those who have worked closely with us on this and many other books, have again proven themselves invaluable in every aspect of producing this book: Rich Altman, Randy Archer, Mike Aronstein, Jerry Bell, Chris Benjamin, Mike Blaisdell, Bill Bossert (Mid-Atlantic Coin Exchange), Todd Crosner (California Sports Card Exchange), Bud Darland, Bill and Diane Dodge, Rick Donohoo, Willie Erving, Fleer (Tim Franz), Gervise Ford, Steve Freedman, Larry and Jeff Fritsch, Jim Galusha, Dick Gariepy, Dick Gilkeson, Mike and Howard Gordon, Sally Grace, Oscar Gracia, George Grauer, John Greenwald, Jess Guffey, George Henn, Mike Hersh, John Inouye, Steven Judd, Edward J. Kabala, Judy Kaye, Lon Levitan, Lew Lipset, Dave Lucey, Paul Marchant, Brian Marcy (Scottsdale Baseball Cards), Dr. John McCue, Mike Mosier (Columbia City Collectibles Co.), Clark Muldavin, B.A. Murry, Steven Panet, Earl N. Petersen, J.C. (Boo) Phillips, Jack Pollard, Racing Champions (Bill Surdock), Pat Quinn, Henry M. Reizes, Gavin Riley, Rotman Productions, John Rumierz, Kevin Savage and Pat Blandford (Sports Gallery), Mike Schechter (MSA), Dan Sherlock, Bill Shonscheck, Glen J. Sidler, John Spalding, Spanky's, Nigel Spill (Oldies and Goodies), Rob Springs, Murvin Sterling, Dan Stickney, Steve Taft, Ed Taylor, Lee Temanson, Topps (Clay Luraschi), Upper Deck (Jake Gonzales), Bill Vizas, Bill Wesslund (Portland Sports Card Co.), Jim Woods, Kit Young, Robert Zanze, Bill Zimpleman, and Dean Zindler.

Many other individuals have provided price input, illustrative material, checklist verifications, errata, and/or background information. At the risk of inadvertently overlooking or omitting these many contributors, we should like to personally thank Joseph Abram, Darren Adams, Harry and Angela Agens, Brett Allen, Alan Applegate, Randy Archer, Jeremy Bachman, Fran Bailey, Dean Bedell, Bubba Bennett, Eric Berger, Stanley Bernstein, Mike Blair, Andrew Bosarge, Naed Bou, David Bowlby, Gary Boyd, Terry Boyd, Nelson Brewart, Ray Bright, Britt Britton, Jacey Buel, Terry Bunt, David Cadelina, Danny Cariseo, Sally Carves, Tom Cavalierre, Garrett Chan, Lance Churchill, Craig Coddling, H. William Cook, Dave Cooper, Ron Cornell, Paul Czuchna, Jeff Daniels, Robert DeSalvatore, Robert Dichiara, Pat Dorsey, Joe Drelich, Brad Drummond, Charles Easterday Jr., Al Eng, Brad Engelhardt, Darrell Ereth, F&F Fast Break Cards, Gary Farbstein, Anthony Fernando, Joe Filas, Tom Freeman, Bob Frye, Alex and Chris Gala, Greg George, Pete George, Arthur Goyette, Dina Gray, Bob Grissett, Jess Guffey, Simon Gutis, Steve Hart, John Haupt, Sol Hauptman, Brian Headrick, Steven Hecht, Rod Heffem, Kevin Heffner, Stephen Hils, Neil Hoppenworth, Bill Huggins, Wendell Hunter, Frank Hurtado, Brett Hyle, John Inouye, Brian Jaccoma, Mike Jardina, David Johnson, Craig Jones, Carmen Jordan, Loyd Jungling, Nick Kardoulias, Scott Kashner, Glenn Kasnuba, Jan Kemplin, Kal Kenfield, John Kilian, Tim Kirk, John Klassnik, Steve (DJ) Kluback, Mike Knoll, Don Knutsen, Mike Kohlhas, Bob and Bryan Kornfeld, George Kruk, Tom Kummer, Tim Landis, Jeff La Scala, Howard Lau, John Law, Ed Lim, Neil Lopez, Kendall Loyd, Fernando Mercado, Bruce Margulies, Scott Martinez, Bill McAvoy, Chris Merrill, Robert Merrill, Blake Meyer, Chad Meyer, Mark Meyer, Midwest Sports Cards, Jeff

Mimick, Jeff Monaco, Jeff Morris, Michael Olsen, Don Olson Jr., Glenn Olson, Arto Paladian, Michael Parker, Jeff Patton, Jeff Prillaman, Paul Purves, Don Ras, Ron Resling, Carson Ritchey, Brent Ruland, Erik Runge, Mark Samarin, Bob Santos, Eric Shilito, Masa Shinohara, Bob Shurtleff, Sam Sliheet, Doug Smith, Doug Spooner, Dan Statman, Geoff Stevers, Brad Stiles, Andy Stoltz, Nick Teresi, Jim Tripodi, Rob Veres, Bill Vizas, Kevin Vo, Mark Watson, Brian Wentz, Brian White, Doc White, Jeff Wiedenfeld, Mike Wiggins, Douglas Wilding, Steve Yeh, Zario Zigler, and Mark Zubrensky.

Every year we make active solicitations for expert input. We are particularly appreciative of help (however extensive or cursory) provided for this volume. We receive many inquiries, comments, and questions regarding material within this book. In fact, each and every one is read and digested. Time constraints, however, prevent us from personally replying. But keep sharing your knowledge. Your letters and input are part of the "big picture" of hobby information we can pass along to readers in our books and magazines. Even though we cannot respond to each letter, you are making significant contributions to the hobby through your interest and comments.

The effort to continually refine and improve this book also involves a growing number of people and types of expertise on our home team. Our company boasts a substantial Sports Data Publishing team, which strengthens our ability to provide comprehensive analysis of the marketplace. Sports Data Publishing capably handled numerous technical details and provided able assistance and leadership in the preparation of this edition.

Our basketball analysts played a major part in compiling this year's book, traveling thousands of miles during the past year to attend sports card shows and visit card shops around the United States and Canada. The Beckett basketball specialist is Keith Hower (price guide editor). His gathering information, entering sets, pricing analysis, and careful proofreading were key contributions to the accuracy of this annual.

Also, key contributors to endless hours of information gathering, pricing, and analysis was Rich Klein.

They were ably assisted by Beverly Melian, who helped enter new sets and pricing information.

Notes

Notes

Notes

Notes

Notes

Notes

Notes

Notes

Notes